The **Rough Guide** to

Canada

written and researched by

Tim Jepson, Phil Lee, Tania Smith and Christian Williams

with additional contributions by

Felicity Aston and Janine Israel

NEW YORK • LONDON • DELHI

www.roughguides.com

Contents

◄◄ Cattle drive in Alberta ◄ Cape Breton Highlands National Park, Nova Scotia

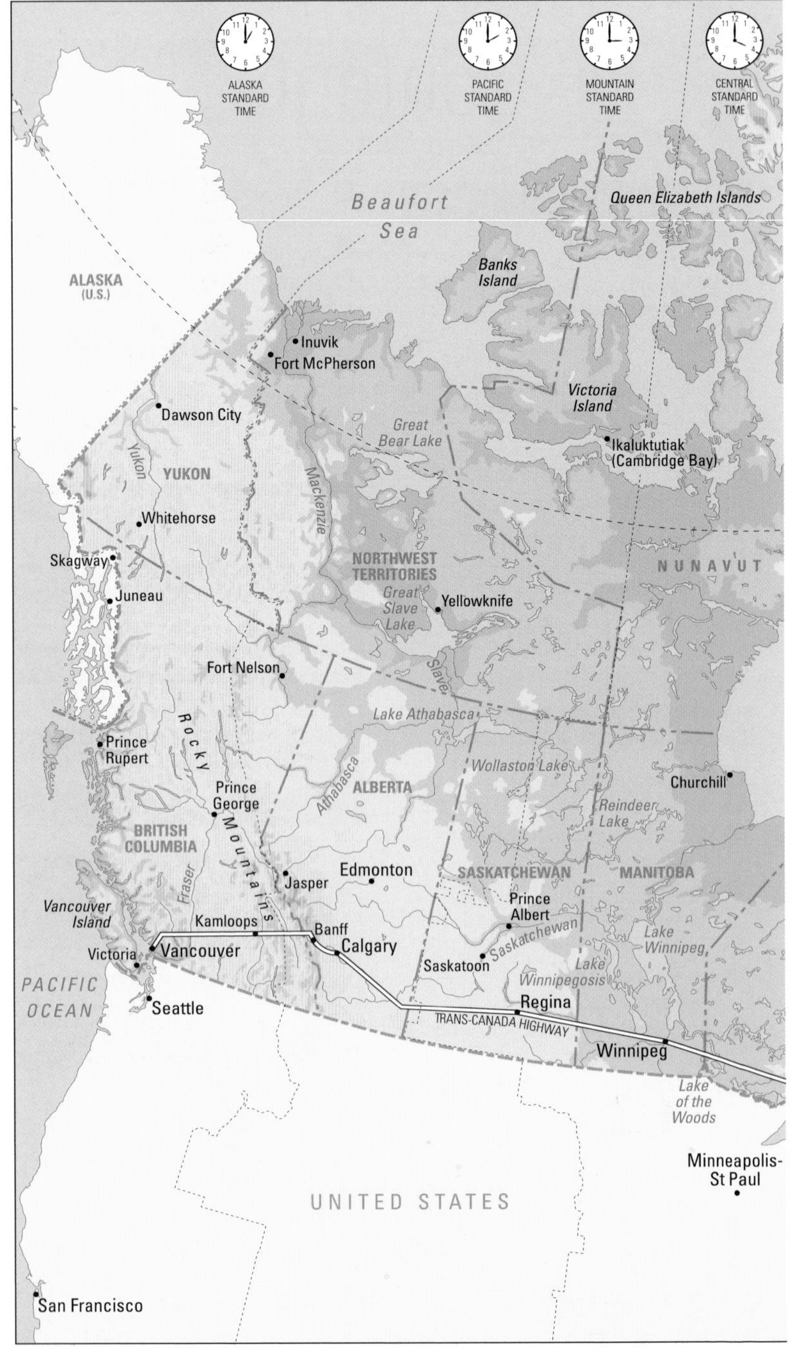
ALASKA STANDARD TIME
PACIFIC STANDARD TIME
MOUNTAIN STANDARD TIME
CENTRAL STANDARD TIME
Beaufort Sea
Queen Elizabeth Islands
Banks Island
ALASKA (U.S.)
Inuvik
Fort McPherson
Victoria Island
Dawson City
Great Bear Lake
Ikaluktutiak (Cambridge Bay)
Yukon
YUKON
Mackenzie
Whitehorse
NORTHWEST TERRITORIES
NUNAVUT
Skagway
Juneau
Great Slave Lake
Yellowknife
Fort Nelson
Slave
Lake Athabasca
Prince Rupert
Rocky Mountains
Wollaston Lake
Athabasca
ALBERTA
Churchill
Prince George
Reindeer Lake
BRITISH COLUMBIA
Fraser
Edmonton
Jasper
SASKATCHEWAN
MANITOBA
Vancouver Island
Prince Albert
Kamloops
Banff
Saskatchewan
Lake Winnipeg
Victoria
Vancouver
Calgary
Saskatoon
Lake Winnipegosis
PACIFIC OCEAN
Seattle
Regina
TRANS-CANADA HIGHWAY
Winnipeg
Lake of the Woods
Minneapolis-St Paul
UNITED STATES
San Francisco

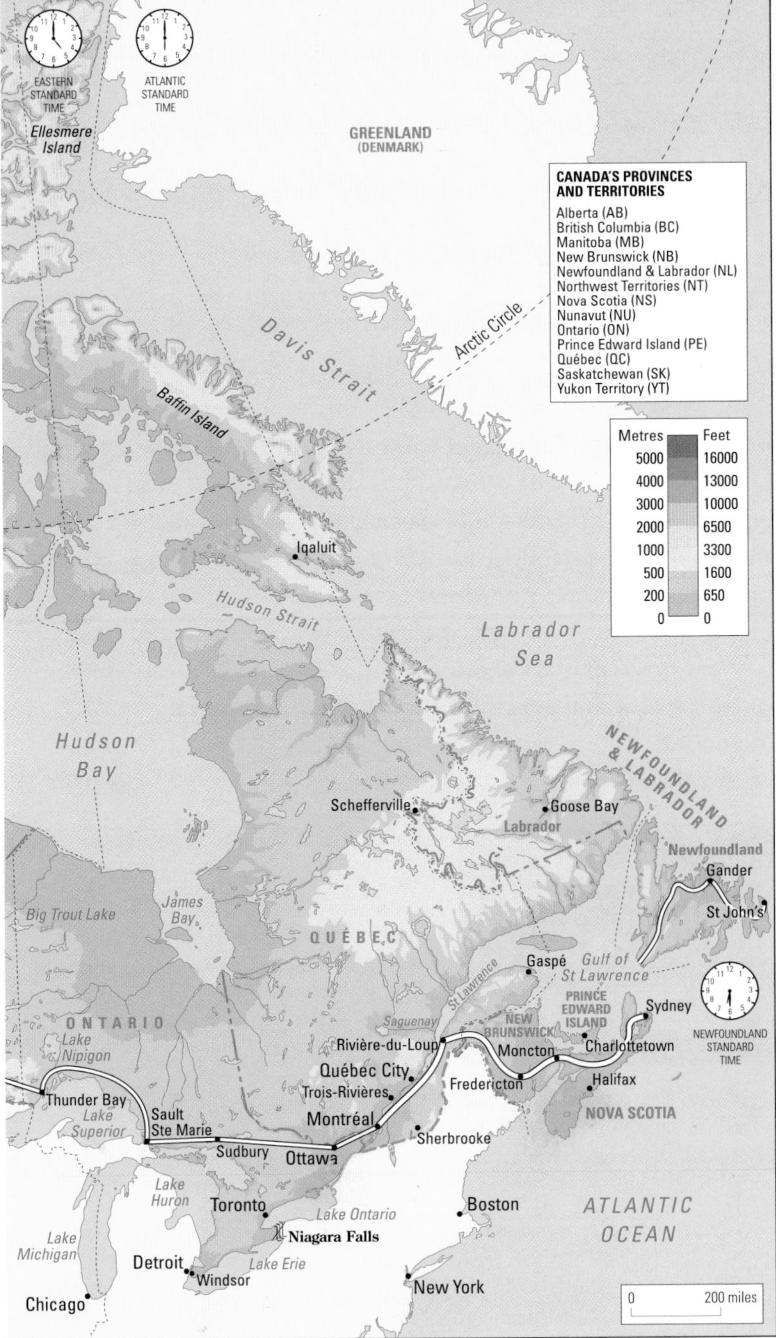

EASTERN STANDARD TIME
ATLANTIC STANDARD TIME
Ellesmere Island
GREENLAND (DENMARK)
CANADA'S PROVINCES AND TERRITORIES
Alberta (AB)
British Columbia (BC)
Manitoba (MB)
New Brunswick (NB)
Newfoundland & Labrador (NL)
Northwest Territories (NT)
Nova Scotia (NS)
Nunavut (NU)
Ontario (ON)
Prince Edward Island (PE)
Québec (QC)
Saskatchewan (SK)
Yukon Territory (YT)
Arctic Circle
Davis Strait
Baffin Island
Metres
Feet
5000
16000
4000
13000
3000
10000
2000
6500
1000
3300
500
1600
200
650
0
0
Iqaluit
Hudson Strait
Labrador Sea
Hudson Bay
NEWFOUNDLAND & LABRADOR
Schefferville
Goose Bay
Labrador
Newfoundland
Gander
St John's
James Bay
Big Trout Lake
QUÉBEC
Gaspé
Gulf of St Lawrence
St Lawrence
PRINCE EDWARD ISLAND
Sydney
NEWFOUNDLAND STANDARD TIME
ONTARIO
Lake Nipigon
Saguenay
NEW BRUNSWICK
Rivière-du-Loup
Moncton
Charlottetown
Québec City
Fredericton
Halifax
Thunder Bay
Trois-Rivières
NOVA SCOTIA
Lake Superior
Sault Ste Marie
Montréal
Sherbrooke
Sudbury
Ottawa
Lake Huron
Toronto
Lake Ontario
Boston
ATLANTIC OCEAN
Niagara Falls
Lake Michigan
Detroit
Windsor
Lake Erie
New York
Chicago
0
200 miles

Introduction to Canada

Canada is almost unimaginably vast. It stretches from the Atlantic to the Pacific and from the latitude of Rome to beyond the Magnetic North Pole. Its archetypal landscapes are the Rockies' lakes and peaks, the endless forests and the prairie wheatfields, but Canada holds landscapes that defy expectations: rainforest and desert lie close together in the southwest corner of the country, while in the east a short drive can take you from fjords to lush orchards. Better still, great tracts of Canada are completely unspoiled: ninety percent of Canadians live within 160km of the US border.

Like its neighbour to the south, Canada is a spectrum of cultures, a hotchpotch of immigrant groups who supplanted the continent's many native peoples. There's a crucial difference, though, between the two countries. Whereas citizens of the US are encouraged to perceive themselves as Americans above all else, Canada's concertedly multicultural approach has fostered an ethnic mosaic. Alongside the French and British majorities live a host of communities who maintain many of the traditions of their homelands – Chinese, Ukrainian, Portuguese, Indian, Dutch, Polish, Greek and Spanish, to name just the most numerous.

For the visitor, the mix that results from Canada's mostly exemplary tolerance is an exhilarating experience, offering such widely differing environments as Vancouver's huge Chinatown and the austere religious

▲ Fresh produce at Jean Talon market

enclaves of Manitoba. Canadians themselves, however, are often troubled by the lack of a clear self-image, tending to emphasize the ways in which they are different from the US as a means of self-description. The question "What is a Canadian?" has acquired a new immediacy with the interminable and acrimonious debate over Québec and its possible secession, but ultimately there can be no simple characterization of a people whose country is not so much a single nation as a committee on a continental scale. Pierre Berton, one of Canada's finest writers, wisely ducked the issue: Canadians, he quipped, are "people who know how to make love in a canoe".

"The typical Canadian" might be an elusive concept, but you'll find there's a distinctive feel to the country. Some towns might seem a touch too well-regulated, but against this there's the overwhelming sense of Canadian pride in their history and pleasure in the beauty of their land. Canada embraces its own clichés with an energy that's irresistible, promoting everything from the Calgary Stampede to maple-syrup festivals and lumberjack contests with an extraordinary zeal and openness. As John Buchan, writer and former Governor General of Canada, once said, "You have to know a man awfully well in Canada to know his surname."

Fact file

- Canada is the world's second-largest country (after the Russian Federation), covering almost ten million square kilometres. A quarter of this is the Inuit homeland of Nunavut.
- Canada extends across six time zones, and shares a border with the US of 8900km. The highest point is Mount Logan (5959m).
- The population is almost 33 million, with an average life expectancy at birth of 80 years. Almost a half claim British ancestry, a quarter French ancestry and just under a million (3.3 percent) claim aboriginal ancestry.
- Canada is a confederation comprising ten provinces and three territories. It has been self-governing since 1867, but retains ties to Britain: the Canadian head of state is Queen Elizabeth II.
- Canada's colossal natural resources help put it among the world's top-ten richest countries. Almost two-thirds of its power is hydroelectric, and it's one of the few developed nations that is a net exporter of energy.

Aboriginal peoples

The British, French and Spanish were latecomers to Canada, a country that for countless thousands of years was home to a vast aboriginal population. Today, almost a million Canadians claim descent from these first peoples, from the so-called "Indians" of the central and western heartlands, to the Inuit, inhabitants of the great sweep of Canada's north. A third group, the Métis – descendants of mixed unions of white and aboriginal people – also have a distinct culture, part of a rich cultural, social and artistic mosaic which provides a beguiling complement to the mainstream. You'll find evidence of Canada's former aboriginal life in many museums and galleries, and plenty of areas nurturing living aboriginal cultures, though there's no escaping the fact that many aboriginal people are among the poorest Canadians.

Where to go

The time and expense involved in covering Canada's immense distances means that most visitors confine their trips to the area around one of the main cities – usually Toronto, Montréal, Vancouver or Calgary for arrivals by air. The attractions of these centres vary widely, but they have one thing in common with each other and all other Canadian towns: they are within easy reach of the great outdoors.

▲ Mural in Toronto

Canada's most southerly region, south **Ontario**, contains not only the country's manufacturing heart and its largest city, **Toronto**, but also **Niagara Falls**, the premier tourist sight. North of Toronto there's the far less packaged scenic attraction of **Georgian Bay**, a beautiful waterscape of pine-studded islets set against crystal-blue waters. Like the forested Algonquin park, the bay is also accessible from the Canadian capital, **Ottawa**, not as dynamic a city as Toronto, but still well worth a stay for its galleries and museums.

Québec, set apart by the depth of its French tradition, focuses on its biggest city, **Montréal**, which is for many people the most vibrant place in the country, a fascinating mix of old-world style and commercial dynamism. The pace of life is more relaxed in the historic provincial capital **Québec City**, and more easygoing still in the villages dotted along the St Lawrence lowlands, where glittering spires attest to the enduring influence of the Catholic Church. For something more bracing, you could continue north to **Tadoussac**, where whales can be seen near the mouth of the splendid **Saguenay fjord** – and if you're really prepared for the wilds, forge on through to **Labrador**, as inhospitable a zone as you'll find in the east.

Across the mouth of the St Lawrence, the pastoral **Gaspé Peninsula** – the easternmost part of Québec – borders **New Brunswick**, a mild-mannered introduction to the three **Maritime Provinces**, whose people have long been dependent on timber and the sea for their livelihood. Here, the tapering **Bay of Fundy** boasts amazing tides – rising and falling by nine metres or more – whilst the region's tiny fishing villages are at their most beguiling near **Halifax**, the bustling capital of **Nova Scotia**. Perhaps even prettier, and certainly more austere, are the land and seascapes

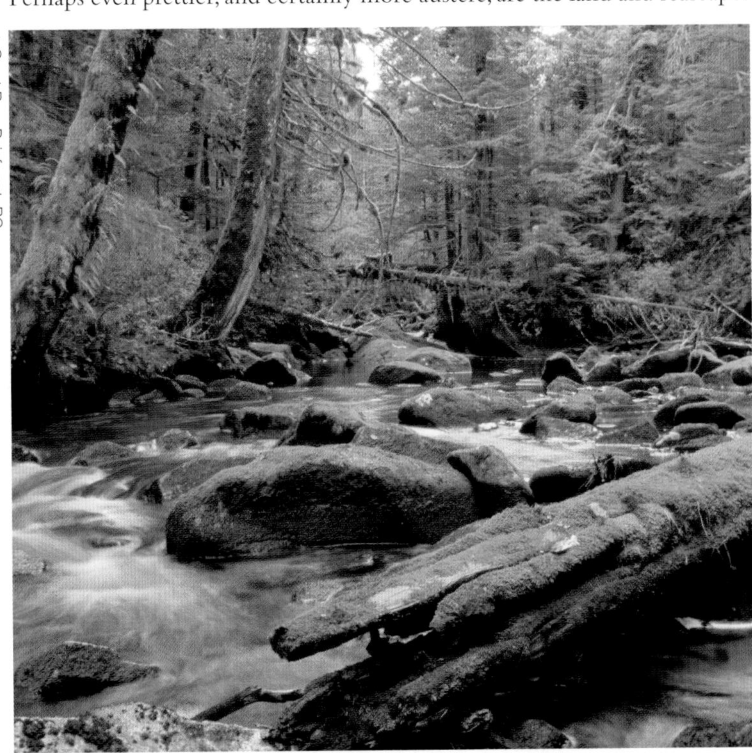

▲ Great Bear Rainforest, BC

Epic journeys

A country the size of Canada lends itself to epic journeys. Travelling by car or bus, you can enjoy some of the world's greatest wilderness drives, from the Icefields Parkway through the heart of the Rockies to routes that push some of North America's last frontiers: the Alaska and Cassiar highways in British Columbia, for example, or the Dempster Highway in the Yukon, the only public road on the continent to cross the Arctic Circle. Trains, too, offer, superlative rides, whether it's the northbound route to Churchill or the classic transcontinental odyssey from Toronto to Vancouver. At sea, ferries also ply routes that provide a dramatic window on glorious scenery, none more so than the boats running up the Inside Passage from Vancouver Island towards Alaska.

of **Cape Breton Island**, whose rugged topography anticipates that of the island of **Newfoundland** to the north. Newfoundland's isolation has spawned a distinctive culture that's at its most lively in **St John's**, where the local folk-music scene is Canada's best. The island also boasts some of the Atlantic seaboard's finest landscapes, particularly the flat-topped peaks and glacier-gouged lakes of Gros Morne.

▲ Forgotten home on Prince Edward island

Back on the mainland, separating Ontario from Alberta and the Rockies, the "prairie provinces" of **Manitoba** and **Saskatchewan** have a reputation for dullness that's unfair: even in the flat southern parts there's the diversion of **Winnipeg**, whose traces of its early days make it a good place to break a trans-Canadian journey. Myriad lakes and gigantic forests offer magnificent canoeing and hiking and in the far north, beside Hudson Bay, the settlement of

▲ Vieux-Montréal

Churchill – remote, but accessible by train – is famous for its polar bears, beluga whales and easy viewing of the Northern Lights.

Moving west, the wheatfields of **Alberta** ripple into ranching country on the approach to the **Canadian Rockies**, whose reputation for natural drama is more than borne out by the reality. The province's two main cities, **Edmonton** and **Calgary**, have both grown fat on the region's oil and gas fields, and provide useful springboards for trips into the mountains – most popularly to the resorts of **Banff**, **Lake Louise** and **Jasper**. Further west **British Columbia** embodies the popular picture of Canada to perfection: a land of snowcapped summits, rivers and forests, pioneer villages, gold-rush ghost towns, and some of the greatest hiking, skiing, fishing and canoeing in the world. Its urban focus, **Vancouver**, is the country's third largest city, known for its spectacular natural setting and a laid-back West Coast hedonism. Off the coast lies **Vancouver Island**, a microcosm of the province's immense natural riches and home to **Victoria**, a devotedly anglophile little city.

Canada embraces its own clichés with an energy that's irresistible

North of British Columbia, wedged alongside Alaska, is the **Yukon Territory**, half grandiose mountains, half subarctic tundra, and full of evocative echoes of the Klondike gold rush. **Whitehorse**, its capital, and **Dawson City**, a gold-rush relic, are virtually the only towns here, each accessed by dramatic frontier highways. The **Northwest Territories** and **Nunavut**, covering the Canadian Arctic, are an immensity of stunted forest, lakes, tundra and ice, the realm of Dene and Inuit aboriginal bands whose traditional way of life is being threatened as oil and gas exploration reaches ever-northwards. Roads are virtually non-existent in the deep north, and only **Yellowknife**, a bizarre frontier city, plus a handful of ramshackle villages, offer the air links and resources necessary to explore this wilderness.

When to go

Canada's **climate** is hugely varied, but it's a safe generalization to say that the areas near the coast or the Great Lakes have milder winters and cooler summers than the interior. **July and August** are reliably warm throughout the country, even in the far north, making these the busiest months to visit. **November to March**, by contrast, is an ordeal of sub-zero temperatures almost everywhere except on the west coast, though winter days in many areas are clear and dry, and all large Canadian towns are geared to the challenge of cold conditions, with covered walkways and indoor malls protecting their inhabitants from the worst of the weather.

More specifically, the **Maritime Provinces** and **eastern Canada** have four distinct seasons: chill, snowy winters; short, mild springs; warm summers (which are shorter and colder in northern and inland regions); and long, crisp autumns. Summer is the key season in the resorts, though late September and October, particularly in New Brunswick, are also popular for the autumn colours. Coasts year-round can be blanketed in mist or fog.

In **Ontario** and **Québec** the seasons are also marked and the extremes intense, with cold, damp and grey winters in southern Ontario (drier and colder in Québec) and a long temperate spring from about April to June. Summers can be hot, but often uncomfortably humid, with the cities often empty of locals but full of visitors. The long autumn can be the best time to visit, with equable temperatures and few crowds.

British Columbia embodies the popular picture of Canada to perfection: a land of snowcapped summits, rivers and forests

The central provinces of **Manitoba**, **Saskatchewan** and **Alberta** experience the country's wildest climatic extremes, suffering the longest, harshest winters but also some of the finest, clearest summers, punctuated by fierce thunderstorms. Winter skiing brings a lot of people to the **Rockies**, but summer is still the busiest time, when July and August offer the best walking weather and the least chance of rain –though this often falls in heavy downpours, the mirror of winter's raging blizzards.

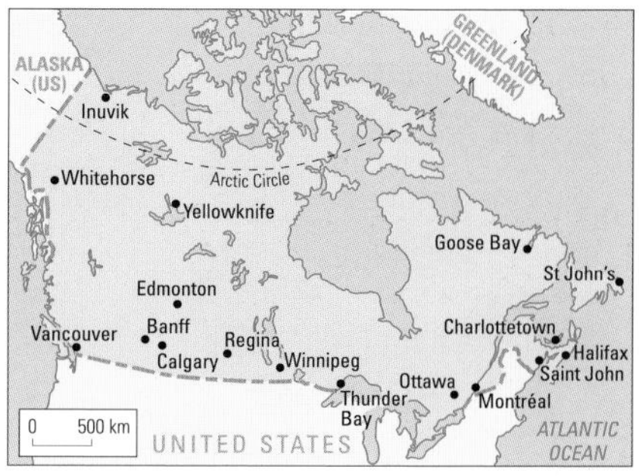

The southwestern parts of **British Columbia** enjoy some of Canada's best weather: the extremes are less marked and the overall temperatures generally milder than elsewhere. Much of the province, though, bears the brunt of Pacific depressions, so this is one of the country's damper regions: visiting between late spring and early autumn offers the best chance of missing the rain.

Across the **Yukon**, the **Northwest Territories** and **Nunavut** winters are bitterly cold, with temperatures rarely above freezing for months on end, though precipitation year-round is among the country's lowest. Summers, by contrast, are short but surprisingly warm. Spring – though late – can produce outstanding displays of wild flowers across the tundra.

Average temperatures and snowfall

	Average daily maximum temperatures				Annual	Duration
	Jan	April	July	Oct	snowfall	of snow cover
Banff, AB	-7°C/19°F	8°C/46°F	22°C/72°F	10°C/50°F	251cm/99in	149 days
Calgary, AB	-6°C/21°F	9°C/48°F	23°C/73°F	12°C/54°F	153cm/60in	116 days
Charlottetown, PE	-3°C/27°F	7°C/45°F	23°C/73°F	12°C/54°F	275cm/108in	122 days
Edmonton, AB	-17°C/1°F	9°C/48°F	22°C/72°F	11°C/52°F	136cm/54in	133 days
Goose Bay, NL	-12°C/10°F	3°C/37°F	21°C/70°F	7°C/45°F	445cm/175in	188 days
Halifax, NS	-1°C/30°F	9°C/48°F	23°C/73°F	14°C/57°F	217cm/85in	99 days
Inuvik, NT	-25°C/-13°F	-8°C/18°F	19°C/66°F	-5°C/23°F	177cm/70in	232 days
Montréal, QC	-6°C/21°F	11°C/52°F	26°C/79°F	13°C/56°F	243cm/96in	116 days
Ottawa, ON	-6°C/21°F	11°C/52°F	26°C/79°F	13°C/56°F	206cm/81in	121 days
Regina, SK	-13°C/9°F	9°C/48°F	26°C/79°F	12°C/54°F	87cm/34in	134 days
Saint John, NB	-3°C/27°F	8°C/46°F	22°C/72°F	12°C/54°F	224cm/88in	104 days
St John's, NL	0°C/32°F	5°C/41°F	21°C/70°F	11°C/52°F	322cm/127in	109 days
Thunder Bay, ON	-9°C/16°F	8°C/46°F	24°C/75°F	11°C/52°F	213cm/84in	132 days
Vancouver, BC	5°C/41°F	13°C/56°F	22°C/72°F	14°C/57°F	51cm/20in	11 days
Whitehorse, YT	-16°C/3°F	6°C/43°F	20°C/68°F	4°C/39°F	78cm/31in	170 days
Winnipeg, MB	-14°C/7°F	9°C/48°F	26°C/79°F	12°C/54°F	126cm/50in	135 days
Yellowknife, NT	-25°C/-13°F	-1°C/30°F	21°C/70°F	1°C/34°F	135cm/53in	210 days

31 things not to miss

It's not possible to see everything that Canada has to offer in one trip – and we don't suggest you try. What follows, in no particular order, is a selective and subjective taste of the country's highlights: beautiful landscapes, alluring cities, great activities and spectacular events. They're arranged in five colour-coded categories to help you find the very best things to see, do and experience. All entries have a page reference to take you straight into the guide, where you can find out more.

01 Dawson City Page **1036** • Dawson City was at the centre of the great 1898 Klondike gold rush.

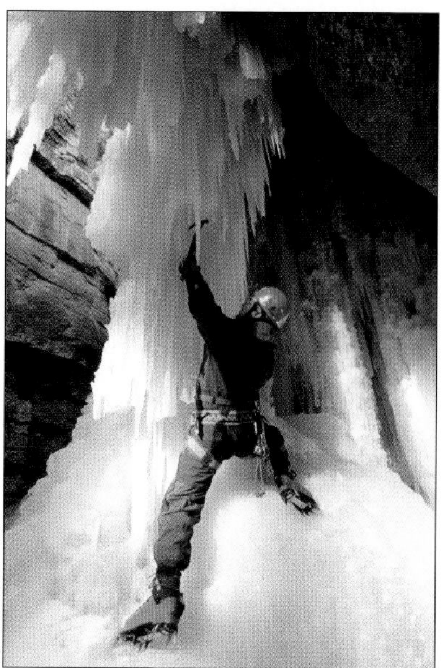

02 **Jasper** Page **742** • Ice-climbing is just one of the activities possible in the largest Rockies' national park – where hiking, biking and skiing trails can take you deep into the backcountry.

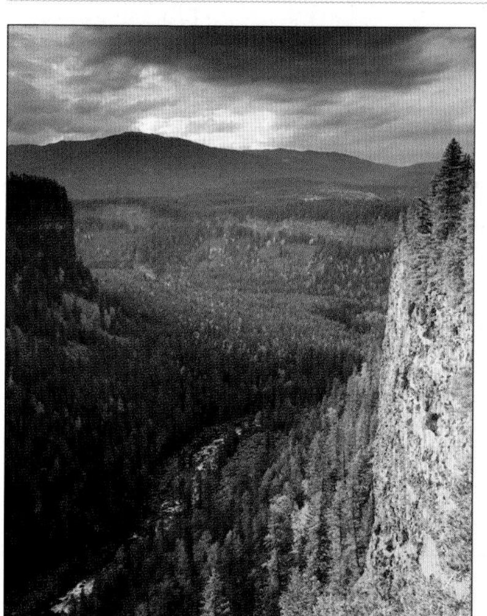

04 **Wells Gray** Page **952** • With the stunning Helmcken Falls, this is among the most appealing of British Columbia's many provincial parks.

03 **Watch polar bears in Churchill** Page **637** • Bleak and solitary, this northern town bills itself as "polar bear capital of the world" – with justification.

05 **Lunenburg** Page **414** • Of all the old fishing towns along the Nova Scotian coast, Lunenburg is the prettiest.

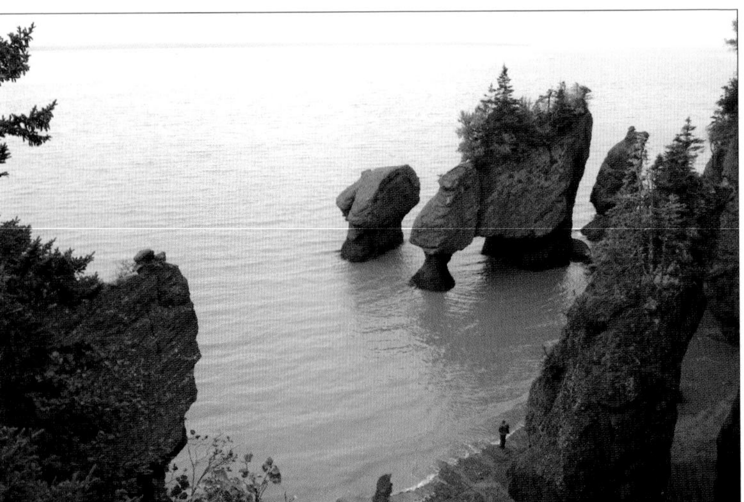

06 **Bay of Fundy** Page **442** • These rugged Nova Scotian sea cliffs and sheltered coves experience the highest tides in the world.

07 **Bird-watching in Newfoundland** Page **513** • Visit the puffins and thousand of other sea birds at the Witless Bay sea bird conserve in Newfoundland.

08 Taking in the coast at Pacific Rim National Park Page **909** • The majestic centrepiece of Vancouver Island is a beguiling mix of islets, rainforests and mountains.

09 Snowboarding in Whistler Page **852** & ***Skiing and snowboarding* colour section** • North America's largest ski resort has hundreds of acres of mind-blowing terrain.

10 Wildlife Page **1093** • Wildlife encounters are virtually assured in all of Canada's national parks and wilderness areas.

11 Niagara Falls Page **128** • Millions come to see the falls – two great sheets of water thundering over a 50m precipice.

12 Stanley Park, Vancouver Page **812** • Stanley Park is a peaceful retreat in this famously relaxed, attractive western city.

13 Ottawa's Parliament buildings Page **180** • Majestic Parliament buildings are the centrepiece of Canada's agreeable capital.

14 **Montréal's waterfront** Page **235** • The stunning waterfront exemplifies vibrant, cultured Montréal – urban Canada at its best.

15 **Hiking in Banff** Page **701** • Hiking is the best way to explore the great outdoors around the Rockies' bustling summer capital of Banff.

16 Mount Robson Page **755** • The highest peak in the Canadian Rockies, set amidst stunning scenery on the Alberta/BC border.

17 Explore Vieux-Quebéc Page **294** • With its clutch of fine old buildings, handsome location and great restaurant scene, Québec City's historic old town feels more European than Canadian.

18 See a glacier up close Page **1032** • One of the most remote spots in Canada's northern wilderness is the Kaskawulsh glacier in the Yukon's St Elias Mountains.

19 Aurora borealis Page **997** • Swirling sheets of iridescent colour, the disconcertingly beautiful Northern Lights can often be seen all across Canada's north.

20 The Laurentians Page **277** • Some of the finest and most diverse scenery in Québec, from rolling farmland to a vast coniferous forest.

21 Canoe in Algonquin Provincial Park Page **168** • The wild tracts of this enormous park – the largest in Ontario – are best explored by canoe; just watch out for the local moose!

22 The art of Emily Carr Page **810** & ***Canadian art* colour section** • One of the most distinguished Canadian artists, Carr loved the forests and villages of the Pacific Northwest.

23 St John's Page **500** • The dramatic approach to St John's old sea port is through a slender channel called The Narrows.

24 Afternoon tea in Victoria Page **882** • High tea at the venerable *Empress Hotel* (the best-known landmark in this genteel west-coast city) is an experience to remember.

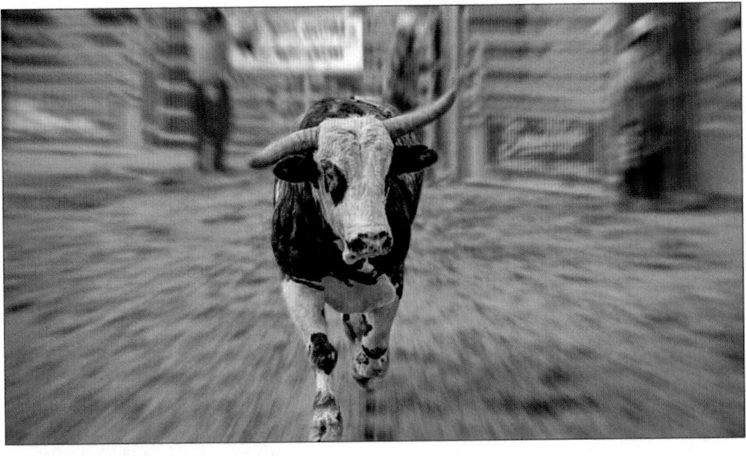

25 Calgary Stampede Page **662** • This annual rodeo lures over a million visitors to the city.

26 Eat your way around the world in Toronto Page **108** • From aromatic Chinatown food stalls to Greek pastry shops, there's no shortage of delicious cuisine from across the globe.

27 Haida Gwaii Page **1006** • Explore this west-coast archipelago of 200 islets for its vibrant aboriginal culture, unique fauna and deep, mossy forests.

28 Drive the Icefields Parkway Page **734** • Taking in the dramatic Rockies for over 200km, this is one of the world's most beautiful drives.

29 **Whale-watching** Page **914** • On both the east and west coasts, venturing out to view whales at close quarters is a popular activity.

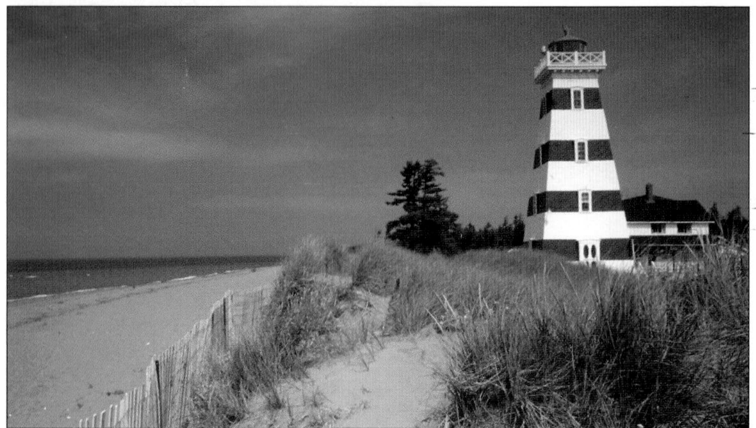

30 **Prince Edward Island** Page **473** • The reddish sands of PEI's National Park band the island's northern shore.

31 **Skiing** Page **684 & *Skiing and snowboarding* colour section** • The resorts of the Canadian Rockies boast great terrain, views and wonderful powder snow but are rarely busy.

Basics

Basics

Getting there

US travellers are spoilt for choice when it comes to deciding how to get to Canada. There are flights from many US airports to the three big Canadian cities, Toronto, Vancouver and Montréal, as well as to a string of smaller Canadian towns and cities, whilst many US citizens live within driving distance of the border. It's also easy to reach Canada from the US by bus, train and – on some routes on the west and east coasts – by ferry. Other travellers, including those from the UK, Australia, New Zealand and South Africa, have little choice but to fly.

Airfares from the UK, Australia and New Zealand to Canada depend on the **season**, with the highest prices applying from around mid-June to early September, the peak tourist season. You'll get the best prices during the low season, mid-November through April (excluding Christmas and New Year, when seats are at a premium and prices are hiked up). If you're flying from the US, the same general strictures apply, though the market is more unpredictable, with airlines constantly moving their prices up and down. Flying on weekends ordinarily adds a substantial amount to the round-trip fare; prices quoted below assume midweek travel.

Flights from the US

From the US to Canada, there are plenty of nonstop **flights** on Air Canada and most US airlines. Montréal, Toronto and Vancouver are the most popular destinations, but there are also services to Halifax, Calgary, Winnipeg and many other cities. Connecting flights within Canada serve some eighty additional destinations. Typical budget **return** fares on major airlines are: New York to Toronto US$200; New York to Montréal US$225; New York to Halifax US$275; Chicago to Winnipeg US$300; LA to Calgary US$250; LA to Vancouver US$200. If you plan only a long weekend trip, you can often find special fares: NY–Toronto for US$150 or Chicago–Winnipeg for US$200. You really need to **shop around** to get the very best deals on the busy US–Canada routes. Your best bet is to first try an **online agent**, who may be able to dig up scheduled return fares for as little as half the prices quoted above. You should also check out low-cost carriers such as Jetsgo and Westjet.

Domestic flights wholly within the US or Canada generally cost less than flights between the two countries, so you may make savings by crossing the border before or after your flight. This is especially true of long-haul flights: a transcontinental flight from New York to Vancouver can be considerably more expensive than a similar flight to Seattle (which lies only a hundred miles south of Vancouver). Typical budget return fares within Canada are Toronto to Montréal C$250; Montréal to Vancouver C$400; Vancouver to Winnipeg C$350; Winnipeg to Toronto C$300. If your main destination is somewhere upcountry you can often save money by buying a separate, domestic flight from the nearest major Canadian destination, rather than treating that leg of the journey as part of an international itinerary.

As for **flight times**, flying north/south is reasonably quick: from New York to Montréal takes around 1hr 15min; New York to Toronto 1hr 30min; New York to Halifax 1hr 50min; Chicago to Winnipeg 2hr 10min; LA to Vancouver 2hr 45min; LA to Calgary 3hr. Flying east/west on domestic routes is fairly painless, too: New York–LA or Montréal–Vancouver takes around 5hr. However, flying east/west between countries usually involves a stopover or onward connection, so New York–Vancouver can take 7–8hr.

From the UK and Ireland

Most nonstop scheduled flights **from Britain** to Canada depart from London Heathrow, with some nonstop scheduled departures from airports around Britain supplemented by holiday charter flights. The main gateways are Montréal, Toronto and Vancouver, but there are also nonstop scheduled flights from Britain to Calgary, Edmonton, Ottawa, Halifax and St John's. Connecting flights from these airports delve into every corner of the country.

As an illustration of potential **fares**, a standard return from London to Toronto with Air Canada can cost anywhere between £400 and £1200 (low/high season), and little more to Vancouver. The only way to cut fares substantially is to fly on a charter or with a budget carrier like Zoom and Flyglobespan.com which fly from major UK cities to up to eight Canadian cities for bargain rates: return fares to eastern destinations start at £250, to western cities from about £350. Most airlines also offer good-value "**open-jaw**" deals that enable you to fly into one Canadian city and back from another – useful if you want to make your own way across the country. Remember to check whether there is a high drop-off fee for returning a rental car in a different location from the one where you picked it up (see p.36).

From Ireland, the only daily nonstop flights are in the summer season (mid-April to mid-Oct) with Air Canada from Dublin and Shannon to Toronto, and on FlyGlobespan; on all other flights you will have to change planes, usually either the UK or US. Typical **fares** on nonstop Dublin–Toronto flights (7hr) are around €700. From Dublin or Belfast to Toronto via London with Air Canada costs slightly more, from €750/£450. Flying to Montréal costs much the same, while you can expect to add around €100 if you're flying to Vancouver. It's often possible to save money by flying to London independently – served by budget carriers including Ryanair and EasyJet – and then taking a separate flight from Heathrow to Canada with BA or Air Canada.

From Australia and New Zealand and South Africa

There are no direct flights **from Australia or New Zealand or South Africa** to Canada. However Air Canada, Qantas, United and Air New Zealand have daily connecting flights from all major Australasian cities to Vancouver via Los Angeles or Hawaii. If you're heading to other parts of Canada, the airlines will quote you through-fares via Vancouver to your chosen destination. The most expensive time to fly is during the northern summer (mid-May to end Aug) and over the Christmas period (Dec to mid-Jan); shoulder seasons cover March to mid-May and September, while the rest of the year is low season.

From **Australia** low season Sydney–Vancouver flights start around A$2300; or A$3000 from Perth and Darwin. Expect to pay an extra A$400 to Edmonton or Calgary, or A$600 to Toronto or Montréal. From **New Zealand**, Air NZ/Air Canada (via LA or Hawaii) and both United and American (via LA) provide daily connections to Vancouver (NZ$2700), Edmonton and Calgary (NZ$2900) and Toronto and Montréal (NZ$3300), as well as other major cities in Canada. It's also possible to fly with Qantas (via Sydney and LA) for similar fares. JAL has daily flights from Auckland to Tokyo, with an overnight connection on to LA and Vancouver (NZ$2600). From **South Africa**, South Africa Airways offer services to Toronto and Vancouver via New York or Washington from around R16,000/R24,000 in low/high season for a return ticket. You will probably find it cheaper, though more time consuming, to fly via London on return flights that cost from R800 and then pick up a direct flight from there (see p.34).

Driving

The **US hwy** system leads into Canada at thirteen points along the border. The busiest corridors are from Blaine, WA to White Rock, BC; from Detroit, MI to Windsor, ON; from Buffalo, NY to Fort Erie, ON; and at Niagara Falls. You may encounter traffic jams at the border and long lines, particularly at the weekends, in the summer months and on US or Canadian holidays. For an idea of **journey times**, from New York to Montréal (383 miles) reckon on eight hours' driving; from San Francisco to Vancouver (954 miles), around nineteen hours. For route advice in the US, check with the AAA (Ⓦwww.aaa.com). It has offices in most major cities, but you probably won't find

Fly less – stay longer! Travel and climate change

Climate change is a serious threat to the ecosystems upon which humans rely, and air travel is among the fastest-growing contributors to the problem. Rough Guides regard travel, overall, as a global benefit, and feel strongly that the advantages to developing economies are important, as is the opportunity of greater contact and awareness among peoples. But each of us has a responsibility to limit our personal impact on global warming, and that means giving thought to how often we fly, and what we can do to redress the harm that our trips create.

Flying and climate change

Pretty much every form of motorized travel generates CO_2 – the main cause of human-induced climate change – but planes also generate climate-warming contrails and cirrus clouds and emit oxides of nitrogen, which create ozone (another greenhouse gas) at flight levels. Furthermore, flying simply allows us to travel much further than we otherwise would do. The figures are frightening: one person taking a return flight between Europe and California produces the equivalent impact of 2.5 tonnes of CO_2 – similar to the yearly output of the average car in the UK.

Fuel-cell and other less harmful types of plane may emerge eventually. But until then, there are really just two options for concerned travellers: to reduce the amount we travel by air (take fewer trips – stay for longer!), and to make the trips we do take "climate neutral" via a carbon offset scheme.

Carbon offset schemes

Offset schemes run by Ⓦwww.climatecare.org, Ⓦwww.carbonneutral.com and others allow you to make up for some or all of the greenhouse gases that you are responsible for releasing. To do this, they provide "carbon calculators" for working out the global-warming contribution of a specific flight (or even your entire existence), and then let you contribute an appropriate amount of money to fund offsetting measures. These include rainforest reforestation and initiatives to reduce future energy demand – often run in conjunction with sustainable development schemes.

Rough Guides, together with Lonely Planet and other concerned partners in the travel industry, are supporting a **carbon offset scheme** run by climatecare.org. Please take the time to view our website and see how you can help to make your trip climate neutral.

Ⓦwww.roughguides.com/climatechange

them much help unless you're a member. For more detailed route enquiries within Canada, try the Canadian Automobile Association (Ⓦwww.caa.ca).

At customs you will probably be asked to declare your citizenship, place of residence and proposed length of stay. Vehicle insurance is compulsory and it's also advisable to obtain a yellow Non-Resident Inter-Province Motor Vehicle Liability Card from your insurance company before you go. Make sure you have your driver's licence, documents establishing proof of insurance and proof of vehicle ownership with you at all times while driving in Canada. If you are renting a car in the US you should mention that you intend to travel to Canada, though this is rarely a problem. Fill the car with gas before going, as US prices are still less than those over the border.

Buses

The scope of North America's **Greyhound bus** service is as vast as the continent itself. The network extends into Canada from three points on the East Coast and one each from the West and Midwest; prices below are approximate. Note also that some of the bus passes (see p.38) are valid in both the US and Canada.

Travelling overland from San Diego to Montréal, say, is no problem: it's an epic, three-day journey, but if you're on a tight budget, the US$209 fare may be compelling

– though be sure to factor in three days worth of food and drink. Plus, of course, you get to see a whole lot of country in between. Buses of both Greyhound and Trailways compete on the popular run **from New York** to Montréal, offering half a dozen trips per day. Fares for the eight-hour journey are US$121 return. Most trips **from Boston** to Montréal are made by Greyhound subsidiary Vermont Transit Lines; tickets cost US$73 one-way and the journey takes around seven hours. Other cross-border connections include **from Buffalo** to Toronto (around 8 daily; 2hr 40min; US$16.20 one-way); **from Burlington**, VT, to Montréal (4 daily; 2hr 30min–3hr; US$30 one-way); and **from Seattle** to Vancouver (5 daily; 4hr; US$27 one-way); and **from Fargo, ND**, to Winnipeg (1 daily; 6hr 10min; US$43 one-way). Be sure to arrive at the terminal one hour before departure.

Green Tortoise – the alternative to long-distance bus hell, with its foam cushions, bunks, fridges and rock music – no longer runs a regular service into Canada, but it does still offer a month-long trip from San Francisco north to Alaska, which includes a ferry ride along the Inside Passage and side-trips into the Canadian Rockies (US$1599, plus $351 for food and park entrance).

Trains

For specific journeys, the **train** is usually more expensive than the bus (and often the plane), though special deals, especially in off-peak periods, can bring the round-trip cost down considerably.

Three routes on **Amtrak** from the north-eastern US have direct connections with **VIA Rail**, Canada's national rail company: the "Maple Leaf" from New York to Toronto via Buffalo and Niagara Falls (1 daily; 12hr; US$88/122 one-way in low/high season); and the "Adirondack" from New York to Montréal via Albany and Plattsburgh (1 daily; 9hr 30min; US$59/72 one-way). In the Northwest, the "Mount Baker International" runs from Seattle to Vancouver (1 daily; 4hr; US$28/40 one-way). All these fares are for travel in economy (the cheapest) class, where pillows are provided for overnight journeys.

You should always **reserve** as far as possible in advance, as it is compulsory to have a seat and some of the eastern-seaboard trains in particular get booked up solid. Some rail passes for the US network are also valid as far as a Canadian gateway like Vancouver or Montréal. For more on these, and train travel within Canada, see p.39.

Ferries

There are four US–Canada **ferry** services: three on the West Coast and two on the East. Quite apart from the enjoyment of the ride, the boats can save you hours of driving on some cross-country routes. You should always **book ahead.**

On the **West Coast**, the *Victoria Clipper* catamaran for foot passengers runs between Seattle and Victoria on Vancouver Island, three times daily from mid-May to mid-September and once daily in spring and fall (2hr 45min; US$86 one-way). The most useful West Coast ferry is the Washington State Ferries service from Anacortes to Sidney, on Vancouver Island. The ferry travels twice daily in summer, once in winter via Washington's beautiful San Juan archipelago (average-sized vehicle with driver $42 each way, extra adult passengers $16 each; 3hr). Further north, Alaska Marine Hwy ferries link several Alaskan towns with Prince Rupert.

On the **East Coast**, a car ferry, *The Cat* alternates daily (June to early-Oct) between sailings to Yarmout, NS from Portland, ME (5hrs; US$79/89 in low/high season) or Bar Harbor, ME (3hrs; US$53/63).

Airlines, agents and operators

Online booking

Ⓦ www.airgorilla.com
Ⓦ www.cheapflights.com (US) Ⓦ www.cheapflights.co.uk (UK) Ⓦ www.cheapflights.ca (Canada)
Ⓦ www.cheapflights.com.au (Australia)
Ⓦ www.cheaptickets.com
Ⓦ www.ebookers.com
Ⓦ www.expedia.co.uk (UK) Ⓦ www.expedia.com (US) Ⓦ www.expedia.ca (Canada)
Ⓦ www.flyaow.com
Ⓦ www.hotwire.com
Ⓦ www.lastminute.com (UK)
Ⓦ www.lastminute.com.au (Australia)
Ⓦ www.lastminute.co.nz (New Zealand)

www.opodo.co.uk (UK)
www.orbitz.com (US)
www.site59.com (US)
www.travelocity.co.uk (UK) www.travelocity.com (US) www.travelocity.ca (Canada)
www.zuji.com.au (Australia) www.zuji.co.nz (New Zealand)

Airlines

Air Canada US 1-888/247-2262, UK 0871/220 1111, Ireland 01/679 3958, Australia 1300/655 767, New Zealand 0508/747 767, www.aircanada.com.
Air New Zealand Australia 13/24 76, www.airnz.com.au, New Zealand 0800/737 000, www.airnz.co.nz.
Air North US 1-800/764-0407, Canada 1-800/661-0407, www.flyairnorth.com.
Air Transat Canada 1-877/872-6728, www.airtransat.com.
American Airlines US 1-800/433-7300, UK 0845/7789 789, Republic of Ireland 01/602 0550, Australia 1300/650 747, New Zealand 0800/887 997, www.aa.com.
ATA (American TransAir) 1-800/435-9282, www.ata.com.
bmi US 1-800/788-0555, UK 0870/607 0555 or 0870/607 0222, Ireland 01/407 3036, www.flybmi.com.
British Airways US and Canada 1-800/AIRWAYS, UK 0870/850 9850, Republic of Ireland 1890/626 747, Australia 1300/767 177, New Zealand 09/966 9777, www.ba.com.
Cathay Pacific US 1-800/233-2742, UK 020/8834 8888, Australia 13 17 47, New Zealand 09/379 0861, www.cathaypacific.com.
Continental Airlines US and Canada 1-800/523-0280, UK 0845/607 6760, Republic of Ireland 1890/925 252, Australia 02/9244 2242, New Zealand 09/308 3350, International 1800/231 0856, www.continental.com.
Delta US and Canada 1-800/221-1212, UK 0845/600 0950, Republic of Ireland 1850/882 031 or 01/407 3165, Australia 1300/302 849, New Zealand 09/379 3370, www.delta.com.
easyJet UK 0905/821 0905, www.easyjet.com.
FlyGlobespan UK 08705/561 522, www.flyglobespan.com.
Frontier Airlines 1-800/432-1359, www.flyfrontier.com.
Harmony Airways US 1-866/868-6789, www.hmyairways.com.

JAL (Japan Air Lines) US and Canada 1-800/525-3663, UK 0845/774 7700, Ireland 01/408 3757, Australia 02/9272 1111, New Zealand 09/379 9906, www.jal.com or www.japanair.com.
JetBlue 1-800/538-2583, www.jetblue.com.
Jetsgo 1-866/440-0441, www.jetsgo.net.
KLM (Royal Dutch Airlines) See Northwest/KLM. US 1-800/225-2525, UK 0870/507 4074, Republic of Ireland 1850/747 400, Australia 1300/303 747, New Zealand 09/921 6040, SA 11/961 6767, www.klm.com.
Korean Air US and Canada 1-800/438-5000, UK 0800/413 000, Republic of Ireland 01/799 7990, Australia 02/9262 6000, New Zealand 09/914 2000, www.koreanair.com.
Lufthansa US 1-800/645-3880, Canada 1-800/563-5954, UK 0870/837 7747, Republic of Ireland 01/844 5544, Australia 1300/655 727, SA 0861/842 538, www.lufthansa.com.
Northwest/KLM US 1-800/225-2525, UK 0870/507 4074, Australia 1-300/767-310, www.nwa.com.
Qantas Airways US and Canada 1-800/227-4500, UK 0845/774 7767, Republic of Ireland 01/407 3278, Australia 13 13 13, New Zealand 0800/808 767 or 09/357 8900, SA 11/441 8550, www.qantas.com.

Ryanair UK ⓣ0871/246 0000, Republic of Ireland ⓣ0818/303 030, ⓦwww.ryanair.com.

Singapore Airlines US ⓣ1-800/742-3333, Canada ⓣ1-800/663-3046, UK ⓣ0844/800 2380, Republic of Ireland ⓣ01/671 0722, Australia ⓣ13 10 11, New Zealand ⓣ0800/808 909, SA ⓣ11/880 8560 or 11/880 8566, ⓦwww.singaporeair.com.

South African Airways US and Canada ⓣ1-800-722-9675, UK ⓣ0870/747 1111, Australia ⓣ1800/221 699, New Zealand ⓣ09/977 2237, SA ⓣ11/978 1111, ⓦwww.flysaa.com.

United Airlines US ⓣ1-800/UNITED-1, UK ⓣ0845/844 4777, Australia ⓣ13 17 77, ⓦwww.united.com.

US Airways US and Canada ⓣ1-800/428-4322, UK ⓣ0845/600 3300, Ireland ⓣ1890/925 065, ⓦwww.usair.com.

USA 3000 Airlines US ⓣ1-877/USA-3000, ⓦwww.usa3000airlines.com.

WestJet US and Canada ⓣ1-888/538-5696, UK and Ireland 0800/5381 5696, ⓦwww.westjet.com.

Zoom US and Canada ⓣ1-866/359-9666) UK 0870/240-0055, ⓦwww.flyzoom.com.

Agents and operators

Adventure World Australia ⓣ02/8913 0755, ⓦwww.adventureworld.com.au, New Zealand ⓣ09/524 5118, ⓦwww.adventureworld.co.nz. Agents for a vast array of international adventure travel compaines that operate trips to every continent.

American Holidays Northern Ireland ⓣ028/9031 0000, Republic of Ireland ⓣ01/673 3840, ⓦwww.american-holidays.com. Offers tour packages from Ireland to the US and Canada.

Backroads US ⓣ510/527-1555, ⓦwww.backroads.com. Cycling, hiking and multi-sport tours. Accommodation ranges from campsites to luxury hotels. Also family-friendly options and singles trips.

British Airways Holidays UK ⓣ0870/850 9850, ⓦwww.baholidays.co.uk. Packages and independent itineries for both long trips and short city-breaks.

Canada's Best Canada ⓣ01502/565648, ⓦwww.best-in-travel.com. Canada specialist offering a wide range of holiday options. Deals in cottages, resorts and inns, as well as hotels. Package and tailor-made holidays.

Cosmos US ⓣ1-800/276-1241, ⓦwww.cosmos.com. Planned vacation packages with an independent focus.

ebookers UK ⓣ0800/082-3000, Republic of Ireland ⓣ01/488-3507, ⓦwww.ebookers.com.

Packages and tours

Package holidays to Canada vary from all-inclusive packages combining plane tickets, bus or train travel, hotel accommodation, meals, transfers and sightseeing tours to land-only deals based around a single specialized activity (bird-watching, for instance). Though they may not sound too appealing to independent travellers – they'll rarely save you money, you'll lose lots of flexibility and you'll probably have to stay in nondescript chain hotels – they do allow you to leave all the organizational hassles to someone else. And if you're intent on backcountry adventure, you'll soon find that the exceptional difficulties inherent in getting to many of Canada's wilderness areas often make a package trip the only practical alternative. These **adventure packages** usually include transport in Canada, accommodation, food and a guide – but not flights. Some of the more adventurous carry small groups around on minibuses and use a combination of budget hotels and camping, providing all equipment. These deals are not cheap, however: a typical package of thirteen days' hiking and camping in the Rockies will cost from £650 plus flights. Operators offering a range of Canadian adventure holidays are listed below; we've listed local companies specializing in the more extreme locations – for example, Labrador – in the appropriate section of the Guide.

Even if you intend to travel independently, you should consider the **fly-drive** deals offered by many travel agents and airlines. These offer cut-price car rental to those buying a transatlantic ticket and are nearly always cheaper than renting a car on the spot: a return flight to Vancouver and a fortnight's car rental might cost as little as $1500 per person

Low fares on an extensive selection of scheduled flights and package deals.

Ecosummer Expeditions Canada ⓣ1-800/465-8884 or 250/674-0102, ⓦwww.ecosummer.com. Wilderness expeditions and ecotourism.

Exodus UK ⓣ0208/8675 5550, ⓦwww.exodus.co.uk. Adventure and action-oriented vacation pacakges focused on low-impact tourism.

Explore Holidays Australia ⓣ02/9423 8080, ⓦwww.exploreholidays.com.au. Accommodation and package tours to Canada.

Frontier Ski ⓣ020/8776 8709, ⓦwww.frontier-ski.co.uk. Leading Canadian ski holiday specialist, with trips to the Rockies and Québec.

Gap Adventures Real Traveller US ⓣ1-800/708-7761, UK ⓣ0870/999 0144 ⓦwww.gapadventures.com. Adventure company taking small groups on specialist programmes that include walking, biking, overlanding, adventure and cultural trips.

Go Fishing Worldwide UK ⓣ020/8742 8299, ⓦwww.go-fishingworldwide.co.uk. Fishing trips to Labrador, New Brunswick, Québec, the Yukon, Alberta, BC, Ontario and NWT.

Great Rail Journeys UK ⓣ01904/521905, ⓦwww.greatrailuk.com. Canada coast-to-coast by Train.

Holiday Shoppe New Zealand ⓣ0800/808 480, ⓦwww.holidayshoppe.co.nz. Great deals on flights, hotels and holidays.

Jetsave UK ⓣ0870/162 3502, ⓦwww.jetsave.co.uk. Escorted packages to North America including airfare, accommodation, and guided tours.

Joe Walsh Tours Republic of Ireland ⓣ01/676 0991, ⓦwww.joewalshtours.ie. Long-established general budget fares and holidays agent.

Kuoni Travel ⓣ01306/742 888, ⓦwww.kuoni.co.uk. Major tour operator running long-haul package holidays. Especially good deals for families.

Moose Travel Network ⓣ604/777-9905 or 1-888/816-6673, ⓦwww.moosenetwork.com. Outfit that runs hop-on and hop-off backpacker mini-coach tours in British Columbia, Alberta, Ontario and Québec.

North America Travel Service UK ⓣ0207/499 7299, ⓦwww.northamericatravelservice.co.uk. Various itineraries cater to city-breaks, cruises, spa vacations, guided tours, and more.

North South Travel UK ⓣ01245/608 291, ⓦwww.northsouthtravel.co.uk. Friendly, competitive travel agency, offering discounted fares worldwide. Profits are used to support projects in the developing world, especially the promotion of sustainable tourism.

Peregrine Adventures UK ⓣ0844/736 0170, Australia ⓣ130/0854 444, ⓦwww.peregrine.net.au. Agent for a multitude of adventure companies all over the world, taking small groups on specialist programmes that include walking, biking, overlanding, adventure and cultural trips.

Rod and Reel Adventures ⓣ1-800/356-6982, ⓦwww.rodreeladventures.com. Fishing holidays.

Ski Independence ⓣ0845/310 3030, ⓦwww.ski-independence.co.uk. Wide range of ski packages, mostly to the Rockies.

Ski Safari ⓣ01273/224 060, ⓦwww.skisafari.com. Sixteen Canadian resorts in the Rockies and Québec.

STA Travel US ⓣ1-800/781-4040, Canada ⓣ1-888/427-5639, UK ⓣ0870/1630 026, Australia ⓣ1300/733 035, New Zealand ⓣ0508/782 872, SA ⓣ0861/781 781, ⓦwww.statravel.com. Worldwide specialists in independent travel; also student IDs, travel insurance, car rental, rail passes, and more. Good discounts for students and under-26s.

Titan HiTours UK ⓣ01293/455345, ⓦwww.titantravel.co.uk. Escorted tours, tailor-made itineraries, cruises, and more.

Trailfinders UK ⓣ0845/058 5858, Republic of Ireland ⓣ01/677 7888, Australia ⓣ1300/780 212, ⓦwww.trailfinders.com. One of the best-informed and most efficient agents for independent travellers.

Travel Cuts US ⓣ1-800/592-2887, Canada ⓣ1-888/246-9762, ⓦwww.travelcuts.com. Popular, long-established student-travel organization.

travel.com.au and **travel.co.nz** Australia ⓣ1300/130 482, ⓦwww.travel.com.au, New Zealand ⓣ0800/468 332, ⓦwww.travel.co.nz. Itineraries, accommodation, and car hire, as well as ski trips, adventure travel, and family vacations.
Travelplan Australia ⓣ1300/130 754, ⓦwww.travelplan.com.au. Holidays in the snow worldwide, plus extreme heli-skiing trips.
Travelsphere UK ⓣ0870/240 2426, ⓦwww.travelsphere.co.uk. Wide-range of options includes, among other things, cruises, activity based vacations, and short trips.
TrekAmerica UK ⓣ0870/444-8735, ⓦwww.trekamerica.co.uk. Offers small-group adventure vacations.
Viator ⓦwww.viator.com. Bookings for local tours and sightseeing trips in destinations around the world.
Wildlife Worldwide UK ⓣ0845/130 6982, ⓦwww.wildlifeworldwide.com. Trips for wildlife and wilderness enthusiasts, including whale and polar-bear watching packages.

Rail contacts

Amtrak US ⓣ1-800/USA-RAIL, ⓦwww.amtrak.com.
VIA Rail ⓣ514/871-6000 or 1-888/842-7245 ⓦwww.viarail.ca.

Bus contacts

Green Tortoise US and Canada ⓣ1-800/867-8647, ⓦwww.greentortoise.com.
Greyhound US ⓣ1-800/231-2222, Canada ⓣ416/367-8747, ⓦwww.greyhound.com.
STA Travel US ⓣ1-800/781-4040, Canada ⓣ1-888/427-5639, UK ⓣ0870/1630-026, Australia ⓣ1300/360 960, New Zealand ⓣ0508/782-872, ⓦwww.statravel.com.
Trailways US ⓣ1-800/776-7548, ⓦwww.trailwaysny.com.
Vermont Transit Lines US ⓣ1-800/552-8737, ⓦwww.vermonttransit.com.

Ferry contacts

Victoria Clipper US ⓣ1-800/888-2535 or 206/448-5000, ⓦwww.victoriaclipper.com.
Alaska Marine Hwy US ⓣ1-800/526-6731, ⓦwww.akferry.org.
Washington State Ferries US ⓣ206/464-6400 or 1-800/84-FERRY, ⓦwww.wsdot.wa.gov/ferries/.
The Cat ferry US ⓣ1-888/359-3760, ⓦwww.catferry.com.

Getting around

Except in the cities, getting around Canada by public transport can be a real pain: train services are limited to a light scattering of routes – and VIA Rail, the national carrier, verges on the skeletal – and although buses are much more plentiful, bus stations and stops can be miles from the nearest hotel or campsite. Flying is predictably more expensive, though increasing competition can throw up some decent bargains, but the vast bulk of visitors hire a car and drive. On the other hand, bus and train transport is relatively inexpensive and there are usually discounted fares for seniors, children and sometimes students.

By plane

Canada's **domestic flight network** is immensely complicated with a plethora of airlines flying to an army of destinations. Throughout the *Guide*, we have given details of the most useful services, but the main carrier remains **Air Canada** (ⓣ1-888/247-2262, ⓦwww.aircanada.com), which, along with its several subsidiaries, flies to more than 100 domestic destinations. A battery of fast changing, no-frills airlines offers the main competition but **prices** remain, for the most part, obdurately high: for example, a single fare from Toronto to Winnipeg with Air Canada costs $212–247. One way to cut costs is to buy an Air Canada **airpass**.

These provide internal air travel at special rates and (usually) have to be bought before you fly to Canada. There are endless permutations, but the principle is that you buy a number of coupons, each of which is valid for an internal flight; the larger the area covered by the pass, the more expensive it is; coupons cost from around $200 each.

By car

Travelling by **car** is the best way to see Canada, even though a vehicle can be a bit of a liability in the big cities, with their stringent parking regulations and rush-hour tailbacks. Any US, UK, Australian or New Zealand national over 21 with a full driving licence is allowed to drive in Canada, though rental companies may refuse to rent to a driver who has held a full licence for less than one year, and under-25s will almost invariably get lumbered with a higher insurance premium. Car-rental companies will also expect you to have a credit card; if you don't have one they may refuse to rent to you.

Most of Canada's vehicles – and almost every rental car – run on **unleaded fuel**, which is sold by the litre. Gas stations are plentiful, though they thin out markedly in the more remote regions, where you should fill up where you can.

On the road

Canada has a superb road network and although **multi-lane highways** radiate out from every city, the bulk of the system is comprised of (lightly used) **two-lane highways**. The **Trans-Canada Highway (TCH)** travels from coast to coast and is marked by maple-leaf signs at regular intervals along its length. Different sections of the TCH do, however, carry different hwy numbers and in some places the TCH forks to offer more than one possible routing. Exits on multi-lane hwys are numbered by the kilometre distance from the beginning of the highway, not sequentially – thus exit 55 is 10km after exit 45. This system works fine, but gets a little confusing when junctions are close together and carry the same number supplemented by "A" and "B". In the north and off the beaten track, hwys may be entirely of **gravel** (cracked windscreens are an occupational hazard on some stretches of the Alaska Highway). Note also that after rain gravel and dirt roads are especially treacherous; if you're planning a lot of dirt-road driving, you'd be well advised to rent a four-wheel-drive.

Rural road hazards include bears, moose and other large animals trundling into the road – particularly in the summer, and at dawn and dusk, when the beasts crash through the undergrowth onto the hwy to escape the flies, and in winter, when they want to lick the road salt. Warning signs are posted in the more hazardous areas. Headlights can dazzle wild animals and render them temporarily immobile.

In cities, parking meters are commonplace, charging 25¢–$1 or more per hour. Car parks charge up to $30 a day. If you park in the wrong place (such as within 5m of a fire hydrant) your car will be towed away – if this happens, the police will tell you where your car is impounded and then charge you upwards of $150 to hand it back. A minor parking offence will set you back around $30; wheel-clamps are also routinely used in major cities. When parking, ensure you park in the same direction as the traffic flow.

Rules of the road

Canadians drive on the **right-hand side** of the road. In most urban areas, streets are arranged on a grid system, with traffic lights at most intersections; at **junctions without traffic lights** there will be either yellow triangular "Yield" signs or red octagonal "Stop" signs ("Arrêt" in Québec) at all four corners. In the latter case, priority is given to the first car to arrive, and to the car on the right if two or more cars arrive at the same time. Except in Montréal, you can **turn right on a red light** if there is no traffic approaching from the left. Traffic in both directions must stop if a **yellow school bus** is stationary with its flashing lights on, as this means children are getting on or off. Roundabouts or rotaries are rare.

Driving laws are made at provincial level, but the uniform maximum speed limit is 100kph on major hwys, 80kph on rural hwys and 50kph or less in built-up areas – though there has been some provincial tinkering with the maximum limit on the hwys. Canadians have a justifiable paranoia about **speed traps** and the traffic-control planes that hover over major hwys to catch offenders. On-the-spot fines are standard for speeding violations, for failing to carry your licence with you, and for having anyone on board who isn't wearing a seat belt. Possession of radar detectors is illegal in most of Canada – even if they aren't being used – and can result in confiscation and/or a hefty fine.

Canadian law requires that any **alcohol** be carried unopened in the boot of the car, and it can't be stressed enough that **drunk driving** is a very serious offence. Bars in some provinces now have designated driver schemes whereby the driver of a group gives the keys to the head barperson and is then given free soft drinks all night; if the driver is spotted taking a sip of alcohol, he or she must pay for all the soft drinks consumed and leave their keys in the bar until the following morning. On the road, **spot checks** are frequently carried out, particularly at the entrances and exits to towns, and the police do not need an excuse to stop you. If you are over the alcohol limit your keys and licence will be taken away, and you may well end up in jail.

Renting a car or RV

Oftentimes, the least expensive way to **rent a car** is either to take a fly-drive package or book in advance with a major rental company (see opposite). Competition is fierce and, as you might expect, special deals are more commonplace in the shoulder and low seasons when there are scores of vehicles lying idle. It's a good idea, when you book your intercontinental flight ticket into Canada, to check whether your airline offers discounted car rental for its passengers.

In Canada itself, expect to pay from around $300 a week for a two-door economy saloon in low season to $450 for a four-door medium car in high season, though throughout the year special promotions are offered by the major companies, which can get rates down to as low as $200 per week. Provincial **taxes** and GST or HST (see p.64) are not included in the rates, but the biggest hidden surcharge is often the drop-off charge, levied when you intend to leave your car in a different place from where you picked it up. This is usually equivalent to a full week's or more rental, and can go as high as $500 – so you may need to haggle. Also be sure to double check if **unlimited mileage** is offered – an important consideration in a country where towns are so widely dispersed. The usual free quota, if you don't get unlimited mileage, is 150–200km per day – woefully inadequate if you're contemplating some serious touring – after which an extra charge of around 20¢ per kilometre is standard. You should also check the

Driving distances in kilometres

The figures shown on this chart represent the total distances **in kilometres** between selected cities in the Canada and the US. They are calculated on the shortest

	Calgary	Chicago	Edmonton	Halifax	Montréal	New York	Ottawa
Calgary							
Chicago	2760						
Edmonton	299	2750					
Halifax	4973	2603	5013				
Montréal	3743	1362	3764	1249			
New York	4294	1280	4315	1270	610		
Ottawa	3553	1220	3574	1439	190	772	
Regina	764	2000	785	4225	2979	3534	2789
St John's	6334	3950	6767	1503	2602	2619	2792
Seattle	1204	3200	1352	5828	4585	4478	4334
Toronto	3434	825	3455	1788	539	880	399
Vancouver	977	3808	1164	5970	4921	5382	4531
Whitehorse	2385	4854	2086	7099	5850	6427	5660
Winnipeg	1336	1432	1357	3456	2408	2966	2218
Yellowknife	1828	4240	1524	6537	5268	5800	5098

insurance policy for the excess applied to claims and ensure that, in general terms, it provides adequate levels of financial cover. Additionally, the **Loss Damage Waiver (LDW)**, a form of insurance that isn't included in the initial rental charge, is well worth the expense. At around $15 a day, it can add substantially to the total cost, but without it you're liable for every scratch to the car – even if it wasn't your fault.

A **"recreational vehicle"** or **RV** (a variation on a motor-home) can be rented through most travel agents specializing in Canadian holidays. It's best to arrange rental before getting to Canada, as RV-rental outlets are not too common there, and travel agents at home will often give competitive rates if you book a flight through them as well. You can rent a huge variety of RVs right up to giant mobile homes with two bedrooms, showers and fully fitted kitchens. A price of around $1400 in low season, $2200 in high season, for a five-berth van for one week is fairly typical, and on top of that you have to take into account the **cost of fuel** (some RVs do less than 25km to the litre), drop-off charges, and the cost of spending the night at designated trailer parks, which is what you're expected to do. Canada also has strict regulations on the size of vehicle allowed; in Ontario, for example, the maximum length for a trailer is 48 feet, 75 feet for trailer plus car – so if you are coming in from the US check that your RV isn't over the limit.

International car rental agencies

Alamo US ⓣ1-800/462-5266, ⓦwww.alamo.com.
Avis US and Canada ⓣ1-800/331-1212, UK ⓣ0870/606 0100, Republic of Ireland ⓣ021/428 1111, Australia ⓣ13 63 33 or 02/9353 9000, New Zealand ⓣ09/526 2847 or 0800/655 111, ⓦwww.avis.com.
Budget US ⓣ1-800/527-0700, Canada ⓣ1-800/268-8900, UK ⓣ0870/156 5656, Australia ⓣ1300/362 848, New Zealand ⓣ0800/283 438, ⓦwww.budget.com.
Dollar US ⓣ1-800/800-3665, Canada ⓣ1-800/229 0984, UK ⓣ 0808/234 7524, Republic of Ireland ⓣ1800/575 800, ⓦwww.dollar.com.
Hertz US & Canada ⓣ1-800/654-3131, UK ⓣ020/7026 0077, Republic of Ireland ⓣ01/870 5777, New Zealand ⓣ0800/654 321, ⓦwww.hertz.com.
Holiday Autos UK ⓣ0870/400 4461, Republic of Ireland ⓣ01/872 9366, Australia ⓣ299/394 433, US ⓣ866-392/9288, South Africa ⓣ11/2340 597, ⓦwww.holidayautos.co.uk. Part of the LastMinute .com group.
National US ⓣ1-800/CAR-RENT, UK ⓣ0870/400 4581, Australia ⓣ0870/600 6666, New Zealand ⓣ03/366 5574, ⓦwww.nationalcar.com.
SIXT Republic of Ireland ⓣ1850/206 088, UK ⓣ0800/4747 4227, US ⓣ1-877/347-3227, ⓦwww.irishcarrentals.ie.

available route by road, rather than straight lines drawn on a map. For conversion, the figure **in miles** is roughly two-thirds of that given in kilometres: 8km equals 5 miles.

Regina							
5581	**St John's**						
1963	7200	**Seattle**					
2670	3141	4050	**Toronto**				
1742	7323	230	4412	**Vancouver**			
2871	8452	2796	5528	2697	**Whitehorse**		
571	5010	2548	2099	2152	3524	**Winnipeg**	
2309	7891	2500	4979	2620	1927	2681	**Yellowknife**

Skycars UK ⓣ0870/789 7789, Republic of Ireland ⓣ1-808 4500, ⓦwww.skycars.com.
Thrifty US and Canada ⓣ1-800/847-4389, UK ⓣ01494/751 500, Republic of Ireland ⓣ01/844 1950, Australia ⓣ1300/367 227, New Zealand ⓣ09/256 1405, ⓦwww.thrifty.com.

Driveaways

A variation on car rental is a **driveaway**, where you deliver a car from one place to another on behalf of the owner. The same rules apply as for renting, but you should look the car over before taking it as you'll be lumbered with any repair costs and a large fuel bill if the vehicle's a gas guzzler. Most driveaway companies will want you to give a personal reference as well as a deposit of up to $500. The most common routes are along the Trans-Canada Hwy and between Toronto or Montréal and Florida in the autumn and winter, although there's a fair chance you'll find something that needs shifting more or less to wherever you want to go. You needn't drive flat out, although not a lot of leeway is given – around eight days is the time allowed for driving from Toronto to Vancouver. We've included details of driveaway companies in some city listings, or check under "**Automobile driveaways**" in the phone directory.

By bus

Greyhound **Canada** runs most of the long-distance **buses** west of Toronto, including a service along the Trans-Canada Hwy from Toronto to Vancouver, and is well represented in the east of the country too, though here a network of smaller companies rules the roost (see the *Guide* for details). Long-distance buses run on a fairly full timetable (at least during the day), stopping only for meal breaks and driver changeovers. All are non-smoking, have toilets and coffee-making facilities and are more comfortable than you might expect.

Any sizeable community will have a main **bus station**, but in smaller places a gas station or restaurant will double as the **bus stop and ticket office** – often inconveniently situated on the edge of town. Seats can be **reserved** but this is rarely necessary: only those services between cities in close proximity, like Montréal and Québec City, are likely to get booked out, and even then you'll have to wait only an hour or two for the next departure. Out in the less populated areas, buses are fairly scarce, sometimes only appearing once or twice a week, and here you'll need to plot your route with care. An increasing number

The Moose Travel Network

Aimed at backpackers, the **Moose Travel Network** (eastern office ⓣ416/504-7514 or 1-888/816-6673, western office ⓣ604/777-9905 or 1-888/244-6673, ⓦwww.moosenetwork.com) provides a completely different experience from regular buses. Their mini-coaches (seating 14–24 people) hit the major destinations on the travellers' circuit in both western and eastern Canada (but not the centre) between May and mid-October; there are some additional winter packages, and also links with VIA Rail. Their jump-on, jump-off services stop three days a week in the major cities and interesting smaller towns. You don't need to book your own accommodation, since Moose ensures that a hostel dorm bed is available for every passenger at all major stopovers (if you want to stay elsewhere, you must make your own arrangements). There's no time limit, so you can take as long as you like to complete a circuit, and you get picked up and dropped off at the door of your hostel. There's also no age limit, although most travellers tend to be in the 19–34 age bracket; to match this, there's an array of adventure activities offered as add-ons, including white-water rafting, bungee jumping and sea kayaking.

They have a range of **bus passes** with their two-week West Pass costing around $900, their East Pass $470; the Mega Moose Pass, covering both east and west and lasting for a month, will also run you about $900.

Selected Canadian bus companies

Acadian Lines buses ⓣ1-800/567-5151, ⓦwww.acadianbus.com. The only significant bus company in the Maritime Provinces.

Coach Canada buses ⓣ1-800/461-7661, ⓦwww.coachcanada.com. Assorted services in Ontario and Québec.

DRL Coachlines ⓣ709/263-2171 or 1-888/263-1854, ⓦwww.drlgroup.com. The only long-distance bus company in Newfoundland.

Greyhound Canada ⓣ1-800/661-8747, ⓦwww.greyhound.ca. Long-distance buses in Ontario, Québec and western Canada.

Ontario Northland buses ⓣ1-800/461-8558, ⓦwww.webusit.com. Long-distance bus (and train) services in Ontario.

Saskatchewan Transportation ⓣ1-800/663-7181, ⓦwww.stcbus.com. Services across Saskatchewan.

of services offer "**seat selection**" for a small fee.

Measured by the kilometre, **fares** are pretty standard from company to company: for example, Toronto to Winnipeg, a distance of 2100km, costs $196 one-way ($161/137, 7/14 days in advance), while Montréal to Toronto, a six-and-a-half hour (540km) ride, costs $96 one-way ($65/45, 7/14 days in advance). The free *Official Canadian Bus Guide*, containing all Canadian (and northern US) bus **timetables**, is produced bimonthly but is not made readily available to travellers. Consequently you'll need to rely on free individual timetables from the major bus stations or local tourist offices. Always double-check routes and times by phoning the local terminal (we've included phone numbers for most cities), or the relevant company.

Bus passes

If you're intending to explore Canada by bus, but the **Moose Travel Network** doesn't appeal (see box, opposite), you may be able to save money by buying a **bus pass** before leaving home. The most comprehensive – and popular – bus pass is the **Greyhound Discovery Pass** (ⓣ800/661-8747, ⓦwww.greyhound.ca), covering almost all of Canada and most of the USA. The pass is valid for 7, 15, 30, or 60 days at US$283/415/522/645 respectively. Canadian and US travellers must buy the pass at least 14 days in advance, others at least 21 days ahead.

By train

The railway may have created modern Canada but, following swingeing cuts in the 1990s, **passenger trains** are now few and far between with the national carrier, **VIA Rail** (ⓣ1-888/842-7245, ⓦwww.viarail.ca), effectively reduced to a rump, though at least VIA services between Montréal and Toronto have remained speedy and efficient. That said, VIA Rail does still run several prestige routes through some of Canada's finest scenery, the long, thrice weekly haul between Toronto and Vancouver, the two-day journey from Jasper to Prince Rupert, and the excursion round Québec's Gaspé peninsula being the prime examples. There's always a choice of **ticket** on these flagship routes. The most basic (Comfort class) entitles passengers to a reclining seat and access to a public coffee lounge and dome car, but not much else, whereas top-of-the-rage tickets include meals in the restaurant car, access to comfortable lounges, hot showers and accommodation in either a bunk-bedded sleeper, a "roomette" for one, or a bedroom for two. For more information, check with VIA Rail or consult the incredibly useful, train-buffs' website, ⓦwww.seat61.com. To give an idea of peak-season **fares**, Toronto to Vancouver tickets cost anywhere between $600 and $2000; expect to pay about 25 percent less for off-peak travel.

VIA Rail sells a number of **rail passes**, which can reduce costs considerably. Perhaps the most tempting, though it's only available to non-North American visitors, is the **Canrailpass**

(June to mid-Oct $890; rest of year $530), which allows unlimited travel for twelve days within a thirty-day period at the basic (i.e. Comfort) class. Alternatively, the **North America Rail Pass** (June to mid-Oct $1150, rest of year $815) – buyable by anyone – allows unlimited travel on VIA trains in Canada and Amtrak trains in the US for thirty days.

Several other, smaller companies offer **scenic rail trips**, including **Rocky Mountaineer** trains (Ⓣ1-877/460-3200 or 604/606-7245, Ⓦwww.rockymountaineer.com) from Vancouver to several western destinations, including Jasper, Kamloops, Banff and Calgary; Ontario Northland's **Polar Bear Express** (Ⓣ1-800/461-8558, Ⓦwww.northlander.ca) from Cochrane to Moosonee, with connections on the **Northlander** train from Toronto to Cochrane; **Algoma Central Railway** (Ⓣ705/946-7300 or 1-800/242-9287, Ⓦwww.agawacanyontourtrain.com;) excursions through the Agawa Canyon (see p.215); and **White Pass & Yukon Railroad** trains (Ⓣ1-800/343-7373 or 907/983-2217, Ⓦwww.whitepassrailroad.com) from Fraser to Skagway (see p.1023).

By bike

City cyclists are reasonably well catered for in Canada: most cities have cycling lanes and produce special maps for cyclists, and long-distance buses, ferries and trains will allow you to transport your bike either free or at a minimal charge. An interesting on-going project is the development of a **coast-to-coat cyclepath**, the Trans Canada trail (Ⓦwww.tctrail.ca), sections of which are already ready for cyclists. The Canadian Cycling Association (CCA; Ⓣ613/248-1353, Ⓦwww.canadian-cycling.com) has information on cycling throughout the country and publishes several books, including the invaluable *Complete Guide to Cycling in Canada*. Standard bike-rental costs are around $15 per day, plus a sizeable cash sum or a credit card as deposit; outlets are listed throughout the guide.

Accommodation

Accommodation isn't particularly expensive in Canada, but it's still likely to take up a good portion of your budget. The least expensive options are camping and dormitory beds in hostels, where prices start at around $15, but be aware that campgrounds and hostels in cities are very popular, so beds go fast. In hotels and motels, double rooms start at around $70 – less in rural areas away from the key attractions – though solo travellers pay more, with single rooms costing around 60 to 70 percent of a double.

Canada is big and sparsely populated. If you're heading into remote parts of the country, always check the availability of accommodation before setting off. Places that look large on the map often have few facilities at all, and US visitors will find motels far scarcer than in similar regions back home.

Wherever you intend to stay, it's best to try to **book a room** before you arrive, particularly in summer and especially in big national parks like Banff and major cities such as Montréal, Québec, Toronto and Vancouver. Also look out for local events and festivals such as the Calgary Stampede, when accommodation is always at a premium. If you're arriving late, let the hotel know, as **reservations** are generally held only until 6pm, or even 4pm in major resorts. Wherever possible take advantage of **toll-free numbers**, but note that some are accessible only in restricted areas, typically a single

Accommodation price codes

Throughout this book, **accommodation prices** have been graded with the **codes** below, corresponding to the cost of the least expensive double room in high season. However, with the exception of the budget motels and lowliest hotels, there's rarely such a thing as a set rate for a room. A basic motel in a seaside or mountain resort may double its prices according to the season, while a big-city hotel in Québec or Vancouver that charges $200 per room during the week will often slash its tariff at the weekend when all the business visitors have gone home. The high and low seasons for tourists vary widely across the country, but as a general rule **high season** refers to July and August, **shoulder season** is May, June, September and October, and **low season** refers to the rest of the year.

Local and federal **taxes** (for more on taxes, see p.64) will also add around fifteen percent to quoted rates. Only where we explicitly say so do the room rates we've indicated include local taxes; everywhere else, they exclude taxes.

1 Up to $40
2 $41–60
3 $61–80
4 $81–100
5 $101–125
6 $126–175
7 $176–240
8 over $241

province, or in Canada only; you can usually dial these numbers from abroad, but at standard international rates. It can also be worth confirming check-in/check-out times, particularly in busy areas, where your room may not be available until late afternoon. Check-out times are generally between 11am and 1pm. Be certain to cancel any bookings you can't make, otherwise the hotel or motel may deduct a night's fee using your credit card details. Most places have a 24-hour-notice cancellation policy, but in places like Banff it can be as much as three days.

Local **tourist information offices** will invariably help out with accommodation if you get stuck: most offer free advice and will book a place free of charge, but few are willing to commit themselves to specific recommendations. Before going to Canada, it's worth picking up the full accommodation and camping listings put out by the provinces (see p.65 for website addresses); they all give details of prices, size and facilities.

Hotels

Canadian **hotels** tend to fall into one of two categories: high-class establishments or plain downtown places, often above a bar. Middle-ground spots are thinner on the ground, their role often being filled by motels, which are basically hotels by another name. **Top-of-the-range** hotels can be very grand indeed, for example those run by Canadian Pacific in busy tourist spots like Québec City, Banff, Ottawa and Lake Louise. In the cities, the emphasis is on the business traveller rather than the tourist. Top-notch hotels charge anywhere between $150 and $500, though $250 would get you a fairly luxurious double in most places. It's always worth enquiring about midweek reductions and out-of-season discounts, as these can reduce rates to as low as $100 a night. If you are going to treat yourself, consider whether you want the sort of old-style comfort and building offered by traditional hotels or the high-tech polish provided by an ultra-modern establishment; most cities and some resorts have both types. **Mid-price** hotels are often part of a chain, such as *Holiday Inn* or *Best Western*, and usually offer a touch more comfort than middling motels. You should be able to find a high-season double in such places from around $90; more if you're in a well-known resort or the downtown area of a major city.

Bottom-bracket hotels – those costing anything from $35–55 – are mostly hangovers from the days when liquor laws made it difficult to run a bar without an adjoining restaurant or hotel. Found in most medium- and small-sized towns, they usually have the advantage of being extremely central – often they've been there since the town first sprang to life – but the disadvantage is that the money-generating bars usually come first, with the rooms mostly an afterthought.

Motels

Motels may be called inns, lodges, resorts or motor hotels, but they all amount to much the same thing: driver-friendly, reasonably priced and reliable places on the main hwys almost always on the edge of town. The simplest rooms start at around $50, with the **average price** nearer $65 – though in resorts and more remote areas it's not unusual to find well over $100 being charged for what are fairly basic rooms. As a rule of thumb, prices drop in the larger centres the further you move from downtown. Many offer **off-season rates**, usually between October and April, some have triple- or quadruple-bedded rooms, and most are fairly relaxed about introducing an extra bed into "doubles" for a nominal charge. Many also offer a **Family Plan**, whereby youngsters sharing their parents' room stay free. You may also be able to negotiate cheaper deals if you're staying more than one night, and especially if you're staying a week – many places advertise weekly rates.

Bed and breakfasts

In recent years, there has been a dramatic increase in the number of **B&Bs** – or **Gîtes du Passant** – both in the big cities and in the towns and villages of the more popular resort areas. **Standards** are generally very high, and prices are around $50 and upwards per couple including breakfast. There are no real savings over cheaper hotels and motels, but that said you may wind up with a wonderful – if often over-homely – room in a heritage building in a great location, with the chance to meet Canadians on closer terms.

Hostels

Canada has about eighty **Hostelling International (HI)** hostels and many more nonaffiliated mini-hostels (also known as Homes or **Backpackers' Hostels**), which may or may not figure in HI literature. Reports suggest certain non-affiliated hostels are slipping in standard as their cheap beds are appropriated by long-stay clients rather than by genuine visitors on a budget. Some are downright unsafe, but we've described most of the good ones in this guide.

Youth Hostel associations

US and Canada

Hostelling International American Youth Hostels US ⓣ301/495-1240, ⓦwww.hiayh.org.
Hostelling International Canada ⓣ1-800/663-5777, ⓦwww.hihostels.ca.

UK and Ireland

Hostelling International Northern Ireland ⓣ028/9031 5435, ⓦwww.hini.org.uk.
Irish Youth Hostel Association Republic of Ireland ⓣ01/830 4555, ⓦwww.irelandyha.org.
Scottish Youth Hostel Association ⓣ01786/891 400, ⓦwww.syha.org.uk.
Youth Hostel Association (YHA) England and Wales ⓣ0870/770 8868, ⓦwww.yha.org.uk.

Australia and New Zealand

Australia Youth Hostels Association Australia ⓣ02/9565 1699, ⓦwww.yha.com.au.
Youth Hostelling Association New Zealand ⓣ0800/278 299 or 03/379 9970, ⓦwww.yha.co.nz.

Ys and student accommodation

Both the **YMCA** and **YWCA** – individually abbreviated to "**the Y**" – have establishments in many Canadian cities. In most cases, the quality of accommodation they offer is excellent, matching that of the cheaper hotels, and invariably exceeding that of most other hostel-type lodgings. Often the premises have cheap cafeterias open to all, and sports facilities, gymnasium and pools for the use of guests. **Prices**, however, reflect the facilities with single, double and family units (with or without private bathrooms), ranging between $50 and $120. This still reflects excellent value, especially in cities, where Ys are usually in central downtown locations. As Ys become more like hotels, so you need to treat them as such, with credit-card **reservations** in advance virtually essential to secure private singles and doubles in high summer. Some places keep a number of rooms available each day for walk-in customers, though in

places like Banff it's not unknown for queues for these to develop around the block first thing in the morning. The old demarcation of the **sexes** is also breaking down, though many YWCAs will only accept men if they're in a mixed-sex couple. Some YWCAs accept women with children, others only in emergencies.

In Canada's university cities it's mostly possible to stay in **student accommodation** during the summer vacation. Often the accommodation is adequate and functional, if soulless, and you'll have access to the campus's sports facilities; on the downside, most places are a good distance from city centres. Prices for single and double rooms start from about $35. Most campuses have a special office to handle such accommodation, and it's a good idea to call well ahead to be sure of a room.

Farm vacations

Farm vacations, where you spend time as a paying guest on a working farm, give you the chance to eat well, sleep cheaply – and even work (if you want) – as well as mingle with your hosts. Ontario has a range of farm-based B&Bs with reasonably priced accommodation. In western Canada, it's possible to stay on a ranch and work as a ranch-hand. Due to the isolation of these places prices are usually for full board and include riding (from £75 per day). For further details, consult tourist offices and provincial accommodation guides. One agency in the UK offering ranch holidays is **Farm Tours** (ⓣ01509/618 800, ⓦwww.itiscanada.co.uk).

Camping

Few countries offer as much scope for **camping** as Canada. Many urban areas have a campsite; all national parks and the majority of provincial parks have government-run sites, and in most wilderness areas and in the vast domain of Canada's federally owned Crown Lands you can camp rough more or less where you please, though you should ask permission where possible and – for your own safety and the sake of the environment – adhere strictly to all rules and recommendations that apply to camping in the backcountry. If you're travelling with a tent, check a campsite's small print for the number of **unserviced** (tent) sites, as many places cater chiefly for recreational vehicles (**RVs**), providing them with full or partial hook-ups for water and electricity (or "**serviced sites**"). Anywhere described as an "RV Park" ought to be avoided completely (unless, of course, you have an RV).

During July and August campsites can become as busy as all other types of accommodation in cities, and particularly near mountain, lake or river resorts. Either aim to arrive early in the morning or book ahead; we've given phone numbers wherever this is possible. Generally reservations can only be made with ease at **private campsites**, not – crucially – at national park or provincial park campsites, where access is often, but certainly not always, on a first-come, first-served basis. Finally, check that your chosen site is open: many campsites only open seasonally, usually from May to October.

Types of campsite

At the bottom of the camping pile are **municipal campsites**, usually basic affairs with few facilities, which are either free or cost only a few dollars – typically $5 per tent, $10 per RV. **Private campsites** run the gamut: some are as basic as their municipal cousins, others are like huge outdoor pleasure complexes with shops, restaurants, laundries, swimming pools, tennis courts, even saunas and Jacuzzis. As for **price**, private campsites have several ways of charging. Some charge by the vehicle, others per couple, comparatively few on a tent or per-person basis. Two people sharing a tent might pay anything between $2.50 and $25 each, though an average price would be nearer $15. You can book places in private campsites but there's often no need outside busy areas as most are obliged to keep a certain number of pitches available on a first-come, first-served basis.

Campsites in national and provincial parks are run respectively by Parks Canada and individual provincial governments. All are immaculately turned out and most, in theory, are open only between May and September. In practice most are available all year round, though key facilities are offered and fees collected only in the advertised period: off season you may be expected to leave fees in an "**honesty box**". You'll usually find at least one site serviced for **winter camping** in the bigger national parks, particularly in the Rockies. **Prices** vary from about $10–25 per tent depending on location, services and the time of year – prices may be higher during July and August. See "Outdoor activities", p.51, for more details.

Primitive camping

Though commonplace in all the larger national and provincial parks, camping rough – or **primitive camping** (or backcountry/wilderness camping) as it's known in Canada – has certain rules that must be followed – check locally for regulations. In particular, check that fires are permitted before you start one: in large parts of Canada they aren't allowed in summer because of the risk of forest fire. If they are permitted, use a fire pit (if provided), or a stove in preference to local materials. In wilderness areas, try to camp on previously used sites. Be especially aware of the precautions needed when in **bear** country (see p.704). Where there are no toilets, bury human waste at least 10cm into the ground and 30m from the nearest water supply and campsite. Canadian parks ask for all rubbish to be carried away; elsewhere burn rubbish, and what you can't burn, carry away. **Never drink** from rivers and streams, however clear and inviting they may look. If you have to drink **water** that isn't from taps, you should boil it for at least ten minutes, or cleanse it with an iodine-based purifier (such as Potable Aqua) or a Giardia-rated filter, available from camping or sports shops.

Food and drink

Right across Canada, except in the far north, the sheer number of restaurants, bars, cafés and fast-food joints is staggering, though at first sight there's little to distinguish mainstream Canadian urban cuisine from that of any American metropolis: the shopping malls, main streets and hwys are lined with pan-American food chains, trying to outdo each other with their bargains and special offers.

However, it's easy to leave the chain restaurants behind for more interesting options – increasingly so, as the general standard of **Canadian cuisine** has improved dramatically in the last few years. In the big cities there's a plethora of ethnic and speciality restaurants; on either seaboard the availability of fresh fish and shellfish enlivens many menus, and even out in the country – once the domain of unappetizing diners – there's a liberal supply of first-rate, family-run cafés and restaurants, especially in the more touristy areas. **Non-smokers** may also be relieved to know that by law almost every café and restaurant has a no-smoking policy.

Breakfast

Breakfast is taken very seriously all over Canada, and with prices averaging between $5 and $13 it's often the best-value and most filling meal of the day. Whether you go to a café, coffee shop or hotel snack bar, the breakfast menu, on offer until around 11am, is a fairly standard fry-up: eggs in various guises, ham or bacon (streaky and fried to a crisp), or bland, skinless sausages (except for Nova Scotia's famous Lunenburg sausage, a hot spicy version pioneered by settlers from Europe). Whatever you order, you nearly always receive a dollop of fried potatoes, called **hash browns** or, sometimes, home fries. Other favourite breakfast options include English muffins or, in posher places, bran muffins, a glutinous fruitcake made with bran and sugar, and waffles or pancakes, swamped in butter with lashings of maple syrup. Also, because the breakfast/lunch division is never hard and fast, mountainous meaty sandwiches are common too.

Whatever you eat, you can wash it down with as much **coffee** as you can stomach: for the price of the first cup, the wait staff will – in many places – keep providing free refills until you beg them to stop. The coffee is either regular or decaf and is nearly always freshly ground, though lots of the cheaper places dilute it until it tastes like dishwater. In the big cities, look out also for specialist **coffee shops**, where the range of offerings verges on the bewildering. As a matter of course, coffee comes with cream or half-and-half (half-cream, half-milk) unless you specifically ask for skimmed milk. **Tea**, with either lemon or milk, is also drunk at breakfast, and the swisher places emphasize the English connection by using imported brands – or at least brands that sound English.

Lunch and snacks

Between about 11.30am and 2.30pm, many big-city restaurants offer special **set menus** that are generally excellent value. In Chinese and Vietnamese establishments, for example, you'll frequently find rice and noodles, or dim sum feasts for $8–12, and many Japanese restaurants give you a chance to eat sushi very reasonably for under $20. Pizza is also widely available, from larger chains like *Pizza Hut* to family-owned restaurants and pavement stalls. Favourites with white-collar workers are café-restaurants featuring wholefoods and vegetarian fare, though few are nutritionally dogmatic, serving traditional meat dishes and sandwiches too; most have an excellent selection of daily lunch specials for around $12.

For quick **snacks**, many **delis** do ready-cooked food, including a staggering range of sandwiches and filled bagels. Alternatively, shopping malls sometimes have ethnic fast-food stalls, a healthier option (just about) than the inevitable burger chains, whose homogenized products have colonized every main street in the land. Regional snacks include fish and chips, especially in Newfoundland; Québec's traditional thick, yellow pea soup, smoked meat sandwiches and poutine, fries covered in melted mozzarella cheese or cheese curds and gravy; and the Maritimes' ubiquitous clam chowder, a creamy shellfish and potato soup.

Some **city bars** are used as much by diners as drinkers, who turn up in droves to gorge themselves on the free hors d'oeuvres laid out between 5pm and 7pm from Monday to Friday in an attempt to grab commuters. For the price of a drink you can stuff yourself with pasta and chilli. **Brunch** is another deal worth looking out for; a cross between breakfast and lunch served up in bars (and elsewhere) at the weekend from around 11am–2pm. For a set price ($10 and up) you get a light meal and a variety of complimentary cocktails or wine.

Regional dishes

Largely swamped by the more fashionable regional European and ethnic cuisines, **traditional Canadian cooking** relies mainly on local game and fish, with less emphasis on vegetables and salads. In terms of price, meals for two without wine average between $25 and $50.

Newfoundland's staple food is the cod, usually in the form of fish and chips, supplemented by salmon, halibut and hake and more bizarre dishes like cod tongues and cheeks, scruncheons (fried cubes of pork fat), smoked or pickled caplin and seal flipper pie. The island's restaurants are not usually permitted to sell moose or seal meat, but many islanders join in the annual licensed shoot and, if you befriend a hunter, you may end up across the table from a hunk of either animal.

In the **Maritimes**, lobster is popular everywhere, whether it's boiled or broiled, chopped up or whole, as are oysters, clams, scallops and herrings either on their own or in a fish stew or clam chowder. Nova Scotia is famous for its blueberries, Solomon Gundy (marinated herring), Annapolis Valley apple pie, fat archies (a Cape Breton molasses cookie) and rappie pie (an Acadian dish of meat or fish and potatoes). New Brunswick is known for its fiddleheads (fern shoots) and dulse (edible seaweed).

Fish is **Ontario**'s most distinctive offering, though the pollution of the Great Lakes has badly affected the freshwater catch. Try the whitefish, lake trout, pike and smelt, but bear in mind that these are easier to come by in the north of the province than in the south. Pork forms a major part of the **Québec** diet, both as a spicy pork pâté known as *creton*, and in *tourtière*, a minced pork pie. There are also splendid thick pea and cabbage soups, beef pies (*cipâte*), and all sorts of ways to soak up maple syrup – *trempette* is bread drenched with it and topped with fresh cream. And, of course, Québec is renowned for its outstanding French-style cuisine.

Northern Saskatchewan and **Manitoba** are the places to try fish like the goldeye, pickerel and Arctic char, as well as pemmican (a mixture of dried meat, berries and fat) and fruit pies containing the Saskatoon berry. The **Arctic** regions feature caribou steak, and **Alberta** is also noted for its prime beef steaks. **British Columbia** features Pacific fish and shellfish of many different types, from cod, haddock and salmon to king crab, oysters and shrimp. Here and there, there's also the odd **native peoples**' restaurant,

Tipping

Almost everywhere you eat or drink, the service will be fast and friendly – thanks to the institution of **tipping**. Waiters and bartenders depend on tips for the bulk of their earnings and, unless the service is dreadful, you should top up your bill by fifteen percent or more. A refusal to tip is considered rude and mean in equal measure. If you're paying by credit card, there's a space on the payment slip where you can add the appropriate gratuity.

most conspicuously at the Wanuskewin Heritage Park in Saskatoon, Saskatchewan, where the restaurant serves venison, buffalo and black-husked wild rice.

Although there are exceptions, like the Ukrainian establishments spread across central Manitoba, the bulk of Canada's **ethnic restaurants** are confined to the cities. Here, amongst dozens of others, Japanese restaurants are fashionable and fairly expensive; Italian food is popular and generally cheap, providing you stick to pizzas and basic pasta dishes; and there's the occasional Indian restaurant, mostly catering for the inexpensive end of the market. East European food is a good, filling standby, especially in central Canada, and cheap Chinese restaurants are common throughout the country. French food, of course, is widely available – though, except in Québec, it's nearly always expensive.

Drinking

Canadian **bars**, like their American equivalents, are mostly long and dimly lit counters with a few customers perched on stools gawping at the bartender, and the rest of the clientele occupying the surrounding tables and booths. Yet, despite the similarity of layout, bars vary enormously, from the male-dominated, rough-edged drinking holes concentrated in the blue-collar parts of the cities and the resource (mostly mining and oil) towns of the north, to more fashionable city establishments that provide food, live entertainment and an inspiring range of cocktails. Indeed, it's often impossible to separate restaurants from bars – drinking and eating are no longer the separate activities they mostly were up until the 1960s.

The **legal drinking age** is 18 in Alberta, Manitoba, Saskatchewan, Québec, Northwest Territories, Nunavut and the Yukon, and 19 in the rest of the country, though it's rare for anyone to have to show ID, except at the government-run liquor stores (closed Sun), which exercise a virtual monopoly on the sale of alcoholic beverages of all kinds direct to the public; the main exception is Québec, where beer and wine are sold at retail grocery stores.

Beer, wine and spirits

By and large, Canadian **beers** are unremarkable, designed to quench your thirst rather than satisfy your palate. Everywhere they're served ice-cold, and light, fizzy concoctions rule the roost. The two largest Canadian brewers, **Molson** and (Belgian-owned) **Labatts**, market a remarkably similar brew under all sorts of names – Molson Canadian, Molson Export, Labatts Blue – that inspire, for reasons that elude most foreigners, intense loyalty. The slightly tastier brews of **Great Western Brewing**, the country's third largest brewer, are produced in Saskatoon, Saskatchewan, while the heavily marketed **Moosehead** beer is, despite its Arctic image, produced in Saint John, New Brunswick. There's also a niche market for foreign beers, although Heineken, the most popular, is made under licence in Canada; American beers like Budweiser and Coors are common, too. A welcome trend is the proliferation of independent small breweries, or microbreweries, whose products are sold in a pub on the premises, but as yet these remain pretty much confined to the bigger cities.

Drinking bottled beer in a bar works out a good deal more **expensive** than the draught, which is usually served by the 170ml glass; even cheaper is a **pitcher**, which contains six or seven glasses.

Once something of a joke, **Canadian wines** are fast developing an excellent reputation, particularly those from Ontario's Niagara-on-the-Lake region, which are subject to the stringent quality control of the Vintners Quality Alliance, the VQA. However, if you don't want to experiment, imported wines from a wide range of countries are readily available and not too pricey.

Copying its giant neighbour, Canada excels with its **spirits**. Even a fairly undistinguished bar will have a startling arrays of gins and vodkas, and usually a good selection of rums. In the more traditional places, the most popular liquor is **whiskey** – either Scottish and Irish imports or the domestically made Canadian Club and VO rye whiskey. In the smarter places you can experiment with all sorts of **cocktails**, costing anywhere between $4 and $13.

The media

Canada's only truly national daily newspapers are the tabloid *National Post* and the outstanding *Globe and Mail*, whose coverage of domestic politics and contemporary issues is second to none. In addition, every major city has at least one daily newspaper focused on local and/or regional issues, and standards are generally high – the *Toronto Star* and *Ottawa Citizen* being two cases in point. In Québec, the French-language *La Presse* is the most widely read newspaper, and there's also the intellectual (and separatist) *Le Devoir*.

Most of Canada's major cities also have **free weekly listings papers**, often with news and features with an alternative slant. The conservative *Maclean's* and *Time Canada* are the most popular weekly news magazines. The monthly *Canadian Geographic* covers the great outdoors through articles and high-quality photographs.

The Canadian Broadcasting Corporation (CBC), with national and regional **TV** broadcasts, has prime place amongst Canadian programmers. The main commercial station is the Canadian Television Corporation (**CTV**), a mix of Canadian, American and regional output. There are many other public-broadcasting channels and private broadcast companies, whose output makes Canada's TV very similar to mainstream American TV. Most US stations can also be picked up in every part of Canada.

The majority of Canadian **radio stations** stick to a bland commercial format. Most are on the **AM** band and display little originality – though they can be good sources of local nightlife and entertainment news, and road and weather reports. On **FM**, on the other hand, the state-subsidised CBC channels provide diverse, listenable and well-informed programmes. Although some of the large cities boast good specialist **music stations**, for most of the time you'll probably have to resort to skipping up and down the frequencies. Driving through rural areas can be frustrating, as for hundreds of kilometres you might only be able to receive one or two very dull stations.

Festivals

The Canadians like their festivals and every province chips in with its share, from pageants and parades celebrating local events and patterns of settlement (Scots, Irish and so forth), through to more prestigious theatrical seasons and film festivals. For further details of the festivals listed below, including more precise dates, see the relevant account in the Guide. The provincial tourist offices listed on p.65 can provide free festival and events calendars for each region.

January

Polar Bear Swim Vancouver, BC. A New Year's Day swim in the freezing waters of English Bay Beach – said to bring good luck for the year (if you survive).

Banff/Lake Louise Winter Festival Banff and Lake Louise, AB. Ski races, skating parties and the incredible International Ice Sculpture Competition on the shores of Lake Louise.

February

Winterlude Ottawa, ON. Winter-warming activities like ice sculpting, snowshoe races, ice boating and skating for all on the canal.
Winter Carnival Québec City, QC. Eleven-day festival of winter-sports competitions, ice-sculpture contests and parades. Includes the Canadian ski marathon when skiers race between Lachute and Gatineau.
Montréal Highlights Festival Montréal, QC. Festival that, like Québec City's, tries to make the most of winter with a multitude of shows and food events.

March

Pacific Rim Whale Festival Vancouver Island, BC. Celebrating the spring migration of grey whales with lots of whale-spotting expeditions as well as music and dance events.

April

TerrifVic Jazz Party Victoria, BC. Dixieland, and other jazz bands, from around the globe.
Shaw Festival Niagara-on-the-Lake, ON. Highly regarded theatre festival featuring the work of George Bernard Shaw and his contemporaries. Performances from April to late October.

May

Apple Blossom Festival Annapolis Valley, NS. Community-oriented festival held in the small towns and villages of this apple-producing valley in Nova Scotia.
Stratford Festival Stratford, ON. The small town of Stratford is well known for its first-class Shakespeare Festival. Runs from May to early November.
Canadian Tulip Festival Ottawa, ON. Three million tulips in a riot of colour all over the city.

June

Jazz City International Festival Edmonton, AB. Ten days of jazz concerts, free outdoor events and workshops.
Banff Festival of the Arts Banff, AB. Young-artist showcase: music, opera, dance, drama, comedy and visual arts.
International Blues Festival Halifax, NS. Big musical event showcasing the best of US and Maritime blues.
International Jazz Festival Montréal, QC. Some 2000 jazz acts, including the world's top names; 75 percent of the performances are free.

July

Canada Day Ottawa, ON, and nationwide. Fireworks, parades and a day off for patriotic shenanigans.
Pow-wows Nationwide. Traditional native Canadian celebrations that take place on reserves across the country in July and August.
Calgary Stampede Calgary, AB. One of the biggest rodeos in the world: all the usual cowboy trappings, plus hot-air-balloon races, chuck-wagon rides, craft exhibitions, native dancing and a host of other happenings. Billed as the "Greatest Outdoor Show on Earth".
Klondike Days Edmonton, AB. Pioneer era in Edmonton revisited with gold panning, raft races, pancake breakfasts and gambling.
Loyalist City Festival Saint John, NB. Celebration of the city's loyalist heritage with parades in period costume.
Antigonish Highland Games Antigonish, NS. All sorts of traditional Scottish sports and activities recall the settlement of the area by Highlanders.
Atlantic Jazz Festival Halifax, NS. First-class jazz festival pulling in big names from round the world.
Caribana Festival Toronto, ON. Large-scale West Indian carnival with music, dance and a flamboyant parade.
Festival d'Été Québec City, QC. Arts performances, live bands and other shows on and off the streets and parks of Québec City.
Juste Pour Rire Montréal, QC. The funniest festival in Canada. Internationally acclaimed comic get-together with comedians from around the world performing in theatres and outdoor stages.
Gay Pride Toronto, ON and Montréal, QC. Gigantic celebration of gay culture. With huge parades and street parties that attract between half and a million spectators.

August

Fringe Theatre Festival Edmonton, AB. One of North America's most prestigious alternative-theatre festivals.
Squamish Days Loggers Sports Festival Squamish, BC. The continent's biggest lumberjacks' convention with impressive logging competitions.
Acadian Festival Caraquet, NB. Celebration of Acadian culture in the northeast of New Brunswick.
Miramichi Folk Song Festival Newcastle, NB. New Brunswick's prestigious folk festival, featuring many of the finest fiddlers in the Maritimes.

Nova Scotia Gaelic Mod South Gut, St Ann's, NS. Seven-day Scottish heritage knees-up with all traditional sports, crafts and contests featured. One of the biggest and best of many similar events in Nova Scotia.
World Film Festival Montréal, QC. Eclipsed by Toronto's film festival, but still a good showcase for new movies.

September

Toronto International Film Festival Toronto, ON. Internationally acclaimed film festival spread over ten days, inundated with Hollywood stars.

October

Vancouver International Film Festival Vancouver, BC. Another of Canada's highly rated film fests.
Okanagan Wine Festival Okanagan, BC. One of the many wine events in this vine-growing region.
Oktoberfest Kitchener-Waterloo, ON. Alcohol and cultural events in honour of the twin towns' roots.
Black and Blue Montréal, QC. Major gay arts festival in Montréal.

November

Canadian Finals Rodeo Edmonton, AB. Pure Canuck rodeo.

December

Carol Ships Vancouver, BC. When carol singers sail around Vancouver harbour in sparkly boats.
New Year's Eve Nationwide, but celebrated in style in St John's, Newfoundland, where everyone heads from the pub to the waterfront for a raucous midnight party.

Outdoor activities

Canada's mountains, lakes, rivers and forests offer the opportunity to indulge in a vast range of outdoor pursuits. We've concentrated on hiking, skiing and canoeing – three of Canada's most popular activities – and on the national parks, which have been established to preserve and make accessible the best of the Canadian landscape.

Other popular activities such as whale-watching, horse riding, fishing and rafting are covered in some detail in the main text but, whatever activity interests you, be certain to check the website of the **provincial tourist office** (see p.65) before you go. Once in Canada you can rely on finding outfitters, equipment rental, charters, tours and guides to help you in most areas; tourist offices invariably carry full details or contact numbers. Also make a point of visiting Canadian bookshops: most have a separate outdoor pursuits section with a wide variety of specialist guides.

The national parks

Canada's twenty-seven **national parks** are administered by Parks Canada (ⓦwww.pc.gc.ca), and local staff based at **park information centres**. Visit these to pick up special **permits** if you intend to fish or camp in the backcountry, and for information and audiovisual displays on flora, fauna and outdoor activities. Many offer talks and nature walks presented by park naturalists, as well as reports on snow, weather and recent bear sightings. The national parks system also administers seventy-eight **National Historic Sites** – small important historical sites dotted around the country.

Supplementing the national parks is a network of **provincial parks** dotted around every province in the country. Entry to these parks is sometimes free, though often you'll have to pay a small fee of around \$5 for three days use; and pay for fishing and hunting permits as well as campsites on top of this; specifics vary from province to province.

For up-to-the-minute **information** on the **national park system**, access the official Parks Canada website at ⓦwww.pc.gc.ca. It features full details of the main attractions of the national parks, plus opening hours, the best times to visit, admission fees, hiking trails, and visitor facilities.

National park permits

All those entering Canada's national sites and parks require a **park permit**, regardless of their mode of transport, though permits are most commonly sold to cover all those entering in a particular vehicle and from a roadside booth on the park boundary. This costs around $5 to $15 per person per day with the concessions for the young and old. If you intend to visit a number of national parks and sites, it might be worth investing in either an annual national pass. An annual pass will provide one adult admission to all parks for $62.40; and to all parks and monuments – called the "Discovery Package" for $77.25; family or group passes, covering a whole car-load of people, cost around double.

Additional permits are also required to fish (see p.54) and backcountry camp (see below) in national parks: both types of pass are generally available from park information centers.

Camping and backpacking

While hotel-style **lodges** are found only in major parks, every park or monument tends to have at least one well-organized **campground** for visitors. Often, a cluster of motels can be found not far outside the park boundaries. With appropriate free permits – subject to some restrictions in popular parks – backpackers can also usually camp in the backcountry (a general term for areas inaccessible by road). Most parks have large, well-run campsites close to the park's main settlement; some for tents or RVs only, others mixed. Fees depend on facilities, and currently run from $7 per tent or per vehicle for semi-primitive sites (with wood, water and pit toilets) up to about $30 for those with electricity, sewage, water and showers. Some park campsites have also introduced another fee (around $3) for use of firewood.

Most parks also have basic **backcountry sites** usually providing only fire pits and firewood. Regulations vary enormously. Some parks allow backcountry camping only in tightly defined sites; others have a special primitive wildland zone where you can pitch a tent within a designated distance of the nearest road or trailhead. Simply ask at park centres or tourist offices for the latest local details. Whether you want to use a backcountry campsite or camp rough in parks, however, the one thing you must do is obtain an overnight permit from the park centre (either free or just a few dollars). When you pick up the permit, but sure to ask about weather conditions and specific local tips. Check whether fires are permitted; even if they are, try to use a camp stove in preference to local materials. In wilderness areas, try to camp on previously used sites. Where there are no toilets, bury human waste at least six inches into the ground and a hundred feet from the nearest water supply and campground.

Hiking

Canada boasts some of North America's finest **hiking**, and whatever your ability or ambition you'll find a walk to suit almost anywhere in the country. All the national and many provincial parks have well-marked and well-maintained trails, and a visit to any park centre or local tourist office will furnish you with adequate **maps** of the usually very well-marked local paths. If you're venturing into the backcountry, though, try to obtain the appropriate 1:50,000 sheet from the Canadian Topographical Series. For key hiking areas we've given a brief summary of the best trails in the appropriate parts of the guide, though with over 1500km of paths in Banff National Park alone, these recommendations only scratch the surface of what's on offer. Park staff can advise on other good walks, and detailed trail guides are widely available for most popular regions.

Before setting off on anything more than a short stroll consider what preparations you should be making. Be properly informed of local conditions but also be **properly equipped** if you're walking in high or rough country: good boots, waterproof jacket and spare warm clothing. For day-long hikes or overnight trips be sure to carry sufficient food and drink – or water purification equipment – to cover emergencies, as well as all the necessary equipment and maps. Hiking at lower elevations should present few problems, though swarms of **mosquitoes** near water can drive you crazy; Avon Skin-so-soft, or anything containing DEET, are fairly reliable repellents. For more on specific health problems, see p.58.

All this equipment and further, more locally specific information can be picked up at Canada's many outdoor stores; one of the best national chains is the **Mountain Equipment Co-op** (Ⓦwww.mec.ca) which has outlets in all the major towns and offers a large range of rental equipment.

Main hiking areas

The most extensive and rewarding hiking trail networks are in the **Rockies national parks** of Alberta and British Columbia. Thousands of kilometres of well-kept and well-tramped paths crisscross the four main parks – Banff, Jasper, Yoho and Kootenay – as well as the smaller enclaves of Glacier, Revelstoke and Waterton lakes. Scope for hiking of all descriptions is almost limitless.

More modest areas dotted all over **British Columbia** boast walking possibilities out of all proportion to their size: we pay less attention to these, but by most relative standards hiking here is still among the best in North America. All the following provincial parks offer a variety of day-hikes, short strolls and longer trails that could keep you happy for a week or more: Wells Gray, north of Kamloops; Kokanee Glacier, near Nelson; Manning, east of Vancouver; Garibaldi, north of Vancouver; and Strathcona, on Vancouver Island.

In **Manitoba**, the Riding Mountain National Park offers about thirty hiking trails, but though there's plenty of upland walking to be had in the so-called prairie provinces, you have to move east to **Québec**'s Mauricie, Forillon and Gatineau parks for a taste of mountains comparable to the western provinces. In **Ontario**, Lake Superior Provincial Park and the Algonquin Park are the most challenging terrains. **New Brunswick**'s Fundy National Park offers coastal walks, while **Newfoundland**'s hiking centres on its two national parks: Terra Nova on the east coast, and the high plateau and fjords of the west coast's Gros Morne. For the truly bold, however, nothing can match the **Arctic** extremes of Baffin Island, whose principal trail lies over an icecap that never melts.

Long-distance footpaths

In areas with highly developed trail networks, seasoned backpackers can blaze their own **long-distance footpaths** by stringing together several longer trails. Recognized long-haul paths, however, are relatively rare, though more are being designated yearly. One of the best is the Chilkoot Trail from Dyea in Alaska to Bennett in British Columbia, a 53-kilometre hike that closely follows the path of prospectors en route to the Yukon during the 1898 gold rush (see p.1038). The most popular is probably Vancouver Island's demanding West Coast Trail, which runs for 80km along the edge of the Pacific Rim National Park (see p.909).

Bears

Make no mistake, **bears** are potentially very dangerous and most people blow a whistle while walking in bear country to warn them off. If confronted don't run, make loud noises or sudden movements, all of which are likely to provoke an attack. Leave the animal an escape route and back off slowly. If you have a backpack, leave it as a distraction. If attacked, climbing a tree or playing dead may save you from a grizzly, but not from black bears. Fighting back only increases the ferocity of an attack. For more on bears, see p.704.

More far-reaching walks include the Rideau Trail, which follows paths and minor roads for 386km from Kingston to Ottawa; the 690-kilometre Bruce Trail from Queenston, on the Niagara River, to Tobermory on the Bruce Peninsula; and the Voyageur Trail along the north shores of lakes Superior and Huron, which is the longest and most rugged route in the province.

Skiing

Wherever there's good hiking in Canada, there's also usually **skiing**. The increasingly popular resorts of the Rockies and British Columbia are the main areas and the country's leading resorts are at Whistler, Banff and Lake Louise. But there's also great skiing in Québec, and a few good runs at the minor day resorts that dot the other provinces too. Most cities are also close to excellent cross-country trail networks.

Canadian ski packages are available from travel agents worldwide, but it's perfectly feasible to organize your own trips, as long as you book well ahead if you're hoping to stay in some of the better-known resorts. **Costs** for food, accommodation and ski passes are still fairly modest by US and European standards: expect to pay $30–60 per day (depending on the quality and popularity of the resort) for lift tickets, plus another $30 or more per day to rent equipment.

Fishing

Canada is **fishing** nirvana. While each region has its specialities, from the Arctic char of the Northwest Territories to the Pacific salmon of British Columbia, excellent fishing can be found in most of the country's super-abundant lakes, rivers and coastal waters. Most towns have a fishing shop for equipment, and any spot with fishing possibilities is likely to have companies running boats and charters. As with every other major type of outdoor activity, most provinces publish detailed booklets on everything that swims within the area of their jurisdiction.

Fishing is governed by a range of **regulations** that vary between provinces and are usually baffling at first glance; but usually boil down to the need for a nonresident permit for freshwater fishing, and another for saltwater fishing. These are obtainable from most local fishing or sports shops for about $35 and are valid for a year. Short-term (one- or six-day) licences are also available in some provinces. In a few places you may have to pay for extra licences to go after particular fish. Additional permits are required to fish in national parks. Available from park administration centres, these cost around $20 annually, $11 weekly or $7 daily. There may well be quotas on the types and numbers of fish you can catch, which you can find out when you buy a permit.

Canoeing

Opportunities for **canoeing** are limited only by problems of access and expertise: some of the rapids and portages on the country's more challenging routes are for real pros only. The most straightforward regions to canoe are in **Ontario**, with its estimated 250,000 lakes and 35,000km of waterways, some 25,000km of which have been documented as practical canoe routes. The key areas are the Algonquin, Killarney and Quetico provincial parks, though the single most popular run is the 190-kilometre Rideau Canal, a tame run from Kingston to Ottawa.

The rivers of **British Columbia** offer generally more demanding white-water routes, though the lake canoeing – in the Wells Gray Provincial Park, for example – is among the country's most beautiful. One of the province's other recognized classics is the 120-kilometre trip near Barkerville on the Cariboo River and the lakes of the Bowron Lakes Provincial Park. More challenging still are the immense backcountry lakes and rivers of the Mackenzie system and the barren lands of the **Northwest Territories**, where you can find one of the continent's ultimate river challenges – the 300-kilometre stretch of the South Nahanni River near Fort Simpson. Growing in popularity, partly because of improved road access, are trips on and around the **Yukon** River system, particularly the South Macmillan River east of Pelly Crossing. Other areas that will test the resources of any canoeist are to be found in **Manitoba** and **Labrador** – all detailed in this guide.

Once you've decided on an area, provincial tourist offices can provide full lists of

outfitters (see p.65). These will rent out equipment, organize boat and plane drop-offs, and arrange provisions for longer trips. Typical **costs** are in the region of $90 for weekly canoe rental, $30 per day for a wetsuit. Most also supply maps. Specialist canoe guides are also widely available in Canadian bookshops, many giving extremely detailed accounts of particular river systems or regions.

Spectator sports

Canadians are sports-mad: ice hockey, baseball and Canadian football matches are all extremely popular – both professional games and intercollegiate competitions, the intensity of whose rivalries are notorious. Lacrosse is the "official" national sport, but ice hockey the real national obsession. Dropping in on a game can give visitors an unforgettable insight into a city and its people. Major-league professional teams almost always put on the most spectacular shows, but games between minor-league teams, college rivals, and even high-school games provide an easy and enjoyable way to get on intimate terms with a place.

Ice hockey

With players hurtling around at nearly 50kph and the puck clocking speeds of over 160kph, **ice hockey** would be a high-adrenaline sport even without its relaxed attitude to combat on the rink (as an old Canadian adage has it: "I went to see a fight and an ice-hockey game broke out"). The North American National Hockey League, or NHL (ⓦwww.nhl.com), consists of thirty teams, of which six are from Canada. Each team plays over eighty games a season, which lasts from October to May. **Ticket prices** start at around $30 for ordinary games and nearly always need to be bought in advance.

Other than the NHL there are also numerous **minor league clubs**. Ontario and Québec both have their own minor leagues; the rest of the country plays in the Western League, all with play-offs for a variety of awards. For college hockey, the University of Toronto and York in Toronto, Concordia in Montréal, St Mary's in Halifax and the University of Alberta in Edmonton all have good teams.

Canadian football

Professional **Canadian football** (similar to the American variety) – played under the aegis of the Canadian Football League, or **CFL** (ⓦwww.cfl.ca) – is largely overshadowed by the National Football League in the US, chiefly because the best home-grown talent moves south in search of better money while NFL castoffs move north to fill the ranks. The two countries' football games vary slightly, but what differences do exist tend to make the Canadian version faster-paced, higher-scoring and more exciting. The season lasts from June to November, each team playing a match a week. The playoffs at the end of the season culminate with the hotly contested Grey Cup. **Tickets** are fairly easy to come by and start at around $30.

Baseball

Baseball, with its relaxed summertime pace and byzantine rules, is generally considered an exclusively American sport – despite the first recorded game taking place in Beachville, Ontario. The Toronto Blue Jays are the only Canadian team to play in the major **North American baseball league** (ⓦwww.mlb.com) and even if you don't understand the rules, visiting a game can be a pleasant day out, drinking beer and eating burgers

Canada's major-league professional sports teams

Specific details for the most important teams in all the sports are given in the various city accounts. They can also be found through the major league websites:

Ice Hockey – NHL
Calgary Flames ⓣ403/777-2177, ⓦwww.calgaryflames.com.
Edmonton Oilers ⓣ780/414-4000, ⓦwww.edmontonoilers.com.
Montréal Canadiens ⓣ514/790-1245, ⓦwww.canadiens.com.
Ottawa Senators ⓣ613/599-0250, ⓦwww.ottawasenators.com.
Toronto Maple Leafs ⓣ416/815-5500, ⓦwww.torontomapleleafs.com.
Vancouver Canucks ⓣ604/899-4600, ⓦwww.canucks.com.

Canadian Football – CFL
BC Lions ⓣ604/589-ROAR, ⓦwww.bclions.com.
Calgary Stampeders ⓣ403/289-0258, ⓦwww.stampeders.com.
Edmonton Eskimos ⓣ403/448-1525, ⓦwww.esks.com.
Hamilton Tiger Cats ⓣ905/547-2287, ⓦwww.tigercats.on.ca.
Montréal Alouettes ⓣ514/871-2255, ⓦwww.montrealalouettes.com.
Saskatchewan Roughriders t306/569-2323, ⓦwww.saskriders.com.
Toronto Argonauts ⓣ416/341-2700, ⓦwww.argonauts.on.ca.
Winnipeg Blue Bombers t204/784-2583, ⓦwww.bluebombers.com.

Baseball – MLB
Toronto Blue Jays ⓣ416/341-1000 ⓦwww.bluejays.ca.

Basketball – NBA
Toronto Raptors ⓣ416/366-DUNK, ⓦwww.nba.com/raptors.

and popcorn in the sun, among a friendly, family-oriented crowd. There are over eighty home games each season, played from April to late September, with play-offs continuing through October. Blue Jays tickets can be hard to come by so it might be worth watching one of the minor league teams, which play in most major cities including Vancouver, Québec City, Edmonton, Calgary and Winnipeg.

Basketball

Basketball was invented by a Canadian, Dr James A. Naismith, in 1891, but since then interest has been at a fairly low-ebb with teams coming and going and national leagues foundering. However, Canada does have one team – the Toronto Raptors – in the US National Basketball Association, or **NBA** (ⓦwww.nba.com). The team has lost more than it's won since 2002, and present prospects aren't good. The season lasts from November to April – tickets cost from $10–130.

Travel essentials

Addresses

Generally speaking, roads in urban Canada are laid out on a grid system, creating "**blocks**" of buildings. The first one or two digits of a specific address refer to the block, which will be numbered in sequence from a central point, usually downtown. For example, 620 South Cedar Ave will usually be six blocks south of downtown. It is crucial, therefore, to take note of components such as "NW" or "SE" in addresses: 3620 King St SW will be a very long way indeed from 3620 King St NE. Where a number is prefixed to the street number, this indicates an apartment or suite number in a block at the same street address. As with US usage, the "**first floor**" is what would be the ground floor in Britain; the "second floor" is one floor above ground level, and so on.

Costs

By western European standards, Canada is very **reasonably priced**, with most basic items – from maps through to food and clothing – costing significantly less than back home. US residents, Australians and New Zealanders, on the other hand, will find prices about the same – maybe a little higher, but not by much. As for dining and drinking, the sheer plethora of restaurants and bars keeps prices down except in the far north, where the high cost of transporting foodstuffs is necessarily passed on to the customer. Accommodation, almost certainly your major outlay, can be very pricey in the country's cities and towns – especially if you're after a degree of comfort – though to be fair there are plenty of bargains to be had, not least in the burgeoning B&B market.

On **average**, if you're prepared to buy your own picnic lunch, stay in hostels, and stick to the least expensive bars and restaurants, you could get by on around £25/US$50/C$57 a day. Staying in a good B&B, eating out in medium-range restaurants most nights and drinking regularly in bars, you'll get through at least £65/US$130/C$150 a day, with the main variable being the cost of your room. On £100/$195/C$230 a day and upwards, you'll be limited only by your energy reserves – though if you're planning to stay in the best hotels and make every night a big night out, this still won't be enough. As always, if you're travelling alone you'll spend much more on **accommodation** than you would in a group of two or more: most hotels do have single rooms, but they're fixed at about seventy percent of the price of a double. See also 'Taxes', p.64.

Crime and personal safety

There's little reason why you should ever come into contact with either **the Royal Canadian Mounted Police** (RCMP), who patrol most of Canada, or their fellow organizations – like the Toronto Police Service – which cover the rest. Canada is one of the safest countries in the world and although there are a few crime hotspots, these are confined to the peripheries of the country's three big cities – Toronto, Montréal and Vancouver. Few Canadian citizens carry **arms**, muggings are uncommon, and even in the cities street crime is infrequent – though the usual cautions about avoiding poorly lit urban areas and so forth stand. Canadian officials are notorious for coming down hard if you're found with **drugs**, especially on non-Canadians. Stiff penalties are imposed, even when only traces of any illegal substance are found. Police are also diligent in enforcing **traffic laws**.

If you are **a victim of crime**, you'll need to go to the police to report it, not least because your insurance company will require a police report. Remember to make a note of the crime report number – or, better still, ask for a copy of the statement itself. Don't expect a great deal of concern if your loss is relatively small, and don't be surprised if the process of completing forms and formalities takes ages. If you are **detained by the**

police, the arresting officer(s) must identify him/herself. At the police station, detainees have the right to free but reasonable use of a phone and legal counsel. For certain sorts of suspected offence – primarily gun- and drug-related – the police are likely to strip-search detainees, though these searches, and the frequency of them, remain controversial.

Electricity

Electricity in Canada is supplied at an alternating current of 110 volts and at a frequency of 60Hz, the same as in the US. Visitors from the UK will need transformers for appliances like shavers and hair dryers, and a plug converter for Canada's two-pin sockets.

Entry requirements

Citizens of the EU, Norway, Iceland and most Commonwealth countries, including the UK, Australia and New Zealand, only need a **valid passport** to enter Canada. **US citizens** simply need some form of photo identification plus proof of US citizenship. This can be a valid US passport, an original US birth certificate (or certified copy), or original US naturalization papers. Note that a US driver's licence alone is **not** sufficient proof of citizenship.

All visitors to Canada have to complete a **Welcome to Canada** form, effectively a customs declaration form, which you'll be given on the plane or at the US–Canadian border. On the form, you have to indicate the purpose of your visit from three options – study, business or personal. At point of entry, the **immigration officer** decides the **length of stay permitted** – usually not more than three months. The officers rarely refuse entry, but they may delve deep, asking you for details of your schedule and likely destinations and enquiring as to how much money you have and what job you do; they may also ask to see a return or onward ticket. If they ask where you're staying and you give the name and address of friends, don't be surprised if they check. Note also that although passing overland between the US and Canada is usually straightforward, there can sometimes be long delays, especially if your vehicle is at the receiving end of a spot search. Officers at the more obscure border entry points can be real sticklers.

For visits of more than six months, study trips and stints of (temporary) employment, contact the nearest Canadian embassy, consulate or high commission for authorization prior to departure. Once inside Canada, if you need an extension of your stay or want to change the basis on which you were admitted, you must apply to the nearest Canada Immigration Centre at least thirty days before the expiry of the authorized visit.

As for **duty-free**, the standard allowance is 1.5 litres of wine or 1.4 litres of liquor or 24 355ml bottles/cans of beer, plus 200 cigarettes, 50 cigars or cigarillos, and 200grms of tobacco.

Health

You'd be daft to visit Canada without a travel insurance policy covering potential **medical**

Canadian high commissions, embassies and consulates abroad

Australia High Commission, Commonwealth Ave, Canberra, ⓣ02/6270 4000, ⓦwww.dfait-maeci.gc.ca/australia. Consulates in Melbourne, Perth & Sydney.

Ireland Embassy, 65 St Stephen's Green, Dublin 2 ⓣ01/417 4100, ⓦwww.canadaeuropa.gc.ca/ireland.

New Zealand High Commission, Level 11, 125 The Terrace, Wellington t04/473 9577, ⓦwww.wellington.gc.ca. Consulate in Auckland.

UK High Commission, Macdonald House, 38 Grosvenor St ⓣ020/7258 6600, ⓦwww.canada.org.uk. Honorary consulates in Belfast, Birmingham, Cardiff & Edinburgh.

USA Embassy, 501 Pennsylvania Ave NW, Washington DC 20001 ⓣ202/682-7726, ⓦwww.can-am.gc.ca/washington. Consulates in Atlanta, Boston, Buffalo, Chicago, Dallas, Detroit, Los Angeles, Miami, Minneapolis, New York, San Francisco, San Jose & Seattle.

expenses. Canada has an excellent health service, but non-residents are not entitled to free health care, and medical costs can be astronomical. If you have an accident, medical services will get to you quickly and charge you later. Doctors and dentists can be found listed in the Yellow Pages. If you are carrying medicine prescribed by your doctor, also bring a copy of the prescription – first, to avoid problems at customs and immigration and, second, for renewing medication with Canadian doctors, if needed. **Pharmacies** are often well equipped to advise on minor ailments and to distinguish between unfamiliar brand names. Most larger towns and cities should have a 24hr pharmacy; many stay open late as a matter of course.

As for **specific health problems**, there are certain dangers out in the **backcountry**. Tap water is generally safe to drink, but it's always prudent to ask, and at campgrounds water is sometimes good for washing only. You should, however, **always boil backcountry water** for at least ten minutes to protect against the Giardia parasite (or "beaver fever"), which thrives in warm water, so equally be careful about swimming in hot springs – if possible, keep nose, eyes and mouth above water. Symptoms are intestinal cramps, flatulence, fatigue, weight loss and vomiting, all of which can appear up to a week after infection. If left untreated, more unpleasant complications can arise, so see a doctor immediately if you think you've contracted it.

Blackfly and **mosquitoes** are notorious for the problems they cause walkers and campers, and are especially bad in areas near standing water and throughout most of northern Canada. **Horseflies** are another pest. Late April to June is the blackfly season, and the mosquito season is from June until about October. If you're planning an expedition into the wilderness, you'd be well advised to take three times the recommended daily dosage of vitamin B complex for two weeks before you go, and to take the recommended dosage while you're in Canada; this cuts down bites by up to 75 percent.

Once you're there, **repellent creams and sprays** may help: the best are those containing DEET. The ointment version of Deep-Woods Off is the best brand, with 95 percent DEET. If you're camping or picnicking you'll find that burning coils or candles containing allethrin or citronella can help. If you're walking in an area that's rife with pests, it's well worth taking a gauze mask to protect your head and neck; wearing white clothes and no perfumed products also makes you less attractive to the insects. Once bitten, an **antihistamine cream** like phenergan is the best antidote. On no account go anywhere near an area marked as a blackfly mating ground – people have died from bites sustained when the creatures are in heat. Also dangerous is **West Nile virus**, a mosquito-born affliction with life-threatening properties; the virus has appeared in a few places as far west as Ontario and will probably spread – so pay attention to local advice.

If you develop a large rash and flu-like symptoms, you may have been bitten by a tick carrying lyme borreliosis (or "**lyme tick disease**"). This is easily curable, but if left untreated can lead to nasty complications, so again see a doctor as soon as possible. It's spreading in Canada, especially in the more southerly and wooded parts of the country, so you should check on its prevalence with the local tourist authority. It also may be advisable to buy a strong tick repellent and to wear long socks, trousers and sleeved shirts when walking.

In backcountry areas, look out for **poison ivy**, which grows in most places, but particularly in a belt across southern Ontario and Québec, where poison-ivy ointment is widely available. If you're likely to be walking in affected areas, ask at tourist offices for tips on where it is and how to recognize it. The ivy causes itchy open blisters and lumpy sores up to ten days after contact. If you do come into contact with poison ivy, wash your body and clothes as soon as possible, smother yourself in calamine lotion and try not to scratch. In serious cases, hospital emergency rooms can give antihistamine or adrenalin jabs.

Also keep an eye open for **snakes** in certain western areas; pharmacists and wilderness outfitters can advise on snakebite kits, and park wardens can give useful

In a medical **emergency**, call ⓣ911.

preventive advice. Should you get bitten without an antidote at hand, get a good look at the culprit so that the doctor can identify the species and administer the right medicine. If walking or climbing, go properly equipped and be prepared for sudden changes of weather. Watch out for signs of **exposure** – mild delirium, exhaustion, inability to get warm – and on snow or in high country during summer take a good **sunblock**.

Insurance

Prior to travelling, you should take out an **insurance policy** to cover against theft, loss and illness or injury. Before paying for a new policy, however, it's worth checking whether you already have some degree of coverage: some all-risks home insurance policies may cover your possessions when overseas; many private medical schemes include cover when abroad; and bank and credit cards often have certain levels of medical or other insurance cover included. In addition, students will often find that their student health coverage extends during vacations and for one term beyond the date of last enrolment.

After exhausting the possibilities above, you'll probably want to contact a **specialist travel insurance company**, or consider the travel insurance deal we offer (see box, below). A typical travel insurance policy provides cover for the loss of baggage, tickets and – up to a certain limit – cash or cheques, as well as cancellation or curtailment of your journey. Most of them exclude so-called **dangerous sports** unless an extra premium is paid: in Canada this can mean white-water rafting, mountain climbing, and so on. Many policies can be chopped and changed to exclude coverage you don't need: for example, sickness and accident benefits can often be excluded or included at will. If you do take **medical insurance**, ascertain whether benefits will be paid as treatment proceeds or only after return home, and whether there is a 24-hour medical emergency number. When securing baggage cover, make sure that the per-article limit will cover your most valuable possession. If you need to make a claim, keep **receipts** for medicines and medical treatment. In the event you have anything stolen, you must obtain a **crime report** statement or number from the police.

Internet

Internet access is commonplace at Canadian hotels, hostels and even B&Bs and there are also oodles of Internet cafés in the cities and towns. Free Internet access is available at all major libraries. The site ⓦwww.kropla.com gives useful details of how to plug your laptop in when abroad, phone codes around the world, and information about electrical systems in different countries.

Mail

Operated by **Canada Post** (ⓦwww.canadapost.ca), every Canadian settlement of any significant size has its own **post office** and opening hours are characteristically Monday to Friday 8.30am to 5.30pm, though a few places open on Saturday between 9am

Rough Guides travel insurance

Rough Guides has teamed up with Columbus Direct to offer you **travel insurance** that can be tailored to suit your needs. Products include a low-cost **backpacker** option for long stays; a **short break** option for city getaways; a typical **holiday package** option; and others. There are also annual **multi-trip** policies for those who travel regularly. Different sports and activities (trekking, skiing, etc) can be usually be covered if required.

See our website (ⓦwww.roughguidesinsurance.com) for eligibility and purchasing options. Alternatively, UK residents should call ⓣ0870/033 9988; Australians should call ⓣ1300/669 999 and New Zealanders should call ⓣ0800/55 9911. All other nationalities should call ⓣ44 870/890 2843.

Metric conversions

All figures are approximate:
1 centimetre = 0.39 inches; 1 inch = 2.5cm; 1 foot = 30cm.
1 metre (100cm) = 1.1 yards or 39 inches; 1 yard = 0.9m.
1 kilometre (1000m) = 0.6 miles; 1 mile = 1.6km; 8km = 5mi.
1 hectare (10,000sq m) = 2.5 acres; 1 acre = 0.4ha.
1 litre = 2.1 US pints; 1 US pint = 0.5 litres; 1 US quart = 0.9 litres.
1 litre = 0.3 US gallons; 1 US gallon = 3.8 litres.
1 litre = 1.8 UK pints; 1 UK pint = 0.6 litres.
1 litre = 0.2 UK gallons; 1 UK gallon = 4.5 litres.
1 kilogram or kilo (1000g) = 2.2lb; 1lb = 45g/0.45kg; 1oz = 28g.

Temperatures

°C	-10	-5	0	5	10	15	20	25	30	35
°F	14	23	32	41	50	59	68	77	86	95

and noon. Much more numerous, however, are Canada Post **service counters** inside larger stores, especially pharmacies, and here opening hours vary considerably, though core hours are the same as those of the post offices. To check for the nearest postal outlet, call ⓣ1-800/267-1177, or consult ⓦwww.canadapost.ca. Apart from Canada Post outlets, **stamps** can be purchased from automatic vending machines, the lobbies of larger hotels, airports, train stations, bus terminals and many retail outlets and newsstands. Current **postal charges** are 52¢ for letters and postcards up to 30g within Canada, 93¢ for the same weight to the US, and C$1.55 for international mail (also up to 30g). If you're posting letters to Canadian addresses, always include the **post code** or your mail may never get there; all codes are six characters long, in the format *letter number letter*, space, *number letter number*. Canada Post's services are very reliable, both inbound and outbound.

Maps

The **free maps** issued by each provincial tourist office (see p.65) are excellent for general driving and route planning, especially as they provide the broad details of ferry connections. The best of the **commercially produced maps** are those published by Rand McNally (ⓦwww.randmcnally.com) and MapArt (ⓦwww.mapart.com).

In the case of **hiking and canoe routes**, all the national and most provincial parks have visitors' centres, which provide free parkland maps indicating hiking and canoe trails. Many of them also sell proper local survey maps, as do lots of outfitters and some of the provincial parks' departments, whose details are given in the guide.

Measurements

Canada uses the **metric system**, though many people still use the imperial system. Distances are in kilometres, temperatures in degrees Celsius, and foodstuffs, petrol and drink are sold in grams, kilograms or litres.

Money

Canadian currency is the **Canadian dollar** ($), made up of 100 cents (¢). Coins come as 1¢ (penny), 5¢ (nickel), 10¢ (dime), 25¢ (quarter), $1 and $2. The $1 coin is known as a "loonie", after the bird on one face; no one's come up with a suitable name for the newer $2 coin – "twoonie" has been tried but hasn't really caught on. There are notes of $5, $10, $20, $50 and $100. **US dollars** are widely accepted, but generally – banks, etc. apart – on a one-for-one basis. It's not a good deal as the US dollar is (usually) worth more than its Canadian counterpart. Approximate **exchange rates** at the time of writing are £1=C$2.27, US$1=C$1.15, €1=C$1.55, A$1=C$0.94, NZ$1=C$0.85. For the most up-to-date rates, check ⓦwww.oanda.com.

All but the tiniest of settlements in Canada has a **bank or savings bank**, the vast majority of which will change foreign currency and traveller's cheques. Many will also give cash advances on credit cards. Banking hours are a minimum of Monday to Friday 10am–3pm, but many have late opening – till 6pm – on one night a week, others are open on Saturday mornings.

ATMs are commonplace. Most accept a host of **debit cards**, including all those carrying the Cirrus coding. If in doubt, check with your bank to find out whether the card you wish to use will be accepted – and if you need a new (international) PIN. You'll rarely be charged a transaction fee, as the banks make their profits from applying different exchange rates. **Credit cards** can be used in ATMs too, but in this case transactions are treated as loans, with interest accruing daily from the date of withdrawal. All major credit and charge cards are widely accepted.

Opening hours and public holidays

Shopping hours vary considerably, but most large and medium-sized retailers open seven days a week, 10am–8/9/10pm Monday to Thursday and often the same on Friday, when quite a few places close a little earlier, at 6pm or 7pm; Saturday is usually 10am–6/7pm and Sunday noon–6pm, though in some parts of Canada Sunday closing remains in operation. In addition,

Public holidays

National holidays

New Year's Day Jan 1
Good Friday Varies; March/April
Easter Sunday Varies; March/April
Easter Monday Varies; March/April - widely observed, but not an official public holiday.
Victoria Day Third Monday in May
Canada Day July 1
Labour Day First Monday in Sept
Thanksgiving second Monday in Oct
Remembrance Day Nov 11 (only a partial holiday; government offices and banks are closed, but most businesses are open).
Christmas Day Dec 25
Boxing Day Dec 26

Provincial holidays

Alberta Third Mon in Feb (Alberta Family Day); first Mon in Aug (Heritage Day).
British Columbia First Mon in Aug (British Columbia Day).
Manitoba First Mon in Aug (Civic Holiday).
New Brunswick First Mon in Aug (New Brunswick Day).
Newfoundland and Labrador March 17 (St Patrick's Day); third Mon in April (St George's Day); third Mon in June (Discovery Day); first Mon in July (Memorial Day); third Mon in July (Orangeman's Day).
Northwest Territories First Mon in Aug (Civic Holiday).
Nova Scotia First Mon in Aug (Civic Holiday).
Nunavut April 1 (Nunavut Day).
Ontario First Mon in Aug (Civic Holiday).
Québec Jan 6 (Epiphany); Ash Wednesday; Ascension (forty days after Easter); June 24 (Saint-Jean-Baptiste Day); Nov 1 (All Saint's Day); Dec 8 (Immaculate Conception).
Saskatchewan First Mon in Aug (Civic Holiday).
Yukon Third Mon in Aug (Discovery Day).

convenience stores, like 7-Eleven, are routinely open much longer, often round the clock. **Office hours** are more restricted, characteristically Monday to Friday 9/9.30am–4.30/5pm. Most major **museums** are open daily from around 10am to 5pm or 5.30pm, with one late-night a week, usually Thursday until 8/9pm. As for **restaurants**, these are usually open daily from 11am to 11pm, with or without an afternoon break, from around 2.30/3pm to 5/6pm. **Bars** are open daily from 11am to 2am. Most businesses are closed on **public holidays**, but not bars, restaurants and hotels. Public transport, where it exists, keeps moving on holidays, too, operating a skeleton service.

Phones

Domestic and international **telephone calls** can be made with equal ease from public and private phones. **Public telephones** are commonplace, though the irresistible rise of the mobile/cell means that their numbers will not increase and may well diminish. All public phones are equipped for the hearing-impaired and take coins. Most also accept pre-paid calling cards, as well as credit cards. Local calls cost 25¢ from a public phone, but are free on private phones (though not usually hotel phones).

When **dialling** any Canadian number, either local or long-distance, you must include the area code. Long-distance calls – to numbers beyond the area code of the telephone from which you are making the call – must be prefixed with "1". On public telephones, this "1" secures an operator intercept; the operator will tell you how much money you need to get connected. Thereafter, you'll be asked to shovel money in at regular intervals – so unless you're making a reverse-charge/collect call you'll need a stack of quarters (25¢ pieces) handy, if your call will be of any length.

To confuse matters, some connections within a single telephone code area are charged at the long-distance rate, and thus need the "1" prefix; a recorded message will tell you this is necessary as soon as you dial the number. To save the hassle of carrying all this change, you could consider either buying a **telephone card** back home or here in Canada. There are a number of Canadian telephone charge cards to choose from with one of the more widely available being Bell's **Prepaid Calling Card**, sold in denominations of C$5, C$10 and C$20. For further details of this and other Bell phone cards, contact their customer service department on ⓣ1-800/668 6878, ⓦwww.bell.ca.

As for **tariffs**, the cheap-rate period for calls is between 6pm and 8am during the week and all the weekend. Detailed rates are listed at the front of all telephone directories. Note also that many businesses, especially hotels, have **toll-free numbers** (prefixed by ⓣ1-800 or 1-888). Some of these can only be dialed from phones in the same province, others from anywhere within Canada, and a few from anywhere in North America; as a rough guideline, the larger the organization, the wider its toll-free net. Finally, remember

Useful phone numbers

Directory enquiries from private phones Local, regional and long-distance within North America ⓣ411; international, call the operator ⓣ0.
Directory enquiries from public phones local/regional ⓣ411; long-distance within North America ⓣ1+ area code + 555-1212; international, call the operator ⓣ0.
Emergencies Police, fire and ambulance ⓣ911.
Operator (Domestic and international) ⓣ0.
Phoning abroad from Canada To Australia: ⓣ011 + 61 + area code minus zero + number; to the Republic of Ireland: ⓣ011 + 353 + area code minus zero + number; to New Zealand: ⓣ011 + 64 + area code minus zero + number; to the UK: ⓣ011 + 44 + area code minus zero + number; to the US: ⓣ1 + area code + number.
Phoning Canada from abroad Dial your country's international access code for Canada, then the area code, followed by the number.

that although most hotel rooms have phones, there is almost always an exorbitant surcharge for their use.

If you want to use your **mobile phone/ cellphone** in Canada, you may need to set up international cellular access with your phone provider before you set out. Also check out their **call charges** as these can be exorbitant, especially as you are likely to be charged extra for incoming calls that originate from back home as the people calling you will be paying the usual (national) rate. The same sometimes applies to text messages, though in many cases these can now be received with the greatest of ease – no fiddly codes and so forth – and at ordinary rates. In Canada, the **mobile network** covers every city and town, but out in the sticks you'll mostly be struggling to get a signal. Canada's network works on GSM 1900 – which means that mobiles bought in **Europe** need to be **triband** to gain cellular access.

Taxes

Virtually all prices in Canada for everything from bubble-gum to hotel rooms are quoted **without tax**, which means that the price you see quoted is not the price you'll end up paying. With the exception of Alberta, the Yukon, Nunavut and NWT, each province levies a **Provincial Sales Tax** (**PST**) of between six and ten percent on most goods and services, including hotel and restaurant bills, and this is supplemented by the **Goods and Services Tax** (**GST**), a seven percent levy applied nationwide. In some provinces, the two taxes are amalgamated into the so-called **Harmonized Sales Tax** (**HST**). As a small mercy, visitors can claim a **GST and PST rebate** on certain outgoings. The rules are complicated, but broadly GST rebates are available on payments of $50 and over that involve hotel accommodation and goods you are taking home with you; the total claimed must be at least $14. PST rebates apply on shopping receipts where you have spent $625 or more. **Claim forms** are available at many hotels, shops and airports. Return them, with **all original receipts**, to the address given on the form. Those returning overland to the US can claim their rebate at selected border duty-free shops. For more information, call either ⓣ905/791-5007, or consult ⓦwww.nationaltaxrefund.com.

Time zones

Canada has six **time zones**, but only four-and-a-half hours separate the eastern extremities of the country from the western.

Newfoundland is on **Newfoundland time** (3hr 30min behind the UK and 1hr 30min ahead of the eastern US).

The Maritimes and Labrador are on **Atlantic** (4hr behind the UK and 1hr ahead of the eastern US).

Québec and most of Ontario are on **Eastern** (5hr behind the UK) – the same zone as New York and the eastern US.

Manitoba, the northwest corner of Ontario, and Saskatchewan are on **Central** (6hr behind the UK; same as US Central).

Alberta, the Northwest Territories and a slice of northeast British Columbia are on **Mountain** (7hr behind the UK – same as US Mountain).

In the west, the Yukon and the remainder of British Columbia are on **Pacific** (8hr behind the UK and 1hr ahead of Alaska – same as US Pacific).

Nunavut spans a number of time zones, from Mountain to Atlantic.

For **daylight saving** (used in all regions except Saskatchewan and northeast BC), clocks go forward one hour on the first Sunday of April, and back one hour on the last Sunday in October.

Toilets

Public toilets are rare, even in cities, but bars, fast-food chains, museums and other public buildings invariably have excellent facilities.

Tourist information

All of Canada's provinces have their own tourist **website** and these, along with the those run by **Canada Parks**, covering the country's national parks and historic sites, and **Travel Canada**'s generic website (ⓦwww.travelcanada.ca), are the most useful source of information before you set out. In addition, each of the provinces operates a **toll-free visitor information line** for use within mainland North America. These lines are staffed by tourist office employees trained to answer all manner of queries and to advise on room reservations; you can usually telephone these numbers from abroad, but at standard international telephone rates. In Canada itself, there are **provincial tourist information centres** along the main hwys, especially at provincial boundaries and along the US border; **information centres** at every national and many provincial parks, selling fishing and backcountry permits and giving help on the specifics of hiking, canoeing, wildlife watching and so forth; and **tourist offices** in every city and town.

Provincial toll-free information numbers and websites

Alberta Within North America toll-free ⓣ1-800/252-3782, from elsewhere ⓣ780/427-4321, ⓦwww.travelalberta.com.
British Columbia ⓣ1-800/663-6000, ⓦwww.hellobc.com.
Manitoba ⓣ1-800/665-0040, ⓦwww.travelmanitoba.com.
New Brunswick ⓣ1-800/561-0123, ⓦwww.tourismnewbrunswick.ca.
Newfoundland and Labrador ⓣ1-800/563-6353, ⓦwww.newfoundlandandlabradortourism.com.
Northwest Territories Within North America toll-free ⓣ1-800/661-0788 or 867/873-5007, ⓦwww.explorenwt.com.
Nova Scotia Within North America toll-free ⓣ1-800/565-0000, from elsewhere ⓣ902/425-5781, ⓦwww.novascotia.com.
Nunavut ⓣ1-866/686-2888, ⓦwww.nunavuttourism.com.
Ontario ⓣ1-800/ONTARIO (668-2746), ⓦwww.ontariotravel.net.
Prince Edward Island Within North America toll-free ⓣ1-800/463-4734, from elsewhere ⓣ902/368-4444, ⓦwww.peiplay.com.
Québec Within North America toll-free ⓣ1-877/266-5687 and from the UK toll-free ⓣ0800/051-7055, from elsewhere ⓣ514/873-2015, ⓦwww.bonjourquebec.com.
Saskatchewan Within North America toll-free ⓣ1-877/237-2273, or ⓣ306/787-9600, ⓦwww.sasktourism.com.
Yukon ⓣ1-800/661-0494, ⓦwww.travelyukon.com

Other useful websites

Assembly of First Nations ⓦwww.afn.ca. Lobbying organization of Canada's native peoples, with plenty to get you briefed on the latest situation.
Canada.Com ⓦwww.canada.com. Canada's number one online news and information service, with content from newspapers, TV, city sites and classified ads.
Canada Eh? ⓦwww.canadianeh.com. Impressive array of links to every conceivable Canada-related site, plus news and views.
Canadian Ice Hockey ⓦwww.hockeycanada.ca. The official site of the amateur governing body for the national obsession.
Gateway to the Arts ⓦwww.artscanadian.com. Good arts information.
The Globe and Mail ⓦwww.theglobeandmail.com. Canada's premier newspaper online.
Government of Canada ⓦwww.canada.gc.ca. The government tells all – or all that it wants its citizens to know?
Infospace ⓦwww.infospace.com. Exhaustive Yellow Pages-like listings. If you want to find a vet in Labrador or a body piercer in Prince Albert, this should have it.
National Atlas of Canada Online ⓦwww.atlas.gc.ca. Maps, stats and plenty of details on Canada's geographic features.
National Library of Canada ⓦwww.nlc-bnc.ca. Information on all things Canadian, ordered by subject. Includes Canadian arts, literature, history.
Northern Stars ⓦwww.northernstars.ca. Tracks the progress of all Canada's film stars, with short bios and lists of credits.
Parks Canada ⓦwww.pc.gc.ca. Excellent website with detailed information on all of Canada's national parks and national historic sites.
Statistics Canada ⓦwww.statcan.ca. A national agency that gives you all the numerical data and analysis on population, economic trends, and more.
Tickets ⓦwww.ticketmaster.ca. Ticket booking service for shows, gigs and sporting events across Canada.

Travellers with disabilities

At least in its cities and towns, Canada is one of the best places in the world to travel if you have limited mobility or other **physical disabilities**. All public buildings are required to be wheelchair-accessible and provide suitable toilet facilities, almost all street corners have dropped kerbs, and public phones are specially equipped for hearing-aid users. Wheelchair users may encounter problems when travelling on urban public transport, but matters are being remedied at a speed of knots. Out in the wilds, things are inevitably more problematic, but almost all the national parks have accessible visitor and information centres and many have specially designed, accessible trails. In addition, VIA Rail offers a good range of services for the traveller with disabilities – and the larger **car-rental companies** (see p.37) can provide cars with hand controls at no extra charge, though these are usually only available on their most expensive models; book one as far in advance as you can as demand can exceed supply. Provincial tourist offices (see p.65) are the prime source of information on accessible hotels, motels and sights. To obtain a parking privilege permit, drivers with disabilities must apply to a provincial authority, though the permit itself, once issued, is valid right across Canada.

Travelling with children

Most of the time, Canada does a good job keeping **children** in good spirits. Many attractions are specifically designed to cater for families; children's menus are commonplace; an extra bed or two will be rolled out in most hotel and motel rooms with a minimum of fuss; swimming pools and assorted sports facilities are ubiquitous; and children get concessionary rates just about everywhere, from buses to museums. The only major problem is distance: few children like to be cooped up in a car for hours, so if you're planning a major expedition get ready with the games and for the questions ('Are we there yet?').

Guide

Guide

1

Toronto

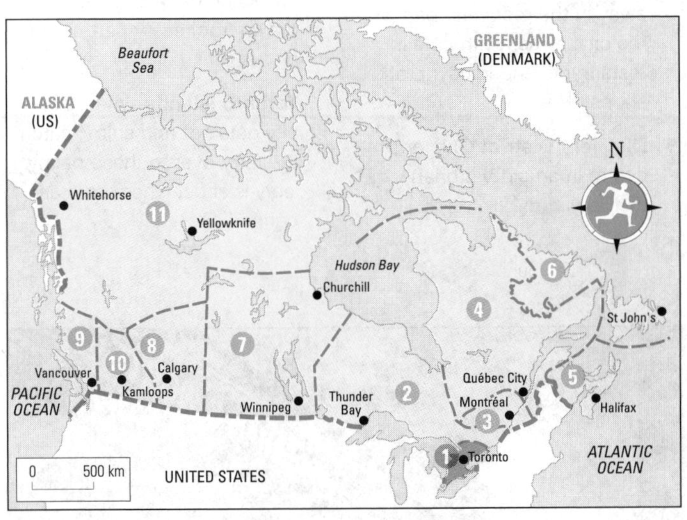
Beaufort Sea
GREENLAND (DENMARK)
ALASKA (US)
N
Whitehorse
11
Yellowknife
Hudson Bay
Churchill
6
4
St John's
9
8
7
10
Calgary
Vancouver
Kamloops
PACIFIC OCEAN
Winnipeg
Thunder Bay
2
Québec City
Montréal
3
5
Halifax
1
Toronto
0 500 km
UNITED STATES
ATLANTIC OCEAN

CHAPTER 1 Highlights

* **Toronto International Film Festival** North America's largest film festival is a star-studded affair held over ten days in September. See p.74
* **Mulberry Tree** Quite simply the best B&B in town. See p.84
* **Queen Street W** Groove away in the grooviest part of the city, awash with cafés, restaurants and idiosyncratic shops. See p.108
* **Distillery District** Chic arts centre in an old Victorian distillery. See p.92
* **The Art Gallery of Ontario** The AGO has a superb collection of Canadian art plus the world's largest assemblage of Henry Moore sculptures. See p.95
* **Gardiner Museum of Ceramic Art** Exemplary museum with a connoisseur's collection of ceramic art drawn from every part of the globe. See p.101
* **Toronto Islands** When the city gets hot and sultry, catch the ferry over to these balmy, leafy islands, where cars are banned. See p.104

△ Distillery District shops

Toronto

The economic and cultural focus of English-speaking Canada, **TORONTO** is the country's largest metropolis with a population of around four and a half million souls. It sprawls along the northern shore of Lake Ontario, its vibrant, appealing centre encased by a jangle of satellite townships and industrial zones that cover (as "Greater Toronto") no less than 100 square kilometres. For decades, Toronto was saddled with unflattering sobriquets ("Toronto the Good", "Hogtown") that reflected a largely deserved reputation for complacent mediocrity, but those dull days are long gone. Since the late 1950s, successive city administrations have lavished millions of dollars on glitzy architecture, slick museums, an excellent public-transport system, and the reclamation and development of the lakefront. As a result, Toronto has become one of North America's most likeable cities, an eminently liveable place whose citizens keep a wary eye on both their politicians and the developers.

Huge new shopping malls and high-rise office blocks reflect the economic successes of the last decades, a boom that has attracted **immigrants** from all over the world, transforming an overwhelmingly Anglophone city into a cosmopolitan one of some sixty significant minorities. Indeed, getting the feel for Toronto's diversity is one of the city's great pleasures. Nowhere is this better experienced than in its myriad **cafés and restaurants**, where standards are high and prices are characteristically low. Toronto also boasts a pulsating **club scene**, not to mention a classy programme of **performing arts**, from dance to theatre and beyond.

Toronto has its share of attention-grabbing sights and the majority are conveniently clustered in the city centre. The most celebrated of them is the **CN Tower**, the world's tallest freestanding structure, which stands next to the modern hump of the **SkyDome** sports stadium, now the **Rogers Centre**. The city's other prestige attractions kick off with the **Art Gallery of Ontario**, which possesses a first-rate selection of Canadian painting, and the **Royal Ontario Museum**, where pride of place goes to the Chinese collection. Yet it's the pick of Toronto's smaller galleries that really add to the city's charm. There is a superb collection of ceramics at the **Gardiner Museum of Ceramic Art**, a fascinating range of footwear at the **Bata Shoe Museum** and the small but eclectic **Gallery of Inuit Art** owned by the Toronto Dominion Bank. There are fascinating period homes too, most memorably the mock-Gothic extravagances of **Casa Loma** and the Victorian gentility of **Spadina House**, not to mention the replica colonial fortress of **Fort York**, where Toronto began. Spare time also for the good-looking buildings of the lively **St Lawrence** neighbourhood and the **Distillery District**, not actually a

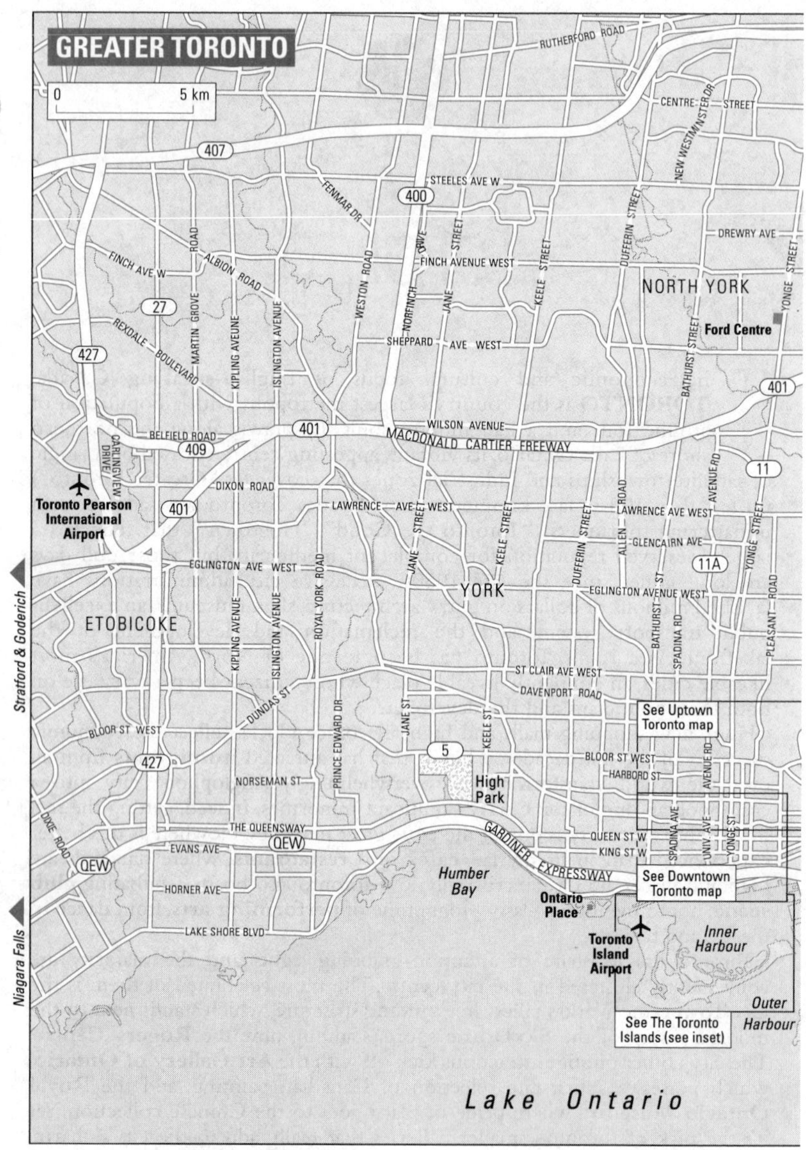

district at all but rather Toronto's brightest arts and entertainments complex, sited in a capacious former distillery.

Toronto's sights illustrate different facets of the city, but in no way do they crystallize its **identity**. The city remains opaque, too big and diverse to allow for a defining personality and this, of course, adds an enticing air of excitement and unpredictability to the place.

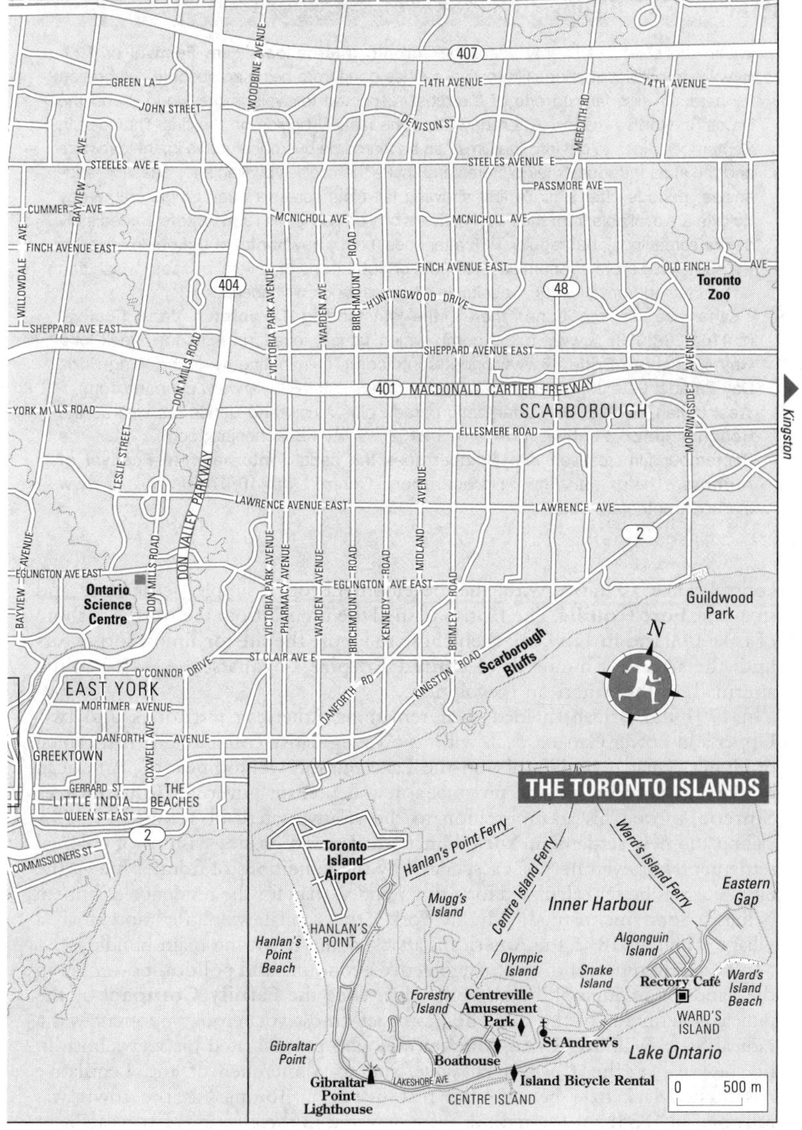

A brief history of Toronto

Situated on the slab of land separating Lake Ontario and Georgian Bay, **Toronto** was on one of the early portage routes into the interior, its name taken from the Huron for "place of meeting". The first European to visit the district was the French explorer Étienne Brûlé in 1615, but it wasn't until the middle of the eighteenth century that the French made a serious effort to

Toronto's leading festivals

Within the space of twenty years the **Toronto International Film Festival** or **TIFF** (Ⓦwww.torontointernationalfilmfestival.ca) has gone from being an obscure celebration for hardcore film fans to one of the most respected festivals in the world – and the largest in North America. A ten-day affair, the festival begins on the first Thursday in September. Lines to get into the films can be fearsome but, once you're in, the directors and the stars introduce their pictures and make themselves available for question-and-answer periods after a film's first showing (all films screen twice). Single, same-day **tickets** are available from the Film Festival's box offices (or as **rush tickets** immediately before screenings), but regular TIFF attendees mostly buy **books of tickets** in advance – a somewhat more economical method – or opt for one of several **passes**, which can be purchased from the TIFF website. In all cases, book well ahead.

Otherwise, in late June, there's the outstanding **Downtown Jazz Festival** (Ⓣ416/928-2033, Ⓦwww.tojazz.com), which usually overlaps with the week-long **Gay & Lesbian Pride** (Ⓦwww.pridetoronto.com), culminating in a whopping Pride Day Parade. Late July sees the **Caribana** (Ⓣ905/799-1630, Ⓦwww.caribana.com), a West Indian carnival with a fantastic parade plus music and dance, as well as the **Beaches Jazz Festival** (Ⓣ416/698-2152, Ⓦwww.beachesjazz.com). After the September film festival, late October sees the sedate **International Festival of Authors**, held at the Harbourfront Centre (Ⓣ416/973-4147, Ⓦwww.harbourfrontcentre.com).

control Lake Ontario with the development of a simple settlement and stockade, **Fort Rouillé**. The British pushed the French from the northern shore of Lake Ontario in 1759, but then chose to ignore the site for almost forty years until the arrival of hundreds of **United Empire Loyalists** (see p.459) in the aftermath of the American Revolution.

In 1791 the British divided their remaining American territories into two, Upper and Lower Canada, each with its own legislative councils. The first capital of Upper Canada was Niagara-on-the-Lake, but this was too near the American border for comfort and the province's new lieutenant governor, **John Graves Simcoe**, moved his administration to the relative safety of Toronto in 1793, calling the new settlement **York**. Simcoe had grand classical visions of colonial settlement, but even he was exasperated by the conditions of frontier life – "the city's site was better calculated for a frog pond… than for the residence of human beings". Soon nicknamed "Muddy York", the capital was little more than a village when, in 1812, the Americans attacked and burnt the main buildings.

In the early nineteenth century, effective economic and political power lay in the hands of an anglophilic oligarchy christened the **Family Compact** by the radical polemicists of the day. The Compact's most vociferous opponent was a radical Scot, **William Lyon Mackenzie**, who promulgated his views both in his newspaper, the *Colonial Advocate*, and as a member of the Legislative Assembly. Mackenzie became the first mayor of Toronto, as the town was renamed in 1834, but the radicals were defeated in the elections two years later and a frustrated Mackenzie drifted towards the idea of armed revolt. In 1837, he staged the **Upper Canadian insurrection**, a badly organized uprising of a few hundred farmers, who marched down the main street, Yonge Street, fought a couple of half-hearted skirmishes and then melted away. Mackenzie fled across the border and two of the other ringleaders were executed, but the British parliament, mindful of their earlier experiences in New England, moved to liberalize Upper Canada's administration instead of taking reprisals. In 1841, they granted Canada **responsible government**, reuniting the two provinces in a loose confederation, prefiguring the final union of 1867 when Upper Canada was redesignated **Ontario**. Even Mackenzie was pardoned and allowed to return, arguably giving the lie to his portrayal of the oligarchs as hard-faced reactionaries: indeed, this same privileged group had even pushed progressive antislavery bills through the legislature as early as the 1830s.

By the end of the nineteenth century, Toronto had become a major manufacturing centre dominated by a conservative mercantile elite, which was exceedingly loyal to the British interest and maintained a strong Protestant tradition. This elite was sustained by the working-class **Orange Lodges**, whose reactionary influence was a key feature of municipal politics, prompting a visiting Charles Dickens to complain about the city's "rabid Toryism". Nevertheless, to be fair, these same Protestants were enthusiastic about public education, just like the Methodist-leaning middle classes, who spearheaded social reform movements, principally Suffrage and Temperance. The trappings, however, remained far from alluring – well into the twentieth century Sunday was preserved as a "day of rest" and Eaton's store drew its curtains to prevent Sabbath window-shopping. Indeed, for all its capital status, the city was strikingly provincial by comparison with Montréal until well into the 1950s, when the opening of the **St Lawrence Seaway** gave the place something of a jolt and the first wave of non-white immigrants began to transform the city's complexion.

In the 1960s, the economy exploded, and the city's appearance was transformed by the construction of a series of mighty, modernistic **skyscrapers**. This helter-skelter development was further boosted by the troubles in Québec, where the clamour for fair treatment by the Francophones prompted many of Montréal's Anglophone-dominated financial institutions and big businesses to up-sticks and transfer to Toronto. Much to the glee of Torontonians, the census of 1976 showed that Toronto had become **Canada's biggest city**, edging Montréal by just one thousand inhabitants, and since then the gap has grown much wider.

In the last twenty years, Toronto's economy has followed the cycles of boom and retrenchment common to the rest of the country, though real estate speculation was especially frenzied in the 1980s until the bottom fell out of the property market in 1988. In the mid-1990s, the **Progressive Conservatives** took control of Ontario, and their hard-nosed leader, **Mike Harris**, pushed through another governmental reorganization, combining the city of Toronto with its surrounding suburbs to create the "Mega City" of today. The change was deeply unpopular in the city of Toronto itself, but Harris still managed to get himself re-elected in 2000 with the large-scale support of small-town and suburban Ontario. A hated figure amongst the province's liberals and socialists, Harris's conservative social policies are often blamed for the dramatic increase in the number of homeless people on the city's streets. In 2002, Harris passed the premiership over to another Progressive Conservative, Ernie Eves, but he proved to be an inconsequential figure, who lost the provincial election of 2003 to the Liberals, heralding a move towards more moderate, consensual politics.

Arrival

Toronto Pearson International Airport, some 25km northwest of the city centre, is linked to almost every important metropolis in the world as well as every major Canadian town and city. The vast majority of visitors to Toronto arrive by plane.

Toronto's **bus and train stations** are conveniently located downtown and they link Toronto to a wide range of Canadian and American cities. Those arriving **by car** will find the city encircled by motorways, a straightforward drive except during rush hour when traffic congestion can be a real pain.

By air

Arriving by **air**, you'll almost certainly land at the city's main airport, **Toronto Pearson International** (ⓦwww.torontoairport.com). There are currently two terminals here (Terminals 1 and 3), though Terminal 3 may soon be decommissioned, and the vast majority of flights use Terminal 1, which has a full range of facilities, including money-exchange offices, ATMs and free hotel hotlines. The **Airport Express bus** service (daily every 20–30min, 5am–1am; $16.45 one-way, $28.35 round-trip valid for one year; ⓣ905/564-6333, ⓦwww.torontoairportexpress.com) picks up passengers outside both terminals and takes forty to sixty minutes to reach downtown, though heavy traffic can make the journey longer. The bus drops passengers at the coach station (see below for details) and several of Toronto's major hotels. You can buy tickets either at the Airport Express bus kiosks or from the driver. Much less expensive, if rather more time-consuming, are the several **bus services** linking the airport with the city's subway network. The two fastest – which leave from designated stops outside both of the terminal buildings – are operated by the TTC (the Toronto Transit Commission, see opposite), which runs all of the city's public transport. Buy tickets from the driver. Their **Airport Rocket** (#192; daily every 20–30min, 5.30am–1.30am; $2.75 one-way) takes about twenty minutes to reach **Kipling subway station**, at the west end of the subway network; from there, it takes another 20min by subway to get downtown. The second option, **bus #58A** (daily every 30min 5.30am–1am; 45mins; $2.75 one-way), links the airport with **Lawrence W subway station**, north of downtown. The **taxi** fare from the airport to the city centre is about $50, a few dollars less if you take the airport **limo service** (a shared taxi system). Unlike taxis, the price of a limo is fixed, an important consideration if you arrive (or leave) during rush hour; the disadvantage is that they mostly only leave when they're full.

The much smaller **Toronto Island Airport** (ⓣ416/203-6942, ⓦwww.torontoairport.com) is close to downtown on Hanlan's Point, in Toronto's harbour, This handles a limited range of domestic flights, principally to Montréal and Ottawa – contact the airport for schedule details. From the airport, there's a **minibus** to the *Royal York Hotel*, on the corner of Front Street W and York Street.

By bus and train

Well connected to most of the major towns of eastern and central Canada, Toronto's **coach terminal** is conveniently located downtown at 610 Bay St, very close to Dundas St W and a five-minute walk from the subway station at the corner of Yonge and Dundas. The two main carriers are Greyhound (ⓣ1-800/661-8747, ⓦwww.greyhound.ca) and Coach Canada (ⓣ1-800/461-7661, ⓦwww.coachcanada.com); for routes to and from the city, see 'Travel details', p.114. If you're arriving late at night, note that the bus station's immediate environs are unsavoury. It only takes a couple of minutes to reach more reassuring parts of downtown, but if you're travelling alone it's probably sound advice to take a taxi.

All incoming and outgoing **trains** use the **Union Railway Station**, at the junction of Bay Street and Front Street W. Most long-distances trains are provided by VIA Rail (ⓣ1-888/842-7245, ⓦwww.viarail.ca), though Ontario Northland

(Ⓣ1-800/461-8558, Ⓦwww.northlander.ca) chips in with the epic Northlander train to and from Cochrane (for Moosonee). The Union station complex is the hub of the city's public transportation system, incorporating a subway station and the main terminal for the **GO** trains and buses (Ⓣ416/869-3200 or 1-888/438-6646; Ⓦwww.gotransit.com) that service the city's suburbs.

By car

From Niagara Falls and points west along Lake Ontario, most **road traffic** arrives via the **QEW** (Queen Elizabeth Way), which funnels into the Gardiner Expressway, an elevated motorway that cuts across the southern side of downtown, just south of Front Street. The Gardiner is notorious for delays. From the east, most drivers opt for the equally busy **Highway 401**, which sweeps along Lake Ontario before veering off to slice through the city's suburbs north of downtown. Driving in from the north, take **Highway 400**, which intersects with Hwy 401 northwest of the centre, or **Highway 404**, which meets Hwy 401 northeast of the centre. To relieve congestion on Hwy 401, an alternative motorway, **Highway 407ETR** (Ⓦwww.407etr.com), has been built further north on the city's edge. It was North America's first all-electronic toll highway: instead of toll booths, each vehicle is identified by an electronic tag (a **transponder**), and the invoice is mailed on later. Toll charges are fixed at around 17¢ per kilometre and there's also a small supplementary charge per trip for any vehicle without a transponder – these vehicles are identified by licence plate photos. If you rent a car, be aware that rental companies slap on an extra administration charge (of around $20) if you take their vehicles on this road.

Information

The excellent **Ontario Tourism Travel Information Centre**, at street level inside the Atrium on Bay mall, 20 Dundas St W at Yonge (Mon–Fri 10am–7pm, Sat 9.30am–7pm, Sun noon–5pm; Ⓣ416/314-5899 or 1-800/ONTARIO, Ⓦwww.ontariotravel.net), stocks a comprehensive range of information. Most of the stuff is free, including reasonably good-quality city maps, the *Ride Guide* to the city's public transport system, and entertainment listings in the monthly magazine *Where*. Ontario Tourism will also book hotel **accommodation** on your behalf in Toronto and across the whole of Ontario and they sell the City Pass (see p.86). Alternatively, **Tourism Toronto**, the city's official visitor and convention bureau, has its own website and operates a telephone information line (Ⓣ416/203-2600 or 1-800/499-2514, Ⓦwww.torontotourism.com), which can handle most city queries and make hotel reservations.

City transport

Fast, frequent and efficient, Toronto's public transportation is operated by the **Toronto Transit Commission**, the **TTC** (Ⓣ416/393-4636, 24hr helpline, Ⓦwww.ttc.ca), whose integrated network of subways, buses and streetcars serves virtually every corner of the city. With the exception of downtown, where all the major sights are within easy walking distance of one another, your best option is to use public transport to hop between attractions – especially in the cold of winter or the sultry summertime. Much to its credit, the TTC has gone to great lengths to assure the safety of its passengers: all subway stations have **DWAs**

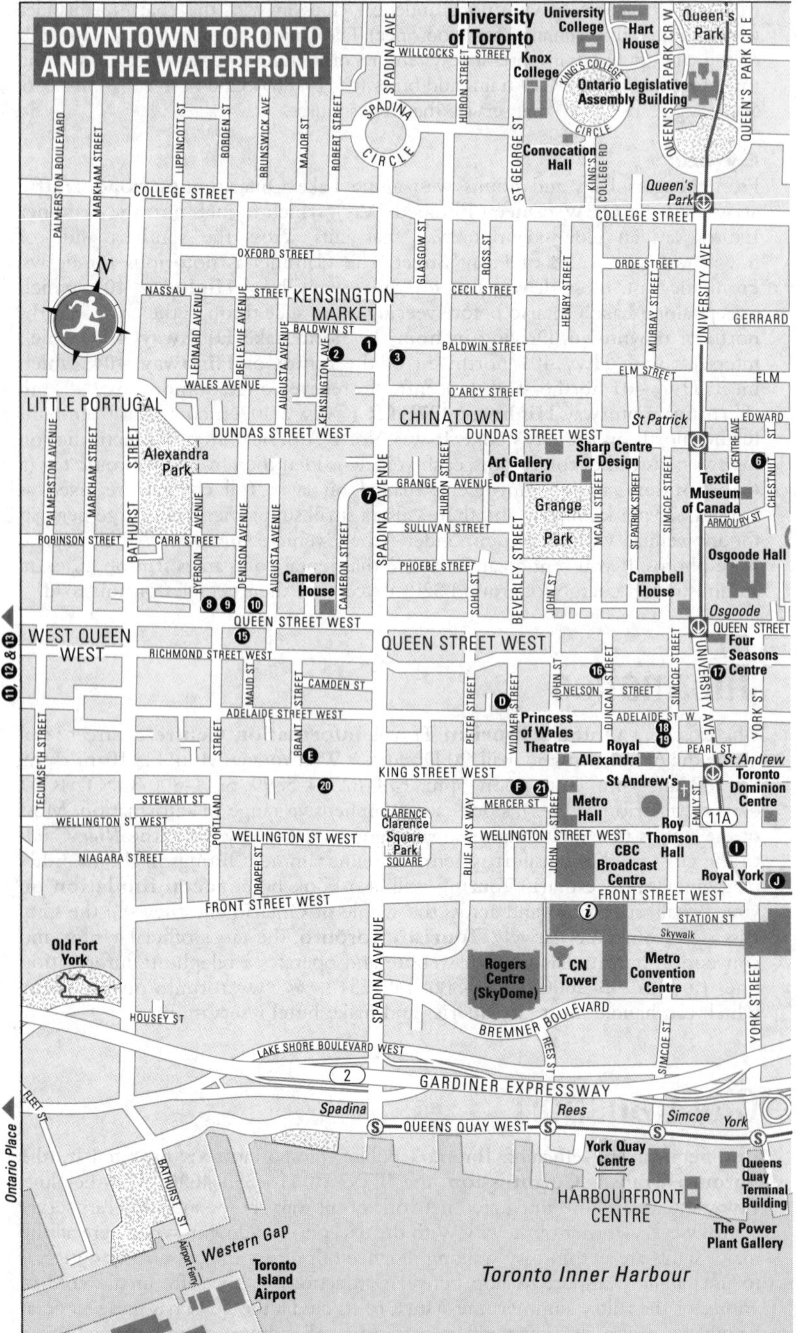

DOWNTOWN TORONTO AND THE WATERFRONT
N
University of Toronto
University College
Hart House
Queen's Park
Knox College
King's College Circle
Ontario Legislative Assembly Building
Convocation Hall
Queen's Park
Spadina Circle
Willcocks Street
Spadina Ave
Huron Street
St George St
King's College Rd
Queen's Park Cr W
Queen's Park Cr E
Palmerston Boulevard
Markham Street
Lippincott St
Borden St
Brunswick Ave
Major St
Robert Street
College Street
Oxford Street
Glasgow St
Ross St
Orde Street
Cecil Street
Henry Street
Murray Street
University Ave
Gerrard
Nassau Street
Kensington Market
Baldwin St
Baldwin Street
Leonard Avenue
Bellevue Avenue
Augusta Avenue
Kensington Ave
Elm Street
Elm
Wales Avenue
D'Arcy Street
Little Portugal
Chinatown
St Patrick
Edward
Dundas Street West
Alexandra Park
Sharp Centre For Design
Art Gallery of Ontario
Textile Museum of Canada
Centre Ave
Chestnut
Grange Avenue
Grange Park
McCaul Street
St Patrick Street
Simcoe Street
Armoury St
Palmerston Avenue
Markham Street
Bathurst Street
Ryerson Avenue
Denison Avenue
Augusta Avenue
Cameron Street
Spadina Avenue
Huron Street
Beverley Street
Sullivan Street
Robinson Street
Carr Street
Phoebe Street
Osgoode Hall
Cameron House
Soho St
John St
Campbell House
Osgoode
Queen Street West
Queen Street
West Queen West
Queen Street West
Four Seasons Centre
Richmond Street West
Maud St
Camden St
Peter Street
Widmer Street
John St
Duncan Street
Nelson Street
Simcoe Street
University Ave
York St
Tecumseth Street
Adelaide Street West
Princess of Wales Theatre
Adelaide St W
Portland Street
Brant Street
Royal Alexandra
Pearl St
St Andrew
King Street West
St Andrew's
Toronto Dominion Centre
Stewart St
Mercer St
Metro Hall
Emily St
Wellington St West
Clarence Square Park
Blue Jays Way
11A
Roy Thomson Hall
Wellington St West
Wellington Street West
CBC Broadcast Centre
John Street
Niagara Street
Draper St
Royal York
Front Street West
Front Street West
Station St
Skywalk
Old Fort York
Spadina Avenue
Rogers Centre (SkyDome)
CN Tower
Metro Convention Centre
York Street
Housey St
Bremner Boulevard
Rees St
Simcoe St
Lake Shore Boulevard West
2
Gardiner Expressway
Fleet St
Spadina
Rees
Simcoe
York
Queens Quay West
York Quay Centre
Queens Quay Terminal Building
Bathurst St
Harbourfront Centre
The Power Plant Gallery
Western Gap
Airport Ferry
Toronto Island Airport
Toronto Inner Harbour
11, 12 & 13
Ontario Place
Hanlan's Point

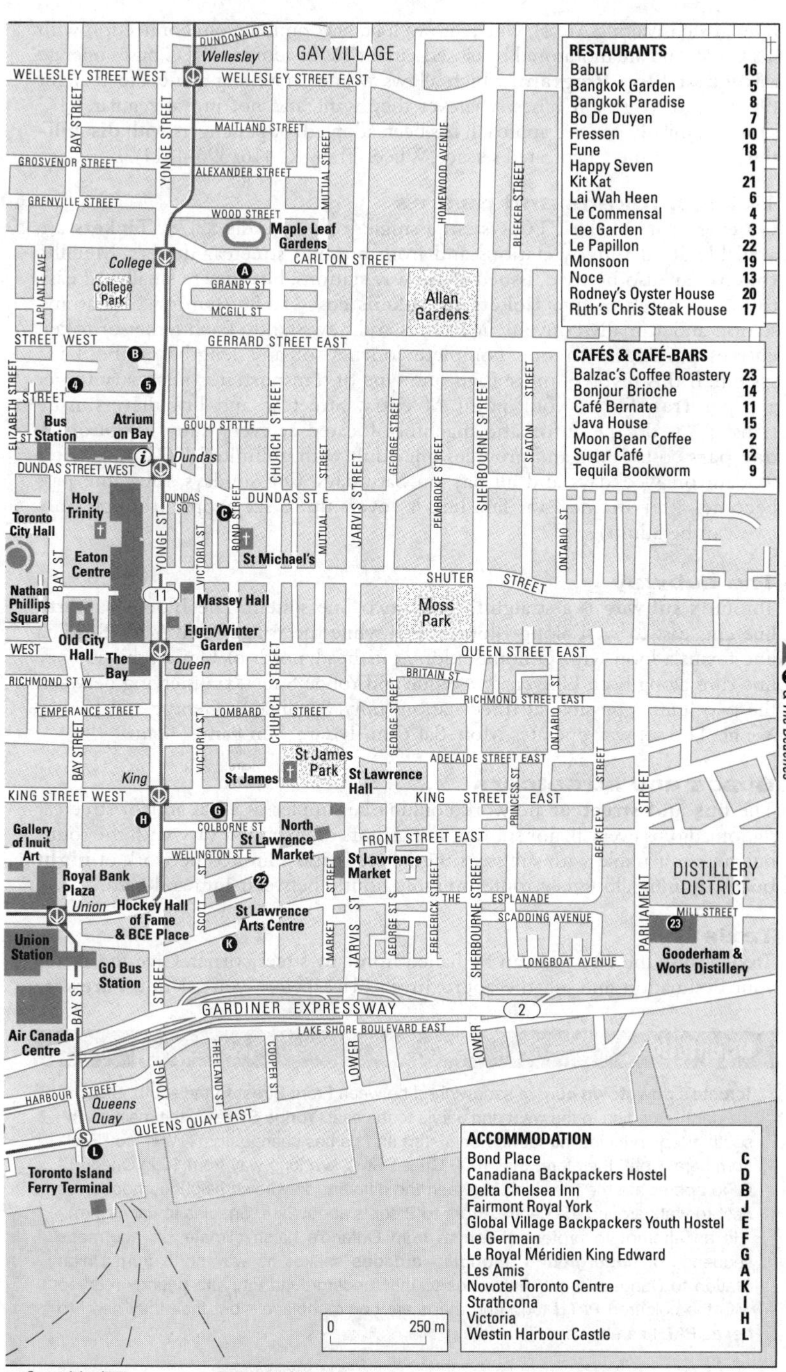

RESTAURANTS
Babur 16
Bangkok Garden 5
Bangkok Paradise 8
Bo De Duyen 7
Fressen 10
Fune 18
Happy Seven 1
Kit Kat 21
Lai Wah Heen 6
Le Commensal 4
Lee Garden 3
Le Papillon 22
Monsoon 19
Noce 13
Rodney's Oyster House 20
Ruth's Chris Steak House 17
CAFÉS & CAFÉ-BARS
Balzac's Coffee Roastery 23
Bonjour Brioche 14
Café Bernate 11
Java House 15
Moon Bean Coffee 2
Sugar Café 12
Tequila Bookworm 9
ACCOMMODATION
Bond Place C
Canadiana Backpackers Hostel D
Delta Chelsea Inn B
Fairmont Royal York J
Global Village Backpackers Youth Hostel E
Le Germain F
Le Royal Méridien King Edward G
Les Amis A
Novotel Toronto Centre K
Strathcona I
Victoria H
Westin Harbour Castle L
GAY VILLAGE
Wellesley
College
Dundas
Queen
King
Union
Queens Quay
Maple Leaf Gardens
College Park
Allan Gardens
Bus Station
Atrium on Bay
Holy Trinity
Toronto City Hall
Eaton Centre
Nathan Phillips Square
Old City Hall
The Bay
St Michael's
Massey Hall
Elgin/Winter Garden
Moss Park
St James Park
St James
St Lawrence Hall
Gallery of Inuit Art
North St Lawrence Market
St Lawrence Market
Royal Bank Plaza
Hockey Hall of Fame & BCE Place
St Lawrence Arts Centre
Union Station
GO Bus Station
Air Canada Centre
DISTILLERY DISTRICT
Goodeherham & Worts Distillery
Toronto Island Ferry Terminal
GARDINER EXPRESSWAY
WELLESLEY STREET WEST
WELLESLEY STREET EAST
YONGE STREET
BAY STREET
CHURCH STREET
JARVIS STREET
SHERBOURNE STREET
QUEEN STREET EAST
KING STREET EAST
KING STREET WEST
FRONT STREET EAST
DUNDAS STREET WEST
CARLTON STREET
GERRARD STREET EAST
LAKE SHORE BOULEVARD EAST
QUEENS QUAY EAST
0 250 m
14 & The Beaches
Centre Island
Ward's Island

(Designated Waiting Areas), which are well lit, have an intercom connection with TTC staff and are monitored by closed-circuit TV. In addition, TTC buses operate a **Request Stop Program**, which allows women travelling alone late at night (9pm–5am) to get off buses wherever they want, and not just at regular TTC stops. A similarly positive approach has been adopted for passengers with **disabilities**, who can use a dedicated service, Wheel-Trans (ⓣ416/393-4111).

Tickets, tokens and passes

On every part of the TTC system a single journey costs $2.75. **Tickets** are available at all subway stations and from bus and streetcar drivers. Metallic **tokens** can also be used, issued at subway stations, but they're small and easy to lose. A batch of **five tickets or tokens** cost $10.50 (ten for $21) at any station and at many convenience stores and newsstands. Each ticket or token entitles passengers to one complete journey of any length on the TTC system. If this involves more than one type of transport, it is necessary to get a paper **transfer** at your point of entry. Streetcar and bus drivers issue transfers, as do the automatic machines located at every subway station. A **day pass** costs $8.50 and provides one adult with unlimited TTC travel after 9.30am on weekdays and all day on Saturdays. On Sundays, the same pass becomes a terrific deal for families: it covers up to six people (though only two can be adults).

The subway

Toronto's **subway** is a straightforward, two-line system. The Bloor–Danforth line cuts east to west along Bloor Street, while the Yonge–University–Spadina line forms a loop with Union Station at its head; north of Union, this subway line runs along both University Avenue and Yonge Street. Transferring between the two lines is possible at three stations only: Spadina, St George and Bloor–Yonge. The subway operates Mon–Sat 6am–1/2am, Sun 9am–1/2am.

Buses and streetcars

The **bus and streetcar** network couldn't be simpler, as a bus and/or streetcar station adjoins every major subway stop. Hours of operation vary with the route, but are comparable with subway times; there is also a limited network of **night buses** running along key routes roughly hourly between 1am and 6am.

Taxis

Taxis cruise the city and can be hailed from any street corner. Give the driver your destination and ask the approximate price before you set out. **Fares** are

Orientation

Toronto's **downtown core** is sandwiched between Front Street to the south, Bloor to the north, Spadina to the west and Jarvis to the east. **Yonge Street** is the main north–south artery: principal street numbers start and names change from "West" to "East" from here. Note, therefore, that 1000 Queen St W is a long way from 1000 Queen St E. To appreciate the transition between the different downtown neighbourhoods, it's best to **walk** around the centre: Front to Bloor is about 2km, Spadina to Jarvis 1km.

In an attempt to protect shoppers from Ontario's harsh climate, an enormous sequence of **underground shopping arcades** snakes its way north from Union Station to Dundas Street. Entrances to this 'underground city' are brightly marked with the coloured **PATH** logo and maps are commonplace – but then they need to be, as PATH can be very disorienting.

generally reasonable with a ride from Union Station to the far side of Cabbagetown, for instance, costing around $12. Of the multitude of cab companies to choose from, two of the most reliable are **Co-op Cabs** (ⓣ416/504-4016) and **Diamond Taxicab** (ⓣ416/366-6868).

Accommodation

As Toronto's popularity as a tourist destination has increased, the availability of **hotel** accommodation, especially in the mid-price range, has shrunk. Indeed, during peak season (late June to Aug) and throughout most of the city's big festivals, it is essential to book well in advance. Most of the city's hotels occupy modern skyscrapers and there is much stylistic uniformity in their standardized fittings and furnishings, though, to be fair, the opening of a string of **boutique hotels** has livened things up considerably. Prices mostly reflect floor space and fluctuate depending on when and for how long you stay, but, in general, a clean, centrally located hotel room starts at $120. **Bed and breakfast** accommodation tends to be a less expensive – even with breakfast thrown in – and although most of these establishments are not as central as the city's hotels, they often take you out into Toronto's quainter neighbourhoods. Budget-conscious travellers might want to consider one of the city's **hostels** or opt instead for a **student room** in one of the university's halls of residence, available – with some variation – from the second week in May to late August. The Ontario Tourism Travel Information Centre (see p.77) will help in **finding a hotel room**, or you can call Tourism Toronto (see p.77).

Hotels

Bond Place 65 Dundas St E; Subway: Dundas ⓣ416/362-6061, ⓦwww.bondplacehoteltoronto.com. This straightforward, tower-block hotel is popular with package-tour operators and handily located, just a couple of minutes' walk from the Eaton Centre. Has simple, unassuming doubles and there are often weekend reductions. ⑤

Days Hotel - Toronto Downtown 30 Carlton St; Subway: College ⓣ416/977-6655 or 1-800/329-7466, ⓦwww.daysinn.com. Routine modern, chain hotel with competitively priced rooms. Occupies a chunky tower block metres from the subway. ⑤

Delta Chelsea Inn 33 Gerrard St W; Subway: Dundas ⓣ416/595-1975 or 1-800/243-5732, ⓦwww.deltachelsea.com. Near the Eaton Centre, this whopping hotel has excellent leisure facilities, including swimming pool, gym, sauna and childcare. The comfortable, attractively furnished rooms are a comparative bargain, with substantial weekend discounts. ⑥

Fairmont Royal York 100 Front St W; Subway: Union ⓣ416/368-2511 or 1-800/257-7544, ⓦwww.fairmont.com/royalyork. When it was completed in 1927, the *Royal York* was the largest hotel in the British Empire and it still retains much of its original grandeur, especially in the sprawling lobby, which is decked out with mosaic floors, coffered ceilings and massive chandeliers. The guest rooms, however, aren't as pricey (or as stylish) as you might expect and there are substantial off-season and weekend discounts. ⑥

Four Seasons 21 Avenue Rd; Subway: Bay ⓣ416/964-0411 or 1-800/819-5053, ⓦwww.fourseasons.com. This well-appointed establishment, situated in the heart of the Yorkville neighbourhood, has a reputation for hosting the city's most famous guests. The hotel's restaurants and wine cellar are as stellar as the impeccable service, and while the prices here are off the charts, this is a fine place to be if you want to splurge. ⑧

Howard Johnson Yorkville 89 Avenue Rd; Subway: Bay ⓣ416/964-1220 or 1-800/446-4656, ⓦwww.hojo.com. This small, chain hotel is tucked away on a busy section of Avenue Rd, just blocks from Yorkville. The helpful staff is attentive, and the large rooms are tidy, comfortable and well-equipped for the business traveller. ⑥

Le Germain 30 Mercer St; Subway: St Andrew ⓣ416/345-9500 or 1-866/345-9501, ⓦwww.germaintoronto.com. Immaculate boutique hotel kitted out in the full flourish of

modern style, from the handsome foyer, with its soaring ceiling, open-fire and acres of glass, through to the stylish, well-appointed guest rooms. A five- to ten-minute walk west from the subway. 8

Le Royal Méridien King Edward 37 King St E; Subway: King ⓣ416/863-9700 or 1-800/543-4300, ⓦwww.starwoodhotels.com. Designed by E.J. Lennox (see p.92) in 1903 and with a long list of famous guests – from Mark Twain to John and Yoko – this distinguished old hotel has recently been restored to its Beaux Arts best. Rooms range from chic minimalism to the faux Edwardian. 8

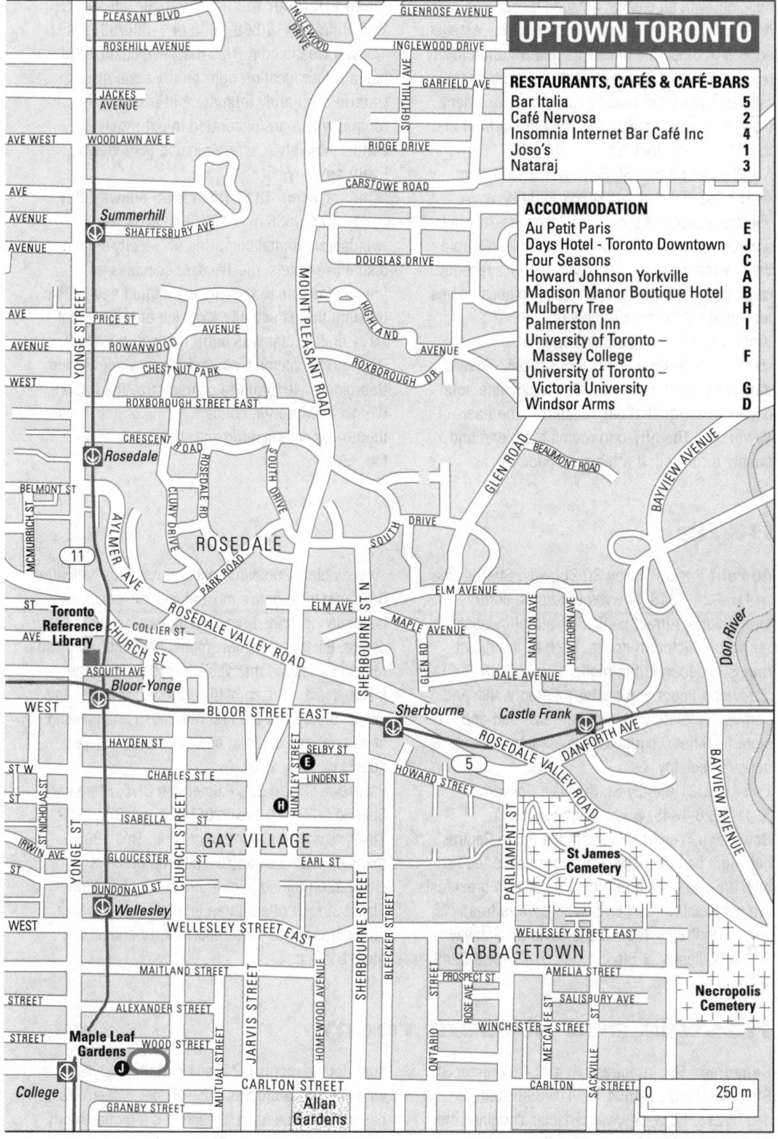

Madison Manor Boutique Hotel 20 Madison Ave; Subway: St George ⓣ416/922-5579 or 1-877-561-7048, ⓦwww.madisonavenuepub.com. Located in the heart of the Annex neighbourhood, this immaculately renovated Victorian inn has 23 comfortable rooms, some with fireplaces and all with en-suite bathrooms as well as the amenities (hair dryers, Internet access) that you would expect in a luxury hotel. A great find. ❹

Novotel Toronto Centre 45 The Esplanade; Subway: Union Station ⓣ416/367-8900, ⓦwww.novotel.com. Located in a splendidly converted old building, with an elegant arcaded facade and other Art Deco flourishes, this chain hotel offers excellent service at moderate prices. Its relative affordability may be linked to its noisy location – it abuts the railway – but otherwise, the location is excellent, close to the downtown core, the Harbourfront and the Distillery District. 6

Strathcona 60 York St; Subway: Union Station ⓣ416/363-3321 or 1-800/268-8304, ⓦwww.thestrathconahotel.com. Great location – about half a block from Union Station, and five minutes from the SkyDome and the CN Tower – for this recently revamped hotel, whose well-equipped guest rooms are kitted out in unfussy, modern style. 6

Victoria 56 Yonge St; Subway: King ⓣ416/363-1666 or 1-800/363-8228, ⓦwww.hotelvictoria-toronto.com. This enjoyable hotel occupies a dignified old building in the heart of downtown. The fifty-odd rooms are clean and crisply furnished, if a tad cramped. 6

Westin Harbour Castle 1 Harbour Square; LRT: York Quay ⓣ416/869-1600 or 1-800/937-8461, ⓦwww.westin.com. This massive, chain hotel has a prime location right on the edge of Lake Ontario. It's hardly intimate, but many of the rooms, which are decorated in extremely comfortable style, offer splendid lake views. Every amenity. 7

Windsor Arms 18 St Thomas St; Subway: Bay ⓣ416/971-9666 or 1-877/999-2767, ⓦwww.windsorarmshotel.com. One of the city's most distinctive hotels, the *Windsor* occupies an immaculate brick-and-stone-trimmed neo-Gothic building that is actually a replica of the original 1911 edifice that was burnt down in the 1990s. Open fires, columns, stained-glass windows and Georgian-style furniture characterize the interior. What's new are the condominiums on top, plus the no-expense-spared spa; top-notch service too. 8

B&Bs

Au Petit Paris 3 Selby St; Subway: Sherbourne ⓣ416/928-1348, ⓦwww.bbtoronto.com/aupetitparis. Attractive B&B in a meticulously renovated Victorian house. Each of the guest rooms is decorated in modern style, with hardwood floors and pastel-painted walls, and comes complete with a queen-size bed and en-suite facilities. Vegetarian breakfasts are the house speciality. 6

Les Amis 31 Granby St; Subway: College ⓣ416/928-1348, ⓦwww.bbtoronto.com. Downtown, a short stroll from the Eaton Centre, holding a handful of pleasantly furnished rooms with a/c and shared facilities. Vegetarian breakfasts are a speciality – the crepes go down a treat. 5

Mulberry Tree 122 Isabella St; Subway: Wellesley or Bloor-Yonge ⓣ416/960-5249, ⓦwww.bbtoronto.com/mulberrytree. This delightful B&B, one of Toronto's most agreeable, occupies a tastefully decorated heritage home close to the city centre. Each of the guest rooms is comfortable and relaxing – indeed the whole atmosphere of the place is just right, combining efficiency and friendliness. Breakfasts are first rate too, home cooking at its best and eaten at one large table where guests can jaw away. 5

Palmerston Inn 322 Palmerston Blvd; Streetcar: College (#506) ⓣ416/920-7842 or 1-877/920-7842, ⓦwww.palmerstoninn.com. This 1906 mansion with a distinctive pillared porch is situated on the edge of the fashionable College Street strip. It offers three en suite guest rooms and extras include afternoon sherry and a daily room service. 6

Hostels and student rooms

Canadiana Backpackers Hostel 42 Widmer St; Streetcar: King St (#504). ⓣ416/598-9090 or 1-877/215-1225, ⓦwww.canadianalodging.com. This hip, clean hostel is right in the midst of Toronto's clubs, steps away from Queen St W and within easy walking distance of downtown. Dorm bed $27, double room $75.

Global Village Backpackers Youth Hostel 460 King St W; Streetcar: King St (#504) ⓣ416/703-8540 or 1-888/844-7875, ⓦwww.globalbackpackers.com. This former hotel (once famed for a free-wheeling Art Deco tap room) has both double rooms ($72) and dormitory-style beds with shared bathrooms ($27–29 per person). Facilities include laundry, a kitchen and a games room. Close to the Richmond St/Queen St W action.

University of Toronto – Massey College 4 Devonshire Place; Subway: St George ⓣ416/946-7843, ⓦwww.utoronto.ca/massey. Apart from being the one-time stomping ground of author Robertson Davies, this old and distinguished college reportedly boasts the presence of at least one ghost. Singles and doubles are available with breakfast included on weekdays from May to early Aug. Single room $50-55, doubles $85–95.

University of Toronto – Victoria University 93 Charles St W; Subway: Museum ⓣ416/585-4524, ⓦwww.vicu.utoronto.ca/. Victoria University's sprawling campus, spreading south from Charles St, offers single and double rooms with breakfast in several of its halls of residence from the middle of May to late Aug. Single room $60, doubles $82.

Toronto's neighbourhoods

One of Toronto's most striking features is its division into distinct **neighbourhoods**, many of them based on ethnic origin, others defined by sexual preference or income. Bilingual street signs identify some of these neighbourhoods, but architecturally they are often indistinguishable from their surroundings. The following rundown will help you get the most from the city's demographic mosaic, whether you want to shop, eat or just take in the atmosphere. But bear in mind that there is a certain artificiality in the nomenclature: Chinatown, for instance, has hundreds of Vietnamese residents, Little Italy many Portuguese.

The Beaches South of Queen St East between Woodbine and Victoria Park Ave. A prosperous and particularly appealing district with chic boutiques, leafy streets and a sandy beach trimmed by a popular boardwalk. Glenn Gould (see box, p.93) was born here.

Cabbagetown East of Jarvis and roughly bounded by Gerrard St East on its south side, Wellesley to the north and the Don River to the east. Renowned for its Victorian housing, the name comes from the district's nineteenth-century immigrants, whose tiny front gardens were filled with cabbages.

Chinatown Concentrated along Dundas between Beverley and Spadina. This is one of Toronto's most distinctive neighbourhoods, with busy restaurants and stores selling anything from porcelain and jade to herbs and pickled seaweed.

The Gay and Lesbian Village Centred around Church and Wellesley, with a plethora of bars, restaurants and bookshops.

Greektown A burgeoning neighbourhood along Danforth Ave, between Pape and Woodbine. Has scores of authentic restaurants, so head here for the city's best Greek cuisine.

Kensington Market Just north of Dundas between Spadina and Augusta. The most ethnically diverse part of town, combining Portuguese, West Indian and Jewish Canadians, who pack the streets with a plethora of tiny shops and open-air stalls.

Little India Along Gerrard Street E, running one block west from Coxwell Avenue. Visually, this neighbourhood is not especially appealing, but it does have a number of first-rate restaurants.

Little Italy This neighbourhood runs along College between Bathurst and Clinton; it's one of Toronto's liveliest neighbourhoods.

Little Portugal A crowded, vital area packed with shops and neighbourhood food joints, focused on Dundas, west of Bathurst as far as Dovercourt Rd.

Queen St W Between University and Spadina. Has one of the highest retail rents in the city and is home to all things trendy and expensive. The students and punks who once hung around here have moved on to what is known as **"West Queen W"**, between Bathurst and Ossington.

Yorkville Just above Bloor between Yonge and Avenue Rd. Was "alternative" in the 1960s, with appearances by the likes of Gordon Lightfoot and Joni Mitchell. Today, the alternative jive is long gone, and the district holds some of Toronto's most expensive clothing shops and art galleries, as well as several good bars and restaurants.

The City

Toronto evolved from a lakeside settlement, but its growth was sporadic and mostly unplanned, resulting in a cityscape that can strike the visitor as a particularly random mix of the run-down, the old and the new. This apparent disarray, when combined with the city's muggy summers, means that most visitors spend their time hopping from sight to sight on the transit rather than walking. If, however, you've the time and determination to get below the surface, take to your feet and the city will slowly unfurl itself. The logical place to start an exploration is **Downtown** (see map, p.78) at the **CN Tower**, whose observation platforms provide panoramic views over the city and its immediate surroundings. From here, it's a brief stroll to the handsome symmetries of **Union Station**, which stands on the edge of the **Business District**, whose striking skyscrapers march north up Yonge as far as Adelaide Street. Beyond Adelaide lies the main shopping area, revolving around the enormous **Eaton Centre**, which is itself but a stone's throw from the neo-Gothic intricacies of the old **City Hall** and the modernism of **Nathan Philips Square**. From the square, it's another short haul to the **Art Gallery of Ontario**, holding the city's finest collection of paintings, and another, slightly longer trek west to **Fort York**, an accurate and intriguing reconstruction of the British outpost established here in 1793.

Moving on into Uptown Toronto (see map, p.82), the northerly reaches of **University Avenue** are framed by a string of bristling, monochromatic office blocks that stomp up to the imposing stonework of the **Ontario Legislative Assembly Building**. This marks the start of what amounts to a museum district, comprising the delightful **Gardiner Museum of Ceramic Art**; the rambling applied arts collections of the vast **Royal Ontario Museum**; and the fascinating **Bata Shoe Museum**. A pair of contrasting Victorian mansions are a short subway ride away too – grandiose **Casa Loma** and genteel **Spadina House**. Finally, save time for the redeveloped **Harbourfront** south of Union Station, which offers flashy shops and galleries as well as the jetty from where **passenger ferries** make the short hop over to the bucolic **Toronto Islands**.

The CN Tower

Much to the dismay of many Torontonians, the **CN Tower**, 301 Front St W (daily Sun–Thurs 9am–10pm, Fri & Sat 9am–10.30pm, sometimes later; observation deck & glass floor $22, Sky Pod $4 extra; Ⓦwww.cntower.ca; Subway: Union Station), has become the city's symbol. It's touted on much of the city's promotional literature, features on thousands of postcards and holiday snaps, and has become the obligatory start to most tourist itineraries. From anywhere in the city, it's impossible to miss its slender form poking high above the skyline, reminding some of French novelist Guy de Maupassant's quip about another

Toronto City Pass

If you are a diligent sightseer, you may be able to save money with the **Toronto City Pass.** Valid for nine days, the pass entitles visitors to free entrance to six of the city's most popular attractions – the CN Tower (see above), the Art Gallery of Ontario (see p.95), the Royal Ontario Museum (see p.100), Casa Loma (see p.102), the Ontario Science Centre (see p.107), and Toronto Zoo (see p.107). It costs $55 ($37 for 4–12 year olds) and can be purchased at any of the six sights.

famous tower: "I like to lunch at the Eiffel Tower because that's the only place in Paris I can't see it."

Unlikely as it may seem, the celebrity status of the CN Tower was entirely unforeseen, its origins plain and utilitarian. In the 1960s, the Canadian Broadcasting Company (CBC) teamed up with the railway conglomerate Canadian National (CN) to propose the construction of a bigger and better transmission antenna. CBC eventually withdrew from the project, but CN, who owned the land, forged ahead. Much to the company's surprise, they found that the undertaking stirred intense public interest – so much so that long before the tower was completed, in 1975, it was clear that its potential as a tourist sight would be huge: today, broadcasting only accounts for about twenty percent of the tower's income, with the rest provided by the two million tourists who throng here annually. Come early (especially on school holidays) to avoid the crowds.

The **tallest freestanding structure in the world**, the sleek and elegant tower tapers to a minaret-thin point 553m (1815ft) above the city centre. Details of its construction are provided in a series of photographs and touch-screen displays on the mezzanine level just beyond the main access ramp and security check-in. The background information is extremely interesting, revealing all sorts of odd facts and figures, though it is hardly reassuring to know that the tower is hit by lightning between sixty and eighty times a year.

From the foot of the tower, **glass-fronted elevators** whisk you up the outside of the building to the indoor and outdoor **Look Out level** galleries at 346m. These circular galleries provide views over the whole of the city, which appears flattened and without much perspective – though markers help by pointing out the most conspicuous sights. This is also where you'll find *360 The Restaurant* (which slowly revolves around the tower, taking 72 minutes to make one revolution), and the reinforced **glass floor** - a vertigo shock that goes some way to justifying the tower's pricey admittance fee. You are, however, still 100m from the top of the tower, with a separate set of lifts to carry visitors up to the **Sky Pod**, a confined little gallery that doesn't justify the extra expense.

The Rogers Centre (SkyDome)

Next door to the CN Tower stands the **Rogers Centre**, formerly the **SkyDome**, which is home to two major Toronto sports teams – the Blue Jays baseball team and the Argonauts, of Canadian football fame. The stadium seats 53,000 and is used for special events and concerts as well as sports. Opened in 1989, it was the first stadium in the world to have a fully retractable roof, an impressive feat of engineering with four gigantic roof panels mounted on rail tracks taking just twenty minutes to cover the stadium's eight acres of turf and terrace. The SkyDome was much touted by the city at the time, but the end result is really rather ugly and when the roof is closed the stadium looks like a giant armadillo. **Guided tours** (call for schedule Ⓣ416/341-2770, Ⓦwww.rogerscentre.com; $13.50), worth it only if you're sticking around for a sporting event, last an hour and begin with a fifteen-minute film about the stadium's construction. The ensuing walking tour takes in a dressing room and a stroll on the playing field.

Union Station

The **Skywalk** is a sheltered walkway that leads from the Rogers Centre to **Union Station**, at Front Street W and Bay Street, a distinguished Beaux Arts structure designed in 1907 and finally completed in 1927. The station's exterior is imposing, with its long serenade of Neoclassical columns, but the interior is the real highlight, the vast **main hall** boasting a coffered and tiled ceiling of graceful design. Like other North American railway stations of the period, Union Station has the flavour of a medieval cathedral, with muffled sounds echoing through its stone cloisters, and daylight filtering through its high arched windows. The station's grandiose quality was quite deliberate. In the days when the steam train was the most popular form of transport, architects were keen to glorify the train station, and, in this case, to conjure up images of Canada's vastness – a frieze bearing the names of all the Canadian cities reachable by rail at the time of construction runs around the hall.

The Banking District: the Royal Bank Plaza and the Toronto Dominion Centre

Opposite the east end of Union Station, the **Banking District,** whose skyscrapers march north as far as Adelaide, kicks off with the **Royal Bank Plaza**, 200 Bay St, where the two massive towers were designed by local architect Boris Zerafa during the architectural boom of the mid-1970s. Each tower is completely coated with a thin layer of gold, and despite Zerafa's assertion that the gold simply added texture to his creation, it's hard not to believe that the Royal Bank wanted to show off a bit too.

To the left of the Royal Bank – and to the right of the *Royal York Hotel* - a gated **stone stairway** climbs up from Front Street W to a tiny plaza overseen by a phalanx of skyscrapers. It's a delightful spot, in a heart-of-the-city sort of way, and Catherine Widgery's *City People* (1989), a folksy set of life-size metal figures attached to the stairway's walls, add a touch of decorative élan. The walkway continues down to Wellington Street W, just a few metres from the southern tower – now the Waterhouse Tower – of the **Toronto Dominion Centre**, whose four reflective black blocks of 1964 straddle Wellington Street between Bay and York. Arguably the most appealing of the city's modern skyscrapers, the four towers are without decoration, but as an ensemble they achieve an austere beauty that can't help but impress.

The Toronto Dominion Gallery of Inuit Art

The **Toronto** Dominion Gallery of Inuit Art, in the South – or Waterhouse – Tower of the Toronto Dominion Centre (Mon–Fri 8am–6pm, Sat & Sun 10am–4pm; free), boasts an outstanding collection of over a hundred pieces of Inuit sculpture. Spread over two levels, the collection is owned by the Dominion Bank, who commissioned

Selling air

In one of the city's stranger ordinances, Toronto's buildings were once decreed to have a "**notional maximum altitude**". Owners of historic properties were not allowed to extend their buildings upwards, but they were permitted to sell the empty space between their roofs and the notional maximum to builders of new structures. Consequently, developers literally bought empty space and added it on to the maximum height they were already allowed for their buildings, thus creating the skyscrapers that the original ordinance seemed to forbid.

The arrangement enhanced neither the old nor the new, and was quickly followed up by an even stranger agreement. By the late 1980s, preservationists had convinced the city that no more of the city's old buildings should be demolished. Developers, however, still wanted to build new downtown buildings, and several deals emerged where a new complex would incorporate or literally engulf the old – the most extreme example being BCE Place at the corner of Yonge and Front sts (see p.91).

a panel of experts to celebrate Canada's Centennial in 1965 by collecting the best of postwar Inuit art. The gallery contains examples of all the favourite themes of Inuit sculpture, primarily animal and human studies supplemented by a smattering of metamorphic figures, in which an Inuit adopts the form of an animal, either in full or in part. Other sculptures depict deities, particularly Nuliayuk the sea goddess (also known as Sedna). Inuit religious belief was short on theology, but its encyclopedic animism populated the Arctic with spirits and gods, the subject of all manner of Inuit folk tales. Christianity destroyed this traditional faith, but the legends survived and continue to feature prominently in native sculpture. Most of the pieces are in soapstone, a greyish-blue stone that is easy to carve, but there are bone, ivory and caribou-antler pieces too. The only problem is the almost total lack of labeling with the free introductory booklet, available from the rack at the start of the gallery, providing only limited assistance.

St Andrew's Presbyterian Church

Crossing over Wellington Street, and walking between the other three towers of the Toronto Dominion Centre, you soon pass **Joe Fafard**'s herd of grazing cows – seven extraordinarily realistic **bronze statues** that have proved immensely popular with the city's office workers. From here, it's a short detour west along King Street to **St Andrew's Presbyterian Church**, 75 Simcoe St (daily 9am–4pm; free; Subway: St Andrew). Marooned among the city's skyscrapers, this handsome sandstone church is a reminder of an older Toronto, and its Romanesque Revival towers and gables have a distinctly Norman appearance. Built in 1876 for a predominantly Scottish congregation, the church has a delightful interior, its cherrywood pews and balcony sloping down towards the chancel with dappled light streaming in through the stained-glass windows.

Roy Thomson Hall and the CBC Centre

Across Simcoe Street from St Andrew's, **Roy Thomson Hall**, the home of the Toronto Symphony Orchestra (for more on whom see p.112), was completed in 1982 to a design by Canada's own Arthur Erickson. The hall looks like an upturned soup bowl by day, but at night its appearance is transformed, its glass-panelled walls radiating a skein of filtered light high into the sky.

From Thomson Hall, it's a brief walk south to the **CBC Broadcasting Centre**, 250 Front St W, a ten-storey edifice whose painted gridiron beams make the building aesthetically bearable, but not much more. Since its foundation in 1936, **CBC** – the Canadian Broadcasting Company – has built up an international reputation for the impartiality of its radio and television news and, although it carries commercials unlike the UK's BBC, it remains in public ownership and directly responsible to the federal Parliament. CBC used to offer guided tours of the Broadcasting Centre, but these have been discontinued at least for the moment, though you can still visit the **CBC museum** (Mon–Fri 9am–5pm, Sat noon–4pm; free; Ⓦwww.cbc.ca/museum), where, amongst a series of modest exhibits, you can look at vintage CBC TV shows in a mini–theatre.

From the CBC Broadcasting Centre, it's a twenty–minute hoof **west** to Fort York, half that **east** to the Hockey Hall of Fame and the St Lawrence district (see p.91).

Fort York

Modern-day Toronto traces its origins to **Fort York** (late May to Aug daily 10am–5pm; Sept to late May Mon–Fri 10am–4pm, Sat & Sun 10am–5pm; $6;

☎416/392-6907), a colonial stockade built in 1793 on the shores of Lake Ontario to bolster British control of the Great Lakes. Since then, landfill has pushed the lakeshore southwards and marooned the fort, which was reconstructed in the 1930s, under the shadow of the (elevated) Gardiner Expressway just to the west of Bathurst Street. There are **two entrances** to the fort – a (well-signed) main entrance off Lakeshore Boulevard W along Fleet Street and then Garrison Road; and a pedestrians' back entrance via a path off Bathurst Street. To get to the latter, head west along Front Street from the CBC Broadcasting Centre, turn left onto Bathurst, walk over the bridge and the path is on the right. To shorten the walk, take the King Street tram west to King and Bathurst. To reach the front entrance, take either the Bathurst streetcar (#511) or streetcar #509 from Union Station, and get off on Fleet Street at the foot of Garrison Road; from here the fort is a ten-minute walk.

Fort York was initially a half-hearted, poorly fortified affair, partly because of a lack of funds, but mainly because it was too remote to command much attention – never mind that the township of York was the capital of Upper Canada. However, in 1811, a deterioration in Anglo-American relations put it on full alert. There was a sudden flurry of activity as the fort's ramparts and gun emplacements were strengthened, but it was still too weak to rebuff the American army that marched on York in 1813, destroying the fort in the process. After the war, Fort York was rebuilt and its garrison made a considerable contribution to the development of Toronto, as York was renamed in 1834. The British army moved out in 1870 and their Canadian replacements stayed for another sixty years; the fort was opened as a **museum** in 1934. Throughout the summer, **costumed guides** give the low-down on colonial life and free plans of the fort are issued at reception.

The fort's carefully restored earth and stone **ramparts** are low-lying and thick and constructed in a zigzag pattern, both to mitigate against enemy artillery and to provide complementary lines of fire. They enclose a haphazard sequence of log, stone and brick buildings, notably a couple of well-preserved **blockhouses**, complete with heavy timbers and snipers' loopholes. In one of them – **Building No.5** on the plan – an introductory video outlines the history of the fort and an exhibit explores the various military crises that afflicted Canada from the 1780s to the 1880s, especially the War of 1812.

Moving on, **Building No.6** started out as a magazine but ended up as a storehouse. Its ground floor now holds a modest display on the role of black soldiers and settlers in the early history of Ontario. Up above, an archeological section displays the various bits and pieces unearthed at the fort – buckles, brooches, plates, clay pipes, tunic buttons and so forth. Across the fort, **Building No.4**, the Blue Barracks, is a 1930s reconstruction of the junior officers' quarters, whilst **Building No.3** is the former Officers' Quarters and Mess. The latter boasts several period rooms and two original money vaults, hidden away in the cellar. Opposite, the stone and brick powder magazine – **Building No.8** – has two-metre-thick walls and spark-proof copper and brass fixtures.

The Hockey Hall of Fame

From the CBC Broadcasting Centre (see p.89), it's a short haul east to the **Hockey Hall of Fame**, 30 Yonge St at Front St W (Mon–Fri 10am–5pm, Sat 9.30am–6pm & Sun 10.30am–5pm; $13, children 4–13 years old & the over-65s $9; ☎416/360-7765, Ⓦwww.hhof.com), a highly commercialized, ultra-modern tribute to Canada's national sport – though you wouldn't think so from the outside: the only part of the Hall visible from the street is the old **Bank of Montréal building**, a Neoclassical edifice dating back to 1885. The bank's doors have been blocked off and the interior bowdlerized to house a collection of hockey trophies that constitutes a small part of the Hockey Hall of Fame, whose **entrance** is below ground in the adjacent **BCE Place** shopping mall.

The St Lawrence District

The **St Lawrence district**, lying just to the east of Yonge Street, between The Esplanade, Adelaide Street East and Frederick Street, is one of the city's oldest neighbourhoods, enjoying its first period of rapid growth after the War of 1812. In Victorian times, St Lawrence became one of the most fashionable parts of the city, and although it hit the skids thereafter, it has recently been revamped and (partly) gentrified. The district is best approached by heading east from Yonge Street along Front Street E. From this direction, you'll soon reach **St Lawrence Market**, at Front and Jarvis (Tues–Thurs 8am–6pm, Fri 8am–7pm & Sat 5am–5pm; Ⓦwww.stlawrencemarket.com), a capacious red-brick building of 1844 that holds the city's best food and drink market. Spread out across the main and lower levels are stalls selling everything from fish and freshly baked bread to international foodstuffs, all sorts of organic edibles and Ontario specialities – cheese, jellies, jams and fern fiddleheads to name but four. The market is at its busiest on Saturday, which also means that you can drop by the **North St Lawrence Market**, an authentic farmers' market (Sat 5am–5pm) housed in the long brick building opposite, on the north side of Front Street.

St Lawrence Hall

Behind North St Lawrence Market, just along Jarvis Street, stands **St Lawrence Hall**, one of the city's most attractive Victorian buildings, a palatial edifice whose columns, pilasters and pediments are surmounted by a dinky little cupola. Dating from 1850, the hall was built as the city's main meeting-place, with oodles of space for balls, public lectures and concerts. Some performances were eminently genteel, others decidedly mawkish – it was here that the "Swedish songbird" **Jenny Lind** (1820–87) made one of her Canadian appearances – and yet others more urgent, like the anti-slavery rallies of the 1850s. The bad taste award goes to the American showman and circus proprietor **P.T. Barnum** (1810–91), one-time mayor of his hometown of Bridgeport, Connecticut, and author of the bizarre *The Humbugs of the World*. It was Barnum who saw the potential of his fellow Bridgeportonian, the diminutive Charles Sherwood Stratton, aka **Tom Thumb** (1838–83), exhibiting him as a curiosity here in St Lawrence Hall as well as anywhere else that would pay. Poor old Stratton was just 60cm (2ft) tall when he first went on tour.

St James Anglican Cathedral

On the other side of King Street, a couple of hundred metres west from St Lawrence Hall, rises the graceful bulk of **St James Anglican Cathedral**, whose yellowish stone is fetchingly off-set by copper-green roofs and a slender spire. An excellent example of the neo-Gothic style once popular in every corner of the British Empire, the cathedral boasts scores of pointed-arch windows and acres of sturdy buttressing. Inside, the nave is supported by elegant high-arched pillars and flanked by an ambitious set of **stained-glass windows** that attempts to trace the path by which Christianity reached Canada from Palestine via England. It's all a little confusing, but broadly speaking, the less inventive windows depict Biblical scenes, whereas those that focus on English history are the more ingenious.

The Distillery District

The **Distillery District** (ⓦ www.thedistillery.com) comprises Toronto's newest arts and entertainment complex, sited in the former **Gooderham and Worts distillery**, an extremely appealing industrial "village" on Mill Street, near the foot of Parliament Street. In use as a distillery until 1990, this rambling network of over forty brick buildings once comprised the largest distillery in the British Empire, and now lays claim to be the best-preserved Victorian industrial complex in the whole of North America. The distillery was founded in 1832, when ships could sail into its own jetty, though landfill subsequently becalmed it in the lee of the railway lines and the tail-end of the Gardiner Expressway. Otherwise unruffled for decades, much of the distillery's machinery has survived, as have its walkways and bottle runways, features that have been carefully integrated into the revamp. Not all the prospective tenants have moved in yet, but when all the work is completed the complex will hold, amongst much else, over thirty art galleries and artists' studios, furniture designers, a chocolatier, bakeries, shops, a microbrewery and a couple of performance venues. The redevelopment of the distillery has been led by a small group of entrepreneurs, who decided (with refreshing integrity) to exclude all multinational chains. As for **opening times**, most of the galleries and shops start daily at 10am and close down at 6pm, whereas the cafés and bars hang on till 8pm, later when things are in full swing. To get there by **public transport**, take the King Street streetcar (#504) east to Parliament and walk from there – it takes about five minutes.

Nathan Phillips Square

Back in the city centre on Queen Street W, **Nathan Phillips Square** is one of Toronto's most distinctive landmarks. Laid out by the Finnish architect Viljo Revell in the 1960s, the square is framed by an elevated walkway and focuses on a reflecting pool, which becomes a skating rink in winter. Toronto's modernist **City Hall** overlooks the square, its curved glass-and-concrete towers fronted by *The Archer*, a Henry Moore sculpture that resembles nothing so much as a giant propeller. Revell won all sorts of awards for this project, which was then considered the last word in urban design, though today its rain-stained blocks look rather dejected. Had Revell's grand scheme been fully implemented, the city would have bulldozed the **old City Hall**, a flamboyant pseudo-Romanesque building on the east side of the square. Completed in 1899, it was designed by Edward J. Lennox, who developed a fractious relationship with his paymasters on the city council. They had a point: the original cost of the building had been estimated at $1.77m, but Lennox spent an extra $750,000 and took all of eight years to finish the project. Nevertheless, Lennox had the last laugh, carving gargoyle-like representations of the city's fathers on the arches at the top of the front steps and placing his name on each side of the building – something the city council had expressly forbidden him to do.

The Eaton Centre

Beginning on the north side of Queen Street W, the **Eaton Centre** (Mon–Sat 9.30am–9.30pm, Sun 11am–7pm) is a three-storey assortment of shops and restaurants that spreads out underneath a glass-and-steel arched roof. By

Glenn Gould

In the 1970s, anyone passing the Eaton's department store around 9pm on any day of the year might have seen the door unlocked for a distracted-looking figure swaddled in overcoat, scarves, gloves and hat. This character, making his way to a recording studio set up for his exclusive use inside the store, was perhaps the most famous citizen of Toronto and certainly the most charismatic pianist in the world – **Glenn Gould**.

Not the least remarkable thing about Gould was that very few people outside the CBS recording crew would ever hear him play live. In 1964, aged just 32, he retired from the concert platform, partly out of a distaste for the accidental qualities of any live performance, partly out of hatred for the cult of the virtuoso. Yet no pianist ever provided more material for the mythologizers. He possessed a memory so prodigious that none of his acquaintances was ever able to find a piece of music he could not instantly play perfectly, but he loathed much of the standard piano repertoire, dismissing romantic composers such as Chopin, Liszt and Rachmaninoff as little more than showmen. Dauntingly cerebral in his tastes and playing style, he was nonetheless an ardent fan of Barbara Streisand – an esteem that was fully reciprocated – and once wrote an essay titled **"In Search of Petula Clark"**. He lived at night and kept in touch by phoning his friends in the small hours of the morning, talking for so long that his monthly phone bill ran into thousands of dollars. Detesting all blood sports (a category in which he placed concert performances), he would terrorize anglers on Lake Simcoe by buzzing them in his motorboat. He travelled everywhere with bags full of medicines and would never allow anyone to shake his hand, yet soaked his arms in almost scalding water before playing in order to get his circulation going. At the keyboard, he sang loudly to himself, swaying back and forth on a creaky little chair made for him by his father – all other pianists sat too high, he insisted. And even in a heatwave he was always dressed as if a blizzard were imminent. To many of his colleagues, Gould's eccentricities were maddening, but what mattered was that nobody could play like Glenn Gould. As one exasperated conductor put it, "the nut's a genius".

Gould's **first recording**, Bach's *Goldberg Variations*, was released in 1956, and became the best-selling classical record of that year. Soon after, he became the first Western musician to play in the Soviet Union, where his reputation spread so quickly that for his final recital more than a thousand people were allowed to stand in the aisles of the Leningrad hall. On his debut in Berlin, a leading German critic described him as "a young man in a strange sort of trance" whose "technical ability borders on the fabulous". The technique always dazzled, but Gould's fiercely wayward intelligence made his interpretations controversial, as can be gauged from an announcement by **Leonard Bernstein**, who, when he was conducting Gould on one occasion, felt obliged to inform the audience that what they were about to hear was the pianist's responsibility, not his. Most notoriously of all, he had a very low opinion of Mozart's abilities – and went so far as to record the **Mozart** sonatas in order to demonstrate that Wolfgang Amadeus died too late rather than too soon. Gould himself died suddenly in 1982 at the age of 50 – the age at which he had said he would give up playing the piano entirely.

Gould's **legacy of recordings** is not confined to music. He made a trilogy of radio documentaries on the theme of solitude: *The Quiet in the Land*, about Canada's Mennonites; *The Latecomers*, about the inhabitants of Newfoundland; and *The Idea of North*, for which he taped interviews with people who, like himself, spent much of their time amid Canada's harshest landscapes. Just as Gould's Beethoven, Bach and Mozart sounded like nobody else's, these were documentaries like no others, each a complex weave of voices spliced and overlaid in compositions that are overtly musical in construction. However, Gould's **eighty-odd piano recordings** are the basis of his enduring popularity, and nearly all of them have been reissued on CD and DVD, spanning Western keyboard music from Orlando Gibbons to Arnold Schoenberg. One of the most poignant is his second version of the *Goldberg Variations*, the last record to be issued before his death.

shopping-mall standards, the design is appealing and the flock of fibreglass Canada geese suspended from the ceiling adds a touch of flair. Maps of the shopping mall are displayed on every floor, but the general rule is the higher the floor, the more expensive the shop. The centre takes its name from **Timothy Eaton**, an Ulster immigrant who opened his first store here in 1869. His cash-only, fixed-price, money-back-guarantee trading revolutionized the Canadian market and made him a fortune. Soon a Canadian institution, Eaton kept a grip on the pioneer settlements in the west through his mail-order catalogue, known as the "homesteader's bible" – or the "wish book" among aboriginal peoples – whilst Eaton department stores sprang up in all of Canada's big cities. In recent years, however, the company has struggled to maintain its profitability and the branch here in the Eaton Centre has been taken over by Sears.

Elgin Theatre and Winter Garden

Across from the Eaton Centre, just north of Queen Street at 189 Yonge St, the **Elgin Theatre and Winter Garden** (guided tours only, Thurs 5pm & Sat 11am; $7; 90min; ⓣ416/314-2871) is one of the city's most unusual attractions. The first part of the guided tour covers the **Elgin**, an old vaudeville theatre, whose ornate furnishings and fittings have been restored after years of neglect. The Elgin was turned into a cinema in the 1930s and, remarkably enough, its accompaniment, the top-floor **Winter Garden**, also a vaudeville theatre, was sealed off. Such double-decker theatres were introduced in the late nineteenth century in New York and soon became popular along the east coast, but only a handful have survived. Even better, when this one was unsealed, its original decor was found to be intact, the ceiling hung with thousands of preserved and painted beech leaves illuminated by coloured lanterns. In the event, much of the decor had to be replaced, but the restoration work was painstakingly thorough and the end result is simply delightful.

West to the Campbell House

Immediately to the west of Nathan Phillips Square, along Queen Street W, stands **Osgoode Hall**, a Neoclassical pile built for the Law Society of Upper Canada early in the nineteenth century. Looking like a cross between a Greek temple and an English country house, it's protected by a wrought-iron **fence** designed to keep cows and horses off the lawn. The elegant Georgian mansion on the opposite side of University Avenue is the **Campbell House** (Tues–Fri 9.30am–4.30pm; also Sat & Sun late May to Sept noon–4pm; $4.50; ⓦwww.campbellhousemuseum.ca), built on Adelaide Street for Sir William Campbell, Chief Justice and Speaker of the Legislative Assembly – it was transported here in 1972. There are regular guided tours of the period interior and these provide a well-researched overview of early nineteenth-century Toronto. At the time, Campbell was a leading figure, and a progressive one too, eschewing the death

Vintage fashion

Toronto has a number of excellent **secondhand** and **vintage fashion** shops and there's a concentration of them down along Queen Street W. Cabaret, 672 Queen St W (ⓣ416/504-7126, ⓦwww.cabaretvintage.com), is one of the best – especially for knock-em-down 1940s hats à la Barbara Stanwyck. Mon–Wed & Sat 11am–6pm, Thurs 11am–7pm & Sun 1–5pm.

The Group of Seven

In the autumn of 1912, a commercial artist by the name of **Tom Thomson** returned from an extended trip to the Mississauga country, north of Georgian Bay, with a bag full of sketches that were to add new momentum to Canadian art. His friends, many of whom were fellow employees of the art firm of Grip Ltd in Toronto, saw Thomson's naturalistic approach to indigenous subject matter as a pointer away from the influence of Europe, declaring the "northland" as the true Canadian "painter's country". World War I and the death of Thomson – who drowned in 1917 – delayed these artists' ambitions, but in 1920 they formed the **Group of Seven**. Initially, the group was comprised of Franklin H. Carmichael, Lawren Harris, A.Y. Jackson, Arthur Lismer, J.E.H. MacDonald, F.H. Varley and Frank Johnston; later, they were joined by A.J. Casson, L.L. Fitzgerald and Edwin Holgate. Working under the unofficial leadership of **Lawren Harris**, they explored the wilds of Algoma in Northern Ontario in the late 1910s, travelling around in a converted freight car, and later foraged even further afield, from Newfoundland and Baffin Island to British Columbia.

They were immediately **successful**, staging forty shows in eleven years, a triumph due in large part to Harris's many influential contacts. However, there was also a genuine popular response to the intrepid frontiersman element of their aesthetic. Art was a matter of "taking to the road" and "risking all for the glory of a great adventure", as they wrote in 1922, whilst "nature was the measure of a man's stature", according to Lismer. Symbolic of struggle against the elements, the Group's favourite symbol was the lone pine set against the sky, an image whose authenticity was confirmed by reference to the "manly" poetry of Walt Whitman.

The **legacy** of the Group of Seven is double-edged. On the one hand, they did indeed establish the autonomy of Canadian art, but on the other their contribution was soon institutionalised, and well into the 1950s it was difficult for Canadian painters to establish an identity that didn't conform to the group's precepts. Among many later painters the Group was – and remains - unpopular, but the Ontario artist Graham Coughtry was, for one, generous: 'They are the closest we've ever come to having some kind of romantic heroes in Canadian painting'.

penalty whenever feasible and even awarding the radical William MacKenzie damages when his printing press was wrecked by a mob of Tories in 1826.

The Art Gallery of Ontario

The **AGO**, the **Art Gallery of Ontario** (opening hours liable to change, but currently Wed–Fri noon–9pm, Sat & Sun 10am–5.30pm; $5, plus extra for special exhibitions; St Patrick subway; ⓣ416/979-6648, ⓦwww.ago.net), a short walk from the Campbell House, just west of University Avenue along Dundas Street W, has long been celebrated both for its wide-ranging collection of foreign and domestic art and its excellent temporary exhibitions. The gallery is, however, in the throes of a major overhaul, which will continue until 2008, and, in the intervening period, only parts of the gallery will be open at any one time. The account below describes some of the more important elements of the permanent collection, at least parts of it that should be displayed – especially the Henry Moore sculptures and the Group of Seven paintings – but for the moment it is all rather hit and miss.

Canadian nineteenth-century paintings

The AGO's collection of early to mid-nineteenth-century Canadian paintings includes the cheery *Passenger Pigeon Hunt* by **Antoine Plamondon** (1802–95). Trained in Paris, Plamondon worked in the Neoclassical tradition, but here he allows some freedom of movement amongst the young hunters, with the St Lawrence River as the backdrop. From eastern Canada comes **John O'Brien** (1832–91), who is well represented by *The Ocean Bride leaving Halifax Harbour*. Self-taught, O'Brien specialized in maritime scenes, turning out dozens of brightly coloured pictures of sailing ships and coastal settings. Look out also for the canvases of one of the era's most intriguing figures, **Paul Kane** (1810–71). Born in Ireland, Kane first emigrated to Toronto in the early 1820s. In 1840, he returned to Europe, where, curiously enough, he was so impressed by a touring exhibition of paintings on the American Indian that he promptly decided to move back to Canada. In 1846, he wrangled a spot on a westward-bound fur-trading expedition, beginning what was, even by the standards of the day, an epic journey: he travelled from Thunder Bay to Edmonton by canoe, crossed the Rockies by horse, and finally returned to Toronto two years later. During his trip, Kane made some seven hundred sketches, which he then painted onto canvas, paper and cardboard. Like many early Canadian artists, Kane's paintings often displayed a conflict in subject and style – that is, the subject was North American but the style European; indeed, it wasn't until the Group of Seven (see box, p.95) that a true Canadian aesthetic emerged. Perfect examples of this conflict are Kane's *Landscape in the Foothills with Buffalo Resting* and *At Buffalo Pound*, where bison are pictured in what looks more like a placid German valley than a North American prairie, plus *Indian encampment on Lake Huron*, a softly hued oil on canvas dating to 1845.

Folksy and/or romanticised country scenes and landscapes ruled the Canadian artistic roost from the 1850s through to the early twentieth century. By and large this is pretty dull stuff, but **Homer Watson**'s (1855–1936) glossy Ontario landscapes, with their vigorous paintwork and dynamic compositions, made him a popular and much acclaimed artist – Queen Victoria even purchased one of his paintings, and Oscar Wilde dubbed him "the Canadian Constable". The AGO possesses several Watson paintings, most memorably *The Old Mill* and *The Passing Storm*, two especially handsome and well-composed canvases, but his

Cornelius Krieghoff

Born in Amsterdam, the prolific **Cornelius Krieghoff** (1815–72) trained as an artist in Düsseldorf before emigrating to New York, where, at the tender age of 21, he joined the US army, serving in the Second Seminole War in Florida. Discharged in 1840, Krieghoff immediately re-enlisted, claimed three months' advance pay and deserted, hot-footing it to Montréal with the French-Canadian woman he had met and married in New York. In Montréal, he picked up his brushes again, but without any commercial success – quite simply no one wanted to buy his paintings. That might have been the end of the matter, but Krieghoff moved to Québec City in 1852 and here he found a ready market for his paintings among the well-heeled officers of the British garrison, who liked his folksy renditions of Québec rural life. This was the start of Krieghoff's most productive period. Over the next eight years he churned out dozens of souvenir pictures – finely detailed, anecdotal scenes that are his best work. In the early 1860s, however – and for reasons that remain obscure – he temporarily packed in painting, returning to Europe for five years before another stint in Québec City, though this time, with the officer corps gone, he failed to sell his work. In 1871, he went to live with his daughter in Chicago and died there the following year, a defeated man. The AGO owns a healthy sample of Krieghoff's paintings, including characteristic winter scenes like his *Settler's Log House* and *The Portage Aux Titres*, whose autumnal colours surround a tiny figure struggling with a canoe, not to mention the light-hearted humour of his *Toll Gate*.

Death of Elaine – inspired by a Tennyson poem – is a bizarrely unsuccessful venture into ancient legend.

The Group of Seven at the AGO

One of the most distinctive artists of the Group of Seven was **Lawren Harris** (1885–1970), whose 1922 *Above Lake Superior* is a pivotal work, its clarity of conception, with bare birch stumps framing a dark mountain beneath Art Deco clouds, quite exceptional. Harris was also partial to city street scenes and the AGO has several – including two of Toronto – each painted in a careful pointillist style very different from his wilderness works. The *West Wind* by **Tom Thomson** (1877–1917) is another seminal work, an iconic rendering of the northern wilderness that is perhaps the most famous of all Canadian paintings. Thomson was the first to approach wilderness landscapes with the determination of an explorer and the sense that they could encapsulate a specifically Canadian identity. A good sample of his less familiar (but no less powerful) works are also part of the AGO collection, including the moody *A Northern Lake*, the sticky dabs of colour of *Maple Springs*, and his *Autumn's Garland*, an oil on panel finished the year before he died. There is also a whole battery of preparatory sketches of lakes and canyons, waterfalls and forests, each small panel displaying the vibrant, blotchy colours that characterize Thomson's work.

J.E.H. MacDonald (1873–1932) was fond of dynamic, sweeping effects, and his panoramic *Falls, Montréal River* sets turbulent rapids beside hot-coloured hillsides. MacDonald also produced the startling sweep of *October Shower Gleam* and the superbly observed *Rowan Berries*. His friend **F.H. Varley** (1881–1969) dabbled in portraiture and chose soft images and subtle colours for his landscapes, as exemplified by *Moonlight after Rain*. The talents of **A.J. Casson** (1898–1992) are perhaps best recalled by the jumble of snow-covered roofs of his *House Tops in the Ward*, and his bright and rather formal *Old Store at Salem*, which offers a break from the scenic preoccupations of the rest of the Seven. There are also the vital canvases of **A.Y. Jackson** (1882–1974), most notably the carpet-like surface of *Algoma Rocks, Autumn*, painted in 1923. Yet another member of the Group of Seven, **Arthur Lismer** (1885–1969) spent every summer at his cottage in Georgian Bay north of Toronto, where he concentrated on painting shoreline and island vistas; the AGO has several prime examples. A contemporary of the Group – but not a member – the gifted **Emily Carr** (1871–1945) focused on the Canadian west coast in general, and its dense forests and native villages in particular, as in her dark and haunting *Thunderbird* of 1930 and the deep green foliage of both *Indian Church* and *Western Forest*, dating to 1929.

Inuit art

Soapstone sculptures form the bulk of the AGO's collection of **Inuit art**. Highlights here include **Pauta Saila**'s (born 1916) *Dancing Bear* and **Joe Talirunili**'s (1906–76) *Migration*, in which a traditional Inuit boat – an *umiak* – is crowded with Inuit seemingly bent on escaping danger. Keep an eye out also for the work of **John Tiktak** (1916–81), generally regarded as one of the most talented Inuit sculptors of his generation. The death of Tiktak's mother in 1962 had a profound effect on him, and his *Mother and Child* forcefully expresses this close connection. Tiktak's *Owl Man* is another fine piece, an excellent example of the metamorphic - half-human, half-animal - figures popular amongst the Inuit, as is **Thomas Sivuraq**'s (born 1941) *Shaman Transformation*.

The European collection

The AGO possesses a marvellous sample of **European fine and applied art**, including ivory and alabaster pieces, exquisite cameos and fine porcelain, as well as **European sculptures** by the likes of Barbara Hepworth. There's also a strong showing for Dutch painters of the Golden Age – Rembrandt, Van Dyck, Frans Hals and Goyen to name but four – as well as **French** artists, with distinguished works including *St Anne with the Christ Child* by Georges de la Tour, and Poussin's *Venus Presenting Arms to Aeneas*. Amongst the **Impressionists**, there's Degas's archetypal *Woman in the Bath*, Renoir's screaming-pink *Concert*, and Monet's wonderful *Vétheuil in Summer*, with its hundreds of tiny jabs of colour, plus more modern work by such luminaries as Picasso and Francis Bacon, among many.

Contemporary art and Henry Moore

The AGO's collection of **contemporary art** showcases work by European, British and American artists. Prime pieces include Warhol's *Elvis I* and *II*, Mark Rothko's strident *No.1 White and Red* and Claes Oldenburg's quirky if somewhat frayed *Giant Hamburger*. The AGO also possesses the world's largest collection of **Henry Moore** (1898–1986) plaster casts and a few bronzes, though it was actually something of an accident that his work ended up here at all. In the 1960s, Moore had reason to believe that London's Tate Gallery was going to build a special wing for him. When the Tate declined, Moore chose the AGO instead, persuaded to do so by the gallery's British representative, **Anthony Blunt**, the art expert who was famously uncovered as a Soviet spy in 1979. Given the sheer size and volume of Moore's AGO sculptures, it is likely that he will have a gallery to himself at the end of all the rebuilding – just as he always has had.

The Grange

Attached to the back of the AGO is **The Grange**, an early nineteenth-century brick mansion built by the Boultons, one of the city's most powerful and reactionary families, who were at the centre of the so-called 'Family Compact', a small group of Anglophile landowners and merchants who controlled the city in the early nineteenth century. The last of the line, William Henry – "a privileged, petted man...without principle", according to a local journalist – died in 1874, and his property passed to his widow, Harriette, who promptly married an English expatriate professor named Goldwin Smith. Goldwin enjoyed Toronto immensely, holding court and boasting of his English connections, and when he died in 1910 (after Harriette) he bequeathed the house to the fledgling Art Museum of Toronto, the predecessor of the AGO. The Grange remains part of the AGO and it is being restored to its mid-nineteenth-century appearance.

Chinatown and Kensington Market

Back on Dundas, the AGO is fringed by **Chinatown**, a bustling and immensely appealing neighbourhood cluttered with shops, restaurants and street stalls selling any and every type of Asian delicacy. The boundaries of Chinatown are somewhat blurred, but its focus, since the 1960s, when the original Chinatown was demolished to make way for the new City Hall, has been Dundas Street W between Bay and Spadina. The first Chinese to migrate to Canada arrived in the mid-nineteenth century to work in British Columbia's gold fields. Subsequently, a portion of this population migrated

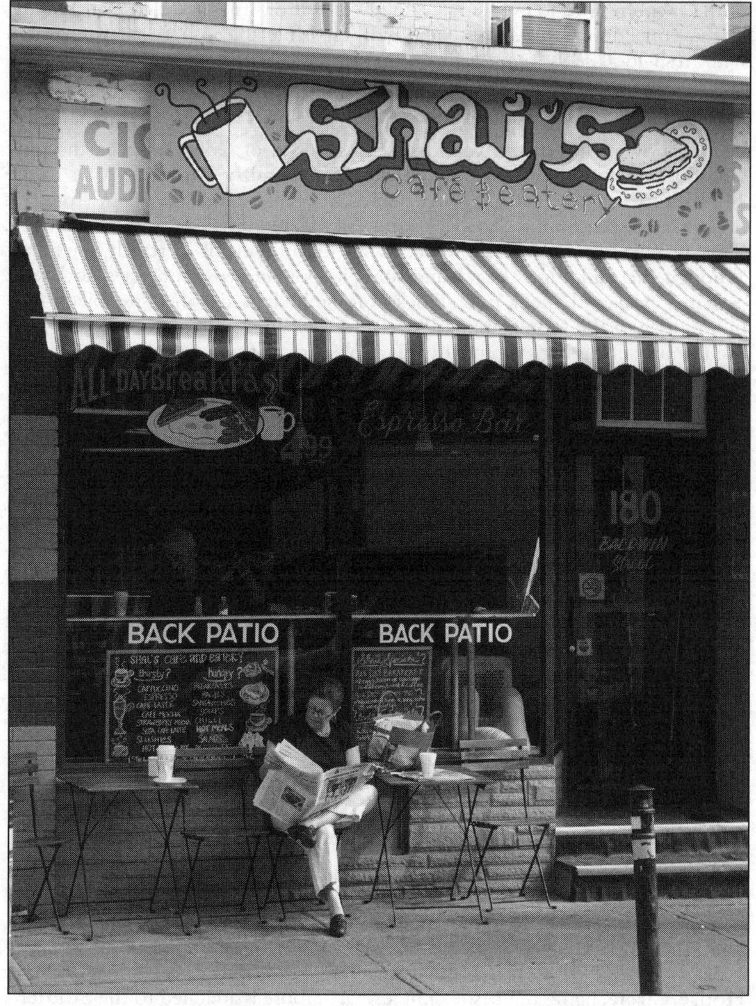

△ Coffee shop at Kensington Market

east, and a sizeable Chinese community sprang up in Toronto in the early twentieth century. Several more waves of migration – the last influx following the handing over of Hong Kong to mainland China by the British in 1997 – have greatly increased the number of Toronto's Chinese, bringing the population to approximately 300,000.

Next door to Chinatown, just north of Dundas Street W between Spadina and Augusta, lies Toronto's most ethnically diverse neighbourhood, pocket-sized **Kensington Market**. It was here, at the beginning of the twentieth century, that Eastern European immigrants squeezed into a patchwork of modest little brick and timber houses that survive to this day. On Kensington Avenue they established a lively **open-air street market** and this has been the main feature of the neighbourhood ever since. The lower half of the market, just off Dundas Street, concentrates on secondhand clothes, while the upper half is crowded with fresh-food stalls (see p.108).

The Ontario Legislative Assembly Building

Peering down University Avenue, from just north of College Street, the pink sandstone mass of the **Ontario Legislative Assembly Building** dates to the 1890s (thirty-minute guided tours: late May to Aug Mon–Fri 10am–4pm, Sat & Sun 9am–4pm; Sept to late May Mon–Fri 10am–4pm; free; Ⓣ416/325-7500, Ⓦwww.ontla.on.ca; Subway: Queen's Park). Elegant it certainly isn't, but although the building is heavy and solid, its ponderous symmetries do have a certain appeal, with block upon block of roughly dressed stone assembled in the full flourish of the Romanesque Revival style. Seen from close up, the design is even more engaging, its intricacies a pleasant surprise: above the chunky columns of the main entrance is a sinuous filigree of carved stone adorned by mythological creatures and gargoyle faces. The main facade also sports a Neoclassical frieze in which the Great Seal of Ontario is flanked by allegorical figures representing art, music, agriculture and so forth. Inside, the foyer leads to the wide, thickly carpeted **Grand Staircase**, whose massive timbers are supported by gilded iron pillars. Beyond, among the long corridors and arcaded galleries, is the **Legislative Chamber**, where the formality of the mahogany and sycamore panels is offset by a series of whimsical little **carvings**: look for the owl overlooking the doings of the government and the hawk overseeing the opposition benches. Under the Speaker's gallery, righteous inscriptions have been carved into the pillars, which is a bit of a hoot considering the behaviour of the building's architect, Richard Waite. Waite was chairman of the committee responsible for selecting an architect; and, as chairman, he selected himself. The provincial assembly typically sits from late September to late June, with breaks at Christmas and Easter, and although guided tours avoid the chamber when the body is in session, the **visitors' gallery** is open to the public during its deliberations; call for further details and times.

The University of Toronto

A short walk to the west of the Ontario Legislative Assembly Building stand the various faculties of the **University of Toronto**, opened in 1843 and the province's most prestigious academic institution. The university's older buildings, with their quadrangles, ivy-covered walls and Gothic interiors, deliberately evoke Oxbridge with **Hart House**, at the west end of Wellesley Street on **Hart House Circle**, being the best example. Hart House is attached to the **Soldier's Tower**, a neo-Gothic memorial erected in 1924 to honour those students who had died in World War I. It adjoins an arcaded **gallery**, which is inscribed with a list of the dead and Canadian **John McCrae**'s *In Flanders Fields*, arguably the war's best-known poem. Optimistically, the builders of the memorial didn't leave any space to commemorate the dead of any further war – so the names of the university students killed in World War II had to be inscribed on the walls under the arches at the foot of the tower.

The Royal Ontario Museum

From both the Legislative Assembly Building and Hart House Circle, it's a short walk north along the boulevard to the **Royal Ontario Museum**, at 100 Queen's Park (Mon–Thurs 10am–6pm, Fri 10am–9.30pm, Sat & Sun

10am–6pm; $15, over–65s $12, children 5–14 years $10, but special exhibitions extra; ⓣ416/586-8000, ⓦwww.rom.on.ca; Subway: Museum). Usually known as the **ROM**, this is Canada's largest and most diverse museum and, among much else, it possesses a vast collection of fine and applied art drawn from every corner of the globe. The museum is, however, being entirely restructured, a process that includes the addition of a large and flashy new extension, whose six crystal–shaped, aluminium–and–glass cubes are the brainchild of the architect Daniel Libeskind. Work is well under way and the redevelopment should be completed by the end of 2007, but in the meantime visitors can only see a small fraction of the collection and have to take potluck as to what's displayed and when. That said, you can pretty much guarantee that the ROM's pride and joy, its internationally acclaimed Chinese collection, will be on display. **Museum plans** are available for free at the entrance.

The ROM's Chinese collection

The ROM owns an exquisite collection of **Chinese Temple Art**, most notably three large and stunningly beautiful Daoist and Buddhist wall paintings dating from around 1300 AD. Two of them are a matching pair of Yuan Dynasty murals depicting the lords of the Northern and Southern Dipper, each of whom leads an astrological procession of star spirits. There is also a superb sample of Buddhist temple figures dating from the twelfth to the fourteenth centuries.

The museum's **South Asian** collection spans six millennia, from 4500 BC to 1900 AD. Among the most important pieces is a remarkable collection of toy-sized tomb figurines – a couple of hundred ceramic pieces representing funerary processions of soldiers, musicians and attendants. Dating from the early sixth to the late seventh century, they re-create the habits of early China – how people dressed, how horses were groomed and shod, changes in armoury and so forth. There is also a fabulous collection of **snuff bottles**, some carved from glass and rock crystal, others from more exotic materials – amber, ivory, bamboo and even tangerine skin. Europeans introduced tobacco to China in the late sixteenth century, and although smoking did not become popular in China until recent times, snuff went down a storm and anyone who was anybody at court was snorting the stuff by the middle of the seventeenth century. Perhaps the most popular component of the Chinese collection, however, is its **Ming Tomb**. The aristocracy of the Ming Dynasty (1368–1644 AD) evolved an elaborate style of monumental funerary sculpture and architecture, and the ROM holds the only example outside of China – though it is actually a composite tomb drawn from several sources rather than an intact, original whole. Central to the Ming burial conception was a Spirit Way, a central avenue with large-scale carved figures of guards, attendants and animals placed on either side. At the end of the alley was the tumulus, or burial mound – in this case the tomb-house of a seventeenth-century Chinese general by the name of Zu Dashou.

Gardiner Museum of Ceramic Art

The **Gardiner Museum of Ceramic Art**, just across the street from the ROM at 111 Queen's Park (daily 10am–6pm, Fri till 9pm; $12, free on Fri 4–9pm; ⓦwww.gardinermuseum.com; Subway: Museum), holds a superb collection of ceramics. Spread over three small floors, the museum's exhibits are beautifully presented, and key pieces are well labelled and explained. An audioguide is also available.

On the main floor, the **pre-Columbian** section is particularly fine, composed of over three hundred pieces from regions stretching from Mexico to Peru. One of the most comprehensive collections of its kind in North America, it provides an intriguing insight into the lifestyles and beliefs of the Mayan, Incan and Aztec peoples. The sculptures are all the more remarkable for the fact that the potter's wheel was unknown in pre-Columbian America, and thus everything on display was necessarily hand-modelled. On this floor also is an exquisite sample of fifteenth- and sixteenth-century tin-glazed **Italian majolica**, mostly dishes, plates and jars depicting classical and Biblical themes designed by Renaissance artists. The early pieces are comparatively plain, limited to green and purple, but the later examples are brightly coloured reflecting technological change: in the second half of the fifteenth century, Italian potters learnt how to glaze blue, yellow and then ochre. The most splendid pieces are perhaps those from the city – and pottery centre – of Urbino, including one wonderful plate portraying the fall of Jericho.

Up above, the second floor has both Japanese and Chinese porcelain plus an especially fine sample of eighteenth-century **European porcelain**, most notably hard-paste wares (fired at very high temperatures) from Meissen, Germany. On this floor also is a charming collection of Italian *commedia dell'arte* figurines, doll-sized representations of theatrical characters popular across Europe from the middle of the sixteenth to the late eighteenth century. The predecessor of pantomime, the *commedia dell'arte* featured stock characters in improvised settings, but with a consistent theme of seduction, age and beauty: the centrepiece was always an elderly, rich merchant and his beautiful young wife.

Bata Shoe Museum

Within easy walking distance of the ROM, the **Bata Shoe Museum**, 327 Bloor St W at St George Street (Tues–Sat 10am–5pm, Thurs until 8pm, & Sun noon–5pm; $8; Ⓦ www.batashoemuseum.ca; subway: St George), was built for Sonja Bata, of the Bata shoe manufacturing family, to house the extraordinary assortment of footwear she has spent a lifetime collecting. A leaflet issued at reception steers visitors around the museum, starting with an introductory section entitled "All About Shoes" on **Level B1**, which presents an overview on the evolution of footwear. Among the more interesting exhibits in this section are pointed shoes from medieval Europe, where different social classes were allowed different lengths of toe, and tiny Chinese silk shoes used by women whose feet had been bound. Banned by the Communists when they came to power in 1949, foot binding was common practice for over a thousand years, and the "ideal" length of a woman's foot was a hobbling three inches. A small adjoining section is devoted to **specialist footwear**, including French chestnut-crushing clogs from the nineteenth century and inlaid Ottoman platforms designed to keep aristocratic feet well away from the mud.

Moving on, **Level G** features a large glass cabinet showcasing all sorts of **celebrity footwear**. The exhibits are rotated regularly, but look out for Buddy Holly's loafers, Marilyn Monroe's stilettos, Princess Diana's red court shoes, Shaquille O'Neal's colossal Reebok trainers and Elton John's ridiculous platforms. **Level 2** and **Level 3** are used for **temporary exhibitions** – some of which are very good indeed.

Casa Loma

From Dupont subway station, it's a five-minute walk north up the slope of Spadina Road to the corner of Davenport Road, where a flight of steps leads to Toronto's most bizarre attraction, **Casa Loma**, 1 Austin Terrace (daily

9.30am–5pm, last admission 4pm; $16, parking $2.75 per hour). A folly to outdo almost every other folly, Casa Loma is an enormous towered and turreted mansion built for Sir Henry Pellatt between 1911 and 1914. Every inch the self-made man, Pellatt made a fortune by pioneering the use of hydroelectricity, harnessing the power of Niagara Falls to light Ontario's expanding cities. Determined to construct a house no one could ignore, Sir Henry gathered furnishings from all over the world and even imported Scottish stonemasons to build the wall around his six-acre property. He spent more than $3m fulfilling his dream, but business misfortunes and the rising cost of servants forced him to move out in 1923, earning him the nickname of "**Pellatt the Plunger**". His legacy is a strange mixture of medieval fantasy and early twentieth-century technology: secret passageways and an elevator, claustrophobic wood-panelled rooms baffled by gargantuan pipes and plumbing.

The clearly numbered route around the house goes up one side and down the other. It begins on the ground floor in the **Great Hall**, a pseudo-Gothic extravaganza with an eighteen-metre-high cross-beamed ceiling, a Wurlitzer organ and enough floor space to accommodate several hundred guests. Hung with flags, heavy-duty chandeliers and suits of armour, it's a remarkably cheerless place, but in a touch worthy of Errol Flynn, the hall is overlooked by a balcony at the end of Pellatt's second-floor bedroom: presumably Sir Henry could, like some medieval baron, welcome his guests from on high.

Pushing on, the **Library** and then the walnut-panelled **Dining Room** lead to the **Conservatory**, an elegant and spacious room with a marble floor and side-panels set beneath a handsome Tiffany domed glass ceiling. Well lit, this is perhaps the mansion's most appealing room, its flowerbeds kept warm even in winter by the original network of steam pipes. The nearby **Study** was Sir Henry's favourite room, a serious affair engulfed by mahogany panelling and equipped with two secret passageways, one leading to the wine cellar, the other to his wife's rooms – a quintessential dichotomy.

On the second floor, **Sir Henry's Suite** has oodles of walnut and mahogany panelling, which stands in odd contrast to the 1910s white-marble, high-tech bathroom, featuring an elaborate multi-nozzle shower. **Lady Pellatt's Suite** wasn't left behind in the ablutions department, either – her bathroom had a bidet, a real novelty in George V's Canada – and she had a lighter decorative touch, too, eschewing wood panelling for walls painted in her favourite colour, Wedgwood Blue.

Up above, the third floor holds a mildly diverting display on Pellatt's one-time regiment, the **Queen's Own Rifles**, tracing their involvement in various campaigns from the 1885 suppression of the Métis rebellion in western Canada (see p.1088) through to World War I and beyond. From the third floor, wooden staircases clamber up to two of the house's **towers**, from where there are pleasing views over the house and gardens.

Back on the ground floor, stairs lead down to the Lower Level, which was where Pellatt's money ran out and his plans ground to a halt. Work never started on the bowling alleys and shooting range he had designed, and the swimming pool only got as far as the rough concrete basin that survives today – never mind that Pellatt conceived a marble pool overlooked by golden swans. Pellatt did, however, manage to complete the 250-metre-long **tunnel** that runs from the house and pool to the **carriage room** and **stables**, where his thoroughbred horses were allegedly better-treated than his servants, chomping away at their oats and hay in splendid iron and mahogany stalls.

The stables are a dead-end, so you'll have to double back along the tunnel to reach the house and the exit. Before you leave, spare time for the **terraced**

gardens (May–Oct daily 9.30am–5pm; no extra charge), which tumble down the ridge at the back of the house. They are parcelled up into several different sections and easily explored along a network of footpaths, beginning on the terrace behind the Great Hall.

Spadina House

Quite what the occupants of **Spadina House** (guided tours: Jan–March Sat & Sun noon–5pm; April–Aug Tues–Sun noon–5pm; Sept–Dec Tues–Fri noon–4pm, Sat & Sun noon–5pm; $6; ⓦwww.toronto.ca/culture/spadina.htm; Subway: Dupont) must have thought when Casa Loma went up next door can only be imagined, but there must have been an awful lot of curtain-twitching. The two houses are a study in contrasts: Casa Loma a grandiose pile, Spadina an elegant Victorian property of genteel appearance dating from 1866. Spadina was built by James Austin, a wealthy banker of Irish extraction whose descendants lived here until 1983, when the house was bequeathed to the city. The Austins' long and uninterrupted occupation means that the house's furnishings are nearly all genuine family artefacts, and they provide an intriguing insight into their changing tastes and interests.

Particular highlights of the **guided tour** include the conservatory trap door that allowed the gardeners to come and go unseen by their employers, an assortment of period chairs designed to accommodate the largest of bustles, the original gas chandeliers and a couple of canvases by Cornelius Krieghoff (see p.106). Pride of place, however, goes to the **Billiard Room**, which comes complete with an inventive Art Nouveau decorative frieze of 1898, and the **Library**, equipped with a sturdy oak bureau and a swivel armchair in the manner of England's William Morris.

The waterfront and the Toronto Islands

There is much to enjoy on the north shore of **Lake Ontario** despite its industrial blotches and the heavy concrete brow of the Gardiner Expressway. Footpaths and cycling trails now nudge along a fair slice of the **waterfront**, the **Harbourfront Centre** offers a year-round schedule of activities – music festivals, theatre, dance and the like – and here also is the adventurous **Power Plant Contemporary Art Gallery**.

Even better are the **Toronto Islands**, whose breezy tranquillity attracts droves of city-dwellers during Toronto's humid summers. It only takes fifteen minutes to reach them by municipal ferry (see opposite), but the contrast between the city and the islands could hardly be more marked, not least because the islands are almost entirely **vehicle-free**: many locals use wheelbarrows or golf buggies to move their tackle, while others walk or cycle.

The Harbourfront Centre

Toronto's grimy docks once disfigured the shoreline nearest the city centre, a swathe of warehouses and factories that was unattractive and smelly in equal measure. Today it's another story: the port and its facilities have been concentrated further east, beyond the foot of Parliament Street, while the **waterfront** west of Yonge Street has been redeveloped in grand style, sprouting luxury condominium blocks, jogging and cycling trails, offices, shops and marinas. The focus of all this activity is the **Harbourfront**

Centre, an expanse of lakefront stretching west from the foot of York Street, whose various facilities include an open-air performance area and the **Power Plant Contemporary Art Gallery** (Tues–Sun noon–6pm, Wed till 8pm; $5, free on Wed after 5pm; ⓣ416/973-4949, ⓦwww.thepowerplant.org). Every year, the gallery presents about a dozen exhibitions of contemporary art, often featuring emerging Canadian artists. It's mostly cutting-edge stuff; indecipherable to some, exciting to others.

To reach the Harbourfront Centre by **public transport**, take streetcar #509 or #510 from Union Station and get off at Queens Quay Terminal, the second stop.

The Toronto Islands

Originally a sandbar peninsula, the **Toronto Islands**, arching around the city's harbour, were cut adrift from the mainland by a violent storm in 1858. First used as a summer retreat by the Mississauga Indians, the islands went through various incarnations during the twentieth century: they once hosted a baseball stadium, where slugger Babe Ruth hit his first professional home run, saw fun fairs featuring horses diving from the pier and even served as training base for the Norwegian Air Force during World War II. Today, this archipelago, roughly 6km long and totalling around 800 acres, seems worlds away from the bustle of downtown, a great day-trip, a haven for rest and relaxation – and a place where visitors' **motor cars are banned**.

The city side of the archipelago is broken into a dozen tiny islets dotted with cottages, leisure facilities, verdant gardens and clumps of wild woodland. By comparison, the other side of the archipelago is a tad wilder and more windswept, consisting of one long sliver of land, which is somewhat arbitrarily divided into three "islands". From the east, these are **Ward's Island**, a quiet residential area with parkland and wilderness; **Centre Island**, the busiest and most developed of the three; and **Hanlan's Point**, which leads round to Toronto's pint-sized Toronto Island Airport (see p.76). Hanlan's Point also holds the city's best **sandy beach** – though, as Lake Ontario is generally regarded as being too polluted for swimming, most visitors stick to sunbathing.

Practicalities

Passenger **ferries** bound for the Toronto Islands depart from the mainland **ferry terminal**, which is located behind the conspicuous Westin Harbour Castle Hotel, between the foot of Yonge and Bay streets. To get to the ferry terminal from Union Station, take the #509 or #510 streetcar and get off at the first stop – Queen's Quay (Ferry Docks). The islands have three **ferry docks** – one each on Ward's Island, Centre Island and Hanlan's Point. The ferries to Ward's Island and Hanlan's Point run year-round, while the ferry shuttling visitors over to Centre Island only operates from spring to fall. During peak season (May to early Sept), ferries to all three islands depart at regular intervals, either every half-hour, every forty-five minutes, or every hour; at other times of the year, it's usually hourly. Ferries begin running between 6.30am and 9am and finish between 9pm and 11.30pm, depending on the service and the season. For schedule details, call ⓣ416/392-8193, ⓦwww.toronto.ca/parks. Regardless of the time of year, a return **fare** for adults is $6. Cyclists are allowed to take their **bikes** with them unless the ferry is jam-packed and **rollerblades** are permitted, but must be removed while on board.

From May to October, **bike hire** is available on Centre Island from **Island Bicycle Rental** (ⓣ416/203–0009), located a five-to ten-minute walk from

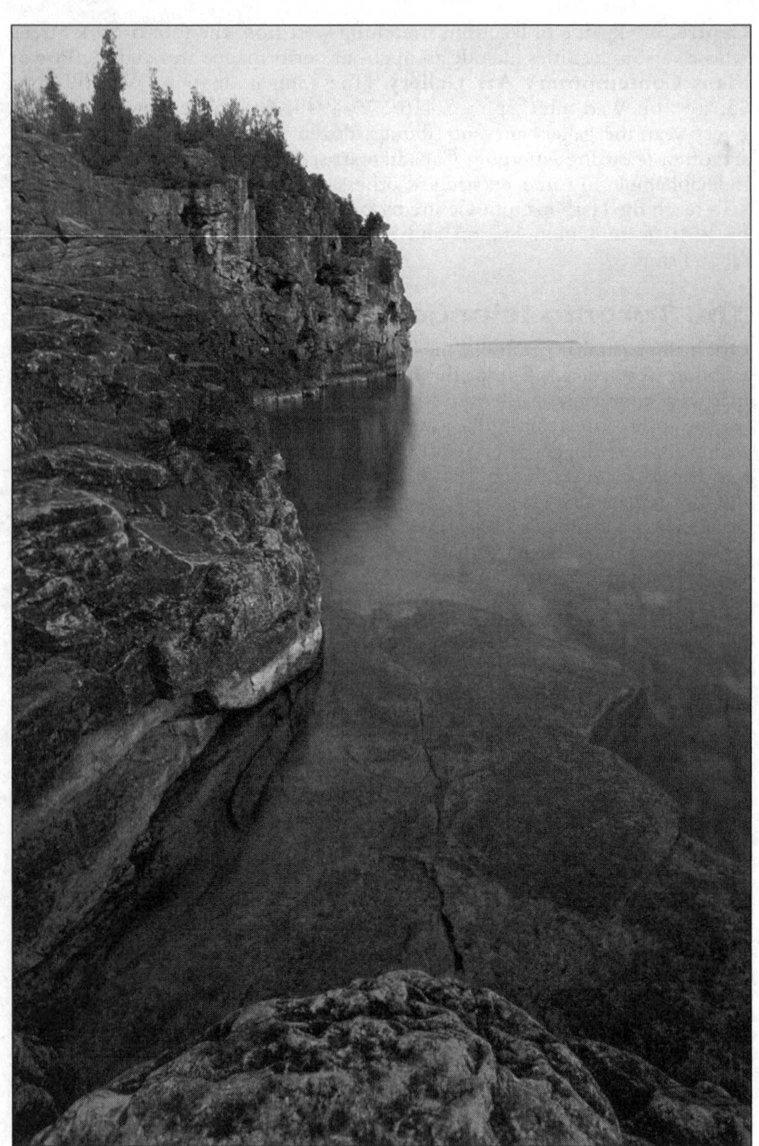

△ Bruce Peninsula National Park Islands

the Centre Island ferry dock at the foot of the pier. They open daily at around 10.30am and stock ordinary bicycles, tandems, and even quadracycles, but they do not take reservations except for groups of ten or more. **Canoe and paddle-boat rental** is available on Centre Island too, from the **Boat House**, a five-to ten-minute walk from the Centre Island ferry dock. Hiring a boat allows you to paddle round the islands' network of mini-lagoons and reach a couple of tiny wooded islets that are otherwise impossible to reach. Aside from walking, cycling and rowing, the other means of conveyance is a free and fairly frequent trackless **train** that runs across the islands throughout the summertime; you can board the train at any point along its circuitous route. As regards eating and drinking, it's all fast-food stuff except for the **Rectory Café** (Mon–Thurs 11am–6pm, Fri–Sun 11am–8pm; high season daily 10am–10pm; ⓣ416/203-2152), on Ward's Island, where they serve tasty snacks and light meals. Several hours are needed to explore the islands by bike, a full day if you are on foot.

The suburbs

The satellite **suburbs** and industrial areas that make up most of Toronto are of little appeal, a string of formless settlements sprawling over a largely flat and dreary landscape that extends from Scarborough in the east to Mississauga in the west and north beyond Steeles Avenue. Nevertheless, the region is home to several prestige attractions, most notably the **Ontario Science Centre**, which showcases dozens of interactive science displays, and the **Toronto Zoo**.

Ontario Science Centre

Featuring over eight hundred exhibits on science and technology, the **Ontario Science Centre**, 770 Don Mills Rd (daily 10am–5pm; $17, children ages 13–17 $12.50, ages 4–12 $10; ⓣ416/696-1000, ⓦwww.ontariosciencecentre.ca), draws more than one million visitors a year with children to the fore. One of the most popular exhibits is **The Human Body**, where visitors can discern the inner workings of human biology through life-sized three-dimensional displays and various quizzes and games. There's also information on complex medical advances like bioengineering, DNA fingerprinting and immunology, all presented in an easily accessible format. Another big pull is the **OMNIMAX Theatre**, which boasts a 24-metre-high wraparound screen with digital sound that hits you right in the solar plexus. Admissions to the Omnimax shows are either separate from the general admission ($12 for adults) or can be combined with general admission, which costs $25 for adults. To reach the Science Centre by **car** from downtown Toronto, take the Don Valley Parkway and follow the signs from the Don Mills Road North exit. By **public transport**, take the Yonge Street subway line north to Eglington station and transfer to the Eglington Avenue East bus; get off at Don Mills Road.

Toronto Zoo

Set on the hilly edge of the Rouge Valley, the **Toronto Zoo** (daily Mar–Sept 9am–6pm; June–Aug 9am–7.30pm; Oct–Feb 9.30am–4.30pm; $19, children aged 4–12 $11; ⓦwww.torontozoo.com) encompasses a 710-acre site that does its best to place animals in their own environments. To this end, **six pavilions** representing different geographic regions are filled with indigenous plants and more than five thousand animals. Hardy species live outside in large paddocks, and an open train, the **Zoomobile**, zips around between the pavilions. The zoo also has an extensive breeding, recovery and reintroduction programme, which has helped a variety of threatened species back into their original environment.

Arriving by **car**, take Hwy 401 to Scarborough (exit 389) and drive north on Meadowvale Road, following the signs for the zoo. Via **public transport** – which takes about fifty minutes from downtown – catch the Sheppard East

#85B bus from the Sheppard subway station. **Eating** at the zoo is dominated by the multi-chains, but there are picnic areas.

Eating and drinking

Toronto heaves with **cafés, café-bars and restaurants**, everything from smart and expensive designer places to informal neighbourhood joints. Some of the best emphasize their use of Canadian ingredients – fish and wild animal meat, particularly – but there's no real distinctive local cuisine: if there is a Toronto dish, it's hamburger, fries and salad. **Prices** range from deluxe restaurants, where a meal will set you back upwards of $60, to bargain-basement cafés, where a decent-sized snack or sandwich works out at just a few dollars. The majority of places fall somewhere in between – a $25 bill per person for a two-course meal, excluding drinks, is a reasonable average in a restaurant, a tad less in a café or café-bar.

For **drinking**, many of Toronto's traditional **bars** are rough-and-ready places that look and feel like beer halls. Until the 1980s, it was common for them to have one entrance for men accompanied by women, the other for men only, and although these formalities have been stripped away, many of the city's bars remain firmly blue collar. In the more prosperous parts of the city especially, the café-bar has supplanted the bar as the place to go, thereby rendering the traditional distinction between eating and drinking places (largely) obsolete.

Cafés and café-bars

Balzac's Coffee Roastery 55 Mill St; Streetcar: King (#504). *Balzac's* has a laid-back, arty feel and occupies the old pump room of the Gooderham & Worts Distillery, at the heart of the Distillery District. Churns out nicely presented espresso-type coffees plus matching cakes and light bites. Mon–Fri 7am–8pm, Sat & Sun 9am–8pm.

Bonjour Brioche 812 Queen St East at Broadview; Streetcar: Queen (#501). This patisserie-café draws hordes from all over the city on account of its fruit tarts, buttery croissants, puffy brioche and delectable *pissaladiere*, a variation on pizza from Provence. The sit-down menu is a blackboard full of soups, sandwiches, omelettes and quiche. There's always a line for Sunday brunch, and almost everything has gone by 2pm – so come early. Tues–Fri 8am–5pm, Sat 8am–4pm & Sun 8am–3pm.

Café Bernate 1024 Queen St W; Streetcar: Queen (#501). The steam machine is in full swing at this neighbourhood spot, and the sunny yellow walls are hung with local artists' work. The menu offers a flock of plump sandwiches for all tastes, and coffee drinkers get free refills. Mon–Sat 11am–4pm.

Café Nervosa 75 Yorkville Ave; Subway: Bay. One of the few reasonably priced café-restaurants left in Yorkville, *Café Nervosa* is strong on Italian-style salads, pastas and pizzas. In particular, don't miss the two-person, regionally named pizzas with thin, crispy crusts and an authentic variety of toppings. Main courses $12 and up. Mon–Sat 11am–11pm, Sun 10.30am–3pm.

Insomnia Internet Bar Café Inc 502 Bloor St W at Lippincott; Subway: Bathurst. This fully licensed Internet café has computer terminals and a kitchen that stays open until 2am, serving up a wide range of dishes from tapas to Canadian. Large screen TV and couches on which to snuggle too. Daily 11am–2am, 4am on the weekend.

Java House 537 Queen St W opposite Denison; Streetcar: Queen (#501). The exterior of this popular local hangout is painted to look like a hut from some sort of South Pacific village, while inside it is all café, steamy and busy serving up light meals and gallons of caffeinated beverages of all descriptions. Daily 8am–midnight.

Moon Bean Coffee 30 St Andrew's St; Subway: St Patrick. One of a dwindling number of cafés that care enough to roast their own beans, *Moon Bean* is a Kensington Market tradition. Its patio is a perfect spot to watch the daily parade go by. A five- to ten-minute walk from the subway.

Sugar Café 942 Queen St W near Ossington. Streetcar: Queen (#501). This little café on the West Queen W strip has all the usual elements –

espresso coffees, sweets and light fare – but presented in a charming, light-hearted way. Thurs–Sat 6–10pm, plus Sat & Sun 10am–3pm.

Tequila Bookworm 490 Queen St W at Denison; Streetcar: Queen (#501). Part second-hand bookshop, part coffee house, this beguiling place has garage-sale armchairs and bare-brick walls. Espresso drinks and simple desserts are served without any fuss. Mon–Wed 8.30am–11pm, Thurs 8.30am–1am, Sat 10am–2am & Sun 11am–11pm.

Restaurants

Babur 273 Queen St W; Subway: Osgoode ☎416/599-7720. Rich, buttery sauces, delicately spiced stews and fluffy naan and pori breads, all delivered to your linen-cloth table by helpful waiters at this pleasing Indian restaurant. Mon–Sat 11.45am–10.30pm, Sun 11.45am–9.30pm. Mains average around $13.

Bangkok Garden 18 Elm St; Subway: Dundas ☎416/977-6748. In one of Elm Street's old brownstones, the menu of this softly lit Thai restaurant covers a take on fresh lake fish as well as a standard selection of salads, noodles and curries. Main courses from $18, less at lunch time. Mon–Fri 11.30am–2.30pm plus Mon–Sat 5–10pm.

Bangkok Paradise 506 Queen St W; Streetcar: Queen (#501) ☎416/504-3210. Informal and usually packed, the menu of the funky *Bangkok Paradise* has all the satay, noodle and curry classics you'd expect, plus a wide range of Thai vegetarian options. Mon–Fri 10.30am–11pm, Sat & Sun noon–11pm. Mains from as little as $8.

Bar Italia 582 College St at Manning; Streetcar: College (#506) ☎416/535-3621. Antipasti, risotto, pasta and panini are dished up here at this appealing Italian restaurant. One of the best buys is a huge antipasti platter that is meant to share – and perfect for a light meal. You can also view the daily selections in a luncheon counter near the front. Chic little patio too. Mains from $12. Mon–Thurs 11am–1am, Fri & Sat 11am–2am, Sun 10am–1am.

Bo De Duyen 254 Spadina Ave; Streetcar: Dundas (#505) ☎416/703-1247. This popular, first-floor joint offers Chinese-Vietnamese cooking for vegetarians. The absence of any animal by-products means that even the strictest vegan can eat here with a clear conscience. Pages and pages of selections, including "mock" meat and seafood items. Mains from $8. Daily 11am–11pm.

Fressen 478 Queen St W at Denison; Streetcar: Queen (#501) ☎416/504-5127. Ultra cool vegetarian restaurant, where regulars ignore the pastas and pizzas and head straight for the entrees. A full meal can also be made of the excellent appetizers, and the juice/smoothie list is extensive. Main courses average $15. Daily 5.30–10pm, plus Sat & Sun 11am–3.30pm.

Fune 100 Simcoe St; Subway: St Andrew ☎416/599-3868. The star turn at this neat and trim Japanese restaurant is the sushi bar, very Tokyo-style with little boats floating by along a channel from the sushi chefs to you and everyone else. The seafood couldn't be fresher and prices are reasonable. Mon–Fri 11.30am–2.30pm & 5–11pm; Fri–Sun 5–10pm.

Happy Seven 358 Spadina Ave; Streetcar: Dundas (#505) ☎416/971-9820. Predominantly Cantonese-style cooking with a few spicy Szechuan dishes, tanks of soon-to-be seafood, and large, attractively presented servings. Bright and spotless, this establishment is extremely popular. Mains from $8. Daily 4pm–5am.

Joso's 202 Davenport Rd ☎416/925-1903. This celebrated restaurant, described at length by Margaret Atwood in her novel *Robber Bride*, is famous for two things: its squid-ink risotto and the plethora of breasts and buttocks in owner Joso Spralja's paintings and statues. Reservations essential. Mains from $25. A fifteen-minute walk north of Bloor St W along Avenue Rd – take a taxi.

Kit Kat 297 King St W at John; Subway: St Andrew ☎416/977-4461. Antipasti, pastas, steaks and seafood dominate the uncomplicated menu of this busy, attractively decorated restaurant, where the cuisine is firmly southern Italian. Main courses hover around $23. Daily 11.30am–11.30pm.

Lai Wah Heen at the Metropolitan Hotel, 108 Chestnut St; Subway: St Patrick ☎416/977-9899. The name means "elegant meeting place", which this Chinese restaurant most certainly is. The high-end dining room atmosphere is matched by the complex menu, best described as Hong Kong *moderne*, with dishes like Lustrous Peacock (a salad of barbecued duck, chicken and jellyfish on slivered melons garnished with eggs). Noted for its dim sum (lunch times only). Main courses range up to $45, starters hover around $18. Daily 11.30am–3pm & 5.30–10.30pm.

Le Commensal 655 Bay St; Subway: Dundas ☎416/596-9364. The cafeteria-style set-up of this large, airy vegetarian restaurant is its only drawback. Otherwise, the variety of offerings is excellent: soups, great salads, hearty pot-pies, stews, casseroles and baked goods are clearly marked for vegans or vegetarians. A large dessert counter too, plus take-out. Lunch or dinner for two costs $16–30. Entrance is on Elm St. Mon–Fri 11.30am–9.30pm, Sat noon–10pm & Sun noon–9.30pm.

Lee Garden 331 Spadina Ave; Streetcar: Dundas (#505) ⓣ416/593-9524. Expect long lines at this much-loved Chinese restaurant. Locals esteem *Lee's* for the boneless chicken with black bean sauce and the large selection of fresh fish dishes. The cuisine is mostly Cantonese with plenty of daily specials that may demand your waiter's translation. Mains from $10. Daily 4pm to midnight.

Le Papillon 16 Church St; Subway: Union Station ⓣ416/363-0838. Large Breton crepes ($9–14), served either sweet or savoury, are the house specialities, though the bistro-style menu covers all the French classics with style and élan. Tues–Thurs noon–2.30pm & 5–10pm, Fri noon–2.30pm & 5pm–midnight, Sat 11am–midnight & Sun 11am–10pm.

Monsoon 100 Simcoe St; Subway: St Andrew ⓣ416/979-7172. Make time to stop for a martini in the slick and chic bar of this Asian fusion restaurant before proceeding to the dining area. Starters are served on delicate *rakku* dishes, and the light, assured cooking boasts imaginative combinations (seared tofu in green tea marinade, maple-ginger grouper etc). Mains $25 and up, less at lunch. Mon–Fri 11.30am–2.30pm & Mon–Sat 5–10.30pm.

Nataraj 394 Bloor St W; Subway: Spadina ⓣ416/928-2925. Delhi-specific dishes with a tandoori twist at this first-rate Indian restaurant. The tandoori oven is on view to diners through a window into the kitchen. Try the spicy stews and shrimp pakoras. Main courses from $9. Mon–Sat 5.30–10.30pm.

Noce 875 Queen St W; Streetcar: Queen (#501) ⓣ416/504-3463. On the corner of Queen W and Walnut (hence the 'nut' name), this little house has become an exceptional Italian restaurant. The pasta is rolled by hand, the beef carpaccio melts on the tongue, and the meat tumbles right off the bone. Main courses begin at $20. Mon–Sat 6–11.30pm.

Rodney's Oyster House 469 King St W; Streetcar: King (#504) ⓣ416/363-8105. Toronto's favourite oyster bar serves up tons of the slippery delicacies, plus scallops, mussels and shrimp. The only regular fish is salmon and trout. Shellfish main courses start at $16. Mon–Sat 11am–1am.

Ruth's Chris Steak House 145 Richmond St W; Subway: Osgoode ⓣ416/955-1455. The decor may be a tad too traditional for some tastes – somber and really rather utilitarian – but the steaks, served on piping hot plates, are quite simply the best in town – make no mistake. Subterranean premises adjoining the *Hilton Hotel* at University Ave. Main courses begin at $40. Daily 5–10/10.30pm.

Nightlife and entertainment

Toronto has its fair share of **live music venues**, even though local bands that hit the big time almost always seem to move to the States. The city's strongest suite is **jazz**, both modern and traditional, with several first-rate jazz joints in and around the city centre. The **club scene** is also strong, if not exactly earth-shattering, but there's more than enough to keep anyone going for days (and nights) on end. For club and live music **listings**, consult *NOW* (ⓦwww.nowtoronto.com), *Eye* (ⓦwww.eye.net), or *TRIBE*, (ⓦwww.tribe.ca), free weekly newspapers which are available in stores, restaurants and street news-boxes. The most comprehensive listings are in *NOW*, which puts the emphasis on live music, while *TRIBE* specializes in dance/rave/house discos, and *Eye* does a bit of both.

As regards the **performing arts**, Toronto sustains a wide-ranging programme of theatre, opera, ballet and classical music. Its particular strength is its **theatre scene**, which is the third-largest in the English-speaking world (after London and New York). As for film, Toronto's mainstream **cinemas** show Hollywood releases before they reach Europe and there is a string of art-house places – as befits a city that hosts what is generally regarded as the world's best film festival, the renowned **Toronto International Film Festival** (see p.74).

Bars, clubs and music venues

Big Bop 651 Queen St W; Streetcar: Queen (#501) ⓣ416/504-6699, ⓦwww.bigbop.com. This vast space is filled with urban rockers and holds several different stages, all of which cater to the live alternative rock scene. The main stage is decorated with sumptuous mural-sized reproductions of famous nineteenth-century paintings – making the walls the best-dressed thing in the joint. Just east of Bathurst.

Cameron House 408 Queen St. W; Streetcar: Queen (#501) ⓣ416/703-0811, ⓦwww.thecameron.com. This old tap house has been a performance space and refuge for members of Toronto's alternative arts scene for two decades, and includes its own vibrant cabaret. The interior is covered with trompe l'oeil skies and angels, while, outside, artists have been rearranging the facade for twenty years now, the only constant being the huge, red metal ants marching up the side of the building. Just west of Spadina.

C'est What? 67 Front St East at Church; Subway: Union Station ⓣ416/867-9499, ⓦwww.cestwhat.com. Located in a dark, low-ceilinged basement in the St Lawrence district, *C'est What* has over twenty micro brews on tap – including the popular house brand, hemp beer – plus an impressive selection of single malt scotches and hearty pub food. The performance space here has seen the likes of Bare Naked Ladies and Jeff Buckley, to name just two. Daily 11.30am–2am.

College St Bar 574 College St; Streetcar: College (#506) ⓣ416/533-2417, ⓦwww.collegestreetbar.com. A laid-back, groovy jazz bar that often dips into R&B. An excellent alternative to some of the city's over-hyped, more sensationalist establishments. Open nightly from 5pm until 2am. West of Bathurst.

El Convento Rico 750 College St; Streetcar: College (#506) ⓣ416/588-7800, ⓦwww.elconventorico.com. Walking into this lively joint, replete with red velvet, flocked wallpaper and baroque spot welding, makes you feel like you've stumbled on the best party in town – and you may well have. The crowd ranges from earnest suburbanites to dishy Latino drag queens, and the DJs spin Latin and disco classics. Mon–Sat until 4am (Sun until 10pm). West of Bathurst, but before Ossington.

El Mocambo 464 Spadina Ave at College; Streetcar: College (#506) T416/777-1777, ⓦwww.elmocambo.ca. The stuff of legends insofar as live acts are concerned, having had visits from luminaries like the Rolling Stones, B.B. King, Blondie, and hometown favourites like Nash the Slash. The tables are sticky and the carpet is scary, but the bands are (usually) great.

Horseshoe Tavern 368 Queen St W; Streetcar: Queen (#501) ⓣ416/598-4753, ⓦwww.horseshoetavern.com. Lots of Toronto bands got their start here, and it's still a favourite place for the newly-famous to sit in for a set or stage a special one-off concert. The interior is relentlessly unglamorous, but the phenomenal bar staff is a major compensation. Just east of Spadina.

Lee's Palace 529 Bloor St W; Subway: Bathurst ⓣ416/532-1598, ⓦwww.leespalace.com. *Lee's* continued popularity has nothing to do with the decor, the food or even the draft beer. Its reputation is entirely based on the outre bands it consistently books. Patrons can also check out the DJ dance action upstairs at the aptly named Dance Cave.

Matador 466 Dovercourt at College; Streetcar: College (#506) ⓣ416/533-9311. This noble institution has been memorialized in song by none other than Leonard Cohen in "Closing Time". When everyone else starts to shut down, the *Matador* opens. Don't think about showing up before 1.30am. A good place to star-watch and catch great bands trying out new material.

The Rex Hotel Jazz & Blues Bar 194 Queen St W, corner of St Patrick ⓣ416/598-2475, ⓦwww.therex.ca. In arguments about which is the best jazz club in town, this one is consistently near the top of the list. A well-primped crowd lounges in the spiffed-up interior, but any reservations about pretensions evaporate once the music – which is always top-notch – begins.

This Is London 364 Richmond St W at Spadina; Streetcar: Queen (#501) ⓣ416/351-9579, ⓦwww.thisislondonclub.com. Yet another club you have to enter off an alleyway (and up a flight of stairs). When it opened, people were appreciative of its stylish interior, DJ selections of disco, soul and good old Top 40, but the real buzz was about the women's washrooms: they take up the whole top floor, and hairdressers and make-up artists are on hand for touch-ups.

Theatre

Princess of Wales Theatre 300 King St W at John; Subway: St Andrew ⓣ416/872-1212, ⓦwww.mirvish.com. Built in 1993 to accommodate the helicopter in *Miss Saigon*, and currently home to the blockbuster musical *The Phantom of the Opera*, this addition to Toronto's more traditional playhouses manages to have a surprisingly intimate feel, despite its 2000-odd seats.

Royal Alexandra Theatre 260 King St W at Simcoe; Subway: St Andrew ⓣ416/872-1212, ⓦwww.mirvish.com. Built in 1906, the "Royal Alex" is a charming Edwardian theatre that has been fully restored to its original, gilt-edged glory. Puts on everything from classical theatre to exuberant musicals like *Mamma Mia*.

St Lawrence Centre for the Arts 27 Front St E; Subway: Union Station ⓣ416/366-7723, ⓦwww.stlc.com. The St Lawrence Centre contains two stages: the Bluma Appel Theatre, which specializes in presenting new works by contemporary artists, and, upstairs, the studio-sized Jane Mallett Theatre showcasing experimental and workshop productions. Opera and dance performances too.

Tarragon Theatre 30 Bridgman St; Subway: Dupont ⓣ416/531-1827, ⓦwww.tarragontheatre.com. A renovated factory space, the Tarragon has contributed much to Toronto's thriving theatrical community, by consistently presenting challenging, innovative performances.

Classical music

Glenn Gould Studio 250 Front St. W; Streetcar: King (#504) ⓣ416/205-5555, ⓦwww.glenngouldstudio.cbc.ca. Named after the great pianist himself (see p.93), this small, boxy hall located downtown in the Canadian Broadcasting Centre (see p.89) is so sprung for sound that enthusiastic performances leave audiences literally vibrating. The programming is first-rate, generally showcasing Canadian talent.

Massey Hall 178 Victoria St; Subway: Dundas ⓣ416/872-4255. A turn-of-the-century recital hall that boasts great acoustics, and has hosted a wide variety of performers – everyone from Maria Callas to Jarvis Cocker. The austere architecture is offset by Moorish details, like the fanciful moulding along the balconies.

Roy Thomson Hall 60 Simcoe St; Subway: St Andrew ⓣ416/872-4255, ⓦwww.roythomson.com. Home to the Toronto Symphony Orchestra (ⓣ416/593-4828, ⓦwww.tso.on.ca), this modern hall looks like an upturned soup bowl during the day, but at night the place is transformed, its glass-panelled walls casting light into the sky and over the reflecting ponds outside. Inside, the circular hall has excellent sightlines, and its acoustics have been tweaked to rave reviews.

Opera and ballet

Canadian Opera Company Four Seasons Centre for the Performing Arts, 145 Queen St W; Subway: Osgoode ⓣ416/363-8231, ⓦwww.coc.ca. Now ensconced in its new and lavish home, Canada's national opera troupe, the COC, has impressed international audiences for years with its ambitious productions, devotion to young talent and the musical erudition of its director, Richard Bradshaw. Seats are often scarce, particularly for the eagerly anticipated season premieres, so reserve as far in advance as possible; ticket prices begin at $60.

National Ballet Company Four Seasons Centre for the Performing Arts, 145 Queen St W; Subway: Osgoode ⓣ416/345-9686, ⓦwww.national.ballet.ca. The NBC's prima ballerinas are much admired, as is the company itself, performing classical ballet and contemporary dance with equal artistry; tickets $40–200.

Cinemas

Bloor Cinema 506 Bloor St W; Subway: Bathurst ⓣ416/516-2331, ⓦwww.bloorcinema.com. Though this cinema won't win any beauty contests, it's still a great place to view second-run films. Frequently plays host to the numerous film festivals that fill up the Toronto calendar.

Carlton 20 Carlton St; Subway: College ⓣ416/598-2309. The Carlton showcases first-run art films on its eleven screens. The café and espresso bar make a nice change from standard concessions fare, although that too is available.

Paramount 259 Richmond St W; Subway: Osgoode ⓣ416/368-5600. Perfect venue for filmgoers who want to feel like extras in 'Blade Runner'. Half the spectacle is the theatre itself, with a mammoth, pixel-board cube showing film clips, an almost vertical ride up the escalator to the cinemas above and, of course, a sound system to blast you out of your seat. Just west of University Ave.

Varsity 55 Bloor St W; Subway: Bloor-Yonge ⓣ416/961-6304. A recent expansion has turned

Spectator sports in Toronto

Baseball The Blue Jays (Ⓣ416/341-1234, Ⓦwww.bluejays.com), of the American Baseball League, play at the Rogers Centre (see p.87).

Canadian football The Argonauts (Ⓣ416/341-2700, Ⓦwww.argonauts.on.ca), of the CFL, also play at the Rogers Centre.

Ice hockey The Maple Leafs (tickets from Ticketmaster Ⓣ416/872-5000, Ⓦwww.mapleleafs.com), of the NHL, play home fixtures in the Air Canada Centre, behind Union Station.

Soccer Toronto FC (Ⓣ416/360-4625; Ⓦtoronto.fc.misnet.com) of the MLS play at BMO Field in Exhibition Place.

this two-screener into an eleven-cinema behemoth, replete with displays of Hollywood costumes, premium prices and full-service (drinks and snacks delivered to your seat) screening rooms. The cinemas are well appointed with deep, comfortable seats.

Listings

Bookshops World's Biggest Bookstore, 20 Edward St, near Yonge and Dundas (Ⓣ416/977-7009), is a huge warehouse-like affair with a vast selection of titles and strong Canada sections. Alternatively, try Indigo (Ⓦwww.chapters.indigo.ca), which has several branches here in Toronto, including one in the Eaton Centre, another at 55 Bloor St W.

Car rental Discount, 134 Jarvis St Ⓣ416/864-0632; National, Union Station, 65 Front St East Ⓣ416/364-4195 and at the airport T905/676-2647; Dollar/Thrifty, 370 King St W Ⓣ416/977-6749 and at the airport T905/673-8811, x6256.

Consulates Australia, 175 Bloor St East Ⓣ416/323-1155; Ireland, 20 Toronto St Ⓣ416/366-9300; New Zealand, 225 MacPherson Ave, Ⓣ416/947-9696; UK, 777 Bay St Ⓣ416/593-1290; US, 360 University Ave Ⓣ416/595-1700.

Internet access Most city hotels provide Internet access for their guests either free or at minimal charge. The Toronto Reference Library also provides free Internet access (see 'Library' below).

Laundry The Laundry Lounge, 527 Yonge St, just north of College (Ⓣ416/975-4747); Splish Splash Cleaning Centre, 590 College St west of Bathurst (Ⓣ416/532-6499).

Left luggage Union Station, Front St at Bay, has lockers, as does the Toronto Coach Terminal, 610 Bay St at Dundas, and the Bloor-Yonge subway station.

Library The main library is the Toronto Reference Library, 789 Yonge St, one block north of Bloor (Mon–Thurs 9.30am–8.30pm, Fri 9.30am–5.30pm & Sat 9am–5pm, & Sun Sept–June 1.30–5pm; Ⓣ416/393-7000, Ⓦwww.torontopubliuclibrary.ca).

Newspapers Toronto has two first-rate newspapers, the *Toronto Star* and the *Globe and Mail*, the latter sold all over Canada.

Pharmacies Shopper's Drug Mart has a string of downtown pharmacies, including outlets at Bay St and Gerrard (Ⓣ416/979-2424) and 728 Yonge St (Ⓣ416/920-0098). For a holistic pharmacy, including herbal and traditional treatments, try the Big Carrot Wholistic Dispensary, 348 Danforth Ave Ⓣ416/466-8432.

Post offices Canada Post operates branches in scores of locations, mostly as a distinct part of a larger retail outlet, mainly pharmacies and stationery stores. One handy location is downtown inside the Royal Bank Plaza, 200 Bay at Front.

Travel details

Trains

Ontario Northland (Ⓣ1-800/461-8558, Ⓦwww.northlander.ca)
Toronto to: Cobalt (6 weekly; 7hr 40min); Cochrane (6 weekly; 11hr); Gravenhurst (6 weekly; 2hr); Huntsville (6 weekly; 3hr); North Bay (6 weekly; 5hr); Temagami (6 weekly; 7hr).
VIA Rail (Ⓣ1-888/842-7245, Ⓦwww.viarail.ca)
Toronto to: Kingston (2–3 daily; 2hr 30min); London (4 daily; 2hr); Montréal (2–3 daily; 4hr 30min); Niagara Falls (2 daily; 2hr); Ottawa (3–5 daily; 4hr 15min); Parry Sound (3 weekly; 4hr); Stratford (2 daily; 2hr 10min); Sudbury Junction (3 weekly; 8hr); Windsor (4 daily; 4hr); Winnipeg (3 weekly; 28hr 45min).

Buses

Coach Canada (Ⓣ1-800/461-7661, Ⓦwww.coachcanada.com)
Toronto to: Brockville (3 daily; 4hr 15min); Kingston (8 daily; 3hr); Montréal (8 daily; 7hr); Niagara Falls (hourly; 1hr 30min–2hr).
Greyhound (Ⓣ1-800/661-8747, Ⓦwww.greyhound.ca)
Toronto to: Collingwood (2 daily; 3hr); Hamilton (4 daily; 1hr); Kitchener (every 30min-1hr; 1hr 45min); London (13 daily; 2hr 30min–3hr); Midland (2 daily; 2hr 45min or 3hr 30min); Montréal (8 daily; 7hr 30min to 9hr); Niagara Falls (hourly; 1hr 30min–2hr); Ottawa (9 daily; 5–6hr); Owen Sound (3 daily; 4hr); Penetanguishene (1 daily; 3hr); Sault Ste Marie (3 daily; 10hr 50min); Thunder Bay (3 daily; 21hr); Wasaga Beach (2 daily; 3hr); Wawa (4 daily; 14hr); Windsor (5 daily; 4–5hr); Winnipeg (3 daily; 30hr 30min).
Ontario Northland (Ⓣ1-800/461-8558, Ⓦwww.webusit.com)
Toronto to: Bracebridge (4 daily; 2hr 45min); Gravenhurst (4 daily; 2hr 30min); Huntsville (4 daily; 3hr); North Bay (4–5 daily; 6hr); Orillia (1 daily; 2hr); Parry Sound (3 daily; 3hr 15min); Port Severn (3 daily; 2hr 45min); Sudbury (3 daily; 6hr).

Flights

Toronto to: Calgary (5–7 daily; 4hr 15min); Edmonton (5–7 daily; 1hr 40min); Fredericton (5–6 daily; 1hr 45min); Halifax (7–9 daily; 2hr); Montréal (15–26 daily; 1hr 15min); Ottawa (11–22 daily; 1hr); Québec City (8–19 daily; 1hr 45min); Saint John (4–5 daily; 1hr 45min); St John's (6–7 daily; 3hr); Saskatoon (2–3 daily; 3hr 30min); Thunder Bay (2–5 daily; 1hr 30min); Vancouver (6–7 daily; 5hr); Winnipeg (5 daily; 2hr 45min).

2 Ontario

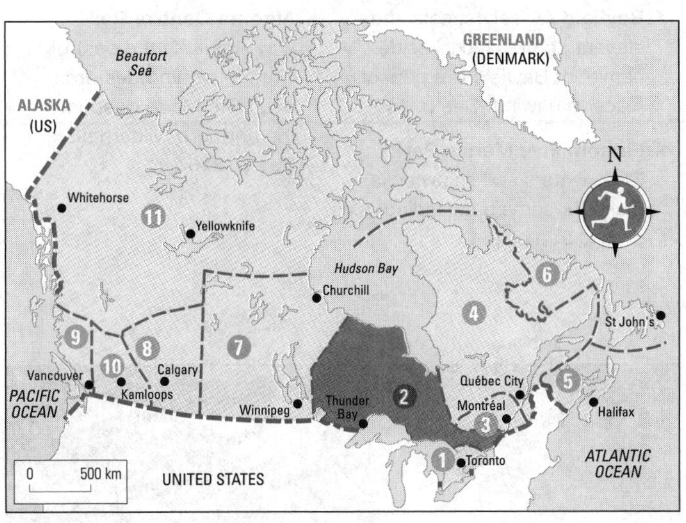
Beaufort Sea
GREENLAND (DENMARK)
ALASKA (US)
N
Whitehorse
11
Yellowknife
Hudson Bay
6
Churchill
4
St John's
9
8
7
10
Calgary
Vancouver
Kamloops
PACIFIC OCEAN
Québec City
5
Thunder Bay
2
Montréal
Winnipeg
3
Halifax
1
Toronto
ATLANTIC OCEAN
0 500 km
UNITED STATES

CHAPTER 2

Highlights

* **Niagara Falls** Quite simply one of the most famous tourist attractions in North America. See p. 128
* **Niagara-on-the-Lake** With its antique clapboard houses and immaculate gardens, this is one of Ontario's prettiest towns. See p. 134
* **Bayfield** All leafy streets and elegant homes, the lakeside hamlet of Bayfield is a perfect place to unwind. See p. 149
* **Fathom Five Marine Park** Clear waters and shipwrecks make for some outstanding diving. See p. 154
* **Georgian Bay Islands** Ontario at its most beautiful – crystal waters studded with pine-dusted islands. See p. 162
* **Ottawa** Amiable capital city, with a lively restaurant and café scene plus a clutch of outstanding museums and galleries. See p. 180
* **Algoma Central Railway** Arguably the best of Ontario's train rides, from Sault Ste Marie deep into the northern wilderness. See p. 215

△ Canoeing in the Georgian Bay Islands

2

Ontario

Ontario, Canada's second-largest province, stretches all the way from the St Lawrence River and the Great Lakes to the frozen shores of Hudson Bay. Some two-thirds of this territory – all of the north and most of the centre – is occupied by the forests and rocky outcrops of the **Canadian Shield**, whose ancient Precambrian rocks were brought to the surface by the glaciers that gouged the continent during the last ice age. The glaciers produced a flattened landscape studded with thousands of lakes and it was the local Iroquois who first coined the name "Ontario", literally "glittering waters". The **Iroquois** – as well as their **Algonquin** neighbours to the north – hunted and fished the Canadian Shield, but their agricultural activities were confined to the more fertile and hospitable parts of southern Ontario, in which the vast majority of the province's ten million people are now concentrated.

Spread along the north shore of **Lake Ontario** is Canada's biggest city, **Toronto** (see Chapter 1), with a population of around four and a half million. To either side of this giant metropolis is the so-called "Golden Horseshoe" – named for its economic clout rather than its looks – comprised of sprawling suburbs and ugly industrial townships. The steel city of **Hamilton**, at the western end of the lake, has one or two interesting historic sights and is also near Canada's premier tourist spot, **Niagara Falls** – best visited on a day-trip from Toronto or from colonial **Niagara-on-the-Lake** nearby. Most of the rest of southwest Ontario, sandwiched between lakes Huron and Erie, is farming terrain that's as flat as a Dutch polder. Nevertheless, the car-producing town of **Windsor** is a lively place to spend a night, and both **Goderich** and **Bayfield** are charming little places tucked against the bluffs along the Lake Huron shoreline. For landscape, the most attractive regions of southern Ontario are the **Bruce Peninsula** and the adjacent **Georgian Bay**, whose **Severn Sound** is the location of the beautiful **Georgian Bay Islands National Park** as well as a pair of top-notch historical reconstructions, **Discovery Harbour** and **Sainte-Marie among the Hurons**.

In **central Ontario**, inland from the coastal strip bordering Georgian Bay, are the myriad **Muskoka Lakes** – the epicentre of what Canadians call "cottage country". Every summer, the province's city folk arrive here in their thousands for a spot of fishing, boating and swimming, hunkering down in their lakeside cottages – though "cottages" is something of a misnomer as these second homes range from humble timber chalets to vast mansions. For all the locals' summer fun, touring the region as an outsider is mostly disappointing. With the notable exception of several superb hotels, there is nowhere in particular to aim for and the main towns – primarily **Gravenhurst** and **Bracebridge** – are far from inspiring. If you get an invite to a cottage things

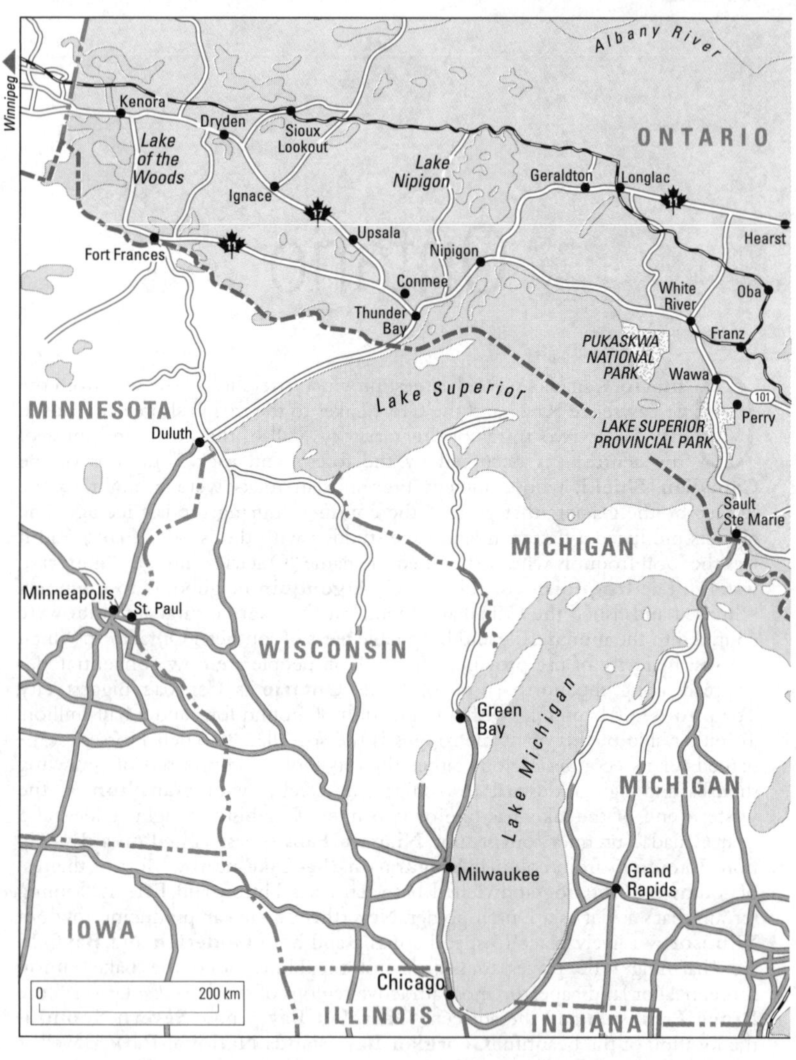

may well seem very different, but otherwise, if you're after the great outdoors, you'd do best to keep going north to **Algonquin Provincial Park**. This consists of a vast wilderness where beavers and black bears roam and you can canoe for days without seeing a soul. Alternatively head east for the towns bordering the St Lawrence River, primarily **Kingston**, a handsome city with a clutch of fine colonial buildings. North of here, within easy striking distance, is **Ottawa**, the nation's capital, but a surprisingly small city of impeccable streets and parks, high-class museums and galleries, plus – and this may be something of a surprise if you're familiar with the city's bureaucratic image – a lively restaurant and bar scene.

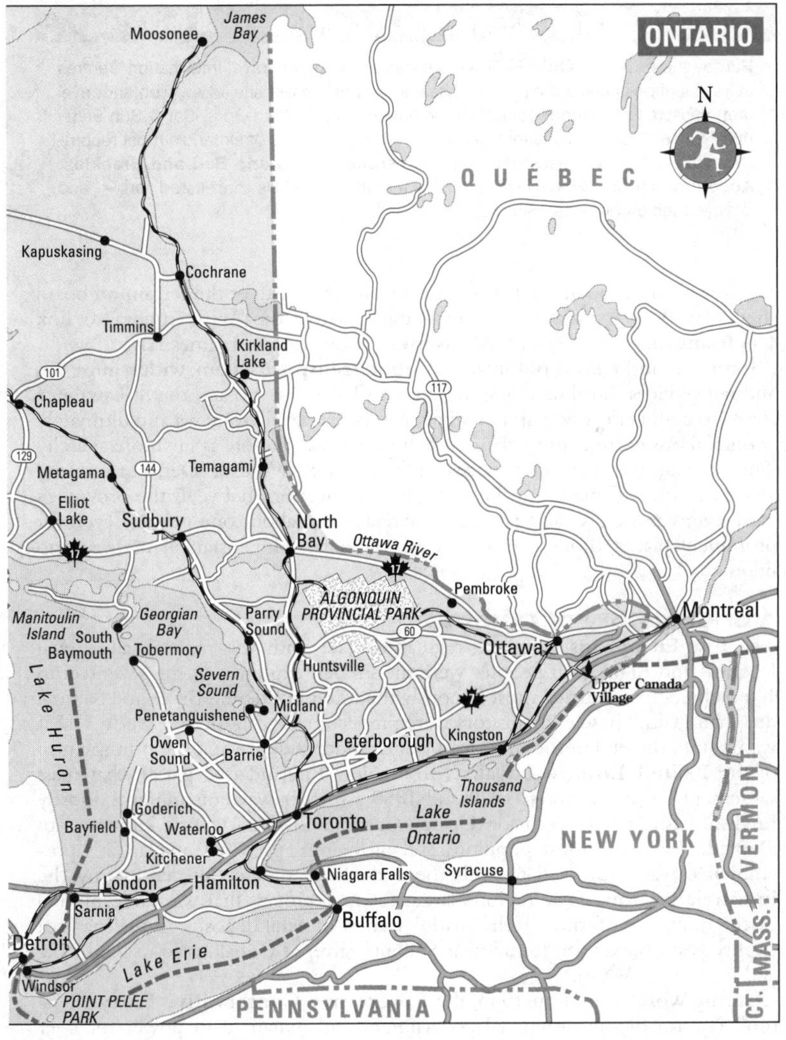

Northern Ontario offers a natural environment stunning in its extremes, but the travelling can be hard and the specific sights too widely separated for comfort. Two main roads cross this sparsely inhabited region, **Highway 11** in the north and **Highway 17** to the south. The former links a series of mining towns and has little to offer, while the latter passes near – or cuts through – a string of parks, including the extravagantly wild **Lake Superior Provincial Park**. Hwy 17 also visits **Sault Ste Marie** – terminus of the **Agawa Canyon** train, which affords a glimpse of the otherwise impenetrable hinterland – as well as the gritty grain port of **Thunder Bay**, an ideal stopping point on the long journey west (or east). North of Hwy 11 lies a brutal country where hunters are the only

Ontario Travel and the Federation of Ontario Bed and Breakfasts

Run by the province, **Ontario Travel** operates a string of Travel Information Centres at key locations across the province, has an exhaustive website (Ⓦwww.ontariotravel.net) and staffs a visitors' telephone help line (Mon–Fri 8am–8pm, Sat & Sun 9am–6pm; Ⓣ1-800/ONTARIO within Canada and the US). Many of Ontario's most recommendable B&Bs are members of the **Federation of Ontario Bed and Breakfast Accommodation** (Ⓦwww.fobba.com); members' details are listed on – and downloadable from – its website.

regular visitors, though the passing tourist can get a taste of the terrain on board the Polar Bear Express train, which tracks across the Arctic tundra to link **Cochrane**, on Hwy 11, with **Moosonee** on the shores of James Bay.

Toronto is at the heart of Ontario's **public transport** system, with regular bus and rail services shuttling along the shore of Lake Ontario and the St Lawrence River to connect every major city between Niagara Falls, Ottawa and ultimately Montréal. Away from this urban core, however, the picture is far more sketchy. There are fairly regular bus services on the London–Windsor–Detroit route and along the Trans-Canada and Hwy 17, but connections between the province's smaller towns are few and far between: reckon on about one per day even for prominent places, though in some cases (Goderich, for instance) there are no buses at all.

A brief history of Ontario

The first **Europeans** to make regular contact with the region's aboriginal Iroquois and Algonquin peoples were the French explorers of the seventeenth and eighteenth centuries, most famously the intrepid Étienne Brûlé and Samuel de Champlain. These early visitors were preoccupied with the **fur trade**, and it wasn't until the end of the American War of Independence and the immigration of the **United Empire Loyalists** from New England (see p.459) that mass settlement began. Between 1820 and 1850 a further wave of migrants, mostly English, Irish and Scots, made **Upper Canada**, as Ontario was known until Confederation, the most populous and prosperous part of Canada. This pre-eminence was reinforced towards the end of the nineteenth century by the **industrialization** of the region's larger towns, a process that was underpinned by the discovery of some of the world's richest mineral deposits: in the space of twenty years, nickel was found near Sudbury, silver at Cobalt, gold in Red Lake and iron ore at Wawa.

During World War II, in 1943, the **Progressive Conservative Party** (PCs) took control of the provincial government and remained in power for over forty years. The PCs followed a right-of-centre, pro-business agenda and their skill in handling the popular vote earned them the nickname the 'Big Blue Machine'. Nevertheless, the PCs did move with the times, passing a string of **progressive acts** such as, for example, Canada's first Fair Employment Practices Act against discrimination and the Female Employees Fair Remuneration Act, both in 1951. In 1985, the PCs finally lost a provincial election, but returned to power ten years later with a flinty right-wing agenda that owed much to Britain's Margaret Thatcher. The PCs were much taken up with privatization and tax cuts (plus endless carping about welfare scroungers), but this did not play well with a sizeable chunk of the population and, much to the relief of the left, the Liberals defeated them in 2003 and remain in power at time of writing.

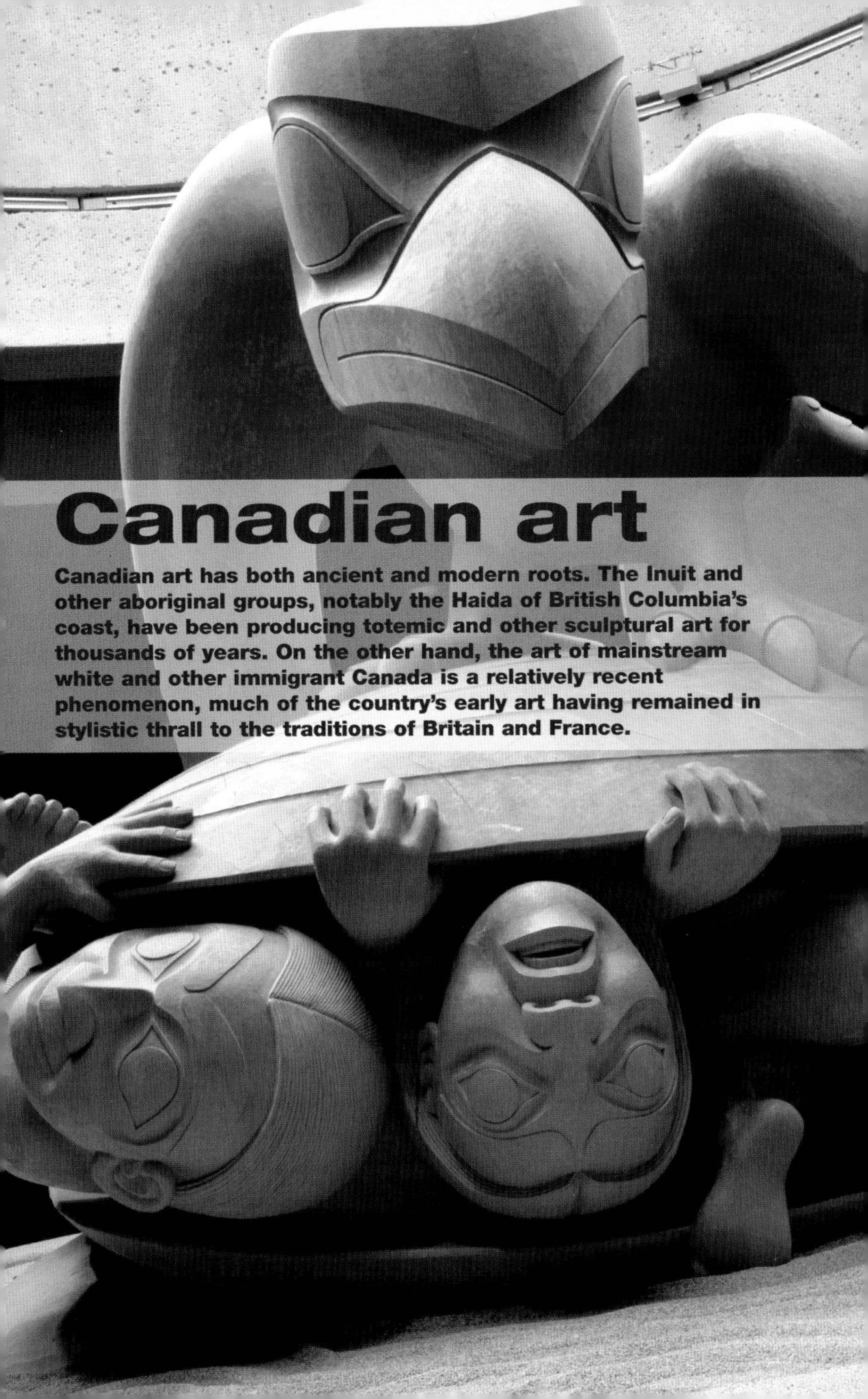

Canadian art

Canadian art has both ancient and modern roots. The Inuit and other aboriginal groups, notably the Haida of British Columbia's coast, have been producing totemic and other sculptural art for thousands of years. On the other hand, the art of mainstream white and other immigrant Canada is a relatively recent phenomenon, much of the country's early art having remained in stylistic thrall to the traditions of Britain and France.

▲ Totems, Vancouver

Aboriginal art

Aboriginal art may be some of Canada's oldest, but it is still some of the country's most vibrant and relevant. Public and private galleries across the country juxtapose the traditional and contemporary, nowhere more so than in Vancouver's peerless Museum of Anthropology, where glorious, but anonymous totems and exquisite jet-black slate jewellery from centuries past sit alongside works such as the majestic *The Raven and the Beast*, 4.5 tonnes of carved cedar by Bill Reid (1920–98), the greatest of recent aboriginal artists.

Today, Inuit art commands particular attention and high prices, especially prints and drawings, media that proliferated in the 1950s but which were already established parts of Inuit culture. Self-taught Pitseolak Ashoona (1904–83) was one of the first whose prints entered the mainstream, paving the way for contemporary artists such as Jessie Oonark (1906–85), whose magnificent panorama of northern life, *When the Days are Long and the Sun Shines Into the Night* (1966–69), is one of the highlights of Ottawa's National Gallery of Canada.

The lure of landscape

The debt to European tradition survived until the middle of the nineteenth century, when painter-explorers such as William Hind (1833–89) and Paul Kane (1810–71) began to depict Canada's landscapes, fauna and – above all – aboriginal cultures. Kane, in particular, embarked on two prodigious journeys west from his Toronto home, and produced some 700 sketches and 100 paintings, the latter often idealized, but the former graphic portrayals of cultures on the brink of calamitous change.

Neither Kane, nor the eminent but often blandly romantic landscape painters who followed him – notably Allan Edson (1846–88) and Lucius O'Brien (1832–99) – completely threw off the shackles of European convention. That job fell to the Group of Seven, a medley of twentieth-century Toronto-based painters who forged Canada's first school of painting and in the process altered the perception of the Canadian wilderness through their iconoclastic approach to art and landscape. Together they pursued the notion of purely "Canadian painting" with almost evangelical zeal. "Only by fostering our own Canadian art," said A. Y. Jackson, one of the Group, "shall we develop ourselves as a people."

Borrowing from the Impressionists, Cézanne, art nouveau and Scandinavian landscape painters, the group, notably Jackson, Frank Johnston and Lawren Harris, used harsh colours and a vivid, iconoclastic style to portray the Canadian wilderness in all its uncompromising beauty.

▲ *Indian Encampment on Lake Huron* by Paul Kane

Group dynamics

In the 1930s – and to this day – artists began to resent the large shadow cast by the Group of Seven, and the feeling that their art and notion of art had become, by default, Canadian art. In Québec, Paul-

Émile-Borduas (1905–60) led a modernist collective in the 1940s known as Les Automatistes, in part a reaction across the Anglophile consensus of the Group of Seven, but also against a linked suspicion on the part of the public and galleries of Modernist movements such as Cubism and Abstract Expressionism.

The Eastern Group of Painters (Eric Goldberg, Jori Smith and John Goodwin Lyman, among others), founded in Montréal in 1938, also shared an antipathy for the notion of a national vision and oeuvre of the Group of Seven and its successors, the Canadian Group of Painters. Their work, however, often remained tied to a notion of place, in this case the landscapes of Québec, exemplified by paintings such as Goldberg's almost naïve image of *Gaspé Village Pier*.

▲ *Lake and Mountains* by Lawren Harris

Free at last

Only in the 1950s can Canadian art be said to have shed both its earlier preoccupations. This freedom was exemplified by Painters Eleven, a collective of eleven artists founded by William Ronald (1926–98) in Toronto in 1954. Its only commitment was to abstract art, and produced influential artists such as Jack Bush (1909–77), who continued to triumph after the group's dismantling in 1960.

More recently, the mantle of Canadian modernism has been borne, among others, by General Idea, a collective of three artists (Felix Partz, Jorge Zontal and AA Bronson), whose witty conceptual and media-based work in the 1990s – often presented as postcards, crests, pins, balloons and other unusual media – subverted popular culture or the media it apparently espoused. A far cry, at last, from the call of the wild and the nationalistic consensus that dominated Canadian art for over 150 years.

Emily Carr

Western Canada's most celebrated artist was born in Victoria in 1871, succeeding at a time when it was difficult for a woman to shine in most activities, never mind an artistic one. Most of the key strands of Canadian art come together in her paintings, notably a preoccupation with landscape; a borrowing from, and celebration of, aboriginal culture; the readiness to look back to the Old World; and a debt to the liberating work of the Group of Seven painters.

Once you've seen a Carr painting, the chances are you'll recognise another, because her themes and treatment, once her style was established, became virtually fixed. Thus there are the motifs and themes – vast trees, sombre landscapes, and the totems, carvings and other aspects of aboriginal culture. Then there is the treatment – dark, or virulent colours, especially greens and browns; violent or almost surreal swirls, patterns and distortions. Finally there is the reaction to them – almost universally negative, at least in her own time. These days she's almost a national treasure. Visit the galleries of Vancouver and Victoria to make up your own mind.

▶ *Western Forest* by Emily Carr

Where to see...

- **Early Canadian art** It's the country's artistic showpiece, so you'd expect a good show, and Ottawa's National Gallery duly delivers, with a superb overview of Canadian art from its earliest days – plus plenty of big names from the Old World.
- **Emily Carr** The Vancouver Art Gallery has the key collection, trumping the handful of works still in her home city of Victoria.
- **Inuit art** Ritzy private galleries country-wide feature Inuit art at eye-watering prices, but visit Winnipeg's Art Gallery for the world's most comprehensive collection of Canadian aboriginal prints, paintings and sculpture.
- **The French-Canadians** Québec City's Musée di Québec offers a comprehensive romp through 300 years of Québécois art, with a sprinkling of outsiders en route.
- **Old Masters** Montréal's wealthy merchants were avid big-name collectors, hence the presence of El Greco, Rembrandt and Memlinc, among others, in the city's dazzling Musée des Beaux Arts.
- **Private bequests** Newspaper tycoon Lord Beaverbrook bequeathed much of his private collection to Fredericton, New Brunswick, where the Beaverbrook Art Gallery features Old Masters, Salvador Dalí and major Canadian works by Kane, Carr and the Group of Seven.
- **The Group of Seven** Start your pilgrimage in Toronto's Art Gallery of Ontario and Thomson Gallery, but keep an eye out for works by the group in galleries across the country.
- **Tom Thomson** The Group of Seven's leading light is represented in several galleries, not least in Toronto, but be sure to visit the excellent McMichael Collection, near Kleinburg, 40km north of the city.
- **Totemic art** Vancouver's Museum of Anthropology has an unparalleled collection not only of totems and other carvings, but also a vast range of decorative arts from the Haida and other Pacific Northwest aboriginal peoples.

▼ *Round Lake, Mud Bay* by Tom Thomson

As for the **economy**, Ontario's highly mechanized timber industry, mineral mines, massive hydroelectric schemes and myriad factories – making more than half the country's manufactured goods – keep the province at the top of the economic ladder. However, this industrial success has created massive **environmental problems**, most noticeable in the wounded landscapes around Sudbury and the polluted waters of lakes Erie and Ontario – problems which the Liberal administration has started to tackle, albeit somewhat cautiously.

Southwest Ontario

The chain of towns to the east and west of Toronto, stretching 120km along the edge of Lake Ontario from Oshawa to Hamilton, is often called the **Golden Horseshoe**, a misleadingly evocative name that refers solely to their geographic shape and economic success. This is Ontario's manufacturing heartland, a densely populated strip whose principal places of interest are in the steel-making city of **Hamilton**, the home of both the Royal Botanical Gardens and the delightful mansion of Dundurn Castle. Further round the lake are the famous **Niagara Falls**, undoubtedly Canada's most celebrated sight and adjoined to an uninspiring town of the same name – opt for the charming town of **Niagara-on-the-Lake** as a base for a visit. At neighbouring Queenston the **Niagara Escarpment** begins its rambling journey across the region to the Bruce Peninsula, the major interruption in a generally flat terrain. To the west of this limestone ridge the main attractions are on the coast, most notably **Point Pelee National Park**, the vigorous town of **Windsor**, and the small-town pleasures of **Goderich** and leafy **Bayfield**. The **Bruce Peninsula** itself boasts dramatic coastal scenery and incorporates two outstanding national parks, which make for some great walking, climbing and scuba diving. To the east of the Niagara Escarpment, along the southern shore of **Severn Sound**, there's a string of lethargic ports, the most agreeable of which is **Penetanguishene**, located a few kilometres from the sturdy palisades of the replica Jesuit mission of **Sainte-Marie among the Hurons**. The northern shore of the Sound boasts the lion's share of the stunningly beautiful **Georgian Bay Islands National Park**, an elegiac land and waterscape of rocky, pine-dotted islets and crystal-blue lake. The park – and its campsites – are best approached by boat from the pocket-sized resort of **Honey Harbour**, but you can sample the scenery on a variety of summer island cruises from Penetanguishene and **Midland** to the south and the dinky little port of **Parry Sound** further north.

There are fast and frequent **buses** and **trains** between Toronto and Niagara Falls, and a similarly efficient service between the region's other major settlements, like Windsor, London and Kitchener. But if you're visiting the smaller towns be aware that transport is much more patchy: Hamilton, Penetanguishene and Midland, for instance, have reasonably good bus connections, but not Niagara-on-the-Lake. Worse still, there are no buses along the east shore of Lake Huron (to Goderich and Bayfield) and up the Bruce Peninsula – where Tobermory has a **car ferry** service to South Baymouth on Manitoulin Island (see p.211), a useful short cut to northern Ontario.

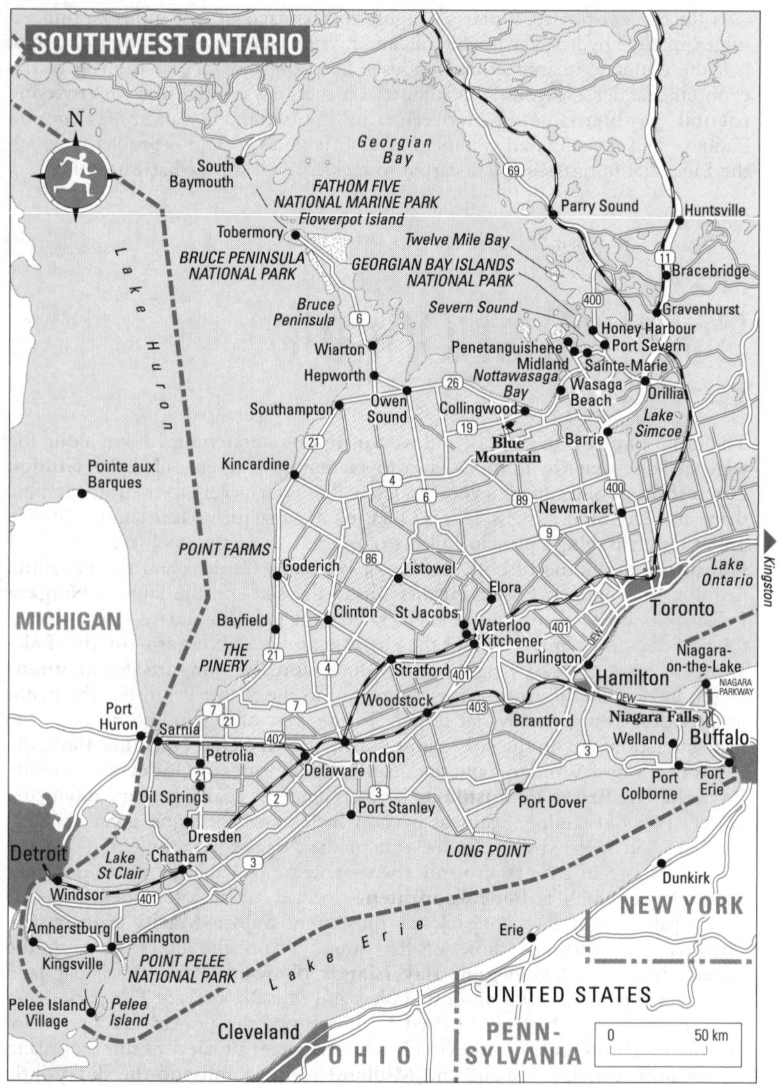

Kitchener, Elora and Stratford

The industrial city of **Kitchener** is southern Ontario at its most prosaic, but amid the prevailing architectural gloom it does have a couple of sights that are worth an hour or so. In marked contrast, **Elora**, 30km north of Kitchener, is a pleasant little village of old stone houses and mills on the periphery of the **Elora Gorge**, a narrow limestone ravine that's a popular spot for a day's walk and picnic. Fifty kilometres west of Kitchener, **Stratford** is different again, a modest country town that hosts one of Canada's most prestigious cultural events, the **Stratford Festival**.

Kitchener and St Jacobs

Just off Hwy 401 about 100km west of downtown Toronto, **KITCHENER** lies at the centre of an industrial belt whose economy has traditionally been based on rubber, textiles, leather and furniture. The town was founded as Sand Hills in 1799 by groups of Mennonites, a tightly knit Protestant sect who came here from the US, where their pacifist beliefs had incurred the wrath of their neighbours during the Revolution. Soon after, German farmers began to arrive in the area, establishing a generally good-humoured trading relationship with the Mennonites. The new settlers had Sand Hills renamed Berlin in 1826, but during World War I it was thought prudent to change the name yet again and to prove their patriotism they chose "Kitchener" after the British field marshal. Today around sixty percent of Kitchener's inhabitants are descendants of German immigrants, a heritage celebrated every year during **Oktoberfest** (Ⓦwww.oktoberfest.ca), nine days of alcoholic stupefaction when even the most reticent of men can be seen wandering the streets in lederhosen. The Mennonites have drifted out of Kitchener itself, and are concentrated in the villages north and west of **Waterloo**, Kitchener's glum northerly neighbour, with a particular concentration in **ST JACOBS**.

The sights

At the heart of Kitchener, on King St E, is the much-lauded **Farmers' Market** (Sat 7am–2pm, year round; Ⓦwww.kitchenermarket.ca), where you should be sure to sample the delicious German sausages. The **Mennonite** traders are unmistakable, with the men wearing traditional black suits and broad-brimmed hats, or deep-blue shirts and braces, the women ankle-length dresses and matching bonnets. The Ontario Mennonites are, however, far from an homogeneous sect – over twenty different groups are affiliated to the **Mennonite Central Committee** (MCC). They all share certain religious beliefs reflecting their Anabaptist origins – the sole validity of adult baptism being crucial – but precise practices and dress codes vary from group to group. Members of the traditional wing of the Mennonite movement, sometimes called **Amish** or Ammanites after the seventeenth-century elder Jakob Ammann, own property communally and shun all modern machinery, travelling to the market and around the back lanes on spindly horse-drawn buggies. To explain their history and faith, the MCC runs The Mennonite Story in the neighbouring village of St Jacobs (see below). Kitchener's only other tourist sight of any real note is **Woodside**, the boyhood home of prime minister William Lyon Mackenzie King (1874–1950), about 1km northeast of the centre at 528 Wellington St North (mid-May to mid-Dec daily 10am–5pm; $3.95, Ⓦwww.pc.gc.ca). Set in a pretty little park, the house has been restored to its late-Victorian appearance and has an interesting display in the basement on King's life and times, though it doesn't give too much away about his eccentricities. A dog lover and spiritualist, he amalgamated the two obsessions by believing his pets were mediums.

The village of **St Jacobs** is home to a popular Mennonite craft shop and **The Mennonite Story**, 1408 King St North (May–Oct Mon–Fri 11am–5pm, Sat 10am–5pm & Sun 1.30–5pm; Nov–April Sat 11am–4.30pm & Sun 2–4.30pm, but times may vary, call Ⓣ519/664-3518; donation), a small but intriguing tourist-office-cum-interpretation-centre that gives the historical low-down on the Mennonites; the introductory DVD is particularly helpful. St Jacobs is just north of Waterloo via Hwy 85.

Practicalities

Kitchener's **bus station** is on Charles Street, one block west of the main street, King, and the town centre. The **VIA train station** is at Victoria and Weber Street West, from where it's a ten-minute walk south to downtown. The Kitchener-Waterloo **tourist office** downtown, opposite the town hall at 191 King St West (June–Aug Mon–Fri 10am–5pm, Sat 10am–4pm & Sun noon–4pm; Sept–May Mon 10am–4pm, Tues–Thurs 9am–5pm, Fri 10am–5pm & Sat noon–4pm; ⓣ519/745-3536 or 1-800/265-6959, ⓦwww.kwtourism.ca), has free maps and **accommodation** listings, including several B&Bs (❶–❷); there's a clutch of **motels** north of the centre along Kitchener's Victoria Street.

Elora

Sloping up from the craggy banks of the Grand River, **ELORA** was founded in the 1830s by settlers who harnessed the river's waters to run their mills. Some of the original limestone cottages have survived, along with a large grist mill, the main landmark, which has been converted into the *Elora Mill Country Inn*, a clever adaptation of what has long been the most important building in town. Nonetheless, most visitors come here to gaze at the **waterfalls** beside the inn – even though they're only a few metres high – and then stroll on to viewpoints overlooking the neighbouring, 3km-long **Elora Gorge**, a forested ravine with limestone cliffs. To get to the gorge from the inn, walk up Price Street to the top of the hill, turn left on James Street and proceed as far as the park area at the end of Henderson, from where footpaths lead across to the gorge.

Elora itself, just ten-minutes' walk from end to end, is most pleasantly approached from the south – along Route 21 – across a narrow bridge that leads into the main street, **Metcalfe**, which cuts across tiny Mill Street, adjoining the falls. Elora is well equipped with **B&Bs**. One of the best is *Tynavon*, 84 Mill St East (ⓣ519/846-6695 or 1-866/334-3305, ⓦwww.bbcanada.com/2481.html; ❺), a smart, modern, lodge-like house with river views and four pleasant guest rooms, all en suite. There's only one **hotel**, the enjoyable *Elora Mill Country Inn*, on Mill St (ⓣ519/846-9118 or 1-866/713-5672, ⓦwww.eloramill.com; ❼), which boasts thirty smooth and polished guest rooms decorated in a modern version of period style with log fires and beamed ceilings. The hotel also has a first-rate **restaurant**.

Stratford

Surrounded by flat and fertile farmland, **STRATFORD** is a likeable little town of 30,000 people, whose downtown core is brightened by the meandering **Avon River** and a grandiose **city hall**, a brown-brick fiesta of cupolas, towers and limestone trimmings. More importantly, the town is also the home of the **Stratford Festival** (see box below), originating in 1953 and now one of the most prestigious theatrical occasions in North America, attracting no fewer than half a million visitors.

From Stratford **VIA train station**, on Shakespeare St, it's a fifteen-minute stroll north via Downie Street to the town's **main crossroads**, where Downie, Ontario and Erie streets meet, just metres from the south bank of the Avon River. Greyhound **buses** use a flag stop on St Patrick Street and from here it's about five minutes' walk north to these same crossroads. There are two tourist offices. The main one is **Tourism Stratford** at 47 Downie St (Jan–March Mon–Fri 8.30am–4.30pm; April & Nov–Dec Mon–Fri 8.30am–4.30pm & Sat 10am–4pm; May–Oct Mon 9am–5pm, Tues–Sat 9am–8pm & Sun 9am–5pm; ⓣ519/271-5140 or 1-800/561-7926, ⓦwww.visitstratfordontario.ca). The second is the seasonal **Visitor Information Centre** located by the river on York Street, immediately northwest of the town's main intersection.

Stratford has over 250 guesthouses and B&Bs plus around a dozen hotels and motels, but **accommodation** can still be hard to find during the Festival's busiest weekends in July and August. The walls of both tourist offices are plastered with pictures and descriptions of many of these establishments. Either tourist office will help you find somewhere to stay, but one good and convenient recommendation is *Avonview Manor B&B*, 63 Avon St (ⓣ519/273-4603, ⓦwww.bbcanada.com/avonview; ❺), which occupies an expansive Edwardian villa overlooking the north bank of the River Avon about 800m northwest of the main crossroads. The four bedrooms here, en suite or with shared facilities, are tastefully decorated and immaculately maintained. Another excellent choice is the *Deacon House B&B Inn*, 101 Brunswick St (ⓣ519/273-2052, ⓦwww.bbcanada.com/1152.html; ❺), whose six lovely guest rooms – all en suite – are centrally located to the southeast of the main crossroads in a good-looking Edwardian villa with a wide veranda. Nearby is a third very recommendable option, the *Duggan Place B&B Inn*, 151 Nile St (ⓣ519/273-7502 or 1-888/394-1111, ⓦwww.dugganplace.com; ❻), set in a well-kept Victorian villa with three en suite rooms kitted out in immaculate period style; two have private balconies overlooking a splendid garden.

The town has a hatful of excellent **cafés and restaurants**, with one of the best being *Fellini's Italian Café & Grill*, 107 Ontario St (daily 11am–8/9pm), which offers a delicious range of fresh pizzas and pastas from $8 and up. Alternatives include the tasty snacks and light meals of *Tango Coffee Bistro*, 104 Ontario St (Sun–Mon 10.30am–5.30pm & Tues–Sat 10.30am–7.30pm), which also has live music on the weekend, and pastries and gourmet coffees at *Balzac's Coffee Ltd*, 149 Ontario St. *Rundles*, 9 Cobourg St (ⓣ519/271-6442; Sat & Sun 11.15am–1.15pm and Tues & Sun 5–7pm, Wed–Sat 5–8.30pm), is arguably the classiest restaurant in town, serving up imaginatively prepared French-style cuisine with full set dinners costing $70, lunches $30; the strikingly modern decor partly compensates for the high prices.

The Stratford Festival

Each season, North America's largest classical repertory company puts on the **Stratford Festival** (ⓣ1-800/567-1600, ⓦwww.stratfordfestival.ca), featuring two of Shakespeare's tragedies and two of his comedies; this programme is augmented by other classical staples – Moliere, Sheridan, Johnson and so forth – as well as by the best of modern and musical theatre. The festival also hosts a lecture series, various tours (of backstage and a costume warehouse, for example), music concerts, an author reading series and meet-and-greet sessions with the actors. The festival runs from mid-April to early November and there are performances in four downtown locations – the Festival, Tom Patterson, Avon and Studio theatres. Regular **tickets** cost anywhere between $45 and $100 depending on the performance and seat category, though there are all sorts of discount deals for students, seniors, same-day performances and previews; many plays are, however, sold out months in advance. Call or consult the website for the latest news.

Hamilton and around

With a population of around 320,000, **HAMILTON** lies at the extreme western end of Lake Ontario, about 70km from Toronto, and it takes its name from George Hamilton, a Queenstown storekeeper-turned-landowner, who surveyed the area after he moved here following the destruction of his homestead during the Anglo-American War of 1812. Strategically located, the town was soon established as a trading centre, but its real growth began with the development of the farm-implements industry in the 1850s. By the turn of the twentieth century, Hamilton had become a major **steel producer** and today its mills churn out about half the country's output, though in general the city's industrial base is on the decline with the recent departure of a string of big companies. Industrial cities are rarely high on tourist itineraries and Hamilton is no exception, but it does rustle up one or two especially good attractions and is within easy striking distance of the **Bell Homestead**, one-time home of the inventor of the telephone, **Alexander Graham Bell**.

The City Centre

An obvious place to start a visit is **Whitehern**, 41 Jackson St West (mid-June to Aug Tues–Sun 11am–4pm; Sept to mid-June Tues–Sun 1–4pm; $6; ⓦwww.tourismhamilton.com), downtown's finest building, a couple of minutes' walk east of Main Street's prominent City Hall. A good example of early Victorian architecture, the house's reworked interior holds an eccentric mix of styles, ranging from a splendid mid-nineteenth-century circular stairway to a dingy wood-panelled 1930s basement – all the garbled legacy of the McQuestern family, who lived here from 1852 until the 1960s. Also in the centre is the **Art Gallery of Hamilton** (Tues & Wed noon–7pm, Thurs & Fri noon–9pm, Sat & Sun noon–5pm; free, but admission charged for exhibitions), which is housed in a brutally modern building at 123 King St W. The gallery displays a representative sample of Canadian painting drawn from the permanent collection, including a good selection of works by the Group of Seven (see box, p.94), most memorably an especially fine *Birch Grove* by Tom Thomson, plus Alex Colville's iconic *Horse and Train* of 1954 and several folksy canvases by Cornelius Krieghoff (see p.96). Nonetheless, the gallery is mainly noted for the high quality of its temporary exhibitions.

Dundurn Castle

From the Art Gallery, it's about twenty minutes' walk northwest along James St North and then York Boulevard to the entertaining **Dundurn Castle** (late May to Aug daily 10am–4pm; Sept to late May Tues–Sun noon–4pm; $10), a handsome villa built in the 1830s for Sir Allan Napier MacNab, a soldier, lawyer and land speculator, who became one of the leading conservative politicians of the day: he was knighted for his loyalty to the Crown during the Upper Canada Rebellion of 1837, when he employed bands of armed Indians to round up supposed rebels and loot their property. Carefully renovated, Dundurn is an impressive, broadly Palladian building with an interior that easily divides into "upstairs" and "downstairs", the former filled with fine contemporaneous furnishings, the latter a warren of poorly ventilated rooms for the dozens of servants. Nearby, the gatekeeper's cottage has been turned into a small **Military Museum** (late May to Aug Tues-Sun 11am–5pm; Sept to late May Tues–Sun 1–5pm; $3, but free admission with castle), detailing local involvement in the War of 1812 and in the Fenian (Irish–American) cross-border raids of the 1860s.

The Royal Botanical Gardens

Heading northwest from Dundurn Castle, York Boulevard clips over the western reaches of Hamilton harbour bound for the neighbouring city of Burlington. The **Royal Botanical Gardens** (Ⓣ905/527-1158, Ⓦwww.rbg.ca) cover some 3000 acres on the far side of the harbour, their several sections spread over 15km of wooded shoreline. The flower displays here are simply gorgeous with highlights including the Hendrie Park Rose Garden (best June–Oct) and the neighbouring Laking Garden with its irises and peonies (May & June). These two gardens adjoin the main **RBG visitor centre** (daily 10am to dusk), where there's a shop, café and several inside areas featuring forced bulbs, orchids, cacti and so forth. Wilder parts of the RBG are round to the west with the 800-hectare Cootes Paradise marsh nature sanctuary latticed with hiking trails.

The outdoor garden areas are **open** daily from 9am to dusk and admission is $8. There are modest additional charges for some of the inside areas, which also close a little earlier – mostly at 5pm. As for transport, most Hamilton–Burlington **buses** stop outside the RBG visitor centre and from here a double-decker **shuttle bus** (May–Aug, every 45min; free) visits all the main sections of the RBG. At other times of the year, you'll need a car.

Hamilton practicalites

Hamilton **bus station** is at the corner of Hunter Street and James Street S, a couple of blocks south of Main Street – which, together with King Street one block further to the north, comprises the **downtown core**. The **tourist information office** is in between Main and King at 34 James St South (Mon–Fri 8.30am–4.30pm; Ⓣ905/546-2666 or 1-800/263-8590, Ⓦwww.tourismhamilton.com). It can supply you with brochures on the city and its surroundings, plus restaurant and hotel lists. Most of the major **hotel** chains have branches in Hamilton, with double rooms starting from around $100; one of the most comfortable is the centrally located *Plaza Hotel Hamilton*, 150 King St East (Ⓣ905/528-3451, Ⓦwww.plazahamilton.com; ❺).

West of Hamilton: Brantford and the Bell Homestead

The modest manufacturing town of **BRANTFORD**, 40km to the west of Hamilton along Hwy 403, takes its name from **Joseph Brant** (1742-1807; also see p.96), who led a large group of Loyalist Iroquois here after the American War of Independence, then worked to form a confederation of Iroquois to keep the United States out of Ohio. His dream was undermined by jealousies amongst the Indian nations, whereupon he withdrew to Burlington and lived the life of an English gentleman. The town was later the birthplace of ice-hockey's greatest player, **Wayne Gretzky**, but no one's built a museum – yet.

The most interesting thing to see in the town itself is the **Brant Museum & Archives**, 10 Charlotte St (Wed–Fri 10am–4pm & Sat 1–4pm; $4; Ⓦwww.brantmuseum.ca), where, amongst the pioneer stuff, there's a reasonable collection of Iroquois artefacts. However, this is really rather small time when compared with Brantford's main sight, the **Bell Homestead**, 94 Tutela Heights Rd (Tues–Sun 9.30am–4.30pm; $5; Ⓦwww.bellhomestead.on.ca), about 4km south of the centre, in the low wooded hills overlooking the Grand River. **Alexander Graham Bell** (1847-1922) left Edinburgh for Ontario in 1870, a reluctant immigrant who came only because of fears for his health after the death of two close relatives from tuberculosis. Soon after his arrival he took a job as a teacher of the deaf, motivated by his mother's loss of hearing and, in his efforts to discover a way to reproduce sounds visibly, he stumbled across the potential of transmitting sound along an electrified wire. The consequence was the first long-distance call, made in 1876 from Brantford to the neighbouring village of Paris and the rest is, as they say, history. The Bell Homestead consists of two simple, clapboard buildings. The first, moved here from Brantford in 1969, housed Canada's original Bell company office and features a series of modest displays on the history of the telephone. The second, the cosy family home, fronts a second small exhibition area devoted to Bell's life and research. There's no public transport from Brantford to the homestead.

Niagara Falls and the Niagara River

In 1860, thousands watched as **Charles Blondin** walked a tightrope across **Niagara Falls** for the third time. Midway, he paused to cook an omelette on a portable grill, and then had a marksman shoot a hole through his hat from the *Maid of the Mist* boat, fifty metres below. As attested by Blondin - and the innumerable lunatics and publicity seekers who have gone over the falls in every craft imaginable - the falls simply can't be beat as a theatrical setting. Yet, in truth, the stupendous first impression doesn't last long and to prevent the twelve million visitors who arrive each year from getting bored by the sight of a load of water crashing over a 52-metre cliff, the Niagarans have ensured that the falls can be seen from every angle imaginable – from boats, viewing towers, helicopters, cable cars and even tunnels in the rock face behind the cascade. The **tunnels** and the **boats** are the most exciting, with the entrance to the former right next to the falls and the latter leaving from the bottom of the cliff at the end of Clifton Hill, 1100m downriver. Both give a real sense of the extraordinary force of the waterfall, a perpetual white-crested thundering pile-up that had Mahler bawling "At last, fortissimo" over the din.

Trains and buses from Toronto and most of southern Ontario's larger towns serve the town of **NIAGARA FALLS**, 3km to the north of the action. The availability of discount excursion fares makes a day-trip a straightforward proposition, although, if you do decide to spend the night, quaint **Niagara-on-the-Lake**, 26km downstream beside Lake Ontario, is a much better option than the crassly commercialized town of Niagara Falls itself. The problem is that hundreds of people agree, the result being that accommodation there can get mighty tight in high season, when you'd be well advised to book up a couple of days in advance. Both the **Niagara Parkway** road and the **Niagara River Recreation Trail**, a jogging and cycle path, stretch the length of the Niagara River from Fort Erie, 32km upstream from the falls, to Niagara-on-the-Lake.

Arrival

Amongst a number of services, there are fast and frequent **Coach Canada buses** (Ⓣ1-800/461-7661, Ⓦwww.coachcanada.com) to the town of Niagara Falls from Toronto and Buffalo. There is also a twice daily VIA **train** service (Ⓣ1-888/842-7245, Ⓦwww.viarail.ca) to Niagara Falls from Toronto. By train or bus, the journey time from Toronto is about two hours. From Toronto, the train is the more scenic way to travel, but delays on the return leg – on which the evening train mostly originates in New York – can be a real pain. If you're travelling by **car**, a day is more than enough time to see the falls and squeeze in a visit to Niagara-on-the-Lake. Trains to Niagara Falls pull in at the **VIA train station** on Bridge Street, in the commercial heart of the town, 3km north of the

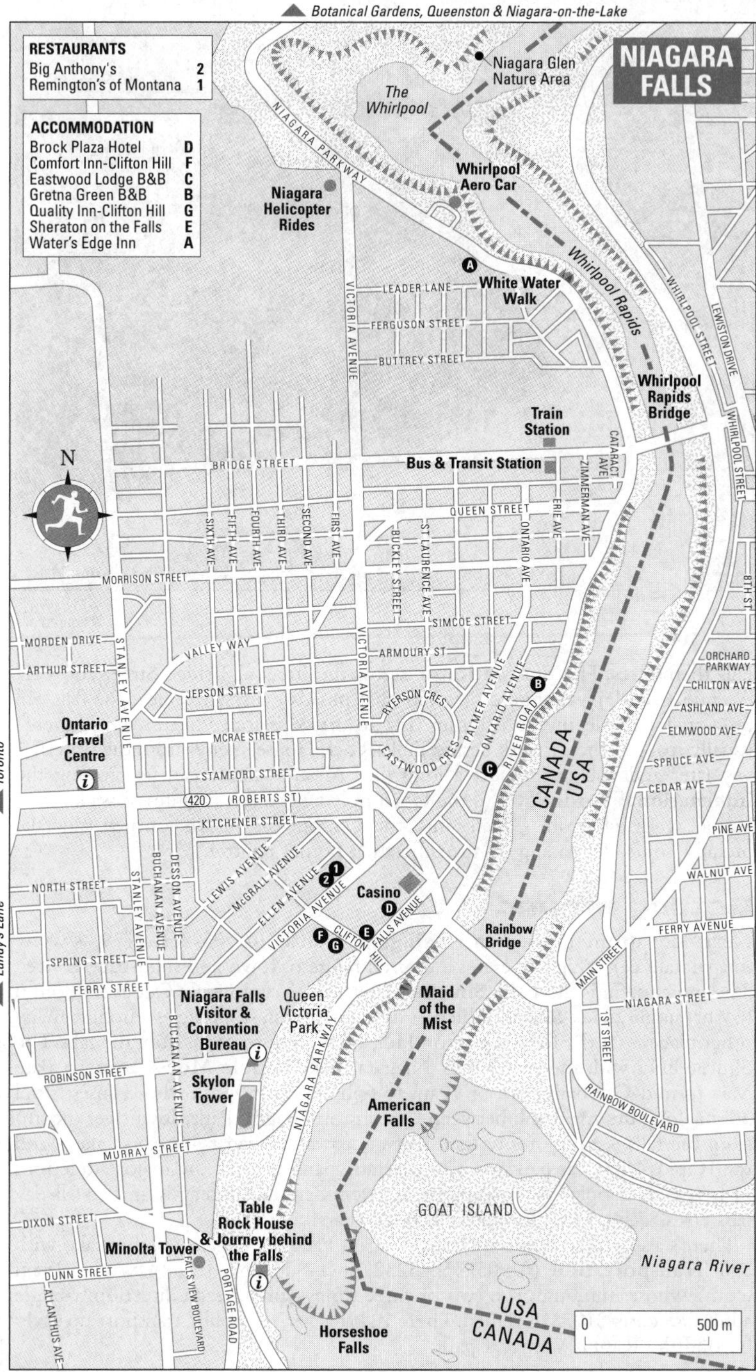
NIAGARA FALLS
RESTAURANTS
Big Anthony's 2
Remington's of Montana 1
ACCOMMODATION
Brock Plaza Hotel D
Comfort Inn-Clifton Hill F
Eastwood Lodge B&B C
Gretna Green B&B B
Quality Inn-Clifton Hill G
Sheraton on the Falls E
Water's Edge Inn A
Botanical Gardens, Queenston & Niagara-on-the-Lake
Niagara Glen Nature Area
The Whirlpool
Whirlpool Aero Car
Niagara Helicopter Rides
White Water Walk
Whirlpool Rapids
Whirlpool Rapids Bridge
Train Station
Bus & Transit Station
Ontario Travel Centre
Toronto
Lundy's Lane
Casino
Rainbow Bridge
Maid of the Mist
Niagara Falls Visitor & Convention Bureau
Queen Victoria Park
Skylon Tower
American Falls
Goat Island
Table Rock House & Journey behind the Falls
Minolta Tower
Horseshoe Falls
Niagara River
CANADA
USA
Fort Erie
0 500 m

△ Niagara Falls

falls themselves. The **bus station** is across the street at Bridge Street and Erie Avenue. **Car drivers** should be aware that **parking** anywhere near the falls can be a major hassle in the summer. Try to arrive before 9.30am when there's usually space in the car park beside Table Rock House, metres from the waterfall; any later and you can expect a long line. Another hassle can be crossing the **international border** over to the US; it only takes a few minutes to walk across Rainbow Bridge from Canada into the US, but the return journey can take literally hours, depending on the officials at border control.

Getting around

Next door to the bus station is **Niagara Transit** (Ⓣ905/356-1179, Ⓦwww.niagarafalls.ca), which operates a limited range of town and suburban services. The most useful is the **Falls Shuttle** (daily: mid-May to early Oct every 30min to 1hr; single ticket $2.25), which runs across town, stopping – amongst many other places – at the foot of Clifton Hill, a few minutes walk from the falls. The Shuttle links with the very handy Niagara Parks' **People Mover System** (late May to mid-Oct daily 9am or 10am to 6pm, 8pm or 9pm), whose buses travel 30km along the riverbank between Queenston Heights Park, downriver (north) from the falls – a little more than halfway towards Niagara-on-the-Lake – and the Rapids'View car park just to the south, pausing at all the major attractions in between. People Movers appear at twenty-minute intervals and an all-day pass costs $7.50, $4.50 for children 6–12 years.

There's also public transport from Niagara Falls to Niagara-on-the-Lake with **5-0 Transportation** (Ⓣ905/358-3232 or 1-800/667-0256, Ⓦwww.5-0taxi.com), whose minibuses run two or three times daily in each direction; a single adult fare costs $10, $18 return. There is, however, no public transport up-river beyond the Rapids'View car park.

Information

For **visitor** information, steer clear of the gaggle of privately run tourist centres that spring up here and there, now and again, and head instead for the main **Niagara Parks information centre** (ⓣ905/371-0254 or 1-877/642-7275, ⓦwww.niagaraparks.com), at the Table Rock complex beside the falls. Here, and elsewhere, but only from mid-May to late October, you can purchase the **Niagara Falls Great Gorge Adventure Pass**, a combined ticket covering four of the main attractions (Journey Behind the Falls, Maid of the Mist, White Water Walk and the Butterfly Conservatory) plus all-day transportation on the People Mover system; the pass can also be purchased at each of the four attractions and currently costs $35 for adults and $22 for children aged 6–12 years.

Other good places to pick up visitor information include the **Ontario Travel Centre**, at the intersection of Hwy 420, the main road to the falls from the QEW freeway, and Stanley Avenue (daily 8.30am–5pm, till 8pm mid-June through Aug; ⓣ905/358-3221), where you'll find a wide range of free literature on the whole of Ontario in general and Niagara Falls in particular. There's also the municipal **Niagara Falls Tourism Office**, just off Stanley Avenue beside the Skylon Tower at 5400 Robinson St (Mon–Fri 8am–6pm, Sat & Sun 10am–6pm; ⓣ905/356-6061, ⓦwww.niagarafallstourism.com), which has a full range of information on the town and the falls and will – if asked – help you find a place to stay.

Accommodation

Niagara Falls is billed as the "Honeymoon Capital of the World", which means that many of its **motels and hotels** have an odd mix of cheap, basic rooms and gaudy suites with heart-shaped bathtubs, waterbeds and the like. Quite what the connection is between water and nuptial bliss is hard to fathom – but there it is. In summer, hotel and motel rooms fill up fast, so either ring ahead or seek help from Niagara Falls Tourism (see above). Out of season it's a buyer's market, which means that haggling can often bring the price way down. For the most part, the least expensive choices are either out along **Lundy's Lane**, an extremely dispiriting motel strip that extends west of the falls for several kilometres, or in the uninteresting town centre near the bus and train stations, 3km from the falls. Neither area is much fun (especially Lundy's Lane) and you're much better off spending a little more to stay either in the **Clifton Hill area**, which has – once you've adjusted to it – a certain kitsch charm, or on leafy **River Road**, running downriver from the foot of Clifton Hill, where there are a couple of good **B&Bs** and a modern **inn**. If you want a room with a decent **view of the falls**, you'll be paying premium rates. The premier hotels on **Falls Avenue**, beside Clifton Hill, and **Fallsview Boulevard**, on top of the ridge directly above the falls, offer the best views but you should always check the room before you shell out: descriptions can be fairly elastic and some rooms claiming to be in sight of the falls require minor gymnastics for a glimpse.

Hotels

Brock Plaza Hotel 5685 Falls Ave ⓣ905/374-4444 or 1-800/263-7135, ⓦwww.niagarafallshotels.com/brock. Just metres from the foot of Clifton Hill, this is one of Niagara's older and most attractive hotels, a tidy tower block with Art Deco flourishes whose upper storeys (and more expensive rooms) have splendid views over the American Falls. Marilyn Monroe stayed here in Room #801 while filming *Niagara* – and you can stay here too for no extra charge. ❻

Comfort Inn – Clifton Hill 4960 Clifton Hill ⓣ905/358-3293 or 1-800/263-2557, ⓦwww.comfortniagara.com. Nothing extraordinary perhaps, but this chain motel has entirely adequate rooms decorated in a brisk, modern style, and is handily located near the falls. ⑥

Quality Inn – Clifton Hill 4946 Clifton Hill ⓣ905/358-3601 or 1-800/263-7137, ⓦwww.qualityniagara.com. Comfortable, pleasantly furnished motel-style rooms in a 300-room inn on its own grounds (or rather car park) on Clifton Hill. ⑥

Sheraton on the Falls 5875 Falls Ave ⓣ905/374-4445 or 1-888/229-9961, ⓦwww.niagarafallshotels.com/sheraton. Walloping skyrise, whose upper floors have wondrous views of the American Falls. Large and well–appointed rooms with supremely comfortable beds. ⑥

Water's Edge Inn 4009 River Rd ⓣ905/356-0131 or 1-800/565-0035, ⓦwww.niagarawatersedgeinn.com. Comfortable if unexceptional motel in attractive location, flanked by parkland near the Whirlpool Aero Car (see opposite). ③

B&Bs

Eastwood Lodge B&B 5359 River Rd ⓣ905/354-8686, ⓦwww.bbcanada.com/585.html. Six commodious, a/c en-suite bedrooms in a rambling old villa with wide balconies and attractive garden. ⑤

Gretna Green B&B 5077 River Rd ⓣ905/357-2081 or 1-888/504-3565, ⓦwww.gretnagreenniagara.com. Pleasant and well-tended B&B in an attractive older house with four guest rooms. ⑥

The Falls

Though you can hear the growl of the falls miles away, nothing quite prepares you for your first glimpse of the deluge, a fearsome white arc shrouded in clouds of dense spray with the river boats struggling down below, mere specks against the surging cauldron. There are two actually cataracts, as tiny Goat Island – which must be one of the wettest places on earth – divides the accelerating water into two channels: on the far side, across the frontier, the river slips over the precipice of the American Falls, 320m wide but still only half the width of the Horseshoe Falls on the Canadian side. The spectacle is, if anything, even more extraordinary in winter, when snow-covered trees edge a jagged armoury of freezing mist and heaped ice blocks.

All this may look like a scene of untrammelled nature, but it isn't. Since the early twentieth century, hydroelectric schemes have greatly reduced the water flow, and all sorts of tinkering has spread what's left of the river more evenly over the crest line. As a result, the process of erosion, which has moved the falls some 11km upstream in 12,000 years, has slowed down from one metre per year to just 30cm. This obviously has advantages for the tourist industry, but the environmental consequences of harnessing the river in such a way are still unclear. More positively, at least the cardsharps and charlatans who overran the riverside in Blondin's day are long gone with the **Niagara Parks Commission** (ⓦwww.niagaraparks.com), which controls the area along the river and beside the falls, ensuring that the immaculately tended tree-lined gardens and parkland remain precisely so.

Beside Horseshoe Falls, **Table Rock House** has a small, free **observation platform** and elevators which travel to the base of the cliff, where tunnels, grandly named the "**Journey Behind the Falls**" (daily 9am to dusk, sometimes later; $11), lead to points directly behind the waterfall. It's a stupendous sight, but for a more panoramic view you might take the pint-sized **Incline Railway** up the hill behind Table Rock House to the **Minolta Tower**, 6732 Fallsview Boulevard (daily: June–Sept 9am–11pm; Oct–May 9am–10pm; $8; ⓦwww.niagaratower.com), which has its own elevated observation decks.

From Table Rock House, a wide path leads north along the edge of the river gorge, with the manicured lawns of **Queen Victoria Park** to the left and views over to the American Falls to the right. At the end of the park is Clifton Hill, the main drag linking the riverside with the town of Niagara Falls. From the jetty below Clifton Hill, **Maid of the Mist boats** edge out into the river and push up towards the falls, an exhilarating and extremely damp trip that no one should miss (daily: April to late June 9.45am–5.45pm; late June to early Sept 9am–7pm;

early Sept to late Oct 9.45am–4.45pm; boats leave every 15min in high season, otherwise every 30min; $14, $9 for children aged 6–12, including waterproofs).

Clifton Hill itself is a tawdry collection of fast-food joints and bizarre attractions, from the innocuous "House of Frankenstein" to the eminently missable "Ripley's Believe It or Not!" where, amongst other wonders, you can spot a cat with two heads. Just off Clifton Hill, near the Rainbow Bridge on Falls Avenue, is one of the town's two 24hr **casinos**, a bristlingly modern structure where – to use the old cliché – college kids can watch their parents fritter away their inheritance; the other is up on Fallsview Boulevard. If you're keen to avoid all this commercialization, then stick to the **riverside** where the Niagara Parks Commission keeps everything in order. There are a string of attractions further downstream, beginning with the White Water Walk, 3km away (see below).

Eating

There are literally dozens of cheap chain **restaurants** and fast-food joints along and around Clifton Hill, but for something rather more distinctive you'll have to venture a little further afield – to **Victoria Avenue** at the top of Clifton Hill, though even here pickings are thin.

Big Anthony's 5677 Victoria Ave ⓣ905/354-9844. Tasty, reasonably priced Italian food at this small, well-known restaurant named after a one-time professional wrestler, pictures of whom decorate the walls. Pizzas from $12. Close to Clifton Hill.

Remington's of Montana 5657 Victoria Ave ⓣ905/356 4410. The restaurant scene in Niagara Falls is hardly pulsating, but this bright, attractively decorated place partly fills the gap, serving tasty and well–prepared steaks and seafood. Steaks from $15 and up.

Downstream from the falls

The Niagara **River Recreation Trail** is a combined bicycle and walking track that travels the entire length of the Niagara River from Lake Erie down to Lake Ontario; for most of its 58km it runs parallel to the main road, the scenic **Niagara Parkway**. Downstream from the falls, trail and parkway cut across the foot of Clifton Hill (see above) before continuing north for a further 3km to reach the **White Water Walk** (daily April to mid-May 9am–4.30pm; mid-May to mid-June 9am–6pm; mid-June to early Sept 9am–7pm; early Sept to late Nov 9am–5pm; $8.50). This comprises an elevator and then a tunnel, which leads to a boardwalk overlooking the Whirlpool Rapids, where the river seethes and fizzes as it makes an abrupt turn to the east.

From here, it's a further 1km along the parkway to the brightly painted **Whirlpool Aero Car** (daily early March to late June 9am–4.45pm; late June to early Sept 9am–7.45pm; early Sept to mid-Nov 9am–4.45pm; $11), a cable-car ride across the gorge that's as near as you'll come to emulating Blondin's tightrope antics. Another 1.5km brings you to **Niagara Helicopter Rides**, 3731 Victoria Ave (ⓣ905/357-5672, ⓦwww.niagarahelicopters.com), which offers a breathtaking twelve-minute excursion over the falls for $110 per person, though costs can be reduced considerably if you are in a group. You don't need to book ahead, as the helicopters whizz in and out with unnerving frequency from 9am until sunset, weather permitting.

Niagara Glen to the Butterfly Conservatory

Pushing on, it's another short hop to the **Niagara Glen Nature Area** (daily dawn to dusk; free), where paths lead down from the clifftop to the bottom of the gorge. It's a hot and sticky trek in the height of the summer, and strenuous at any time of the year, but rewarding for all that – here at least (and at last) you get a sense of what the region was like before the tourist hullabaloo. Nearby, about 800m further downstream along the parkway, lies the Niagara Parks Commission's pride and joy, the immensely popular **Niagara Parks Botanical Gardens** (daily dawn to dusk; free), whose various themed gardens – rose, parterre and so forth – flank the huge, climate-controlled **Butterfly Conservatory** (daily early March to mid-June 9am–6pm; mid-June to early Sept 9am–9pm; early Sept to early Oct 9am–6pm; early Oct to early March 9am–5pm; $11), which houses over 2000 exotic butterflies in a tropical rainforest setting.

Queenston Heights Park and Queenston

About 3km further on, **Queenston Heights Park** marks the original location of the falls, before the force of the water – as it adjusts to the hundred-metre differential between lakes Erie and Ontario – eroded the riverbed to its present point, 11km upstream. Soaring above the park is a grandiloquent monument to **Sir Isaac Brock**, the Guernsey-born general who was killed here in the War of 1812, leading a head-on charge against the invading Americans. To honour the man, his statue has been plonked on top of an enormous Neoclassical plinth with guardian lions at its base.

From beside the park, the Niagara Parkway begins a curving descent down to the little village of **QUEENSTON**, whose importance as a transit centre disappeared in 1829 when the falls were bypassed by the Welland Canal, which runs west of the river between lakes Erie and Ontario. In the village, on Queenston Street, the **Laura Secord Homestead** (guided tours: early May to June Mon–Fri 9.30am–3.30pm, Sat & Sun 11am–5pm; July to early Sept daily 11am–5pm; $4) is a reconstruction of the substantial timber-frame house of Massachusetts-born Laura Ingersoll Secord (1775–1868). It was from here, during the War of 1812, that Secord proved her dedication to the imperial interest by walking 30km through the woods to warn a British platoon of a surprise attack planned by the Americans. As a result, the British and their native allies laid an ambush and captured over 500 Americans at the Battle of Beaver Dams. Secord had good reason to loathe the Americans – during the war they looted her house and her husband was badly wounded at the battle of Queenston Heights – but in the years following her dramatic escapade she kept a low profile, possibly fearing reprisals in what was then a wild, frontier area. Indeed, it was only in 1861, after her deeds came to the attention of the Prince of Wales, the future King Edward VII, that she received any real credit, plus a reward of one hundred golden sovereigns. The house itself is of elegant proportions and equipped with period furnishings and fittings, and the tour provides an intriguing introduction to Secord's life and times.

From Queenston, it's about 12km to Niagara-on-the-Lake.

Niagara-on-the-Lake

Boasting elegant clapboard houses and verdant, mature gardens, all spread along tree-lined streets, **NIAGARA-ON-THE-LAKE**, 26km downstream from the falls, is one of Ontario's most charming little towns, much of it dating from the early nineteenth century. The town was originally known as Newark and became the first capital of Upper Canada in 1792, but four years later it lost this distinction to York (Toronto) because it was deemed too close to the American frontier, and therefore vulnerable to attack. The US army did, in fact, cross the river in 1813, destroying the town, but it was quickly rebuilt and renamed. Even better, it has managed to avoid all but the most

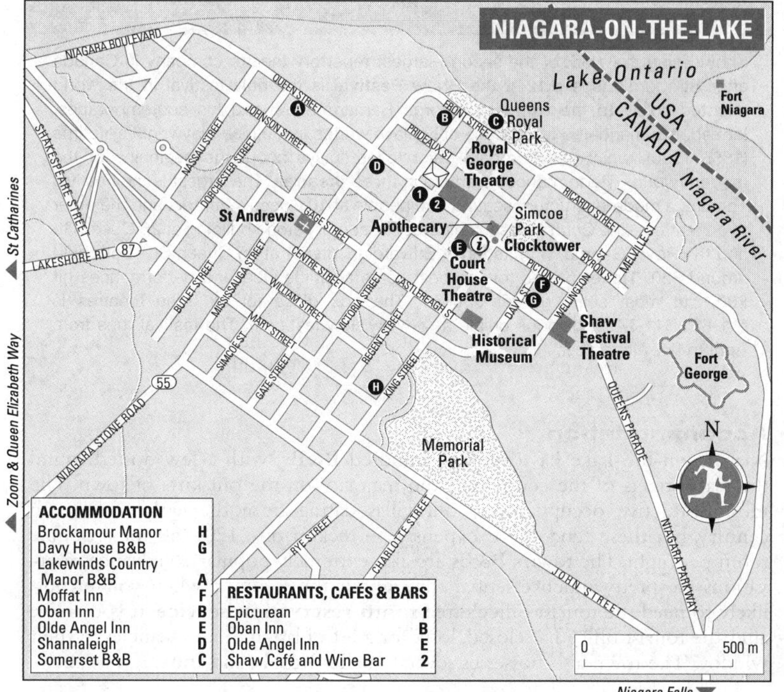

sympathetic of modifications ever since, except just away from the centre down on Melville Street, where a rash of new development and a marina add nothing to the appeal of the place. Niagara-on-the-Lake attracts a few too many day-trippers for its own good, but the crowds are rarely oppressive, except at weekends in July and August. The town is also popular as the location of one of Canada's most acclaimed theatre festivals, the **Shaw Festival**, which celebrates the works of George Bernard Shaw with performances from April to late October, and is surrounded by **wineries**, many of which encourage visitors (see box, p.139).

Arrival and information

A reliable **minibus service** linking Niagara Falls and Niagara-on-the-Lake is provided two or three times daily by **5-0 Transportation** (Ⓣ905/358-3232 or 1-800/667-0256, Ⓦwww.5-0taxi.com), who charge $10 for the one-way fare, $18 return. The Niagara-on-the-Lake **tourist office** is on the main drag at 26 Queen St, in the lower level of the Court House (daily May–Oct 10am–7.30pm, Nov to April 10am–5pm; Ⓣ905/468-1950, Ⓦwww.niagaraonthelake.com). It issues town maps and operates a free **room reservation service**, which can be a great help in the summer when the town's hotels and B&Bs – of which there are dozens – get very busy.

It only takes a few minutes to stroll from one end of town to the other, but to venture further afield – especially to the falls – you might consider renting a **bicycle** from Zoom, out at 2017 Niagara Stone Rd, which doubles as Hwy 55 (Ⓣ905/468-2366 or 1-866/811-6993, Ⓦwww.zoomleisure.com).

The Shaw Festival

Showcasing the work of the second-largest repertory theatre company in Canada after Stratford's (see p.124), the **Shaw Festival** is the only festival in the world devoted solely to the works of George Bernard Shaw and his contemporaries. Indeed, it is mandated to produce only plays written in the Irish playwright's lifetime (1856–1950), which the company refer to as "plays about the beginning of the modern world". Performances are held in **three theatres**. The largest is the Festival Theatre, a modern structure seating 850 people at 10 Queen's Parade, and the other two theatres – the Court House, a nineteenth-century stone building at 26 Queen St, and the Royal George, with its fancy Edwardian interior at 85 Queen St – both hold around 320. **Ticket prices** for the best seats at prime weekend performances hit $80, but most seats go for $50–60. The box office for all three theatres is ⓣ1-800/511-7429, or book online at ⓦwww.shawfest.com. The festival runs from April to late November.

Accommodation

Niagara-on-the-Lake has over one hundred **B&Bs**, with a few dotted round the leafy streets of the centre and the majority on the outskirts of town. The most distinctive occupy lovely old villas dating from the early nineteenth century, but these tend to be expensive – reckon on $120–150 for a double room per night. The town's B&Bs are also extremely popular, so advance reservations are pretty much essential throughout the summer, when you're most likely to need the tourist office's free **room reservation service**. If you arrive after the tourist office has closed, look for a list of last-minute vacancies in their window. The town also possesses several quality **hotels** and **inns**.

Hotels and B&Bs

Brockamour Manor 433 King St at Mary ⓣ905/468-5527, ⓦwww.brockamour.com. This elegant B&B has six en-suite guest rooms ranging from the commodious Sir Brock's Bedchamber to the two smaller rooms in the old servants' quarters. With its high gables and wide veranda, the house itself is a splendid affair dating from 1812, surrounded by an attractive wooded garden. ❼

Davy House B&B 230 Davy St ⓣ905/468-5307 or 1-888/314-9046, ⓦwww.davyhouse.com. Cosy two-storey clapboard house with a verandah for relaxing. Within easy strolling distance of the town centre. Doubles ❻.

Lakewinds Country Manor B&B 328 Queen St at Dorchester ⓣ905/468-1888 or 1-866/338-1888, ⓦwww.lakewinds.ca. Expansive Victorian mansion with six a/c guest rooms and suites, each of which is decorated in a particular style – Florentine or Singaporean, for example. The house possesses a handsome veranda and is surrounded by a well-kept garden. Two nights minimum stay on the weekend. ❼

Moffat Inn 60 Picton St T905/468-4116, ⓦwww.moffatinn.com. This modest hotel is located in a modernized building close to the centre of town. The rooms are pleasant but undistinguished – which means that its prices are lower than most of its rivals and there is sometimes space here when everyone else is full. ❺

Oban Inn 160 Front St ⓣ905/468-2165 or 1-866/359-6226, ⓦwww.obaninn.ca. A delightful and luxurious hotel across from the lake and within easy walking distance of the town centre. The original *Oban* burnt to the ground in 1992, but its replacement was built in full-flush colonial style, with an elegant wooden veranda. The gardens are beautiful and the breakfasts are first-rate. Doubles ❼.

Olde Angel Inn 224 Regent St just off Queen St ⓣ905/468-3411, ⓦwww.angel-inn.com. Dating from the 1820s, this is the oldest inn in town. Offers a handful of simple but perfectly adequate rooms in the main building and a couple of annexe-cottages too. Doubles ❹

Shannaleigh 184 Queen St at Simcoe ⓣ905/468-2630 or 1-866/511-1263, ⓦwww.shanna.ca. This rambling mock-Tudor mansion of 1910 has six spacious, en-suite guest rooms and splendid gardens. ❼

Somerset B&B 111 Front St at Victoria ⓣ905/468-5565, ⓦwww.somersetbb.info. This flashy brick villa of modern design looks almost shocking when compared with the old wooden houses that characterize the rest of the centre, but it is one of only a couple of places actually on the lake. Great views and very comfortable, a/c guest rooms. ⑧

The Town

It's the general flavour of Niagara-on-the-Lake that appeals, rather than any specific sight, but **Queen Street**, the main drag, does hold a pretty **clock tower** and the **Apothecary** (mid-May to Sept daily noon–6pm; free), which is worth a peep for its beautifully carved walnut and butternut cabinets, crystal gasoliers and porcelain jars. Nearby, the town's finest building is the church of **St Andrews**, at Simcoe and Gage sts, a splendid illustration of the Greek Revival style dating to the 1830s. The church has a beautifully proportioned portico and the interior retains the original high pulpit and box pews. From here, it's a brief stroll to the **Niagara Historical Museum**, at 43 Castlereagh St and Davy St (daily May–Oct 10am–5pm, Nov–April 1–5pm; $5), whose accumulated tackle relates the early history of the town and includes mementoes of the Laura Secord family (see p.134). Also of interest is the fenced **burial plot in Simcoe Park**, at King and Byron sts, which holds the earthly remains of 25 Polish soldiers who died here during the great influenza epidemic of 1918–19.

Fort George

There is more military stuff not too far away at the one-time British outpost of **Fort George** (May–Nov daily 10am–5pm; $10.90; ⓦwww.pc.gc.ca), 700m southeast of the town centre via Picton Street. In the early nineteenth century, so many of the fort's soldiers were hightailing it off to the States that the British had to garrison it with the Royal Canadian Rifle Regiment, a troop of primarily married men approaching retirement who were unlikely to forfeit their pensions by deserting. If they did try and were caught, they were branded on the chest with the letter "D" (for "Deserter"), and were either lashed or transported to a penal colony – except in wartime, when they were shot.

Built in the 1790s as one of a line of stockades that was slung across the Great Lakes to protect Canada from the US, the original Fort George was destroyed

Polish soldiers in Niagara-on-the-Lake

In the later stages of World War I, over twenty thousand **Poles** mustered in the US to form a Polish brigade. It was a delicate situation, as the Allies needed the soldiers but the Poles were committed to the creation of an independent Poland at a time when their country was ruled by Russia, an ally of the US. In the event, policy differences with the US government prompted the Poles to move over the border to Niagara-on-the-Lake, where they established a base camp. Paid and equipped by France, the Poles were trained by Canadian officers and then shipped off in batches to fight on the Western front, thereby deferring their attempts to create an independent Poland. At the end of the war, with the Tsar gone and the Bolsheviks in control of Russia, the Polish brigade – or "Blue Army" as it was called from the colour of their uniform – crossed Germany to return to their homeland, where they played a key role in the foundation of an independent Poland. The graves of the 25 soldiers here in Niagara recall these historical complexities, and a wooden shrine has been erected in their honour.

during the War of 1812, but the site was thoroughly excavated and the fort reconstructed in splendid style in the 1930s. Today the palisaded **compound** with its protective bastions holds about a dozen buildings, among them the officers' quarters and two log blockhouses, which doubled as soldiers' barracks. The difference between the quarters and the barracks is striking. The former are comparatively spacious and were once – as recorded on shipping lists – furnished with fancy knick-knacks, while the latter housed the men and some of their wives (six wives out of every hundred were allowed to join the garrison) in the meanest of conditions. A tunnel links the main part of the fort with one of the exterior bastions, or ravelins, which is itself the site of a third, even stronger blockhouse. The only original building is the **powder magazine** of 1796, its interior equipped with wood and copper fittings to reduce the chances of an accidental explosion; as an added precaution, the soldiers working here went barefoot. There are also ninety-minute lantern-light **ghost tours** of the fort – good fun with or without an apparition (May–June Sun 8.30pm; July & Aug Sun, Mon, Wed, Thurs & Fri 8.30pm; Sept Sun 7.30pm; $10; ⓣ905/468-6621). Tours begin at the car park in front of the fort; **tickets** can be purchased either in advance at the fort's gift shop, or from the guide at the beginning of the tour.

Eating and drinking

By sheer weight of numbers, the day-trippers set the gastronomic tone in town, but one or two good **cafés and restaurants** have survived the flood to offer tasty meals and snacks.

Epicurean 84 Queen St. Inexpensive but very competent café, featuring Mediterranean dishes. Vegetarian options offered most days; sandwiches $6–9. Daily 9am–9pm.

Oban Inn 160 Front St ⓣ905/468-2165. This hotel restaurant is nicely decorated and comparatively formal and the food – steak, salmon and so forth – is reliably good. Mains from $20.

 **Olde Angel Inn** 224 Regent St. With its low-beamed ceilings and flagstone floors, this is the town's most atmospheric pub, serving a first-rate range of draught imported and domestic beers. Also offers filling and very affordable bar food – Guinness steak-and-kidney pies from $8 – and has a smart à la carte restaurant at the back. Just off Queen St.

Shaw Café and Wine Bar 92 Queen St at Victoria. This café-restaurant caters to theatre-goers rather than day-trippers. The decor is a tad overdone, but the pastas and salads (from $9) are tasty and well prepared. Closes 8pm.

Upstream from Niagara Falls to Fort Erie

Heading upstream from the falls, the **Old Scow** soon comes into view – it's the rusting barge stuck against the rocks in the middle of the river. In 1918 the barge was being towed across the Niagara River when the lines snapped and the barge – along with the two-man crew – hurtled towards the falls. There must have been an awful lot of praying going on, because – just 750m from the precipice – the barge caught against the rocks, and it's stayed there ever since.

Pressing on past the Old Scow, both the **Niagara Parkway** road and the **Niagara River Recreation Trail** stay close to the river giving pleasant views over to the US. Nonetheless, this portion of the river is much less appealing than the stretch to the north of the falls – especially so beyond humdrum **CHIPPAWA**, which is where America's Grand Island divides the river into two drowsy channels. Further upriver, just 32km from the falls, the Niagara Parkway peters out at **FORT ERIE**, a small industrial town that also marks the end of the Queen Elizabeth Way linking Toronto with the American city of Buffalo. The one noteworthy site here is **Fort Erie** (daily:

Ontario wines

Until the 1980s **Canadian wine** was something of a joke. The industry's most popular product was a sticky, fizzy concoction called "Baby Duck", and other varieties were commonly called "block-and-tackle" wines, after a widely reported witticism of a member of the Ontario legislature: "If you drink a bottle and walk a block, you can tackle anyone." This state of affairs was, however, transformed by the **Vintners Quality Alliance** (VQA; Ⓦwww.vqaontario.com), who have, since 1989, come to exercise tight control over wine production in Ontario, which produces around eighty percent of Canadian wine. The VQA's appellation system distinguishes between – and supervises the quality control of – two broad types of wine. Those wines carrying the **Provincial Designation** on their labels must be made from one hundred percent Ontario-grown grapes from an approved list of European grape varieties and selected hybrids; those bearing the **Geographic Designation** (ie, Niagara Peninsula, Pelee Island or Lake Erie North Shore), by comparison, can only use *Vitis vinifera*, the classic European grape varieties, such as Riesling, Chardonnay and Cabernet Sauvignon. As you might expect from a developing wine area, the results are rather inconsistent, but the **Rieslings** have a refreshingly crisp, almost tart flavour with a mellow, warming aftertaste – and are perhaps the best of the present range, white or red.

More than twenty **wineries** are clustered in the vicinity of **Niagara-on-the-Lake**, and most are very willing to show visitors around. Local tourist offices carry a full list with opening times, but one of the most interesting is **Inniskillin**, Line 3 (Service Road 66), just off the Niagara Parkway, about 5km south of Niagara-on-the-Lake (daily: May–Oct 10am–6pm, Nov–April 10am–5pm; Ⓣ905/468-2187, Ⓦwww.inniskillin.com). Here you can follow a self-guided tour or take a free guided tour, sip away at the tasting bar and buy at the wine boutique. Inniskillin has produced a clutch of award-winning vintages and played a leading role in the improvement of the industry. They are also one of the few Canadian wineries to produce **ice wine**, an outstanding sweet dessert wine made from grapes that are left on the vine till December or January, when they are hand-picked at night while frozen; there is also a slightly tarter sparkling ice wine. The picking and the crushing of the frozen grapes is a time-consuming business and this is reflected in the price – from about $60 per 375ml bottle of either sparkling or regular.

early May to June 10am–5pm; July & Aug 10am–6pm; Sept to early Oct 10am–4pm; $8.50; Ⓦwww.niagaraparks.com), which overlooks Lake Erie from the mouth of the Niagara River just 2km south of town. The Americans razed the original fort in 1814, but it was painstakingly rebuilt in the 1930s as a Depression make-work scheme. The layout is similar to that of Fort George (see p.137) with a dry ditch, earth-and-stone ramparts and protruding bastions encircling a central compound, though here the outer gate is much more imposing, comprising a pair of huge double doors strengthened by iron studs. The central compound holds the usual spread of army buildings, including officers' quarters, barracks and a powder magazine, plus a modest museum that explores the fort's history.

London

The citizens of **LONDON**, 125km west of Hamilton, are justifiably proud of their clean streets, efficient transport system and neat suburbs, but to the outsider the main attractions are the leafiness of the centre and two of the city's **music festivals** – the three-day Bluesfest (Ⓣ519/488-1240, Ⓦwww.thebluesfest.com) and the three-day Home County Folk Music Festival (Ⓣ519/432-4310, Ⓦwww.homecounty.ca), both held in mid- to late July. London owes its existence to a one-time governor of Upper Canada, **John Graves Simcoe**, who arrived in 1792 determined to develop the wilderness west of Lake Ontario. Because of its river connections to the west and south, he chose the site of London as his new colonial capital and promptly renamed its river the Thames. Unluckily, Simcoe's headlong approach to his new job irritated his superior, Governor Dorchester, who vetoed his choice with the wry comment that access to London would have to be by hot-air balloon. When York (present-day Toronto) was chosen as the capital instead, Simcoe's chosen site lay empty until 1826, yet by the 1880s London was firmly established as the economic and administrative centre of a prosperous agricultural area. With a population of some 340,000, it remains so today.

The Town

London's **downtown core** is laid out as a grid to either side of its main east–west thoroughfares, Dundas Street and, one block to the north, Queens Avenue. At the west end of Dundas, close to the river, is the chunkily modernist **Museum London**, 421 Ridout St North (Tues–Sun noon–5pm; donation; Ⓦwww.londonmuseum.on.ca), designed by Raymond Moriyama of Toronto. A once fashionable architect, Moriyama favoured dramatic concrete buildings

characterized by a preference for contorted curves and circles rather than straight lines, but here the end result isn't all that successful. Inside, the gallery's permanent collection features a somewhat indeterminate mix of lesser eighteenth- and nineteenth-century Canadian painters and there's a modest local history section too, but the temporary modern art exhibitions – some of which come here straight from Toronto – are usually excellent.

London's oldest residence, the **Eldon House** (Jan–April Sat & Sun noon–5pm; May Wed–Sun noon–5pm; June–Sept Tues–Sun noon–5pm; Oct–Dec Wed–Sun noon–5pm; donation suggested) is a couple of minutes' walk north from the museum at 481 Ridout St N. Built in the 1830s by John Harris, a retired Royal Navy captain, the house is a graceful clapboard dwelling, whose interior has been returned to its mid-nineteenth-century appearance. The British influence is also easy to pick out in the nearby **St Paul's Anglican Cathedral**. A simple red-brick structure built in the English Gothic Revival style in 1846, it's in marked contrast to the rival **St Peter's Catholic Cathedral**, just to the north at Dufferin Avenue and Richmond Street, a flamboyant, high-towered, pink-stone edifice typical of the French Gothic style that was popular amongst Ontario's Catholics in the late nineteenth century.

Though not exactly required viewing, the replica **Ska-Nah-Doht Iroquoian village** (late May to early Sept daily 9am–4.30pm; early Sept to late May Mon–Fri 9am–4.30pm; donation; ⓣ519/264-2420), situated 32km southwest of London on Hwy 2, makes for a mildly enjoyable jaunt. Built in 1972, the complex contains a resource centre, where you can gather background information before walking out to the village, which is enclosed by a timber palisade. Inside the palisade are storage areas, drying and stretching racks, a sweat house and three long-houses; outside are a deer run, burial area, a cultivated field and three log cabins dating from the 1850s. The arrangement of the village accurately reflects the archaeological evidence unearthed at several prehistoric settlements, one of which was close by. The village also has a lovely rural setting and – if the school groups that come here begin to wear – you can stroll out into the woods. To get here, head south from downtown London onto Hwy 401, then go west onto Hwy 402. Come off Hwy 402 (at Exit 86) and follow Hwy 2 south for about 6km.

Practicalities

London's **train station** is centrally situated at York and Richmond, a couple of minutes' walk from the **bus depot** at York and Talbot. The most central **tourist office** is at 267 Dundas St (Mon–Fri 8.30am–4.30pm & Sat 10am–5pm; ⓣ519/661-5000, ⓦwww.londontourism.ca). As regards accommodation, the best **hotel** in town is the smart and polished *Delta London Armouries Hotel*, 325 Dundas St and Waterloo (ⓣ519/679-6111 or 1-877/814-7706, ⓦwww.deltahotels.com; ❻), part of which occupies an old Edwardian drill hall with a robust, crenellated facade. A less expensive but equally convenient option is the *Comfort Hotel Downtown*, a standard-issue chain hotel at 374 Dundas St and Colborne (ⓣ519/661-0233 or 1-800/424-6423, ⓦwww.choicehotels.ca; ❺). Incidentally, the cheapest hotels in town are in the vicinity of the bus station, but these are little more than flop-houses and are best avoided. London also has a handful of **B&Bs**, several of which are in Victorian or Edwardian villas. The tourist office has the complete list, but one recommendation is the extremely fetching *Idlewyld Inn*, to the south of the centre at 36 Grand Ave (ⓣ519/433-2891 or 1-877/435-3466, ⓦwww.idlewyldinn.com; ❻). The inn occupies a rambling Victorian mansion that retains many of its original fittings and its graceful public rooms come complete with fine open fireplaces. Each of the 23 en-suite guest rooms beyond is attractively furnished in a modern rendition of period style.

When **eating out**, choose among the string of café-restaurants along and around Richmond Street; the majority offer versions of Mediterranean cuisine at affordable prices. The best **deli** sandwiches, coffees and finger-licking cakes are sold at *Café One*, 551 Richmond St. Tempting **restaurants** include *Garlic's*, 481 Richmond (daily 11.30am–11pm; ⓣ519/432-4092), where the emphasis is firmly Italian, and the riverside *Michael's on the Thames*, 1 York St (Mon–Fri 11.30am–11pm, Sat 5-midnight & Sun 5–9pm; ⓣ519/672-0111), which features a wide range of dishes though once again the emphasis is on Italian cuisine with main courses averaging $25-30. For something rather different, try *Budapest*, 348 Dundas St at Waterloo St (ⓣ519/439-3431), a family-run establishment offering first-rate Hungarian food – the goulash is a treat – with mains from $17. London has a **music** scene too: try the *Old Chicago Speakeasy & Grill* (Tues–Sat 7pm–2am; ⓣ519/434-6600), 153 Carling St, a short side street off Richmond just north of Dundas, where quality R&B, soul and blues bands sometimes perform.

Windsor and around

"I'm going to Detroit, Michigan, to work the Cadillac line," growls the old blues number, but if the singer had crossed the river from Detroit he'd have been equally at home amongst the car plants of **WINDSOR**, 190km southwest of London. The factories are American subsidiaries built as part of a complex trading agreement which, monitored by the forceful Canadian United Automobile Workers Union, has created thousands of well-paid jobs. Living opposite Detroit makes the "Windsors" feel good in another way too: they read about Detroit's problems – the crime and the crack – and the dire difficulties involved in rejuvenating that city, and shake their heads in disbelief and self-congratulation. A robustly working-class place, Windsor has a clutch of good restaurants, a lively café-bar nightlife, and is also a good base for visiting both the remains of the British **Fort Malden** in Amherstburg, 25km to the south, and **Point Pelee National Park**, some 50km away to the southeast. The main local shindig is the Windsor SummerFest with all sorts of folksy events spread over a thirteen-day period at the back end of June.

Windsor itself has few specific sights, but **Dieppe Gardens**, stretching along the waterfront from the foot of Ouellette Avenue – and part of a longer riverside park – is a good place to view the audacious Detroit skyline. Close by, just to the east of Ouellette at the bottom of McDougall Street, is the fantastically popular and ultra-glitzy **Casino Windsor**, which is open 24hrs a day, 365 days of the year. The casino's boosters claim it has played a leading role in the rejuvenation of downtown Windsor, whose formative years are recalled at the **Windsor Community Museum**, one block south of the riverfront at 254 Pitt St West (Tues–Sat 10am–5pm, plus May–Sept Sun 2–5pm; free). The museum occupies a pretty brick house built in 1812 by François Baby (pronounced *Baw-bee*), scion of a powerful French-Canadian clan who proved consistently loyal to the British interest after the fall of New France, an example of the money going with the power. Back on the riverfront, the **Art Gallery of Windsor**, 401 Riverside Drive West (Wed 11am-8pm, Thurs & Fri 11am–9pm, Sat & Sun 11am–5pm; $3; ⓦwww.artgalleryofwindsor.com), has a well-deserved reputation for the excellence of its temporary exhibitions. The

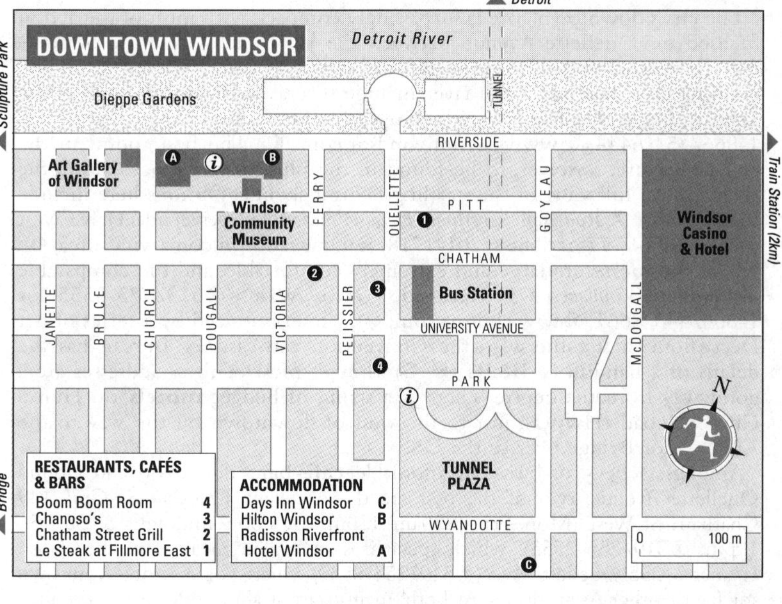

permanent collection is first-rate too, its forte being late nineteenth- and early twentieth-century Canadian paintings. In particular, look out for some good examples from the Group of Seven (see p.94) – including Lawren Harris's skeletal *Trees and Snow* and the dramatic perspectives of Arthur Lismer's *Incoming Tide, Cape Breton Island.* Also on display is a goodly sample of Inuit art, with a particular highlight being *Hunters and Polar Bear*, a dark and elemental soapstone carving by Juanasialuk. Finally, there's more art at the open-air, open-access **Odette Sculpture Park**, a whimsical assortment of thirty-one modern sculptures dotted along the riverfront lawn between Curry Avenue and the Ambassador Bridge, about 1.2km west of Ouellette Avenue.

Practicalities

With daily Greyhound buses arriving from Chicago, London and Toronto, Windsor's **bus** station is right in the centre of town on University Avenue, just east of the main street, Ouellette Avenue, which runs south from the river. From the bus station, **Transit Windsor** (ⓣ519/944-4111) runs a shuttle service (1–3 hourly) over to downtown Detroit via a tunnel whose entrance is bang in the middle of town at Goyeau and Park; vehicles bypassing Windsor en route to Detroit use the Ambassador Bridge, on Hwy 3. Windsor **train station** is some 2km east of the city centre, near the waterfront at 298 Walker Rd and Riverside Drive E; to get into the centre from here, take a taxi ($8). The Windsor **Convention and Visitors' Bureau**, Suite 103, City Centre Mall, 333 Riverside Drive West (Mon–Fri 8.30am–4.30pm; ⓣ519/255-6530 or 1-800/265-3633, ⓦwww.visitwindsor.com), is located just west of Ouellette Avenue and issues free maps and glossy local brochures. It also runs a tourist information kiosk (open daily) in the casino. In addition, there's an **Ontario Travel Information Centre** just off Ouellette and beside the Detroit tunnel at 110 Park St East (mid-May to Aug daily 8am–8pm; Sept to mid-May daily 8.30am–5pm; ⓣ519/973-1338).

The city's downtown core is surprisingly compact, with most of the action focused on Ouellette Avenue between the river and Wyandotte Street – merely five-minutes' stroll from top to bottom. If you're staying the night, convenient options near the river include several chain **hotels** such as the *Days Inn Windsor*, 675 Goyeau St (T519/258-8411 or 1-866/454-6444, Wwww.daysinnwindsor.com; 4). The best rooms in the city centre are, however, to be found in the plush tower blocks along the riverfront in full view of the startling Detroit skyline. Options here include the splendid *Radisson Riverfront Hotel Windsor*, 333 Riverside Drive West (T519/977-9777 or 1-888/201-1718, Wwww.radisson.com/windsorca; 7), where the rooms are large and extremely comfortable; and the comparable *Hilton Windsor*, 277 Riverside Drive West (T519/973-5555 or 1-800/445-8667, Wwww.hilton.com; 7), which is graced by a series of Art Deco flourishes. Otherwise, the Convention and Visitors' Bureau has the details of a handful of **B&Bs** (2–3), though most of their addresses are a good way from the centre. There is a string of budget **motels** on Huron Church Road (Hwy 3), just to the west of downtown on the way to the Ambassador Bridge over to the US.

Amongst a bevy of busy but affordable **café-bars** dotted on and around Ouellette Avenue, two of the best are the excellent *Chatham St Grill*, 149 Chatham St West (Mon–Fri 11.30am–11pm, Sat noon–midnight & Sun 5–10pm; T519/256-2555), which specializes in grilled meats, and the stylish *Chanoso's*, 255 Ouellette Ave. (T519/254-8530), where you assemble your own stir fry or other Asian dishes. At both, mains start at about $20 in the evening, $10 at lunch.

Windsor has a bustling **club and live music** scene. In the city centre, *Le Steak at Fillmore East*, 53 Pitt St East (T519/971-0457, Wwww.fillmoreeast.ca), is a self-styled 'Jazz Supper Club' with live music at the end of the week, whereas the *Boom Boom Room*, 315 Ouellette Ave (T519/971-0000, Wwww.boomboomroom.ca) is a raucously groovy spot with lots of house music and star DJs. Nonetheless, this is still small musical beer compared with what's happening over the river: Detroit remains one of the USA's premier musical cities, so watch out for flyers and posters in Windsor advertising what's on and where or drop by the Visitors' Bureau.

Amherstburg and Fort Malden

Highway 20 runs south from Windsor, slicing through the industrial region that edges the Detroit River, whose murky waters form the border with the US. The one-time enmity of the Americans prompted the British to build a fort here, close to the mouth of the Detroit River at **AMHERSTBURG** in 1796, but it proved difficult to supply and they were forced to abandon the stockade during the War of 1812. Reoccupied after the war, the British made half-hearted attempts to improve the fort's defenses, but it probably would have been abandoned had it not been for the Upper Canada Rebellion of 1837. In a panic, the colonial powers rebuilt what was now called '**Fort Malden**' and garrisoned it with four hundred soldiers, stationed here to counter the efforts of the insurgents and their American sympathizers. The last troops left in 1859 and the fort was handed over to the provincial government, who promptly turned it into a lunatic asylum.

Now renovated and restored, the early nineteenth-century ditches and bastions of **Fort Malden National Historic Site**, beside the Detroit River in Amherstberg (May–Oct daily 10am–5pm; $3.95; Wwww.pc.gc.ca), comprise a sequence of grassy defensive lines that surround the excavated foundations of several buildings and a single-storey brick **barracks** of 1819. The interior of the barracks, complete with British army uniforms, is deceptively neat and trim for, as the guides explain, conditions were appallingly squalid. Across from the barracks, the asylum's old laundry and bakery has been turned into an **interpretive centre** with intriguing accounts of the various episodes of the fort's history, including the War of 1812 and the Rebellion of 1837. Original artefacts are few and far between, but you'll spy the powder horn of the **Shawnee** chief and staunch British ally, **Tecumseh**, one of the most formidable and renowned of the region's leaders. Born in what is now Ohio in 1769, Tecumseh spent the better part of his life struggling to keep American settlers from spreading west into Shawnee territory. To this end he allied himself to the British, who were, he felt, less of a territorial threat than the colonials. By the sheer force of his personality, he managed to hold together an aboriginal army of some size. He was killed in the War of 1812 at Moraviantown and his army promptly collapsed.

Leamington and Pelee Island

Around 400km from one end to the other, the largely flat and often tedious northern shoreline of **Lake Erie** is broken up by a string of provincial parks and a handful of modest port-cum-resorts, such as Port Stanley, whose popularity declined when the more beautiful landscapes around Georgian Bay became accessible. **LEAMINGTON**, with a population of 27,000 – and 50km southeast of Windsor – is the largest agricultural centre in this fertile region and also the nearest town to the north shore's most distinctive attraction, the elongated peninsula of **Point Pelee National Park** (see p.146). Leamington's centre is itself uninspiring, though the **tourist office** (late May to Sept daily 10am–5pm; ⓣ519/326-2721, ⓦwww.leamington.ca) always raises a smile: it's sited in a large plastic tomato, a reminder that Leamington is billed as the "tomato capital of Canada" – there's a massive Heinz factory here. Much more enticing is the revamped **dock area** just south of the centre at the foot of Erie Street. It's here you'll find the town's best **hotel** – the spick-and-span and very modern *Seacliffe Inn*, at 388 Erie St South (ⓣ519/324-9266, ⓦwww.seacliffeinn.com; ❻). Less expensive accommodation is available back towards the town centre on Erie Street in several chain **motels**: the *Comfort Inn*, at no. 279 (ⓣ519/326-9071, ⓦwww.choicehotels.ca; ❹) is as good as any. Greyhound **buses** from London and Windsor pass through Leamington once daily in each direction, pulling in at Macleods Family Restaurant, 57 Erie St S; there are, however, no connections on to Point Pelee Park, which begins 8km to the south of town.

From Leamington docks, **ferries** (early April to mid-Oct 2–3 daily; 1hr 30min; one-way: $7.50 per person, bicycles $3.75, cars $16.50; ⓣ519/724-2115 or 1-800/661-2220, ⓦwww.ontarioferries.com) sally out across Lake Erie to **Pelee Island**, whose quiet country roads are flanked by orchards and vineyards. Some 15km long and 6km wide, the island possesses a pair of nature reserves – Lighthouse Point and Fish Point – at its northern and southern extremities and one significant settlement, **PELEE ISLAND village**, where the boat docks, but it's the rural atmosphere that is of most appeal. The best way to explore the island is by **bike** and these can be rented from Comfortech (ⓣ519/724-2828; advance booking required), metres from the dock. Ferry schedules usually make it easy to visit the island on a day-trip, but there are several **places to stay**: the pick is the *Blueberry Hill B&B*, in a neat and trim,

There is a **ferry service** from the mainland to Pelee Island from the end of March to mid-December and there are two departure ports – Leamington and Kingsville, about 10km to the west of Leamington. The same company runs both ferries and the tariffs are the same too, but – depending on the date and the time – it's worth checking with the ferry company to see which sailing suits you most.

modern timber dwelling on the north side of the island, near Scudder at 86 North Shore Rd (ⓣ519/724-1109, ⓦwww.pelee.org; ❸). Island maps and information are available at Leamington tourist office.

Point Pelee National Park

Occupying the southernmost tip of Canada's mainland – and rather surprisingly set on the same latitude as Rome and Barcelona – **Point Pelee National Park** (daily April–Oct 6am–9.30pm; Nov–March 7am–6.30pm; April–Oct; $6.90, otherwise free; no camping) fills the southern half of a twenty-kilometre sandspit. The park boasts a variety of habitats rarely matched in Canada, including marshlands and open fields, but most remarkably it is one of the few places where the ancient **deciduous forest** of eastern North America has survived. One-third of the park is covered by this jungle-like forest, packed with a staggering variety of trees, from hackberry, red cedar, black walnut and blue ash to vine-covered sassafras. The park's mild climate and its mix of vegetation attract thousands of **birds** on their spring and autumn migrations. In September, the sandspit also funnels thousands of southward-moving **monarch butterflies** across the park, their orange and black wings a splash of colour against the greens and browns of the undergrowth.

From the **park entrance** it's a three-kilometre drive down behind the shore to the start of the Marsh Boardwalk nature trail, where there's bike and canoe rental during the summer. It's a further 4km to the **visitor centre** (April–June daily 10am–5pm; July–Aug daily 10am–6pm; Sept–Oct daily 10am–5pm; Nov–March Sat & Sun only 10am-5pm; ⓣ519/322-2365), at the beginning of the Tilden's Wood and Woodland trails. From April to early October propane-powered "trains" shuttle the last 3km from the visitor centre to the start of the short footpath leading to the tip of the peninsula. However, the tip itself is merely a slender wedge of coarse brown sand that can't help but seem a tad anticlimactic – unless, that is, a storm has piled the beach with driftwood.

Highway 21: Dresden to Sarnia

The large chunk of farmland rolling 100km west from London to the inconsequential border town of **Sarnia** is one of the less absorbing parts of the province. It was also one of the last parts of southern Ontario to be cleared and settled, its heavy clay soil being difficult to plough and becoming almost impassable in rain. The district is bisected by **Highway 21**, which serves as a handy short cut between both Windsor and Point Pelee (see above) and the good-looking towns of the Lake Huron shoreline, primarily Bayfield and Goderich (see p.149). Fortunately, Hwy 21 also passes by the area's three points of interest. These are – from south to north – **Uncle Tom's Cabin Historic Site**, where a group of escaped US slaves found refuge in the 1830s; the **Oil Museum of Canada**, recalling the local oil boom of the middle of the nineteenth century; and small-town **Petrolia**, also a result of the oil rush. You'll need a car for Hwy 21 as there are **no buses**.

Uncle Tom's Cabin

Highway 401 trucks east from Windsor to intersect with Hwy 21 after about 100km. Turn north onto Hwy 21 and it's a further 30km to the agricultural town of **DRESDEN**, which is itself just 2km from **Uncle Tom's Cabin Historic Site** (late May to late Oct Tues–Sat 10am–4pm, Sun noon–4pm; also July & Aug Mon 10am–4pm; $6.25; ⓦwww.uncletomscabin.org), comprising a handful of old wooden buildings, most notably a plain and simple church. Here also is the clapboard house that was once the home of the **Reverend Josiah Henson**, a slave who fled from Maryland to Canada in 1830 by means of the Underground Railroad (or UGRR; see box below). Henson and a group of abolitionist sympathizers subsequently bought 200 acres of farmland round Dresden and founded a vocational school for runaway slaves known as the "British American Institute". Unable to write, Henson dictated his life experiences and in 1849 these narrations were published as *The Life of Josiah Henson – Formerly a Slave*. It's a powerful tract, unassuming and almost matter of fact in the way it describes the routine savagery of slavery – and it was immediately popular. One of its readers was **Harriet Beecher Stowe**, who met Henson and went on to write the most influential abolitionist text of the day, *Uncle Tom's Cabin* (1852), basing her main character on Henson's accounts. Most of the Dresden refugees returned to the US after the Civil War, but Henson stayed on, accumulating imperial honours that must have surprised him greatly. He was even presented to Queen Victoria and, in commemoration of this royal connection, a crown surmounts his tombstone, which stands outside the complex; he died in 1883. Henson's book is hard to get hold of, but copies are sold here at the **interpretive centre**, where there's also a small museum on slavery and the UGRR plus an intriguing video giving more details on Henson's life and times.

Oil Springs

Some 25km north of Dresden, Hwy 21 scuttles past the Oil Museum of Canada (see p.148) just before it reaches tiny **OIL SPRINGS**, which once formed the nucleus of a rough-and-ready frontier district whose flat fields were packed with hundreds of eager oil-seekers and their hangers-on. The first prospectors were attracted to the area by patches of black and sticky oil that had seeped to the surface through narrow fissures in the rock. These **gum beds** had long been used by local native peoples for medicinal and ritual purposes, but it was not until Charles and Henry Tripp of Woodstock incorporated their oil company in

The Underground Railroad

The **Underground Railroad** – the UGRR – started in the 1820s as a loose and secretive association of abolitionists dedicated to smuggling slaves from the southern states of America to Canada. By the 1840s, the UGRR had become a well-organized network of routes and safe houses, but its real importance lay not so much in the number of slaves rescued – the total was small – but rather in the psychological effect it had on those involved in the smuggling. The movement of a runaway usually involved very few people, but many more, particularly neighbours and friends, knew what was happening and therefore were complicit in the breaking of the law. To the extent that white Americans could be persuaded to accept even the most minor role in the Railroad, the inclination to compromise with institutional slavery was undermined, though the psychology of racism remained intact: like Beecher Stowe's Uncle Tom, the freed negroes were supposed to be humble and grateful, simulating childlike responses to please their white parent-protectors.

1854 that serious exploitation began. Four years later, James Miller Williams dug North America's **first commercial oil well**, and in 1862 a certain Hugh Shaw drilled deeper than anyone else and, at 49m, struck the first **gusher**. The shock of seeing the oil fly up into the trees prompted Shaw, a religious man, to use the words of his Bible – "And the rock poured me out rivers of oil" (Job 29:6). Shaw became rich, but his luck ran out just one year later when the gas and sulphur fumes of his own well suffocated him. At the height of the boom, the oilfields produced about 30,000 barrels of crude a day, most of it destined for Sarnia, transported by stagecoach and wagon along a specially built plank road. The **Oil Museum of Canada** (May–Oct daily 10am–5pm; Nov–April Mon–Fri 10am–5pm; $5; Ⓦwww.tourismsarnialambton.com) has been built next to the site of James Williams' original well 1km south of Oil Springs. Highlights of the open-air display area include a nineteenth-century blacksmith's shop, with some fascinating old sepia photos taken during the oil boom, and an area of gum bed. The inside of the museum has a motley collection of oil-industry artefacts and background geological information. Oil is still produced in the fields around the museum, drawn to the surface and pushed on into an underground system of pipes by some seven hundred low-lying pump jacks.

Petrolia

Located some 10km to the north of Oil Springs, just off Hwy 21, the grand stone-and-brick buildings of tiny **PETROLIA** speak volumes about the sudden rush of wealth that followed the discovery of oil in Oil Springs. This was Canada's first oil town and as the proceeds rolled in so the Victorian mansions and expansive public buildings followed. Several have survived, dotted along and around the main drag, Petrolia Line. Three prime examples are the **Municipal Offices**, at Petrolia Line and Greenfield St; **Nemo Hall**, an impressive brick building decorated by splendid wrought-iron trimmings at 419 King St and Victoria St; and **St Andrew's Presbyterian church**, close by at Petrolia Line and Queen St, which is awash with neo-Gothic gables and towers. To emphasize the town's origins, its streetlamps are cast in the shape of oil derricks, but once you've had a scout round the architecture there's no strong reason to hang round.

Sarnia

Pushing on along Hwy 21 from Petrolia, it's about 10km to **Highway 402**, (the motorway linking London to the east and Sarnia away to the west), and a further 80km to Lake Huron's Bayfield. Given these rival destinations, there's precious little reason to detour to **SARNIA**, but the town does offer several places to stay and is one way to get into Michigan without having to pass through Detroit. Established as a lumber port in 1863, Sarnia is a negligible sort of place with a workaday gridiron of streets making up its modest centre. The **VIA Rail train station** (Ⓣ1-888/842-7245, Ⓦwww.viarail.ca), with daily services to and from London and Toronto, is on the southern edge of town at the end of Russell Street, a $10 taxi ride from the centre. The (moveable) Greyhound **bus stop** (Ⓣ1-800/661-8747, Ⓦwww.greyhound.ca) is currently located beside Mac's Convenience Store, some 5km east of Sarnia's waterfront at 580 Murphy Rd – but long-distance services are few and far between. There's a useful **Ontario Travel Information Centre** on the northern side of Sarnia, beside the approach road to the Bluewater Bridge over to the US (mid-May to mid-June Sun–Thurs 8.30am–6pm, Fri & Sat 8am–8pm; mid-June to early Sept daily 8am–8pm; early Sept to mid-May Mon–Sat 8.30am–5pm; Ⓣ519/344-7403). This has details of local **accommodation**, which includes a reasonable selection of chain **motels** strung out along London Road, one of the main drags running south of (and parallel to) Hwy 402.

Bayfield and Goderich

A popular summer resort area, the southern section of the **Lake Huron shoreline** is trimmed by sandy beaches and a steep bluff, which is interrupted by the occasional river valley. The water is much less polluted than Lake Ontario, the sunsets are fabulously beautiful, and in **Bayfield** and **Goderich** the lakeshore possesses two of the most appealing places in the whole of the province. You will, however, need your own transport to get to either: there are no **buses** at all.

Bayfield

Beguiling **BAYFIELD** is a wealthy and good-looking village whose handsome timber villas nestle amongst well-tended gardens beneath a canopy of ancient trees – all about 90km north of London. The villagers have kept modern development at arm's length – there's barely a neon sign in sight, never mind a concrete apartment block – and almost every old house has been beautifully maintained: look out for the scrolled woodwork, the fanlights and the graceful verandas. Historical plaques give the lowdown on the older buildings that line Bayfield's short **Main Street**, and pint-sized **Pioneer Park** on the bluff overlooking the lake at the west end of Main Street is a fine spot to take in the sunset. If you have the time, venture down to the **harbour** on the north side of the village and from there ramble up along the banks of the Bayfield River where, in season, you can pick wild mushrooms and fiddleheads. The Mara Street footpath down to the harbour begins just behind Pioneer Park – it's signposted. In winter there's ice fishing and skating to enjoy here too.

The **tourist office** (May–Sept daily 10am–6pm; ⓣ519/565-2499 or 1-866/565-2499, ⓦwww.bayfieldchamberofcommerce.on.ca), in the booth by Hwy 21 just north of the Bayfield River bridge, has a full list of local **accommodation** and staff will help you find a room, though their assistance is only really necessary in July and August when most places – including the B&Bs – are heavily booked. At other times of the year, it's easy enough to find a place yourself. The best **hotel** for miles around is the outstanding *Little Inn of Bayfield*, Main St (ⓣ519/565-2611 or 1-800/565-1832, ⓦwww.littleinn.com; ❼), a tastefully modernized early nineteenth-century timber-and-brick building with a handsome second-floor veranda and delightfully furnished rooms, most of which have whirlpool baths. The hotel has an annexe just across the street and, once again, the rooms here are simply splendid. Incidentally, do not confuse this hotel with the *Bayfield Village Inn*, a very different proposition. Other good places to stay include the pleasant *Albion Hotel*, in another old building on Main Street (ⓣ519/565-2641, ⓦwww.thealbionhotel.com; ❺), and several charming **B&Bs**. Amongst the latter, the pick is *Clair on the Square*, in a handsome and sympathetically renovated old house beside the village green at 12 The Square (ⓣ519/565-2135, ⓦwww.claironthesquare.ca; ❻). Alternatively, there's **camping** at **Pinery Provincial Park** (reservations on ⓣ1-888/668-7275, ⓦwww.pinerypark.on.ca; $22.25–35.50 depending on site), a popular chunk of forested sand dune beside Lake Huron about 40km south of Bayfield.

Bayfield has several great places to **eat**, but it's hard to beat the smart and chic restaurant of the *Little Inn of Bayfield*, which is the best place to sample fish from Lake Huron – perch, white fish, pickerel or steelhead. Footsteps away on Main St, the *Red Pump Restaurant* (Ⓣ519/565-2576) is similarly classy, whilst the *Albion Hotel* has more routine, but still appetizing bar food and meals.

Goderich

Just 20km north of Bayfield at the mouth of the Maitland River, **GODERICH** is a delightful country town of eight thousand inhabitants that has both postcard appeal and a working harbour. It began life in 1825, when the British-owned Canada Company bought two and a half million acres of southern Ontario – the **Huron Tract** – from the government at the ridiculously low rate of twelve cents an acre, amid rumours of bribery and corruption. Eager to profit on their investment, the company pushed the **Huron Road** through from Cambridge in the east to Goderich in the west, an extraordinary effort that was witnessed by a certain Mr Moffat – "The trees were so tall, the forest was eternally dark and with the constant rains it was endlessly damp… Clearing the centuries of undergrowth and tangled vines was only the beginning, the huge rotted deadfalls of hardwood had to be hauled deeper into the bush, already piled high with broken pine. Since each man was responsible for cooking his own food after a hard day's work, the men sometimes ate the fattest pork practically raw… To make up for such fare, a barrel of whiskey with a cup attached always stood at the roadside." Completed in 1828, the road attracted the settlers the company needed. Indeed, within thirty years, the Huron Tract had two flourishing towns, Stratford (see p.124) and Goderich, and was producing large surpluses of grain for export, as it continues to do today.

The wide, tree-lined avenues of Goderich's geometrically planned centre radiate out from a grand octagonal central circle dominated by the town's white-stone courthouse. From here, the four main streets follow the points of the compass with North Street leading in a couple of minutes to the compendious Huron County Museum (mid-April to Dec Mon–Sat 10am–4.30pm & Sun 1–4.30pm; Jan to mid-April Mon-Fri 10am-4.30pm & Sat 1-4.30pm; $5, $7.50 with Gaol, see below; Ⓦwww.huroncountymuseum.on.ca), which concentrates on the district's pioneers. Highlights include a fantastic array of farm implements, from simple hand tools to gigantic, clumsy machines such as the steam-driven thresher, a beautifully restored Canadian Pacific steam engine, and lots of old sepia photos.

A ten-minute walk up to the far end of North Street and right along Gloucester Terrace brings you to the high stone walls of the **Huron Historic Gaol** at 181 Victoria St (mid-May to early Sept daily 10am–4.30pm; $5, $7.50 with Huron County Museum). One of the province's most intriguing attractions, the gaol was constructed as a combined courthouse and jail between 1839 and 1842. Start on the third floor of the main block, whose claustrophobic courtroom and council chamber were originally situated next to a couple of holding cells. There were two problems: the design was most unpopular with local judges, who felt threatened by the proximity of those they were sentencing; the other was the odour emanating from the privies in the exercise yard below. Several judges even refused to conduct proceedings because of the smell. In 1856, the administration finally gave way and built a new courthouse in the town centre, thereby separating the jail and the judiciary once and for all. Moving on from the third floor, the jail's second and first floors hold the original jailer's apartment and a string of well-preserved prison cells, reflecting various changes in design between 1841 and 1972, when the prison was finally closed. The worst is the leg-iron cell for "troublesome" prisoners, where unfortunates were chained to the wall with neither bed nor blanket. End your tour at the **Governor's House**, with its attractively restored late Victorian interior.

Back in the centre, **West Street** leads the 1km through a cutting in the bluffs to the Lake Huron shoreline at the south end of the **harbour** and salt works. A footpath leads northeast round the harbour, passing the grain elevators on its way to the **Menesetung Bridge**, the old CPR railway bridge that now serves as a pedestrian walkway across the Maitland River. On the north side of the river you can pick up the **Maitland Trail** for the brief but enjoyable jaunt along the river's north shore. In the opposite direction – south from the harbour – some 1.5km of shoreline has been tidied up to create a picnic area, but although the sunsets are spectacular the sandy **beach**, right at the end, is unenticingly scrawny.

Practicalities

Goderich **tourist office** sits beside Hwy 21 at the intersection of Nelson and Hamilton, a couple of minutes' walk to the northeast of the central circle (mid-May to Sept daily 9am–7pm; Oct to mid-May Mon–Fri 9am–4.30pm; ⓣ519/524-6600 or 1-800/280-7637, ⓦwww.goderich.ca). It has details of the town's twenty-odd **B&Bs**, which average out at about $70 per double per night. One of the more appealing options is the *Colborne B&B*, 72 Colborne St (ⓣ519/524-7400 or 1-800/390-4612, ⓦwww.colbornebandb.com; ④), in a large, plain-brick building dating from the early twentieth century and located just to the west of the central circus. There are four guest rooms here, all en suite, and each is decorated in a simple, straightforward manner. Also near the central circus and perhaps even more appealing is *Twin Porches B&B*, 55 Nelson St East at Victoria (ⓣ519/524-5505, ⓦwww.bbcanada.com/3694.html; ②; May–Oct), in an immaculate Victorian house of buff-coloured brick embellished with fine gingerbread scrollwork; this B&B, with its period décor, has three air-conditioned guest rooms with shared bathroom. The **hotel** scene is less varied, but the reasonably priced *Hotel Bedford*, right in the centre at 92 Court House Square (ⓣ519/524-7337 or 1-519/524-7337, ⓦwww.hotelbedford.on.ca; 3), is certainly distinctive. Built in 1896, the *Bedford* has an enormous open stairwell fitted with a grandiose wooden staircase just like a saloon in a John Ford movie – though the modernized rooms beyond are a tad disappointing. Much better is the plush *Benmiller Inn* (ⓣ519/524-2191 or 1-800/265-1711, ⓦwww.benmiller.on.ca; ⑥), which occupies a converted 1830s wool mill in an attractive wooded dell east of Goderich. To get there, take Hwy 8 out of town and watch for the sign after about 6km. There's **camping** near Goderich, too, just 7km north along the lakeshore at **Point Farms Provincial Park** (mid-May to early Oct; ⓣ519/524-7124; reservations on ⓣ1-888/668-7275).

Goderich is no gourmet's paradise, but there is a handful of **cafés and restaurants**, including *Robindale's Fine Dining*, a comparatively formal place in the centre at 80 Hamilton St (ⓣ519/524-4171), where the pork dishes are delicious. The *Park House Tavern & Eatery*, 168 West St, is the town's liveliest bar and offers wide views of Lake Huron.

The Bruce Peninsula and Nottawasaga Bay

Separating the main body of Lake Huron from Georgian Bay, the **Bruce** Peninsula holds two of Ontario's national parks. The more distinctive is the

Orientation in Owen Sound

Owen Sound's street plan can be more than a little confusing, but it does follow a plan: *avenues* run in one direction (north-south), *streets* the other, while the river, which bisects the compact town centre, separates avenues and streets *East* from those marked *West*.

Fathom Five National Marine Park, at the northern tip of the peninsula, where extraordinary rock formations, plentiful shipwrecks and crystal-clear waters provide wonderful sport for divers. The second is the **Bruce Peninsula National Park**, comprising two slabs of forested wilderness on either side of Hwy 6, its northern portion offering magnificent coastal hiking on a small section of the Bruce Trail (see opposite). There's camping at both parks and a reasonable choice of hotel and motel accommodation at lively **Tobermory**, an amiable combination of fishing village, port and resort, though note that advance booking is strongly recommended at the height of the season (mid-July to mid-Aug) - and the same applies to the ferry from Tobermory to Manitoulin Island in northern Ontario (see p.210). Spare time also for a quick zip round the interesting old port of **Owen Sound** at the base of the peninsula.

East of Owen Sound the southern curve of Georgian Bay forms **Nottawasaga Bay**, one of the province's most popular holiday areas. In summer the focus of attention is the crowded resort of **Wasaga Beach**, where a seemingly endless string of chalets and cottages fringe the several kilometres of protected sand that make up **Wasaga Beach Provincial Park**. To the west of Wasaga Beach, inland from the gritty port of **Collingwood**, is the **Blue Mountain ski area**, whose slopes utilize the Niagara Escarpment, the limestone ridge that weaves its way from near Niagara Falls to the Bruce Peninsula.

Public transport hereabouts is thin on the ground. Greyhound (Ⓣ1-800/661-8747, Ⓦwww.greyhound.ca) operates one **bus** five days a week from Toronto to Owen Sound, and a comparable service from Toronto to Collingwood, but the Bruce peninsula has no bus services at all.

Owen Sound

Just under 200km northwest of Toronto, **OWEN SOUND** occupies the ravine around the mouth of the Sydenham River, at the foot of the Bruce Peninsula. In its heyday, Owen Sound was a rough and violent port packed with brothels and bars, prompting the Americans to establish a consulate whose main function was to bail out drunk and disorderly sailors. For the majority it was an unpleasant place to live, and the violence spawned an especially active branch of the Women's Christian Temperance Organization, whose success was such that an alcohol ban was imposed in 1906 and only lifted in 1972. The town was in decline long before the return of the bars, its port facilities undercut by the railways from the 1920s, but it's managed to reinvent itself and is now an amiable sort of place well worth at least a pit stop. There are also three central sights of some interest, kicking off with the **Marine-Rail Museum**, overlooking the harbour in the old railway station at 1155 1st Ave West (June–Aug daily 10am–4pm; Sept–May Tues–Fri 10am–4pm & Sat–Sun 11am–3pm; $3). The museum has photos and scale models of old trains and ships and there is an old log tug and a caboose outside. Perhaps more diverting, however, are the **Tom Thomson Memorial Art Gallery**, 840 1st Ave West (July & Aug Mon–Sat 10am–5pm & Sun noon–5pm; Sept–June Tues–Fri 11am–5pm, Sat &

Sun noon–5pm; $5 donation), which features temporary exhibitions by Canadian artists and a clutch of Thomson's less familiar paintings; and the **Billy Bishop Museum**, 948 3rd Ave West (July–Aug daily 10am–4pm; Sept–Dec & April–June Tues–Sun noon–4pm; Jan & Feb Tues–Fri noon–4pm; $4), concentrating on the military exploits of Canada's Victoria Cross-winning air ace.

Owen Sound **bus station** is on 3rd Ave East at 10th St E, ten-minutes' walk from the **tourist office**, which is next door to the Marine-Rail Museum at 1155 1st Ave West (Mon–Fri 9am–4.30pm; June–Aug also Sat & Sun noon–4pm; Ⓣ519/371-9833 or 1-888/675-5555, Ⓦwww.e-owensound.com). They have a list of local accommodation, including details of a dozen **B&Bs** (❶–❸) with one of the handiest being the *Brae Briar*, 980 3rd Ave West (Ⓣ519/371-0025, Ⓦwww.bbcanada.com/622.html; ❹), which occupies a pleasant, two-storey, detached house with two guest rooms downtown off 10th Street. The town's **motels** are strung out along hwy 6/10 on the south side of town.

For downtown **food**, stick to *Jazzmyns Tapas & Taps*, 261 9th St E, where they serve up excellent, inexpensive meals – anything from tapas to pizzas and burgers.

The Bruce Peninsula National Park and Tobermory

Heading north from Owen Sound, **Highway 6** scoots up the middle of the Bruce Peninsula to reach – after about 100km – the turning for the **Bruce Peninsula National Park** at **Cyprus Lake**. The park is a mixture of limestone cliff, rocky beach, wetland and forest that's best visited in June when the wild flowers are in bloom and it's not too crowded. At Cyprus Lake are the park's headquarters and all-year **campsites**, which operate on a first-come, first-served basis in winter, by reservation from May to September (Ⓣ1-877/737-3783, Ⓦwww.pccamping.ca). Four hiking trails start at the northern edge of Cyprus Lake and three of them connect with one of the most dramatic portions of the **Bruce Trail**.

Just 11km or so beyond the Cyprus Lake turning, Hwy 6 slips into **TOBERMORY**, a bustling fishing village and holiday resort at the northern tip of the peninsula. There are no sights as such, but it's a pleasant spot with Tobermory's tiny centre focused on a slender inlet, **Little Tub harbour**. Here, **car ferries** (May to mid-Oct 2–4 daily; $15 one-way, cars $31; 2hr; Ⓣ1-800/265-3163, Ⓦwww.ontarioferries.com) leave for South Baymouth on Manitoulin Island (see p.210) and passenger boats shuttle out to Fathom Five National Marine Park (see below). At the back of the harbour, the **National Park office** (Mon–Fri 9am–4.30pm; Ⓣ519/596-2233, Ⓦwww.pc.gc.ca) covers both of the Bruce Peninsula's national parks, issuing maps and free brochures. The Fathom Five National Marine Park is known across Canada for the excellence of its diving; the waters are clear and they are dotted with around twenty shipwrecks. Prospective divers must register in person at the harbourfront **Registration Office** (April to early Oct daily 8am–4.30pm; Ⓣ519/596-2503). Diving gear can be rented footsteps away at G&S Watersports (Ⓣ519/596-2200, Ⓦwww.gswatersports.com), who also offer diving lessons and kayak rental.

There are a dozen or so **hotels** and **motels** in and around Tobermory, mostly brisk, modern affairs that are comfortable without being especially distinctive. The pick is the *Grandview Motel* (Ⓣ519/596-2220, Ⓦwww.grandview-tobermory.com; ❺), with eighteen spick-and-span rooms on the east side of the harbour at the junction of Bay and Earl streets. A second good choice, also on the east side of the harbour, is the two-storey, balconied *Blue Bay Motel*, 32 Bay St (☎519/596-2392, Ⓦwww.bluebay-motel.com; ❺). The *Grandview Motel* has the town's best **restaurant** with views out across the harbour and tasty, reasonably priced dishes with seafood a speciality – try the whitefish and ocean perch. There are also several lively **bars** and **cafés** beside the harbour – the *Crow's Nest* is as good as any.

Fathom Five National Marine Park

Fathom Five National Marine Park (Ⓦwww.pc.gc.ca) comprises nineteen uninhabited islands and the waters that surround them at the end of the Bruce Peninsula, offshore from Tobermory. To protect the natural habitat, only **Flowerpot Island**, 4km from the mainland, has any amenities, with limited space for **camping** – six sites only – and a couple of short hiking trails that explore its eastern reaches. A delightful spot, Flowerpot takes its name from two pink-and-grey rock pillars that have been eroded away from its eastern shore, and are readily seen on the islet's hiking trails. From May to mid-October, Flowerpot Island is easily reached by **boat** from Tobermory. Several operators run regular boats out to the island, either dropping passengers off and then collecting them later or pausing at Flowerpot as part of a longer excursion – just stroll along Little Tub harbour until you find the service that suits. One reliable company is Blue Heron (☎519/596-2999, Ⓦwww.blueheronco.com). The return fare from Tobermory to Flowerpot is around $30, a few dollars more for the longer trips. Prospective campers need to make reservations at and get permits from the Diver Registration office (see p.153). Both hikers and campers need to pack in their own food and drink.

Collingwood and the Blue Mountain ski area

The small-time port of **COLLINGWOOD**, 65km east of Owen Sound on Nottawasaga Bay, has a clutch of fine early twentieth-century buildings dotted along its main street, **Hurontario** – red-brick facades decorated with geometric designs and roughly dressed sandstone sills. More importantly, the town is also the gateway to the **Blue Mountain**, a segment of the Niagara Escarpment whose steepish slopes are now a major winter sports area, mainly for **alpine skiing** though several cross-country trails have also been developed. To get there from Collingwood, take the **Blue Mountain Road** (Hwy 19) which reaches – after about 10km – the **downhill ski slopes** at the *Blue Mountain Resort* (☎705/445-0231 or 1-877/445-0231, Ⓦwww.bluemountain.ca; ❹), a large and modern lodge that is the centre of wintertime activity. In total, the Blue Mountain ski area has 34 downhill ski slopes of varying difficulty with a maximum vertical drop of 219m. The prime season is from mid-December to mid-March.

Wasaga Beach and around

With its amusement parks and fast-food joints, there's nothing subtle about **WASAGA BEACH**, 20km east along the bayshore from Collingwood, but the beach is of fine golden sand, the swimming is excellent and you can rent out all manner of watercraft from jet skis to canoes. There's also one historical curiosity at the **Nancy Island Historic Site** (late May to mid-June Sat & Sun 10am–6pm; mid-June to early Sept daily 10am–6pm; early Sept to mid-Oct Sat & Sun 11am–5pm; free, but parking charge), on the main drag – Mosley Street

– behind Beach Area 2. In the War of 1812 the Americans managed to polish off the few British ships stationed in the upper Great Lakes without too much difficulty, and the last Royal Navy vessel, the supply ship *Nancy*, hid out here just off the bay at the mouth of the Nottawasaga River. The Americans tracked down and sunk the *Nancy*, but silt subsequently collected round the sunken hull to create Nancy Island. In 1927, the hull was raised from the silt and today it forms the main exhibit of the island's museum, whose imaginative design resembles the sails of a schooner.

Wasaga Beach makes for a good day's swimming and sunbathing, but if you do decide to stay the night you have the choice of lots of reasonably priced **motels** as well as cottages and campsites; just drive along Mosley Street until some place takes your fancy. Alternatively, the local Chamber of Commerce's year-round **information centre** at 550 River Rd W, in Beach Area 1 (Mon–Sat 9am–5pm, Sun 10am–4pm; ⓣ705/429-2247 or 1-866/292-7242, ⓦwww.wasagainfo.com), will help you find accommodation.

Severn Sound

Severn Sound, the southeastern inlet of Georgian Bay, is one of the most beautiful parts of Ontario. The bay's sheltered southern shore is lined with tiny, homely ports and its deep-blue waters are studded by the outcrops of the **Georgian Bay Islands National Park**, whose glacier-smoothed rocks and wispy pines were celebrated by the Group of Seven painters. In **Discovery Harbour**, on the edge of **Penetanguishene**, and **Sainte-Marie among the Hurons**, outside **Midland**, Severn Sound also possesses two of the province's finest historical reconstructions – the first a British naval base, the second a Jesuit mission. Leaving Severn Sound, there's more lovely Canadian Shield scenery on the road north to **Parry Sound**, an agreeable little port that also serves as a convenient stopping point on the long road north to Sudbury and Northern Ontario. Alternatively, you can head southeast from Severn Sound to **Orillia**, home of the Stephen Leacock Museum – and just 120km from Toronto on hwys 11 and 400.

There's a reasonably good **bus** service running north from Toronto to Midland and Penetanguishene on the southern shore of Severn Sound, and it's operated by Greyhound (ⓣ1-800/661-8747, ⓦwww.greyhound.ca). Ontario Northland buses (ⓣ1-800/461-8558, ⓦwww.webusit.com) link Toronto with Orillia (for North Bay and points north) and Orillia, Port Severn and Parry Sound (for Sudbury and points north).

Penetanguishene

The most westerly town on Severn Sound, amenable **PENETANGUISHENE** – "place of the rolling white sands" in Ojibwa – was the site of one of Ontario's first European settlements, a Jesuit mission founded in 1639, then abandoned in 1649 following the burning of Sainte-Marie (see p.159). Europeans returned some 150 years later to establish a trading station, where local Ojibwa exchanged pelts for food and metal tools, but the settlement remained insignificant until just after the War of 1812, when the British built a naval dockyard that attracted a bevy of French and British shopkeepers and suppliers. Today Penetanguishene is one of the few places in southern Ontario that maintains a bilingual tradition.

The town's **Main Street** is a pleasant place for a stroll, its shops and bars installed behind sturdy red-brick facades. It's the general atmosphere that appeals rather than

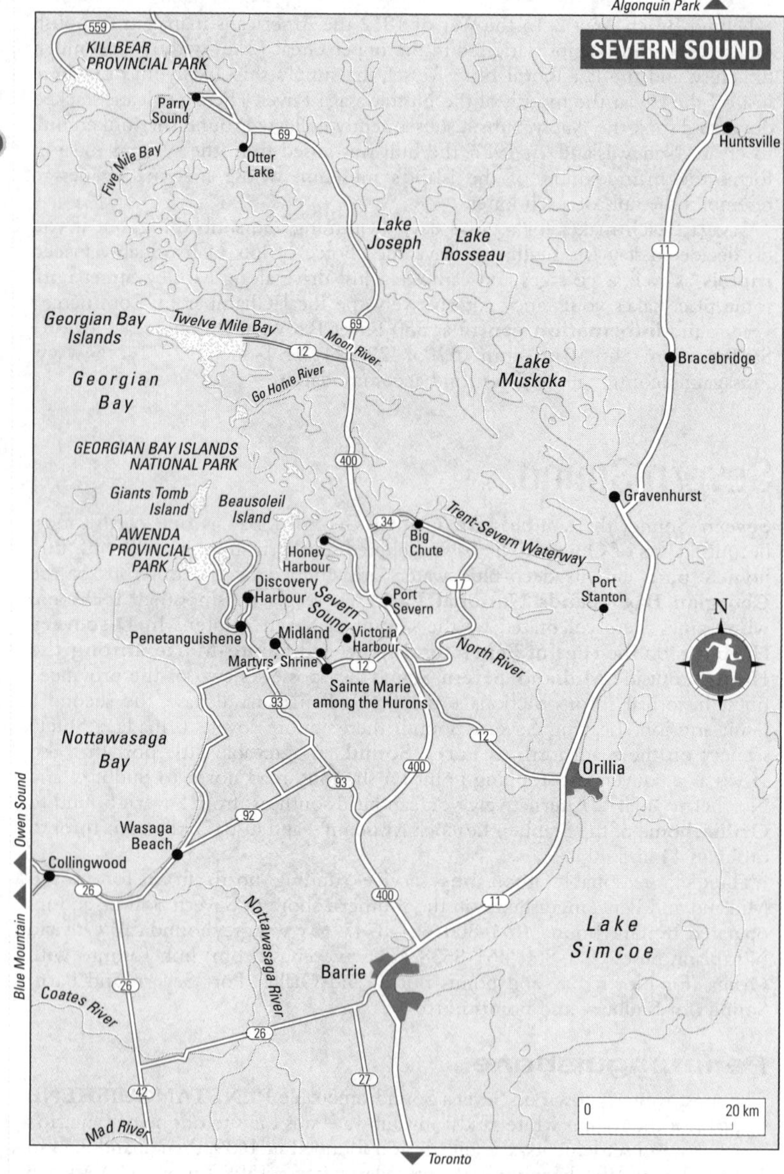

any particular sight, but the **Centennial Museum**, 13 Burke St (Mon–Sat 9am–4.30pm, Sun noon–4.30pm; $4.50; Ⓦwww.pencemuseum.com), a couple of minutes' walk east of Main Street along Beck Boulevard, is worth a quick visit. The museum occupies the old general store and offices of the Beck lumber company, whose yards once stretched right along the town's waterfront. The company was founded in 1865 by Charles Beck, a German immigrant who made himself immensely unpopular by paying his men half their wages in tokens that were only redeemable at his stores. The museum has several displays on the Beck lumber company, including examples of these "Beck dollars", and there's also a fascinating selection of old photographs featuring locals at work and play in the town and its forested surroundings. Doubling back, it's a short walk to the jetty at the north end of Main Street, from where there are enjoyable, three-hour **cruises** of the southern stretches of Georgian Bay and its myriad islands – known collectively as the **Thirty Thousand Islands** (mid-June to Aug 1–2 cruises daily; May & early June, Sept & early Oct occasional sailings; $22-25; ⓣ705/549-7795 or 1-800/363-7447, ⓦwww.georgianbaycruises.com).

Discovery Harbour

Penetanguishene's prime attraction, **Discovery Harbour** (late May to June Mon–Fri 10am–5pm; July & Aug daily 10am–5pm; $6.50; ⓦwww.discoveryharbour.on.ca), situated about 5km north of the town centre, is an ambitious reconstruction of the important British naval base that was established here in 1817. The principal purpose of the base was to keep an eye on American movements on the Great Lakes following the War of 1812, and between 1820 and 1834 up to twenty Royal Navy vessels were stationed here. Ships from the base also supplied the British outposts further to the west and, to make navigation safer, the Admiralty decided to chart the Great Lakes. This monumental task fell to Lieutenant Henry Bayfield, who informed his superiors of his determination "to render this work so correct that it shall not be easy to render it more so". He lived up to his word, and his charts remained in use for decades. The naval station was more short-lived. By 1834, relations with the US were sufficiently cordial for the Navy to withdraw, and the base was turned over to the Army, who maintained a small garrison here until 1856.

Now staffed by enthusiastic costumed guides, the sprawling site spreads along a hillside above a tranquil inlet, its green slopes scattered with accurate reconstructions of everything from a sailors' barracks to several period houses, the prettiest of which is the **Keating House**, named after the base's longest-serving adjutant, Frank Keating. Only one of the original buildings survives – the dour limestone **Officers' Quarters**, dating from the 1840s. However, pride of place goes to the working harbour-cum-dockyard, where a brace of fully rigged **sailing ships**, the HMS *Bee* and HMS *Tecumseth*, have been rebuilt to their original nineteenth-century specifications. In addition, Discovery Harbour also accommodates the **King's Wharf Theatre** (ⓣ705/549-5555 or 1-888/449-4463, ⓦwww.kingswharftheatre.com), which offers a season of plays as well as concerts and musicals from mid-June to August.

Awenda Provincial Park

Just 11km northwest of Penetanguishene, **Awenda Provincial Park** (ⓣ705/549-2231, ⓦwww.ontarioparks.com) is one of Ontario's larger parks, its delightful mainland portion dominated by a dense deciduous forest that spreads south from the Nipissing Bluff on the edge of Georgian Bay. The other section, Giants Tomb Island, lies offshore, but you need your own boat to get there. Awenda has a few small rock-and-pebble beaches, four good **campsites** (mid-May to early Oct), and a handful of hiking trails starting near the park office, which issues trail guides and maps.

Practicalities

Greyhound's daily bus service from Toronto and Midland pauses at the **bus stop** on Robert Street East at Peel Street, immediately to the east of Main Street.

From here, it's a five- to ten-minute walk down Main Street to the harbour, where the **tourist office** (Mon–Fri 9am–5pm plus summer weekends 9am–5pm; ⓣ705/549-2232, ⓦwww.penetanguishene.ca) has details of local **hotels** and **B&Bs**. Amongst them, easily the pick is the delightful *No.1 Jury Drive B&B*, 1 Jury Drive (ⓣ705/549-6851, ⓦwww.jurydrbb.huronia.com; ❺), whose five comfortable en-suite guest rooms occupy an attractive modern house built in traditional style near Discovery Harbour; the leafy suburban setting is very relaxing and the breakfasts are superb – especially the home-made carrot muffins. A second good choice is the *Hillside Inn B&B*, 27 Church St (ⓣ705/549-5462 or 1-866/806-3508, ⓦwww.bbcanada.com/6483.html; ❸), where the four cosy, period-style guest rooms, both en suite and with shared facilities, are in a handsome old house with a veranda; the B&B is about 900m northeast of the bus stop and offers wide views of the bay from its hillside location. If you decide to use Penetanguishene as a base, you can zip off to other local attractions with Union Taxi, 2 Robert St East (ⓣ705/549-7666). For **food**, the *Blue Sky Family Restaurant*, 32 Main St, is a most agreeable small-town diner offering good-quality snacks and meals at very affordable prices.

Midland

MIDLAND, just east along the bay from Penetanguishene, lost its engineering plants in the 1930s, its shipyards in 1957 and much of its flour-mill capacity in 1967. Yet it has bounced back, shrugging off these setbacks with the help of provincial and federal grants, and nowadays the town has a sprightly air, its main drag – **King Street** – an amenable parade of shops and cafés with the occasional mural to brighten up the sturdy brick buildings. Efforts to cash in on the tourist industry have included the construction of a marina and the redevelopment of the harbourfront, where sightseeing **cruises** of the Thirty Thousand Islands that necklace Georgian Bay leave from mid-May to mid-October (1–3 daily; $22; 2–3hr; reservations on ⓣ705/549-3388 or 1-888/833-2628, ⓦwww.midlandtours.com). Sooner or later, every school kid in Midland gets taken to the **Huronia Museum & Huron–Ouendat Village** (July & Aug daily 9am–6pm, Sept–June daily 9am–5pm, but phone to confirm winter times on ⓣ705/526-2844; $6; ⓦwww.huroniamuseum.com), a twenty-minute walk south of the harbour via King Street on Little Lake Park Road. Highlights of the **museum** include a large number of Huron artefacts and a series of photos tracing the pioneer settlement of Midland. The adjacent **village** is a replica of a sixteenth-century Huron settlement, its high palisade encircling storage pits, drying racks, a sweat bath, a medicine man's lodge and two long houses. These long houses are characteristic Huron constructions, their bark-covered walls of cedar poles bent to form a protective arch. They hold tiers of rough wooden bunks, draped with furs, whilst up above herbs, fish, skins and tobacco hang from the roof to dry. It's all very interesting and feels surprisingly authentic, though it still lags behind the comparable section of the nearby Sainte-Marie among the Hurons (see opposite).

Practicalities

Greyhound buses to Midland pull in at the **bus depot**, which they share with Central Taxi (ⓣ705/526-2218), at 207 King St. From here, it's the briefest of walks to the waterfront and the **tourist office**, at the foot of King Street (June daily 9am-6pm, July & Aug daily 9am-8pm, Sept–May Mon–Fri 9am–5pm; ⓣ705/526-7884, ⓦwww.town.midland.on.ca). They have the details of local and regional **accommodation** – anything from cottage rental through to a handful of downtown **B&Bs** (②–③). Amongst the latter, one perfectly adequate and fairly central option is the *Victorian Inn B&B*, in a good-looking Victorian house with wraparound veranda at 670 Hugel Ave and 6th St (☎705/526-4441 or 1-877/450-7660, Ⓦwww.victorianinn.on.ca; ④); to get there, take King Street up from the harbour and turn right along Hugel. A second recommendation is the unusual and rather engaging *Little Lake Inn B&B*, 669 Yonge St at 5th St (☎705/526-2750 or 1-888/297-6130, Ⓦwww.littlelakeinn.com; ⑥), where the modern front part of the house leads to an older section at the back with high-beamed ceilings and park views. There are three well-appointed guest rooms here, all en suite and as for directions, Yonge Street cuts across King about 600m south of the harbourfront.

For **food**, the *Daily Perk*, 292 King St, serves first-class deli-style sandwiches and meals; *Midland Fish & Chips*, 311 King St, does what it does rather well; and *Scully's Waterfront Grill*, by the town dock, is a popular, boisterous place with bar food.

Sainte-Marie among the Hurons

One of Ontario's most arresting historical attractions is **Sainte-Marie among the Hurons** (early to late May & mid- to late Oct Mon–Fri 10am–5pm; late May to mid-Oct daily 10am–5pm; Ⓦwww.saintemarieamongthehurons.on.ca; $12), the carefully researched and beautifully maintained site of a crucial episode in Canadian history. It's located 5km east of Midland beside Hwy 12 – and although there are no buses, the taxi fare from Midland is only $8 or so.

In 1608, the French explorer and trader **Samuel de Champlain** returned to Canada convinced that the only way to make the fur trade profitable was by developing alliances with native hunters. The **Huron** were the obvious choice, as they already acted as go-betweens in the exchange of corn, tobacco and hemp from the native bands to the south and west of their territory, for the pelts collected to the north. In 1611, having participated in Huron attacks on the Iroqouis, Champlain cemented the alliance by a formal exchange of presents. However, his decision to champion one tribe against another – and particularly his gifts of firearms to his allies – disrupted the balance of power amongst the native societies of the St Lawrence and Great Lakes area and set the stage for the destruction of Sainte-Marie almost forty years later. Meanwhile, the **Jesuits**, who established their centre of operations at Sainte-Marie in 1639, had begun to undermine social cohesion within the Huron community itself, by then enfeebled by three European sicknesses: measles, smallpox and influenza. The priests succeeded in converting a substantial minority of the Huron. Furthermore, in 1648 the Dutch on the Hudson River began to sell firearms to the **Iroquois**, who launched a full-scale invasion of Huronia in March 1649, slaughtering their enemies as they moved in on Sainte-Marie. Fearing for their lives, the Jesuits of Sainte-Marie burnt their settlement and fled. Eight thousand Hurons went with them; most starved to death on Christian Island, in Georgian Bay, but a few made it to Québec. During the campaign two Jesuit priests, fathers **Brébeuf and Lalemant**, were captured at the outpost of Saint-Louis, near present-day Victoria Harbour, where they were bound to the stake and tortured, as per standard Iroquois practice. The image of Catholic bravery and Indian cruelty lingered in the minds of French-Canadians long after the sufferings of the Hurons had been forgotten.

A visit to Sainte-Marie starts in the **reception centre** with an audiovisual show that provides some background information before the screen lifts dramatically away to reveal the painstakingly restored **mission site**. There are

25 wooden buildings here, divided into two sections: the Jesuit area with its watchtowers, chapel, forge, living quarters, well-stocked garden and farm buildings, complete with pigs, cows and hens; and the native area, including a hospital and a pair of bark-covered long houses – one for Christian converts, the other for heathens. Fairly spick-and-span today, it takes some imagination to see the long houses as they appeared to Father Lalemant, who saw "...a miniature picture of hell... on every side naked bodies, black and half-roasted, mingled pell-mell with the dogs... you will not reach the end of the cabin before you are completely befouled with soot, filth and dirt". Costumed guides act out the parts of Hurons and Europeans with great gusto, answering questions and demonstrating crafts and skills, though they show a certain reluctance to eat the staple food of the region, sagamite, a porridge of cornmeal seasoned with rotten fish. The grave in the simple wooden **church of St Joseph** between the Christian and native areas is the place where the (remaining) flesh of Brébeuf and Lalemant was interred after the Jesuits had removed the bones for future use as reliquaries.

A path leads from the site to the excellent **museum**, which traces the story of the early exploration of Canada with maps and displays on such subjects as fishing and the fur trade, seen in the context of contemporary European history. This leads into a section on the history of the missionaries in New France, with particular reference to Sainte-Marie. Information on the archaeology of the site follows: the mission's whereabouts were always known even though Victorian settlers helped themselves to every chunk of stone – from what was known locally as "the old Catholic fort" – because the Jesuits had deposited the necessary documentation in Rome. Excavations began on the site in the 1940s and work is still in progress.

The Martyrs' Shrine and Wye Marsh

The eight Jesuits who were killed in Huronia between 1642 and 1649 are commemorated by the **Martyrs' Shrine** (mid-May to mid-Oct daily 9am–9pm; $3; ⓦwww.martyrs-shrine.com), a twin-spired, 1920s church which overlooks Sainte-Marie from the other side of Hwy 12. Blessed by Pope John Paul II in 1984 – when he bafflingly remarked that it was "a symbol of unity of faith in a diversity of cultures" – the church, along with the assorted shrines and altars in its grounds, is massively popular with pilgrims. Inside, the transepts hold a number of saintly reliquaries, most notably the skull of Brébeuf, and a stack of crutches discarded by healed pilgrims. Back across Hwy 12 and next door to Sainte-Marie is the **Wye Marsh Wildlife Centre** (daily 9am–5pm; $6.50; ⓦwww.wyemarsh.com), whose footpaths explore a patch of wetland and woodland.

Orillia

If you're heading south from Severn Sound towards Toronto, you might consider a brief detour to **ORILLIA**, set beside Lake Couchiching, which is separated from the much larger Lake Simcoe by a short and narrow promontory; the town is also on Hwy 11, the road to Algonquin Provincial Park (see p.168). Orillia lies just to the west of the narrow channel – **The Narrows** – that connects the two lakes, a waterway that was once a centre of Huron settlement. When **Samuel de Champlain** arrived here in 1615, he promptly handed out muskets to his Huron allies, encouraging them to attack their Iroquois rivals to secure control of the fur trade; this intervention was to lead to the destruction of the Jesuit outpost at Sainte-Marie in 1649 (see p.159). Two hundred years later, a second wave of Europeans cleared the district's forests, and today Orillia is a trim little town of 27,000 citizens – part lakeside resort, part farming centre.

Orillia's humdrum **town centre** spreads out on either side of the main drag, Mississaga Street, which runs east from Hwy 11 to Lake Couchiching. At the foot of Mississaga, **Centennial Park** incorporates a marina, a harbour and a boardwalk that runs north to **Couchiching Beach Park**, complete with an Edwardian bandstand and a bronze statue of Champlain. However, the town's principal attraction, the **Stephen Leacock Museum** (Mon–Fri 9am–5pm; $5; Ⓦwww.leacockmuseum.com), is located some 3km southeast of the centre along the lakeshore – just follow the signs. Built in 1928 in the colonial style, with symmetrical pitched roofs and an ornate veranda, this was the summer home of the humorist and academic Stephen Leacock until his death in 1944. His most famous book, *Sunshine Sketches of a Little Town*, gently mocks the hypocrisies and vanities of the people of Mariposa, an imaginary town so clearly based on Orillia that it caused great local offence. Some of the rooms contain furnishings and fittings familiar to Leacock, others shed light on his career, interests and attitudes. Indeed, although the books may be engagingly whimsical, you can't help but wonder about a man who had concealed spyholes in his library so that he could watch his guests and, perhaps worse, carefully positioned his favourite living-room chair so that he could keep an eye on his servants in the pantry via the dining-room mirror. After you've explored the house, take a few minutes for the easy stroll out along the adjacent wooded headland and drop by the giftshop, which sells almost all of his works.

Ontario Northland buses arrive and depart from Orillia **bus station**, sited in the former railway station at the southern end of the town centre on Front Street S. From here it's 2km south to the Leacock Museum and around 800m north along Front Street South to the seasonal **tourist office** (June–Aug Mon–Fri 8.30am–5pm, Sat 10am–4pm & Sun 10am–3pm), right by the harbour. The Chamber of Commerce year-round tourist office is at 150 Front St South (Mon–Fri 9am–5pm; Ⓣ705/326-4424, Ⓦwww.orillia.com). There's no special reason to hang around after you've done the sights, but if you do decide to stay you can get details of local accommodation from either office.

Port Severn and around

Sitting on the northern shore of Severn Sound at the mouth of the Severn River, minuscule **PORT SEVERN** is the gateway to the **Trent–Severn Waterway**, a 400km canalized route that connects Georgian Bay with Lake Ontario. With a maximum depth of only 2m, it's of little commercial importance today, but until the late nineteenth century this was one of the region's principal cargo routes. It's open from the middle of May to the middle of October and takes about a week to travel from one end to the other. If you've the inclination for a serious **boating trip**, your first port of call should be Parks Canada (Ⓣ1-888/773-8888, Ⓦwww.pc.gc.ca), whose website provides the nautical low-down, and then the Friends of the Trent–Severn Waterway, who will help with cruise planning (Ⓣ1-800/663-2628, Ⓦwww.ftsw.com). In addition, **taster cruises** (early to mid-Oct 1 daily; $20; Ⓣ1-888/833-2628, Ⓦwww.midlandtours.com) lasting 2hrs and 30min leave from Lock #45 in Port Severn, travelling as far as the **Big Chute Marine Railway**, where boats are lifted over the eighteen-metre drop between the upper and lower levels of the river. Frankly, the Big Chute is something of a yawn, but it certainly attracts its share of visitors, most of whom drive here – just follow the signs off Hwy 400 (Exit 162) north of Port Severn.

There are two recommendable **hotels** in Port Severn, beginning with the smart and briskly modern *Inn at Christie's Mill*, 263 Port Severn Rd North (ⓣ705/538-2354 or 1-800/465-9966, ⓦwww.christiesmill.com; ❼), which also has the district's best **restaurant** with views out across the river. Even better, however, is the delightful *Severn Lodge*, 116 Gloucester Trail (ⓣ705/756-2722 or 1-800/461-5817, ⓦwww.severnlodge.on.ca), which has a wonderful solitary location amongst dense forests overlooking a wide and quiet section of the Trent–Severn Waterway. The main lodge and chalets have all the facilities of a mini-resort, including canoe and motorboat rental, an artificial beach, a restaurant and an outside swimming pool, and is extremely popular with families. Rates vary enormously, and there's usually a minimum stay of two nights, but a lodge room for two nights including meals works out at about $300 per person in summer. To get there, leave Hwy 400 at Exit 162 (also the turning for the Big Chute Marine Railway – see p.161) and it's 7km along Route 34.

The Ontario Northland **bus** service from Toronto to Parry Sound and Sudbury drops passengers at the gas station on Hwy 400 on the edge of Port Severn; there are no connections on to Honey Harbour.

Honey Harbour

It's 13km northwest from Port Severn across the mouth of the river and along Route 5 to **HONEY HARBOUR**, the nearest port – with water taxis – to the Georgian Bay Islands National Park. Little more than a couple of shops, a liquor store and a few self-contained hotel resorts, the village achieved some notoriety in the 1970s when the bar of the *Delawana Inn* was the site of violent confrontations between Toronto's Hell's Angels and local Ojibwa; the feud ended with the Angels walking home after their bikes had been dynamited. Things are much more civil today, but Honey Harbour is still a lively place in summer, with motorboats whizzing in and out as cottagers drop by to collect supplies. If you decide to stay here – eschewing the offshore campsites of the national park (see opposite) – the best place is the lakeside *Delawana Inn* (ⓣ705/756-2424 or 1-888/335-2926, ⓦwww.delawana.com; ❽ for full board in high season, with discounts on package deals; mid-May to mid-Oct). The inn comprises an extensive, resort complex with spacious chalet cabins dotted round its pine-forested grounds and its own little island patterned with hiking trails. Guests have use of the resort's canoes, kayaks and windsurfing boards.

Georgian Bay Islands National Park

A beautiful area to cruise, the **Georgian Bay Islands National Park** (ⓦwww.pc.gc.ca) consists of a scattering of about sixty islands spread between Honey Harbour and Twelve Mile Bay, about 50km to the north. The park's two distinct landscapes – the glacier-scraped rock of the Canadian Shield and the hardwood forests and thicker soils of the south – meet at the northern end of the largest and most scenic island, **Beausoleil**, a forty-minute boat ride west of Honey Harbour. Beausoleil has twelve short **hiking trails**, including two that start at the **Cedar Spring landing stage**, on the southeastern shore. These are the Treasure Trail (3.8km), which heads north behind the marshes along the edge of the island, and the Christian Trail (1.5km), which cuts through beech and maple stands to the balsam and hemlock groves overlooking the rocky beaches of the western shoreline. At the northern end of Beausoleil, within comfortable walking distance of several other **jetties**, are the Cambrian (2km) and Fairy (2.5km) trails, two delightful routes through the harsher scenery of the Canadian Shield. Nearby, just to the west, is the Dossyonshing Trail (2.5km), which tracks through a mixed area of wetland, forest and bare granite in the transitional zone between the two main landscapes. The (very informal) **national park office** in Honey Harbour (late May to early Sept Mon–Fri 8am–4.30pm, Sat 8am–4pm & Sun 8am–noon; ☎705/756-2415 or 705/526-9804) provides a full range of information on walking trails and flora and fauna. In winter, a visit to the park office is essential as the wardens will advise on where it's safe to ski across the ice to the islands – ring ahead to check their when they are around; weather permitting, the wardens maintain a marked ski trail out to Beausoleil.

The park has eleven **campsites** on Beausoleil Island. The charge is $14 a night and all of them operate on a self-registration, first-come, first-served basis, with the exception of Cedar Spring ($23), where the visitor centre (☎705/756-8907) takes reservations on half the 87 sites for bookings between May and September; there is an additional $10 fee for this service. For everywhere else, ask about availability at the Honey Harbour park office before you set out – and don't forget the insect repellent. Several Honey Harbour operators run a **water taxi** service over to three of the park's islands – Beausoleil ($40–45 one-way), Centennial Island ($45–50) and Island 95 ($45–50). Honey Harbour Boat Club (☎705/756-2411), about 700m from the park office at the marina at the end of Route 5, is as good as any. Water taxi prices are fixed – the park office has the list – but times are negotiable; be sure to arrange an agreed pick-up time before you get dropped off. If you want to head southwest, a one-way water-taxi trip to Midland (see p.158) costs around $100. The park also organizes its own boat trips to Beausoleil, a fifteen-minute journey each way (and around four hours on the island) with the **Georgian Bay Islands Day Tripper** (July & Aug Thurs–Mon 3 daily; $16 return plus $5.50 park admission; ☎705/526-8907). Advance reservations are essential for both the day trip and the water taxis.

Parry Sound

A cheerful little place, **PARRY SOUND**, beside an inlet of Georgian Bay 80km north of Port Severn, was named after the Arctic explorer Sir William Edward Parry, but it earned the nickname "Parry Hoot" because the water-bound log-drivers hereabouts chose this as the place to get drunk in. Things are more genteel today and the town has become a popular stopover for boats roaming the Thirty Thousand Islands out in the bay: Parry Sound is the home port of the "Island Queen", which squeezes through these islands in a spectacular **cruise** that has become one of the region's most popular attractions (June to mid-Oct 2 daily; 3hr for $30, 2hr $24; ☎705/746-2311 or

The Massasauga rattlesnake

The endangered **Massasauga rattlesnake** is the only venomous snake in eastern Canada and a small population of them slither around the Georgian Bay Islands National Park. Tan-coloured with dark brown blotches, an adult specimen is 50 to 70cm long with a heavy body and triangular head. In the unlikely event you stumble across one, give it a wide berth. The snake prefers marsh and mixed forest, so if you are hiking in this kind of habitat, be sure to pick up one of the advisory leaflets at the park office.

1-800/506-2628, Ⓦwww.island-queen.com). The jetty for the Island Queen is at Government Wharf, just below the centre of town at the end of Bay Street. Otherwise, Parry Sound is short of specific sights, though its pocket-sized harbour is overshadowed by a splendid Edwardian railway **trestle bridge** and the few blocks that make up the commercial centre – along and around **James Street** – are dotted with good-looking, old brick and stone buildings. In addition, the town rustles up the well-respected **Festival of the Sound** of classical music (details on Ⓣ705/746-2410 or 1-866/364-0061, Ⓦwww.festivalofthesound.on.ca), in the second half of July and early to mid-August.

Practicalities

Parry Sound is on the Ontario Northland (Ⓣ1-800/461-8558, Ⓦwww.webusit.com) **bus** route from Toronto to Sudbury. Buses pull into Richard's Coffee House, 119 Bowes St, 1km or so to the east of the town centre. To get downtown from here, call Parry Sound Taxi (Ⓣ705/746-1221). The **tourist office** is in the former railway station at 70 Church St (May–Sept Mon–Thurs 8am–4pm, Fri 8am–6pm & Sat 10am–2pm; Ⓣ705/746-4213 or 1-800/461-4261, Ⓦhttp://chamber.parrysound.com). From here, it's 800m south along Church Street to the centre and 300m more to Government Wharf. The tourist office has details of local accommodation including several central **B&Bs**. One especially enticing option is the *Victoria Manor B&B*, in the centre at 43 Church St and Rosetta (Ⓣ705/746-5399, Ⓦwww.solutionsforu.com/victoria; ❹). This occupies a handsome old house of 1907 that comes complete with turrets, a grand portico and immaculate gardens; there are four guest rooms here, one en suite, and each is kitted out in pleasant period style. Alternatively, routine chain-style rooms are available at the *Comfort Inn*, 120 Bowes St (Ⓣ705/746-6221, Ⓦwww.choicehotels.ca; ❸), east of the centre on the way out to Hwy 69.

For **food**, head for *The Country Gourmet*, in the centre at 65 James St (Mon–Fri 7am–5pm & Sat 8am–4pm; Ⓣ705/746-5907) – a smashing deli and bakery selling the tastiest of meals and snacks. In the evening, try the *Bay St* Café, 22 Bay St (Ⓣ705/746-2882), down by Government Wharf, where the menu runs from pizza and sandwiches to fish and chips.

Killbear Provincial Park

The wild and rugged Georgian Bay shoreline, formed by glaciers that scoured the rock and dumped mighty boulders onto its long beaches, is seen to fine advantage in **Killbear Provincial Park**, reached by driving 18km north from Parry Sound on Hwy 69 then 20km southwest on Route 559. The park occupies a tapering peninsula, with spindly cedars and black spruce clinging precariously to a shoreline of pink-granite outcrops, the classic Canadian Shield scenery that was so beloved by Tom Thomson (see p.96). The best of the park's three short hiking trails is the easy 3.5-km loop of the **Lookout Point Trail**, which slips through the maple, beech and yellow birch forest of the park's rugged interior to reach a lookout across Parry Sound; allow a couple of hours. Killbear has seven **campsites**, (mid-May to early Oct; reservations on Ⓣ519/826-5290 or 1-888/668-7275, Ⓦwww.ontarioparks.com; $27–36), some by the water, others in the forest, some with showers, others not.

From Killbear, it's about 180km north to Sudbury (see p.209) along the Trans-Canada (Hwy 69).

Central Ontario

Lying between Lake Ontario's northern shore and the Ottawa River Valley, **central Ontario** is largely defined by the **Canadian Shield**, whose endless forests, myriad lakes and thin soils dip down from the north in a giant wedge. This hostile terrain has kept settlement down to a minimum, though latterly the very wildness of the land has attracted lots of Canadian holiday-makers, who come here to hunker down in their lakeside cottages. The centre of all this holiday activity is the **Muskoka Lakes**, a skein of narrow lakes and rivers whose main supply towns – **Gravenhurst** and **Bracebridge** – lie on Hwy 11. Staying in a cottage or a resort is the one sure-fire way of appreciating the beauty of the area, but passing visitors are better off heading further north to the wondrous expanse of **Algonquin Provincial Park** with its abundant wildlife and extraordinarily large network of canoe routes. The implacability of the Shield breaks up as it approaches the **St Lawrence River** at the east end of Lake Ontario and it's here you'll find a string of interesting historic towns. The pick is **Kingston**, founded by United Empire Loyalists (see p.459) and renowned for its fine limestone buildings, not to mention its good restaurants and quality B&Bs. Kingston is also useful as a stepping stone on the road east to either Montréal (see p.235) or **Ottawa**, Canada's engaging capital city, which boasts some of the country's finest museums and a first-rate restaurant and bar scene.

Public transport along Lake Ontario's north shore and the St Lawrence River is excellent by bus and quite good by rail. Things get trickier in the Muskoka Lakes area, but Ontario Northland (Ⓣ1-800/461-8558, Ⓦwww.webusit.com) operates two bus routes from Toronto, one linking Orillia, Parry Sound and Sudbury, the other Orillia, Gravenshurst, Bracebridge, Huntsville (for Algonquin Park) and North Bay; they also operate the **Northlander train** (once daily except Sat; Ⓦwww.northlander.ca) from Toronto to Cochrane with stops at Gravenshurst, Bracebridge and Huntsville.

The Muskoka Lakes

The main route from Toronto to Algonquin Provincial Park passes through the **Muskoka Lakes**, a region of more than 1500 lakes and hundreds of urbanites' **cottage** retreats. Named after an Ojibwa chief, Mesqua-Ukee, who settled here with his people after aiding the British during the War of 1812, the area was opened to tourism in 1860, when two hikers made the two-day trek from Toronto to a small Ojibwa settlement at what is now the town of Gravenhurst. By the 1890s, the lakes had become the haunt of wealthy families from southern Ontario and although things are more democratic today, this is still primarily the preserve of the well heeled. The main access towns to the Muskoka Lakes – **Gravenhurst**, **Bracebridge** and **Huntsville** – are strung out along Hwy 11. None has much to offer the passing visitor and neither, for that matter, do the lakes. Just driving round is well-nigh pointless and you're much better off heading for one of the area's splendid hotel resorts, one of the best being the Sherwood Inn near **Port Carling**.

Public transport is limited to Hwy 11, with Ontario Northland **buses** (Ⓣ1-800/461-8558, Ⓦwww.webusit.com) going to all three major Muskoka towns on their way from Toronto to North Bay. The three can also be reached on the same company's **Northlander train** (once daily except Sat; Ⓦwww.northlander.ca).

Gravenhurst

The gateway to Muskoka is humdrum **GRAVENHURST**, sited at the southern end of Lake Muskoka, some 170km north of Toronto. Cottagers whizz in and out to collect supplies and arrive in numbers for the **Music on the Barge** season of big band, jazz and C&W music held here from late June to late August (Ⓣ705/687-3412, Ⓦwww.gravenhurst.ca). Otherwise, the main attraction is the **Bethune Memorial House National Historic Site**, 235 John St North (June–Aug daily 10am–4pm; Sept & Oct Sat-Wed 10am–4pm; $3.95), the birthplace of Norman Bethune (1890-1939), a doctor who introduced Western medicine to the Chinese in the 1930s and invented mobile blood-transfusion units. The house has been restored to its appearance in 1890 and has displays on Bethune's considerable accomplishments – he was even praised by Chairman Mao – all detailed in English, French and Chinese. Afterwards, you could hop aboard one of **Muskoka Steamships**' (Ⓣ705/687-6667 or 1-866/687-6667) three vessels – including an authentic 1887 steamship, the *RMS Segwun* – for a cruise up Lake Muskoka from the town wharf, giving fine views of the hills and its many mansions (June & Oct 5 weekly; July–Aug 2–4 daily; $16 for a 1hr cruise up to $42 for 4hr).

In the unlikely event you decide **to stay**, aim for the *Pinedale Inn*, 200 Pinedale Lane (Ⓣ705/687-2822, Ⓦwww.pinedaleinn.com; ④), a well-maintained motel on the shore of Gull Lake surrounded by pine trees and with rooms that have kitchenettes and bathrooms. For **food**, head for either the

The beaver

The **beaver** is Canada's national animal: it appeared on the first postage stamp issued by the colony in 1851, and now features on the back of the 5¢ piece. There was nothing sentimental about this choice – beaver pelts kick-started the colonial economy – and only recently has the beaver been treated with restraint and protected from being indiscriminately bumped off.

Beavers are aquatic rodents, growing to around 75cm long and weighing about 35kg. Native Canadians hunted the beaver for its thick, soft **pelt**, composed of long guard hairs and a dense undercoat, to use for clothing. Thereafter, European fur traders soon realized the value of beaver pelts, particularly in the manufacture of the all-weather, all-purpose **hat** worn by every man of any substance. To keep up with demand the beaver was extensively trapped, and the French *voyageurs* pushed further and further west along the lake and river systems in pursuit of the animal, thereby opening up much of the interior. The beaver was hunted to the point of extinction in much of eastern Canada, but was reprieved when the beaver hat went out of fashion in the late nineteenth century; today beavers are comparatively commonplace.

Beavers start to build their **dams**, which can be up to 700m wide, by strategically felling one tree across a stream. This catches silt and driftwood and the beaver then reinforces the barrier with sticks and stones plus grass and mud, which is laboriously smoothed in as a binding element. The **lodge** is constructed simultaneously; sometimes it forms part of the dam and sometimes it is fixed to the shore or an island in the pond. It is about 2m in diameter and has two entrances – one accessible from land and one from underwater – both for its own convenience and to be able to escape its predators in any emergency. Lodges are topped with grass thatch and a good layer of mud, which freezes in winter, making them virtually impenetrable. During the autumn, the beaver stocks its **pond** with the soft-bark trees and saplings that make up its diet. It drags them below the water line and anchors them to the mud at the bottom before retiring to the lodge for the winter, only emerging to get food from the pond or repair the dam. Beaver lakes are not, however, the tree-fringed paradises portrayed by some nature-film makers; nearer the mark is a mud-banked pond, surrounded by untidily felled trees and with a bedraggled-looking domed heap of sticks and sludge somewhere along its banks.

pleasant *White Pine Café*, on the main street in a tastefully converted old general store at 195 Muskoka Rd S, or *Sloan's*, 155 Muskoka Rd S, which has been here as long as Gravenhurst, and serves a divine blueberry pie.

Bracebridge and Port Carling

BRACEBRIDGE, 25km north of Gravenhurst, prides itself on being "Halfway to the North Pole" – and on that basis bills itself as the summer home of Santa Claus, who hangs out amongst the theme-park rides of **Santa's Village** just southwest of town (late June to Aug daily 10am–6pm; adults and children over 5 $27, 2–4s $22, under 2s and reindeer free; Ⓦ www.santasvillage.ca). There's not much else, though the short main drag, **Manitoba Street**, is lined with a pleasant ensemble of Victorian red-bricks, worth at least a few minutes. The **tourist office**, in the mews by the bridge at the foot of Manitoba Street (April–Sept Mon–Sat 9am–5pm & Sun 10am–4pm; Oct–March Mon–Fri 9am–5pm & Sat 10am–4pm; Ⓣ 705/645-8121 or 1-866/645-8121, Ⓦ www.tourismbracebeidge.com), has town maps and buckets of local information.

Driving west from Bracebridge along Hwy 118, it's about 25km to the lakeside hamlet of **PORT CARLING**, the nearest settlement to one of the region's finest hotel–resorts, the *Delta Sherwood Inn*, 1090 Sherwood Rd (705/765-3131 or 1-866/844-2228, www.deltahotels.com; 8 all inclusive), a handsome complex of luxurious chalet-villas set deep in the Muskoka woods – call for directions. Each of the guest rooms is kitted out in smart modern style and the food, served in the main lodge, is first-rate.

Huntsville

Workaday **HUNTSVILLE**, 35km beyond Bracebridge on Hwy 11, is as near as the buses and trains get to Algonquin Park. **Ontario Northland buses** pull into the bus depot, on the north side of town at 377 Centre St N, and their **Northlander train** pauses at the train station about 600m away to the south (and across the river) at 2 Centre St S. As for **moving on** to Algonquin Park, the best bet is Hammond Transportation's thrice weekly minibus service to the park, which operates from July to early September (705/645-5431, www.hammondtransportation.com). If you find yourself marooned here in Huntsville, head for the inexpensive chain **motels** lined up along King William Street. Reliable options here include the *Comfort Inn*, at no. 86 (705/789-1701 or 1-800/424-6423, www.choicehotels.ca; 4), and the *King William Inn* at no. 23 (705/789-9661 or 1-888/995-9169, www.kingwilliaminn.com; 4).

Algonquin Provincial Park

Created in 1893 at the behest of logging companies keen to keep the farmers out, **Algonquin Provincial Park** (www.algonquinpark.on.ca) is Ontario's oldest and largest provincial park and for many it comprises the quintessential Canadian landscape. Located on the southern edge of the Canadian Shield, the park straddles a **transitional zone**, with the hilly two-thirds to the west covered in a hardwood forest of sugar maple, beech and yellow birch, whilst in the drier eastern part jack pines, white pines and red pines predominate. Throughout the park, the lakes and rocky rounded hills are interspersed with black spruce bogs, a type of vegetation typical of areas far further north. **Canoeing** is very popular here and with an astounding 1600km of routes there's a good chance of avoiding all contact for days on end. **Wildlife** is as varied as the flora – any trip to Algonquin is characterized by the echo of birdsong, from the loons' ghostly call to the screech of ravens. Beavers, moose, black bears and raccoons are all resident, as are white-tailed deer, whose population thrives on the young shoots that replace the trees felled by the park's loggers. Public "howling parties" – which can attract up to 2000 people – set off into the wilderness during August in search of **timber wolves**, or rather their howls: many of the rangers are so good at howling that they can get the animals to reply.

Access to the park is via either the **West Gate**, 45km from Huntsville on Hwy 60, or – if you are arriving from Ottawa and points east – the **East Gate**. A day-pass costs $13 per vehicle. The two gates are linked by the 56km-long **Parkway Corridor** – also known as the Frank McDougall Parkway – the park's only road. Away from the corridor, walking and canoeing are the only means of transport. The well-signposted main **visitor centre** is 43km inside the park from the West Gate (late April to June & Sept–Oct daily 10am–5pm; July & Aug daily 9am–9pm; Nov to late April Sat & Sun 10am–4pm; 705/633-5572). Besides the inevitable gift shop, it holds a series of dioramas explaining the park's general and natural history. The visitor centre also has a comprehensive range of literature describing every aspect of the park, from maps and detailed hiking trail and canoeing route guides through to booklets on native folklore. The **park offices** at both the West and East gates have trail descriptions and other park information, but there's not so wide a range; individual trail guides are also available at most trailheads. If you're heading for the backcountry, pick up **food and water** before you get here as outlets in the park are few and far between. In all cases, **backcountry camping** requires a permit. These are available at both the West and East gates and at the visitor centre ($10 per person per night).

For **all-in tours**, Call of the Wild, 23 Edward St in Markham, a suburb of Toronto (Ⓣ905/471-9453 or 1-800/776-9453, Ⓦwww.callofthewild.ca), runs personalized and relaxed adventure canoe trips in the park (three/four/five days: $350/460/580). Prices include all meals, permits, equipment and transport from Toronto. It's essential to book in advance. If you're reliant on **public transport**, the nearest you'll get by train or bus is Huntsville (see opposite). However, Hammond Transportation (Ⓣ705/645-5431, Ⓦwww.hammondtransportation.com) operates an Algonquin Park shuttle from Huntsville to points along the Parkway Corridor from July to early September (3 weekly).

The Parkway Corridor

Along the Parkway Corridor, the location of trailheads and campsites is indicated by distances from the West Gate. No less than fourteen **day-hikes** begin beside the road and of these the 2km **Beaver Pond Trail** (km 45) is a rugged but easy trail that takes you past huge beaver dams, while the equally short but somewhat steeper **Lookout Trail** (km 39) gives a remarkable view of the park. For a longer trail with greater chances of spotting wildlife, the 11km **Mizzy Lake Trail**

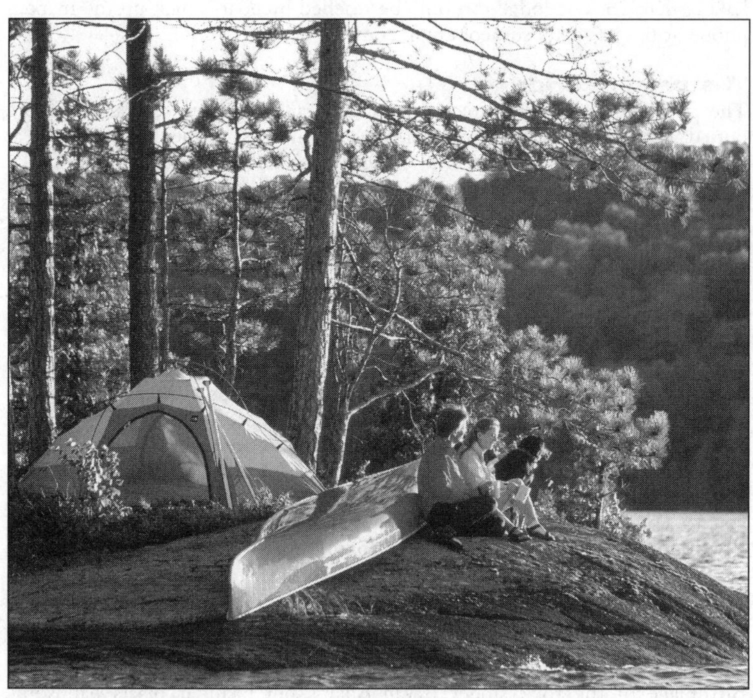

△ Campers in Algonquin Provincial Park

(km 15) is recommended. Spare time also for the illuminating **Algonquin Logging Museum** (late May to early Oct daily 9am–5pm; free with day-pass), just inside the East Gate at Km 54.5. Here, an easy 1.3-km loop trail threads past some fascinating old logging leftovers, including a tugboat, a locomotive, sawlog camp and sleighs.

Strung along the Parkway Corridor are eight park **campsites**. The less crowded sites tend to be those that prohibit motorboats, namely Canisbay Lake (km 23; mid-May to early Oct); Mew Lake (km 30; all year); Pog Lake (km 37; early June to early Sept); Kearney Lake (km 37; early June to early Sept); and Coon Lake (km 40; mid-June to Aug) Mew Lake is the only park campsite to be open all year. The cost of a pitch, covering a car and up to six people, is $26–35, and **reservations** are well-nigh essential (Ⓣ519/826-5290 or 1-888/668-7275, Ⓦwww.ontarioparks.com). In addition, note that the rangers who roamed the park in its early years built dozens of **log cabins**, some of which have survived and are now rented out for $50–80 per person per night; consult the park website for precise details.

Also lining the Parkway Corridor are several privately owned **lodges and mini-resorts**, ranging from the simple and unaffected to the comparatively lavish. Perhaps the best is *Killarney Lodge* (Ⓣ705/633-5551, Ⓦwww.killarneylodge.com; ❽ including meals; May to mid-Oct), whose cosy, prettily painted log cabins dot a spindly promontory that hooks out into the Lake of Two Rivers (at Km 32). A second good option is *Bartlett Lodge* (Ⓣ705/633-5543 or 1-866/614-5355, Ⓦwww.bartlettlodge.com; ❼ including meals; mid-May to mid-Oct), comprising a scattering of older cabins overlooking Cache Lake at Km 23. The lodge can only be reached by boat – pick up the marked phone at the jetty and someone will come to get you.

The park interior

The park interior is best explored by **canoe**, and there are several **outfitters** dotted along the Parkway Corridor. One of the best is the Portage Store at Canoe Lake (km 14; summertime Ⓣ705/633-5622, in winter 705/789-3645, Ⓦwww.portagestore.com). **Rates** vary enormously depending on the sort of canoe you rent, but the simplest models cost about $25 per day, $17 per day for five days and more. The Portage Store also rents out tents, life vests and all the associated canoeist's tackle, and organizes guided canoe trips; in all cases, advance reservations are pretty much essential. Note also that given Algonquin's immense popularity, canoeing is best avoided at holiday weekends: horror stories abound of three-hour jams of canoeists waiting their turn to tackle the portages between some of the more accessible lakes. Incidentally, Canoe Lake was where the artist Tom Thomson (see p.96) drowned in 1917 – and there's a monument to him about forty-minutes' canoe paddle from the Portage Store.

If you don't fancy canoeing, the interior can also be experienced on one of two main long-distance hiking trails. These are the **Western Uplands Backpacking Trail** (km 3), which is composed of a series of loops that allow you to construct a hike of between 32km and 88km; and the **Highland Backpacking Trail** (km 29; 19km or 35km).

Kingston

Birthplace of the rock singer Bryan Adams but prouder of its handsome limestone buildings, the city of **KINGSTON**, a fast 260km east of Toronto along Hwy 401, is the largest and most enticing of the communities along the northern shore of Lake Ontario. The town occupies an attractive and strategically important position where the lake narrows into the St Lawrence River, its potential first recognized by the French who built a fortified fur-trading post here in 1673. It was not a success. The commander of this **Fort Frontenac**, the Comte de Frontenac, managed to argue with just about everybody, and his deputy, Denonville, pursued a risky sideline in kidnapping, inviting local Iroquois to the fort and then forcibly shipping them to France as curiosities. Nevertheless, the fort struggled on until 1758 when it fell to a combined force of British, Americans and Iroquois, a victory soon followed by an influx of United Empire Loyalists (see p.459), who promptly developed Kingston – as they renamed it – into a major shipbuilding centre and naval base. The money rolled in and the future looked rosy when the completion of the Rideau Canal (see p.177), linking Kingston with Ottawa in 1832, opened up its hinterland. Indeed, Kingston became the **capital** of Canada in 1841 and although it lost this distinction just three years later it remained the region's most important town until the end of the nineteenth century. In recent years, Kingston – and its 155,000 inhabitants – has had as many economic downs as ups, but it does benefit from the presence of **Queen's University**, one of Canada's most prestigious academic institutions, and of the **Royal Military College**, the country's answer to Sandhurst and West Point rolled into one.

Central Kingston's medley of old buildings displays every architectural foible admired by the Victorians, from neo-Gothic mansions with high gables and perky dormer windows to elegant Italianate villas. Yet, the cream of the stylistic crop are the city's Neoclassical limestone buildings, especially **City Hall** and the **Cathedral of St George**. Kingston also holds the first-rate **Agnes Etherington Art Centre** gallery and **Bellevue House**, once the home of Prime Minister Sir John A. Macdonald. Add to this several delicious **B&Bs**, a cluster of good **restaurants** and scenic **boat trips** round the **Thousand Islands** just offshore, and you have a city that is well worth a couple of days.

Arrival and information

Trains from Toronto (4–6 daily; 2hr 10min) pull into the **VIA Rail station** beside Hwy 2, an inconvenient 7km northwest of the city at the junction of Princess Street and Counter Boulevard; Kingston Transit buses #2 and #6 (Mon–Fri every 30min, Sat every 30min-1hr; no Sun service) connect with downtown Kingston. The terminus for long-distance **Greyhound** (Ⓣ1-800/661-8747, Ⓦwww.greyhound.ca) and **Coach Canada buses** (Ⓣ1-800/461-7661, Ⓦwww.coachcanada.com) is on the corner of Division Street and Counter Boulevard, about 6km to the north of the city centre; Kingston Transit bus #12 (Mon–Sat only; hourly) runs downtown from here. Kingston Transit's **local bus** information line is Ⓣ613/546-0000.

Kingston's helpful **tourist office** is in the centre of the city, across from the waterfront at 209 Ontario St (June–Aug daily 9am–6pm; May & Sept–April daily 9am–5pm; Oct–April Mon–Fri 9am–5pm; Ⓣ613/548-4415 or 1-888/855-4555, Ⓦwww.kingstoncanada.com). It has a wide range of local and regional information and operate a free room reservation service.

Guided tours

Kingston offers a full complement of **guided tours**. Top of the list is **cruises** out amongst the **Thousand Islands** from the dock at the foot of Brock Street.

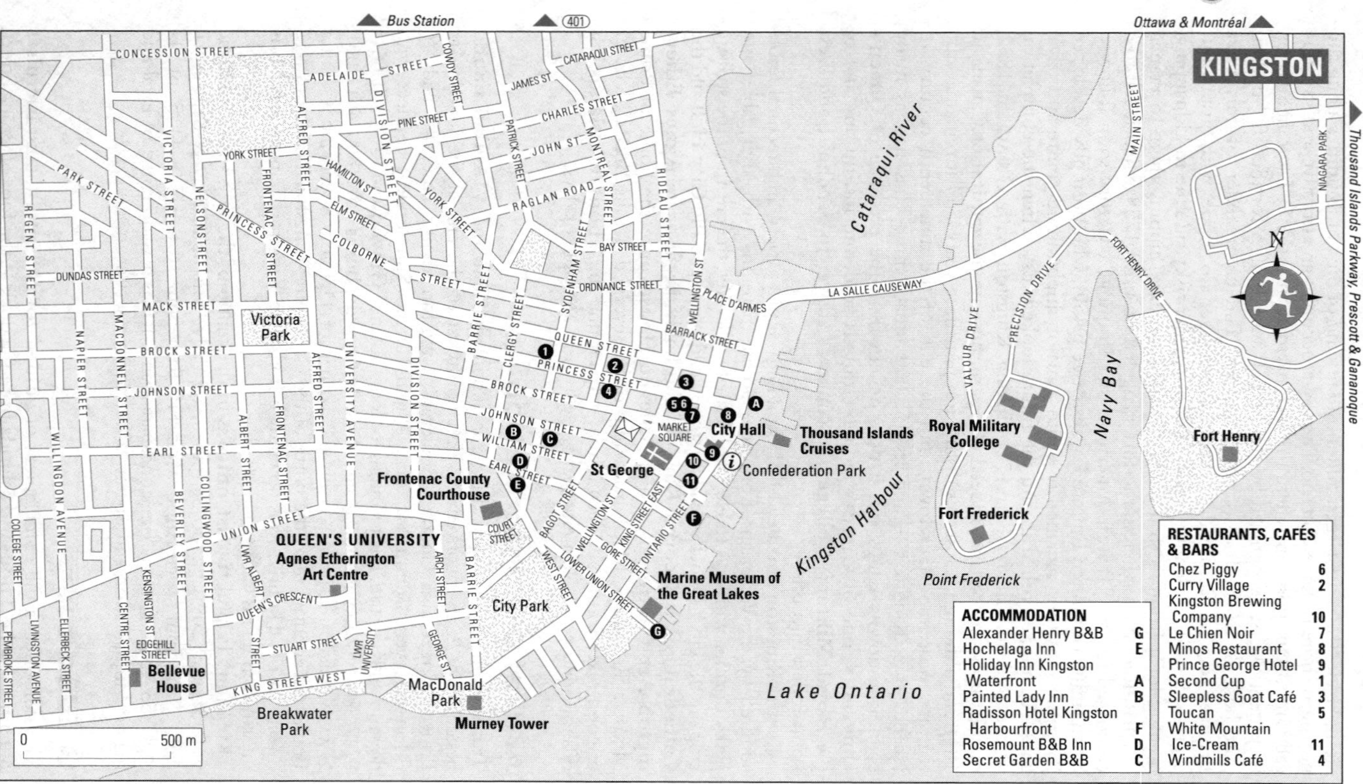
KINGSTON
Thousand Islands Parkway, Prescott & Gananoque
Ottawa & Montréal
401
Bus Station
Train Station
ACCOMMODATION
Alexander Henry B&B G
Hochelaga Inn E
Holiday Inn Kingston Waterfront A
Painted Lady Inn B
Radisson Hotel Kingston Harbourfront F
Rosemount B&B Inn D
Secret Garden B&B C
RESTAURANTS, CAFÉS & BARS
Chez Piggy 6
Curry Village 2
Kingston Brewing Company 10
Le Chien Noir 7
Minos Restaurant 8
Prince George Hotel 9
Second Cup 1
Sleepless Goat Café 3
Toucan 5
White Mountain Ice-Cream 11
Windmills Café 4
Fort Henry
Navy Bay
Royal Military College
Fort Frederick
Point Frederick
Cataraqui River
Kingston Harbour
Lake Ontario
Thousand Islands Cruises
Confederation Park
City Hall
Market Square
St George
Marine Museum of the Great Lakes
Frontenac County Courthouse
Queen's University
Agnes Etherington Art Centre
City Park
Victoria Park
MacDonald Park
Murney Tower
Breakwater Park
Bellevue House
La Salle Causeway
Fort Henry Drive
Precision Drive
Valour Drive
Main Street
Niagara Park
Place d'Armes
Wellington St
Barrack Street
Rideau Street
Ordnance Street
Bay Street
Montreal Street
Sydenham Street
Queen Street
Princess Street
Brock Street
Johnson Street
William Street
Earl Street
Clergy Street
Barrie Street
Division Street
University Avenue
Alfred Street
Frontenac Street
Albert Street
Collingwood Street
Beverley Street
Kensington St
Centre Street
Edgehill Street
Pembroke Street
Livingston Avenue
Ellerbeck Street
Willingdon Avenue
Napier Street
Macdonnell Street
Mack Street
Victoria Street
Nelsonstreet
Concession Street
Regent Street
Dundas Street
Park Street
College Street
Colborne Street
York Street
Elm Street
Hamilton St
Adelaide Street
Cowdy Street
Pine Street
Patrick Street
John St
Charles Street
James St
Cataraqui Street
Raglan Road
Bagot Street
Wellington St
King Street East
Ontario Street
Gore Street
Lower Union Street
West Street
Court Street
Union Street
Arch Street
Lwr Albert St
Queen's Crescent
Stuart Street
Lwr University
George St
King Street West
0 500 m

Freshwater diving

In the 1950s, the creation of the **St Lawrence Seaway** regulated the depth of Lake Ontario and flooded its various rapids. Before then, the waters off Kingston had been extremely treacherous and the bottom of the lake hereabouts is dotted with **shipwrecks**. The tourist office (see p.171) publishes an excellent booklet explaining what is where and several companies rent out **diving** gear and organize **diving trips**. One of them is Kingsdive, 121 Princess St (Ⓣ613/542-2892).

The islands, which speckle the St Lawrence River as it leaves Lake Ontario, range from tiny hunks of rock to much larger islets with thick forest and lavish second homes. It's a pretty cruise at any time of the year, but especially so in autumn when the leaves turn. Several companies offer cruises, but the benchmark is set by **Kingston 1000 Islands Cruises** (Ⓣ613/549-5544, Ⓦwww.1000islandscruises.ca), whose three-hour sightseeing excursions are as good as any with – or preferably without – the live entertainment (mid-May to mid-Oct 1–4 daily; $27). Another enjoyable outing is the **Haunted Walk of Kingston**, a ninety-minute narrated stroll through the older parts of town beginning in the centre outside the Prince George Hotel (early May to Oct 1–2 daily; $12.50; Ⓣ613/549-6366, Ⓦwww.hauntedwalk.com).

Accommodation

Kingston has an excellent range of **accommodation**, much of it in or near the city centre. The best places are those **inns and B&Bs** that occupy grand old buildings, but there are less expensive options too, most distinctively beds/berths in a decommissioned **coastguard ship**. At the top end of the market at least, advance reservations are advised in July and August.

Alexander Henry Bed and Breakfast 55 Ontario St Ⓣ613/542-2261, Ⓦwww.marmuseum.ca. Kingston's most unusual lodgings are provided here in this former coast-guard ice-breaker, moored downtown next to the Marine Museum. Berths vary from a bunk in a tiny cabin ($45 per person) to more comfortable quarters ($95–125 per person in a two-berth cabin). The ship itself dates from the 1950s and is a sturdy affair with narrow stairways and corridors, all to the salty taste of the sea. Open mid-May to early Oct. ❹

Hochelaga Inn 24 Sydenham St Ⓣ613/549-5534 or 1-877/933-9433, Ⓦwww.hochelagainn.com. This sprawling inn occupies a good-looking Victorian mansion with a playful central tower, bay windows and wraparound veranda. There are 23 guest rooms, all en suite, and although the furnishings and fittings are rather pedestrian, each is very comfortable. In a residential area within easy walking distance of the centre. ❺

Holiday Inn Kingston Waterfront 2 Princess St Ⓣ613/549-8400 or 1-800/465-4329, Ⓦwww.hikingstonwaterfront.com. Not the most distinctive of the city's hotels, for sure, but the rooms are comfortable enough and it couldn't be more convenient for the centre. Most rooms have lake views. ❻

Painted Lady Inn 181 William St Ⓣ613/545-0422, Ⓦwww.paintedladyinn.on.ca. This appealing, three-storey Victorian redbrick, with its inviting porch, has seven well-maintained guest rooms, all en suite. Central location. ❺

Radisson Hotel Kingston Harbourfront 1 Johnson St Ⓣ613/549-8100 or 1-800/333-3333, Ⓦwww.radisson.com/kingstonca. Smart, chain hotel with standard-issue modern furnishings and fittings, but great views out over Lake Ontario and the marina. ❻

Rosemount B&B Inn 46 Sydenham St South Ⓣ613/531-8844 or 1-888/871-8844, south Ⓦwww.rosemountinn.com. An eminently appealing B&B, which occupies a strikingly handsome, distinctively Italianate old limestone villa – one of Kingston's finest buildings. The *Rosemount* has ten guest rooms, all en suite, decorated in immaculate period style. The breakfasts are delicious too. ❻

Secret Garden B&B 73 Sydenham St Ⓣ613/531-9884 or 1-877/723-1888, Ⓦwww.the-secret-garden.com. One of Kingston's most enjoyable B&Bs, there are seven extremely comfortable guest rooms here, all en suite and each decorated in charming antique style. The house itself is a fetching Victorian building of timber and brick with verandas and porches and a splendid bay-windowed tower. Faces the slender limestone symmetries of Sydenham St United Church. ❺

The City

The obvious place to start a visit is **City Hall** (guided tours: June to Sept Mon–Fri 10am–4pm, plus Sat & Sun in July & Aug 11am–3pm; 30mins; free), a copper-domed, stone extravagance which, with its imposing Neoclassical columns and portico, dominates the waterfront as was intended – a suitably grand structure for what was scheduled to be the Canadian Parliament. By the time the building was completed in 1844, however, Kingston had lost its capital status and – faced with colossal bills – the city council had to make some quick adjustments, filling the empty corridors with shops and stalls and even a saloon. Things are more sedate today, with municipal offices occupying most of the space, but the tour does provide a fascinating insight into the development of the city and includes a trip up the **clock tower** via a magnificent circular stairway.

Back outside, the **Market Square**, at the back of City Hall, is home to an excellent open-air **market** (Mon–Sat) and on summer Sundays the square is given over to craft and antiques stalls. In front of City Hall is the site of the original French outpost and this is now marked by the waterfront **Confederation Park**, whose manicured lawns run behind the harbour with its marina and squat, nineteenth-century Martello tower. Here also, from the dock at the foot of Brock Street, there are regular **cruises** out amongst the Thousand Islands (see p.178).

Anglican Cathedral and Marine Museum

It's a couple of minutes' walk west from Confederation Park to Kingston's finest limestone building, the **Anglican Cathedral of St George**, at King Street and Johnson (Tues–Fri 9am–3pm & some Sat 10am–1pm; free; ⓣ613/548-4617). Dating from the 1820s, the graceful lines of the cathedral, with its Neoclassical portico and dainty domes, are deceptively uniform, for the church was remodelled on several occasions, notably after severe fire damage in 1899. The capacious interior holds some delightful Tiffany stained-glass windows and, attached to the wall of the nave, a plain **memorial** to Molly Brant (1736–97), a Mohawk leader and sister of Joseph Brant (see p.96). From the cathedral, it's a brief stroll to the main commercial drag, **Princess Street**, whose assorted shops, offices and cafés stretch up from the lakeshore. Alternatively, it's a short hop back to the waterfront and the **Marine Museum of the Great Lakes** (March to late May Wed-Fri 10am–4pm & Sat noon–4pm; late May to Sept daily 10am–4pm; $6.50), a somewhat dowdy accumulation of maritime bygones, where the shipbuilders' gallery is of some mild interest. Moored alongside is the unusual *Alexander Henry Bed and Breakfast* (see p.173).

Murney Tower

From the Marine Museum, it's a five- to ten-minute stroll west to **Murney Tower**, at the foot of Barrie Street (late May to Aug daily 10am–5pm; $3). The most impressive of four such towers built in Kingston to defend the dockyards against an anticipated US attack during the Oregon Crisis of 1846–47, this one holds incidental military memorabilia including old weapons, uniforms and re-created nineteenth-century living quarters. The design of the tower, built as a combined barracks, battery and storehouse, was copied from a Corsican tower (at Martello Point) that had proved particularly troublesome to the British navy. A self-contained, semi-self-sufficient defensive structure with thick walls and a protected entrance, the Martello design proved so successful that towers like this were built throughout the empire, only becoming obsolete in the 1870s with advances in artillery technology. Incidentally, on Christmas Day 1885, members of the Royal Canadian Rifles regiment set out to skid around the frozen lake equipped with their field **hockey sticks and a lacrosse ball**, thereby inventing the sport that has become a national passion/obsession.

Queen's University and the Agnes Etherington Art Centre

Striking inland up Barrie Street, with City Park on the right, it's a ten-minute walk to the top of the park, where the **Frontenac County Courthouse** of 1858 is another grand limestone pile whose whopping Neoclassical portico is fronted by a fanciful water fountain and surmounted by a copper dome. Head west from here, along Union Street, and you'll soon be in the midst of the **Queen's University campus**, whose various sturdy stone college buildings fan out in all directions. The place to aim for is the first-rate **Agnes Etherington Art Centre**, on the corner of University Avenue and Queen's Crescent (Tues–Fri 10am–4.30pm, Sat & Sun 1–5pm; $4; Ⓦwww.aeac.ca). The gallery has an excellent reputation for its temporary exhibitions, so paintings are regularly rotated, but the first room (Room 1) usually kicks off in dramatic style with a vivid selection of Canadian Abstract paintings (1940–60), with French-speaking artists on one side and English-speaking artists on the other. Beyond, there is a strong showing for the **Group of Seven**, including a striking *Evening Solitude* by **Lawren Harris** and the carpet-like, rolling fields of **Lismer**'s *Québec Village*, while **Tom Thomson** weighs in with his studied *Autumn, Algonquin Park*. Other exhibits to look out for are the **Inuit** prints of Kenojuak and Pitseolak – two of the best-known Inuit artists of modern times – as well as heritage **quilts** from eastern Ontario, which date back to the 1820s.

West of the centre: Bellevue House

Born in Glasgow, **Sir John Alexander Macdonald** (1815–91) emigrated to Canada in his youth, settling in Kingston, where he became a successful corporate lawyer, an MP – representing the town for nearly forty years – and ultimately prime minister (1867–73 and 1887–91). A shrewd and forceful man, Macdonald played a leading role in Canada's Confederation, with a little arm-twisting here and a little charming there, to ensure the grand plan went through. In the 1840s, Macdonald rented **Bellevue House** (daily: April–May & Sept–Oct 10am–5pm; June–Aug 9am–6pm; $3.95; Ⓦwww.pc.gc.ca), a bizarrely asymmetrical, pagoda-shaped building located about 2km to the west of the city centre, beyond the university campus, at 35 Centre St. The idea was that the country air would improve the health of Macdonald's wife, Isabella, whose tuberculosis was made worse by the treatment – laudanum. Isabella never returned to good health and died after years as an invalid, leaving Macdonald alone (with the bottle). Both the house and gardens have been restored to the period of the late 1840s, when the Macdonalds lived here.

East of the centre: Fort Henry and Fort Frederick

The twin headlands over the Lasalle Causeway to the east of downtown Kingston have long been used by the military. The first is home to the **Royal**

Military College, the training academy for officers of all three services; the second to **Fort Henry** (late May to Sept daily 10am–5pm; $11; programme info on ⓣ613/542-7388, ⓦwww.forthenry.com), a large and imposing fortress built to keep the Americans at bay after the War of 1812. The fort's thick stone-and-earth ramparts are flush with the lie of the land to protect against artillery bombardment, but as it turned out it was all a waste of time and money. Anglo-American relations improved and the fort never saw a shot fired in anger, so when the last garrison upped sticks at the end of the nineteenth century, the fortress fell into disrepair. Restored in 1938, the fort's focus is now the large **parade ground**, where students periodically dress up in military gear and fill the fort with the smoke of muskets and cannons and the racket of bugles, drums and fifes. These period enactments are firmly aimed at families, and there's lots for kids to do, from joining in on drill parades and helping with the gun salute, to participating in lessons in a Victorian schoolroom and doing the laundry. If this doesn't appeal you can explore the ramparts, with their vistas of Lake Ontario and the Thousand Islands, and examine the fort's magazines, kitchens and officers' quarters. Proto-militarists can also double their fun by visiting the **RMC Museum** (Royal Military College Museum; July & Aug daily 10am–5pm; donation; ⓦwww.rmc.ca) in Fort Frederick, a Martello tower on the more westerly headland, which is stuffed with military bric-a-brac.

Eating and drinking

For a city its size, Kingston has a good supply of quality **restaurants** and a wide range of inexpensive **cafés**, many of which prosper from its large student population. The city also has several lively British- and Irish-style **pubs** and a modest live music scene: for **listings**, see the bi-monthly freebie *Key to Kingston*, available from major hotels, restaurants and the tourist office.

Cafés and restaurants

Chez Piggy 68 Princess St at King St East ⓣ613/549-7673. Kingston's best restaurant is housed in restored stables dating from 1810. The patio is packed in summer and the attractive interior has handcrafted pine and limestone walls. The wide-ranging menu features all manner of main courses, from Thai and Vietnamese through to South American and standard North American dishes. Main courses average around $20. Mon–Sat 11.30am–11.30pm, Sun 11am–10pm.

Curry Village 169A Princess St ⓣ613/542-5010. Popular, reasonably priced Indian restaurant above a shoe shop. Just north of Bagot St. Reservations recommended; mains from as little as $8. Mon–Fri 11.30am–2pm & 5–10pm, Sat & Sun 2-9pm.

Le Chien Noir 69 Brock St ⓣ613/549-5635. Spirited bar-cum-bistro with smart, modern decor and a fancy – some would say over-elaborate – menu featuring some unusual combinations. Main courses average around $20. Mon–Sat 11am–10pm

Minos Restaurant 248 Ontario St at Brock ⓣ613/548-4654. All the Greek favourites at this long-established downtown restaurant. Don't be deterred by the ugliness of the building. Main courses $10–20. Mon–Fri 4.30–10pm & Sun 5–9pm, closed Sat.

Second Cup 251 Princess St. Downtown branch of this reliable Canadian coffee-house chain. Daily 7am–11pm.

The Sleepless Goat Café 91 Princess St at Wellington. Laid-back bakery-cum-café serving good sandwiches, delicious breads and rolls, and great desserts, all at affordable prices. Fair trade coffee – and a workers' co-operative to boot. Mon–Fri 7am–11pm, Sat & Sun 8am–11pm.

White Mountain Ice-Cream 176 Ontario St. Seriously rich home-made ice cream and waffle cones. Try the White Mountain special – vanilla dotted with chocolate, pecan and maple brittle. Yum, yum.

Windmills Café 184 Princess St at Montréal. Good cakes and a wide-ranging menu at this agreeable café-restaurant, which serves up everything from tapas and pizzas to salads and noodles. Inexpensive. Daily 8am–10pm.

Kingston to Ottawa via the Rideau Canal

Heading on **from Kingston to Ottawa**, the obvious route is east along Hwy 401 and then north up Hwy 416, a fast journey of 175km. With more time, however, it's worth considering taking **Hwy 15** and then, at Smiths Falls, **Hwy 43** (and ultimately hwys 2, 5, 13 and 73) inland from Kingston as these minor roads follow much of the route of the **Rideau Canal** (mid-May to mid-Oct; www.pc.gc.ca). Completed in 1832 after a mere six years' work, the 202-km canal – and its 27 lock stations – cuts through the slab of coniferous and deciduous forest, bogs, limestone plains and granite ridges that separate Ottawa and Kingston. It was intended to provide safe inland transport at a time of poor Anglo-American relations, but after the political situation improved it developed as an important route for regional commerce. The canal's construction led to the development of **Bytown**, renamed Ottawa in 1855, but in the second half of the nineteenth century the railways made it obsolete. Today, it is plied by holiday traffic and motorists visit its **locks**. The two most interesting are **Kingston Mills** (Locks 46–49), 12km inland from Kingston on Hwy 15, and, even better, **Jones Falls** (Locks 39–42), about 50km from Kingston. At the latter, the complex includes four locks, a dam, a former blacksmith's forge and a defensible lockmaster's house.

To break the journey, aim for the pleasant little canalside town of **MERRICKVILLE** (Locks 21–23), 100km or so from Kingston. A popular tourist spot, there are several places to stay here, including *Sam Jakes Inn*, which occupies a good-looking Victorian building with thirty guest rooms at 118 Main St East (613/269-3711 or 1-800/567-4667, www.samjakesinn.com; ⑥). The *Nicholson House B&B* is in an attractive old building with spick and span period decor – and five en suite guest rooms – 4km north of Merrickville at 378 Heritage Drive (613/866-5971, www.bbcanada.com/2202.html; ④). Alternatively, it takes five days to get from Kingston to Ottawa **by boat** on the Rideau Canal with Ontario Waterways (705/327-5767 or 1-800/561-5767, www.ontariowaterwaycruises.com) at a cost of $1500; there are between three and six cruises monthly from mid-May to mid-October and advance reservations are essential.

Pubs

Kingston Brewing Company 34 Clarence St. The best pub in town, serving natural ales and lagers brewed on the premises, as well as tasty bar food. Cosy premises and outside patio area too.

Prince George Hotel 200 Ontario St. Opposite the tourist office, the ground floor of this old inn is subdivided into three bars. There's *Tir Nan Óg*, an Irish pub with Irish brews, *Monte's Lounge*, which specializes in Belgian beers and cocktails, and the English-style *Old Speckled Hen*.

The Toucan 76 Princess St 613/544-1966. Student pub with excellent live music from blues to traditional Irish, and also filling bar food. Guinness is their speciality. Till 2am nightly.

The upper St Lawrence River

To the east of Kingston, Hwy 401 and the prettier Hwy 2 strip along the northern shore of the **St Lawrence River**, whose island-studded waters were tricky-going until the 1950s when the US and Canadian governments created the **St Lawrence Seaway**. An extraordinarily ambitious project, the Seaway extends 3790km inland from the Atlantic by means of lakes, rivers and locks to the west end of Lake Superior. Fifteen locks were installed on the St Lawrence alone, each big enough to handle massive ocean-going freighters, whilst a string of dams harnessed the river's hydroelectric potential. But it all came at a price: the Seaway necessitated the relocation of many riverside towns, a process which one local newspaper bewailed with the headline "once again another patch of Ontario is sicklied o'er with the pale cast of progress". There were long-term **environmental** costs, too, with the ships transporting species previously unknown here on their hulls and in their bilge. What's more, the Seaway has been something of a flop, its decline directly related to the move towards road and air.

Leaving Kingston, **Highway 2** begins by cutting across rolling farmland and offering fleeting views of the region's scenic highlight, the **Thousand Islands**. Native Canadians called these tiny, lightly forested granite chunks Manitouana – the "Garden of the Great Spirit" – in the belief they were created when petals of heavenly flowers were scattered on the river; more prosaically the islands later gave their name to a salad dressing. Geologically, they form part of the Frontenac axis, a ridge of million-year-old rock that stretches down into New York State. The islands are seen to best advantage on a **cruise** and these are available at most riverside towns, including Kingston (see p.170), though those from **Gananoque** are often rated the best. In themselves, the towns that dot the river are not especially enthralling – the pick is probably low-key **Prescott** – and this is especially true as the varied charms of Ottawa (see p.180) are within easy distance: from Kingston to Ottawa is only 175km. The most scenic part of the drive is along the **Thousand Islands Parkway**, a 40km stretch of Hwy 2 beginning just to the east of Gananoque where the road is shadowed by a combined cycle and footpath.

There are fast and frequent **Greyhound** (Ⓣ1-800/661-8747, Ⓦwww.greyhound.ca) and **Coach Canada buses** (Ⓣ1-800/461-7661, Ⓦwww.coachcanada.com) along Hwy 401 and VIA **trains** (Ⓣ1-888/842-7245, Ⓦwww.viarail.ca) shadow the north bank of the river too, on their way from Kingston to Montréal or Ottawa via Brockville.

Gananoque

Workaday **GANANOQUE**, some 30km east of Kingston, doesn't have too much going for it, but it does offer several Thousand Islands boat cruises. The **Thousand Islands** first hit the headlines in the late 1830s, when they were the haunt of an irascible Canadian pirate, one William Johnston, whose irritation with the British prompted him and his gang to spend several years harrying British shipping and Canadian farmers until he retired (with his booty) to New York state. Thereafter, the islands became a popular retreat for the rich and famous – Irving Berlin and Jack Dempsey, to name but two – but it was George Boldt, the owner of New York's *Waldorf Astoria*, who outdid himself. In 1899, he bought one of the islands and reshaped it into a heart as a tribute to his wife – hence the name Heart Island. He then plonked the whopping, $2m, pseudo-medieval **Boldt Castle** on top of his island (mid-May to June & Sept to mid-Oct daily 10am–6.30pm, July & Aug daily 10am–7.30pm; US$5.75; Ⓦwww.boldtcastle.com), but promptly abandoned it when his wife died, taking his new salad-dressing recipe back with him to New York.

In Gananoque, the main **cruise boat** operator is Gananoque Boat Line (Ⓣ613/382-2144 or 1-888/717-4837, Ⓦwww.ganboatline.com), which runs one-hour (May to mid-Oct 3–6 daily; $17) and three-hour (May to mid-Oct 3–6 daily; $24) excursions out into the Thousand Islands. Highlights of the longer cruise include a good look at Just Room Enough Island, with its single tiny home, and, at the other extreme, Millionaire's Row on Wellesley Island. The same company also does five-hour cruises (mid-May to late Sept 1 daily; $27, but castle extra), which include a two-hour overlay at Boldt Castle; note that the castle is over the international frontier in US waters, so Canadians and US citizens need proof of citizenship and everyone else needs a **passport**.

Rockport and Brockville

Moving on from Gananoque, it's a pleasant 25km drive east via the leafy **Thousand Islands Parkway** to tiny **ROCKPORT**, the nearest Canadian dock to Boldt Castle. Rockport Boat Line, 23 Front St (ⓣ613/659-3402 or 1-800/563-8687, ⓦwww.rockportcruises.com; late May to late June Sat & Sun 1 daily; late June to Aug 1 daily; Sept to early Oct Wed–Sun 1 daily; $18), does the nautical honours.

From Rockport, it's another short hop to **BROCKVILLE**, a substantial little town that takes its name from the Canadian general Isaac Brock, who was killed near Niagara Falls during the War of 1812. Brockville was at its busiest in the second half of the nineteenth century, when it became a prosperous river port and holding station for thousands of immigrants, who were temporarily detained here in enormous sheds on the waterfront Hospital Island. Today the town centre is somewhat careworn, but the harbourfront is pleasant enough and the **main square** remains suitably commanding, fanning out from an ambitious war memorial. The square is flanked by sturdy stone buildings, notably the neo-Romanesque pinkish former **post office** and, at the top, the rambling Neoclassical **County Courthouse** to either side of which are no less than three good-looking Victorian **churches**. The other Victorian building of note is **Fulford Place**, east of the centre at 287 King St East (guided tours: June–Aug Tues–Sun 11am–4pm; Sept–May Sat & Sun 11am–4pm; $5; ⓣ613/498-3003), a vast mansion built in lavish style for George Taylor Fulford, who made his fortune with a cure-all remedy that he marketed brilliantly as "Pink Pills for Pale People". Nevertheless, most visitors skip the architecture in favour of a Thousand Islands **cruise** with Brockville's 1000 Islands Seaway Cruises (ⓣ613/345-7333 or 1-800/353-3157, ⓦwww.1000islandscruises.com). They provide one-hour (early May Mon–Fri 1 daily; late May to June Sat & Sun 2 daily; July & Aug 1 daily; Sept to late Oct 1–4 daily; $14) and three-hour (late May to mid-Sept Sat & Sun 1–2 daily; $24) excursions, which sail west to cover pretty much the same itinerary as boats departing Gananoque.

Prescott

Pocket-sized **PRESCOTT**, trailing along the riverside some 20km east of Brockville, was rendered well-nigh obsolete by the St Lawrence Seaway, but previously it had been important as a deep-water port and trans-shipment centre. Beside Hwy 2 on the east side of town, the crumbling, dark-black **timbers** of the old town jetty that poke up out of the water and the imposing bulk of **Fort Wellington** (mid-May to Sept daily 10am–5pm; $4; ⓦwww.pc.gc.ca) recall busier days. Work started on the fort in 1812 during the Anglo-American war, but by the time it was finished the war was over. There was another spurt of (fairly fruitless) imperial activity after the Upper Canada Rebellion of 1837, when the British strengthened the earthen ditches and ramparts surrounding the fort and placed a set of military buildings in the middle. These included a two-storey blockhouse-cum-barracks, an officers' quarters, powder magazine and a cookhouse. The military moved out in 1869 and, after years of neglect, the fort has been returned to its 1830s appearance, complete with a miscellany of period furnishings and fittings.

The Americans never attacked Fort Wellington, but it did serve as the muster station for the militia in the lead-up to the **Battle of the Windmill** in 1838. In the aftermath of the shambolic Upper Canada Rebellion, hundreds of refugee rebels took off into the Ontario bush or fled to the US. One of the larger groups hunkered down in the Thousand Islands and, together with their American sympathizers, planned an attack on Canada, hoping that this would stir a general rebellion. Two hundred of them landed beside a stone windmill 2km east of Prescott, but there was no widespread uprising and the invaders ended up occupying the windmill instead. Here, the militia surrounded them and eventually – after a dogged fight – they were forced to surrender: eleven were executed and most of the rest were transported to Australia. The **windmill**, which later became a lighthouse, has survived and makes for a pleasant, albeit brief, excursion – it's signed from Hwy 2.

Prescott has one excellent **place to stay**, the *Blue Heron Inn*, just west of the handful of shops that passes for the town centre at 1648 Hwy 2 (Ⓣ613/925 0562, Ⓦwww.blueheroninn.on.ca; ④). Occupying an attractively revamped old stone house, the inn has two well appointed en-suite guest rooms decorated in attractive, unfussy style and the breakfasts are first rate. For **food**, try the *Blue Stone Café* (Ⓣ613/925-0255), just off the main drag, where a simple but tasty range of pasta dishes are served and main courses average $13. Opening times vary, especially out of season, so ring ahead to confirm.

Heading east from Prescott, it's just 5km to **JOHNSTOWN**, where there's a **choice of routes**: the bridge leads south over the river to the US; Hwy 416 cuts north to Ottawa and Hwy 401 ploughs on east along the riverside, passing the Upper Canada Village on its way to Montréal (see p.235).

Upper Canada Village

In the 1950s, the construction of the St Lawrence Seaway raised the river level, threatening many of the old buildings that dotted the river bank. The best were painstakingly relocated to a purpose-built complex some 40km east of Prescott, creating the **Upper Canada Village** (late May to early Oct daily 9.30am–5pm; $17; Ⓦwww.uppercanadavillage.com), one of the region's most popular attractions. Covering a sixty-acre site, the village re-creates rural Ontario life as of 1860 and contains a wide range of buildings, from farmhouses and farm outhouses to a bakery, a parsonage, a church, a wool factory, a saw mill and a blacksmiths. It is all very well done and the staff dress up in period gear to demonstrate traditional skills, producing cheeses, quilts, brooms, bread and cloth in exactly the same way as their pioneer ancestors. Finally, in the adjacent riverside park is the **Battlefield Monument**, which – along with a visitor centre – commemorates the Battle of Crysler Farm in 1813, when a small force of British and Canadian soldiers drove off American invaders; Crysler Farm was itself submerged by the Seaway.

From the Village, it takes about an hour and a half to drive to Ottawa.

Ottawa

The capital of the second-biggest country on the planet, **OTTAWA** wrestles with its reputation as a bureaucratic labyrinth of little charm and character. The problem is that many Canadians who aren't federal employees – and even some who are – blame Ottawa for all the country's woes. All too aware of this, the Canadian government has spent lashings of dollars to turn Ottawa into "a city of urban grace in which all Canadians can take pride" (so the promotional literature runs) and despite the undoubted success of the policy, this very investment is often resented. The innate hostility is deeply rooted, dating back as far as 1857 when **Queen Victoria**, inspired by some genteel watercolours, declared Ottawa the capital, leaving Montréal and Toronto smarting at their rebuff.

In truth, Ottawa is neither grandiose nor tedious, but a lively cosmopolitan city of over one million inhabitants that boasts a clutch of outstanding **national museums**, a pleasant riverside setting and superb cultural facilities like the National Arts Centre. Throw in acres of parks and gardens, miles of bicycle and jogging paths, lots of good **hotels** and **B&Bs** and a busy **café-bar** and **restaurant** scene and you have enough to keep the most diligent sightseer going for a day or three, maybe more. It's here that Canada's bilingual laws make sense: French-speaking **Gatineau**, just across the river in Québec, is commonly lumped together with Ontario's Ottawa as the

Ottawa's festivals

Ottawa uses every excuse in the book to put on a **festival**. Federal funding ensures that national holidays – especially Canada Day – are celebrated in style, while seasonal shindigs like the Winterlude and the Canadian Tulip Festival are as lavish as any in the country. Ethnic festivals embracing the city's diverse population are smaller but equally entertaining and there's a wide variety of musical festivals too. The tourist office (see p.185) has the full calendar of events. The list below is arranged chronologically.

Winterlude ⓣ613/239-5000, ⓦwww.canadascapital.gc.ca/winterlude/. A ten-day snow-and-ice extravaganza spread over most of February. Concentrated around the frozen Rideau Canal, it includes ice sculptures at Confederation Park – renamed the Crystal Garden for the duration – and snow sculptures around Dows Lake. Other events include speed skating, bed- and dog-sled races.

Canadian Tulip Festival ⓣ613/567-4447 or 1-800/6688547, ⓦwww.tulipfestival.ca. Held over three weeks from early May, this is the oldest of Ottawa's festivals. It began in 1945 when the Dutch sent 100,000 tulip bulbs to the city both to honour those Canadian soldiers who had liberated the Netherlands and as a thank you for sheltering Queen Juliana, who had taken refuge in Ottawa during the war. The bulbs are planted around Parliament, along the canal and around Dows Lake, a gigantic splash of colour that's accompanied by concerts, parades, fireworks and a huge craft show. The major events take place in Major's Hill Park and Dows Lake – but few are free, and the festival now has a reputation for being rather touristy.

Franco-Ontarien Festival ⓣ613/321-0102, ⓦwww.ffo.ca. Held over three days in the middle of June, this joyous celebration of French culture features bands and street dancers.

Canada Day ⓣ613/239-5000. July 1, the country's national day, is celebrated with vim and gusto. Parades, processions and much flag waving are the hallmarks.

Ottawa Jazz Festival ⓣ613/241-2633 or 1-888/226-4495, ⓦwww.ottawajazzfestival.com. Late June. One of Ottawa's most popular festivals, showcasing more than 400 musicians. The main stage is in Confederation Park with concerts several times daily. In addition, local bands play around Byward Market and at city clubs.

Bluesfest ⓣ613/247-1188 or 1-866/258-3748, ⓦwww.ottawa-bluesfest.ca. Held over ten days in July, this is Canada's largest festival of blues and gospel with concerts held in various venues and free shows in Confederation Park.

Ottawa Chamber Music Festival ⓣ613/234-8008, ⓦwww.chamberfest.com. Late July to early Aug. North America's largest classical chamber music festival, with concerts in venues (and churches) across the city.

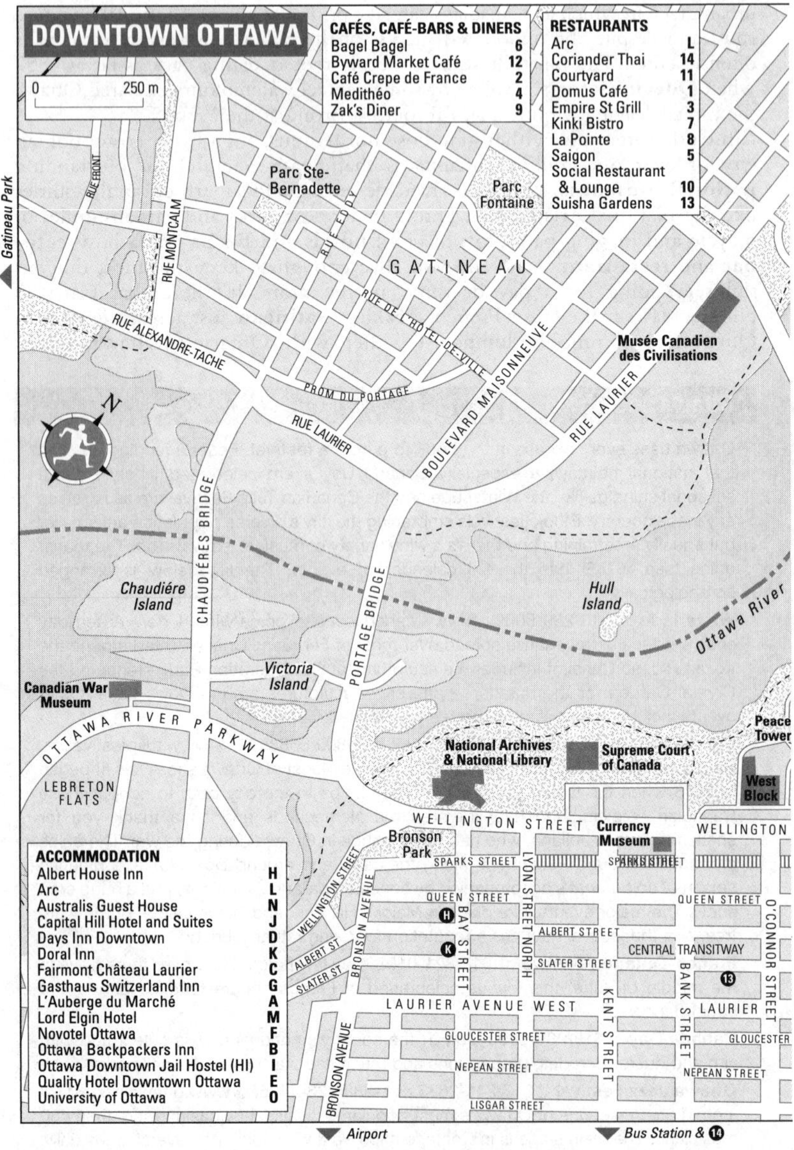

"Capital Region", and on the streets of Ottawa you'll hear as much French as English.

A brief history of Ottawa

The one-time hunting ground of the Algonkian-speaking Outaouais, **Ottawa** received its first recorded European visitor in 1613 in the shape of Samuel de Champlain. The French explorer pitched up, paused to watch his aboriginal

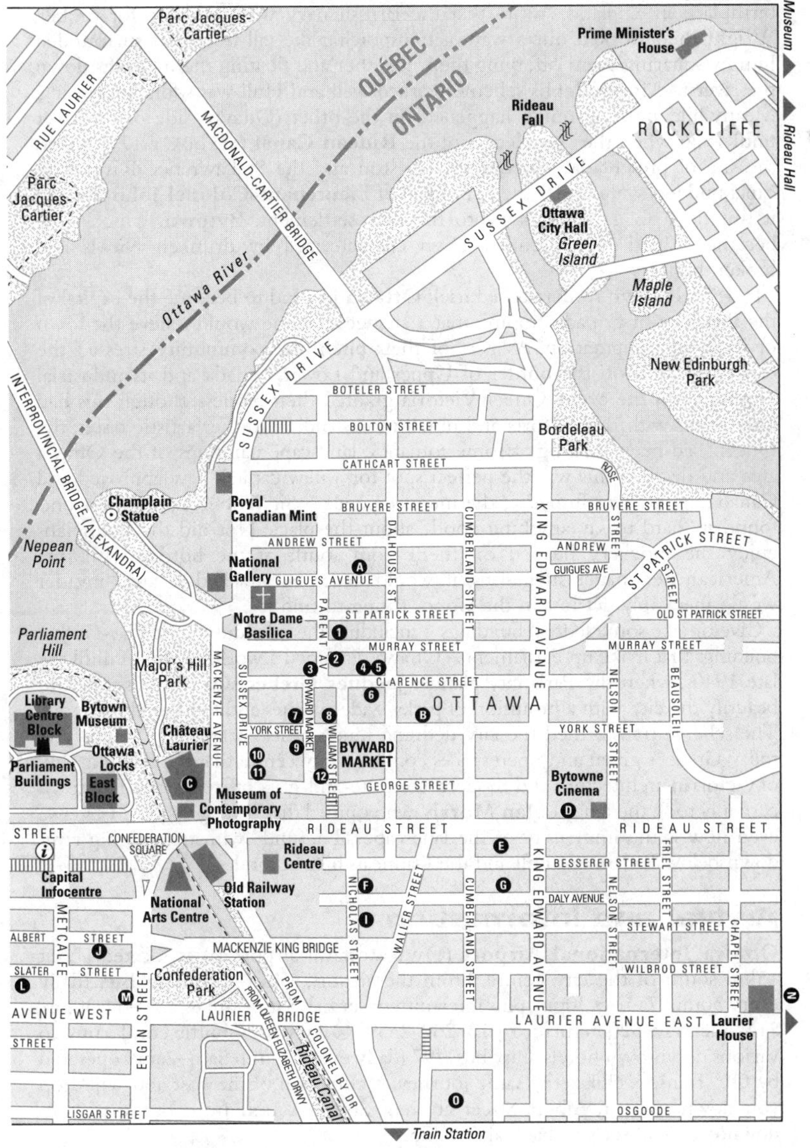

guides make offerings of tobacco to the misty falls which he christened Chaudière (French for "cauldron") and then took off in search of more appealing pastures. Later, the **Ottawa River** became a major transportation route, but the Ottawa area remained no more than a camping spot until 1800, when **Philemon Wright** snowshoed up here along the frozen Ottawa River from Massachusetts. Wright founded a small settlement, which he called Wrightstown and subsequently **Hull** (now **Gatineau**) after his parents' birthplace in England. Aware that the British navy was desperate for timber, Wright then worked out a way of transporting the tall trees that surrounded him by squaring them off, tying them together and floating them as rafts down the river to Montréal. His scheme worked well and Hull was soon flourishing. Meanwhile, nothing much happened on the other (Ottawa) side of the river until 1826 when the completion of the **Rideau Canal** (see box, p.177) linked the site of present-day Ottawa to Kingston and the St Lawrence River. The canal builders were under the command of **Lieutenant-Colonel John By** and it was he who gave his name to the new settlement, **Bytown**, which soon became a hard-edged lumber town characterized by drunken brawls and broken bones.

In 1855 Bytown re-christened itself **Ottawa** in a bid to become the capital of the Province of Canada, hoping that a change of name would relieve the town of its tawdry reputation. As part of their pitch, the community stressed the town's location on the border of Upper and Lower Canada and its industrial prosperity. In the event, Queen Victoria granted their request, though this had little to do with their efforts and much more to do with her artistic tastes: the Queen had been looking at some romantic landscape paintings of the Ottawa area and decided this was the perfect spot for a new capital. Few approved and Canada's politicians fumed at the inconvenience – Sir Wilfred Laurier, for one, found it "hard to say anything good" about the place. Nor did the politicians enjoy the mockery heaped on them from south of the border with one American newspaper suggesting it would never be attacked as any "invader would inevitably get lost in the woods trying to find it".

Give or take some federal buildings – including the splendid trio of neo-Gothic buildings that make up Parliament – Ottawa remained a workaday town until the late 1940s, when the Paris city planner **Jacques Greber** was commissioned to beautify the city with a profusion of parks, wide avenues and tree-lined pathways. The scheme transformed the city, defining much of its current appearance, and today Greber's green and open spaces confine a city centre that is a fetching mix of Victorian architecture and modern concrete-and-glass office blocks. The town certainly took the fancy of **Jan Morris**, who opined that "ever palpable in Ottawa even now is the immensity of the landscape all around" with the surging river down below Parliament Hill and the Gatineau hills beyond.

Arrival and information

Ottawa International Airport (Ⓦwww.ottawa-airport.ca) is located about 15km south of the city centre. From the airport, a **hotel shuttle bus** (daily every 30min 7am–5.30pm, plus intermittent service 5am–7am & 5.30–11.30pm; $14 one-way, $20 return; Ⓣ613/260-2359, Ⓦwww.yowshuttle.com) runs to various downtown hotels. City bus #97 (daily every 20min 5am–2am), operated by OC Transpo, makes the same journey at a fraction of the cost and will drop you downtown on Albert Street at Kent Street. A **taxi** from the airport to downtown will set you back about $25.

Ottawa's **VIA train station** (Ⓣ1-888/842-7245, Ⓦwww.viarail.ca) is on the southeastern outskirts of the city, about 4km from the centre, off the Queensway (Hwy 417) at 200 Tremblay Rd. There are direct VIA Rail services to and from Kingston, Montréal and Toronto. OC Transpo bus #95 goes downtown from the train station; the same journey by taxi costs about $15. Long-distance buses, including Greyhound (Ⓣ1-800/661-8747, Ⓦwww.greyhound.ca), use the **bus station**, 3km south of the city centre at 265 Catherine St and Kent, just off the Queensway (Hwy 417). Take OC Transpo bus #4 to get downtown.

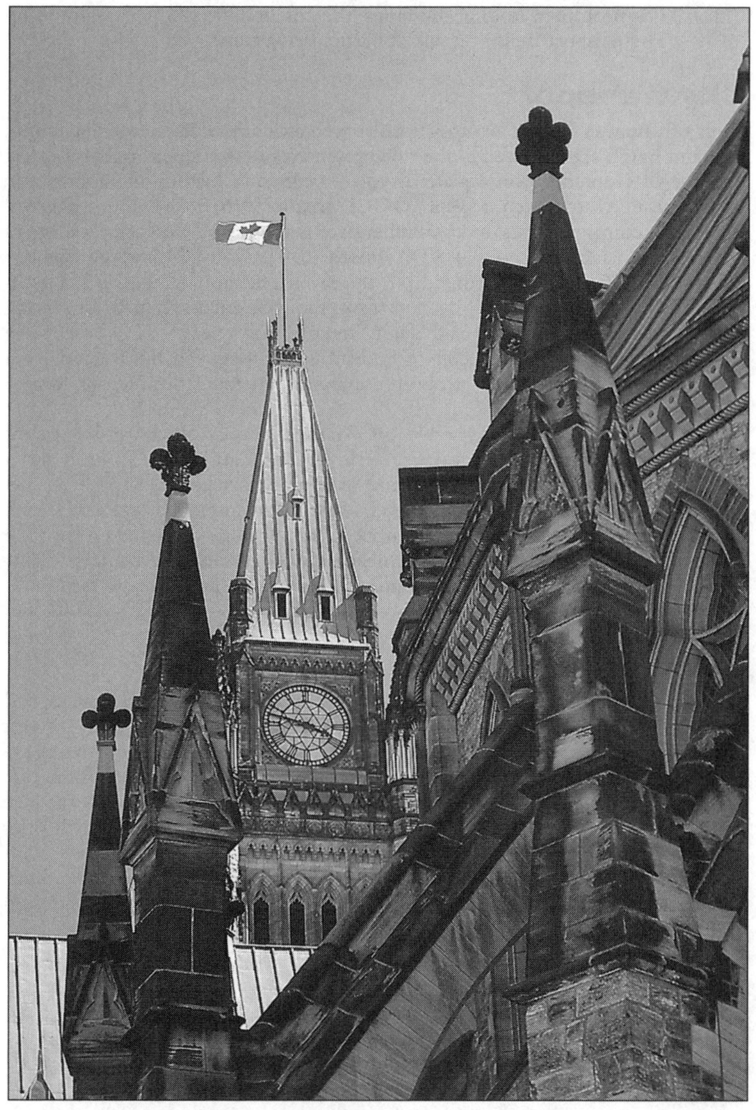

△ Parliament Building, Ottawa

The **Capital Infocentre**, 90 Wellington St at Metcalfe (daily: mid-May to Aug 8.30am–9pm; Sept to mid-May 9am–5pm; ⓣ613/239-5000 or 1-800/465-1867, ⓦwww.canadascapital.gc.ca), is handily located right opposite the Parliament Buildings. It's a busy place, but the staff will help you find accommodation and hand you masses of free literature, including a useful *Visitor Guide* plus city and public transport maps. They also sell the **Capital Museums Passport**, which is valid for seven days and allows the bearer free admission into

Ottawa/Gatineau's ten leading museums; the cost is $30 ($75 per family of up to five). The passport is also on sale at participating museums.

City transport

Most of Ottawa's important attractions as well as many of its better restaurants, bars and hotels are clustered in the downtown area within comfortable walking distance of Confederation Square. If you're venturing further afield, however, you may need to catch a **bus**. **OC Transpo** (Ⓣ613/741-4390, Ⓦwww.octranspo.com) provides a comprehensive network of bus services across Ottawa and its suburbs, while **STO buses** (Ⓣ819/770-3242, Ⓦwww.sto.ca) cover Gatineau and the north side of the river. The hub of the OC Transpo system is the **Transitway**, which runs from the Mackenzie King Bridge along Albert Street (one-way west) and Slater Street (one-way east). STO buses leave for Gatineau from the west end of Rideau Street, between Sussex and King Edward Avenue. Key buses with both companies operate from 5am or 6am to around midnight daily.

Ticket prices are very reasonable. OC Transpo tickets, which can be bought at corner stores, the tourist office and many hotels, cost just $0.95 each and a standard single fare within the city limits (costing two tickets) is $1.80 – a good bit more if you pay cash to the driver (exact fare only). A **DayPass**, which allows unlimited travel on the OC Transpo system for one day, costs $7. If you're travelling on an ordinary ticket and need to change buses to complete your journey, ask for a free transfer at the point of embarkation. There are **taxi** ranks outside major hotels and nightspots.

Accommodation

As the federal honeypot, Ottawa hosts dozens of business conferences and conventions, and consequently, although there are hundreds of rooms in the city, things can still get tight – with **hotel** prices rising accordingly. At other times – especially when parliament is in recess and at the weekend – it's much more of a buyer's market and even the poshest hotels offer big discounts. That said, the best bet for a reasonably priced room is in an **inn or B&B**, the pick of which offer prime lodgings close to the centre. The tourist office (see p.185) will assist with finding accommodation, though note that staff won't actually make a booking. The cheapest beds in town are at two **hostels**, both of which are open year-round and right downtown, and there are inexpensive **student rooms** too.

Hotels, inns and motels

Albert House Inn 478 Albert St at Bay Ⓣ613/236-4479 or 1-800/267-1982, Ⓦwww.albertinn.com. Occupying a good-looking Victorian villa with a sweeping portico, this inn has seventeen en-suite guest rooms, each of which is pleasantly furnished. Full breakfast included. Light sleepers may prefer the rooms at the back, away from busy Albert St. ❺

Arc 140 Slater St Ⓣ613/238-2888 or 1-800/699-2516, Ⓦwww.arcthehotel.com. Immaculate, medium-sized designer hotel with minimalist decor and a sharp decorative theme. The guest rooms are kitted out in style, too, all wood and leather with Egyptian cotton sheets. ❼

Capital Hill Hotel and Suites 88 Albert St Ⓣ613/235-1413 or 1-800/463-7705, Ⓦwww.capitalhill.com. This smart, high-rise hotel is furnished in brisk, modern style and all 150 rooms are spacious and comfortable. Handy downtown location, just off Confederation Square. Very competitive prices. ❺

Days Inn Downtown 319 Rideau St Ⓣ613/789-5555 or 1-800/329-7466, Ⓦwww.daysinn.com. Nothing special, perhaps, but this reliable chain motel offers good quality accommodation at reasonable prices downtown. ❺

Fairmont Château Laurier 1 Rideau St Ⓣ613/241-1414 or 1-800/257-7544,

ⓦwww.fairmont.com. This superb hotel, Ottawa's finest, has pretty much everything. It was opened in 1912 as a prestige railway hotel for the Grand Trunk Pacific Railway, whose president, Charles Hayes, lavished millions on its construction. A fine example of the French Renaissance – or château – style, the exterior is a forest of copper-clad turrets, spires and towers. Inside, the grand public areas boast marble floors, high ceilings, chandeliers and soaring columns, plus extravagantly embossed lifts. The rooms themselves are not quite as grand, but they are thoroughly comfortable and the best offer delightful views over the river. ❼

Lord Elgin Hotel 100 Elgin St at Laurier Ave West ⓣ613/235-3333 or 1-800/267-4298, ⓦwww.lordelginhotel.ca. Occupying a fine château-style-meets-Art-Deco 1940s high-rise close to Confederation Square, this classy hotel has comfortable rooms decked out with crisp, modern furnishings. Reasonable prices and discounts on the weekend. ❻

Novotel Ottawa 33 Nicholas St ⓣ613/230-3033 or 1-800/668-6835, ⓦwww.novotelottawa.com. This hotel doesn't win any beauty contests – it's overshadowed by a hulking brick high-rise – but the public areas are done out in sharp, modernistic style and the 280 rooms are tastefully and cheerfully decorated; the service is excellent too. Downtown location. ❻

Quality Hotel Downtown Ottawa 290 Rideau St ⓣ613/789-7511 or 1-800/424-6423, ⓦwww.choicehotels.ca. Spick-and-span modern, chain hotel in a handy downtown location. ❻

B&Bs

Australis Guest House 35 Marlborough Ave ⓣ613/235-8461, ⓦwww.bbcanada.com/1463.html. Straightforward B&B with three rooms in a 1920s detached house about 2km southeast of Parliament Hill. Price includes full breakfast. ❸

Gasthaus Switzerland Inn 89 Daly Ave at Cumberland ⓣ613/237-0335 or 1-888/663-0000, ⓦwww.gasthausswitzerlandinn.com. Twenty-two, pleasant en-suite rooms in this long-established, three-storey inn. Central location and good (Swiss-style) breakfasts, but the streets nearby are seedy. ❻

L'Auberge du Marché 87 Guigues Ave ⓣ613/241-6610 or 1-800/465-0079, ⓦwww.aubergedumarche.ca. In the heart of Byward Market, this extremely appealing B&B occupies an unassuming two-storey nineteenth-century brick house, whose interior has been renovated in sympathetic style. Often full, the very popular B&B has four air-conditioned bedrooms, with shared facilities, and serves great breakfasts too. ❸

Hostels

Ottawa Backpackers Inn 203 York St ⓣ613/241-3402 or 1-888/394-0334, ⓦwww.ottawahostel.com. Spartan, medium-sized hostel in the Byward Market area. Self-catering facilities, Internet access and linen supplied (free). Thirty two beds, mostly in four-, six- and eight-bed dormitories at $22 per person per night. Doubles cost $65. ❶–❸

Ottawa Downtown Jail Hostel (HI) 75 Nicholas St at Daly ⓣ613/235-2595 or 1-866/299-1478, ⓦwww.hihostels.ca. Stay in cells complete with bars on the windows in Ottawa's converted nineteenth-century jail. The old admissions area is now a kitchen, but Death Row remains the same with its 1m-by-2m cells. There are a few single and double rooms, but most of the 150-odd beds are in four-, five- and six-bed rooms, costing $27 per person per night, non-members $32. The hostel is handily located downtown, just south of Rideau Street's Rideau Shopping Centre. Advance reservations strongly recommended. ❶–❸

Student rooms

University of Ottawa 100 University St ⓣ613/562-5771, ⓦwww.uottawa.ca. From May–Aug, student rooms in the Stanton Residence, on the University of Ottawa campus off Nicolas St, are rented out to visitors. Double rooms cost $60, singles $40 ($46/30 for students). The campus has sports and laundry facilities, a pool and café and is located about 1km southeast of Parliament Hill. ❶–❸

The City

Ottawa's major sights are clustered on the steep south bank of the Ottawa River to either side of the Rideau Canal. It's here you'll find the monumental Victorian architecture of **Parliament Hill**, the outstanding art collection of the **National Gallery**, the military memorabilia of the **Canadian War Museum**, the imposing **Notre Dame Basilica** and **Byward Market**, the hub of the restaurant and bar scene. Many visitors only cover these, but there are a clutch of other, lesser attractions too, beginning with the **Laurier House**, packed with the possessions of the former prime minister William Lyon Mackenzie King and located 2km or so east of downtown. Northeast of the centre, on the far side of the Rideau River, is the ritzy suburb of **Rockcliffe**, home to both the governor-general's mansion, **Rideau Hall**, and the **Canada Aviation Museum**.

Parliament Hill

Perched on the limestone bluff of Parliament Hill, high above the Ottawa River, Canada's handsome **Parliament Buildings** (Ⓣ613/239-5000, Ⓦwww.parl.gc.ca) have, with their spires, pointed windows and soaring clock tower, a distinctly ecclesiastical air – "a stupendous splodge of Victoriana" as Jan Morris put it, though they certainly didn't overawe the original workmen, who urinated on the copper roof to speed up the oxidization process. Comprising a trio of sturdy neo-Gothic structures, the complex was begun in 1859 after the land was purchased from the British army, who had erected a barracks here during the construction of the Rideau Canal. **Centre Block** (guided tours when parliament is in session: mid-May to Aug Mon–Thurs 9am–12.50pm & 3.30–7.20pm, Fri 9.20–9.50am & 12.50–7.20pm, Sat & Sun 9am–4.20pm; Sept to mid-May Mon–Thurs 9.20am–12.50pm, Fri 9.20–9.50am & 12.50–3.20pm, Sat & Sun 9.20am–3.20pm; when parliament is not in session: mid-May to Aug Mon–Fri 9am–7.20pm, Sat & Sun 9am–4.20pm; Sept to mid-May daily 9.20am–3.20pm; free), home of the Senate and the House of Commons, dominates proceedings, though it is actually a replacement for the original building, which was destroyed by fire in 1916. This second structure was supposed to be the same as its predecessor, but it ended up about twice the size. The **Peace Tower**, rising from the middle of the facade, was added in 1927 as a memorial to Canadians who served in World War I. Highlights of the guided tour – though itineraries do change - include a quick gambol round the **House of Commons**, where the Speaker's chair is made of English oak from Westminster Hall and from Nelson's flagship *Victory*, and the red-carpeted **Senate** with its murals of scenes from World War I surmounted by a beautiful gilded ceiling. At the back of the Centre Block is the **Library**, the only part of the building to have survived the fire of 1916; the circular design and the richly carved wooden galleries make this the most charming part of the building. The **debates** in both the House of Commons and the Senate are open to the public, who can observe proceedings from the visitors' galleries. Passes are required and are issued by security at the main Peace Tower entrance. Parliament's liveliest debates are held during **Question Period**, when the Opposition interrogates the Prime Minister; call ahead (Ⓣ613/239-5000) for details as to what is being debated when.

Flanking Centre Block are **West Block** (no public access) and **East Block** (July & Aug daily 10am–5pm; free), where the guided tour pops into four Confederation-era rooms: the original governor general's office, the offices of Sir John A. Macdonald and Sir George Étienne Cartier, and the Privy Council Chamber. Costumed guides provide the history. The manicured lawns surrounding the Parliament Buildings are dotted with **statues** of the great and the good with two of the more interesting occupying a tiny hillock just to the west of Centre Block. Here, **Queen Victoria** has been stuck on a plinth guarded by a lion and offered laurels from below, whilst **Lester Pearson** (Prime

Parliament Hill tickets

In the summer, tickets for guided tours of Centre Block are available at the **Info-Tent** (mid-May to late June daily 9am–5pm; late June to early Sept Mon–Fri 9am–8pm, Sat & Sun 9am–5pm), which is erected behind West Block and to the left of Centre Block every year. From early September to mid-May, head instead for the Visitor Welcome Centre at the base of the Peace Tower.

Minister 1963–68) lounges in an armchair, the epitome of the self-confident statesman. Round the back of Centre Block there are pleasant views across the Ottawa River to Gatineau (see p.195) and of the Library's handsome design.

Two events pull the tourist crowds onto Parliament Hill, beginning with the **Changing of the Guard**, when the Governor General's Foot Guards march onto the Hill dressed in full ceremonial uniform – bright-red tunics and bearskins (late June to late Aug daily between 10am and 10.30am). The second is a free summer-evening **sound and light show** (early July to early Sept), illustrating Canada's history with alternate French and English performances nightly.

Wellington Street and around

Behind West Block, in between the river and Wellington Street, are supplementary **federal buildings**, château-style monoliths with perky dormer windows and green-copper roofs that culminate in the **Supreme Court of Canada building**, a sturdy 1930s Art Nouveau edifice which blends in neatly with its neighbours. Turn inland from Wellington Street and you'll soon reach Sparks Street, where the **Sparks Street Mall** – one of the country's earliest pedestrianized shopping streets – runs from Confederation Square to Lyon Street. The design can't help but look a little jaded today, despite serious efforts to jazz it up, but the main reason to visit is the **Currency Museum**, 245 Sparks St (May–Sept Mon–Sat 10.30am–5pm, Sun 1–5pm; Oct–April Tues–Sat 10.30am–5pm, Sun 1–5pm; free), housed in the old HQ of the Bank of Canada. When it expanded the premises, the bank encased the original 1937 stone building within its new offices, which were themselves enclosed by two green-glass towers with an indoor jungle-like garden court. Within the garden, in front of the museum, is a huge Yap stone, a symbol of wealth in the South Pacific; such stones usually remain at the bottom of the sea, their possession simply changing hands among the islanders by agreement. Inside, the museum focuses on Canadian currencies, from the small beads and shells known as wampum to playing cards, beaver pelts and modern banknotes.

Confederation Square and the Rideau Canal

The eastern end of the Sparks Street Mall empties into the triangular **Confederation Square**, a breezy open space dominated by the magnificent **National War Memorial**, in which a soaring stone arch is surmounted by representations of liberty and peace. Down below, a swirling, finely executed bronze of 1926 depicts returning service men and women passing through the arch – from war to peace – and manages to convey both their exultation and sorrow. On the southeast side of the square is the complex of low concrete buildings that houses the **National Arts Centre** (see p.198), which clunks down to the **Rideau Canal**, a narrow sliver of water that becomes the world's longest skating rink in winter, with hot chocolate and muffin stands warming everyone up. Opposite, across the canal, rise the stirring lines of

Ottawa's former **railway station**, a grand Beaux Arts edifice of 1911 that has now – rather sadly – been recycled as a conference centre.

Following the west side of the Rideau Canal north towards the Ottawa River, it only takes a minute or two to reach the pretty flight of **locks** that connects canal and river with Parliament Hill rising directly above. Beside the locks is the **Bytown Museum** (April to mid-May & mid-Oct to late Nov Mon–Fri 10am–2pm; mid-May to mid-Oct daily 10am–5pm; $5; Ⓦwww.bytownmuseum.com), Ottawa's oldest building, where military supplies were stored during the construction of the canal. Here, a short video display explains the history of the waterway, while the rest of the museum features assorted Ottawan memorabilia, including some of Colonel By's belongings. During the summer, **canal boat trips** leave from the top of the locks, **river trips** from the bottom. There are several operators, but Paul's Boat Lines (Ⓣ613/225-6781, Ⓦwww.paulsboatcruises.com) is as good as any, charging $16 for an hour-long canal cruise, $18 for the river. There are departures every couple of hours or so from May to October; reservations are advised.

The Museum of Contemporary Photography to Nepean Point

Doubling back from the Bytown Museum, climb up the steps to the **bridge** abutting Confederation Square and it's the briefest of strolls to the splendid *Château Laurier Hotel* (see p.186) and the adjacent **Canadian Museum of Contemporary Photography** (closed for refurbishment until further notice) whose collection of around 160,000 photographs is (usually) displayed in changing exhibitions.

From the *Château Laurier*, it's a brief walk east to **Sussex Drive**, whose southern section holds some of Ottawa's oldest buildings: the stone houses between George and St Patrick hark back to Ottawa's pioneer days and now house expensive shops and galleries. Nearby, **Major's Hill Park** rolls across a small hill above the Ottawa River. This was where Colonel By decided to build his house and the extant foundations bear a plaque attesting to its history. Major's Hill Park slopes down towards **Nepean Point**, a pint-sized headland that nudges out into the river bisected by the main road – and bridge – to Gatineau (see p.195). On the far side of the road a path climbs up the headland to an outside theatre and, at the tip, a statue of Champlain, from where there are wide river views. The statue is actually a foul-up: erected in 1915, Champlain holds his astrolabe – his navigational aid – aloft, but it is in fact upside down.

National Gallery of Canada

Back on Sussex Drive, the **National Gallery of Canada** (May–Sept daily 10am–5pm, Thurs till 8pm; Oct–April Tues–Sun 10am–5pm, Thurs till 8pm; $6, but free Thurs after 5pm; Ⓦwww.national.gallery.ca) occupies a cleverly conceived building whose acres of glass, designed by Moshe Safdie, reflect the turrets and pinnacles of Parliament Hill. The collection was founded in 1880 by the Marquis of Lorne, then the governor general, who persuaded each member of the Royal Canadian Academy to donate a painting or two. Over the next century artworks were gathered from all over the world, resulting in a permanent collection that now numbers more than 25,000 pieces – too many to be exhibited at any one time. This means that the exhibits are rotated, so although the paintings mentioned below will probably be on display, there are no guarantees. The National Gallery also holds world-class **temporary exhibitions** for which an extra admission fee is usually charged. The collection spreads over two levels and **free plans** are issued at the reception desk; the gallery shop sells useful guides to both the permanent collection and the exhibitions.

The Canadian galleries – early days

The **Canadian** galleries, laid out in roughly chronological order on Level 1, are the finest in the building, following the history of Canadian painting from the mid-eighteenth century to modern times. They begin with religious art from Québec, including a flashy gilded high altar by Paul Jourdain, followed by a room showing the emergence of secular art in the early nineteenth century, with paintings by immigrant artists trained in Europe. The most notable of these was **Joseph Légaré** (1795-1855), who was not only a painter but also a politician and nationalist – his *Cholera Plague, Québec* is a fine example of his fastidiously romantic work. For popularity, though, none could match **Cornelius Krieghoff** (1815-72), who could turn his hand to anything requested by his middle class patrons – as illustrated by his *Winter Landscape* and *White Horse Inn by Moonlight*. Close by is the gallery's most unusual exhibit, the **Rideau Street Chapel**, rebuilt piece by intricate piece after it was threatened with demolition in 1972. Designed in 1887 by the architect and priest Canon Georges Bouillon for a convent school in Ottawa, it has slender cast-iron columns supporting a fan-vaulted ceiling – one of the few examples of its kind in North America. Contained in the chapel is a modest collection of ecclesiastical silverware and mawkish wooden sculptures from Québec.

Moving on, a small collection of early nineteenth-century paintings from the Maritimes and Ontario kicks off with John Poad Drake's *Port of Halifax* and **John O'Brien**'s (1831-91) dramatic depiction of a storm-tossed frigate. The native population makes an appearance too in the evocative portraits of **Paul Kane** (1810-71), Canada's first artist-explorer. Also here is the unique **Croscup Parlour** from Nova Scotia. Once the living room of a shipping family, it is covered in murals that juxtapose images from mid-nineteenth-century North America and Europe – portraits of Micmac Indians next to bagpipe-playing Scots and so forth.

The Canadian galleries – 1880s to 1960s

In the second half of the nineteenth century, the construction of the railroads made it much easier for artists to explore the wilder reaches of Canada, a development encapsulated by **Lucius O'Brien**'s (1832-1899) *Sunrise on the Saguenay* of 1880. However, painters of this period were still in thrall to European masters – the Royal Canadian Academy of Arts sent its students to Paris to complete their training – and this state of affairs continued into the twentieth century. Illustrative of this is the impressionistic work of Newfoundland's **Maurice Cullen** (1866-1934) and the soberly romantic rural scenes of George A. Reid and **Homer Watson** (1855-1936), both of whom were inspired by contemporary Dutch landscape painters.

Ultimately, it was to be the **Group of Seven** (see box, p.94) who developed a Canadian aesthetic in a style that aimed to capture the spirit and vastness of the northern landscape, rather than rendering it into a tamer European version and vision. That said, the Group was influenced by the work of contemporary Scandinavian painters, who were wrestling with similar problems of scale on the other side of the Atlantic. The two rooms devoted to the Group's works feature the seminal paintings of **Tom Thomson** (1877-1917), whose startling *Jack Pine* of 1916 was in effect the Group's clarion call – trees, often windswept or dead, are a constant symbol in the Group's paintings of Canada's wilderness. Using rapid, brash, often brutal brushstrokes, the Group's works are faithful less to the landscape itself than to the emotions they evoked – **Lawren Harris**'s (1885-1970) ejaculatory *North Shore, Lake Superior*, A.Y. Jackson's *Red Maple* and J.E.H. Macdonald's *The Solemn Land* are all memorable examples.

Following Macdonald's death in 1932, the Group of Seven formed the **Canadian Group of Painters**, embracing all Canadian artists of the time whatever their style. Initially landscape remained the dominant genre, but the effects of the Depression forced politics to the fore – *Ontario Farm House* by **Carl Schaefer** (1903-95) turns a landscape into a social statement, while Jack Humphrey, Miller Brittain and Sam Borenstein depict the harsh realities of urban life.

A subsequent section focuses on **abstract** works produced in Montréal from the 1940s to the 1970s. In Canada, abstraction was first explored by the Montréal Automatistes, whose emphasis on the expressive qualities of colour was rejected by the Platiciens, for whom geometrical and analytical forms were the preoccupations. Both groups are represented here, as are postwar artists from British Columbia and Ontario – look out for the aggressive abstractions of **William Ronald** (1926-98), as in his *Monarch*.

The contemporary art and Inuit collections

Beginning with the 1960s, the **Contemporary Art collection** is spread over Levels 1 and 2. The highlights here are almost exclusively the work of American artists, most notably Andy Warhol's *Brillo* sculpture, George Segal's life-size assemblage *The Gas Station* and a couple of distinctive pieces by Claes Oldenburg. Canadians pop up here and there, but they almost always seem to take the lead from foreigners – witness the shadow of New York's Abstract Expressionists falling over Charles Gagnon's *Cassation/Open/Ouvert*.

Also displayed on Level 1 is the gallery's small but eclectic collection of **Inuit art and sculpture**. The kernel of the Inuit material is soapstone sculptures, but there are whale bone and ivory pieces too, as well as brightly coloured drawings. One particular sculptor to look out for is **Charlie Inukpuk** (b.1941), who carved the elemental *Woman who Killed a Bear with a Mitten*.

The European galleries

Currently located on Level 2, the **European galleries** begin with a medley of medieval and **Renaissance** paintings and panel paintings from Northern Europe. There's a strong showing for religious works produced in Siena and Florence, though the Italian highlight is Filippino Lippi's *Triumph of Mordecai* and *Esther at the Palace Gate*, painted for chests that contained a bride's dowry. The Low Countries are well represented too, with works by Hans Memling, Bouts and Quentin Matsys, who was responsible for a *Crucifixion*, in which Jerusalem looks like a Flemish town encircled by ramparts, and an especially sorrowful *Lamentation*. The collection of works from **seventeenth-century** Europe is, however, even more impressive. There's Bernini's sculpture of his patron Pope Urban VIII, Claude Lorrain's *Landscape with a Temple of Bacchus*, an *Entombment* by Rubens, Rembrandt's sumptuous *Heroine from the Old Testament* and Van Dyck's *Suffer the Little Children to Come Unto Me*, an early, finely observed work that includes portraits thought to be of Rubens and his family. Venetian genre paintings include Canaletto's elegaic *Campo di Rialto* and Guardi's *Santa Maria Della Salute*.

From Britain in the **eighteenth century** there are portraits by Reynolds and Gainsborough, and Romney's *Joseph Brant (Thayendanega)*, a portrait of the anglophile Mohawk chief made when he was on a visit to London. Also here is the iconic *Death of General Wolfe* by **Benjamin West**, an American who became

George III's official painter. West depicts Wolfe in a Christ-like pose, lying wounded and surrounded by his adjutants; the painting made Wolfe a British hero. The **nineteenth-century** selection is basically a show of minor paintings by great artists: Delacroix's romantic *Othello and Desdemona*; Corot's orderly *The Bridge at Narni*; Constable's *Salisbury Cathedral from the Bishop's Grounds*; and Turner's *Mercury and Argus*, with a sunset that anticipates the exquisite qualities of his later works. In stark contrast, the gritty realism of a later generation of European painters is well represented by Courbet's *The Cliffs at Étretat* and Millet's *The Pig Slaughter*, though tranquillity is soon restored by Monet's *Waterloo Bridge: The Sun through the Fog*, beautifying London's notorious fog, and two canvases by Pissarro. Van Gogh's *Iris* and Cézanne's *Forest* are the two most noteworthy Post-Impressionist works. The final European galleries push on into the twentieth century, featuring a diverse and top-quality range of paintings and sculptures from the disturbing *Hope I* by Gustav Klimt and Matisse's *Nude on a Yellow Sofa*, through to Francis Bacon's macabre *Study for Portrait No. 1* and pieces by Picasso, Léger, Epstein, Mondrian, Dali and Duchamp.

The Abstract Expressionists

One room on Level 2 is devoted to American **Abstract Expressionists**. This is where you'll find **Barnet Newman**'s *Voice of Fire*, the very mention of which causes some Canadians to break out in a cold sweat – not because of its artistic significance but because it cost a cool $1.76m. The artist intended the 5.5-metre-high piece to give the viewer a "feeling of his own totality, of his own separateness, of his own individuality, and at the same time of his connection to others, who are also separate". Such blandishments did not, however, satisfy everyone with one Manitoba Tory MP ranting that it could have been "done in ten minutes with two cans of paint and two rollers". The same room contains lesser works by Jackson Pollock and Mark Rothko.

Notre Dame and the Royal Canadian Mint

The twin silver spires of the capital's Catholic cathedral, the **Notre Dame Basilica** (Mon 11.30am–6pm, Tues–Sat 7.30am–6pm & Sun 8am–6pm; free), poke high into the sky across the street from the National Gallery. Completed in 1890, the cathedral is broadly neo-Gothic in style, its long and slender nave reaching a sort of ecclesiastical crescendo in a massive high altar piece, which is surrounded by dozens of pious wooden sculptures, many of which were carved by the carpenters and masons who worked on the Parliament Buildings.

From the basilica, it's a brief stroll north along Sussex Drive to the castellated **Royal Canadian Mint** (May–Aug Mon–Fri 9am–8pm, Sat & Sun 9am–5.30pm; Sept–April daily 9am–5pm; $5), where you can view different aspects of currency production and design – though the printing and the minting is now done in Winnipeg.

West of the centre: the Canadian War Museum

The ambitious and gleamingly new **Canadian War Museum** (May–June & Sept to early Oct daily 9am–6pm, Thurs till 9pm; July–Aug daily 9am–6pm, Thurs & Fri till 9pm; early Oct to April Tues–Sun 9am–5pm, Thurs till 9pm; $10, but free on Thurs after 4pm; Ⓦwww.warmuseum.ca) is located at 1 Vimy Place, on Lebreton Flats, a parcel of land by the river about 2km west of Confederation Square – and is easily reached by OC Transpo bus: get off at Lebreton station on the Transitway. The museum prides itself on its temporary exhibitions, featuring everything from Canada's current involvement in Afghanistan to obscure imperial campaigns its soldiers conducted with – and sometimes on behalf of – the British. Spread over one large floor, the well-researched and well-considered **permanent collection** is divided into seven main areas, beginning in Gallery 1 with Canada's First Peoples and the Franco-British and then American-British colonial wars of the eighteenth century. Gallery 2 deals with the Boer war and World War I, Gallery 3 World War II and Gallery 4 the Cold War and Canadian Peacekeeping. For many Canadians, World War I is the centre of attention for it was then that the country sustained enormous losses in a string of fruitless battles, especially at the storming of Vimy Ridge in 1917. The historical orthodoxy has long been that these very losses made Canada 'come of age' as an independent country beyond its ties with – and dependency on – the mother country.

Laurier House and Points East

About 2km east of Byward Market is the **Laurier House**, 335 Laurier Ave East (April to mid-May Mon–Fri 9am–5pm; mid-May to early Oct Mon–Sat 9am–5pm, Sun 1–5pm; $3.95; Ⓦwww.pc.gc.ca), former home of prime ministers Sir Wilfred Laurier and William Lyon Mackenzie King. **Laurier**, Canada's first French-speaking prime minister, served from 1896 to 1911, while **Mackenzie King**, his self-proclaimed "spiritual son", was Canada's longest-serving (1921–30 and 1935–48). Notoriously pragmatic, King enveloped his listeners in a fog of words through which his political intentions were barely discernible. The perfect illustration – and his most famous line – was "Not necessarily conscription, but conscription if necessary", supposedly a clarification of his plans at the onset of World War II. Even more famous than his obfuscating rhetoric, however, was his personal eccentricity. His fear that future generations would view him simply as the heir of his grandfather William Lyon Mackenzie – who led the Upper Canada rebellions of the 1830s (see p.336) – eventually led him into spiritualism. He held regular séances to tap the advice of great dead Canadians, including Laurier, who allegedly communicated to him through his pet dog.

The house is dominated by King's possessions, including his crystal ball and a portrait of his obsessively adored mother, in front of which he placed a red rose every day. Other mementoes include the programme Abraham Lincoln held the night of his assassination, a painting by Rogier van der Weyden and a guest book signed by Churchill, Roosevelt, de Gaulle, Nehru, the Dionne quintuplets (see p.201) and Shirley Temple. The house also contains a reconstruction of a study belonging to Prime Minister **Lester B. Pearson**, who was awarded the Nobel peace prize for his role in the 1956 Arab–Israeli dispute. Pearson also had a stab at devising a new flag for his country and, although it was rejected, the mock-up he commissioned, with blue stripes at either end to symbolize the oceans, is on display.

Rideau Falls and Rockcliffe

Laurier Avenue East ploughs onto the **Rideau River**, which is itself escorted north by walkways and bicycle paths to **Rideau Falls**, whose twin cataracts are separated by Green Island – the site of Ottawa City Hall, an unattractive building dating from the 1950s. The falls themselves were once enveloped in an industrial complex, but this has now been cleared away to allow excellent views across the river to Gatineau. Northeast of the falls lies **Rockcliffe**, Ottawa's ritziest district, a leafy suburb colonized by parliamentary bigwigs and diplomats – and in the evening by local lovers, who canoodle in the pavilions on the river shore, looking across to the Gatineau Hills. The prime minister lives here too, holed up in a stately stone mansion that is barely visible through the trees on the river bank at 24 Sussex Drive (no public access), whilst nearby, inland from Sussex Drive, is the stately, Neoclassical **Rideau Hall** (free guided tours, call ⓣ613/991-4422 or 1-866/842-4422, ⓦwww.gg.ca for schedule), home of Canada's governors general since Confederation. The hall's **gardens** of maples and fountains are usually open from 8am to one hour before sunset – but call ahead if you want to be certain.

Canada Aviation Museum

At the east end of Rockcliffe Parkway, 5km from downtown, is the huge hangar of the **Canada Aviation Museum** (May–Aug daily 9am–5pm; Sept–April Wed–Sun 10am–5pm; $6; ⓣ613/993-2010, ⓦwww.aviation.technomuses.ca). Highlights include a replica of the *Silver Dart*, which made the first powered flight in Canada in 1909; it flew for a full nine minutes, a major achievement for a contraption that seems to be made out of spare parts and old sheets. There are also bombers and fighters from both world wars and after, including a British Harrier.

Gatineau

Though firmly incorporated within the Capital Region, **GATINEAU** (formerly **Hull**), lying just across the river from Ottawa in Québec, remains quite distinct and predominantly francophone. For years it served mainly as Ottawa's nightspot as its bars were open two hours longer than those in the capital, but with this alcoholic advantage now gone – and its paper mills relegated to minor importance – Gatineau struggles to compete with Ottawa. It does have one key museum, the **Musée Canadien des Civilisations**, and the handsome scenery of the V-shaped **Gatineau Park**, whose assorted lakes and forested hills cover no less than 360 square kilometres.

As regards public transport, STO buses (ⓣ819/770-3242, ⓦwww.sto.ca) operates a fast and frequent service from the west end of Rideau Street to the Musée Canadien des Civilisations or you can walk – it only takes ten minutes to get there from the National Gallery. There are no buses to Gatineau Park.

Musée Canadien des Civilisations

Gatineau's pride and joy, standing on the far side of the Alexandra Bridge from the National Gallery, is the whopping **Musée Canadien des Civilisations** (May to June & Sept to early Oct daily 9am–6pm, Thurs until 9pm; July–Aug daily 9am–6pm, Thurs & Fri till 9pm; early Oct to April Tues–Sun 9am–5pm, Thurs until 9pm; $10; ⓦwww.civilization.ca), whose curvy limestone contours are supposed to represent the rocky sweep of the Canadian Shield. Not everyone was convinced, but the architect – Douglas Cardinal, a Blackfoot from Red Deer, Alberta – certainly mounted a spirited argument and the building is undoubtedly distinctive; the best view is from the Ottawa side of the river.

The museum spreads over four floors and the entrance, where you can pick up a **free plan**, is on Level 2. Also on **Level 2** is a mixed bag of attractions, including a Canadian Postal Museum, a Children's Museum, offering an interactive "world tour", a theatre and a giant IMAX cinema screen showing nature and adventure films (for a supplementary fee of $7–10). Upstairs, **Level 3** holds **Canada Hall**, which tracks through Canada's history from the Viking colony on Newfoundland (see p.495) to the 1970s. It's an ambitious affair, featuring life-size reconstructions of historical environments, from an Acadian settlement and a fur-trading post to a Métis camp, a frontier farm, a Maritime shipyard, an Ontarian Main Street circa 1900, a Canadian Pacific train station, a Union Hall and a Chinese laundry. **Level 4** holds temporary exhibitions and then it's down to **Level 1** for the **Grand Hall**, easily the largest room in the museum and perfectly designed to display a magnificent collection of around twenty Pacific Coast **totem poles** – more properly house posts. The main line of poles stands outside six native "houses" which explore Pacific Coast native culture, including displays on trade, religious beliefs, tribal gatherings and art.

Gatineau Park

The second good reason to venture north from Ottawa is the rolling forested hills and lakes of **Gatineau Park**, which extends northwest from Gatineau and has long been a favourite with the region's hikers and cyclists, who troop off here in their hundreds every summer weekend. From the Musée Canadien des Civilisations, it's just 3km west – follow the signs – to the park's southern entrance. The park was founded in 1934 when the government snapped up the land to stop its deforestation for firewood during the hard years of the Depression. The park is latticed with **hiking trails** and many of these are readily reached along the park's most scenic road, the **Champlain Parkway**, a turning off the park's main road, the **Gatineau Parkway**. The Champlain meanders its way across the south-eastern reaches of the park before reaching its conclusion at the **Champlain Lookout**, 24km from the park entrance. The belvedere here provides a grand view of a distinctive landscape, where the granite outcroppings of the Canadian Shield shelve down to the rich green fields of the St Lawrence lowlands. Among the **trail heads** passed by the Champlain Parkway, one of the most appealing is the short and easy, one-hour hoof through the woods to **Larriault Falls and Mulvihill Lake**. From the Gatineau Parkway, there's also the easy 2.5-km gambol to the geologically rare meromictic **Pink Lake** – named for an early settler, not its colour; meromictic lakes have high-density lower waters. Trail leaflets and park maps are available at the **Welcome Area** (June to mid-Oct daily 9am–5pm), just beyond the southern entrance to the park, and at the main **Visitor Centre**, off the Gatineau Parkway beyond the Champlain Parkway turning (daily 9am–5pm; ⓣ819/827-2020, ⓦwww.canadascapital.gc.ca/gatineau).

Cocooned within the park – and signed from the Gatineau Parkway – is the **Mackenzie King Estate** (mid-May to mid-Oct Mon–Fri 11am–5pm; Sat & Sun 11am–6pm; $8 per car), once the summer retreat of prime minister William Lyon Mackenzie King. In a characteristically eccentric manner, King littered the grounds of his estate with architectural follies – chunks of the old Ottawa Parliament buildings and so forth – and his former house, the otherwise inaccessible **Moorside**, now offers light meals and high teas (advance reservations on ⓣ819/827-3405).

Eating and drinking

As you might expect of a capital city, Ottawa has a good range of **restaurants**, some geared firmly to the expense account, but the majority informal, reasonably priced affairs – surprisingly so considering the amount of political money floating around – and a main course should rarely cost more than $25. Ethnic restaurants are commonplace – from Italian through Mexican, Chinese and Spanish – and although there is no distinctive Ottawa cuisine as such, the city's chefs borrow strongly from the French-Québecois tradition – Québec is, after all, just across the river. The trendiest joints are in the Byward Market area (see box, opposite), but there are also a number of first-rate places in the few blocks to the south of Parliament Hill, and a small Chinatown on Somerset West and Bronson. In addition, Ottawa has sprouted dozens of **café-bars**, some offering little more than glorified bar food, but many dip into Asian, French and Italian

Byward Market

Since the 1840s, the **Byward Market** neighbourhood, just east of Sussex and north of Rideau Street, has been a centre for the sale of farm produce, but in the last few years it has become Ottawa's hippest district. At its heart, the 1920s **Byward Market building** (Mon–Thurs 9.30am–6.30pm, Fri 9.30am–8pm, Sat 9am–6pm & Sun 10am–5.30pm) is home to cafés and delis, specialist food and fresh fruit and vegetables stalls and these merge with the street stalls outside. Many of Ottawa's best restaurants and bars are located here too, and at night the area buzzes until the early hours.

cuisines to provide excellent food at affordable prices – $10–15 should see you through in all but the priciest ones.

These café-bars have dented Ottawa's **bar and pub** scene, but there is still a reasonable range of downtown drinking places with a particular concentration in and around the Byward Market, which heaves with revellers on the weekend. Byward Market is also home to the city's best **delicatessens** and fresh produce stalls, and **fast-food** vans provide sustenance at night. These are something of an Ottawa institution, mainly on account of their *poutine* – fries covered in gravy and cheese curds. Another municipal institution, albeit a recent one, is "**Beavertails**", a half-pizza, half-doughnut snack, fried and covered either in garlic butter and cheese or cinnamon and sugar, and on sale at **Hooker's All Canadian Beavertails**, a fast-food kiosk in Byward Market at the junction of George and William streets.

Cafés, café-bars and diners

Bagel Bagel 92 Clarence St. Nine different types of bagel with an assortment of fillings from $3. Open late every night. Byward Market.

Byward Market Café Byward Market. Straightforward café inside Byward Market (at the south end) selling a wide range of snacks and light meals – sandwiches, salads and so forth – at very reasonable prices.

Café Crepe de France 76 Murray St at Parent. Divine crepes from $10 in a distinctive French-style café. Byward Market.

Medithéo 77 Clarence St. Fashionable Byward Market hangout with stone walls, angular modern furniture and a good menu with a Mediterranean slant. daily 11am–11pm.

Zak's Diner 16 Byward Market. A 1950s-style time warp with chrome decor, rock'n'roll blaring from the jukebox and good all-American food. Open 24hrs, seven days a week.

Restaurants

Arc 140 Slater St ☎613/238-2888. In immaculate, modernistic surroundings – see hotels, p.186 – this attractive little restaurant serves a tasty line in Asian food alongside Canadian dishes, all featuring local ingredients. Main courses average $25. Mon–Fri 11.30am–2pm & Mon–Sat 6–10pm.

Coriander Thai 282 Kent St at Somerset ☎613/233-2828. Arguably the best Thai in Ottawa. Amazing satays, rich green and red curries, lemongrass tea and other classic dishes at fair prices. Not far from Parliament Hill, but still off the tourist track – and none the worse for that. Main courses $10–14.

Courtyard 21 George St ☎613/241-1516. This long-established restaurant has a wide-ranging, very inviting menu with mains from $25. It's best to visit in sunny weather as the outside terrace enjoys a particularly pleasant location in an attractive cobbled courtyard. Byward Market area. Daily 5.30–9pm.

Domus Café 85 Murray St at Parent ☎613/241-6007. Part of the deluxe Domus houseware store, this chi-chi, pastel-painted restaurant serves top-quality food from an imaginative menu. Local ingredients are a feature too. Main courses hover around $25–35. Near Byward

Market. Mon–Sat 11.30am–2pm & 5.30–10pm, plus Sun 11am–2pm

Empire St Grill 47 Clarence St at Parent ⓣ613/241-1343. Smart and polished restaurant in the Byward Market area. First-rate steaks and an extensive wine list. The bar, chic and appealing, offers smooth background music, with jazz the particular favourite. Entrées from $15. Daily 11.30am–1am

Kinki Bistro 41 York St ⓣ613/789-7559. Smart Asian fusion restaurant with a creative menu – mango-dusted scallops for one. Main courses around $18. Daily noon–1am.

La Pointe 55 York St ⓣ613/241-6221. Atmospheric Byward Market restaurant serving quality seafood at reasonable prices in informal, basement premises. Mon–Sat 11am–11pm

Saigon 85 Clarence St ⓣ613/789-7934. First-rate and inexpensive Vietnamese cuisine in the Byward Market. Daily 11.30am–11pm.

Social Restaurant & Lounge 537 Sussex Drive ⓣ613/789-7355. Stylish restaurant-cum-bar graced by slick modern furnishings and fittings, plus a good, wide-ranging menu with a Mediterranean slant. Near Byward Market. Mains from $17. Daily 11.45am to midnight, until 2am Thurs–Sat.

Suisha Gardens 208 Slater St ⓣ613/236-9602. Tasty sushi, tempura, sukiyaki and teriyaki. There's also a *tatami* room where you can sit on rush mats and eat Japanese-style. Good deals at lunchtime, sushi combinations $17–22 at night. South of Parliament Hill. Mon–Fri 11.30am–2pm & 5–10pm, plus Sat 5–10pm.

Nightlife and entertainment

Ottawa is a major port of call for big-name rock and pop acts, most of whom appear at Scotiabank Place, about 15km southwest of downtown in Kanata (ⓣ613/599-3267 or 1-877/788-3267, ⓦwww2.scotiabankplace.com). Otherwise, things aren't too exciting, though downtown is home to a number of busy **bars** and several good **clubs**, featuring both live music and DJ sounds. For **listings**, the free *Where Ottawa* is a monthly promotional magazine that details what's coming up and where, but the reviews are cursory. It's available at the tourist office as is the *Xpress* (ⓦwww.ottawaxpress.ca), a weekly freebie that provides much better reviews and is a good deal hipper. The Friday edition of the *Ottawa Citizen* newspaper also provides listings and perceptive reviews.

Ottawa's cultural focus is the **National Arts Centre**, 53 Elgin St (ⓣ613/947-7000, ⓦwww.nac-cna.ca), which presents plays by its resident **theatre** company as well as touring groups, **concerts** by its resident orchestra, **operas** and **dance** from (among others) the National Ballet of Canada and the Royal Winnipeg Ballet. The acoustics are outstanding. Quality **theatre** is also on offer from the mainstream Great Canadian Theatre Company, 910 Gladstone Ave (ⓣ613/236-5192, ⓦwww.gctc.ca), and the Ottawa Little Theatre, 400 King Edward Ave (ⓣ613/233-8948, ⓦwww.o-l-t.com), presenting avant-garde Canadian plays with strong social or political overtones.

Ottawa has a good selection of **cinemas**. Options include the Bytowne Cinema, 325 Rideau St (ⓣ613/789-3456, ⓦwww.bytowne.ca), the capital's most popular repertory cinema, and the Canadian Film Institute, 2 Daly Ave (ⓣ613/232-6727, ⓦwww.cfi-icf.ca), which shows art-house and mainstream films arranged by theme.

Bars

Blackthorn Café 15 Clarence St at Sussex. In the Byward Market area, this trendy spot incorporates an English-style pub and has a pleasant outside terrace.

Blue Cactus 2 Byward Market. Hectic bar with a good line in cocktails and stylish modern decor.

Centretown Pub 340 Somerset St W. Popular gay bar, ten minutes' walk south of Laurier Ave West along O'Connor Street.

The Collection 56 Byward Market. Busy modern bar at the heart of the Byward Market that is strong on cocktails.

Heart and Crown 121 Parent Ave. Popular Irish-style bar with large outside terrace.

Clubs and music venues

Barrymore's Music Hall 323 Bank St ☎613/233-0307, ⓦwww.barrymores.on.ca. Former Vaudeville theatre converted into a huge seven-level venue with commercial, mainstream and local bands performing most nights. Showcases big names too: both U2 and Tina Turner have played here.

Mercury Lounge 56 Byward Market, ☎613/789-5324, ⓦwww.mercurylounge.net. Big loft with great Martinis and vinyl couches. House, hop and techno with DJs from all over Canada along with weird and wacky live acts. Above *The Collection* bar.

Rainbow Bistro 76 Murray at Parent St 613/241-5123, ⓦwww.therainbow.ca. Atmospheric blues and jazz club with regular jam sessions and good side lines in reggae, funk, rock and ska. Downtown, above a restaurant. Open nightly, sometimes during lunch too.

Zaphod Beeblebrox 27 York St at Sussex Drive ☎613/562-1010 ⓦwww.zaphodbeeblebrox.com. The whole spectrum of live bands from C&W to alternative, plus featured DJ slots. Nightly.

Listings

Airport enquiries ☎613/248-2000, ⓦwww.ottawa-airport.ca.

Bike rental Rent-A-Bike, East Arch, Plaza Bridge, Rideau St and Colonel By Drive (mid-April to Oct; ☎613/241-4140, ⓦwww.rentabike.ca).

Bookshops Chapters, 47 Rideau St (☎613/241-0073), has a good selection of Canadian literature and nonfiction. A World of Map and Travel Books, 1235 Wellington St at Holland Ave (☎613/724-6776), specializes in travel books.

Car rental Discount, 1749 Bank St (☎613/667-9393); Hertz, in the Crowne Plaza Hotel, 101 Lyon St North at Queen (☎613/230-7607) and at the airport (☎613/521-3332); National, at the airport (☎613/737-7023).

Embassies Australia, 50 O'Connor St (☎613/783-7665); Ireland, 130 Albert St (☎613/233-6281); Netherlands, 350 Albert St (☎613/237-5030); New Zealand, 99 Bank St (☎613/238-5991); Poland, 443 Daly Ave (☎613/789-0468); UK, 80 Elgin St (☎613/237-2008); US, 490 Sussex Drive (☎613/238-5335).

Gay & lesbian life Gayline Information & Counselling, 177 Nepean St ☎613/238-1717.

Ice hockey From Sept to April, the Ottawa Senators play NHL games at Scotiabank Place (formerly the Corel Centre), 1000 Palladium Drive, Kanata, Ottawa (☎613/599-0250, ⓦwww2.ottawasenators.com), about 15km southwest of downtown.

Internet access Chapters, 47 Rideau St at Sussex (Mon–Sat 9.30am–11pm, Sun 9.30am–10pm; ☎613/241-0073).

Laundry Rideau Coinwash, 436 Rideau St (daily 8am–10pm; ☎613/789-4400).

Left luggage Coin-operated lockers at the train and bus stations.

Outdoor equipment The Expedition Shoppe, 43 York St (☎613/241-8397).

Pharmacy Rideau Pharmacy, 390 Rideau St (Mon–Fri 9am–9pm, Sat 9am–6pm, Sun noon–6pm; ☎613/789-4444).

Post office 59 Sparks St, corner of Confederation Sq (Mon–Fri 8am–6pm).

Taxis Blue Line ☎613/238-1111; Capital Taxi ☎613/744-3333.

White-water rafting Owl Rafting (☎1-800/461-7238, ⓦwww.owl-mkc.ca/owl/) offers an excellent programme of white-water rafting on the Ottawa River, near Pembroke, about 170km west of Ottawa. A one-day excursion costs $110–130 with rental of all the necessary tackle and a buffet lunch included.

Northern Ontario

Stretching north from the shores of Lake Huron and Lake Superior to the frozen reaches of Hudson Bay, **northern Ontario** is a land of sparse population and colossal distances. Give or take the odd ridge and chasm, the landscape is almost entirely flat, an endless expanse of forest and lake pouring over the mineral-rich rocks of the **Canadian Shield**. To the anglophile elite of the south, the region was (and still is) seen as barbarous and crude – Canadian humourist Stephen Leacock, for one, dismissed it with "The best that anyone could say of the place was that it was a 'sportsman's paradise', which only means a good place to drink whiskey in." Such disdain always ignored the economic facts. The north once produced the furs that launched Canada's economy and its raw materials – gold, silver, nickel, timber – paid (and pay) for Toronto's gleaming skyscrapers. The extractive nature of the northern economy and the harshness of the climate have defined the locals' attitude to their surroundings. **Hunting and fishing** are extremely popular – and most visitors who come here join in – but other types of appreciation have been slow to grow.

Given that the distances are so great, it's important to plan an itinerary carefully. Northern Ontario is traversed by two main hwys, Hwy 11 and the much more interesting Hwy 17. **Highway 11** begins by slicing through mundane **North Bay**, 345km north of Toronto, before pushing on to the hunting and fishing resort of **Temagami**. From here, it's a manageable hop onto **Cochrane**, notable as the starting point for the lonely rail line that strikes north beyond the road network to **Moosonee** on the bleak and barren shores of James Bay, an extension of Hudson Bay. This rail line, plied by Ontario Northland's Polar Bear Express train, makes for one of the most unusual excursions in the province and is a comfortable way of seeing something of the Arctic north, way beyond the tree line. From Cochrane, Hwy 11 leads west to a series of mining towns. This part of the hwy holds little of interest but dramatically demonstrates the vast emptiness of the greater part of northern Ontario.

There are two obvious ways to join **Highway 17**. The faster route comes up from Parry Sound (see p.163) to meet Hwy 17 at the mining town of **Sudbury**, or you can catch the ferry from Tobermory (see p.153) to reach **Manitoulin Island** on Hwy 6 and join Hwy 17 west of Sudbury. Whichever route you choose (and both have their scenic advantages), your first port of call on Hwy 17 should be **Sault Ste Marie**. In itself, this industrial town is only of middling interest, but it is the terminus for a splendid wilderness train trip on the **Algoma Central Railway**. From Sault Ste Marie, Hwy 17 begins its long haul round **Lake Superior** passing by, or through, a string of parks, notably **Lake Superior Provincial Park** and **Pukaskwa National Park**, both of which have dramatic lakeshore hiking trails and campsites. Beyond lies the inland port of **Thunder Bay**, home to the replica fur trading post of Fort William and the last place of much appeal before Winnipeg (see p.560), a further 680km away to the west.

Public transport is sketchy across northern Ontario, but Ontario Northland does operate regular **buses** (Ⓣ1-800/461-8558, Ⓦwww.webusit.com) from Toronto to North Bay and points north to Cochrane. They also run the **Northlander train** (Ⓣ1-800/461-8558, Ⓦwww.northlander.ca) along a parallel route, also from Toronto to North Bay and Cochrane, which is where passengers change for the same company's **Polar Bear Express** (July & Aug) or **Little Bear** to Moosonee on James Bay. **Greyhound buses** (Ⓣ1-800/661-8747, Ⓦwww.greyhound.ca) make a showing in the region too, with their busiest route being along the Trans-Canada Hwy between Toronto and Winnipeg, and **VIA Rail** (Ⓣ1-888/842-7245, Ⓦwww.viarail.ca) links Toronto with Sudbury Junction and points west to Winnipeg. Note, however, that if you're heading for a particular park, hotel, motel or campsite, you should check to see how near you'll get by bus or train – towns and even villages hereabouts can sprawl over several kilometres. Hardy souls who visit in winter should be aware that driving on both Hwy 11 and Hwy 17 can be – and often is – perilous, but at least they dodge the mosquitoes and **blackfly** that can make

> **Train journeys in northern Ontario**
>
> Two outstanding **train rides** Carry much pride in nothern Ontario. One is the journey from Cochrane to Moosonee in the far north on James Bay with Ontario Northland's (Ⓣ1-800/461-8558, Ⓦwww.northlander.ca) **Polar Bear Express** (July & Aug) or **Little Bear** (see p.207); the second is the **Algoma Canyon excursion** (see p.215) operated by Algoma Central Railway, 129 Bay St, Sault Ste Marie (Ⓣ705/946-7300 or 1-800/242-9287, Ⓦwww.agawacanyontourtrain.com). Advance booking is strongly recommended for all three.

life absolutely miserable in the summertime: be sure to pack the repellant and get all the gear. The best time to go hiking is either at the start of spring or in the autumn.

North Bay and points north to Moosonee

Highway 11 cuts a 1000km arc through Northern Ontario, eventually meeting up with Hwy 17 as it nears Thunder Bay. En route, it links a string of gritty resource towns that endure a climate which is, away from the moderating effects of Lake Superior, as savage as any in the world. Passing through a wilderness of lakes and swampy forest, or '**muskeg**', Hwy 11 is subject to ferocious blizzards during the winter – quite enough to make the road impassable to ordinary vehicles. The first, more manageable, stretch covers the 400km from **North Bay**, a small lakeshore town, to **Cochrane**, even smaller but the starting point for one of the region's star attractions, the train ride to **Moosonee**, beyond the road network and close to the frozen shores of James Bay.

Ontario Northland **trains** and **buses** connect most of the larger settlements between North Bay and Cochrane, but you really need a car to be sure of getting where you want, when you want – and you certainly don't want to be hanging around for ages waiting for a connection. The train from Cochrane to Moosonee is operated by Ontario Northland (see p.226) and should be booked in advance.

North Bay

Once an important halting point on the canoe route running from Montréal to the West, and now a useful place to break your journey on the long drive north, the cluttered town of **NORTH BAY**, some 160km from Bracebridge (see p.167), is a relative giant hereabouts with a population of about 55,000. Glued to the shores of Lake Nipissing, it is the embarkation point for the *Chief Commanda II*, a modern passenger vessel that makes scheduled **cruises** around the Manitou Islands in the middle of the lake (June–Sept Mon–Sat 1pm; Ⓣ705/494-8167 or 1-866/660-6686, Ⓦwww.chiefcommanda.com; $16). The other notable attraction is the **Dionne Quints Museum**, handily located where Hwy 11 hits the south side of town (daily: mid-May to June 9am–5pm; July & Aug 9am–7pm; Sept to mid-Oct 9am–4pm; $3). The museum is housed in the small log cabin transported here from Corbeil, just west of North Bay, where the Dionne quintuplets were born of French-speaking parents on May 28, 1934. Born two months prematurely, the quintuplets were considered miracle children by the Depression-hit nation, and at the age of three months the government took custody of them, removing them from their parents and

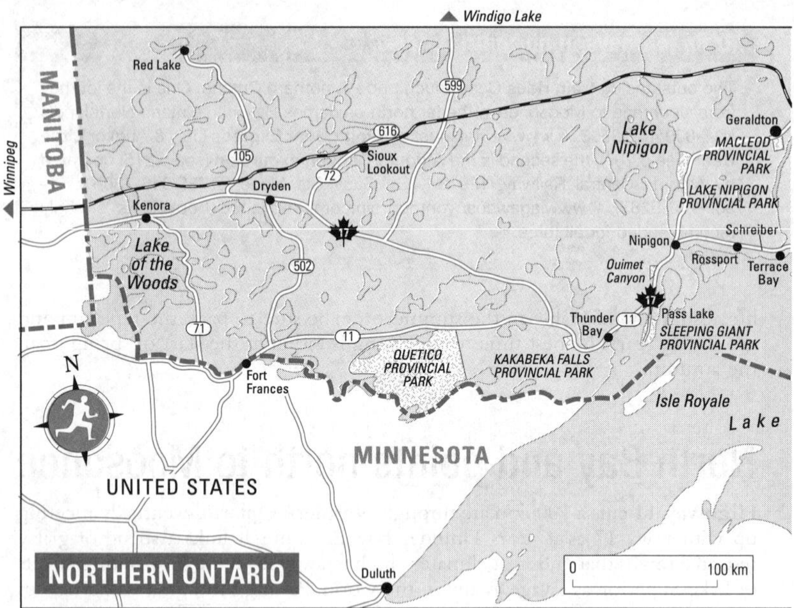

five other siblings. Until they were nine years old, the quintuplets were put on display in a glassed-in playground, to the delight of up to 6000 sightseers who turned up each day to watch them and to pay for a gaggle of souvenirs, including "birth-promoting" stones. The girls were educated in a synthetic "normal school atmosphere" provided by ten classmates, five of whom were English to help the quins with their second language. This bizarre childhood eventually caused a highly publicized estrangement between the quins and their parents, and doubtless contributed to the unhappiness of their later lives, a story dominated by illness, depression and failed marriages. Indeed, three of the quins – Yvonne, Annette and Cécile – published a shared autobiography accusing their father of sexual abuse, their mother of verbal abuse and the Ontario government of exploitation. The small museum contains dresses, toys, photographs, advertising hoardings and souvenirs of the quins' childhood, including the bed they were born in.

Practicalities

Ontario Northland **trains and buses** from Cochrane and Toronto terminate at the Intermodal station at 100 Station Rd, to the east of – and a local bus ride from – the downtown core, which zeroes in on Main Street, one block from the lakeshore. The town's **tourist office** beside Hwy 11 is next door to the Dionne Quints Museum at 1375 Seymour St (daily: mid-June to Aug 8.30am–8.30pm; Sept to mid-June 9am–5pm; ⓣ705/472-8480, ⓦwww.northbaychamber.com).

Most of North Bay's **accommodation** is concentrated on Lakeshore Drive, a crowded strip of motels and fast food joints along the sandy shore of Lake Nipissing. Proficient chain **motels** here include the *Comfort Inn*, 676 Lakeshore Drive (ⓣ705/494-9444 or 1-877/449-4484, ⓦwww.comfortnorthbay.com; ④), and the *Lakeshore (North Bay) Travelodge*, 718 Lakeshore Drive (ⓣ705/472-7171, ⓦwww.travelodge.com; ④). For somewhere with a little more soul, try the *Eagle*

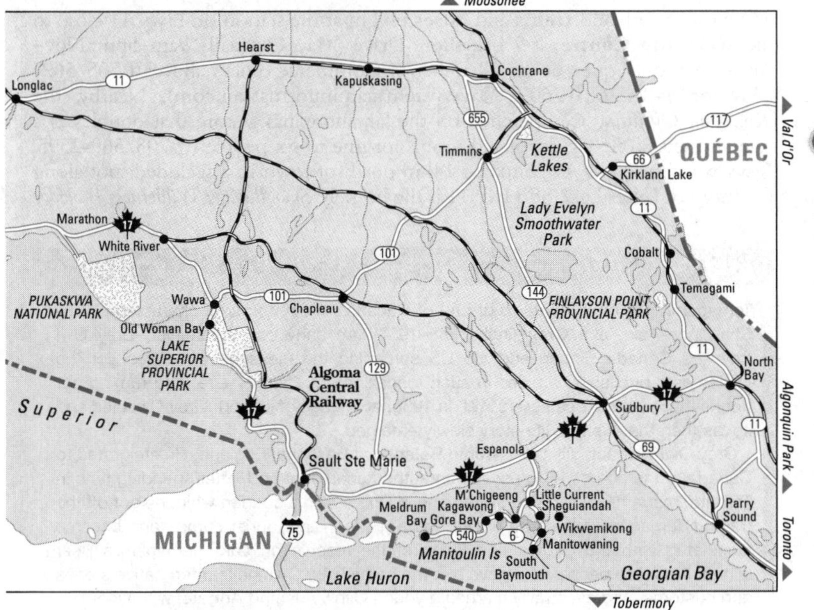

Lake B&B, 425 Jim Young Rd, South River (ⓣ705/386-7764, ⓦwww.eaglelakebedandbreakfast.ca; ❷), with immaculate rooms, a country-lodge feel and an uncommonly large wildlife pond in the backyard. South River is south of North Bay; the B&B lies about 14km from the town center.

For **food**, *Churchill's* at 631 Lakeshore Drive is close to North Bay's motels (ⓣ705/476-7777; mains start at $24), with intimate tables and smart clientele. A more casual, and central, option is *Café Chicago*, 167 Main St (ⓣ705/472-9510; mains $18 and up), which specializes in Asian dishes as well as grills.

Temagami

Surrounded by lakes and forests, the pleasant resort village of **TEMAGAMI**, 100km beyond North Bay on Hwy 11, started life as a rest stop on the long portage from Snake Lake to Lake Temagami. It has been attracting tourists since the turn of the twentieth century, when it was the site of the region's first grand hotel with a steamship company and rail line to bring holiday-makers here. Nowadays, it serves as a base for extended forays into the wilderness – mostly hunters and fishermen travelling by float plane and/or canoe, but note that the terrain is much too wild for the novice and you have to be well equipped to be safe. To get a view of this wilderness, climb the 30-metre-high **Temagami Tower** ($2) just before you hit town; you may even spot a peregrine falcon – they were reintroduced in 1997 after previously being polished off by DDT. A unique way to get a closer view of the country during the winter is to join a guided dog-sledding trip with **Wolf Within Adventures** (Dec–March; ⓣ705/840-9002, ⓦwww.wolfwithin.ca; $375 for a weekend expedition) based in Temagami. Guests learn how to care for and work with the dog teams, which are famous locally for their obedience.

Ontario Northland **trains** and **buses** pull in at the station on Hwy 11 close to the **Welcome Centre**, at 7 Lakeshore Drive (May–Oct daily 9am–5pm; Nov–April open on request at the Chamber of Commerce offices above; ⓣ705/569-3344 or 1-800/661-7609, ⓦwww.temagamiinformation.com). Nearby, the *Temagami Outfitting Co.*, perched on the lakeshore, has a store that doubles as a café and several newly decorated rooms for one to six people (ⓣ705/569-2595, ⓦwww.icanoe.ca; ❶–❹). Situated 14km north of town in a secluded spot along the shore of James Lake off Hwy 11 is the homely *Smoothwater Wilderness Ecolodge*

Grey Owl

Temagami was once home to of one of Canada's most colourful characters: Wah-Sha-Quon-Asin, aka **Grey Owl** (1888–1938). An early conservationist, Grey Owl travelled Canada, Britain and the US spreading the message of respect for the wilderness, publishing articles in such magazines as *Country Life*, and turning out books that became bestsellers. Yet, in 1938, at the age of just 50, Grey Owl died and it was then that his true life story slowly emerged.

Grey Owl was actually born **Archie Belaney** in Hastings, England. He emigrated to Canada at the age of 17 to escape an authoritarian aunt and, after spending time in Toronto, made his way to the silver mine in Cobalt. On a sudden whim he got off the train at Temagami, where he worked as a guide in the tourist camps and became fascinated with the Ojibwa population of the reserve on Lake Temagami's Bear Island. From the people who gave him the name Grey Owl, he learned native stories and customs, and eventually married a young Ojibwa named **Angele**, with whom he had a daughter. Taking on the persona of the son of an Apache and a Scotsman, Belaney was prone to drinking and rowdiness and was finally run out of town after a brawl. He moved to **Biscotasing**, a railway stop and Hudson Bay trading post north of Sudbury, where he became a forest ranger, but soon his arrest warrant caught up with him and he had to leave town again – though not before making **Marie Girard**, another native woman, pregnant. She died of consumption shortly after giving birth to their child.

During World War I, Belaney fought with the Canadian army in Flanders, where he was wounded in the foot. During his convalescence in England, he married his nurse, thereby adding **bigamy** to his many accomplishments. In the event, however, the call of the Canadian wilderness proved his marriage's undoing and Belaney returned to Biscotasing, stopping en route to see Angele for four days, during which another child was conceived. Back in Biscotasing, Belaney became the town drunk, living an anarchic life of fighting, drinking and trapping under his Wah-Sha-Quon-Asin persona. For reasons that remain obscure, Belaney seems then to have had a change of heart, returning to Temagami to live with Angele and their two children in 1925. It was then that he met **Anahereo**, a 19-year-old Iroquois. Angele was duly dumped as Grey Owl eloped with Anahereo to a hut in northern Québec, where their only companions were two beavers. It was these two animals (and a third that followed) that inspired much of Grey Owl's writing and prompted him to start a beaver colony. To raise money for the project Grey Owl began writing and lecturing about his (fictional) life, a publicity campaign that secured him the post of warden of Riding Mountain National Park and later Prince Albert National Park in Manitoba.

Grey Owl's long absences and the days spent writing led to the collapse of his relationship with Anahereo, but it didn't take long for him to meet and marry a replacement, this time a French-Canadian who adopted the Indian name **Silver Moon**. Grey Owl made a lecture tour of Britain and the US in 1938, which included an audience with King George and the princesses Elizabeth and Margaret, but it left him so exhausted that he died later the same year. Only then did his wives, friends and family find out the full truth.

(Ⓣ705/569-3539, Ⓦwww.smoothwater.com; ❷), which provides bed and breakfast and/or a spot to camp on the lakeshore. It also serves excellent organic meals using local produce. There is more **camping** (mid-May to late Sept; Ⓣ705/569-3205, Ⓦwww.ontarioparks.com; $23–33.50) at **Finlayson Point Provincial Park**, beside Lake Temagami, just south of town.

Cobalt

Local legend has it that the silver boom at **COBALT**, just off Hwy 11 some 50km north of Temagami, started when a blacksmith named Fred La Rose threw a hammer at a fox and hit a rock instead, breaking off a great hunk of silver in the process. Whatever the truth, mining began here in earnest in 1903. Subsequently, in the frantic search for silver, new mine shafts were dropped every few weeks and within a decade the haphazard collection of tents, log cabins and huts had swollen to contain seven thousand people. Life in Cobalt was perilous: typhoid, smallpox and influenza were common and many of the homes were built from wooden dynamite boxes prone to fire. The high times ended with the Great Depression, but Cobalt struggled on until the last mine closed in 1990. Cobalt today is designated a national historic site but is hardly compulsive viewing. The best you'll do is Canada's oldest **Mining Museum** (May–Sept daily 9am–5pm; Oct–April Mon–Fri 9am–5pm; $3.25), which includes a collection of luminous stones. There is more information about Cobalt's mining past in the **Welcome Centre** at 1 Station St (May–Sept daily 9am to 5pm, Oct–April weekdays only; Ⓣ705/679-5191, Ⓦwww.historiccobalt.com).

North to Cochrane

Some 100km north of Cobalt, Hwy 11 passes over the **Arctic Watershed**, or 'Height of Land', a slight elevation in the Canadian Shield that divides Ontario's water flow: to the north, all water flows to Hudson Bay, to the south it flows to the Great Lakes and the St Lawrence.

Beyond, it's a tedious haul on Hwy 11 to **COCHRANE**, 280km from Temagami. Cochrane, hometown of Tim Horton – one-time hockey player and founder of the ubiquitous coffee and doughnut chain – is a modest place that grew up as a repair and turntable station for the railroad companies serving the far north. Most of the workshops have closed down, but this is still the departure point for Ontario Northland's **Polar Bear Express train**, which ventures north beyond the road network to Moosonee, on James Bay, an appendage of Hudson Bay (see p.207). Despite the name of the train you won't see any Polar Bears but at the **Cochrane Polar Bear Conservation and Education Habitat** (July & Aug Mon–Thurs 8am–6pm, Fri–Sun 8am–7pm, Sept–June daily 9am–5pm; Ⓣ705/272-2327 or 1-800-354-9948, Ⓦwww.polarbearhabitat.ca; $20 for a 3 day pass) you have the opportunity to swim next to them. A glass partition separates a small wading pool from a large bear enclosure in which three orphaned Polar Bears, Nakita, Aurora and Nanook, regularly splash about. Even if you don't want to swim, the pool's underwater windows offer magnificent views of these majestic animals.

Less majestic is the oversized Polar Bear statue on the way into town marking the entrance to the **Information Centre** (daily late June–Aug 8am–8pm, Sept–June 9am–4.30pm; Ⓣ705/272-4926, Ⓦwww.town.cochrane.on.ca). The most convenient place to stay in Cochrane is the *Station Inn* right above the train station itself (Ⓣ705/272-3500 or 1-800/265-2356, Ⓦwww.northlander.ca; ❹), but for more character head to the *North Adventure Inn* west of town on

Kirkland Lake and Sir Harry Oakes

The mining community of **Kirkland Lake**, off Hwy 11 between Cobalt and Cochrane, isn't much to look at, but it does have an interesting tale to tell. To begin with, the town produces one-fifth of Canada's **gold** and the main street, Government Road, is actually paved with gold – the construction crew used the wrong pile of rocks: gold ore instead of waste rock. The town also featured in one of the most sensational stories of Canada's recent past – the tale that Nicolas Roeg made into the film *Eureka* with Gene Hackman and Rutger Hauer. In the summer of 1911, **Sir Harry Oakes** arrived in Swastika, close to Kirkland Lake, with $2.65 in his pocket. He left in 1934 with $20 million, the largest fortune ever gained through mining in Canada. Oakes began his quest for gold in 1898, his search taking him to Alaska, where his vessel was blown into the Bering Strait and then captured by Cossacks. He escaped under rifle fire and continued his explorations in Australia, West Africa, Mexico and California until, fleeing a revolution in South America, he joined the **gold rush in northern Canada**. In 1912, he founded a mine here in what was later to become Kirkland Lake. It soon produced $100,000-worth of gold a month, but not content, in 1928 Oakes also opened up the Lake Shore gold mine to exploit the most lucrative ore ever discovered in Canada. Obsessed with keeping his wealth from the tax man, Oakes then emigrated to the tax-free Bahamas and it was there that he came to a sticky end.

Around midnight on July 8, 1943, Oakes was murdered in his bed in Nassau, a crime that momentarily knocked World War II off the front pages. Detectives immediately arrested **Alfred de Marigny**, a handsome playboy who had eloped with Oakes's daughter, Nancy, two years previously. The case against him was thin, resting on the presence of a single fingerprint in Oakes's bedroom and a clear motive – with Oakes dead, his daughter would inherit a shed load of money. During the trial it became obvious that the detectives had planted the fingerprint and de Marigny was acquitted. The case was never reopened, but the murder of Sir Harry Oakes has prompted a variety of theories. Alfred de Marigny implicated Oakes's debt-ridden friend Harold Christie, who had defrauded Oakes in a property deal that was about to be exposed by the auditors. Rumours of voodoo and Mafia involvement were rife at the time, but more intriguing is a possible cover-up involving Oakes's confidant, the **Duke of Windsor**. Apparently, the Duke and Oakes were involved in a money-laundering operation with a Swedish industrialist and alleged Nazi agent. The suggestion is that the Duke, terrified that the scam would come to light in the course of a prolonged police investigation, might have wanted de Marigny's quick arrest in order to throw people off the scent.

Oakes's 1919 Frank Lloyd Wright-style Château is now the **Museum of Northern History** (Mon–Sat 10am–4pm, Sun noon–4pm; ⓣ705/568-8800; $4.50), located near the west end of Kirkland Lake. The museum details his climb from rags to riches and displays antique mining equipment, ores, minerals and stuffed animals.

Hwy 11 (ⓣ705/272-6683; ④), which has four fibre-glass igloos, each complete with bathroom and kitchenette. Ten kilometres south of town on Hwy 11 is the splendid and very welcoming *Betty's B&B* in (ⓣ705/272-4085; ②–③). A friendly place to eat is *JR's Bar and Grill*, easily spotted at 63 3rd Ave (ⓣ705/272-4999). Their specialty, BBQ ribs, starts at $15.

Cochrane to Moosonee by train

A popular excursion, Ontario Northland's (ⓣ1-800/461-8558, ⓦwww.northlander.ca or ⓦwww.polarbearexpress.ca) **Polar Bear Express** (July & Aug Tues–Sun 1 daily) cuts across 300km of Arctic tundra on its way from

Cochrane to Moosonee, on the Moose River as it empties into James Bay. This is as far north as anyone can easily (or reasonably) go in Ontario – but, despite the name, you won't see any polar bears. The train departs Cochrane at 8.30am and arrives in Moosonee at 12.50pm, departing Moosonee 6pm and arriving back in Cochrane at 10.05pm. The return fare is $95 and reservations are compulsory. Also linking Cochrane with Moosonee is Ontario Northland's year-round **Little Bear train**, one of Canada's last remaining flagstop trains (departs Cochrane Mon, Wed & Fri 10.45am, arrives Moosonee 3.45pm; departs Moosonee Tues, Thurs & Sat 9am, arrives Cochrane 2.30pm; $43.45 one way), taking freight and halting along the way to pick up trappers, fishers, hunters and local Crees.

Moosonee and Moose Factory Island

The Crees have been hunting and fishing Hudson Bay for several thousand years and they make up the majority of the population of **MOOSONEE**, which was founded in 1903 by a French fur-trading company, Révillon Frères – today's Revlon. The **Révillon Frères Museum** (late June to Aug daily 9am–5pm; free), in one of the original company buildings, traces the history of the settlement and its largely unsuccessful attempt to challenge the local monopoly of the **Hudson's Bay Company**. The latter had established the trading post of **Moose Factory Island**, just offshore from Moosonee, in 1673, which makes it the oldest English-speaking community in Ontario. **Water taxis** ($8 one way) zip travellers from the jetty at Moosonee to the island, where the **Moose Factory Centennial Museum Park** (late June to early Sept; free) holds the original blacksmith's shop, graveyard, powder magazine (the island's only stone building), and a tepee where the locals sell bannock (freshly baked bread). South of here, **St Thomas Anglican Church**, built in 1860, has an altar cloth of beaded moose hide, prayer books written in Cree, and removable

△ Moose Factory Island

The Hudson's Bay Company

In 1661 two Frenchmen, **Medard Chouart des Groseilliers** and **Pierre-Esprit Radisson**, reached the southern tip of Hudson Bay overland and realized it was the same inland sea described by earlier seafaring explorers. They returned to the St Lawrence laden down with furs and the French governor arrested them for trapping without a licence. Understandably peeved, they turned to England, where Charles II's cousin, Prince Rupert, persuaded the king to finance and equip two ships, the *Eaglet* and the *Nonsuch*. After a mammoth voyage, the *Nonsuch* returned with a fantastic cargo of furs and this led to the incorporation of the **Hudson's Bay Company** by Charles II on May 2, 1670. The Company was granted wide powers, including exclusive trading rights to the entire Hudson Bay watershed, now re-named **Rupert's Land**.

The HBC was a joint-stock company, its shareholders annually electing a governor and committee to hire men, order trade goods and arrange fur auctions and shipping. By 1760, **trading posts** had been built at the mouths of all the major rivers flowing into Hudson Bay and these were commanded by **factors**, who took their policy orders from London. The orders were often unrealistic and based on the concept of native trappers bringing furs to the posts – the direct opposite to the Montréal-based North West Company, whose mainly Francophone employees spent months in the wilderness working with the natives. Unsurprisingly, the NWC undercut the HBC's trade and there was intense competition between the rival concerns right across the north of the continent, occasionally resulting in violence. In 1821 a compromise was reached and the two companies **merged**. They kept the name Hudson's Bay Company and the British parliament granted the new, larger company a commercial monopoly from Hudson Bay to the Pacific. Parliament also refined the administrative structure of the company. A North American chief factor was appointed and his councils dealt increasingly with local trading concerns, though the London governor and committee continued to have the last word.

The extensive **monopoly** rights ceded to the new company were fiercely resented by local traders, and, in a landmark case of 1849, a Manitoban jury found a Metis trader guilty of breaking the monopoly, but then refused to have him punished. Thereafter, in practice if not by law, the Company's stranglehold on the fur trade was dead and gone. Furthermore, the HBC's quasi-governmental powers seemed increasingly anachronistic and when a company official, **James Douglas**, became governor of British Columbia in 1858, the British government forced him to resign from the HBC. This marked the beginning of the end of the company's colonial role.

In 1870 the HBC sold Rupert's Land to Canada. In return it received a cash payment, but, more importantly, retained the title to the lands on which the trading posts had been built and one-twentieth of the fertile land open to settlement. Given that the trading posts often occupied land that was to be the nucleus of the new cities that were sprouting in the west, this was a remarkably bad deal for Canada – and a great one for the HBC. Subsequently, the HBC became a major real-estate developer and retail chain, a position it maintains today.

floor plugs to prevent the church floating away in floods. The **Cree Cultural Interpretive Centre** (June–Sept, daily 10am-5pm; ⓣ705/658-2733; $5), at the other end of the island, is run by locals and has several exhibits about native life on the island including a replica campground. **Two Bay Tours**, 16 Ferguson Rd, Moosonee (ⓣ705/336-2944, ⓦwww.twobay.com), operates a guided tour of Moose Factory Island from Moosonee (late June to early Sept daily; 3hrs; $26) that is timed to coincide with the arrival and departure of the Polar Bear Express. They also run an afternoon tour to **Fossil Island** (late June to early Sept, daily 2hrs; $21), 10km upriver, where 375-million-year-old fossils have been found; or a longer excursion on the Polar Princess **cruise boat**, down the

Moose River to James Bay (late June to early Sept daily except Tues 9am–3pm; $56 including lunch). All tours should be reserved in advance.

Practicalities

One interesting **place to stay** is the *Cree Village Ecolodge* (ⓣ705/658-6400, ⓦwww.creevillage.com; ⑥), on Moose Factory Island, which occupies an attractive wood and glass structure and has light and spacious rooms with fabulous views of the river. Its restaurant offers a mix of contemporary and native fare including baked trout and caribou. In Moosonee itself, the *Polar Bear Lodge* (ⓣ416/244-1495, ⓦwww.polarbearlodge.com; ⑤) is handily located opposite the public jetty, but its rooms are as bland as its exterior. A little way out of the centre at 5 Pisew St, there's also the *Busy Bee B&B* (ⓣ705/336-3467 or 1-800/883-9935, ⓦwww.bbcanada.com/busybee; ④), in a modern chalet with two cosy rooms; they offer a shuttle service from the railway station. Finally, **camping** is available in *Tidewater Provincial Park* (mid-June to early Sept; ⓣ705/336-1209, ⓦwww.ontarioparks.com; ①), on Charles Island halfway between Moosonee and Moose Factory Island. There are no facilities but the small park office sells bottled water.

Sudbury

The economic centre of northeastern Ontario, sprawling **SUDBURY**, some 165km north of Parry Sound (see p.163), is parked on the edge of the **Sudbury Basin**, a pit created either by a volcano or, the preferred theory, by a giant **meteor**. Whatever did the damage, the effect was to throw one of the world's richest deposits of **nickel and copper** towards the surface. It was the nickel – used to temper steel – that made Sudbury's fortune, but its by-products caused acute environmental degradation. Most of the damage was done by a smelting method known as heap roasting, used until the 1920s, which spread clouds of sulphurous fumes over forests already ravaged by lumber firms and mineral prospectors, who often started fires to reveal the traces of metal in the bare rocks. Likened to Hell and Hiroshima, the bleak landscape had only one advantage: in 1968 it enabled Buzz Aldrin and Neil Armstrong to practise their great leap for mankind in a ready-made lunar environment. Having continued to produce sulphur-laden smoke from the stacks of their nickel smelters, the mining companies were finally forced to take action when a whole community of workers from **Happy Valley**, just northeast of Sudbury (and now ringed off by a large steel fence), were evacuated in the 1970s because of the number of sulphur-induced illnesses. Since then, pollutants have been greatly reduced and the city has implemented an ambitious re-greening programme, which has been widely acclaimed by environmentalists. One result is that large chunks of wasteland have spluttered back to life and the thirty lakes in the vicinity of Sudbury, including one in the middle of town, are no longer stagnant pools.

The town

Sudbury's key attractions are located to the south and west of the **downtown core**, which is focused on Elm Street between Notre Dame Avenue and Durham Street. Making the most of the city's unusual geology, **Science North** (opening times vary, call ⓣ705/523-4629 or 1-800/461-4898; $18 for Science Centre, $30 for all attractions; ⓦwww.sciencenorth.ca), a huge snowflake-shaped structure south of the centre on Ramsey Lake Road, is installed in a cavern blasted into the rock of the Canadian Shield. The hands-on displays enable you to simulate a miniature hurricane, gauge your fitness, lie on a bed of nails, learn to lip-read, call up amateur radio hams worldwide, tune in to weather-tracking stations and try different sensory tests, all under the guidance of students from the city's Laurentian University. The museum also has a collection of insects and animals, some of which can be handled, an **IMAX Theatre**, and various virtual-reality rides.

The town's symbol, a nine-metre-high steel replica of a five-cent piece, known as the **Big Nickel**, stands by the Trans-Canada on the western approach to town. The nickel marks the entrance to **Dynamic Earth** (daily early March to Oct, call for hours: ⓣ705/523-4629 or 1-800/461-4898, ⓦwww.dynamicearth.ca; $16), where an imaginative range of attractions has been located in an old nickel mine, from multimedia features on the world's cultures through to an exploration of old mine shafts and stories exploring Sudbury's bumpy history.

Practicalities

Sudbury's principal **train station** – Sudbury Junction – is about 10km northeast of the town centre on Lasalle Boulevard, with services south to Toronto and west to Winnipeg. There are no buses into town: you have to take a taxi (ⓣ705/673-9999). The Greyhound **bus** depot is at 854 Notre Dame, about 3km north of the centre. Sudbury **tourist office** is about 10km south of downtown beside Hwy 69 (Mon–Fri 8.30am–6pm, Sat & Sun 10am–6pm; ⓣ1-877/304-8222, ⓦwww.sudburytourism.ca).

As regards **accommodation**, Sudbury has a number of proficient chain **motels** with one of the more encouraging being the central *Best Western Downtown Sudbury Centreville*, 151 Larch St (ⓣ705/673-7801, ⓦwww.bestwestern.com; ④). For **food**, *The Red Lobster*, 1600 Lasalle Blvd (ⓣ705/560-9825), does a good line in local pickerel as does the more expensive *Teklenburg's* (ⓣ705/560-2662), just down the street at no. 1893. Alternatively, there's good quality Italian food – and smashing homemade pasta – at *Pasta & Vino*, 118 Paris St (ⓣ705/674-3050).

Manitoulin Island

The **Ojibwa** believed that when Gitchi Manitou (the Great Spirit) created the world he reserved the best bits for himself and created **Manitoulin** (God's Island) – the world's largest freshwater island (at over 2700 square km) – as his home. A continuation of the limestone Niagara Escarpment (see p.121), Manitoulin is strikingly different from the harsh grey rocks of the Canadian Shield, its white cliffs, wide lakes, gentle woodland and stretches of open, prairie-like farmland presenting an altogether more welcoming aspect. This rural idyll has long attracted hundreds of summer sailors, who ply the lakes that punctuate the island, and has proved increasingly popular with motorized city folk, who arrive here in numbers on the car ferry from Tobermory (see p.153) in southwest Ontario. Nevertheless, it's easy enough to escape the crowds, either by driving along the north shore, the prettiest part of the island, or by hunkering down in one of Manitoulin's secluded **resorts**.

About a quarter of the island's 12,000 inhabitants are aboriginals, descendants of groups believed to have arrived here over 10,000 years ago. Archeologists have uncovered evidence of these Paleo-Indians at **Sheguiandah**, on the east coast, and the small display of artefacts at the museum here contains some of the oldest human traces found in Ontario. Much later, in 1836, the island's aboriginal peoples – primarily, Ojibwa and Odawa – reluctantly signed a treaty that turned Manitoulin into a refuge for several Georgian Bay bands who had been dispossessed by white settlers. Few of them came, which was just as well because the whites soon revised their position and wanted the island for themselves. In 1862, this pressure culminated in a second treaty that gave most of the island to the newcomers. It was all particularly shabby and, to their credit, the Ojibwa band living on the eastern tip of the island at **Wikwemikong** refused to sign. Their descendants still live on this so-called "unceded reserve" and, during the third Weekend in August, hold the largest **powwow** in the country.

Manitoulin can be reached from the north by **road** (and bridge) from Hwy 17 or by **car ferry** from Tobermory to the south (May to mid-Oct 2–4 daily; $15 one-way, cars $31; 2hr; ⓣ1-800/265-3163, ⓦwww.ontarioferries.com). Ferries arrive on the island's south coast at South Baymouth; there are no bus or train services to or around the island.

East Manitoulin

Heading north from the South Baymouth ferry dock, **Highway 6** cuts inland before veering east to reach – after 30km – the lakeshore hamlet of **MANITOWANING**, where the treaty of 1836 was signed. There's nothing much to detain you here, though you might drop by the modest **Assiginack Museum** (June–Sept daily 10am–5pm; ⓣ705/859-3905; $2), whose pioneer bygones are mostly housed within the sturdy limestone building that once served as the local jail.

From Manitowaning, a side road runs east to the village of **WIKWEMIKONG**, on Smith Bay 14km from Hwy 6 – and the focus of the eponymous Indian Reserve. Canada's foremost native theatre group, **De-Ba-Jeh-Mu-Jig** (meaning 'story teller') is based here and holds regular bilingual (English & Ojibway) performances of native legends and contemporary plays by native playwrights during the summer (July & Aug; call for dates, venues and reservations, ⓣ705/859-2317, ⓦwww.debaj.ca).

Back at Manitowaning, Hwy 6 pushes north cutting across rolling farmland en route to **SHEGUIANDAH**, where the homely **Centennial Museum of**

△ Manitoulin island lighthouse

Sheguiandah (mid-May to Sept daily 10.30am–4.30pm, May & Oct daily except Mon 12.30–4.30pm; ⓣ705/368-2367, ⓦwww.visitamuseum.com; $4) is mainly concerned with the pioneer families who first farmed and traded here. Named photographs tell you who was who – and who was related to whom – in what was once an extremely isolated and tightly knit community, where the inhabitants were called "Haweaters" by outsiders after their liking for the scarlet fruit of the hawthorn tree. It was in this wooded bayshore setting that archeologists found the remains of a Paleo-Indian settlement around 10,000 years old. It was a remarkable find but most of the artefacts were carted off to big museums elsewhere, leaving this museum with a display case of crudely fashioned quartzite tools – a weak display for something so important.

From the museum, it's another short hop to **LITTLE CURRENT**, Manitoulin's largest settlement with a population of just 1500. The town is the site of the island's main **tourist office** (early May to late Oct daily 9am–8pm; ⓣ705/368-3021, ⓦwww.manitoulintourism.com), located beside the swing bridge from where Hwy 6 continues north to the mainland over a series of inter-island causeways.

North Manitoulin

Heading west from Little Current, **Highway 540** ducks and weaves its way right along the northern edge of Manitoulin, giving long, lingering views over the North Channel. It also accesses several popular **hiking trails**, notably the **Cup and Saucer Lookout Trail**, which starts near – and is signposted from – the junction of Hwy 540 and Bidwell Road, about 18km west of Little Current. The eight-kilometre-long trail reaches the highest point of the island (460m) and involves climbing rough wooden ladders and squeezing through natural rock chimneys.

KAGAWONG, about 45km from Little Current, is arguably the best-looking settlement along the north shore, comprising an attractive ensemble of old timber houses draped around a wide, sheltered bay – perfect for swimming. It also possesses **Bridal Veil Falls**, the place for cool dips on hot days, which has given its name to one of Kagawong's best B&Bs, the *Bridal Veil B&B* (ⓣ705/282-3300, ⓦwww.manitoulin-island.com/bridalveil; ③), a century-old home with two guest rooms in the centre of the village.

Pushing on along Hwy 540, **GORE BAY** zeroes in on its busy marina and is home to the first-rate *Rocky Racoon Café* (ⓣ705/282-8111; lunch $6, dinner including dessert $25), where the Nepalese chef/owner has injected some Asian spice into standard Canadian fare creating such marvels as Indian Maple Spice Bread – simply delicious.

From Gore Bay, it's about 80km to the western tip of the island, where the **Mississagi Lighthouse** (May–Sept daily 8am-8pm; ⓣ705/282-8503; free) has safeguarded passing ships since 1873, but not without mishap – the clear waters hereabouts are popular with divers set on exploring the many shipwrecks. There is a café in one of the lighthouse buildings and a basic but stunningly located campsite right on the rocky headland; sites cost $17–20 per night.

Sault Ste Marie

Strategically situated beside St Mary's River, the tortuous link between lakes Superior and Huron, industrial **SAULT STE MARIE** – more popularly **The Soo** – sits opposite the Michigan town of the same name and sees constant two-way traffic, with two sets of tourists keen to see how the other lot lives. The Soo is northern Ontario's oldest community, originally settled by Ojibwa fishing parties, who gathered here beside what was then – before the river was canalized – a set of rapids. The French called these Ojibwa *Saulteux* – "people of the falls" – and the Jesuit missionaries who followed added the Christian sobriquet to give the town its present name. Initially, The Soo flourished as a gateway to the fur-rich regions inland, but it was the construction of a **lock and canal** in the nineteenth century that launched its career as a Great Lakes port and industrial centre, churning out pulp, paper and steel. Too industrial to be pretty, The Soo rustles up a reasonable range of attractions and motels, but its real appeal is as the starting point for a splendid wilderness train ride on the **Algoma Central Railway**.

The City

Some 2km long and three blocks wide, The Soo's **downtown** runs parallel to the waterfront to either side of the main drag, Queen Street E. All the principal sights are here, beginning with the enjoyable **Ermatinger Old Stone House**, right at the east end of the town centre at 831 Queen St East and Pim (June–Oct daily 9.30am–4.30pm; Oct–May Mon–Fri 9.30am–4.30pm; ⓣ705/759-5443; $5). Built in 1814, the house was originally home to the fur trader Charles Ermantinger and his Ojibwa wife Manonowe – also known as Charlotte – and their thirteen children. Since then the house has served as a hotel, the sheriff's house, a meeting hall for the YWCA and a social club. Restoration has returned its early nineteenth-century appearance and the period-costumed staff bake tasty cakes in the summer. Across the street, and entirely different, is the special-interest **Canadian Bushplane Heritage Centre** (daily: mid-May to mid-Oct 9am–6pm; mid-Oct to mid-May 10am–4pm; ⓣ705/945-6242; ⓦwww.bushplane.com) $10.50; whose collection of antique bushplanes is stored within a giant hangar. Bushplanes are of particular use in locating forest fires and there are several sections dealing with this aspect of their work. There's even a replica fire tower to climb.

The waterfront

The spruced-up section of The Soo's elongated **waterfront** begins just five-minutes' walk away to the west of the Bushplane Heritage Centre, at the foot of East Street – and a block or two from Queen Street E. First up is the **Art Gallery of Algoma**, 10 East St (Mon–Sat 9am–5pm; ⓣ705/949-9067, ⓦwww.artgalleryofalgoma.on.ca; $3), whose temporary exhibitions usually feature local artists. It's a couple of minutes more to the **Museum Ship Norgoma** (guided tours daily June–Aug 12pm–7.30pm; ⓣ705/256-7447; $5), an old Great Lakes' passenger ferry that has ended up moored here, and the **Roberta Bondar Pavilion**, a prominent tent-like permanent structure named after Canada's first woman astronaut, who came from The Soo. The pavilion is used for concerts and exhibitions and locals are proud of the murals running round its exterior. From here, it's another short stroll to the jetty where cruises of The Soo lock system depart (see p.214) and beyond that is the **Station Mall**, a sprawling shopping centre that has sucked the commercial heart out of downtown Soo; in front of the mall is the Algoma Central Railway station (see box, p.215).

A good twenty-minute walk west of Station Mall, Canal Drive crosses one of the river's narrow channels to reach St Mary's Island, home to the **Sault Ste Marie Canal National Historic Site** (open access; free). Here, you can stroll along the lock and investigate the old stone buildings that surround it with the help of a series of explanatory plaques. It's all mildly interesting – and if your nautical interest is stimulated there are two-hour **canal cruises** through The Soo lock system with Lock Tours Canada (late May to mid-Oct 2 daily at 12.30pm and 3pm; ⓣ705/253-9850 or 1-877-226-3665, ⓦwww.locktours.com; $26). Cruises leave from beside the Roberta Bondar Pavilion (see p.213).

Practicalities

The Soo's Greyhound **bus station** is handily located at 73 Brock St and Bay, in between Queen Street East and the waterfront. Local and provincial information is available at the **Ontario Travel Centre**, 261 Queen St West (daily: mid-May to early June 8am–6pm; mid-June to early Sept 8am–8pm; mid-Sept to mid-Oct 8.30am–6pm; late Oct to mid-May 8.30am–5pm; ⓣ705/945-6941 or 1-800/668-2746, ⓦwww.ontariotravel.net), a ten-minute walk west from the bus station along Queen Street.

Amongst the town's many chain **motels and hotels**, the *Best Western Great Northern*, 229 Great Northern Rd (ⓣ705/942-2500 or 1-800/563-7262, ⓦwww.bestwesternsault.com; ❺), stands out if only for its five-storey indoor water slide and bowling alley. More historic is *Eastbourne Manor B&B*, 1048 Queen St East (ⓣ705/942-3648 or 1-888/431-5469, ⓦwww.bbcanada.com/3010.html; ❸), one-time home of an Ontario premier and a grand Edwardian mansion with beautiful gardens and surround-sound video lounge. The town's cheapest accommodation is in the *Algonquin Hotel* **HI hostel**, a stern-looking brick building at the east end of the centre at 864 Queen St East and Pim (ⓣ705/253-2311 or 1-888/269-7728, ⓦwww.hihostels.ca; $28 dorm beds, doubles ❶).

If you ask any local to name The Soo's gastronomic speciality they'll tell you it's **pizza** – which is apparently quite unlike pizza anywhere else. The most popular place is *Mrs. B's*, 76 East St (ⓣ705/942-9999), where large pizzas begin at $13. The finest downtown restaurant is *A Thymely Manner*, 531 Albert St at Brock (ⓣ705/759-3262; Tues–Sun), which is well known for its local lamb – from nearby St Joseph's Island – and its great Caesar salad; reservations are a must. Along the Great Northern Rd, at no. 357, *The Steamy Bean Café* (ⓣ705/253-9690) serves up coffee and cakes in a relaxed setting with sofas and Internet terminals.

Lake Superior's north shore

With a vast surface area of no less than 82,000 square kilometres, **Lake Superior** is the largest freshwater lake in the world, and one of the wildest. Its northern shore between Sault Ste Marie and **Sleeping Giant Provincial Park** is a windswept, rugged region formed by volcanoes, earthquakes and glaciers, its steep, forested valleys often overhung by a steely canopy of grey sky. In 1872 Reverend George Grant wrote of Superior: "It breeds storms and rain and fog, like a sea. It is cold… wild, masterful and dreaded." The native Ojibwa lived in fear of the storms that would suddenly break on the lake they knew as Gitche Gumee, the Big-Sea-Water, and white sailors were inordinately suspicious of a lake whose icy waters caused its victims to sink like stones: Lake Superior never gives up its dead. For the most part, **Highway 17** sticks close to the north shore of Lake Superior between Saulte Ste Marie and Sleeping Giant Provincial Park, but a screen of trees almost

The Algoma Central Railway

The 500km-long **Algoma Central Railway** (ACR) was constructed in 1901 to link The Soo's timber plants with the forests of the interior. The first recreational users were members of the Group of Seven (see box, p.94), who shunted up and down the track in a converted boxcar, stopping to paint whenever the mood took them. The ACR's timber days are long gone, but today the railway offers one of Ontario's finest excursions, with the train snaking through a wonderfully wild wilderness of deep ravines, secluded lakes and plunging gorges. To see it all, sit on the left-hand side – otherwise you'll end up looking at an awful lot of rock.

There are **three tours** to choose from and all depart from the Algoma Central Railway Terminal, in downtown Soo at 129 Bay St and Dennis (ⓣ705/946-7300 or 1-800/242-9287, ⓦwww.agawacanyontourtrain.com). The **Agawa Canyon Tour Train** takes the whole day to cover the first 200km of track and back (late June to mid-Oct departs daily at 8am, returns 5.30pm; $65–85 in the fall). Advance reservations are strongly advised and are pretty much essential in the autumn, when the leaves turn. A two-hour stop within the canyon's 180-metre-high walls allows for a **lunch break** and a wander around the well-marked nature trails, which include a lookout post from where the rail line appears as a thin silver thread far below. Unless you are properly equipped don't miss the train back – the canyon gets very cold at night, even during the summer, and the flies are merciless. During the winter when the lakes are frozen and the trees are bent low with ice, the **Snow Train** (late Jan to mid-March Sat only; departs 8am, returns 5pm; $65) travels a little further north. It passes right through the canyon to the dramatic exit, where the walls are only 15m apart, before returning to The Soo. The third and longest trip is the **Tour of the Line** (all year Wed & Fri & Sun departs 9am or 9.20am, arrives Hearst 6.40pm or 7pm; $187 return, excluding accommodation), a return trip that takes two days with an overnight stay in **Hearst**, the ACR's northern terminus. This is arguably the weakest of the three excursions as the scenery north of the canyon is dreary pine forest and small-town Hearst is hardly riveting. Note also that passengers are responsible for arranging their own accommodation in Hearst – ring the Hearst Chamber of Commerce (ⓣ1-800/655-5769) well ahead of time for details of availability; or contact the *Companion Hotel*, 930 Front St, Hearst (ⓣ705/362-4304 or 1-888/468-9888, ⓦwww.companion-hotel-motel.ca; ❸).

In addition to these well-publicized tourist jaunts, the ACR runs a regular **passenger train** from The Soo to Hearst four times weekly from early May to October, three times weekly in winter. Passengers on this train, which is commonly called the "moose meat special" on account of its popularity with hunters and trappers, get off and on at various points along the line and pay as little as $16 for a short journey up to $115 for the whole trip up to Hearst. This service enables serious hikers to step out into the great unknown comforted by that they can always flag down the next train up. Schedule details are available from the ACR, which also has information about renting **boxcars** and details of the several **outback lodges** that dot the line.

always keeps the lake out of view. This stretch of road is about 690km long so, unless you're up for a gruelling thrash or have to reach Thunder Bay (see p.220) or bust, it's much better to dally and dawdle. Along the way are three magnificent parks, **Lake Superior Provincial Park**, **Pukaskwa National Park** and **Sleeping Giant Provincial Park**, where there's camping and hiking – though the insects can be unbearable from May to August, sometimes longer. The small towns dotted along the hwy mostly fail to inspire, but low-key **Wawa**, about a third of the way along, has several good places to stay, while diminutive **Rossport**, a further 300km west, is easily the prettiest settlement hereabouts.

Greyhound **buses** regularly travel Hwy 17 between Toronto and Winnipeg, but don't expect them to drop you exactly where you want. If you are aiming for a specific motel or campsite, check how far you'll have to walk.

Lake Superior Provincial Park

Heading north from Sault Ste Marie on Hwy 17, it's about 120km to the southern perimeter of **Lake Superior Provincial Park** (April–Oct; day-use fee $11), which offers ready access to Lake Superior's granite shoreline and its immediate hinterland. Autumn is the best time to visit, when the blackflies have abated and the forests of sugar maples and yellow birch flash with colour, but the scenery and wildlife are enthralling throughout the year. Moose, chipmunks and beavers are the most common mammals, sharing their habitat with more elusive species including white-tailed deer, woodland caribou, coyote, timber wolves and black bears, as well as myriad migratory and resident birds. Hwy 17 cuts through the park for around 100km, passing three campsites, the magnificent cliffs of **Old Woman's Bay**, a series of trailheads and, after about 70km, the **park office** (May–Oct daily 9am–6pm; ⓣ705/856-2284), which sells hiking and canoe route maps as well as backcountry camping permits ($8.50), which are compulsory if you're heading off into the wilderness. The office also has information on vacancies at the park's three major **campsites**. These are the basic **Crescent Lake** (mid-June to mid-Sept; $23–29.50) on the southern boundary, popular **Agawa Bay** (May to early Oct; $27–36), 8km further north and right on Lake Superior, plus **Rabbit Blanket Lake** (May to late Oct; $27–33.50) just north of the park office and ideal for forays into the interior. The last two campsites have electrical hook-ups, showers and laundry facilities. The rangers will warn you if weather conditions look perilous, but always expect the worst – the park receives more rain and snow than any other area in Ontario. There are no park services of any kind from November to April, when service roads (but not of course Hwy 17) are barred and gated.

For thousands of years the Ojibwa used this stretch of the Lake Superior shoreline for hunting and fishing and their presence is recalled by a number of **rock carvings**. Most are inaccessible, but an exception is **Agawa Rock**, where the carvings represent a crossing of the lake by Chief Myeegn and his men, during which they were protected by Misshepexhieu, the horned lynx demigod of Lake Superior. To reach Agawa Rock, take the short, signed access road west of Hwy 17 about 16km from the southern border of the park; from here a 400-metre trail leads to a rock ledge from where the pictographs can be viewed.

The finest of the park's trails – the **Coastal Trail** – begins some 140km from Sault Ste Marie at Sinclair Cove and runs north to Chalfant Cove and comprises a challenging forty-eight-kilometre-long route of high cliffs, sand and cobbled beaches, sheltered coves and exposed granite ledges. There are numerous designated backcountry campsites on the trail and the burnt-out fires on the beaches indicate where most people choose to pitch. The entire trek takes about five to seven days but access points enable you to do shorter sections of the trail; the southern part of the trail is not as demanding, with fewer climbs and easier going on sand rather than cobbled beach. Maps and trail guides are available at the park office.

Wawa

The unassuming former iron-mining town of **WAWA**, just 14km north of the park, was named after the Ojibwa word for wild goose – and to hammer home the point there's a great big steel model of the bird at the entrance to town, outside the **Visitor Information Centre** (late June–Aug daily 8am–8pm, May, Sep & early Oct daily 9am–5pm; ⓣ1-800/367-9292, ⓦwww.wawa.cc). The model has helped to make Wawa a busy stopping point on the Trans-Canada Hwy (Hwy 17), which was just the idea. In the 1960s, much to the chagrin of local businessfolk, the TCH was routed a couple of kilometres to the west of town – hence the goose to pull passing motorists in. Modern **motels** line up along Wawa's main street, Mission Road. Amongst them, the *Wawa Motor Inn* (ⓣ705/856-2278 or 1-800/561-2278, ⓦwww.wawamotorinn.com; ④) ignited furious speculation after its original owner died in 1987, taking with him the code to the huge safe he'd had built in the hotel; to this day nobody knows what is locked inside. More scenic is the secluded *Rock Island Lodge* (ⓣ705/856-2939 or 1-800/203-9092; ⓦwww.rockislandlodge.ca; ④), 10km from Wawa – take the TCH south from town and turn right (west) after 5km along Michipicoten River Village Road; the lodge is perfectly located on a sandy beach, its wooden patio literally hanging over Lake Superior. The lodge's three guest rooms have no phones and no TV, but it's a popular spot and advance reservations are advised.

A stay in Wawa isn't complete without eating at the *Kinniwabi Pines Restaurant*, Hwy 17 South (ⓣ705/856-7226; $15 for dinner, $5 for breakfast), which is famous hereabouts for its Caribbean cuisine, a specialty of the Trinidadian chef.

White River

Beyond Wawa, the mixed deciduous–coniferous forest gives way to a boreal forest of balsam fir, white birch, trembling aspen, and white and black spruce – and you have plenty of time to observe it on the 90km haul to the next settlement of any interest, **WHITE RIVER**. There's nothing much to the place, but it does have two claims to fame. First, in 1935 the temperature here dropped to a mind-boggling -57°C (-72°F), the lowest ever recorded in the whole of Canada – and hence the whopping thermometer hanging by Hwy 17. Second, this was the home of a small bear cub named Winnipeg who was exported to London Zoo in 1914 and became the inspiration for Winnie-the-Pooh. To emphasize the connection, you'll spot a fibreglass Winnie up a tree beside the highway. **Winnie's Hometown Festival** on the third weekend of August is a relatively local affair with fireworks and a parade but there is plenty of Pooh-paraphenalia on sale, year round, at the White River **Tourist Information Centre** (ⓣ1-888/517-1673).

Pukaskwa National Park

Pushing on from White River, Hwy 17 loops round to the west, heading back towards the Lake Superior shoreline. After about 85km, just short of the little lakeshore town of Marathon, Hwy 17 clips past **Highway 627**, the 15km-long sideroad that provides the only access to **Pukaskwa National Park** (open year-round with limited services in winter; ⓦwww.pc.gc.ca), a chunk of hilly boreal forest interspersed by muskeg and loch that fills out an enormous headland with a stunningly beautiful coastline. Hwy 627 goes to **Hattie Cove**, the site of the park's one and only serviced **campsite** (from $13.85 plus park entry fee of $5.45), three sandy beaches and a **visitor centre** (late June to mid-Sept daily 10am–5pm; ⓣ807/229-0801), which sells trail guides and backcountry camping permits ($9 per night). From Hattie Cove, the **Coastal Hiking Trail** travels 60km south through the boreal forest and over the ridges and cliffs of the Canadian Shield. It is not an easy hike by any means, but it is simply magnificent and there are regular backcountry campsites on the way. In the summer, **McCuaig Marine Services** offers a water shuttle to the head of the trail at Swallow River, so you can just hike one-way back to Hattie Cove; the visitor centre has the details or call ⓣ807/229-0193. A one-way trip for up to 12 people will cost around $500. The same company also operates tours along the Pukaskwa coast to White River where a suspension bridge crosses narrow rapids (every Sat in Aug from the visitor center; $60).

Rossport

Some 130km from the Pukaskwa turning, Hwy 17 passes close to **ROSSPORT**, a picture-perfect village draped around a tiny, sheltered bay. Originally a Hudson's Bay Company trading post, the settlement prospered as a fishing port until the 1960s, when a combination of overfishing and a sea-lamprey attack on the lake trout led to the industry's decline. The railway station was closed down too and today Rossport is the quietest of villages and one that makes for a perfect **overnight stay** on the long trek north. The tiny *Rossport Inn* (ⓣ807/824-3213 or 1-877/824-4032, ⓦwww.rossportinn.on.ca; ❸), whose mock-Tudor flourishes date from the 1880s, occupies a fine lakeside setting. It has seven bedrooms in the main house and ten wooden cabins, with double beds, in the garden. The inn has a good restaurant, but the **place to eat** is the *Serendipity Café* (ⓣ807/824-2890, ⓦwww.serendipitygardens.ca; closes 7pm), a surprisingly sophisticated spot with feta cheese, rocket salad, smoked salmon and the like – all at reasonable prices. You can stay here too, in four stylish self-catering studios with views of the lake (❹).

Ouimet Canyon Provincial Park

From Rossport, it's 80km to **NIPIGON**, where Hwy 11 finishes its mammoth trek across northern Ontario to merge with Hwy 17. After a further 35km or so, Hwy 17 reaches the 11km-long turning that leads north away from the lake to one of the region's more spectacular sights in **Ouimet Canyon Provincial Park** (mid-May to early-Oct daily, daylight hours; ⓣ807/977-2526, ⓦwww.ontarioparks.com; free). The canyon was formed during the last ice age, when a sheet of ice 2km thick crept southward, bulldozing a fissure 3km long, 150m wide and 150m deep. Nearly always deserted, the canyon has two lookout

Terry Fox

West of Nipigon, hwys 17 and 11 merge to become the Terry Fox Courage Highway, named after **Terrance Stanley Fox** (1958–81), one of modern Canada's most remarkable figures. At the age of 18, Terry developed cancer and had to have his right leg amputated. Determined to advance the search for a cure, he nevertheless planned a money-raising run from coast to coast and on April 12, 1980, he set out from St John's in Newfoundland. For 143 days he ran 26 painful miles a day, covering five provinces by June and raising $34m. In September, at mile 3339, just outside Thunder Bay, lung cancer forced Terry to abandon his run; he returned home to Port Coqitlam in British Columbia, where he died the following summer. More than $85m has now been raised for cancer research in his name and in his honour the **Terry Fox Monument**, a finely crafted bronze statue, has been placed on top of a ridge in a little park above the hwy just to the east of Thunder Bay. From the monument, there are panoramic views over Lake Superior; Thunder Bay tourism has its main office here too.

points that hang over the terrifyingly sheer sides with the permanently dark base lurking below – an anomalous frozen habitat whose perpetual snow supports some very rare arctic plants. On the way back from the canyon, about 4km short of Hwy 17, **Eagle Canyon Adventures** (mid-March to mid-Nov, daily, 9am–9pm; ⓣ807/857-1475, ⓦwww.eaglecanyonadventures.ca; $25 per night) has a well-sited **campground** which includes a 600ft suspension footbridge spanning the canyon. In the winter, water is pumped over the canyon sides to form huge ice-falls transforming the area into a dedicated ice-climbing park.

West from Ouimet Canyon to Sleeping Giant Provincial Park

Doubling back to Hwy 17 from Ouimet Canyon, it's about 25km west along the main hwy to Hwy 587, which branches south to scuttle down the 42km-long **Sibley Peninsula**. Almost all of the peninsula is given over to the dramatically scenic **Sleeping Giant Provincial Park**, so named because of four flat-topped mountains that resemble a recumbent giant. Established in 1944 to protect what the logging companies had left of the red and white pines, the park covers 243 square kilometres of high, barren rocks and lowland bogs, criss-crossed with 100km of hiking trails. Acting as a sort of catch net for animals, the peninsula is inhabited by beaver, fox, porcupine, white-tailed deer and moose. There are also wolves in the more remote areas and on a still night you can hear them howling.

Hwy 587 enters the park about 6km beyond the village of **PASS LAKE**. Admission is $10 per vehicle, payable at the gatehouse kiosk. Pick up maps and hiking trail details either here or 20km further along the road at the visitor centre (late June–Aug daily 10am–6pm, May & Sept weekends only 10am–4pm; ⓣ807/977-2526, ⓦwww.ontarioparks.com). The park's one and only **campsite** (mid-May to early Oct; $27–33) is close to the gatehouse on the shores of Lake Marie Louise; reservations are advised in high season. Backcountry camping is possible too – pick up a permit at the visitor centre. Of the park's hikes, the 40-kilometre **Kaybeyun Trail** is the most spectacular and the longest, running around the tip of the peninsula finishing up at Thunder Bay lookout. Several of the parks other, shorter trails, such as the tough but rewarding five-kilometre-long **Talus Lake Trail**, branch off to reach various viewpoints that boast superb views of Lake Superior. Of these, the **Top of the Giant Trail** is popular because you can bike the first 20km, completing the last, short slog up to the highpoint, known as the Giant's knees, on foot.

At the southern tip of Hwy 587, but still within the park, is the curious **Silver Islet**, not an island at all, but the ice-blasted remains of a thriving silver town, some fifty houses in all, including a customs house, a log jail, and a weathered general store, plus a population of two. Mining magnate Alexander Sibley founded Silver Islet in 1872 and his ambitious plans involved building a causeway from his new town to Burnt Island just offshore to get at a silver deposit – you can still see bits of the causeway today. Over the years the town exhausted the local firewood supply and had to rely on coal for fuel – and this was to be its undoing. One winter, the coal boat got stuck in the ice and, rather than freeze to death, the miners were forced to leave; they never came back.

Doubling back to the top of Hwy 587, it's 30km west on Hwy 17 to Thunder Bay.

Amethysts

Amethyst, a purple-coloured variety of quartz, was first discovered near the shores of Lake Superior between the Ouimet Canyon and Thunder Bay in the middle of the nineteenth century. It is still mined hereabouts and particular deposits have been turned into well-signposted tourist attractions; Hwy 17 whizzes past a string of them. One of the best is **Blue Points Amethyst Mine**, about 4km east of the city (mid-May to mid-Oct daily). Tours of the open-pit mine are free, but you can pick up a bucket and digging tool to gather as many lumps of rock as you want, and pay a minimal amount for your booty on the way out. Amethysts can be polished with baking soda.

Thunder Bay and around

The Lake Superior port of **THUNDER BAY** is much closer to Winnipeg than to any city in Ontario, and consequently its 120,000 inhabitants are prone to see themselves as westerners. Economics as well as geography define this self-image, for this was until recently a booming **grain-handling port**, and the grain, of course, is harvested in the Prairies. Some grain still arrives here by rail to be stored in the town's gigantic grain elevators on its way to the Atlantic, but since the 1990s the economics of the grain trade have favoured Canada's Pacific ports and many of the grain elevators that dominate the harbourfront are now literally rotting away. This reversal of fortunes has encouraged Thunder Bay to reinvent itself through manufacturing and tourism. To boost the latter, the city council has created a cheerful **marina** and built a spanking new **casino**, though this proved very controversial. Such was the opposition that the casino was, in a rather bizarre compromise, called the "Charity Casino" to remind the citizenry that the profits are and will be spent on good causes.

Thunder Bay was created in 1970 when the two existing towns of Fort William and Port Arthur were brought together under one municipal roof. **Fort William** was the older of the two, established in 1789 as a fur-trading post and subsequently becoming the upcountry headquarters of the North West Company. It lost its pre-eminent position when the North West and Hudson's Bay companies merged, but it remained a fur-trading post until the end of the nineteenth century. Meanwhile, in the middle of the nineteenth century, rumours of a huge **silver** lode brought prospectors to the Lake Superior shoreline just north of Fort William and here they established **Port Arthur**. But the silver didn't last and the Port Arthur, Duluth and Western railway (PD&W), which had laid the lines to the mines, was soon nicknamed "the Poverty, Distress and Welfare". The Canadian Northern Railway, which took over the abandoned PD&W lines, did much to rescue the local economy, but did not bring Fort William and Port Arthur closer together. Rudyard Kipling noted that, "The twin cities hate each other with the pure, passionate, poisonous hatred that makes cities grow. If Providence wiped out one of them, the other would pine away and die." The 1970 amalgamation bypassed Kipling's prediction and nowadays these parochial rivalries have all but vanished.

Scarred by industrial complexes and crisscrossed by rail lines, Thunder Bay is not immediately enticing, but it does have enough of interest to make a pleasant stopover on the long journey to or from Winnipeg. The most agreeable part of

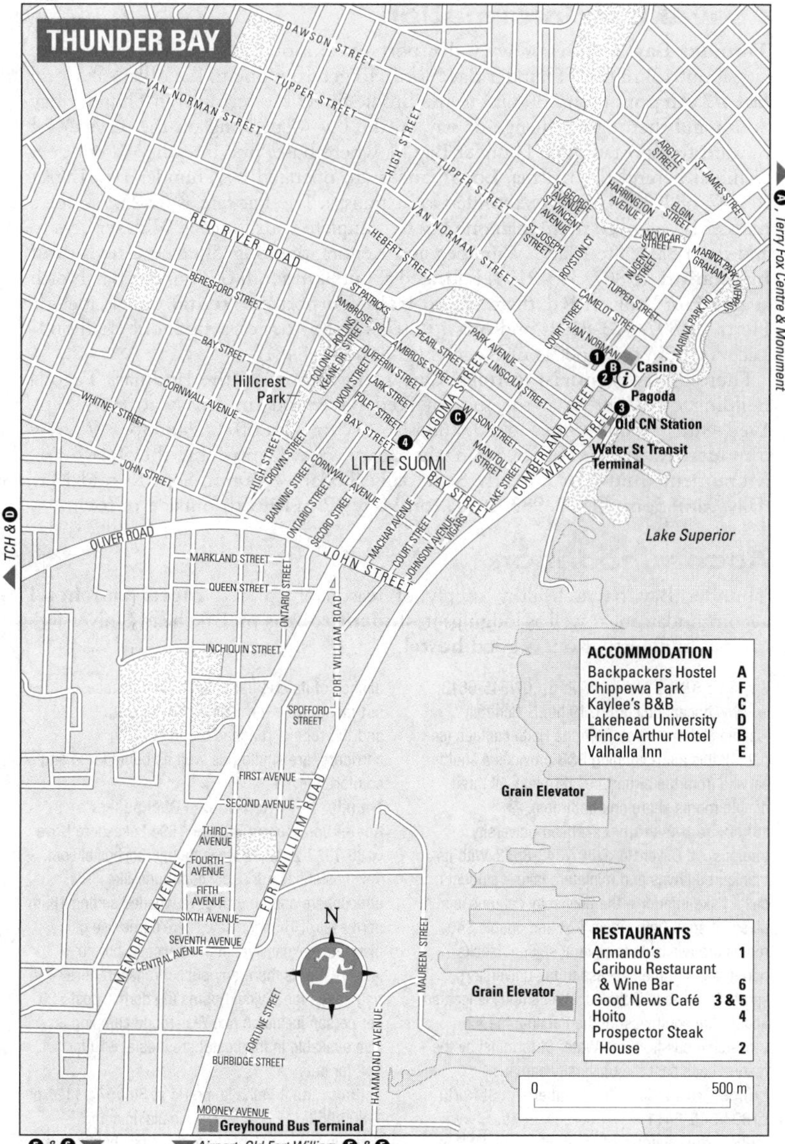

town is the few blocks stretching inland from behind the marina in **Thunder Bay North** – north of Central Avenue – and here you'll also find several good cafés and restaurants. **Thunder Bay South** is much less appealing, but on its outskirts is the city's star turn, the replica fur-trading post of **Old Fort William**, or you could plump instead for the waterfalls of **Kakabeka Falls Provincial Park**, 30km or so west of Thunder Bay

Arrival and information

Thunder Bay Airport (Ⓦwww.tbairport.on.ca) is on the southwest edge of the city, about 13km from Thunder Bay North. To get from one to the other, take local **bus #3 Airport** (every 30min) to the Brodie Street bus terminal in Thunder Bay South and then either change or stay on the bus (depending on the service) for onward transportation to Thunder Bay N, where buses pull into the Water Street terminal behind the marina. **Local buses** are operated by Thunder Bay Transit (Ⓣ807/684-3744, Ⓦwww.thunderbay.ca/transit). The flat fare is $2.25; ask for a transfer if you need more than one bus to complete your journey. With services to and from Sault Ste Marie, Winnipeg and Kenora, the long-distance **Greyhound bus station** (Ⓣ807/345-2194) is located about 3km south of Thunder Bay North at 815 Fort William Rd; there are no **trains**. Airport **car rental** outlets include Hertz (Ⓣ807/473-8111) and Avis (Ⓣ807/473-8572). For a **taxi**, call Diamond-Laceys (Ⓣ807/622-6001) or Roach's (Ⓣ807/344-8481).

There are two **tourist offices**. One is downtown in the landmark Pagoda building on Water St at the foot of Red River Rd (mid-May to early Sept, Wed–Sun 10am–6pm; Ⓣ807/684-3670 or 1-800/667-8386, Ⓦwww.thunderbay.ca); the other is in the Terry Fox Centre by the Terry Fox Monument (mid-May to early Sept, daily 8.30am–8.30pm; Sept to mid-May, daily 9am–5pm; Ⓣ807/983-2041), on Hwy 17 just north outside of town.

Accommodation

Thunder Bay has a healthy supply of reasonably priced **motel and hotel** accommodation, as well as lodgings in **student rooms** on Lakehead University's campus and, further out, a good **hostel**.

Kaylee's B&B 2 Machar Ave Ⓣ807/345-6813, Ⓦwww.bbcanada.com/3719.html. Centrally located just one block from the Hoito canteen (see p.224), this long-standing B&B provides a shuttle service from the airport/bus terminal. All three double rooms share one bathroom. ❷

Lakehead University Lakehead University Campus, off Oliver Rd Ⓣ807/343-8612. With its manicured lawns and miniature lake – students call it Lake Inferior – the university campus is a pleasant spot. Both single $28 and double $40 rooms are available in several student blocks during the summer. Access to the university's sports facilities is included. The campus is located about 4km southwest of the Pagoda; the #2 Crosstown bus from the Water St terminal by the marina goes past the university campus.

Prince Arthur Hotel 17 Cumberland St North Ⓣ807/345-5411 or 1-800/267-2675, Ⓦwww.princearthurwaterfront.ca. Built by the CNR in 1908, this imposing stone-and-brick block is bang in the centre of town. Inside, there are flashes of its original Edwardian elegance, but most of the furnishings are modern and the rooms, reached along echoing corridors, are similar, as well as being large and comfortable. ❹

Thunder Bay International Backpacker's Hostel Longhouse Village 1594 Lakeshore Drive Ⓣ807/983-2042, Ⓦwww.thunderbayhostel.com. This hostel has a friendly commune-like atmosphere and an attractive wooded setting 18km northeast of Thunder Bay. There's free use of bicycles, inexpensive Internet access, but no laundry. Nor is there any public transport here – ring ahead for advice. Rooms (no dorms) cost $20 per person including tax. Year-round camping is also available in the hostel grounds at $19 for two, $12 for one.

Valhalla Inn 1 Valhalla Inn Rd Ⓣ807/577-1121 or 1-800/964-1121, Ⓦwww.valhallainn.com. Perhaps the best-looking of the city's hotels, this brick-and-timber modern hotel offers over two hundred spacious and well-equipped rooms. ❺

The Town

Thunder Bay's 5km-long **waterfront** is home to a string of **grain elevators**, whose striking architecture – all modernist lines and pure functionalism – can't fail to impress. In the middle of the industrial jangle is the **marina** and behind that is the old **CN railway station**, whose distinctive high-pitched gables, turrets and dormer windows were built to resemble a French Château. The station was erected in 1906 and three years later CN dipped into their pockets again to create the **Pagoda**, a fanciful bandstand just across the street that now houses a tourist office (see opposite).

Thunder Bay North's most appealing enclave is the Finnish district of **Little Suomi**, focused on the Bay and Algoma streets intersection, about ten minutes' walk southwest from the Pagoda. There are over forty ethnic groups in Thunder Bay and several of them maintain their own institutions, but none more so than the Finns. Arriving in the 1870s, the first Finns to get here were left-wing refugees escaping the tender mercies of the Tsar, whereas those who arrived after 1917 were right-wing opponents (plus the odd anarchist) of the Bolsheviks, leading to a political divide within the

△ Thunder Bay, Ontario

community that still echoes today. Little Suomi's architecture is resolutely suburban, but the town's most atmospheric restaurants are here (see below). Keep on going west along Bay Street from Algoma Street and you'll soon reach **Hillcrest Park**, perched on a low ridge, offering great views out across the lake.

Southwest of Thunder Bay: Old Fort William

Thunder Bay's tour de force is the reconstructed fur-trading post of **Old Fort William** (late May to mid-Oct daily 10am–5pm; ⓣ807/473-2344, ⓦwww.fwhp.ca; $14), in a loop of the Kaministiquia River about 15km southwest of the town centre – and 13km upriver from its original site. At the entrance is a **visitor centre**, where a first-rate film traces the history of the fort and explains its workings. From here, it's a quick stroll or bus ride to the fort, a large palisaded compound which has been restored to its appearance in 1815, when it was the inland headquarters of the North West Company and their major trans-shipment base. Impeccably researched and staffed by students dressed in period gear, the forty-odd buildings that fill out the compound illuminate the fort's original purpose with everything from simple storehouses to the capacious Great Hall. Look out also for the fur warehouse, festooned with the pelts of beaver, lynx and arctic fox, and the canoe workshop, where exquisite birch-bark canoes are made to traditional designs for museums all over Canada. There are demonstrations of contemporary trades and crafts, as well as a working kitchen, kitchen garden and a farm complete with sheep, pigs and cows.

West of Thunder Bay: Kakabeka Falls

Kakabeka Falls Provincial Park (all year ⓣ807/473-9231, ⓦwww.ontarioparks.com; entry $8–11), some 32km west of Thunder Bay, is named after the powerful 39-metre waterfall at its heart. The erosion caused by the scouring water has exposed layers of rock over a billion years old, allowing scientists to examine some of the oldest fossils ever found. There are two viewing platforms above the falls and a roped off area for swimming.

Cafés and restaurants

Thunder Bay's choicest places to **eat** are concentrated in Little Suomi, on Cumberland Street, just up from the Pagoda, and around the Marina near the old CN station.

Armando's 28 Cumberland St North ⓣ807/344-5833. Trim Italian restaurant offering good pizzas, pastas and a baritone performance at your table with your order. Closed Sun.

Caribou Restaurant and Wine Bar 727 Hewitson St ⓣ807/628-8588. An unlikely location in the industrial wilderness that is South Thunder Bay provides an oasis of tapas, imaginative pizza and dishes like oven-roasted barramundi. Lunch is served on Thurs & Fri for $14 while dinner averages $25.

Good News Cafe 116 South Syndicate Ave ⓣ807/623-5001. A fabulous place for a light bite. All ingredients are sourced locally and there is a wide variety of vegetarian options from just $6. The cakes and desserts are mouthwatering.

Hoito Restaurant 314 Bay St at Algoma ⓣ807/345-6323. Established in 1918, Thunder Bay's best-known Finnish café-cum-canteen is always full and the specials on the board should not be missed. The salt fish, potatoes and viili (clabbered milk) is delicious. Breakfasts start at $5, dinners at $10 including beverages. Mon–Fri 7am–8pm, Sat & Sun 8am–8pm.

Prospector Steak House 27 Cumberland St South ⓣ807/345-5833. A local favourite, the *Prospector* has pictures of old-time Thunder Bay on the walls and serves chowder from brass prospector's vats. Ribs and locally caught fish from $20.

West of Thunder Bay

Heading west from Thunder Bay on Hwy 17 towards Manitoba, it's a long, gruelling drive of almost 500km through the interminable pine forests of the Canadian Shield to the next town of any real interest, **Kenora**, where hundreds of fishermen gather every summer before sidling off into the vast **Lake of the Woods** in their quest to reel in walleye, among other species. The lake straddles the Ontario–Manitoba border and Kenora is itself just 200km from Winnipeg (see p.560). Regular long-distance Greyhound buses ply Hwy 17.

Kenora and the Lake of the Woods

KENORA used to be known as "Rat Portage" until a flour company refused to build a mill here, arguing that the word "rat" on their sacks wouldn't do much for sales. Nowadays the permanent population of 9000 quadruples in the summer, when droves of Americans arrive with their fishing tackle – no wonder the town has a twelve-metre statue of a fish at its entrance. Rod or not, Kenora is a pleasant enough spot to break the long journey west (or east), especially in summer when there's a really laid-back feel to the place.

From the foot of Main Street, the *MS Kenora* **cruises** the Lake of the Woods' islands and channels for two hours (Aug to mid-Sept 2 daily; ⓣ807/468-9124, ⓦwww.mskenora.com; $21.50), offering an opportunity to see **Devil's Gap Rock** at the entrance to the town harbour. In 1884, the rock was painted to resemble a human face and it has been regularly repainted ever since. This is not, however, a gimmicky attraction: Devil's Gap is an Ojibwa spirit rock, to which food and tobacco offerings were once made to propitiate Windigo, the large and threatening personification of winter. Windigo's powers could only be controlled by powerful shamen, and when hunters disappeared in the bush they were thought to have been eaten by him. As an introduction to the **Lake of the Woods**, the boat trip does just fine, but the sheer vastness of the lake – and its 14,000 islands – is hard to grasp. One way of sampling much more is to rent a **houseboat** with Houseboat Adventures, at the Main Street wharf (ⓣ1-800/253-6672, ⓦwww.houseboatadventures.com). Their boats have all modern conveniences – from toasters through to freezers – and the onboard fish-cleaning stations reveal the predilections of their customers. Prices range from $1275–4000 per week per boat for up to six people.

Practicalities

Kenora's **bus terminus** is at 1350 Hwy 17 East (ⓣ807/468-7172), not far from the **tourist office**, also on Hwy 17 East (ⓣ1-800/535-4549, ⓦwww.kenora.ca). First choice for **accommodation** is the landmark, eleven-storey *Best Western Lakeside Inn*, 470 1st Ave South (ⓣ807/468-5521, ⓦwww.bestwestern.com; ❺), from where there are panoramic views over the town and its surroundings. There are several other chain **motels** dotted along Hwy 17 just east of town as well as a number of **B&Bs**, including the *Kendall House B&B*, 127 5th Ave South (ⓣ807/468-4645, ⓦwww.bbcanada.com/3568.html; ❹), in a tastefully restored Victorian property complete with period furniture. In both cases, reservations are strongly advised in summer.

Remember to put your watch back one hour when you cross into the **Central time zone**, about 60km west of Thunder Bay.

Travel details

Trains

Ontario Northland trains (ⓣ1-800/461-8558, ⓦwww.northlander.ca)
Cochrane to: Moosonee on the Polar Bear Express (July & Aug 1 daily except Mon; 4hr 20min); Moosonee on the Little Bear (3 weekly in winter; 5hr).
VIA Rail (ⓣ1-888/842-7245, ⓦwww.viarail.ca)
Kingston to: Montréal (3 daily; 2hr 15min); Ottawa (2–4 daily; 2hr); Toronto (2–3 daily; 2hr 30min).
London to: Stratford (2 daily; 1hr)
Ottawa to: Gananoque (1 daily; 1hr 35min); Kingston (2–4 daily; 2hr); Montréal (3–5 daily; 2hr); Toronto (3–5 daily; 4hr 15min).

Buses

Greyhound (ⓣ1-800/661-8747, ⓦwww.greyhound.ca)
Kenora to: Winnipeg (3 daily; 2hr 30min).
Kingston to: Montréal (2 daily; 5hr); Ottawa (2 daily; 2hr 45min).
London to: Hamilton (5 daily; 2hr); Kitchener (4 daily; 2hr); Owen Sound (1 daily; 4hr 30min, including 2 changes); Stratford (2 daily; 1hr 20min); Windsor (5 daily; 2hr 40min).
North Bay to: Ottawa (3 daily; 5hr); Sudbury (3 daily; 2hr).
Ottawa to: Kingston (2 daily; 2hr 45min); Montréal (hourly; 2hr 30min); North Bay (3 daily; 5hr); Sudbury (3 daily; 7hr 30min); Toronto (9 daily; 5-6hr).
Sault Ste Marie to: Kenora (3 daily; 16hr); Thunder Bay (3 daily; 9–10hr); Toronto (3 daily; 10hr 30min); Wawa (3 daily; 3hr); White River (2 daily; 4hr); Winnipeg (3 daily; 20hr).
Sudbury to: Montréal (3 daily; 11hr); North Bay (3 daily; 2hr); Ottawa (3 daily; 7hr 30min); Sault Ste Marie (4 daily; 4–5hr).; Thunder Bay (3 daily; 15hr).
Thunder Bay to: Kenora (3 daily; 6hr); Sault Ste Marie (3 daily; 9–10hr); Sudbury (3 daily; 15hr); Toronto (3 daily; 20hr); Winnipeg (3 daily; 9hr).
Ontario Northland (ⓣ1-800/461-8558, ⓦwww.webusit.com)
North Bay to: Bracebridge (4 daily; 2hr); Cobalt (2 daily; 1hr 50min); Cochrane (5 daily; 6hr 15min); Gravenhurst (4 daily; 2hr 10min); Hearst (2 daily; 10hr); Huntsville (4 daily; 1hr 30min); Kirkland Lake (2 daily; 4hr); Orillia (4 daily; 3hr 15min); Temagami (2 daily; 1hr 10min); Toronto (4-5 daily; 6hr).
Sudbury to: Cochrane (1 daily; 2hr 45min); Hearst (1 daily; 8hr 15min); Orillia (1 daily; 4hr); Parry Sound (3 daily; 2hr); Port Severn (3 daily; 3hr 15min); Toronto (3 daily; 6hr).
Coach Canada (ⓣ1-800/461-7661, ⓦwww.coachcanada.com)
Kingston to: Montréal (8 daily; 3hr 20min); Toronto (8 daily; 3hr).

3

Montréal and Southwest Québec

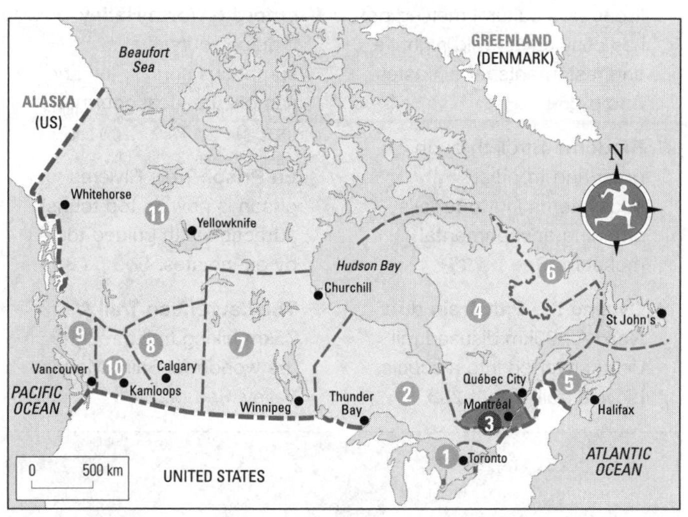

CHAPTER 3

Highlights

* **Montréal Jazz Festival** From late June, crowds gather for free outdoor shows. See p.239
* **Vieux-Montréal** Wander through narrow streets lined with centuries-old buildings. See p.245
* **Plateau Mont-Royal** Montréal's cultural melting pot has cosy cafés, wild nightlife and restaurants for all tastes. See p.259
* **Biodôme** Stroll through polar and tropical ecosystems in Montréal's stunning environmental museum. See p.263
* **Cycling the P'tit Train du Nord** A 200km disused rail bed converted into a scenic bicycle trail. See p.280
* **Mont-Tremblant** Eastern Canada's premier ski resort is a great spot year-round for outdoor pursuits. See p.281
* **Abbaye Saint-Benoît-du-Lac** Listen to the Gregorian chants of Benedictine Monks amid spectacular countryside. See p.284
* **Orford & North Hatley** Indulge yourself at a sumptious country inn and sample the local gourmet fare. See p.284
* **En Prison** Trois Riviéres' old prison is now its top tourist attraction with guided tours by ex-inmates. See p.288
* **The Laurentian Trail** A 75km hiking trail through the wonderful Saint-Maurice Valley. See p.289

△ Abbaye Saint-Benoit-du-lac, Québec

Montréal and Southwest Québec

As home to the only French-speaking society in North America, Québec is totally distinct from the rest of the continent – so distinct, in fact, that its political elite have been obsessed with the politics of secession for decades. The province was ceded to the British after the conquest of the French in 1759 and yet more than 200 years later the legacy of 'New France' is as tangible as ever. After the colony was transferred to British rule, the Québecois were allowed to maintain their language and Catholic religion, which ensured large families and a prevalence of French-speakers throughout the following generations – a political move termed the *revanche du berceau* ("revenge of the cradle"). Centuries later, the result is a unique blend of North American and European influence and a province with an interesting dual-personality. Nowhere is this more evident than in **Montréal and Southwest Québec**. Within striking distance of Ottawa, and pressed hard against the US border with Vermont, New Hampshire and Maine, this one tiny corner of the province has led both the economic and political resurgence of French-speaking Canada throughout the last century. Home to over a third of all Québecois, the island metropolis of **Montréal** is fiercely proud of both its European heritage and its reputation as a truly international city. There can be few places in the world where people on the street flit so easily between two or more languages – sometimes within the same sentence – or whose cafés and bars ooze such a cosmopolitan feel.

From downtown Montréal the mirrored skyscrapers that vie for space between colony-era cathedrals and historic buildings have a view across to the St Lawrence River and the wilderness beyond that was once the source of the city's wealth and power. These days the vast wilds of Southwest Québec are admired for their natural beauty rather than their promise of furs and minerals

Information and hotel reservations

Fédération des Agricotours Ⓦwww.agricotours.qc.ca. An excellent service listing quality-inspected bed and breakfasts throughout Québec.

Tourisme Québec Ⓣ1-877/266-5687, Ⓦwww.bonjourquebec.com. Information and a province-wide accommodation booking facility.

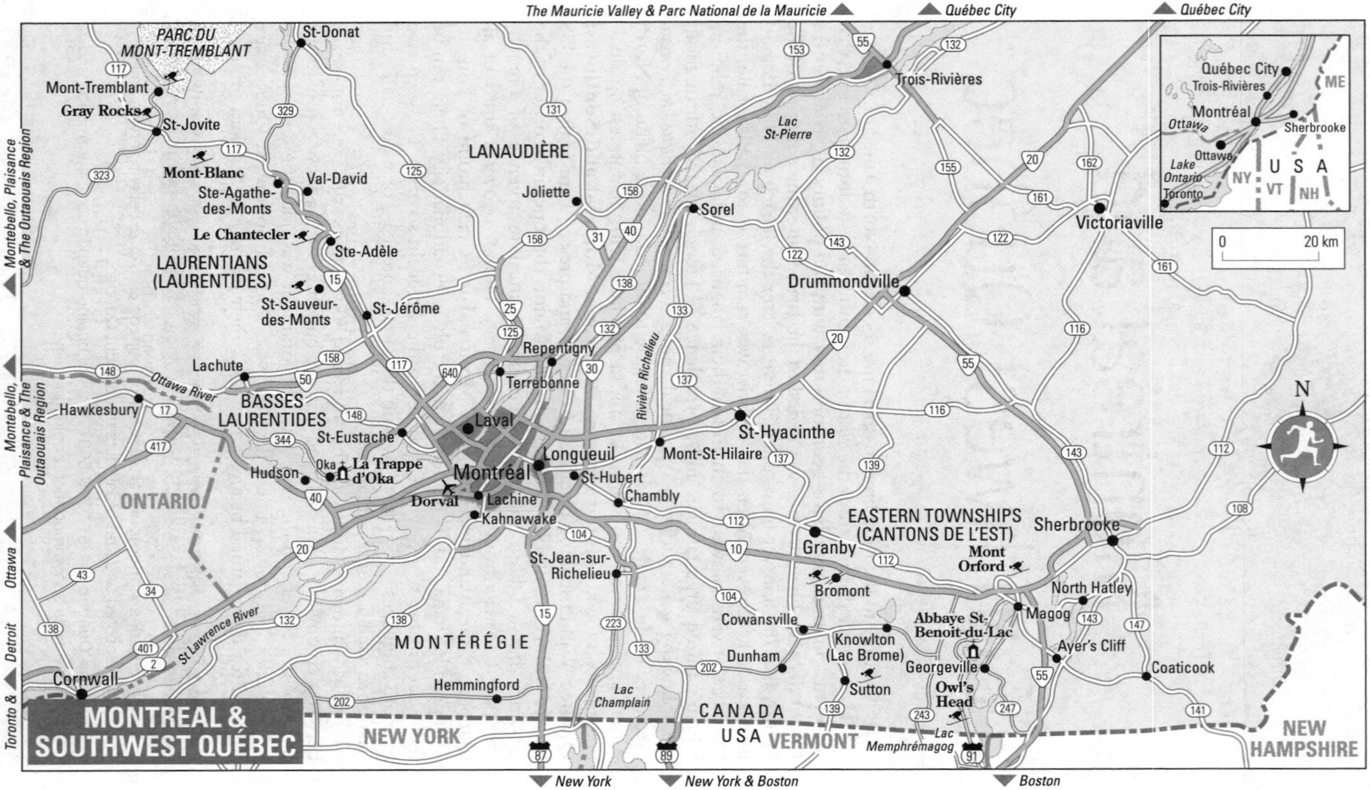

MONTREAL & SOUTHWEST QUÉBEC

The Mauricie Valley & Parc National de la Mauricie
Québec City
Québec City
Montebello, Plaisance & The Outaouais Region
Montebello, Plaisance & The Outaouais Region
Ottawa
Detroit
Toronto &
New York
New York & Boston
Boston

PARC DU MONT-TREMBLANT
St-Donat
Mont-Tremblant
Gray Rocks
St-Jovite
Mont-Blanc
Ste-Agathe-des-Monts
Val-David
Le Chantecler
Ste-Adèle
LAURENTIANS (LAURENTIDES)
St-Sauveur-des-Monts
St-Jérôme
LANAUDIÈRE
Joliette
Repentigny
Terrebonne
Lachute
Ottawa River
Hawkesbury
BASSES LAURENTIDES
St-Eustache
Oka
La Trappe d'Oka
Hudson
ONTARIO
Laval
Montréal
Dorval
Lachine
Kahnawake
Longueuil
St-Hubert
Chambly
Mont-St-Hilaire
St-Hyacinthe
Rivière Richelieu
Sorel
Lac St-Pierre
Trois-Rivières
Drummondville
Victoriaville
St-Jean-sur-Richelieu
MONTÉRÉGIE
Hemmingford
Cornwall
St Lawrence River
NEW YORK
Lac Champlain
CANADA
USA
VERMONT
EASTERN TOWNSHIPS (CANTONS DE L'EST)
Granby
Bromont
Cowansville
Dunham
Knowlton (Lac Brome)
Sutton
Abbaye St-Benoit-du-Lac
Georgeville
Owl's Head
Lac Memphrémagog
Mont Orford
Magog
North Hatley
Ayer's Cliff
Coaticook
Sherbrooke
NEW HAMPSHIRE
N
0 20 km

Québec City
Trois-Rivières
Montréal
Ottawa
Ottawa
Sherbrooke
Lake Ontario
Toronto
ME
USA
NY
VT
NH

and there are two carefully groomed rural getaways just an hours drive out of the city. To the north, the hilly and forested **Laurentians** offer easily accessible outdoor activities all year round including over 500kms of dedicated cycling, hiking and horse riding trails in the summer and 8 downhill ski centers and 2000kms of prepared cross-country ski routes in the winter. To the south of Montréal, the **Eastern Townships (Cantons-de-l'Est)**, which spread across the foothills of the Appalachian mountains, lure city dwellers into the country with a more opulent approach to the outdoors. Originally a place of refuge for Americans wanting to stay loyal to the British Crown both during and after the American War of Independence in 1775–1810, the area has an Anglophone veneer. The initial settlers formed small towns and villages rather than adopting the French Seigneurie system used elsewhere in Québec, but within two generations the majority of the population were French Canadian. Today the townships, despite their very British-sounding names, are 94 percent Francophone. The Gallic ancestry of most Townshippers is clear in their attitude towards hedonistic pleasures: surrounding themselves with specialized eateries, vineyards and expert cheese makers, they eat and drink in a style that combines the simplicity of the first Norman settlers with the rich tastes of the contemporary French. This is Disney-perfect France with flawless country inns and dreamy spas flaunting impeccable gardens and unbelievable views.

Train services within the region run from Montréal to Ontario, New Brunswick and into the US as well as connecting Québec City and the north of Québec. Though a little slower, the **jetfoil** makes an interesting alternative for the Montréal to Québec City run. For most destinations, though, **buses** are your best bet for getting around, with the major places connected by Orléans Express and Intercar services, supplemented by a network of smaller local lines.

A brief history of Québec

Although various **First Nations** have lived in pockets of the province for millennia and there had been sporadic European contact to the east, Québec's history really begins with Jacques Cartier's 1535 voyage. He sailed up the St Lawrence stopping at Stadacona and Hochelaga, where settlements in the early seventeenth century have evolved into present-day Québec City and Montréal – see p.237 and p.296 for a detailed history of those two cities. The early days of the colony revolved around the fur trade and attempts to convert the natives to **Christianity**. The Récollets (reformed Franciscans) and Jesuit missionaries – called the "Black Robes" by the natives who suspected them of sorcery – were more often than not put to death. The priests' tasks were not made any easier by the fact that the French had aligned with the Algonquin and Huron nations to gain access to their **fur-trading networks**, while those groups' traditional enemies, the Iroquois Confederacy, had formed alliances with the Dutch and subsequently the British. Periodic bouts between the factions over control of the industry would continue over the next half-century. Louis XIV made New France a royal province in 1663 despatching troops and, subsequently, unmarried Frenchwomen, the so-called **filles du roi**, who were shipped over by the boatload. Periodic skirmishes between the French and British and their native allies continued to be a destabilizing factor, stunting the growth of the colony. Matters were resolved somewhat when 1200 colonists met with an even greater number of natives from across eastern North America at Pointe-à-Callière in Montréal to sign **La Grande Paix**, the Great Peace treaty of 1701. The signing of the Treaty of Utrecht with the British a decade later further allowed the fur trade to flourish.

Aboriginal peoples in Québec

Francophone–anglophone relations may be the principal concern of most Québecois – eighty percent of them have French as their mother tongue – but the province's population also includes eleven nations of **aboriginal** peoples, the majority of whom live on reservations "granted" them by the early French settlers. Resentment and racism are as rife here as elsewhere in Canada, but aboriginal grievances are particularly acute in Québec as most of the province's tribes are English-oriented – the **Mohawks** near Montréal even fought on the side of the British during the conquest. Still, relations are even bad between the authorities and French-speaking groups. The **Hurons** (see p.1084) near Québec City, for example, battled in courts for eight years to retain their hunting rights, while around James Bay the **Cree** fought and won the right to block the expansion of Québec's hydroelectric network which, had it been completed as planned, would have covered an area the size of Germany. Begun in 1971, the project nonetheless resulted in the displacement of Cree and **Inuit**, due to flooded lands as well as the pollution of rivers that had not been safely channelled.

Aboriginal peoples have categorically voted against separation and have used mostly peaceful methods to register their land claims, which amount to 85 percent of the province's area. There was violence at the Mohawk uprising at Oka near Montréal in 1990 (see p.276), which, though condemned by most Canadians and aboriginals, drew attention to the concerns of aboriginal Canadians. This led to the creation of the Royal Commission on Aboriginal Peoples, a nationwide examination of the issues at stake. In 1996, the commission recommended a revamping of the aboriginal welfare system, greater self-government and a settlement of land-claims negotiations. Some of these have been enacted – such as the Nisga'a treaty in British Columbia – but scarcely any movement has been made on other issues. First Nations have also been asserting ownership of natural resources, especially in the eastern provinces where fishing rights are a hotly contested issue, and these have also been upheld by the Supreme Court of Canada. Each decision in favour of aboriginal land claims carries implications for Québec's aboriginal groups who have repeatedly refused to join their territories to a sovereign Québec state in the event of secession.

It wasn't until mid-century that further serious conflict broke out, with the British and French again at odds in the **Seven Years' War** (also known as the French and Indian War). Although the early years of fighting were concentrated in the Atlantic colonies, the turning point took place in 1759 with the Battle of the Plains of Abraham (see p.312). The British consolidated their hold with the 1774 Québec Act, allowing the Québecois to maintain their language, civil code, seigneurial system and religion, a pre-emptive move that helped resist American attempts to take over the colony. After the Americans won independence from Britain in their own land, however, a flood of **United Empire Loyalists** fled across the Canadian border, settling primarily in the Eastern Townships and present-day Ontario.

The creation of Lower and Upper Canada in 1791 emphasized the inequalities between anglophones and francophones, as the French-speaking majority in Lower Canada were ruled by the so-called **Château Clique**, an assembly of francophone priests and seigneurs who had to answer to a British governor and council appointed in London. Rebellions against this hierarchy by the mainly French *Patriotes* in 1837 led to an investigation by Lord Durham who concluded that English and French relations were akin to "two nations warring within the bosom of a single state". His prescription for peace was immersing French-Canadians in the English culture of North America, and the subsequent establishment of the Province of Canada in 1840 can be seen as a deliberate attempt to marginalize francophone opinion within an English-speaking state.

French-Canadians remained insulated from the economic mainstream until nineteenth-century **industrialization**, financed and run by the better-educated anglophones, led to a mass francophone migration to the cities. By the mid-twentieth century, a French-speaking middle class had begun to articulate the grievances of the workforce and to criticize the suffocating effect the Church was having on francophone opportunity. The shake-up of Québec society finally came about with the so-called **Quiet Revolution** in the 1960s, spurred by the provincial government under the leadership of Jean Lesage and his Liberal Party of Québec. The provincial government took control of welfare, health and education away from the Church and, under the slogan *Maîtres chez-nous* ("Masters of our own house"), established state-owned industries that reversed anglophone financial domination by encouraging the development of a francophone entrepreneurial and business class.

In order to implement these fiscal policies, Québec needed to administer its own taxes, and the provincial Liberals, despite being staunchly federalist, were constantly at loggerheads with Ottawa. Encouraged and influenced by other nationalist struggles, Québecois' desire for recognition and power reached a violent peak in 1970 with the terrorist actions of the largely unpopular **Front de Libération du Québec** (FLQ) in Montréal. The kidnapping of Cabinet Minister Pierre Laporte and British diplomat James Cross, with Laporte winding up dead in the trunk of a car, led then-Prime Minister Pierre Trudeau to enact the War Measures Act and send Canadian troops into the streets of Montréal. Six years later a massive reaction against the ruling provincial Liberals brought the separatist **Parti Québécois** (PQ) to power in Montréal. Led by René Lévesque, the PQ accelerated the process of social change with the *Charte de la langue française*, better known as **Bill 101**, which established French as the province's official language. With French dominant in the workplace and the classroom, many Québecois thought they were on the brink of cultural and social independence. In 1980, a **referendum** on sovereignty was held but, still reeling from the terrorist activities of the FLQ and scared that separatism would leave Québec economically adrift, the 6.5-million population voted 60:40 against. Prime Minister Trudeau then set about repatriating the country's **constitution**. In 1981 he called a late-night meeting on the issue and did not invite Lévesque, literally denying Québec a seat at the table. "The night of the long knives", as the event became known, wound up imposing a Constitution on the province that placed its language rights in jeopardy and removed its veto power over constitutional amendments. The provincial government refused to sign it – and still hasn't to this day.

In 1993, Québec's displeasure with federalism was evident in the election of Lucien Bouchard's Bloc Québécois to the vastly ironic status of Her Majesty's Loyal Opposition in Ottawa. The cause received added support in 1994 when the PQ was returned to provincial power after vowing to hold a province-wide **referendum** on separation from Canada. The referendum was held a year later and the vote was so close – Québec opted to remain within Canada by a margin of less than one percent – that calls immediately arose for a third referendum (prompting pundits to refer to the process as the "neverendum").

Bouchard left federal politics in 1996 to take the leadership of the PQ, determined to become the leader of a new country. After further steps at constitutional reform got nowhere, the federal Liberals enacted the **Clarity Act** in 1999 – a sharp departure from their previous kowtowing tactics: the act laid out the requirements Québec needed to meet in order to secede.

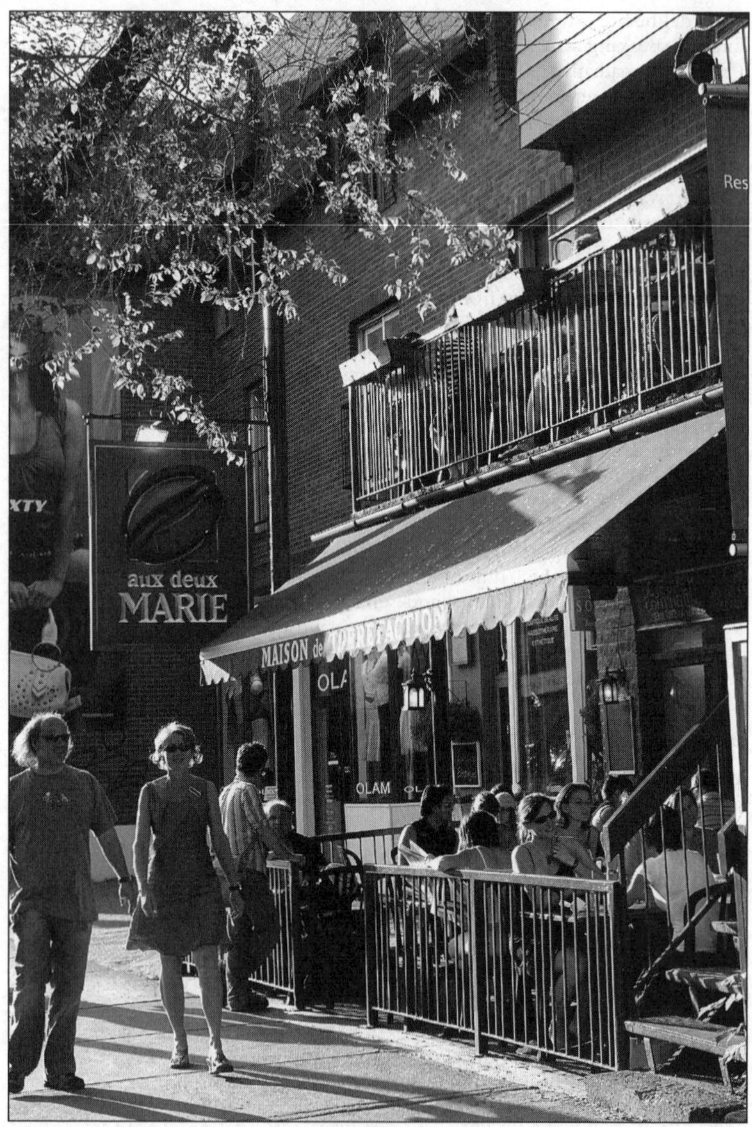

△ Café terraces on rue St Denis

Matters stumbled on until Bouchard's sudden resignation as Premier of Québec in 2001; his successor, Bernard Landry, couldn't match Bouchard's powers of oratory and charisma and marked the beginning of a slump in support for the sovereignist cause.

After suffering through a long recession (due, in large part, to the political battles) Québecois tired of the constitutional wrangling and appeared to be more interested in maintaining political peace than encouraging old fights – an attitude that no doubt led Jean Charest and his Liberals to victory on mainly bread-and-butter issues in 2003. Charest initially proved to be a deeply unpopular Premier due to his failure to deliver on pre-election pledges, which included promises of tax cuts and the demerger of cities that had been forcibly amalgamated by the previous PQ government. Electing a new leader, André Boisclair, in November 2005, the PQ looked strong enough, once again, to vie for power but instead they have been blighted by internal frictions and very public leadership bickering. Still waiting for a third referendum, the PQ has found itself fighting for survival on two fronts – accused by its own hard line supporters of going soft on the idea of independence and increasingly being forced by everyone else to justify its existence. Meanwhile, in recent years, Charest has gained a grudging acceptance, if not modest popularity, in the province. Boosted by his insistence that Québec set its own Kyoto targets (after a wider Federal decision to opt out of the Kyoto Protocol) and his campaign to win Québec more money from the Federal purse, his Liberals are once again beating the PQ in the polls.

Today, little hope remains of achieving the dream of a sovereign Québec in the near future – if ever – and yet, 'The National Question' rumbles on. Charest was recently accused of using the name 'Jean' rather than his legal name 'John' to appeal to the francophone vote. Although there is still no evidence of majority support on either side of the debate, the current political climate suggests that Québecois would now rather see a new deal that keeps them in Canada and view the threat of sovereignty as a way to strengthen their position in federal matters.

Montréal

MONTRÉAL, Canada's second-largest city, is geographically as close to the European coast as to Vancouver, and in look and feel it combines some of the finest aspects of the two continents. Its North American skyline of glass and concrete rises above churches and monuments in a melange of European styles as varied as Montréal's social mix. This is also the world's third-largest French-speaking metropolis after Paris and Kinshasa, but only two-thirds of the city's three and a half million people are of French extraction, the other third being a cosmopolitan mishmash of *les autres*, including British, Eastern Europeans, Chinese, Italians, Greeks, Jews, Latin Americans and Caribbeans. The result is a truly multidimensional city, with a global variety of eateries, bars and clubs, matched by a calendar of festivals that makes this the most vibrant place in Canada.

It is also here that the two main linguistic groups – anglophones and francophones – come into greatest contact with one another. In the wake of the "francization" of Québec, English-Canadians hit Hwy 401 in droves, tipping the nation's economic supremacy from Montréal to Toronto. Though written off by Canada's English-speaking majority, the city did not sink into oblivion. Instead, it has undergone a resurgence, becoming the driving force behind the high-tech industries that are transforming Canada's economy.

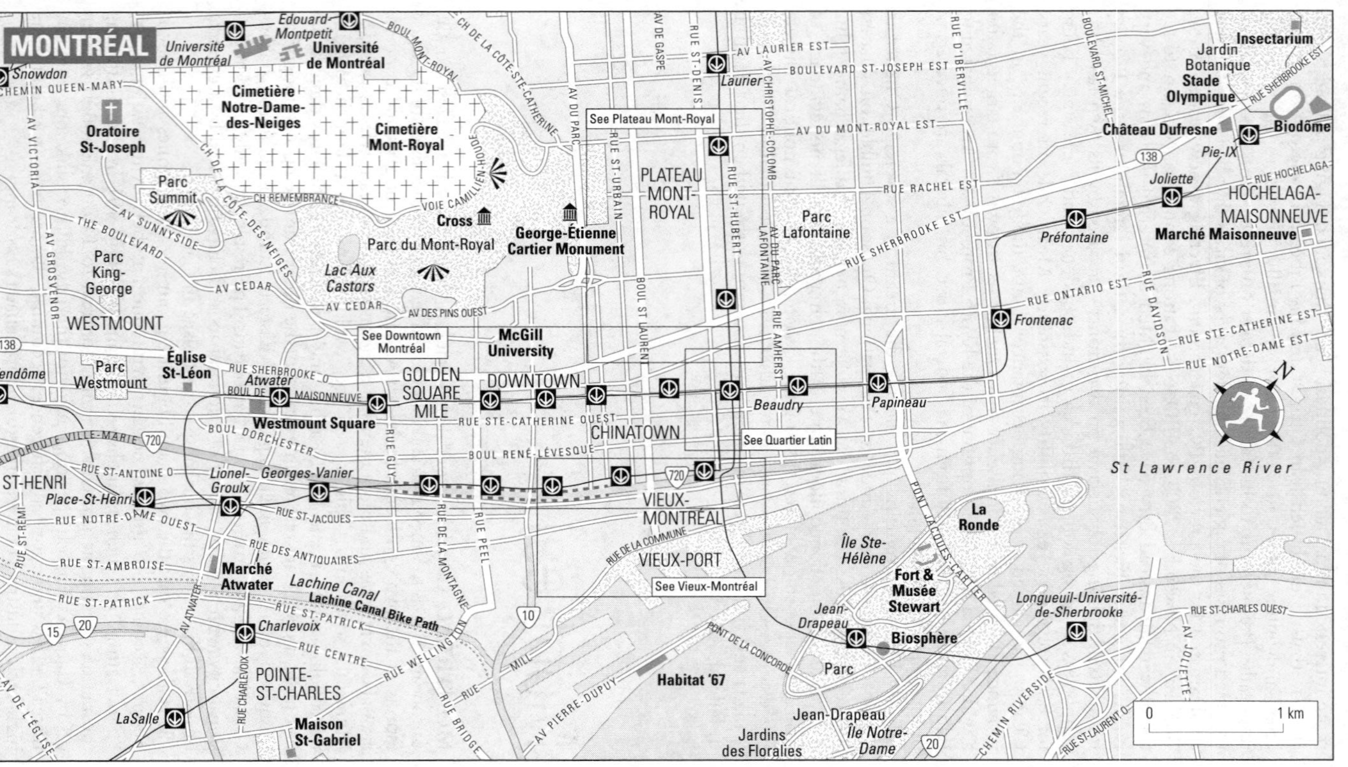
MONTRÉAL
Snowdon
Université de Montréal
Edouard-Montpetit
Université de Montréal
CHEMIN QUEEN-MARY
Oratoire St-Joseph
Cimetière Notre-Dame-des-Neiges
Cimetière Mont-Royal
BOUL MONT-ROYAL
CH DE LA CÔTE-STE-CATHERINE
AV DU PARC
See Plateau Mont-Royal
AV DE GASPE
RUE ST-DENIS
AV LAURIER EST
Laurier
BOULEVARD ST-JOSEPH EST
AV CHRISTOPHE-COLOMB
AV DU MONT-ROYAL EST
RUE D'IBERVILLE
BOULEVARD ST-MICHEL
Jardin Botanique
Insectarium
Stade Olympique
RUE SHERBROOKE EST
Château Dufresne
Biodôme
Pie-IX
138
Joliette
RUE HOCHELAGA
HOCHELAGA-MAISONNEUVE
Marché Maisonneuve
AV VICTORIA
Parc Summit
CH DE LA CÔTE-DES-NEIGES
CH REMEMBRANCE
VOIE CAMILLIEN-HOUDE
Cross
George-Étienne Cartier Monument
RUE ST-URBAIN
PLATEAU MONT-ROYAL
RUE ST-HUBERT
AV DU PARC LAFONTAINE
Parc Lafontaine
RUE RACHEL EST
RUE SHERBROOKE EST
Préfontaine
AV SUNNYSIDE
THE BOULEVARD
AV GROSVENOR
Parc King-George
AV CEDAR
Parc du Mont-Royal
Lac Aux Castors
AV DES PINS OUEST
BOUL ST LAURENT
RUE AMHERST
RUE ONTARIO EST
RUE DAVIDSON
Frontenac
WESTMOUNT
138
See Downtown Montréal
McGill University
RUE STE-CATHERINE EST
RUE NOTRE-DAME EST
Vendôme
Parc Westmount
Église St-Léon
RUE SHERBROOKE O
Atwater
BOUL DE MAISONNEUVE
GOLDEN SQUARE MILE
DOWNTOWN
Beaudry
Papineau
Westmount Square
RUE STE-CATHERINE OUEST
CHINATOWN
See Quartier Latin
BOUL DORCHESTER
AUTOROUTE VILLE-MARIE
720
RUE GUY
BOUL RENÉ-LÉVESQUE
St Lawrence River
ST-HENRI
RUE ST-ANTOINE O
Lionel-Groulx
Georges-Vanier
720
Place-St-Henri
RUE NOTRE-DAME OUEST
RUE ST-JACQUES
RUE DE LA MONTAGNE
RUE PEEL
VIEUX-MONTRÉAL
PONT JACQUES-CARTIER
La Ronde
RUE ST-REMI
RUE DES ANTIQUAIRES
RUE DE LA COMMUNE
VIEUX-PORT
Île Ste-Hélène
RUE ST-AMBROISE
Marché Atwater
Lachine Canal
Lachine Canal Bike Path
See Vieux-Montréal
Fort & Musée Stewart
RUE ST-PATRICK
AV ATWATER
RUE ST-PATRICK
Jean-Drapeau
Longueuil-Université-de-Sherbrooke
RUE ST-CHARLES OUEST
15
20
Charlevoix
10
Biosphère
RUE CENTRE
RUE WELLINGTON
MILL
PONT DE LA CONCORDE
Parc
AV JOLIETTE
POINTE-ST-CHARLES
RUE BRIDGE
AV PIERRE-DUPUY
Habitat '67
CHEMIN RIVERSIDE
AV DE L'ÉGLISE
LaSalle
RUE CHARLEVOIX
Maison St-Gabriel
Jean-Drapeau
Jardins des Floralies
Île Notre-Dame
20
RUE ST-LAURENT O
0
1 km
N

Everywhere you look there are the signs of civic pride and prosperity. In the historic quarter of **Vieux-Montréal**, on the banks of the St Lawrence River, the streets and squares are flanked by well-tended buildings, from the mammoth **Basilique Notre-Dame** and steepled **Chapelle de Notre-Dame-de-Bon-Secours**, to sleek and stately commercial buildings and chic new boutique hotels. Old houses have been converted into lively restaurants and shops, abandoned warehouses into condos and the disused **Vieux-Port** into a summer playground with landscaped parklands facing onto the St Lawrence. Beneath the forested rise of **Mont Royal**, the boulevards and leafy squares of **downtown** are alive from the morning rush hour right through to the wee hours, when revellers return from the clubs of **rue Ste-Catherine** and the more intimate bars and lounges of the nearby **Plateau** and **Quartier Latin** districts. Below ground are the walkways of the **Underground City** and the outstanding **Métro** system, while towards the eastern outskirts the **Stade Olympique**'s leaning tower overshadows the vast **Jardin Botanique**, second in international status only to London's Kew Gardens.

In addition, the city boasts some excellent museums. The **Centre Canadien d'Architecture** has one of the continents most impressive specialist collections, focusing on the role of architecture in society, innovative design practice and the history of ideas. The **Musée d'Art Contemporain** is Canada's only museum devoted entirely to contemporary art and the **Musée des Beaux-Arts** is the oldest fine-arts museum in the country. Equally outstanding are the museums devoted to Montréal and Canadian history; of these, the **Musée McCord** has a mint collection of native artefacts, while the **Musée d'Archéologie et d'Histoire de Montréal** delivers a state-of-the-art presentation of archeological findings at the site of Montréal's founding in 1642.

Some history

The island of Montréal was first occupied by the St Lawrence **Iroquois**, whose small village of Hochelaga ("Place of the Beaver") was situated at the base of Mont Royal. The first European contact occurred in 1535 when Jacques-Cartier was led here while searching for a northwest route to Asia. However, a permanent European presence was not instigated until 1611; the French settlement was little more than a small garrison, and it wasn't until 1642 that the colony of Ville-Marie was founded. The soldiers were on orders from Paris to "bring about the Glory of God and the salvation of the Indians", a mission that predictably enough found a frosty response from the aboriginal peoples. Bloody conflict with the Iroquois, fanned by the European fur-trade alliances with the Algonquins and Hurons, was constant until the **Great Peace treaty** of 1701 prompted the growth of Montréal into the main embarkation point for the fur and lumber trade. When Québec City fell to the British in 1759, Montréal briefly served as the capital of New France. The ensuing **British occupation** saw a flood of Irish and Scottish immigrants who soon made Montréal North America's second-largest city. It was not a harmonious expansion, however, and in 1837 the predominantly French *Patriotes* led by Louis-Joseph Papineau rebelled against the British ruling class. Their insurgency failed and was followed by hangings and exiles.

With the creation of the **Dominion of Canada** in 1867, Montréal emerged as the nation's premier port, railroad nexus, banking centre and industrial producer. Its population reached half a million in 1911 and doubled in the next two decades with an influx of émigrés from Europe. It was also during this period that Montréal acquired its reputation as Canada's "sin city". During Prohibition in the US, Québec became the main alcohol supplier to the entire continent: the Molsons and their ilk made their fortunes here, while prostitution and gambling thrived under the protection of the authorities. Only in the wake of World War II and the subsequent economic boom did a major anti-corruption operation begin, tied in with rapid architectural growth. The most glamorous episode in the city's face-lift came with **Expo '67**, the World's Fair that attracted fifty million visitors to Montréal. However, it was the city's anglophones who were benefiting from the prosperity, and beneath the smooth surface francophone frustrations were reaching dangerous levels.

The crisis peaked in 1970, with the terrorism of the **Front de Libération du Québec** (FLQ), who kidnapped a British diplomat and then a Québec cabinet minister, Pierre Laporte. As ransom, the FLQ demanded the publication of their manifesto, the transportation to Cuba of 25 FLQ prisoners and $500,000 in gold bullion. Prime Minister Pierre Trudeau responded by suspending civil liberties and putting troops on the streets of Montréal. The following day, Laporte's body was found. Although the Briton was later released, and his captors and Laporte's murderers arrested, the reverberations shook the nation.

Recognizing the need to redress social imbalances, the federal government poured money into schemes to promote French-Canadian culture. Francophone discontent was further alleviated by the provincial election of the Parti Québécois (PQ) in 1976, the year Montréal staged the **Olympic Games**. The consequent language laws, known as **Bill 101**, have made French a compulsory part of the school curriculum and banned English signs on business premises, only allowing them inside establishments – providing the signs are bilingual and the French is printed twice as large as the English. Businesses that fail to comply are at the mercy of the "language police", inspectors of the Office de la Langue Française (OLF) who can go to extraordinary lengths – such as measuring signs and checking business cards – to ensure that French is the dominant form of communication. This, for many anglophones, combined with the threat of sovereignty, prompted an exodus in the tens of thousands from Montréal, chiefly to Toronto.

A Canada-wide economic recession in the mid-1990s saw Québec lag behind the rest of the country in economic growth. But the turning point came after 1995, when a tacit truce was made on the issue of separation. The boarded-up shops that lined rue Ste-Catherine in the mid-1990s have reopened and now do good business. Derelict pockets on the edges of downtown and Vieux-Montréal were renovated to house the booming multimedia industry. And with **rising prosperity**, popular residential areas like the Plateau are being gentrified; apartment developments abound. Even the city's nightlife scene is changing, as working people opt for the weekday *cinq à sept* early-evening cocktail hour rather than partying late into the night. But perhaps the most enduring change is that the gaps left by departing anglophones have been filled by young **bilingual** francophones, who feel in charge of their own culture and economy. At the same time, many anglophones that stayed have also become bilingual, and these days it's perfectly normal to hear the two languages intermingling with one another wherever you may be.

Arrival, information and city transport

Montréal's main international **airport** is the Aéroport International Pierre-Elliott-Trudeau de Montréal (occasionally referred to by its old name of **Dorval**), or just **Montréal-Trudeau** for short (code YUL; ⓣ 514/394-7377 or 1-800/465-1213, ⓦ www.admtl.com), is located 22km southwest of the city.

Montréal's festivals and events

Montréal has a different festival every week throughout the summer months (pick up the quarterly *What to do in Montréal* guide at the tourist office for a comprehensive list or visit Ⓦwww.tourism-montreal.org). Most event **tickets** can be purchased through Admission (Ⓣ514/790-1245 or 1-800/361-4595, Ⓦwww.admission.com).

The **Festival International de Jazz de Montréal** (Ⓦwww.montrealjazzfest.com) is North America's largest, with more than 400 shows in late June and early July, most of them free at huge open-air stages surrounding Place des Arts. The mid-July **Juste pour Rire** ("Just For Laughs"; Ⓦwww.hahaha.com) is the world's largest comedy festival, with past headliners including Tim Allen, Rowan Atkinson, Jim Carrey, John Candy and Lily Tomlin. Just afterwards, the **Francofolies** (Ⓦwww.francofolies.com) brings French musicians from around the world to various downtown stages. The most visually spectacular of the city's shindigs is the **International Fireworks Competition** late in July, whose participants are competing to get contracts for the July 4 celebrations in the US. The music-coordinated pyrotechnics are a breathtaking sight. The action takes place at the La Ronde amusement park and tickets are around $40 (including ride pass), but across the water and on the Jacques-Cartier Bridge the spectacle is free, and the music for the displays is broadcast live on local radio. There are many food-tasting events and, in some cases, boozy ones, like the June **Mondiale de la Bière** (Ⓦwww.festivalmondialbiere.qc.ca) in the Gare Windsor, which offers the opportunity to sample more than 250 brands of beer from around the world. In late January, Île Ste-Hélène hosts ice-sculpting and general carousing with the **Fête des Neiges de Montréal** (Ⓦwww.fetedesneiges.com). Of the many film festivals, the most notable is the **Montréal World Film Festival** in late August (Ⓦwww.ffm-montreal.org). The late-April **Vues d'Afrique** (Ⓦwww.vuesdafrique.org) is gaining prominence for bringing African and Caribbean films to Montréal. Finally, the **Cirque du Soleil** (Ⓦwww.cirquedusoleil.com) is a world-renowned circus company that travels all over the world; every other year it has a big-top season in its home city. Refusing to exploit animals, the circus's acrobats, trapeze artists, clowns, jugglers and contortionists present an incredible show, with original music scores, extravagant costumes and mind-blowing stunts.

The Aérobus airport shuttle service (daily every 30min 7am–1am; takes 35–45 min; $13 one-way, Ⓣ514/631-1856, Ⓦwww.autobus.qc.ca) links to the Station Centrale d'Autobus Montréal and the Gare d'Aérobus, adjacent to the train station, from where you can take the complimentary shuttle service to major downtown hotels (some hotels also have vans that pick up guests directly from the airport – ask when booking). Several local buses run from the airport to downtown but they take ages. A taxi downtown is $35.

Montréal's main **train station**, Gare Centrale, is below the *Queen Elizabeth Hotel* on the corner of boul René-Lévesque and rue Mansfield, and is entered at 895 rue de la Gauchetière ouest. The station is the major terminus for Canada's VIA Rail trains from Halifax, Toronto, Ottawa, Québec and the Gaspé, as well as US Amtrak trains from Washington and New York. The Underground City links it to Bonaventure Métro station and the rest of downtown. Long-distance **buses** use the Station Centrale d'Autobus Montréal, at 505 boul de Maisonneuve est (Ⓣ514/842-2281 for info on all bus lines). The Berri-UQAM Métro station is beneath it. A number of bus lines – including Orléans Express (Ⓣ1-888/999-3977, Ⓦwww.orleansexpress.com), Québec's main coach company – serve various destinations.

Montréal's main information centre, **Infotouriste** (daily June to early Sept 8.30am–8pm; rest of year 9am–6pm; Ⓣ514/873-2015 or 1-877/266-5687,

Ⓦwww.bonjourquebec.com), is at 1001 rue du Square-Dorchester on the corner of rue Metcalfe. The nearest Métro is Peel: walk south on rue Peel past rue Ste-Catherine. In addition to masses of useful free information, it offers an accommodation service, which will make any number of free calls to find vacancies for you. The **Tourist Information Centre of Old Montréal**, on the northwest corner of Place Jacques-Cartier at 174 rue Notre-Dame est (April–June & Sep–Oct daily 9am–5pm, Jun–Aug daily 9am–7pm, Nov–March Wed–Sun 9am–5pm; Ⓦwww.tourism-montreal.org) provides information on the city only.

Transport

The **public transport** system is one of the city's greatest assets, linking the 65-station **Métro** to 150 bus routes, all run by the STM (Société de transport de Montréal; Ⓣ514/288-6287, Ⓦwww.stm.info). The clean, speedy, reliable and cheap Métro system has four colour-coded lines; the major interconnecting stations are **Berri-UQAM** (which links the orange, green and yellow lines), **Lionel-Groulx** (green and orange), and **Snowdon** and **Jean-Talon** (blue and orange). Coloured signs indicate the direction of each line by showing the name of the end-station. A **correspondance**, available from machines beyond the turnstiles at the Métro stations, allows you to complete your journey by bus at no extra cost, but you must get one at the beginning of your journey, not as you depart the Métro. The transfer system also works in reverse, from buses to Métro: ask the driver for one as you board. Most **buses** stop running at 12.30am, shortly before the Métro, though some run all night.

A one-way **fare** on either Métro or bus is $2.50 (exact change required on buses), and a strip of six tickets costs $11.50. The STM **tourist pass** allows

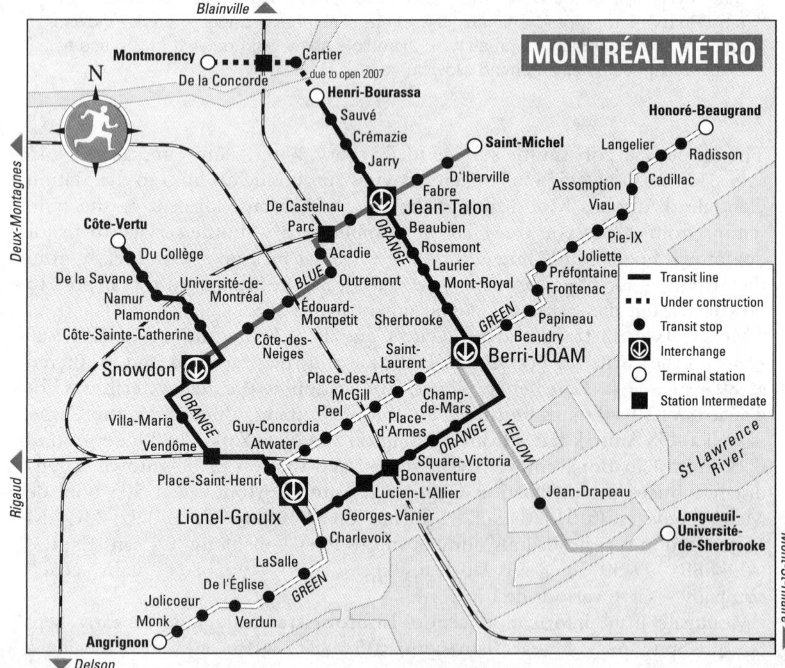

Ridesharing

Allô-Stop, 4317 rue St-Denis (ⓣ514/985-3032, ⓦwww.allo-stop.com) is a **carpool** service matching drivers with passengers for destinations within Québec and the Maritime Provinces only. Membership costs $6 per year plus your share of petrol. Typical prices from Montréal are: Québec City $16, Rimouski $32, Gaspé around $47 (but plan ahead for Gaspé trips, as they're not common: most cars only go as far as Rimouski).

unlimited travel in a day for $9 (or $17 for three consecutive days); it's available from the information centres, Berri-UQAM and Bonaventure Métro stations and, from April to October, at all downtown Métro stations. For longer stays, the weekly CAM-Hebdo pass is a better deal at $18.50, but note that it is only valid from a Monday through to a Sunday.

It is rarely necessary to take a **taxi**. They cost $3.15 plus $1.45 per kilometre, and an additional fifteen percent tip is normal. You can pick one up from the ranks outside hotels and transport terminals, by flagging it down in the street, or by ordering by phone: Taxi Diamond (ⓣ514/273-6331) and Taxi Co-op (ⓣ514/725-9885) are two reliable services.

Accommodation

Much of Montréal's **accommodation** is geared towards expense-account travellers in the downtown hotels, although a recent growth in boutique hotels in Vieux-Montréal offers more atmospheric options. Moderately priced hotel rooms are concentrated around the livelier St-Denis area, with even cheaper options in the rundown area along rue St-Hubert east of the bus terminal. A better option is one of the growing number of **B&Bs**, which offer budget accommodation in interesting neighbourhoods like the Plateau. Rock-bottom prices are charged in the city's **hostels** and **university residences**. The **campsites** are at least twenty-minutes' drive off the island, with no public transport.

Hotels

Abri du Voyageur 9 rue Ste-Catherine ouest; Métro: St-Laurent ⓣ514/849-2922 or 1-866/302-2922, ⓦwww.abri-voyageur.ca. While the location could be better – it is smack in the middle of the red-light district – the rooms are clean, several have exposed brick walls, and it is just steps away from Chinatown and Vieux-Montréal. ❷

Anne ma Soeur Anne 4119 rue St-Denis; Métro: Mont-Royal ⓣ514/281-3187, ⓦwww.annemasoeuranne.com. On a prime stretch of rue St-Denis, this stylish seventeen-room hotel is a great find. The sunny, yellow rooms feature kitchenettes, large bathrooms and some have "Eurobeds" that tuck up into the wall. ❹–❺

Auberge Bonaparte 447 rue St-François-Xavier; Métro:: Place-d'Armes ⓣ514/844-1448, ⓦwww.bonaparte.com. A handsome upscale inn, steps from the Basilique Notre-Dame, built in 1886 and shaded by smart burgundy awnings. Inside, the quarters are decked out with wrought-iron headboards, hardwood floors, high ceilings and French dormer windows. Breakfast included. ❻

Auberge Casa de Mateo 440 rue St Francois-Xavier; Métro: Place d'Armes. ⓣ514/286-9589, ⓦwww.casademateo.com. Offering bright, spacious and clean rooms, the best thing about this auberge is undoubtedly its location – right in the heart of Vieux-Montréal. ❹

Auberge Les Passants du Sans Soucy 171 rue St-Paul ouest; Métro: Place-d'Armes ⓣ514/842-2634, ⓦwww.lesanssoucy.com. Brass beds and hardwood floors contribute to the romantic atmosphere at this charming inn, and some rooms have wooden beams and stone walls.

Breakfast, served in a skylit nook, is included. ⑥

Le Breton 1609 rue St-Hubert; Métro: Berri-UQAM Ⓣ514/524-7273, Ⓦwww.lebreton.ca. Near the bus station, this clean and friendly European-style hotel has smallish rooms; half have a/c, and most have private bath. ①–③

Castel Saint-Denis 2099 rue St-Denis; Métro: Berri-UQAM or Sherbrooke Ⓣ514/842-9719, Ⓦwww.castelsaintdenis.qc.ca. One of the better small hotels in Montréal, it's right in the trendy St-Denis area, but quiet. ③

Château de l'Argoat 524 rue Sherbrooke est; Métro: Sherbrooke Ⓣ514/842-2046, Ⓦwww.hotel-Chateau-argoat.qc.ca. A fanciful cream-coloured fortress offering 25 spacious and attractive rooms with high ceilings, quaint chandeliers and private bath. Breakfast and parking included. ④

Château Versailles 1659 rue Sherbrooke ouest; Métro: Guy-Concordia Ⓣ514/933-8111 or 1-888/933-8111, Ⓦwww.versailleshotels.com. A unique, beautifully furnished hotel located in four stone buildings on the northwestern edge of downtown. Book well in advance, as it is one of the city's most popular hotels; family discounts and cheap winter weekend rates also available. ⑦

Hôtel Gault 449 rue Ste-Hélène; Métro: Square-Victoria Ⓣ514/904-1616 or 1-866/904-1616, Ⓦwww.hotelgault.com. Most glamorous of the recent crop of boutique hotels, the Gault is the place to stay – if you can afford it. The 30 individually designed loft-style rooms in this 1871 warehouse are a design-junkie's dream, with Arne Jacobsen fixtures, white-oak panelling and custom-made linens. ⑧

Manoir Ambrose 3422 rue Stanley; Métro: Peel Ⓣ514/288-6922, Ⓦwww.manoirambrose.com. Two adjoining Victorian houses a couple of blocks from the heart of downtown. Cheap rooms, some with a/c and private bathrooms. Continental breakfast included. ③–④

Manoir des Alpes 1245 rue St-André; Métro: Berri-UQAM Ⓣ514/845-9803 or 1-800/465-2929, Ⓦwww.hotelmanoirdesalpes.qc.ca. This Victorian building near the bus station is a three-star hotel with Swiss overtones but rates include buffet breakfast and parking. ③

Hôtel de Paris 901 rue Sherbrooke est; Métro: Sherbrooke Ⓣ514/522-6861 or 1-800/567-7217, Ⓦwww.hotel-montreal.com. An old mansion near rue St-Denis with a balcony café to hang out in, with other rooms in two nearby properties. The cheaply furnished rooms have tiny beds but all are en suite with TVs, telephone and most have a/c. ③–④

Hôtel St-Paul 355 rue McGill; Métro: Square-Victoria Ⓣ514/380-2222 or 1-866/380-2202, Ⓦwww.hotelstpaul.com. Housed in a former bank, this most minimalist of Vieux-Montréal's new boutique hotels has a very trendy restaurant, *Cube*. Upstairs, white walls and linens contrast with the dark wood floors and elegantly simple furnishings of the rooms and suites. ⑦

B&Bs

Boulanger Bassin B&B 4293 rue Brébeuf; Métro: Mont-Royal Ⓣ514/525-0854, Ⓦwww.bbassin.com. The chatty owner of this B&B north of Parc Lafontaine will tell you all about the Plateau neighbourhood over extravagant breakfasts. The three bright and colourful rooms are simple but nicely furnished and all have private bath. Kids under 12 stay free. ⑤

À la Maison de Pierre et Dominique 271 Square St-Louis; Métro Sherbrooke Ⓣ514/286-0307, Ⓦwww.pierdom.qc.ca. In a lovely house facing a picturesque square, the three rooms are tastefully decorated, though none has private bathroom. ③

La Maison du Patriote 169 rue St-Paul est; Métro: Champ-de-Mars Ⓣ514/397-0855. Unbeatable location, just around the corner from Place Jacques-Cartier, and friendly student ambience with free wireless Internet connection but dorms are a crowded open space with air mattresses rather than beds. ③

Petite Auberge les Bons Matins 1393 av Argyle; Métro: Lucien-l'Allier Ⓣ514/931-9167 or 1-800/588-5280, Ⓦwww.bonsmatins.com. Located on a tree-lined street near downtown and busy rue Crescent, this well-appointed B&B-style inn has fifteen large rooms and six apartments (⑦), each with special architectural features (archways, exposed brick, fireplace), large windows, and private bathroom. ⑤

Le Petit Prince Bed and Breakfast 1384 Overdale; Métro: Lucien L'Allier. Ⓣ514/938-2277 or 1-877/938-9750, Ⓦwww.montrealbandb.com/petit. If you are searching for a place to sweep your sweetheart off their feet in downtown Montréal, this is it. Each individually decorated room has its own double whirlpool bath and either a functioning fireplace or a private balcony. ⑦

Aux Portes de la Nuit 3496 av Laval; Métro: Sherbrooke Ⓣ514/848-0833, Ⓦwww.auxportesdelanuit.com. Well situated on one of the Plateau's most attractive streets, this Victorian house has five rooms, all with private bath. ④

Bed-and-breakfast agencies

These agencies can be big time savers if you're looking to stay at a B&B, as each represents several guesthouses across town in a range of prices – and offers booking too.

Downtown B&B Network in Montréal ⓣ514/289-9749 or 1-800/267-5180, ⓦwww.bbmontreal.qc.ca. Almost always has a vacancy in one of their hundred or so homes downtown or in the Quartier Latin, starting at $55 for a single and $65 for a double, and ranging from quaint Victorian homes to modern apartments.

Fédération des Agricotours ⓦwww.agricotours.qc.ca. An excellent service listing quality-inspected B&Bs throughout Montréal and Québec – you must book directly with the B&Bs, however. The information is also published in the annual *Inns and Bed & Breakfasts in Québec* guide ($17.95), which can be ordered online or by calling ⓣ514/252-3138. Rates for B&Bs start at $65.

Montréal Downtown Network ⓣ514/287-9635 or 1-800/363-9635, ⓦwww.martha-pearson.com. A service offering placement in a number of B&Bs situated in downtown or Vieux-Montréal. They also list apartments for longer stays.

Hostels

Auberge Alternative du Vieux-Montréal 358 rue St-Pierre; Métro: Square-Victoria ⓣ514/282-8069, ⓦwww.auberge-alternative.qc.ca. Montréal's finest hostel is located in a refurbished 1875 Vieux-Montréal warehouse. Rooms for six to sixteen people and some doubles. You don't need to be a member to stay here. ❶–❷

Auberge Chez Jean 4136 av Henri-Julien; Métro: Mont-Royal ⓣ514/843-8279, ⓦwww.aubergechezjean.com. You'll either love or hate this very unofficial hostel. Guests bunk down all over the common rooms on its three floors, making it a great place to make new friends quickly, but forget about privacy unless you take one of the closed rooms or sleep in the van out back. ❶

Auberge de Jeunesse Internationale de Montréal (HI) 1030 rue Mackay; Métro: Lucien-L'Allier ⓣ514/843-3317 or 1-866/843-3317, ⓦwww.hostellingmontreal.com. With 250 beds, this is a large, well-located hostel with single, family or shared rooms that all have a/c and their own showers. Very sombre coloured rooms but staff are friendly and helpful. Book ahead from June–Sept. Check-in 1pm–2am. ❶–❷

Gîte Plateau Mont-Royal 185 rue Sherbrooke est; Métro: Sherbrooke ⓣ514/284-1276 or 1-877/350-4483, ⓦwww.hostelmontreal.com. Bright six- to eight-bed dorms and private rooms (with shared bath), an extremely chill common room and great Plateau location make this one of the city's best backpacker options. The main drawback is that the kitchen is only open 5–8pm. ❶–❸

Le Sous-bois 431 rue St-Vincent; Métro: Berri UQAM. ⓣ514/879-1394, ⓦwww.lesousbois.com. Bunk down on air matresses in the main dorm or hire a private wooden cabin in the courtyard. Cosy, friendly and great value for its vieux-Montréal location at $19 per night including free Internet, laundry, phonecalls, tea, coffee, breakfast, linen and towels. ❶

Hôtel Y des Femmes (YWCA) 1355 boul René-Lévesque ouest; Métro: Lucien L'Allier or Guy-Concordia ⓣ514/866-9942, ⓦwww.ydesfemmesmtl.org. Single, double and triple rooms for men and women in this rather pricey downtown YWCA, but only women have access to the pool and gym facilities. Kitchen and laundry facilities and Internet access also available. ❷–❸

Student rooms

La Maison du Prêt d'Honneur 1 boul René-Lévesque est; Métro: Place-d'Armes or St-Laurent ⓣ514/982-3420 ext 5501 or 5502, ⓦwww.mph.sat.qc.ca. A college residence on the edge of Chinatown that has studios with one or two single beds as well as a few two-bedroom apartments. All have kitchenette, private bath, phone and Internet access. Summer only. ❸

McGill University Residences 3935 rue University; Métro: McGill ⓣ514/398-5200, ⓦwww.residences.mcgill.ca/summer.html. Popular residences for visiting anglophones and consequently often full. Four of the buildings are on the slopes of Mont Royal but Royal Victoria College is on the edge of downtown. Good weekly rates. Summer only. ❶–❷

Les Résidences Universitaires UQAM 303 boul René-Lévesque est; Métro: Berri-UQAM ⓣ514/987-6669, ⓦwww.residences-uqam.qc.ca. Over a hundred clean and simply furnished studios with double bed, kitchenette and private bath, as well as apartments, in this Quartier Latin student residence. Summer only. ❷

Vacances Canada 5155 av de Gaspé; Métro: Laurier ⓣ514/270-4459, ⓦwww.vacancescanadamd.montrealplus.ca. Two hundred beds available all year, and 550 in July and August in two locations: the Collège Français residence has rooms with one to seven beds that are popular with school groups, so often booked up. Check in 9am–2pm & 5–7pm. Second location has good deals for longer stays. Ⓣ

Campsites

Camping Alouette 3449 rue de l'Industrie, Saint-Mathieu-de-Beloeil ⓣ450/464-1661 or 1-888/464-7829, ⓦwww.campingalouette.com. Exit 105 off Hwy 20 East. With 300 sites this is the largest of the city's campsites with a store, washing machines, hook-ups and outdoor swimming pool. Sites $28–36.

Camping La Cle des Champs 415 montée St-Claude. Saint-Philippe ⓣ450/659-3389, ⓦwww.campinglacledeschamps.com. Hwy 30 west, exit 104, Hwy 104 east. Big, charmless campsite with hook-ups, playground, showers, washing machines and restaurant. Sites $20.

KOA Montréal Sud 130 boul Monette. St-Philippe-de-la Prairie ⓣ450/659-8626 or 1-800/562-8636, ⓦwww.koa.com. About 20km south of downtown; take exit 38 off Hwy 15, turn left, and it's 3km further on. Full facilities at well-kept campsite. Open from May to Oct. Sites from $22.

The City

Though the island of Montréal is a large 51km by 16km, the heart of the city is very manageable, and is divided into Vieux-Montréal along the St Lawrence River, a downtown high-rise business core on the south side of the hill of Mont Royal, and the lively Plateau and Quartier Latin neighbourhoods to the east. The main east–west arteries are Rue Sherbrooke, boulevard de Maisonneuve, rue Ste-Catherine and boulevard René-Lévesque, all divided into east (*est*) and west (*ouest*) sections by the north–south **boulevard St-Laurent**, known locally as "The Main". North–south street numbers increase as you progress north from the St Lawrence River.

You're most likely to start by sampling the old-world charm of **Vieux-Montréal**. The narrow streets, alleys and squares are perfect for strolling, and every corner reveals an architectural gem, from monumental public edifices to the city's early steep-roofed homes. Close by, the parklands of the **Vieux-Port** adjoin a child-friendly science centre and departure points for getting onto the water. To the northwest, in the compact **downtown** area, the glass frontages of the office blocks reflect Victorian terraces and the spires of numerous churches, underlain by the passages of the **Underground City**, which link hotels, shopping centres and offices with the Métro. Rising above downtown, the city's landmark, **Mont Royal** – which the residents simply call "The Mountain" – is best accessed from the easterly Plateau Mont-Royal. This is the spot where the city's pulse beats fastest, as the cafés, restaurants and bars of **The Main** and rue St-Denis throng with people day and night. Further out to the east, the enormous **Stade Olympique** complex and the vast green space of the **Jardin Botanique** are the main pull. For a breath of fresh air, the islands facing the Vieux-Port that make up Parc Jean-Drapeau

Museum passes

The **Carte Musées Montréal** (Montréal Museums Pass $35; including transport $45) grants free admission to 25 museums in the city on any two of three consecutive days at a significant discount; buy it at tourist offices or participating museums. In addition, the Nature Package covers admission to the Botanical Garden, Insectarium and Biodôme for $20.50, while the Get an Eyeful package ($31.50) covers all three plus a trip up the Olympic Tower; none of these four is covered by the Carte Musées.

and the westerly Lachine Canal offer all manner of activities, many of them family-friendly.

Vieux-Montréal

Severed from downtown by the Autoroute Ville-Marie, the gracious district of **Vieux-Montréal** was left to decay until the last couple of decades, when developers stepped in with generally tasteful renovations that brought colour and vitality back to the area. North America's greatest concentration of seventeenth, eighteenth- and nineteenth-century buildings has its fair share of tourists, but it's popular with Montréalers, too – formerly as a symbolic place to air francophone grievances; more recently as a spot to wander around, take in the sights and, increasingly, to inhabit the condos converted from the old warehouses. Place d'Armes is the most central Métro station, although Square-Victoria or Champ-de-Mars are handier for the western and eastern ends of the district.

Place d'Armes and around

The focal point of Vieux-Montréal is **Place d'Armes**, its centre occupied by a century-old statue of Maisonneuve, whose missionary zeal raised the wrath of the displaced Iroquois. The mutt among the luminaries represents the animal who warned the French of an impending attack in 1644; legend has it that the ensuing battle ended when the supposedly unarmed Maisonneuve killed the Iroquois chief on this very spot.

Despite the addition of an ugly skyscraper on its west side, the square is still dominated by the twin-towered, neo-Gothic **Basilique Notre-Dame** (Mon–Fri 8am–4.30pm, Sat 8am–4.15pm, Sun noon–4.15pm; $4, light show $10; Ⓦwww.basiliquenddm.org; Métro: Place-d'Armes), the cathedral of the Catholic faithful since 1829. Its architect, the Protestant Irish-American James O'Donnell, was so inspired by his creation that he converted to Catholicism in order to be buried under the church. The western of the two towers, named Temperance, holds the ten-tonne Jean-Baptiste bell, whose booming could once be heard 25km away. The breathtaking gilt and sky-blue interior, flooded with light from three rose windows unusually set in the ceiling, and flickering with multicoloured votive candles, was designed by Montréal architect Victor Bourgeau. Most notable of the detailed furnishings are Louis-Philippe Hébert's fine wooden carvings of the prophets on the pulpit and the awe-inspiring main altar by French sculptor Bouriché. Imported from Limoges in France, the stained-glass windows depict the founding of Ville-Marie. Behind the main altar is the **Chapelle Sacré-Coeur**, destroyed by a serious fire in 1978 but rebuilt with an impressive modern bronze reredos by Charles Daudelin. Time your visit for the "And then there was light" *son et lumière* show for a history lesson and a chance to see the architectural details

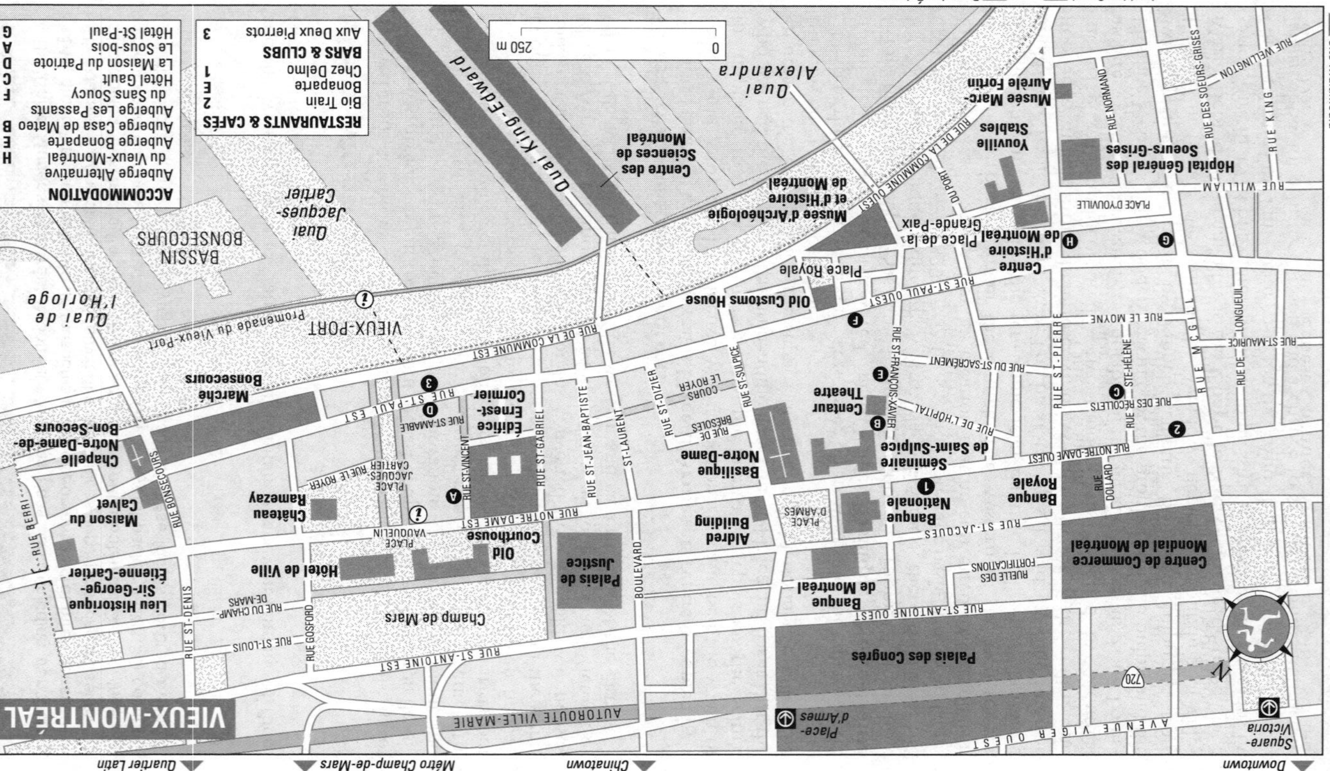
VIEUX-MONTRÉAL
ACCOMMODATION
Auberge Alternative du Vieux-Montréal H
Auberge Bonaparte E
Auberge Casa de Mateo B
Auberge Les Passants du Sans Soucy F
Hôtel Gault C
La Maison du Patriote D
Le Sous-bois A
Hôtel St-Paul G
RESTAURANTS & CAFÉS
Bio Train 2
Bonaparte E
Chez Delmo 1
BARS & CLUBS
Aux Deux Pierrots 3
0
250 m
Tour de L'Horloge
Quartier Latin
Métro Champ-de-Mars
Chinatown
Downtown
Cité Multimédia
Lachine Canal
Parc des Écluses
Quai de l'Horloge
BASSIN BONSECOURS
Quai Jacques-Cartier
Quai King-Edward
Quai Alexandra
VIEUX-PORT
Promenade du Vieux-Port
Centre des Sciences de Montréal
Musée d'Archéologie et d'Histoire de Montréal
Place Royale
Old Customs House
Centre d'Histoire de Montréal
Place de la Grande-Paix
Youville Stables
Musée Marc-Aurèle Fortin
Hôpital Général des Soeurs-Grises
PLACE D'YOUVILLE
Marché Bonsecours
Chapelle Notre-Dame-de-Bon-Secours
Maison du Calvet
Lieu Historique Sir-George-Étienne-Cartier
Château Ramezay
Hôtel de Ville
Champ de Mars
Old Courthouse
Édifice Ernest-Cormier
Palais de Justice
Aldred Building
Basilique Notre-Dame
Banque de Montréal
Banque Nationale
Séminaire de Saint-Sulpice
Centaur Theatre
Banque Royale
Centre de Commerce Mondial de Montréal
Palais des Congrès
Place-d'Armes
Square-Victoria
PLACE D'ARMES
PLACE VAUQUELIN
PLACE JACQUES-CARTIER
RUE BERRI
RUE ST-DENIS
RUE BONSECOURS
RUE ST-LOUIS
RUE DU CHAMP-DE-MARS
RUE GOSFORD
RUE LE ROYER
RUE ST-ANTOINE EST
RUE ST-ANTOINE OUEST
AUTOROUTE VILLE-MARIE
RUE NOTRE-DAME EST
RUE NOTRE-DAME OUEST
RUE ST-VINCENT
RUE ST-AMABLE
RUE ST-PAUL EST
RUE ST-PAUL OUEST
RUE DE LA COMMUNE EST
RUE DE LA COMMUNE OUEST
RUE ST-GABRIEL
RUE ST-JEAN-BAPTISTE
BOULEVARD ST-LAURENT
RUE ST-DIZIER
RUE DE BRÉSOLES
COURS LE ROYER
RUE ST-SULPICE
RUE ST-FRANÇOIS-XAVIER
RUE ST-JACQUES
RUELLE DES FORTIFICATIONS
RUE DE L'HÔPITAL
RUE DU ST-SACREMENT
RUE ST-PIERRE
RUE DOLLARD
RUE DES RÉCOLLETS
RUE STE-HÉLÈNE
RUE LE MOYNE
RUE MCGILL
RUE DE LONGUEUIL
RUE ST-MAURICE
DU PORT
RUE NORMAND
RUE DES SOEURS-GRISES
RUE WILLIAM
RUE KING
RUE WELLINGTON
AVENUE VIGER OUEST
720
N

artfully lit up; otherwise take advantage of one of the 20-minute guided tours (half-hourly from 9am–4.30pm; included in entry).

Behind the fieldstone walls and wrought-iron gates to the right of Notre-Dame is the low-lying, mock-medieval **Séminaire de St-Sulpice**, saved from blandness by a portal that's topped by North America's oldest public timepiece, which began chiming in 1701. Generally considered Montréal's oldest building, the seminary was founded in 1685 by the Paris-based Sulpicians, who instigated the establishment of Montréal by Maisonneuve as a religious mission. They liked the place so much that they bought the whole island, and until 1859 were in charge of religious and other affairs as the *seigneurs* of the colony. The seminary is still the Canadian headquarters of the Sulpicians (and thus not open to the public), but their duties are now limited to maintaining the basilica.

The domed shrine of Montréal's financial rulers, the **Banque de Montréal**, stands opposite. This grand, classical-revival building still houses the headquarters of Canada's oldest bank, which rose from its foundation by a few Scottish immigrants to serve the entire nation until the creation of the Bank of Canada in the 1930s. Erected in 1837, it was built to resemble the Roman Pantheon. The interior marble counters, black granite pillars and gleaming brass and bronze fittings ooze wealth and luxury. A small **numismatic museum** (Mon–Fri 10am–4pm; free) displays early account books, banknotes, coins and pictures. British names once controlled the finances of the continent from the stately limestone, griffin-capped institutions along **rue St-Jacques**, once the Wall Street of Canada, but French businesses now rule the roost. The red-sandstone building on the northeast corner of Place d'Armes and rue St-Jacques was built for the New York Life Insurance Co. in 1888 and, at eight storeys high, was the city's first skyscraper. Next door at 501 Place d'Armes, the Aldred Building is among the city's finest examples of the Art Deco style. Both are dwarfed today by the black monolith on the west side of the square that houses the Banque Nationale, built in 1967 as a symbol of new-found francophone business strength. Transformations have also occurred alongside the basilica, in the area around **rue St-Sulpice**, where the warehouses constructed in the Victorian era to cope with the growing trade of Montréal's harbour have been converted into luxurious flats and offices, as well as a couple of boutique hotels. Many of the continent's first explorers once lived here, including Pierre Gaulthier de Varennes, who charted South Dakota, the Rockies and Wyoming, and Daniel Greysolon, Sieur du Lhut, who roamed over Minnesota. Peek along rue le Royer, extending eastward, an austere courtyard lined with late-nineteenth-century warehouses that recall Montréal's past as a major shipping port and whose conversion into offices and apartments was the first development in the revival of Vieux-Montréal.

Along rue Notre-Dame

Ville-Marie's first street, **rue Notre-Dame**, was laid out in 1672 and runs east–west across Vieux-Montréal. Other than the financial buildings of rue St-Jacques, there is little of particular interest to the west of Place d'Armes; it's more rewarding to head east along Notre-Dame from the top of rue St-Sulpice, past the black glass behemoth of the **Palais de Justice** on the corner of boulevard St-Laurent. It overshadows its forerunner, the imposing **Old Courthouse**, erected by the British to impress upon the French population the importance of abiding by their laws. It went on to become the site of civil trials under the Napoleonic Code after the courts were divided in 1926, and today serves as municipal offices. Criminal trials took place across the street, at 100 rue Notre-Dame est, in the **Édifice Ernest Cormier**, which was built in 1925 and only recently returned to its calling as the appellate court; step inside to admire the impressive colonnade and unique Art Deco lamps. Further along, the 1800 Maison de La Sauvegarde at no. 160, with its rough-hewn limestone facade, high chimneys and steeply pitched roof and dormers, was among the last homes to be built in the local French vernacular. Opposite, on the eastern side of the Old Courthouse, **Place Vauquelin**, centred on a pretty fountain and statue of the naval commander Jean Vauquelin, gives views of the **Champ de Mars** to the north. Excavations to build a car park here hit rock, which turned out to be the original city walls. After a public vote, the car park scheme was abandoned, the walls were excavated and restored, and the area was transformed into a pleasant grassy space.

East of Place Vauquelin, the ornate **Hôtel de Ville** (City Hall) was built in the 1870s and is a typical example of the area's civic buildings of the time when French-speaking architects looked to the mother country for inspiration. On a visit to Expo '67, General de Gaulle chose its second-floor balcony to make his "Vive le Québec libre!" speech, which left the city's anglophones reeling at the thought that Québec was on its way to independent status and infused francophones with a political fervour that ended in the October Crisis (see p.1090).

The cobbled **Place Jacques-Cartier** opposite City Hall slopes down towards the river and offers spectacular views of the Vieux-Port, but is overrun with buskers, street artists and hair-braiders throughout the summer months. The city-run **tourist office** (April–June & Sept–Oct daily 9am–5pm, June–Aug daily 9am–7pm, Nov–March Wed–Sun 9am–5pm; ⓦwww.tourism-montreal.org) occupies a stone building at the northwest corner. Restaurants and cafés surrounding the square hustle for business, while the narrow **rue St-Amable** to the west is choked with struggling artists selling quaint watercolours and tinted photos of Montréal scenery alongside garish caricatures of film and music stars. Your best bet for souvenirs here is the small courtyard market hidden away from the street, where jewellery stalls offer some decent artisan-crafted pieces. A few buildings on the square – Maison Vandelac, Maison del Vecchio and the Maison Cartier – show the architectural features typical of Montréal architecture in the 1800s, with pitched roofs designed to shed heavy snowfall and small dormer windows to defend against the cold. At the top of the square itself, the controversial **Nelson Monument** stands above the few stalls that serve as the only reminders that this was once Montréal's main marketplace. The city's oldest monument – the column is a third the height of its more famous London counterpart, but predates it by a few years – was funded by anglophone Montréalers delighted with Nelson's defeat of the French at Trafalgar in 1805. Québec separatists adopted it as a rallying point in the 1970s. Ironically, the anglophones never liked the monument much either, because it faced away from the water.

East of Place Jacques-Cartier, the long and low fieldstone manor of the **Château Ramezay** (June to mid-Oct daily 10am–6pm; mid-Oct to May Tues–Sun 10am–4.30pm; $7; ⓣ514/861-3708, ⓦwww.Chateauramezay.qc.ca; Métro Champ-de-Mars) looks much as it did in 1705 when it was built for the eleventh governor of Montréal, Claude de Ramezay – it was the finest of the colony's 200 homes at the time. It then served as the North American headquarters for the Compagnie des Indes, before passing into the hands of the British after the Conquest in 1760. During the fleeting American invasion fifteen years later, Benjamin Franklin stayed here in an attempt to persuade Montréalers to join the United States, but he lost public and church support by not promising the supremacy of the French language in what would have been the fourteenth state. Nowadays, after a variety of other uses, it is an historical museum; the collection of oil paintings, domestic artefacts, tools, costumes and furniture from the eighteenth and nineteenth centuries is thorough and informative. The most impressive room is a reconstruction of the *Salle des Nantes*, complete with mahogany walls and woodwork imported from the Compagnie des Indes headquarters in France. Other rooms are furnished in the bourgeois style of New France, while in the whitewashed stone vaults below, the exhibits take on more of an educational slant, re-creating domestic scenes of the early European settlers that include a kitchen with a dog-powered roasting spit.

At the intersection of rues Notre-Dame and Berri, a five-minute walk east, the **Lieu historique national de Sir-George-Étienne-Cartier** (late May to Aug daily 10am–6pm; April to late May & Sept to late Dec Wed–Sun 10am–noon & 1–5pm; $6.25; Ⓦwww.pc.gc.ca/cartier; Métro Champ-de-Mars) comprises two adjoining houses that were inhabited by the Cartier family from 1848 to 1871. The cocky Sir George-Étienne Cartier was one of the fathers of Confederation, persuading the French-Canadians to join the Dominion of Canada by declaring: "We are of different races, not for strife but to work together for the common welfare." Today, leaders of French-Canadian nationalism decry Cartier as a collaborator, and the displays in the east house diplomatically skirt over the issue of whether he was right or wrong and emphasize instead his role in the construction of Canada's railways. This collection is decidedly bizarre, however, with Muppet-like figures representing the founding fathers on the main floor, while eight white-painted papier-mâché models of Cartier himself sit at a round, glass-domed table upstairs. The stuffily decorated rooms in the west house are more interesting, furnished with more than a thousand original artefacts to evoke the period when Sir George lived here. Strangely, part of the display is concentrated around a dinner theme, and recordings of conversations between fictitious house staff automatically start playing once the infrared sensor catches movement in the room.

Rue St-Paul

A block south of rue Notre-Dame, **rue St-Paul**, one of Montréal's most attractive thoroughfares, is lined with nineteenth-century commercial buildings and Victorian lampposts, the buildings little changed from when Charles Dickens stayed here, although they now house restaurants, art galleries and specialist shops selling everything from Inuit crafts to kites.

Mark Twain noted that, in Montréal, "you couldn't throw a brick without hitting a church", and near rue St-Paul's eastern end is Montréal's favourite: the delicate and profusely steepled **Chapelle Notre-Dame-de-Bon-Secours** (Tues–Sun: May–Oct 10am–5.30pm; mid-March to April & Nov to mid-Jan 11am–3.30pm; free), or the Sailors' Church. The outstretched arms of the Virgin on the tower became a landmark for ships on the St Lawrence and, once safely landed, the mariners would endow the chapel with wooden votive lamps in the shape of ships, many of which are still here. The chapel dates back to the earliest days of the colony, when Maisonneuve helped cut the wood for what was Ville-Marie's first church, under the instigation of Marguerite Bourgeoys, who had been summoned to Ville-Marie to teach the settlement's children. The devout Bourgeoys also founded the nation's first religious order and was in charge of the *filles du Roi* – orphaned French girls sent to marry bachelor settlers and multiply the colony's population. She was canonized in 1982, becoming Canada's first saint. Today's chapel, postdating Bourgeoys by some seventy years, contains a small **museum** devoted to her life (same hours; $6; Ⓣ514/282-8670, Ⓦwww.marguerite-bourgeoys.com; Métro Champ-de-Mars). The entry price is worth it mainly for the chance to climb the narrow stairs leading to the summit of the tower above the apse, where the "aerial chapel" affords excellent views over the port and the old town.

Opposite the chapel is the three-storey, high-chimneyed **Maison du Calvet**, built in 1725 and one of Montréal's best examples of French domestic architecture. Photographed, painted and admired more than any other house in the district, it was the home of a Huguenot draper and justice of the peace called Pierre Calvet, a notorious turncoat who changed his allegiances from the French to the British and then to the Americans. Today it houses a pricey inn and restaurant (La Maison Pierre du Calvet; 405 rue Bonsecours; ⓣ1-866/544-1725, 514/282-1725, ⓦwww.pierreducalvet.ca; rooms from $265 including breakfast; dinner from $30).

Rue Bonsecours, which links rue St-Paul to rue Notre-Dame, is another typical Vieux-Montréal street. The grey-painted, many-dormered **Maison Papineau** at no. 440 was home to four generations of the Papineau family, including Louis-Joseph who, as Speaker of the Assembly, championed the *habitants* of the St Lawrence farmlands against the senior Catholic clergy, the British government and Montréal's business class. Calling for democratic election of the executive officers of church and government, he fuelled the rage of the *Patriotes* – the leaders of Lower Canada reform – but deserted the scene as the 1837 rebellion reached a bloody climax (see p.275). The house remains a private residence, but renovations have significantly altered its exterior facade from the days when the Papineaus lived here. The silver-domed **Marché Bonsecours** (daily from 10am; ⓣ514/872-7730, ⓦwww.marchebonsecours.qc.ca), with its long facade of columns, extends beyond the intersection of rue Bonsecours and rue St-Paul. For years this elegant building was used for municipal offices, but for the city's 350th birthday in 1992 it was restored and transformed to house restaurants, designer boutiques, expensive artworks and special exhibitions.

Vieux-Port

The south side of the Marché Bonsecours faces onto the **Vieux-Port de Montréal**, once the import and export conduit of the continent. When the main shipyards shifted east in the 1970s they left a lot of vacant space, which has since been renovated for public use, with biking, cross-country skiing and jogging paths and exhibitions in the quayside hangars.

At the Vieux-Port's easternmost point, the **Tour de l'Horloge** on the Quai de l'Horloge rises 51m above sea level. The clock tower was built in 1922 to commemorate the men of the Merchant Fleet who died in World War I; ships were recorded as having entered the harbour as soon as they had passed it. If you can stand the walk up the 192 steps leading to the observatory, you'll be rewarded with excellent views of the harbour, the St Lawrence Seaway, Vieux-Montréal, the islands and Mont Royal. Westward, across the pedalboat-filled Bassin Bonsecours, there's a seasonal information centre (see ⓦwww.quaysoftheoldport.com for seasonal opening times) located at the northeast corner of the **Pavillon Jacques-Cartier**, which is a good place to find out about weekend activities and performances portside. The main events of the Vieux-Port are clustered in and around the next hangar westward, the **Quai King-Edward**. There's an IMAX cinema here, with eye-popping films on the seven-storey-high screen (English screening times vary), which is part of the **Centre des Sciences de Montréal** (Mon–Fri 8.30am–5pm, Sat & Sun 9.30am–5pm; exhibit or film $10, both $17; ⓣ514/496-4629 or 1-800/349-4629, ⓦwww.montrealsciencecentre.com;

Boat trips in and around Montréal

The Vieux-Port is the major departure point for various **boat trips**. The best by far is the **jet boat** run by Saute-Moutons, departing every two hours from the Quai de l'Horloge (May to Oct daily 10am–6pm; $60; ⓣ514/284-9607, ⓦwww.jetboatingmontreal.com). Scooting through the Lachine Rapids, the trip will leave you wet, exhilarated and terrified. Meandering Bâteau Mouche **cruises** leave from the Quai Jacques-Quartier (mid-May to mid-Oct 4 daily; $20.46; ⓣ514/849-9952 or 1-800/361-9952, ⓦwww.bateau-mouche.com). The glass-topped boats offer lovely views of the surrounding islands and the river. Most tours last around two hours, though there are longer dinner cruises. A more unique way to see the area is the **Amphi-bus** (June–Sept hourly departures 10am–midnight, May & Oct 4 daily; $20.75; ⓣ514/849-5181, ⓦwww.Montreal-amphibus-tour.com), which leaves from the corner of rue de la Commune and boulevard St-Laurent, or the Centre Infotouriste downtown. In true James Bond style, this customized military landing craft sails on water and drives along the streets of Vieux-Montréal.

Métro: Place-d'Armes), an interactive science and entertainment complex that is heavy on new technology. Divided into three exhibition halls, focusing on themes of life, information and matter, the massive rooms contain little that will keep you occupied, but most kids will enjoy some of the hands-on exhibits, including how to design the perfect paper airplane, record a radio show and stay balanced on a tightrope. At the end of the pier itself there is a **lookout point** up a few flights of stairs, with explanatory panels showcasing a panorama of Vieux-Montréal and the islands.

Place Royale and Place d'Youville

Once the site of duels, whippings and public hangings amidst the peddlers and hawkers who sold wares from the incoming ships, **Place Royale** is dominated by the neat classical facade of the Old Customs House. After a nine-day journey from Québec City, Maisonneuve and his posse moored their boats at nearby **Pointe-à-Callière**, now landlocked after the changes in the Vieux-Port.

The **Musée d'Archéologie et d'Histoire de Montréal**, 350 Place Royale (late June to early Sept Mon–Fri 10am–6pm, Sat & Sun 11am–6pm; rest of year Tues–Fri 10am–5pm, Sat & Sun 11am–5pm; $11; ⓣ514/872-9150, ⓦwww.pacmuseum.qc.ca; Métro: Square-Victoria), occupies the striking modern Éperon building on the Pointe, visible across the parkland from the Quai King-Edward. The $27m centre, which spreads underground below Place Royale as far as the Old Customs House, focuses on the development of Montréal as a meeting and trading place, as told through the archeological remains excavated here at the oldest part of the city. The high-tech audiovisual presentation gives an excellent introduction to the museum, to archeology generally, and to that of Montréal in particular. Early remnants of the city include a cemetery from 1643, eighteenth-century water conduits and sewage systems, and walls dating from different centuries: you can see from the foundations of each subsequent building how the street level has risen three metres over the years and traces of the variety of roles Place Royale has played. The underground sections emerge into the Old Customs House, which holds a dull exhibition and a gift shop. The layout is terribly confusing: time your visit for one of the free but infrequent guided tours, or look for the interactive map downstairs near the cemetery. Be sure to leave time for the generally excellent temporary shows, all with an archeological theme, on the Éperon building's upper floors.

Directly behind the museum is **Place d'Youville**, a charming public square that includes the Founder's Obelisk, a monument to the city founders. The square's eastern portion was renamed **Place de la Grande-Paix** in 2001, to mark the tercentennial of the Great Peace of Montréal, a treaty signed here in 1701 to end the conflict between the Natives and French settlers. On the south side of the square, the **Youville Stables**, with its shady courtyard, gardens, restaurants and offices, was one of the first of the area's old buildings to be gentrified. (The complex was in fact a warehouse; the stables were next door.) Dating from 1825, the courtyard layout is a throwback to a design used by the earliest Montréal inhabitants as a protection against the hostilities of the Iroquois.

Halfway along the square, a century-old red-brick fire station has been converted into the **Centre d'Histoire de Montréal** (Tues–Sun 10am–5pm; $4.50; ⓣ514/872-3207, ⓦwww.ville.montreal.qc.ca/chm; Métro Square-Victoria). The multimedia exhibits of the city's history, from its first days of European settlement to its present expansions under and above ground, aren't terribly interesting, but are fine for a sketchy overview. The competing soundtracks of films shown in the warren of rooms upstairs (including a locker room and a kitchen circa 1950) attempt to capture daily life in Montréal. Kids will love the mock tram: enter it and images start running past the windows while a recording of a bus driver calls out stops in French and English. Temporary exhibitions, too, are usually quite stimulating. Ask for an English-language guidebook when you enter the museum. The barren car park covering the western half of Place d'Youville gives no indication that this was once a marketplace, which also served as the Parliament of United Canada from 1844 until it was torched by Tory rioters in 1849.

Square Victoria and around

To reach downtown (in a roundabout fashion), head back towards the archeology museum and detour up rue St-François-Xavier to find the **Centaur Theatre**. Located at no. 453, and housed in the former Montréal Stock Exchange – Canada's first – it is the main English-language theatre in Montréal today. Continue north to reach rue St-Jacques, where to the west you'll pass the sumptuous **Molson and Royal banks** at nos. 360 and 362. When it was built in 1866, the 23-storey Royal Bank was the tallest building in the British Empire.

At the northwestern end of Vieux-Montréal, the entire block of rue St-Jacques between rue St-Pierre and Square Victoria is taken up by the **Centre de Commerce Mondial**, an architectural gem and prominent business address. Inaugurated in 1991 with the hope of reviving the former business district, the structure incorporates the facades of the centuries-old buildings that formerly stood there. Inside, the **ruelle des Fortifications**, so named because the former alley marked the location of the city's stone walls, was transformed into a lofty interior arcade adorned with boutiques, restaurants, a soothing fountain and a statue of Amphitrite, Poseidon's wife. At its easternmost end is a chunk of the Berlin Wall.

Across the street, renovations to **Square Victoria** have made it a more welcoming space, but it's still a far cry from its heyday when it was surrounded by Second Empire and neo-Renaissance buildings and bustling with activity from the city's haymarket. The imposing skyscraper bracketing the west side of the square used to be the digs of the **Montréal Stock Exchange**, but futures are traded there now instead of shares. Also of note is the **Art Nouveau grill** adorning the Métro station entranceway – which once graced a station on the Paris Métro – donated to the city for Expo '67.

Downtown Montréal

Montréal's **downtown** lies roughly between rue Sherbrooke and rue St-Antoine to the north and south, towards rue St-Denis in the east and overlapping with the Golden Square Mile as it stretches west beyond rue Guy.

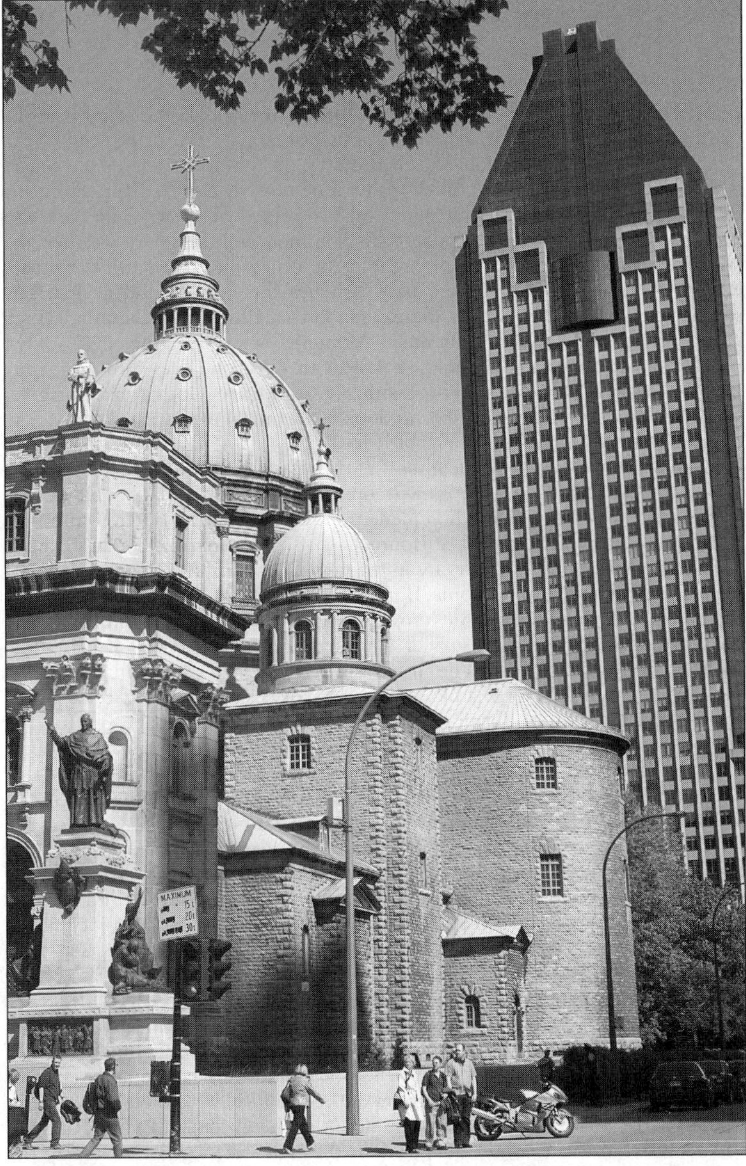

△ Basilique-Cathédrale Marie-Reine-du-Monde

Of the main streets, **rue Ste-Catherine** offers the most in the way of shopping, dining and entertainment, while **boulevard de Maisonneuve** is more business-oriented. A number of Métro stations on the green and orange lines provide easy access to downtown's attractions – most are linked to the so-called Underground City (see box opposite). Though the main sights are the high-rises and shopping complexes, the area is also dotted with old churches, museums and public squares filled with activity from buskers, artists and market vendors.

Square Dorchester and around

Formerly a Catholic cemetery, **Square Dorchester** is a leafy spot right in the centre of downtown that is as good a place as any to get your bearings – the Art Deco-inspired Dominion Square Building on the north side of the square is the site of the Infotouriste office (daily: June to early Sept 8.30am–8pm; rest of year 9am–6pm) and the starting point for guided bus tours. The park also hosts occasional lunchtime concerts in summer, and in good weather the wedding-cake-like Sun Life building and the office blocks around the square empty their personnel onto the park benches for a snack and a chat. The southern half of the square is partitioned off as **Place du Canada**, which commemorates the 1967 centennial. Along its west side, the area's oldest building is the Victorian **St George's Anglican Church** (Tues–Sun 9am–4pm; ⓣ514/866-7113, ⓦwww.st-georges.org). Its solid Neo-Gothic exterior gives way to a lofty interior with vaulting double hammer-beam trusses that rise in a series of arches to support the gabled roof.

Dwarfed by its high-rise neighbours, the **Basilique-Cathédrale Marie-Reine-du-Monde** (Mon–Fri 7am–7.30pm, Sat 7.30am–8.30pm, Sun 8.30am–7.30pm, ⓦwww.cathedralecatholiquedemontreal.org; Métro Bonaventure) was commissioned by Bishop Ignace Bourget in 1875 as a reminder that Catholicism still dominated the largest city in the new Dominion of Canada. Impressed by St Peter's while visiting Rome, Bourget created a scaled-down replica of the famous church. While the statues crowning St Peter's facade are of the Apostles, the thirteen statues atop its smaller cousin represent the patron saints of the parishes that donated them. The inside is not as opulent as you might expect, though the high altar of marble, onyx and ivory is surmounted by a gilded copper reproduction of Bernini's baldachin over the altar in St Peter's. To your left on entering is the Chapelle des Souvenirs, which contains various relics, including the wax-encased remains of the obscure St Zoticus.

The city's legendary ice-hockey team, the **Montréal Canadiens**, play in the 21,000-seat **Centre Bell** (ⓦwww.centrebell.ca; ⓣ514/932-2582), at 1260 rue de la Gauchetière ouest, two blocks west of the Place du Canada. The centre is also the venue for rock concerts, classical-music performances and family entertainment. English guided tours take place daily at 11.15am and 2.45pm ($8). If you fancy a puck souvenir or a hockey jersey, head inside to the Canadiens' Souvenir Boutique (Mon–Wed 9.30am–6pm, Thurs & Fri until 9pm, Sat until 5pm).

A few blocks west of the Centre Bell, the **Centre Canadien d'Architecture** (CCA), 1920 rue Baile (Wed–Sun 10am–5pm, Thurs to 9pm and free after 5.30pm; ⓣ514/939-7026, ⓦwww.cca.qc.ca; Métro Guy-Concordia) inhabits a wonderfully sleek building with a curiously windowless facade and vast glass doors. The Peter Rose design incorporates the beautifully restored Shaughnessy Mansion (the former residence of a president of the Canadian Pacific Railway) and its Art Nouveau conservatory, while the light-filled galleries display the museum's vast collection of prints, drawings and books in exhibitions ranging from individual masters to whole movements from all cultures and periods. Behind the museum on the south side of boulevard René-Lévesque are the whimsical **CCA Sculpture Gardens** (daily 6am–midnight; free). Designed by prominent Montréal artist and architect Melvin Charney, the sculptures are a wacky mishmash of architectural references, arranged in a way reminiscent of ancient stone circles.

Rue Ste-Catherine and around

Proceeding north for two short blocks brings you to **rue Ste-Catherine**, the city's main commercial thoroughfare since the early 1900s. The street stretches for 15km across the island of Montréal, with the part east of rue Guy serving as the main shopping artery, featuring department stores interspersed with exclusive boutiques, souvenir shops and fast-food outlets. For all its consumerist gloss the road still has its seedy bits, peepshows and strip clubs enlivening the streetscape. Further along, the street passes through the Quartier Latin, forms the heart of the gay village, and extends into the working-class neighbourhoods of east Montréal.

From the intersection of rues Peel and Ste-Catherine you can see the elegant **Cours Mont-Royal**. Formerly the largest hotel in the British Commonwealth, it now contains four floors of shops (including those of expensive designers), topped by apartments and offices. Peek inside and gawk up at the fourteen-storey-high atria and chandeliers preserved from the hotel. One of these hangs from the coffered ceiling over a permanent catwalk – a testament to the fashion aspirations of the shopping centre. Standing out amongst the skyscrapers and malls, the cross-shaped, 46-storey **Place Ville Marie** has been a Montréal landmark since the 1960s, its rooftop searchlight visible for miles around, while below ground its shopping mall was one of the main catalysts of the Underground City (see box below). It marks one end of **avenue McGill College**, a broad boulevard lined with skyscrapers that frame a view of McGill University and the mountain beyond.

A block or so further east, the grounds of the 1859 Anglican **Christ Church Cathedral**, 635 rue Ste-Catherine ouest (daily 10am–6pm; ⓣ514/843-6577, ⓦwww.montreal.anglican.org/cathedral; Métro McGill) and Square Phillips, opposite, provide a break in the commercial strip. By 1927, the church's slender stone spire was threatening to crash through the wooden roof and was replaced with the peculiar aluminium replica. Inside, the soaring Gothic arches are

The Underground City

Place Ville Marie marks the beginning of Montréal's famous **Underground City**, planned as a refuge from the city's weather – outrageously cold in the winter and humid in the summer. The underground network began with the construction of the cruciform Place Ville Marie in the 1960s. Montréalers flooded into the first climate-controlled shopping arcade, and the Underground City duly spread. Today its 33km of passages provide access to the Métro, major hotels, shopping malls, transport termini, thousands of offices, apartments and restaurants, and a good smattering of cinemas and theatres. Everything underground is signposted, but you're still likely to get lost on your first visit – pick up a map of the ever-expanding system from the tourist office. However, while the pamphlets make the Underground City sound somewhat exotic, it's a pretty banal place – most Montréalers just use it to get from place to place, or drop in on a number of fairly standard shopping malls. If you're on a budget, check out the inexpensive food courts on the lowest floor of any of the malls (also handy for public toilets).

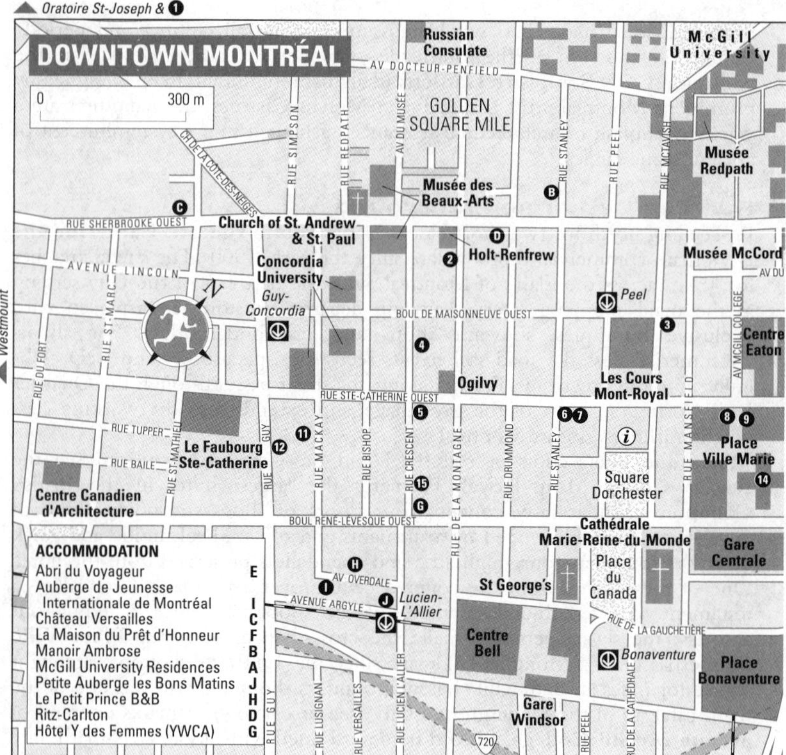

decorated with heads of angels and the evangelists, but the most poignant feature is the Coventry Cross, made from nails salvaged from England's Coventry Cathedral, which was destroyed by bombing during World War II. With the decline in its congregation, the cathedral authorities' desperation for money led them to lease all the land around and beneath the church. For nearly a year, Christ Church was known as "the floating church" – it was supported on concrete struts while the developers tunnelled out the glitzy Promenades de la Cathédrale, a boutique-lined part of the Underground City.

A couple of blocks east of Square Phillips, Ste-Catherine slopes down towards **Place des Arts**, Montréal's leading performing-arts centre and the site of major festivals throughout the summer. The layout tends to throw newcomers: the entrances to all the performance halls are via an underground concourse. Atop that is a large plaza, with a series of gardens and fountains. The wide steps create a seating area for use during outdoor concerts, and the walls around the fountains are a popular snoozing spot for nearby office workers during the summer. Occupying the west side of the Place des Arts plaza, the **Musée d'Art Contemporain de Montréal** (Tues–Sun 11am–6pm, Wed till 9pm; $8, free Wed evenings; ⓣ514/847-6226, ⓦwww.macm.org; Métro Place-des-Arts) is Canada's first museum devoted entirely to contemporary art. The city's foremost showcase for work by Québecois artists, such as Paul-Émile Borduas and Jean-Paul Riopelle, the museum also has works by other Canadian

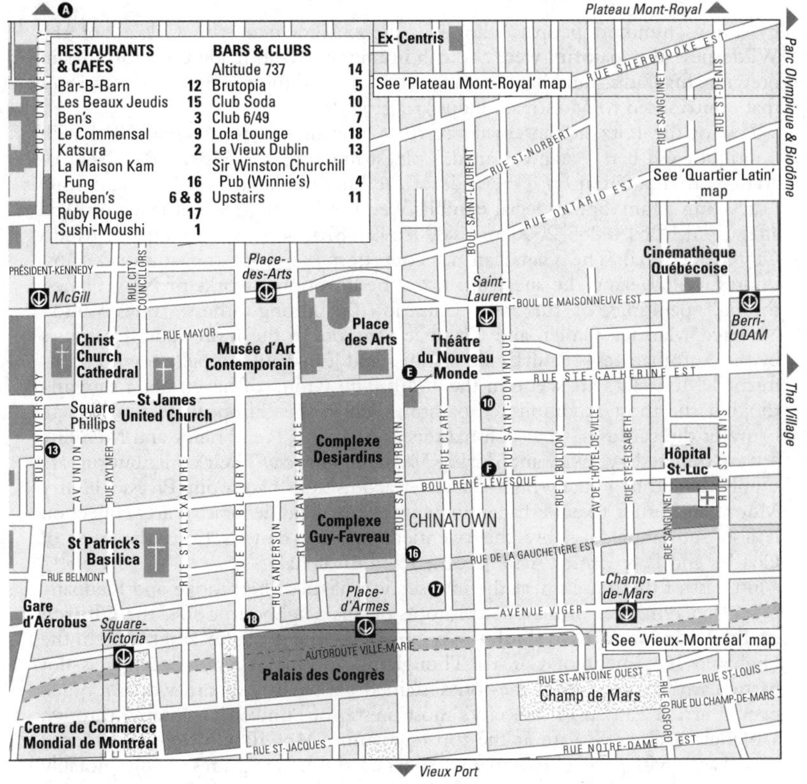

and international artists. One wing is devoted to the permanent collection; the other stages temporary exhibitions. There's a nice restaurant terrace, often filled with live music, and a small sculpture garden – though difficult to find, it holds a Henry Moore sculpture amidst the greenery.

Rue Sherbrooke and around

Rue Sherbrooke crosses half of the island of Montréal but, other than the Stade Olympique far out east, its most interesting part is the few blocks from McGill University to rue Guy, an elite stretch of private galleries, exclusive hotels and boutiques – the likes of Yves Saint-Laurent, Ralph Lauren and Giorgio Armani. At the corner of rue Drummond is the **Ritz-Carlton Hotel**, Montréal's most ornate hotel; Elizabeth Taylor married Richard Burton here. Inside, the small **Claude Lafitte Art Gallery** (Mon–Sat 10.30am–5pm, Sun noon–5pm; ⓣ514/842-1270, ⓦwww.lafitte.com) has works by Picasso, Miro, Chagall and Canadian artists Riopelle, Fortin, Lemieux, Borduas and Pellan. The hotel remains a symbol of what was once known as the **Golden Square Mile**; although downtown has encroached upon its southern precincts, the area between rue Sherbrooke, chemin de la Côte-des-Neiges, the mountain and McGill University retains many of the sumptuous mansions (though many now do duty as commercial or university buildings). From the late nineteenth century to World War II, about seventy percent of Canada's wealth was owned by a few hundred people who lived here. Known as the Caesars of the Wilderness, the majority were Scottish immigrants who made their fortunes in brewing, fur trading and banking, and who financed the railways and steamships that contributed to Montréal's industrial growth.

West of the Ritz, at the corner of rue Crescent – a lively street filled with boutiques and bars – stands Canada's oldest museum, the **Musée des Beaux-Arts**, with a pavilion on either side of rue Sherbrooke at nos. 1379 and 1380 (Tues–Sun 11am–5pm, special exhibits Wed until 9pm; $15, half price on Wed after 5pm; ⓣ514/285-2000 or 1-800/899-6873, ⓦwww.mmfa.qc.ca; Métro Guy-Concordia). The Canadian art collection is one of the country's most impressive, covering the spectrum from the devotional works of New France, through paintings of the local landscape by, among others, James Wilson Morrice, Maurice Cullen and Clarence Gagnon, to the more radical canvases by the Automatistes – Paul-Émile Borduas and Jean-Paul Riopelle – who transformed Montréal's art scene in the 1940s. The Group of Seven get a showing too, but the most accomplished paintings are in the European section, where many of the canvases – by such masters as El Greco, Rembrandt and Memling – were donated by merchants during Montréal's heyday. Their contributions are supplemented by equally high-class later acquisitions by Rodin, Picasso, Henry Moore and other twentieth-century luminaries. The decorative arts collection is also substantial, notably the twentieth-century designs from the likes of Charles and Ray Eames, Arne Jacobsen and Alvar Aalto.

Just east of the museum, at the intersection of rues Sherbrooke and Redpath, is another reminder of the Scottish roots of this neighbourhood – the **Church of St Andrew and St Paul**, the regimental church of the Black Watch, the Highland Regiment of Canada. Though the Gothic Revival building is not particularly impressive, Burne-Jones' stained-glass windows are worth a quick peek. Further east still is the city's most prestigious university, entered through a Neoclassical stone gate at the top of **avenue McGill College**, a principal boulevard with wide pavements adorned with sculptures, most notably Raymond Mason's *The Illuminated Crowd*, portraying a mass of larger-than-life people – generally faced by an equally large crowd of tourists. The leafy campus of **McGill University** was founded in 1813 from the bequest of James McGill, a Glaswegian immigrant fur trader, and the university is now world-famous for its medical and engineering schools. The ornate limestone buildings and their modern extensions are perfect for relaxing or for a walk above the street level of downtown. A boulder on the campus near Sherbrooke marks the spot where the original Iroquois village of Hochelaga stood before European penetration. In the middle of the campus is the **Musée Redpath** (Mon–Fri 9am–5pm, Sun 1–5pm, closed Sat all year; late June to Aug closed Fri also; free; ⓣ514/398-4086, ⓦwww.mcgill.ca/redpath; Métro McGill), the first custom-built Canadian museum, with an eclectic anthropological collection that includes a rare fossil collection, crystals, dinosaur bones and two Egyptian mummies.

Facing the campus, in the handsome early twentieth-century McGill Union building at 690 rue Sherbrooke ouest, is the **Musée McCord d'Histoire Canadienne** (Tues–Fri 10am–6pm, Sat–Mon 10am–5pm; winter closed Mon; $10, free on Sat before noon; guided tours Sat 2pm; ⓣ514/398-7100, ⓦwww.mccord-museum.qc.ca; Métro McGill), an extensive museum of Canadian history. The main part of the collection was amassed by the rich and worthy Scots-Irish McCord family over an eighty-year period from the mid-nineteenth century and represents a highly personal vision of the development of Canada, which they saw as a fusion of colonial and declining native elements. The museum is particularly strong on native artefacts, textiles, costumes and photographs, and examples of these are found in the high quality temporary shows as well as in the "Simply Montréal" exhibition on the second floor. Highlights include First Nations items such as furs, ivory carvings and superb beadwork. Nearby, ornate jewellery and other memorabilia from elite Montréal families contrast with the gritty floor-to-ceiling black-and-white photographs of the city taken by William Notman at the turn of the nineteenth century.

Mont Royal and the Plateau

Boulevard St-Laurent – **The Main** – leads all the way up from Vieux-Montréal to the northern extremities of the city. North of rue Sherbrooke is the absorbing **Plateau Mont-Royal** district, where Montréal's cosmopolitan diversity is evident in distinct enclaves of immigrant neighbourhoods. Running parallel to **rue St-Denis**, the Plateau's other main artery and, at its southern end, the heart of the upbeat studenty **Quartier Latin**, this zone is where the most fun can be had in Montréal, with a huge array of ethnic food outlets and bars spilling out onto the streets. If the party atmosphere is too much, you can head for the landscaped expanse of **Mont Royal** or the reverent hush of the **Oratoire St-Joseph** on the mountain's northwest flank.

Plateau Mont-Royal and the Quartier Latin

Traditionally, **boulevard St-Laurent** divided the English in the west from the French in the east of the city. Montréal's immigrants, first Russian Jews, then Greeks, Portuguese, Italians, East Europeans and, more recently, Latin Americans, settled in the middle and, though many prospered enough to move on, the area around The Main is still a cultural mix where neither of the two official languages dominates. Delis, bars, nightclubs, hardware stores, bookshops and an increasing number of trendy boutiques provide the perfect background to a wonderful jumble of sights, sounds and smells.

Wandering north from rue Sherbrooke on The Main, you'll pass through the strip's flashiest block, filled with see-and-be-seen restaurants and clubs, before arriving at one of Montréal's few pedestrianized streets, **rue Prince-Arthur**, thronged with buskers and caricaturists in the summer. Its eastern end leads to the beautiful fountained and statued **Square St-Louis**, the city's finest public square. Designed in 1876, the square was originally the domain of bourgeois Montréalers, and the magnificent houses were subsequently occupied by artists, poets and writers. The east side of the square divides the lower and upper areas of **rue St-Denis**. The part of rue St-Denis leading south from rue Sherbrooke to rue Ste-Catherine – the **Quartier Latin** – has long had a rather grubby reputation, but has become increasingly colonized by terrace cafés and bars crammed with students from the nearby Université du Québec à Montréal (UQAM) well into the early hours. By contrast, the Plateau stretch of rue St-Denis north of the square is the stamping ground of the francophone intellectual set, where a different yet equally heady atmosphere pervades the sidewalks. Here you'll find some of the city's most upscale boutiques and restaurants.

Mont Royal

Little more than a hill to most tourists but a mountain to Montréalers, **Mont Royal** reaches just 233m but its two square kilometres of greenery are visible from almost anywhere in the city. Mont Royal holds a special place in the history of the city – it was here that the Iroquois established their settlement and that Maisonneuve declared the island to be French – but for centuries the

ACCOMMODATION

- Anne ma Soeur Anne C
- Auberge Chez Jean B
- Boulanger Bassin B&B A
- Château de l'Argoat G
- Gîte Plateau Mont-Royal H
- À la Maison de Pierre et Dominique D
- Hôtel de Paris F
- Aux Portes de la Nuit E

RESTAURANTS & CAFÉS

- Amelio's 31
- Beauty's 2
- La Binerie Mont-Royal 3
- Brulerie St-Denis 11
- ChuChai 9
- Eurodeli 25
- Fonduementale 7
- La Iguana 19
- La Jardin de Panos 12
- Laïka 10
- Laloux 20
- Maestro SVP 26
- Moishe's 16
- Pizzédélic 4
- Red Thai 29
- Café Santropol 13
- Schwartz's 17
- Senzala 1
- Toqué! 18

mountain was privately owned. Then, during an especially bitter winter, one of the inhabitants cut down his trees for extra firewood. Montréalers were outraged at the desecration and in 1875 the land was bought by the city for the impressive sum of $1 million. Frederick Law Olmsted, designer of New York's Central Park and San Francisco's Golden Gate Park, was hired to landscape the hill, which now provides 56km of jogging paths and 20km of skiing trails to keep city inhabitants happy year-round. The city has steadfastly refused any commercial developments on this lucrative site, the only construction being **Lac aux Castors**, built in the 1930s as a work-creation scheme for the unemployed; it now serves as a skating rink in the winter and pedal-boat playground in the summer. In the 1950s, protection of the mountain reached a puritanical extreme when a local journalist revealed that young couples were using the area for amatory pursuits and, even worse, that people were openly drinking alcohol. Consequently all of the underbrush was uprooted, which only succeeded in killing off much of the ash, birch, maple, oak and pine trees. Within five years Mont Royal was dubbed "Bald Mountain" and a replanting campaign had to be instigated.

There are various access points for a walk up the mountain but the most popular starting point is at the **George-Étienne Cartier monument** along avenue du Parc, most easily accessed by following rue Rachel westward from boulevard St-Laurent. You can also take the Métro to Mont-Royal station, walk west along avenue du Mont-Royal and turn left on avenue du Parc, or get off the Métro at Place-des-Arts and take bus #80, disembarking halfway along the park. However you get there, the angel-topped monument is hard to miss on summer Sundays, when buskers and people of all ages congregate with "tam tam" drums until the sun goes down, in a display out of a Woodstock love-in. From here, several paths lead towards the summit and the illuminated cross that commemorates Maisonneuve placing a wooden cross here in 1642. The gentlest slope is along chemin Olmsted, a carriage trail that winds lazily up from the monument, past the top of rue Peel (the easiest access from downtown), and along the summit. In addition to the aforementioned Lac aux Castors, chemin Olmsted provides access to the **Maison Smith** (daily 9am–5pm; free; Ⓣ514/843-8240, Ⓦwww.lemontroyal.com), which houses an information centre and exhibition on the mountain, and proceeds to the Chalet, fronted by a **lookout point** offering fine views of downtown and the St Lawrence beyond.

On the northwest side of the mountain the awesome **Oratoire St-Joseph** (daily late June to late Aug 6.30am–9.30pm; rest of year 7am–9pm; Ⓦwww.saint-joseph.org) rises from its green surroundings near Montréal's highest point. If you don't want to walk across the summit, the nearest Métro is Côte-des-Neiges, from where the way to the oratory is signposted; buses #51, #165, #166 and #535 also stop nearby. In 1904, Brother André – a sickly and long-serving brother of the Congregation of the Holy Cross in Montréal - built a small chapel here to honour St Joseph, Canada's patron saint. Before long, Brother André's ability to heal people had earned him the sobriquet "The Miracle Man of Montréal", and huge numbers of patients took to climbing the outside stairs on their knees to receive his grace. Satisfied clients donated so much money that in 1924 he could afford to begin work on this immense granite edifice, which was completed in 1967, thirty years after his death. It is topped by a dome second in size only to St Peter's in Rome. The interior of St Jo's (as it's known locally) does not live up to the splendour of the Italianate exterior, though the chapel in the apse is richly decorated with green marble columns and a gold-leaf ceiling. In the adjoining anteroom, thousands of votive candles burn along the walls, and proof of Brother André's curative powers hang everywhere: crutches, canes and braces are crammed into every available space. The roof terrace, above the portico, has excellent views of the city and provides access to the gardens. A small upstairs museum displays items relating to Brother André's life, including the room in which he died, which was shifted here from a local hospice. Brother André's heart is enclosed in a glass case; the devout believe it quivers occasionally. Outside, the **Way of the Cross** has some particularly beautiful sculptures in smooth, white Carrara marble and Indiana buff stone by Montréal artist Louis Parent – a tranquil site used as a setting for the Denys Arcand film *Jésus de Montréal*. You can also visit the small building a few metres away from the Oratory that contains the original chapel and Brother André's tiny room.

The Parc Olympique and Jardin Botanique

It's best to take the Métro to Pie-IX (pronounced "pee-nuhf") station in order to view Montréal's most infamous architectural construction, the **Parc Olympique**. The main attraction, the **Stade Olympique**, is known by Montréalers as the "Big O" for three reasons: its name, its circular shape and the fact that the city owes so much money for its construction. The main facilities for the 1976 Summer Olympics were designed by Roger Taillibert, who was told that money was no object. Mayor Jean Drapeau declared, "It is as unlikely that Montréal will incur a debt as for a man to bear a child." The complex ended up costing $1.4 billion (over $2 billion with subsequent interest and maintenance),

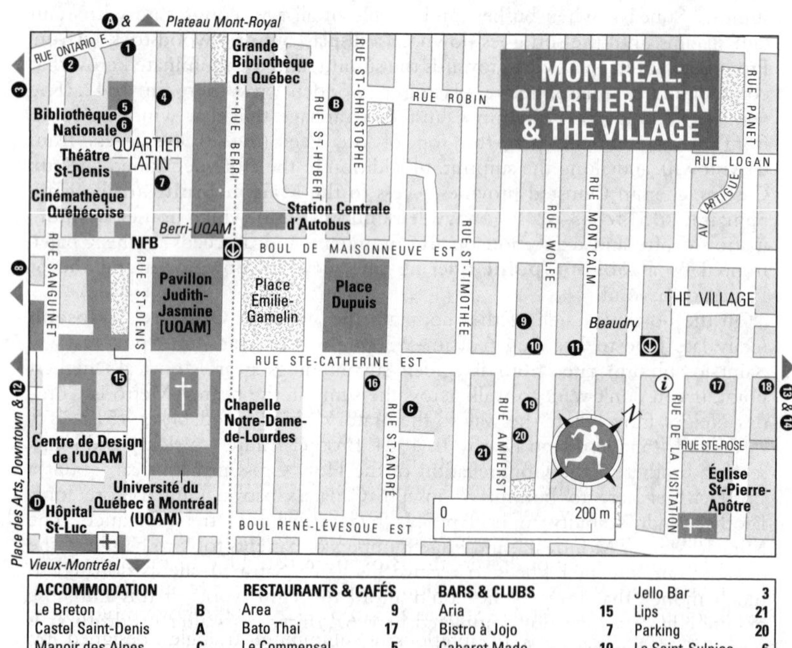

ACCOMMODATION		RESTAURANTS & CAFÉS		BARS & CLUBS			
Le Breton	B	Area	9	Aria	15	Jello Bar	3
Castel Saint-Denis	A	Bato Thai	17	Bistro à Jojo	7	Lips	21
Manoir des Alpes	C	Le Commensal	5	Cabaret Mado	10	Parking	20
Les Résidences Univ UQAM	D	Kilo	13	Le Drugstore	18	Le Saint-Sulpice	6
		Mikado	4	Foufounes Électriques	12	Le Ste-Élisabeth	8
		La Paryse	2	L'Île Noire	1	Sky	14
		Le Resto du Village	19			Stereo	16
						Unity 2	11

of which a large chunk is *still* outstanding – and it was not even completed in time for the games. It's now one of the most heavily used stadiums in the world: in a desperate attempt to pay the debts, the ceaseless schedule features everything from monster truck races to baseball games played by the Montréal Expos. Daily **guided tours** are available ($8; ⓣ514/252-4737 or 1-877/997-0919 for schedule, ⓦwww.rio.gouv.qc.ca) but for just a few bucks more you can take it in from the cheap seats at an Expos game. The stadium's 175-metre **tower** is a major engineering feat – the highest inclined tower in the world. Its main function was to hold a retractable 65-tonne roof, but the 45-minute retraction process never really worked properly, and today sections of the roof are prone to falling in. The attraction is the **funicular** that takes you up the tower to an observation deck with sixty-kilometre views and an exhibition of historic photos of Montréal (daily mid-June to early Sept 9am–7pm; otherwise 9am–5pm; $14; ⓦwww.rio.gouv.qc.ca).

In the stadium's shadow is the **Biodôme** (late Feb–early Sept daily 9am–5pm, otherwise Tues–Sun only; $12.75; ⓣ514/868-3000, ⓦwww.biodome.qc.ca; Métro Viau), housed in a building shaped like a bicycle helmet that started life as a venue for the Olympic cycling events. Now it is a stunning environmental museum comprising four ecosystems: tropical, Laurentian forest, St Lawrence maritime and polar. You can wander freely through the different zones, which are planted with appropriate flourishing vegetation and inhabited by the relevant birds, animals and marine life. It's all highly educational and good fun, but try to avoid visiting on Sundays, when, it seems, the entire population of Québec and its children head there.

Just north of the stadium and linked by a free shuttle bus (mid-May to mid-Sept daily every 30min 11am–5pm) is the **Jardin Botanique de Montréal**, 4101 rue Sherbrooke est (mid-May to Nov daily: 9am–6pm; rest of the year Tues–Sun 9am–5pm, guided tours daily 10am and 1.30pm; $12.75 May–Oct, $9.75 rest of year; ⓣ514/872-1400, ⓦwww.ville.montreal.qc.ca/jardin; Métro Pie-IX). The grounds and greenhouses contain some thirty types of gardens from medicinal herbs to orchids. Highlights include a Japanese garden, its ponds of water lilies bordered by greenish sculptured stone and crossed by delicate bridges. Especially resplendent during the autumn lantern festival is the nearby Chinese garden. Other attractions include the Insectarium (same hours and ticket), a bug-shaped building containing insects of every shape and size. If you visit in November, you'll get a chance to eat some of the insects at the Insectarium's annual bug fry.

Parc Jean-Drapeau

The former Parc des Îles, renamed **Parc Jean-Drapeau** following the death of the colourful and long-time mayor who served from 1954 to 1957 and again from 1960 to 1986, comprises Île Ste-Hélène and the artificial Île Notre-Dame, constructed from fill dredged from the river and from the construction of the Métro (whose yellow line includes the Jean-Drapeau stop, located on Île Ste-Hélène). Bus #167 links the Métro with the attractions on both islands.

Not far from the station hovers the **Biosphère** (late June to mid-Sept daily 10am–6pm; mid-Sept to late June Mon–Fri noon–5pm, Sat & Sun 10am–5pm; $8.50; joint ticket with Musée Stewart $15; ⓣ514/283-5000, ⓦwww.biosphere.ec.gc.ca), a giant sphere of interlocking aluminum triangles designed by Buckminster Fuller for Expo '67. Today, it's an interactive museum focusing on the St Lawrence Seaway and the Great Lakes. The exhibits change yearly and there are lots to amuse children, from interactive touch-screens to skill-testing games, movies and multimedia displays. On the fourth floor, a stupendous lookout point takes in the St Lawrence River and the city, foregrounded by the giant Alexander Calder stabile, *Man* – one of many pieces of public art dotted about the island. A twenty-minute walk from the Biosphère around the winding chemin du Tour de l'Île will get you to the grounds of Montréal's only **fort**, a U-shaped building situated close to the river's edge. Built by the British between 1820 and 1824 as a defence against the threat of American invasion – which never came – it played a number of roles, including a World War II prison camp, before opening as the **Musée Stewart** (daily 10am–5pm; $10, joint ticket with Biosphère $15; Ⓦ www.stewart-museum.org). In the fortified arsenal commissioned by the Duke of Wellington, the museum contains a collection of weapons and assorted domestic and scientific artefacts. The fort is also the summer venue for the re-enactment of seventeenth- and eighteenth-century military manoeuvres by actors dressed as the Fraser Highlanders and Compagnie Franche de la

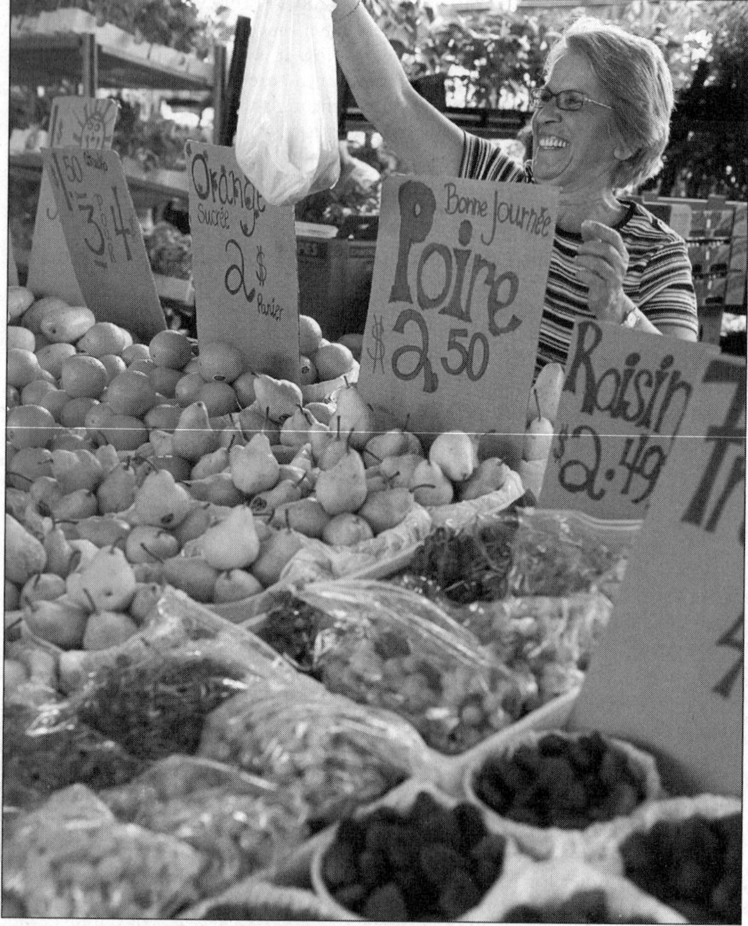

△ Fruit stalls at the Jean-Talon Market

Marine. The shrieking sounds that can be heard all over the island's eastern point, beyond the Jacques-Cartier bridge, emanate from **La Ronde** (mid-June to Sept daily 10am–10.30pm, otherwise see website for schedule; rides $36, grounds only $22.60; ⓣ514/397-2000, ⓦwww.laronde.com). The city's amusement park is the venue for various celebrations throughout the year, including the annual Fireworks Competition from June to July.

Île Notre-Dame, with its beach, canals and gardens, seems quieter than its neighbour – unless you venture here during one of the big motorsports weekends, when cars tear their way along the Circuit Gilles-Villeneuve, which rings the island.

Eating

Montréalers conduct much of their business and their social lives in the city's **eating places**, and Montréal food is as varied as its population, ranging from the rich meat dishes of typical Québecois cuisine to bagels bursting with cream cheese: Montréal comes a close second to New York as the **bagel** capital of the world, and they are sold everywhere from grimy outlets to stylish cafés – particularly delicious when fresh, warm and crammed with cream cheese and lox (smoked salmon).

Montréal's ethnic diversity is amply displayed by the variety of **cuisines** available and Montréalers try to outdo each other by indulging in exotic fare from Japanese rotis to earthy Portuguese nosh. The city has its own **Chinatown** just north of Vieux-Montréal, a **Little Italy** around Jean-Talon Métro, a **Greek** community whose cheaper restaurants are concentrated along Prince Arthur – but for more traditional Greek cuisine head further north along avenue du Parc where a number of Greek-Canadians live. Most prominent of the ethnic eateries are the **Eastern European** establishments dotted around the city. Opened by Jewish immigrants who came to work in the garment factories, their speciality is **smoked meat**, which has become a Montréal obsession, served between huge chunks of rye bread with pickles on the side. Masses of restaurants line the area around rue Ste-Catherine downtown, though American fast-food chains seem to be taking over, while Vieux-Montréal has an ever-expanding number of places to eat, but here most are touristy and slightly overpriced. The best for food, and upbeat atmosphere, is in the more French area of the metropolis, around the Plateau and Quartier Latin. *Apportez votre vin* ("bring your own wine") establishments, of which there are many on rue Prince Arthur and av Duluth, are the cheaper restaurant alternatives serving good ethnic cuisine.

Cafés and snack outlets

Bagel Etc. 4320 boul St-Laurent; Métro: Mont-Royal or bus #55. Trendy New York-type diner. Excellent bagels from the simple cream cheese to caviar and extravagant breakfasts. Daily 8am–5pm.

Beauty's 93 av du Mont-Royal ouest; Métro: Mont-Royal or bus #55 ⓦwww.beautys.ca. A brunch institution with wonderful 1950s decor. Be prepared to get up early on the weekend to avoid the lineup.

Ben's Delicatessen 990 boul de Maisonneuve ouest; Métro: Peel. Lithuanian Ben Kravitz opened his deli in 1908 and his sons and grandsons still run this Montréal institution. Its gaudy 1930s interior still draws a few people in the wee hours for delicious smoked meat and diner fare, but the wall of fame attests to happier days.

La Binerie Mont-Royal 367 av du Mont-Royal est; Métro: Mont-Royal. Four tables and a chrome counter seat the hundreds of people who visit this well-known café daily. The menu consists of beans, beans and more beans with ketchup, vinegar or maple syrup. Also served is pork, beef, *tourtière* (a minced pork pie) and *pouding chômeur* ("unemployed pudding"), a variation on bread pudding.

Bio Train 410 rue St-Jacques; Métro: Square-Victoria. Self-serve health-food restaurant with tasty soups and hearty sandwiches. The muffins – especially the tangy cranberry ones – make great snacks.

Brulerie St-Denis 1587 rue St Denis; Métro: Berri-UQAM. A nirvana for those that obsess over their coffee beans. Hundreds of varieties, roasted and ground on site, with plenty of tables on the terrace to sit and savour the perfect caffiene hit.

Café Santropol 3990 rue St-Urbain; bus #55 or Métro: Sherbrooke or Mont-Royal Ⓦwww.santropol.com. Mostly vegetarian café on the corner of av Duluth. Spectacular during the summer when its blooming back terrace is a welcome oasis from the busy streets, *Santropol* still retains its charm in winter thanks to its cozy atrium. Huge sandwiches, quiches and salads are offered as well as various herbal teas and coffees. Killer milkshakes, too.

Chez Claudette 351 av Laurier est; Métro: Laurier. Cheap family bistro, great for a big breakfast fry-up.

Euro Deli 3619 boul St-Laurent; Métro Sherbrooke or bus #55. Busy deli where you can stuff yourself for about $5 on sandwiches, calzone, pasta and veggie food.

Fairmount Bagel Bakery 74 av Fairmount ouest; Métro: Laurier or bus #55. Possibly the best bagel outlet in Montréal, offering a huge variety of bagels. There is nowhere to sit, but arm yourself with a bag of bagels, a pot of cream cheese and some smoked salmon (lox), perch on the nearest curb and you'll soon be in bagel heaven. Open daily 24hr.

Faubourg Ste-Catherine 1616 rue Ste-Catherine ouest; Métro: Guy-Concordia Ⓦwww.lefaubourg.com. A gigantic restored building on the corner of rue Guy. Downstairs is a wealth of food stalls from cookies to fresh veg; upstairs a fastfood mall to surpass all others – everything from fresh salmon to crepes and cookies.

Kilo 5206 boul St-Laurent; Métro: Laurier or bus #55. Creating the most divine cakes, particularly the cheesecake, this patisserie is expensive but worth every cent. Open late on weekends. There's a second location in the Village at 1495 rue Ste-Catherine (Métro Beaudry).

Laïka 4040 boul St-Laurent; bus #55 or Métro: Sherbrooke or Mont-Royal. The sleek interior draws urbane hipsters from the Plateau for daily specials and *cafés au lait.*

Reuben's Deli 1116 rue Ste-Catherine ouest; Métro: McGill. An excellent deli with great jars of pimentos in the window and a wealth of smoked meats. Frantic atmosphere and friendly service. A favourite with local business types, and thus packed at lunchtime. A second outlet, a couple of blocks east at no. 888, is cheaper as it's in a (cosy) basement.

Schwartz's 3895 boul St-Laurent; bus #55 or Métro: Sherbrooke. A Montréal institution: a small, narrow deli serving up colossal smoked-meat sandwiches, with surly service thrown in as part of the package. Line-up out the door on weekends.

Senzala 177 rue Bernard ouest; Métro: Outremont. If your taste buds need a wake-up call in the morning head to this Brazilian café in Mile End for brunch and sample lively concoctions such as poached eggs in advocado and tomato sauce.

Wilensky's Light Lunch 34 av Fairmount ouest; Métro: Laurier or bus #55. Used for countless film sets because the decor hasn't changed since 1932 and that includes the till, the grill and the drinks machine. The Wilensky Special includes bologna and three types of salami and costs around $3. Mon–Fri 9am–4pm only.

Restaurants

Asian

Azuma 5263 boul St-Laurent; Métro: Laurier or bus #55 Ⓣ514/271-5263. A popular Japanese restaurant that looks a little run down from the outside but there is nothing shabby about the food. Unusual traditional dishes to experiment with and a reasonable $20 a head menu.

Chu Chai 4088 rue St-Denis; Métro: Mont-Royal or Sherbrooke Ⓣ514/843-4194. Excellent, fresh vegetarian Thai with lunch menus from $11 and dinner from $20.

Katsura 2170 rue de la Montagne; Métro: Peel Ⓣ514/849-1172. Large and popular downtown Japanese restaurant. Fairly expensive but they serve cheaper bento boxes ($13) and the like for weekday lunch.

La Maison Kam Fung 1111 rue St-Urbain; Métro: Place-d'Armes; Ⓣ514/878-2888. Hard to find (tucked away on the third floor of a shopping complex) but worth the search, this large dim sum restaurant offers over 30 varieties of the popular delicacy for $8–20.

Pho Bang New York 970 boul St-Laurent; Métro: Place-d'Armes Ⓣ514/954-2032. The servings of *pho* (tonkinoise) noodle soup are huge and delicious, and extremely affordable – a large lunch or dinner will only set you back $10–12. If it's full, try the similar *Pho Bac 97* up the street at no. 1016.

Red Thai 3550 boul St-Laurent; Métro: Sherbrooke or St-Laurent ☎514/289-0998. This resto serves up exquisite Thai in a dodgy decor straight out of *Anna and the King*. Most dishes around $17.

Ruby Rouge 1008 rue Clark; Métro: Place-d'Armes ☎514/390-8828. Montréal's vast temple to dim sum, right in the heart of Chinatown. At around $4 a serving it's well-priced but not dirt-cheap. There are often long queues so get there early.

Sushi-moushi 3193 boul Decarie; Métro: Plamondon ☎514/369-8860. In a town where sushi is an obsession, Sushi-moushi is a locals favourite. Specializes in decorative Maki at around $5 for a full selection of 10.

Soy 5258 boul St-Laurent; bus #55 ☎514/499-9399. Deliciously prepared light dishes from the Orient. *Soy* is especially good for lunch, when a three-course meal costs under $10.

Thai Express 3710 boul St-Laurent; Métro: Sherbrooke ☎514/287-9957. The name says it all: speedy Thai at low prices – for around $8, you'll get a seriously hearty serving of rice or noodles with wonderfully aromatic spices.

French

Au 917 917 rue Rachel est; Métro: Mont-Royal ☎514/524-0094. An inexpensive bistro (table d'hote from $10) with a reliable menu in a comfortable atmosphere. Bring your own wine.

Les Beaux Jeudis 1449 rue Crescent; Métro: Guy-Concordia ☎514/288-5656. Classy, but unpretentious, Parisian-style bistro with a flower-decked terrace in summer. Great value all-you-can-eat weekday specials for $24 including roast leg of lamb on Tuesdays and shrimps on Wednesdays.

Bonaparte 443 rue St-François-Xavier; Métro: Place d'Armes ☎514/844-4368. Moderately priced, well-situated French restaurant in Vieux-Montréal. The fish is good and there are tables on the balconies. Evening table d'hote around $26.

Fonduementale 4325 rue St-Denis; Métro: Mont-Royal ☎514/499-1446. Set in a historic two-storey house with a warm fireplace in winter and a blooming outdoor terrace in summer. The fondue, starting at just $17, is divine and the meals are long and languid. Generous table d'hote menu's from $35.

Laloux 250 av des Pins est; Métro: Sherbrooke ☎514/287-9127. This Parisian-style bistro serves pricey *nouvelle cuisine* but most people come simply to enjoy the wood panel and polished brass décor. Expect to pay $50 for lunch and up to $150 for dinner with a bottle of wine.

Au Petit Extra 1690 rue Ontario est; Métro: Papineau ☎514/527-5552. Large, lively and affordable bistro (lunch from $12 and dinner around $20) with great food and authentic French feel but it's a bit of a hike east.

Toqué! 3842 rue St-Denis; Métro: Sherbrooke ☎514/499-2084. Renowned chef Normand Laprise holds court here and the dining experience is ultra chic, high-end and unforgettable – if you can get a seat and afford the price tag. Reservations are essential and dinner starts at $91.

Mediterranean

Amelio's 201 rue Milton; Métro: Place-des-Arts or bus #24 ☎514/845-8396. Basic and hearty pasta and pizza from $8 in a tiny half-basement restaurant in the heart of the McGill University student ghetto. The prices are excellent and the service friendly. Bring your own wine.

Arahova Souvlaki 256 rue St-Viateur ouest; bus #80 ☎514/274-7828. Superb, authentic Greek cuisine for under $10. Popular with the after-clubbing crowd.

Bottega 67 rue St-Zotique est; Métro: Laurier ☎514/277-8104. Dominated by the huge authentic pizza oven, this back-to-basics pizza place is run by a master baker that trained in Naples. The results are divine, all for $10–15. Reservations essential.

La Jardin de Panos 521 av Duluth est; Métro: Sherbrooke or Mont-Royal ☎514/521-4206. Beats out the numerous cheap Greek *brochetteries* on rue Prince Arthur in taste and has a garden to boot. An average meal will cost $15–30. Bring your own wine.

Maestro SVP 3615 boul St-Laurent; Métro: Sherbrooke or bus #55 ☎514/842-6447. When oysters are in season, this is the place to go to get them, served in a myriad of ways for $30 per dozen. Try one in a shooter with vodka and horse-radish sauce for a quick kick.

Milos 5357 av du-Parc; bus #80 ☎514/272-3522. Expensive, but the finest Greek restaurant in the city, especially notable for its fresh seafood. Early-bird and Sunday dinners are cheaper at $35.

Pizzédélic 3467 boul St-Laurent; Métro: St-Laurent or bus #55 ☎514/845-0404. A whole chain has been spawned from the reputation of this one restaurant serving tasty and experimental square pizza's for under $16. The daily lunch special is a bargain at $6.99.

Pizzeria Napoletana 189 rue Dante; bus #55 ☎514/276-8226. Authentic Little Italy pizzeria where nothing is over $15; take your own alcohol and expect to queue at the weekend.

North American

L'Anecdote 801 rue Rachel est; Métro: Mont-Royal ⓣ514/526-7967. Small, cosy hamburger and sandwich joint with meals around $9.

Bar-B-Barn 1201 rue Guy; Métro: Guy-Concordia ⓣ514/931-3811. Top chicken and ribs from $4 to $20 (depending on how much 'hawg' you can eat) served amidst yeee-haa decor; a favourite with the local "cowboy" business world – hundreds of business cards are stuck in the log rafters. Just south of rue Ste-Catherine.

Chez Delmo 211 rue Notre-Dame ouest; Métro: Place-d'Armes ⓣ514/849-4061. Popular with anglophones and workers from the nearby stock exchange in Vieux-Montréal, the food doesn't come cheap – expect to pay $30–45. Eat in the first room with its two long oyster bars. Fish and seafood dishes are the speciality, and the chowder is a treat. No lunch Sat, closed Sun, no dinner Mon.

Le Commensal 1204 av McGill College; Métro: McGill ⓣ514/871-1480. Cheap vegetarian with hot or cold buffet paid for by weight ($1.69 per 100g). The St-Denis location has the best atmosphere. Open daily until late. Also in the Quartier Latin at 1720 rue St-Denis (ⓣ514/854-2627; Métro Berri-UQAM).

La Iguana 51 rue Roy; Métro: Mont-Royal ⓣ514/844-0893. Traditional Mexican in sumptious surroundings for $10–25. Try the giant shrimps flambeed in Tequila Gold.

Laurier BBQ 381 av Laurier ouest; bus #80 ⓣ514/273-3671. Great hunks of Québec-style barbecued chicken and huge salads for around £12; a Montréal favourite for half a century.

Moishe's 3961 boul St-Laurent; bus #55 or Métro: Sherbrooke ⓣ514/845-3509, ⓦwww.moishes.ca. Favourite haunt of Montréal's business community. Excellent (and huge) steaks, upwards of $30, with notoriously bad-tempered service. Reservations recommended.

Patati Patata 4177 boul St-Laurent; bus #55 ⓣ514/844-0216. With only enough room for a dozen people this is a tiny place with excellent and cheap home-made food. The Poutine is supposedly the best in Montréal and for $4 it's worth a try.

Shed Café 3515 boul St-Laurent; Métro: St-Laurent or Sherbrooke ⓣ514/842-0220. Hamburger, salad and sandwich joint ($10–15) with sumptious cheesecakes, where trendy Montréalers come to see and be seen. Avant-garde, wacky interior and a DJ after 8pm. Open until 1am (weekend 3am).

Nightlife and entertainment

Montréal's **nightlife** keeps going into the small hours of the morning, and its bars and clubs cater to everyone – from the students of the Quartier Latin and the punks who hang out on the corner of rue Ste-Catherine and boul St-Laurent to the anglophone yuppies of rue Crescent. The **bars** listed here are the best of the bunch and are open until 3am unless stated otherwise. Always tip the bar staff: the perks constitute most of their wages. Many bars have regular music nights, with **jazz** being especially popular. Other than the bars, there are numerous venues in the city, with top-name touring bands playing at the Centre Bell and other large venues. For up-to-date **information**, the *Mirror* (ⓦwww.montrealmirror.com) and *Hour* (ⓦwww.hour.ca) are free English alternative weekly newspapers with excellent listings sections. The English-language daily *Montréal Gazette* also carries comprehensive listings; the Friday weekend guide is particularly good.

Bars

Bar Fly 4062 boul St-Laurent; Métro: Saint Laurent. This bar revels in live music, featuring local bands – from punk to blues – nearly every night of the week. Unpretentious and deliciously sleazy, it's popular with elabourately tattooed and pierced teens and twenty-somethings.

Le Bifteck 3702 boul St-Laurent; Métro: Sherbrooke or bus #55. Perenially popular studenty, cheap beer bar with taped music from grunge to hip-hop that overflows onto two floors at the weekend and outside in the summer.

Bily Kun 354 av du Mont-Royal est; Métro: Mont-Royal. Packed brasserie-pub, with stuffed ostrich heads on the minimalist walls overlooking tables and booths. DJ's and occasional live bands.

Blizzarts 3956a boul St-Laurent; bus #55. Funked-out lounge-bar with retro furnishings, Sputnik-lighting, and a tiny dance floor. Draws a late-twenty-something Plateau crowd.

Brutopia 1219 Crescent St; Métro: Lucien Allier. A welcoming pub spread over three floors with a terrace and balcony that has a huge range of exotic beers brewed on-site in the copper drums behind the bar. Live bands most nights of the week, open mic on Sun.

Jello Bar 151 rue Ontario est; Métro: St-Laurent. Enjoy live jazz and blues at this bar furnished with 1960s and 1970s novelties – kitch but irresistibly slinky. Martini cocktails are the house speciality.

Laïka 4040 boul St-Laurent. bus #55. Café by day, lounge by night, heaven-sent haven by early morning, *Laïka*'s stark décor attracts a casually chic crowd at any time of day, though the service can be a bit spotty.

Lola Lounge 1023 rue de Bleury; Métro: Square-Victoria. With plenty of sofas to sink into and specialist DJs creating chilled out vibes every night of the week, this is a place to sit, chat with friends and soak up the atmosphere.

L'Île Noire 342 rue Ontario est; Métro: Berri-UQAM. A homage to the Scottish pub complete with mahogany bar stools and traditional pint glasses. Popular with British ex-pats, it stocks over 140 types of whisky from $5 to $500 a shot.

Sir Winston Churchill Pub 1459 rue Crescent; Métro: Peel or Guy-Concordia. Known locally as *Winnie's*, this large English-style pub is part of a complex of nine bars that attracts an older crowd of local and visiting anglophone professionals. Pool tables and a small dance floor. Prime pick-up joint.

Le Ste-Élisabeth 1412 rue Ste-Élisabeth; Métro: Berri-UQAM. Don't miss the secluded outdoor courtyard with ivy-covered walls lit by stained glass lamps or the glass terrace upstairs. This is a bar that seems to transport you far away from the city, perfect for an intimate drink with friends.

Le St-Sulpice 1680 rue St-Denis; Métro: Berri-UQAM. A bar complex over 3 floors with a warren of often-crowded rooms, each playing its own music genre. In the basement is a chill room with chairs that are perfect for lounging and widescreen TVs playing music videos.

Sofa 451 rue Rachel est; Métro: Mont-Royal. ⓦwww.sofa-bar.com; A sophisticated bar-lounge where well-dressed twenty and thirty somethings smoke cigars and drink port while appreciating groovy music from acid jazz to house.

Le Swimming 3643 boul St-Laurent; Métro: Sherbrooke or bus #55. ⓦwww.leswimming.com; Don't let the dodgy-looking entrance put you off. This is a modern pool hall that is just as popular for socialising with live ska, reggae and jazz acts at the weekend. Pool is free until 5pm.

Le Vieux-Dublin 1219 rue University; Métro: McGill. As comfortable as an old shoe, the "Old Dublin" is an example of what an Irish pub should be with a relaxed, lively crowd, loud music and a massive choice of draught beers. Popular with students and a more mature crowd alike.

Whisky Café 5800 boul St-Laurent; Métro: Outremont or bus #55 ⓦwww.whiskycafe.ca. Featuring the only ladies urinal in Montréal this is actually an expensive and elegant bar that attracts a young wealthy clientele. With themed spirit tasting menu's and gourmet snacks, it's the perfect place to round off a special evening.

Clubs and music venues

Altitude 737 1 Place Ville Marie; Métro: McGill or Bonaventure. Popular with a financial district crowd, the main selling point of this club on the top three floors of Montréals tallest building is the stunning panoramic view of the city, not the sordid meat-market atmosphere.

Aria 1280 rue St-Denis; Métro: Berri-UQAM ⓦwww.arianightclub.com. From 1.30am until 10am, Montréal's club kids dance the night and morning away to house music, with occasional detours into techno and trance, led by big-name guest DJs in the main room making the most of the famously impressive sound system. Fri & Sat only; $20–25.

Le Balattou 4372 boul St-Laurent; bus #55. Montréal's only African nightclub, *Balattou* is resolutely dark, smoky, crowded, hot and loud, but also friendly. Live acts every night; entrance $5 on weekdays, $7 at weekends (includes one drink), closed Mondays.

Bistro à Jojo 1627 rue St-Denis; Métro: Berri-UQAM ⓦwww.bistroajojo.com. Low ceilings and stone walls give this unpretentious blues cave an intimate feel. Shows nightly from around 10pm.

Café Campus 57 rue Prince-Arthur est; Métro Sherbrooke. Notorious as a place that knows how to party Café Campus has live acts every night. Particularly recommended is Retro Tuesday (which attracts a young crowd) and Blues Wednesday. Francophone Sunday's are free.

Casa del Popolo 4873 boul St-Laurent. bus #55 or Métro Laurier ⓣ514/284-3804. "The House of the People" is a sofa-strewn, low-key Plateau spot where high-calibre spoken-word evenings and folk and other bands perform for a marginal fee. A good spot to mingle with the locals any time from noon until 3am.

Club 6/49 1112 rue Ste-Catherine ouest; Métro Peel. Long-running Latin dance club with plenty of tables to sit at and simply enjoy the spectacle if you don't have the spirit for salsa, merengue or bachata. Free lessons on Mon and Thurs nights.

Club Soda 1225 boul St-Laurent; Métro: St-Laurent. Large live music venue that attracts all the best acts and has reached almost legendary status in Montréal. Cover charge of $25.

Aux Deux Pierrots 104 rue St-Paul est; Métro: Champ-de-Mars. Québecois folk singers are the mainstay of this club and everyone sings along. There's usually a good crowded atmosphere but don't expect to understand a word unless your French is excellent. Outside terrace in the summer.

Exit 3553 boul St-Laurent; Métro: Sherbrooke or bus #55 ⓦwww.exit3553.com. The hip-hop sessions (Thurs–Sat) attract a mostly under-25 crowd to this long and narrow space; older clubbers head to the top floor (open Sat only) for Christian Pronovost's popular house set. Cover $10.

Les Foufounes Électriques 87 rue Ste-Catherine est; Métro: St-Laurent ⓦwww.foufounes.qc.ca. A bizarre name ("The Electric Buttocks") for a bizarre and wonderful bar-club venue. Known as *Foufs*, it's the best place in Québec for alternative bands, attracting a young crowd from ravers to punks. Huge outside terrace perfect for summer evenings. Tickets for bands $5–15, club nights free–$8; admission to the bar is free and pitchers of beer are cheap.

Orchid 3556 boul St-Laurent; Métro Sherbrooke or bus #55. Playing mostly house with a mix of soul, salsa and R&B this popular club is just big enough to strutt your stuff without getting lost in the crowd. Dress beautiful to get in. Tuesday nights is gay men's night. Cover charge of $10.

Saphir 3699 boul St-Laurent; Métro: St Laurent or bus #55. Friday's are the biggest night at this Morrocan influenced club, serving everything from 80's glam to gothic rock. Enthusiastic funk and break dancing shows entice clubbers back during the week. Cover charge $3–$5.

Stereo 858 rue Ste-Catherine est; Métro: Beaudry ⓦwww.stereo-nightclub.com. Known as the best after-hours club in the city and said to have the best sound system, the stereo in question kicks techno, house and drum'n'bass from 2am until whenever. Fri & Sat only. $25–30.

Gay Montréal

Montréal has an excellent **gay** scene, with the action concentrated in the area known as **The Village** – roughly located on rue Ste-Catherine est between rue Amherst and the Papineau Métro station. There's a **tourist information centre** here, at 1260 rue Ste-Catherine est, Suite 209 (late June to early Sept Mon–Thurs 11am–6pm, Fri–Sun 10am–8pm; rest of year Mon–Fri and weekends during major events 10am–6pm; ⓣ514/522-1885 or 1-888/595-8110). As well, two **help lines** can provide up-to-date news on the latest events: Gay Line (daily 7–11pm; ⓣ514/866-5090, ⓦwww.gayline.qc.ca) is in English; Gai Écoute (ⓣ514/866-0103) in French. Priape, 1311 rue Ste-Catherine est, is a Village-based sex shop and clothing store that also sells tickets to most events. *Fugues* (ⓦwww.fugues.com) is the city's monthly French gay and lesbian magazine (there's usually a small English section hidden among the ads and pictures). In early August, **Divers Cité** (ⓦwww.diverscite.org), the gay and lesbian pride parade, is the event of the year; also popular are the September **image + nation** film festival (ⓦwww.image-nation.org) and the week of events leading up to the massive **Black & Blue** circuit party (ⓦwww.bbcm.org) on Thanksgiving weekend.

Cafés and restaurants

Most of the **restaurants** and hangouts in The Village cater to a lesbian, bisexual and gay crowd in the evening, but are more mixed during the day. Unless noted otherwise, Métro Beaudry is the nearest station.

Area 1429 rue Amherst ⓣ514/890-6691. Well-designed, if rather small, restaurant with a stylish and airy atmosphere reflected in the exquisite French and Asian fusion dishes at around $20. Dinner only; closed Sun & Mon.

Bato Thai 1310 rue Ste-Catherine est ⓣ514/524-6705. An elegant, nautical themed (Bato means boat in Thai) Thai restaurant, but with slow service. Cheap lunch deals from $14 during the week. Don't leave without trying the spectacular fried ice-cream.

Le Club Sandwich 1560 rue Ste-Catherine est. Boasting over 60 varieties of sandwiches and clubs this relaxed 24-hour diner also serves breakfast around the clock. Brunch from $14. Famous for its coleslaw.

Tokyo Bar 3709 boul St-Laurent; Métro: St-Laurent or bus #55. With plush Asian décor, low lighting and resident DJs playing uncomplicated favourites, this is a great place to let your hair down either on the dancefloor, in the lounge or on one of the two rooftop terraces.

Upstairs 1254 rue Mackay; Métro: Guy-Concordia Ⓦwww.upstairsjazz.com. Upstairs is actually downstairs in a cosy half-basement with fresh jazz and blues on tap nightly in a wonderfully attitude-free atmosphere. Predominently thirty-something crowd. Cover charge of $10.

The performing arts and cinema

Montréal's most prestigious centre for the **performing arts** is the Place des Arts, 175 rue Ste-Catherine ouest (Ⓦwww.pdarts.com), a five-hall complex with a comprehensive year-round programme of dance, music and theatre. The Théâtre de Verdure in Parc Lafontaine is an outdoor theatre with a summer-long programme of free plays, ballets and concerts. Another eclectic venue is the Théâtre St-Denis, 1594 rue St-Denis (Ⓦwww.theatrestdenis.com), which presents blockbuster musicals and other shows. The Saidye Bronfman Centre for the Arts, 5170 chemin de la Côte-Ste-Catherine (Ⓦwww.saidyebronfman.org), contains an exhibition centre and a three-hundred-seater venue for English (and Yiddish) music, dance, film and theatre.

La Paryse 302 rue Ontario est; Métro: Berri-UQAM. Lesbian-owned retro diner with an extraordinary and exotic range of burger fillings all for less than $10. Tasty veggie-burgers too.

Piccolo Diavolo 1336 rue Ste-Catherine est Ⓣ514/526-1336. Devilishly hip place to eat Italian; dimly lit with plenty of hell-themed touches. Pizzas, pastas and meatier dishes, including good veal *osso buco*. Dinner for around $20.

Le Resto du Village 1310 rue Wolfe. Just off rue Ste-Catherine, this small diner serves filling comfort food such as *pâté chinois* (shepherd's pie) and *poutine* for less than $15 to a largely gay crowd. Open 24hr.

Bars, clubs and discos

Cabaret Mado 1115 rue Ste-Catherine est Ⓦwww.mado.qc.ca. Local drag celebrity Mado and her cohorts camp it up for a mixed, fun-loving clientele, who enevitably end the evening on the huge dancefloor partying the night away.

Le Drugstore 1366 rue Ste-Catherine est. An extravagant six-floor bar complex complete with pool lounge, rooftop terrace and even a popcorn machine. With homely 60's decor it is busiest before 11pm and popular with both lesbians and gay men.

Lips 1294 Amherst St. Montréal's newest night-spot purely for lesbians promises a raunchy dancefloor plus plenty of space to chill out and an all-important pool table.

Parking 1296 Amherst St. Set in an old auto-repair shop, complete with mechanic tools and spare auto parts, Montréals best gay club has several dancefloors and lounges catering to all genre's and tastes. Men-only on Friday and Saturday nights. Cover charge $3–5.

Sky 1474 rue Ste-Catherine est. Choose between the café bar on the first floor, the male strip club on the second floor or the unfailingly pounding dancefloor and cabaret on the 3rd floor. Attracts the beautiful-people set after work during the week. Cover charge $4.

Unity II 1171 rue Ste-Catherine est. A young, mixed and outgoing crowd fill the large dance floor here, though the *Bamboo Bar* upstairs tends to get more packed and sweaty – head to the rooftop terrace to cool off and take in an unforgettable view of the city.

The Orchestre Symphonique de Montréal (Ⓦwww.osm.ca) and Orchestre Métropolitain (Ⓦwww.orchestremetropolitain.com) stage regular **concerts** at Place des Arts and the Basilique Notre-Dame. The city also has a programme of free summer concerts in various city parks. L'Opéra de Montréal (Ⓦwww.operademontreal.com) produces five bilingually surtitled productions a year at Place des Arts. The city's foremost French-language **theatre** is the Théâtre du Rideau Vert, 4664 rue St-Denis (Ⓦwww.rideauvert.qc.ca), which gives prominence to Québec playwrights, while the Théâtre du Nouveau Monde, 84 rue Ste-Catherine ouest (Ⓦwww.tnm.qc.ca), presents a mix of contemporary and classic plays in French. Montréal's main English-language theatre is the Centaur Theatre, 453 rue St-François-Xavier (Ⓦwww.centaurtheatre.com). Montréal has more than ten excellent **dance** troupes, from Les Grands Ballets Canadiens (Ⓦwww.grandsballets.qc.ca) and Les Ballets Jazz de Montréal (Ⓦwww.balletsdemontreal.com) to the avant-garde La La La Human Steps and O Vertigo, who perform at various times at the Place des Arts, Théâtre de Verdure and during the festivals.

Films in English, usually the latest releases from the US, can be caught at most cinemas; the Paramount, 977 rue Ste-Catherine ouest, features armchairs and a wide screen. The main repertory cinema in English is the NFB (National FilmBoard) Cinema, 1564 rue St-Denis (Ⓦwww.nfb.ca). The Cinémathèque Québécoise, 335 boul de Maisonneuve est (Ⓦwww.cinematheque.qc.ca), has excellent screening and exhibition programmes; Ex-Centris, 3536 boul, St-Laurent (Ⓦwww.ex-centris.com), has a penchant for alternative French film and experimental digital works. Check online (Ⓦwww.cinemamontreal.com) or in the *Montréal Gazette* or the free weeklies for show times – make sure to verify that the English film you want to see is playing in **v.o.** (*version originale*), not v.f. (*version français*); the latter means it's dubbed.

Listings

Airport enquiries Ⓣ514/394-7377 or Ⓣ1-800/465-1213, Ⓦwww.admtl.com.

Bike and blade rental Cycle Pop, near Parc Lafontaine at 1000 rue Rachel est (Ⓣ514/526-2525, Ⓦwww.cyclepop.ca), rents from $25 per day. In the Vieux-Port, Ça Roule, 27 rue de la Commune est, facing Quai King-Edward (Ⓣ514/866-0633, Ⓦwww.caroulemontreal.com); both offer lessons and guided tours. The Maison des Cyclistes, 1251 rue Rachel est (Ⓣ514/521-8356, Ⓦwww.velo.qc.ca), is an excellent resource for cycling information and organized tours out of the city but does not rent bikes.

Books and maps English books can be bought from most major bookshops. Paragraphe, 2220 av McGill College, is one of the best bookstores in town. Double Hook, 1235a av Greene, specializes in English-Canadian authors. Chapters, 1171 rue Ste-Catherine ouest, is huge, as is Indigo, 1500 av McGill College; both have large travel sections. Travel books in English and French are also available at Librairie du Voyage Ulysse, 4176 rue St-Denis and 560 av du President-Kennedy. Aux Quatre Points Cardinaux, 551 rue Ontario est (Ⓦwww.aqpc.com; Métro Berri-UQAM), carries 1:50,000 topographic maps of Québec.

Camping equipment You can rent or buy all you need for the outdoors at Altitude Sports Plein-Air, 4140 rue St-Denis (Ⓣ514/847-1515 or 1-800/729-0322, Ⓦwww.altitude-sports.com; Métro Mont-Royal).

Car rental Avis, 1225 rue Metcalfe (Ⓣ514/866-7906); Budget, 1240 rue Guy (Ⓣ514/938-1000); Discount, 607 boul de Maisonneuve ouest (Ⓣ514/286-1554); Hertz Canada, 1073 rue Drummond (Ⓣ514/938-1717); Thrifty, 845 rue Ste-Catherine est (Ⓣ514/845-5954); and Via Route, 1255 rue Mackay (Ⓣ514/871-1166), which charges a bit less than the majors.

Consulates UK, 1000 rue de la Gauchetière ouest Ⓣ514/866-5863; US, 1155 rue St-Alexandre Ⓣ514/398-9695. For Australia, Ireland, New Zealand and South Africa, contact the embassy in Ottawa; see p.199.

Spectator sports in Montréal

Canadian football The Montréal Alouettes (Ⓦwww.montrealalouettes.com) represent the city in the Canadian Football League (CFL). Home games are at McGill University's Molson Stadium, 475 av des Pins ouest. Tickets cost $21–125.

Ice hockey The Montréal Canadiens, known as the Habs (Ⓦwww.canadiens.com), play at the Centre Bell, 1250 rue de la Gauchetière ouest (Métro: Lucien L'Allier or Bonaventure). Tickets start at $22.

Currency exchange American Express, 1141 boul de Maisonneuve ouest (Ⓣ514/284-3300); Bureau de Change du Vieux-Montréal, 230 rue St-Jacques (Ⓣ514/284-8686); Calforex, 1250 rue Peel (Ⓣ514/392-9100); Thomas Cook, Centre Eaton, 705 rue Ste-Catherine ouest (Ⓣ514/284-7388). Most large downtown banks will change currency and travellers' cheques. You can also withdraw money at ATMs throughout the city, so long as your card is Cirrus or Plus compatible.

Internet access CyberGround, 3672 boul St-Laurent ($7/hr), open until 11pm; L'Inter-Café.net, 1455 rue Amherst ($6/hr), open until 8pm (weekends 7pm); and a number of places clustered around Concordia University, including Net 24, 2157 rue Mackay ($4/hr), which has free coffee to keep you going 24 hours a day. Larger post offices have free access but a 15min limit.

Laundry Net-Net, 310 av Duluth est Ⓣ514/844-8511, will wash, dry and fold your clothes for you within 24 hours for 77¢ per pound; doing it yourself works out to around $4–5. Buanderie du Village, 1499 rue Amherst Ⓣ514/526-4084, will wash your clothes in a few hours for $6/load, around $4 if you do it yourself.

Left luggage There are $2 lockers at the main bus terminal (24hr only; $5/day charge thereafter) accessible until 11pm, as well as left-luggage storage ($4–6 with hefty late charges) open 7am to 7pm. The train station has left-luggage facilities for passengers only ($2.50/24hr, $5 oversized); open until 11pm.

Medical emergencies Central English-language hospitals that are part of the McGill University Health Centre "superhospital" (Ⓣ514/934-1934) are the Montréal General Hospital, 1650 av Cedar, on the mountain's slope northwest of downtown, and Royal Victoria Hospital, 687 av des Pins ouest, up the hill from McGill University. Centre Dentaire, 3546 av Van-Horne (Ⓣ514/342-4444) is a 24hr dental clinic, and there's a walk-in dental clinic on the 3rd floor of Montréal General Hospital (Mon–Fri 8am–noon & 1–4pm, but go as early as possible; after-hour emergencies call Ⓣ514/934-8075).

Pharmacies Most downtown outlets of Jean Coutu (Ⓦwww.jeancoutu.com) and Pharmaprix (Ⓦwww.pharmaprix.ca) are open until 11pm and midnight, respectively. The Pharmaprix near the Oratory, at 5122 chemin de la Côte-des-Neiges, is open 24hr (Ⓣ514/738-8464).

Post office 1250 rue University (Mon–Fri 8am–5.45pm).

Taxis Co-op Ⓣ514/725-9885; Diamond Ⓣ514/273-6331.

Weather and road conditions Environment Canada (Ⓣ514/283-3010, Ⓦwww.weatheroffice.ec.gc.ca) for info on weather and winter road conditions; Transports Québec (Ⓣ514/284-2363, Ⓦwww.mtq.gouv.qc.ca) for roadworks. Up-to-the-minute traffic reports are also on radio stations such as CJAD (800 AM). Skiers can check snow conditions at Ⓦwww.quebecskisurf.com.

Southwest Québec

Beyond the city limits, Montréalers are blessed with superb holiday regions, most within an hour or two of the metropolis. The lake-dotted countryside of **Southwest Québec** offers a range of recuperative pleasures for the city-dweller, from relaxing country drives and nosing about historic sites, to cycling and hiking in summer and a plethora of ski hills to choose from come winter.

Information for Southwest Québec

Eastern Townships ⓣ819/820-2020 or 1-800/355-5755, ⓦwww.easterntownships.org.
Laurentides ⓣ450/436-8532 or 1-800/561-6673, ⓦwww.laurentides.com.
Mauricie ⓣ819/536-3334 or 1-800/567-7603, ⓦwww.tourismemauricie.com.
Outaouais ⓣ819/778-2222 or 1-800/265-7822, ⓦwww.outaouais-tourism.ca.

Just across the river to the northwest of Montréal, along the fertile banks of the St Lawrence, the **Basses Laurentides** (Lower Laurentians) are dotted with whitewashed farm cottages and manor houses, a monastery and a provincial park that all make an easy day-trip from Montréal. Continue along to the largely wilderness stretch of the **Outaouais** region beginning around 130km west of Montréal and extending along the north side of the Rivière Outaouais (Ottawa River). Once the domain of Algonquin tribes, the region was not developed until the 1800s, when it became an important centre for the lumber industry. While the bulk of the activities in the region are of an outdoorsy nature – hiking, canoeing, snowmobiling, cycling and cross-country skiing – it's worth stopping in **Montebello** for its atmosphere and historical heritage.

Extending along the north side of the St Lawrence from the Ottawa River to the Saguenay are the **Laurentians** – one of the world's oldest ranges – where five hundred million years of erosion have moulded a rippling landscape of undulating hills and valleys. The most accessible stretch lies north of Montréal but, unlike the more historic Basses Laurentides, settlement in the upper Laurentians did not begin until the 1830s, when the construction of the P'tit Train du Nord railway tracks let in the mining and lumber industries. When the decline in both industries left the area in a depression, salvation came in the form of the recreational demands of the growing populace of Montréal. The region is now one of North America's largest ski areas, with the number of resorts increasing annually, and the train tracks have been replaced by a terrific cycling trail.

Along the US border to the east of Montréal, the charm of the **Cantons-de-l'Est** (Eastern Townships) lies in the acres of lush farmlands, vineyards, orchards, maple woods and lakeshore hamlets popular among antique collectors. Like the Laurentians, the region is also a popular getaway for city dwellers in search of active pursuits on the lakes, trails and pistes.

Along the north shore of the St Lawrence, the rather dull drive to Québec City (see p.287) provides access to a couple of worthwhile distractions. The **Mauricie** valley, home to the province's smallest national park, has a web of waterways and lakes amidst a landscape of mountainous forest. Spanning the mouths of the Rivière Mauricie, **Trois-Rivières** is a seemingly unprepossessing town unless you detour to its historic centre.

The Lower Laurentians (Les Basses Laurentides)

Once the domain of various aboriginal groups, the **Lower Laurentians** (Basses Laurentides) were granted by Ville-Marie's governors to the colony's first seigneurs, who, using a modified version of the feudal land system of the motherland, oversaw the development of the land by their tenants, or *habitants*. As the rivers were the lifeline of the colony, these tenant farms were laid out perpendicular to the water in long, narrow, rectangular seigneuries that shaped life under the long regime.

St-Eustache and Oka

The first town of note in the region is **ST-EUSTACHE**, about forty-minutes' drive through the suburbs northwest of Montréal by Hwy 13 or 15, then Hwy 640; the main tourist office is en route, just off exit 14 from Hwy 640 (daily late June to late Aug 8.30am–7pm; rest of year 9am–5pm; ⓣ450/491-4444, Ⓦwww.basseslaurentides.com). Alternatively, take bus #46 from Métro Henri-Bourassa in Montréal ($2.85; 1hr). Most of the town is a dull sprawl, except for the riverside historic centre, **Vieux St-Eustache**, where the frustrations of the *habitants* with the British occupancy met a tragic end in the 1837 Rebellion. About thirty buildings survived the battle that put down the rebellious *Patriotes* led by Louis-Joseph Papineau (see box below) and these are located along two narrow streets in Vieux St-Eustache. Most are simply marked with heritage signs, and inaccessible to the public, but the **church**, at 123 rue St-Louis, still bears a few scars and offers free guided tours (late June to late Aug Tues–Fri 9.30am–4.30pm, Sun noon–4.30pm). The cross street, rue St-Eustache, has two sights worth visiting, the most impressive being the wedding-cake Manoir Globensky at no. 235 (May–Oct daily 9am–5pm; Ⓦwww.moulinlegare.com, ⓣ450/974-5170; $5 including entrance to the Moulin Legare), which doubles as the **Musée de St-Eustache et des Patriotes** and includes displays, films and temporary exhibitions on local history. Opposite, the eighteenth-century **Moulin Légaré**, at no. 232, is the oldest water-powered flour mill in continuous operation in North America; guided tours are available (May-Oct daily 9am-5pm; $5 including entrance to the Manoir Globensky; ⓣ450/974-5170, Ⓦwww.moulinlegare.com) but you can get a glimpse of the works from the bakery shop in front. *Café Bistro Coincidence*, a block back towards the church at 198 rue St-Eustache (ⓣ819/623-8094), is a good spot for ciabatta sandwiches and salads in a house dating from 1812.

Southwest of St-Eustache, on Hwy 344, lies the small lakeside town of **OKA**. Although associated with the armed stand-off between the Mohawks and police (see box, p.276), there isn't much to see in the town itself, though worth a visit is the **Abbaye Cistercienne d'Oka**, 1600 chemin d'Oka (Mon–Sat 4am–8pm; ⓣ450/479-8361, Ⓦwww.abbayeoka.com), one of North America's oldest

The rebellion of 1837

In the early 1800s, British immigrants to Lower Canada were offered **townships** (*cantons*), while the francophones were not allowed to expand their holdings, exacerbating the resentment caused by the favouritism extended to English-speaking businesses in Montréal. The situation was worsened by high taxes on British imports and a savage economic depression in 1837. Wearing Canadian-made garments of *étoffe du pays* as a protest against British imports, the leaders of Lower Canada reform – known as **the Patriotes** – rallied francophones to rebel in Montréal. As Louis-Joseph Papineau, the Outaouais region seigneur whose speeches in the Assembly had encouraged the rebellions, fled the city, fearful that his presence would incite more rioting, the government sent military detachments to the countryside, the hotbed of the *Patriotes*. Two hundred *Patriotes* took refuge in Saint-Eustache's church, where eighty of them were killed by British troops, who went on to raze much of the town.

monasteries. Commanding a spectacular site just outside town, its century-old bell tower rises amidst the hills. The Trappists arrived here from France in 1880, their life in Canada beginning in a miller's house that's now overshadowed by the rest of the complex and the landscaped gardens of the abbey. The nearby monastery shop (closed Sun) sells organic Trappist products, from maple syrup and chocolates to variations on the delicious Oka cheese. Between the town and monastery, the **Calvaire d'Oka** with its seven mid-eighteenth-century stone chapels is best visited on September 14, when native pilgrims hold the Feast of the Holy Cross along the banks of Lac des Deux Montagnes. The Calvaire is reached by a 5.5km trail up the Colline d'Oka, a hill that gives views of the region, and is set within the **Parc National d'Oka** (open year-round; $3.50 plus $6.25 parking; Ⓣ450/479-8365 or 1-888/727-2652, Ⓦwww.parcsquebec.com), a magnificent provincial park with 45km of hiking and cycling trails and a long stretch of sandy beach. Bicycles and watercraft can be rented, while in winter cross-country skis and snowshoes are available for exploring the trails. There are serviced campsites ($31) and more rustic spots to pitch a tent ($16.30).

Montebello and around

The drive from Montréal to Gatineau (see p.195) on scenic Hwy 148 takes in a few riverside villages that used to be thriving logging towns. The first stop en route, 135km west of Montréal, is **MONTEBELLO**, a picturesque village named after seigneur and Rebellion leader Louis-Joseph Papineau's estate. Today, the town is the Outaouais' star attraction thanks to a resort-like atmosphere that includes horseback riding, boating, upscale boutiques and the inimitable *Fairmont Le Château Montebello*, 392 rue Notre-Dame (Ⓣ819/423-6341 or 1-800/441-1414,

The Oka Mohawk standoff

In the summer of 1990, Oka became the stage for a confrontation between **Mohawk** warriors from Kanesatake and the provincial government. The crisis began when Oka's town council decided to expand its golf course onto a sacred burial ground, a provocation to which the Mohawks responded by arming themselves and staking out the territory. Québec's public security minister sent in the provincial police to storm the barricades. In the ensuing fracas a policeman was killed – no one knows by whom, but the autopsy established it was not by a police bullet. Hostilities reached a new pitch and the two sides became ever more polarized. As sympathetic Mohawks from the Kahnawake reserve south of Montréal set up barricades across the Mercier Bridge, one of Montréal's main commuter arteries, groups of white Québecois attacked them with stones, while other groups of aboriginal people showed solidarity with the Mohawks throughout Canada and the USA. The federal government offered to buy the land for the natives on the condition that they surrender, but the standoff continued as negotiators failed to agree on terms. The crisis lasted 78 days, until the core of fifty Mohawks was encircled by 350 Canadian army soldiers and forced to give up. The fate of the disputed land, along with hundreds of other similar claims, is still being negotiated (though there have been other improvements for the Kanesatake community). However, many believe that the natives went too far at Oka, and the existing distrust between aboriginal Canadians and other Canadians seems to have deepened. As Georges Erasmus, former national chief of the Assembly of First Nations, said: "Our demands are ignored when we kick up a fuss – but they are also ignored if we do not."

ⓦwww.fairmont.com; ⑧), the world's largest log building. Built by the Seigneury Club in 1930 in 90 days, the original three buildings are made up of 10,000 red-cedar logs. Today, it's a five-star hotel; even if you can't afford to stay, check out the six-hearthed fireplace in the massive hexagonal lobby and tour the photo gallery. The *Château* abuts the **Site historique national du Manoir Papineau** (mid-May to June Wed–Sun 10am–5pm, July & Aug daily 10am–5pm, Sept–late Oct Sat & Sun only; site free; house tour $7; ⓣ819/423-6965, ⓦwww.pc.gc.ca/papineau), Papineau's tranquil estate comprising his spectacular manor house, chapel and granary over a sizeable tract of land. The ticket office is on the main road at 500 rue Notre-Dame in an old train station shared with the tourist information centre. A ten-minute forested walk leads to the verandah-fronted **house**, which contains a ground-floor ballroom, a turreted library tower and another tower that was formerly a three-storey greenhouse, and which can only be seen on a guided tour. Along the path to the house, the **Papineau Memorial Chapel**, a modest stone building (1855) nestled among tall pines and maples, is especially remarkable for being of Anglican, not Catholic, denomination: Papineau's son converted to Anglicanism after his father was refused a Catholic burial. Papineau senior and eleven other family members are buried here, and the Patriotes' flag is on display.

Tourist information is available in an old train station at 502 rue Notre-Dame (late June to early Sept daily 10am–7pm; rest of year daily 9am–4pm; ⓣ819/423-5602). Voyageur **buses** drop passengers off twice daily down the street at no. 535. The most reasonable **accommodation** in Montebello is *Gîte des 3D Chez Dodo*, an unremarkable B&B at 493 rue Notre-Dame (ⓣ819/423-5268; ②). *Le Clos des Cèdres*, 227 rue St-Joseph (ⓣ819/423-1265, ⓦwww.leclosdescedres.ca; ⑤), has more character. Otherwise, try the attractive *Motel l'Anse de la Lanterne*, 646 rue Notre-Dame (ⓣ819/423-5280; ③), which has a good restaurant for dinner. Most **restaurants** are on the main drag; *Le Pot au Feu*, 489 rue Notre-Dame (ⓣ819/423-6901), serves Italian and French for under $20; and the cheaper resto-bar *Le Zouk*, at no. 530, has a pub-bistro menu and sunny terrace.

The only other stop of interest between Montréal and Gatineau is **PLAISANCE**, 15km west of Montebello (and 30km east of Gatineau). Once the region's main lumber centre, the main draw today is the **Parc National de Plaisance** (late April to mid-Oct; $3.50; ⓣ819/427-5334 or 1-800/665-6527, ⓦwww.parcsquebec.com), a tiny provincial park made up of three *presqu'îles* replete with hiking and cycling trails, picnic areas and footbridges. A dull interpretation centre in the old presbytery on Hwy 148 tells the town's history (June to Sept daily 10am–6pm; $4; ⓦwww.ville.plaisance.qc.ca); admission also allows access to see the 67m-high waterfall. **Camping** is available at the provincial park (ⓣ819/427-5334 or 1-877/752-4726; from $20.87 for a two-person site); bikes, canoes and kayaks can be rented on-site.

If you're not planning to head any further west, you can follow **Highway 323** northeast from Montebello to Mont-Tremblant (see p.281) and return to Montréal via the Laurentians. It's a pleasant trip – a flat valley laced with rivers gives way to rising terrain where the road twists through forested hills – and there's a lake with a sandy beach half-way along.

The Laurentians (Les Laurentides)

The slopes of the **Laurentians**, a vast sweep of coniferous forest dotted with hundreds of tranquil lakes and scored with rivers, was once Montréal's "wilderness back yard". Nowadays, winter sports have done away with the region's former tranquillity as thousands of Québecois take to the slopes at more than 25 ski resorts, causing mind-numbing traffic jams. Still, much of the land has remained relatively untouched – like the **Parc National du Mont Tremblant** – and the area is a must when autumn colours take over. The Laurentians really cater to families on a week's sporty vacation, and much of the **accommodation** is pricey, as it includes gyms, tennis courts, golf courses and the like. However, a smattering of B&Bs and numerous motels offer an alternative to those on a tight budget, as do the hostels in Val-David and Mont-Tremblant itself.

Two **roads** lead from Montréal to this area of the Laurentians: the Autoroute des Laurentides (Hwy 15) and the slower Hwy 117, which is the one to choose if you want to go antique-hunting, as there are a number of large shops around Piedmont. Limocar Laurentides (ⓣ514/842-2281 or 1-866/692-8899, ⓦwww.limocar.ca) offers a regular **bus** service from the Station Centrale d'Autobus de Montréal to most of the towns. Other than Tremblant – which costs a small fortune – rates for **ski passes** are around $40 a day in the decent areas, a few dollars more at weekends.

Saint-Sauveur-des-Monts

The ski resorts start 60km from Montréal and can be visited easily as day-trips. The first is **SAINT-SAUVEUR-DES-MONTS**, with 46 pistes in the immediate vicinity and an ever-increasing number of apartment complexes. Its resident population of seven thousand is boosted to a peak-season maximum of thirty thousand, and the main drag, rue Principale, reflects the influx by boasting every type of restaurant imaginable, as well as designer boutiques and craft shops. Come nightfall, skiers take to the numerous glitzy clubs and discos.

Information on shopping and skiing is available from the Bureau Touristique, 605 chemin des Frênes near exit 60 from Hwy 15 (Mon–Fri 9am–5pm, late May to early Sept until 9pm; ⓣ450/227-3417 or 1-800/898-2127, ⓦwww.saint-sauveur.net or ⓦwww.tourismepdh.org); there's also a kiosk near the church on rue Principale in the warmer months. For those with money, Saint-Sauveur is the top place to be seen, and **hotel** prices reflect the fact: the excellent *Le Relais St-Denis*, 61 rue St-Denis (ⓣ450/227-4766 or 1-888/997-4766, ⓦwww.relaisstdenis.com; ⑥), leads the way for class with a pool and beautifully decorated rooms. For home comforts, there are **B&Bs** like *Aux Petits Oiseaux*, at

△ Cyclist on the P'tit Train du Nord

Laurentians information and hotel reservations

The Laurentians has a free **accommodation booking service** for the region (ⓣ1-800/561-6673, ⓦwww.laurentides.com). You can pick up information on the resorts at the regional **tourist office** (late June to Aug daily 8.30am–9pm; rest of year Sat–Thurs 8.30am–5pm, Fri 9am–6pm), located at exit 51 off Hwy 15. During the ski season, you can get information on snow conditions at ⓦwww.quebecskisurf.com, as well as on the radio and in the local newspapers.

no. 342 rue Principale (ⓣ819/227-6116 or 1-877/227-6116, ⓦwww.bbcanada.com/auxpetitsoiseaux; ❸–❻) with a private pool for summer and stone fireplace for winter, and the pricier *Le Bonnet d'Or* at no. 405 (ⓣ450/227-9669, ⓦwww.bbcanada.com/bonnetdor; ❺–❻) where each room has its own fireplace and therapeutic bath. For **eating** on a budget you'll be pretty well limited to the food (and excellent coffee) at *Brûlerie des Monts*, 197 rue Principale, or branches of Montréal outfits like *Pizzédélic*, 16 rue de la Gare, or *Mexicali Rosa's* average Mexican fare at no. 61. Mid-price local spots are a better bet: try *La Bohème*, 251 rue Principale (ⓣ450/227-6644), which serves French specialities like frog's legs and bœuf bourguignon under $20, or the lively Italian restaurant *Papa Luigi*, 155 rue Principale (ⓣ450/227-5311) with Italian and seafood dishes from $25.

Val-David

Further north along Hwy 117, **VAL-DAVID** is the bohemian resort of the Laurentians, favoured by artists and craftspeople; the main street, rue de l'Église, has galleries and shops run by the artisans themselves. The town also has some non-ski-related activities come summertime, with plenty of hiking trails and rock climbing faces in the area and the P'tit Train du Nord bicycle path (see box, p.280). On a wholly different note, the tackiest attraction in the Laurentians, the **Village du Père Noel**, 987 rue Morin (early June to early Sept daily 10am–6pm; ⓣ819/322-2146, ⓦwww.noel.qc.ca; $10), is a Santa's village that features games and animals. Save your money.

The **tourist office** is at 2501 rue de l'Eglise (mid-April to mid-Oct Sun–Thurs 9am–5pm, Fri & Sat 9am–6pm; mid-Nov to mid-March daily 9.30am–5pm; other times Wed–Sun 9.30am–5pm; ⓣ819/322-3104 or 1-888/322-7030 ext 235, ⓦwww.valdavid.com). Val-David's excellent but noisy **hostel**, *Le Chalet Beaumont*, 1451 rue Beaumont (ⓣ819/322-1972, ⓦwww.chaletbeaumont.com; ❷; dorms $24), is a massive chalet with roaring fires in the winter and great views all year. A twenty-minute walk from the bus station, the hostel offers a pick-up service. Other **accommodation** is fairly expensive: the most affordable options are **B&Bs** – at *La Maison de Bavière*, 1470 chemin de la Rivière (ⓣ819/322-3528, ⓦwww.maisondebaviere.com; ❹), you can watch the river rapids from the fireplace-warmed sitting room after an extravagant breakfast. More basic is *La Tagine*, 868 rue Hillside (ⓣ819/322-5764, ⓦwww.latagine.com; ❸) where the two rooms (which share a bathroom) are almost as floral as the carnation-decked balcony. At the other end of the scale, the swishest ski lodge, *La Sapinière*, by Mont Alta at 1244 chemin de la Sapinière (ⓣ819/322-2020 or 1-800/567-6635, ⓦwww.sapiniere.com; ❽), is built of logs. At the one **campsite** along Hwy 117, *Camping Laurentien* (ⓣ819/322-2281, ⓦwww.campinglaurentien.com), pitches start at $24. Rue de l'Église has decent, well-priced **restaurants**, including the friendly *Le Grand Pa*, at no. 2481 (ⓣ819/322-3104), which serves simple French food for around $10 and has live music at the weekend; and *L'Express* (Mon–Fri 8am–4pm, Sat & Sun 8am–6pm), a café-bistro at rue de l'Eglise and de la Sapinière that's great for

The P'tit Train du Nord bicycle trail

The bed of **Le P'tit Train du Nord**, a disused railway line that once ferried Montréalers to the Laurentians' resorts, now sees brisk business as a major **bicycle trail** as thousands of cyclists pedal their way among the mountains throughout the summer. The former stations have been renovated as well, now often housing tourist information centres, some with facilities such as showers and snack bars for cyclists taking a break. Access to the 200km trail, which runs north from St-Jérôme to Mont-Laurier, costs $5/day, or $15 for the whole May to October season. In winter, the snow-covered route is equally in demand by **crosscountry skiers** ($7/day), who can explore numerous side-trails branching off into the hills between St-Jérôme and Val-David, and to **snowmobilers** – the Ste-Agathe to Mont-Laurier stretch is part of the network of thousands of kilometres of trails that crisscross the province. **Information**, as well as a guide with maps and list of services (including cycle repair, baggage transport and accommodation) along the route, is available from the Association Touristique des Laurentides (see p.278).

Les Excursions Rivière du Nord (Ⓣ450/229-1889 or 1-866/342-2668, Ⓦwww.riviere-du-nord.ca) gives you the chance to **canoe or raft** downriver for a couple of hours from Mont Rolland station (near Ste-Adèle) to Piedmont (just east of St-Sauveur) and then cycle the 7km back north, starting at $22. Similar trips are available for the 4-hour return trip between Val-David and Mont Rolland from Pause Plein Air, 1381 chemin de la Sapinière, Val-David (Ⓣ819/322-6880 or 1-877/422-6880, Ⓦwww.pause-plein-air.com); they also rent bikes, canoes and kayaks.

breakfast, as well as specials like *tourtière*. Vegetarians are well catered for at the co-operative restaurant *Aux Vivres d'en Haut*, 2360 rue de l'Eglise, where they serve fair-trade coffee and organic vegan dishes in a ramshackle house.

Ste-Agathe-des-Monts

On the shores of Lac des Sables is **STE-AGATHE-DES-MONTS**, a luxurious resort since the 1850s and the largest town in the Laurentians. Situated 97km from Montréal and almost entirely quashed by commercialism, there is little to do here but it's a good base for exploring the less developed towns and wildlife reserves further north.

For **information** and facilities for cyclists on the P'tit Train du Nord (see box), go to the old train station at 24 rue St-Paul est (late June to early Sept daily 8am–9pm; early Sept to late June 9am–5pm), across the street from the **bus** stop. The least expensive **accommodation** is the clean if unexciting *Motel Clair-Mont*, out along Hwy 117 at 1591 rue Principale (Ⓣ819/326-1444 or 1-800/520-1444, Ⓦwww.motelclair-mont.com; ❷). Of the five **B&Bs**, the *Auberge de la Tour-du-Lac*, nearby at 173 chemin Tour du Lac (Ⓣ819/326-4202 or 1-800/622-1735, Ⓦwww.aubergedelatourdulac.com; ❹), is one of the town's most beautiful historic homes with its pointed roof and wraparound veranda. The nearest **campsite** is *Parc des Campeurs* (Ⓣ819/324-0482 or 1-800/561-7360, Ⓦwww.parcdescampeurs.com; from $25), 1.5km south of town (take exit 83 off Hwy 15 and follow signs), an enormous place with a beach on Lac des Sables and cross-country skiing in winter. Most of Ste-Agathe's **restaurants and bars** are near the lakefront, the most attractive part of town: *Del Popolo*, at 1 rue Principale est (Ⓣ819/326-4422), serves Italian, and *Chez Girard*, at 18 rue Principale ouest (Ⓣ819/326-0922), has reasonably priced, delicious *cuisine du terroir* (regional market cuisine). *La Sauvagine*, 1592 Hwy 329 nord (Ⓣ819/326-7673 or 1-800/787-7172, Ⓦwww.lasauvagine.com), is a chapel converted into a gastronomic Belgian restaurant with comfy **rooms** upstairs (④–⑥).

Mont-Tremblant

Situated some 130km north of Montréal, **MONT-TREMBLANT** is the Laurentians' oldest and most renowned ski area, focused on the range's highest peak, **Mont Tremblant** (960m), so called because the native population believed it was the home of spirits that could move the mountain. In 1997, the company that developed British Columbia's ski resort of Whistler (see p.852) pumped some $50m into Tremblant, and the resulting European-style ski village has made it a premier ski destination. The 92 runs are for all levels, with a maximum vertical drop of more than 640m and the longest ski run in Québec. One-day **ski passes** cost $55.

Mont-Tremblant comprises the resort itself plus the merged town of **St-Jovite**, the area's commercial centre, and tiny **Mont-Tremblant Village**, 10km north. The main **tourist information** office is just off Hwy 117 as you enter St-Jovite, at 48 chemin de Brébeuf (June–Sept Sun–Thurs 9am–7pm, Fri & Sat 9am–8pm; Oct–May daily 9am–5pm; ⓣ819/425-3300 or 1-800/322-2932, ⓦwww.tourismemonttremblant.com); a second tourist office is located further north at 5080 montée Ryan (ⓣ819/425-2434). Mont-Tremblant Village has only the most basic services but some cheap accommodation, including a **hostel** – the *Auberge de Jeunesse International du Mont-Tremblant*, 2313 chemin du Village (ⓣ819/425-6008 or 1-866/425-6008, ⓦwww.hostellingtremblant.com), with dorms for $29, double rooms (②–④) and plenty of organized activities. Throughout the area are a variety of **lodges**, though two of the most glamorous in the Laurentians are both slope-side: *Fairmont Tremblant*, by Lac Tremblant facing the base of the mountain (ⓣ819/681-7000 or 1-800/441-1414, ⓦwww.fairmont.com; ⑧), and *Auberge Gray Rocks*, at the smaller resort midway to St-Jovite (ⓣ819/425-2771 or 1-800/567-6767, ⓦwww.grayrocks.com; ⑧). Less pricey **rooms** are available at *Hôtel Mont Tremblant*, 1900 chemin du Village (ⓣ819/425-3232 or 1-888/887-1111, ⓦwww.hotelmonttremblant.com; ④ including breakfast), right where the P'tit Train du Nord bike path (see box opposite) passes Lac Mercier. On the lakeshore facing the hotel, *Tremblant Onwego*, 112 chemin Plouffe (ⓣ819/429-5522 or 1-866/429-5522, ⓦwww.tremblantonwego.com; ⑤), provides coanoes, kayaks and pedal-boats free of charge and is one of a dozen **B&Bs** in the area.

For **eating**, there are plenty of options at Tremblant resort itself in all price brackets. In the St-Jovite sector, there's a cheap pub-style restaurant, *Bagatelle Saloon*, at 852 rue de St-Jovite, and a decent-priced café-bar, *Le Bistro Brunch Café*, at no. 814, in the same complex as La Crémerie du Hameau, a candy store. For dinner, *Chez Roger*, 444 rue St-Georges (ⓣ819/429-6991), offers rich French cuisine at slightly elevated prices – the three-course *table d'hôte* starts at $30. The best **party scene** is at the resort's *après-ski* spots; elsewhere, you can kick things off at *Le Saint Georges*, a relaxed pub with a terrace at 890 rue de St-Jovite.

The **Parc National du Mont Tremblant**, a large wilderness area spreading northwards from the villages, is a favourite with Québecois. Skiing, snowmobiling and snowshoeing are favoured winter sports; in summer the park attracts campers, canoeists, hunters and hikers – in remote areas you may see bears (see box, pp.704–705), deer and moose. The park's three lakeside **campsites** must be reserved in advance (ⓣ819/688-2281 or 1-800/665-6527, ⓦwww.sepaq.com; park entry $3.50, sites $16.30 and up). There's no public transport.

The Eastern Townships (Cantons-de-l'Est)

Beginning about 80km east of Montréal and extending to the US border, the **Eastern Townships** were once Québec's best-kept secret, but the nineteenth-century villages are fast becoming no more than shopping arcades fringed with vacation complexes for Montréal weekenders. A growing ski industry – concentrated around Mont Sutton, just north of the Vermont border – is making its mark on the land, too. However, the region's agricultural roots are still evident, especially in spring, when the maple trees are tapped for syrup. At this time of year, remote *cabanes à sucre* offer sleigh rides and Québecois fare such as maple taffy – strips of maple syrup frozen in the snow.

The land, once the domain of scattered groups of aboriginal peoples, was later settled by United Empire Loyalists hounded out of the US after the American Revolution. Their loyalty to the crown resulted in freehold land grants from the British, and townships with very English names like **Sherbrooke** and **Granby** were founded. In the mid-nineteenth century the townships opened up to industry, which attracted an influx of French-Canadians seeking work: today, nearly 95 percent of the 400,000 population are francophone. For the most part, relations between the linguistic groups have been amicable, though pockets like the towns and villages around **Knowlton** and **North Hatley** remain staunchly tied to their anglophone heritage, and the English-language cultural scene is much stronger than the size of the population would suggest.

You can reach the region from Montréal by the Autoroute des Cantons-de-l'Est (Hwy 10), which has a useful **information centre** for the whole region at exit 68, southwest of Granby (daily June–Sept 10am–7pm; Oct–May 9am–5pm; ⓣ819/820-2020 or 1-800/355-5755, ⓦwww.easterntownships.org). Slower Hwy 112 wends through small villages and past forests and lakes; if you've got plenty of time, detour south onto the secondary roads nearer the US border that pass rustic barns, duck under covered bridges and wind through the province's fledgling vineyards. A dozen or so Limocar **buses** a day from Montréal (ⓣ514/842-2281 or 1-866/700-8899, ⓦwww.limocar.ca) stop in Magog and Sherbrooke; less often in Granby (4/day) and Bromont (2/day).

Granby and Bromont

Approached from Montréal, the Cantons-de-l'Est begins at the unappealing city of **GRANBY**. The **Zoo de Granby** (late May to late June & late Aug to early Sept daily 10am–5pm, late June to Late Aug till 7pm; ⓦwww.zoodegranby.com; $24.99) is Québec's best-known zoo and has just placed significant investment into improving its animal enclosures. The zoo shares the site with the **Parc Aquatique Amazoo** (same schedule and entry price) a popular water park with pools and slides. The **Centre d'interprétation de la Nature du Lac Boivin**, 700 Drummond (Mon–Fri 8.30am–4.30pm, weekends 9am–5pm; ⓣ450/375-3861, ⓦwww.cinlb.org; free) has observation towers allowing a terrific vantage point for watching birds peck and preen on the marsh. Granby's **information centre** is at 650 rue Principale (daily June to early Sept 8am–6pm; rest of year 9am–5pm; ⓣ450/372-7056, ⓦwww.granbybromont.com).

Just south of Granby, **BROMONT** is much more pleasant, focused on the 405m ski and snowboarding hill at its centre, **Ski Bromont** (ⓣ450/534-2200 or 1-866/276-6668, ⓦwww.skibromont.com; $52). In summer, the hill metamorphoses into a hiking and mountain biking centre and watery playground thanks to the slides and pools of the **Bromont Aquatic Park** (early to late June daily 10am–5pm; late June to late Aug daily 10am–6.30pm; ⓦwww.skibromont.com; $29). Less energetic options include the large **flea market** alongside Hwy 10 (May–Oct Sun 9am–5pm) and the tiny **Musée du Chocolat**, 679 rue Shefford (Mon–Fri 9.30am–6pm, Sat & Sun 8.30am–5.30pm; ⓣ450/534-3893, ⓦwww.bromont.com/chocolat; free), where you can learn about chocolate-making while nibbling on some fine specimens from the attached candy store. Cross the street to the 1889 **Église St-Francois-Xavier**, with a delicate tin-clad tiered steeple and a vault decorated in minty pastels.

Of the many **B&B's** *La Maison aux Pignons Verts*, at 129 rue Adamsville in the village of Adamsville, 10km southwest of Bromont (ⓣ450/260-1129, ⓦwww.lamaisonauxpignonsverts.com; ④) is notable for its large outdoor whirlpool, while *Auberge Nuits de St-Georges*, 792 rue Shefford (ⓣ450/534-0705 or 1-888/534-0708, ⓦwww.aubergenuitsdestgeorges.com; ⑤), is a handsome red-brick house with six suites. Though pricier, it includes a five-course breakfast. Otherwise, try the *du Badouillard*, 871 rue Shefford (ⓣ450/534-2502, ⓦwww.aubergedubadouillard.ca; ④ including breakfast) for more traditional hotel accommodation. For **eating**, *L'Âme du Pain*, 702 rue Shefford, is a bakery serving good sandwiches and salads on a shady terrace; pizza and more substantial dishes are available later on. *Auberge Le Madrigal*, 46 boul de Bromont (ⓣ450/534-3588), serves expensive regional cuisine from $30, such as duck and sweetbread in Madeira sauce.

Magog and around

The summer resort town of **MAGOG**, about 40km east of Bromont, gets its name from a corruption of an aboriginal word meaning "great expanse of water" – the expanse of which is one of the township's largest lakes, **Lac Memphrémagog**, on which it borders. A strange beast known as Memphré supposedly lurks in its waters (the subject of various fishy tales since 1798). A cruise boat plies the lake (mid-May to Aug daily; Sept & Oct Sat & Sun only; 1hr 45min tour; $15). You can also opt for a day-long cruise south over the border to Newport, Vermont (June–Sept; $55; ⓣ819/843-8068 or 1-888/842-8068, ⓦwww.croisiere-memphremagog.com; passport needed). Magog is a lively spot fairly teeming with bars and restaurants along its main street, rue Principale. One quirky diversion is at the **Labyrinthe Memphrémagog** on the westernmost of the beaches fronting the lake – you can navigate a maze on blades or on foot (May to mid-Oct daily 10am–dusk; ⓣ819/868-4188, ⓦwww.easterntownships.org/labyrinthe_memphremagog; $7.75). Explore the area on numerous well-kept bike trails; Ski-Vélo Vincent Renaud, set back from the main drag at 395 rue Principale ouest (ⓣ819/843-4277, ⓦwww.skivelo.com), rents bicycles for $17 per half-day.

The **bus** stops on rue Sherbrooke, near its intersection with rue Principale. The **information centre**, midway between the town and the labyrinth at 55 rue Cabana, is accessed by Hwy 112 (June to mid-Oct daily 8.30am–8pm; mid-Oct to May daily 9am–5pm, Fri until 7pm; ⓣ1-800/267-2744, ⓦwww.tourisme-memphremagog.com). There are many places to stay. Among the **B&Bs** are a few century-old houses clustered together: *Ô Bois Dormant*, 205 rue Abbot (ⓣ819/843-0450, ⓦwww.oboisdormant.qc.ca; ⑤), comes with a veranda and pool; *Au Coeur de Magog*, 120 rue Merry Nord (ⓣ819/868-2511, ⓦwww.aucoeurdemagog.com; ③), is a fine old house with pink shutters and charming rooms; *La Belle Victorienne*, 142 rue Merry Nord (ⓣ819/847-0476 or 1-888/440-0476, Ⓦwww.bellevic.com; ❹), has beautiful gardens and comfy rooms. **Hotels** are expensive: *Le Manoir St-Christophe*, 2316 Hwy 112 (Ⓣ819/843-3355 or 1-877/447-3355, Ⓦwww.manoirsaintchristophe.ca; ❺), is a modern country inn with ten rooms just west of town. *L'Auberge du Grand Lac*, 40 rue Merry Sud (Ⓣ819/847-4039 or 1-800/267-4039, Ⓦwww.grandlac.com; ❺–❼), is nearer the centre of things, with a rooftop terrace for sunsets, full facilities and a continental breakfast. Several **bars** and **restaurants** are clustered along rue Principale ouest: *Le Panier à Pain*, at no. 382, serves up healthy sandwiches, soups and home-made ice cream, while *Le Martimbeault*, at no. 341 (Ⓣ819/843-3182), is a good dinner option that charges about $30 for a meal of rich French food. Alternatively, get a veggie fix at *La Petite Place* at 108 Place du Commerce, opposite the bistro-bar *La Grosse Pomme* at 276 rue Principale. A better bet for drinking and eating is *La Memphré*, 12 rue Merry Sud, a pleasant bar with views of the lake from the veranda where they serve quality pub food and a tasty local beer.

Abbaye Saint-Benoît-du-Lac

About 25km southwest of Magog via Hwy 245 along the lakeshore is the **Abbaye Saint-Benoît-du-Lac**, its presence signalled by white-granite turrets. Occupied by some sixty Benedictine monks renowned for their Gregorian chants (daily 7.30 & 11am; also Mon–Wed & Fri–Sun 5pm, Thurs 7pm) and their Ermite blue cheese (shop Mon–Sat 9am–4.30pm, till 6pm in July and Aug), it often serves as a refuge for flustered politicians and prominent figures who need time for contemplation. The abbey's doors are open to anyone who needs a retreat for spiritual reflection. Food and **accommodation** are free, though a donation of $35 is expected (Ⓣ819/843-4080 men or 843-2340 women; appropriate clothing required; Ⓦwww.st-benoit-du-lac.com). There is no public transport to the abbey; a taxi costs about $30 from Magog.

Mont Orford

A mature sugar maple forest blankets three-quarters of the small **Parc National du Mont-Orford**, 10km north of Magog via Hwy 141. Ski on Mont Orford (859m) in winter (passes $45) or hike in the summer: the chair-lift operates year-round. There's not much to see in the tiny town of **ORFORD** itself, but the summertime **hostel** on Hwy 141, *Auberge du Centre d'Arts Orford*, 3165 chemin du Parc (Ⓣ819/843-3981 or 1-800/567-6155, Ⓦwww.arts-orford.org; ❶; May–Oct), is a great base for exploring the park and Magog. You can also **camp** at one of the park's sites or off in the woods (Ⓣ819/843-9855 or 1-800/655-6527, Ⓦwww.sepaq.com; $16–32). The only other accommodation options are more upscale in price and service: *Auberge de la Tour*, 1837 Alfred-Desrochers (Ⓣ819/868-0763, Ⓦwww.auberge-de-la-tour.com; ❹), is a charming country inn, while the *Auberge Au Lion d'Or*, 2240 chemin du Parc (Ⓣ819/843-6000 or 1-877/843-6000, Ⓦwww.auliondor.com; ❹), has a health spa and a heated outdoor pool. For **dining**, *Tonnerre de Brest*, 2197 chemin du Parc (Ⓣ819/847-1234), serves up crêpes, mussels and fries, and *La Mérise*, at no. 2329 (Ⓣ819/843-6288; dinner $10–$20), has regional cuisine, crêpes and, in winter, fondue.

North Hatley

The region east of Magog holds its Loyalist connections dear, and this is one of the few areas in Québec where you'll encounter vestiges of the snobbish anglophone attitudes that once pervaded the whole province. **NORTH HATLEY**,

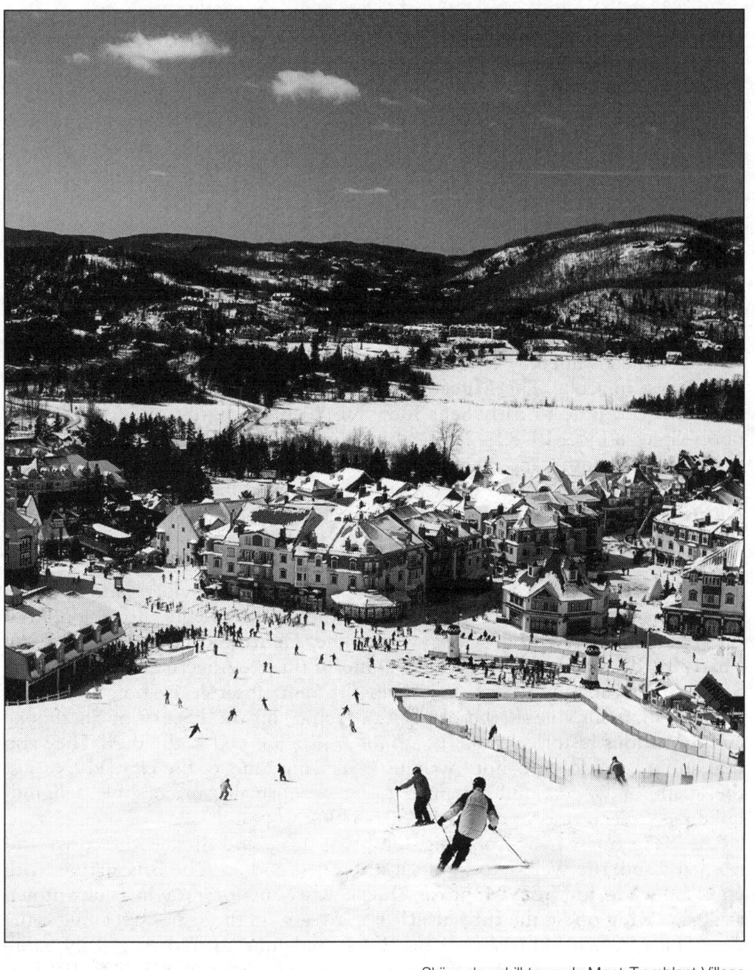

△ Skiing downhill towards Mont-Tremblant Village

a thirty-minute drive east from Magog along Hwy 108, is an anglophone bastion, with boutiques selling Lipton teas, Liberty products, tweeds and Aran jumpers; the resident population steadfastly refuses to change the town's name to "Hatley Nord". Otherwise the village is home to Québec's longest-running English-language **theatre**, The Piggery (Ⓣ819/842-2431, Ⓦwww.piggery.com), which puts on several quality productions throughout the summer, and there are several art galleries and antique shops clustered along the waterfront.

North Hatley boasts one of Québec's classiest **inns**: the romantic *Manoir Hovey* (Ⓣ842-2421 or 1-800/661-2421, Ⓦwww.manoirhovey.com; ❽), nestled along the lake with its private beach and boats. Cheaper and in the village itself, *Serendipity Bed & Breakfast*, 340 chemin de la Rivière (Ⓣ819/842-2970, Ⓦwww.serendipitybb.qc.ca; ❹), is a century-old house; the owner runs fly-fishing trips on the lake. Decent **food** can be had at either the English-style gastro-pub *Le Pilsen*, 55 rue Principale, with its locally brewed Massiwippi ales and large meals for as little as $10, or *Café de Lafontaine*, which serves standard salads, burgers and the like next door at no. 35. The expensive but exquisite *Café Massawippi*, 3050 chemin Capelton (Ⓣ819/842-4528), serves original variations on international classics such as tartar of red stag but is open in the evenings only. Expect to pay over $30 for a main dish.

Sherbrooke

The 100,000-strong university town of **SHERBROOKE**, 147km east of Montréal, revels in the title "Queen of the Eastern Townships", a strange accolade for a town that's no great shakes and has just a few minor attractions, clustered in Vieux-Sherbrooke around the 1.5km gorge carved by the Rivière Magog, which is lined by walkways and lookouts. The city's two main museums are modest in scope. The **Musée des Beaux Arts de Sherbrooke**, 241 rue Dufferin (late June to early Sept Tues–Sun 10am–5pm, rest of year Tues–Sun noon–5pm; $6; Ⓣ819/821-2115, Ⓦwww.mbas.qc.ca), the better of the two, displays nineteenth- and twentieth-century pieces by Québecois artists and visiting collections of good quality. The hands-on exhibits at the **Musée de la Nature et des Sciences**, 225 rue Frontenac (Wed–Sun 10am–5pm; $7.50; Ⓣ819/564-3200, Ⓦwww.mnes.qc.ca), will keep kids occupied for a couple of hours. The largest section explores the flora and fauna of Québec's forests throughout the seasons, with both live and stuffed animals, videos and bird calls kids can activate. There's also an interactive theatre for an educational look into the brain and how the senses work. The **Centre d'interprétation de l'histoire de Sherbrooke**, 275 rue Dufferin (July & Aug Tues–Fri 9am–5pm, Sat & Sun 10am–5pm; Sept–June Tues–Fri 9am–noon & 1–5pm, Sat & Sun 1–5pm; $6; Ⓦshs.ville.sherbrooke.qc.ca), focuses on the history of Sherbooke and on various historical subjects; ask for an English text at the desk. They also rent audio tapes for two-hour walking or driving tours of the city ($10, or just the map for $2.50) and organize tours of normally inaccessible religious buildings (call to reserve on Ⓣ819/821-5406).

Rue King ouest is like one big, long strip mall, and divides the town into nord and sud; rue Wellington splits it into ouest and est. The **bus** station, with connections to and from Montréal, Québec City and local towns, is downtown at 20 rue King ouest; the **information centre** is on the same street, but at the west end of town 5km away at no. 2964 (mid-June to mid-Aug daily 9am–7pm; rest of year Mon–Sat 9am–5pm, Sun 9am–3pm; Ⓣ819/821-1919 or 1-800/561-8331). Sherbrooke's **accommodation** lacks charm; the few inexpensive options include the student residence at 2500 boul de l'Université (Ⓣ819/821-8000, ext 2851; summer only; Ⓦwww.usherbrooke.ca/sa/residences; ❶). Otherwise, you could try one of the numerous modern motels along rue King ouest: the three-star *L'Ermitage* at no. 1888 (Ⓣ819/569-5551 or 1-888/569-5551; ❸) or *Hôtellerie Jardins de Ville* at no. 4235 (Ⓣ819/566-6464 or 1-800/265-7119, Ⓦwww.hotelleriejardinsdeville.com; ❹). The *Delta Sherbrooke*, 2685 rue King ouest (Ⓣ819/822-1989 or 1-800/268-1133, Ⓦwww.deltahotels.com; ❽), is the plushest hotel in town, while the *Marquis de Montcalm* (Ⓣ819/823-7773, Ⓦwww.marquisdemontcalm.com; ❹) is an atmospheric B&B near the gorge. For **restaurants**, *Café Bla-Bla*, 2 rue Wellington sud, has a good selection of imported beers in addition to its well-priced bistro fare. Well to the east, *Délia Egg-xtra*, 661 rue King est, has more than a hundred breakfast options, while *Au Four à Bois*, opposite the tourist office at 3025 rue

King ouest, is a sound pizza joint. For dining downtown, *Le Petit Parisien*, 243 rue Alexandre (☎819/822-4678), is an ambient bring-your-own-wine resto where plates of boar and bison will set you back $20–30; regional produce is the focus of the French cuisine at *La Falaise St-Michel* at 100 rue Webster (☎819/346-6339).

Montréal to Québec City

Two **autoroutes** (expressways) cover the 270km between Montréal and Québec City, though plenty of VIA Rail **trains** and Voyagueur **buses** also trawl the route: the boring Hwy 20 cuts along the south shore of the St Lawrence, and the even more banal Hwy 40 takes to the north side with very few rest-stops en route, so fill up before leaving Montréal. Hwy 138, the old chemin du Roi (King's Highway), also meanders along the north shore but gives a closer look at rural Québec and farms left over from the seigneurial regime, like the **Seigneurie de Terrebonne** (May to early Sept Wed–Sat 10am–9pm, Sun 10am–5pm, early Sept–late Dec Thurs & Fri 1–9pm, Sat & Sun 10am–5pm, rest of the year weekends only; free, guided tours $5; Ⓦwww.ile-des-moulins.qc.ca), on the Île des Moulins about thirty minutes northeast of downtown Montréal via Hwy 25 (exit 22 est). A seigneury from 1673 to 1883, the restored nineteenth-century buildings – including the manor house of the area's last seigneur and Canada's first francophone millionaire, Joseph Masson – powerfully evoke life under the old regime.

Trois-Rivières

The major town between Montréal and Québec City is **TROIS-RIVIÈRES**, located midway between the two, at the point where the Rivière St-Maurice splits into three channels – hence the name "Three Rivers" – before meeting the St Lawrence. The European settlement dates from 1634, when the town established itself as an embarkation point for the French explorers of the continent and as an iron-ore centre. Lumber followed, and today Trois-Rivières is one of the world's largest producers of paper, the delta chock-full of logs to be pulped. It's often dismissed as an industrial city and little else, but its shady streets of historic buildings – neither as twee as Québec City, nor as monumental as Vieux-Montréal – are well worth a wander, and the town is a good starting point for exploring the Mauricie Valley.

Trois-Rivières' compact downtown core branches off from the small square of **Parc du Champlain** and extends south down to the waterfront. Facing the park to the east, at 363 rue Bonaventure, the **Cathédrale de l'Assomption** (Mon–Fri 7–11.30am & 1.30–5.45pm, Sat 7am–8pm, Sun 9.30am–noon & 2–5.45pm; free), is notable for its stained-glass windows by Guido Nincheri and massive Gothic Revival style reminiscent of Westminster Abbey. Head south,

By jetfoil from Montréal to Québec City

The long journey from Montréal to Québec City is best experienced from the **jetfoil** – a unique way to experience the St Lawrence River with a bit of commentary thrown in. From late May to mid-October, Les Dauphins du St-Laurent (☎1-877/648-4499 or 514/288-4499, Ⓦwww.dauphins.ca) runs daily trips, with a stop in Trois-Rivières en route, for $109 (July & Aug $149, when there are two sailings a day).

past the pretty **Manoir de Niverville** at no. 168, one of the town's oldest buildings and the home of the local seigneur, until the water is in sight. Take a left turn to reach the narrow and ancient rue des Ursulines, the city's most attractive thoroughfare; two art galleries, at nos. 802 and 864, are especially worth a visit for contemporary printmaking during the Biennale Internationale d'Estampe Contemporain (odd-numbered years, mid-June to Aug). Further along is the **Musée des Ursulines**, whose slender, silver dome dominates the street. A former convent established by a small group of Ursuline nuns who arrived from Québec City in 1697, it includes a chapel with attractive frescoes and gilt sculptures. The nunnery's treasures are displayed in a little museum in the old hospital quarters (May–Nov Tues–Sun 10am–5pm; March & April Wed–Sun 1–5pm; Nov–Feb by appointment only; $3 including chapel visit; Ⓦwww.musée-ursulines.qc.ca). Just east of the cathedral, the **Musée Québécois de Culture Populaire**, 200 rue Laviolette (late June to early Sept daily 9.30am–6.30pm; rest of year Tues–Sun 10am–5pm; museum or prison $8, both $12; Ⓦwww.culturepop.qc.ca or www.enprison.com) has entertaining folk and pop culture exhibitions but the real highlight is the old **prison** that adjoins it. Dating from 1822, the stone structure housed up to eighty inmates at a time until 1980, and while the decades of graffiti tell a story, it's nothing compared to the tales of the guides – they all once served time here.

You may want to make a pilgrimage across the river east of downtown to the **Sanctuaire Notre-Dame-de-Cap**, 626 rue Notre-Dame (free; Ⓦwww.sanctuaire-ndc.ca; bus #2), in the merged town of Cap-de-la-Madeleine, accessible from Hwy 40 (exit 205); a few of the Québec–Montréal buses also stop here. Adjacent to a pleasant park marked by the Stations of the Cross is the 1720 Petit Sanctuaire; the fieldstone chapel is "the oldest church in Canada to retain its primitive state" (ignoring the jarring modern addition, presumably). It's overshadowed, though, by the massive octagonal basilica, a mid-twentieth-century concrete structure with a vertigo-inducing 38m-high vault best experienced when the 75-stop Casavant organ reverberates throughout the space. Finally, the ruins of **Les Forges du Saint-Maurice**, 10,000 boul des Forges (mid-May to early Sept daily 9.30am–5.30pm, early Sept to early Oct til 4.30pm; $4; Ⓣ1-888/773-8888 or 819/378-5116, Ⓦwww.pc.gc.ca/forges), which put the town on the map as a supplier to the farmers and arsenals of Québec and Europe, is now a national historic site. Its pretty riverside grounds are 12km north of Vieux Trois-Rivières, linked to downtown by bus #4 – get on at the bus terminal on rue Badeaux – and Hwy 55 (exit 191).

Practicalities

The **information centre** at 1457 rue Notre Dame (late June to early Sept daily 8am–8pm; rest of year Mon–Fri 9am–5pm; Ⓣ819/375-1122 or 1-800/313-1123, Ⓦwww.tourismetroisrivieres.com) gives out maps and has an accommodation service. For a place **to stay**, the cheapest option is the clean and comfortable **hostel**, *La Flottille*, in the heart of downtown at 497 rue Radisson (Ⓣ819/378-8010, Ⓦwww.hihostels.ca; dorms $20). A number of attractive **B&Bs** are situated in heritage homes in Vieux Trois-Rivières: *Le Fleurvil* at no. 635 rue des Ursulines, has five rooms in a low-lying house (Ⓣ819/372-5195 or 1-877/375-5190, Ⓦwww.fleurvil.qc.ca; ❸); and the gorgeous *Manoir DeBlois*, 197 rue Bonaventure, an 1828 stone house with original wood floors and an antique-strewn salon (Ⓣ819/373-1090 or 1-800/397-5184, Ⓦwww.multimania.com/manoirdeblois; ❹–❻). Centrally located, modern **hotels** include the high-rise *Delta*, 1620 rue Notre-Dame (Ⓣ819/376-1991 or 1-800/268-1133, Ⓦwww.deltahotels.com; ❺), and *Hôtel*

Gouverneur, 975 Hart (☎819/379-4550 or 1-888/910-1111, Ⓦwww.gouverneur.com; ⑥).

Most of the city's **restaurants** are located in the downtown core, their terraces lining rue des Forges between the waterfront and rue Royale. *Le Bolvert*, 1556 rue Royale, is a hearty, affordable breakfast option and *Angeline*, 313 rue des Forges, has imaginative pasta and pizza choices for under $10. The nearby *Gaspard* at no. 475 offers steak, fish and chicken, plus some cheaper lunch specials. *Le Zenob*, 171 rue Bonaventure, is a chilled **bar** with two leafy terraces that also sells sandwiches; for coffee and a snack, head to *Café Morgane*, at 100 rue des Forges, a sleek coffee shop with three other outlets around town. For **nightlife**, the multistorey *Le Temple*, 300 rue des Forge, caters to all types.

Parc National de la Mauricie

Some 60km north of Trois-Rivières lies the mountainous area of the Saint-Maurice valley – known as the **Mauricie** – where the best of the landscape is demarcated by the **Parc National du Canada de la Mauricie** (year round; $6.90; ☎819/533-7272, Ⓦwww.pc.gc.ca/mauricie). Situated on the southernmost part of the Canadian Shield, the park comprises soft-contoured hills, lakes and rivers, waterfalls and sheer rock faces. The one drawback is the lack of public transport; to get there, take Hwy 55 north of Trois-Rivières to exit 226 and follow the signs to the St-Jean-des-Piles entrance.

The park offers numerous hiking trails of various lengths and abilities, ranging from the Cache Trail, a mere 1km walk leading to the Lac du Fou where a raised platform has a telescope for marine and wildlife watching, to the Laurentian Trail, a 75km trek which takes five to eight days to complete (reservation required; camping permit $35.65 for four nights). Information centres at the park's entrances have excellent maps and booklets about the park's well-maintained trails, canoe routes and bike paths, and also provide canoe rentals (for $18/day). The park has hundreds of **camping** places (from $22.75 a pitch; May–Oct) allocated on a first-come, first-served basis, and they're rarely filled to capacity. If you'd rather sleep under a roof, there are also two **lodges** located 3.5km from the nearest parking lot: the *Wabenaki*'s two dormitories sleep up to 24 people and *Andrew*'s four rooms each sleep four (☎819/537-4555 for both lodges; weekdays $24 per person, weekends $50–54 per person). Both open again in winter (mid-Dec to March) to accommodate cross-country skiers who use the park (trail permit $8.90).

Travel details

Trains

Montréal to: Bonaventure (3 weekly; 13hr 10min); Carleton (3 weekly; 12hr); Cornwall (4–5 daily; 1hr 5min); Gaspé (3 weekly; 17hr 30min); Jonquière (3 weekly; 8hr 55min); Kingston (4–5 daily; 2hr 30min); Matapédia (6 weekly; 10hr 10min); New York (1 daily; 9hr 40min); Ottawa (4–6 daily; 2hr 10min); Percé (3 weekly; 16hr 5min); Québec City (4–5 daily; 3hr); Rimouski (6 weekly; 7hr 40min); Rivière-du-Loup (6 weekly; 5hr 55min); Toronto (4–5 daily; 4hr 30min–5hr 30min; express daily except Sat; 4hr; sleeper daily except Sat; 8hr 50min); Washington, DC (1 daily; 16hr 10min including bus to St Alban's, Vermont).

Buses

Montréal to: Bromont (2 daily; 2hr); Chicoutimi (4 weekly; 4hr 55min); Chicoutimi via Québec City (5–6 daily; 6hr 30min); Granby (4–8 daily; 1hr 30min); Jonquière (4 weekly; 5hr 25min); Jonquière via Québec City (3–5 daily; 6hr 15min); Kingston (7 daily; 3hr); Magog (7–11 daily;

1hr 30min); Mont-Tremblant (3 daily; 2hr 40min); New York (6 daily; 8hr 30min); North Bay (2 daily; 7hr 40min); Orford (3 daily; 3hr); Ottawa (hourly; 2hr 20min); Québec City (hourly; 3hr); Rimouski (3 daily; 7hr); Rivière-du-Loup (4 daily; 5hr 30min); Ste-Adèle (6 daily; 1hr 25min); Ste-Agathe (6 daily; 1hr 45min); St-Jovite (5 daily; 2hr 15min); St-Sauveur (6 daily; 1hr); Sherbrooke (7–11 daily; 2hr 5min); Tadoussac (2 daily; 7hr 30min); Toronto (8 daily; 6hr 45min); Trois-Rivières (6–8 daily; 2hr); Val-David (6 daily; 1hr 30min), Montebello (6 daily; 1hr 30 min).

Sherbrooke to: Trois-Rivières (4 weekly; 2hr 10min); Québec City (2 daily; 3hr 30min).

Trois-Rivières to: Grand-Mère (3 daily; 1hr).

Flights

Montréal to: Baie-Comeau (3–4 daily; 1hr 30min); Bathurst (2–3 daily; 1hr 45min); Calgary (3–4 daily; 4hr 30min); Chicoutimi (5 daily; 1hr 5min); Fredericton (3–4 daily; 1hr 30min); Gaspé (2–3 daily; 2hr 40min); Halifax (10–12 daily; 1hr 25min); Îles-de-la-Madeleine (1–3 daily; 3hr 50min); Moncton (3–4 daily; 1hr 20min); Mont Joli (3–4 daily; 1hr 25min); Ottawa (9–11 daily; 40min); Québec City (13–20 daily; 50min); Saint John, NB (3–5 daily; 1hr 35min); St John's, NL (1–2 daily; 2hr 35min); Sept-Îles (3–6 daily; 2hr 45min); Toronto (19–40 daily; 1hr 15min); Vancouver (4–6 daily; 5hr 20min); Wabush (2 daily; 4hr 5min); Winnipeg (2–3 daily; 2hr 55min).

Québec City and Northern Québec

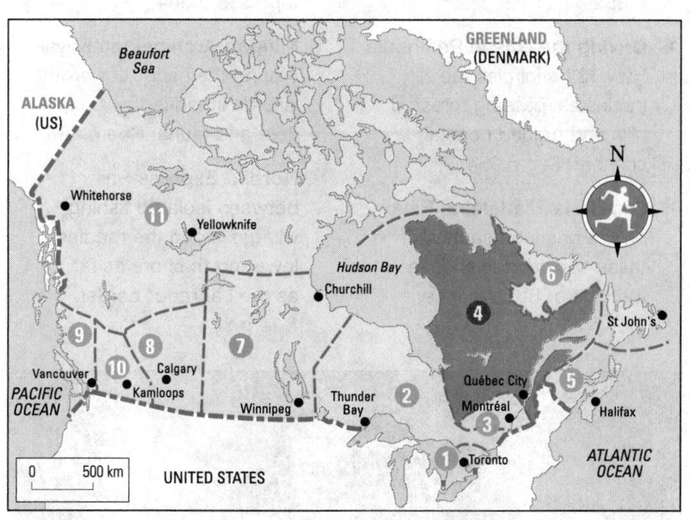

CHAPTER 4

Highlights

* **Québec City** Vieux-Québec, the only walled city in North America, is full of romantic nooks and crannies. See p.294

* **Mont St Anne** ski resort offers varied ski terrain in the winter as well as world class mountain biking and hiking during the summer. See p.332

* **Driving the Gaspé Peninsula** Hwy 132 encircles the peninsula, passing forested hills and rugged coastal scenery. See p.334

* **Iles-de-la-Madeleine** Relax on the pristine beaches of these secluded islands in the Gulf of St Lawrence. See p.353

* **Traversée de Charlevoix** A long distance hiking, mountain biking and cross-country skiing route across the Parc des Hautes-Gorges-de-la-Rivière-Malbaie. See p.360

* **Tadoussac** A lively base for exploring the Saguenay fjord or joining a whale-watching trip. See p.364

* **Mingan Archipelago** Kayak around the eerie "flowerpot" islands inhabited by unique flora and fauna. See p.383

* **Nordik Express** Sail between isolated fishing villages along the roadless lower north shore as far as the Labrador border. See p.384

△ Ice Hotel, Québec City

Québec City and Northern Québec

Forming the greater part of Canada's largest province, **Northern Québec** stretches from the temperate farmland in the south to the Arctic tundra in the north, covering over one million square kilometres. Much of this area is a monotonous blanket of dense boreal forest grafted onto a thin layer of soil spread over the Canadian shield – a horseshoe of ancient rock scoured clean during the last Ice Age. Nature rules supreme in northern Québec and the influence of the Arctic is strong. Winters, cooled by northern air and ocean currents, are long and amongst the coldest in eastern Canada, and the blazing summers are clipped short by northern frosts. Moose, caribou, wolverine and bears fill the forest while humans have barely made inroads. Civilisation clings tenaciously to the north shore of the **St Lawrence**, clustered around the main coastal hwy that radiates eastward from Québec City. Mining communities, groups of indiginous peoples and the hardy characters that man the immense hydroelectric installations on many of northern Québec's rivers are among the few that have the will to penetrate deeper into this imposing wilderness.

However, the coast has its own allure, not least the **whales** that come to feed and breed in the Gulf of St Lawrence from mid-May to mid-October, making it one of the best places in the world to learn about these incredible creatures. Away from the rural farmlands of **Charlevoix**, the further north you travel along the **Côte Nord** from Québec City, the greater the distances between communities and the more self-contained they become. The isolation brings a noticeable change in attitude and you will find the northern Québecois genuinely interested in your travels and keen to demonstrate the tradition of 'northern hospitality'. In order to reach the more remote parks and settlements on secondary roads a **car** is pretty much essential but the effort is worth it for a glimpse of the natural richness that initially drew settlers here in the first place.

Historic **Québec City** is the undisputed highlight of the region, sitting at the narrowing of the St Lawrence like a symbolic gateway to the north (the word québec actually means 'narrowing' in the Algonquin language). It is also the most easterly point that connects the north and south shores of the St Lawrence. Beyond the city, the river broadens dramatically and the only connection between the shores is by ferry. The mountainous **Gaspé Peninsula** forms the south shore of the St Lawrence and presents a clear contrast to the flat wilds of the north. The **Chic Choc Mountains** create a rocky backbone along the centre of the

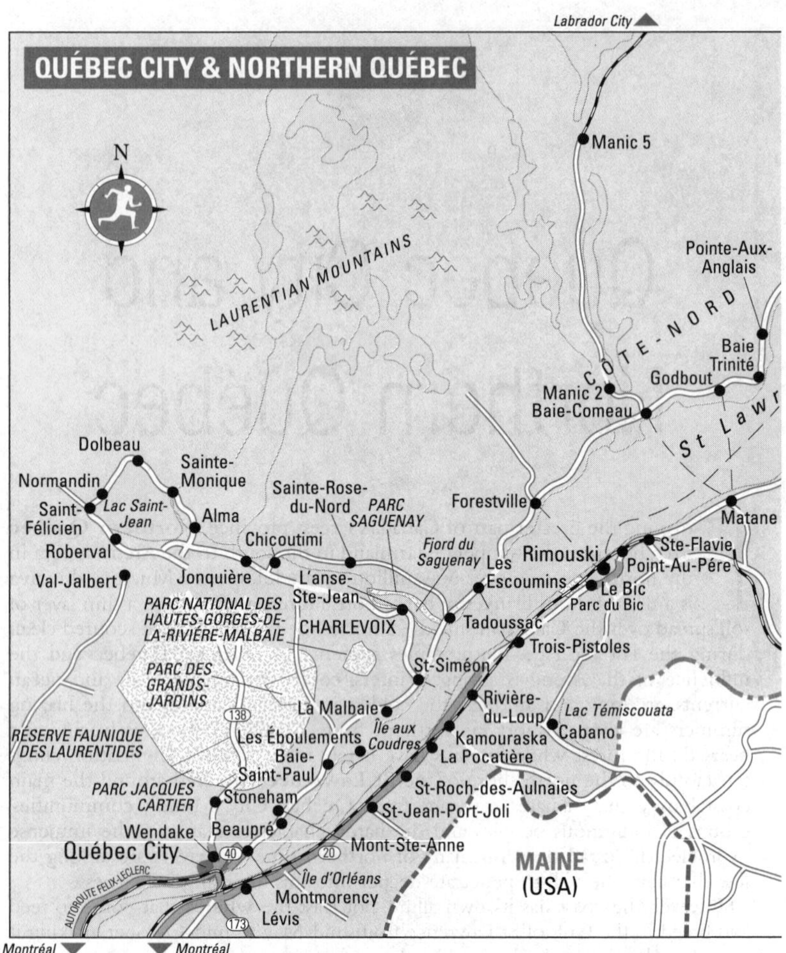

peninsula and mark the end of the famous Appalachian Chain. More populated than the north shore, the Gaspé Peninsula can be easily negotiated by public transport or car and makes for a pleasing circuit out of Québec City.

Québec City

Spread over Cap Diamant and the banks of the St Lawrence, **QUÉBEC CITY** (sometimes referred to just as "Québec") is Canada's most beautifully located

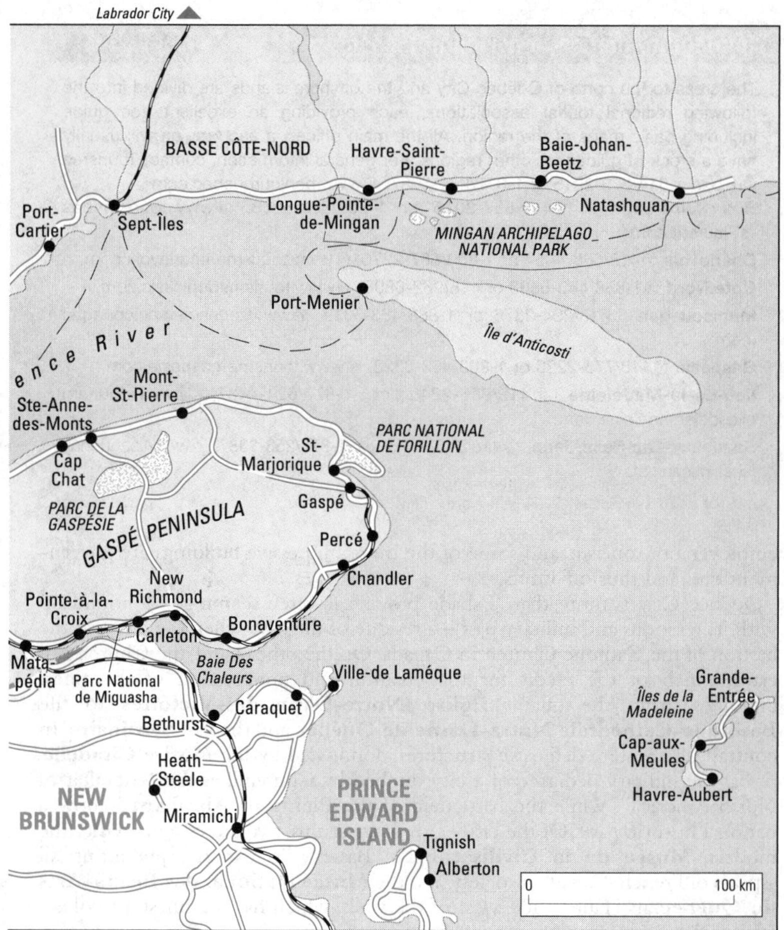

and most historic city. Vieux-Québec, surrounded by solid fortifications, is the only walled city in North America, and a UNESCO World Heritage Site. In both parts of the Old City – Haute and Basse-Ville (Upper and Lower Town) – the winding cobbled streets are flanked by seventeenth- and eighteenth-century stone houses and churches, graceful parks and squares, and countless monuments. Although some districts have been painstakingly restored to give tourists as seductive an introduction to Québec as possible, this is nevertheless an authentically and profoundly French-Canadian city: 95 percent of its 600,000 population are French-speaking, and it is often difficult to remember which continent you are in as you tuck in to a croissant and a steaming bowl of *café au lait* in a Parisian-style café. Moreover, despite the fact that the city's symbol is a hotel, the **Château Frontenac**, the government remains the main

For a brief history of Québec, see p.231.

Tourist information in northern Québec

The areas to the north of Québec City and the offshore islands are divided into the following regional tourist associations, each providing an excellent free guide including basic maps of the region. All the main offices in each region will usually have a stock of guides for other regions. For general information, contact Tourisme Québec ⓣ514/873-2015 or 1-877/266-5687, ⓦwww.bonjourquebec.com.

Bas Saint-Laurent ⓣ418/867-3015 or 1-800/563-5268, ⓦwww.tourismebas-st-laurent.com.

Charlevoix ⓣ418/665-4454 or 1-800/667-2276, ⓦwww.tourisme-charlevoix.com.

Cote Nord ⓣ1-888/463-0808 or 418/962-0808, ⓦwww.tourismeduplessis.com.

Manicouagan ⓣ418/294-2876 or 1-888/463-5319, ⓦwww.tourismemanicouagan.com

Gaspésie ⓣ418/775-2223 or 1-800/463-0323, ⓦwww.tourisme-gaspesie.com.

Îles-de-la-Madeleine ⓣ418/986-2245 or 1-877/624-4437, ⓦwww.tourismeilesdelamadeleine.com.

Saguenay–Lac-Saint-Jean ⓣ418/543-9778 or 1-877/253-8387, ⓦwww.saguenaylacsaintjean.net.

employer, not tourism, and some of the more impressive buildings are government-run and thus off-limits.

Québec City is more than a shade provincial, often seeming too bound up with its religious and military past – a residue of the days when the city was the bastion of the Catholic Church in Canada. On the other hand, the Church can claim much of the credit for the creation and preservation of the finest buildings, from the quaint **Église Notre-Dame-des-Victoires** to the **Basilique-Cathédrale Notre-Dame de Québec** and the vast **Séminaire**. In contrast, the austere defensive structures, dominated by the massive **Citadelle**, reveal the military pedigree of a city dubbed by Churchill as the "Gibraltar of North America", while the battlefield of the **Plains of Abraham** is now a national historic park. Of the city's rash of museums, two are essential visits: the modern **Musée de la Civilisation**, in Basse-Ville, expertly presenting all aspects of French-Canadian society, and the **Musée National des Beaux-Arts du Québec**, in Haute-Ville, west of the walls, which has the finest art collection in the province.

Outside the city limits, the town of **Lévis** and the Huron reservation, **Wendake**, make worthwhile excursions, whilst the churches and farmland of the **Côte-de-Beaupré** and the **Île d'Orléans** hark back to the days of the *seigneurs* and *habitants*. The gigantic **Basilique de Ste-Anne-de-Beaupré**, attracting millions of pilgrims annually, is one of the most impressive sights in Québec, and for equally absorbing natural sights there are the spectacular waterfalls at **Montmorency** and in the **Canyon Ste-Anne**, and the wildlife reserve in the **Laurentian mountains** where they arc north of the city.

Some history

For centuries the clifftop site of what is now Québec City was occupied by the **Iroquois** village of Stadacona, and although Cartier visited in the sixteenth century, permanent **European settlement** did not begin until 1608, when Samuel de Champlain established a fur-trading post here. To protect what was rapidly developing into a major inland trade gateway, the settlement shifted to the clifftop in 1620 when Fort St-Louis was built on the present-day site of the

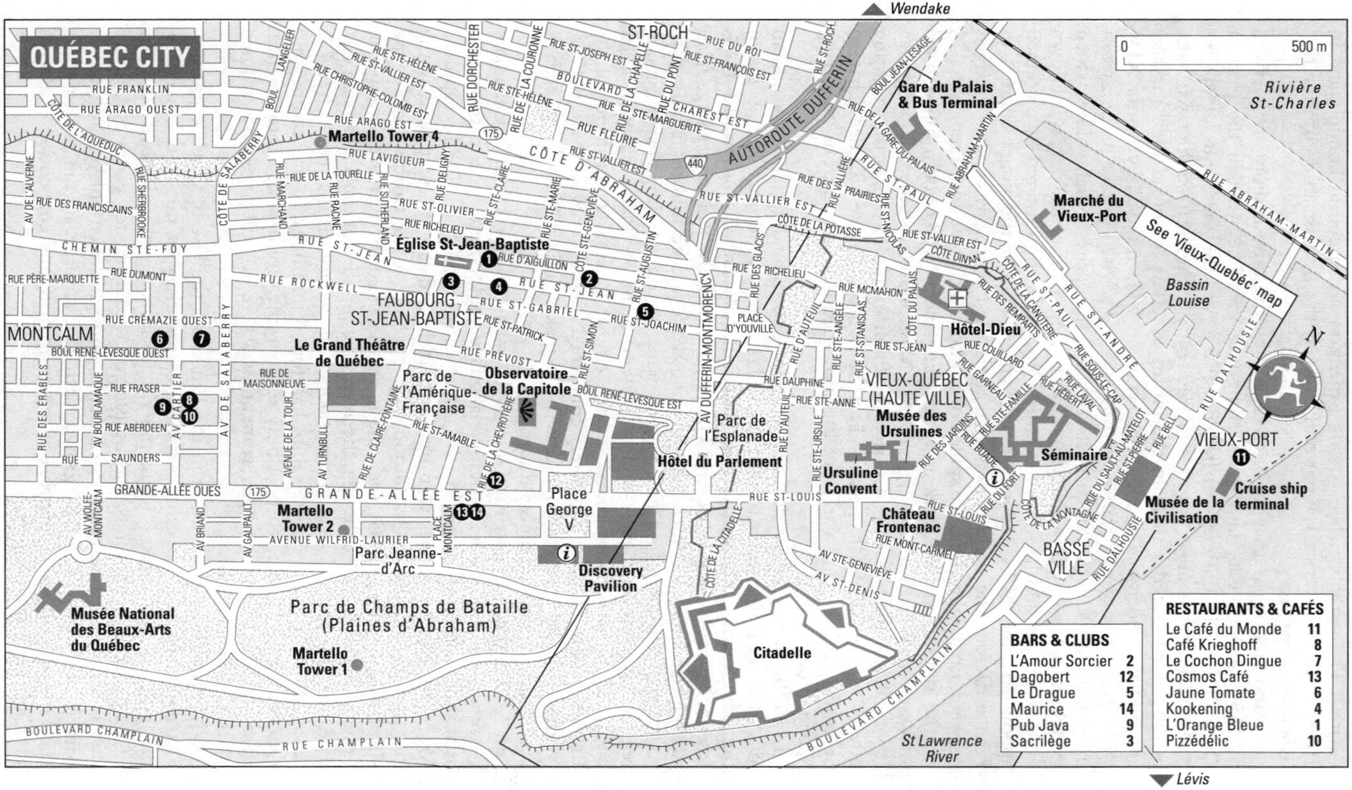

QUÉBEC CITY

BARS & CLUBS

L'Amour Sorcier	2
Dagobert	12
Le Drague	5
Maurice	14
Pub Java	9
Sacrilège	3

RESTAURANTS & CAFÉS

Le Café du Monde	11
Café Krieghoff	8
Le Cochon Dingue	7
Cosmos Café	13
Jaune Tomate	6
Kookening	4
L'Orange Bleue	1
Pizzédélic	10

Wendake
Lévis
0 500 m
N
Rivière St-Charles
St Lawrence River
Gare du Palais & Bus Terminal
Marché du Vieux-Port
See 'Vieux-Québec' map
Bassin Louise
VIEUX-PORT
Cruise ship terminal
Musée de la Civilisation
Séminaire
Hôtel-Dieu
Musée des Ursulines
Ursuline Convent
Château Frontenac
BASSE VILLE
VIEUX-QUÉBEC (HAUTE VILLE)
Citadelle
Parc de l'Esplanade
Hôtel du Parlement
Place George V
Discovery Pavilion
Observatoire de la Capitole
Parc de l'Amérique-Française
Le Grand Théâtre de Québec
Église St-Jean-Baptiste
FAUBOURG ST-JEAN-BAPTISTE
ST-ROCH
MONTCALM
Martello Tower 4
Martello Tower 2
Martello Tower 1
Parc Jeanne-d'Arc
Parc de Champs de Bataille (Plaines d'Abraham)
Musée National des Beaux-Arts du Québec
Place d'Youville
Autoroute Dufferin
Côte d'Abraham
Rue St-Jean
Grande-Allée Est
Av Dufferin-Montmorency
Boulevard Champlain
Rue Champlain

Château Frontenac. Québec's steady expansion was noted in London, and in 1629 Champlain was starved out of the fort by the **British**, an occupation that lasted just three years.

Missionaries began arriving in 1615, and by the time Bishop Laval arrived in 1659 Québec City and the surrounding province were in the grip of **Catholicism**. In the city's earliest days, however, the merchants of the fur trade wielded the most power and frequently came into conflict with the priests, who wanted a share in the profits in order to spread their message amongst the aboriginal peoples. The wrangles were resolved by **Louis XIV**, who assumed power in France in 1661 and was advised to take more interest in his kingdom's mercantile projects. By 1663 the entire French colony, which stretched all the way from Newfoundland to the Gulf of Mexico, was known as New France and had become a royal province, administered by a council appointed directly by the crown and answerable to the king's council in France. Before the century was out, the long-brewing European struggles between England and France spilled over into the colony, with French attacks on the English in New York and New England in 1689 and a foiled naval attack by Sir William Phipps, governor of Massachusetts, in the following year. It was at this time that the **Comte de Frontenac**, known as the "fighting governor", replaced Champlain's Fort St-Louis with the sturdier Château St-Louis, and began work on the now-famous fortifications that ring Vieux-Québec.

In 1759, during the Seven Years' War (also known as the French and Indian War), the most significant battle in Canada's history took place here, between the British under General **James Wolfe** and the French commander Louis Joseph, **Marquis de Montcalm**. The city had already been under siege from the opposite shore for three months when Wolfe and his four thousand troops scaled the cliff of Cap Diamant and crept up on the unprepared French regiment from behind. The twenty-minute battle on the Plains of Abraham left both leaders mortally wounded and the city of Québec in the hands of the English, a state of affairs ultimately confirmed by the Treaty of Paris in 1763. Madame de Pompadour commented: "It makes little difference; Canada is useful only to provide me with furs."

In 1775 – the year after the Québec Act, which allowed French-Canadians to retain their Catholic religion, language and culture – the town was attacked again, this time by the Americans, who had already captured Montréal. The battle was won by the British, and for the next century the city quietly earned its livelihood as the centre of a **timber-trade** and **shipbuilding** industry. By the time it was declared the provincial capital of Lower Canada in 1840, though, the accessible supplies of timber had run out. The final blow came with the appearance of steamships that could travel as far as Montréal (earlier sailing ships had found it difficult to proceed beyond Québec City). Ceasing to be a busy seaport, the city declined into a centre of small industry and local government, its way of life still largely determined by the Catholic Church.

With the Quiet Revolution in the 1960s and the rise of Québec **nationalism**, Québec City became a symbol of the glory of the French heritage: the motto *Je me souviens* ("I remember"), for instance, placed above the doors of its parliament buildings, was transferred to the licence plates of Québec cars, to sweep the message across Canada. Though the city played little active part in the changes, it has grown with the upsurge in the francophone economy, developing a suburbia of shopping malls and convention centres as slick as any in the country.

Arrival, information and accommodation

Québec City's **Aéroport Jean-Lesage** (Ⓦwww.aeroportdequebec.com), 20km west of the city, caters almost exclusively for domestic flights; most international flights arrive at Montréal. The twenty-minute trip to Vieux-Québec by taxi is a fixed rate of $24.50. VIA Rail **trains** from Montréal arrive at the central Gare du Palais in Basse-Ville, while services from the Atlantic provinces stop at Charny, across the St Lawrence, occasionally at inconvenient times; a shuttle is available from Charny to Gare du Palais but reservations must be made in advance. The long-distance **bus terminal** is at 320 rue Abraham-Martin (Ⓣ418/525-3000), adjoining the Gare du Palais. Other options include **ridesharing** and the **jetfoil** (see p.287), which docks at the Vieux-Port. **Parking** downtown can be a real pain: it's best to leave your vehicle outside the walls, near the tourist office off Grande-Allée or in the Vieux-Port area (for parking details, see "Listings" on p.323).

For **information**, the main tourist office is beside the Voltigeurs de Québec armoury, off Place Georges V at 835 av Wilfrid-Laurier (late June to early Sept daily 8.30am–7.30pm; early Sept to mid-Oct daily 8.30am–6.30pm; mid-Oct to late June Mon–Sat 9am–5pm, Fri until 6pm, Sun 10am–4pm; Ⓣ418/641-6290, Ⓦwww.quebecregion.com), in the same building as the Discovery Pavilion of the Plains of Abraham. Information on the whole province (as well as Québec City) is available at the **Centre Infotouriste** on the other side of Place d'Armes from the Château Frontenac, at 12 rue Ste-Anne (daily: late June to early Sept 8.30am–7.30pm; rest of year 9am–5pm; Ⓣ1-877/266-5687, Ⓦwww.bonjourquebec.com).

Québec City's sights and hotels are packed into a small area, so **walking** is the best way to get around. Motorcycles are banned from Vieux-Québec. For sights further out, like the Musée National des Beaux-Arts du Québec, RTC **local buses** (Ⓣ418/627-2511, Ⓦwww.rtcquebec.ca) are efficient and run from around 6am to 1am (certain routes until 3am Fri & Sat). Fares are a standard $2.05 per journey by prepaid ticket, available at newsstands, grocery stores and

Québec City festivals

Québec City is renowned for its large annual **festivals**. The **Carnaval de Québec** (Ⓣ418/626-3716, Ⓦwww.carnaval.qc.ca) is in freezing early February, when large quantities of the warming Caribou – a lethal mix of red wine, spirits and spices – are consumed amid parades and ice-sculpture competitions, all presided over by the mascot snowman called Bonhomme Carnaval. In early July, the ten-day **Festival d'Été** (Ⓣ1-888/992-5200, Ⓦwww.infofestival.com) is an equally cheery affair, especially as the provincial law prohibiting alcohol on the streets is temporarily revoked. The largest festival of francophone culture in North America attracts hundreds of artists, and everyone is roped in to the celebration, with restaurants offering discounts and all of Québec's major performers pitching up to dance, make music and lead the party from massive open-air stages all over town. A month later, the **Fêtes de la Nouvelle France** (Ⓣ418/694-3311, Ⓦwww.nouvellefrance.qc.ca) returns Basse-Ville to the seventeenth and eighteenth centuries. It's great fun if you're in the mood: thousands of Québecois from around the province dress up in period costume, often ones they've sewn themselves. It's also worth being in the city on **St-Jean Baptiste Day** (June 24), the provincial holiday, when an outpouring of Québecois pride spills onto the streets in a massive celebration, with the entire city decked with thousands of fleur-de-lis flags.

supermarkets across town, as are one-day passes ($5.80; valid for two people Sat & Sun); the cash fare per journey is $2.50, exact fare only. If you need more than one bus to complete your journey, pick up a **transfer** (*une correspondance*) from the driver, which enables you to take the second bus for no extra charge. The main bus stop in Vieux-Québec is on its west side at Place d'Youville, near Porte St-Jean. The main transfer points for RTC buses are here and at Place Jacques-Cartier; many buses stop at both locations.

Accommodation

Delightful **accommodation** in the historic heart of Québec City is easy to find and surprisingly affordable. In Vieux-Québec two **hostels**, and many budget **hotels** are as well located as those at the top end. As the city is one of Canada's most frequented tourist destinations, try to reserve in advance, particularly during the summer months and the Carnaval in February. Even at those times, though, you're not likely to find the city completely full, as there are plenty of standard chain hotels outside the walls and the suburbs have masses of **motels** and **B&Bs**, all of them just a local bus ride away. All of Québec City's **campsites** are around 20km from the old town, convenient only for those with their own transport; we've listed the closest.

The hotels in Vieux-Québec are usually renovated townhouses with the rooms fitted to provide a variety of accommodation. For cheaper rooms in the $40–80 range, head for the area around rue Ste-Ursule; the more upmarket places are around the Jardin des Gouverneurs, in the shadow of the prestigious Château Frontenac. With such a variety of characterful places to stay in the old parts of town, we've focused on accommodation within the walls and a couple of special places in the old part of Basse-Ville.

Hotels and B&Bs

Basse-Ville

Auberge St-Antoine 10 rue St-Antoine ⓣ418/692-2211 or 1-888/692-2211, ⓦwww.saint-antoine.com. Contemporary hotel divided into two buildings next to the Musée de la Civilisation. All rooms are tastefully decorated (some with a historic theme) and several have views of the river. Massage therapy, a private cinema, babysitters, indoor valet parking and free high-speed Internet access available. ❽

Hôtel Belley 249 rue St-Paul ⓣ418/692-1694 or 1-888/692-1694, ⓦwww.oricom.ca/belley. Eight-bedroom hotel near the Gare du Palais with spacious rooms full of period features. Breakfast is served next to a roaring fire in winter and on a sunny terrace in summer. ❹

Hôtel Dominion 1912 126 rue St-Pierre ⓣ418/692-2224 or 1-888/833-5253, ⓦwww.hoteldominion.com. Fabulous boutique hotel with all the touches – feather pillows and duvets, subdued lighting, stylish modern decor and cool frosted-glass sinks lit from below. Some rooms have river views. ❼

Hôtel Le Priori 15 rue du Sault-au-Matelot ⓣ418/692-3992 or 1-800/351-3992, ⓦwww.hotellepriori.com. Tastefully modernized old house on the 'oldest street in North America' with a large courtyard for breakfast. Many rooms have open fires or roll top baths and the suites are so comfortable that you may just want to move in permanently. ❻

Jardin des Gouverneurs area

B&B des Grisons 1 rue des Grisons ⓣ418/694-1461, ⓦwww.bbcanada.com/2608.html. A late-nineteenth century home with high ceilings, wood-strip floors and antiques from various epochs. The larger of the five rooms have sofa-beds and all have shared bath. ❹

Hôtel Cap-Diamant 39 av Ste-Geneviève ⓣ418/694-0313, ⓦwww.hcapdiamant.qc.ca. Nine-bedroom guesthouse with Victorian furnishings and a courtyard for breakfast. All rooms are en suite, and have a/c, minifridges and TVs. ❻

Hôtel Château Bellevue 16 rue de la Porte ⓣ418/692-2573 or 1-800/463-2617, ⓦwww.vieux-quebec.com/bellevue. Quality, but unexciting, modern hotel lurking behind the facades of a row of town houses facing the Jardin. Free wireless

Internet, continental breakfast and morning paper. Parking is available. ❼

Le Château Frontenac 1 rue des Carrières ⓣ418/692-3861 or 1-800/441-1414, ⓦwww.fairmont.com. This opulent Victorian "castle", built for William Van Horne, president of CP Railways, opened in 1893, and has accommodated such dignitaries as Churchill, Roosevelt, Madame Chiang Kai-shek and Queen Elizabeth II. Thanks to its location and history it's the most expensive place in town, with splendid rooms and views, antique furnishings and first class service. There's no wireless Internet (although there are guest computers in the Business Centre) and parking is extra. (See p.323) ❽

Hôtel Château de Léry 8 rue de la Porte ⓣ418/692-2692 or 1-800/363-0036, ⓦwww.quebecweb.com/Chateaudelery. A rather functional-looking exterior conceals bright and attractively furnished rooms with hardwood floors in this large 19th century house with an enviable location just round the courner from the Château Frontenac. Includes breakfast. ❺

Hôtel Le Château de Pierre 17 av Ste-Geneviève ⓣ418/694-0429 or 1-888/694-0429, ⓦwww.Chateaudepierre.com. An 1853 mansion with fifteen plush rooms; all are en suite and those without a/c have balconies. ❺

Hôtel Au Jardin du Gouverneur 16 rue Mont-Carmel ⓣ418/692-1704 or 1-877/692-1704, ⓦwww.quebecweb.com/hjg. On the corner of the Jardin. Seventeen decent-sized rooms with modern furnishings and adjoining bathrooms. ❸

Hôtel Manoir Ste-Geneviève 13 av Ste-Geneviève ⓣ418/694-1666 or 1-877/694-1666, ⓦwww.quebecweb.com/msg. A Victorian hotel dating from 1820 with alarmingly floral décor but large, comfortable beds and a superb location. Rates include breakfast and there are a few very cheap basement rooms with kitchenettes. ❷–❻

Hôtel Manoir sur le Cap 9 av Ste-Geneviève ⓣ418/694-1987 or 1-866/694-1987, ⓦwww.manoir-sur-le-cap.com. Fourteen bright rooms with exposed beams or stone walls. All have private bath and TVs; a few have kitchenettes. ❺

Hôtel Terrasse-Dufferin 6 place Terrasse-Dufferin ⓣ418/694-9472 or 1-800/694-9472, ⓦwww.terrasse-dufferin.com. The better rooms (❻) in this 1830 private mansion have the best views in town, overlooking the St Lawrence, which makes up for the slightly plain decor – book months ahead. ❹

Rue Ste-Ursule area

Auberge St-Louis 48 rue St-Louis ⓣ418/692-2424 or 1-888/692-4105, ⓦwww.aubergestlouis.ca. A simple inn comprising two, three-storey houses dating from the 1830s. Muted olive-coloured rooms feature IKEA-style furnishings but are comfy nonetheless. ❹–❻

Hôtel Le Clos St-Louis 69 rue St-Louis ⓣ418/694-1311 or 1-800/461-1311, ⓦwww.clossaintlouis.com. Elegant hotel in two interconnected 1840s houses with Victorian decor – four-poster beds in some of the rooms, gilt mirrors and lots of antiques. Hot breakfast. ❼

Hôtel Acadia 43 rue Ste-Ursule ⓣ418/694-0280 or 1-800/463-0280, ⓦwww.hotelacadia.com. Three ancestral dwellings with bare brick walls, original fireplaces, period furniture and the odd stained glass window. A few have shared bathrooms. ❺–❽

Hôtel La Maison Demers 68 rue Ste-Ursule ⓣ418/692-2487 or 1-800/692-2487. Parking and breakfast included in the price of this family-run old house. A few of the rooms have balconies. ❸–❹

Hôtel La Maison Ste-Ursule 40 rue Ste-Ursule ⓣ418/694-9794, ⓦwww.quebecweb.com/maisonste-ursule. Built in 1759, with green shutters and tiny doors, this is a clean hotel with bare-bones furnishing. There's also a small courtyard with picnic tables. ❷–❹

Maison Historique James Thompson 47 rue Ste-Ursule ⓣ418/694-9042, ⓦwww.bedandbreakfastquebec.com. B&B in historic 1793 house with sleigh beds, antiques throughout and a lovely sitting room. ❹

Hôtel Le Manoir d'Auteuil 49 rue d'Auteuil ⓣ418/694-1173 or 1-866/662-6647, ⓦwww.manoirdauteuil.com. Lavish 1835 townhouse by the city walls, with Art Deco rooms. Free breakfast and a cheery owner. ❹–❼

Hôtel Manoir La Salle 18 rue Ste-Ursule ⓣ418/692-9953. Small century-old red-brick hotel. Only two of the eleven rooms are en suite, one of which has a kitchenette. ❷–❹

Au Petit Hôtel 3 ruelle des Ursulines ⓣ418/694-0965, ⓦwww3.sympatico.ca/aupetithotel. Situated in a peaceful cul-de-sac just off rue Ste-Ursule. Beds and rooms are a bit small but all are en suite. ❸–❺

Rue Ste-Anne

Auberge de la Place d'Armes 24 rue Ste-Anne ⓣ418/694-9485, ⓦwww.aubergeplacedarmes.com. Perfectly situated opposite the Anglican Cathedral, on the pedestrianized part of rue Ste-Anne. Upper floor a bit stuffy in summer; others have a/c. All rooms have shower but some shared WCs. ❻

Hôtel Clarendon 57 rue Ste-Anne ⓣ418/692-2480 or 1-888/554-6001, ⓦwww.hotelclarendon.com. Québec City's oldest hotel, dating from 1870.

Renovated in the 1930s, it has a classic Art Deco reception area. ❼

Hôtel Jardin Ste-Anne 109 rue Ste-Anne ⓣ418/694-1720 or 1-866/694-1720, ⓦwww.jardinsteanne.com. Century-old house with 18 small but characterful rooms with a/c and a courtyard. ❺

Elsewhere in Vieux-Québec

Hôtel Manoir des Remparts 3 1/2 rue des Remparts ⓣ418/692-2056, ⓦwww.manoirdesremparts.com. At the north end of Vieux-Québec on the ramparts, with views of the St Lawrence from the third-floor terrace. Simple hotel with bland mostly en-suite rooms; others have dorm-type showers. ❸–❺

Hôtel Manoir Victoria 44 Côte du Palais ⓣ418/692-1030 or 1-800/463-6283, ⓦwww.manoir-victoria.com. A very grand, rambling manor off rue St-Jean with a pool to die for, sauna, gym and luxuriously furnished rooms. A hotel that will not fail to impress. ❺–❽

Motels, hostels, student rooms and campsites

Motels

Auberge Michel Doyon 1215 chemin Ste-Foy ⓣ418/527-4408 or 1-800/928-4408, ⓦwww.aubergemicheldoyon.com. One of the cheapest motels around, in the suburb of Ste-Foy. Basic but clean, with free parking. Ten-minute bus ride to Vieux-Québec. ❸–❺

Hostels and the YWCA

Auberge de la Paix 31 rue Couillard ⓣ418/694-0735, ⓦwww.aubergedelapaix.com. Situated just off rue St-Jean, this is by far the better of the city's two hostels. Large courtyard to hang out in; rate includes breakfast. ❶

Centre International de Séjour de Québec (HI) 19 rue Ste-Ursule ⓣ418/694-0755, ⓦwww.aubergeinternationaledequebec.com. The 300-bed HI hostel, in a former hospice run by nuns, is often full and can be impersonal, though it offers laundry facilities, Internet access ($3 per hour), luggage lockers, kitchens and a bar. No curfew, but you need to be buzzed in after 11pm. ❶–❻

YWCA 855 av Holland ⓣ418/683-2155, ⓦwww.ywcaquebec.qc.ca. Men are accepted as well as women here, though there are no double beds. Just off chemin Ste-Foy, about a 15-min bus ride from the Old Town. ❶

Student rooms

Services des Résidences de l'Université Laval Pavillon Alphonse-Marie-Parent, Room 1618, Cité Universitaire, Ste-Foy ⓣ418/656-5632, ⓦwww.sres.ulaval.ca. Single and double rooms are available in the student residences, a fifteen-minute bus ride from Vieux-Québec. Cheap breakfast in cafeteria, but it's best avoided. Early May to mid-Aug. Check-in after 2pm. ❶

Campsites

Camping Aéroport 2050 rte de l'Aéroport ⓣ418/871-1574 or 1-800/294-1574, ⓦwww.campingaeroport.com. Take exit 305 nord off Hwy 440 onto rte de l'Aeroport – the campsite is around 5km north of the airport itself. Sites from $22.

Camping Municipal de Beauport 95 rue Sérénité, Beauport, off boul Rochette ⓣ418/641-6112 or 1-877/641-6113, ⓦwww.campingbeauport.qc.ca. Take exit 322 off Hwy 40. Bus #800 to Beauport, then #50 or #55. Mid-June to early Sept. $21 per site.

The City

Québec City spreads from its historic heart into a bland suburbia but the highlights lie beside the St Lawrence, with main attractions being evenly distributed between the upper and lower portions of what is known as **Vieux-Québec** (Old Québec). On the Cap Diamant, **Haute-Ville** (Upper Town) continues along the St Lawrence from the old city walls and the furthest you need to wander from here is to the Musée National des Beaux-Arts du Québec, set in the extensive parkland of the Plains of Abraham that unfurls west of the magnificent Citadelle. The Terrasse Dufferin is also worth a stroll to watch street entertainers, unproductive students or the views over the river, but it gets overcrowded in the evening. It overlooks the second part of the old city, **Basse-Ville** (Lower Town), connected to Haute-Ville by funicular and several winding streets and stairs. One of the main pleasures of the area, besides the wonderful old houses and small museums, is the Musée de la Civilisation.

This itinerary begins at Vieux-Québec's Place d'Armes and then explores the upper part of Vieux-Québec and the rest of Haute-Ville as far west as the Musée National des Beaux-Arts du Québec. To finish the tour, you can explore Vieux-Québec's compact Basse-Ville, which can be reached directly from Place d'Armes. Strapped between the cliffs and the St Lawrence, this district is of considerable interest and is a pleasant area to wander around; if you're only in Québec City for a short while, head here straight from Place d'Armes and then return to the upper town for the remainder of the sights as time permits.

Place d'Armes and around

The ten square kilometres of Vieux-Québec's Haute-Ville, encircled by the city walls, form the Québec City of the tourist brochures. Its centre of gravity is the main square, the **Place d'Armes**, with benches around the central fountain serving in the summer as a resting place for weary sightseers. It was here that Champlain established his first fort in 1620, on the site now occupied by the gigantic **Château Frontenac**, probably Canada's most photographed building. New York architect Bruce Price drew upon the French-Canadian style of the surroundings to produce a pseudo-medieval red-brick pile crowned with a copper roof. Although the hotel he designed was inaugurated by the Canadian Pacific Railway in 1893, its distinctive main tower was only added in the early 1920s – during which time the hotel never closed – resulting in an over-the-top design that makes the most of the stupendous location atop Cap Diamant. Numerous notables, including Queen Elizabeth II, have stayed here, and the hotel has hosted one pair or more of newlyweds every night since it opened. The hotel has fifty-minute guided tours departing on the hour from the lower level (May to mid-Oct daily 10am–6pm; mid-Oct to April Sat & Sun noon–5pm, call for weekday times; reservations preferable ⓣ418/691-2166, ⓦwww.toursChateau.ca; $8).

Beside the Château Frontenac, where rue St-Louis enters the square, is the **Maison Maillou**, which houses the Québec chamber of commerce. Dating from 1736, this grey-limestone house, with metal shutters for insulation and a steeply slanting roof, displays the chief elements of the climate-adapted architecture brought over by the Norman settlers. On the west side of the square, on the spot where the Récollet missionaries built their first church and convent, stands the former **Palais de Justice**, a Renaissance-style courthouse designed in 1877 by Eugène-Étienne Taché, architect of the province's Parliament Buildings.

On the northeast corner of Place d'Armes, where rue Ste-Anne intersects with rue du Fort, is the **Musée du Fort** (April–Oct daily 10am–5pm, Feb, Mar & Nov Thurs–Sun 11am–4pm; ⓣ418/692-2175, ⓦwww.museedufort.com; $7.50), whose sole exhibit is a 37-square-metre model of Québec City circa 1750. You can only see it as part of the quaint thirty-minute sound and light show, when the city's six major battles, including the battle of the Plains of Abraham and the American invasion of 1775, are re-enacted – a fairly pricey, if engaging, history lesson.

Parallel to rue du Fort is the narrow alley of **rue du Trésor** where French settlers paid their taxes to the Royal Treasury; nowadays it is a touristy artists' market. You're better to visit the row of stalls manned by local artisans in the churchyard that runs alongside the portraitists on the pedestrianized stretch of rue Ste-Anne. Nearby, the Centre Infotouriste occupies the former Union Hotel at

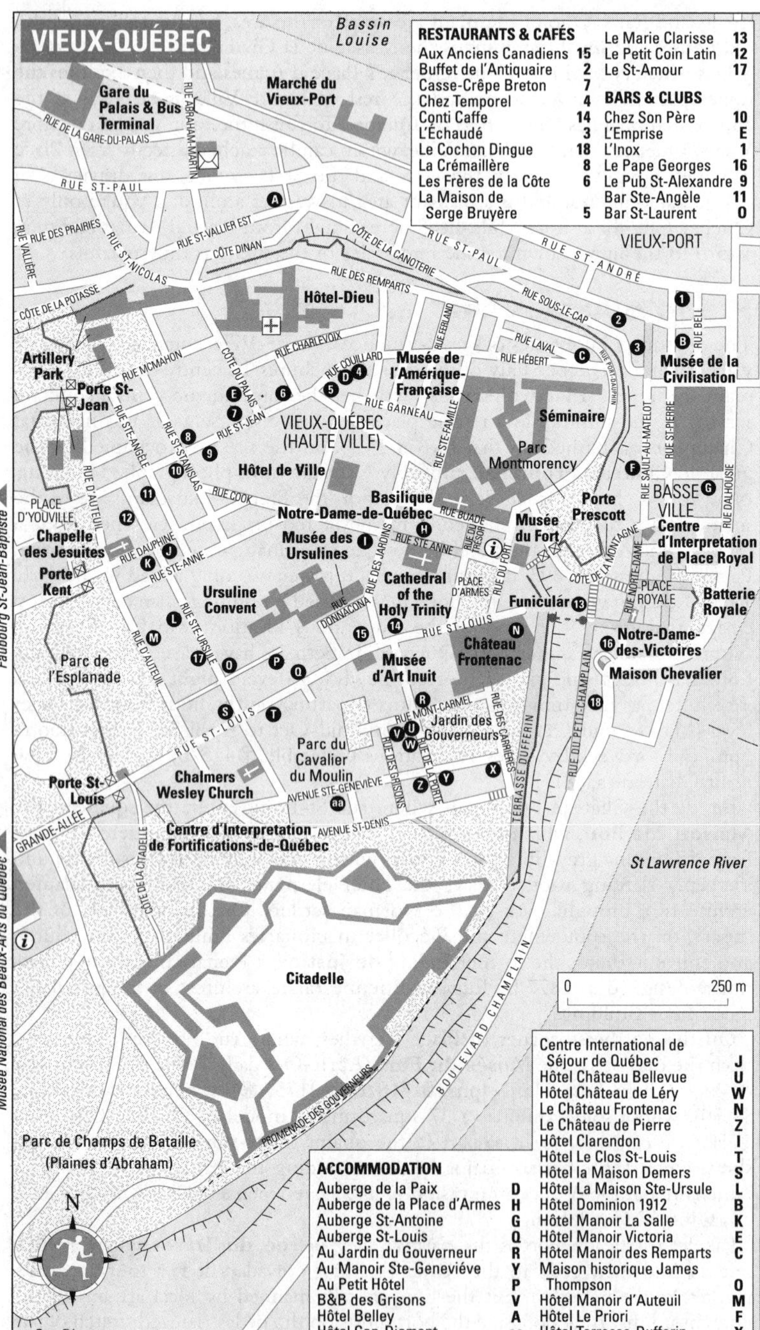
VIEUX-QUÉBEC
RESTAURANTS & CAFÉS
Aux Anciens Canadiens 15
Buffet de l'Antiquaire 2
Casse-Crêpe Breton 7
Chez Temporel 4
Conti Caffe 14
L'Échaudé 3
Le Cochon Dingue 18
La Crémaillère 8
Les Frères de la Côte 6
La Maison de Serge Bruyère 5
Le Marie Clarisse 13
Le Petit Coin Latin 12
Le St-Amour 17
BARS & CLUBS
Chez Son Père 10
L'Emprise E
L'Inox 1
Le Pape Georges 16
Le Pub St-Alexandre 9
Bar Ste-Angèle 11
Bar St-Laurent 0
ACCOMMODATION
Auberge de la Paix D
Auberge de la Place d'Armes H
Auberge St-Antoine G
Auberge St-Louis Q
Au Jardin du Gouverneur R
Au Manoir Ste-Geneviéve Y
Au Petit Hôtel P
B&B des Grisons V
Hôtel Belley A
Hôtel Cap-Diamant aa
Centre International de Séjour de Québec J
Hôtel Château Bellevue U
Hôtel Château de Léry W
Le Château Frontenac N
Le Château de Pierre Z
Hôtel Clarendon I
Hôtel Le Clos St-Louis T
Hôtel la Maison Demers S
Hôtel La Maison Ste-Ursule L
Hôtel Dominion 1912 B
Hôtel Manoir La Salle K
Hôtel Manoir Victoria E
Hôtel Manoir des Remparts C
Maison historique James Thompson O
Hôtel Manoir d'Auteuil M
Hôtel Le Priori F
Hôtel Terrasse-Dufferin X
Bassin Louise
Gare du Palais & Bus Terminal
Marché du Vieux-Port
VIEUX-PORT
Hôtel-Dieu
Artillery Park
Porte St-Jean
Musée de l'Amérique-Française
Séminaire
Musée de la Civilisation
VIEUX-QUÉBEC (HAUTE VILLE)
Parc Montmorency
Hôtel de Ville
BASSE VILLE
Basilique Notre-Dame-de-Québec
Porte Prescott
Musée du Fort
Centre d'Interpretation de Place Royal
PLACE D'YOUVILLE
Chapelle des Jesuites
Porte Kent
Musée des Ursulines
Ursuline Convent
Cathedral of the Holy Trinity
PLACE D'ARMES
Funicular
PLACE ROYALE
Batterie Royale
Château Frontenac
Notre-Dame-des-Victoires
Maison Chevalier
Parc de l'Esplanade
Musée d'Art Inuit
Jardin des Gouverneurs
Parc du Cavalier du Moulin
Porte St-Louis
Chalmers Wesley Church
Centre d'Interpretation de Fortifications-de-Québec
St Lawrence River
Citadelle
Parc de Champs de Bataille (Plaines d'Abraham)
Cap Diamant
Faubourg St-Jean-Baptiste
Musée National des Beaux-Arts du Québec
Lévis
0 250 m
N
RUE DE LA GARE-DU-PALAIS
RUE ABRAHAM-MARTIN
RUE ST-PAUL
RUE DES PRAIRIES
RUE VALLIÈRE
RUE ST-VALLIER EST
RUE ST-NICOLAS
CÔTE DINAN
CÔTE DE LA CANOTERIE
RUE ST-ANDRÉ
RUE DES REMPARTS
CÔTE DE LA POTASSE
RUE SOUS-LE-CAP
RUE CHARLEVOIX
RUE FERLAND
RUE LAVAL
RUE HÉBERT
RUE MCMAHON
CÔTE DU PALAIS
RUE COUILLARD
RUE BELL
RUE PORT-DAUPHIN
RUE GARNEAU
RUE ST-JEAN
RUE STE-ANGÈLE
RUE ST-STANISLAS
RUE STE-FAMILLE
RUE SAULT-AU-MATELOT
RUE ST-PIERRE
RUE DALHOUSIE
RUE D'AUTEUIL
RUE COOK
RUE BUADE
RUE DU TRÉSOR
RUE DAUPHINE
RUE STE-ANNE
RUE DES JARDINS
RUE DU FORT
CÔTE DE LA MONTAGNE
RUE NOTRE-DAME
RUE DONNACONA
RUE STE-URSULE
RUE ST-LOUIS
RUE MONT-CARMEL
RUE DES CARRIÈRES
RUE DES GRISONS
RUE DE LA PORTE
TERRASSE DUFFERIN
RUE DU PETIT-CHAMPLAIN
AVENUE STE-GENEVIÈVE
AVENUE ST-DENIS
GRANDE-ALLÉE
CÔTE DE LA CITADELLE
BOULEVARD CHAMPLAIN
PROMENADE DES GOUVERNEURS

12 rue Ste-Anne, while at no. 22 the impressive 1732 Maison Vallée houses a missable waxworks museum. Production values are a bit higher at the **Québec Expérience** show back around the corner at 8 rue du Trésor (mid-May to mid-Oct 10am–10pm, rest of year 10am–5pm; 30min; Ⓣ418/694-4000, Ⓦwww.quebecexperience.com; $7.50), where a 3D multimedia extravaganza, complete with holographic characters and animatronics, gives a potted history of Québec.

△Château Frontenac, Québec City

Terrasse Dufferin and the ramparts

Fronting the Château Frontenac the wide clifftop boardwalk of the **Terrasse Dufferin** overlooks the narrowing of the river that was known to the aboriginal peoples as the *kebec* – the source of the province's name. Underlying part of the boardwalk are the foundations of Frontenac's Château St-Louis, which served as the governor's residence for two centuries until a fire destroyed it in 1834. The leafy park running alongside the boardwalk was the château's garden – hence its name, the **Jardin des Gouverneurs** (see p.309). To the south, a long flight of stairs leads up to the Promenade des Gouverneurs, a narrow boardwalk perched precariously on the cliff face below the Citadelle that leads to the Plaines d'Abraham (see p.312).

At the north end of the terrace – which offers charming views of the river – stands a romantic statue of **Champlain** and, beside it, a modern sculpture symbolizing Québec City's status as a UNESCO World Heritage Site. From here a **funicular** descends to Vieux-Québec's Basse-Ville (see p.315); save that for the weary walk back up and instead take the stairs down at the north end of the terrace to the **Porte Prescott**, one of the city's four rebuilt gates.

Rather than descending to street level, you can continue across the top of the gate to **Parc Montmorency**; tucked between the upper and lower parts of the old city, its monuments recall the historic figures of the area. This land was granted by Champlain to Canada's first agricultural settler and seigneur, Louis Hébert, and was later the meeting place of Québec's first legislature in 1694. The park gives wonderful views of Québec's port and its massive grain elevators, as does the flanking rue Port Dauphin, which becomes **rue des Remparts**, where the cannons that once protected the city still point across to Lévis.

The ten-minute walk along rue des Remparts circles around the north side of the Séminaire past nineteenth-century homes to the **Hôtel-Dieu du Précieux Sang**, the oldest hospital north of Mexico. At the end of rue Remparts, turn left onto Côte du Palais; from here, you can turn right on rue McMahon to reach Artillery Park, or left on rue St-Jean and continue up the hill to the basilica.

Basilique-Cathédrale Notre-Dame de Québec

From Place d'Armes, you can follow rue du Trésor directly north towards the impressive bulk of the **Basilique-Cathédrale Notre-Dame de Québec** (daily 8am–4pm; free; ⓣ418/694-0665, ⓦwww.patrimoine-religieux.com). The oldest parish north of Mexico, the church was burnt to the ground in 1922 – one of many fires it has suffered – and was rebuilt to the original plans of its seventeenth-century forebear. Absolute silence within the cathedral heightens the impressiveness of the Rococo-inspired interior, culminating in a ceiling of blue sky and billowy clouds. The altar, a gilded replica of St Peter's, is surmounted by an elaborate baldachin uncharacteristically supported by angelic caryatids rather than columns due to the narrow space, and is topped by a statue of Jesus standing on a gilded sphere. The pewter sanctuary lamp, to the right of the main altar, was a gift from Louis XIV and is one of the few treasures to survive the fire. In the crypt more than nine hundred bodies, including three governors and most of Québec's bishops, are interred. Champlain is also rumoured to be buried here, though archeologists are still trying to work out which body is his. Unfortunately, the only part of the crypt you can see on the informative **guided tours** (daily every 30min 8.30am–3.30pm) is a mundane modern corridor – skip the Crypt part and the tour is free; otherwise it's a dollar.

In the afternoons, access to the cathedral is limited to half an hour at a time unless you pay for the half-hour Heavenly Lights **sound and light show** (May to mid-Oct Mon–Fri 6 shows daily from 3.30pm, Sat & Sun 3 shows daily from 6.30pm; $7.50). Architectural details are illuminated and isolated in the darkness to give you a sense of the volumes that make up the church's interior.

Séminaire de Québec

Next door to the cathedral and sprawling to the north is the old **Séminaire de Québec**, founded by the aggressive and autocratic Monseigneur François de Laval-Montmorency in 1663 (see box below). At its construction, the seminary was the finest collection of buildings the city had seen, leaving Governor Frontenac muttering that the bishop was now housed better than him. Primarily a college for priests, the seminary was also open to young men who wanted to follow other professions, and in 1852 it became Laval University, the country's first francophone Catholic university. Today, only the school of architecture remains; most of the other departments were moved to the western suburb of Ste-Foy.

Public access is limited mainly to the ever-expanding **Musée de l'Amérique Française** (late June to early Sept daily 9.30am–5pm; Sept–June Tues–Sun 10am–5pm, ⓣ418/692-2843, ⓦwww.mcq.org; $5; Nov–May free on Tues), whose four sections occupy a small part of the old Séminaire. The entrance – and departure point for one-hour guided tours of the seminary – is in the Welcome Pavilion in the Maison du Coin, next to the basilica. It has a small exhibition on the early colonists upstairs and adjoins the Roman-style **chapel**, whose Second Empire interior houses Canada's largest collection of religious relics – bones, ashes and locks of hair of various saints, a few of which are on display. Laval's memorial chapel contains his ornate marble tomb, but not his remains, which were moved to the basilica when the chapel was deconsecrated in 1993. The whole interior is a bit of a sham, though: fed up with rebuilding after the chapel burnt down yet again in 1888, the church authorities decided to construct the pillars and coffered ceilings out of tin and paint over them; the stained-glass windows have been painted on single panes of glass and even the tapestries are the result of some deft brushwork.

Monseigneur Laval

François-Xavier de Montmorency-Laval was born into a wealthy aristocratic family in North East France. Educated by Jesuits, he briefly studied in Paris before giving up his hefty patrimony to join the church, and was ordained a priest in 1647 at the age of 24. Ten years later the Pope needed someone to oversee the spiritual development of New France and the Jesuits proposed Laval. He was swiftly made a bishop and sent to Québec. In the three decades of his incumbency, from 1659 to 1688, Laval secured more power than the governor and intendant put together, and any officer dispatched from France found himself on the next boat home if Laval did not care for him. Even the Royal Governers had to tread carefully. Frontenac himself was recalled in 1682 after Laval travelled to France to protest at the governer's actions. Laval objected to the trade of alcohol with the Iroquois (it undermined his proselytizing) that Frontenac and his 'Brandy Government' failed to discourage. Laval retired early due to ill health (brought on by a religious fervour that denied him blankets and proper food) but, unhappy with his successor, Bishop de St Valier, he continued to exert a stubborn influence on the running of the colony well into his dotage. Death finally came in 1708 after his feet froze on the stone floor of the chapel during his morning prayer session.

The wrought-iron gates between the Welcome Pavilion and the basilica lead into a vast courtyard flanked by austere white buildings with handsome mansard roofs, through which you can pass to visit the rest of the museum. Alternatively, take the underground corridor directly from the chapel; a photo exhibit fills in the history of the Séminaire's buildings. Either way, you end up at the museum's **Pavillon Jérôme-Demers**, which displays mostly well-presented, historical exhibitions. A tiny sample of the eclectic items gathered by Québec's bishops and the academics at Laval – scientific instruments, an Egyptian mummy (with a remarkably well-preserved penis) – as well as ecclesiastical silverware and some of Laval's personal belongings are on display. The museum's name derives from the exhibition on the second floor, **The Settling of French America**, which illustrates the history of the emigration and settlement of the more than nineteen million North Americans of French stock.

Around the Hôtel de Ville

The edifices of the colony's once-powerful Church face the home of democratic power in the city today – the **Hôtel de Ville** (City Hall), which dates from 1883 and is surrounded by the park space of the Jardins de l'Hôtel de Ville, scene of numerous live shows in the summer. To the north, the shops on Côte de la Fabrique extend down the hill to the lively restaurants and bars of rue St-Jean; while to the south, the Hôtel de Ville is overlooked by the far more impressive Art Deco buildings of the **Hôtel Clarendon** and the **Édifice Price** (the city's first skyscraper), at nos. 57 and 65 rue Ste-Anne, respectively.

By the corner of rue Ste-Anne and rue des Jardins stands the first Anglican cathedral built outside the British Isles, the **Cathedral of the Holy Trinity** (daily late May to Oct 10am–5pm; free guided tours; Ⓣ418/692-2193, Ⓦwww.cathedral.ca). The king of France gave the site to the Récollet Fathers but their church burnt down in the late eighteenth century. Its replacement, constructed in 1800–04 on orders from George III, followed the lines of London's church of St Martin-in-the-Fields. The simple interior houses the 1845 bishops' throne, reputedly made from the wood of the elm tree under whose branches Samuel de Champlain conferred with the Iroquois. Many of the church's features came from London, including the silverware from George III and Victorian stained glass, shipped in vats of molasses for protection. The brass bars on the balcony denote the seats for the exclusive use of British sovereigns (or their representatives); humbler parishioners had wooden doors on the box pews to keep the winter cold out. In the courtyard are Les Artisans de la Cathédrale, Québec-based artisans whose small crafts and clothes stalls avoid tourist tack.

Couvent des Ursulines and around

Heading south along rue des Jardins brings you to the narrow rue Donnacona, where a sculptured hand holding a quill – a monument to the women who, since 1639, have dedicated their lives to teaching young Québecois – rests on a pedestal. It seems to point the way to the **Couvent des Ursulines**, built by a tiny group of Ursuline nuns who arrived in Québec in 1639 calling themselves "the Amazons of God in Canada". Their task was to bring religion to the natives and later to the daughters of the settlers, a mission carried out in the classrooms of North America's first girls' school – the buildings still house a private school. They also cared for the *filles du roi*, marriageable orphans and peasant girls imported from France to swell the population. These girls were kept in separate rooms in the convent for surveillance by the local bachelors, who were urged to select a wife within fifteen days of the ship's arrival – a fine of three hundred livres was levied on any man who failed to take his pick within the period. Fat girls were the most desirable, as it was believed they were more inclined to stay at home and be better able to resist the winter cold.

The Ursulines' first mother superior, Marie Guyart de l'Incarnation, was widowed at age 19 and left her son with family when she entered the Ursulines de Tours monastery twelve years later. Her letters to him once she finally made it to Québec give some sharp insights into the early days of the city: "It would be hard to live here an hour without having the hands protected and without being well covered. Although the beds are covered well with quilts or blankets, scarcely can one keep warm when lying on them." Her likeness can be seen in a posthumous portrait attributed to Pommier in the interesting little **museum** (May–Sept Tues–Sat 10am–noon & 1–5pm, Sun 1–5pm; Oct–April Tues–Sun 1–4.30pm; ⓣ418/694-0694, ⓦwww.museocapitale.qc.ca/014.htm; $6), housed in the former home of one of the first nuns. A painting by Frère Luc, though executed in France, pictures a Canadian version of the Holy Family: Joseph is shown presenting a Huron girl to Mary, while through the window one can glimpse Cap Diamant and the St Lawrence flowing past. Other paintings, documents and household items testify to the harshness of life in the early days of the colony, but lace-work and embroidery are the highlights, particularly the splendid liturgical ornaments and vestments produced by the early Ursulines and shot through with gold and silver thread.

Marie de l'Incarnation's remains are entombed in the oratory adjoining the **chapel** (May–Oct Tues–Sat 10–noon & 1pm–5pm, Sun 1pm–5pm; free), rebuilt in 1902 but retaining the sumptuous early eighteenth-century altar and sculptures by Pierre-Noël Levasseur. A plaque indicates General Montcalm's former resting place below the chapel (only his skull was found there during renovations, and this has subsequently been re-interred in a suburban military cemetery). The collection of seventeenth and eighteenth-century paintings were acquired from post-Revolution France in the 1820s. Next to the museum, the **Centre Marie-de-l'Incarnation** (Feb–Nov Tues–Sat 10am–11.30am & 1.30pm–4.30pm, Sun 1.30pm–4.30pm; ⓣ418/694-0413; free) sells religious and historical books, and displays a few of Marie's personal effects.

On the corner of rue des Jardins and rue St-Louis – a touristy restaurant strip – stands **Maison Jacquet**, occupied by the restaurant *Aux Anciens Canadiens*. The name comes from Québec's first novel, whose author, Philippe Aubert de Gaspé, lived here for a while in the middle of the nineteenth century. Dating from 1677, the house is another good example of seventeenth-century New France architecture, as is the blue and white **Maison Kent** at no. 25 on the other side of rue St-Louis, which was built in 1649. Maison Kent was once home to Queen Victoria's father, the Duke of Kent but it's best known as the place where the capitulation of Québec was signed in 1759 and now ironically houses the French consulate.

Jardin des Gouverneurs and around

Rue Haldimand, around the corner from the Musée d'Art Inuit, leads to the **Jardin des Gouverneurs**, whose wonderful prospect of the St Lawrence was once the exclusive privilege of the colonial governors who inhabited the Château St-Louis, upon whose foundations the Terrasse Dufferin was built. The garden's Wolfe–Montcalm obelisk monument, erected in 1828, is rare in paying tribute to the victor and the vanquished. Converted merchants' houses border this grandiose area, and the nearby streets are some of the most impressive in Vieux-Québec – check out rue de la Porte and the parallel rue des Grisons on the park's west side, which boasts some fine eighteenth-century homes.

To escape the tourist hordes for a bit, follow rue Mont-Carmel, on the northern side of the square, to the almost unnoticed **Parc du Cavalier du Moulin**, a quiet little park that's perfect for a picnic. The remnant of a defensive bastion built atop Mont Carmel hill, this was part of the seventeenth-century French fortifications that protected the city's western side. You can't really see the walls from this angle, but you can see the rear facades of the houses on rue St-Louis.

From the Jardin des Gouverneurs, av Ste-Geneviève runs west past handsome nineteenth-century houses towards Porte St-Louis. En route, turn right onto rue Ste-Ursule for the **Chalmers-Wesley United Church** at no. 78 (late June–late Aug daily 10am–5pm; ⓣ418/692-2640; free), built in 1852 and one of the most beautiful in the city. Its slender, Gothic Revivalist spires are a conspicuous element of the skyline and, inside, the stained-glass windows are worth a look. During summer there are weekly organ concerts on Sunday evenings at 6pm. Opposite, the 1910 **Sanctuaire de Notre-Dame du Sacré-Coeur** (daily 7am–8pm; ⓣ418/692-3787; free) also has impressive stained-glass windows.

The fortifications and Artillery Park

A left turn onto rue St-Louis leads to the Porte St-Louis, one of the four gates in the city wall. It's surrounded by **Parc de l'Esplanade**, the main site for the Carnaval de Québec, and departure point for the city's smart horse-drawn calèches. The park's **Centre d'interprétation des Fortifications-de-Québec**, 100 rue St-Louis (May to Oct daily 10am–5pm; ⓣ418/648-7016, ⓦwww.pc.gc.ca/fortifications; $4), includes a powder house constructed in 1815 and a dull exhibition on the fortifications. Most visitors start their 4.5-kilometre stroll around the city wall from here. You can also take a 90-minute tour focusing on the fortifications' military history with a costumed guide for $10.

The entrance to the Citadelle lies south of here along the Côte de la Citadelle. Alternatively, head north on rue d'Auteuil as it descends alongside the fortifications to Porte Kent, next to the **Chapelle des Jésuites**, 20 rue Dauphine (Mon–Fri 11am–1pm; Guided visits late June to Sept Thurs–Mon; free). Framed by the rose and powder-blue vault, the church's delicately carved altar and ecclesiastical sculptures are by **Pierre-Noël Levasseur**, one of the most illustrious artists to work on the early Québec parish churches.

Immediately north of the **Porte St-Jean** lie the defensive structures of **Artillery Park**, raised in the early 1700s by the French in expectation of a British attack from the St Charles River, and subsequently a barracks for the Royal Artillery Regiment for more than a century. In 1882 it became a munitions factory, providing the Canadian army with ammunition in both world wars. The foundry, added in 1902, now houses an interpretation centre (April–Oct daily 10am–5pm; ⓣ418/648-4205, ⓦwww.pc.gc.ca/artillerie; $4.90), which has displays on the military pedigree of the city, including a vivid model of Québec City in 1808. It's also the starting point for one-hour guided tours ($3 extra) and visits of the site's four buildings, including the Officers' Quarters furnished as it was in 1830 and the massive Dauphine Redoubt. The latter typifies the changes of fortune here: used by the French as the barracks for their garrison, it became the officers' mess under the British and then the residence of the superintendent of the Canadian Arsenal.

The Citadelle

Dominating the southern section of Vieux-Québec, the massive star-shaped **Citadelle** can only be visited on one of the worthwhile **guided tours** (every 30min: July & Aug 9am–6pm; every hour: April 10am–4pm, May, June & Sept 9am–5pm, Oct 10am–3pm; once daily: Nov–March daily 1.30pm; ⓣ418/694-2815, ⓦwww.lacitadelle.qc.ca; $8). The *tour de force* of Québec City's fortifications, the Citadelle occupies the highest point of Cap Diamant, 100m above the St Lawrence. This strategic site was first built on by the French, but most of the buildings were constructed by the British under orders from the Duke of Wellington, who was anxious about American attack after the War of 1812.

The complex of 25 buildings covers forty acres and is the largest North American fort still occupied by troops – it's home to the Royal 22nd Regiment, Canada's only French-speaking regiment. Around the parade ground are ranged various monuments to the campaigns of the celebrated "Van-Doos" (*vingt-deux*), as well as the summer residence of Canada's governor general and two buildings dating back to the French period: the Cap Diamant Redoubt, built in 1693 and thus one of the oldest parts of the Citadelle, and the 1750 powder magazine, now a mundane museum of weaponry and military artefacts.

In addition to the mandatory but entertaining hour-long guided tours, the admission price includes the colourful Changing of the Guard (late June to early Sept daily 10am), which you can catch at the end of a 9am tour (otherwise arrive by 9.45am), and the Beating of the Retreat tattoo (early July to early Sept Fri–Sun 7pm, at the end of the 6pm tour).

Grande-Allée and the Parliament Buildings

Sweeping out from Porte St-Louis and flanked by grand Victorian mansions, the tree-lined boulevard of **Grande-Allée** is proclaimed the city's equivalent of the Champs-Élysées, with its bustling restaurants, hotels and bars. Adjacent to the *Loews Le Concorde* hotel, Place Montcalm has a monument to Montcalm and a more recent statue of Charles de Gaulle, the French president who declared

Faubourg St-Jean-Baptiste

If you want to take a break from the tourist sights, head through the Porte St-Jean and across Place D'Youville to where rue St-Jean picks up again in the former *faubourg* – the name given to the settlements that once stood undefended outside the city walls – of **St-Jean-Baptiste**. The quarter's studenty atmosphere is more laid-back than the rest of Québec, with cheaper restaurants and great nightlife spots. A five-minute walk will bring you to the **Protestant Burying Ground** (May to mid-Nov daily 7am–11pm), Québec City's first Protestant cemetery and now the oldest one remaining in the province. Many historical figures were buried here between 1772 and 1860, including Lt Col James Turnbull, Queen Victoria's presumed half-brother. Further along on the same side of the street, **Maison Jean-Alfred Moisan** has been in the grocery trade since 1871, making it the oldest grocery store in North America. The tin ceilings and wooden furnishings provide a backdrop for fine foods and baked goods. The district's namesake, the **Église St-Jean-Baptiste**, 410 rue St-Jean (late June to mid-Sept Mon–Fri & Sun 11am–4pm, Sat 9am–4pm), dominates the *faubourg*, its spire rising to 73m. When reconstruction began after a fire destroyed the original church in 1881, local architect Joseph Ferdinand Peachy looked to France for inspiration – the facade is a close reproduction of the Église de la Trinité in Paris.

"Vive le Québec libre" in the 1960s, much to the separatists' delight. This area is now known as Parliament Hill, a new name that caused a lot of controversy, as Canada's Parliament area in Ottawa has the same title and anglophones thought it presumptuous of Québec City to label itself like a capital city.

However, there is indeed a hill here, and upon it, at the eastern end of Grande-Allée, stand the stately buildings of the **Hôtel du Parlement** (late June to early Sept Mon–Fri 9am–4.30pm, Sat & Sun 10am–4.30pm; early Sept to late June Mon–Fri 9am–4.30pm; Guided tours every 30 minutes; ⓣ418/643-7239 or 1-866/337-8837, ⓦwww.assnat.qc.ca; free), designed by Eugène-Étienne Taché in 1877 in the Second Empire style using the Louvre for inspiration. The ornate facade includes niches for twelve bronze statues by Québecois sculptor Louis-Philippe Hébert of Canada's and Québec's major statesmen, while finely chiselled and gilded walnut panels in the entrance hall depict important moments in Québec's history, coats of arms and other heraldic features. From here the corridor of the President's Gallery, lined with portraits of all the Legislative Assembly's speakers and presidents, leads to the Chamber of the National Assembly, where the 125 provincial representatives meet for debate. You can't see much, though, unless you take one of the free half-hour guided tours.

Among the government buildings clustered to the west of here, the Édifice Marie-Guyart, 1037 rue de la Chevrotière, is the tallest structure in the city. On its 31st floor, the **Observatoire de la Capitole** (late June to mid-Oct daily 10am–5pm; mid-Oct to late June Tues–Sun 10am–5pm; ⓣ418/644-9841, ⓦwww.observatoirecapitale.org; $5) offers a 360-degree panoramic view over Vieux-Québec, the Citadelle and beyond, with panels usefully providing background info on what you can see.

Battlefields Park

Westward of the Citadelle are the rolling grasslands of the **Battlefields Park** (Parc des Champs-de-Bataille), a sizeable chunk of land stretching along the cliffs above the St Lawrence. The park encompasses the historic **Plains of Abraham**, which were named after Abraham Martin, the first pilot of the St Lawrence River in 1620. The Plains were to become the site on which Canada's history was rewritten. In June 1759 a large British force led by **General Wolfe** sailed up the St Lawrence to besiege **General Montcalm** in Québec City. From the end of July until early September the British forces shuttled up and down the south side of the river, raking the city with cannon fire. Montcalm and the governor, Vaudreuil, became convinced that Wolfe planned a direct assault on the citadel from Anse de Foulon (Wolf's Cove), the only handy break in the cliff face – opinion confirmed when lookouts observed a British detachment surveying Cap Diamant from across the river in Lévis. Montcalm thus strengthened the defences above Anse de Foulon, but made the mistake of withdrawing the regiment stationed on the Plains themselves. The following night the British performed the extraordinary feat, which even Wolfe had considered "a desperate plan", of scaling the cliff below the Plains via Anse de Foulon, and on the morning of September 16 Montcalm awoke to find the British drawn up a couple of kilometres from the city's gate. The hastily assembled French battalions, flanked by aboriginal warriors, were badly organized and rushed headlong at the British, whose volleys of gunfire mortally wounded Montcalm. On his deathbed Montcalm wrote a chivalrous note of congratulations to Wolfe, not knowing that he was dead. Québec City surrendered four days later. The park's **Discovery Pavilion**, below the tourist office at 835 av Wilfrid-Laurier est (late June to early Sept daily 8.30am–5.30pm, early

Sept to late June Mon–Fri 8.30am–5pm, Sat 9am–5pm, Sun 10am–5pm; ⓣ418/648-4071, ⓦwww.ccbn-nbc.gc.ca; $8 or $10 for a day pass including other attractions), has maps, information panels and a multimedia show, which does a reasonable job of covering the after-effects of the Conquest, marred by irksome 3D-enhanced "interviews" with Wolfe, Montcalm and other historical personages.

The dead of 1759 are commemorated by a statue of Joan of Arc in a beautifully maintained sunken **garden** just off av Wilfrid-Laurier at Place Montcalm by the Ministry of Justice. More conspicuous, standing out amid the wooded parklands, scenic drives, jogging paths and landscaped gardens, are two Martello towers, built between 1805 and 1812 for protection against the Americans. Martello Tower 2, on the corner of Wilfrid-Laurier and Taché, hosts period dinner events (call ⓣ418/649-6157 for information and tickets), whilst **Martello Tower 1** (late June to early Sept 10am–5pm; $4), further south in the park, has superb views of the St Lawrence from its rooftop lookout. The views are almost as good from the base of the tower, and you don't have to pay for an unmemorable exhibition in order to reach the top; children get to dress up in costumes for the optional tour, though. Further west, outside the Musée National des Beaux-Arts du Québec, there's a monument to General Wolfe, whose body was shipped back to England for burial, pickled in a barrel of rum. Beyond the park's western peripheries, cannons ring the perimeter of a large playing field and there's another lookout point above where Côte Gilmour winds down the cliffs at Anse de Foulon.

Musée National des Beaux-Arts du Québec

Canadian art had its quiet beginnings in Québec City and the full panoply of this output can be found on the western edge of the Parc des Champs-de-Bataille in the **Musée National des Beaux-Arts du Québec** (June to early Sept daily 10am–6pm, rest of the year Tues–Sun 10am–5pm, all year Wed until 9pm; $12; ⓣ418/643-2150 or 1-866/220-2150, ⓦwww.mnba.qc.ca; bus #11). The Grand Hall, with its cruciform skylight, connects the museum's two buildings (its original home, the Pavillon Gérard-Morisset, and a renovated Victorian prison renamed the Pavillon Charles-Baillairgé) and also serves as the main entrance.

For a chronological tour, start with Gallery 7 on the second floor of the **Pavillon Gérard-Morisset**, which provides a good survey of Québecois art from the early seventeenth to late nineteenth centuries. As Québec churches were the primary art commissioners at the time, most of the earliest works are **religious art**, including the output of **Frère Luc**, represented here by *The Guardian Angel*. The most notable contributions to the collection are by two dynasties: the works of brothers **Pierre-Noël** and **François-Noël Levasseur** from the mid-1700s and the three generations of **Baillairgés** who succeeded them, their copious output including the architecture of churches as well as their interior decoration. Under the British, the subject matter broadened to include portraiture, seen here in **Antoine Plamondon**'s poised *Madame Tourangeau*, and Canadian landscapes by Québec-born **Joseph Légaré** and, more famously, Amsterdam-born **Cornelius Krieghoff**, noted for his romanticized landscapes of landmarks in the region.

Gallery 8, opposite, covers the period from 1860 to 1945, from the late-nineteenth-century **salons** to the development of **modernist art**. In the first room, paintings fight for space on the walls; one that grabs your attention as you enter is **Horatio Walker**'s *Ploughing, the First Gleam at Dawn*, a romantic vision of the lives of the French-Canadian *habitants* who so engrossed him that he repudiated his Ontario roots. The tug-of-war of styles in Europe is played out in many of the subsequent works, including **Maurice Cullen**'s Impressionist-influenced view onto Basse-Ville, *Wolfe's Cove*, and the evocative scene of a horse-drawn carriage in a snowstorm, *Craig Street, Montréal*. Urban life is also admirably recorded by **Adrien Hébert**'s *Rue St-Denis*, which wonderfully captures the spirit of Montréal in the 1920s.

Downstairs, in gallery 2, the impact of **Alfred Pellan**, who returned from Paris in 1940 to teach at Montréal's École des Beaux-Arts, plays out in the development of post-war **figurative** and **abstract art**. His comparative radicalism, evident in his Cubist-influenced still life, *Flowers and Dominoes*, was the catalyst for a generation of Québecois artists to pick up on the avant-garde movements of the time. The move to non-figurative representation can be seen in **Jean Dallaire**'s softly muted abstract figures in his 1957 *Julie*, which contrasts with his surreally colourful and strident *Coq Licorne* (Unicorn Rooster) painted five years earlier. The process reaches its apogee with the Neo-Plasticism represented by **Fernand Leduc**'s boldly coloured geometric abstract *The Mountain Climber*.

At the same time, two of Québec's best-known artists were developing their signature styles. **Paul-Émile Borduas** applied the automatic writing technique of the surrealists to painting – his *Cabalistic Signs* is almost a doodle in oils. His progression to the increasingly spare canvases that have rooms devoted to them in Montréal's museums (see pp.256-258) can also be noted here. Gallery 3, across the hall, is devoted solely to the work of **Jean-Paul Riopelle**. The gallery's highlight is his *L'Hommage à Rosa Luxemburg* (1992), a 40-metre-long triptych in thirty segments, with ghostly spray-painted outlines of birds and man-made objects.

In the **Pavillon Charles-Baillairgé**, the red brick interior walls of the former jail have been spruced up, creating a warm atmosphere surprisingly conducive to displaying art. Vaillancourt's *Tree on rue Durocher* sweeps up into the atrium, which then leads visitors into the galleries and a few of the old prison cells. These lie en route to gallery 10, where "Je me souviens" portrays the personages and events in Québec's history through paintings and sculptures by some of the province's leading artists, and includes the studies for public works by sculptors Louis-Philippe Hébert and Alfred Laliberté. In the prison's tower, Montréal sculptor David Moore has created a unique two-storey sculpture of bodies scaling walls – just what you might expect in an old prison.

Gallery 12 on the third floor is devoted to Québec-born painter Jean-Paul Lemieux. His style varies wildly, from landscapes inspired by the Group of Seven such as the Charlevoix-set *Afternoon Sunlight*, through a phase of folk-art-style painting (including a fun look at the Corpus Christi parade winding down côte de la Montagne), to end with a series of uncluttered Expressionist portraits.

A new, but permanent, addition to the museum is the remarkable **Brousseau collection of Innuit Art**. Collected over 50 years from across the Arctic, the collection traces the development of Inuit art from the naive works of the mid-twentieth century to the highly narrative and intricately carved sculptures by contemporary artists. The few ancient items include simple ivory works from the nomadic Dorset and Thulé cultures. Stone sculpture really began in the 1940s, replacing the declining fur and hunting industries as a source of income – the Inuit artists used aspects of everyday life such as animals and hunting for inspiration.

Basse-Ville

The birthplace of Québec City, **Basse-Ville** (Lower Town), can be reached from Terrasse Dufferin either by the steep **escalier casse-cou** (Breakneck Stairs) or by the **funicular** alongside (daily 7.30am–11pm, until midnight in summer; Ⓣ418/692-1132, Ⓦwww.funiculaire-quebec.com; $1.50). The Basse-Ville station of the funicular is the 1683 **Maison Louis-Jolliet**, 16 rue du Petit-Champlain, built for the retired discoverer of the Mississippi, Louis Jolliet; it now houses a second-rate souvenir shop.

Dating back to 1685, the narrow, cobbled **rue du Petit-Champlain** is the city's oldest street, and the surrounding area – known as **Quartier du Petit-Champlain** – is the oldest shopping area in North America. The boutiques and art shops in the quaint seventeenth- and eighteenth-century houses are not too overpriced and offer an array of excellent crafts, from Inuit carvings to the products of the glass-blowing workshop and gallery, **Verrerie La Mailloche** (July–Oct daily 9am–10pm, Nov–June Sat–Wed 9.30am–5.30pm, Thurs & Fri till 9pm; Ⓣ418/694-0445, Ⓦwww.lamailloche.com), at the base of the escalier casse-cou. Older artefacts can be seen closer to the river, on the corner of rue du Marché Champlain and rue Notre-Dame, in the 1752 **Maison Chevalier** (May to late June & early Sept to mid-Oct Tues–Sun 10am–5pm; late June to early Sept daily 9.30am–5pm; Nov–April Sat & Sun 10am–5pm; Ⓣ418/646-3167, Ⓦwww.mcq.org; free), a grand town house and one-time London Coffee House, where merchants would meet throughout the nineteenth century. Its rooms excellently depict interior scenes comprising period furniture, costumes and domestic objects – compare the plush drawing room of a nineteenth-century bourgeois family with the all-in-one common room a tradesman and his family might have occupied a century earlier. Take a peek, too, into the vaulted cellars, where local artisans sell traditional works.

Place Royale and around

From here it's a short walk along rue Notre-Dame to **Place Royale**, where Champlain built New France's first permanent settlement in 1608, to begin trading fur with the aboriginal peoples. The square – known as Place du Marché until the bust of Louis XIV was erected here in 1686 – remained the focal point of Canadian commerce until 1759, and after the fall of Québec the British continued using the area as a lumber market, vital for shipbuilding during the Napoleonic Wars. After 1860 Place Royale was left to fall into disrepair, a situation reversed as recently as the 1970s, when the scruffy area was renovated. Its pristine stone houses, most of which date from around 1685, are undeniably photogenic, with their steep metal roofs, numerous chimneys and pastel-coloured shutters, but it's a Legoland townscape, devoid of the scars of history. Fortunately, the atmosphere is enlivened in summer by entertainment from classical orchestras to juggling clowns, and by the Fêtes de la Nouvelle-France (see box, p.299), when everyone dresses in period costume and it once again becomes a chaotic marketplace.

In Maison Hazeur, a merchant's house dating in part to 1684, the **interpretation centre** at 27 rue Notre-Dame (late June to early Sept daily 9.30am–5pm; early Sept to late June Tues–Sun 10am–5pm; Ⓣ418/646-3167, Ⓦwww.mcq.org; $4), outlines the stormy past of Place Royale, the mercantile aspects and the changes in the look of the square from the days when it was inhabited by the Iroquois to its recent renovation – search out the tucked away exhibit on level one rather than sitting through the hokey multimedia show. Domestic objects and arrowheads are on the upper floors, from where you can see Gille's

Girard's *À rebrousse-temps*, an enigmatic three-storey sculpture that plays with the idea of determining an artefact's original purpose. The vaulted cellars have modern-looking displays of 1800s domestic scenes and kids can try on period costumes and act out a role.

The **Église Notre-Dame-des-Victoires** (daily May to mid-Oct 9.30am–5pm, rest of the year 10am–4pm; ⓣ418/692-1650; free), on the west side of the square, nearly always has a wedding in progress during the summer. It was built by Laval in 1688 but has been completely restored twice – after being destroyed by shellfire in 1759 and a fire in 1969. Inside, the fortress-shaped altar alludes to the two French victories over the British navy that gave the church its name: the destruction of Admiral Phipps' fleet by Frontenac in 1690 and the sinking of Sir Hovenden Walker's fleet in 1711. Paintings depicting these events hang above the altar, while the aisles are lined with copies of religious paintings by Van Dyck, Van Loo and Rubens, gifts from early settlers to give thanks for a safe passage. The large model ship suspended in the nave has a similar origin.

Place Royale exits to the east past rue St-Pierre – the heart of the old financial district – onto **Place de Paris**, where a white cubic sculpture called *Dialogue with History* marks the disembarkation place of the first settlers from France. Visible to the south (but accessible only from rue St-Pierre), the **Batterie Royal**, a crenellated rampart trimly restored in the 1970s, was used to defend the city during the siege of 1759. The **ferry to Lévis** (6.30am–2am; ⓣ1-877/787-7483, ⓦwww.traversiers.gouv.qc.ca; $2.60 one-way; see p.326) leaves from the waterfront just to the southeast.

Musée de la Civilisation

A walk north along rue Dalhousie from Place de Paris brings you to one of Québec City's most impressive museums, the **Musée de la Civilisation**, 85 rue Dalhousie (late June to early Sept daily 9.30am–6.30pm; otherwise Tues–Sun 10am–5pm; $8; Nov–May free on Tues; ⓣ418/643-2158, ⓦwww.mcq.org). Designed by prominent Canadian architect Moshe Safdie, the museum references the steep-pitched roofs of the early settlers in a structure that incorporates a rooftop terrace with great views and three historic buildings – be sure to check out the vaulted cellars in the 1751 **Maison Estèbe**, which survived the British bombardment to eventually become the museum's gift shop (ask for the leaflet detailing the house's history). In the main foyer, a 1730s barque discovered on the site is displayed between a stone wall (the edge of the quay built a couple of decades later) and Astri Reusch's *La Débâcle*, a sculpture that symbolizes the break-up of the ice in the spring thaw.

Concentrating primarily on Canadian subjects but also diversifying into a worldwide perspective, the museum presents engaging temporary exhibitions that have ranged from whimsical pop culture interests to serious looks at earlier historical periods. The first of the two permanent exhibitions upstairs, **Memories**, expertly displays life in Québec from the early days of the settlers to the present (pick up an English-language text at the entrance). Cross the atrium for the **Encounter with the First Nations** exhibition, set up in consultation with all eleven of the First Nations of Québec. It presents the history and culture of these earlier residents using artefacts and videotaped oral histories; the larger items – including a *rabaska*, an enormous birch-bark canoe – were crafted in recent years.

Vieux-Port and around

To the east and north, near the confluence of the St Charles and the St Lawrence rivers, lies the **Vieux-Port de Québec**, the busiest harbour in the province until its gradual eclipse by Montréal at the end of the 19th century. Much of the harbour has been renovated as a recreational area, with theatres, yuppie flats, sheltered walkways, restaurants and a marina packed with pleasure boats and yachts. The **Marché du Vieux-Port** (March–Nov daily from 8am) is a throwback to how the port used to be – its busy market stalls selling cheap, fresh produce from the local area.

Also on the south side of the Bassin Louise, the next street down from St-André is rue St-Paul, heart of Québec's **antiques district**. Numerous cluttered antique shops, art galleries, cafés and restaurants now occupy warehouses and offices abandoned after the demise of the port. From rue St-Paul the steep Côte du Colonel Dambourgès leads to rue des Remparts on the northern borders of Haute-Ville (see p.308).

Cartier-Brébeuf National Historic Site

Northwest of Vieux-Québec, on the banks of the St-Charles River (bus #4), the **Cartier-Brébeuf National Historic Site**, 175 de l'Espinay (daily early May to early Sept 10am–5pm; Sept 1–4pm; ⓣ418/648-4038, ⓦwww.pc.gc.ca/brebeuf; $4) has a double claim to fame. It marks the spot where Jacques Cartier spent the winter of 1535–36 in friendly contact with the people of the surrounding Iroquoian villages – a cordial start to a relationship that Cartier later soured by taking a local chief and nine of his men hostage. It is also where Jean de Brébeuf, with his Jesuit friends, built his first Canadian residence in 1625: Brébeuf is best known for his martyrdom near today's Midland in Ontario (see p.158). The **interpretation centre** features an excellent account of Cartier's voyages and of the hardship he and his crew endured during the winter and a backgrounder on the Jesuits' role in New France. The guided tour of the site (included in the entrance fee) leads to a mock-up of an Iroquoian longhouse and sweat lodge set within a palisade, where costumed guides demonstrate daily tasks, mostly to the benefit of the kids. Keep an eye out for the resident muskrat.

Eating

It is when you start **eating** in Québec City that the French ancestry of the Québecois hits all the senses: the city's eateries present an array of culinary delights adopted from the mother country, from beautifully presented gourmet dishes to humble baguettes. Whether you are on a tight budget or not, the lively **cafés** are probably where you will want to spend your time, washing down bowls of soup and *croûtons* (toasted baguettes dripping with cheese) with plenty of coffee.

As you might expect, Vieux-Québec (both upper and lower) is home to most of the gourmet **restaurants** and cafés; within Haute-Ville's walls you'll generally find better value along rue St-Jean than rue St-Louis. Other areas have their fair share of eating spots as well – notably along rue St-Jean (quirky and cheaper) and, just outside the walls, Grande-Allée (generally touristy and expensive). Your best bet for good-value mid-price restaurants is to head for the numerous terrace-fronted establishments on avenue Cartier, near the Musée National des Beaux-Arts du Québec. Although prices in the city tend to be rather high, even the poshest restaurants have cheaper lunch-time and table d'hôte menus. For a change of taste, the dishes of other countries are also represented, including Italian, Greek and Thai. Strangely though, typical French-Canadian cooking – game with sweet sauces followed by simple desserts with lashings of maple syrup – is available at very few places in town, although the many *cabanes à sucre* on Île d'Orléans (see p.326) offer typical meals to tourists.

Cafés and snack outlets

A.L. Van Houtte 995 Place D'Youville. Reliable chain with sandwiches and salads until late evening. Internet access $6/hr.

Brûlerie Tatum Café 1084 rue St-Jean. All-day omelettes and light snacks. Exposed brick walls and roasting coffee beans provide ambience. Open 8am–11pm.

Buffet de l'Antiquaire 95 rue St-Paul. An old-school diner popular with locals for breakfast (from 6am) and home-cooked comfort food like *poutine* and *pâté chinois* (shepherd's pie).

Café Buade 31 rue Buade. In a central location, with good light breakfasts and passable bistro fare throughout the day. It's nicer upstairs. Open from 7am; evening table d'hote around $20.

Café Dépot 36 Côte de la Fabrique. Basic wraps, filled baguettes and pastries at the front of a convenience store. Open 24hr.

Le Casse-Cou 90 rue du Petit-Champlain. Cute little spot at the end of pedestrianized rue du Petit-Champlain for $5 breakfast fry-ups and decent light meals until 9pm.

Chez Temporel 25 rue Couillard. Bowls of steaming *café au lait*, croissants and *chocolatines* make this café, a few doors from the *Auberge de la Paix* hostel, a perfect place for breakfast. Soups and sandwiches are also available until 1.30am.

Kookening 565 rue St-Jean. Chilled-out café-bar with bright walls and board games. Mainly Tex-Mex menu with some eclectic choices like *Mole de canard confit* (duck with Aztec chocolate sauce) and kaiser rolls filled with tandoori chicken. Daily from 4pm.

L'Omelette 66 rue St-Louis. Adequate tourist joint with omelette specialities; breakfast from 7am, evening meals from $10.

L'Orange Bleue 526 rue St-Jean. A tiny cooperative vegetarian café with changing art displays and music acts on various nights. Closed Mon; no lunch weekends.

Tutto Gelato 716 rue St-Jean. Fantastic Italian ice cream (with a few soya varieties thrown in) five minutes west of the walls. There's another at 1190 av Cartier.

Restaurants

Haute-Ville (within the walls)

L'Apsara 71 rue d'Auteuil ⓣ418/694-0232. Cambodian, Vietnamese and Thai food in a muted dining room near the Porte St-Louis. Three-course lunch is around $20, dinners in the $30 region.

Aux Anciens Canadiens 34 rue St-Louis ⓣ418/692-1627. This overly expensive and touristy restaurant (table d'hôte around $35) is in one of the oldest homes in Québec City. It serves refined Québecois specialities like *tourtière* (meat pie) and *pattes de cochon* (pigs' trotters) and house inventions such as duck glazed with maple syrup and caribou in blueberry-wine sauce.

Café de la Paix 44 rue des Jardins ⓣ418/692-1430. The desserts in the front window taste as good as they look, and the rest of the menu – pricey French classics and game for around $30 – is equally delicious. Closed Sun.

Casse-Crêpe Breton 1136 rue St-Jean ⓣ418/692-0438. Diner-style restaurant where crepes are made in front of you with two or three fillings, costing around $5. There's often a queue, but it moves quickly. 7am to around 11pm.

Charles Baillairgé At *Hôtel Clarendon*, 57 rue Ste-Anne ⓣ418/692-2480. Opened in 1870, this is supposedly Canada's oldest restaurant and serves classic French cuisine. Expect to pay upwards of $40 for dinner and dress is formal.

Conti Caffe 32 rue St-Louis ⓣ418/692-4191. Sharing the kitchen of *Le Continental* next door, this casual Italian eatery is the best choice on a street swamped with mediocre, touristy restaurants. Veal is a speciality – the medallions in porcini mushroom sauce are rich and succulent. The evening table d'hôte is great value at around $25.

Le Continental 26 rue St-Louis ⓣ418/694-9995. Old-fashioned place down the street from the *Château Frontenac*. Seafood, veal and flambéed dishes appear on the three-course table d'hôte for $34–41.

La Crémaillère 21 rue St-Stanislas ⓣ418/692-2216. Superior French and Italian cuisine in a romantic, stone-walled 1829 residence that feels miles away from busy rue St-Jean just beyond the windows. Prices star at $30.

Les Frères de la Côte 1190 rue St-Jean ⓣ418/692-5445. A friendly and crowded bistro that draws locals as well as tourists for steaks, smoked salmon and great mussels moderately priced between $10 and $20. Make sure to check the daily specials on the blackboard.

Gambrinus 15 rue du Fort ⓣ418/692-5144. Good Italian and French food on the corner of Place d'Armes, with seafood specialities and a table d'hote regularly around $25. Musicians nightly.

La Maison de Serge Bruyère 1200 rue St-Jean ⓣ418/694-0618. Three restaurants under one roof: the *Restaurant la Grande Table* is one of the best in the city, serving fresh produce, beautifully prepared and presented. The eight-course *ménu découverte* ($85 per person, $145 with wine) is a French nouvelle cuisine extravaganza. Closed Sun & Mon. The adjacent *Bistro Livernois* is more affordable and the streetfront café even cheaper.

Au Petit Coin Breton 1029 rue St-Jean ⓣ418/694-0758. A pretty good and reasonably priced specialist creperie, where servers wear traditional Breton costume, serving dishes from $10.

Le Petit Coin Latin 8.5 rue Ste-Ursule ⓣ418/692-2022. Cosy café-bistro with a secluded courtyard. Raclette is a speciality, but they also serve steaks and a caribou *tourtière* (meat pie) for heartier appetites. Breakfast (7.30–11.30am, until 4pm weekends) ranges from straightforward fry-ups to eggs Benedict.

Le Rétro 1129 rue St-Jean ⓣ418/694-9218. Well-priced if touristy café-restaurant; serves everything from spaghetti to *filet mignon.*

Le St-Amour 48 rue Ste-Ursule ⓣ418/694-0667. Romantic French restaurant with a glass-roofed winter garden. Excellent food at around $85 for two – the foie gras is exquisite.

Haute-Ville (outside the walls)

L'Astral 1225 Place Montcalm ⓣ418/647-2222. Rotating restaurant on the top floor of the *Hôtel Loews Le Concorde.* The international menu is generally expensive, starting at $30, but the views can't be beaten. The all-you-can-eat Buffet Royal costs $40, half that at lunch.

Café Krieghoff 1089 av Cartier ⓣ418/522-3711, ⓦwww.cafekrieghoff.qc.ca. A typical French bistro *à la Québécois* that serves up some of the city's best coffee, big breakfasts and light meals, including traditional *croûtons* (a baguette topped with garlic butter and melted cheese), for around $16. Good spot to sit and read or write in the day, especially on the terrace.

Le Cochon Dingue 46 boul René-Lévesque ouest ⓣ418/523-2013. Close to av Cartier, this branch draws locals rather than tourists, as in Basse-Ville. Mains from $15.

Le Commensal 860 rue St-Jean ⓣ418/647-3733. Great spot for vegetarians five minutes from Vieux-Québec's gates. Buffet where the food is sold by weight.

Cosmos Café 575 Grande-Allée est ⓣ418/640-0606. By far the best spot on the Grande-Allée – cool decor, great breakfasts and imaginative menu from $10. Crowded and lively at lunch and for the *cinq à sept* cocktail hour.

Garam Massala 1114 av Cartier ⓣ418/522-4979. Indian restaurant in a cosy basement specializing in tandoori chicken. Dinner for two is around $38, lunch for $10 or less a head.

Le Graffiti 1191 av Cartier ⓣ418/529-4949. Chic French-Italian restaurant with decent lunch specials that also does a good Sunday brunch (10am–3pm). Table d'hote from $20.

Le Hobbit 700 rue St-Jean ⓣ418/647-2677. A popular local spot where a mixed studenty crowd come for the great vegetarian options, as well as burgers, pasta and bistro dishes like steak and trout filet.

Jaune Tomate 120 boul René-Lévesque ouest ⓣ418/523-8777, ⓦwww.jaunetomate.com. Terrace-fronted house with tasty and reasonably priced Italian dishes like *osso bucco, linguini del mare* and a range of pizzas. The two-course lunch is a good filler-upper at around $10.

Piazzetta 707 rue St-Jean ⓣ418/529-7489. Trendy pizzeria with funky furnishings – the pizzas come close to perfection and are quite cheap – a good meal for 2 plus drinks will come to less than $40. There's another in Basse-Ville at 63 rue St-Paul (ⓣ418/529-7489).

Pizzédélic 1145 av Cartier ⓣ418/525-5981. Trendy spot with creative pizzas and pastas for as little at $11 and a large, packed terrace.

Basse-Ville

Aviatic Club Gare du Palais ⓣ418/522-3555. Surprisingly good international cuisine from $20 including sushi, Thai and Tex-Mex in a historic train station with a large patio alongside.

Le Café du Monde 84 rue Dalhousie ⓣ418/692-4455, ⓦwww.lecafedumonde.com. This large and sleek Parisian-style bistro may be in the cruise ship terminal, but it's a hit with locals for its brash atmosphere and fantastic terrace overlooking the St Lawrence. And the food – mussels, veal sweetbreads, *confit de canard*, steak tartare and the like – is quite good, too.

Le Délice du Roy 33 rue St-Pierre ⓣ418/694-9161. Around the corner from Place Royale, this place dishes up hearty if plain traditional Québecois food for between $10 and $20.

L'Échaudé 72 rue du Sault-au-Matelot ⓣ418/692-1299. Upscale but unpretentious bistro with a terrace on the pedestrian portion of the street. A good selection of wines accompanies bistro classics like *confit de canard*, steak tartare and stuffed quail for around $30.

Initiale Le Restaurant 54 rue St-Pierre ⓣ418/694-1818. One of Québec City's best restaurants, and priced accordingly ($49 table d'hôte). A chic place with a lighter take on fine French classics.

Le Lapin Sauté 52 rue du Petit-Champlain ⓣ418/692-5325. Very popular, informal bistro specializing in rabbit – even the breakfast menu ($10) includes a rabbit dish. Dinner for $20–30.

Laurie Raphael 117 rue Dalhousie ⓣ418/692-4555, ⓦwww.laurieraphael.com. Warm but formal atmosphere in a restaurant focusing on *cuisine du marché* (market cuisine). Specialities include fish, sweetbreads, Québec venison and scallops from the Mingan Islands. The three course Chef Menu startes at $23 for lunch and $60 for dinner.

Le Marie Clarisse 12 rue du Petit-Champlain ⓣ418/692-0857. Fine fish and market-fresh seafood in a tiny stone-walled restaurant at the foot of the *escalier casse-cou*. A four-course meal goes for $40–45; advance booking advised. A good spot for people-watching.

Poisson d'Avril 115 quai St-André ⓣ418/692-1010. Seafood and grilled steaks in the $30 plus range near the Vieux-Port.

Bars and nightlife

Nightlife in Québec City is far more relaxed than in Montréal: an evening spent in an intimate bar or a jazz or blues soiree is more popular than a big gig or disco, except among the younger set. Few major bands tour here, except during the Festival d'Été in July, when everyone lets their hair down. Québec City's main bar and nightclub strip is around rue St-Jean; the stretch outside the city walls in the Faubourg St-Jean-Baptiste has studenty bars and gay nightspots. Places on Grande-Allée tend to cater to tourists, but there are a few decent clubs at either end of the strip. For up-to-date **information** check the local media.

Bars and music venues

L'Amour Sorcier 789 Côte Ste-Geneviève. Popular, intimate lesbian bar with cheap beers, soft music (which gets louder and more danceable later on) and a great roof terrace.

Chez Son Père 24 rue St-Stanislas ⓦwww.barchezsonpere.qc.ca. Overlooking rue St-Jean in Vieux-Québec. Québecois folk singers create a great thigh-slapping atmosphere. Free admission and drink specials.

Le Drague 815 rue St-Augustin ⓦwww.ledrague.com. A gay bar, café and nightclub, with cheap imported beers. Sunday night drag shows are great fun.

L'Emprise *Hôtel Clarendon*, 57 rue Ste-Anne. Art Deco surroundings attract a sophisticated touristy crowd to evenings of smooth jazz and blues (nightly 9.30pm, weekends only in winter; free).

L'Étrange 275 rue St-Jean ⓦwww.etrange.qc.ca. Relaxed upstairs bar with regular two-for-one specials and a mix of rock tunes from the speakers. Twenty-something crowd.

Le Fou Bar 525 rue St-Jean. Packed studenty hangout with table football and cheap beer.

L'Inox 37 quai St-André. The city's original brewpub, serving artisanal cheeses and European sausages to go with the fine ales.

Jules et Jim 1060 av Cartier. Long-time local hangout, it's a small, quiet place amidst all the restaurants on av Cartier.

Le Pape-Georges 8 rue Cul-de-Sac ⓦwww.papegeorges.com. Tiny cellar of a bar near Place Royale with acoustic acts and pavement terrace serving cheeses and smoked meats. Popular with the locals.

Pub Java 1112 av Cartier. Good selection of imported and draught beers and you can even come back for breakfast. The Irish pub *Salon Galway* upstairs has large armchairs by the fireplace.

Le Pub St-Alexandre 1087 rue St-Jean ⓦwww.pubstalexandre.com. More than 200 beers and 40 single malts in this yuppie English-style pub.

Sacrilège 447 rue St-Jean. Friendly and cheap watering hole with a popular terrace in back. In the Faubourg St-Jean-Baptiste.

Bar Ste-Angèle 26 rue Ste-Angèle. A dark and smoky neighbourhood bar with a beamed ceiling and cozy nook that hasn't noticed it's in the middle of tourist central. Open from 8pm.

Bar St-Laurent 1 rue des Carrières ⓣ418/692-3861. The Château Frontenac address may be a bit stuffy and alcohol pricey at the polished octagonal bar, but you don't need to dress to the nines and the view from the terrace is stupendous.

Les Yeux Bleus 1117 rue St-Jean. Despite the name, there's no blues at this *boîte à chansons* tucked down an alleyway. You can catch acoustic acts in the dark and smoky interior or hang out on the crowded and lively terrace.

Clubs and discos

Casablanca 1169 rue St-Jean Weekend dance club playing reggae, African and Arabic beats hidden away down a passageway off rue St-Jean. Only gets going around 11pm (Fri & Sat only). No cover.

Dagobert 600 Grande-Allée est ⓦwww.dagobert.ca. This sprawling old house has been one of the city's most raucous nightspots for decades. Young dressed-up-for-it clubbers head upstairs for the large Eighties-ish dance floor. Downstairs a slightly older crowd sit at tiered tables to catch cover bands from 10.30pm. There's rarely a cover charge.

Kashmir 1018 rue St-Jean. Loud and packed full some nights, dead others, depending on the DJ or the band playing. Very young crowd, usually.

Maurice 575 Grande-Allée est ⓦwww.mauricenightclub.com. Happening club with a rotating crew of DJs that attracts a stylish 20s to mid-30s crowd for R&B and house nights (Wed–Sun only in winter). Dress up to get by the selective door policy. The $3 cover ($4 on weekends) includes the more laid-back *Charlotte* upstairs, with couches for chilling out or smoking a cigar, though on the funk and latino nights it can be just as hopping.

Sonar 1147 av Cartier. Swish basement club-lounge that grooves to R&B on Thursdays and house on the weekend after the tapas plates have been cleared away. Mid-20s to mid-30s crowd.

Zazou 811 rue St-Jean. Mixed gay club with a mezzanine-encircled dance floor and a chilled bar and packed terrace off to the side.

Performing arts and cinema

Québec City is not especially renowned for its high culture, but from May to September there are dance, theatre and music events at various outdoor venues, and throughout the year performances can be caught at the city's theatres. The liveliest periods are in February and July, when the entire city is animated by its two principal **festivals**: the excellent Carnaval and the equally frenzied Festival d'Été (see box, p.299). **Tickets** for most events can be purchased through the Admission agency (ⓣ1-800/361-4595, ⓦwww.admission.com) and Réseau Billetech (ⓦwww.billetech.com). For up-to-date **information** on the city's goings-on, check out the listings section in the French daily newspapers *Le Soleil* and *Journal de Québec* and the free weekly newspaper *Voir* (ⓦwww.voir.ca). The quarterly bilingual magazine for tourists *Voilà Québec* also carries information, as does the English *Québec Chronicle Telegraph* (ⓦwww.qctonline.com), published every Wednesday.

Québec City has a fair smattering of **theatres**, all producing plays in French only. The city's main theatre for the performing arts is the Grand Théâtre de Québec, 269 boul René-Lévesque est (ⓣ418/643-8131, ⓦwww.grandtheatre.qc.ca), which has a sound programme of drama, as well as opera, dance shows and classical music concerts. For small-scale dramatic productions, check out the Théâtre de la Bordée, 315 rue St-Joseph est (ⓣ418/694-9721, ⓦwww.bordee.qc.ca), while Théâtre Le Capitole, 972 rue St-Jean (ⓣ418/694-4444 or 1-800/261-9903, ⓦwww.lecapitole.com), hosts dinner theatre, cabaret and flashy musicals. Canada's oldest symphony **orchestra**, L'Orchestre Symphonique de Québec (ⓦwww.osq.org), performs at the Grand Théâtre, as does the Opéra de Québec (ⓦwww.operadequebec.qc.ca) and the chamber ensemble Les Violons du Roy (ⓦwww.violonsduroy.com). Other **classical concerts** can be caught at the Bibliothèque Gabrielle-Roy, 350 rue St-Joseph est. Seventeenth- and eighteenth-century music is performed at the chapel in the Séminaire in summer. In summer,

Spectator sports in Québec City

Ice hockey Les Remparts de Québec (ⓦwww.remparts.qc.ca), of the Québec Major Junior Hockey League, play at the Colisée Pepsi, 250 boul Wilfred-Hamel (tickets ⓣ418/691-7211 or 1-800/900-SHOW). Season is mid-Sept to April and tickets start at $12.

open-air venues are particularly popular in Québec. The largest is the Agora, in the Vieux-Port at 120 rue Dalhousie, a huge amphitheatre used for a range of productions from comedies to classical music. A summer-long programme of activities is also enacted on open stages in the Jardins de l'Hôtel de Ville; at the Parc de la Francophonie beside Grande-Allée, just beyond the Parliament Buildings; and in the Place D'Youville. In Place Royale and at the Kiosque Edwin-Bélanger bandstand on the Plains of Abraham, there are various free classical music concerts in the summer.

Most **cinemas** are out in the suburbs – the most convenient are the multiplexes in Ste-Foy's shopping malls, which occasionally have some undubbed English films. Films are often listed under their English titles, but make sure that it says "**v.o.a.**" (original English version) or "**s-t.f.**" (in the original language but with French subtitles); The city's rep cinema, Cinéma le Clap, also in Ste-Foy at no. 2360 chemin Ste-Foy (ⓦwww.clap.qc.ca; bus; #7), has the odd English film, too – pick up their monthly programme at cafés and bookstores.

Listings

Airport enquiries ⓣ418/640-2700, ⓦwww.aeroportdequebec.com.

Banks and currency exchange American Express, Place Laurier, 2700 boul Laurier, Ste-Foy (ⓣ418/658-8820); Banque Royale, 700 Place d'Youville and 140 Grande-Allée est. Caisse Populaire Desjardins du Vieux-Québec, 19 rue des Jardins (summer daily 9am–6pm; winter Mon–Fri 10am–3pm, Thurs until 6pm) has exchange facilities and a 24hr cashpoint (ATM) in Vieux-Québec; as does Banque Nationale, 1199 rue St-Jean (summer: Mon–Fri 9am–8pm, Sat & Sun 9.30am–8pm (May, June, Sept & Oct daily until 6pm only); winter: Mon–Thurs 9am–5pm, Fri 9am–4.30pm).

Bike and blade rental Vélo Passe-Sport Plein Air, 22 Côte du Palais (ⓣ418/692-3643) is conveniently situated, but Cyclo Services, in the Marché du Vieux-Port, 160 quai St-André (ⓣ418/692-4052; ⓦwww.cycloservices.net), is cheaper and is next to the bike trail. Information on cycle trails from Promo-Vélo (ⓣ418/522-0087).

Bookshops The two main English bookshops are in the suburb of Ste-Foy: Librairie Smith, Place Laurier, 2700 boul Laurier; and La Maison Anglaise, Place de la Cité, 2600 boul Laurier. In Vieux-Québec there's a small selection at Pantoute, 1100 rue St-Jean, and a counter selling travel books inside the tourist office on Place d'Armes.

Car rental Avis, *Hôtel Hilton*, 900 boul René-Lévesque est ⓣ418/523-1075, and at the airport ⓣ418/872-2861; Budget, 380 boul Wilfred-Hamel ouest ⓣ418/687-4220, 29 Côte du Palais ⓣ418/692-3660, and at the airport ⓣ418/872-9885; Discount, 12 rue Ste-Anne ⓣ418/692-1244; Hertz, airport ⓣ418/871-1571, 44 Côte du Palais ⓣ418/694-1224, and 580 Grande-Allée est ⓣ418/647-4949; Thrifty, near the airport at 6375 boul Wilfred-Hamel ⓣ418/877-2870.

Consulate US, 2 Place Terrasse-Dufferin ⓣ418/692-2095.

Gay and lesbian life Gai Écoute and Gay Line (ⓣ1-888/505-1010; in English 7–11pm only).

Laundry Lavoir la Lavandière, 625 rue St-Jean (Mon–Sat 8am–9pm, Sun 9am–6pm); Lavoir Ste-Ursule, 17B av Ste-Ursule (daily 8am–9pm).

Left luggage $2 lockers in the bus station.

Medical emergencies 24hr medical advice and referral service ⓣ418/648-2626. Hôtel-Dieu Hospital, 11 Côte du Palais (ⓣ418/691-5042), is in Vieux-Québec; Jeffrey Hale Hospital, 1250 chemin Ste-Foy (ⓣ418/683-4471), is better for English-speakers. Dental emergencies ⓣ418/653-5412

(Mon 8am–8pm, Tues 8am–7pm, Wed & Thurs 8am–5pm, Fri 8am–4pm) or ⓣ418/656-6060 (Sat 10am–3pm, Sun 10am–1pm; emergencies only).

Parking In Vieux-Québec off rue Pierre-Olivier Chauveau (below the Hôtel de Ville); rue Haldimand (near the Jardin des Gouverneurs). Outside the walls at av Wilfrid-Laurier outside Porte St-Louis; near Place D'Youville; rue Dalhousie in the Vieux-Port. Long-term parking is opposite the bus terminal.

Pharmacy The only late-closing pharmacy is Pharmacie Brunet, Les Galeries Charlesbourg, 4250 av 1ère, in the northwesterly suburb of Charlesbourg (daily 8am–10.30pm; ⓣ418/623-1571).

Post office 300 rue St-Paul and 5 rue du Fort. All are open Mon–Fri 8am–5.30pm and have a free internet station (max 15min).

Ridesharing Allo-Stop, 665 rue St-Jean (ⓣ418/522-0056, ⓦwww.allostop.com).

Taxis Taxi Coop ⓣ418/525-5191; Taxi Québec ⓣ418/525-8123.

Weather and road conditions Environment Canada (ⓣ418/648-7766, ⓦwww.weatheroffice.ec.gc.ca) for recorded weather forecast; Transports Québec (ⓣ1-888/355-0511, ⓦwww.mtq.gouv.qc.ca) for roadworks and winter road conditions. Skiers can check snow conditions at ⓦwww.quebecskisurf.com.

Around Québec City

Options for day-trips on the fringes of the city include **Wendake**, to see the past and present crafts of Canada's only surviving Huron community and **Lévis**, on the opposite shore of the St Lawrence – less inundated by visitors than Québec City and with great views of its more illustrious neighbour. Also in easy striking distance of the city is tranquil, charming **Île d'Orléans** where the agricultural landscape is dotted with gîtes and auberges, and the homes of the well heeled. Slightly further afield the tiny island of **Grosse Ile** has served as a secretive quarantine station for more than a century and is now a National Historic Site. Both the islands are just offshore of the **Côte-de-Beaupré** further to the northeast, which, though something of a city annexe, boasts the spectacular waterfalls of **Chute Montmorency** and the **Canyon Ste-Anne**. For those in search of a longer jaunt into the great outdoors, the **Réserve Faunique des Laurentides** is within easy reach and there are a number of **ski hills** in the area.

City **buses** and bicycle paths run to Chute Montmorency and Wendake, a quick **ferry** trip lands you in Lévis and Intercar buses go daily to **Ste-Anne-de-Beaupré**.

Wendake

Just to the northwest of Québec City lies **WENDAKE**, the only **Huron reserve** in Canada. Its name derives from the Hurons' own name for their people – *Wendat*, meaning "people of the island". In 1650, French Jesuit missionaries led three hundred Huron from Ontario's Georgian Bay to the shores of the St Lawrence around today's Vieux-Québec, thereby saving the smallpox-weakened population from extermination at the hands of the Iroquois. As more French settlers arrived, the Hurons were successively relocated, ending up here beside the St-Charles River in 1697. Today, with a population of 1600, the central village core of the reserve retains typical Québecois wooden houses with sloping and gabled roofs, but is rather dilapidated – the main activities for visitors are at Onhoüa Chetek8e (see below), though there is also a pretty waterfall.

In nice weather, the best way to get here is by bike – a 25km round trip along the bike path (La Route Vert 6) from the Vieux-Port; all the climbing is on the way there, making the journey back to town an easy cycle. The STCUQ #801 bus runs from Place D'Youville to its terminus at Charlesbourg, from where the

#72 goes to Wendake; get a transfer (*une correspondance*) and the 45-minute or so journey will set you back $2.50. The bus arrives at the 1730 church of **Notre Dame-de-Lorette** on boul Bastien. This is Canada's only Huron church, and you'll find snowshoes on the altar and a small museum displaying old manuscripts

Winter sports around Québec City

As you'd expect for a region that spends half its life under several feet of snow, winter activities are well developed around Québec City. You'll find good opportunities for just about every imaginable winter sport, particularly **cross-country skiing** and **ice-climbing**, but the most popular activites are **skiing** and **snowboarding** at three varied and challenging ski resorts – Stoneham, Mont-Sainte-Anne and Le Massif, which all lie within easy striking distance of Québec City. All are superbly equipped for intermediate skiers, while beginners will also find many good runs and excellent-value lesson, rental and lift ticket packages. Some experts in search of big bowls and deep powder snow might find the terrain a little limited, but for most, the fine steep mogul fields, tricky glades, well thought-out terrain parks and extensive night-skiing more than compensate. The resorts all get plenty of good snow. Le Massif and Mont-Sainte-Anne in particular are on the front line for storms travelling up the Saint-Lawrence Seaway laden with heavy Atlantic clouds. Yet at all three the combination of wind and busy weekend traffic – all the resorts are primarily day use areas – can polish many runs to an icy glaze.

The resorts

Nearest to town, only 6km beyond the city limits off Rte 73, is the pleasantly casual **Stoneham** (late Nov to early April Mon–Fri 9am–10pm, Sat 8.30am–10pm, Sun 8.30am–9pm; ⓣ418/848-2411 or 1-800/463-6888, ⓦwww.ski-stoneham.com; day pass $43), a locals' mountain with limited expert terrain, but loved for its closeness to the city as well as its position in a wind-protected horseshoe valley - a good place to shelter from cold temperatures and the harsh winds of the region's more brutally cold winter days. Despite a minimal vertical drop of 1,380ft and a modest 322 acres of terrain, the resort has been sculpted into an impressive ski area, thanks in part to its huge night skiing operation, which keeps around two-thirds of the resort open after dark, and attracts crowds from Québec City particularly at weekends, when the après ski can get wild.

The largest of Québec City's major ski areas is **Mont-Sainte-Anne** (mid-Nov to early May Mon 9am–4pm, Tues–Fri 9am-10pm, Sat 8.30am–10pm, Sun 8.30am–4pm; ⓣ418/827-4561 or 1-888/827-4579, ⓦwww.mont-sainte-anne.com; day pass $53) – 40km away via Rte 440, which becomes Rte 138, northeast out of town. It offers a well-balanced mix of terrain and comprehensive base area facilities. Centred on single peak and covering a mere 428 acres, it's easily navigable yet still provides a remarkably varied high-density trail system. The presence of novice runs extending from summit to base on both sides of the mountain is particularly pleasing, while first-timers can benefit from free access to bunny slopes conveniently adjoining the base area. The resort's greatest strength, however, is its wealth of intermediate-level pistes that make up almost half the ski zone. Most start from the resort's rapid gondola to follow a consistently smooth and steep grade back to the minimal lift queues at its base. The resort's smoothly efficient night-skiing operation even keeps fifteen of these runs open until 10pm. Those hunting for steeps, moguls, trees and high-speed carving will quickly find their niche among a cluster of black diamonds on the south side of the trail map. Here steep terrain ensures empty pistes, even though the fall-line is beautifully even.

The third main mountain in the area is **Le Massif** (early Dec to early April opening hours vary throughout the season but are at least 9am–3pm, longer at weekends;

and religious objects. To get into the church, you must first visit the **Maison Aroüanne** opposite (late June to late Aug daily 10am–5pm; free), an early wooden house displaying a collection of Huron cultural objects, including ceremonial attire beaded with pearls and porcupine quills, drums of moose hide

Ⓣ418/632-5876 or 1-877/536-2774, Ⓦwww.lemassif.com; day pass $52), around an hour's drive from Québec City, 73km along Rte 138. Towering above the majestic ice floes that speckle the vast expanse of the St Lawrence Seaway to the horizon, Le Massif has some of the most spectacular views of any resort in the world, so stunning that it can be distracting as you make your way down the resort's more taxing slopes. In spite of the presence of a couple of narrow, tricky and busy beginner runs, Le Massif is best at providing wonderful intermediate-level carving slopes. In addition, the mountain's painstaking grooming regime puts several black diamond runs well within the capacity of intermediates. But to ski Le Massif's moguls, or its pride, the terrifying triple-diamond La Charlevoix, you'll need plenty of talent and you'll find yourself rubbing shoulders with international athletes on this hugely steep racecourse.

Many **other sports** are also possible: tubing, ice-skating and an indoor climbing wall at Stoneham; and ice-skating, snowshoeing, dog-sledding, paragliding, sleigh riding and snowmobiling at Mont-Sainte-Anne. From mid-December to mid-April the **Mont-Sainte-Anne Nordic Center**, 7km east of the ski area base, is a splendid local resource – the largest of its kind in Canada. It boasts over 223km of trails, of which over half are set up for skating. There are plenty of trails through hardwoods and evergreens, also expert possibilities to ascend and ski down some double-black diamond rated terrain. Day tickets to the network cost $17, rentals another $15, and lessons are also available. For more of a wilderness experience cross-country skiers should also explore the rolling hills around Camp Mercier (see p.333) which are suitable for every level of skier. Back down the highway, and just on the fringes of Québec City at Montmorency Falls (see p.330), is the world's largest **ice-climbing** school, L'Ascensation Ecole d'escalade (Ⓣ1-800/762-4967, Ⓦwww.rocgyms.com), which charges from around $95 per day to tutor novices.

Practicalities

Both Mont-Sainte-Anne and Stoneham have slopeside **accommodation** with this and ski packages available through their websites, or you can conveniently stay in one of Beaupré's motels (see p.332) most of which also offer ski packages. If you have your own transport and fancy a novel splurge on your accommodation, consider staying in the **Ice Hotel** (Ⓣ418/875-4522 or 1-877/505-0423, Ⓦwww.icehotel-canada.com; ❽; Jan to early April; day visit $15) in Sainte-Catherine-de-la-Jacques-Cartier, beyond Wendake on Rte 367. Carved afresh each winter from ice and snow, its interior temperatures hover around -5°C, making the deer pelt mattresses and thick sleeping bags all the cosier. Far more convenient are hotels in Québec City (see p.300), which are linked to the resorts via a top-notch **ski shuttle**, the Hiver Express (Ⓣ418/525-5191, Ⓦwww.taxicoop-quebec.com; round trips $23). Services run the duration of the ski season from sixteen downtown hotels and the tourist information office to both Stoneham and Mont-Sainte-Anne. Le Massif runs a complimentary shuttle designed to link with the Hiver Express service, which departs from Mont-Sainte-Anne's shuttle parking area. You don't need your own gear, with all three resorts offering stock **equipment for rent** at reasonable prices: skis for around $22/day, snowboards $31. For a better selection of higher end gear and lower prices – allowing significant savings if you're renting for several days – check the stores scattered along the hwy in Beaupré.

and feathered headdresses used for festive occasions. The waters of the **Chute Kabir-Kouba** tumble into a 42m-deep canyon visible from the bridge just west of the church. For a closer look, take the path, which starts at the end of the car park directly opposite the church and leads to the slippery rocks below.

From Maison Aroüanne head along boul Valcartier and past the bike path Vert 6 (there's parking here) to follow signs to the **Onhoüa Chetek8e** site, 575 rue Stanislas Kosca (May–Oct daily 8.30am–5pm, rest of the year call to arrange; $10; ⓣ418/842-4308, ⓦwww.huron-wendat.qc.ca), a thirty-minute walk north. This replica of a seventeenth-century Huron village constructed for the benefit of tourists consists of wooden long houses, with Hurons in traditional garb and delicious native foods such as bison, caribou, trout and sunflower soup at the *Nek8arre* restaurant (May–Oct noon–3pm). These are available in six different table d'hôte combinations ($30). You're greeted by a traditional welcome dance; participatory activities such as shooting arrows cost extra. The few souvenirs – mini totem poles, suede bags, moccasins and the like – in the shop not made by Huron artisans come from other First Nations reserves.

Lévis

It's hard to think of any commuters who have as pleasant a morning trip as those who cross the St Lawrence from **LÉVIS** to Québec City. Lévis itself is an attractive Victorian town, but the views of Québec make the visit a treat. The regular ferry leaves day and night (until 2am) from near Québec City's Place Royale, and costs $2.60 (ⓣ418/644-3704, ⓦwww.traversiers.gouv.qc.ca) for the fifteen-minute crossing – double that if you go back (whether or not you disembark). Most tourists stay on the ferry for the return trip, but those dauntless enough to scale the staircase (five-minutes' walk, to the right as you exit the ferry terminal) to the **Terrasse** on the heights of Lévis are rewarded with an even greater panorama. That vantage point is also accessible via the half-hour bus tour ($1) available at the tourist office in the Lévis terminal.

The Terrasse and its landscaped park lie at the northwestern end of the old quarter, **Vieux-Lévis**, whose main drag, avenue Bégin, has a small-town feel with low-rise modernized buildings. For a quick pastry, sandwich or salad, stop at the café and fine-foods grocery, *Aux P'tits Oignons*, 45 avenue Bégin, or at the patrician house opposite, where you can purchase home-made chocolates and ice cream. The streets between here and the river are wider than those in Québec City, lined with large single-family homes – on rues Notre-Dame, Wolfe and Guénette, look out for examples of elaborate brickwork and ornate roof lines that are as fine as those across the water. The **Maison Alphonse-Desjardins**, 6 rue du Mont-Marie (Mon–Fri 10am–noon & 1–4.30pm, Sat & Sun noon–5pm; ⓣ418/835-2090, ⓦwww.desjardins.com; free), is a particular delight with its cake-frosting-like façade facing onto a leafy park whose centrepiece is a statue of Father Joseph David Déziel, founder of Lévis. Inside, a permanent exhibition explains the evolution of the *caisse populaire* (cooperative credit union) in Québec, and the early twentieth-century interior furnishings convey the family lifestyle of the period. From here you can walk east a couple of blocks to rue St-Jean, where a second staircase leads back to the ferry terminal.

Île d'Orléans

From just northeast of Québec City to a short distance beyond Ste-Anne-de-Beaupré, the St Lawrence is bottlenecked by the **ÎLE D'ORLÉANS**, a fertile islet whose bucolic atmosphere and handy location have made it a popular spot for holiday-making Québecois. More than most places on the mainland, Île d'Orléans, with its old stone churches, little cottages and seigneurial manors, has kept a flavour of eighteenth-century French Canada. This is largely because it was cut off from the mainland until 1935, when a suspension bridge was constructed from Hwy 440, about 10km out of the city, connecting it to the west end of the island.

To its first inhabitants, the **Algonquins**, the island was known as Minigo, which means "enchanting place". Jacques Cartier christened it Île de Bacchus because the wild grapes he saw here were "such as we had seen nowhere else in the world". (He was soon to change the name to Île d'Orléans in honour of the king's son.) Tourism and agriculture are the mainstays for the population of seven thousand: roadside stalls heave under the weight of fresh fruit and vegetables, jams, dairy products, home-made bread and maple syrup, and the island's restaurants and B&Bs are some of the best in the province, thanks to the supplies from local farms.

Around the island

Encircling the island, the 67-kilometre Hwy 368 – called the chemin Royal for most of its length – dips and climbs over gentle slopes and terraces past acres of neat farmland and orchards, passing through the six villages with their churches evenly spaced around the island's periphery.

Following a counter-clockwise route around the island, the first village you come to is **STE-PÉTRONILLE**, the island's oldest and most beautifully situated settlement and a district still characterized by the grand homes of the merchants who made their fortunes trading farm produce with Québec City. Wolfe observed the city from this spot before his bombardment. The white **Maison Gourdeau-de-Beaulieu** at no. 137 chemin Royal was the island's first permanent dwelling, built in 1648 and still the private residence of the Beaulieu

△ Île d'Orléans house

family. Some of the best views can be had from rue Horatio Walker, named after the landscape painter who had his home and studio here. Known unofficially as the grand seigneur of Ste-Pétronille, **Horatio Walker** lived here from 1904 until his death in 1938. He despised his English heritage, continually emphasizing a French branch in his ancestry and refusing to speak English. His subject matter was almost entirely based on the Île d'Orléans, which he viewed as a "sacred temple of the muses and a gift of the gods". Many of his paintings now grace Canada's larger galleries. Until the 1950s the south shore of the island was the domain of sailors and navigators, with the village of **ST-LAURENT** being the island's supplier of *chaloupes*, the long rowing boats that were the islanders' only means of getting to the mainland before the bridge was built. At the **Parc maritime de St-Laurent interpretation centre**, 120 chemin de la Chalouperie (mid-June to early Sept daily 10am–5pm; ⓣ418/828-9672; $2), you can get details of attractions like **La Forge à Pique-Assaut**, 2200 chemin Royale (June to mid-Oct daily 9am–5pm; rest of year Mon–Fri 9am–noon & 1.30–5pm; ⓣ418/828-9300, ⓦwww.forge-pique-assaut.com; free), which features a blacksmith's shop and an eighteenth-century bellows and sells forged metal crafts.

ST-JEAN, on the east side of the island, was similarly nautical; the cemetery of its red-roofed local church contains gravestones of numerous mariners. In the prettiest village on the island, most of the mid-eighteenth-century mariners' homes have dormer windows and wide porches, with Victorian-inspired filigree. St-Jean's museum of antique furniture and domestic objects, housed in the stately 1734 **Manoir Mauvide-Genest**, 1451 Royal (ⓣ418/829-2630, ⓦwww.manoirmauvidegenest.ca; $6). At this one-time home of Louis XV's surgeon, the metre-thick walls withstood the impact from Wolfe's bombardment – you can still see dents in the wall. From St-Jean, the road continues to the island's easterly tip and the village of **ST-FRANÇOIS**, where a precarious observation tower offers a view of both shores of the St Lawrence. The village church was rebuilt in the early 1990s after a suicidal driver wrecked the 1734 church; the wall in front was added to avoid a repeat. Among the French-Regime stone buildings in **STE-FAMILLE**, the **Maison Canac-Marquis**, 4466 chemin Royal, is a particularly fine example, but only the 1675 **Maison Drouin**, at no. 4700 (mid-June to mid-Aug daily 10am–6pm; ⓣ418/829-0330, ⓦwww.fondationfrancoislamy.org; $2), with its exhibits on the architecture of these early houses, is open to the public. The richly decorated **church**, built in 1743, includes a painting of the Holy Family by Québec's foremost early painter, Frère Luc. **ST-PIERRE**, to the west of Ste-Famille, is notable for its **church**, the oldest in rural Québec; constructed in 1718, it has pews with special hot-brick holders for keeping bottoms warm on seats. The town, by far the largest on the island, is however best know as the long-time home and final resting place of Félix Leclerc (1914-88), the poet and singer–songwriter who penned "P'tit Bonheur" and the first musician to bring Québecois music international acclaim. The **Espace Félix Leclerc**, 682 chemin Royal (mid-Feb to mid-Dec Tues–Sun 9am–6pm; ⓣ418/828-1682, ⓦwww.felixleclerc.com; $3) covers a site that not only pays homage to the life and work of Leclerc, but also has several hiking trails and picnic tables.

Practicalities

The island's **information office**, 490 côte du Pont (mid-June to early Sept Sun–Thurs 8.30am–7.30pm, Fri & Sat to 8pm; April to mid-June & early Sept to Oct daily 9am–5pm; rest of the year Mon–Fri 9am–5pm Sat & Sun 11am–3pm; ⓣ418/828-9411, ⓦwww.quebecweb.com/tourismeiledorleans), is on the right at the top of the hill after the bridge from the mainland. It's well set up for finding a B&B; it has descriptions with photos and prices and a free phone for bookings. The centre also has self-guided driving tours (cassette or CD; English available) for $10. Budget travellers wanting to stay on the island should head straight for *Auberge Le P'tit Bonheur*, 183–186 Côte Lafleur (T 418/829-2588, W www.leptitbonheur.qc.ca; 3), a **hostel** in an old stone manor with dorm beds ($20) and bike and cross-country ski rental. For others, the choice of good **B&Bs** is more bewildering but try *Le Vieux Presbytère*, 1247 av Monseigneur D'esgly (T 418/828-9723 or 1-888/828-9723, W www.presbytere.com; 3-6), in St-Pierre – a charming inn with low ceilings, beams and antiques in an old presbytery just behind the village church. It has terrific river views and rents bicycles ($6/hr, $25/day). To **camp** head to St-François, to the lovely and convenient *Camping Orléans*, 357 chemin Royal (T 418/829-2953; $23.50 unserviced, $36.50 for hookup; mid-May to early Oct), near the village jetty, which has a small onsite pool.

The island is replete with **restaurants** serving fine French cuisine, but particularly good bets are *La Goéliche*, 22 chemin du Quai (T 418/828-2248), in Ste-Pétronille, where table d'hôte starts at $30 and always includes great views. In St-Laurent, for similar prices, *Canard Huppé*, 2198 Chem Royal (T 418/828-2292), is a gourmand's treat with local duck, trout and maple on the menu. *Le Vieux Presbytère* (see p.above) in St-Pierre also has a good restaurant that serves game dishes. *Le Bistro de bout de Lîlle*, 148 du Bout de l'Île opposite rue Horatio Walker in Ste-Pétronille, serves salads, pizza and *croque monsieur* (all around $10). The *Chocolaterie* in the basement has exquisite chocolates and ice creams – a good accompaniment to a stroll along the rocky waterfront here. In St-Laurent, beside the Parc Maritime interpretation centre, the open-air seafood restaurant *Les Honerdises de Lîle* is on the waterfront; the table d'hôte menu is $11. On the opposite side of the island in Ste-Famille the local *boulangerie*, G.H. Blouin, 3967 chemin Royal, is one of the island's oldest and best, with irresistable bread and pastries.

Grosse Île

Beyond Île d'Orléans an archipelago of 21 islands trail into the current of the wide St Lawrence. Despite its name, Grosse Île is not the biggest island in the group but, 48km downstream from Québec City, it served as Canada's main quarantine station for over a century. First opened in 1832 the island was soon processing up to 100,000 European immigrants a year, most of them Irish. The immigrants arrived in overcrowded vessels that came to be known as 'coffin ships' because so few survived the journey. Those that did survive were described as 'cadaverous' on arrival. Medical facilities on the island, which had never been more than rudimentary, were soon completely overwhelmed by the numbers passing through. First cholera, then typhus swept through the station, exacerbated by the crowded and unsanitary living conditions. At its worst, the epidemic claimed 40 to 50 lives a day and an estimated 7500 people are buried on Grosse Île alone, not including those that died at sea. Visiting the island in 1847, the Anglican Bishop of Montréal described invalids abandoned on the beach screaming for water, inmates covered in vermin. He describes watching a child that 'sat down for a moment, and died.' After the outbreaks, conditions improved on the island when Dr Frederick Montizambert, who was Medical Superintendant of the station from 1869 to 1899, introduced stringent controls. Vessels and luggage were inspected and disinfected and passengers examined and vaccinated. A new disinfection building and infirmary was built as well as

1st, 2nd and 3rd class hotels so that the healthy could wait out their quarantine in comfort, away from the infected. Eventually improvements in microbiology as well as a decline in the number of immigrants caused the closure of the centre in 1937 but the island's disturbing history was far from over. From 1937 until 1957 it was used as a secretive military base for biological warfare experiments including, allegedly, the development of Anthrax. After a further 23 years as an animal quarantine and vetenarian research centre it was finally declared a historic site in 1983 and taken over by Parcs Canada 10 years later.

There are regular ferry departures to **Grosse Île National Historic Site** (Ⓣ418/248-888 or 1-800/463-6769, Ⓦwww.pc.gc.ca/grosseile; entry included in ferry fee) from Berthier-sur-Mer, 40-minutes out of Québec City on the south shore of the St Lawrence (**Croisières Lachance**; May–Oct daily 9.45am & 1pm; Ⓣ1-888/476-7734, Ⓦwww.croisiereslachance.com; $41). On the island you can wander around the infirmary, accomodation buildings and workshops as well as the disinfection building, which now houses a poignant multi-media exhibition about the history of the station. There is also a large memorial and 50ft Celtic cross, erected in 1909, with insciptions in English, French and Gaelic to commemorate the large number of Irish casualties in the 1847 epidemic.

Côte-de-Beaupré

Dubbed the "coast of fine meadows" by Jacques Cartier, the **Côte-de-Beaupré** stretches along the St Lawrence past the **Basilique de Ste-Anne-de-Beaupré**, 40km northeast of Québec City, as far as the migratory bird sanctuary on Cap Tourmente, where you can see the greater snow goose in spring and autumn. There are two roads along the coast: the speedy Autoroute Dufferin-Montmorency (Hwy 440, then Hwy 138) and the slower Avenue Royale (Hwy 360), which is served by local buses. The latter gives a far better introduction to the province's rural life, passing through little villages with ancient farmhouses and churches lining the way. Beyond Ste-Anne-de-Beaupré, Hwy 360 leads to one of the best ski resorts in the province – **Mont Ste-Anne** (see box, p.324), which has everything from golf to world-championship mountain biking in summer.

Chute Montmorency

Some 9km northeast of Québec City the waters of the Montmorency River cascade 83m down from the Laurentians into the St Lawrence, which makes the **Chute Montmorency** one and a half times the height of Niagara, though the volume of water is considerably less. The falls, named by Champlain in honour of the governor of New France, were the site of Wolfe's first attempt on the colony. However, Wolfe and his men were driven off by Montcalm's superior forces. In those days – before a hydroelectric dam cut off much of the flow – the falls were far more impressive, but the cascade remains an awesome spectacle, especially in winter, when the water and spray become a gigantic cone of ice, known locally as the "sugar loaf". Inevitably, the falls attract droves of tourists, especially now that the site has been thoroughly developed. From the main car park ($8.75 payable from mid-April to late Oct, otherwise free), a **cable car** (late Jan to early April Sat & Sun 9am–4pm; mid-April to early June & late Aug to mid-Oct daily 8.30am–6.45pm; mid-June to late Aug until 7.30pm; closed Nov–Jan; $8 return) shoots up to the **interpretation centre** (daily 9am–8pm; June–Aug until 10pm; Ⓣ418/663-3330, Ⓦwww.sepaq.com/chutemontmorency; free), in the Manoir Montmorency, which also has a bar and restaurant with a terrace. You can also walk up to the centre, but be warned this involves 487 steps. From the centre, a cliffside walkway leads to the bridge over the falls (wooded trails follow the river upstream) and onto the zigzag path down the other side. Local STCUQ bus #53 stops at the bottom of the falls, #50 at the top; both buses leave from Place Jacques-Cartier in Québec and take around fifty minutes, each costing $2.50. You can also cycle here – 25km round-trip from the Vieux-Port, and the path passes the **Domaine Maizerets** park, where you can have a pleasant break.

Ste-Anne-de-Beaupré

Québec's equivalent of Lourdes, the **Basilique de Ste-Anne-de-Beaupré**, 39km northeast of Québec City (25min by Intercar coach from Gare Centrale; 3 daily; $6), dominates the immediate area, its twin spires soaring proudly above the St Lawrence shore. The church began in 1658 as a small wooden chapel devoted to St Anne (the Virgin Mary's mother). During its construction a crippled peasant was cured but the legend of St Anne's intercession didn't really get going until some Breton sailors were caught in a storm on the St Lawrence in 1661 and vowed to build a chapel to St Anne if she saved them. The ship capsized at nearby Cap Tourmente but the sailors survived. Word of this miracle spread, and from then on everyone caught in the St Lawrence's frequent storms prayed to St Anne and donated *ex votos* to the shrine. In 1876, the same year that St Anne was declared patron saint of Québec, the church was distinguished as a basilica (or pilgrimage church), to which the devout came on their knees from the beach or walked shoeless from Québec City; now, one and a half million pilgrims flock to the site every year in comfortable coachloads.

The neo-Romanesque granite cathedral with lofty symmetrical spires is the fifth church to stand here, fires and floods having destroyed the first four. The statue of St Anne between the steeples miraculously survived the 1922 destruction of the fourth church, even though the roof and both steeples fell in the blaze. The basilica seats 1500, though on St Anne's feast day (July 26) up to 5000 pilgrims crowd inside. Most of its decoration – countless stained-glass windows and massive murals – depict the miraculous powers of St Anne, though the wooden pews bear delightful animal carvings. Behind the ornate golden statue of St Anne, depicted holding her daughter Mary, is a chapel said to contain a portion of Anne's forearm, donated by the pope in 1960. Those who have been cured by her intervention have left a vast collection of crutches and wooden limbs hanging on the basilica's pillars near the entrance. The **information centre** in front of the basilica (daily 8.30am–4.30pm; Ⓦ www.ssadb.qc.ca) runs pious, free, guided tours daily at 1pm from the basilica entrance. The hours of the basilica itself vary, but it is open 8am–4.30pm at a minimum, and 6am–10pm at the height of the midsummer pilgrimage. The church is open to all even during Mass although photos are prohibited at that time. The information centre has a schedule of Masses conducted in English.

Several little chapels are hidden in the basilica's shadow. The simple **Chapelle Souvenir** (early May to mid-Sept daily 8am–7pm), across the street behind the basilica, contains some of the stones from the second chapel and was built in the nineteenth century on the foundations of the transept of the third church (1676–1877), hence its north–south orientation. Nearby, the small white chapel of the **Scala Santa** (same hours) contains stairs that replicate those climbed by Christ on his meeting with Pontius Pilate. Glass boxes, embedded in each stair, contain lumps of earth from various holy places, and the devout accomplish the ascent on their knees. Another obligatory part of the penitential route is the nearby **Way of the Cross**, which curves steeply up the hillside. There are two daytime processions, and on some summer evenings torchlit processions wend their way through each station. Less athletic visitors can pay their respects to the basilica's collection of *ex votos* and treasures in the **Musée de Ste-Anne** (June to early Sept daily 9am–5pm; $4), which contains displays on the early churches and some of the surviving furnishings.

The vaguely Middle Eastern building at the other end of the car park contains the **Cyclorama de Jerusalem** (daily May–Oct 9am–6pm; Ⓦwww.cyclorama.com; $8), an enormous 360-degree painting set at the time of Christ's crucifixion. It has been there longer than the present basilica, though the 3D cutouts were added in the 1950s in a misguided attempt to make it more realistic.

Practicalities

There's a glut of inexpensive **motels** sprawling along Rte 138 in Ste-Anne-de-Beaupré, with prices and standards fairly uniform between them. *Motel des Berges* (Ⓣ418/827-8578 or 1-888/827-2484; Ⓦwww.moteldesberges.com; ❷–❹) offers large and clean rooms with and without kitchenettes, looks out over the St Lawrence River and is within walking distance of the Basilica. Alternatives to motels include free **camping** (without facilities) in especially set-aside parkland opposite the basilica itself, a basic but welcoming **hostel**, *The Basilica Inn* (Ⓣ418/827-4475; dorms $17, or private rooms ❷) primarily designed for pilgrims and several pleasant **B&Bs**, including *Auberge Baker,* 8790 av Royale (Ⓣ418/824-4478 or 1-866/824-4478, Ⓦwww.auberge-baker.qc.ca; ❹), a wonderfully atmospheric B&B occupying a 150-year-old farmhouse set well back from the busy Rte 138. Rooms have rough-hewn beams and gloriously mismatched antique furnishings; guests have use of a communal kitchen. More central in Ste-Anne-de-Beaupré, *Auberge La Camarine*, 10947 boul Ste-Anne (Ⓣ418/827-5703 or 1-800/567-3939, Ⓦwww.camarine.com; ❹), offers pleasant hotel units, stylishly decorated with surreal art, in a large wooden lodge beside Rte 138. Many are equipped with wood-burning fires. The inn's **restaurant** is the best in the area, serving an eclectic variety of French, Italian and Asian dishes, often fused and off a frequently changing menu. The food is of the highest standard but a four-course meal starts at $28 and the *Bistro Bar* has its own menu starting at $9. Reservations are essential. For more modest prices but almost as satisfying a meal try *Auberge Baker* (see above), a classy but relaxed restaurant serving hearty traditional items: *Migneron de bai St Paul* ($6.50), a local cheese in filo pastry with maple syrup sauce, earthy yellow pea soup ($4) and entrees that include meat pies, pork meatball stew, duck or salmon (around $16). The $27 table d'hôte keeps tabs on spending.

Mont-Sainte-Anne and around

On the fringes of Beaupré, the **MONT STE-ANNE** ski resort (see box, p.324) has successfully marketed itself as an off-season destination and it's now the longest-standing venue on the **mountain bike** world-cup circuit. In summer you can explore the extensive cross-country mountain bike trails ($10), either staying around the base area to test your trials skills on the North-Shore-style wooden obstacles, or using the gondola ($28 per day) to explore one of the hardest downhill mountain bike courses in the world – though there are easier routes down the mountain too. Bikes can be rented at the base area by the hour with front-suspension mountain bikes going for $17.39 for two hours; full-suspension for $56.51. The gondola up the mountain is also open to and hikers wanting to enjoy the remarkable views over the St Lawrence and Québec City as well as several marked trails. But one of the best hiking trails leaves out of the car park at the base area – head down the hill and over the bridge – to the **Chutes Jean-Larouse**, a twenty-minute walk. The trail leads to a series of dramatic waterfalls, though the latticework stairway that's been constructed alongside is just as dizzying and almost more impressive. The resort also operates a respectable golf course, and has a pleasant campsite (Ⓣ418/827-5281 or 1-800/463-1568, Ⓦwww.mont-sainte-anne.com; sites from $24). At the resort, *Au Café Suisse*, 1805 boul Les Neiges (Ⓣ418/826-2184), is a twee place with fondues (from $20), raclettes ($24) and some more unusual items like Japanese-style steak with noodles and a curry broth.

For even grander waterfalls head some 6km east of Ste-Anne-de-Beaupré along Hwy 138 to **Canyon Ste-Anne** (daily May to late June & early Sept to Oct 9am–4.45pm; late June to early Sept 9am–5.45pm; $9.50; Ⓦwww.canyonste-anne.qc.ca) about a thirty-minute drive from Québec City. Here, the river has carved a gorge where the water tumbles 74m in a waterfall flanked by a chasm fringed with woodlands and short nature trails. A bridge crosses just before the precipice, giving views down the canyon, while in front of the falls a precarious suspension bridge allows for splendid and terrifying views. With your own transport you can head 2km from the canyon towards the coast via Saint-Joachim to the **Cap-Tourmente National Wildlife Area** (mid-April to early Nov daily 8.30am–5pm, Jan–March weekends only 8.30am–4pm; Ⓦwww.qc.ec.gc.ca; $6). It's a favourite with snow geese, who stop to gather strength on its sandbars during their spring and autumn migrations. Another 250 species of bird also inhabit the park and naturalists are on hand to answer questions.

Réserve Faunique des Laurentides

The zone of the Laurentians 40km to the north of Québec City – via Hwy 73 and 175 – is considerably wilder than the mountains near Montréal, thanks to the creation of the **Réserve Faunique des Laurentides**. The vast wooded terrain, with summits of more than 1000m towards the east, was once a hunting ground of the Montagnais, until the Hurons, armed by the French, drove the small population further north. The wildlife reserve became a protected area in 1895 to conserve the caribou herds, an intervention that was not a great success – very few exist today. However, though it allows controlled moose-hunting, the reserve's main function is still to preserve native animals such as the beaver, moose, lynx, black bear and deer, all of which you may see in remote areas. Intercar (Ⓣ418/525-3000 or 1-888/861-4592) runs a **bus** service through the park from Québec City's bus station to Alma (3 daily; 2hr 45min) and Chicoutimi (4–5 daily; 2hr 30min).

In 1981, the southernmost portion of the reserve was set off as the **Parc National de la Jacques-Cartier** (Ⓦwww.sepaq.com; $3.50). A visitor centre (mid-May to late Oct), 10km from Hwy 175, serves as the gateway to the Jacques-Cartier river valley, enclosed by 550m-high forested slopes. The park is ideal for canoeing, although the river runs beside the road for most of the way, detracting from the wilderness experience. Rent canoes, kayaks, inflatable rafts and bicycles from Les Excursions Jacques-Cartier (Ⓣ418/848-7272, Ⓦwww.excursionsj-cartier.com), who also manage the park's **campsites**. Pitches are available from $15.65, both near the visitor centre and in more peaceful spots further into the park.

The reserve proper begins further north along Hwy 175 where **Camp Mercier** (daily 8.30am–4pm; Ⓣ418/848-2422 or 1-800/665-6527, Ⓦwww.sepaq.com) near its southern perimeter gives out **information**. The heavy snowfall makes the park an excellent place for cross-country skiing on a 192km network ($11/day). Hwy 175 traverses the reserve; halfway through is **L'Étape**, the only spot to fill your tank (or yourself) until just before Chicoutimi or Alma. Nearby there's **camping** beside Lac Jacques-Cartier at the *La Loutre* campsite (late May to early Sept; Ⓣ418/846-2201; $23.47), and chalets available.

Northern Québec

Northern Québec stretches out as two separate entities on either side of the St Lawrence River. The southern shore is the less remote, with the agricultural **Bas Saint-Laurent** (Lower St Lawrence) the gateway to the rugged and lightly populated **Gaspé Peninsula**. East of here, stuck out in the middle of the Gulf of St Lawrence, the **Îles-de-la-Madeleine** are most easily reached by ferry from Prince Edward Island. This windswept archipelago has majestic, treeless landscapes, fringed by fine beaches and crazily eroded sandstone cliffs, and appeals particularly to cyclists, walkers and people who just want to lie on a beach in complete solitude.

The north shore of the St Lawrence covers an area that changes from trim farmland to a vast forest bordering the barren seashore. Further north, communities take on an isolated feel and the dominant role of nature in day-to-day life becomes more conspicuous. Immediately northeast of Québec City is the beautiful **Charlevoix** region of peaceful villages and towns that bear the marks of Québec's rural beginnings – both in the architecture of the seigneurial regime and in the layout of the land. Often the winding hwys and back roads pass through a virtually continuous village, where the only interruptions in the chain of low-slung houses are the tin-roofed churches. The beguiling hills and valleys give way to dramatic ravaged rock just beyond the Charlevoix borders, where the **Saguenay River** crashes into the immense fjord that opens into the St Lawrence at the resort of **Tadoussac**. Protected as a marine park these waters are popular for whale-watching, while the adjacent cliffs are superb for hiking. Inland, **Lac Saint-Jean** – source of the Saguenay – is an oasis of fertile land in a predominantly rocky region, and its peripheral villages offer glimpses of native as well as Québecois life. Adventurous types following the St Lawrence can head beyond Tadoussac along the **Côte Nord** through a sparsely populated region of spectacular empty beaches and dramatic rockscapes where the original livelihoods of fishing and lumber have largely given way to ambitious mining and hydroelectric projects. In the far northeast the supply ship *Nordik Express* serves the **Île d'Anticosti** and the roadless lower north shore as far as the Labrador border – the ultimate journey within Québec. The remoteness of the **Île d'Anticosti** and the sculptured terrain of the **Mingan archipelago** – a national park well served by boats from Havre-St-Pierre – is matched by the isolation of the fishing communities along the **Lower North Shore**, where no roads penetrate and visits are possible only by supply ship, plane or snowmobile.

Bas Saint-Laurent and the Gaspé Peninsula

Heading east from Québec City along the southern shore of the **St Lawrence**, the most scenic route is Hwy 132, which sticks close to the shoreline showcasing the highlights of a region of fertile lands with farming and forestry covering gently rolling hills. The landscape is an agricultural one and dominated by long, narrow fields that are remnants of the old seigneurial system (see box, p.337), and the road passes through a string of quiet villages overshadowed by their oversized, silver spired, Catholic churches. The stops worth making on the 180-kilometre trip to Rivière-Du-Loup are the woodcarving centre of **St-Jean-Port-Joli**, the seigneurial **St-Roche-des-Aulnaies** and the architecturally quaint **Kamouraska**.

Running parallel to Hwy 132, the Trans-Canada (Hwy 20) is a much faster route to the attractive town of **Rivière-du-Loup**, effectively the start of the **Gaspé Peninsula**. Bounded by the Gulf of St Lawrence to the north and west, and by the Baie des Chaleurs to the south and east, the Gaspé Peninsula is roughly 550km long, with a chain of mountains and rolling highlands dominating the interior and the northern shore. It has always been sparsely inhabited and poor, its remote communities eking out an existence from the turbulent seas and the rocky soil. But the landscape provides some wonderful scenery. Forested hills cut with deep ravines and vistas of craggy mountains tumble to a jagged coastline fronted by the St Lawrence where the winding coastal drive along Hwy 132 is a delight. The principal towns strung along this shore – **Rimouski**, **Matane** and **Gaspé** – are less appealing than its many smaller villages or the peninsula's two outstanding parks: the extravagantly mountainous **Parc de la Gaspésie**, inland from **Ste-Anne-des-Monts**, and the **Parc National de Forillon**, at the tip of the peninsula, with its mountain and coastal hikes and wonderfully rich wildlife. Just to the south of the Forillon park, the village of **Percé** is famous for the offshore **Rocher Percé**, an extraordinary limestone monolith that has been a magnet for travellers for more than a hundred years.

The **south coast** of the peninsula runs along the **Baie des Chaleurs**, a long wedge of sheltered ocean with relatively warm waters that separates the Gaspé from New Brunswick. For the most part, it's flatter and duller than the north here, though some of the seaside resorts-cum-fishing villages and farming communities that dot the coast are an agreeable place to break your journey. **Carleton**, where the mountains return to tower over the coast, is tempting, especially as it's near the extraordinary fish and plant fossils of the **Parc de Miguasha**, a UNESCO World Heritage Site. This, along with **Bonaventure** further up the coast, is also one of the few long-established English-speaking settlements on the peninsula which is otherwise predominantly and proudly Québecois – another pocket of Anglophones exists in and around **Gaspé** town. Both Carleton and Bonaventure are centres of Acadian culture, established in 1755 in the wake of the British deportation of some 10,000 Acadians from around the Bay of Fundy in Nova Scotia (see p.442). Neither of these communities has created visually distinctive villages or towns, however, so even this part of the Gaspé looks as French as the heartlands of rural Québec.

The Gaspé is well served by **bus**, with regular services travelling both the north and south coasts of the peninsula from Rimouski, Rivière-du-Loup and Québec City. The interior and the peninsula's parks are, however, difficult to explore without a car. VIA Rail links Montréal by **train** with Rivière du Loup and Rimouski, then follows the southern coast of the peninsula to Carleton and Percé, terminating in Gaspé town after more than 17 hours – there's no service between Gaspé and Rimouski on the northern coast, though. Be warned: some stations (like Percé) are miles from the towns they serve. Note that as a major summer holiday spot the Gaspé gets especially busy during the last two weeks of July for Québec's **construction holiday**; if you travel during this period, book your accommodation and activities well in advance.

St-Jean-Port-Joli

The first settlement of any note along Hwy 132, some 80km east of Lévis, is **ST-JEAN-PORT-JOLI**, where the long main street accommodates the galleries of the region's most popular **woodcarvers**. A traditional Québecois folk art, woodcarving flourished in the eighteenth and nineteenth centuries, but had almost expired by the 1930s, when the 3 Bourgault brothers (Médard, Jean-Julien and André) established their workshop here. Initially, religious statuary was their main source of income, but their folksy style and Francophile themes were adopted and popularized by the nationalists in the 1960s.

Along the main road, on the west side of the village, the ugly **Musée des Anciens Canadiens**, 332 av de Gaspé ouest (daily May–June 9am–5.30pm, July–Aug 8.30am–9pm, Sept–Oct 8.30am–6pm; ⓣ418/598-3392 or 1-866/598-3392, ⓦwww.quebecweb.com/ancienscanadiens; $5), has an interesting collection of woodcarvings cut in white pine and walnut, many of which are the work of the Bourgaults. The most impressive piece is the giant *Les Patriotes*, a tribute to the Québecois rebels of 1837 who, under the leadership of Louis-Joseph Papineau, tried to drive out the British (see p.275). The studied romance of the woodcarving bears little relation to the actual rebellion, though, which was badly organized and easily suppressed. A few doors down the same road at no. 322, the **Maison Médard-Bourgault** (mid-June to early Sept daily 10am–6pm; $4) concentrates on the life and work of Médard Bourgault. He was the most talented of the brothers – he even carved the walls and furniture. The delicate and ornate interior of the village church, **Église St-Jean Baptiste** at no. 2, celebrates the work of an earlier generation of Québecois woodcarvers from the 1770s, the Baillairgé brothers. Any of the dozen or so galleries along the main road sell woodcarvings; the shop adjoining the museum is one of the best.

There are some pleasant **B&Bs**, of which *La Maison de L'Ermitage*, 56 rue de l'Ermitage (ⓣ418/598-7553, ⓦwww.maisonermitage.com; ❸), has a lovely, turreted, red and white roof – if you're feeling particularly flush you can stay in one of the turrets (❹). Numerous motels line Hwy 132, but one of the cheapest options is the **campsite** *De La Demi-Lieue*, on the grounds of a former seigneury farther down the road at no. 589 Hwy 132 est (ⓣ418/598-6108 or 1-800/463-9558, ⓦwww.campingunion; $23–35; May to late Sept). For **food** try the inexpensive *La Boustifaille*, 547 av de Gaspé ouest, (ⓣ418/598-3061) for gigantic portions of Québecois fare for around $15, or the pricier *Café la Coureuse des Greves*, 300 Hwy 204, (ⓣ418/598-9111; dinner $18) where tables are arranged on a lushly-flowered outdoor terrace and good breakfasts served. For upscale regional dining with views of the river, try the *Auberge du Faubourg*, 280 Hwy 132 ouest (late April to Oct; ⓣ418/598-6455, ⓦwww.aubergedufaubourg.com; ❹)

St-Roch-des-Aulnaies and beyond

About 14km east of St-Jean-Port-Joli is the village of **ST-ROCH-DES-AULNAIES**, where a gorgeous water mill and manor house have survived on a nineteenth-century seigneurial estate formerly the home of a rich merchant. Offering a fascinating glimpse into that era, **La Seigneurie des Aulnaies** (daily late June to early Sept 9am–6pm; early June & Sept weekends only 10am–4pm; ⓣ418/354-2800, ⓦwww.laseigneuriedesaulnaies.qc.ca; $8.75), is named after the alder trees that grow along the banks of the Ferrée River. The river powered Québec's largest bucket wheel in the estate's three-storey communal grist mill. Now refurbished and in full working order, the mill has frequent flour-grinding displays and mouth-watering muffins and pancakes in

The seigneurial system

In the seventeenth century the agricultural settlement of New France – now Québec – was conceived as an extension of European-style feudalism with the granting of **seigneuries** to religious orders, nobleman, merchants and, in a break from tradition, others of humble birth. The average seigneury covered around fifty square kilometres and part of the land was owned by the seigneurs, the rest rented by **habitants**, who were secure in their tenancy (they could sell the land or pass it on to their children) provided they met certain obligations. They had to pay a yearly tithe for the upkeep of the parish church, pay rent in kind (usually grain, as the seigneurs had a monopoly on milling), work on the roads and make themselves available for the militia.

In the early days the waterways provided the easiest form of transportation and so each *habitant's* farm had a river frontage of around a couple of hundred metres in length, with the rest of his land extending back in a narrow strip. One result of this was that *habitants* lived near their neighbours and, content with this decentralized way of life, long resisted the development of nuclear settlements. You can still see these ribbon farms and villages, which are very much in evidence along the St Lawrence today.

The seigneurial system was **abolished** in 1854 by legislation that passed land-ownership rights to the *habitants*.

the café. Just upstream from the mill, the veranda-wrapped manor house has period rooms, guides in costume and diverting interactive displays on the seigneurial system. A few minutes' drive from St-Roch, agricultural **LA POCATIÈRE** sits on a ridge above the coastal plain, bereft of charm. It's worth stopping if you want information on the Bas Saint-Laurent region that stretches from here to Rimouski. The **information centre** is at exit 439 from Hwy 20 (daily: late June to early Sept 9am–8pm; mid-May to late June & early Sept to mid-Oct 9am–5pm; ⓣ418/856-5040), and signposted from Hwy 132.

Some 40km further east along Hwy 132 is **KAMOURASKA**, a pretty village where well-heeled citizens of Québec City once congregated to take the air. While they no longer visit to the same degree, it's not for lack of good air, which still has its way with the town's current residents, many of whom live to more than 100 years of age. The village boasts many examples of the Bas-St-Laurent region's most distinctive architectural feature, the Kamouraska roof. Extended to keep the rainwater off the walls, the arched and rounded eaves project from the houses in a design borrowed from the shipyards. One of the best examples is the **Villa St-Louis**, at 125 av Morel, a private residence that was once the home of Adolphe Basile-Routhier, the man who scripted the words to Canada's national anthem. You may also spot several nets attached to wooden stakes emerging out of the river – these ensnare eels, traditionally the village's economic mainstay. Learn something about the industry at the slightly bizarre **Site d'interprétation de l'anguille**, 205 av Morel (June to mid-Oct daily 9am–5pm; ⓣ418/492-3935; $5); aside from a barn filled with nets, there's not much to see here except the taxidermy collection of various non-eel animals ensnared in the nets, which is particularly morbid. The enormous **Palais de Justice**, 111 av Morel (June–Sept, Tues–Sun 10am–noon & 1–5pm; ⓣ418/492-9458; $4), at the centre of town, once served as the region's superior court, but today merely displays early registries, maps and various pictures of the village. A better collection of artefacts – crockery, farming tools and the like – is at the **Musée de Kamouraska**, 69 av Morel (June to mid-Oct daily 9am–5pm, mid-Oct to mid-Dec Tues–Fri 9am–5pm Sat & Sun 1pm–4.30pm; ⓣ418/492-9783; $5), housed in a former convent. Kamouraska has a host of charming **B&Bs**. *Gîte Chez Nicole et Jean*, at 81 av Morel (Ⓣ418/492-2921; ❹), is one of the best, with cheerful rooms and a bountiful breakfast of regional and organic food. For views of the river, try the simple *Motel Cap Blanc*, 300 av Morel (May–Nov; Ⓣ418/492-2919; Ⓦwww.quebecweb.com/motelcapblanc; ❸). If you are curious to try the local eel, **Café du Clocher** at no. 88 av Morel (Ⓣ418/492-7365) serves smoked eel as well as a good range of vegetarian dishes under $20. For similar prices *Au Relais de Kamouraska* at no. 253 (Ⓣ418/492-6246) is more family-orientated but also makes eel a speciality.

Rivière-du-Loup

A prosperous-looking place, whose hilly centre is complete with broad streets and handsome Victorian villas, **RIVIÈRE-DU-LOUP** owes its development to the timber industry and the coming of the railway in 1859. This established Rivière-du-Loup as a crossroads for traffic between the Maritimes, the Gaspé peninsula and the rest of Québec. Its significance as an administrative and commercial centre has grown accordingly and today it has a population of around 18,000.

The river that gives the place its name crashes down a thirty-metre drop close to the centre, at the top of rue Frontenac, near **Parc de la Croix Lumineuse**, which offers a panoramic view of the mountains on the north shore. The town's **waterfall** is disappointing, however: although it generates a lot of noise and spray, even the specially built platform that crosses it fails to make the view enthralling. Similarly modest are the town's three museums. The central **Musée du Bas-St-Laurent**, 300 rue St-Pierre (June to mid-Oct daily noon–5pm; mid-Oct to May Wed–Sun 1–5pm; Ⓣ418/862-7547; $5), combines ethnological displays of the region with historical exhibits and works of modern art by local artists. On the eastern edge of town the **Musée des Carillons**, 393 rue Témiscouata (late June to early Sept daily 9am–8pm; Sept & Oct daily 9am–5pm; $5), is a unique collection of 250 bells of all types from around the world. The **Musée de bateaux miniatures et légendes du Bas-St-Laurent**, 80 boul Cartier (daily May to late June & late Aug to mid-Oct 11am–7pm, late June to late Aug 8.30am–9.30pm; Ⓣ418/868-0800; $4), houses an interesting collection of model boats built by local craftspeople. If you're interested in the architectural heritage pick up the interpretation booklet ($1) from the **tourist office**, at 189 boul de l'Hôtel-de-Ville (daily mid-June to Sept 8.30am–9pm, otherwise closed weekends; Ⓣ418/862-1981 or 1-888/825-1981) and stroll round the centre: although there's nothing special, it's a pleasant way to pass an hour. The most

Boat trips from Rivière-du-Loup

Rivière-du-Loup is a good place for **boat trips** on the St Lawrence River. Beginning at around $40 per person, these excursions are not cheap, but they are well organized and you may see beluga, minke and finback whales throughout the summer. All the companies are located by the marina at 200 rue Hayward; Croisières AML (Ⓣ418/867-3361 Ⓦwww.croisieresaml.com, or 1-800/563-4643) specializes in three-hour **whale-watching** trips on large boats, while Exceptionelle Aventure (Ⓣ418/862-7775) takes in the river's aquatic life in twelve-person zodiacs – inflatable raft-type boats that get you very close to the whales. Alternatively, La Société Duvetnor (Ⓣ418/867-1660, Ⓦwww.duvetnor.com; June to mid-Sept) has daily cruises to various midstream sea-bird and mammal sanctuaries, with overnight stops offered ($25–200 per person; reservations required).

intriguing historical site in town is **Le Manoir Fraser**, 32 rue Fraser (daily mid-June to mid-Oct 10am–5pm; ⓣ418/867-3906; $5), the home of Seigneur Fraser; instead of costumed guides, a computer-animated seigneur introduces you to his life and times. The red-brick manor house also has a fancy tearoom and garden.

Highway 132 runs through the centre of Rivière-du-Loup. The town's **bus station** is on boul Cartier, beside the junction of Hwys 132 and 20, about ten minutes' walk northeast of the centre. The **train** station (ⓣ1-888/842-7245) is on Rue Lafontaine and Rue Fraserville and only open when VIA Rail trains arrive here from destinations including Montréal, Gaspé and Halifax. A **car ferry** (mid-April to Jan; 2–5 trips daily; 65min; ⓣ418/862-5094, ⓦwww.travrdlstsim.com; $13.80, cars $35) provides service to and from the marina to

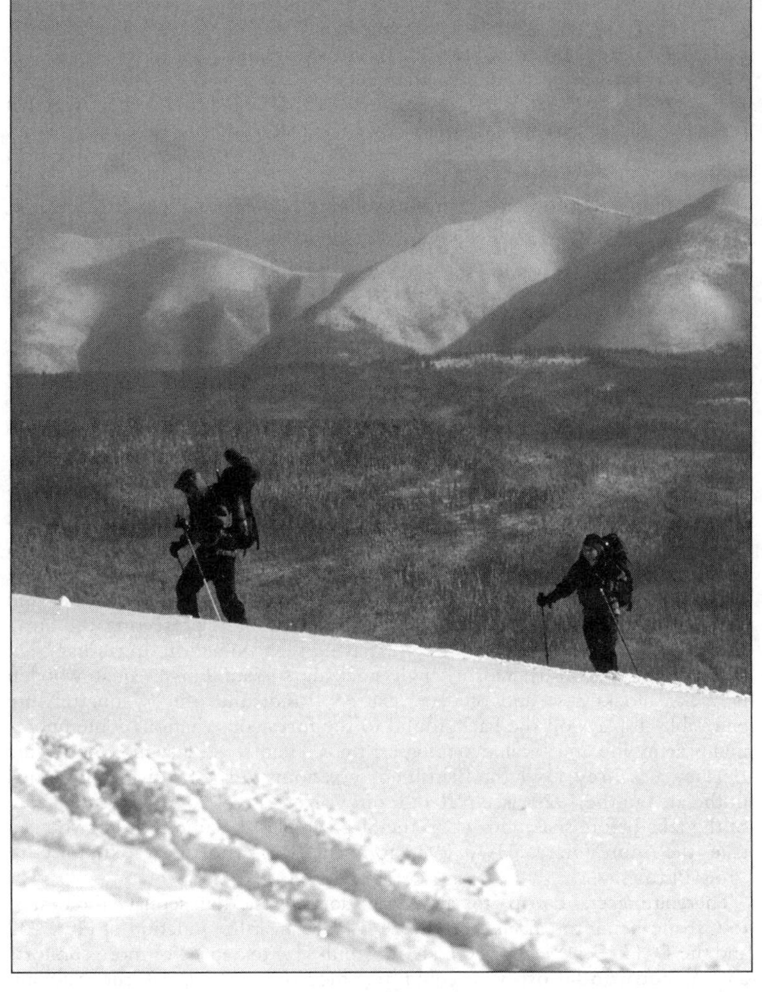

△ Hikers in the Réserve Faunique

St-Siméon on the north shore (see p.362). For cheap accommodation the **HI hostel** *Auberge Internationale de Rivière du-Loup* (Ⓣ418/862-7566 or 1-800/461-8585, Ⓦwww.aubergerdl.ca), at 46 Rue de l'Hôtel-de-Ville, occupies an attractive wooden building. Dorm beds are $22, breakfast included. An equally convenient option is the *CÉGEP*, 325 rue St-Pierre (Ⓣ418/862-6903 ext 282), a college residence offering a hundred spartan rooms for $25 throughout the summer. **Motels** and **hotels** include the *Auberge de la Pointe*, 10 boul Cartier (Ⓣ418/862-3514 or 1-800/463-1222, Ⓦwww.aubergedelapointe.com; ❺), with comfortable rooms and its own health spa. Two magnificent **B&Bs** are virtually across from each other on a gorgeous tree-lined stretch of Hwy 132 west of town: *Auberge La Sabline*, 343 rue Fraser (Ⓣ418/867-4890, Ⓦwww.bbcanada.com/lasabline; ❸), and the summer residence of Canada's first prime minister, Sir John A. MacDonald, *Les Rochers*, at no. 336 (Ⓣ418/868-1435; ❹). The municipal **campsite**, exit 507 from Hwy 20 (Camping Municipal De La Pointe De Rivière-Du-Loup; Ⓣ418/862-4281, Ⓦwww.campingquebec.com/rivieredulou p; $20–32; mid-May to late Sept), is off Hwy 132, near the harbour.

Pricey **restaurants** abound in the centre of town – *Le St-Patrice*, 169 rue Fraser (Ⓣ418/862-9895), is among the best, devoted to serving regional produce – dishes start at $25. A walk down rue Lafontaine, near the river, reveals less expensive alternatives – the best value is *La Gourmande* at no. 120 (Ⓣ418/862-4270), where salads and vegetarian meals average about $13, though things get more pricey in the evenings. *L'Estaminet*, 299 rue Lafontaine, is a bar with 150 types of beer and good pub food, including mussels with fries (from $7).

Cabano and Lac Témiscouata

The area southeast of Rivière-du-Loup, along the Trans-Canada Hwy towards Edmundston, New Brunswick (see p.442) – just beyond which is the US border – is saved from mediocrity by the graceful sweep of **Lac Témiscouata**, where a combination of lake, river, woods and hills is adorned by a dazzling display of wild flowers in spring. The Trans-Canada Hwy offers glimpses of the lake, but it's Hwy 232 that tracks along the prettiest stretches, leaving the main road at the sprawling lakeside village of **CABANO**. Aside from **Fort Ingall** (late June to early Sept daily 9.30am–5pm; Ⓣ418/854-2375, Ⓦwww.roseraie.qc.ca; $7), a restored British fortification dating from 1839, there's little to do here except hang out by the lake. Built during a border dispute with the Americans, the fort was part of a series of schemes that strengthened the land link between the St Lawrence and the Bay of Fundy, protecting the area's timber resources. Abandoned in 1842, having seen no action, Ingall has been painstakingly reconstructed, its high stockade surrounding a squat wooden barracks, blockhouse and officers' quarters. Inside the officers' quarters are enjoyable displays on the background to the fort's construction, contemporaneous army life and local archeological finds. There's also a section on Archie Belaney, aka **Grey Owl**, the British conservationist turned native, who settled in the area in the 1920s (see p.204). From Cabano, Hwy 232 follows the shore of the lake before snaking back to the St Lawrence at Rimouski – or you can take the more direct Hwy 293 from the lake's northern extremity to Trois-Pistoles.

There are several **campsites** along the shores of Lac Témiscouata, the nearest to Cabano being the *Témilac*, 33 rue de la Plage, near the junction of Hwy 232 and the TCH (Ⓣ418/854-7660; $18–25; mid-May to Sept). For more comfortable **accommodation** you could try the *Motel Royal*, 19 rue St-Louis

(☎418/854-2307 or 1-888/854-2307, Ⓦwww.motelroyal.net; ❸), a decent and inexpensive place to stay. For **food**, *Le Quai des Brumes*, 140 rue Commercial (☎418/854-1888), is a cheerful place with a terrace and a wide selection of salads and sandwiches. *Auberge de la Gare*, 5 rue de la Gare, specializes in crêpes and pasta and offers **B&B** accommodation upstairs (☎418/845-9315 or 1-888/463-4273; 2).

Trois-Pistoles and beyond

Heading northeast from Rivière-du-Loup along Hwy 132, with the far bank of the St Lawrence clearly visible, the coastal hwy passes through a succession of farming and fishing villages on its way to **TROIS-PISTOLES**, said to be named after a silver goblet worth three *pistoles* (gold coins) that a French sailor dropped into the river while trying to fill it with water in 1621. The town is dominated by the enormous church of **Notre Dame-des-Neiges-de-Trois-Pistoles** (late June to early Sept daily 9am–4.30pm; ☎418/851-1391; $2), built between 1882 and 1887. From a distance the church looks like something out of Disneyland, as the roof, surmounted by four pinnacles, is painted silver. Inside, the vaulted Italianate ceiling is supported by massive trompe-l'oeil marble columns with ornate gilded capitals, while the walls are dotted with nineteenth-century devotional paintings. The most interesting museum in town is the **Parc de l'Aventure Basque en Amérique**, 66 Rue du Parc (daily late June to early Sept 10am–8pm; mid-May to late June & early Sept to mid-Oct noon–4pm; ☎418/851-1556 or 1-877/851-1556, Ⓦwww.paba.qc.ca; $6). Built on the site of the first Basque village in Québec, the informative displays examine their early history in the region. An accompanying English-language booklet is available for the museum. The first weekend of July sees the centre host a Basque festival, during which the traditional stick-and-ball game of pelote is played. The town's other main museum is the **Musée St-Laurent**, 552 rue Notre Dame ouest (late June to early Sept daily 9am–5pm; ☎418/851-2345; $4), which has a great ensemble of cars, with vehicles from the 1930s to the 1970s and an eclectic collection ranging from old packs of cigarettes to harpoons. You can **sea-kayak** at sunset with Kayak de Mer des Îles, 60 av du Parc (mid-May to mid-Sept 11am & 5pm; ☎418/851-4637 or 1-877/851-4637, Ⓦwww.kayaksdesiles.com; $35).

The town's **information centre** is on Hwy 132 with a miniature windmill and lighthouse outside (late June to early Sept daily 9am–7pm; ☎418/851-3698). A **car ferry** crosses to Les Escoumins (mid-May to Oct 2–3 daily; 90min; ☎418/851-4676 or 1-866/851-4676, Ⓦwww.info-basques.com/traverse; $11.50, cars $29) on the Côte-Nord (see p.377). Should you want to break your journey here, try *Motel Trois-Pistoles*, 64 Hwy 132 ouest (☎418/851-2563 or 1-888/999-5599; ❹), which has 32 comfortable rooms, some with views of the river. There's not much in the way of **B&Bs** in the downtown area, with the exception of *Le Pistolois*, 15 rue Rousseau (☎418/851-4481; ❹). *L'Ensoleillé*, at 138 rue Notre Dame ouest (☎418/851-2889), serves up fine vegetarian and fish cuisine on an outdoor terrace for $25 or more. For a picnic

> Edmundston, New Brunswick (see p.468) – just beyond Cabano – is on **Atlantic time**, one hour ahead of Québec's **Eastern time**. However, note that if you carry on over the bridge at Edmundston, which marks the border with the US state of Maine, you have to switch back to Eastern.

lunch head to *La Fromagerie des Basques*, 69 Hwy 132 ouest (ⓣ418/851-2189) for artisan cheeses, bread, pastries and traditional beer, all made on site.

Parc du Bic and Le Bic

Heading east from Trois-Pistoles, Hwy 132 crosses a comparatively tedious landscape of fertile agricultural land, until it reaches the rocky wooded hummocks of the shoreline's **Parc du Bic**. At this naturalists' paradise, whose headlands push up tight against the river, it's possible to see herds of grey seals, especially at dusk. The park (entry $3.50) has three short hiking trails, a beach and a visitors' centre (mid-May to mid-Oct daily 10am–5pm; ⓣ418/869-3333, ⓦwww.sepaq.com) – from which shuttle buses head up to the highest peak, Pic Champlain (late June to late Aug departures every half hour 12.30-3pm; $5.70 return trip), and around the park (3 departures daily; 2hr; $14). You can also view the park from a **bicycle** (rental $26/day) or a **sea kayak** from Rivi-Air Aventure (ⓣ418/723-5252, ⓦwww.rivi-air.qc.ca; from $20 per person). The **campsite** (ⓣ418/736-4711 or 1-800/665-6527, ⓦwww.sepaq.com; $18–38; early June to early Sept) is pleasant, but hwy noise is a problem.

Just beyond the park along Hwy 132, the elongated village of **LE BIC**, perched on a low ridge above its snout-shaped harbour, is a handsome medley of old and modern architectures. Samuel de Champlain named the place "Pic" (for peak), but the name morphed. The *Auberge du Mange Grenouille*, 148 rue Ste-Cécile (ⓣ418/736-5656, ⓦwww.aubergedumangegrenouille.qc.ca; ❸–❻; May to mid-Oct), has a superb **restaurant** (reservations advised) with table d'hote from $29 to $46 per person and attractively furnished double **rooms**. *Aux Cormorants,* 213 chemin du Golf (ⓣ418/736-8113; ❷) is a serene waterside **B&B** nestled along Pointe des Anglais. The **bakery**, *Folles Farines*, at 113 rue St-Jean Baptiste, has a wicked selection of tasty breads, croissants and thin-crust pizzas. Up the hill and facing the handsome church, *Chez Saint-Pierre*, 129 du Mon St-Louis (ⓣ418/736-5051), is a sunny bistro with an imaginative menu and a terrace overlooking the town's rooftops.

Rimouski

Some 20km northeast of Bic, **RIMOUSKI** – "Riki" to its residents – appears quite unattractive from Hwy 132 thanks to a major fire that destroyed one-third of the buildings from the river to midtown in 1950, forcing the city to rebuild in 1960s strip-mall style. But forge past the hwy and into the town, the administrative capital of eastern Québec, and you'll find a youthful city – thanks to the number of educational institutions here – and the interesting **Musée régional de Rimouski**, at 35 rue St-Germain (June–Sept Wed–Fri 9.30am–8pm, Sat–Tues until 6pm; rest of year Wed–Sun noon–5pm, Thurs until 9pm; ⓣ418/724-2272, ⓦwww.museerimouski.qc.ca; $4). It's housed in the oldest church in eastern Québec whose exterior has stayed intact, while the the three floors inside have been renovated and now focus on rotating exhibits on local history and contemporary art.

The Orléans Express **bus** station is at 90 av Léonidas (ⓣ418/723-4923), the **train** station at 57 de l'Évêché est (ⓣ418/722-4737 or 1-800/361-5390) and the rideshare outfit Allô-Stop at 106 rue St-Germain est (ⓣ418/723-5248, ⓦwww.allo-stop.com). There's a **car ferry** to Forestville on the Côte-Nord (late April–Oct 2–4 trips daily; ⓣ418/725-2725 or 1-800/973-2725, ⓦwww.traversier.com; 55min; $18, cars $38), which only holds thirty cars so reservations are essential. The Relais Nordick departs Rimouski every week.

Rimouski's **tourist office**, 50 rue St-Germain ouest (mid-June to early Sept daily 9am–8pm; early Sept to early Oct daily 9am–noon & 1–4.30pm; rest of the year closed weekends; ⓣ418/723-2322 or 1-800/746-6875), is in the centre of town, on the waterfront. It has **accommodation** listings, including the college rooms available during the summer vacation at *CÉGEP Residences*, 320 rue St-Louis (ⓣ418/723-4636 or 1-800/463-0617, ⓦwww.cegep-rimouski.qc.ca/residenc; $22–33). For **B&B** accommodation, *Chez Charles et Marguerite*, 686 boul St-Germain ouest (ⓣ418/723-3938; ❸), has cheery rooms looking out onto fields that lead down to the St Lawrence. The town's cheapest motel is the *Motel St-Laurent*, 740 boul St-Germain ouest (ⓣ418/723-9217 or 1-888/440-9241; ❷). For **camping**, *Le Bocage*, 124 Hwy 132 (ⓣ418/739-3125; $20), is 13km east of Rimouski in Sainte-Luce, a quiet village that's become a lively beach resort. Rimouski has a number of affordable places to **eat**, not least the *Central Café*, 31 rue de l'Évêché ouest (ⓣ418/722-4011; dinner from $20), a bistro with great salads and pizza in a home decorated with birdcages. The *Maison du Spaghetti* at 35 boul St-Germain est (ⓣ418/723-6010) serves up hearty pasta at a reasonable $13; and if you're into kitsch, plump for *Retro 50* across the street at no. 38 (ⓣ418/723-4858), a themed 1950s diner.

A few kilometres east from Rimouski along Hwy 132, the small town of **POINTE-AU-PÈRE** holds not much more than the **Maison Lamontagne**, 707 boul du Rivage (late June to early Sept daily 10am–6pm; ⓣ418/722-4038, ⓦwww.maisonlamontagne.com; $5), the oldest house in eastern Québec; though there's not much inside that's worth your time or money, the gardens are free and quite educational. Further down the road, the **Musée de la Mer** (daily June–Aug 9am–6pm; Sept & Oct until 5pm; ⓣ418/724-6214, ⓦwww.museedelamer.qc.ca; $10.50) is housed in a modern building that resembles a tilting ship. The exhibit includes a 3D film on the *Empress of Ireland*, a luxury liner that sank offshore here in 1914, a disaster second only to the *Titanic*, with more than a thousand lives lost.

Sainte-Flavie and Matane

From Rimouski to Matane a few places are worth a stop. The first is **SAINTE-FLAVIE**, a small coastal town that's home to Gaspésie's **regional tourist office**, 357 rue de la Mer (daily mid-June to mid-Sept 8am–8pm; rest of year 8.30am–4.30pm; ⓣ418/775-2223 or 1-800/463-0323). Nearby at no. 564, the **Centre d'art Marcel Gagnon** (daily: early May to mid-Oct 7.30am–10pm; mid-Oct to April 8am–9pm; ⓣ418/775-2829 or 1-866/775-2828, ⓦwww.centredart.net; free) offers a unique and memorable sight. The artist's outdoor work, *Le Grand Rassemblement* (The Great Gathering), groups more than eighty life-size statues and seven rafts, starting on a strip of land and then leading into the water. The works are especially remarkable at high tide, as the statues emerge out of the river, and the rafts seem to float. Another visual feast lies 9km further east down Hwy 132. Here the **Jardins de Métis** (June & Sept 8.30am–6pm, July & Aug until 8pm; ⓣ418/775-2222, ⓦwww.jardinsmetis.com; $14) is a gigantic aristocratic mansion and garden complex with over 100,000 introduced species of plants neatly presented among forty acres of features such as miniature bridges and tumbling brooks. Whatever your tastes, it's an impressive horticultural feat.

MATANE, 98km from Rimouski, appears to be dominated by oil refineries and cement works, but in fact fishing and forestry have long been the mainstays of the local economy. The Matane River, which bisects the town, is spanned by a pair of bridges – one beside the harbour (part of Hwy 132), the other a shorter affair a few hundred metres north, next to the fish ladder, which was built to help salmon head upstream to spawn. At the **Barrage Mathieu-d'Amours** (mid-June to Sept 7.30am–9.30pm; ⓣ418/562-7006) the dam's observation area allows visitors to watch salmon battling to get upstream. Matane's **tourist office** (late June to mid-Sept daily 8.30am–8.30pm; rest of year Mon–Fri 8.30am–5pm; ⓣ418/562-1065 or 1-877/762-8263) is beside Hwy 132, just west of the centre, in the lighthouse at 968 av du Phare ouest. Simple institutional **accommodation** can be rented at *CÉGEP de Matane*, 616 av St-Rédempteur (ⓣ418/562-1240, ⓦwww.cgmatane.qc.ca; ❶), while *Gite des Îles*, at 29 av Desjardins (ⓣ418/562-6688, ⓦwww.bbcanada.com/legitedesiles; ❸) is a homely **B&B** right by the Matane River with comfortable rooms. Most of Matane's **hotels** and **motels** are pricey: *Auberge la Seigneurie*, at 621 av St-Jérôme (ⓣ418/562-0021 or 1-877/783-4466, ⓦwww.aubergelaseigneurie.com; ❹), is one of the best and *Motel Le Beach*, 1441 rue Matane-sur-Mer (ⓣ418/562-1350 or 1-888/570-1350, ⓦwww.welcome.to/motel_lebeach; ❷), is one of the least expensive; it has sea views but is nothing special. There's a huge **campsite** at 150 rte Louis-Félix-Dionne (ⓣ418/562-3414, ⓦwww.ville.matane.qc.ca; $16–22; mid-June to Aug) southwest of the centre of town – follow the river past the industrial park – where sites are pleasant amid trees. A casual **restaurant** decorated by local artists, *Restaurant Le Rafiot*, 1415 av du Phare ouest (ⓣ418/562-8080; dinner $20–30), alongside Hwy 132, is the best bet for shrimp, while *Bistro de l'Estuaire*, 50 rue d'Amours (ⓣ418/562-2939), is the place to go for mussels. *Italia Pizzeria*, 101 St-Pierre, serves great, moderately priced pizza.

From Matane, **car ferries** (ⓣ418/562-2500 or 1-877/562-6560, ⓦwww.traversiers.gouv.qc.ca) cross to the Côte-Nord (see p.377) on two routes: to Godbout (April–Dec 1–2 trips daily; Jan–March 1 daily except Thurs & Sun; 2hr 10min; $13, cars $30); and to Baie-Comeau (April–Dec 1–2 trips daily; Jan–March daily except Thurs & Sun; 2hr 20min; same fares).

Sainte-Anne-des-Monts and around

East of Matane the hwy hugs the shoreline, passing through increasingly rugged scenery where the forested hills of the interior push up against the fretted, rocky coast. A string of skimpy fishing villages breaks up this empty landscape – places like Capucins, with its fine headland setting, and **Cap Chat**, whose 76 towering wind turbines are visible for miles around. Of these, the 110m-tall **Éole de Cap-Chat** (mid-June to Oct daily 9am–5pm; ⓣ418/786-5719, ⓦwww.eolecapchat.com; $6) is the tallest and most powerful vertical-axis wind tower in the world.

Just 16km beyond Cap-Chat, unenticing **SAINTE-ANNE-DES-MONTS** sprawls along the coastline, its untidy appearance only offset by its relaxed atmosphere and its convenience – it's an easy place to break your journey before heading on to the cape, or inland to the Parc de la Gaspésie. The lone sight is the **Exploramer** at 1 rue du Quai (mid-June to mid-Oct daily 9am–6pm; ⓣ418/763-2500, ⓦwww.exploramer.org; $8), a marine and birdlife discovery centre on two floors. Head to the aquarium downstairs, where you can handle starfish, sea cucumbers and scallops. The **HI hostel** *Auberge internationale Ste-Anne-des-monts*, 295 1ère av est (ⓣ418/763-7123, ⓦwww.aubergegaspesie.com; dorm beds $24), has great views over the river and offers bike rental and transportation to Parc de la Gaspésie, while the *Motel Manoir sur Mer*, 475 1ère av ouest (ⓣ418/763-7844; ❷–❸), has rooms backing onto the beach. For **B&B** accommodation, try *La Villa des Roses*, 500 1ère av ouest (ⓣ418/763-3529; ❷).

Parc de la Gaspésie

As you travel south from Ste-Anne-des-Monts on Hwy 299, the snowcapped **Chic-Choc Mountains** – which make up most of the **Parc de la Gaspésie** – can be spotted in the distance, a stark and forbidding backdrop to the coastal plain. The Chic-Chocs are the most northerly protrusions of the Appalachian Ridge, which extends deep into the US, and the serpentine road reveals the full splendour of their alpine interior. The sequence of valleys framed by thickly wooded slopes culminates in the staggering ravine that lies at the foot of the towering **Mont Albert**. In this ravine, 40km from Sainte-Anne-des-Monts, the park's extremely helpful reception and interpretation centre (mid-June to mid-Sept daily 8am–10pm, otherwise until 8pm; ⓣ418/763-5435 or 1-866/727-2427, ⓦwww.sepaq.com; park admission $3.50) rents out hiking equipment and has details and maps of half a dozen well-signposted **hiking trails**; most are about a day's duration, though a couple around the base are shorter. Prospective hikers should come equipped with warm clothes, food and water, and log their intended route at the centre. The trails ascend to the summits of the area's three highest mountains – Mont Jacques-Cartier, Mont Richardson and Mont Albert – and are remarkable in that they climb through three distinctive habitats. Herds of Virginia deer thrive in the rich vegetation of the lowest zone, while moose live in the boreal forest, and caribou in the tundra near the peaks. This is the only place in Québec where the three species exist in close proximity. The park is linked by **shuttle bus** to Ste-Anne-des-Monts (late June to early Oct daily 8am; $6 roundtrip) with buses travelling between the town's tourist office and the interpretation centre.

The park has four **campsites**, two of which, *Camping La Riviere and Camping Mont Albert* (ⓣ418/763-1333; from $20.87 per site), are conveniently near the interpretation centre. Close by is the smart, modern *Gîte du Mont-Albert* (ⓣ418/763-2288 or 1-866/727-2427, ⓦwww.sepaq.com; ❺-❼) which offers the only fixed **lodgings** in the park; room prices rocket during the summer and skiing seasons, but you couldn't wish for a handier location. The *Gîte* has an excellent but pricey restaurant specializing in regional produce such as pan-seared rabbit, caribou medallions and the Gite's own home smoked salmon. The Gite also controls a number of **chalets** (from $35 per night per person) around the park, offering simple but reliable facilities.

Mont-Saint-Pierre

Heading east from Sainte-Anne-des-Monts towards the tip of the Gaspé Peninsula, the road often squeezes between the ocean and the sheer rock faces of the mountains, its twists and turns passing tumbling scree and picturesque coves.

The view as you approach **MONT-SAINT-PIERRE** is particularly majestic, the curving seashore and the swelling mountains together framing this little community set at the mouth of a wide river valley. This low-key resort is dedicated to bathing and sea fishing, except during the ten-day **hang-gliding festival** at the end of July (ⓣ418/797-2222, ⓦwww.mont-saint-pierre.ca). During the rest of the summer you can fly in tandem with Carrefour Aventure (ⓣ418/797-5033 or 1-800/463-2210) who also rent out sea kayaks and mountain bikes. There are several inexpensive **motels** along rue Prudent-Cloutier: try *Chalets Auberge Bernatchez* at no. 12 (ⓣ418/797-2733, ⓦwww.mont-saint-pierre.ca; ❶) or *Motel Restaurant au Délice* at no. 100 (ⓣ1-888/797-2955, ⓦwww.audelice.com; ❸). *Auberge les Vagues*, at no. 84 (ⓣ418/797-2851; ❷), is a motel that doubles as a hostel (dorm beds $19). For **camping**, there's

Du Pont on Hwy 132 (☎418/797-2951; $19; June–Sept) and a larger **municipal campsite** at 103 rue Pierre-Godfroie-Coulombe (☎418/797-2250; $20–30; mid-June to early Sept). There are a couple of good places to **eat**: *Le Croissant d'Art*, on the main thoroughfare, is an inexpensive artsy café ideal for light lunches, while *Les Joyeux Naufragés*, 7 rte Pierre-Mercier, offers more substantial fare at equally affordable prices.

Parc National de Forillon

At the very tip of the peninsula, the **PARC NATIONAL DE FORILLON** is the scenic culmination of the Gaspé, encompassing thick forest and mountains, crossed by hiking trails and fringed by stark cliffs along a deeply indented coastline. The splendour of the landscape is complemented by the **wildlife**: black bears, moose, beavers, porcupines and foxes are all common to the area. To chance sighting them, you're best to arrive early in the morning or at dusk. More than two hundred species of birds have also been seen, ranging from sea birds like gannets, cormorants and guillemots, to songbirds such as the skylark and chaffinch. From the coastal paths around Cap Gaspé itself, **whales and porpoises** can also be spotted (May–Oct). As Thomas Anburey, a British soldier, observed in the 1770s, "They cause most beautiful fireworks in the water: for being in such abundance, and darting with amazing velocity, a continued stream of light glides through the water, and as they cross each other, the appearance is so picturesque that no description can reach it." Roughly triangular in shape, the park is sandwiched between the Gulf of St Lawrence and the Baie de Gaspé and encircled by Hwys 197 and 132, the former crossing the interior to delineate the park's western limits, the latter mostly keeping to the seashore and threading through Anse-au-Griffon and Cap-des-Rosiers – tiny coastal villages with views onto the river and Forillon's wooded parkland. Make the time to take this route as the views are spectacular. You can also stop for a cup of tea at the **Manoir Le Boutillier**, a restored 1850s house at 578 boul Griffon, in Anse-au-Griffon (mid-June to early Oct daily 9am–5pm; ☎418/892-5150; $7; guided tours only) with a café serving period desserts. Closer to the park, the **lighthouse** at Cap-des-Rosiers is the tallest in Canada.

Parc Forillon has numerous hiking trails, the best of which takes you to the tip of **Cap Gaspé**, otherwise known as "land's end". The ninety-minute (8km) return trip starts a few kilometres south of the **interpretation centre** (see below). The trail extends from the end of the paved road beyond Grande-Grave, a restored fishing village founded by immigrants from Jersey – the inhabitants were relocated as recently as 1970, when the park was established. Their historical presence is enshrined in two sites situated along the trail that follows the southern coast of the cape. The first, **Hyman & Son's General Store and Warehouse** (early June to mid-Oct 10am–5pm; free with park entry) is a marvellous restoration of a 1920s general store; nearby **Anse-Blanchette** (mid-June to early Sept 10am–5pm; free with park entry), a fisherman's house dating from the same era, has also been painstakingly restored; the onsite barn frequently does duty as a stage for storytelling and musical acts. You'll also note unfinished buildings down near the edge of the cliff: these are the remnants of the set for the popular Québec television series *L'Ombre de l'Épervier*. After these, the path rises and falls until it makes the final steep ascent to the **lighthouse**, which is set on a 150m cliff with the ocean on three sides.

Park practicalities

Admission to Parc Forillon costs $7. The park's **interpretation centre** (daily early June & late Aug to mid-Oct 10am–5pm; late June to late Aug 9am–6pm;

☎418/892-5572, Ⓦwww.pc.gc.ca/forillon) is close to the lighthouse, near the village of Cap-des-Rosiers on the park's north side. Here, you can get an imaginative overview of the natural and human history of the area and a wealth of suggestions as to how to spend your time. There are also two **visitors' centres** off Hwy 132 – one at Anse-au-Griffon (daily mid-June to Aug 8.30am–9.30pm; Sept to mid-Oct 9am–4pm; ☎418/368-5505 or 1-800/463-6769), the other on the south coast at Penouille (same hours; ☎418/892-5661). **whale-watching** excursions depart from Grande-Grave (June–Oct 1–4 daily; ☎418/892-5500, Ⓦwww.baleines-forillon.com; $40).

The park's half-dozen **campsites** (all ☎418/368-6050, Ⓦwww.pccamping.ca; from $22.75) are pleasantly situated and well maintained; *Camping Cap Bon-Ami* (early June to early Sept) has a particularly delightful setting just south of the interpretation centre. Alternatively, the villages edging the park offer plain accommodation that includes Anse-au-Griffon's *Motel le Noroît*, 589 boul Griffon (☎418/892-5531; ❷), and Cap-aux-Os's HI **hostel**, 2095 boul Grande-Grève (☎418/892-5153, Ⓦwww.gaspesie.net/aj-gaspe; $24), with a café, laundry facilities and a **mountain-bike rental** shop.

Gaspé

The town of **GASPÉ**, straddling the hilly estuary of the York River – its name derived from *Gespeg*, "the end of the land" in the Micmac language – is a disappointment after the scenic drama of the national park, a humdrum settlement of about 17,000 people whose hard-pressed economy is reliant on its deep-water port. This is the spot where the French navigator and explorer **Jacques Cartier** landed in July 1534, on the first of his three trips up the St Lawrence. He stayed here for just eleven days, time enough to erect a wooden cross engraved with the escutcheon of Francis I, staking out the king's – and Christianity's – claim to this new territory. Cartier's first aim was to find a sea route to the Orient, but he also had more extensive ambitions – to acquire land for himself and his men, exploit the Indians as fur gatherers and discover precious metals to rival the loot the Spaniards had taken from the Aztecs. Naturally, Cartier had to disguise his real intentions on the first trip and his initial contacts with the Iroquois were cordial. Then, in the spring of 1536, he betrayed their trust by taking two of the local chief's sons back with him to Francis I. They were never returned, and when Cartier made his third trip in 1541 the Iroquois were so suspicious that he was unable to establish the colony he had been instructed to found. Desperate to salvage his reputation, Cartier sailed back to France with what he thought was a cargo of gold and diamonds. His cargo turned out to be iron pyrite and quartz crystals.

Just to the east of the town centre, at 80 boul Gaspé, the **Jacques Cartier monument** looks out over the bay from the grounds of the town museum. It consists of six striking bronze dolmens carved in relief that record Cartier's visit and treatment of the natives in ambivalent terms, along with anodyne homilies on the nature and unity of humankind. The **museum** itself, 80 boul Gaspé (late June to early Oct daily 9am–5pm; otherwise Tues–Fri 9am–noon & 1–5pm, Sat & Sun 1–5pm; ☎418/368-1534; $4), illuminates the social issues that have confronted the inhabitants of the peninsula to the present – isolation from the centres of power, depopulation and, more recently, unemployment. Temporary displays concentrate mostly on local subjects, like the peninsula's artists and musicians. A good ten-minutes' walk west, near the top of rue Jacques-Cartier, stands the **Gaspé Cathedral**. Built in 1970, it's the only wooden cathedral in North America and its barn-like exterior has an extraordinarily dour and industrial appearance. The interior is completely different: the nave – all straight lines and symmetrical simplicity – is bathed in warm, softly coloured light that pours in through an enormous stained-glass window.

Just outside town, the white **Sanctuaire Notre Dame-des-Douleurs** (early June to mid-Sept daily 9am–5pm, rest of the year Mon–Fri 9am–4.30pm, Sunday 1–4pm; ⓣ418/368-2133; $3) is a popular pilgrimage site due to the healing powers it's said to have, supported by the collection of crutches, braces and canes found in the chapel entombing Father Watier, the sanctuary's founder. Up a slight incline behind the church, the replica of the Lourdes Grotto (replete with outdoor altar) and the Garden of Mary's Sorrows are both attractive gardens with remarkable religious sculptures. Next door, the **Site Historique Micmac de Gespeg**, 783 boul Pointe Navarre (June–Sept daily 9am–5pm; guided tours only; ⓣ418/368-7568; $5), is a replica of the aboriginal village that stood here in 1675, when aboriginal trading with Europeans was in full swing. The site offers interesting insight into how to build tepees and animal traps and carve utensils, but the visit is overlong at 2½ hours.

Practicalities

Buses to Gaspé stop on the main street, rue Jacques-Cartier, at the *Motel Adams*. The **tourist office** (daily 8am–8pm; ⓣ418/368-6335) is on the far side of the river from the town centre along Hwy 132; it has accommodation listings and maps of the town. **College rooms** are available during the summer at the *CÉGEP de la Gaspésie et des Îles*, 94 rue Jacques-Cartier (ⓣ418/368-2749, ⓦwww.cgaspesie.qc.ca/logis_vacances; ❶–❹; mid-June to mid-Sept). Most of the town's **B&B** accommodation is of high quality, but *Les Petits Matins*, 129 rue de la Reine (ⓣ418/368-1370; ❷), is the best, located in an old bank building and with excellent breakfasts. Bargain-basement **motel** accommodation is available at *Motel Plante*, 137 rue Jacques-Cartier (ⓣ418/368-2254 or 1-888/368-2254, ⓦwww.motelplante.com; ❶–❺).

Le Bourlingueur, next to the Jacques-Cartier mall opposite the main bridge at 207 de la Reine, is recommended for **breakfast** (around $4), though the Chinese and Canadian dishes on the evening menu are rather pricey, with main courses costing $13. *Brise-Bise*, 135 rue de la Reine (ⓣ418/368-1456), is a great bistro and a swinging bar at night. If you can afford to splurge, do it at the *Café des Artistes*, 249 boul Gaspé (ⓣ418/368-2255; table d'hote from $30) – it's one of the best restaurants on the peninsula for French cuisine. The upstairs cigar room nestled under the eaves is worth a visit whether you eat or not.

Percé and around

Once a humble fishing community, **PERCÉ** is a prime holiday spot, thanks to the tourist potential of the gargantuan limestone rock that rears up from the sea here facing the reddish cliffs of the shore. One of Canada's most celebrated natural phenomena, the **Rocher Percé** – so named for the hole at the western end – is nearly 500m long and 90m high, and is a surreal sight at dawn, when it appears bathed in an eerie golden iridescence. The town is now replete with tacky gift shops and mediocre restaurants and bars; off-season, when much of the resort closes down, Percé maintains a delightfully relaxed and sleepy feel. At low tide it's possible, if you hurry, to walk around most of the rock – ideally wearing waterproof shoes with good treads – starting from the lookout beyond the red-roofed houses at the end of rue Mont-Joli. Access to the rock now costs $1 – allegedly for upkeep of the belvedere and stairway leading to the stone beach – tide times

△ Percé, Gaspé Peninsula

are posted at the top. One of the most spectacular longer-range views of the monolith is from the top of **Mont Sainte-Anne**, which rises directly behind Percé town; the path is signposted from behind the church on avenue de l'Église. The steep 3km walk takes about an hour each way. A separate trail leads to the **Grotto**, a lovely spot with waterfalls and statues of the Virgin Mary nestled into the mountain's crevasses.

Apart from the rock, there's precious little to see in Percé, though the **Centre d'Interprétation du Parc de l'Île-Bonaventure-et-du-Rocher-Percé** (late May to mid-Oct daily 9am–5pm; free), some 2km to the south of the centre (exit Hwy 132 at route des Failles and turn left along route d'Irlande), has some enjoyable displays on the area's flora and fauna. In the middle of town, in the old Charles Robin Company building formerly used for processing and storing fish, the **Musée la Chafaud**, 145 Hwy 132 (daily late June to late Sept 10am–8pm; $5), displays traditional and contemporary art and occasionally gets high-calibre exhibitions. A small room downstairs has some old pictures of Percé. A few kilometres west of Percé, **La Vieille Usine de l'Anse-à-Beaufils** (June to mid-Sept daily 10am–10pm; ⓣ418/782-2777, ⓦwww.lavieilleusine.qc.ca) showcases a wide range of local art in a renovated fish-packing plant that fronts a decent beach. Otherwise, Percé makes a useful base for visiting several natural attractions, including the **Grande Crevasse**, a volcanically formed split in a rocky outcrop that's just a few millimetres wide but several hundred metres deep. The clearly marked path takes about an hour to walk in each direction and begins behind the *Auberge de Gargantua*, a first-class restaurant on route des Failles.

Hwy 132 bisects Percé and passes just to the north of the main wharf, close to the **tourist office** (late May to late-Oct daily 9am–7pm; ⓣ418/782-5448), which operates a free room-reservation service and keeps boat and tide timetables. Arriving from Carleton or Gaspé, **buses** drop passengers in the centre of Percé at the Petro-Canada service station, but the VIA Rail **train** station is 10km south of town on Hwy 132. Most of Percé's **accommodation** is open

Boat trips from Percé

From the wharf in the centre of Percé, frequent **boat trips**, operated by Les Traversiers de l'Île (1hr 30min to 3hr; ⓣ418/782-2750; $20–30), go around the nearby **Île Bonaventure** bird reserve (daily: late May–June & Sept to mid-Oct 8.15am–4pm; July & Aug 8.15am–5pm; $3.50), whose precipitous cliffs are favoured by gannets in particular, as well as kittiwakes, razorbills, guillemots, gulls, cormorants and puffins. You can also arrange to disembark at the island's tiny jetty, where all of the lengthy walking trails lead to the clifftops above the gannet colonies, and one includes a visit to **Le Boutillier**, a restored nineteenth-century fisherman's home.

The wharf is also the departure point for **whale-watching** excursions – between May and October the blue and humpback whales are often in the area, and you may also see porpoises, seals and the rarer white-sided dolphins. Zodiacs speed out with Observation Littoral Percé (ⓣ418/782-5359; $40), but as they fill up quickly, you may have to opt for a larger glassed-in boat with Les Croisières Julien Cloutier (ⓣ418/782-5606 or 1-877/782-2161; $20). Trips last two or three hours and should be reserved in advance at the various ticket kiosks lining the main drag.

during the summer months only, when advance booking is advised; in the off-season, you'll likely have to stay in Gaspé. Charming **motels** dot Hwy 132 – including *Le Macareux*, no. 262 (ⓣ418/782-2414 or 1-866/602-2414, ⓦwww.members.lycos.fr/motelmacareux; ❶–❸), and *Le Mirage*, no. 288 (ⓣ418/782-5151 or 1-800/463-9011, ⓦwww.hotellemirage.com; ❸–❻). Rather more upmarket, the *Hôtel la Normandie*, 221 Hwy 132 ouest (ⓣ418/782-2112 or 1-800/463-0820, ⓦwww.normandieperce.com; ❺–❼), has a clutch of bright, modern bedrooms with superb views along the coast. Also on Hwy 132 is the town's dynamic **hostel** *La Maison Rouge*, 125 Rte 132 (ⓣ418/782-2227; ❸; dorm beds $20), which has kayaks for rent. *Camping Gargantua*, 222 rte des Failles (ⓣ418/782-2852; $22–30), is one of five nearby campgrounds and has great views of the rock.

La Maison du Pêcheur, 155 Place du Quai (ⓣ418/782-5624) just up from the wharf, has fine **seafood** dishes, with evening table d'hote from $25 upwards; while similarly priced *Le Matelot*, 7 rue de l'Église (ⓣ418/782-2569), serves candlelit lobster with live entertainment. Substantial **snacks**, coffees and vegetarian dishes for under $20 are best in the faintly bohemian atmosphere of *Les Fous de Bassan*, 162 Rte 132 (ⓣ418/782-2266), also on the main street. For very fine food, dine at *Auberge Gargantua*, 222 rte des Failles (ⓣ418/782-2852; dinner around $30), with gourmet French cuisine and great panoramas over town, or *La Normandia*, 221 Hwy 132 (ⓣ418/782-2112 or 1-800/463-0820), for such delights as lobster baked in champagne.

Chandler and Bonaventure

To the southwest of Percé, Hwy 132 follows the coast as the dramatic mountains that dominate the north and east of the peninsula are replaced by a gently undulating landscape of wooded hills and farmland. **CHANDLER**, the first town of any size on this route, is an ugly lumber port notable solely for the wreck of the Peruvian freighter *Unisol* in the mouth of the harbour. It ran aground in a gale in 1983, allegedly because its captain, unable to negotiate entry into the port for his cement-laden vessel, got drunk and allowed the vessel to run onto the sandbank where it remains today. The most easterly resort on the bay is **BONAVENTURE**, whose tiny centre, beside Hwy 132, edges the marshy delta and man-made lagoon of the river that sports its name. A wildlife observation centre, **Bioparc de la Gaspésie**, 123 rue des Vieux Ponts (daily June–Sept 9am–6pm; ⓣ1-866/534-1997, ⓦwww.bioparc.ca; $12.50), showcases the region's animals – caribou, lynx, otters and mountain lions – in their respective ecosystems. But Bonaventure is really known for being a stronghold of **Acadian** culture. Their traditions and heritage are celebrated at the **Musée Acadien du Québec**, 95 av Port-Royal (late June to early Sept daily 9am–6pm; early Sept to mid-Oct daily 9am–5pm; mid-Oct to early May Mon–Fri 9am–noon & 1–4.30pm, Sun 1–4.30pm; early May to late June Mon–Fri 9am–noon & 1–4.30pm, Sat & Sun 1–4.30pm; ⓣ418/534-4000, ⓦwww.museeacadien.com; $7), set in an imposing blue and white wooden building, once the church hall, in the town centre. Highlights of the collection include some delightful handmade furniture dating from the eighteenth century and a range of intriguing photographs that encapsulate something of the hardships of Acadian rural life. On the opposite side of the main street **Cur de la mer** is, uniquely, a centre for the production of fish-leather products such as purses and wallets. The small shop sells a variety of examples and is worth a browse.

Next door to the Musee Acadien, Bonaventure's **tourist office**, 91 av Port-Royal (mid-June to Aug daily 9am–6pm; ⓣ418/534-4014), has background information on the town and **accommodation** lists. The latter includes *Motel Grand Pré*, 118 av Grand-Pré (ⓣ418/534-2053 or 1-800/463-2053, ⓦwww.fortune1000.ca/grandpre; ❻), and more reasonable **B&Bs** like the bohemian *Au Foin Fou*, 204 rte de la Rivière (ⓣ418/534-4413, ⓦwww.foinfou.qc.ca; ❷), and *Auberge du Café Acadien*, 168 av Beaubassin (ⓣ418/534-4276; ❷) – above the excellent *Café Acadien*, which serves imaginative French-Canadian **food**. *Cime Aventure*, 200 chemin Arsenault (ⓣ418/534-2333 or 1-800/790-2463, ⓦwww.cimeaventure.com), has campsites ($25), tepees ($50) to sleep in alongside the Bonaventure river and runs adventure trips into the local area (3hr to 6 days; prices vary). *Camping Plage Beaubassin*, 154 av Beaubassin (ⓣ418/534-3246, ⓦwww.bonaventuregaspesie.com/dec_beaubassin.aspx; $19–28; early June to Aug), is a municipal **campsite** on the spit of land between the lagoon and the bay.

New Richmond and around

NEW RICHMOND, 30km from Bonaventure, has only one worthy attraction, the **Centre d'Héritage Britannique de la Gaspésie**, beside the bay towards the west end of town, 7km from the highway, at 351 boul Perron ouest (daily mid-June to mid-Sept 9am–5pm; last admission 4pm; ⓣ418/392-4487; $10). Set in wooded parkland around the old lighthouse at Duthie's Point, near the mouth of the Rivière Cascapédia, it's a kind of Loyalist theme park-cum-ghost town made up of a collection of wooden buildings assembled from the surrounding region. Although they were all restored to their nineteenth- or early twentieth-century appearance, many are ill-kept and falling into disrepair today. Even so, the centre is spacious enough for a pleasant stroll along the shore. It even has its own tiny beach.

Carleton and the Miguasha Peninsula

Just west of New Richmond, Hwy 299 runs north along the banks of the Cascapédia towards the Parc de la Gaspésie (see p.345), while the coastal Hwy 132 continues on to the popular bayside resort of **CARLETON**, where the mountains of the interior return to dominate the landscape. Founded in 1756 by Acadian refugees, Carleton is an unassuming little place that stands back from the sea behind a broad lagoon, linked to the narrow coastal strip by a couple of long causeways. The town has a bird sanctuary – a favourite haunt of wading species like the sandpiper and plover – and several accessible bathing beaches where you can rent kayaks (ⓣ418/364-7802). But what makes the place special is the contrast between the coastal flatlands and the backdrop of wooded hills that rise up behind the town. At 582m, **Mont Saint-Joseph** is the highest of these and is presided over by the **Oratoire Notre Dame-du-Mont-Saint-Joseph** (daily mid-June to early Sept 8am–7pm, early Sept to Oct 9am–5pm; ⓣ418/364-2256; $4), a disappointing church that incorporates the walls of a stone chapel built on the site in 1935. A 3km maze of steep footpaths slip past streams and waterfalls before they reach the summit. You can also take the less adventurous option and drive up to see the splendid panoramic views over the bay and across to New Brunswick.

Carleton is a good place to stay overnight and, while you're here, the hilly **Miguasha Peninsula**, some 20km to the west off Hwy 132, makes a pleasant excursion. Famous for its fossils, this tiny peninsula is home to the **Parc de Miguasha**, where the cream of the fossil crop is displayed at the combined **research centre and museum** (daily June to Aug 9am–6pm; Sept to mid-Oct 9am–5pm; otherwise Mon–Fri 8.30am–noon & 1–4.30pm; $11). Frequent and free guided tours take in the museum, the research area and a walk along the beach and cliffs. About 800m from the museum is the jetty for the little **car ferry** (late June to early Sept hourly 7.30am–7.30pm; 20min; ⓣ506/684-5107; $12 one-way for driver and car, $1 per additional passenger), a two-minute ride to Dalhousie in New Brunswick, a short cut that avoids the tip of the Baie des Chaleurs.

Carleton's many **motels** line the main street, boul Perron: *Manoir Belle Plage*, no. 474 (ⓣ418/364-3388 or 1-800/463-0780, ⓦwww.manoirbelleplage.com; ❸–❻) has a touch of class. A **B&B**, *Gite Les Leblanc*, is at no. 346 (ⓣ418/364-7601, ⓦwww.giteetaubergedupassant.com/Leblanc; ❷). The town has a well-situated **campsite**, *Camping Carleton*, on the causeway, Banc de Larocque (mid-June to Aug; ⓣ418/364-3992, ⓦwww.carletonsurmer.com; from $21). *Le Bleu Marine*, 203 rte du Quai, offers affordable lunchtime menus overlooking the beach, while more substantial seafood **meals** are available at *Restaurant le Héron*, at no. 561 (where the **bus** stops), and the expensive but superb *La Maison Monti*, at 840 boul Perron (ⓣ418/364-6181). If you're heading off to the Parc de Miguasha, pack up a picnic lunch at the bakery *La Mie Véritable*, 578 boul Perron.

Pointe-à-la-Croix and around

Some 50km west of Carleton, humdrum **POINTE-À-LA-CROIX** is the site of the inter-provincial bridge over to Campbellton, New Brunswick. During the summer, a **tourist booth** in the tiny wooden house by the turn-off for the bridge on Hwy 132 (daily 8am–8pm) offers a full range of information on the Gaspé Peninsula.

Just before the bridge, a right turn leads to the little waterside community of **LISTUGUJ** (Restigouche), the heart of a Micmac Indian reservation that functions on New Brunswick time because the children go to school in Campbellton. The village is home to the Micmacs, an Algonquian-speaking people who spread across the Atlantic seaboard from Nova Scotia through to the Gaspé and east Newfoundland. Their history is a familiarly sad one: trading furs for European knives, hatchets and pots, the Micmacs quarrelled with other aboriginal groups over hunting grounds until there was a state of perpetual warfare. In later years, the Micmacs proved loyal allies to the French military

New Brunswick is on **Atlantic time**, one hour ahead of Québec.

cause, but, as with all other aboriginal groups, their numbers were decimated by European diseases and they remain a neglected minority. However, the reserve is self-governing and one of the five richest in Canada (of 800-odd reserves). The **Listuguj Arts and Cultural Centre** (May–Sept daily 9am–5pm; $5) offers a small display of traditional crafts and buildings from before European contact. The clothing, canoes and porcupine quill boxes are all made locally to rekindle interest in Micmac culture and traditional skills.

A couple of kilometres west of the bridge, back along Hwy 132, **La Bataille-de-la-Restigouche**, a national historic site, commemorates the crucial naval engagement of 1760, which effectively extinguished French hopes of relieving their stronghold in Montréal, the year after the fall of Québec City. The French fleet, which had already taken casualties in evading the blockade of Bordeaux, was forced to take refuge in the mouth of the Rivière Restigouche and then, despite assistance from local Micmacs and Acadians, was overpowered by superior British forces. The site's excellent **interpretation centre** (daily June to early Oct 9am–5pm; Ⓦwww.pc.gc.ca/ristigouche; $4) contains relics of the French fleet, especially the frigate *Le Machault*, which has been partly reconstructed. An audiovisual display provides a graphic account of the battle and of its strategic significance.

There's no need to stay in Pointe-à-la-Croix, but if you're marooned here, try an unusually regal **hostel**, *Auberge du Château Bahia* (Ⓣ418/788-2048; ❷; dorms $24), in **POINTE-À-LA-GARDE**, some 6km east of Listuguj and signposted off Hwy 132. It's in an eccentric Renaissance-style wooden castle built by the owner and his father – and the food is excellent. Rates include breakfast, and banquet-style dinners are served ($12).

Matapédia

At the western tip of the Baie des Chaleurs, at the confluence of the Restigouche and Matapédia rivers, the tiny village of **MATAPÉDIA**, a Micmac term meaning "there where the two rivers meet", is surrounded by steep green hills and lies at the centre of an excellent salmon-fishing region. Not a lot else happens here aside from canoe trips down the river which can be organized by Nature Aventure (Ⓣ418/865-2100, Ⓦwww.matapediaaventure.com). A two-hour canoe trip departing from Matapedia costs $25 per person while a multi-day canoe-camping trip starts at $65 per person. For eating there isn't a great choice of **restaurants**; *La Vieille Gare*, at 50 boul Perron ouest, (Ⓣ418/865-2007) has somewhat pricey seafood fare and, close by, the *Motel Restigouche*, at no. 5 (Ⓣ418/865-2155 or 1-877/865-2848, Ⓦwww.matapedia.com; ❸), is the place to **stay** if you're into fishing and hunting. From Matapédia, Hwy 132 cuts north across the interior of the peninsula through Amqui, a dreary little town that serves as a ski resort in the winter, before heading back up to Ste-Flavie (see p.343).

Îles-de-la-Madeleine

The archipelago of the **Îles-de-la-Madeleine** (Magdalen Islands), in the middle of the Gulf of St Lawrence some 200km southeast (and one hour ahead) of the Gaspé Peninsula and 100km east of Prince Edward Island (see p.473), consists of twelve main islands, seven of which are inhabited. Six of these are connected by narrow sand spits and crossed by paved and gravel roads, while the last is only accessible by boat. Together these dozen islands form a crescent-shaped series of dunes, lagoons and low rocky outcrops that measures about 80km from end to end, with the main village and ferry port roughly in the middle at **Cap-aux-Meules**. The islands lie in the Gulf Stream, which makes the winters warmer than those of mainland Québec, but they are subject to almost constant winds, which have eroded the red-sandstone cliffs along parts of the shoreline into an extraordinary array of arches, caves and tunnels. These rock formations, the archipelago's most distinctive attraction, are at their best on the central **Île du Cap-aux-Meules** and the adjacent **Île du Havre-aux-Maisons**.

In 1534, **Jacques Cartier** stumbled across the Îles-de-la-Madeleine on his way west to the St Lawrence River. Cartier, always keen to impress his sponsors with the value of his discoveries, wrote with characteristic exaggeration, "The islands are full of beautiful trees, prairies, fields of wild wheat, and flowering pea plants as beautiful as I've ever seen in Brittany." Despite Cartier's eulogy, the islands attracted hardly any settlers until the Deportations of 1755, when a few Acadian families escaped here to establish a mixed farming and fishing community. Remote and isolated, the **Madelinots**, as the islanders came to be known, were unable to control their own economic fortunes, selling their fish at absurdly low prices to a series of powerful merchants who, in turn, sold them tackle and equipment at exorbitant rates. The most notorious of these men was **Isaac Coffin**, who was granted the land in 1798 by the British Crown in return for services rendered during the American Civil War. Coffin developed a classically colonial form of oppression by forcing most of the islanders to pay him rent for their lands. Only in 1895 did a provincial statute allow the Madelinots to buy them back, and Québec purchased the islands outright in 1958.

Today the 15,000 inhabitants are largely dependent on **fishing** in general, and the lobster catch in particular. Herring, mackerel, scallops and halibut are also mainstays, and most people work at local companies that freeze, can, smoke, ship or market the catch. Until recently, when international pressure brought it to an end, the annual seal hunt supported many islanders (in March, the seals can be easily spotted on the ice floes). Other sectors of the fishery are now suffering because of fish-stock depletion, and the community's future livelihood revolves around tourism. Many residents worry about preserving their way of life and the fragile ecology of their beautiful islands. Tourists come to the archipelago for its wide-open landscapes and sense of isolation – it's easy to find a dune-laden beach where you can be alone with the sea. Bear in mind, though, that throughout the islands powerful currents and changeable weather conditions can make sea bathing dangerous, and the waters are occasionally home to stinging jellyfish.

Île du Cap-aux-Meules

The ferry from Souris, Prince Edward Island (PEI) (see p.473), docks in the middle of the archipelago, at **Île du Cap-aux-Meules**, which boasts the islands' largest community – **CAP-AUX-MEULES**, on the eastern shore. A useful base for exploring the neighbouring islands, the town is the islands' administrative and business centre and their least attractive enclave. However, just a couple of kilometres west of the village, there are fine views of the entire island chain from the **Butte du Vent**, the area's highest hill. Further west, on the other end of the island near the fishing port of **ÉTANG-DU-NORD**, you'll find some extravagant coastal rock formations and a port where kayaking tours take off. In the opposite direction, the main road skirts the southern tip of the islands' longest lagoon before heading on across the Île du Havre-aux-Maisons.

Accommodation options include the *Motel Bellevue*, 40 chemin Principal (Ⓣ418/986-4477, Ⓦwww.ilesdelamadeleine.com/bellevue; ❹), and the large *Château Madelinot*, 323 Hwy 199 (June-Sept; Ⓣ418/986-3695 or 1-800/661-4537, Ⓦwww.quebecweb.com/Chateaumadelinot; ❺), which offers fine sea views, great food and comfortable rooms. There are several **campsites**: try the peaceful *Le Barachois*, chemin du Rivage, Fatima (Ⓣ418/986-6065; $20 for two; May–Oct), or *Hostel and Camping Gros Cap*, 74 chemin du Camping, Étang du Nord (Ⓣ418/9886-4505 or 1-800/986-4505, Ⓦwww.leradar.qc.ca/parcdesgroscap.htm; dorms $24, camping site $18 for two; May–Sept).

For outstanding but pricey **food**, try the seafood at *La Table des Roy*, 1188 Hwy 199 (Ⓣ418/986-3004; closed Mon) in La Vernière just west of Cap-aux-Meules; dinner will set you back over $50. Better everyday choices are the *Petit Café* (Ⓣ418/986-2130) in the Château Madelinot, 323 Hwy 199, open all year, with a menu that ranges from hamburgers to lobsters (evening specials cost about $25), and *La Factrie*, 521 chemin Gros Cap (Ⓣ418/986-2710), a fun and inexpensive cafeteria-style lobster restaurant attached to a lobster-processing plant.

Île du Havre-aux-Maisons

Île du Havre-aux-Maisons' smooth green landscapes contrast with the red cliffs of its southern shore. Crisscrossed by narrow country roads and littered with tiny straggling villages, this island is best known for a unique oral tradition. The Acadians that settled here post-deportation were so irate with their treatment they decided never to utter the word "king" (*roi* in French) again; over the years, they wound up dropping the letter "r" altogether from their language. The weird shapes of the coastal rocks around **Dune-du-Sud** are well worth a visit, as is the **Fumoir d'Antan**, 27 chemin du Quai (daily 9am–5pm; Ⓦwww.ilesdelamadeleine.com/fumoir; free tour), the last remaining traditional herring smokehouse on the islands. Down by the lagoon, the hodgepodge collection of artefacts at the **Centre d'interprétation de Havre-aux-Maisons** (June to mid-Sept daily 9am–9pm) is on loan from local families and offers an excellent introduction to the local lore. Next door, **Les Excursions de la Lagune** takes off three times daily for a two-hour tour of the lagoon on a glass-bottom boat (Ⓣ418/969-2088; $20) that's both highly entertaining and educational. Deserted twin beaches edge the hamlet islet of **Pointe-aux-Loups** north of here, across the sand spit and along Hwy 199.

Should you want to **stay**, the *Auberge la P'tite Baie*, 187 Hwy 199 (Ⓣ418/969-4073, Ⓦwww3.sympatico.ca/auberge.petitebaie; ❸), with its lovely rooms and sea vistas, is your best bet. Or **camp** by the beach on the east side of the island at *Camping Les Sillons* (May to mid-Oct; Ⓣ418/969-2134, Ⓦwww.ilesdelamadeleine.com/sillons; $19-28 per site) which also has chalets (❸–❺). For great **seafood**, try the restored convent *Au Vieux Couvent*, 292 Hwy 199 (Ⓣ418/969-2233), which also has a lively basement **bar** with regular live music acts – even without, the place gets packed nightly until 11pm.

Grosse-Île and Île de la Grande-Entrée

At the far end of the archipelago, the twin islets of anglophone **Grosse-Île** and francophone **Île de la Grande-Entrée** border the wildlife reserve of the **Pointe-de-l'Est**, whose entrance is beside the main road. On its south side, the reserve is edged by the enormous sandy expanse of La Grande Échouerie **beach**, whose

Îles-de-la-Madeleine practicalities

Time zone

The Îles-de-la-Madeleine and Prince Edward Island are on **Atlantic time**, one hour ahead of Québec's **Eastern time**.

Getting there

Every month except February and March a CTMA **ferry** goes to Cap-aux-Meules **from Souris** on Prince Edward Island (Souris ⓣ902/687-2181; Cap-aux-Meules ⓣ418/986-6600; Montréal ⓣ514/937-7656, ⓦwww.ctma.ca/traversier-madeleine) – the number of weekly departures varies from five to ten depending on the season (takes 5hr). A return trip costs $327 for a car with two passengers. Reservations are mandatory in July and August and need to be made several months in advance. The *Voyageur*, a cargo and fifteen-passenger ship, also operated by CTMA, departs **from Montréal** for the islands every Friday (takes 48hr; around $470 one-way; plus $150 for a car).

Daily scheduled **flights** on Air Canada leave Gaspé town, Québec City, Montréal (around $600 roundtrip) and Halifax, NS. Book two weeks in advance, and include a Saturday overnight stay for discount flights. The only alternative airline is Pascan Aviation (ⓣ418/877-8777 or 1-888/313-8777, ⓦwww.pascan.com) which flies from Montréal and Québec City.

Arrival and information

The islands' **airport** is inconveniently situated at the north end of Île du Havre-aux-Maisons, some 20km from Cap-aux-Meules. Some flights have connecting buses to Cap-aux-Meules, but otherwise you'll have to take a **taxi** (about $35), or **rent a car** from National (ⓣ418/969-4209) or Thrifty (ⓣ418/969-9006) at the airport; book in advance in the summer. The **ferry terminal** at Cap-aux-Meules is near the **tourist office**, 128 chemin Principal (late June to Aug daily 7am–9pm; Sept to mid-Oct daily 9am–9pm; mid-Oct to late June Mon–Fri 9am–5pm; ⓣ418/986-2245 or

southern end is framed by yet more splendid rock formations at Old Harry's Point. This is where Europeans first came to the islands in order to slaughter walruses, depleting the stock by 1800. Nowadays, the 10km walk down the beach offers a good chance to spot seals, and there have been renewed – albeit very rare – walrus sightings. A kilometre past the rustic wharf at **Old Harry**, a pretty white church with beautifully sculptured doors uses the islands as backdrop for biblical tales. A little further, the old red schoolhouse is home to the Council for Anglophone Magdalen Islanders and a **museum** (July & Aug Mon–Fri 9am–4pm, Sat & Sun 1–4pm; Sept–June by appointment; ⓣ418/985-2116; free) tells the history of the anglophone population, most of whom are of Scottish descent. To learn more about seals head to the **Centre d'interprétation du Phoque**, 377 Hwy 199 (June–Sept daily 10am–6pm; rest of year by appointment; ⓣ418/985-2833 or 1-888/537-4537, ⓦwww.ilesdelamadeleine.com/cip; $5.75).

The lobster port of **Île de la Grande-Entrée**, the last island to be inhabited, has a couple of **accommodation** options: *Domaine de la Grenouille sur Mer*, 83 chemin des Pealey (ⓣ418/985-2365 or 514/645-9855; ❸), and *Club Vacances "Les Îles"*, 377 Hwy 199 (ⓣ418/985-2833 or 1-888/537-4537, ⓦwww.clubiles.qc.ca; ❸), which is open all year and has camping space as well as rooms and a great cafeteria. The **food** is expensive but you can save money by opting to pay for full board; it's also open to non-guests. The club also offers various activities, like trips to the caves on offshore Île Boudreau and seal-spotting excursions in the summer.

1-877/624-4437, Ⓦwww.tourismeilesdelamadeleine.com). They have masses of free leaflets and operate a free room-reservation service with a special emphasis on B&Bs. With few **inns, motels** and **hotels** on the islands, it's a good idea to book a bed before you arrive. The tourist office also has details of cottage and apartment rentals, starting at roughly $250 per week. The cheapest way to stay is either at the **hostel** – where you can also camp – or one of the other half-dozen commercial **campsites** on the islands.

Transport, boat trips and water sports

The best way to tour the principal islands is by a **bike**, which may be rented at Le Pédalier, 365 chemin Principal, Cap-aux-Meules (Ⓣ418/986-2965). **Mopeds** can be rented from Cap-aux-Meules Honda, Hwy 199 at La Vernière, southwest of Cap-aux-Meules (Ⓣ418/986-4085).

Departures for **boat** and **fishing trips** are near the ferry terminal throughout the summer by Aventure en zodiac (Ⓣ418/986-4745, Ⓦwww.excursiosenmer.com) and Explorivage (Ⓣ418/986-3255, Ⓦwww.ilesdelamadeleine.com/explorivage).

In the past many of the visitors to these out-of-the-way islands have been hippies and drifters looking for a break from the mainstream and the mainland, and some elements of this still exist among the some of the islands' artsy newer inhabitants. But recently the bigger attraction for many adventurous visitors has been the strong winds that blow here. Between late August and late October conditions for **windsurfing** and **kite-surfing** are exemplary and the Canadian Professional and Amateur Windsurf Championship heads here every year. Aerosport Carrefour d'Aventures 1390 route 199 (Ⓣ418/986-6677, Ⓦwww.aerosport.ca) in Etang-du-Nord can be contacted for advice and rentals for all things kite. Winds have also played their part in leaving so many ships to founder around the coast – leaving behind some superb **wreck-diving** for scuba fans. For information and trips contact Le Repère du Plonger, 18 Allée Léo Leblanc (Ⓣ418/986-3962, Ⓦwww.repereduplongeir.com).

Île du Havre-Aubert

To the south of Île du Cap-aux-Meules, **Île du Havre-Aubert** has one significant community, **HAVRE-AUBERT**, that's edged by round, sloping hills. It's the most attractive of the islands' communities, and its picturesque location and undoubtable charm attract a lot of visitors. It is situated around **La Grave**, a pebbly beach flanked by a boardwalk and wooden buildings once used by sailors and fishermen and now transformed into bars, cafés, restaurants, souvenir shops and an art gallery for the island's new trade in tourists; for the best spot to buy things, from lampshades and fish-heads to household decorations made of sand, try *Les Artisans du Sable*. On the beach the **Aquarium** (early June to mid-Aug daily 10am–6pm; mid-Aug to mid-Oct 10am–5pm; Ⓦwww.ilesdelamadeleine.com/aquarium; $5.50) displays fish and crustaceans found in the waters around the island, and there's a small seal tidal pool out back. Overlooking La Grave, the **Musée de la Mer** (mid-June to mid-Sept Mon–Fri 9am–6pm, weekends from 10am; Sept–Nov Mon–Fri 9am–noon & 1–5pm, Sat & Sun 1–5pm; Ⓦwww.ilesdelamadeleine.com/musee; $5) has a series of displays on local fishing techniques and the history of the islands. Especially interesting is the exhibit focused on the more than 400 shipwrecks that have occurred just offshore.

Set apart from Havre-Aubert, in the community of Bassin, the **Site d'Autrefois** (daily: mid-June to Sept 9am–5pm; Sept 10am–4pm; $10) is a fanciful spot that tells the story of Madelinot life through life-sized mannequins of fishermen, boats and model houses. La Chevauché des Iles (Ⓣ418/937-2368 or 937-5453; $25–40) also in Bassin, offers **horseback riding** tours of the island.

You can **stay** on La Grave at *Chez Charles Painchaud*, 930 Hwy 199 (Ⓣ418/937-2227, Ⓦwww.aubergechezcharles.ca; ❸), or *Le Berceau des Îles*, 701 chemin principal in Havre-Aubert (Ⓣ418/937-5614, Ⓦwww.berceaudesiles.com; ❸) which has some more luxurious rooms. Both are **B&Bs** and can arrange for pick-ups from the airport or ferry as well as organize winter and summer activities – they even rent cars. *Auberge Chez Denis à François*, 404 chemin d'en Haut (Ⓣ418/937-2371, Ⓦwww.ilesdelamadeleine.com/auberge; ❸), offers fine views of the strip. **Restaurants** are of good quality in Havre-Aubert: even if you don't stay at *Auberge Chez Denis à François*, you should definitely try the seafood – they even have seal on the menu. *La Saline*, 1009 Hwy 199 (Ⓣ418/937-2230) in La Grave, is open for delicious evening fare – there's also live music in the adjoining bar. The much more expensive *La Marée Haute*, 25 chemin des Fumoirs (Ⓣ418/937-2492), is also only open at night and serves up some of Canada's finest seafood, including sea urchins and smoked seal. For chunky sandwiches and clam chowder served in bread, head for the atmospheric *Café de la Grave* (Ⓣ418/937-5244) in the old general store. *Le Petit Mondrain* on chemin de La Grave is popular with locals, and its seafood is among the islands' cheapest.

Île d'Entrée

To the southeast, tiny anglophone **Île d'Entrée** is the only inhabited island not linked by land to the rest of the archipelago. Home to 175 people, this grassy hillock is encircled by footpaths and makes a pleasant day out, providing the sea is calm on the **ferry** trip from Cap-aux-Meules (May–Dec 2 daily; Ⓣ418/986-8452 or 986-5705, Ⓦwww.traversiers.gouv.qc.ca; $22 return). Horses and cows roam freely on the slopes of the Îles-de-la-Madeleine's highest point, **Big Hill** (174m), accessible from the port by taking chemin Main and then chemin Post Office, and following the path across the fields to the top for a view of the whole archipelago. On your way towards the path, a tiny **museum** (June–Sept hours vary Ⓣ418/986-6622; free) displays island artefacts and historical household items. The only official lodging is the basic **B&B** *Chez McLean* (Ⓣ418/986-4541; ❷). Otherwise, you'll probably end up in someone's home – ask around. For **food**, there's a bar-restaurant and a grocery store near the port.

Charlevoix

Stretching along the **north shore** of the St Lawrence east of Québec City, from the Beaupré coast to the Saguenay Fjord, the area of **Charlevoix**, named after the Jesuit historian Francois Xavier de Charlevoix, is a UNESCO World Biosphere Reserve. Species like the arctic caribou and great wolf, not usually associated with such southerly latitudes, can be seen in the more remote areas, and because the Ice Age that shaped the rest of eastern Canada missed this breathtaking portion of the Canadian Shield, numerous pre-glacial plants still thrive here. It consists of gently sloping hills, sheer cliffs and vast valleys veined with rivers, brooks and waterfalls, a landscape that Québec's better known artists – Clarence Gagnon, Marc-Aurèle Fortin and Jean-Paul Lemieux – chose for inspiration. Though Charlevoix has been a tourist destination for years and especially popular with people from Québec City on weekend breaks, the land has been carefully preserved, and quaint villages and tin-roofed churches still nestle in an unspoiled countryside. The tourist office produces a brochure, *La Route des Saveurs de Charlevoix*, which is useful on a gastronomic trip: it lists agricultural producers and the restaurants that use local products in regional cuisine.

Highway 138, the main route through Charlevoix, travels 225km from Québec City to Baie-Ste-Catherine on the Saguenay. The main towns along this hwy are served by Intercar **buses** from Québec City, but many of the quintessential Charlevoix villages – in particular those along the coastal Hwy 362 – are not served by public transport. Be prepared to rent a car or bike; the expense is well worth it.

Baie-Saint-Paul and around

One of Charlevoix's earliest settlements and longtime gathering place for Québec's landscape painters, the picture-perfect **BAIE-SAINT-PAUL** is tucked into the Gouffré valley at the foot of the highest range of the Laurentian mountains. Dominated by the twin spires of the church, the streets wind from the centre of town flanked by houses that are more than two hundred years old – and just wandering around Baie-Saint-Paul is the main attraction. For an overview of the works of art produced in Charlevoix, visit the plush **Centre d'Exposition** (Tues–Sun 10am–7pm; ⓣ418/435-3681, ⓦwww.centredexpo-bsp.qc.ca; $4) at 23 rue Ambroise-Fafard, which has established an international reputation for the excellence of its temporary exhibitions of Québecois and international art. Also every August to early September, at a symposium, the public can watch young Canadian and European artists at work in the nearby arena. From beside the church, the rue St-Jean-Baptiste slips through the commercial heart of the town edged by numerous quaint cottages characteristic of Québec's earliest houses, with curving roofs and wide verandas, many converted into commercial galleries. At 58 rue St-Jean-Baptiste, the **Maison de René Richard** (ⓣ418/435-5571; daily 10am–6pm; free, guided tour $4) offers an insight into the works of René Richard, an associate of the Group of Seven. The 1852 house has been left exactly the same since Richard died in 1982; bilingual guided tours take you around his studio and living quarters, a rare glimpse at the Charlevoix of the 1940s when some of Québec's finest painters hung out here.

The **information centre** for Baie-Saint-Paul and the whole Charlevoix area is at the Belvédère Baie-Saint-Paul off Hwy 138 before you descend into town from the west (daily; mid-June to early Sept 9am–7pm; rest of year 9am–4.30pm; ⓣ418/435-4160 or 1-800/667-2276, ⓦwww.baiestpaul.com), where there's a free museum detailing the geography of the area. The Intercar **bus** stops at *Restaurant La Grignote*, 2 rte de l'Equerre (ⓣ418/435-6569), in the shopping centre by Hwy 138, twenty minutes' walk from downtown.

Baie-Saint-Paul has an excellent variety of **accommodation**. The best hotels are the 1840 *Auberge la Maison Otis*, 23 rue St-Jean-Baptiste (ⓣ418/435-2255 or 1-800/267-2254, ⓦwww.maisonotis.com; ⑤) with its floral rooms, some with exposed beams and a country-house feel, and the *Auberge La Pignoronde*, 750 boul Mgr-de-Laval (ⓣ418/435-5505 or 1-888/554-6004, ⓦwww.aubergelapignoronde.com; ③) with spacious modern rooms, pool and attractive gardens. Next door to each other on the waterfront and run by the same company, the *Domaine Belle-Plage*, 192 rue Ste-Anne (ⓣ418/435-3321, ⓦwww.belleplage.ca; ③) and the *Auberge le Cormoran* at no. 196 (ⓣ418/435-6030, ⓦwww.lecormoran.ca; ③), both have comfortable doubles with fussy decor, while in the centre of town the beautiful *Auberge La Muse*, 39 rue St-Jean-Baptiste (ⓣ418/435-6839 or 1-800/841-6839, ⓦwww.lamuse.com; ④) has large, prettily decorated rooms with a warm welcome. The town has numerous **B&Bs** including *A La Lune Bleue*, 44 chemin de la Martine (ⓣ418/435-5102; ⓦwww.gites-classifies.qc.ca/lunebleue2; ❸–❹) a few minutes out of the centre in peaceful wooded grounds. Its 4 brand new designer rooms each have their own bathroom and TV. The town's best bargain is the **hostel** and **campsite** *Le Balcon Vert* (ⓣ418/435-5587, ⓦwww.balconvert.com; mid-May to early Oct) up a gravel road about 3km out on Hwy 362 to Malbaie, with four-berth cabins ($45), camping ($20 for a four-person site) and dorm beds ($20). The views are tremendous from here and the on-site bar and restaurant (there are no guest kitchens) ensure a sociable vibe. Summer **camping** is also available at the heavily wooded riverside *Camping du Gouffre*, 439 chemin St-Laurent (ⓣ418/435-2143, ⓦwww.campingdugouffre.com; $17–27), or the larger *Camping le Genévrier*, 1175 boul Mgr-de-Laval (ⓣ418/435-6520 or 1-877/435-6520, ⓦwww.genevrier.com; $24–40).

Food is plentiful within a block or two of the church: *Café d'Artistes*, 25 rue St-Jean-Baptiste, has desserts, coffees and thin-crust pizzas, while *Les Deux Soeurs* is an excellent patisserie-café across the street at no. 48. *Le Mouton Noir*, 43 rue Ste-Anne (ⓣ418/240-3030), serves hearty country cooking, like smoked sausages with maple syrup and dishes range from $10 to $30. The restaurant of the *Belle-Plage* (ⓣ418/435-3321) also serves traditional Québecois cuisine, with a buffet for around $15. Two good spots combine eating and **drinking**: *Le Saint-Pub*, 2 rue Racine (corner of St-Jean-Baptiste), a terrific brewpub with delicious bistro fare, and *Cuore di Lupo*, 29 rue Ambroise-Fafard, which has a terrace and reasonably priced pizza and pasta.

Around Baie-Saint-Paul

At 41 rue St-Jean-Baptiste in Baie-Saint-Paul, Randonnées Nature-Charlevoix (ⓣ418/435-6275) runs excellent **bike tours** of the environs (2hr; $6; or $4 if you rent a bike for $20/day), as well as hiking tours in the Parc des Grands-Jardins and tours around the **Charlevoix Crater** – one of the planet's largest craters, made by a meteorite – by bus (late June to early Sept; 1 daily; 2hr; $15). Down at the marina, L'Air du Large, 210 rue Ste Anne (ⓣ418/435-2066, ⓦwww.quebecweb.com/airdularge) rent bicycles, kayaks, canoes and paragliders and offer courses in kayaking and paragliding. They also run boat trips to explore nearby islands.

Some of the province's most dramatic **skiing** can be found at **Le Massif** perched over the St Lawrence to the west of town. Baie-Saint-Paul also makes a good base to explore the **Parc des Grands-Jardins** (daily June–Aug 8am–8pm; Sept–May 9am–5pm; ⓦwww.sepaq.com; $3.50), 42km away on Hwy 381 but with no public transport. Within the forests and lakes of the park, the 900m Mont du Lac des Cygnes gives the best of all Charlevoix panoramas; it's a four-hour (10km) climb to the top and back along a clear but rocky path. You will need proper footgear. The trailhead is just beyond the **Thomas-Fortin reception centre** at the park entrance on Hwy 381. (Hwy 381 continues to Chicoutimi on the Rivière Saguenay; see p.372) You can rent canoes ($34/day) here and **chalets** (❷), huts (❶) and campsites ($20) are also available but must be reserved in advance (ⓣ1-800/665-6527).

Attracting hikers, mountain bikers and cross-country skiers, the long-distance **Traversée de Charlevoix** (ⓣ418/639-2284, ⓦwww.charlevoix.net/traverse) begins near the park on Hwy 381, crossing 100km of mountainous terrain including the Parc des Hautes-Gorges-de-la-Rivière-Malbaie before ending at Mont Grand-Fonds near La Malbaie. Accommodation in cabins or cottages starts at $145 for the six nights needed to complete the hike.

Les Éboulements and around

From Baie-Saint-Paul the main route onwards is Hwy 138, but if you have your own transport you should opt for the coast-hugging detour of Hwy 362, which twists and turns through a succession of cliff-top villages along the shore of the St Lawrence.

The first settlement on this route is **LES ÉBOULEMENTS**, which means "landslides" – named after the massive earthquake of 1663, one of many that shaped this region. Just west of the village at no. 157 rue Principale is the eighteenth-century **Moulin Banal** (late June to early Sept daily 10am–5pm; $3), an operating flour mill atop a pretty waterfall on the well-kept grounds of the **Manoir de Sales-Laterrière**. The manor and mill are among the few intact structures left from the seigneurial regime of New France. The manor (a school) is not actually open to the public but a path leads up from the mill, with interpretation panels on the grounds. At the entrance to the grounds is a charming chapel (1840) built of wood and relocated here from St-Nicholas, a village on the St Lawrence. Further down the road, in the village itself, the **Centre d'interprétation de la Forge Tremblay**, 214 rue Principale (Nov to mid-May; free but reservations required), dating from 1888, is still used by blacksmiths.

From Les Éboulements, a steep secondary road leads to the pretty coastal village of **SAINT-JOSEPH-DE-LA-RIVE**, once a shipyard; some heritage can be seen in the **Exposition Maritime**, 305 rue de l' Eglise (late June to early Sept daily 9am–7pm, rest of the year Mon-Fri until 4pm, weekends 11am–4pm; ⓣ418/635-1131, ⓦwww.musee-maritime-charlevoix.com; $3), a museum with a few nautical displays, a workshop and boat-building yards. Pop into the local **church** (June–Oct daily 9am–8pm; free) on chemin de l'Église, where anchors prop up the altar and the font is a huge seashell from Florida. *Le Loup-Phoque*, 188 rue Félix-Antoine-Savard, a funky spot good for **food** and views, has occasional live music.

Île aux Coudres

The 16km-long island of **Île aux Coudres** is said to have been formed when an earthquake shook it from the escarpment at Les Éboulements. Cartier celebrated Canada's first Mass here in 1535 and named the island after its numerous hazelnut trees. Missionaries were the first permanent settlers, arriving in 1748, and the growing population came to depend on shipbuilding and beluga-whale hunting for their livelihoods. Ship- and canoe-building still takes place here, but the main industry of its 1600 inhabitants is harvesting peat moss from the bogs in the centre of the island.

Access is on a free **car ferry** (8–24 trips daily 7am–11.30pm; takes 15min; ⓣ418/438-2743, ⓦwww.traversiers.gouv.qc.ca) from Saint-Joseph-de-la-Rive. The island's stone manors and cottages nowadays attract huge numbers of visitors, who drive and **cycle** around the 26km peripheral road that connects – in a clockwise direction – the three villages of **ST-BERNARD**, **LA BALEINE** and **ST-LOUIS**. Of the incidental attractions along the way, the only real diversions are the restored wind and adjacent water mills – **Les Moulins de l'Islè-aux-Coudres** (late May to early Oct daily 9.30am–5.30pm; ⓣ418/438-2184, ⓦwww.lesmoulinsiac.com; $8) – in the southwest corner of the island, both of which are in full working order. There is an **information centre** (mid-June to Aug daily 10am–7pm) near the ferry dock in St-Bernard, with maps of the island. **Bikes** can be rented from Gérard Desgagnés, near the jetty at 34 rue du Port (ⓣ418/438-2332), or Vél 'O'-Coudres, 743 chemin des Coudriers in La Baleine

(Ⓣ418/438-2118), which has a wider selection but is 5km from the dock, linked by free hourly shuttle. Rent **kayaks** for $29 per half-day at Kayak de Mer, down the road at no. 783 (Ⓣ418/438-4388); they also offer guided trips for $25–70.

Places **to stay** are unexciting, but many have reasonable restaurants. In La Baleine the best deals are the *Motel la Baleine*, 138 rue Principale (Ⓣ418/438-2453, Ⓦwww.charlevoix.net/motellabaleine; ❷), and *Motel Écumé*, 808 chemin des Coudriers (Ⓣ418/438-2733, Ⓦwww.maisoncroche.com; ❷), a bizarre place with deliberately tilted windows and mismatched furniture in very basic rooms. The best bargain is the *Motel l'Islet*, 10 chemin de l'Islet (Ⓣ418/438-2423, Ⓦwww.quebecweb.com/lislet; ❷; May to mid-Oct), in an isolated spot near St-Louis, on the west tip of the island. The posh hotel *Cap-aux-Pierres*, 246 rue Principale in La Baleine (Ⓣ 418/438-2711 or 1-888/554-6003, Ⓦwww.hotelcapauxpierres.com; ❺), provides half-board accommodation and has a good restaurant. **Campsites** include *Camping Leclerc*, 183 rue Principale, La Baleine (Ⓣ418/438-2217, Ⓦwww.charlevoix.net/famille-leclerc; $17–24) and *Camping Sylvie*, 191 rue Royale ouest, St-Bernard (Ⓣ418/438-2420, Ⓦwww.campingsylvie.zip411.net; tents $12–18, chalets $40), where you can rent canoes. For good local **meals** head to *La Mer Veille*, 160 des Coudriers in St-Louis; the lunch menu is $10.

La Malbaie

Hwys 362 and 138 converge about 50km from Baie-Saint-Paul at **LA MALBAIE** ("Bad Bay"), so called because Champlain ran aground here in 1608. Situated at the mouth of the Malbaie River, the town – an amalgamation of five villages – sprawls along the riverfront with little to detain you, though it's a good base for a day trip to the Hautes-Gorges; and the ritzy resort area **POINTE-AU-PIC** – back along Hwy 362 – is worth a quick look for its late nineteeth-century tourist-château. Originally built in 1899 for the Richelieu and Ontario Navigation Company, who ferried tourists here from New York and Montréal, the hotel was rebuilt after a fire in the 1920s, and has been recently renovated. It makes for a delightful overnight stay – and you can wager the rest of your travel budget at the *Casino de Charlevoix* next door.

Descente Malbaie (Ⓣ418/439-2265, Ⓦwww.descentmalbaie.com), who are based just north of St Aimé des Lacs halfway to the Hautes-Gorges, run white-water **rafting** in summer (around $50 for 2hr); overnight trips are also available. In winter the Rac du Mont Grand Fords has **downhill skiing** and **snowboarding** (Ⓣ418/664-0095 or 1-877/667-0095; day pass $28) on fourteen trails or **cross-country skiing** at the Centre de Plein Aire Les Sources Joyeuses (Ⓣ418/665-4858; $8) where 82km of trails – and 5km of ice-skating trails – are maintained. Instruction and equipment rental is available at both ski centres.

The **tourist office**, beside the main road at 630 boul de Comporté (mid-June to Sept daily 8.30am–9pm; rest of year Mon–Fri 8.30am–4.30pm, Sat & Sun 9am–5pm; Ⓣ418/665-4454), has a full range of regional tourist info. **Buses** arrive nearby at Dépanneur Otis, 46 rue Ste-Catherine (Ⓣ418/665-2264). The nearest **car ferry** service across the St Lawrence leaves from the hillside village of **Saint-Siméon** 25km northeast on Hwy 138 towards Rivière du Loup (see p.338). Much of the classiest **accommodation** is in Pointe-Au-Pic, home to the luxurious château-like *Le Manoir Richelieu*, 181 rue Richelieu (Ⓣ418/665-3703 or 1-800/441-1414, Ⓦwww.fairmont.com; ❽) and many manor houses that have been converted into charming country inns. The *Auberge des 3 Canards*, 115 Côte Bellevue (Ⓣ418/665-3761 or 1-800/461-3761, Ⓦwww.auberge3canards.com; ❻), is an inn with 49 comfortable rooms, most with their own private balcony overlooking the St Lawrence and a restaurant of the same name widely regarded as one of the finest in the area. It specializes in high French cuisine using local products such as Deer carpaccio and wild Charlevoix mushrooms. The Victorian **B&B** *Gîte Harrop's*, 400 rue Richelieu (Ⓣ418/665-4120, Ⓦwww.harrops.com; ❸), has gardens overlooking the St Lawrence. In the main part of La Malbaie is *Motel Murray Bay*, 40 rue Laure-Conan (Ⓣ418/665-2441; ❷), and *Gîte E. T. Harvey* (Ⓣ418/665-2779, Ⓦwww.bbcanada.com/2779; ❷) on the same street at no. 19. Cap-à-l'Aigle, an agricultural village to the east, has an excellent B&B, *Claire Villeneuve*, 215 rue St-Raphaël (Ⓣ418/665-2288, Ⓦwww.quebecinformation.com/clairevilleneuve; ❷), a great example of Québecois rural architecture. If you have transport, head for Charlevoix's oldest and most beautifully situated **campsite**, *Camping Chutes Fraser*, 500 chemin de la Vallée (Ⓣ418/665-2151, Ⓦwww.campingchutesfraser.com $18–28, chalets $40; mid-May to mid-Oct), by the falls of the same name about 3km north of La Malbaie. For **food** try the *Manoir Richelieu's Winston* bar and restaurant for inexpensive breakfasts. At the La Malbaie marina *Café de la Gare*, 100 chemin du Havre (Ⓣ418/665-4272), has a limited menu of items like paninis, mussels and nachos (mains $10–30). For pub food head to *Club des Monts*, 110 Ruisseau des Frênes (Ⓣ418/439-3711), a busy bar with frequent live music.

The Hautes-Gorges

One sight not be missed in the Charlevoix region is the **Parc des Hautes-Gorges-de-la-Rivière-Malbaie**, a network of valleys that slice through a maze of lofty peaks 45km west of La Malbaie. To get there take Hwy 138 to **SAINT-AIMÉ-DES-LACS**, a small town 13km northwest of La Malbaie from where the way to the park is well marked. Admission to the park is $3.50 and the park's **information centre**, Chalet l'Écluse (daily mid-May to early Oct 7am–9pm; Ⓣ418/439-1227 or 1-800/665-6527), is located beside the Malbaie River just off rue Principale. You must leave your car here and rent a bike ($29/day) or take the frequent, free shuttle bus into the park as far as the l'Écluse dam.

As you enter the park, cliff faces on all sides rise up to more than 700m, making it Canada's deepest canyon east of the Rockies, formed by a slip in the earth's crust 800 million years ago. Its uniqueness lies not just in this astounding geology but also in the fact that all of Québec's forest species grow in this one comparatively small area. From the Chalet l'Écluse a tiring but rewarding five-kilometre hike on the **Mont des Érables trail** leads to the canyon's highest point, passing through a Laurentian maple grove on the way to the arctic–alpine tundra of the 800m summit; reckon on six hours for the round-trip. Other shorter trails from the **l'Écluse dam** offer less strenuous alternatives. From here you can take a leisurely ninety-minute river cruise ($26) or rent **canoes or kayaks** ($12/hr; $35/day) for the six-kilometre paddle along the calm "Eaux Mortes" of the river. All these must be paid for first at the park information centre where you can also reserve sites at the park's one **campsite**, *Camping du Pin Blanc* ($20; June–Aug), and get permits for wild camping – some of which is only accessible by canoe.

The Saguenay and Lac Saint-Jean

The **Saguenay** is Québec's most schizophrenic region, encompassing some of the province's most spectacular scenery, tremendous marine life and also the dreariest of industrial towns. Fortunately, the two extremes are kept nicely separate along the Saguenay River, so that you can explore the rich landscapes along its fjord and source – **Lac Saint-Jean** – in peace. Best known for its **whale-watching** opportunities, the region is also exceptional for canoeing, backcountry hiking and cycle touring.

The main tourist centre of the region is **Tadoussac**, 78km north of La Malbaie and 227km from Québec City via Hwy 138. It lies at a pretty spot at the neck of the Saguenay Fjord and its confluence with the St Lawrence. Many come here just to catch a boat to head out to the whales. It's a pretty town in its own right, from which you can often see the whales, and it also makes a great base to explore a number of other outdoor attractions in the vicinity. Many of these are centered on the national parks along the **Fjord du Saguenay** where both the land and sea are protected (as the Parc du Saguenay and Parc Marin du Saguenay–St-Laurent; ⓣ418/235-4703 or 1-800/463-6769, ⓦwww.sepaq.com). The marine park contains six different ecosystems and supports hundreds of marine species, but as part of the hydrographic basin of the Great Lakes and the St Lawrence – once the most polluted waterway in Canada thanks to toxic waste discharges – it had its work cut out protecting the area. Since the creation of the park, government initiatives have eliminated ninety percent of the pollutants from industrial plants in the immediate vicinity. The damage has already been done, though: pollutants remain in the sediment and the number of St Lawrence **beluga whales** is down from five thousand a century ago to one thousand today, placing them on Canada's list of endangered species. That said, the area continues to attract the whales because the mingling of the cold Labrador Sea waters with the highly oxygenated freshwater of the Saguenay produces a uniquely rich crop of krill and plankton. The white St Lawrence beluga lives in the area all year round, and from May to October it is joined by six species of migratory whales including the minke, finback and gigantic **blue whale**, the largest animal on earth.

If you have the time, continue west to the **Upper Saguenay** past the industrial centres of **Chicoutimi** and **Jonquière** and make a circuit of the flat farming country of **Lac Saint-Jean**. It's an ideal location to cycle, and the recently completed **Véloroute des Bleuets** allows you to travel the 256km around the lake without trucks forcing you off the road.

Tadoussac and around

One of Canada's oldest villages, **TADOUSSAC** is beautifully situated beneath the rounded hills that gave the place its name; the Algonquian word *tatoushak* means "breasts". Basque whalers were the first Europeans to live here and by the time Samuel de Champlain arrived in 1603 Tadoussac was a thriving trading post. The mid-nineteenth century saw Tadoussac evolve into a popular summer resort for the anglophone bourgeoisie: the first hotel opened in 1846 and by the 1860s steamer-loads of rich anglophones were arriving every summer to escape the heat of the city. Nowadays it's the best place in Québec, along with Bergeronnes and Les Escoumins just north along the coast, for **whale-watching** (see box, p.366). Late June is a good time to be here, when traditional Québecois folk singers, jazz pianists and rock guitarists all play a part in the popular **Festival de la Chanson**.

The waterfront rue de Bord-de-l'Eau is dominated by the red roof and green lawns of the *Hôtel Tadoussac*, a landmark since 1864 and the focus of the historic quarter. Across the road is the oldest wooden church in Canada, the tiny **Chapelle de Tadoussac** (mid-June to early Sept daily 9am–8pm, Sept to early Oct until 6pm; ⓣ418/235-1415; $2), built in 1747; visits are possible out of season by reservation (ⓣ418/235-4324). Tucked on the other side of the hotel,

△ Tadoussac ferry

the steep-roofed wooden **Poste de Traite Chauvin** (early June to early Oct daily 9am–8pm, otherwise 10am–6pm; ⓦwww.tadoussac.com; $3) exactly replicates – right down to the handmade nails – the first trading post on the north shore of the St Lawrence as described in Champlain's 1603 diary. It houses a small museum of beaver pelts and bits and pieces pertaining to the fur trade, but a peek in from the doorway will suffice. Following the waterfront towards the harbour brings you to the modern **Centre d'Interprétation des Mammifères Marins**, 108 rue de la Cale-Sèche (daily: mid-May to mid-June & late Sept to late Oct noon–5pm; mid-June to late Sept 9am–8pm; ⓦwww.gremm.org; $8), run by the nonprofit Group for Research and Education on Marine Mammals (GREMM). This is a must if you intend to go whale-watching, as its excellent documentary films and displays explain the life cycles of the whales in the St Lawrence and the efforts being made to save their ever-diminishing numbers. The small but informative **Musée Maritime de Tadoussac**, back near the ferry terminal at 145 rue du Bateau-Passeur (late June to Aug daily 10am–4pm; $2.50), has exhibits on the history of shipbuilding and navigation in the area.

The Tadoussac sector of the Parc du Saguenay offers some easy **hikes** around the village and a 42km trek to Baie-Ste-Marguerite further along the fjord; an **information office** (mid-June to Sept daily 9am–5pm) in the car park just after the ferry terminal supplies maps of the trails. From near the Chapelle there is a two-hour walk along the beach; check what time the tide rolls in as you'll have to clamber over rocks at high tide. It ends northeast of Tadoussac at the long terraced **sand dunes** on the Baie du Moulin-Baude, known locally as *le désert*. To reach the 112m-high dunes, you can also follow chemin du Moulin-Baude for 5km to the interpretation centre, the Maison des Dunes (early June to mid-Oct daily 9am–5pm; ⓣ418/272-1556 or 1-877/272-5229; $3.50).

Practicalities

Traffic crosses the neck of the fjord by a free **car ferry** from Baie-Ste-Catherine to Tadoussac, but you may have to wait as long as an hour or two to board in midsummer. The nearest ferries across the St Lawrence depart and arrive from Les Escoumins in the north (see p.368) and Saint-Siméon in the south (see p.362). Tadoussac's **bus** terminus is at 443 rue du Bâteau-Passeur on Hwy 138 by the campsite (Ⓣ418/235-4653). The excellent **information** centre for the entire Côte-Nord is in the smart red-brick manor at 197 rue des Pionniers (daily: late June to early Sept 8am–9pm; early Sept to late June 9am–noon & 1–5pm; Ⓣ418/235-4744 or 1-866/235-4744). They have a load of leaflets, an accommodation service and next door you can watch videos of the area.

The pick of Tadoussac's wealth of **accommodation** is the red-roofed *Hôtel Tadoussac*, 165 rue du Bord de l'Eau (Ⓣ418/235-4421 or 1-800/561-0718, Ⓦwww.hoteltadoussac.com; ❼), with surcharged riverview rooms, swimming pool, miniature golf and tennis courts. Cheaper is the *Motel de l'Anse-à-l'Eau*, 173 rue des Pionniers (Ⓣ418/235-4313; ❸), which does a fine breakfast. A number of the town's **B&Bs** are ranged along rue des Pionniers, including *Maison Clauphi* at no. 188 (Ⓣ418/235-4303, Ⓦwww.clauphi.com; ❸), a B&B-cum-motel. *Maison Hovington*, at no. 285 (Ⓣ418/235-4466, Ⓦwww.maisonhovington.com; ❹; mid-May to Oct), is a century-old B&B with five beautifully decorated rooms; the bilingual owners will pick you up from the bus station. *La Maison Boularch*, near the harbour at 118 rue de la Cale Sèche (Ⓣ418/235-2000; ❷), is another friendly bilingual place, with comfy beds in mostly tiny rooms. The beatnik **hostel** *Maison Majorique*, 158 rue du Bateau-Passeur (Ⓣ418/235-4372, Ⓦwww.fjord-best.com/ajt; dorms $19) is

Whale-watching from the Tadoussac area

Every season more companies appear offering **whale-watching trips** from Tadoussac and the surrounding communities (mid-May to mid-Oct). Prices for two- to three-hour trips from Tadoussac are around $45 in a large, sturdy and comfortable boat, and $52 in a zodiac, which provides a more exciting ride. The price drops the more northerly the starting-point: similar excursions from Bergeronnes and Les Escoumins cost around $35 in a zodiac. Pop into **La Croisière**, 231 rue des Pionniers in Tadoussac, who have full information and sell tickets (at the same price as the companies) for all the available trips; you can also compare directly down at the quay. Officially, boats are not allowed to stray within 400m of the protected belugas, but the whales don't know that and often come thrillingly close to the craft.

If you can't afford a boat trip, or would rather leave the whales in peace, take the short **hike** around the Pointe de l'Islet from the marina in Tadoussac, which has lookout points for beluga-spotting where you may be lucky to see whales. Or improve your chances by heading to even better lookout points along the shore: the two best are at **Baie-Ste-Marguerite** west of Tadoussac (see p.371) and **Cap-de-Bon-Désir** just past Bergeronnes (see p.368). A bewildering array of interpretation centres supplement the whale-watching adventures, but don't miss the excellent Centre d'Interprétation des Mammifières Marins in Tadoussac (see p.364).

Aviation du Fjord, 231 rue des Pionniers in Tadoussac (Ⓣ418/235-4640, Ⓦwww.fjord-best.com/aviation.du.fjord), can take you up in a **seaplane** (mid-July to mid-Oct; $55 for 20min) to view whales, the fjord and backcountry from the air.

From south of Tadoussac

Croisières Famille-Dufour (Ⓣ418/692-0222 or 1-800/463-5250, Ⓦwww.familledufour.com) offers a ten-hour trip from **Québec City** for $169, with pick-ups and drop-offs in **Ste-Anne-de-Beaupré**, **Île aux Coudres** and **Pointe-au-Pic**. A coach trip and cruise package is the other option from Québec City: Croisières AML (Ⓣ418/692-1159 or 1-800/563-4643, Ⓦwww.croisieresaml.com) charges $100. They also run a boat from **Rivière-du-Loup** on the south shore of the St Lawrence (Ⓣ418/867-3361; 3 daily; 3hr 30min; $42).

one of the best in Québec and – thanks to its own bar – determinedly lively and sociable. Canoes, cross-country skis, skidoos and snowshoes are all available for rent; various activities such as guided hikes, snowshoe excursions and dog-sleigh trips are organized in their relative seasons. All-you-can-eat breakfasts for $3.50 are optional, and camping ($6) is available in the hostel grounds. Family-style **camping** away from the hostel is available in summer at *Camping Tadoussac*, 428 rue du Bateau-Passeur (late May to mid-Sept; ⓣ418/235-4501, ⓦwww.essipit.com; $20–35), 2km from the ferry terminal on Hwy 138 – arrive early in summer for a spot.

For a unique stay, opt for the keeper's house at the **lighthouse** on Île Rouge in the middle of the St Lawrence (ⓣ418/237-5050). The rooms are more luxurious than what the keeper would have been used to, and it's reflected in the price – an expensive $530 for two people ($299 if you go solo), that includes transport by zodiac (including an hour whale-watching), breakfast, a five-course dinner and tour of the island. Day-trips (2 daily; 2hr 30min; $23) will suffice for most people.

Eating possibilities include: the *Hôtel Tadoussac*, which has a vast dining room and a reasonably priced set menu ($20–30); *Chez Georges*, 135 rue du Bateau-Passeur, which is in Tadoussac's oldest house and has seafood and steaks on the table d'hôte for $21; *La Bolée*, 164 rue Morin (ⓣ418/235-4750), which is a

From Tadoussac

If you're worried about missing a reservation in **Tadoussac** because of the ferry queue, it's worth asking if you can board at the quay in **Baie-Ste-Catherine** instead – many of the companies fill up their boats on both shores of the mouth of the Saguenay before heading off to see the whales. Some firms also run cruises up the Saguenay fjord, as well as combined whale/fjord packages. Load up with brochures at the tourist office and compare what's on offer.

For trips in zodiacs contact Les Croisières Express, 161 rue des Pionniers (ⓣ418/235-4770 or 1-888/235-6842); Compagnie de la Baie de Tadoussac, 145 rue du Bord de l'Eau (ⓣ418/235-4548 or ⓣ1-800/757-4548); or Otis Excursions, 431 rue Bateau-Passeur (ⓣ418/235-4197). Croisières AML (ⓣ418/237-4274 or 1-800/563-4643) gives you the option of a large boat or 24-person zodiac, and the other big outfit, Croisières Famille-Dufour at the *Hôtel Tadoussac*, 165 rue du Bord de l'Eau (ⓣ418/235-4421 or 1-800/561-0718), offers whale safaris aboard a catamaran, a 48-person zodiac or a more sedate 1922 schooner. *Tayout*, 148 rue du bord de L'Eau (ⓣ418/235-1056), offers whale-watching trips in sea kayaks.

From north of Tadoussac

Although you'll spend less time on the water with the following companies, their points of departure on the Côte-Nord are closer to where the whales are most likely to be, so you get about the same amount of contact time for less money. Heading north on Hwy 138, there's a turn-off on the right just after the overpass at **Bergeronnes**, where Les Croisières Neptune has a ticket office at 507 rue du Boisé (ⓣ418/232-6716, ⓦwww.croisieresneptune.net) for trips in zodiacs only. The Montagnais company Croisière Essipit, 498 rue de la Mer (ⓣ418/232-6778 or 1-888/868-6666, ⓦwww.essipit.com), uses the quay in Bergeronnes as well and has a wider variety of craft. Les Pionniers des Baleines, 41 rue des Pilotes (ⓣ418/233-3274), is the least expensive in the area and launches its zodiacs from Les Escoumins, at the northern limit of the marine park.

pricey place with crêpes, salads and a takeaway deli underneath with delicious breads; and *Le Bâteau*, 246 rue des Forgerons, a popular place that churns out an all-you-can-eat buffet of Québecois food for $17, but has the atmosphere of a school cafeteria. Cheaper food and great evenings of **drinking** can be had at *Le Gibard*, 135 rue Bord de l'Eau, which stays open until 3am, and at *Café du Fjord*, 154 rue du Bateau-Passeur (ⓣ418/235-4626) near the hostel, a young hangout with good music; they also have food, including a good $16 dinner buffet. The best spot is *Le Père Coquart Café*, 115 rue Coupe de L'Islet (ⓣ418/235-1170; early June to Oct), with its large terrace, around the corner from *Le Gibard*. They serve light meals until 9pm when the place morphs into an intimate place to hear Québecois and other music.

North of Tadoussac

The landscape **north of Tadoussac** takes in lakes surrounded by granite outcroppings and boreal forest, interspersed with stretches of sandy beaches and salt marshes. The craggy terrain is the chief attraction here with lookout points and short trails in many of the villages, as well as interpretation centres for just about everything. The area is particularly known for cheaper and more convenient whale-watching, spectacular diving and first-rate birding, particularly during the migratory seasons.

As accommodation fills up in Tadoussac in high season, you may wind up having to stay in the community of **BERGERONNES**, 22km along the road. Otherwise if you're here its generally for the good lookout post by a popular whale-feeding ground beside the Cap de Bon Désir lighthouse which now serves as the **Centre d'Interprétation et d'Observation de Cap-de-Bon-Désir**, 13 chemin du Cap-Bon-Désir (mid-June to mid-Oct daily 8am–8pm; ⓦwww.parcmarin.qc.ca; $5), which has displays on whales. Also in town is the Archéo Topo, 498 rue de la Mer (mid-May to mid-Oct daily 9am–8pm; ⓦwww.archeotopo.qc.ca; $4.50), a worthwhile research and exhibition centre devoted to archeology along the Côte-Nord, where finds date back eight thousand years. **Accommodation** is available at *Le Bergeronnette*, 65 rue Principale (May–Oct ⓣ418/232-6642 or 1-877/232-6605, ⓦwww.bergeronnette.com; ❸), which has simple rooms and a reasonable restaurant – and there's a **campsite**, off the hwy east of town, whose beautiful site has views over the St Lawrence: *Camping Bon Désir* (ⓣ418/232-6297, ⓦwww.campingbondesir.com; $21–29; June–Oct), which charges more for a pitch with a view.

Though whale-watching is also popular at **LES ESCOUMINS**, the big deal here is the diving, especially at night when the phosphorescence creates an eerie underwater landscape. **Le Centre des Loisirs Marins**, 41 rue des Pilotes (interpretation centre: 9.30–11am & 1.30–3.30pm; $5), is only worthwhile if you intend to dive (diving card required). The dive shop downstairs, Centre de plongée Atlan (ⓣ418/233-4242), rents out a complete set of gear for $55 a day. The only other reason to visit is for the excellent **birding**: the Promenade du Moulin brings you to a rugged shoreline with hundreds of birds. The town's **hostel**, *Auberge de la plongée*, 118 rue St-Marcelin (ⓣ418/233-3289 or 1-800/375-3465; dorms $18), is a bit shabby. If you want to **eat**, try the excellent burgers at *Auberge Manoir Bellevue*, 27 rue de l'Église (ⓣ418/233-3325 or 1-888/233-3325, ⓦwww.manoirbellevue.com; ❸), which also does a pricey table d'hôte for dinner and has comfortable rooms.

About 152km north of Les Escoumins on Hwy 138 – and 20km short of Baie-Comeau – is the tip of a broad peninsula where the **Parc Nature de Pointe-aux-Outardes** (daily June–Oct 8am–5pm; ⓣ418/567-4226, ⓦwww.parcnature.com; $5), is worth the admission price when migratory birds flock here around May and mid-September. Easy trails take in a variety of ecosystems including salt marshes and sand dunes, and ninety-minute guided tours of the plant- and birdlife are included in midsummer. If you want to visit the beach (where the water is warm enough for swimming after a few hot sunny days), there's access at the Quai municipale on rue Labrie.

From Les Escoumins there's a **ferry** to Trois-Pistoles (see p.341), while the seasonal **ferry** to Rimouski (see p.342 for details) leaves 59km along the coast from Forestville. While waiting in Forestville you can picnic next to the river or hang out on a pleasant beach, where camping is permitted.

Fjord du Saguenay

One of the world's longest, the **Fjord du Saguenay** cuts through the Canadian Shield before merging with the St Lawrence. A stupendous expanse of rocky outcrops, sheer cliffs and thick vegetation, the land flanking the fjord on both sides is protected as the provincial Parc du Saguenay. The walls of the fjord extend to a depth of 270m in places, almost as much as the height of the cliffs above the waterline. Wedged between the two halves of the Parc du Saguenay are some of the most attractive parts of the Parc Marin du Saguenay–St-Laurent. But since **no bridges** cross the Saguenay for the 126km between Tadoussac and Chicoutimi, you may need to backtrack to explore both shores. For a taste of both the terrestrial and marine parks, drive as far as **Rivière-Éternité** on the south shore, and then double back. From Tadoussac, Hwy 172 runs parallel to the north side of the fjord past the turn-offs to Baie Ste-Marguerite and the pretty waterside village of **Ste-Rose-du-Nord** before reaching the bridge to **Chicoutimi**.

The southern shore

Coming from Charlevoix, the best approach to the Parc du Saguenay is to drive along the wriggling Hwy 170 from Saint-Siméon, a road that strikes the **southern shore** of the Saguenay fjord after about 50km, close to L'Anse-St-Jean. Both this town and Rivière-Éternité, 33km further west, are easy entry points to the park and arguably the most attractive places on the fjord to take a boat trip.

The only village on the Saguenay when it was founded in 1838, **L'ANSE-ST-JEAN** is famous for its Pont du Faubourg, the covered bridge that was featured on the back of the now-retired $1000 note and which managed to survive the flood of 1996, though the rest of the village was badly affected. The town's other claim to fame is that, on January 21, 1997, it became a monarchy following a local referendum. The new ruler, King Denys I, an artist and professor, also known as "l'Illustre Inconnu" (the Illustrious Unknown), didn't reign for long, though. In the face of local political wrangling he lost much of his popularity and consequently abdicated in 2000. Though clearly difficult to rule, at least this kingdom has a terrific view of the Saguenay fjord and surrounding hills from the marina, and makes a good base to explore the park. L'Anse-St-Jean also boasts a particularly fine view of the Saguenay from the **L'Anse-de-Tabatière lookout**; the 500m trail begins at the lookout's car park. From the quay in L'Anse-St-Jean you can take a two- or four-hour **cruise** (June–Oct 1–3 daily; from $35) or join Fjord en kayak, 4 rue du Faubourg (May–Oct; ⓣ418/272-3024, ⓦwww.fjord-en-kayak.qc.ca) – three-hour trips are $52, two- to five-day excursions start at $350. Alternatively, ride along the fjord on **horseback**: the Centre équestre des Plateaux, 31 chemin des Plateaux (ⓣ418/272-3231, ⓦwww.aei.ca/~cep), offers three-hour rides for $55, as well as multiday excursions. Inland from L'Anse-St-Jean, **Mont-Edouard** (ⓣ418/272-2927, ⓦwww.montedouard.com), with a 450m vertical and 28 trails, attracts skiers in the winter. L'Anse-St-Jean's cheapest **accommodation** is a medicinal plant farm doubling as a hostel – the laid-back *Auberge Chez Monika*, 12 chemin des Plateaux (ⓣ418/272-3115; dorms $10), at the top of a steep hill. The village has a few **B&Bs** – *Le Nid de l'Anse*, the last house on rue St-Jean-Baptiste (ⓣ418/272-2273; ❸; June–Sept), overlooks the fjord and is close to the quay and walking trails. Other options are the clifftop cottages and condos at *Gîtes du Fjord*, 344 rue St-Jean-Baptiste (ⓣ418/272-3430 or 1-800/561-8060, ⓦwww.quebecweb.com/gitesdufjord; ❺–❽), as well as a couple of **campsites** – *Camping de l'Anse* (ⓣ418/272-2554, ⓦwww.campingdelanse.ca; $18–25) is in a good position close to the fjord and has excellent facilities. For moderately priced **seafood** try *Le Maringoinfre*, 212 rue St Jean Baptiste (ⓣ418/272-2385; $20–30 for dinner).

Continuing along the fjord, scrappy **RIVIÈRE-ÉTERNITÉ**, 83km from Saint-Siméon on Hwy 138 and 61km east of Chicoutimi, is the main gateway to the Parc du Saguenay (admission $3.50). The park's **information centre** (mid-May to late-Sept daily 9am–9pm; late Sept to mid-Oct weekends only; ⓣ418/272-3008 or 1-877/272-5229, ⓦwww.parcsquebec.com), 8km from the village, has maps of hiking trails ($3) and kayak routes ($4) – and expert naturalists on hand. A smaller information post lies 1.5km from the village, on the park's border. Halfway between the two is the park's main **campsite** (sites $20-27); reservations are available from the information centre. Beware: blackflies love this area, though the worst is over by late July. From the main information centre, a couple of short **hikes** and a long one are laid out through this sector of the park. The best short hike is the Statue Hike, an easy four-hour (7km) round trip up the massive bluff of Cap Trinité, which flanks the deep-blue water of the Baie Éternité. The summit is topped by a huge statue known as *Our Lady of the Saguenay*, erected in 1881 by Charles-Napoléon Robitaille after he was saved from drowning in the river. The long-distance Les Caps hike (25km) follows the bay of the Éternité River back to L'Anse-St-Jean via massive plateaus, ravines, waterfalls and stunning views. It is an intermediate walk along clear paths and takes about three days. There are wilderness campsites and a couple of refuges along the way; registration with the information centre is a must. A number of companies offer **water-taxi** services for backpackers, enabling you to hike as far as Tadoussac (it takes a week) – and you can even have your vehicle sent on to your destination by boat. Ninety-minute **cruises** of the Cap Trinité, one of the prettiest spots on the fjord, are offered by Croisières du Cap Trinité (May–Sept 2–3 daily; $20; ⓣ418/272-2591); boats leave from near the information centre. Guided **kayak** trips are available from next to the information centre at *Explo-Fjord* (ⓣ418/545-3737 or 1-877/272-5229; 3 daily; 2–3hr; $29–39), which also runs zodiac cruises (same prices and times).

The northern shore

Running parallel to the Saguenay fjord, Hwy 172 is a dramatic route along the less-frequented **northern shore** of the Saguenay that gives occasional panoramas over the water and provides access to a couple of pretty towns en route, where cruises are available or kayaks can be rented. The daily (except Sat) Intercar **bus** from Tadoussac follows the highway, terminating at Chicoutimi.

A 42-kilometre hiking trail from Tadoussac (follow the signs for 'Sentier Le Fjord') ends at **BAIE-STE-MARGUERITE**, where the main interpretation centre (early June to mid-Oct daily 9am–5pm; ⓣ418/236-1162 or 1-877/272-5229, ⓦwww.sepaq.com) for the northern part of the Parc du Saguenay ($3.50) is located. To get here by car, you need to travel 3km down a dusty gravel road that exits the hwy just after tiny Rivière-Ste-Marguerite, itself worth a quick stop for its covered bridge. The main draw here is **belugas**, and the interpretation centre has displays that cover all facets of them as well as the fjord in general; ask at the desk for an English-language guidebook. An easy three-kilometre trail leads through the woods to an observation platform where the belugas can frequently be spotted. Despite its appearances, the centre's cafeteria serves up good, hearty grub for hungry hikers from 7am in summer.

About 80km from Tadoussac is the turn-off for **STE-ROSE-DU-NORD**, a tiny village of white houses crammed beneath the precipitous walls of the fjord, 3km from the main road. The seasonal **tourist office**, 213 rue du Quai (late June to mid-Sept 9.30am–7.30pm), has free maps of **hiking trails**, including the Plate-Forme trail that leads to a fabulous panoramic viewpoint above the town. The **Musée de la Nature**, 199 rue de la Montagne (May to mid-Oct daily 8.45am–8.30pm, otherwise until 7pm; ⓦwww.musee-de-la-nature.com; $5), is a small but surprisingly informative museum housing an eclectic range of exhibits from stuffed animals to knotty roots from the local region. The church of **Ste-Rose-de-Lima** (daily 8am–8pm), with its interior of wood, birch bark, branches and roots, is also worth a peek. Explo-Fjord (ⓣ418/545-3737) offers boat excursions on zodiacs and Croisière Marjolaine runs three-hour **cruises** of the fjord's most stunning stretch (late June to early Oct 10.15am & 1.15pm; $45; ⓣ418/543-7630 or 1-800/363-7248, ⓦwww.croiseremarjolaine.com). The boat then travels on to Chicoutimi from Ste-Rose-du-Nord in the late afternoon (2hr; $37), useful if you intend to visit Lac Saint-Jean. Sometimes there's a boat connection with Tadoussac as well; enquire at the information centre for details. Should you want to **stay** over, you could try *Auberge le Presbytère*, 136 rue du Quai (ⓣ418/675-1362 or 1-866/303-1326, ⓦwww.aupresbytere.com; ❸), converted from an old presbyterian sanctuary. It has an outstanding **restaurant**, but a full menu will cost over $30. Rooms are also available above the Musée de la Nature (ⓣ418/675-2348; ❷), while *Camping la Descente des Femmes* (ⓣ418/675-2581; June to mid-Oct) has sites for $17–22 and incredible views.

The Upper Saguenay and Lac Saint-Jean

The Saguenay fjord's source – the vast **Lac Saint-Jean** – sits 210km inland, linked by the Rivière Saguenay. Along this stretch, a glut of aluminium and paper plants using the river as a power source has resulted in the growth of characterless industrial towns, the largest of which is **Chicoutimi**. Further west, beyond **Jonquière**, the lake's farmland periphery is still relatively untouched and offers the opportunity to stay on the Montagnais reserve at **Mashteuiatsh** near Roberval, a unique zoo at **Saint-Félicien** and the strange sight of **Val-Jalbert**, Québec's most accessible ghost town. A bike route connects the lake's towns and is an increasingly popular option for travellers from Montréal or Québec who pop their bike on the train or bus for a three- to five-day tour of the lake. In 1996, the Saguenay–Lac-Saint-Jean region was devastated by one of the biggest catastrophes in Canada's recent past – a flood that wiped out homes and businesses in several towns. As the flood was an "act of God" no one received insurance, but those who lost their homes were helped out by donations from across the country.

From the Lac Saint-Jean's southern shore it's about five hours to Montréal on Hwy 155 (via Trois-Rivières); from the southeast, you can take the moose-infested Hwy 169 until it joins up with Hwy 175 on its way to Québec City.

Chicoutimi

Since its founding by a Scottish immigrant in 1842, the regional capital of **CHICOUTIMI** has grown from a small sawmill centre into one of the province's largest towns. It's not a particularly enticing place, though the pedestrianized port area is pleasant enough. The town is, however, host to one of Québec's best **festivals** – the mid-February ten-day **Carnaval Souvenir** when what seems like the entire population dresses in costumes from circa 1900; lumber camps, can-can clubs, operetta shows and period-authentic heavy drinking augment the pioneer atmosphere. Outside this time, the main local attraction is **La Pulperie de Chicoutimi**, 300 Dubuc (June & Sept to mid-Oct Wed–Sun 9am–5pm; late June to Sept daily 9am–6pm; mid-Oct to early June Wed–Sun 10am–4pm; Ⓦwww.pulperie.com; $8.50), five austere brick buildings built along the rapids by the Chicoutimi Pulp Company, which was founded in 1896 and quickly became Canada's largest producer of paper pulp. Left to rot in 1930, these gigantic ghosts of Chicoutimi's industrial past had been restored to prime condition but the flood of 1996 caused $1m damage and the site lost its restaurant and summer theatre. Exhibits explain the mill's history and include the strange **Maison du Peintre Arthur Villeneuve** which was relocated here in 1994. The former home of naive painter Arthur Villeneuve, the house is in effect one big painting, with murals covering inside and out. The subject matter is unadventurous, but the artist's work is bright and cheery, while scenes of 1950s Chicoutimi – when Villeneuve started his project after retiring as a barber – are intriguing.

Chicoutimi's **bus station**, 55 rue Racine est (Ⓣ418/543-1403), is on the corner of Tessier and Racine, right in the centre of town. Buses from Montréal, Québec City, Lac Saint-Jean and Tadoussac all connect here. The CITS local bus (Ⓣ418/545-2487) links with Jonquière's **train station** (arrival point for trains from Montréal), running at least hourly from 7.15am to 9.45pm. There's a municipal **tourist office** at 295 Racine est (Mon–Fri 8am–noon & 1.30pm–4.30pm; Ⓣ418/698-3167 or 1-800/463-6565). **Accommodation** is readily available as the town hosts business conferences all year round. Budget rooms can be obtained through the college *CÉGEP de Chicoutimi*, 534 rue Jacques-Cartier est (Ⓣ418/549-9520 ext 258 or 257; Ⓦwww.cegep-chicoutimi.qc.ca; ❶). *Auberge Centre-Ville*, 104 rue Jacques-Cartier est (Ⓣ418/543-0253; ❷), is a small, central **hotel**, while *Le Montagnais*, 1080 boul Talbot (Ⓣ418/543-1521 or 1-800/463-9160, Ⓦwww.lemontagnais.qc.ca; ❹), is a modern hotel further out. There are numerous small **restaurants** on rue Racine, east of the tourist office. Recommended is *La Cuisine Café-Resto* at no. 387, which has French food in the $10–20 range, though for a better class of meal try the elegant *La Bourgresse*, 260 rue Riverin (Ⓣ418/543-3178), where French cuisine is $20–40. Most **nightlife** is also on rue Racine, in lively bars.

If you're using Chicoutimi as a gateway to the Saguenay Fjord, you might be tempted by a **cruise** with Croisière Marjolaine (Ⓣ418/543-7630 or 1-800/363-7248, Ⓦwww.croisieremarjolaine.com; $37; late June to Aug) as far as Cap Trinité, stopping both ways at Ste-Rose-du-Nord (see p.371), where they provide a coach back to Chicoutimi on the morning run (in the afternoon, the first Chicoutimi–Ste-Rose-du-Nord leg is by coach).

Jonquière

Some 15km west of Chicoutimi, **JONQUIÈRE** thrives due to its Alcan aluminium smelter, one of the largest in the world, and its two paper mills. The smelter brought many Eastern European immigrants to the area when it was first opened in 1925, and the industry overtook the Price sons and their wood empire as the largest employer. A modern town with wide avenues and the world's only large-scale aluminium bridge (across the Saguenay), it can make a good stop for budget travellers because of an Allo-Stop office and train connections with Montréal; it also has a better nightlife than Chicoutimi.

The **tourist office** is at 2665 boul du Royaume in the Centre des Congrès (Mon–Fri 8am–noon & 1.30pm–4.30pm; ⓣ418/548-4004 or 1-800/561-9196). **Buses** terminate at 2249 rue St-Hubert (ⓣ418/547-2167) and **trains** arrive at the VIA Rail station (ⓣ1-800/361-5390, ⓦwww.viarail.ca). To **stay**, try *CÉGEP*, 2505 rue St Hubert (ⓣ418/542-2643, ⓦwww.cjonquiere.qc.ca/cegep_jonquiere; ❶), which has good, clean, college rooms. The *Auberge des Deux Tours*, 2522 rue Saint-Dominique (ⓣ418/695-2022 or 1-888/454-2022, ⓦwww.aubergedeuxtours.qc.ca; ❸), is reasonable, or there's the *Holiday Inn Saguenay*, 2675 boul du Royaume (ⓣ418/548-3124 or 1-800/363-3124, ⓦwww.saguenay.holiday-inn.com; ❻). You can **eat** at the stately 1911 *Auberge Villa Pachon*, 1904 rue Perron (ⓣ418/542-3568 or 1-888/922-3568), whose very expensive restaurant is excellent with meals starting at $30. Another pricey option is *L'Amandier*, 5219 chemin St-Andre (ⓣ418/542-5395), out of town but worth the trip for the bizarre dining room of carved plaster and wood. For an everyday meal head to the Rue St-Dominique: *Le Puzzle*, no. 2497, is a fun place with cool decor; *Les Pâtes Amato*, 2655 boul de Royaume, has coffees, pasta and Italian desserts to die for. The tawdry nightclubs and gritty **bars** along the same road are a good laugh.

Lac Saint-Jean

To the west of Chicoutimi, around **Lac Saint-Jean**, stretches a relatively untouched area whose tranquil lakeshore villages are linked by the circular route of Hwy 169. Named after Father Jean Duquen, the first European to visit the region in 1647, the huge glacial lake is fed by most of the rivers of northeastern Québec and – unusually for an area of the rocky Canadian Shield – is bordered by sandy beaches and a lush, green terrain that has been farmed for over a century. The local cuisine, especially the delicious coarse meat pie called a *tourtière* and the thick blueberry pie, is renowned throughout the province.

A relatively flat 256km **bike route** – the **Véloroute des Bleuets** (ⓦwww.veloroute-bleuets.qc.ca) – encircles the whole lake, mostly as a wide paved shoulder, but a total of 60km of the route is completely free of cars. The path passes close to most of the major attractions and through many of the villages around Lac Saint-Jean and there are beaches all along the lakeshore where you can cool off after a hard day's ride. It's well set up for getting there: the **train** from Montréal to Jonquière stops at Chambord on the south shore near Val-Jalbert and there's a **bus** from Québec City to Alma. A growing number of **B&Bs** and other services are popping up to serve the two-wheeled visitors, and even the locals are laying out a warm welcome – some have even set up garden chairs to rest on near the bike path. A minivan service, Gilles Girard (ⓣ418/342-6651) can even help take the strain by transporting your luggage around the lake for $20 per trip. An annual **bike marathon** is held for three days in early June.

Alma and west around the lake

The dull aluminium-producing city of **ALMA**, 50km west of Jonquière, is useful for its **buses** – to Chicoutimi and Québec City and various points around Lac St-Jean – and is a practical starting point for the cycle ride around Lac St-Jean. Liberté à Vélo (ⓣ418/668-8430 1-877/668-8430, ⓦwww.liberteavelo.ca) provides guided **tours** along the cycle route – a service which includes luggage transport. Should you need to **rent** a bicycle try Vélo Jeunesse, 1691 av du Pont Alma (ⓣ418/662-9785, ⓦwww.velo-jeunesse.com; $20/day). The **information centre** is at 1682 av du Pont Nord (Mon–Fri 8am–noon & 1.30pm–4.30pm; ⓣ418/668-3611 or 1-877/668-3611). A number of motels along avenue du Pont Sud provide predictable **accommodation**, including *Motel Rustik* at no. 1350 (ⓣ418/668-2373, ⓦwww.motelrustik.com; ❷).

In a clockwise direction beyond Alma, the cycle path follows along shoreline inaccessible by highway, joining up with Hwy 170 beyond **SAINT-GÉDÉON**, a popular beach town. To treat yourself, head for the lakefront *Auberge des Îles*, 250 rang des Îles (ⓣ418/345-2589 or 1-800/680-2589, ⓦwww.aubergedesiles.com; ❸), a lovely inn just north of St-Gédéon with a four-course menu of game and local flavours for $35.

One of the main attractions of the region, the historical village of **VAL-JALBERT** (daily: early June & late Aug to early Oct 10am–5pm; mid-June to late Aug 9.30am–5.30pm; ⓣ418/275-3132 or 1-888/675-3132, ⓦwww.valjalbert.com; $17) is 52km beyond Alma along the cycle route and 92km west of Chicoutimi along Hwy 170 and 169. The 72m-high Ouiatchouan waterfall, which dominates the town, led to the establishment of a pulp mill here a century ago, and by 1926 the village had around 950 inhabitants. In the following year, the introduction of chemical-based pulping made the mill redundant, and the village was closed down. Val-Jalbert was left to rot until 1985, when the government decided to renovate it as a tourist attraction. From the site entrance a bus (with on-board French commentary) runs around the main sights of the village, ending at the mill at the base of the falls. You can then wander around whatever catches your eye along the way – the abandoned

△ Homes in Val-Jalbert

wooden houses, a former convent (now a museum) or the general store (now a souvenir shop). From the mill, itself converted into an excellent crafts market and cafeteria, a **cable car** leads to the top of the falls, from where there are stunning views of the village and Lac Saint-Jean beyond. It is possible to stay in Val-Jalbert's renovated **hotel** above the general store (③), in apartments in the converted houses on St George St ($72–112 for one to six people), or in the **campsite** ($20–26) just outside the village. From late October to April, when the site is officially closed, you can still gain access for free – it is a beautifully tranquil place to spend some time.

Mashteuiatsh

Some 10km west of Val-Jalbert, at **Roberval**, a turn-off leads to the Montagnais reserve of **MASHTEUIATSH**, also known as **Pointe-Bleue**. Before European contact the Montagnais ("Ilnu" in the local language) were a migratory people who split into small family groups for summer hunting. When the Europeans arrived they found the Montagnais in bitter conflict with the Iroquois, an enmity that Champlain intensified by allying himself with the Montagnais for trade. By the late seventeenth century their population had been greatly weakened by warfare, European diseases, depletion of game and displacement from their lands. This reserve was created in 1856, and today around 1800 of eastern Québec's 14,000 Montagnais live here. Like many Canadian reserves, Mashteuiatsh is dry, in an attempt to reduce alcoholism and its attendant problems, yet the Montagnais suffer a great deal of prejudice from the surrounding white communities – so much so that there's no bus service, because Québecois bus drivers refuse to go there.

The village is situated right on the lake, and has an **information centre** on the main street at 1427 Ouiatchouan (mid-June to Sept daily 8am–8pm). At the end of July a **powwow** is held on the waterfront by the four concrete tepee sculptures that represent the seasons. Up the hill, at 1787 rue Amishk, is the recently renovated **Musée Amérindien** (mid-May to mid-Oct daily 10am–6pm; rest of year Mon–Thurs 9am–noon & 1–4pm, Fri 9am–noon & 1–3pm; Ⓦwww.museeilnu.ca; $8), where you start with a twenty-minute film showing traditional Montagnais life, much of it revolving around hunting and fishing. The permanent exhibition Pekuakami Ilnuatsh, which translates as "the Lac St-Jean Montagnais", continues the theme with artefacts and interpretation panels that also describe domestic life and the impact of European contact; temporary exhibitions highlight the works of aboriginal artists.

From August to September, Ashuapmushuaniussi, at 1562 Ouiatchouan (Ⓣ418/275-2473), organizes **adventure trips** into the bush where you are immersed in the traditional way of life, relying on the resources of the surrounding woodlands and rivers to build shelters, make fires and prepare food (from $150 per person per day).

Saint-Prime and Saint-Félicien

The village of **Saint-Prime**, 13km west of Roberval, has a surprising little museum, the **Musée du fromage cheddar**, 148 av Albert-Perron (daily: early June 10.15am–5.30pm; late June to Aug 9.15am–5.30pm; Sept 10.15am-5pm; Ⓦwww.museecheddar.org; $7.95), where four generations of cheese-makers have worked their craft since 1895. The one-hour guided tour covers the whole process of producing cheddar here – almost all of which was shipped to England. The unexpected part of the tour is upstairs, where the Perron family residence appears as it would have in 1922 and a very convincing "Marie Perron" tells about her life, how the best piece of furniture was reserved for the priest who visited but once a year, and why kitchen counters used to be so low – so the children could make themselves useful. You also get to try a bit of the cheese produced by the modern cheese factory.

Situated on the western extremity of the lake on the Ashuapmushuan River, **SAINT-FÉLICIEN** is the site of Québec's best zoo, the **Zoo Sauvage de Saint-Félicien** (daily late May–Aug 9am–6pm; early May & Sept to mid-Oct 9am–5pm; Nov–May by appointment; ⓣ418/679-0543 or 1-800/667-5687, ⓦwww.borealie.org; $29), located on Chamouchouane Island. Don't let the giant car park put you off: the first part of the zoo is in a beautiful riverside setting. The rest mimics a number of ecosystems where around eighty, mainly Canadian, species roam free all over the site. It is the humans who are the ones in cages, hauled around on the back of a mini-train (provisions are made for disabled travellers). The Arctic environment for the polar bears allows you to see the magnificent beasts swim underwater; they put on their best show at feeding time. The zoo also has an historical angle, with mock-ups of an Indian village, trading post, loggers' camp and settlers' farm, staffed by costumed guides performing everyday tasks to match the setting. An English guidebook is available at the entrance. Saint-Félicien's **information office** is at 1209 boul Sacré-Coeur (late June to early Sept Mon–Fri 8.30am–8pm, Sat & Sun 9am–8pm; rest of year Mon–Fri 8.30am–noon & 1–4.30pm; ⓣ418/679-9888). For **accommodation**, try *Hôtel Bellevue*, 1055 boul Sacré-Coeur (ⓣ418/679-0162; ❷), or one of the ten **B&Bs** (❶–❷) in the town and surrounding farmland.

From Saint-Félicien to Alma

From Saint-Félicien the hwy and bike path separate, rejoining 15km inland at **NORMADIN**, where **Les Grands Jardins de Normandin**, 1515 av du Rocher (daily late June to early Sept 9.30am–6pm; ⓦwww.lesgrandsjardinsdenormandin.com; $11) is an overpriced and over-hyped formal garden. More worthwhile is one of the local **B&Bs**: at *Les Gîtes Makadan*, 3km off the hwy at 1728 rue St-Cyrille (ⓣ418/274-2867 or 1-877/625-2326, ⓦgitemakadan.cjb.net; ❷), where the owners serve up huge portions of local country dishes, much of which is fresh produce from their farm down the road; you need to tell them ahead of time that you want dinner ($15).

Continuing clockwise around the lake brings you to **DOLBEAU-MISTASSINI**, 28km further on. Dolbeau, the western half of town, is at its best during mid-July's ten-day **Western Festival**, with rodeos and people wandering around in stetsons and spurs. Mistassini, the region's blueberry capital, outdoes its neighbour in early August, with the **Festival du Bleuet** – one big blowout on blueberries dipped in chocolate, blueberry pie, blueberry cheesecake and a potent blueberry wine. Over the Mistassini River 7km up the road to St Eugéne d'Argentenay the **Monastère des Pères Trappistes** sells its own organic produce; a large quantity of the berries are on offer in season along with their home-made chocolates (the chocolate-covered blueberry bar is regionally famous). Another worthwhile trip out of town is south in the direction of Ste-Marguerite-Marie, following route de Vauvert to its end where you'll find the 7km **beach** at the Centre Touistique Vauvert (ⓣ418/374-2746). Here, there's a restaurant and a few free places to pitch a tent; discreet no-trace camping on the beach is also tolerated. Of **accommodation** in Dolbeau-Mistassini the *Hôtel du Boulevard*, 1610 boul Wallberg (ⓣ418/276-8207 or 1-800/268-1061, ⓦcf.geocities.com/hotelduboulevard; ❸), is passable, but the *Auberge La Diligence*, 414 av de la Friche (ⓣ418/276-6544 or 1-800/361-6162,

Ⓦwww.hotelier.qc.ca; ④), is nicer. *Gîte Bonjour, Bienvenue*, 1824 boul Wallberg (Ⓣ418/276-1291; ②), is a good, inexpensive **B&B**.

Another 20km round the shore, a short walk just west of the village of **SAINTE-MONIQUE**, is a **hostel** and **campsite** on it's own little island: the *Auberge de l'Île du Repos de Péribonka* (Ⓣ418/347-5649, Ⓦwww.iledurepos.com; ②; dorms $19, camping from $17). Its location is useful for an excursion to **Parc de la Pointe-Taillon** (Ⓣ418/347-5371, Ⓦwww.sepaq.com; $3.50, parking $5), which also has rustic camping available 2–4km from the car park ($16 per site, no services); they'll give you a lift if you need one. Occupying a finger of land that juts into Lac Saint-Jean, the park is bordered by long and often deserted beaches, and there are 45km of cycle trails, a portion of which coincides with the Véloroute des Bleuets. From Sainte-Monique, it's 29km round to Alma.

The Côte-Nord

The St Lawrence River was the lifeline of the wilderness beyond Tadoussac until the 1960s, when **Highway 138** was constructed along the **Côte-Nord** to Havre-St-Pierre, 625km away. In 1996, the road was extended a further 145km, to Natashquan. The road sweeps from high vistas down to the rugged shoreline through the vast regions of Manicouagan and Duplessis, the few distractions offered in the villages and towns en route being supplemented by panoramas of spruce-covered mountains, the vast sky and the mighty river. **Bears** and **moose** often lumber out of the stunted forest onto the highway, and in the summer you can frequently spot the shiny backs of **whales** arching out of the water.

Basque whalers were the first Europeans to penetrate this chilly shore in the sixteenth century, but later, when they began to trade fur with the aboriginal Montagnais, Naskapi and Inuit, they were ousted by French merchants. After the British conquest the fur trade continued but fishing remained the main industry until the twentieth century, when mining, lumber and hydroelectric projects led to the growth of a few settlements into fair-sized towns. Despite this, the region has a population density of just five people per square mile, and the distances between communities become longer and longer the further you travel.

The Intercar **bus** from Québec City to Tadoussac serves the Côte-Nord as far as Baie-Comeau, from where another travels to Sept-Îles, where you have no choice but to spend the night before continuing on to Havre-St-Pierre. At the time of writing there is no public transport to Natashquan, but a bus service is expected – ask at tourist information for details. At Natashquan the hwy gives out altogether and the only onward transport is by snowmobile, plane or the supply **ship** from Rimouski, which serves the wildlife haven of Île d'Anticosti and undertakes a breathtaking journey along the inlets of the windswept coastline of the Basse Côte-Nord (Lower North Shore).

Manicouagan

The Manicouagan refers largely of a string of settlements along the side of the St Lawrence. The stretch between the two major industrial conurbations, **Baie-Comeau** and **Sept-Îles**, is rugged and desolate, the road twisting over passes and down to the occasional pretty fishing village like **Godbout**, but attractions are thin on the ground and most travellers here are just passing through on their way to the Mingan Coast (see p.383) or Labrador City (see p.549) via the Hwy 389 from Baie-Comeau or the railway from Sept-Îles. If you are on your way through, stop for a quick look at the gigantic **Manic dams** and pause at Sept-Îles to explore some first-rate **Innu** museums and events – they will help to make more sense of the indigenous culture, which becomes more evident as you travel north.

Baie-Comeau

The road into the western sector of **BAIE-COMEAU** may be a fairly drab landscape of strip malls, but it's nothing compared to the eastern sector, where a monstrous newsprint mill plant churns out poisonous emissions 24 hours a day. It was established in 1936 by Colonel Robert R. McCormick, the publisher of the *Chicago Tribune*, and Baie-Comeau has done nothing but boom ever since: with a population of 26,000, it dwarfs the communities around it. There's no reason to hang around here, but while waiting for a northward bus or a ferry to Gaspé's Matane you might stroll through the quartier Sainte-Amélie in the eastern Marquette sector, where the streets are lined by grand houses dating from the 1930s. The **Église Sainte-Amélie**, 37 av Marquette (daily June to mid-Sept 9am–6pm; rest of year 10am–5pm; free), is worth a peek for its frescoes and stained-glass windows, designed by the Italian artist Guido Nincheri.

There's a seasonal **tourist information** office on the western edge of town at 3503 boul Laflèche (June–Aug daily 8am–8pm; ⓣ418/589-3610). **Buses** terminate at 212 boul Lasalle (ⓣ418/296-6921); the departure point for the **car ferry** to Matane (see p.343) is beyond the eastern end of boul Lasalle on rue Cartier. **Accommodation** is available at the rambling stone hotel *Le Manoir*, 8 Cabot (ⓣ418/296-3391 or 1-800/463-8567, ⓦwww.manoirbc.com; ④), which overlooks the St Lawrence. Less expensive **motels** are along boul Lasalle; try the modern *Hôtel-Motel La Caravelle*, at no. 202 (ⓣ418/296-4986 or 1-800/463-4986, ⓦwww.hotelmotellacaravelle.com; ②). The cheapest place in town is *Motel du Rosier*, 228 boul Lasalle (ⓣ418/296-6696, ⓦwww.acomba.net/durosier; ②), but for a few dollars more there are a few **B&Bs**, like *Gîte Le Champlain*, 67 rue Champlain (ⓣ418/296-3814; ③) that offer a cosier experience. For **camping**, *Camping Manic 2* at Km 24 on Hwy 389 (June–Sept; ⓣ418/296-3951 or 2810, ⓦwww.campingquebec.com/manic2) near the dam has six-person sites for $17–25. The hotel *Le Manoir* is pricey for **eating** ($30) but excellent. For down-to-earth eats, try *Brasserie Le Boucannier*, 720 boul Laflèche in the western sector, for surf-and-turf and pizza ($10–20).

The Manic Dams

One of the few roads to penetrate the bleak terrain north of the St Lawrence is the partly paved Hwy 389 (Manic Road), which runs 215km into the forest from the east sector of Baie-Comeau. The road was built as a supply route for the hydroelectric company that built the colossal **dam system** on the Rivière Manicouagan, the only artificial site to rival the landscape in these parts. The first dam in the system, **Manic 2**, is 22km from Baie-Comeau, a journey that takes in great views of the rocky Canadian Shield. A free guided tour takes you inside the massive wall (late June to early Sept daily 9am, 11am, 1.30pm & 3.30pm), but an even more stupendous structure awaits two and a half hours' drive further north at the end of the paved stretch of the road – the awesome **Manic 5,** or Daniel Johnson Dam, 214km north of Baie-Comeau. Constructed in 1968, it is named after the premier of Québec who died here on the morning of the opening ceremony. With a length of 1314m and a central arch of 214m, this is the world's largest multiple-arch structure, and apparently contains enough concrete to build a pavement from pole to pole. Free guided tours (same hours as Manic 2) take visitors to the foot of the dam and across the top, giving panoramic views of the Manicouagan Valley and the huge reservoir. The 90km-wide donut-shaped depression was created by a massive meteor impact more than 200 million years ago, but the water level only became high enough to fill in the entire depression after the dam was constructed. You can **fly** here with Air Satellite (Ⓣ418/589-8923) from Baie-Comeau for around $150 round-trip, which is great for the overhead views of the dam. There's **accommodation** 2km before Manic 5 at the *Motel de L'Énergie* (Ⓣ418/584-2301 or 1-800/760-2301; ❸).

Beyond Manic 5, it's another 385km along a gravel hwy to Labrador City (see p.549), a six-hour journey through the wilderness with very little in the way of services. For road and weather conditions call Ⓣ418/589-6911.

Godbout and beyond

The attractive village of **GODBOUT**, situated on a crescent-shaped bay 54km from Baie-Comeau, is not just the most pleasant place hereabouts and excellent for salmon fishing, it also has an excellent **Musée Amérindien et Inuit**, 134 rue Pascal-Comeau (June–Oct daily 9am–9pm; Ⓣ418/568-7306; $4). The museum was founded by Claude Grenier, who spent ten years in the frozen north in the 1970s on a government scheme to boost the Inuit economy by promoting aboriginal culture. Consequent commercialism has diluted the output since then, but the private collection of Grenier features nothing but genuine pieces, from the characteristic soapstone carvings to domestic artefacts. Just down the road, the old general store houses a seasonal **tourist office** (mid-June to early Sept Mon–Fri 8am–6pm, Sat & Sun 9am–6pm; Ⓣ418/568-7647) with a few relics from its former life on display. The village is linked to Matane on the south shore by **car ferry** (see p.343). For **accommodation**, you can get a simple room above a convenience store Dépanneur Proprio, 156 rue Pascal Comeau (Ⓣ418/568-7535; ❶), where fishing licences are sold. Or, try one of the **B&Bs** facing the water, like the pretty, century-old *La Maison du Vieux Quai*, 142 rue Pascal-Comeau (Ⓣ418/568-7453, Ⓦwww.gitemaisonduvieuxquai.com; ❸). There's **camping** at *Camping de la Traverse*, 180 rue Pascal-Comeau (May to mid-Sept; Ⓣ418/568-7816; Ⓦwww.maisonettes-chalets-quebec.com; $12–20).

Situated where the St Lawrence River merges into the Gulf of St Lawrence, scenic **POINTE-DES-MONTS**, 28km from Godbout (and a further 11km off the highway), has changed little since the nineteenth century. Mind you, there's not a lot to change – all that stands on this rocky outcrop is Canada's oldest **lighthouse** dating from 1830 and a small missionary **chapel** built in 1898. The lighthouse now contains a small **museum** (mid-June to mid-Sept daily 9am–5pm; Ⓦwww.pharepointe-des-monts.com; $5), whose nautical displays and history of the lighthouse-keeper and his family provide adequate distraction as you make your way to the top. The adjacent house contains a fairly expensive seafood **restaurant** and a **B&B**, while nearby chalets handle the overflow of this popular spot (Ⓣ418/939-2242; 2; June–Oct). **Camping** is available at *Domaine de l'Astérie* (Ⓣ418/939-2327, Ⓦwww.campingquebec.com/domaindelasterie; mid-May to mid-Sept; $17–20), 2km before the lighthouse. Back on the hwy the tiny hamlet of **BAIE TRINITÉ** would be easily missable if not for the **Centre national des naufrages du Saint-Laurent** (June to mid-Sept, daily 9am–8pm; Ⓣ418/939-2679; $8). This fascinating museum tells the story of every shipwreck along the St Lawrence through films and multimedia displays. After browsing the museum, a self-guided trail along the nearby shoreline allows you to visit the site of several of the shipwrecks and has designated wilderness campsites for those who would like to stay longer in the secluded bays. You can also camp for free on the public beach at **POINTE-AUX-ANGLAIS** 40km northeast along Hwy 138; there are no facilities, but the nearby restaurant will let you shower for $5.

From Pointe-aux-Anglais it's another 63km to the lumber and iron-ore centre of **PORT-CARTIER**. The town is the entrance to the **Réserve Faunique de Port-Cartier-Sept-Îles** (admission $3.50), a wildlife reserve with more than a thousand lakes, popular for its hunting and salmon and trout fishing. Information, permits and reservations are available from the administration offices, 24 boul des Îles in Port-Cartier (Ⓣ418/766-2524, Ⓦwww.sepaq.com). It's a bumpy 27km drive to the **reception post** (May–Sept 7am–7pm; Ⓣ418/766-4743) at the southern tip of Lac Walker, where **campsites** ($18–23) and **chalets** (❺) are available, as well as canoe rentals and hiking trails.

Sept-Îles

The largest ore-exporting port in eastern Canada, **SEPT-ÎLES** is a good base for trips further north, owing to its **rail** links with Labrador. The town itself has as much character as a pile of iron ore, but it's pleasantly situated on the St Lawrence shore and you could spend an enjoyable day here thanks to two museums that explore native culture and, in August, the presence of one of Québec's foremost native-music festivals nearby. A trip to Île Grande Basque is also a worthwhile, easy adventure.

The town is best appreciated along the waterfront. A 27km bike path leads from **Parc Rivière des Rapides**, with a three-kilometre walking trail and ice fishing in winter, to the beaches east of town. The road down to the third beach, **Plage Routhier**, offers the best view of the seven islands that gave Sept-Îles its name. Along the way, the path passes through the Jardins de l'Anse – a good spot for bird-watching – and along the riverfront promenade in the **Parc du Vieux Quai**, where evening concerts of Québecois music are held under the yellow tent (late June to Aug Thurs–Sun; free). Rent **bikes** from Rioux Vélo Plein Air, 391 av Gamache (Ⓣ418/968-8356). An interesting overview of local history is offered by **Le Vieux-Poste**, on boulevard des Montagnais, west of the centre (late June to mid-Aug daily 9am–5pm; Ⓣ418/968-2070, Ⓦwww.mrcn.qc.ca; $3). Prior to the British conquest, when the Hudson's Bay Company took over the trade here, Sept-Îles was leased by the French crown to merchant traders. Settlements like these opened up

Innu Nikamu festival

One of the more offbeat Canadian music chart successes of recent years was the local aboriginal group Kashtin, the only nationally known band to perform in a native tongue. Although Claude McKenzie and Florent Vollant have gone on to solo careers, they still appear occasionally at the excellent **Innu Nikamu Festival** of song and music (information Ⓣ418/927-2985), held in early August, 14km east of Sept-Îles in the Montagnais reserve of **Maliotenam**. Inspired by Kashtin's success, numerous other groups travel to the four-day festival to produce some of the best of Canada's contemporary and traditional native music. As well as the music, the festival includes native food and craft stalls; despite the reserve's alcohol ban, there is always a good buzz. There is no public transport to the reserve: by car, take Hwy 138 towards Havre-St-Pierre and turn right at the Moisie intersection for the Maliotenam entrance. Tickets, available at the gate, cost around $10.

Québec for the Europeans but practically destroyed the lives of the native Montagnais. Converted to Christianity and overwhelmed by their desire for and subsequent need of European goods – particularly firearms, which aided them in their battles against the feared Iroquois – the Montagnais were forced by market pressure to hunt more and more fur-bearing animals. The resulting depletion of game was worsened so much by the later lumber and mining industries that the Montagnais were obliged to live on official reserves in order to become eligible for state hand-outs. The reconstructed Vieux-Poste, with its small chapel, store and postmaster's house, presents an absorbing portrayal of the Montagnais culture and is staffed by local Montagnais who produce crafts and food, which are sold at a decently priced handicrafts store.

The excellent **Musée Shaputuan**, 290 boul des Montagnais (All year Mon–Fri 8am–4.30pm; late June to early Sept Sat & Sun 10am–4pm; ⓣ418/962-4000, ⓦwww.museeshaputuan.org; $4), presents the traditional life of the Innu (Montagnais) people as it is shaped by the seasons. Unlike most descriptive museums, the exhibits speak to the viewer – often literally via audio and video recordings. Artefacts and sculptures on display illustrate the myths and folk tales of the Innu. However, the museum is primarily a space for Innu who want to learn more about their own culture.

Just offshore, the largest island in the archipelago, **Île Grande Basque**, has 12km of easy walking trails and picnic spots; you can buy camping permits for $7 at the kiosk in Parc du Vieux Quai. From June to September, the quay is the departure point for regular **passenger ferries** (10 daily 10min; $15) and **cruises** offered by Les Excursions La Petite Sirène (ⓣ418/968-2173, ⓦwww.freewebs.com/la_petite_sirene; 1–3 daily; 2–4hr) and Croisière Petit Pingouin (ⓣ418/968-9558, ⓦwww.geocities.com/gtocpp; June–Sept 1–3 daily; 20min–3hr). Whales and a sea-bird sanctuary are the main attractions, but fishing trips are also available; you can also catch herring right from the quay in early summer. **Kayak tours** are another possibility: Vêtements des Îles, 637 av Brochu (ⓣ418/962-7223 or 1-800/470-7223, ⓦwww.vetementsdesiles.com), offers two-day guided tours for $194 per person.

Practicalities

Sept-Îles has a seasonal **tourist office**, 516 rue Arnaud (mid-June to Aug daily 9am–6pm; ⓣ418/968-1818), down by the waterfront in the Parc du Vieux-Quai, and another on the outskirts of town at 1401 boul Laure (daily late May to mid-Sept 7.30am–9.30pm; rest of year 8.30am–5pm; ⓣ418/968-0022 or 1-888/880-1238, ⓦwww.ville.sept-iles.qc.ca/tourisme). The **bus** station, 126 rue Monseigneur-Blanche (ⓣ418/962-2126), has buses east to Havre-St-Pierre; the QNS&L **train** station, with 2–3 trains a week to Labrador City and Schefferville (see p.550), is on rue Retty at the east end of town. The *Nordik Express* supply **ship** (see box, p.384) from Rimouski leaves Sept-Îles every Wednesday morning at 6am, arriving at Port-Menier on the Île d'Anticosti ($48) that afternoon and Havre-St-Pierre ($67) in the evening, before continuing along the Basse Côte-Nord to Blanc-Sablon near the Labrador border. It does not stop in Sept-Îles on the return trip.

The *Le Tangon* **hostel**, 555 rue Cartier (ⓣ418/962-8180 or 1-800/461-8585, ⓦpages.globetrotter.net/tangon; June to mid-Oct; dorms $20–28), is a cheap, cramped, family-run place with breakfast for $3.50; you can camp in the grounds for $10. Alternatively, try the luxurious *Hôtel Gouverneur Sept-Îles*, 666 boul Laure (ⓣ418/962-7071 or 1-888/910-1111, ⓦwww.gouveneur.com; ❺), or the *Hotel Sept-Îles*, 451 av Arnaud (ⓣ418/962-2581 or 1-800/463-1753, ⓦwww.hotelseptiles.com; ❷), on the waterfront. The town's **B&Bs** are more attractive than the motels along the highway: *Gîte Les Tournesols*, 388 rue Évangéline (ⓣ418/968-1910, ⓦ7tournesols.com; ❸), is nearest the quay. Two **campsites** lie 27km to the east, off Hwy 138 next to the salmon-filled Rivière Moisie: *Camping Laurent-Val* (ⓣ418/927-2899; $16–27; mid-May to late Sept) and *Camping de la rivière Moisie* (ⓣ418/927-2021; $16–28; late May to early Sept).

For **eating**, Sept-Îles has great seafood restaurants such as the rather expensive *Chez Omer*, 372 av Brochu (ⓣ418/962-7777) where dishes cost between $20 and $30. Get cheaper seafood, pizza and pasta (as well as a few rounds of **drinks**) at nearby *Café du Port* at no. 495 (ⓣ418/962-9311), while further down the road *Pub St-Marc,* 588 av Brochu (ⓣ418/962-7770), is a surprisingly stylish bar serving microbrews, with a more expensive restaurant upstairs where there's great pasta and a vast selection of salads all under $20.

The Mingan coast

There is little of specific interest along the stretch of shore east of Sept-Îles, known as the **Mingan coast** – blackfly-ridden from May to June – until you reach **Longue-Pointe-de-Mingan**, but the scenery changes constantly with sand dunes followed by granite outcroppings of the Canadian Shield, then eerie landscapes of rounded grey boulders surrounded by scrubby vegetation. Most visitors make the journey for the stunning islands of the **Mingan Archipelago**, a unique environment of sculptured rock formations and profuse wildlife lying off the coast between Longue-Pointe-de-Mingan and **Havre-St-Pierre**, the region's largest town and a good base for visiting the archipelago. As the tourist season is short here, accommodation can be at a premium – it's a good idea to book ahead.

If you want to break up the journey, park your car at the small tourist office 86km east of Sept-Îles (just after the marker for Km 61 – distances are measured from the Rivière Moisie) and visit the **Chutes Manitou** (May–Oct daily 8.30am–7.30pm; $2). Cross the river via the hwy bridge and walk five minutes on the marked trail along the river to a viewing point beside the rocky cascades. A more substantial waterfall is ten minutes further down the trail, with secluded pebble beaches along the way. It's dangerous to swim here, though; a couple of drownings have occurred.

Longue-Pointe-de-Mingan

Although Havre-St-Pierre is the more popular departure point for cruises of the Mingan Archipelago, it is worth stopping in **LONGUE-POINTE-DE-MINGAN** for the Centre de Recherche et d'Interprétation de la Minganie, or CRIM, 625 rue du Centre (mid-June to mid-Oct daily 9am–9pm; $7), a joint venture between Parks Canada and the Mingan Island Cetacean Study. In addition to a film and displays on whales and other marine life, the centre provides information on excursions to the islands, issues camping permits and, for the more adventurous, offers a day with one of the **whale researchers** (ⓣ418/949-2845; June–Oct; $105). The latter are not cruises – you are with a marine biologist in a small boat from dawn until whenever their work is finished – but they are a unique experience. Less taxing cruises are offered by Excursions du Phare, 126 rue de la Mer (ⓣ418/949-2302, ⓦwww.minganie.info/croisieres), who lead trips to the westernmost islands – an important consideration if you want to see **puffins**, as most of the cruises from Havre-St-Pierre only visit the islands in the centre sector.

Longue-Pointe-de-Mingan has little accommodation and isn't much of a gourmet hot spot, but adequate **accommodation** and **seafood** is available at the restaurant of the basic *Hôtel-Motel de la Minganie*, 860 chemin du Roi (Ⓣ418/949-2992; ❷). Across the road are a few beachside campsites that are free if you book an excursion, otherwise $10. Alternatively you can camp a few metres down the road where the sites and facilities are larger at *Camping de la Minganie* (Ⓣ418/949-2320 or 1-866/949-2307, Ⓦwww.tourisme-loiselle.com; $15–22)

Havre-St-Pierre

The community of **HAVRE-ST-PIERRE** would have remained a tiny fishing village founded in 1857 by fleeing Acadaians but for the discovery in the 1940s of a huge deposit of ilmenite, the chief source of titanium. The quarries are 45km north of the town itself, where fishing and tourism provide employment for the non-miners, the latter industry having received a major boost when the forty islands of the **Mingan Archipelago** were made into a national park in 1983. Before setting off to the park, check out the **interpretation centre**, which shares a building with the information centre on the wharf, 1010 Promenade des Anciens (mid-June to Aug hours vary; Ⓣ418/538-5264; free). The centre has temporary photographic displays and information on the flora, fauna and geology of the islands. It opens around 8.30am if the weather is too poor for the tour boats to depart. You can book cruises to the archipelago here or at one of the smaller kiosks further along the wharf.

Away from the wharf, Havre-Saint-Pierre's old general store, the **Maison de la Culture Roland-Jomphe**, 957 rue de la Berge (daily late June to early Sept 9am–9pm; Ⓣ418/538-2512; $2) houses a *centre d'interprétation* that depicts the local history. The **bus station** is at 843 rue de l'Escale (Ⓣ418/538-2033). The wharf is the departure point for the *Nordik Express* (see box, p.384). The *Auberge de la Minganie* **hostel** (Ⓣ418/538-1538; ❹; dorms $25, camping $10; May–Nov) is inconveniently situated 17km west of town, but the bus from the west will let you off nearby, leaving you to walk the remaining 700m. An old fishing camp on a pretty bay with minimum renovations and lots of bugs, the hostel doesn't serve breakfast, but does have kitchen facilities and canoes for rent. In town, you could try the *Hôtel-Motel du Havre*, 970 rue de l'Escale (Ⓣ418/538-2800 or 1-888/797-2800; ❸), or *Camping Municipal* (Ⓣ418/538-2415, Ⓦwww.havresaintpierre; $17–23) at the east end of av Boréal. The tourist office can provide a list of **B&Bs** which includes the *Gîte Chez Francoise*, 1122 rue Boréale (Ⓣ418/538-1329, Ⓦwww.gitechezfrancoise.has.it; ❸), which has a room with its own private bathroom and kitchenette for $75 per night including breakfast, as well as three other impeccable rooms that share a bathroom. For good seafood and smoked-salmon pizza for under $30, try the **restaurant** *Chez Julie*, 1023 Dulcinée (Ⓣ418/538-3070). *Resto-Bar Les Moutons Blancs*, 1121 av Boréale, has occasional live music and also serves seafood.

The Mingan Archipelago

Immediately offshore from Havre-St-Pierre, the **Mingan Archipelago National Park Reserve** (Ⓦwww.pc.gc.ca; $5.45) offers some of the most beautiful landscapes in Québec. Standing on the islands' white-sand shorelines are innumerable eight-metre-high **rocks** like ancient totem poles, with bright orange lichen colouring their mottled surfaces and bonsai-sized trees clinging to their crevices. These formations originated as underwater sediment near the equator. The sediment was thrust above sea level more than 250 million years ago and then covered in an icecap several kilometres thick. As the drifting ice melted, the islands emerged again, seven thousand years ago, at their present location. The sea and wind gave the final touch by chipping away at the soft limestone to create the majestic monoliths of today. But bizarre geology isn't the archipelago's only remarkable feature. The **flora** constitutes a unique insular garden of 452 arctic and rare alpine species, which survive here at their southerly limit due to the limestone soil, long harsh winters and cold Gulf of Labrador current. As for **wildlife**, other than the Gulf's whale populations, the permanent inhabitants of the national park include puffins, who build nests in the scant soil of three of the islands from early May to late August, and 199 other species of birds.

Information is available from two visitor centres: 625 rue du Centre in Longue-Pointe-de-Mingan and 1010 Promenade des Anciens in Havre-St-Pierre. Biologists on some islands meet passengers from the cruise boats (mid-June to Aug) to explain aspects of the geology and flora.

One of the best ways to see the islands is by **sea kayak** or **two-man sail boats**. The friendly folks at Expédition Agaguk, 1062 av Boréale in Havre-St-Pierre (ⓣ418/538-1588, ⓦwww.expedition-agaguk.com), organize one- to six-day excursions (May–Sept) for $79 a day, $129 a day if you want them to supply camping equipment and local cuisine. Even if you have your own gear, this is an excellent place for tips on currents and other conditions. On prior request, they will also organize backcountry trips to the lakes and rivers to the north.

The Nordik Express

When the road peters out at Natashquan, access further up the Basse Côte-Nord is by snowmobile in winter, floatplane, or boat. The **Nordik Express supply ship** (April–Jan; ⓣ418/723-8787 or 1-800/463-0680, ⓦwww.relaisnordik.com) makes a weekly journey here on a trip that affords stunning views of a rocky, subarctic landscape, which is so cold that icebergs occasionally float past the ship even in the height of summer. The boat is evenly split between its role as a freighter and passenger ship; the majority of its passengers are locals skipping between settlements or heading for a longer jaunt to Québec's bigger towns. Its voyage begins in **Rimouski** on Tuesdays, stopping in **Sept-Îles**, **Port-Menier** on Île d'Anticosti, **Havre-St-Pierre** and **Natashquan**, before calling in at the roadless communities along the Basse Côte-Nord, reaching **Blanc-Sablon** (see p.542), Québec's most easterly village on the Labrador border, on Fridays. The same route is then followed in reverse – though the boat does not stop in Sept-Îles on the way back – to arrive back in Rimouski on Monday.

The journey up this stretch of the St Lawrence is far more impressive than the destinations. During the day, whales, dolphins and seals along with a wealth of sea birds are a common sight; while at night the northern lights often present an unforgettable display. At some stops the village inhabitants surround the boat, as its twice-weekly arrival is about all that happens hereabouts. With careful planning you can arrange to spend a couple of days in one community and catch the boat on the return voyage. Plan ahead, though: although each village receives at least one daytime visit, either the upstream or downstream stop may be in the middle of the night. But the vast majority of travellers just hop off at each port of call for the couple of hours that the boat needs to load and unload freight. A rented bicycle is particularly handy if you want to see much.

Stops include the village of **Kegaska** with its large sandy beach and **La Romaine**, a scrappy Innu town further on. Beyond here the land becomes increasingly rocky and picturesque, the coastline cut with many intriguing inlets. **Harrington Harbour**, a pretty village and easily one of the sightseeing highlight of the trip, is set on an

Boat tours (June–Sept) around portions of the archipelago are available from the wharf at Havre-St-Pierre, but they must be booked in advance; *La Relève II* operates from kiosk no. 3 (3 daily; $33; ⓣ418/538-2865), while Tournée des Îles at kiosk no. 2 (ⓣ418/538-2547, ⓦwww.tourismecote-nord.com/minisite/tournee) runs the *Perroquet de Mer* (3 daily; $33) and *Le Calculot* (3 daily; $33), a small boat whose captain's unrelenting commentary may spoil your trip. Cruises to see the puffins in the western sector of the park depart from Longue-Pointe-de-Mingan (see p.382).

Camping is allowed on Île Quarry and five other islands ($14–16) but the only transport besides a sea kayak is the *Bateau-Mouche* sea bus (ⓣ418/538-3427; $17–34 depending on destination). Obtain permits from the interpretation centre in Longue-Pointe or the wharfside kiosk in Havre-St-Pierre.

Île d'Anticosti

In the Gulf of St Lawrence between the Jacques Cartier and Honguedo straits, the remote 220km-long **Île d'Anticosti** was once known as the "Graveyard of the Gulf", as more than four hundred ships have been wrecked on its shores, including Admiral Phipp's fleet, retreating from Québec City in 1690. The island's vast expanse is made up of windswept sea cliffs and forests of twisted pine, crisscrossed by turbulent rivers and sheer ravines. Known as Notiskuan – "the land where we hunt bears" – by the

island whose topography of large rounded rocks made it necessary to make the pavements out of wood. Harrington Harbour is best seen on the upstream journey, when the boat arrives in the daytime rather than at midnight. **Accommodation** is available at *Amy's Bed & Breakfast* (ⓣ418/795-3376; ⑤), which includes three meals a day; they also have a shop selling local handicrafts. Tête-à-la-Beleine and, later on, Saint Augustin have similarly picturesque settings. At Tête-à-la-Beleine local boatmen are usually on hand to transport tourists from the ship out to the incongruous Chapelle de l'île Providence perched on a nearby hill. There is also a youth hostel here (June–Oct; ⓣ418/242-2015; $35) At some villages – particularly those some distance from the boat – a shuttle bus and tour of the local village is offered, but in all cases this doesn't really add much to the experience. And the bus tour of Blanc Sablon ($20) in particular is a bare-faced, if good-humoured, money-making exercise: the bus spends most of its time at the driver's souvenir shop. You are better off hiring a local taxi to show you the sights. The website of the local residents' group, the Coasters Association (ⓦwww.htmlweb.com/LNS), has a comprehensive listing of what you can do in each village.

Fares on the ship are reasonable and it's possible either to travel all-inclusive (with three surprisingly good daily meals and a cabin berth) or to bed down on the aircraft-style seats and picnic on the deck or in the cafeteria. You can start and finish your journey from any of the stops along the coast, but the basic fare to travel the entire length of the route on a return trip to Rimouski is $387. This with a spot in the most basic four-berth cabin is $762, while you pay $1256 to do the trip in a two-berth cabin with porthole and shower. Food is extra: breakfast $7, lunch $15, dinner $18. As another example, a round trip to Blanc-Sablon from Havre-St-Pierre costs $223, or from Natashquan $184 ($447 and $363 respectively for a basic cabin). You can also bring your car, although it is inaccessible during the voyage; fares are based on distance and the weight of the car. A one-way journey from Natashquan to Blanc-Sablon – useful if you are continuing or returning from Newfoundland and Labrador – costs at least $221 for the car. A bike adds a flat rate of $20 to the fare.

natives, and a walrus- and whale-fishing ground for the Basques, Île d'Anticosti became the private domain of Henri Menier, a French chocolate millionaire, in 1873. He imported white-tailed Virginia deer, red fox, silver fox, beaver and moose to his domain in order to gun them down at his leisure. Nowadays a less exclusive horde of hunters and fishers comes here to blast the deer from the back of their four-wheel-drives and to hoist the salmon from the rivers, which now fall under the jurisdiction of the province. For other travellers it presents an opportunity to explore an area that's untamed and still practically deserted, with a population of just 340.

Menier established the tiny village of Baie Ste-Claire on the western tip in 1873; fewer than thirty years later the settlers moved to **PORT-MENIER** on the south side of this tip, and Baie-Ste-Claire's homes were left to the ravages of the salt air. The human population is now concentrated in the blue-roofed houses of Port-Menier, where the *Nordik Express* comes in once a week each from Havre-St-Pierre and from Sept-Îles (see p.380).

Port-Menier edges the westerly portion of the **Parc national d'Anticosti** (Ⓣ418/535-0156, Ⓦwww.sepaq.com; $3.50) whose protected landscapes are continued further east in the reserve's two other sectors – one deep in the interior, the other covering the island's eastern tip. The twisting gravel road that crosses the island, jokingly called the "Trans-Anticostian", provides access to the central and eastern portions of the reserve. Driving is the only way to get there: a four-wheel-drive is necessary, and it's not uncommon to get a few dents or a flat tyre. You can rent a car in Port-Menier at Location Pelletier (Ⓣ418/535-0204). En route, a rough track leads from the "main" road to Québec's largest cave. Discovered in 1982, the glacial **Caverne de la Rivière à la Patate**, 120km east of Port-Menier, has a modest opening that leads into a cathedral-like chamber and a warren of 500-metre-long passages. Some 10km further on you can glimpse the impossible canyon of the **Rivière Observation**, whose bleak walls rise to over 50m. The reserve's scenery is equally impressive and a good basis for its attempt to encourage **adventure tourism** during the summer months. SÉPAQ Anticosti, the government body responsible for the Réserve Faunique, runs a variety of ecologically sound packages which, although pricey (starting at around $560 a week per person, based on two people flying from Sept-Îles; Ⓣ418/535-0156, Ⓦwww.sepaq.com), include transport to the island, accommodation (Inn, cabin or campground) and four-wheel-drive vehicles. Other outfits offer similar fly-in packages starting around $250 for a 24-hour excursion from Sept-Îles. Safari Anticosti has 24-hour packages starting at $219 from Havre-St-Pierre (Ⓣ418/538-1414, Ⓦwww.safarianticosti.com), and $259 from the Îles-de-la-Madeleine.

The *Nordik Express* **supply ship** from Havre-St-Pierre costs $37 one-way, from Sept-Îles $47. You can also stop off for two hours en route. There is no boat from Port-Menier to Sept-Îles – it goes straight on to Rimouski instead. A number of local **airlines** serve the island from Gaspé, Baie-Comeau, Sept-Îles and Havre-St-Pierre. **Accommodation** is available in Port-Menier at *Auberge Port-Menier* (Ⓣ418/535-0122, Ⓦwww.sepaq.com; ⑤) or at the two **hostels**: *Auberge Au Vieux Menier*, 26 chemin de la Faune (Ⓣ418/535-0111; ①; mid-June to mid-Oct), which also has camping for $10, will pick you up from the airport or wharf and organize excursions; or *Auberge Pointe-Ouest*, 20km west of Port-Menier (Ⓣ418/535-0155; ①), which also has camping ($10/day).

Basse Côte-Nord

Until 1996, Hwy 138 terminated at Havre-St-Pierre, leaving the dozen or so villages along the rugged **Basse Côte-Nord** (Lower North Shore) cut off from the rest of Québec, as they had been for centuries – to such an extent that many inhabitants speak only English. Now a section of Hwy 138 links Havre-St-Pierre with **Natashquan** and three other villages on the 145-kilometre stretch. If you make the lonely journey by car – as yet there is no bus – you will receive a welcome unique to a people that have only recently been connected by road to the rest of Canada.

The original inhabitants of the area were Montagnais, Naskapi and Inuits, who were invaded by Vikings in the year 1000. Cartier saw the coast in 1534 but did not register it as a discovery because it was already seasonally occupied by Basque, Spanish and Portuguese fishermen, and fishing is still the only industry on this desolate coast. The current 7500 inhabitants are descendants of fishermen from the Channel Islands and Newfoundland.

The first settlement, 65km east of Havre-St-Pierre, is the 100-strong village of **BAIE-JOHAN-BEETZ**, named after the painter and sculptor whose extraordinary and enormous house is open to the public (late June to late Aug daily 10am–noon & 1.30–4pm; reservations recommended ⓣ418/539-0137, ⓦwww.baiejohanbeetz.com; $5); you can also sleep in one of its seven historic bedrooms; 🏃(❸).

Beyond, you pass through the tiny hamlets of **Aguanish** and **Île-à-Michon**. At the end of the 780km road from Tadoussac, a small church, wooden houses and the old fishing huts are about all there is to see in **NATASHQUAN**, the one-time home of highly revered Québecois poet Gilles Vigneault. The century-old general store has been reborn as yet another **centre d'interprétation** that focuses on local history (late June to Aug daily 9am–5pm; ⓣ418/726-3233, ⓦpages.globetrotter.net/lebordducap; $3.50) and is less impressive than the town's long sandy beach. **Accommodation** is available in the ten rooms of *Auberge la Cache*, 183 chemin d'en Haut (ⓣ418/726-3347 or 1-888/726-3347, ⓦwww.tourismecote-nord.com/minisite/lacache; ❸), whose seafood restaurant is open from June to August, or in a number of **B&B's** including *Maison Chevarie*, 77 rue du pre, (ⓣ418/726-3541; ❷). There is also camping along Hwy 138 at *Camping Municipal Chemin Faisant* (mid-June to Sept; ⓣ418/726-3697, ⓦwww.campingquebec.com/municipalcheminfaisant; $15–23)

Travel details

Trains

Sept-Îles to: Labrador City (2–3 weekly; 8hr 30min–10hr 30min); Schefferville (1 weekly; 11hr 15min).

Buses

Baie-Comeau to: Baie-St-Paul (2 daily; 5hr 30min); Godbout (1 daily; 50min); Port-Cartier (1 daily; 2hr 15min); Sept-Îles (1 daily; 3hr 30min).
Chicoutimi to: Alma (2 daily; 1hr); Dolbeau (2–3 daily; 3hr 30min); Jonquière (9 daily; 25min); St-Félicien (2 daily; 2hr 55min); Val-Jalbert (2 daily; 2hr 15min).
Dolbeau to: Alma (1 weekly; 1hr 15min); Péribonka (1 weekly; 30min).
Québec City to: Alma (3 daily; 2hr 45min); Baie-Comeau (2 daily; 6hr 5min); Baie St-Catherine (2 daily; 3hr 20min); Baie-St-Paul (3 daily; 1hr 15min); Chicoutimi (5-6 daily; 2hr 30min); Dolbeau (2 daily; 5hr 25min); Forestville (2 daily; 4hr 45min); Jonquière (3–5 daily; 3hr); La Malbaie (3 daily; 1hr 50min); Les Escoumins (2 daily; 4hr 10min); Rimouski (5 daily; 3hr 55min); Rivière-du-Loup (4 daily; 2hr 20min); St-Félicien (2 daily; 4hr 25min); St-Siméon (2 daily; 2hr 20min); Sherbrooke (2 daily; 3hr 30min); Tadoussac (2 daily; 4hr); Val-Jalbert (2 daily; 3hr 45min).
Rimouski to: Bonaventure (2 daily; 6hr); Cap-aux-Os (summer 1 daily; 6hr 50min); Carleton (2 daily; 4hr 15min); Gaspé via Carleton (2 daily; 9hr 10min); Gaspé via Matane (2 daily; 6hr 50min); Matane (2–3 daily; 1hr 30min); Matapédia (2 daily;

2hr 50min); Mont St-Pierre (2 daily; 4hr 20min); New Richmond (2 daily; 5hr 30min); Percé (2 daily; 8hr 20min); Ste-Anne-des-Monts (2–3 daily; 2hr 50min); Ste-Flavie (2–3 daily; 30min).
Rivière-du-Loup to: Edmundston, NB (3 daily; 3hr).
Sept-Îles to: Baie-Comeau (1 daily; 3hr 30min); Havre-St-Pierre (1 daily; 2hr 30min).
Sherbrooke to: Trois-Rivières (4 weekly; 2hr 10min).
Tadoussac to: Chicoutimi (1 daily; 1hr 40min); Rivière Ste-Marguerite (6 weekly; 30min); Ste-Rose-du-Nord (6 weekly; 55min).
Trois-Rivières to: Grand-Mère (3 daily; 1hr).

Ferries

Baie-Ste-Catherine to: Tadoussac (1–3 hourly; 10min).
Blanc-Sablon to: St Barbe, NL (May–Dec 1–3 daily; 1hr 30min).
Matane to: Baie-Comeau (4 weekly–2 daily; 2hr 20min); Godbout (1–3 daily; 2hr 10min).
Québec City to: Lévis (1–3 hourly; 15min).
Rimouski to: Forestville (April–Oct 2–4 daily; 55min).
Rivière-du-Loup to: St-Siméon (April–Dec 2–5 daily; 1hr 15min).
St-Joseph-de-la-Rive to: Île-aux-Coudres (8 daily–2 hourly; 15min).
Trois-Pistoles to: Les Escoumins (May–Oct 2–3 daily; 1hr 15min).

Nordik Express

Continuous voyage (see p.385). Broken down into segments here for clarity.
Havre-St-Pierre to: Natashquan (1 weekly; 6hr 15min); Kegaska (1 weekly; 11hr 30min); La Romaine (1 weekly; 16hr); Harrington Harbour (1 weekly; 24hr 45min); Tête-à-la-Baleine (1 weekly; 29hr 15min); La Tabatière (1 weekly; 32hr 45min); St-Augustin (1 weekly; 37hr 15min); Blanc-Sablon (1 weekly; 43hr 45min).
Rimouski to: Blanc-Sablon (1 weekly; 78hr 30min); Sept-Îles (downstream only; 1 weekly; 11hr 30min).
Sept-Îles to: Havre St-Pierre (1 weekly; 15hr 15min); Port-Menier (1 weekly; 7hr 45min).

Flights

Québec City to: Baie-Comeau (1–3 daily; 1hr 35min); Gaspé (1–2 daily; 2hr 10min); Halifax (1 daily; 1hr 40min); Îles-de-la-Madeleine (1–2 daily; 3hr 20min); Ottawa (2–7 daily; 1hr 10min); Sept-Îles (2–3 daily; 1hr 30min); Toronto (6 daily; 1hr 30min); Wabush (1–2 daily; 2hr 50min).

5

The Maritime Provinces

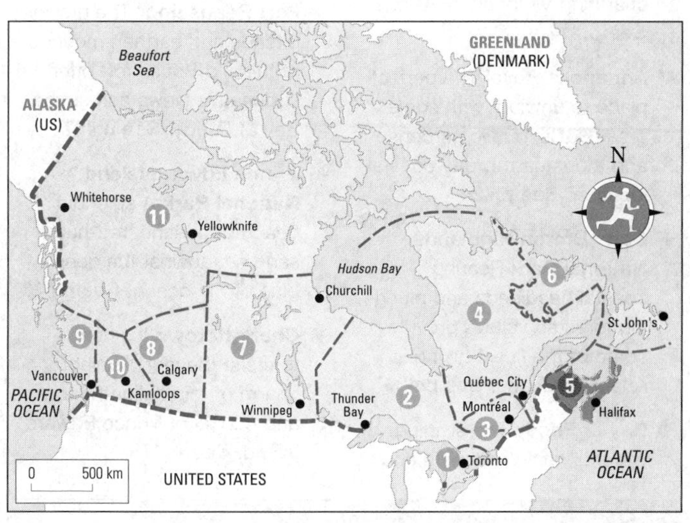

CHAPTER 5 Highlights

* **Halifax** The British lost the US, but they intended to hold on to Canada – as the stirring militarism of the Citadel demonstrates. See p.397

* **Lunenburg** This handsome fishing port is small-town Nova Scotia at its prettiest, its hilly streets dotted with charming Victorian mansions. See p.414

* **Annapolis Royal** The perfect place to unwind, with some great B&Bs, public gardens and a postcard-pretty coastal location. See p.424

* **Cape Breton Highlands National Park** Rearing coastal headlands and plunging forested valleys provide some of the finest hiking in Atlantic Canada. See p.436

* **Bay of Fundy** The swirling waters, whale-watching and record setting tides of the bay are at their most pristine in Fundy National Park. See p.442

* **The Beaverbrook Art Gallery** This beguiling gallery in Fredericton has an outstanding collection of Canadian paintings. See p.447

* **Fort Beauséjour** The grassy ditches and earthen mounds of this old British fort offer superlative views across the Bay of Fundy. See p.467

* **Prince Edward Island National Park** A splendid beach of pristine, red-hued sand set against the deep blue of the ocean. See p.473

* **Charlottetown** It's hard to resist the leafy, amiable charm of this delightful town and capital of Prince Edward Island. See p.476

△Harbour, Blue Rocks, NS

5

The Maritime Provinces

Canada's Maritime Provinces – **Nova Scotia**, **New Brunswick** and **Prince Edward Island** – are the country's three smallest provinces, and their combined population of around two million has been largely confined to the coasts and river valleys by the thin soils of the forested interior. Even today, the bulk of the Maritimes remains intractable – 84 percent of New Brunswick, for example, is covered by pine, maple and birch forest – and this rough and ready **wilderness** combines with a ruggedly beautiful **coastline** to form one of Canada's most scenic regions. The chunks of fertile **farmland** that punctuate the forests are also appealing, principally in the undulating fields of Prince Edward Island (PEI) and the lowlands around New Brunswick's Grand Falls, both of which produce massive crops of potatoes, and in Nova Scotia's Annapolis Valley, a major fruit-producing area.

Most visitors to the Maritimes come for the coastal scenery and the slow pace of the "unspoilt" fishing villages, but the Maritimes were not always as sleepy as they appear today. When the three provinces joined the Dominion in the middle of the nineteenth century, their economies were prospering from the export of fish and timber and the success of their **shipyards**. But, as opponents of the confederation had argued, the Maritimers were unable to prevent the passage of protectionist measures favouring the burgeoning industries of Ontario and Québec. This discrimination, combined with the collapse of the shipbuilding industry as steel steamers replaced wooden ships, precipitated a savage and long-lasting recession. Within the space of thirty years, the economic collapse transformed most of the Maritimes from a prosperous, semi-industrialized region to a pastoral backwater dependent on the sale of its raw materials – chiefly wood and fish. In recent years, **tourism** has helped to keep the region's economy afloat – the tourist industry is extremely well organized, though out of season – before mid-May and after mid-October – many attractions and B&Bs are closed.

Bypassed economically, many of the region's villages still retain their nineteenth-century appearance, with pastel-shaded clapboard houses set around rocky coves and bays. However, the Maritimes offer much more variety than this bucolic image suggests. In **Nova Scotia**, the southwest coast does indeed have a clutch of quaint fishing ports, but it also harbours the busy provincial capital of **Halifax**, whilst **Annapolis Royal**, with its genteel mansions, is only a few kilometres from **Port Royal** and its reconstruction of the fort Samuel de

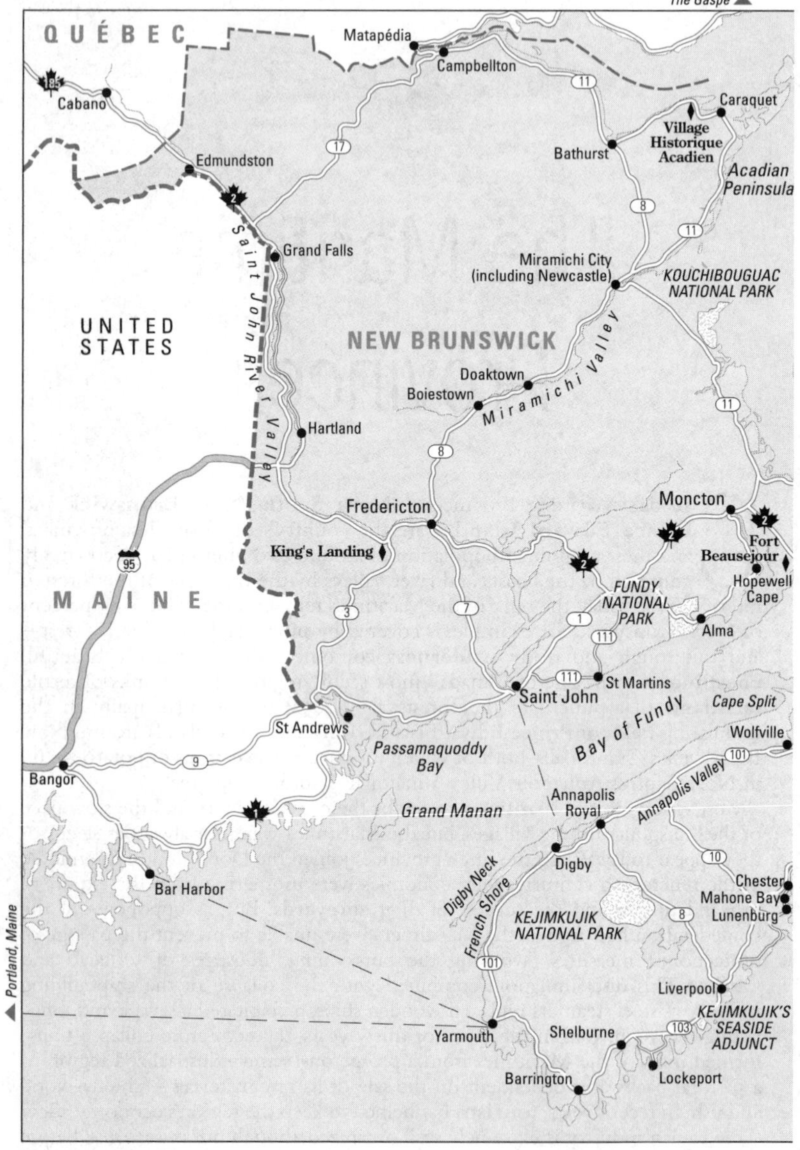

Champlain built in 1605. Further east, **Cape Breton Island**, connected to the mainland by a causeway, is divided in two by **Bras d'Or Lake**: the forested plateau flanking industrial **Sydney** is unremarkable, but in the west the elegiac hills and lakes framing the resort of **Baddeck** lead into the mountainous splendour of **Cape Breton Highlands National Park** – a rare chunk of mountain in a region that is predominantly flat.

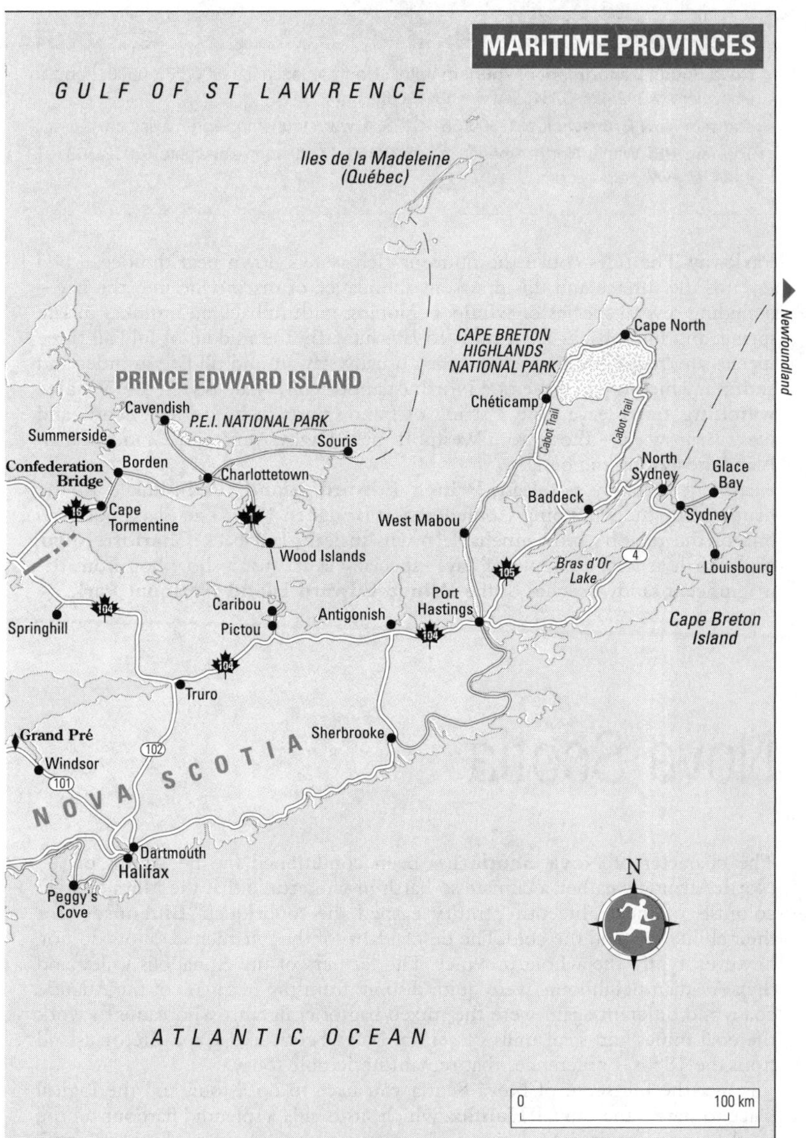

Moving on, **New Brunswick** has urban pleasures in the shape of its cosy capital **Fredericton** and the gritty, revitalized port of **Saint John** (never "St John", and not to be mixed up with St John's, Newfoundland) – but its star turn is the **Bay of Fundy**, whose taper creates tidal variations of up to 12m. This phenomenon is observable right along the shoreline, but has a spectacularly scenic setting at both **Fundy National Park** and along the **Fundy Trail**

Regional information

Nova Scotia Department of Tourism Within North America ⓣ1-800/565-0000, from elsewhere ⓣ902/425-5781, ⓦwww.novascotia.com.

Tourism New Brunswick ⓣ1-800/561-0123, ⓦwww.tourismnewbrunswick.ca.

Tourism PEI Within North America ⓣ1-800/463-4734, from elsewhere ⓣ902/368-4444, ⓦwww.peiplay.com.

Parkway. The tides churn the nutrient-rich waters down near the ocean bed towards the surface and this draws an abundance of marine life into the bay – including several species of **whale**, beginning with finback and minkes in late spring, and humpbacks from mid- to late June. By the middle of July all three species are frequently sighted and they usually stay around till late summer and autumn, which is when the rare North Atlantic right whale is seen too. **Whale-watching trips** leave from a string of Fundy ports in both Nova Scotia and New Brunswick – those from Westport, near Digby, Alma and Grand Manan Island are among the best.

Last but certainly not least, **Prince Edward Island** (**PEI**), linked to the mainland by the whopping Confederation Bridge in 1997. The island possesses one of the region's most amenable towns in leafy, laid-back **Charlottetown**, well worth at least a couple of days especially as it's just a short hop from the magnificent sandy beaches of the **Prince Edward Island National Park**.

Nova Scotia

The character of **Nova Scotia** has been conditioned by the whims of the North Atlantic weather, a climate so harsh in wintertime that the Nova Scotian colonists of the eighteenth century earned the soubriquet "**Bluenoses**" for their ability to stand the cold. The descendants of these hardened sailors do not, however, typify the whole province. The farmers of the Annapolis Valley and their Acadian neighbours were quite distinct from the mariners of the Atlantic coast, and different again were the mixed bag of emigrants who came to work the coal mines and steel mills of central Nova Scotia and Cape Breton Island from the 1880s – differences that remain noticeable today.

To get the full sense of Nova Scotia you have to do a tour, and the logical place to start is the capital, **Halifax**, which sits beside a splendid harbour on the south coast. With its international airport, excellent restaurants, lively nightlife and handful of historic attractions, the city can easily fill a couple of days. To continue, it's best to take in the beguiling fishing villages of the southwest shore, amongst which handsome **Lunenburg** and solitary **Lockeport** stand out. Between them is **Liverpool**, where you turn inland for both the remote forests and lakes of **Kejimkujik National Park** and, beyond, on an arm of the Bay of Fundy, the delightful little town of **Annapolis Royal**. Heading east from here along the Annapolis Valley, it's a further 110km to the amenable college town of **Wolfville** and another 90km back to Halifax.

Nova Scotia's other outstanding circular tourist route is the **Cabot Trail**. Named after the explorer John Cabot, who is supposed to have landed here in 1497, it encircles the more northerly half of **Cape Breton Island**, where the mountainous landscapes of **Cape Breton Highlands National Park** constitute some of eastern Canada's most stunning scenery. Cape Breton Island – and the strip of Nova Scotia coast bordering the Northumberland Strait – attracted thousands of Scottish highlanders at the end of the eighteenth century, mostly tenant farmers who had been evicted by Scotland's landowners when they found sheep-raising more profitable than renting farmland. Many of the region's settlements celebrate their Scots ancestry and Gaelic traditions in one way or another – museums, Highland Games and bagpipe-playing competitions – and in **South Gut St Ann's**, on the Cabot Trail, there's even a Gaelic college. The final attraction of Cape Breton is the reconstructed eighteenth-century French fortress of **Louisbourg**, stuck in splendid isolation on the southeast coast.

Southwest Nova Scotia is reasonably well served by **bus**, with daily connections running between Halifax and Yarmouth via the south shore and another daily service linking Halifax and Digby via the Annapolis Valley. There are also frequent buses from Halifax to Baddeck and Sydney as well as to Truro, for connections on to New Brunswick and PEI. VIA Rail **trains** run between Halifax and Truro, then continue on to New Brunswick's Miramichi and Québec. Elsewhere, however, you'll need a **car**, particularly if you're keen to see anything of the wilder sections of the Cabot Trail. **Car ferries** link Yarmouth with Bar Harbor and Portland in Maine; North Sydney with Newfoundland; Caribou, near Pictou, with PEI; and Digby with Saint John, New Brunswick, which often makes a useful short cut.

A brief history of Nova Scotia

The original inhabitants of the Maritime Provinces were the **Micmacs** and **Malecites**, Algonquian-speaking peoples who lived a semi-nomadic life based on crop cultivation, fishing and hunting. Never numerous, both groups were ravaged by the diseases they contracted from their initial contacts with Basque and Breton fishermen in the late sixteenth century. Consequently, they were too weak to contest European colonization, although the Micmacs were later employed by the French to harass and attack the colonists of northern Maine.

Eating a lobster

Throughout Nova Scotia and PEI, **lobsters** are a favourite dish and they appear, in various guises, on many a restaurant menu. For whole lobster, you pay by weight, with the smaller lobsters averaging 450g and costing about $20–25. Also, look out for all-you-can-eat **lobster suppers**, rural community events held in village halls and the like, though these are now something of a rarity. Given that the Maritimers are so familiar with eating lobster, it's particularly embarrassing if you don't know how. There are eight main steps:

1. Twist off the claws.
2. Crack each claw with the nutcracker you receive with the lobster.
3. Separate the tailpiece from the body by arching the back until it breaks.
4. Bend back and break off the flippers from the tailpiece.
5. Insert a fork where the flippers broke off and push.
6. Unhinge the back from the body – the meat in the back, the tomalley, is considered by many to be the choicest part of a lobster.
7. Open the remaining part of the body by cracking it apart sideways.
8. Suck out the meat from the small claws.

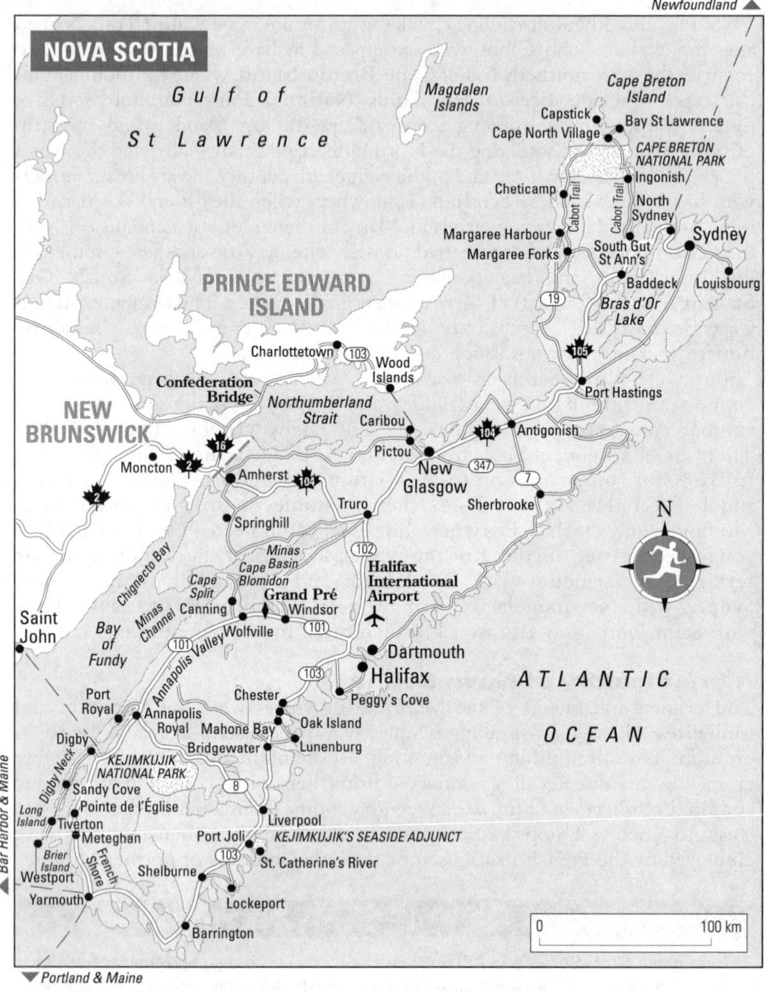

Founded by the French in 1605, **Port Royal**, on the south shore of the Bay of Fundy, was Nova Scotia's first European settlement, but in 1613 it was razed by Virginian raiders and abandoned the following year. In 1621, James I, King of England and Scotland, granted "**Nova Scotia**" – as New Scotland was termed in the inaugural charter – to William Alexander, whose colony near Port Royal lasted just three years. The French returned in the mid-1630s, establishing themselves on the site of today's Annapolis Royal and colonizing the surrounding area, which they called **Acadie**. These competing claims were partly resolved by the **Treaty of Utrecht** in 1713 – when Britain took control of all the Maritimes except Cape Breton Island and today's PEI – and finally determined after the fall of New France in 1759. The British victory was subsequently tarnished by the cruel expulsion of the Acadians from their farms along the Bay of Fundy.

With France defeated and the British keen to encourage **immigration** there was a flood of settlers from Ireland, England and Scotland as well as United Empire Loyalists escaping New England during and after the American War of Independence. This increase in the population precipitated an administrative reorganization, with the creation of Prince Edward Island in 1769 and New Brunswick in 1784. The new, streamlined Nova Scotia prospered from the development of its agriculture and the expansion of its fishing fleet. Further profits were reaped from shipbuilding, British-sanctioned privateering and the growth of Halifax as the Royal Navy's principal North Atlantic base. In 1867 Nova Scotia became part of the Dominion of Canada confident of its economic future. However, the province was too reliant on shipbuilding and, when this industry collapsed, Nova Scotia experienced a dreadful recession, whose effects were only partly mitigated by the mining of the province's coalfields and the industrialization of Cape Breton's **Sydney**, which became a major steel producer. Most of the pits and steel mills were closed in the 1950s, and the province is now largely dependent on farming, logging, fishing and tourism, though there is a new kid on the economic block – **oil and gas**. The first oil and gas reserves were discovered off Nova Scotia's coast in the 1970s, but production did not commence until the early 1990s. Reserves are substantial and promise a considerable, long-term injection into the provincial economy.

Halifax

HALIFAX, set on a steep and spatulate promontory beside one of the world's finest harbours, has become the focal point of the Maritimes, the region's financial, educational and transportation centre, whose metropolitan population of over 500,000 makes it four times the size of its nearest rival, New Brunswick's Saint John. This pre-eminence has been achieved since World War II, but long before then Halifax was a naval town *par excellence*, its harbour defining the character and economy of a city which rarely seemed to look inland.

The British were the first to develop Halifax, founding a base here in 1749 to counter the French fortress of Louisbourg (see p.441) on Cape Breton Island. When New France was captured shortly afterwards, the town became a heavily fortified guarantor of the Royal Navy's domination of the North Atlantic, a role reinforced when the British lost control of New England. The needs of the garrison called the tune throughout the nineteenth century: the waterfront was lined with brothels; martial law was in force till the 1850s; and most **Haligonians**, as the local citizenry are known, were at least partly employed in a service capacity.

In the twentieth century Halifax acted as a key supply and convoy harbour in both world wars, but since then its military importance has declined, even though the ships of the Canadian navy still dock here. Workaday office blocks reflect the city's new commercial successes, but interrupt the sweep of the town as it tumbles down to the harbour from the **Citadel**, the old British fortress that is the town's most significant sight. Nevertheless, Halifax retains a compact, bustling centre whose appealing and relaxing air is a far cry from the tense industriousness of many a metropolis.

Arrival and information

Halifax International Airport is located 35km northeast of the city centre and it has its own extremely efficient **provincial tourist information office**

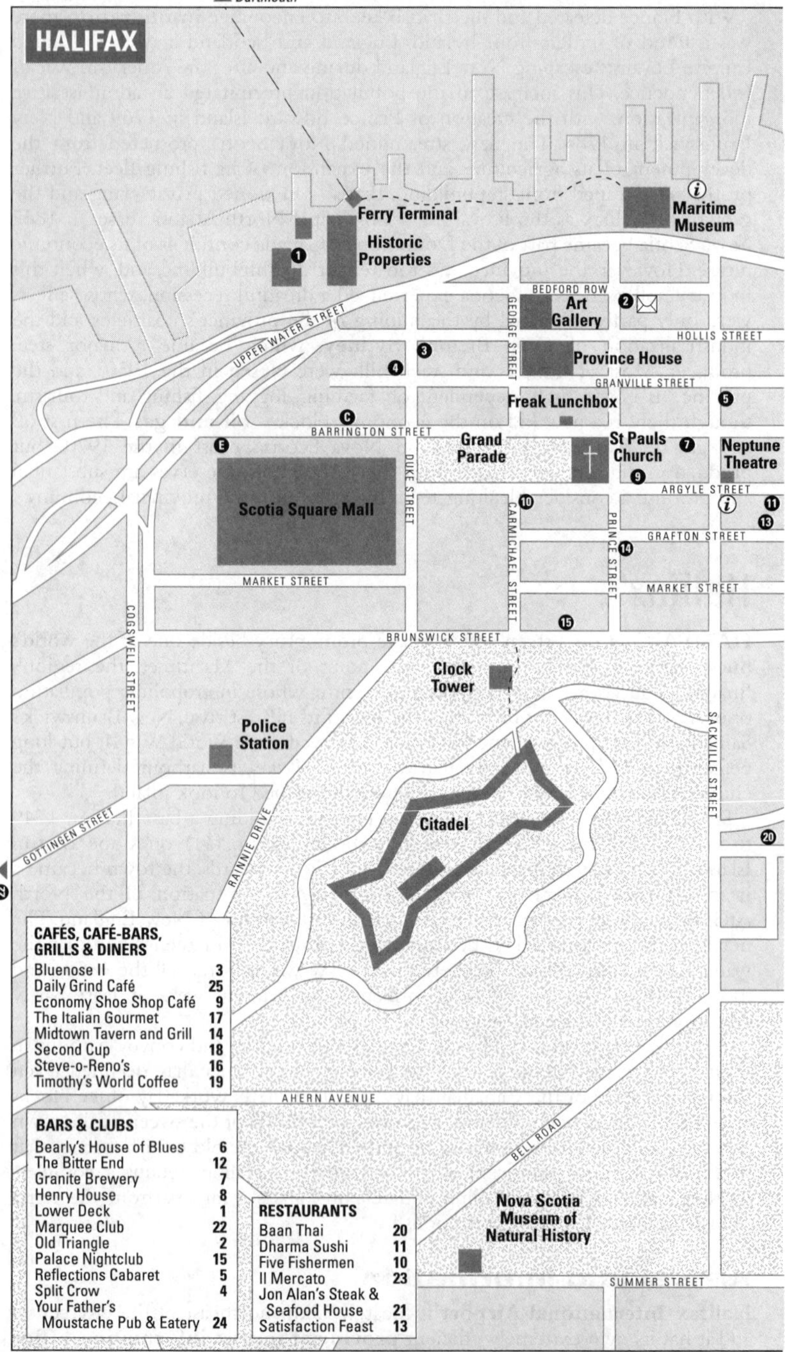

CAFÉS, CAFÉ-BARS, GRILLS & DINERS

Bluenose II	3
Daily Grind Café	25
Economy Shoe Shop Café	9
The Italian Gourmet	17
Midtown Tavern and Grill	14
Second Cup	18
Steve-o-Reno's	16
Timothy's World Coffee	19

BARS & CLUBS

Bearly's House of Blues	6
The Bitter End	12
Granite Brewery	7
Henry House	8
Lower Deck	1
Marquee Club	22
Old Triangle	2
Palace Nightclub	15
Reflections Cabaret	5
Split Crow	4
Your Father's Moustache Pub & Eatery	24

RESTAURANTS

Baan Thai	20
Dharma Sushi	11
Five Fishermen	10
Il Mercato	23
Jon Alan's Steak & Seafood House	21
Satisfaction Feast	13

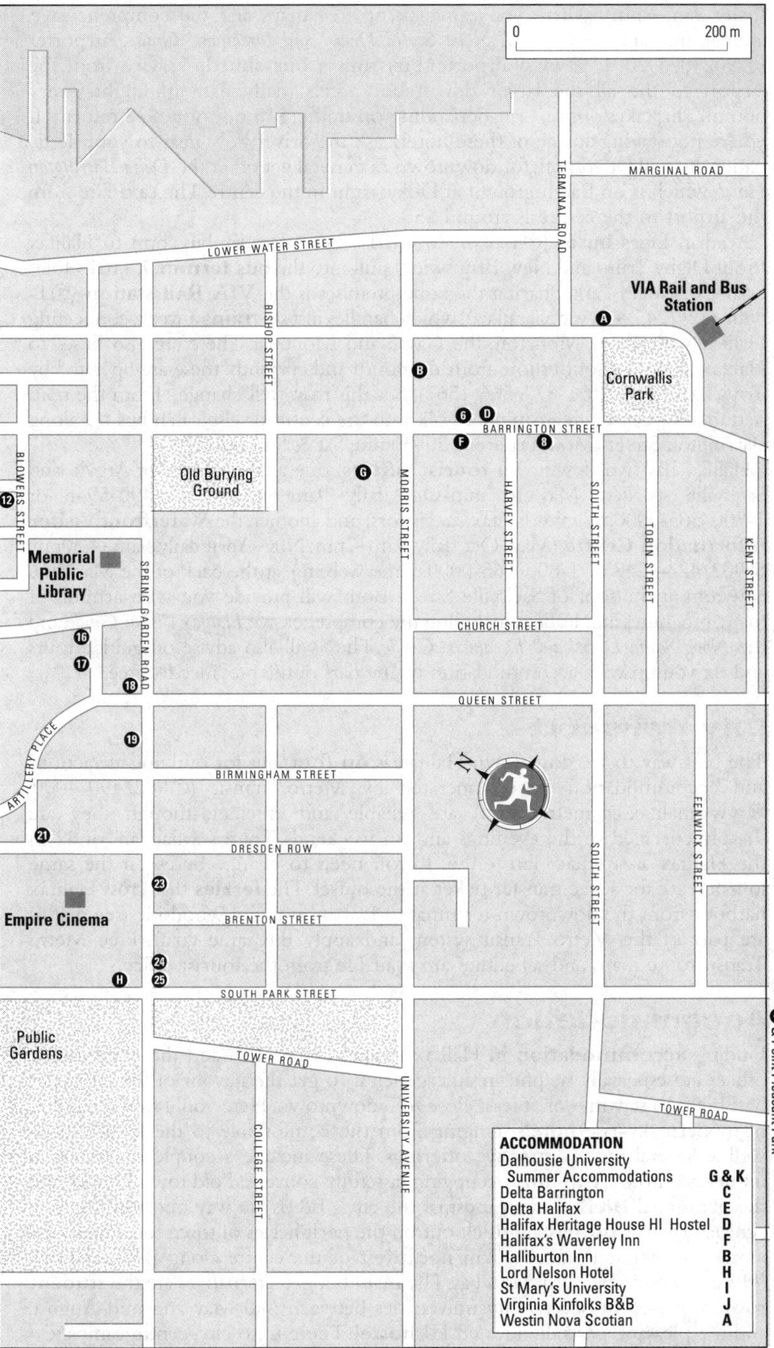
0
200 m
MARGINAL ROAD
TERMINAL ROAD
LOWER WATER STREET
VIA Rail and Bus Station
BISHOP STREET
Cornwallis Park
BARRINGTON STREET
Old Burying Ground
BLOWERS STREET
MORRIS STREET
HARVEY STREET
SOUTH STREET
TOBIN STREET
KENT STREET
Memorial Public Library
SPRING GARDEN ROAD
CHURCH STREET
QUEEN STREET
ARTILLERY PLACE
BIRMINGHAM STREET
DRESDEN ROW
FENWICK STREET
Empire Cinema
BRENTON STREET
SOUTH PARK STREET
Public Gardens
TOWER ROAD
UNIVERSITY AVENUE
COLLEGE STREET
I & Point Pleasant Park
K
ACCOMMODATION
Dalhousie University Summer Accommodations G & K
Delta Barrington C
Delta Halifax E
Halifax Heritage House HI Hostel D
Halifax's Waverley Inn F
Halliburton Inn B
Lord Nelson Hotel H
St Mary's University I
Virginia Kinfolks B&B J
Westin Nova Scotian A

(daily 9am–9pm), where you can pick up free maps and the comprehensive, annual, free and very useful *Nova Scotia Doers' and Dreamers' Guide*. Airporter (ⓣ902/873-2091, ⓦwww.airporter.biz) runs a **bus shuttle** service from the airport to the all the larger downtown hotels (daily 5am–midnight, every 30min/1hr; takes 40min–1hr depending on traffic; $16 one-way, $28 return). If you're not staying at one of these hotels, ask the driver how near to your destination he will let you off; for downtown in general get off at the *Delta Barrington Hotel*, which is on Barrington St at Duke, right in the centre. The **taxi** fare from the airport to the centre is around $55.

Acadian Lines **buses** (ⓣ1-800/567-5151, ⓦwww.acadianbus.com) to Halifax (from Digby, Truro and New Brunswick) pull into the **bus terminal**, 1161 Hollis St at Cornwallis Park. Sharing the same premises is the **VIA Rail station** (ⓣ1-888/842-7245, ⓦwww.viarail.ca), which handles just six **trains** a week, connecting Halifax with Truro, Moncton, the Gaspé and Montréal. There are also buses to Halifax along the south shore from Yarmouth and currently these are operated by Trius Coachlines (ⓣ1-877/566-1567), but this may well change. From the train station, it's an easy fifteen-minute walk into the centre, or else catch bus #9 along Barrington Street (Mon–Fri every 20–30min, Sat & Sun hourly).

Halifax has two downtown **tourist offices**: one at the corner of Argyle and Sackville sts (late May to mid-Oct daily 9am–6pm; ⓣ902/490-5946 or 1-800/565-0000, ⓦwww.halifax.ca/visitors) and another, the **Waterfront Visitor Information Centre** (May–Oct daily 9am–7pm; Nov–April daily 9am–4.30pm; ⓣ902/424-4248 or 1-800/565-0000, same website), at the back of the Maritime Museum at the foot of Sackville Street. Both will provide you with armfuls of maps, brochures and leaflets, including the comprehensive *Halifax Visitor Guide* and the *Nova Scotia Doers' and Dreamers' Guide*. They will also advise on guided tours and fix you up with accommodation in any part of the province for free.

City transport

The best way to see downtown Halifax is **on foot**, but for outlying attractions and accommodation **buses** operated by Metro Transit (ⓣ902/490-4000, ⓦwww.halifax.ca/metrotransit) are reliable and efficient, though they are sharply curtailed in the evenings and on weekends. There's a flat fare of $2 in the Halifax area (exact fare only). If you need to change buses on the same journey, ask for a free transfer ticket at the outset. The **ferries** that cross Halifax harbour from the downtown terminal to Dartmouth and Woodside (see p.406) are part of the Metro Transit system and apply the same tariff. Free Metro Transit route maps and schedules are available from the tourist office.

Accommodation

Finding **accommodation** in Halifax is rarely a problem and the city's tourist offices are especially helpful in emergencies. To get the flavour of the city your best bet is to stay in – or at least close to – downtown. Here you'll find a number of modern sky-rise **hotels**, ranging from the comfortable to the luxurious, as well as several more distinctive offerings. These include a couple of Art-Deco influenced hotels, two **inns** occupying tastefully converted old town houses, and the occasional **B&B**, though most of the city's B&Bs are way out from the city centre. Halifax's **motels** are stuck out on the peripheries of town too, inconveniently concentrated about 10km northwest of the centre along Bedford Hwy (Hwy 2), beside Bedford Basin bay. The main budget alternatives are the **student rooms** offered by several city universities between mid-May and mid-August, and the pleasant, centrally located HI **hostel**. There is no city-centre campsite.

Hotels and inns

Delta Barrington 1875 Barrington St ⓣ902/429-7410 or 1-877/814-7706, ⓦwww.deltabarrington.com. Modern luxury, bang in the middle of downtown, with weekend discounts of up to thirty percent. Attached to one of the city's larger shopping malls. ❻

Delta Halifax 1990 Barrington St ⓣ902/425-6700 or 1-877/814-7706, ⓦwww.deltahalifax.com. Large, modern downtown hotel occupying a concrete-and-glass tower block with attractive, spacious rooms and frequent weekend discounts. ❻

Halifax's Waverley Inn 1266 Barrington St ⓣ902/423-9346 or 1-800/565-9346, ⓦwww.waverleyinn.com. Elegant Victorian mansion, with thirty a/c rooms, that's been sympathetically refurbished with splendid period furnishings. Oscar Wilde stayed here on a North American lecture tour, apparently turning up in green velvet pantaloons – outlandish gear that only seems to have added to his popularity amongst the locals. The inn is situated about a five-minute walk from the train station; reservations advised. All rooms are en-suite. Rates include breakfast. ❻

Halliburton Inn 5184 Morris St ⓣ902/420-0658 or 1-888/512-3344, ⓦwww.thehalliburton.com. Near the railway station off Barrington St, this long-established thirty-room inn occupies three adjacent buildings. The oldest, the original inn, has a Victorian period look to its public rooms, but the bedrooms beyond are firmly modern. The nicer – and larger – bedrooms, many of which have balconies, are in the other two buildings. ❻

Lord Nelson Hotel 1515 South Park St ⓣ902/423-6331 or 1-800/565-2020, ⓦwww.lordnelsonhotel.com. Opposite the Public Gardens at the corner of Spring Garden Rd. With its high coffered ceiling, the lobby of this popular brown-brick hotel is spacious and elegant, with Art Deco details dating from its 1920s construction. The 200-odd rooms do not quite live up to the lobby, but they are spacious, comfortable and furnished in smart modern style – and certainly compare well with those of their rivals. ❻

Westin Nova Scotian 1181 Hollis St ⓣ902/421-1000 or 1-877/993-7846, ⓦwww.westin.ns.ca. Massive, luxurious, chain hotel in the upgraded premises of the old railway hotel, which – with its Art Deco touches – is next door to the train station. Located a fifteen-minute stroll along Barrington or Hollis sts from the city centre. ❻

B&Bs and hostels

Halifax Heritage House HI Hostel 1253 Barrington St ⓣ902/422-3863, ⓦwww.hihostels.ca. Only 300m from the train station, this clean and agreeable HI hostel with family rooms (doubles $40–50) and dorm beds (from $20) has Internet facilities, a laundry, kitchen, patio and parking.

Virginia Kinfolks B&B 1722 Robie St at Jubilee ⓣ902/423-6687 or 1-800/668-7829, ⓦwww.bbcanada.com/6930.html. Situated beside a busy main road about 1.5km west of downtown – opposite the Halifax Infirmary – this well-kept B&B occupies a suburban house with garden and rear sun deck. Four spacious en-suite rooms and full breakfast. ❺

Student accommodation

Dalhousie University Summer Accommodations Room 1024 Risley Hall, 1233 Le Marchant St ⓣ902/494-8840, ⓦwww.dal.ca/confserv. Halifax's premier academic institution, Dalhousie University is geared up for conferences during the summer recess, and also offers rooms to tourists from mid-May to mid-August. There are several locations, including **Gerard Hall**, a twelve-storey block just south of the centre at 5303 Morris St. Guests have access to the university's sports facilities. Single and double rooms available, usually with shared bathrooms. Singles $42, doubles ❸

St Mary's University 923 Robie St ⓣ902/420-5485 or 1-888/347-5555. About 2km southwest of the centre, on the way to Point Pleasant Park; singles and doubles available with shared bathrooms plus full, en suite apartments. Open mid-May to mid-August. Singles $40, doubles ❸

The City

With its shopping malls and brusque tower blocks, the commercial and social heart of modern Halifax clambers up the steep hillside from the harbourfront, its gridiron streets dotted with scores of bustling bars and restaurants. The city's main attractions – most notably the **Art Gallery**, with its eclectic collection of modern Canadian paintings, the **Maritime Museum** and the Georgian **Province House** – all huddle close together in the lower part of town beneath Halifax's star turn, the Vaubanesque **Citadel**. On a sunny day a pleasant diversion is a trip to see a couple of the **outer fortifications** built to defend Halifax harbour, and you can also catch the ferry over to neighbouring **Dartmouth**, home of the old **Quaker House**.

The Citadel

The distinctively bright-white Georgian **Clock Tower**, a solitary landmark sitting at the top of Carmichael Street beside the path up to the Citadel, looks somewhat confused, its dainty balustraded tower set on top of the dreariest of rectangular shacks. Completed in 1803, the tower is a tribute to the architectural tastes of its sponsor, Edward, Duke of Kent and father of Queen Victoria, who was sent here as military commandant in 1794. The Duke insisted on having a clock on each of the tower's four faces so none of the garrison had an excuse for being late, a preoccupation typical of this unforgiving martinet.

Up above the Clock Tower, the present fortifications of **Halifax Citadel National Historic Site** (daily early May to June & Sept–Oct 9am–5pm; July & Aug 9am–6pm; $10.90, $7.15 in shoulder season; Nov to early May 9am–5pm, free but all the exhibits are closed; ⓦ www.pc.gc.ca) are Victorian, the fourth in a series dating from Edward Cornwallis's stockade of 1749. It's a star-shaped fortress, constructed flush with the crest of the hill to protect it from artillery fire, a design that makes it seem insignificant until you reach the massive double stone and earth walls which flank the deep encircling ditch. Close up, it's a forbidding approach to one of Britain's most important imperial strongholds, but despite their apparent strength, the walls, faced with granite and ironstone, were a source of worry to a succession of British engineers. The sunken design simply didn't suit the climate – in winter the earth in the ramparts and the water in the mortar froze and the spring melt brought regular collapses.

A slender footbridge spans the ditch and leads into the fort, whose expansive **parade ground** is flanked by stone walls and dominated by the three-storey general **barracks**, whose long, columned galleries now mostly hold offices, though one particular barrack room has been returned to its appearance as of 1869. Here also is an **Army Museum**, which adopts an earthy soldier's outlook in the labelling of its wide collection of small arms. Ancient and sometimes rare photos track the Canadian army through its various imperial entanglements – from the Boer War onwards – and there's an interesting section tracing Canadian involvement with the Anglo-French attack on Bolshevik Russia after World War I. The **walls** themselves contain a string of **storehouses** stuffed with military bric-a-brac. Here you'll find a couple of reconstructed powder magazines, the former garrison school room and several exhibits exploring the Citadel's history, including a small theatre where a fifty-minute-long film, *The Tides of History*, details the development of Halifax. Also of interest is the **Communications Exhibit**, which explains the niceties of the Admiralty's signalling system – a complicated affair with, for instance, different flags for different types of ship and flags distinguishing whether vessels had been sighted or had actually arrived.

Free and entertaining half-hour **guided tours** (early May to Oct) of the Citadel depart from the information office in the barracks building every hour or so. Throughout the summer bagpipe bands and marching "soldiers" perform on the parade ground in period uniform and one of the cannons is ceremoniously fired every day at noon. If all this militarism leaves you cold, the Citadel is still worth a visit for the grand view from its ramparts over the city and harbour.

Grand Parade and the Province House

Retracing your steps down past the Clock Tower, keep straight along Carmichael Street to reach the tree-lined, elongated square known as **Grand Parade**, the social centre of the nineteenth-century town. For the officer corps, this was the

△ Bagpiper at the Citadel

place to be seen walking on a Sunday, when, as one obsequious observer wrote, "their society generally [was] sought, frequently courted, and themselves esteemed" – a judgement rather different from that of the radical journalist Joseph Howe, who hated their "habits of idleness, dissipation and expense". The southern edge of the Grand Parade borders the handsome **St Paul's Church** (Mon–Fri 9am–4.30pm; free), whose chunky cupola and simple timber frame date from 1750, making it both the oldest building in town and the first Protestant church in Canada. Inside, the church's simple symmetry – with balcony and sturdy pillars – is engaging, an unpretentious garrison church enlisting God to the British interest, its nave studded with memorial plaques to those steadfast Victorians who led Nova Scotia through good times and bad – like Sampson Salter Blowers, long-time chief justice who died in 1842 at the age of 100. Look out, also, for the piece of wood embedded in the plaster above the inner entrance doors, a remnant of the 1917 Halifax Explosion (see box, p.406). Following the disaster the vestry was used as an emergency hospital and the bodies of hundreds of victims were laid in tiers around the walls.

Charles Dickens, visiting in 1842, described the graceful sandstone **Province House**, a couple of minutes' walk from Grand Parade down George Street on Hollis (July & Aug Mon–Fri 9am–5pm, Sat & Sun 10am–4pm; rest of year Mon–Fri 9am–4pm; free), as "a gem of Georgian architecture" whose proceedings were "like looking at Westminster through the wrong end of a telescope". Highlights of the free **guided tour** – self-guided in winter – include a peek into the old upper chamber, now the Red Chamber, with its ornate plasterwork and assorted portraits, including a dandified King George III and Queen Charlotte and, at the other end of the room, George I and his daughter-in-law Caroline: George I should have been pictured with his wife, Sophia, rather than his daughter-in-law, but no one ever bothered to rectify this costly decorative error. The present legislature meets in the Assembly Chamber, a cosy room that partly resembles a Georgian bedroom rather a provincial seat of government.

Art Gallery of Nova Scotia

Across the road from the Province House, the **Art Gallery of Nova Scotia**, 1741 Hollis St (daily 10am–5pm, Thurs till 9pm; $12, ⓦ www.agns.gov.ns.ca), occupies two adjacent buildings – one a stern Art Deco structure, the other an embellished Victorian edifice that has previously served as a courthouse, police headquarters and post office. The gallery is attractively laid out and although there is some rotation of the exhibits most of the pieces described here should be on view. Pick up a free **gallery plan** at the entrance in the more southerly of the two buildings, Gallery South.

The ground floor – Floor 1 – of **Gallery South** contains a delightful section devoted to the Nova Scotian artist **Maud Lewis** (1903–70). The daughter of a Yarmouth harness maker, Lewis overcame several disabilities, including rheumatoid arthritis, to become a painter of some regional renown, creating naive, brightly coloured works of local scenes. Lewis's tiny cabin – awash with her bright paintwork – has been moved here intact from the outskirts of Digby.

An underground passageway connects the Lower Floor of Gallery South with the Lower Floor of **Gallery North**. Both the passageway and Gallery North's Lower Floor hold temporary exhibitions of modern sculpture and painting plus a sample of the museum's most recent acquisitions. Upstairs, Gallery North's Level 1 has further temporary displays plus – concentrated in Room 8 – an enjoyable selection of **Canadian historical paintings** with the Maritimes to the fore. The earlier canvases are distinguished by four intriguing views of Halifax in the 1760s produced by Dominique Serres in the minutely observed

Dutch land- and seascape tradition. Surprisingly, Serres never actually visited Canada, but painted Halifax while in Europe, from drawings produced by a camera obscura. In the same gallery, there's also Joshua Reynolds' flattering *Portrait of George Montagu Dunk, 2nd Earl of Halifax*. As the man responsible for colonial trade, Dunk permitted his recently acquired title to be used in the naming of Halifax – what would have happened but for his timely ennoblement is anyone's guess ("Dunktown", "Dunkville", who knows).

Close by, Room 4 holds several canvases by Cornelius Krieghoff (see p.96) and a small sample of the work of the **Group of Seven** (see p.94). In particular, look out for Lawren Harris's haunting *Algoma* landscape and J.E.H. MacDonald's diminutive *Lake O'Hara*. Moving on, Room 6 features an eclectic selection of modern Canadian paintings drawn from the permanent collection: the egg tempera on masonite *Island in the Ice* by the Nova Scotian artist Tom Forrestall (b.1936) is perhaps the most striking painting here, its sharp, deep-hued colours and threatening ice- and seascape enhanced by a tight control of space. Look out also for the work of Forrestall's mentor, **Alex Colville** (b.1920), whose disconcerting paintings demonstrate a sort of Magic Realism of passive, precisely juxtaposed figures caught, cinema-like, in mid-shot.

Up above, Levels 2, 3 and 4 are devoted to temporary exhibitions with the emphasis on modern Atlantic Canadian and European painters.

The Maritime Museum of the Atlantic

From the bottom of George Street, it's one block south to the **Maritime Museum of the Atlantic**, 1675 Lower Water St (May & Oct Mon–Sat 9.30am–5.30pm, Tues until 8pm, Sun 1–5.30pm; June–Sept daily 9.30am–5.30pm, Tues until 8pm; Nov–April Tues 9.30am–8pm, Wed–Sat 9.30am–5pm, Sun 1–5pm; $8), which contains a fascinating exhibition covering all aspects of Nova Scotian seafaring from colonial times to the present day spread over two large floors. Beyond the entrance, the **ground floor** holds a series of small displays, including one on the Allied convoys that used Halifax as a port during both World Wars; a second on the Halifax Explosion (see box, p.406), illustrated by a first-rate video, *One Moment in Time*; and a third on the perilously sited Sable Island lighthouse, stuck out in the Atlantic southeast of Nova Scotia. **Upstairs**, a collection of small boats and cutaway scale models details the changing technology of shipbuilding in the 'Days of Sail', but it is the neighbouring '**Shipwreck Treasures**' section that attracts most attention, mainly because of its well-presented display on the **Titanic**, which sank east of Halifax in 1912. Curiously enough, several pieces of fancy woodwork found floating in the ocean after the sinking have ended up in the museum, a poignant epitaph to the liner's grand Edwardian furnishings and fittings. Another salvaged item is the wooden effigy of a turbaned Turk that started out as the figurehead of a British barque, the *Saladin*. In 1844, the *Saladin*'s crew mutinied in mid-Atlantic, killed the captain and ran the boat aground near Halifax, thinking they could escape the long arm of the Royal Navy. They were wrong: the surviving mutineers were all rounded up, tried and hung. Close by, a remarkable assortment of nautical knick-knacks is stored in the '**Visible Storage**' section, everything from tricorn hats, ships' clocks, ships' bells, sextants, compasses, foghorns to the piano used to entertain passengers on the ferry from Pictou to Prince Edward Island.

Docked **outside** the museum are an early twentieth-century steamship, the CSS *Acadia*, and a World War II corvette, HMCS *Sackville*. The first is part of the museum, the second is a (free) attraction in its own right; both can only be boarded in the summer

The Halifax Explosion

Nothing in the history of the Maritimes stands out like the 1917 **Halifax Explosion**, the greatest man-made cataclysm of the pre-atomic age. It occurred during World War I when Halifax was the departure point for convoys transporting troops and armaments to Europe. Shortly after dawn on December 6, a Norwegian ship called the *Imo*, a vessel carrying relief supplies to Belgium, and a French munitions carrier called the *Mont Blanc* were manoeuvring in Halifax harbour. The Norwegian ship was steaming for the open sea, while the *Mont Blanc*, a small, decrepit vessel, was heading for the harbour stuffed with explosives and ammunition, including half a million pounds of TNT – though it flew no flags to indicate the hazardous nature of the cargo. As the ships approached each other, the *Imo* was forced to steer into the wrong channel by a poorly positioned tugboat. With neither ship clear about the other's intentions and each attempting to take evasive action, they collided, and the resulting sparks caused the ignition of the drums of flammable liquid stored on the *Mont Blanc*'s deck. A fire took hold, and the crew abandoned their vessel, which drifted under the force of the impact towards the Halifax shore.

A large crowd had gathered on the waterfront to witness the spectacle when the TNT **exploded**. The blast killed 2000 people instantly and flattened over 300 acres of north Halifax, with fire engulfing much of the rest. Windows were broken in Truro over 90km away and the shock wave was felt in Cape Breton. Nothing remained of the *Mont Blanc*, and part of its anchor, a piece of metal weighing over half a ton, was later found more than 4km away. To make matters worse, a **blizzard** deposited 40cm of snow on Halifax during the day, hampering rescue attempts. The bodies of many victims were not recovered until the spring.

It's hard to appreciate today the vision of Armageddon that haunted Halifax after the explosion, but haunt the city it did, as the poignant newspaper cuttings in the Maritime Museum show.

The waterfront's Historic Properties

From the Maritime Museum, it's an agreeable 400m stroll north along the waterfront to the much-vaunted **Historic Properties**, comprising an area of refurbished wharves, warehouses and merchants' quarters situated below Upper Water Street – and just beyond the Dartmouth and Woodside ferry terminal. The ensemble has a certain charm – all bars, boutiques and bistros – and the narrow lanes and alleys still maintain the shape of the harbourfront during the days of sail, but there's not much to see unless the schooner **Bluenose II** is moored here, as it often is during the summer. The original *Bluenose*, whose picture is on the 10¢ coin, was famed throughout Canada as the fastest vessel of its kind in the 1920s, although she ended her days ingloriously as a freighter, foundering off Haiti in 1946. The replica has spent several years as a floating standard-bearer for Nova Scotia, but it's now on its last sea legs and its future is uncertain. Pressure groups are campaigning either to have it refurbished or berthed permanently here at Halifax or at its home port of Lunenburg (see p.414).

The Old Burying Ground and the Nova Scotia Museum

Mysterious and spooky at dawn and dusk, the **Old Burying Ground** is a five-minute walk south of Grand Parade at Barrington Street and Spring Garden Road. The cemetery manages to look something like the opening shot of David Lean's *Great Expectations* despite the best efforts of the over-blown memorial by the gates in honour of a brace of Canadian officers killed in the Crimean War. Many of the tombstones are badly weathered, but enough inscriptions survive to give an insight into the lives (and early deaths) of the colonists and their offspring. The oldest tomb is that of a certain John Connor, who ran the first ferry service over to Dartmouth and died in 1754.

Walking west up Spring Garden Road from the Burying Ground, it's about 800m to South Park Street, where a set of handsome iron gates announces the main entrance into the city's **Public Gardens** (dawn–dusk; free). First planted in the 1870s, the gardens cover sixteen acres of meticulously maintained exotic shrubs, flowerbeds and trees set around ornamental statues, water fountains, ponds and a brightly painted bandstand. All together, the gardens are a pleasant interlude on the way to the **Nova Scotia Museum of Natural History**, 1747 Summer St – to the rear of the old grassy commonland that trails back from the Citadel (June to mid-Oct Mon–Sat 9.30am–5.30pm, Wed till 8pm, Sun 1–5.30pm; mid-Oct to May Tues–Sat 9.30am–5pm, Wed till 8pm, Sun 1–5pm; $5; Ⓦwww.museum.gov.ns.ca/mnh). The museum is compact, but still manages to touch all its bases, from an acrylic honeybee hive through to illuminating sections on whales and the province's land-based wildlife. There's also a modest display of Micmac (or, more properly, Mi'kmaq) archaeological finds.

The outer fortifications

In the eighteenth century the British navy protected the seven-kilometre-long sea passage into **Halifax harbour**, and the Bedford Basin behind it, with a string of coastal gun batteries. Two of these are worth a visit, though more for their commanding views than the ragbag of military remains. The first is at **Point Pleasant**, at the tip of the Halifax peninsula about 3km south of the city, whilst the other is on **McNab's Island**, sitting in the middle of the main seaway, 4km south of the city.

Point Pleasant Park

At the end of South Park Street and its continuation, Young Avenue, **Point Pleasant Park** (bus #9 from Barrington Street) incorporates the remains of four gun batteries and the squat **Prince of Wales Martello Tower** (July to early Sept daily 10am–6pm; free), which was built at the end of the eighteenth century as a combined barracks, battery and storehouse. One of the first of its type, the design was copied from a Corsican tower (at Martello Point) that had proved particularly troublesome to the British. Indeed, these self-contained, semi-self-sufficient defensive fortifications with their thick walls and protected entrances proved so successful that Martello towers were built throughout the empire, only becoming obsolete in the 1870s with advances in artillery technology. Path and **walking trails** crisscross the surrounding park, 200 acres of wooded hills and shoreline that were unlucky enough to be badly mauled by a hurricane in 2003. Incidentally, this is one of the few places in North America where heather grows, supposedly originating from seeds shaken from the bedding of Scots regiments stationed here.

McNab's Island

McNab's Island (Ⓦwww.mcnabsisland.ca), 5km long and 2km wide, contains the remnants of five different fortifications, the earliest dating from the middle of the eighteenth century and the last being **Fort McNab** (free), which was built in 1890. The island, most of which is parkland, is laced with hiking trails and dotted with picnic spots, making it a relaxing retreat from the city, though here again "Hurricane Juan" ripped up many of the island's trees in 2003. During the summer, there is a **passenger ferry** over to the island from Fisherman's Cove on the east (Dartmouth) side of the harbour with McNab's Island Ferry (Ⓣ902/465-4563; return fare $10), but without your own transport

Fisherman's Cove is a pain to get to: either ask the operator for a lift or check at the tourist office to see if there are any island tours beginning downtown.

Dartmouth

Humdrum **DARTMOUTH**, across the harbour from Halifax, is often ignored by visitors as it lacks the more obvious appeal of its neighbour. Nevertheless, it is the province's second largest town, with 70,000 inhabitants, and although it's primarily an industrial centre the ferry ride over there does provide wide views of the harbour and downtown Halifax – and there are a couple of minor attractions to further justify a sortie. The Dartmouth **ferry** leaves the Halifax waterfront from beside the Historic Properties at the foot of George Street and the journey takes about ten minutes (Mon–Sat 6.45am–11.30pm every 15–30min; Sun, except Jan & Feb, 10.30am-6pm every 30min-1hr; $2). Two road **bridges** also connect the twin cities: the Macdonald, running just to the north of both city centres, and the Mackay, part of the outer ring road. Metro Transit bus #1 from Barrington Street at Duke uses the MacDonald.

In Darmouth, turn left outside the ferry terminal and then take the first right for the five-minute stroll to the **Quaker House**, 57 Ochterloney St (early June to Aug Tues–Sun 10am–1pm & 2–5pm; $2), a small, grey-clapboard residence sitting three blocks up the hill from the dock at King Street. After the American War of Independence, several Quaker whaling families emigrated from Nantucket Island, off Cape Cod, to Dartmouth, but this is the only one of their houses to survive. The interior has been painstakingly restored to its late eighteenth-century appearance, its spartan fittings reflecting Quaker values. Among the exhibits are a two-hundred-year-old pair of shoes found under the floorboards during renovations in 1991, and the eye of a Greenland whale preserved in formalin – though the staff won't show you this if they think you're squeamish.

From here, it's another five-minute walk along – and left at the end of – **King Street** to a very short stretch of the **Shubenacadie Canal**, which once connected the Bay of Fundy to Dartmouth, a distance of 90km. Begun in 1826, this monumental feat of engineering, linking a dozen existing lakes with new watercourses and locks, was completed in 1860, but the canal only made a profit for ten years before it was superseded by the railways – and then left to rot.

To return to the Dartmouth ferry terminal, double back across the end of King Street and keep straight until you reach the **park** that leads round the harbourfront – in all, a five- to ten-minute walk.

Eating

It's easy to **eat** well and inexpensively in Halifax. There's a wide selection of **downtown** cafés, diners, café-bars and restaurants within easy walking distance of Grand Parade – with particular concentrations along Spring Garden Road from Queen Street to South Park and along Argyle Street. Both of these areas mostly cater to locals, whereas the more touristy spots are clustered down on the waterfront in the Historic Properties. At the majority of restaurants, a substantial meal will only set you back about $15–20, excluding drinks. **Seafood** is the leading local speciality, with **lobster** being a particular favourite – expect to pay about $30 for a medium-sized specimen. Bear in mind also that most kitchens start to finish up at around 9.30–10pm and that some restaurants close on Sunday, sometimes Monday too.

For something a bit different, head for *Freak Lunchbox*, 1723 Barrington St (Mon–Sat 10am–9pm & Sun noon–6pm), which boasts a phenomenal range of **sweets** and **candy** – from the traditional to the kitsch via the bizarre.

Cafés, café-bars, grills and diners

Bluenose II 1824 Hollis at Duke St. Something of an institution, this long-established diner serves filling and fairly tasty meals with lobster, in various guises, being the speciality along with Greek dishes. Lobster dinners cost $25. Mon–Fri 6.30am–10pm, Sat & Sun 8am–10pm.

Daily Grind Café 5684 Spring Garden Rd at South Park. Respectable coffee house at the back of a bookshop serving up a small range of pasta and vegetarian dishes at very affordable prices. Mon–Fri 7am–10pm, Sat 8am–8pm & Sun 8am–6pm.

Economy Shoe Shop Café 1663 Argyle St. Everything here is imaginative – from the name and the off-beat decor through to the menu, offering tapas to Italian. One of a cluster of fashionable café-bars on Argyle. Daily 11am–2am.

The Italian Gourmet 5431 Doyle St. A wide selection of good quality Italian meals, snacks, salads and cakes at this large and relaxed deli-café. Mon–Sat 9am–7pm, Sun 10am–5pm.

Midtown Tavern and Grill At Prince and Grafton. One of the most enjoyable places in town, this blue-collar favourite serves up tasty steaks at amazingly reasonable prices (as little as $11). It's a far cry from the tourist-industry niceties down on the waterfront, and none the worse for it. Mon–Sat 11am–10pm.

Steve-o-Reno's 1532 Brunswick St, just off Spring Garden Rd. New Age-ish café-bar with bohemian decor and laidback vibes. The breakfasts are tip-top, with a bewildering range of coffees. Daily 9am–6pm.

Second Cup 5417 Spring Garden Rd at Queen St. National chain with first-rate coffees. Daily 7am–11pm.

Timothy's World Coffee 5475 Spring Garden Rd at Queen St. This competent coffee house sells great coffees and delicious pastries plus cakes and muffins. Part of a chain, there's also a branch at 1791 Barrington St. Mon–Fri 7am–11pm & Sat–Sun 8am–11pm.

Restaurants

Baan Thai 1569 Dresden Row ☎902/446-4301. There's often a queue here to sample the city's best Thai food, but it's well worth the wait. Hidden away upstairs. Inexpensive with main courses at around $12. Daily 5–10pm.

Dharma Sushi 1576 Argyle St ☎902/425-7785. First-rate Japanese restaurant serving all the favourites. Faded decor, but very easy on the pocket with main courses from around $12. Mon–Fri noon–3pm & Mon–Sat from 6.30pm.

Five Fishermen 1740 Argyle St at Carmichael ☎902/422-4421. One of Halifax's best restaurants, where the house speciality is seafood with main courses $30 and up – expensive perhaps, but the food is delicious and the all-you-can-eat mussel bar is included in the price. The restaurant is on the first floor of an old building and its cosy interior, with its booths and stained glass, is decked out in antique nautical style. Reservations required. Daily from 5.30pm.

Il Mercato 5650 Spring Garden Rd at Dresden Row ☎902/422-2866. Busy, neatly decorated restaurant featuring well-prepared, mouthwateringly tasty Northern Italian dishes of every persuasion. Main courses $15–20, pizzas and pastas from $9. Mon–Sat 11am–11pm.

Jon Alan's Steak and Seafood House Corner Dresden Row & Artillery Place ☎902/422-5267. Smart, modern restaurant, where the steaks are the big deal – excellently done and attractively presented ($25 and up). Mon–Thurs 11.30am–10pm, Fri 11.30am–11pm, Sat 5–11pm & Sun 5–10pm. There's an adjoining cigar and martini bar too.

Satisfaction Feast 1581 Grafton St at Sackville ☎902/422-3540. Vegetarian restaurant with a wide-ranging, imaginative menu, featuring everything from nutloaf and bean burritos to curry and lasagne. Vegan options too. Main courses around $12. Open Mon–Sat 11.30am–8.30pm.

Nightlife and entertainment

They say Halifax has more **bars** per head than anywhere else in Canada except St John's, Newfoundland, and although cafés and café-bars have made substantial inroads, there are still plenty of good, old bars, many of which offer pub food (of variable quality). Incidentally, bars and restaurants sometimes occupy different floors of the same premises - and this can be a tad confusing.

If you want to go out and groove, Halifax has a vibrant **live music scene** with around forty of its café-bars and bars offering everything from blues and jazz through to indie and techno. Many of these places have live music on just a couple of nights a week, and detailed **entertainment listings**, along with reviews and well-written local news features, are given in a free weekly newssheet, *The Coast* (Ⓦwww.thecoast.ca), which is available at record shops, bars and the tourist office. The local newspaper *The Chronicle-Herald* (Ⓦwww.herald.ns.ca) carries reviews and listings on Thursdays, and *Where*, a free monthly magazine supplied by the tourist office, has a section describing the city's most popular bars and giving some opening hours. The venues listed on below are places where you can expect to see live music on most nights of the week. The main **musical event** is the eight-day Atlantic Jazz Festival (Ⓣ1-800/567-5277, Ⓦwww.jazzeast.com), held in mid-July and featuring many of the biggest international names. Halifax, as the provincial capital, also attracts major touring acts in key **classical** and theatrical performances and has a well-regarded **theatre** scene.

Bars

The Bitter End 1572 Argyle St. Well known for their martinis, this polished cocktail bar provides a quietly cool beginning to – or end of – a night on the tiles. Mon–Thurs 4.30pm–2am, Fri–Sun 11.30am–2am

Granite Brewery 1662 Barrington St at Sackville. Deep and dark bar with an antique pressed-tin roof and an excellent range of its own brews – try the Granite Best Bitter to get you started.

Henry House 1222 Barrington St at South. In the style of a British pub, this charmingly intimate bar occupies a nineteenth-century stone building not far from the train station. Most of the ale is brewed on the premises – try the Peculiar, a fair approximation of the sultry grandeur of the legendary British ale. Open daily.

Old Triangle 5136 Prince St at Hollis Ⓣ902/492-4900. An Irish-style pub with a whole network of cosy snugs and a warm and welcoming atmosphere. Live Gaelic music on the weekend.

Split Crow 1855 Granville St at Duke Ⓣ902/422-4366, Ⓦwww.splitcrow.com. Large and lively English-style pub. Very central and often featuring live Maritime folk and fiddle music.

Your Father's Moustache Pub & Eatery 5686 Spring Garden Rd at South Park Ⓣ902/423-6766 Ⓦwww.yourfathersmoustache.ca. Good range of ales with frequent live acts – blues a speciality. Seasonal rooftop patio.

Live music and clubs

Bearly's House of Blues 1269 Barrington St Ⓣ902/423-2526, Ⓦwww.bearlys.ca. Near the train station, this low-key bar has regular acts with the emphasis – you guessed it – on blues and bluegrass. Jam sessions on Sun nights. Open Tues–Sun.

Lower Deck In the Privateer's Warehouse, one of the Historic Properties down on the waterfront Ⓣ902/425-1501, Ⓦwww.lowerdeck.ca. Traditional Maritime folk music is the speciality here with regular live acts weekly.

Marquee Club 2037 Gottingen St Ⓣ902/429-2442, Ⓦwww.themarqueeclub.ca. Upstairs, rock bands play to an energetic and enthusiastic audience. Downstairs, it's laid-back acoustic jazz and blues. A ten-minute walk from the centre off Cogswell Street.

Palace Nightclub 1721 Brunswick St Ⓣ902/420-0015, Ⓦwww.thenewpalace.com. Massive, brash and noisy nightclub where Halifax's young more than get acquainted. Open Thurs–Sun until 3.30am.

Reflections Cabaret 5184 Sackville St Ⓣ902/422-2957, Ⓦwww.reflectionscabaret.com. Halifax's biggest dance club with themed nights, both by music and disposition, though house tends to predominate. Mon–Sat 1pm–4am, Sun 4pm–4am.

Classical music

Symphony Nova Scotia Box office at the Dalhousie Arts Centre, 6101 University Ave Ⓣ902/494-3820, Ⓦwww.symphonynovascotia.ca. Professional orchestra that usually performs at the university's Rebecca Cohn Auditorium (University Ave and Le Marchant St). Concert season from Sept to April. Everything from Beethoven to Piaf.

Film

Empire 5657 Spring Garden Rd ⓣ902/422-2022, ⓦwww.empiretheatres.com. Mainstream cinema in the Park Lane Mall, just west of Dresden.

Drama

Neptune Theatre 1593 Argyle St ⓣ902/429-7070, ⓦwww.neptunetheatre.com. The doyen of Halifax's live theatres, offering a wide range of mainstream dramatic productions; closes for three months in summer.

Listings

Airlines Air Canada ⓣ1-888/247-2262, ⓦwww.aircanada.com; Air St-Pierre ⓣ902/873-3566, ⓦwww.airsaintpierre.com; Provincial Airlines ⓣ902/873-3575, ⓦwww.provincialairlines.com.
Banks Amongst many downtown branches, there's a Bank of Nova Scotia in the Scotia Square Mall, Barrington St and Duke.
Bike rental Idealbikes, 1678 Barrington St at Prince (Mon–Fri noon–6pm, Sat 10am–6pm & Sun noon–4pm; ⓣ902/444-7433, ⓦwww.idealbikes.ca).
Bookshops As befits a university town, Halifax has several good bookshops on and around Barrington St, both new and secondhand. The Book Room, 1546 Barrington at Blowers (Mon & Tues 9am–5.30pm, Wed–Fri 9am–7.30pm, Sat 9am–5pm & Sun noon–5pm; ⓣ902/423-8271, ⓦwww.bookroom.ca), opened in 1839 (making it Canada's oldest) and has a good selection of new and used books, with its Maritimes section especially noteworthy. There also giant piles of used books at the charmingly bookish John Doull Bookshop, 1684 Barrington at Prince (Mon & Tues 9.30am–6pm, Wed–Fri 9.30am–9pm & Sat 10am–9pm; ⓣ902/429-1652, ⓦwww.doullbooks.com).
Buses From Halifax's combined bus and train station, 1161 Hollis St at Cornwallis Park, Acadian Lines buses (ⓣ1-800/567-5151, ⓦwww.acadianbus.com) depart Halifax for Truro and New Brunswick as well as Sydney on Cape Breton Island; change at New Brunswick's Moncton for PEI. Trius (ⓣ1-877/566-1567) currently run a bus down along the southwest shore from Halifax to Yarmouth. See Travel details p.488 for further information.
Car rental Discount, at the airport ⓣ902/468-7171; Dollar, at the airport ⓣ902/873-2075; National, at the airport ⓣ902/873-3505 and at the Westin Nova Scotian Hotel 1181 Hollis St, ⓣ902/422-4439
Consulate US, 1969 Upper Water St ⓣ902/429-2480.
Internet access Free Internet access at the Memorial Public Library, 5381 Spring Garden Rd at Grafton (Tues–Thurs 10am–9pm, Fri & Sat 10am–5pm, plus Sun in winter 2–5pm; ⓣ902/490-5700)
Post office 1680 Bedford Row and Prince (Mon–Fri 7.30am–5.15pm).
Taxis Yellow Cab ⓣ902/420-0000, Casino Taxi ⓣ902/425-6666.
Trains VIA Rail ⓣ1-888/842-7245, ⓦwww.viarail.ca.
Weather Up-to-date bulletin on ⓣ902/426-9090, ⓦwww.weatheroffice.ec.gc.ca.

Southwest Nova Scotia

The jagged coastline running southwest of Halifax to **Yarmouth**, a distance of 340km, boasts dozens of tiny fishing villages pressed tight against the shore by the vast forest that pours over the interior. Most were of these villages were founded by United Empire Loyalists, whose dedication to the British interest both during and after the American War of Independence obliged them to hotfoot it out of the US, often as penniless refugees. Today, the most beguiling of these villages are **Peggy's Cove**, an incredibly picturesque smattering of higgledy-piggledy clapboard houses dotted along a wild shore, and lesser-known **Lockeport**, with its old-fashioned air and fine sandy beaches. Equally diverting are the towns of **Lunenburg**, with its stunning Victorian architecture, and ritzy, leafy **Chester**, both of which derived their former prosperity, like their coastal neighbours, from the now-defunct shipbuilding business and from privateering.

Travelling the shoreline is the **Lighthouse Route**, a tourist trail that winds through everything of any possible interest, but you're better off sticking to the main road, **Highway 103**, and dropping down to the coast for the highlights. At workaday **Liverpool**, there's a choice of routes: you can cut across the peninsula to charming Annapolis Royal (see p.424) on Hwy 8, past the wilderness splendours of **Kejimkujik National Park**, or – with more time – you can press on along the coast, sampling the fine coastal scenery of the clumsily named **Seaside Adjunct of Kejimkujik National Park** before arriving at Lockeport and ultimately **Yarmouth**. Beyond Yarmouth, a second tourist route, the **Evangeline Trail**, pushes up the **French Shore** to **Digby**, where the finger of land known as the **Digby Neck** offers whalewatching tours of national repute.

The southwest coast is popular with tourists, but not oppressively so, and almost every settlement has at least a couple of fine old Victorian mansions that have been converted into **inns** or **B&Bs**. These provide first-rate accommodation at reasonable prices and reservations are only essential in the height of the season and on holiday weekends. In terms of **restaurants**, seafood is the big deal around here – usually simply prepared and perfectly delicious.

Public transport is limited. **Acadian Lines bus** (ⓣ1-800/567-5151, ⓦwww.acadianbus.com) operates a once daily service from Halifax to Digby via the Annapolis Valley, though currently this doesn't leave until 6.45pm, reaching Digby at 11pm, which is far from ideal. **Trius Coachlines** (ⓣ1-877/566-1567) runs the other bus route, from Halifax to Yarmouth along the southern shore, but again it's only once daily and the operator is liable to change – check at Halifax tourist office for the latest news. Trius and Acadian buses depart from Halifax bus station, next to the train station on Hollis Street.

Peggy's Cove

Highway 333 leaves Hwy 103 a few kilometres west of Halifax to make its slow progress through the forested hinterland that so successfully confined the region's early settlers to the coast. Once at the shoreline, the road slips through ribbon fishing villages, past glacial boulders and round rocky bays to reach tiny **PEGGY'S COVE**, 45km from Halifax. Founded in 1811, the hamlet, with a resident population of just sixty souls, surrounds a rocky slit of a harbour, with a spiky timber church, a smattering of clapboard houses and wooden jetties on stilts. It's a beautiful spot, the solitary **lighthouse** set against the sea-smoothed granite of the shore, and it attracts swarms of tourists; try to visit at sunrise or sunset, when the coach parties leave the village to the locals. Behind the lighthouse, *The Sou'wester* dispenses mundane meals, while the three-roomed *Peggy's Cove B&B,* overlooking the harbour from the end of Church Road (ⓣ902/543-2233 or 1-800/725-8732, May–Oct; ④), provides simple but perfectly adequate accommodation – advance reservations are advised.

Beyond Peggy's Cove Hwy 333 sticks closely to the coastline, meandering through a magnificently desolate landscape of stunted firs and cumbersome seashore boulders. Pull in at any of several places for a stroll along the shore or press on north through the gentler scenery that leads back to Hwy 103.

Chester

It's a thirty-minute drive north from Peggy's Cove to Hwy 103 and a further 40km west to **CHESTER**, a handsome and prosperous-looking town tumbling over a chubby little peninsula. Founded by New Englanders in 1759, the town, with its fine old trees and elegant frame houses, has long been the favoured resort of yachting enthusiasts, whose principal shindig is the **Chester Race Week** regatta held in mid-August. Chester is also home to the first-rate **Chester Playhouse**, right in the centre on Pleasant Street which offers a lively programme of concerts and plays from mid-March to December (Ⓣ902/275-3933 or 1-800/363-7529, Ⓦwww.chesterplayhouse.ns.ca), with a crescendo of activity in July and August during a festival of contemporary music and Canadian-oriented drama. Finally, a **passenger ferry** (Mon–Fri 4 daily, Sat & Sun 2 daily; 50min; $5 return) sallies out from Chester bound for the offshore islet of **Big Tancook** (as distinct from neighbouring Little Tancook), whose quiet country roads and benign scenery are popular with walkers, who pop across for a day's ramble. There's somewhere to eat here too – *Carolyn's Café & Crafts* (Ⓣ902/228-2749, Ⓦwww.tancookislandrestaurantandcrafts.ca; June–Oct), just opposite the jetty; the café sells island maps and its website carries both a map and the ferry schedule.

Chester **tourist office** (July & Aug Mon–Sat 9am–7pm, Sun 10am–5pm; June, Sept & Oct Mon–Sat 10am–5pm, Sun noon–5pm; Ⓣ902/275-4616, Ⓦwww.chesterns.com) is located in the old train station on the northern edge of town, beside Hwy 3. They issue free town maps, which are very useful as Chester's layout is a tad confusing, plus Tancook island ferry timetables. They will also arrange accommodation, though there's only one **B&B** in town, the affordable if really rather modest *Mecklenburgh Inn*, whose four guest rooms – three en suite – are in a good-looking Victorian house in the centre at 78 Queen St (Ⓣ902/275-4638, Ⓦwww.bbcanada.com/298.html; ④). For delicious **seafood** head for the *Rope Loft* (Ⓣ902/275-3430; May–Sept) down by the jetty, where main courses average around $15, half that for fish and chips.

Mahone Bay

In 1813, the wide waters of **Mahone Bay** witnessed the destruction of the splendidly named American privateer the *Young Teaser*, which had been hounded into the bay by a British frigate. On board was a British deserter who knew what to expect if he was captured, so he blew his own ship up instead – a tribute to the floggers of the Royal Navy. Legend has it that the ghost of the blazing vessel reappears each year - and this is not the only strange story attached to the area. In 1795, three boys discovered the top of an underground shaft on tiny **Oak Island**, a low-lying, offshore islet a few kilometres west of Chester. The shaft, or "Money Pit", soon attracted the attentions of treasure hunters, who were convinced that this was where a vast horde of booty had been interred. At first the betting was on Drake, Kidd or Morgan, but present favourites include the Templars and even the Rosicrucians. No treasure has ever been found, but the diggings became so dangerous that the island's owners have closed it to the public. If you go – the 1.3km turning is clearly signed on Hwy 3 – you can only get to the chain at the start of the causeway over to the island.

Beyond Oak Island, the **village of MAHONE BAY** spreads along the seashore just 25km west of Chester, its elongated waterfront dominated by three adjacent **church towers**, which combine to create one of the region's most famous vistas. There's not much else to the place, though you might drop by the **Settlers' Museum**, 578 Main St (June–Sept Tues–Sat 10am–5pm, Sun 1–5pm; free), to examine its hotchpotch of period furniture and early nineteenth-century ceramics. The village also possesses one of the best **delis-cum-cafés** hereabouts, *Jo-Ann's Deli & Bakeshop*, beside the main crossroads and selling a

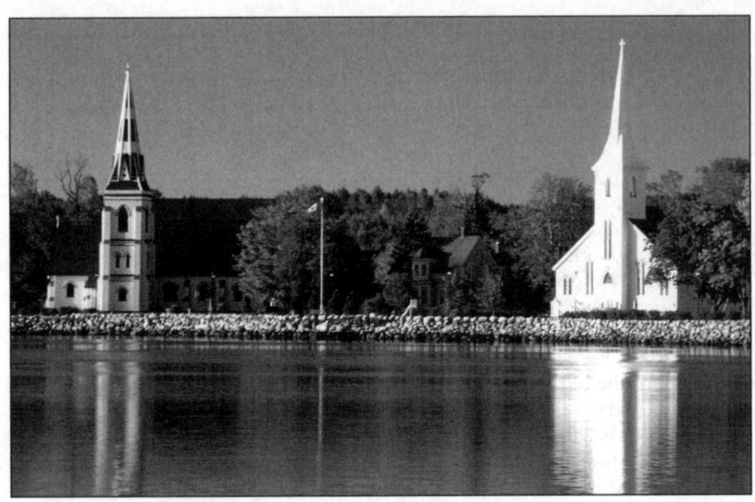

△ Church at Mahone Bay

superb selection of filled rolls and baguettes. Another good option is the *Mimi's Ocean Grill Restaurant*, a five- to ten-minute walk south from the crossroads at 662 Main St ⓣ902/624-1342), where they serve up delicious lunches in attractive waterfront surroundings. If you decide to **stay the night**, the well-tended *Heart's Desire B&B*, at 686 Main St (ⓣ902/624-8470, ⓦwww.heartsdesirebb.com; ❸), occupies an attractive older building with pleasant views out across the bay.

Lunenburg

Comely **LUNENBURG**, 10km south of Mahone Bay village, perches on a narrow, bumpy peninsula, its central gridiron of streets clambering up from the main harbourfront flanked by brightly painted wooden houses. Dating from the late nineteenth century, the most flamboyant of these mansions display an arresting variety of architectural features varying from Gothic towers and classical pillars to elegant verandas, high gables and peaked windows, all embellished with intricate scrollwork. Amidst the virtuousity, a distinctive municipal style is noticeable in the so-called "Lunenburg Bump", where triple-bell cast roofs surmount overhanging window dormers – giving the town a vaguely European appearance, which is appropriate considering its original settlement. Lunenburg was founded in 1753 by German and Swiss Protestants, who of necessity soon learned to mix the farming of their homeland with fishing and shipbuilding. They created a prosperous community with its own fleet of trawlers and scallop-draggers, although nowadays the town earns as much from the tourist industry as from fishing.

Arrival, information and accommodation

Double check, but Trius **buses** from Halifax and Yarmouth should pull in at the Bluenose Mini-Mart, a five- to ten-minute walk from the main harbourfront at 35 Lincoln St. The town's **visitor centre** (daily: May–Sept 9am–8pm, Oct 9am–6pm; ⓣ902/634-8100, ⓦwww.explorelunenburg.ca) occupies an imitation blockhouse high up on Blockhouse Hill Road, a stiff 700m walk up

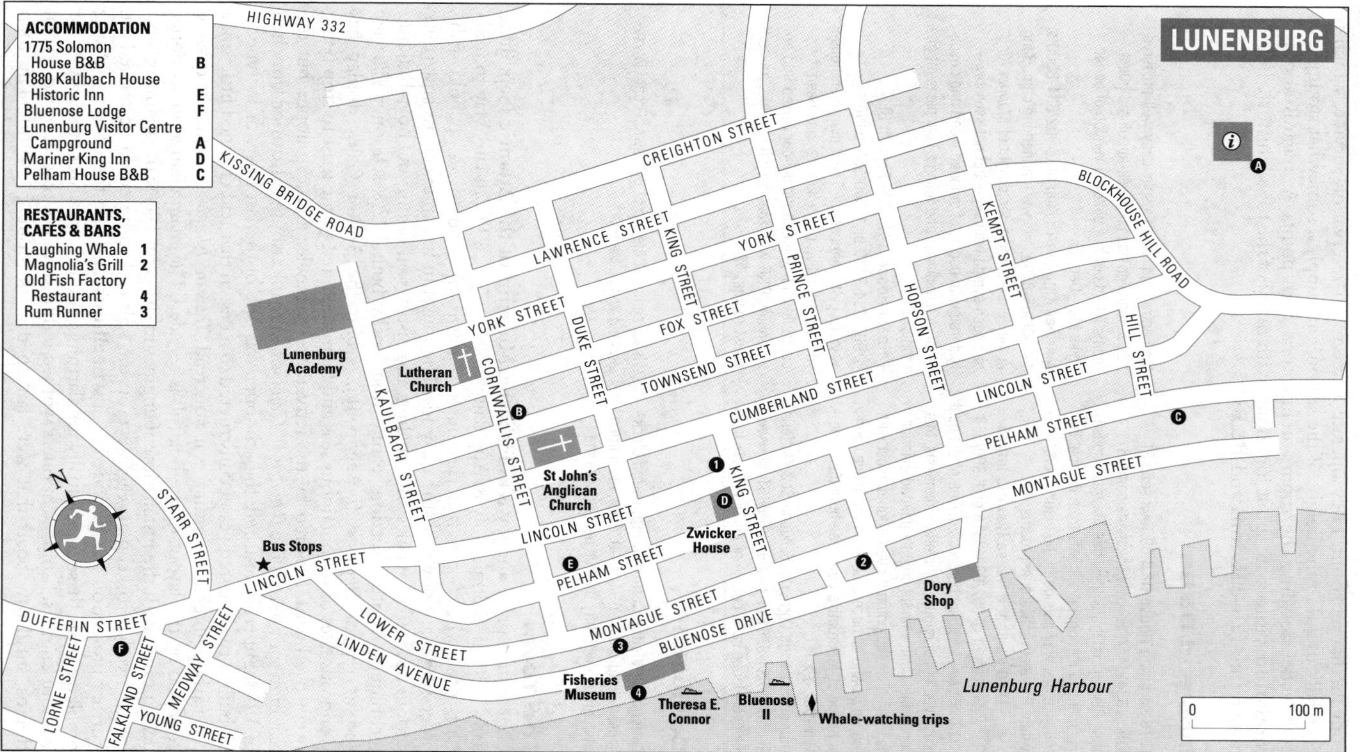
LUNENBURG
ACCOMMODATION
1775 Solomon House B&B B
1880 Kaulbach House Historic Inn E
Bluenose Lodge F
Lunenburg Visitor Centre Campground A
Mariner King Inn D
Pelham House B&B C
RESTAURANTS, CAFÉS & BARS
Laughing Whale 1
Magnolia's Grill 2
Old Fish Factory Restaurant 4
Rum Runner 3
HIGHWAY 332
KISSING BRIDGE ROAD
CREIGHTON STREET
BLOCKHOUSE HILL ROAD
LAWRENCE STREET
YORK STREET
KING STREET
PRINCE STREET
HOPSON STREET
KEMPT STREET
HILL STREET
DUKE STREET
FOX STREET
TOWNSEND STREET
CUMBERLAND STREET
LINCOLN STREET
PELHAM STREET
MONTAGUE STREET
CORNWALLIS STREET
KAULBACH STREET
Lunenburg Academy
Lutheran Church
St John's Anglican Church
Zwicker House
Dory Shop
Bus Stops
STARR STREET
LOWER STREET
LINDEN AVENUE
BLUENOSE DRIVE
DUFFERIN STREET
LORNE STREET
FALKLAND STREET
MEDWAY STREET
YOUNG STREET
Fisheries Museum
Theresa E. Connor
Bluenose II
Whale-watching trips
Lunenburg Harbour
0
100 m
N

5 THE MARITIME PROVINCES

from the harbourfront. They operate a free room-reservation service, which is especially useful in the height of the season, and supply a somewhat stodgy (but free) leaflet detailing the town's architectural high points. As regards **accommodation**, visitors are spoilt for choice with many of the town's historic houses turned into first-class **inns** and **B&Bs**.

Inns and B&Bs

1775 Solomon House B&B 69 Townsend St ⓣ902/634-3477, ⓦwww.bbcanada.com/5511.html. Clad in cedar shingles, this Georgian house has many of its original features from its double entrance stairway outside to the plank floors within. Three attractive guest rooms. ❹

1880 Kaulbach House Historic Inn 75 Pelham St ⓣ902/634-8818 or 1-800/568-8818, ⓦwww.kaulbachhouse.com. One of the best preserved of Lunenburg's Victorian mansions, this comfortable inn, with its brightly painted exterior, has seven well-appointed guest rooms, most with sea views and all decorated in an attractive version of period style. Creative European breakfasts too. May–Dec. ❺

Bluenose Lodge Corner of Falkland St & Dufferin St ⓣ902/634-8851 or 1-800/565-8851, ⓦwww.bluenoselodge.ca. A couple of minutes' walk from the central gridiron, this splendidly well-preserved 1860s mansion has nine well-appointed guest rooms kitted out in a pleasing version of period style. May–Dec. ❻

Mariner King Inn 15 King St ⓣ902/634-8509 or 1-800/565-8509, ⓦwww.marinerking.com. Bang in the centre of town, the delightful *Mariner King* has been sympathetically – but not slavishly – restored with oodles of stripped wood and crisply modern furnishings and fittings. Five pleasant guest rooms. ❺

Pelham House B&B 224 Pelham St ⓣ902/634-7113 or 1-800/508-0446, ⓦwww.pelhamhouse.ca. This Edwardian house, with its attractive bay windows, has been carefully and sympathetically converted into an amenable B&B with four broadly period, en-suite guest rooms. ❹

Campsite

Lunenburg Visitor Centre Campground Blockhouse Hill Rd ⓣ902/634-8100. Plain, unadorned campground with fifty pitches next door to the visitor centre at the top of the town. Great views – and big winds. May–Oct.

The Town

Lunenburg's pride and joy is its **Fisheries Museum of the Atlantic** (Sept–June daily 9.30am–5.30pm; July & Aug daily 9.30am–7pm; $9 from late May to mid-Oct, otherwise $4; ⓦfisheries.museum.gov.ns.ca), housed in an old fish-processing plant down by the quayside. The museum has an excellent aquarium, a room devoted to whales and whaling, and displays on fishing and boat-building techniques. Another section features the locally built 1920s schooner *Bluenose* and its replica *Bluenose II* (see p.406), whilst the August Gales display has wondrous tales of mountainous seas and helmsmen tied to the mast to stop being swept overboard. Moored by the jetty, there's a trawler and a scalloper, but the real high spot here is the *Theresa E. Connor*, a saltbank fishing **schooner** launched in 1938. Superbly restored, the schooner was one of the last boats of its type to be built, a two-masted vessel constructed to a design that had changed little since the early eighteenth century – if you read *Treasure Island* as a child and were confused by the layout of the boat, all is revealed. The main change in schooner design came with the installation of engines in the early 1900s: the helmsman no longer needed to keep an eagle-eye on the sails and so he could be moved aft. Further protection was provided by a **wheelhouse**, though there were teething problems with these and initially an alarming number were lost at sea. With or without engines, fishing schooners worked in the same way: each carried several **dories**, small row boats that were launched at the fishing grounds. The men rowed the dories away from the schooner, fanning out to trail long hand-lines with baited hooks over the ocean – line-fishing. At the end of the day, the catch would be brought back to the schooner. Dory fishing was a dangerous business – the transfer of the catch was especially risky and there was always the chance of being caught in the dory by a sudden squall. Not surprisingly, therefore, local fishermen didn't need much persuading to abandon their schooners and dories for the larger **trawlers** that replaced them in the 1950s. The *Theresa E. Connor* soldiered on, but her last voyage was an ignominious failure: in 1963 she sailed out of Lunenburg bound for Newfoundland to raise the rest of her 25-man crew. No one turned up and the schooner had to return home empty-handed.

There's more of maritime interest down along the harbourfront at the **Dory Shop**, where they make wooden boats in traditional style and hire out sail and row boats. If you haven't the confidence/experience to sail out on your own, regular boat trips leave the jetty near the museum throughout the summer. There are also two- to three-hour **whale-watching** trips operated four times daily from May to October by Lunenburg Whale Watching Tours (Ⓣ902/527-7175, Ⓦwww.whalewatchingnovascotia.com; $45).

The rest of the centre

Take King Street from the harbourfront and it's a couple of blocks to one of the finest of Lunenburg's mansions, the **Zwicker House** – now the Mariner Inn (see opposite) – at no.15. The house was built in the 1820s, but its exterior, including a fine illustration of the Lunenburg bump, was added later, probably in the 1870s. From here, it's a couple of minutes walk to the **Kaulbach Inn**, at 75 Pelham St (also see opposite), which has changed little since its construction for one of the town's premier families in the 1880s. At heart, the house is a simple clapboard frame, but perky dormer windows have been tacked on as has the triple-bell cast roof of the "bump".

From the inn, it's another short stroll to Lunenburg's fanciest building, **St John's Anglican Church**, whose original oak frame was imported lock, stock and barrel from Boston in 1754. This first church was plain and simple and by the early nineteenth century this just didn't match the expectations of the town's increasingly prosperous burghers, so they had it remodelled, once in the 1840s and again fifty years later. The end result is a superb illustration of decorative Gothic, its frilly wooden scrollwork punctuated by slender pinnacles that poke up from every one of its façades, though the church did suffer substantial fire damage in 2001. All this Anglican brouhaha stimulated the Lutherans, who, in 1890, erected a **Lutheran Church** in grand Victorian Gothic style, from its pointed windows through to its soaring spire, nearby at Cornwallis and Fox Street Round the corner from the Lutheran church, on Gallows Hill at the far end of Kaulback Street, is **Lunenburg Academy**, a whopping maroon, black and white timber school building of 1895. Three storeys high, with towers and a mansard roof, the construction costs were enormous, partly because the interior was finished in ash and birch – a clear indication of the importance the townsfolk attached to education. From the academy, it takes about five minutes to walk back to the harbourfront.

Eating and drinking

Lunenburg has a goodly supply of restaurants and cafés, though standards do vary considerably, partly because of the number of summer day-trippers. While you're here, look out for two local culinary delights, the **Lunenburg sausage**, traditionally served at breakfast, which is made of lean pork and beef, flavoured with coriander and allspice, and the **Solomon Gundy**, marinated herring with sour cream or occasionally mustard.

Easily the best **café** in town is the *Laughing Whale*, at the corner of King and Lincoln, a large, modern place with contemporary paintings and offering tasty snacks and zippy coffees. For **restaurants**, the prime spot has long been considered the *Old Fish Factory Restaurant* (Ⓣ902/634-3333; May–Oct), on the waterfront next to the Fisheries Museum, but although it still serves a splendid range of seafood, it's become a tad canteen-like. Instead, you're much better off heading for the moderately priced *Magnolia's Grill*, just off the waterfront at 128 Montague St (Ⓣ902/634-3287; closed Sun). This cosy little place, with its diner-like booths, has a wide and inventive menu, featuring everything from burgers through to lobster, mussels and fish cakes. A good reserve choice is the *Rum Runner* (Ⓣ902/634-9200), opposite the Fisheries Museum: the modern decor is a bit tacky, but the food is well prepared and served, fish being its forte; main courses here average $20.

Liverpool

Like its British namesake, **LIVERPOOL**, 150km from Halifax along Hwy 103 and 70km from Lunenburg, skirts the mouth of a Mersey River and has a strong seafaring tradition, but there the similarities end. Nova Scotia's Liverpool was founded in 1759 by Cape Cod emigrants, who established a fearsome reputation for privateering during both the American Revolution and the War of 1812. Their most famous ship, the *Liverpool Packet,* claimed no less than a hundred American prizes and, to rub salt into the wound, these piratical endeavours were cheekily celebrated in a local broadsheet as upholding "the best tradition of the British Navy". Nowadays, Liverpool is a minor fish-processing and paper-making town, a desultory sort of settlement only cheered by the fine old houses grouped around the eastern end of **Main Street**. One of these, the **Perkins House** (June to mid-Oct Mon–Sat 9.30am–5.30pm, Sun 1–5.30pm; $2), has been restored to its late eighteenth-century condition, when it was the home of Simeon Perkins, who moved here from New England in 1762. A local bigwig, Perkins was a shipowner, a merchant, a colonel in the militia and a justice of the court, but he still had time to keep a detailed diary from 1766 until his death in 1812. The diaries provide an insight into the life and times of colonial Nova Scotia and they show Perkins as a remarkably unflappable man: in 1780 Liverpool was attacked by Americans, who Perkins outwitted and drove off, describing the dangerous emergency as just a "dubious and difficult affair". Copies of the four-volume diary are on display at the house, whilst the adjacent **Queens County Museum** (June to mid-Oct Mon–Sat 9.30am–5.30pm, Sun 1–5.30pm; mid-Oct to May Mon–Sat 9am–noon & 1–5pm; $2 June to mid-Oct, otherwise free) sometimes sells excerpts for a couple of bucks – and also possesses a diverting collection of early local photographs.

Liverpool has one recommendable **place to stay**, *Lane's Privateer Inn*, just across the bridge from the centre of town at 27 Bristol Ave (Ⓣ902/354-3456 or 1-800/794-3332, Ⓦwww.lanesprivateerinn.com; ④). The inn occupies a spick and span, two-storey, motel-like structure built in the general style of an old timber house and the guest rooms, of which there are twenty-seven, are in the annexe. The inn is also the **place to eat**, either in the restaurant, where well-prepared steak and seafood dishes average $17, or in the adjoining café, which serves a good line in coffees, teas and gourmet treats, including hand-made Belgian chocolates.

Inland to Kejimkujik National Park

There's no better way to experience the solitude and scenery of the southwest Nova Scotian hinterland than to head northwest 70km from Liverpool along Hwy 8 to Maitland Bridge and the entrance to the **Kejimkujik National Park**. This magnificent tract of rolling wilderness has a rich variety of forest habitats – both hardwood and softwood – interrupted by rivers and brooks linking about a dozen lakes. In the spring and autumn the park is alive with wild flowers, whose brilliant colours provide cover for an abundance of porcupines, black bears, white-tailed deer and beavers, as well as three sorts of turtle: the Painted and Snapping turtle and, rarest of all, the Blanding's turtle, a green and yellow amphibian that grows to around 25cm. The best time to visit is in the early spring and autumn, when the insects aren't too troublesome: the blackfly peak between mid-May and late June. A park **entrance fee** of $5.45 per adult per day is levied from mid-May to mid-October.

Hiking trails crisscross Kejimkujik, but the easiest way to explore the park and its flat-water rivers and lakes is by **canoe**. These can be rented from **Jakes Landing** (Ⓣ902/682-5253; reservations recommended), roughly 10km by road from the entrance to the park. A couple of clearly defined, day-long **canoe trips** begin here, namely the delightful paddle amongst the islets of Kejimkujik Lake and an excursion up the Mersey River beneath a canopy of red maples. For overnight trips, the park has around fifty primitive **campsites** ($21) dotted along its canoe routes and hiking trails – and these are a better bet than the large year-round campsite at **Jeremys Bay** ($23; reservations Ⓣ1-877/737-3783, Ⓦwww.pccamping.ca), also 10km by road from the main entrance. For backcountry camping, you must register at the **information centre** (mid-June to Aug daily 8.30am–9pm; Sept to mid-June Mon–Fri 8.30am–4.30pm; Ⓣ902/682-2772, Ⓦwww.pc.gc.ca), near the park entrance, where you can also pick up detailed maps and trail advice.

If camping out isn't your thing, the nearest **beds** are at the *Whitman Inn* (Ⓣ902/682-2226 or 1-800/830-3855, Ⓦwww.whitmaninn.com; ❹), which occupies a two-storey, white and yellow former farmhouse dating back to the 1910s. The inn is set in its own grounds 2km south of the park entrance on Hwy 8 and has eight guest rooms. The nearest town to Kejimkujik is Annapolis Royal (see p.424), 50km to the north.

Kejimkujik's Seaside Adjunct

Back on Hwy 103, heading southwest from Liverpool, it's about 25km to tiny **Port Joli**, from where a bumpy, 6.5km-long gravel road leads to **St Catherines River** and the more accessible, western side of **Kejimkujik National Park Seaside Adjunct**, a parcel of pristine coastline that provides an ideal half-day or day's hike. The Adjunct straddles the end of a beautiful but inhospitable peninsula where the mixed forests and squelchy bogs of the interior back onto the tidal flats, lagoons, headlands and beaches of the coast. If you're lucky, you'll catch sight of the rare piping plover, which nests here between May and early August. From the parking lot, the **Harbour Rocks Trail** follows the route of an old cart track straight down to the seashore, a fairly straightforward if sometimes wet and squelchy 3km (40min) hike. At the coast, the main hiking trail then loops around the headline that comprises the southwest tip of the park, taking in Macleods Cove and Port Joli Head. Access to the Adjunct is free, but there are no facilities, so be sure to carry in food and water.

Lockeport

Well off the beaten track, 65km southwest of Liverpool via Hwy 103 and then Hwy 3, the sleepy fishing village of **LOCKEPORT** sits on a tiny island that's connected to the mainland by a 1.5-kilometre-long causeway, fringed by the white sands of **Crescent Beach**. The beach is never crowded, the sea is deep and clear, and the village features a row of five contrasting houses built by the prosperous Locke family over a forty-year period in the nineteenth century. It's a lovely, relaxing spot, where nothing much seems to happen except for the comings and goings of the odd fishing smack. It also boasts one first-rate **B&B**, *Seventeen South B&B*, 17 South St (Ⓣ902/656 2512 Ⓔshorebb@ns.sympatico.ca; ❸), a tastefully modernized Cape Cod-style house with two spacious guest rooms perched on a wooded knoll in sight of the seashore and not far from the harbour; it's open all year and the owners even throw in a canoe if you fancy a paddle. If it's full, the seasonal tourist office (Ⓣ902/656-3123), in the brash building at the end of the causeway, has details of a several beachside cottages. Lockeport has a good **restaurant** too, in the seasonal *Locke's Island Dining*, 18 North St (Ⓣ902/656-2294).

Shelburne

SHELBURNE, 35km northwest of Lockeport and 70km southwest of Liverpool on Hwy 103, took heart when it was chosen as the backdrop for the 1994 cinematic version of Nathaniel Hawthorne's classic *The Scarlet Letter*, but the film was such a dodo that it did the town no favours at all. Indeed, despite the well-kept shingle and clapboard houses that string down from **Water Street**, the main drag, to Dock Street and the waterfront, Shelburne manages a vaguely disconsolate air. It does, however, boast the third largest harbour in the world, after Halifax and Sydney – easily big enough, so the plan went, to accommodate the British fleet if Hitler managed to launch a successful invasion of Great Britain. The British would have been welcome: Shelburne has been intensely anglophile ever since thousands of Loyalists fled here in the 1780s – including two hundred free blacks, ancestors of the town's present black community.

Shelburne is home to the **Nova Scotia Museum Complex** (Ⓦwww.historicshelburne.com; combined ticket $8), centred on Dock St, which has four distinct elements. First up is the **Shelburne County Museum**, on Maiden Lane (June to mid-Oct daily 9.30am–5.30pm; mid-Oct to May Mon-Fri 10am-noon & 2–5pm; $3), which provides a broad overview of the town's history and its maritime heritage, whilst the adjacent **Ross-Thomson House** (June to mid-Oct daily 9.30am–5.30pm; $3) is a Loyalist merchant's store and home, pleasingly restored to its appearance circa 1800. The nearby **Dory Shop** (June to mid-Sept daily 9.30am–5.30pm; $3) comprises a waterfront boat factory/museum. The flat-bottomed **dory**, rarely more than 5m long and built to ride the heaviest of swells, was an integral part of the fishing fleet during the days of sail. Each schooner carried about six of them; manned by a crew of two, they were launched from the deck when the fishing began, fanning out to maximize the catch. The Dory Shop produces three a year, but only for private use for hand-fishing – the few dories used today in the offshore fishery are steel-hulled. Allow about an hour to visit the three sites, a little more if you throw in the **Muir-Cox Shipyard Interpretive Centre** (June–Sept daily 9.30am–5.30pm; $3), at the south end of Dock St. Finally, while you're here in Shelburne, you may as well take a peek at the handful of heavyweight shingle buildings left over from the film set – you'll find them just off Dock Street.

There's no special reason to stay in Shelburne, but the **tourist office** (summer daily 9am–7pm; ⓣ902/875-4547), at the north end of Dock Street, does operate a free room-reservation service. The most agreeable **hotel** in town is the *Cooper's Inn*, which occupies a lavishly refurbished old shingle house at 36 Dock St (ⓣ902/875-4656 or 1-800/688-2011, ⓦwww.thecoopersinn.com; ❺; April–Oct). Wooded, lakeside **camping** is available 5km west round the bay at the *Islands Provincial Park* (ⓣ902/875-4304; mid-May to Aug). As regards **food**, the *Charlotte Lane Café*, down an alley – Charlotte Lane – off Water Street (mid-May to late Dec Tues–Sat 11.30am–2.30pm & 5–8pm), serves wholesome meals and smashing salads; and there's first-rate cuisine at the *Cooper's Inn* restaurant – try the steaks ($19 and up).

Barrington

There's not much to delay you on the 100-kilometre journey west from Shelburne to Yarmouth, but you should make a brief stop at minuscule **BARRINGTON**, where the **Old Meeting House** (June–Sept Mon–Sat 10am–6pm, Sun 1–6pm; $3), with its simple wooden pews and severe pulpit, reflects the intellectual rigour of the Nonconformist settlers who migrated here from New England in the mid-eighteenth century. In its simplicity, it's a beautiful building, which is more than can be said for the adjacent **Lighthouse Museum** (same hours; free), where a smattering of lightkeepers' memorabilia is housed in a replica of the lighthouse that once stood on remote Seal Island – though this version stands on a hillside apropos of nothing in particular.

Yarmouth

Arriving by ferry from Maine, many American visitors get their first taste of Canada in **YARMOUTH** – and they can be excused for feeling distinctly underwhelmed. To all intents and purposes, Yarmouth is a mundanely modern place, though gallant efforts have been made to freshen up the waterfront and the town's deep, tidal bay provides a modicum of scenic interest. It's also a good place for tourist information with the **Nova Scotia Visitor Centre**, just uphill from the ferry terminal (daily: July & Aug 8am–7pm; late May to June & Sept to late Oct 9am–5pm; ⓣ902/742-5033), issuing bucketloads of free leaflets and brochures. There's also a comfortable **B&B** right opposite the visitors' centre, the *Murray Manor*, in an attractive Regency-style house at 225 Main St (ⓣ902/742-9625 or 1-877/742-9629, ⓦwww.murraymanor.com; ❹), where travelers can break their journey in one of three pleasant bedrooms. Alternatively, the rather more humdrum *Midtown Motel*, 13 Parade St (ⓣ902/742-5333 or 1-877/742-5600; ❸), which offers simple but adequate rooms a ten-minute walk north along Main Street from the ferry terminal.

Ferries between Yarmouth and Maine

From Yarmouth, **Bay Ferries** (ⓣ1-877/359-3760, ⓦwww.catferry.com) operates high-speed, car-carrying **catamarans** to both Bar Harbor, Maine (late May to mid-Oct 1–2 daily on 4 days a week; 3hr; passengers one-way $60–75, vehicles one-way $110–140); and Portland, Maine (late May to mid-Oct 3 weekly; 6hr; passengers $95–105, cars $150–175). Special deals and discounts on return fares and midweek sailings are commonplace.

The French Shore

North from Yarmouth, **Highway 101** and the much slower **Highway 1** slip across the flat littoral of the 100-kilometre **French Shore**, whose straggling villages house the largest concentration of Acadians in the province (see p.428 for more on the Acadians). Their gold-starred, red, white and blue flags are everywhere, but there's nothing worth stopping for – **METEGHAN**, the main town, is noticeably ugly – until you reach **POINTE DE L'EGLISE** (Church Point). Here, right next to the sea, is the massive church of **St Mary's**, whose stolid tower and steeple, finished in 1905, reach a giddy 56m. Unfortunately, the fastidiously clean interior holds some of the worst religious paintings imaginable, nineteenth-century dross with none of the medievalism suggested by the reliquaries beside the altar, amongst which are wooden shards purportedly from the Holy Cross. Some 10km further north is the church of **St Bernard**, a cumbersome granite pile that took 32 years to complete (1910–42) – and is, if nothing else, certainly a tribute to the profound Catholicism of the local Acadians.

Digby and Digby Neck

It's around 30km from St Bernard to the fishing port of **DIGBY**, whose workaday centre spreads over a hilly headland that pokes out into the Annapolis Basin. The latter is connected to the Bay of Fundy by a narrow channel known as the **Digby Gut**, thereby subjecting Digby **harbour** to the swirling effects of the Fundy tides – and it's the pocket-sized harbour, with its rickety wooden piers, which is the most appealing part of town. Otherwise, Digby is notable for two things: its **smoked herrings** or "Digby chicks" – chewy, dark and salty delicacies on sale beside the north end of the harbour at the Royal Fundy Seafood Market; and its delicious, world-beating **scallops**, which you can sample at the popular *Fundy Restaurant*, 34 Water St (ⓣ902/245-4950), the pick of several restaurants lining the harbourfront's Water Street and its continuation, Montague Row.

Acadian Lines **buses** to Digby stop at 77 Montague Row, from where it's a couple of minutes walk north along the waterfront to the **tourist office** (ⓣ902/245-5714), which operates a room-reservation service and gives information on Digby Neck whale-watching trips. Digby has several pleasant **places to stay**, beginning with the agreeable *Thistle Down Inn*, in an old two-storey house with a motel-style annexe at 98 Montague Row (ⓣ902/245-4490 or 1-800/565-8081, ⓦwww.thistledown.ns.ca/theinn; ④; May–Oct). There's also the *Bayside Inn*, 115 Montague Row (ⓣ902/245-2247 or 1-888/754-0555, ⓦwww.baysideinn.ca; ③), which occupies an old timber house, has eleven rooms – seven en suite – and is equipped with an airy patio.

Digby's **ferry port** is located 5km north of town; from here Bay Ferries (ⓣ1-888/249-7245, ⓦwww.bayferries.com) runs regular **car ferries** (1–3 daily; 3hr; passengers $25–39 one-way, cars $75–95, bicycles $10–12) across the Bay of Fundy to Saint John in New Brunswick (see p.442), thereby saving a long drive.

Digby Neck

Heading west from Digby, the 70km-long **Digby Neck** comprises a narrow finger of land that gingerly nudges out into the Bay of Fundy, sheltering the French Shore from the full effects of the ocean. The Neck's further reaches are broken into two little islands – **Long Island** and, at the tip, **Brier Island** – and a pair of **car ferries** shuttle across the narrow channels between them, running every hour, 24 hours a day and charging $4 each for the return trip. Ferry times are coordinated, so it takes about two hours to reach Brier Island from Digby - and ferry timetables are available at Digby tourist office. For the most part, the road along the Neck travels inland and is fairly monotonous, but then most people only venture down here to join a **whale-watching trip** (see box below).

From either Digby or (even better) Annapolis Royal (see p.424), it's easy enough to complete both the drive along the Neck and the whale-watching cruise in a day, but if you do decide to stay the night, there are two good options. The first, on the main part of the Neck, before you reach the first of the two ferries, is the *Olde Village Inn* (Ⓣ902/834-2202 or 1-800/834-2206, Ⓦwww.oldevillageinn.com; ❹; May to mid-Oct), a cosy nineteenth-century inn set among the densely wooded coastal hills of **SANDY COVE**, a picturesque little place of old white-painted houses about 30km from Digby; the inn has six rooms in the old building and seven more in the annexe. The second is the appealing *Seacliff B&B* (Ⓣ902/839-2241 or 1-866/722-2445, Ⓦwww.bbcanada.com/seacliffbb; ❸; mid-June to mid-Sept), in a pretty Victorian house overlooking the harbour and with two guestrooms – and shared bath – in **TIVERTON**, a quiet sprawl of wooden houses dotted round a forested bay at the north end of the first of the Neck's two islands, Long Island.

The Annapolis Valley

The **Annapolis Valley**, stretching 110km northeast from Annapolis Royal to Wolfville, is sheltered from the winds and fog that afflict much of the central part of the province by a narrow band of coastal hills. This factor, combined with the fertility of the soil, makes the valley and the coast as far as Windsor – another 25km to the east – ideal for **fruit growing**. As a consequence, the brief weeks of apple-blossom time, from late May to early June, are the subject of much sentimental and commercial exploitation – as well as the communal

Digby Neck whale watching

The nutrient-rich waters of the **Bay of Fundy** attract dozens of whales and several local companies organize daily **whale-watching excursions** from late May to mid-Oct or thereabouts. They are heavily subscribed, so advance reservations are highly recommended; if the weather is poor, check to see if a sailing has been cancelled before you set out. Trips usually last between two and three hours and cost in the region of $50, though those from Westport tend to last longer - between three and five hours. To state the obvious, no one can guarantee you'll spy a whale, but there's every chance, beginning with finback and minkes in late spring, and humpbacks from mid- to late June. By the middle of July all three species are sighted and usually hang around the Bay of Fundy till late summer and autumn, which is when the rare North Atlantic right whale is seen too - see p.1099 for more.

Amongst several Digby Neck whale-watching companies, one of the most proficient is **Ocean Explorations Whale Cruises** (Ⓣ902/839-2417 or 1-877/654-2341, Ⓦwww.oceanexplorations.ca), which uses zodiac boats and is based in tiny Tiverton on Long Island. Further along the Neck, based in the forlorn little fishing village of Westport, on Brier Island, are **Brier Island Whale & Seabird Cruises** (Ⓣ902/839-2995 or 1-800/656-3660, Ⓦwww.brierislandwhalewatch.com) and **Mariner Cruises** (Ⓣ902/839-2346 or 1-800/239-2189, Ⓦwww.novascotiawhalewatching.ca).

knees-up of the **Apple Blossom Festival** (ⓦwww.appleblossom.com). The string of little towns that dot the valley were settled by Loyalists from New England after the expulsion of the Acadians, but although several of them are pretty places where old wooden houses are sheltered by mature trees only two stand out. These are delightful **Annapolis Royal**, with its handsome Victorian mansions and proximity to the historic site of **Port Royal**, and **Wolfville**, an amiable university town of some charm. Wolfville is also within easy striking distance of **Grand Pré National Historic Site** and the harsh scenery of **capes Blomidon** and **Split**. Further east, **Windsor** is no great shakes, but it is the site of the Haliburton House Museum, the former home of the nineteenth-century humorist Thomas Haliburton.

Annapolis Royal and Wolfville – but not Windsor – are both reachable on the once daily Acadian Lines **bus** (ⓣ1-800/567-5151, ⓦwww.acadianbus.com) service between Halifax and Digby, though currently this doesn't leave until 6.45pm, reaching Digby at 11pm.

Annapolis Royal

With a population of just six hundred, the township of **ANNAPOLIS ROYAL**, 40km northeast of Digby and 120km northwest of Liverpool, spreads across a podgy promontory that lies tucked in between the Annapolis River and its tributary, the Allain River. The long main drag, **St George Street**, part of Hwy 8, sweeps through the leafy southern outskirts to reach the end of the promontory, where it turns right to run parallel to the waterfront through the commercial heart of town. Here, restaurants and shops have replaced the merchants and shipwrights of yesteryear and there's a tourist-oriented boardwalk near the jetty, but it's all very low-key and the town maintains a relaxed and retiring air that's hard to resist.

Edging St George Street just before it swings right are the substantial remains of **Fort Anne** (open access), whose grass-covered ramparts surround the old parade ground. A few military remains are encased within the ramparts – namely a couple of powder magazines and a sally port – but the most significant survivor is the old **officers' quarters** right in the middle. The British built these quarters during the Napoleonic Wars and, surmounted by three outsize chimney stacks, they now house a small **museum** (mid-May to mid-Oct daily 9am–5.30pm; $3.95) comprising a ragbag of military memorabilia, a reconstruction of an Acadian domestic interior and an outline of the fort's development. There's also a copy of the original charter by which James I incorporated "Nova Scotia" in 1621, and a cheerful community tapestry tracing the town's history. Back outside, the **view** downriver is simply delightful and it's a lovely peaceful spot too, but it wasn't always so. Both colonial powers, France and England, neglected the fort and its garrison, and when a new military governor arrived here in 1708 he told his superiors back in Paris that his officers were "more in need of a madhouse than a barracks". If you want more of the flavour of early Annapolis Royal, ask at the museum (or your B&B) for details of the candlelight tours of the **old graveyard** (June to mid-Oct 4 weekly; 1hr) next to the fort – good fun, and a snip at $7.

Five-minutes' walk from the fort – back along St George Street – lie the ten-acre **Annapolis Royal Historic Gardens** (daily: mid-May to June & Sept to mid-Oct 9am–5pm; July & Aug 8am–dusk; ⓦwww.historicgardens.com; $9). These feature a string of enjoyable "theme gardens", from the formality of a Victorian garden to an extensive rose collection in which the different varieties are arranged broadly in chronological order. The whole site slopes gently down towards the Allain River, with a dyke-walk offering views of mud flats and salt marshes and also twisting through elephant grass, a reed imported by the Acadians to thatch their cottages.

Practicalities

In each direction, one **bus** a day on the Acadian Lines route between Halifax and Digby stops at the Annapolis Royal Inn on Hwy 1, an inconvenient 1.3km west of St George Street and the town centre. The **tourist office** is on the other side of town, inside the generating station on the Hwy 1 bridge, about 1.4km north of the centre (daily: July & Aug 8am–8pm; mid-May to June & Sept to mid-Oct 10am–5pm; ⓣ902/532-5454). They can arrange **accommodation** – and the town's best options are its B&Bs, several of which occupy immaculately maintained heritage properties. One such is the *Hillsdale House Inn*, 519 St George St (ⓣ902/532-2345 or 1-877/839-2821, ⓦwww.hillsdalehouse.ns.ca; ❺), and a second is the *Queen Anne Inn*, opposite at no. 494 (ⓣ902/532-7850 or 1-877/536-0403, ⓦwww.queenanneinn.ns.ca; ❻; May–Nov): the former occupies an elegant villa of 1849, the latter a grand turreted and towered extravagance of the 1860s. All the rooms at both inns are en suite and kitted out in attractive period style – as they are at the well-tended *Bread and Roses Inn*, a spiky late Victorian mansion at 82 Victoria St (ⓣ902/532-5727 or 1-888/899-0551, ⓦwww.breadandroses.ns.ca; ❻; April–Nov). Finally, the well-equipped *Dunromin* **campsite** (ⓣ902/532-2808, ⓦwww.dunromincampsite.com; May to mid-Oct), 1km beyond the tourist office on the far side of the Annapolis River, occupies a wooded, riverside location.

There are several **cafés** along the town's waterfront, including *Leo's Café*, 222 St George St (June–Sept Mon–Sat 9am-8pm & Sun noon–5pm, otherwise Mon–Sat 9am–4.30pm), which serves up first-rate snacks and lighter meals, while the inexpensive *Fort Anne Café*, opposite the entrance to the fort, sells tasty and substantial meals from a traditional Canadian menu – don't be put off by the downbeat decor. *Ye Olde Towne Pub* at 9 Church St – just down the street from Leo's and across from the boatyard – serves good draught **beer**. The King's Theatre, 209 St George St (ⓣ902/532-7704, ⓦwww.kingsthetre.ca), showcases everything from films and drama through to folk music, storytellers, comedians and mime artists.

Port Royal

Port Royal National Historic Site (mid-May to mid-Oct daily 9am–5.30pm; $3.95), on the north side of the Annapolis River 12km west of Annapolis Royal, was where Samuel de Champlain and Pierre Sieur de Monts first set up camp in 1605 after their dreadful winter on the island of Saint-Croix in Passamaquoddy Bay. Scared of English attack, the scurvy-ridden party hastily constructed an *habitation* similar in design to the fortified farms of France, where a square of rough-hewn, black-painted timber buildings presented a stern, partly stockaded face to any enemy. The stronghold dominated the estuary from a low bluff, as does today's **replica**, a painstaking reconstruction relying solely on the building techniques of the early seventeenth century. The *habitation* was captured by roving Virginians in 1613 and passed over to the British, who, led by Sir William Alexander, settled the district in 1629. This venture was enthusiastically supported by King James I, who wished to found a New Scotland – "Nova Scotia" in the Latin of the deeds – near Port Royal, but after three years of hardship and starvation, the Scots settlers were forced to withdraw, like their French predecessors.

For both French and Scot settlers alike, the problem of survival was compounded by acute boredom during the months of winter isolation. To pass the time Champlain constituted the **Order of Good Cheer**, whose "entertainment's programme" starred the poet Marc Lescarbot – though the role hardly filled him with colonial zeal, to judge from a poem he wrote for a gang of departing buddies:

We among the savages are lost
And dwell bewildered on this clammy coast
Deprived of due content and pleasures bright
Which you at once enjoy when France you sight.

Note that there are **no buses** from Annapolis Royal to the site.

Wolfville and around

The orderly and well-heeled university town of **WOLFVILLE**, 110km northeast from Annapolis Royal, was originally called Mud Creek until the daughter of a local dignitary, a certain Justice DeWolf, expressed her embarrassment at the hick-sounding name. He modestly had the place renamed after himself, but the mud flats surrounding the tiny harbour, which now abuts a parklet located just off Main Street on Harbourside Drive, remain the town's most distinctive feature. They are the creation of the Fundy tides, which rush up the Cornwallis River from the Minas Basin to dump the silt that is home to hundreds of herons and waders, with thousands of sandpipers arriving in early August on their annual migration from Arctic breeding grounds. If you're prepared to ignore the keep away signs, you can walk west from the harbour out along the causeway that encircles a portion of the wetland with pleasing views of Acadia University, whose three thousand students double the resident population, on the way. Wolfville's other curiosity is the Robie Tufts Nature Centre, down Elm Avenue from Main Street, which is best visited an hour before sunset on a summer's evening – usually from the second or third week in May till late August – to see the chimney swifts. These brown-grey birds give an amazing performance. After a long day hunting for insects, an enormous flock of them fly in ever-decreasing circles above the centre, which is no more than a wooden shelter built around an old chimney, before suddenly swooping en masse into the chimney to roost for the night.

Practicalities

Wolfville is on the Acadian Lines **bus** route connecting Halifax and Digby, but buses pull in on Highland Avenue, on the west side of town on the edge of the Acadia University campus, a good ten-minute walk from the tiny town centre - which consists of a few blocks of Main Street and several subsidiary side streets. The **tourist office** is located on the east side of the town centre, just off Main Street in Willow Park on Willow Avenue (daily: July & Aug 9am–7pm; May–June & Sept–Oct 9am–5pm; ⓣ902/542-7000, ⓦwww.wolfville.info). They have information on the whole of the Annapolis Valley as well as local accommodation lists and – a necessary preparation – details of the hike along Cape Split (see opposite).

The town has several splendid **inns and B&Bs**, the cream of the crop in attractively renovated old mansions. Tempting choices start with the *Blomidon Inn*, a five-minute walk east of downtown at 195 Main St (ⓣ902/542-2291 or 1-800/565-2291, ⓦwww.blomidoninn.com); the *Blomidon* occupies an ornate sea captain's mansion of 1882 that comes complete with oodles of period detail. The rooms in the main house are in similar style (❺), but the rooms (❹) in the modern annexe behind are less endearing, whilst the suites (❻) in the two-storey chalet at the back of the property are the epitome of modern luxury, albeit in retro style. Alternatively, *Victoria's Historic Inn & Carriage House* is an immaculately maintained grand mansion with fancy gingerbread scrollwork just 800m or so west of the centre at 600 Main St (ⓣ902/542-5744 or 1-800/556-5744, ⓦwww.victoriashistoricinn.com; ❺). There are sixteen guest rooms here, both in the inn and the adjacent carriage house, and each is decorated in a plush version of period style. Finally, a third and less expensive option is the three-roomed *Garden House B&B*, 220 Main St (ⓣ902/542-1703, ⓦwww.gardenhouse.ca; ❸), in an attractive old property of 1830 also just east of downtown.

For **food**, there are good snacks, lip-smacking muffins and great coffee at *Just Us! Café*, in the front of the old Art Deco Acadia Cinema at 450 Main St (Mon–Fri 7am–9pm, Sat 8am–6pm & Sun 10am–7pm); and delicious salads, meats and seafood at the smart, perhaps even a little formal *Acton's Grill & Café*, at 406 Main St (daily from 5pm; ⓣ902/542-7525); main courses here hover around $20.

East of Wolfville: Grand Pré

In 1847, Henry Wadsworth Longfellow chose **GRAND PRÉ**, 5km east of Wolfville along Hwy 1, as the setting for his epic poem *Evangeline – A Tale of Acadie*, which dramatized the Acadian deportations through the star-crossed love of Evangeline for her Gabriel. Horribly sentimental and extremely popular, the poem turned the destruction of this particular community into a symbol of Acadian suffering and British callousness. Yet, the **Grand Pré National Historic Site** (May–Oct daily 9am–6pm; $7.15; ⓦwww.pc.gc.ca), located amidst the dykelands of the Minas Basin, is a strangely antiseptic tribute. The visitor centre explains the history and describes Acadian culture very competently, but the rest of the site, with its trim lawns, planted trees and statues of Longfellow and Evangeline, only plods along and the main building, the **chapel**, which stands on the site of the original church, is uninspiring.

North of Wolfville: Cape Blomidon and Cape Split

The rugged, hook-shaped peninsula stretching north of Wolfville encompasses the dramatic scenery of **Cape Blomidon**, which, local legend has it, takes its name from the sailors' phrase "Blow me down", and of wilder and bleaker **Cape Split** beyond. To reach the peninsula from Wolfville, begin by taking Hwy 1 west for a couple of kilometres and then turn north along **Highway 358** for the 10km drive to the township of **CANNING**. Just after Canning, there's a choice of routes. Stay on Hwy 358 for Cape Split (see p.429) or take the signed 13km-long turning that leads down to **Blomidon Provincial Park**, a narrow slice of seashore where steep sea cliffs back onto a lush, coastal forest of maple, birch, fir and beech. It's a lovely spot with around 14km of footpaths and the park has a popular, shaded **campsite** (ⓣ902/582-7319, ⓦwww.parks.gov.ns.ca; mid-May to Aug).

Beyond the Blomidon turning, Hwy 358 clambers the 3km up to the peninsula's highest point, the **Look-off Provincial**, from where the views over the Annapolis Valley and the Minas Basin are truly spectacular – and you can savour the scenery at length if you bed down at the *Look-off Camping Park* (ⓣ902/582-3022; mid-May to Sept), one of the best-sited in the province. From the Look-off, it's a further 17km to **SCOTS BAY**, a scattered farming village that straggles along the edge of a wide and muddy bay. The

The Acadians

Acadia – *Acadie* in French – has at different times included all or part of Maine, New Brunswick and Nova Scotia. The etymology of the name is as vague as the geographical definition, derived from either the local Micmac word *akade*, meaning "abundance", or a corruption of *Arcadia*, an area of Greece that was a byword for rural simplicity when transient French fishermen first arrived here in the early 1500s. Whatever the truth, the origins of **Acadian settlement** date to 1604, when a French expedition led by Pierre Sieur de Monts and Samuel de Champlain built a stockade on the islet of **Saint-Croix**, in Passamaquoddy Bay, on the north side of the Bay of Fundy. It was a disaster: with the onset of winter, the churning ice floes separated the colonists from the fresh food and water of the mainland, and many died of malnutrition. The following spring the survivors straggled over to the sheltered southern shore of the bay, where they founded **Port Royal** (see p.425), considered Canada's first successful European settlement.

However, Champlain and Sieur de Monts quickly despaired of Port Royal's fur-trading potential and transferred to the banks of the St Lawrence, which soon became the main conduit of French colonization, leaving **Acadia** a remote and neglected backwater. Port Royal was **abandoned** in 1614 and, although it was refounded on the site of present-day Annapolis Royal in 1635, there were few immigrants. Indeed, the bulk of today's Acadians are the descendants of just forty French peasant families who arrived in the 1630s. Slowly spreading along the **Annapolis Valley**, the Acadians lived a semi-autonomous existence in which trading with their English-speaking neighbours was more important than grand notions of loyalty to the French Empire. Consequently, when the British secured control of Port Royal under the Treaty of Utrecht in 1713, the Acadians made no protest.

But then, in the 1750s, the tense standoff between the colonial powers highlighted the issue of Acadian loyalty. In **1755**, at the start of the Seven Years War, British government officials attempted to make the Acadians swear **an oath of allegiance** to the Crown. They refused, so Governor Lawrence decided – without consultation with London – to **deport** them en masse to other colonies. The process of uprooting and removing a community of around 13,000 was achieved with remarkable ruthlessness. As Lawrence wrote to a subordinate, "You must proceed with the most vigorous measures possible, not only in compelling them to embark, but in depriving those who should escape of all means of shelter or support, by burning their houses and destroying everything that may afford them the means of subsistence in the country."

By the end of the year over half the Acadians had arrived on the American east coast, where they faced a cold reception – the Virginians even rerouted their allocation to England. Most of the rest spread out along the North Atlantic seaboard, establishing communities along New Brunswick's Miramichi Valley, on Prince Edward Island and in St-Pierre et Miquelon. Many subsequently returned to the Bay of Fundy in the 1770s and 1780s, but their farms had been given to British and New England colonists and they were forced to settle the less hospitable lands of the **French Shore**, further west. For other deportees, the expulsion was the start of wider wanderings. Some went to Louisiana, where they were joined in 1785 by over 1500 former Acadian refugees who had ended up in France – these were the ancestors of the **Cajuns**, whose name is a corruption of "Acadian".

The Acadian communities of the Maritime Provinces continued to face discrimination from the English-speaking majority for many years and even today they remain firmly planted at the bottom of the economic pile. Nevertheless, the Acadians have resisted the pressures of assimilation and have recently begun to assert their cultural independence, most notably in New Brunswick, where Moncton University has become their academic and cultural centre.

road ends abruptly just beyond the village at the start of one of the region's most popular and not-too-difficult hiking trails that leads the 7km to the tip of **Cape Split**. Reckon on two hours each way and be sure to pick up trail information and maps at Wolfville tourist office (see p.426) before you set out. The trail begins by threading up through thick forest beneath towering cliffs and passes heavily eroded rock formations before emerging onto a small open area, from where there are wondrous views across the Bay of Fundy.

Windsor

Sloping along the shore of an inlet of the Minas Basin 25km from Wolfville, pint-sized **WINDSOR** was originally settled by Acadians and it was here in 1750 that the British built a fort to overawe them. The stockade was subsequently used to hold Acadians during the deportations, but all that remains today is a sorry-looking timber blockhouse conserved as the **Fort Edward National Historic Site** (mid-June to Aug Tues–Sat 10am–6pm, Sun & Mon noon–6pm; free). The blockhouse, complete with musket loopholes and cannon portholes, perches on a grassy, treeless hill at the east end of town, overlooking Hwy 101 and the tidal mud flats that stretch out towards the basin. On the other side of town, set in its own leafy grounds on a hillside 1km west of the centre, is the **Haliburton House Museum** (June to mid-Oct Mon–Sat 9.30am–5.30pm, Sun 1–5.30pm, Ⓦwww.museum.gov.ns.ca/hh/; $3), one-time home of Thomas Chandler Haliburton, a mid-nineteenth-century judge and humorist. The house has been returned to something akin to its appearance when Haliburton lived here, writing the short stories that made him famous – cuttingly sarcastic tales whose protagonist, the itinerant Yankee clock pedlar **Sam Slick of Slickville**, travels Nova Scotia meanly defrauding its gullible, unenterprising inhabitants. Immensely popular at the time, the stories are interesting as literary history, but leave a nasty High-Tory taste, although it was through Slick that Haliburton coined a bucketload of epigrams that remain in use: "six of one and half a dozen of the other"; "facts are stranger than fiction"; "raining cats and dogs"; "the early bird gets the worm"; and "as quick as a wink" – plus many more – all came from his pen. Most of Haliburton's work is out of print, but the museum has a small supply; if you're keen to sample his stories, begin with *The Clockmaker.* From Windsor, it's about 90km back to Halifax.

Central Nova Scotia

Most visitors hurry through **central Nova Scotia**, the chunk of forested land north and east of Halifax, on their way to Cape Breton Island, PEI or New Brunswick. By and large they're right to do so, but there is the odd pleasant diversion hereabouts, and a couple of places make for a convenient overnight stay. One place difficult to avoid is humdrum **TRURO**, the region's largest town and major crossroads, situated at the east end of the Minas Basin and so subject to the Bay of Fundy tides. The most appealing parts of the bay are well to the west in New Brunswick (see p.442), but if time is tight view the **tidal bore** here at Truro – the municipal Welcome Centre, right in the centre on Victoria Square, Commercial St (Ⓣ902/893-2922), has tide tables and will provide directions.

Heading northwest from Truro, the Trans-Canada Hwy heads off to New Brunswick's Fort Beauséjour (see p.467), scooting past the old coal-mining centre of **Springhill**, home to the Anne Murray Centre detailing the life and times of the town's most famous daughter. Beyond Springhill on the north Fundy Coast – though there's absolutely no need to actually go there – is **Spencers Island**, not an island at all, but a former shipbuilding centre and homeport of the *Mary Celeste*. This vessel posed one of the most celebrated mysteries of Victorian times when she was discovered in mid-Atlantic without a crew – and with the table set for dinner – and although all sorts of theories have been promulgated, no one has ever really worked out what happened. In the opposite direction from Truro, the Trans-Canada travels just inland from the northeast shore, whose rolling countryside was a centre of Scottish settlement from the end of the eighteenth century. The Scots first landed in **Pictou**, and this is the pick of the fishing, lumber and agricultural communities hereabouts – especially as it's both conveniently close to the PEI ferry terminal at **Caribou** and midway between Halifax and Cape Breton.

An alternative route between Halifax and Cape Breton is along the **southeast shore**, an isolated region of skinny bays and the tiniest of fishing villages connected by a tortuous 320-kilometre road. The coastal scenery is often quite delightful, but the villages don't deserve their redolent names – Spanish Ship Bay, Ecum Secum, Mushaboom – and the only place worthy of attention is **Sherbrooke**, where around thirty old buildings have been preserved to create an enjoyable village museum. Sherbrooke lies some 200km east of the capital on the coastal road, but is more rapidly reached from the Trans-Canada Hwy from outside either New Glasgow or Antigonish.

Acadian Lines **buses** (Ⓣ1-800/567-5151, Ⓦwww.acadianbus.com) run eight times daily from Halifax to Truro, with three buses daily continuing northeast to Cape Breton Island and three buses pressing on northwest to New Brunswick's Moncton. VIA Rail's Halifax–Montréal **trains** (Ⓣ1-888/842-7245, Ⓦwww.viarail.ca) pass through Truro en route to Moncton. There's no public transport to either Pictou or Sherbrooke.

Springhill

Just off the Trans-Canada, 200km from Halifax and 30km from the New Brunswick border, **SPRINGHILL** is an Appalachian lookalike, its tangle of modern buildings set amidst a vast forest that rolls over the surrounding hills. A coal mine was first sunk here in 1872 and it was coal that dominated the local economy until the last mine closed in the 1970s, leaving the town's population – which now numbers about 4000 – pretty much high and dry. Of all the coalfields in Canada, Springhill's was the most disaster-prone, with three major tragedies grabbing national headlines: 125 miners perished in an underground explosion in 1891, 39 died in a gas explosion in 1956 and in 1958 a tunnel collapse – or "bump" as it is known locally – accounted for 75 more. As if this wasn't enough, in 1957 and again in 1975 fires wiped out the town's commercial district. A **memorial** in the centre of town – beside the junction of hwys 142 and 2 – remembers the dead miners and there are contemporary photographs of the sites of the two later disasters at the **Tour a Mine, Springhill Miners' Museum**, on Black River Rd, 2.5km south of town just off Hwy 2 (late May to mid-Oct daily 10am–6pm; $5). The museum's outdoors section contains several wooden shacks looking exactly as they did when the pit closed in the 1970s. One is the lamp room and another the wash house, outside of which is what the miners themselves called the Liars' Bench – after, no doubt, a certain tendency to exaggerate coal-cutting feats. What you won't see is winding gear: Springhill's coal seams were near the surface and the miners walked down to the coalface – as visitors can do today in the company of a guide.

Coalface or not, it's the **Anne Murray Centre**, 36 Main St (mid-May to mid-Oct daily 9am–5pm; ⓦwww.annemurray.com; $6), which pulls the crowds to Springhill – an exercise in organized sycophancy that tracks through the extraordinarily successful career of the Springhill-born balladeer. Murray (b.1945) shot to fame with her sugary song *Snowbird* in 1970 and her later releases keep up the easy listening. Naturally enough, if you're a fan you'll love it – and you can feel good that all the centre's proceeds go to the local community.

Pictou

Signs proclaim **PICTOU**, 170km from Halifax, as the "Birthplace of New Scotland" on the basis of the arrival in 1773 of the ship *Hector*, loaded with settlers from the County of Ross, the advance guard of the subsequent Scots migrations. To maintain the connection, the town has its own middle-of-August **Hector Festival (**ⓦwww.decostecentre.ca**)**, a five-day affair featuring Scottish traditional dancing and the playing of the bagpipes – and very good it is too. Pictou has also spent years building itself a replica of the *Hector*, an expensive and time-consuming project because they stuck to the original shipbuilding techniques. The boat was finally launched in 2000 and now either bobs around the harbour or sallies forth along the Nova Scotian coast. The dock where the boat was built forms part of the **Hector Heritage Quay Interpretative Centre** (mid-May to mid-Oct Mon–Sat 9am–5pm, Sun noon–5pm; July & Aug Tues–Thurs 9am–7pm & Sun 10am–5pm; ⓦwww.townofpictou.com; $7), which gives the historical lowdown on the original voyage, complete with nautical sound effects. It's all excellently done and spruces up Pictou's unassuming centre, where the narrow streets slope up from the harbour dotted with stone buildings of Scottish demeanour. A second sight is the **Northumberland Fisheries Museum** (mid-May to mid-Oct daily 9am–5pm; ⓦwww.northumberlandfisheriesmuseum.com; $4), just along the waterfront from the *Hector* in the old train station at 71 Front St.

Pictou is a convenient place to spend the night and there are several quality **inns and hotels** to choose from. One of the best is the ornately decorated *Consulate Inn*, 115 Water St (ⓣ902/485-4554 or 1-800/424-8283, ⓦwww.consulateinn.com; ④), housed in an elegant early nineteenth-century mansion that once served as a US consulate and with ten comfortable suites and guest rooms. There's also the *Customs House Inn*, 38 Depot St (ⓣ902/485-4546, ⓦwww.customshouseinn.ca; ④), which has eight spacious rooms with exposed brick walls and hardwood floors, all in a stately redbrick down on the waterfront. A third good and central choice is the *Willow House Inn*, 11 Willow St (ⓣ902/485-5740, ⓦwww.willowhouseinn.com; ④), whose four suites and two guest rooms, in a well-kept timber house built in 1840, are kitted out in a fetching version of period style.

The best of Pictou's **restaurants** is *Fougere's*, 91 Water St (ⓣ902/485-1575), where both the seafood and the steaks are delicious; mains here average around $20. Alternatively, and amongst several rather average town-centre **cafés**, try the filling snacks of the *Stone House Café*, just up from the Hector Quay at 13 Water St. The town also possesses a **performing arts** centre, the deCoste Entertainment Centre, 85 Water St (ⓣ902/485-8848 or 1-800/353-5338, ⓦwww.decostecentre.ca), where much of the summer season is taken up by ceilidhs, pipe bands and Highland dancing.

Ferries from Caribou, Nova Scotia, to PEI

Some 8km north of Pictou is **Caribou**, from where Northumberland Ferries operates frequent **car ferries** over to Wood Islands on Prince Edward Island (May to late June 5 daily, late June to mid-Oct 7 daily, mid-Oct to late Dec 3–5 daily; 1hr 15min; $13 return, $57 for car and passengers; ⓣ902/566-3838 or 1-888/249-7245, ⓦwww.nfl-bay.com). Note that the full return fare is only collected on the way off the island – either on the ferry or the Confederation Bridge (see p.485). Ferries operate on a first-come, first-served basis and queues are common in high season, when you should arrive about an hour and a half before departure to be safe. There are no ferries from late Dec to April.

Sherbrooke

Developed as a timber town in the early nineteenth century, **SHERBROOKE** boomed when gold was found near here in 1861, the start of a short-lived gold rush that fizzled out within the space of twenty years, though a handful of mines struggled on until the 1940s. Most of the population checked out after the gold rush and Sherbrooke returned to the lumber trade, but without much success: the decline of the industry gradually whittled the population down to the 400 of today. One result has been the creation of the open-air museum of **Sherbrooke Village** (June to mid-Oct daily 9.30am–5.30pm; ⓦwww.museum.gov.ns.ca; $9), which encompasses those late nineteenth- and early twentieth-century buildings that are, for the most part, now surplus to requirements. It's a large site, several streets situated just beyond the modern part of the village beside St Mary's River - and costumed "interpreters" preside. Amongst the eighty-odd buildings highlights include the surprisingly grand Neoclassical Court House of the 1850s and the Victorian luxury of the high-gabled Greenwood Cottage nearby. Also of special note are the assorted baubles and throne-like chairs of the **Masonic Lodge**, which still meets on the second floor of the Masonic Hall, the Temperance Hall of 1892, and the good-looking Cummings Bros General Store. Take a peek too at the jail, where jailer and prisoner lived cheek by jowl right up until the 1960s, and the replica nineteenth-century water-powered sawmill, built about 600m outside the village. Allow two to three hours to do the place justice.

There are three main ways **to reach** Sherbrooke: from the west along Nova Scotia's southeast shore and from the north by turning off Hwy 104 (the Trans-Canada) either along Hwy 347 just east of New Glasgow or down Hwy 7 about 50km further east near Antigonish. The most agreeable of the three **places to stay** is *Daysago B&B*, 15 Cameron Rd (ⓣ902/522-2811 or 1-866/522-2811, ⓦwww.bbcanada.com/daysago; ❷; May–Sept), in a 1920s house with lovely river views and four homely rooms. The tiny *St Mary's Riverside Campground* (ⓣ902/522-2913; mid-May to mid-Oct) is near the sawmill. There's not much choice about where to eat, but fortunately the central *Bright House* (ⓣ902/522-2691) is an excellent **restaurant** – be sure to try the seafood casserole. The *Main Street Café* sells competent snacks and pizzas.

Cape Breton Island

"I have travelled the globe. I have seen the Canadian and American Rockies, the Andes and the Alps and the Highlands of Scotland, but for simple beauty

Cape Breton outrivals them all." With these words Alexander Graham Bell summed up a part of Nova Scotia whose scenery continues to attract its share of hyperbole. From the lakes, hills and valleys of the southwest to the ripe, forested mountains of the north, **CAPE BRETON ISLAND** – or at least its more westerly half – offers the most exquisite of landscapes, reaching its melodramatic conclusion along the fretted, rocky coast of the **Cape Breton Highlands National Park**. Encircling the park and some of the adjacent shore is the **Cabot Trail**, a 300-kilometre loop that is reckoned to be one of the most beguiling drives on the continent – and one that is best approached in a clockwise direction. Allow time also for a **whale-watching cruise**: these are big business hereabouts and they are available at almost every significant settlement – usually three-hour trips cost about $30.

By contrast, the more easterly half of Cape Breton – east, that is, of **Bras d'Or Lake** and its subsidiary channels – was once a busy coal-mining and steel-milling region, centred on the town of **Sydney**. It was here in the early 1920s that the struggles of the miners against the pit companies grabbed national headlines. The worst of several disputes began when the owners, the British Empire Steel Corporation (BESCO), decided to cut the men's wages by a third. The miners went on strike and the dispute escalated until BESCO persuaded prime minister King to send in the militia – and the colliers were driven back to work. Today the area's industries have largely collapsed and a de-industrialized sprawl blotches the landscape, only relieved by the splendid reconstruction of the French fortress town of **Louisbourg**, stranded out on the east coast.

The scenic delights of Cape Breton attract thousands of summer tourists and, consequently, although there's a liberal sprinkling of **accommodation** across the island – especially in the west – it's still a good idea to make a reservation a day or two beforehand. Failing that, all the island's tourist offices offer a free room-reservation service. Most visitors stay in the tiny ribbon villages that dot the island, but two of the more enjoyable spots are undoubtedly the busy resort of **Baddeck** and the quieter coastal community of **Chéticamp**.

Without your own transport, getting around much of Cape Breton is a struggle, but Acadian Lines **buses** (Ⓣ1-800/567-5151, Ⓦwww.acadianbus.com) from Halifax and Truro bomb along Hwy 105 en route to Sydney twice daily. On the way, they shoot through Baddeck and **North Sydney**, the departure port for ferries to Newfoundland. There are no buses to either Louisbourg or

Music on Cape Breton Island

Cape Breton is not just about scenery and sights: the Scottish Highlanders who settled much of the island in the late eighteenth and early nineteenth centuries brought with them strong cultural traditions and today these are best recalled by the island's **musicians**, especially the fiddle players. Names to watch out for include Buddy MacMaster, Ashley MacIsaac, Natalie MacMaster and the Rankin family, not to mention Glenn Graham, Rodney MacDonald and Jackie Dunn – though it's impossible to pick out the "best" as each fiddler has their own particular style. Local tourist offices will gladly advise you on **gigs**, whether it be a ceilidh, concert or square dance, and listings are given in the weekly *Inverness Oran* (Ⓦwww.oran.ca), a local newspaper available at tourist offices and convenience stores. During the summer there's something happening almost every day – the Saturday night **Family Square Dance** at West Mabou Hall is especially well regarded. The largest festival is **Celtic Colours** (Ⓣ902/562-6700 or 1-877/285-2321, Ⓦwww.celtic-colours.com), with performances all across Cape Breton held over ten days in early to mid-Oct.

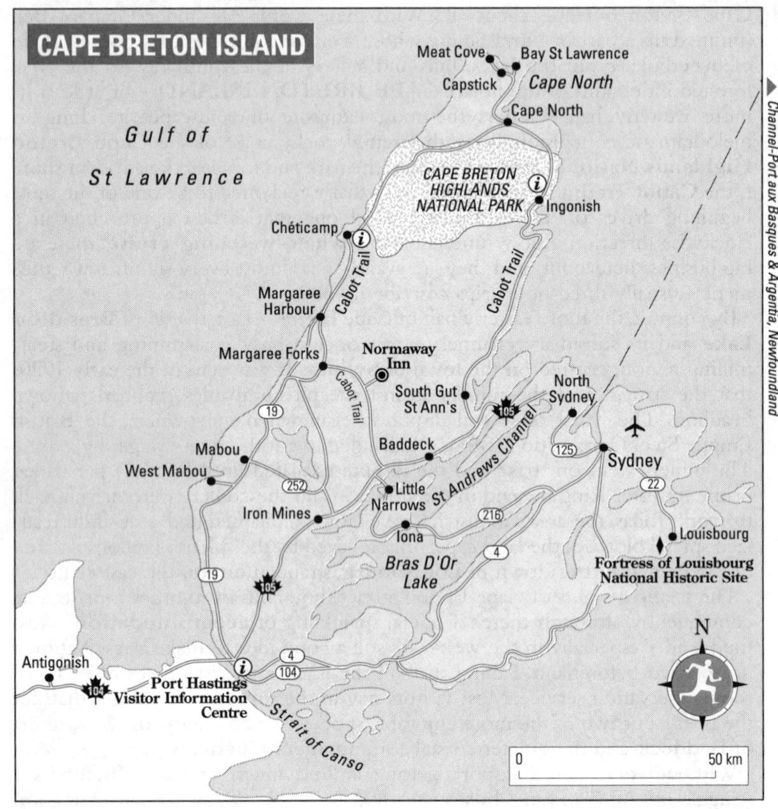

the Cape Breton Highlands National Park, though several local companies run minibus excursions to the park from Baddeck, starting from around $40. To get onto Cape Breton, all traffic has to cross the **Strait of Canso causeway**.

Finally, note that Cape Breton's **weather** is notoriously unpredictable, even in summer. The Cabot Trail is pretty miserable in mist and rain, so if possible you should build a bit of flexibility into your itinerary.

The Cabot Trail

Just up the hill from the Canso causeway is the **Port Hastings Visitor Information Centre** (daily: May & Sept 9am–6pm; June–Aug 8.30am–7pm; Oct to early Dec 9am–5pm; ⓣ902/625-4201), where you can get your bearings and make advance room reservations on all of Cape Breton Island. From here it's about 45km on Hwy 105 (the Trans-Canada) through low, forested hills to the hamlet of **IRON MINES**, overlooking a small inlet at the western limit of Bras d'Or Lake – a pleasant foretaste of the splendours beyond. From Iron Mines, it's a further 30km to the **Cabot Trail**, which begins at Hwy 105 (Exit 7) by weaving its way northwest over the hills before slipping along the **Margaree River Valley**, whose soft, green landscapes are framed by bulging hills. The road veers north at the hamlet of Margaree Forks and then pushes on to the coast at

MARGAREE HARBOUR, 50km from the Trans-Canada. This is handsome scenery indeed – all rolling fields and wooded hills – and there's a great place to stay too, the *Normaway Inn* (☎902/248-2987 or 1-800/565-9463, Ⓦwww.normaway.com; mid-June to mid-Oct), 4km off the Cabot Trail along Egypt Road, about 28km from Hwy 105. Deep in the countryside, the inn occupies a tastefully maintained 1920s farmhouse and stands in its own estate. There are nine rooms (❺) in the main lodge and nineteen one- and two-bedroomed cabins (❻), mostly with wood stoves. The inn has contacts with local ghillies, so you can try your hand at fishing, and it also hosts folk-music concerts and serves a delicious evening meal by prior reservation.

Chéticamp

North from Margaree Harbour, the Cabot Trail offers lovely views of land and sea as it slices across the wide grassy littoral with a band of forested hills looming inland. The scattered dwellings hereabouts are home to an **Acadian** community whose earliest members hid out in the woods during the troubles of 1755 (see p.428). As news filtered through of their survival, returning deportees joined them and – in a dramatic change of policy – the British formally ceded the land to them in 1790. After 30km or so, the road slips into the district's main village, **CHÉTICAMP**, where the towering Catholic church of **St-Pierre**, with its soaring silver steeple, was built in 1893 of stones lugged across the ice from Chéticamp Island, just offshore. Inside, the lines of the cavernous nave are interrupted by two long galleries and oceans of elaborate wood and plasterwork. The striking frescoes were added later – in the 1950s – and, even though they're awfully sanctimonious, they do have a certain cheery charm. Below the church – 200m back down the road – is the **Co-operative Artisanale** (daily: mid-June to Sept 8am–9pm; early May to mid-June & Oct 9am–6pm; ☎902/224-2170, Ⓦwww.co-opartisanale.com), where a tiny **Musée Acadien** features a selection of the crudely patterned hooked rugs that are a characteristic craft of the area. The display is hardly spellbinding, but the co-operative's simple café-style **restaurant** *Acadien* is excellent and great value. In particular, the *poulet fricot*

△ Square dancing on Cape Breton Island

(chicken stew) is mouthwatering, and so are the fruit pies and pea soup. There's a much better exhibition of Acadian crafts at the north end of the village in **Les Trois Pignons** (daily: mid-May to June & Sept to mid-Oct 9am–5pm; July & Aug 8am–7pm; Ⓦwww.lestroispignons.com; $4), a cultural centre that proudly displays the hooked mats of Elizabeth LeFort, an artist of some local renown. LeFort's hooked mats often depict religious and historical scenes, mostly large-scale, multi-coloured affairs that took as long as a year to complete, but her portraits are perhaps more unusual, pushing the limits of mat-making with admittedly mixed results – though her *Jackie Onassis* of 1962 is quite delightful.

Practicalities

Chéticamp straggles along the main road for about 5km. In between the church – at the south end of the village – and Les Trois Pignons, at the north, is a seashore **tourist kiosk** (July–Sept; Ⓣ902/224-3349), where they have the latest details on a variety of boat trips, several of which leave from the adjacent jetty. One especially appealing option is to go **whale-watching** with the highly reputable Whale Cruises (mid-May to mid-Oct 2–3 daily; 3hr; Ⓣ902/224-3376 or 1-800/813-3376, Ⓦwww.whalecruises.com; $30).

There are around twenty **motels and B&Bs** in and around Chéticamp with one of the best being *Ocean View Chalets & Motel* (Ⓣ902/224-2313 or 1-877/743-4404, Ⓦwww.oceanviewchalets.com; ❹; May to mid-Oct), whose well-maintained, shingle-clad chalets sit right by the seashore on the main road opposite Les Trois Pignons. Another option is *L'Auberge Doucet Inn* (Ⓣ902/224-3438 or 1-800/646-8668, Ⓦwww.aubergedoucetinn.com; ❸; May–Oct), above the main road on the south side of the village, which has eleven straightforward, modern rooms. More distinctive is *Chéticamp Outfitters Inn B&B* (Ⓣ902/224-2776, Ⓦwww.cheticampns.com/chéticampoutfitters; ❷; April–Nov), perched on a hilltop just off the main road about 4km south of the village and with splendid views over the surrounding shoreline. The rooms may be plain and simple, but the breakfasts (and views) are good and the Acadian family who run the place offer bike rental. A fourth choice, the *Parkview Motel* (Ⓣ902/224-3232 or 1-877/224-3232, Ⓦwww.parkviewresort.com; ❹; May to mid-Oct), occupies a pair of well-kept but routine motel blocks on the main road about 8km north of Chéticamp – in a pretty wooded dell across the Chéticamp River from the national park.

For **food**, stick to the *Restaurant Acadien* (see p.435); a reserve option is the *L'Auberge Doucet Inn* (see above), where the crab dinners are well known all along the coast.

Cape Breton Highlands National Park

The extensive **Cape Breton Highlands National Park** (Ⓦwww.pc.gc.ca), beginning 9km north of Chéticamp, offers some of the most gorgeous scenery anywhere in the Maritimes – a mix of deep wooded valleys, rocky coastal headlands, soft green hills and boggy upland. Although visitors get a sniff of the park travelling by car – 120km of hwy trimming all but its southern edge – the essence of the place is only revealed on foot: twenty-five **hiking trails** are signposted from the road, some of them the easiest of woodland strolls, others striking deep into the interior to the small lakes and wetlands of the central plateau. One of the most popular is the 9km-long **Skyline Loop Trail** (2–3hr), which clambers up the coastal mountains north of Corney Brook, a few kilometres up the coast from Chéticamp. Another good trail is the 7km **Franey Loop Trail** (3–4hr), a steep walk up through the mountains and lakes north of Ingonish Beach. Most of the wildlife inhabits the inner reaches of the park:

garter snakes, red-backed salamanders, snowshoe hares and moose are common, while bald eagles, black bear and lynx are rarer. The only artificial sight is the **Lone Sheiling**, a somewhat battered replica of the stone shelters once built by Highlanders beside their mountain pastures. The hut is on the northern perimeter of the park in a valley that was settled by Scots in the early 1800s; it is accessible along a short and easy footpath from the road.

The park has two **information kiosks** – one at the west-coast entrance just beyond Chéticamp (daily: late June to late Aug 8am–8pm; mid-May to late June & late Aug to mid-Oct 9am–5pm; ⓣ902/224-2306), the other at the east-coast entrance near Ingonish Beach (same details). There's also a **visitor centre** (same details) at the west-coast entrance with displays on local flora and fauna and a well-stocked bookshop. Both the visitor centre and the east-coast kiosk sell 1:50,000 maps, have details of the park's hiking trails (which are in peak condition from July to September), and issue backcountry camping permits ($18). There is a daily park entrance fee of $6.90 when the kiosks are staffed. The park has six serviced **campsites** ($22–31), all within easy reach of the road, and one **wilderness campsite** – Fishing Cove – along one of the more arduous trails. Campsite services are only available from mid-May to mid-October, but you can camp in the park at any time of the year. Reservations are not accepted.

Cape North

Beyond the northern perimeter of the national park is **Cape North**, a forested hunk of hill and valley that juts out into the sea where the Gulf of St Lawrence meets the Atlantic Ocean. The Cabot Trail threads its way across the base of the cape, passing through the tiny village of **CAPE NORTH**, no more than a few lonely buildings straggling along the road. There are, however, several **places to stay** round here, beginning with the handy *Macdonald's Motel & Cabins* (ⓣ902/383-2054; ❸; mid-May to mid-Oct), a modern affair at the village crossroads. Much more enticing, however, is *Oakwood Manor B&B* (ⓣ902/383-2317, ⓦwww.capebretonisland.com/oakwood; ❹; May–Oct), whose en-suite guestrooms are in a charming 1930s timber farmhouse. The 200-acre farm occupies a gentle valley and is dotted with shingle-clad barns and outbuildings. To get there, take the Bay St Lawrence road north from Cape North village and, after about 1.3km, turn left at the sign, down the 1.2km-long gravel road leading to the farm. The best place to **eat** is *Morrison's Restaurant*, a casual café serving tasty seafood at the village crossroads.

There aren't many reasons to push on up the North Cape, away from the Cabot Trail, but one of them is to join a **whale-watching trip** at tiny **BAY ST LAWRENCE**, 17km from Cape North village. Several operators lead trips from the harbour and one of the most dependable is Captain Cox, whose cruises depart from here throughout the summer (mid-June to Sept 2–3 daily; 2–3hr; $25; ⓣ902/383-2981 or 1-888/346-5556, ⓦwww.whalewatching-novascotia.com). Just before you reach Bay St Lawrence, there's a 5km-long turning to the hamlet of **CAPSTICK**, where a string of houses spreads out along a wide bay with wooded hills pressing in from behind. Beyond, at the end of a bumpy, occasionally hairy 8km-long gravel road, lies **MEAT COVE**, which passing sailors once raided for moose and caribou – hence the name. The small **campsite** here (ⓣ902/383-2379; June–Oct; sites $18) is full of the roar of the ocean.

Ingonish and the Gaelic Coast

Back at Cape North village, heading east, the main road skirts the edge of the national park, cutting across the interior before veering south along the coast to reach the series of roadside resorts that make up **INGONISH**. Amongst several

places to stay here, the *Glenghorm Beach Resort* (T 902/285-2049 or 1-800/565-5660, W www.glenghormbeachresort.com; mid-May to late Oct) is as good as any – and better than most – its neat and trim motel rooms (4) and cabins (6) spreading out along a pleasant slice of seashore. The attractions of Ingonish, however, pale in comparison with *Keltic Lodge* (T 902/285-2880 or 1-800/565-0444, W www.signatureresorts.com; mid-May to mid-Oct), one of the province's finest hotel complexes, perched high above the cliffs amidst immaculate gardens on a rocky promontory some 40km from Cape North village – and close to the national park's east entrance. The lodge has a comprehensive range of facilities, from beaches, restaurants and tennis courts through to hiking trails that explore the locale's scenic nooks and crannies. You can stay in the main lodge (8), a handsome Edwardian mansion with high gables and brick chimneys, or the modern *Keltic Inn* (8), but the cottages (8) are perhaps more enjoyable, the best of them prettily located amongst the woods that cover much of the promontory.

Leaving the national park, the Cabot Trail threads its way down the 80km-long **Gaelic Coast** – named after the Scottish Highlanders who first settled here – passing through **SOUTH GUT ST ANN'S**, the location of the **Gaelic College of Celtic Arts and Crafts**. Standing on its own campus in the hills, the college offers courses in the Gaelic language and all manner of Highland activities – bagpiping, tartan-weaving, dancing and Scots folklore. The main focus of a visit here is the **Great Hall of the Clans** (June & Sept Mon-Fri 9am–5pm, July & Aug daily 9am–5pm; $3), which provides potted clan descriptions alongside wax models dressed in the appropriate tartan.

From the college, it is a few hundred metres to the Trans-Canada for either Baddeck to the southwest or Sydney (see opposite) to the east.

Baddeck

The amenable resort and yachting town of **BADDECK**, some 90km east of the Canso causeway along Hwy 105, enjoys an attractive lakeside setting on St Patrick's Channel, an inlet of the tentacular Bras d'Or Lake. It is also home to the fascinating **Alexander Graham Bell Museum and National Historic Site** (daily: May & late Oct 9am–5pm; June 9am–6pm; July to mid-Oct 8.30am-6pm; $7.15, W www.pc.gc.ca), which overlooks the waterfront from a tiny park and whose excellent exhibits do full justice to the fertility of the great man's mind. The museum is a mine of general biographical information about Bell (1847–1922) and gives detailed explanations of all his inventions – both successful and unsuccessful. Most famous for the invention of the **telephone**, Bell also made extraordinary advances in techniques for teaching hearing-impaired children, a lifelong interest inspired by the deafness of his mother, and undertook pioneering experiments in animal husbandry. He also worked on aircraft and boats, and his nautical adventures culminated in 1919 with the launch of the world's first hydrofoil, the **HD-4** (of which there's a full-scale replica in the museum), which reached a speed of 70mph on the lake right in front of town. Bell spent his last 37 years in Baddeck, working away at **Beinn Bhreagh** (no public access), the family mansion that still stands amongst the trees just across the bay from town.

The museum is Baddeck's only significant sight, but the town's waterfront makes for an enjoyable stroll and in July and August the local Lion's Club runs a free shuttle-boat service from the municipal jetty to **Kidston Island**, a couple of hundred metres offshore, where you can take a walk in the woods.

Practicalities

Baddeck is on the Acadian Lines **bus** route between Halifax and Sydney, with two buses daily in each direction stopping at the Ultramar gas station 3.5km west of town on Hwy 105 (Exit 8). The **tourist office** (June–Oct daily 9am–7pm; ⓣ902/295-1911, ⓦwww.visitbaddeck.com) has lots of useful local information and sits by the side of the resort's main intersection – at Shore Road and the top of the short main drag, Chebucto Street. Baddeck is a popular holiday spot, so there's a wide range of **accommodation**, but it fills up fast in the height of the season. Amongst several downtown **B&Bs**, one good bet is the *Tree Seat* (ⓣ902/295-1996, ⓦwww.baddeck.com/treeseat; ❸; May–Oct), in a pleasant old timber building next door to the Bell Museum at 555 Chebucto St; there are four guest rooms here, two en suite, and the home-cooked breakfasts are first rate. A second handy option is *Heidi's B&B* (ⓣ902/295-1301; ❷; June to late Oct), in a large timber house with a new wing and wide terrace about 400m from the tourist office at 64 Old Margaree Rd; this has six rooms, three en-suite. In addition, several smart **resort-hotels** line up along Shore Road, west of the town centre. These include the *Silver Dart Lodge* (ⓣ902/295-2340 or 1-888/662-7484, ⓦwww.maritimeinns.com; ❹; mid-May to mid-Oct), whose spacious chalets spread over a hillside in view of the lake; and *Auberge Gisele's Inn* (ⓣ902/295-2849 or 1-800/304-0466, ⓦwww.giseles.com; ❻; May to late Oct), where the commodious bedrooms are decked out in brisk, modern style. Pick of the bunch, however, is the *Inverary Resort* (ⓣ902/295-3500 or 1-800/565-5660, ⓦwww.inveraryresort.com; May–Nov), an extensive and immaculately maintained complex that spreads down from Shore Road to the bay. The *Inverary* offers rooms in the main lodge (❺) and in several different types of cottage (from ❻). The nearest **campsite** is the *Bras d'Or Lakes* (ⓣ902/295-2329; mid-June to Sept), about 6km west on Hwy 105.

Most visitors **eat** where they sleep: Baddeck is surprisingly short on cafés and restaurants. The best café in town is the *High Wheeler*, on Chebucto St (May–Oct daily 6am–10pm), which serves up a reasonable range of wholefood snacks and cakes, whilst the *Bell Buoy*, further down Chebucto Street, at no.536, is OK for steaks and seafood (May–Oct daily).

For those without their own transport, **Bannockburn Tours** (ⓣ902/295-3310 or 1-888/577-4747, ⓦwww.bannockburntours.com) runs day-long **excursions** in summer along the Cabot Trail through the Cape Breton Highlands National Park; tours cost $75 per person. **Car rental** is available in Baddeck with Macaulay's, 404 Shore Rd (ⓣ902/295-2500).

Sydney

Poor old **SYDNEY**, sprawling along the east bank of the Sydney River 430km from Halifax and 80km from Baddeck, was once the industrial dynamo of eastern Canada. From the late nineteenth century to the 1950s, its steel mills processed Newfoundland iron ore with Nova Scotian coke, but as gas and oil came on stream this arrangement became uneconomic and the subsequent decline has been severe and long-lasting: the city has regularly recorded an unemployment rate twice the national average. It's hardly surprising, therefore, that the town lacks charm, though brave efforts have been made to reinvigorate the **North End** waterfront, along and around the **Esplanade**, downtown between Prince and Amelia streets. This is the district to head for and it's here you'll find Sydney's oldest buildings, including the early nineteenth-century **St Patrick's Church**, 87 Esplanade, a broadly Gothic structure that now holds a local history museum (June–Aug Mon–Sat 9.30am–5pm, Sun 1–5pm; suggested donation). Nearby, the **Cossit House**, 75 Charlotte St (June to mid-Oct, same hours), was built for the town's first Anglican minister in 1787.

Arriving from Halifax either via Hwy 105 (and Baddeck) or Hwy 4, Acadian Lines buses pull into the **bus station** at 99 Terminal Rd, off Prince St. From here, it's a good fifteen-minute walk west to the Esplanade. Sydney **tourist office** (Ⓣ902/539-9876) is on the southern edge of town beside Hwy 125 (Exit 6). Staff have details of all the town's accommodation and can also advise on local minibus services to Louisbourg fortress (see opposite). There are several **hotels** along the Esplanade, easily the pick of them being the *Delta Sydney* (Ⓣ902/562-7500 or 1-800/268-1133, Ⓦwww.deltasydney.com; ❺), a large and well-equipped chain hotel at no. 300.

Around Sydney: North Sydney

Ferries to Newfoundland (see box below) leave from **NORTH SYDNEY**, 21km northwest of Sydney along Hwy 125. North Sydney is itself unremarkable, but if for some reason you get stuck here, the *Best Western North Star Inn*, on the hill next to the ferry terminal at 39 Forrest St (Ⓣ902/794-8581 or 1-800/561-8585, Ⓦwww.bestwestern.com; ❹), is a comfortable chain hotel. Acadian Lines **buses** on their way to and from Sydney drop off and pick up passengers at the very same *North Star Inn*.

Fortress of Louisbourg National Historic Site and Louisbourg

Beginning work in 1719, the French constructed the coastal **Fortress of Louisbourg**, 37km southeast of Sydney, to guard the Atlantic approaches to New France and salvage their imperial honour after the humiliation of the Treaty of Utrecht six years earlier. The result was a staggeringly ostentatious stronghold covering a hundred acres and encircled by ten-metre-high stone walls; it took so long to build and was so expensive that Louis XV said he was expecting its towers to rise over the Paris horizon. Yet, Louisbourg was wildly ill-conceived: the humid weather stopped the mortar from drying, the fort was overlooked by a score of hillocks – and anyway developments in gunnery had already made high stone

Ferries and flights from North Sydney and Sydney

Marine Atlantic (Ⓣ1-800/341-7981, Ⓦwww.marine-atlantic.ca) operates two **car ferry** routes to Newfoundland from **North Sydney**, 21km northwest of Sydney. The first, **to Channel-Port aux Basques** (2–4 daily), takes between five and six hours (6–8hr at night). One-way tickets cost $28 for passengers and $78 for a car up to 20 feet. A four-berth cabin, which should be reserved in advance, cost $54 ($99 at night); there are also dormitory bunks for $16. The second car ferry connects North Sydney **to Argentia**, 130km southwest of St John's (late June to early Sept 3 weekly, mid-June & late Sept 1 weekly; 14–15hr). One-way tickets cost $77 for passengers and $160 for a car up to 20 feet. Vehicles must be booked in advance as must (four-berth) cabins, which cost $140; there are also dormitory bunks for $28.

Sydney airport, 10km northeast of Sydney, offers the shortest and least expensive flights (2 weekly; $125 one-way, $225 return) from the mainland to St-Pierre et Miquelon (see p.518) with **Air St-Pierre** (Ⓣ011/508/41 00 00 or 1-877/277-7765, Ⓦwww.airsaintpierre.com). There are also regular flights from here to Halifax with Air Canada

walls an ineffective means of defence. As Charles Lawrence, the British governor, confirmed, "the general design of the fortifications is exceedingly bad and the workmanship worse executed and so disadvantageously situated that…it will never answer the charge or trouble." And so it proved: Louisbourg was only attacked twice, but it was captured on both occasions, the second time by the celebrated British commander, James Wolfe, on his way to Québec in 1758.

A visit to the **Fortress of Louisbourg National Historic Site** (daily: May–June & Sept to mid-Oct 9.30am–5pm; July & Aug 9am–5.30pm; Ⓦwww.pc.gc.ca; $16.35) begins just 2km beyond the modern village of Louisbourg (see below) at the Reception Centre, where there's a good account of the fort's history and its reconstruction in the 1960s. From here, a free shuttle bus runs to the fort, whose stone walls rise from the sea to enclose more than four dozen restored buildings, a mid-eighteenth-century fortress town set beneath a soaring church spire. There are powder magazines, forges, guardhouses, warehouses, barracks and, last but not least, the chilly abodes of the soldiers, all attached to costumed guides to provide extra atmosphere. It's an extraordinary reconstruction in a lovely coastal setting and particular care has been taken with the **governor's apartments**, which have been splendidly furnished according to the inventory taken after the death of Governor Duquesnel here in 1744. It's amazing the man hadn't died before: already minus a leg from early in his military career, Duquesnel's body was buried under the chapel floor and when it was exhumed in the 1960s the remains showed him to have been suffering from a bewildering variety of ailments from arthritis and arteriosclerosis through to dental abscesses. Allow at least three hours to look round the fortress and sample the authentic refreshments that are available at the taverns and eating houses; the most sustaining food of all is the soldiers' bread (wheat and rye wholemeal), sold by the loaf at the bakery.

Louisbourg

Stringing along the seashore down along the bay from the fortress, the modern **village of LOUISBOURG** has a cheerful setting and several good **places to stay**. Choices include the *Stacey House B&B*, 7438 Main St (Ⓣ902/733-2317 or 1-866/924-2242, Ⓦwww.bbcanada.com/thestaceyhouse; ❷; June to mid-Oct), an attractive, high-gabled old home with just four guest rooms; the fiercely pink *Cranberry Cove Inn*, 12 Wolfe St (Ⓣ902/733-2171 or 1-800/929-0222, Ⓦwww.louisbourg.com/cranberrycove; ❺; May–Oct), a lavishly refurbished old house on the edge of the village on the way to the fort; and the *Louisbourg Manse B&B*, 10 Strathcona St (Ⓣ902/733-3155 or 1-866/733-3155, Ⓦwww.bbcanada.com/lsbgmanse; ❸; May–Oct), which occupies a comely Victorian house with a capacious verandah down an alley just off Main Street. There's a spartan **campsite**, the *Louisbourg Motorhome Park* (Ⓣ902/733-3631 or 1-866/733-3631; mid-May to mid-Oct), down by the harbour in the centre of the village.

Amongst several **cafés** and **restaurants**, the *Grubstake*, 7499 Main St (Ⓣ902/733-2308; mid-June to early Oct), is recommended for its fish platters and home-baked pastries. Both the breakfast and dinner at the *Cranberry Cove Inn* are excellent.

From Louisbourg to the Canso causeway via Iona

From Louisbourg, it's a dreary 200km thrash north then west along hwys 22 and 4 back to the Canso causeway. Instead, if you have the time, leave Hwy 4 about 20km west of Sydney and take **Highway 216** over the hills and along a tapering arm of Bras d'Or Lake to **IONA**, a remote hamlet where some of the inhabitants still speak Gaelic. Iona is home to the **Highland Village Museum** (daily: June to mid-Oct 9am–5.30pm; Ⓦwwwmuseum.gov.ns.ca/hv; $9), a modest collection of old pioneer buildings brought here from all over Cape Breton. The views from the museum, over the lake, are, however, quite delightful – as they are from the neighbouring *Highland Heights Inn* (Ⓣ902/725-2360 or 1-800/565-5660, Ⓦwww.capebretonresorts.com/highland.asp; ④; mid-May to mid-Oct), a smart modern place with thirty well-appointed, motel-style rooms.

Iona is 25km from the Trans-Canada Hwy 105 (Exit 6) between Baddeck and the Canso causeway.

New Brunswick

The province of **NEW BRUNSWICK**, roughly 350km long and 270km wide, attracts less tourist attention than its Maritime neighbours, and it's hard to understand quite why. It's true that the forested upland that makes up the bulk of the province is a trifle repetitious, but the long river valleys that furrow the landscape at least partly compensate and the funnel-shaped **Bay of Fundy**, with its dramatic tides and delightful coastline, is no less than outstanding. Equally, in **Fredericton**, the capital, the province has one of the region's most appealing towns, a laidback sort of place which, besides offering the bonus of the Beaverbrook Art Gallery, also possesses strings of fine old villas and a good-looking cathedral. Handsome scenery is within easy reach of the capital too – most obviously it's a short journey south to scenic **Passamaquoddy Bay**, an island-studded inlet of the Bay of Fundy that's home to the likeable resort of **St Andrews**.

Southeast of Fredericton, the Saint John River snakes a tortuous route to the Bay of Fundy at the busy port of **Saint John**. Like most of the settlements of southern New Brunswick, Saint John was founded by **United Empire Loyalists**, whose descendants, mingled with those of British colonists, account for around sixty percent of the province's 756,000 inhabitants. Some 126,000 people live here in Saint John, making this the province's big city – it's much larger than Fredericton – and, although hard times have left the place frayed at the edges, the city does boast a splendid sample of Victorian architecture. Also, although industry has scarred the Fundy coast near Saint John, there's still no denying the rugged charms of the city's setting, and not far away are the more pristine land- and seascapes of both the coastal **Fundy Trail Parkway** and **Fundy National Park**.

The remaining forty percent of New Brunswick's population are **French-speakers**, the descendants of those Acadians who settled in the region after the deportations of 1755 (see p.428). To avoid further persecution, these refugees clustered in the remote northern reaches of the province, though since the 1960s they have become more assertive, following the example set by their Québecois cousins. As a result, they have made **Moncton**, in southeast New Brunswick, the effective capital of modern Acadia, with a French-speaking university as their cultural centre. Moncton is, however, of limited interest to the

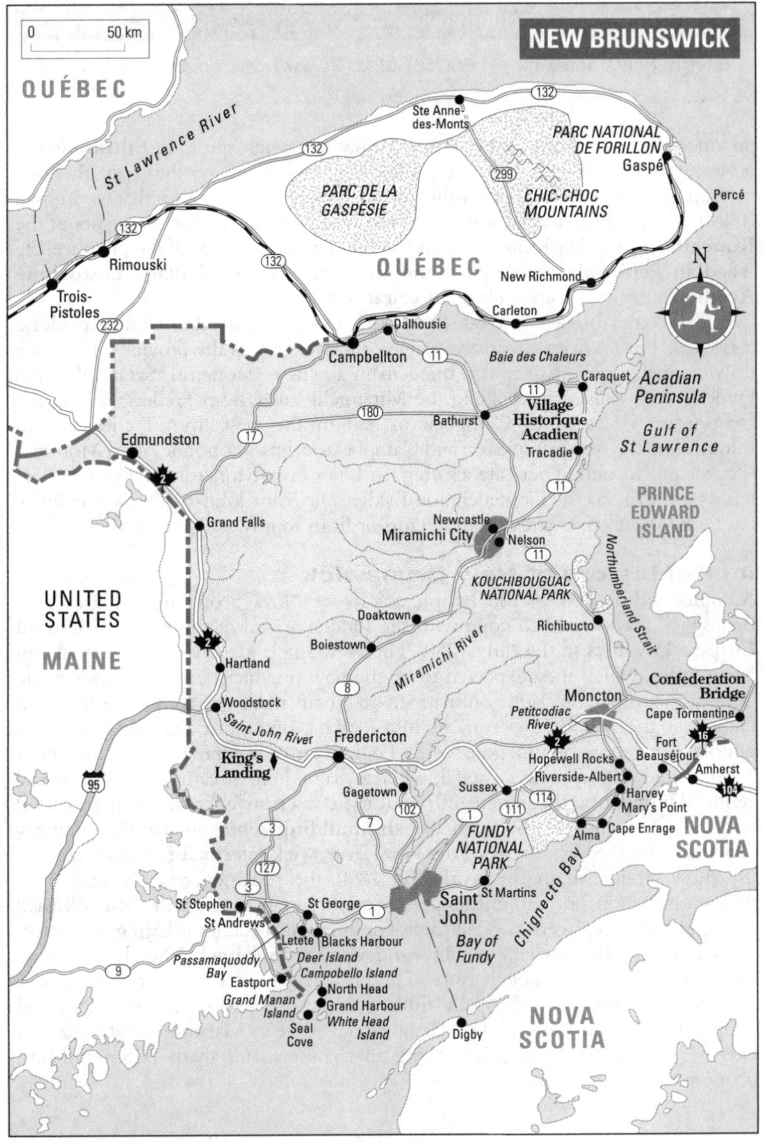

passing visitor – it's a modern, brassy, breezy sort of place – and is chiefly of use as a stepping stone either west to Fundy National Park or east to the beautifully remote remains of **Fort Beauséjour**.

As for the other Acadian districts, they are best visited on the way to Québec. Two main roads link Fredericton with its northern neighbour. The first – which is both more scenically diverting and more direct – slices up the western edge of the

New Brunswick information

Tourism New Brunswick ⓣ1-800/561-0123, ⓦwww.tourismnewbrunswick.ca.

province along the **Saint John River Valley** to French-speaking **Edmundston**, en route to Rivière-du-Loup (see p.338). The second cuts northeast for the long haul up the **Miramichi River Valley** to the cluster of small towns that are known collectively as **Miramichi City**. Near here are the untamed coastal marshes of the **Kouchibouguac National Park** and, in the northeast corner of the province, the **Acadian Peninsula**, whose pride and joy is the re-created **Village Historique Acadien**, near the fishing village of **Caraquet**.

Acadian Lines **buses** (ⓣ1-800/567-5151, ⓦwww.acadianbus.com) provides a reasonable but far from exhaustive range of services across the province. There are daily connections between the three main towns – Moncton, Saint John and Fredericton – plus services along the Miramichi valley from Fredericton, up the coast from Moncton to Campbellton and in the west from Fredericton to Edmunston. Beyond Edmunston and Campbellton, buses continue on to Montréal, Ottawa and Toronto. There are also regular buses from Moncton over to Charlottetown on PEI, via the Confederation Bridge. The Saint-John-to-Digby **car ferry** is a useful short cut if you're travelling to or from southwest Nova Scotia.

A brief history of New Brunswick

Administered as part of the British colony of Nova Scotia until 1784, New Brunswick was created to cope with the sudden arrival of thousands of **United Empire Loyalists** in the early 1780s. The New Englanders were concentrated in **Saint John**, which they expected to be the new provincial capital. However, the governor's aristocratic claque outmanoeuvred them, managing to get **Fredericton** chosen as the seat of government instead. This unpopular decision led to an unusual separation of functions, with Fredericton developing as the province's political and administrative capital, whereas Saint John became the commercial centre. Throughout the nineteenth century, conservative Fredericton stagnated whilst liberal Saint John boomed as a **shipbuilding** centre, its massive shipyards, dependent on the vast forests of the New Brunswick interior, becoming some of the most productive in the world. By 1890, the province was Canada's most prosperous region, but within the space of twenty years its economy had collapsed as steel steamers replaced wooden ships. The **recession** was long-lasting, ultimately reflecting New Brunswick's inability to develop a diversified industrial economy, and this remains the problem today. The province splutters along on the profits from its raw materials, principally timber, fish and potatoes, plus zinc, lead and copper from the northeast around Bathurst, but – like its Maritime neighbours – it exercises no control over price-setting mechanisms, and sharp boom-and-bust economic cycles continue.

Fredericton

Situated 100km or so inland from the Bay of Fundy on the banks of the Saint John River, **FREDERICTON**, the capital of New Brunswick, has a well-padded air, the streets of its tiny centre graced by well-established elms and genteel villas. There's scarcely any industry here and the population of 81,000 mostly work for the government or the university, at least partly fulfilling the

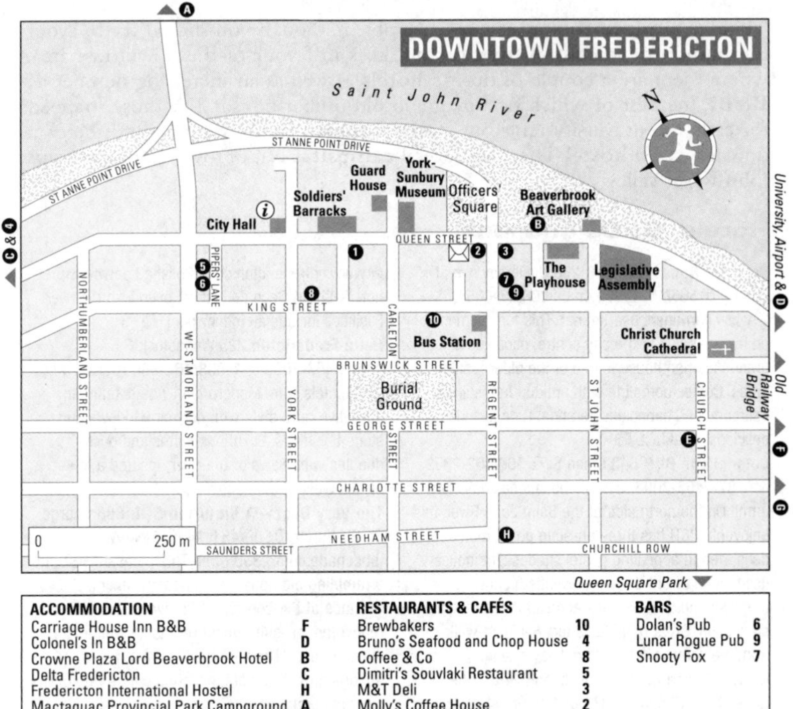

aims of one of the town's aristocratic sponsors, who announced in 1784: "it shall be the most gentlemanlike place on earth". Fredericton has few specific sights, but the **Beaverbrook Art Gallery**, the gift of that crusty old reactionary Lord Beaverbrook (1879–1964), is outstanding and there are several intriguing reminders of the British army in the handful of buildings that have survived from the old **Military Compound**.

Arrival, information and accommodation

The Acadian Lines **bus station** is at 101 Regent St at King, about five-minutes' walk south of the river and one block south of the main drag, Queen Street. There are no **trains** to Fredericton: the nearest service is to Moncton. Air Canada provides a wide range of domestic flights into Fredericton **airport**, 16km southeast of town; the taxi fare into the centre will cost you around $20.

Fredericton's main **Visitors Information Centre** is downtown in City Hall on the corner of Queen and York sts (daily: May to late June & Sept–Oct 8am–4.30pm; late June to Aug 8am–8pm; ⓣ506/460-2129 or 1-888/888-4768, ⓦwww.tourismfredericton.ca). They will call ahead to reserve accommodation for free and have all manner of leaflets on the city and its surroundings. In winter, information is available at the **Fredericton Tourism Office**, 11 Carleton St (Mon–Fri 8.15am–4.30pm; ⓣ506/460-2041 or 1-888/888-4768, ⓦwww.tourismfredericton.ca).

Finding a **place to stay** is rarely a problem, though you should try to avoid the humdrum motels on the city's outskirts in favour of the downtown area, where there are a couple of tip-top **hotels** as well as an increasing number of **B&Bs**, the best of which occupy grand old timber houses. For those strapped for cash, the university rents out **student rooms** in the summer and there's a downtown HI **hostel**. There are several **campsites** out of town along the Saint John River Valley.

Hotels, B&Bs and inns

Carriage House Inn B&B 230 University Ave at George ⓣ506/452-9924 or 1-800/267-6068, ⓦwww.carriagehouse-inn.net. This ten-room inn, on the east side of the city centre, occupies a grand Victorian house in one of the older residential areas. Comes complete with antique furnishings, ballroom, and capacious veranda. Rate includes delicious breakfast. ❺

Colonel's In B&B 843 Union St ⓣ506/452-2802 or 1-877/455-3003, ⓦwww.bbcanada.com/1749.html. On the north side of the Saint John River, this enjoyable B&B has three en-suite guest rooms decorated in appealing pastel shades. The house itself, dating from the early twentieth century, offers splendid views back across to Fredericton's downtown. Great breakfasts too. A 15min-walk from the centre via the old railway bridge. ❹

Crowne Plaza Lord Beaverbrook Hotel 659 Queen St ⓣ506/455-3371 or 1-866/444-1946, ⓦwww.cpfredericton.com. Polished downtown hotel with Art Deco flourishes; overlooks the river. Facilities include an indoor pool. ❻

Delta Fredericton 225 Woodstock Rd ⓣ506/457-7000 or 1-888/462-8800, ⓦwww.deltahotels.com. Modern high-rise hotel in an attractive retro style with dormer windows and stone finishings. Luxurious suites and posh doubles with views of the river; located a few blocks west of the centre. ❺

The Very Best – A Victorian B&B 806 George St at Church ⓣ506/451-1499, ⓦwww.bbcanada.com/2330.html. This pleasant B&B, in a rambling old house within easy walking distance of the centre, offers five tastefully renovated, en-suite guest rooms as well as an outside pool. "The very best" is a common aphorism in Miramichi, which is where one of the owners comes from. ❺

Hostel

Fredericton International Hostel (HI) 621 Churchill Row ⓣ506/450-4417, ⓦwww.hihostels.ca. Friendly HI hostel in a sparse, but well-kept older building about 500m south of downtown at the corner of Regent St. Kitchen facilities, laundry, and Internet access. Dorm beds for $20 (non-members $24). Also doubles.

Student rooms

UNB Residence Accommodation Residence Administration Building, University of New Brunswick, 20 Bailey Drive ⓣ506/453-4800, ⓦwww.unbf.ca/housing. Over a thousand single ($24) and double ($40) rooms for rent on the university campus, at the south end of University Ave just beyond Beaverbrook St, about 2km south of the river. Late May to mid-Aug.

Campsite

Mactaquac Provincial Park Campground 1256 Route 105, Mactaquac ⓣ506/363-4747. Large, popular and well-equipped campsite some 20km west of Fredericton, on the north side of the Saint John River off Route 105. Sites $21–24. May–Oct.

The City

The **Saint John River**, running from northern Maine to the Bay of Fundy, was long the fastest way to reach **Fredericton**, whose early streets, bounded by Brunswick Street to the south and York Street to the west, were laid out close to a curve of the river bank. Here the provincial administration set up shop and the garrison, stationed to counter the threat of American attack, paraded on the **Officers' Square**, at the foot of Regent Street. Mostly grassed over today, the square still has space for the **Changing of the Guard**, a re-enactment of British drill that takes place during the summer (July & Aug Fri–Sun at 11am & 4pm, Mon–Thurs 11am & 7pm; ⓣ506/460-2041). If you miss it, the sentry changes every hour on the hour, a brief march between the square and City Hall just along the street.

The square formed the eastern perimeter of the **Military Compound**, which once stretched over to York Street between Queen Street and the river. It was a large garrison for such a small place and, once Canada–US relations were on a secure footing, the attitude of the local citizenry towards the antics of the military hardened. They could put up with the grog shops and brothels discreetly located on the other side of the river, but they were infuriated by a huge brawl between soldiers and sailors that swept right across town – and indeed when the British regulars finally departed in 1869 many were relieved. One reminder of the British presence is the elegant three-storey **Officers' Quarters**, on the square's west side, whose symmetrical columns and stone arches follow a design much used by Queen Victoria's Royal Engineers. Inside, the **York-Sunbury Historical Museum** (April–June Tues–Sat 1–4pm; July & Aug Mon–Sat 10am–5pm & Sun noon–5pm; Sept–Nov Tues–Sat 1–4pm; $3) possesses an intriguing assortment of local bygones, which fills every nook and cranny of this warren-like building. The ground floor kicks off with displays on Fredericton under the British and up above – on the second floor – are military uniforms, armaments and a reconstruction of a World War I trench. Moving on, the third floor holds a couple of Native Canadian rooms, with a ragbag of archeological finds, plus the stuffed remains of the twenty-kilo "Coleman Frog", a giant-sized amphibian of dubious origins. It's not known whether the creature is real or not, but the local innkeeper, who produced it in the 1880s, claimed to have fed it on beer and buttermilk.

A few metres west along Queen, at the foot of Carleton Street, is the **Guard House** (June–Aug daily 10am–6pm; free), where guides in period British uniforms show you round a restored orderly room, a guardroom and detention cells that create a fearsome picture of military life in the middle of the nineteenth century: the guardroom is little different from the airless cells where villains were locked up waiting to be flogged, branded and/or transported. Directly opposite, with its back to Queen Street, is the **Soldiers' Barracks** (same times) a sturdy three-storey block that at one time accommodated more than two hundred squaddies. Most of the building has been turned into offices and its street-level arcades house arts and craft stalls, but one room has been restored to its appearance in the early 1800s.

Beaverbrook Art Gallery

Lord Beaverbrook (1879–1964), the newspaper tycoon and champion of the British Empire, was raised in New Brunswick's Newcastle (see p.470), and although he moved to England in 1910 – becoming a close friend of Churchill and a key member of his war cabinet – he sustained a sentimental attachment to his homeland. In Fredericton his largesse was extended to the university, the Playhouse Theatre, and the **Beaverbrook Art Gallery**, by the river at the foot of St John Street (daily 9am–5.30pm, Thurs till 9pm; $8, Thurs after 5.30pm voluntary donation; ⓦwww.beaverbrookartgallery.org). It's a first-rate gallery, where an eclectic and regularly rotated collection of mostly British and Canadian art is squeezed into a dozen or so rooms, sharing space with an imaginative programme of temporary exhibitions; free plans are issued at reception.

Salvador Dali's monumental *Santiago El Grande*, depicting St James being borne up towards a vaulted firmament on a white charger, usually takes pride of place at the **entrance** – a Dali blitzkrieg after which it takes time to adjust to the subtler works beyond. Here, Hogarth, Reynolds, Gainsborough, Constable, Turner, Landseer, Augustus John, Francis Bacon and Lowry represent the British and there's also a small sample of medieval paintings plus a haunting *Lady Macbeth Sleep-Walking* by Delacroix.

The extensive **Canadian collection** features well-known artists like Paul Kane (see p.96), the Group of Seven (see p.94) and Emily Carr, as well as lesser figures like the early nineteenth-century artist George Chambers, whose *"The Terror" Iced-in off Cape Comfort* is a wonderfully melodramatic canvas, the creaking ship crushed by the ice underneath a dark and forbidding sky. Dominique Serres (1722–93), a favourite of George III, never visited Canada, but he saw sketches made by returning naval officers that proved sufficient for him to produce *The Bishop's House with Ruined Town of Québec* and *The Intendant's Palace, Québec*, townscapes in the soft-hued Italian style. There's also a good selection of the works of the prolific **Cornelius Krieghoff** (1815–72), who made a living churning out souvenir pictures of Indians and French Canadians from the time of his arrival in Canada in 1840. Krieghoff had a roller-coaster life. Born to a German father and Dutch mother, he emigrated to New York in 1836 and promptly joined the US army, serving in the Second Seminole War down in Florida. Discharged in 1840, Krieghoff immediately re-enlisted, claimed three months' advance pay and deserted, hotfooting it to Montréal with the French-Canadian woman he had met and married in New York. Montréal was a disaster – no one would buy his paintings – but when he moved to Québec City he found a ready market for his work amongst the British officers of the large garrison and their well-heeled friends. This was Krieghoff's most productive period and the finely detailed, carefully composed anecdotal scenes

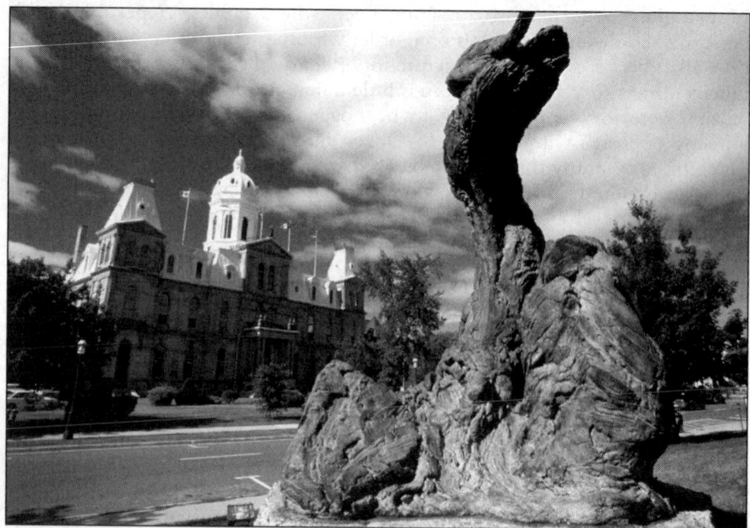

△ Beaverbrook Art Gallery

of French-Canadian life he painted during these years are his best. Two of the finest, *Merrymaking* and *Coming Storm at the Portage*, can be seen here amongst no fewer than 27 of his paintings.

Legislative Assembly Building and around

The **Legislative Assembly Building** (guided tours: early June to mid-Aug daily 9am–7pm; mid-Aug to early June Mon–Fri 9am–4pm; free), the home of New Brunswick's parliament, stands opposite the art gallery, its robust and imposing exterior topped by a ponderous tower and cupola. The interior holds a sumptuously decorated Assembly Chamber, adorned with portraits of George III and Queen Charlotte by Joshua Reynolds, as well as a splendid oak and cherry spiral staircase leading to the chamber's visitors' gallery. The Reynolds were rescued from the previous parliament building, which burnt down in 1880.

The Legislature occupies the grandest building in Fredericton, but the nearby **Christ Church Cathedral**, King Street and Church (mid-June to Aug Mon–Fri 9am–6pm, Sat 10am–5pm, Sun 1–5pm; Sept to mid-June Mon–Fri 9am–4pm; free guided tours from mid-June to Aug), comes a close second. A mid-Victorian copy of the fifteenth-century parish church of Snettisham, in Norfolk, England, it's distinguished by the elegance of its tapering spire and the intricate grace of its red-pine hammerbeam ceiling. The church also marks the beginning of the smartest part of town, whose leafy streets, lined by handsome Victorian mansions complete with gingerbread scrollwork and expansive verandas, stretch south towards tiny **Queen Square Park**. Near here too – at the east end of Brunswick Street – the old **railway bridge** has been pedestrianized and is easily the nicest way to cross the Saint John River. The bridge is actually part of a system of hiking trails that loops through and around Fredericton focused on the river. There are several jetties dotted along the trails and in the summertime **passenger boats** ($3 per trip, $4 return) link them several times daily, except in bad weather. Maps of the hiking trails and boat timetables are available from the tourist office.

Eating and drinking

Downtown Fredericton offers a reasonable range of informal **cafés** and **restaurants** and there are enough **bars** to entertain for a night or two. In the summer, there's also free outdoor theatre and live music down on Officers' Square. The Playhouse (Ⓣ506/458-8344 or 1-866/884-5800, Ⓦwww.theplayhouse.nb.ca), beside the Legislative Assembly Building, puts on a good variety of shows and is home to the province's only professional English-speaking **theatre** company, Theatre New Brunswick (Sept–April season). The tourist office has the details of all up-and-coming events.

Cafés and restaurants

Brewbakers 546 King St between Regent and Carleton Ⓣ506/459-0067. First-rate wood-fired pizzas at affordable prices ($12 and up), plus steaks and seafood. Jam-packed at the weekend. Open Mon–Fri 11.30am–10pm, Sat 4–11pm & Sun 4–9pm.

Bruno's Seafood and Chop House At the Delta Hotel, 225 Woodstock Rd Ⓣ506/451-7935. One of the most popular spots in town, this café-restaurant is noted for its lavish help-yourself buffets where the emphasis is on pasta and seafood. Eat either inside the hotel or outside on the large riverside patio and watch the sunset. Daily 6.30am–10pm.

Coffee & Co 415 King St at York. Great coffees – probably the best range in town – plus tasty cakes and sandwiches. Open Mon–Fri 7am–6pm, Sat 8am–6pm & Sun 9.30am–6pm.

Dimitri's Souvlaki Restaurant Pipers Lane, 349 King St Ⓣ506/452-8882. Good, standard-issue

Greek restaurant amongst the café-bars crowding Pipers Lane, in between King and Queen sts, just west of York. Mon–Sat 11am–10pm.

M&T Deli 602 Queen at Regent St. Fredericton's best deli, specializing in New York-style bagels and Montréal smoked meat. Mon–Fri 7.30am–4pm.

Molly's Coffee House 554 Queen St. Fine coffee and tasty snacks in this pocket-sized, touch-of-New-Age café. Opposite Officers' Square.

The Palate Restaurant 462 Queen St ⓣ506/450-7911. Bright and breezy café-cum-restaurant with a lively, inventive menu featuring everything from baby spinach salad to porcini and escargot brie. In the evening, main courses range from $16–22, and there's a tasty "pasta of the day" too. Mon–Thurs 10am–9pm, Fri & Sat 10am–10pm.

Bars

Dolan's Pub Pipers Lane, 349 King St ⓣ506/454-7474. Bustling bar with imported and domestic beers on draught. Regular live folk music. Closed Sun.

Lunar Rogue Pub 625 King St ⓣ506/450-2065. Busy bar serving British and Maritime ales as well as an extensive range of malt whiskeys. Live music on most weekends. Summer patio.

Snooty Fox 66 Regent St at Queen. Filling bar food as well as a good range of draught beers, both domestic and imported, at this bustling downtown bar.

Southeast of Fredericton: Gagetown

When it comes to **moving on from Fredericton**, you're spoiled for choice: you could head northwest up the Saint John River Valley to Edmundston (see p.468) and Québec, northeast along the Miramichi River Valley to Miramichi City and the Acadian Peninsula (see p.472), or southwest a short way to Passamaquoddy Bay (see below).

A fourth option is to head **southeast** to Saint John (see p.455), either on the fast and direct Hwy 7 or along the more leisurely **Highway 102**, which weaves its way along the rusticated banks of the Saint John River. If you choose Hwy 102, be sure to spend an hour or two in **GAGETOWN**, a pretty little village whose graceful old houses are sprinkled along the riverside about 60km from Fredericton – and 100km from Saint John. There are several enjoyable craft and pottery shops here, including **Grimross Crafts**, where thirty artists exhibit under one roof, as well as gentle riverside walks, a prim and proper Anglican church, and a grand old courthouse of 1836. *Beamsley's Coffee House*, 44 Front St, offers tasty snacks and sandwiches and there are several **places to stay**. The pick of Gagetown's several B&Bs is the well-kept *Step-Aside B&B* (ⓣ506/488-1808; ❸; May–Dec), whose four guest rooms are in an 1880s house down by the river at 58 Front St.

Passamaquoddy Bay

In the southwest corner of New Brunswick, abutting the US state of Maine, lies **Passamaquoddy Bay**, a deeply indented inlet of the Bay of Fundy whose sparsely populated shoreline is a bony, bumpy affair of forest, rock and swamp. Easily the prettiest of the region's coastal villages is **St Andrews**, a Loyalist settlement turned seaside resort, 135km south of Fredericton and equipped with a battery of great inns and B&Bs. The other main attraction is the **Fundy Islands** archipelago at the mouth of Passamaquoddy Bay. Here, accessible from the US by road and from mainland New Brunswick by ferry (via **Deer Island**), lies **Campobello Island**, the site of Franklin Roosevelt's immaculately maintained country home. Finally, stuck out in the bay two hours by ferry from the Canadian mainland, is the far larger **Grand Manan Island**, a much wilder and remoter spot that is noted for its imposing sea cliffs and rich birdlife.

St Andrews

ST ANDREWS was once a busy fishing port and trading centre but is now a leafy resort with a laid-back air that makes for a restful place to spend a night or two. The town is at its prettiest amongst the antique clapboard houses flanking King Street – which leads up the hill from the busy little pier – while **Water Street**, the main drag, tracks along the waterfront lined with cafés and craft shops. The only sights as such are the **Kingsbrae Horticultural Garden** (mid-May to early Oct daily 9am–6pm; $9) on the crest of King Street and the squat, minuscule **St Andrews blockhouse**, a replica of the original wooden fort built in 1813 to protect the area from the Americans. It's at the west end of Water Street, and at low tide you can scramble around the reefs and rock pools just below. The pier is packed with boat-tour companies. Amongst several, Quoddy Link Marine (Ⓣ506/529-2600 or 1-877/688-2600, Ⓦwww.quoddylinkmarine.com) operates first-class **whale-watching** cruises (late June to Sept 1–3 daily; 3hr; $50), each of which has a naturalist on board; and Seascape runs regular **kayak trips** from $65 per half-day (early May to late Sept; Ⓣ506/747-1844 or 1-866/747-1884, Ⓦwww.seascapekayaktours.com). Of particular interest also are the guided tours of **Minister's Island** (mid-May to mid-Oct 1–2 daily; 2hr; Ⓣ506/529-5081; Ⓦwww.ministersisland.org; $8), whose undulating farmland is reached by car along a tidal causeway. The island was once the property of William Van Horne, a Victorian railway baron, who built a grand stone mansion here alongside a clutter of farm buildings. Highlights of the two-hour tour include a romp round the dilapidated mansion and inspection of the windmill, with its kerosene-powered reserve engines. You also get to check out the tidal bathhouse down on the seashore and the magnificent, state-of-the-art livestock barn, where Horne pampered his horses and cattle – treating them, according to local lore, rather better than he did his workforce.

Practicalities

St Andrews is accessible by Acadian Lines **bus** from Saint John (1 daily; 1hr 15min) and passengers are dropped on Water Street, a couple of blocks east of the pier. The **tourist office** is on Hwy 127 as you enter the town (daily: early May to June 9am–5pm; July & Aug 8am–8pm; Sept to early Oct 9.30am–5.30pm; Ⓣ506/529-3556, Ⓦwww.townofstandrews.ca). They issue free tide tables and town maps, supply information on local bike rental, have the schedule for visits to Minister's Island, and will happily help you with accommodation, though advance bookings are a good idea during the height of the season. Most illustrious of the **hotels** is the *Kingsbrae Arms*, 219 King St (Ⓣ506/529-1897, Ⓦwww.kingsbrae.com; ❽), a sumptuous, immaculately maintained mansion overlooking the botanical gardens. There are just eight guest rooms here, six of them suites with balconies offering wide views of the gardens and the bay, and each is decorated in lavish modern style. An excellent second choice is the *Windsor House*, on the seafront at 132 Water St (Ⓣ506/529-3330 or 1-888/890-9463, Ⓦwww.windsorhouseinn.com; ❽; April–Dec), a beautifully restored eighteenth-century inn with antiques in the public rooms and six opulent guest rooms beyond. The largest hotel in town is the *Fairmont Algonquin* (Ⓣ506/529-8823 or 1-800/441-1414, Ⓦwww.fairmont.com; ❻), a sprawling and well-equipped resort complex whose turrets and gables, dating from 1915, dominate the northwest of town, about 1.5km from the waterfront on Prince of Wales Street.

More affordable are the **B&Bs**, beginning with the *Harris Hatch Inn*, an elegant, broadly Georgian mansion with shutters, fanlight and Neoclassical columns a short walk from the pier at 142 Queen St (Ⓣ506/529-4995, Ⓦwww.bbcanada.com/1439.html; ❹). Another good bet is the *Garden Gate B&B*, whose wide Edwardian verandas and lovely garden are in a quiet part of town at 364 Montague St (Ⓣ506/529-4453, Ⓦwww.bbgardengate.com; ❺). Very different is *Salty Towers*, 340 Water St (Ⓣ506/529-4585; ❷), where guests are encouraged to treat this charmingly ramshackle old house as their own in what can only be described as a cross between a 1960s commune and a 1940s guest-house; it's unique and great fun. Finally, the popular *Kiwanis Oceanfront Camping* (Ⓣ506/529-3439; May to mid-Oct) has a great seaside location just over 1km east of the town centre along Water Street.

St Andrews has an excellent range of **cafés** and the occasional good **restaurant**. The inexpensive *Gables Restaurant Bar & Patio*, 143 Water St (Ⓣ506/529-3440), is a funky little place serving tasty food from its bayshore location, while the *Lobster Bay Eatery,* just along the street at no. 113 (Ⓣ506/529-4840), is a family-oriented restaurant offering up delicious lobsters. The *Windsor House*, 132 Water St (Wed–Sat noon–2pm & 6–9.30pm; Ⓣ506/529-3330), gets into the gastronomic act too, offering tasty lunches and dinners in smart, period surroundings; main courses here start for as little as $10.

Deer Island

Deer Island, a pocket-sized member of the Fundy archipelago, is uninspiring – its handful of ribbon villages straggling amongst low forested hills – but you do have to cross it to reach Campobello Island from the rest of New Brunswick. **Ferries** to Deer Island (Mon–Sat every 30min 7am–7pm, then hourly till 10pm; Sun same hours, hourly; 20min; free; first-come first-served; Ⓣ506/453-3939 or 1-888/747-7006) leave from **Letete** on the southeast shore of Passamaquoddy Bay, 14km south of Hwy 1 (and the village of St George). They dock at the island's northern shore, from where it's a 16km drive south to the **Deer Island–Campobello ferry** (late June to mid-Sept hourly 8.30am–5.30/6.30pm; 35min; car & driver $14, foot passenger $3; Ⓣ506/747-2159; first-come first-served). Ferries also sail from this jetty to **Eastport in Maine** (late June to mid-Sept hourly 9am–7pm; 20min; car & driver $11).

Metres from the jetty, at the southern tip of the island, is **Deer Island Point Park**, which overlooks a narrow sound where it's sometimes possible to hear the whirlpool known as the Old Sow; it's caused by the Fundy tides as they sweep round the island and is at its noisiest three hours before high tide. There's a well-appointed seashore campsite in the park (Ⓣ506/747-2423; June–Sept).

Campobello Island

Franklin D. Roosevelt (1882–1945) loved **Campobello Island** for its quiet wooded coves, rocky headlands and excellent fishing. Those sleepy days are long gone, but although the island, which is just 16km long by 5km wide, is now sprinkled with second homes and busy with day-trippers, the southern half is protected as the **Roosevelt Campobello International Park**. Here, mixed forests, marshes, tidal flats, beaches and gullies are explored by 24km of gravel road, which give access to a variety of gentle hiking trails. Several of these – including the enjoyable, 1.5km-long walk over to Friar's Head – begin beside the island's star turn, the red and green **Roosevelt Cottage** (late May to mid-Oct daily 10am–6pm; free), set amongst the woods by the seashore about 3km south of the ferry dock. One look at the place and you'll see that "cottage" is

Remember that Maine is on **Eastern Time**, one hour behind New Brunswick's **Atlantic Time**.

an understatement – it's a 35-room mansion built in a Dutch colonial style and packed with memorabilia, from the great man's childhood potty and the Christmas list he made when he was knee-high through to the megaphone with which the children were summoned to dinner. It was at the cottage in 1921 that Roosevelt contracted polio and, poignantly, the stretcher on display was the one used to carry him off the island.

Reached from the north by means of the Deer Island ferry (see opposite) and from the south over the bridge from Lubec in Maine, Campobello Island is easily seen in a day, but, if you do decide **to stay**, head for *Lupine Lodge* (ⓣ506/752-2555 or 1-888/912-8880, ⓦwww.lupinelodge.com; ❹; late May to mid-Oct), whose delightful log cabins, with their Art Deco lines, occupy a clearing in the woods, in sight of the sea about 500m north of Roosevelt Cottage. The lodge itself dates from 1915 and holds a first-class and reasonably priced **restaurant** featuring local ingredients – Fundy haddock, Maine shrimp and so forth.

Grand Manan Island

At the mouth of the Bay of Fundy lies **Grand Manan Island**, a rugged nature hotspot some 30km from tip to toe. The unique geology, wildlife and atmosphere of the place make it a popular destination for day-trippers as well as holiday-makers, with ornithologists and geologists leading the way. A geological fault essentially splits the island in two: the west side of the island is dominated by dark, imposing craggy cliffs of volcanic origin, the east by reddish sedimentary rock, whose crumblings have created some beautiful sandy – and occasionally magnetic – beaches. The ferry docks towards the north end of the island at **NORTH HEAD**, a tiny settlement that is home to the **Whale and Seabird Research Station** (daily: June, Sept & Oct 10am–4pm; July & Aug 9am–5pm; donation suggested), which operates several research and release programmes for seabirds, porpoises and the endangered right whale. The centre provides an excellent introduction to the several sorts of whale that hunt the waters hereabouts – Grand Manan is a popular place to come whale-watching (see p.454). North Head also has a **tourist office** about 1.5km from the ferry terminal, in the Business Centre on the main coastal road at no.130 Hwy 776 (May to mid-Oct daily 9am–5pm; ⓣ506/662-3442 or 1-888-525-1655, ⓦwww.grandmanannb.com). They provide an invaluable booklet of trails and footpaths and will also help with booking accommodation, although it's advisable to book in advance before you catch the ferry in high season. The rocky coast to the north of North Head provides some of the island's best **hiking** with both the Swallows Tail Lighthouse and the Hole in the Wall rock formation being just over a kilometre from the ferry terminal. Alternatively, you can hire a **sea kayak** or **bike** from Adventure High, also on Hwy 776 at no.83 (ⓣ506/662-3563 or 1-800/732-5492, ⓦwww.adventurehigh.com).

From North Head, the main road hugs the coast southwards to **GRAND HARBOUR**, the main settlement, where the **Grand Manan Museum**, 1141 Hwy 776 (mid-June to mid-Sept Mon–Fri 9am–5pm; $5) houses a large collection of stuffed birds, including many of the 300-plus species that congregate on the island throughout the year. The naturalist and painter James John Audubon first documented the island's assembly of puffins, gannets,

Ferries to Grand Manan

To get to Grand Manan Island, catch the **car ferry** from **Blacks Harbour**, located 10km south of Hwy 1 between St Andrews and Saint John (late June to mid-Sept 6–7 daily; mid-Sept to late June 3–4 daily; 1hr 30min–2hr; cars $32 return, passengers $12 return; ⓣ506/662-3724, ⓦwww.coastaltransport.ca). Spaces are allocated on a first-come, first-served basis so it is advisable to arrive at least an hour before the departure time, and be prepared to queue, especially in July and Aug; no fares are collected on the outward journey – you pay the whole deal on the way back.

guillemots, stormy petrels and kittiwakes during his visit in 1831. The best bird-watching times are in the spring migratory period (early April to early June), the summer nesting season and the autumn migration (late Aug through Sept).

Pushing on south from Grand Harbour, it's 3.5km to **Ingalls Head**, from where a toll-free **ferry** (4–10 daily; 25min) scuttles over to **White Head Island**, a tiny islet whose delightfully quiet beach makes for a pleasant day trip. Back on Grand Manan, it's a brief drive southwest from Grand Harbour to **SEAL COVE**, a fishing village that still bears the signs of the once-thriving smoked herring industry. Restored smokehouses and rickety wharves crowd the small harbour, where the prize catch now is lobster. The village is also home to the dependable Sea Watch Tours (ⓣ506/662-8552 or 1-877/662-8552, ⓦwww.seawatchtours.com), who run **whale-watching** trips from mid-July to late Sept; they also offer **bird-watching** tours from late June to mid-August; both cost around $55 per person.

Practicalities

There's a healthy supply of **accommodation** on Grand Manan, though there's nothing pretentious or grand – it's all pleasantly low-key and distinctly folksy. Just outside **North Head**, one especially good choice is the *Swallowtail Inn B&B*, whose six guest rooms are in the two former homes of the lighthouse keeper at 50 Lighthouse Rd (ⓣ506/662-1100, ⓦwww.swallowtailinn.com; ❹; June–Oct); the neighbouring lighthouse is still operational – as you will no doubt come to realize when the fog comes down and the fog horn goes off. A second appealing North Head choice is *The Inn at Whale Cove Cottages*, 26 Whale Cove Cottage Rd (ⓣ506/662-3181, ⓦwww.holidayjunction.com/whalecove; ❺), where there are three cosy, shaker-furnished en-suite rooms in a peaceful seashore location. To get there, turn off the main road in North Head and head 700m up Whistle Road. Also in North Head, just up from the post office, is the unassuming *Marathon Inn,* 19 Marathon Lane (ⓣ506/662-8488 or 1-888/660-8488, ⓦwww.marathoninn.com; ❹; May–Oct), a wing of which was won in a poker game at the turn of the twentieth century and then promptly transported here 1km along the road. There are 15 rooms, with basic comforts and many have sea views; note that the Marathon bills itself as an 'Elder Hostel'. At the opposite end of the island, **Seal Cove** chimes in with *McLaughlin's Wharf Inn* (ⓣ506/662-8760; ❹; June–Sept), which occupies an old post office on the harbour with a large deck where great home- cooked meals are served. As regards **camping**, the *Hole-in-the-Wall Park Campground* near North Head (ⓣ506/662-3152 or 1-866/662-4489, ⓦwww.grandmanancamping.com; May–Oct) offers some breathtaking cliff-top pitches, but they are popular, so arrive early or book ahead.

The island has a fair crop of **cafés** and **restaurants**, but the seasonal dining room of *The Inn at Whale Cove* (reservations required on ⓣ506/662-3181) is the best. They do excellent lunches and evening meals with an abundance of fresh produce and they also run a gourmet take-away lunch shop. Not far away, the *North Head Bakery,* 199 Hwy 776, bakes French artisan bread and pastries and is a great place to stock up for a picnic. Don't forget to sample a true Grand Manan treat– **dulse** (edible seaweed). It grows on the western shore, in the shade of the cliffs, and is sold all over the island – just look for the signs.

Saint John

At first sight **SAINT JOHN** (never "St John", and not to be mixed up with St John's, Newfoundland) seems a confusing hotchpotch of industrial and residential zones spread over the bluffs, valleys and plateaus where the Saint John River twists and turns its way into the Bay of Fundy, 100km southeast of Fredericton. In fact, the downtown area is squeezed onto a chubby peninsula immediately east of the river mouth – a surprisingly compact centre for a city of 126,000 people with the focus firmly on the short main drag, **King Street**. In 1877, a fire wiped out most of the town, but as a major shipbuilding centre Saint John was sufficiently wealthy to withstand the costs of immediate reconstruction. Consequently, almost all the city's older buildings – at their most resplendent along and around **Prince William Street** – are late Victorian. Most of the shipyards have now gone and the place survives as a modest seaport and manufacturing town – hence the belching chimneys – with a good range of restaurants. Apart from its diverting Victorian architecture, Saint John's leading attractions are the **New Brunswick Museum** and the **Reversing Falls Rapids**; the latter is a good place to see the effects of the Fundy tides. The town's most famous son is actor Donald Sutherland; its most celebrated product, Moosehead beer.

Arrival

From the Acadian Lines **bus depot**, at 19 Chesley Drive, it's a fifteen-minute walk east to Market Slip. There are no **rail** services; the nearest you'll get is Moncton (see p.465). Saint John's **ferry terminal**, 5km west of the centre across the mouth of the Saint John River, is served by Bay Ferries (ⓣ1-888/249-7245, ⓦwww.bayferries.com), which has services across the Bay of Fundy to Digby, Nova Scotia (1–3 daily; 3hr; passengers $25–39 one-way, cars $75–95, bicycles $10–12). There are no buses direct to the centre from the terminal – take a waiting cab or call Diamond Taxi (ⓣ506/648-8888). **Driving** into downtown Saint John can be a baffling experience; the easiest route is to keep on Hwy 1 and follow the signs from Exit 122.

Information and city transport

The main **tourist office** is right in the centre of town in the Market Square mall, beside Market Slip at the foot of King Street (daily: early June to Aug 9.30am–8pm; rest of year 9.30am–6pm; ⓣ506/658-2855 or 1-866/463-8639, ⓦwww.tourismsaintjohn.com). They will help with accommodation and have a wide range of local and provincial information. This is also the best place to get the latest details of local **boat trips**: the two most appealing are jetboat rides up the Reversing Falls Rapids (see p.460) and Bay of Fundy whale-watching

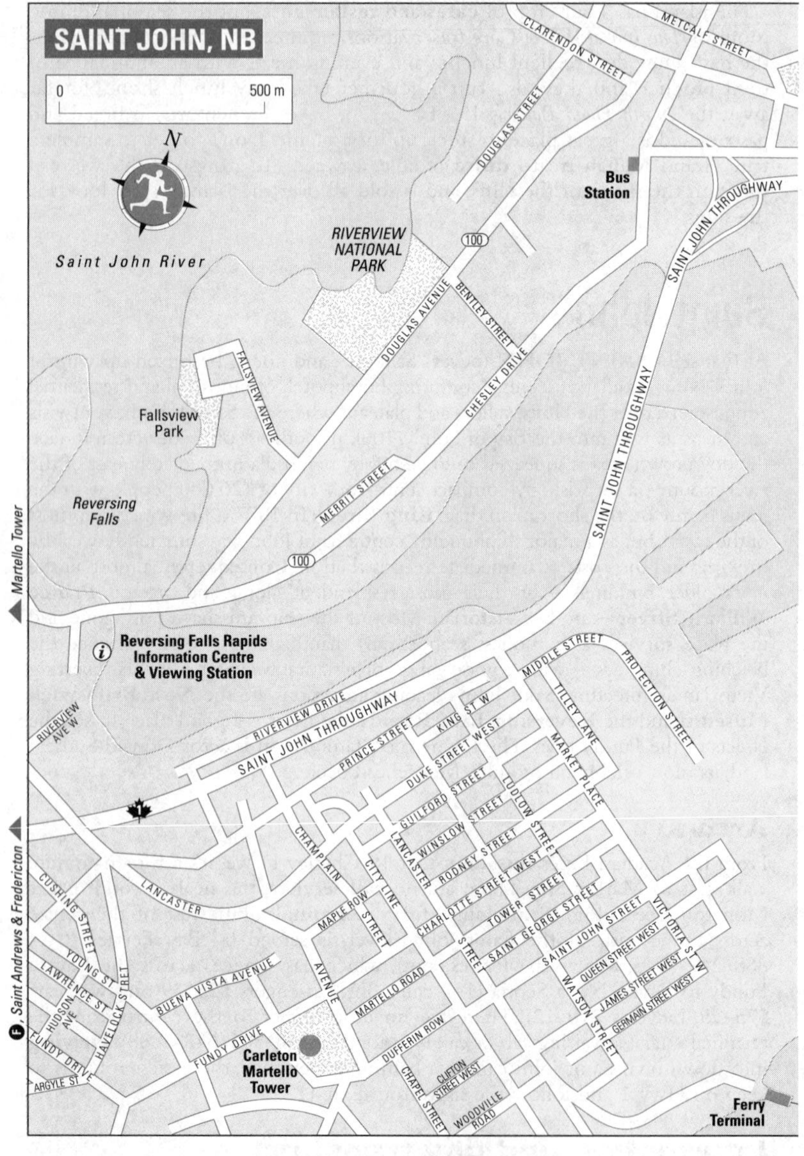

excursions. Of particular note, too, is the tourist office's excellent (and free) walking-tour leaflet on the city's architectural heritage. As for **city transport**, Saint John Transit (Ⓣ506/658-4700, Ⓦwww.saintjohntransit.com) operates a reasonable range of bus services; most start and finish downtown at King's Square. The East–West bus (#1, #2, #3 or #4), running from King's Square to the Reversing Falls Rapids, is the one you're most likely to use.

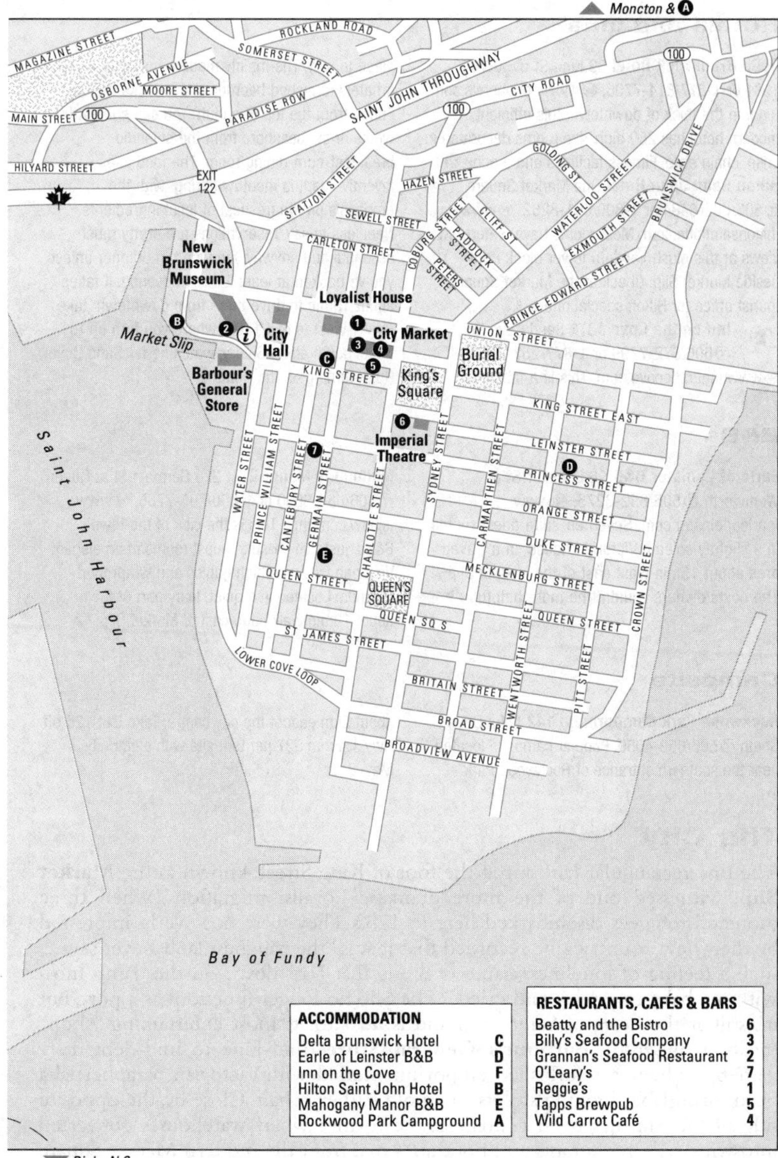

Accommodation

There's no shortage of **accommodation** in Saint John. Budget motels line up along the main routes into the city, but for something more interesting – and often no more expensive – you're much better off staying in a downtown hotel or B&B. There is also an outstanding inn a short drive just west of the city, beside the Bay of Fundy.

Hotels and inns

Delta Brunswick Hotel 39 King St ⓣ506/648-1981 or 1-877/814-7706, ⓦwww.deltahotels.com. Right in the thick of downtown, this efficient, modern hotel has 250 high-rise rooms decorated in crisp, chain style. Fitness facilities and a pool. ❻

Hilton Saint John Hotel One Market Square ⓣ506/693-8484 or 1-800/561-8282, ⓦwww.hiltonsaintjohn.com. Most rooms have waterfront views at this plush, modern tower block right beside Market Slip. Check at the Market Square tourist office for Hilton special offers. ❻

Inn on the Cove 1371 Sand Cove Rd ⓣ506/672-7799 or 1-877/257-8080, ⓦwww.innonthecove.com. This is a fabulous place to stay. The mainly modern inn, with its six ornately furnished bedrooms, overlooks the Bay of Fundy from the top of a bluff. You can survey the whole of the seashore from the splendid breakfast-cum-dining room. The food is as inventive as it is mouthwatering, with the emphasis on the freshest of local ingredients. Needless to say, reservations are pretty much essential and anyway you won't get dinner unless you've booked at least 24hr in advance. It takes about 10min to drive there from downtown: take Hwy 1 west to exit 119A, where you turn off to travel south along Bleury, watching for Sand Cove Rd, a turning on the right. ❻

B&Bs

Earle of Leinster B&B 96 Leinster St at Wentworth ⓣ506/652-3275, ⓦwww.earleofleinster.com. Seven en-suite guest rooms in a slightly solemn Victorian house, in a frayed area about 15min walk east of the Market Slip. The hosts/owners couldn't be more helpful. ❹

Mahogany Manor B&B 220 Germain St at Queen ⓣ506/636-8000 or 1-800/796-7755, ⓦwww.sjnow.com/mm. This is the pick of the town's B&Bs, just five en-suite guest rooms in an elegant Victorian villa with high gables and wrapround veranda. Located in a quiet, leafy part of town about 10min walk southeast of Market Slip. ❹

Campsite

Rockwood Park Campground 142 Lake Drive South ⓣ506/652-4050. Popular campsite located near the southern entrance of Rockwood Park about 2km east of the city centre. Take Exit 125 off Hwy 1. From $27 per tent site with electricity. May–Sept.

The City

The tiny rectangular harbour at the foot of King Street, known as the **Market Slip**, witnessed one of the more dramatic Loyalist migrations, when three thousand refugees disembarked here in 1783. They were not overly impressed by their new country; one recorded that it was "the roughest land I ever saw… such a feeling of loneliness came over me that I sat down on the damp moss with my baby in my lap and cried." The Slip no longer functions as a port, but it's still at the heart of Saint John and is next to its most entertaining "shop" (really a museum), **Barbour's General Store** (mid-June to mid-Sept daily 9am–6pm; free), a refurbished emporium stuffed with Victorian paraphernalia from formidable-looking sweets to an old barber's chair. Close by, the opposite side of the Slip has been gentrified, the former wharf warehouses converted into wine bars, restaurants and boutiques that front the modern Market Square shopping mall behind. Inside the mall, the **New Brunswick Museum** (Mon–Wed & Fri 9am–5pm, Thurs 9am–9pm, Sat 10am–5pm & Sun noon–5pm; $6) is devoted to the province's human, natural and artistic life and has a particularly revealing section on the Age of Sail as well as a fine collection of Chinese decorative and applied art. In addition, there's much on the region's marine life, including the skeleton of a rare North Atlantic Right whale in the "Hall of Great Whales" and a thirteen-metre-high tidal tube constructed to illustrate the rise and fall of the Bay of Fundy tides.

From Market Slip, it's a five-minute walk east on King Street and left along Germain to the white wooden **Loyalist House**, at 120 Union St (mid-May to June Mon–Fri 10am–5pm; July to mid-Sept daily 10am–5pm; $3). Built in 1820 for merchant David Merritt – whose descendants lived here for six generations – the house boasts an attractive interior kitted out with early nineteenth-century furnishings and fittings, most notably a fine, sweeping staircase, cleverly worked curved doors and hand-carved mouldings. Costumed guides give the lowdown on Loyalist life. Just down the hill, back along Germain, is the entrance to the lively **City Market** (Mon–Thurs 7.30am–6pm, Fri 7.30am–7pm & Sat 7.30am–5pm), heaped with the characteristic foods of New Brunswick – **fiddleheads**, a succulent fern tip that tastes rather like asparagus, and **dulse**, a dried seaweed that enlivens the chowders hereabouts. Behind the market are the Union Jack paths and fanciful Edwardian bandstand of **King's Square**.

Prince William Street

After the fire of 1877, the city's merchant class funded a rebuilding programme that would, they believed, properly reflect Saint John's status as a major seaport and shipbuilding centre. Blissfully unaware of the hard years ahead, they competed with each other in the construction of grand offices and banks, brimmingly self-confident structures that line up along **Prince William Street**, south of the Market Slip. There's an extraordinary attention to detail here, the careful symmetries of each red brick facade patterned with individualistic

The Loyalists

The forty thousand **United Empire Loyalists** who streamed north to British Canada in the aftermath of the American War of Independence accounted for a sizeable chunk of the New England population. Many had been subjected to reprisals by their revolutionary neighbours and most arrived virtually penniless. All but eight thousand settled in the Maritime Provinces, where they and their descendants formed the kernel of powerful commercial and political cliques. As a result, the Loyalists have frequently – and not altogether unfairly – been pilloried as arch-conservatives, but in fact they were far from docile royalists: indeed shortly after their arrival in Canada they were pressing the British for their own elective assemblies. Crucially, they were also to instil in their new country an abiding dislike for the American version of republican democracy – and this has remained a key sentiment threading through Canadian history.

Before their enforced exile, the Loyalists conducted a fierce debate with their more radical compatriots, but whereas almost everyone today knows the names of the revolutionary leaders, the Loyalists are forgotten. The Loyalist argument had several strands: loyalty to Britain, fear of war, the righteousness or otherwise of civil obedience and, rather more subliminally, the traditional English Tory belief that men live most freely in a hierarchical society where roles are clearly understood. One of their most articulate spokesmen was **Daniel Leonard**, who during his epistolatory debate with John Adams wrote: "A very considerable part of the men of property in this province are at this day firmly attached to the cause of government... [and will,] if they fight at all, fight under the banners of loyalty... And now, in God's name, what is it that has brought us to this brink of destruction? Has not the government of Great Britain... been a nursing mother to us? Has she not been indulgent almost to a fault?... Will not posterity be amazed, when they are told that the present destruction took its rise from a three-penny duty on tea, and call it a more unaccountable frenzy... than that of the witchcraft?"

designs – everything from angular stone trimmings and dog-tooth window ledges through to hieroglyphic insets and elaborately carved window arches. Amongst the predominate red-brick are the grandiose Neoclassical and Second Empire facades of the Old Post Office at no. **115**, the Old City Hall at no. **116**, and the Nova Scotia Bank's Palatine Building at no. **124**. These finely worked stone extravagances, with their columns, pediments and arcades, were built as institutional confirmation of the city's excellent prospects. To the middle class of the time this was all in good taste, but there were limits. The Chubb building, **111** Prince William St at the corner of Princess, was – and still is – decorated by a singular series of mini-gargoyles: "We trust no more of our buildings will be adorned by such buffoonery," thundered the local newspaper.

The outskirts

Like just about everywhere else on the shores of the Bay of Fundy, Saint John is proud of its tides. What you have here are the **Reversing Falls Rapids**, created by a sharp bend in the Saint John River about 3km west of the centre. At low tide, the river – still some 60m deep – flows quite normally, but the incoming tide forces it into reverse, causing a brief period of equilibrium when the surface of the water is totally calm, before a churning, often tumultuous, surge upstream. You need to stick around for a couple of hours to see the complete process, and there's a viewing station (mid-May to mid-Oct daily 8am–7pm; free) high above the river at the far end of the bridge on Hwy 100. To get there by public transport, take the East–West transit bus (#1, #2, #3 or #4) from King's Square. The attached information centre shows a film telescoping a day's tidal flow into fifteen minutes. There are also a couple of mini-parks beneath the bridge where you can view the phenomenon from near the riverbank: one upstream in eyeshot of a noxious paper mill, the other downstream and reached via a short, steep path from the car park. Better still, Reversing Falls Jet Boat operates 'thrill rides' through the Reversing Falls during the summer from their jetty near the bridge on Fallsview Avenue (June to mid-Oct; 20min; ⓣ506/634-8987 or 1-888/634-8987, ⓦwww.jetboatrides.com; $37).

When you've finished with the river, it's another short drive west via Hwy 100 to the **Carleton Martello Tower** on Fundy Drive (June to early Oct daily 10am–5.30pm; $3.95): beyond the viewing station, take the first left along Lancaster Avenue and follow the signs. This stone tower was raised as one of a chain of strongholds designed to protect the Fundy coast from American attack, its squat design – and that of several hundred others dotted across the empire – copied from a Corsican tower that had previously proved especially troublesome to the British navy. Completed in 1815, too late to be of much use in the struggle against the States, the tower was soon abandoned, though it was eventually recycled as a detention centre for deserters in World War I. Later still, in World War II, it became the focal point of the coastal defence system protecting Saint John harbour – hence the ungainly concrete structure plonked on top. Inside, there's a reconstruction of a nineteenth-century barrack room and displays on World War II – plus splendid views over town and bay.

The tower is perched on the same headland as the ferry port linking Saint John with Nova Scotia (for ferry details, see p.489) and beyond the port – just 1km out in the bay – you'll spy **Partridge Island**, where the first quarantine station in North America was established in 1785. By the middle of the nineteenth century, the island had accumulated several hospitals and a full complement of medical staff, but they were simply overwhelmed by the flood of Irish immigrants who arrived during and after the Great Irish Famine of the late 1840s. A Celtic cross commemorates the Irish who died here and the island's lighthouse has survived too, but the quarantine station, which was closed in 1938, has all but disappeared. The island is uninhabited now and usually inaccessible, but sometimes there are boat trips here – check with the tourist office.

Eating, drinking and nightlife

Saint John is a boisterous, lively place to **eat and drink**. One good place to start is *Reggie's*, a well-lived-in diner near the city market at 26 Germain St (daily 6am–5pm), which serves up superb chowders, all sorts of sandwiches, and whopping breakfasts. Alternatively, inside the market, try the *Wild Carrot Café*, which provides wholesome snacks, or *Billy's Seafood Company* (Mon–Sat 11am–10pm & Sun 4–10pm), where they serve up fine fresh seafood and there's an oyster bar. Down by the Market Slip, amongst a string of bars and cafés, the pick is *Grannan's Seafood Restaurant* (daily 11am to midnight; ⓣ506/634-1555), where the catch of the day is a treat, or you might stroll over to *Beatty and the Bistro*, 60 Charlotte St (Mon–Fri 11.30am–3pm & 5–9.30pm, plus Sat 5–9.30pm; ⓣ506/652-3888), a café-restaurant offering crepes, pasta and seafood through to delicious New Brunswick lamb.

As for **bars**, *O'Leary's*, 46 Princess St (ⓣ506/634-7135) has draught imported and domestic beers and features live music towards the end of the week – mostly folk, Irish or Maritime; and *Tapps Brewpub*, 78 King St (ⓣ506/634-1957), the city's first microbrew pub, offers several especially tasty light ales as well as regular live music. For **performance arts**, the city's leading venue is the Imperial Theatre, a refurbished Edwardian theatre at 24 King Square South (ⓣ506/674-4100 or 1-800/323-7469, ⓦwww.imperialtheatre.nb.ca).

The Fundy Coast east of Saint John

One of the most beautiful portions of New Brunswick's coastline has been opened up by the **Fundy Trail Parkway**, a 13km-long scenic hwy that drifts along a dramatic stretch of seashore about 40km east of Saint John on Hwy 111. The parkway begins at the attractive seaside village of **St Martins**, which boasts two covered bridges and where there are several first-rate places to stay. There is, however, even prettier and much wilder coastal scenery much further to the east in the **Fundy National Park**, whose rugged sea cliffs, bays and coves are patterned with superb hiking trails. Hwy 114 cuts a diagonal through the park, branching off the Trans-Canada about 100km east of Saint John to access its trails and campsites, before finally emerging at the seaside hamlet of **Alma**, the only sizeable settlement hereabouts and a handy spot to break your journey. If you're after visiting both the parkway and the park, allow at least a couple of days especially as the drive between the two is a time-consuming, wearying business – though there are long-term plans to build a coastal road between St Martins and Alma.

East of Alma, a lovely coastal drive passes by turnings for tide-battered **Cape Enrage**, the bird sanctuary of **Mary's Point**, and the curiously shaped **Hopewell Rocks** on the way to bustling **Moncton**, the province's third city. Beyond Moncton, the chubby isthmus linking New Brunswick with Nova Scotia is pierced by Chignecto Bay, an easterly arm of the Bay of Fundy. The isthmus has long been a sleepy backwater of tiny fishing and marshland farming villages, but following the Treaty of Utrecht of 1713, which gave Nova Scotia to the British and left the French in Québec, its possession became of great if albeit brief strategic significance. The splendid windswept remains of **Fort Beauséjour** recall these tawdry imperial disputes.

The Fundy coast is a popular holiday spot, so it's a good idea to book **accommodation** ahead of time. Also, pick up a tide table at any local tourist office – the tides rise and fall by about nine metres, making a spectacular difference to the shoreline – and be prepared for patches of pea-soup fog: the Bay of Fundy is notoriously prone to them.

There is **no public transport** to either St Martins or the national park.

St Martins and the Fundy Trail Parkway

The fishing village of **ST MARTINS** drizzles along the Bay of Fundy shoreline about 40km to the east of Saint John. To get there from downtown Saint John, take Hwy 100 and exit at Loch Lomond Road (Hwy 111). First impressions of St Martins aren't especially favourable, but things improve when you finally (after 3km) reach the **harbour**, a compact affair of lobster pots and skiffs set within a ring of hills. A matching pair of **covered bridges** flanks the harbour and you drive through one of them for the journey 8km east to the **Fundy Trail Parkway** (mid-May to mid-Oct daily 6am-8pm; Ⓦwww.fundytrailparkway.com; $3 per adult), one of the province's more recent tourist initiatives. It works very well. The 13km-drive is a pleasurable jaunt along the seashore, threading past craggy headlands, and the road is shadowed by a multi-use trail that offers fine and comparatively easy hiking as well as access to several beaches. The Parkway ends at the **Big Salmon River Interpretive Centre** (mid-May to mid-Oct daily 8am–8pm; Ⓣ506/833-2019), whose exhibits provide lots of details about the Parkway and give the historical low-down on the lumber town of Big Salmon River, whose inhabitants packed up shop in the 1940s; the centre is actually built on the site of an old bunkhouse. From the centre, you can stroll down the hillside and cross the suspension bridge to the river below or negotiate the steep ninety-minute hike up into the hills to the hunting and fishing **lodge** built here by the Hearsts – of newspaper fame – in the 1960s. The Interpretive Centre will advise on routes and conditions.

Exploring the Parkway properly takes time (a day is about long enough), which means you'll need to overnight in St Martins. **Accommodation** here includes the first-rate *St Martins Country Inn* (Ⓣ506/833-4534 or 1-800/565-5257, Ⓦwww.stmartinscountryinn.com; ⑤; April–Dec), whose high Victorian gables and fancy gingerbread scrollwork are at 303 Main Street, which doubles as Hwy 111; the inn has sixteen, en suite guest rooms decorated in broadly period style. A good, second bet – and it's less expensive – is the *Waterfront B&B*, in a modern house of traditional design built down by the bay at 296 Main St (Ⓣ506/833-9010, Ⓦwww.bbcanada.com/thewaterfront; ④); there are three en suite guest rooms here with bayside balconies.

Fundy National Park

Bisected by Hwy 114, **Fundy National Park** (Ⓦwww.pc.gc.ca/fundy) encompasses a short stretch of the Bay of Fundy shoreline, all jagged cliffs and tidal mud flats, and the forested hills, lakes and river valleys of the central plateau

> **Moving on from St Martins** currently involves a long, looping drive inland along Hwy 111, though the provincial government does have plans to bulldoze a link along the coast east from St Martins to Fundy National Park.

behind. This varied scenery is crossed by more than 100km of **hiking trails**, mostly short and easy walks taking no more than three hours to complete – though the 45km Fundy Circuit links several of the interior trails and takes between three and five days. The pick of the hiking trails are, however, along the Fundy shore and it's here you'll find the spectacular **Point Wolfe Beach Trail**, a moderately steep, 300-metre hike down from the wooded headlands above the bay to the beach below. Of equal appeal is the 4.5km loop of the **Coppermine Trail**, which meanders through the forests with breathtaking views out along the seashore.

All the park's trails are described in a free booklet issued on arrival at either of the two Hwy 114 **entrance kiosks** (mid-May to mid-Oct $7 entry per adult; free at other times). One is at the west entrance near Lake Wolfe, about 20km south of the Trans-Canada (mid-May to mid-Oct daily 8am–6pm); the other is about 20km to the east, on the coast next door to Alma (same details). In addition, there is a **visitor centre** (daily: mid-May to mid-June & Sept to early Oct 8am–4.30pm; mid-June to Aug 8am–10pm; ⓣ506/887-6000) on Hwy 114 near the east entrance. The visitor centre features displays on local flora and fauna, organizes guided walks, issues backcountry permits and sells hiking maps and trail descriptions. The park is well equipped for **camping**, with two serviced ($27–30) and two unserviced ($18–22) campsites as well as a string of backcountry sites ($9). Both serviced campsites – Chignecto North (mid-May to early Oct) and Headquarters (late June to Aug) – are located near the east entrance (close to Alma) along with most of the park's tourist facilities. For the most part, they operate on a first-come, first-served basis, though reservations are taken for a minority of pitches on ⓣ1-877/737-3783, ⓦwww.pccamping.ca. **Backcountry** sites require reservations with the visitor centre: you can either take pot luck and register on arrival or ring ahead, which is certainly the better option in July and August. For a greater degree of isolation, take the 10km-long byroad southwest from the visitor centre to **Point Wolfe**, where a medium-sized, unserviced campsite (late June to Aug) is tucked in amongst the wooded hills above the coast – and near the starting point of the Point Wolfe Beach and Coppermine trails (see above).

If you're after a roof over your head, there are a couple of modern **chalet complexes** just inside the park near the visitor centre. These are *Fundy Park Chalets* (ⓣ506/887-2808 or 1-877/887-2808, ⓦwww.fundyparkchalets.com; ❸; May–Oct); and the marginally more comfortable, air-conditioned *Fundy Highlands Inn & Chalets* (ⓣ506/887-2930 or 1-888/883-8639, ⓦwww.fundyhighlandchalets.com; ❹; May–Oct). In both, the rooms come with kitchenettes. Note that there's more accommodation close by in Alma (see below).

East to Alma and Cape Enrage

Across the Salmon River from the east entrance to the national park is **ALMA**, a pleasant little village whose 300 inhabitants make a tidy living from fishing, farming and tourism. All of Alma's facilities are clustered on a short stretch of its Main Street including several **motels** and **hotels**. The pick is the trim *Captain's Inn B&B* (ⓣ506/887-2017, ⓦwww.captainsinn.ca; ❹) with nine cosy rooms in a modern building of traditional design. There is also the spick-and-span, bayshore *Alpine Motor Inn* (ⓣ506/887-2052 or 1-866/887-2052, ⓦwww.alpinemotorinn.ca; ❸; May–Oct); and the two-storey, motel-like *Parkland Village Inn* (ⓣ506/887-2313 or 1-866/668-4337, ⓦwww.parklandvillageinn.com; ❸; April–Nov). **Food** is a bit of a problem, but the *Parkland* has a (just about) competent restaurant – stick to the simpler dishes. *Kelly's Bake Shop* is well known for its enormous, delicious sticky buns.

On the east edge of Alma, **Highway 915** branches off Hwy 114 to stick close to the coast, threading over the hills and along the valley past isolated farmsteads sheltering behind rugged sea-cliffs. Here and there the coast comes into view – wide vistas of beach and cliff – but the most dramatic scenery is at **Cape Enrage**, 6km down a side road off Hwy 915, where the lighthouse is glued to a great shank of rock soaring high above the sea. It's remarkable that you can drive down to the cape at all. When the lighthouse was automated in 1988, the keepers moved away, abandoning their old house to the elements. Offended by the neglect, a Moncton schoolteacher initiated an ambitious plan to protect and develop the site with the enthusiastic help of his students. In the last decade, they've transformed the place. There's now a wooden walkway up to the foot of the lighthouse and the old keepers' house has been converted into a pleasant café (try the fish chowder). The students staff the cape in the summer and help run a programme of **adventurous pursuits**, principally sea-kayaking (half-day, $60; full day $85) and rappelling (2–3hr; $55). There's **hostel**-style accommodation here too – in Chignecto House ($25 per person); two cabana-style structures ($5 per person); and on tent decks ($15 per tent). In all cases, book ahead on ⓣ506/887-2273 or 1-888/280-7273, ⓦwww.capenrage.com.

East from Cape Enrage to Mary's Point bird reserve and Riverside-Albert

Doubling back to Hwy 915, it's a short drive east to the two country lanes that lead down to **Mary's Point bird reserve** – though only the second turning is currently signposted; the two lanes connect to form a (partly gravel) 6km-long loop off Hwy 915. Mary's Point is the prettiest of headlands, a varied terrain of forest, beach, marsh and mud flat that attracts thousands of migrating shorebirds on their way south from the Arctic in the late summer. The migration begins in July and continues until early October, depending on the age of the particular

△ Cape Enrage

bird and the species. Of all the birds, it's the **semipalmated sandpiper** that attracts most attention, a small grey and white creature with black bill and legs. They appear in late July and peak in the first two weeks of August, tearing round in formation, the greyish white of their undersides flashing in the sun. They can't swim, so the best time to see them – and it is an extraordinary sight – is a couple of hours either side of high tide when they fly closest to the shore. The reserve's **information office** (Ⓣ506/882-2544) will advise on what birds are around and when is best to see them. Even if the birds are gone, Mary's Point makes for some delightful walking with a network of **footpaths** running down from the information office to explore its various nooks and crannies.

If you're after **accommodation** hereabouts, head for the minuscule hamlet of **HARVEY** at the junction of Hwy 915 and the second lane to Mary's Point as you approach from the west. Here you'll find two good options, beginning with the *Sandpiper's Rest B&B* (Ⓣ506/882-2744, Ⓦwww.sandpipersrest.nb.ca; ❸; May–Oct), which occupies an appealing nineteenth-century cottage and has three unassuming, en suite guest rooms. The other recommendation is the *Florentine Manor* (Ⓣ1-800/665-2271, Ⓦwww.florentinemanor.com; ❺), set in a large Victorian house in its own grounds and with period furnishings. The manor has nine guest rooms, all en suite.

Some 3km north of Harvey, Hwy 915 rejoins Hwy 114. At the crossroads is the local **tourist office**, distinctively housed in the old bank building, a Victorian extravagance that comes complete with its original vault and wickets. The tourist office marks the start of **RIVERSIDE-ALBERT**, an elongated village that trails along the bayshore for several kilometres.

Onto the Hopewell Rocks

Beyond Riverside-Albert, Hwy 114 travels northeast passing through farmland and offering attractive views of headlands and tidal flats on its way to Hopewell Cape, where the Petitcodiac River flows into the bay. The cape is the site of the red-sandstone **Hopewell Rocks** (daily: mid-May to early June & Sept to early Oct 9am–5pm; early June to Aug 8am–7pm; $8), gnarled pinnacles rising up to 15m above the beach and snared within a coastal park – an 'Ocean Tidal Exploration Site' if you will – that attracts too many visitors for its own good. The interpretive centre explains the cape's geological wherewithal and the marine complexities of the Bay of Fundy, but you'll soon be wandering down the footpath – past several vantage points – to the rocks. The rocks were pushed away from the cliff face by glacial pressure during the Ice Age, and the Bay of Fundy tides have defined their present, eccentric shape. At high tide they resemble stark little islands covered in fir trees, but at low tide they look like enormous termite hills. Steps lead down to the beach and you can safely walk round the rocks two to three hours either side of low tide, or you can paddle round them at high tide by hiring a kayak for a nominal fee.

From the Hopewell Rocks, it's 50km along the west bank of the Petitcodiac River to Moncton.

Moncton

MONCTON, some 80km from Alma, was named after Colonel Robert Monckton [sic], though the Acadians had originally called the place *Le Coude* ("the elbow"), which at least hinted at its setting on a sharp bend of the Petitcodiac River. Indeed, the river provides Moncton with its most singular attraction, the tidal bore, which sweeps up from the Bay of Fundy, 35km downstream. Otherwise, Moncton is a minor commercial centre and major transport junction surrounded by marshy flatlands. This may sound unpromising, but the downtown area has recently been spruced up and there are now enough good restaurants, bars and hotels to make an overnight stay enjoyable, and the town is a convenient stop on the journey between Fundy National Park and PEI via the Confederation Bridge. Moncton's rejuvenation partly reflects the increasing confidence of local Acadians: the town hosts the province's only French-speaking university and is proud of its **bilingualism** – the result of Acadian ex-deportees settling here in the 1790s.

Arrival and information

Moncton **bus station** is on the west side of the town centre – about 1km west of Tidal Bore Park – at 961 Main St. **Acadian Lines buses** (ⓣ1-800/567-5151, ⓦwww.acadianbus.com) arrive here from most major settlements in New Brunswick and twice or three times daily from PEI's Charlottetown; there are also buses to and from Halifax in Nova Scotia. Moncton's **train station** is nearby – behind the shopping mall, a couple of blocks further west along Main Street – with services running to Halifax and Montréal. Moncton's main **tourist office** is in Tidal Bore Park (daily: May & Sept 8.30am–4.30pm, June–Aug 9am–8pm; ⓣ506/853-3590, ⓦwww.gomoncton.com). They'll book accommodation for free, provide free city maps and give information on forthcoming events.

The town

Moncton's **tidal bore** is a wave that varies from a few centimetres to a metre in height, depending on weather conditions and the phase of the moon. At low tide you'll be in no doubt as to why the locals called the Petitcodiac the "chocolate river", but the mud flats disappear after the bore arrives and the river level rises by up to 8m. Tiny **Tidal Bore Park**, downtown at Main and King sts, has information plaques on the tide times and a small grandstand so you can watch the phenomenon in comfort. The town's other oddity is **Magnetic Hill** (mid-May to mid-Sept daily 8am-8pm, $5, otherwise free), an extraordinarily popular motorized attraction where your car appears to travel uphill when it is in neutral along an otherwise ordinary bit of road. Local farmers first observed this optical illusion in the nineteenth century, when they noticed their horses were straining to go uphill just as they felt they were going down. The idea today is that you drive to what appears to be the bottom of the hill, put your vehicle in neutral and then coast backwards, apparently uphill – which is really rather weird. Magnetic Hill is located just off the Trans-Canada Hwy (Exit 450) about 9km northwest of downtown.

Accommodation

Moncton has a healthy supply of convenient downtown **accommodation**. The most lavish is the *Delta Beauséjour*, 750 Main St (ⓣ506/854-4344 or 1-800/268-1133, ⓦwww.deltahotels.com; ❻), a big modern high-rise right in the middle of town. However, the motel-style rooms of the much more modest *Rodd Parkhouse Inn*, beside Tidal Bore Park at 434 Main St (ⓣ506/382-1664 or 1-800/565-7633, ⓦwww.rodd-hotels.ca; ❹), are both much less expensive and perfectly adequate if rather routine. Alternatively, several pleasant **B&Bs** are dotted amongst the leafy residential avenues to the north of Main Street. The pick of the bunch is the four-room *Bonaccord House B&B*, 250 Bonaccord St (ⓣ506/388-1535, ⓦwww.bbcanada.com/4135.html; ❷), north of the bus station in an attractive Victorian villa with picket fence and portico. A good reserve is the nearby *Archibald B&B*, 194 Archibald St (ⓣ506/382-0123 or

1-877/389-0123, ⓦwww.archibaldbed-breakfast.com; ❸), which offers six comfortable guest rooms in a wide-verandahed house on a quiet leafy street just to the north of Main Street.

Eating and drinking

For **food**, *Le Château à Pape*, 2 Steadman St (ⓣ506/855-7273), serves the finest of Acadian cuisine from its premises in a big old house a couple of minutes' walk west along the river bank from Tidal Bore Park; mains start at $18. Less expensive places include *Jean's Diner*, 369 St George St, about three blocks north of Main St, which is worth a trip for its clams not to mention its 1950s booths, and *Graffiti*, 897 Main St (ⓣ506/382-4299), which specializes in moderately priced Greek food.

Bars throng the centre – try the popular *Pump House Brewpub*, at 7 Orange Lane, just off Main Street a few metres east of City Hall. *Kramer's Corner*, 700 Main St (ⓣ506/857-9118), is a combined restaurant and bar with a massive outdoor patio and regular live music, mostly jazz. Both Theatre New Brunswick and the provincial symphony orchestra perform at the **Capitol Theatre**, 811 Main St (ⓣ506/856-4379 or 1-800/567-1922, ⓦwww.capitol.nb.ca), which has been impressively restored to its original 1920s vaudeville glory, all gold leaf and plush velvet.

Fort Beauséjour

Providing gorgeous views over the broad sweep of Chignecto Bay, **Fort Beauséjour National Historic Site** (June to mid-Oct daily 9am–5pm; $3.95) is stuck on a grassy, treeless hill about 50km south of Moncton and just 2km from the junction of Trans-Canada hwys 2 and 16. The fort stands on the isthmus connecting New Brunswick and Nova Scotia and its strategic value was first recognized by the French, who fortified the site in 1751. Four years later, the British captured the fort and promptly strengthened it with a beady eye fixed firmly on the local Acadians, who they thought might rebel against them. In the event, the Acadians did no such thing, but they were deported anyway and the British garrison stayed on until 1835 as a defence against the Americans.

Flush with the brow of the hill, the **remains** of the star-shaped fort include much of the original earthwork, the concentric ditches and mounds typical of the period, as well as a sally port and a couple of deeply recessed casements, used for general storage. The site also has a delightful **museum** with excellent displays on the history of the fort and of the Acadian farmers who settled the region in the 1670s. Some of the most interesting exhibits, like ancient clogs and farm tools, were recovered when the fort was repaired and restored in the 1960s. The Acadians enclosed and drained the marshes below the fort to produce hay, grain crops and vegetables – and the lines of their dykes and ditches are still visible from the hill.

From Fort Beauséjour, it's just a few kilometres south to central Nova Scotia (see p.394) and about 50km east to the Confederation Bridge over to PEI (see p.473).

The Saint John River Valley

The **Saint John River Valley**, running west by northwest from Fredericton to **Edmundston**, a distance of 270km, is not consistently beautiful but it does have its moments, especially when it slips through maple and pine forests or, to

the north, where its low-lying hills and farmland are replaced by a more mountainous, heavily forested terrain. Neither are the valley towns, which dot the Trans-Canada, particularly memorable, but the restored pioneer village of **King's Landing** is first-rate and well worth at least a couple of hours, as is the waterfall at **Grand Falls**.

Acadian Lines (Ⓣ1-800/567-5151, Ⓦwww.acadianbus.com) operates a twice-daily **bus** between Moncton, Fredericton and Edmundston, with services continuing on to Rivière-du-Loup, Québec City, Montréal, Ottawa and Toronto.

King's Landing and beyond

Some 25km west of Fredericton on Hwy 102 lies the **Mactaquac dam**, part of a hydroelectric project whose reservoir stretches 75km up the valley. **King's Landing Historical Settlement** (June to mid-Oct daily 10am–5pm; $15; Ⓦwww.kingslanding.nb.ca), 10km west of the dam, exists because of the project. Making a virtue of necessity, several nineteenth-century buildings were carefully relocated here to form the nucleus of an open-air museum of rural life as of about 1850. Since then, further judicious purchases have added to the housing stock and, supplemented by a handful of replicas, there are now no fewer than seventy buildings spread out amidst delightful waterside woods and fields. Like similar reconstructions, King's Landing aims to provide a total experience to its visitors, with its "inhabitants" engaged in bread-making, horseshoeing, logging, milling, weaving, cattle-driving, and so on. Themed villages are not to everyone's taste, but this one works very well and several of the buildings are fascinating in their own right – particularly the **Jones House**, a stone dwelling built into the hillside in a manner typical of this area; the **Ingraham House**, once the property of a well-to-do farmer; and the fully operational sawmill.

Surrounded by forest, **HARTLAND**, some 90km beyond King's Landing, advertises itself exclusively on the size of its **wooden bridge**, which at 391m is by far the longest covered bridge in the world. It was completed in 1901, the idea being to protect the timbers of the bridge from the elements by means of a long shed-like affair built in the manner of a barn. It's not graceful – but it is long.

North of Hartland, the scenery changes as the maples give way to a great undulating belt of potato fields. There's a surprise in store here at **GRAND FALLS**, 105km from Hartland, where, right in the centre of what is otherwise a nondescript town, a spectacular weight of water squeezes through hydroelectric barriers to crash down a 23-metre pitch. Even if the diversion of water through nearby turbines has deprived the falls of their original vigour, they're still impressive, as is the 2km-long gorge they've carved downstream, a steep-sided ravine encircling half the town. A 253-step **stairway** (daily: mid-May to June & Sept to mid-Oct 9am–6pm; July & Aug 9am–9pm;, July & Aug 9am–9pm) leads down into the gorge; it begins just across the bridge from the conspicuous **Visitor Centre** (Ⓣ506/475-7788, Ⓦwww.grandfalls.com), which perches on the bridge above the falls. There's nothing much else to see in Grand Falls, but straightforward **accommodation** is available right by the gorge and the waterfall at the *Hill Top Motel*, 131 Madawaska Rd (Ⓣ506/473-2684 or 1-800/496-1244, Ⓦwww.sn2000.nb.ca/hilltop; ③).

Edmundston

Lying at the confluence of the Saint John and Madawaska rivers, wood-pulping **EDMUNDSTON** is the largest town in the north of New Brunswick, with a population of nearly eighteen thousand. It's a brash, modern place, where a profusion of flashing neon signs proclaim the proximity of the USA, which lies just over the biggest of the town's three bridges. Edmundston is mainly French-speaking and, curiously, regards itself as the capital of an enclave known as the **Republic of Madawaska**, the snout-shaped tract of Canadian territory jutting out into the state of Maine. While the idea of an independent state here is preposterous, the "Republic" is more than a publicity stunt: it signifies the frustration of a population over whom the British and Americans haggled for thirty years until 1842, and who still feel ignored by Fredericton. Yet the town also packages the Republic frivolously, with Ruritanian touches such as a coat of arms, a flag, honorary knights and a president (otherwise the mayor).

Acadian Lines **buses** pull in at 169 Victoria St, just off Blvd Hébert before the Fournier Bridge over the Madawaska River into the town centre. There's a seasonal **tourist office** (late June to early Sept daily 9am–8pm) just off the Trans-Canada (Exit 18) near the top of Boulevard Hébert, which runs downtown. For central **accommodation**, head for the standard-issue comforts of the *Quality Inn*, 919 Canada Rd (Ⓣ506/735-5525 or 1-800/563-2489, Ⓦwww.choicehotels.ca/cn529; ❸). A second, less expensive option is the homely, motel-style *Praga Hotel*, near the marina at 127 Victoria St (Ⓣ506/735-5567; ❷).

The Miramichi Valley

Running northeast from Fredericton, Hwy 8 traverses the **Miramichi River Valley**, passing endless stands of timber en route to the **City of Miramichi**, an amalgamation of the six tiny logging ports that flank the mouth of the river – and amongst which **Newcastle** is easily the most diverting. The 180-kilometre trip takes three to four hours, longer if you pause at the one sight of any real interest, the Woodmen's Museum in **Boiestown**. The river valley is, however, much more famous for its **salmon fishing**, which draws anglers from all over the world. The season begins anywhere between April and July, depending on the waters to be fished, and every angler has to buy a licence. A veritable raft of regulations controls the sport but any local tourist office will have the details. The other big deal hereabouts is the **Miramichi Folksong Festival** (Ⓣ506/622-1780, Ⓦwww.miramichifolksongfestival.com), held over five days in early August in Miramichi City and generally reckoned to be one of the best of its kind, with fiddle music its forte. Miramichi City is also within easy striking distance of **Kouchibouguac National Park**, a slab of protected coastline noted for its superb sandy beach.

Acadian Lines **buses** ply Hwy 8 once daily, passing through Miramichi City bound for Campbelltown. At Miramichi City, there are also connecting bus services (1 daily) south along the coast past the Kouchibouguac National Park to Moncton.

Boiestown and Doaktown

Some 70km north of Fredericton, **BOIESTOWN** was once a rowdy loggers' settlement whose drunken "goings-on" inspired the region's balladeers – "If you're longing for fun and enjoyment, or inclined to go out on a spree, come

Québec (just north of Edmundston) and Maine (just south, across the bridge) both run on **Eastern Time**, one hour back from New Brunswick's **Atlantic Time**.

along with me to Boiestown, on the banks of the Miramichi."The **Woodmen's Museum**, beside Hwy 8 (late May to mid-Oct daily 9am–5pm, Ⓦwww.woodsmenmuseum.com; $5), recalls these rougher days beginning with a pair of large huts jam-packed with loggers' artefacts, from all sorts of strange-looking tools to fascinating photographs of the men floating the logs downstream. There are more intimate exhibits too: the loggers collected resin from spruce trees, chewed it until it was smooth and sweet and then placed it in "gumbooks", a couple of which are on display, to give to their kids back home. After the huts, it only takes a few minutes to wander the rest of the site, where there's an incidental assortment of old lumber-industry buildings, including a sawmill, pitsaw, an earthy bunkhouse and cookhouse, and a fire tower. For some obscure reason, an old and well-built fur-trapper's cabin has ended up here as well, and a small train, the *Whooper*, runs round the edge of the museum.

DOAKTOWN, 20km further down the valley, is a favourite spot for fishermen, who congregate here to catch the **Atlantic salmon** as it struggles up the Miramichi on the last leg of its complex life cycle (see box below). Doaktown's **Atlantic Salmon Museum** (mid-April to May Mon–Fri 9am–5pm; June to mid-Oct daily 9am–5pm; $5; Ⓣ506/365-7787, Ⓦwww.atlanticsalmonmuseum.com), beside Hwy 8, illustrates the salmon's arduous life cycle, has a small aquarium, and looks at different fishing techniques – but you're much better off having a go at fishing yourself: there are lots of outfitters and guides in and around town; ask for information at the museum.

Miramichi City: Newcastle and Nelson

Now incorporated within sprawling **MIRAMICHI CITY**, the old shipbuilding centre of **NEWCASTLE** sits on the north bank of the Miramichi River as it nears the sea. Its compact centre is cheered by a pleasant little park at **Ritchie Wharf** and by the trim town square which, with its Italian gazebo and English garden seats, was spruced up at the whim of

Atlantic salmon

The life cycle of the **Atlantic salmon** is a complicated affair, which culminates in the battle upriver to spawn; the Miramichi is one of the salmon's major spawning rivers, hence the fishermen who gather here every year.

Early each spring, thousands of tiny fish emerge from pea-sized orange eggs deposited in the riverbed the previous autumn. These young fish – or **fry** – soon acquire dark markings and are then known as **parr**. The parr remain in the river for two to six years (determined by water temperature and the availability of insects and other aquatic food) before a springtime transformation when their internal systems adapt for saltwater life and they turn silver, becoming **smolt**. It seems that the odours of the smolt's native river are imprinted in its memory before it heads out to sea, to be recalled when it returns to spawn. Some fish, the **grilse**, return to spawn after a year, but the majority, the **salmon**, swim back after two years or more, entering the Miramichi between April and Nov and weighing anywhere between 4kg and 20kg. Once they're back in the fresh water, the salmon stop feeding and their bodies deteriorate in favour of egg or sperm production, with the male developing a hooked lower jaw or kype. After they spawn in late autumn, the adults (by then known as **kelt**, or black salmon) return to the ocean to begin the cycle again – unlike their Pacific cousins, all of whom die after their first and only spawning. It's an unfortunate fact that the kelt are nowhere near as tasty as the smolt.

local-lad-made-good Max Aitken, otherwise Lord Beaverbrook, whose bust sits in the square too. There's nothing much else to the place, but it is a convenient stopping point on the long drive north to Québec's Gaspé Peninsula (see p.334) and there are a handful of reasonable **places to stay**. These include the modern, motel-like *Wharf Inn On The River*, near the bridge at 1 Jane St (ⓣ506/622-0302 or 1-866/612-8600, ⓦwww.wharfinnontheriver.com; ❹), and the *Comfort Inn*, 201 Edward St (ⓣ506/622-1215 or 1-800/228-5150, ⓦwww.choicehotels.ca/cn243; ❹). Alternatively, across the river from Newcastle in **NELSON**, the *Governor's Mansion B&B*, at 62 St Patrick's Drive (ⓣ506/622-3036 or 1-877/647-2642, ⓦwww.governorsmansion.ca; ❸), occupies a handsome Victorian villa that was once the Lieutenant-Governor's residence. The mansion is graced by antique furnishings and holds eight guest rooms on the two upper floors; there are four additional rooms in a second old house, Beaubear Mansion.

The *Wharf Inn*'s **restaurant** offers a tasty range of seafood and meat dishes. If you're in town for the Miramichi Folksong Festival (see p.469), go to the **visitor centre**, in the Lighthouse on Ritchie Wharf (late June to late Aug daily 9am–9pm; ⓣ506/623-2152 or 1-800/459-3131, ⓦwww.miramichi.org), which has gig details.

Kouchibouguac National Park

From the southeast edge of Miramichi City, **Highway 11** slices across the interior for the 50km trip to the coastal forests, bogs, salt marshes, lagoons and sandy beaches of the **Kouchibouguac** ("Koo-she-boo-gwack") **National Park**. Near the park's main **entrance** (April–Nov $7, free at other times) is the **visitor centre** (mid-May to early June & Sept to mid-Oct daily 9am–5pm; early June to Aug 8am–8pm; ⓣ506/876-2443), where displays explore the area's complex ecology and the habits of some of its rarer inhabitants. From here, it's a few kilometres' drive, past the trailheads of several woodland walks, to the turning down to the sandy expanse of **Kellys beach** – the park's main attraction. The sea water here is, you're assured, the warmest north of Virginia, with temperatures between 18°C and 24°C. Further on, past the turning, there's a restaurant as well as bike, kayak and canoe rental at seasonal **Ryans Rental Centre**, on the south bank of the Kouchibouguac River. Just upriver is the trailhead of the park's longest trail, the 13km-long **Kouchibouguac River Trail**, which wriggles west along the river bank passing one of the park's few wilderness campsites. Hikers have to use the same trail in both directions - allow at least six hours and check trail conditions at the visitor centre before you set out as superactive beavers have closed the trail on several occasions. Another and much shorter option is the 1km **Cedars Trail** loop, which offers wide views over salt marshes, lagoons and dunes. Hikers should on no account forget the insect repellent.

The park has one fully serviced **campsite**, South Kouchibouguac (mid-May to mid-Oct; $23–27), and one unserviced campsite, Cote-à-Fabien (early June to early Sept; $14). Reservations (on ⓣ1-877/737-3783, ⓦwww.pccamping.ca) are advised for South Kouchibouguac, but Cote-à-Fabien is first-come, first-served, so arrive early in the day to be sure of a spot. If you're not camping, the park is easily visited on a day-trip from Miramichi, or you can stay in one of the settlements nearby. The modern and straightforward *Habitant Hotel,* 9600 Main St (ⓣ506/523-4421 or 1-888/442-7222, ⓦwww.habitant.nb.ca; ❸), is located in **RICHIBUCTO**, a short drive south of the park entrance off Hwy 11 (Exit 64) on Hwy 134.

The Acadian Peninsula

The **Acadian Peninsula**, which protrudes some 130km into the Gulf of St Lawrence in the northeast corner of New Brunswick, is promoted as a part of the province where the twentieth century has yet to gain a foothold. For the Acadians who fled here to avoid the deportations (see p.428), this isolation was a life-saver, and more than anywhere else in the Maritimes this is where they have maintained their traditional way of life. Many locals are still reliant on fishing and marshland farming, though frankly there's precious little actually to see: the countryside is uniformly dull and the ribbon villages are hardly enticing. The mundane port of **Caraquet**, on the north shore, serves as the peninsula's cultural focus and is the best base for a visit to the replica **Village Historique Acadien**, the one sight of any note.

There are **no buses** along the peninsula.

Caraquet

Heading east from the mining town of **BATHURST**, Hwy 11 bobs along the Acadian Peninsula's northern shore, trimming the edge of rolling countryside before reaching, after about 50km, the district's pride and joy, the **Village Historique Acadien** (June to early Sept daily 10am–6pm, Ⓦwww.villagehistoriqueacadien.com; $15). This holds around forty old Acadian buildings relocated from other parts of New Brunswick – only the church was built specifically for the village. Costumed "inhabitants" emphasize the struggles of the early settlers and demonstrate traditional agricultural techniques as well as old methods of spinning, cooking and so on – all in an attractive rustic setting.

From the historic village, it's a further 16km east on Hwy 11 to **CARAQUET**, a fishing port that was founded by Acadian fugitives in 1758 and now straggles along the seafront for some 13km. It may not be much to look at, but Caraquet does have one or two sights, beginning with **Le Musée Acadien de Caraquet**, at 15 Blvd St-Pierre East, also Hwy 145 (May, June & early Sept Mon–Fri 10am–6pm; July & Aug Mon–Sat 10am–8pm & Sun 1–6pm; $3; Ⓣ506/726-2682), which chronicles the life and times of the early settlers and has a small gallery devoted to the work of local artists. At the west end of town, there's also the shrine of **Ste-Anne-de-Bocage** built to commemorate the founding families' trials and tribulations. Finally, Caraquet is the setting for the region's most important **Acadian Festival** (Ⓣ506/727-2787), a two-week programme of music and theatre held in early August, which begins with the blessing of the fishing fleet by a local bishop.

Amongst a bevy of Caraquet **motels, inns and B&Bs**, the pick is the *Hotel Paulin*, 143 Blvd St-Pierre West (Ⓣ506/727-9981 or 1-866/727-9981, Ⓦwww.hotelpaulin.com; ❹), a smart and comfortable, family-operated inn with eight guest rooms in an attractive Victorian building graced by an expansive verandah. The restaurant here is first-rate, too, featuring traditional Acadian cuisine – the pea soup is a real treat. Slightly less expensive rooms are on offer at *Le Pignon Rouge*, a B&B in a sympathetically renovated old house at 338 Blvd St-Pierre East (Ⓣ506/727-5983; ❹; June–Sept).

Prince Edward Island

The freckly face and pert pigtails of Anne of Green Gables are emblazoned on much of **PRINCE EDWARD ISLAND**'s publicity material, and her creator, local-born novelist Lucy Maud Montgomery, was the island's most gushing propagandist, depicting the place floating "on the waves of the blue gulf, a green seclusion and haunt of ancient peace... invested with a kind of fairy grace and charm". Radical William Cobbett, who soldiered here in the 1780s, was not so dewy-eyed, and saw instead "a rascally heap of sand, rock and swamp... a lump of worthlessness [that] bears nothing but potatoes". Each had a point. The economy may not be as uniform as Cobbett suggested, but PEI does remain thoroughly agricultural – Million-Acre Farm, as it's sometimes called – and it can often be beguiling: Canada's smallest province – a crescent-shaped slice of land separated from Nova Scotia and New Brunswick by the Northumberland Strait – boasts a long and complicated shoreline that is serrated by dozens of bays and estuaries, where the ruddy soils and grassy tones of the rolling countryside are set beautifully against the blue of the sea, with gorgeous sandy **beaches** banding much of the north shore.

Charlottetown, the capital and only significant settlement, sits on the south coast beside one of these inlets, the tree-lined streets of its tiny centre occupying a chunky headland that juts out into a wide and sheltered harbour. With its graceful air, wide range of accommodation and good restaurants, this is easily the best **base** for exploring the island, especially as almost all of PEI's villages are formless affairs whose dwellings ribbon the island's roads. One exception is **Victoria**, a tiny old seaport southwest of Charlottetown, which makes a peaceful overnight stay. Otherwise, **Orwell Corner Historic Village**, just to the east of the capital, is an agreeable attempt to re-create an island village as of 1890; **Cavendish**, on the north coast, boasts the house that Montgomery used as the setting for her books; and, close by, **Prince Edward Island National Park**, the island's busiest tourist attraction, has kilometres of magnificent sandy beach. Further east is the careworn township of **Souris**, the ferry port for the Îles-de-la-Madeleine (Magdalen Islands, see p.353) and but a short hop down along the coast from the intriguing beach and fishery museum of **Basin Head**. In the west, the chief interest is social: descendants of PEI's **Acadian** settlers – once the majority of the population – today constitute some fifteen percent of the island's inhabitants and many of them live on the wedge of land that runs down from the village of Wellington to **Cap-Egmont**.

PEI is a major holiday spot, so there's plenty of **accommodation** to choose from with B&Bs, inns, cottages and campsites liberally sprinkled across the whole of the island – though it's still a good idea to make advance reservations during July and August. Note, also, that although it's easy to reach Charlottetown by Acadian Lines **bus** the rest of PEI has hardly any public transport at all. On a culinary note, PEI has a reputation for the excellence of its **lobsters**, which are trapped on the west side of the island during August and September and in the east from June to July. A number of restaurants specialize in lobster dishes, but keep a look out for local posters advertising **lobster suppers**, inexpensive buffet meals served in several church and community halls during the lobster season.

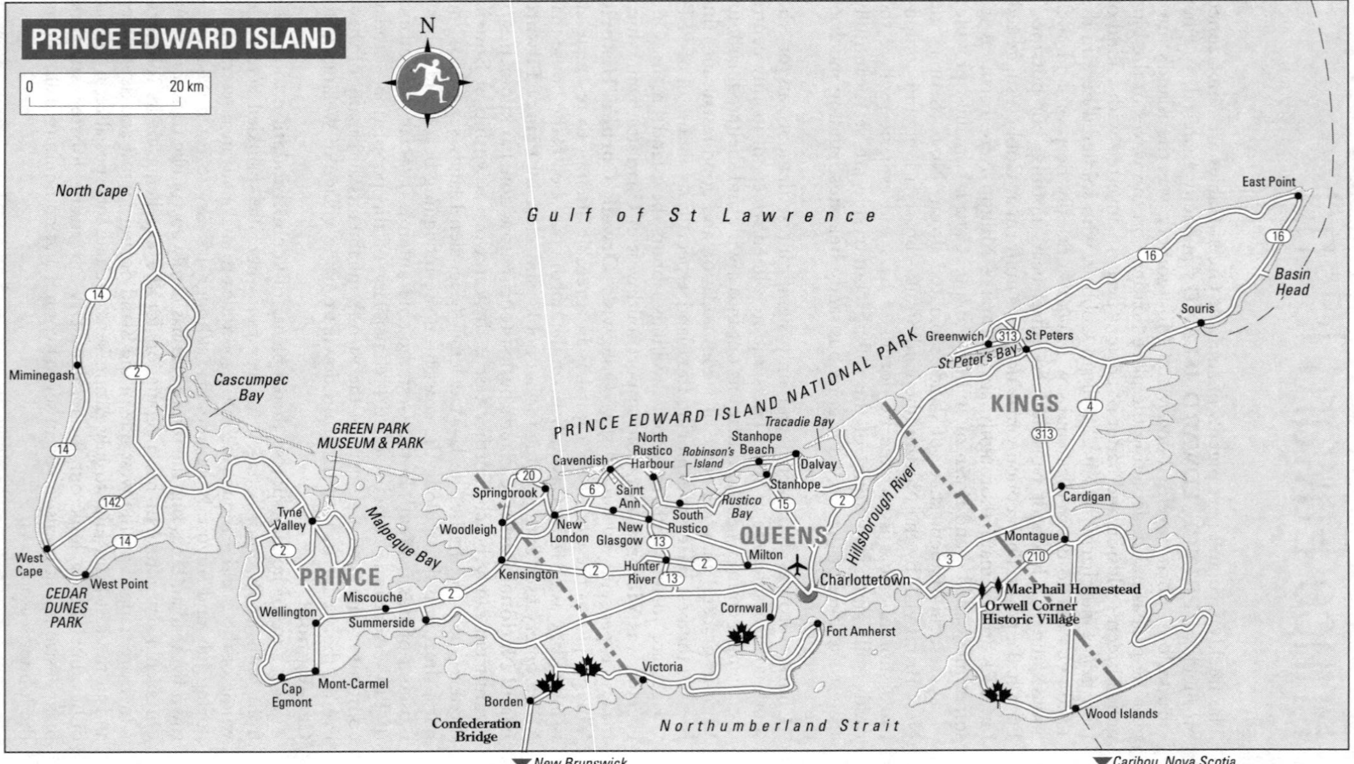
PRINCE EDWARD ISLAND
0
20 km
N
Îles-de-la-Madeleine
Gulf of St Lawrence
North Cape
Miminegash
West Cape
West Point
CEDAR DUNES PARK
Cascumpec Bay
GREEN PARK MUSEUM & PARK
Tyne Valley
Malpeque Bay
PRINCE
Miscouche
Wellington
Summerside
Cap Egmont
Mont-Carmel
Borden
Confederation Bridge
New Brunswick
Woodleigh
Springbrook
Kensington
Cavendish
New London
New Glasgow
Saint Ann
North Rustico Harbour
South Rustico
Robinson's Island
Rustico Bay
Hunter River
Stanhope Beach
Stanhope
Tracadie Bay
Dalvay
Milton
QUEENS
Charlottetown
Hillsborough River
Cornwall
Victoria
Fort Amherst
Northumberland Strait
PRINCE EDWARD ISLAND NATIONAL PARK
Greenwich
St Peters
St Peter's Bay
KINGS
Cardigan
Montague
MacPhail Homestead
Orwell Corner Historic Village
Wood Islands
Caribou, Nova Scotia
Souris
Basin Head
East Point
14
2
142
20
6
13
15
3
210
313
4
16

Getting to PEI

There are regular domestic **flights** (ⓦwww.flypei.com) to Charlottetown airport from several cities in eastern Canada, primarily Halifax, Montréal and Toronto, with the principal carriers being West Jet (ⓣ1-888/937-8538, ⓦwww.westjet.com) and Air Canada Jazz (ⓣ1-888/247-2262, ⓦwww.aircanada.com). Nevertheless, the majority of visitors arrive via the 13km-long **Confederation Bridge** (ⓣ902/437-7300, ⓦwww.confederationbridge.com) spanning the Northumberland Strait between New Brunswick's Cape Tormentine and Borden, 60km west of Charlottetown. A **toll** of $40.75 is levied on each standard-size vehicle, but this is only collected as you leave the island partly to encourage visitors to use the ferry (see below). Cycling is a popular pastime on PEI, but cyclists aren't allowed on the bridge; instead, they are transported across in a shuttle bus ($8 per cyclist), which operates 24/7; advance reservations are not accepted. The bridge is used by the twice- or three times daily **Acadian Lines bus** service (ⓣ1-800/567-5151, ⓦwww.acadianbus.com) connecting Charlottetown with Moncton in New Brunswick and by the minibuses of the **PEI Express Shuttle** (ⓣ902/462-8177 or 1-877/877-1771) between Charlottetown and Halifax (4hr; $50; advance reservations are essential).

The alternative to the bridge is the Northumberland Ferries (ⓣ902/566-3838 or 1-888/249-7245, ⓦwww.nfl-bay.com) **car ferry** from **Caribou**, Nova Scotia, to **Wood Islands**, 61km east of – and a 45-minute drive from – Charlottetown (May to late June 5 daily; late June to mid-Oct 7 daily; mid-Oct to late Dec 3-5 daily; 1hr 15min; $13 passenger return, $57 for car & passengers). There's no ferry from late Dec to April. Ferries operate on a first-come, first-served basis and queues are common in high season, when you should arrive about an hour and a half before departure to be safe. Just like the Confederation Bridge, fares are only collected when you leave the island. Finally, note that if you are driving to Charlottetown from Halifax, the bridge is quicker than the ferry, but the drive is longer by about 80km (320km against 240km).

Operated by CTMA, a second **car ferry** (ⓣ418/986-3278 or 1-888/986-3278, ⓦwww.ctma.ca) does the five-hour hop between **Cap-aux-Meules** on the Magdalen Islands (Îles-de-la-Madeleine, see p.353) and **Souris**, 81km northeast of Charlottetown from April to January (April–June & Sept 6 weekly, July & Aug 7–11 weekly; Oct–Jan 3–4 weekly). A one-way adult fare is $44 ($28 in winter), plus $80 ($57) per car.

A brief history of Prince Edward Island

Jacques Cartier claimed Prince Edward Island for France on the first of his voyages across the Atlantic, naming it the **Île-St-Jean** in 1534. However, the French and the Acadian farmers he brought with him from the Bay of Fundy made little impact on the island until they were reinforced in 1720 by three hundred French colonists, who founded a tiny capital at **Port La Joye**, near the site of present-day Charlottetown. In 1754 there were about three thousand settlers, but their numbers doubled the following year with the arrival of refugees from the Fundy deportations (see p.428), a sudden influx with which the island was unable to cope. After the capture of Louisbourg in 1758, the British army turned its attention to Île-St-Jean and its starving, dispirited population. Lord Rollo, the local British commander, rounded up and shipped out all but three hundred of the Acadians and the colony was subsequently renamed the Island of St John in 1763, and **Prince Edward Island** in 1799.

After the expulsion of the Acadians, the island was parcelled out to wealthy Englishmen on condition that they organized settlement, but few did. Consequently, when the island's population climbed from around seven thousand to eighty thousand in the first half of the nineteenth century, the majority of the colonists were tenant farmers or squatters, victims of an **absentee landowning**

Prince Edward Island information

Tourism PEI Within North America ⓣ1-800/463-4734, from elsewhere ⓣ902/368-4444, ⓦwww.peiplay.com.

system that was patently unjust and transparently inefficient. Although most of these immigrants were drawn from the poor of the Scottish Highlands and Ireland, the new citizens had come here in the hope of owning land. Their ceaseless petitioning eventually resulted in the compulsory **Land Purchase Act** of 1875, and within a decade PEI became a land of freeholders.

With the agricultural, fishing, shipbuilding and logging industries buoyant, the late 1870s marked the high point of the island's fortunes, but this prosperity was short-lived. The Canadian government's protectionist **National Policy** discriminated in favour of the manufactured goods of Ontario and Québec and the result was a long-lasting recession that helped precipitate a large-scale emigration with PEI now a forgotten backwater, derisively nicknamed **Spud Island**. Since the 1960s, the successful exploitation of the island's tourist potential has brought much relief, as has the modernization of its agriculture and fishery. It was also hoped that the completion of the **Confederation Bridge** between PEI and the mainland in 1997 would provide a further economic boost, though the long-term consequences are proving hard to assess: many were disappointed to see the initial rise in day visitors subside, but there again it's now much easier for the islanders to export their produce to the mainland and fears that the island's farms would be snaffled up as second homes have not materialised.

Charlottetown

Pocket-sized **CHARLOTTETOWN**, the administrative and business heartbeat of PEI, is the most urbane spot on the island, the comfortable streets of its centre – principally Grafton and Kent – hemmed in by leafy avenues of clapboard villas, the most opulent of which spread west of the centre towards **Victoria Park**. Yet although these well-disposed streets give the place a prosperous and sedate appearance, this is not the whole truth: Charlottetown has a relatively high rate of unemployment and this is reflected in some of the bargain-basement department stores – in contrast to the upmarket tourist shops on the snazzily developed harbourfront. That said, Charlottetown is an exceptionally amiable place to spend a couple of days and it also has, in small-island terms, a reasonable **nightlife**, with a handful of excellent restaurants and a clutch of good bars.

Arrival and information

Charlottetown **airport** is 8km north of town; the **taxi** fare into the centre is just $11. Acadian Lines **buses** (ⓣ1-800/567-5151, ⓦwww.acadianbus.com) from Moncton via the Confederation Bridge arrive and depart from the **bus depot**, an inconvenient 3km north of downtown out along Longworth Ave/ Mount Edward Road at 156 Belvedere Ave.

Inside the airport, a seasonal **tourist information desk** has buckets of information and provides a free room-reservation service – as does PEI's main

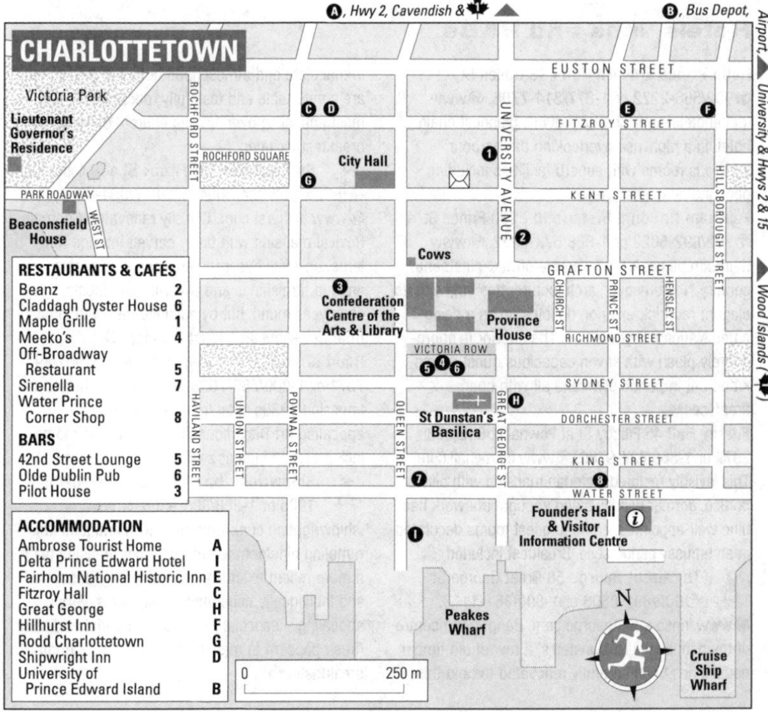

Visitor Information Centre, on the harbourfront in the same building as Founders' Hall (see p.479), a couple of minutes' walk from the town centre at the foot of Prince Street (mid-May to mid-June & mid-Sept to early Oct daily 9am–6pm; mid-June to mid-Sept daily 9am–7pm; early Oct to Nov & Feb to mid-May Mon–Fri 10am–4pm; Ⓣ902/368-4444 or 1-888/734-7529, Ⓦwww.peiplay.com). Both have copies of the comprehensive and free annual *Island Guide,* but the Charlottetown office has much more on the island's B&Bs, national park and farm-holiday spots as well as free town maps. The main local daily **newspaper**, *The Guardian* ("covers PEI like the dew"), makes for an enjoyable read, and there's a good quality, free entertainment **listings magazine** too, *The Buzz* (Ⓦwww.isn.net.buzzon).

Accommodation

Charlottetown has a wide range of **accommodation** and things only get tight in the height of the season (July & Aug). To get the flavour of the place, you're much better staying in the oldest part of town – between Fitzroy Street and the waterfront. Options here include several reasonably priced **inns** and **B&Bs**, the best of which occupy grand late nineteenth-century houses, as well as a smattering of **hotels**, mostly expensive places that are either smart, modern high-rises or well-conceived conversions of some of the town's oldest properties. At the other end of the market are a handful of small **guesthouses** – only some of which accept credit cards – and, to the north of town, **student rooms**, available in the summer at the university.

Hotels, inns and B&Bs

Delta Prince Edward Hotel 18 Queen St ⓣ902/566-2222 or 1-877/814-7706, ⓦwww.deltahotels.com. Charlottetown's plushest chain hotel, in a high-rise overlooking the harbour; luxurious rooms with superb facilities including pool and health centre. ❼

Fairholm National Historic Inn 230 Prince St ⓣ902/892-5022 or 1-888/573-5022, ⓦwww.fairholm.pe.ca. A fine example of mid-nineteenth century "Picturesque" architecture, this inn, with its elegant redbrick exterior, doubles up as a designated National Historic Site. The interior is appropriately plush with seven capacious guest rooms kitted out in period style and all with open fireplaces. ❻

Fitzroy Hall 45 Fitzroy St at Pownal ⓣ902/368-2077 or 1-866/627-9766, ⓦwww.fitzroyhall.com. This lavishly restored Victorian mansion with pillars, portico, dormer windows and wrought ironwork has nine well-appointed, en-suite guest rooms decorated in an unfussy period style. Breakfast included. ❻

The Great George 58 Great George St ⓣ902/892-0606 or 1-800/361-1118, ⓦwww.innsongreatgeorge.com. Bang in the centre of town, opposite St Dunstan's, a row of old timber houses has been carefully renovated to hold this immaculate and atmospheric hotel. All the rooms are comfortable and tastefully decorated – the most appealing overlook the church. Continental breakfast included. ❼

Hillhurst Inn 181 Fitzroy St at Hillsborough ⓣ902/894-8004 or 1-877/994-8004, ⓦwww.hillhurst.com. Classily renovated Georgian Revival mansion with finely carved interior. Nine large, en-suite guest rooms, each with ornate antique furnishings and two with whirlpools. It is open year-round, but by advance reservation only from Dec–April. Breakfast included. ❻

Rodd Charlottetown Kent at Pownal ⓣ902/894-7371 or 1-800/565-7633, ⓦwww.rodd-hotels.ca. Imposing 1930s hotel (part of a chain) with appealing Art Deco flourishes, though the rooms lack a certain intimacy. ❻

Shipwright Inn 51 Fitzroy St ⓣ902/368-1905 or 1-888/306-9966, ⓦwww.shipwrightinn.com. Crammed with antiques, this rambling nineteenth-century timber mansion (with a more recent extension) has nine well-appointed and individually decorated guest rooms. Very appealing – especially with its thoughtful additions (fresh popcorn to mention one) and its superlative breakfasts. ❻

Guesthouse

Ambrose Tourist Home 17 Passmore St, off University Ave ⓣ902/566-5853 or 1-800/665-6072, ⓦwww.ambrosetouristhome.com. Six unassuming but neat and trim, en suite guest rooms in a duplex on a quiet street. Ten minutes' walk from downtown. May–Oct. ❷

Student rooms

University of Prince Edward Island 550 University Ave. May–Aug: ⓣ902/566-0442; Sept–April: ⓣ902/566-0568; ⓦwww.upei.ca/housing. Single ($55) and double ($70) rooms available on the university campus, 3km north of town. Advance reservations required; breakfast included. May–Aug.

The Town

The island's most famous historical attraction is the **Province House** (May to early Oct daily 9am–5pm; July & Aug daily 9am–6pm; Oct–May Mon–Fri 9am–5pm; free), which sits right at the heart of Charlottetown, at the foot of University Avenue. A squat brownstone structure dominated by an overlarge portico, it hosted the first meeting of the **Fathers of Confederation** in 1864, when representatives of Nova Scotia, New Brunswick, Ontario, Québec and PEI met to discuss a union of the British colonies in North America. Today it's used by the island's legislature, but some of its rooms are open to visitors. On the ground floor, a fifteen-minute film provides a melodramatic account of that original meeting and explains its historical context, whilst the balconied Confederation Chamber up above looks pretty much like it did in 1864, though frankly it's not overly riveting – just a large table and some heavy-duty chairs.

Next door, the **Confederation Centre of the Arts** (daily 9am–5pm, June–Sept till 8pm; free; ⓦwww.confederationcentre.com) is housed in a glass and concrete monstrosity built in 1964 to commemorate the centenary of the epochal meeting. Each of Canada's provinces paid fifteen cents for each of its residents to cover its construction and they continue to contribute towards its upkeep. The centre contains the island's main library, a couple of theatres, and a combined **museum and art gallery** (mid-June to mid-Oct daily 9am–5pm; mid-Oct to mid-June Wed–Sat 11am–5pm, Sun 1–5pm; donation suggested), whose changing exhibitions are often first-rate and always have a Canadian emphasis. Items from the permanent collection are also regularly displayed, and although much is fairly average look out for the manuscripts, papers and scrapbooks of Lucy Maud Montgomery and the portraits of Robert Harris, who painted most of PEI's business elite in the 1880s. Harris also painted the iconic *Fathers of Confederation*, a picture of bewhiskered representatives in debate that has been reproduced for everything from postage stamps to postcards, though the original was actually lost in a fire in 1916.

From the Confederation Centre, it's a couple of hundred metres south to the pretty terraced houses of Great George Street, which face the twin spires and imposing facade of **St Dunstan's Catholic Basilica** (daily 8am–5pm; free). Finished in 1897 and ten years in the making, the church has all the neo-Gothic trimmings, from blind arcaded galleries and lancet windows through to heavy-duty columns and a mighty vaulted ceiling. There were, however, some economies – tap the marble inside and you'll find it's mostly wood painted like marble. The basilica marks the centre of the oldest part of Charlottetown and the surrounding side streets are lined with rows of simple wood and brick buildings, mostly dating from the middle of the nineteenth century. Some of the best ensembles are concentrated on and around **King Street** to either side of Great George Street, whilst pedestrianized **Victoria Row**, also near the church, has the city's finest example of commercial architecture, a long and impressive facade that now holds a series of restaurants and bars.

Below Water Street, the sequence of jetties that make up the **harbourfront** has been neatly refurbished with ice-cream parlours and restaurants, a yacht club, the lavish *Delta Prince Edward Hotel* and the souvenir shops of Peake's Wharf. Big cruise liners are often moored here too, disgorging hundreds of day-trippers, many of whom make a beeline for **Founders' Hall**, at the foot of Prince St (early

△ Charlottetown

May & early Oct to Nov Tues–Sat 9am–3.30pm; late May to early June daily 9am–4pm; late June daily 9am–6pm; July to mid-Aug Mon–Sat 9am–8pm, Sun 9am–5pm; mid-Aug to early Sept Mon–Sat 9am–6.30pm, Sun 9am–5pm; early Sept to early Oct daily 9am–5pm; closed Dec & Jan; $7; Ⓦwww.foundershall.ca), whose various multimedia displays, complete with a battery of sound effects, give the background to the deliberations of the Fathers of Confederation.

From Founders' Hall, it's a pleasant ten-minute stroll northwest to **Beaconsfield House** (regular guided tours; Ⓣ902/368-6603; $4.25), a resplendent late Victorian mansion whose fancy wooden trimmings, capacious porch and peaked roof overlook the harbour from the corner of West and Kent streets. The house was built for James Peake, one of Charlottetown's leading shipbuilders in the 1870s, but he went bust shortly after its completion and thereafter the house was passed from hand to hand with alarming rapidity until finally a local conservation society got a grip, returning it to its former splendour. Across the way, the assorted greenery of **Victoria Park** edges the grandiose lieutenant-governor's residence. Within the park are the scant remains of the gun battery built to overlook the harbour in 1805.

Eating, drinking and nightlife

Charlottetown has a reasonable range of **restaurants** – quite enough to keep you going for a day or two, and several are excellent. The best are downtown, with particular concentrations along Victoria Row, beside the Confederation Centre and on Sydney Street at Queen. The best **cafés** and **bars** are here too, nothing amazingly exciting, but still amenable, easygoing places to enjoy a drink. Note also that in several cases restaurants share their premises with bars: food below, booze up above. *Cows*, something of an island institution, makes delicious **ice cream**; there are outlets down on the harbourfront and on the corner of Grafton and Queen, opposite the Confederation Centre.

As regards the **performing arts**, the programme of events at the Confederation Centre of the Arts (Ⓣ902/566-1267 or 1-800/565-0278, Ⓦwww.confederationcentre.com) encompasses an extensive variety of acts, from rock and jazz through to comedians, magicians, theatre, opera and ballet. The centre is also the home to the main show of the annual **Charlottetown Festival** (mid-June to Sept; Ⓦwww.confederationcentre.com/festival.asp), which – surprise, surprise – is a musical adaptation of *Anne of Green Gables*. The musical has been running for years, though modifications are made every year to freshen it up. During festival time in particular, Charlottetown also offers all sorts of comedy revues and shows both indoors and out. *The Buzz* (Ⓦwww.isn.net.buzzon), a free monthly newssheet available all over town and at the tourist office, carries comprehensive listings and reviews.

Cafés and restaurants

Beanz 38 University Ave and Grafton. Great coffee and a range of tasty sandwiches and snacks from around $8 at this agreeable little café. Especially popular at lunch times with the town's office workers. Mon–Fri 7.30am–6pm, Sat 8am–6pm & Sun 9am–4pm.

Claddagh Oyster House 131 Sydney at Queen Ⓣ902/892-9661. Attractive modern restaurant, where they specialize in PEI oysters – and delicious they are too; a ten-piece tasting plate costs a very reasonable $17. Otherwise, the menu offers a competent selection of seafood and meat dishes with mains averaging $26. Daily from 5pm; it's beneath the *Olde Dublin Pub* (see opposite).

Maple Grille 67 University Ave Ⓣ902/892-4411. Cosy and intimate family-style restaurant with carefully prepared dishes from a small but well-chosen menu. Main courses at around $15. Mon–Thurs 11am–9pm, Fri & Sat 11am–10pm.

Meeko's Victoria Row, 146 Richmond St at Queen ⓣ902/892-9800. For something a little different, try this cheerfully decorated Mediterranean café and grill. Locals are apt to praise the moussaka. Daily from 11am.

Off-Broadway Restaurant 125 Sydney St at Queen ⓣ902/566-4620. Arguably the best restaurant in town, *Off-Broadway* features a creative menu of traditional and modern dishes – including the illustrious lobster ($35 for 1.5lb). Two other house specialities are exotic crêpes and home-made desserts. The decor is good fun too – customers sit in dinky little wooden booths. Prices are reasonable with main courses averaging about $20, $16 for the pastas. Daily from 4.30pm.

Sirenella 83 Water St ⓣ902/628-2271. The decor may be somewhat pedestrian, but there's good quality north Italian cuisine here, featuring the usual suspects from pastas and grilled meats through to seafood. Mains around $15. Mon–Fri 11.30am–2pm & Mon-Sat 5–10pm.

Water Prince Corner Shop 141 Water St ⓣ902/368-3212. It may look like a corner shop, but many locals swear by the seafood here - even if they are usually outnumbered by the tourists. The lobster dinners and chowders are perhaps the best on the island, but then the scallop burger is a real groove too. Booking is essential. Moderately priced with mains from as little as $10. May–June & Sept to early Oct daily 10am–8pm; July & Aug daily 10am–10pm.

Bars

42nd Street Lounge 125 Sydney St at Queen ⓣ902/566-4620. Laidback lounge bar above the *Off-Broadway Restaurant.* A good range of brews too.

Olde Dublin Pub 131 Sydney ⓣ902/892-6992, ⓦwww.oldedublinpub.com. Intimate and justifiably popular spot with imported and domestic ales. Live folk music – mostly Irish – nightly from May to September. Above the *Claddagh* (see opposite).

Pilot House 70 Grafton St. Traditional pub-cum-diner with booths to sit in and fish and chips (from its bar menu) to devour. Mon–Sat 11.30am–10pm.

Listings

Airlines Air Canada ⓣ1-888/247-2262, ⓦwww.aircanada.com.

Bike rental Smooth Cycle, 308 Queen St (ⓣ902/566-5530 or 1-800/310-6550, ⓦwww.smoothcycle.com); MacQueen's, 430 Queen St (ⓣ902/368-2453 or 1-800/969-2822, ⓦwww.macqueens.com).

Bus companies The Shuttle (2–4 daily; ⓣ902/566-3243) connects Charlottetown with Cavendish, whilst the East Connection Shuttle (late June to Sept daily; ⓣ902/393-5132) links the capital with Souris. Long-distance buses to and from Moncton, in New Brunswick, are provided by Acadian Bus Lines, whose depot is at 156 Belvedere Ave (ⓣ1-800/567-5151, ⓦwww.acadianbus.com). PEI Express Shuttle (ⓣ902/462-8177) operates a minibus service between Charlottetown and Halifax (4hr; $50); advance reservations are essential.

Car rental Avis, at the airport ⓣ902/892-3706; Hertz, at the airport ⓣ902/894-5774 & 417 University Ave ⓣ902/566-5566; National, at the airport ⓣ902/628-6990 & on the harbourfront at the Visitor Information Centre ⓣ902/628-990. All these companies do good deals on short-term rentals.

Internet access Free at the harbourfront Visitor Information Centre (mid-May to mid-June & mid-Sept to early Oct daily 9am–6pm; mid-June to mid-Sept daily 9am–7pm; early Oct to Nov & Feb to mid-May Mon-Fri 10am-4pm) and at the Confederation Public Library, Richmond St (Mon 10am–5pm, Tues–Thurs 10am–9pm, Fri & Sat 10am–5pm, Sun 1–5pm).

Pharmacy Shoppers Drug Mart, 128 Kent St ⓣ902/566-1200 and 670 University Ave ⓣ902/566-3211.

Post office 135 Kent St (Mon–Fri 8am–5.15pm).

Taxis City Cab, 168 Prince St ⓣ902/892-6567; Co-op Taxi, 91 Euston St ⓣ902/628-8200.

The rest of PEI

Prince Edward Island is divided into three counties. In the middle is **Queens County**, which incorporates the province's most popular tourist attractions and has some of its prettiest scenery. It also boasts the island's finest **beaches**, stretching along a goodly portion of the northern shore and protected within the **Prince Edward Island National Park**. To the east of Queens lies **Kings County**, comprising two broad geographical areas, with the tree-dotted farmland and estuary townships of the south preceding the wilder scenery further north. To the west of Queens is **Prince County**, which makes up the flattest part of PEI, its broad-brimmed, sparsely populated landscapes curving round a handful of deep bays. The provincial government has worked out three **scenic drives** covering each of the counties: the Points East Coastal Drive to the east, the Blue Heron Coastal Drive in the centre, and the North Cape Coastal Drive to the west. However, although these drives visit everything of interest, they are frequently dreary, so unless you really love driving it's better to be more selective.

Getting around the island by public transport

PEI's **public transport** system is rudimentary, but from early June to late September there is a **minibus shuttle** (2–4 daily; $20 day return; ⓣ902/566-3243) between Charlottetown's harbourfront Visitor Information Centre and pint-sized Cavendish, on the north shore and the site of Green Gables House (see p.484); there's also the East Connection Shuttle (late June to Sept daily; ⓣ902/393-5132) linking the capital with Souris, where ferries leave for the Magdalen Islands. Alternatively, several Charlottetown companies operate **sightseeing tours**; the busiest is Abegweit, 157 Nassau St (ⓣ902/894-9966, ⓦwww.peisland.com/abegweit/tours.htm), which offers tours of the southern and northern shores ($65 each) as well as Charlottetown ($10).

Cycling and hiking

Prince Edward Island is good for all manner of outdoor sports with specialist companies offering everything from diving and deep-sea fishing to canoeing and sailing. The island's quiet roads and gentle terrain also make it a great place to go **cycling**, but although there are several **cycle-tour operators**, it's much less expensive (and entirely straightforward) to plan your own route: in Charlottetown, both Smooth Cycle, 308 Queen St (ⓣ902/566-5530 or 1-800/310-6550, ⓦwww.smoothcycle.com), and MacQueen's, 430 Queen St (ⓣ902/368-2453 or 1-800/969-2822, ⓦwww.macqueens.com), rent out all the necessary gear and will advise on routes. The most popular is the **Confederation Trail**, a combined hiking and cycling trail that weaves its way right across the island from east to west, partly following the route of PEI's old railway, which was closed in the 1980s.

Queens County

Pulling in thousands of visitors every summer, **Queens County**'s principal attraction is the **Prince Edward Island National Park**, whose gorgeous sandy beaches, extending along much of the north shore for some 40km, are ideal for swimming and sunbathing. Rarely more than one or two hundred metres wide, the main body of the park incorporates both the beaches and the sliver of low red cliff and marram-covered sand dune that runs behind – a barrier which is occasionally interrupted by slender inlets connecting the ocean with a quartet of chubby little bays. A narrow road runs behind the shoreline for most of the length of this part of the park, spanning several of these inlets, but forced into a detour when it reaches the main channels into Rustico Bay and Tracadie Bay. Indeed, **Rustico Bay** effectively divides the main body of the park into two: the smaller, more **westerly portion** runs from Cavendish – site of Green Gables House – to North Rustico Harbour; the **easterly section**, which is wilder and more untrammelled, goes from Robinson's Island to Tracadie Bay, with a third, smaller section lying further east still at **Greenwich**, at the mouth of St Peter's Bay. In the main body of the park, it's easy enough to drive along the shore road behind a goodly proportion of the beach until you find a place to your liking.

There's a seasonal **visitor centre** or **information kiosk** at every entrance to the park and from early June to August they levy an entrance fee of $6.90 per adult per day. On arrival, you're issued with a free and comprehensive guide and out of season this is available at Charlottetown's Visitor Information Centre (see p.477). The park has eleven short **hiking trails**, easy strolls that take in different aspects of the coast from its tidal marshes and farmland through to its woodlands and dunes. The most strenuous is the 5km-long Woodlands Trail, up through a red-pine plantation near Dalvay, though perhaps the most scenic is the partly-boardwalked 5km-long Greenwich Dunes Trail. Cyclists will find the journey from Charlottetown to the main body of the park easy enough, but **bike rental** is available amongst the many tourist facilities on the park's peripheries.

The park has two **campsites**. The larger is the well-equipped, fully serviced Cavendish Campground (mid-June to late Aug), where there's a supervised sandy beach that's great for swimming. The quieter Stanhope Campground (mid-June to Sept), a short walk from the beach near the hamlet of Stanhope, is similarly well equipped and appointed. A few sites are allocated on a first-come, first-served basis, but most can be reserved (Ⓣ1-877/737-3783, Ⓦwww.pccamping.ca) – and reservations are strongly advised. Pitches cost $22–30.

PEI National Park east: Robinson's Island to Tracadie Bay and Greenwich

The fastest route from Charlottetown to the more easterly section of the national park is the half-hour, 23-kilometre thump along **Highway 15**, which branches off Hwy 2 on the north side of town. This takes you past long ranks of chalet-style second homes and, as you near the park, the delightful *Dunes Studio Gallery and Café*, located just 600m beyond the Hwy 6 and Hwy 15 junction. The *Dunes* is a combined **café** (mid-June to Sept daily 11.30am–4pm & 5.30–10pm; Ⓣ902/672-2586, Ⓦwww.dunesgallery.com), pottery shop and art gallery, which serves mouthwatering and reasonably priced snacks and meals from an imaginative menu of seafood and vegetarian dishes; it's one of the best places to eat on the island. Close by, another 1km or so north on Hwy 15, is the pick of the resort and cottage complexes hereabouts, the charmingly rustic *Shaw's Hotel and Cottages* (Ⓣ902/672-2022, Ⓦwww.shawshotel.ca), whose hotel rooms (June–Sept; full board ❼) and all-year chalets and cottages occupy extensive grounds and farmland about ten-minutes' walk from the beach; *Shaw's* also does **canoe**, **kayak** and **bike rental** for guests and non-guests alike.

Inside the park, at the end of Hwy 15, turn left along the coast for the causeway over to wooded **Robinson's Island** and right for the 5km trip along the seashore to **Stanhope Beach**, the setting for a string of perfectly placed beachside cottage complexes. These include the little red and white *Del-Mar Cottages* (Ⓣ902/672-2582 or 1-800/699-2582; ❹, sleeps up to 4 people; June–Sept) and *Surf Cottages* (Ⓣ902/651-3300, Ⓦwww.peisland.com/surfcottages; ❹, sleeps up to 3 people; mid-June to Sept).

Heading east from Stanhope Beach, it's about 6km to the end of the beach road and the pocket-sized hamlet of **DALVAY**, whose most conspicuous asset is the recently revamped *Dalvay-by-the-Sea Inn* (Ⓣ902/672-2048 or 1-888/366-2955, Ⓦwww.dalvaybythesea.com; full board ❼; mid-June to late Sept). By any standard, the inn is an especially grand affair, a Victorian mansion that comes complete with high gables, rough-hewn stonework, a magnificent wraparound veranda, a yawning wood-panelled and balconied foyer, and even a croquet lawn. The inn holds just 26 tastefully decorated rooms and has an ideal location inside the park just a couple of hundred metres from the beach. Advance reservations are well-nigh essential.

Along the coast to the east of Dalvay are two more segments of the national park, the first being the slender sandspit that shelters much of **Tracadie Bay** from the ocean. There are no roads to this part of the park – just hiking trails – and a similar caution applies to the second segment, the spatulate, partly wooded headland at the mouth of **St Peter's Bay**. In this case, Hwy 313 travels west from Hwy 2 along the north shore of the bay, slipping through **GREENWICH** before grinding to a halt at the car park. From here, hiking trails head across the headland, exploring its wild and especially beautiful beaches, dunes and wetlands.

To PEI National Park west via New Glasgow

The 40km-long journey from Charlottetown to Cavendish and the western portion of the National Park covers some of PEI's prettiest scenery – take **Highway 2** west from the capital and, after about 23km, turn north along **Highway 13** at **Hunter River**. Every inch a country road, Hwy 13 wends over hill and dale before threading its way through the tiny settlement of **NEW GLASGOW**, whose matching pair of black and white clapboard churches sit on opposite sides of an arm of Rustico Bay. In the centre of the village, the Prince Edward Island Preserve Company (June to early Oct 9am-4.30pm, till 9pm at peak periods; ⓣ902/964-4300, ⓦwww.preservecompany.com) is a great place to buy local jams, mustards and maple syrups, and the attached **café** serves first-rate breakfasts, lunches and – in the summer – evening meals: try the Atlantic salmon. There are **lobster suppers** available in the village too, at *New Glasgow Lobster Suppers*, on Hwy 258 (June to early Oct daily 4–8.30pm; reservations ⓣ902/964-2870), though those at the church of **SAINT ANN**, a neighbouring hamlet about 5km west of New Glasgow along Hwy 224 – follow the signs – are generally considered better (mid-June to late Sept Mon–Sat 4–9pm; reservations ⓣ902/621-0635). At both, reckon a 500g (1lb) lobster in its shell will set you back about $30.

From New Glasgow, it's 10km to Cavendish along Hwy 13.

PEI National Park west: Cavendish and around

Straggling **CAVENDISH**, clumped around the junction of Hwy 6 and Hwy 13, is in itself an inconsequential village, but it is no more than a stone's throw from the long sandy beaches of the National Park and home to the wildly popular (greatly over-visited) **Green Gables House** (daily: May to late June & late Aug to Oct 9am–5pm; late June to late Aug 9am–8pm; $7.15, ⓦwww.pc.gc.ca), situated in a dell just 500m west of the crossroads. Part of a tourist complex, with a gift shop and visitor centre, the two-storey timber Green Gables House was once occupied by the cousins of **Lucy Maud Montgomery** (1874-1942), one of Canada's best-selling authors. In 1876, when Montgomery was just two years old, her mother died and her father migrated to Saskatchewan, leaving her in the care of her grandparents in Cavendish. Here she developed a deep love for her native island and its people and, although she spent the last half of her life in Ontario, PEI remained the main inspiration for her work. Completed in 1905 and published three years later, *Anne of Green Gables* was her most popular book, a tear-jerking tale of a red-haired, pigtailed orphan girl that Mark Twain dubbed "the sweetest creation of child life ever written". As for the house itself, the mildly diverting period bedrooms and living rooms – supposedly the setting for *Anne* – are worth a quick look, though you may think twice when you see the crowded car park. Surprisingly, many of the tourists are Japanese: the book has been on school curricula there since the 1950s and remains extremely popular.

If you decide **to stay** in Cavendish, head for *Shining Waters Country Inn & Cottages* (Ⓣ902/963-2251 or 1-877/963-2251, Ⓦwww.shiningwatersresort.com; May–Oct), 200m north of the crossroads on the way to the National Park. They have rooms in the old inn (❸), a pleasant, homely structure with a wide verandah, as well as in a motel-style annexe (❺) and a string of modern chalet/cottages (❻ for two). The National Park's **Cavendish campground** (see p.483) is another possibility – it's located just off – and signed from - Hwy 6 just to the west of Green Gables House.

From the Cavendish Hwy 13/6 crossroads, it's about 600m to the National Park and a few more to the coastal byroad that travels east, sticking close to the beach and its swelling dunes on the way to the scrawny fishing port of **NORTH RUSTICO**, the home of the *Fisherman's Wharf Restaurant* (Ⓣ902/963-2669; mid-May to mid-Oct daily noon–6pm, 9pm in peak periods), another good place to sample the island's lobsters. Beyond the port, Hwy 6 leaves the park, slipping round the peaceful waters of **Rustico Bay** on its way to meet – after 15km – Hwy 15 from Charlottetown (see p.476).

West from Cavendish - Woodleigh

West of Cavendish, **Highway 6** passes through the most commercialized part of the island, an unappealing tourist strip stretching as far as **New London**. Here, **Highway 20** branches north along the coast and you'll soon spot signs to PEI's most bizarre sight, the large-scale reproductions of famous British buildings that make up **Woodleigh** (early June to late Sept daily 9am–5pm, July & Aug till 7pm; $8.50). Built by a certain Colonel Johnston, who developed an obsessional interest in his ancestral home in Scotland, it features models of such edifices as the Tower of London, York Minster and Anne Hathaway's cottage. Some of the structures are even big enough to enter and their interiors have been painstakingly re-created, right down to the Crown Jewels in the Tower.

South Queens County - west of Charlottetown

The deep inlet of Charlottetown harbour splits the southern reaches of Queens County into west and east. In the west, the **Confederation Bridge** has become a major attraction in its own right and the tourist facilities of the adjoining Gateway Village take a stab at introducing visitors to the island. Elsewhere, **Port-La-Joye/Fort Amherst National Historic Site** (mid-June to late Aug daily 9am–5pm; $3), perched on an isolated promontory across the bay from Charlottetown, marks the spot where the Acadians established their island headquarters, Port-La-Joye, in 1720. The British subsequently built Fort Amherst here, but all that survives today is a scattering of grass-covered earthworks. Much more diverting is the old seaport of **VICTORIA**, overlooking the Northumberland Strait about 30km west of Charlottetown along the Trans-Canada Hwy – on the main route between the capital and the Confederation Bridge. There's nothing remarkable about Victoria's gridiron of nineteenth-century timber houses, but it's a pretty spot and a relaxing place to while away a couple of hours. Victoria also has an attractive old **hotel**, the *Orient* (Ⓣ902/658-2503 or 1-800/565-6743, Ⓦwww.theorienthotel.com; ❹; mid-May to mid-Oct), and is home to the

Victoria Playhouse (Ⓣ902/658-2025 or 1-800/925-2025, Ⓦwww.victoriaplayhouse.com), where a good range of modern plays and musical evenings are performed from late June through to late September. There are several places to **eat**, the pick of the bunch being the *Landmark Café* (daily mid-May to late Sept), near the playhouse in the centre of the village, where they serve excellent and moderately priced home-made meals.

South Queens County – east of Charlottetown

Some 30km east of Charlottetown just off the Trans-Canada Hwy lies the delightfully rustic **Orwell Corner Historic Village** (late May to June Mon–Fri 9am–5pm; July to Aug daily 9.30am–5.30pm; Sept to mid-Oct Sun–Thurs 9am–5pm; $7.50; Ⓦwww.orwellcorner.isn.net), which was originally settled by Scottish and Irish pioneers in the early nineteenth century. At first the village prospered as an agricultural centre, but by the 1890s it was undermined by the expansion of Charlottetown and mass emigrations to the mainland. Orwell was finally abandoned in the 1950s, but the historic graveyard and a handful of buildings remained, principally the main farmhouse-cum-post-office-cum-general-store, the schoolhouse and the church. In recent years, these have been restored and supplemented by replicas of some of the early buildings, like the blacksmith's shop, barns and shingle mill. Even better, care has been taken to give the interiors the authentic flavour of Orwell's rusticated past, from the farmhouse's darkened, cluttered living rooms and the austerity of the Presbyterian church to the cheeky graffiti carved into the schoolhouse desks. In addition, the gardens are splendidly maintained in period style, farm animals root around purposefully, and the village hosts a wide variety of special events – ploughing contests, ceilidhs and so forth.

Close by – just 1.4km further up the same side road as the village – is the **Sir Andrew MacPhail Homestead** (mid-June to mid-Sept Tues–Sun 11am–5pm; free). This features MacPhail's farmhouse, a comfortable nineteenth-century building whose period furnishings and fittings have a real sense of Victorian gentility, albeit in what was then the backcountry. It was from here that MacPhail (1864–1938) ran his farm, dabbled in medical research, and wrote as a journalist, banging on about the decline of the hierarchical, rural society he (as a Tory) loved. The veranda accommodates a pleasant **tearoom** (Ⓣ902/651-2789), where they serve lunches and afternoon tea daily from the middle of June to the middle of September, except on Mondays (Tues–Sat 11am–4.30pm, Sun noon–5pm); advance reservations are recommended. Bordered by the Orwell River, the homestead's woods and meadows offer several nature trails; details at the farmhouse.

Kings County

Just 600m beyond the Orwell/MacPhail turning, **Highway 210** branches off the Trans-Canada to weave its way east across the rich farmland bordering the Montague River en route to the little town of **Montague**. From here, Hwy 4 – **Kings County**'s principal north–south road – leads the 40km or so northeast to **SOURIS**, a busy fishing port and harbour, which curves round the shore of Colville Bay and has a regular car ferry service to the Magdalens (Îles-de-la-Madeleine; see p.353). The docks are a few hundred metres north of the scrabble of older houses that passes for the town centre and the stretch of shoreline between the two sees Souris at its best. Here you'll find a sequence of Victorian mansions, including the first-rate *Matthew House Inn B&B*, 15 Breakwater St (Ⓣ902/687-3461, Ⓦwww.matthewhouseinn.com; ❺; late June to early Sept), which has eight attractive guest rooms with a period feel. Alternatively, the nearby *Dockside B&B*, at 37 Breakwater St (Ⓣ902/687-2829 or 1-877/687-2829, Ⓦwww.bbcanada.com/4010.html; ❷; mid-June to mid-Oct), is a more economical option, occupying a 1960s house of expansive, open design with views out across the ferry terminal and ocean; there are four guest rooms here, two en suite.

The **Basin Head Fisheries Museum** (daily: early to late June & most of Sept 9am–5pm; July & Aug 9am–6pm; $4), a 15km drive up the coast from Souris, has a lovely setting, lodged on a headland overlooking a wedge of sandy beach which is, in turn, trapped between the sea, the dunes and a narrow stream that drains an elongated lagoon. Too isolated and barren for any settlement, Basin Head was never more than a fishermen's outpost, and the museum details the lives of these itinerant workers with displays of equipment, photographs of boats and miniature dioramas showing the fishing techniques they employed. However, it's the setting that really appeals and several timber huts have been built here to provide shelter, picnic and changing facilities, erected alongside the original timber cannery building.

From Basin Head, it's possible to drive right round the island's northeast corner along **Highway 16** but, with the possible exception of the mid-nineteenth-century lighthouse at **East Point**, there's nothing much to see.

Prince County

Some 40km west of Charlottetown, Hwy 2 crosses the **Prince County** boundary, from where it's another 20km to **SUMMERSIDE**, PEI's second largest settlement, a sprawling and uninspiring bayside city of fifteen thousand people that was once the island's main port. If you're in town, pop into the curious **International Fox Museum and Hall of Fame**, a couple of blocks from the harbourfront at 286 Fitzroy St (June–Sept Mon–Sat 10am–5pm; donation). This traces the history of the island's fox-ranching industry from its beginnings in 1894 to its heyday in the 1920s, when fox-fur collars reached the height of their popularity in the cities of Europe and the US. There are potted biographies of the leading fox-ranchers, some of whom grew extremely rich from the furs of the silver fox, a rare variety of the common red fox, whose pelts momentarily reached astronomical values – up to $35,000 each. At one time, indeed, fox pelts became PEI's leading export.

Heading west from Summerside, it's a few minutes' drive along Hwy 2 to **MISCOUCHE**, where the **Acadian Museum** (July & Aug daily 9.30am–7pm; rest of year Mon–Fri 9.30am–5pm, Sun 1–4pm; $4.50) is devoted to the island's French-speaking community. Miscouche was the site of the second Acadian Convention in 1884, when the assembled representatives boldly chose their own flag – the French tricolour with a gold star, the *Stella Marae* ("Star of Mary"), inserted onto the blue stripe. The museum's exhibits are, however, rather paltry, no more than a series of modest displays outlining Acadian history from pioneer days and deportations (see p.428) through to today, though the interesting fiftees-minute video partly saves the day. There are around 17,000 Acadians on PEI, of whom only 7000 speak French as their first language, a state of linguistic affairs that has made Acadian community leaders apprehensive of the future. The museum aims to support the Acadian identity and houses an Acadian Research Centre, complete with a library and archives.

Continuing west, the headland south of the village of **WELLINGTON** is a centre of Acadian settlement, but it doesn't look any different from the surrounding districts until you reach **MONT-CARMEL**. This tiny coastal village is dominated by the hulking red-brick mass and mighty spires of the **Église**

Notre-Dame, whose fantastically ugly appearance is made bizarre by a series of peculiarly sentimental statues and statuettes dotted around the entrance.

Malpeque Bay to West Point

After the church, there's nothing else of any real interest around here, and it's a time-consuming drive north before you leave the flattened farmland of this part of Prince County for the slightly hillier scenery along the northwest shore of **Malpeque Bay**. The bay's reedy waters were once fringed by tiny shipbuilding yards and the scant remains of one of them have been conserved as part of the **Green Park Shipbuilding Museum** (June–Sept daily 9.30am–5.30pm; $5). The museum also incorporates an interpretive centre, focusing on PEI's shipbuilding industry, and the **James Yeo house**. The most successful of the island's shipbuilders, the Yeos were the descendants of Cornish immigrants and they maintained close contacts with their Cornish relatives, the two branches of the family combining to develop a prosperous transatlantic shipping business. Some of the proceeds were spent on the Yeo House, whose slender gables and mini-tower date from the 1860s. The interior, with its fetching Victorian furnishings and fittings, is a real delight: look out for the beautiful wax fruit in the parlour.

There's no strong reason to hang around once you've visited the museum, but there is a bayshore **campsite** in the Green Park Provincial Park next door (ⓣ902/831-7912; June to late Sept). Furthermore, the minuscule village of **TYNE VALLEY**, just 4km away, is home to the pleasant *Doctor's Inn B&B* (ⓣ902/831-3057, ⓦwww.peisland.com/doctorsinn; ❸), which occupies a big old house and has three modest but still pleasantly appointed guest rooms. The owners run the adjoining two-acre organic garden, whose produce is well known hereabouts, and you can have dinner at the inn providing you make an advance booking.

It's about 50km from Green Park to the western tip of the island – via hwys 12, 2 and 14 – where the remote and windswept **West Point Lighthouse** (June to late Sept daily) holds a small collection of photographs and memorabilia portraying the lives of the lighthouse keepers. One room in the lighthouse and eight more in the adjoining building, all en suite and decorated in cheery modern style, comprise the *West Point Lighthouse Inn* (ⓣ902/859-3605 or 1-800/764-6854, ⓦwww.westpointlighthouse.com; ❺; late May to Sept), which makes the most of a great seaside location, overlooking a long sandy beach. The lighthouse is surrounded by the **Cedar Dunes Provincial Park**, which has a **campsite** about 500m down the coast (ⓣ902/859-8785; June to mid-Sept).

Travel details

Trains

Schedules and ticket prices from **VIA Rail** ⓣ1-888/842-7245, ⓦwww.viarail.ca.

Halifax to: Moncton (1 daily except Tues; 4hr 20min); Montréal (1 daily except Tues; 20hr); Truro (1 daily except Tues; 1hr 30min).

Moncton to: Halifax (1 daily except Tues; 4hr 20min); Montréal (1 daily except Tues; 15hr).

Buses

Acadian Lines (ⓣ1-800/567-5151, ⓦwww.acadianbus.com) operates the following services. Note that not all of these services are direct; some involve a change.

Charlottetown to: Moncton (2–3 daily; 3hr 15min).

Edmundston to: Fredericton (3 daily; 4hr 30min); Halifax (3 daily; 12hr); Moncton (3 daily;

6hr 45min); Montréal (3 daily; 8hr); Québec City (2 daily; 5hr 30min); Rivière-du-Loup, Québec (3 daily; 3hr).
Fredericton to: Edmundston (3 daily; 4hr 30min); Halifax (3 daily; 7hr); Moncton (3 daily; 2hr 30min); Montréal (2 daily; 12hr); Miramichi City (1 daily; 2hr 30min); Saint John (2 daily; 1hr 30min).
Halifax to: Annapolis Royal (1 daily; 4hr); Baddeck (2 daily; 6hr); Digby (1 daily; 4hr 30min); Edmundston (3 daily; 12hr); Fredericton (3 daily; 7hr); Moncton (3 daily; 4hr); Montréal (2 daily; 20hr); North Sydney (2 daily; 7hr 30min); Sydney (2 daily; 8hr); Truro (5 daily; 1hr 30min); Wolfville (2–3 daily; 1hr 30min).
Moncton to: Bathurst (1 daily; 3hr 30min); Charlottetown (2–3 daily; 3hr 15min); Edmundston (3 daily; 6hr 45min); Fredericton (3 daily; 2hr 30min); Halifax (3 daily; 4hr); Miramichi City (1 daily; 2hr 10min); St Andrews (1 daily; 3hr); Saint John (3 daily; 2hr).
Sydney to: Halifax (2 daily; 8hr); North Sydney (2 daily; 30min); Truro (3 daily; 5hr 45min).
Currently, **Trius Coachlines** (℡1-877/566-1567) operates a once daily service from Halifax to Yarmouth along Nova Scotia's southwest shore.
Halifax to: Chester (1 daily; 1hr); Liverpool (1 daily; 2hr 40min); Lunenburg (1 daily; 1hr 30min); Mahone Bay (1 daily; 1hr 15min); Port Joli (1 daily; 3hr); Shelburne (1 daily; 3hr 40min); Yarmouth (1 daily; 5hr 30min).
Yarmouth to: Chester (1 daily; 4hr 30min); Halifax (1 daily; 5hr 30min); Liverpool (1 daily; 2hr 40min); Lunenburg (1 daily; 4hr); Mahone Bay (1 daily; 4hr); Port Joli (1 daily; 2hr 20min); Shelburne (1 daily; 1hr 45min).

Ferries

Caribou, Nova Scotia to: Wood Islands, PEI (May to late June 5 daily, late June to mid-Oct 7 daily, mid-Oct to late Dec 3–5 daily; 1hr 15min) with **Northumberland Ferries** (℡902/566-3838 or 1-888/249-7245, Ⓦwww.nfl-bay.com).
Digby, Nova Scotia to: Saint John, New Brunswick (1–3 daily; 3hr) with **Bay Ferries** (℡1-888/249-7245, Ⓦwww.bayferries.com).
North Sydney, Nova Scotia to: Channel-Port aux Basques, Newfoundland (2–4 daily; 5–6hr or 6–8hr) and Argentia, Newfoundland (late June to early Sept 3 weekly, mid-June & late Sept 1 weekly; 14–15hr).) with **Marine Atlantic** ℡1-800/341-7981; Ⓦwww.marine-atlantic.ca.
Saint John, New Brunswick to: Digby, Nova Scotia (1–3 daily; 3hr) with **Bay Ferries** (℡1-888/249-7245, Ⓦwww.bayferries.com).
Souris, PEI to: Cap-aux-Meules, on the Magdalen Islands (Îles-de-la-Madeleine), in Québec (April–June & Sept 6 weekly, July & Aug 7–11 weekly; Oct–Jan 3–4 weekly; 5hr) with **CTMA** (℡418/986-3278 or 1-888/986-3278, Ⓦwww .ctma.ca).
Wood Islands, PEI to: Caribou, Nova Scotia (May to late June 5 daily, late June to mid-Oct 7 daily, mid-Oct to late Dec 3–5 daily; 1hr 15min) with **Northumberland Ferries** (℡902/566-3838 or 1-888/249-7245, Ⓦwww.nfl-bay.com).

Catamarans

Yarmouth, Nova Scotia to: Bar Harbor, Maine (late May to mid-Oct 1–2 daily on 4 days a week; 3hr) and Portland, Maine (late May to mid-Oct 3 weekly; 6hr) with **Bay Ferries** (℡1-888/249-7245, Ⓦwww.catferry.com).

6

Newfoundland and Labrador

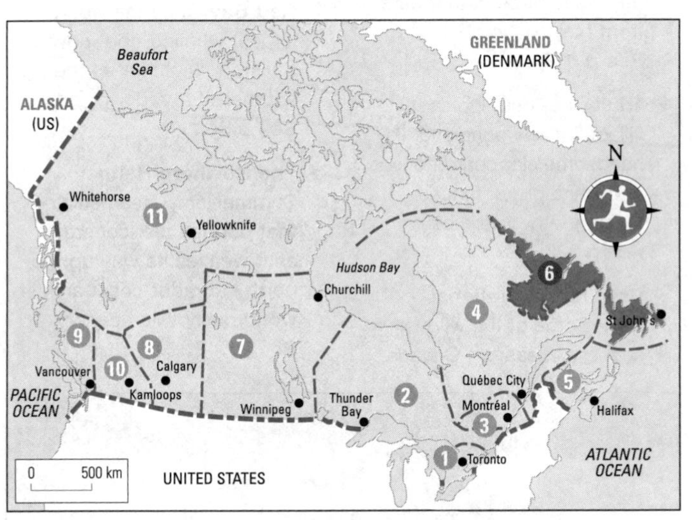

CHAPTER 6

Highlights

* **St John's** This lively port, with its fine coastal setting and bustling nightlife, provides the best introduction to Newfoundland's life and times. See p.500

* **Witless Bay sea-bird reserve** Puffins galore as well as thousands of other sea birds gather here from May to October. See p.513

* **Trinity** The best-looking village in Newfoundland, its handsome clapboard houses and white picket fences sitting pretty by the bay. See p.523

* **Gros Morne National Park** Some of the wildest scenery in eastern Canada, a wonderful mix of plunging fjords and rearing mountains. See p.530

* **L'Anse aux Meadows** The Vikings reached North America long before Columbus and the archeological evidence is here to prove the point. See p.534

* **Red Bay** Once the world's largest whaling port, now a historic highlight of the southern Labrador coast. See p.543

* **The Northern Ranger** Summer-only steamship that dodges the icebergs as it weaves its way up the north Labrador coast amidst wondrously wild scenery. See p.548

△ Norse house replicas in L'Anse aux Meadows

6

Newfoundland and Labrador

In 1840 an American clergyman named Robert Lowell described **Newfoundland** as "A monstrous mass of rock and gravel, almost without soil, like a strange thing from the bottom of the deep, lifted up, suddenly, into sunshine and storm", an apt evocation of this fearsomely beautiful island, which is still referred to – by Newfoundlanders and mainlanders alike – as "The Rock". The island's distant position between the Atlantic Ocean and the Gulf of St Lawrence has fostered a distinctive culture, distinguished by a close sense of community and a remarkable **dialect**, in essence an eclectic and versatile mix of old Irish and English. The dialect developed because the **outports** – the ancient fishing settlements that were home to the first Europeans – could only be reached by boat, though today almost all are connected to the skein of side roads that plug into the principal highway, the **Trans-Canada**. This sweeps 900km from the southwest corner of the island to the Avalon Peninsula, where **St John's**, the capital of the province (of "Newfoundland and Labrador"), sits on the northeast shore, the region's largest settlement by a long chalk.

Ferries from North Sydney in Nova Scotia (see p.394) plough across the turbulent waters of the Atlantic, bound for Channel-Port aux Basques in the southwest and Argentia much further to the east on the Avalon Peninsula, but most visitors fly straight to **St John's**, which provides the best introduction to island life, not least for its museums, good restaurants, bars and flourishing folk music scene. The city is also within easy striking distance of the **Witless Bay sea-bird reserve**, the lighthouses of **Cape Spear** and the **East Coast Trail**, which runs for several hundred kilometres from Topsail to Trepassey, providing opportunities for everything from a short ramble to a full-scale expedition

Neither do Newfoundland's attractions end on the Avalon – far from it. Tiny **Trinity**, on the Bonavista Peninsula, is perhaps the most beguiling of all the old outports, though **Twillingate** comes a close second, while **Gros Morne National Park**, in the west, features wondrous mountains and glacier-gouged lakes. Furthermore, to the north of the park, at **L'Anse aux Meadows**, lie the scant but evocative remains of an eleventh-century Norse colony, the only such site in North America, as well as a remarkable hotel in the old lighthouse on **Quirpon** island. The southern coast of Newfoundland chips in with the wild and windswept Burin Peninsula, which is a quick ferry ride from French-speaking **St-Pierre et Miquelon**, a tiny archipelago with a light scattering of fishing villages that is – as an imperial oddity – a *département* of France.

Iron ore mines and hydroelectric schemes drive the **Labrador** economy, but these industrial blemishes are mere pinpricks in the barely explored **wilderness** that defines this part of the province. Unimaginably vast, Labrador boasts some of Canada's highest mountains, wonderful fjords, crashing rivers, a spectacular shoreline with minuscule coastal settlements and a forested hinterland teeming with wildlife. A trip here is not something to be undertaken lightly, but Labrador's intimidating landscapes match anything in Canada's far north – recommendation indeed. The biggest hydro scheme in Labrador is at **Churchill Falls**, completed in the 1970s despite being the subject of a bitter dispute between Newfoundland and Québec. Neither side could agree on the allocation of the profits, forcing some surprisingly bellicose exchanges. In one, a Newfoundland senator, a certain Alexander Baird, was roused to declare, "We Newfoundland-Canadians don't

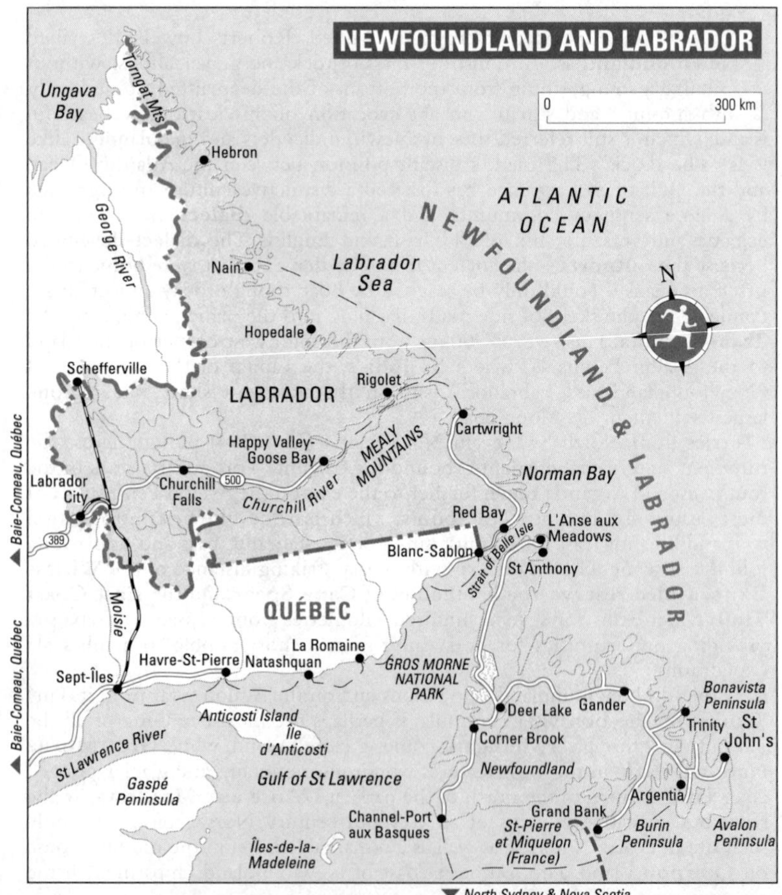

Regional information and time zones

Newfoundland and Labrador Tourism ⓣ1-800/563-6353, ⓦwww.newfoundlandandlabradortourism.com. All of Newfoundland, as well as the Labrador coastal communities south of Cartwright (from L'Anse au Claire, on the Québec border, to Norman Bay), is on **Newfoundland Time**. However, most of Labrador (Cartwright itself, plus Happy Valley-Goose Bay, Labrador City and elsewhere), as well as the Maritime Provinces, is on **Atlantic Time**, half-an-hour behind Newfoundland time. St Pierre et Miquelon also has its own time zone – half-an-hour ahead of Newfoundland Time.

want to fight, but, by jingo, if we have to, then I say we have the ships, the money and the men", to which Québecois senator Maurice Bourget added sneeringly – "and the fish".

Newfoundland

The first Europeans to settle on **Newfoundland** – mostly English and Irish – were kept glued to the coast by the inhospitality of the interior and the fertility of the ocean when they founded scores of tiny **outports** in the sixteenth and seventeenth centuries. These remote fishing villages were only linked to each other by boat and were named, in the manner of the times, after geographical features, notable events and even emotional responses – from Tickle Harbour and Cape Race to Heart's Content, Witless Bay and Chance Cove. The new settlers were largely reliant on the codfish of the **Grand Banks**, whose shallow waters, concentrated to the south and east of the island, constituted the richest fishing grounds in the world, though in winter they did hunt **seals** on the pack ice for meat, oil and fur. It was a singularly harsh life, prey to vicious storms, dense fogs and the whims of the barter system operated by the island's merchants, who exercised total control of the trade price of fish until as late as the 1940s in some areas. The arrival of several thousand servicemen in World War II did much to break down Newfoundland's long-standing isolation, but this was nothing compared with the development of a **road network** in the years that followed. Finally the outports could be reached with ease, providing their inhabitants with opportunities their ancestors could barely have imagined.

Distances within Newfoundland are considerable, so it's worth weighing up itineraries carefully. The weather is also notoriously unreliable, so try not to be too ambitious; the last thing you want to be doing is thrashing across the island through dense fog or blinding rain. The obvious place to start a visit is **St John's**, whose varied attractions could easily fill out two or three days. St John's is also a good base for day-tripping out into the **Avalon Peninsula**, the most populated part of Newfoundland. Pick of the Avalon day trips are **Cape Spear** and **Bay Bulls**, from where there are regular whale-watching boat trips, though the attractive little outport of **Brigus** runs a close third. Here as

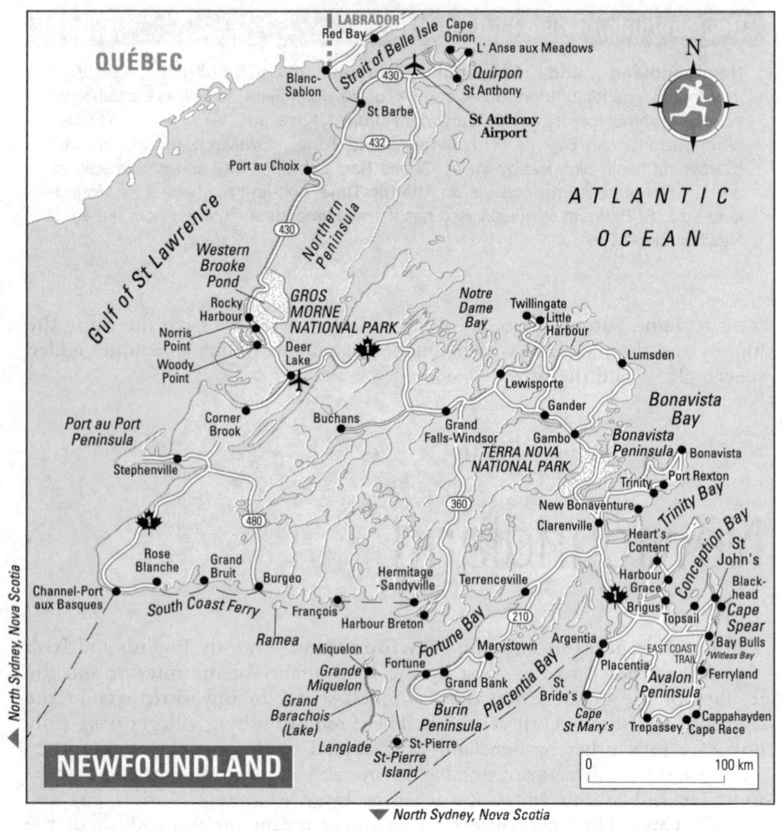

elsewhere it is, however, the rocky, craggy coast that makes the most lasting impression: the **East Coast Trail**, running through St John's, offers endless hiking opportunities. Further afield, but still within a half-day's drive from the capital, is the **Bonavista Peninsula**, where the prime objective is the picture-postcard prettiness of **Trinity**, and the stirring fjords of **Terra Nova National Park**. Thereafter, distances between the island's highlights get much longer. From Clarenville, on the Trans-Canada at the foot of the Bonavista Peninsula, it's 230km south to Fortune and the ferry to the **St-Pierre et Miquelon**; or 250km to the handsomely craggy coastline surrounding **Twillingate**; or 500km to the spectacular scenery of **Gros Morne National Park**; or a whopping 900km to the former Viking colony of **L'Anse aux Meadows** at the tip of the Northern Peninsula.

To get anything like the best from the island you pretty much have to have a **car** as public transport is extremely thin on the ground. There are no trains and the only long-distance **bus** is the once daily DRL Coachlines service running the length of the Trans-Canada from Channel-Port aux Basques to St John's (see p.500). Otherwise, a number of **minibus** companies provide a limited service across much – but certainly not all – of the island (see p.499 for further details).

A brief history of Newfoundland

The Vikings may have established an outpost here, but it was **John Cabot**, sailing out of England on behalf of Henry VII in 1497, who stirred a general interest in Newfoundland when he reported back that "the sea is swarming with fish, which can be taken not only with the net, but in baskets let down with a stone". This was the effective start of the **migratory ship fishery**, with boats sailing out from France and England in the spring and returning in the autumn, an industry that was soon dominated by the merchants of the English West Country, who grew fat on the profits. In the early 1700s, the English fishery began to change its modus operandi, moving towards an **offshore bank fishery** based in the coves of the eastern coast. This encouraged greater permanent settlement, with the British concentrated in St John's and the French around Placentia, their main fishing station since the 1660s. Mirroring the wars of Europe, these rival nationalities fought a series of desultory skirmishes until the **Treaty of Utrecht** finalized matters in 1713. Under its terms, France gave up her claims to the island in return for the right to catch, land and dry fish on the northwest coast, the so-called **French Shore** – an arrangement that lasted until 1904. In 1763 the French also swapped Labrador for St-Pierre et Miquelon.

Meanwhile, in 1729 the British government had introduced a bizarre system whereby the commanders of the naval convoy accompanying the fishing fleet became the temporary **governors** of Newfoundland, even though they returned home in the autumn. Largely left to their own devices, the English and Irish settlers, who numbered about thirty thousand by 1790, spread out along the coasts, massacring the native **Beothuks** who were completely wiped out by the end of the 1820s. A permanent governor was eventually appointed in 1817; the island was recognized as a colony in 1824; and representative, ultimately responsible government followed shortly after.

The Beothuks

The Algonquian-speaking **Beothuks**, who reached Newfoundland in about 200 AD, were semi-nomadic, spending the summer on the coast catching fish, seals and sea birds, and moving inland during the winter to hunt caribou, beaver and otter. They were also the first North American natives to be contacted by British explorers, who came to describe them as "**Red Indians**" from their habit of covering themselves with red ochre, perhaps as some sort of fertility ritual or simply to keep the flies off. Initial contacts between the two cultures were quite cordial, but the British soon began to encroach on the Beothuks' ancient hunting grounds, pushing them inland, a process that the Beothuks were unable to resist, partly because they had no immunity to the diseases the Europeans had brought with them, primarily smallpox, measles and chicken pox.

In the late eighteenth century, British attitudes hardened and the Beothuks were casually slaughtered in a manner summarized by a contemporary observer named Joseph Banks: "The English fire at the Indians whenever they meet them, and if they happen to find their houses or wigwams, they plunder them immediately." With the Beothuks fast disappearing, some white settlers organized expeditions into the interior to catch one or two alive – John Peyton of Twillingate being a case in point (see p.527) – but the last of the tribe, a young woman by the name of **Shanawdithit**, died of tuberculosis aged 29 in 1829. She spent the last years of her life in the protective custody of the attorney general in St John's, and it was here that she built a small model of a Beothuk canoe and made ten simple drawings of her people and their customs.

Struggling through a period of sectarian violence, Protestant English against Catholic Irish, Newfoundlanders decided not to join newly formed Canada in the 1860s, opting instead for self-governing **dominion** status. However, by the 1910s class conflict had replaced religious tension as the dominant theme of island life, reflecting the centralization of the economy in the hands of the bourgeoisie of St John's – a process that impoverished the outports and fuelled the growth of the trade unions. The biggest of these, the **Fishermen's Protective Union**, launched a string of hard-fought campaigns that greatly improved the working conditions of the deep-sea fishermen and sealers. These were steps in the right direction, but Newfoundland's export-oriented economy collapsed during the Great Depression of the 1930s, and the bankrupt dominion turned to Great Britain for help. The British suspended the legislative chamber and replaced it with a London-appointed commission, whose efforts were favoured by international events: the outbreak of World War II boosted demand for the island's exports and things got even better when the Allies, recognising Newfoundland's strategic importance, garrisoned it with 16,000 American and Canadian servicemen.

After the war, a narrow majority voted in favour of **confederation** with the rest of Canada in a referendum of 1948. It was a close-run race and the result might well have been different had it not been for the tireless campaigning of **Joe Smallwood** (1900–92), who became Newfoundland's first provincial premier. Smallwood remained in office until 1972, dominating the political

Getting to and around Newfoundland

Air Canada (☎1-888/247-2262, ⓦwww.aircanada.com) operates flights to St John's international airport (see p.502) from a variety of foreign and domestic destinations, including London Heathrow (May–Sept) and Halifax, Nova Scotia. In addition, Air Canada's **Jazz Air** (☎1-888/247-2262, ⓦwww.flyjazz.ca) links St John's and Deer Lake with both Halifax and Montréal. Regional carriers include **Air Labrador** (☎1-800/563-3042, ⓦwww.airlabrador.com), which has flights between St John's and Deer Lake, St John's and Wabush in Labrador, Deer Lake and Goose Bay, St Anthony and Blanc Sablon. **Provincial Airlines** (inside Newfoundland ☎1-800/563-2800, elsewhere ☎709/576-1666, ⓦwww.provincialairlines.ca) provides a regular service between St John's and two other island airports, Deer Lake and St Anthony, with other flights to Labrador's Goose Bay, Blanc Sablon and Churchill Falls. Finally, **Air St-Pierre** (☎(International prefix) (0)508/41 00 00 or 1-877/277-7765, ⓦwww.airsaintpierre.com) links St-Pierre et Miquelon with Montréal, Nova Scotia's Halifax and Sydney, New Brunswick's Moncton, and St John's, Newfoundland.

Marine Atlantic (☎1-800/341-7981, ⓦwww.marine-atlantic.ca) operates two **car ferry** routes to Newfoundland from North Sydney, Nova Scotia (see p.489). The first, **to Channel-Port aux Basques** (2–4 daily), takes between five and six hours (six to eight hours at night). One-way tickets cost $28 for passengers and $78 for a car up to 20 feet. A four-berth cabin, which should be reserved in advance, cost $54 ($99 at night); there are also dormitory bunks for $16. The second car ferry connects North Sydney **to Argentia**, 130km southwest of St John's (late June to early Sept 3 weekly, mid-June & late Sept 1 weekly; 14–15hr). One-way tickets cost $77 for passengers and $160 for a car up to 20 feet. Vehicles must be booked in advance as must (four-berth) cabins, which cost $140; there are also dormitory bunks for $28. Newhook's Transportation (see p.499) runs minibuses from Argentia to downtown St John's for $35 per person, but be sure to confirm minibus departure details before you set out. **Labrador Marine** (☎709/724-9173 or 1-866/535-2567, ⓦwww.labradormarine.com) operates a roll-on, roll-off car ferry service from Québec's **Blanc Sablon to St Barbe**,

landscape, though he was an extremely controversial figure. The root of his popularity was in the outports, where he was seen – with much justification – as the champion of the working man and woman against the merchant middle class of St John's. In this regard, it's certainly true that he tried hard to diversify the island's economy and save his fellow islanders from their over-reliance on the fishery, but the results were very mixed. Some of Smallwood's efforts to attract industry proved successful, but most did not. There were ill-considered social initiatives too, most notoriously a **resettlement programme** in which the government persuaded 28,000 Newfoundlanders to move to designated "growth centres", thereby abandoning over 300 of the smaller outports. The scheme began in 1954 and finally fizzled out in 1975, leaving behind a sorry tale of community dislocation.

In 1977, the Canadian government extended the country's territorial waters to two hundred nautical miles, partly to restrict access to its fishing grounds and partly as a prelude to large-scale investment in eastern Canada's **offshore fishery**. At first, it worked a treat – catches increased and so did the number of Newfoundlanders involved in the fishery – but within a decade fish stocks were down and there were dire warnings about the future of the entire cod fishery. The crisis came to a head in 1992 when a **moratorium** on most cod fishing was imposed; it remains in place today, and was widened in scope as recently as 2003. Newfoundland was hit terribly hard and there were bitter recriminations. Some thought the demise of the cod was brought about by foreign deep-sea

on Newfoundland's Northern Peninsula (mid-April to mid-Jan 1–3 daily; 1hr 30min; $11.25 one-way, car $23). There are sixteen other ferry routes connecting the remoter outports of both Labrador and Newfoundland; timetables and prices are given online at Ⓦwww.gov.nl.ca/ferryservices.

The only long-distance **bus** on Newfoundland is operated by **DRL Coachlines** (Ⓣ709/263-2171 or 1-888/263-1854, Ⓦwww.drlgroup.com). It's a once-daily service running the 900km east from Channel-Port aux Basques to St John's via the Trans-Canada Highway, stopping at over twenty points on the way. The one-way fare costs $110 and the whole trip takes 14 hours; be sure to confirm bus tickets and departure details before you set out. Otherwise, a patchy public transport network is provided by a string of **minibus/taxi** companies, most of whom are based in St John's. Amongst them, **Marsh's Transportation** (Ⓣ709/747-2225) provides a once daily minibus service from St John's to Bonavista via Trinity with the journey to either costing $30; **Foote's Taxi** (Ⓣ709/832-0491 or 1-800/866-1181) operates a once-daily service to Grand Bank and Fortune from the capital for $40 per person; and **Newhook's Transportation** (Ⓣ709/682-4877) charges $35 for the trip from St John's to the Argentia ferry (see p.551). As for **maps**, the free road maps issued by the province and available from just about every tourist office are really pretty good, but you might want to buy a copy of **MapArt**'s (Ⓦwww.mapart.com) first-rate provincial road map, which is on sale for a few dollars at bookshops and major gas stations.

One final word about the **moose**: Newfoundland has thousands of them and they present a real danger to the motorist at dawn and dusk and to a lesser extent at night – so much so that many locals prefer not to drive at these times. The problem is that this large and powerful animal is drawn to vehicle headlights as if hypnotized and the results of a collision can be devastating for beast and human alike: on impact, cars typically knock the moose's legs away, leaving the animal's body to come barrelling through the windscreen.

trawlers, others blamed the burgeoning seal population, some scientists put it down to a change in sea temperature and some islanders denied there was a problem at all, pointing out that cod had always been prone to appear and disappear. Whatever the truth – and Mark Kurlansky's book *Cod* convincingly points the finger of blame at the development of Canada's offshore fishery after 1977 – the moratorium put 30,000 Newfoundlanders out of work. The federal government dispensed $26 billion in aid over the ensuing decade, but many islanders decided to **emigrate**: in the years from 1994 to 2001, Newfoundland's population dropped by sixty thousand (to 512,000).

Given these problems, many Newfoundlanders regarded Ottawa's preoccupation with Québec's claims to distinct status – the dominant political theme of the 1990s and early 2000s – with a mix of contempt and incredulity. There was, however, some good news: **oil and gas** had been discovered in significant quantities some 300km southeast of Newfoundland and this **Hibernia** oil field (Ⓦwww.hibernia.ca) began to produce in 1997 with a dedicated fleet of tankers transporting the oil from a massive mobile offshore drilling unit (MODU) to an onshore storage terminal on the Avalon Peninsula. Hibernia now produces an average of 150,000 barrels of oil a day and the field itself is reckoned to hold reserves of 610 million barrels. The profits – not to mention several hundred jobs – have provided a welcome boom to the island's economy – as have developments in the fishing industry: after the collapse of the cod, many inshore fishermen diversified, fishing other species, most profitably snow crab, shrimp and scallops. Indeed, Newfoundland's future looks rosier now than it has for years and there were smiles all round when it was revealed that between 2003 and 2006 the population had started to increase.

St John's

For centuries life in **ST JOHN'S** has focused on its **harbour**, a dramatic jaw-shaped inlet approached through the 200-metre-wide channel of **The Narrows**. In its salad days, the port was packed with sailing ships from a score of nations and still today, although traffic is not as brisk, it draws a mixed maritime bag of trawlers, container ships and oil construction barges. St John's is not, however, the tempestuous seaport of yesteryear. It still possesses a boisterous nightlife, no mistake, but the rough houses of the waterfront have been replaced by shops and offices and its inhabitants – of whom there are about 170,000 – are less likely to be seafarers than white-collar workers. These squirrel away in a string of downtown skyscrapers and in the Confederation Building, the huge government complex on the western outskirts, far – in Newfoundland terms – from the swell of the sea. Yet although the city's gravity has moved inland, the waterfront remains the social hub, sprinkled with good **restaurants** and lively **bars** that feature the pick of Newfoundland **folk music** – one good reason for visiting in itself.

Devastating fires in the nineteenth century and developers in the twentieth have taken their toll on the fine old buildings of St John's, but much has survived, most notably the imposing **Courthouse**, the handsomely proportioned **Colonial Building** and the grand Catholic **Basilica of St John the Baptist**. Nonetheless, it's the overall appearance of the centre that pleases most, its higgledy-piggledy mix of the old and new clambering up the hillside to the brightly painted clapboard houses that are the hallmark of the older residential districts with **Gower Street** being a prime example. Beside the basilica are

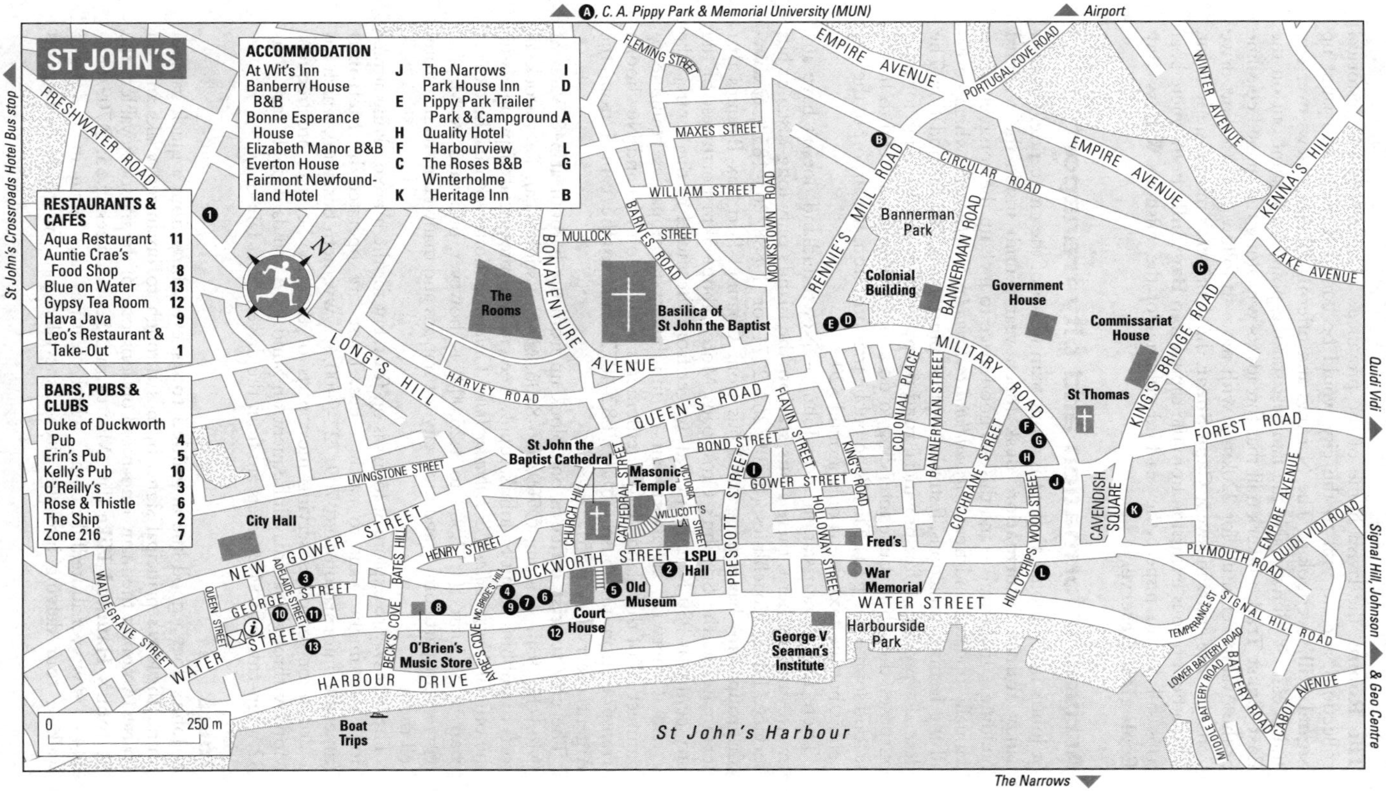

ST JOHN'S

ACCOMMODATION

At Wit's Inn	J	The Narrows	I
Banberry House B&B	E	Park House Inn	D
Bonne Esperance House	H	Pippy Park Trailer Park & Campground	A
Elizabeth Manor B&B	F	Quality Hotel	H
Everton House	C	Harbourview	L
Fairmont Newfoundland Hotel	K	The Roses B&B	G
		Winterholme Heritage Inn	B

RESTAURANTS & CAFES

Aqua Restaurant	11
Auntie Crae's Food Shop	8
Blue on Water	13
Gypsy Tea Room	12
Hava Java	9
Leo's Restaurant & Take-Out	1

BARS, PUBS & CLUBS

Duke of Duckworth Pub	4
Erin's Pub	5
Kelly's Pub	10
O'Reilly's	3
Rose & Thistle	6
The Ship	2
Zone 216	7

The Rooms, the lavish home of the province's excellent art and historical collections, and no visit to the city would be complete without a jaunt up **Signal Hill**, overlooking The Narrows and offering fabulous views over city and ocean. St John's is also the handiest starting point for a jaunt out on the **East Coast Trail**, a hiker's trail that threads its way along the rugged coastline of the Avalon Peninsula for 220km – with more to follow – and a short drive from the bare and windswept **Cape Spear**, the continent's most easterly point. The other obvious excursion from the capital is to **Bay Bulls**, from where boat trips sail out to inspect the sea-bird colonies of the offshore **Witless Bay Ecological Reserve.**

Arrival, information and city transport

St John's international **airport** is about 6km north of the city centre. There's a handy **tourist information desk** (open year round) inside the terminal building – in Arrivals – and this is a good place to pick up the comprehensive, annually updated and free *Newfoundland & Labrador Travel Guide*, which covers all the leading attractions, festivals, outdoor pursuits and accommodation. The desk also provides a free provincial **road map**, which is good enough for most purposes, though if you're intending to do a lot of driving it's useful to have a second source (see p.61). There's no public transport from the airport to the city centre, but the **taxi** fare is only around $20.

There isn't a train station in St John's – Newfoundland doesn't have any trains – and neither is there a **bus station**: the island's only long-distance bus service, DRL Coachlines (Ⓣ709/263-2171 or 1-888/263-1854, Ⓦwww.drlgroup.com) has a once daily bus from Channel-Port aux Basques that terminates at the St John's Crossroads Motel, about 5km northwest of the city centre at 980 Kenmount Rd. To get from the motel to the centre, take a taxi. Otherwise, an assortment of minibus/taxi companies combine to connect all of the island's larger settlements with St John's – and Newhook's Transportation minibuses (Ⓣ709/682-4877) run to the capital from the Argentia ferry (see p.551).

The **city tourist office** is one block up from the harbour at 348 Water St (Mon–Fri 9am–4.30pm; Ⓣ709/576-8106, Ⓦwww.stjohns.ca). They stock all sorts of gubbins about St John's, supply free city and provincial maps, and issue the official *Newfoundland & Labrador Travel Guide* mentioned above. The clearest **map** of St John's (1:12,500 to 1:25,000) is, however, published by MapArt (Ⓦwww.mapart.com) – and most city gas stations and many convenience stores sell them.

The best way to explore St John's is on **foot**, but for the more outlying attractions you might want to catch a bus. These are operated by **Metrobus** (timetable information on Ⓣ709/722-9400, Ⓦwww.metrobus.com), which has a dozen or so routes serving most parts of the city. Services are frequent Monday through Saturday, infrequent on Sundays. A standard single **fare** costs $2, a ten-ride pass $18; tickets are from the driver, exact fare only.

Tours

St John's does a good line in **guided tours**, everything from a quick gambol round the city's principal sights by bus through to organized walks and sea cruises. Amongst the many land-based options, one of the most enjoyable is the **St John's Haunted Hike** (late May to mid-Sept 5 weekly; $5; Ⓣ709/685-3444, Ⓦwww.hauntedhike.com), which features an intriguingly spooky walking tour delving into the city's dishevelled past. Alternatively, **Legend**

Tours (reservations ⓣ709/753-1497, ⓦwww.legendtours.ca) provides three-hour bus trips round the city centre, Signal Hill, Quidi Vidi and Cape Spear for $42; they operate all year, weather permitting.

Summer produces a whole fleet of **boat trips** that promise whales, icebergs, sea birds and dramatic coastal scenery – or different permutations of these depending on the month. The boats line up along the harbourfront to either side of the foot of Beck's Cove with two- to three-hour excursions costing in the region of $40. **Scademia Adventure Tours** (May–Oct; ⓣ709/726-5000, ⓦwww.nfld.com/scademia) are slightly more expensive, but they sail out to Cape Spear on the *Scademia*, a refurbished two-masted schooner.

Accommodation

As you might expect of a provincial capital, St John's has a healthy supply of downtown **hotels**, but – with one or two notable exceptions – its **B&Bs** are rather more distinctive, the pick occupying fine Victorian houses. For those on a tighter budget, there are several chain **motels** (❷–❸) along Kenmount Road, one of the main approach roads running east into the city from the Trans-Canada, and a **campsite** within easy striking distance of the centre, though camping is something of an acquired taste, given the climate.

Hotels

Fairmont Newfoundland Hotel 115 Cavendish Square ⓣ709/726-4980 or 1-800/441-1414, ⓦwww.fairmont.com. The exterior of this chain hotel is all modern clunkiness, but the interior has a real sense of itself – as befits the city's most famous hotel, whose earliest incarnation dates back to 1926. All the rooms are kitted out in top-whack chain style and most have great views over the harbour and The Narrows in particular. Indoor pool, fitness facilities and 24hr Internet access. Convenient location at the northern end of Duckworth St. Weekend and off-season discounts of up to thirty percent. ❼

Quality Hotel Harbourview 2 Hill O'Chips ⓣ709/754-7788 or 1-800/228-5151, ⓦwww.choicehotels.ca. Great address and location – right by the waterfront – but otherwise no surprises at this standard-issue, modern chain. ❺

Inns and B&Bs

At Wit's Inn 3 Gower St ⓣ709/739-7420 or 1-877/739-7420, ⓦwww.atwitsinn.ca. Sympathetically renovated Victorian row house with a handy central location. Four pleasant en-suite guest rooms turned out in attractive, period style; Internet access too. ❺

Banberry House B&B 116 Military Rd ⓣ709/579-8006 or 1-877/579-8226, ⓦwww.banberryhouse.com. Six en-suite guest rooms here in this appealing Victorian house of 1892. Each room is attractively decorated, comfortable without being fussy, and the atmosphere is a pleasing mix of friendliness and efficiency. ❻

Bonne Esperance House 18-22 Gower St ⓣ709/726-3835 or 1-888/726-3835, ⓦwww.bonneesperancehouse.ca. Central B&B spread over three Victorian terrace houses that date to the 1890s. The interiors are decked out in broadly period style and each of the guest rooms, all en-suite, are well appointed; good breakfasts as well. ❻

Elizabeth Manor B&B 21 Military Rd ⓣ709/753-7733 or 1-888/263-3786, ⓦwww.elizabethmanor.nl.ca. Long-established, but recently revamped (and renamed) B&B in a good-looking, double-bayed clapboard house of 1894. Has four nicely furnished double rooms decorated in period style. Convenient central location, at the north end of Military Road. ❹

Everton House 23 Kingsbridge Road ⓣ709/754-1326 or 1-866/754-1326, ⓦwww.evertonhouse.com. Set in its own grounds, about fifteen minutes' walk from the harbour, this classy B&B occupies a good-looking mansion of 1891. The interior has been revamped in sympathetic style and the four en-suite guest rooms are very well appointed. ❺

The Narrows 146 Gower St ⓣ709/739-4850 or 1-866/739-4850, ⓦwww.thenarrowsbb.com. Infinitely cosy B&B in an old terrace house a short walk from the centre. Four en-suite guest rooms decorated in a neat and trim version of period style. ❸

Park House Inn 112 Military Rd ⓣ709/576-2265 or 1-866/303-0565, ⓦwww.newfoundlandbedandbreakfast.nl.ca. This handsome old house, dating back to the 1870s, has been intelligently revamped with all modern conveniences grafted onto all manner of period detail, from the wide wooden staircase to the expansive bay windows. Four en-suite, a/c bedrooms and a handy location, just five minutes' walk from the town centre. The owner also operates the *Banberry House* (see p.503). ❺

The Roses B&B 9 Military Rd ⓣ709/726-3336 or 1-877/767-3722, ⓦwww.therosesbandb.com. Pleasing conversion of an old Edwardian house into a four-bedroom B&B. Breakfast is served in the third-floor kitchen, which has harbour views. Downtown location. ❹

Winterholme Heritage Inn 79 Rennie's Mill Rd ⓣ709/739-7979 or 1-800/599-7829, ⓦwww.winterholme.com. Twelve splendidly luxurious rooms with all modern conveniences in an intelligently renovated and especially handsome Queen Anne revival mansion of 1905. Set in its own grounds facing Bannerman Park and within comfortable walking distance of the centre. ❻

Campsite

Pippy Park Trailer Park and Campground Nagle's Place, Pippy Park ⓣ709/737-3669, ⓦwww.pippypark.com. Around 130 sites, both serviced and unserviced, located about 4km west of the city centre, near the Confederation Building. To get there, proceed west along Allandale Road and Nagle's Place is on the left, just beyond Prince Philip Drive. Clean, accessible washrooms. Convenience store. Open May–Sept.

The City

Running the length of the centre, a stone's throw from St John's all-important harbour, **Water Street** has long been the city's commercial hub, though the chandlers and tanners, ship suppliers and fish merchants that once clustered here are gone, replaced by an engaging mix of shops, restaurants and bars. Along with neighbouring **George Street**, this is the centre of the city's nightlife and there's one outstanding building too – the grand and domineering **Courthouse**. Nearby stand several other handsome old structures, but St John's finest buildings string along **Military Road**, culminating in the gargantuan **Basilica of St John the Baptist** and the new museum of **The Rooms**. Further afield, the prime objective is **Signal Hill**, not so much for the conspicuous Cabot Tower perched on top but for the panoramic views. With the exception of Signal Hill, which is a fair old hoof out from the centre, all the main downtown attractions are within easy walking distance of each other. Incidentally, the appellation "cove", which is commonplace here, means a short side street, not a bay.

Harbourside Park and the War Memorial

Tiny **Harbourside Park**, on Water Street, is the logical place to start a visit to the city for it was here – or at least hereabouts – that Sir Humphry Gilbert landed in 1583 to claim the island for England, thereby kick-starting the British Empire. Quite what the itinerant fishermen who had already been harvesting the Grand Banks for several decades made of the claim and the simple ceremony that accompanied it is unknown, as is the reaction of the Beothuks, if any were unwise enough to be hanging around. Both may have been surprised by some of the things Gilbert packed in his bags – hobby horses and Morris dancing bells "to delight the savage people, whom we intend to winne by all faire means possible". A series of historical plaques in the park gives all the background and behind are two bronze dogs, a Newfoundland and a Labrador. The early settlers were very reliant on their dogs and the

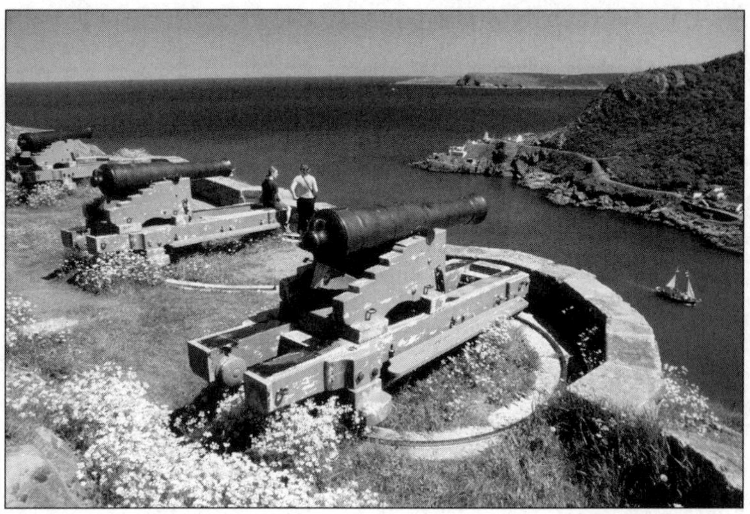

△ English cannons at St John's port entrance

Newfoundland breed, with its double-layered waterproof coat and webbed feet, was perfect for their requirements, though the Labrador – a cross between a Newfoundland and a Pointer – proved better for hunting. The gloomy brick building next to the park, the **George V Seaman's Institute**, was funded by public subscription for the welfare of local seafarers. As a plaque records, the foundation stone was laid on George V's Coronation Day in 1911 by the King's representative as authorised by "the agency of an electric current from Buckingham Palace".

Across Water Street from the park a short flight of granite steps climbs up to the **War Memorial**, which was unveiled in 1924 in front of a crowd of thousands. The island suffered grievous losses in World War I, especially during the battle of the Somme, but nevertheless the imperial-minded authorities placed the figure of Victory on top and invited Field Marshal Haig to unveil it, the very man whose ineptitude many soldiers blamed for the slaughter. Before the battle Haig wrote "I feel that every step in my plan has been taken with the Divine help" – a monstrous hoot considering the imperial army sustained nearly 60,000 casualties on the first day.

From the Courthouse to Gower Street

Back on Water Street, it's a five-minute walk south from the War Memorial to the **Courthouse**, the city's most impressive structure, a monumental Romanesque Revival building of 1901 made of granite and equipped with rounded turrets, a tumble of different gables and a clock tower. Take the steps that run up beside the Courthouse and at the top, on Duckworth Street, turn right and it's a few metres to the **old museum** (no access). The main body of the building is sullen red brick, but the facade boasts a coat of arms and three finely cast panels – one each for the island's miners, loggers and fishermen. Opposite, Cathedral Street scuttles up to the **Masonic Temple**, whose cliff-face of a facade looks challengingly across to the bluestone **Anglican Cathedral of St John the Baptist** (mid-June to Sept Mon–Fri 10am–2pm, Sat 11am–noon &

Sun 11am–3pm; free) designed in Gothic Revival style by the English architect Sir George Gilbert Scott. Begun in 1847, much of the church burnt down in 1892 but Scott's son rebuilt it to the original plans, though the work was never fully completed. Inside, the stone walls are capped by a handsome vaulted timber ceiling and the stained glass is of exceptionally high quality.

Immediately below the Masonic Temple, wooden stairs climb up to a huddle of old clapboard houses set around a tiny **courtyard** at the end of Willcott's Lane. The city once possessed dozens of these little hideaway courtyards and this is one of the very few to have survived. Willcott's Lane leads to **Gower Street**, one of the city's prettiest residential streets, its long line of brightly painted clapboard (or vinyl imitation) houses festooned by a quaint cobweb of power and telephone cables. Some of the houses are the simplest of structures, no more than wooden rectangles with doors set right on the street, but others have bay windows, outside stairways (once a real status symbol) and fancy gingerbread scrollwork – altogether a pleasing streetscape that leads north to Military Road.

The Commissariat House and Military Road

From the north end of Gower Street, it's a couple of minutes' walk over to the perky dormer windows and pastel-painted clapboard of the **Commissariat House Provincial Historic Site** on Kings Bridge Road (June–Sept daily 10am–5.30pm; $3). Dating from the early nineteenth century, this comprises the home and offices of the assistant commissary general, who was responsible for keeping the British garrison paid, fed, watered and clothed. The most intriguing rooms are the clerk's office, into which the soldiers entered by a side door to collect their wages, and the small sewing room upstairs, where there are two tiny paintings by Turner. The coach house out at the back completes the ensemble. The British garrison left St John's once and for all in 1871 and the Commissariat House then became the rectory for the adjacent Anglican **Church of St Thomas** (early July to Aug daily 9.30am–4pm; free), a wooden structure of 1836 whose sturdy tower and main entrance face onto **Military Road**. The church's unusual shape – the nave seems unnaturally long with outhouse-like structures tacked onto the side – is no accident: in 1846 a gale moved the whole church six inches and, in a panic, the commander of the garrison had his men add what amounted to stabilizing tail fins.

From the church, it's the briefest of walks along Military Road to the elegant red sandstone symmetries of **Government House**, which was completed at great expense in 1831 to serve as the residence of the Governor-General, the Queen's representative on the island. Initially, the Governor-General had extensive powers, but by the time Newfoundland joined Canada in 1949 the position had become almost entirely ceremonial. Just along the street stands the limestone **Colonial Building**, a perfectly proportioned Neoclassical edifice fronted by a stirringly grand portico. It was here that the island's legislature met in session from 1850 until the 1950s, but despite the serenity of the architecture things could get mighty rough: in 1932 the disgruntled citizenry attacked the place and made a determined if unsuccessful effort to lynch the Prime Minister, one Richard Squires.

Continuing along Military Road, it's only a few minutes to the grandest of the city's churches, the **Catholic Basilica of St John the Baptist** (Mon–Fri 9am–4.30pm, Sat 9am–1.30pm, Sun 9am–noon; free), whose twin-towered limestone and granite mass overlooks the harbour from the crest of a hill. The church was completed in 1855, but there was no ecumenical rejoicing: the church's prominent position irritated the Protestants no end. The facade of the basilica makes a competent attempt to mimic the Romanesque churches of Italy, but the interior is rather better, the stained-glass windows illuminating a delightfully ornate and embossed gold, maroon and deep-green ceiling. Look out also for the ceremonial arch in front of the church, an over-egging of the architectural pudding, where the statue of St John the Baptist is blessed with strangely lopsided buttocks.

The Rooms

Across from the basilica, on Bonaventure Avenue, **The Rooms** (June to mid-Oct Mon–Sat 10am–5pm, Wed & Thurs till 9pm, & Sun noon–5pm; mid-Oct to May Tues–Sat 10am–5pm & Sun noon–5pm; $5 plus extra charges for major exhibitions; Ⓦwww.therooms.ca) are lavish new premises built to exhibit in one setting the various historical, ethnographic and fine art collections that were previously distributed across the city. The Rooms are divided into two main sections, the **art gallery** and the **museum**, both of which spread over two floors, and the exhibits are beautifully presented and thoughtfully composed. The emphasis is very much on all things local, though some of the art displays have more international themes, and a rolling programme of temporary exhibitions occupies every nook and cranny with one exception, Floor 3 of the museum, which has a permanent display that zips through the island's history at speed. Floor plans are available at reception.

Floor 3 of the museum kicks off with a mock-up of a Newfoundland sea cliff complete with stuffed birds and bird sound recordings – press a button and you can hear their various calls. Behind is a modest display on the island's earliest inhabitants, the Maritime Archaic Peoples, and their successors, the Dorset Inuit and the Beothuks. Subsequent displays provide easy-to-digest details on the island's early fishery, whaling, the arrival of the Vikings and early European settlement, all illustrated with an assortment of archeological artefacts – there's even a miniature Norse boat-patching kit. Perhaps most interesting of all, however, and stored in the draws of a small wooden cabinet, are the crude but particularly poignant drawings made by **Shanawdithit** (see box, p.497), the last of the Beothuks, who, half-starved and desperate, surrendered herself to a European trapper, a certain William Cull, in 1823.

Signal Hill

Rearing up above The Narrows, **Signal Hill National Historic Park** (open access) is a protuberant, grass-covered, lake-studded chunk of rock with views that are dramatic enough to warrant the strenuous half-hour (2km) walk up from the northern end of Duckworth Street – there's no city bus. Originally known as The Lookout, Signal Hill took its present name in the middle of the eighteenth century, when it became common practice for flags to be hoisted here to notify the city of impending arrivals. The signallers would also indicate whose ship or ships were approaching, thereby giving the city's merchants a couple of hours to prepare docking and supplies – or time for city folk to gather down at the harbour to celebrate the arrival of the highliner, the first ship back from the seal hunt (see box, p.508). The hill was also an obvious line of defence for the garrison of St John's, and the simple fortifications that were first established during the Napoleonic Wars were embellished every time there was a military emergency, right up until World War II.

The views from the top of Signal Hill may be the main reason to journey out here, but the road to the summit is dotted with a string of attractions, beginning with the flashy **Johnson Geo Centre** (mid-May to mid-Oct Mon–Sat 9.30am–5pm, Sun 1–5pm; mid-Oct to mid-May Tues–Sat 9.30am–5pm, Sun

1–5pm; $10.25; Ⓦwww.geocentre.ca), which is devoted to earth sciences. An introductory film illustrates various natural phenomena and then there's a section each on the Earth, Newfoundland and Labrador's geology, the Earth's peoples, and the future, including a so-called Stellarium, examining the stars. In addition, side exhibits focus on geothermal heating, the *Titanic* and icebergs, and on oil and gas (the last funded by ExxonMobil).

Moving on, you soon reach Parks Canada's **Signal Hill Visitor Centre** (daily; mid-June to early Sept 8.30am–8pm; early Sept to Dec and April to mid-June 8.30am–4.30pm; $3.95), whose well-chosen displays explore the history of the city and the island. Beside the centre is **Gibbet Hill**, where the bodies of hanged criminals were once left to rot as a grisly warning to sailors passing through The Narrows – just in case they were harbouring mutinous thoughts. Just up the road a bit is the **Queen's Battery**, whose antiquated guns peer over the entrance to the harbour. The plot of ground beside the battery is used for 1790s period military tattoos from the middle of July to the middle of August (call for times Ⓣ709/772-5367) and down below, by the water, is **Chain Rock**, from where a chain used to be dragged across The Narrows in times of danger.

Sealing

The Newfoundland **seal hunt** has always been dependent on the **harp seal**, a gregarious animal that spends the summer feeding around the shores of Greenland, Baffin Island and northern Hudson Bay. In the autumn they gather in a gigantic herd that surges south ahead of the arctic ice pack, passing the coast of eastern Labrador before dividing into two. One group pushes down the Strait of Belle Isle into the Gulf of St Lawrence to form the **Gulf herd**, the other continues south as far as Newfoundland's northeast coast, where they congregate as the **Front herd**. From the end of February to early March, the seals of the Front herd start to breed, littering the ice with thousands of helpless baby seals or **whitecoats**, as they're known. It's just two or three weeks before the pups begin to moult and their coats turn a shabby white and grey.

From early days, the Front herd provided the people of northeast Newfoundland with fresh meat during the winter, but it was the value of the whitecoats' fur that spawned a clutch of hunting centres – primarily Bonavista, Trinity and Twillingate – and thousands of jobs. In 1853, the seal fleet consisted of 4000 ships manned by 15,000 sailors, who combined to kill no fewer than 685,000 harps. However, in the 1860s **steamers** made the old sailing ships obsolete and provoked a drastic restructuring of the industry. The new vessels were too expensive for the shipowners of the smaller ports and control of the fleet fell into the hands of the wealthy merchants of St John's. By 1870, the bulk of the fleet was based in the capital and hundreds of Newfoundlanders were obliged to travel here for work every winter.

For those "lucky" enough to get a berth, conditions on board were appalling: as a government report noted, a captain could "take as many men as he could squeeze onto his ship... When the seal pelts began to come aboard, the crew had to make way until, by the end of a successful voyage, the men would be sleeping all over the deck, or amongst the skins piled on the deck, even in the most savage weather conditions." All this hardship was endured on a basic diet of "hardtack", hard bread or ship's biscuit, and "switchel", black unsweetened tea, enlivened by the odd plate of "duff", a boiled-up mixture of old flour and water. "Small wonder," as one of the sealers – or **swilers** – recalled, "that most of us learned to eat raw seal meat. The heart, when it was cut out and still warm, was as good as steak to we fellows." There were two compensations: money and status – as it left for the Front herd the seal fleet was cheered on its way and the men of the first ship back, the **highliner**, dispensed seal flippers, an island delicacy, and got free drinks all round.

Cabot Tower

Plonked on top of Signal Hill is **Cabot Tower** (daily; June–Aug 8.30am–9pm; Sept to mid-Oct 9am–7pm; rest of year 9am–5pm; free), a short and stout stone structure built at the end of the nineteenth century to commemorate both John Cabot's landing of 1497 and Queen Victoria's Diamond Jubilee. The tower holds a small display on electronic signalling, and outside in the car park there's a **plaque** honouring Guglielmo **Marconi**, who confirmed the reception of the first transatlantic radio signal here in December 1901. The views back over the city and out to sea are nothing short of fabulous and half a dozen **hiking trails** are outlined on a notice board at the other end of the car park from the Cabot Tower. The shortest is the comfortable 500m stroll back down Signal Hill to the Queen's Battery, another is the wild and windswept trek down the headland to The Narrows and onto Outer Battery Road, by means of which you can return to the city centre. For a longer hike, you can pick up the East Coast Trail (see box, p.513) on the south side of the harbour at **Fort Amherst Lighthouse**, which is clearly visible across The Narrows from the top of Signal Hill.

In the early 1900s, the wooden-walled steamships were, in their turn, replaced by **steel steamers**. Once again, the traders of St John's invested heavily, but the shrinking seal population reduced their profit margins. Increasingly, they began to cut corners, which threatened the safety of the swilers. The inevitable result was a string of disasters that culminated in 1914 in the loss of the *Southern Cross* with all 173 hands. Shortly afterwards, a further 78 men from the *Newfoundland* died on the ice as a consequence of the reckless greed of one of the captains, who was trying to secure his catch in excessively dangerous conditions. These twin catastrophes destroyed the hunt's communal popularity, and a decade later the economics of the industry collapsed during the Great Depression. By 1935 most of the sealing firms of St John's had gone broke.

After World War II sealing was dominated by the ships of Norway and Nova Scotia, with the Newfoundlanders largely confining their activities to an inshore cull of between 20,000 and 40,000 whitecoats per year – enough work for about four thousand people. Thus, sealing remained an important part of the island's economy up until the 1960s, when various conservationist groups, spearheaded by **Greenpeace**, started a campaign to have it stopped. Slowly but surely the pressure built up on the Canadian government until, in 1965, it implemented the first seal protection regulations, restricting the number of juvenile and adult seals the islanders were allowed to kill. This remains the position today with the annual cull restricted to 350,000 seals per year, worth about $17m in meat and pelt sales.

The **conservationists** have always objected to the cruelty of the cull, and it's certainly true that the killing of a hapless seal is a brutal act. Yet the furore has much to do with the doleful eyes and cuddly body of the baby seal, an anthropomorphism that doesn't wash with an island people whose way of life has been built on the hunting of animals. To add grist to the mill, many islanders are convinced that the decline in fish stocks has everything to do with the increasing number of seals and there are frequent attempts to get the hunting restrictions removed or at least lessened. As a consequence of all this, nothing angers many Newfoundlanders more than the very mention of Greenpeace, whose supporters are caricatured as well-heeled, urban outsiders who have no right to meddle in traditional hunting practices.

Quidi Vidi village

Tiny **QUIDI VIDI** ("kiddy-viddy"), a couple of kilometres north of the city centre, is a well-known beauty spot, where a handful of old fishing shacks are backdropped by sharp-edged cliffs and set beside the deep-blue waters of a slender inlet. A spate of new construction has robbed the village of much of its charm, but it is home to both **Mallard Cottage Antiques** (May–Sept daily 10am–5pm), in an attractive old building dating from the 1750s, and **Quidi Vidi Brewery**, which occupies the old fish plant. The brewery offers tours and tastings year-round (times and bookings on ⓣ709/738-4040; $5) and you should look out for their well-regarded "1892 Traditional Ale". From the centre of the village, it's a short walk east to **Quidi Vidi battery** (late May to late Sept daily 10am–5.30pm; $3), which overlooks the narrow channel that connects the inlet to the sea from the side of a hill. The gun battery has been restored to its 1812 appearance, when it was readied against potential attack from the US.

To get to Quidi Vidi from the city centre, take Forest Road from beside the Fairmont Newfoundland Hotel and keep going – or take Metrobus service #15 from Plymouth Road on the harbourside of the same hotel. En route, you'll travel the length of **Quidi Vidi Lake**, the site of the annual Royal St John's Regatta, held every August. This is one of the oldest sporting events in North America, featuring fixed-seat rowing races and a huge garden party.

Eating, drinking and entertainment

St John's **café and restaurant** scene is very much on the up, with a string of good places dotted round the city centre and a particular concentration down on Water Street. Seafood remains the key ingredient on many menus, but, with

Newfoundland folk music

The English and Irish settlers who first colonized Newfoundland brought their music with them: party nights would typically begin with step dances and square sets performed to the accompaniment of the **fiddle** and the **button accordion**, followed by the unaccompanied **singing** of locally composed and "old country" songs. The music was never written down, so as it passed from one generation to the next a distinctive Newfoundland style evolved, whose rhymes and rhythms varied from outport to outport – though its Irish and English roots always remained pronounced.

Newfoundland's traditional music was in fine fettle until the advent of radio and the arrival of thousands of soldiers in World War II began to modify and influence many of the island's leading musicians. Country & western was the key catalyst with, for example, an old story or ballad given a C&W melody and rhythm, the accordion supported by lead and bass guitar and drum. Nonetheless, the traditional style of folk music lingered on, as exemplified by the island's most famous fiddlers, **Rufus Guinchard** and **Émile Benoit**. The two died in the 1980s, but their approach was adopted, albeit in modified form, by younger artists like singer-songwriters Jim Payne and Ron Hynes, musician-producer Kelly Russell and groups such as **Figgy Duff**. At present, Celtic music – mainly Irish – is the big deal in the bars of St John's, but local musicians regularly perform in a more traditional idiom. In particular, look out for **Dermot O'Reilly**, **Phyllis Morrissey** and **Anita Best**, not to mention two of the most popular bands, **Great Big Sea** and the **Irish Descendants**.

St John's has two good specialist record shops – **O'Brien's Music Store**, 278 Water St (ⓣ709/753-8135, ⓦwww.obriens.nf.ca), and **Fred's**, 198 Duckworth St (ⓣ709/753-9191, ⓦwww.freds.nf.ca).

the exception of fish and chips, traditional Newfoundland dishes – most notably cods' tongues (throats), toutons (fried bread dough with molasses) and seal-flipper pie – can be hard to track down.

The city has dozens of **bars and pubs** – indeed St John's is said to have more drinking places per square kilometre than any other city in the country. Most of the more popular joints are on Water and adjoining George streets and they can get mighty crowded (and boisterous) on the weekend. The vast majority are small with no-frills decor, and the pick offer regular live **folk music**, anything from C&W with an idiosyncratic nautical twist through to traditional unaccompanied ballads and more generic Celtic music. If you're content to take pot luck, follow the crowds along George Street, but otherwise either pick up a copy of the free (and particularly well-written) weekly listings magazine *The Scope* (Ⓦwww.thescope.ca) or ask at O'Brien's Music Store, 278 Water St (Ⓣ709/753-8135, Ⓦwww.obriens.nf.ca), where you can get a comprehensive list of up-and-coming gigs. Another good contact is the **St John's Folk Arts Council**, 155 Water St (Ⓣ709/576-8508, Ⓦwww.nlfolk.com), which organizes regular folk-music concerts and folk dances. The best of the island's dozen folk festivals, the **Newfoundland and Labrador Folk Festival** (Ⓣ709/576-8508, Ⓦwww.nlfolk.com), is held in Bannerman Park in St John's in early August. Finally, the **LSPU Hall**, in the centre on Victoria St (Ⓣ709/753-4531, Ⓦwww.rca.nf.ca), offers an inventive programme of **theatre** and **cinema**.

Cafés and restaurants

Aqua Restaurant 310 Water St Ⓣ709/576-2782. One of the new breed of restaurants to appear on the island with cool decor and an ambitious menu featuring the likes of chicken with mangoes and a raspberry vinaigrette. Main courses hover around $20. Open Mon–Fri noon–2pm & daily 5.30–10pm.

Auntie Crae's Food Shop 272 Water St. It's worth popping in here for the premises alone – a good old-fashioned general store that has been updated with a minimum of fuss. Selling food is the main event, but there is a small and basic café and they do inexpensive soups and salads, croissants and muffins plus filled sandwiches to order. Daily 8am–7pm.

Blue on Water 319 Water St Ⓣ709/574-2583. Chic restaurant decorated in sharp modern style that features local ingredients on its inventive menu – for instance, a delicious rabbit and partridgeberry soup. First-rate cuisine with mains hovering around $25. Daily from 4.30pm.

Gypsy Tea Room 195 Water St Ⓣ709/739-4766. Not a tea room at all, but perhaps the best restaurant in town, a lively informal place with a groovy sound track and an amazingly creative menu with a dozen or so specials every day – seafood and grilled meats often Greek in inspiration. Main courses average around $25. Daily noon–3pm & 6–10pm, midnight on Thurs & Fri.

Hava Java 216 Water St. The best coffee in town, plus veggie sandwiches, light lunches and bagels. A fashionable spot, so the flyers here are likely to give good ideas about what's on and where. Mon–Fri 7.30am–11pm, Sat & Sun 9am–10pm.

Leo's Restaurant and Take-Out 27 Freshwater Rd Ⓣ709/726-2658. Good spot to try some of the local specialities like cods' tongues and, in season, seal-flipper pie, as well as first-rate fish and chips. Closed Sun.

Bars, pubs and clubs

Duke of Duckworth Pub 325 Duckworth St. Popular bar just down the steps from Duckworth towards Water St. Serves a wide range of Newfoundland ales and lagers, but its speciality is English pints.

Erin's Pub 186 Water St Ⓣ709/722-1916. Popular and well-established, no-frills bar, showcasing the best of folk acts several nights a week.

Kelly's Pub 25 George St at Adelaide Ⓣ709/753-5300. Lively spot with a youthful (drunken) clientele. Good range of beers and frequent live music too.

O'Reilly's 13 George St Ⓣ709/722-3735, Ⓦwww.oreillyspub.com. Irish pub with Irish booze and a mixed bag of live entertainment including an open mike night once a week.

Rose & Thistle 208 Water St ⓣ709/579-6662. Small and long-established pub that pulls in the punters with live bands – and folk at the fore.

The Ship Solomon's Lane, at 265 Duckworth St ⓣ709/753-3870. Down the steps from Duckworth St, this dark, earthy pub showcases an eclectic mix of live music that attracts everyone from grizzled old-timers who love their folk music to arty, black-clad students.

Zone 216 216 Water St ⓦwww.hello.to/zone216. St John's only gay bar. Dark, cramped and sweaty. Fri & Sat only. Above *Hava Java* (see p.511).

Listings

Bike rental Canary Cycles, 294 Water St ⓣ709/579-5972, ⓦwww.canarycycles.nfnet.com.

Bookshops Afterwords, 245 Duckworth St (ⓣ709/753-4690), has a large range of Newfoundland titles, both new and used. If the island dialect intrigues you, this is also the place to pick up the substantial *Dictionary of Newfoundland English* edited by Story, Kirwin and Widdowson.

Buses DRL Coachline buses (ⓣ709/263-2171 or 1-888/263-1854; ⓦwww.drlgroup.com) operates a once daily bus from Channel-Port aux Basques to St John's along the Trans-Canada Highway, with halts at over twenty places on the way. In St John's, this DRL service terminates at the St John's Crossroads Motel, about 5km west of the city centre at 980 Kenmount Road. To get from the motel to the centre, take a taxi. In addition, an assortment of minibus companies combine to connect St John's with all of the island's larger settlements and the Argentia ferry – see p.551 for more details.

Camping equipment The Outfitters, 220 Water St ⓣ709/579-4453, ⓦwww.theoutfitters.nf.ca.

Car rental Budget, at the airport ⓣ709/747-1234; Discount, 350 Kenmount Rd ⓣ709/722-6699; National, at the airport ⓣ709/722-4307.

Consulates UK ⓣ709/579-2002.

Laundry Mighty White's, 152 Duckworth St ⓣ709/753-7947, near the Fairmont *Newfoundland Hotel.*

Newspapers St John's racks up two first-rate daily newspapers – the *Telegraph* and the *Independent.*

Pharmacy Water Street Pharmacy, 337 Water St at George ⓣ709/579-5554.

Police ⓣ709/729-8333.

Post office 354 Water St and Queen (Mon–Fri 8am–5pm).

Shopping Good places to purchase Newfoundland handicrafts, knitwear and jewellery include The Cod Jigger, 245 Duckworth St; Devon House Craft Shop and Gallery, 59 Duckworth St; and Nonia, 286 Water St.

Taxis Bugden's ⓣ709/726-4400; Jiffy Cabs ⓣ709/722-2222. There's a rank outside the *Fairmont Newfoundland Hotel.*

Weather Up-to-date bulletins ⓣ709/772-5534.

Around St John's

By car, St John's is within easy striking distance of three enjoyable attractions, each of which can occupy half a day. The nearest is **Cape Spear**, where a Victorian lighthouse guards the island's easternmost point, followed by **Bay Bulls**, the starting point for boat trips out to **Witless Bay Ecological Reserve**. From Bay Bulls, it's another short haul to **Ferryland**, where archeologists are exploring the site of the seventeenth-century English colony of **Avalon**, from which the whole peninsula received its name. St John's is also where the **East Coast Trail** begins (see box, p.513).

The East Coast Trail is **linear**, which means that if you're after a day's hiking you really need two cars and at least two people, but there are places to stay along the trail and it is possible to arrange to be picked up (and/or taken out) by taxi. The Association is always glad to help and advise and also organizes a programme of group hikes for free. As for particular recommendations, the 3.7km hike from the former fishing village of **Blackhead to Cape Spear** is one of the easier and more accessible portions of the trail and it covers a handsomely rugged stretch of coastline; allow one and a half to two hours. The trailhead is clearly signed.

The East Coast Trail

Negotiating much of the length of the Avalon Peninsula, the **East Coast Trail** has brought together backcountry routes and hunting paths to create a long-distance **hiking trail** that passes through fishing communities, provincial parks, national historic sites and a couple of ecological reserves. At present, the 220km stretch from Fort Amherst, on St John's harbour, to Cappahayden has been completed – along with nearly forty trailheads – but construction is under way to extend the trail another 320km - to Topsail, on Conception Bay in the north, and Trepassey in the south. It's an extraordinarily ambitious enterprise and one that is largely reliant on volunteer labour – in itself a real tribute to the Newfoundlanders. To assist hikers, the **East Coast Trail Association** (Ⓣ709/738-4453, Ⓦwww.eastcoasttrail.com) is in the process of preparing five guide books ($23 each) covering different sections of the trail and including first-rate 1:25,000 topographical maps. The first two – from St John's to Petty Harbour, and from Petty Harbour to Bay Bulls – have already been published and are superb, beautifully illustrated and with all sorts of advice and information on everything from flora and fauna through to historical anecdotes and biographical snippets.

Cape Spear

In St John's, take the signposted turning off Water Street south of the centre and it's a 15km-drive via Route 11 to **Cape Spear National Historic Site** (open access), a rocky, windswept headland which is a popular day-trip mainly because it's nearer to Europe than any other part of mainland North America. To cater for tourists, the cape is crisscrossed by boardwalks, the most obvious of which leads up from the car park past the heritage shop and the modern lighthouse to the squat and rectangular Victorian **Lighthouse** (mid-May to mid-Oct daily 10am–6pm; $3.95), at the cape's highest point. Built in the 1830s, the lighthouse's interior has been pleasantly decked out in period style, down to imitation barrels of sperm oil and the neatly made bed, though there's surprisingly little on the lighthouse-keepers themselves. The other specific attraction is the substantial remains of the World War II **gun emplacement** at the tip of the cape, but the views are really the main event, right along the coast and up to The Narrows of St John's. In spring and early summer, the waters off the cape are a great place to spy the blue-tinged icebergs that have floated south from the Arctic pack ice and there's a reasonable chance of spotting a whale too. If you're really lucky, you'll see entire pods of whales in pursuit of the capelin (smelt), which roll onto the Avalon Peninsula's sandier coves to spawn in their millions from about the middle of June to mid-July. This can be a truly remarkable sight, but there's no way of knowing which cove and when, and the capelin don't appear as frequently as they used to; the rangers may be able to point you in the right direction.

Bay Bulls and the Witless Bay Ecological Reserve

Doubling back from Cape Spear, turn left along the road to **Petty Harbour** and, after about 18km, you'll reach Route 10 just 16km or so short of **BAY BULLS**. Joe Smallwood (see p.527) had Bay Bulls designated a town, but really it's only a village, which straggles around the head of a deep and pointed bay. It was here that one of the last active German U-boats surrendered in 1945 – much to the amazement of the locals – and today the town makes much of its living from boat tours around the four tiny offshore islets that comprise the **Witless Bay Ecological Reserve**. The best time to visit is between mid-June

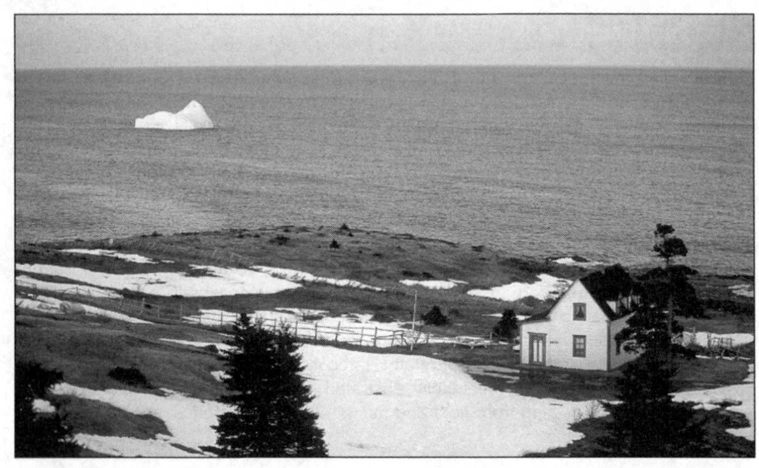

△ Iceberg at Witless Bay

and mid-July, when over 800,000 birds gather here – the reserve has the largest puffin colony in eastern Canada and there are also thousands of storm petrels, common murres, kittiwakes, razorbills, guillemots, cormorants and herring gulls. In addition, the area is home to the largest population of **humpback whales** in the world, and finback and minke whales are often spotted between June and August.

From May to September, several companies offer daily **boat trips** to the waters surrounding the reserve. These include O'Brien's Whale & Bird Tours (ⓣ709/753-4850 or 1-877/639-4253, ⓦwww.obriensboattours.com); Mullowney's Puffin and Whale Tours (ⓣ709/334-3666 or 1-877/783-3467, ⓦwww.puffinswhales.com); and Gatheralls Puffin and Whale Watch (ⓣ709/334-2887 or 1-800/419-4253, ⓦwww.gatheralls.com). All three companies run two-hour sea trips ($40–50) and reservations are advised. They will also provide transport to and from major hotels in St John's for roughly $30 return, though this has to be arranged ahead of time. O'Brien's also offers **sea kayaking** in the (relatively) sheltered waters of Bay Bulls harbour.

From Bay Bulls, it's 30km straight back to St John's or you can press on south the 45km to Ferryland.

Ferryland

George Calvert (1580–1632), the first Baron Baltimore, was a favourite of King James I of England, who gave him a slab of land in Newfoundland to settle as a colony. Calvert obligingly sailed out to what is now **FERRYLAND** in 1620 and took a shine to the place, naming it **Avalon** and dispatching a band of prospective colonists the following year. The settlers sent him such wonderful reports that he decided to move there himself a few years later, but he only lasted one winter. Everything that could go wrong did, as Calvert penned to a friend back home: "I have sent [my family] home after much sufferance in this woful country, where with one intolerable wynter were wee almost undone. It is not to be expressed with my pen what wee have endured."

Archeologists have set about unearthing the remains of Calvert's colony, which lies at the base of a narrow and low-lying headland that hooks out into the ocean opposite today's Ferryland. They have discovered a surprising amount, including the foundations of several buildings, part of the original sea wall, a well and – a real surprise – a small strip of cobblestone street. The whole site has been attractively landscaped and afterwards you can follow the gravel road that leads along the headland to the stumpy Victorian **lighthouse** on Ferryland Head – allow twenty-five minutes each way for the walk. At the lighthouse, two enterprising young Newfoundlanders have established *Lighthouse Picnics* (Tues–Sun 11.30am–6pm; ⓣ709/363-7456, ⓦwww.lighthousepicnics.ca), offering tasty spreads that feature local ingredients and lip-smacking homemade lemonade; as you might expect, picnics have to be pre-booked. Finally, back at the base of the headland, some 400m from the archeological site, there's also a **Visitor Centre** (daily mid-May to June & Sept to early Oct 10am–5pm; July & Aug 9am–7pm; $6), which gives the historical background to Calvert's colony.

The Avalon Peninsula

St John's sits on the northeast corner of the **Avalon Peninsula**, a jagged, roughly rectangular slab of land connected to the rest of Newfoundland by a narrow, tapering isthmus. Almost invariably, the Avalon's towns and villages stick resolutely to the coast and there's a particular concentration around populous **Conception Bay**, whose eastern shore lies just 15km west of the capital. Setting aside Cape Spear, Bay Bulls and Ferryland (see opposite), the peninsula has half a dozen places that are well worth a visit, a varied bunch including **Brigus**, home to the delightful Hawthorne Cottage; **Heart's Content**, with its antique cable station; **Castle Hill**, from where there are panoramic views over Placentia Bay; and the sea-bird colonies of **Cape St Mary's**. With the exception of the cape, which is a tad too far away for comfort, all make good day-tripping destinations from St John's.

Brigus

Captain Robert Bartlett (1875–1946) was no ordinary seaman, but a much sought-after ice navigator and Arctic explorer who helped get Peary to his base camp prior to his dash to the North Pole in 1909. Captain Bob was also a Newfoundlander and his old home in **BRIGUS**, on the south shore of Conception Bay, about 80km from St John's, has become the **Hawthorne Cottage National Historic Site** (daily mid-May to late June and Sept to mid-Oct 9am–5pm; late June to Aug 9am–7pm; $3.70). The house is littered with his keepsakes, but just as interesting is the architecture. Bartlett was a man of substance and style and the family home, built in 1830, eschewed the clapboard of the traditional Newfoundland house for a decorative Regency style, complete with an elevated, wrought-iron, wraparound balcony. The Cottage is in the old part of Brigus, a pint-sized pocket of good-looking Victorian houses that backs onto the bay.

Harbour Grace

HARBOUR GRACE, one of Conception Bay's prettiest settlements, sits on the bay's western shore, tucked in against Route 70, 30km or so from Brigus. The village stretches out along **Water Street**, which is at its most attractive near its northern end, where a handful of elegant clapboard houses flank a slender inlet and are overseen by two **churches**, a handsome silver and green-spired

Catholic effort and the pretty stonework of the Anglicans. The old red-brick Customs House has been turned into a mildly entertaining **museum** (mid-June to early Sept daily 10am–5pm; $2), featuring sepias of the village and its Victorian inhabitants, and an outdoor plaque commemorates **Peter Easton** (1570–1620), the so-called "Pirate Admiral". Easton, who was based here at the beginning of the seventeenth century, ran a phenomenally successful fleet, which was manned by five thousand sailors, who made their leader rich enough to retire to a life of luxury in the south of France. Next door, the tiny park has another plaque, this one in honour of the early aviators who flew across the Atlantic from the Harbour Grace area, including **Amelia Earhart**, the first woman to complete the journey solo in 1932.

Heart's Content

In the middle of the nineteenth century, **HEART'S CONTENT**, 30km northwest of Harbour Grace on the shores of Trinity Bay, was packed with engineers attempting to connect North America with Britain by **telegraph cable**. The project had begun when the USS *Niagara* had hauled the first transatlantic line ashore here in 1858, but after Queen Victoria and the American president James Buchanan had swapped inaugural jokes the cable broke. It was eight years before an improved version, running from Valentia in Ireland, could be installed and thereafter Heart's Content became an important relay station to New York, a role it performed until technological changes made it obsolete in the 1960s. Tight against the waterfront, in the centre of the village, the **Cable Station Provincial Historic Site** (mid-June to Oct daily 10am–5.30pm; $3) contains an intriguing old cable operating room that has been preserved in pristine condition. It also houses a series of displays on the history of telecommunications, including a replica of the original Victorian cable office and details of the problems encountered during the laying of the first telegraph lines.

From Heart's Content, it's a pleasant 60km south along the eastern shore of Trinity Bay to the Trans-Canada Hwy just near the turning for Castle Hill National Historic Site.

Castle Hill National Historic Site

The thumb-shaped promontory filling out the southwest corner of the Avalon Peninsula is a foggy wilderness of marsh and rock, whose westerly shoreline is negotiated by **Route 100**, branching off the Trans-Canada some 80km from St John's. Route 100 begins by whistling across the interior for the 50km dash to the ferry terminal of **ARGENTIA**, and most people drive straight past the turning for the tiny **Castle Hill National Historic Site**, just 5km short of the port (open access; free). This is a pity, because Castle Hill is magnificently located overlooking the watery web of channel and estuary that edges **Placentia Harbour**, one of Newfoundland's finest anchorages. The harbour's sheltered waters first attracted the French, who established their regional headquarters, "Plaisance", here in 1662, with Fort Royale (now Castle Hill) up above as the key defensive position. As the fortunes of war seesawed, so harbour and fort were successively occupied and re-fortified by the British and the French, a turbulent history skillfully explored at the **visitor centre** (mid-May to mid-Oct daily 10am–6pm; $3.95). Little remains of these works today – just a few stone walls and ditches – but make the trip for the views and maybe have a look at one of the historical re-enactments that take place in the summer – ring ⓣ709/772-5367 or 709/227-2401 for programme details.

St Bride's and Cape St Mary's

Viewed from Castle Hill, the village of **Placentia** way down below looks a pretty affair, a ribbon of buildings sandwiched between the green of the hills and the blue of the bay. However, on closer inspection, the village doesn't live up to its setting and you'll soon be continuing along on Route 100 as it sets out on its 45km journey to the quiet outport of **St Bride's** (see below). From here, it's a further 20km to **Cape St Mary's Ecological Reserve**, which is best visited between early May and early August, when thousands of sea birds, principally gannets, kittiwakes, razorbills and murres, congregate on its rocky sea cliffs and stumpy sea stacks. An **interpretive centre** (daily May & Oct 9am–5pm; June–Sept 8am–8pm; $5) close to the parking lot provides all the background information and from here a clearly marked footpath cuts across the cape. The best vantage point is generally considered to be at **Bird Rock**, a twenty-minute (1km) walk away, though note a few cautions: wear good walking shoes, carry or wear warm clothing and stick to the footpath as the cape can be engulfed by fog as quick as a wink. If that sounds intimidating, then join one of the reserve's **guided walks** – details from the interpretive centre on Ⓣ1-800/563-6353.

Cape St Mary's is just over 200km from St John's, which makes it rather too far away for a comfortable day-trip, but there are three **places to stay in ST BRIDE'S**, beginning with the motel-style *Bird Island Resort*, whose assorted modern buildings spread out along the seashore (Ⓣ709/337-2450 or 1-888/337-2450, Ⓦwww.birdislandresort.com; ❸). The alternatives are the spick and span *Capeway Motel* (Ⓣ709/337-2163 or 1-866/337-2163, Ⓦwww.thecapeway.ca; ❷), which has seven unassuming en-suite rooms in what was once a convent; and the *Atlantica Inn* (Ⓣ709/337-2860 or 1-888/999-2860; ❷), which has just three guest rooms.

The Burin Peninsula

The bony mass of the **Burin Peninsula** pokes out into the Atlantic from the north end of the isthmus connecting the Avalon Peninsula with the rest of Newfoundland. Much of the Burin is crossed by **Route 210**, which forks off the Trans-Canada about 160km from St John's, but although the road starts promisingly with the handsome scenery of the **Piper's Hole River estuary**, thereafter it's a singularly lonely journey across boggy plateaux. Eventually, about 140km from the Trans-Canada, Route 210 sidles into the shipyard town of **Marystown**, easily the biggest settlement hereabouts with a population of around 7000 souls. From here, it's a further 50km to the peninsula's most interesting spot, the fishing village of **Grand Bank**, and a couple more to **Fortune**, the departure point for **passenger ferries** over to St-Pierre et Miquelon (see p.519).

Foote's Taxi (Ⓣ709/832-0491 or 1-800/866-1181) operates a once-daily service to Grand Bank and Fortune; the fare is $40 and the journey takes six hours. Given the length of the journey and the scarcity of accommodation on the Burin, both car drivers and minibus passengers should book their overnight stay before they set out. Note that Foote's schedule does not necessarily coincide with the times of the ferry over to St Pierre.

Grand Bank and Fortune

Looking firmly out to sea, the older streets of **GRAND BANK** incorporate a charming assortment of late nineteenth-century timber houses, a few of which are equipped with the so-called "widow's walks", rooftop galleries from where the women watched for their returning menfolk. Some of these houses are truly splendid, reflecting a time when the village's proximity to the Grand Banks fishing grounds brought tremendous profits to the shipowners, if not to the actual fishermen. Nowadays the Grand Banks fishery is in an acute state of decline, much to the frustration of local people, who apportion blame amongst a number of old enemies: foreigners who overfish, big marketing corporations who are indifferent to local interests, greedy seals and a government that imposes unrealistic quotas. What makes it particularly hard to bear is the affinity many locals have for the fishing – as one of their representatives declared: "Without fish there is no soul, no pride, no nothing."

To see something of this tradition, visit the **Seamen's Museum** (late April to late Oct daily 9am–4.45pm; $2.50), situated on Marine Drive in a modern building shaped like the sails of a schooner. It has all sorts of models, paintings and photographs of different types of fishing boat, and a relief model of Newfoundland and the surrounding ocean that shows exactly where the illustrious "Banks" are. The Banks comprise a great belt of shallow ocean lying to the southeast of Newfoundland. It's here that the cold waters from Labrador bump into the much warmer Gulf Stream, creating pea-soup fogs and, more importantly, a density of plankton that attracts fishes by the million. For four and a half centuries, the Banks teemed with **cod** but trawling – as distinct from line fishing – eventually took care of that, though admittedly there are lots of competing theories as to quite why the cod has declined; the results in places like the Burin are not, however, in dispute.

Grand Bank has one very recommendable **B&B**, the *Thorndyke*, an especially well-maintained old sea captain's house with five en-suite period rooms at 33 Water St (Ⓣ709/832-0820 or 1-866/882-0820, Ⓦwww.thethorndyke.com; ④; May to mid-Sept). There's also the *Inn by the Sea* (Ⓣ709/832-0202, Ⓦwww.theinnbythesea.com; ④; June–Sept), whose four en-suite guest rooms occupy a 1940s clapboard house down by the seashore on the north side of town on Blackburn Road, and a **motel**, *Granny's Motor Inn*, on Grandview Blvd, which doubles as Route 220 (Ⓣ709/832-2180 or 1-888/275-1098; ③).

From Grand Bank, it's 5km or so to **FORTUNE**, a slightly smaller village and the departure point for ferries over to St-Pierre et Miquelon (see opposite). These are passenger ferries only and there's a **car park** near the ferry terminal.

St-Pierre et Miquelon

The tiny archipelago of **St-Pierre et Miquelon**, 20km west off the coast of the Burin, became a fully fledged *département* of mainland France in 1976 and a *collectivité territoriale* in 1985, justifying the billing of the islands as "a little bit of France at your doorstep". The tag certainly pulls in several thousand visitors each year and also manages to put a gloss on the lack of actual attractions and the wetness of the climate, though the islands are still worth a day or two. The main appeal is the francophone atmosphere of the main settlement, the **Ville de St-Pierre**, whose good restaurants and simple guesthouses have a genuinely European flavour. All but 700 of the 6500 islanders live here, with the remainder – mainly of Acadian and Basque descent – marooned on **Grande Miquelon** to the north. The third and middle island, **Langlade**, or **Petite Miquelon**, has just a scattering of houses and is only inhabited in summer.

A brief history of St-Pierre et Miquelon

The Portuguese stumbled across the archipelago in 1520, but it was **Jacques Cartier** who claimed it for the French in 1536. Subsequently settled by fishermen from the Basque provinces, Normandy and Brittany, the islands were alternately occupied by Britain and France until the British gave them to the French as a commercial sop after the loss of the rest of their North American colonies in 1763. St-Pierre et Miquelon soon became a vital supply base and safe harbour for the French fishing fleet, and provided France with a yearly harvest of salted cod.

After World War I, the French colonial authorities wanted to expand the local fishing industry, but their efforts became irrelevant with **Prohibition** in 1920. Quite suddenly, St-Pierre was transformed from a maritime backwater into a giant transit centre for booze smuggling: even the main fish-processing plant was stacked high with thousands of cases of whisky destined for Boston and Long Island. It was an immensely lucrative business, but when Prohibition ended thirteen years later the St-Pierre economy dropped through the floor. Those were desperate days, but more misery followed during World War II, when the islands' governor remained controversially loyal to the collaborationist **Vichy regime**. Both the Canadians and the Americans considered invading, but it was a **Free French** naval squadron that got there first, crossing over from their base in Halifax and occupying the islands in late 1941 without a shot being fired.

There was further trouble in 1965 when a **stevedores' strike** forced the administration to resign. **De Gaulle** promptly dispatched the navy, who occupied the islands for no fewer than nine years. Perhaps surprisingly, the St-Pierrais remained largely loyal to France, and they certainly needed the support of Paris when the Canadians extended the limit of their territorial waters to 200 nautical miles in 1977. The ensuing wrangle between Canada and France over the islands' claim to a similar exclusion zone was finally resolved in 1994, although the tightening of controls on foreign vessels has largely ended St-Pierre's role as a supply centre.

Arrival

Air St-Pierre (ⓣ0508/41 00 00 or 1-877/277-7765, ⓦwww.airsaintpierre.com) **flies** to St-Pierre et Miquelon from Montréal, Halifax and Sydney in Nova Scotia, Moncton in New Brunswick, and St John's, Newfoundland. The least expensive flights are from St John's (3 weekly; 45min), where the company has a desk at the airport (ⓣ709/726-9700); in summer a return flight costs in the region of €180/CDN$261. The St-Pierre et Miquelon **airport** is located just south of the town of St-Pierre; taxis run into the centre.

SPM Express (Newfoundland ⓣ709/832-0429 or 1-800/563-2006; St-Pierre ⓣ0508/41 53 93, ⓦwww.spmexpress.net) operates **passenger**

St-Pierre currency and customs control

Since St-Pierre is part of France, local currency is the **euro** (€), made up of 100 cents. Canadian and US dollars are also widely accepted, but you'll usually get change in euros. Approximate **exchange rates** at the time of writing are €1=CDN$1.50 or CDN$1 = €0.65. For up-to-date rates, check ⓦwww.oanda.com.

To clear St-Pierre et Miquelon's **customs control**, Canadians need only present an official photo identity, but EU and US nationals need a passport. For **medical emergencies**, dial ⓣ15, police ⓣ17.

ferries (May to mid-Oct 3 weekly to 1 daily; 1hr 30min; $64 one-way, $94 return) from Fortune in Newfoundland to the town of St-Pierre, but be aware that the crossing can get mighty rough. The ferry schedule means that you almost always have to spend the night on St-Pierre – book your accommodation ahead. To sample St-Pierre on a **day-trip** from Fortune, contact St Pierre Tours (ⓣ1-800/563-2006, ⓦwww.spmtours.com), who organize nine-hour ferry and bus excursions (July & Aug Mon–Sat 1 daily) for $95.

Information and getting around

The main St-Pierre et Miquelon **tourist office** is in the centre of Ville de St-Pierre, just metres from the ferry dock on place du Général de Gaulle (June–Sept daily 8.30am–6pm; Oct–May Mon–Fri 8.30am–noon & 1.30–5pm; ⓣ0508-410-200, ⓦwww.st-pierre-et-miquelon.com). They supply all sorts of information about the archipelago, issue free maps, and also have the timetable of the **local passenger ferry** that links Ville de St-Pierre with Miquelon village at the other end of the archipelago (1–2 daily, on 3 days a week; 1hr). It is, however, much easier to join a **guided tour** if you're after venturing beyond St-Pierre and in the summer, from mid-June to late September, there are several excellent bus and boat **day-trips** to choose from. As an example, the nine-hour excursion to Miquelon village via Langdale and the Grand Barachois lagoon costs about CDN$50. The islands' area **telephone code** is ⓣ0508; for international dialling, use the international prefix, then ⓣ508, followed by a six digit number.

Ville de St-Pierre

The tidy streets of the **VILLE DE ST-PIERRE** nudge back from the harbour, altogether a pleasant ensemble of plain stone and brightly-painted timber buildings with a quintessentially French demeanour. The central area makes for an enjoyable stroll, though there's nothing special to aim for, with the possible exception of the early twentieth-century **cathédrale**, on place Maurier, which does at least attempt to look imposing with its large stone bell tower. A short walk away, just to the north on rue Gloanec, is the **Zazpiak Bat**, a court on which the game of *pelote basque* is played – a reflection of the islands' strong Basque heritage. From here, it's about 700m southwest to the **Musée de l'Arche** (June–Aug Tues–Sun 10am–noon & 2–5.30pm; rest of year daily 2–5.30pm), home to the islands' archives and featuring temporary displays on local history and culture. To the rear of the building is the flamboyant **Le Monument aux Morts** (War Memorial), raised in honour of the dead of the two world wars. From the war memorial, it's a short walk back to the harbourfront and the main square, **place du Général de Gaulle**.

Across the harbour from the town quayside lies the minuscule **Île aux Marins** (Dog's Island), where the rocks were once strewn with thousands of drying cod fish. After centuries of use, the islet was abandoned in 1964, its assorted buildings pretty much left to their own weather-beaten devices. **Guided tours** (May–Sept 2 daily; €20 including 10min boat trip; reservations on ⓣ0508/410-200) take in the church, the town hall, the old school (now a museum), the lighthouse, and a garish Stations of the Cross that leads to a small cemetery perched on the windiest of promontories. Along the shore from the cemetery is the rusted hulk of the German ship *Transpacific*, which was wrecked there in 1971. The church, **Notre Dame des Marins**, is the islet's most intriguing building, a large and good-looking structure whose original furnishings, dating from 1874, have survived, including a large black-wrapped catafalque, used for carrying coffins.

Ville de St-Pierre accommodation and restaurants

Ville de St-Pierre has a good supply of **accommodation**, though most of it is both modern and modest and reservations are strongly recommended from July to early September. Smarter **hotels** include the *Hôtel Île de France*, 6 rue Maître Georges-Lèfvre (Ⓣ0508/410-350, Ⓦwww.hoteliledefrance.net; doubles €90), and the workaday *Hôtel Robert*, 10 rue du 11 Novembre (Ⓣ0508/412-419; doubles €70–80), which was where Al Capone stayed during Prohibition; a small museum off the foyer has one of his straw hats and other memorabilia. For **pensions**, try the comfortable *Chez Hélène*, 15 rue Beaussant (Ⓣ0508/413-108; doubles €42).

St-Pierre's **restaurants** are splendid, combining the best of French cuisine with local delicacies such as *tiaude*, a highly seasoned cod stew. Prices are fairly high – reckon on about €25 for a main course – but it really is worth splashing out. Perhaps the best spot in town is *Le Cabestan*, 2 rue Marcel Bonin (Ⓣ0508/412-100), which features *nouvelle cuisine* at its most subtle; if your pocket book looks thin, head instead for *Le Maringouin'fre*, 22 rue Général-Leclerc, where they serve delicious crêpes as well as steaks and burgers at very affordable prices.

Grande Miquelon and Langlade

At the north end of the archipelago, the stubby little island of **Grande Miquelon** comprises peat bog, marsh and a couple of hills which slope away from the only village – **MIQUELON**. The village has a couple of sights of some modest interest, beginning with **L'Eglise** (church) of 1865, whose sombre exterior hides a folksy interior filled with faux-marble columns and containing a good copy of a Murillo *Virgin* donated by Napoléon III – it's above the altar. Just down the street from the church is the cramped **musée** (museum), which displays all manner of items salvaged from local shipwrecks. Otherwise, the **tourist office** (call St-Pierre tourist office for hours) can provide you with details of local walks or you can rent a bicycle from them and cycle off towards Grand Barachois (see below). Of the handful of **places to stay** in Miquelon village, the modest, modern *Maxotel*, 42 rue Sourdeval (Ⓣ0508/416-457; €70) has the advantage of a seashore location.

The archipelago's most unusual feature is the **Isthme de Langlade**, a sweeping ten-kilometre sandy isthmus that links Grande Miquelon with **LANGLADE**, otherwise **PETITE MIQUELON**. The isthmus began to surface above the ocean two hundred years ago as a result of sand collecting around a shipwreck and is now anything up to 2500m wide. There's a road along the length of the Dune, but note that heavy seas can swamp parts of it, so be sure to stick to the guided tours. These stop at the **Grand Barachois**, a large saltwater pool at the northern end of the isthmus that's a favourite haunt of breeding seals. Langlade itself has a more varied landscape than the other islands – high hills, deciduous forests and rushing brooks – and is at its liveliest in summer, when the St-Pierrais arrive in droves to open up their summer homes.

The Bonavista Peninsula

Crossed by **Route 230**, which leaves the Trans-Canada 200km west of St John's near Clarenville (see p.496), the thickly wooded **Bonavista Peninsula** pokes out into the ocean for some 120km, its shredded shoreline confettied with bays, coves and islands. The English settled here in numbers during the seventeenth

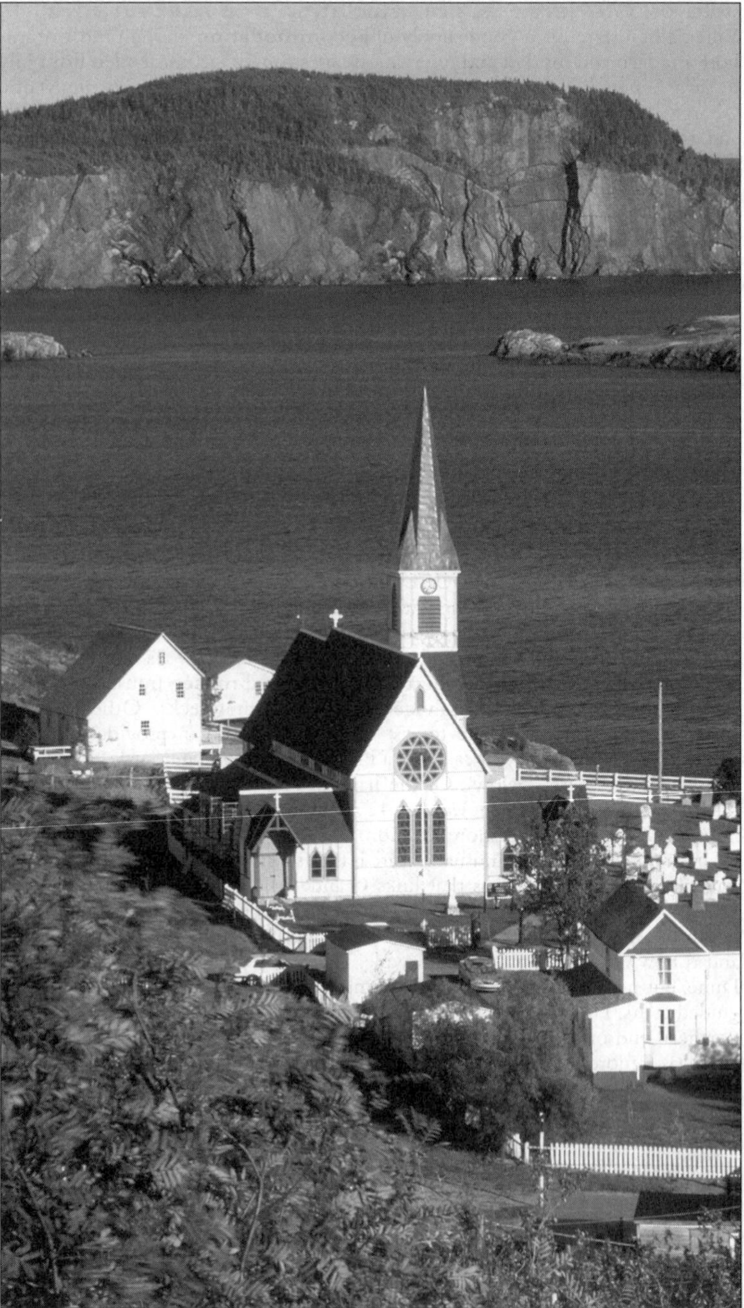

△ Bonavista Peninsula

century, establishing dozens of tiny outports and one administrative centre, **Trinity**, whose handsome headland setting and medley of fine old buildings make it the most beguiling of all Newfoundland's towns. Trinity is also the ideal base for exploring the rest of the peninsula: it's close to several first-rate hiking trails and is within comfortable striking distance of the wild and windswept **Cape Bonavista**, right at the tip of the peninsula. Trinity also offers **whale-watching tours** and possesses a clutch of **B&Bs**, though the best accommodation is in neighbouring **Port Rexton** – another of the twelve settlements that are collectively known as **Trinity Bight**. If you're intent on **hiking**, look out for the *Hiking on the Discovery Trail* booklet, which describes a dozen or so local trails supported by photos, potted descriptions of the peninsula's outports, flora and fauna plus some (pretty rudimentary) maps. The problem is getting hold of a copy – try the district's shops and museums or your B&B.

As regards public transport, Marsh's Transportation (Ⓣ709/747-2225) provides a once daily **minibus** service from St John's to Bonavista via Trinity with the journey to either costing $30. However, before you catch the minibus check to see exactly where you'll be dropped off, otherwise you might be facing an awful long hike to the nearest hotel.

Trinity and around

Situated about 70km from the Trans-Canada, just off Route 230, the narrow lanes of tiny **TRINITY** are edged by a delightful ensemble of white and pastel-painted clapboard houses, all set between a ring of hills and the deep and intricate Trinity Bight. The architectural high point is **St Paul's Anglican Church** of 1892, whose perfectly proportioned exterior is adorned by elaborate scrollwork. Inside, the graceful and dignified nave is divided into three, the side aisles entered through arches carved to resemble whale bones and the ceiling up above fashioned in the shape of an upturned boat. A series of **memorial plaques** tacked to the walls witnesses both the dedication of the islanders to the British imperial interest, with many a young man killed on a foreign battle field, and the dangers of the sea, drowning and shipwrecks being all too commonplace. Opposite the church, there's the modest but entertaining **Trinity Historical Museum** (mid-June to mid-Sept daily 10am–5.30pm; $4.50, including the forge and the interpretation centre – see below), which crowds together an eccentric collection of bygones, such as an old shoemaker's kit, sealing gear, an early cooperage and a fire engine of 1811.

From the church, it's a few paces to both the cream and green **Hiscock House Provincial Historic Site** (mid-May to late Sept daily 10am–5.30pm; $3), where guides in period costume explain the intricacies of early twentieth-century life in this old merchant's house, and the uncommonly grand **Parish Hall**. Beyond, West Street chalks up no fewer than four minor sites, beginning with the **Green Family Forge** (mid-June to mid-Sept daily 10am–5.30pm), which focuses on the town's blacksmiths, and the **Trinity Interpretation Centre** mid-June to mid-Sept daily 10am–5.30pm), where the emphasis is on local history. Next up are the **Lester-Garland House Provincial Historic Site** (mid-May to late Sept daily 10am–5.30pm; $3), a reconstructed three-storey Georgian brick house with period rooms, and the **Ryan general store** (same hours; free), returned to something like its appearance circa 1910.

Practicalities

Trinity has several appealing **B&Bs**, foremost of which is the *Campbell House*, in a good-looking Victorian building on High Street (Ⓣ709/464-3377 or 1-877/464-7700, Ⓦwww.trinityvacations.com; ⑤; mid-May to mid-Oct).

Trinity whale-watching tours

Based at the *Village Inn*, in the centre of Trinity, Ocean Contact (Ⓣ709/464-3269, Ⓦwww.oceancontact.com) runs an extensive programme of **whale-watching** excursions, or rather, as they insist, whale "contact" trips designed to encourage close encounters between whales and humans. They can't, of course, guarantee contact, but there is an excellent chance of sighting minke, finbacks and humpbacks, particularly between mid-June and early August. Expertly run, these excursions take place daily during the whale season from June to October, and prices begin at $60 for a half-day trip with an introductory talk thrown in. If the sea is too rough for a boat trip, Ocean Contact will provide escorted whale-watching walks along the nearby cliffs at half the price.

There are three guest double rooms here, all en-suite, and the breakfasts are first-class, featuring such local delicacies as partridgeberry crepes. A second good choice, also in an older property, is the *Eriksen Premises B&B*, West St (Ⓣ709/464-3698 or 1-877/464-3698, Ⓦwww.trinityexperience.com; ❹; May–Oct), which has seven en-suite guest rooms, mostly with sea views. The finest accommodation hereabouts is, however, in Port Rexton (see opposite).

The best **restaurant** in town is the waterside *Twine Loft* (Ⓣ709/464-3377), just off High Street near the *Artisan Inn*; seafood is the speciality here with main courses averaging $22. Another good bet is the *Dock Marina Restaurant* (Ⓣ709/464-2133), on the water's edge near the Parish Hall, where both the seafood and the meat are well prepared and they do a good line in traditional Newfoundland cuisine. Afterwards, you can stroll up to *Rocky's Place* for a drink.

In summer, Trinity plays host to a professional **theatre** company, Rising Tide Theatre (Ⓣ709/464-3847, Ⓦwww.risingtidetheatre.com), which puts on an excellent programme of Canadian plays in the **Summer in the Bight Theatre Festival** running from late June to September. They are also involved in the **Trinity Pageant**, a sort of community street theatre performed on various days from late June to August with costumed actors strolling the town relating and enacting scenes from yesteryear.

South of Trinity: New Bonaventure

Interrupted by four spindly headlands, **Trinity Bight** is a particularly pretty slice of coastline, its rough, bulging hills decorated with woods and brightened by the odd patch of farmland, bright green after the grass has been mown. Trinity sits on one of these headlands and you have to double back a kilometre or so to the west to pick up **Route 239**, which weaves its way south, passing through a string of lonely outports. Eventually, after about 15km, the road slips into **NEW BONAVENTURE**, a haphazard assortment of clapboard houses edging a rocky bay. On a rainy day it seems like the end of the world, but a side road pushes on even further – fork right over the hill as you descend into the village and continue for another 500m until you reach the church at the end of the road. The **church** seems surprisingly large considering the size of New Bonaventure, even larger when you realise the locals had to roam far and wide to collect the wood for its construction in the 1920s.

Beginning at the church, a six-hundred-metre-long gravel road leads down to the **Cape Random Passage film set** (mid-May to mid-Oct daily 9.30am–7.30pm; Ⓦwww.randompassagefilmset.com; free), which consists of a replica early-1800s outport with fishing stages, shacks, a church and a school. Built in

2000, the set was used for filming *Random Passage* and *Waiting for Time*, two romantic novels written by Newfoundland's Bernice Morgan (b.1935) and telling the tale of the Andrews family who settled here in the 1820s. Beyond the film set, a **hiking trail** proceeds to the abandoned outport of **Kerley's Harbour**, a charming and fairly straightforward coastal walk of 2km (40min each way) along the old cart road.

East of Trinity: Port Rexton and Trinity East

From Trinity, it's about 8km round Trinity Bight – via Route 230 – to **PORT REXTON**, which actually consists of two pocket-sized outports (Robin Hood and Ship Cove) on either side of a headland. These twin communities once flourished on the back of the Labrador fishery, but things are very quiet today with a haphazard jigsaw of houses rambling across the foreshore. Overlooking Ship Cove from the side of a hill is the *Fishers' Loft Inn* (ⓣ709/464-3240 or 1-877/464-3240, ⓦwww.fishersloft.com; ❺; May–Oct), whose five separate houses – and 21 en-suite guest rooms and suites – are of recent construction, though they are built in various versions of traditional Newfoundland style. It's an extraordinarily successful ensemble and the interiors are simply superb, a well-conceived balance of the intimate and the smart from the wooden floors through to the handmade furniture and the large and comfortable beds. The views over Ship Cove and out across Trinity Bay are similarly delightful and breakfasts, which feature local ingredients, are tasty and filling, but note that their splendid, four-course **dinners** are by prior arrangement only.

The signposted side road that leads from Route 230 past the turning to the Fishers' Loft Inn carries on for another 2km to reach the hamlet of **TRINITY EAST**, the starting point of the popular **Skerwink Trail**, a 5.4km loop trail that negotiates the jutting headland that lies beyond. It's a lovely two-hour walk offering handsome coastal views and lots of wildlife.

Cape Bonavista and Bonavista

Cape Bonavista, some 50km north of Trinity, is violently beautiful, a desolate headland of dark-grey rock and pounding sea inhabited by hundreds of puffins. This is supposed to be the spot where the English-sponsored Genoese explorer **John Cabot** first clapped eyes on the Americas in 1497, exclaiming – or so it's claimed – "O buona vista!" ("O, happy sight") and, true or not, a statue has been erected in his honour. The cape has always been hazardous to shipping and it's overseen by a red-and-white-striped **lighthouse** (mid-May to late Sept daily 10am–5.30pm; $3), which has been attractively restored to its appearance in 1870 when it was occupied by an 80-year-old lighthouse keeper, Jeremiah White, and his family; costumed guides give the background.

The cape is 5km from the sprawling fishing village of **BONAVISTA**, which spreads out across the flattish headlands surrounding its double harbour. Settled by the English in the seventeenth century, Bonavista was long a successful trading centre and fishing station, a history explored at the **Ryan Premises National Historic Site** (mid-May to late Oct daily 10am–6pm; $3.95), sited in the old fish-processing complex. There's more nautical stuff nearby at the docks in the form of a replica of **Cabot's ship**, the *Matthew* (mid-May to Sept daily 10am–6pm; $6.50), with tours above and below deck; the attached interpretation centre has the historical low-down. Bonavista's other noteworthy sight is the plain white clapboard **Mockbeggar Property** on Roper Street (mid-May to late Sept daily 10am–5.30pm; $3), once the home of F. Gordon Bradley, one of the island's first representatives in the Canadian Senate. The house has been returned to its appearance in the 1930s and comes complete with a full set of heavy-duty, English-made Victorian and Edwardian furniture.

The best **accommodation** in Bonavista is provided by *Elizabeth J. Cottages* (☎709/468-5035 or 1-866/468-5035, Ⓦwww.elizabethjcottages.com; ❼), comprising two oceanside cottages on Harris Street. Of modern construction, but built in traditional saltbox style, each cottage has two bedrooms and an outside deck, and is attractively furnished with hardwood floors, Persian rugs and all modern conveniences. Bonavista also has a handful of **B&Bs**, with one of the better options being *Butler's by the Sea*, whose two well-appointed, en-suite guest rooms overlook the sea at 15 Butler Crescent (☎709/468-2445 or 1-877/968-2445, Ⓦwww.bbcanada.com/1412.html; ❸). **Restaurants** are thin on the ground – try the *Baie-Vista*, in the centre on Main Street (☎709/468-2169).

Terra Nova National Park to Deer Lake

The **Trans-Canada Highway** cuts a long and lonely course across central Newfoundland on its way west from Clarenville, at the base of the Bonavista Peninsula, to Deer Lake, a distance of 450km. Of the towns it encounters, **Grand Falls-Windsor** has an intriguing museum and **Deer Lake** is a handy starting point for the journey up the Northern Peninsula (see p.530). The hwy also threads its way through **Terra Nova National Park**, with its handsome coastal scenery. The most obvious detour is the 100km dash north to the old fishing port and trading centre of **Twillingate**, set amidst a craggy broken coastline that attracts icebergs by the score from May to August.

Terra Nova National Park

Heading north from Clarenville along the Trans-Canada, it's about 40km to the southern edge of **Terra Nova National Park** (admission fee of $5.45 per adult charged from mid-May to early Oct), whose coniferous forests, ponds and marshes border a deeply indented slice of rugged coastline. The Trans-Canada slices right through the park, giving clearly signed access to its various facilities, most of which are concentrated about 40km into the park at the head of **Newman Sound** – though technically it's not a sound at all, but a channel linking the ocean with an estuary. The Sound is the best place to start a visit to the park as it's here you'll find the **Salton's Brook Marine Interpretation Centre** (daily: mid-May to late June & early Sept to early Oct 10am–5pm; late June to early Sept 9am–8pm; no extra charge; ☎709/533-2942), whose excellent displays explain and illustrate the park's flora and fauna. The Centre also supplies oodles of information about guided walks, boat trips, safe swimming areas, canoeing and sea kayaking. The **boat trips** are operated by **Ocean Watch Tours** (mid-May to Oct 2–4 cruises daily; ☎709/533-6024, Ⓦwww3.nf.sympatico.ca/oceanwatch), who offer a varied programme from cruises around the Sound to trips out into the Atlantic and along the coast; trips cost $40 or more per person. The Marine Centre also has the details of over a dozen **hiking trails**, from short strolls to full-scale expeditions, including the strenuous **Outport Loop Trail**, a 46km endurance test that takes sixteen hours to complete. En route are several primitive **campsites** ($14), permits for which must be arranged at the Centre before you set out. The most stunning part of the Outport Trail is the first 18km (5hr), with the trail snaking its way along the south shore of Newman Sound to **South Broad Cove**, where Ocean Watch **water taxis** will pick you up or drop you off – again details at the Marine Centre.

The national park also has several serviced **campsites**, the largest being the all-year *Newman Sound Campground* (reservations advised on ⓣ1-877/737-3783 or 905/426-4648, ⓦwww.pccamping.ca; $16–25), reached along a side road off the Trans-Canada just to the south of the Salton's Brook Marine turning. If camping seems too daunting a prospect, then aim for the village of **CHARLOTTETOWN**, about 15km south of Newman Sound – and 50km from Clarenville - where there's a **motel**, the *Clode Sound* (ⓣ709/664-3146, ⓦwww.clodesound.com; May–Oct; ③), with a reasonably priced **restaurant** known for its apple pies and apple crisps.

Gambo and Gander

The Trans-Canada Hwy leaves Terra Nova National Park to reach, after 32km, the logging and former railway town of **GAMBO**, where the **Smallwood Interpretation Centre** (daily 11am–5pm; $3) celebrates the life and times of its most famous son, Joe Smallwood (1900–92). Smallwood, the larger-than-life Newfoundland premier who dominated the political scene from 1949 to 1972, was a controversial figure, whose various grand designs had very mixed consequences. Most islanders would now agree that his main contribution was in squeezing through the vote for Confederation in the referendum of 1948, but his attempts to diversify the economy by attracting industry were often ill-considered and very costly. Even worse, his resettlement programme, in which the inhabitants of dozens of the remoter outports were pushed into so-called "growth centres", was well-nigh disastrous – though Smallwood was so formidable a party boss that few would have said so to his face.

From Gambo it's just 40km to **GANDER**, a workaday town built around an airport, whose site was chosen carefully by the British in the 1930s – it was far enough inland to escape Newfoundland's coastal fogs, but still near enough to Europe to facilitate the introduction of regular transatlantic flights. During World War II, the airport was a major staging point for American planes on their way to England and later, in the 1960s and 1970s, it became a major re-fuelling stop for incoming flights from Europe. It lost this role years ago and has developed into an important air-traffic control centre for much of the northwest Atlantic instead, though its past was reprised when over twenty jets were diverted here after the attack on the World Trade Center in New York on September 11, 2001.

Twillingate

Heading north from Gander, away from the Trans-Canada, **Route 330** weaves across the inhospitable wastes of the interior before slipping down to the coast at the mouth of the River Gander. From here, Route 331 shuffles north through a string of outports before meeting **Route 340**, which cuts an improbable course, its causeways and bridges negotiating the jigsaw of islets, headlands and inlets that distinguishes this part of the coast. Eventually, 100km from Gander, the road meanders into **TWILLINGATE**, where a scattering of bright-white houses strings along the seashore. One of Newfoundland's oldest settlements, Twillingate was settled by the English in the early eighteenth century after several decades of use by itinerant French fishermen, who gave the place its original name, "Toulinguet", from an island back home in

Brittany. By the 1780s Twillingate had become the most important cod fishing station on the north coast and a flourishing seaport on account of its fine, sheltered harbour. As elsewhere on Newfoundland, the merchants kept an economic stranglehold on the fishermen, who could only barter their catch in return for food, provisions and equipment – at a rate set by these very same merchants. The merchants also brought a compulsion for respectability and, by the 1820s, there was a whole set of churches, masonic lodges and schools, several of which survive to this day. What really got the locals going, however, was the "**Great Haul**" of 1862, when ice floes carrying thousands of seals drifted into the shore close to Twillingate harbour. This provided a bonanza of seal meat, skins and cash – seals were beyond the barter system and the town's fishermen and women could sell what they could kill. Twillingate's boom times ended in the 1880s, when the switch from sail to steam curtailed its role as a fishing station, but it remained a busy fishing port until the demise of the cod fishery in the 1990s. The best time to be in Twillingate is during the four-day **Fish, Fun and Folk Festival** (Ⓦwww.fishfunfolkfestival.com), held over the last full weekend of July and attracting folk musicians from all over the province.

There are about ten **B&Bs** in and around Twillingate as well as a couple of inns. One of the best options is the *Hillside*, an attractive, well-kept B&B in an 1870s timber house that overlooks the harbour at 5 Young's Lane (Ⓣ709/884-1666, Ⓦwww.bbcanada.com/nfhillside; ❸; June–Sept); there are three en-suite guest rooms here, each decorated in brisk modern style. Alternatively, the *Toulinguet Inn*, down on the waterfront at 56 Main St (Ⓣ709/884-2080 or 1-877/684-2080, Ⓦwww.bbcanada.com/9127.html; ❸; mid-May to Sept), is sited in a 1920s building and has three smart, en-suite guest rooms. Finally, there's the *Beach Rock B&B* (Ⓣ709/884-2292; ❸; May–Oct), which occupies a charmingly renovated, two-storey timber house of 1904. There are three guest rooms here as well, all en-suite and breakfasts feature home-made bread and muffins; it is located on the seashore about 5km south of Twillingate, just off

Twillingate iceberg-spotting

Every year, from May to August, the myriad headlands and inlets of the coast near Twillingate ensnare dozens of **icebergs** as they float down from the Arctic. Tinted in shades of blue and white by reflections from the sea and sun, they can be wondrously beautiful and, if you're particularly lucky, you might witness the moment when one of them rolls over and breaks apart, accompanied by a tremendous grating and wheezing and then an ear-ringing bang. Several local companies offer **iceberg-watching boat tours** with one of the best known being Twillingate Adventure Tours (mid-May to mid-Sept 3 daily; 2hr; $30; Ⓣ709/884-5999 or 1-888/447-8687, Ⓦwww.daybreaktours.com). A second recommended operator is Twillingate Island Boat Tours (mid-May to Sept 3 daily; 2hr; $30; Ⓣ709/884-2242 or 1-800/611-2374, Ⓦwww.icebergtours.ca), which also operates the **Iceberg Shop**, an arts and crafts shop and iceberg interpretive centre in an old barn in **DURRELL**, a couple of kilometres north of Twillingate. With both companies, boat tours should be booked ahead of time.

Landlubbers still stand a good chance of spotting an iceberg from the bright red and white **Long Point Lighthouse**, which occupies a commanding position on a high rocky cliff at the north end of Main Street – incidentally the approach is rocky and often slippery, so you'll need appropriate footwear. The **Long Point Centre**, across the street from the lighthouse (daily mid-May to mid-Oct 10am–9pm; free), has a tearoom, crafts shop and a small display on local culture and natural history.

Route 340 in the hamlet of **Little Harbour**. For **food**, head for the fish at the brusquely modern *Anchor Inn Motel*, on Main St (Ⓣ709/884-2777).

Grand Falls-Windsor

GRAND FALLS, 91km west of Gander along the Trans-Canada, sits amongst some of the island's best stands of timber, an expanse of **forest** that's been intensively exploited ever since Alfred Harmsworth, later Lord Northcliffe, had a paper mill built here in 1905. Harmsworth, the founder of Britain's *Daily Mirror* and *Daily Mail* newspapers, funded the project to secure a reliable supply of newsprint well away from Europe, which he believed was heading towards war. It was an immensely profitable venture, which also established the first Newfoundland community sited, as one contemporary put it, "out of sight and sound of the sea". For many of Northcliffe's employees, who hailed from the outports, it was the first time they had ever received a cash wage, though this particular pleasure was countered by some bitter disputes between management and unions. The worst was in 1959, when the Mounties broke a well-supported strike with appalling barbarity, at the behest of Newfoundland's premier Joe Smallwood.

Grand Falls remains a timber town, an unprepossessing place built around the hulking mass of the paper mill that towers over the Exploits River. Nevertheless, there is one pleasant surprise, the **Mary March Provincial Museum**, 16 St Catherine St (May to late Oct daily 9.30am–4.45pm; $2.50), just to the south of the Trans-Canada – come off at Cromer Avenue (Exit #18), where the hwy separates Grand Falls from the adjacent (and unremarkable) township of **WINDSOR**. The museum has a good section on the history of the town and an intriguing series of displays on the **Beothuks** (see p.497). The focus is on one of the last of the tribe, Mary March or Demasduit, who was captured near here in March 1819. The story makes depressing reading. An Englishman by the name of John Peyton settled in Twillingate in 1812 and, over the next few years, became increasingly irritated with the Beothuks, who he thought were damaging his traps and stealing his fish. Peyton wanted to teach the Beothuks a lesson and he set about organizing an expedition into the interior. The end result was the capture of Mary March – named after the month of her seizure – and thereafter Peyton carted the hapless woman around the island, first to St John's and then to Twillingate, where she was deposited for safe-keeping with the local minister; she died of tuberculosis shortly afterwards.

Deer Lake

More than anything else, **DEER LAKE**, 210km west of Grand Falls, is a convenient pitstop on either the long road west to Channel-Port aux Basques – and the Nova Scotia ferry (see p.551) – or the journey north to Gros Morne National Park (see p.530) and ultimately L'Anse aux Meadows (see p.534). It has the added advantage of having an **airport**, with both Air Labrador (Ⓣ1-800/563-3042, Ⓦwww.airlabrador.com) and Provincial Airlines (inside Newfoundland Ⓣ1-800/563-2800, elsewhere Ⓣ709/576-1666, Ⓦwww.provincialairlines.ca) providing regular services to and from St John's: a flight in or out is one way of reducing the driving considerably. As a sample fare, Provincial Airlines flights from St John's to Deer Lake cost around $200 one-way, double that for a return. In addition, Air Canada's *Jazz Air* (Ⓣ1-888/247-2262, Ⓦwww.flyjazz.ca) links Deer Lake with Montréal and Halifax. There are currently four **car-rental** offices inside the Deer Lake terminal building, including Budget (Ⓣ709/635-3211), Hertz (Ⓣ709/635-4442) and National (Ⓣ709/635-3282).

DRL Coachline **buses** (Ⓣ709/263-2171 or 1-888/263-1854, Ⓦwww.drlgroup.com) from St John's and points on the Trans-Canada pull into Deer Lake's Irving Big Stop gas station on the hwy just outside town – you'll need a taxi to move on. The **tourist office** (daily June–Aug 8.30am–9pm; Sept & Oct 10am–7pm; Ⓣ709/635-2202) is also beside the Trans-Canada and supplies free town maps. As regards **accommodation**, Deer Lake has half a dozen places, one of the more convenient being the workaday *Deer Lake Motel* (Ⓣ709/635-2108 or 1-800/563-2144, Ⓦwww.deerlakemotel.com; ④), on the Trans-Canada just 2km from the airport. Alternatively, there are several B&Bs in the centre of town amongst the grid of streets that stretch east from the Trans-Canada as it sweeps round the edge of the lake that gave the town its name. Options here include the *Lakeview B&B*, in a modern, chalet-like building at 1 Young's Ave (Ⓣ709/635-8104 or 1-888/635-8104; Ⓦwww.lakeviewbb.ca; ③) with five, straightforward but pleasant en-suite guest rooms. Much fancier is the *Humberview B&B*, which occupies a large and well-appointed, modern, two-storey brick house on the north side of the Trans-Canada (Exit 15) at 11 Humberview Drive (Ⓣ709/635-4818 or 1-888/635-4818, Ⓦwww.thehumberview.com; ④).

The Northern Peninsula

Stretching out between Deer Lake and the township of St Anthony, a distance of about 450km, the **Northern Peninsula** is a rugged, sparsely populated finger of land that separates the Gulf of St Lawrence from the Atlantic. Its interior is dominated by the spectacular **Long Range Mountains**, a chain of flat-topped peaks that are some of the oldest on earth, punctuated by the starkest of glacier-gouged gorges above the bluest of lakes – or "ponds" as the locals incongruously call them. Most of the region remains inaccessible to all except the most experienced of mountaineers, but **Route 430** trails along the western edge of the peninsula, connecting the small fishing villages of the narrow coastal plain. This hwy also connects with the minor roads that lead to the region's most remarkable sight, the remains of the Norse colony at **L'Anse aux Meadows**, at the tip of the peninsula some 50km beyond St Anthony.

Travelling around the peninsula by **minibus** is just too difficult to contemplate for all but the most energetic (or foolhardy), but Viking Express (Ⓣ709/688-2113) has a service from Deer Lake to St Anthony, and Pittman's (Ⓣ709/634-4710) connects Deer Lake and Rocky Harbour. The nearest **car rental** is at Deer Lake airport (see p.529).

Gros Morne National Park

Beginning about 30km from Deer Lake, the southern section of the Long Range Mountains has been set aside as the **Gros Morne National Park**, a UNESCO World Heritage Site that incorporates a large chunk of the peninsula's finest and most approachable scenery. Indeed, the imposing beauty of the park can be almost overpowering, its bays, scrawny beaches, straggling villages and wizened sea stacks backclothed by bare-topped, fjord-cut mountains, whose forested lower slopes are home to moose, woodland caribou and snowshoe hare. It's possible – weather permitting – to drive into the park at any time, but from mid-May to mid-October there's an entry charge of $9 per car.

△ Fjord in Gros Morne National Park

The best place to start a visit is the main **visitor information centre** (daily: late June to Aug 9am–9pm; mid-May to late June and Sept to mid-Oct 9am–4pm; ⓣ709/458-2417, ⓦwww.pc.gc.ca), situated beside Route 430 as it approaches Rocky Harbour, just 70km from Deer Lake. The centre has a series of excellent displays on the geology, botany, biology and human history of the park, and also issues free maps, brochures on the park's key hiking trails and details of local boat excursions. It also runs a programme of guided walks and has all the gubbins on the park's five **campsites** (advance reservations on ⓣ1-877/737-3783, ⓦwww.pccamping.ca). The park also has a number of backcountry **primitive campsites** dotted along the longer trails and for these you have to register here first. If all this sounds too much like hard work consider Gros Morne Adventures (ⓣ709/458-2722, ⓦwww.grosmorneadventures.com) which offers a wide-ranging programme of guided hikes, cycling, sea kayaking and winter sports.

Rocky Harbour

It's a brief drive from the visitor centre to **ROCKY HARBOUR**, the park's largest and prettiest village, which curves around a long and sweeping bay with the mountains lurking in the background. Although there's nothing special to do or see here, the long walk round to the **Lobster Cove Head Lighthouse** is a pleasant way to spend an afternoon. Rocky Harbour is also near several of Gros Morne's **hiking trails**, notably the lung-bursting, 16km Gros Morne Mountain Trail. The trail – for experienced hikers only – begins **at the signed trailhead** beside Route 430, just 7km east of the village, and climbs to the top of Gros Morne Mountain where, at 806m above sea level, the views are stupendous. There's a primitive **campsite** on the way down from the summit (July–Oct) should you decide to stay on the mountain overnight.

Rocky Harbour is the best place to stay in the park, not least because it's relatively compact and has a reasonable range of tourist facilities. **Accommodation** includes the modest, modern but comfortable *Ocean View Motel*, beside the waterfront on Main Street (Ⓣ709/458-2730 or 1-800/563-9887, Ⓦwww.oceanviewmotel.com; ❹), and *Bottom Brook Cottages* (Ⓣ709/458-2236 or 1-866/922-2236; ❹), also on Main Street and consisting of six fully equipped chalets. In both cases advance booking is recommended in July and August. Of the **campsites** hereabouts, the pick is *Berry Hill* (June to mid-Oct), whose 150 unserviced sites are located 5km north of Rocky Harbour along Route 430. For **food**, either stick to the restaurant of the *Ocean View Motel*, where they serve very good seafood dishes for around $17, or head off to *Java Jack's*, on Main Street (Ⓣ709/458-3004), where there's a good café downstairs and a very good restaurant up above.

Norris Point, Bonne Bay and Woody Point

From Rocky Harbour, it's just 11km south to **NORRIS POINT** on the north shore of **Bonne Bay** at the point where this deep and mountainous fjord divides into two inlets – East Arm and South Arm. The best way to see the bay is by **boat** with Bontours (early June to late Sept 1–2 daily; 2hr; $35; Ⓣ709/458-2016 or 1-888/458-2016, Ⓦwww.bontours.ca), departing from Government Wharf in Norris Point. The same company also operates a **water taxi** (foot passengers only; 3 daily; 15min; $10 return) across Bonne Bay from Norris Point to minuscule **WOODY POINT**, where tasty seafood and traditional island dishes are served up at the *Old Loft Restaurant*, on Water St (Ⓣ709/453-2294). On the edge of the village – some 3km west along Route 431 – is the **Discovery Centre** (daily mid-May to late June and Sept to mid-Oct 9am–5pm; late June to Aug 9am–6pm; free), operated by the national park and examining the area's geology, plant and animal life. The Centre is also close to the trailhead for the **Tablelands Hiking Trail**, a 4km-long circular track that cuts across a forbidding landscape of bare and barren rock. Another 8km along Route 431 brings you to the 16km-long loop of the **Green Gardens Trail**, which twists its way to some secluded coves, caves and sea stacks and is equipped with three primitive campsites. Continuing down Route 431, it's a further 4km to **Trout River Pond**, sandwiched by the yellowed bareness of the Tablelands and the massive cliffs bordering the Gregory Plateau. Here, in dramatic profile, you can see the extraordinary force of the uplift created by the collision of the North American and European continents 450 million years ago. The views are splendid, but the best way to see the lake is on the **Trout River Pond Boat Tour** (mid-June to late Sept 1–3 daily; 2hr 30min; $35; Ⓣ709/451-7500).

Western Brook Pond

The remote **Western Brook Pond**, reached by just one access point, 25km north of Rocky Harbour beside Route 430, is one of eastern Canada's finest landscapes, 16km of deep, dark-blue water framed by mighty mountains and huge waterfalls. From the access-point car park it's a forty-minute (3km) walk on a well-maintained trail through forest and over bog to the edge of the lake's gorge along the **Western Brook Pond Trail**, which crosses the narrow coastal plain. When you get to the end, don't skimp on the **boat trip** (reservations required; July & Aug 3 daily; June & Sept 1 daily; 2hr; $40) operated by Bontours, the same company who run trips on Bonne Bay (see above). The boat inches its way between the cliffs right to the extreme eastern end of the lake, past several huge rockslides, dramatic hanging valleys and former sea caves now marooned high above the water.

Port au Choix

The tiny fishing village of **PORT AU CHOIX** sits on a bleak headland about 160km north of Rocky Harbour. Its main claim to fame is the **Port au Choix National Historic Site** (mid-June to early Sept daily 9am–6pm; also early June & early Sept to early Oct daily 9am–5pm; $7.15), established where a mass of prehistoric bones, tools and weapons were accidentally discovered in the 1960s. The ensuing archeological dig unearthed three ancient cemeteries, confirming the area as a centre of settlement for the **Maritime Archaic Peoples**, hunter-gatherers who lived here around 2000 BC. Begin at the visitor centre, which details what is known of these peoples by means of an assortment of artefacts and touch-screen presentations. It also examines two later groups of settlers, the **Groswater** and **Dorset Paleoeskimo**, whose scant remains, dating from between two and three thousand years ago, have also been unearthed near here at what seems to have been their most southerly place of settlement. Afterwards, you can head over to **Philip's Garden** to take a look at the exposed remains of a Dorset settlement; a dig is in progress.

Port au Choix has several unassuming **places to stay**, the pick being *Jeannie's Sunrise B&B* (ⓣ709/861-2254 or 1-877/639-2789, ⓦwww.jeanniessunrisebb.com; ②), a trim modern place in the centre on Fisher Street and with views out to sea. For **food**, choices are limited, but the *Anchor Café*, also on Fisher Street, offers heaped plates of fresh cod, salmon and the local speciality, shrimp, for just $14.

St Barbe and St Anthony

Pressing on from Port au Choix, it's about 100km to the hamlet of **ST BARBE**, from where Labrador Marine (ⓣ1-866/535-2567, ⓦwww.tw.gov.nl.ca/ferryservices) runs a **car ferry** (mid-April to Oct 1–3 daily; 2hr; $11.25 one-way, vehicle $22.75) across the Strait of Belle Isle to Blanc Sablon (see p.542) on the Québec–Labrador border; reservations are not required, but they are recommended and all traffic must check in at the dockside one hour before departure.

Beyond St Barbe, Route 430 slips through a handful of fishing villages and then cuts east across the peninsula, passing the byroad to L'Anse aux Meadows (see p.534) before thumping on to the fishing and supply centre of **ST ANTHONY**. With a population of around four thousand, this is the area's largest settlement, but it's not much more than a humdrum port stretched out around the wide sweep of its harbour. It does, however, possess one worthwhile attraction, the **Grenfell House Museum** (June–Sept daily 9am–8pm; $4), tucked behind the Charles S. Curtis Hospital. The house, a dark-green shingled structure in New England cottage style, is the restored home of the pioneering missionary doctor, Sir Wilfred Grenfell, an Englishman who first came here on behalf of the Royal National Mission to Deep Sea Fishermen in 1892. He never moved back home and, during his forty-year stay, he established the region's first proper hospitals, nursing stations, schools and cooperative stores. Behind the house, there's a pleasant woodland path that leads – in twenty minutes – to the top of Tea House Hill, where Grenfell and his wife were buried. Back down the hill, beyond the hospital, the **Grenfell Interpretation Centre** (same hours; $6 including museum) expands upon its subject with two floors on Grenfell's life and times and a shop that sells local handicrafts.

Practicalities

Provincial Airlines (inside Newfoundland ⓣ1-800/563-2800, elsewhere ⓣ709/576-1666, ⓦwww.provincialairlines.ca) has regular **flights** to St Anthony from St John's. **St Anthony airport** is near Seal Bay, a rather distant 55km west of town on Hwy 430 – and 60km from L'Anse aux Meadows. Onward transport is by taxi only; reckon on $50–60 to either. Bargain short-term **car-rental** deals are available at St Anthony airport – try National (℡709/454-8522).

For **accommodation** in St Anthony, the best bet is *Lynn's Bed & Breakfast*, 340 West St (℡709/454-2677 or 1-877/510-2287; ❷), a pleasant place with two guest rooms surrounded by flowerbeds and with views of the harbour. Alternatives include the *Spruce Inn B&B*, 1 Spruce Lane St, off East Street (℡709/454-3402 or 1-877/454-3402; ❷; May–Nov), and the modern, motel-like *Haven Inn*, 14 Goose Cove Rd (℡709/454-9100 or 1-877/428-3646, Ⓦwww.haveninn.ca; ❹). As regards **food**, the *Lightkeeper's Café* (℡877/454 4900), on Fishing Point, at the end of West Street, serves up a tasty line in seafood.

L'Anse aux Meadows

L'Anse aux Meadows National Historic Site (mid-June to early Sept daily 9am–6pm; also early June & early Sept to early Oct daily 9am–5pm; $10.40) is a UNESCO World Heritage Site comprising the scant remains of the earliest verified European settlement in the Americas. It's also a tribute to the obsessive drive of **Helge Ingstad**, a Norwegian writer and explorer who from 1960 onwards hunted high and low to find Norse settlements on the North Atlantic seaboard. His efforts were inspired by two medieval Icelandic sagas, which detailed the establishment of the colony of **Vinland** somewhere along this coast in about 1000 AD.

At L'Anse aux Meadows, a local – a certain George Decker – took Ingstad to a group of grassed-over bumps and ridges beside Epaves Bay. It was an unremarkable location, beside a peat bog, but in the event the bumps contained

Vinland and the Vikings

Sailing out from every part of coastal Scandinavia, the first **Viking** voyages, dating to the eighth century, had no wider purpose than the plunder of nearby lands and neighbours, but by the start of the ninth century overpopulation at home had pushed the Vikings towards migration and colonization. By 870 they had settled on the shores of Iceland, and by the start of the eleventh century there were about three thousand Norse colonists established in Greenland. As good farmland became scarce, so it was inevitable that there would be another push west.

The two **Vinland sagas** – the *Graenlendinga* and *Eirik's Saga* – give us the only extant account of these further explorations, recounting the exploits of Leif Eiriksson the Lucky and Thorfinn Karlsefni, his merchant brother-in-law, who founded a colony they called **Vinland** in North America around 1000 AD. Crucially, the Norse settlers failed to establish reasonable relations with their native neighbours – whom they called *skraelings*, literally "wretches" – and the perennial skirmishing that ensued eventually drove them out of Vinland, though they did return to secure raw materials for the next few decades; it seems likely that **L'Anse aux Meadows** is the result of one of these foragings.

The Norse carried on collecting timber from Labrador up until the fourteenth century, when a dramatic deterioration in the climate made the trip from Greenland too dangerous. Attacks from the Inuit and the difficulties of maintaining trading links with Scandinavia then took their toll on the main Greenland colonies. All contact between Greenland and the outside world was lost around 1410 and the last of the half-starved, disease-ridden survivors died out towards the end of the fifteenth century – just as Christopher Columbus was eyeing up his "New World".

the remnants of the only **Norse village** ever to have been discovered in North America. These comprised the foundations of eight turf and timber buildings and a ragbag of archeological finds, including a cloak pin, a stone anvil, nails, pieces of bog iron, an oil lamp and a small spindle whorl. Ingstad concluded that these were left behind by a group of about one hundred sailors, carpenters and blacksmiths who probably remained at the site for just one or maybe two years, using it as a base for further explorations.

The site was thoroughly excavated between 1961 and 1968, and again in the 1970s, and there followed an acrimonious academic debate about whether it was actually "Vinland". The geographical clues provided in the sagas are extremely vague, so the argument is essentially linguistic. They hinge on the various possible interpretations of the old Icelandic word "Vinland": one side insists it means "Wine-land" and therefore cannot refer to anywhere in Newfoundland, the other suggests the word means "fertile land" and therefore could.

Whatever the truth, thousands of tourists come here every summer and begin at the **visitor centre**, where the Norse artefacts appear alongside changing exhibitions on Viking life and culture, all beefed up by an excellent (if somewhat melodramatic) thirty-minute film entitled *The Vinland Mystery*. From here it's a few minutes' walk to the cluster of gentle mounds that make up what's left of the original village, and another short stroll to a group of full-scale replicas of a **long house**, storage shed, workshop and a *faering*, a small boat used in coastal waters.

Practicalities

Getting to L'Anse aux Meadows **by car** can seem like an endurance test, but you can save yourself oodles of time by **flying** from St John's to St Anthony with Provincial Airlines (inside Newfoundland ⓣ1-800/563-2800, elsewhere ⓣ709/576-1666, ⓦwww.provincialairlines.ca), and then working your way back – or the other way round. As a sample fare, Provincial Airlines flights from St John's to St Anthony cost around $250 one-way, double that for a return.

The tourists visiting L'Anse aux Meadows have fuelled a mini-boom in local **B&Bs** and **inns**. There are two star turns, kicking off with the *Tickle Inn* (ⓣ709/452-4321, off-season 709/739-5503, ⓦwww.tickleinn.net; ❸; June–Sept), whose four, infinitely cosy guest rooms share an attractive 1890s house in a superb location on the shores of a secluded cove at remote **Cape Onion**. Reservations are essential and evening meals – as well as boat trips along the rugged coast nearby – need to be booked in advance. The Cape is about 45km from L'Anse aux Meadows – backtrack along Route 436, turn down Route 437 and keep going.

Perhaps even better, and certainly closer to L'Anse aux Meadows, is the *Quirpon Lighthouse Inn* (ⓣ709/634-2285 or 1-877/254-6586, ⓦwww.linkumtours.com; ❸; May–Oct), where eleven rooms in the two old lighthouse keeper's houses have been intelligently upgraded. The inn boasts a spectacular location, standing on its own islet next to the lighthouse with the cliffs jagging down below. A double room costs $325 per night, but this does include the forty-five minute boat trip over and all meals; the islet is 8km from L'Anse aux Meadows along a short gravel turning off Route 436.

One other possibility is the all-year, four-room *Viking Nest B&B* (ⓣ709/623-2238 or 1-877/858-2238, ⓦwww.bbcanada.com/vikingnest; ❷), in a modern brick chalet in Hay Cove, just 1km from L'Anse aux Meadows.

Channel-Port aux Basques and the southwest coast

From Deer Lake (see p.529), it's a long-winded 270km along the Trans-Canada to **Channel-Port aux Basques**, from where Marine Atlantic car ferries (see p.551) sail to North Sydney in Nova Scotia. En route, nowhere special commands attention, though you might pause at industrial **Corner Brook**, Newfoundland's second-largest city. Neither is Channel-Port aux Basques particularly riveting, but it is a short drive from the handsomely appointed outport of **Rose Blanche**, which is itself the starting point for ferries to the remote outports of the **southwest coast**, most of which are still beyond the road network. The submerged rocks and jutting headlands of this southwest coast have witnessed the shipwreck of hundreds of vessels, which foundered as they attempted to steer round Newfoundland into the Gulf of St Lawrence, some running aground in a fog bank, others driven ashore by tremendous gales. Such was the frequency of these disasters that many locals came to rely on washed-up timber for firewood and building materials, a bonus for communities all too dependent on the trade price of fish. The flotsam and jetsam days are long gone, but if you're after a slice of traditional outport life, then this is the nearest you'll come, though pre-planning is crucial.

In many outports – though not the ones mentioned below – the Newfoundland tourist office has no listed accommodation and instead you'll have to hunt down the details of the simple **guesthouses** (usually in price category ❷, including all meals) that almost every outport possesses. Unfortunately, there's no central agency with lists of which families in which outports take guests, but you might consider checking the phone book for each community to see if there's a chamber of commerce – or at least a town office – and give them a call. If you do express interest in a particular outport, you shouldn't have any problem finding accommodation: the locals will be pleased you're coming and will set you up for a couple of days or a week.

With regard to public transport, DRL Coachline **buses** (Ⓣ709/263-2171 or 1-888/263-1854, Ⓦwww.drlgroup.com) link Deer Lake and the ferry terminal at Channel-Port aux Basques once daily, though buses do arrive late in the evening (at 9pm). On the southwest coast, **ferry schedules** (Ⓣ709/292-4302, Ⓦwww.tw.gov.nl.ca/ferryservices) require careful attention. In theory it's still possible to travel by boat from **Rose Blanche to Hermitage-Sandyville**, about 180km to the east, but this is – in terms of time – a mammoth commitment involving several changes of ferry and several overnight stays of two or three days, as boats run to irregular timetables. Consequently, it's best to limit your ambitions and aim for **Ramea**, arguably the most dramatic of the coast's outports and just 83 nautical miles from Channel-Port aux Basques. Ramea lies just offshore from **Burgeo**, from where Route 480 makes the heroic 150km journey north across the interior to the Trans-Canada; Stew's Bus Line (Ⓣ709/886-2955) links Burgeo with Corner Brook.

Corner Brook

CORNER BROOK, 50km south of Deer Lake, is magnificently sited, surrounded by steep wooded hills dropping down to the blue waters of the Humber Arm, which funnels into the Bay of Islands. The city is Newfoundland's second biggest, a workaday pulp-and-paper town supplying newsprint to much of the world, and with the mill to prove it. The coast hereabouts was charted by Captain Cook, who now accounts for the city's most enjoyable attraction, the **Cook Monument**, to the west of the centre in a small park at the top of Crow Hill Road. Otherwise aim for **Main Street**, about 500m long and lined by several of the city's better-looking old buildings. Main Street intersects with West Street, where *13 West*, at no. 13, is an excellent bistro serving reasonably priced food from a creative, international menu.

DRL Coachline buses pause at Irving Big Stop station on Confederation Drive to the north of Main Street.

Channel-Port aux Basques and beyond

An important port and ferry terminal, **CHANNEL-PORT AUX BASQUES** divides into two distinct sections, an older part stuck on a bare and bumpy headland about 1.5km seaward from the ferry dock and a newer section spread out along Grand Bay Road about 3km to the west. Most people drive straight through the town, but it does have a **tourist information office** (Ⓣ709/695-2262), on the outskirts beside the Trans-Canada, and a substantial supply of affordable **accommodation**. In the newer part of the port, two options are the *Caribou Bed and Breakfast*, 42 Grand Bay Rd (Ⓣ709/695-3408, Ⓦwww.home.thezone.net/~gibbons; ❷; May–Sept), with five en-suite guest rooms; and the large, chalet-like *Hotel Port aux Basques*, 2 Grand Bay Rd (Ⓣ709/695-2171 or 1-877/695-2171, Ⓦwww.hotelpab.com; ❸).

From Channel-Port aux Basques, it's a 45km drive east to end-of-the-road **ROSE BLANCHE**, a postcard-pretty village of steep lanes, brightly coloured houses and a fine old, granite lighthouse (May–Oct daily 9am–9pm; $3), set high above the seething sea and dating to 1871. Nearby, in these harsh rocky surroundings, is a **B&B**, the *Hook, Line & Sinker* (Ⓣ709/956-2005; ❸; May–Oct).

From Rose Blanche, **passenger ferries** (6 weekly; 2hr 30min) head east to **GRAND BRUIT**, where there is one listed lodging, the *Blue Mountain Cabins* (Ⓣ709/492-2753, Ⓦwww.bluemountaincabins.ca; ❸; June–Oct). Here at Grand Bruit, you change for the ferry (1 weekly; 3hr) to **BURGEO**, a much larger community that has a road link with the Trans-Canada. There are frequent ferries from Burgeo (mid-May to mid-Oct Sun–Fri 1–3 daily; rest of year 1–3 daily; 1hr 20min) to **RAMEA**, which perches on a tiny rugged island; there are a couple of B&Bs here, too, including the *Four Winds* (Ⓣ709/625-2002; ❷).

Labrador

Labrador, a huge swathe of sub-arctic wilderness on the northeastern edge of the Canadian Shield, is a place so desolate that it provoked Jacques Cartier to remark, "I am rather inclined to believe that this is the land God gave to Cain". Cartier's assessment was perhaps rather cruel, but Labrador is certainly a land full of rocky expanses and precious little vegetation, all set against soaring mountains and cool, clean rivers that seem to run forever. Much of it is an unspoiled, barely accessible wilderness where **caribou** roam, well

outnumbering the people of Labrador – by thirty to one - with the largest herd being around 800,000 head.

Labrador divides into two zones. Half the population of 29,000 live along the **coast** – the traditional preserve of fisherman and whalers since the sixteenth century. Most are scattered along the more accessible south coast, while the (largely native Canadian) communities dotted along the northern coast are small and remote. The other half live in the towns of the **interior** - **Happy Valley-Goose Bay**; **Churchill Falls**; and **Labrador City-Wabush**. These settlements have emerged since the 1960s (the products respectively of military bases, dam projects and mining operations) and are populated chiefly by white southerners with a very different outlook on the use of natural resources from that of the indigenous population. The original owners of this land, the **Naskapi**, **Innu** and **Inuit**, who collectively number around five thousand, were pretty much left alone until the middle of the twentieth century, excepting for the work of **Moravian** missionaries between the 1770s and 1950s, but in the last few decades the region's natural resources have attracted enormous attention, prompting the development of dams and mines that have played havoc with the local ecology. The Labrador Trough, in the west, has the highest concentration of **iron ore** in North America, and in 1997 Inuit and Innu set up blockades in an (unsuccessful) attempt to disrupt the construction of a **nickel mine** and mill at Voisey Bay, in northern Labrador.

This barren terrain was also long a bone of contention between Québec and Newfoundland, whose current **common border** was fixed in the 1920s, although these days the disputes (concerning Newfoundland's jurisdiction over Labrador, and then again over its hydroelectric potential) have been patched up and more or less consigned to history.

The Labrador coast

According to local lore, God built the world in six days and on the seventh he pelted Labrador with rocks, leaving a wind-cracked and ice-chiselled **coast** that is inhospitable to say the least, with barely a twig in sight never mind a tree along its entire, jagged length.

Inhabited for over nine thousand years, the Labrador coast was first used by caribou-hunters and then by Basque whalers, but permanent settlements did not develop until the turn of the eighteenth century, long after fishermen from Newfoundland first began summer migrations to these well-stocked waters. Those who chose to live here all year – often of English West Country origin – were known as "**livyers**" (literally "we live 'ere"); they generally married "Esquimaux" women, and led terribly harsh lives, their incomes curtailed by the English merchants' iniquitous truck system, by which the merchants fixed both the price of exported fish and all imported goods. **Wilfred Grenfell** (1865-1940), the superintendent of the Mission to Deep Sea Fishermen from 1892, did his best to ameliorate conditions by establishing hospitals, orphanages and nursing stations all along the coast, and improved economic conditions by bringing the hated truck system to an end. The livyers, incidentally, were the first to train **Labrador retriever dogs** to catch any fish that fell off the hook.

Today, the subsistence farming and fishing once common here has all but disappeared, thanks to overfishing - and consequent government moratoriums. Hunting and trapping still play a role, giving shape to the annual calendar of many communities, but unemployment along the coast is high, and government subsidies underpin many local economies. The character of local people, the majority an ethnic mix of European and Native American, is generally marked by dogged determination and resilience. By and large, they're a friendly bunch, who have developed a distinct vocabulary, referring to the multitude of narrow inlets along the coast as "tickles" and dolphins as "jumpers", and they still use ancient phrases like "heaken!" and "dout the lights". The history of the area is at its most evocative in some of the old settlements along the **Labrador Straits**, the most temptingly accessible portion of the region. This is particularly so at **Red Bay**, unquestionably the historic highlight hereabouts, though the newly rebuilt fishing centre of **Battle Harbour** further up the southern coast, runs a close second. There is a road along the southern Labrador coast, but the **northern coast** is still only accessible by plane and passenger ferry (see box, p.548), which makes for a remarkable trip, with lots of opportunity to spy whales, seals and all manner of northern wildlife plus **icebergs**. Around three thousand icebergs drift over from Greenland every year, taking two years to reach Labrador, and they make for a stunning, if ghostly, sight – but have also sounded the death knell for many boats along the coast here, including the *Caron* – once the passenger ferry here before it sank in 1977.

Labrador practicalities

The harsh **climate** and **remoteness** make Labrador one of Canada's most forbidding areas for travellers. January temperatures in Happy Valley-Goose Bay average -16°C (3°F) and the annual snowfall is around five metres – with much of it covering the ground for half the year. Further inland and up north the climate is even colder. Most major roads are unpaved and can close for days in snowy or rainy conditions. Tourist facilities are generally scarce and costly, though most major towns have formal accommodation of some sort. In many smaller towns you'll have to ask around to find a room for rent in someone's home and the same goes for local boat trips. Any trip needs a fair amount of organization – especially if you are heading for the hinterland.

Most visitors to Labrador are **adventure** seekers who come to trek, paddle the coastline, or hunt and snowmobile in the interior. Be warned that unless you have extensive backcountry experience it's best to join an organized **tour** (see opposite), which makes the exploration of Labrador's wilds as safe and trouble-free as possible. With good camping equipment, an adventurous spirit and a healthy budget, there are few landscapes that match the untouched, rugged beauty of the area. This is particularly so when it comes to the **Aurora borealis** (northern lights; see also p.997), visible in Labrador on average 243 nights per year. The location of magnetic north here makes it the best place in Canada to experience the lights – though at the height of summer the long daylight hours mitigate against seeing the lights. Wherever you go, and whenever you go, make sure to take the strongest insect repellent you can find and heavy winter clothing, as even in the height of summer fierce snowstorms can occur.

Getting to Labrador

Labrador is connected to the rest of the world by **flights** from Newfoundland, Nova Scotia and Québec. The major carrier is Air Canada (Ⓣ1-888/247-2262, Ⓦwww.aircanada.ca), which flies to Goose Bay from Halifax and to Wabush from Montréal, Québec City and Sept-Îles. Air Labrador (Ⓣ709/896-8113 or 1-800/563-3042, Ⓦwww.airlabrador.com) flies from St John's, Deer Lake, Stephenville and St Anthony in Newfoundland to their hub at Goose Bay; and Provincial Airlines (Ⓣ1-800/563-2800, Ⓦwww.provair.ca) flies from these and from Halifax to Goose Bay and Blanc Sablon. Expect to pay around $800 for the longer flights from Montréal, Québec City and Halifax; around half that for shorter hops from Newfoundland.

Labrador has **ferry** links from St Barbe, about 80km north of Port au Choix, to Blanc-Sablon (mid-April to mid-Jan 1–3 daily; 1hr 45min; Ⓣ1-866-535-2567; Ⓦwww.labradormarine.com; $11, car $22.75); reservations are generally advised. Bear in mind that Blanc-Sablon is on Atlantic time – half an hour behind the neighbouring southern Labrador coastal communities. There are also the less frequent sailings of the *Nordik Express* (see p.384), which takes several days to find its way here from Rimouski via numerous communities on the north shore of the St Lawrence.

Trains operated by the Québec North Shore and Labrador Railway (QNS&L; Ⓣ709/944-8205 or 418/962-5530) follow the 416km line from Sept-Îles on Québec's North Shore to Labrador City and Schefferville. It's primarily an industrial link, but there is limited space for passengers and the journey is an exhilarating ride over high bridges, through dense forest and tundra, past waterfalls, deep gorges and rocky mountains; a special dome car allows passengers to appreciate the views. Trains

The Labrador Straits and southern coast

The most accessible portion of Labrador is the **Labrador Straits**, a short ferry ride from St Barbe in Newfoundland (see box, p.533) across the 18km-wide Strait of Belle Isle to Blanc-Sablon. The trip is an experience in itself, with the

leave Sept-Îles for Labrador City (Thurs 9am; 8hr; $115 return) and for Schefferville (Mon 9am; 11hr; $156 return); in both cases the return journey is the following day.

It's also possible to **drive** to Labrador from Québec, via the 580-kilometre Route 389 from Baie-Comeau to Labrador City and Wabush; the road is partly paved and partly gravel and has fuel, food and accommodation services along much of its length.

Specialist tour companies

BreakAway Adventures ⓣ709/896-9343. Guided or unguided wilderness river trips in a kayak, with instruction available. Also offered are 5–14 day all-inclusive hiking expeditions from April to Oct.

Experience Labrador ⓣ709/938-7444 or 1-877/938-7444, ⓦwww.experiencelabrador.com. Outdoor adventure company operating out of Cartwright, offering local kayak, open boat and walking tours. July to Sept.

Labrador Scenic Limited ⓣ709/497-8326. Wilderness tours lasting up to two weeks, from around $180 per day. Also canoe and kayak rentals from March to Oct and half or full day snowmobile tours in winter.

Nature Trek Canada ⓣ250/653-4265, ⓦwww.naturetrek.ca/Labrador. Offers custom hiking tours in the Torngat Mountains and along the coast as well as a regular 16-day inland wilderness tour that tries to catch the Caribou on their summer migration. July–Sept.

Information and local transport

Advance **information**, maps and timetables are available in advance from the Department of Tourism, Culture and Recreation in St John's, Newfoundland (ⓣ1-800/563-6353, ⓦwww.newfoundlandandlabradortourism.com). This government site also contains a section run by the Department of Works Services and Transportation (ⓣ709/896-7840, ⓦwww.gov.nl.ca), which has up-to-date information on road conditions and ferry schedules. An even better bet for advance information – as well as a comprehensive collection of links - is ⓦwww.explorelabrador.nf.ca. For information on the snowmobiling trail system contact Labrador Winter Trails (ⓣ1-877/884-7669, ⓦwww.labradorwintertrails.com).

With the exception of the **rail line** between Labrador City and Schefferville, there is no land-based public transport in Labrador and **driving** on the region's unpaved roads can be extremely difficult. That said, some roads have improved dramatically in recent years and it is now possible to drive around the southern coast and across the interior with regular vehicles. In addition, Labrador Marine (ⓣ1-866/535-2567, ⓦwww.labradormarine.com) operates a coastal **car ferry**, the *Sir Robert Bond* (June to Oct 2–3 weekly; 12hr; ⓣ1-866/535-2567 or 1-709/724-9173; $48.75 one-way, car $79.25, 2-berth cabin $51.75) between two sections of the road network - Cartwright and Happy Valley-Goose Bay. The passenger-only *Northern Ranger* steamship, also operated by Labrador Marine, sails weekly from Cartwright and is the main lifeline for the northern coast, providing a bare-bones transport link between coastal communities in the north (see p.548). If you want to reach the distant outposts quickly, the only choice is by **internal flights** with Air Labrador or Provincial Airlines (see opposite). Between them they serve 14 coastal communities, most with daily flights; reckon on paying around $400 to fly from Happy Valley-Goose Bay to Nain and back.

vessel dwarfed by icebergs floating down the strait from Greenland, and minke and humpback whales a common sight. From Blanc-Sablon **Route 510** joins coastal villages for 83km to Red Bay, before turning into a gravel road and heading inland along the **southern Coast** a further 350km to Cartwright.

If you don't have your own transport, the only way to get around is to **rent a car** from National in Blanc-Sablon (☎418/481-2777 or 1-877/461-2777) or Eagle River Rent-a-Car in L'Anse Au Clair (☎709/931-2352). Exploring the coast is easily done in a couple of days and some visitors even head back to Newfoundland the same day.

Blanc-Sablon to L'Anse-au-Loup

On the south coast, just across the border in Québec, **BLANC-SABLON** is the main transport hub between Newfoundland and Labrador with an airport (see p.540) and car ferries (see p.540) shuttling over the Strait of Belle Isle from St Barbe (see p.533) – the ferry terminal is 2km east of town. From Blanc-Sablon, most travellers head **east** into Labrador along **Route 510**, which connects a string of villages that were once fishing camps and are now modest, little places huddling against the coastal cliffs. The first community along the way is **L'ANSE-AU-CLAIRE**, 8km east of the ferry terminal, which has the main visitor centre (see Practicalities below) and a relatively good range of hotels and restaurants. From the visitor centre a 3km trail follows the original settlers path along the coast to the **Jersey Rooms**, an ongoing excavation of one of the first eighteenth-century sealing settlements. Another 13km along Route 510 is **FORTEAU**, the largest community hereabouts, at its liveliest during the annual three-day Bakeapple Festival in mid-August that celebrates the locally-abundant cloudberry. A worthwhile hike out of Forteau is the 4km long Overfalls Brook Trail, which leads to a 30m-high waterfall. Also east of town, the **Labrador Straits Museum** (mid-June to mid-Sept Mon–Sat 9.30am–5.30pm; ☎709/927-7307, Ⓦwww.labradorstraitsmuseum.ca; $5) traces the area's history, with particular emphasis on the important contributions made by Labrador women.

The most significant sights in the area are the 7500-year-old **burial mound** of a 12-year-old Indian boy at **L'ANSE-AMOUR** – the oldest-known funeral monument in North America – and the 36m-high **Point Amour lighthouse** (mid-June to mid-Oct daily 10am–5.30pm; ☎709/927-5826; $3), further along the same side road. This mid-nineteenth-century lighthouse is Canada's second largest, offering spectacular views from the top of its 128-step tower and providing some informative displays on the locality in a museum that's staffed by costumed guides.

Further up the coast, **L'ANSE-AU-LOUP** has all basic services (including fuel) and the Schooner Cove Trail, a 3km hike to a cove used by prehistoric tribes. Beyond the village, and 10km short of Red Bay, the **Pinware River Provincial Park** (late May to mid-Sept; ☎709/927-5516 or 1-800/563-6353, Ⓦwww.env.gov.nl.ca/parks) is one of the most scenic stretches in the Labrador Straits, with the rushing, white-water Pinware River as its centrepiece.

Practicalities

For **information** head to the "Gateway to Labrador" Visitor Centre (mid-June to Sept Mon–Sat 9.30am–6pm, Sun 2pm–6pm; ☎709/931-2360, Ⓦwww.labradorstraits.net), housed in a 1909 church at L'Anse au Claire.

Most of the **places to stay** on this stretch of coast are either basic hotels or B&Bs; most offer dinner at an additional charge (to which non-guests are welcome). In Blanc-Sablon *Pension Quatre Saisons*, 2 Beaudoin St (☎428/461-2024; ③) has motel rooms, but there's a greater selection at L'Anse au Claire: the *Northern Light Inn* (☎709/931-2332 or 1-800/563 3188, Ⓦwww.northernlightinn.com; ④) is a modern motel with a restaurant that serves simple meals for around $13, while the inexpensive *Beachside Hospitality*

Home, 9 Lodge Rd (☎709/931-2338; ❷), has three rooms sharing two bathrooms with a whirlpool tub and free entertainment in the evenings, on request, from the owner, Norm, who is a master of the accordion.

In Forteau, the *Grenfell Louie A Hall B&B*, 3 Willow Ave (☎709/931-2916, Ⓦwww3.nf.sympatico.ca/peggy.hancock; ❷), has pleasant rooms, a common room and occupies a 1946 nursing home; and the *Sea-View Restaurant and Cabins*, 33 Main St (☎709/931-2840 or 1-866-931-2840; ❸–❹), has basic motel rooms and a good restaurant known for its seafood (scallops under $15). Further northeast, the *Lighthouse Cove B&B* (☎709/927-5690, Ⓦwww.lighthousecovebb.labradorstraits.net; ❶) in L'Anse-Amour and *Barney's Bed & Breakfast*, 122 Main St (☎709/927-5634; ❷) in L'Anse-au-Loup are both excellent value, with ocean views and tasty home cooking.

In West St Modeste, a few kilometres north of L'Anse-au-Loup, overlooking Pinware Bay, the *Oceanview Resort* (☎709/927-5288, Ⓦwww.oceanviewresort.ca; ❹–❺) has cottages, pleasant hotel rooms and several serviced RV sites. You can **camp** ($10) up the valley in the *Pinware River Provincial Park* (May to mid-Sept; ☎709/729-2424 or 1-877/214-2267, Ⓦwww.env.gov.nl.ca/parks). Facilities are basic but there is drinking water and pit toilets.

Red Bay to Cartwright

The world's largest whaling port in the late sixteenth century, **RED BAY** is the most worthwhile place to visit on Labrador's southern coast. Finds from extensive land and marine archeological surveys can be viewed at the **Red Bay National Historic Site Interpretation Centre** (daily: June to early Oct 9am–6pm; ☎709/920-2142, Ⓦwww.pc.gc.ca/redbay; $7.15). The most impressive find is one of the Basque whaling vessels that foundered in the bay and was beautifully preserved in its ice-cold waters. The story of its discovery and excavation is told in an hour-long documentary film in the **Welcome Centre** a short walk away and here also is one of the small *Chalupas* (see box, p.544) used by the whalers and also recovered from the bay (entry included in Interpretation Centre admission fee). If you're feeling adventurous, take a **boat trip** to Saddle Island (hourly departures from the Interpretation Centre daily 9am–4pm July-Sept; $2), where you can roam around the whaler's cemetery on a self-guided tour. If you are lucky you may also spot a few whales in the distance.

△ Fishing houses at Red Bay

Beyond Red Bay, Route 510 switches from asphalt to well-maintained gravel and heads inland to re-emerge 85km later at the coast by **MARY'S HARBOUR**, a settlement which was only founded in 1955 after fire wiped out offshore **BATTLE HARBOUR**, Labrador's most significant settlement in the early nineteenth-century and now rebuilt as an historic village (June–Sept; ⓣ709/921-6325 or 921-6216, ⓦwww.battleharbour.com; $7). Today, Battle Harbour has a clutch of old buildings, a visitor centre and several walking trails; you can also stay here in some of the old houses (see below). To get from Mary's Harbour to Battle Harbour island, contact Jones Charters and Tours (May–Oct, twice daily departures from Mary's Harbour 11am and 7pm; ⓣ709/921-6249 or 921-6948; $40 round-trip).

CARTWRIGHT, the northern terminus of Route 510, around 240km from Mary's Harbour, is named after Captain George Cartwright. He was one of the first Europeans to coexist with the natives, even taking several locals back to England in 1772 to visit the king and Dr Johnson, though smallpox finished them all off and none returned to tell the tale. In recent years Cartwright has become a relatively busy port, with **ferries** to Goose Bay and along the coast, but it's still best known for nearby **Porcupine Strand**, a 56km-long sandy beach that can only be visited by boat or ATV.

Practicalities

For **accommodation**, Red Bay's *Whaling Station Cabins*, 61 East Harbour Drive (May–Oct; ⓣ709/920-2156; ④), offers en-suite rooms with cable TV,

Basque whalers at Red Bay

At its peak in the late sixteenth century, over two thousand men lived in Red Bay during the **whaling** season, producing half a million gallons of whale oil that was subsequently shipped back to Europe on a month-long voyage. Whale oil was used for light, lubrication and as an additive to drugs, soap and pitch, and one 55-gallon barrel could fetch a price equal to $10,000 today – so for the **Basques** the discovery of Labrador's right-whale stocks was equivalent to striking gold. However, as well as the treacherous journey from Spain to what they knew as Terranova, the Basques withstood terrible hardships to claim their rich booty. Once in Labrador, they rowed fragile wooden craft called *chalupas* into these rough seas and then attached drogues to the whales to slow them down. It was then a matter of following their prey for hours until the whale surfaced and could be lanced to death. Three factors brought the whale boom to an end: first, the Basques were so successful that within thirty years they had killed off more than 15,000 whales; second, the industry became more hazardous with early freeze-ups in the 1570s; and, finally, the Basque ships and men were absorbed into the ill-fated Spanish Armada of 1588.

Serious study of Red Bay area began in 1977, when marine archeologists discovered the remains of three Basque **galleons** and several *chalupas*. Most notable of these vessels was the *San Juan* galleon, which was split in half by an iceberg in 1565, with the loss of one black rat – its bones were found in a wicker basket with a scattering of codfish bones, which showed that the heading and splitting techniques were identical to those used by the Labrador fishermen of today. On land, excavations uncovered try-works (where the whale blubber was boiled down into oil), personal artefacts and, in 1982, a cemetery on Saddle Island where the remains of 160 young men were found. Many were lying in groups, indicating that they died as crew members when chasing the whales, but some had not been buried – which suggests that at least part of the community had died of starvation when an early freeze dashed their chances of getting home.

some with their own catering facilities and a restaurant serving traditional Labrador dishes for around $15, while the *Basinview Bed & Breakfast*, 145 Main (☎709/920-2002 or 1-866/920-2001; ❷), is more basic but run by friendly owners with a good knowledge of the town's Basque whaling history.

At Mary's Harbour you can stay and eat at the *Riverlodge Hotel* (☎709/921-6948, Ⓦwww.riverlodgehotel.com; ❹), but it's more pleasant, if less convenient, to stay in Battle Harbour itself where the options include a two-storey restored fishing house – the *Battle Harbour Inn* (❹) – and a hostel-style fisherman's bunkhouse ($❷–❺ per person). Meals are provided at an extra cost of $8 for breakfast and $18 for dinner. Alternatively, several old self-catering cottages around the village are available from $150 for 2 to 4 adults.

In Cartwright the *Cartwright Hotel* (☎709/938-7414, Ⓦwww.cartwrighthotel.ca; ❹) is a friendly place near the airport that also serves good local cuisine, while *Harbourview B&B* (☎709/938-7325; ❸), a few doors along, offers a slideshow of historic sites and guided tours of the surrounding area as well as comfortable rooms.

Happy Valley-Goose Bay and around

Located on the westernmost tip of the huge Hamilton Inlet – also called Lake Melville – the adjacent towns of **HAPPY VALLEY-GOOSE BAY** are the principal transport and service hub for the entire Labrador Coast. Nevertheless, there's not much to tempt you either here or to neigbouring **North West River**, but a couple of museums and some short hikes into the surrounding spruce forest that's interspersed with sparkling lakes and rivers. One of the liveliest times to visit is the first weekend in August during **Labrador Canoe Regatta**, the area's most important festival. This hectic, carnival-like event is held over a weekend and features canoe races, musical performances and pavilions serving traditional food.

The former trapping community of **Happy Valley**, where most of the shops and restaurants are located, is a fairly quiet, laid-back sort of place, which peters out into dirt and gravel tracks at the edges of town. Until recently, it lived to service Goose Bay, which has been a sprawling NATO military airbase, housing up to 12,000 military personnel, since World War II. However, in 2006 NATO left, leaving the base all but abandoned and Happy Valley struggling to adjust to the massive change, socially and economically.

The town's two museums largely focus on its military heritage: the **Northern Lights Military Museum**, 170 Hamilton River Rd (Mon–Sat 10am–5.30pm, Thurs & Fri until 9pm; free), occupies a room in the basement of a general store and is stuffed with military memorabilia; and the **Labrador Military Museum**, in a large hangar on C Street on the old base (June–Sept Mon–Fri 9am–noon & 1–4pm, Sat noon–4pm, closed Wed & Sun; rest of year by appointment; ☎709/897-4093), documents the history of the British, American, Dutch and German – as well as Canadian – military presence with displays of flags, insignia and radar apparatus. Particularly poignant are the references to the all-too-frequent fatal air crashes that have occurred here in past decades.

To experience the countryside around Happy Valley-Goose Bay at its most striking, make a trip to **Muskrat Falls**, a thunderous falls on the Churchill River. To get there, drive out of Happy Valley on the Trans-Labrador Route 500. After about 40km, watch for a small sign on the left indicating a narrow dirt road, down which you drive about 10km. From here it's a twenty-minute hike on a rough, unmarked trail down to the bank of the river, where you can view the falls from a spray-covered rocky outcrop. Be sure to take good walking shoes, plenty of drinking water and insect repellent. Both Labrador Scenic Limited and (BreakAway Adventures) (see box, p.541) offer tours here.

Practicalities

The tiny Happy Valley-Goose Bay **airport** is located on the recently vacated military base, a couple of kilometres north of town. As there's no shuttle bus or public transport, you'll have to rely on **taxis** (T709/896-3333) to move on to either Goose Bay ($10) or Happy Valley ($15). National (T709/896-1072) and Budget have booths at the airport and charge about $60 per day, with the first 100km per day free. To get to town, head along Loring Drive and turn right at the traffic lights (the only ones in town) onto Hamilton River Road. Right on the corner is the **Visitor Centre**, 365 Hamilton River Rd (June–Aug daily; rest of year closed weekends 8.30am–4pm; T709/896-3489, Wwww.tourismlabrador.com), which can provide brochures and help you plan trips out of town. You can also get tips and gear from **Labrador Aquatic Rentals**, at T&R Marina, 1 Hamilton River Rd (T709/896-2766 or 896-4885), which rents out boats, canoes, bicycles and ATVs; snowmobiles are available in winter too.

Happy Valley-Goose Bay has a reasonable range of **accommodation**. The least expensive options are the B&Bs in town, particularly *TMT's B&B*, 451 Hamilton River Rd (T709/896-4404; 1), located close to the ferry terminal. The more central *Davis' B&B*, 14 Cabot Crescent (T709/896-5077, Wwww.bbcanada.com/davisbandb; 2) has rooms with private bathrooms while *Bradley's B&B*, 13 Mackenzie Divre (T709/896-8006 or 1-877/884-7378, Wwww.bbcanada.com/bradleybb; 2) boasts homemade breads and jams for breakfast. A few minutes drive out of town *Goose River Lodges*, Route 520 (T709/896-2600 or 1-877/496-2600, Wwww.gooseriverlodges.ca) has chalets ($95 per night for 4 adults) as well as tent and serviced RV sites ($17–24) all year round. They also rent snowmobiles in winter. The *Royal Inn*, 5 Royal Ave (T709/896-2456 or 1-888/440-2456, Wwww.royalinnandsuites.ca; 3), is a modern hotel where continental breakfasts and Internet access are free but the town's fanciest lodging choice is *Hotel North*, 25/27 Loring Drive (T709/896-9301 or 1-877/996-9301, Wwww.atyp.com/hotelnorth; 5) with bygones in its lobby and locally recommended restaurant, the *Mariners Galley*, that features a wooden ship centerpiece.

Apart from Hotel North, the best places to **eat** are *Tricia Dee's*, 96 Hamilton River Rd (T709/896-4441), specializing in steaks and ribs, and *Trappers Cabin Bar and Grill*, 1 Aspen Rd, (T709/896-9522; steak from $12), where you cook your steak yourself on their grill. Happy Valley-Goose Bay is a lively **drinking** town: the busiest bars are *Mulligan's Pub*, 368 Hamilton River Rd, a tiny place that is always full to bursting and *Maxwell's II/Bentley's*, 97 Hamilton River Rd, the town's main nightspot located right on the waterfront.

North West River

From Happy Valley-Goose Bay a paved road heads north 30km to **NORTH WEST RIVER**. A pleasant diversion on the way is **Simeon Falls**, a forest waterfall in the middle of a dense, moss-covered thicket. It's easy to miss: watch for a sign on the side of the road, just past the Port turn-off, that says "Scenic waterfall" and then walk along a short winding trail over a tangle of tree roots. In winter, cross-country skiers should head to the 30km of trails groomed by the Birch Brook Nordic Ski Club (T709/896-2718, Wwww.birchbrook.com), 13km from Happy Valley-Goose Bay on Northwest River Road. They can also rent snowshoes and have a map of various snowshoe trails.

NORTH WEST RIVER itself is a small, former fur-trading station – the oldest in Central Labrador - picturesquely sited on a broad isthmus surrounded by three vast bodies of water: Grand Lake, Little Lake and the briney Lake Melville. For a panoramic **view**, drive the 2km up to **Sunday Hill** on a rather rough, potholed road; you'll be rewarded with sweeping vistas of both lakes, the lumpy outline of mount Mokami and, in the distance, the Mealy Mountains. In the village, the main attraction is the **Labrador Heritage Museum** on River Rd (daily 9am–noon & 1–5pm; ⓣ709/497-8858, ⓦwww3.nf.sympatico.ca/lab.heritage; $2), which incorporates the 1923 Hudson Bay store and a trapper's cabin along with a potted history of the area. The museum also has an intriguing account of the ill-fated 1903 Wallace-Hubbard expedition into the Labrador interior. Leonidas Hubbard, his friend Dillon Wallace and guide George Elson hoped to cross from Lake Melville to Ungava Bay on the northern fringe of Québec, but misunderstanding directions from the natives, they travelled up the wrong river valley. Eventually running out of food, Hubbard died in the wilderness, but his wife Mina – who never forgave Wallace for abandoning him – completed the spectacular trek two years later. She documented the trip in the book *A Woman's Way Through Unknown Labrador*, a 1983 edition of which is still in print. If the museum whets your appetite for more information on Labrador's history pick up a copy of *Them Days, Them Days*, a quarterly publication that presents an oral history largely through interviews with old-timers, at the **Heritage Craft Shop** further along River Road. If the shop isn't open, call Audrey on ⓣ709/497-8251 or Marguerite on 709/497-8386. From the jetty next to the museum, **Campbell Adventure Tours** (ⓣ709/497-8731; hourly tour $30 per person) runs daily boat trips along the trap lines used by the old timers. Also on River Road is the house and **studio of John Goudie**, a local artist who makes furniture and jewellery out of Labradorite, a lustrous crystallized stone. If he is at work he'll show you his studio where he crafts the stone and then take you into his house to see the furniture he's made, as well as a huge Labradorite-studded fireplace.

In the heart of town, at the end of Portage Road, the houses stop abruptly to reveal a long sandy **beach** curling around the shore – just one of many that surround Lake Melville. At the far end of Portage Road, the **Labrador Interpretion Centre** (early June to late Sept Mon & Wed 1–4pm, otherwise 10am–4pm, rest of the year daily 1–4pm; ⓣ709/497-8566) has four separate displays presenting local history and culture. The guides are extremely knowledgeable and are happy to explain the significance of the artefacts, sculptures and ceremonies included in the exhibits. Particularly interesting is the Innu shaking tent ceremony and the 300-year-old jacket made of caribou leather that was used for hunting rituals.

The northern Labrador coast

The **north** is the most untouched part of Labrador and few visitors venture this far: the coastal boat from Happy Valley-Goose Bay (see box, p.548) takes three days to reach **Nain** – and a sudden storm can leave you stranded for days in one of the tinier midway settlements. But the desolate, rocky coast and floating icebergs are spectacular and the mixed native-white communities and their history is intriguing. To some extent traditional patterns of life have been preserved here. There are no cars in most of the settlements, arctic char are still hung in the street to dry, and activities change according to what is in season to hunt or trap – but similarly conspicuous is the unemployment and alcoholism. North of Nain, the **Torngat Mountains** beckon the adventurous – and are destined to be protected within a national park.

North from Happy Valley-Goose Bay to Nain and beyond

Most of the coastal villages beyond Happy Valley-Goose Bay began as fur-trading posts in the nineteenth century, though some date back to the eighteenth-century missionary work of the **Moravian Brethren**, a small German evangelical sect active along the Labrador coast from the late 1700s to the 1950s. The Moravians were originally invited to settle in 1762 by the government in London, who considered the people of the area to be some of the world's most savage. The group did its best to undermine traditional spirituality, while helping the local population make better sense of their contacts with the outside world. The prim, white Moravian mission – consisting of a 1782 church, residence, store, storehouse and small huts to house visiting native peoples – still stands at **HOPEDALE**, 150km south of Nain (June–Sept by appointment; $5; ⓣ709/933-3777), its hymn-books printed in Inuktitut, the language of the Inuit. Close by, the site of the former American radar base serves as a superb lookout to watch the icebergs below. In town the *Amaguk Inn* (ⓣ709/933-3750; ⑤) provides comfortable motel-quality rooms and food, as well as small self-catering units.

NAIN, despite its picturesque setting in a deep fjord, is sometimes dubbed "Viet-Nain" by Labradorians for its social problems. Fishing is the main industry and centuries-old hunting and trapping traditions continue, but the Moravian mission, which had been converted into a museum called Piulimatsivik (Inuit for "place where we keep the old things"), burnt down in 1999. Some artefacts were rescued, however – ask around to find where they are currently displayed. You can stay in town at the *Atsanik Lodge*, Sand Banks Rd (ⓣ709/922-2910; ⑤).

From Nain you can travel onwards to the treeless tundra of the flat-topped **Torngat Mountains**, the highest range east of the Rockies. The region is best visited with experienced guides like Torngat Mountain Labrador Tours in Nain

The Northern Ranger

Northern Labrador is the region at its most remote, yet the coast is fairly easy to explore, thanks to the weekly, summer-only **ferry service** of the **Northern Ranger**, which is becoming popular as a budget cruise. The foot-passenger only steamship, run by Coastal Labrador Marine (ⓣ1-866-535-2567, ⓦwww.labradormarine.com), leaves once-weekly from Cartwright on a route that takes it to Nain via Happy Valley-Goose Bay, with stops at every larger community along the way. In most cases the hour or so the ferry spends at every stop is plenty to have a look around. Should you decide to stop for longer, you'll have to stay for several days until the ferry docks in again, and will have to ask around for somewhere to stay, though it's generally not too hard to find accommodation. The ferries run from mid-June to late November; soon after this, the Arctic ice pack closes in to seal up the area for the rest of year. The late-season schedule is notoriously unreliable since storms can delay sailings, sometimes for days. It's late in the season that the sea can also be at it's roughest; the naturalist Sir Joseph Banks noted that his 1766 voyage down the coast was "one continual puke".

Fares are very reasonable, based on the number of nautical miles travelled, with supplements for cabin space, which you should reserve well in advance, otherwise it's likely you'll have no option but to make yourself as comfortable as possible on the aircraft-style seats. A round-trip from Happy Valley-Goose Bay to Nain costs around $416 return in an economy cabin. Prices at the **onboard canteen** are reasonable but choice is limited and the meals are reminiscent of over-cooked school dinners so it's worth stocking up on provisions beforehand.

(☎709/896-0184 or 579-0995, ⓔwinstonw@nl.rogers.com), which offers canoeing, kayaking, walking and camping trips year-round – in igloos in the winter. At Nain you can also charter a boat to sail up the coast with Webb Services (☎709/922-2865 or 922-2960), who will show you the deserted mission at Hebron and take you to the **Nachvak Fjord**, near Labrador's northernmost extremity, where the razorback mountains soar out of the sea at an angle of nearly eighty degrees to a height of 915m. En route you're likely to spot grey seals, whales, peregrine falcons and golden eagles.

Western Labrador

Only developed in the last fifty years, **western Labrador**, a vast expanse of low, rolling, forested mountains and tracts of tundra, is punctuated by towns that live to serve the remarkable mining and engineering projects that have sprouted up here. Consequently, unless you have a deep interest in exploring some of the world's largest mines and hydroelectric projects, it's hard to find a reason to come here – although for some the spectacular **rail journey** to Labrador City from Sept-Îles in Québec (see p.380) is reason enough. You can also **drive** here from Québec via **Route 389**, from Baie-Comeau (see p.378) – a route which has services at Manic 5 and Gagnon. The other road into the region is the Trans-Labrador Route (**Route 500**), though this is of poorer quality – 526 kilometres of rough, unpaved road linking Happy Valley-Goose Bay (see p.545) to **Labrador City-Wabush** via **Churchill Falls**. This is one of the least frequented stretches of major road in eastern Canada and before driving it you should make enquires about its current condition at the Department of Works Services and Transportation. On average it takes at least nine hours to traverse and, as there are no services along the route, you'll need to take all necessary supplies (including fuel) with you.

Churchill Falls

Rising from a spring high on the Labrador plateau, the **Churchill River** plunges 75m into McLean Canyon as **Churchill Falls**, located about 300km west of Happy Valley-Goose Bay. In order to exploit the massive power of this cascade, 6700 square kilometres – an area three and a half times the size of Lake Ontario – was dammed for the Churchill Falls hydroelectric development, a project conceived by the then premier, Joe Smallwood, in 1952 to boost Newfoundland's economy. Wrangling with possible US backers, and then with the Québec government, delayed its construction until 1967, when a workforce of thirty thousand finally began the largest civil engineering project in North America. The Churchill Falls Hydro-Electricity Facility (Mon–Fri 8am–noon & 1–4.30pm, 3-hour tours thrice daily; ☎709/925-3335; free but book in advance) now offers two-and-a-half-hour **tours** of the resulting 550 megawatt plant which provides enough power for most of New England. The town of **CHURCHILL FALLS** – simply an outgrowth of the power plant – contains two **accommodation** options: the *Black Spruce Lodge*, 23 Cabot St (☎709/925-3233; ❸) which has a common area and kitchen, and the smarter *Churchill Falls Inn* (☎709/925-3211 or 1-800/229-3269; ❹–❺), which also serves **food**.

Labrador City-Wabush

Some 260km west of Churchill Falls it's a shock to come across **LABRADOR CITY** and neighbouring **WABUSH**, two planned mining communities of wide streets and a couple of malls in the middle of nowhere. Both were established in the 1950s and, with a population of 12,000, make up the largest concentration of people in Labrador. Half of Canada's iron ore output is produced here from vast open pit mines that are serviced by oversized 20m-long dump trucks adorned with giant 3m tires. The mines can be toured by appointment with Labrador West Tourism (Ⓣ709/944-7631, Ⓦwww.exploringlabrador.com).

Given the relatively sizeable population, a few recreation facilities have been developed in the vicinity of the towns. **Duley Lake Park** (late June to early Sept; Ⓣ709/282-3660; $4), 10km from town, has excellent facilities for swimming and boating, while the **Menihek Interpretive Trails** make an appealing place to hike in summer and snowshoe or cross-country ski in winter, with 34km of trails groomed for all ability levels by the Menihek Nordic Ski Club (Nov–April; Ⓣ709/944-5842, Ⓦwww.crrstv.net/menihek). There's more skiing, though of the downhill variety, at **Smokey Mountain** in the Wapusakatto Mountains 5km from town. The ski hill offers nineteen runs with a 300m vertical drop and some night-skiing too. But the most popular local winter activity is **snowmobiling**, which can conveniently be done from the Northern Lights Lodge (Ⓣ709/944-7475, Ⓦwww.northernlightsfishhunt.com), which lies beside a network of trails and offers rentals, guided tours and custom packages.

The helpful Destination Labrador **information office**, 118 Humphrey Rd (Ⓣ1-800/563-6353), can point you in the right direction for all of these attractions and provides a full list of in-town **accommodation**. For a cheap room, try the *Tamarack B&B*, 852 Tamarack Drive (Ⓣ709/944-6002; ②), where three functional rooms share a bathroom, or head to the *Two Seasons Inn*, Avalon Drive (Ⓣ709/944-2661 or 1-800/670-7667; ④), a good-value, if uninspiring, hotel. To **camp**, head to the Duley Lake Family Park (Ⓣ709/282-3660; $10), with an onsite store and a swimming beach. Alternatively *Grand Hermine Camping* (Ⓣ709/282-5369, Ⓦwww.explorelabrador.com; $12) is 45km from Labrador on the Québec road (Route 389).

Good choices for **eating** are *Jed's Pub* (Ⓣ709/282-5522) on Grenfell Drive, for tasty pub food (and, occasionally caribou) from $8 and the restaurant at the *Two Seasons Inn* for regular Canadian Fare (main meals around $12).

Schefferville

Journey's end for the railway from Sept-Îles is **SCHEFFERVILLE**, 190km north of Labrador City. When the IOC mining operation opened the first Labrador iron-ore mine here in the 1950s they recruited a band of migratory Naskapi as cheap labour, so beginning a particularly woeful episode in the history of Canada's native peoples. In 1978, the natives signed an agreement, finally giving them compensation for their lost land and exclusive hunting and fishing rights, but by that time the majority were so debilitated by alcohol that a return to their former existence was impossible. When the mine closed in the late 1980s, the Naskapi were left to fend for themselves, while the white workers moved on to employment in other mines. Schefferville is now a run-down, blackfly-ridden reserve, where houses can be bought for less than $10. Lying just over the border in Québec, the town is essentially a dead-end spot and only worth visiting as the terminus of the spectacular train journey; there's no vehicular road access. The only **accommodation** is the *Hotel-Motel Royal*, 182 Rue Montagnais (Ⓣ709/585-2605; ④).

Travel details

Trains

Labrador City to: Sept-Îles (1 weekly; 8hr).
Schefferville to: Sept-Îles (1 weekly; 11hr).

Buses

St John's to: Channel-Port aux Basques (1 daily; 14hr); Clarenville (1 daily; 2hr 30min); Corner Brook (1 daily; 10hr 15min); Deer Lake (1 daily; 9hr); Grand Falls (1 daily; 6hr 30min); Lewisporte (1 daily; 5hr 40min).
For further details, contact **DRL Coachlines** (☎709/263-2171 or 1-888/263-1854; Ⓦwww.drlgroup.com).

Ferries

North Sydney, Nova Scotia to: Channel-Port aux Basques (2–4 daily; 5-6hr, 6-8hr at night).
North Sydney, Nova Scotia to: Argentia (late June to early Sept 3 weekly, mid-June & late Sept 1 weekly; 14–15hr).
For further details, contact **Marine Atlantic** (☎1-800/341-7981, Ⓦwww.marine-atlantic.ca).
Cartwright to: Happy Valley-Goose Bay (4–6 weekly; 12hr); Nain (1 weekly; 84hr).
St Barbe to: Blanc-Sablon (mid-April to mid-Jan 1–3 daily; 1hr 30min).
For further details, contact **Labrador Marine** (☎709/724-9173 or 1-866/535-2567, Ⓦwww.labradormarine.com).
Fortune to: St-Pierre (May to mid-Oct 3 weekly to 1 daily; 1hr 30min).
For further details, contact **SPM Express** (Newfoundland ☎709/832-0429 or 1-800/563-2006; St-Pierre ☎0508/41 53 93, Ⓦwww.spmexpress.net)
There are sixteen **other ferry routes** connecting the remoter outports of both Labrador and Newfoundland; timetables and prices are given online at Ⓦwww.gov.nl.ca/ferryservices.

National parks

Landscape and wilderness are Canada's defining features. While Toronto, Montréal and Vancouver are compelling urban spaces, the extent and variety of the country's great outdoors, its rich fauna and flora, the countless opportunities for outdoor activities and the sublime rivers, lakes, coasts and mountains of its national and provincial parks are likely to provide the most abiding memories of any Canadian visit.

▼ Ellesmere Island National Park, Nunavut

Landscapes

Canada's national parks embrace virtually every possible landscape and natural habitat, from the near-desert badlands of Saskatchewan's **Grasslands National Park** and the temperate rainforests of British Columbia's **Gwaii Haanas** to the desolate, often icy beauty that defines the arctic wilderness of the Northwest Territories' **Aulavik National Park**, or the tundra of Nunavut's **Ukkusiksalik**, the country's newest national park.

Between these extremes are parks that protect Canada's classic landscapes, the mountain and forests ensembles of popular imagination. First and foremost of these are the Big Four of the Rockies in the west, **Banff**, **Jasper**, **Yoho** and **Kootenay**, closely followed by **Kluane National Park** in Yukon, home to the country's highest and most inaccessible peaks, or less well-known **Prince Albert National Park**, which protects part of the great coniferous forests of the north.

Across the country, in the complex medley of landscapes making up Québec, Ontario and the Maritimes, the story is different. Here variety is the watchword, with parks such as Ottawa's **Pukaskwa**, which protects part of the rugged landscapes typical of the **Canadian Shield**, an ancient upland of 500-million-year-old granites and gneiss that extends over 43 percent of the country.

Then there is **Terra Nova**, which protects the almost equally ancient remnants of Newfoundland's share of the Appalachian Mountains, or smaller parks such as **Kouchibouguac** in New Brunswick, which embraces an intimate blend of Acadian maritime and inland habitats.

Easy to forget in a country dominated by mountain and forest (50 percent of Canada is forest) are the coastal parks. In the west, the **Pacific Rim National Park** features Long Beach, one of the continent's greatest stretches of wild shoreline, while in the east the parks of Prince Edward Island, Forillon, the Cape Breton Highlands and Mingan Archipelago embrace a stunning collection of cliffs, bluffs, beaches, rockpools, coves, inlets, headlands, briny fishing villages and other maritime landscapes.

▼ Yoho National Park

Outdoor activities

▲ Kayaking at sunset

Where there are national and provincial parks, there is a wealth of **outdoor activities**. Which is to say that pretty much anywhere in the country you're never far from the chance to hike, ride, camp or mountain-bike. You may have to plan a little more carefully, or travel a little farther, if you want to ski or snowboard, or indulge in more extreme winter sports such as ice-climbing, dog-sledding or snow-shoeing, but even then there are numerous parks, and vast swathes of the country, where you can indulge.

Fishing, canoeing, kayaking, surfing and other watery activities are also widely available – after all, its coastal parks aside, Canada's interior has 15 percent of the world's fresh water, while Ontario alone has an estimated 250,000 lakes and 35,000km of waterways, 25,000km of which have been documented as canoe routes.

Complementing the varied terrain and spectacular scenery is the invariably excellent infrastructure of the country's parks system. In any park you can be sure you'll be able to turn up, ask some questions, rent some gear and get going.

The best national parks to...

Admire aboriginal culture Gwaii Haanas, in the Haida Gwaii (Queen Charlotte Islands), protects ancient Haida villages and sacred sights in a sublime rainforest setting.

Brave the world's highest tides Fundy National Park embraces the best of Canada's wild Atlantic coast.

Canoe Take to the rivers and winding lakes of the Le Mauricie National Park in Québec, ideal for canoe and portage activities.

Drive Jasper's Icefields Parkway is one of the world's ultimate mountain drives, but the coastal scenery of the Cabot Trail in the Cape Breton Highlands provides a fine maritime alternative.

Hike You're spoiled for choice, but Banff, with 1500km of trails and the cream of the Rockies scenery, takes some beating.

Island-hop Jump around the Gulf Islands off Vancouver Island or mosey among the islets of Québec's Mingan Archipelago, both national park reserves.

Raft Jasper National Park has its fans, but for wild white-water thrills it has to be Nahanni in the Northwest Territories.

Soak in a hot spring Kootenay National Park in the Rockies was founded in part to protect the natural hot pools of Radium Hot Springs.

Watch sunsets and storms Head for Long Beach in Vancouver's Pacific Rim National Park and take shelter in the *Wickaninnish Inn* or settle back on a headland above the crashing surf.

Flora and fauna

▼ Grizzly bear in the Yukon

No one's done the sums, but you can be sure there are an awful lot more animals in Canadian national parks than there are people. The variety of **flora and fauna** is as great as the variety of landscapes the parks protect – our "Natural Environment" section on pp.1093–1101 has more specific detail on the vast range of Canada's wildlife – but some of the best parks for sightings are those that were wholly, or in part, designated to help protect specific plants or animals. Among these are Wood Buffalo National Park in the Northwest Territories (NWT), designed to conserve the eponymous **buffalos** (bison), or Tuktut Nogait, also in the NWT, which protects the calving grounds of the Bluenose **caribou** herds. But almost any park guarantees a sighting of some sort, whether it's a swathe of spring **wild flowers** or **black bear** disappearing into the trees at the side of the highway in Banff National Park.

Top ten attractions of Canada's natural world

Ancient cedars The rainforest of British Columbia's Mount Revelstoke National Park has cedars that are over 1000 years old.

Bears You don't want to encounter them face to face, but you'll often catch sight of black bears near the highway in Banff, Jasper or Glacier national parks.

Buffalos Make for Alberta and the Northwest Territories' Wood Buffalo park – but be prepared: it's the size of Switzerland.

Dall's sheep No need to trek to the high peaks to see these guys: they'll probably be grazing happily near the highway in the Yukon's Kluane National Park.

▼ Dall's sheep

Elk Rangers try to discourage them, but elk still amble around the golf course and streets of downtown Banff in Banff National Park.

Muskox These majestic, lumbering beasts can be seen in Ukkusiksalik, along with caribou and polar bears.

Polar bears Head for Wapusk in Manitoba, one of the world's largest polar bear denning areas.

Sea otters and sea lions Both can be seen enjoying the seas off British Columbia's Pacific Rim National Park.

Whales Plenty swim in the waters of Pacific Rim National Park in the right season and as well off the coastal parks of Québec and the Maritime Provinces.

Wild flowers Spring brings a carpet of flowers to most parks, especially high alpine meadows, but visit the Auyuittuq or Sirmilik national parks in Nunavut for the remarkable June or July flowering of the otherwise barren tundra.

Manitoba and Saskatchewan

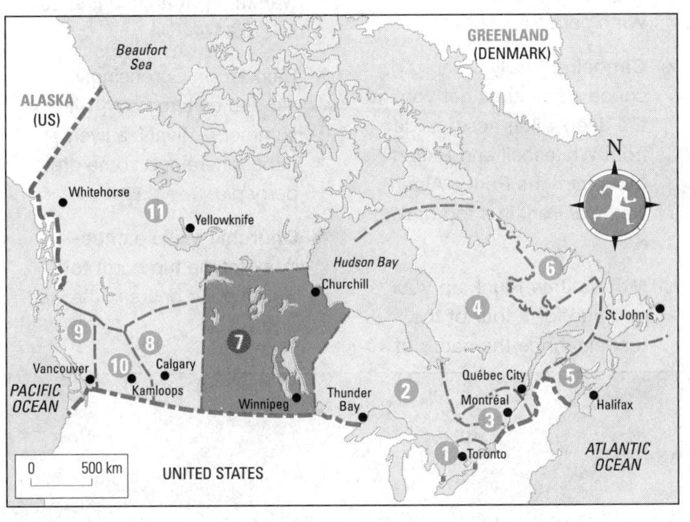

7 MANITOBA AND SASKATCHEWAN

CHAPTER 7 Highlights

* **Winnipeg** The region's biggest city, with an array of museums and some excellent restaurants. See p.560
* **Small-town rodeos** Alberta's Calgary Stampede aside, there are hundreds of rodeos across the prairies with a more authentic vibe – the biggest is at Morris, near Winnipeg. See p.581
* **Canoeing** Easily organized canoe adventures get you into the deep wilderness; aside from Whiteshell and Riding Mountain, the Prince Albert National Park is a top draw. See p.582
* **Moose Jaw** Pluck up your courage for a tour of the tunnels, once the haunt of Chicago gangsters. See p.599
* **Grasslands** Strike out off the beaten track to this beautiful but under-visited national park. See p.602
* **Little Manitou Lake** Experience near-weightlessness while floating in the salty lake waters, or at adjacent spas. See p.616
* **Saskatoon** Surprisingly hip and cultured city, with summer festivals, a lively atmosphere and some great berry pie. See p.616
* **Churchill** Make a once-in-a-lifetime trip north to watch polar bears in the wild. See p.637

△ A polar bear at Cape Churchill

7

Manitoba and Saskatchewan

The provinces of **Manitoba** and **Saskatchewan** (and eastern Alberta) together form a vast tract bounded by the Ontario border to the east and the Rocky Mountains to the west. Although commonly known as "**the prairies**", this area in fact has flat treeless plains only in its southernmost part, and even then they are broken up by the occasional river valley and range of low-lying hills, which gradually raise the elevation from sea level at Hudson Bay to nearly 1200m near the Rockies. Furthermore, the plains themselves are divided into two broad geographical areas: the semi-arid short **grasslands** that border the United States in Alberta and Saskatchewan, and the **wheat-growing belt**, a crescent-shaped expanse to the north. In turn, this wheat belt borders the low hills, mixed farms and sporadic forests of the **aspen parkland**, a transitional zone between the plains and the **boreal forest**, whose trees, rocky outcrops, rivers and myriad lakes cover well over half of the entire central region, stretching to the Northwest Territories and as far as the treeless **tundra** beside Hudson Bay.

The prairie provinces are certainly not one of Canada's glamour areas, the main cities caricatured as dull, the scenery as monotonous. To some extent, these prejudices stem from the route of the Trans-Canada Highway, which treks through a desultory prairie landscape, avoiding nearly everything of interest: many Canadians prefer to do the long and boring drive to Calgary at night when, so it's said, the views are better. Yet, in truth, this image is grossly unfair. Busy **Winnipeg** – the largest city in central Canada – is well worth a visit for its museums, restaurants and nightlife. And many of Manitoba's most significant

Information and time zones

Travel Manitoba is on ⓣ1-800/665-0040, ⓦwww.travelmanitoba.com. **Tourism Saskatchewan** is on ⓣ1-877/237-2273, ⓦwww.sasktourism.com.

Manitoba and Saskatchewan are both on **Central time**. In winter, both provinces run one hour behind Ontario and one hour ahead of Alberta. However, in summer, Manitoba adopts daylight saving but Saskatchewan does not: this means that between April and October Saskatchewan runs on the same time as Alberta and is one hour behind Manitoba.

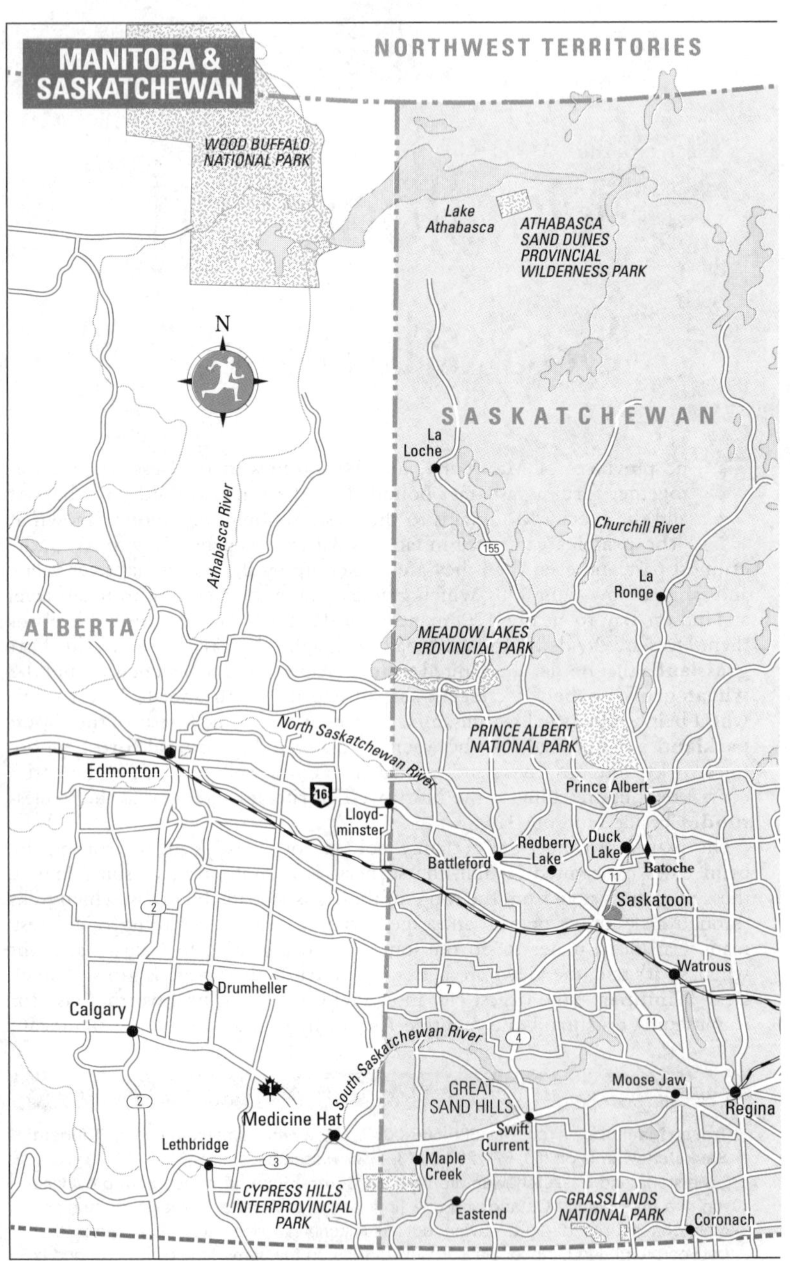
MANITOBA & SASKATCHEWAN
NORTHWEST TERRITORIES
WOOD BUFFALO NATIONAL PARK
Lake Athabasca
ATHABASCA SAND DUNES PROVINCIAL WILDERNESS PARK
N
SASKATCHEWAN
La Loche
Athabasca River
Churchill River
155
La Ronge
ALBERTA
MEADOW LAKES PROVINCIAL PARK
North Saskatchewan River
PRINCE ALBERT NATIONAL PARK
Edmonton
16
Lloydminster
Prince Albert
Redberry Lake
Duck Lake
Battleford
Batoche
11
Saskatoon
2
Watrous
Drumheller
7
Calgary
South Saskatchewan River
4
11
GREAT SAND HILLS
Moose Jaw
Regina
2
Medicine Hat
Swift Current
Lethbridge
3
Maple Creek
CYPRESS HILLS INTERPROVINCIAL PARK
Eastend
GRASSLANDS NATIONAL PARK
Coronach

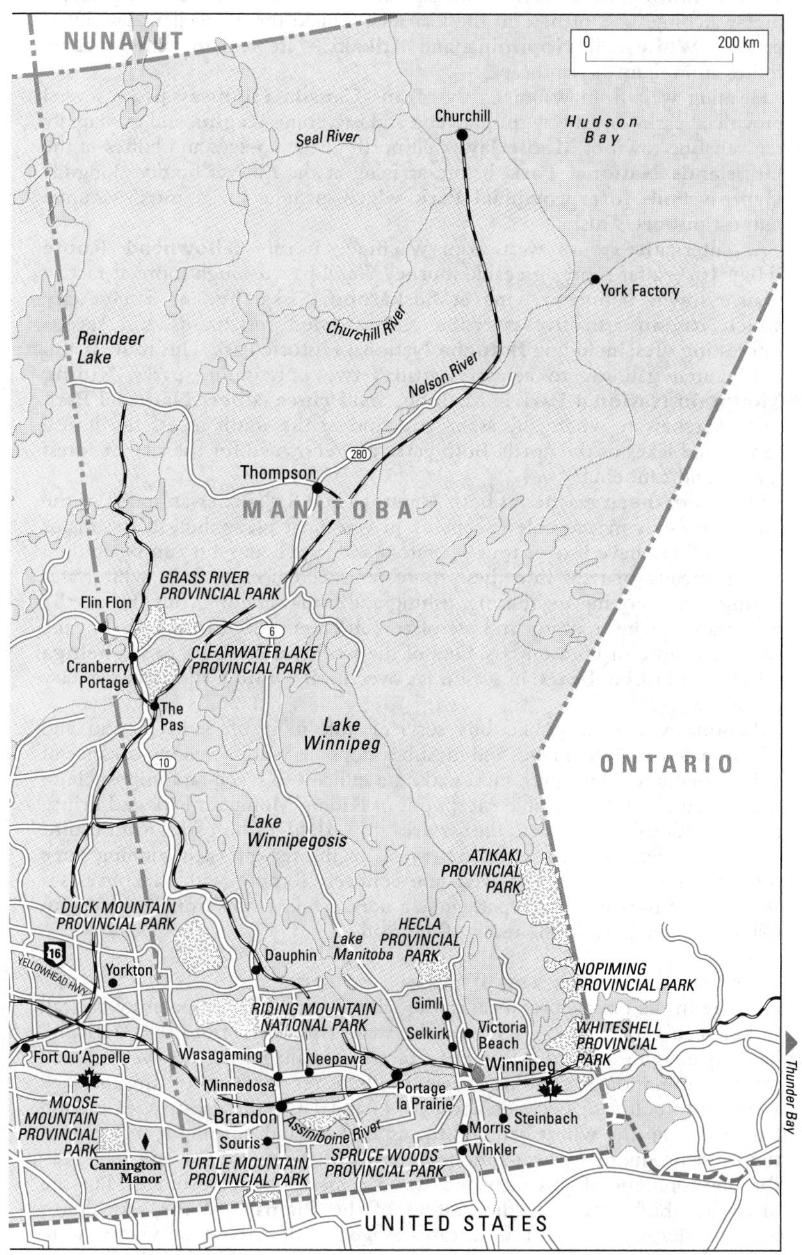
NUNAVUT
0
200 km
Churchill
Hudson Bay
Seal River
York Factory
Churchill River
Reindeer Lake
Nelson River
280
Thompson
MANITOBA
GRASS RIVER PROVINCIAL PARK
Flin Flon
6
CLEARWATER LAKE PROVINCIAL PARK
Cranberry Portage
The Pas
Lake Winnipeg
10
ONTARIO
Lake Winnipegosis
ATIKAKI PROVINCIAL PARK
DUCK MOUNTAIN PROVINCIAL PARK
HECLA PROVINCIAL PARK
16
YELLOWHEAD HWY
Dauphin
Lake Manitoba
Yorkton
NOPIMING PROVINCIAL PARK
RIDING MOUNTAIN NATIONAL PARK
Gimli
Victoria Beach
Selkirk
WHITESHELL PROVINCIAL PARK
Fort Qu'Appelle
Wasagaming
Neepawa
Winnipeg
Thunder Bay
1
Minnedosa
Portage la Prairie
1
MOOSE MOUNTAIN PROVINCIAL PARK
Brandon
Assiniboine River
Steinbach
Morris
Souris
Winkler
Cannington Manor
TURTLE MOUNTAIN PROVINCIAL PARK
SPRUCE WOODS PROVINCIAL PARK
UNITED STATES

attractions lie within easy striking distance, along the **Red River Corridor** to **Lake Winnipeg**, whose lakeside marshes and forests of Hecla Park are great for bird-watching. East of here in the Canadian Shield three excellent provincial parks – **Whiteshell**, **Nopiming** and **Atikaki** – are replete with canoeing routes amid dramatic landscapes.

Heading west from Winnipeg the **Trans-Canada Highway** passes several provincial parks on its way to sprawling and easygoing **Regina** and the rapidly rejuvenating town of **Moose Jaw**, well north of the coulees and buttes of the **Grasslands National Park**, before arriving at the Alberta border alongside **Cypress Hills Interprovincial Park**, which includes the restored Mountie outpost of **Fort Walsh**.

An alternative route west from Winnipeg is the **Yellowhead Route** (Hwy 16) – a far more agreeable journey. You'll pass through more attractive prairie towns before arriving at **Saskatoon**, Saskatchewan's largest city, which has an attractive riverside setting, good restaurants and several interesting sites, including **Batoche** National Historic Park. This route is also the natural gateway to central Canada's two outstanding parks, **Riding Mountain National Park** in Manitoba and **Prince Albert National Park** in Saskatchewan, where the aspen parkland of the south meets the boreal forests and lakes of the north. Both parks are renowned for their lakes, forest hiking and canoeing.

In the **northern** reaches of both Manitoba and Saskatchewan much of the boreal forest is inaccessible except by private float plane, but all the major tourist offices have lists of tour operators and suppliers who run or equip a whole variety of trips into these more remote regions – from whitewater rafting and canoeing to hunting, fishing and bird-watching. But the north's big draw is the remote and desolate settlement of **Churchill**, on the southern shore of Hudson Bay. One of the world's best places to see **beluga whales** and **polar bears**, in season it's overrun by visitors and documentary film crews.

Reasonably regular public **bus** services link most of Saskatchewan and Manitoba's main settlements, and most bus stops are within walking distance of at least one hotel. However, most parks are difficult to reach and impossible to tour by bus, with the notable exceptions of Riding Mountain Park and Prince Albert National Park, where the services stops right at the parks' main centre. VIA Rail operates just two **train** services in the region, each running three times weekly: the main east–west line connects Toronto with Vancouver via Winnipeg, Saskatoon and Jasper, while a northern line runs from Winnipeg to Churchill, well beyond the reach of the road.

A brief history of the prairie provinces

If you're in the prairie provinces in the winter, when the temperature can fall to between -30°C and -40°C, and the wind rips down from the Arctic, it's hard to imagine how the European pioneers managed to survive, huddled together in remote log cabins or even sod huts. Yet survive they did, and they went on to cultivate, between about 1895 and 1914, the great swath of land that makes up the wheat belt and the aspen parkland, turning it into one of the most productive wheat-producing areas in the world. By any standards, the development of this farmland was a remarkable achievement, but the price was high: the nomadic culture of the **Plains Indians** was almost entirely destroyed and the disease-ravaged, half-starved survivors were dumped in a string of meagre reservations. Similarly, the **Métis** – descendants of white fur traders and native women – who for more than two centuries

Provincial parks

Manitoba and to a lesser extent Saskatchewan are distinguished principally by their **parks**: thousands of acres of wilderness, lake, river and forest that boast wonderful scenery, great hikes and hundreds of kilometres of canoe routes.

Entry to any of **Manitoba's** provincial parks is $6 per car (good for 3 consecutive days); entry by foot or bike is free. Park campsites ($7–14) can be reserved from April to September by calling the Parks Reservation Service (Ⓣ204/948-3333 or 1-888/482-2267). There is a charge of $7.75 for each reservation. For detailed information and to obtain complimentary **maps** contact or visit Manitoba Conservation, 200 Saulteaux Crescent in Winnipeg (Mon–Fri 8am–4.30pm; Ⓣ204/945-6784 or 1-800/214-6497, Ⓦwww.manitobaparks.com). They are the people to turn to for specialist advice on anything from weather conditions to outfitters and guides. Those planning a backcountry hike, wilderness canoeing, rafting or kayaking can get topographic, angling and illustrated maps and aerial photographs of thirteen major canoe routes from Manitoba Conservation, Land Information Centre, 1007 Century St in Winnipeg (Ⓣ204/945-6666 or 1-877/627-7226, Ⓦwww.canadamapsales.com).

Entry to any of **Saskatchewan's** provincial parks is $7 for a day, $17 for three days, $25 weekly, $50 annual. Information is on Ⓣ306/953-3751 in Regina or 1-800/205-7070, Ⓦwww.saskparks.net. Between mid-May and August you can reserve a campsite ($11–24, plus $3 per night campfire fee) in advance at most of the parks for a $5 fee – see individual sections for phone numbers. A good walking guide is *Saskatchewan Trails – A Guide to Nature Walks and Easy Hikes* by Robin and Arlene Karpan, which outlines over a hundred hikes in the province.

had acted as intermediaries between the two cultures, found themselves overwhelmed, their desperate attempts to maintain their independence leading to a brace of futile rebellions under the leadership of Louis Riel in 1869–70 and 1885 (see box, p.624).

With the Métis and the Indians out of the way, thousands of European immigrants concentrated on their wheat yields, but they were the victims of a one-crop economy, their prosperity dependent on the market price of grain and the freight charges imposed by the railroad. Throughout the twentieth century, the region's farmers experienced alarming changes in their fortunes as bust alternated with boom, and this situation continues to dominate the prairie economies. Saskatchewan in particular remains as dependent on agriculture as it was when the province was established in 1905, today producing 45 percent of Canada's grain, particularly wheat. Saskatchewan's farmers often struggle to make ends meet when international prices fall, and consequently they have formed various **Wheat Pools**, which attempt to control freight charges and sell the grain at the best possible time. The political spin-off has been the evolution of a strong socialist tradition, built on the farmers' mistrust of the market. For many years Saskatchewan was a stronghold of the **Cooperative Commonwealth Federation** (**CCF**), the forerunner of the New Democratic Party (NDP), and in 1944 the CCF formed the country's first leftist provincial government, pushing through bills to set up state-run medical and social security schemes.

Winnipeg

With 706,900 inhabitants, **WINNIPEG** accounts for two-thirds of Manitoba's population, and lies at Canada's geographic centre, sandwiched between the US frontier to the south and the infertile Canadian Shield to the north and east. The city has been the gateway to the prairies since 1873, and became the transit point for much of the country's transcontinental traffic when the railroad arrived twelve years later. From the very beginning, Winnipeg was described as the city where "the West began", and its polyglot population, drawn from almost every country in Europe, was attracted by the promise of the fertile soils to the west. But this was no classless pioneer town: as early as the 1880s the city had developed a clear pattern of residential segregation, with leafy prosperous suburbs to the south along the **Assiniboine River**, and "Shanty Town" to the north. The long-term effects of this division have proved hard to erase, and today the dispossessed still gather round the cheap dorms just to the north of the business district, a sad rather than dangerous corner near the main intersection at Portage Ave and Main St. Winnipeg's skid row is only a tiny part of the downtown area, but its reputation has hampered recent attempts to reinvigorate the city centre as a whole: successive administrations have refurbished warehouses and built walkways along the **Red River** and Assiniboine River, but the new downtown apartment blocks remain hard to sell, and most people stick resolutely to the suburbs.

That apart, Winnipeg makes for an enjoyable stopover, and all of the main attractions are within easy walking distance of each other. The **Manitoba Museum of Man and Nature** has excellent displays on the history of the province and its various geographic areas; the **Exchange District**, recently declared a National Historic Site, features some good examples of Canada's early twentieth-century architecture; the Winnipeg **Art Gallery** has the world's largest collection of Inuit art; and, just across the Red River, the suburb of **St Boniface** has a delightful museum situated in the house and chapel of the Grey Nuns, who arrived here by canoe from Montréal in 1844. Winnipeg is also noted for the excellence and diversity of its restaurants, while its flourishing performing-arts scene features everything from ballet and classical music through to Country & Western and jazz.

The city also makes a useful base for exploring the region's immediate attractions (see p.575), the most popular of which – chiefly **Lower Fort Garry** – are on the banks of the Red River as it twists its way north to **Lake Winnipeg**, 60km away. On the lake itself, **Grand Beach Park** has the province's finest stretches of sandy beach, just two hours' drive from the city centre.

A brief history of Winnipeg

Named after the **Cree** word for murky water ("win-nipuy"), Winnipeg owes much of its history to the Red and Assiniboine rivers, which meet just south of today's city centre at the confluence called **The Forks**. The first European to reach the area was **Pierre Gaultier**, Sieur de la Vérendrye, an enterprising explorer who founded Fort Rouge near the convergence of the two rivers in 1738. This settlement was part of a chain of fur-trading posts he built to extend French influence into the west. Prospering from good connections north along the Red River to Lake Winnipeg and Hudson Bay, and west along the Assiniboine across the plains, the fort became one of the region's most important outposts within twenty years.

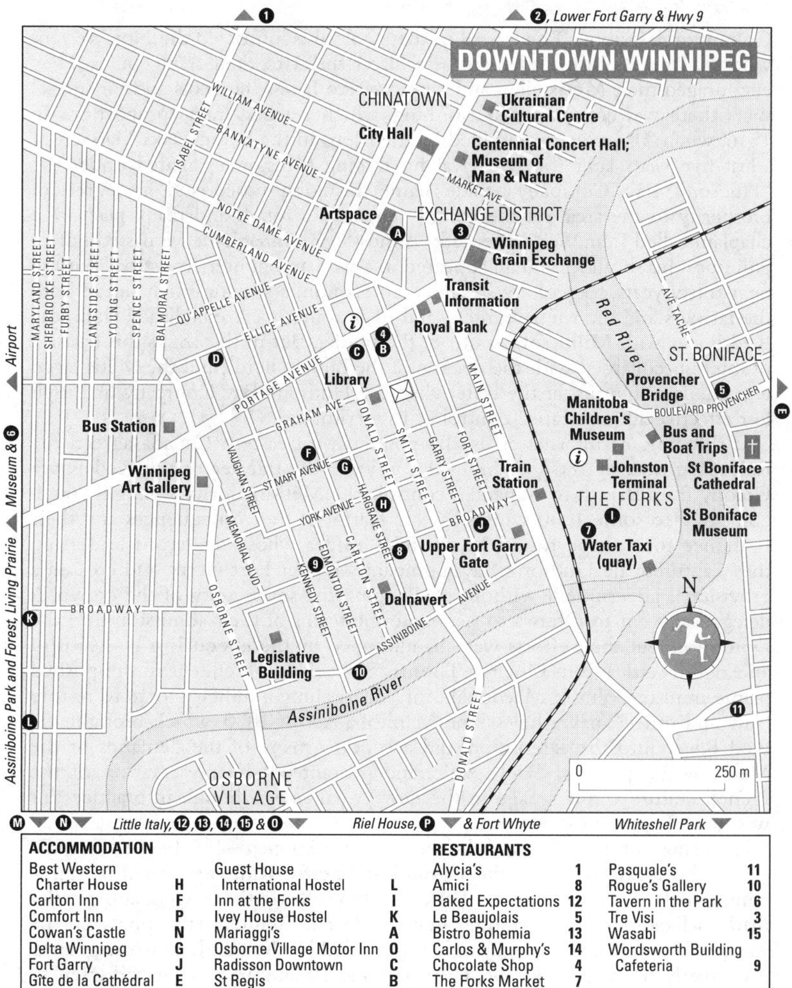

After the defeat of New France in 1763, local trading activity was absorbed by the Montréal-based **North West Company**, which came to dominate the fur trade at the expense of its rival, the Hudson's Bay Company. The latter continued to operate from fortified coastal factories staffed by British personnel, expecting their Indian trading partners to bring their pelts to them – unlike their rivals, who were prepared to live and travel among the natives. This inflexible policy looked like the ruination of the company until it was rescued by Thomas Douglas, the **Earl of Selkirk**, who bought a controlling interest in 1809.

In the three years Lord Selkirk took to turn the business round, he resettled many of his own impoverished Scottish crofters around The Forks, buying from his own company a huge tract of farmland, which he named the Red River

Colony, or Assiniboia. The arrival of these colonists infuriated the Nor'Westers, who saw the Scottish settlement as a direct threat to their trade routes. They encouraged their **Métis** allies and employees to harass the Scots and for several years there was continuous skirmishing, which reached tragic proportions in 1816, when 21 settlers were killed by the Métis in the Seven Oaks Massacre.

Just five years later the two rival fur-trading firms amalgamated under the "Hudson's Bay Company" trade name, bringing peace and a degree of prosperity to the area. Yet the colony remained a rough-and-ready place, as a chaplain called John West lamented: "Almost every inhabitant we passed bore a gun upon his shoulder and all appeared in a wild and hunter-like state." For the next thirty years, the colony sustained an economic structure that suited both the farmers and the Métis hunters, and trade routes were established along the Red River with Minnesota, south of the border. But in the 1860s this balance of interests collapsed with the decline of the buffalo herds, and the Métis faced extreme hardship just at the time when the Hudson's Bay Company had itself lost effective administrative control of its territories.

At this time of internal crisis, the politicians of eastern Canada agreed the **federal union** of 1867, opening the way for the transfer of the Red River Colony from British to Canadian control. The Métis majority – roughly 6000 compared to some 1000 whites – were fearful of the consequences and their resistance took shape round **Louis Riel**, under whose dexterous leadership they captured the Hudson's Bay Company's Upper Fort Garry and created a provisional government without challenging the sovereignty of the crown. A delegation went to Ottawa to negotiate the terms of their admission into the Dominion, but their efforts were handicapped by the **execution** by Métis of an English settler from Ontario, Thomas Scott. The subsequent furore pushed prime minister John A. Macdonald into dispatching a military force to restore "law and order"; nevertheless, the Manitoba Act of 1870, which brought the Red River into the Dominion, did accede to many of the demands of the Métis, at the price of Riel's exile, and guaranteed the preservation of the French culture and language in the new province – although in practice this was not effectively carried out.

The eclipse of the Métis and the security of Winnipeg – as it became in 1870 – were both assured when the **Canadian Pacific Railway** routed its transcontinental line through The Forks in 1885. With the town's commodity markets handling the expanding grain trade and its industries supplying the vast rural hinterland, its population was swelled by thousands of **immigrants**, particularly from the Ukraine, Germany and Poland; in 1901 it had risen to 42,000. By World War I, Winnipeg had become the third-largest city in Canada and the largest grain-producing centre in North America, and by 1921 the population had reached 192,000. More recently, the development of other prairie cities, such as Regina and Saskatoon, has undermined something of Winnipeg's pre-eminence, but the city is still the economic focus and transport hub of central Canada.

Arrival, information and getting around

Winnipeg **airport** (ⓦ www.waa.ca) is some 7km west of the city centre. There's a tourist **information** desk inside the airport concourse, which has a good range of leaflets on the city and its principal attractions along with accommodation listings. Close by, there's a complimentary hotel-booking phone and display board. From outside the terminal building, Winnipeg Transit bus #15 (daily every 20–30min 6.15am–12.45am; $1.80) runs downtown, dropping passengers at or near most of the larger hotels; buy tickets from the driver. Taxis charge around $20. The Mall Centre **bus station**, for Greyhound and other long-distance buses, is on the west side of the downtown area at Portage Avenue and Memorial Boulevard (daily 6.30am–midnight; ⓣ204/783-8857). Union Station, the city's **train station**, is on Main Street, just south of Portage, and has connecting VIA Rail (ⓣ1-888/842-7245, ⓦwww.viarail.ca) trains to Churchill, Toronto and Saskatoon for Vancouver.

Tourism Winnipeg has an information office at 279 Portage Ave (Mon–Fri 8.30am–4.30pm; ⓣ204/943-1970 or 1-800/665-0204, ⓦwww.destinationwinnipeg.ca), as well as at the airport. A comprehensive range of leaflets on both the city and province is also available at the **Explore Manitoba** Centre (daily 10am–6pm; ⓣ204/945-3777 or 1-800/665-0040, ⓦwww.travelmanitoba.com), adjacent to the Johnston Terminal at the Forks, where travel counsellors can also help plan your itinerary. All outlets provide free city maps, a Winnipeg Transit bus plan, accommodation listings, a restaurant guide, an historic and architectural guide to the downtown area and free listings of activities and attractions.

Although you can stroll across the downtown core in twenty minutes, the suburbs and more outlying attractions are easy to reach by bus. **Winnipeg Transit** (ⓣ204/986-5700, ⓦwww.winnipegtransit.com) has an excellent range of citywide services (flat fare $1.80 per journey), with tickets and transfers for trips involving more than one bus available from the driver (exact fare only). For details of bike rental, car rental and taxis, see "Listings", p.575.

Accommodation

Most of Winnipeg's **hotels** are within walking distance of the bus and train stations, and there's rarely any difficulty in finding somewhere to stay. The modern hotels are standard-issue skyscrapers that concentrate on the business clientele; some offer weekend discounts and up to twenty percent reductions if you stay for three or four nights. At a lower budget, avoid the "flophouses", the cheap dorms calling themselves "hotels" on Main Street, just north of Portage Avenue. Breakfast is extra almost everywhere. The major approach roads are dotted with **motels** (from ❶ up to ❹), of which the largest concentrations are along the Pembina Highway, which runs south from the city centre as Donald Street and Route 42, and along Portage, which runs west forming part of the Trans-Canada Hwy (Route 1).

Tourism Winnipeg (see above) will help arrange hotel and B&B accommodation and has details of some thirty **B&B** addresses (mostly ❷), with breakfasts that vary from frugal continental to a complete meal. Most of these are marketed by Bed and Breakfast of Manitoba (ⓦwww.bedandbreakfast.mb.ca): a good place to look for B&Bs throughout the province. The **hostels** are within easy walking distance of the bus station.

Hotels and motels

Best Western Charter House 330 York Ave at Hargrave St ⓣ204/942-0101 or 1-800/782-0175, ⓦwww.bwcharterhouse.com. A good location in the heart of downtown, one block from the Convention Centre – reasonable rates make up for the absence of character. ❸

Carlton Inn 220 Carlton St ⓣ204/942-0881 or 1-877/717-2885, ⓦwww.carltoninn.mb.ca. One of the more agreeable budget hotels, centrally located opposite the city's Convention Centre, with motel-style rooms, restaurant and pool. ❸

Comfort Inn 3109 Pembina Hwy ⓣ204/269-7390 or 1-800/228-5150. One of a clutch of no-frills motels around the junction of the TransCanada and Pembina hwys 11km south of downtown. Restaurant and free local calls. ❹

Delta 350 St Mary Ave at Hargrave St ⓣ204/944-7243 or 1-800/268-1133, ⓦwww.deltahotels.com. Stay in tasteful, opulent rooms adjoining the Convention Centre, with restaurants and pools. ❹

Fort Garry 222 Broadway ⓣ204/942-8251 or 1-800/665-8088, ⓦwww.fortgarryhotel.com. Built in Neo-Gothic style between 1911 and 1914 near the train station and lavishly refurbished, with an elegant, balconied foyer leading to 250 rooms. Rates include a breakfast buffet. ❺

Gordon Downtowner 330 Kennedy St ⓣ204/943-5581. Probably Winnipeg's most comfortable budget hotel, with restaurant and bar and in a central location. ❷

Inn at the Forks 75 Forks Market Rd ⓣ204/942-6555 or 1-877/377-4100, ⓦwww.innforks.com. Self-consciously hip boutique hotel in tremendous central location overlooking the confluence of the Assiniboine and Red rivers. Rooms are decorated with local art and have hi-speed Internet; slick spa and innovative restaurant also on site. ❻

Mariaggi's Theme Suite Hotel 231 McDermot Ave ⓣ204/947-9447, ⓦwww.mariaggis.com. Pay through the nose but reap the rewards of Hawaiian, Mexican, Moroccan or African themed suites or a tropical penthouse. Couples only. ❼

Osborne Village Motor Inn 160 Osborne St ⓣ204/452-9824, ⓦwww.osbornevillage.com. Basic but decent choice in the heart of lively Osborne Village. Bands often play downstairs and the rooms (none are non-smoking) are not soundproofed. ❶

Radisson Hotel Winnipeg Downtown 288 Portage Ave at Smith St ⓣ204/956-0410 or 1-800/333-3333, ⓦwww.radissonhotel.com. One of the city's largest and most recently renovated hotels, with fine views from the top floors, as well as a gym, saunas, whirlpool, swimming pool, plus baby-sitting services. Offers big discounts at weekends. ❹

St Regis 285 Smith St ⓣ204/942-0171 or 1-800/663-7344, ⓦwww.stregishotel.net. An historic hotel (dating from around 1900) in the downtown area. Tastefully furnished with dining room and coffee shop. The honeymoon suites have hot tubs. Under-18s stay free. ❷

B&Bs

Bob & Margaret's 950 Palmerston Ave ⓣ204/774-0767, ⓔbm950@mts.net. A fifteen-minute ride on bus #10 from downtown, this riverside B&B has one bedroom suite only, with TV room and private bathroom. Bikes and canoes can be rented. ❷

Cowan's Castle 39 Eastgate ⓣ204/786-4848, ⓦwww.cowanscastle.tripod.com. A 1907 four-bed heritage home on the Assiniboine River, twenty minutes' walk to downtown. Serves delicious home-cooked breakfasts. ❷

Gîte de la Cathédrale 581 rue Langevin, St Boniface ⓣ204/233-7792. Run by French Manitobans, this B&B in the heart of St Boniface offers Québecois breakfasts of pancakes and maple syrup, omelettes and French toast, with service in French. Five flowery bedrooms with shared bathroom. ❷

West Gate Manor 71 West Gate ⓣ204/772-9788, ⓦwww.westgatemanor.ca. Pleasant rooms with Victorian period furnishings in Armstrong Point, within walking distance of downtown. ❷

Hostels

Guest House International Hostel 168 Maryland St ⓣ204/772-1272 or 1-800/743-4423, ⓦwww.backpackerswinnipeg.com. A restored Victorian house with six comfortable dorms (beds $20), four private bedrooms (doubles $42) and walls decorated with art by aboriginal children. Bus #29 from the train station, or a nine-block walk from the bus station. The area, though residential, can be a bit dodgy at night. Facilities include a laundry, kitchen, game room and Internet access. Reservations recommended in summer. April–Nov.

Ivey House International Youth Hostel 210 Maryland St at Broadway ⓣ204/772-3022. A friendly, forty-room hostel a short walk from the Guest House International Hostel (above), clean and well run with dorm beds ($20) and some private rooms (sleeping 2–4; doubles $42). There's also a lounge, a big kitchen, sun deck, lockers and bike rental.

Campsites

Conestoga Campground 1341 St Anne's Rd at Perimeter Hwy ⓣ204/257-7363. Located 13km southeast of town beside the TransCanada City ByPass (Hwy 100); most sites have electricity and water. Mid-May to mid-Oct. $14–22.

Welcomestop 588 Trans-Canada Hwy, St François Xavier ⓣ & ⓕ204/864-2201. In a small town on the Assiniboine River, 15km west of Winnipeg, this campsite has 44 unreserved sites, most with water and electricity as well as toilets, showers and a BBQ area. May–Sept. $15–25.

Traveller's RV Resort 870 Murdock Rd ⓣ204/864-2721. Just off the Trans-Canada, some 14km southeast of the centre, with over fifty unreserved sites and facilities that include mini-golf and a swimming pool. May–Sept. $17–25.

The City

The traditional centre of Winnipeg is the intersection of **Portage Avenue** and **Main Street** just north of **The Forks**, close to the Red River at the start of what was once the main Métis cart track (the Portage Trail) west across the prairies to the Hudson's Bay Company posts, and the principal trail north to Lake Winnipeg linking the riverside farm lots and Lower and Upper Fort Garry. While you're here, have a look at the grand Neoclassical **Bank of Montréal** on the southeast side of the intersection, its fussily carved capitals in stark contrast to the sharp, clean lines of its skyscraper neighbours. The intersection is also known as the **windiest** of any town in Canada.

The Exchange District

Just north of the Portage and Main intersection, the **Exchange District National Historic Site** is a rough rectangle of well-preserved old warehouses, former commodity exchanges and commercial buildings. Many of them were converted, from the late 1970s onwards, into art galleries, boutiques, antique shops and restaurants. The district is also one of the city's principal cultural centres, home to such buildings as the Manitoba Museum of Man and Nature, the Ukrainian Cultural and Educational Centre and the artist-run Artspace.

The effective centre of the district is the **Old Market Square** at King and Albert streets and Bannatyne Avenue with its weekend produce market, flea markets and buskers. This part of town was built during Winnipeg's boom, a period of frenzied real-estate speculation and construction that peaked in 1882, but lasted only until the outbreak of World War I. The standard architectural design, used for most of the office buildings and nearly all the warehouses, was simple and symmetrical, the plain brick walls topped off by decorative stone cornices. However, one or two companies financed extravagant variations, notably the Electric Railway Chambers Building at 213 Notre Dame Ave, an imaginative blend of Italian Renaissance and early twentieth-century motifs, its terracotta facade lined with some six thousand electric lights. Possibly the most gracious building in the Exchange District is the former Winnipeg Grain Exchange, opposite the *Lombard Hotel* on Lombard Ave. It was built between 1906 and 1928 and was the largest building of its type in Canada; grain offices still occupy some of the floors. Other imposing buildings are the ten-storey Confederation Life Building, 457 Main St, which has a curved facade of white terracotta, and the massive Royal Bank Building at the corner of Main Street and William Avenue.

The Manitoba Museum

In the heart of the Exchange District, at 190 Rupert Ave, the **Centennial Centre** incorporates the **Manitoba Museum** (late May to early Sept daily 10am–6pm; rest of year Tues–Fri 10am–4pm, Sat & Sun 11am–5pm; Ⓦwww.manitobamuseum.mb.ca; $8), an excellent introduction to the province's geography, history and peoples.

Highlights of the **natural history** galleries include an imposing polar bear diorama, a well-illustrated explanation of the Northern Lights and the evocative Boreal Forest gallery, where you'll find a waterfall, a family of moose, and a diorama of Cree gathering food and painting sacred designs on rocks. There's also a disconcerting section devoted to the more malicious insects of Manitoba – starring the "no-see-um", a deer fly that specializes in burrowing into the nostrils of caribou. The **Grasslands Gallery** has a small display of Assiniboine Indian artefacts, along with a reconstruction of a tepee and a copy of a pioneer

The history of the railway in Canada

Even before Confederation in 1867, Sir John A. Macdonald, Canada's first prime minister, grasped the need to physically link the disparate provinces of the new nation. Each area needed lines of communication to the east and west to counteract the natural tug of the neighbouring parts of the USA to the south. Both the Maritime Provinces and British Columbia joined the Confederation on the condition that **rail** links would be built to transport their goods throughout the land. Railway construction of this scale was a huge undertaking for such a young country and outside finance was the only answer.

From 1855, lines were constructed in eastern Ontario and Québec, culminating in the completion in 1876 of the **Intercolonial Railway**, which linked central Canada with the Maritime Provinces. Progress of the transcontinental line to the Pacific, however, was impeded by the Riel rebellion at the Red River in 1869–70, and in 1871 the Parliamentary Opposition labelled the entire scheme "an act of insane recklessness". Two years later Macdonald's Conservative government fell after implication in scandals involving the use of party funds in railway contracts, and Alexander Mackenzie's subsequent Liberal ministry proceeded so slowly with the railway plans that British Columbia openly spoke of secession if construction was not speeded up. The eventual completion of the **Canadian Pacific Railway** (**CPR**) in 1885 finally made Canada "more than a geographical expression", and by the early twentieth century another coast-to-coast line had been completed.

Passage across the hitherto virtually impenetrable Canadian Shield was now feasible and the full agricultural potential of the prairies to the west could be realized. Between 1896 and 1913 more than one million people arrived by train to settle in the prairies, and wheat production rose from 20 million to more than 200 million bushels a year. Additionally, some of the first major mineral finds in northern Ontario were brought to light during the construction of the railway. The years following World War I were a period of economic consolidation, which culminated in the union of various smaller lines into a nationwide system: the **Canadian National Railways** (**CNR**), a government-controlled organization.

What has been called "the bizarre project" of the **Hudson Bay Railway** stemmed from the prairie farmers' desire to create an outlet for trade with the rest of the world that was not dependent on the bankers back east. A first attempt in 1886 foundered when the promoters ran out of money after the first 65km. After many delays this major engineering feat was accomplished in 1929, just in time for the Great Depression.

The impact of the Depression on Canadian railways was particularly severe, leading to stringent economies and pooling of competing lines. World War II saw a rise in profits, but over the subsequent decades the story has been one of gradual decline, with freight increasingly travelling by road and air, and passenger services pruned almost to extinction on some lines. By 1992, passengers could no longer cross Canada on the CPR, and one of the world's great train rides was gone forever. Grain and minerals are still moved by train, however, and the privately owned CPR is now exclusively a freight line. **VIA Rail**, the passenger branch of CNR, operates virtually all of Canada's passenger services, including the Hudson Bay line in roadless northern Manitoba – probably the only rail route in North America still to exist primarily as a passenger service.

log cabin. There's also an example of the sod houses that the pioneers were forced to build in many parts of the treeless southern plains, and a replica of the odd-looking Red River cart, the Métis's favourite form of land transportation, with massive wheels that could tackle the prairie mud and mire.

The museum's most popular exhibit, moored in a massive display area that reproduces a seventeenth-century River Thames dockside, is an impressive full-scale working replica of **the Nonsuch**, the ship whose fur-collecting voyage to

Hudson Bay in 1668 led to the creation of the Hudson's Bay Company. The new Hudson's Bay Company Gallery comprises more than 10,000 artefacts and documents amassed by the Company and which form a record of its links with Manitoba and its impact on Canada as a whole. A reconstructed trading post showcases goods that were exchanged for furs – everything from beads and guns to canned foods. There's also the last surviving York boat used for river and lake travel from the 1800s to the early 1900s, including relics from the ill-fated Franklin Expedition's search for the Northwest Passage and beautiful artworks and crafts produced by the First Nations, Métis and Inuit, among them carved ivory and immaculate beadwork that can't fail to impress. At the end of the gallery a reconstruction of the Hudson's Bay Company's boardroom in London includes a huge ram's head used, unbelievably, as a snuff holder and passed around at dinner parties. The last section of the museum is the **Urban Gallery**, which re-creates the Winnipeg of the early 1920s, a street complete with pharmacy, barber shop, dentist, promenade and cinema showing period films. The **Parklands Gallery** houses displays and dioramas on the province's largest region.

Also in the Centennial Centre are the **Planetarium** (May to early Sept daily; schedule varies; call ⓣ204/956-2830 for hours; $6.50) and the "Touch the Universe" **Science Gallery** (same hours as museum; $6.50), where more than sixty interactive exhibits focus on the way the universe is perceived by the five senses. A Value Pass for the museum, planetarium and science centre costs $18, and allows 3-day all-inclusive admission.

The Ukrainian Centre, Artspace and Chinatown

Two blocks north of the Centennial Centre, the **Ukrainian Cultural and Educational Centre** (Oseredok), 184 Alexander Ave East at Main St (Mon–Sat 10am–4pm; July & Aug also Sun 1–5pm; $2; ⓣ204/942-0218, ⓦwww.oseredok.org), occupies a 1930s office building on the edge of the Exchange District. The second largest ethnic group in Manitoba, the Ukrainians arrived here around 1900, a peasant people united by language and custom, but divided by religion and politics – Orthodox against Catholic, nationalist against socialist. By 1940, the various factions managed to amalgamate to create the Ukrainian Canadian Committee, a loose coalition committed to the country's institutions and the promotion of Ukrainian interests. Their collection of folk art in the fifth-floor museum of the complex is an excellent introduction to their strongly maintained traditions, with delightful examples of embroidery, weaving, woodcarving and the exquisite designs of *pysanky*, Easter egg painting. There's also an art gallery, library and gift shop.

Artspace, in a warehouse building at the corner of Arthur Street and Bannatyne Avenue, is the largest artist-run centre in Canada and houses a cinema (see p.575), several galleries and offices for art groups. All this gives it an artsy vibe and makes it a great place to see contemporary local and Canadian art, photography and wacky multimedia installations.

Adjacent to the Exchange District, north of Rupert Street and west of Main Street, is **Chinatown**, originally settled in the 1920s by immigrants brought to Manitoba to help build the railway into the west. The area has many good restaurants and groceries, as well as shops selling silk fabrics and exotic herbs and spices – though, other than that, not much in the way of sights.

The Forks

South of Portage Avenue along Main Street (take bus #38 or #99 from Portage Avenue) rises the ponderous dome of the Beaux Arts-style Union

Station, designed by the same architects as Grand Central Station in New York; it has an indoor market and the **Winnipeg Railway Museum** upstairs (June–Aug Fri–Sun noon–5pm; Sept–May Sat & Sun noon–4pm; Ⓦwww.wpgrailwaymuseum.com; $3), dedicated to the preservation of Manitoba's rail heritage. Immediately south of the station is the present headquarters of the Hudson's Bay Company. Across the street, in a small park, is the stone gate that's the sole remnant of Upper Fort Garry, a Hudson's Bay Company fort from 1837 to 1870 and thereafter the residence of Manitoba's lieutenant governors until 1883, when the fort was dismantled. The pointed dormers and turrets behind it belong to the *Hotel Fort Garry*, a château-like structure built for the Grand Trunk Railroad.

Behind the station, the chunk of land bordering the Red River as it curves round to **The Forks** (Ⓦwww.theforks.com) was, until recently, one of the country's largest railway yards – as the CNR freight cars and cabooses that dot the grounds remind. Subsequent redevelopment has turned The Forks into Winnipeg's most visited sight due to its **Explore Manitoba Centre** (see p.563), half tourist information point, half museum, with six reasonably interesting themed displays covering the province's tourist areas. It's worth a quick visit, if only to pick the brains of the very helpful staff and admire the magnificent stuffed polar bear from Churchill, a persistent and dangerous marauder of the town's dump who came to a sticky end. Just east along the river from here is **The Forks National Historic Site**, bearing plaques to celebrate the role of the fur traders and pioneers who first settled here.

Nearby, the 1889 rail maintenance shed houses the **Manitoba Children's Museum** (Sun–Thurs 9.30am–4pm, Fri & Sat 9.30am–6pm; Ⓦwww.childrensmuseum.com; $6.25), a hands-on, state-of-the-art enterprise that appeals equally to adults. Five different sections cover aspects of history, science, nature and technology. A vintage steam-engine with a couple of Pullman carriages and a mail office is equipped with tickets, luggage, uniforms and mail; close by, bear, lynx and raccoon costumes are on hand for kids to don while they explore a huge model of an oak tree and its ecosystem. Visitors to the museum can be filmed and have their activities shown simultaneously on two huge video screens, with added optical effects. For older kids, the highlight is probably the fully functioning TV studio where they can experiment with lights

Boat tours around Winnipeg

On the banks of the Red River there's a quay beside Provencher Bridge where you can take sightseeing **boat trips** (May–Oct daily 1pm; 2hr; $15; ⓣ204/944-8000, Ⓦwww.paddlewheelcruises.com) as well as various evening dinner cruises. All run parallel to the attractive riverwalk path, back along the Assiniboine River as far as the Legislative Building on Broadway and in the opposite direction up the Red River. The **Historic Fort Cruise** (July & Aug Wed–Fri 9am–4.30pm; $23) takes you to Lower Fort Garry (see p.576) and back. One of the boats is a replica paddlewheel vessel. **Water taxis** also leave every fifteen minutes from a quay closer to the market (daily 11am–sunset; 30min; ⓣ204/783-6633; $9) and run along the same route. They are also handy for getting about, charging $2.50 one-way to a number of different spots along the river. If you'd rather do the work yourself, you can **rent canoes** (daily 11am–9pm, weather permitting; $7.50/30 min; ⓣ204/783-6633) at the Johnston Terminal. Alternatively check the river out for an hour aboard a 26-foot replica of a **birch-bark canoe** paddled by a guide in *voyageur* garb; tickets cost $30 and are available from the Explore Manitoba Centre or from Wild-Wise Wilderness Adventures on ⓣ204/788-1070.

△ The Forks market

and cameras; at certain times, staff conduct interviews with them on their views of current events, which are relayed by one of the local stations.

A couple of minutes' walk away, **The Forks Market** (July & Aug Mon–Sat 9.30am–9pm, Sun 9.30am–6pm; rest of year daily 9.30am–6.30pm Fri until 9pm) and the Johnston Terminal, both old railway buildings, house shops, food stalls, bars and restaurants. Paths from the two buildings lead down to the **Assiniboine River** via an outdoor amphitheatre, where buskers entertain the gathered crowds with anything from hard rock to bagpipe music. Nearby is **The Wall Through Time**, a curving brick barricade covered with plaques and inscriptions recording the historic events of the area.

Downtown

Lined by department stores and offices, **downtown Portage Avenue** is the city's main shopping street, with a web of underground passageways and glass-enclosed overhead walkways linking the various malls and large stores and providing welcome relief from the summer heat and winter cold. The largest complex is the ugly mall **Portage Place** (Mon–Sat 10am–6pm, Thurs & Fri until 9pm, Sun noon–5pm), on the north side of the avenue. There are over 160 shops and services here, plus a giant-screen IMAX cinema on the third level (information ⓣ204/956-IMAX, tickets ⓣ204/780-SEAT, ⓦwww.imaxwinnipeg.com). Among the many modern buildings that line Portage are some earlier ones that are architecturally attractive: the Paris Building at no. 259, with a splendid tiered facade and delicate cornice, and the Boyd Building at no. 388, with cream and bronze terracotta decoration.

The uncompromisingly modern **Winnipeg Art Gallery** (WAG), a wedge-shaped building at 300 Memorial Blvd and Portage Ave (Tues & Thurs–Sun 11am–5pm, Wed 11am–9pm; $6; ⓣ204/786-6641, ⓦwww.wag.mb.ca), is the home of the largest public collection of Inuit art in the world, a decent selection of Gothic and Renaissance paintings and a reasonable assortment of modern European art, including works by Miró, Chagall and Henry Moore. The problem is that little of these collections is on display at any one time: much of the available space is taken up by offices while the main display area, on the third floor, is given over to temporary (and often dire) exhibitions of modern Canadian art. The mezzanine level, and often the third floor galleries, are devoted to the Inuits, each temporary display developing a particular theme – from the symbolic significance of different animals to the role of women sculptors in the isolated communities. The gallery also has an open-air sculpture court and a rooftop restaurant.

Legislative Building, Osborne Village and Dalnavert

A few minutes' walk south of the Art Gallery, along Memorial Boulevard, is the **Manitoba Legislative Building** (July & Aug hourly tours 9am–6pm; rest of year Mon–Fri by appointment; ⓣ204/945-5813; free), built between 1913 and 1919 and surrounded by trim lawns and flower borders. The building, made of local Tyndall stone embedded with fossils, has a central pediment decorated with splendidly pompous sculptures representing the ideals of Canadian nationhood. A half-kneeling figure, symbolizing progress, beckons his lazy neighbour to come to the land of promise, whilst a muscular male, with a team of powerful horses, idealizes the pioneer spirit. High above, a central square tower rises to a copper-green dome that's topped by the **Golden Boy**, a four-metre-high gold-plated bronze figure that's supposed to embody the spirit of enterprise and eternal youth. Inside, the marble columns and balconies of the foyer house two magnificent life-size buffalo bronzes by the French sculptor Charles Gardet, framing a staircase of brown-veined Carrara marble. The mural over the entrance to the legislative chamber depicting World War I scenes is by the English artist Frank Brangwyn.

Just behind the Legislative Building, across the Assiniboine, lies **Osborne Village**, the bohemian part of town, whose inexpensive bars, restaurants and music joints – strung along Osborne Street – are favourites with the city's students. West off Osborne Street is Corydon Avenue, whose several blocks and side streets comprise **Little Italy**, known for its cappuccino bars and restaurants.

A couple of blocks east of the Legislative Building, **Dalnavert**, 61 Carlton St (Wed–Fri 11am–4pm, Sat 11am–6pm, Sun noon–4pm; guided tours every 30min; $5; ⓦwww.mhs.mb.ca), was the home of Hugh John Macdonald, the son of Canada's first prime minister and, briefly, premier of Manitoba. Built in 1895 in Queen Anne Revival style, the house has been painstakingly restored, its simple red-brick exterior engulfed by a fanciful wooden veranda, the interior all heavy, dark-stained woods and strong deep colours. Macdonald's conservatism, reflected in the decor, was mellowed by a philanthropic disposition – he even reserved part of his basement for some of the city's destitute.

St Boniface

The suburb of **St Boniface**, a ten-minute walk east of the downtown area just across the Red River (or by bus #10 or #56 from Portage Avenue), was a centre of early French-Canadian and Métis settlement. Founded by two French-Canadian Catholic priests in 1818, it retains something of its distinctive character. Even today, decades after its incorporation into the city of Winnipeg, roughly a quarter of its population speaks French as a first language. Free walking tours of St Boniface are regularly organised by its Chamber of Commerce (June–August; 1hr; ⓣ204/235-1406 or 945-1715).

St Boniface's principal historic sights are situated beside the river, along **avenue Taché**. Walking south from the Provencher Bridge, the massive white-stone facade on the left is all that remains of St Boniface Cathedral, a huge neo-Romanesque structure built in 1908 and largely destroyed by fire in 1968. Its replacement, just behind, was designed with an interior in the style of a giant tepee. The large silver-domed building immediately to the east is the **Collège Universitaire** de Saint-Boniface, formerly a Jesuit college and now the French-speaking campus of the University of Manitoba. Here you'll see a controversial modern statue of Louis Riel that portrays him as naked and deformed. Its original location was on the grounds of the Legislative Building, but it caused such a storm of protest that it was moved here in 1994. In front of the cathedral is the cemetery containing Riel's grave, whose modest tombstone gives little indication of the furore surrounding his execution in Regina on November 16, 1885. Only after three weeks did the authorities feel safe enough to move the body, which was then sent secretly by rail to St Boniface. The casket lay overnight in Riel's family home in the suburb of St Vital (see below) before its transfer to the cathedral, where a Requiem Mass was attended by most of the Métis population. That same evening, across the river, Riel's enemies burnt his effigy on a street corner, a symptom of a bitter divide that was to last well into the twentieth century.

The **Musée de Saint-Boniface** (May–Sept Mon–Fri 9am–noon, Sat & Sun 10am–5pm; Oct to mid-May Mon–Fri 9am–noon Sun noon–4pm; $2; guided tours available by reservation on ⓣ204/237-4500) is housed in an attractive whitewashed building across from the cathedral. The oldest building in Winnipeg and the largest squared-oak log building in North America, it was built between 1846 and 1851 as a convent for the Grey Nuns, a missionary order whose four-woman advance party had arrived by canoe from Montréal in 1844. Subsequently, the building was adapted for use as a hospital, a school and an orphanage. Inside, a series of cosy rooms are devoted to the Red River Colony, notably an intriguing collection of Métis memorabilia that includes colourful sashes – the most distinctive feature of Métis dress. You can also see the battered wooden casket used to transport Riel's body from Regina to St Boniface. There's also a lovely little chapel, whose papier-mâché Virgin was made from an old newspaper that one of the original Grey Nuns found outside Upper Fort Garry when she walked across the frozen river to buy food.

Out of the centre

The **Riel House National Historic Site**, 330 River Rd (mid-May to Aug daily 10am–6pm; $4; ⓣ204/257-1783; bus #16 from the Portage Place Mall), in the suburb of **ST VITAL**, about 10km south of the city centre, is just about worth the trip. The main feature of the site is a tiny clapboard house that was built by the Riels in 1880–81 and stayed in their possession until 1968. Louis Riel never actually lived here, but this was where his body was brought after his execution in 1885, and the house has been restored to its appearance at that time, complete with black-bordered photographs and a few artefacts left by his wife, Marguerite. Other period furnishings and fittings give a good idea of the life of a prosperous Métis family in the 1880s. The railway had reached St Boniface in 1877, a time when the simple products of the Red River could be supplemented by manufactured goods from the east with relative ease: the iron stove, the most obvious import, improved the quality of the Riels' life immeasurably. Costumed guides provide an enjoyable twenty-minute tour of the house and garden, the sole remnant of the once sizeable Riel landholdings.

Across the Red River from St Vital, at the city's southern limits, is the **Fort Whyte Centre**, 1961 McCreary Rd (Mon–Fri 9am–5pm, Sat & Sun 10am–5pm; ⓦwww.fortwhyte.org; $5), an environmental education centre dealing with the diversity of plants and animals of the prairie ecosystem. It's a real outdoors experience, with a wildlife observation tower, herd of bison, deer enclosure and a maze of self-guiding trails through woodlands and marsh, plus an interpretive centre. There's no public transport to Fort Whyte.

Assiniboine Park and the Living Prairie Museum

Some 8km west of the city centre, to the south of Portage Avenue, a great chunk of land has been set aside as **Assiniboine Park** (daily 9am–sunset; free; bus #66 from Broadway at Smith Street), whose wooded lawns, gardens, cycling paths, playing fields and zoo attract hundreds of visitors every summer weekend. The park's English gardens of daisies, marigolds, roses and begonias bloom beneath columns of spruce trees and blend into the excellent **Leo Mol Sculpture Garden**, which contains the works of Ukrainian artist Leo Mol, who moved to Winnipeg in 1949. Dozens of his graceful sculptures – deer, bears, nude bathers and other whimsical figures – are featured here reflecting in the pond. More can be seen in the nearby glass-walled **gallery** (June to late Sept Tues–Sun 10am–8pm; free). Mol's studio, just behind the gallery, is also on view. The park's best-known feature is a large, half-timbered pavilion in mock-Tudor style – a favourite meeting place for Winnipeggers at the weekend and home to the **Pavilion Gallery Museum** (Tues–Sun 11am–5pm; free) with a permanent collection of three local artists: Ivan Eyre, Walter J. Phillips and Clarence Tillenius. By the pavilion, completed in 1999, the similarly Tudoresque bandshell of the **Lyric Theatre** (Ⓣ204/268-3552) has free performances by the Royal Winnipeg Ballet and the Winnipeg Symphony Orchestra, and hosts jazz, folk and drama festivals. The **zoo** (daily 10am–sunset; $3; Ⓣ204/982-0660, Ⓦwww.zoosociety.com) has over 1300 animals and a giant tropical conservatory with a foyer displaying local artwork, a steamy Palm House, floral displays and a restaurant. A statue of Winnie the Pooh on the zoo grounds is a reminder that the fictitious bear was named after a real bear called Winnipeg. Adjoining the park to the south, the 700-acre nature reserve of Assiniboine Forest (sunrise–sunset; free), the largest in Canada, is home to deer, ruffled grouse and waterfowl.

A couple of kilometres further west, the **Living Prairie Museum**, 2795 Ness Ave (April–June Sun 10am–5pm; July & Aug daily 10am–5pm; free; guided tours $2.25; bus #24 along Portage), is worth a brief visit, its thirty acres of land forming the largest area of unploughed tall-grass prairie in Manitoba. A small visitor centre provides a wealth of background information on the indigenous plants, whose deep-root systems enable them to withstand both the extreme climate and prairie fires. There's a daily programme of half-hour guided walks, or you can pick up a brochure and stroll alone. Come prepared with insect repellent: the native bugs that thrive among the grass and wild flowers are particularly vicious.

Eating, drinking and entertainment

Winnipeg boasts literally dozens of good, inexpensive places **to eat**, though many of them in truth emphasize quantity over finesse. The wide variety of ethnic restaurants are the exception, ranging from deluxe establishments serving fine French and Italian delicacies to Ukrainian and French-Canadian restaurant-bars that cater mainly to their own communities. In the more expensive places it's possible to pay upwards of $60 per person for a full dinner, but $25 per head is a reasonable average elsewhere. Many of Winnipeg's more staid restaurants and restaurant-bars are concentrated in and around the downtown shopping malls, but there's a cluster of more interesting ones in Osborne Village and the Exchange District. Several other good places are dotted around the edges of the centre, notably the Jewish delis and Ukrainian restaurants in the North End, around Selkirk Ave. For **drinking**, many of the city's bars are cheerless places, so it's best to stick to the restaurant-bars.

Restaurants and restaurant-bars

Alycia's 559 Cathedral Ave ⓣ204/582-8789. A long-established Ukrainian restaurant, 4km north of the centre, which also serves as an informal social centre with cheap, filling food, including borscht and *holubchi* (stuffed cabbage rolls); dishes for $5–8. Closed Sun.

Amici 326 Broadway ⓣ204/943-4997. Expensive but superb and elegant restaurant with Italian food – the desserts are sensational. Dishes for $15–36.

Baked Expectations 161 Osborne St ⓣ204/452-5176. Delicious burgers and salads, but especially known for its cheesecakes. Dishes for $3–8.

Bistro Bohemia 159 Osborne St ⓣ204/453-1944. Czech restaurant with great herring. Dishes for $8–14.

Carlos & Murphy's 129 Osborne St ⓣ204/284-3510. Huge portions of Mexican food are $5–10; eat out on the pleasant patio or inside adjacent to the raucous and dingy bar.

The Chocolate Shop 268 Portage Ave ⓣ204/942-4855. Winnipeg's oldest restaurant, dating its roots to 1918, where you can have your tea leaves and tarot read from 1 to 9pm. Diner-style establishment with great desserts. Popular karaoke night on Tues.

The Forks Market The Forks. A converted railway shed incorporating some cheap, pleasant bars selling a variety of fast food from Caribbean to Greek; try *Yudyta's* for Ukrainian and *Tavola Calda* for Italian food, both of which are dirt cheap.

Kelekis 1100 Main St. Another true Winnipeg institution, located around 1km north of town and dishing out greasy fries, hotdogs and enormous hamburgers to people from all walks of life – including Pierre Trudeau – since 1931. Dishes $3–9. Closes 9.45pm.

Le Beaujolais 131 Blvd Provencher, St Boniface ⓣ204/237-6276. Winnipeg's premier French restaurant, with prices to match; reservations recommended. Dishes for $19–26.

Le Café Jardin Centre Culturel Franco-Manitobain, 340 Blvd Provenche, St Boniface. A large cultural complex housing an attractive open-air restaurant featuring traditional French-Canadian food – try the meat pies (*tourtière*) and the bread pudding. Open Mon–Fri 11.30am–2pm. A full meal costs around $15.

Pasquale's 109 Marion St, St Boniface ⓣ204/474-2750. Delightful, busy little place with well-prepared Italian dishes from $6.

Rogue's Gallery 432 Assiniboine Ave ⓣ204/947-0652. Hip coffee house serving light meals like falafels and burgers, and decorated with local art.

Sofia's Caffè 635 Corydon Ave ⓣ204/452-3037. In the heart of Little Italy, this restaurant, with outdoor patio, serves large portions of veal, pasta and the like from $7.

Tavern in the Park The Pavilion in Assiniboine Park. Perfectly situated in a glass atrium on the back of the fake Tudor Pavilion, and a favourite with Winnipeggers. Expensive, with a lavish buffet on Sundays. Dishes for $18–28.

Tre Visi 173 McDermot Ave ⓣ204/949-9032. Tiny, extremely popular Italian restaurant with good atmosphere and food. Reservations essential. Dishes for $7.50–18.

Wordsworth Building Cafeteria 405 Broadway Ave ⓣ204/944-8927. Overrun by lunching office workers thanks to the excellent, well-priced specials and extensive salad bar. Open for breakfast and lunch only.

Wasabi 105–121 Osborne St ⓣ204/474-2332. Buzzing, trendy sushi bar in Osborne Village. Sushi from 95¢, $18.95 for a combo platter.

Nightlife, entertainment and festivals

Winnipeg tries hard to be the cultural centre of the prairies, and generous **arts** sponsorship arrangements support a good range of theatre, ballet, opera and orchestral music. The city also has some lively **nightlife**, featuring the best of local and national rock and jazz talent. For listings, consult the free news sheet *Uptown* (ⓦwww.uptownmag.com), available from self-serve kiosks all over the city and issued every Thursday or check out the Thursday editions of the *Winnipeg Sun* or the *Winnipeg Free Press* newspaper.

Spectator sports in Winnipeg

Baseball The Winnipeg Goldeyes (Ⓣ204/982-2273, Ⓦwww.goldeyes.com) play Northern League games (mid-May to early Sept) at the CanWest Global Park adjacent to The Forks. Tickets cost $4–15.

Canadian football The Winnipeg Blue Bombers (Ⓣ204/784-2583 or 1-888/780-7328, Ⓦwww.bluebombers.com), ten-time winners of the Grey Cup, play at the Canad Inns Stadium, 1430 Maroons Rd (June–Nov).

Ice hockey The Manitoba Moose (Ⓣ204/780-7328, Ⓦwww.moosehockey.com) play American Hockey League games at Winnipeg Arena (Oct–April).

Major performances by the **Winnipeg Symphony Orchestra** ($20–56; Ⓦwww.wso.mb.ca) as well as the **Manitoba Opera** (Nov–April; $29–84; Ⓦwww.manitobaopera.mb.ca) take place at the Centennial Concert Hall, 555 Main St (Ⓣ204/956-1360) in the Exchange District. The **Royal Winnipeg Ballet** ($12–35; Ⓦwww.rwb.org) – Canada's finest dance company – also performs at the Concert Hall and has an extensive programme of traditional and contemporary ballets.

Winnipeg has an ambitious summer programme of open-air concerts, notably the nine-day **Jazz Winnipeg Festival** in late June (Ⓦwww.jazzwinnipeg.com), and the **Winnipeg Folk Festival** (Ⓦwww.winnipegfolkfestival.ca), a three-day extravaganza featuring over a hundred concerts, held in early July at Birds Hill Provincial Park, 25km northeast of the city. Apart from the music festivals, the biggest festival in Manitoba is **Folklorama** (Ⓦwww.folklorama.ca), held during the first two weeks in August to celebrate Winnipeg's multiethnic population. The festival has over forty pavilions spread out over town, each devoted to a particular country or region. The **Winnipeg Fringe Festival** (Ⓦwww.mtc.mb.ca) is a ten-day event of theatrical productions, held in mid-July in the Exchange District. St Boniface's French-Canadian heritage is honoured annually in the **Festival du Voyageur** (Ⓦwww.festivalvoyageur.mb.ca) – ten days of February fun, whose events lead up to a torchlit procession and the Governor's Ball, where everyone dresses up in period costume.

Music venues and clubs

Au Bar 65 Rorie St. Small, swank and lively Osbourne Village martini bar.

Centre Culturel Franco-Manitobain 340 Blvd Provencher, St Boniface Ⓣ204/233-8972, Ⓦwww.ccfm.mb.ca. Hosts free weekly concerts (Fri) by French-Canadian musicians. Also jazz sessions (Tues 9pm).

Club 200 190 Garry St Ⓣ204/943-6045 Ⓦwww.club200.ca. A popular gay and lesbian club with karaoke nights and other weekly events.

The Empire 436 Main St Ⓣ204/943-3979. Roman-themed upscale dance club in an old bank building. Has a non-smoking lounge.

Jazz on the Rooftop Winnipeg Art Gallery, 300 Memorial Blvd Ⓣ204/786-6641. Showcases frequent performances by some of Canada's best-known jazz musicians.

Kokonut Club 114 Market Ave Ⓣ204/944-1117. Live music venue with a huge aquarium.

Mezzo 291 Bannatyne Ave Ⓣ204/987-3399. Ultra-swank, high-tech club with catwalks and fashionably offhand patrons.

Ms Purdy's 226 Main St Ⓣ204/989-2344. Long-running women-only lesbian bar.

Palomino Club 1133 Portage Ave Ⓣ204/722-0454, Ⓦwww.palominoclub.ca. Best place for a good boot-scoot if you're looking for line dancing.

Times Change Cafe Main and St Mary Ⓣ204/957-0982. Rough-and-ready jazz and blues place. Live entertainment Thurs–Sun.

Toad in the Hole 112 Osborne St. Osborne Village's busy pub with British beer and dance floor upstairs.

The Zoo 160 Osborne St Ⓣ204/452-9824. Alter-native/rock bar in *Osborne Village Inn* with live metal and rock acts.

Cinema and theatre

Winnipeg's best downtown **cinema** is Cinémathèque, 100 Arthur St (ⓣ204/925-3457), in the Artspace building, concentrates on art-house and Canadian releases and plays host to much of **Film Exchange**, an all-Canadian film festival, organized by the National Screen Institute Canada (ⓦwww.nsi-canada.com) in late February.

The city has several professional **theatre** groups: principally the Prairie Theatre Exchange, Portage Place (ⓦwww.pte.mb.ca; $20–34), which performs traditional and avant-garde comedy and drama and the Manitoba Theatre Centre, 174 Market Ave (ⓦwww.mtc.mb.ca; $20–59). Both tend to feature local talent, while Winnipeg's main theatrical events are performed by international touring companies in the Centennial Concert Hall.

Listings

Bike rental Corydon Cycle Sports, 753 Corydon Ave at Cockburn St ⓣ204/452-6531; Portage Cycle & Sports, 1841 Portage Ave ⓣ204/837-6785.
Bookshops McNally Robinson, 393 Portage Ave ⓣ204/943-8376.
Car rental Avis (ⓣ204/989-7521) and at the airport (ⓣ204/956-2847); Budget (ⓣ204/989-8500); Hertz, 276 Colony St (ⓣ204/925-6615); National (ⓣ204/925-3525); Thrifty (ⓣ204/949-7620).
Consulates UK, 229 Athlone Drive ⓣ204/896-1380.
Internet access Centennial Library, 251 Donald St ⓣ204/986-6450. Osborne Cyber Café, 118 Osborne St (daily until midnight).
Laundries Zip-Kleen, 110 Sherbrook St at Westminster Ave T204/772-5247.
Left luggage 24hr coin-operated lockers at the train and bus stations.
Medical emergencies Health Sciences Centre, 820 Sherbrook St ⓣ204/233-8563. For dental emergencies, Broadway Dental Centre, 640 Broadway ⓣ204/772-3523.
Pharmacy Shoppers Drug Mart, 43 Osborne St ⓣ204/958-7000.
Post office 266 Graham Ave at Smith St ⓣ1-800/267-1177.
Taxis Unicity ⓣ204/925-3131.
Weather information ⓣ204/983-2050.

Around Winnipeg

The area **around Winnipeg** contains quite a few tempting day-trip destinations, with most attractions north of the city, en route to **Lake Winnipeg**. With extra days to spare, try spending a pleasant day nosing around the small prairie towns **south of town** and experiencing something of the local **Mennonite** culture, or head to some of Manitoba's **Eastern Parks** (see p.582) where the canoeing is simply superb – particularly if you have the time and energy for an overnight or multi-day trip.

As Winnipeg's dreary suburbs fade into the seamless prairie landscape to the north, the only major interruption is provided by the course of the **Red River**. And on it's banks are the trading posts of **Lower Fort Garry** and the area's only major settlement, **Selkirk**. Ornithologists should make a beeline to the marshlands to the west of these: **Netley Marsh** and the **Oak Hammock Marsh Wildlife Area**. The latter is home to thousands of migrating birds, particularly snow and Canada geese, between April and September.

At its northern end the Red River empties out into **Lake Winnipeg**, a giant finger of water some 400km long that feeds the Nelson River on its way to the Hudson Bay. It's a shallow lake, subject to violent squalls and, aboriginal reservations aside, the only settlement has been around its southern rim. Here, on the east shore, Winnipeg's wealthy have built their cottages in and around **Victoria Beach** and **Hillside Beach**, but **Grand Beach Provincial Park** still has the lake's finest bathing and long lines of sand dune stretching as far as the eye can see. The beaches of the west shore are poor by comparison, and the old fishing and farming villages that trail up the coast are not of major interest. But **Gimli**, on the west side of Lake Winnipeg, has its own windblown charm and a pleasant museum tracing its Icelandic history. Nearby, the **Narcisse Wildlife Management Area** is a must-see attraction in April and May when thousands of red-sided garter snakes gather to mate. Further north, scattered on islands in the centre of Lake Winnipeg, **Hecla Provincial Park** is more agreeable for the squeamish; the developed facilities of Gull Harbour Resort supplemented by unspoilt marsh and forest.

Striking out in the opposite direction – **south** of the city – the town of **Steinbach** is of particular interest for its **Mennonite Heritage Village** and **Morris** is not to be missed in late July during its annual **rodeo**.

Relying on public transport to explore the area around Winnipeg is awkward, but just about workable, with most key places having one or two bus services per day. The only exception to this is the frequent Beaver Bus (Ⓣ204/989-7007, Ⓦwww.beaverbus.com) service from the Winnipeg bus station to **Lower Fort Garry** and Selkirk (Mon–Fri 12 daily; Sat 7 daily; Sun 5 daily; $3 one way) – though it's more fun to catch the boat (see p.568). Other useful buses from Winnipeg include the Greyhound bus to **Steinbach** (2 daily; 1 hr); and the Grey Goose (operated by Greyhound; May–Aug Thurs & Fri; 1 daily) to **Grand Beach**.

Lower Fort Garry

Driving out from the city on Main Steet, which becomes Hwy 9, it's about 32km from to **Lower Fort Garry National Historic Site** (grounds open daily until sunset; visitor centre: mid-May to Aug daily 9am–5pm; $7.15), built as the new headquarters of the Hudson's Bay Company between 1830 and 1847. It was the brainchild of George Simpson, governor of the company's northern department, an area bounded by the Arctic and Pacific oceans, Hudson Bay and the Missouri River Valley. Nicknamed the "Little Emperor" for his autocratic style, Simpson selected the site because it was downriver from the treacherous waters of the St Andrew's Rapids but not prone to flooding, as Upper Fort Garry had been. However, the settlers around The Forks were reluctant to cart their produce down to the new camp and when the governors of Assiniboia refused to move here his scheme collapsed. Sandwiched between Hwy 9 and the Red River, Lower Fort Garry begins at the visitor reception centre, where there's a comprehensive account of the development of the fort and its role in the fur trade. A couple of minutes' walk away, the low, thick limestone walls of the fort protect reconstructions of several company buildings, including the retail store, where a small museum is devoted to Inuit and Indian crafts. Several of the exhibits here are exquisite, particularly the decorated skin pouches and an extraordinary necklace fringed by thin strips of metal cut from a sardine can. Next door, the combined sales shop and clerk's quarters has a fur loft packed with pelts, while the middle of the compound is dominated by the Big House with its low sloping roof, built for Governor Simpson in 1832. People in 1850s period costume stroll the grounds, ensuring the right atmosphere. The **restaurant** sells good *tortière* – a Québecois meat pie – and bannock (freshly baked bread).

Selkirk

About 8km north of the fort, along Hwy 9A, you can visit the modest town of **SELKIRK** whose only real attraction is the **Marine Museum of Manitoba** (mid-May to Aug Mon–Fri 9am–5pm, Sat & Sun 10am–6pm; $3.50), situated on the edge of Selkirk Park at Eveline and Queen streets. The museum consists of seven passenger and freight ships, dragged out of the water and parked on a lawn, as well as a lighthouse, plus a mildly interesting video on the history of Lake Winnipeg's shipping and fishing industries. In **Selkirk Park** there's a bird sanctuary and a 6.5-metre-high oxcart, said to be the world's largest. If you're in Selkirk in early July, you could take in the **Manitoba Highland Gathering**, a Scottish festival honouring the original settlers.

Places to stay include the *Selkirk Motor Hotel*, 219 Manitoba Ave (ⓣ204/482-1900; ❷), and the *Evergreen Gate B&B*, 1138 River Rd (ⓣ204/482-6248 or 1-877/901-0553, ⓦwww.evergreengate.ca; ❷), with three guestrooms. You can camp at the *Willow Springs Campground*, 13km north of Selkirk on Hwy 320 (ⓣ204/482-1344; $14–16; May–Oct). For **food**, try *Barney Gargles*, 185 Main St, which has delicious main courses from $7, or *The Garden on Eaton*, 205 Eaton Ave (closed Sun), for its fresh home-cooked food.

Netley Marsh

From Selkirk, Provincial Road 320 heads north 16km to the edge of **Netley Marsh**, a huge swampy delta formed by the Red River as it seeps into Lake Winnipeg. At the end of the road, there's a small recreation park with a snack bar, an observation tower and a series of plaques that detail the way of life of the area's native peoples. The marsh is an impenetrable maze for the inexperienced, but you can hire a boat and guide at the park for about $120 a day. On the lake side of the delta, the Bird Refuge is one of North America's largest waterfowl nesting areas and there are lots of good fishing spots; the pickerel, or wall-eye, are delicious.

Oak Hammock Marsh

The **Oak Hammock Marsh Wildlife Management Area** (daily: May–Aug 10am–8pm; Sept & Oct 8.30am to dusk; Nov–April 10am–4.30pm; ⓣ204/467-3300, ⓦwww.ducks.ca/ohmic; $5) is all that remains of the wetlands that once stretched from St Andrews, near the Red River, up to the village of Teulon, and to the west of Netley Creek. Most of this wetland was drained and farmed around the beginning of the twentieth century, but in the 1960s some of the area was restored to its original state and protected by a series of retaining dykes. In addition, a number of islands were built to provide marshland birds a safe place to nest. To get there from Winnipeg take Hwy 7 or Hwy 8 north for 10km, turn east along Hwy 67; from Selkirk take Hwy 67 west, from just south of town. In both cases, follow the signs to the Main Mound Area, where an excellent interpretive centre has hands-on displays about the local environment and wildlife, a picnic site and a couple of observation decks, all connected by a system of dykes and boardwalk trails. The best time to come is in spring or autumn, when the grebes, coots and other residents are joined by thousands of migrating birds, including Canada geese. Another part of the Wildlife Area has been returned to tall-grass prairie, carpeted from mid-June to August with the blooms of wild flowers such as the purple Blazing Star and the speckled red Prairie Lily.

Grand Beach Provincial Park and around

Approached along Hwy 59, the southeast shore of Lake Winnipeg has one major attraction, **Grand Beach Provincial Park**, whose long stretch of powdery white sand, high grass-crowned dunes and shallow bathing water make it the region's most popular day-trip. The beach, a favourite swimming spot with Winnipeggers since the 1920s, is divided into two distinct parts, separated by a narrow channel that drains out of a knobbly lagoon, set just behind the lakeshore. The channel is spanned by a tiny footbridge: on the beach to the west are privately owned cottages, sports facilities, motor- and rowboat rental, grocery stores and a restaurant; the eastern section of the beach is less developed, although it does have the large *Grand Beach Campground* (ⓣ1-888/482-2267; $15–18; May–Sept) tucked away amongst the dunes. Both parts of the beach get very crowded on summer weekends. By the campsite office, the **Ancient Beach Trail** follows the line of the prehistoric lake that dominated southern Manitoba in the last Ice Age; allow about an hour for the walk. At **GRAND MARAIS**, just outside the park, you'll find an array of motels, beachside cottages and cabins (❷–❹; most May–Sept).

Roughly 20km north of Grand Beach Provincial Park, the twin townships of **HILLSIDE BEACH** and prettier **VICTORIA BEACH** have good sandy beaches, but their well-heeled inhabitants avoid catering for outsiders. There are no campsites and the only **motel** is the *Birchwood* (ⓣ204/754-2596; ❷) on the highway, 6km south of Victoria Beach at Traverse Bay; the motel's star facility is the huge patio overlooking the bay.

Gimli and Narcisse

In 1875, some two hundred Icelanders moved to the southwestern shore of Lake Winnipeg, where they had secured exclusive rights to a block of land that stretched from today's Winnipeg Beach to Hecla Island, named after a volcano in their homeland. The next year the colonists were struck by a smallpox epidemic, yet they managed to survive and founded the **Republic of New Iceland**, a large self-governing and self-sufficient settlement with its own Icelandic-language school, churches and newspaper. Their independence lasted just twenty years, for in 1897 they acquiesced in the federal government's decision to open their new homeland to other ethnic groups. An identifiable Icelandic community ceased to exist by the 1920s, but this part of Manitoba still has the largest number of people of Icelandic descent outside Iceland. The residents celebrate their heritage during the Islendingadagurinn (Icelanders' Day) festival, on the first weekend in August, when they dress up in Viking helmets and organize beauty pageants, concerts and firework displays. This rather commercial festival is held in the largest township, **GIMLI** (literally "paradise"). There's little else to attract visitors to this part of the lake, though Gimli's harbourside, with a fibreglass Viking statue and a massive wharf, is modestly attractive. The **New Iceland Heritage Museum**, at 62 2nd Ave (Mon–Fri 10am–4pm, Sat & Sun 1pm–4pm; ⓣ204/642-4001, ⓦwww.nihm.ca; $5), chronicles the history of New Iceland. The **tourist office** is located downtown on 7th Ave (May–Aug daily 10am–8pm; ⓣ204/642-7974). Gimli doesn't have a lot of **places to stay**, but the best of the lot is the *Lakeview Resort*, 10 Centre St (ⓣ204/642-8565 or 1-877/355-3500; ❺), which has comfortable suites and rooms, each of which has a balcony overlooking either Gimli or the lake. There's also a campsite near the beach, 8km south of town, *Idle-Wheels Trailer Park* (ⓣ204/642-5676; $17; mid-May to Oct). *Seagull's*, 10 Centre St (ⓣ204/642-4145), serves Icelandic **food** like gyro and deep-fried fish, which you can wash down with potent schnapps; eat in the large dining room or on the beachside patio.

Known as the **Interlake**, the marginal farmland that lies between Lake Winnipeg to the east and lakes Manitoba and Winnipegosis to the west is pancake-flat and one of the most boring parts of the prairies. The only significant attraction is at the **Narcisse Wildlife Management Area**, 25km west of Gimli on Hwy 231 or 90km north of Winnipeg on Hwy 17, where thousands of red-sided garter snakes gather to mate in late April and early May, writhing around the bottom of a series of shallow pits in slithering heaps. It's not for the squeamish.

Hecla Provincial Park

Roughly 100km north of Gimli, **Hecla Provincial Park** consists of several islands and a slender peninsula that jut out into Lake Winnipeg, almost touching the eastern shore. The park is approached along Hwy 8, which runs across a narrow causeway to the largest of the islands, **Hecla**, where the tourist township of **GULL HARBOUR** has a comprehensive range of facilities. Nearby, on the east side of the island, the original **Hecla Village** has a number of old houses, a church and a school dating from the early years of Icelandic settlement; a short heritage trail covers the highlights (guided tours available in summer), or you can strike out on one of the island's hiking trails through forest and marsh. For **accommodation**, there's the *Solmundson Gesta Hus*, in Hecla Village (Ⓣ204/279-2088, Ⓦwww.heclatourism.mb.ca; ③), a B&B with home-cooked dinners, and a medium-size **Gull Harbour Campground** (Ⓣ204/948-3333 or 1-888/482-2267; $14–16; May–Sept) on the neck of land between Gull Harbour and the lake.

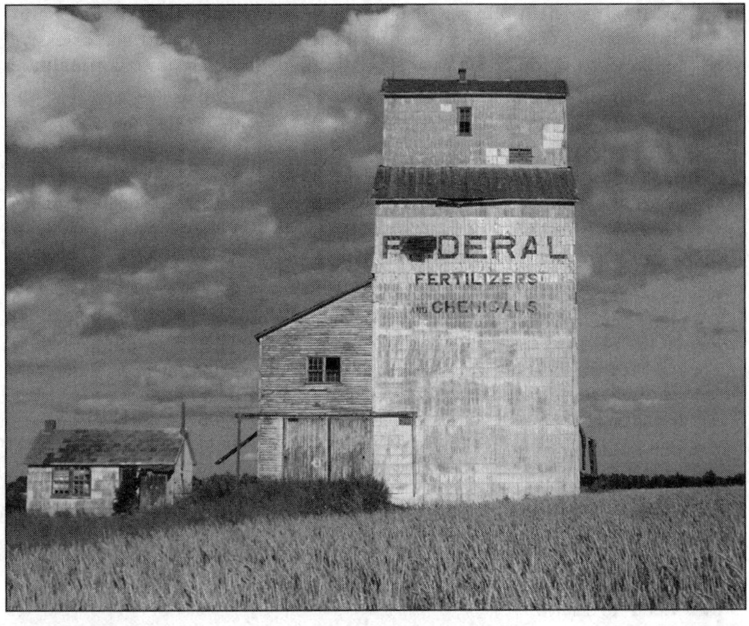

△ A classic grain elevator

South of Winnipeg

It's easy to have an enjoyable day-out from Winnipeg driving a loop through the settlements that dot the prairies **south** of the city. It's here that you'll find the quintessential prairie town: squat false-gabled buildings lining a wide main street, parked half-ton trucks filled with bales of hay, sacks of horsefeed, a sleeping dog or two, and quiet side streets bordered by tall Manitoba oaks or trembling aspen. The drive takes you along part of the Red River and across vast golden wheatfields punctuated only by **grain elevators**, huge storage silos situated at the edge of almost every town, usually with the town's name painted high up in large white letters – though most of these may soon disappear to be replaced by massive concrete terminals (see box below).

A good first stop is the sprawling town of **STEINBACH**, about 60km southeast of Winnipeg (2 buses daily), where the **Mennonite Heritage Village** (July & Aug Mon–Sat 10am–7pm, Sun noon–6pm; May, June & Sept 10am–5pm; Oct–April 10am–4pm; ⓣ204/326-9661 or 1-866-280-874, ⓦwww.mennoniteheritagevillage.com; $8), on the north edge of town off Hwy 12, is worth a peek for its good reconstruction of a nineteenth-century pioneer settlement. This includes a church, a windmill and a couple of stores and farmhouses, but it's the general flavour of the place that appeals rather than any particular structure. The **Mennonites**, a Protestant sect, were founded in the Netherlands under the leadership of Menno Symons in the early sixteenth century. Subsequently the movement divided into two broad factions, with one group refusing to have anything to do with the secular state and sustaining a hostile attitude to private property, and the more "liberal" clans being inclined to compromise. Many of the former – the Ammanites – moved to the United States and then Ontario, settling in and around Kitchener-Waterloo, while the more liberal Untere migrated to Russia and then Manitoba in the 1870s. There are about 100,000 Mennonites in Canada today. Few of the Manitoba Mennonites, who congregated in and around Steinbach, wear the traditional black and white clothes or live on communal farms, but like all Mennonite communities

Grain elevators

Canada hasn't exactly set the world afire with its contributions to the field of architecture; in fact, it's most distinctive form of building may be the ubiquitous **grain elevators** found throughout the prairies, warehouses built to store wheat before it was shipped off by the railroad. Most are wooden, while the more modern ones are made of steel – but both have the same simple, functional lines rising above the flat prairie land that have earned them the nickname "prairie sentinels".

The first grain elevators were built in the 1880s. By 1938 there were 5800 dotted across the region emblazoned with the names of the small towns they mark. However, as transportation of grain switched from rail to road their numbers dwindled to the present seven hundred. In 2000, the Canadian Wheat Board decided to build massive central concrete terminals at main transit points, a move that will make the old-style elevator redundant and no doubt dramatically alter the rural prairie-scape. Grain will now travel by trucks from the new terminals, much to the detriment of the region's already abysmal roads.

In **Inglis**, a tiny town on the west side of Riding Mountain National Park, about 20km east of the Saskatchewan border, a row of 1920s elevators beside an abandoned railway line has been declared a National Historic Site. With very little local concern to preserve the grain elevators, these may be the only "castles of the New World" to survive.

△A rider at the Manitoba Stampede

they maintain a strong pacifist tradition. Costumed guides at the Heritage Village provide an intriguing account of their history, augmented by displays in the tiny museum and the interpretive centre. For a Mennonite **meal**, eat at the cafeteria-style *Livery Barn* in the Heritage Village, with borscht, stone-ground bread, smoked sausages and other delights priced inexpensively. For a more formal meal try the *Dutch Connection*, 88 Brandt St (Ⓣ204/326-2018), one of the province's better places serving Dutch and Indonesian food at reasonable prices; a **motel** (❷) has sprung up around this successful restaurant. To **camp** try the RV-orientated *Steinbach Campground* just west of Hwy 12 on Park Road (Ⓣ204/326-6892).

The pleasant small town of **MORRIS**, 59km west of Steinbach via hwys 52, 29 and 23, is home to the annual **Manitoba Stampede** and Exhibition, one of Canada's largest, which takes place during the third week of July in and around a huge recreational complex dominating the town. The area where the Morris River joins the Red River is great for catching wall-eye and catfish, and a Catfish Derby is held here in August. Following Hwy 75 a bit further south, **ST JEAN BAPTISTE** is an attractive French-speaking community known for producing the type of pea that's used in French-Canadian pea soup. **EMERSON**, 30km south, right on the border with Minnesota and North Dakota, has some interesting architectural titbits, like the log customs house, Fort Dufferin (the original site of the North West Mounted Police), and the 1917–18 town hall and courthouse, at the corner of Church Street and Winnipeg Avenue (Mon–Fri 9am–4pm; free) done in the Neoclassical Prairie style. For lunch or afternoon tea, the place to visit is *Aunt Maud's Tea Room*, 57 4th St (closed Mon–Wed). **GRETNA**, 25km west of Emerson, is another Mennonite community, as is **WINKLER**, to the northwest, which has several arts and crafts shops, a farmers' market (July–Sept Fri evening), and the August Harvest Festival. It's also a great place to sample genuine Mennonite food, served in almost all the cafés and restaurants; be sure to try *platz*, a rhubarb dessert.

West of Winkler is the large town of **MORDEN**, site of the annual Corn and Apple Festival in August, and **DARLINGFORD**, 20km farther west, where a large granite boulder marks the route taken by the eighteenth-century French explorer Sieur de la Vérendrye on his way west in search of a reputed vast "western sea". The land to the south and west of Darlingford begins to descend into the Pembina River Valley, which offers magnificent, sweeping views of the prairies. Kaleida, a tiny village about 15km southwest of Darlingford, has a charming pioneer stone church and an attractive cemetery.

The Eastern Parks

Wedged between the eastern edges of Lake Winnipeg and the Ontario border, Manitoba's **Eastern Parks** protect an inhospitable and sparsely inhabited region of lake, river and forest that occupies the granite landscapes of the Canadian Shield. This is the home of three of the province's largest parks: **Whiteshell**, **Nopiming** and **Atikaki Provincial Parks**. **Whiteshell** is the oldest and by far the most developed, with a relatively extensive road system, fifteen campsites and one-quarter of Manitoba's holiday lodges, and gets busy on summer weekends – but all have an excellent network of canoe routes which link multiple backcountry campsites.

The only park you don't absolutely need your own transport to reach is **Whiteshell National Park**, thanks to a twice-daily Greyhound **bus** service between Winnipeg and West Hawk Lake.

Whiteshell Provincial Park

Whiteshell Provincial Park takes its name from the small, white seashell, the *megis*. The *megis* was sacred to the Ojibwa, who believed the Creator blew through the shell to breathe life into the first human being. These shells, left by the prehistoric lake that covered the entire region, were concentrated along the park's two main rivers, the Whiteshell to the south and the Winnipeg to the north, the latter an important part of the canoe route followed by the *voyageurs* of the North West Company on their way from Montréal to the Red River.

Most of the park's visitors head for **FALCON LAKE** and **WEST HAWK LAKE**, two well-developed tourist townships situated on either side of the Trans-Canada Highway, near the Ontario border. Crowded throughout the summer, neither has much to recommend it, though each has a full range of facilities from serviced campsites ($12–17), resort hotels – try the *Penguin Resort* at Falcon Lake (Ⓣ204/349-2218; ❷–❺) – fuel stations, grocery stores and miniature golf through to boat and water-sports equipment rental. The best places to **eat** are in West Hawk Lake: the *Nite Hawk Café*, for home-made burgers, and the *Landing Steak House*, which serves juicy steaks and prime rib.

West Hawk Lake, which was formed by a meteorite, is the deepest lake in Manitoba and particularly good for scuba diving. On its south side the sixteen-kilometre loop of the **Hunt Lake Hiking Trail** passes through cedar and white-pine forests, across sticky, aromatic bogs and over rocky outcrops, all in the space of about eight hours. There's a primitive campsite on the trail at Little Indian Bay, but be sure to register at the West Hawk Lake **park office** (May–Sept daily 8.30am–4.30pm; Oct–April Mon–Fri same hours; Ⓣ204/349-2245) if you're planning to stay overnight.

From West Hawk Lake, Route 44 cuts north towards **CADDY LAKE** (with campsites and two holiday lodges), the starting point for one of the area's most

Wilderness trips

The **Manitoba Naturalists' Society** runs an excellent programme of Whiteshell Wilderness Adventures during July and August. The trips last for five days, cost $310, and are based at a cabin on secluded Lake Mantario. All equipment is provided, as are the services of fully experienced guides, who organize classes in canoeing and survival skills. Reservations are essential: check Ⓦwww.manitobanature.ca for details.

beautiful **canoe routes**, the 160-kilometre journey along the Whiteshell River to Lone Island Lake, in the centre of the park. Experienced walkers could tackle the sixty-kilometre loop of the **Mantario Hiking Trail** just to the east of Caddy Lake, along Provincial Road 312. For beginners, there are the **Bear Lake trail** (8km) and **McGillivray trail** (4km), clearly signposted from Hwy 44 to the west of Caddy Lake; they reveal a good sample of the topography of the park – dry ridges dominated by jack pine, bogs crammed with black spruce, and two shallow lakes brown from algae and humic acid. Opposite the start of the Bear Lake Trail, the **Frances Lake** canoe route makes for a pleasant overnight excursion, a twenty-kilometre trip south to the Frances Lake campsite, with three portages past the rapids, and twelve hauls round beaver dams.

Further west, 32km from West Hawk, the village of **RENNIE** is home to the **park headquarters** (Mon–Fri 8am–noon & 1pm–4pm; Ⓣ204/369-5246), which has a comprehensive range of information on local trails and canoe routes. The nearby **Alf Hole Goose Sanctuary** (late May to mid-Oct Mon–Fri 10am–5pm, also Sat & Sun until early Sept 10.30am–6pm; free) is best visited in spring or autumn, when the Canada geese pass through on their migration. If you need to **stay** in Rennie as a base for excursions into the park, your choices are the rather primitive *Rennie Hotel* (Ⓣ204/369-5308; ❷) or the *Rocky Ridge Campground* (Ⓣ204/369-5507; $12–15; May–Sept). From Rennie, the eighty-kilometre stretch of Route 307 passes most of the park's other campsites, lodges, trails and canoe routes.

Nopiming Provincial Park

Just north of Whiteshell Park, **Nopiming Park** is more isolated, with a handful of lakeside campsites that can be reached along two bumpy gravel roads. Separated from the Whiteshell by the Winnipeg River, **Nopiming Provincial Park** is a remote rocky area whose granite shoreline cliffs spread out above black-spruce bogs and tiny sandy beaches; the name is Ojibwa for "entrance to the wilderness". The park's four campsites (all May–Sept; Ⓣ1-888/482-2267 or 204/948-3333 for camping reservations; Ⓣ1-800/214-6497 for park information; $7–10) lie close to its two gravel roads: Route 314, which meanders across the 80km of its western edge, and the shorter Route 315, a thirty-kilometre track that cuts east below Bird Lake to the Ontario border. Nopiming Park is crossed by the Oiseau and Manigotagan waterways, whose creeks and rivers trickle or rush from lake to lake, forming no less than 1200km of possible canoe route. Towards the south of the park, **BIRD LAKE** is a useful base, with a main settlement on the south shore that's equipped with a campsite ($7), a grocery store and the cabins of the *Nopiming Lodge* (Ⓣ204/884-2281, Ⓦwww.nopiminglodge.com; ❹). There's also motorboat rental, as well as canoe and guide rental for excursions to Snowshoe Lake, around falls and over rapids (55km). Near **Bissett**, in the north of the park, there are several abandoned gold-mining shafts from the 1930s.

Atikaki Provincial Wilderness Park

North of Nopiming, the **Atikaki Provincial Wilderness Park** is the most remote of the three eastern parks. The Atikaki's mile upon mile of rugged forest and granite outcrop are connected to the east shore of Lake Winnipeg by the Bloodvein and Leyond rivers, two of Manitoba's wildest white-water canoe routes. Accessible by float plane from Winnipeg and Lac du Bonnet, Atikaki has half a dozen holiday cottages and fishing lodges dotted across some of the finest Canadian Shield scenery in the province. There are no campsites or roads through the park, but the rough gravel track that makes up most of Route 304 does reach Wallace Lake, at the park's southern tip, via the east shore of Lake Winnipeg or Nopiming Park's Route 314. The Atikaki is crisscrossed by canoe routes that give glimpses of the region's ancient pictograph sites, but they all include difficult white-water stretches that should only be attempted by experienced canoeists.

The park's more popular canoe routes include the dramatic journey down the **Bloodvein River** to Lake Winnipeg, its rapids, falls and wild twistings balanced by peaceful drifts past quiet lakes and wild-rice marshes, and the **Kautunigan Route**, a 500-kilometre excursion that starts at Wallace Lake and threads its way to the mouth of the Berens River on Lake Winnipeg, well to the north of the park. Both routes pass stands of white birch, black spruce, jack pine, elm, oak and maple, and you may catch sight of moose, timber wolves, coyotes and black bears.

To obtain **information** on canoe routes, call the Manitoba Recreational Canoeing Association (ⓣ204/925-5078, ⓦwww.paddle.mb.ca). **Maps** are available from Manitoba Conservation (ⓣ204/945-6666 or 1-877/627-7226), and you should file trip plans with the Lac du Bonnet Natural Resource Office (ⓣ204/345-1454). Alternatively, several of the outfitters in Winnipeg and Lac du Bonnet organize **guided excursions**: Atikaki Canoe Outfitters (ⓣ651/483-1920 or 1-807/727-2797, ⓦwww.geocities.com/atikaki.geo), offers all manner canoeing excursions in the park starting from $357 per week, and details of other operators are on the Travel Manitoba website (ⓦwww.travelmanitoba.com).

Trans-Canada Highway

Slicing east–west across both Manitoba and Saskatchewan, the **Trans-Canada Highway** (Hwy 1), rushes past brilliant yellow canola (rapeseed) fields, for around 1000km before hitting the Alberta border. Dotted with campsites and fast-food joints, it follows the route of the original transcontinental railroad, pushing past a series of charmless towns that are at the heart of the province's most fertile farming region. Driving across, the novelty of the big skies and vast spaces quickly wears off and the journey can easily become dull. But this needn't be so if you're prepared to leave the hwy for breaks along the way. Several **Provincial Parks** offer the chance to stretch your legs and put the monotonous asphalt out of mind and a few attractions such as **Cannington Manor** and the **Tunnels of Moose Jaw** are genuinely entertaining. Surrounding the latter, **Moose Jaw** is a pleasant small town for an overnight break, as is **Regina** – the largest town en route. However, the only sight for which it's genuinely worth travelling in from afar is the pristine and wonderfully empty **Grasslands National Park**.

Winnipeg to Regina

West of Winnipeg, the Trans-Canada soon hits the workaday agricultural town **Portage La Prairie**, located roughly halfway en route to **Brandon**, the province's second largest city, which has a handful of Victorian mansions and a lively arts centre. Between them, **Spruce Woods** Provincial Park, contains the exceptional dune landscape of Manitoba's only desert, while other easy day-trips from Brandon include the pleasant little prairie town of **Souris** and **Turtle Mountain** Provincial Park on the US border. Over the provincial border in the southeast corner of Saskatchewan, the lakes, hillocks and aspen, birch and poplar forests of **Moose Mountain** Provincial Park come complete with campsites, nature trails and a resort village and are close to the delightful **Cannington Manor** Provincial Historic Park.

Portage La Prairie

The first major settlement west of Winnipeg is the food-processing centre of **PORTAGE LA PRAIRIE**, Manitoba's third largest city, located in the richest agricultural land in the province. East of the town is the mildly interesting **Fort la Reine Museum and Pioneer Village** (mid-May to mid-Sept daily 9am–6pm; $5), located at the junction of hwys 1A and 26, which remembers an original fort that served as the headquarters of Pierre Gaultier, Sieur de la Vérendrye, during his explorations in the 1740s. The present complex re-creates nineteenth-century life through a trading post, a log homestead, a trapper's cabin, a schoolhouse and a railway caboose. In the city centre, the limestone **city hall**, on the main drag, Saskatchewan Avenue, is the most attractive building; it was built in the 1890s by the same architect who designed the Parliament Buildings in Ottawa. On the same street is the **Portage Arts Centre and Gallery** (Tues–Sat 11am–5pm; free), featuring frequent exhibitions. Just south of the centre, the large **Island Park** is worth a stroll. It's almost completely surrounded by Crescent Lake, an oxbow of the Assiniboine River, formed when a river cuts across the narrow end of a loop in its course and creates an isolated crescent of water.

You'll find the **tourist bureau** (Mon–Fri 8.30am–5pm; ⓣ204/857-7778) in the Glesby Centre at 11 2nd St NE. The library next door also keeps a stock of tourist pamphlets and has public Internet access. For **accommodation**, your best bet is the 61-room *Westward Village Inn*, 2401 Saskatchewan Ave West (ⓣ204/857-9745 or 1-800/817-7855, ⓦwww.westwardvillageinn.com; ④), with a pool and hot tub, or the recently renovated *Westgate Inn Motel*, 1010 Saskatchewan Ave East (ⓣ204/239-5200, ⓦwww.westgateinn.com; ②). The well-equipped *Portage Campground* (ⓣ204/267-2191 or 1-866/887-330; $17–23; mid-April to Sept) is 16km east of the city on the Trans-Canada, with a playground, store and hiking trails. The range of good **restaurants** in Portage is limited; try *Bill's Sticky Fingers*, a local rib joint at 210 Saskatchewan Ave East, or *Essence Tea House*, 818 Saskatchewan Ave East, for great cheesecake.

Around Portage La Prairie

Delta Marsh, 25km north of the city on Provincial Road 240, is a wetland extending for some 40km along the southern shore of Lake Manitoba, and is one of the largest waterfowl marshes in North America. From May to mid-September, Delta Marsh Canoe Trips (☎204/243-2009) arranges guided tours.

West of town, near **Austin**, 3km south of the Trans-Canada on Hwy 34, the **Manitoba Agricultural Museum** (mid-May to Sept daily 9am–5pm; Ⓦwww.ag-museum.mb.ca; $5) has an exhaustive collection of early twentieth-century farm machinery, from gigantic steam tractors through to threshing machines and balers. The site also includes a homesteaders' village, which simulates village life of the late nineteenth century and has the province's largest collection of pioneer household articles. The immensely popular **Manitoba Threshermen's Reunion and Stampede** is held here every year in mid-July, featuring all things "Western" – four days of rodeo riding, threshing displays, ploughing competitions, square dancing, jigging and Central Canada's Fiddle Festival. You can camp in the museum grounds ($12–15; mid-May to Oct); otherwise, B&B **accommodation** is available next door at *The Oak Tree* (☎204/637-2029, Ⓦwww.bedandbreakfast.mb.ca; ❷).

Spruce Woods Provincial Park

Between Austin and Brandon, about 15km south of the Trans-Canada along Hwy 5, **Spruce Woods Provincial Park** falls on either side of the Assiniboine River, whose confused loops twist slowly south and west. The park has several walking trails that begin beside or near the road. To the north, the **Epinette Creek Trails** run through woodland and marsh, the longest being the 25km Newfoundland Trail. There are a number of unserviced campsites along the various paths.

Roughly 5km south of the Epinette Creek Trails, the **Spirit Sands Trails** cross an area of mixed-grass prairie before entering the shifting sand dunes and pots of quicksand that constitute Manitoba's only **desert**. These "Spirit Sands" were of great religious significance to the Ojibwa who, according to one of the earliest fur traders, Alexander Henry, told "of the strange noises heard in its bowels, and its nightly apparitions". Hire a guide or, if it's too hot to walk, try one of the horse-drawn **wagon tours** that leave from the start of the trail throughout the summer (May–Sept; 1hr 30min; for times call ☎204/827-2800, or off-season 379-2007; $8). The park is filled with strange, bluish-green ponds formed by the action of underground streams, and has some rare animals, notably the hognose snake and the prairie skink (a lizard); there's also a lot of poison ivy about, so take care. About 1km south of the start of the Spirit Sands, there's a **visitor centre** (mid-May to early Sept daily; summer ☎204/827-8850, rest of year ☎204/834-8800) and a range of tourist facilities at **KICHE MANITOU LAKE**, including a large campsite (☎204/948-3333 or 1-888/482-2267; $14–16; mid-May to Sept), a caravan park, grocery stores, restaurants, a beach and canoe rental.

CARBERRY is the nearest community of any size to Spruce Woods, and you can use it as a base to explore the park. Other than the **Seton Centre**, 116 Main St (June–Aug Mon–Sat 9am–5pm; $2), displaying the artwork and memorabilia of the naturalist Ernest Thompson Seton, and the local history **Carberry Plains Museum** (July & Aug daily 1–6pm; June & Sept by appointment ☎204/834-2284; free), there's not much to see. You can **stay** at the no-frills *4-Way Motel* (☎204/834-2878; ❷) or the more comfortable *Carberry Motor Inn* (☎204/834-2197; ❷).

Brandon

In 1881, when the CPR decided to route the transcontinental railroad through Winnipeg, it was clear that they would need a refuelling depot in the western part of the province. The ideal location was on the east bank of the Assiniboine

River, opposite today's **BRANDON**, 160km from Winnipeg, but a certain Dugald McVicar was already established here. The sudden arrival of all sorts of speculators encouraged McVicar to overreach himself, and he attempted to sell his farm and sod hut to the CPR for around $60,000, prompting a railway negotiator to exclaim, "I'll be damned if a town of any kind is built here." It wasn't, and Brandon was founded 4km to the west. Nowadays, the city is a major agricultural centre, home to several research institutions, Manitoba's largest livestock show – the Royal Manitoba Winter Fair – in late March, the huge First Nations Winter Celebration in January, rodeo finals in November and the Brandon Film Festival in February.

If you want to know what's going on in Brandon and the surrounding region, visit the swish **Riverbank Discovery Centre** (May–Sept Mon–Fri 8.30am–8.30pm, Sat & Sun 10.30am–8.30pm; Oct–April Mon–Fri 8.30am–5pm; ⓣ204/729-2141 or 1-888/799-1111, ⓦwww.brandon.com) a short drive south of the Trans-Canada Hwy along 18th St North. The bureau is also the starting point of several trails along the Assiniboine River and can provide leaflets on self-guided tours, including the one downtown that highlights historic buildings. Some of these are on the south side of Rosser Avenue where a terrace in the Romanesque Revival style includes the former Mutter Brothers Grocery Store, whose interior has been removed to the **Daly House Museum**, 122 18th St (Tues–Sun 10am–noon & 1–5pm; $3), the restored home of Brandon's first mayor. The highlight of the house is an illuminated four-storey doll's house in one of the upstairs bedrooms, complete with minuscule mice and mousetraps. Other imposing late nineteenth-century residences are located on the stretch of Louise Avenue as you walk west to **Brandon University**. The university itself has a small campus dotted with a mix of old and new buildings, most impressive of which is the original college building, with its ragged silhouette facing you to the right as you approach from Louise Avenue. The former **courthouse** topped by an octagonal cupola, at 11th St and Princess Ave, is Brandon's grandest building. The **Art Gallery of Southwestern Manitoba**, 710 Rosser Ave (Mon, Tues & Fri–Sun 10am–6pm, Thurs 10am–9pm; ⓦwww.agsm.ca; free), has changing exhibitions concentrating on the work of Manitoba artists and craftspeople.

Brandon's **bus terminal**, at 141 6th St (ⓣ204/727-0643 or 1-800/661-8747), handles Greyhound buses running to Winnipeg, Regina and Saskatoon, as well as smaller places in southwest Manitoba, and also Grey Goose Lines, which runs buses south on Hwy 10. VIA Rail **trains** on the thrice-weekly Winnipeg to Vancouver run stop north of Brandon along Hwy 10, from where it's a twenty-minute taxi ride into town ($15).

Brandon has lots of good places to **stay**. Just off the Trans-Canada is the eccentric *Barney's Motel*, 105 Middleton Ave (ⓣ204/725-1540 ⓦwww.barneysmotel.com; ❷), a place so scrupulously clean that it'll cut your bill by ten cents for every dead fly you find. Some rooms have kitchenettes. The *Super 8 Motel*, 1570 Highland Ave, just off the Trans-Canada (ⓣ204/729-8024 or 1-800/800-8000, ⓦwww.super8.com; ❹), is good value, with a free continental breakfast, plus a pool and hot tub. Other recommended places are the *Royal Oak Inn*, 3130 Victoria Ave (ⓣ204/728-5775; ❹), the city's most reputable accommodation, with a 1930s theme restaurant. There are two **campsites** just outside town: *Curran Park Campground* (ⓣ204/729-2486; $15–25; May–Sept), beside the Assinibione River 2km west of the visitor centre on Grand Valley Road, and smaller *Meadowlark Campground* (ⓣ204/728-7205 or 1-800/363-6434; $20–21), just off the Trans-Canada Hwy west of *Barney's Motel*. The city's selection of **restaurants** is poor. The best are along Rosser Avenue and include *Oliver's Bistro and Steakhouse* at no. 935 (ⓣ204/727-3333) where chandeliers hang among red drapes and classical melodies, but meat entrees start at a reasonable $12 – veggie options are a bit cheaper still. More expensive but excellent *Jerry's Bistro* (☎204/727-7781), at no. 926, serves up such exotic fare as emu and ostrich. Also on Rosser is the favourite meeting place of Brandon's sophisticates, the *Casteleyn*, at no. 908, where you can sip cappuccinos in minimalist splendour; they also sell beautiful chocolates. Around the corner at 139 110th St, *Timothy Beans* has Internet access as well as coffees and great sandwiches. The bland *Double Decker Tavern & Restaurant*, 943 Rosser Ave, regularly has live music.

Around Brandon: Souris and Turtle Mountain Provincial Park

An easy 43km drive southwest of Brandon, **SOURIS** is a pretty tree-shaded town on the steep banks of the Souris River and easily reached by Greyhound. Its main attraction is the vertigo-inducing cable **suspension bridge**, which is the longest in Canada. Beside the bridge is the charming local history **Hillcrest Museum**, 26 Crescent Ave (May & June Sun 2–5pm; July & Aug daily 10am–6pm; $3). You can prospect for agates, jaspers and other semi-precious stones at the pits outside town. The Rock Shop, 8 1st St South (May–Sept Mon–Fri 9.30am–6pm, Sat 10am–6pm, Sun noon–5pm; Oct–April Mon–Fri 10am–5pm, Sat 11am–5pm), sells some of the stones as well as the permit ($10.70), and can direct you to the pits. You can take away as much as you can carry.

Turtle Mountain Provincial Park

Ninety-seven kilometres south of Brandon along Hwy 10 you come to **Turtle Mountain Provincial Park**, a mixed area of marsh, rolling hills and deciduous forest, whose four hundred shallow lakes form an ideal habitat for the western painted turtle, after which the park takes its name. There's also a substantial moose population, most visible in late September. Turtle Mountain's main facilities are beside the main road at **ADAM LAKE**, where there's the large *Adam Lake Campsite* (☎1-888/482-2267 or 204/948-3333; $13–15; mid-May to mid-Sept), a beach, a store, a **park office** (Mon–Thurs 10am–noon & 1–6pm, Fri & Sat 10am–10pm, Sun 1–4pm; ☎204/534-2578) and a number of walking and cross-country skiing trails. There's a smaller, prettier campsite at **MAX LAKE** ($10; May–Sept), south of Hwy 3 on Provincial Road 446. This campsite gives easy access to the **Oskar Lake Canoe Route**, a nineteen-kilometre paddle and portage excursion across ten of the park's lakes. Best in the spring or autumn, the route should be tackled in an anticlockwise direction to eliminate the need to climb steep hills, and can be completed in one or two days. There's an overnight cabin at James Lake – register at the district office of the Manitoba Department of Natural Resources in **Boissevain**, 40km north (☎204/534-7204) if you intend to use it. Oddly, there are no canoe-rental facilities in the park.

On the southeastern edge of Turtle Mountain Park, and straddling the US border, is the landscaped shrub and formal flower garden of the **International Peace Garden** (☎204/534-2510). The dubious attractions on offer here include a Peace Chapel (built right on the border), the starkly modern Peace Tower and a large, floral clock. You can also take one of three self-guided **walking tours**. The garden costs $10 per vehicle (useful if you want to drive around the outlying trails) or $5 per pedestrian.

Moose Mountain and Cannington Manor

Moose Mountain Provincial Park in southeastern Saskatchewan – 60km south of the Trans-Canada on Route 9 – is a rough rectangle of wooded hills and lakes whose main resort, **KENOSEE LAKE**, is packed with holidaymakers throughout the season. There's a full range of amenities here, including a **parks office** (Mon–Fri 8am–5pm; ⓣ306/577-2600), restaurants, bars, sports facilities, waterslides and canoe and paddleboat rental, but it's still easy enough to escape the crowds and wander off into the surrounding poplar and birch groves. For **accommodation**, *Kenosee Condos and Gardens* (ⓣ306/577-2331 or 584-1028), in the resort village, has luxurious two-bedroom units (❺), and there are also a number of **campsites** spread out around the lake. Hotel rooms and cabin rentals are also available through the *Kenosee Inn* (ⓣ306/577-2099, ⓦwww.kenoseeinn.com; ❸–❹), which is near two golf courses, tennis courts and waterslides. The *Fish Creek* and *Lynwood* **campsites** (ⓣ306/577-2611 or 577-2600; $17–23; mid-May to early Sept) have the advantage of being right on the western edge of the developed area, a good 2km from the busiest part of the park. For **food**, try the *Moose Head Dining Room*, on the lake, which serves pizza, pasta, steaks and Saskatoon berry pie.

A short-lived experiment in transplanting English social customs to the prairies is the subject of the **Cannington Manor Provincial Historic Park** (mid-May to Aug Mon & Wed–Sun 10am–5pm; $2.50), a partly reconstructed Victorian village about 30km east of Kenosee Lake. Founded in 1882 by Edward Pierce, the would-be squire, the village attracted a number of British middle-class families determined to live as "gentlemen farmers", running small agricultural businesses, organizing tea and croquet evenings and even importing a pack of hounds to stage their own hunts. Their efforts failed when the branch rail line was routed well to the south of Cannington Manor, and by 1900 the settlement was abandoned.

The Qu'Appelle River Valley

The slow-moving **Qu'Appelle River** flows 350km from Lake Diefenbaker – 160km west of Regina – to the border with Manitoba, its lush, deep and wide valley filled with a series of lakes coming as a welcome break from the prairies. You can leave the Trans-Canada at its junction with Hwy 9 to explore the pleasantly quiet Round and Crooked lakes (both have several good campsites) or head on to the river's main township, the pleasant **Fort Qu'Appelle**, which sits sandwiched between Hwy 10 and the grooved escarpments of the neighbouring lakes, an hour's drive northeast of Regina.

Roughly ten minutes' walk from end to end, **FORT QU'APPELLE** has leafy gridiron streets that fall on either side of Broadway Street, the main drag, whose attractively restored red-brick **Hudson's Bay Company store**, on the corner of Company Avenue, dates from 1897 – the oldest original Hudson's Bay store in Canada. Nearby, at the top end of Bay Avenue, the **museum** (June–Aug daily 10am–noon & 1–5pm; other times by appointment; ⓣ306/332-4319; $2.50) has a small display on the area's European pioneers and the North West Mounted Police and is joined to the Hudson's Bay Company trading post of 1864. Three blocks to the south, the stone **obelisk** at Fifth Street and Company Avenue commemorates the signing of Treaty Number 4 between the Ojibwa, Cree and Assiniboine of the southern prairies and Lieutenant-Governor Morris in 1874. It was a fractious process. The Ojibwa insisted that the Hudson's Bay Company had stolen "the earth, trees, grass, stones, all that we see with our eyes", hectoring Morris to the point where he finally snapped. He confined the more militant Indian leaders to their tents, an authoritarian manoeuvre that undermined the unity of the Indians, who then signed the treaty in return for various land grants, pensions and equipment.

Buses make the seventy-kilometre journey from Regina to Fort Qu'Appelle two or three times daily. The **tourist information centre** is in the old CNR station at the junction of Boundary Avenue and Hwy 10 (June–Aug daily 9am–7pm; ⓣ306/332-4426). One of the town's three **motels**, the *Country Squire Inn* (ⓣ306/332-5603, ⓦwww.fortquappelle.com; ❷), is beside Hwy 10 at the bottom end of Bay Street. There's also an attractive **B&B** in the town: *Company House*, 172 Company Ave (ⓣ306/332-6333 or 332-7393; ❷), which serves up hearty home-cooked breakfasts and is near beaches and fishing, hiking and canoeing areas. On the north side of town, beside Echo Lake and near the golf course, is the *Fort* **campsite** (ⓣ306/332-4614; $11–15; mid-May to mid-Sept). There are several **restaurants** on Broadway Street, including the Chinese *Jade Palace* at no. 215, and *Bubba's* next door. For more imaginative food, head for the *Off Broadway Bistro*, 12 Boundary Ave, where you can dine on turkey lasagne or *tourtière*.

Near Fort Qu'Appelle, the river bulges into a chain of eight little lakes known collectively as the **Fishing Lakes**. It's possible to drive alongside all of them, but the pick of the bunch is the nearest, **Echo Lake**, which affords pleasant views over the river valley. Between this lake and Pasqua Lake is the scenic **Echo Valley Provincial Park** (year-round; visitor centre and Parks office mid-May to Aug ⓣ306/332-3215; $7 entry fee, camping $13–20), while **Katepwa Point Provincial Park**, an even tinier park (mid-May to Sept; free), sits at the southernmost point of the chain of lakes.

About 35km east of Fort Qu'Appelle, just off Hwy 22 south of the village of Abernethy, is the **Motherwell Homestead National Historic Site** (late May to Sept daily 9am–5pm; ⓣ306/333-2116; $7.15). This large, square house, with its odd assortment of multicoloured fieldstones embedded in the exterior walls, and lacy wrought-iron "widow's walk" on the roof, was built in 1898 for W.R. Motherwell, a local farmer and politician who moved to Saskatchewan from Ontario in 1882. He brought with him his knowledge of domestic architecture, for the six-bedroom building is similar to the gracious stone farmhouses of southern Ontario and looks a bit incongruous in its prairie surroundings. Just behind the house, which is restored to its 1912–14 appearance, there's a large red 1907 barn, with farm equipment and roaming farm animals to complete the rustic setting.

Regina

REGINA, 575km west of Winnipeg, is the capital city of Saskatchewan, its commercial and administrative services anchoring a vast network of agricultural villages and towns. Yet despite its status, its brash shopping malls and 200,000-plus population, Regina acts and feels like a small prairie town. It's a comfortable, if unremarkable, place to spend a couple of days, with the offbeat attraction of the **Royal Canadian Mounted Police Training Academy and Museum**, and more hours of sunshine than any other major city in Canada.

In 1881 the Indian Commissioner **Edward Dewdney** became lieutenant-governor of the Northwest Territories, a vast tract of land that spread west from Ontario as far as the Arctic and Pacific oceans. Almost immediately, he decided to move his capital south from the established community of Battleford to **Pile o'Bones**, an inconsequential dot on the map that took its name from the heaps of bleached buffalo bones left along its creek by generations of native hunters. The reason for Dewdney's decision was the routing of the Canadian Pacific transcontinental railroad across the southern plains: the city was renamed Regina (Latin for "queen") after Queen Victoria, and Dewdney petitioned for it to be expanded on land to the north of the creek, a plot coincidentally owned by him. The site was terrible: the sluggish creek provided a poor water supply, the clay soil was muddy in wet weather and dusty in the summer, and there was no timber for building. Accordingly, the railway board refused to oblige, and the end result was farcical: Government House and the Mounted Police barracks were built where Dewdney wanted them, but the train station was a three-kilometre trek to the south.

In 1905 Regina became the capital of the newly created province of **Saskatchewan**, and settlers flocked here from the United States and central Europe. At the heart of an expanding wheat-growing district, the city tripled its population during its first fifteen years. It also overcame its natural disadvantages with an ambitious programme of tree-planting, which provided shade and controlled the dust, and by damming the creek to provide a better source of water. However, the city's success was based on the fragile prosperity of a one-crop economy, and throughout the twentieth century boom alternated with bust.

Arrival, information and getting around

Regina's **airport** (ⓣ306/761-7555, ⓦwww.yqr.ca) is about 5km west of the city centre. The taxi trip downtown costs roughly $10, or you can take the Hobo Express Shuttle bus (ⓣ306/949-2121 or 1-877/828-4626) to Regina's downtown hotels or locations in Moose Jaw ($25). A ten-minute walk east of the airport brings you to the junction of Regina Avenue and Pasqua Street, from where Regina Transit's **buses** #11 and #13 head for the city centre (Mon–Sat every 25min 6am–12.30am, Sun hourly 11am–6pm). The **bus station** is downtown at 2041 Hamilton St, just south of Victoria Avenue, with

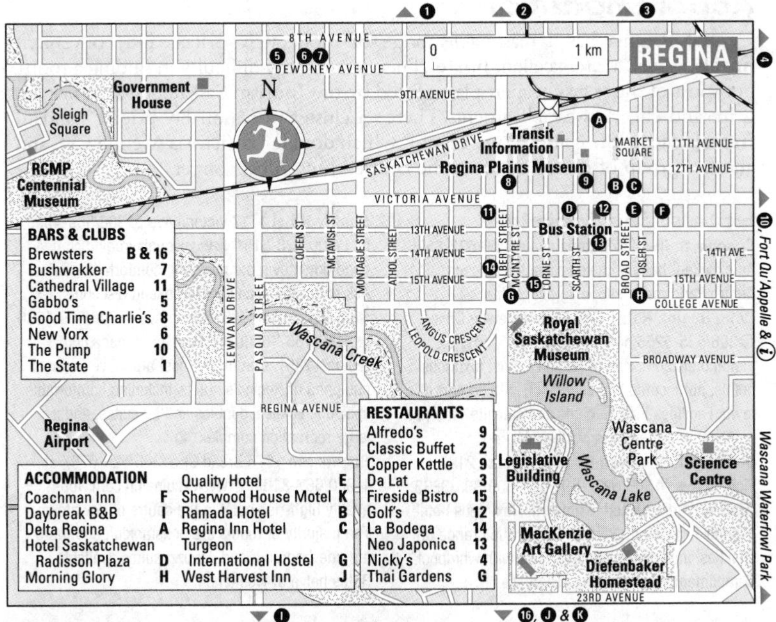

Tours in and around Regina

Great Western Adventure Tours, 41 Wesley Rd (☎306/584-3555), runs **tours** of the city (4hr 30min; $16), as well as to Moose Jaw (6hr; $24) and the Qu'Appelle Valley (7hr; $37 including lunch). Heritage Regina Tours (☎306/585-4214) has free guided walking tours of the city (July to mid-Sept Sun). RC Tours (☎306/545-0555) has minibus tours of the city's highlights including the Legislative Building, Royal Canadian Mounted Police Museum and Government House (10am & 1pm, pick-up from downtown hotels; 3hr 30min; $24). The Saskatchewan History & Folklore Society, 1860 Lorne St (☎306/780-9204 or 1-800/919-9437), organizes one- to four-day tours of the province's historic sites.

services from Greyhound and the provincial carrier, the Saskatchewan Transportation Company (☎306/787-0101 or 1-800/663-7181).

Tourism Regina operates a tourist bureau east of town on Hwy 1, really only accessible by car (mid-May to early Sept Mon–Fri 8am–7pm, Sat & Sun 10am–6pm; rest of year Mon–Fri 8am–5pm; ☎306/789-5099 or 1-800/661-5099, Ⓦwww.tourismregina.com). The **Tourism Saskatchewan** office, in the Leaderpost building at 1922 Park St (Mon–Fri 8am–5pm; ☎306/787-2300 or 1-877/237-2273, Ⓦwww.sasktourism.com), has a comprehensive range of leaflets and booklets and can help with specific info on Regina.

The best way to see the centre is on **foot**, though the area around McIntyre Street and Saskatchewan Drive, and sections of Osler Street, six blocks east, are rundown neighbourhoods that are best avoided. Similarly accessible is the **Wascana Centre**, a large multipurpose park and recreational area, whose northern boundary is a few minutes' stroll south of the centre. **Regina Transit** runs bus services; a standard one-way fare is $2.10 (Ⓦwww.reginatransit.com).

Accommodation

Central Regina has a reasonable range of moderately priced and convenient **hotels**, as well as an excellent **hostel**. There's rarely any difficulty in finding a room, but most of the very cheapest places listed by the Tourism Saskatchewan office are grim and cheerless establishments. There's a cluster of reasonably priced, standard **motels** east of the centre along Hwy 1, which doubles as Victoria Avenue East, and another group of motels south of the centre, along Albert Street.

Hotels and motels

Coachman Inn 835 Victoria Ave ☎306/522-8525. An excellent budget choice close to Wascana Centre Park, major shopping and sights. ❷

Delta Regina Hotel 1919 Saskatchewan Drive ☎306/525-5255 or 1-800/209-5255, Ⓦwww.deltahotels.com. One of Regina's most luxurious hotels, but located in a slightly off-putting part of town. Facilities include cable and satellite TV, and a pool with a three-storey waterslide. ❺

Hotel Saskatchewan Radisson Plaza 2125 Victoria Ave ☎306/522-7691 or 1-800/333-3333, Ⓦwww.hotelsask.com. This large, luxurious hotel, overlooking Victoria Park, provides a full range of facilities, including a fitness centre with whirlpool. Complimentary pick-up at airport. ❹

Quality Hotel 1717 Victoria Ave ☎306/569-4656 or 1-800/228-5151 Ⓦwww.qualityregina.com. A good downtown bargain, with comfortable rooms. Ask about the occasional weekend discounts. ❸

Ramada Hotel 1818 Victoria Ave ☎306/569-1666 or 1-800/667-6500, Ⓦwww.the.ramada.com.regina/11851. One of the most attractive and well equipped of Regina's hotels, including comfortable, spacious singles, doubles and en suites, and a large recreation complex. ❹

Regina Inn 1975 Broad St ☎306/525-6767 or 1-800/667-8162, Ⓦwww.reginainn.com. Top-quality high-rise hotel in the centre of downtown. The majority of rooms are nonsmoking and there are one-bedroom and Jacuzzi suites available. Rates halve at weekends. ❹

Sherwood House Motel 3915 Albert St ⓣ306/586-3131, ⓦwww.sherwoodhousemotel.com. Budget motel on the Albert Street strip; nothing fancy but clean and good value, with adjoining restaurant and bar. ❸

West Harvest Inn 4025 Albert St ⓣ306/586-6755 or 1-800/853-1181, ⓦwww.westharvestinn.com. One of the best bargains in the Regina area. Singles, doubles and en suites all come with free in-room coffee and local calls. The inn also has a health spa and gym. ❹

B&Bs

Daybreak B&B 316 Habkirk Drive ⓣ306/586-0211. In the south of the city, east of Albert St, near the Trans-Canada. Two rooms with a nice old-fashioned feel and the owners offer free pick-up and delivery to airport or bus station. ❶

Morning Glory Manor 1718 College Ave ⓣ306/525-2945 ⓦwww.morningglorymanor.ca. Charming 1920s home, minutes from downtown and Wascana Centre Park. Off-street parking. ❷

Hostels

Turgeon International Hostel (HI) 2310 McIntyre St ⓣ306/791-8165, ⓦwww.hihostels.ca. Extremely clean HI hostel in a restored heritage house, immediately south of the downtown core, with cooking and laundry facilities and a small library. Dorm beds $24; one double room $52.

Campsites

Buffalo Lookout Campground Hwy 1 East ⓣ306/525-1448 or ⓣ306/757-6389, ⓦwww.buffalolookoutrvcampground.com. Located 5km east of downtown off the Hwy to Winnipeg. Includes a store, shower house, phones and indoor recreation facilities, as well as a 24hr on-site manager. $22–31.

Kings' Acres Campground Hwy 1 East ⓣ306/522-1619. Located on a spacious property 1km east of town, behind the Tourism Regina Bureau. With a full range of serviced and unserviced sites, with store, phone, pool, and TV and games room. $19–28. March–Oct.

The City

Fifteen minutes' walk from end to end, Regina's downtown business and shopping core is known as the **Market Square**, a simple gridiron bounded by Saskatchewan Drive and 13th Avenue to the north and south, Osler and Albert streets to the east and west. The rather mundane **Regina Plains Museum** (Mon–Wed & Fri 10am–4pm, Thurs 10am–5.30pm, Sat call for hours; free; ⓣ306/780-9435, ⓦwww.reginaplainsmuseum.com) is within Market Square, on the fourth floor of the mall at 1801 Scarth St and 11th Ave – its modest displays on the city's history are less diverting than the stories of the elderly volunteers who staff the museum. Exhibitions of innovative, and often controversial, contemporary art can be seen at the **Dunlop Art Gallery**, in the Public Library, west of the museum at 2311 12th Ave (Mon–Thurs 9.30am–9pm, Fri 9.30am–6pm, Sat 9.30am–5pm, Sun 1.30–5pm; free; ⓦwww.dunlopartgallery.org). If the museum and gallery has whetted your appetite you should visit the **Antique Mall**, the largest in western Canada, located beyond the railway tracks north of Market Square, at 1175 Rose St (Mon–Sat 10am–6pm, Wed & Thurs until 9.30pm, Sun 1.30–5pm; free).

Immediately to the west of the Market Square district, across Albert Street, is **Cathedral Village**, with 13th Avenue as its heart. It's an old area with an eclectic mix of boutiques, coffee shops, craft shops and classy restaurants.

Wascana Centre Park

Roughly eight times the size of the Market Square, Regina's most distinctive feature is **Wascana Centre Park** (ⓦwww.wascana.sk.ca), which begins three blocks south of 13th Avenue and extends southeast to the city limits, following the curves of **Wascana Lake**, which was created as part of a work project for the unemployed in the 1930s. The city's main recreation area, the park is equipped with a bandstand (performances Sun 2–4pm), barbecue pits, snack bars, boating facilities and waterfowl ponds, but for the most part it's a cheerless combination of reed-filled water and bare lawn.

In the northwest corner of the park, near College Avenue and Albert Street, the **Royal Saskatchewan Museum** (daily May–Aug 9am–5.30pm; Sept–April 9am–4.30pm; suggested donation $2; ⓦwww.royalsaskmuseum.ca) is devoted to the province's geology and wildlife, starring a giant animated dinosaur called Megamunch. Informative dioramas portray aspects of aboriginal life in the First Nations Gallery, including storytelling, shown in the scene of a grizzled grandfather recounting stories to a couple of rapt youths. In the new Life Sciences Gallery the relationships between habitat, plants and animals are explored with a multitude of skilfully stuffed animals and plastic flora set against backdrops that evoke the diverse eco-regions of Saskatchewan. A couple of minutes' walk to the east is the ferry boat to **Willow Island** (mid-May to Aug Mon–Fri noon–4pm; $2), a favourite picnic spot. **Boat tours** are available, departing from the observation deck, near the swimming pool (mid-June to Aug Sun 1–5pm; 20min; $2).

Further east, reached by the winding Wascana Drive, is perhaps Regina's main tourist attraction, the **Saskatchewan Science Centre** (May to early Sept Mon–Thurs 9am–6pm, Fri 9am–8.30pm, Sat & Sun 11am–6pm; rest of year Tues–Fri 9am–5pm, Sat & Sun 11am–6pm; ⓣ306/522-4629 or 1-800/667-6300, ⓦwww.sciencecentre.com; $7). The open, airy building houses more than a hundred interactive scientific exhibits, live stage shows and demonstrations; of particular interest is a display on uranium mining and a room which has a direct video link to NASA headquarters in Houston, enabling you to watch the live proceedings when a mission is under way. Another gallery is devoted to the soils and weather of Saskatchewan, and here you can learn about what's involved in running a farm. Also on the premises is an IMAX cinema (Mon 6–9pm, Tues–Sun 12.30–9.30pm; $7, or joint ticket with centre $12).

On the other side of the lake, accessible from Albert Street, is the grand **Legislative Building** (daily late May to Sept 8am–9pm; rest of year 8am–5pm; free tours every 30min; 2hr), a self-confident cross-shaped structure of Manitoba limestone with an impressive domed tower at its centre. Guided tours take in the oak-and-marble-panelled Legislative Chamber and six small art galleries, the best of which houses Edmund Morris's portraits of local Indian leaders, presented to the province in 1911. A neighbouring corridor is occupied by the paintings of the **Native Heritage Foundation**, some thirty canvases featuring the work of contemporary Métis and native artists, notably Allen Sapp from North Battleford, who has won some international acclaim for his softly coloured studies of life on Saskatchewan's Indian reserves as he remembers them from the 1930s. A few minutes' walk south of the Legislative Building, just off Albert Street at 23rd Avenue, the **MacKenzie Art Gallery** (daily 11am–6pm, Wed & Thurs until 10pm; free) has several spacious modern galleries devoted to temporary exhibitions by modern Canadian artists, plus a good permanent collection. It's also the stage for the city's principal theatrical event, **The Trial of Louis Riel** (mid-July to Aug Wed–Fri; $12), whose text is based on the transcripts of the trial in Regina in September 1885. No other single event in Canada's past has aroused such controversy: at the time, most of English-speaking Canada was determined he should hang as a rebel, whereas his French-Canadian defenders saw him as a patriot and champion of a just cause. Though Riel was subject to visions and delusions, the court rejected the defence of insanity on the grounds that he knew what he was doing. As he exclaimed: "No one can say that the North-West was not suffering last year… but what I have done, and risked, rested certainly on the conviction [that I was] called upon to do something for my country." The jury found him guilty, but the execution was delayed while Prime Minister John A. Macdonald weighed the consequences; in the end, he decided against clemency.

The **Diefenbaker Homestead** (mid-May to Aug daily 10am–8pm; free), about 1km east of the gallery but still within the park, was the boyhood home of John Diefenbaker, Conservative Prime Minister of Canada from 1957 to 1963. Moved from the township of Borden, SK in 1967, the tiny wooden house has been decked out with original and contemporary furnishings and memorabilia reflecting both Diefenbaker's homespun philosophies and the

The Mounties

The heroes of a hundred adventure stories, from *Boys' Own* yarns to more eccentric epics such as the movie *Canadian Mounties versus the Atomic Invaders*, the **Mounties** have been the continent's most charismatic good guys ever since Inspector James Morrow Walsh rode into Chief Sitting Bull's Canadian encampment to lay down the law. Coming straight after the Sioux's victory at the battle of the Little Bighorn in 1876, this was an act of extraordinary daring, and it secured the future of the Mounties. The **North West Mounted Police**, as the Mounties were originally called, had been created in Ottawa during the autumn of 1873, simply in order to restore law and order to the "Whoop-up Country" of southern Saskatchewan and Alberta in the aftermath of the Cypress Hills Massacre (see box, p.607). There was no long-term strategy: the force's areas of responsibility were undecided, and even their uniforms had been slung together from a surplus supply of British army tunics that happened to be handy. However, they did a brilliant job of controlling the whiskey traders who had created pandemonium through the unscrupulous sale of liquor to the Plains Indians, and it was soon clear – after Walsh's dealings with Sitting Bull – that they were to become a permanent institution.

The Mounties came to perform a vital role in administering the west on behalf of the federal government, acting both as law enforcement officers and as justices of the peace. From the 1880s their patrols diligently crisscrossed the territory, their influence reinforced by a knowledge of local conditions that was accumulated in the exercise of a great range of duties – from delivering the mail to providing crop reports. Despite this level of autonomy, the Mounties saw themselves as an integral, if remote, part of the **British Empire**, their actions and decisions sanctioned by the weight of its authority. In this sense, they despised the individualism of the American sheriff and marshal, for the Mounties expected obedience because of the dignity of their office, not because of their speed with a firearm.

The officer corps, most of whom were recruited from the social elite of the eastern provinces, became respected for an even-handedness that extended, remarkably for the period, to their dealings with the Plains Indians. **Crowfoot**, the Blackfoot leader, was even moved to remark, "If the police had not come to the country, where would we all be now? They have protected us as the feathers of a bird protect it from the frosts of winter." Yet the officers' class prejudices had a less positive influence on their approach to law and order: socially disruptive crimes of violence were their main priority, whereas prostitution and drunkenness were regarded as predictable and inevitable nuisances that were confined to the "lower orders". They had a cohesive view of the society they wanted to create, a WASP-ish patriarchy where everyone knew their place.

After 1920, when the force lost its exclusively western mandate to become the **Royal Canadian Mounted Police**, this conservative undertow became more problematic. Time and again the RCMP supported reactionary politicians who used them to break strikes – like prime ministers Bennett in Saskatchewan in 1933 and 1934, and Joey Smallwood in Newfoundland during 1959 – and they have often been accused of bias in their dealings with the Québecois. That said, although the Mounties are seen by some as a bastion of reaction at odds with multicultural definitions of Canada, for the most part they remain a potent symbol of nationality.

immense self-confidence that earned him the nickname "Dief the Chief". In the extreme southeast corner of the park, reached by buses #10 or #12 or by car along Arcola Avenue East and Prince of Wales Drive from the city centre, is the **Wascana Waterfowl Park** (May–Nov daily 9am–9pm; free; guided tours Mon–Fri 9am–4pm), a group of ponds that's a habitat for ducks, pelicans and Canada geese.

Royal Canadian Mounted Police Training Academy

All Mounties do their basic training at the **Royal Canadian Mounted Police Training Academy**, 4km west of the city centre at Dewdney Avenue West, accessible by bus #8 from 11th Avenue at Cornwall Street. Beside the main parade ground of Sleigh Square – site of the closely choreographed Sergeant Major's parade (late May to Aug Mon–Fri 12.50pm) and Sunset Retreat Ceremony (July to mid-Aug Tues 6.45pm) – is the RCMP **Centennial Museum** (daily mid-June to Aug 8am–6.45pm; rest of year 10am–4.45pm; free tours Mon–Fri 9am (summer only), 10am, 11am, 1.30pm, 2.30pm & 3.30pm; Ⓦwww.rcmpmuseum.com; free). This traces the history of the force, from early contacts with the Plains Indians and Métis through to its present role as an intelligence-gathering organization.

Inside the museum, a series of contemporary quotations illustrates the **Long March** that first brought the Mounties to the west from Ontario in 1874. Their destination was Fort Whoop-up, near present-day Lethbridge, AB where they intended to expel the American whiskey traders. However, by the time they arrived they were in a state of complete exhaustion, and it was fortunate that the Americans had already decamped. Another small section deals with **Sitting Bull**, who crossed into Canada after his victory at the Battle of the Little Bighorn in 1876. Fearing reprisals from the furious American army, Sitting Bull spent four years in and around the Cypress Hills,

△ Trainees at the RCMP Academy

where he developed a friendship with Police Inspector James Walsh. A picture of the chief and his braves, taken at Fort Walsh in 1877, shows an audience of curious Mounties in their pith helmets. To reinforce the romantic Hollywood image of the Mounties, an onsite cinema has continuous free runnings of such glorified interpretations as *Rose Marie* (1936), starring Nelson Eddy and Jeanette MacDonald.

On the **tour** of the grounds you're shown the various buildings, including mock-ups of houses where recruits practise family arrests, search warrants and surveillance techniques; the drill hall where new recruits are put through their paces; and the 1883 chapel – Regina's oldest building – a splendid structure furnished in dark, polished oak where you can escape the intense training activity outside.

Government House

Government House, a couple of kilometres west of the city centre at 4607 Dewdney Ave and Lewvan Drive (Tues–Sun 10am–4pm; tours every 30min; free; bus #1, #11 or #13), was the residence of the lieutenant-governors of the Northwest Territories and subsequently Saskatchewan from 1891 to 1945. A stolid yellow-brick building, it has been delightfully restored to its appearance at the end of the nineteenth century, with offices and reception areas downstairs and a splendid, balconied staircase leading up to the bedrooms. The men's billiards room is decorated with an enormous bison head and a lemon-water stand, where the governor and his cronies would dip their fingers to hide the smell of the cigars. There are also a couple of mementos of one of the more eccentric governors, Amédée Forget, whose specially designed "salesman's chair", beside the entrance, was meant to be uncomfortable, with protruding gargoyles sticking into the visitor's spine, legs shorter at the front than the back and a flesh-pinching crack cut across the middle of the seat. The rocking horse in the office was for Forget's pet monkey. High tea, complete with finger sandwiches and fragile china cups, is served in the ballroom one weekend each month between 1.30pm and 4pm.

Eating, drinking and entertainment

Regina has a clutch of good downtown **restaurants**, lively places whose prices are usually very reasonable. However, many of them close early and don't open at all on Sundays; in emergencies try the big hotels whose standard-issue snack bars are nearly always open daily to 9.30pm.

The city's **nightlife** is hardly inspiring, but the university students provide a little stimulation for the couple of downtown clubs, whilst local roustabouts and government workers alike tend to stick to Country & Western. As a general rule, avoid the downtown **bars**, which are really not very pleasant, and try one of Regina's **brewpubs**, though most are a bit far from the centre. A couple are on the city's main strip of – fairly unexciting – clubs on Dewdney Avenue, which is just north of downtown in Regina's Old Warehouse District.

For **theatre**, the Regina Performing Arts Centre, 1077 Angus St (Ⓣ306/779-2277), stages work by the Saskatchewan Community Theatre and the Regina Little Theatre. The Regina Symphony Orchestra (Ⓦwww.reginasymphonyorchestra.sk.ca) performs at the Saskatchewan Centre of the Arts, 200 Lakeshore Drive (Ⓣ306/525-9999 or 1-800/667-8497). The *Prairie Dog* is Regina's free weekly entertainment newspaper and useful for listings; pick it up at roadside dispensers or in cafés and bars. **Buffalo Days** is a week-long festival (late July & early Aug) of craft and livestock exhibitions and music shows, ending with a fireworks display.

The **Kinsmen Rock in the Valley**, held in Craven, a 20min drive north of town, is a four-day contemporary and classic rock festival in mid-July. The mid-June **Folk Festival** is held in Victoria Park; and the **Mosaic Multicultural Festival**, held in early June at various locations throughout the city, is a multiethnic celebration featuring folk dancing and pavilions serving food and drink. On the first weekend of September, Chinese dragon boats rowed by large teams race each other in Wascana Park.

Cafés and restaurants

Alfredo's Fresh Pasta and Bistro 1801 Scarth St ⓣ306/522-3366. Specializes in home-made pasta dishes and combines a tasty and imaginative menu with good-value main courses from $8. Closed Sun.

Classic Buffet Co. 100 Albert St ⓣ306/545-6955. Help yourself to the table laid out with pizza, roast beef and fifteen other hot dishes. Early closing.

The Copper Kettle 1953 Scarth St ⓣ306/525-3545. Central Greek-Canadian place overlooking Market Square; pick the fabulous spinach and feta pizza over the very average pasta ($9).

Da Lat by Night 1312 Broad St ⓣ306/757-7291. Popular place for huge helpings of Vietnamese or Chinese food. Filling set meals run from $15 for two people. Take out and delivery available.

Fireside Bistro 2305 Smith St ⓣ306/761-2305. Great bistro tucked away in a leafy residential neighbourhood close to Wascana Park. A reliable mix of burgers, sandwiches, salads and wraps (around $10) emerge for lunch; best enjoyed out on the sunny terrace in summer. Evenings the chef gets more experimental with bison spring rolls and crab stuffed mushrooms among the appetizers; fine cuts of bison and beef, seafood and pasta forming the entrees; the pork tenderloin with blue cheese and pears ($23) is a house specialty.

Golf's Steak House 1945 Victoria Ave ⓣ306/525-5808. Special-occasion steakhouse with top-notch prime rib and charbroiled steaks.

La Bodega 2228 Albert St ⓣ306/546-3660. Hip restaurant with great patio where movies are screened on a neighbouring wall and which hosts a drum night (Tues). Food is equally adventurous, with Thai mango and palm salads available and a confusing array of tapas and so-called tappetizers that include odd bedfellows like sushi and bannock bruschetta. But execution is excellent and prices consequently fairly steep.

Neo Japonica 2167 Hamilton St ⓣ306/359-7669. Among the best Japanese restaurants in Canada; excellent tempura and sushi.

Nicky's Café & Bake Shop 1005 8th Ave. Good Canadian menu at reasonable prices, especially their breakfasts, Saskatoon berry pie and bread. Fresh turkey served daily. Closed Sun.

Thai Gardens 2317 Albert St ⓣ306/584-0345. Huge portions of tasty, well-priced Thai and pan-Asian food; served on the same block as the hostel on the south side of town. Take out available.

Bars and clubs

Brewster's 1832 Victoria Ave East. One of a chain of three brewpubs known for their extensive range of beer; branch also at 4180 Albert St.

The Bushwakker 2206 Dewdney Ave ⓣ306/359-7276. Successful chain brewpub with twelve types of beer and a large selection of single-malt scotches; excellent hearty bar food including pierogies and buffalo steaks. Live music frequently livens things up later on.

Cathedral Village Free House 3062 Albert St at 13th ⓣ306/359-1661. Busy bar and restaurant with locally brewed beers and good wood-fired pizzas, sandwiches and burritos. Try something a bit fancier like the excellent Freehouse Bouillabaisse that combines halibut, salmon, scallops, shrimp, walleye and tiger prawns.

Gabbo's 2338 Dewdney Ave. One of several fairly basic nightclubs in a row of old warehouses; choose between them by following the crowds. Small cover Sat & Sun.

Good Time Charlie's In *Plains Hotel*, 1965 Albert St. Biker bar – the best blues club in Regina. Jam sessions Thurs, Sat & Sun nights, plus Sat afternoons. $3–5 cover charge.

OUTside Bar 2070 Broad St. Popular gay venue.

New Yorx Lounge 2300 Dewdney Ave ⓣ306-359-7772. A current favourite on the Dewdney strip, this multi-level nightclub has sociable outdoor deck, three bars and two dance floors that draws twenty-somethings in droves and attracts touring bands. Check out the extraordinary scale model of Manhattan and come early for the great bar food.

The Pump 641 Victoria Ave East. ⓦwww.thepumproadhouse.com. C&W venue with a huge dance floor.

The State 1326 Hamilton St. Alternative rap, pop, 1980s hits – all on a jammed multi-level dance floor. Great live bands most nights. $7 cover charge on Fri. Closed Sun.

Listings

Bike rental Western Cycle, 1550 8th Ave ☎306/522-5678.
Bookshops Book and Brier Patch, 4065 Albert St ☎306/586-5814.
Car rental Avis ☎306/757-1653, airport ☎306/751-5460; Budget ☎306/791-6810; Hertz ☎306/791-9139; Thrifty ☎306/525-1000.
Internet access Central library 2311 12th Ave ☎306/777-6000.
Laundries Cathedral Laundromat, 2911 13th Ave ☎306/525-2665.
Medical Regina General Hospital, 1440 14th Ave ☎306/766-4444. Cathedral Dental Clinic, 3032 13th Ave ☎306/352-9966.
Pharmacy 11th Ave Pharmacy,11th Ave ☎306/569-981.
Police ☎306/777-6500.
Post office 2200 Saskatchewan Drive.
Taxis Capital Cab ☎306/791-2222; Co-op Taxi ☎306/586-6555.

Southern Saskatchewan

From Regina the 400km drive west across **southern Saskatchewan** on the Trans-Canada Hwy is monotonous, and the only town worth a stopover is **Moose Jaw**, once a Prohibition hangout of American gangsters. Otherwise the rest of southern Saskatchewan is mostly undulating farmland, broken up by a handful of lakes and rivers, stretches of arid semi-desert and the odd range of wooded hills. South of Moose Jaw near the US border are the **Big Muddy Badlands**, weathered buttes and conical hills that can easily be explored on the tours that leave the tiny town of Coronach throughout the summer. Directly west of here, the **Grasslands National Park** is still being developed and extended, two separate slices of prairie punctuated by coulees and buttes that add a rare touch of drama to the landscape.

Back along the Trans-Canada, beyond the small city of Swift Current and just north of the quintessential cowboy town of Maple Creek – the market town for several Hutterite colonies – are the **Great Sand Hills**, a starkly beautiful desert landscape. Finally, straddling the Alberta border, **Cypress Hills Interprovincial Park** is also well worth a visit, its heavily forested hills and ridges harbouring a restored Mountie outpost, **Fort Walsh**.

Apart from the daily bus services along the Trans-Canada, the region's **public transport** system is dismal; to see the parks, you'll need a car.

Moose Jaw

MOOSE JAW, 70km west of Regina, was founded as a railway depot in 1882 and is now Saskatchewan's fourth largest city, with 35,000 inhabitants – a number that has remained almost static since the 1940s. Its name may have come from a local word for "warm breezes", or the jaw-like turn that the river takes just outside town, or even the repairs made to a cartwheel by an early pioneer with the assistance of a moose's jawbone.

Moose Jaw achieved some notoriety during Prohibition in the 1920s, when liquor was smuggled south by car or by train along the Soo Line, which ran from here to Chicago. For most locals this period of bootleggers, gangsters, gamblers and "boozoriums" (liquor warehouses) was not a happy one, and for years various schemes to attract tourists by developing the "Roaring Twenties" theme met with considerable opposition from the substantial portion of the population that actually experienced them. Those suffering from aches and pains, however, welcomed the 1995 opening of the wonderful **Temple**

The tunnels of Moose Jaw

A network of **tunnels** in Moose Jaw runs underneath River Street from the basements of the old buildings. No one knows who built the tunnels, or why. What is known is that they were extended and used in the early 1900s by Chinese railway workers and their families hoping to escape the $500 "head tax", a measure designed to force them to return to famine-stricken China after the completion of their work on the railway. Later, during Prohibition, Chicago gangsters used the tunnels to negotiate their deals for Canada's liquor supplies and to hide out when things got too "hot" in Chicago.

The city runs two entertaining 45-minute **Tunnels of Moose Jaw tours** (hours vary every month: approximately summer Mon–Fri 10am–7pm, Sat & Sun 10am–9pm; Oct–May daily noon–5.30pm; tours every 20min; ⓣ306/693-5261, ⓦwww.tunnelsofmoosejaw.com; one tour $13, two tours $21). These are entitled the **Chicago Connection**, a light-hearted look at the capers of Al Capone's men in the tunnels, complete with a speakeasy, a police bust and an actor playing the particularly slimy Chief of Police; and the more serious **Passage to Fortune**, which tells the horrific story of the Chinese immigrants, with re-creations of a Chinese laundry, sweatshops, a herbalist and an opium den. Costumed guides ham it up through the network of narrow tunnels beneath Main St, helped by old movies and state-of-the-art animatronics: moving, talking mannequins.

Tours begin at **Tunnel Central**, 16 Main St North, in a reception area with a beautiful copper ceiling and walls adorned with local photos from the early decades of the twentieth century.

Gardens Mineral Spa, 24 Fairford St East (Sun–Thurs 9am–11pm, Fri & Sat 9am–midnight; $13.50; ⓦwww.templegardens.sk.ca) where you can soak in pools of mineral-rich hot waters piped from an underground spring 1km away. For a treat, take a dip in the outdoor pool when it's snowing or at sunset.

The **downtown** area is bisected by Main Street, running from north to south, and Manitoba Street, the east–west axis, which is adjacent to the railway line and the Moose Jaw river. The central area is dispiriting, though a string of **murals** of early pioneer days, concentrated along 1st Avenue NW between Manitoba and Hochelaga streets, do their best to cheer things up. That apart, some of the streets look as if they haven't changed much since the 1920s, the wide treeless avenues framed by solemn brick warehouses and hotels and porticoed banks. One block north of Manitoba, the best example is **River Street**, whose rough-and-ready *Royal* and *Brunswick* hotels were once favourite haunts of the gangsters; the street is earmarked for redevelopment as a cobbled, partly pedestrian street with an amphitheatre for shows.

Next door to "Tunnel Central" (see box above), Joyner's General Store, 30 Main St North, is worth a quick look for the complicated **cash carrier system** used by department stores, before the invention of the till, that carried shoppers' cash by cable to the accountants upstairs. It's one of only two in the world still operating and was kept in Moose Jaw despite Euro-Disney's attempts to purchase it.

A replica of one of Moose Jaw's original electric trams, the **Moose Jaw Trolley**, travels the local sights with a guide who dwells on the town's shady past (May–Sept 3 daily; Oct–Dec Thurs–Sat 2 daily; 1hr 15min; $8); it leaves from opposite Temple Gardens and from the *Heritage Inn* on Main St. You can also ride the trolley without a guide (May–Dec Thurs–Sat 11am–3pm; $2) to Moose Jaw's branch of the **Western Development Museum** (Jan–March Tues–Sun 9am–5pm; April–Dec daily 9am–5pm; ⓦwww.wdmuseum.sk.ca; $7.25), about 2km from the centre, beside the Trans-Canada as it loops around the northern edge of town. Divided into sections covering air, land, water and rail transport, the museum exhibits include a replica of a steamship, several Canadian Pacific railway coaches, a number of fragile old planes, and a 1934 Buick car converted to carry the chief superintendent up and down the rail line.

Practicalities

Moose Jaw's **bus station**, 63 High St East (ⓣ306/692-2345), is a couple of minutes' walk from Main Street and two blocks north of Manitoba Street, served by four to six buses daily from Regina. There are no trains. The **Tourism Moose Jaw** bureau (July & Aug daily 9am–5pm; rest of year Mon–Fri 9am–5pm; ⓣ306/693-8097 or 1-866/693-8097, ⓦwww.citymoosejaw.com/tourism) is on the east side of town alongside the Trans-Canada. Out-of-province visitors get **free parking** at any of the town's meters.

The town has several reasonably priced, central **hotels** and **motels**, including the renovated, good-value *Capone's Hideaway*, 1 Main St North opposite the defunct train station (ⓣ306/692-6422 or 1-877/443-3003; ❷), where the rooms have been given a 1920s feel. Further out there's a *Super 8 Motel*, 1706 Main St North (ⓣ306/692-8888 or 1-800/800-8000; ❸). Book well in advance for the four-star *Temple Gardens Mineral Spa*, 24 Fairford St East (ⓣ306/694-5055 or 1-800/718-7727, ⓦwww.templeparkgardens.sk.ca; ❺), which has luxurious rooms (each with its own Jacuzzi) and spa suites, geothermal pools and facilities for massage, facials, reflexology and hydrotherapy treatments; guests receive a free rubber duck, too. The *Redland Cottage* **B&B** in a tree-lined residential area at 1122 Redland Ave (ⓣ306/694-5563, ⓦwww.bbcanada.com/3418.html; ❸) has comfortable bedrooms and full breakfasts. The *River Park Campground* (ⓣ306/692-5474; $14–19; mid-April to mid-Oct) is 2km southeast of the centre at 300 River Drive.

There are a few worthwhile **places to eat**. The *Copper Café*, part of the Yvette Moore Gallery in the 1910 Land Titles building at 76 Fairford St West, has wonderful daily specials, and the adjacent gallery (Jan–April Mon–Sat 10am–5pm; May–Dec Mon–Sat 10am–5pm, Sun 1–4pm; free) features work by Yvette Moore and her prairie contemporaries. *Houston Pizza and Steak House*, 117 Main St North, has Italian dishes from $6; the *National Café*, 20 Main St, has a good-value daily smorgasbord; the *Prairie Oasis Restaurant*, junction of Hwy 1 East and Thatcher Drive, specializes in freshly baked pies; and the *Hopkins Dining Parlour*, 65 Athabasca St West, located in a pleasant Victorian house, is a more formal affair with a wide-ranging menu and main courses from $18. For something more exotic, try the very good *Nit's Thai Food*, 124 Main St North, which has main courses from $6.

The Big Muddy Badlands

At the end of the last Ice Age, torrents of meltwater produced a massive gash in the landscape to the south of the site of Moose Jaw, near the US border. Edged by rounded hills and flat-topped buttes that rise up to 200m above the valley floor, the **Big Muddy Valley** can best be explored with organized tours from dreary **CORONACH**, about 200km from Regina (July & Aug Sat & Sun; at other times June–Sept, tours by appointment; $30 by minibus, $10 in your own car with a guide; ⓣ306/267-3312 or 267-2150). The tours include visits to Indian burial cairns, the dramatic **Castle Butte**, a sandstone formation rising above the plains that resembles the backdrop for a Western movie (without a guide you'll find it by turning west off Hwy 34 in the Big Muddy Valley along the only road), the small prairie town of **BIG BEAVER** where Aust's general store ("If we don't have it you don't need it") is the social centre, and a couple of outlaw caves, the refuge of American rustlers and robbers like Butch Cassidy and Dutch Henry. Cassidy and his Wild Bunch gang established an outlaw trail that connected the Big Muddy with Mexico via a series of safe houses; their antics were curtailed by the arrival of a detachment of Mounties in 1904 led by a certain Corporal Bird, known ruefully as the "man who never sleeps". The **tourist information** centre on the hwy (mid-June to Aug 9am–7pm; ⓣ306/267-3312) can provide information on the history and geography of the area. **Accommodation** in Coronach includes the *Country Boy Motel* (ⓣ306/267-3267; ❷) at the junction of hwys 18 and 36, opposite the Pioneer Grain elevator, with complimentary coffee and fridges in each of its 21 rooms. The trailer-based *Schwab B&B* is outside Big Beaver, north along Hwy 34 (ⓣ306/267-4554; ❶). The only place worth **eating** at is the coffee shop in the small Coronach Mall, 111 Centre St.

Grasslands National Park

Directly west of the Big Muddy, accessible along Hwy 18, the **Grasslands National Park** is predominantly mixed-grass prairie, a flat, bare badlands landscape broken up by splendid coulees, buttes and river valleys – notably the wide ravine edging the Frenchman River in the western block. Far from the moderating influence of the oceans, the area has a savage climate, with an average low in January of -22°C and temperatures that soar to 40°C in summer. Even so, this terrain is inhabited by many species that are adapted to cope with the shortage of water, from flora such as prairie grasses, greasewood, rabbit brush, sagebrush and different types of cacti, to fauna like the graceful pronghorn antelope, the rattlesnake and Canada's only colonies of black-tailed prairie dog.

At present, Grasslands National Park consists of east and west sections separated by private ranches and farms, which the federal government eventually intends to buy, creating a single park stretching from Hwy 4 in the west to hwys 2 and 18 in the east. The **west** section is both more scenic and accessible, its limited system of gravel tracks and roads cutting in from hwys 8 and 4, south and east of **VAL MARIE**. This tiny township houses the **Grasslands National Park Reception Centre**, at the junction of Hwy 4 and Centre St (late May to Aug daily 8am–6.30pm; Sept to late May Mon–Fri 8am–4.30pm; ⓣ306/298-2257, ⓦwww.parkscanada.gc.ca/grasslands), whose rangers provide advice on weather and road conditions, hand out maps, arrange for guided or self-guided eco-tours, issue camping permits and give tips on animal-spotting and hiking. The few places to **stay** in town include the *Val Marie Hotel*, 221 Centre St (ⓣ306/298-2007 or 298-2003; ❶), with seven basic rooms, and the far more attractive *Convent B&B*, 4515 Hwy 4 (ⓣ306/289-4515; ❷), a converted convent with lots of character that is also the best place to eat in town. Opposite is a well-worn **campsite** (ⓣ306/298-2022; $14; May–Oct). There are no campsites within the park, but camping is allowed within 1km of its roads if you have purchased a $9 backcountry permit; take a good supply of water, a stout pair of walking shoes and a stick to sweep in front of you in tall grass or brush as a warning to **rattlesnakes**. Animal activity is at its height at dawn and dusk and during spring and autumn; whatever the season, you'll need a pair of binoculars.

One of the best **hikes** is the one to the 70 Mile Butte, a massive flat-topped promontory that is the highest point of land in the region, rising 100m above the valley floor with wonderful views of the waving prairie grasslands all around.

To get there, drive south of Val Marie on Hwy 4 and turn east at Butte Road and continue to the end of the road. While there is no marked trail, the way becomes obvious as you begin walking over the hills from the end of the road. Even just a couple of hours' walk will take you through exceptional country.

Swift Current

Driving west from Moose Jaw along the Trans-Canada Highway, it's about 180km to **SWIFT CURRENT**, a small industrial city and farm-research centre that's a convenient stopoff on the long journey between Regina and Calgary. It has limited attractions, but if you decide to stay here drop in to the helpful **tourist office**, at the junction of hwys 1 and 4 (May–Sept daily 9am–7pm; Oct–April Mon–Fri 9am–noon & 1–5pm; ⓣ306/773-7268). The **bus**

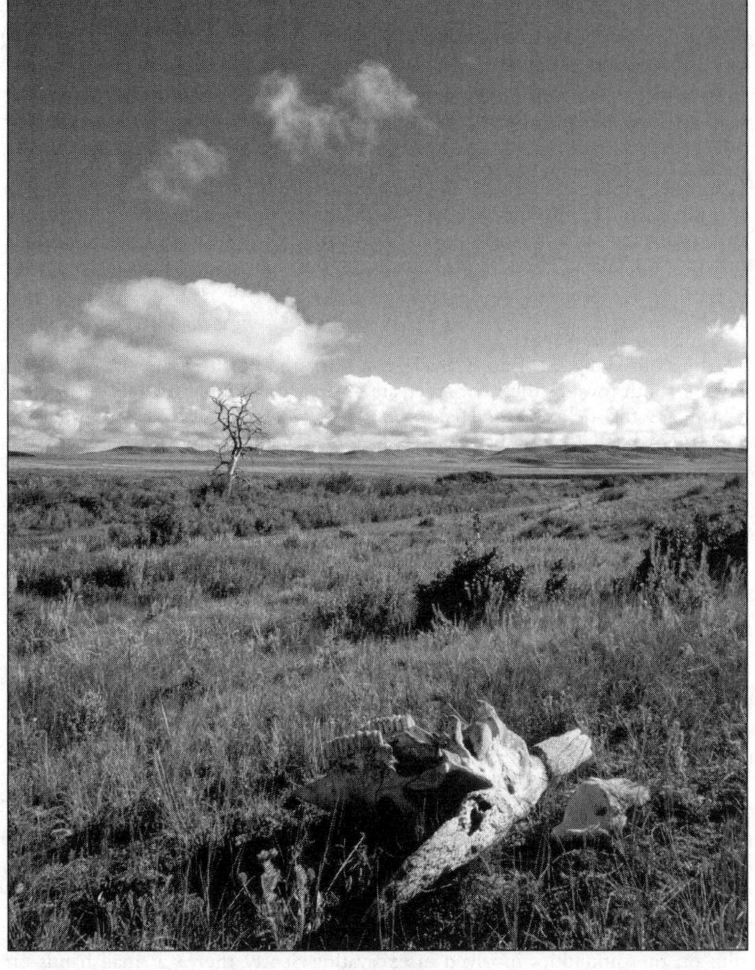

△ Grasslands National Park

station is at 143 4th Ave NW, serviced by three buses daily from Regina and one from Saskatoon.

In Kinetic Park, at 17th Ave and South Railway St East, is a **Mennonite Heritage Village** (June–Sept Fri–Sun 2–8pm; other times by appointment ⓣ306/773-7685 or 773-6068; free), consisting of a long, rectangular house and adjoining barn built in 1911–15, and six buildings comprising **Doc's Town** (July & Aug Fri–Sun 2–6pm; other times by appointment ⓣ306/773-2944; $2), a replica of an early twentieth-century prairie village – highlights are a fully functioning windmill, a one-room prairie schoolhouse and an old dancehall (now a tearoom), transported here from a rural Saskatchewan town. The only other worthwhile stopoff is the **Art Gallery of Swift Current**, 411 Herbert St East (Mon–Thurs 2–5pm & 7–9pm, Fri–Sun 1–5pm; July & Aug closed Sun; free), where you'll see exhibitions of paintings, sculpture and ceramics by artists from Saskatchewan and elsewhere in Canada.

Reached by Hwy 4, around 40km north of Swift Current is the pretty little **Saskatchewan Landing Provincial Park**, situated on both banks of the South Saskatchewan River, where it emerges from razorback hills and opens out into the large, finger-like artificial **Lake Diefenbaker**. The park area was once an important river crossing for Native Canadians and early white settlers, and the staff at the park's **Goodwin House Visitors' Centre** (June–Sept Mon–Fri 8am–4pm, Sat & Sun 10am–6pm; Oct–May Mon–Fri 8am–4pm), a beautiful century-old stone house built by a retired member of the North West Mounted Police, can organize nature-trail hikes through coulees and explain the significance of the crossing – once one of the most difficult river crossings in western Canada. There are remains of several ancient tepee encampments in the area. You can **camp** in the north of the park at the *Bear Paw Campground* (ⓣ306/375-5525 or 375-5527; $15–20; mid-May to Oct) and rent kayaks at the small marina ($6/hr).

Strung out along the Trans-Canada as it skirts the north of the city, and along Hwy 4 south towards the US border, are several comfortable **motels**, the best of which are the deluxe *Best Western Inn*, 105 George St (ⓣ306/773-4660 or 1-800/773-8818, ⓦwww.bestwestern.sk.ca; ❸–❻), just off the Trans-Canada; the enormous *Imperial 400*, 1150 Begg St East (ⓣ306/773-2033 or 1-800/781-2268; ❷–❸), also near the Trans-Canada, which has waterslides; and the *Super 8 Motel*, 405 North Service Rd East (ⓣ306/778-6088 or 1-800/800-8000; ❸–❹), which has a pool and whose rates include a small breakfast. Just north of the Trans-Canada is a small but convenient **campsite**, *Trail Campground* (ⓣ306/773-8088; $12–15; May to mid-Oct). For **restaurants**, try *Carol's Diner*, 914 Central Ave North, specializing in Belgian waffles, or *Humpty's*, at the junction of hwys 1 and 4 East, which does a low-priced all-day breakfast. *Gramma Bep's* on the east side of town on Hwy 1 does berry pies and coffee, while a shop inside also sells jams, soups and sauces made to traditional Saskatchewan recipes.

Eastend

In 1994, one of only thirteen Tyrannosaurus Rex skeletons in the world was discovered 40km south of the 695-strong town of **EASTEND**, 150km west of the park. The T-Rex was named Scotty, after the bottle of scotch its discoverers consumed in celebration, and there is now a swish **T-Rex Discovery Centre** (July & August daily 9am–9pm; Sept–June 9am–5pm; ⓣ306/295-4009, ⓦwww.dinocountry.com; $7.50) on the gravel Grid Road no. 614, about 1km north of town – worth hitting if you're travelling with children. After seeing a film on the difficulties involved in excavating Scotty, there's a small hands-on museum in which to view replica bones of various dinosaurs. In the town itself is a **museum and cultural centre** with a small information centre, located in the old theatre on Red Coat Drive (July & Aug daily 10am–8pm; mid-May to June by appointment ⓣ306/295-3375; $2), featuring paleontological exhibits and a pioneer log house from a century ago.

If you want to base yourself in Eastend for a more thorough exploration of the Grasslands park and the Frenchman River Valley, you could **stay** at the *Riverside Motel*, just west of town on Hwy 13 (ⓣ306/295-3630 or 295-3773; ❷–❸), which also has **camping** on its grounds for $15, or at the basic but comfortable *Cypress Hotel*, 343 Red Coat Drive (ⓣ306/295-3505; ❶), in the middle of town. For **food**, *Alleykatz,* 115 Fir Ave, offers up coffees and bagels and has a gift shop that sells pottery made from the local white clay. For more substantial meals head to *Jack's Café* on Red Coat Drive.

Maple Creek and the Great Sand Hills

From Swift Current it's another 130km along the Trans-Canada to **MAPLE CREEK**, situated 8km south of the highway. Nicknamed "old cow town", Maple Creek lies at the heart of ranching country, and its streets are full of pickup trucks, cowboy boots and stetsons, reaching wild heights in early September for the **Cowboy Poetry Gathering**, a literary celebration of the wrangler that draws cowboys from across North America. Some of the late nineteenth-century brick storefronts have survived, and the trim and tidy **Old Timers' Museum**, 218 Jasper St (May–Sept Tues–Sat 9am–5.30pm, Sun & Mon 1–5pm; $3), has good displays on pioneer life and the Mounties. The place is also the market town for a number of **Hutterite colonies**, whose women stand out with their floral dresses and headscarves (see box below).

Perhaps the best reason for stopping at Maple Creek is its proximity to the Cypress Hills (see p.606) and the **Great Sand Hills**. The latter incorporate a large area of giant sand dunes, home to hordes of kangaroo rats as well as mule deer and antelope. The best place to view the dunes is east off Hwy 21. From the village of **LIEBENTHAL** follow the road east in the direction of Fitters Ranch for 17.6km before turning off north for the final 2km to the dunes

The Hutterites

The **Hutterites**, the only prairie community to have maintained a utopian communal ideal, are members of an Anabaptist sect that takes its name from their first leader, Jacob Hutter. Originating in central Europe (in the Tyrol and Moravia) in the sixteenth century, they gradually moved east, ending up in Russia, which they abandoned for South Dakota in the 1870s. It was fifty years before they felt obliged to move again, their pacifism recoiling from the bellicosity that gripped their American neighbours during World War I. They moved north between 1918 and 1922, and established a series of **colonies** where they were allowed to educate their own children, speak their own language and avoid military service. In these largely self-sufficient communities tasks are still divided according to ability and skill, property is owned communally, and social life is organized around a common dining room and dormitories. Economically prosperous, they continue to multiply, a new branch community being founded whenever the old one reaches a secure population of between one hundred and two hundred. Apart from the occasional skirmish with the outside world when they buy new land, the Hutterites have been left in peace and have resisted the pressures of assimilation more staunchly than their kindred spirits, the Mennonites and the Doukhobors (see box, p.969).

parking lot. You can also get here from **SCEPTRE**, 18.4km to the north of the dunes where the small **Great Sandhills Museum** on Hwy 32 (June–Sept Mon–Sat 9am–noon & 1–4pm, Sun 1–5pm; $3) has displays on the ecology of the hills and can provide printed directions.

The Cypress Hills

South of the Trans-Canada Highway, between Maple Creek and Irvine, AB, the wooded ridges of the **Cypress Hills** rise above the plains in a 130-kilometre-long plateau that in places reaches a height of 1400m – the highest point in Canada between Labrador and the Rockies. Because of its elevation, this area was untouched by glaciers as they moved south during the Ice Age, scouring the land bare of vegetation. The Cypress Hills are an anomaly in the landscape of the prairies, having a wetter and milder climate than the treeless plains that surround them, creating a rich variety of woodland, wetland and grassland. In turn, this comparatively lush vegetation supports a wealth of wildlife, from the relatively rare elk, lynx, bobcat and coyote through to the more common gopher and raccoon, plus about two hundred species of bird, over half of whom breed in the hills. (Watch out for the colonies of long-necked wild turkeys, as well as the sage grouse, whose bizarre courting rituals involve the male swelling out his chest and discharging air with a sound akin to a gunshot.) One surprise – considering the name – is the absence of cypress trees: the early French *voyageurs* seem to have confused the area's predominant lodgepole pines with the jack pines of Québec, a species they called *cyprès*. Literal-minded translation did the rest.

There are a variety of guided **tours** of both the Centre and West blocks of the Cypress Hills Interprovincial Park that will help you to better appreciate the rugged beauty of the area and the high-altitude flora and fauna – much of which is found nowhere else in western Canada except the Rocky Mountains. A tour of the **Centre Block** (2hr $70) includes trips to Lookout Point and Bald Butte on the edge of the park, where there are panoramic views north down into the valleys and plains. The more rugged **West Block** can be experienced on longer tours (4hr $150; 6hr $185) that take you over the bone-rattling Gap Road to points of interest such as Fort Walsh and the Conglomerate Cliffs. All tours are led by trained local guides; to book, call ⓣ306/662-5411 (Mon–Fri 8am–5pm).

Cypress Hills Interprovincial Park

In amongst the cattle ranches two separate sections of the Hills have been set aside to form the **Cypress Hills Interprovincial Park**: Saskatchewan's Centre Block lies to the south of Maple Creek along Hwy 21, and the larger West Block spans the Saskatchewan–Alberta border, accessible from Maple Creek along Hwy 271 in the east and via Alberta's Hwy 41 in the west. The Saskatchewan part of the West Block is also attached to Fort Walsh National Historic Park, incorporating a partly refurbished Mountie station and a replica of one of the Battle Creek trading posts. The three north–south access hwys present no problems, but it's difficult to drive across the park from east to west as the paved road, known as the Gap Road, is interrupted by two long stretches of gravel and clay track suitable only for high clearance four-wheel drive vehicles in dry weather.

Just 30km south of Maple Creek, on Hwy 21, a paved side road heads into the park's **Centre Block** (entry fee $7), a rough rectangle of hilly land dominated by a forest of lodgepole pines. At the centre, a pleasant tourist resort surrounds tiny **Loch Leven**, complete with canoe- and bike-rental facilities, shops and a

The Cypress Hills massacre

From the mid-eighteenth century, the Cypress Hills lay in a sort of neutral zone between the **Blackfoot** and the **Cree**, whose intermittent skirmishing was small-scale until the 1860s, when the depletion of the Crees' traditional hunting grounds forced them to move west. Some three thousand Cree reached the Cypress Hills in 1865 and the violence began just four years later with the murder of the Cree peace-maker, Maskepetoon. The ensuing war was overshadowed by the Red River rising of 1869–70 in Manitoba, but casualties were high and its effects were compounded by two smallpox epidemics. In 1871 the Cree sued for peace, but both sides were exhausted, their morale, health and social structures further undermined by the whiskey traders who had moved into the region.

These **whiskey traders**, who were mostly American, brought their liquor north in the autumn, returning south in late spring laden with furs and buffalo robes. Though it was illegal to supply the Indians with booze, the traders spread out across the southern plains, aptly nicknamed **Whoop-up Country**, establishing dozens of trading posts whose occupants were protected from their disorderly customers by log stockades. (They needed to be, as the stuff they sold was adulterated with such substances as red ink, gunpowder and strychnine.) In the spring of 1873, there were two such outposts beside **Battle Creek**, deep in the Cypress Hills, owned by a certain Abel Farwell and his rival Moses Solomon. For reasons that remain obscure, though the prevailing drunkenness played a part, this was the scene of a violent confrontation between a group of white wolf-hunters, whiskey traders and a band of Assiniboine. Equipped with the latest fast-action rifles, the hunters riddled an Assiniboine camp with bullets, killing up to seventy (according to some sources) before returning to the trading posts to celebrate. News of the incident, known as the **Cypress Hills Massacre**, filtered back to Ottawa, and this speeded up the recruitment of the newly formed **North West Mounted Police**, who in the autumn received their first posting west as a detachment to Fort MacLeod, near today's Lethbridge, Alberta. They reached it in early 1874, where they set about suppressing the whiskey trade and establishing law and order.

To consolidate their control of the area, the Mounties built **Fort Walsh**, near Battle Creek, the following year. An unpopular posting, the fort was considered "unhealthy, isolated and indefensible", but it could not be abandoned until 1883, when the last of the restless Indian bands were moved to reservations further north. It was during this period that the fort's first inspector, **James Morrow Walsh**, was faced with an extremely delicate situation. In 1876, **Chief Sitting Bull's** Sioux had exterminated General Custer's army at the battle of the Little Bighorn. Fearing reprisals, five thousand Sioux moved north, establishing their camp at Wood Mountain, 350km east of Fort Walsh. Aware of the danger, Walsh rode into the Sioux encampment with just four other constables to insist that they obey Canadian law. This act of bravery established a rough rapport between the two leaders, and by his tactful dealings with the Sioux Walsh enhanced the reputation of the Mounties, whose efficiency ensured there were no more massacres in the Canadian west.

petrol station. There's also a modest nature centre adjoining the park's **administration office** (Mon–Thurs 8am–8pm, Fri–Sun 8am–10pm; ⓣ306/662-5411 or 1-800/205-7070, ⓦwww.cypresshills.com), which has useful maps and trail brochures. The resort is a popular holiday destination, but it's easy to escape the crowds along the half-dozen hiking trails. There's one **hotel**, the modern *Cypress Park Resort Inn* (ⓣ306/662-4477), with rooms and cabins (both ❷–❸) and apartments (❸–❻). Close by, there are several busy summer **campsites** (all $14–25), which have to be booked at the campsite office on Pine Avenue, west of the centre (mid-May to Aug daily 8.30am–10pm; ⓣ306/662-4459).

The eastern side of the park's **West Block** has alternating areas of thick forest and open grassland broken up by steep hills and deep, sheltered ravines. Hwy 271 enters this section from the east and becomes increasingly bumpy as it twists south towards the **Fort Walsh National Historic Park** and Visitors Information Centre (mid-May to Aug daily 9.30am–5.30pm; ⓣ306/662-3590, off-season 662-2645; $9.15), which has excellent displays on the Plains Indians, the history of the fort and the development of the RCMP. A five-minute walk behind the information centre, Fort Walsh sits in a wide, low-lying valley, its trim stockade framed by pine forests. Built in 1875, the fort was abandoned in favour of Maple Creek just eight years later; in 1942 the RCMP acquired the land, and most of the present buildings date from that decade. Guides in period costumes enliven a tour of whitewashed log buildings, the whole site having returned to its original appearance. Close to the fort is a cemetery containing the tombstones of several North West Mounted Police officers. Every 45 minutes a minibus makes the trip from the information centre over the hills to Battle Creek, where Abel Farwell's whiskey trading post has been reconstructed to commemorate the 1873 Cypress Hills Massacre (see box, p.607). Guides will also take you to the actual site of the Massacre. The main **accommodation** in this part of the park is the *West Block Campground* (ⓣ306/662-5489 or 1-800/205-7070; $14; May–Sept), 5km north of Fort Walsh, in a dense stand of lodgepole pines and with a brook running through it. It's in an isolated spot, so take your own food and drink. From the campsite you can make an expedition to the **Conglomerate Cliffs**, a few kilometres to the northeast near Adams Lake. These are strange-looking walls of rock, some 150m high, composed of multicoloured cobblestones.

The lodgepole forests and deep coulees of the Alberta section of the park's West Block are centred on the tourist resort of **ELKWATER**, 34km south of the Trans-Canada on Hwy 41. Curving round the southern shore of Elkwater Lake, the village has a comprehensive range of facilities, from boat and bike rental through to a sandy beach and sauna baths. There's also a **park office** (Mon–Fri 8.15am–noon & 1–4.30pm; ⓣ403/893-3777) and a **visitors' centre** (mid-May to early Sept Mon–Fri 10am–6pm; ⓣ403/893-3833), which has maps and hiking brochures and runs guided walks throughout the summer. For **accommodation**, there's the *Green Tree Motel* (ⓣ403/893-3811; ❷–❸), which also has self-contained cabins, while the *Elkwater Campground* is relatively luxurious, with both simple and hooked-up sites. Southwest of Elkwater a paved road leads to Horseshoe Canyon and **Head of the Mountain**, where there are striking views over the hills towards Montana; other roads lead east to Reesor Lake and Spruce Coulee Reservoir. Beside the roads there are twelve other campsites, bookable through the visitors centre.

Yellowhead Route (Hwy 16)

Highway 16, one of central Canada's most appealing long-distance drives, is better known as **the Yellowhead Route** – taking its name from a light-haired Iroquois explorer and guide who was called *Tête Jaune* ("yellow head") by the *voyageurs*, the

French-speaking boatmen who plied the waterways transporting people, furs and supplies. It's a good alternative to the Trans-Canada Highway, with more interesting sights along the way – including several towns, like **Dauphin**, where some of the culture of original groups has been preserved – and also more varied scenery. This not only includes vast tracts of prairie, but also some of the aspen parklands and boreal forest to the north. And if you have the time you can easily make a foray into the enticingly wild **Prince Albert National Park**. The Yellowhead route also runs through **Saskatoon**, 781km from Winnipeg, which makes a good point at which to break a journey and has several important historic sites in the vicinity that help bring alive the region's history.

Winnipeg to Saskatoon

The Yellowhead Route follows the Trans-Canada Hwy west out of Winnipeg as far as Portage la Prairie (see p.585), from where it cuts northwest from the Trans-Canada to form a more attractive route across the prairies. It passes through the pretty little villages of **Neepawa** and **Minnedosa** before running south of **Riding Mountain National Park** which protects attractive areas of deciduous and boreal forest, lake and grassland. Just north of the park is the strongly Ukrainian town of **Dauphin** which can form a base for exploring **Duck Mountain Provincial Park**, noted for its fishing canoe routes. This park continues over the border in Saskatchewan and is close to the intriguing Doukhobor settlement of **Veregin** and the dreary prairie hub of **Yorkton**. From here the Yellowhead embarks on one of its dullest stretches across the prairies towards Saskatoon, though if you have time to spare be sure to investigate **Little Manitou Lake** – Saskatchewan's Dead Sea.

Neepawa and around

About 90km along the road from Portage la Prairie lies one of Manitoba's more pleasant townships, tiny **NEEPAWA**, whose streets are lined with elms and cottonwoods. The oldest buildings are spread along and around the principal drag, Mountain Avenue – notably the cosy neo-Romanesque Knox Presbyterian Church at Mill St and 1st Ave, with an unusual thick, turreted bell tower, and the tidy, late-Victorian County Court House, close to Mountain Avenue and Hamilton Street. Also in the centre, in the old CNR station at the west end of Hamilton Street, the **Beautiful Plains Museum** (mid-May to Aug Mon–Fri 9am–5pm; July & Aug also Sat & Sun 1–5pm; other times by appointment; $1; ☎204/476-3896 or 476-5292 off-season) has diverting displays on the life of the district's pioneers. Margaret Laurence (1926–87), one of Canada's best-known writers, lived in Neepawa in her early years and used the town (renamed Manawaka) as a setting for many of her novels, which portray strong women struggling against small town life, beginning with the highly acclaimed *The Stone Angel* (1964) and ending with *The Diviners* (1974). You can visit her home, now the **Margaret Laurence Museum**, at 312 1st Ave North (mid-May to Aug Mon–Fri 10am–6pm, Sat & Sun noon–6pm; July & Aug daily 10am–6pm; other times by appointment; ☎204/476-3612; $2). Laurence is buried in the Riverside Cemetery, in the north of town.

The Yellowhead Hwy doubles as Neepawa's Main Street, marking the southern perimeter of the town centre. The **tourist office** (June–Aug daily 11am–7pm, Tues & Wed closes 5pm; ☎204/476-5292) is on the Yellowhead just east of town, beside the Whitemud River. The **bus station** is attached to the Petro Canada fuel station at 52 Main St. For accommodation, there's a central riverside **campsite** on Hamilton Street, the *Lions Riverbend Park* (Ⓣ204/476-7607; $9–12; May–Sept) with fishing, a playground and a pool. The down-at-heel *Hamilton* **hotel** is convenient at Mountain Ave and Mill St (Ⓣ204/476-2368; ①), with bars beneath, but you'd do better at the three **motels**, all west of town on Hwy 16, particularly the spotlessly clean *Westway Inn* (Ⓣ204/476-2355; ② including breakfast). Or try the *Garden Path B&B*, 536 2nd Ave at Main St (Ⓣ204/476-3184; ③), in a beautiful 1903 former lumber merchant's home. The **restaurants** downtown are unappealing but the best of the bunch on Hwy 16 (Main Street) is the busy *Mr Ribs*, which offers dinners from $7. Better to head out to the *Prairie Orchard Tea House* (Ⓣ204/368-2486), 13.6km east on Hwy 16, which serves locally grown organic food.

More varieties of lilies grow in the area around Neepawa than any other part of the world. To see the flowers in bloom, visit the **Lily Nook** (July to mid-Aug daily 9am–6pm; donation suggested), 4km south of town on Hwy 5. There's also a **Lily Festival** in Neepawa in the third week of July.

Minnedosa

The approach to **MINNEDOSA**, 28km west of Neepawa, is stunning, as the attractive town sits on the flat of a long valley that slowly rises up at each end. The relaxing small-town atmosphere of the place is most appealing and, as it's about halfway between Winnipeg and the Saskatchewan border, it can make for a convenient stopoff. It's also only thirty minutes from Riding Mountain National Park (see below). There's not much to see here except for a **bison compound** near the Little Saskatchewan River (March–Oct; free), reached by crossing the swinging bridge over the river or turn off Main Street onto 2nd Avenue SE, and then drive five minutes along Beach Road; you can view the bison from a platform in a public car park. You can also reach the compound and Minnedosa's pleasant **public beach** by following the two-kilometre **Heritage Village Walk** from a 1920s CPR caboose and diesel engine, located beside the boulder-strewn river at the bridge on Main Street. The walk takes you on a pretty amble along the riverbank, past a salmon ladder to a small collection of heritage buildings, none of which are particularly inspiring.

Minnedosa's **tourist information** centre (daily 11am–7pm; Ⓣ204/867-2741, Ⓦwww.minnedosa.com/chamber) is west of town at a rest stop where Hwy 10 meets Hwy 16. In town there's a handful of acceptable **motels**, including the *Minnedosa Inn*, 138 Main St (Ⓣ204/867-2777; ②). One of the more attractive **B&Bs** in western Manitoba, *The Castle*, is at 149 2nd Ave SW (Ⓣ204/867-2830; ③), a Queen Anne-style house on the banks of the Little Saskatchewan River. Delicious German and French food is available at *Brede's*, 121 Main St South (Wed–Sun dinner); otherwise the choice is limited to nondescript places along Main Street.

Riding Mountain National Park

One of the region's best parks is **Riding Mountain National Park** ($6.90 per person per day; $34.65 per year), 250km northwest of Winnipeg and bisected by Hwy 10 on its way from Hwy 16 to Dauphin. The park derives its name from the fur trappers who changed from canoe to horseback to travel across its wooded highlands and it's still a vast expanse of wilderness, roughly 50km long and 100km wide, providing some of Manitoba's finest hiking and biking trails and most beautiful scenery. Its **eastern perimeter** is formed by a 400-metre-high ridge studded with a dense evergreen forest of spruce, pine, balsam fir and tamarack. This soon gives way to a **highland plateau** whose mixed forests and lakes form the central, and most scenic, part of the park, bordered to the west by an area of aspen woodland, meadow and open grassland. There are moose, elk and a carefully tended herd of buffalo, best viewed in the morning or evening, near Lake Audy (45min drive northwest of Wasagaming on a gravel road; no public transport; open year-round; free).

Wasagaming

For Riding Mountain National Park, the tourist village of **WASAGAMING** is the only settlement of any significance and so a useful base. Located beside the main hwy on the southern edge of the park, beside Clear Lake, it has a campsite, motels and restaurants, grocery stores, petrol stations, a 1930s log theatre, and boat and canoe rental. But its narrow, scrawny **beach** is desperately overcrowded in July and August, while the lake, though spring-fed, is infested with a parasitic flatworm that can cause the painful skin irritation "Swimmer's Itch".

Beside the beach, the park **visitor information centre** (daily late May to June & Sept to mid-Oct 9am–5.30pm, July & Aug 9.30am–8pm; ⓣ204/848-7275 or 1-866/787-6221, ⓦwww.pc.gc.ca) has a collection of stuffed animals and environmental displays, and publishes *The Bugle*, a free broadsheet guide to the park's amenities. The staff organizes a programme of summer events, featuring free day-long **walks** and **hikes**. The centre also issues fishing permits ($9) and backcountry permits ($9), which are compulsory for overnight stays in the bush. From mid-October to mid-May, when the centre is closed, the **administration office** opposite (Mon–Fri 8am–noon & 12.30pm–4pm) provides a similar service.

Most of the trails that begin in or near Wasagaming are short and easy, the longest being the newly completed Clear Lake Trail around Clear Lake's shore (24km). The best of the park's trails is the eight-kilometre **Grey Owl Trail** to Beaver Lodge Lake from Hwy 19, where Grey Owl (see p.204) lived for six months in 1931. This trail connects with the nearest of the overnight routes, the **Cowan Lake Trail**, which branches off to pass through a region of dense forest, small lakes and meadows. All the overnight trails have primitive campsites. To get deep into the rugged beauty of the park, contact Riding Mountain Nature Tours (ⓣ204/636-2968, ⓦwww.churchillnaturetours.com), which offers a variety of longer **tours**, including horseback riding, hiking, bird-watching and wildlife safaris. To learn more about the history of the park – including Grey Owl's stay here – visit the **Pinewood Museum** at 154 Wasagaming Drive (July & Aug daily 2–4pm; free).

Served by daily buses from Winnipeg, Brandon and Dauphin, Wasagaming's main **bus stop** is on the corner of Wasagaming Drive and Mooswa Drive. For **accommodation**, the *Mooswa Resort*, Mooswa Drive (ⓣ204/848-2533; ❷), has modern chalets, motel rooms and bungalows, but the basic bungalows and log cabins at *Johnson Cabins*, 109 Ta-Wa-Pit Drive (ⓣ204/848-2524 or 1-888/848-2524, ⓦwww.johnsoncabins.com; ❷), are a bit cheaper. *Clear Lake Lodge*, at Ta-Wa-Pit Drive and Columbine St (ⓣ204/848-2345, ⓦwww.clearlakelodge.com; ❸), is a comfortable, nonsmoking hotel, but to save money head for the *Manigaming Resort*, 137 Ta-Wa-Pit Drive (ⓣ204/848-2459, ⓦwww.manigaming.com; ❷), or the *Southgate Motor Hotel* in Onanole, 5km south of the park (ⓣ204/848-2158; ❷). Most accommodation in the park is open from May to September or October only; one of the few year-round possibilities is the *New Chalet*, 116 Wasagaming Drive (ⓣ204/848-2892; ❸), with its kitchenette units. There's only one **campsite**, *Wasagaming Campground*,

(Ⓣ905/426-4648 or 1-877/737-3783, Ⓦwww.pccamping.ca; $24–33; May to mid-Oct; reservations advised) in the village just beyond the main park gate.

Wasagaming's **restaurants** are poor, with the notable exception of *TR McKoys* in the same log building as the Park Theatre on Wasagaming Drive – it has lunch and dinner menus with pasta dishes from $10 and delicious sandwiches from $7. You can also try the *Mooswa*, where a delicious fresh fish meal will set you back about $20. The best of the cheaper establishments is the *Whitehouse*, also on Wasagaming Drive with burgers, sandwiches and other fast food. The Tempo fuel station opposite rents out **bikes** (Ⓣ1-800/816-2524; $14/hr, $52/day), while **canoe** and **powerboat** rentals ($18/hr) are available from the jetty on Clear Lake. **Horse riding** is available at the riding stables at Triangle Ranch ($18/hr; Ⓣ204/848-4583).

Dauphin and around

Despite the diverse backgrounds of the European immigrants who cleared and settled Manitoba in the late nineteenth century, there is little evidence of this in most of the province's virtually indistinguishable settlements – except for clues left in place names. Most cultures were rapidly and almost entirely assimilated, but at least the onion domes of the Ukrainians' Orthodox churches in and around **DAUPHIN** are still a reminder of their ancestry. Dauphin was founded as a fur-trading post by the French in 1739 and is now a pleasant town that straggles across the flat prairie landscape just to the east of the Vermilion River. Its long Main Street features some good examples of early twentieth-century Canadian architecture, but there's only one real attraction, the **Fort Dauphin Museum** (May, June & Sept Mon–Fri 9am–5pm; July & Aug daily 9am–5pm; Oct–April by appointment Ⓣ204/638-6630; $3). This tidy wooden replica of a North West Company trading outpost, located by the river at the end of 4th Avenue SW, fifteen-minutes' walk from Main Street, holds the stockade where there are reconstructions of several sorts of pioneer building, including a trapper's cabin. If you have time to kill, nose around the huge CNR **railway station** on 1st Ave NW and the modest **arts centre** and gallery at 104 1st Ave NW (Mon–Fri noon–5pm; free), in a striking Romanesque Revival building. At the corner of 1st Street SW and 11th Avenue SW is the Ukrainian **Church of the Resurrection**, with its distinctive clustered domes (call for hours Ⓣ204/638-5511 or 638-4196).

The fertile river valley that runs west of Dauphin towards Roblin was a centre of Ukrainian settlement between 1896 and 1925, and its village skylines are still dominated by onion-domed church spires. There's a modest collection of Ukrainian pioneer artefacts and traditional handicrafts in Dauphin at the **Selo Ukraina Office**, 119 Main St South (call for hours Ⓣ204/638-9401; free), but their main task is to organize the **National Ukrainian Festival**, which takes place on the first weekend of August at a purpose-built complex 12km south of Dauphin, just off Hwy 10 on the edge of Riding Mountain Park. The complex has a tiny heritage village dedicated to the early Ukrainian settlers (call for hours Ⓣ204/638-9401; free) and a splendid amphitheatre built into a hillside, ideal for the festival's music and dance performances.

If you want to absorb still more Ukrainian ambience, visit the **Wasyl Negrych Pioneer Farmstead**, near the village of Gilbert Plains, 30km west of Dauphin. Here you'll find Canada's best-preserved and most complete Ukrainian homestead (June–Aug daily 1–5pm; rest of year by appointment; Ⓣ204/548-2477 or 548-2689; $3). Wasyl and Anna Negrych arrived here in 1897 with their seven children from the Carpathian Mountains. Over the next few years they built the farmstead, which now has ten buildings: an 1899 home that replaced their first log house after it burnt down, three granaries, barns, a chicken coop, pigsty, garages and a bunkhouse with a fully preserved, working *peech* (the log and clay cookstove that was once the heart of every Ukrainian household). Amazingly, two of Wasyl and Anna's children ran the farmstead according to traditional practices until their deaths in the 1980s, never introducing electricity, sewers or phone lines.

Practicalities

Dauphin's **bus station**, 404 Main St North (☎204/622-9500), is a couple of minutes' walk from the town centre. The **Chamber of Commerce**, 21 3rd Ave NE (Mon–Fri 8.30am–4.30pm; ☎204/638-4838), provides tourist information. There's also a **tourist bureau** (mid-May to Aug Mon–Thurs 10am–6pm, Fri–Sun 9am–7pm; ☎204/638-5295), 2km away on the southern edge of town on Hwy 10, beside the airport.

For **accommodation**, the *Boulevard Motor Hotel*, 28 Memorial Blvd (☎204/638-4410 or 1-877/999-2228; ❷), and the *Dauphin Community Inn*, 104 Main St North (☎204/638-4311; ❶), are both fairly seedy downtown **hotels**; you may opt instead for either the *Canway Inn Motel and Suites* (☎204/638-5102 or 1-888/325-3335; ❸), about 4km south of town near the junction of hwys 5 and 10, with a pool, a sauna and more appealing rooms – four of them have Jacuzzis en suite. The *Touch of Africa B&B* (☎204/638-7936; ❷), on Hwy 10, south of Dauphin opposite the tourist information centre, keeps ostriches on its grounds. The *Vermilion Trailer Park & Campground*, 21 2nd Ave NW (☎204/638-3740 or 622-3109; $12–17; May–Oct), is ten minutes' walk north of Main Street. You can **eat** at *Irving's Steak House & Lounge*, 26 1st Ave NW, which has a real honky-tonk feel, or *Zamrykut's Ukrainian Family Restaurant*, 119 Main St N, a plain establishment that serves delicious home-made food, from borscht through to pierogies and kielbossa (sausage).

Duck Mountain Provincial Park

Straddling the Manitoba–Saskatchewan border, **Duck Mountain Provincial Park** is a large slice of the Manitoba Escarpment run as two separate and strikingly different entities by the park authorities of each province.

In Manitoba

On the **Manitoba side** the park is huge and wild, comprising several thousand acres of thickly wooded rolling hills punctuated by meadows, bogs, streams and hundreds of tiny lakes. Most of the park is boreal forest, a mixture of white spruce, jack pine, balsam fir, aspen and birch, but many of its eastern slopes are covered by maple, burr oak and elm, which are usually found further south. Portions of this are regularly harvested for lumber, but care is taken not to disturb the black bears, moose, white-tailed deer and lynx that inhabit the park; it's not unusual to hear the cries of coyotes and wolves at night or the unmistakeable bugling of a bull elk amongst the dense woodland. The park is noted for its fishing, with pickerel, pike and trout in most of its lakes, and the delicious arctic char to the north.

Access, some 100km northwest of Dauphin, is along two partly paved roads: the east–west Route 367, which branches off Hwy 10 just north of Garland and cuts across the middle of the park to Hwy 83, a distance of 80km; and the south–north Route 366, connecting the town of Grandview, on Hwy 5 just 45km west of Dauphin, with the village of Minitonas, 130km away. Approached along Route 366, the park's best section is in the southeast corner, where **Baldy Mountain** (831m) is the highest point in Manitoba, complete with an observation tower which provides views over the forest. A few kilometres to the north, the twin **West** and **East Blue Lakes** are among the park's finest – curving strips of clear water fed by underground springs. Between the lakes is the *Blue Lakes Campground* (Ⓣ1-888/482-2267; May to mid-Sept), close to both are the **Blue Lakes Trail**, a six-kilometre cross-country hike, and the **Shining Stone Trail**, a short path along the peninsula that juts out into West Blue Lake. The campsite has a beach, a grocery store and fuel station; the camp office advises on boat rental and fishing. There are only unserviced sites here ($10). For serviced sites, try *Childs Lake Campground* (Ⓣ204/546-2463; $12–14; May to mid-Sept), with similar facilities; it's on Route 367 on the west edge of the park. Great West Trails (Ⓣ204/734-2321) organizes **horseback riding** excursions through the park that include camping and fishing. High Mountain Outfitters (Ⓣ204/967-2077), based in Kelwood on the east edge of the park, can also arrange a variety of one- to seven-day camping trips.

In Saskatchewan

By contrast, the **Saskatchewan side** of the Duck Mountain park is a highly regulated environment with much better, but far more crowded, facilities. It has toll booths at park entrances, a more extensive system of walking trails – including one trail that is wheelchair-accessible – and is open year-round. In winter, it has some of the best snowmobiling and cross-country skiing in the province.

Located some 100km northeast of Yorkton on hwys 9 and 5, Saskatchewan's part of the park centres on the roughly circular **Madge Lake**, ringed with aspens, where you'll find a beach, several stores, canteens, recreational and picnic areas, and places that rent canoes, paddleboats and ski equipment. The **parks office** is near the lake (year-round; Ⓣ306/542-3482) and has full information on dates and times of the various activities. Some of the most popular attractions are the various **horseback-riding** excursions organized by Coyote Creek Stables, located on Lakeshore Drive, just inside the park's main entrance ($16/hr; Ⓣ306/542-3439). The chalet-style *Duck Mountain Lodge*, overlooking the lake (Ⓣ306/542-3466; ❷–❹), is a relaxing place to stay; you can sleep in the large lodge, the two-bedroom town-house units with fireplaces, or the woodland cabins nearby. There's also a campsite at Pickerel Point, 4km east of the main Saskatchewan entrance (Ⓣ306/542-3479; $9–17; mid-May to Aug).

KAMSACK, a small Saskatchewan town about 10km west of Duck Mountain, is the best place to **stay** if you want to explore the park but not camp in it. The *Woodlander Inn*, corner of Railway Ave and 3rd St (Ⓣ306/542-2125 or 542-2105; ❶), and the *Duck Mountain Motel and Campground*, 335 Queen Elizabeth Blvd East (Ⓣ306/542-2656; ❷), are the only two options in town and fairly basic. Better is the *Border Mountain Country Bed & Breakfast* (Ⓣ306/542-3072, Ⓦwww.bbcanada.com/bordermountaincountry; ❷), 15km southeast of Kamsack.

Yorkton

Heading west along Hwy 16 into Saskatchewan, **YORKTON** is the first town of any note – and the last sizeable place before you come to Saskatoon 333km away. It was founded as an agricultural community in the 1880s by farmers from Ontario, although – as with so many other places hereabouts – it's the Ukrainian community that features most strongly in the town and the surrounding area. The silver-painted dome and barrel roof of the nave of the white-brick **St Mary's Ukrainian Catholic Church**, at 155 Catherine St, is the town's most distinctive feature. Inside, there's a large illusionistic painting of the Coronation of the Virgin (1939–41) on the surface of the dome – about as close as you'll get in western Canada to the Baroque painted domes in Italian and German churches. The Ukrainian community features strongly in Yorkton's branch of the **Western Development Museum** (June–Aug daily 9am–6pm, Sept–May Mon, Tues & Wed 2pm–5pm; Ⓦwww.wdm.ca; $7.25), devoted to the various ethnic groups who have settled in the region. You'll also find a replica of the interior of a 1902 Catholic church and a superb collection of early twentieth-century Fords and Buicks. However, the most startling sights are the bright-red, huge-wheeled early fire trucks, looking entirely too fragile for their function. If you want to see farmworkers and their fierce-looking machines in action, you could attend the **Threshermen's Show**, held in the grounds of the museum in early August. Also in the city, at the corner of Smith Street and 3rd Avenue, is the **Godfrey Dean Cultural Centre** (Mon–Fri 1–5pm, Sat & Sun 2–5pm; free), which has a small but striking permanent collection of the work of Saskatchewan artists, plus several galleries which display temporary exhibitions; the **Sports Hall of Fame** (10am–noon & 1–4pm; free), located in the older part of the building is also part of the centre. After the long winter, the town is ready to host the **Yorkton Short Film and Video Festival** (Ⓦwww.yorktonshortfilm.org) in May, the oldest festival of its kind in North America, started in 1947.

Veregin and the Doukhobors

An hour's drive northeast of Yorkton, and 12km west of Kamsack, the tiny town of Veregin is named after **Peter Veregin**, the leader of the pacifist Doukhobor sect whose seven thousand members migrated to Saskatchewan at the end of the nineteenth century. The town is home to the **National Doukhobor Heritage Village** (mid-May to mid-Sept daily 10am–6pm; rest of year by appointment; Ⓣ306/542-4441 or 542-4370; $3).

The first **Doukhobors** developed their dissenting beliefs within the Russian Orthodox Church during the eighteenth century, rejecting both the concept of a mediatory priesthood and the church's formal hierarchy. Later they established an independent sect, but their pacifist and protocommunist views made them unpopular with the tsars, who subjected them to periodic persecution. In the late 1890s they fled Russia for Saskatchewan under the leadership of **Peter Veregin**, a keen advocate of communal labour and the collective ownership of property. Veregin maintained his authority until 1907, when the Canadian government insisted that all Doukhobor homesteads be registered as private property. The colonists were divided, with over one-third accepting the government's proposals despite the bitter opposition of the collectivists, who showed their contempt for worldly possessions by destroying their belongings; some even burnt their clothes and organized Canada's first nude demonstrations. Irretrievably divided, Veregin and his supporters left for British Columbia, but the rest stayed behind to create a prosperous, pacifist and Russian-speaking community, which remained separate and distinct until the 1940s.

A modest museum in the **Heritage Village** traces the history of the sect and a large, square, refurbished two-storey prayer home contains the living quarters of their leader, complete with many original furnishings. The building, with its encircling veranda and wrought-iron adornment on both levels, dominates a large green lawn and faces the other buildings of the village, most of which were moved here from Doukhobor colonies in other parts of the province. Lined up in a neat row are a farmhouse, blacksmith's shop, granary, bakery, and bathhouse equipped with dried oak leaves that were used to cleanse the skin and make it fragrant. Another smaller prayer home features a Russian library and a display on Tolstoy, whose financial support helped the Doukhobor to migrate. On the grounds is an imposing bronze statue of the writer, donated by the Soviet Union.

Just south of the city, on the Yellowhead Hwy near Rokeby, is the **Parkland Heritage Centre** (mid-May to Sept Mon–Fri 1–8pm, Sat 1–5pm; $3), a modest but interesting group of nineteenth-century pioneer buildings brought here from other parts of Saskatchewan. Much further out, 48km northwest of Yorkton off the Yellowhead Hwy, **Good Spirit Lake** Provincial Park is an attractive area noted for its ecologically fragile sand dunes and the warm, shallow lake itself, which has exceptionally clear water. Here you'll find fine sandy beaches on the south shore, a fuel station, miniature golf course, tennis courts, riding stables, dining and snacking facilities, plus a **campsite** (ⓣ306/792-4750 or 786-1463; $15–20; mid-May to Sept).

Practicalities

Yorkton's **bus station**, served by three buses daily from Saskatoon, is located downtown on 1st Avenue. The smart **Visitors' Information Centre** is located at the junction of hwys 9 and 16 (Mon–Fri 9am–noon & 1pm–5pm; ⓣ306/783-8707 or 1-877/250-6454, ⓦwww.tourismyorkton.com) and can supply a good range of information and maps. There are several reasonably priced central **hotels**, including the *Holiday Inn*, 100 Broadway St East (ⓣ306/783-9781 or 1-800/667-1585; ❸–❺); and the *Imperial 400 Motel*, 207 Broadway St East (ⓣ306/783-6581 or 1-800/781-2268; ❸), both of which serve great Ukrainian food; and the basic *City Limits Inn*, off Broadway St at 8 Betts Ave (ⓣ306/782-2435; ❶). A pleasant **B&B** is *Lazy Maples*, 111 Darlington St West (ⓣ306/783-7078; ❷); the owner is an excellent cook and can serve you Ukrainian pierogies for breakfast. You can **camp** in town at the well-shaded *City of Yorkton Campground* (ⓣ306/786-1757 or 786-1750; $17–22; mid-May to mid-Oct), on Hwy 16A near the Western Development Museum. Yorkton's dining scene is drab, with several predictable places along Broadway.

Little Manitou Lake

Some 260km west of Yorkton and 120km east of Saskatoon on the Yellowhead Hwy is **Little Manitou Lake**. Set in a rather arid landscape, it looks just like any other lake, until you submerge yourself in its murky waters – or try to, for it has a saline content three times saltier than ocean water and denser than that of the famous Dead Sea in the Middle East. You couldn't sink if you tried, and you'll inevitably find yourself floating on the surface, feet up. The lake has long been known for its healing properties, even by the Indians in the eighteenth and nineteenth centuries, who camped on its shores and called it "lake of the healing waters".

Today, most people head to the tiny, rather ramshackle resort town of **Manitou Beach** on the lake's south shore to bathe in heated indoor mineral pools. Here you can experience near-weightlessness and sooth any rheumatic or arthritic pains in the heated comfort of *Manitou Springs Mineral Spa* (daily 9am–10pm; ⓣ306/946-2233, ⓦwww.manitousprings.ca; $9), one of the largest and oldest mineral **spas** in Canada. You can also stay and eat in their **hotel**, whose rates (❹) include a swim in the spa.

Saskatoon

Set on the wide South Saskatchewan River at the heart of a vast wheat-growing area, **SASKATOON**, 781km west of Winnipeg, is a commercial, manufacturing and distribution centre with a population of around 236,000 – making it Saskatchewan's largest city and, in the opinion of many of its inhabitants, a better claimant to the title of provincial capital than Regina. Ontario Methodists founded the town as a temperance colony in 1883 and named it after the purple berry that grows in the region, but in spite of their enthusiasm the new settlement made an extremely slow start, partly because the semi-arid farming conditions

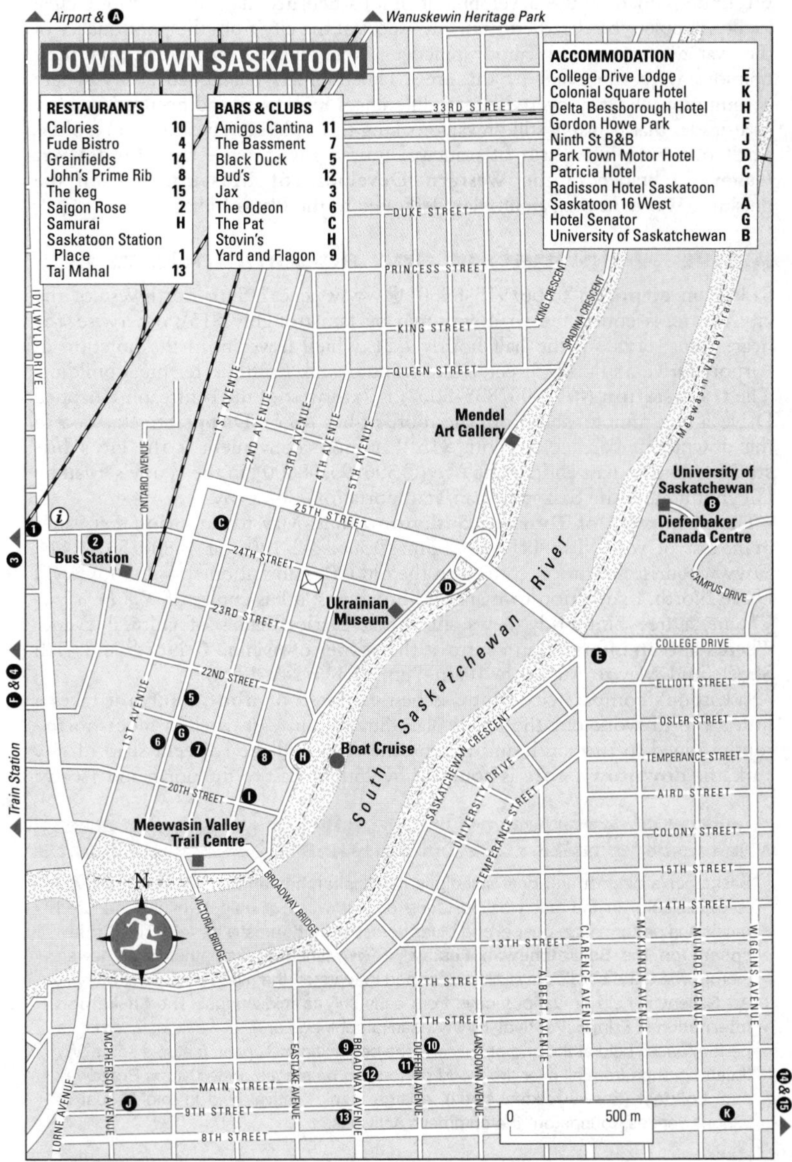

were unfamiliar to them and partly because the Northwest Rebellion of 1885 raised fears of Indian hostility. Although the railroad reached Saskatoon in 1890, there were still only 113 inhabitants at the beginning of the twentieth century. In the next decade, however, there was a sudden influx of European and American settlers and, as the agricultural economy of the prairies expanded, so the city came to be dominated by a group of entrepreneurs nicknamed **boomers**, under whose management Saskatoon became the economic focus of the region. This success was underpinned by the development of a particularly sharp form of municipal loyalty: people who dared criticize any aspect of the city, from the poor quality of the water to tyrannical labour practices, were dubbed **knockers**, and their opinions were rubbished by the press. The boomers established a city where community solidarity overwhelmed differences in income and occupation, a set of attitudes that palpably still prevails, making this a pleasant, well-groomed place, albeit one with just a trio of principal tourist attractions – the **Mendel Art Gallery**, a branch of the **Western Development Museum** and, on the outskirts, **Wanuskewin**, a complex dedicated to the Plains Indians.

Arrival, information and accommodation

Saskatoon **airport** (ⓣ306/975-8900, ⓦwww.yxe.ca), 5km northwest of the city centre, is connected to downtown by taxi (roughly $15); otherwise, the nearest bus service is the half-hourly #21, which leaves from the junction of Airport Drive and 45th Street, a five-minute walk from the terminal building. The **train station** (ⓣ1-800/835-3037) is 7km west of the centre, on Chappell Drive, a five-minute walk from the route of bus #3 on Dieppe Street; a taxi to the downtown core costs about $15. Far more convenient is the city's **bus station**, 23rd St East and Pacific Ave (ⓣ306/933-8000), in the centre served by Greyhound and the Saskatchewan Transportation Company.

The main office of **Tourism Saskatoon** (mid-May to Aug Mon–Fri 9am–5pm; rest of year Mon–Fri 9am–5pm; ⓣ306/242-1206 or 1-800/567-2444, ⓦwww.tourismsaskatoon.com) is in the old CP train station at 6-305 Idylwyld Drive North. In addition to maps and brochures, it has copies of *The Broadway Theatre*, a free bimonthly news sheet that carries details of cultural events. There's also an information centre at the corner of Avenue C North and 47th Street (mid-May to Aug daily 10am–7pm; ⓣ306/242-1206).

Saskatoon's compact city centre is best explored **on foot**, though it takes a little time to work out the street plan. Streets run east–west, avenues north–south. Edged to the south and east by the river and the adjacent strip of city park, the **downtown core** is bounded by 25th St East to the north and 1st Ave

Saskatoon's festivals

Saskatoon's biggest and best shindig is the **Saskatchewan Jazz Festival** (ⓦwww.saskjazz.com) in the last week of June or first week of July; over five hundred musicians perform jazz, gospel and blues across the city, mostly for free. The **Shakespeare on the Saskatchewan Festival** (ⓦwww.shakespeareonthesaskatchewan.com), where the bard's plays are performed in tents on the riverbank by the Mendel Art Gallery, is held on various days from early July to mid-August. The **Saskatoon International Fringe Festival** (ⓦwww.saskatoonfringe.org), a week of alternative performances held at the end of July and the beginning of August, features some fifty theatre groups from all over the world performing on stages dotted along Broadway Ave. **Folkfest** (ⓦwww.folkfest.sk.ca), a large ethnic festival held in mid-August at various venues, rounds out the summer's activities.

to the west. Numbered sequentially, these central streets are all suffixed "East", with their western extensions starting at either 1st Avenue or Idylwyld Drive. However, the avenues change from "South" to "North" right in the centre at 22nd Street East. For the suburbs, Saskatoon Transit (ⓣ306/975-3100) operates an efficient and fairly comprehensive **bus** system, with a standard adult fare of $2.25 (pay on board). **Cruises** along the South Saskatchewan River, with its weir, sand bars and fast-flowing currents, are organized by Shearwater Boat Cruises on its ship, the *Saskatoon Lady* (May–Sept daily; for times call ⓣ306/549-2452 or 1-888/747-7572, ⓦwww.shearwatertours.com; $15); the boat departs for the one-hour trip from the wharf at the Mendel Art Gallery.

Saskatoon has a good choice of downtown **hotels**. There are also lots of reasonably priced **motels** on Hwy 11 south of town and Hwy 16 going east, with standard facilities (❷–❹) and a couple of fairly central **campsites.**

Hotels and motels

Colonial Square Motel 1301 8th St East ⓣ306/343-1676 or 1-800/667-3939, ⓦwww.colonialsquaremotel.com. Eighty simple singles and doubles, all with cable TV & free Wifi. Close to the Broadway Ave area. ❹

Delta Bessborough Hotel 601 Spadina Crescent & 21st St East ⓣ306/244-5521 or 1-800/268-1133, ⓦwww.deltahotels.com. Built for the CNR in 1931, the Bessborough is an enormous turreted and gabled affair that has been tastefully refurbished in a French château style that makes it the city's most striking building. Set in Kiwanis Memorial Park, beside the river. ❼

Hotel Senator 243 21st St East at 3rd Ave ⓣ306/244-6141, ⓦwww.hotelsenator.ca. One of the cheapest places in town, but with fairly primitive rooms. ❹

Park Town Motor Hotel 924 Spadina Crescent & 25th St East ⓣ306/244-5564 or 1-800/667-3999, ⓦwww.parkhotel.com. Large hotel with standard rooms and river views. Better weekend rates. ❹

Radisson Hotel Saskatoon 405 20th St East ⓣ306/665-3322 or 1-800/333-3333, ⓦwww.radisson.com. Tower block with luxurious rooms. Fourteen en suites. Good weekend rates. ❺

B&Bs

College Drive Lodge 1020 College Drive ⓣ306/665-9111, ⓦwww.collegedrivelodge.com. Budget air-conditioned rooms; laundry, kitchen, complimentary coffee and tea; free parking. Close to the university. ❶

Ninth St Bed & Breakfast 227 9th St East ⓣ306/224-3754, ⓦwww.bbcanada.com/949.html. Three attractive suites with shared bath, great gourmet breakfasts and bike rental. In the historic Nutana district and near the Broadway Ave area. ❷

Hostels & Student rooms

Patricia Hotel 3458 2nd Ave North ⓣ306/242-8861. Low-budget downtown hotel above a noisy nightclub with basic dorms ($14), singles and doubles ($40–50). Free parking but no other facilities and no showers for those staying in dorm rooms.

University of Saskatchewan 91 Campus Drive ⓣ306/966-8600. Dorm accommodation – private rooms with shared washrooms – in student residences available to those who call at least a day in advance. Mid-May to mid-Aug. ❶

Campsites

Gordon Howe Campsite Ave P South, off 11th St ⓣ306/975-3328 or 1-866/855-6655. Most comfortable and central of the three city campsites, located near the South Saskatchewan River, 4km southwest of the centre – take 22nd out of town and follow Avenue P to it's southern end. Over 130 serviced sites, with barbecue, picnic area, laundry and on-site manager. Mid-April to Sept. $25–28.

Saskatoon 16 West RV Park Hwy 16, 1.5km northwest of the city ⓣ306/931-8905 or 1-800/478-7833, ⓦwww.saskatoonrvpark.com. Twenty-five pull-through sites, plus fifty serviced sites with hook-ups and free Wifi. Convenience shop on grounds selling Saskatchewan crafts. April–Oct. from $23.

The City

Most of Saskatoon's principal sights are on or near the **Meewasin Valley Trail**, a circular, nineteen-kilometre walking and cycle route that follows the narrow strip of park along both banks of the river between the Idylwyld Drive and Circle Drive bridges. At the start of the trail, the **Meewasin Valley Centre**, 402 3rd Ave South at 19th St East (daily 9am–5pm; free; ⓦwww.meewasin.com), provides a useful introduction to the region's history and geography with the aid of maps, old photographs and a video film; a tourist information office is part of the centre. A few minutes' walk from the Valley Centre, along the west bank, the **Ukrainian Museum of Canada**, 910 Spadina Crescent East at 24th St East (Tues–Sat 10am–5pm, Sun 1–5pm; Ⓦwww.umc.sk.ca; $5), is the more interesting of the city's two Ukrainian museums, representing the Orthodox as distinct from the Catholic tradition. Displays cover the history of Ukrainian migration, traditional textile design, festivals and Easter-egg painting. The **Mendel Art Gallery**, overlooking the river from Spadina Crescent, just north of 25th St East (daily 9am–9pm; free; Ⓣ306/975-7610, Ⓦwww.mendel.ca), features temporary shows of modern Canadian and international art. The gallery is named after local magnate Fred Mendel, whose personal collection includes paintings by many of the country's renowned artists – Emily Carr, Lawren Harris and David Milne – and a good selection of Inuit sculpture, a small sample of which is always on display. The building also has a delightful conservatory full of plants, a snack bar and an excellent gift shop.

Across the river from the Mendel Art Gallery, over University Bridge, the campus of the **University of Saskatchewan** (Ⓦwww.usask.ca), with a number of dignified grey-stone buildings in Gothic Revival style, occupies a prime riverbank site just to the north of College Drive. Departmental collections include a **Museum of Antiquities** (mid-Jan to mid-Dec Mon–Fri 9am–4pm; free), in the Murray Building and the small **Kenderdine Gallery** (Mon–Fri 11.30am–4pm; free). Neither of these draws as many visitors as the **Diefenbaker Canada Centre** (Mon, Tues, Thurs & Fri 9.30am–4.30pm, Wed 9.30am–8pm, Sat & Sun noon–4.30pm; $5), a museum, archive and research centre at the west end of the campus, beside the river. Prime Minister from 1957 to 1963, John Diefenbaker was a caricaturist's dream with his large flat face, protruding teeth and wavy white hair, and the museum's high point is its assortment of newspaper cartoons. He was buried just outside the centre in 1979. One of the finest **views** of the city, across the river, is from the grounds of the centre.

On the south side of the river, 8km from the centre, is the Saskatoon branch of the **Western Development Museum**, 2610 Lorne Ave South (Jan–March Tues–Sun 9am–5pm; April–Dec daily 9am–5pm; Ⓦwww.wdm.ca; $7.25), a few minutes' walk from the route of bus #1 from 2nd Avenue in downtown. The principal exhibit here is Boomtown, an ambitious reconstruction of a typical Saskatchewan small-town main street circa 1910, complete with boardwalk sidewalks and parked vehicles. More like a film set than a museum, its mixture of replica and original buildings includes a school, a general store, a church, a theatre, a train station and a combined pool hall and barbershop. There's a shop with a range of unusual gifts, and the *Boomtown Café* serves delicious home-cooked meals with a pioneer flavour.

Wanuskewin Heritage Park

Wanuskewin Heritage Park (April to late May & Sept daily 9am–5pm; late May to Aug daily 9am–9pm; Oct–March Wed–Sun 9am–5pm; Ⓦwww.wanuskewin.com; $8.50), twenty minutes' drive north of the city centre – along Hwy 10 then Warman and Wanuskewin roads – is designed to be Saskatoon's principal tourist attraction, a lavish tribute to the culture of the Northern Plains Indians. It's well worth the trip out here, as the commercial aspect is played down in favour of a sensitive interpretation of the Indians' spiritual relationship to the land and to living creatures. Bordering the South Saskatchewan River in the attractive wooded Opamihaw Valley, the park embraces a string of marshy creeks and wooded ridges that have been used by native peoples for more than six thousand years. All along the trails are ecologically fragile plants and flowers that must not be picked. The nineteen sites are connected by trails and walkways to a visitor centre that features reconstructions of tepees, a buffalo pound and a buffalo jump as well as displays on traditional skills as diverse as tool-making and storytelling. The park can also arrange for overnight camping in tepees with breakfast, dinner cooked on the fire and interpretive programmes including storytelling and bannock-making (mid-May to Sept; reservation essential), plus longer sessions of two or three nights. The attached **restaurant** specializes in indigenous foodstuffs such as buffalo meat and bannock bread, and a gift shop has a full range of authentic arts and crafts by native people. Wanuskewin has been developed with the cooperation of local native peoples, who provide most of the interpretive staff. There is no public transport; a **taxi** from downtown costs around $20.

Eating, drinking and nightlife

Saskatoon has a useful assortment of **restaurants** clustered in and around the downtown core and along the first couple of blocks of Broadway Avenue, which lies just across the river via the bridge at 4th Avenue South and 19th Street East. Broadway is the nearest thing the city has to a "cultural centre", the home of the Broadway Theatre and a handful of vaguely alternative shops and cafés. **Nightlife** is a little slow, but there are a few pubs and clubs which can reward the determined, with a concentration in the old warehouse district around corner of 24th Street and Pacific Avenue. The local newspaper, *The Star Phoenix*, has bland reviews and nightlife listings at the weekend. While you're in town try a bottle of Great Western Beer (especially the Brewhouse brand), the product of a local factory whose future was threatened by the merger of two of Canada's giant brewing companies, Molson and Carling O'Keefe. The workers bought the factory themselves and can now barely keep up with demand.

△ Canadian Plains First Nations men on horseback

Saskatoon berry pie

The thing to try while in town is **Saskatoon berry pie**, made with berries grown on the outskirts of the city. Arguably the best place for this is the *Berry Barn*, 830 Valley Rd (May–Sept daily 10am–9pm; Oct–Dec Mon–Thurs 10am–5pm, Fri–Sun 10am–9pm; ⓣ306/978-9797), located 11km southwest of town off Hwy 11. It's one of a number of places along this road that allows you to pick your own fruit, and also has a good restaurant serving hearty home-made food.

The Broadway Theatre, 715 Broadway Ave (ⓣ306/652-6556, ⓦwww.broadwaytheatre.ca), has the best of foreign and domestic **films**. For **theatre**, the Persephone, 2802 Rusholme Rd (ⓣ306/384-7727, ⓦwww.persephonetheatre.org; tickets $16–25), is the best known of the city's professional companies; their season runs from October to May. Visiting ballet, theatre and opera stars appear at the TCU Place, 35 22nd St East (ⓣ306/975-7770, ⓦwww.tcuplace.com).

Restaurants

Calories Bakery & Restaurant 721 Broadway Ave ⓣ306/655-7991. An atmospheric French-style bistro, with a great wine list and main courses around $8.

Fude Bistro 119 Ave B ⓣ306/652-2028. Expensive but stylish place for classy regional cooking; mains (like the grilled beef tenderloin with cardamom spiced pumpkin, Saskatoon berry relish and roast potatoes) average $20.

Grainfields Pancake and Waffle House Grosvenor Park Centre, 2105 8th St East ⓣ306/955-1989. Huge, mouthwatering selections of pancakes and waffles with a multitude of toppings.

John's Prime Rib and Steakhouse 401 21st St East ⓣ306/244-6384, ⓦwww.johnssaskatoon.com. Probably the best steaks in town, done any way you want in a fine-dining environment. Closed Sun.

The Keg Steakhouse & Bar 1110 Grosvenor Ave ⓣ306/653-3633. Popular chain serving standard steak and seafood dishes for $10–20.

Saigon Rose 69 24th St East ⓣ306/242-1351. Simple place with plastic tablecloths and fantastic cheap and filling Vietnamese and Chinese food; most dishes are $7–10.

Samurai 601 Spadina Crescent East ⓣ306/683-6926. Good but pricey Japanese sushi restaurant inside the *Delta Bessborough Hotel*.

Saskatoon Station Place 221 Idylwyld Drive North ⓣ306/244-7777, ⓦwww.saskatoonstationplace.com. Eat steak and prime rib in Pullman cars in a converted train station. Great Sun brunches.

Taj Mahal 1013 Broadway Ave ⓣ306/978-2227. Outstanding Indian restaurant, arguably the best in Canada. The most delicious dishes are those made with coconut (*naryal*); the menu has a large vegetarian section. The chutneys are home-made as is the mango ice cream, whilst the lassis are made with buttermilk. A meal for two will cost around $40. Closed Mon.

Bars and clubs

Amigos Cantina 806 Dufferin Ave ⓦwww.amigoscantina.com. Mexican restaurant that becomes a club at night with local bands often playing.

The Bassment 245 3rd Ave South ⓣ306/683-2277, ⓦwww.saskatoonjazzsociety.com. Great jazz venue attracting international performers. Live jazz performances every Sat evening from mid-Sep to mid-May usually starting at 8:30pm.

Black Duck Freehouse 154 2nd Ave S. Comfortably familiar pub, with the biggest selection of scotch and beer in Saskatchewan.

Buds 817 Broadway Ave. Rough-and-ready bar with nightly R&B acts, plus jam sessions Sat afternoon. $3–5 cover charge.

Jax Nite Club 302 Pacific Ave. One of several middling dance clubs in the warehouse area; follow the crowds.

Odeon 241 2nd Ave S, ⓣ306/651-1000 ⓦwww.theodeon.ca. Saskatoon's hippest club, attracting the city's chic crowd. Occasional live music but mostly dance and techno.

The Pat 345 2nd Ave N. Vast middle-of-the road nightclub catering to just about everybody, though the college crowd dominates. Mostly Top 40.

Stovin's Lounge 601 Spadina Crescent E. The *Bessborough Hotel*'s quiet and comfortable lounge: ideal for chatting and unwinding when all the other options sound like too much effort.

Yard and Flagon Pub 718 Broadway Ave. Broadway bar with a lively rooftop that pulls in the college crowd.

Listings

Bike rental Bike Doctor, 623 Main St ☎306/664-8555.
Car rental Avis ☎306/652-3434; Budget ☎306/224-77925; Discount ☎306/242-1098; Enterprise ☎306/651-4114 or ☎306/244-6900; Thrifty, 2130 Airport Drive ☎306/244-1833.
Hospitals Saskatoon City Hospital, 701 Queen St ☎306/655-8000.
Laundries Off-Broadway Laundromat, 835b Broadway Ave ☎306/244-1344.
Police 130 4th Ave North ☎306/975-8300.
Post office 202 4th Ave N.
Taxis United Cabs ☎306/652-2222.
Weather line ☎306/975-4266.

Around Saskatoon

North of Saskatoon, Hwy 11 cuts across the narrow slice of prairie that separates the final stretches of the North and South Saskatchewan rivers, before they flow together further to the northeast. There's nothing to see on the road itself, but on the way the briefest of detours will take you to one of the province's more interesting attractions, **Batoche National Historic Site**, where the Métis rebellion of 1885 reached its disastrous climax. Setting out early and with your own transport, this can be visited as part of an exceptional day-trip that also includes Wanuskewin (see p.620) on the north side of town, a museum at **Duck Lake** and the reconstructed **Fort Carlton** where you can camp overnight. If you have more days to spare exploring the Saskatoon area, be sure to head to the spas and healing waters of **Little Manitou Lake** (see p.616) and, for a weekend or more away try heading up to wilds of **Prince Albert National Park** (see p.631).

Batoche National Historic Site

The site of the Métis's last stand – and the last place where Canadians fought against Canadians – **Batoche National Historic Site** (May–Sept daily 9am–5pm; $7.15) occupies a splendid site beside the east bank of the South Saskatchewan River, 90km from Saskatoon, just off Provincial Hwy 225. At the entrance to the park, a **visitor reception centre** (☎306/423-6227) has displays on the culture of the Métis and provides a detailed account of the rebellion, supplemented by a glossy brochure and an exceptional 45-minute audiovisual presentation combining clips of re-enactments, spoken narration, music and tableaux of realistic mannequins. This is great for an insight into the Métis way of life and a blow-by-blow account of the battle, but rather glosses over the cause of the actual conflict; the displays are perhaps too sympathetic to the Métis, instead of appreciating the government's concern to avoid Canada being split in half – the west was still very much an open territory at the time.

Behind the centre, the main footpath leads to a refurbished Catholic church and adjacent rectory, all that's left of the original village. A few minutes' walk away, in the cemetery perched above the river bank, memorials inscribed with the hoary commendation "a credit to his race" contrast with the rough chunk of rock that commemorates Riel's commander in chief **Gabriel Dumont**. A stern and ferocious man, Dumont insisted that he be buried standing up, so that he could enjoy a good view of the river.

The church and cemetery are at the centre of the park's **walking trails**, which extend along the river bank in both directions. Roughly 1km to the

The Northwest Rebellion

The 1869–70 Red River rebellion in Manitoba, led by **Louis Riel**, won significant concessions from the Canadian government but failed to protect the Métis's way of life in subsequent years against the effects of increasing white settlement. Many Métis moved west to farm the banks of the **South Saskatchewan River**, where the men worked as freighters, traders, horse breeders and translators, acting as intermediaries between the Indians and the Europeans. In itself, the development of these homesteads was a recognition by the Métis that the day of the itinerant buffalo hunter was over. However, when the government surveyors arrived here in 1878, the Métis realized, as they had on the Red River twenty years before, that their claim to the land they farmed was far from secure.

Beginning with the Métis, a general sense of instability spread across the region in the early 1880s, fuelled by Big Bear's and Poundmaker's increasingly restless and hungry **Cree** and by the discontent of the white settlers at the high freight charges levied on their produce. The leaders of the Métis decided to act in June 1884, when they sent a delegation to Montana, where Riel was in exile. Convinced that the Métis were God's chosen instrument to purify the human race, and he their Messiah, Riel was easily persuaded to return to Canada, where he spent the winter unsuccessfully petitioning the Ottawa government for confirmation of Métis rights.

In March 1885, Riel and his supporters declared a provisional government at **Batoche** and demanded the surrender of the nearest Mountie outpost, **Fort Carlton**, just 35km to their west on the North Saskatchewan River. The police superintendent refused, and the force he dispatched to re-establish order was badly mauled at **Duck Lake**. When news of the uprising reached Big Bear's Cree, some 300km away, they attacked the local Hudson's Bay Company store and killed its nine occupants in the so-called **Frog Lake Massacre**. Within a couple of weeks, no fewer than three columns of militia were converging on Big Bear's Cree and the meagre Métis forces at Batoche. The total number of casualties – about fifty altogether – does not indicate the full significance of the engagement, which for the Métis marked the end of their independence and influence. Riel's execution in Regina on November 16, 1885, was bitterly denounced in Québec and remains a potent symbol of the deep divide between English- and French-speaking Canada. In Ontario there was a mood of unrepentant triumphalism, the military success – however paltry – stirring a deep patriotic fervour that excluded Métis and Indian alike.

south, there's a military graveyard, a Métis farmhouse and the remains of some rifle pits; about the same distance to the north, there's the site of the old ferry crossing, more rifle pits and the foundations of several Métis buildings. With a knowledge of the history, the park becomes an extremely evocative spot.

Duck Lake and Fort Carlton

Back on Hwy 11, on the west side of the South Saskatchewan, the tiny farming community of **DUCK LAKE** – many of whose buildings have outdoor murals depicting local history – is home to a **Regional Interpretive Centre**, 5 Anderson Ave (late May to early Sept daily 10am–5.30pm; Ⓦwww.dlric.org; $4.50), with displays on Indian, Métis and pioneer society from 1870 to 1905. Prize exhibits include some elaborate Cree costumes; an outfit that belonged to the Sioux chief Little Fox, an adviser to Sitting Bull; and Gabriel Dumont's gold watch, presented to him in New York where he was appearing in Buffalo Bill's Wild West Show. The buildings huge tower gives views a long way over the prairies.

Continuing 26km west along Hwy 212, you'll reach **Fort Carlton Provincial Historic Park** (mid-May to Aug daily 10am–6pm; Ⓦwww.se.gov.sk.ca; $2.50), a reconstruction of a Hudson's Bay Company trading post circa 1860. Founded in 1810, the riverbank station was fortified in successive decades and became an important centre of the fur and pemmican trade, until the demise of the buffalo brought an end to its success. Reduced to a warehouse facility in the early 1880s, the fort was garrisoned by the Mounties during the Northwest Rebellion (see box opposite), but it was finally burnt down and abandoned in 1885. The **visitors' centre** provides an historical introduction to the fort, whose stockade shelters replicas of the clerk's quarters, a sail and harness shop, a fur and provisions store with piles of colourfully striped Hudson's Bay Company blankets and bottles of bright Indian trading beads, and a trading shop, where the merchandise included gunpowder – which meant the clerks were forbidden to light a stove here, no matter what the temperature. Just outside the walls of the stockade are three tepees, neatly aligned along a path. The centre, also offers guided **trail walks**, which allow you to see the remains of rutted wagon trails made by carts carrying supplies to and from the fort. There's also an on-site **campsite** ($11–24; mid-May to early Sept). Take care when hiking or camping as the wooded gullies of the North Saskatchewan River are home to a number of **black bears**.

Saskatoon to Alberta

From Saskatoon it's only another 275km to the Alberta border and the dull town of **Lloydminster** which straddles it. But **Redberry Lake** is a must for keen birders, and the **Battlefords** make another good short stop to see a refurbished Mountie stockade.

Redberry Lake

The **Redberry Lake World Biosphere Reserve** (ⓦwww.redberrylake.ca; free), about 100km northwest of Saskatoon via hwys 16, 340 and 40, is one of the province's best areas to view over two hundred species of birds. The north shore of Redberry Lake is home to several rare species, including piping plovers and white pelicans. There are trails around the lakeshore, as well as the Stuart Houston Ecology Centre (mid-May to mid-Sept daily 9am–5pm), an interpretive centre with videos and dioramas on the lake's fragile ecosystem. You can book guided walking tours ($4 per person) and get information on a driving tour of the region at the centre. Within the reserve, the **Redberry Lake Regional Park** (May–Sept; $5) has **camping** ($10–18).

The Battlefords

Following the Yellowhead Hwy towards Edmonton, you'll come to the **Battlefords**, roughly 150km from Saskatoon. These twin townships consist of grimy and impoverished **North Battleford** and, facing it from the opposite bank of the North Saskatchewan River, sedate little **Battleford** with its trim riverside streets and refurbished Mountie stockade.

From the middle of the eighteenth century, this stretch of the North Saskatchewan River formed a natural boundary between the **Blackfeet** to the south and the **Cree** to the north. These two groups were temporary trading partners, the Cree and their Ojibwa allies controlling the flow of European goods, the Blackfeet providing the horses. However, with the arrival of **white traders** at the start of the nineteenth century, the Blackfeet developed a flourishing trade direct with the Europeans, and by 1870 the Cree and Blackfeet were waging war across the entire length of their frontier, from the Missouri River to Fort Edmonton. In the 1870s, apprehensive after the Cypress Hills Massacre and the arrival of Sitting Bull and his warriors (see box, p.607), the government speeded its policy of containment and control, determined to push the Plains Indians into reservations and thereby open the area for European settlers. Their chosen instrument was the North West Mounted Police, who in 1876 established a post at Battleford, which then became the regional capital.

With the virtual **extinction of the buffalo** herds in the late 1870s, the Plains Indians began to starve and Lieutenant Governor Dewdney used his control of emergency rations to force recalcitrant Indians onto the reservations. Several bands of Cree resisted the process, fighting a series of skirmishes at the same time as the Métis rebellion in Batoche, but by the mid-1880s their independence was over. Meanwhile, Battleford had lost its pre-eminence when the Canadian Pacific Railway routed its transcontinental line through Regina, which became the new capital in 1883. Twenty years later, its prospects were further damaged by the Canadian Northern Railway, which laid its tracks on the other side of the river, creating the rival town of North Battleford. Since then, Battleford has stagnated and shrunk, while its rival has become a moderately successful industrial and distribution centre, with a population of around fourteen thousand.

The townships

Situated on the east side of the river valley, North Battleford's downtown core is arranged into streets running north–south and avenues running west–east, forming a central gridiron that intersects with Railway Avenue, which runs southeast to northwest. Across the river, some 5km away, Battleford sprawls next to Hwy 4, its streets running from west to east and avenues from north to south. There are two roads between the two: a modern flyover that's part of Hwy 16, and the shorter old Route 16A.

On the Yellowhead Hwy, just east of **NORTH BATTLEFORD**, this town's branch of the **Western Development Museum** (May–Aug daily 9am–5pm, Sept–April Mon–Fri 10am–4pm; Ⓦwww.wdm.ca; $7.25) deals with the farming history of Saskatchewan. Inside, vintage vehicles and a "Jolly Life of the Farmer's Wife" exhibit of old ranges and laundry equipment recall older, and harder, times, while outside is the Heritage Farm and Village, which contains 36 buildings, saved from around the province, including tiny churches and homesteads, banks, a general store, creaky barns and a grain elevator from 1928. The museum is an excellent way to acquaint yourself with prairie history and realize the harshness and the changes in farming life over the last century. Try to visit on the second weekend in August when the "ghost" village comes alive in the "Those Were the Days" event, which features costumed locals bread-baking and craft-making.

The old municipal library in the centre of North Battleford, 1091 100th St at 11th Ave, now houses the **Allen Sapp Gallery** (June–Sept daily 11am–5pm; Oct–May Wed–Sun noon–4pm; Ⓦwww.allensapp.com; free), showcase for the work of Allen Sapp, a local Cree. Perhaps the best known of Canada's contemporary native artists, Sapp trawls his childhood recollections of life on the Red Pheasant reserve in the 1930s for most of his material. His simply drawn figures are characteristically cast in the wide spaces of the prairies, whose delicately blended colours hint at a nostalgic regard for a time when his people had a greater sense of community.

In **BATTLEFORD**, the **Fred Light Museum**, 11 20th St East at Central Ave (mid-May to Aug daily 9am–8pm; free), has a substantial collection of early

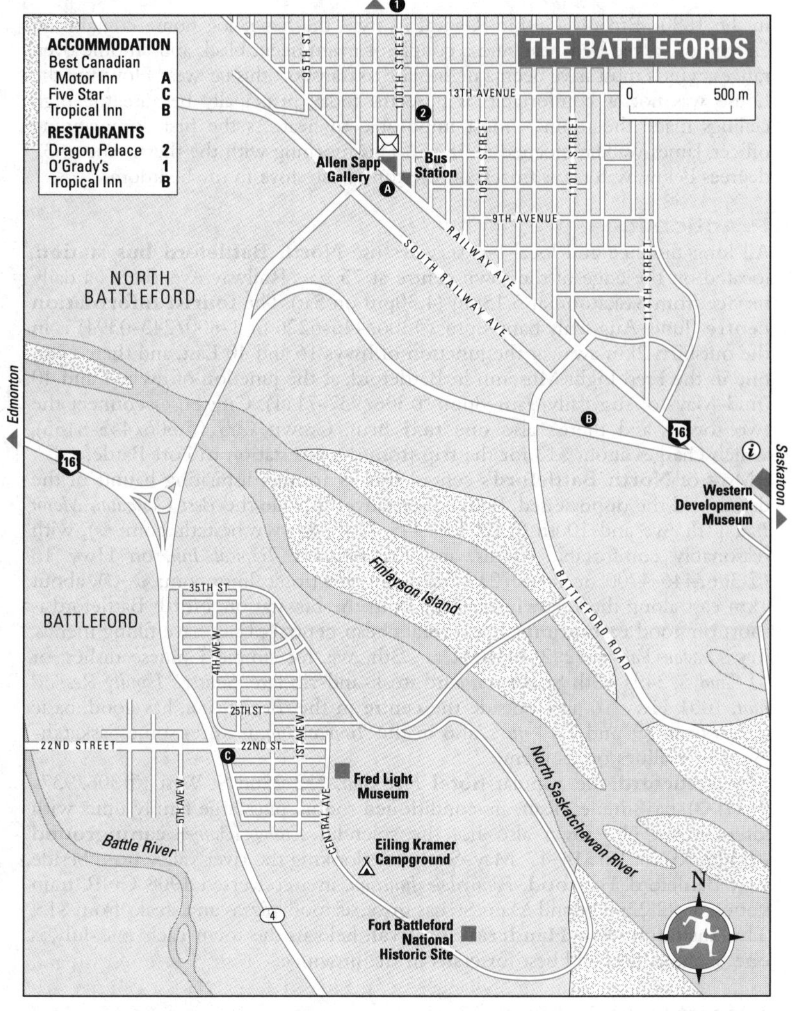

firearms and military uniforms and a replica of an old general store, but is thoroughly upstaged by **Fort Battleford National Historic Site** (mid-May to early Sept daily 9am–5pm; Ⓦwww.parkscanada.gc.ca/battleford; $7.15), overlooking the river valley from the top of a steep bluff just down the road, accessed from Central Ave. At the entrance to the park, the visitors' information centre provides a general introduction to the fort and, next door, the restored barracks contains a display explaining its history, assisted by well-informed, costumed guides. Within the replica stockade stand four original buildings, including the **Sick Horse Stable**, where the delicate constitutions of the Mounties' horses – most of which came from Ontario – were coaxed into accepting the unfamiliar prairie grasses. Centrepiece of the park is the **Commanding Officer's Residence**, which has been returned to its appearance in the 1880s. Broadly Gothic Revival in style, the hewn-log house contains an enormous carved bed-head and a couple of magnificent black and chrome oven ranges, which must have been a nightmare to transport this far west. However, the house was not as comfortable as it seems today, principally because the high ceilings made the rooms almost impossible to heat. As the first commanding officer, James Walker, moaned in 1879, "This morning with the thermometer 37 degrees below, water was frozen on the top of the stove in my bedroom."

Practicalities

All long-distance and local bus services use **North Battleford bus station**, located on the edge of the town centre at 75 East Railway Ave; there's a daily service from Saskatoon at 5.15pm (4.30pm on Sat). The **tourist information centre** (June–Aug daily 8am–8pm; ⓣ306/445-6226 or 1-800/243-0394) is in the outskirts 2km away, at the junction of hwys 16 and 40 East, and there's also one in the Fred Light Museum in Battleford, at the junction of hwys 4 and 40 (mid-May to Aug daily 9am–8pm; ⓣ306/937-7111). City buses connect the two towns, and there's also one **taxi** firm, Crown Cab (ⓣ306/445-8155), which charges about $13 for the trip from the bus station to Fort Battleford.

Most of **North Battleford**'s central **hotels** are the dispiriting haunts of the drunk and the dispossessed. Better alternatives include the *Best Canadian Motor Inn*, 11th Ave and 100th St (ⓣ306/445-7747, ⓦwww.bestcdn.com; ❷), with reasonably comfortable rooms, and the pleasant *Tropical Inn*, on Hwy 16 (ⓣ306/446-4700 or 1-800/219-5244, ⓦwww.tropicalinns.com; ❸–❻), about 1km east along the Yellowhead Hwy from the bus station. North Battleford is short on good **restaurants**, but several cheap, central places have filling menus. Try *Dragon Palace*, 1292 101st St at 13th Ave, for simple Chinese dishes; or *O'Grady's*, 2491 99th St, for standard steak-and-rib fare. *Smitty's Family Restaurant*, 1001 Hwy 16, just outside the centre in the *Tropical Inn*, has good, basic dishes from $9, and *Da Vinci's*, also in the *Tropical Inn*, features some Saskatchewan specialities on its menu.

In **Battleford**, the popular **hotel** *Five Star*, 322 22nd St West (ⓣ306/937-2651; ❷), has simple, clean, air-conditioned rooms, plus large family units with kitchenettes. The town also has the splendid *Eiling Kramer* **campground** (ⓣ306/937-6212; $14–17; May–Sept), overlooking the river valley from beside Fort Battleford. For **food**, *Pennydale Junction*, in a converted 1908 CNR train station at 92 22nd St and Main St, has great seafood, pizzas and steaks from $13. The **Saskatchewan Handcraft Festival**, held in the town each mid-July, is one of the largest and best for crafts in the province.

Lloydminster

Some 140km northwest of the Battlefords you hit the Saskatchewan–Alberta border, and the drab city of **LLOYDMINSTER**, which was founded in 1903 by a group of two thousand British pioneers known as the Barr colonists. Top draw is the underwhelming **Barr Colony Heritage Cultural Centre** (late May to early Sept daily 9am–8pm; Sept to late May Wed–Fri 9am–5pm, Sat & Sun 1–5pm; $6), located in Weaver Park beside the Yellowhead Hwy at 44th St and 45th Ave, featuring a small display on the founders, together with a couple of art galleries and a wildlife exhibition. Perhaps the most interesting aspect of the city is its geographical location: the 4th Meridian runs right down 50th Avenue, the main street. Thirty-metre-high metal border markers, shaped like the survey stakes used by the original surveyors when they laid out the border between the two provinces, line Hwy 16 on the north and south sides, and smaller markers line the main street.

Yet Lloydminster is a popular town for a break in the journey, and has a **tourist office** at 5001 50th Ave (Mon–Fri 8am–5pm; ⓣ306/825-6180 or 1-800/825-6180). Both Tourism Saskatchewan and Alberta Tourism run seasonal **visitor reception centres** on either side of the border. The **bus station** is on the Alberta side at 50th Street and lots of **hotels** and **motels** line its two main streets, 44th Street (the Yellowhead) and 50th Avenue (Hwy 17). The pick of these are the *Best Canadian Motor Inn*, 4320 44th St (ⓣ306/825-4400 or 1-888/700-2264, ⓦwww.bestcdn.com; ❸) with an indoor pool and cable TV; and the *Best Western Wayside Inn* (ⓣ780/875-4404 or 1-800/658-4404; ❸), a sprawling complex just west of the city on Hwy 16 on the Alberta side. For **camping**, *Weaver Park Campground* (ⓣ306/825-3726; May to mid-Oct; $16–22), next door to the heritage centre, has a full range of facilities, including showers and a playground. Options for **eating out** are limited: try *David's Steak House*, 5501 44th St, or one of the pizza chains around town.

Northern Manitoba and Saskatchewan

Stretching from the edges of Lake Winnipeg and the Northern banks of the North Saskatchewan River all the way to the Northwest Territories and Nunavut, **northern Manitoba and Saskatchewan** are inhospitable and sparsely inhabited expanses that account for roughly half the two provinces. The region divides into two slightly different zones, with the marginally richer flora and fauna of the **Interior Plains** lying south of the more spartan landscapes of the **Canadian Shield**. The shield stretches north of a rough curve drawn between Flin Flon, La Ronge and La Loche – whose shallow soils support a gigantic coniferous forest broken up by a complex pattern of lakes and rivers. Both regions are hostile environments, with deep, cold winters alternating with brief, bright summers, when the first few centimetres of topsoil thaw out above the permafrost to create millions of stagnant pools of water; ideal conditions for mosquitoes and blackflies. There are compensations: out in the bush or along the shores of Hudson Bay you'll find a sense of desolate **wilderness** that's hard to find elsewhere – crossed by a staggering number of first-rate backcountry **canoe routes** – and a native **wildlife** that includes caribou, **polar bear** and all sorts of migratory birds.

Most of the region is inaccessible and the bulk of its limited hwy system was built to service the resource towns whose wealth is founded on mining or logging. These tend to provide the only convenient bases – don't expect much more – for the region's provincial and national parks. In **Saskatchewan** the town of **Prince Albert** provides a gateway to the north, with all major hwys or bus journeys passing through or beginning here. Yet while there's nothing worth stopping for here, just beyond it's backdoor is **Prince Albert National Park** and, further still, the uranium mining town of **La Ronge**, beside the lakes and forests of the appealing **Lac La Ronge Provincial Park** and some of the north's longest and most varied canoe routes on the nearby **Churchill River**. There's more challenging white-water canoeing further northwest along Saskatchewan's Alberta border, in **Clearwater River** Provincial Park, but some of the most extraordinary backcountry adventures and landscapes are found in the far northwest of the province, where the **Athabasca Sand Dunes Provincial Wilderness Park** provides a unique getaway for well-heeled wilderness-fans.

The layout of Manitoba's far north is quite different, with Lake Winnipeg and Winnipegosis creating a vast natural barrier between it and the southerly portions of the province. The largest towns up here are **Flin Flon** and **The Pas**, which provide bases for the region's two main provincial parks, **Clearwater Lake** and **Grass River**. Even further north is **Thompson**, which along with The Pas has a rail-link with the entire region's key tourist centre: **Churchill**. This remote and windswept township, on the southern shore of Hudson Bay, is far beyond the reach of the hwy network, and the main attractions here are the **beluga whales** and **polar bears** that congregate around the town from late June to early November.

With distances so vast and the population so thin, public transport in Northern Saskatchewan and Manitoba is understandably poor, yet it's still possible to get to many places by bus or train. The **Saskatchewan Transportation Company** (Ⓣ306/787-3340 or 1-800-663-7181, Ⓦwww.stcbus.com) provides two useful bus services: one connecting Saskatoon, Prince Albert, Waskesiu (mid-May to mid-Sept only) and La Ronge (daily; 6hrs; $61); the other heading up to The Pas (daily 11hrs; $97) and Flin Flon in Manitoba. The latter two are also connected by a daily Greyhound to Winnipeg (to Flin Flon; 12hrs; $90) as is Thompson (2 daily 9hrs; $92). The only rail service in the region operates between Winnipeg, The Pas, Thompson and Churchill, with three departures in each direction every week.

Prince Albert

Founded as a Presbyterian mission in 1866, **PRINCE ALBERT**, 144km north of Saskatoon along Hwy 11, has a thriving timber industry, is a major transport centre and is the province's oldest and third-largest city. But it's a dull spot, its long main drag, **Central Avenue** (Hwy 2), lined with fast-food joints, fuel stations and shopping malls. Apart from the Northern Lights Casino, which brings thousands of visitors to town, the only conceivable attractions are the **Historical Museum** at River St and Central Ave (mid-May to Aug Mon–Sat 10am–6pm, Sun 10am–9pm; $1), given over chiefly to the area's first farmers and loggers, and **Diefenbaker's House**, 246 19th St West (May–Sept Mon–Sat 10am–6pm, Sun 10am–8pm; free), where the politician John Diefenbaker lived from 1947 until he donated it to the city in 1975.

The appeal of the town is that it has the only **bus** to Prince Albert National Park (see opposite) and La Ronge (see p.632), a daily service leaving from the station at 99 15th St East (Ⓣ306/953-3700). A daily bus also arrives here from Saskatoon. The **tourist office** 3700 2nd Ave West (daily June–Aug 9am–8pm; Sept–May Mon–Fri 9am–5pm; Ⓣ306/953-4385, Ⓦwww.patourism.ca) in the south of town provides free town maps and brochures and can provide accommodation and dining listings if you really have to stay or eat in town.

There's no reason **to stay**; the town's central hotels are either grim or – thanks to the casino – noisy. At the south end of Hwy 2 is the comfortable *South Hill Inn*, 3245 2nd Ave West (☎306/922-1333 or 1-800/363-4466; ③), which also has some outlandish Jacuzzi suites (⑥) and a popular bar downstairs. For **campers**, the *Mary Nisbit Campground* (☎306/953-4880; $13–16; mid-May to Sept) is about 2km north of town, across the river beside Hwy 2. There's not much choice for good **eating** places, but the most expensive and renowned place is *Amy's on Second*, 2990 2nd Ave West (☎306/763-1515), with three-course lunches from $30, and local fish such as pickerel. There's also *Diggers Road House*, 2901 2nd Ave W, with inexpensive specials, and *WK Kitchen*, 2840 2nd Ave W, which dishes up big Chinese buffets at reasonable prices.

Prince Albert National Park

Some 230km north of Saskatoon **Prince Albert National Park** is a great tract of wilderness where the aspen parkland of the south meets the boreal forest of the north, a transitional landscape that incorporates a host of rivers and creeks, dozens of deep lakes, pockets of pasture and areas of spruce bog. The shift in vegetation is mirrored by the wildlife, with prairie species such as coyote and wild bison giving way to black bear, moose, wolf, caribou, osprey and eagle further north. There's an entry fee of $7 to the park, with reductions for groups and longer stays.

The tourist village of **WASKESIU**, approached from the south by Hwy 263 and from the east by hwys 2 and 264, is the only settlement in the park. Spread out along the southern shore of Waskesiu Lake, it has all the usual facilities, a narrow sandy beach that gets ridiculously overcrowded in summer, and the park's **nature centre**, on Lakeview Drive (mid-May to Sept daily noon–4pm; ☎306/663-4522 or 1-877/255-7267), which has a hands-on display on the southern boreal forest and its inhabitants. In the centre of Waskesiu, at the junction of Lakeview Drive and Waskesiu Drive, the park's main **information office** (mid-May to Aug daily 8am–8pm; Sept to mid-Oct daily 8am–5pm; mid-Oct to mid-May Mon–Sat 8am–4pm; ☎306/663-4522, ⓦwww.pc.gc.ca) gives advice on wildlife and the condition of the hiking trails, along with weather forecasts. The information office also runs a programme of **guided walks** in July and August and issues backcountry camping permits ($9), which allow visitors to use the primitive, seasonal **campsites** dotted along most of the more substantial trails. Shearwater Boat Cruises runs **boat** trips on the lake (July to mid-Sept daily 1pm, 3pm, 5pm & 7pm; 1hr; $15; ☎306/982-4478 or 1-888/747-7572). Whatever you do in the park, remember to take insect repellent.

Several of the park's easier **hiking trails** begin in or near Waskesiu, most notably the thirteen-kilometre Kingfisher Trail, which loops through the forest just to the west of the resort. However, the best trails and **canoe routes** begin roughly 15km further north at the bottom end of Kingsmere Lake, accessible by boat or car from Waskesiu. They include a delightful week-long canoe trip that skirts the west shore of Kingsmere Lake before heading through a series of remote lakes amidst dense boreal forest. There's also a twenty-kilometre hike or canoe (a good overnight trip) to the idyllic spot of **Grey Owl's Cabin** (May–Sept), situated beside tiny Ajawaan Lake, near the northern shore of Kingsmere Lake. Grey Owl (see p.204) lived in this cabin from 1931 until 1937, the year before his death, and it was here that he wrote one of his better books, *Pilgrims of the Wild*, and where he, his wife Anahereo and daughter Shirley Dawn are buried. For further information on the trip to the cabin, and on other canoe routes in the park, call the park information office.

Park practicalities

Connected by bus to La Ronge to the north (see below) and Prince Albert to the south, Waskesiu's **bus stop** is right in the centre, beside a **tourist kiosk** (mid-May to Aug daily 8am–10pm; Sept–Dec & April to mid-May Mon–Fri 8am–4pm; Jan–March daily 8am–4pm; ⓣ306/663-5410), which provides free maps of the town. Waskesiu's stores sell a full range of outback **equipment**, but no one rents out camping gear. **Canoe** and **kayak rentals** (ⓣ306/663-5994) are available at three marinas within the park.

Waskesiu's main street, Waskesiu Drive, runs roughly parallel to and just south of the lake, its western section curving round behind Lakeview Drive. Almost all the **hotels** and **motels** are on or near these two streets, including the *Lakeview Hotel*, Lakeview Drive (ⓣ306/663-5311 or 1-877/331-3302, ⓦwww.lakeviewhotel.com; ③), and the more luxurious *All Season Waskesiu Lake Lodge*, Lakeview Drive (ⓣ306/663-6161, ⓦwww.waskesiulakelodge.com; ⑤; May to mid-Oct), with one- and two-bedroom apartments that include lakeside decks and barbecues. For **bungalow** and **cabin** accommodation try *Kapasiwin Bungalows* (ⓣ306/663-5225, ⓦwww.kapasiwin.com; ④; May to mid-Oct), 2km round the lake to the east of the resort, which has cabins that form a quiet mini-resort with its own private beach.

Waskesiu has two **campsites**: the centrally situated *Trailer Park* (ⓣ306/663-4522 or 1-877/255-7267; $30; mid-May to Sept) on the north end of Waskesiu Drive near *Waskesiu Lodge*, and the nearby *Beaver Glen Campground* (ⓣ306/663-4522 or 1-877/255-7267; $20–25; mid-May to Sept), near Waskesiu Lake. The basic, unserviced *Kingsmere Lake Campgrounds* (ⓣ306/663-4522 or 1-877/255-7267; $9 backcountry permit from park office; year-round) is near Grey Owl's Cabin. For reservations at all other Prince Albert campsites, call ⓣ1-800/333-7267.

There are several low-priced **restaurants** and **snack bars** in the centre, while on the beachfront, *The Beach House* is good for cappuccinos, wraps, desserts and sunsets. For more expensive dining, try the Mackenzie's Dining Room at the *Hawood Inn*, 851 Lakeview Drive, where main courses start at around $15, and include good cuts of local beef.

La Ronge and around

Some 350km west of Flin Flon and 242km north of Prince Albert along Hwy 2, the scrawny, straggling resort of **LA RONGE** is sandwiched between the road and the western edge of Lac La Ronge. It was home to an isolated Cree community until the road reached here in 1948. Since then, gold mines and forestry operations have started just to the north of town and the area's lakes and rivers have proved popular with visiting canoeists and anglers.

Falling on either side of Boardman Street, the town is fronted by La Ronge Avenue, which runs parallel to the waterfront, the location of the **bus depot**. A few minutes' walk away, in Mistasinihk Place, is the office of the **Saskatchewan Parks Department** (Mon–Fri 8am–noon & 1–5pm; ⓣ306/425-4234 or 1-800/772-4064) and an interpretive centre (same days and hours) with exhibits on northern lifestyles, crafts and history. The nearest **visitor reception centre** (mid-May to mid-Sept Mon–Fri 8am–9pm, Sat & Sun 10am–8pm; ⓣ306/425-3055 or 1-866/527-6643) is 2km south of town beside Hwy 2.

A good base for exploring the region, La Ronge has several reasonably priced and central **hotels** and **motels**. These include the *La Ronge Motor Hotel*, 1120 La Ronge Ave (ⓣ306/425-2190 or 1-800/332-6735, ⓦwww.lrhotel.sk.ca; ③). There are a series of **campsites** strung along Hwy 102 north of town, the nearest of which is *Nut Point* (☎306/425-4234 or 1-800/772-4064; $13–18; mid-May to Aug), 1km north via La Ronge Avenue. One of the few places to **eat** that isn't run-of-the-mill is the vaguely Greek *Kostas II*, 707 La Ronge Ave.

La Ronge is on the western edge of **Lac La Ronge Provincial Park**, which incorporates Lac La Ronge itself and extends north to encompass a number of smaller lakes and a tiny section of the **Churchill River**, once the main route into the northwest for the voyageurs. The Churchill swerves across the width of the province, from west to east, before heading on into Manitoba, its waterways providing some of the region's longest canoe routes. The parks department in La Ronge (see opposite) provides a detailed description of the river and its history in the booklet *Saskatchewan's Voyageur Highway: A Canoe Trip*. The park is one of the few areas in the province where you can hike the Canadian Shield. The 15km **Nut Point Hiking Trail** leaves the campsite and runs along a narrow peninsula that juts into Lac La Ronge, crossing rock ridges through forests and over high, open ridges where you can view the enormous island-studded lake. Less strenuously, these waters are also good for fishing – the walleye, pike and lake trout are delicious. A number of La Ronge **tour operators** and **outfitters** run and equip fishing and canoeing trips into the park, most of them using its web of lakeside holiday **lodges** and **cabins**; the parks department office has the details. There are also several **campsites** along Hwy 102 including the *Missinipe* (☎306/425-4234 or 1-800/772-4064; $9–22; mid-May to Aug) on Otter Lake, where the hwy crosses the Churchill River.

North of La Ronge, Hwy 102 deteriorates long before it reaches **MISSINIPE**, 80km away, the home of Horizons Unlimited/Churchill River Canoe Outfitters (☎1-877/511-2726, Ⓦwww.churchillrivercanoe.com), a highly recommended wilderness-holiday company. Beyond here, the road joins Route 905, a bumpy 300-kilometre track that leads to the uranium mines around Wollaston Lake.

La Loche and Clearwater River Provincial Park

Apart from Hwy 2/102, the only other paved road running into the heart of northern Saskatchewan is Hwy 155, which extends as far as the tiny town of **LA LOCHE**, near the Alberta border. From here, a rough, gravel track, Route 955 (the Semchuk Trail), passes through **Clearwater River Provincial Park** before continuing on to the uranium mines of Cluff Lake. The park's main feature is the rugged **Clearwater River Valley**, whose turbulent waters are recommended only to the experienced white-water canoeist – you have to navigate 28 sets of rapids. There's a small and simple free **campsite** where the river meets the road, but otherwise the nearest accommodation is back in La Loche, 60km to the south. The town has one **motel**, the *Pines Motel* (☎306/822-2600; ❷), located beside the highway, and a parks department office (Mon–Fri 8am–5pm; ☎306/236-7672).

Lake Athabasca

The shallow soils of northern Saskatchewan are unable to support any form of agriculture, and its native peoples, the Woodland Cree, have traditionally survived by hunting, trapping and fishing. In recent times, this precarious and nomadic existence has been replaced by a more settled and restricted life on the reservations concentrated around **Lake Athabasca** in the extreme northwest corner of the province close to the 60th parallel. The area has become a

Wilderness canoeing in northern Saskatchewan

Northern Saskatchewan has an abundance of **canoe routes** sprinkled across its thousands of lakes. It's important, though, that prospective canoeists come fully prepared both in terms of equipment and knowledge of the proposed route. For independent and experienced wilderness travellers, Saskatchewan Environment (Ⓦ **www.se.gov.sk.ca**) issues a comprehensive range of free material that includes route descriptions, lists of outfitters, details of campsites and information on climate, wildlife and potential hazards. Some park offices also sell detailed local maps. The department has offices in a number of towns, but the best point of contact after its website is its **toll-free advice line** on Ⓣ1-800/567-4224 (or Ⓣ306/953-3750 if outside Saskatchewan). You can also get information on canoe routes from Horizons Unlimited/Churchill River Canoe Outfitters (Ⓣ1-877/511-2726, Ⓦwww.churchillrivercanoe.com) and on other canoe outfitters from the Saskatchewan Outfitters Association (Ⓣ306/763-5434, Ⓦwww.soa.ca). Saskatchewan has a host of **tour operators** running hunting, fishing and canoe excursions into the north of the province from the middle of May to September. A full list of hunting and fishing outfitters is provided in the *Saskatchewan Fishing and Hunting Guide*, while the *Saskatchewan Vacation Guide* lists operators offering canoeing, bird-watching and wildlife-viewing excursions throughout the province. Both books are available through Tourism Saskatchewan (see p.592) and at most tourist offices. For a complete range of topographic maps and canoe-route charts and booklets, plus secondary road maps, contact SaskGeomatics, 260-10 Research Drive, Regina (Ⓣ306/787-2799 or 1-866-420-6577, Ⓦwww.isc.ca).

particular favourite of the hook-and-bullet brigade – and, in recent years, ecotourists – but can only be reached only by private float plane. The most amazing landscapes in the area, not least because of their incongruity, are within the **Athabasca Sand Dunes Provincial Wilderness Park**, the world's most northerly sand dunes. Several companies organize excursions to the area that include flights, food, accommodation and boat rental; if you can afford $2000–3000 for a six-day trip, try Athabasca Camps in Saskatoon (Ⓣ1-800/922-0957, Ⓦwww.athabascalake.com).

Flin Flon

The mining township of **FLIN FLON** – 138km from The Pas on Manitoba's Hwy 10, or 409km from Prince Albert on Saskatchewan's Hwy 106 – gouges copper, gold, lead and zinc from a massive seam that was discovered in 1914. Straddling the Manitoba–Saskatchewan border, it's a stark, rough-looking town, full of precipitously steep streets, where the houses are built on sheer rock in a barren landscape. Flin Flon takes its unusual name from the hero of an obscure dime-novel entitled *The Sunless City*, which one of the first prospectors was reading at the time of the discovery. In the book, Josiah Flintabbatey Flonatin builds a submarine and enters the bowels of the earth, where he discovers that everything is made of gold. The nearest you'll come to his trip here is on the free guided tours of the town's **HudBay Minerals Inc** smelting plant (by appointment; ask at the tourist office). Surprisingly, you'll see greenhouses in the depths of the mine, where warm and humid conditions are perfect for growing flowers such as orchids. The mine was due to shut down in 2004, a move that would have meant the end of Flin Flon, but in the summer of 2000 some $400 million from mining companies (the biggest industrial investment in Manitoba) ensured the mine's, and the town's, future. There's not much else to see, except in July, when the town hosts the **Trout Festival**, with a parade, a Queen Mermaid Pageant, the

Great Northern Duck Race – and the tantalizing smell of frying fish.

Flin Flon's **bus station** is right in the centre at 63 3rd Ave. About 1km to the east, along Hwy 10A, the **tourist office** (May–Sept daily 8am–8pm; ⓣ204/687-7511, ⓦwww.cityofflinflon.com) runs the main **campsite** ($14–16; May–Sept) opposite a large statue of the intrepid Flintabbatey Flonatin. Otherwise try the central **hotel** *Royal*, 93 Main St (ⓣ204/687-3437 or 1-800/308-2224; ❶–❸), or, for dorm accommodation, the *Flin Flon Friendship Centre Hostel*, 57 Church St (ⓣ204/687-3900; ❶). For a basic **meal**, try *Mugsy's*, on Main St, or the *Victoria Inn*'s restaurant, 160 Hwy 10.

Grass River Provincial Park

A 40km drive southeast from Flin Flon along Hwy 10 brings you to **Grass River Provincial Park**: several thousand square kilometres of evergreen forest, lake and river interspersed by the granite outcrops of the Canadian Shield. Its channels and lakes were first charted in the 1770s by Samuel Hearne, an intrepid employee of the Hudson's Bay Company, and are still noted as excellent **canoe routes**. Hearne, who became the first European to reach the Arctic Ocean by land, witnessed both the development of the Grass River's fur trade and the cataclysmic effects of the smallpox epidemic that followed. He estimated that about ninety percent of the local Chipewyan population was wiped out in the space of a decade, an indication of the scale of a tragedy whose results were compounded by other European diseases, particularly whooping cough and measles. On this and other matters Hearne was an acute observer of Indian culture and customs. His *Journey to the Northern Ocean* records, for example, the comments of his Chipewyan guide concerning the importance of women:

> **" 'Women', added he, 'were made for labour; one of them can carry, or haul, as much as two men can do. They also pitch our tents, make and mend our clothing, keep us warm at night; and, in fact, there is no such thing as travelling any considerable distance in this country without their assistance.' "**

The most popular canoe route in the park runs 180km from the **Cranberry Lakes**, on the park's western perimeter, to its eastern boundary, where the southern tip of **Tramping Lake** is located near Hwy 39. It's an excursion of about ten days – all of the route's portages are short and fairly easy and there are lots of basic campsites on the way. The start of the canoe route, on the first of the three Cranberry Lakes, is situated close to **CRANBERRY PORTAGE**, a straggling township on Hwy 10, which runs along the western edge of the park. The settlement has its own park **information kiosk**; the small *Cranberry Portage Park* **campsite** (ⓣ204/472-3219; $18; mid-May to Sept), 1km west of Hwy 10 with its own beach; a couple of **hotels**, including the *Northern Inn*, 112 Portage Rd (ⓣ204/472-3231; ❶); and a handful of holiday **lodges** (mid-May to early Oct) along its lakeshore, such as the *Viking Lodge* (ⓣ204/472-3337; ❹). Most of the lodges have boat and canoe rentals, and can arrange guided trips and flights to the more remote lakes. There are other access points to Grass River Park along Hwy 39, which runs along its southern boundary. This road passes three small summer **campsites** (all $10) – *Gyles* (24km east of Hwy 10), *Iskwasum* (40km) and *Reed Lake* (56km) – where park entry points lead to circular canoe trips that can be accomplished within one day.

A worthwhile side-trip can be made from the park to **Wekusko Falls**, about 35km beyond the east boundary of the park along Hwy 39 and then south along a short stretch of gravel road (Hwy 596). Here the Mitishto River drops dramatically in a series of falls and rapids. You can view the spectacle from two suspension footbridges or along the walking trails below. A campground here has showers (May–Sept; $14)

The Pas

Situated 400km north of Dauphin on Hwy 10, on the southern bank of the Saskatchewan River, **THE PAS** – a former fur-trading and missionary centre founded in 1750 – is a town with no specific sights. However, it does host the annual **Northern Manitoba Trappers' Festival** in the third week of February, four days of revelling that include competitions in a number of traditional pioneer skills like tree-felling, trap-setting, ice-fishing and muskrat-skinning, with the highlight being the World Championship Sled Dog Races and its 50km mushes. If you're in town in mid-August, you can join in the aboriginal celebrations honouring the Cree people during **Opasquiak Indian Days**.

The town's **bus** and **train stations** are right in the centre, a few minutes' walk from the Municipal Offices, 324 Ross Ave (Mon–Fri 9am–1pm; ⓣ204/623-7256, ⓦwww.thepasarea.com), where you can get basic tourist information. There's also a summer **tourist booth** (June–Aug daily 9am–5pm) at the foot of Edwards Ave, beside the tiny Devon Park and *Kinsmen Kampground* (ⓣ204/627-1134; $12–19; mid-May to early Oct) and close to **accommodation** on Gordon Avenue: the *Rupert House Hotel* (ⓣ204/623-3201; ❶) and the three-star *Kikiwak Inn* (ⓣ204/623-1800 or 1-888/545-4925; ❹). Back in the centre, near the train station, the comfortable *Wescana Inn*, 439 Fischer Ave (ⓣ204/623-5446, ⓦwww.wescanainn.com; ❸), is also a good **place to eat**.

Clearwater Lake Provincial Park

Just 19km north of The Pas, the square-shaped lake and adjoining strip of coniferous forest that constitute **Clearwater Lake Park** are a favourite haunt of the region's anglers, who come here to catch northern pike, whitefish and highly prized lake trout. The park's amenities are concentrated along Route 287, a turning off Hwy 10, which runs along the lake's southern shore past The Pas airport. Beside the road there are two summer **campsites** (ⓣ204/482-2267 or 1-888/482-2267; mid-May to mid-Sept; $15), and the *New Vickery Lodge* (ⓣ204/624-5429 or 1-888/624-5429, ⓦwww.newvickerylodge.com; ❺; May–Oct) where you can arrange to go on a bear hunt. For a **wilderness excursion**, Clearwater Canoe Outfitters (ⓣ204/624-5606 or 624-5467) rents out a full range of equipment and organizes canoe trips from $25 a day.

Thompson

The sprawling nickel-mining town of **Thompson** at the end of Hwy-6 and 399km from The Pas is as far north as you can go on Manitoba's network of sealed hwys and a long haul from anywhere. Driving here you'll pass through hundreds of kilometres of boreal forest, with barely another vehicle in sight and part of the reason for this is that there's little reason to come here other than to catch the overnight train to Churchill; thereby cutting the cost and journey time of picking up the service in Winnipeg.

Thompson's highway-side **visitor information centre** (June–Sept 10am–5pm, Oct–May 1pm–5pm; ⓣ204/677-2216, ⓦwww.thompson.ca) is on the south-eastern edge of town – walking distance from the Greyhound **bus depot** – and can organise tours of local mines and suggest other ways in which to kill a few hours before your train leaves if you're not busy stocking up on groceries in the large downtown malls. The **railway station** is just southeast of the centre of town – take Station Road, just south of Wal-Mart – but its not recommended that you leave a car in this desolate spot due to vandalism problems. It's better to either park at City Hall, 226 Mystery Lake Rd (just off the main drag), for free and take a taxi with Thompson Cab (ⓣ204/677-6262) or park at the lakeside and pleasantly wooded *McReedy Campground* (ⓣ204/778-8810; tent and RV sites $15) at the northern fringes of town for $7 per day and use their courtesy shuttle service to and from the station. If you need a **room** for the night try the dreary-looking but reasonable and very central *Interior Inn* (180 Thompson Dr ⓣ204/778-5535 or 1-866/778-5535; ❺) where the ample rooms are clean and free wifi is provided.

Churchill

Sitting on the east bank of the Churchill River where it empties into Hudson Bay, **CHURCHILL** has the neglected appearance of many of the settlements of the far north, its unkempt open spaces dotted with the houses of its mixed Inuit, Cree and white population. These grim buildings are heavily fortified against the biting cold of winter and the insects of the summer: ample justification for a local T-shirt

Churchill's flora and fauna

Churchill occupies a transitional zone where the stunted trees of the taiga (subarctic coniferous forest) meet the mosses of the tundra. Blanketed with snow in the winter and covered by thousands of bogs and lakes in the summer, this terrain is completely flat until it reaches the sloping banks of the Churchill River and the ridge around Hudson Bay, whose grey-quartzite boulders have been rubbed smooth by the action of the ice, wind and water.

This environment harbours splendid **wildlife**, including Churchill's premier attraction, the **polar bears**, which start to come ashore when the ice melts on the bay in late June. They must then wait for the ice to form again to support their weight before they can start their seal hunt; a polar bear can detect scent from 32km away and can pick up the presence of seals under a metre of snow and ice. The best months to spot bears are September, October and early November, just before the ice re-forms completely.

In mid-June, as the ice breaks on the Churchill River, the spreading patch of open water attracts schools of white **beluga whales**. As many as three thousand of these intelligent, inquisitive and vocal mammals spend July and August around the mouth of the river, joining the **seals**, who arrive in late March for five months. The area around the town is also on one of the major migration routes for **birds** heading north from April to June and returning south in August or early September. Nesting and hatching take place from early June until early July. A couple of hundred species are involved, including gulls, terns, loons, Lapland longspurs, ducks and geese. The star visitor is the rare Ross's Gull, a native of Siberia, which has nested in Churchill for some years now. The *Birder's Guide to Churchill* ($7) by Bonnie Chartier lists them all and is available in the town and at the Eskimo Museum.

Churchill is also a great place to see the **aurora borealis** (Northern Lights), whose swirling curtains of blue, green and white are common in the skies between late August and April; occasionally it's seen all year round, and is at its best from January to March. Finally, in spring and autumn the tundra is a colourful sheet of moss, lichens, flowers and miniature shrubs and trees that include dwarf birch, spruce and cranberry.

△ Polar bear warning sign in Churchill

featuring a giant mosquito above the inscription "I gave blood in Churchill". That said, the town has long attracted a rough-edged assortment of people with a taste for the wilderness, and nowadays tourists flock here for the wildlife, particularly the polar bears – a lifeline, now that Churchill's grain-handling facilities are underused.

In 1682, the Hudson's Bay Company established a fur-trading post at **York Factory** (see p.641), a marshy peninsula some 240km southeast of today's Churchill. The move was dictated by the fact that the direct sea route here from England was roughly 1500km shorter than the old route via the St Lawrence River, while the Hayes and Nelson rivers gave access to the region's greatest waterways. Within a few years, a regular cycle of trade had been established, with the company's Cree and Assiniboine go-betweens heading south in the autumn to **hunt and trade** for skins, and returning in the spring laden with pelts they could exchange for the company's manufactured goods. Throughout the eighteenth century, before the English assumed control of all facets of the trade and laid off their native intermediaries, both sides seem to have benefited economically, and the reports of the company's traders are sprinkled with bursts of irritation at the bargains forced on them by the natives. The company was always keen to increase its trade, and it soon expanded its operations to Churchill, building the first of a series of forts here in 1717.

In the nineteenth century the development of faster trade routes through Minneapolis brought decline, and by the 1870s both York Factory and Churchill had become remote and unimportant. Then the development of agriculture on the prairies brought a reprieve. Many of the politicians and grain farmers of this new west were determined to break the trading monopoly of Sault Ste Marie in northern Ontario and campaigned for the construction of a new port facility on Hudson Bay, connected **by rail** to the south through Winnipeg. In the 1920s the Canadian National Railway agreed to build the line, and it finally reached Churchill in 1929. Unfortunately, despite all the efforts of the railway workers in the teeth of the ferocious climate, the port has never been very successful, largely because the bay is ice-free for only about three months a year.

The Town

The obvious place to start any exploration of town – not least if you've arrived by train – is the railway station which Parks Canada has refurbished into a swish visitor centre (Mon–Sat 10am–8.30pm; ⓣ204/675-8836, ⓦwww.pc.gc.ca). Displays on the history of the fur trade and the Hudson's Bay Company are jazzed up by films dealing with arctic wildlife, **Prince of Wales' Fort** and the construction of the railway. These are supplemented by free evening lectures on archaeological history and climate change. As Churchill's only formal information centre, this is also the place to pick up information on local tours (see box below).

Exiting the railway station you quickly arrive in the middle of **Kelsey Boulevard**, the town's main street. For a quick orientation simply walk straight on from here to the large and rather forlorn **Town Centre Complex** overlooking the Hudson Bay. The town's admin is based here as are its library (with free Internet connection) and various recreational facilities that include a curling rink, hockey rink, swimming pool, bowling alley and a cinema.

Just east down the road, the **Eskimo Museum**, 242 La Vérendrye Ave (June–Aug Mon 1–5pm, Tues–Sat 9am–noon & 1–5pm; Sept–May Mon & Sat 1–4.30pm; donation suggested), houses the Inuit collection of the Oblate Fathers of Mary Immaculate, whose missionary work began around here around 1900. The museum's one large room is dominated by animal-hide canoes and stuffed Arctic animals, with Inuit art arranged in cases round the walls. It's a fine range of material, from caribou-antler pictographs and highly stylized soapstone figurines through to walrus-tooth scrimshaws and detailed ivory and stone carvings. The sculptures fall into two distinct periods. Up until the 1940s, the artistic work of the local Inuit was essentially limited to the carving of figurines in walrus ivory, modelled on traditional designs. However, in 1949 a Canadian painter, James Houston, travelled the east coast of Hudson Bay in Québec, encouraging the Inuit to vary their designs and experiment with different materials – which led, in particular, to the development of larger and more naturalistic sculptures carved in soapstone. One corner of the

Churchill tour operators

Local wildlife **tour operators** have proliferated in Churchill over the past few years, offering everything from diving with the whales to viewing the polar bears from helicopters. They are all listed in the indispensable *Travel Manitoba* pamphlet which you can pick up at all major tourist information centres, and usually at the Churchill Parks Canada Visitor Centre as well.

The best place to get a feel for what's on offer at any time of year is at **North Star Tours** (ⓣ204/675-2356 or 1-800/665-0670) based in the Bayport Plaza on Munck Street. The outfit is run by jolly third-generation locals who organize an excellent mini-bus tour of local sites (3hrs; $75) – which includes a good look for polar bears – but they won't hesitate to suggest, and even call, other companies for you if you have particular activities in mind. One company they'll happily contact is whale-watching specialist **Sea North Tours**, 39 Franklin St (mid-June to late Aug; ⓣ204/675-2195 or 1-888/348-7591 ⓦwww.seanorthtours.com), who offer trips by either zodiac or kayak (no experience necessary) and who can listen in on the belugas using stereo hydrophones (tours 3hr; $85). They also organise snorkelling trips, when visibility in the bay is good enough.

In prime polar bear season it's worth hopping on a tour with **Tundra Buggy Tours** (July–Nov; ⓣ204/675-2121 or 1-800/663-9832, ⓦwww.tundrabuggy.com) who have a range of excursions in vehicles specially designed to avoid damaging the tundra (starting from $85 for a half-day tour) – some trips offer overnight lodge accommodation in the heart of the wilderness wildlife area. If you've arrived outside the main polar bear season consider splashing out on a flight with **Hudson Bay Helicopters** (ⓣ204/675-2576 or 1-867/873-5146, ⓦwww.hudsonbayheli.com), who can all but guarantee polar bear sights for $460 per hour.

museum functions as a **gift shop** selling a wide range of prints and carvings, plus a good collection of books on the north.

A couple of minutes' walk from the town centre, Churchill's grain elevators and silos stand at the base of a narrow peninsula that sticks out into the mouth of the Churchill River. At the tip, approached along a track, **Cape Merry National Historic Site** (check with Parks Canada for times of guided tours – see p.638) has the remains of an eighteenth-century gun emplacement and a cairn commemorating the Danish explorer Jens Munck, who led an expedition that was forced to winter here in 1619; most of the crew died from cold and hunger. The cape is about a half-hours' walk from town and a brilliant spot at high tide to watch belugas in the bay, but take local advice first as to whether the area is currently safe; polar bears often potter among the rocks here.

On the other side of the estuary, **Prince of Wales' Fort National Historic Site** (June to early Nov daily 1pm–5pm & 6pm–9pm; $7.90) is a partly restored eighteenth-century stone fortress that was built to protect the trading interests of the Hudson's Bay Company from the French. Finished in 1771, this massive structure took forty years to complete, but even then it proved far from impregnable. When a squadron of the French fleet appeared in the bay in 1782 the fort's governor, Samuel Hearne, was forced to surrender without firing a shot because he didn't have enough men to form a garrison. The French spiked the cannon and undermined the walls, and after this fiasco the Company never bothered to repair the damage. The fort is only accessible as part of a guided tour of the Churchill River organized by Sea North Tours (see box, p.639).

East of town, a road runs behind the shoreline past a series of rather eccentric attractions. Near the airport, the **polar bear "prison"** is a large hangar-like compound where dangerous bears are kept until they can be released safely. The problem is that some of the beasts wander into town in search of food and, although most can be scared off quite easily, a handful return. These more persistent specimens are shot with tranquillizers and transported to the compound. It's a necessary precaution, as polar bears can run and swim faster than humans and there are occasional horror stories, such as the owner of a fire-damaged house returning to empty his freezer, only to be trapped and killed by a bear. Repeat bear offenders are given three chances, after which they are humanely destroyed.

Practicalities

Churchill is well beyond the reach of Manitoba's hwys, but it is connected to Winnipeg, The Pas (see p.636) and Thompson (see p.636) **by train** along one of the longest railway lines in the world. VIA Rail (Ⓣ1-888/842-7245, Ⓦwww.viarail.ca) runs a service from Winnipeg (three weekly; takes 34hr). The train station and adjoining Parks Canada Centre **information centre** is right in the centre of town (see p.638). There are also regular **flights** from Winnipeg with Calm Air (Ⓣ204.675-8858 or 1-888/225-6247, Ⓦwww.calmair.com) and Kivalliq Air (Ⓣ204/675-2086 or 1-877/855-1500). Churchill's **airport** is 7km from the centre, and around a $13 cab ride from town with Churchill Taxi (Ⓣ204/675-2345).

There are no campsites or hostels in Churchill, so visitors are dependent on the town's **hotels**, which are so uniformly drab it's hard to see why they vary in price. All are within easy walking distance of the train station, and all should be booked in advance. The best of the bunch are the *Northern Nights Lodge*, 101 Kelsey Blvd (Ⓣ204/675-2403, Ⓦwww.northernlightslodge.com; ❻; June–Nov), with an adjacent restaurant, and the *Polar Inn*, 15 Franklin St (Ⓣ204/675-8878, Ⓦwww.polarinn.com; ❺), with mountain bikes for rent. The hotels can get

Canoeing the Seal River

The wild rivers that drain into Hudson Bay constitute some of the most challenging **canoe routes** in Canada, their long stretches of white water demanding considerable planning, experience and skill. One of the more popular is the **Seal River**, whose principal canoe route begins at the tiny Chipewyan village of Tadoule, and then passes through regions of boreal forest and tundra before emptying into Hudson Bay, just 45km west of Churchill. In the summer the estuary is a gathering place for several thousand beluga whales, an amazing sight to witness. There's float-plane transportation to the start of the canoe route and from the mouth of the river at the end, which can take between two and four weeks to reach. For details, contact Dymond Air Services, 23 Selkirk St, Churchill (Ⓣ204/675-8875). For something a bit shorter, you can stay at the *Churchill Wild Lodge* (Ⓣ204/778-3700 or 1-888/778-3730, Ⓦwww.churchillwild.com) on a three-day ($1450) or six-day package ($2300) including all meals, services of a guide, whale-watching expeditions, canoeing trips and wildlife tours.

booked up by tour groups so you may prefer to stay at the friendly **B&Bs** run by Vera Gould and her family: *Vera's* is at 87 Hearne St (Ⓣ204/675-2544; ❸); and her son Donald runs the *Polar Bear Bed & Breakfast,* 26 Hearne St (Ⓣ204/675-2819; ❸), lending out bikes to guests for free.

Churchill's handful of **restaurants** leave a lot to be desired, with the exception of the budget bistro and local's hangout *Gypsy's Bakery*, 253 Kelsey Blvd, where you can get basic burger-and-fries fare or splash out a bit and sample delicious cuts of local caribou, or try the popular local fish, arctic char, for around $18. All the hotels also have their own restaurants.

York Factory

The remote **York Factory National Historic Site** (June to mid-Sept daily 8am–5pm, depending on river conditions) lies 240km southeast of Churchill, at the mouth of the Hayes and Nelson rivers. This was the central storehouse of the northwestern fur trade throughout the eighteenth century, its wooden palisades the temporary home of soldiers and explorers, travellers and traders, and settlers bound for the Red River Colony at present-day Winnipeg. With the amalgamation of the North West and Hudson's Bay companies in 1821, it was here that the new governor **George Simpson** set about the delicate task of reconciling the feuds stirred by a generation of inter-company rivalry. In October he arranged his first formal joint banquet, 73 traders facing each other across two long and narrow tables. It was, according to a contemporary, "dollars to doughnuts [whether it would be] a feed or fight", but Simpson's diplomatic skills triumphed, leading to a successful reorganization of trading operations. In its heyday, there were some fifty buildings within the stockade, including a guesthouse, fur stores, trading rooms, living quarters and shops, but they were all destroyed in the 1930s, with the exception of the **main warehouse** (1832), a sturdy wooden building that serves as a reminder of the fort's earlier significance. Wandering around the desolate site today, it's hard to imagine that it was once the largest community in western Canada. Guided tours of the site are available (June to mid-Sept daily 8am–5pm; contact the Parks Canada Visitor Reception Centre in Churchill Ⓣ204/675-8863; $7.90).

This remote spot can only be reached by **charter flight** – weather permitting – from Thompson, Churchill or Gillam, a hydroelectric centre on the rail line between Winnipeg and Churchill. Or you can get there by **canoe** along the Hayes River from Norway House on the north shore of Lake Winnipeg – an arduous journey of 600km, which should not be undertaken without advice from the Manitoba Parks Department in Winnipeg (Ⓣ204/945-3744 or 1-866/626-4862, Ⓦwww.manitobaparks.com). Because of the disturbance to polar bears in the area, camping is not allowed at York Factory. The only **place to stay** is the *Silver Goose Lodge*, and this must be arranged in advance with the owners (Ⓣ204/652-2776; ❹). There are no services, and all supplies must be brought in.

Travel details

Trains

Winnipeg to: Churchill (3 weekly; 36hr); Edmonton (2 weekly; 16hr); Jasper (3 weekly; 21hr 15min); Saskatoon (3 weekly; 9hr); Sioux Lookout (3 weekly; 6hr 20min); The Pas (3 weekly; 12hr); Toronto (3 weekly; 30hr); Vancouver (3 weekly; 40hr).

Buses

Regina to: Calgary (6 daily; 11hr); Coronach (4 per week; 4hr); Medicine Hat (4 daily; 6hr 30min); Moose Jaw (4 daily; 1hr); Prince Albert (3–5 daily; 6hr); Saskatoon (3 daily; 3hr); Swift Current (3 daily; 3hr 30min); Yorkton (2 daily; 2hr 35min).
Saskatoon to: Calgary (4 daily; 11hr); Edmonton (4 daily; 7hr); La Ronge (1 daily; 6hr); Lloydminster (3 daily; 3hr 15min); North Battleford (4 daily; 1hr 30min); Prince Albert (1 daily; 1hr 50min); Swift Current (3 daily; 3hr 30min); The Pas (1 daily 11hrs); Waskesiu (mid-May to mid-Sept 1 daily; 3hr); Yorkton (2 daily; 3hr 30min).
Swift Current to: Eastend (2 week; 2hr).
Winnipeg to: Flin Flon (1 daily; 12hrs); Gimli (1 daily; 1hr 30min); Grand Beach Provincial Park (1 daily; 1hr 15min); Kenora (3 daily; 2hr 30min); Lac du Bonnet (1 daily; 2hr); Neepawa (2 daily; 2hr 30min); Portage La Prairie (6 daily; 1hr 10min); Regina (4 daily; 8hr); Riding Mountain (3 daily; 3hr); Saskatoon (2 daily; 12hr); Sault Ste Marie (3 daily; 19hr); Sudbury (3 daily; 25hr); Thompson (2 daily; 9hr); Thunder Bay (3 daily; 10hr 35min); Toronto (3 daily; 31hr); West Hawk Lake (2 daily; 2 hr).

Flights

Regina to: Calgary (9 daily; 1hr 25min); Saskatoon (4 daily; 50min); Toronto (6 daily; 3hr); Vancouver (5 daily; 3hr 30min).
Saskatoon to: Calgary (3 daily; 1hr); Regina (8 daily; 40min); Toronto (5 daily; 4hr); Vancouver (4 daily; 2hr 10min).
Winnipeg to: Calgary (8 daily; 2hr 10min); Churchill (1–4 daily; 3hr); Regina (4 daily; 1hr 10min); Saskatoon (4 daily; 1hr 20min); The Pas (Mon–Fri 2 daily; 1hr 15min); Toronto (8 daily; 2hr 20min); Vancouver (3 daily; 4hr).

8

Alberta and the Rockies

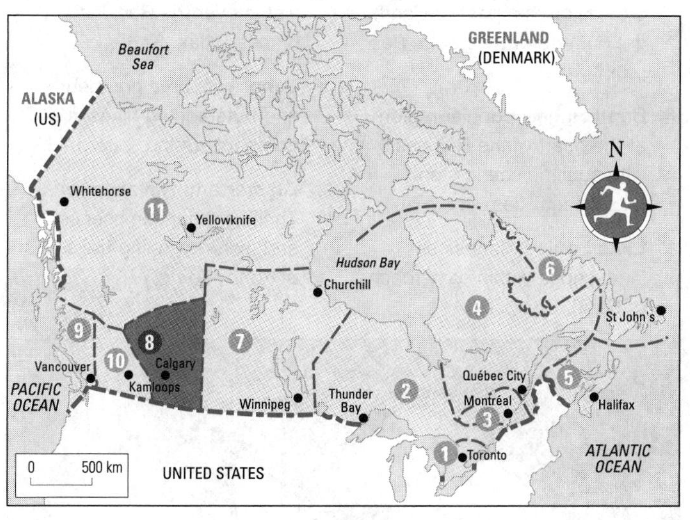

CHAPTER 8

Highlights

- **Calgary** Let your inner cowboy or cowgirl out at the annual Stampede in this likeable plains city. See p.662
- **Waterton Lakes** Superb hiking and stunning scenery at this small park on the US border. See p.686
- **Kananaskis Country** As the crowds stream past to Banff, get out and draw breath. See p.695
- **Banff** Hugely popular region at the heart of the Rockies, with sublime scenery and tons of activities. See p.701
- **Lake Louise** Magnificent landscapes within easy reach of Banff. See p.724
- **Rafting** Get up close and personal with the mountains, out on the water. See p.740
- **Jasper** Head north on the legendary Icefields Parkway for some memorable backcountry walks. See p.742
- **Mount Robson** Explore west of Jasper for breathtaking vistas over the Rockies' highest peak. See p.756
- **Yoho** Awesome grandeur and outstanding hikes in a compact setting. See p.759
- **Glacier and Revelstoke** Thrilling mountain scenery and award-winning trails west of Yoho. See p.770

△ Downtown Banff

8

Alberta and the Rockies

The vast majority of Alberta is given over to endless prairies, where isolated farms act as sentinels for thousands of acres of swaying wheat or giant herds of cattle, or where endless pine forests carpet the oil and gas-rich wilderness in the north of the province. But the focus of most visitors is, quite rightly, the Canadian Rockies, which stud the province's eastern border with British Columbia. This is where you'll find archetypal Canada: lands where craggy peaks tower over iridescent turquoise lakes and conifer valleys where bears scavenge for berries and elk quietly graze.

Such is their scenic quality that almost the whole region is protected one way or another as parks or wilderness areas. The dual wonders of **Banff** and **Jasper National Parks** are the best known among them, though the series of parks on the BC side of the border are equally magnificent, in part because they're more lightly visited. But together these protected areas form a nirvana for outdoor enthusiasts of all stripes – particularly those who like to hike, bike, paddle, ski or snowboard.

The bustling oil-towns of **Edmonton** and **Calgary** form the main gateways to the entire Rockies region, by acting as transport hubs for northern and southern Alberta respectively. Though similar in feel and appearance the two are intense rivals; as apparent as anywhere in the fierce competition between their ice hockey teams.

Edmonton tends to be the bleaker of the two; its weather is harsher and it lies on the edge of an immense expanse of low hills and boreal forest that stretches to the border of the Northwest Territories and beyond. Yet the current oil boom in these areas has made Edmonton's economy one of Canada's most dynamic, attracting droves of young workers. But to travellers the city's main importance is as a gateway to **Jasper National Park** and **Mount Robson Provincial Park** – via the **Yellowhead Highway** – and Canada's remote Northwest: via the far flung communities that dot Alberta's **Mackenzie Highway** or British Columbia's **Alaska Highway** to the remote Arctic extremities of the North West Territories and Yukon. Whether you're starting a long drive into these areas, or simply changing planes, you'll likely as not pass through Edmonton.

Far more on the track beaten by most visitors is **Calgary**, just ninety minutes west of **Banff National Park** along the **Trans-Canada Highway** – which

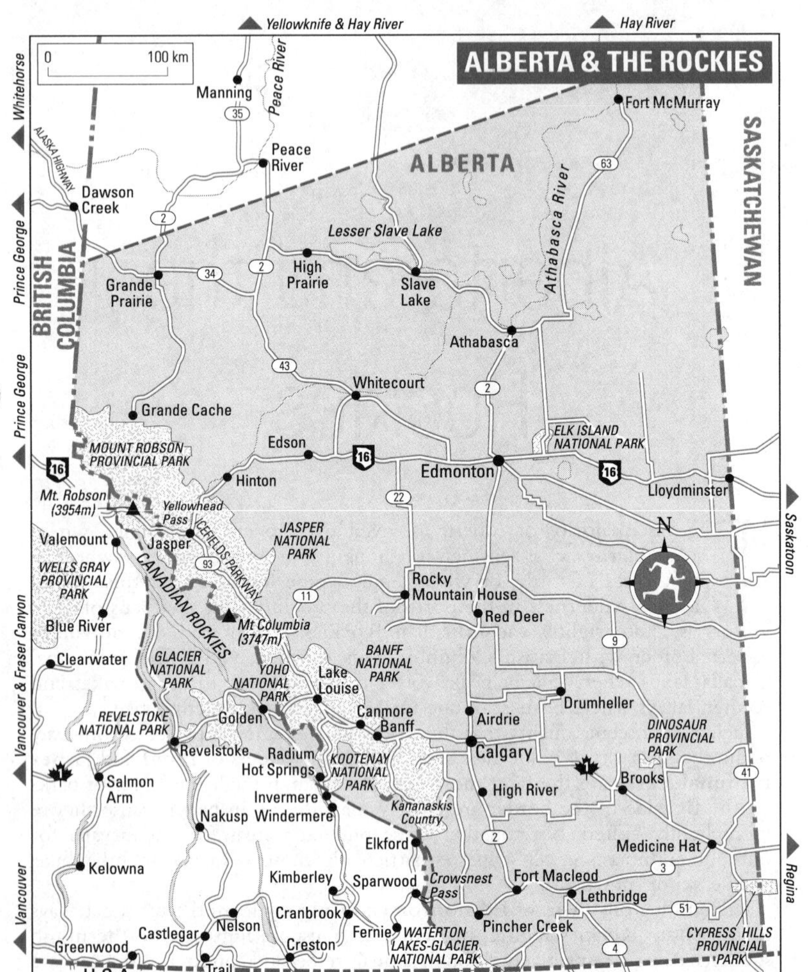

goes on towards **Yoho, Kootenay, Glacier** or **Revelstoke National Parks** – and three hours from **Waterton National Park** on the southern edge of the province. To the east of Calgary a ranching belt gives way to arid Badlands – where dinosaurs once roamed and have left abundant traces. The city is also famous for the **Calgary Stampede**, a July rodeo festival that's one of the country's rowdiest shindigs – a reminder that above all Alberta is cowboy country; where devotion to Alberta beef takes on religious proportions and rodeos form the high points of social calendars.

Edmonton and around

Apart from making the pilgrimage to its world-class Folk Music Festival in August, there's really scant reason to visit **Edmonton**. Even so, the city may well end up on your itinerary if you're bound for Jasper National Park, or heading to the unimaginable vastness of Northern Canada (covered in Chapter 11 – see p.991). It's the main gateway for both, so if you do find yourself overnighting in Edmonton, you'll find a proud and bustling city choc full of shopping (not least at the massive West Edmonton Mall), a couple of reasonable attractions, particularly the **TELUS World of Science,** and a restaurant, bar and nightlife scene that's booming thanks to a huge recent injection of oil money – and young workers – into the city.

The rippling hills of dreary prairie country that surround Edmonton are dotted by parochial but very welcoming little towns, though none call out for a special trip. The only place worth making a beeline for is the **Elk Island National Park,** a half-hour's drive east of the city. Otherwise, most travelers will want to just head west: either along Canada's last transcontinental **railway** link or the **Yellowhead Highway** to Jasper National Park. Far fewer people head north and, unless you're fishing or boating, simply into sheer untrammelled wilderness, or on your way to Yellowknife (p.1064) or the Alaska Hwy (see p.1018), little here is worth detouring for – with the possible exception of the giant Wood Buffalo National Park (see p.1062) that straddles the border with the Northwest Territories.

Edmonton

Alberta's provincial capital, **EDMONTON** is among Canada's most northerly cities, and at times – particularly in the teeth of its bitter winters – it can seem a little too far north for comfort. Situated above the waters of the North Saskatchewan River, whose park-filled valley winds below the high-rises of downtown, the city tries hard with its festivals, parks, restaurants and urban-renewal projects. Yet, given the somewhat unfinished feel of its downtown, it's perhaps appropriate that the premier attraction for the vast majority of visitors is a shopping centre, the infamous **West Edmonton Mall.** This certainly has curiosity value, but not enough to merit a special journey here. Downtown has a handful of modest sights, though most enjoyment in the city is to be had in **Old Strathcona**, a rejuvenated "historic" district south of the North Saskatchewan River filled with heritage buildings, modest museums and plenty of eating and drinking venues. Edmonton lacks the big set-piece

Edmonton addresses

Addresses in Edmonton can look complicated. Avenues run east–west, with numbers increasing as you travel further north, while streets run north–south, the numbers increasing as you move westwards. This is easy enough, but note that building numbers tend to be tacked onto the end of street numbers: for instance, 10021-104th Ave is building number 21 on 100th St, at the intersection with 104th Ave.

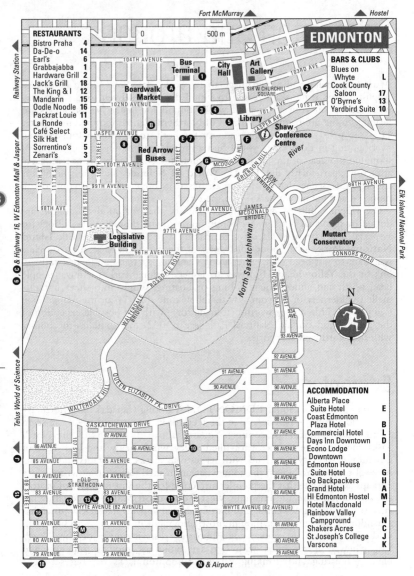

museums of Calgary or Vancouver, but its **TELUS World of Science** is a sight within a whisker of the first rank.

Some history

Aboriginal peoples were attracted to the site where Edmonton lies today for thousands of years before the arrival of white settlers, thanks to the abundance of local **quartzite**, used to make sharp-edged stone weapons and tools. **Fur traders** arrived in the eighteenth century, attracted by river and forest habitats that provided some of Canada's richest fur-producing territory. Better still, the area lay at the meeting point of the territory patrolled by the Blackfoot to the south and the Cree, Dene and Assiniboine to the north. Normally these aboriginal peoples would have been implacable enemies, but around Edmonton's future site they were able to coexist when trading with intermediaries like the North West Company, which built Fort Augustus on Edmonton's present location in 1795. The fort was joined later the same year by **Fort Edmonton**, a redoubtable log stockade built by William Tomison for the Hudson's Bay Company (and named in fine sycophantic fashion after an estate owned by Sir James Winter Lake, the Hudson's Bay Company's deputy governor).

Though the area soon became a major trading district, **settlers** arrived in force only after 1870, when the HBC sold its governing right to the Dominion of Canada. The decline of the fur trade around 1880 made little impact, as the settlement continued to operate as a staging point for travellers heading north. Worldwide demand for grain also attracted settlers to the region, now able to produce crops despite the poor climate thanks to advances in agricultural technology. Crucially, though, the first trans-Canada railway was pushed through Calgary at Edmonton's expense, and when a spur was built by the Edmonton Railway Company in 1891 it finished south of the town at Strathcona, where a new settlement developed. The city only became firmly established with the Yukon gold rush of 1897, and only then through a scam of tragic duplicity. Prompted by the city's outfitters, newspapers lured prospectors with the promise of an "All Canadian Route" to the gold fields that avoided Alaska and the dreaded Chilkoot Trail (see p.1024). In the event, this turned out to be a largely phantom trail across 3000km of intense wilderness. Hundreds of men perished as they pushed north; many of those who survived, or who never set off, ended up settling in Edmonton. World War II saw the city's role reinforced by its strategic position relative to Alaska, while its postwar growth was guaranteed by the **Leduc oil strike** in 1947. By 1956 some three thousand wells were in production within 100km of the city. If Edmonton has achieved any fame since, it has been in the field of **sports**, as the home of Wayne Gretzky, the greatest player in ice-hockey history. Oil money continues to bankroll all sorts of civic improvements, though never quite manages to disguise the city's rather rough-and-ready pioneer roots.

Arrival, information and transport

Edmonton is one of the easiest places to reach in western Canada. Its road and rail links are excellent, and the international **airport** (Ⓦwww.edmontonairports.com), 29km south of downtown off Hwy 2 (Calgary Trail), is served by many airlines. There's a small **visitor information desk** (Mon–Fri 8.30am–10.30pm, Sat & Sun 9am–10.30pm; Ⓣ780/890-8382 or 1-800/268-7134) in the arrivals area; **foreign exchange** facilities (daily 10am–12.30am) are upstairs in departures. A shuttle **bus**, the Sky Shuttle (daily every 30mins 6am–midnight; $15 one-way; Ⓣ780/465-8515 or 1-888/438-2342), runs to downtown hotels, the university district and the western part of the city on three different routes; the bus leaves from outside arrivals, and you can buy tickets from the driver. A taxi costs around $45. The Jasper Express service links Edmonton airport directly with Jasper (daily at 4.30pm; $55 one way; Ⓣ403-762-9102 or 1-800-661-4946).

The VIA Rail **station** is some 3km northwest of downtown at 12360-121st St (Ⓣ1-888/842-7245, Ⓦwww.viarail.ca). The Greyhound **bus terminal** (Ⓣ780-420-2400, Ⓦwww.greyhound.ca) is also central at 10324-103rd St,

Edmonton festivals

There's almost always something good on in Edmonton, the self-proclaimed "Festival City" even has a website solely dedicated to goings-on: Ⓦwww.festivalcity.ca. However, the finest event is easily the **Edmonton Folk Music Festival** (Ⓣ780/429-1899, Ⓦwww.edmontonfolkfest.org) held at Gallagher Park (near the Muttart Conservatory) in early August. Also well regarded are the **International Street Performers Festival** (Ⓣ780/425-5162, Ⓦwww.edmontonstreetfest.com), which attracts over 1000 street performers in early July; the **International Jazz City Festival** (Ⓣ780/432-7166) at the end of June; and the increasingly popular August **Fringe Festival**, or Fringe Theatre Event (Ⓣ780/448-9000, Ⓦwww.fringetheatreadventures.ca), a ten-day theatrical jamboree that's turned into one of the largest festivals of its kind in North America. The more contrived and commercial **Capital Ex** (Ⓣ780/471-7210 or 1-888/800-7275) is a less compelling blowout that has been cobbled together to steal some of Calgary's Stampede thunder. Held for ten days during July, this popular outing revolves around a re-creation of the 1890s gold-rush era, with plenty for kids, and a panoply of events: one of the best is "A Taste of Edmonton", where 40-odd local restaurants set up stalls and let you taste tidbits from their menus.

within easy walking distance of central downtown. **Red Arrow** buses serving Calgary (four daily; Ⓣ780/425-0820 or 1-800/232-1958, Ⓦwww.redarrow.ca) use their terminal at the *Holiday Inn Express Plaza* hotel at 10014-104th St.

Tourist information centres can be found at the airport in arrivals and dotted around the city, including one in Gateway Park south of downtown on Hwy 2. But the most central is the **Downtown Visitor Information Centre** at 9990 Jasper Ave (Mon–Fri 6am–9pm, Sat & Sun 9am–5pm; Ⓣ780/496-8400 or 1-800/463-4667, Ⓦwww.edmonton.com).

The downtown area is easily negotiated **on foot**. Longer journeys can be made using Edmonton Transit (route and timetable **information** Ⓣ780/496-1611), an integrated **bus and light-rail** (LRT) system. Interchangeable tickets for bus and LRT cost $2.25; day-passes cost $6.75. You can buy tickets on buses or from machines in the ten LRT stations. Transfers are available from drivers on boarding for use on other services for ninety minutes.

Accommodation

Due to its importance among business travellers Edmonton has no shortage of **hotels**, but there's quite a bit of reasonable budget accommodation too. **Motels** dot the arterial roads on unlovely outskirts of the city, the main concentrations being along Stony Plain Road (northwest of downtown) and on the Calgary Trail (south).

For details of **B&B** lodgings – which virtually all reside well outside the centre – contact the visitor centre or browse the listings of the Alberta Central Bed & Breakfast Association (Ⓦwww.bbcanada.com). Note that since hotel beds in the city are generally inexpensive, you won't necessarily make much of a saving by opting for a B&B.

Hotels and motels

Alberta Place Suite Hotel 10049-103rd St Ⓣ780/423-1565 or 1-800/661-3982, Ⓦwww.albertaplace.com. Large, well-equipped suites with kitchens and extra facilities; weekly rates available. ④

Coast Edmonton Plaza Hotel 10155-105th St Ⓣ780/423-4811 or 1-800/663-1144, Ⓦwww.coasthotels.com. Uninspired 299-room downtown hotel, handy for the LRT and with all the usual features of a smart big hotel, including reasonable spa, pool and fitness facilities; room service and high-speed Internet Rooms are spotless if a bit dingy, but are often substantially discounted online. ❻

Commercial Hotel 10329-82nd Ave ⓣ780/439-3981. A friendly no-frills, but clean, place above a blues bar in the happening Old Strathcona neighbourhood. Some rooms share a bathroom, but those that don't are only $10 more. ❷

Days Inn Downtown 10041-106th St ⓣ780/423-1925 or 1-800/267-2191, ⓦwww.daysinn.com. Mid-sized and renovated central motel with parking just off Jasper Ave. ❹

Econo Lodge Downtown 10209-100th Ave ⓣ780/428-6442 or 1-800/613-7043. Reliable downtown motel with covered parking, TV, phone and usual facilities. ❹

Edmonton House Suite Hotel 10205-100th Ave ⓣ780/420-4000 or 1-888/962-2522, ⓦwww.edmontonhouse.com. Bigger (300 suites) and more expensive than the *Alberta Place*, but rooms have balconies and views – some with high-speed Internet. There's also an indoor pool and a free shuttle to the West Edmonton Mall. ❺

Grand Hotel 10266-103rd St ⓣ780/422-6365 or 1-888/422-6365. Handily located near the bus terminal, this hotel is anything but grand: its 65 rooms, only some with private bath, are used mainly by long-stay residents. ❷

Hotel Macdonald 10065-100th St ⓣ780/424-5181 or 1-800/441-1414, ⓦwww.fairmont.com. One of the big historic "railway" hotels run by Canadian Pacific, and undoubtedly the first choice if you want to stay in Edmonton in traditional style. Some rooms are a little small for the price, but there are lots of facilities including pool and health club. ❼

Varsonca 8208-106th St ⓣ780/434-6111 or 1-888/515-3355, ⓦwww.varscona.com. Plush Old Strathcona boutique hotel, with every thinkable business amenity and many luxuries which include a fitness centre and nightly wine and cheese tastings, served by the ever-attentive staff. ❺

Hostels

Go Backpackers 10815 Jasper Ave ⓣ780-423-4146, ⓦwww.gohostels.ca. Cheerful new downtown hostel with dorm beds ($22) and private rooms ($70), some with kitchenettes ($85) and all with private washrooms. Also has sociable communal areas and decent kitchen facilities.

HI-Edmonton Hostel 10647-81st Ave ⓣ780/988-6836 or 1-877/467-8336, ⓦwww.hihostels.ca. This 104-bed Hostelling International hostel in a former convent in the Old Strathcona district is not so convenient for downtown, though the airport shuttle will drop you close by if you ask. Plenty of smart facilities, including laundry, library, bike rental and roomy kitchen. Check-in after 11am; open 24hr with no curfew. Dorm beds $22, plus some private rooms ($40).

St Joseph's College 11325-89th Ave ⓣ780/492-7681. Small, cheap and popular student rooms ($20 per night); reservations required in summer. Out of the centre but well served by buses, and only a ten-minute walk from the Old Strathcona district.

Campsites

Rainbow Valley Campground 13204-45th Ave NW ⓣ780/434-5531. The only site within the city limits: 85 sites off the Whitemud Freeway at 119th St and 45th Ave, in Whitemud Park. It's full by afternoon in summer, so arrive early or be sure to book in advance. Mid-April to early Oct. Sites $20–26.

The City

Edmonton feels oddly dispersed, even in the six-block **downtown** area around Sir Winston Churchill Square and along the main east–west drag, **Jasper Avenue** (101st Avenue). Bounded to the south by the North Saskatchewan River, this grid holds a few assorted points of interest, though most of the younger and more cosmopolitan Edmonton resides south of the river in **Old Strathcona**. For the **West Edmonton Mall**, TELUS World of Science, and the **Provincial Museum**, you'll need to take transport west from downtown. To stretch your legs, wander up and down the big string of attractive parks that protects the river, or cross the Low Level Bridge to the **Muttart Conservatory**, another worthwhile sight consisting of four space-age glass pyramids filled with flora and natural-history displays.

Downtown

Downtown Edmonton only really comes alive as a place to wander on sunny days when office workers pour out for lunch; otherwise it's really not much of a place to linger unless you're in town for one of the city's many festivals. However, with time to kill the following low-key sites could keep you occupied. The **Art Gallery of Alberta** (Mon–Wed & Fri 10.30am–5pm, Thurs 10.30am–8pm, Sat, Sun & holidays 11am–5pm; $7, free after 4pm; ⓣ780/422-6223, ⓦwww.artgalleryalberta.com), part of the Civic Centre on 99th St and 102nd Ave on the north edge of Sir Winston Churchill Square, deals mainly in modern Canadian artists, though it also hosts many visiting exhibitions. More satisfyingly offbeat is the **Edmonton Police Museum and Archives** on the third floor of the central police station at 9620-103A Ave (Mon–Sat 9am–3pm, closed public holidays; free; ⓣ780/421-2274), which traces the long arm of Albertan law enforcement from the formation of what would become the RCMP (Royal Canadian Mounted Police) in 1873 to the city's current flatfoots. Marvel at handcuffs, old jail cells and a stuffed rat that served time as an RCMP mascot.

Walk across the Low Level Bridge to the distinctive glass pyramids of the **Muttart Conservatory**, 9626-96A St (Mon–Fri 9am–5.30pm, Sat & Sun 11am–5.30pm; $8.75; ⓣ780/496-8735), just south of downtown and the river. Three high-tech greenhouses reproduce tropical, temperate and arid climates, complete with the trees and plants (and occasional exotic birds) which flourish in them; a fourth houses a potpourri of experimental botanical projects and temporary exhibitions. If you don't want to walk, take **bus** #51 (Capilano) travelling south on 100th Street just south of Jasper Ave as far as 98th Avenue and 97A Street, then walk one block south. Finally, you might stop by for a free guided tour of the domed sandstone **Alberta Legislature Building** (May to mid-Oct Mon–Fri 9am–5pm, Sat & Sun 9am–5pm; mid-Oct to April Mon–Fri 9am–4.30pm, Sat & Sun noon–5pm; free; ⓣ780/427-7362, ⓦwww.assembly.ab.ca) south of Jasper Avenue on 97th Avenue and 107th Street (the nearest LRT station is Grandin). Set in the manner of a medieval cathedral over an ancient shrine, it was built in 1912 on the original site of Fort Edmonton. Topped by a vaulted dome, it's a big city landmark, its interior reflecting the grandiose self-importance of the province's early rulers, who imported wood for their headquarters from as far afield as Belize: the marble came from Québec, Pennsylvania and Italy, the granite from rival British Columbia. Just to the north, amidst parkland that flanks the building, stands the **Alberta Legislative Assembly Interpretive Centre**, where you can learn more than you probably want to know about Alberta's political history and the building in which much of it took place (same hours and contact).

Old Strathcona

The **Strathcona** district south of the North Saskatchewan River grew up at the end of the nineteenth century, thanks to a decision by the Calgary and Edmonton Railway Company (C&E) to avoid the expense of a bridge across the North Saskatchewan River by concluding a rail spur from Calgary south of the river and Edmonton proper. In 1912, when its population had reached about 7500, the new town was incorporated into the city. Today the streets and many of the older buildings have been spruced up in a manner typical of urban-renewal projects – lots of new pavements and fake period street furniture. This said, it's still the city's best-preserved old quarter, and the nicest to wander around on a sunny day and – as the city's most vibrant district of café culture, nightlife and alternative arts – the best evening hangout too. Plenty of buses run here from downtown, or you can walk across the river via the Walterdale or High Level bridges. The best approach is to take the LRT to University station and board buses #8, #43 or #46 to 104th Street and 82nd Avenue.

The area centres on **Whyte Avenue** (82nd Avenue) between 109th Street and 103rd, making the **Old Strathcona Foundation** office, 10324 Whyte Ave (summer Mon–Fri 8.30am–4.30pm; rest of year Tues & Wed 8.30am–4.30pm ⓣ780/439-9166, ⓦwww.strathcona.org), a sensible first port of call. Here you can pick up pamphlets detailing walks that take in the area's historic buildings. Just to the north, on 83rd Avenue, is the **Old Strathcona Farmers' Market** (July & Aug, Tues noon–5pm, Sat 8am–3pm; free), a happy hunting ground for picnic supplies and craft goods. If you tire of wandering or sitting in cafés, you can give a little structure to your exploration by heading for one or both of the area's two small museums. Rail buffs should check out the **C&E Railway Station Museum**, 10447-86th Ave (June to Aug Tues–Sat 10am–4pm; winter by appointment; $2 donation suggested; ⓣ780/433-9739), a collection of railway memorabilia, costumes and photos housed in a replica of Strathcona's original 1891 station.

Royal Alberta Museum

Housed in a drab building well out in the western suburbs – a ten-minute drive from downtown – at 12845-102nd Ave, the **Royal Alberta Museum** (daily 9am–5pm; $10; ⓣ780/453-9100, ⓦwww.royalalbertamuseum.ca) makes a reasonable introduction to the history, culture, flora and fauna of western Canada, worthwhile if Edmonton is your first stop in the region. To reach it by **bus**, take the #1 or #120 buses heading west to "Jasper Place" on Jasper Avenue. **Natural history** exhibits include painted dioramas and stuffed animals; by far the best section concerns the virtual extinction of region's bison herds. Other displays include a humdrum collection of domestic appliances, a couple of beautiful chrome stoves and vintage jukeboxes and a rundown of the **native peoples** of the province. This last collection includes a series of state-of-the-art multimedia displays that do justice to the history and culture of the Blackfoot and other aboriginal cultures with displays of art, artefacts and other exhibits. Other engaging parts of the museum are the Bug, a showcase of live and often exotic insects, and "Earth's Changing Face", a geological display of gems, minerals, rocks and dinosaur exhibits. The museum also comes into its own when hosting temporary and travelling exhibitions from collections and museums around the world – ask at the visitor centre for current details.

Fort Edmonton Park and the Space Centre

Located southwest of the city on a deep-cut bend of the North Saskatchewan River at the southwest end of Quesnell Bridge and Fox Drive, the 158-acre **Fort Edmonton Park** (daily late May to late June Mon–Fri 10am–4pm, Sat & Sun 10am–6pm; late June to early Sept daily 10am–6pm; rest of Sept Mon–Sat 11am–3pm, Sun 11am–6pm; $13; ⓣ780/496-8787, ⓦwww.edmonton.ca/fort) recreates the history of white settlement in Edmonton during the nineteenth century. Everything has been built from scratch and, while you can't fault the attention to detail, the pristine woodwork of the supposedly old buildings hardly evokes period authenticity (though the carpentry methods are apparently those used around 1846). To get here take the LRT to University station and there pick up buses #4 or #106 to Fox Drive, about ten-minutes' walk from the site, which is off the Whitemud Freeway near the Quesnell Bridge. The heart of the complex is a facsimile of **Fort Edmonton**, a fur-trading post dominated by the Big House, former home of the Chief Factor, John Rowland, head of the (then) ill-defined Saskatchewan District between 1828 and 1854. Arranged around the house are the quarters of the 130 or so people who called the fort home and who are now represented by appropriately dressed guides pretending to be blacksmiths, shopkeepers and schoolteachers from the era. Edmonton's later, pre-railway age is represented by a rendition of Jasper Avenue as it appeared in 1885, while two other streets simulate 1905 and 1920, complete with working steam engines and trams, which you can ride at no additional cost, to bolster the period effect.

The splendid **TELUS World of Science**, 11211-142nd St (July & Aug daily 10am–9pm, Sept–June Sun–Thurs 10am–5pm, Fri & Sat 10am–9pm; $10, Combo Pack $16 includes Zeidler Star Theatre Shows, exhibits and scientific demonstrations or one IMAX film presentation; Ⓦwww.odyssium.com), in Coronation Park, is one of the city's principal attractions. The complex has two main attractions: the **Margaret Zeidler Star Theatre** (daily 11am–7pm) houses Canada's largest planetarium dome and several galleries, and presents different laser and star shows hourly; and the **IMAX Theatre**, housed with a café and shop in the so-called Lower Gallery, is a large-screen cinema with special-format films and laser shows (prices and times vary according to shows). Elsewhere, the Middle Gallery features a range of temporary exhibitions on scientific and technological themes, while the Upper Gallery contains the **Challenger Centre** and its "Astronaut Missions", designed to allow you to make simulated space missions. There are also assorted displays on advanced communications technology, and a selection of the various science demonstrations you can expect to see around the centre throughout the day. Computers are dealt with in the Dow Computer Lab, while budding astronomers can check in to the centre's **Observatory** (weather allowing). To get here on public transport take a #5 (Westmount) bus travelling west on 102nd Avenue and then north on 124th Street – ask the driver to tell you when you're close.

West Edmonton Mall

"Your Adventure Awaits" announces the brochure to **West Edmonton Mall** (Ⓦwww.westedmall.com), preparing you for a place that has had eleven mentions in the *Guinness Book of World Records*, including its main claim to fame as the largest shopping mall in the world. Built at a total cost of $1.2 billion, the complex extends over the equivalent of 115 American football fields (or 48 city blocks) and boasts more than 800 shops – of which some 110 are restaurants – plus twenty-one cinemas, and eleven department stores. There's almost a queue of superlatives. Its car park is the world's largest, with room for 20,000 cars; it has the world's largest water park (fifty million litres of water); it uses enough power to run a town of 50,000 people. The mall's effect on Edmonton has been double-edged: it employs 15,000 people but has captured thirty percent of the city's retail business, thus crippling the downtown shopping area, though it has also succeeded, to everyone's surprise, in attracting twenty million visitors a year (that's 55,000 a day).

Funnily enough, many of the shops are rather downmarket (retail hours are Mon–Fri 10am–9pm, Sat 10am–6pm, Sun noon–6pm), though the sheer size of the place is enough to keep you browsing all day. But its size aside it's the clutch of extra attractions that make the mall unique. These include the world's largest indoor lake (122m long) as part of a cluster of attractions known as **Deep Sea Adventure** that contains a full-sized replica of Columbus's *Santa Maria* and some 200 different species of marine life. Other distractions here include sea lion shows ($4.95 an underwater aquarium ($4.95) laced with the inevitable sharks.

Then there's Galaxyland (Mon–Thurs noon–8pm, Fri & Sat 10am–10pm, Sun 11am–7pm; day-pass $29.95), the world's largest indoor **amusement park**, which features such attractions as the *Drop of Doom*, a thirteen-storey "free-fall experience", and the fourteen-storey *Mindbender* triple-loop roller coaster. The latter, it comes as no surprise to learn, is the world's largest indoor roller coaster. The **World Waterpark**, by contrast, is a superb collection of vast swimming pools, immense water slides and wave pools (Mon–Thurs noon–7pm, Fri & Sat 10am–7pm, Sun 11am–6pm; day-pass $29.95 or $19.95 during last three hours each day). If you've still any energy, you can also ice-skate on a National Hockey League-size skating rink ($5.95 a session, skate rental $4). You could round off the day or indulge yourself further in one of the mall's many **cinemas** (including IMAX), the Ice Palace, Sea Life Caverns, Professor Wem's Golf Adventure, or a variety of clubs.

If you want to go the whole hog, spend the night in the 354-room **Fantasyland Hotel** (ⓣ780/444-3000 or 1-800/737-3783, ⓦwww.fantasylandhotel.com; ⑦) where 118 of the rooms are intricately equipped and decorated to fulfil various assorted fantasies: Roman, Hollywood, Arabian, Victorian Coach, African, Igloo, Canadian Rail and, most intriguing of all, Truck. Cheaper rooms are available without Jacuzzis and mirrored ceilings. There are over a hundred places to **eat** – the best of which are listed below, some lined up on two "theme" streets: Europa Boulevard and a New Orleans-style Bourbon Street.

Bus services to the mall heading west out of downtown include #100, #109, #111 and #113. The monster's location, so far as it has an address (it has five different postal codes and 58 entrances – remember which one you parked by if you've come by car), is 170th Street and 87th Avenue. Maps are available throughout the main building at information booths, where you can also get **information** and any number of facts and figures. To save tired feet, you can rent a scooter (ⓣ780/444-5330) for $8 an hour from beside the ice rink at the centre of the mall.

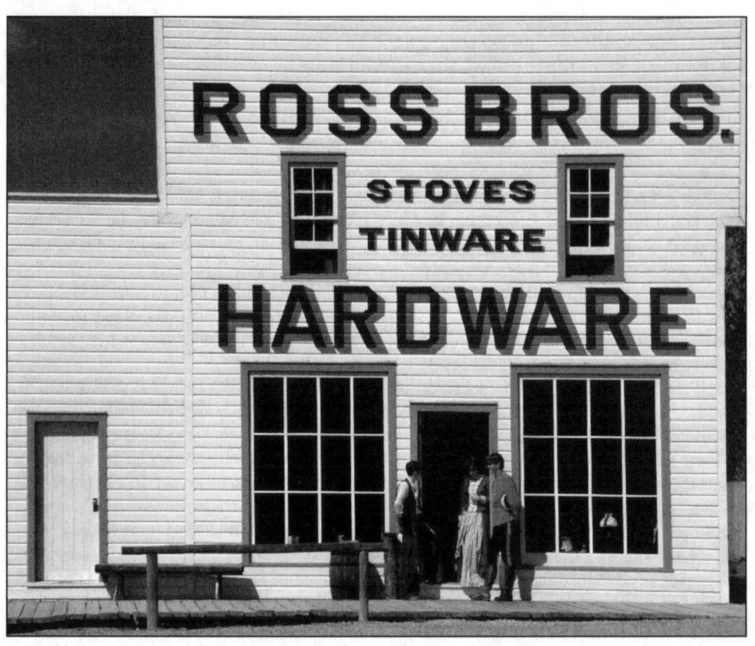

△ Edmonton's historic district

Eating, drinking and nightlife

Edmonton has 2000-odd **restaurants**, some of them very good. There's plenty in or near downtown, but if you want a bit of nocturnal zip to go with your meal you'd do best to head out to **Old Strathcona** (see p.652). Ethnic options – notably restaurants serving Edmonton's populations of Ukrainian and Eastern European origin – complement the standard Italian-influenced cuisine or steak-and-salmon offerings. Otherwise, the stalls in the downtown mall and street-front snack bars are lively at lunchtime, and all the usual fast-food, snack and breakfast options are available. **Beer** drinkers should be sure to try the local real ale, Big Rock.

There are any number of small-time **nightspots**, especially in Old Strathcona, putting on live music, but larger clubs capable of attracting big names are thin on the ground. The big-name acts and theatre companies that do appear tend to use the University of Alberta's **Jubilee Auditorium**, 87th Ave and 114th St (Ⓣ780/451-8000, Ⓦwww.jubileeauditorium.com) – venue for the Edmonton opera – and the **Citadel Theatre**, 9828-101A Ave (Ⓣ780/425-1820 or 1-888/425-1820, Ⓦwww.citadeltheatre.com), the latter being a five-theatre complex which allows it to run a number of varied performances simultaneously. Some companies, plus the **Edmonton Symphony Orchestra** (Ⓣ780/428-1414 or 1-800/563-5081, Ⓦwww.edmontonsymphony.com), use the excellent **Francis Winspear Centre for Music**, 4 Sir Winston Churchill Square (Ⓣ780/428-1414 or 1-800/563-5081, Ⓦwww.winspearcentre.com). The season for most of the city's dozen or more theatre companies runs from May to September. For revivals, foreign films and art-house **cinema**, try the old Princess Theatre, 10337-82nd Ave (Ⓣ780/433-0728). The best **listings** source is the free weekly *Vue* (published Thurs; from stores, hotels and kiosks), as well as the entertainment sections of the city's main newspaper, the *Edmonton Journal*. **Tickets** for most classical music, dance, opera, theatre and other events – including big-name concerts and Edmonton Oilers **ice hockey** games, which are played in the Skyreach Centre (formerly the Edmonton Coliseum), 118th Ave and 74th St – are available from Ticketmaster outlets (Ⓣ780/451-8000, Ⓦwww.ticketmaster.ca) around the city including at 9930-102 Ave, downtown on Churchill Square.

Cafés and restaurants

Bistro Praha 10168-100A St Ⓣ780/424-4218. A good opportunity to sample Eastern European cuisine, Edmonton-style, in the city's oldest European-style restaurant. Slightly highbrow and expensive, though – best for lunch or a late-night meal.

Café Select 10018-106th St Ⓣ780/423-0419. An excellent, intimate place, trendy without being intimidating. Serves fine, simple, moderately-priced bistro-type food, and is one of downtown's best choices for a late-night treat; book ahead.

Da-De-O 10548A-82nd Ave Ⓣ780/443-0903. Upbeat Cajun diner with chrome-rimmed tables and great southern food. All the old favourites are here – oysters, gumbo, jambalaya and southern fried chicken – very good and reasonably priced with entrees around $15; be sure to start off with the excellent sweet potato fries.

Earl's 11830 Jasper Ave Ⓣ780/448-6582. This invariably excellent chain of relaxed and popular mid-range restaurants has no fewer than eight Edmonton outlets serving modern North American cuisine. This branch, known as the *Tin Palace*, is the most central.

Grabbajabba Coffee 82nd Ave and 104th St. Coffee, cake and the works at this very popular café in the heart of Old Strathcona; other outlets around the city.

Hardware Grill 9698 Jasper Ave Ⓣ780/423-0969. The seasonally inspired Canadian cuisine in the best restaurant in Edmonton is served in a chic modern environment with dark hardwood floors, simple lines, elegant linen and prices to match. Be sure to reserve in advance.

Jack's Grill 5842-111th St Ⓣ780/434-1113. Probably a tad too south of the city centre unless you have a car, but this is one of the top places in Edmonton for modern, innovative Pacific Rim cuisine. Many local ingredients are offered on the reassuringly short menu; entrees cost around $30 and include oddities like wild-boar shoulder. Vegetarian dishes are entirely absent.

The King and I 8208-107th St ⓣ780/433-2222. If you want a change from steaks, salmon and the Italian-based cuisine of many Edmonton restaurants, then you can't do better than this superlative Thai restaurant, where prices are nonetheless moderate.

La Ronde 10111 Bellamy Hill ⓣ780/428-6611. Stunning views of Edmonton from the city's only revolving dining room (atop the *Crowne Plaza Château Lacombe*). The expensive (mains from $25) Albertan cooking – steaks, bison, berries – is good too. Dancing nightly, live entertainment Fri–Sun.

Mandarin 11044-82nd Ave ⓣ780/433-8494. Edmonton's best Chinese buffet-restaurant, located on the western side of the Old Strathcona district, serves up inexpensive specialties like Szechwan beef and fried dumplings. Closed Sun.

Oodle Noodle 10803-82nd Ave. Excellent, inexpensive Asian noodle house, where the food's speedily cooked to order and boxed for a quick chow down on the premises or a take away.

Packrat Louie 10335-83rd Ave ⓣ780/433-0123. Bright, young and welcoming bistro in Old Strathcona with generous portions of steaks, salads, chicken and other more sophisticated international dishes. Closed Sun & Mon. Inexpensive to moderate.

Silk Hat 10251 Jasper Ave ⓣ780/425-1920. A fine place to knock back a Molson from the brewery up the road, this local institution's dim interior hasn't altered in forty years. Best known for the 1950s jukeboxes at each booth, but the inexpensive, basic food is as good as the ambience. Great milkshakes, too.

Sorrentino's 10162-100th St ⓣ780/424-7500. Downtown branch of an enormously successful local chain of family-run Italian restaurants with great atmosphere and service serving good affordable food in a pleasant, stylish setting.

Zenari's Kitchen 10180-101 St NW ⓣ780/423-5409. Great Italian deli/houseware shop with a tremendous lunch counter for soups, salads, sandwiches, pasta, pizza and other Italian staples.

Bars and clubs

Blues on Whyte 10329-82nd Ave ⓣ780/439-3981. At the *Commercial Hotel*, this is one of the city's better live music clubs; bands most nights; jam sessions Sat.

Cook County Saloon 8010-103rd St ⓣ780/432-2665. Deservedly popular Old Strathcona C&W venue, cited many times as Canada's best country nightclub, attracting twentysomethings in droves and packing out on weekend nights. Cover $4.

O'Byrne's Irish Pub 10616-82nd Ave ⓣ780/414-6766. Old Strathcona's popular version of an Irish pub has good food, live music, drink and reasonably authentic atmosphere. If this doesn't take your fancy, there are dozen or so other bars an easy stagger away along Whyte Ave.

Yardbird Suite 10203-86th Ave ⓣ780/432-0428. Live groups nightly (10pm–2am) in the city's top jazz venue; admission is lower for the Tues night jam session. Nonsmoking rule enforced on Friday.

Listings

Bike rental Redbike, 10918-88 Avenue NW (ⓣ780/435-2674) at the southwest corner of Kinsmen Park has mountain bikes for $20/day.

Bookshops Old Strathcona is renowned for its many stores selling new and secondhand books: Greenwood's (ⓣ780/439-2005), on 82nd Ave between 103rd and 104th, is one of the city's best; Old Strathcona Books, 8104 Gateway Blvd (ⓣ780/436-2265), is a quality secondhand outlet. For maps and guides, go to Map Town, 10344-105th St (ⓣ780/429-2600).

Car rental Avis (ⓣ780/962-9493); Budget (ⓣ780/448-2000); Driving Force (ⓣ780/483-9559); Hertz (ⓣ780/890-4566); National (ⓣ780/422-6097); Rent-a-Wreck (ⓣ780/433-0999).

Laundry Jasper Place Coin Laundry, 11122-153rd St (daily 7.30am–8pm).

Left luggage Lockers ($2) at the Greyhound station.

Library Stanley A. Milner Library, 7 Sir Winston Churchill Square (Mon–Fri 9am–9pm, Sat 9am–6pm, Sun 1–5pm).

Medical Royal Alexandra Hospital, 10240 Kingsway (ⓣ780/477-4111) has a 24-hr emergency centre. Whyte Ave Dental Care, 10712-82 Avenue NW (ⓣ780/433-3131) is a dental surgery.

Outdoor equipment Mountain Equipment Co-op, 12328-102nd Ave (ⓣ780/488-6614).

Police ⓣ780/423-4567.

Post office 9808-103A Ave ⓣ780/944-3271.

Road conditions ⓣ780/471-6056, ⓦwww.ama.ab.ca.

Taxis Alberta Co-op (ⓣ780/425-2525); Laidlaw Transit (ⓣ780/465-8546).

Weather Information ⓣ780/468-4940.

Around Edmonton

Surrounded by a landscape of rippling hills, rivers, lakes, lonely farms and open prairie that slowly pass into an unending mantle of northern Albertan forest, Edmonton's hinterland has few real attractions. Certainly compared with the spectacular mountain scenery to the west, the region's landscape is more akin to the monotony of the central plains in Saskatchewan and Manitoba. The only really worthwhile attractions in the immediate vicinity of the city are **Elk Island National Park** and the **Ukrainian Cultural Village**, both to the east. Head west, in contrast – en route to Jasper or the Alaska Hwy (see p.1018) and you'll find diversions almost nonexistent. Northbound travellers on their way along Hwy 2 to Peace River and the Mackenzie Hwy (see p.1056) fare a little better, particularly if they are keen **birders**.

Greyhound **buses** run on all these routes from Edmonton, supplemented by the VIA Rail **train** service from Edmonton to Jasper (with connections on to Vancouver or Prince Rupert).

Elk Island National Park and the Ukrainian Cultural Village

Scenically, the beautifully preserved rolling aspen parklands of **Elk Island National Park** (dawn–dusk; $5; ⓣ780/922-5790, ⓦwww.parkscanada.gc.ca/elk), 45km east of Edmonton along Hwy 16 (the Yellowhead Highway) are a bit dull, so what draws visitors here in numbers is the concentration of wildlife. The herds of both plains and wood bison – a combined population of about eight hundred beasts – are a particular highlight, but there are also good numbers of elk, moose, deer, beavers and coyotes in the park. Seeing many of these animals is generally easy, the chances of watching free-roaming bison at close quarters to your vehicle along the main road, very good. And if not here, then you'll almost certain to see them, and possibly other mammals, along some of the 16km of hiking paths that criss-cross the park – early mornings and late evenings are, as ever, the best time to see the wildlife at its most active. Be sure to stop off at the parks interpretive centre on arrival for some interesting background info on the animals as well as the hiking, cycling, canoeing, skiing and snowshoeing opportunities in the park. They can also advise on what **camping** is possible here between October and May (bookable in advance on ⓣ1-877/737-3883, ⓦwww.pccamping.ca) which costs $6 for a backcountry site and $18 for a spot for a tent or RV in a campground.

A good accompaniment to any jaunt to Elk Island National Park is a visit to the **Ukrainian Cultural Heritage Village** (mid-May to early Sept daily 10am–6pm, early Sept to early Oct Sat & Sun 10am–4pm; $8; ⓣ780/662-3640, ⓦwww.cd.gov.ab.ca/uchv), 5km further east of Edmonton along Hwy 16. This reconstructed thirty-building village celebrates the culture of the 250,000 Ukrainians who migrated here in the late nineteenth and early twentieth centuries, attracted by the familiar landscape and climate. The village centrepiece is an impressive Ukrainian Greek Orthodox Church, which is surrounded with many seemingly authentic pioneer homes and businesses where costumed guides provide explanations and insights to bring the experience to life.

The Yellowhead Highway to Jasper

The town of Jasper (see p.742), 357km west of Edmonton along **Yellowhead Highway**, is an easy four-hour journey by car, though until the final hour the scenery is fairly dull – after which it picks up considerably. Numerous **campsites** and **motels** service the road at regular intervals, the main concentrations being at **EDSON**, halfway to Jasper, and **HINTON,** 79km from Jasper. The motels at both are pretty standard, yet fill up by 5pm almost every day thanks to the local needs of transient oil industry employees.

Highway 43 to Dawson Creek and the Alaska Highway

Highway 43 out of Edmonton to BC rolls through terminally unexceptional towns, hills and prairie scenery on its 602km way west to Dawson Creek, the mile-zero of the **Alaska Highway** (p.1018). It's a mind-numbing day's journey by car or **bus**, making the unfocused sprawl of **GRANDE PRAIRIE**, 463km from Edmonton, a relative highlight. If you end up stopping here, go first to the slick **infocentre** (June to early Sept daily 8.30am–8.30pm; ⓣ780/539-7688 or 1-866-202-2202, ⓦwww.northernvisitor.com), on Hwy 43 which bypasses the main part of town to the west. It's a good place to stock up on regional information and use the Internet for free. The centre also organises a free bison barbeque (June–August Wed 4pm–6pm) and is the departure point for the rotary club's jovial bus tours of the city (June–Aug Mon, Tues & Thurs 7pm; free). Otherwise, the town's only real attraction is the reasonable Grand Prairie Museum and Heritage Discovery Centre (June–Aug Mon–Fri 9am–5pm, Sat & Sun 10am–5pm; $8; ⓣ780/523-5482), in Heritage Park on the western side of downtown. Local history from the year dot is related here, with a few reconstructed pioneer buildings to helping to shed light on recent times.

Grand Prairie's **bus** depot is at 9918-121st St (ⓣ780/539-1111), while most of its many **motels** are on the strip known as Richmond Avenue (100th Ave), which links the southern part of the hwy bypass to downtown. If you decide to stay in Grand Prairie, and have your own vehicle, try to make the trip to **CLAIRMONT** on the north side of town where *Kelly's Bar* in the *Clairmont Inn,* 9811 - 101 Ave. (ⓣ780/567-3778) has to be one of Canada's ultimate **cowboy bars**. Owned by a Calgary Stampede chuck-wagon champion, it's the sort of place that has saddles for bar stools and serves up shooters in bull-semen collection tubes.

Highway 2 to Peace River and the Mackenzie Highway

It's almost 500km from Edmonton to Peace River (see p.1060) along Hwy 2; a long day watching a slow transition from prairie to boreal forests along a route which passes through little more than a handful of small towns. Luckily all are welcoming and deserve at least a quick stop to soak up a bit of small-town life and to stretch legs around a museum or nature reserve; and all have a motel or two in case you need to break your journey.

Westlock

Not long after you've broken free of Edmonton's suburbs and satellite towns – 88km along Hwy 2 from downtown – is the prairie town of **WESTLOCK**. Its archetypal small-town feel is only accentuated by a visit to its cheerfully cluttered **Museum and Information Centre** (late May to Aug daily 10am–5pm; free; ⓣ780/349-4444), where the collection of artefacts and nick-knacks that chart the course of the town's history include an antique treshing machine, aged Native American carvings and a lovingly restored 1920 automobile – with accompanying photos showing the forty-year process.

Slave Lake and Lesser Slave Lake Provincial Park

Another 165km northwest of Westlock on Hwy 2, you arrive at the 100km-long **Lesser Slave Lake** and it's gateway community **Slave Lake**. The sleek highway-side Lesser Slave Lake Regional Information Centre (Fri 9am–9pm, Sat–Mon 10am–6pm, Ⓦwww.lesserslavelake.ca), on the southern side of town is helpful and well-stocked, though it doesn't take long to realise that the **Lesser Slave Lake Provincial Park** (Ⓣ780/849-7100), stretching out along Hwy 88 on the north side of Slave Lake, is virtually the only attraction. Here you can join locals for the day on its long white-sand Devonshire Beach, or explore inland parts of the park. Highlights there include the **Lesser Slave Lake Bird Observatory** (July–Aug Sun–Thurs 8.15am–4.30pm, Fri & Sat 8.15am–6pm, free; Ⓣ780-849-8240, Ⓦwww.lslbo.org), which provides an excellent introduction to the area's extraordinarily rich bird life. The **Marten Mountain Lookout**, some 30km north of Slave Lake along Hwy 88, has grand views spread over an otherwise relatively flat region. From the lookout you can also **hike** out to the pretty little **Lily Lake** – that's ideal for swimming and trout fishing – along a rough 6km trail (allow at least two hours). Another good active option is **kayaking** on the Lesser Slave Lake, with the bird refuge of **Dog Island**, 5km from the shore, the most tempting destination. Rentals and guided tours can be organised through Wildside (rentals from $27 per day; Ⓣ780/849-8375 or 1-877-305-2925, Ⓦwww.wildside.ca).

Among the best of the slew of Slave Lake's highway-side **motels** is the *Sawridge Hotel* (Ⓣ780/849-4101 or 1-800/661-66571, Ⓦwww.sawridge.com; ❸) which has rooms in just about every price bracket as well as a sauna and exercise room; fishing and kayaking packages are also available. **Campers** should head to the Marten River Campground in the Provincial Park ($20 per night). Head-and-shoulders above all the very average **restaurants** and fast food chains in town is the *Point Steakhouse* (Ⓣ780/849-4133) off Albert Ave on the north side of town, not least for its great lake views.

McLennan and the Kimiwan Lake Bird Sanctuary

If the bird observatory in the Lesser Slave Lake Provincial Park whetted your appetite, then make a point of stopping in the small rag-tag town of **McLennan**, 166km from Slave Lake. It's not an over-statement to say that its **Kimiwan Lake Bird Sanctuary** (May–Aug 10am–5.30pm; Ⓣ780/324-2004) is of international importance, with white pelicans among the hundreds of species – and 300,000 birds – that stop here on their migration routes. The reserve and centre is easily found beside the hwy on the eastern edge of downtown.

Calgary and southern Alberta

Located an easy hour's drive from where the prairies buckle into the Rockies, **Calgary** is the obvious focus of **southern Alberta**, and is the best point from which to strike out west into the mountains. Yet, with some of the continent's most magnificent scenery practically on its doorstep, it takes some self-restraint to give the city the couple of days it deserves. Within day-tripping distance lie two unexpected gems: the dinosaur exhibits of the **Royal Tyrrell Museum**,

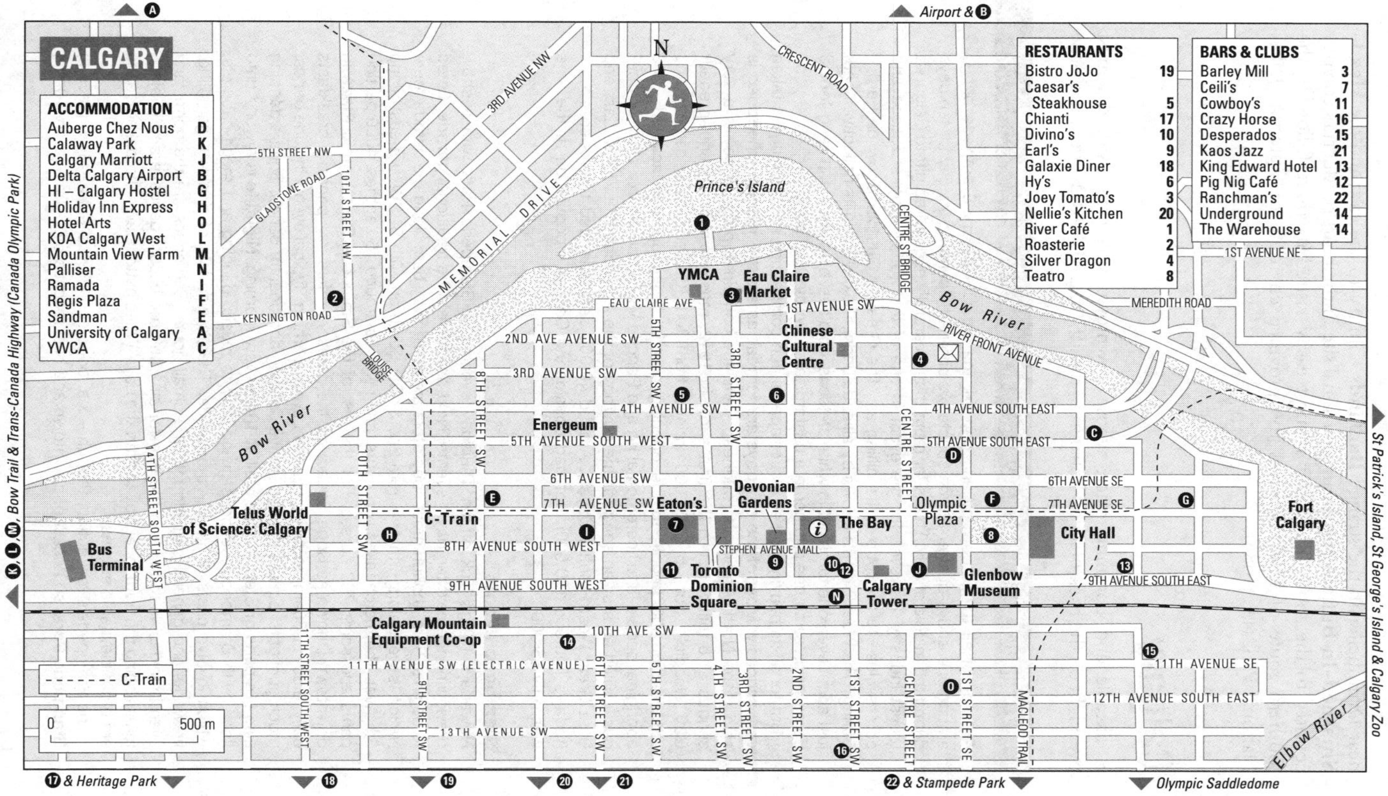

CALGARY

ACCOMMODATION

Auberge Chez Nous	D
Calaway Park	K
Calgary Marriott	J
Delta Calgary Airport	B
HI – Calgary Hostel	G
Holiday Inn Express	H
Hotel Arts	O
KOA Calgary West	L
Mountain View Farm	M
Palliser	N
Ramada	I
Regis Plaza	F
Sandman	E
University of Calgary	A
YWCA	C

RESTAURANTS

Bistro JoJo	19
Caesar's Steakhouse	5
Chianti	17
Divino's	10
Earl's	9
Galaxie Diner	18
Hy's	6
Joey Tomato's	3
Nellie's Kitchen	20
River Café	1
Roasterie	2
Silver Dragon	4
Teatro	8

BARS & CLUBS

Barley Mill	3
Ceili's	7
Cowboy's	11
Crazy Horse	16
Desperados	15
Kaos Jazz	21
King Edward Hotel	13
Pig Nig Café	12
Ranchman's	22
Underground	14
The Warehouse	14

A
Airport & B
N
Crescent Road
3rd Avenue NW
5th Street NW
Gladstone Road
10th Street NW
Kensington Road
Memorial Drive
Prince's Island
Louise Bridge
Centre St Bridge
1st Avenue NE
Meredith Road
Bow River
River Front Avenue
YMCA
Eau Claire Market
Eau Claire Ave
1st Avenue SW
Chinese Cultural Centre
2nd Ave Avenue SW
3rd Avenue SW
4th Avenue SW
4th Avenue South East
5th Avenue South West
5th Avenue South East
6th Avenue SW
6th Avenue SE
7th Avenue SW
7th Avenue SE
8th Avenue South West
Stephen Avenue Mall
9th Avenue South West
9th Avenue South East
10th Ave SW
11th Avenue SW (Electric Avenue)
11th Avenue SE
12th Avenue South East
13th Avenue SW
14th Street South West
11th Street South West
10th Street SW
9th Street SW
8th Street SW
6th Street SW
5th Street SW
4th Street SW
3rd Street SW
2nd Street SW
1st Street SW
Centre Street
1st Street SE
Macleod Trail
Energeum
Telus World of Science: Calgary
C-Train
Bus Terminal
Eaton's
Devonian Gardens
The Bay
Olympic Plaza
City Hall
Fort Calgary
Toronto Dominion Square
Calgary Tower
Glenbow Museum
Calgary Mountain Equipment Co-op
Elbow River
St Patrick's Island, St George's Island & Calgary Zoo
K, L, M, Bow Trail & Trans-Canada Highway (Canada Olympic Park)
17 & Heritage Park
18
19
20
21
22 & Stampede Park
Olympic Saddledome
- - - - C-Train
0 500 m

near Drumheller in the strange **Badlands** country to the east; and the **Head-Smashed-In Buffalo Jump**, an aboriginal site in the heart of Alberta's cowboy country to the south. The latter is most easily visited if you're following the southern route of Hwy 3 across the province en route to Waterton Lakes National Park (see p.686).

Calgary

A likeable and booming place, whose downtown skyscrapers soared almost overnight on the back of an oil bonanza in the 1970s, **CALGARY**'s tight high-rise

The Calgary Stampede

An orgy of all things cowboy and cowgirl, the annual **Calgary Stampede** brings around one-and-a-quarter-million spectators and participants to the city for ten days during the middle of July. This is far more than a carefully engineered gift to Calgary's tourist industry, however, for the event is one of the world's biggest rodeos and comes close to living up to its billing as "The Greatest Outdoor Show on Earth". During "The Week", as it's known by all and sundry, the city loses its collective head; just about everyone turns out in white stetsons, bolo ties, blue jeans and hand-tooled boots, addressing one another in a bastardized cowboy C&W slang.

But for all its heavily worked visitor appeal, the competition end of things is taken very seriously. Most of the cowboys are for real, as are the injuries – the rodeo is said to be North America's roughest – and the combined prize money is a very serious $1.6 million. Even the first show in 1912, masterminded by entrepreneur Guy Weadick, put up $100,000 (raised from four Calgary businessmen) and attracted 60,000 people to the opening parade, a line-up that included 2000 aboriginal people in full ceremonial rig and Pancho Villa's bandits in a show erroneously billed as a swan song for the cowboy of the American West ("The Last and Best Great West Frontier Days"). Around 40,000 daily attended the rodeo events (today's figure is 100,000), not bad considering Calgary's population at the time was only 65,000.

Stampede events

Nowadays things kick off on Thursday evening at Stampede Park with a show previewing the next ten days' events. Next day there's the traditional **parade**, timed to begin at 9am, though most spectators are in place by 6am along the parade route (which is west along 6th Ave from 2nd St SE, south on 10th St SW and east along 9th Ave). The march takes two hours, and involves around 150 entries, 4000 participants and some 700 horses. For the rest of the Stampede the **Olympic Plaza** in downtown (known as Rope Square for the duration) offers free pancake breakfasts daily (8.30–11.30am) and entertainment every morning. Typical events include bands, mock gunfights, square dances, native dancing and country bands. Square dancing also fills parts of Stephen Ave Mall at 10am every morning. **Nightlife** is a world unto itself, with Stampede locations giving way to music, dancing and mega-cabarets, which involve casts of literally thousands. There's also lots of drinking, gambling, fireworks and general partying into the small hours. Barbecues are the norm, and even breakfast is roped into the free-for-all – outdoor bacon, pancake and flapjack feasts being the traditional way to start the day. "White hatter stew" and baked beans are other inevitable staples.

The Stampede's real action, though – the rodeo and allied events – takes place in **Stampede Park**, southeast of downtown and best reached by C-Train (every 10min)

core is good for wandering, and holds the prestigious **Glenbow Museum**. The wooden houses of the far-flung suburbs, meanwhile, recall the city's pioneering frontier origins, which are further celebrated in the annual **Calgary Stampede**, a hugely popular cowboy carnival in which the whole town – and hordes of tourists – revel in a boots-and-stetson image that's still very much a way of life in the surrounding cattle country. Year-round you can dip into the city's lesser museums and historic sites, or take time out in its scattering of attractive city parks.

Some history

Modern Calgary is one of the West's largest and youngest cities, its present population of almost one million having grown from almost nothing in barely 130 years. Long before the coming of outsiders, however, the area was the

to Victoria Park–Stampede Station. This vast open area contains an amusement park, concert and show venues, bars and restaurants and a huge range of stalls and shows that take the best part of a day to see. Entrance is $12, which allows you to see all the **entertainments** except the rodeo and chuck-wagon races. Things to see include the aboriginal village at the far end of the park, where members of the Five Nations peoples (Blackfoot, Blood, Sarcee, Stoney and Piegan) set up a tepee village (tours available); the John Deere Show Ring, scene of the World Blacksmith Competition; the Centennial Fair, which hosts events for children; the Agricultural Building, home to displays of cattle and other livestock; the outdoor Coca-Cola Stage, used for late-night Country shows; and the Nashville North, an indoor Country venue with bar and dancing until 2am.

If you want to see the daily **rodeo** competition – bronco riding, bull riding, native-buffalo riding, branding, calf-roping, steer-wrestling, cow-tackling, wild-cow milking and the rest – you need another ticket ($12 on the day), though unless you've bought these in advance (see below) it's hardly worth it: you'll probably be in poor seats miles from the action and hardly see a thing. Rodeo heats are held each afternoon from 1.30pm for the first eight days, culminating in winner-takes-all finals on Saturday and Sunday (prize money that weekend accounts for $1 million of the total). If you want to watch the other big event, the ludicrously dangerous but hugely exciting **chuck-wagon** races (the "World Championship"), you need yet another ticket ($12) on the day, though again you need to buy these in advance to secure anything approaching decent seats. The nine contests are held once-nightly at 8pm, the four top drivers going through to the last-night final.

Stampede practicalities

It's worth planning ahead if you're coming to Calgary for Stampede. **Accommodation** is greatly stretched – be certain to book ahead – and prices for most things are hiked for the duration. **Tickets** for the rodeo and chuck-wagon races go on sale anything up to a year in advance. They're sold for the Stampede Park grandstand, which is divided into sections. "A" is best and sells out first; "B" and "C" go next. Then comes the smarter Clubhouse Level (D–E are seats; F–G are Clubhouse Restaurant seats, with tickets sold in pairs only). This is enclosed and air-conditioned, but still offers good views and the bonus of bars, lounge area and restaurants. The top of the stand, or Balcony (J–K) is open, and provides a good vantage point for the chuck-wagon races as you follow their progress around the length of the course. Rodeo tickets range from about $23 to $49, chuck-wagon races from $34 to $75; tickets for the finals of both events are a few dollars more in all seats.

For ticket order forms, **advance sales** and general information, check ⓦwww.calgarystampede.com.

domain of the **Blackfoot**, who ranged over the site of present-day Calgary for several thousand years. About 300 years ago, they were joined by **Sarcee**, forced south by war from their northern heartlands, and the **Stoney**, who migrated north with Sitting Bull into southern Saskatchewan and then Alberta. Traces of old campsites, buffalo kills and pictographs from all three peoples lie across the region, though these days local aboriginal lands are confined to a few reserves.

Whites first began to gather around the confluence of the Bow and Elbow rivers at the end of the eighteenth century. Explorer **David Thompson** wintered here during his travels, while the Palliser expedition spent time nearby en route for the Rockies. Settlers started arriving from around 1870, when hunters moved into the region from the United States, where their prey, the buffalo, had been hunted to the edge of extinction. Herds still roamed the Alberta grasslands, attracting not only hunters but also **whiskey traders**, who plied their dubious wares among whites and aboriginal peoples alike. Trouble inevitably followed, leading to the creation of the West's first North West Mounted Police stockade at Fort Macleod (see p.680). Soon after, in 1875, a second fort was built further north to curb the lawlessness of the whiskey traders. A year later it was christened **Fort Calgary**, taking its name from the Scottish birthplace of its assistant commissioner. The word *calgary* is Gaelic for "clear running water", and it was felt that the ice-clear waters of the Bow and Elbow rivers were reminiscent of the "old country".

By 1883 a station had been built close to the fort, part of the new trans-Canadian **railway**. The township laid out nearby quickly attracted **ranchers** and British gentlemen farmers to its low, hilly bluffs – which are indeed strongly reminiscent of Scottish moors and lowlands – and cemented an enduring Anglo-Saxon cultural bias. Ranchers from the US – where pasture was heavily overgrazed – were further encouraged by an "open grazing" policy across the Alberta grasslands. Despite Calgary's modern-day cowboy life – most notably its famous annual **Stampede** – the Alberta cattle country has been described as more "mild West" than Wild West. Research suggests that there were just three recorded gunfights in the nineteenth century, and poorly executed ones at that.

By 1886 fires had wiped out most of the town's temporary wooded and tented buildings, leading to an edict declaring that all new buildings should be constructed in sandstone (for a while Calgary was known as "Sandstone City"). The fires proved no more than a minor historical hiccup and within just nine years of the railway's arrival Calgary achieved official city status, something it had taken rival Edmonton over a hundred years to achieve. Edmonton was to have its revenge in 1910, when it was made Alberta's provincial capital.

Cattle and the coming of the railway generated exceptional growth, though the city's rise was to be nothing compared with the prosperity that followed the discovery of **oil**. The first strike, the famous Dingman's No. 1 Well, took place in 1914 in the nearby Turner Valley. An oil refinery opened in 1923 and since then Calgary has rarely looked back. In the 25 years after 1950 its population doubled. When oil prices soared during the oil crisis of the 1970s, the city exploded, becoming a world energy and financial centre – headquarters for some four hundred oil and related businesses – with more American inhabitants than any other Canadian city.

Falling commodity prices subsequently punctured the city's ballooning economy, but not before the city centre had been virtually rebuilt and acquired improved and oil-financed cultural, civic and other facilities. Today only Toronto is home to the headquarters of more major Canadian corporations, though the city's optimism is tempered, as elsewhere in Canada, by the notion of **federal**

Shuttles to Banff

Direct **buses** from the airport to **Banff** and Lake Louise mean you can be in Banff National Park a couple of hours after collecting your baggage. Services include those run by Banff Airporter (18 daily; $50 to Banff; ⓣ403/762-3330 or 1-888/449-2901, ⓦwww.banffairporter.com); Brewster Transportation (2 daily to Banff and Lake Louise, 1 daily to Jasper in summer; $50 to Banff, $65 to Lake Louise, $120 to Jasper; ⓣ403/762-6767 in Banff, ⓣ403/221-8242 in Calgary, ⓣ780/852-3332 in Jasper, ⓦwww.brewster.ca).

Tickets are available from separate desks adjacent to the Airporter desk in Arrivals.

disintegration. Much of the West, which still harbours a sense of a new frontier, is increasingly impatient with the "old East", and happy – if election results are anything to go by – to become increasingly self-sufficient.

Arrival, information and transport

Approaching Calgary **by air** you're rewarded (in the right weather) with a magnificent view of the Rockies stretching across the western horizon. **Calgary International Airport** (ⓦwww.calgaryairport.com), a modern, often half-deserted strip, is about 15km northeast of downtown. There's a small **information centre** (daily 10am–10pm) in Arrivals. The Arrivals level also offers courtesy phones to hotels and car-rental agencies, though most of the hotels are well away from the centre but at least usually served by courtesy shuttles. The cheapest way downtown is with Calgary Transit service #57 (every 20–30mins 6am–11pm) which costs only $2.25 but takes around an hour. You can halve the journey time by taking a shuttle bus: the Airporter (every 30mins; $9; ⓣ403/531-3907) drops you off at major downtown locations, while the Airport Shuttle Express (call to book; $12; ⓣ403/509-4799) will pick you up and drop you off at virtually anywhere. A taxi downtown costs $30.

Calgary's Greyhound **bus terminal** (ⓣ403/265-9111 or 1-800/661-8747, ⓦwww.greyhound.ca) is comfortable but not convenient. It's located west of downtown at 8th Avenue SW and 850-16th St, an uninspiring thirty-minute walk to the city centre. Fortunately free transit buses operate to the C-Train at 10th Street SW, the key to the city's central transport system (free from this point through the downtown area). The shuttles leave from Gate 4 within 20 minutes of every bus arrival to the terminal and are announced over the loudspeaker: keep your ears open. Shuttles return from the same point more or less hourly on the half-hour. Alternatively, taxis for the short run to downtown ($6) are plentiful outside the terminal.

The main **Visitor Information Services** is rather pitiful and located downtown in the front of the Riley & McComick Western Store, 220 8th Ave SW (daily 8am–5pm; ⓣ403/263-8510 or 1-800/661-1678, ⓦwww.tourismcalgary.com).

City transport

Almost everything in Calgary, barring Stampede locations and a few minor diversions, is a comfortable walk away – except in winter, when low temperatures can make any excursion an ordeal. The city's much-vaunted **Plus 15 Walking System**, a labyrinthine network of enclosed walkways 4.5m above ground, is designed to beat the freeze. It enables you to walk through downtown without setting foot outside, but is too confusing to bother with when the weather's fine.

Calgary's **public transport** system is cheap, clean and efficient, comprising an integrated network of buses and the **C-Train** (every 15 to 30min; no late-night service), the latter a cross between a bus and a train, which is free for its downtown stretch along the length of 7th Avenue SW between 10th Street and City Hall at 3rd Street SE. An on-board announcement tells you when the free section is coming to an end. **Tickets**, valid for both buses and C-Train, are available from machines on C-Train stations, shops with a Calgary Transit sticker, and from the main Information and Downtown Sales Centre, also known as the **Calgary Transit Customer Service Centre**, 224-7th Ave SW (Mon–Fri 10am–5.30pm), which also has free schedules and route planners. The one-way fare is $2.25, a day-pass $6.75. You can pay on the bus if you have the exact change. Request a transfer from the driver (valid for 90min) if you're changing buses. The sales centre also provides timetables and an invaluable **information line** (Mon–Fri 6am–11pm, Sat & Sun 8am–9.30pm; ⓣ403/262-1000): tell them where you are and where you want to go, and they'll give you the necessary details.

You can easily get a **taxi** from outside the bus terminal, or see p.674 for numbers of cab companies.

Accommodation

Budget and mid-priced **accommodation** in downtown Calgary is not plentiful, but the little that exists is rarely at a premium except during Stampede (mid-July) when prepaid reservations, in central locations at least, are essential months in advance. Remember that even smart hotels are likely to offer vastly reduced rates on Friday nights and over the weekend, when their business custom drops away. In addition to the recommendations given below, motels abound, mostly well away from the centre along Macleod Trail heading south and on the Trans-Canada Hwy heading west. "Motel Village" is a cluster of a dozen or so motels in the $65–75 a night bracket, grouped together at the intersection of 16th Avenue NW and Crowchild Trail; a taxi ride out here costs about $10. If you run into difficulties or a looking for a B&B, try the search engine provided on the website of the Bed and Breakfast Association of Calgary (ⓦwww.bbcalgary.com).

Hotels and motels

Calgary Marriott 110-9th Ave SE ⓣ403/266-7331 or 1-800/228-9290, ⓦwww.calgarymarriott.com. Not the most expensive of Calgary's smart hotels, but probably the best for its extremely central location, helpful staff and cleanliness. Try to request a room high up on the east side for the best views. Parking can be a hassle here though, making the hotel's $28 per day valet service worth considering. ❼

Delta Calgary Airport Hotel 2001 Airport Rd ⓣ403/291-2600 or 1-800/441-1414, ⓦwww.deltacalgaryairport.com. Soundproofed hotel right at the airport – ideal if you arrive late or have an early flight out – but it's not cheap. ❻

Holiday Inn Express Calgary Downtown 1020-8th Ave SW ⓣ403/269-8262 or 1-800/661-6017, ⓦwww.hiexpress.com/calgarydt. A ten-storey modern but slightly faded block with 56 rooms close to the more expensive *Sandman*, to which it is inferior. Just a block from the free C-Train. ❹

Hotel Arts 119-12th Ave SW ⓣ403/266-4611 or 1-800/661-9378, ⓦwww.hotelarts.ca. Stylish amenity-loaded modern boutique hotel, three few blocks off the centre of town. ❼

Palliser 133-9th Ave SW ⓣ403/262-1234 or 1-800/441-1414, ⓦwww.fairmont.com. Built in 1914, this is the hotel royalty chooses when it comes to Calgary, and is as smart as you can find in the city if you want traditional style and service (though avoid the back rooms overlooking the rail tracks). ❼

Ramada Hotel Downtown 708-8th Ave SW ⓣ403/263-7600 or 1-800/661-8684, ⓦwww.ramadacalgary.com. A large, comfortable hotel with 200 predictably good rooms and a swimming pool at the heart of downtown. ❺

Regis Plaza Hotel 124-7th Ave SE ⓣ403/262-4641, ⓦwww.regisplazahotel.com. An old and fairly unappealing hotel, but handy for the desperate, since it's cheap and just two blocks from the Calgary Tower. Many rooms share bathrooms; beware the rough bar. ❸

Sandman Hotel Downtown Calgary 888-7th Ave SW ⓣ403/237-8626 or 1-800/726-3626, ⓦwww.sandmanhotels.com. An excellent and first-choice mid-range hotel, with 300 totally dependable clean, modern rooms with private bathrooms in a high-rise block: extremely handy for the free C-Train. ❺

Travelodge 2750 Sunridge Blvd NE ⓣ403/291-1260 or 1-800/578-7878; 2304-16th Ave ⓣ403/289-0211 or 1-888/294-6444; and 7012 Macleod Trail ⓣ403/253-7070 or 1-888/314-1444. Inexpensive out-of-town chain motels; the first is convenient to the airport; the second north of town along the Trans-Canada Highway; the third south along the arterial Macleod Trail. ❸

Hostel and student rooms

Auberge Chez Nous 149-5th Ave SE ⓣ403-232-5475, ⓦwww.auberge-cheznous.com. Clean and friendly hostel with Francophone owners in quiet neighbourhood a five minutes walk from the C-Train. Less sociable but more relaxing and safer than the HI hostel. Beds in 5–7 bed dorms go for $26; private rooms for $65.

Calgary YWCA 320-5th Ave SE ⓣ403/263-1550. Hotel comfort for women and children only in quiet, safe area; food service, pool, gym, health club and squash courts; book in summer. Singles available from about $45 for singles ($55 double) without bath.

HI-Calgary Hostel 520-7th Ave SE ⓣ403/269-8239, ⓦwww.hihostels.ca. Sociable hostel in seedy area close to downtown; two blocks east of City Hall and the free section of the C-Train. Laundry, six- and eight-bed dorms (120 beds in total), four double/family rooms, cooking facilities, bike storage, snack bar. Dorms $20–22; family rooms/doubles add $5 per person. The hostel organizes some evening activities.

University of Calgary 3456-24th Ave NW 104 Cascade Hall ⓣ403/220-3202 or 1-877/498-3203, ⓦwww.ucalgary.ca/residence. Way out in the northwest suburbs, but cheap with a huge number private rooms (around $45–60) and apartments ($75–90) from early May to late Aug. All the student facilities – including great sports facilities are on hand, as is a free Internet connection. Take the C-Train or bus #9. By car, from downtown head west along Hwy 1 then northwest on University Drive. The 24hr room-rental office (call first) is in the lobby of Cascade Hall on campus.

Campsites

Calaway Park 245033 Range Rd 33 ⓣ403/240-3822, ⓦwww.calawaypark.com. About 10km west of the city on the Trans-Canada Hwy to Banff and the Rockies. It's also within walking distance of the Calaway Park amusement park – western Canada's largest. Full facilities, including showers. Late May to Sept; $23–35.

KOA Calgary West 221-101 St SW ⓣ403/288-0411 or 1-800/562-0842. Off the south side of Hwy 1 at the western end of the city, close to Canada Olympic Park: 400 sites, laundry, store and outdoor pool. Shuttle services to downtown. Mid-April to mid-Oct; $24–35.

Mountain View Farm Campground ⓣ403/293-6640, ⓦwww.calgarycamping.com. A 202-site full service campsite situated on a farm 3km east of the city on the Trans-Canada (Hwy 1). April-Oct; $26.50–36.

The City

Downtown Calgary lies in a self-evident cluster of mirrored glass and polished granite facades bounded by the Bow River to the north, 9th Avenue to the south, Centre Street to the east and 8th Street to the west. A monument to oil money, the area is about as sleek as an urban centre can be: virtually everything is brand-new, and the modern architecture is easy on the eye. The **city centre**, so far as it has one, is traditionally 8th Avenue between 1st Street SE and 3rd Street SW, a largely pedestrianized area known as **Stephen Ave Mall**.

Any city tour, though, should start with a trip to the **Glenbow Museum**, while a jaunt up the **Calgary Tower**, across the street, gives a literal overview of the Calgarian hinterland. Thereafter a good deal of the city lends itself to wandering on foot, whether around the mall-laden main streets or to **Prince's Island**, the nearest of many parks, and gentrified **Kensington**, a busy shopping and café district. The appeal of attractions further afield – **Fort Calgary**, **Heritage Park** and the **Calgary Zoo** – will depend on your historical and natural-history inclinations. These sights, together with a crop of special interest **museums**, can be easily reached by bus or C-Train.

Glenbow Museum

The excellent and eclectic collection of the **Glenbow Museum** (Fri–Wed 9am–5pm, Thurs 9am–9pm; $12; Ⓦ www.glenbow.org) is, the Stampede apart, the only sight for which you'd make a special journey to Calgary. Although it's opposite the Calgary Tower at 130-9th Ave SE, the main entrance is hidden alongside the Skyline Plaza complex a short way east down the street (there's another entrance from the Stephen Ave Mall). Built in 1966, the no-expense-spared museum is a testament to sound civic priorities and the cultural benefits of booming oil revenues. Its three floors of displays make a fine introduction to the heritage of the Canadian west.

The permanent collection embraces the eclectic approach, starting with a section devoted to ritual and **sacred art** from around the world and an **art gallery** tracing the development of western Canadian indigenous art. Better still is the European art depicting the culture of aboriginal peoples. Two outlooks prevail – the romantic nineteenth-century image of the Indian as "noble savage", and the more forward-looking analysis of artists from the same period such as Paul Kane, a painter determined to make accurate representations of aboriginal peoples and cultures before their assimilation by white expansion. The second floor runs the gamut of western Canadian history and heritage, including an outstanding exhibit on First Nations or **aboriginal peoples**. In the treaties section, hidden in a corner almost as if in shame, the museum text skates over the injustices with a glossary of simple facts. On display are the original documents that many chiefs were tricked into signing, believing they were peace treaties, when in fact the contracts gave away all land rights to those who drafted them in deliberately incomprehensible legalese. All facets of **native crafts** are explored on this floor, as well, with stunning displays of carving, costumes and jewellery; whilst their emphasis is on the original inhabitants of Alberta – with a special new display on the Blackfoot – the collection also forays into the Inuit and the Métis – the latter being the offspring of native women and white fur traders, and the most marginalized group of all, since for centuries they were neither recognised as Canadians or aboriginals, denying them rights and causing many to wander the country in poverty with nowhere to settle. Following a historical chronology, the floor moves on to exhibits associated with the fur trade, Northwest Rebellion, the Canadian Pacific, pioneer life, ranching, cowboys, oil and wheat – each era illustrated by interesting and appropriate artefacts of the time – adding up to a glut of period paraphernalia that includes a terrifying exhibit of frontier dentistry, an absurdly comprehensive display of washing machines, and a solitary 1938 bra. The eccentric top floor kicks off with a pointless display of Calgary Stampede merchandising, before moving on to a huge collection of **military paraphernalia** and a dazzling display of **gems and minerals**, said to be among the world's best. These exhibits are mainly for genre enthusiasts, though the gems are worth a look if only to see some of the extraordinary and beautiful things that come out of the drab mines that fuel so much of western Canada's economy.

Other downtown sights

The **Calgary Tower** (daily May–Sept 7.30am–11.30pm; Oct–April 9am–10pm; $12.95 Ⓦ www.calgarytower.com), the city's favourite folly, is a good deal shorter and less imposing than the tourist material would have you believe.

An obligatory tourist traipse, the 190m-tall sceptre (762 steps if you don't take the lift) stands in a relatively dingy area at the corner of Centre St–9th Ave SW, somewhat overshadowed by downtown's more recent buildings. Nevertheless its unusual shape has made it a long-term landmark, and as good a starting point as any for a tour of the city. The Observation Terrace offers outstanding views, especially on clear days, when the snowcapped Rockies fill the western horizon, with the ski-jump towers of the 1988 Canada Olympic Park in the middle distance. Up on the observation platform after your one-minute elevator ride you'll find a snack bar (good value and reasonable food), cocktail bar and revolving restaurant (expensive).

Any number of shopping malls lurk behind the soaring high-rises, most notably Toronto Dominion Square (8th Avenue SW between 2nd & 3rd sts), the city's main shopping focus and the unlikely site of **Devonian Gardens** (daily 9am–9pm; free). Like something out of an idyllic urban Utopia, the three-acre indoor gardens support a lush sanctuary of streams, waterfalls and full-sized trees, no mean feat given that it's located on the fourth floor of a glass and concrete glitter palace (access by elevator). Around 20,000 plants round off the picture, comprising some 138 local and tropical species. Benches beside the garden's paths are perfect for picnicking on food bought in the takeaways below, while impromptu concerts are held on the small stages dotted around.

The **TELUS World of Science: Calgary** is located one block west of the 10th Street SW C-Train at 701-11th St and 7th Ave SW (Tues–Thurs 10am–4pm, Fri–Sun 10am–5pm; $15; ⓣ403/268-8300, ⓦwww.calgaryscience.ca). Here you can look through the telescopes of its small observatory, which are trained nightly on the moon, planets and stars (weather permitting). Other daytime highlights here include the interactive exhibits of the Discovery Hall (these change regularly) and the **Discovery Dome**, a multimedia theatre complete with cinema picture images, computer graphics, slide-projected images and a vast speaker system. To get here, take the C-Train along 7th Avenue SW and walk the last block.

△ Downtown Calgary

Eau Claire Market, Prince's Island, the Bow River and Kensington

At the north end of downtown and 3rd Street SW (six blocks north of the free C-Train), the wonderful **Eau Claire Market** (Mon–Wed & Sat 10am–6pm, Thurs & Fri 10am–8pm, Sun and holidays 11am–5pm – though shops and restaurants have varying hours; ⓦwww.eauclairemarket.com) is a bright and deliberately brash warehouse mix of food and craft market, cinemas (including a 300-seat IMAX large-screen complex), buskers, restaurants, walkways and panoramic terraces. All in all it brings some heart to the concrete and glass of downtown – the large communal eating area, in particular, is a good place to people-watch and pick up bargain takeaway Chinese, Japanese, wholefood and burger snacks. A footbridge on the market's northern side connects **Prince's Island**, a popular but peaceful retreat offering plenty of trees, flowers, an outstanding restaurant (the *River Café* – see p.673), a kids' playground and enough space to escape the incessant stream of joggers pounding the walkways. Swimmers might be tempted by the adjacent broad and fast-flowing **Bow River**, but it's for passive recreation only – the water is just two hours' drive from its icy source in the Rockies. The river is the focus for Calgary's civilized and excellent 210-kilometre system of recreational **walkways**, asphalt paths (also available to cyclists) that generally parallel the main waterways: maps are available from the visitor centre. Just east of the market and five blocks north of the C-Train at 197-1st St SW lies the **Calgary Chinese Cultural Centre** (daily: centre 9am–9pm, museum 11am–5pm; $2; ⓣ403-262-5071, ⓦwww.culturalcentre.ca), its big central dome modelled on the Temple of Heaven in Beijing and it claims to be one of the largest Chinese centres in Canada. It forms the focus for Calgary's modest Chinatown and large Chinese-Canadian population, most of whom are descendants of immigrants who came to work on the railways in the 1880s. It contains a small museum and gallery, and a gift shop and restaurant.

A twenty-minute jaunt along the walkway system from Prince's Island in the other direction from the market, **Kensington** is a gentrified café district on 10th Street NW and Kensington Road. Shops here sell healing crystals and advertise yoga and personal-growth seminars, though the older cafés, bookshops and wholefood stores are beginning to give way to trinket shops. As an eating area, though, Kensington has been superseded by the increasingly trendy section of 4th Street SW, beyond 17th Avenue.

Fort Calgary

Fort Calgary, the city's historical nexus, stands at 750-9th Ave SE (daily 9am–5pm; ⓣ403/290-1875, ⓦwww.fortcalgary.ab.ca; $10.50), a manageable eight-block walk east of downtown; you could also take bus #1 to Forest Lawn, bus #14 (East Calgary) from 7th Avenue, or the C-Train free to City Hall and walk the remaining five blocks. Built in under six weeks by the North West Mounted Police in 1875, the fort was the germ of the present city, and remained operative as a police post until 1914, when it was sold – inevitably – to the Canadian Pacific Railway. The whole area remained buried under railway tracks and derelict warehouses until 1974 when the city bought back the land and began to reclaim it. Period photographs in the adjoining interpretive centre provide a taste of how wild Calgary still was in 1876. Even more remarkable was the ground that men in the fort were expected to cover: the log stockade was a base for operations between Fort Macleod, 160km to the south, and the similar post at Edmonton, almost 400km to the north. It's not as if they had nothing to do: Crowfoot, most prominent of the great Blackfoot chiefs of the time, commented, "If the Police had not come to the country, where would we all be now? Bad men and whiskey were killing us so fast that very few of us indeed would have been left. The Police have protected us as the feathers of a bird protect it from the winter." Only a few forlorn stumps of the original building remain, much having been torn down by the developers, and what survives is its site, now a pleasant forty-acre park contained in the angled crook of the Bow and Elbow rivers. Moves have recently been made to begin construction of an exact replica of the original log stockade. The interpretive centre traces Calgary's development with the aid of artefacts, audiovisual displays and "interpretive walks" along the river. Among the more kitsch activities on offer is the opportunity to dress up as a Mountie.

Across the river to the east is **Hunt House**, built in 1876 for a Hudson's Bay official and believed to be Calgary's oldest building on its original site. Close by, at 750-9th Ave SE, on the same side of the Elbow River, is the renovated **Deane House Historic Site and Restaurant** (free tours Mon–Fri 11am–3pm, Sat & Sun 10am–3pm; ⓣ403/269-7747), built in 1906 by the Mountie Captain Superintendent Richard Deane. It subsequently served time as the home of an artists' co-operative, a boarding house and a stationmaster's house. Today it's a teahouse and restaurant.

St George's Island

St George's Island is home to Calgary's most popular attractions, the **Calgary Zoo, Botanical Gardens and Prehistoric Park**, all at 1300 Zoo Rd (daily 9am–6pm; last admission 5pm; $16; ⓣ403/232-9300 or 1-800/588-9993, ⓦwww.calgaryzoo.org). It can be reached from downtown and Fort Calgary by riverside path, by C-Train northeast towards Whitehorn, or by car (take Memorial Drive East to just west of Deerfoot Trail). Founded in 1920, this is now Canada's largest zoo (and one of North America's best), with 850,000 annual visitors and some 1200 animals, 400 species and innovative and exciting displays in which the animals are left as much as possible in their "natural" habitats. There are underwater viewing areas for polar bears and sea creatures, darkened rooms for nocturnal animals, a special Australian section, greenhouses for myriad tropical birds, and any number of pens for the big draws like gorillas, tigers, giraffes and African warthogs. Check out the extended North American and Canadian Wilds, Aspen Woodlands and Rocky Mountains sections for a taste of a variety of fauna. Also worth a look are the Tropical, Arid and Butterfly gardens in the conservatory. A fast-food concession and picnic areas can help you make a day of it. The **Botanical Gardens** are dotted throughout the zoo, while the **Prehistoric Park** annexe – a "re-created Mesozoic landscape" – is accessible by suspension bridge across the Bow River (June–Sept daily; free with general admission). Its nineteen life-size dinosaur models, none too convincing in their incongruous settings, are a poor substitute for the superb museum at Drumheller (see p.675), and only the fossils in two adjoining buildings are of more than fleeting interest.

Natural-history enthusiasts might also want to visit the **Inglewood Bird Sanctuary** (dawn–dusk; free), on the Bow River's forested flats at 9th Avenue and 20A Street SE, 3km downstream of the zoo and east of downtown. Some 230 species are present year-round – more during migratory cycles, around 266 species having been recorded across the sanctuary, a portion of land once owned by Colonel James Walker, one of Calgary's original North West Mounted Police. Some of the birds you might see include bald eagles, Swainson's hawks, ring-necked pheasants, warblers, grey partridges and great horned owls. Numerous duck, geese and other waterfowl are also present, and you may catch sight of muskrats, beavers, white-tailed and mule deer, foxes and long-tailed weasels. A visitor centre (May–Sept daily 9am–5pm) offers information, details of the year-round walking trails, and occasional natural history courses to guide nonexperts. To get here, follow 9th Avenue SE to Sanctuary Road and follow signs to the parking area on the river's south bank. On weekdays the #14 bus (East) turns off 9th Avenue at 17th Street SE, leaving you just a short walk from the Sanctuary.

Heritage Park Historical Village

A sixty-acre theme park centred on a reconstructed frontier village 16km southwest of downtown, **Heritage Park** (mid-May to Aug daily 9am–5pm; Sept to early Oct Sat & Sun 9am–5pm; $22.95 admission with rides, $13.95 without rides; free pancake breakfast with admission 9–10am; Ⓦwww.heritagepark.ca) replicates life in the Canadian West before 1914 and panders relentlessly to the myth of the "Wild West". Full of family-oriented presentations and original costumes, this "heritage" offering – the largest of its type in Canada – is thorough enough for you never to feel obliged to see another. The living, working museum comprises more than 150 **restored buildings**, all transported from other small-town locations. Each has been assigned to one of several communities – fur post, native village, homestead, farm and c.1900 – and most fulfil their original function. Thus you can see a working blacksmith, buy fresh bread, buy a local paper, go to church, even get married. Transport, too, is appropriate to the period, including steam trains, trams, horse-drawn bus and stagecoaches. If you're here for the day you can pick up cakes and snacks from the traditional *Alberta Bakery*, or sit down to a full meal in the old-style *Wainwright Hotel*. To get there by car, take either Elbow Drive or Macleod Trail south and turn right on Heritage Drive (the turn-off is marked by a huge, maroon steam engine); or you can take the C-Train to Heritage Station and then a free shuttle bus that operates during park hours.

Eating

Alberta claims, with some justification, to have some of the best **steaks** in the world; so Calgary's cuisine can be heavily meat-oriented. Given its immigration history, the city lacks the Ukrainian influences that often grace prairie cooking, preferring instead to follow the fusion and Pacific Rim trends popular in western Canada. Most bars and even the live-music venues double up as restaurants (see p.674) and invariably serve perfectly good, and often well-priced, food. The Toronto Dominion Square and Stephen Avenue malls, on 8th Avenue SW between 1st and 3rd, are riddled with ethnic **takeaways** and café-style restaurants – hugely popular and perfect for lunch or snacks on the hoof. The nicest thing to do is buy food and eat it either in the superb Eau Claire Market, which is packed with food stalls and restaurants, or amid the greenery of Devonian Gardens.

Cafés and restaurants

Bistro Jo Jo 917-17th Ave SW ⓣ403/245-2382. If you want to eat good French food, but balk at the typically high prices, try the exceptional cuisine in this marble-tiled and red-banquette-filled restaurant. Here you can choose between entrées like halibut in creamy white wine and lemon sauce with capers ($22) or duck with blackcurrant berries and Calvados ($25).

Caesar's Steakhouse 512-4th Ave SW ⓣ403/264-1222. Best place for a huge, perfect steak ($30–45) in the sort of wonderfully cheesy steakhouse – think dimly lit "Roman" decor – that's been around for decades. The rib-eye is considered by many to be the finest slab of meat in town. Closed Sun.

Chianti Café and Restaurant 1438-17th Ave SW ⓣ403/229-1600. A favourite local spot for years: dark, noisy, well priced and extremely popular (try to book ahead), with no-nonsense pasta basics and the odd fancy dish (mains $8–16). Patio for summer dining outdoors.

Divino's 1st St and 9th Ave SW. Café and wine bar opposite the *Palliser* hotel with rather faux mahogany-Tiffany chandelier interior, but good Italian food (entrées $8–21) and particularly noteworthy desserts.

Earl's 315-8 Ave SW ⓣ403/265-3275. Ever-reliable mid-range chain, serving North American food at average prices.

Galaxie Diner 1413-11th St SW ⓣ403/228-0001. Very popular place with authentic diner decor, great breakfasts and fine open grill served at moderate prices. Daily 8am–4pm.

Hy's 316-4th Ave SW ⓣ403/263-2222. This deep red-carpeted institution has been serving prime Albertan beef in vast quantities since 1955; charbroiled steaks are the house specialty. Fairly expensive, with steaks priced from around $30, and reservations recommended.

Joey Tomato's 208 Barclay Parade ⓣ403/263-6336. This inexpensive Mediterranean-style grill is part of a small chain, but no worse for that, and is a lively, informal place for a good meal among the plethora of choices in and around the Eau Claire market.

Nellie's Kitchen 738B-17 Ave SW. A laid-back, popular and informal café. Especially busy at breakfast – which they do superbly; try its notoriously good eggs Benedict ($8.25), two poached eggs on an English muffin with hollandaise sauce, hash browns and fruit. Daily 8am–3pm.

River Café Prince Island Park ⓣ403/261-7670, ⓦwww.river-cafe.com. With *Teatro* (see below), this is the best of Calgary's restaurants: innovative Canadian cuisine – including game, smoked fish, roasted beet and crab apple borscht and flatbreads – and an informal atmosphere on Prince's Island Park, across the bridge from the Eau Claire Market. Be sure to book ahead. Entrees average $20.

The Roasterie 314-10th St NW near Kensington Rd. Nice café and hangout attracting an artsy crowd – no meals, but newspapers, notice board and twenty kinds of coffee and snacks.

Silver Dragon 106-3rd Ave SE ⓣ403/264-5326. The first choice in town for a Chinese meal: this place has been around for over 30 years and uses a team of 15 Hong Kong-trained chefs to conjure up a menu of some 200 dishes. Dim sum is served from 9.30am–2.45pm, and involves no ordering, just picking hot, tasty tidbits off circulating carts and chasing them down with a bottomless pot of tea. Prices are moderate.

Teatro 200-8th Ave SE ⓣ403/290-1012, ⓦwww.teatro-rest.com. This is the place to come if you want to dress up a little and drop a little money: the fine Italian-influenced food (mains start at $20) is on a par with that of the less formal *River Café*. Booking is essential.

Drinking, nightlife and entertainment

Calgary is rarely a party town, except during Stampede and a brief fling in summer when the weather allows barbecues and nighttime streetlife. Nonetheless, its **bars, cafés and clubs** are all you'd expect of a city of this size, the vast majority of them found in five distinct areas: **Kensington**, with its varied cafés; "**Electric Avenue**", as 11th Avenue SW between 5th and 6th streets is called, which has lost most of its brash and mostly trashy bars, night-time action having moved more to **17th Avenue SW**, a more varied collection of pubs, bars, high-quality restaurants, speciality shops and ethnic eating, and **4th Street SW**, a similarly more refined restaurant area. **Downtown** cafés and pubs are fine during the day but fairly desolate in the evening. In the specialist clubs the quality of **live music** is good – especially in jazz, blues and the genre closest to cowtown Calgary's heart, country. Major **festivals** include an annual jazz festival (third week in June) and a folk festival at the end of July on Prince's Island.

Much of the city's highbrow cultural life focuses on the **Epcor Centre for the Performing Arts**, 205-8th Ave SE (ⓣ403/294-7455, ⓦwww.epcorcentre.org), a dazzling modern downtown complex with five performance spaces close to the Glenbow Museum, where six of the city's professional theatre companies perform along with the acclaimed Calgary Philharmonic Orchestra (ⓦwww.cpo-live.com) and often the excellent Alberta Ballet Company (ⓦwww.albertaballet.com). **Opera** is the preserve of Calgary Opera (ⓣ403/262-7286, ⓦwww.calgaryopera.com), whose home base is the Jubilee Auditorium at 1415-14th Ave NW (ⓦwww.jubileeauditorium.com). The season runs from October to April. For repertory, art-house, classic and foreign **films**, try the restored Uptown Stage & Screen, 612-8th Ave (Ⓣ403/265-0120, Ⓦwww.theuptown.com) or Plaza Theatre at 1113 Kensington Rd NW (Ⓣ403/283-3636, Ⓦwww.theplaza.ca). The **Museum of Movie Art** at the University of Calgary, 9-3600-21st St NE (Tues–Sat 9.30am–5.30pm), is home to some 4000 cinema posters, some dating back to 1920.

More modest, and often free, classical concerts and theatre performances pop up all over downtown in the summer – contact the visitor information centre for the schedules. Tickets for virtually all events are available through Ticketmaster Ⓣ403/777-0000, Ⓦwww.ticketmaster.ca) which has an office in the Epcor Centre for the Performing Arts. You'll find events listings in the *ffwd* (Ⓦwww.ffwdweekly.com) and Calgary's main dailies, the *Herald* and the *Sun*.

Bars

Barley Mill Eatery & Pub 201 Barclay Parade. Busy neighbourhood pub that looks and feels the part in Eau Claire Market with an outside patio and a 100-year-old bar imported from Scotland inside; 24 draught beers, 40 bottled brews and lots of whiskies.

Ceili's 513 8th Ave SW. Large and lively "Irish" pub, with fish 'n' chips, pies and stews on the menu and standing room only after work.

Ship and Anchor 17th Ave SW on the corner of 5th St. Long-established neighbourhood pub – friendly and laid-back but jumping, with darts, fine music and excellent pub food. A good place to start a big night out, or simply while away an evening.

Clubs and music venues

Cowboy's 826-5th St SW. Holds over 1000 people on two levels with nightly live entertainment; usually heaving thanks to promotions that involve 25¢ beers and the club's policy to pay for breast implants of female employees!

Crazy Horse 1311-1st St SW. Popular dance venue with live music on Thursday nights. Small dance floor.

Desperados 1088 Olympic Way. This huge sports and "cowboy" bar, a Calgary institution supposedly with room for 3500 people.

Kaos Jazz and Blues Bistro 718-17th Ave. Best location in the city for nightly jazz, with blues, acoustic and soul also on offer. Occasional afternoon performances, otherwise daily 6pm–2am.

The King Edward Hotel 438-9th Ave SE. Much-loved, down-at-heel location, with consistently good C&W and R&B bands. The Sat jam session – the blues event of the city – is invariably packed.

Piq Niq Café 811-1st St SW. This place isn't bad as a café, but it really comes into its own Thurs–Sat with good live jazz acts in the basement. Cover $10 average.

Ranchman's Steak House 9615 Macleod Trail South Ⓦwww.ranchmans.com. A classic honky-tonk and restaurant, 8km south of downtown, known throughout Canada for the live, happening C&W. Free dance lessons at 7pm Mon–Fri. Free admission before 8pm on Thurs. Closed Sun. Packed with cowboys during the Stampede.

Underground 731-10th Ave SW. Hardcore, punk and metal bar with live bands every Fri and Sat and the cheapest beer in the city: jugs for $5.25.

The Warehouse 731-10th Ave SW. Calgary's only truly late-night dance club, opens at 9pm and on weekend nights doesn't close until 7am. Drink specials help keep the party going. Located above *Underground*; the entrance is around the back.

Listings

Bookshops McNally Robinson Booksellers 120 8th Ave SW. For maps and travel books, check out Mountain Equipment Co-op.

Car rental Avis, 211-6th Ave SW Ⓣ403/269-6166; Budget, 140-6th Ave SE Ⓣ403/226-1550; Rent-A-Wreck Ⓣ403/287-9703, Ⓦwww.rentawreck.ca.

Hospital Foothills Hospital, 1403-29th Ave Ⓣ403/944-1110.

Library Central Library, 616 Macleod Trail SE (Mon–Thurs 10am–9pm, Fri–Sat 10am–5pm, Sun noon–5pm).

Outdoor gear Mountain Equipment Co-op, 830-10th Ave SW (Ⓣ403/269-2420) is Calgary's largest camping and outdoor store.

Pharmacy Chinook Mall Ⓣ403/253-2605 (24hr).

Police 316-7th Ave SE Ⓣ403/266-1234.

Post office 227-9th Ave SW Ⓣ403/974-2078.

Taxis Associated Cabs Ⓣ403/299-1111; Checker Ⓣ403/299-9999; Yellow Cab Ⓣ403/974-1111.

Weather Information Ⓣ403/299-7878; road conditions Ⓣ403/246/5853.

The Alberta Badlands

Formed by the meltwaters of the last Ice Age, the valley of the Red Deer River cuts a deep gash through the prairie about 140km east of Calgary, creating a surreal landscape of bare, sunbaked hills and eerie lunar flats dotted with sagebrush and scrubby, tufted grass. On their own, the **Alberta Badlands** – strangely anomalous in the midst of lush grasslands – would justify a visit, but what makes them an essential detour is the presence of the **Royal Tyrrell Museum of Paleontology**, one of North America's greatest natural history museums. It's located 8km outside the old coal-mining town of **Drumheller**, a dreary but obvious base if you're unable to fit the museum into a day-trip from Calgary. Drumheller is also the main focus of the **Dinosaur Trail**, a road loop that explores the Red Deer Valley and surrounding badlands; you'll need your own transport for this circuit, and for the trip to the **Dinosaur Provincial Park**, home to the Tyrrell Museum Field Station and the source of many of its fossils.

Drumheller

A downbeat town in an extraordinary setting, **DRUMHELLER** is roughly ninety minutes' drive northeast of Calgary. As you approach it from the west, the town is hidden until you come to a virulent-red water tower and the road suddenly drops into a dark, hidden canyon. The otherworldliness of the gloomy, blasted landscape is heightened by its contrast to the vivid colours of the earlier wheat and grasslands. Drumheller sits at the base of the canyon, surrounded by the detritus and spoil heaps of its mining past, the Red Deer River having exposed not only dinosaur fossils but also (now exhausted) coal seams. The coal attracted the likes of Samuel Drumheller, an early mining pioneer after whom the town is named. The first mine opened in 1911, production reaching a peak after the opening of a rail link to Calgary two years later. In less than fifty years it was all over, coal's declining importance in the face of gas and oil sounding the industry's death knell. These days Drumheller is sustained by agriculture, oil – there are some 3000 wells dotted around the

The Dinosaur Trail from Drumheller

The **Dinosaur Trail** is a catch-all circular road route of 51km from Drumheller embracing some of the viewpoints and lesser historic sights of the badlands and the Red Deer Valley area. The comprehensive *Drumheller Valley Visitor's Choice* (free from the Drumheller infocentre) lists thirty separate stopoffs, mostly on the plain above the valley, of which the key ones are: the **Little Church** (6km west of Drumheller), the "Biggest Little Church in the World" (capacity six); **Horsethief Canyon** (17.6km west of the museum) and **Horseshoe Canyon** (19km southwest of the museum on Hwy 9), two spectacular viewpoints of the wildly eroded valley, the latter with good trails to and along the canyon floor; the **Hoodoos**, slender columns of wind-sculpted sandstone, topped with mushroom-like caps (17km southeast of Drumheller on Hwy 10); the still largely undeveloped **Midland Provincial Park**, site of the area's first mines and crisscrossed by badland trails, now home to an interpretive centre (daily 9am–6pm; free; ⓣ403-823-1749); and the **Atlas Coal Mine** (guided tours May–June daily 9.30am–5.30pm, July–Aug daily 9.30am–8.30pm, Sept daily 10am–5pm; $6 for guided tour; ⓣ403/822-2220, ⓦwww.atlascoalmine.ab.ca), dominated by the teetering wooden "tipple", once used to sort ore and now a beautiful and rather wistful piece of industrial archeology.

surrounding farmland – and tourism, the Tyrrell Museum of Paleontology ranking as one of Alberta's biggest draws.

The town is best reached by taking Hwy 2 north towards Edmonton and branching east on Hwy 72 and Hwy 9 around 70km north of Calgary. It's an easy day-trip with your own transport, and most people make straight for the Tyrrell Museum, signposted from Drumheller on Hwy 838. Using one of the daily **Greyhound buses** from Calgary to Drumheller (around $62 return) makes a day-trip more of a squeeze: the bus arrives at 10am and leaves at 3pm. The depot at 308 Centre St (Ⓣ403/823-7566) is in the town centre but it's too far to walk from here to the museum, particularly on a hot day, but Jack's Taxi (Ⓣ403/823-2220) will run you there for about $10.

There's not much to do in the town, despite the best efforts of its **infocentre** at the corner of Riverside Drive and 2nd St West (daily 10am–6pm; Ⓣ403/823-1331). For all its half million visitors a year, Drumheller has just 350 or so beds; you don't really want to spend a night here. If you have no choice, try to book well in advance. The least expensive option is to camp at the *River Grove Campground and Cabins*, 25 Poplar St (Ⓣ403/823-6655) with it's well-shaded campsites (May–Sept; $20) and collection of basic cabins (❸) a short walk northwest of downtown. Another friendly no-frills option is the well-kept *Badlands Motel*, 801 Dinosaur Trail (Ⓣ403/823-5155; ❹) on the fringes of the town en-route to the Tyrell Museum. For a little more you can stay at southeast of town at the *Super 8 Motel*, 680 2nd St SE (Ⓣ403/823-8887 or 1-888/823-8882; ❺). The visitor centre has lists of the many other hotels and campsites up and down the valley (*Little Fish Lake Provincial Park*, 50km southeast of Drumheller on Hwy 573, in prairie landscape of rolling grassy hills a peaceful well-shaded place to camp). As good a place as any to start the day with a homemade breakfast is *Whif's Flapjack House* (Ⓣ403/823-7595), beside the *Badlands Motel*. Though there's always a reasonable choice, Drumheller's **restaurants** come and go with alarming regularity, one of the few places that's been around a while is the reasonably priced *Sizzling House*, 160 Centre St (Ⓣ403/823-8098), reckoned to be one of Alberta's best Chinese restaurants; which offers a good line in Thai dishes too.

Royal Tyrrell Museum

Packed with high-tech displays, housed in a sleek building and blended skilfully into its desolate surroundings, the **Royal Tyrrell Museum**, 6km outside Drumheller, (daily: late May to Aug 9am–9pm; Sept to early Oct 10am–5pm; early Oct to late May Tues–Sun 10am–5pm; $10; Ⓦwww.tyrrellmuseum.com) is an object lesson in museum design. It attracts half a million-plus visitors a year, and its wide-ranging exhibits are likely to appeal to anyone with even a hint of scientific or natural curiosity. Although it claims the world's largest collection of complete dinosaur skeletons (fifty full-size animals and 80,000 miscellaneous specimens), the museum is far more than a load of old bones, and as well as tracing the earth's history from the year dot to the present day it's also a leading centre of study and academic research. Its name comes from Joseph Tyrrell, who in 1884 discovered the Albertosaurus, first of the dinosaur remains to be pulled from the Albertan badlands.

Laid out on different levels to suggest layers of geological time, the open-plan exhibit guides you effortlessly through a chronological progression, culminating in a huge central hall of over two hundred dinosaur specimens. If there's a fault, it's that the hall is visible early on and tempts you to skip the lower-level displays, which place the dinosaurs in context by skilfully linking geology, fossils, plate tectonics, evolution and the like with Drumheller's own landscape. You also get a chance to peer into the preparation lab and watch scientists working on fossils in one of the world's best-equipped paleontology centres.

By far the most impressive exhibits are the **dinosaurs** themselves. Whole skeletons are immaculately displayed against three-dimensional backgrounds that persuasively depict the swamps of sixty million years ago. Some are paired with full-size plastic dinosaurs, which appear less macabre and menacing than the freestanding skeletons. Sheer size is not the only fascination: Xiphactinus, for example, a four-metre specimen, is striking more for its delicate and beautiful tracery of bones. Elsewhere the emphasis is on the creatures' diversity or on their staggeringly small brains, sometimes no larger than their eyes. The museum naturally also tackles the problem of the dinosaurs' extinction, pointing out that around ninety percent of all plant and animal species that have ever inhabited the earth have become extinct. Leave a few minutes for the wonderful **paleoconservatory** off the dinosaur hall, a collection of living prehistoric plants, some unchanged in 180 million years, selected from fossil records to give an idea of the vegetation that would have typified Alberta in the dinosaur age.

Dinosaur Provincial Park

Drivers can feasibly fit in a trip to **Dinosaur Provincial Park** (daily: mid-May to mid-Sept 9am–6pm; mid-Sept to mid-May 10am–5pm; free; ⓣ403/378-4342), 174km southeast of Drumheller, on the same day as the Tyrrell Museum, and still be able to head back to Calgary on the Trans-Canada Highway, which runs just south of the park. The nearest town is **BROOKS**, 48km west of the **Royal Tyrrell Museum Field Station** (mid-May to early Sept daily 8.30am–9pm; rest of year Mon–Fri 9am–4pm; $2.50; ⓣ403/378-4344), the park's obvious hub. The excellent Dinosaur Provincial Park **campsite** in the park beside Little Sandhill Creek is open year-round, but only serviced from May to September ($15) – book on ⓣ403/378-3700.

Nestled among some of the baddest of the badlands, the region's landscape is not only one of the most other-worldly in Canada, but also one of the world's richest fossil beds, a superb medley of prairie habitats and ecosystems and a UN World Heritage Site. Over 300 complete skeletons have been found and

△ Royal Tyrrell Museum

dispatched to museums across the world, representing 35 (or ten percent) of all known dinosaur species. The field station has five self-guided **trails**, the Badlands Trail and Cottonwood Flats Trail being the most worthwhile, and giving a good taste of this extraordinary region. The centre also has a small museum that goes over the same ground as its parent in Drumheller, leaving the real meat of the visit to the **Badlands Bus Tour**, an excellent ninety-minute guided tour of the otherwise out-of-bounds dinosaur dig near the centre of the park (late May to Oct Mon–Fri 3 or more tours daily; Sat & Sun 7 tours daily; $4.50). A few exposed skeletons have been left *in situ*, with panels giving background information. The station also organizes two-hour guided **hikes**, most notably the Centrosaurus Bone Bed Hike (Tues, Thurs, Sat & Sun 9.15am; $4.50), which visits a restricted area where some 300 centrosaurus skeletons have been uncovered. All tours fill up quickly, so it's worth trying to book ahead. **Reservations** for both hiking and bus tours are highly recommended, call ⓣ404/378-4342.

Highway 3: Medicine Hat to Crowsnest Pass

The most travelled route across southern Alberta is the Trans-Canada Highway, through Calgary; **Highway 3**, branching off at **Medicine Hat**, takes a more southerly course across the plains before finally breaching the Rockies at Crowsnest Pass. This quieter and less spectacular route into the mountains holds a couple of worthwhile diversions: the new **Carriage Centre** near Cardston and **Head-Smashed-In Buffalo Jump** heritage site.

Medicine Hat

Though **MEDICINE HAT** is barely a hundred years old, the origin of its wonderful name has already been confused. The most likely story has to do with a Cree medicine man who lost his headdress while fleeing a battle with the Blackfoot; his followers lost heart at the omen, surrendered, and were promptly massacred. These days you rarely see the town mentioned without the adage that it "has all hell for a basement", a quotation from Rudyard Kipling coined in response to the huge reserves of natural gas that lurk below the town. Discovered by railway engineers drilling for water in 1883, the gas fields now feed a flourishing petrochemical industry which blots the otherwise park-studded downtown area on the banks of the South Saskatchewan River. Medicine Hat may claim that its 1440 hours of summer sunshine make it Canada's sunniest city, but its main function is as a major staging post on the Trans-Canada Highway. The world's **tallest tepee** (twenty storeys tall and actually made of metal), on the hwy close to the visitor centre, and the excellent **Riverside Waterslide** at Hwy 1 and Powerhouse Rd (mid-May to early Sept daily 10am–8pm; $12.50; ⓣ403/529-6218) – where twelve slides beckon – are the only attractions of note.

Inexpensive motels are not hard to find around the fringes of town, but the main downtown accommodation is the *Medicine Hat Inn*, 530 4th St SE (ⓣ403/526-1313 or 1-800/730-3887; ❷) a clean but basic motel. Meanwhile, the best place around is the smart and comfortable *Medicine Hat Lodge*, 1051 Ross Glen Drive (ⓣ403/529-2222 or 1-800/661-8095, ⓦwww.medhatlodge.com; ❺), with it's own health centre, pool and gamut of other 4-star facilities.

The best place for coffee and snacks is *Café Mundo*, 579 3rd St SE; for lunch try *Caroline's*, 101 4th Ave SE (ⓣ403/529-5300); and for a novelty "Wild West" setting the place to go is the historic *Rustler's*, 901 8th St SW (☎403/526-8004), one of the town's oldest restaurants.

Lethbridge

Alberta's third city, **LETHBRIDGE** is booming on the back of oil, gas and some of the province's most productive agricultural land; none of which is of much consequence to people passing through, whom the city attempts to sidetrack with the **Nikka Yuko Centennial Gardens** (early May to June & Sept daily 9am–5pm; July & Aug daily 9am–8pm; $7; ☎403/328-3511, Ⓦwww.japanesegarden.ab.ca) in its southeastern corner at 7th Avenue and Mayor Macgrath Drive in Henderson Lake Park. Built in 1967 as a symbol of Japanese and Canadian amity, the gardens were a somewhat belated apology for the treatment of Japanese-Canadians during World War II, when 22,000 were interned, 6000 of them in Lethbridge. Four tranquil Japanese horticultural landscapes make up the gardens, along with a pavilion of cypress wood handcrafted in Japan perpetually laid out for a tea ceremony. Far removed from the gardens' decorum is **Fort Whoop-Up** (March–May & Sept–Nov Wed–Sun 1–4pm; June–Aug daily 9am–5pm, Sun noon–5pm; Dec–Feb Sat & Sun 1pm–4pm; $7; ☎403/329-0444, Ⓦwww.fortwhoopup.com) at Indian Battle Park (Scenic Drive at 3rd Ave), a reconstruction of the wild whiskey-trading post set up in 1869 by American desperadoes from Fort Benton, Montana (the first of several in the region). It became the largest and most lucrative of the many similar forts which sprang up illegally all over the Canadian prairies, and led directly to the arrival of the North West Mounted Police in 1874. Aboriginal peoples came from miles around to trade anything – including the clothes off their backs – for the lethal hooch, which was fortified by grain alcohol and supplemented by ingredients such as red peppers, dye and chewing tobacco. The fort was also the scene of the last armed battle in North America between aboriginal peoples (fought between the Cree and Blackfoot nations in 1870). Lethbridge's other significant sight is the **Sir Alexander Galt Museum** (daily 10am–4.30pm; donation suggested) at the western end of 5th Avenue South off Scenic Drive, one of Canada's better small-town museums. It's named after a Canadian high commissioner who in 1882 financed a mine that led to the foundation of Lethbridge. Revamped at vast expense in 1985, the museum offers an overview of the city's history, with displays that cover coal mining, irrigation, immigration and the shameful internment episodes during the 1940s. There are also a couple of galleries devoted to art and other temporary exhibitions.

Four Greyhound **buses** operate daily from Calgary; the Lethbridge bus terminal is at 411-5th St South (☎403/327-1551). Two buses run daily to Fort Macleod, and two to Medicine Hat and the US border for connections to Great Falls and Helena in Montana. The **tourist office** is at 2805 Scenic Drive at the corner of Hwy 4 and Hwy 5 (summer daily 9am–8pm; winter Mon–Sat 9am–5pm; ☎403/320-1222 or 1-800/661-1222). Most of the city's **motels** line Hwy 5, including the top-of-the-pile *Sandman Hotel Lethbridge* (☎403/328-1111 or 1-800/726-3626; ❹). Downtown the best value is the *Days Inn*, 100 3rd Ave South (☎403/327-6000 or 1-800/661-8085; ❸). The *Henderson Lake Campgrounds* (☎403/328-5452; $18; May–Oct) are near Henderson Lake on 7th Ave South alongside the Nikka Yuko gardens. The best downtown **eating** is to be found in the *Lethbridge Lodge Hotel*, 320 Scenic Dr (☎403/328-1123 or 1-800/661-1232), which boasts *Anton's*, an upmarket restaurant with modern American food, and the cheaper but pleasant and popular *Garden Café*. For downtown coffee and snacks, make for *The Penny Coffee House*, 331 5th St South.

Fort Macleod and around

FORT MACLEOD catches traffic coming north from the US and south from Calgary on Hwy 2, which eases around the town centre via the largely rebuilt wooden palisade of the **Fort Museum**, 219 25th St (early to mid-May, Sept & Oct Wed–Sun 10am–4pm; late May to June 9am–5pm July & Aug daily 9am–6pm; $7.50). One for die-hard Mountie fans, this was the first fort established in Canada's Wild West by the North West Mounted Police, who got lost after being dispatched to raid Fort Whoop-Up in Lethbridge, allowing the whiskey traders to flee; finding Whoop-Up empty, they continued west under Colonel James Macleod to establish a permanent barracks here on Oldman Island on the river in 1874. The RCMP "musical ride", a display of precision riding, is performed four times daily in July and August by students in replica dress. **Buses** serve the town from Lethbridge and from Calgary, the latter continuing west to Cranbrook, Nelson and eventually to Vancouver in British Columbia. The depot is at 2302 2nd Ave (Ⓣ403/553-3383). The town has several similarly priced **motels**, the most central being the *Fort Motel* on Main St (Ⓣ403/553-3606; ❷). Top choice is the *Sunset Motel* (Ⓣ403/553-4448; ❹), located on Hwy 3 at the western entrance to town. All fill up quickly in summer.

Head-Smashed-In Buffalo Jump

The image of Indians trailing a lone buffalo with bow and arrow may be Hollywood's idea of how aboriginal peoples secured their food, but the truth, while less romantic, was often far more effective and spectacular. Over a period of 10,000 years, Blackfoot hunters perfected a technique of luring buffalo herds into a shallow basin and stampeding them to their deaths over a broad cliff, where they were then butchered for meat (dried to make pemmican, a cake of pounded meat, berries and lard), bone (for tools) and hide (for clothes and shelter). Such "jumps" existed all over North America, but the **Head-Smashed-In Buffalo Jump**, in the Porcupine Hills 18km northwest of Fort Macleod on Hwy 785, is the best preserved (daily mid-May to early Sept 9am–6pm, mid-Sept to mid-May 10am–5pm; $9; Ⓣ403/553-2731, Ⓦwww.head-smashed-in.com). Its name is a literal description of how a nineteenth-century Blackfoot met his end after deciding the best spot to watch the jump was at the base of the cliff, apparently unaware he was about to be visited by some five hundred plummeting buffalo. The modern **interpretive centre**, a seven-storey architectural tour de force, is built into the ten-metre-high and 305-metre-wide cliff near the original jump. Below it, a ten-metre-deep bed of ash and bones accumulated over millennia is protected by the threat of a $50,000 fine for anyone foolish enough to rummage for souvenirs. All manner of artefacts and objects have been discovered amidst the debris, among them knives, scrapers and sharpened stones used to skin the bison. Metal arrowheads in the topmost layers, traded with white settlers, suggest the jump was used until the early nineteenth century. The multilevel facility delves deep into the history of the jump and native culture in general, its highlight being a film, *In Search of the Buffalo*, which attempts to re-create the thunderous death plunge using a herd of buffalo, which were slaughtered, frozen and then somehow made to look like live animals hurtling to their deaths (shown half-hourly on Level Four). Around the centre the jump is surrounded by a couple of kilometres of **trails**, the starting point for tours conducted by Blackfoot native guides. No public transport serves the site; taxis from Fort Macleod cost about $20.

Remington-Alberta Carriage Centre

The **Remington Carriage Centre**, 623 Main St (daily mid-May to early Sept 9am–6pm; rest of year 10am–5pm; $8; ⓦwww.remingtoncarriagemuseum.com), lies immediately south of **CARDSTON** (across the river from the town centre), just off Hwy 2 about 50km south of Fort Macleod. Although brilliantly executed, the museum's appeal is more limited, centring on horse-drawn vehicles and evoking the atmosphere of their nineteenth-century heyday. The main hall boasts around sixty working carriages – the core of a private collection begun by Don Remington in the 1950s – and around 140 in passive display, the exhibits cleverly integrated with 25 "stories" that place the carriages in their social and cultural context. Additionally there's the chance to ride the carriages (usually for free), see working stables and admire the magnificent Quarters and Clydesdales that make up the centre's horse herd. Guides are often in period dress, and you can watch craftspeople in the process of building and renovating various carriages. Free guided tours run regularly around the site.

Highway 3: Fort MacLeod to Crowsnest Pass

Crowsnest Pass (1382m) is the most southerly of the three major routes into the Rockies and British Columbia from Alberta, and far less attractive than the Calgary and Edmonton approaches. As Hwy 3 pushes west out of Fort Macleod across glorious windblown prairie, it augurs well: the settlements are bleaker and more backwoods in appearance, and the vast unbroken views to the mountain-filled horizon appear much as they must have to the first pioneers. As the road climbs towards the pass, however, the grime and dereliction of the area's mining heritage make themselves increasingly felt. Hopes a century ago that Crowsnest's vast coal deposits might make it the "Pittsburgh of Canada" were dashed by disasters, poor-quality coal, complicated seams, cheaper coal from British Columbia and rapid obsolescence. Today much of the area has been declared an Historic District and turned into Alberta's only "ecomuseum", a desperate attempt to bring life and tourist cash back to economically blighted communities (many people commute to work in British Columbia's mines over the Pass or have left altogether). To a limited extent they've succeeded. If mines and disaster sites don't appeal, the Crowsnest route west is of most use as a direct route if you're hurrying to Vancouver or aim to explore the Kootenays in southern British Columbia. After breasting the pass, Hwy 3 drops into BC passing through Fernie (see p.985) and following the often spectacular Elk River Valley to join Hwy 95 at Cranbrook (see p.984).

Bellevue and the Frank Slide

Sleepy **BELLEVUE** is the first village west of Fort Macleod worthy of a stop; an oddball and close-knit spot with an old-world feel unusual in these parts. It's distinguished by a church the size of a dog kennel and a wooden tepee painted lemon yellow. Nonetheless, it supports a small summer-only **infocentre** by the campsite and provides visitors with the opportunity to explore – complete with hard hat and miner's lamp – a wonderfully dark and dank 100m or so of the old **Bellevue Mine** (30min tours every half-hour mid-May to early Sept daily 10am–5.30pm; $7). The only mine open to the public locally, it ceased production in 1962, but remains infamous for an explosion in 1910 that destroyed the ventilator fan. Thirty men died in the disaster, though not from the blast, but by breathing so-called "afterdamp", a lethal mixture of carbon dioxide and carbon monoxide left after fire has burnt oxygen from the atmosphere. As if this wasn't enough, Canada's worst mining disaster ever had occurred five years earlier at **HILLCREST**, a village immediately south of Bellevue (signed from Hwy 3), when 189 men were killed by an explosion and the effects of "afterdamp". All were buried together a few centimetres apart in mass graves, now the Hillcrest Cemetery on 8th Avenue.

Bellevue has a quaint **campsite**, the *Bellecrest Community Association Campground* (Ⓣ403/564-4696; donation suggested), located off the hwy just east of the village: it's open May to October and has toilets, tap water and an on-site ten-seat church with recorded sermons. The site is also handy for the **Leitch Collieries Provincial Historic Site** (mid-May to mid-Sept daily 10am–4pm; winter site unstaffed; $2), just off the main road to the north before the campsite. This was once the region's largest mining and coking concern; it was also the first to close (in 1915). Today there's little to see in the way of old buildings, but displays and boardwalk interpretive trails past "listening posts" fill you in on mining techniques. The overgrown site is also enthusiastically described by interpretive staff.

The Crowsnest Pass trail of destruction, death and disaster continues beyond Bellevue. Dominating the skyline behind the village are the crags and vast rock fall of the **Frank Slide**, an enormous landslide that has altered the contours of Turtle Mountain, once riddled with the galleries of local mines. On April 29, 1903 an estimated 100 million tonnes of rock on a front stretching for over 1km and 700m high trundled down the mountain, burying 68 people and their houses in less than two minutes. Amazingly none of the miners working locally were killed – they dug themselves out after fourteen hours of toil. The morbidly interesting **Frank Slide Interpretive Centre** (daily mid-May to mid-Sept 9am–6pm; rest of year 10am–5pm; Ⓦwww.frankslide.com; $9), situated 1.5km off the hwy about 1km north of the village, highlights European settlement in the area, the coming of the Canadian Pacific Railway to Alberta and the technology, attitudes and lives of local miners. It's well worth wandering around the site and slide area – there's a 1.5-kilometre trail or you can walk up the ridge above the car park for good views and an idea of the vast scale of the earth movement: no one to this day quite understands the science of how boulders travelled so far from the main slide (several kilometres in many cases). "Air lubrication" is the best theory, a device by which the cascading rock compressed the air in front of it, creating a hovercraft-like cushion of trapped air on which it "rode" across the surface.

Blairmore and Crowsnest Pass

BLAIRMORE, 2km beyond the slide, is a scrappy settlement redeemed for the casual visitor only by the walks and dozen ski runs on Pass Powder Keg Ski Hill (day pass $20, ski rentals from $17; Ⓣ403/562-8334, Ⓦwww.passpowderkeg.ca) above it. Beyond Blairmore the road climbs towards **Crowsnest Pass** itself and, after a rash of sawmills, the natural scenery finally takes centre stage in a reassuring mix of lakes, mountains and trees protected by **Crowsnest Provincial Park**. A rustic provincial **campground** ($8) overlooks the lake at Crowsnest Creek, about 21km west of Blairmore,

The Canadian Rockies

Rising with overwhelming majesty from **Alberta's** rippling plains, the **Canadian Rockies** are one of the main reasons people come to Canada. Their beauty is legendary and few North American landscapes come this loaded with expectation. So, it's a relief to find that superlatives are scarcely able to do credit to the splendour or immensity of the forests, lakes, rivers and snowcapped mountains here.

Joined with their smaller cousins in the US, the Canadian Rockies extend north of the US border almost 1500km to Canada's far north where they merge with ranges in the Yukon and Alaska, forming the Continental Divide in the process – a vast watershed which separates rivers flowing to the Pacific and Arctic oceans from those flowing into the Atlantic. But the range is best known for its virtually unbroken north-south chain of national and provincial parks and glut of world-class ski resorts at its heart (see p.684).

At the southern end of the range and coupled with Glacier National Park in the US is small but impressive **Waterton Lakes National Park**. North of here lie a series of less-restrictively managed provincial parks, collectively known as **Kananasksis Country**. These exist partly to take the pressure off the adjacent **Banff National Park**, the region's best known and most touristy park. Beyond its northern boundary the range is protected by the much less busy **Jasper National Park,** by far the largest park in the region. The western boundary of both Banff and Jasper parks is also the provincial border, so that adjacent lands are protected in a separate set of parks managed by British Columbia: **Mount Robson Provincial Park**, just west of Jasper – which protects Mount Robson, the highest and most dramatic peak in the Canadian Rockies – and **Yoho** and **Kootenay** west of Banff. Two smaller parks, **Glacier** and **Mount Revelstoke**, lie separate and firmly in BC.

There's not a great deal to choose between the parks in terms of scenery – they're all sensational – and planning an itinerary that allows you to fit them all in neatly is just about impossible. It is also rather unnecessary, since to really experience the Rockies you're best off homing in on just one or two parks and then heading into the backcountry. But if you're here to see as much of the highlights as possible, it's best to start with Banff National Park, then head north along the otherworldly Icefields Parkway to Jasper and Mount Robson before doubling back – no hardship, given the scenery – to the Lake Louise and Banff area. Then, if you've time to spare, it's easy to head out to Yoho, Kootenay or Kananaskis or pick up the Trans-Canada Hwy – a particularly enticing option if you're travelling to or from Vancouver – west to the smaller Glacier and Revelstoke national parks. Similarly, a visit to Waterton Lakes is most tempting if you are on your way to or from the US.

Though you can get to all the parks by **bus**, travelling by **car** is the obvious way to get the most out of the region. Once there, you'd be foolish not to tackle some of the 3000km of hiking and biking trails that crisscross the mountains, the vast majority of which are well worn and well signed. We've highlighted the best short walks and day-hikes in each area, and you can get more details from the excellent **park visitor centres**, which sell 1:50,000 topographical maps and usually offer small reference libraries of trail books; *The Canadian Rockies Trail Guide*, by Brian Patton and Bart Robinson, is invaluable for serious hiking or backpacking. Other activities – fishing, skiing, canoeing, whitewater rafting, cycling, horse riding, rock climbing and so on – are comprehensively dealt with in visitor centres, and you can easily **rent equipment** or sign up for organized tours in the bigger towns.

A word of warning: don't underestimate the Rockies. Despite the impression created by the summer throngs in centres like Banff and Lake Louise, excellent roads and sleek park facilities, the vast proportion of parkland is wilderness and should be respected and treated as such. See Basics, pp.52–55, for more.

National Park passes

In common with most other Canadian National Parks, anyone entering any of the Rockies parks must buy a permit ($9 per day, or $62 for an annual pass – see Basics p.52), most conveniently available at the road entrances to all parks and park information centres. Park infocentres are also the place to pick up the separate **Backcountry Wilderness Pass** ($9 per person per night, or $62 for an annual pass; plus $12 reservation fee), required for overnight backcountry use. Note that all backcountry areas in all parks have a quota and that it's vital to make bookings well in advance (up to three months) if you wish to walk – and camp on – some of the most popular trails requiring overnight stops. Reservations can made by phone via park information offices.

Wintersports in the Rockies

With terrific terrain, reliable snow cover, uncrowded slopes and relatively low prices the Rockies are phenomenally tempting for a **ski or snowboard** vacation. The area is also ideal for a host of other **winter sports** like cross-country skiing, snowshoeing, dog sledding and snowmobiling (though the latter is not allowed in national parks). Opportunities for ice climbing, skating, canyon crawling and ice fishing are also plentiful. The season at most resorts runs from mid-December until the end of May, with the best conditions usually in March, when the days are getting warmer and longer, the snow is deepest and resort accommodation – hard to come by during Christmas week, the mid-February school holidays and at Easter – easier to find.

Best known and invariably the busiest and most expensive resorts are those in **Banff National Park**. All within easy reach of the town of Banff, the best hub, these include the small, steep and taxing **Mount Norquay**; the well-rounded intermediate-friendly **Sunshine Village**; and the vast, varied and hugely challenging **Lake Louise**. The three promote themselves with a common lift-ticket system. Locals make up a sizeable chunk of the business: weekends and holidays are peak times, leaving working weekdays particularly quiet. Smaller-scale alternatives within striking distance of Banff are in Kananaskis Country. Here **Nakiska** is one of the most user-friendly resorts on the continent, with state-of-the-art facilities and plenty of fine cross-country skiing. **Fortress Mountain**, 15km south, is a much smaller area, where you're likely to share the slopes with school groups and families. A glorious three-hour drive north of Banff into **Jasper National Park** through craggy montane scenery along the Icefields Parkway lies **Marmot Basin**. A far more modest affair than the ski areas surrounding Banff, it nevertheless has the advantage of being both quieter and less expensive. The town of Jasper, centre of the skiing area, is less commercial than Banff, and its surroundings remain more conspicuously wild, with almost limitless cross-country skiing possibilities.

Aside from these big names the region also contains many other equally worthy, though less accessible resorts, further west in the British Columbia Rockies. Blessed with much the same light snow that's made the whole region famous – with the added advantage of much milder temperatures – this area has the extra benefit of being located outside strictly regulated national park lands. The result has been not only the emergence of the world's highest concentration of heli-skiing operations, but also both heavy investment in the industry and an ongoing programme of rapid expansion at resorts here. The newest and closest to Banff is **Kicking Horse**. Though still in its early stages of growth, given the fabulous quality of its expert terrain, it is tipped by many to steal much of Banff's business. South along the western fringe of the Rockies, **Panorama** is a fantastic mountain for cruising and carving, with a superlative setting for its quiet resort village. Another couple of hours' drive south is the cheerful family-orientated ski hill **Kimberley**, where the quantity of spacious ideal beginner and intermediate terrain almost distracts from the presence of a few incredible bump runs. Multi-day tickets here are interchangeable with those at **Fernie**, with its bountiful mountain bowls and ridges, becoming Banff's greatest regional competitor for the international ski trade. With all four resorts

The creation of the Canadian Rockies

About 600 million years ago the vast granite mountains of the Canadian Shield covered North America from Greenland to Guatemala (today the Shield's eroded remnants are restricted largely to northeast Canada). For the next 400 million years, eroded debris from the Shield – mud, sand and gravel – was washed westward by streams and rivers and deposited on the offshore "continental slope" (westward because the Shield had a very slight tilt). Heavier elements such as gravel accumulated close to the shore; lighter deposits like sand and mud were swept out to sea or left in lagoons. The enormous weight and pressure of the sediment, which built up to a depth of 20km, converted mud to shale, sand to sandstone and the natural debris of the reefs and sea bed – rich in lime-producing algae – into limestone. Two further stages were necessary before these deposits – now the strata so familiar in the profile of the Rockies – could be lifted from the sea bed and left several thousand metres above sea level to produce the mountains we see today.

The mountain-building stage of the **Rockies** took just 100 million years, with the collision of the North American and Pacific continental plates (gigantic 50-kilometre-thick floating platforms of the earth's crust). About 200 million years ago, two separate strings of volcanic Pacific islands, each half the size of British Columbia, began to move eastward on the Pacific Plate towards the North American coast. When the first string arrived off the coast, the heavier Pacific Plate slid beneath the edge of the North American Plate and into the earth's molten interior. The lighter, more buoyant rock of the islands stayed "afloat", detaching itself from the plate before crashing into the continent with spectacular effect. The thick, orderly deposits on the continental slope were crumpled and uplifted, their layers breaking up and riding over each other to produce the coast's present-day interior and Columbia Mountains. Over the next 75 million years, the aftershock of the collision moved inland, bulldozing the ancient sedimentary layers still further to create the Rockies' Western Main Ranges (roughly the mountain edge of Yoho and Kootenay national parks), and then moving further east, where some 4km of uplift created the Eastern Main Ranges (the mountains roughly on a line with Lake Louise). Finally the detached islands "bonded" and mingled with the new mainland mountains (their "exotic" rocks can be found in geological tangles as far east as Salmon Arm in BC).

Behind the first string of islands the second archipelago had also now crashed into the continent, striking the debris of the earlier collision. The result was geological chaos, with more folding, rupturing and uplifting of the earlier ranges. About 60 million years ago, the aftershock from this encounter created the Rockies' easternmost Front Ranges (the distinct line of mountains that rears up so dramatically from the prairies), together with the foothills that spill around Kananaskis and Waterton lakes. The third stage of the Rockies' formation – erosion and glaciation – was relatively short-lived, at least three Ice Ages over the last 240,000 years turning the mountains into a region resembling present-day Antarctica. While only mountain summits peeked out from ice many kilometres thick, however, glaciers and the like were applying the final touches, carving sharp profiles and dumping further debris.

no more than a couple of hours' drive from their nearest neighbour, they make for an ideal multi-resort trip tackled as a loop from Calgary; a loop which can, of course include Banff.

Waterton Lakes National Park

Located in an isolated position well to the south of the other Canadian Rockies parks, **WATERTON LAKES NATIONAL PARK** appears at first glance to be simply an addendum to the much larger Glacier National Park, which joins it across the US border. Despite its modest size, however, it contains scenery – and trails – as stupendous as any of the bigger Canadian Rockies parks. In particular this is a great place to come for day-hikes, most of which – unlike equivalent walks in Banff and Jasper – can be easily accessed from the park's principal focus, **Waterton Village** (or just Waterton).

Founded in 1895, the park was relaunched in 1932 as an "International Peace Park" to symbolize the understated relationship between Canada and its neighbour. The two parks remain separate, but Canadian and US citizens who are backpacking can cross the border without formalities. However, if you're not a national of either country you're limited to using trails that begin and end in the same park unless you have secured visas in advance. To drive from one to the other, everyone has to exit the park and pass through immigration controls, which are as stringent as anywhere else. A **park permit** is required between April and the end of September for all who enter the park: a day-pass is $6.90 (yearly $34.65) – see p.52 for more details concerning Canadian park entry fees.

A history of the park

These days Waterton is on the road pretty much to nowhere. It was a different story in the past, for the region provided a happy hunting ground for **Ktunaxa** (Kootenay) First Peoples, whose home base was across the Continental Divide in the Kootenay region of present-day British Columbia. Around 200 archeological sites betraying their presence have been found in the park. Up to 9000 years ago aboriginal peoples crossed the mountains to fish and hunt bison on the prairie grasslands fringing the Waterton region, foodstuffs denied to them in their own aboriginal heartlands. By about 1700 the diffusion of the horse across North America (introduced by the Spanish) allowed rival peoples, namely the Blackfoot, to extend their sphere of influence from central Alberta into the area around Waterton. Their presence and increased mobility made it increasingly difficult for the Ktunaxa to make their habitual incursions, though Blackfoot supremacy in turn was to be cut short by the arrival of pioneer guns and white homesteads. By the mid-nineteenth century the Blackfoot had retreated eastwards, leaving the Waterton area virtually uninhabited. The region was named by Lieutenant Thomas Blakiston, a member of the famous Palliser expedition, in honour of the eighteenth-century British naturalist Charles Waterton.

The area's first permanent white resident, **John George Brown** – or "Kootenai Brown" – was a character straight out of a Wild West fantasy. Born in England and allegedly educated at Oxford, he spent time with the British Army in India, decamped to San Francisco, chanced his arm in the gold fields of British Columbia and worked for a time as a pony express rider with the US Army. While moving to the Waterton region he was attacked by Blackfoot

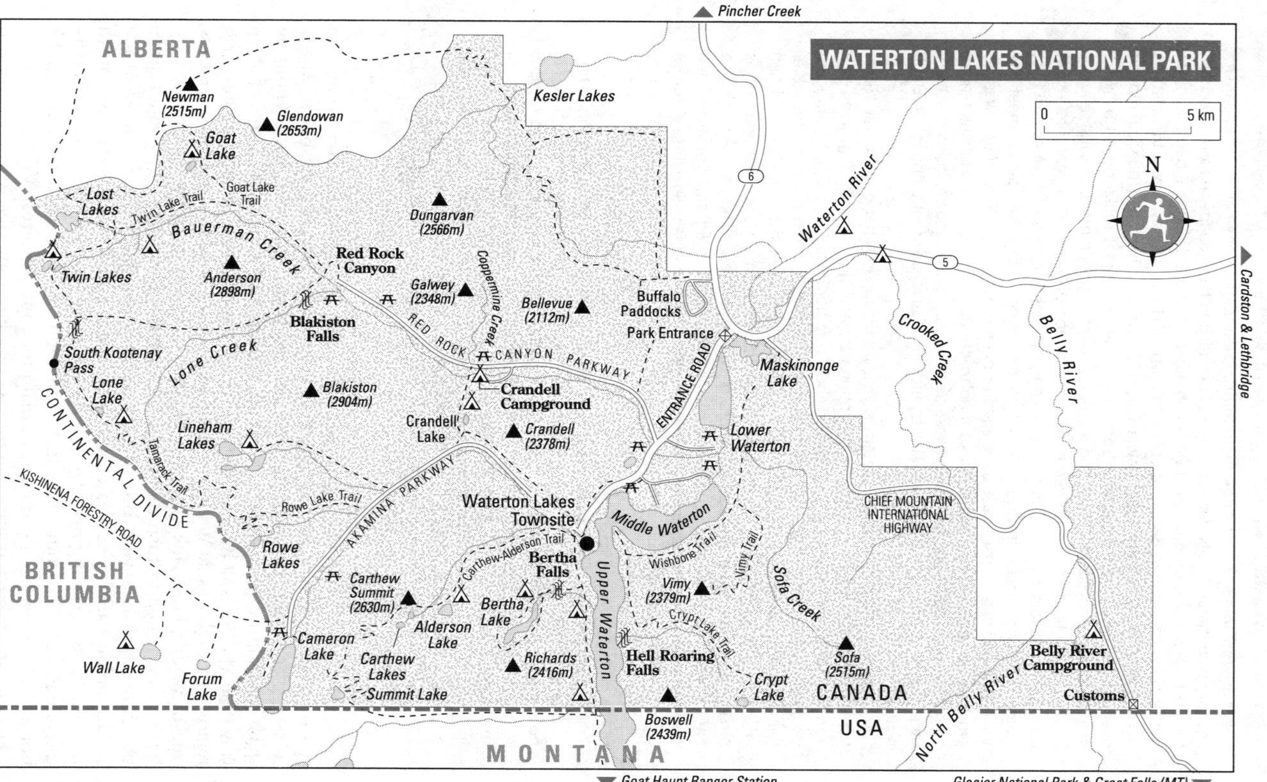
WATERTON LAKES NATIONAL PARK
0
5 km
N
Pincher Creek
Cardston & Lethbridge
Goat Haunt Ranger Station
Glacier National Park & Great Falls (MT)
ALBERTA
BRITISH COLUMBIA
MONTANA
CANADA
USA
CONTINENTAL DIVIDE
KISHINENA FORESTRY ROAD
Newman (2515m)
Glendowan (2653m)
Goat Lake
Goat Lake Trail
Lost Lakes
Twin Lake Trail
Twin Lakes
Bauerman Creek
Anderson (2898m)
Dungarvan (2566m)
Kesler Lakes
Red Rock Canyon
Galwey (2348m)
Coppermine Creek
Bellevue (2112m)
Buffalo Paddocks
Park Entrance
Blakiston Falls
RED ROCK CANYON PARKWAY
South Kootenay Pass
Lone Creek
Lone Lake
Blakiston (2904m)
Crandell Campground
Crandell Lake
Crandell (2378m)
Lineham Lakes
Tamarack Trail
Rowe Lake Trail
Rowe Lakes
AKAMINA PARKWAY
ENTRANCE ROAD
Maskinonge Lake
Lower Waterton
Middle Waterton
Waterton Lakes Townsite
Carthew-Alderson Trail
Bertha Falls
Bertha Lake
Upper Waterton
Wishbone Trail
Vimy Trail
Vimy (2379m)
Crypt Lake Trail
Hell Roaring Falls
Crypt Lake
Carthew Summit (2630m)
Alderson Lake
Cameron Lake
Carthew Lakes
Summit Lake
Richards (2416m)
Boswell (2439m)
Wall Lake
Forum Lake
Waterton River
Crooked Creek
Belly River
6
5
CHIEF MOUNTAIN INTERNATIONAL HIGHWAY
Sofa Creek
Sofa (2515m)
Belly River Campground
North Belly River
Customs

The natural environment of Waterton Lakes National Park

The Waterton area's unique **geological history** becomes clear when you compare its scenery with the strikingly different landscapes of Banff and Jasper national parks to the north. Rock and mountains in Waterton moved eastward during the formation of the Rockies (see box, p.685), but unlike the ruptured strata elsewhere it travelled as a single vast mass known as the Lewis Thrust. Some 6km thick, this monolith moved over 70km along a 300-kilometre front, the result being that rocks over 1.5 billion years old from the Rockies' "sedimentary basement" – now the oldest surface rocks in the range – finally came to rest undisturbed on *top* of the prairies' far more recent 60-million-year-old shales. Scarcely any zone of transition exists between the two, which is why the park is often known as the place where the "peaks meet the prairies", and its landscapes as "upside-down mountains". The effect was to produce not only slightly lower peaks than to the north, but also mountains whose summits are irregular in shape and whose sedimentary formations are horizontal (very different from the steeply tilted strata and distinctive sawtooth ridges of Banff National Park).

The classic glacial U-shaped Waterton Valley and Upper Waterton Lake (at 150m, the Rockies' deepest lake) are more recent phenomena, gouged out 1.9 million years ago by Ice Age **glaciers** as they carved their way northwards through the present Waterton valley before expiring on the prairies. Upper Waterton Lake and the other two Waterton lakes are residual depressions left after the ice's final retreat 11,000 years ago. Cameron Lake, by contrast, was created when a glacial moraine (debris created by a glacier) dammed the waters of Cameron Creek. The flat townsite area has different origins again, consisting of deposits of silt, mud and gravel washed down from the mountains over the millennia and deposited as an alluvial "fan" across Upper Waterton Lake.

Flora and fauna

The huge variety of altitude, habitats and climate within the park – a combination of prairie, montane and alpine – mean that plants and wildlife from prairie habitats co-mingle with the species of the purely montane, subalpine and alpine regions found elsewhere. The result is the greatest diversity of **flora and fauna** of any of the western national parks: 1200 plant species – well over half of all those grown in Alberta – and 250 species of birds. The variety is immediately noticeable. As you approach the park on Hwy 5 from the north, a route almost as scenic as the park, you pass through dry prairie **grassland**. This is home to native grasses such as

natives, supposedly wrenching an arrow from his back with his own hands. He was then captured by Chief Sitting Bull and tied naked to a stake, but managed to escape at the dead of night to join the rival Ktunaxa natives, with whom he spent years hunting and trapping, until their virtual retreat from the prairies. Marriage in 1869 calmed him down, and encouraged him to build a cabin (the region's first) alongside Waterton Lake. In time he was joined by other settlers, one of whom, Frederick Godsal, a rancher and close personal friend, took up Brown's campaign to turn the region into a **federal reserve**. In 1895 a reserve was duly established, with Brown as its first warden. In 1910 the area was made a "Dominion Park"; a year later it was designated a **national park**, the fourth in Canada's burgeoning park system. Brown, then aged 71, was made its superintendent, but died four years later, still lobbying hard to extend the park's borders. His grave lies alongside the main road into Waterton Village.

For all Brown's environmental zeal it was he, ironically, who first noticed globules of **oil** on Cameron Creek, a local river, a discovery that would bring

grama and rough fescue, local species now rapidly disappearing, displaced over the years by cultivated crops. Here, too, you should see the prickly wild rose (Alberta's floral emblem), sagebrush, buckbrush (yellow rose) and pincushion cactus. Entering the park you pass the **wetlands** of Maskinonge Lake on your left, while in the Blakison Valley and around *Belly River Campsite* you are in the realms of **aspen parkland**, a transitional zone between prairie and forest habitats dominated by aspen, willow, white spruce, balsam poplar and flowers such as prairie crocus, snowberry and lily of the valley. Higher up you encounter **montane forest** and subalpine zones, fecund zones rich in plant and animal life easily explored on hikes such as the Bertha Lake and Carthew Lakes trails (see p.692). On the eastern slopes above Cameron Lake are copses of 400-year-old subalpine trees (lodgepole pine, larch, fir, whitebark pine and Engelmann spruce), the oldest forest growth in the park. Here, too, you'll see vast spreads of so-called bear grass, a bright flower-topped grass which can grow up to a metre in height. Trees largely give out in the **alpine zone**, an area of which the park's Crypt Lake is a good example. It is the preserve of heathers, hardy lichens, flower-strewn meadows and rarer high-altitude alpine plants. See Contexts p.1098 for more on these various habitats.

If you want to see **fauna**, inquire at the park centre for likely locations and times – autumn days at dawn and dusk are usually best. **Birds** are best seen on Maskinonge and Lower Waterton lakes, Linnet Lake, Cameron Lake and along the easy 45-minute Wishbone Trail off Chief Mountain Highway. The best time to look is during the migratory season between September and November, as the park lies under two major migration routes. Ospreys also nest close to Waterton Village. Maskinonge Lake is the place to sit in the hope of seeing mink and muskrats. As for **mammals**, beavers can be seen on the Belly River, and golden-mantled ground squirrels around Cameron Lake and on the Bear's Hump above town; Columbian ground squirrels are ubiquitous. The park has about fifty black bears, but you'll be lucky to see them: your best bet is to scan the slopes of Blakison Valley in July and August as they forage for berries in readiness for hibernation. Grizzlies, moose and cougars are also prevalent, but rarely seen. White-tailed deer nibble up and down the Red Rock Canyon Parkway, while elk and mule deer often wander in and around Waterton town itself. Mountain goats are shy and elusive, but you may glimpse one or two in the rocky high ground above Bertha, Crypt and Goat lakes. Bighorn sheep congregate above the Visitor Centre and the northern flanks of the Blakison Valley.

oil and other mineral entrepreneurs to ravage the region. Brown himself actually skimmed oil from the river, bottled it, and sold it in nearby settlements. In 1901 a forest road was ploughed into Cameron Creek Valley. In September of the same year the Rocky Mountain Development Company struck oil, leading to western Canada's first commercial oil well. The oil soon dried up, a monument on the Akamina Parkway (see p.690) now marking the well's original location. Tourists meanwhile were giving the park a conspicuously wide berth, thanks mainly to the fact that it had no railway (unlike Banff and Jasper), a situation that changed in the 1920s when the Great Northern Railway introduced a bus link here from its Montana to Jasper railway. Visitors began to arrive, the *Prince of Wales* hotel was built, and the park's future was assured. In 1995, some time after the other big parks, UNESCO declared Waterton a World Heritage Site. Today, the park is becoming ever more popular, with souvenir shops lining Waterton Avenue, Waterton Village's main street, much as they do in Banff.

Waterton Village

WATERTON VILLAGE, the park's only base, accommodation source and services centre, is beautifully set on Upper Waterton Lake, but offers little by way of cultural distraction. Most people are here to walk (see box, p.692), windsurf, horse ride or take boat trips on the lake (see p.694). There are also a handful of town trails, and a trio of great hikes – Bertha Lake, Crypt Lake and the Upper Waterton Lakeshore – which start from the village (see box, p.692). Having long been a poor relation to the "big four" national parks in the Rockies, Waterton is now so popular that it's essential to book accommodation well in advance for much of July and August.

Two wonderfully scenic access roads from Waterton probe west into the park interior and provide picnic spots, viewpoints and the starting point for most other trails: the **Akamina Parkway** follows the Cameron Creek valley for 20km to Cameron Lake, a large subalpine lake where you can follow easy trails or rent canoes, rowing boats and paddleboats. The **Red Rock Canyon Parkway** weaves up Blakiston Creek for about 15km to the mouth of the

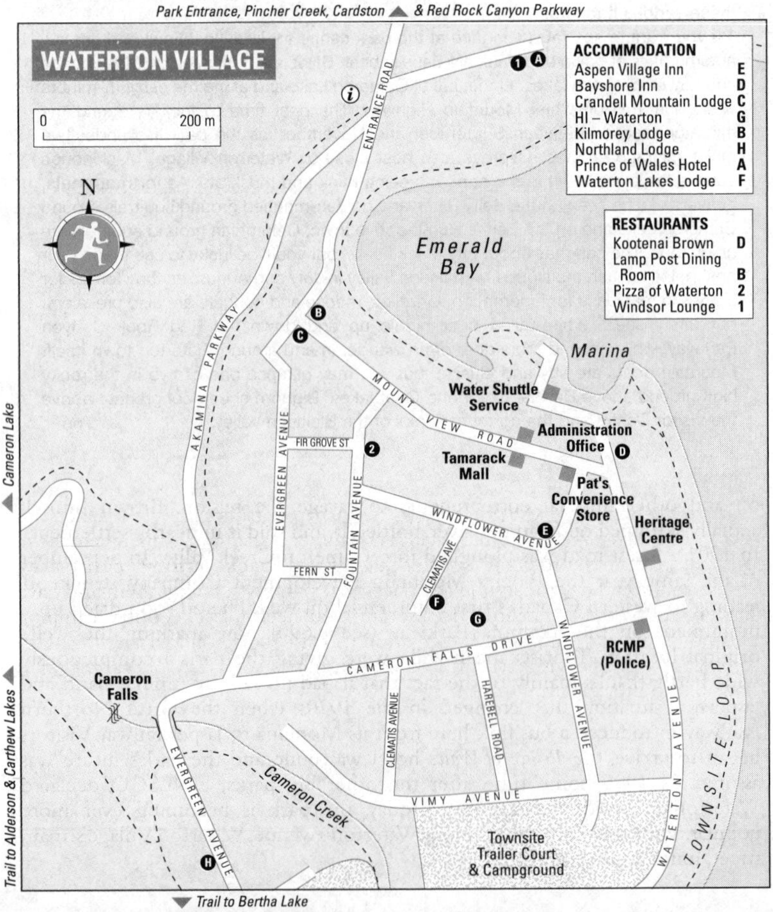

Park Entrance, Pincher Creek, Cardston ▲ & Red Rock Canyon Parkway

WATERTON VILLAGE

0 200 m

N

ACCOMMODATION	
Aspen Village Inn	E
Bayshore Inn	D
Crandell Mountain Lodge	C
HI – Waterton	G
Kilmorey Lodge	B
Northland Lodge	H
Prince of Wales Hotel	A
Waterton Lakes Lodge	F

RESTAURANTS	
Kootenai Brown	D
Lamp Post Dining Room	B
Pizza of Waterton	2
Windsor Lounge	1

Entrance Road
Emerald Bay
Marina
Water Shuttle Service
Administration Office
Tamarack Mall
Pat's Convenience Store
Heritage Centre
RCMP (Police)
Akamina Parkway
Mount View Road
Fir Grove St
Evergreen Avenue
Fountain Avenue
Windflower Avenue
Clematis Ave
Fern St
Cameron Falls Drive
Cameron Falls
Clematis Avenue
Harebell Road
Waterton Avenue
Townsite Loop
Vimy Avenue
Cameron Creek
Townsite Trailer Court & Campground
◀ Cameron Lake
◀ Trail to Alderson & Carthew Lakes
▼ Trail to Bertha Lake

water-gouged Red Rock Canyon, so called because of the oxidation of local argillite, a rock with a high iron content that turns rust-red on exposure to the elements. The road is one of the best places to see wildlife in the park without too much effort and, like the Akamina Parkway, has the usual pleasant panoply of picnic sites, trailheads and interpretive notice boards. If you're without transport for these roads see below for details of hiker shuttle services and car and bike rentals. The third named road in the park, the **Chief Mountain International Highway** (25km), runs east from the park entrance at Maskinonge Lake along the park's eastern border. After 7km it reaches a fine **viewpoint** over the mountain-backed Waterton Valley and then passes the park-run *Belly River Campground* (see p.964) before reaching the US–Canadian **border crossing** (open June to late Sept 7am–10pm). When this crossing is closed, depending on your direction of travel, you have to use the crossings on Alberta's Hwy 2 south of Cardston or Hwy 89 north of St Mary in Montana.

Arrival and information

Canadian **access** to Waterton by road is from Fort Macleod via either Hwy 3 west then Hwy 6 south (via Pincher Creek) or on Hwy 2 south to Cardston and then west on Hwy 5. Calgary is 264km and three hours' drive away; Lethbridge (which has the nearest airport), 130km (75min); and St Mary, Montana, 60km (45min). More than other Rockies' parks this is somewhere you really need your own transport to reach. A small taxi-bus service, the **Southwest Alta Bus Lines** (usually three times daily, but call for services; ⓣ403/627-5205), runs between Waterton and the nearest Greyhound depot at Pincher Creek 50km away ($20 one-way); a cab from Crystal Taxi (ⓣ403/627-4262) will cost around $60 for the same run, otherwise there's no public transport to the town or within the park.

Waterton Village has all the accommodation (bar the campsites) and the national park **visitor centre**, on Entrance Road at the road junction just to the north (daily May–Oct 8am–7pm; ⓣ403/859-5133). Further information is available from the Chamber of Commerce (ⓣ403/859-2224, ⓦwww.watertonchamber.com) and, outside the visitor centre's summer hours, at the park's administration office at 215 Mount View Rd (Mon–Fri 8am–4pm; ⓣ403/859-2477). The Canadian Parks Service 1:50,000 **map** *Waterton Lakes National Park*, is very useful if you're going to do any serious walking. It's usually available from the visitor centre and outdoor stores in Waterton Village.

Accommodation and eating

Waterton has a range of **hotel** accommodation. In addition to the private campsites – and three Canadian Parks Service park-run campsites, which are first-come, first-served, and fill quickly in summer – that are detailed below, the national park has provided thirteen designated **backcountry campsites**, where you'll find dry toilets and a surface-water supply; a few of them also have shelters and cooking facilities. To use any, you need a backcountry camping permit ($9 per person plus $12 reservation fee) also issued on a first-come, first-served basis by the visitor centre or administration office. A quota system is operated to prevent overcrowding.

Hotels and motels

Aspen Village Inn Windflower Ave ⓣ403/859-2255 or 1-888/859-8669, ⓦwww.aspenvillageinn.com. Quiet spot with mountain views opposite the municipal pool; 35 motel rooms and 16 "cottage" rooms, some with kitchenettes. May to mid-Oct. ❺

Bayshore Inn 111 Waterton Ave ⓣ403/859-2211 or 1-888/527-9555, ⓦwww.bayshoreinn.com. Just south of the marina; very comfortable hotel, with 49 of its seventy units on the lakefront; two-unit and deluxe suites available. Mid-April to mid-Oct. ❻

Hikes in Waterton Lakes National Park

Waterton Lakes' 255km of trails are among the best constructed in the Canadian Rockies, and also some of the most easily graded, well marked and scenically routed. Like Moraine Lake in Banff National Park – and unlike Banff and Jasper – you can also access superb walks easily without a car. Bar one or two outlying hikes, three key areas contain trails and trailheads: the **townsite** itself, which has two magnificent short walks; the **Akamina Parkway**; and the **Red Rock Canyon Parkway**. Most walks are day-hikes, climaxing at small alpine lakes cradled in spectacular hanging valleys. Options for backpacking are necessarily limited by the park's size, though the 36km **Tamarack Trail**, following the ridges of the Continental Divide between the Akamina Parkway (same trailhead as for Rowe Lakes – see opposite) and Red Rock Canyon, is rated as one of the Rockies' greatest high-line treks (maximum elevation 2560m); the 20km Carthew–Alderson Trail from Cameron Lake to Waterton (maximum elevation 2311m), a popular day's outing, can be turned into a two-day trip by overnighting at the Alderson Lake campsite. To do it in a day, take advantage of the hiker shuttle service to the trailhead offered by Park Transport (☎403/859-2378) based in the Tamarack Village Square on Mount View Road.

In short, this is a great park in which to base yourself for a few days' hiking: details of hikes are given below, but as a general guide to do the best of the hikes you'd first stroll the **Bear's Hump** for views of Waterton town and the lakes; then walk all or part of the **Bertha Lake Trail** (day or half-day) from the townsite. Next day take a boat to Goat Haunt and walk back on the **Waterton Lakeshore Trail**. Then try the **Crypt Lake Trail** from the townsite and/or the **Rowe Lake–Lineham Ridge Trail**, both ranked among the best day-walks in the Rockies. Finally, gird your loins for the longer **Carthew–Alderson Trail**, possible in a day.

Walks from Waterton Village

In and around the town there are various short loops: stroll to Cameron Falls, try the Prince of Wales from the Visitor Centre (2km; 45min) or climb the more demanding **Bear's Hump**, also from the centre (1.2km; 200m vertical; 40min one-way); the latter is one of the park's most popular short walks, switchbacking up the slopes to a rocky outcrop with great views of the Waterton Valley. More surprisingly good views can be had from the easily reached viewpoint near the Bison Paddock. Another obvious, and very simple, walk from the town is the Waterton Lakeshore Trail (13km one-way; 100m ascent; 4hr), which follows Upper Waterton Lake's west shore across the US border to Goat Haunt; regular lake ferries sail back to the townsite ($18), completing a lovely round trip (ferry details from the marina or ☎403/859-2362, ⓦwww.watertoncruise.com; see p.694). Alternatively, catch an early boat and walk back so as not to worry about making a boat connection.

The single most popular half-day or day's walk from the townsite is the classic **Bertha Lake Trail** from Waterton, 5.8km each way with an ascent of 460m (allow 3–4hr for the round trip). It's a short, steep hike beginning on Evergreen Drive to a busy but remarkably unsullied mountain-ringed lake. There is an easy trail that runs right around the lakeshore (adding about another 5km to the trip). If you're not up to this, you can just do the first part of the trail and break off at Lower Bertha Falls (2.9km from the townsite; 150m ascent; 1hr); this deservedly popular section corresponds to the route of the *Bertha Falls Self-Guiding Nature Trail* pamphlet available from the Visitor Centre.

Another excellent, if challenging, walk out of Waterton is the unique **Crypt Lake Trail**, often touted as one of the best in Canada. The 8.7km hike (one-way; 675m

Crandell Mountain Lodge 102 Mount View Rd, corner of Evergreen Ave ☎403/859-2288, ⓦwww.crandellmountainlodge.com. Seventeen nicely finished nonsmoking rooms (two with special wheelchair access) in a pretty lodge; more intimate than some of the town's hotels, with kitchenette and fireplace units available. Easter–Oct. ❻

ascent) involves a boat trip ($15 round trip) across Upper Waterton Lake to the trailhead on the east side of the lake, a (perfectly safe) climb up a ladder, a crawl through a rock tunnel and a section along a rocky ledge with cable for support. The rewards are the crashing waterfalls and the great glacial amphitheatre containing Crypt Lake (1955m); rock walls tower 600m on three sides, casting a chill shadow that preserves small icebergs on the lake's surface throughout the summer. Allow time to catch the last boat back to Waterton (ferry details see p.694), and note that it's a good idea to make reservations in summer.

Trails from the Akamina Parkway

Most of the trails accessed by the Akamina Parkway leave from the road's end near Cameron Lake. To stretch your legs after the drive up, or if you just want a stroll, try either the Akamina Lake (0.5km; 15min) or Cameron Lakeshore (1.6km; 30min) trails. The best of the longer walks is to Carthew Summit (7.9km one-way; 660m ascent), a superb trail that switchbacks through forest to Summit Lake (4km), a good target in itself, before opening out into subalpine meadow and a final climb to a craggy summit (2310m) and astounding viewpoint. The trail can be followed all the way back to Waterton Village (another 12km) – it's then the **Carthew–Alderson Trail** (see opposite), most of whose hard work you've done in getting up to Carthew Summit; from the summit it's largely steeply downhill via Carthew and Alderson lakes (1875m) to Cameron Falls and the townsite (1295m).

Another highly rated trail from the Akamina Parkway is equally appealing – the **Rowe Lakes Trail** (5.2km one-way; 555m ascent), which is accessed off the Parkway about 5km before Cameron Lake (it is also the first leg of the Tamarack Trail – see opposite). Most people make their way to the Rowe Basin (where there's a backcountry campsite) and then, rather than pushing on towards the Upper Rowe Lakes (1.2km beyond), either camp, turn around or – for stronger walkers – take the trail that branches right from the Upper Rowe path to walk to Lineham Ridge (another 3.4km and 540m ascent). This **Rowe Lake–Lineham Ridge** combination has been cited as one of the top five day-hikes in the Rockies. The stiffish walk is rewarded by Lineham Lake, sapphire blue in the valley far below, and a vast sea of mountains stretching to the horizon. Only come up here in good weather, as it's particularly hazardous when visibility's poor and the winds are up.

Trails from the Red Rock Canyon Parkway

Most trails on the Red Rock Canyon Parkway, such as the short Red Rock Canyon Trail (700m loop) and Blackiston Falls (1km; 30min), leave from Red Rock Canyon at the end of the road. The most exhilarating option from the head of the road, however, is the **Goat Lake Trail** (6.7km; 550m ascent), which follows Bauerman Creek on an old fire road (flat and easy, but a little dull) before peeling off right at the 4.3-kilometre mark for the climb to tranquil Goat Lake and ever-improving views (there's a backcountry campsite at the lake). If you ignore the lake turn-off and follow the fire road for another 4km, you come to a junction: one trail leads north to Lost Lake (2km), the other south to the spectacular Twin Lakes area (3.2km). This latter option will bring you to the long-distance Tamarack Trail (see opposite). Walk south on this from Twin Lakes (3.1km) and you can pick up the **Blackiston Creek Trail**, which will take you back to the head of the Red Rock Canyon Parkway.

Kilmorey Lodge 117 Evergreen Ave ⓣ403/859-2334 or 1-888/859-8669, ⓦwww.kilmoreylodge.com. At the northern entrance to town on Emerald Bay; 23 antique-decorated rooms with a lakefront setting and historic old-fashioned feel. Some rooms are small for the price, while others score by virtue of their views (book in advance for these); there's also an excellent restaurant (the *Lamp Post*) and nice *Gazebo Café on the Bay* with outdoor waterfront deck for snacks and light meals. Open all year. 5

Northland Lodge Evergreen Ave ⓣ403/859-2353, ⓦwww.northlandlodgecanada.com. Nine nonsmoking and cosy rooms, seven with private bathroom, east of the town site in the lee of the mountains one block south of Cameron Falls; some with kitchenettes. Mid-May to mid-Oct. 5

Prince of Wales Hotel Waterton Lake ⓣ403/859-2231, ⓦwww.glacierparkinc.com. Famous and popular old hotel – the best in town – whose 1927 Gothic outline is in almost every picture of Waterton; worth it if you can afford it. Lakeside rooms with views are pricier, but some are rather small, so check what you're getting for $275. Mid-May to mid-Sept. 8

Waterton Lakes Lodge Cameron Falls Drive and Windflower Ave ⓣ403/859-2150 or 1-888/985-6343, ⓦwww.watertonlakeslodge.com. Smart 80-room resort hotel; health spa with indoor pool, recreational centre with 18m pool and lots of extra facilities such as kitchenettes in certain deluxe rooms. Mid-May to Oct. 7

Hostels

HI-Waterton Corner of Cameron Falls & Windflower Avenue ⓣ403/859-2151. Well-equipped and spotless Hostelling International place, with dorm beds for $35 and rooms from $105. Facilities include internet, laundry and sauna.

Campsites

Belly River Campground 29km from the townsite, 1km off Chief Mountain Parkway on Hwy 6. Smallest (24 sites) and simplest of the park-operated campsites. First-come-basis with Self-registration; tap water; kitchen shelters; fireplaces; chemical and pit toilets. Late May to early Sept. $14.

Crandell Mountain Campground 8km west of Waterton on the Red Rock Canyon Parkway off Hwy 5. Semi-serviced park-run campsite with 129 sites available on a first-come basis. Tap water, fireplaces, no showers. Late May to August. $19.

Waterton Village Campground Off Vimy Ave ⓣ1-877/737-3783, ⓦwww.pccamping.ca. On the southern side of Waterton Village, this busy 238-site park-run campsite is the only one which can be booked in advance. Showers, no open fires; wheelchair-accessible. Mid-April to late Oct. $20–32.

Restaurants

Kootenai Brown Dining Room Waterton Ave at the *Bayshore Inn* ⓣ403/859-2211. One of the better and more elegant spots in town to treat yourself; the dining room overlooks the lake. Open all day for breakfast, lunch and dinner. Moderate.

Lamp Post Dining Room 117 Evergreen Ave at the *Kilmorey Lodge* ⓣ403/859-2334. Old-world appeal and tempting good food without the stuffiness of *Windsor Lounge*; the moderate prices are lower too (entrées $6–12). Open daily 7.30am–10pm. The hotel's *Gazebo* café on the waterfront is also good for snacks (open 10am–10pm).

Pizza of Waterton 103 Fountain Ave ⓣ403/859-2660. Dough made daily on the premises; good, cheap pizzas ($7–12) to eat in or take away. Open daily 4.30–10pm.

Windsor Lounge At *Prince of Wales Hotel* ⓣ403/859-2231. One of several lounges, bars and dining rooms in this posh hotel open for nonpatrons to enjoy afternoon tea, a good breakfast or a refined hour with a drink and great lake views. Dress well, as the place is fairly smart. The *Garden Court* is the most elegant restaurant in the hotel (reservations required).

Park activities

If you want to **cruise the lakes**, the most popular summer activity round these parts, contact Waterton Shoreline Cruises at the marina (ⓣ403/859-2362). It runs scenic two-hour cruises (June–Aug 5 daily, fewer in May & Sept; $25 or $18 one-way) up and down the lake across the US–Canadian border to Goat Haunt in Montana, little more than a quayside and park ranger station, where there is a scheduled thirty-minute stop before the return to Waterton (note that after the ranger station closes in mid-Sept boats no longer stop at Goat Haunt). No immigration procedures are required, but if you wish to camp overnight in the backcountry you need to register with the ranger station. You can take an early boat to Goat Haunt and then return on foot to Waterton on the **Waterton Lakeshore Trail**, an easy four-hour walk (13km one-way). The same company runs a ferry to various trails around the lake, most notably a passage to the trailhead of the famed Crypt Lake walk (see box, p.692) and the myriad longer hikes from Goat Haunt in the US. Park Transport in Tamarack Mall on Mount View Rd (Ⓣ403/859-2378) organizes two-hour tours round the park ($30), but will also lay on a **taxi** shuttle (from $10) to trails on the area's two Parkways; the most popular drop-off is the beginning of the Carthew-Alderson trail (see box, p.692).

Windsurfing is also surprisingly popular locally, thanks to the powerful winds – anything up to 70kph – which often roar across the lakes (Waterton is wetter, windier and snowier than much of Alberta). Winds generally gust south to north, making the beach at Cameron Bay on Upper Waterton Lake a favourite spot for surfers to catch the breeze. The water is cold and deep, though, so you'll need a wet suit. If you want to **swim**, head for the cheap outdoor heated pool on Cameron Falls Drive. **Fishing** is good on the lakes, but remember to pick up the compulsory national park permit ($8.90 a day, $29.70 annual) from the visitor centre or park administration office. Off the water, **horse riding** is available from the Alpine Stables (Ⓣ403/859-2462, Ⓦwww.alpinestables.com), located just east off the hwy about 1km north of the visitor centre. On offer are one-hour outings (hourly on the hour; from $25) and two-hour (3 daily; $42), daily and overnight treks. Four kilometres north of town on the main hwy is the beautiful eighteen-hole **Waterton Lakes Golf Course** (Ⓣ403/859-2114); green fees are $33 and club rental $11.

Kananaskis Country

Most first-time visitors race straight from Calgary to Banff, ignoring **Kananaskis Country**, a dramatic foothill area that sprawls along the eastern boundary of Banff National Park. Created out of existing provincial parks to take pressure off Banff, Kananaskis remains almost the exclusive preserve of locals, who come to ski in the winter and to hike, bike and camp in the summer. The mountain scenery rivals that of parks and the possibilities for outdoor pursuits even better, thanks to more liberal protection policies. **Canmore** is the region's natural focus, much as Banff is in the neighbouring national park – though in many other ways the towns are dissimilar. The scope and variety of facilities and services are far more limited at Canmore, but then so are the levels of crowds and commercialism, and accommodation is cheaper and easier to find. Plenty of excursions are possible on foot from the town itself, but to get deep into adjacent **provincial parks** you'll need your own transport.

Canmore

Long considered a gateway to the parks, youthful and outdoorsy **CANMORE** has begun to compete with Banff, 28km away, for visitors, and it's a decent alternative if you'd rather stay in a less touristy place and can live without Banff's huge selection of restaurants and shops. Canmore began life in 1883 as a supply point for the CPR railroad, before booming as a mining centre after the company was delighted to discover coal in surrounding hills. It quickly became a boom town and lived off mining for almost a century until the last mine closed in 1979. Things looked bleak, but not for long as it was soon decided that the town would host all the Nordic skiing events for the 1988 Calgary Olympics, which gave the town its impressive **Canmore Nordic Centre**. On the back of this and thanks to the town's splendid location between rows of towering mountains and outside the tight restrictions of the national parks, the town grew. Over the last twenty years its

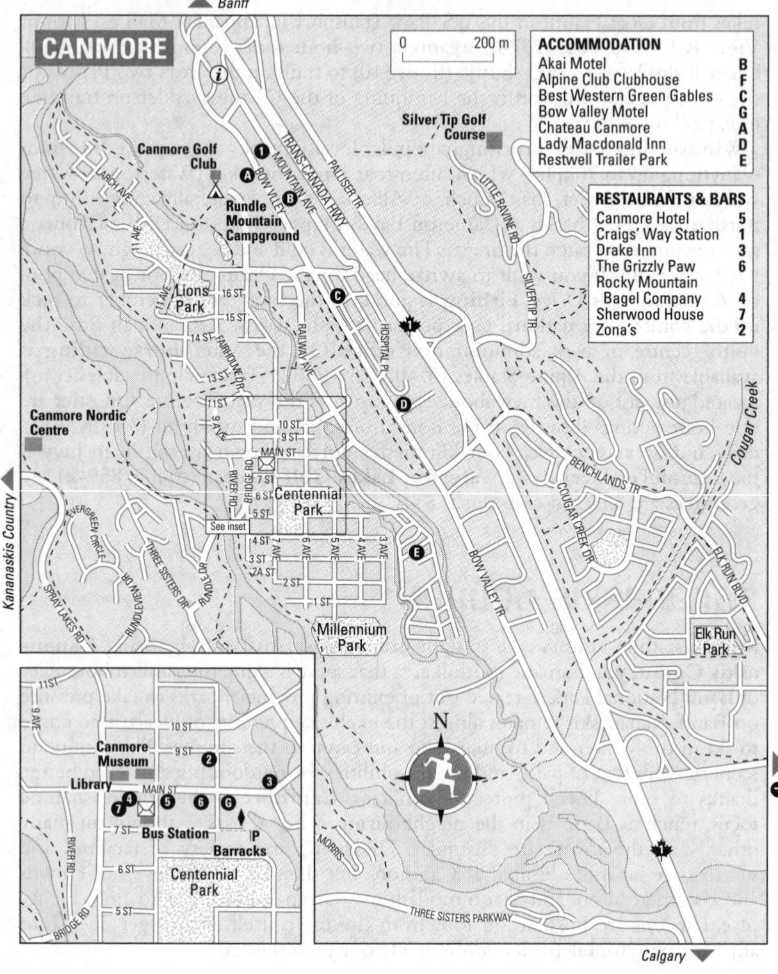

population has tripled to 11,000 and it's expected to double again in the next twenty. Occasional references to it as the "Aspen of Alberta" overstate the case, but certainly many young adventurous types and artists are relocating here to escape cities. It's a good place to visit as well as live, with good hiking, climbing, biking, skiing and fishing on the fringes of town – and opportunities for many more activities, including caving and rafting, not much further away.

Arrival, information and accommodation

Most shuttles between Calgary Airport and Banff (see p.665) make a stop at Canmore, with fares around $45 one-way. You can also take the Greyhound here from Calgary and Banff, with services arriving at the **bus station**, 801 8th St (☎403/678-4465). From here it's a long walk to the town's information centre, part of the **Travel Alberta Visitor Information Centre**, 2801 Bow

Valley Trail (June–Aug 8am–8pm; Sept–May 9am–6pm; ⓣ403/678-5277 or 1-800/661-8888, ⓦwww.discoveralberta.com) just off the Trans-Canada. The centre is an excellent place to pick up information about the whole Rocky Mountain region as well as Canmore.

Downtown Canmore can easily be explored **on foot**, though a bike is useful on the extensive trail network in and around town. Gear Up, 1302 Bow Valley Trail (ⓣ403/678-1636), is one of several places that **rents bikes**. The only car rental outlet in town is Hertz (ⓣ403/678-1630) in the *Radisson Hotel*, 511 Bow Valley Trail. For a taxi call Apex (ⓣ403/609-0030).

The bulk of Canmore's **accommodation** is in new hotels and motels squatting beside the Trans-Canada Hwy and the parallel road, the Bow Valley Trail. In summer prices are a little steep for what's offered, though levels are much saner than in Banff. In winter rates are typically cut by at least a third. For a less anonymous experience you can stay in one of around fifty B&Bs in and around town that are brought together by the Canmore Valley Bed and Breakfast Association (ⓣ403/609-7224, ⓦwww.bbcanmore.com).

Hotels and motels

Akai Motel 1717 Mountain Ave ⓣ403/678-4664 or 1-877/900-2524. Small basic motel on the northern edge of town with some of the cheapest rooms around. ❹

Best Western Green Gables Inn 1602 2nd Ave ⓣ403/678-5488 or 1-800/661-2133, ⓦwww.bestwestern.com. Reliable mid-range chain hotel where many rooms have a whirlpool. ❻

Bow Valley Motel 610 8th St ⓣ403/678-5085 or 1-800/665-8189, ⓦwww.bowvalleymotel.com. Average motel, but with a location – downtown and an easy walk from the restaurants and bars – that sets it apart from the rest. ❸

Château Canmore 1720 Bow Valley Trail ⓣ403/678-6699 or 1-800/261-8551, ⓦwww.Chateaucanmore.com. Chain hotel with big, well-equipped rooms with kitchenettes, fitness facilities, pool and hot tub. ❼

Lady Macdonald Inn 1201 Bow Valley Trail ⓣ403/678-3665 or 1-800/567-3919, ⓦwww.ladymacdonald.com. Highly recommended friendly twelve-room B&B, with hot tub and great breakfasts. ❻

Hostel

Alpine Club Clubhouse Indian Flats Rd ⓣ403/678-3200, ⓦwww.alpineclubofcanada.ca. Run by the Alpine Club of Canada, this hostel at the base of Grotto Mountain, 5km southeast of downtown via Indian Flats Road, has a wonderful mountaineering feel, exceptional valley views and the usual facilities – with the library and sauna definite plus points. Dorm beds $21.

Campsites

Bow River Campground ⓣ403/673-2163, ⓦwww.bowvalleycampgrounds.com. A good option at the Three Sisters Overpass 3km east of Canmore. Sites $20–30.

Restwell Trailer Park ⓣ403/678-5111, ⓦwww.restwelltrailerpark.com. A regimented and unattractive place, on the northern edge of downtown. Sites $30–47.

The town and around

Canmore straddles the Trans-Canada Highway, though its downtown area is entirely south of the road, and centred on laid-back Main Street (8th St). The **Canmore Centennial Museum and Geoscience Centre**, 907 7th Ave (Mon–Fri 9am–5pm, Sat & Sun noon–4pm; free), is a good wet-weather option, doing a fine job of rooting around the town's past from its geological and First Nation origins to its Olympic glory days. At the far end of Main Street is a spur of the extensive network of local **bike paths**, which leads down to and alongside the Bow River. Parts of it are reasonable for **fishing** for bull trout, brown trout and whitefish; the Green Drake Fly Shop, 102-512 Bow Valley Trail (ⓣ403/678-9522), can provide tackle and advice. The other main form of recreation in town is **golf**. The most modest of the three courses is run by the Canmore Golf and Curling Club (ⓣ403/678-4785), on the north side of town; greens fees are around $50. Far more impressive is the Silver Tip course

(Ⓣ403/678-1600, Ⓦwww.silvertipresort.com), which offers a unique and challenging course just east of town; greens fees run $90–130.

West of downtown and the Bow River the land begins to rise and the town starts to thin out, so that by the time Spray Lakes Road has climbed to **Canmore Nordic Centre** (Ⓣ403/678-2400), you're only left with views of the urban area. This state-of-the-art former Olympic facility is as popular in summer as in winter, since 70km of the total 300km cross-country network is maintained for mountain biking and suitable for every level of rider. Free trail maps are available, as are bike rentals ($30/day). Beyond the Nordic Centre Spray Lakes Road soon loses its asphalt cover and begins to climb in earnest, but just before it does there's a small turn-off to a parking lot beside a reservoir. This is the trailhead for an easy 2km hike up to **Grassi Lakes**, a series of small picture-book lakes high above town on a route that affords exceptional views over the valley. The trail up is rough and steep, though there's also the option of descending back down a rough access road, which is much easier going. On reaching the upper lake, be sure to take an easy scramble up the scree slope to four **pictographs** of human figures painted onto the first large boulder of the gorge. The surrounding cliffs are invariably busy with rock climbers testing their skill; along with Heart Creek, Cougar Creek and Grotto Canyon this is one of the best local areas for the sport. For a local guiding service, contact the Yamnuska Mountain School (Ⓣ403/678-4164, Ⓦwww.yamnuska.com), which also offers novice rock-climbing courses from $230.

High above Grassi Lakes, Spray Lakes Road climbs out of view of Canmore to enter **Spray Valley Provincial Park**, the most accessible part of high-mountain Kananaskis Country. The main feature of the park is its 16km-long Spray Lakes Reservoir, which is used to generate electricity. Despite its industrial use the lake is a tranquil spot and surrounded by huge, impressively contorted mountains. A campground (late May to early Sept; no reservations; $20) is strung out along the western shore and is an exceptionally attractive spot to pitch a tent, though facilities are basic and you need to bring all your own supplies except firewood ($6 per bundle). An added bonus is the great hiking trail that heads out from the campground to the small **Jakeroy Glacier**, perched high up in the goat range. The trail (4km; 4hr round-trip) begins opposite campsite no. 17 and is fairly well marked – at the only river crossing be sure to head straight on up the scree slope rather than right up to the waterfall – and climbs steeply through pine, willow, spruce and larch forests to a narrow hanging valley.

The east side of Canmore is also good for shorter hikes: an easy informal trail with good views follows the course of **Cougar Creek**. It's possible to follow this all the way to the boundary of Banff National Park. An even better trail starts from Grotto Pond, 12km east of Canmore on Hwy 1a. It starts fairly unpromisingly, following a powerline road, but soon cuts into the woods to **Grotto Canyon**. There's no formal trail but the way up the steep-sided canyon is clear enough; look for pictographs around 300m into the canyon – on the left at about head-height at one of its narrowest points. Another 100m or so into the canyon is an impressive little waterfall. Beyond this the valley opens up, passing a cave and some hoodoos. If these strange landforms whet your appetite, be sure to tour **Canmore Caverns** (Ⓣ403/678-8819, Ⓦwww.canadianrockies.net/wildcavetours) in the base of Grotto Mountain. Groups are shuttled to the limestone caves here from Canmore, with easy half-day tours costing $94 per person. Even more fun is the full day tour ($121) which involves some rappelling through the extensive cave network; dress warmly and expect to get dirty.

Eating, drinking and nightlife

Recently, several smarter **restaurants** serving imaginative regional food have opened up in Canmore, alongside a number of long-standing dependable downtown **pubs** for bar food. Though there is one very average nightclub in town – *Hooligan's*, 103 Bow Valley Trail – the most popular form of **nightlife** is the deliberately cheesy theatrical performance *Oh Canada Eh!* (☎403/609-0004 or 1-800/773-0004). A musical dinner show, it's a slapstick celebration of Canada using costumed performers, staged nightly at 125 Kananaskis Way; the food served alongside is hearty local fare.

Canmore Hotel 738-8th St ☎403/678-5181. Wild bar that looks likes it's straight off the set of a Western and is barely more refined inside. Honky-tonk atmosphere and regular live music keeps the locals coming.

Craigs' Way Station 1727 Mountain Ave ☎403/678-2656. Cheerful family-oriented place amid the motels on the north side of town. Good full breakfasts and inexpensive diner food.

Drake Inn 909 Railway Ave. Locals' pub with outdoor patio, nonsmoking section, pool and occasional live music.

The Grizzly Paw Brewing Company 622 Main St. The Rockies' only microbrewery, with decent pub grub and reasonable beers; the Grumpy Bear Honey Wheat Ale is the most refreshing after a day in the outdoors.

Rocky Mountain Bagel Company 830 Main St. One of several decent cafés on Main St that's ideal for a simple breakfast, light lunch or just hanging out.

Sherwood House 838 Main St ☎403/678-5211. Log cabin that's a long-standing local favourite with lots of Rocky Mountain charm. The huge patio-cum-beer-garden catches the sun until late and there lots of game served – including a great buffalo stew – along with decent pizza.

Zona's 710-9th St ☎403/609-2000. Chic bistro with earthtone decor and highly inventive meals like the Moroccan molasses lamb curry or the Thai vegetable lasagne. Main courses $12–18. On Thursdays the place is open late, has a DJ and is packed with locals.

The Kananaskis Valley

The **Kananaskis Valley** is the mainstay of Kananaskis Country. Hwy 40, which intersects with the Trans-Canada Hwy 30km east of Canmore, travels south along its length, bisecting the high-mountain country, linking all the most significant provincial parks, and providing a ribbon to which most of the trails, campsites and scattered service centres cling. About 3km down the hwy is the **Barrier Lake Information Centre** (daily June to mid-Sept 9am–6pm; rest of year 9am–4pm; ☎403/673-3985), where you can get a full breakdown on outdoor activities.

Kananaskis Village

The only real settlement around is **KANANASKIS VILLAGE**, a rather soulless resort-village based around a golf course and ski area (see box, p.700) which can be used as a useful base. A number of hiking and biking trails radiate from here. Peregrine Sports (☎403/591-7453) offers rentals of mountain bikes, fishing rods and canoes and can advise on local conditions for these pursuits. Of the hiking trails, the 9km hike to **Ribbon Falls** is deservedly popular and arrives at the eponymous campsite, which in common with all Kananaskis backcountry campsites costs $8 per person; buy permits from the Barrier Lake Information Centre or on ☎403/678-3136. From here you can either head back, or with basic rock climbing skills head on and complete a loop by following the Galetea Creek trail below the hulking Mt Kidd. If you're fit and want to bag a peak, **Mount Allan**, just north of Kananaskis Village beckons: it's one of the few maintained trails in the Rockies that leads to a summit at 2990m. Other than excellent **golf**

Nakiska and Fortress Mountain ski areas

Generally written off in favour of the local headline acts Sunshine Village and Lake Louise, **Nakiska** and **Fortress Mountain** are two ski areas in Kananaskis Country Provincial Park which, in good conditions (the snowphone for both is ⓣ403/244-6665), have skiing and riding of a quality that justifies a trip even from Banff. Lift passes at the two are interchangeable.

Developed specifically for the 1988 Winter Olympics, **Nakiska** (ⓣ403/591-7777, ⓦwww.skinakiska.com) lies 25km south of the Trans-Canada Highway, around an hour's drive from either Calgary or Banff, and beside Kananaskis Village. Designed from scratch, the ski area has vertical drop of 735m (2412ft), is one of the most user-friendly on the continent, and includes all the usual rental, instruction and childcare facilities. Intended for downhill racers to fly down, the runs here are mostly smooth and steep, making it a great intermediate mountain for cruising – seventy percent of the runs are blue – and a useful schoolroom for beginner boarders. The lack of snow at the ski area – only 250cm (98 inches) annually – is rarely a problem, since snowmaking covers 85 percent of the mountain, and though conditions can be a little crusty, the ski area's grooming helps with this. The area also maintains two competition-standard half-pipes and a terrain park.

Located 15km south of Nakiska on Hwy 40, **Fortress Mountain** (ⓣ403/591-7108, ⓦwww.skifortress.com) is a very different ski area. In place of smart regimented runs is largely untamed terrain, huddled beneath several vast, craggy rock outcrops. Particularly renowned for its tree-skiing, gullies and many natural obstacles as well as its well-maintained half pipe, Fortress Mountain offers a vertical drop of 280m (918ft) and spreads over 328 acres. The majority of its 47 trails are intermediate. In contrast with Nakiska, the snowfall at Fortress is a reassuring 630cm (23 feet) which, coupled with a sixty-percent snowmaking capacity, means decent conditions are virtually guaranteed.

(ⓣ403/591-7272 or 1-877/591-2525, ⓦwww.kananaskisgolf.com), the other organized pursuit in the area is **whitewater rafting**, run by the Canmore Rafting Centre (ⓣ403/678-4919 or 1-888-312-7238, ⓦwww.canmoreraftingcentre.com).

The best **accommodation** choice in Kananaskis Village itself is the comfortable *Delta Lodge* (ⓣ403/591-771 or 1-800/268-1133, ⓦwww.deltahotels.com; ❼) with its huge rooms, great mountain views and facilities with include gym, spa, pool and outdoor hot tub. A family-friendly place, the hotel organizes a range of activities for kids, as well as offering an adult-only section for those who want to enjoy a bit of peace.

Other options include the *Kananaskis Wilderness Hostel* (ⓣ403-670-7580 or 1-866/762-4122, ⓦwww.hihostels.ca; dorms $24, private room $66), beside Ribbon Creek just off the Village access road. There are two good **campsites**: *Sundance Lodges* (ⓣ403/591-7122, ⓦwww.sundancelodges.com; mid-May to Sept), which has regular sites ($19) hidden in the trees as well as cheerful hand-painted furnished tepees (❷); and the impressive *Mount Kidd RV Park* (ⓣ403/591-7700, ⓦwww.mountkiddrv.com; sites $20–32), which boasts hot tubs, saunas and tennis courts.

Peter Loughead Provincial Park

Around 40km south of Kananaskis Village on Hwy 40, a short spur leads to Upper Kananaskis Lake, the head of the valley and the main focus of **Peter Loughead Provincial Park**. This has the biggest concentration of accessible boating, fishing, camping and hiking possibilities in the region. Around

4km off Hwy 40 en route to the lake is the excellent Peter Loughead Park **Information Centre** (daily mid-May to Aug 9am–7pm; rest of year 9am–5pm; ☎403/591-6322), whose staff are only too happy to give you information on the plentiful camping and hiking. Top trails include the rewarding half-day jaunt to Rawson Lake and the magnificent multi-day backpacking adventure over Burstall Pass to Banff, easily one of the best in the region. This hike is well detailed, along with many others in the Kananaskis area, in the definitive *Where Locals Hike in the Canadian Rockies* by Kathy and Craig Copeland, which is widely available.

Banff National Park

BANFF NATIONAL PARK is the most famous of the Canadian Rockies' parks and Canada's leading tourist attraction – so be prepared for the crowds that throng its key centres, **Banff** and **Lake Louise**, as well as the best part of its 1500km of trails, most of which suffer a continual pounding during the summer months. That said, it's worth putting up with every commercial

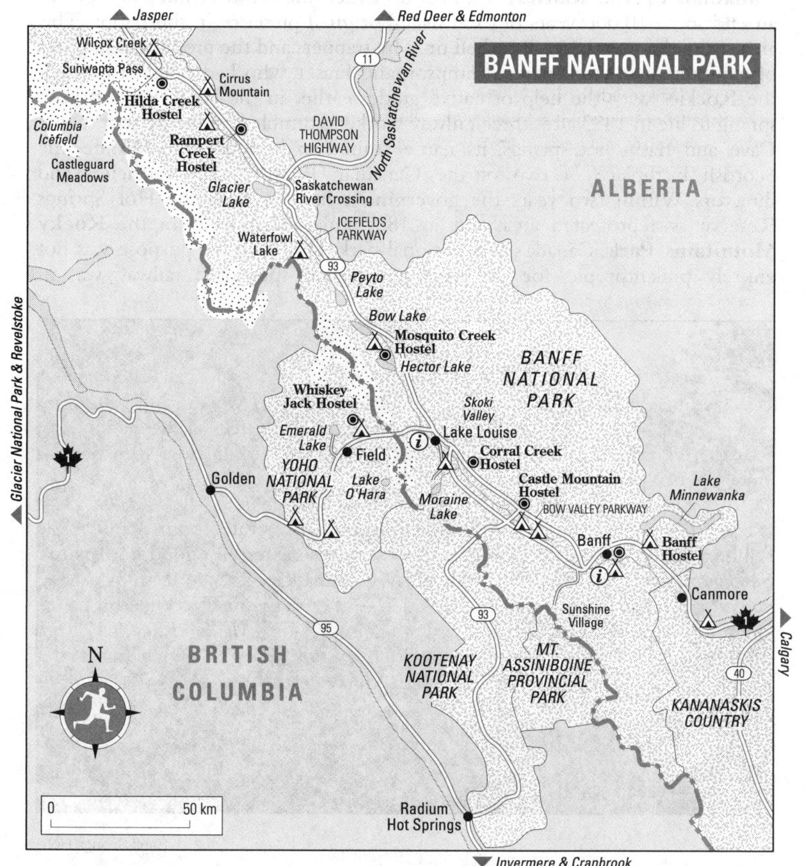

indignity to enjoy the sublime scenery – and if you're camping or are prepared to walk, the worst of the park's excesses are fairly easily left behind. The best plan of attack if you're coming from Calgary or the US is to make straight for Banff, a busy and commercial town where you can pause for a couple of days to soak up the action and handful of sights, or stock up on supplies and make for somewhere quieter as quickly as possible. Then head 58km north along Hwy-1 to Lake Louise, a much smaller but almost equally busy centre with some unmissable landscapes plus readily accessible short trails and day-hikes if you just want a quick taste of the scenery. Two popular hwys within the park offer magnificent vistas: the **Bow Valley Parkway** from Banff to Lake Louise is a far preferable route to the parallel Hwy 1 (Trans-Canada), and the much longer **Icefields Parkway** leads from Lake Louise to Jasper. Both are lined with trails long and short, waterfalls, lakes, canyons, viewpoints, pull-offs and a seemingly unending procession of majestic mountain, river, glacier and forest scenery.

A history of the park

The modern road routes in the park provide transport links that have superseded the railway that first brought the park into being. The arrival of the **Canadian Pacific Railway** at the end of the nineteenth century brought to an end some 10,000 years of exclusive aboriginal presence in the region. This area had previously been disturbed only by trappers and the prodigious exploits of explorers like Mackenzie, Thompson and Fraser, who had sought to breach the Rockies with the help of native guides earlier in the century. Banff itself sprang to life in 1883 after three railway workers stumbled on the present town's Cave and Basin hot springs, its name coined in honour of Banffshire, the Scottish birthplace of two of the Canadian Pacific's early financiers and directors. Within two years the government had set aside the Hot Springs Reserve as a protected area, and in 1887 enlarged it to form the **Rocky Mountains Park**, Canada's first national park. However, the purpose was not entirely philanthropic, for the new government-sponsored railway was in

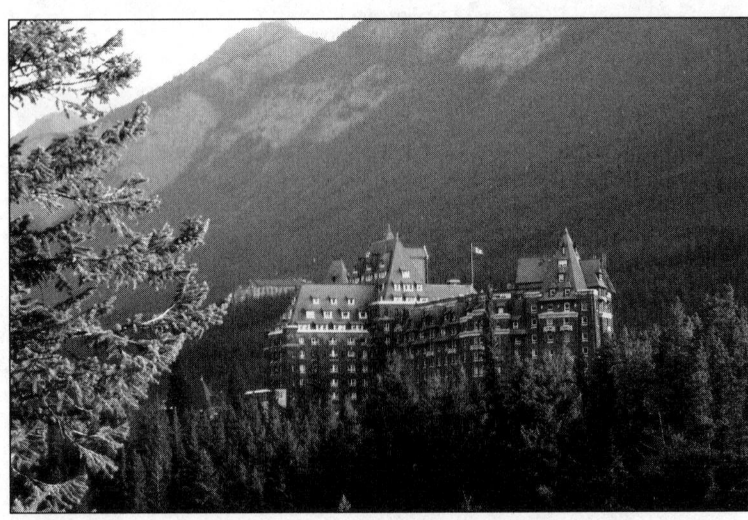

△ Banff Springs Hotel

desperate need of passengers and profit, and spectacular scenery backed up by luxurious hotels was seen – rightly – as the best way to lure the punters. Cars were banned from the park until 1916.

Today the park is not quite at crisis point, but some hard decisions need to be made. Around four-and-a-half million visitors come to Banff every year and another four million pass through. Together they pump a staggering $800m or more annually into the local economy. Such numbers, despite the best efforts and intentions of the park authorities, inevitably have an effect on the environment. Scientists believe, for example, that the black and grizzly bear populations are dying out (combined numbers of both types of bear here are probably just 100 to 130), while numbers of wolves are declining at only a slightly lower rate than in areas where they have no protection at all (the park has just 35 or 40). Conversely, elk numbers have exploded beyond internally sustainable limits to about 3200, almost entirely because they've realized the town offers food (tasty suburban grass) and total safety from their natural predators. In the past, there have been about sixty usually provoked elk attacks on humans in Banff every year. The sight of elk nibbling on verges in downtown Banff will soon be a thing of the past, however, for around 120 of the beasts have been removed and relocated elsewhere, and there are plans to remove the remainder.

These are just a handful of symptoms of a greater ecological malaise. In response, a ceiling of 10,000 has been put on Banff's human population (it's currently around 7100), building is strictly controlled and areas are being closed to the public: even the famous Bow Valley Parkway is closed to traffic for parts of the year. The airport, too, is now all but closed, for it – like much of Banff town and the Bow River Valley – lies right in the path of major wildlife routes. Many of the big mammals require large areas to survive, larger even than the park. Experts suggest that Banff's ecosystem is on a knife edge: it may be saved and previous damage restored only if action is taken. There's much more work to be done.

Banff

BANFF is the unquestioned capital of the Canadian Rockies, and with its intense summer buzz it can be a fun, bustling and likeable base – but if you've come to commune with nature, you'll want to leave as soon as possible. Although the town is quite small, it handles an immense amount of tourist traffic, much of it of the RV and coach-tour variety. Anything up to 50,000 visitors arrive daily in high season, making this the largest and busiest urban focus of any national park anywhere in the world. Backpackers are abundant in summer, and an East Asian presence is also marked, with a huge number of Japanese signs and menus in shops and restaurants. Around a third of the town's accommodation is Japanese-owned, including two of the largest hotels; this investment is an ongoing bone of contention among some townspeople who would prefer local money.

What's rather odd, given all the people, however, is that there's next to nothing to do or see in Banff, save a couple of small museums, a cable-car ride and the chance to gape at the crowds on **Banff Avenue**, a thoroughfare lined with probably more souvenir stores and upmarket outdoor clothing and equipment shops than anywhere in North America. Whether or not your main aim is to avoid the crowds, however, some contact with the town is inevitable, as it contains essential shops and services almost impossible to come by elsewhere in the park. Many of the more rewarding **walks** locally are some way from the town – you'll need a car or have to rent a bike to explore properly – but some surprisingly good strolls start just minutes from the main street.

Bears

Two types of **bears** roam the Rockies – black bears and grizzlies – and you don't want to meet either. They're not terribly common in these parts (sightings are all monitored and posted at park centres) and risks are pretty low on heavily tramped trails, but if you're camping or walking it's still essential to be vigilant, obey basic rules, know the difference between a black bear and a grizzly (the latter are bigger and have a humped neck), know how to avoid dangerous encounters, and understand what to do if confronted or attacked. Popular misconceptions about bears abound – that they can't climb trees, for example (they can, and very quickly) – so it's worth picking up the parks service's pamphlet *You are in Bear Country*, which cuts through the confusion and lays out some occasionally eye-opening procedures. Be prepared, and if you don't want to be attacked, follow the cardinal rules: store food and garbage properly, make sure bears know you're there, don't approach or feed them, and, if you find yourself approached by one, don't scream and don't run.

When hiking, walk in a group – bears rarely attack more than four in a group – and make noise, lots of it, as you traverse the wilderness; bears are most threatened if surprised, so warning of your approach will give them time to leave the area. Many people shout, rattle cans with stones in or carry a whistle; be warned, the widely touted hand-held, tinkling bells are not loud enough. Be especially alert and noisy when close to streams, in tall vegetation, crossing avalanche slopes or when travelling into the wind, as your scent won't carry to warn bears of your approach: move straight away from dead animals and berry patches, which are important food sources. Watch for bear signs – get out quick if you see fresh tracks, diggings and droppings – and keep in the open as much as possible.

Camp away from rushing water, paths and animal trails, and keep the site scrupulously clean, leaving nothing hanging around in the open. Lock food and rubbish in a car, or hang it well away from a tent between two trees at least 4m above ground (many campsites have bear poles or steel food boxes). Take all rubbish away – don't bury it (bears will just dig it up) and certainly don't store it in or near the tent. Avoid smelly foods, all fresh, dried or tinned meat and fish, and never store food, cook or eat in or near the tent – lingering smells may invite unwanted nocturnal visits. Aim to cook at least 50m downwind of the tent: freeze-dried meals and plastic-bag-sealed food is best. Likewise, keep food off clothes and sleeping bags, and sleep in clean clothes at night. Bears have an acute sense of smell, so avoid *anything* strongly scented – cosmetics, deodorant, shampoo, gel, lip balm, insect repellents, toothpaste, sun screen. Bears can be attracted to women during menstruation, so dispose

Arrival and information

Banff is a ninety-minute **drive** from Calgary along the Trans-Canada Hwy (Hwy 1). Several operators offer efficient shuttle services **from Calgary Airport** (see p.665). Daily **Greyhound buses** (ⓣ403/762-1092 or 1-800/661-8747, ⓦwww.greyhound.ca) also ply the route from the centre of Calgary (5 daily; 1hr 40min; $23 one-way), arriving in Banff's bus terminal at 100 Gopher St (7.30am–10.45pm; ⓣ403/762-6767 or 1-800/661-1152). Buses also arrive from Vancouver (4 daily; 13hr; $115).

Once in Banff it's easy to get around **on foot**, though a frequent town **bus** service, operated by Banff Transit ($1; ⓣ403/760-8294), provides transport to outlying areas, including the campgrounds on Tunnel Mountain Road and the *Banff Springs Hotel*.

The showpiece **Banff Information Centre** is at 224 Banff Ave (daily: mid-May to late June and Sept 8am–6pm; late June to Aug 8am–8pm; Oct to

of tampons in an airtight container; they're also attracted by the smell of sex, so watch what you do in your tent if you don't want a rather drastic *coitus interruptus*.

Bears are unpredictable, and experts simply can't agree on best tactics: there's no guaranteed life-saving way of coping with an aggressive bear. Calm behaviour, however, has proved to be the most successful strategy in preventing an attack after an encounter. Bears don't actually want to attack; they simply want to know you're not a threat. Mothers with cubs are particularly dangerous and prone to suspicion. A bear moving towards you can be considered to have it in for you, other signs being whoofing noises, snapping jaws, and the head down and ears back. A bear raised on its hind legs and sniffing is trying to identify you: if it does it frequently, though, it's getting agitated; ideally, on first encounter you want first to stand stock still, never engage in direct eye contact (perceived as aggressive by the bear) and – absurd as it sounds – start speaking to it in low tones. Whatever you do, don't run, which simply sets off an almost inevitable predator–prey response in the bear (a bear can manage 61kph – that's easily faster than a racehorse or the fastest Olympic sprinter); instead, back away quietly and slowly at the first encounter, speaking gently all the while to the bear. If the backing off seems to be working, then make a wide detour, leave the area or wait for the bear to do so – and always leave it an escape route. If things still look ominous, set your pack gently on the ground as a distraction as you continue to back away.

If you're attacked, things are truly grim, and quack tactics are unlikely to help you. With grizzlies, playing dead – curling up in a ball, protecting face, neck and abdomen – may be effective. Fighting back will only increase the ferocity of a grizzly attack, and there's no way you're going to win. Keep your elbows in to prevent the bear rolling you over, and be prepared to keep the position for a long time until the bear gets bored. You may get one good cuff and a few minutes' attention and that's it – injuries may still be severe but you'll probably live. With a black bear the playing dead routine won't wash, though they're not as aggressive as grizzlies, and a good bop to the nose or sufficient frenzy on your part will sometimes send a black bear running: it's worth a try. Don't play dead with either species if the bear stalks or attacks while you're sleeping: this is more dangerous, as bears are often after food. Instead, try and get away or intimidate – people who have survived such attacks have often had a brave companion who has attacked the bear in return with something big and heavy.

Chemical repellents are available, but of unproven efficacy, and in a breeze you're likely to miss or catch the spray yourself. If this all sounds too scary to make you even contemplate walking or camping, remember that attacks are very rare.

mid-May 9am–5pm; ⓣ403/762-8421, ⓦwww.banfflakelouise.com; park information ⓣ403/762-1550, ⓦwww.pc.gc.ca/banff). The centre is also the place to pick up a **park permit** if you haven't already done so (see box p.684). Among the many free handouts, make a point of asking for the *Banff and Vicinity Drives and Walks* and *The Icefields Parkway* for **maps** of park facilities, the *Backcountry Visitors' Guide* for an invaluable overview of backpacking **trails** and campsites, and *Trail Bicycling in the National Parks* for conditions and a full list of mountain-bike trails. In the centre is a selection of maps and guides you can consult free; you can also buy excellent topographical maps from the "Friends of Banff National Park" shop (ⓣ403/762-8918) on the left, but many of the shorter and more popular trails are signed and well trodden, so you won't really need detailed maps unless you're venturing into the backcountry. You can also pick up details or book a place on the various **events** offered by the "Friends", which in past years have included free

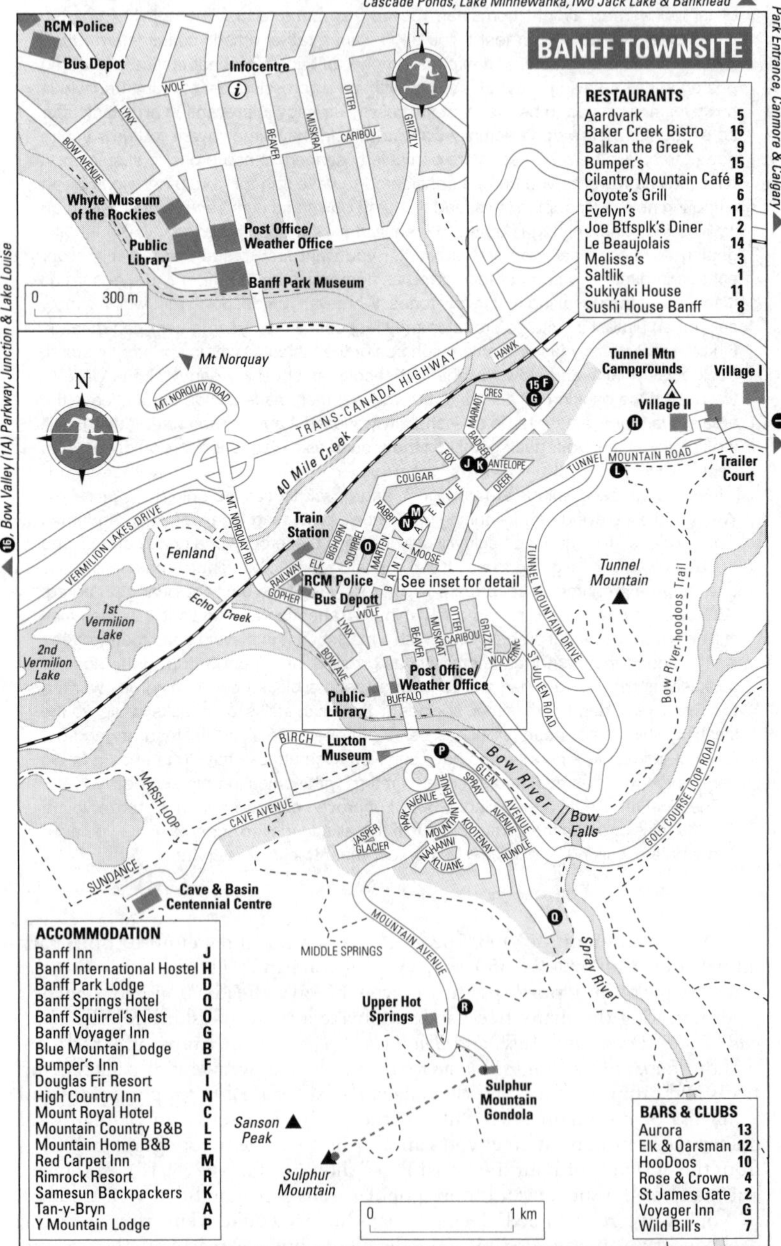
BANFF TOWNSITE
Cascade Ponds, Lake Minnewanka, Two Jack Lake & Bankhead
Park Entrance, Canmore & Calgary
16, Bow Valley (1A) Parkway Junction & Lake Louise
RESTAURANTS
Aardvark 5
Baker Creek Bistro 16
Balkan the Greek 9
Bumper's 15
Cilantro Mountain Café B
Coyote's Grill 6
Evelyn's 11
Joe Btfsplk's Diner 2
Le Beaujolais 14
Melissa's 3
Saltlik 1
Sukiyaki House 11
Sushi House Banff 8
ACCOMMODATION
Banff Inn J
Banff International Hostel H
Banff Park Lodge D
Banff Springs Hotel Q
Banff Squirrel's Nest O
Banff Voyager Inn G
Blue Mountain Lodge B
Bumper's Inn F
Douglas Fir Resort I
High Country Inn N
Mount Royal Hotel C
Mountain Country B&B L
Mountain Home B&B E
Red Carpet Inn M
Rimrock Resort R
Samesun Backpackers K
Tan-y-Bryn A
Y Mountain Lodge P
BARS & CLUBS
Aurora 13
Elk & Oarsman 12
HooDoos 10
Rose & Crown 4
St James Gate 2
Voyager Inn G
Wild Bill's 7
RCM Police
Bus Depot
Infocentre
Whyte Museum of the Rockies
Public Library
Post Office/ Weather Office
Banff Park Museum
0 300 m
Mt Norquay
Trans-Canada Highway
Mt. Norquay Road
40 Mile Creek
Train Station
Fenland
Vermilion Lakes Drive
1st Vermilion Lake
2nd Vermilion Lake
Echo Creek
See inset for detail
Bus Depott
Tunnel Mtn Campgrounds
Village I
Village II
Trailer Court
Tunnel Mountain Road
Tunnel Mountain
Tunnel Mountain Drive
Bow River-hoodoos Trail
St Julien Road
Luxton Museum
Bow River
Bow Falls
Golf Course Loop Road
Cave Avenue
Marsh Loop
Sundance
Cave & Basin Centennial Centre
Middle Springs
Mountain Avenue
Spray River
Upper Hot Springs
Sulphur Mountain Gondola
Sanson Peak
Sulphur Mountain
0 1 km

guided walks daily in the summer to Vermilion Lakes (10am; 2hr 30min), a Discovery Tour of the Cave and Basin Hot Springs (45min) and a Park Museum Wildlife Tour (45min).

Accommodation

It's almost impossible to turn up after midday in Banff during July and August and find reasonably priced **accommodation**: preplanning is essential. Anything that can be booked has usually been snapped up – Banff has over 3500 beds at its disposal nightly – and many visitors are forced to accept top-price places ($150 plus) or backtrack as far as Canmore or even Calgary to find space. The Tourism Bureau maintains a constantly updated vacancies board (though staff aren't allowed to make specific recommendations) and a free courtesy phone. There are also several fee-based alternatives (see box, p.708).

The Bed & Breakfast and Private Home accommodation list at the infocentre lists forty-plus places with **private rooms** and **B&Bs**, but don't expect too much – they're usually cheapish by Banff standards (typically around $90–125) and among the first places to go each day. Note, too, that "breakfast" usually means just toast, coffee and cereal. Most of the town's **motels** are on the busy strip-cum-spur from the Trans-Canada into town, and charge high rates for basic lodgings – typically from $150 for doubles. Off-season (Oct–May), rates are usually considerably lower. **Campsites** are not quite as bad (the town offers over a thousand pitches), but even these generally fill up by 2pm or 3pm in summer – especially the excellent government campsites. Try to beat the crowds by booking ahead on the Parks Canada reservation service (ⓣ1-877/737-3783, ⓦwww.pccamping.ca). In addition to the places listed here, remember that there are lovely and less-developed park-run sites available along both the Bow and Icefields parkways to the north.

Hotels and motels

Banff Inn 501 Banff Ave ⓣ403/762-8844 or 1-800/667-1464, ⓦwww.banffinn.com. Fancy-looking 99-unit motel, a five-minute walk from town, whose gables, loft windows, stucco and stone-clad walls make it stand out from neighbouring complexes. The smart and spacious rooms are much more run-of-the-mill, though some have fireplaces and Jacuzzi tubs. Other amenities include a steam room, hot tub and underground parking. ⑥

Banff Park Lodge 222 Lynx St ⓣ403/762-4433 or 1-800/661-9266, ⓦwww.banffparklodge.com. Quietly sophisticated, low slung cedar and oak hotel, a block from the town centre and offering the best downtown deal. Scandinavian-style rooms are simple and airy; some have whirlpools and fireplaces. Hotel facilities include hot tub, steam room, indoor pool, laundry and dry cleaning service. ⑧

Banff Springs Hotel Spray Ave ⓣ403/762-2211 or 1-800/441-1414, ⓦwww.fairmont.com. One of the continent's most famous hotels – built in Scots Baronial style with turrets and cornices towering above its thick nine-storey granite walls – offering luxurious service that borders on pageantry. The glut of facilities, which include a world-class fitness and spa complex, several stores and restaurants, make the hotel almost entirely self-contained. Rates are extravagant but the winter season offers a chance to stay here for around half price. ⑧

Banff Voyager Inn 555 Banff Ave ⓣ403/762-3301 or 1-800/879-1991, ⓦwww.banffvoyagerinn.com. Predictably comfortable motel; one of the last of a number that line the road from the town centre. With chilly outdoor pool, hot tub, sauna and the cheapest bar in town. ⑤

Bumper's Inn Banff Ave and Marmot Crescent ⓣ403/762-3386 or 1-800/661-3518, ⓦwww.bumpersinn.com. Small, well-priced, 1970s motel on the northeastern fringe of town but only 50m from the nearest ski shuttle stop. Facilities are limited to the basics, though some units have kitchenettes. ⑥

Douglas Fir Resort Tunnel Mountain Rd ⓣ403/762-5591 or 1-800/661-9267, ⓦwww.douglasfir.com. Collection of low-rise wood-clad condo blocks in secluded wooded area on Tunnel Mountain, a fifteen-minute walk from the town centre. Ideally equipped for families or groups, units have a kitchen and lounge with fireplace as well as access to a host of leisure facilities, including squash

Room and ski package operators

Banff Accommodation (rooms and ski packages) ⓣ403/762-0260 or 1-877/226-3348, ⓦwww.banffaccommodations.com.

Banff Central Reservations (rooms and ski packages) ⓣ403/705-4020 or 1-877/542-2633, ⓦwww.banffreservations.com.

Good Earth Travel (ski packages) ⓣ403/678-9358 or 1-888/979-9797, ⓦwww.goodearthtravel.com.

Resorts of the Canadian Rockies (ski packages) ⓣ403/256-8476 or 1-800/256-7669, ⓦwww.skircr.com.

Ski Banff–Lake Louise (ski packages) ⓣ403/762-4561 or 1-800/754-7080, ⓦwww.skibig3.com.

courts and pool with waterslides. Laundromat and small convenience store on-site. 6

High Country Inn 419 Banff Ave ⓣ403/762-2236 or 1-800/661-1244, ⓦwww.banffhighcountryinn.com. Mid-range 1980s motel with some luxury suites in a great central location. Facilities include two hot tubs and an indoor pool – rare in Banff. 6

Mount Royal Hotel 138 Banff Ave ⓣ403/762-3331 or 1-877/422-2623, ⓦwww.mountroyalhotel.com. Bland, three-storey building amid downtown shops at the centre of town. Most guests in the newly renovated rooms have mountain views; all have access to a large health club with whirlpool and exercise equipment. 7

Red Carpet Inn 425 Banff Ave ⓣ403/762-4184 or 1-800/563-4609, ⓦwww.banffredcarpet.com. Pastel shaded inside and out, this no-frills 1970s motel is a clean, central and decent value option for those looking for no more than very soft mattresses and the most basic in-room facilities. 6

Rimrock Resort Mountain Ave ⓣ403/762-3356 or 1-800/661-1587, ⓦwww.rimrockresort.com. Elegant and richly furnished hotel in imposing, ten-storey angular building that nestles alone among thick stands of trees on the lower slopes of Sulphur Mountain, 3km south of town. The smart, modern rooms come with views of Bow Valley. Excellent and extensive fitness facilities are offered, as is a free shuttle into town. 8

B&Bs

Banff Squirrel's Nest 332 Squirrel St ⓣ403/762-4432, ⓦwww.banffsquirrelsnest.com. Pleasant rooms on a quiet residential side street an easy walk from downtown. Rooms have queen beds and bathrooms en suite. Continental buffet breakfast included. 4

Blue Mountain Lodge 137 Muskrat St ⓣ403/762-5134, ⓦwww.bluemtnlodge.com. Friendly budget place in centre with ten small rooms all equipped with private bathrooms and spectacular mountain views. Common amenities include a guest kitchen and lounge, and laundry facilities. 4

Mountain Country Bed & Breakfast 427 Marten St ⓣ403/762-3288, ⓦwww.banffmountaincountry.com. Large barn-shaped house close to downtown Banff and a block from the ski shuttle route. The large, dark-wood furnished rooms are equipped with private Jacuzzi tubs, queen-size beds and duvets. Light continental breakfast. 3

Mountain Home Bed & Breakfast 129 Muskrat St ⓣ403/762-3889, ⓦwww.mountainhomebb.com. Elegant 1940s tourist lodge converted into a B&B a couple of minutes' walk to downtown Banff. Spacious, antique-furnished en-suite guest rooms have down comforters on king-size beds. Delicious cooked breakfasts with daily menu. 5

Tan-y-Bryn 118 Otter St ⓣ403/762-3696. Eight simple and extremely reasonable B&B rooms (and one cheap "emergency" room) with private or shared bathrooms and in-room continental breakfast. Quiet residential district three blocks from downtown. No credit cards. 2

Hostels

Banff International Youth Hostel (HI) Tunnel Mountain Rd ⓣ403/762-4122, ⓦwww.hihostels.ca. Friendly modern 216-bed hostel in great setting, but 3km from downtown and a $8 cab ride from the bus depot. Great facilities include large kitchen, laundry, lounge with fireplace, ski workshop and an adjoining inexpensive restaurant that can save trips downtown. Dorm beds are $32.50; private doubles ($87) also available. Ski packages cost $575 per person for five nights. No curfew.

SameSun Backpackers 449 Banff Ave ⓣ403/762-5521 or 1-888/844-7875, ⓦwww.samesun.com. Bohemian, sociable and chaotic 100-bed hostel on the strip just north of town, with a hot tub and sauna and all the more usual hostel facilities. Dorm beds cost $31, doubles available ($96).

Y Mountain Lodge 102 Spray Ave ⓣ403/762-3560 or 1-800/813-4138, ⓦwww.ywca-banff.ab.ca. Clinically clean, but reasonably relaxed, hostel a short walk from downtown. Dorms cost $31, but if there are two of you a large spartan private room ($75) costs little more (some en-suite). In addition to a huge living room with gigantic stone fireplace, the hostel has a café with reasonable food as well as a kitchen, laundry facilities and showers ($3 for nonresidents).

Campsites

Bow Valley Parkway There are three park campsites on or just off the Bow Valley Parkway road between Banff and Lake Louise, all within easy reach of Banff if you have transport (less than 30-minutes' drive): Johnston Canyon, Castle Mountain and Protection Mountain. See p.724 for full details.

Tunnel Mountain Village I 4.3km from town and 1km beyond the hostel on Tunnel Mountain Rd. Huge 622-pitch government-run campsite ($24 plus optional $8 for firewood and fire permit), the nearest to downtown, on the Banff Transit bus from Banff Ave. Arrive early – like all frontcountry park campsites, it's first-come, first-served. Electricity and hot showers. The nearby 322-site *Tunnel Mountain Trailer Court* ($28–33) is only for RVs. May to Sept.

Tunnel Mountain Village II 2.4km from town and close to *Village I* site. In the summer, available for group camping and commercial tenting only. However, after *Tunnel I* shuts (in late Sept) this government-run 189-pitch site becomes available for general walk-in winter camping ($24–32 plus optional $8 fire permit). Electricity and hot showers. The two sites are set amid trees, with lovely views, plenty of space and short trails close at hand. Bighorn sheep, elk and even the odd bear may drop in. Year-round.

Two Jack Lakeside 12km northeast of town on the Lake Minnewanka Rd. Fully serviced eighty-site park-run campsite ($24 plus optional $8 fire permit) with showers. Open mid-May to mid-Sept.

Two Jack Main 13km northeast of town on Lake Minnewanka Rd. Semi-serviced 381-site park campsite ($19 plus optional $8 fire permit); no showers. Open mid-May to Aug.

In and around Banff

With some of the world's most spectacular mountains on your doorstep, sightseeing in Banff might seem an absurd undertaking, yet it's good to have some rainy-day options. The **Banff Heritage Passport** ($8) gives entry to the Banff Park Museum, the Whyte Museum and the Cave & Basin National Historic Site.

The downtown **Banff Park Museum** at 93 Banff Ave (daily mid-May to Sept 10am–6pm; Oct to mid-May 1–5pm; $4), near the Bow River bridge, bulges with two floors of stuffed animals, many of which are indigenous to the park. In many ways the museum chronicles the changes of attitudes to wildlife in the park over the years. Many Victorians wanted to see the park's animals without the tiresome business of having to venture into the backcountry – so they killed and stuffed the beasts for permanent display. The hunting of game animals was eventually banned in the park in 1890, but not before populations of moose, elk, sheep, goats and grizzlies had been severely depleted. Game wardens only arrived to enforce the injunction in 1913, and even then they didn't protect the "bad" animals – wolves, coyotes, foxes, cougars, lynx, eagles, owls and hawks – which were hunted until the 1930s as part of the park's "predator-control program". Many of the stuffed victims in the museum date from this period. Sixty years ago a hapless polar bear was even displayed in the park behind the museum, one of sixty species of animals kept in the Banff Zoo and Aviary between 1904 and 1937. Until as recently as the 1970s hotels were organizing trips to the town's rubbish dumps to view foraging bears. Oddly enough, the museum – a fine building whatever your views on what's inside it – might have gone the same way as the animals. In the 1950s, changing attitudes saw the exhibits considered dated, and plans were mooted for the museum's demolition. However, it survived as a fine piece of frontier Edwardiana, distinguished, in particular, by its preponderance of skylights, essential features at a time when Banff was still without electricity. The lovely wood-panelled **reading room** – a snug retreat, full of magazines and books on nature and wildlife – makes a perfect spot to while away a cold afternoon. In summer, by contrast, the beautiful **riverside park** behind the museum is ideal for a snooze or picnic.

Nearby, the excellent **Whyte Museum of the Canadian Rockies** (daily 10am–5pm; $6; ⓦwww.whyte.org), next to the library at 111 Bear St, contents itself, among other things, with a look at the Rockies' emergence as a tourist destination through paintings and photographs, and at the early expeditions to explore and conquer the interior peaks. Pictures of bears foraging in Banff rubbish bins and of park rangers grinning over a magnificent lynx they've just shot give some idea of how times have changed. The museum, which opened in 1968, forms part of the Whyte Foundation, created in the 1950s by artists Peter and Catherine Whyte to collate and preserve as great a range of material as possible relating to the Rockies. The gleaming complex is also home to the 2075-volume Alpine Club of Canada library and the 4000-volume Archives of the Canadian Rockies – the largest collection of artistic and historical material relating to the mountains. The museum also hosts temporary exhibitions by local, national and international artists, as well as presenting lectures and walking, nature and gallery tours.

Across the river, dated displays of native history, birds and animals fill the **Luxton Museum**, an aboriginal peoples-run enterprise attractively housed in a huge wooden stockade at 1 Birch Ave (daily 9am–5pm; $8). The museum takes its name from Norman Luxton, a local who ran a trading post here and forged a close relationship with Banff's Stoney native population over the course of sixty years. The exhibits aren't exciting, but the museum shop has some good crafts and other items if you're in spending mode.

The Banff Springs Hotel

At around $1000 a night for some suites – $1800-plus for the presidential ensemble and its personal glass-sided elevators – the **Banff Springs Hotel** may be way out of your league, but you can't spend much time in town without coming across at least one mention of the place, and it's hard to miss its landmark Gothic superstructure. Initiated in 1888, it got off to a bad start when the architect arrived to find the place being built 180 degrees out of kilter: while the kitchens enjoyed magnificent views over the river the guestrooms looked blankly into thick forest. When it finally opened, with 250 rooms and a rotunda to improve the views, it was the world's largest hotel. The thinking behind the project was summed up by William Cornelius Van Horne, the larger-than-life vice-president of the Canadian Pacific Railway, who said of the Rockies, "if we can't export the scenery we'll import the tourists". One of the best ways to make the railway pay, he decided, was to sell people the idea of superb scenery and provide a series of jumbo hotels from which to enjoy it: the *Banff Springs* was the result, soon followed by similar railway-backed accommodation at Lake Louise and Yoho's Emerald Lake. Horne was also the man who, when he discovered the *Banff Springs* was being built back to front, pulled out a piece of paper and quickly sketched a veranda affair, which he decided would put things right: he was no architect, but such was his overbearing managerial style that his ad hoc creation was built anyway.

Today the 828-room luxury pile, largely rebuilt between 1911 and 1928, costs around $100,000 a day just to run, but boasts an extraordinary hundred percent occupancy – or over 1700 guests nightly – for half of the year. The influx has prompted further rebuilding, including a spa centre talked of as one of North America's best and a ballroom for 1600 people. Don't bother with the hotel's guided tours: a voyeuristic hour or so can be spent looking around the hotel's first three floors on your own (pick up a map in reception) or taking a coffee, beer or afternoon tea in the second-floor café and Sunroom off the main reception; prices for anything else in most of the sixteen various eating places are ludicrous. It's also worth walking out onto the terrace beyond the Sunroom for some truly spectacular views.

If you have the time and money try and visit the hotel's vast **spa complex**, The Willow Stream Spa (Ⓣ403/762-1772 or 1-800/404-1772), which competes with the Upper Hot Springs (see p.714). It centres on a circular mineral pool beneath a high-topped glass ceiling and offers outdoor saltwater hot tubs, steam rooms, lounges, fireplaces, and complimentary drinks and snacks, with an extensive array of therapeutic services on offer. Rates for using the facility are steep at $59 per day, but this fee is waived if you buy a service – say an hour's massage for $155.

You can get out to the hotel either by walking along the south bank of the Bow River (taking in Bow Falls) or picking up the Banff Transit bus from downtown ($2.25).

Sulphur Mountain Gondola

Banff is rightly proud of the **Sulphur Mountain Gondola** on Mountain Ave (daily: Feb–Mar 10am–5pm; April–May 8.30am–6pm; June–Aug 7.30am–9pm; Sept to mid-Oct 8.30am–6.30pm; mid-Oct to Nov 8.30am–4.30pm; Dec & Jan 10am–4pm; $25; Ⓦwww.banffgondola.com), some 5km south of town. High-price tickets buy you crowds, great views and a commercialized summit (2255m), but also the chance to do some high-level hiking without the slog of an early morning climb – a glimpse of the remote high country if you're short of time or unable to walk the trails. The best times to take a ride are early morning or evening, when wildlife sightings are more likely, and when the play of light gives an added dimension to the views.

The gondola trundles 700m skywards at a stomach-churning 51 degrees to immense panoramas from two observation terraces. It takes just eight minutes for the glass-enclosed four-passenger cars to reach the high point, where there's an ugly but surprisingly good-value summit restaurant, Canada's highest. (Far too much of its food ends up being eaten by bighorn sheep which gather here for handouts; don't encourage them – feeding wildlife is against park regulations and can land you with a stiff fine.) From the restaurant a one-kilometre path, the **Summit Ridge Trail**, has been blazed to take you a bit higher, while the short **Vista Trail** leads to the restored weather station and viewpoint on Sanson Peak. Norman Betheune "N.B." Sanson was first curator of the Banff Park Museum, and between 1903 and 1931 made around a thousand ascents of the mountain – that's before the gondola was built – to take his weather readings. Note that if, like him, you slog the 5.5km up from the car park you can ride the gondola down for free.

If you're without transport note that the only options for getting to the base station are to walk (dull and tiring) or take a taxi from downtown. In summer Brewster Transportation (Ⓣ403/762-8400, Ⓦwww.brewster.ca) runs a short **tour shuttle** from the town centre (mid-May to mid-Aug daily on the hour 9am–4pm; mid-Aug to early Oct until 6pm); the price ($29) includes the cost of the gondola ticket and return bus shuttle, which leaves the base station hourly on the half-hour.

Cave & Basin Hot Springs

Banff boasts eight **hot springs**, and the next stop on the standard itinerary after the gondola ride was, for a long time, a plunge into their waters. In their early days

Banff activities

The information centre carries extensive lists and contact information for guides and outfitters for all manner of **outdoor activities**; the box on p.716 details some of the best **walks** in and around Banff, while for all kinds of **winter sports** turn to p.720.

For general **bus tours**, contact Brewster Transportation (Ⓣ403/762-8400, Ⓦwww.brewster.ca), who've been running trips for decades. There's **golf** at the stunning Banff Springs Golf Course (Ⓣ403/762-6801; from $40 for nine holes, $125 for eighteen holes, club rental from $30). You'll need to book well in advance. Free shuttles run to the clubhouse from the *Banff Springs Hotel*.

Indoor climbing and swimming

Indoors, some of the best **fitness facilities** in town are in the Banff Recreation Centre, St Julien Rd (daily 6am–10pm; $10 admission, $4.25 swim only), and in the less expensive Community Fitness Centre (3–10pm) which also has a six-metre **climbing wall**. Climbers should additionally investigate the free climbing and bouldering walls at Mountain Magic, 224 Bear St, where gear rental is also offered (rock shoes, harness and helmet $20 per day). Another large pool complex is at the Douglas Fir Resort Tunnel Mountain Drive (Mon–Fri 4–9.30pm, Sat & Sun 10am–9.30pm; $8), which also has two massive indoor **waterslides.** Note that the only swimmable lake in the park is Johnson Lake northeast of town off Lake Minnewanka Rd: the others are usually glacier-fed and thus too cold.

Biking and skating

Mountain biking is popular, with plenty of rental places around town. One of the cheapest, Bactrax Bike Rentals, 225 Bear St, (from $8/hr or $30 per day; Ⓣ403/762-8177) has easy bike tours from one to four hours (from $20) on paved routes around Sundance Canyon and Vermilion Lakes. More ambitious rides on the Icefields and Bow Valley parkways or around Moraine Lake can be arranged in Lake Louise at the *Château Lake Louise* hotel (see p.726). If you're exploring on a bike under your own steam, pick up the *Trail Bicycling Guide* from the infocentre, which outlines some of the dedicated cycling trails: the best known are Sundance (3.7km one-way); Rundle Riverside (8km one-way); Cascade Trail (9km one-way); and the Spray River Loop (4.3km). The paved Sundance Canyon Trail near the Cave and Basin centre is a popular **inline skate** run.

Boating and fishing

Boat trips can be taken on Lake Minnewanka, as can **fishing** trips, which can be arranged through Lake Minnewanka Boat Tours (see p.714). Monod Sports, 129 Banff Ave (Ⓣ403/762-4571, Ⓦwww.monodsports.com), has all-day drift-boat fishing trips on the Bow River and Nakoda Lake for cutthroat and bull trout plus brown and

these springs were vital to Banff's rise and popularity, their reputedly therapeutic effects being of great appeal to Canada's ailing Victorian gentry. Dr R.G. Brett, chief medical officer to the Canadian Pacific Railway, used his position to secure an immensely lucrative virtual monopoly on the best springs. In 1886 he constructed the Grandview Villa, a money-spinning sanatorium promising miracle cures and wonders such as "ice-cold temperance drinks". Its handrails were reinforced by crutches abandoned by "cured" patients, though the good doctor reputedly issued crutches to all arrivals whether they needed them or not.

There may be quieter places in western Canada to take the waters, but hot springs always make for a mildly diverting experience, and even if the crowds are a pain the prices are reasonable. On the face of it, the springs at the recently renovated **Cave & Basin National Historic Site** (mid-June to Aug daily 10am–6pm; Sept–April Mon–Fri 11am–4pm, Sat & Sun 9.30am–5pm; $4;

brook trout (both are catch and release, meaning you have to put any caught fish back into the water) at $400 for two people, and walk and wade trips ($130 per person); trips include guide, instruction, tackle, waders, drinks and food. Beginner fly-fishers can take an instructional tour with the company. Banff Fishing Unlimited (ⓣ403/762-4936, ⓦwww.banff-fishing.com) has Bow River float trips and walk and wade trips (from $110 per person) and half-day fishing cruises on Lake Minnewanka ($90 per person in a group of six). Tackle can be rented from Performance Ski and Sports, 208 Bear St (ⓣ403/762-8222). Remember you need a national park licence to fish, available for $8.90 a day, $29.70 a year, from tackle shops, most of the above companies or the infocentre. If you want to **rent canoes** for paddling on the Vermilion Lakes or quiet stretches of the Bow River, contact Bow River Canoe Docks ($25/hr, $50/day; ⓣ403/762-3632); the dock is on the river at Wolf Street.

Horse riding

Horse riding is easy to organize, with anything from one-hour treks to two-week backcountry expeditions available. The leading in-town outfitters are Holiday on Horseback, 132 Banff Ave (ⓣ403/762-4551, ⓦwww.horseback.com). One-, two- and three-hour rides start at about $36, while a five-hour trip up the Spray River Valley costs about $136. You can also take overnight trips either camping or with nights spent in a lodge.

Whitewater rafting

Best among adrenaline-rush activities is **whitewater rafting** on the Kicking Horse River, located a few kilometres up the road in Yoho but accessed by some eight companies in Banff and Lake Louise, most of them providing all necessary gear and transportation. Other gentler "float" trip options with the same companies are available on the Kananaskis, Kootenay and Bow rivers. Long-established Hydra River Guides, 209 Bear St (ⓣ403/762-4554 or 1-800/644-8888, ⓦwww.raftbanff.com), has two daily trips ($99) in paddle or oar rafts on the Kicking Horse. Wet 'n' Wild Adventures (ⓣ403/344-6546 or 1-800/668-9119, ⓦwww.wetnwild.bc.ca/rafting) has full ($110 including shuttle from Lake Louise) and half-day ($65) trips in the Kicking Horse Canyon, a half-day trip ($65) in the wilder lower part of the canyon for more advanced rafters, as well as easier, child-friendly trips, two-day trips and raft and horse-riding packages. For half-day trips ($64) on the Kootenay River, contact Kootenay River Runner (ⓣ250/347-9210 or 1-800/599-4399, ⓦwww.raftingtherockies.com), who also run various parts of the Kicking Horse canyon. For gentle float trips, contact Canadian Rockies Rafting (ⓣ403/678-6535 or 1-877/226-7625, ⓦwww.rafting.ca): who charge $45 for half a day on the Bow River.

guided tours free with admission summer daily 11am, winter weekends only), southwest of downtown at the end of Cave Avenue, are the best places to indulge. The original cave and spring here are what gave birth to the national park, discovered on November 8, 1883 by three railway navvies prospecting for gold on their day off. Having crossed the Bow River by raft they discovered a warm-watered stream, which they proceeded to follow to a small eddy of sulphurous and undergrowth-clogged water. Close by lay a small hole, the water's apparent source, which on further exploration turned out to be the entrance to an underground cave and warm mineral pool. The government quickly bought the three out, promoting travel to the springs as a means of contributing to the cost of the railway's construction. A small reserve was established in 1885, from which the present park eventually evolved. The first bathhouse was built in 1887, but over the years succumbed to the corrosive effects of chlorine and the pool's natural minerals. The pools finally closed in 1975, were restored (at a cost of $12m), opened in 1985 and closed again in 1993 – again because of corrosion and low visitor numbers.

Today the pools are still shut to bathers, leaving a popular **interpretive centre** to delve into their history and geology. You can walk here in a few minutes from town. From the foyer, where the faint whiff of sulphur is unmistakable, a short tunnel leads to the original cave, where the stench becomes all but overpowering. Smell aside, it's still a rather magical spot, with daylight shining in from a little hole in the roof and the limpid water inviting but tantalizingly out of bounds. Back down the tunnel and up the stairs brings you to a few rooms of displays, with a film show, some illuminating old photographs and several pertinent quotations, among which is the acidic comment of an early travel writer, Douglas Sladen: "Though it consists of but a single street," he grumbled about Banff in 1895, "it is horribly overcivilized." Down the stairs from the displays at the rear brings you to the "basin", a small outdoor hot spring that's separate from the cave-spring system, but no less inviting. Alongside is a wooden hut theatre with a half-hour film show.

Immediately outside the centre, the short Discovery Trail (15min) heads up the hill for a view over the site, together with the nearby start of the excellent **Sundance Canyon** surfaced path (see box, p.716). Just below the centre is the **Marsh Loop Trail** (2km; 25min), a treat for bird-watching enthusiasts in particular. The area's low-elevation wetlands teem with waterfowl during the winter and spring migrations, with the chance to see – among others – Barrow's goldeneye and all three species of teal: cinnamon, blue-winged and green-winged. The warm microclimate produced here by the springs' warm waters supports mallards over the winter, as well as attracting seasonal rarities such as killdeer, common snipe and rusty blackbird. During the summer you might see belted kingfisher, common yellowthroat, willow flycatcher and red-winged blackbird. Just across the river from here on Vermilion Lakes is the single most important area for bird-watching in the entire park, accessed via trails and the Vermilion Lakes Road. Ospreys and bald eagles both nest here, and other highlights include tundra swan, hooded merganser and northern shoveler.

Upper Hot Springs

Unlike the Cave & Basin, there's no problem with swimming in the **Upper Hot Springs**, 4.5km from Banff town centre on Mountain Avenue (mid-May to mid-Oct daily 9am–11pm; rest of year Fri & Sat 10am–11pm, Sun–Thurs 10am–10pm; $7.50, rental of lockers, towel and swimming costumes is extra; ⓣ403/762-1515 or 1/800-767-1611). Originally developed in 1901, the springs have since undergone several renovations and now offer soaking at 38°C in a large outdoor pool. Sadly, the flow of natural spring water has recently dwindled so that currently the pool is topped up using tap water – with a clear loss of therapeutic benefits. Other attractions include a steam room and cold plunge, and the possibility of signing up for relaxing therapeutic massages ($50 for half an hour) and other treatments. There's a good poolside restaurant with outside terrace, fresh juice bar and hot and cold snacks.

Lake Minnewanka

Lake Minnewanka lies a few kilometres north of Banff town centre and is easily accessed by bike or car from the Trans-Canada and the northern end of Banff Avenue on Lake Minnewanka Road. The largest area of water in the national park, its name means "Lake of the Water Spirit", and with the peaks of the Fairholme Range as backdrop it provides a suitably scenic antidote to the bustle of downtown. Various dams augmented the lake to provide Banff with hydroelectric power, though they've done little to spoil the views, most of which are best enjoyed from the various **boat trips** run by Lake Minnewanka Boat Tours (mid-May to Sept sailings at 10am, 12.30pm, 3pm & 5pm, late June to Aug there's an extra sailing at 7pm; $40; ⓣ403/762-3473, ⓦwww.minnewankaboattours.com) that depart regularly from the quay in summer. This lake is the only one in the national park where public motorboats are allowed. Fishing trips can be arranged through the same company. Brewster Transportation offers an inclusive bus tour and cruise from Banff for around $54 (mid-May to early Oct).

Eating and drinking

Banff's hundred-plus **restaurants** run the gamut from Japanese and other ethnic cuisines to nouvelle-frontier grub. For cheap eats you're best sticking to hostel cafés, though Banff Ave is lined with good little spots for coffee and snacks, many with pleasant outdoor tables; some of the bars in town are also decent value. For **groceries** try the big Safeway supermarket at 318 Marten St and Elk (daily 9am–10pm).

Cafés and restaurants

Aardvark Pizza and Sub 304a Caribou St. Tiny takeaway place with subs, wings, tacos, nachos, poutine (french fries with cheese curd, the favorite Québécois comfort food and fantastic thick-crust pizzas. There's virtually nowhere to sit but with the best takeout food in town, and open until 4am, popularity's assured.

Baker Creek Bistro Baker Creek Chalets, Bow Valley Parkway ⓣ403/522-2182. Romantic dining in softly lit log cabin outfitted with deer-antler chandeliers midway between Banff and Lake Louise on the Bow Valley Parkway. The menu has innovative steaks and pastas, and good game dishes ($25–31); apple cake is the house speciality.

Balkan the Greek 120 Banff Ave ⓣ403/762-3454. Cheerful blue and white Greek place, best known for frantic belly dancing on Tuesdays and large portions of decent, if rather curious, Greek-style food: choose from the likes of Greek ribs (pork ribs in a lemon sauce) for $27; Greek spaghetti; or better, stick to the traditional favourites like *souvlaki* ($19) or if you're ravenous the two-person Greek platter ($54) which includes beef *souvlaki*, ribs, *moussaka*, lamb chops and salad.

Banff Springs Hotel 405 Spray Ave ⓣ403/762-6860. With around fifteen dining options under one roof, the *Banff Springs* has plenty of variety; all are open to non-guests. The *Bow Valley Grill* is the largest restaurant, its menu focused around reliably popular seafood and rotisserie-grilled meats. The Sunday brunch ($40) here is legendary for its variety and value, while some of the other buffets offered include a tour of the hotel. Other places to eat range from the 24-hour deli serving pizza, to the super-luxurious *Banffshire Club*, which stipulates formal attire and includes *Castello Ristorante* for top-class Italian foods and the *Samurai*, which serves excellent sushi. For light snacks try *Grapes Wine Bar* which has good salads, a fine selection of pâtés and cheese and a highly esteemed fondue.

Bumper's 603 Banff Ave ⓣ403/762-2622. Busy, good-value steakhouse with adjoining laid-back bar located a little outside downtown. Entrée prices start at around $20 and vegetarians can console themselves with a decent salad bar.

Cilantro Mountain Café At *Buffalo Mountain Lodge*, Tunnel Mountain Rd ⓣ403/760-3008. A good café-restaurant, with the usual North American fare that's ideal if you're staying at the hostel or campsite and want a modest treat; has a nice outside terrace for the summer. Inexpensive.

Coyote's Grill 206 Caribou St. Small, simple café just off the main drag, serving top-notch breakfasts. One of the best is the cream-cheese-filled French Toast with fruit ($9). But the hungry should try the huge Mountain Man Breakfast ($9.50) which includes two eggs, two pancakes, bacon or sausage and roasted potatoes. Evenings see fine renditions of pizza, pasta and Southwestern Tex-Mex entrees ($15–25).

Elk and Oarsman Upstairs at 119 Banff Ave ⓣ403/762-4616. Refined pub with a fine roof terrace, with excellent, if obvious, food – pizza, steaks, burgers and salads – albeit with a "gourmet" twist at good prices. There's also a good range of beers on tap – many of them local.

Evelyn's 201 Banff Ave ⓣ403/762-0352. A superb range of coffees wash down pastries and muffins here in a café that's popular enough to justify a second outlet, *Evelyn's Too*, at 229 Bear Ave. Both

Hikes around Banff

Walks from Banff downtown

Banff Townsite is one of two obvious bases for walks in the park (the other is Lake Louise), and trails around the town cater to all levels of fitness. The best short stroll from downtown – at least for flora and fauna – is the **Fenland Trail**, a 1.5-kilometre loop west through the montane wetlands near the First Vermilion Lake (there are three Vermilion lakes, fragments of a huge lake that once probably covered the whole Bow Valley at this point; all can be accessed off Vermilion Lakes Drive). Marsh here is slowly turning to forest, creating habitats whose rushes and grasses provide a haven for wildlife, birds in particular. Ospreys and bald eagles nest around the lake, together with a wide range of other birds and waterfowl. You may also see beaver, muskrat, perhaps even coyote, elk and other deer. You can walk this and other easy local trails in the company of the "Friends of Banff" – see p.705 for more.

For a shorter walk, and a burst of spectacular white water, stroll the level and very easy **Bow Falls Trail** (1km) from beneath the bridge on the south side of the river, which follows the river bank east to a powerful set of waterfalls and rapids just below the *Banff Springs Hotel*. The **Hoodoos Trail** on the other side of the river (starting at the eastern end of Buffalo St) offers similar views with fewer people, eventually linking up to Tunnel Mountain Road (3km) – making it a good way to walk into town for the hostel and campsites – and beyond to viewpoints above the hoodoos (4.6km).

The **Marsh Loop Trail** (2km) from Cave Avenue leads along a boardwalk through a marshy habitat renowned for its flora and birds (see p.714): warm waters from the Cave and Basin hot springs immediately above have created a small, anomalous area of lush vegetation. In winter Banff's own wolf pack has been known to hunt within sight of this trail. The **Sundance Canyon Trail** (3.7km), an easy and deservedly popular stroll along a paved path (also popular with cyclists and rollerbladers – be warned) to the picnic area at the canyon mouth, also starts from close to the springs; you can extend your walk along the 2.1km loop path up through the canyon, past waterfalls and back down a peaceful wooded trail. Finally, the most strenuous walk near town is to the summit of Tunnel Mountain. It's approached on a windy track (300m ascent) from the southwest from Tunnel Mountain Drive, culminating in great views over the townsite, Bow River and flanking mountains.

Day-hikes near Banff

Day-hikes from the town centre are limited – you need transport and usually have to head a few kilometres along the Trans-Canada to reach trailheads that leave the flat valley floor for the heart of the mountains. Only a couple of longish ones strike out directly from town: the **Spray River Circuit**, a flat, 13km round trip past the *Banff Springs Hotel* up the Spray River; and the Sulphur Mountain Trail, a 5.5-kilometre switchback that climbs 655m up to the Sulphur Mountain gondola terminal at 2255m (you're better off simply taking the gondola).

are open 7am–11pm, and put together deli sandwiches (around $5) that make ideal picnic food.

Joe Btfsplk's [sic] Diner 221 Banff Ave ☎403/762-5529. Red vinyl seats and black and white tiles help make this 1950s-style diner feel authentic, as do the dependable and giant portions of classic, comfort foods like meatloaf ($9). And yes, the name is *Joe Btfsplk's* – named after a comic book character.

Le Beaujolais 212 Banff Ave at Buffalo St ☎403/762-2712. Longstanding gourmet restaurant whose reputation for fine French renditions of regional cuisine extends all over western Canada. Pick from a choice of three set-price menus between $55 and $90, which help keep tabs on spending and range from two to six courses – though only the six course meal includes drinks from the lavish wine list.

Melissa's 218 Lynx St ☎403/762-5511. Probably Banff's most popular daytime destination, set in an old log cabin: big breakfasts, superb mignon steaks, salads and burgers, plus a good upstairs

Park wardens at the infocentre seem unanimous in rating the **Cory Pass Trail** (5.8km; 915m ascent), combined with the Edith Pass Trail to make a return loop, as the best day-hike close to Banff. The trailhead is signed 6km west of the town off the Bow Valley Parkway, 500m after the junction with the Trans-Canada. The stiff climbing involved, and a couple of scree passages, means that it's not for the inexperienced or faint-hearted. The rewards are fantastic, with varied walking, a high-mountain environment and spine-tingling views. From the pass itself at 2350m you can return on the Edith Pass Trail (whose start you'll have passed 1km into the Cory Pass walk), to make a total loop of a demanding 13km.

Another popular local day-hike, the trail to **Cascade Amphitheatre** (2195m), starts at Mount Norquay Ski Area, 6km north of the Trans-Canada Mount Norquay Road. This offers a medley of landscapes, ranging from alpine meadows to deep, ice-scoured valleys and a close view of the knife-edge mountains that loom so tantalizingly above town. Allow about three hours for the walk (7.7km; 610m ascent). For the same amount of effort you could tackle **Elk Lake** (2165m) from the ski area, though at 13.5km each way it's a long day's hike; some people turn it into an overnight hike by using the campsite 2.5km short of Elk Lake. Shorter, but harder on the lungs, is the third of Banff's popular local walks, **C Level Cirque** (1920m), reached by a 4km trail from the Upper Bankhead Picnic Area on the Lake Minnewanka road east of Banff. Elsewhere, the Sunshine Meadows area has five high trails of between 8km and 20km, all possible as day-hikes and approached either from the Sunshine Gondola (if running) or its parking area, 18km southwest of Banff. There are also some good short trails off the Bow Valley Parkway, most notably the **Johnston Canyon** path (see box, p.723).

The best **backpacking** options lie in the Egypt Lake area west of Banff Townsite, with longer trails radiating from the lake's campsite. Once you're in the backcountry around Banff, however, the combination of trails is virtually limitless. The keenest hikers tend to march the routes that lead from Banff to Lake Louise – the Sawback Trail and Bow Valley Highline, or the tracks in the Upper Spray and Bryant Creek Valley south of the townsite.

If you're planning long walks and overnight trips in backcountry you must have a **Wilderness Pass** ($9 a night from park centres). You should also book backcountry campsites (contact Parks Canada at Lake Louise or Banff visitor centres – see p.726 and p.704) and walks well in advance ($12 nonrefundable booking fee), as **quotas** operate for all backcountry areas – if the quotas fill, you won't be able to walk or camp or may have to make do with a second-choice hike. The most popular of the fifty-odd campsites are Marvel Lake, Egypt Lake, Luellen Lake, Aylmer Pass, Mystic Meadow, Fish Lakes, Paradise Valley, Hidden Lake, Baker Lake, Merlin Meadows, Red Deer Lakes and Mount Rundle. Be sure to pick up or send for the Parks Canada *Backcountry Visitors' Guide* pamphlet for further details of the system and of recommended routes.

bar, *Mel's*, for a leisurely drink, and a summer patio for food and beer in the sun. Recommended, particularly for lunch. Moderate prices with most main dishes in the $8–15 range.

Saltlik 221 Bear St ⓣ403/762-2467. Swanky second-floor restaurant with wacky lamps and loud art in an otherwise understated but stylized interior. A nouvelle-steakhouse, it does Alberta proud with its almost finicky preparation of the 10oz prime sirloin ($20). But most entrees, including rotisserie chicken, smoked Alaskan black cod and sea bass, are under the $20 mark – but the price doesn't include the tasty sides (mushrooms, spinach, corn, shrimp) that you use to assemble your own meal. The wide selection of wines suffer little markup and the trendy first-floor bar is a good place for a drink before or after dinner – or with dinner as it has the best bar menu in town; don't miss the crisp, seasoned shoestring fries.

Sushi House Banff 304 Caribou Street. Sushi delivered by train – a toy train that is – that circulates around the counter. Take what you fancy and get charged by the number of your dirty plates. Fresh and good fun for a quick and inexpensive bite, if you don't mind being elbow-to-elbow with the other diners. All of Banff's other budget dining options line the same street.

Sukiyaki House 211 Banff Ave ⓣ403/762-2002. Sit low among Japanese visitors at the squat tables of this chic Japanese restaurant. With a broad menu, it's hard to choose, but almost impossible to go wrong; the easy option is to pick the Love Boat ($35), a well-priced and varied selection for two people.

Drinking and nightlife

Given Banff's huge number of summer travellers and a large young seasonal workforce, there are plenty of people around looking for **nightlife** (winter is rarely as busy) and the town has no shortage of **bars** – most within a short walk of one another – and several late-night clubs to stagger to afterwards. Among the less boozy entertainments are **billiards** upstairs at the ten-pin **bowling** at the *Banff Springs Hotel* ($6 a game, $3 shoe rental) and new-release **films** at the Lux Cinema, 229 Bear St (ⓣ403/762-8595).

Aurora 110 Banff Ave. Loud, pricey and popular bar, nightclub and pick-up joint usually gets going around midnight when twentysomethings gather to dance until 2am. Occasional live music on Fri and Sat evenings.

Banff Springs Hotel ⓣ403/762-6892. The giant hotel has a selection of bars, including the neighbourhood-style *Waldhaus Pub*, the cigar-friendly *Ramsay Lounge*, the *Rundle Balcony* with its own pianist, and wine bar *Grapes*.

HooDoos 137 Banff Ave. Basement bar and nightclub that's the main competition for Banff's other major nightspot, the *Aurora*. If it's dead here it won't be in the Aurora and vice-versa. Live music or DJ nightly, small cover.

Rose and Crown 202 Banff Ave. Victorian-style pub with family-oriented restaurant serving decent bar food, which include fantastic hot wings. There's pool here and occasionally live music, particularly blues and funk, making it a cornerstone of town nightlife.

St James Gate 205 Wolf St. Genuinely dingy dark-wood pub, originally built in Ireland then reassembled here to become hugely popular with locals and visitors alike. The thirty beers on tap include good Guinness, as do many of the dishes on the satisfying bar menu; Guinness, crab and asparagus soup ($6), or Guinness, steak and mushroom pie ($11). Other menu items are equally earthy like the tasty Kilpatrick's cabbage and sausage soup ($6) and the juicy halibut fish and chips ($11) and decent meatloaf $12. Occasional live Celtic music.

Voyager Inn 555 Banff Ave. Workaday bar adjoining eponymous motel on the edge of town. Locals who appreciate the cheapest drinks in town – along with nightly specials – converge here.

Wild Bill's Legendary Saloon 203 Banff Ave. Lively country-and-western bar with live bands (country Wed–Sat; rock & blues Sun–Thurs) and weekly line-dancing lessons (Wed 8.30pm). There's also a pool hall and games room here, and before 8pm good Tex-Mex and vegetarian food is served in a more family-oriented atmosphere.

Listings

Bookshop Banff Book & Art Den, Clock Tower Mall, 94 Banff Ave (daily 9am–9pm; ⓣ403/762-3919).

Car rental Book well in advance. Avis ⓣ403/762-3222; Banff Rent-a-Car, 230 Lynx St ⓣ403/762-3352, for lower-priced older vehicles; Budget ⓣ403/762-4546; Hertz ⓣ403/762-2027; National ⓣ403/762-2688.

Internet Public library, 101 Bear St (Mon–Thurs 10am–8pm, Fri 10am–6pm, Sat 11am–6pm, Sun 1–5pm; ⓣ403/762-2661).

Laundries Cascade Coin Laundry, Lower Level, Cascade Plaza, 317 Banff Ave ⓣ403/762-3444.

Medical Mineral Springs Hospital, 301 Lynx St ⓣ403/762-2222. A dentist is at 210 Bear St ⓣ403/762-3144. Gourlay's pharmacy is at 229 Bear St ⓣ403-762-2516.

Outdoor equipment Tents, outdoor gear and ski equipment to rent from Bactrax, 225 Bear St ⓣ403/762-8177. Other rental stores and outlets line the same strip.

Police ⓣ403/762-2228.

Post office 204 Buffalo St (Mon–Fri 9am–5.30pm, ⓣ403/762-2586).

Road conditions ⓣ403/762-1450.

Taxis Banff Taxi (ⓣ403/762-4444; Mountain ⓣ403/762-3351.

Weather ⓣ403/762-1550 or 762-2088 (24hr recording).

Highway 1 and the Bow Valley Parkway

Two roads run parallel through the Bow Valley from Banff to Lake Louise (58km): the faster **Highway 1** (the Trans-Canada); and the quieter **Bow Valley Parkway**, on the north side of the river, opened in 1989 as a special scenic route. After Banff, there's only one link between the two roads, at Castle Junction, 30km from Lake Louise. Both routes are staggeringly beautiful as the mountains start to creep closer to the road. For the entire run, the mighty Bow River, broad and emerald green, crashes through rocks and forest. Despite the tarmac and heavy summer traffic, the surroundings are pristine and suggest the immensity of the wilderness to come. Sightings of elk and deer are common, particularly around dawn and sundown, and occasionally you'll spot moose.

Both roads offer some good **trails**: if you want to tackle one of the most highly rated day-walks in Banff National Park, make for the Bourgeau Lake Trail off Hwy 1 (see box, p.723); for a shorter walk, make for the Johnston Canyon on the Parkway.

Highway 1

Most people tend either to cruise **Highway 1**'s rapid stretch of the Trans-Canada without stopping – knowing that the road north of Lake Louise is more spectacular still – or leap out at every trail and rest stop, overcome with the grandeur of it all. On Greyhound or Brewster **buses** you're whisked through to Lake Louise in about forty minutes; if you're driving, try, for the sake of wildlife, to stick to the 90kph speed limit. The vast fences that march for kilometre after kilometre along this section of the road are designed to protect animals, not only from traffic, but also from the brainless visitors who clamber out of their cars to get close to the bears occasionally glimpsed on the road. You won't have to be in the Rockies long during the summer before you're caught in a **bear jam**, when people – contrary to all park laws, never mind common sense – abandon their cars helter-skelter on the road to pursue hapless animals with cameras and camcorders.

Sunshine Meadows

A beautiful and unusually large tract of alpine grassland, **Sunshine Meadows**, 18km southwest of Banff off Hwy 1, is cradled by Sunshine Village ski resort and straddles the continental divide. The area may be better known for its winter sports, but for the short summer season the valley is replete with hundreds of wild flowers and ideal for high-mountain hiking. Access to the valley is on foot on an arduous 6km access trail from the resort's car park, but a much better option is to take a shuttle bus. A service is run between early June and the end of September by White Mountain Adventures (Ⓣ403/678-4099 or 1-800/408-005, Ⓦwww.canadiannatureguides.com; $23 one-way from the car park, $43 from Banff), departing from both Banff (currently at 8.30am, returning at 2.30pm & 5.30pm) and the Sunshine Village parking lot (hourly from 9am, returning hourly). Once you're in Sunshine Meadows two connecting gravel trails can be followed. The **Rock Isle Trail** loop starts at the Sunshine Meadows Nature Centre. After 1km, branch right to pass Rock Isle Lake on the left (take the left fork and you'd eventually come to Lake Assiniboine). Around 600m after the branch right you come to a fork: turn left and you loop around the Garden Path Trail (3.8km) past Larix Lake, the Simpson Viewpoint and Grizzly Lake back to the fork. From here it's 500m to a 1.2-kilometre detour to the right to Standish Viewpoint (a dead end). Otherwise head straight on and after 2.8km you come to a junction and the

Winter sports in and around Banff

As enticing in winter as it is the rest of the year, Banff National Park comes close to paradise if you're a skier or snowboarder. The terrain here is some of the best and most varied in North America and three world-class resorts lie in the park: two close to Banff – **Mount Norquay** and **Sunshine Village** – and one in **Lake Louise** (see p.734). On top of great snow and pristine runs, you get crisp air, monumental mountains, sky-high forests, and prices and space that make a mockery of Europe's crowded and exorbitant winter playgrounds. You're also pretty certain of snow, sensational views, plenty of nightlife and comfortable hotels – much cheaper than in summer and connected to the ski hills via frequent shuttle buses. On top of this the park also offers the full gamut of **winter activities**, embracing everything from skating, ice-fishing and toboggan trips to dog-sledding, snowshoeing and sleigh rides. However, what the brochures don't tell you is that here – as in Lake Louise – it can be bitterly cold for much of the skiing season.

Mount Norquay

Mount Norquay (ⓣ403/762-4421, ⓦwww.banffnorquay.com) is the closest resort to Banff, just 6km and ten minutes' drive from downtown. Skiing started on the mountain's steep eastern slopes in the 1920s. In 1948 it gained Canada's first-ever chairlift, immediately gaining a reputation as an experts-only resort thanks largely to horrors like the double-black diamond Lone Pine run. This reputation has only recently disappeared, the result of a complete revamp and the opening of a new network of lifts on and around Mystic Ridge to provide access to intermediate terrain and 31 runs suitable for all levels of skiers and boarders alike.

As a result Norquay is now equally renowned for its uncrowded beginners' slopes as for its expert runs, the terrain breaking down as follows: Novice (20 percent), Intermediate (36 percent) and Expert (44 percent). The average snowfall is 300cm, and there's snow-making on ninety percent of the terrain. The season runs from December to mid-April. The highest elevation is 2133m, giving a vertical drop of 503m to the resort's base elevation at 1636m. Amenities include a visitor centre, ski school, rental shop, day-care and – on Fridays – the promise of night skiing. Lift tickets are around $53 a day.

Sunshine Village

Sunshine Village (ⓣ403/277-7669, ⓦwww.skibanff.com) is a stunning resort, situated way up in the mountains at 2160m, 18km southwest of Banff. If anything the scenery's better than at Norquay – you're higher – and you have the plus of the national park's only on-hill accommodation. There's also an incredible 10m of snow a year – so there's no need for snow-making machines – with superb soft, light powder that *Snow Country* magazine has repeatedly voted "The Best Snow in Canada". Skiing started here in 1929 when two locals got lost on Citadel Pass and came back with tales of fantastic open bowls and dream slopes just made for skiing. In 1938 the Canadian National Ski Championships were held here, and by 1942 a portable lift had been installed on site. The biggest change in the area's fortunes came in 1980, when a gondola (cable car) was built to carry skiers (and occasionally summer walkers) the 6km from the Healy Creek parking area to the self-contained Sunshine Village resort.

Today some 107 uncrowded runs can be accessed on the gondola, three high-speed detachable quads, a triple chair, four double chairs, two T-bars and two beginner rope tows. There's as much here for the advanced skier as at Norquay, as well as plenty for the beginner and competent intermediate. Terrain breaks downs as follows: Novice (20 percent), Intermediate (55 percent) and Expert (25 percent). The top elevation is an incredible 2730m at Lookout Mountain and there's 3168 acres of terrain to choose from. Lift tickets are around $70 a day.

Amenities include a day-lodge, day-care, outdoor hot pool, ski school, rental shop and overnight rooms in the Village at the 85-room *Sunshine Inn*, the Rockies' only on-slope accommodation (Ⓣ403/277-7669; Ⓦwww.skibanff.com; ⑧). Ski packages are available here, with two nights' skiing and lodging around $280 per person.

Other winter activities

If you really want to see the park, head out on either **cross-country skis** or **snowshoes** on the myriad summer walking trails groomed for these purposes. Details of the full network are given in the *Nordic Trails in Banff National Park* pamphlet ($3) available from the town's visitor centre. Popular areas include Johnston Lake, Golf Course Road, Spray River and Sundance Canyon, along with several areas around Lake Louise (see p.735). An additional 300km of cross-country trails crisscross the Kananaskis region, many developed for Olympic competitions, radiating from Canmore Nordic Centre (see p.698). But if these networks aren't enough and you're interested in ski tours of Banff's backcountry, it's best to have the company of an experienced guide; Banff Alpine Guides (Ⓣ403/678-6091) is a reliable local company. Good local sources of rentals, repairs, accessories and advice are Trail Sports (Ⓣ403/678-6764) at the Canmore Nordic Centre and Mountain Magic (Ⓣ403/762-2591). Both stores also rent out snowshoes and can help with suggestions for local hikes.

One of the best **winter walks** in the area is the hike through the fairytale scenery of Johnston Canyon, on boardwalks suspended from its limestone walls to impressive pillars of glassy ice. Though icy, the boardwalks are navigable in winter with the right gear and knowledge. White Mountain Adventures (Ⓣ403-760-4403 or 1-800/408-0005, Ⓦwww.whitemountainadventures.com) can offer a 3.5hr trip down the canyon. Similar packages, down the less spectacular Grotto Canyon, are offered by Discover Banff tours (Ⓣ403/760-5007 or 1-877/565-9372, Ⓦwww.banfftours.com), which only take an hour. One of the highlights of this trip is to watch the ice-climbers in this canyon, as this is one of the area's most popular intermediate pitches. Other popular sites in the area include Goat Mountain, past Yamnuska, a fairly moderate area, and Cougar Canyon, a more intermediate challenge. Beginners should head to Canmore Junkyards, past Nordic Centre turn-off in Canmore, while death-defying experts might like to explore the internationally notorious Terminator just outside the Banff National Park boundary. For detailed **ice climbing** information visit the National Park desk in Banff's Information Centre (see p.704) where climbers should also register.

Of the large selection of local commercial tours one of the best is **dog-sledding**. Thrilling trips are offered for a rather steep fee by Discover Banff Tours (see above; around $280 for two people for four hours) or Snowy Owl Sled Dog Tours (Ⓣ403/678-4369). For less adrenaline-filled **sleigh rides** on the frozen Bow River, again contact Discover Banff Tours or Holiday on Horseback (from 45mins for $24; Ⓣ403/762-4551, Ⓦwww.horseback.com), while those who seek the positively calming experience of **ice-fishing** on surrounding lakes should contact Banff Fishing Unlimited (Ⓣ403/762-4936, Ⓦwww.banff-fishing.com).

For a session of **ice-skating** or **tobogganing**, head to the *Banff Springs Hotel* where the outdoor rink is made particularly appealing by a fire beside it. Ice skates can be rented from The Ski Shop (Ⓣ403/762-5333) in the hotel for $7/hr; you can also rent sleds here ($5/hr) for use on the unofficial run beside the rink. Many other hotels in town also provide sleds for toboggan runs, of which there are several unofficial examples around town and an alternative venue for ice-skating is the rinks of Banff High School, on the Bow River (off Bow St).

Note that in past years the 17km of the Bow Valley Parkway between Johnston Canyon and the east entrance off the Trans-Canada (that is, the entrance closest to Banff) has been **closed** every day from March 1 to June 25 between 6pm and 9am. This lets animals forced down to look for food at lower altitudes by late snow to graze. Access at these times to the Johnston Canyon trails and campsite is from Hwy 1 only. Consult the visitor centre in Banff to confirm the latest arrangements.

Monarch Viewpoint, where a 1.6-kilometre walk takes you back to the Nature Centre (11.5km total with all loops and detours). Ask for a sketch map of this area from the information centre.

The Bow Valley Parkway

If anything, the **Bow Valley Parkway** boasts more scenic grandeur than Hwy 1 – which is saying something – and offers more distractions if you're taking your time: several trails, campsites, plus plenty of accommodation choices and one excellent eating option. The largest concentration of sightseers is likely to be found at the Merrent turn-off, enjoying fantastic views of the Bow Valley and the railway winding through the mountains.

If you have the time, therefore, the Parkway is the preferable route, and you should budget some time to walk one of the **trails** en route, in particular the easy but impressive Johnston Canyon Trail (see box opposite). En route, some of the various viewpoints and signed pull-offs deserve more attention than others. Around 8km down the highway, look out for the **Backswamp Viewpoint**, where views one way extend to the mountains and the other across a river swamp area where you might see beaver, muskrat, ospreys and other birds, as well as the common butterwort, a purple-flowered carnivorous plant whose diet consists largely of marsh insects. In winter Backswamp Viewpoint is also known locally as one of the most likely areas to spot wolves; at other times of the year you might also see bighorn sheep or mountain goats on the mountain slopes above. About 3km further on you come to **Muleshoe Picnic Area**, also noted for its birds and wildfowl. Some of the area around shows signs of having been burnt in forest fires, though the park authorities deliberately torched these areas to encourage fresh undergrowth and the return of wildlife excluded from more mature forests. Some 11km on, a 400m trail takes you to a lovely little lake once known as Lizard Lake after the long-toed salamanders that thrived here. These were eaten when the lake was stocked with trout, and the name's now been changed to Pilot Lake. About 3km beyond is the trailhead for the **Johnston Canyon Trail,** deservedly the most popular in the area; 3km beyond that is **Moose Meadows**, where – name notwithstanding – you'll be mighty lucky to see any moose: habitat changes have forced them out.

Of interest to **bird-watchers**, Johnston Canyon is one of only two known breeding sites in Alberta of the black swift – you may see the birds flitting back to their nests at dusk – and is also a breeding place for American dippers, buxom grey birds that have the ability to walk along stream beds underwater and habitually nest below waterfalls. Elsewhere on the Parkway the various turn-offs give you the opportunity to spot species associated with montane forest and meadow zones, notably at the Muleshoe Picnic Area, 21km southeast of Castle Junction, where you might spot western tanagers, pileated woodpeckers and orange-crowned warblers. At various points on the Bow River along the entire run from Banff to Lake Louise you may spot harlequin ducks on the river's islands and gravel bars, as well as spotted sandpipers and common mergansers.

Practicalities

The road's **accommodation** possibilities make a more rural alternative to Banff and Lake Louise, and are close enough to both to serve as a base if you have transport; as ever, you should book rooms well in advance. Four **lodges** are spaced more or less equally en route and, though expensive, they may have room when Lake Louise's hotels are stretched. First is the *Johnston Canyon Resort*, 26km west of Banff and close to the trail that leads to the canyon (Ⓣ403/762-2971, Ⓦwww.johnstoncanyon.com; ❺; mid-May to late Sept), which consists of rustic cabins (some with fireplaces and some with kitchenettes), a shop, garage, tennis court and basic groceries. Next come the chalets, laundry and grocery store of *Castle Mountain Chalets*, 32km west of Banff near Castle Junction (Ⓣ403/762-3868, Ⓦwww.castlemountain.com; ❼; year-round); the log chalets for four with kitchenettes and fireplaces are more expensive, but the best options of all here are the delightful deluxe cabins for four, five or six people (complete with full kitchens, dishwashers and Jacuzzis). Some 5km south of Hwy 1 on Hwy 93 to Radium (27km from Banff) is *Storm Mountain Lodge* (Ⓣ403/762-4155; ❻; late May to late Sept), with highly appealing log cabins. Finally there's *Baker Creek Guest Lodge & Bistro*, 12km east of Lake Louise (Ⓣ403/522-3761, Ⓦwww.bakercreek.com; ❻; year-round), with 25 one- and two-room log cabins and lodge rooms for between one and six people; there's also an excellent **restaurant** here that comes with local recommendations and an annex with eight smart motel-type rooms. By far the least expensive possibility is the Parkway's charming HI **hostel**, *Castle Mountain Youth Hostel*, 1.5km east of Castle Junction (Ⓣ403/762-2367 or 762-4122, Ⓦwww.hihostels.ca; dorms for members $19–23 Oct–June, $23 July–Sept; non-members $23–27 & $27 over the same periods; ❶; year-round but closed Wed).

Bow Valley Trails

Five major trails branch off the Bow Valley Parkway. The best short walk is the **Johnston Canyon Trail** (2.7km each way), 25km from Banff, an incredibly engineered path to a series of spray-veiled waterfalls. The Lower Falls are 1.1km, the Upper Falls 2.7km from the trailhead on the Parkway. From the upper falls you can continue on to the seven cold-water springs of the Ink Pots, which emerge in pretty open meadows, to make a total distance of 5.8km (215m ascent). Another short possibility is the **Castle Crags Trail** (3.7km each way; 520m ascent) from the signed turn-off 5km west of Castle Junction. Short but steep, and above the tree-line, this walk offers superb views across the Bow Valley and the mountains beyond. Allow ninety minutes one-way to take account of the stiff climb.

The best day-hike is to **Rockbound Lake** (8.4km each way), a steepish climb to 2210m with wild lakeland scenery at the end; allow at least two and a half hours one-way, due to the 760m ascent. Another fifteen-minutes' walk beyond Rockbound and Tower lakes at the end of the trail lies the beautiful Silverton waterfall. The other Parkway trails – **Baker Creek** (20.3km) and **Pulsatilla Pass** (17.1km) – serve to link backpackers with the dense network of paths in the Slate Range northeast of Lake Louise.

The two outstanding trails along Hwy 1 are the trek to **Bourgeau Lake** (7.5km one-way), considered by many to be among the top five day-hikes in Banff: it starts from a parking area 10km west of Banff – allow two and a half to three hours for the 725m ascent – and the long day-hike to **Shadow Lake** (14.3km each way), where the lakeside campsite (at 1840m), in one of the Rockies' more impressive subalpine basins, gives access to assorted onward trails. The main trail starts from the **Redearth Creek** parking area 20km west of Banff (440m ascent; allow 4hr).

Three national park **campsites** provide excellent camping retreats. In order of distance from Banff these are the very popular 140-pitch *Johnston Canyon* ($23.75; mid-May or early June to mid-Sept), 25km from Banff – the best equipped, with full facilities including showers and wheelchair access; the 43-pitch *Castle Mountain*, 32km from Banff in a beautiful wooded area near Castle Junction ($18.80; mid-May to early Sept), with no facilities beyond water, kitchen shelters and flush toilets (but close to a small store and restaurant); and the similarly simple 89-pitch *Protection Mountain*, 5km north of Castle Junction, with flush toilets, piped water and kitchen shelters ($18.80; late June to early Sept). An additional $7.90 fee is payable at all three if you wish to use firewood.

Lake Louise

The Banff National Park's other main centre, **LAKE LOUISE**, is very different from Banff – less a town than two distinct artificial resorts. The first is a small mall of shops and hotels just off the Trans-Canada known as **Lake Louise Village**. The second is **the lake** itself, 4.5km from the village (and 200m higher) on the winding Lake Louise Drive, the self-proclaimed "gem of the Rockies" and – despite its crowds and monster hotel – a sight you have to see. You can walk between the two, the uphill hike from the townsite to the lake totalling 2.7km on the Louise Creek Trail or 4.5km along the Tramline Trail. But, really, you're better off saving the walking for around the lake and taking a taxi (ⓣ403/522-2020; around $10) from the village (if anything, save the two linking trails for coming down from the lake).

A third area, **Moraine Lake**, 13km south of the village, has almost equally staggering scenery and several magnificent and easily accessed trails. All three areas are desperately busy in summer while in winter things slow down a little, though crowds still turn up for some of Canada's best powder **skiing** at the nearby resort (see box, p.734).

Nonetheless, the mountains around offer almost unparalleled **hiking country** and the park's most popular day-use area. You'll have to weigh awesome scenery against the sheer numbers, for these are some of the most heavily used trails on the continent – 50,000-plus people in summer – though longer backpacking routes lead quickly away to the quieter spots.

If you do intend to hike – and the trails are all a little more accessible and manageable than at Banff – then in an ideal world you'd spend two or three days here: one to walk the loop around above Lake Louise (Lake Agnes–Big Beehive–Plain of the Six Glaciers–Lake Louise Shoreline) or the more demanding Saddleback (at a push you could do both in a day if you were fit and keen). Then you'd bike, taxi or drive (or take the shuttle bus) to Moraine Lake (if you're not staying there), where in a day you could easily walk to Consolation Lake, return to Moraine Lake and then tackle the Moraine Lake–Larch Valley–Sentinel Pass or Moraine Lake–Larch Valley–Eiffel Lake trail. A third day could be spent in Paradise Valley between Lake Louise and Moraine Lake.

If, on the other hand, you merely want to take in the scenery and enjoy **modest strolls** in the course of a day, then cruise up to Lake Louise, walk up and down the shore, then drive the twenty minutes or so to Moraine Lake and do the same.

Arrival and information

Four Greyhound **buses** a day ($13.25) link Banff and Lake Louise (50min) and stop in the Samson Mall car park at the little office known as The Depot (ⓣ403/522-2080); three continue to Vancouver and the west. Four buses a

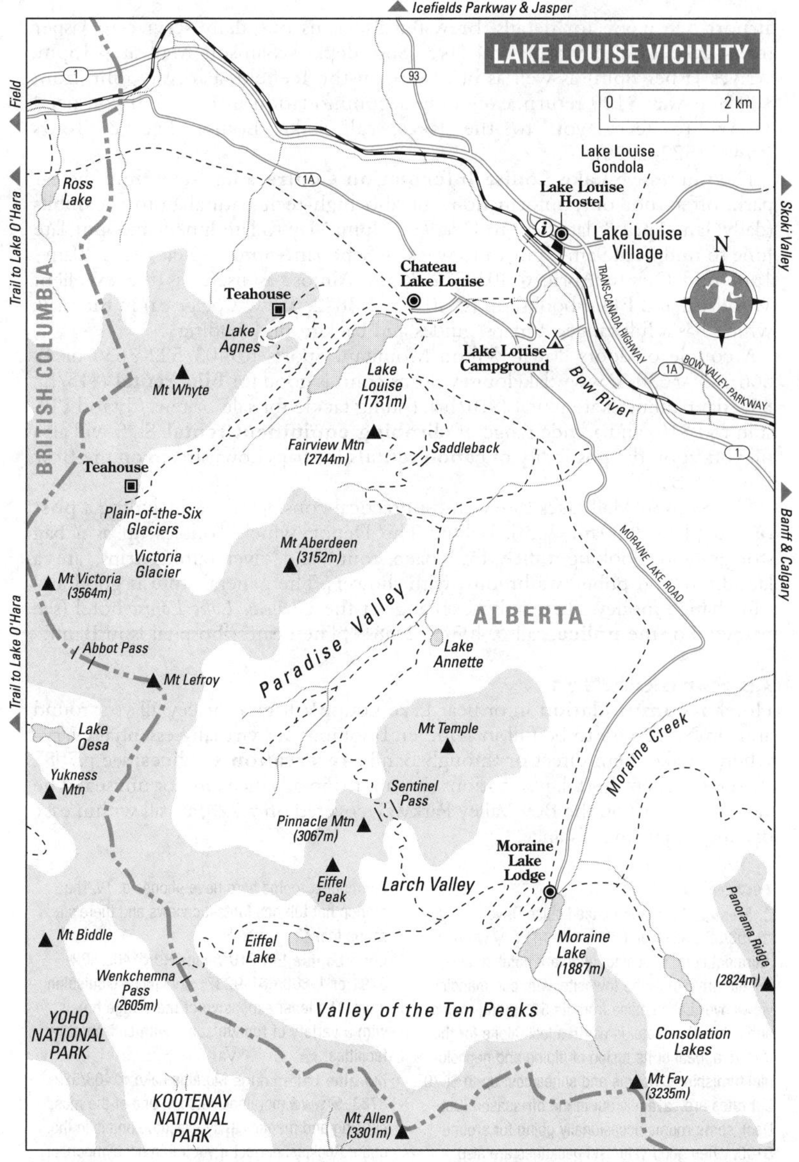

day return from Lake Louise to Banff and Calgary. Brewster Transportation (Ⓣ403/762-6700 or 1-800/760-6934, Ⓦwww.Brewster.ca or www.sightseeingtourscanada.ca) has three buses a day from Banff ($16), its services continuing to the *Château Lake Louise* (a good way to get up here if you're without transport – you can walk back down to the village). There are also direct Brewster and other connections to and from Lake Louise and Calgary airport; see p.665 for details. Brewster also runs one daily service to Jasper from Lake Louise village and lake ($60; departs Samson Mall at 4.15pm, arrives Jasper 8pm) as well as bus tours on the Icefields Parkway (8hr; from $90 one-way, $120 return, excluding accommodation in Jasper). If you need a taxi to ferry you to the lakes, call Lake Louise Taxi & Tours (ⓣ403/522-2020).

The impressive **Lake Louise Information Centre**, a few steps from the car park, offers not only information but also high-tech natural history exhibits (daily: Jan–April & late Sept to Dec 9am–4pm; May to late June 9am–5pm; late June to mid-Sept 9am–7pm; third week of Sept 9am–5pm; also closes 12.30am–1pm mid-Oct to April; ⓣ403/522-3833). Almost as useful is the excellent Woodruff and Blum bookshop (ⓣ403/522-3842, ⓦwww.pc.gc.ca) in the mall, which has a full range of maps, guides and background reading.

A couple of doors down, Wilson Mountain Sports (ⓣ403/522-3636 or 1-866/929-3636, ⓦwww.lakelouisewilsons.com) is good for **bike rental** ($15/hr, $39/day), inline skate rental ($10/hr), fishing tackle for sale or rent (fly rod $19, spin rod $10) and a wide range of **climbing equipment rental**. Staff will also fill you in on the possibility of **canoe rentals** for trips downstream on the Bow River to Banff.

The Samson Mall takes care of most practical considerations including a **post office** (daily 6.30am–7pm). Behind The Depot, which doubles up as a bag storage and booking office for coach tours and river-rafting trips, are a laundrette and public washrooms with showers. The general store is good and can change money. There's also exchange at the *Château Lake Louise* hotel (see below). For the **police**, call ⓣ403/522-3811. The nearest hospital is in Banff.

Accommodation

Hotel **accommodation** in or near Lake Louise Village is pricey all year round and almost certain to be full in summer. Bookings are virtually essential everywhere (make them direct or through Banff's **reservation services**; see p.708). At the excellent hostel, reservations six months in advance are not unusual. The various options on the Bow Valley Parkway, covered on p.723, are all within easy driving or cycling distance.

Hotels

Château Lake Louise Lake Louise Drive ⓣ403/522-3511 or 1-800/441-1414, ⓦwww.fairmont.com. Imposing landmark hotel, a five-minute drive from the townsite, with commanding views over Lake Louise from its 511 grand rooms and suites. The hotel is worth a look alone for the bizarre appeal of its fusion of alpine and neocolonial furnishings. Rooms and suites cost up to $579, but rates are savagely cut in the off-season (Oct–Dec), some rooms occasionally going for around $100, when good value ski packages are also offered. The hotel's battery of five-star facilities includes an exercise room, pool, and several bars and restaurants. ❽

Deer Lodge Lake Louise Drive ⓣ403/522-3747 or 1-800/661-1595, ⓦwww.crmr.com. Labyrinthine lodgings in a 1920s log teahouse. Contrasting with the pomp of its neighbour, *Château Lake Louise*, a short walk away, it's far more laid back and few of the modest rooms here have phones or TV. The rooftop hot tub has fantastic views and there's a sauna too. ❻

Lake Louise Inn 210 Village Rd ⓣ403/522-3791 or 1-800/661-9237, ⓦwww.lakelouiseinn.com. The least expensive of the village hotels, with a variety of rooms, some with self-catering facilities. ❼

Moraine Lake Lodge Moraine Lake ⓣ403/522-3733, ⓦwww.morainelake.com. One of the most enticing and magnificently executed hotels in the entire Rockies: perfect if you're on honeymoon, or just want to splash out. Accommodation consists of a nicely landscaped collection of high-quality cabins and lodge rooms designed by eminent architect Arthur Erickson (also responsible for Vancouver's UBC Museum of Anthropology and the Canadian Embassy in Washington DC). Their open fires probably make the cabins best. The friendly staff and great privacy here gives it an edge over the more lacklustre hotels in the village and near Lake Louise. May–Oct. 8

Paradise Lodge and Bungalows Lake Louise Drive ⓣ403/522-3595, ⓦwww.paradiselodge.com. A short walk from Lake Louise, this is the pricier of the near-lake options, but with reasonable off-season rates for its 21 self-contained bungalows and 24 one- and two-bedroom suites (some with kitchens). Mid-May to mid-Oct. 7

Post Hotel Village Rd ⓣ403/522-3989 or 1-800/661-1586, ⓦwww.posthotel.com. Grand log chalet-hotel that is the top hotel in the village, with a noted restaurant and bar but expect to pay $300-plus for a room here in summer. 8

Hostels

Castle Mountain Youth Hostel (HI) 1.5km east of Castle Junction on Hwy 93 South ⓣ403/762-4122, ⓦwww.hihostels.ca. Well situated for the Bow Valley Parkway and its trails. Sleeps just 36, with bookings possible through the Banff hostel. Dorm beds members $19–23 Oct–June, $23 July–Sept; non-members $23–27 & $27 over the same periods.

Lake Louise International Hostel (HI) Village Rd ⓣ403/522-2200, ⓦwww.hihostels.ca. Standard-setting, mountain chalet-style 150-bed hostel just north of the village mall, offering dorm beds ($23) and private rooms. Clean, superior-quality facilities include communal kitchen, laundry, Internet access, a mountaineering library and a handy restaurant. Reservations are virtually essential (up to six months in advance) for summer and winter ski weekends. Dorm beds for members $23 April–May & Oct–Jan, $27 June & Feb–March, $34 July–Sept; non-members $27, $31 and $38 respectively over the same periods. Private doubles in the same periods cost $85, $99 and $106.

Campsites

Lake Louise Campground Lovely park-run site with 210 pitches close to the village – follow the signs off Fairview Rd up to the lake. Gets busy in summer. It's open between mid-May and early Oct, is partially serviced (it has showers, flush toilets, kitchen shelters and provision for food storage) and sites cost $23.75. Sites are close together, though the trees offer some privacy and, with the railway close by, it can be noisy. This is one of the national park campgrounds where reservations have been possible in past years from March of the year in question. Visit ⓦwww.pccamping.ca or call ⓣ1-877/737-3783 to book or for latest details.

Lake Louise Trailer Site Near to the above, but for RVs only. 189 sites. Year-round. $27.70.

Lake Louise Village

Lake Louise Village doesn't amount to much, but it's an essential supply stop, with more or less everything you need in terms of food, shelter (at a price), information and equipment rental. Most of it centres round the Samson Mall and car park, with a smart hostel and a few outlying motels dotted along the service road to the north.

A short way from the village, the **Lake Louise Gondola** (the "Friendly Giant"; daily: May 9am–4pm, June & Sept 8.30am–6pm; July & Aug 8am–6pm; $23) takes thirteen minutes to get to 2042m, partway up Mount Whitehorn (2669m). To reach it, pick up the free shuttle which operates from some village hotels or return to and cross over the Trans-Canada, and follow the road towards the ski area; the gondola is signed left after about 1km. You can choose between enclosed gondola cars, open chairs, or chairs with bubble domes. At the top are the usual sensational views – rated some of the best in the Rockies – a self-service restaurant, sun decks, picnic areas, souvenir shops and several trailheads through the woods and meadows. One takes you to the summit of Mount Whitehorn.

Lake Louise

Before you see **Lake Louise** you see the hotel: *Château Lake Louise*, a grandiose monstrosity that would surely never get planning permission today. Yet even so intrusive an eyesore fades into insignificance beside the immense beauty of its surroundings. The lake is brilliant turquoise, the mountains sheer, the glaciers vast; the whole ensemble is perfection. Outfitter Tom Wilson, the first white Canadian to see Lake Louise when he was led here by a local native in 1882,

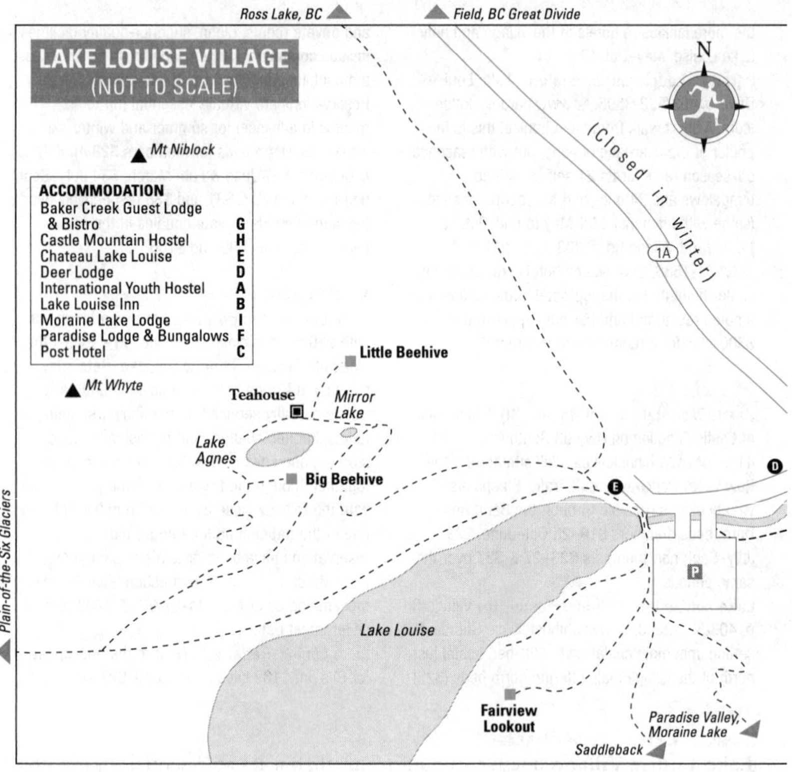

wrote: "I never, in all my explorations of these five chains of mountains throughout western Canada, saw such a matchless scene… I felt puny in body, but glorified in spirit and soul."

You can't help wishing you could have been Tom Wilson, and seen the spot unsullied by the hotel and before the arrival of the tourists and general clutter. Around 10,000 people come here daily in peak season to gawp (car parks often fill by noon), while noticeboards on the waterfront seem obsessed with the profoundly dull account of how the lake came by its name – it was named in honour of the fourth daughter of Queen Victoria. The native name translates as the "Lake of the Little Fishes". Wilson, showing precious little wit, originally called it Emerald Lake. More interesting is the account of Hollywood's discovery of the lake in the 1920s, when it was used to suggest exotic European locations. After Wilson's "discovery" all access was by rail or trail – the station, then known as Laggan, was 6km away.

The first hotel appeared in 1890, a simple two-bedroom affair which replaced a tumbledown cabin on the shore. Numerous fires, false starts and additions followed until the present structure made its unwelcome appearance; the final wings were added as recently as 1988. The first road was built in 1926. Be sure to walk here, despite the paths' popularity (see box, p.732). Alternatively, escape the throng by renting an old-style canoe from the office to the left as you face the lake (June–Sept daily 10am–8pm; $38/hr; maximum of three adults per

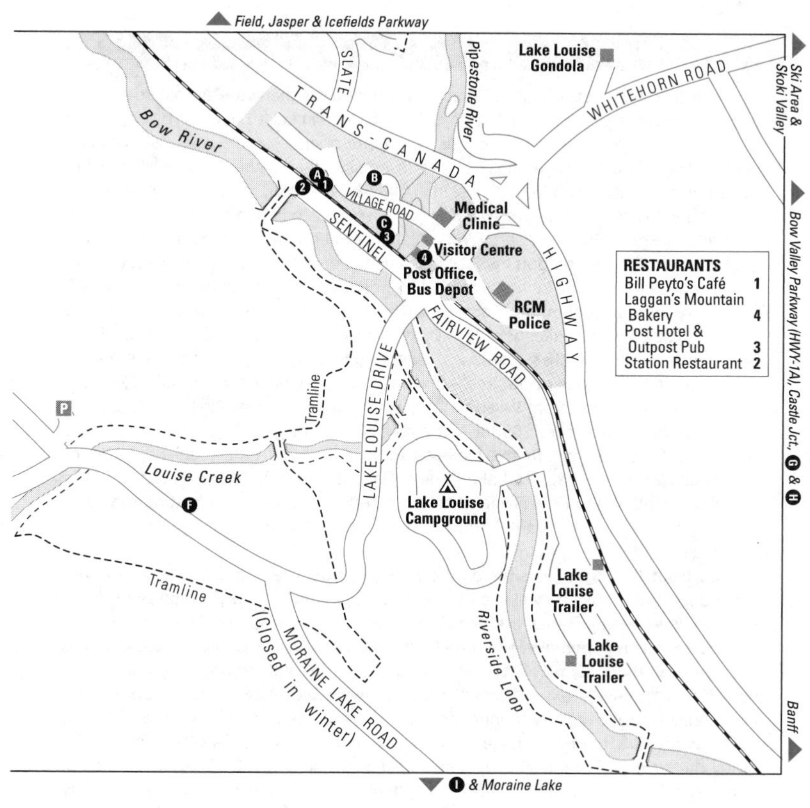

boat). Don't think about swimming: the water's deep and cold – highest temperature in summer is a numbing 4°C.

Moraine Lake

Not quite so many people as visit Lake Louise make the road journey 13km to **Moraine Lake**, which is smaller than its neighbour although in many ways its scenic superior. If you're without your own transport, you'll have to rely on a bike or taxi ($35) to get here or the park-run "Vista" bus shuttle (daily every 30min from outside the hostel and Lake Louise campsite; free on production of park pass). The last has been introduced because of the sheer number of visitors in cars and RVs trying to cram into the tiny car park and clogging the approach road.

No wonder they come, for this is one of the great landscapes of the region, has some cracking trails (see box, p.732) and the splendid yet discreet *Moraine Lake Lodge,* which is one of the best places to stay in the region (see p.726). Bar the *Lodge*, with its good little café and top-notch restaurant, nothing disturbs the lake and its matchless surroundings. Until comparatively recently the scene graced the back of Canadian $20 bills, though the illustration did little justice to the shimmering water and the jagged, snow-covered peaks on the eastern shore that inspired the nickname "Valley of the Ten Peaks". The peaks are now officially christened the Wenkchemna, after the Stoney native word for "ten".

Lake Louise activities

As for **activities**, most operators – especially rafting companies – are based in Banff or elsewhere (see p.712), though many offer pick-ups in Lake Louise, typically with a $10 add-on to their listed Banff prices; a handful operate trips directly out of Lake Louise itself. Companies actually based in or near the village include Wild Water Adventures (☎403/678-5058, 522-2211 or 1-888/771-9453, Ⓦwww.wildwater.com), which runs half-day, full-day or two-day "gentle-water" or whitewater rafting trips on the Kicking Horse River in nearby Yoho National Park (half-day trips at 8.30am and 1.30pm, from $79). If you don't want to hike alone, or wish to know more about what you're walking past, the national park and Friends of Banff (Ⓦwww.friendsofbanff.com) runs **guided walks** (from around $15) three or four times a week in July and Aug: the Lake Louise Lakeshore Stroll (2hr) and the Plain of the Six Glaciers (6hr). Drop by the visitor centre's Friends of Banff store to confirm latest timings and to reserve a place (do so in good time – the walks are popular) or call ☎403/522-3833. Cyclists can rent bikes from Wilson Mountain Sports in the mall (see p.727), or sign up for **cycling tours** (from $65 for half a day, $95 full day) and transfers that'll take you up to Bow Summit on the Icefields Parkway so you can pedal down hill or freewheel all the way back to Lake Louise. Serious canoeists can rent canoes from Wilson for trips on the Bow River, while more sedate paddlers can **rent canoes** and kayaks (daily in summer 10am–7pm; $38 per hour) at *Château Lake Louise* to dabble on Lake Louise itself (☎403/522-3511).

Good **trout fishing** is possible on the Bow River between Lake Louise and Banff, with support and advice available at the *Castle Mountain Chalets* on the Bow Valley Parkway (see p.722). Rental equipment is again on offer at Wilson Mountain Sports. Compulsory fishing permits ($8.90 daily) are available from the visitor centre. If you fancy **horse riding**, contact Brewster Lake Louise Stables at the *Château Lake Louise* hotel (☎403/522-3511 ext 1210, or 762-5454, Ⓦwww.brewsterlakelouisestables.com) and enquire about their two-hour trips along the shores of Lake Louise ($71.50), half-day tours ($105) to the Lake Agnes or Plain of the Six Glaciers (see box, p.732) or full-day treks to Paradise Valley and Horseshoe Glacier ($170.50, including lunch). Timberline Tours (☎403/522-3743, Ⓦwww.timberlinetours.ca) runs similar if slightly cheaper treks from the Lake Louise Corral behind the *Deer Lodge* hotel; 90-minute rides locally ($55), three-hour rides to Lake Agnes ($75), four- to five-hour trips to the Plain of the Six Glaciers ($90/$105) and all-day trips to the Skoki Valley ($130) east of Lake Louise.

The lake itself, half the size of Lake Louise, is the most vivid turquoise imaginable. Like Lake Louise and other big Rockies lakes (notably Peyto on the Icefields Parkway), the peacock blue is caused by fine particles of glacial silt, or till, known as rock flour. Meltwater in June and July washes this powdered rock into the lake, the minute but uniform particles of flour absorbing all colours of incoming light except those in the blue–green spectrum. When the lakes have just melted in May and June – and are still empty of silt – their colour is a more normal sky-blue.

You can admire the lake by walking along the east shore, from above by clambering over the great glacial moraine dam near the lodge (though the lake was probably created by a rock fall rather than glaciation), or from one of the **canoes for rent** on the right just beyond the *Lodge* and car park. For the best overall perspective, tackle the switchback trail through the forest on the east shore (see box, p.732), but check with the visitor centre at Lake Louise for the latest on bear activity – a young grizzly has made the Moraine Lake region its home, and areas are sometimes closed to avoid its coming into contact with humans.

Eating and drinking

Excellent basic **food** – snacks and coffee – can be had in Lake Louise Village at the always busy *Laggan's Mountain Bakery* (daily 6am–7pm) on the corner of the mall opposite the general store. For something more substantial than snacks, wander to the relaxed and reasonably priced *Bill Peyto's Café* for full and varied meals from around $10 (daily 7am–9pm; ⓣ403/522-2200), within the hostel but open to all; in summer the nice outdoor eating area is a good place to meet people. The unique *Lake Louise Station Restaurant* (ⓣ403/522-2600) is housed in the restored 1909 station building; choose between hearty Canadian fare in the informal station building (garden dining in summer) and the more formal and expensive restored railway-dining carriages. Some of the best (and pricier)

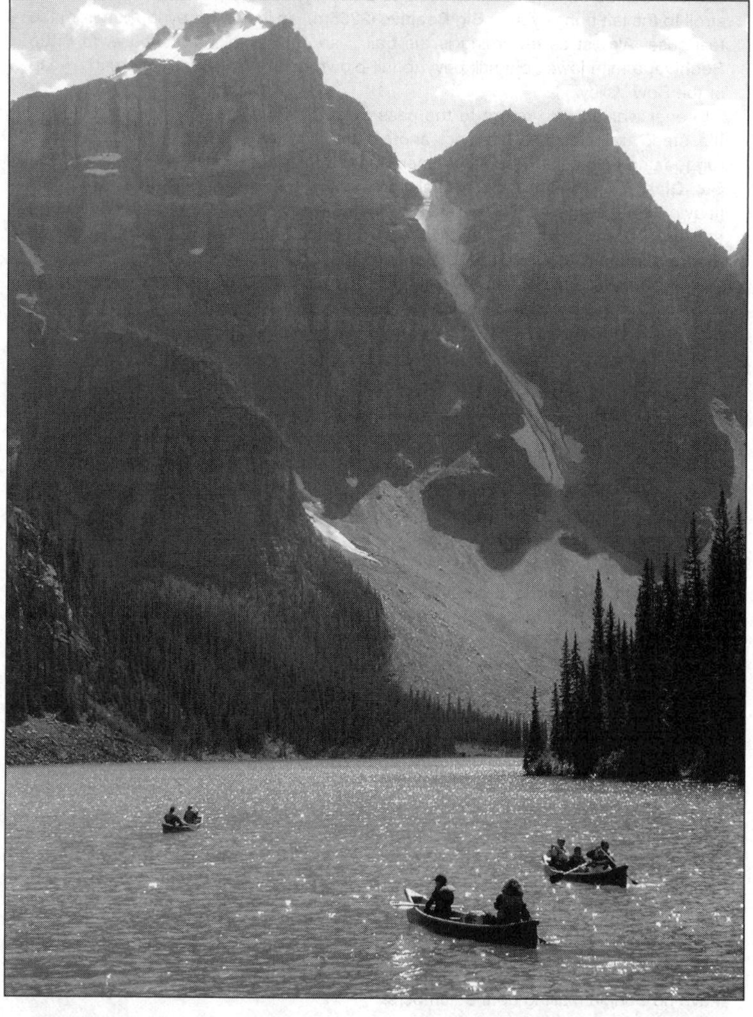

△ Canoeing on Moraine Lake

Hikes around Lake Louise

All the Lake Louise **hiking trails** are busy in summer, but they're good for a short taste of the scenery. They're also well worn and well marked, so you don't need to be a seasoned hiker or skilled map-reader. The two most popular finish up at teahouses – mountain chalets selling welcome, but rather pricey, snacks.

The signed **Lake Agnes Trail** (3.4km), said to be the most-walked path in the Rockies (but don't let that put you off), strikes off from the right (north) shore of the lake immediately past the hotel. It's a gradual 400m climb, relieved by ever more magnificent views and a teahouse beautifully situated beside mountain-cradled Lake Agnes (2135m); allow one to two hours. Beyond the teahouse, if you want more of a walk, things quiet down considerably. You can continue on the right side of the lake and curve left around its head to climb to an easily reached pass. Here a 200-metre stroll to the left brings you to **Big Beehive** (2255m), an incredible eyrie, 1km from the teahouse. Almost as rewarding is the trail, also 1km from the teahouse, to **Little Beehive**, a mite lower, but still privy to full-blown panoramas over the broad sweep of the Bow Valley.

Keener walkers can return to the pass from Big Beehive and turn left to follow the steep trail down to intersect another trail; turning right leads west through rugged and increasingly barren scenery to the second teahouse at the **Plain of the Six Glaciers** (2100m). Alternatively, the more monotonous Six Glaciers Trail (leaving out the whole Lake Agnes–Big Beehive section) leads from the hotel along the lakeshore to the same point (5.3km to the teahouse; 365m ascent). However, a better option is to follow the Lake Agnes and Big Beehive route to the Plain, then use the Six Glaciers Trail for the return to *Château Lake Louise*, which neatly ends the day's loop with a downhill stroll and an easy but glorious finale along the shore of Lake Louise (see our map to make sense of what is a pretty straightforward and very well-worn loop).

The main appeal of the less-used **Saddleback Trail** (3.7km one-way) is that it provides access to the superlative viewpoint of Fairview Mountain. Allow from one to two hours to Saddleback itself (2330m; 595m ascent); the trail to the summit of Fairview (2745m) strikes off right from here. Even if you don't make the last push, the Saddleback views – across to the 1200m wall of Mount Temple (3544m) – are staggering. Despite the people, this is one of the park's top short walks.

Skoki Valley

The **Skoki Valley** region east of Lake Louise offers fewer day-hikes; to enjoy it you'll need a tent to overnight at any of the six campsites. The main access trail initially follows a gravel road forking off to the right of the Lake Louise Ski Area, off Hwy 1. Many people hike as far as Boulder Pass (2345m), an 8.6-kilometre trek and 640-metre ascent from the parking area, as a day-trip, and return the same way instead of pushing on to the *Lodge*, 8km beyond. Various well-signposted long and short trails from the *Lodge* or the campsites are documented in the *Canadian Rockies Trail Guide*, found at the visitor centre.

Moraine Lake

Each of the four basic routes in the **Moraine Lake** area are easily accomplished in a day or less, two with sting-in-the-tail additions if you want added exertion; all start from the lake, which lies 13km from Lake Louise Village at the end of Moraine Lake Rd. Before hiking, check with the visitor centre in Lake Louise on the latest restrictions imposed to protect both the bears known to have made the area part of their territory as well as the tourists who hope to catch a glimpse of them. At the time of writing, walks in the Larch Valley and around were restricted. You must walk in groups of at least six people (there are often people waiting to join a group, so you should have no trouble making up the numbers).

The easiest walk is the 1km amble along the lakeshore – hardly a walk at all – followed by the 3km stroll to **Consolation Lake**, an hour's trip that may be busy but can provide some respite from the frenzy at Moraine Lake itself. This almost level walk ends with lovely views of a small mountain-circled lake, its name coined by an early explorer who thought it a reward and "consolation" for the desolation of the valley that led up to it. If you're tenting, fairly fit, or can arrange a pick-up, the highline **Panorama Ridge Trail** (2255m) branches off the trail (signed "Taylor Lake") to run 22km to the Banff–Radium hwy 7km west of Castle Junction.

The most popular walk (start as early as possible) is the Moraine Lake–**Larch Valley–Sentinel Pass Trail**, one of the Rockies' premier hikes, which sets off from the lake's north shore 100m beyond the lodge. A stiffish hairpin climb through forest on a broad track, with breathtaking views of the lake through the trees, brings you to a trail junction after 2.4km and some 300m of ascent. Most hikers branch right, where the track levels off to emerge into Larch Valley, broad alpine upland with stands of larch (glorious in late summer and autumn) and majestic views of the encircling peaks. If you have the energy, push on to Sentinel Pass ahead, in all some two hours' walk and 720m above Moraine Lake. At 2605m, this, along with the Wenkchemna Pass, is the highest point reached by a major trail in the Canadian Rockies. You can see what you're in for from the meadows – but not the airy views over Paradise Valley from the crest of the pass itself. You could even continue down into Paradise Valley, a tough, scree-filled descent, and complete an exceptional day's walk by picking up the valley loop (see below) back to the Moraine Lake Road. Otherwise return to the 2.4-kilometre junction and, if legs are still willing – you'll have done most of the hard climbing work already – think about tagging on the last part of the third Moraine Lake option.

This third option, the less-walked Moraine Lake–**Eiffel Lake–Wenkchemna Pass Trail**, follows the climb from the lake as for the Larch Valley path before branching off left instead of right at the 2.4-kilometre junction. It's equally sound, virtually level and if anything has the better scenery (if only because less barren than Sentinel Pass) in the stark, glaciated grandeur to be found at the head of the Valley of the Ten Peaks. It's also much quieter once you're beyond the trail junction. At 2255m, Eiffel Lake is a 5.6-kilometre hike and 370-metre climb in total (allow 2–3hr) from Moraine Lake, and you don't need to go much further than the rock pile and clump of trees beyond the lake to get the best out of the walk. Ahead of you, however, a slightly rougher track continues through bleak terrain to Wenkchemna Pass (2605m), clearly visible 4km beyond. Having got this far, it's tempting to push on; the extra 350-metre climb is just about worth it, if lungs and weather are holding out, for the still broader views back down the Valley of the Ten Peaks. The views beyond the pass itself, however, over the Great Divide into Yoho and Kootenay parks, are relatively disappointing.

Paradise Valley

In 1894, the mountaineer Walter Wilcox deemed **Paradise Valley** an appropriate name for "a valley of surpassing beauty, wide and beautiful, with alternating open meadows and rich forests". North of Moraine Lake, it's accessed via Moraine Lake Rd about 3km from its junction with Lake Louise Drive. The walk here is a fairly straightforward hike up one side of the valley and down the other, a loop of 18km with a modest 385m of vertical gain. Most people take in the Lake Annette diversion for its unmatched view of Mount Temple's 1200-metre north face (unclimbed until 1966), and many overnight at the campsite at the head of the valley (9km from the parking area), though this is one of the busiest sites in the park. Others toughen the walk by throwing in the climb up to Sentinel Pass on the ridge south of the valley, which gives the option of continuing down the other side to connect with the Moraine Lake trails.

meals can be found in the *Post Hotel* (daily 7am–2pm & 5–10pm; ⓣ403/522-3989) – reservations are essential in the evening. Reckon on $30–50 for a three-course dinner, less at lunch, when there is a restricted menu. The best local's hangout is the hotel's *Outpost Pub* (ⓣ403/522-3989), a snug **bar** that serves light meals from late afternoon. Other good drinking spots include the *Lake Louise Bar and Grill* (ⓣ403/522-3879) upstairs in the mall, and the lively *Explorers Lounge* (ⓣ403/522-3791) in the *Lake Louise Inn*, 210 Village Rd.

The Icefields Parkway

The splendour of the **Icefields Parkway** (Hwy 93) can hardly be overstated: a road 230km from Lake Louise to Jasper through the heart of the Rockies, it ranks as one of the world's best drives. Its unending succession of huge peaks, immense glaciers, iridescent lakes, wildflower meadows, wildlife and

Winter sports in and around Lake Louise

In a region already renowned for its **skiing** Lake Louise stands out, regarded by many as among the finest winter resorts in North America. In addition to skiing and snowboarding there are hundreds of kilometres of cross-country trails, numerous other winter activities, and landscape that's earned the area the title of "North America's Most Scenic Ski Area" from *Snow Country* magazine. It's also Canada's largest ski area, with over forty square kilometres of trails, plenty of mogul fields, lots of challenging chutes, vast open bowls and some of the best "powder" on the continent.

Skiing started here in the 1920s. The first chalet was built in 1930, the first lift in 1954. The resort's real birth can be dated to 1958, when a rich Englishman, Norman Watson – universally known as the "Barmy Baronet" – ploughed a large part of his inheritance into building a gondola on Mount Whitehorn. Further lifts and other developments followed. More would have materialized had it not been for environmental lobbying. Further protests forestalled a bid for the 1968 Winter Olympics and put an end to a plan for a 6500-bed megaresort in 1972. Even so, the resort has grown, and now regularly hosts World Cup skiing events. The only drawback is the phenomenally low temperatures during January and February.

For further information on skiing in and around Lake Louise, visit the official website (ⓦwww.skilouise.com) or call ⓣ1-877/754-5462.

Ski areas

Naturally dividing into three distinct zones, the core of the Lake Louise ski area is the **Front Side** (sometimes called the South Face). Climbing from the base area, this is particularly attractive to beginners and intermediates, who will find all the best groomed green and blue runs here. Tucked behind the Front Side, the **Back Bowls** are a very different proposition; flecked with above-tree-line black diamonds that offer wide-open runs particularly rewarding for those prepared to hike. From the Back Bowls a long, fairly flat run-out leads to the base of the **Ptarmigan** and **Larch** area, and some of the mountain's best glade runs. Slopes here face in several directions allowing you to follow the sun, and trees can give shelter from winds, a combination that makes this the best area to zero in on when conditions are harsh.

The 4200 acre terrain divides as follows: Novice (25 percent), Intermediate (45 percent) and Expert (30 percent) and sees an average annual snowfall (early Nov to mid-May) of 360cm. The top elevation is 2637m, giving a 1000m drop to the base

forests – capped by the stark grandeur of the Columbia Icefield – is absolutely overwhelming. Fur traders and natives who used the route as far back as 1800 reputedly christened it the "Wonder Trail", though in practice they tended to prefer the Pipestone River Valley to the east, a route that avoided the swamps and other hazards of the Bow Valley. Jim Brewster made the first recorded complete trek along the road's future route in 1904. The present hwy was only completed in 1939 and opened in 1940 as part of a Depression-era public-works programme. Although about a million people a year make the journey to experience what the park blurb calls a "window on the wilderness", for the most part you can go your own way in relative serenity.

After 122km, at about its midway point, the Icefields Parkway crosses from Banff into Jasper National Park (about a 2hr drive); you might turn back here, but the divide is almost completely arbitrary, and most people treat the Parkway as a self-contained journey, as we do here. Distances in brackets are from Lake Louise, which is virtually the only way to locate places on the road, though everything mentioned is clearly marked off the hwy by distinctive brown-green

elevation at 1645m. Lift tickets are around $69 a day ($55 half-day) and $74 ($60) in peak holiday periods and key weekends, but bear in mind that you can invest in the Ski Banff/Lake Louise **Tri-Area Pass**, which you can buy for between three and 14 days' skiing in Lake Louise, Mount Norquay and Sunshine Village (see p.720). A three-day Tri-Area Pass is $198, six days $350. Call ⓣ403/762-4561 or 1-800/661-1431, or visit ⓦwww.skibig3.com for further information.

Facilities in the ski area include three day-lodges, each of which has a restaurant and bar, a ski school, ski shop, rental shop, day-care, nursery and lockers. Free shuttles run from Lake Louise, while transfers from Banff cost around $15 return: however, these transfers are included free if you buy the Tri-Area Pass. Free tours of the mountain are also available three times daily.

Cross-country skiing in Lake Louise is also phenomenal, with plenty of options around the lake itself, on Moraine Lake Rd and in the Skoki Valley area north of the village. For **heli-skiing**, contact RK Heli-Ski (ⓣ403/342-3889) who have a desk in the *Château Lake Louise* hotel (winter daily 4–9pm); one of their shuttle buses leaves from the hotel daily for the two-hour drive to the Purcell Mountains in BC (the nearest heli-skiing).

Other activities

The *Château* is also the hub for other winter activities, particularly **ice-skating** and **sleigh rides**, while several tour operations also offer pickups here for **dog sled** or **snowmobiling** tours. Brewster Lake Louise Sleighrides (ⓣ403/762-5454 or ⓣ403/522-3511 ext 1210 in *Château Lake Louise*; ⓦwww.brewsteradventures.com) offers 45-minute sleigh rides from outside the *Château*, hourly departures from 1pm to 4pm, night rides at 7 and 8pm Monday to Saturday, and morning rides at 10am and 11am on weekend days. The ride costs $27.50 per person and reservations are necessary. The hotel is also the place to hire skates (at Monod Sports in the *Château* ⓣ403/522-3837; from $12 per day) for **ice-skating** on the floodlit lake, probably one of the most inspirational spots imaginable for the activity.

For more exciting adventures you need to look further afield. Kingmik Dog-Sled Tours (ⓣ250/344-5298 or 1-877/919-7779, ⓦwww.kingmikdogsledtours.com) runs **dog sled tours** – from 35 minute romps ($125) to multi-day adventures ($255–$275/day) – while Wet 'n' Wild adventures in Golden (ⓣ250/344-6546 or 1-800/668-9119, ⓦwww.wetnwild.bc.ca) offers all-inclusive **snowmobiling** trips for $180 per person for half a day, $245 for a full day.

national park signs. Pick up the Parks Canada *In the Shadow of the Great Divide* pamphlet from visitor centres for a detailed map and summary of all the sights and trailheads.

You could drive the whole hwy in about four hours, but to do so would be to miss out on the panoply of short (and long) trails, viewpoints and the chance just to soak up the incredible scenery.

Access, transport and accommodation

Tourist literature often misleadingly gives the impression that the Icefields Parkway is highly developed. In fact, the wilderness is extreme, with snow often closing the road from October onwards, and there are only two points for **services**, at Saskatchewan Crossing (the one place campers can stock up with groceries, 77km from Lake Louise), where the David Thompson Hwy (Hwy 11) branches off for Red Deer, and at the Columbia Icefield (127km).

Brewster Transportation (ⓣ403/762-6767, ⓦwww.brewster.ca) runs several tours and a single scheduled bus daily in both directions between Banff or Lake Louise and Jasper from late May to mid-October ($70 one-way from Banff, $60 from Lake Louise), though services at either end of the season are often weather-affected. A word with the driver will usually get you dropped off at hostels and trailheads en route. If you're **cycling** – an increasingly popular way to tackle the journey – note that the grades are far more favourable if you travel from Jasper to Banff (Jasper's 500m higher than Banff).

Four **hostels** and twelve excellent park **campsites** (two year-round) are spaced along the Parkway at regular intervals; we've given details of each in the account below. It's essential to book the hostels as far in advance as you can, either direct if they have contact details, through the hostel at Banff or online at ⓦwww.hihostels.ca. As ever, the frontcountry park campsites are available on a first-come, first-served basis. If you want more comfort, you'll have to overnight at Banff, Lake Louise or Jasper, as the only other accommodation – invariably booked solid – is hotels at Bow Lake, Saskatchewan Crossing, the Columbia Icefield and Sunwapta Falls.

North from Lake Louise

One of the biggest problems in the Rockies is knowing what to see and where to walk among the dozens of possible trails and viewpoints. The Parkway is no exception. We've picked out the must-sees and must-dos along the 122-kilometre stretch of the Parkway from Lake Louise to the Columbia Icefield: the best view is at Peyto Lake; the best lake walk is at Bow Lake; the best waterfalls are the Panther–Bridal Falls; the best quick stroll is at Mistaya Canyon; the best short walk is at Parker Ridge; and the best walk if you do no other is Wilcox Pass.

The first **hostel** north of Lake Louise is *Mosquito Creek* (28km; no phone, reservations ⓣ403/762-4122; $20 for members, $24 for non-members; year-round, but closure dates may apply; check-in 5–11pm), four log cabins which sleep 38 and have basic food supplies, a kitchen, large common room and a wood-fired sauna. Private doubles are available for $58 ($66 for non-members). Slightly beyond is the first park **campsite**, *Mosquito Creek* ($13.85; mid-June to mid-Sept; 32 sites; hand-pumped well water, fire rings and wood and dry toilets, but no other facilities) and one of the Parkway's two winter campsites (free after mid-Sept; 32 walk-in sites only). You're near the Bow River flats here, and the mosquitoes, as the campsite name suggests, can be a torment.

Two hikes start from close to the site: **Molar Pass** (9.8km; 535m ascent; 3hr), a manageable day-trip with good views, and **Upper Fish Lake** (14.8km; 760m ascent; 5hr), which follows the Molar Pass trail for 7km before branching off and crossing the superb alpine meadows of North Molar Pass (2590m).

On the *Num-Ti-Jah Lodge* (see below) access road just beyond (37km), a great short trail sets off from beside the lodge to **Bow Lake** and **Bow Glacier Falls** (4.3km; 155m ascent; 1–2hr), taking in the flats around Bow Lake – one of the Rockies' most beautiful – and climbing to some immense cliffs and several huge waterfalls beyond (the trail proper ends at the edge of the moraine after 3.4km, but it's possible to pick your way through the boulders to reach the foot of the falls 900m beyond). If you don't want to walk, take a break instead at the picnic area on the waterfront at the southeast end of the lake.

The *Num-Ti-Jah Lodge* itself, just off the road, is one of the most famous old-fashioned lodges in the Rockies, built in 1920 by legendary guide and outfitter Jimmy Simpson (who lived here until 1972). It's the only privately owned freehold in the park – all other land and property is federally owned and leased; be sure to book well in advance to have any chance of securing a room (Ⓣ403/522-2167, Ⓦwww.num-ti-jah.com; ❻; May–Sept). There's a **coffee shop** here if you need a break, or want to admire the *Lodge*'s strange octagonal structure, forced on Jimmy because he wanted a large building but only had access locally to short timbers. You aren't allowed in the lodge (so guests can enjoy their privacy), but you can take dinner here, or sign up for **horse riding**; rides include a one-hour trip to Bow Lake, a three-hour ride to Peyto Lake (see below) and a full-day excursion to Helen Lake.

Peyto Lake and beyond

Another 3km up the Parkway comes the pass at Bow Summit, source of the Bow River, the waterway that flows through Banff, Lake Louise and Calgary. (At 2069m this is the highest point crossed by any Canadian highway.) Just beyond is the unmissable twenty-minute stroll to **Peyto Lake Lookout** (1.4km; elevation loss 100m), one of the finest vistas in the Rockies (signed from the road). The beautiful panorama only unfolds in the last few seconds, giving a breathtaking view of the vivid emerald lake far below; mountains and forest stretch away as far as you can see. Another 3km along the Parkway lies a viewpoint for the Peyto Glacier, part of the much larger Wapta Icefield.

After 57km you reach the *Waterfowl Lakes* **campsite** (116 sites with water, flush toilets, kitchen shelter and food storage but no showers; $18.80; mid-June to mid-Sept) and the **Chephren Lake Trail** (3.5km; 80m ascent; 1hr), which leads to quietly spectacular scenery with a minimum of effort. The next pause, 14km further on, is the **Mistaya Canyon Trail**, a short but interesting 300m breather of a stroll along a river-gouged "slot" canyon. *Mistaya* is a Cree word meaning "grizzly bear".

Saskatchewan Crossing and beyond

SASKATCHEWAN CROSSING (77km) is the lowest point on the road before the icefields; the 700m descent from Bow Summit brings you from the high subalpine ecoregion into a montane environment with its own vegetation and wildlife. Largely free of snow, the area is a favourite winter range for mountain goats, bighorn sheep and members of the deer family. The bleak settlement itself offers expensive food (restaurant and cafeteria), petrol, a spectacularly tacky gift shop and a 66-room **hotel-restaurant**, *Crossing*, that is surprisingly comfortable (Ⓣ403/761-7000, Ⓦwww.thecrossingresort.com; ❻; early March to mid-Nov).

Some 12km north is the *Rampart Creek* **hostel** (Ⓣ403/439-3139; members $20, non-members $24; June–Oct open daily all day, check-in 5–11pm; Nov–May Sat & Sun only with reservation), with thirty beds, two cabins, the "best sauna in the Rockies", a basic food store and a fifty-pitch park-run **campsite** ($13.85; late June to early Sept). Apparently this area is one of the best black bear habitats close to the road anywhere in the park. The last of the Banff National Park campsites is the tiny sixteen-pitch *Cirrus Mountain* site at the 103km mark ($10; late June to early Sept), but its position is precarious, so check at the Lake Louise visitor centre or visit Ⓦwww.pc.gc.ca if it's open before planning a stay. At the time of going to press it was not in operation.

Shortly before the spectacular **Panther Falls** (113.5km) the road makes a huge hairpin climb (the so-called "Big Hill"), to open up yet more panoramic angles on the vast mountain spine stretching back towards Lake Louise. The unmarked and often slippery one-kilometre trail to the falls starts from the lower end of the second of two car parks on the right.

Beyond it (117km) is the trailhead to **Parker Ridge** (2.4km one-way; elevation gain 210m; allow 1hr one-way, less for the return), which, at 2130m, commands fantastic views from the summit ridge of the Saskatchewan Glacier (at 9km, the Rockies' longest). If you're only going to do one walk after the Peyto Lake Lookout, make it this one: it gets cold and windy up here, so bring extra clothing.

Nearby **Sunwapta Pass** (2023m) marks the border between Banff and Jasper national parks and the watershed of the North Saskatchewan and Sunwapta rivers: the former flows into the Atlantic, the latter into the Arctic Ocean. From here it's another 108km to Jasper.

The Columbia Icefield

Just beyond, covering an area of 325 square kilometres, the **Columbia Icefield** is the largest collection of ice and snow in the entire Rockies, and the largest glacial area in the northern hemisphere outside the Arctic Circle. It's also the most accessible of some seventeen glacial areas along the Parkway. Meltwater flows from it into the Arctic, Atlantic and Pacific oceans, forming a so-called "hydrological apex" – the only other one in the world is in Siberia. This is fed by six major glaciers, three of which – the Athabasca, Dome and Stutfield – are partially visible from the highway.

The ugly and extremely busy **Icefield Centre** (Ⓣ1-877/423-7433 or Parks Canada 780/852-6288, Ⓦwww.columbiaicefield.com; daily May to mid-June & early Sept to mid-Oct 9am–5pm; mid-June to early Sept 9am–6pm) provides an eerie viewpoint for the most prominent of these, the Athabasca Glacier, as well as offering the Parks Canada Exhibit Hall and information and slide shows on the glaciers and Canada's most extensive cave system – the Castleguard Caves, which honeycomb the ice but are inaccessible to the public. This is not a place to linger, however, thanks to the legions of people and dozens of tour buses.

You can walk up to the toe of the **Athabasca Glacier** from the parking area at Sunwapta Lake, noting en route the date-markers, which illustrate just how far the glacier has retreated (1.5km in the last 100 years). You can also walk onto the glacier, but shouldn't, as it's riddled with dangerous crevasses. People are killed and injured every year on the glacier: even a slip can rip off great slivers of skin. Full-scale expeditions are the preserve of experts but you can join an **organized trip**. Brewster's special "Snocoaches" run ninety-minute, five-kilometre rides over the glacier with a chance to get out and walk safely on the ice (daily every 15min or 30min: early May to Sept 9am–5pm; Oct 10am–5pm depending on weather; $33.95; book tickets at the Centre or call Ⓣ1-877/ICE

RIDE). They're heavily subscribed, so aim to avoid the peak midday rush by taking a tour before 10.30am or after 3pm.

More dedicated types can sign up for the two Athabasca Glacier ice walks (3hr "Ice Cubed" walk mid-June to early Sept daily at 11am, except Thurs & Sun, $55; 5hr "Icewalk Deluxe" Thurs & Sun 11am, $65), led by licensed guides. Sign up on the spot at the front desk of the Icefields Centre – be sure to bring warm clothes, boots and provisions. Visit Ⓦwww.icewalks.com for more information.

The 32-room *Columbia Icefields Chalet* (Ⓣ780/852-6550; ❺–❼) provides excellent but much-sought-after **accommodation** in the Icefields Centre between May and mid-October (note that rooms cost $225 from mid-June to Sept but half that the rest of the year). Brewster bus services between Jasper and Banff stop here: it's possible to take a Banff-bound Brewster bus out of Jasper at lunchtime (arrives at the Icefields at 3pm), see the Icefield, and pick up the evening Jasper-bound bus (leaves Icefield at 6.30pm) later the same day.

Two unserviced but very popular **campsites** lie 2km and 3km south of the Icefield Centre respectively: the tent-only 33-site *Columbia Icefield* ($13.85; mid-May to mid-Oct, or until the first snow) and the 46-site *Wilcox Creek*, which takes tents and RVs ($13.85; early June to mid-Sept). The latter is also the trailhead for one of the very finest **hikes** in the national park, never mind the highway: the **Wilcox Pass Trail** (4km one-way; 335m ascent; allow 2hr round trip), highly recommended by the park centres and just about every trail guide going. The path takes you steeply through thick spruce and alpine fir forest before emerging suddenly onto a ridge that offers vast views over the Parkway and the high peaks of the icefield (including Mount Athabasca). Beyond, the trail enters a beautiful spread of meadows, tarns and creeks, an area many people choose to halt at or wander all day without bothering to reach the pass itself. You could extend the walk to 11km by dropping from the pass to Tangle Creek further along the parkway.

Beyond the Columbia Icefield

If there's a change **beyond the Columbia** Icefield, it's a barely quantifiable lapse in the scenery's awe-inspiring intensity over the 108-kilometre stretch towards Jasper. As the road begins a gradual descent the peaks retreat slightly, taking on more alpine and less dramatic profiles in the process. Yet the scenery is still magnificent, though by this point you're likely to be in the advanced stages of landscape fatigue. It's worth holding on, though, for two good, short trails at Sunwapta and Athabasca falls. About 17km beyond the icefield is the 24-berth, two-cabin *Beauty Creek* **hostel** (reservations Ⓣ780/852-3215; $10; May–Sept; hostel open all day, check-in 5–11pm; partial closure possible Oct–April). Some 9km further is the unserviced 25-site *Jonas Creek* **campsite** ($13.85; mid-May to first snowfall).

A one-kilometre gravel spur leads off the hwy to **Sunwapta Falls** (175km from Banff, 55km from Jasper), fifteen minutes' walk through the woods from the road: they're not terribly dramatic unless in spate, but are interesting for the deep canyon they've cut through the surrounding valley. A short trail along the riverbank leads to more rapids and small falls downstream. The 35-pitch *Honeymoon Lake* **campsite** with kitchen shelter, swimming and dry toilets is 4km further along the Parkway ($10; mid-June to first snowfall).

The last main stop before you're in striking distance of Jasper Townsite, **Athabasca Falls** (30km from Jasper) is impressive enough, but the platforms and paths show the strain caused by thousands of tramping feet, making it hard to feel you're any longer in wilderness. One kilometre away, however, is the excellent *Athabasca Falls* **hostel** (Ⓣ780/852-5959; $11; closed Nov & Tues Oct–April; check-in 5–11pm; members $15, non-members $20), with forty

Rafting in the Rockies

If lazing around Maligne Lake in Jasper, or walking the odd trail elsewhere in the Rockies, sounds a bit tame, think about **whitewater rafting** – currently all the rage in the national parks, and Jasper in particular. Many operators, notably in Jasper, Golden (near Yoho National Park) and in Banff, cater to an ever-growing demand. Not all trips are white-knuckle affairs. Depending on the river and trip you choose, some rafting tours are just that – gentle rafting down placid stretches of river. Others require that you be fit and a strong swimmer. Trips last anything from a couple of hours to a couple of days.

While no previous experience is required for most tours, one or two things are worth knowing; the most important is how rivers are **graded**. White water is ranked in six classes: Class 1 is gentle and Class 6 is basically a waterfall. The **season** generally runs from May to mid-Sept, with the "biggest" water in June and July, when glacial meltwater is coursing down rivers. Operators are licensed by the park authorities and invariably supply you with everything you need, from the basics of helmet and life jacket to wet suits, wool sweaters and spray jackets depending on the likely severity of the trip. They also provide shuttle services from main centres to the rivers themselves, and many on longer trips include lunch, snack or barbecue in the tour price. Bigger operators may also have on-site shower and changing facilities if you're on a run where you're likely to get seriously wet. On any trip it's probably a good idea to have a change of clothes handy for when you finish, wear training shoes or something you don't mind getting wet, and have a towel and bag for any valuables. Many people sport swimming costumes beneath clothing. Often you can choose between trips – gentle or severe – where you sit back and hang on while others do the work in oared boats, or you join a trip where everyone who wants a paddle gets one.

At Banff the **Bow River** has no major rapids, so gentle one-hour float trips are offered through pretty scenery by several operators. Most companies in Banff or Lake Louise offer trips on one of two rivers to the west of the park. The **Kootenay River** in Kootenay National Park, two hours from Banff, is a Class 2–3 river. The **Kicking Horse River**, a premier destination just an hour from Banff, is a much more serious affair. In and just outside Yoho National Park, it has Class 4 sections (Cable Car, Man Eater Hole, Goat Rapid, Twin Towers and the Roller Coaster) in its upper sections and stretches in the Lower Kicking Horse Canyon which give even seasoned rafters pause for thought.

Jasper has perhaps the most possibilities on its doorstep. The Class 2 **Athabasca River** (from Athabasca Falls, 35km south of the town) is scenic and provides gentle

beds in three cabins. About 3km back down the road is the 42-site *Mount Kerkeslin* **campsite**, with swimming, kitchen shelter and dry toilets, spread over a tranquil riverside site ($13.85; mid-June to early Sept).

Highway 93A, the route of the old Parkway, branches off the Icefields Parkway at Athabasca Falls and runs parallel to it for 30km. This alternative route has less dramatic views than the Parkway, as dense trees line the road, but the chances of spotting wildlife are higher.

Jasper National Park

Although traditionally viewed as the second-ranking of the Rockies' big-four parks after Banff, **JASPER NATIONAL PARK** covers an area greater than Banff, Yoho and Kootenay combined, and looks and feels far wilder and less

rafting for families or those who just want a quiet river trip from May–Oct, but it also has one or two harmless whitewater sections. The **Sunwapta River** nearby, 55km south of Jasper, is a Class 3 river with some thrilling stretches of water, magnificent scenery and good chances to spot wildlife. The **Maligne River**, 45km from town, is Class 2–3+, offering a wide variety of trips between July and Sept for the many operators who use this river (including a lively 1.6-kilometre stretch of rapids). Yet the most riotous local river is the **Fraser**, accessed an hour west of Jasper in Mount Robson Provincial Park. This is Class 4 in places, but also has some gentle sections where the chance to watch salmon spawning at close quarters from mid-August to September provides an added attraction.

Operators in Jasper include **Maligne Rafting Adventures**, 627 Patricia St (ⓣ780/852-3370 or 1-866/625-4463, ⓦwww.mra.ab.ca), which runs a range of trips to suit all ages and abilities, including some of the wildest trips in the park: the four-hour "Sunwapta Challenge" uses six-passenger paddle-assisted rafts to ride parts of the Sunwapta – which means "turbulent river" in the local Stoney language. All equipment is supplied as are changing rooms and hot showers. They also offer two-hour "Mile 5 Run" (3 daily; $49) raft trips (3 daily) on the Athabasca River on small but lively rapids and three-hour "Heritage Run" trips (small paddle raft $62) on the same river suitable for families and children, as well as two different overnight trips to the Kakwa and Athabasca rivers (2 days $350, three days $599). There are also Class-3 rides on the Sunwapta River (4hr; $72) and Class 3 on the Fraser (5hr; $72), with two departures on each trip daily.

Jasper Raft Tours at Jasper Adventure Centre, Chaba Movie Theatre, 604 Connaught Drive (ⓣ780/852-2665 or 1-888/553-5628, ⓦwww.jasperrafttours.com) offers good trips for first-timers: two- to three-hour jaunts twice daily in summer on the Athabasca River in comfortable oar rafts. Tickets cost $47 and include shuttle to and from the river, with possible pick-ups from your hotel by prior arrangement; tickets are also available from the Brewster office in the train station. Another long-established company offers similar trips at similar prices to suit all ages and courage levels on several rivers: White Water Rafting (Jasper) Ltd (ⓣ780/852-7238 or 1-800/557-7328, ⓦwww.whitewaterraftiober and make special provisions for visitors with disabilities. Mile 5 rides on the Athabasca cost $51, Athabasca Falls is $62, Sunwapta River $62 and the Heritage Route tour $110. Trips last between two and four hours except for the Heritage Route, which is six hours plus and requires at least two days' notice and a minimum of six on the tour.

commercialized than its southern counterparts. Its backcountry is more extensive and less travelled, and **Jasper Townsite** (or Jasper), the only settlement, is more relaxed and far less of a resort than Banff and has just half Banff's population. Most pursuits centre on Jasper and the **Maligne Lake** area about 50km southeast of the townsite. Other key zones are **Maligne Canyon**, on the way to the lake; the Icefields Parkway (covered on p.734); and the **Miette Hot Springs** region, an area well to the east of Jasper and visited for its springs and trails.

The park's **backcountry** is a vast hinterland scattered with countless rough campsites and a thousand-kilometre trail system considered among the best in the world for backpackers. Opportunities for day and half-day-hikes are more limited and scattered than in other parks. Most of the shorter strolls from the townsite are just low-level walks to forest-circled lakes; the best of the more exciting day-hikes start from more remote points off the Maligne Lake road, Icefields Parkway (Hwy 93) and Yellowhead Hwy (Hwy 16).

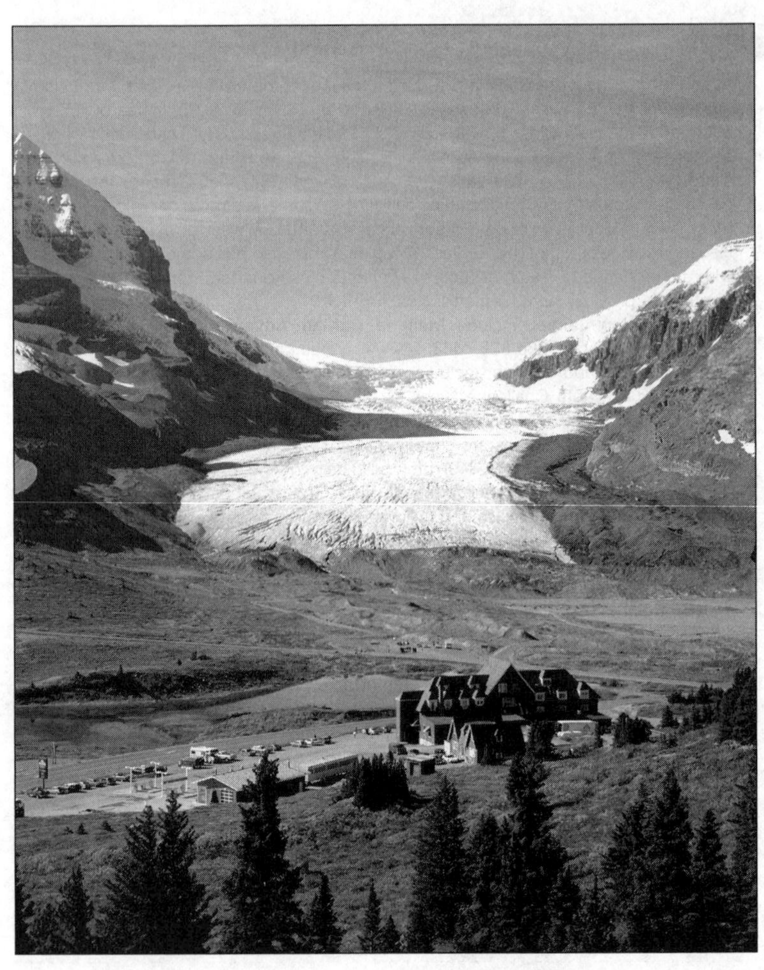

△ Athabasca Glacier, Icefields Parkway

A history of the park

Permanent settlement first came to the Jasper area in the winter of 1810–11. The great explorer and trader David Thomson left **William Henry** at Old Fire Point (just outside the present townsite), while he and his companions pushed on up the valley to blaze a trail over the Athabasca Pass that would be used for more than fifty years by traders crossing the Rockies. In the meantime, Henry established **Henry House**, the first permanent European habitation in the Rockies (though its exact location has been lost). Two years later the North West Company established Jasper House at the eastern edge of the park's present boundary. Named after Jasper Hawes, a long-time company clerk there, it moved closer to Jasper Lake in 1829, when the North West and Hudson's Bay companies were amalgamated. By 1880, and the collapse of the fur trade, the post had closed. By 1900, the entire region boasted just seven homesteads.

Like other parks and their townsites, Jasper traces its real origins to the coming of the railway in the late nineteenth century. The Canadian Pacific had brought boom to Banff and Yoho in 1885 when it spurned a route through the Jasper region in favour of a more southerly route. The **Grand Trunk Pacific Railway** hoped for similar successes in attracting visitors when it started to push its own route west in 1902, and the Jasper Forest Park was duly created in 1908. The government bought up all land locally except for the homestead of Lewis Swift, which remained in stubborn private hands until 1962: the town is now "run" by Parks Canada.

By 1911 a tent city known as **Fitzhugh**, named after the company's vice president, had grown up on Jasper's present site, and the name "Jasper" was adopted when the site was officially surveyed. Incredibly, a second railway, the **Canadian Northern Railway** (CNR), was completed almost parallel to the Grand Trunk line in 1913, the tracks at some points running no more than a few metres apart. Within just three years, the line's redundancy became obvious and consolidation took place west of Edmonton, with the most favourably graded portions of the two routes being adopted. The ripped-up rails were then shipped to Europe and used in World War I, and Jasper became a centre of operations for the lines in 1924, greatly boosting its importance and population.

The first tourist accommodation here was ten tents on the shores of Lac Beauvert, replaced in 1921 by the first *Jasper Lake Lodge*, forerunner of the present hotel. The first road link from Edmonton was completed in 1928. Official national-park designation came in 1930. Today Jasper's still a rail town, with around a third of the population employed by the CNR.

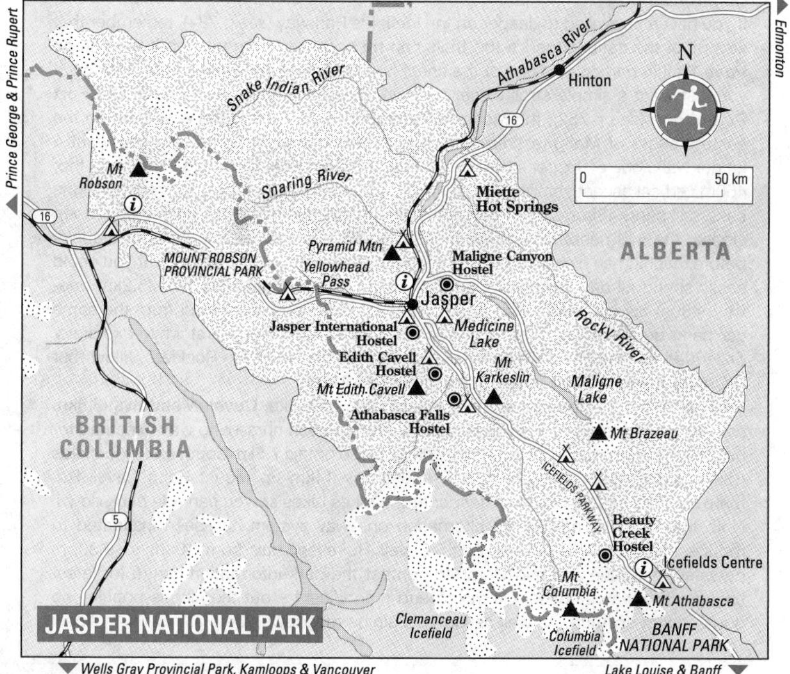

Arrival and information

Where Banff's strength is its convenience from Calgary, Jasper's is its ease of access from Edmonton, with plenty of **transport** options and approaches, as well as a wide range of onward destinations. Driving time from Edmonton (362km) or Banff (287km) is around four hours; from Kamloops (443km) and Calgary (414km) it's five or six hours; from Vancouver nine or ten hours (863km). Greyhound (ⓣ780/852-3926 or 1-800/661-8747, ⓦwww.greyhound.ca) runs four **buses** daily from Edmonton (5hr; $56.80 one-way) along the Yellowhead Hwy (Hwy 16), plus onward services (2–4 daily) to Kamloops (5hr; $61.05) and Vancouver (11hr 30min; $115.90) via scenic Hwy 5, and Prince George (2–4 daily; $61.05).

Brewster Transportation (ⓣ780/852-3332 or 1-800/661-1152, ⓦwww.brewster.ca) operates services to Banff (4hr 45min; $70) via Lake Louise (3hr

Hiking in Jasper National Park

The range of hiking trails on offer in and around Jasper is vast – far more than we could possibly outline here. We've sketched out some ideas in this box; at a glance, the best walks in Jasper are:

- Best stroll: Maligne Canyon
- Best short walk: Wilcox Pass
- Best day-hike (easy): Cavell Meadows
- Best day-hike (moderate): Opal Hills
- Best day-hike (strenuous): Sulphur Skyline
- Best backpacking trail: Skyline Trail

Day-hikes

If you haven't travelled to Jasper on the Icefields Parkway (see p.734), remember that several of the national park's top trails can be accessed from this road: the **Wilcox Pass Trail** in particular is one of the finest half-day-hikes anywhere in the Rockies. If you just want a simple stroll closer to town, then think about walking the **Old Fort Point Loop** (see p.752), the **Maligne Canyon** (see p.752) and the easy path on the eastern shore of **Maligne Lake** (see p.754). If you're at Maligne Lake and want a longer walk, one of Jasper's best day-hikes, the **Opal Hills Circuit** (8.2km round trip; 460m vertical ascent), starts from the picnic area to the left of the uppermost Maligne Lake car park, 48km east of Jasper. After a heart-pumping haul up the first steep slopes, the trail negotiates alpine meadows and offers sweeping views of the lake before reaching an elevation of 2160m; the trip takes about four hours, but you could easily spend all day loafing around the meadows. The **Bald Hills Trail** (5.2km one-way; 480m ascent) starts with a monotonous plod along a fire road from the same car park, but ends with what Mary Schaffer, one of the area's first white explorers, described as "the finest view any of us had ever beheld in the Rockies"; allow four hours for the round trip, which goes as high as 2170m.

To get to the trailhead for another outstanding day-hike, **Cavell Meadows** (3.8km one-way; 370m ascent) – which is named after a British nurse who was executed for helping the Allies during World War I – drive, cycle or taxi 7.5km south on the Icefields Parkway, then 5km along Hwy 93A and finally 14km up Mount Edith Cavell Rd; there's a daily shuttle bus from Jasper and it takes bikes so you can ride back down. Note that if you're driving, an alternating one-way system has been instigated to reduce traffic flow up Mount Edith Cavell Rd every day from 10am to 9.30pm between mid-June and mid-October: contact the park information centre for latest timings. The walk's scenery is mixed and magnificent – but the hike is popular, so don't expect solitude. As well as Cavell's alpine meadows, there are views of Angel

45min; $60) and continuing to Calgary and Calgary Airport (1 daily; 8hr 40min; $120), and also runs day-trip tours to Banff, taking in sights on the Icefields Parkway; note, however, that weather can play havoc with Brewster's schedules in October and April. Both companies share the same **bus terminal** (daily 6am–8pm; outside regular hours, the terminal opens briefly a few minutes before bus departures), located in the train station building at 607 Connaught Drive.

There are also left-luggage lockers here and **car rental** offices for Hertz (Ⓣ780/852-3888 or 1-800/263-0600, Ⓦwww.hertz.com) and National (Ⓣ780/852-1117). Be sure to have booked cars in advance if you're hoping to pick up vehicles at these outlets: all cars go very quickly, especially on days when trains come in from Vancouver and Edmonton. Other car-rental agencies in town include Avis at the Sundog Tours office, 414 Connaught Drive (Ⓣ780/852-3970 or 1-800/879-2847, Ⓦwww.avis.ca).

Glacier and the dizzying north wall of Mount Edith Cavell. Allow two hours for the round trip; the maximum elevation reached is a breathless 2135m.

Further afield – you'll need transport – another superlative short, sharp walk starts from Miette Hot Springs, 58km northeast of Jasper. The **Sulphur Skyline** (4km one-way; 700m ascent) offers exceptional views of knife-edged ridges, deep gorges, crags and remote valleys. Be sure to take water with you, and allow two hours each way for the steep climb to 2070m. The trailhead is signed from the Miette Hot Springs complex, reached from Jasper by heading 41km east on Hwy 16 and then 17km south; in the past the shuttles have made the trip in summer – check latest timetables. More soothing, and a good way to round off a day, are the **springs** themselves, the hottest in the Rockies – so hot in fact they have to be cooled for swimming; there's one pool for soaking, another for swimming, with massages by appointment and not included in pass price (mid-June to early Sept daily 8.30am–10.30pm, mid-May to mid-June and early Sept to mid-Oct daily 10.30am–9pm, $6.15 or $8.65 day-pass; Ⓣ780/866-3939 or 1-800/767-1611, Ⓦwww.pc.gc.ca). You can rent bathing suits, towels and lockers for an extra $4–6. Other trails from the springs make for the **Fiddle River** (4.3km one-way; 275m ascent) and **Mystery Lake** (10.5km one-way; 475m ascent).

Backpacking trails

Jasper's system of **backpacking trails** and 111 backcountry campsites makes it one of the leading areas for backcountry hiking in North America. To stay overnight in the backcountry, pick up a Wilderness Permit ($8.90) within 24 hours of your departure, from the park information centre in Jasper Townsite or at the Columbia Icefield. All trails and campsites operate quota systems; contact the park information office for details and book yourself a backcountry campsite(s) – and thus trail place – as soon as you can. Reservations cost $11.85 (nonrefundable). Trails remain busy even into Sept: the busiest are Skyline, Maligne Lake, Brazeau and Tonquin Valley.

The office staff offer invaluable advice, and issue excellent low-price strip maps of several trails. Overnight hikes are beyond the scope of this book – talk to staff or get hold of a copy of *The Canadian Rockies Trail Guide* – but by general consent the finest long-distance trails are the **Skyline** (44km; 820m ascent) and **Jonas Pass** (19km; 555m ascent), with the latter often combined with the **Nigel** and **Poboktan** passes (total 36km; 750m ascent) to make a truly outstanding walk. Not far behind come two hikes in the Tonquin Valley – **Astoria River** (19km; 445m ascent) and **Maccarib Pass** (21km; 730m ascent) – and the **Fryat Valley** (3–4 days). Others to consider are Maligne Pass and the long-distance North and South Boundary trails (the latter both over 160km).

VIA Rail **trains** operate to Jasper from Winnipeg and Edmonton and continue to Vancouver (via Kamloops) or Prince Rupert (via Prince George). As this is the only scheduled rail route through the Rockies, summer places are hard to come by, but at other times there's little need to book a seat. Fares are considerably more than those of equivalent buses, and journey times considerably longer. The **ticket office** is open on train days only (Ⓣ780/852-4102 or 1-888/VIA-RAIL, Ⓦwww.viarail.ca).

Jasper's superb national park **visitor centre** is at 500 Connaught Drive, 50m east of the station, back from the road on the left in the open grassy area (daily Jan–March & Nov–Dec 9am–4pm, April to mid-June & Oct 9am–5pm, mid-June to early Sept 8.30am–7pm, early Sept to the end of Sept 9am–6pm; Ⓣ780/852-6176, Ⓦwww.pc.gc.ca). This is for park-related and campsite information only, and sells compulsory **national park permits** ($8.90 daily, $62.40 annual) and backcountry wilderness permits ($8.90), and lets you register for backpacking trails.

For weather reports, call Environment Canada (Ⓣ780/852-3185). The centre also has a shop (good for **maps**) run by the Friends of Jasper (Ⓣ780/852-4767), who offer a couple of **guided walks** which delve into the history of the town and some of the legends and stories of the region. You should register at the centre for both; payment is by donation. Other popular Friends' activities include performances at the Whistler's Campground Theatre (July–Sept daily) and wildlife talks at the Wabasso Campground Campfire Circle (July–Sept).

For information on the town of Jasper, and accommodation in particular, contact the Jasper Chamber of Commerce **infocentre** behind the park office about 100m east on Patricia St at no. 409 (June to early Sept daily 9am–7pm; rest of year Mon–Fri 9am–5pm; Ⓣ780/852-3858, Ⓦwww.jaspercanadianrockies.com).

Accommodation

Beds in Jasper are not as expensive or elusive as in Banff, but hotel rooms are still almost unobtainable in late July and August. The Chamber of Commerce

Taxis and shuttle services

One of the problems you're likely to have in Jasper if you're without transport is getting to some of the more outlying sights, strolls and trailheads. One option is to rent a bike (see p.754). Another is take advantage of a variety of small-scale **shuttle services** that run to various sights. These tend to come and go year by year, but there's always someone prepared to start up a service. Currently services include the **Sundog Tour Shuttle**, also known as the **Tramway Shuttle** (Ⓣ780/852-4056 or 852-8255 or 1-888/786-3641, Ⓦwww.sundogtours.com), which runs nine times daily in summer from outside the VIA Rail-bus depot to the Jasper Tramway (cable car) at a cost of $29, including Tramway ticket; more importantly, it also takes in the *Jasper International* (or *Whistlers*) *Hostel*.

Or there's the long-established **Maligne Lake Shuttle**, run by Maligne Tours, 616 Patricia St (Ⓣ780/852-3370, Ⓦwww.malignelakeshuttle.com; 4 departures daily late June to late Sept, 3 daily mid-May to late June and last week of Sept), which will run you all the way to Maligne Lake ($16.05 or $32.10 round trip) to coincide with the company's boat cruises on the lake (see p.753), or drop off at Maligne Canyon ($10.70) and other points on the Maligne Lake Road such as the Maligne Canyon hostel and Skyline trailheads.

For a **taxi**, call Heritage Cab (Ⓣ780/852-5558), Michael Angelo (Ⓣ780/852-7277) or Jasper Taxi (Ⓣ780/852-3600).

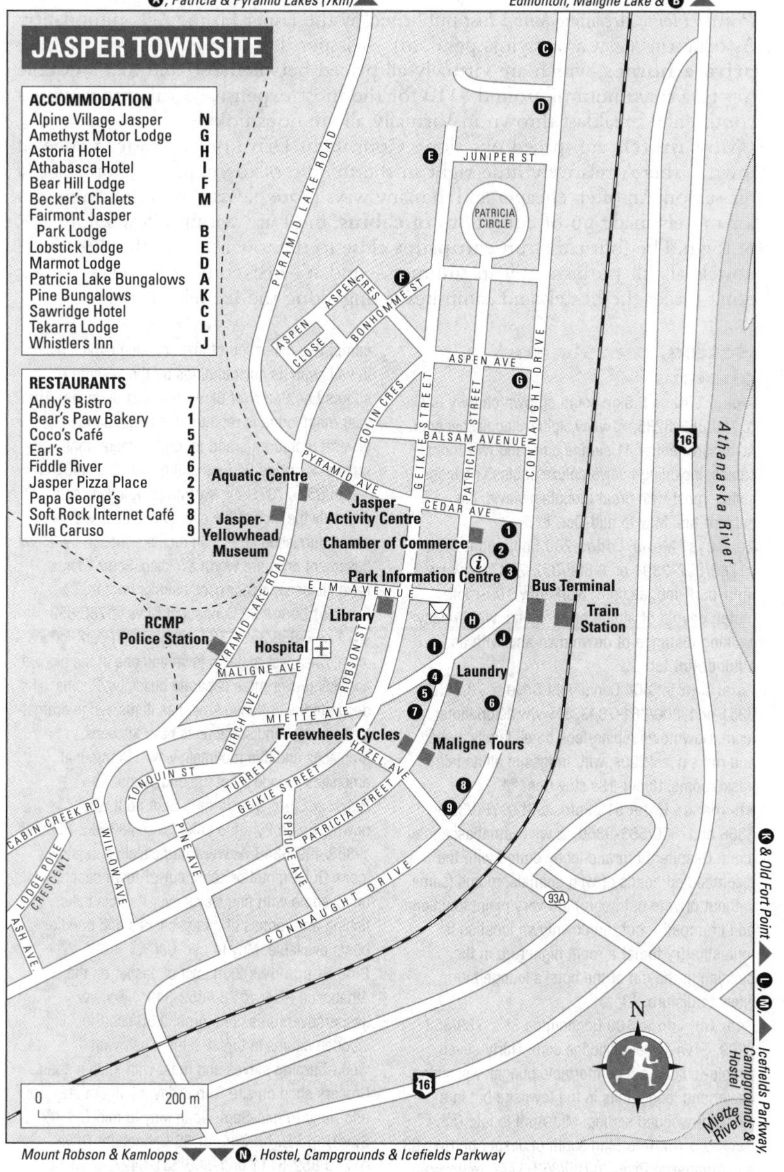

will help with accommodation, but does not offer a booking service. If you're desperate, try Jasper Adventure Centre, 604 Connaught Drive (moves to 306 Connaught Drive in winter), which offers an accommodation service (Ⓣ780/852-5595 or 1-877/902-9455, Ⓦwww.jasperadventurecentre.com). So, too, does Sundog Tours, 414 Connaught Drive (Ⓣ780/852-4056, Ⓦwww.sundogtours.com). You could also ask the Chamber of Commerce for the

Private Home Accommodation List published by the Jasper Home Accommodation Association (ⓦ www.stayinjasper.com) – Jasper has rooms in around sixty **private homes**, which are virtually all priced between $60 and $75 a double (up to a maximum of around $110 for the most expensive), sometimes with a continental breakfast thrown in. Virtually all are nonsmoking.

Most **motels** are spaced out along Connaught Drive on the eastern edge of town – there's relatively little right in the middle of town; prices drop sharply off-season. An often cheaper and in many ways more pleasant option is to plump for motels made up of collections of **cabins**; most are within a few kilometres of town. The four park-run **campsites** close to the townsite and the three local hostels all fill up promptly in summer – and it's first-come, first-served – but don't forget the hostels and campsites strung along the Icefields Parkway.

Hotels, motels and chalets

Alpine Village 2.5km south of town on Hwy 93A ⓣ 780/852-3285, ⓦ www.alpinevillagejasper.com. An assortment of 41 serene one- and two-room cabins, including twelve deluxe cabins and lodge suites, most with great mountain views; big outdoor tub. May to mid-Oct. ❻

Amethyst Motor Lodge 200 Connaught Drive ⓣ 780/852-3394 or 1-888/852-7737, ⓦ www.mtn-park-lodges.com. Workaday 100-room motel, devoid of alpine pretensions, within easy walking distance of downtown and with an outdoor hot tub. ❼

Astoria Hotel 404 Connaught Drive ⓣ 780/852-3351 or 1-800/661-7343, ⓦ www.astoriahotel.com. Downtown Alpine-look hotel, family owned and run since 1920s, with fridges in all its fairly basic rooms. Under-18s stay free. ❼

Athabasca Hotel 510 Patricia St ⓣ 780/852-3386 or 1-800/563-9859, ⓦ www.athabascahotel.com. Despite the grand lobby dotted with the disembodied heads of wild animals, rooms (some without private bathroom) are very plain, functional and cramped – but the downtown location is fantastic. Try to get a room higher up in the building, if the din of the hotel's lounge bar is likely to disturb. ❻

Bear Hill Lodge 100 Bonhomme St ⓣ 780/852-3209, ⓦ www.bearhilllodge.com. Thirty-seven simple-looking but comfortable bungalows, suites, chalet and lodge units in the townsite but in a pleasant wooded setting. Mid-April to late Oct. ❺

Becker's Chalets 5km south of Jasper on Hwy 93 and Athabasca River ⓣ 780/852-3779, ⓦ www.beckerschalets.com. Ninety-six of the best local one-, two-, three- and four-bedroom log cabins, most with wood-burning stoves and kitchenettes. May to mid-Oct. ❹

Fairmont Jasper Park Lodge Lac Beauvert ⓣ 780/852-3301 or 1-800/441-1414, ⓦ www.jasperparklodge.com. Reminiscent of a summer camp, this collection of luxurious log cabins blends in well with its surroundings on the secluded shores Lac Beauvert 6km northeast of Jasper. The vast main lodge is replete with large lounges, several restaurants and an underground mall. ❽

Lobstick Lodge 94 Geikie St ⓣ 780/852-4431 or 1-888/852-7737, ⓦ www.mtn-park-lodges.com. Arguably the pick of the east end motels, with large, simply furnished and clean rooms – though the dingy basement ones are worth avoiding. Some rooms have kitchens; indoor pool, outdoor hot tub. ❼

Marmot Lodge 92 Connaught Drive ⓣ 780/852-4471 or 1-888/852-7737, ⓦ www.mtn-park-lodges.com. Cheapest motel in town and one of the biggest; spreading over three separate buildings. Rooms, all decorated with Native American items, range dramatically in size, and some units have kitchens, fireplaces and fine mountain views. Communal amenities include a hot tub and sauna. ❻

Patricia Lake Bungalows 5km northwest of downtown on Pyramid Lake Rd ⓣ 780/852-3560 or 1-888/499-6848, ⓦ www.patricialakebungalows.com. Quiet motel or cabin out-of-town base; 35 units, some with fine views over Patricia Lake; fishing and rentals of boats, canoes and paddle boats available. May to mid-Oct. ❸

Pine Bungalows 2km east of Jasper on the Athabasca River ⓣ 780/852-3491, ⓦ www.jasperadventures.com. Around 80 good-looking wooden cabins in forest setting, half with wood-burning stoves and most with kitchenettes. Grocery shop on site. Three-day minimum stay from mid-June to mid-Sept. Open May to mid-Oct. ❹

Sawridge Hotel Jasper 82 Connaught Drive ⓣ 780/852-5111 or 1-800/661-6427, ⓦ www.sawridge.com/jasper. Plush and expensive 154-room hotel on the eastern edge of town. ❽

Tekarra Lodge 1km south of town on the Athabasca River off Hwy 93A. ⓣ 780/852-3058 or 1-888/404-4540, ⓦ www.tekarralodge.com. Forty-two quiet, nicely kitsch wood cabins with wood-burning stoves. Open May–Oct. ❻

Whistlers Inn 105 Miette Ave ⓣ780/852-3361 or 1-800/282-9919, ⓦwww.whistlersinn.com. Central but unexciting 41-room motel, opposite the station. ❼

B&Bs

A-1 Tourist Rooms 804 Connaught Drive ⓣ780/852-3325, ⓔlwhitema@telusplanet.net. Two rooms with shared bathroom on Main St close to bus and train. Two-night minimum stay for advance reservations. ❷

Aspen Lodge 8 Aspen Crescent ⓣ780/852-5908, ⓔaspnlodg@telusplanet.net. Two clean, comfortable rooms with private bathrooms on a quiet street 10min walk from downtown. ❹

B&G Accommodation 204 Colin Crescent ⓣ780/852-4345, ⓔwgunrau@telusplanet.net. Three well-priced rooms with shared bathroom three blocks from downtown. ❷

Creekside Accommodation 1232 Patricia Crescent ⓣ780/852-3530, ⓔrushacom@telusplanet.net. Two bright, clean rooms (shared bath) near Cabin Creek and trails. ❷

Kennedy's Mountain Holiday Rooms 1115 Patricia Crescent ⓣ780/852-3438. Pair of rooms that share bath, patio, living room and great views.❷

Rooney's Accommodation 1114 Patricia St ⓣ780/852-4101, ⓔmismaeil@telusplanet.com. Just out of the town centre comprising two nice rooms with and without private baths. ❷

Tasson Inn 706 Patricia St ⓣ780/852-3427, ⓔtassinn@incentre.net. Two bright and newly renovated rooms with shared bathroom less than a block from the town centre. ❹

Hostels

Jasper International Hostel (HI) Whistlers Mountain Rd ⓣ780/852-3215, ⓦwww.hihostels.ca. Large, sterile and highly institutional hostel, the biggest of three in the vicinity of Jasper, and located 7km south of town via the Icefields Parkway (Hwy 93). The 4km uphill walk from Hwy 93 is a killer, but shuttles run from downtown, as do taxis (about $15). Check-in operates from noon to midnight when HI members are charged $21–23 for dorm beds, non-members $26–28. Private doubles cost from $50–80. It has all the usual hostel facilities and no curfew. The eighty beds fill up quickly in summer, so arrive early or book.

Maligne Canyon Hostel (HI) ⓣ780/852-3215, ⓦwww.hihostels.ca. Two cabins in lovely setting with beds for 24 in six-bed rooms 11km east of town near Maligne Canyon; the Maligne Lake Shuttle from downtown or Alberta Hostel Shuttle drop off here daily in summer. Dorms $15 for members, $20 for non-members. Open all day, year-round but check-in 5–11pm and may have closures in winter.

Mount Edith Cavell Hostel (HI) Edith Cavell Rd, 13km off Hwy 93A, 26km south of Jasper ⓣ780/852-3215, ⓦwww.hihostels.ca. Check-in 5–11pm. Cosier than the *Jasper International*, close to trails and with great views of the Angel Glacier. Sleeps 32 in two cabins; outdoor wood-burning sauna. Dorms $15 for members, $20 for non-members. Mid-June to Oct. Occasionally opens up with key system for skiers in winter.

Campsites

Pocahontas 45km east of Jasper and 1km off Hwy 16 on Miette Rd. One of two to the northeast of Jasper on this road; 130 pitches, hot and cold water and flush toilets but no showers. Mid-May to mid-Oct. $18.80 plus $7.90 for use of firewood.

Snaring River 16km east of Jasper on Hwy 16. Simple 66-site park-run facility. The other simple park campsite east of Jasper; tap water, kitchen shelter, dry toilets only and no showers. Mid-May to early Sept. $13.85 plus $7.90 for use of firewood. There's also a basic overflow site at $8.90.

Wabasso 16km south of Jasper on Hwy 93A. A 228-pitch riverside park-run site with flush toilets, hot water but no showers. Wheelchair-accessible. Mid-June to early Sept. $18.80 plus $7.90 for use of firewood.

Wapiti 4km south of the townsite and 1km south of *Whistlers* campsite (see below) on Hwy 93. Big 362-pitch park-run place with flush toilets and coin showers that accepts tents but also caters for up to forty RVs. Wheelchair-accessible. Some ninety sites remain open for winter camping from October – the park's only year-round serviced campsite. Summer $23.75 plus $7.90 for use of firewood; winter, when there are no showers or other services save water and flush toilets, $14.85 plus $7.90 for use of firewood. RV sites cost $27.70 in summer, $17.80 in winter.

Whistlers 3km south of Jasper just west off Hwy 93. Jasper's main 781-site park-run campsite is the largest in the Rockies, with three sections, and prices depending on facilities included. Wheelchair-accessible. If you're coming from Banff, watch for the sign; Brewster buses also usually stop here if you ask the driver. Taxis and shuttles run from Jasper. Early May to early Oct. $23.75 plus $7.90 for use of firewood. RV sites with electrical hookups are $32.65

Jasper Townsite and around

JASPER's small-town feel comes as a relief after the razzmatazz of Banff: its streets still have the windswept, open look of a frontier town and, though the mountains don't ring with quite the same majesty as Banff, you'll probably feel the town better suits its wild surroundings. Situated at the confluence of the Miette and Athabasca rivers, its core centres around just two streets: **Connaught Drive**, which contains the bus and train terminal, restaurants, motels and park information centre, and – a block to the west – the parallel **Patricia Steet**, lined with more shops, restaurants and the odd hotel. The rest of the central grid consists of cosy little houses and the fixtures of small-town life: the post office, library, school and public swimming pool.

Apart from the **Yellowhead Museum & Archives** at 400 Pyramid Rd, with its fur trade and railroad displays (mid-May to early Sept daily 10am–9pm; early Sept to Oct daily 10am–5pm; Nov to mid-May Thurs–Sun 10am–5pm; $4) and a cable car (see below), nothing here even pretends to be a tourist attraction; this is a place to sleep, eat and stock up. If you're interested in getting to know a little more about the town or park from the locals, contact the Friends of Jasper National Park (Ⓣ780/852-4767, Ⓦwww.friendsofjasper.com), which offers guided walks between July and August, or pick up *Jasper: A Walk in the Past* from local bookshops. A lot of people head 58km northeast of town for a dip in Miette Hot Springs (see box, p.745).

With little on offer in town you need to use a bike, car or the shuttle services to get anything out of the area. The obvious trip is on Canada's longest and highest cable car, the **Jasper Tramway**, 7km south of town on Whistlers Mountain Rd, off the Icefields Parkway (daily April to mid-May and late Aug

Operation Habbakuk

Behind every triumph of military ingenuity in World War II there were probably dozens of spectacular and deliberately obfuscated failures. Few have been as bizarre as the one witnessed by Jasper's Patricia Lake. By 1942, Allied shipping losses in the North Atlantic had become so disastrous that almost anything was considered that might staunch the flow. One Geoffrey Pike, institutionalized in a London mental hospital, managed to put forward the idea of a vast aircraft carrier made of ice, a ship that would be naturally impervious to fire when torpedoed, and not melt in the icy waters of the North Atlantic.

Times were so hard that the innovative scheme, despite its odd source, was given serious consideration. Louis Mountbatten, one of the Allied Chiefs of Staff, went so far as to demonstrate the theories with ice cubes in the bath in front of Winston Churchill at 10 Downing St. It was decided to build a thousand-tonne model somewhere very cold – Canada was ideal – and **Operation Habbakuk** was launched. Pike was released from his hospital on special dispensation and dispatched to the chilly waters of Patricia Lake near Jasper. Here a substance known as pikewood was invented, a mixture of ice and wood chips (spruce chips were discovered to add more buoyancy than pine). It soon became clear, however, that the 650m-long and twenty-storey-high boat stood little chance of ever being seaworthy (never mind what the addition of 2000 crew and 26 aircraft would do for its buoyancy). Pike suggested filling the ice with air to help things along. Further complications arose when the labourers on the project, mostly pacifist Doukhobors (see p.969), became aware of the boat's proposed purpose and refused to carry on working. Spring thaws brought the project to a halt. The following season, with $75m budgeted for it, the scheme was moved to Newfoundland, where it died a quiet death.

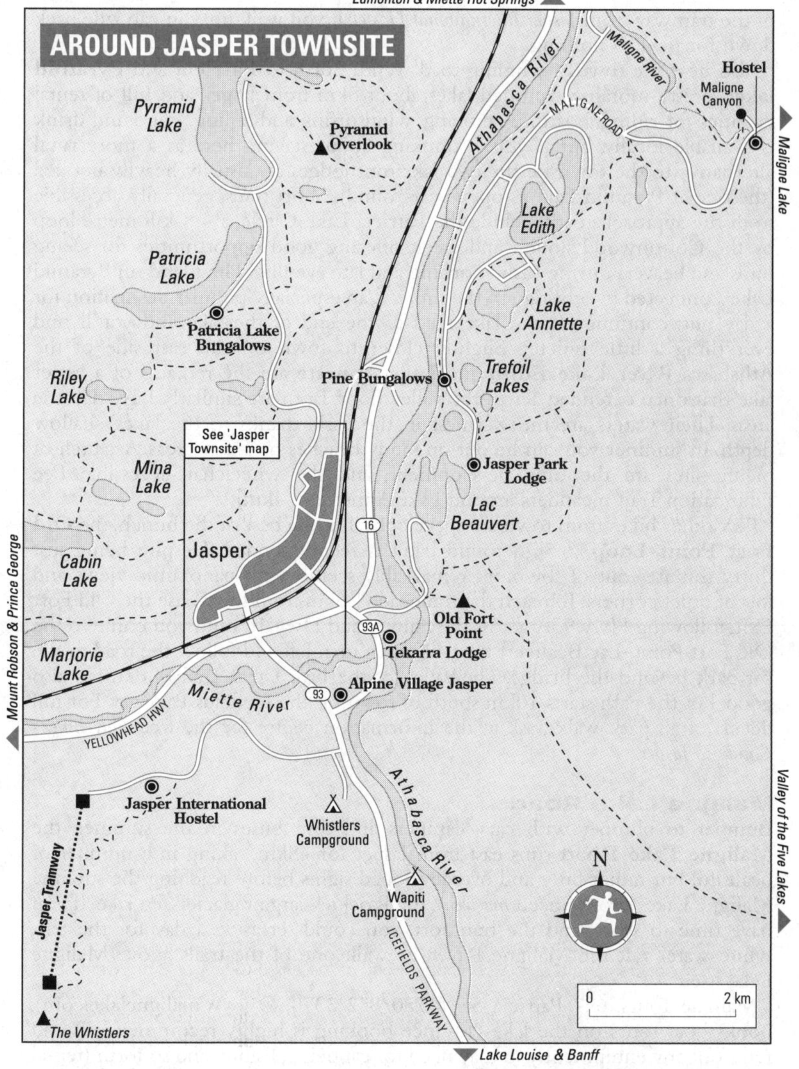

to early Oct 10am–5pm; mid-May to late June 9.30am–8.30pm; late June to late Aug 9am–8pm; $24 return or $29 including Sundog Tours shuttle from Jasper; see box, p. 746). In peak season you may well have a long wait in line for the 2.5-kilometre cable-car ride, whose two thirty-person cars take seven minutes to make the 1000m ascent (often with running commentary from the conductor). It leaves you at an interpretive centre, expensive restaurant, and an excellent viewpoint (2285m) where you can take your bearings on much of the park. A steep trail ploughs upwards and onwards to the Whistlers summit (2470m), an hour's walk that requires warm clothes year-round and reveals even more stunning views. A tough but rather redundant 10km trail follows the route of the tramway from *Jasper International Hostel*; if you walk up, you can ride back down for next to nothing.

Also near the town, a winding road wends north to **Patricia** and **Pyramid lakes**, pretty moraine-dammed lakes about 5km from Jasper and full of rental facilities for riding, boating, canoeing, windsurfing and sailing. Food and drink is available locally, but if you're thinking about staying here as a more rural alternative to the townsite the two lakefront lodges are usually heavily booked (the one at Pyramid Lake is open year-round). Short trails, generally accessible from the approach road, include the Patricia Lake Circle, a 4.8-kilometre loop by the Cottonwood slough and creek offering good opportunities for seeing birds and beavers during early morning and late evening. The island on Pyramid Lake, connected by a bridge to the shore, is an especially popular destination for a day out: continue on the lake road to the end of the lake and you'll find everything a little quieter. Slightly closer to town on the east side of the Athabasca River, **Lake Edith** and **Lake Annette** are the remains of a larger lake that once extended across the valley floor. Both are similarly busy day-use areas. Their waters are the warmest in the park, thanks to the lakes' shallow depth. In summer you can lie out on sandy beaches or grassy areas. A clutch of picnic sites are the only development, and the wheelchair-accessible Lee Foundation Trail meanders around Lake Annette (2.4km).

Few other hikes from town are spectacular, but the best of the bunch, the **Old Fort Point Loop** (6.5km round trip), is recommended. Despite being just thirty minutes out of town, it's remarkably scenic, with panoramic views and lots of quiet corners. To reach the trailhead (1.6km from town) use the Old Fort Exit, following Hwy 93A across the railway and Hwy 16 until you come to the Old Fort Point–Lac Beauvert turn-off, then turn left and follow the road to the car park beyond the bridge. The Valley of the Five Lakes Trail (4.6km) is also good, but the path starts 10km south of town off the Icefields Parkway. For full details of all park walks, ask at the information centre for the free *Day-hiker's Guide to Jasper.*

Maligne Lake Road

Bumper to bumper with cars, campers and tour buses in the summer, the **Maligne Lake Road** runs east from Jasper for 48km, taking in a number of beautiful but rather busy and overdeveloped sights before reaching the sublime Maligne Lake (pronounced *ma-leen*), the Rockies' largest glacier-fed lake. If you have time to spare, and the transport, you could set aside a day for the trip, white-water raft the Maligne River, or walk one of the trails above Maligne Lake itself.

Maligne Tours, 627 Patricia St (ⓣ780/852-3370, ⓦwww.malignelake.com), books boat tours on the lake (advance booking is highly recommended) and rents out any equipment you may need for canoeing, fishing and so forth (rental reservations are also essential in summer). The company also runs a **bus**, the Maligne Lake Shuttle (ⓦwww.malignelakeshuttle.com), to the lake eight times daily ($16.05 one-way, $32.10 return), with drop-offs (if booked) at *Maligne Canyon* hostel and the northern and southern ends of the Skyline Trail, one of the park's three top backpacking trails (see box, p.744). Joint tickets are offered for the shuttle and other activities organized by the company, notably the cruises, raft trips and horse rides on and around Maligne Lake.

The often rather crowded **Maligne Canyon** is a mere 11km out of Jasper, with an oversized car park and a tacky café/souvenir shop. This heavily sold excursion promises one of the Rockies' most spectacular gorges: in fact the canyon is deep (50m), but almost narrow enough to jump across – many people have tried and most have died in the attempt. In the end the geology is more interesting than the scenery; the violent erosive forces that created the canyon are explained on the main trail loop, an easy twenty-minute amble that can be extended to 45 minutes (few people do this, so the latter part of the trail is often quiet), or even turned into a hike back to Jasper. In winter, licensed guides lead tours (more like crawls) through the frozen canyon.

Next stop is picture-perfect **Medicine Lake**, 32km from Jasper, which experiences intriguing fluctuations in level. Its waters have no surface outlet; instead the lake fills and empties through lake-bed sink holes into the world's largest system of limestone caves. They re-emerge some 17km away towards Jasper (and may also feed some of the lakes around Jasper Townsite). When the springs freeze in winter, the lake drains and sometimes disappears altogether, only to be replenished in the spring. The lake's strange behaviour captivated local natives, who believed spirits were responsible, hence the name. Few people spend much time at the lake, preferring to press on to Maligne Lake, so it makes a quietish spot to escape the headlong rush down the road.

Maligne Lake

At the end of Maligne Lake Road, 48km from Jasper, is the stunning **Maligne Lake**, 22km long and 92m deep, and surrounded by snow-covered mountains. The largest lake in the Rockies, its name comes from the French for "wicked", and was coined in 1846 by a Jesuit missionary, Father de Smet, in memory of the difficulty he had crossing the **Maligne River** downstream. The road peters out at a warden station, three car parks and a restaurant flanked by a picnic area and the start of the short, self-explanatory Lake Trail along the lake's east side to the Schäffer Viewpoint (3.2km loop; begin from Car Park 2).

A small waterfront area is equipped with berths for glass-enclosed boats that run ninety-minute narrated **cruises** on the lake to Spirit Island: the views are sensational (daily hourly on the hour: first ice-free period to early June 10am–3pm; early June to late June 10am–4pm; late June to early Sept to late Sept 10am–5pm; early to end of season 10am–4pm; $41). The boats are small, however, and reservations are vital during peak times, especially as tour companies often block-book entire sailings; again, contact Maligne Tours (see p.746).

Riding, fishing, rafting and guided hiking tours are also available, as are fishing tackle, rowing boat and canoe rentals ($26.75/hr, $80.25/day) and sea kayaks ($32.10/hr, minimum 2hr; $96.30/day). Guided fishing with Maligne Tours costs $192.60 for a full day (assuming two or more people) and $144.45 for a half-day. There are no accommodation or camping facilities here, but two backcountry campsites on the lakeshore can be reached by canoe; get details from Jasper's information centre.

Eating and drinking

Though a far cry from the selection in Banff, Jasper has just about enough **restaurants** to ensure variety and a reasonable choice for a week-long vacation, though hearty North American food dominates local menus.

Wholly unpretentious, generally gritty and regularly raucous, **nightlife** in Jasper's limited number of **bars** tends to make up in enthusiasm what it lacks in style. And with the presence of plenty of friendly local folk to share a beer with, a good night out is easy to come by. Yet many of the hostels and campsites are too far out of town for people to get in, so the fun there is generally of the make-your-own variety. For alternative evening entertainment – local theatre, music, dance performances and movies – consult the

Jasper activities

Tours and excursions

Tours and activities can be accessed through several operators around town, amongst whom the most wide-ranging is **Sundog Tours**, 414 Connaught Drive (Ⓣ780/852-4056, Ⓦwww.sundogtours.com), who run their own tours and act as a one-stop booking agent for a huge range of others, including seeing the park by **helicopter** ($199 for a 25-minute flight; involves 1hr road transfer to Mount Robson), guided nature hikes (3hr locally $45, 6hr on Mount Edith Cavell Meadows $55) or white-water rafting ($45 and up).

The town's other big operator is **Maligne Tours**, 616 Patricia St (Ⓣ780/852-3370, Ⓦwww.malignelake.com), which do boat cruises on Maligne Lake, guided hiking and fishing trips, canoe rentals and rafting excursions.

For free walking tours run by the Friends of Jasper National Park in the summer, contact the park visitor centre and see p.746. If you need to **rent outdoor equipment**, the best bet is On-Line Sport & Tackle, 600 Patricia St (Ⓣ780/852-3630), or the Totem Ski Shop, 408 Connaught Drive (Ⓣ780/852-3078 or 1-800/363-3078, Ⓦwww.totemskishop.com).

Bikes, skates and camping

You can **rent bikes** in town from On-Line Sport & Tackle ($9/hr, $24/3hr, $35/day) or from Freewheel Cycles, 618 Patricia St (same rates; Ⓣ780/852-3898, Ⓦwww.freewheeljasper.com). At the latter, drop in and ask for their *Mountain Biking Trail Guide*, a summary of trails to suit all types of riders. Out of town you can rent bikes at the *Jasper International Hostel*; at the *Fairmont Jasper Park Lodge* on the shore of Lac Beauvert); and at Patricia Lake Bungalows, 4.8km northwest of town on Pyramid Lake Rd). Most of the above outlets offer **in-line skate rental**. To rent **camping equipment** (plus bikes and fishing tackle) make for Source for Sports, 406 Patricia St (Ⓣ780/852-3654, Ⓦwww.jaspersports.com). A three-man tent, for example, costs $15/day.

Fishing, golf and horse riding

For **fishing** tours, info and advice, Maligne Tours or On-Line Sport & Tackle (see above) are the operators to look at, along with Currie's Guiding, 414 Connaught Drive

town's summer or winter guide available from the tourist office. Every second year (odd years) the town hosts the **Jasper Heritage Folk Festival** (Ⓣ780/852-3615, Ⓦwww.jasperfolkfestival.com), with performers from across North America playing in Centennial Park. The town's biggest **cinema** is the Chaba Movie Theatre, 604 Connaught Dr (Ⓣ780/852-4749).

Cafés and restaurants

Andy's Bistro 606 Patricia St Ⓣ780/852-4559. Staid but popular and unpretentiously upscale place serving good Swiss food and some interesting gamey options (main courses cost $16–34). Arrive early for a seat on Wed or Fri (Nov–April), when a three-course set meal is offered for $28. At other times, finding space is usually easy, thanks to the big *Stammtisch*, a sociable communal table seating up to ten where people come and go independently. Open daily from 5pm.

Bear's Paw Bakery 4 Cedar Ave Ⓣ780/852-3233. Slightly tucked away, but always busy with locals. Freshly baked buns, cakes and pastries with coffee, plus big sandwiches, other snacks and great trail food such as date squares and carrot cake. Has just a couple of tables and most people here take away. Daily 6am–8pm.

Coco's Café 608 Patricia St Ⓣ780/852-4550. Tiny, earthy and fun café with a glut of fabulous home-made items including tasty egg (free range) breakfasts, wraps, sandwiches, cakes and smoothies. Most items are available to take away and great for picnic lunches. Daily 7am–7pm or later.

Earl's 600 Patricia St Ⓣ780/852-2393. Branch of Canada-wide chain with cheerful staff and a

(☎780/852-5650, ⓦwww.curriesguiding.com). A full day's (8hr) fishing will cost around $300, $190 if there are two of you; a half-day costs $249/$149.

Golf on a highly rated eighteen-hole course is available at the *Jasper Park Lodge* (greens fees $169, cheaper twilight and off-season fees available; ☎780/852-6090). **Horse-riding** enthusiasts should contact Pyramid Stables, 4km from Jasper on Pyramid Lake Rd (☎780/852-3562), who run day-treks and one-, two- and three-hour trips (from $25/45/70; full-day rides from $130) around Patrician and Pyramid lakes. Ridgeline Riders at Maligne Tours and Skyline Trail Rides (☎780/852-4215 or 1-888/852-7787, ⓦwww.skylinetrail.com) at *Jasper Park Lodge* also organize rides.

Winter sports

The park has plenty of winter activities and a first-rate ski area in **Marmot Basin** (early Dec to late April; ☎780/852-3816, ⓦwww.skimarmot.com), a twenty-minute drive from the townsite, and a resort that has the advantages of cheaper skiing and far less crowded runs than its Banff rivals. Scenically it's every bit as spectacular, and the quality of the snow is superb; it's best for intermediate skiers and riders.

A total of eight lifts serve 1500 acres of terrain with a vertical drop of 700m and a choice of 75 trails. Lift passes cost $58.50 per day ($42.46 in January) and equipment rental is available at the resort. Daily shuttle buses head here from downtown hotels; for local taxis call Jasper Taxi ☎780/852-3600 or Heritage Cabs ☎780/852-5558.

Where Jasper rates as highly, if not more so, than Banff National Park is in the range and quality of its **cross-country skiing**, for its summer backcountry trails lend themselves superbly to winter grooming. Pick up the *Cross-Country Skiing* leaflet from the park information centre. To buy or rent cross-country skis try Totem Ski Shop, 408 Connaught Drive (☎780/852-3078, ⓦwww.totemskishop.com), and for a guiding service contact Beyond the Beaten Path (☎780/852-5650). You can **ice-skate** on parts of Pyramid Lake and Lac Beauvert that are cleared for the purpose. Source for Sports, 406 Patricia St (☎780/852-3654, ⓦwww.jaspersports.com), and most other rental shops and hotels offer skate rentals.

dependable, mid-priced and generally North American menu (main courses from $10), though the burgers, a huge rib platter and perfectly broiled salmon steaks are offset by the presence of some eclectic options like sushi and Thai stir-fry. There's also a cocktail bar here. Open daily 11am–11pm.

Fiddle River 620 Connaught Drive ☎780/852-3032. Stylish restaurant with dried flower and oil lamp decor, mountain panoramas and excellent fresh seafood at prices that reflect its distance from the sea; expect to pay $35–40 per person for three courses (or a set $25 during the ski season). Main courses range from basic beer-battered cod fish and chips to more exotic seafood jambalaya and green curry grilled swordfish. Open from 5pm daily.

Jasper Park Lodge Lac Beauvert ☎780/852-3301, ⓦwww.jasperparklodge.com. The area's most prestigious lodging address has several restaurants to chose from, all under one roof. Choices include fresh sushi at the small basic *Oka Sushi*, a large bar menu at the *Tent City Sports Lounge* and the 500-seater *Beauvert Dining Room*, an everyday choice, particularly recommended for its buffet breakfast and Sun brunch (from $20). A notch above these, the *Moose's Nook* serves local mountain fare, which generally includes excellent whiskey-soaked salmon and, occasionally, musk ox (main courses cost around $27). But the lodge's best restaurant – and the only one really worth the trek out here if you are based in town – is the *Edith Cavell Room*, a fine dining establishment with white glove service, where you can expect to part with around $80 for five courses from an expertly crafted menu that's basically French with some Canadian accents. Daily 6–10pm.

Jasper Pizza Place 402 Connaught Drive ☎780/852-3225. Despite the open kitchen and everyday bar furnishings that make for a chain-restaurant ambience, the wood-fired pizzas (from $10.50) here are little short of unique. The choice of zany toppings include Dijon mustard, escargot, smoked oysters and palm hearts. The small salads like the spinach, mushroom and citrus and honey ($5.25) combination are less exciting but still good. Other options include a gargantuan lasagne ($11), burgers and pita-pizzas that are ideal for a quick snack. Pool tables in the basement invite you to hang out after your meal. Daily 11am–11pm. Closed Nov.

Papa George's 406 Connaught Drive ☎780/852-3351. Though it looks plain and dowdy this locals' favourite is one of the town's oldest restaurants (opened in 1924); it has excellent very varied food and gargantuan portions. Dinner mains cost from $15 ($12 in winter) but a quick lunch comes in at around $6–10, dinner up to about $35. Breakfasts are also good and inexpensive. Daily 7am–2.30pm & 5–9.30pm (later in summer).

Soft Rock Internet Café 622 Connaught Drive ☎780/852-5850. Good breakfast choice with encyclopedic selection of coffee and mouth-watering waffles heaped with fresh fruit and cream and satisfying all-day breakfasts. The best place in town to both browse the web and pick up fantastic, massive cinnamon buns. Daily 7.30am–10pm (7am–4pm in winter).

Villa Caruso 640 Connaught Drive ☎780/852-3920. Upmarket steakhouse with subdued lighting, wood accents and orange hues the backdrop for meat feasts, largely focused on flame-grilling Alberta's best cuts, though seafood, pasta and pizzas (main courses cost $18–37, $10–13 at lunch) are also available. Execution of dishes is unexciting but the pleasant ambience compensates; the adjoining fireside lounge is particularly tempting for a drink before or after your meal.

Bars

Atha-B At *Athabasca Hotel*, 510 Patricia St. Uninspired, but large and occasionally rowdy, this is Jasper's most reliably busy venue, with nightly dancing – mostly to mainstream chart hits – and regular live music. Small cover.

Bonhomme Lounge At *Château Jasper*, 96 Geikie St. With a harpist most nights, ideal if you want a smoochy evening.

De'd Dog Bar and Grill 404 Connaught Drive. Regularly unruly sports bar that's almost inevitably full of extrovert, 30-something locals. Other diversions here include pool, darts, big-screen sports and a bar menu with great burgers. The generous happy hour runs 5–7pm.

Downstream Grill 620 Connaught Drive. Funky, spacious, airy and nonsmoking bar with several laid-back sofas, below the *Fiddle River* restaurant (see p.755). Good bar food at reasonable prices.

Pete's Bar 614 Patricia St. Big bustling young bar with big screens – frequently for snowboarding videos – pool, darts and, on weekend nights, live music, varying from blues to Irish; locals jam here on Tuesdays.

Villa Caruso 640 Connaught Drive. Elegantly laid-back fireside martini and cocktail bar (adjoining a restaurant) with piped jazz and blues; as relaxing and stylish a place as you'll find to sip a drink in town.

Listings

Bookshop Jasper Camera and Gift, 412 Connaught Drive ☎780/852-3165, has a small selection.

Hospital Seton General, 518 Robson St ☎780/852-3344.

Internet access Soft Rock Internet Café, 633 Connaught Drive (☎780/852-5850).

Laundry Coin Clean, 607 Patricia St ☎780/852-3852.

Library Elm Ave (Mon–Thurs 2–5pm & 7–9pm, Fri 2–5pm, Sat 10am–3pm). Has a huge number of books on the park.

Pharmacy Cavell Drugs, 602 Patricia St ☎780-852-4441.

Police ☎780/852-4848.

Post office 502 Patricia St ☎780/852-3041.

Mount Robson Provincial Park

The extensive **MOUNT ROBSON PROVINCIAL PARK** borders Jasper National Park to the west and protects Mount Robson, at 3954m the highest peak in the Canadian Rockies. Its scenery equals anything anywhere else in the Rockies, and Mount Robson itself is one of the most staggering mountains you'll ever encounter. Facilities are thin on the ground, so stock up on food and fuel before entering the park. Around 16km beyond the park's western boundary Hwy 16 comes the Tête Jaune Cache, where you can pick up one of two immensely scenic

Yellowhead Pass marks the boundary between the Jasper park, which is in Alberta (on **Mountain time**), and the Mount Robson park, which is in British Columbia (on **Pacific time**, one hour behind).

roads: the continuation of Hwy 16 north to Prince George (for routes to Prince Rupert, northern BC and the Yukon), or Hwy 5, which heads south past Wells Gray Provincial Park to Kamloops and a whole range of onward destinations; the latter route is covered on p.950.

Both road and rail links to the park from Jasper climb through **Yellowhead Pass** (1131m), 20km west of Jasper Townsite, long one of the most important

Hiking in Mount Robson Provencial Park

Starting 2km north of the park visitor centre, the **Berg Lake Trail** (22km one-way; 795m ascent) is perhaps the most popular short backpacking trip in the Rockies, and the only trail that gets anywhere near Mount Robson. You can do the first third or so as a comfortable and highly rewarding day-walk, passing through forest to lovely glacier-fed Kinney Lake (6.7km; campsite at the lake's northeast corner). Many rank this among the Rockies best day-hikes and it's particularly good for naturalists. Trek the whole thing, however, and you traverse the stupendous Valley of a Thousand Waterfalls – the most notable being sixty-metre Emperor Falls (14.3km; campsites 500m north and 2km south) – and eventually enjoy the phenomenal area around Berg Lake itself (17.4km to its nearest, western shore). Mount Robson rises an almost sheer 2400m from the lakeshore, its huge cliffs cradling two creaking rivers of ice, Mist Glacier and Berg Glacier – the latter, one of the Rockies' few "living" or advancing glaciers, is 1800m long by 800m wide and the source of the great icebergs that give the lake its name.

Beyond the lake you can pursue the trail 2km further to Robson Pass (21.9km; 1652m ascent; campsite) and another 1km to Adolphus Lake in Jasper National Park. The most popular campsites are the *Berg Lake* (19.6km) and *Rearguard* (20.1km) campsites on Berg Lake itself; but if you've got a Jasper backcountry permit you could press on to Adolphus where there's a less-frequented site with more in the way of solitude.

Once you're camped at Berg Lake, a popular day-trip is to Toboggan Falls, which starts from the southerly *Berg Lake* campsite and climbs the northeast (left) side of Toboggan Creek past a series of cascades and meadows to eventual views over the lake's entire hinterland. The trail peters out after 2km, but you can easily walk on and upward through open meadows for still better views.

The second trail in the immediate vicinity is Robson Glacier (2km), a level walk that peels off south from the main trail 1km west of Robson Pass near the park ranger's cabin. It runs across an outwash plain to culminate in a small lake at the foot of the glacier; a rougher track then follows the lateral moraine on the glacier's east side, branching east after 3km to follow a small stream to the summit of Snowbird Pass (9km total from the ranger's cabin).

Two more hikes start from Yellowhead Lake, at the other (eastern) end of the park. To get to the trailhead for **Yellowhead Mountain** (4.5km one-way; 715m ascent), an excellent day-hike, follow Hwy 16 for 9km down from the pass and then take a gravel road 1km on an isthmus across the lake. After a steep two-hour climb through forest, the trail levels out in open country at 1830m, offering sweeping views of the Yellowhead Pass area.

The **Mount Fitzwilliam Trail** (13km one-way; 945m ascent), which leaves Hwy 16 about 1km east of the Yellowhead Mountain Trail (but on the other side of the highway), is a more demanding walk, especially over its last half, but if you don't want to backpack to the endpoint – a truly spectacular basin of lakes and peaks – you could easily walk through the forest to the campsite at Rockingham Creek (6km).

native and fur-trading routes across the Rockies. This stretch of road is less dramatic than the Icefields Parkway, but then most roads are, given over to mixed woodland – birch interspersed with firs – and mountains that sit back from the road with less scenic effect. The railway meanders alongside the road most of the way, occasionally occupied by epic freight trains hundreds of wagons long – alien intrusions in the usual beguiling wilderness of rocks, river and forest. Just down from the pass, **Yellowhead Lake** is the park's first landmark. Look for moose around dawn and dusk at aptly named **Moose Lake**, another 20km farther west.

Even if the first taste of the park seems relatively tame, the first sight of **Mount Robson** itself is among the most breathtaking in the Rockies. The preceding ridges creep up in height hiding the massive peak itself from view until the last moment. The British explorer W.B. Cheadle described the mountain in 1863: "On every side the mighty heads of snowy hills crowded round, whilst, immediately behind us, a giant among giants, and immeasurably supreme, rose Robson's peak... We saw its upper portion dimmed by a necklace of light, feathery clouds, beyond which its pointed apex of ice, glittering in the morning sun, shot up far into the blue heaven above."

The overall impression is of immense size, thanks mainly to the colossal scale of Robson's south face – a sheer rise of 3100m – and to the view from the road, which frames the mountain as a single mass isolated from other peaks. A spectacular glacier system, concealed on the mountain's north side, is visible if you make the popular backpacking hike to the Berg Lake area (see box, p.757).

The source of the mountain's name has never been agreed on, but could be a corruption of Robertson, a Hudson's Bay employee who was trapped in the region in the 1820s. Local natives called the peak Yuh-hai-has-hun (the "Mountain of the Spiral Road"), an allusion to the clearly visible layers of rock that resemble a road winding to the summit. Not surprisingly, this monolith was one of the last major peaks in the Rockies to be conquered: it was first climbed in 1913, and is still considered a dangerous challenge.

Practicalities

Trains don't stop anywhere in the park, but if you're travelling by bus you can ask to be let off at Yellowhead Pass or the **Mount Robson Information Centre** (June to early Sept daily 9am–7pm; ⓣ250/566-4325 or 1-800/689-9025), located at the Mount Robson viewpoint near the western entrance to the park.

Most of the park's few other facilities are found near the infocentre: a **café/garage** (May–Sept) and a fully serviced commercial **campsite** – *Robson*

Provincial campsites in BC

Tent and RV sites at many public **campsites** in British Columbia's provincial parks can now be reserved in advance through Discover Camping (March to mid-Sept Mon–Fri 7am–7pm, Sat & Sun 9am–5pm Pacific time; ⓣ1-800/689-9025 or ⓣ604/689-9025). Reservations can be made up to three months in advance but no later than 48 hours before the first day of arrival. Cancellations can be made after 7pm by following the recorded instructions. A nonrefundable booking fee of $6.36 per night, up to a maximum of three nights ($19.08), is charged. Reservations can also be made at ⓦwww.discovercamping.ca. You can stay in any single BC provincial park for up to fourteen days; advance payment by Visa or MasterCard only, and additional nights once at a campsite are cash only. General information on the parks is on ⓣ250/387-4550 or 1-800/663-7867, ⓦwww.elp.gov.bc.ca/bcparks.

Shadows Campground (☎250/566-9190 or 1-888/566-4821; $15; mid-May to early Oct), 30 nice sites on the Fraser River side of Hwy 16, 5km west of the park boundary. The 144-site *Mount Robson Provincial Park Campground* (☎250/566-4325; $17; mid-May to early Oct) comprises two closely adjacent campsites – *Robson River* and *Robson Meadows* – and is situated further afield on Hwy 16, 22km north of Valemount. It offers hot showers and flush toilets; reservations can be made in advance (see box opposite). Another park campsite with the same name and the tag "Lucerne" (which has no reservations, dry toilets only and no showers; $14; May–Sept) is situated 10km west of the Alberta border on Hwy 16, just west of the eastern boundary of the Mount Robson Provincial Park.

The only other beds in or near the park are *Mountain River Lodge* (☎250/566-9899 or 1-888/566-9899, Ⓦwww.mtrobson.com; ❹), a B&B with five different rooms; the eighteen log-sided riverfront units (some with kitchens for $5 extra) at the *Mount Robson Lodge* (☎250/566-4821 or 1-888/566-4821, Ⓦwww.mountrobsonlodge.com; ❺; May–Oct), which also organizes meals, river rafting, helicopter tours and horse riding. **Backcountry camping** in the park is only permitted at seven wilderness campsites dotted along the Berg Lake Trail (see box p.757); to use these you have to register and pay an overnight fee at the infocentre.

Yoho National Park

Wholly in British Columbia on the western side of the Continental Divide from Lake Louise, **YOHO NATIONAL PARK**'s name derives from a Cree word meaning "wonder" – a fitting testament to the awesome grandeur of the region's mountains, lakes and waterfalls. At the same time it's a small park, whose intimate scale makes it perhaps the finest of the four parks and the one favoured by Rockies' connoisseurs. The Trans-Canada Hwy divides Yoho neatly in half, climbing from Lake Louise over the **Kicking Horse Pass** to share the broad, glaciated valley bottom of the Kicking Horse River with the old Canadian Pacific Railway. The only village, **Field**, has the park centre, services and limited accommodation (the nearest full-service towns are Lake Louise, 28km east, and **Golden**, 54km west). Other expensive accommodation is available at the central hubs, **Lake O'Hara**, the **Yoho Valley** and **Emerald Lake**, from which radiate most of the park's stunning and well-maintained trails – **hiking** in Yoho is magnificent – and a couple of lodges just off the Trans-Canada. Thus these areas – not Field – are the focal points of the park, and get very busy in summer. Side roads lead to Emerald Lake and the Yoho Valley, so if you choose you can drive in, do a hike and then move on at night.

Access to Lake O'Hara is far more difficult, being reserved for those on foot, or those with lodge or campsite reservations, who must book for a special bus (full details are on p.765). The other five park-run campsites are all much more readily accessible, and there's a single road-accessible hostel in the Yoho Valley. The park also operates six backcountry campsites (see p.763). The Trans-Canada also gives direct access to short but scenic trails; as these take only an hour or so, they're the best choice if you only want a quick taste of the park before moving on.

Although in BC, Yoho runs on **Mountain time.**

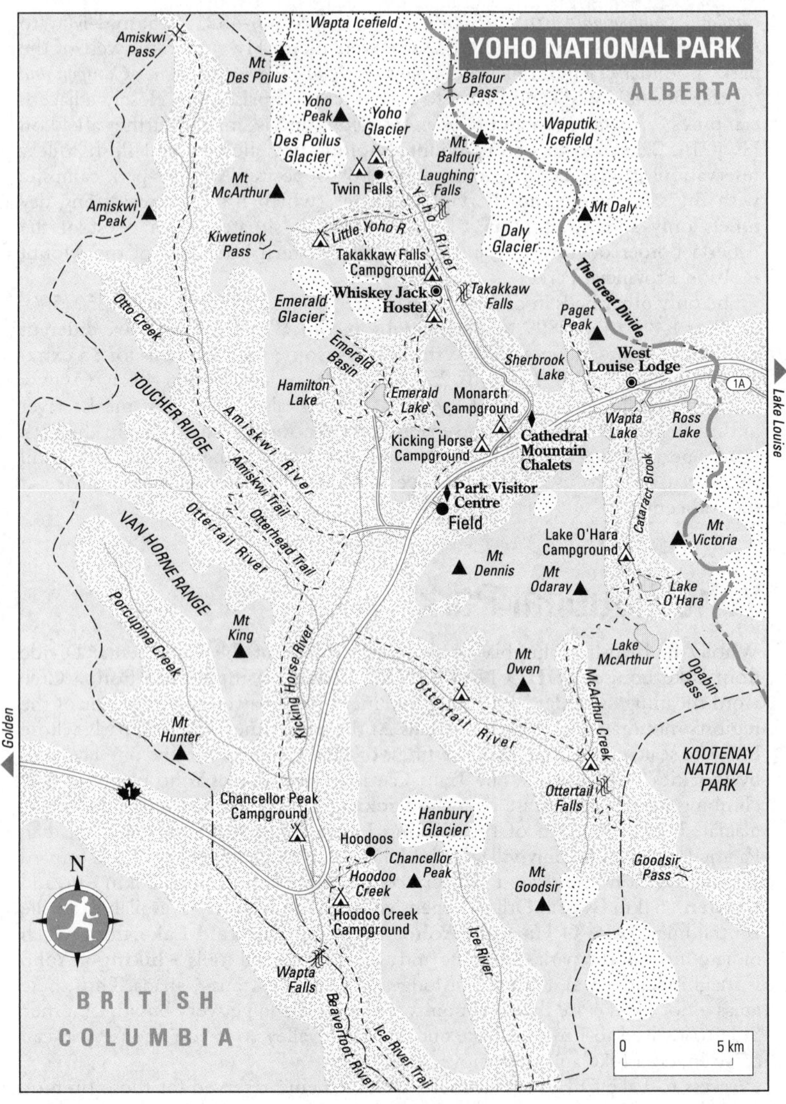

If you have time for just a single day walk, make it the **Iceline–Whaleback–Twin Falls Trail**, rated among the top five day-hikes in the Rockies (see p.766). If you're cycling, note that **mountain biking** – very popular in the park – is restricted to several designated trails only: these are Kicking Horse (19.5km); the Amiskwi Trail to the Amiskwi River crossing (24km); the Otterhead Trail to Toche Ridge junction (8km); Ice River to Lower Ice Ridge warden cabin (17.5km); the Talley-Ho Trail (3km); and the Ottertail Trail as far as the warden cabin (14.7km).

Field

No more than a few wooden houses backed by an amphitheatre of sheer-dropped mountains, **FIELD** looks like an old-world pioneer settlement, little changed from its 1884 origins as a railroad-construction camp (named after Cyrus Field, sponsor of the first transatlantic communication cable, who visited Yoho that year). As in other national parks, it was the railway that first spawned tourism in the area: the first hotel in Field was built by Canadian Pacific in 1886, and within a few months sixteen square kilometres at the foot of Mount Stephen (the peak to Field's east) had been set aside as a special reserve. National park status arrived in 1911, making Yoho the second of Canada's national parks.

Passenger services (other than private excursions) no longer come through Field, but the **railway** is still one of the park "sights", and among the first things you see whether you enter the park from east or west. That it came this way at all was the result of desperate political and economic horse trading. The Canadian Pacific's chief surveyor, Sandford Fleming, wrote of his journey over the proposed Kicking Horse Pass route in 1883: "I do not think I can forget that terrible walk; it was the greatest trial I ever experienced." Like many in the company he was convinced the railway should take the much lower and more amenable Yellowhead route to the north.

The railway was as much a political as a transportational tool, and designed to unite the country and encourage settlement of the prairies. A northerly route would have ignored great tracts of valuable prairie near the US border (around Calgary), and allowed much of the area and its resources (later found to include oil and gas) to slip from the Dominion into the hands of the US. Against all engineering advice, therefore, the railway was cajoled into taking the Kicking Horse route, and thus obliged to negotiate four-percent grades, the greatest of any commercial railway of the time.

The result was the infamous **Spiral Tunnels**, two vast figure-of-eight galleries within the mountains; from a popular viewpoint about 7km east of Field on Hwy 1, you can watch the front of goods trains emerge from the tunnels before the rear wagons have even entered. Still more notorious was the **Big Hill**, where the line drops 330m in just 6km from Wapta Lake to the flats east of Field (the 4.5 percent grade was the steepest in North America). The very first construction train to attempt the descent plunged into the canyon, killing three railway workers. Runaways became so common that four blasts on a whistle became the standard warning for trains careering out of control (the rusted wreck of an engine can still be seen near the main *Kicking Horse Park Campground*). Lady Agnes MacDonald, wife of the Canadian prime minister, rode down the Big Hill on the front cowcatcher (a metal frame in front of the locomotive to scoop off animals) in 1886, remarking that it presented a "delightful opportunity for a new sensation". She'd already travelled around 1000km on her unusual perch; her lily-livered husband, with whom she was meant to be sharing the symbolic trans-Canada journey to commemorate the opening of the railway, managed just 40km on the cowcatcher. Trains climbing the hill required four locomotives to pull a mere fifteen coaches; the ascent took over an hour, and exploding boilers (and resulting deaths) were recurrent.

The Burgess Shales

Yoho today ranks as highly among geologists as it does among hikers and railway buffs, thanks to the world-renowned **Burgess Shales**, a unique geological formation situated close to Field village. The shales – layers of sedimentary rock – lie on the upper slopes of Mount Field and consist of the fossils of some

120 types of soft-bodied marine creatures from the Middle Cambrian period (515–530 million years ago), one of only three places in the world where the remains of these unusual creatures are found. Soft-bodied creatures usually proved ill-suited to the fossilization process, but in the Burgess Shales the fossils are so well preserved and detailed that in some cases scientists can identify what the creatures were eating before they died.

Plans are in hand to open a major new museum in Field devoted to the shales, but in the meantime access is restricted to protect the fossils, and fossil-hunting, needless to say, is strictly prohibited. The area can only be seen on two **guided hikes** to Walcott's Quarry (760m ascent; 20km round-trip; departs 8am Fri–Mon; $65) and the trilobite beds on Mount Stephen (780m ascent; 6km round-trip; departs 10am Sat & Sun; $45). The walks – note the considerable ascents involved – are led by qualified guides, limited to fifteen people and run between late June and October. For details and reservations, contact the Yoho Burgess Shale Foundation (ⓣ1-800/343-3006, ⓦwww.burgess-shale.bc.ca). Phone reservations can be made only Mon–Fri 10am–3.30pm.

Practicalities

Yoho's **park information centre**, marked by a distinctive blue roof about 1km east of Field (daily: May to late June 9am–5pm; late June to Aug 9am–7pm; first two weeks of Sept 9am–5pm; mid-Sept to April 9am–4pm ⓣ250/343-6783, ⓦwww.pc.gc.ca), sells park permits ($8.90 daily), makes backcountry registrations (nightly fee $8.90, reservations $11.85), takes bookings for Lake O'Hara (see p.765), has displays, lectures and slide shows (notably on the famous Burgess Shales), and advises on trail and climbing conditions. It also gives out a useful *Backcountry Guide* with full details of all trails and sells 1:50,000 **maps** of the park. Backcountry camping requires a permit, and if you intend to camp at Lake O'Hara it's essential to make **reservations** at the information centre.

Enquire at the park centre for details of activities arranged by the "Friends of Yoho" (ⓣ250/343-6393, ⓦwww.friendsofyoho.ca; information also available on Parks Canada website) and the two free guided walks: "Emerald Lakeshore Stroll" (July to late Aug Sat 10am; 2hr 30min; 5km; meet at Emerald Lake Trailhead) and "Walk into the Past" (July & Aug Mon & Thurs 7pm; 1hr 30min; meet at the Old Bake oven at *Kicking Horse Campground*). Other park-run activities include Kicking Horse Campground talks and presentations some summer evenings and other talks at the *Hoodoo Creek Campfire* Circle.

Whatever other literature may say, there are now no VIA Rail passenger **trains** to Field. The village is, however, a flag stop for Greyhound **buses** (5 daily in each direction) – wave them down from the Petro-Canada just east of the turn-off from the hwy to the village, though most stop anyway to drop packages.

Accommodation

Yoho's popularity and accessibility mean there is huge pressure on **accommodation** in late July and August: if you're really stuck, you can always make for one of the motels in Golden (see p.770). The only officially listed **rooms** in Field itself, a fine base if you have transport, are at the excellent *Kicking Horse Lodge*, 100 Centre St (ⓣ250/343-6303 or 1-800/659-4944, ⓦwww.kickinghorselodge.net; ⑥). Just across from the lodge you can **eat** well at the *Truffle Pigs Café*, 318 Stephen Ave (ⓣ250/343-6462), a relaxed and funky spot for snacks, all-day breakfasts and home-baked breads and cakes.

If you don't stay at the lodge, you can also try one of the recent spate of fully furnished suites in **private homes** – of which there were a dozen or so dotted around the village at last count. Bar one or two exceptions, these are all similarly priced – from $85 or $125 for a double – and of a similar arrangement: a private entrance, usually only one or two rooms; non-smoking; some cooking provisions; and all within a few minutes' walk of each other in Field's small grid of streets.

They are: *Alpine Guesthouse* (no address – call for directions; ⓣ250/343-6878 or 1-866/634-5665, ⓦwww.alpineguesthouse.ca; ⑤–⑦); *Alpenglow Guesthouse* 306 Kickinghorse Ave (ⓣ250/343-6356 or 1-800/992-6356, ⓔalpenglow@redshift.bc.ca; ④); *Bear's Den Guesthouse*, 414 1st St W (ⓣ250/343-6439, ⓦwww.bearsdenguesthouse.ca, ⓔzirke@rockies.net ④–⑥; *Canadian Rockies Inn and The Village Shop*, 308 Stephen Ave (ⓣ250/343-6046, ⓔcdnrockies@telus.net; ⑤); *Coyote's Den Guesthouse*, 213 2nd Ave (ⓣ250/343-6034, ⓔcoyotesden@redshift.bc.ca; ④); *Lynx Lair*, 412 1st Ave (ⓣ250/343-6421; ⑤); *Mount Burgess Guesthouse*, 314 Kickinghorse Ave (ⓣ250/343-6480, ⓦwww.mtburgessguesthouse.ca; ④); *Mount Stephen Guesthouse*, 343 Kickinghorse Ave (ⓣ250/343-6441, ⓦwww.mountstephen.com; ④); *Old Church Guesthouse*, 308 Kickinghorse Ave (ⓣ250/343-6345, ⓦwww.oldchurchguesthouse.ca; ⑥); *Spiral Tunnels Guesthouse*, 306 1st Ave (ⓣ250/343-6067 or 1-877/FIELD-BC, ⓔspirals@rockies.net; ⑤); *Sunset Guesthouse*, 416 1st Ave (ⓣ250/343-6333, ⓔsunsetgh@uniserve.com; ④); *Wildflower Guesthouse*, 303 Kickinghorse Ave (ⓣ250/343-6707, ⓦwww.wildflowerguesthouse.com; ④); and *Yoho Accommodation*, 310A 1st Ave (ⓣ250/343-6444 or 343-6445; ④). All are easily found in the tiny village, most lying on the central 1st Avenue or parallel Kickinghorse Avenue.

Away from the village, but on or just off the Trans-Canada (Hwy 1), are the 21 units of *Cathedral Mountain Lodge* (ⓣ250/343-6442 or 1-866/619-6442, ⓦwww.cathedralmountain.com; ⑧; June to mid-Oct), 4km east of Field and fifteen minutes' drive from Lake Louise (leave the hwy at the Takakkaw Falls turn-off), and the bigger and less expensive fifty-room *West Louise Lodge* (ⓣ250/343-6311, 1-888/682-2212 or 1-800/258-7669, ⓔwestlouiselodge@skilouise.com; ⑤) just inside the park boundary, 11km west of Lake Louise (with café, restaurant and indoor pool). There's also the **hostel** in the Yoho Valley (see p.769), perfectly situated for many superb walks, and an expensive lodge at Emerald Lake.

The most central of the five park-run **campsites**, the 92-site *Kicking Horse* ($23.75; late June to Sept), lies 3km east of Field just off the Trans-Canada (Hwy 1) near the junction with Yoho Valley Road for Takakkaw Falls. It's fully serviced (coin showers) and pleasingly forested, though it echoes somewhat with goods trains rumbling through day and night. In summer a separate overflow site is often opened (no showers), but even this fills up and you should aim to arrive extremely early. Remember: all park campsites are first-come, first-served.

A short distance east up Yoho Valley Road is the second of the park's major campsites, the 46-site *Monarch* ($15.85; mid-May to early Sept); the third, the 35-site *Takakkaw Falls* ($15.85; late June to first snow), lies at the end of the same road (17km from Field and 300m from the falls' day-use car park) by the eponymous falls (great views from many pitches) and is the best-placed for local hikes (see box p.766). The remaining site is close to the park's western border, lying just north of the Trans-Canada: the 106-site *Hoodoo Creek* (no showers; $18.80; late June to early Sept. An additional fee of $7.90 is charged at all campsites for use of firewood.

The six **backcountry campsites** ($8.90 each nightly) are *McArthur Creek* (ten sites); *Float Creek* (four sites); *Yoho Lake* (eight sites); *Laughing Falls* (eight sites); *Twin Falls* (eight sites); and *Little Yoho* (ten sites). The only facilities are

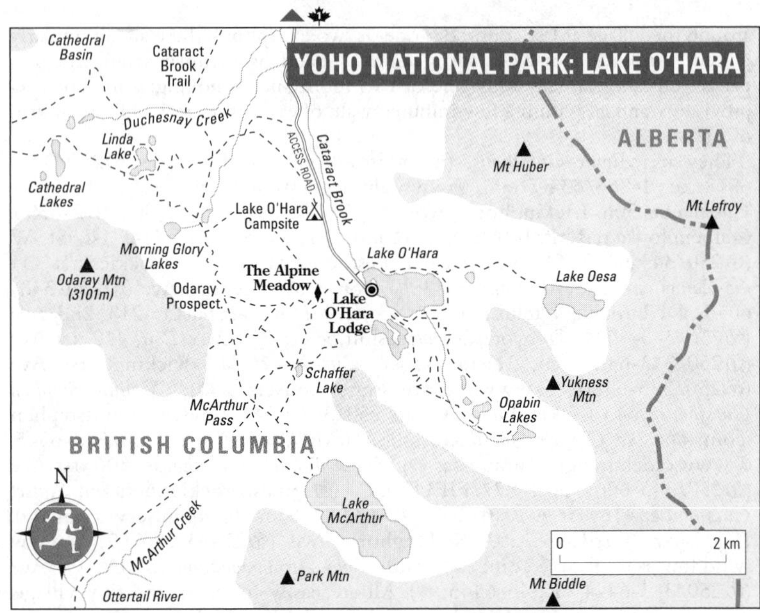

privies (except *Float Creek*) and bear poles. All of these campsites are popular, but unlike the front country campsites (where it's first-come, first-served) between one and three sites at each campsite can be reserved ($11.85 fee) up to 21 days in advance through the park centre at Field. **Random camping** is allowed in the Amiskwi, Otterhead, Lower Ice River and Porcupine valleys, but check current closures: you must be at least 3km from any road, 100m from water, 50m from a trail and purchase the usual $8 backcountry pass.

Lake O'Hara

Backed up against the Continental Divide at the eastern edge of the park, **Lake O'Hara** is one of the Rockies' finest all-round enclaves – with staggering scenery, numerous lakes, and an immense diversity of alpine and subalpine terrain. It's a great base for concentrated hiking: you could easily spend a fortnight exploring the well-constructed trails that strike out from the central lodge and campsite. The setting is matchless, the lake framed by two of the peaks that also overlook Lake Louise across the ridge – mounts Lefroy (3423m) and Victoria (3464m). The one problem is **access**, which is severely restricted to safeguard the mountain flora and fauna.

To get there, turn off the Trans-Canada onto Hwy 1A (3.2km west of the Continental Divide), cross the railway and turn right onto the gravel road leading to the parking area (1km). This fire road continues all the way up to the lake (13km), but it's not open to general traffic (or bikes: **no bikes** are allowed on the road or anywhere else in the Lake O'Hara region). Getting up here, therefore, is quite a performance, but worth it if you want to hike some of the continent's most stunning scenery.

Anybody can walk the 13km up the road ($9.90 user fee), or the more picturesque **Cataract Brook Trail** (12.9km), which runs roughly parallel to the road, but a quota system applies for the bus up here (42 people daily plus campers in the 30-site campground at the end; and, after 13km, of course, you'd need to be very fit to get in any meaningful walking in the area where it matters.

Aim instead for the special **bus** from the car park up to the lake, but note that priority is given to those with reservations or those with reservations for the lodge, campsite or Alpine Club huts. **Reservations** for bus and campsite can be made three months in advance by phone only (mid-March to mid-April Mon–Thurs 8am–noon & 1–4pm; mid-April to mid-May Mon–Fri 8am–noon & 1–4pm; mid-May to Sept daily 8am–noon & 1–4pm; Oct reduced hours; ⓣ250/343-6433).

△ Lake O'Hara

Hikes in Yoho National Park

Hikes from Lake OíHara

For walking purposes the **Lake O'Hara region** divides into five basic zones, each of which deserves a full day of exploration: Lake Oesa, the Opabin Plateau (this area and others are often closed to protect their grizzlies), Lake McArthur, the Odaray Plateau and the Duchesnay Basin.

If you have time to do only one day-hike, the classic (if not the most walked) trails are the **Wiwaxy Gap** (12km; 495m ascent), rated by some among the top five day-walks in the Canadian Rockies, or the **Opabin Plateau Trail** (3.2km one-way; 250m ascent), from the *Lake O'Hara Lodge* to Opabin Lake. Despite the latter's brevity, you could spend hours wandering the plateau's tiny lakes and alpine meadows on the secondary trails that crisscross the area. Most people return to O'Hara via the **East Circuit Trail**, but a still more exhilarating hike – and a good day's outing – is to walk the **Yukness Ledge**, a section of the Alpine Circuit (see below) that cuts up from the East Circuit just 400m after leaving Opabin Lake. This spectacular high-level route leads to the beautiful Lake Oesa, from where it's just 3.2km down to Lake O'Hara. Oesa is one of many beautiful lakes in the region, and the **Lake Oesa Trail** (3.2km one-way; 240m ascent) from Lake O'Hara is the single most walked path in the O'Hara area. Close behind comes the **Lake McArthur Trail** (3.5km one-way; 310m ascent) that leads to the largest and most photographed of the lakes in the Lake O'Hara area. The **Odaray Plateau Trail** (2.6km one-way; 280m ascent) is another highly rated, but rather overpopular hike.

The longest and least-walked path is the **Linda Lake–Cathedral Basin** trip, past several lakes to a great viewpoint at Cathedral Platform Prospect (7.4km one-way; 305m ascent). The most challenging hike is the high-level **Alpine Circuit** (11.8km), taking in Oesa, Opabin and Schaffer lakes. This is straightforward in fine weather, and when all the snow has melted; very fit and experienced walkers should have little trouble, though there's considerable exposure, and some scrambling is required. At other times it's best left to climbers, or left alone completely.

Yoho Valley and Emerald Lake hikes

Most trails in the **Yoho Valley area** start from the *Takakkaw Falls campsite* and car park at the end of the Yoho Valley Rd. Many of the area's trails connect, and some run over the ridge to the Emerald Lake region, offering numerous permutations. We've tried to highlight the very best. If you want a stroll from the main trailhead at the campsite after a drive or cycle, then walk to **Point Lace Falls** (1.9km one-way; minimum ascent) or **Laughing Falls** (3.8km one-way; 60m gain). Another shortish, extremely popular walk from the same car park is the **Yoho Pass** (10.9km; 310m ascent, 510m height loss), which links to Emerald Lake and its eponymous lodge (though you'll need transport arranged at the lake). A southern branch from this hike will take you over the Burgess Pass and down into Field, another manageable day-trip with fine overviews of the entire area.

If you want to follow the most tramped path in the Yoho Valley, however, take the **Twin Falls Trail** (8.5km one-way; 290m ascent) from the Takakkaw Falls car park. This easy six-hour return journey passes the Laughing Falls and has the reward of the Twin Falls cataract at the end, plus fine scenery and other lesser waterfalls en route. Stronger walkers could continue over the highly recommended **Whaleback Trail** (4.5km one-way; 1hr 30min) to give some quite incredible views of the glaciers at the valley head. A complete circuit returning to Takakkaw Falls with the Whaleback is 20.1km.

If you're allowing yourself just one big walk in Yoho it's going to be a hard choice between the Takakkaw Falls–Twin Falls–Whaleback Trail just described or the **Iceline–Little Yoho Valley–(Whaleback)–Twin Falls** combination. The latter is often cited as one of the top five day-walks in the Rockies, and on balance might be the one to go for, though both options duplicate parts of one another's route. The Iceline (695m vertical gain), specially built in 1987, also starts close to the Takakkaw Falls car park at the *Whiskey Jack* hostel, climbing west through a large avalanche path onto a level bench with jaw-dropping views of the Emerald Glacier above and the Daly Glacier across the valley. It contours above Lake Celeste (a trail drops to this lake, making a shorter 17km circuit in all back to the car park) and then drops to the Little Yoho Valley and back to Takakkaw Falls for a 19.8-kilometre circuit. If you're very fit (or can camp overnight to break the trip), tagging on the Whaleback before returning to Takakkaw Falls makes a sensational 27-kilometre walk with 1000m of ascent. Most people will want to do this as a backpacking option (there are four backcountry sites up here) – and they don't come much better – though the Iceline–Little Yoho walk coupled with the trek west to the **Kiwetinok Pass** (30km; 1070m) is also in many people's list of top-five day/backpacking Rocky Mountain walks. Juggling further with the permutations brings the Whaleback into this last combination to make one of the best backpacking routes in the Rockies: Iceline–Little Yoho Valley–Kiwetinok Pass–Whaleback (35.5km; 1375m ascent), a route up there with the Rockwall Trail in Kootenay, Skyline in Jasper and Berg Lake in Mount Robson Provincial Park.

From Emerald Lake, if you just want a stroll, then follow the self-guided and wheelchair-accessible **nature trail** (4.6km circuit; minimal ascent) around the lake from the parking area to the bridge at the back of the lake. Even shorter is the trail from the entrance to the parking area to **Hamilton Falls** (1.6km return; minimal ascent). The best day-trip is the comparatively underused but interesting **Hamilton Lake Trail** (5.5km one-way; 850m vertical; 2–3hr), again leaving from the parking area at the end of Emerald Lake Road. It's demanding and steep in places, and confined to forest for the first hour or so – thereafter it's magnificent, culminating in a classic alpine lake. The more modest climb to **Emerald Basin**, which you could manage in half a day (4.3km one-way; 300m vertical; 1–2hr), also gives relative peace and quiet, following the lakeshore before climbing through a forest of yew and hemlock, and ending in a small, rocky amphitheatre of hanging glaciers and avalanche paths.

Hikes from the Trans-Canada

Five short walks can be accessed off the **Trans-Canada Highway** as it passes through Yoho. From east to west these are: **Ross Lake** (1.3km), a stunning little walk given the loveliness of the lake and the ease with which you reach it (accessed 1km south of the Great Divide picnic area); **Sherbrooke Lake** (3.1km), a peaceful subalpine lake accessible from the Wapta Lake picnic area (5km west of the Great Divide), where stronger walkers can peel off after 1.4km to Paget Lookout for huge views of the Kicking Horse Valley (3.5km; 520m ascent); **Mount Stephen Fossil Beds** (2.7km), a short but very steep trail, for fossil lovers only, from 1st St East in Field; **Hoodoo Creek** (3.1km), on the western edge of the park (22km west of Field), accessed from the 600-metre gravel road from the *Hoodoo Creek* campsite (the steep path leads to the weirdly eroded hoodoos themselves, pillars of glacial debris topped by protective capping stones); and finally **Wapta Falls** (2.4km), an excellent and almost level forty-minute walk on a good trail to Yoho's largest waterfalls (by volume of water), accessed via a 1.6-kilometre dirt road 25km west of Field.

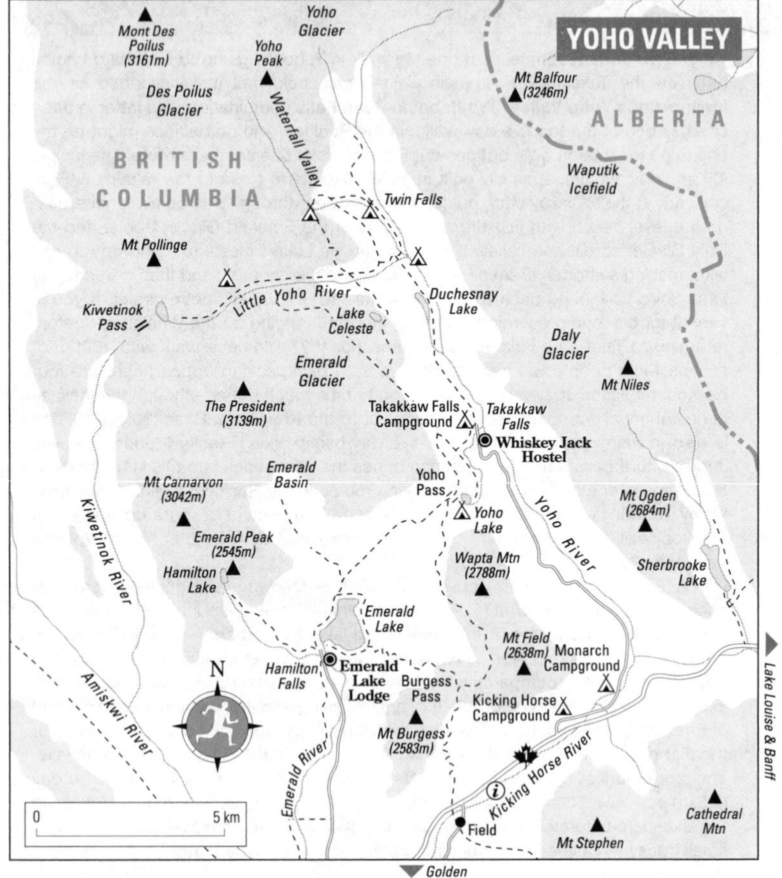

If you're going **for the day**, your only feasible buses leave at 8.30am and 10.30am (there are also 3.30pm and 5.30pm departures, with returns at 9.30am, 11.30am, 2.30pm, 4.30pm and 6.30pm from mid-June to early Oct; and outbound at 10am and 3pm and returns at 11am and 4pm for the rest of Oct), and the maximum number in a party is six. If you want to use the campsite you have to have dates ready (up to a maximum of four nights), state the number of people, the number of sites required (maximum of two per party, one tent per site) and your preferred bus time (mid-June to Sept; first and second choices from 8.30am, 10.30am, 3.30pm or 5.30pm). The reservation fee for bus (day-use or camp) is $11.85 and the return bus fare $14.85, payable by credit card over the phone.

Cancellation must be made to an answering machine (Ⓣ250/343-6344); you forfeit your booking fee, and you can't just cancel the first day of several you booked to camp and expect to come later. Cancellations made less than three days in advance mean you lose the booking fee, half the bus fare and, if you're camping, the first night's campsite fee ($8.90 per person per night). Cancel after 4pm on the day before your trip and you lose everything.

If all this sounds horribly complicated, remember the park does merit attention, but if you don't manage to plan in advance there are arrangements for **stand-bys**: six day-use places are available daily and three to five sites are kept available each night. You must reserve at the Field park information centre in person the day *before* you wish to take the bus and/or camp; these places are *not* available over the phone, and you'll have to get to the centre early.

To stay in one of the 23 rooms at *Lake O'Hara Lodge* (Ⓣ250/343-6418, Ⓦwww.lakeoharalodge.com; ❽; mid-June to late Sept & Feb to mid-April), you need to reserve weeks in advance and be prepared to part with a large amount of money. Out of season you can book on Ⓣ250/678-4110.

The Yoho Valley and Emerald Lake

Less compact an area than Lake O'Hara, the **Yoho Valley** and nearby **Emerald Lake** are far more accessible for casual visitors, and offer some great sights – the Takakkaw Falls in particular – and a variety of top-rated trails. Both areas were formerly used by the Cree to hide their women and children while the men crossed the mountains into Alberta to trade and hunt buffalo. The eradication of the buffalo herds, and the arrival of the railway in 1884, put paid to such ways. The lake was "discovered" by Tom Wilson, the same Canadian Pacific employee who first saw Lake Louise. He named it Emerald Lake after its colour. Now the lake and valley combine to form one of the Rockies' most important backpacking zones. Though popular and easily reached – access roads head north from the Trans-Canada to both the Emerald and Yoho valleys – the region is not, however, quite as crowded as its counterpart to the south. The scenery is equally mesmerizing, and if fewer of the trails are designed for day-hikes, many of them interlock so that you can tailor walks to suit your schedule or fitness (see box on, p.766).

Most trails start from the end of the Yoho Valley Road at the **Takakkaw Falls** parking area; the road leaves the Trans-Canada about 5km east of Field (signed from the *Kicking Horse* campsite), a narrow and switchbacking route unsuitable for trailers and RVs and open in the summer only. It's 14km from the Trans-Canada to the parking area. The cascades' total 254-metre drop makes them among the most spectacular road-accessible falls in the mountains: *takakkaw* is a Cree word roughly meaning "it is wonderful".

The *Whiskey Jack* HI **hostel**, ideally placed just beyond the end of the Yoho Valley Road, 500m south of Takakkaw Falls, has room for 27 in three dorms (Ⓣ250/670-7580 or 1-888/762-4122, Ⓦwww.hihostels.ca; dorms $23 for members, $27 for non-members; late June to Sept). Close by is the park-run *Takakkaw Falls* **campsite** with 35 unserviced sites ($15.85; mid-June to mid-Sept). Trails to the north (see box, p.766) lead to four further backcountry campsites.

The Emerald Lake Road leaves the Trans-Canada about 2km west of Field and ends, 8km on, at the *Emerald Lake Lodge* (Ⓣ250/343-6321 or 1-800/663-6336, Ⓦwww.crmr.com; ❽), which has a **restaurant** where walking boots are certainly not in order, and a less formal **bar** for drinks and snacks. If you want to stay, advance reservations are essential and prices are steep – $300 and over in high season, less outside summer. Like the Yoho Valley Rd, this road offers access to easy strolls and a couple of good day- or half-day hikes (see box, p.766).

Golden

GOLDEN, 54km west of Field and midway between Yoho and Glacier national parks, is the nearest town to either. Despite its name and mountain backdrop, the part of Golden most people see is little more than an ugly ribbon of motels and garages at the junction of Hwy 1 and Hwy 95. The town proper occupies a semi-scenic site down by the Columbia River, way below the hwy strip, but only if you use the municipal campsite, use one of the enormous number of motels, or book one of the many rafting and other **tours** based here will you do anything but look down on it from above. Note that finding places in Golden can be difficult if you don't know that all the "South" streets are on one side of the river, all the "North" streets on the other.

Much is likely to change here in the next few years, however, following approval of plans to develop **Kicking Horse** (ⓣ1-888/706-1117, ⓦwww.kickinghorseresort.com), the most significant new BC **ski resort** in decades since the creation of Blackcomb at Whistler. The resort is still expanding, but there is already enough here to suggest that it will one day be in the same league as Lake Louise or Whistler, but without – at least for a while – the crowds. The resort is 13km from Golden itself, with a state-of-the-art eight-person gondola (12 minutes to a pair of fine alpine bowls) and a vertical rise of 1245m. On-hill accommodation is planned.

The main **infocentre** is at 500-10th Ave North (year-round; ⓣ250/344-7125 or 1-800/622-4635, ⓦwww.goldenchamber.bc.ca), but a small infocentre also usually opens in summer at the strip's southern end (June–Sept). Some 200m north is the **bus terminal**, next to the Chinese-Canadian *Golden Palace Restaurant* – open 24 hours a day, like several of the local joints. All the **motels** on the strip, like the *Selkirk Inn*, Hwy 1 (ⓣ250/344-6315 or 344-5153, ⓦwww.selkirkinn.com; ❸), look over the road or onto the backs of garages opposite. None has anything you could call a view of the mountains, but at least the big *Sportsman*, 1200-12th St North (ⓣ250/344-2915 or 1-888/477-6783, ⓦwww.sportsmanlodge.com; ❸), is off the road.

Around 16km northwest of Golden, the *Blaeberry Mountain Lodge*, on Moberly School Rd (ⓣ250/344-5296, ⓦwww.blaeberrymountainlodge.bc.ca; ❹), is first-rate and beautifully situated; accommodation consists of simple but comfortable log cabins and a lodge. There are also plenty of outdoor activities and the owners will often pick you up in Golden if you're travelling without your own transport. Down in the town proper, a good place to **eat** standard Canadian fare like salads, chicken, pasta and seafood is the *Eleven 22 Grill*, 1122 10th Ave South (ⓣ250/344-2443; from 5pm daily), with a wide range of dishes (everything from Greek and Asian to fondues). A full meal will cost around $28, often less.

Campsites in Golden have prettier settings, particularly the *Whispering Spruce* (ⓣ250/344-6680, ⓦwww.whisperingspruce.net; $16–19; mid-April to mid-Oct) at 1430 Golden View Rd on Hwy 1 2km east of the Hwy 95 intersection. The town's own site, the *Golden Municipal Campground* (ⓣ250/344-5412, ⓔesutter@redshift.bc.ca; $15–20; mid-May to mid-Oct), is on the banks of the river at 1407 9th St, three blocks east of the main street. It has flush toilets, hot showers, washhouses, firewood and is adjacent to a swimming pool and tennis courts.

Glacier National Park

Strictly speaking, **GLACIER NATIONAL PARK** is part of the Selkirk and Columbia Mountains rather than the Rockies, but on the ground little sets it apart

The Glacier and Revelstoke parks, like most of the rest of BC, run on **Pacific time**, one hour behind Yoho NP and Alberta.

from the magnificence of the other national parks, and all the park agencies include it on an equal footing with its larger neighbours. It is, however, to a great extent the domain of ice, rain and snow; the weather is so atrocious that locals like to say that it rains or snows four days out of every three, and in truth you can expect a soaking three days out of five. As the name suggests, **glaciers** – 422 of them – form its dominant landscape, with fourteen percent of the park permanently blanketed with ice or snow. Scientists have identified 68 new glaciers forming on the sites of previously melted ice sheets in the park – a highly uncommon phenomenon. The

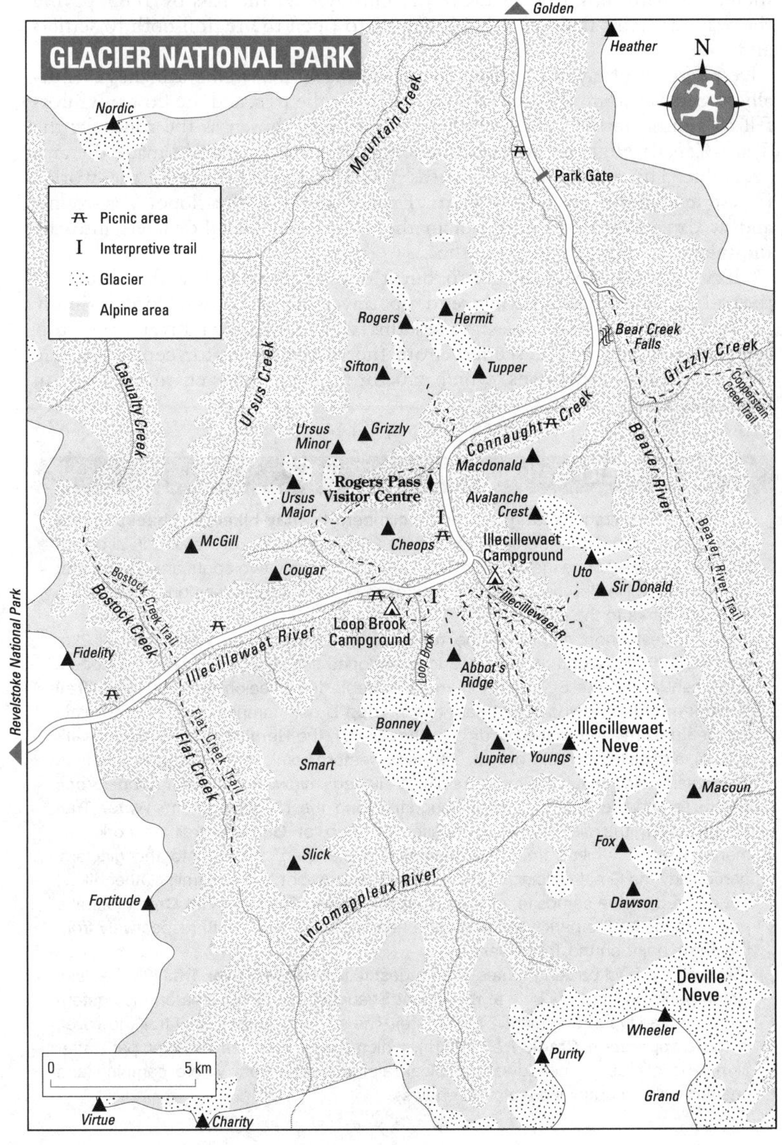

main ice sheet, the still-growing **Illecillewaet Neve**, is easily seen from the Trans-Canada Hwy or from the park visitor centre.

The Columbia range's peaks are every bit as imposing as those of the Rockies – Glacier's highest point, **Mount Dawson**, is 3390m tall – and historically they've presented as much of a barrier as their neighbours. Aboriginal peoples and then railwaymen shunned the icefields and the rugged interior for centuries until the discovery of **Rogers Pass** (1321m) in 1881 by Major A.B. Rogers, the chief engineer of the Canadian Pacific. Suffering incredible hardships, navvies drove the railway over the pass by 1885, paving the way for trains that, until 1916, helped to open the region both to settlers and tourists.

Despite the railway's best efforts the pounding of repeated avalanches eventually forced the company to bore a tunnel under the pass, and the flow of visitors fell to almost nothing. In the 1950s the pass was chosen as the route for the Trans-Canada Highway, whose completion in 1962 once again made the area accessible. This time huge snowsheds were built, backed up by the world's largest **avalanche-control system**. Experts monitor the slopes year-round, and at dangerous times they call in the army, who blast howitzers into the mountains to dislodge potential slips.

Glacier is easy enough to get to, but it doesn't tie in well with a circuit of the other parks; many people end up traversing it at some point simply because the main route west passes this way, but comparatively few stop, preferring to admire the scenery from the road. The visitor centre is a flag stop for Greyhound **buses**, which zip through up to seven times a day in each direction.

Hiking in Glacier National Park

Glacier's primary renown is among serious climbers, but **day-hikers** and **backpackers** have plenty of options. Some of the park's 21 trails (140km of walking in all) push close to glaciers for casual views of the ice – though only two spots are now safe at the toe of the Illecillewaet – and the backcountry is noticeably less busy than in the Big Four parks to the east.

The easiest short strolls off the road are the **Abandoned Rails Trail** (1.2km one-way; 30min), along old rail beds to abandoned snowsheds between the Rogers Pass centre and the Summit Monument (suitable for wheelchairs); the **Loop Trail** (1.6km) from the viewpoint just east of the Loop Brook campsite, full of viewpoints and features relating to the building of the railway; the **Hemlock Grove Boardwalk** (400m), a stroll through old-growth stands of western hemlock trees, some more than 350 years old (wheelchair-accessible; trailhead midway between *Loop Brook* campsite and the park's western boundary); and the **Meeting of the Water Trail** (30min) from the *Illecillewaet* campsite, the hub of Glacier's trail network. Six manageable day-hikes from the campsite give superb views onto the glaciers, particularly the Great Glacier, Avalanche Crest and Abbott's Ridge trails. Other hikes, not centred on the campsite, include **Bostock Creek** (9km) and **Flat Creek** (9km), a pair of paths on the park's western edge heading north and south respectively from the same point on the Trans-Canada.

Among the backpacking routes, the longest is the **Beaver River Trail** (30km-plus), which peels off from the hwy at the Mount Shaughnessy picnic area on the eastern edge (also a favourite mountain-bike route). The single best long-haul trail, however, is the **Copperstain Creek Trail** (16km), which leaves the Beaver River path after 3km, and climbs to meadows and bleak alpine tundra from where camping and onward walking options are almost endless.

Practicalities

The **Rogers Pass visitor centre** (daily April to mid-June & early Sept to Oct 9am–5pm; mid-June to early Sept 8am–7pm; Nov closed; Dec–March 7am–5pm; ⓣ250/837-6274 or 837-7500, ⓦwww.pc.gc.ca), 1km west of Rogers Pass, is a draw in itself, attracting some 160,000 visitors annually. It sells park permits ($6.90) and houses a variety of high-tech audiovisual aids, including a fun video on avalanche control called *Snow Wars*. In summer (July & Aug), book here for **guided walks** (1–6hr) featuring flowers, wildlife and glaciers, some of them fairly strenuous. Walks start at the Illecillewaet Campground Welcome Station. Also ask about trips to the **Nakimu Caves**, some of the largest in Canada; they were opened to the public (in the company of experienced guides only) in 1995. If you're heading for the backcountry, pick up *Footloose in the Columbias*, a hiker's guide to Glacier and Revelstoke national parks; you can also buy good walking **maps**. Next to the visitor centre, a **garage** and a **shop** are the only services on the Trans-Canada between Golden and Revelstoke, an hour's drive east and west respectively.

Accommodation is best sought in Golden (see p.769). The sole in-park **hotels** are the excellent fifty-room *Best Western Glacier Park Lodge* (ⓣ250/837-2126 or 1-800/528-1234, ⓦwww.glacierparklodge.ca; ❻), located just east of the visitor centre, and the 24-unit *Heather Mountain Lodge* (ⓣ250/344-7490, ⓦwww.heathermountainlodge.com; closed Oct & Nov ❺, 20km east of the Pass; both tend to be full in season. The latter has a useful 24-hour service and cafeteria.

Other places close to Glacier's borders are the ten-unit *Purcell Mountain Lodge* (ⓣ250/344-2639; ❻; July–Sept & Dec to April; three-night minimum stay), a remote lodge at 2180m on the eastern border accessible only by hiking trail, scheduled helicopter flights or winter ski trails – prices are a prohibitive $1,160 inclusive for three days. Slightly more manageable is the *Canyon Hot Springs Resort Campground*, 35km east of Revelstoke (ⓣ250/837-2420, ⓦwww.canyonhotsprings.com; cabins ❼, tent sites $28–36; May–Sept), which has mineral hot and warm springs, 200 secluded sites, café, firewood and sixteen cabins with B&B deals available. Cheaper is the *Hillside Lodge*, 1740 Seward Front Rd (ⓣ250/344-7281, ⓦwww.hillsidechalets.com; ❹), nine cosy cabins set in sixty acres 13km west of Golden at Blaeberry River with breakfast included.

The park-run **campsites** are the 57-site *Illecillewaet* ($18.80; mid-June to early Oct; also winter camping), 3.4km west of the visitor centre just off the Trans-Canada (and the trailhead for eight walks), and the twenty-site *Loop Brook*, 2km farther west ($18.80; mid-June to mid-Oct; self-serve check-in), which provides the luxuries of wood ($7.90), water and flush toilets only on a first-come, first-served basis. If you don't manage to get into these, or want more facilities, there are three commercial campsites west of the park on the Trans-Canada towards Revelstoke. Wilderness camping is allowed anywhere if you register with the visitor centre, pay for a nightly backcountry camping permit ($8.90) and pitch more than 5km from the road.

Mount Revelstoke National Park

The smallest national park in the region, **MOUNT REVELSTOKE NATIONAL PARK** is a somewhat arbitrary creation, put together at the request of local people in 1914 to protect the Clachnacudainn Range of the Columbia Mountains. The lines on the map mean little, for the thrilling scenery in the 16km of no-man's-land between Glacier and Revelstoke is largely the same as that within the parks. The mountains here are especially steep, their slopes often scythed clear of trees by

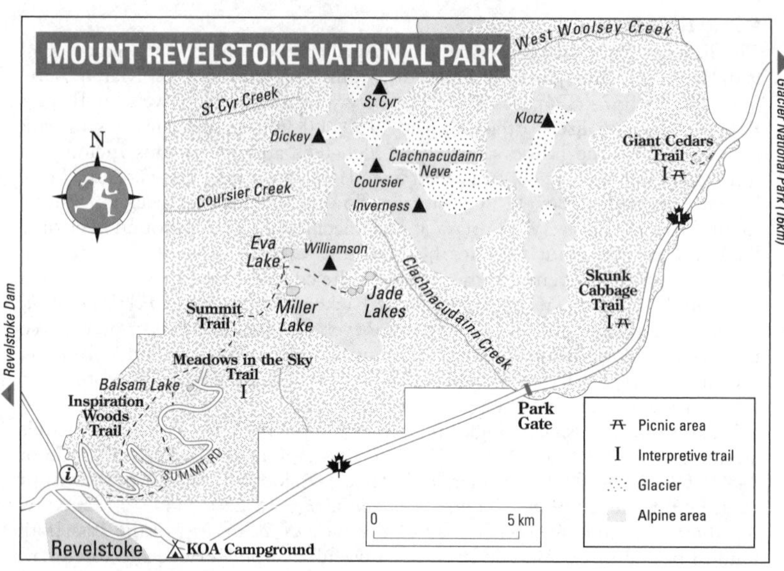

avalanches. The views from the Trans-Canada, as it peeks out of countless tunnels, are of forests and snowcapped peaks aplenty and, far below, the railway and the Illecillewaet River crashing through a twisting, steep-sided gorge.

The main access to the park interior is the very busy **Summit Road**, or **Meadows-in-the-Sky-Parkway** (mid-June to Aug long weekend 7am-10pm; rest of Aug 7am–8.30pm; May to early June & Sept to early Oct 9am–5pm), which strikes north from the Trans-Canada at the town of Revelstoke and winds 26km almost to the top of Mount Revelstoke (1938m) through forest and alpine meadows noted for glorious displays of wild flowers (best during July and Aug). Note that a gate across the road is locked outside opening hours.

You can also walk this stretch on the **Summit Trail** (10km one-way; 4hr) from the car park at the base of Summit Road. Damage to the delicate ecosystem has prompted park authorities to rethink access, and often the last 2km of the road is closed to cars, leaving the choice of a walk or regular shuttle bus (daily 10am–4.20pm during snow-free periods) to the summit from a car park at Balsam Lake.

There is a park "**welcome station kiosk**" at the start of the road for park information (daily mid-June to Aug long weekend 9am–10pm; information the rest of the year from the small office in Revelstoke post office at 300-3rd St West; year-round Mon–Fri 8.30am–noon & 1–4.30pm; Ⓦ www.pc.gc.ca). The Summit Parkway itself is open limited hours (mid-June to Aug 9am–10pm; the rest of Aug 7am–8pm; early June, Sept and early Oct 9am–5pm). The daily **park fee** is $6.90.

Park trails

Many of the longer of the park's ten official **trails** start from the top of Summit Road; serious backpackers prefer to head to **Eagle Lake**, off Summit Road, rather than take the more popular **Miller Lake Trail** (6km one-way). The award-winning **Giant Cedars Trail** is a wooded one-kilometre jaunt with ten interpretive exhibits off the road on the park's eastern edge, its boardwalks negotiating a tract of ancient forest crammed with 800-year-old western red cedars and rough-barked western hemlock (the trailhead begins at the Giant Cedars Picnic Area). You could also try the **Skunk Cabbage Boardwalk** (1.2km), an easy trail through temperate forest and wetland inhabited by muskrat, beaver, numerous birds and the eponymous skunk cabbage. **Meadows in the Sky Trail**, by contrast, is a quick one-kilometre paved loop through alpine meadows at the top of Summit Road. Look out for the so-called Icebox, a shaded rock cleft that contains what is reputedly the world's smallest glacier. The *Footloose in the Columbias* booklet, available from Glacier's Rogers Pass visitor centre, has further trail information.

Revelstoke

REVELSTOKE, the only community within striking range of the park, sits just outside the western boundary, but in its promotional pitch chooses to ignore its scenic appeal in favour of a somewhat unimpressive claim to be "Home of the World's Largest Sculpted Grizzly Bears" (they stand at Mackenzie Ave at the entrance to downtown). Like many mountain towns, it's divided between a motel-and-garage strip along the Trans-Canada and a dispersed, frontier-type collection of houses some distance away. The river and rugged scenery round about redeem it, and the downtown area also has a nice feel, having been spruced up as a placatory measure following the disaster at the dam site (see p.776). If you're without your own vehicle, note that it's a good twenty-minute walk from the strip.

In downtown, you might dip into the small but polished **Revelstoke Railway Museum** (May, June, Sept daily 9am–5pm; July & Aug daily 9am–8pm; March–April & Oct–Nov Thurs–Tues 9am–5pm; Dec–Feb Fri–Tues 11am–4pm; $6), which has a steam engine, snowploughs and assorted memorabilia relating to the building of the stretch of the CPR between Field and Kamloops. If you want to relax close to town, try warm-watered **Williamson Lake**, a favourite swimming spot for locals with mini-golf and campsite 4km south of town east of Airport Way.

Seven daily Greyhound **buses** stop at the town of Revelstoke between Kamloops and Calgary; the terminal is at the west end of the strip, just after the big blue Columbia River bridge (Ⓣ250/837-5874). The **infocentre** is 200m beyond on the left at 204 Campbell Ave (daily May & June 10am–6pm; July & Aug 8am–8pm; shorter winter hours Ⓣ250/837-5345, Ⓦwww.seerevelstoke.com). Between May and September there's a small additional office where the Trans-Canada and Hwy 23N meet (Ⓣ250/837-3522; same hours). Get park information at these offices, or visit the **Park Administration Office** on 3rd Street in the **post office** building (park office: Mon–Fri 8.30am–noon & 1–4.30pm; Ⓣ250/837-7500) or the Rogers Pass visitor centre. The park office also has a store for the Friends of Glacier and Mount Revelstoke (Ⓣ250/837-2010, Ⓦwww.friendsrevglacier.com) that is useful for **maps** and guides.

Eating possibilities include the *Frontier Restaurant* on the Trans-Canada, part of the eponymous motel near the infocentre, which serves up superior steak-and-salad meals at reasonable prices, with friendly service and a genuine cowpoke atmosphere. In town, the *One-Twelve Restaurant & Lounge* in the *Regent Inn* at 112 Victoria Rd (Ⓣ250/837-2107; daily 11.45am–2pm & 5.30–9pm) is a favourite, with good food (mains cost $15–30), a lively pub and dance floor. For something even cheaper in downtown there's *Tony's Roma*, 306 Mackenzie (Ⓣ250/837-4106; daily 11am–10pm, closed Sun in winter), where basic pastas and the like cost from $9.

A far more amenable place to stay than Golden, the town of Revelstoke has plenty of **accommodation** – fifteen-plus motels and half a dozen campsites. Backcountry camping in the park is free, with tent-pads, outhouses and food-storage poles provided at Eva and Jade lakes, but no camping is allowed in the Miller Lake area or anywhere within 5km of the Trans-Canada and Summit Road. Registration at the Park Administration Office is obligatory. The park is so small, however, that you might be better off at some of the area's more developed private campsites.

Hotels and motels

Best Western Wayside Inn 1901 Laforme Blvd ⓣ250/837-6161 or 1-800/528-1234, ⓦwww.bestwestern.com. The priciest and best of the town's hotels. ⑤

Frontier Motel and Restaurant 122 North Nakusp Hwy ⓣ250/837-5119 or 1-800/382-7763, ⓔwelcome@revelstoke.net. On the main Trans-Canada near the junction with Hwy 23 away from the town centre; good motel and first-rate food. ②

Nelles Ranch Bed and Breakfast Hwy 23 South ⓣ250/837-3800 or 1-888/567-4177, ⓦwww.nellesranch.com. Just six units on a working horse and cattle ranch 2km off the Trans-Canada Hwy. ③

Peaks Lodge 5km west of Revelstoke off Hwy 1 ⓣ250/837-2176 or 1-800/668-0330, ⓦwww.peakslodge.net. Nice small place (15 units) in a reasonably rustic setting convenient for hikes, bird-watching and the like. Open mid-May to mid-Oct & mid-Nov to mid-April. ③

'R' Motel 1500 1st St ⓣ250/837-2164, ⓦwww.rmotel.com. One of the cheapest motels in town, but some rooms still have kitchenettes and a/c. ②

Samesun Budget Lodge 400 2nd St W ⓣ250/837-4050 or 1-877/562-2783, ⓦwww.samesun.com. Cheap private, semi-private and dorm beds convenient for local restaurants and supermarkets. Well run and offers Internet access, bike rentals and kitchen facilities. ①

Sandman Inn 1821 Fraser St ⓣ250/837-5271 or 1-800/726-3626, ⓦwww.sandmanhotels.ca. Part of a usually reliable mid-range hotel chain. Has 83 comfortable, modern rooms, so a good chance of finding space. ⑤

Campsites

Lamplighter Campground ⓣ250/837-3385. Off Hwy 1 before the Columbia River bridge; take Hwy 23 south towards Nakusp and turn into Nixon Rd (first left). A peaceful, fully serviced tent and RV site within walking distance of downtown. Fifty fully-serviced sites. Mid-April to mid-Oct. $18–26.

Williamson Lake Campground 1818 Williamson Lake Rd ⓣ250/837-5512 or 1-888/676-2267, ⓦwww.williamsonlakecampground.com. Nice 41-site lakeside campsite 4km south of the town centre. Free hot showers, canoe and rowboat rentals, flush toilets and beach. Mid-April to Oct. $16–21.50.

Revelstoke Dam

A trip to Canada's largest dam may sound dull, but the **Revelstoke Dam** (daily mid-March to mid-June & early Sept to late Oct 9am–5pm; mid-June to early Sept 8am–8pm; free) makes an interesting outing. Located 4km north of the town on Hwy 23, the 175m-tall barrier holds back the waters of the Columbia River, around 500km from its source. Its sleek, space-age **visitor centre** offers a two-hour self-guided tour, which omits to tell you that insufficient mapping during the construction caused a landslide that threatened to swamp Revelstoke: millions had to be spent or it would have been curtains for the town. The boring bits of the tour can be skipped in favour of a lift to the top for a great view of the dam and surrounding valley.

Kootenay National Park

KOOTENAY NATIONAL PARK, lying across the Continental Divide from Banff in British Columbia, is the least known of the four contiguous parks of the Rockies, and the easiest to miss out – many people prefer to follow the

Trans-Canada through Yoho rather than commit themselves to the less enthralling westward journey on Hwy 3 imposed by Kootenay. The park's scenery, however, is as impressive as that of its neighbours – it draws three million visitors a year – and if you're not determined to head west you could drive a neat loop from Banff through Kootenay on Hwy 93 to **Radium Hot Springs** (the only town in this area), north on Hwy 95, and back on the Trans-Canada

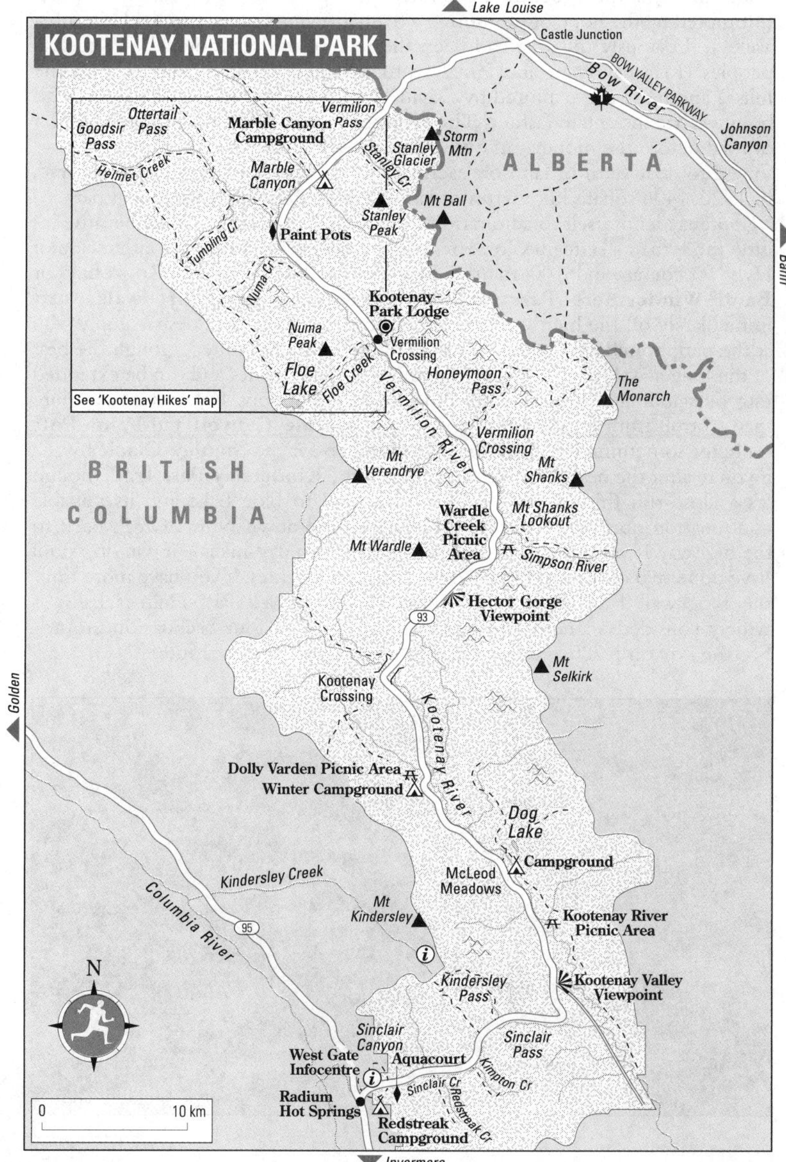

through Yoho to Lake Louise and Banff. You could drive this in a day and still have time for a few short walks and a dip in Radium's hot springs to boot.

In many ways the park's mountains seem closer at hand and more spectacular than on the Icefields Parkway, partly because the road climbs higher over the Continental Divide, and partly because the park's origins guaranteed it an intimate link with the highway. In 1910 Randolph Bruce, a local businessman, persuaded the Canadian government and Canadian Pacific to push a road from Banff through the Rockies to connect the prairies with western seaports (prompted by the hope of promoting a fruit-growing industry in the Columbia Valley). Previously the area had been the reserve of the Kootenai or Ktunaxa peoples (*Kootenay* is an aboriginal word meaning "people from beyond the hills") and had been explored by David Thompson, but otherwise it was an all but inviolate mountain fastness. The project began in 1911 and produced 22km of road before the money ran out. To wangle more cash British Columbia was forced to cede 8km of land on each side of the hwy to the government and, in 1920, 1406 square kilometres of land were established as a national park.

Kootenay lends itself to admiration from a car, bus or bike, mainly because it's little more than a sixteen-kilometre-wide ribbon of land running either side of Hwy 93 for around 100km (the hwy here is known as the **Kootenay** or **Banff–Windermere Parkway**). All its numerous easy **short walks** start immediately off the highway, though the scenery, of course, doesn't simply stop at the park boundary. Options for **day-hikes** are more limited, though the best of the longer walks are as good as anything in the Rockies and can be extended into outstanding two-day (or more) backpacking options. If you want no more than a stroll from a car or bike follow the **Marble Canyon** and **Paint Pots** trails; for something longer but not too long go for the **Stanley Glacier** walk; if you're after the best day-hike the choice is the **Kindersley Pass Trail**, though it's a close-run thing with the Floe Lake Trail to Floe Lake and its possible continuation northwest over the Numa Pass and down Numa Creek back to the highway. If you have time do both of these two day-hikes – if you do, you'll have done two of the top ten or so walks in the Rockies. If you have more time, the Rockwall Trail (Floe Lake–Numa Pass–Rockwell Pass–Helmet Falls) is widely considered among the Rockies' top three or four backpacking routes. See the box on p.780 and our maps to make sense of these routes.

△ Kootenay National Park

Park information

The only practicable access to Kootenay is on Hwy 93, a good road that leaves the Trans-Canada at Castle Junction (in Banff National Park), traverses Kootenay from north to south, and joins Hwy 95 at Radium Hot Springs at the southern entrance. Radium offers the only practical accommodation options, bar a trio of park-run campsites and handful of rooms at Vermilion Crossing, a summer-only huddle of shop, cabins and petrol station midway through the park. The two daily Greyhound **buses** east and west on the southern British Columbia route between Cranbrook, Banff and Calgary stop at Vermilion Crossing and Radium. **Park permits** are required for entry unless you already have a valid permit from Banff, Jasper or Kootenay: $8.90 per person per day, or $62.40 for an annual pass valid for 27 Canadian national parks.

If you come from the east you'll hit the *Marble Canyon* campsite about 15km from Castle Junction, where occasionally in summer there's a simple information kiosk (mid-June to early Sept Mon & Fri–Sun 8.30am–8pm, Tues–Thurs 8.30am–4.30pm; no phone); coming the other way, the main **park visitor centre** is at the corner of Main Street East and Redstreak Road at 7556 Main St in the town of Radium Hot Springs (daily mid-May to late June & early Sept to early Oct 9am–5pm; late June to early Sept 9am–7pm; closed 12.30am–1pm mid-Sept to early Oct; ⓣ250/347-9505, ⓦwww.pc.gc.ca). Main Street East is a turn south off Hwy 93 close to its junction with Hwy 95. The park entrance, however, is on Hwy 93 itself farther east close to the Radium Hot Springs Pools (see p.783). The centre provides a free *Backcountry Guide to Kootenay National Park*, all you need walk-wise if you're not planning anything too ambitious. There is a seasonal visitor centre at the Kootenay Park Lodge (see p.780), 68km north of Radium on Hwy 93 (no phone; mid-May to June & Sept 10am–5pm; July–Aug 9am–7pm).

Kootenay, like the other major Rockies parks, has a "Friends" organization (ⓣ250/347-6525, ⓦwww.friendsofkootenay.com), which helps run **guided walks** and other activities: walks should be booked at the visitor centre. In Kootenay, there are usually good walks in July and August to Stanley Glacier (5hr; 10km; meet at Stanley Glacier trailhead on Hwy 93) and two walks in Sinclair Canyon – "Walk of the Two Lions" (July; 2hr) and "Into the Secret Canyon" (Aug; 1hr 30min). Meet for both walks at the front entrance of the Radium Hot Springs Pools – call or visit the website for latest days and start times.

Accommodation

Park staff is also usually on hand at the park's only two roadside **campsites**: the 98-site *McLeod Meadows*, 25km north of Radium ($18.80; mid-May to mid-Sept; no showers), and the 61-site *Marble Canyon* ($18.80; mid-June to early Sept; no showers). If you want more comforts (including hot showers) and easier access use the big 242-site *Redstreak* campsite, Kootenay's major park tent and RV campsite. It's located 3km north of Radium Hot Springs (tents $23.75, RVs $27.70–32.65; firewood $7.90; May–Sept; ⓣ250/347-9567); the turn-off for the site is Redstreak Road. To reach it, carry on along Main St East from the park visitor centre until Main Street becomes Redstreak Road.

If you're staying at the campsite, incidentally, note that the Redstreak Campground Trail (2.2km) takes you from the northwest corner of the site to the Radium Hot Springs Pools. The Valleyview Trail (1.4km) takes you from the campsite entrance into Radium village, avoiding Redstreak Road. A dozen or more **backcountry sites** with pit toilets and firewood are scattered within easy backpacking range of the highway, for which you need a **permit** from the infocentres ($8.90). The small seven-site *Dolly Varden* park campsite just north of McLeod Meadows opens for **winter camping** (Sept–May; flush toilets only; $13.85).

Hikes in Kootenay National Park

If you have time and energy for only one long walk in Kootenay, make it the **Kindersley Pass Trail**, a strenuous 9.8-kilometre trail that climbs to **Kindersley Pass** and then cuts northeast for the steep final push to Kindersley Summit (2210m). Here you can enjoy the sublime prospect of an endless succession of peaks fading to the horizon away to the northeast. Rather than double back down through the open tundra, many people push on another 2km (trail vague) and contour around the head of the Sinclair Creek valley before dropping off the ridge (the Kindersley–Sinclair Col) to follow the well-defined **Sinclair Creek Trail** (6.4km) down to meet the hwy 1km from the starting point (be sure to do the hike this way round – the Sinclair Creek Trail is a long, dull climb).

Most of Kootenay's other longish day-walks are in the park's northern half, accessed on the west side of the hwy from the Marble Canyon, Paint Pots, Numa Creek and Floe Lake parking areas. The **Rockwall Trail**, an incredible thirty-kilometre (54km including approach trails; 1450m ascent), backpacking high-level trail, follows the line of the mountains on the west side of the highway, and can be joined using four of the six trails described below. You could walk it in two days, but could easily spend longer, particularly as there are five backcountry campsites en route.

From north to south on the highway, the trails start with the **Kaufmann Lake Trail** (15km one-way; 570m ascent; allow 4–6hr one-way), which climbs to one of the park's loveliest high-mountain lakes (there's also a campsite here). A trail from the Paint Pots runs for 2km before dividing to provide three onward options: the first to the dull **Ottertail Pass**, the second up **Tumbling Creek** (10.3km; 440m ascent to the intersection with the Rockwall Trail), and the third and best option the **Helmet Creek Trail** (14.3km; 310m ascent), a long day-hike to the amazing 365-metre **Helmet Waterfalls** (another intersection with the Rockwall Trail). The best of the day-hikes after Kindersley Pass is the easier **Floe Lake Trail** (10.5km; 715m ascent), up to a spellbinding lake edged by a 1000m sheer escarpment and a small glacier. There are campsites on the route, and another tie-in to the Rockwall Trail. The **Numa Creek Trail** (6.4km; 115m ascent) to the north is less enthralling – though you could use it as a downhill leg to add to the Floe Lake Trail – as are the series of fire-road walks advertised in the park: unless you're mountain biking, therefore, ignore the Simpson River, West Kootenay, Honeymoon Pass and East Kootenay trails.

The only indoor **accommodation** in the heart of the park is ten rustic cottages of the *Kootenay Park Lodge* at Vermilion Crossing (ⓣ250/762-9196, ⓦwww.kootenayparklodge.com; ❺; mid-May to Sept). You'll need to book these well in advance.

Vermilion Pass

Vermilion Pass (1637m) marks the northern entrance to the park, the Continental Divide's watershed and the border between Alberta and British Columbia. Little fanfare, however, accompanies the transition – only the barren legacy of a huge forest fire (started by a single lightning bolt) that ravaged the area for four days in 1968, leaving a 24-square-kilometre blanket of stark, blackened trunks. Take the short **Fireweed Trail** (1km) through the desolation from the car park at the pass to see how nature deals with such disasters, indeed how it seems to invite lightning fires to promote phoenix-like regeneration. The ubiquitous lodgepole pine, for example, specifically requires the heat of a forest fire to crack open its resin-sealed cones and release its seeds. Strange as it seems, forests are intended to burn, at least if a healthy forest is to be preserved: in montane regions the natural "fire return cycles" are a mere 42–46 years; in lower subalpine habitats, 77–130 years; and in upper subalpine areas, 180 years. Forests

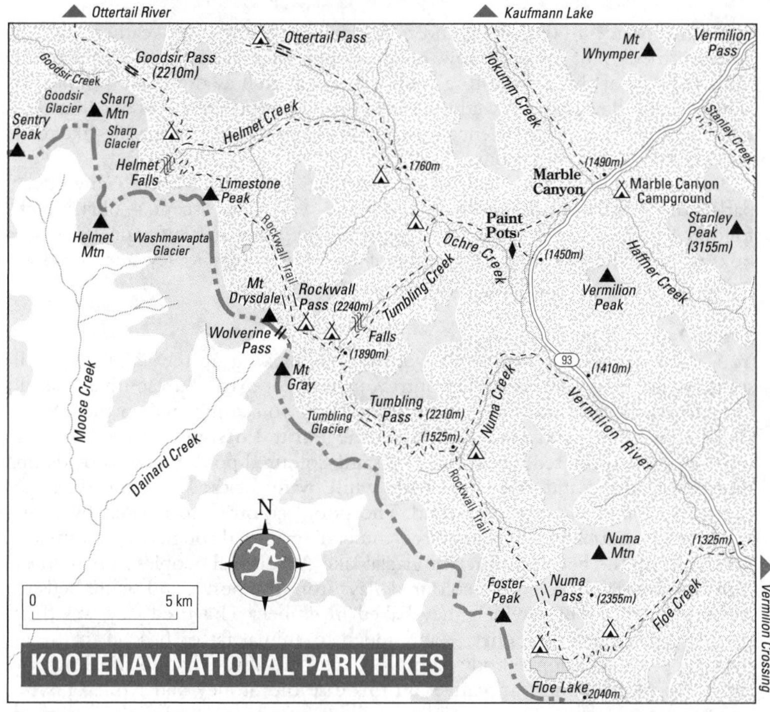

any older are actually in decline, providing few species and poor wildlife habitats. Ironically, as a result of the national parks' success in preventing forest fires over the last fifty years, many woods are now over-mature and the need for controlled burning is increasingly being addressed. At Vermilion Pass a broad carpet of lodgepole pines have taken root among the blasted remnants of the earlier forest, while young plants and shrubs ("doghair forest") are pushing up into the new clearings. Birds, small mammals and deer, elk and moose are being attracted to new food sources and, more significantly, black and grizzly bears are returning to the area. Burning takes place in the park, and some trails may be closed as a result: latest details are posted at the park centre or the Parks Canada website.

Stanley Glacier and Marble Canyon

About 3km south of Vermilion Pass, the small, well-defined **Stanley Glacier Trail** (4.2km; 365m ascent; 1hr 30min) strikes off up Stanley Creek from a parking area on the eastern side of the highway. In its first 2km the trail provides you with a hike through the Vermilion Pass Burn (see opposite), but more to the point pushes into the beautiful hanging valley below Stanley Peak. Here you can enjoy close-up views of the Stanley Glacier and its surrounding recently glaciated landscapes. The area is also known for its fossils, and for the chance to see marmots, pikas and white-tailed ptarmigan.

Marble Canyon, 8km south of Vermilion Pass, the site of a park-run **campsite**, has an easy trail (800m) that's probably the most heavily trafficked of Kootenay's shorter hikes. The track crosses a series of log bridges over Tokumm Creek, which has carved through a fault in the limestone over the last 8000 years to produce a 600m-long and 37m-deep gorge. In cold weather this is a fantastic medley of ice and snow, but in summer the climax is the viewpoint from the top of the path onto a thundering waterfall as the creek pounds its way through the narrowest section of the gorge. The rock here was once mistakenly identified as marble – hence the canyon's name; the white marble-like rock is actually dolomite limestone.

One of the park's better long hikes also starts from the Marble Canyon car park – the **Kaufmann Lake Trail** (15km one-way; 570m ascent; 4–6hr), which follows Tokumm Creek towards the head of the valley at Kaufmann Lake (see box, p.780). The first few kilometres of the trail – easy valley and meadow walking – make an appealing hour or so's stroll.

The Paint Pots

You could extend the Marble Canyon walk by picking up the Paint Pots Trail south, which puts another 2.7km onto your walk, or drive 2km south and stroll 1km to reach the same destination. Either way you come first to the Ochre Beds (after 800m) and then (1.5km) to the **Paint Pots**, one of the Rockies' more magical spots: red, orange and mustard-coloured pools prefaced by damp, moss-clung forest and views across the white water of the Vermilion River to the snowcapped mountains beyond. The pools' colours are created by iron-laden water bubbling up from three mineral springs through clay sediments deposited on the bed of an ancient glacial lake. Aboriginal peoples from all over North America collected the coloured clays from the ponds and ochre beds to make into small cakes, which they baked in embers. The fired clay was then ground into powder – **ochre** – and added to animal fat or fish oil to use in rock, tepee or ceremonial body painting. Ochre has always had spiritual significance for North American natives, in this case the Stoney and Ktunaxa, who saw these oxide-stained pools and their yellow-edged surroundings as inhabited by animal and thunder spirits. Standing in the quiet, rather gloomy glade, particularly on overcast days, it's easy to see why – not that the atmosphere or sanctity of the place stopped European speculators in the 1920s from mining the ochre to manufacture paint in Calgary.

The car park is the trailhead for three longer (day or backpack) trails, all of which kick off along the Ochre Creek Valley: Tumbling Creek Trail, Ottertail Pass Trail and the Helmet Creek–Helmet Waterfalls Trail (see box, p.780).

Vermilion Crossing and Kootenay Crossing

VERMILION CROSSING, 20km south of the Paint Pots Trail, is gone in a flash, but it's the only place, in summer at least, to find lodgings, petrol and food in the park. It also has a new visitor centre, built on the site of a 1920 CPR railway camp. You can also stop to walk the **Verendyre Creek Trail** (2.1km), accessed west off the highway, an easy stroll, but forest-enclosed, and with only limited views of Mount Verendrye as a reward. One of the Rockies' tougher walks heads east from the Crossing, up over Honeymoon Pass and Redearth Pass to Egypt Lake and the Trans-Canada Hwy in Banff National Park, while to the south equally demanding trails provide the only westside access into the wilderness of **Mount Assiniboine Provincial Park**. Sandwiched between Kootenay and Banff, this wilderness park was created in honour of Mount Assiniboine (3618m), a sabre-tooth-shaped mountain with one of the most dramatic profiles imaginable, whose native Stoney name means "those who cook by placing hot rocks in water". The **Simpson Road Trail** (8.2km) leads to the park boundary, and then divides into two paths (20km and 32km) to Lake Magog in the heart of Assiniboine. Some 8.5km beyond the Crossing look out for the Animal Lick, a spot where animals come down to lick nutrients from a natural mineral source: with luck you may see elk, mule deer and even moose here. Over the next few kilometres, for similar reasons, you might also see mountain goats by banks at the side of the road.

Kootenay Crossing is no more than a ceremonial spot – it was where the ribbon was cut to open Hwy 93 in 1923 – though a clutch of short trails fan out from its park warden station, and the nearby *Dolly Varden* campsite (see p.779) is the park's only specific site for winter camping. **Wardle Creek** nearby is a good place to unpack a picnic if you're determined to stick to the road.

Around 11km south of the Kootenay Crossing is the **McLeod Meadows** campsite (see p.779), and immediately behind it to the east the easy **Dog Lake Trail** (2.7km), much tramped as an after-dinner leg-stretcher by campers (the trail can also be accessed from the hwy at the picnic area 500m south). The path offers glimpses of the Kootenay Valley through the trees, and ends in a marsh-edged lake whose temperate microclimate makes it ideal for nature study. You may see deer, elk and coyotes, and – if you're lucky – bears and moose. Several types of orchid also bloom here in early summer (June & July), including white bog, round-leafed, calypso and sparrow's egg. About 11km further on, the **Kootenay Valley Viewpoint** offers one of the broadest views on the highway, with great vistas of the Mitchell and Vermilion mountain ranges, and with them the inevitable hordes in search of a photo opportunity.

Sinclair Pass

For its final run down out of the park, the hwy doglegs west through the **Sinclair Pass**, a red-cliffed gorge filled with the falling waters of Sinclair Creek and the start of the **Kindersley Pass Trail**, possibly the most scenic day-hike in the park (see box, p.780). If this seems too much of a slog, Sinclair Pass offers three far easier short trails, all marked off the hwy to the west. The best is the **Juniper Trail** (3.2km), accessed just 300m inside the park's West Gate. The trail drops to Sinclair Creek and over the next couple of kilometres touches dry canyon, arid forest slopes of juniper and Douglas fir, and thick woods of western red cedar, before emerging at the hot springs, or Aquacourt, 1.4km up the road from the start. The **Redstreak Creek Trail** (2.7km), 4.5km east of the West Gate, starts off as a good forest walk, but tails off into dullness subsequently, as does the **Kimpton Creek Trail** (4.8km), also on the south side of the road and canyon, accessed 7.5km east of the West Gate.

Radium Hot Springs

RADIUM HOT SPRINGS is far less attractive than its evocative name suggests but, as the service centre for Kootenay, its tacky motels and garages are likely to claim your attention and money. The town spreads across the flats of the Columbia Valley, 3km from the southern/western entrance at the junction of Hwy 93 and Hwy 95. For **information** visit the park centre, which has a Chamber of Commerce desk (hours as for park centre – see p.779; ⓣ250/347-9331 or 1-800/347-9704, ⓦwww.radiumhotsprings.com).

The **hot springs** (or Aquacourt) themselves – plus park visitor centre – are nicely away from the settlement, 2km north of town off the Banff–Windermere Parkway (Hwy 93) and are administered by the park authorities. There is a hot pool and cool pool with a single admission ($6.40, unlimited day use $9.65) but slightly different opening times: hot pool (daily mid-May to mid-Oct 9am–11pm; mid-Oct to mid-May Sun–Thurs noon–9pm, Fri & Sat noon–10pm); cool pool (daily mid-May to late June & early Sept to mid-Oct noon–9pm; late June to early Sept 9am–11pm; mid-Oct to mid-May Fri 6–9pm, Sat & Sun noon–9pm; ⓣ250/347-9485).

Aboriginal peoples used the springs for centuries, and commercial white development started as early as 1890 when Roland Stuart bought the area for $160. Traces of supposedly therapeutic radium found in the water turned Stuart's investment into a recreational gold mine. When the government appropriated the springs for inclusion in the national park, it paid him $40,000 – a small fortune, but considerably less than what they were worth, which at the time was estimated to be $500,000. The pools today are outdoors, but serviced by a large, modern centre. In summer, 4000 people per day take the plunge into the odourless 45°C waters, enough to discourage any idea of a quiet swim, though in late evening or off-season (when the hot pool steams invitingly) you can escape the bedlam and pretend more easily that the water is having some sort of soothing effect. The radium traces sound a bit worrying, but 300,000 visitors a year don't seem to mind.

If you have the choice, aim **to stay** in Invermere (see p.988) or one of the newer **motels** creeping up the Sinclair Valley around the hot springs area away from downtown: they're more expensive, but far more attractively sited than the thirty-odd mirror-image motels in town (where there are any number of rooms in the $60–90 bracket). Try the big 120-room *Radium Resort* for something of a treat, 1km south of the springs at 8100 Golf Course Rd (Ⓣ250/347-9311 or 1-800/667-6444, Ⓦwww.radiumresort.com; ❻), for all the trimmings (including swimming pool and massage therapist). Almost alongside the park entrance are the fourteen-room *Alpen Motel* (Ⓣ250/347-9823 or 1-888/788-3891, Ⓦwww.alpenmotel.com; ❺), sixteen-room *Kootenay* (Ⓣ250/347-9490 or 1-877/908-2020; ❸) and nine-room *Crescent* (Ⓣ250/347-9570 or 1-888/295-8822; ❸) motels. The *Radium International Hostel*, located at the Misty River Lodge at the edge of the park (Ⓣ250/347-9912, Ⓦwww.radiumhostel.bc.ca; ❶), has a kitchen, common room, bicycle storage and rental and two dorms with five or six beds ($18 a head) and one private room (❸).

Travel details

Trains

Calgary to: Vancouver with private Rocky Mountaineer Railtours (see Basics, p.40).
Edmonton to: Prince Rupert via Jasper and Prince George (3 weekly; 30hr); Vancouver (3 weekly; 24hr); Winnipeg via Saskatoon (3 weekly; 24hr).
Jasper to: Edmonton (3 weekly; 5hr 30min); Prince Rupert via Prince George (3 weekly; 20hr); Vancouver (3 weekly).

Buses

Calgary to: Banff (6 daily; 1hr 40min); Coutts in the US (connections for Las Vegas and Los Angeles) via Fort Macleod and Lethbridge (1 daily; 4hr 30min); Creston via Banff, Radium Hot Springs and Cranbrook (1 daily; 7hr 30min); Dawson Creek (2 daily; 7hr 15min); Drumheller (2 daily; 1hr 50min); Edmonton (14 daily; 3hr 30min); Fort St John (2 daily; 9hr 15min); Lake Louise (6 daily; 2hr 35min); Prince George (2 daily; 14hr); Saskatoon (2 daily; 9hr); Vancouver via Fort Macleod, Cranbrook, Nelson, Osoyoos and Hope (2 daily; 24hr); Vancouver via Kamloops (7 daily; 13hr); Vancouver via Vernon, Kelowna and Penticton (3 daily; 16hr); Winnipeg via Lethbridge, Medicine Hat and Regina (2 daily; 24hr).
Edmonton to: Calgary (14 daily; 3hr 30min); Drumheller (1 daily; 4hr 45min); Grande Prairie (4 daily; 6hr); Hay River via Peace River (1 daily; 17hr); Jasper (6 daily; 4hr 30min); Peace River (3 daily; 6hr 30min); Saskatoon (4 daily; 5hr); Vancouver (6 daily; 14hr); Whitehorse (mid-May to mid-Oct 1 daily; rest of year 3 weekly; 28hr); Winnipeg (2 daily; 21hr).

Flights

Calgary to: Edmonton (every 30min; 50min); Montréal (12 daily; 5hr); Toronto (14 daily; 4hr); Vancouver (every 30min; 1hr 20min).
Edmonton to: Calgary (every 30min; 50min); Montréal (9 daily; 5hr); Toronto (10 daily; 4hr 10min); Vancouver (every 30min; 1hr 25min).

Vancouver and Vancouver Island

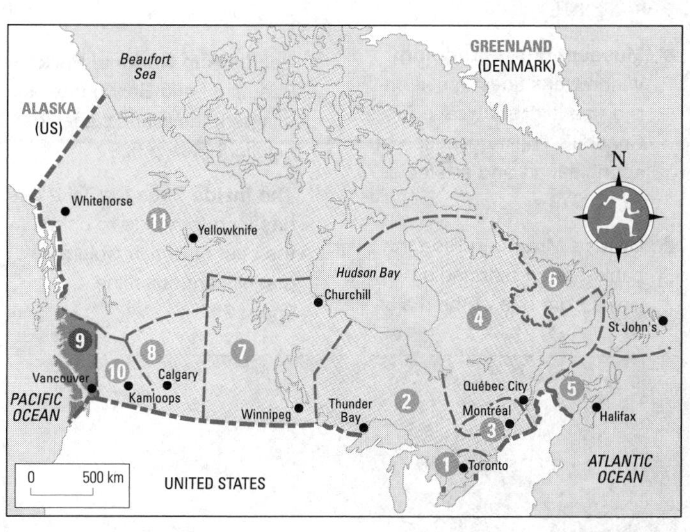

CHAPTER 9 Highlights

✱ **Stanley Park** North America's largest urban park is an oasis of ancient forest, beaches, gardens and peaceful trails. See p.812

✱ **Granville Island** A superb market and specialist stores are the main attractions of this hugely popular enclave. See p.815

✱ **Museum of Anthropology** Vancouver's finest museum is a beautiful showcase for Canada's finest collection of aboriginal art and artefacts. See p.819

✱ **Grouse Mountain** Ride the cable-car for astounding views from one of the major peaks on Vancouver's North Shore. See p.822

✱ **Whistler** Come here for superlative outdoor activities in summer or winter. See p.852

✱ **Victoria** British Columbia's Anglophile capital is one of Canada's most charming cities. See p.870

✱ **Pacific Rim National Park** Beautiful Long Beach makes this park the island's scenic highlight. See p.909

✱ **The Inside Passage** Take this day-long ferry ride to enjoy the best of British Columbia's magnificent coastline. See p.934

△ The Inside Passage ferry

9

Vancouver and Vancouver Island

V**ancouver and Vancouver Island** stand apart from the rest of British Columbia, the big-city outlook and bustling, cosmopolitan streets of Vancouver, Canada's third-largest metropolis, and Victoria, the provincial capital, dramatically at odds with the interior's small towns, remote villages and vast tracts of wilderness. And while Vancouver Island has scenery that occasionally matches that of the interior, its landscapes are generally more modest, the island's intimate and self-contained nature and relatively small extent creating a region that feels very different to the great continental land mass of which mainland British Columbia is a part.

In **Vancouver** you have one of the world's great scenic cities, its watery and mountain-ringed setting on a par with those of Sydney and Rio de Janeiro. Long after the many fine galleries and museums, notably the Museum of Anthropology, North America's finest collection of aboriginal art and artefacts, and the even better restaurants, have faded, the memory of the Coast Mountains rearing above the Burrard Inlet, or the beaches and semi-wilderness of Stanley Park, will probably linger. Vancouver is also a sophisticated and famously hedonistic city, having more in common with the West Coast ethos and outlook of San Francisco than, say, Toronto or Ottawa to the east. It also gives the lie to the stereotype of the Canadian west as an introverted, cultural wasteland, its combination of glittering skyline and generous open spaces.

With all its natural advantages, not to mention one of the world's finest ports, it is no wonder most of Vancouver is booming, the Downtown core growing rapidly in a waves of gleaming new condominiums, for all that the city's eastern fringes remain grittier and, in places, downright impoverished. The boom, and Vancouver's enhanced international profile, looks set to continue, for the city is to host the 2010 Winter Olympics, the honour in no small part due to the proximity of **Whistler**, 125 km north of the Vancouver, a modern centre for skiing, boarding and other winter sports, and for hiking, in-line skating, golf and, above all, mountain biking, in the summer (the resort now has as many summer as winter visitors). Beyond Whistler stretch the endless forests and ranch country of the Fraser valley and **Cariboo** region, not without interest, but not one of British Columbia's most compelling destinations.

The so-called Sea to Sky Hwy (Hwy 99) to Whistler is the tempting of two obvious road excursions from Vancouver. The other is the 150-kilometre **Sunshine Coast**, distinguished by occasional stretches of fine coastal scenery, but experienced by most travellers only as far as Horseshoe Bay, one of several points of embarkation for ferries to Vancouver Island.

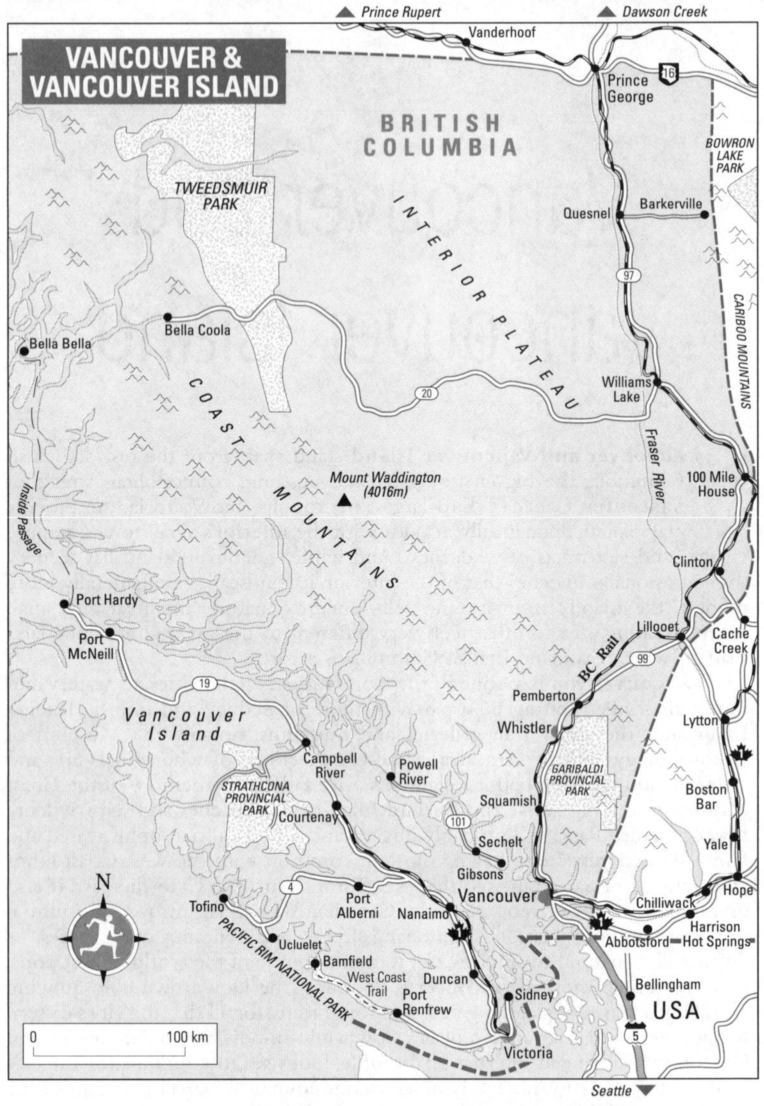

Most visitors to the island start in Victoria, easily reached by ferry or seaplane from Vancouver or nearby ferry terminals. Few break their journey en route between the cities, missing out on the **Gulf Islands**, an archipelago scattered across the Strait of Georgia between the mainland and Vancouver Island. If you have time, though, the islands' laid-back vibe, numerous small galleries, glorious seascapes and often bohemian population, make them great places in which to catch your breath for a few days.

You can also reach the islands from **Victoria**, a city that pre-dates Vancouver and which was the focus of the earliest white settlement in the region, only surrendering its primacy after the mainland gold rushes of the mid-19th century and the eventual arrival of the transcontinental railway in Vancouver in 1887. Today, the city is considerably smaller than Vancouver, a comfortable and easy-going place of solid, small-town values, a pretty waterfront, numerous gardens, excellent restaurants, one superb museum and a decidedly English ambience that it rather overplays to lure its (mostly US) visitors.

Away from Victoria, Vancouver Island moves quickly from the gentle, pastoral country of the south to the jagged peaks of **Strathcona Provincial Park** and the ravishing landscapes of the **Pacific Rim National Park**, one of the region's undoubted highlights. Of the visitors that venture farther north, most are either fishermen or whale-watchers bound for **Campbell River** or **Telegraph Cove** respectively, or those intending to catch a ferry from Port Hardy along the **Inside Passage** or **Discovery Passage** to Prince Rupert or Bella Coola, two of western Canada's most stunning journeys.

Vancouver

Cradled between the ocean and snowcapped mountains, **VANCOUVER** has a dazzling Downtown district that fills a narrow peninsula bounded by Burrard Inlet to the north, English Bay to the west and False Creek to the south. Greater Vancouver sprawls south to the Fraser River. Edged around its idyllic waterfront are fine beaches, a dynamic port and a magnificent swath of parkland, not to mention the mirror-fronted ranks of skyscrapers that look across Burrard Inlet and its bustling harbour to the residential districts of North and West Vancouver. Beyond these comfortable suburbs, the Coast Mountains rise in steep, forested slopes to form a dramatic counterpoint to the Downtown skyline and the most stunning of the city's many outdoor playgrounds. Small wonder, given Vancouver's surroundings, that Greenpeace was founded in the city.

Vancouver's over two million residents exploit their spectacular natural setting to the hilt, and when they tire of the immediate region can travel a short distance to the unimaginably vast wilderness of the BC interior. Whether it's sailing, swimming, fishing, hiking, skiing, golf or tennis, locals barely have to move to indulge in a plethora of **recreational whims**. Summer and winter the city oozes hedonism and healthy living – it comes as no surprise to find that you can lounge on beaches Downtown – typically West Coast obsessions that spill over into its sophisticated **arts and culture**. Vancouver claims a world-class museum and symphony orchestra, as well as opera, theatre and dance companies at the cutting edge of contemporary arts. Festivals proliferate throughout its mild, if occasionally rain-soaked, summer while numerous music venues provide a hotbed for up-and-coming rock bands and a burgeoning jazz scene.

Business growth continues apace in Canada's third-largest city, much of its prosperity stemming from a **port** so laden with the raw materials of the Canadian interior – lumber, wheat and minerals – that it ranks as one of North America's largest, handling more dry tonnage than the West Coast ports of

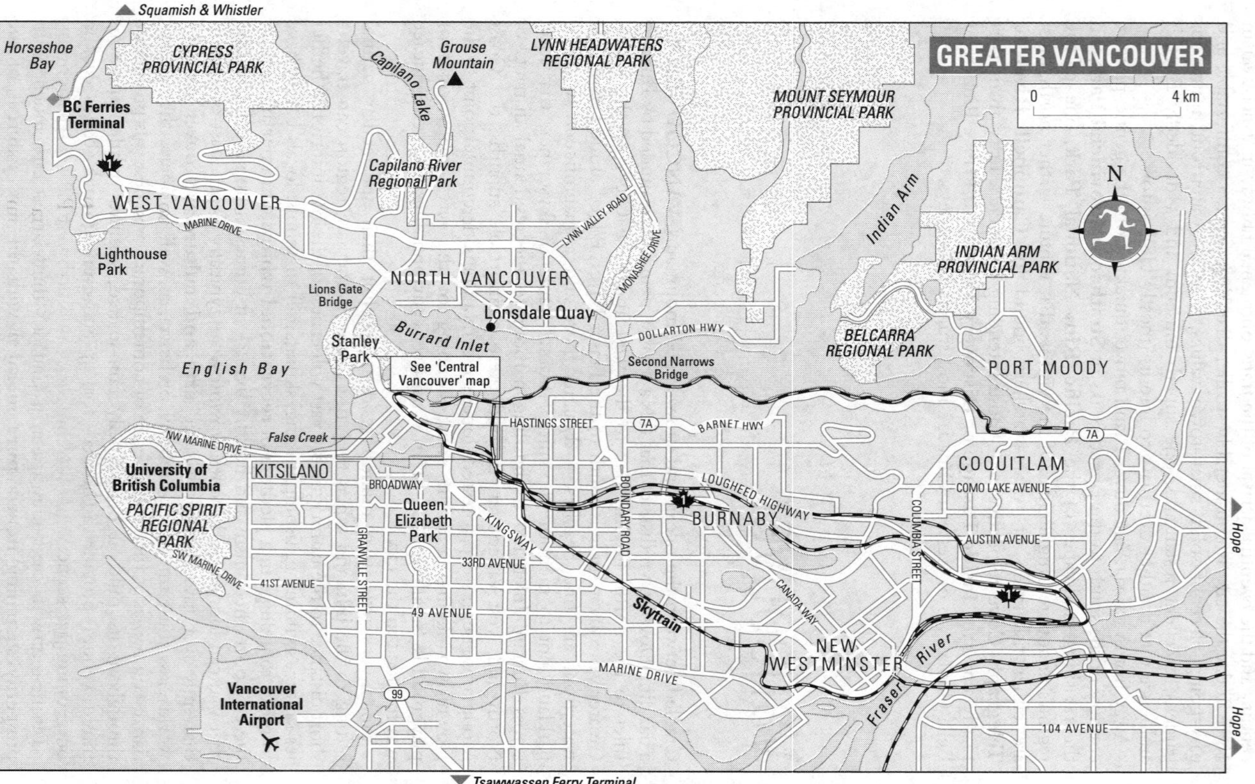
GREATER VANCOUVER
0
4 km
N
Squamish & Whistler
Horseshoe Bay
BC Ferries Terminal
CYPRESS PROVINCIAL PARK
Capilano Lake
Grouse Mountain
LYNN HEADWATERS REGIONAL PARK
MOUNT SEYMOUR PROVINCIAL PARK
Capilano River Regional Park
WEST VANCOUVER
MARINE DRIVE
Lighthouse Park
LYNN VALLEY ROAD
MONASHEE DRIVE
Indian Arm
INDIAN ARM PROVINCIAL PARK
NORTH VANCOUVER
Lions Gate Bridge
Lonsdale Quay
Burrard Inlet
DOLLARTON HWY
BELCARRA REGIONAL PARK
Stanley Park
See 'Central Vancouver' map
English Bay
Second Narrows Bridge
PORT MOODY
HASTINGS STREET
7A
BARNET HWY
7A
False Creek
NW MARINE DRIVE
University of British Columbia
KITSILANO
BROADWAY
COQUITLAM
LOUGHEED HIGHWAY
COMO LAKE AVENUE
BOUNDARY ROAD
BURNABY
Queen Elizabeth Park
PACIFIC SPIRIT REGIONAL PARK
KINGSWAY
GRANVILLE STREET
COLUMBIA STREET
AUSTIN AVENUE
Hope
SW MARINE DRIVE
41ST AVENUE
33RD AVENUE
CANADA WAY
49 AVENUE
Skytrain
NEW WESTMINSTER
River
MARINE DRIVE
Fraser
Vancouver International Airport
99
104 AVENUE
Hope
Tsawwassen Ferry Terminal

Seattle, Tacoma, Portland, San Francisco and San Diego put together. The port in turn owes its prominence to Vancouver's much-trumpeted position as a gateway to East Asia, and its increasingly pivotal role in the new global market of the **Pacific Rim**. This lucrative realignment is strengthened by a two-way flow in traffic: in the 1990s Vancouver was inundated with Hong Kong Chinese (the so-called "yacht people"), an influx that pushed up property prices and for a while strained the city's reputation as an ethnically integrated metropolis.

Much of the city's earlier immigration focused on Vancouver's extraordinary **Chinatown**, just one of a number of ethnic enclaves – Italian, Greek, Indian and Japanese in particular – which lend the city a refreshingly gritty quality that belies its sleek, modern reputation. So too do some of the city's semi-derelict eastern districts, whose worldly lowlife characters, addicts and hustlers are shockingly at odds with the glitzy lifestyles pursued in the lush residential neighbourhoods. Low rents and Vancouver's cosmopolitan young have also nurtured an unexpected **counterculture**, distinguished by varied restaurants, secondhand shops, avant-garde galleries, clubs and bars – spots where you'll probably have more fun than in many a Canadian city. And at the top of the scale there are **restaurants** as good – and as varied – as any in North America.

These days Vancouver is more dynamic than ever, its growth and energy almost palpable as you walk the streets. The Downtown population, currently around 600,000, is the fastest growing on the continent. In response the Downtown area is spreading to the older and previously run-down districts southeast of the old city core. Development over the last decade is symbolized by a superb library and performing-arts complex that constitutes the most expensive capital project ever undertaken in the city. Real estate here is now more expensive than in Toronto, and the city is North America's largest **film and TV** production centre after Los Angeles and New York. Yet, in the peculiar way that seems second nature to Canadians, the changes are being handled in a manner that's enhancing rather than compromising the city's beguiling combination of pleasure, culture, business and natural beauty.

A brief history of Vancouver

Vancouver in the modern sense has existed for a little under 120 years. Over the course of the previous nine millennia the Fraser Valley was home to the Tsawwassen, Musqueam and another twenty or so native tribes, who made up the **Stó:lo Nation**, or "people of the river". The fish, particularly salmon, of this river were the Stó:lo lifeblood. Over the millennia these people ventured relatively little into the mountainous interior, something that remains true to this day. One of the things that makes modern Vancouver so remarkable is how wild and empty British Columbia remains beyond the Fraser's narrow corridor. The Stó:lo inhabited about ten villages on the shores of Vancouver's Burrard Inlet before the coming of the Europeans. A highly developed culture, the Stó:lo were skilled carpenters, canoe-makers and artists, though little in the present city – outside its museums – pays anything but lip service to their existence. Vancouver Island is the nearest best bet if you're in search of latter-day tokens of aboriginal culture.

Europeans appeared on the scene in notable numbers during the **eighteenth century**, when Spanish explorers charted the waters along what is now southwestern British Columbia. In 1778 **Captain James Cook** reached nearby Nootka Sound while searching for the Northwest Passage, sparking off immediate British interest in the area. In 1791 José Maria Narvaez, a Spanish pilot and surveyor, glimpsed the mouth of the Fraser from his ship, the *Santa Saturnia*. This led to wrangles between the British and Spanish, disputes quickly settled in Britain's favour when Spain became domestically embroiled in the aftermath of the French Revolution. **Captain George Vancouver** officially claimed the land for Britain in 1792, but studying the Fraser from a small boat decided that it seemed too shallow to be of practical use. Instead he rounded a headland to the north, sailing into a deep natural port – the future site of Vancouver – which he named "Burrard" after one of his companions. He then traded briefly with several Squamish tribespeople at X'ay'xi, a village on the inlet's forested headland (the future Stanley Park). Afterwards the Squamish named the spot Whul-whul-Lay-ton, or "place of the white man". Vancouver sailed on, having spent just a day in the region – scant homage to an area that was to be named after him a century later.

Vancouver's error over the Fraser was uncovered in 1808, when Scottish-born **Simon Fraser** made an epic 1368-kilometre journey down the river from the Rockies to the sea. In 1827 the Hudson's Bay Company set up a fur-trading post at **Fort Langley**, 48km east of the present city, bartering not only furs but also salmon from the Stó:lo, the latter being salted and then packed off to company forts across Canada. Fort Langley was kept free of homesteaders, despite being the area's first major white settlement, their presence deemed detrimental to the fur trade. Major colonization of the area only came after the Fraser River and Cariboo gold rushes in 1858, when **New Westminster** bustled with the arrival of as many as 25,000 hopefuls, many of whom were refugees from the 1849 Californian rush. Many also drifted in from the US, underlining the fragility of the national border and the precarious nature of British claims to the region. These claims were consolidated when British Columbia was declared a crown colony with New Westminster as its capital. Both were superseded by Fort Victoria in 1868, by which time the gold rush had dwindled almost to nothing.

In 1862, meanwhile, three British prospectors, unable to find gold in the interior, bought a strip of land on the southern shore of Burrard Inlet and – shortsightedly, given the amount of lumber around – started a brickworks. This soon gave way to the Hastings Sawmill and a shantytown of bars that by 1867 had taken the name of **Gastown**, after "Gassy" – as in loquacious – Jack Leighton, proprietor of the site's first saloon. Two years later Gastown became incorporated as the town of **Granville** and prospered on the back of its timber and small coal deposits. The birth of the present city dates to 1884, when the **Canadian Pacific Railway** decided to make it the terminus of its transcontinental railway. In 1886, on a whim of the CPR president, Granville was renamed Vancouver, only to be destroyed on June 13 that year when fire razed all but half a dozen buildings. The setback proved short-lived, and since the arrival of the first train from Montréal in 1887 the city has never looked back.

Arrival

Vancouver International Airport (Ⓣ604/207-7077, Ⓦwww.yvr.ca) is situated on Sea Island, 13km south of the city centre. Its often-used coded abbreviation is YVR. International flights arrive at the majestic main terminal; domestic flights at the smaller and linked old Main Terminal. If you're an international passenger, you'll find a **tourist information** desk (daily 7am–midnight; Ⓣ604/688-5515) as you exit customs and immigration and before entering the terminal's public spaces. Close by are desks for direct bus services from the airport to Victoria (Pacific Coach Lines) and Whistler. There are also services for Bellingham Airport and Sea-Tac Airport (Seattle) in the US available outside Arrivals; see below. You will find plenty of **foreign exchange** and other facilities as well. Domestic passengers also have a tourist information desk (daily 7am–midnight) just before the terminal exit.

The best way to get into Vancouver is on the private **Airporter bus** (6.45am–1.10am; $12 single, $18 return; ⓣ604/946-8866 or 1-800/668-3141, ⓦwww.yvrairporter.com), which leaves every 15 minutes from a bay to the left immediately outside the main door of the international arrivals; from domestic arrivals you can walk here if you need Airporter information or wait at the domestic arrivals pick-up outside the terminal. You can buy **tickets** from the driver or at the bus stop by international arrivals. Resourceful staff and a pamphlet with a useful map help you figure out which drop-offs on the shuttle's three routes are most useful. Note that if you're headed straight for the bus depot (see below) on route #3 you need to transfer to another Airporter service closer to Downtown: the driver will tell you all you need to know. Returning to the airport, buses run round the same pick-up points, including the bus depot.

Taxis into town cost about $25–30, limos $42. **Public transport** is cheaper but slower and involves a change of bus – from the domestic terminal, take the BC Metro Transit bus #100 (roughly every 30min) to the corner of 70th Street and Granville, then change to the #20 or #21 which drops off Downtown on Granville Street. Tickets cost $3.25 during rush hour, $2.25 off-peak (Mon–Fri after 6.30pm, Sat & Sun all day), and exact change is required to buy tickets on board: make sure you get a transfer if the driver doesn't automatically give you one (see "City transport", p.795, for more on peak and off-peak hours and transfers).

Pacific Coach Lines (ⓣ604/662-7575 or 1-800/661-1725, ⓦwww.pacificcoach.com) runs direct buses from the airport **to Victoria** (7 daily; $41 single, $78 return). Ask for details at the bus desk in international arrivals, or go straight to the hotel shuttle bus stop outside the international terminal. Other **bus services from the airport** are run by Perimeter (ⓣ604/266-5386 or 905-0041, ⓦwww.perimeterbus.com) for services **to Whistler**; Quick Shuttle (ⓣ604/940-4428 or 1-800/665-2122, ⓦwww.quickcoach.com) to **Bellingham** Airport, Downtown **Seattle** and Sea-Tac Airport; and Malaspina Coach Lines (ⓣ604/885-2217 or 1-877/227-8287, ⓦwww.malaspinacoach.com) to the **Sunshine Coast**, Powell River, Whistler, Pemberton and **Nanaimo** on Vancouver Island.

By bus

Vancouver's main **bus terminal** is used by **Pacific Coach Lines** (ⓣ604/662-7575 or 1-800/661-1725, ⓦwww.pacificcoach.com; for Victoria, Vancouver Island), **Malaspina Coach Lines** (ⓣ604/885-2217 or 1-877/227-8287, ⓦwww.malaspinacoach.com; for the Sunshine Coast) and all **Greyhound** services (ⓣ604/482-8747 or 1-800/661-8747, ⓦwww.greyhound.ca; for BC, Alberta, Yukon and long-haul destinations including Seattle and the US). It is in a slightly dismal area alongside the VIA Rail Pacific Central train station at 1150 Station St; ticket offices for all companies are inside on the right as you enter. There are **left-luggage** facilities here and a useful **hotel board**, whose freephone line connects to some of the city's genuine cheapies (but check their locations) – some of whom will deduct the taxi fare from the terminal from your first night's bill.

It's too far to walk to Downtown from the bus terminal, so bear left from the station through a small park to the Science World–Main Street SkyTrain station, from where it's a couple of stops to Downtown (take the train marked "Waterfront"); tickets ($2.25) are available from platform machines. Alternatively, you could take a taxi Downtown from the station for about $7–9.

△ Vancouver skyline

By train

Skeletal **VIA Rail** services operate out of Pacific Central Station (Ⓣ1-888/ VIA-RAIL, Ⓦwww.viarail.ca); they run to and from Jasper (3 weekly; see p.937), where there are connections (also 3 weekly) for Prince George and Prince Rupert, and on to Edmonton and the east. There is one service run by **VIA–Amtrak** (Ⓣ253/931-8917 or 1-800/872-7245, Ⓦwww.amtrak.com) between Vancouver and Seattle (departs both stations daily 6pm; arrives Vancouver 9.30pm, arrives Seattle 9.55pm).

A second train station, belonging to the provincial **BC Rail**, at 1311 West 1st St, in North Vancouver (Ⓣ604/984-5246 or 1-800/339-8752 in BC, 1-800/663-8238 in the rest of North America, Ⓦwww.bcrail.com), once provided passenger services to and from Whistler, Lillooet and Prince George via 100 Mile House, Williams Lake and Quesnel. This service, however, has been suspended indefinitely, as have their popular excursion trips to Squamish aboard the *Royal Hudson* steam train.

Information and city transport

The excellent Vancouver visitor centre – most commonly called the "**Touristinfo Centre**" – is almost opposite Canada Place (see p.806) at the foot of Burrard Street in the Waterfront Centre, 200 Burrard St at the corner of Canada Place Way (mid-May to Sept daily 8am–6pm; rest of year Mon–Sat 8.30am–5pm; Ⓣ604/683-2000 or 1-800/663-6000 or 1-800/435-5622, Ⓦwww.tourismvancouver.com). Besides information on the city and much of south-

For information on moving on from Vancouver, see p.846.

eastern British Columbia, the office provides **foreign exchange** facilities, BC TransLink (transit or **public transport**) tickets and information, and tickets to sports and entertainment events through a separate Ticketmaster booth. Same-day tickets for events are often available at a discount. It also has one of the most comprehensive **accommodation services** imaginable, backed up by bulging photo albums of hotel rooms and B&Bs: the booking service is free.

Smaller **information kiosks** open in the summer (July & Aug daily 9.30am–5.30pm, Thurs & Fri till 9pm) in a variety of locations, usually including Stanley Park and close to the Vancouver Art Gallery on the corner of Georgia and Granville.

City transport

Vancouver's **public transport** system is an efficient, integrated network of bus, light rail (known as SkyTrain), SeaBus and ferry services that are operated by TransLink, formerly – and occasionally still – known as BC Transit (daily 6.30am–11.30pm; ⓣ604/953-3333, ⓦwww.translink.bc.ca).

Tickets are valid across the system for bus, SkyTrain and SeaBus. Generally they cost $2.25 for journeys in the large, central Zone 1, and $3.25 or $4.25 for longer two- and three-zone journeys – though you're unlikely to go out of Zone 1 unless you're travelling to the airport from Downtown, which involves crossing from Zone 1 to 2. These regular fares apply in **peak hours**: Monday to Friday from start of service until 6.30pm. In **off-peak hours** – after 6.30pm and all day Saturday, Sunday and public holidays – a flat $2.25 fare applies across all three zones. Tickets are valid for **transfers** throughout the system for ninety minutes from the time of issue; on buses you should ask for a transfer ticket if the driver doesn't automatically give you one. Otherwise, you can buy tickets individually (or in books of ten for $18 for Zone 1) at station offices or machines, 7-Eleven, Safeway and London Drugs stores, or any other shop or newsstand displaying a blue TransLink sticker (so-called "FareDealer" outlets). You must carry tickets with you as proof of payment.

Probably the simplest and cheapest deal if you're going to be making three or more journeys in a day is to buy a **DayPass** ($8), valid all day across all three zones (weekly passes are not available). If you buy these over the counter at stores or elsewhere (not in machines) they're "Scratch & Ride" – you scratch out the day and month before travel.

See "Listings" on p.844 for details of **car and bicycle rental** and **taxis**.

Buses

The useful *Transit Route Map & Guide* ($1.95) is available from the Touristinfo Centre and FareDealer shops, while free **bus** timetables can be found at the Touristinfo Centre, 7-Eleven stores and the central library. You can buy tickets on the bus, but make sure you have the right change (they don't carry any) to shovel into the box by the driver; ask specially if you want a transfer ticket. If you have a pass or transfer, simply show the driver. Normal buses stop running around midnight, when a rather patchy "Night Owl" service comes into effect on major routes until about 4am. Note that blue **West Van buses** (ⓣ604/985-7777) also operate in the city (usually to North and West Vancouver destinations, including the BC Ferries terminal at Horseshoe Bay) – TransLink tickets are valid on these buses as well.

SeaBuses

The **SeaBuses** ply between Downtown and Lonsdale Quay in North Vancouver, and they're a ride definitely worth taking for its own sake: the views

Information and hotel reservations

Tourism British Columbia ⓣ1-800/HELLO-BC (435-5622) Toll-free in North America, or ⓣ604/435-5622 or ⓣ250/387-1642 outside North America, ⓦwww.HelloBC.com.
Tourism Vancouver ⓣ604/683-2000, ⓦwww.tourismvancouver.com.

of the mountains across Burrard Inlet, the port and the Downtown skyline are superb. The Downtown terminal is Waterfront Station in the old Canadian Pacific station buildings at the foot of Granville Street. There is no ticket office, only a ticket machine, but you can get a **ticket** (same price as bus tickets) from the small newsagent immediately on your left as you face the long gallery that takes you to the boats. Two 400-seat catamarans make the thirteen-minute crossing every fifteen to thirty minutes (6.30am–12.30am). Arrival in North Vancouver is at Lonsdale Quay, where immediately to the left is a bus terminal for connections to Grouse Mountain and other North Vancouver destinations. Bicycles can be carried on board.

Ferries

The city also has a variety of small **ferries** – glorified bathtubs – run over similar routes by two rival companies: Aquabus (ⓣ604/689-5858, ⓦwww.aquabus.bc.ca) and False Creek Ferries (ⓣ604/684-7781, ⓦwww.granvilleislandferries.bc.ca). These provide a useful, very frequent and fun service (daily 7am–10.30pm, winter until 8.30pm). Aquabus runs boats in a continuous circular shuttle from the foot of Hornby Street to the Fish Docks on the seawalk to Vanier Park and the museums ($2.50), to Granville Island ($2.50), and to the Yaletown dock by the road loop at the east foot of Davie Street ($3). False Creek Ferries also runs to Granville Island ($2.50) and to Vanier Park ($3.50 from Granville Island, $2.50 from the Aquatic Centre) just below the Maritime Museum – this is a good way of getting to the park and its museums (see p.817). You buy **tickets** on board with both companies. They also offer what amount to **mini-cruises** up False Creek, with connections from Granville Island to Science World and the Plaza of Nations. You can pick up the Aquabus boat at the Arts Club Theatre on Granville Island, the foot of Hornby Street Downtown or – with False Creek Ferries – below the Aquatic Centre at the foot of Thurlow and northern end of Burrard Bridge, on Granville Island, or below the spit and small harbour near the Maritime Museum in Vanier Park.

SkyTrain

Vancouver's single light-rail line – **SkyTrain** – is a model of its type: driverless, completely computerized and magnetically propelled, half underground and half on raised track. It links the Downtown Waterfront Station (housed in the CPR building with the SeaBus terminal) and the southeastern suburb of New Westminster. Only the first three or four stations – Waterfront, Burrard, Granville and Stadium – are of any practical use to the casual visitor.

Accommodation

Vancouver has a surprisingly large number of inexpensive **hotels**, but some – mainly in the area east of Downtown – are of a dinginess at odds with the city's highly polished image. If you're on a low budget, you're better off in the **hostels** or the excellent **YWCA**. Mid-range hotels are still reasonable, but Vancouver is a tourist city and space can get tight in summer: you'll need to **book ahead**. A lot of the nicer options (including the *Sylvia*) are in the West End, a quiet residential area bordering Vancouver's wonderful Stanley Park, only five or ten minutes' walk from Downtown. Another option, if you're here to explore the parks on the city's fringe, is to take advantage of the hotels and **B&Bs** on the North Shore. Vancouver is not a camper's city: the majority of the in-city **campsites** are for RVs only and will turn you away if you only have a tent.

Hotels

Gastown, Chinatown and the area between them hold central Vancouver's cheaper **hotels**, often located on top of a bar where live bands and late-night drinking will keep you awake till the small hours. These areas are not safe for women at night, and everyone needs to avoid the backstreets. If you really need to stick to the rock-bottom price bracket, and don't fancy the hostels or YWCA, as a last resort go for one of the invariably dodgy hotels north of the Granville Street Bridge, a tame but tacky red-light area. Further up the scale, you should book in advance for the best and most popular places such as the *Sylvia* and *Kingston*.

The **North Shore** embraces North Vancouver – the area across the Burrard Inlet opposite the Downtown peninsula – and West Vancouver, the mix of residential and open country along Marine Drive and the Trans-Canada Hwy (Hwy 1) towards Lighthouse Park and Horseshoe Bay. The main reasons you may want to stay here are to access the BC Ferries terminal at Horseshoe Bay easily (see p.846) or to be more handily placed for the hikes and other outdoor activities afforded by Grouse Mountain and the Capilano River, Mount Seymour and Lyon

Vancouver bus routes

Some of the more important Vancouver **bus routes** are:
#1 Gastown–English Bay loop.
#3 and #8 Gastown–Downtown (Robson at Granville)–Marine Drive at Main.
#4 UBC and #10 UBC Granville Street–University of BC–Museum of Anthropology.
#17 and #20 Downtown–Marine Drive; transfer at Granville and 70th Street to #100 (for the airport).
#19 Pender Street (Downtown)–Stanley Park (Stanley Park Loop).
#23, #35, #123 and #135 Downtown (Pender and Burrard)–Stanley Park.
#50 Gastown–False Creek–Broadway.
#51 SeaBus Terminal–Downtown–Granville Island.
#236 Lonsdale Quay terminal (North Vancouver)–Capilano Suspension Bridge–Grouse Mountain.

Some scenic routes

These are some **scenic bus routes**, worth travelling for their own sakes:
#52 "Around the Park" service through Stanley Park (April–Oct Sat & Sun only); board at Stanley Park Loop (connections from #23, #35 or #135) or Denman Street (connections from #1, #3 or #8).
#210 Pender Street–Phibbs Exchange; change there for the #211 (mountain route) or **#212** (ocean views) to Deep Cove.
#250 Georgia Street (Downtown)–North Vancouver–West Vancouver–Horseshoe Bay.
#351 Howe Street–White Rock–Crescent Beach (1hr each way).

Bed and Breakfasts

B&B accommodation can be booked through agencies, but most of them operate as a phone service only and require two days' notice – it's better to try the Touristinfo Centre's accommodation service first (see p.794). Though seldom central or cheap – reckon on $80-plus for a double – B&Bs are likely to be relaxed and friendly, and if you choose well you can have beaches, gardens, barbecues and as little or as much privacy as you want. **B&B agencies** have accommodation throughout the city, in Victoria (see p.870), the Gulf Islands and beyond: one of the best is the Western Canada Bed and Breakfast Innkeepers' Association (ⓣ604/952-0982, ⓦwww.wcbbia.com).

Canyon parks. If this is your intention, there are some delightful **B&B** options close to the parks. However, there's no point staying here if you want to get to grips with Downtown, even if you have a car, as traffic across the Lions Gate Bridge – the only vehicular access – is often bad. Despite this, there are several reasonably priced **motels** in the area, mostly just over the Lions Gate Bridge on or close to the junction of Capilano Road and Marine Drive. If you're relying on public transport, then you'll need to use buses or the SeaCat. The city's reservation services (see p.794) can help out with North Shore lodging, but North Vancouver also has its own **visitor centre** at 102–124 West 1st St (ⓣ604/987-4488, ⓦwww.nvchamber.bc.ca) with information on the area's accommodation.

Out of season, hotels in all categories offer reductions, and you can reckon on thirty percent discounts on high-season prices. Even the smartest hotels will introduce an extra bed into a double room at very little extra cost if there are three of you.

Central Vancouver

Barclay Hotel 1348 Robson St between Jervis and Broughton sts ⓣ604/688-8850, ⓦwww.barclayhotel.com. A good bargain, the *Barclay* is one of the nicer of several hotels at the north end of Robson St, with ninety rooms and a chintzy French rustic ambience. ❹

Buchan Hotel 1906 Haro St between Chilco and Gilford sts ⓣ604/685-5354 or 1-800/668-6654, ⓦwww.buchanhotel.com. Some smallish rooms, past their prime, but still a genuine bargain given the peaceful residential location, only a block from Stanley Park and English Bay Beach. ❸–❻

Budget Inn-Patricia Hotel 403 East Hastings St near Gore St ⓣ604/255-4301, ⓦwww.budgetpathotel.bc.ca. A well-known and widely advertised budget choice with 92 rooms, but far from Downtown in the heart of Chinatown (too far to walk comfortably): an exciting or grim location, depending on your point of view, though some women have reported feeling distinctly unsafe in the area. Generally clean and reasonably renovated, it's the best of the many in this district. ❸

Burrard Motor Inn 1100 Burrard St near Helmcken St ⓣ604/681-2331 or 1-800/663-0366, ⓦwww.vancouver-bc.com/burrardmotorinn. A fairly central and pleasantly dated motel with standard fittings: some rooms look onto a charming garden courtyard, and some have kitchens. ❹

Comfort Inn Downtown 654 Nelson St ⓣ604/605-4333 or 1-888/605-5333, ⓦwww.comfortinnDowntown.com. There have been lodgings of sorts in this heritage building for years – the last was the *Hotel Dakota* – but after a 1950s retro-inspired refit, complete with lots of black and white photographs and period neon, this 82-room boutique hotel now has a hip and stylish look. Rooms all come with high-speed Internet access, voicemail, dataports and a/c. The location isn't the best but is convenient for the restaurant and clubs of both Yaletown and the lower end of Granville St. ❺

Days Inn Vancouver Downtown 921 West Pender St at Burrard St ⓣ604/681-4335 or 1-877/681-4335, ⓦwww.daysinnvancouver.com. A city institution, this old seventy-room, seven-storey block in the central financial district has more character than most and lots of original Art Deco touches. While it looks tatty from the outside, the interior is more appealing and the rooms are clean and comfortable; streetfront rooms are likely to be noisy. ❼

Dominion Hotel 210 Abbott St at Water St ⓣ604/681-6666 or 1-877/681-1666, ⓦwww.dominionhotel.bc.ca. A nice, refurbished old hotel on the edge of Gastown let down by its thunderous live music: it's almost impossible to find a room where you're not kept awake, but at least try to ask for one of the newer rooms with private bathroom as far away as possible from the live bands that play in the bar downstairs. ❸

Dufferin Hotel 900 Seymour St ⓣ604/683-4251 or 1-877/683-5522, ⓦwww.dufferinhotel.com. This 72-room hotel is not far from the preferable *Kingston* (see below), and tends to pick up its overflow. It's not as calm, cheap or pleasant as its near rival, but does offer free parking, dining room and a choice of family rooms and rooms with and without private bathrooms. Noise and late-night bustle can be an issue here, as there is a (predominantly gay, but straight-friendly) pub on the premises. ❹

Fairmont Hotel Vancouver 900 West Georgia St at Burrard St ⓣ604/684-3131 or 1-800/441-1414, ⓦwww.fairmont.com. This traditional old hotel is the city's most famous and prestigious. It's the place to stay if money's no object and you want old-world style and Downtown location. Whether you stay here or not, the ground floor *900 West* restaurant and bar is good, as are the various other restaurants, including *Griffins* on the same floor. Doubles among the 550 rooms range from $269–589, but low-season rates around $190 are available. ❽

Fairmont Waterfront 900 Canada Place Way ⓣ604/691-1991 or 1-800/441-1414, ⓦwww.fairmont.com. Another prestigious *Canadian Pacific* hotel, this time a fabulous multistorey affair on the dazzling Downtown waterfront. It's more modern than its sister hotel, the Hotel Vancouver, and has the benefit of fine outdoor pool. ❽

Four Seasons Hotel Vancouver 791 Georgia St at Howe ⓣ604/689-9333 or 1-800/332-3442, ⓦwww.fourseasons.com. A Four Seasons hotel rarely disappoints, and Vancouver's is no exception. The location is central, a block from Robson and the Vancouver Art Gallery, and the 385 rooms occupy a 28-storey high-rise building above the Pacific Centre mall. Rooms are enormous, the service immaculate, and the common parts stunning. If you're staying or not, you should definitely think about taking the buffet breakfast which is served on the Garden Terrace – it's one of the best in the city (from $13). Doubles start from about $400 for an executive suite. ❽

Granville Island Hotel 1253 Johnson St ⓣ604/683-7373 or 1-800/663-1840, ⓦwww.granvilleislandhotel.com. A polished, modern hotel, with good bar and restaurants. You're away from central Downtown, but on the other hand you're in the heart of one of the city's trendiest and most enjoyable little enclaves. You pay a premium for this and for the spectacular waterfront setting. ❼

Holiday Inn Hotel & Suites Downtown 1110 Howe St between Helmcken and Davie sts ⓣ604/684-2151 or 1-800/663-9151 in Canada and the US (also 1-800/HOLIDAY), ⓦwww.hivancouverDowntown.com. Reasonably central, large and – unlike the dingier hotels nearby – you'll know what to expect, though at this price there's plenty of alternative choice around town. Lots of facilities, including sauna, pool and kids' activity centre, plus rooms with kitchenettes for self-catering. ❻

Kingston Hotel 757 Richards St at Robson St ⓣ604/684-9024 or 1-888/713-3304, ⓦwww.kingstonhotelvancouver.com. This popular bargain is handily sited for Downtown and its clean and nicely decorated interior affects the spirit of a "European-style" hotel. Rooms are available with or without private bathroom and there's a modest but free breakfast to start the day. Along with the *Sylvia*, it's by far the best hotel at its price in the city, so book well ahead. Long-stay terms available. ❸

Opus Hotel 322 Davie St ⓣ604/642-6787 or 1-866/642-6787, ⓦwww.opushotel.com. It was only a matter of time before Yaletown aquired a hyper-trendy hotel, and in the *Opus*, opened in 2002, it has a stylish, contemporary place to stay that lives up to its hip reputation. Outside it's just another seven-storey former warehouse, but inside is a bold palette of decorative colours and materials (mosaic, marble and expensive fabrics). The 97 rooms are equally fetching – expensive linens, firm beds, CD players, big windows and great bathrooms. The cool *Opus Bar* and *Elixir* French brasserie mean you need never leave the hotel precincts for food, drink and evening relaxation – though with the temptations of Yaletown just seconds away, this would be a mistake. Rooms start from $290, with suites coming in at $479, but off-season rates are far more manageable. ❽

Pan Pacific 300–999 Canada Place ⓣ604/662-8111 or 1-800/663-1515 in Canada, 1-800/937-1515 in the US, ⓦwww.panpacific.com. If you walk around Canada Place and wonder what happens in the magnificent white high-rise that rises above the complex's famous "sails" then wonder no more, for it's occupied by the *Pan Pacific*, the most expensive and spectacularly situated of Vancouver's modern luxury hotels. An eight-storey atrium and lobby set the tone, with vast 12m picture windows that look out over the harbour. All 504 rooms enjoy great views (the hotel rooms start on the building's eighth floor),

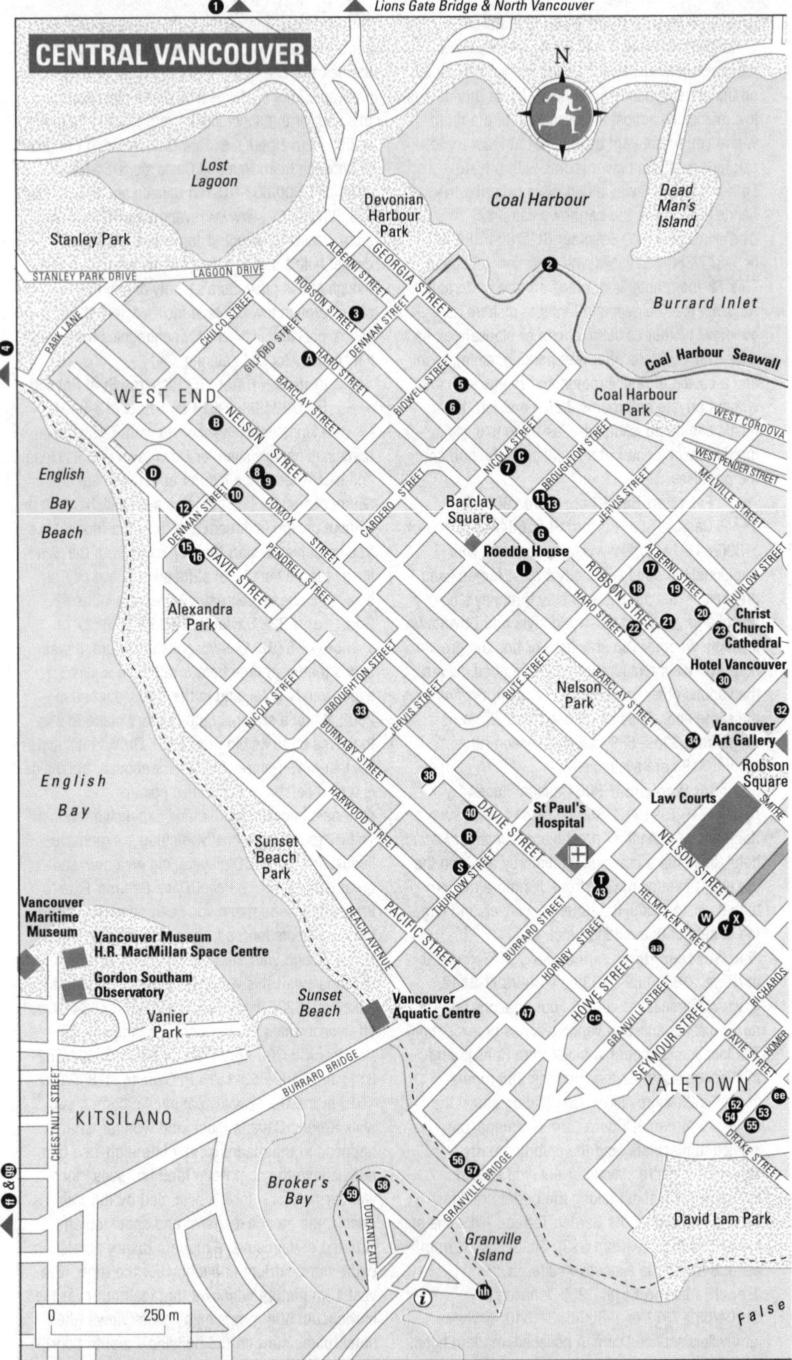
CENTRAL VANCOUVER
Lions Gate Bridge & North Vancouver
N
Lost Lagoon
Stanley Park
STANLEY PARK DRIVE
LAGOON DRIVE
Devonian Harbour Park
Coal Harbour
Dead Man's Island
Burrard Inlet
Coal Harbour Seawall
Coal Harbour Park
WEST CORDOVA
WEST PENDER STREET
MELVILLE STREET
GEORGIA STREET
ALBERNI STREET
ROBSON STREET
DENMAN STREET
CHILCO STREET
PARK LANE
GILFORD STREET
HARO STREET
BARCLAY STREET
BIDWELL STREET
WEST END
NELSON STREET
COMOX STREET
NICOLA STREET
BROUGHTON STREET
JERVIS STREET
THURLOW STREET
CARDERO STREET
English Bay Beach
Barclay Square
Roedde House
PENDRELL STREET
DAVIE STREET
Alexandra Park
Christ Church Cathedral
Hotel Vancouver
BUTE STREET
Nelson Park
Vancouver Art Gallery
Robson Square
Law Courts
SMITHE
BURNABY STREET
HARWOOD STREET
English Bay
St Paul's Hospital
Sunset Beach Park
HELMCKEN STREET
PACIFIC STREET
BEACH AVENUE
BURRARD STREET
HORNBY STREET
Vancouver Maritime Museum
Vancouver Museum H.R. MacMillan Space Centre
Gordon Southam Observatory
Vanier Park
Sunset Beach
Vancouver Aquatic Centre
HOWE STREET
GRANVILLE STREET
SEYMOUR STREET
RICHARDS
HOMER
YALETOWN
DRAKE STREET
BURRARD BRIDGE
KITSILANO
CHESTNUT STREET
Broker's Bay
DURANLEAU
GRANVILLE BRIDGE
Granville Island
David Lam Park
False
0 250 m

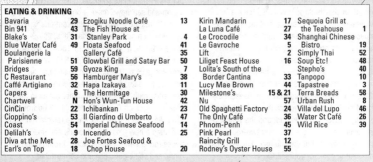

EATING & DRINKING

Name	Key
Bavaria	29
Bin 941	43
Blake's	31
Blue Water Café	49
Boulangerie la Parisienne	51
Bridges	59
C Restaurant	56
Caffé Artigiano	32
Capers	6
Chartwell	N
CinCin	22
Cioppino's	53
Coast	54
Delilah's	9
Diva at the Met	28
Earl's on Top	18
Ezogiku Noodle Café	13
The Fish House at Stanley Park	4
Floata Seafood	41
Gallery Café	35
Glowbal Grill and Satay Bar	50
Gyoza King	7
Hamburger Mary's	38
Hapa Izakaya	11
The Hermitage	30
Hon's Wun-Tun House	42
Ichibankan	23
Il Giardino di Umberto	47
Imperial Chinese Seafood	14
Incendio	25
Joe Fortes Seafood & Chop House	20
Kirin Mandarin	17
La Luna Café	27
Le Crocodile	34
Le Gavroche	5
Lift	2
Liliget Feast House	16
Lolita's South of the Border Cantina	33
Lucy Mae Brown	44
Milestone's	15 & 21
Nu	57
Old Spaghetti Factory	24
The Only Café	36
Phnom-Penh	45
Pink Pearl	37
Raincity Grill	12
Rodney's Oyster House	55
Sequoia Grill at the Teahouse	1
Shanghai Chinese Bistro	19
Simply Thai	52
Soup Etc!	48
Stepho's	40
Tanpopo	10
Tapastree	3
Terra Breads	58
Urban Rush	8
Villa del Lupo	46
Water St Café	26
Wild Rice	39

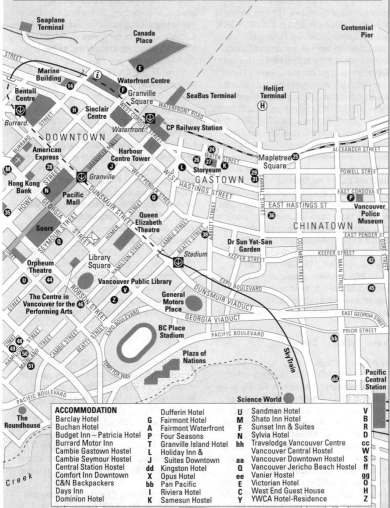

ACCOMMODATION

Name	Key
Barclay Hotel	G
Buchan Hotel	A
Budget Inn – Patricia Hotel	P
Burrard Motor Inn	T
Cambie Gastown Hostel	L
Cambie Seymour Hostel	J
Central Station Hostel	dd
Comfort Inn Downtown	X
C&N Backpackers	bb
Days Inn	I
Dominion Hotel	K
Dufferin Hotel	U
Fairmont Hotel	M
Fairmont Waterfront	F
Four Seasons	N
Granville Island Hotel	hh
Holiday Inn & Suites Downtown	aa
Kingston Hotel	Q
Opus Hotel	ee
Pan Pacific	E
Riviera Hotel	C
Samesun Hostel	Y
Sandman Hotel	V
Shato Inn Hotel	B
Sunset Inn & Suites	R
Sylvia Hotel	D
Travelodge Vancouver Centre	cc
Vancouver Central Hostel	W
Vancouver Downtown Hostel	S
Vancouver Jericho Beach Hostel	ff
Vanier Hostel	gg
Victorian Hotel	O
West End Guest House	H
YWCA Hotel-Residence	Z

and if you can snaffle rooms 10 and 20 on each floor, then your bathroom will also have a sweeping panorama. Service and facilities are impeccable, and the heated outdoor pool and health centre are both state of the art. Rooms start at around $490. ⑧

Riviera Hotel 1431 Robson St between Nicola and Broughton sts ⓣ604/685-1301 or 1-888/699-5222, ⓦwww.rivieraonrobson.com. Reasonably priced central motels such as this place, around midway between Stanley Park and the Vancouver Art Gallery, are rare; the one- and two-room suites are slightly dated, but they do have kitchenettes if you want to cook for yourself. ⑥

Sandman Hotel Downtown 180 West Georgia St at Beatty St ⓣ604/681-2211 or 1-800/726-3626, ⓦwww.sandmanhotels.com. Flagship of a mid-price chain with hotels all over western Canada and well placed at the eastern edge of Downtown. Rooms are bland but fine and spacious as far as chain hotels go, which makes this first choice if you want something one up from the *Kingston*. ⑥

Shato Inn Hotel at Stanley Park 1825 Comox St between Gilford and Denman sts ⓣ604/681-8920. A small, quiet, family-run place two blocks from the park and the beach. Some of the rooms have balconies and/or kitchen units. ⑤

Sunset Inn & Suites 1111 Burnaby between Davie and Thurlow sts ⓣ604/688-2474 or 1-800/786-1997, ⓦwww.sunsetinn.com. One of the best West End "apartment" hotels and a good spot for a longer stay – spacious studio, double or triple rooms (all with kitchens and balconies) with on-site laundry and many nearby shops. Ten minutes' walk to Downtown. ⑤

Sylvia Hotel 1154 Gilford St ⓣ604/681-9321, ⓦwww.sylviahotel.com. A local landmark located in a "heritage" building, this is a popular place with a high reputation, making reservations essential. It's by the beach two blocks from Stanley Park, and its snug bar, quiet, old-world charm and sea views make it one of Vancouver's best. Rooms are available at different prices depending on size, view and facilities. ④–⑦

Travelodge Vancouver Centre 1304 Howe St ⓣ604/682-2767 or 1-800/578-7878, ⓦwww.travelodge.com. This 66-room chain hotel has seen better days, and at $129 upwards, the rates are rather high, but like many other hotels in the area – a block off Granville and a block up from the Granville Street Bridge – extensive restoration work is putting a new gloss on the place and making the prices rather better value. Ask for a refurbished room, and you'll get clean and comfortable interiors, air-conditioning, TV, free local phone calls, free parking and access to a restaurant and heated outdoor pool. Despite the "Centre" in the name, it's not terribly central, but is convenient for the Granville Island ferry jetty. ⑤

Victorian Hotel 514 Homer St on the corner of Pender ⓣ604/681-6369 or 1-877/681-6369, ⓦwww.victorianhotel.com. The family-run *Victorian* is situated about as far east as you'd want to be, but remains within easy walking distance of Gastown and the rest of Downtown. It was built in 1898 as one of the city's first guesthouses, and has been carefully restored, so that many of its 26 rooms have a period feel, with high ceilings, hardwood floors, elegant bathrooms and old features such as original fireplaces and mouldings. Prices vary by up to $60 between double rooms, depending on whether they have private bathrooms and/or kitchenettes. All rooms have phones and small TVs, and a continental breakfast is included in the rate. ④

West End Guest House 1362 Haro St at Jervis St ⓣ604/681-2889, ⓦwww.westendguesthouse.com. A wonderful, small guesthouse with an old-time parlour and bright rooms, each with private bathroom; book well in advance. Full breakfast included. No smoking. ⑥

The North Shore

Best Western Capilano Inn & Suites 1634 Capilano Rd ⓣ604/987-8185 or 1-800/644-4227, ⓦwww.bestwesterncapilano.com. Virtually on the junction of Marine Drive and Capilano Rd, this 74-room is one of several chain motels just east of the Lions Gate Bridge. Standard rooms or rooms with kitchenettes for an additional $20, as well as laundry, restaurant and outdoor summer pool. ④

Lonsdale Quay Hotel 123 Carrie Cates Court ⓣ604/986-6111 or 1-800/836-6111, ⓦwww.lonsdalequayhotel. Tastefully appointed rooms and a location right on the Lonsdale Quay waterfront (with fabulous harbour views) and above the quay's superb market (see p.822): escalators from the market itself lead you to the hotel reception on the third floor. Posted room rates are as low as $80 off season, but you are far more likely to pay up to $225. ⑥

Lynn Canyon House B&B 3333 Robinson Rd ⓣ604/986-4741, ⓦwww.vancouverinn.com. A Tudor-style home with two cosy guest rooms 13km from Downtown a lovely garden and wooded setting close to the eponymous park and its hiking trails. ④

Mountainside Manor B&B at Grouse Mountain 5909 Nancy Greene Way ⓣ604/990-9772 or

1-800/967-1319, ⓦwww.mtnside.com. Situated off the road to Grouse Mountain (exit Hwy 1 at Capilano Rd exit north and follow the Grouse Mountain signs for about 2.5km), this ultramodern contemporary home offers four bright and airy B&B rooms. Best rooms are the Panorama Room (with Jacuzzi and views of the city, mountains and the ocean as far as Vancouver Island) and the City Room (with a four-poster bed and view of the city skyline). ❺

Ramada Inn Vancouver-North Shore 1800 Capilano Rd ⓣ604/987-4461 or 1-800/663-4055 in Canada and the US (also 1-800/HOLIDAY), ⓦwww.ramadavan.com. One block north of the Capilano Rd and Marine Drive intersection. Rates include continental breakfast, and some rooms have kitchens and/or microwaves and fridges. ❺

The Grouse Inn 1633 Capilano Drive ⓣ604/988-7101 or 1-800/779-7888, ⓦwww.grouseinn.com. Close to Downtown road links – one block east of the Lions Gate Bridge and one block south of Hwy 1 at Exit 14. Choose between 80 regular or larger superior rooms and one or two-bedroom kitchen suites (the kitchens cost an extra $29). ❺

Thistledown House B&B 3910 Capilano Rd ⓣ604/986-7173 or 1-888/633-7173, ⓦwww.thistle-down.com. A 1920 heritage building immediately east of the Capilano River park (just north of Edgemont Blvd) and en route for Grouse Mountain, offering easy access to trails; en-suite rooms are tastefully restored and furnished with antiques; there are lovely gardens; and the room rate includes a full breakfast and afternoon tea. ❻

Travelodge Vancouver Lions Gate 2060 Marine Drive ⓣ604/985-5311 or 1-800/578-7878, ⓦwww.lionsgatetravelodge.com. Noise can be a problem at this 61-room chain motel, given its busy (but convenient) position between the Lions Gate Bridge and Capilano Rd. In its favour is the fact that it was refurbished in 2002, the rooms have a/c, there's an outdoor pool, and rates are reasonable. ❸

Hostels

Vancouver has three good Hostelling International (HI) **hostels**, plus a handful of other reasonable privately run hostels. Be warned, though, that there are a rash of dirty, badly run and occasionally dangerous "hotels", "hostels" and "rooming houses", particularly on Hastings Street a few blocks either side of Main Street: don't be tempted into these. In addition to the hostels, relatively low-price accommodation is available in summer at the *Vanier Hostel* of the **University of British Columbia**, though this is a long way from Downtown.

Cambie Gastown Hostel 300 Cambie St at Cordova ⓣ604/684-6466 or 1-888/395-5335, ⓦwww.cambiehostels.com. A private hostel located in Vancouver's oldest hotel and pub (built in 1897) just off Gastown's main streets, and so with a much nicer and more central position than many of the city's hostels. Beds are arranged in two-, four- or six-bed bunk rooms, and there are laundry, luggage-storage and bike-storage (but no cooking) facilities. There's a deservedly popular and inexpensive bar-grill with good patio (the *Cambie Saloon & Grill*) downstairs, so aim for beds away from this area if you want a relatively peaceful night's sleep. Also check out the linked and good-value *General Store & Bakery* nearby at 312 Cambie. No curfew. $20 per person in a dorm room (Oct–April $18); private double or quad rooms $25 person (off season $22.50). Weekly rates available.

Cambie Seymour Hostel 515 Seymour St at West Pender ⓣ604/684-7757 or 1-888/395-5335, ⓦwww.cambiehostels.com. This is the second, newer, calmer and more central of the *Cambie*'s hostels. Like the Gastown hostel (see above), the management has made an effort to ensure that rooms in this heritage building are pleasant, secure and well kept, and provide laundry, storage, Internet and food and drink in the shape of café and *Malone's Bar & Grill* next door. No curfew. Pricing is slightly different to the Gastown hostel. Doubles in a bunk room cost $23 per person (Oct–April $20) and $27.50 per person for a double bed ($22.50 off season).

Central Station Hostel 1038 Main St ⓣ604/681-9118 or 682-2441 or 1-800/434-6060, ⓦwww.cnnbackpackers.com. This hostel opened near the main railway station in 2001 in the former *Ivanhoe Hotel*, a location that can be most kindly be described as "edgy". Each of the 104 rooms (renovated when the hostel opened) comes with sink, fridge and TV, and there's Internet access and an inexpensive restaurant and bar (with pool and darts) on site. Beds in six-bed dorm $18 ($90 weekly), singles $20, private doubles from $45 ($210 weekly).

C&N Backpackers Hostel 927 Main St ⓣ604/682-2441 or 1-888/434-6060, ⓦwww.cnnbackpackers.com. Not exactly dazzling and its location on the eastern edge of Downtown is hardly the best and so far from anything but the Pacific Central Station and bus depot – which is 150m away – that it's hard to see why anyone should want to stay here unless you'd just got in on a late bus. This said, it's convenient for the SkyTrain station, and buses #3 or #8 from Downtown run along Main St. Book or arrive early (office open 8am–midnight). No curfew. Bunks at $18 (maximum of three- or four-bed dorms) and rooms at $45 and $55 for a single and double respectively. Weekly rates available.

Samesun Hostel 1018 Granville St at Nelson ⓣ604/682-8226 or 1-888/844-7875, ⓦwww.samesun.com. *Samesun* has followed up the success of a popular hostel in Toronto with a zippy, bright hostel in Vancouver, although their chosen location on Granville St – while central and away from the worst of this street's tawdriness – is not the quietest in the city. The hostel has 250 beds in two- and four-bed rooms, and offers a free shuttle from the bus/train station, secure lockers, modern kitchen and common area, games room and Internet access. No curfew. From $27 per person ($24 Oct–May), doubles from $65.

Vancouver Central Hostel (HI) 1025 Granville St ⓣ604/685-5335 or 1-888/203-8333, ⓦwww.hihostels.ca. Vancouver's newest and smartest HI hostel on busy Granville St is a far cry from the humble days of hostelling. It offers 226 beds in private double rooms with TV and en-suite bathrooms, four-bed dorms and air-conditioning in most rooms. Family rooms are also available. Facilities include a kitchen, pub, reading lounge and shuttle runs to the other city HI hostels and the Pacific Central Station. Check-in is at noon and check-out 11am. Dorm beds start at $25 for members and $29 for non-members. Private doubles for members start at $62 ($70 for non-members).

Vancouver Downtown Hostel (HI) 1114 Burnaby St at the corner of Thurlow ⓣ604/684-4565 or 1-888/203-4302, ⓦwww.hihostels.ca. Located in a former nunnery and health-care centre in the city's West End. There are 223 beds split up between shared and private rooms (maximum of four per room). Bike rental and storage as well as laundry, kitchen, Internet access and storage lockers are available. A free shuttle (look for the blue HI logo) operates between this hostel, the Jericho Beach hostel (see below) and the Pacific Central railway and bus terminal; if there's no bus, call the hostel to find when the next one is due. No curfew. Check-in 24 hours a day; check out by 11am. Reservations are essential. Beds cost $25–28 for members ($29–32 for non-members), private doubles $70 for members, $85 for non-members.

Vancouver Jericho Beach Hostel (HI) 1515 Discovery St off NW Marine Drive ⓣ604/224-3208 or 1-888/203-4852, ⓦwww.hihostels.ca. Canada's biggest HI hostel has a superb and safe position surrounded by lawns by Jericho Beach south of the city. A former barracks, the 286-bed hostel fills up quickly, occasionally leading to a three-day limit in summer. There are dorm beds and ten private rooms (sleeping up to six) which go quickly, with reductions for members and free bunks occasionally offered in return for a couple of hours' work. Family rooms are available. Facilities include kitchen, licensed café (April–Oct), bike rental and storage, storage lockers, Internet access and an excellent cafeteria. There is no curfew, but a "quiet time" is encouraged between 11pm and 7am. Check-in 24 hours a day. Dorm beds cost $18.50 for members, $22.50 for non-members. Doubles are $58.50 for members, $67.50 for non-members.

Vanier Hostel University of British Columbia (UBC), 5961 Student Union Blvd ⓣ604/822-1000, ⓦwww.conferences.ubc.ca. This "hostel" is on the UBC campus, which means it's a long way from Downtown (see p.797 for transport details), but close to the Museum of Anthropology and trails and sights such as Wreck Beach (see p.817). You get clean, safe accommodation (bed linen included), TV lounge, laundry, an Internet kiosk in the lobby, affordable campus food outlets and pubs and access to the university's fitness facilities, tennis courts and indoor and outdoor pools. No curfew. Additional discounts are available for HI and ISIC cardholders on the room rates which start at around $25 single, $50 double. Open early May to late Aug only.

The YWCA

YWCA Hotel-Residence 733 Beatty St between Georgia and Robson ⓣ604/895-5830 or 1-800/663-1424, ⓦwww.ywcahotel.com. Vancouver's main "Y" – open to men, women, couples and families – is an excellent place, offering the best inexpensive accommodation in the city. It was purpose-built in 1995 in a handy east Downtown location close to the stunning central library. The nearest SkyTrain station is Stadium, a five-minute walk. Top-value rooms (especially for small groups) are spread over eleven floors with a choice of private, shared or hall bathrooms. There are no dorm beds. Most rooms have TVs, plus there are sports and cooking facilities, Internet access, lounges, a/c, laundry rooms as well as a cheap cafeteria and rooms with mini-kitchens. Check-in is 3pm, check-out by 11am. Rates for the various configurations of rooms come in three bands: A (from mid-Oct to April), B (May) and C (June to mid-Oct). Singles cost $53/55/61 in the three bands; doubles $57/69/75 with shared bathroom or $76/99/117 with private bathroom. Four-person rooms (two double beds) are also available from $85/115/134, plus $5 for each additional adult.

Campsites

In a city famed for its natural beauty and opportunities for outdoor activities it's something of a disappointment – and a municipal failing – that not only are there no public or private **campsites** in or near the city centre, but also none of the handful of sites that do exist could be described as memorable. To pitch a tent or hook up an RV you'll have to head to North Vancouver or the suburbs of Richmond and Burnaby, neither of which are places you'd choose to camp.

Burnaby Cariboo RV Park 8765 Cariboo Place, Burnaby ⓣ604/420-1722, ⓦwww.bcrvpark.com. This 237-pitch site about 16km east of the city centre has luxurious facilities (indoor pool, Jacuzzi, laundry, free showers and convenience store) and a separate tenting area away from the RVs (for which there are full hook-up facilities). Take the Gaglardi Way exit (#37) from Hwy 1, turn right at the traffic light, then immediately left. The next right is Cariboo Place. Open year-round. $31 per tent site, $44–47 per RV site.

Capilano RV Park 295 Tomahawk Ave, North Vancouver ⓣ604/987-4722, ⓦwww.capilanorvpark.com. This is a pretty unattractive place – think car park rather than verdant pastures – but it is the city's most central site for trailers and tents, located beneath the north foot of the Lion's Gate Bridge and a short walk from the Park Royal Shopping Centre: exit Capilano Rd South or Hwy 99 exit off Lion's Gate Bridge. There are full RV facilities and hookups, plus swimming pool, free showers, washrooms and laundry, ice and water. Reservations (with deposit) are essential June–Aug. $30–45 per site.

Park Canada Recreational Vehicles Inn 4799 Hwy 17, Delta ⓣ604/943-5811 or 1-877/943-0685, ⓦwww.parkcanada.com. Convenient for the Tsawwassen ferry terminal to the southwest, this 145-pitch site has partial and three-way hookups for RVs and – despite the name – some separate tent sites. There are free showers, washrooms, laundry, heated pool, grocery store and, if this is your thing, the site's right next to a waterslide and golf course. Tent sites $18.50, RV sites $21–27.50.

Peace Arch RV Park 14601-40 Ave, Surrey ⓣ604/594-7009, ⓦwww.peacearchrvpark.com. Calling this a city campsite is a bit of a stretch as it's about 30km southeast of Downtown near the junctions of Hwy 99 and the King George Highway. However, it's a good place to pause before hitting Vancouver if you've driven up from the US. There are 250 tent and RV sites with full hookups, a games room and a swimming pool. $22.50 per site.

The City

Vancouver is not a city that offers or requires lots of relentless sightseeing. Its breathtaking physical beauty makes it a place where often it's enough just to wander and watch the world go by – "the sort of town", wrote Jan Morris, "nearly everyone would want to live in". In summer you'll probably end up doing what the locals do, if not actually sailing, hiking, skiing, fishing or whatever, then certainly going to the beach, lounging in one of the parks or spending time in waterfront cafés.

In addition to the myriad leisure activities, however, there are a handful of sights that make worthwhile viewing by any standards. You'll inevitably spend a good deal of time in the **Downtown** area and its Victorian-era equivalent, **Gastown**, now a renovated and less than convincing pastiche of its past. **Chinatown**, too, could easily absorb a morning, and contains more than its share of interesting shops, restaurants and rumbustiously busy streets. For a taste of the city's sensuous side, hit **Stanley Park**, a huge area of semi-wild parkland

and beaches that crowns the northern tip of the Downtown peninsula. Take a walk or a bike ride here and follow it up with a stroll to the **beach**. Be certain to spend a morning on **Granville Island**, by far the city's most tempting spot for wandering and people-watching. If you prefer a cultural slant on things, hit the formidable **Museum of Anthropology** or the museums of the Vanier Park complex, the latter easily accessible from Granville Island.

At a push, you could cram the city's essentials into a couple of days. If you're here for a longer stay, though, you'll want to venture further out from Downtown: trips across Burrard Inlet to **North Vancouver**, worth making for the views from the SeaBus ferry alone, lend a different panoramic perspective of the city, and lead into the mountains and forests that give Vancouver its tremendous setting. The most popular trips here are to the Capilano Suspension Bridge, something of a triumph of PR over substance, and to the more worthwhile cable-car trip up **Grouse Mountain** for some staggering views of the city.

Downtown

You soon get the hang of Vancouver's **Downtown** district, an arena of streets and shopping malls centred on **Robson Street**. On hot summer evenings it's like a latter-day vision of *La Dolce Vita* – a dynamic meeting place crammed with bars, restaurants, late-night stores, and bronzed youths preening in bars or cafés, or ostentatiously cruising in open-topped cars. At other times a more sedate class hangs out on the steps of the Vancouver Art Gallery or glides in and out of the two big department stores, Sears and The Bay. Downtown's other principal thoroughfares are **Burrard Street** – all smart shops, hotels and offices – and **Granville Street**, partly pedestrianized with plenty of shops and cinemas, but curiously seedy in places, especially at its southern end near the Granville Street Bridge. New development, however, is taking Downtown's reach farther east, and at some point in your stay you should try to catch the **public library**, opened in 1995, at 350 West Georgia, a focus of this growth and a striking piece of modern architecture to boot.

For the best possible introduction to Vancouver, though, you should walk down to the waterfront and **Canada Place** (walkways open daily 24 hours, information ⓣ604/775-7200, ⓦwww.canadaplace.ca; free), the Canadian pavilion for Expo '86, the huge world exhibition held in the city in 1986, and another architectural tour de force that houses a luxury hotel, cruise-ship terminal and two glitzy convention centres. For all its excess, however, it makes a superb viewpoint, with stunning vistas of the port, mountains, sea and buzzing boats, helicopters and floatplanes. The port activity, especially, is mesmerizing. One of North America's busiest **ports** began by exporting timber in 1864 in the shape of fence pickets to Australia. Today it handles around seventy million tonnes of cargo annually, turns over $40 billion in trade and processes some 3000 ships a year from almost a hundred countries. Canada Place's design, and the manner in which it juts into the port, is meant to suggest a ship, and you can walk the building's perimeter as if "on deck", stopping to read the boards that describe the immediate cityscape and the appropriate pages of its history. Inside are expensive shops, an unexceptional restaurant and an IMAX cinema ($9–16; ⓣ604/682-IMAX or 1-800/582-4629, ⓦwww.imax.com/vancouver).

An alternative to Canada Place's vantage point, the nearby **Harbour Centre Building** at 555 West Hastings, is one of the city's tallest structures, and is known by locals either as the "urinal" or, more affectionately, the "hamburger", after its bulging upper storeys. On a fine day it's definitely worth paying to ride the stomach-churning, all-glass SkyLift elevators that run up the side of the tower – 167m in a minute – to the fortieth-storey observation deck, known as "The Lookout!", with its staggering 360-degree views (daily: May–mid-Oct 8.30am–10.30pm; mid-Oct–April 9am–9pm; $11; ⓣ604/689-0421, ⓦwww.vancouverlookout.com). Admission is valid all day so you can return and look out over the bright lights of Vancouver at night.

Much of the **Expo site** here and at other points to the south and east has been levelled or is undergoing rigorous redevelopment, and to see its remaining sights requires a long walk from central Downtown (take the SkyTrain or ferries from Granville Island instead). The geodesic dome is the main survivor, and has become a striking city landmark – but the museum it now houses, **Science World** at Québec St–Terminal Ave, near the Science World–Main Street SkyTrain station – is something of a disappointment (Mon–Fri 10am–5pm, Sat & Sun 10am–6pm; Science World $14.50, Omnimax $11.25 for a single feature; joint ticket for Science World entry and one Omnimax film $19.50; ⓣ604/443-7440 or 24-hour recorded line ⓣ604/443-7443, ⓦwww.scienceworld.bc.ca). Probably only children, at whom the place seems largely aimed, will be satisfied by the various high-tech, hands-on displays, which include the opportunity to make thunderous amounts of noise on electronic instruments and drum machines. Galleries deal with all manner of science-related themes, but probably the best things here if you're an adult are the building itself and the vast screen of the Omnimax Cinema at the top of the dome – though as with the similar screen at Canada Place, only a limited range of quality movies have been produced to suit the format.

The Vancouver Art Gallery

Centrally located in the imposing old city courthouse is the rather exorbitant **Vancouver Art Gallery**, at the corner of Howe and Robson sts (daily 10am–5.30pm, Tues & Thurs until 9pm; $15; ⓣ604/662-4700, ⓦwww.vanartgallery.bc.ca). The permanent collection has over 8000 works and is valued at over $100 million – but there's a problem: the only part of the collection you can be sure of seeing is the Emily Carr portion on the top floor. The other three floors are given over to (admittedly excellent) touring shows and a rotating display of parts of the permanent collection: you can never be sure quite what you will see.

The permanent collection features a rather sparse international assortment, with some of the lesser works of Warhol and Lichtenstein, and Italian, Flemish and British paintings spanning the sixteenth to twentieth centuries. In recent years, though, the gallery has made a determined effort to concentrate on contemporary works – videos, sculptures, installations and, in particular, photo-based and photoconceptual art. In the last area the gallery boasts the largest such collection in North America, including wonderful pieces by Cindy Sherman (notably her "self" portraits), Jeff Wall, Rachel Whiteread, Jenny Holzer and the magnificent monumental photographs by Andreas Gursky.

But, of course, you can't be sure you'll see these, although the fact that there are three or four temporary shows means there's often something of interest. The steep admission fee means casual visitors are taking a rather expensive chance unless you know you want to see a particular exhibition. What ultimately redeems the place are the powerful and almost surreal works of **Emily Carr** (see box p.810), who was born on Vancouver Island in 1871 and whose paintings – characterized by deep greens and blues – evoke something of the scale and intensity of the West Coast and its native peoples. The **gallery café** is also excellent, with a sun-trap of a terrace if you want to sit outside.

△ The steam clock in Gastown

where the pathologist conducting the autopsy is said to have removed a piece of Flynn's penis and placed it in formaldehyde to keep as a souvenir. The horrified chief coroner Glen McDonald, a rather more fastidious operator, is said to have pulled rank and reattached the missing piece of member to the corpse with sticky tape. The body was then dispatched to Los Angeles for burial. This was not the end of the story, for it emerged that somewhere between the

Gastown

An easy walk east of Downtown – five minutes from Canada Place and concentrated largely on Water Street – **Gastown** is a determined piece of city rejuvenation aimed fair and square at the tourist, distinguished by new cobbles, fake gas lamps, *Ye Olde English Tea Room*-type cafés and a generally over-polished patina. The name derives from "Gassy" (as in loquacious) Jack Leighton, a retired sailor turned publican and self-proclaimed "mayor", who arrived on site by canoe with his native wife and a mangy yellow dog in 1867, quickly opening a bar to service the nearby lumber mills, whose bosses banned drinking on or near the yards. Leighton's statue stands in **Maple Tree Square**, Gastown's heart, focus of its main streets and reputed site of this first tavern. Trade was brisk, and a second bar opened, soon followed by a village of sorts – "Gassy's Town" – which, though swept away by fire in 1886, formed in effect the birthplace of modern Vancouver. Over the years, the Downtown focus moved west and something of Gastown's boozy beginnings returned to haunt it, as its cheap hotels and warehouses turned into a skid row for junkies and alcoholics. By the 1970s the area was declared a historic site – the buildings are the city's oldest – and an enthusiastic beautification programme was set in motion.

The end product never quite became the dynamic, city-integrated spot the planners had hoped, and was slated for years by locals as something of a tourist trap, though recent signs suggest that interesting cafés, clubs and restaurants are slowly beginning to make themselves felt. It's certainly worth a stroll for its buskers, Sunday crowds and occasional points of interest. These do not include the hype-laden two-tonne **steam-powered clock**, the world's first (and hopefully last), at the west end of Water Street. It's invariably surrounded by visitors armed with cocked cameras, all awaiting the miniature Big Ben's toots and whistles every fifteen minutes, and bellowing performances on the hour that seem to presage imminent explosion. The steam comes from an underground system that also heats surrounding buildings.

Probably the most surprising aspect of Gastown, however, is the contrast between its manicured pavements and the down-at-heel streets immediately to the south and east. The area between Gastown and Chinatown is both a thoroughly unpleasant skid row and, nearer Gastown, a haven for secondhand clothes shops, bookshops, galleries, new designers and cheap five-and-dimes. In places, however, this area recalls Gastown's bad old days: unpleasantly seedy, pocked with the dingiest of dingy bars and hotels, and inhabited by characters to match.

The Police Centennial Museum

One sight that is worth hunting out in the area between Gastown and Chinatown is Vancouver's **Police Centennial Museum** at 240 East Cordova St (Mon–Sat 9am–5pm; shorter hours possible in winter; $7; ⓣ604/665-3346, ⓦwww.vancouverpolicemuseum.ca), a bizarre and fascinating little museum that is easily seen and leaves you well placed for a short two-block walk south to the centre of Chinatown. It's housed in the city's old Coroner's Court Building and takes its name from the fact that it was established in 1986 to celebrate the centennial of the Vancouver police force.

The building has its own place in Vancouver folklore, not least for the fact that it was here that the actor **Errol Flynn** was brought after he died in Vancouver in 1959. Flynn arrived in the city in October 1959 with his best acting days well behind him. With him was his "personal assistant", a 17-year-old blonde girl not known for her secretarial skills. Within two days Flynn had dropped dead in his rented West End apartment. The body was brought to the Coroner's Court,

West End and the morgue, a key to a Swiss safety-deposit box that Flynn wore round his neck had disappeared. When Flynn's lawyers opened the box three years later, the stock certificates and half a million dollars in cash they had expected to find were nowhere to be seen.

The **autopsy room** is still there, together with a suitably macabre selection of mangled and preserved body parts arranged around the walls. Check out the **morgue**'s cooler, penultimate resting place of many over the years. Other rooms include a **forensics lab**, a simulated autopsy room, police cell and radio room, while a variety of themed displays include sections on notorious local criminals, weapons seized from criminals (some pretty unusual), crime-scene reconstructions, gambling, uniforms, counterfeit money and a sizeable collection of firearms. More light-hearted exhibits include a collection of model police cars from around the world. Finally, the museum's "**Cop Shoppe**" has an interesting line in police-related gifts and souvenirs.

To get here by public transport, take buses #10, #16, #20, #23, #35 or #150 along Hastings Street to Main then walk one block north to East Cordova.

Chinatown

Vancouver's vibrant **Chinatown** – clustered mainly on Pender Street from Carrall to Gore and on Keefer Street from Main to Gore (buses #22 or #19 east from

Emily Carr

Emily Carr is western Canada's most celebrated painter. Born into a prosperous Victoria family in 1871, she led an almost caricatured artistic life – one that was eccentric, thwarted, ridiculed, bohemian and impoverished by turn, but also one that was ultimately successful and triumphant.

Carr's life got off to a bad start. Having been orphaned at an early age, her remaining family tried to persuade her against an artistic career, a way of life that was then deemed unsuitable for a woman. Ignoring their advice, she made her own way to San Francisco's California School of Art in 1890, aged just 19. Here, unable to make ends meet, she was forced to teach for a living, an activity she continued on her return to Victoria in 1893.

The event that sparked her creative life came in 1899, when she travelled to Ucluelet on the west coast of Vancouver Island. Here she came into contact with the aboriginal art and culture of the indigenous Nuu-chah-nulth, an experience that would influence and feature in Carr's own work for the rest of her life. She quickly realized she needed formal instruction in landscape painting, and used her teaching to finance a trip to London and further training at art schools in Westminster and Cornwall. Her sojourn in England, however, was marked by illness, and was a less than happy time. She returned to Victoria in 1904.

By now her lifestyle was what in later decades would be called artistic, but which in the provincial and largely hidebound world of early twentieth-century British Columbia was viewed as wildly eccentric or worse. Carr often travelled with either a dog or parrot for company, and in time acquired a menagerie that included cats, cockatoos, a white rat named Susie and a capuchin monkey known as Woo. Carr made pinafores for her charges to wear on walks in the park with their owner. In 1906, after travelling in Europe and Canada, she moved to a studio in Vancouver at 570 Granville St. A year later she travelled with her sister to Alaska, and for the first time encountered the aboriginal cultures and northern landscapes that would change the focus of her art. Four years later, still feeling her work lacked power and technique, she travelled to Paris where she absorbed the lessons of the new art movements

Pender, or #22 north from Burrard) – is a city apart. Vancouver's 100,000 or more Chinese make up one of North America's largest Chinatowns and are the city's oldest and largest ethnic group after the British-descended majority. Many crossed the Pacific in 1858 to join the Fraser Valley gold rush; others followed under contract to help build the Canadian Pacific Railway. Most stayed, only to find themselves being treated appallingly. Denied citizenship and legal rights until as late as 1947, the Chinese community sought safety and familiarity in a ghetto of their own, where clan associations and societies provided for new arrivals and the local poor – and helped build the distinctive houses of recessed balconies and ornamental roofs that have made the area a protected historic site.

Unlike Gastown's gimmickry, Chinatown is all genuine: shops, hotels, markets, tiny restaurants and dim alleys vie for attention amidst an incessant hustle of jammed pavements and the buzz of Chinese conversation. Virtually every building replicates an Eastern model without a trace of self-consciousness, and written Chinese characters feature everywhere in preference to English. Striking and unexpected after Downtown's high-rise glitz, the district brings you face to face with Vancouver's oft-touted multiculturalism, and helps explain why Hong Kong immigrants continue to be attracted to the city. It is, however, a district with a distinct edge, and visitors should avoid the area's dingier streets at night and parts of East Hastings near Main Street just about any time.

sweeping the city. Chief of these was the Fauve ("wild beast") school of painters, so called for the frenzied distortions, patterns and bright, almost violently coloured nature of its exponents' works. This was one of the most fertile artistic periods of the century, and in one of Europe's most febrile cities, but Carr, unable to speak French and with a dislike of big cities, seems not to have met the likes of Picasso and the other ground-breaking artists of the time.

Returning to Vancouver in 1911, Carr exhibited work from her French sojourn. The show – and another in 1913 – was panned, and her work rejected as impenetrable or offensive by British Columbia's staid critics. Ridiculed and outcast at 42, Carr retired to land inherited from her family, where she built a home, bred sheepdogs, and became a landlady to pay her bills. She also began making pottery, digging her own clay and wheeling it home in a dilapidated pram-cum-shopping trolley.

It would be almost another twenty years, in the late 1920s, before Carr's work began to find fame. Her change of fortune followed a meeting with the Group of Seven painters, a celebrated assembly of eastern Canadian artists who, like Carr, looked to the Canadian landscape for much of their inspiration. Working with renewed confidence, and gaining a degree of international recognition in the process – but little financial gain – she made repeated visits to aboriginal villages and settings. Over the next ten years she completed some of her most accomplished work, often working in the wilderness from a ramshackle caravan equipped with improvised shelters for her pets. With her health failing – she would suffer four heart attacks – she began to write during a period of convalescence. Her first book, *Klee Wyck*, was published when she was 70, taking its name – "the laughing one" – from the name given to her by the Kwakiutl people of the Pacific coast. The book dealt with her travels and life among aboriginal people, and won the Canadian Governor General's medal for literature. Three other books followed – *The Book of Small* (a chronicle of her Victoria childhood), *The House of All Sorts* (about her career as a landlady), and *Growing Pains* (her autobiography). Carr died in 1945, secure in her status as Canada's first major female artist.

Apart from the obvious culinary temptations (see "Eating and drinking", beginning on p.825), Chinatown's main points of reference are its **shops**. Some of the best boast fearsome butchery displays and such edibles as live eels, flattened ducks, hundred-year-old eggs and other stuff you'll be happy not to identify. Check out the open-air **night market** at Main and Keefer streets (May–Sept Fri–Sun 6pm–midnight), a wonderful medley of sights. Keefer Street is **bakery** row, with lots of tempting stickies on offer like moon cakes and *bao*, steamed buns with a meat or sweet-bean filling. On the corner of Keefer and Main is the Ten Ren Tea and Ginseng Company, with free tastings of a vast range of teas, many of which promise cures for a variety of ailments. In a similar vein, it's worth dropping in to one of the local **herbalists** to browse amongst their panaceas: snakeskins, reindeer antlers, buffalo tongues, dried sea horses and bears' testicles are all available if you're feeling under the weather. Ming Wo, 23 East Pender, is a fantastic cookware shop, with probably every utensil ever devised, while China West, 41 East Pender, is packed with slippers, jackets, pens, cheap toys and the like. Most people also flock dutifully to the 1913 **Sam Kee Building**, at the corner of Carrall and Pender; at just 1.8m across, it's officially the world's narrowest building.

Chinatown's chief cultural attraction is the small **Dr Sun Yat-Sen Garden**, at 578 Carrall St near Pender Street, a 2.5-acre park billed as the first authentic, full-scale classical Chinese garden ever built outside China (May to mid-June & Sept daily 10am–6pm; mid-June–Aug daily 9.30am–7pm; Oct daily 10am–4.30pm; Nov–April Tues–Sun 10am–4.30pm; $8.75; Ⓦwww.vancouverchinesegarden.com). Named after the founder of the first Chinese Republic, who was a frequent visitor to Vancouver, the park was created for Expo 86. The whole thing is based on classical gardens developed in the city of Suzhou during the Ming dynasty (1368–1644) to achieve a subtle balance of Yin and Yang: small and large, soft and hard, flowing and immovable, light and dark. Every stone, pine and flower was carefully placed and has symbolic meaning. Hourly free guided tours on the half-hour explain the Taoist philosophy behind the carefully placed elements. After a time the chances are you'll find the garden working its calm and peaceful spell.

Alongside the entrance to the gardens, the **Chinese Cultural Centre Museum & Archives** (Tues–Sun 11am–5pm; $3), Chinatown's community focus and a sponsor of New Year festivities, offers classes and hosts changing exhibitions. It also has a museum – the first of its kind dedicated to Chinese-Canadian history – which focuses on early Chinese pioneers and Chinese veterans who served Canada in the two world wars. Next to the gardens and centre is a small and slightly threadbare Dr Sun Yat-Sen Park (free), which, though less worked than the main garden, is still a pleasant place to take time out. Hours are the same as for the garden, and there's an alternative entrance on Columbia Street and Keefer.

Stanley Park

One of the world's great urban spaces, **Stanley Park** is Vancouver's green heart, helping lend the city its particular character. At nearly 1000 acres, it's the largest urban park in North America – a semi-wilderness of dense rainforest, marshland and beaches. Ocean surrounds it on three sides, with a road and parallel cycleway/pedestrian promenade following the sea wall all the way round the peninsula for a total of 10.5km (see p.814 for the park practicalities). From here, views of the city and across the water to the mountains are particularly worthwhile. Away from the coastal trail network and main draw – the aquarium – the interior is nearly impenetrable scrub and forest, with few paths and few people. At the same time there are plenty of open, wooded or flower-decorated spaces to picnic, snooze or watch the world go by.

The peninsula was partially logged in the 1860s, but in 1886 the newly formed city council – showing typical Canadian foresight and an admirable sense of priorities – moved to make what had become a military reserve into a permanent park. Thus its remaining first-growth forest of cedar, hemlock and Douglas fir, and the swamp now known as Lost Lagoon, were saved for posterity in the name of Lord Stanley, Canada's governor general from 1888 to 1893.

In the park

Taking time in the park, especially on a busy Sunday, gives a good taste of what it means to live in Vancouver. The first thing you see is the **Lost Lagoon**, a fair-sized lake that started life as a tidal inlet, and got its name because its water all but disappeared at low tide. Dozens of waterfowl species inhabit its shoreline. Just east are the pretty Rose Garden and Vancouver Rowing Club, before which stands a statue of Scottish poet Robbie Burns. From here you can follow the sea-wall path all the way, or make a more modest loop past the **totem poles** and round Brockton Point.

Walking all the way round the **sea-wall path** takes about two hours at a brisk lick. Moving around anticlockwise, odd little sights dot the promenade, all signed and explained, the most famous being the *Girl in a Wetsuit* statue, a rather lascivious update of Copenhagen's *Little Mermaid*. If you want a more focused walk, the **Cathedral Trail**, northwest of the Lost Lagoon, takes you past some big first-growth cedars. **Beaver Lake**, carpeted green with water lilies, is a peaceful spot for a sleep or a stroll. **Lumberman's Arch**, near the aquarium (see below) was raised in 1952 to honour those in the lumber industry, an odd memorial given that the industry in question would probably give its eyeteeth to fell the trees in Stanley Park. Its meadow surroundings are a favourite for families and those looking for a good napping spot. **Prospect Point**, on the park's northern tip, is a busy spot but worth braving for its beautiful view of the city and the mountains rising behind West Vancouver across the water. There's a café-restaurant here, popular for its outdoor deck and sweeping views. West of here lies **Siwash Rock**, an outcrop which has defied the weather for centuries, attracting numerous native legends in the process, and which is distinguished by its solitary tree (not visible from the road, but quickly reached by path). Further around the wall there are various places to eat and drink, the best being the *Sequoia Grill at the Teahouse* at Ferguson Point, about a kilometre beyond Siwash Rock.

Though people do swim in the sea at beaches around the park's western fringes, most bathers prefer the **swimming pool** next to Second Beach (see box, p.816). Facilities of all sorts – cafés, playgrounds, golf, outdoor dancing – proliferate near the Downtown margins. Guided **nature walks** are also occasionally offered around the park; ask at the Touristinfo Centre for details.

Vancouver Aquarium Marine Science Centre

Stanley Park Zoo, home to some all too obviously distressed animals, has now thankfully closed, leaving the **Vancouver Aquarium Marine Science Centre** as the park's most popular destination (daily: late June to early Sept 9.30am–7pm; rest of year 10am–5.30pm; $18.50; Ⓦ www.vanaqua.org). At its entrance at 845 Avison Way stands a vast killer whale in bronze, the work of celebrated Haida artist Bill Reid, whose famous *Raven and the Beast* sculpture forms the centrepiece of the Museum of Anthropology (see p.819). The aquarium is ranked among North America's best, and with over a million visitors a year claims to be the most-visited sight in Canada west of Toronto's CN Tower. It contains over 8000 living exhibits representing some 600 different species, though in truth this is a relatively modest summation of the eighty percent of the world's creatures that live in water. Like the zoo before it, the complex has been targeted by animal-rights campaigners for its treatment of performing beluga and killer whales, not to mention cooped-up seals and otters. Given the aquarium's reputation as a tourist attraction, however, as well as its claims as a research centre, the campaigners have a long, uphill battle. The whales in particular are huge draws, but you can't help but feel they should really be in the sea, for all the hoopla surrounding their $14 million marine-mammal area.

There are several key areas to see in the aquarium. The **Arctic Canada** section concerns itself with the surprisingly fragile world of the Canadian north, with a chance to see whales face to face through glass and hear the sounds of whales, walruses, seals and other creatures in this icy domain. The **Amazon Gallery** displays the vegetation, fishes, iguanas, sloths and other creatures of the rainforest in a climate-controlled environment, while the **Pacific Northwest Habitat** performs a similar role for otters, beavers and other creatures of the waters of BC. The **BC Waters Gallery** and **Ducks Unlimited Wetlands** displays are fairly self-explanatory.

Park practicalities

The park is a simple though rather dull **walk** from most of Downtown: Beach Avenue to the south and Georgia to the north are the best approaches if you're on foot, leading to either end of the sea wall. Alternatively, grab a Stanley Park **bus** #19 from the corner of Burrard and Pender streets Downtown, which drop you just inside the park by Lost Lagoon. Other buses that will take you close to the park are the #1 (Beach) to Davie and Beach Avenue and the #3 (Robson) to Denman Street. A neat **itinerary** would be to stroll or cycle all or part of the sea wall and then walk back to Denman Street, where you can

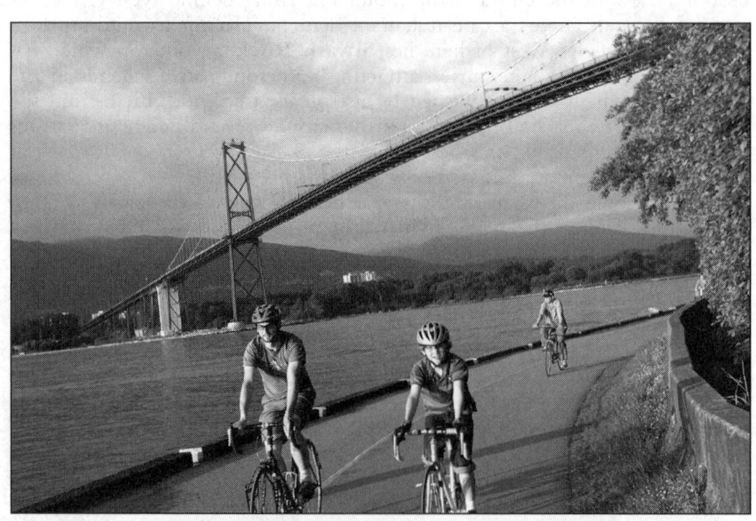

△ Biking the Stanley Park seawall

pause at one of several cafés before heading on down Denman to the grass or sand at English Bay Beach.

The corner of Denman and Georgia streets has a cluster of **bike rental** outlets. Spokes, 1798 West Georgia (Ⓣ604/688-5141, Ⓦwww.vancouverbikerentals.com), is a big, busy place established in 1938 (from $3.75/hr for a wide variety of bikes, including children's bikes and tandems with child trailers). You need to leave ID, and a cash or credit-card deposit. Helmets, which are compulsory in BC, and locks are included in the rental. A few metres up the street, Bikes 'n' Blades (Ⓣ604/602-9899)is smaller, less busy, a touch cheaper and rents **blades** as well. Directly opposite at 745 Denman St is Bayshore Bicycle & Rollerblade Rentals (Ⓣ604/688-2453, Ⓦwww.bayshorebikerentals.ca). From Denman it's just a minute's pedalling to the park, but watch the traffic.

A special TransLink "Stanley Park Shuttle" **bus**, which makes fourteen stops around the park, runs on a fifteen-minute schedule in summer (June–Aug/early Sept daily 9/10am–6.30pm; Ⓣ604/257-8400). You can transfer to the service from the #1 and #5 buses on Denman or the #19: both Denman and the Loop are a few moments' walk from the shuttle's stops at Stanley Park Entrance, Pipeline Road or the Rowing Club. The service is free, though fees may be introduced. Don't bother taking a **car** into the park, especially at weekends, when parking is just about impossible.

Granville Island

Granville Island, huddled under the Granville Street Bridge south of Downtown, is the city's most enticing "people's place" – the title it likes for itself – and pretty much lives up to its claim to be the "heart of Vancouver". Friendly, easy-going and popular, its shops, markets, galleries, marina and open spaces are juxtaposed with a light-industrial setting whose faint whiff of warehouse squalor saves the area from accusations of pretentiousness. The island was reclaimed from swampland in 1917 as an ironworks and shipbuilding centre, but by the 1960s the yards were derelict and the place had become a rat-infested dumping ground for the city's rubbish. In 1972 the federal government agreed to bankroll a programme of residential, commercial and industrial redevelopment that retained the old false-fronted buildings, tin-shack homes, sea wall and rail sidings. The best part of the job had been finished by 1979 – and was immediately successful – but work continues unobtrusively today, the various building projects only adding to the area's sense of change and dynamism. Most people come here during the day, but there are some good restaurants, bars and the Arts Club Theatre, which are all enough to keep the place buzzing at night.

Virtually the first building you see on the island walking from the bus stop augurs well: the **Granville Island Brewery**, 1441 Cartwright St (tours only: daily noon, 2pm & 4pm; $9.75; Ⓣ604/687-2739, Ⓦwww.gib.ca), a small but interesting concern which offers guided tours that include tastings of its additive-free beers. Dominant amongst the maze of shops, galleries and businesses, the **Granville Island Public Market** (daily 9am–6pm; closed Mon in winter) is the undisputed highlight of the area. On summer weekends it's where people go to see and be seen and it throngs with arts-and-crafts types, and a phalanx of dreadful buskers. The quality and variety of **food** is staggering, with dozens of kiosks and cafés selling ready-made titbits and potential picnic ingredients. Parks, patios and walkways nearby provide lively areas to eat and take everything in. Other spots to look out for include Blackberry Books, the Water Park and Kids Only Market (a kids-only playground with hoses to repel intruders) and the bright-yellow *Bridges* pub/restaurant/wine bar, which has a nice outdoor drinking and eating area. You can also **rent canoes** for straightforward paddling in False Creek and English Bay, from Ecomarine Ocean Kayak on the island at 1688 Duranleau St (ⓣ604/689-7575).

The island also has a trio of small, linked **museums** almost opposite the brewery at 1502 Duranleau St (all daily 10am–5.30pm; $7.50 for all three; ⓦwww.modeltrainsmuseum.bc.ca): these are the self-explanatory Granville Island Model Trains Museum, Model Ships Museum and Sport Fishing museum – all of limited appeal. The Model Trains Museum claims to contain the largest collection of toy trains in the world on public display.

Island practicalities

The most direct approach to Granville Island is to take **bus** #50 from Gastown or Granville Street. The walk down Granville Street and across the bridge is deceptively long, not terribly salubrious, and so probably only worthwhile on a fine day when you need the exercise. Alternatively, and more fun, private **ferries** ($2, pay on board) ply back and forth almost continuously between the island and little quays at the foot of Hornby Street or the Aquatic Centre at the foot of Thurlow Street. They also connect from Granville Island to Science World (hourly) and,

Vancouver's beaches

Vancouver, it's rather surprising to find, has **beaches** – even if much of the sand comes from Japan in container ships. All are clean and well kept; the clarity of the water is remarkable given the size of the city's port and the majority have lifeguards during the summer months.

English Bay Beach and north

The best face each other across False Creek and English Bay, starting with Stanley Park's three adjacent beaches: **English Bay Beach**, ranged along Beach Avenue is the most readily accessible, and easily visited after seeing Stanley Park; **Second Beach**, to the north, which also features a shallow onshore swimming pool (mid-May to mid-June Mon–Fri noon–8.45pm, Sat & Sun 10am–8.45pm; mid-June to mid-Sept daily 10am–8.45pm; $4.75); and **Third Beach**, further north still, least crowded of the three and the one with the best views of West Vancouver and the mountains.

Kitsilano Beach

Across the water to the south and west of the Burrard Bridge, **Kitsilano Beach**, or "Kits", is named – like the district behind it – after Chief Khahtsahlano, a Squamish chieftain of a band who once owned the area. Walk here from Vanier Park and the museums on the coast path (30min) or, from downtown, take **bus** #22 southbound on Burrard Street. Kits is the busiest and most self-conscious of the beaches. It's especially popular with the university, volleyball and rippling torso crowds. Families also come here to take advantage of the warm and safe swimming area, while sunbathers can take up a position on the grass to the rear. Vancouver's largest and most popular outdoor heated pool is the **lido** at Yew and Cornwall (mid-May to mid-June Mon–Fri noon–8.45pm, Sat & Sun 10am–8.45pm; mid-June to mid-Sept Mon–Fri 7am–8.45pm, Sat & Sun 10am–8.45pm; $4), while the **shoreline path** is a lovely place for an evening stroll, cycle or time out on a bench to watch the street life. Follow the path all the way east and it takes you to Granville Island by way of Vanier Park and the museums. A former hippie and alternative-lifestyle hangout, Kits still betrays shades of its past and, with nearby bars and restaurants to fuel the party spirit, there's always plenty going on.

more significantly, to Vanier Park (half-hourly). A logical and satisfying day's **itinerary** from Downtown, therefore, would take you to Granville Island, to the museums and back by ferry. You might also choose to **walk** from the island along the False Creek sea wall (east) or west to Vanier Park and Kitsilano Beach.

There's a good **infocentre** at the heart of the island for Island-related information only (daily 9am–6pm; ⓣ604/666-5784, ⓦwww.granvilleisland.bc.ca), with a **foreign exchange** facility in the same building and ATM machines on the wall outside. Stamps are available from the LottoCentre inside the Public Market Building. Note that many of the island's shops and businesses close on Mondays, and that if you want a **bus back** to Downtown you should *not* take the #51 from the stop opposite the infocentre (it will take you in the wrong direction): walk out of the island complex's only road entrance, and at the junction the #50 stop is immediately on your right.

Vanier Park museum complex

A little to the west of Granville Island, **Vanier Park** conveniently collects most of the city's main museums: the **Vancouver Museum**, the **Maritime**

Jericho Beach and west

Jericho Beach, west of Kits and handy for the hostel, is a touch quieter and serves as a hangout for the windsurfing crowd. Still further west, Jericho blurs into **Locarno Beach** and **Spanish Banks**, progressively less crowded, and the start of a fringe of sand and parkland that continues round to the University of British Columbia (UBC) campus. Locals rate Spanish Banks the most relaxed of the city's beaches, while Locarno is one of its most spectacular, especially at low tide, when the sand seems to stretch for ever. Bikers and walkers use the dirt track at the top of Locarno, beyond which a broad sward of grass with picnic tables and benches runs to the road. You can **rent canoes** from Ecomarine Ocean Kayak, 1668 Duranleau St (ⓣ604/689-7575 or 1-888/425-2925, ⓦwww.ecomarine.com). It also has an office at the Jericho Sailing Centre at 1300 Discovery St on Jericho Beach itself. At low tide the more athletically inclined could walk all the way round to UBC (otherwise take the bus as for the Museum of Anthropology; see p.819), where the famous clothing-optional **Wreck Beach** lies just off the campus area below NW Marine Drive – ask any student to point you towards the half-hidden access paths. It's inevitably aroused a fair bit of prudish criticism in the past, but attitudes seem more relaxed now. The atmosphere is generally laid-back – though women have been known to complain of voyeurs – and nude hawkers are often on hand to sell you anything from pizza and illegal smokeables to (bona fide) massage and hair-braiding. The beach's reputation shouldn't hide the fact that it's also a very beautiful and broad strand, edged by the ocean on one side (with many shallow and often warm pools) and bordered by lofty trees on three other flanks. It's also well looked after, thanks to the Wreck Beach Preservation Society (ⓦwww.wreckbeach.org). The best of the Wreck Beach sand is below trail #6, the trailhead for which you'll find just beyond the Nitobe garden heading away from the Museum of Anthropology.

North Vancouver

Finally, **Ambleside**, west of the Park Royal Mall along Marine Drive (turn south at 13th St W), is the most accessible beach if you're in North or West Vancouver.

Museum and the **H.R. MacMillan Space Centre** (the last combines the old planetarium and observatory). The complex sits on the waterfront at the west end of the Burrard Bridge, near Kitsilano Beach and the residential-entertainment centres of Kitsilano and West 4th Avenue; Vanier Park itself is a fine spot to while away a summer afternoon. You could easily incorporate a visit to the museums with a trip to Granville Island using the **ferry**, which docks just below the Maritime Museum. Coming from Downtown, take the #22 Macdonald **bus** south from anywhere on Burrard or West Pender – get off at the first stop after the bridge and walk down Chester Street to the park. The park is pleasant but open – there's little shade – and has a few nice patches of sandy beach on its fringes.

The Vancouver Museum

The **Vancouver Museum**, 1100 Chestnut St (daily 10am–5pm, Thurs until 9pm; $8; ⓦwww.vanmuseum.bc.ca), traces the history of the city and the lower British Columbian mainland, and invokes the area's past in its very form: the flying-saucer shape is a nod to the conical cedar-bark hats of the Northwest Coast natives, former inhabitants of the area. The fountain outside, looking like a crab on a bidet, recalls the animal of native legend that guards the port entrance.

Though it's the main focus of interest at Vanier Park, the museum is not as captivating as you might expect. It claims 300,000 exhibits, but it's hard to know where they all are, and a visit needn't take more than an hour or so. A patchy collection of baskets, tools, clothes and miscellaneous artefacts of aboriginal peoples – including a huge whaling canoe, the only example in a museum – homes in on the 8000 years before the coming of white settlers. After that, the main collection, weaving in and out of Vancouver's history up to World War I, is full of offbeat and occasionally memorable insights if you have the patience to read the material – notably the accounts of early explorers' often extraordinary exploits, the immigration section (which re-creates what it felt like to travel steerage) and the forestry displays. The twentieth-century section is a disappointment, much of it looking more like an antique shop than a museum.

The H.R. MacMillan Space Centre

The **H.R. MacMillan Space Centre**, also sometimes known as the Pacific Space Centre (daily 10am–5pm; Sept–June closed Mon; evening laser shows at varying times Thurs–Sun; Space Centre $14, additional Virtual Voyage rides $6, prices and times vary for the evening laser shows; ⓣ604/738-7827, ⓦwww.hrmacmillanspacecentre.com), incorporates the MacMillan Planetarium and a range of space-related displays and shows. Like the Vancouver Museum – which is nearby – it lies in Vanier Park and can be accessed at 1100 Crescent St or from the small ferry landing in the park. Its main draws are its 40-minute star shows – the standard planetarium fare, held several times daily – and very loud, very brash evening laser and music extravaganzas, which are very popular: arrive in good time or make reservations.

Many of the centre's exhibits are high-tech and hands-on, especially in the so-called Cosmic Courtyard, where interactive displays allow you to battle an alien, design a spaceship, guide a lunar robot or plan a voyage to Mars. Many displays also involve lots of impressive computer and other audiovisual effects, notably the Virtual Voyages Simulator, a flight simulator complete with the "motion" you might encounter during space travel and other journeys. The "rides" on the simulator last about five minutes (entrance is included with admission) and experiences range from collisions with a comet to trips on a roller coaster and simulated space flights to the planets. The GroundStation Canada Theatre shows 20-minute films on aspects of space roughly hourly from mid-morning.

The Maritime Museum

The **Maritime Museum**, 1905 Ogden Ave (May–Sept daily 10am–5pm; Oct–April Tues–Sat 10am–5pm, Sun noon–5pm; $10; Ⓦwww.vmm.bc.ca), is a short 150-metre walk from the Vancouver Museum and features lovely early photographs evoking turn-of-the-century Vancouver, though the rest of the presentation doesn't quite do justice to the status of the city as one of the world's leading ports. The less arresting displays, however, are redeemed by the renovated *St Roch*, a two-masted schooner that was the first vessel to navigate the famed Northwest Passage in a single season; it now sits impressively in its own wing of the museum, where it can be viewed by guided tour only. Special summer shows spice things up a little, as do the recent Pirates' Cove and Children's Maritime Discovery Centre, both aimed at making the museum more attractive to children. Outside, just below the museum on **Heritage Harbour** (quay for ferries to and from Granville Island), you can admire, free of charge, more restored old-fashioned vessels.

The Museum of Anthropology and around

Located well out of Downtown on the University of British Columbia campus, the **Museum of Anthropology**, 6393 NW Marine Drive is far and away Vancouver's most important museum (mid-May to early Sept daily 10am–5pm, Tues until 9pm; rest of year Tues 11am–9pm, Wed–Sun 11am–5pm; $9, free on Tues 5–9pm; Ⓦwww.moa.ubc.ca). Emphasizing the art and culture of the natives of the region, and the Haida in particular, its collection of carvings, totem poles and artefacts is unequalled in North America.

Much is made of the museum's award-winning layout, a cool and spacious collection of halls designed by Arthur Erickson, the eminent architect also responsible for converting the Vancouver Art Gallery. Particularly outstanding is the huge **Great Hall**, inspired by native cedar houses, which makes as perfect an artificial setting for its thirty-odd **totem poles** as you could ask for. Huge windows look out to more poles and Haida houses, which you're free to wander around, backed by views of Burrard Inlet and the distant mountains. Most of the poles and monolithic carvings, indoors and out, are taken from the coastal tribes of the Haida, Salish, Tsimshian and Kwakiutl, all of which share cultural elements. The suspicion – though it's never confessed – is that scholars really don't know terribly much of the arcane mythology behind the carvings, but the best guess as to their meaning is that the various animals correspond to different clans or the creatures after which the clans were named. To delve deeper into the complexities, it's worth joining an hour-long, all-year **guided walk**.

One of the museum's great virtues is that none of its displays is hidden away in basements or back rooms; instead they're jammed in overwhelming numbers into drawers and cases in the galleries to the right of the Great Hall. Most of the permanent collection revolves around **Canadian Pacific** cultures, but the **Inuit** and **Far North** exhibits are also outstanding. So, too, are the jewellery, masks and baskets of Northwest native tribes, all markedly delicate after the blunt-nosed carvings of the Great Hall. Look out especially for the argillite sculptures, made from a jet-black slate found only on BC's Haida Gwaii or

Queen Charlotte Islands. The **African** and **Asian** collections are also pretty comprehensive, if smaller, but appear as something of an afterthought alongside the indigenous artefacts. A small, technical archeological section rounds off the smaller galleries, along with a new three-gallery wing designed to house the Koerner Collection, an assortment of six hundred European ceramics dating from the fifteenth century onwards.

The museum saves its best for last. Housed in a separate rotunda, **The Raven and the Beast**, a modern sculpture designed by Haida artist Bill Reid, is the museum's pride and joy and has achieved almost iconographic status in the city. Carved from a 4.5-tonne block of cedar and requiring the attention of five people over three years, it describes the Haida legend of human evolution with stunning virtuosity, depicting terrified figures squirming from a half-open clam shell, overseen by an enormous and stern-faced raven. However, beautiful as the work is, its rotunda setting makes it seem oddly out of place – almost like a corporate piece of art.

To get to the museum, catch **bus** #10 or #4 bus south from Granville Street and stay on until the end of the line. The campus is huge and disorienting: to find the museum, turn right from the bus stop, walk along the tree-lined East Mall to the very bottom (10min), then turn left on NW Marine Drive and walk till you see the museum on the right (another 5min). In the foyer pick up a free mini-guide or the cheap larger booklet – a worthwhile investment, given the exhibits' almost total lack of labelling, but still pretty thin.

Around the museum

There are a number of odds and ends dotted around the museum, but they amount to little of real interest. For the exception, turn right out the front entrance and a five-minute walk leads to the **Nitobe Memorial Garden**, a small Japanese garden that is good for a few minutes of peace and quiet (daily: mid-March to mid-May & Sept to mid-Oct 10am–5pm; mid-May to Aug 10am–6pm; mid-Oct to mid-March Mon–Fri 10am–2.30pm; $5, joint ticket with Botanical Garden $10, free from mid-Oct to mid-March; Ⓦwww.nitobe.org). This is considered the world's most authentic Japanese garden outside Japan (despite its use of many non-Japanese species), and is full of gently curving paths, trickling streams and waterfalls, as well as numerous rocks, trees and shrubs placed with Oriental precision.

Beyond the garden lies the greater seventy-acre area of the university's **Botanical Garden**, 16th Ave and SW Marine Drive (daily 10am–6pm; mid-Oct to mid-March closes 3pm; $6, joint ticket with Nitobe Garden $8; Ⓦwww.ubcbotanicalgarden.org), established in 1916, making it Canada's oldest such garden. Non-gardeners will probably be interested only in the macabre poisonous plants of the Physick Garden, a re-created sixteenth-century monastic herb garden – though most plants here are actually medicinal rather than lethal – and the swaths of shrubs and huge trees in the Asian Garden. Dip in, as well, to the BC Native Garden, the Alpine Garden and the Food Garden.

While you're out at the university, you might also take advantage of the **University Endowment Lands**, on the opposite, west side of the museum. A huge tract of wild parkland – as large as Stanley Park, but used by a fraction of the number of people – the endowment lands boast 48km of trails and abundant wildlife (including blacktail deer, otters, foxes and bald eagles). Best of all, there are few human touches – no benches or snack bars, and only the occasional signpost.

North Vancouver

Perhaps the most compelling reason to visit **North Vancouver** (known colloquially as North Van) is the trip itself – preferably by SeaBus – which provides views of not only the Downtown skyline but also the teeming port area, a side of the city that's otherwise easily missed. Most of North Van itself is residential,

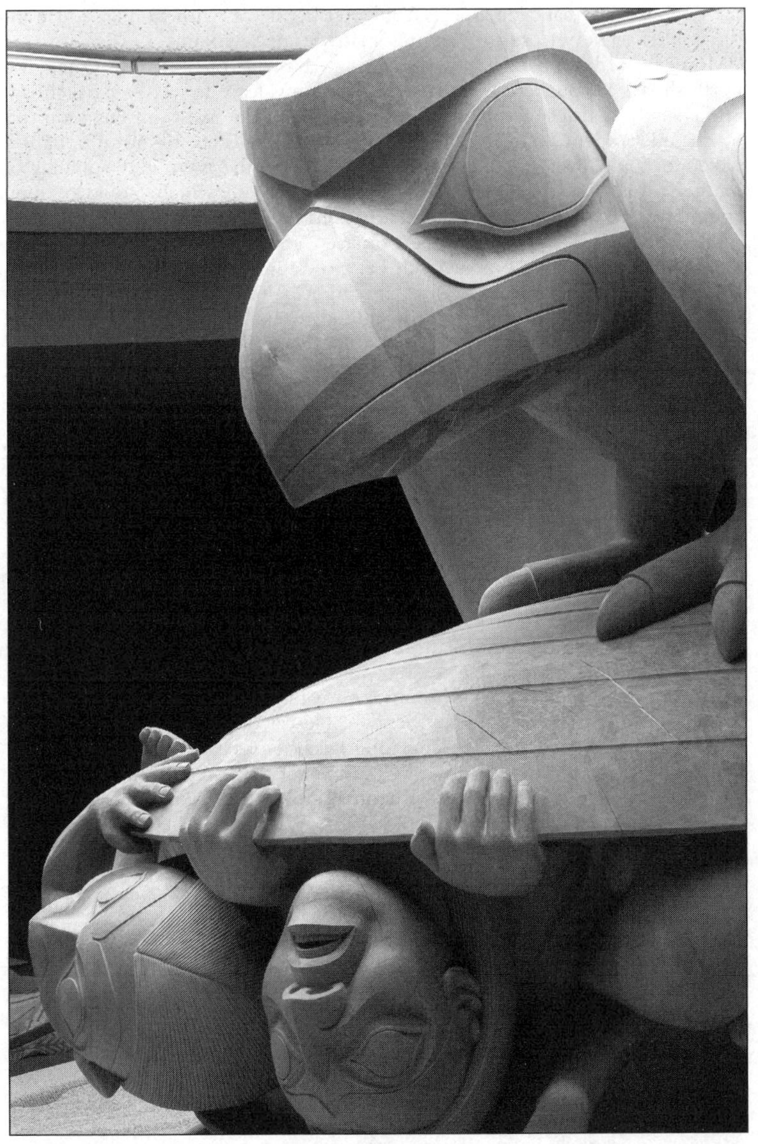

△ The Raven and the Beast

as is neighbouring **West Vancouver**, whose cosseted citizens boast the highest per capita income in Canada. You'll probably cross to the north shore less for these leafy suburbs than to sample the outstanding areas of natural beauty here: **Lynn Canyon**, **Grouse Mountain**, **Capilano Gorge** (the most popular excursion), **Mount Seymour** and **Lighthouse Park**. All are found in the mountains that rear up dramatically almost from the West Van waterfront, the proximity of Vancouver's residential areas to genuine wilderness being one of the city's most remarkable aspects. Your best bet if you wish to hike, and want the wildest scenery close to Downtown, is Mount Seymour.

Most of North Vancouver is within a single bus ride of **Lonsdale Quay**, the north shore's SeaBus terminal. **Buses** to all points leave from two parallel bays immediately in front of you as you leave the boat; blue West Van buses are run by an independent company but accept TransLink tickets. If you've bought a ticket to come over on the SeaBus, remember you have ninety minutes of transfer time to ride buses from the time of purchase, which should be long enough to get you to most of the destinations below.

The **Lonsdale Quay Market**, 123 Carrie Cates Court (Sat–Thurs 9.30am–6.30pm, Fri 9am–9pm; Nov–March Fri closes 8pm; restaurants remain open later; Ⓦwww.lonsdalequay.com), to the right of the buses, is worth making the crossing for whether or not you intend to explore further. While not as vibrant as Granville Island Market, it's still an appealing place, with great food stalls and takeaways, plus walkways looking out over the port, tugs and moored fishing boats.

Grouse Mountain

The trip to **Grouse Mountain**, named by hikers in 1894 who stumbled across a blue grouse, is a popular one. This is mainly due to the Swiss-built **cable cars** – North America's largest – which run from the 290-metre base station at 6400 Nancy Greene Way to the mountain's 1250-metre summit (daily 9am–10pm; $29.95; Ⓦwww.grousemountain.com). A favourite among people learning to **ski** or **snowboard** after work, the mountain's brightly illuminated slopes and dozen or so runs are a North Vancouver landmark on winter evenings. A day-pass costs $39; for more information call Ⓣ604/984-0661 or visit the website above. In summer, it's possible to walk up on the aptly named Grouse Grind Trail from the base station, but it's not a great hike, so you'd do better to settle instead into the inevitable queue for the cable-car ticket office (get here early if you can). After two stomach-churning lurches over the cables' twin towers you reach the summit, which, with its restaurants and allied tourist paraphernalia, is anything but wild. The views, though, are stunning, sometimes stretching as far as the San Juan Islands 160km away in Washington State. Have a quick look at the interpretive centre off to the right when you leave the cable car. A 3-D film is shown in the theatre downstairs (admission covered by your cable-car ticket). Of the two cafés, *Altitudes Bistro* has panoramic views, but fills up quickly. The smarter restaurant *The Observatory* (Ⓣ604/998-4403) serves dinner accompanied by a fine prospect of the sunset and city lights below. Rides up on the cable car are free with a restaurant booking. Ask at the centre, or small information desk just beyond the centre, about easy **guided walks** (summer daily 11am–5pm); the "Tribute to the Forest" (30min) leaves on the hour, the "Walk in the Woods" on the half-hour (35min).

Walk up the paved paths away from the centre for about five minutes and you pass a cabin office offering guided "gravity assisted" (read downhill) **bike tours** from the summit (May–Oct 3 daily; 20km trips cost from around $85, 30km $95, including cable-car fee); behind the office you can sign up for expensive

Information

Vancouver's main visitor centre (see p.792) has plenty of **information** and accommodation listings for North Van, but you might also want to consult the area's own office, the North Vancouver Visitor Infocentre, 102–124 West 1st St, North Vancouver (Mon–Fri 9am–5pm; ⓣ604/987-4488 or 980-5332, ⓦwww.nvchamber.bc.ca). Two smaller offices open daily 9am to 5pm from mid-May to early September at the bottom of Lonsdale Road by the Lonsdale Quay (ⓣ604/984-8588) and at the junction of Marine Drive and Capilano Road (ⓣ604/980-5332).

helicopter tours. On the left up the path lies the scene of the "Logging Sports" shows (twice daily; free); involving various crowd-pleasing sawing and wood-chopping displays. Just beyond this is the **Peak Chairlift** (also included in your ticket), which judders upwards for another eight minutes to the mountain's summit; views of the city and Fraser delta are even better. Check with the office at the lower cable-car base station for details of long **hikes** – many are down below rather than up at the summit proper. The best easy stroll is to **Blue Grouse Lake** (15min); the Goat Ridge Trail is for experienced hikers. More rugged paths lead into the mountains of the West Coast Range, but for these you'll need maps.

To get directly to the base station of the cable car from Lonsdale Quay, take the special #236 Grouse Mountain **bus** from Bay 8 to the left of the SeaBus terminal. You can also take a #246 Highland bus from Bay 7 and change to the #232 Grouse Mountain at Edgemount Village.

Lynn Canyon Park

Among the easiest targets for a quick taste of backwoods Vancouver is **Lynn Canyon Park** (open all year dawn to dusk), a quiet, forested area with a modest ravine and suspension bridge which, unlike the more popular Capilano Suspension Bridge (see below), you don't have to pay to cross. Several walks of up to ninety minutes take you through fine scenery – cliffs, rapids, waterfalls and, naturally, the eighty-metre-high bridge over Lynn Creek – all just twenty minutes from Lonsdale Quay. Take bus #228 from the quay to its penultimate stop at Peters Street, from where it's a ten-minute walk to the gorge; alternatively, take the less-frequent #229 Westlynn bus from Lonsdale Quay, which drops you about five minutes closer. Before entering the gorge, it's worth popping into the **Ecology Centre**, 3663 Park Rd, off Peters Rd (daily 10am–5pm; closes 4pm Oct–Feb; donation; ⓦwww.dnv.org), a friendly and informative place where you can pick up maps and pamphlets on park trails and wildlife.

Capilano River Regional Park

Lying just off the approach road to Grouse Mountain, **Capilano River Park**'s most publicized attraction is the inexplicably popular seventy-metre-high and 137-metre-long **suspension bridge** – the world's longest pedestrian suspension bridge – over the vertiginous Capilano Gorge (daily: mid-March to mid-April & late Oct 9am–6pm; late April 9am–6.30pm; early May & Sept to mid-Oct 9am–7.30pm; mid-May to Aug 8.30am–8pm; Nov to mid-March 9am–5pm; admission May–Oct $25.95, Nov–April $10.25; ⓦwww.capbridge.com). The first bridge here was built in 1889, making this Vancouver's oldest "attraction", though the present structure dates from 1956. Although part of the park, the footbridge is privately run as a money-making venture. Elsewhere in the park stick to the paths – and avoid the pedestrian toll, which buys you miscellaneous tours, forestry exhibits, trails and a visit to a native carving centre, which frankly don't amount to much. More interesting is the **salmon hatchery** just upstream (daily June–Aug 8am–8pm; May & Sept 8am–7pm; April & Oct 8am–4.45pm; Nov–March 8am–4pm; free; Ⓦwww-heb.pac.dfo-mpo.gc.ca), a provincial operation dating from 1977 designed to help salmon spawn and thus combat declining stocks. The building is well designed and the information plaques interesting, but it's a prime stop on city coach tours, so the place can often be packed.

Capilano is probably best visited on the way back from Grouse Mountain: from the cable-car station it's an easy downhill **walk** (1km) to the north end of the park, below the Cleveland Reservoir, source of Vancouver's often disconcertingly brown drinking water. From there, marked trails – notably the **Capilano Pacific Trail** – follow the eastern side of the gorge to the hatchery (2km). The area below the hatchery is worth exploring, especially the Dog's Leg Pool (1km), which is along a swirling reach of the Capilano River, and if you really want to stretch your legs you could follow the river the full 7km to its mouth on the Burrard Inlet. Alternatively, you could ride the #236 Grouse Mountain bus to the Cleveland Dam or the main park entrance – the hatchery is quickly reached via a side road (or the Pipeline Trail) from the signed main entrance left off Nancy Greene Way. This comes not far after the busy roadside entrance to the Capilano Suspension Bridge (on the bus, ring the bell for the stop after the bridge).

Mount Seymour Provincial Park

At 8668 acres, **Mount Seymour Provincial Park** is the biggest of the North Vancouver parks, the most easterly and the one that comes closest to the flavour of high-mountain scenery. It's 16km north of Vancouver and named after the short-serving BC provincial governor, Frederick Seymour (1864–69). Four major **trails** here are manageable in a day, but you should be aware that conditions can change rapidly and snow lingers as late as June. The easiest hikes go out to Goldie Lake, a half-hour stroll, and to Dog Mountain, an hour from the parking area (one-way), with great views of the city below. Still better views, requiring more effort, can be had on the trails to First and Second Pump. The wildest and most demanding hike by-passes Mount Seymour's summit and runs by way of an intermittently marked trail to the forest- and mountain-circled Elsay Lake.

Adjacent to the park to the northwest is the **Lower Seymour Conservation Reserve**, still occasionally known by its old name, the **Seymour Demonstration Forest** (Ⓦwww.gvrd.bc.ca/lscr), a 14,000-acre area of mostly temperate rainforest, nestled in the lower part of a glacier-carved valley. It's situated at the northern end of Lillooet Road and, if going by public transport, you need to take the #229 Lynn Valley bus to Dempsey Road and Lynn Valley Road. From here it's a ten-minute walk over Lynn Creek via the bridge on Rice Lake Road. You're far better off coming up here on a bike, for the 40km of trails in the area offer some of the best **mountain biking** close to Downtown. Forestry education is the area's chief concern, as the area's name suggests, and you can follow various sixty- and ninety-minute marked **hiking trails** that will top up your general knowledge about local trees, soils, fish and wildlife.

For **information** on the park, call Ⓣ604/924-2200, visit Ⓦwww.gov.bc.ca/bcparks, or ask at the city Touristinfo Centre for the blue *BC Parks* pamphlet. To get here by **bus**, take the #239 from Lonsdale Quay to Phibbs Exchange and then the #215 to the Mount Seymour Parkway (1hr) – from there you'll have to walk or cycle up the thirteen-kilometre road to the heart of the park. The road climbs to over 1000m and ends at a car park where boards

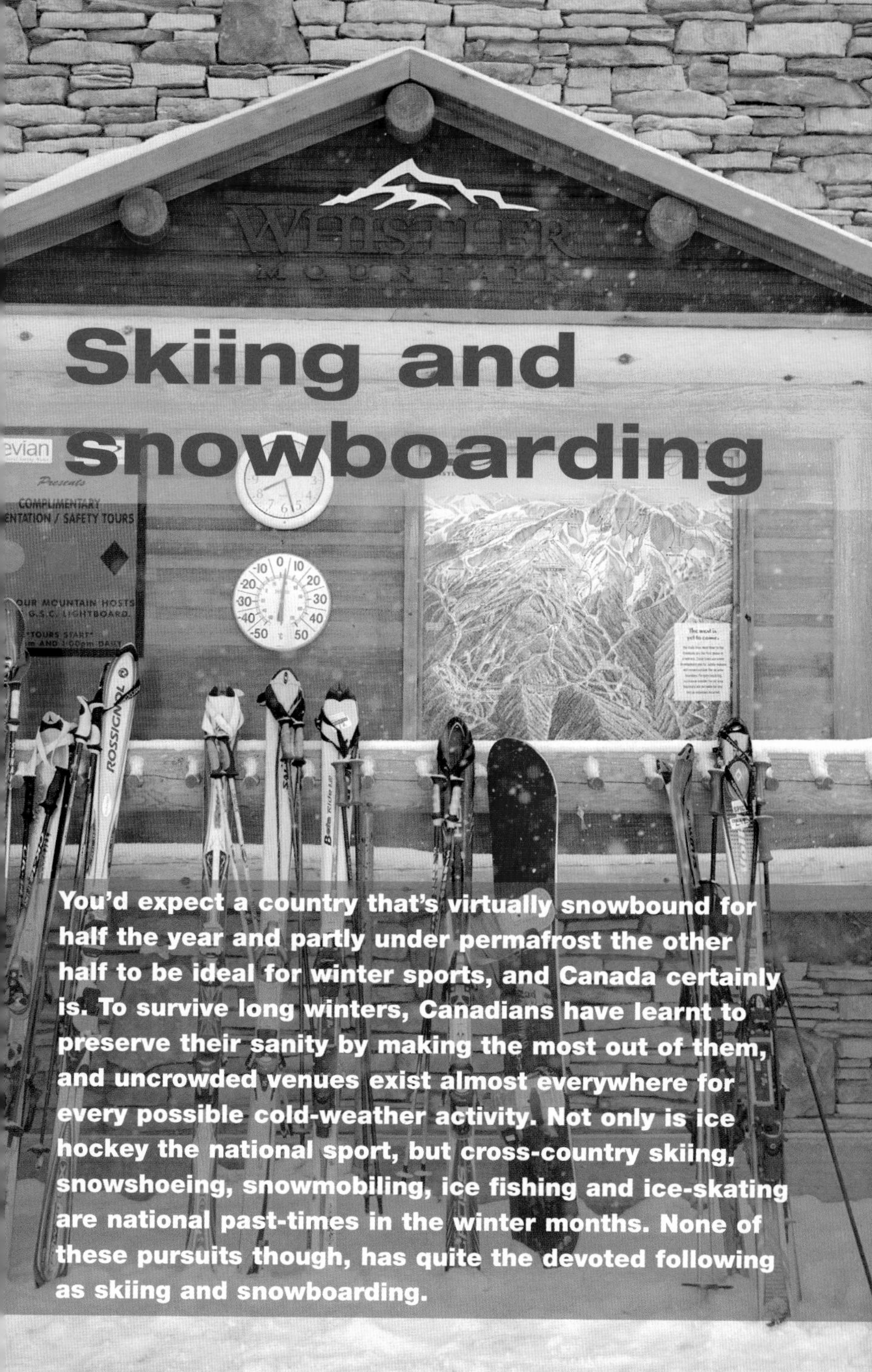

Skiing and snowboarding

You'd expect a country that's virtually snowbound for half the year and partly under permafrost the other half to be ideal for winter sports, and Canada certainly is. To survive long winters, Canadians have learnt to preserve their sanity by making the most out of them, and uncrowded venues exist almost everywhere for every possible cold-weather activity. Not only is ice hockey the national sport, but cross-country skiing, snowshoeing, snowmobiling, ice fishing and ice-skating are national past-times in the winter months. None of these pursuits though, has quite the devoted following as skiing and snowboarding.

▲ Skiing at Lake Louise

The Rocky Mountains

Most of Canada's best skiing and snowboarding is in the Rocky Mountains, and much of that around Banff. A trio of resorts – Norquay, Sunshine and Lake Louise – are served by shuttles from town, while another half-dozen are within day trip distance along with some of Canada's best heliskiing operations. Despite this, Banff is largely a summer destination and in winter you benefit from off-season prices and a more relaxed pace. This also makes the nightlife subdued, but perhaps the area's biggest drawback is its temperatures which, particularly in the early season, can be bitterly cold (-30°C is not unknown), making for uncomfortable lift rides. Yet as every experienced skier or boarder knows, these low temperatures preserve the quality of the snow; and in any case the beauty of the surrounding national park lands – where herds of elk and big-horn sheep roam streets and roadsides – more than compensate.

British Columbia

The scenery is not any less stunning in the **British Columbian Rockies**, where a series of slightly smaller resorts on the western side of the range are ideal for shorter vacations

Other winter sports

While skiing and snowboarding are, hands down, Canada's most popular winter pursuits, there are plenty of other outdoor activities to provide action on a day away from the pistes. It's never hard to find places for low-tech activities like **sledding**, **ice-skating** or **snowshoeing**; and the activities desk at most resorts will happily refer you operators providing guided horse-drawn **sleigh rides** and **snowmobile trips**. In some areas, particularly around Banff and Jasper, there's also a good chance to go **ice climbing**, **canyon crawling** or **ice-fishing**. Another option is to join the many locals who **cross-country ski**. It's especially popular in the flatter areas of the country, with ski trails maintained in and around many Canadian towns and cities. Dedicated centres also exist in many forest areas, with Canmore's **Nordic Centre** one of the best.

▶ Ice-skating, Ottawa

An overview of Canada's resorts

Almost three hundred **ski resorts** dot Canada, yet most skiers visiting from abroad head to just a handful in three main groupings: the **Rocky Mountains**, interior **British Columbia** and southern **Québec**. The season runs from mid-December until the end of May, with the **best conditions** usually in March, when the snow is at its deepest, the days get warmer and longer, and resort accommodation – hard to come by during Christmas week, the mid-February school holidays and at Easter – is easy to find.

What all Canada's resorts have in common is their great **balance of terrain,** with each ski area offering loping green-graded runs with names like *Strawberry Fields* to terrifying black-runs like *Vertigo*. The emphasis on **service** and **courtesy** is also a strong point: fast chairlifts whisk you away from tiny lift queues, and cheery mountain hosts are on hand to guide you around the resorts' invariably immaculately **groomed** and **managed** slopes where efficient snow-making equipment is at the ready in case nature fails to provide. All this makes the experience broadly similar to skiing in the US, but what distinguishes Canadian resorts – those in the Rockies, particularly – is that the mountains are far more **scenically stunning**, in league with the Alps.

▲ Mount Tremblant by night

or a trip hopping between them. Among them are: **Kicking Horse**, known for its epic backcountry-style terrain, near the town of Golden; **Panorama**, with a big vertical drop, impressive range of slopes and cosy purpose-built village; and **Kimberley**, where a good mix of uncrowded blue and black runs lie close to the eponymous Bavarian-themed town. The most remote of these resorts – yet still only two hours' drive from Calgary and three hours' from Banff – is the excellent **Fernie** with its deserved reputation for varied terrain and great powder.

With much of Canada's best snow and terrain in the Rockies, it's perhaps surprising to find Canada's biggest ski town, **Whistler**, far away on the country's western shores – close to the Pacific Ocean and Vancouver, with whom it will host the 2010 Winter Olympics. Whistler boasts the continent's biggest vertical drop, highest piste mileage and a lot of exciting runs above the tree line as well as through woodland. Whistler is also the best resort to party, with a thriving nightlife in its village. This can make the place a bit hectic and pricey, but its greatest weakness is the bad weather that rolls in from the ocean. This can provide good snow, but often it also brings rain at resort level, and days on end without the sun in sight.

To swap rain for sun head into BC's interior to the resorts clustering the **Okanagan Valley**. Northernmost of these is **Sun Peaks**, near Kamloops, where a

▲ Snowboarders sizing up a run at Whistler

large investment has created a Tirolean-style slope-side village and good intermediate and beginner terrain to go with its fabulous steeps. South along the valley, **Silver Star** is based around a tiny 'gaslight-era' 1890s-style village and offers a wooded mountain with many easy and intermediate slopes and a splendid bowl of expert trails. Further south, near Kelowna, **Big White** is BC's highest ski area, peaking at 2318m, and the province's biggest after Whistler – with a reputation for powder snow (as well as thick fog) on its many great runs. Southeast of the Okanagan Valley on the US border is the remote but exceptional **Red Mountain**, a no-nonsense resort that's a worthy pilgrimage for all lovers of steep tree runs coupled with superb powder.

▲ Flying high in Québec

Québec

Though the snow is not considered to be nearly as good as British Columbia's and conditions are often bitterly cold, eastern Canada has world-class skiing, most notably in **Québec** where the Francophone culture, language and cuisine become an extra attraction, as does the shorter flight time for Europeans and east coast Americans. Québec's single most popular resort, **Mont Tremblant**, is 120km west of Montréal and rivalled only by the cluster of resorts around Québec City: **Monte-Ste-Anne**, **Stoneham**, and **Le Massif**. In February Québec City's two-week carnival is worth a trip in itself, but otherwise winter is off-season, bringing hotel room prices tumbling.

Heliskiing

The British Columbian Rockies are still one of the best places on earth to do the terrifically expensive and fairly dangerous activity of **heliskiing**. It's a pristine mountain wonderland filled with open bowls and endless tree runs, all coated in a layer of untouched light and fluffy powder snow. Accessing these areas by helicopter intensifies the feeling of exploration and isolation – easily elevating the trip there to a once-in-a-lifetime experience.

A glut of heliski operators make access to nature's snowy bounty easy, with many one to five- or six-day trips on offer, and prices close to $1000 per day, including accommodation and meals. A more affordable option is cat-skiing, using snow cats to transport you uphill. Though less glamorous, this provides a similar experience at around a third of the price.

The heli- and cat-skiing seasons run late-November to mid-May, and with numbers small and spaces strictly limited, booking well in advance is usually essential. Most heliski operations are concentrated in the southern Rockies around Golden and Panorama; at the northern end of the range, just west of Jasper National Park; and further into British Columbia's interior around Revelstoke.

spell out clearly the trails and mountaineering options available. Views are superb on good days, particularly from the popular **Vancouver Lookout** on the parkway approach road, where a map identifies the city landmarks below. There's also a café, toilets and a small infocentre (summer only). In winter this is the most popular family and learners' **ski area** near Vancouver (Ⓣ604/986-2261, Ⓦwww.mountseymour.com; a day pass is $33).

Cypress Provincial Park

Cypress Provincial Park, most westerly of the big parks that part-cover the dramatic mountains and forest visible from Vancouver's Downtown, is among BC's most visited day-use park and probably the most popular of the north shore's protected areas. It takes its name from the huge old red and yellow cedars that proliferate here. Something of a hit with locals who prefer their wilderness just slightly tamed, its trails can be rugged and muddy, but they're always well marked, and even just a few minutes from the parking area you can feel in the depths of the great outdoors. There are several good trails, including the three-kilometre **Yew Lake Trail** – wheelchair-accessible – and the main park trail, which climbs through forest and undergrowth, occasionally opening up to reveal views. The trail also shadows part of Cypress Creek, a torrent that has cut a deep and narrow canyon. For more **information**, ask for the relevant *BC Parks* pamphlet at the Touristinfo Centre, call Ⓣ604/926-6007 or visit Ⓦwww.gov.bc.ca/bcparks. To get here, take the #253 Caulfield/Park Royal **bus**. The park also has two closely linked **ski** and **snowboard** areas: the Alpine skiing area at Cypress Bowl (Ⓣ604/926-5612, Ⓦwww.cypressmountain.com) and the Nordic ski area (Ⓣ604/922-0825) at Hollyburn just to the southwest. Day passes cost $42.

Lighthouse Park

Lighthouse Park, just southwest of Cypress, offers a seascape semi-wilderness at the extreme western tip of the north shore, 8km from the Lion's Gate Bridge. Smooth granite rocks and low cliffs line the shore, backed by huge Douglas firs up to 1500 years old, some of the best virgin forest in southern BC. The rocks make fine sun beds, though the water out here is colder than around the city beaches. A map at the car park shows the two trails to the 1912 Point Atkinson **lighthouse** itself – you can take one out and the other back, a return trip of about 5km which involves about two hours' walking. Although the park has its secluded corners (no camping allowed), it can be disconcertingly busy during summer weekends. For more **information**, contact the Touristinfo Centre or call Ⓣ604/925-7200 or 925-7000. The West Van #250 **bus** makes the journey all the way from Georgia Street in Downtown.

Eating and drinking

Vancouver's **restaurants** are some of Canada's finest, and span the price spectrum from budget to blowout. If you want to eat well, you'll be spoilt for choice – and you won't have to spend a fortune to do so. As you'd expect, the city offers a wide range of ethnic eateries. **Chinese** and **Japanese** cuisines have the highest profile (though the latter tend to be expensive), followed by **Italian**, **Greek** and other European imports. **Vietnamese** and **Thai** are more recent arrivals and can often provide the best starting points if you're on a tight budget. Specialist **seafood** restaurants are surprisingly thin on the ground, but those that exist are of high quality and often remarkably cheap. In any case, seafood does crop up on most menus and salmon is heavily featured. **Vegetarians** are well served by a number of specialist places.

Countless **cafés** are found mainly around the beaches, in parks, along Downtown streets, and especially on Granville Island. Many sell light meals as well as coffee and snack staples. The city also has a commendable assortment of **bars**, many a cut above the functional dives and sham pubs found elsewhere in BC.

Note that the definitions of bar, café, restaurant and nightclub can be considerably blurred: food in some form – usually substantial – is available in most places, while daytime cafés and restaurants also operate happily as night-time bars. In this section we've highlighted places whose main emphasis is food and drink; entertainment venues are listed under "Nightlife". Note, too, that Vancouver has a handful of places that stay open all night or until the small hours; a selection of these is given below.

Cafés and snack outlets

Little Italy, the area around Commercial Drive (between Venables and Broadway), is good for cheap, cheerful and downright trendy cafés, though as new waves of immigrants fill the area Little Italy is increasingly becoming "Little Vietnam" and "Little Nicaragua". The heavily residential **West End**, notably around Denman and Davie streets – Vancouver's "gay village" – is also booming, having gained a selection of interesting shops and restaurants.

Bavaria 203 Carrall St. A simple, no-frills Gastown place with a couple of tables outside on Maple Tree Square almost in front of Gassy Jack's statue. Particularly recommended for its inexpensive all-day breakfast: if you want something a touch more upmarket, then head for the fine *Pistol Burnes* café on the corner to the right (with lots more outside seating) or *Blake's* (see below) and *The Irish Heather* (see p.835), both just a few doors away.

Blake's 221 Carrall St near Water St. One of several cosy and relaxed places on this short Gastown stretch of Carrall St for a coffee, sandwich or snack; a good place to while away an hour writing a postcard or reading the newspaper.

Boulangerie la Parisienne 1076 Mainland St near Helmcken. A Yaletown café and bakery with striking and very pretty all-blue interior that – true to its name – opens up French-style on to the pavement in summer.

Caffè Artigiano 763 Hornby St at Robson St ⓣ604/696-9222, ⓦwww.caffeartigiano.com. Across from the Vancouver Art Gallery, this café serves the best coffee in town. You can also choose from a full crop of criossants and other pastries, plus grilled sandwiches and light pasta dishes – though quality here is not on the level of the coffee. There is an older, less cosy branch at 1101 West Pender St on the corner of Thurlow plus branches further afield at 740 West Hastings St and 2154 West 41st St.

Capers 1675 Robson, and outlets. Capers is a three-branch chain of pristine supermarkets selling natural and organic foods, many of which can be bought as sandwiches and snacks in the on-site cafés. There is a branch in West Vancouver (too far from Downtown to be useful to most casual visitors) and at 2285 West 4th Ave.

Flying Wedge 3499 Cambie ⓣ604/874-8284. If you want pizza this is the place; cheap, thin-crust pizza by the slice (but no alcohol) at five outlets, including Library Square (lunch only), Cornwall Ave (for Kits beach) and just south of the Burrard St Bridge.

Gallery Café Vancouver Art Gallery, 750 Hornby St. Relaxed, stylish and pleasantly arty place at the heart of Downtown for coffee, good lunches and healthy, high-quality food (especially desserts); also has a popular summer patio.

Hamburger Mary's 1202 Davie St between Bute and Jervis sts ⓣ604/687-1293. These may well be the best burgers in the city, though there are plenty of other things on the menu. Lots of people end the evening for a snack at this former West End diner. Outside tables when the weather is fine. Open very late (usually until 3am).

La Luna Café 117 Water St between Cambie and Abbot sts. One of only a couple of places on Gastown's main street that has the character to raise it above the usual tourist-oriented cafés in this part of the city.

The Only Café 20 East Hastings and Carrall St. One of Vancouver's most famous institutions, founded in 1912, and worth the trip to the less than salubrious part of town to sample the food and old-world atmosphere. This counter-seating greasy spoon has little more than seafood (perhaps the best in town) and potatoes on its menu. No toilets, no credit cards, no licence and no messing with the service. Mon–Sat 11am–8pm.

Sophie's Cosmic Café 2095 West 4th Ave at Arbutus St ⓣ604/732-6810. This excellent 1950s-style diner is a Kits institution and is packed out for weekend breakfasts and weekday lunch; renowned for its vast, spicy burgers, milkshakes and whopping breakfasts.

Soup Etc! 1091 Hamilton St at Helmcken St ⓣ604/689-4505, ⓦwww.soupetcetera.com. A fast-expanding chain of small oulets that draws on a range of around fifty healthy soups to present eight rotating daily specials to eat in or take out, including at least one stew, one chilli and two vegetarian options daily. Breakfasts, puddings, salads and sandwiches are also available. Other locations include Granville Mall, 575 Granville St, Lonsdale Quay, 143 Chadwick Court in North Van, and 1550 West Broadway at Fir St in Kits. Open Mon–Fri 8am–6pm, Sat & Sun 10am–5pm.

Soupspoons 2278 West 4th Ave at Vine St ⓣ604/328-7687, ⓦwww.soupspoons.com. The Joinville family came to Vancouver from Paris and brought a slew of great soup recipes with them, now sold at a small chain of deli-style soup bars. About ten daily specials (all made on the premises) are available, along with pastries and panini, focaccia and croque monsieur. There are other locations, including 1055 West Georgia St in Downtown and 990 Denman St in the West End.

Terra Breads Granville Island Public Market and branches. Tremendous rustic, grainy and fresh-baked breads are the speciality here, with black olive, rosemary, focaccia, cheese, onion, rye, raisin, grape, pine nut and other variations also available. You can also pick up the odd accompaniment and sandwich to combine with a drink from elsewhere.

Urban Rush 1040 Denman St at Comox ⓣ604/685-2996. Also in Kitsilano at 1880 West 1st at Cypress; and at 812 Bute, Downtown, off Robson. Locals love to moan about the slow service, but food in these hypertrendy deli-cafés is some of the best – and best looking – in the city. Great for people-watching.

Restaurants

Restaurants are spread around the city – check locations carefully if you don't want to travel too far from Downtown – though are naturally thinner on the ground in North and West Vancouver. Places in Gastown are generally tourist-oriented, with some notable exceptions, in marked contrast to Chinatown's bewildering plethora of authentic and reasonably priced options. Downtown also offers plenty of chains and huge choice, particularly with top-dollar places and fast-food fare: the local *White Spot* chain was founded in 1928 and has some thirty locations in Vancouver, offering good and glorified fast food if time and money are tight – the branch at 1616 West Georgia St between Seymour and Granville is the most central Downtown outlet. Superior chains like *Earl's* and *Milestones* are highly commendable, and provide a reliable choice for Downtown eating right on Robson (see "West Coast" restaurants, p.833). The old warehouse district of **Yaletown**, part of Downtown's new southeasterly spread, is also a key – and still developing – eating and nightlife area. Similar places line 4th Avenue in Kitsilano and neighbouring West Broadway, though these require something of a special journey if you're based in or around Downtown: perhaps try them for lunch if you're at the beach or visiting the nearby Vanier Park museums.

Chinese

Floata Seafood Restaurant 400-180 Keefer St ⓣ604/602-0368, ⓦwww.floata.com. Canada's largest Chinese restaurant, and one of the city's most popular places for dim sum (from $3 to $6 a shot). Despite its size – the main dining area is nearly the length of a city block – it is not easy to find: it's on the third floor of a mall close to the Dr Sun Yat-Sen Garden. Dim sum is popular – and cheap – at lunch (choose from the carts being wheeled around by countless waitresses), but in the evening menu items become more adventurous and more expensive (shark-fin and bird's-nest soups, Peking duck and so forth), with a set menu for two from $54. Daily 7.30am–10pm.

Hon's Wun-Tun House 108-268 Keefer at Gore St ⓣ604/688-0871. Started life as a cheap, basic and popular place known for the house specialities, "potstickers" – fried meat-filled dumplings – and ninety-odd soups (including fish ball and pig's feet). Success has spawned other branches and a slight smartening-up, but the encouraging queues, good food and low prices (with mains from around $6–$11) are mercifully unchanged. No alcohol or credit cards. Daily 11am–11pm.

Imperial Chinese Seafood Restaurant 355 Burrard St near Pender St ⓣ604/688-8191, ⓦwww.imperialrest.com. A grand and opulent spot in the old Marine Building with good views and busy atmosphere, serving fine, but pricey, food. Set menus start at $38 per person. Mon–Fri 11am–10.30pm, Sat & Sun 10.30am–10pm.

Kirin Mandarin 1166 Alberni near Bute St ⓣ604/682-8833, ⓦwww.kirinrestaurant.com. Among the first of the city's smart Chinese arrivals with an elegant decor that's a world away from old-fashioned Chinatown. The superior food is relatively costly, with mains from $15, but you're repaid with great views of the mountains. Daily 11am–2.30pm, 5–10.30pm.

Pink Pearl 1132 East Hastings near Glen St ⓣ604/253-4316, ⓦwww.pinkpearl.com. Big, bustling and old-fashioned with a highly authentic feel but in a dingy part of town. The moderately priced food (mains from $11–25, dim sum from about $3–6) has a Cantonese slant, strong on seafood and great for dim sum. It frequently emerges as the city's top Chinese restaurant in dining polls. Sun–Thurs 11am–9pm, Fri–Sat 11am–10pm.

Shanghai Chinese Bistro 1128 Alberni St and Thurlow St ⓣ604/683-8222. A modern-looking but less ostentatious and more reasonably priced alternative to the *Imperial*, if you want to eat Chinese Downtown. The handmade noodles are a must. Main courses come in around $20. Sun–Thurs 11.30am–11pm, Fri & Sat 11am–midnight.

Sun Sui Wah 3888 Main Street, East Vancouver ⓣ604/872-8822, ⓦwww.sunsuiwah.com. This elegant and sophisticated restaurant has won deserved rave reviews from critics and locals alike, especially for its seafood, with numerous regular dishes and special catches of the day (pick from the tank or order from the menu if you are squeamish). Main dishes start at around $12, but prices for the more exotic offerings can be three or four times this figure. Dim sum is available (also with a seafood emphasis), as are meat and vegetarian options, but when all's said and done, this place is about seafood. Open daily for dim sum 10.30am–3pm and dinner 5–10.30pm.

Wild Rice 117 West Pender St ⓣ604/642-2882, ⓦwww.wildricevancouver.com. A western take on Chinese food from a former chef at Bin 941 (see p.831), with dishes and ingredients from across China refined and reworked for Canadian consumption. Go for bite-size tasters or platters to share and don't worry too much about cost – this is high quality food at reasonable prices (mains from around $15). Dishes might include wild boar with jasmine rice and plantain, rabbit wontons, winter melon salad, crispy fried duck and warm rice pudding with chocolate and ginger. Good, short wine list and a choice of teas and martinis. Open Mon–Thurs 11.30am–midnight, Fri 11.30am–1am, Sat 5pm–1am, Sun 5pm–midnight.

Fish and seafood

Blue Water Café 1095 Hamilton St ⓣ604/688-8078, ⓦwww.bluewatercafe.net. This big restaurant has quickly become one of Yaletown's most popular fixtures, thanks to the sushi, fish and seafood, and to the attractive terrace and long interior, the last a dark, comfortable space of exposed beams and brick originally used as ballast in ships that sailed to Vancouver in the 1890s. There's an open kitchen for the fish and seafood staples, with mains around $23 (great halibut dishes, BC sablefish or salmon with pumpkin seed gnocchi), plus Eastern and Western bars (for sushi or ceviche, caviar and other treats respectively), and an Ice Bar, where you can indulge in chilled vodkas and freshly squeezed fruit juices. Service is amiable and unstuffy and quality is excellent, as you'd expect from a place run by James Walt, who has had stints at two other superb BC restaurants – *Sooke Harbour House* on Vancouver Island (see p.894) and *Araxi* in Whistler (see p.860). Daily 5am–midnight.

Coast 1257 Hamilton St near Drake St, Yaletown ⓣ604/685-5010, ⓦwwwcoastrestaurant.ca. Opened in May 2004, by the owners of the *Glowbal Grill* (see p.833), *Coast* quickly became a star of the booming Yaletown dining scene. The vibrant dining room is on two levels: bright, airy and angular, with lots of pale wood and hard surfaces. Foodies or single diners might want to go for the the "community table", edged around an open cooking area where you can watch food being prepared at close quarters. The food here is fish and seafood from various "coasts" of the world, not just that of BC, all divinely cooked and presented but at rather eye-watering prices. Thus you might choose from swordfish from New Zealand (at $27), Indian Ocean Tiger Prawns ($29), Alaska King Crab Gnocchi ($31) or "Liverpool-style" fish and chips ($23) – though it is doubtful fish and chips in Liverpool have ever been served with wild rice barley cake, lobster ragout and roasted roma tomatoes. A good choice of simply grilled fish is always available, along with a handful of "On Shore" meat dishes. Open daily 4.30pm–11pm or later.

C Restaurant 2-1600 Howe St near Pacific Blvd ⓣ604/681-1164. The *Fish House at Stanley Park* (see below) is *C*'s only serious rival for the title of best fish and seafood restaurant. The lengthy menu, which contains Southeast Asian influences, might include a choice from the "raw bar" – say a trio of scallop, wasabi salmon and smoked chilli tuna – and unusual fish such as Alaskan arctic char. Views from the dining room are good, too. Bank on around $28 for main courses. Mon–Fri 11.30am–2.30pm & 5.30–11pm, Sat 5.30–11pm, Sun 11am–2pm & 5.30–11pm.

Joe Fortes Seafood and Chop House 777 Thurlow St near Robson, Downtown ⓣ604/669-1940, ⓦwww.joefortes.ca. This long-established oyster bar-cum-chophouse and seafood restaurant (named after the Caribbean seaman who became English Bay's first lifeguard) is a city institution, noted as a hip place for high-spirited singles, Robson Street shoppers, visitors and workers, partly seduced by the great bar (drinks and oysters) upstairs on the year-round heated roof garden and terrace. The restaurant plays it straight food-wise: fish and seafood presented simply and without contemporary frills – and in generous portions. There are many varieties of oyster available, plus ever-reliable fish dishes – the trio of grilled fish (choose from several types) is always a winner. Mains cost from $20. The atmosphere is lively and casual, the saloon-style décor heavy on the mahogany and stained glass. Open daily 11am–11pm.

Rodney's Oyster House 1228 Hamilton St, Yaletown ⓣ604/609-0080. Not one of the most up-front Yaletown locations – it's tucked away in a relatively quiet dead-end street – but if you're after oysters, this fishing-shack lookalike is the place. "The lemon, the oyster and your lips are all that's required" is the pitch here. Expect anything up to 18 varieties, from locally harvested bivalves to exotic Japanese kumamotos, all laid out on ice, and priced from about $1.50 to $3.50 each. More substantial main courses cost from $15–20. There are also chowders and other dishes, plus other fresh seafood, notably Louisiana wild white shrimp and tremendous Fundy scallops. Or grab an appetizer and martini in the adjoining Mermaid Lounge. Open Mon–Sat 11am–11pm, Sun 3–10pm.

The Fish House at Stanley Park 2099 Beach Ave and Stanley Park Drive, at the north end of Beach Ave ⓣ604/681-7275. The leafy setting in the southwest corner of Stanley Park is almost that of a country estate, and the seafood arguably the city's best. Indulge at the oyster bar, order any available fish baked, broiled, steamed or grilled, and check out the daily specials. Excellent wine list and main dishes from about $20. Mon–Sat 11.30am–4pm & 5–10pm, Sun 11am–4pm & 5–10pm.

French

Cioppino's Mediterranean Grill 1133 Hamilton St ⓣ604/688-7466, ⓦwww.cioppinosyaletown.com. It's hard to categorize this inviting Yaletown restaurant with warm, cherrywood interior – the name comes from San Francisco's *cioppino* fish stew, but some food is French-influenced, other Italian. It's an attractive and convenient place if you are in this part of town. If the food seems too expensive (main courses cost from about $20–45), make instead for the *Cioppino* wine bar next door for a drink. Mon-Fri noon–2.30pm & 5.30–11pm, Sat 5.30–11pm.

The Hermitage 115-1025 Robson near Thurlow St ⓣ604/689-3237, ⓦwww.thehermitagevancouver.com. Warm brick walls, a big fireplace, crisp linen, French-speaking waiters and a courtyard setting give this central and very highly rated restaurant a cosy, almost European feel. The chef here once cooked for King Leopold of Belgium, so he knows his way around food – the onion soup is unbeatable and prices, with mains from $13, aren't bad either. Mon–Fri 11.30am–2.15pm, 5.30–10.30pm.

Le Crocodile 100-909 Burrard St, entrance on Smithe St ⓣ604/669-4298, ⓦwww.lecrocodilerestaurant.com. Plush French-Alsace upmarket bistro establishment that pushes *Bishop's* (see below) close for the title of the city's best restaurant and, unlike its rival, it's located Downtown. The menu has something for traditionalists and the more adventurous alike. A memorable meal is guaranteed, but at a price, with main courses ranging from $20 to $40. Mon–Sat 11.30am–2pm, 5.30–10pm.

Le Gavroche 1616 Alberni St at Cardero St ⓣ604/685-3924, ⓦwww.legavroche.com. The similarly priced *Le Crocodile* may just take the culinary plaudits, but this other top French restaurant (with a West Coast twist) is not far behind. A formal but amiable place and rated as one of the most romantic places in the city. Daily from 5.30pm.

Lucy Mae Brown 862 Richards St ⓣ604/899-9199, ⓦwww.lucymaebrown.ca. This intimate, moderately priced restaurant is currently one of the most popular in the city, and takes its name from the owner of a former brothel and boarding house on the site. The appealing decor is a rhapsody of blues, offset by stone and wood floors and high ceilings. Food changes regularly with the seasons, but is always lusty (lamb shanks, ahi tuna with capers) without forgetting its sophisticated French and West Coast inspiration. Reckon on between $15 and $35 for main courses. Downstairs is a secret, club-like little bar that opens late and has a simplified menu. Daily 5.30pm–2am.

Lumière 2551 West Broadway near Trafalgar St, Kitsilano ⓣ604/739-8185, ⓦwww.lumiererestaurant.ca. Local food critics regularly name this Vancouver's best restaurant. Cooking here is "contemporary French", and a touch lighter than *Le Crocodile*, though prices are equally elevated. Visitors based in Downtown will need to take a cab here; you'll also need to book, for the simple, tasteful dining room accommodates just fifty diners. Tues–Sun 5.30–11pm.

Greek

Ouzeri 3189 West Broadway at Trutch St, Kitsilano ⓣ604/739-9995, ⓦwww.ouzeri.ca. A friendly and fairly priced restaurant (mains from $10) that is the first port of call if you're at the hostel or beach in Kitsilano. Tues–Sat 11.30am–3.30pm, Mon & Sun 4.30–10pm.

Stepho's 1124 Davie St between Thurlow and Bute sts ⓣ604/683-2555. This West End restaurant has simple interior, fine food, efficient service and is very popular, thanks in part to the fair prices, with mains from $5–10. Daily 11am–11.30pm.

Indian

Vij's 1480 West 11th Ave near Granville St, Fairview ⓣ604/736-6664. The Indian cooking here has won just about every award going in Vancouver for Best Ethnic Cuisine. The menus change regularly and always include some excellent vegetarian options. Main courses cost from $15–25. The only problem – you can't book. Daily 5.30–10pm.

Italian

CinCin 1154 Robson St at Bute St ⓣ604/688-7338, ⓦwww.cincin.net. An excellent Downtown option, with stylish, buzzy setting (try to book an outside table in summer), food that merits the prices (mains from $16) and includes top-grade home-made pastas and desserts. Check the wine list – it's one of the best in the city. Mon–Fri 11am–11pm, Sat 9am–10.30pm.

Il Giardino di Umberto 1382 Hornby St at Pacific St ⓣ604/669-2422, ⓦwww.umberto.com. Sublime and expensive food (mains from $15–35) with a bias towards pasta and game served to a trendy and casually smart thirty-something clientele. Weekend reservations are essential, especially for the nice vine-trailed outside terrace. Mon–Fri 11.30am–3pm, 6–11.30pm, Sat 6.30–11pm.

Incendio 103 Columbia St near Alexander St, Gastown ⓣ604/ 688-8694. This vividly painted pizzeria is in a heritage building decorated with funky local art just a block east of Maple Tree Square, making hidden enough to escape the attention of the crowds rampaging through central Gastown. It features excellent wood-fired thin-crust pizzas (over 20 varieties), calzone, good salads and a range of well-made and inventive pastas such as fettucine with capers and a tomato and lime-butter sauce. Pizzas and main courses start at around $9. A second, more recent branch has opened in Kits at 2118 Burrard St (ⓣ604/736-2220). Open Mon–Thurs 11.30am–3pm & 5-10pm, Fri 11.30am–3pm & 5-11pm, Sat 5-11pm, Sun 4.30–10pm

The Old Spaghetti Factory 55 Water St at Abbot St ⓣ604/684-1288, ⓦwww.oldspaghettifactory.ca. Part of an inexpensive chain and hardly *alta cucina*, but a standby if you're in Gastown and better than the tourist trap it appears from the outside, with its spacious 1920s Tiffany interior and main courses from $12. Daily 10am–10pm.

Villa del Lupo 869 Hamilton St near Smithe St ⓣ604/688-7436, ⓦwww.villadellupo.com. Authentic and expensive, high-quality food in a renovated country house – unfussy and elegant – on the eastern edge of Downtown midway between the library and Yaletown: there's not a better *osso bucco* in Vancouver. However, you pay for quality with mains from about $29–36. Daily 5.30–10.30pm.

Japanese

Ezogiku Noodle Café 1329 Robson St at Jervis St ⓣ604/685-8608. This tiny Japanese noodle house is a perfect place for quick food Downtown. The queues are prohibitive, but the turnover's speedy and it's hard to spend more than $10 on a filling meal.

Gyoza King 1508 Robson St near Nicola St, Downtown ⓣ604/669-8278. Fight through groups of homesick Japanese students and visitors to enjoy the great food (very little sushi), casual atmosphere and funky, dark-walled interior. Choose, tapas-style, from more than 20 types of gyoza – succulent fried dumplings with a variety of fillings (the vegetable and spinach are great) with a soy dipping sauce. Or go for noodle and robust o-den soups, katsu-don (breaded pork chop with rice). Chase them down with one of many choices of beer and sit at the bar, the low front table or the higher Western tables. If you can't follow what is going on, or understand the menu, the waiters are helpful. Main courses cost from $8–18. Open Mon–Thurs 5.30pm–1am, Fri 5.30pm–1.30am, Sat 6pm–1.30am, Sun 6–11.30pm.

Hapa Izakaya 1479 Robson St near Broughton St, Downtown ⓣ604/689-4272. The archytypal and most popular of Vancouver's latest Japanese import, the "izakaya" restaurant (see box opposite). Small, individual dishes and low prices are the lure, along with a boistrous, busy and entertaining atmosphere. There are sushi-like raw fish options (try the fresh tuna with chopped spring onions and garlic bread), as well as tasty hotpots and other meat dishes. For sheer drama, try the seared mackeral, where the searing is done at your table with a blowtorch. Mains cost from about $8–12, and the opening times mean you can eat and drink (sake, martinis, wine) long and late. Open Sun–Thurs 5.30pm–midnight, Fri & Sat 5.30pm–1am.

Ichibankan 770 Thurlow St at Robson St ⓣ604/682-6262, ⓦwww.ichibankanrestaurant.com. You can't argue with the credentials of a place that's been turning out no-nonsense sushi (plus tempura and teriyaki) for over twenty years – and at reasonable prices (less than $15 for mains). The basement dining room, decked out in striking red and black, is handy for Robson St shoppers and stollers, and you can eat in, sit at the sushi bar, sample a light menu or buy food to take out. Open Mon–Thurs 11am–10.30pm, Fri & Sat 11am–11pm, Sun 11.30am–10pm.

Koji 630 Hornby St, Downtown ⓣ604/685-7355. Gardens are rare enough Downtown, let alone in restaurants, so the very pretty Japanese patio with pines and river rocks here is a treat. Sushi here isn't the city's best by any means, but Japanese visitors and locals come here for the setting, fair prices ($30 for plenty of sushi, $10–20 for combinations of non-sushi dishes) and other outstanding dishes, notably smoky black cod and grilled shiitake with bonito flakes, and for the generous boxed lunch at around $10. Open Mon–Fri 11.30am–2.30pm & 5.30–10pm, Sat & Sun 5.30–10pm.

Tanpopo 1122 Denman St at Pendrell St ⓣ604/681-7777. A popular favourite, as you'll see from the almost nightly queues for the second-floor dining room – you could be waiting 30 minutes. You can try booking ahead – they take the occasional reservations – or opt to sit at the sushi bar to cut down waiting time. The reason for the queues is the quality and quantity of the sushi – this is an all-you-can-eat place for a set price (currently $22). Open daily 11.30am–10pm.

Mexican

Bin 941 941 Davie St, West End ⓣ604/683-1246, ⓦwww.bin941.com. Also at 1521 West Broadway ⓣ604/734-9421. It's not surprising that no one seems to have a bad word for *Bin 941*. Both outlets are tiny, on the slightly crazy side of funky, and packed long and late with people drawn by the up-tempo bars (the West Broadway location is marginally more subdued) and some of the city's best – and best-value – bite-size food. The menu's "tapatizers" include great fries ($3 for a mountain of hand-cut Yukon Gold potato fries), jumbo scallops, tiger-prawn tournedos, crabcakes, charred bok choy and many more. Open for dinner daily until 2am.

Lolita's South of the Border Cantina 1326 Davie St near Jervis St ⓣ604/696-9996, ⓦwww.lolitasrestaurant.com. One glance from outside at the boldly-coloured dining room here gives you a pretty good idea of what to expect inside: a rather self-conscious but fun, funky and friendly neighbourhood café-restaurant that requires no dressing up, offers filling and unfancy Mexican (and other) food and prices (from $6) that aren't going to hurt your pocket. That said, it's stranded in a residential part of town, and you're unlikely to be passing by unless you're travelling the length of Davie St. If you are nearby, it's a good place for a snack, light meal or invigorating late-night beer or tequila cocktail. Open daily 5pm–2am.

Tapastree 1829 Robson St between Denman and Gilford, West End ⓣ604/606-4680,

Izakaya

When it comes to Japanese food, sushi's crown is being challenged, at least in Vancouver, where links across the Pacific ensure the rapid takeup of most Japanese culinary trends. **Izakaya** is the latest thing, a word that means "eat-drink place", and refers to informal and inexpensive establishments where you can eat a variety of small Japanese dishes (and sometimes Korean and Chinese ones as well), rather in the manner of sushi, tapas or dim sum. Dishes may not always be traditional and there are some Western-influenced inventions such as asparagus wrapped in bacon, or deep-fired chicken. The restaurants are usually small, diner-type places, with open kitchens. Beer and sake are the main liquid accompaniments to the food. The other defining quality is noise, and the bustle of an izakaya can take the unwary by surprise. First the entire staff, or lively head waiter, may greet anyone walking over the threshold with a bellowed irashimase, or "welcome". Waiters will call out orders, chefs will acknowledge them, and the maitre d' keeps all and sundry informed of the progress of anything from dishes to the size of the queue outside. Izakayas started life as places for students to eat and drink, so prices are always good (main courses shouldn't cost more than $8). It's rare for places to accept reservations, though service and turnover is brisk and accommodating.

Hapa Izakaya on Robson Street (see review p.831) is one of the most popular, but also check out Shiru Bay (1193 Hamilton St) – both are rather refined, upscale isakayas – or Guu (838 Thurlow St and other locations) or the Korean E-Hwa (1578 Robson St).

ⓦwww.tapastree.org. Vancouver's tapas craze of the 1990s has faded, but the best Spanish bars and restaurants (see also *La Bodega* on p.835) are still great places for inexpensive food and a relaxed early evening or wind-down late night. *Tapastree* has a vast choice of tapas from $7–15 whose inspiration goes way beyond Spain to include pork ribs with Chinese barbecue sauce, Asian seafood salad, lamb with sun-dried tomatoes and Gorgonzola, and Japanese aubergine with pesto. Late in the evening patrons are likely to include chefs from other restaurants who have just got off their shift – so you know the quality's got to be good. Open Sun–Thurs 5.30–10.30pm, Fri–Sat 5.30–11.30pm.

Topanga Café 2904 West 4th Ave near Macdonald St, Kitsilano ⓣ604/733-3713. A small but extremely popular and moderate Mexican restaurant that has become a Vancouver institution, not least because of the prices – mains start at just $10 – and the always reliably good food. Mon-Sat 11.30am–10pm.

Southeast Asian

Phnom-Penh 244 East Georgia near Gore St ⓣ604/682-5777; also at 955 West Broadway near Oak St ⓣ604/734-8988. Excellent, cheap Vietnamese and Cambodian cuisine, especially seafood, in a friendly, family-oriented restaurant. Most dishes come in at around $5–10. Daily 10am–10pm.

Pho Hoang 3610 Main at 20th ⓣ604/874-0810; also at 238 East Georgia near Gore St ⓣ604/682-5666. The first and perhaps friendliest of the many Vietnamese *pho* (beef soup) restaurants now springing up all over the city. Choose from thirty soup varieties with herbs, chilis and lime at plate-side as added seasoning. Open for breakfast, lunch and dinner. The new Chinatown branch is right by the *Phnom-Penh* (see above). Daily 11am–10pm.

Simply Thai 1211 Hamilton St, corner of Davie St ⓣ604/642-0123, ⓦwwwsimplythairestaurant.com. This plain, modern but inviting Yaletown restaurant is packed at lunch (11.30am–3pm) and dinner, thanks to the keen prices (mains from $7) and good, authentic food – the chefs are all from Bangkok.

Vegetarian

The Naam 2724 West 4th Ave near Stephens St, Kitsilano ⓣ604/738-7151. The oldest and most popular health-food and vegetarian restaurant in the city. Comfortable and friendly ambience with live folk and other music and outside eating some evenings. Choose right, and you can fill up here from as little as $5. Open 24hr.

West Coast

Bishop's 2183 West 4th near Yew St, Kitsilano ⓣ604/738-2025. Consistently ranked one of Vancouver's best restaurants, though it's some way from Downtown. Although there's a frequent film-star and VIP presence, the welcome is as warm for everyone. The light and refined "contemporary home cooking" – Italy meets the Pacific Rim – commands high prices (mains start at around $30) but is worth it. First choice for the big, one-off splurge, but booking is essential. Mon–Sat 5.30–11pm, Sun 5.30–10pm.

Bridges 1696 Duranleau, Granville Island ⓣ604/687-4400. Unmissable big, yellow restaurant upstairs, pub and informal bistro (the best option) downstairs, with a large outdoor deck and decent prices (mains from about $13). A reliable and very popular choice for a drink or meal on Granville Island. Bistro daily 11am-11pm, restaurant daily 5.30–10pm.

Delilah's 1789 Comox St near Denman St, West End ⓣ604/687-3424, ⓦwww.delilahs.ca. With a name like *Delilah's* you somehow know you're in for a little bit of kitsch, and the hand-painted decorative cherubin cavorting on the ceiling and glamourous, if slightly camp velvet banquettes don't disappoint. First task here is to order one of the martinis for which the place is famous, and which doubtless contribute to the cheerful, buzzy atmosphere. *Delilah's* has been around for over 20 years, and has always been fun, but the food has recently picked up, and the mostly traditional (occasionally French-influenced) main courses (from $22) such as grilled beef tenderloin with foie gras butter and fresh horseradish are well worth trying. Or perhaps dip into the tapas menu, with dishes (house-cured elk carpaccio) that have almost certainly never appeared on a Spanish menu (tapas from $8). Open daily 5.30pm–10pm or later.

Diva at the Met At *Metropolitan Hotel*, 645 Howe St ⓣ604/602-7788, ⓦwww.metropolitan.com. Like the *Chartwell* (see above), *Diva* has carved out a character completely separate to the hotel in which it's lodged. This is among Vancouver's leading restaurants, thanks to the punchy, imaginative food and the modern, clean-lined dining room. Starters might include smoked salmon with Québec foie gras, followed by a main course of halibut cheeks with black-olive tapinade. Expensive (mains start at about $25 at dinner, $12 at lunch), but a great place for a treat or full-on brunch. Daily 6.30am–1am.

Earl's On Top 1185 Robson St near Bute St ⓣ604/669-0020. Come here first if you don't want to mess around scouring Downtown for somewhere to eat. The mid-priced, and often innovative, high-quality food (main courses range from around $10–20) is served in a big, open and casual dining area, with outside terrace in the summer. Daily 11.30am–1am.

Glowbal Grill & Satay Bar 1079 Mainland St near Helmcken St, Yaletown ⓣ604/602-0835, ⓦwww.glowbalgrill.com. This is the perfect place to catch up on the hip, buzzy dining typical of Vancouver, and of Yaletown in particular – not to mention the classic fusion of Asian and West Coast cuisines that characterizes so much of the city's cooking. The simple, clean-lined Modernist-inspired dining room is divided between a long raised bar and semi-isolated tables with banquettes below. An open kitchen, satay bar and lots of illuminated cubes add to the dashing, vibrant air. Food is fusion to a fault, with dishes such as Italian and Japanese coming together in spaghetti with truffles and Kobe meatballs ($24). But there are also reasonably straight steaks, fish and mainstream Italian dishes, with mains from $18–35 for lobster. Around twenty wines by the glass are available, but the best place to drink at leisure, or to enjoy smaller, lighter meals is in the more recently opened *Afterglow* lounge, with suitably funky music and inventive cocktails. Daily 11.30am–1am.

Liliget Feast House 1724 Davie St at Bidwill St ⓣ604/681-7044. This West End aboriginal restaurant – the only one in Vancouver – serves types of food you'll get nowhere else in the city: seaweed, steamed ferns, roast caribou and barbecued juniper duck. However, the cedar tables and benches, designed to resemble a Coast Salish long house, making the dining room a mite austere. Main courses cost from $12–30. Daily 5–10pm.

Lift 333 Menchions Mews, on the Coal Harbour waterfront behind the Westin Bayshore Resort, West End-Stanley Park ⓣ604/689-5438, ⓦwww.liftbarandgrill.com. You have to hope this place continues to prosper, because it cost someone eight million dollars to build. The omens are good. For a start, the position is divine: part of the gleaming new waterfront taking shape just east of Stanley Park, while its super-modern and design-conscious interior, complete with vast glass walls, is at one with the ranks of gleaming new condominiums close by. The food and service had an uneven start, but as things settled down the tunas, steaks, salmon and other West Coast staples – with the inevitable sophisticated twists – came good. Prices are highish, however – with mains from around $25 – but you can go for smaller portions (between a starter and a main) to keep costs down, or simply come here for a drink. The rooftop patio on a fine day is the place to be. Open Mon–Fri 11.30am–11pm, Sat & Sun 11am–11.30pm (Sun brunch until 2.30pm).

Milestone's 1145 Robson St between Bute and Thurlow sts ⓣ604/682-4477, also at 1210 Denman St ⓣ604/662-3431 and 1109 Hamilton on the corner of Helmcken ⓣ604/684-9112. Popular mid-market chain restaurants with cheap drinks and food (especially good breakfasts) in very generous portions and reasonable prices (a pasta main dish costs around $15). Located at the heart of Downtown (fast and noisy), the English Bay Beach end of Denman St (more laid-back) and in Yaletown (popular, with outdoor terrace). Mon–Fri 10.30am–10.30pm, Sat & Sun 9.30am–midnight.

Nu 1661 Granville St, Downtown, near Granville Island ⓣ604/646-4668, ⓦwww.whatisnu.com. Not "new", as the name might suggest, but from the French for "naked". One of Vancouver's newest restaurants it's quickly made its mark, and by general consent is currently one of the city's best. It is under the same management as the *C Restaurant*, though here the "naked", or unadorned approach, is decidedly lighter and more simple, with easy-to-eat finger food and classic West Coast meat and fish staples from around $18 for a main course. The dining room has a vaguely nautical, cruise-ship theme, appropriately enough, given its location on the north shore of False Creek opposite Granville Island. Open Mon–Fri 11am–1am, Sat 10.30am–1am, Sun 10.30am–midnight.

Raincity Grill 1193 Denman St ⓣ604/685-7337, ⓦwww.raincitygrill.com. The candles and a position in the West End near Davie St overlooking English Bay make for a romantic dining experience, but it is the food and wine, both of which make the most of BC and Pacific Northwest ingredients (more than 100 varieties of Northwest and Californian wines by the glass are available), which are the main attraction here. The regional menu, with mains from about $20, changes regularly, but you can always be sure to find salmon, seafood and other locally sourced food (much of it organic) and at least four vegetarian options. Each dish comes with a suggestion for wine. Mon–Fri 5–10pm, Sat & Sun 10.30am–2pm & 5–10pm.

Sequoia Grill at the Teahouse Ferguson Point, Stanley Park ⓣ604/669-3281, ⓦwww.vancouverdine.com. A very pretty and romantic spot on the west side of Stanley Park with ocean views and outside dining that started life in 1928 as a barracks. Formerly a teahouse, it has become less twee since 2004 under its new owners. The revamped terrace is an obvious place for a lunch or brunch during a walk or ride round the park. The food embraces predictable West Coast and French–Italian staples (seafood and steaks, pastas, small-plate selections of Asian-influenced starters), with main courses from around $10–35. The food is not quite as good as the sea views, but this is still a fine spot for a drink and light meal while watching the sun go down over the ocean. Book a table on the terrace a day or so in advance. Open Mon–Sat 11.30am–9.45pm, Sun 10.30am–9.45pm.

Water Street Café 300 Water St at Cambie St ⓣ604/689-2832. The café-restaurant of choice if you wind up in Gastown (located close to the famous steam clock). An airy and casual atmosphere that offers a short but well-chosen menu and decent prices – a pasta main course will cost around $13; consider booking an outside table if you're going to be here for lunch.

West 2881 Granville St near West 13th Ave ⓣ604/738-8938, ⓦwww.westrestaurant.com. Year after year, *West* challenges *Bishop's* and *Lumière* for the title of Vancouver's best restaurant. It's owned by the same people that run *CinCin* and the *Blue Water Café* (and *Araxi* in Whistler), all excellent restaurants, and it's to them that credit goes for the smart but never stuffy dining room and the attention to detail. Plaudits for the food go to executive chef David Hawksworth, who spent more than ten years in the UK working alongside top-rank chefs such as Raymond Blanc at the *Quat'Saisons* and Marco Pierre White at *The Canteen*. The restaurant's credo – "True to our region, true to the seasons" – is a shorthand way of saying what most of the city's West Coast and many other restaurants are saying: that the emphaisis is on exceptional, locally sourced ingredients, and a menu that changes according to what is seasonally available. Main courses cost from $30, but high prices bring consistently high-quality food, with menus changing three or four times a week. Indulge in one of the tasting menus (from $70) for a full taste of what this exceptional restaurant can offer. Mon–Fri 11.30am–11pm, Sat & Sun 5.30–11pm.

Pubs and bars

900 West 900 West Georgia St ⓣ604/684-3131. Hotel bars and lounges can be bland and anonymous affairs – not the bar of the *Hotel Vancouver*. Despite leading off the main lobby of one of the city's biggest and grandest hotels, this is a cosy space of dark wood, comfortable chairs and low lighting. It's at its best immediately after businesses close, when it fills with an animated crowd catching a drink before heading home or moving on to a restaurant or club. Later in the evening it tends to be used more by hotel guests and the atmosphere becomes more mellow.

Alibi Room 157 Alexander St between Columbia and Main ⓣ604/623-3383, ⓦwww.alibiroom.com. Various movie-makers and shakers put money into this unashamedly hip bar-restaurant – and the result is a crowd that is trendy, but not so trendy that it spoils what is a good place for drinks and – perhaps – dinner. Excellent and eclectic food is served upstairs, with a short, modern menu at surprisingly reasonable prices; downstairs you can drink and venture onto the small dance floor.

Afterglow 1079 Mainland St near Helmcken ⓣ604/642-0577. The very mellow bar attached to the *Glowbal Grill* (see review p.833), with its candlelight, intimate seating and easy listening grooves, is a good place for a pre- or post-dinner drink – or for a night's drinking without pause for food.

Arts Club 1585 Johnston on Granville Island ⓣ604/687-1354. The *Arts Club*'s popular *Backstage Lounge*, part of the theatre complex, has a waterfront view, easy-going atmosphere, decent food and puts on blues, jazz and other live music Friday and Saturday evenings.

Bar None 1222 Hamilton St ⓣ604/689-7000. Busy, reasonably smart and hip New York-style Yaletown bar and club where you can eat, drink, watch TV, smoke cigars (walk-in humidor), play backgammon or shoot pool and listen to live music.

Bin 941 941 Davie St between Burrard and Hornby ⓣ604/683-1246, ⓦwwwbin941.com. This is a great place to eat (see review on p.831), but vast numbers of people come here (be prepared to wait in line – there are no reservations) primarily to drink, attracted by the place's high-energy and cramped good vibes.

Blarney Stone 216 Carrall near Water St ⓣ604/687-4322. A lively Irish pub and restaurant in Gastown, complete with live Irish music and dance floor. Closed Sun.

Bridges 1696 Duranleau St on Granville Island ⓣ604/687-4400. You can eat here, but when the sun's shining it's a close-run thing between the busy patio here and the *Dockside Brewing Company* as to which is the nicest place to have a waterside drink on Granville Island: *Bridges* is more central and thus more convenient.

The Cambie 300 Cambie St ⓣ604/684-6466. An obvious place to drink if you're staying at the linked hostel (see p.803), but the roomy (and invariably crowded) outdoor area and cheap pitchers of beer bring in a fair number of locals and other passing trade. Inside, it's all smoke, pool tables and down-to-earth drinking.

C9 Live Lounge At the *Empire Landmark Hotel*, 1400 Robson St at Nicola St ⓣ604/687-0511. Vancouver has several bars with a view – notably the lounge in the *Sylvia* and *Bridges* on Granville Island – but none can match the panorama from this super-sleek lounge bar on the 42nd floor of the *Empire Landmark Hotel*. The bar rotates, so your view changes by six degrees every sixty seconds. There's a modest cover charge for entry on Fri and Sat, but it's worth paying for the panorama.

Darby's Pub 2001 Macdonald St and 4th Ave ⓣ604/731-0617. A pub handy for Kits Beach and the hostel. People often start the evening here, meals are served 11.30am–7pm, snacks till 10pm, and then move on to the *Fairview* for live blues (see p.837). Live music is only played on Fri and Sat evenings with jam sessions on Sat afternoons.

Dockside Brewing Company 1253 Johnston St, Granville Island ⓣ604/685-7070. Beer buffs may want to try this stylish lounge in the *Granville Island Hotel* to sample some of the establishment's on-site microbrewery's ales. The atmosphere is relaxed and the generally well-heeled crowd thirty-something. Things tend to be livelier early in the evening, and in summer there's a fine outdoor patio.

George 1137 Hamilton St at Helmcken St ⓣ604/628-5555, ⓦwww.georgelounge.com. If you want a smart, urban bar, this is a good bet, a place that appeals to a young, beautiful set, with easy-on-the-palate cocktails, well-priced wines by the glass, just-right subdued lighting and a choice between sitting at the long bar or on the sofas of the lounge.

Gerard Lounge 845 Burrard at Robson St ⓣ604/682-5511. The smooth wood-panelled lounge and piano bar with leather chairs and tapestries, all make this very elegant Downtown drinking. Also, the place to spot the stars currently filming in town.

The Irish Heather 217 Carrall St near Water St ⓣ604/688-9779. A definite cut above the usual mock-Irish pub, with an intimate bar, live Irish music some nights, excellent food, good Guinness (apparently it sells the second largest number of pints of the stuff in Canada); and an unexpectedly pretty outdoor area in the back.

La Bodega 1277 Howe near Davie St ⓣ604/684-8815. One of the city's best and most popular places, with tapas and excellent main courses, but chiefly dedicated to lively drinking. It's packed later on, so try to arrive before 8pm. Closed Sun.

Shark Bar & Grill At *Sandman Hotel*, 180 West Georgia ⓣ604/687-4275, ⓦwww.sharksclub.com.

The best and busiest of several sports bars in the city. There are 30 screens, a 180-seat oak bar, 22 beers on tap, Italian food from the kitchen, and lots of testosterone.

SkyBar 670 Smithe St at Granville St ⓣ604/697-9199, ⓦwww.skybarvancouver.com. A slick spot off a busy Downtown street, the *SkyBar* occupies three levels, with martini bar, nightclub and Vancouver's largest rooftop terrace that's great in the summer – if you can get on to it, as it's popular, with long queues. This place requires a certain pose and effort, however, so go elsewhere if you want a quiet, relaxed drink.

Sylvia Hotel 1154 Gilford and Beach ⓣ604/688-8865. This nondescript but easy-going hotel bar is popular for quiet drinks and superlative waterfront views, and pleasant after a stroll on English Bay Beach.

Yaletown Brewing Company 1111 Mainland St ⓣ604/681-2739. An extremely large and unmissable bar and restaurant with their own six-beer on-site brewery. Very popular, and leading the way in the funky Yaletown revival.

Nightlife and entertainment

Vancouver gives you plenty to do come sunset, laying on a varied and cosmopolitan blend of **live music**. **Clubs** are more adventurous than in many other Canadian cities, particularly the fly-by-night alternative dives on and around Main Street and Commercial Drive, and in the backstreets off Gastown and Chinatown. There's also a choice of smarter and more conventional clubs, a handful of discos and a selection of **gay** and **lesbian** clubs and bars. Summer nightlife often takes to the streets in West Coast fashion, with outdoor bars and (to a certain extent) beaches becoming venues in their own right. Fine weather also allows the city to host a range of **festivals**, from jazz to theatre, and the **performing arts** are as widely available as you'd expect in a city as culturally self-conscious as Vancouver.

The most comprehensive **listings** guide to all the goings-on is *Georgia Straight* (ⓦwww.straight.com), a free weekly published on Thursday and available in larger stores and street boxes around the city. Many other free magazines devoted to different musical genres and activities are available at the same points, but they come and go quickly. Selected club listings can also be found at ⓦwww.clubvibes.com, while ⓦwww.vancouverjazz.com/directory offers a list of jazz venues, but no critical commentary.

Tickets for many major events are sold through Ticketmaster, based at 1304 Hornby St, which has forty outlets throughout the city (ⓣ604/280-4444 for concerts, 280-4400 for sporting events and 280-3311 for the performing arts; ⓦwww.ticketmaster.ca); they'll sometimes unload discounted tickets for midweek and matinee performances. Half-price and last-minute same-day tickets are available via "Tickets Tonight" (ⓦwww.ticketstonight.ca) at participating venues, or through the outlet at the main TouristInfo visitor centre at 200 Burrard St (see p.794).

Live music and clubs

Vancouver's live-music venues showcase a variety of musical styles, but mainstream **rock** groups are the most common bill of fare; the city is also a fertile breeding ground for **punk** bands, with particularly vocal audiences. **Jazz** is generally hot news in Vancouver, with a dozen spots specializing in the genre (ring the Jazz Hot Line at ⓣ604/682-0706 for current and upcoming events). And, while Vancouver isn't as cowpoke as, say, Calgary, it does have several clubs dedicated to **country music**, though many are in the outer suburbs. Many venues also double as **clubs** and discos, and as in any city with a healthy alternative scene there are also plenty of fun, one-off clubs that have an irritating habit of cropping up and disappearing at speed. Cover charges are usually nominal, and tickets are often available (sometimes free) at record shops. At the other end of the spectrum, the 60,000-seat Pacific Coliseum is on the touring itinerary of many international acts.

Rock

Commodore Ballroom 870 Granville St at Smithe St ⓣ604/681-7838, ⓦwww.commodoreballroom.com. Still fresh from a one million dollar face-lift – which retained its renowned 1929 dance floor – the *Commodore* is the city's best mid-sized venue. There is an adventurous music policy and both local and national DJs frequently spin.

Lamplighter 210 Abbott St at Water St ⓣ604/681-6666, ⓦwww.thelamplighter.ca. This Gastown bar had little to recommend it, other than its claim to be the city's oldest, until a refurb in 2004. Now it's a better place for a beer, and a better place for live music, with an informed and adventurous booking policy that means a pleasing selection of local bands in all manner of musical styles often fill the 200-person capacity venue. There are musically themed nights plus karaoke throughout the week.

Media Club 695 Cambie St at West Georgia St ⓣ604/608-2871, ⓦwww.themediaclub.ca. A pleasing and intimate 150-person capacity that books key touring bands most nights, plus an open-mike night (currently Mon) and comedy night on Sun.

Pub 340 340 Cambie St at West Hasting St ⓣ604/602-0644. A 110-person capacity venue that never pretends to be other than what it is: a no-nonsense pub, with cheap beer and food, and live music nightly from loud and enthusiastic rock, punk, electronic and hardcore metal bands. There's also the inevitable karaoke, currently on Wedn nights.

Piccadilly Pub 620 West Pender near Granville ⓣ604/682-3221. The "Pic" is a long-established pub with a guarantee of raucous music of some description (garage, rock, punk, rockabilly) most nights, usually Thurs–Sat. It's a laid-back, non-posey sort of place aimed at those who simply want beer, music and a good time.

Railway Club 579 Dunsmuir St at Seymour St ⓣ604/681-1625. Long-established favourite with excellent bookings, wide range of music (folk, blues, jazz) and a casual atmosphere. Has a separate "conversation" lounge, so it's ideal for a drink (and weekday lunches). Arrive before 10pm at weekends – the place is tiny.

Roxy 932 Granville St at Nelson St ⓣ604/684-7699, ⓦwww.roxyvan.com. Nightly live bands with emphasis on retro 1950s to 1970s music. Casual and fun place for college crowd and people in from the burbs.

Sonar 66 Water St at Abbott St ⓣ604/683-6695, ⓦwww.sonar.bc.ca. Central Vancouver's best-known music venue, with live bands nightly. Convenient mid-Gastown location attracts a varied clientele – it's also known as something of a pick-up spot. Bar food and piano lounge until 9pm, when the band strikes up.

Jazz and blues

Arts Club Theatre Backstage Lounge 1585 Johnston, Granville Island ⓣ604/687-1354. The lounge is a nice spot to hear R&B, jazz and blues, or watch the boats and sunset on False Creek.

Capone's 1141 Hamilton St ⓣ604/684-7900. This Yaletown spot is primarily a restaurant, but has a stage for live jazz renditions while you eat.

Cellar Restaurant & Jazz Club 3611 West Broadway ⓣ604/738-1959, ⓦwww.cellarjazz.com. Kitsilano has only recently acquired clubs, and this tiny 70-seat red-walled basement with black booths and low tables is one of the most popular, frequently offering the best live jazz in the city four or more nights a week (generally Wed–Sat). Join the enthusiastic crowd for top local outfits or big international names.

Fairview 898 West Broadway at the *Ramada Inn* ⓣ604/872-1262. Good local blues and 1950s rock in a pub atmosphere with only a small dance floor. Snacks are served during the day and good-value meals in the evening. Closed Sun.

Hot Jazz 2120 Main St and 5th Ave ⓣ604/873-4131, ⓦwww.hotjazzvancouver.com. *Hot Jazz* is the oldest and most firmly established jazz club in the city. Music is mainly traditional – swing, Dixieland and New Orleans – performed by both local and imported bands. On Sat nights you'll occasionally be treated to a big band. A jumping (and invariably full) dance floor and large bar ensures the place swings past midnight. This is a club, so you'll have to pay a nominal annual membership fee unless you manage to be signed in as a guest by a member. Wed is jam night; closed Mon and Sun.

Purple Onion 15 Water St near Abbot St ⓣ604/602-9442, ⓦwww.purpleonion.com. Casual club right in the heart of Gastown: top-notch jazz and live Latin music upstairs, dance floor, cigars, oysters and cabaret downstairs. Currently a very popular choice, so expect to wait in line on Fri and Sat.

Yale 1300 Granville St at Drake St ⓣ604/681-9253. An outstanding venue: the top place in the city to hear hardcore blues and R&B. Relaxed air, big dance floor and occasional outstanding international names. Often jam sessions with up to fifty players at once, on Sat (3–8pm) and Sun (3pm–midnight). Closed Mon & Tues.

Country

Boone County Cabaret 801 Brunette Ave, Coquitlam ⓣ604/523-3144. Just off the Trans-Canada (take bus #151) this is suburbia's favourite country music club and it shows – it's typically raucous and crowded. There's no cover Mon–Thurs, and free dance lessons Mon, Tues & Thurs 8pm. Closed Sun.

Clubs and discos

Atlantis 1320 Richards St at Pacific Blvd ⓣ604/662-7707, ⓦwww.atlantisclub.net. This large and recently renovated Yaletown club ($1.5 million was spent) has cutting-edge music, lights and dance floor, and a sharp clientele to match. There's plenty of room at the rear bar (one of eight) for a drink and a break from the music, with hip-hop currently on Sat and a wide range of sounds on theme nights the rest of the week.

Au Bar 674 Seymour St ⓣ604/648-2227. Downtown club for suits and miniskirts, with martinis the (expensive) drink of choice. Strict dress code and vetting on the door (you'll spot the Seymour St queues from afar), but the exclusive air is what attracts punters. If you get in, people-watching may prove the most entertaining part of your evening. Three bars and small dance floor with safe Top 40, hiphop and R&B.

Plaza Club 881 Granville St ⓣ604/646-0064, ⓦwww.plazaclub.net. A popular, no-nonsense dance club with great sound and lighting in a former cinema in central Granville St location. Music has a strong British bias, but there are also theme nights. Saturday is very popular, so expect to queue.

Richard's on Richards 1036 Richards St at Nelson St ⓣ604/687-6794. A well-known club and disco, but pretentious and aimed at the BMW set. Long waits and dress code. Open Thurs–Sat.

Shine 363 Water St ⓣ604/408-4321. Conveniently located and happening Gastown club which attracts some of the city's top DJs, notably Dicky Doo. Understated decor, with comfortable retro 1960s couches and all-white colour scheme provide a sophisticated setting for house, reggae, soul, R&B, hiphop and other sounds. Dress up a bit.

Tokoyo Lounge 350-1050 Alberni St between Burrard and Thurlow sts, beside *Kobe* 3rd-floor lift access ⓣ604/689-0002, ⓦwww.tokyolounge.ca. Queues are inevitable for the big three nights at this red-lighted, Asian-themed Downtown club: All Good on Thur, Get Up Get Down on Fri and Sumo on Sat, all three seeing DJs spinning lashings of hip-hop, reggae, funk, soul and R&B. There are plenty of cosy booths to which to retreat when it all becomes too much.

Urban Well 888 Nelson St at Hornby ⓣ604/638-6070, ⓦwww.urbanwell.com. The combination of club-like bar and restaurant, with nightly DJs and comedy and other event nights, has proved so successful that there are two Urban Wells in town – the one here in Downtown just two blocks from Robson and the other in Kitsilano at 1516 Yew St (ⓣ604/737-7770). You'll probably have to queue for both at busy times.

Voda At *Westin Grand Hotel*, 783 Homer St ⓣ604/684-3003, ⓦwww.voda.com. Arrive early in this very roomy hotel lounge near the central library and chances are it'll be empty. Come later and you'll find it heaving, for this is one of the newer and most popular of the city's clubs. The sleek look and fittings – wood panelling, back-lit bar, lots of candles, waterfalls, rocks, angled beams – are offset by the generally very elegant and fashion-conscious clientele. Don't wear your jeans, Music for the smallish dance floor covers most bases, from R&B and funk to electro and old-school house. Closed Sun & Mon.

Comedy

Balthazar's House of Comedy 1215 Bidwell St ⓣ604/689-8822. Small venue that usually hosts just one night of professional standup a week, currently on Mon.

Darby's 2001 Macdonald St and West 4th Ave ⓣ604/803-8429 for information. Fun bar (see p.835 for review) that hosts a Mon night comedy show with a different host and headliner each week.

Jupiter Lounge ⓣ604/609-6665. A West End bar that showcases professional standups once weekly, currently on Mon.

Urban Well 1516 Yew St at Cornwall Ave ⓣ604/737-7770, ⓦwww.urbanwell.com. There's generally only comedy one or two nights a week (currently improvisations on Mon plus Tues or Wed depending on venue) at this small Kits venue, but a good bar and good value have proved a successful combination. Chances are you'll have to queue for both at busy times.

Yuk Yuk's Century Plaza Hotel & Spa, 1015 Burrard St at Helmcken St ⓣ604/696-9857, ⓦwww.yukyuks.com. Vancouver's longest-established central comedy club presents top US and Canadian stand-up acts. Shows generally kick off at 9pm, with extra performances on Sat & Sun at around 11.30pm. It's worth booking at weekends. Closed Mon and Tues.

Performing arts

Vancouver serves up enough highbrow culture to suit the whole spectrum of its cosmopolitan population, with plenty of unusual and avant-garde performances to spice up the more mainstream fare you'd expect of a major North American city. The main focus for the city's performing arts is the **Queen Elizabeth Theatre**, 600 Hamilton St at Georgia (ⓣ604/299-9000, ⓦwww.city.vancouver.bc.ca/theatres), which plays host to visiting theatre, opera and dance troupes and even the occasional big rock band, along with the **Centre in Vancouver for the Performing Arts** opposite the central library at 777 Homer St (ⓣ604/602-0616, ⓦwww.centreinvancouver.com). The refurbished **Orpheum Theatre**, 884 Granville at Smithe (ⓣ604/665-3050, ⓦwww.city.vancouver.bc.ca/theatres), is Vancouver's oldest theatre and headquarters of the Vancouver Symphony Orchestra. Farther afield, the **Chan Centre for the Performing Arts**, 6265 Crescent Rd at the University of British Columbia (ⓣ604/822-2697, ⓦwww.chancentre.com), has the 1400-seat Chan Shun Concert Hall, the main space of the three-hall UBC performance complex. It has the best acoustics in the city, and hosts shows by outside and university music, drama and other groups, as well as fashion shows, world-music and other events. The UBC has a smaller Recital Hall at Gate 4, 6361 Memorial Rd. **Tickets** can be obtained from individual box offices or through the Ticketmaster agency (see p.836).

Classical music

Early Music Vancouver ⓣ604/732-1610, ⓦwww.earlymusic.bc.ca. Early music with original instruments where possible; concerts all over the city, and at the UBC during the Early Music Festival in July & Aug.

Festival Concert Society ⓣ604/736-3737. Often organizes cheap Sun morning concerts (jazz, folk or classical) at the Queen Elizabeth Playhouse.

Music-in-the-Morning Concert Society 125 East 4th Ave ⓣ604/873-4612, ⓦwww.musicinthemorning.org. This began modestly in someone's front room over a decade ago but now organizes innovative and respected concerts of old and new music with local and visiting musicians.

University of British Columbia School of Music Recital Hall, Gate 4, 6361 Memorial Rd ⓣ604/822-5574, ⓦwww.music.ubc.ca. The UBC presents around eight major and many smaller performances during Jan & Feb and also Sept–Nov. Many are free.

Vancouver Bach Choir ⓣ604/921-8012, ⓦwww.vancouverbachchoir.com. The city's top non-professional choir performs three major concerts yearly at the Orpheum Theatre.

Vancouver Cantata Singers 5115 Keith Rd ⓣ604/921-8588, ⓦwww.cantata.org. Various locations are used by this 40-strong, semi-professional choir for performances of traditional and contemporary choral music.

Vancouver Chamber Choir ⓣ604/738-6822, ⓦwww.vancouverchamberchoir.com. One of two professional, internationally renowned choirs in the city. They perform at the Orpheum and on some Sunday afternoons at the *Hotel Vancouver*.

Vancouver New Music Society 837 Davie St ⓣ604/663-0861, ⓦwww.newmusic.org. Responsible for the several annual concerts of cutting-edge twentieth-century music, usually at the East Cultural Centre (see "Drama" opposite).

Vancouver Opera 500-845 500-845 Cambie St ⓣ604/638-0222, ⓦwww.vanopera.bc.ca. Four operas are produced annually at the Queen Elizabeth Theatre and productions currently enjoy an excellent reputation.

Vancouver Recital Society 304-873 Beatty St ⓣ604/736-0363, ⓦwww.vanrecital.com. Hosts two of the best and most popular cycles in the city: the summer Chamber Music Festival (at St George's School) and the main Vancouver Playhouse recitals (Sept–April). Catches up-and-coming performers plus a few major international names each year.

Vancouver Symphony Orchestra 601 Smithe St ⓣ604/876-3434, ⓦwww.vancouversymphony.ca. Presents most concerts at the Orpheum or Chan Shun Hall on Crescent Rd off NW Marine Drive, but also sometimes gives free recitals in the summer at beaches and parks, culminating in a concert on the summit of Whistler Mountain.

Drama

Arts Club Theatre ⓣ604/687-1644, ⓦwww.artsclub.com. A leading light in the city's drama scene, performing at three venues: the main stage, at 1585 Johnston St on Granville Island, offers mainstream drama, comedies and musicals; the next-door bar presents small-scale revues and cabarets; and a third stage, at 1181 Seymour and Davie sts, focuses on avant-garde plays and Canadian dramatists – a launching pad for the likes of Michael J. Fox. The theatre has cult status for its "theatre sports", in which teams of actors compete for applause with improvization. Beware, as audience participation features highly.

Firehall Arts Centre 280 East Cordova at Gore St ⓣ604/689-0926, ⓦwww.firehall.org. The leader of Vancouver's community and avant-garde pack, presenting mime, music, video and visual arts.

Theatre Under the Stars (TUTS) Malkin Bowl, Stanley Park ⓣ604/687-0174 or 257-0366, ⓦwww.tuts.bc.ca. Summer productions here are fun and lightweight, but can suffer from being staged in one of Canada's rainiest cities.

Vancouver East Cultural Centre 1895 Venables St at Victoria St ⓣ604/251-1363, ⓦwww.vecc.bc.ca. Renowned performance space housed in an old church, used by a highly eclectic mix of drama, dance, mime and musical groups.

Vancouver Playhouse Theatre Company Hamilton St at Dunsmuir St ⓣ604/665-3050. One of western Canada's biggest companies. It usually presents six top-quality shows with some of the region's premier performers and designers during its Oct–May season.

Waterfront Theatre 1411 Cartwright St, Granville Island ⓣ604/685-6217. Home to three resident companies that also hold workshops and readings.

Dance

Anna Wyman Dance Theatre 707-207 West Hastings St ⓣ604/685-5699, ⓦwww.annawyman.com. Although their repertoire is wide, this group specializes in contemporary dance. As well as standard shows, they occasionally put on free outdoor performances at Granville Island and at Robson Square near the Art Gallery.

Ballet British Columbia Sixth Floor, 677 Davie St ⓣ604/732-5003, ⓦwww.ballet.bc. The province's top company performs – along with major visiting companies – at the Queen Elizabeth Theatre.

EDAM Western Front Lodge, 303 East 8th Ave ⓣ604/876-9559, ⓦwww.edamdance.org. Experimental Dance and Music present modern mixes of dance, film, music and art.

Karen Jamieson Dance Company 4036 West 19th Ave ⓣ604/893-8807. Award-winning company and choreographer that often use Canadian composers and artists, and incorporates native cultural themes.

Scotiabank Dance Centre 677 Davie St ⓣ604/689-0926. This new dance centre in a former bank building was converted by Arthur Erickson, architect of the Museum of Anthropology and other Vancouver buildings. It provides studio and rehearsal space for around 30 companies, and is open to the public for workshops, classes, exhibitions and other events. It also houses the Vancouver Dance Centre, a major source of information on dance in Vancouver and beyond (ⓣ604/606-6400, ⓦwww.thedancecentre.ca). Contact it for details of the major Dancing on the Edge Festival in July.

Film

The western capital of Canada's **film** industry, Vancouver is increasingly favoured by Hollywood studios in their pursuit of cheaper locations and production deals. It's therefore no surprise that the spread of cinemas is good. Home-produced and Hollywood first-run films play in the Downtown cinemas on Granville St and other big complexes, and there's no shortage of cinemas for more esoteric productions.

Cinemark Tinseltown 88 Pender St at Abbott ⓣ604/806-0799, ⓦwww.cinemark.com. Just two blocks south of Water St and the heart of Gastown, this multi-screen in the International Village complex has the most modern and high-tech of the city centre's first-run cinemas, with big screens, underground parking and good seating.

Denman Cinema 1737 Comox St at Denman ⓣ604/683-2201, ⓦwww.denmancinema.com. A good choice in the West End if you need a break after Stanley Park or want to catch a movie before or after hitting the cafés and bars on Denman St. Expect second-run or near first-run films at good prices.

Fifth Avenue Cinemas 2110 Burrard St at West 5th Ave ⓣ604/734-7469. Fiveplex cinema in south Vancouver run by the founder of the Vancouver Film Festival. It is one of the better in the city for art-house or more arty first-run films.

Granville Cineplex 855 Granville St between Robson and Smithe ⓣ604/684-4000,

Ⓦwww.cineplex.com. What's happened to Granville St? Once there were a dozen or so cinemas on the strip: now this is the last one, a multiplex that's also known locally as the Granville 7, and an obvious Downtown choice to catch a big-budget first-run movie.

Hollywood 3123 West Broadway between Tutch and Barclay sts Ⓣ604/738-3211, Ⓦwww.hollywoodtheatre.ca. A Kitsilano repertory cinema that can also always be relied on for good (and good-value) double bills and second-run (or just over first-run) movies.

Pacific Cinémathèque 1131 Howe St near Helmcken St Ⓣ604/688-3456, Ⓦwww.cinematheque.bc.ca. The non-profit film society that runs this screen is devoted to furthering the understanding of cinema and contemporary visual arts. As part of its brief, it shows a good range of arthouse, overseas and experimental films. All of which makes it the best non-mainstream cinema in the city. The programmes can be hit or miss, but any film buff will find something to tempt them.

Raja Cinema 639 Commercial Drive at Georgia Ⓣ604/253-0402. The place to come when only Bollywood will do.

Ridge Theatre 3131 Arbutus St at West 15th Ave Ⓣ604/738-6311, Ⓦwww.ridgetheatre.com. A little too far south to catch its target Kits audience, but still a great neighbourhood place for second-run, classic and other films. Look out for its provocatively paired double bills and late-lunch (1.30pm) "Movies for Mommies" screenings. Built in 1950, it's virtually unchanged – there's even an enclosed "crying room" for parents with boisterous children or howling infants.

Festivals

Warm summers, outdoor venues and a culture-hungry population combine to make Vancouver an important **festival** city. To learn more about events and shows, contact Tourism Vancouver (Ⓣ604/683-2000, Ⓦwww.tourismvancouver.com), or pick up *The Vancouver Book*, an annually updated listing of festivals and general information available free from the Touristinfo Centre (see p.794). Other listings can be found by visiting Ⓦwww.foundlocally.com/vancouver and Ⓦwww.bcpassport.com/festivals.

Among the major festivals is the annual **Du Maurier International Jazz Festival** (late June to early July), organized by the Coastal Jazz and Blues Society (Ⓣ604/872-5200, Ⓦwww.coastaljazz.ca). Past line-ups have featured such luminaries as Wynton Marsalis, Youssou N'Dour, Ornette Coleman, Carla Bley and John Zorn. Some 800 international musicians congregate annually, many offering workshops and free concerts in addition to paid-admission events. The **Vancouver International Folk Music Festival** (Ⓣ604/602-9798 or 1-800/985-8363, Ⓦwww.thefestival.bc.ca) hosts a bevy of international acts centred on Jericho Park and the Centennial Theatre for several days during the third week of July. Vancouver loses its collective head over the July **Sea Festival** (Ⓣ604/684-3378) – nautical fun, parades and excellent fireworks around English Bay. Farther afield in Whistler (see p.852), there's a **Country & Bluegrass Festival** in mid-July.

Theatre festivals come thick and fast, particularly in the summer. The chief event is the **Fringe Festival** (Ⓣ604/257-0350, Ⓦwww.vancouverfringe.com), modelled on the Edinburgh equivalent. It currently runs to more than 550 shows, staged by some ninety companies at ten venues. There's also an annual **Bard on the Beach Shakespeare Festival** (Ⓣ604/739-0559, Ⓦwww.bardonthebeach.org; June–Aug) in Vanier Park and an **International Comedy Festival** (Ⓣ604/683-0883, Ⓦwww.comedyfest.com) in early August on Granville Island. Many of the city's art-house cinemas join forces to host the **Vancouver International Film Festival** (Ⓣ604/685-0260, Ⓦwww.viff.org), an annual showcase for more than 150 films running from late September to mid-October.

Gay and lesbian Vancouver

Vancouver is a tolerant and welcoming city for **gays and lesbians**. It may not have the profile or élan of San Francisco, but it enjoys the same laid-back West Coast attitudes. There is a large, vibrant and unabashed gay and lesbian community, much of which is culturally and politically active and aware. There's also a lively and diverse scene when it comes to entertainment and nightlife, with plenty of clubs – theme nights are a popular phenomenon – drag shows and up-to-the-minute bars and discos. **Davie Village**, which runs from Burrard along Davie to Denman, is where you will find the highest concentration of long-established gay clubs, pubs and stores, though there are plenty of other venues throughout the city, while lesbians have traditionally hung out on **Commercial Drive** ("The Drive"). Most clubs are late-night opening, usually until 4am. British Columbia has also legalized same-sex marriage. For more information, visit ⓦwww.gayvan.com/marriage.

For detailed information on gay and lesbian **events**, check out *X-tra* (ⓣ604/684-XTRA, ⓦwww.xtra.ca),m a regular free magazine available at clubs, bookshops and many of the Georgia Straight distribution points.

Bars, pubs and restaurants

Café Luxy 1235 Davie St ⓣ604/669-5899, ⓦwww.cafeluxy.com. Davie Village and the West End have no shortage of gay-friendly places to eat and drink, but this stands out by virtue of its fresh, home-made pastas and jazz-groove DJ nights, currently every Tues.

Dufferin 900 Seymour St and Smithe St ⓣ604/683-4251, ⓦwww.dufferinhotel.com. This is one of the city's key places for gay men to shake their stuff on the dance floor, but it also hosts a lot of drag-nights – the Buff at the Duff drag shows (Mon–Thurs) are an institution – as well as providing strippers, go-go boys (Fri and Sun) and karaoke.

Fountainhead Pub 1025 Davie ⓣ604/687-2222, ⓦwww.thefountainheadpub.com. A popular and pleasantly buzzing place at the heart of Davie Village for good food, drink (including microbrewed beers) and a large, heated patio from which to spy on all the street action. Also has a pool table, darts and multiple TV screens. Tends to attract a slightly older, more mellow crowd.

Global Beat 1249 Howe St ⓣ604/689-2444. A gay-owned restaurant and lounge with billiard tables that makes a good place for an inexpensive meal (fine Italian-influenced food) or a drink -- there's no heavy cruising – to start the evening, especially if you're heading to *Odyssey*, a club which stands right next door (see opposite).

Oasis 1240 Thurlow ⓣ604/685-1724, ⓦwww.theoasispub.com. Vancouver's only gay piano bar. Comfortable upstairs place for people who want to be heard above the music. Long list of martinis and a tapas menu, with daily specials and a roof-top patio. Daily 9pm until late.

Pump Jack Pub 1167 Davie ⓣ604/685-3417, ⓦwww.pumpjackpub.com. A spacious spot and Vancouver's leather bar of choice: it's favoured by Western Canada Leather Pride and the BC Bears, a gay affiliation for those with a penchant for the hirsute. Arrive early to guarantee a cruisey window-side bar stool to watch the men go by. There are pool tables and uniform nights. Expect queues at the weekends.

Sugar Daddy's 1262 Davie St ⓣ604/632-1646. Another West End gay rendezvous of some standing, thanks to video sports, big-screen TVs, and good burgers, beer and margheritas. Open for lunch and dinner daily.

Clubs

816 Granville 816 Granville St Ⓔsublimenightclub@hotmail.com. A good place to wind up in the small hours if you're still raring to go at the weekend: the after-hours dance club runs Fri & Sat night 1–6am.

Celebrities 1022 Davie St near Burrard St ⓣ604/681-6180, Ⓦwww.celebritiesnightclub.com. Currently Vancouver's current high-profile and showcase gay and lesbian club, completely renovated and overhauled in 2005, with Davie St's largest dance floor, the latest lighting and sound systems and a roster of the city's top DJs. Also numerous theme and one-off nights, plus excellent entertainers. Cover charge most nights.

Club 23 West 23 West Cordova ⓣ604/662-3277. A cool, dark split-level club, perfect for the various theme nights held here, such as the naked parties held by the Pacific Canadian Association of Nudists, "Lesbians on the loose" and "Sin City" fetish nights.

Lotus Sound Lounge 455 Abbott St ⓣ604/685-7777. The bars here host a number of gay and lesbian nights, with men-only, women-only and various theme nights: call for latest details. Some of the most popular dyke nights come courtesy of the Lick Club (Ⓦwww.lickclub.com), a women-run club. There are some mixed nights and occasional fetish and other theme nights. Call before you go for latest permutations and times.

Numbers 1042 Davie St and Burrard St ⓣ604/685-4077. This is a cruisy multilevel venue which has been in business for over twenty years, with a gay disco, kitsch mirrored dance floor, movies and pool tables upstairs, men and women downstairs – but with very few women. Tends to attract a slightly more mature crowd. As with virtually all other clubs listed here, there are a wide variety of theme nights.

Octane 1188 Davie ⓣ604/688-0677. A hip club and bar with DJs and a happening, youngish crowd. Best of the spinning is at the late-night event on Sun. There's currently live jazz on Sat.

Odyssey 1251 Howe St near Davie St ⓣ604/689-5256, Ⓦwww.theodysseynightclub.com. A young gay and bisexual club with house and techno disco and theme shows on most nights. Expect to queue on Fri & Sat as it currently has the reputation as the hippest and wildest place in town.

Events and festivals

While there are no vast **events** or **festivals** in the manner of Sydney's Mardi Gras, there are plenty of one-off and occasional events that have become, or are becoming, permanent fixtures. The main draw in Vancouver's gay calendar is **Pride** (ⓣ604/687-0955 or 737-7433, Ⓦwww.vancouverpride.bc.ca), which celebrates 30 years in 2008. It usually takes place over three days during the first long weekend in August. Special events are held in clubs across the city, while the traditional parade along Denman and Beach has, by general consent, become bigger and better each year, with ever-more exuberant floats. Over the years, the parade has spawned stalls and stages at Sunset Beach up to Davie Street, with lots of beer gardens and live performances. It has also spawned the Vancouver Dyke March (Ⓦwww.vancouverdykemarch.com) in the same week. Special **club events** can be found in the *Georgia Straight* or *Xtra West* (see opposite) free magazines in the week or so preceding Pride. The **Queer Film and Video Festival** (Ⓦwww.outonscreen.com) takes over the city's movie theatres shortly after Pride in August. It will mark its 20th anniversary in 2008. Other noteworthy events include **Gay Ski Week** (Ⓦwww.outontheslopes.com), which has attracted thousands every year since its inception in 1991. Event organizers also now have a summer event, with riding, biking and rafting among warmer-weather activities.

Listings

American Express Park Place Building, 666 Burrard St, enter at Hornby and Dunsmuir (ⓣ604/669-2813 or 1-800/772-4473), and is open Mon–Fri 8.30am–5.30pm, Sat 10am–4pm.
Area code The area code for the greater Vancouver area is ⓣ604.
BC Parks ⓣ604/924-2200, ⓦwww.gov.bc.ca/bcparks.
Bike rental Bayshore Bicycles & Rollerblade Rentals, 745 Denman St (ⓣ604/688-2453) and 1610 West Georgia St at Cardero St and the Westin Bayshore Hotel (ⓣ604/689-5071); Harbour Air, Harbour Air Terminal at the waterfront west of Canada Place (ⓣ604/688-1277) – also rents blades and motorcycles; Spokes, 1798 Georgia at Denman (ⓣ604/688-5141, ⓦwww.vancouverbikerental.com).
Buses Airporter (ⓣ604/946-8866 or 1-800/668-3141, ⓦwww.yvrairporter.com) for shuttle from Vancouver Airport to bus depot and Downtown; BC Transit for city buses, SeaBus and SkyTrain (ⓣ604/953-3333, ⓦwww.translink.bc.ca); Greyhound (ⓣ604/662-3222, 482-8747 or 1-800/661-8747, ⓦwww.greyhound.ca, ⓦwww.malaspinacoach.com) for BC, Alberta, Yukon and long-haul destinations including Seattle and the US; Malaspina Coach Lines (ⓣ1-877/227-8287) for the Sunshine Coast, Powell River, Whistler, Pemberton and Nanaimo on Vancouver Island; Pacific Coach Lines (ⓣ604/662-8074 or 1-800/661-1725, ⓦwww.pacificcoach.com) for Victoria, Vancouver Island; Perimeter (ⓣ604/266-5386 or ⓣ604/717-6600, ⓦwww.perimeterbus.com) for services between Whistler and Vancouver Airport; Quick Shuttle (ⓣ604/940-4428 or 1-800/665-2122, ⓦwww.quickcoach.com) for Bellingham Airport, Downtown Seattle and Sea-Tac Airport.
Car rental Alamo, 1132 West Georgia St at Thurlow St (ⓣ604/684-2869, ⓦwww.Alamo.ca); Avis, 757 Hornby St at West Georgia St (ⓣ604/606-2869, ⓦwww.avis.ca); Budget, airport, 416 West Georgia St at Richards St and 1705 Burrard St (ⓣ604/668-7000 or 1-800/268-8900 in Canada, 1-800/527-0700 in US, ⓦwww.bc.budget.com); Hertz, 1128 Seymour St at Helmcken St (ⓣ604/606-4711 or 1-800/263-0600, ⓦwww.hertz.com); Lo-Cost, 1835 Marine Drive (ⓣ604/986-1266 or 1-800/986-1260, ⓦwwwlocost.com); National (ⓣ1-800/227-7368), airport (ⓣ604/207-3730) and 1130 West Georgia St at Thurlow St (ⓣ604/609-7150, ⓦwww.nationalcar.com); Rent-a-Wreck, 1349 Hornby St (ⓣ604/688-0001 or 1-888/665-3777, ⓦwww.rentawreckvancouver.com).
Currency exchange Custom House Currency, Unit 60-200 Granville St (ⓣ604/608-1763, ⓦwww.customhouse.com); International Securities Exchange, 1169 Robson St near Thurlow (ⓣ604/683-9666); Travelex-Thomas Cook, Suite 130, 999 Canada Place (ⓣ604/641-1229); Vancouver Bullion & Currency Exchange, 402 Hornby St (ⓣ604/685-1008, ⓦwww.vbc.ca).
Dentists Many major hotels have a dentist on call. Otherwise, for your nearest dentists, call the College of Dental Surgeons for a referral (ⓣ604/736-3621) or the British Columbia Dental Association (ⓣ604/736-7202, ⓦwww.bcdentalorg). Drop-in dentist, Dentacare (Mon–Fri 8am–5pm only; ⓣ604/669-6700), is in the lower level of the Bentall Centre at 1055 Dunsmuir and Burrard.
Directory enquiries ⓣ411.
Doctors The College of Physicians can provide names of three doctors near you (ⓣ604/733-7758). Drop-in service (no appointments necessary) at Bentall Centre, Vancouver Medical Clinics, 1055 Dunsmuir (ⓣ604/683-8138; Mon–Fri 8am–4.45pm); Carepoint, 1175 Denman St (ⓣ604/681-5338; daily 9am–9pm); Stein Medical Clinic, Bentall 5 Lobby, 188-550 Burrard St at West Pender St (ⓣ604/688-5924, ⓦwww.steinmedicalclinic.com; Mon–Fri 8.30am–5.30pm); or Ultima Vancouver Airport Medical Clinic, Vancouver International Airport, Domestic Terminal (ⓣ604/207-6900, ⓦwww.ultimamedical.ca).
Electricity Canada uses 110-volt, 60-cycle electricity, which means that travellers from the US should find that their appliances work without a hitch, but Europeans and others will need an adapter.
Emergency services (police, fire and ambulance) ⓣ911.
Hospitals Emergency Room, St Paul's Hospital, 1081 Burrard Street (ⓣ682-2344). Vancouver General Hospital, 855 West 12th Avenue (ⓣ604/874-4111) or British Columbia's Children's Hospital, 4480 Oak St. (ⓣ604/875-2345). In North Van there is the Lions Gate Hospital, 231 East 15th St (ⓣ604/988-3131).
Internet access Free access at the Vancouver Central Library, 350 West Georgia St (ⓣ604/331-3600, ⓦwww.vpl.ca; access not available on Sun); or from about $4 an hour at the *Internet Café*, 1104 Davie St at Thurlow (ⓣ604/682-6668), which opens daily until 11pm.
Laundry Davie Laundromat, 1061 Davie St (ⓣ604/682-2717); Scotty's One Hour Cleaners, 834 Thurlow near Robson (ⓣ604/685-7732).

Left luggage At Pacific Central Station ($2 per 24hr) and at CDS Baggage at the city airport national and international arrivals (from $2 per item for 24hr).
Liquor laws The legal drinking age in British Columbia is 19.
Lost property BC Transit, Stadium SkyTrain station, 590 Beatty St (Ⓣ604/682-7887); West Vancouver Transit (Ⓣ604/985-7777); police (Ⓣ604/717-2726); airport, Customer Service Counter, Level 3, International Departures (Ⓣ604/276-6104). If you leave items in a taxi, call the appropriate cab company.
Maps Geological Survey of Canada, 101-605 Robson near Richards (Mon–Fri 8.30am–4.30pm; Ⓣ604/666-0529). Superb source of official survey maps, including *all* 1:50,000 maps of BC and Yukon.
Optician Opticana Eyewear, 455 Granville St (Ⓣ604/685-1031, Ⓦwww.opticana.ca).
Parking Main Downtown garages are at The Bay (entrance on Richards near Dunsmuir), Robson Square (on Smithe and Howe), and the Pacific Centre (on Howe and Dunsmuir) – all are expensive and fill up quickly. A better idea might be to leave your car at the free Park'n'Ride in New Westminster (off Hwy 1).
Pharmacies Shopper's Drug Mart, 1125 Davie and Thurlow (Ⓣ604/669-2424), is open 24hr and has five other outlets open Mon–Sat 9am–midnight, Sun 9am–9pm. London Drugs, 1650 Davie St (Ⓣ604/669-2884) is open daily until 11pm. Carson Midnite Drug Store, 6517 Main at 49th, is open daily until midnight. Safeway supermarket pharmacies are also often open late: the store at Robson and Denman sts is open until midnight.
Police Non-emergency 24-hr (Ⓣ604/717-3321). RCMP (Ⓣ604/264-3111); Vancouver City Police, 2120 Cambie St (Ⓣ604/665-3535 or 717-3535, Ⓦwww.Vancouver.ca/police).
Post office Main office at 349 West Georgia and Homer (Mon–Fri 8am–5.30pm; Ⓣ604/662-5722 or 1-800/267-1177). Post-office information (Ⓣ1-800/267-1177, Ⓦwww.canadapost.ca). Post office outlets with longer hours can be found in many 7-Eleven and Shopper's Drug Mart stores.
Smoking All indoor public transport and other public spaces, including bars and restaurants, are non-smoking. Smoking is generally allowed on restaurant and bar terraces and patios. You need to be 19 to purchase tobacco.
Student cards Most places will accept a school ID for student discounts; an ISIC card, however, is the most widely recognized and accepted card of all.
Tax Provincial Sales Tax (PST) is 7.5 percent on most goods and services, rising to eight percent on hotel bills and ten percent in restaurants and bars; this is supplemented by the nationwide Goods and Services Tax (GST), a seven percent levy equivalent to VAT in Europe.
Taxis Black Top (Ⓣ604/731-1111 or 681-2181); Vancouver Taxi (Ⓣ604/871-1111); Yellow Cab (Ⓣ604/681-3311 or 604/681-1111).
Train enquiries VIA Rail (Ⓣ604/669-3050 or toll-free in Canada only Ⓣ1-888/842-7245, 1-800/561-3949 in the US, Ⓦwww.viarail.ca); Amtrak (Ⓣ1-800/872-7245, Ⓦwww.amtrak.com); Rocky Mountain Railtours (Ⓣ604/606-7200 or 1-800/665-7245, Ⓦwww.rockymountaineer.com) for expensive rail tours through the Rockies.
Weather information Ⓣ604/664-9010.

The Sunshine Coast, Whistler and the Cariboo

Apart from Vancouver Island, Victoria and the Southern Gulf Islands, covered in the next section, two other major excursions from Vancouver are possible, each of which can easily be extended to embrace longer itineraries out of the city. Both are part of mainland southern British Columbia, but owing to the lie of the land and the paucity of roads in this region, both can only realistically be accessed from Vancouver.

The first, and less enticing, is the 150-kilometre **Sunshine Coast**, the only stretch of accessible coastline on mainland British Columbia, and a possible

Moving on from Vancouver

Vancouver is at the hub of transport links to many parts of western Canada. Deciding where to move **onward from the city** – and how to go – presents a wealth of possibilities. We've listed the basic alternatives, together with cross-references to more detailed accounts of the various options.

The Yukon and Alaska

You can **fly** to **Whitehorse** (see p.1043) in the Yukon directly from Vancouver, but there are no nonstop flights to Alaska from the city: all go via Seattle in the US. Flying to Seattle or taking a bus to Sea-Tac Airport takes around three hours from Vancouver Airport or various downtown hotels and other locations (see p.797 for bus details). You can **drive** to Alaska through southern British Columbia to **Dawson Creek**, where you can pick up the **Alaska Hwy** (see p.1018), which runs through the Yukon to Fairbanks. Allow at least three days. Alternatively drive to Prince George, head west towards Prince Rupert and then strike north up the more adventurous **Cassiar Hwy** (see p.1014) to connect with the Alaska Hwy in the Yukon. Using **public transport** you could take a Greyhound bus to Prince George (one day), connecting with another Greyhound to Dawson Creek and Whitehorse (two days). Buses link Whitehorse with other Yukon and Alaskan destinations. To travel to Alaska **by boat** from Vancouver you need to go via Bellingham (in the US), Prince Rupert, or Port Hardy on Vancouver Island (see p.933).

BC, Calgary and the Canadian Rockies

Two main **road** routes strike east from Vancouver towards Alberta and the Canadian Rockies – the **Trans-Canada Highway** and **Hwy 3**, both served by regular Greyhound buses. Both give access to **the Okanagan** (see p.957), known for its warm-watered lakes and summer resorts, and to the beautiful mountain and lakes enclave of the **Kootenays** (see p.971). VIA trains run three times weekly through the region via Kamloops to **Jasper** (for the Rockies) and **Edmonton**. Buses also serve the **Cariboo** region, the duller central part of the province (see p.864). Several mouthwatering itineraries can be put together by combining car or public transport journeys in the **BC interior** with BC Ferries' connections from Port Hardy on Vancouver Island to either Bella Coola or Prince Rupert.

It takes between ten and twelve hours to drive to **Calgary** on the Trans-Canada Hwy, and about ninety minutes less to reach the heart of the Canadian Rockies, **Banff**. Special express-service Greyhound buses operate over the same route. There is no longer a VIA Rail passenger service to Calgary. Very frequent one-hour flights connect Vancouver and Calgary, and charter operators and no-frills airlines offer highly competitive rates on this route (though cheap flights often leave very early or very late in the day).

Vancouver Island

Numerous **ferries** ply between Vancouver and three points on **Vancouver Island** – Swartz Bay (for Victoria), Nanaimo and Comox. Most leave from Tsawwassen and Horseshoe Bay, terminals about thirty minutes' drive south and west of downtown respectively. As a foot passenger you can buy inclusive bus and ferry tickets from Vancouver to Victoria or Nanaimo. Car drivers should make reservations well in advance for all summer crossings (see p.872 for full details of getting to Vancouver Island). **Public transport** connects to the Pacific Rim National Park, the island's highlight, and to Port Hardy on the island's northern tip for ferry connections to Prince Rupert and Bella Coola.

springboard to Vancouver Island: ferries depart from Powell River, the coast's largest town, to Comox on Vancouver Island. Most people on short trips, however, make the run to Powell River and then turn tail for Vancouver – there is no alternative route back to the city and no onward road route after the village of Lund and the end of Hwy 101 beyond Powell River.

The second, and far more tempting trip is the inland route to **Garibaldi Provincial Park**, which contains by far the best scenery and hiking country within striking distance of Vancouver, and then on to the famous world-class summer and winter resort of **Whistler**. The latter is well worth visiting at any time of the year, with winter an obviously busy time and summer almost equally popular, thanks to the area's many outdoor activities. En route to whistler you'll pass through **Squamish**, nothing to rave over scenically, but one of North America's premier destinations for windsurfing, climbing and – in season – eagle-watching.

Beyond Whistler the roads and countryside empty quickly, picking up the Fraser River at **Lillooet**, a striking scenic interlude before the more workaday ranching country and immense forests of the **Cariboo** region. On the coast, and only accessible via a single mountain road or by sea, is **Bella Coola**, best seen as part of a longer itinerary that takes in Vancouver Island and the Discovery Coast ferry service (see p.935). Continuing north from the Cariboo provides access to Prince George and the north (see p.997), but be warned – it's a long and pretty dull haul.

The Sunshine Coast

A mild-weathered stretch of sandy beaches, rugged headlands and quiet lagoons running northwest of Vancouver, the **Sunshine Coast** receives heavy promotion – and heavy tourist traffic as a result – though in truth its reputation is considerably overstated and the scenic rewards are slim compared to the grandeur of the BC interior. Even as a taste of the province's mountain scenery it leaves much to be desired, and the best that can be said of the region is that in summer it offers some of western Canada's best diving, boating and fishing. If you are just coming out for the day, the best parts of the trip are the various **ferry crossings** en route: the first is from Horseshoe Bay at the western extreme of West Vancouver to Langdale and Gibsons Landing, where you pick up Hwy 101 for the 79-kilometre run along the coast to Earl's Cove, and the beautiful (and slightly longer) crossing to Saltery Bay, where the boat provides views of some fine maritime landscapes. The road then continues 35km to Powell River before coming to an abrupt conclusion 23km later at the village of Lund.

Highway 101

Highway 101 runs almost the length of the coast from Gibsons Landing, often known simply as Gibsons, which is just 5km from the ferry terminal at Langdale for boats coming from **Horseshoe Bay** at the end of Marine Drive and the western edge of West Vancouver. You can reach the ferry terminal here from the city by taking bus #250 or the #257 express westbound from points on West Georgia Street downtown. Given that the coast is hardly worth full-scale exploration by car, and that the two ferry crossings provide two of the trip's highlights, you might consider saving the price of a rental and going by **bus**; it's perfectly feasible to get to **Powell River** in a day. Malaspina Coachlines (Ⓣ1-888/227-8287, Ⓦwww.malaspinacoach.com) runs two buses to Powell River at 8.15am (Fri–Sun) and daily at 4.15pm (5hr 45min; $49 one way). Returns leave at 6.45am daily and 2.45pm Friday to Sunday. Bus tickets include the price of the

△ An aerial view of the Sunshine Coast

ferry crossings en route. Buses also run from the airport daily at 3.15pm and Friday to Sunday at 7.15am (6hr 45min; $62).

Gibsons to Powell River

Soon reached and well signposted from North and West Vancouver, **Horseshoe Bay** is the departure point for the first of the Hwy 101 **ferry** crossings, a 30–40-minute passage through the islands of fjord-like Howe Sound. There are regular sailings year-round, and tickets cost $9.15 ($8.90 off peak) for adults and $32.65 for cars: bikes cost $2.50; all tickets cost a little less outside the late-June to early September peak period. Note that each ticket is valid for one Horseshoe Bay-Langdale (return), Earl's Cove-Saltery Bay (return) or single journeys on both the Horseshoe Bay-Langdale and Earl's Cove-Saltery Bay crossings. Ferries also ply from here to Nanaimo on Vancouver Island, with hourly sailings in summer and every other hour off-season. Tickets cost $10.80 per adult and $37.80 for cars (less off-season and less for cars year-round outside weekends). For information on either of these services, contact BC Ferries in Vancouver (Ⓣ604/669-1211, 250/386-3431 or 1-888/223-3779, Ⓦwww.bcferries.com), or pick up a timetable from the Vancouver infocentre.

Gibsons, the terminal on the other side of Howe Sound, is spread widely over a wooded hillside – the nicest area is around the busy marina and public wharf, a better bet if you're pausing than Upper Gibsons a little further down the highway, which is little more than a busy strip. If you have time to kill, check out the town's two modest museums: the **Sunshine Coast Maritime Museum & Archives** on Molly's Lane (June–Aug Tues–Sat 10.30am–4pm; free; Ⓦwww.sunshinecoastmuseum.ca), which contains predictable displays of maritime and frontier memorabilia. For more on the town and details of local trails, beaches and swimming areas, visit the **infocentre** at 417 Marine Drive (daily 9am–6pm; Ⓣ604/886-2374 or 1-866/222-3806, Ⓦwww.gibsonschamber.com).

Farther west on Hwy 101 is Pender Harbour, a string of small coastal communities of which **Madeira Park** is the most substantial; whales occasionally pass this section of coast – which, sadly, is the source of many of the whales in the world's aquariums – but the main draws are fishing and boating. **Earl's Cove** is nothing but the departure ramp of the second ferry hop – a longer crossing (45min) that again offers fantastic views, including an immense waterfall that drops off a "Lost World"-type plateau into the sea.

From Jervis Bay, the opposite landing stage, it's a couple of kilometres up the road to the best of all the provincial parks in this region, **Saltery Bay Provincial Park**. Everything here is discreetly hidden in the trees between the road and the coast, and the campsite ($14) – beautifully situated – is connected by short trails to a couple of swimming beaches. Farther along on the main road, various **campsites** give onto the sea, notably the big *Oceanside Resort Motel* site which also has 11 cabins, 7km short of Powell River, which sits on a superb piece of shoreline (ⓣ604/485-2435 or 1-888/889-2435, ⓦwww.oceansidepark.com; sites $16 per two persons; ❸).

Powell River and beyond

Given its seafront location, **Powell River** has its scenic side, but like many a BC town its unfocused sprawl and nearby sawmill slightly dampen the overall appeal. If you're catching the **ferry** to Courtenay on Vancouver Island (4 daily; 75min), you might not see the town site, as the terminal is 2km to the east at Westview, and some of the **buses** from Vancouver are timed to coincide with the boats; if your bus doesn't connect, you can either walk from the town centre or bus terminal or call a taxi (ⓣ604/483-3666). The local **infocentre** (summer daily 9am–5pm, winter Mon–Fri 9am–5pm; ⓣ604/485-4701 or 1-877/817-8669, ⓦwww.discoverpowellriver.com), which is at 111-4871 Joyce Ave, can supply a visitors' map showing the many trails leading inland from the coast hereabouts; they can also advise on boat trips on Powell Lake, immediately inland, and tours to Desolation Sound farther up the coast. The most central of several **campsites** is the 81-site *Willingdon Beach Municipal Campground* on the seafront off Marine Avenue at 6910 Duncan St (ⓣ604/485-2242, ⓦwww.willingdonbeach.ca; $17–23).

The northern end-point of Hwy 101 – which, incidentally, starts in Mexico City, making it one of North America's longest continuous routes – is the hamlet of **Lund**, 28km up the coast from Powell River. **Desolation Sound Marine Provincial Park**, about 10km north of Lund, offers some of Canada's best boating and scuba diving, plus fishing, canoeing and kayaking. There's no road access to the park, but a number of outfitters in Powell River run tours to it and can hire all the equipment you could possibly need – try Westview Live Bait Ltd, 4527 Marine Ave, for **canoes**; Coulter's Diving, 4557 Willingdon Ave, for **scuba gear**; and Spokes, 4710 Marine Drive for **bicycles**. The more modest **Okeover Provincial Park**, immediately north of Lund, has an unserviced campsite ($14).

The Sea to Sky Highway

A fancy name for Hwy 99 between North Vancouver and Whistler, the **Sea to Sky Highway** has a slightly better reputation than it deserves. It undoubtedly scores in its early coastal stretch, where the road clings perilously to an almost sheer cliff and mountains come dramatically into view on both sides of Howe Sound. Views here are better than along the Sunshine Coast, though plenty of campsites, motels and minor roadside distractions fill the route until the mountains of the Coast Range rear up beyond **Squamish** for the rest of the way to Whistler.

If you've a **car** you're better off driving the hwy only as far as **Garibaldi Provincial Park** – the section between Pemberton and Lillooet, the Duffy Lake Road, is very slow going and often impassable in winter, though the drive is a stunner, with wonderful views of lakes and glaciers. Regular buses (see "Perimeter bus" details on p.844) connect Vancouver and Whistler (some continue to Pemberton), which you can easily manage as a day-trip (it's 2hr 30min one-way to Whistler from Vancouver by bus).

Britannia Beach

Road and rail lines meet with some squalor at tiny **Britannia Beach**, 53km from Vancouver, whose **BC Museum of Mining** is the first reason to take time out from admiring the views (early May to mid-Oct daily 9am–5.30pm, mid-Oct to early May Mon–Fri 9am–4.30; $14.98; ⓣ1-800/8964044, ⓦwww.bcmuseumofmining.org). Centring on what was, in the 1930s, the largest producer of copper in the British Empire – 56 million tons of ore were extracted here before the mine closed in 1974 – the museum is housed in a huge, derelict-looking building on the hillside and is chock-full of hands-on displays, original working machinery, a 235-ton monster mine truck and archive photographs. You can also take guided underground tours (every 30min) around about 350m of the mine's galleries on small electric trains. And if parts of the complex look familiar it's because the mine has been used as a location in *The X-Files* and numerous other films and TV programmes.

Continuing north you pass several small coastal reserves, the most striking of which is **Shannon Falls Provincial Park**, 7km from Britannia Beach, signed right off the road and worth a stop for its spectacular 335-metre **waterfall**. Six times the height of Niagara, you can see it from the road, but it's only five minutes' walk to the viewing area at the base, where the proximity of the road, plus a campsite and diner, detract a touch.

Squamish

The sea views and coastal drama end 11km beyond Britannia Beach at **SQUAMISH**, whose houses spread out over a flat plain amidst warehouses, logging waste and old machinery. However, if you want to climb, windsurf or mountain bike, there's nowhere better in the region to do so. At a glance, all the town has by way of fame is the vast granite rock overshadowing it, "The Stawamus Chief", which looms into view to the east just beyond Shannon Falls and is claimed to be the world's "second-biggest free-standing rock" (after Gibraltar, apparently). The town rates as one of Canada's top – if not *the* top – spot for **rock climbing**. Around 200,000 climbers from around the world come here annually, swarming to more than four hundred routes covering the 625-metre monolith: the University Wall and its culmination, the Dance Platform, is rated Canada's toughest climb.

The rock is sacred to the local Squamish, whose ancient tribal name – which means "place where the wind blows" – gives a clue as to the town's second big activity: **windsurfing**. There are strong, consistent winds to suit all abilities, but the water is cold, so a wet suit's a good idea (there are rental outlets around town). Most people head for the artificial **Squamish Spit**, a dyke separating the waters of the Howe Sound from the Squamish River. The area is run by the Squamish Windsports Society (small fee; ⓣ604/926-WIND, ⓦwww.squamishwindsurfing.org) and is 3km from town.

Rounding out Squamish's outdoor activities is the tremendous **mountain biking** terrain – there are 63 trails in the area ranging from gnarly single-track trails to readily accessible deactivated forestry roads. The best areas are the Valley Cliff Trails (stream-bed, single-track and woodland trails); Mamquam Forest Service roads (active logging roads with fine views of the Mamquam Glacier); the Cat Lake and Brohm Lake trails; and the Alice Lake trails, which include an abandoned railway for an easy ride.

The town has one more unexpected treat, for the Squamish River, and the tiny hamlet of Brackendale in particular (10km to the north on Hwy 99), which is the world's best place to see **bald-eagles**. In winter around 2000 eagles congregate here, attracted by the migrating salmon. The best places to see them are the so-called Eagle Run just south of the centre of Brackendale, and on the river in the Brackendale Eagles Provincial Park.

If you want to base yourself locally while seeing the eagles, contact the Sunwolf Outdoor Centre (Ⓣ604/898-1537 or 1-877/806-8046, Ⓦwww.sunwolf.net), signposted off Hwy 1 – take a left onto Squamish Valley Road at the Alice Lake junction 2km past Brackendale, continue for 4km and the centre is on the right. It has ten great three-person cabins on the shore of the Cheakamus River for $90; some have kitchens for an extra $10. To see the eagles from a raft costs $99 per person, including light lunch; a raft trip plus cabin accommodation costs $134 per person, if two share a cabin.

Practicalities

Most of the relevant parts of the town are concentrated on or near Cleveland Avenue, off Hwy 99, including the **infocentre** (May–Sept daily 9am–5pm; Oct–April Mon–Fri 9am–5pm, Sat & Sun 10am–2pm; Ⓣ604/892-9244 or 1-866-333.2010, Ⓦwww.squamishchamber.com), a big supermarket and the most central **accommodation** if you're not at the hostel (see below), the *August Jack Motor Inn* (Ⓣ604/892-3504 or 1-888-892-3502, Ⓦwww.augustjack.com; ❸). Alternatively, the *Garibaldi Budget Inn*, 38012-3rd Ave (Ⓣ604/892-5204 or 1-888-313-9299; ❷), is excellent value. If you can afford more, then definitely plump for the Howe Sound Inn & Brewing Company, 37801 Cleveland Ave (Ⓣ604/892-2603 or 1-800-919-2537, Ⓦwww.howesound.com; ❺), which has 20 simple but modern rooms, great food and plenty of beer from its own microbrewery. The superlative *Squamish Hostel* at Mamquam Blind Channel on Hwy 99 (Ⓣ 604/892-9240 or 1-800/449-8614, Ⓦwww.hostels.com/squamish; ❶) is clean and friendly, with a kitchen, common room and 18 beds including two private rooms. Beds are $25.50 a night (three nights cost $60) and private rooms are $55.

If you're looking into **renting equipment**, Vertical Reality Sports Centre at 37835 2nd Ave (Ⓣ604/892-8248, Ⓦwww.verticalrealitysports.com) rents climbing shoes ($10 a day) and mountain bikes ($15–40 a day). For other **mountain bike hire**, contact Tantalus (Ⓣ604/898-2588), by the Greyhound depot at 40446 Government Road, or Corsa Cycles (Ⓣ604/892-3331, Ⓦwww.corsacycles.com) at 800-1200 Hunter Place: rates for both start at about $45 for a day's hire. If you are here to climb, there are several **guides**, available from bookstores in Vancouver as well as the climbing shops in Squamish: Kevin McLane is the author of several books, including *The Climbers' Guide to Squamish* (Elaho, $34.95).

Garibaldi Provincial Park

After about 5km, the road north of Squamish enters the classic river, mountain and forest country of the BC interior. The journey thereafter up to Whistler is a joy, with only the march of electricity pylons to take the edge off an idyllic drive.

Unless you're skiing, **Garibaldi Provincial Park** is the main incentive for heading this way. It's a huge and unspoilt area that combines all the usual breathtaking ingredients of lakes, rivers, forests, glaciers and the peaks of the Coast Mountains (Wedge Mountain, at 2891m, is the park's highest point). Four rough roads access the park from points along the hwy between Squamish and Whistler, but you'll need transport to reach the trailheads at the end of them. Other than camping, the only accommodation close to the park is at Whistler.

There are five main areas with trails, of which the **Black Tusk/Garibaldi Lake** region is the most popular and probably most beautiful, thanks to its high-mountain views. Further trails fan out from Garibaldi Lake, including one to the huge basalt outcrop of **Black Tusk** (2316m), a rare opportunity to reach an alpine summit without any rock climbing. The other hiking areas from south to north are **Diamond Head**, **Cheakamus Lake**, **Singing Pass** and **Wedgemount Lake**. Outside these small, defined areas, however, the park is untrammelled wilderness. For more **information**, including good advice on trails, visit Ⓦwww.garibaldipark.com or pick the dedicated BC Parks pamphlet from infocentres in Vancouver and elsewhere, whose information can also be accessed at Ⓦwww.gov.bc.ca/bcparks.

Whistler

WHISTLER, 56km beyond Squamish and 125km from Vancouver, is Canada's finest four-season resort, and frequently ranks among most people's world top-five winter ski resorts. Skiing and snowboarding are clearly the main activities, but all manner of other winter sports are possible and in summer the lifts keep running to provide supreme highline hiking and other outdoor activities (not to mention North America's finest summer skiing). It is a busy place, be warned – over two million lift tickets are sold here every winter, more than at any other North American resort. Fortunately it also has one of the continent's largest ski areas, so the crowds are spread thinly over the resort's 200-plus trails and twelve alpine bowls.

The resort consists of two adjacent but separate mountains – **Whistler** (2182m) and **Blackcomb** (2284m) – each with their own extensive lift and chair systems (but a joint ticket scheme). The mountains can be accessed from a total of five bases, including lift systems to both mountains from the resort's heart, the purpose-built and largely pedestrianized **Whistler Village**, the tight-clustered focus of many hotels, shops, restaurants and après-ski activity. The gondola (cable-car) for Whistler Mountain also leaves from the Village. Around this core are two other "village" complexes, **Upper Village** (for the gondola to Blackcomb Mountain), about a kilometre to the northeast and the newer Village North about 700m to the north. Around 6km to the south of Whistler Village is **Whistler Creekside** (also with a gondola and lift base), which has typically been a cheaper alternative but is now undergoing a fifty-million dollar redevelopment that will see its accommodation and local services duplicating those of its famous neighbour. Such sums, and such development, are likely to be repeated in the build-up to the 2010 Winter Olympics, which will be largely based in and around Whistler. Property prices, especially around Whistler Village have already soared.

Arrival, information and getting around

There are several ways of **getting to** Whistler. If you're driving from Vancouver, allow about two and a bit hours for the 125-kilometre run on the hwy – the road was only completed as recently as 1965: before that the area was little visited. Note that a 600-million dollar upgrade to the hwy for the 2010 Winter Olympics means that delays of up to 30 minutes and occasional closures should be expected. It is hoped the upgrading will knock an hour off the current two- to three-hour trip.

Perimeter (Ⓣ604/266-5386 or 1-877/317-7788, Ⓦwww.perimeterbus.com) runs a shuttle **bus** from Vancouver airport and various Vancouver hotels to Whistler Bus Loop and a selection of Whistler hotels. Reservations are required year-round for the service (April–mid-Dec 7 daily, 3 of which are express services and do not stop at Vancouver hotels – there are 8 southbound departures, including 3 express runs; mid-Dec–April 11 daily, including 8 express services; 2hr 30min–3hr; $67 plus tax one-way). Note that winter schedules can be affected by bad weather on the Sea to Sky Hwy.

Greyhound (Ⓣ604/482-8747 in Vancouver, Ⓣ604/932-5031 in Whistler, 1-800/661-8747 from anywhere in North America, 604/904-7060 from outside North America and 0800 731 5983 from the UK; Ⓦwww.greyhound.ca or Ⓦwww.whistlerbus.com) runs eight daily bus services from Vancouver's bus depot (see p.795) to the Village (2hr 30min; $18.45 one-way) via Britannia Beach, Whistler Creek and other stops. In winter (Dec–April) Greyhound's ski express leaves Vancouver at 6.30am and goes non-stop to Whistler arriving at 8.30am.

After years as a freight-only operation, part of the old BC Rail line from North Vancouver to Prince George has been reopened to the passenger traffic. The Whistler Mountaineer departs daily from May to mid-October from North Vancouver station at 8am, arriving in Whistler at 11.30am. The return trip leaves at 2pm. It's designed as an excursion trip rather than a passenger service, however, and it costs a steep $99 one way. Bookings must be made in advance by phone only (Ⓣ1-888/403-4727).

Faster still is a helicopter with Helijet (Ⓣ604/273-1414, Ⓦwww.helijet.com), which costs around $150 one-way from Vancouver Airport (2 daily; 45min) or the terminal at Coal Harbour in downtown Vancouver (2 daily; 30min).

If you're staying in or near the Village, then you won't really need **local transport**, but WAVE (Ⓣ604/932-4020) runs a shuttle bus service around Whistler Village, Village North and Upper Village as well as buses to Whistler Creek and other destinations ($1.50 flat fare, five-day pass $5). Buses have racks for skis and bikes. If you need taxis to get around locally, try Whistler Taxi (Ⓣ604/932-3333) or Airport Limousine Service (Ⓣ1/800-278-8742 or 604/273-1331).

Information

For recorded **information** on Whistler-Blackcomb call Ⓣ1-800/766-0449 (Ⓣ604/664-5614 from Vancouver, Ⓣ604/932-3434 from Whistler or 1-866/218-9690 toll-free in North America, Ⓦwww.whistlerblackcomb.com). Tourism Whistler (Ⓣ604/932-3928) is another source of information, though they cater towards the top end of the market; they also run the Whistler Activity and Information Centre, in the green-roofed Conference Centre near the Village Square (daily 9am–5pm; Ⓣ604/932-2394 or 1-800/WHISTLER, Ⓦwww.tourismwhistler.com). The more down-to-earth and friendly **Chamber of Commerce** is in Whistler Village at 4230 Gateway Drive, off Village Gate Blvd (Mon–Thu 8.30am–6.30pm, Fri–Sat 8.30am–7.30pm; Ⓣ604/932-5592, Ⓦwww.whistlerchamber.com). This office can assist with general information, tickets for events and last-minute accommodation. **Information kiosks** open

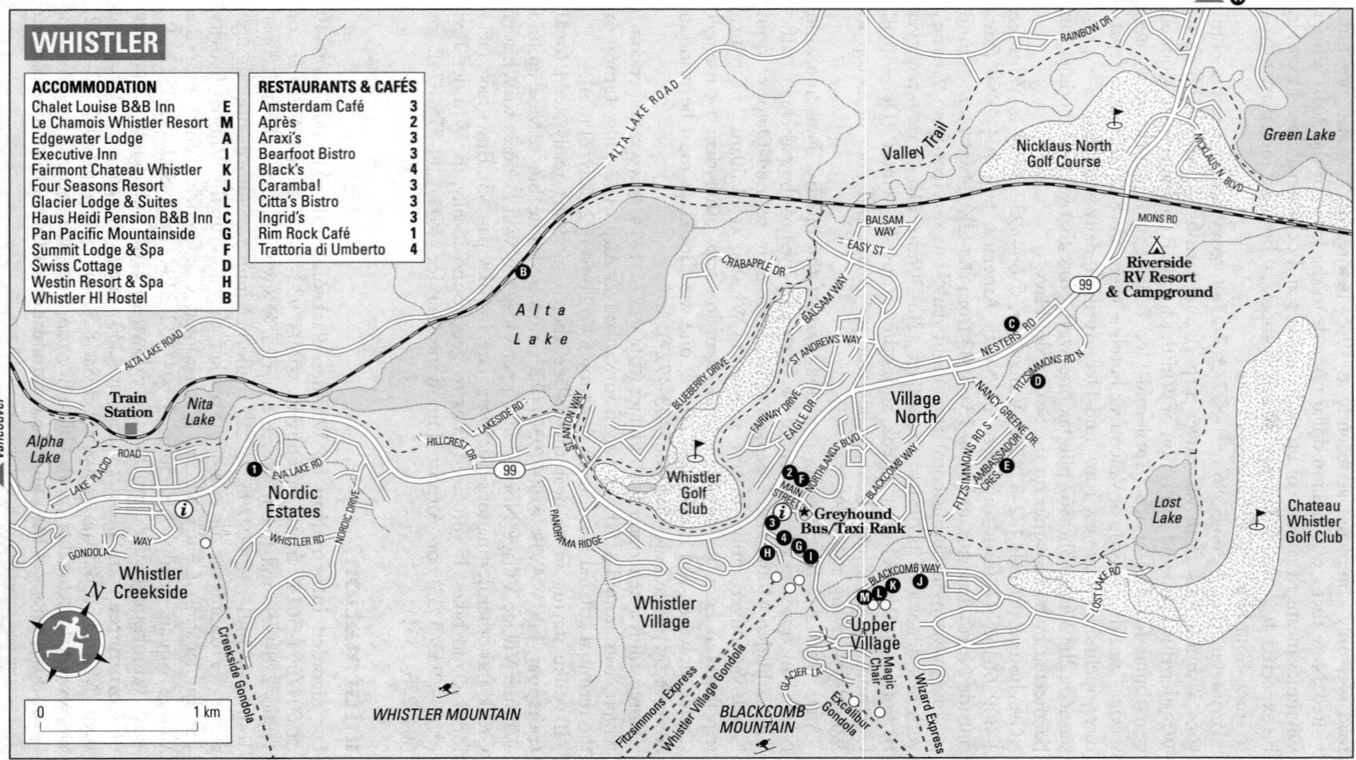
WHISTLER
ACCOMMODATION
Chalet Louise B&B Inn E
Le Chamois Whistler Resort M
Edgewater Lodge A
Executive Inn I
Fairmont Chateau Whistler K
Four Seasons Resort J
Glacier Lodge & Suites L
Haus Heidi Pension B&B Inn C
Pan Pacific Mountainside G
Summit Lodge & Spa F
Swiss Cottage D
Westin Resort & Spa H
Whistler HI Hostel B
RESTAURANTS & CAFÉS
Amsterdam Café 3
Après 2
Araxi's 3
Bearfoot Bistro 3
Black's 4
Caramba! 3
Citta's Bistro 3
Ingrid's 3
Rim Rock Café 1
Trattoria di Umberto 4
Pemberton
Vancouver
Green Lake
Nicklaus North Golf Course
Valley Trail
Riverside RV Resort & Campground
Alta Lake
Nita Lake
Alpha Lake
Train Station
Nordic Estates
Whistler Creekside
Whistler Golf Club
Village North
Greyhound Bus/Taxi Rank
Whistler Village
Upper Village
Lost Lake
Chateau Whistler Golf Club
WHISTLER MOUNTAIN
BLACKCOMB MOUNTAIN
Creekside Gondola
Fitzsimmons Express
Whistler Village Gondola
Excalibur Gondola
Magic Chair
Wizard Express
ALTA LAKE ROAD
RAINBOW DR
NICKLAUS N. BLVD
MONS RD
BALSAM WAY
EASY ST
CRABAPPLE DR
NESTERS RD
FITZSIMMONS RD N
FITZSIMMONS RD S
NANCY GREENE DR.
AMBASSADOR CRES
ST ANDREWS WAY
BLUEBERRY DRIVE
FAIRWAY DRIVE
EAGLE DR
NORTHLANDS BLVD
BLACKCOMB WAY
MAIN STREET
LOST LAKE RD
GLACIER LA
LAKESIDE RD
ST ANTON WAY
HILLCREST DR
PANORAMA RIDGE
EVA LAKE RD
NORDIC DRIVE
WHISTLER RD
LAKE PLACID ROAD
GONDOLA WAY
99
0 1 km

daily 9am to 5pm between May and early September at several points, including the main bus stop and the Village Gate Boulevard at the entrance to Whistler Village.

For information on, and bookings for **activities** visit the **Tourism Whistler Activity Centre** in front of the TELUS Conference Centre near the Whistler Mountain gondola (ⓣ604/938-2769 or 1-877/991-9988).

Accommodation

If you're here in summer and not on a package tour, all local **accommodation** can be booked through the excellent Whistler Central Reservations (ⓣ604/664-5625, 1-800/944-7853 toll-free in North America and toll-free in the UK ⓣ0800/731 5983, ⓦwww.tourismwhistler.com or www.mywhistler.com). In winter, reservations for those not on a package tour should be made well in advance (Sept at least), as many hotels have a thirty-day cancellation window and may insist on a minimum of three days' stay; prices are highest at this time, too. In winter there's no such thing as budget accommodation, unless you stay at the hostel, and with ever greater numbers of visitors in the summer, prices – and availability – of beds are increasingly a problem outside the ski season. But bear in mind that you don't have to stay in a "conventional" hotel, as there is a wide range of chalets, condos, apartments and houses to rent. These, as well as many hotels, often have kitchen facilities, enabling you save money on dining out. Virtually all types of accommodation, from B&B to condo, list nightly and weekly rates, and in season there's likely to be a minimum stay.

Hotels

Alpine Lodge 8135 Alpine Way ⓣ604/932-5966 or 905-8766, ⓦwww.Alpinelodge.com. A casual but reasonably elegant lodge, with eight rooms and beds for 32 people, which means that much of the accommodation can be taken by groups or families, so book early. ❸

Chalet Luise B&B Inn 7461 Ambassador Crescent ⓣ604/932-4187 or 1-800/665-1998, ⓦwww.chaletluise.com. Open May–Nov. Eight rooms in a peaceful garden setting that is convenient for the Village, lifts and various summer hiking trails. The European owners pride themselves on providing big, homemade breakfasts. ❺

Edgewater Lodge 8841 Hwy 99, 3km north of the Village ⓣ604/932-0688, ⓦwww.edgewater-lodge.com. Set on a lovely forested waterfront promontory that pushes into Green Lake. As a result the 12 luxurious rooms enjoy sublime views, and you can canoe and hike virtually from the front door. ❼

Executive Inn at Whistler Village 4250 Village Stroll ⓣ604/932-3200 or 1-800/663-6416, ⓦwww.executiveiinnwhistler.com. Located at the heart of the Village, this "European-style" hotel has 37 rooms, each with big picture windows, kitchenettes, fireplaces and two-person Jacuzzis. ❹

Fairmont Château Whistler 4599 Château Boulevard, Upper Village ⓣ604/938-8000 or –800/257-7544; ⓦwww.fairmont.com. This was the resort's obvious first choice until the arrival of the *Four Seasons* (see across), which has left the vast English-manor-house-meets-French-château affair looking a little dated and its vast lobby and overall stylistic effect a little bombastic (the colossal lobby and its redoubtable wooden beams are a sightseeing attraction in themselves for some visitors). You won't be disappointed here, certainly not in the fine spa, but if you have the money, the Four Seasons is the preferred choice. ❾

Four Seasons Resort Whistler 4591 Blackcomb Way, Upper Village ⓣ604/935-3400 or 1-888/935-2460, ⓦwww.fourseasons.com. Opened in June 2004, the *Four Seasons* stole the *Château Whistler's* upmarket thunder, quickly emerging as Whistler's luxury resort hotel of choice. Service reaches the *Four Seasons*' group's usual elevated standards, and the fabulous panoramic rooms, black-slate bathrooms, suites and town-house-style accommodation are the largest and most polished of their sort in town. Gas-burner fireplaces in the cosy wood-interior rooms are typical nice touches. All manner of facilities are available, along with every aid and guidance imaginable when it comes to skiing or indulging in other outdoor (or indoor) activities. ❾

Glacier Lodge & Suites 4573 Château Blvd ⓣ604/905-4144 or 1-866/580-6644, ⓦwww.glacierlodge.com. Situated in the quieter Upper Village, at the base of Blackcomb Mountain, with 89 simple hotel rooms and some three-bedroom suites with kitchens. There is a pub, deli and spa on site. ❼

Haus Heidi Pension B&B Inn 7115 Nesters Rd ⓣ604/932-3113 or 1-800/909-7115, ⓦwww.hausheidi.com. An eight-room inn that has been run by the same family for over 25 years, close to the Village, lifts and valley trails. A generous breakfast is included in the price. ❹

Le Chamois Whistler Resort Hotel 4557 Blackcomb Way ⓣ604/932-8700 or 1-888/560-9453, ⓦwww.lechamoishotel.com. A mid-range choice in the Upper Village next to the Blackcomb Mountain liftbase, with 46 rooms and a choice of studios, one- and two-bedroom suites and three-bedroom condos. ❻

Pan Pacific Mountainside 4320 Sundial Crescent ⓣ604/905-2999 or 1-888/905-9995, ⓦwww.panpacific.com. There's nowhere closer to the lifts than the older of Whistler's two Pan Pacifics– you can ski from the front door to the Whistler Mountain gondola station a few steps away. The contemporary lodge style is pleasant, and the 121 units include compact studios and one- and two-bedroom suites with kitchens. There's an outdoor pool, and the "Irish" pub and lounge are popular après-ski locations. ❺

Summit Lodge & Spa 4359 Main St ⓣ604/932-2778 or 1-888/913-8811, ⓦwww.summitlodge.com. A peaceful boutique-style hotel, with 81 rooms, all with kitchenettes, balconies and fireplaces. Granite worktops and cherry-wood décor add more than a dash of style, along with details such as free hot chocolate nightly, a ski shuttle, heated outdoor pool and above-average spa. ❾

Swiss Cottage 7321 Fitzsimmons Rd ⓣ604/932-6062 or 1-800/718-7822, ⓦwww.swisscanada.com. Off Nancy Greene Way, the three rooms here in a Swiss Alpine-style house are reasonably close to the action, with a quiet location, generous breakfast and bright, ensuite facilities. ❺

Westin Resort & Spa 4090 Whistler Way ⓣ604/905-5000 or 1-888/634-5577, ⓦwww.westinwhistler.com. The Westin chain came relatively late to Whistler (in 2000), but still managed to snaffle a prime location on the mountainside below the main run into the Village. With almost 1,000 beds, this is not an intimate place, but the rooms are spacious and well finished, with granite and cedar trim providing luxurious touches. Facilities include a spa and indoor and outdoor pools. ❾

Hostels

Hostelling International Whistler 5678 Alta Lake Rd ⓣ604/932-5492, ⓦwww.hihostels.ca; beds for members $24, non-members $28). A 32-bed hostel with four- and eight-bed dorms 7km from the Village right on the shores of Alta Lake. One of the nicest hostels in BC, it's a signposted fifty-minute walk from Whistler Creek or ten-minute drive to the Village centre; local buses leave the gondola base in the Village four times a day for the hostel 15min; $1.50). As it's popular year-round, reserve many weeks, if not months ahead. Check-in is between 4 and 10pm.

Campsites

Riverside RV Resort and Campground ⓣ604/905-5533 or 1-877/905-5533, ⓦwww.whistlerlogcabins.com. Whistler's only central campsite is 1.4km north of Whistler Village at 8018 Mons Rd, and also has 14 five-person log cabins for $125–205 and 107 RV/tent sites for $28–48 per two persons.

Whistler Village

WHISTLER VILLAGE is the key to the resort, a rather characterless and pastel-shaded conglomeration of hotels, restaurants, mountain-gear shops and more loud people in fluorescent clothes than are healthy in one place at the same time. It's all a far cry from February 1966 when what was then known as London Mountain (local population 25) first started skiing operations. Apparently the International Olympics Committee (IOC) had let drop in the early 1960s that the region satisfied all the criteria for a successful Winter Olympic bid, and development began soon after. Someone on the IOC was obviously making mischief, however, for over the years, Whistler would make no fewer than three failed bids, losing out to Sapporo in 1972, Innsbruck in 1976 and Lake Placid in 1980. But the fourth time was lucky, and Whistler will be one of the major centres for the 2010 winter games.

The brouhaha that accompanied the awarding the games has led to a fury of investment, building and upgrading, especially in Whistler Village, which took shape in the late 1970s (until then its site had been the community's rubbish tip), and where the price of an average home is over one million dollars, making

Skiing and snowboarding practicalities

The **skiing and snowboarding season** for Whistler and Blackcomb is one of the longest in North America, often running for almost 200 days from Nov to early June, weather permitting. The yearly average snowfall is a whopping ten metres (for **snow conditions** call ⓣ604/932-4211 in Whistler or ⓣ604/687-7507 from Vancouver), while the average winter alpine temperature rarely falls below –5C (compare this with a chillier –12C in Banff). Whistler sits in an area of temperate rainforest, and rain can certainly be a problem at lower altitudes. This said, what falls as rain in the Village is often falling as snow higher up.

Blackcomb closes at the end of April, while Whistler stays open until early June. Then the mountains switch places, as Whistler closes and Blackcomb reopens in early June for glacier skiing and snowboarding. Lifts open at 8.30am (9am from mid-April) and close at 3pm until late Jan, 3.30pm until late Feb, and at 4pm from late Feb. The Tube Park on Blackcomb is open Mon–Fri noon–8pm and 11am–8pm at weekends and holidays. **Summer hours** (June 5–July 30), for glacier skiing or high-level hiking are noon–3pm daily.

Lift tickets give you full use of both Whistler and Blackcomb mountains, and it will take days for even the most advanced skier or snowboarder to cover all the terrain. The best advice is to pick one mountain and stick to it for the day, at least until the completion of a planned $50-million, 4.4-kilometre gondola 415m above the valley floor that should link the mountains by around 2008. See the main text below for the relative merits of each mountain. Tickets are available from the lift base in Whistler Village, but the queues can be horrendous. Instead, plan ahead and purchase your tickets and check all lift and other information online at ⓦwww.whistlerblackcomb.com. Or book by phone on ⓣ1-888/403-4727. Discounts are available for online booking, but you must book another element as well as a pass, such as rentals, lessons or accommodation. Your hotel can often set you up with tickets if you pre-book far enough in advance.

Prices increase slightly in peak season – over Christmas and New Year and from mid-Feb to mid-March – and lift tickets are subject to a seven-percent tax. Regular/peak season tickets are $70/75 daily for adults, $60/64 for seniors and youth aged 13–18; passes for children 7–12 are $36/39. Two-day passes are simply double daily rates. Prices come right down from late April to early June, so that adult one-day passes cost $46, seniors and youth $37 and child $23.

You can rent equipment from outlets at the Whistler and Blackcomb lifts, but it is first-come, first-served, and you need to be there first thing (8am) to beat the queues. Alternatively, Summit Ski (ⓣ604/932-6255, ⓦwww.summitsport.com) has several outlets around the Village, including the Delta Whistler Resort and Market Pavilion.

Intermediate and expert skiers can join the **free tours** of the mountains: contact the infocentre for latest departure times.

it Canada's single most expensive municipality. Whistler's name is said to derive either from the distinctive shriek of the marmot (a small, chubby mammal), or the sound of the wind whistling through Singing Pass up in the mountains. Whatever its origins, almost 40 years' worth of investments, plus the money pouring in anticipation of 2010, have paid off; the resort's services, lifts and general overall polish are almost faultless, and those of its nearby satellites are not far behind.

Whistler Mountain

Winter-sports enthusiasts can argue long and late over the relative merits of **WHISTLER MOUNTAIN** and its rival, Blackcomb Mountain (see p.859), both accessed from lifts at Whistler Village's lifts (the Blackcomb base is a little closer to the Upper Village). Both are great mountains, and both offer top-notch skiing and boarding, as evidenced by world-class events like the annual Snowboard FIS World Cup in December and the World Ski and Snowboard Festival in April – both held on Whistler. If this makes the slopes sound big-scale and intimidating, they're not, and if you become lost, confused or just want advice, there are 80 or so red-jacketed "Mountain Hosts" to answer questions.

Each mountain has its own distinctive character, and traditionally Whistler has been seen as the more homely of the two mountains, somewhere you can ski or board for days on end and never have to retrace your steps. One of Whistler's great advantages over Blackcomb is the sun, which the mountain catches much earlier: Seventh Heaven run aside, much of Blackcomb doesn't see the sun until after 11.30am.

The ski area is 3657 acres and there are over a hundred marked **trails** and seven major bowls. The breakdown of terrain is twenty percent beginner, fifty-five percent intermediate and twenty-five percent expert. Common consent has Whistler as the better mountain for beginners and intermediates – if you're attending ski school it's a mid-station. Blackcomb is steeper and has more narrow roads, which can test beginners' stopping abilities to the limit. The exception for beginners is for **children**, where the under-sixes should learn at the small hill at the base of Blackcomb, avoiding the bustle of the lift to mid-station on Whistler. Under-sixes ski free on the mountains. Day-care is available for toddlers aged three months to 48 months, for around $100, but should be booked well in advance. Contact the infocentre or visit Ⓦ www.whistlerblackcomb.com.

Whistler's **lifts** include two high-speed gondolas, six high-speed quads, two triple and one double chairlift, and five surface lifts. Helicopter drops make another 100 runs and glacier runs available. If you want the fast track to the best skiing on a quality powder day, take the Harmony and Peak chairlifts. Snowboarders are blessed with a half-pipe and park, though most boarders prefer

△ Whistler Mountain trails

Blackcomb, if only because it has fewer dull traverses where you have to unbuckle your board. Total vertical drop is 1530m and the longest run is 11km.

Blackcomb Mountain

BLACKCOMB MOUNTAIN, the "Mile-High Mountain", is a ski area laden with superlatives: the most modern resort in Canada, North America's finest summer skiing (on Horstman Glacier), the continent's longest unbroken fall-line skiing and the longest *and* second longest lift-serviced vertical falls in North America (1609m and 1530m).

Mountain biking

Figures show that over the last few years the number of people visiting Whistler in summer has actually exceeded those coming in winter. One of the main reasons for this upsurge of warm-weather interest has been the phenomenal rise in the popularity of **mountain biking** in and around the resort, with an estimated 100,000 visitors annually coming to the resort specifically to take to two wheels. Free riding was all but invented in the mountains above Vancouver, so its proliferation in Whistler, an hour or so to the north is no surprise. The oft-made observation is what Hawaii is to the worldwide surfing community, Whistler is to the mountain-biking fraternity. Some are predicting that by the time the Winter Olympics come round in 2010, biking could actually be bigger in Whistler than skiing.

The resort's popularity is not all down to terrain and happy accident. It always did have hundreds of free trails, with a total of 100km of single-track and 80km of double-track trails, plus around 200km of lift-serviced trails, the last factor vital, for there's nothing better than having a ski lift do all the hard work of carrying your bike up the mountain and letting gravity do the work – and provide the pleasure – coming down. What has made a big difference, however, is the opening of the deservedly celebrated **Whistler Mountain Bike Park** (Ⓣ604/938-7275, Ⓦwww.whistlerbike.com; open daily late May to early Sept, 10am–5pm, plus 5–8pm on some lifts mid-June to early Sept, depending on the light). This includes those 200km of lift-serviced trails, two jump park areas, three or four access lifts (Whistler Gondola, Fitzsimmons, Magic and Garbanzo), three skills centres for all abilities (green circle, blue square and black diamond), expert staff on site, banked cruisers and dirt trails through canopied forest, a BikerCross park (fun to watch even if you don't take part), and self-guided rides over 1200-metre vertical trails.

Prices for the park aren't cheap: it'll cost you $45 for a day pass in high season ($39 the rest of the time), and $39/34 for seniors and youth 13–18. Children 10–12 are charged $23/20 – note that children under 12 must be accompanied by adults. These prices cover riding, entry to the Magic Bike Park and access to the lifts from 10am–8pm. You can also rent a high-quality "Park" bike from $69.99 for half a day from the park's various outlets, or $99.99 for the whole day. Lesser "Youth Park" models cost $39.99/49.99. You can also rent individual bits of protective gear, or a full armour package (arm, leg, glove, chest and helmet) for $44.99 ($39.99 with a bike rental).

Of course, you don't have to sign up to the Bike Park to ride locally, or rent equipment from designated outlets. You can buy lift-only passes and do your own thing, and visit other rental outfits such as Cross Country Connection (Ⓣ604/905-0071, Ⓦwww.crosscountryconnection.com), which has bikes from $12 an hour, and also offers tours and lessons. If you want to research routes and further information, then Ⓦwww.whistlermountainbike.com is an excellent resource.

If you're a beginner, then you can stick with the **Valley Trail**, the 30km paved pedestrian and cycle route in the valley around Whistler Village. You can rent bikes from outlets around the resort, including so-called "cruiser" bikes designed for beginners or those who want a more sedate and comfortable ride.

Blackcomb is slightly smaller than Whistler, at 3341 acres, and has a similar breakdown of **terrain** (fifteen percent beginner, fifty-five percent intermediate and thirty percent expert). **Lifts** are one high-speed gondola, six express quads, three triple chairlifts, and seven surface lifts. There are over a hundred marked trails, two glaciers and five bowls along with two half-pipes and a park for snowboarders. Runs such as Ruby, Sapphire, Garnet and Diamond are some of the world's best steep and avalanche-controlled powder, but note that it takes two chairlifts to reach them. Even if you're not skiing, come up here (summer or winter) on the ski lifts to walk, enjoy the **view** from the top of the mountain, or to eat in the restaurants like *Rendezvous* or *Glacier Creek*. The *Crystal Hut*, a cosy log cabin, is one of the best, and is deservedly popular at lunch.

Eating

When it comes to **food**, Whistler Village and its satellites are loaded with cafés and around a hundred restaurants, though none really Has an "address" as such. These can come and go at an alarming rate, and none – given the resort's purpose-built nature – can be said to have much in the way of original interiors or atmosphere. Most hotels have one or more restaurants, always open to non-residents. In smarter places such as the Four Seasons, where the *'Fifty Two 80 Bistro* (ⓣ604/966-5280) – named after Whistler and Blackcomb Mountain's "vertical mile" – has been winning plaudits, these can be of very high quality, if rather expensive.

Amsterdam Café ⓣ604/932-8334. You don't come here for sophisticated dining, but for reliable and no-nonsense pub food (burgers, fries, chicken, salmon and so forth) at no-nonsense prices (around $10 for mains).

Après Restaurant 103-4338 Main St ⓣ604/935-0200, ⓦwww.apresrestaurant.com. If you want a treat, but the rather traditional setting of *Araxi's* and *Bearfoot Bistro* (see below) is not for you, then the cool, contemporary approach of Après offers a distinct alternative. The cuisine is Pacific Rim, the recipes ambitious and the flavours bold. Prices are high, however – from about $30 to $60 for a main.

Araxi's Restaurant 4222 Village Square ⓣ604/932-4540, ⓦwww.araxi.com. A top-rated restaurant of long standing that serves up expensive Italian and West Coast-style food, with inventive pasta and very high-quality seafood bar and dishes – try the amazing mussels in chilli, vermouth and lemongrass followed by a perfect crème brûlée for dessert. The wine list runs to 27 pages and 12,000 bottles, but there's a good choice of wines by the glass. A meal for two here will cost $80-plus, with mains from about $30 – expensive, but you're paying for probably the best food in town.

Bearfoot Bistro 4121 Village Green ⓣ604/932-3433, ⓦww.bearfootbistro.com. A few years ago this was a simple French bistro: today it has a reputation of one of Canada's best restaurants, with superlative French food served in a variety of tasting menus (from $90–200-plus) that change from day to day. Reservations are essential.

Black's Dining Room Mountain Square ⓣ604/932-6408. Pizza, pasta and other slightly over-priced Mediterranean food (mains $10 and up) are the staples here, but it's the snug bar, *Black's Pub*, upstairs that provides the lure for most people here.

Caramba! Restaurante 12-4314 Main St ⓣ604/938-1879, ⓦwww.caramba-restaurante.com. On the face of it, the Mediterranean food in this casual but buzzy Lower Village spot – pastas, pizzas, roast meats – might seem unremarkable, but the regular queues out of the door bear witness to the quality of the food and dining experience. Main courses start at about $12, but run as high as $32.

Citta's Bistro Village Square ⓣ604/932-4177. *Citta's* – pronounced "Cheetas" – is an American-style bistro offering a predictable but well-prepared variety of pizzas, gourmet burgers and the like at fair prices – main courses range from about $7–16. It opens at 9am and closes at 1am, which means it is also a busy and appealing late-night spot. During the day, the terrace, with its umbrella tables, is a great place for people-watching.

Ingrid's Village Café 4305 Skiers Approach-Village Square ⓣ604/932-7000. *Ingrid's* is a favourite among locals and resort workers for breakfast (it opens 7.30am–6.30pm), coffee and snacks. Prices are fair – the daily soup special will cost around $5, a veggie burger a dollar or so more – and the quality good.

Rim Rock Café & Oyster Bar 2117 Whistler Rd. ☎604/932-5565, Ⓦwww.rimrockwhistler.com. This place is excellent for seafood, and for the traditional log-cabin-style atmosphere created by the long, narrow room and redoubtable fireplace at one end. Oysters are predictably good – try them in the house style: broiled with béchemal sauce and smoked salmon. Expect to pay between $20–40 for main courses.

Trattoria di Umberto in the *Mountainside Lodge*, beside the *Pan Pacific Mountainside*. ☎604/932-5858. You can pay less for Italian food in Whistler, but this well-established place scores by virtue of its cosy setting and accomplished, straightforward cooking. Expect to part with up to about $50 for three courses for two, without wine.

Nightlife

Winter or summer, Whistler enjoys a lot of **nightlife** and après-ski activity, with visitors being bolstered by the large seasonal workforce. Like restaurants, clubs can come and go, but certain clubs and bars have established well-defined niches on the nightlife circuit. These include Moe Joe's, Buffalo Bill's, Savage Beagle and Tommy Africa's for dancing (and more) and the Boot Pub, Crabshack and Dubh Linn Gate for live music. For peace and quiet, hit any of the bars and lounges in the luxury hotels such as the *Four Seasons* and *Fairmont Château Whistler* hotel. Note that some clubs may charge a cover on busy night, or for live music – anything from $10 to $30.

Boot Pub 7124 Nancy Greene Drive ☎604/932-3338. There's beer, live punk some nights (generally Sun & Mon) and various other stage "shows" or dubious import on other nights. You might not like it, but it's a local institution.

Buffalo Bill's Bar & Grill ☎604/932-6613 Across from the Whistler gondola, is a thirty-something bar/club with comedy nights, hypnosis shows, video screens, a moderate dancefloor and live music.

Crabshack, Whistler Village ☎604/932-4451. Sunnights here mean cheap drinks, cheap chicken wings and music from local Whistler bands.

Dubh Linn Gate Pan Pacific Mountainside, 4320 Sundial Crescent ☎604/905-4047. An "Irish" pub with Whistler's largest selection of whiskies and draught beers, plus live modern and traditional Irish music every night (no cover charge).

Garfinkels Club 1-4308 Main St, Village North ☎604/932-2323. If you fancy yourself hip, are over 20 but under 25, and don't mind sports bars, then "Garf's" is for you. It's a good dance place week round, but Thurs is the big night, with indie, funk and classic dance tracks.

Longhorn Saloon and Grill 4280 Mountain Square ☎604/932-5999. Its position near the lifts make the Longhorn an obvious après-ski favourite, but don't expect too much beyond that, sports TV aside. Particularly lively on Sun.

Merlin's ☎604/938-7700. A lively and beer-heavy place in the Blackcomb Daylodge near the Wizard skilift and Blackcomb Mountain base. It has a good patio, with plenty of après-ski eating and cheap drinking options. Later, things liven up with a staff that "encourages bar-top dancing", live music some nights, theme parties, karaoke and pay-per-view sports on a giant screen. Popular with resort workers.

Moe Joe's 4115 Golfer's approach ☎604/935-1152. Fri nights are popular at *Moe Joe's*, one of the best places in Whistler for dancing. It's smaller and more intimate than *Garf's* (see opposite) but attracts a similar clientele and expouses a similar musical policy.

Savage Beagle 4222 Village Stroll ☎604/938-3337. Like *Buffalo Bill's*, the long-established and split-level *Savage Beagle* appeals to a slightly older, 30-something crowd, with a good little pub upstairs (with a great selection of drinks) and a dance floor downstairs. Tues is the key night.

Tommy Africa's 4216 Gateway Drive ☎604/932-6090. "Tommy's" is the best-known dance club in the Village and usually the most musically adventurous. The big night here is Mon.

North to Lillooet

Hwy 99 funnels down to two slow lanes at **PEMBERTON,** 25km northeast of Whistler, known primarily for its potatoes, of all things, where apartments are now mushrooming in the wake of Whistler's popularity. Beyond, you're treated to some wonderfully wild country in which Vancouver and even

Outdoor activities

In addition to skiing (see p.857) and mountain biking (see p.859), Whistler offers a wealth of **outdoor activities** year-round. For further information on the activities below, contact the various visitor centres (see p.853) or the Whistler Activity and Information Centre (☎604/938-2769 or 1-877/991-9988, which can book and advise on most activities. Numerous **rental outlets** around the resort provide bikes, blades and other equipment.

Hiking

You can ride the ski lifts up both mountains for tremendous views and easy access to high-altitude **walking** trails (June to early Sept daily 10am–8pm; early Sept to late Sept daily 10am–5pm, late Sept to mid-Oct Sat & Sun only 10am–5pm; $24.95).

Pick up the sheet of hiking trails from the infocentres (see p.853), or better yet buy the 1:50,000 *Whistler and Garibaldi Region* **map**. The two most popular high-level day walks are the **Rainbow Falls** and **Singing Pass** trails (both five to six hours). Other good choices are the easy and mostly level 4km trail to Cheakamus Lake or any of the high-alpine hikes accessed from the Upper Gondola station (1837m) on Whistler Mountain or the Seventh Heaven lift on Blackcomb. Among the eight walks from Whistler Mountain gondola station, consider the **Glacier Trail** (2.5km round trip; 85m ascent; 1hr) for views of the snow and ice in Glacier Bowl. The slightly more challenging **Little Whistler Trail** (3.8km round trip; 265m ascent; 1hr 30min–2hr) takes you to the summit of Little Whistler Peak (2115m) and gives grand views of Black Tusk in Garibaldi Provincial Park. Remember to time your hike to get back to the gondola station for the last ride down (times vary according to season).

If the high-level hiking seems too daunting (it shouldn't be – the trails are good and less than 4km, save the Musical Bumps trail at 19km) – then there are plenty of trails (some surfaced) for bikers, walkers and in-line skaters around the Village. The **Valley Trail** system starts on the west side of Hwy 99 by the Whistler Park Golf Course and takes you through parks, golf courses and peaceful residential areas: the 30km of trails on and around **Lost Lake**, entered by the northern end of the Day Skier car park at Blackcomb Mountain, wend through cedar forest and past lakes and creeks; the eponymous lake is just over a kilometre from the main trailhead. There are also numerous operators offering guided walks to suit all abilities.

Other summer activities

Between May and September, Whistler River Adventures (☎604/932-3532 or 1-888/932-3532, ⓦwww.whistlerriver.com; from $75 for a short cruise to $145 for a six-hour trip) has **jet boating** on the Green River to below the Nairn Falls, with a good chance of spotting wildlife such as moose and bears. It also has a range of **rafting** trips from gentle to extreme priced from $89 for four-hour trips (one hour on the river) and $154 for full-day tours: beginners are taken to the Green River, while experts can plump for the Class-IV thrills of the Elaho or Squamish River rapids. Bear in mind, though, that it can take two hours round-trip just to reach the water: only three hours of the six-hour ride, for example, are spent on the river. The same company offers half- and full-day catch-and-release **fishing** trips in surrounding rivers from about $150 per person.

If you want to rock climb, The Great Wall, 4340 Sundial Crescent (☎604/905-7625, ⓦwww.greatwallclimbing.com; daily 10am–10pm, except autumn noon-9pm) offers indoor facilities for climbing year-round and an outdoor summer climbing wall. The indoor centre is located near the Pan Pacific Mountainside, and the outdoor is near the Wizard lift in the Upper Village. A day's drop-in indoor climbing costs $16. Tours are also offered: a four-hour trip cost $95.

You can **play tennis** at several public courts, or ask at the visitor centre for details of hotels such as the *Delta Whistler Resort*, *Fairmont Château Whistler* and *Château*

Whistler Resort that allow players to use their courts and provide racket rental (from $10 an hour). Free public courts (☎604/938-7529), include Meadow Park Sports Centre Myrtle Public School, Brio, Blackcomb Benchlands, White Gold, Emerald Park, Miller's Pond and Alpha Lake Park. The *Whistler Racquet & Golf Resort*, 4500 Northland Boulevard (☎604/932-1991, ⓦwww.whistlertennis.com) has three indoor and seven outdoor courts open to drop-in players from $16 an hour outdoor, $32 indoor. It also offers summer three-day camps for adults and children in summer, but they fill quickly, so book early.

The area has four great **golf** courses, including one designed by Jack Nicklaus. For further information on all, visit ⓦwww.golfbc.com. Despite a recent upgrade, the Whistler Golf Club course remains the cheapest to play, ranging from $90 to $159 (☎1-800/376-1777 or 604/932-4544), while the others, including Nicklaus North (☎604/938-9898), cost from about $85 to $185. After any of these activities there are umpteen **spas** for massage, mud baths and treatments that soothe all aches and pains – for utter luxury – the top-of-the-range spa at the *Fairmont Château Whistler* (☎604/938-2086, ⓦwww.fairmont.com).

Winter activities

Snowshoe rental and tours are available to get you across some of the safer snowfields in summer. For **snowshoe tours** for novices contact Outdoor Adventures@Whistler (☎604/932-0647, ⓦwww.adventureswhistler.com; from $69 for 90 minutes' snowshoeing or $109 for an evening tour by Green Lake followed by dinner) or Whistler Cross Country Ski & Hike (☎604/932-7711 or 1-888/771-2382, ⓦwww.whistlerhikingcentre.com).

Cougar Mountain Adventures (☎1-888/297-2222, ⓦwww.cougarmountain.com) also offers snowshoeing tours around Cougar Mountain (from around $50 for two hours or from $120 for three hours in the backcountry with snowshoe and snowmobile combination), and also offers **dog-sled rides** in the backcountry from $140 for two hours, but you need a minimum of two people for the tour.

For gentle **sleigh rides**, contact Blackcomb Horsedrawn Sleigh Rides (☎604/932-7631, ⓦwww.blackcombsleighrides.com). Four tours (hourly from 5pm) run every evening in winter ($49 for 40–50 min), and follow the ski trails to the woods for great views and a stop in a cabin for a mug of hot chocolate. For $99 you get a sleigh ride and dinner.

You can ride **snowmobiles** with Blackcomb Snowmobile (☎604/932-8484, ⓦwww.blackcombsnowmobile.com). The trips are a 15-minute road transfer south of Whistler and you can choose between two- and three-hour rides in Family, Scenic, Wilderness, Extreme and Fondue (dinner included) categories. Two-hour Scenic rides (five daily) cost $119 for a single driver, $89 per person for two sharing (driver and passenger); the three three-hour trips daily hours cost $159/119. Children under 12 go free on Family tours. Similar tours and prices, including Family tours, are offered by Canadian Snowmobile Adventures (☎604/938-1616, ⓦwww.canadiansnowmobile.com), weather allowing. Two-hour rides in the Fitzsimmons Creek area start from $119 and $89 for a passenger; similar-length "Mountain Safari" trips on Blackcomb Mountain cost from $159 and $119 respectively.

If you want some **cross-country skiing**, the best spots are the 32km of groomed trails around Lost Lake and the *Château Whistler* golf course, all very easily accessible from Whistler Village, beginning just a block from the Blackcomb Mountain car park. The routes are suitable for beginners to experts and are groomed and patrolled. The visitor centre and resort websites have lots more background information. Visit ⓦwww.crosscountryconnection.com for more details and rental information.

Whistler seem a long way away. Patches of forest poke through rugged mountainsides and scree slopes, and a succession of glorious lakes culminate in Sefton Lake, whose hydroelectric schemes feed power into the grid as far south as Arizona, accounting for the pylons south of Whistler.

At the lumber town of **LILLOOET**, founded as Mile 0 of the 1858 Cariboo Wagon Road to the goldfields to the north (see below), the railway meets the Fraser River, which marks a turning point in the scenery as denuded crags and hillsides increasingly hint at the *High Noon*-type ranching country to come. In July and August, the rocky banks and bars of the sluggish, mud-coloured river immediately north of town are dotted with vivid orange and blue tarpaulins. These belong to aboriginal Canadians who still come to catch and dry salmon as the fish make their way upriver to spawn. It's one of the few places where this tradition is continued and it is well worth a stop to watch. The town's name, changed from Cayoosh Flat in the 1860s, is a misrendering of Leel-wat, one of the aboriginal peoples who lived to the north.

The town boasts a handful of central **hotels and motels** if you need to stay: the best are the *Mile 0 Motel*, 616 Main St (Ⓣ604/256-7511 or 1-888/766-4530, Ⓦwww.mileomotel.com; ❸), downtown, overlooking the river and mountains (kitchenettes available in some units for self-catering); and the *4 Pines Motel* on the corner of 8th Avenue and Russell Street at 108 8th Ave, also with kitchenettes (Ⓣ604/256-4247 or 1-800/753-2576, Ⓦwww.4pinesmotel.com; ❷). The **infocentre/museum** is in the old church at 790 Main St (mid-May to Sept Mon–Sat 9am–5pm, longer hours July & Aug; Ⓣ604/256-4308, Ⓦwww.lillooetbc.com), with displays of local life past and present. The nearest **campsite** is the riverside *Cayoosh Creek* on Hwy 99 within walking distance of downtown (Ⓣ604/256-4180 or 1-877/748-2628, Ⓦwww.cayooshcampground.com; $18–23; mid-April to mid-Oct). To **eat**, make for the *Lillooet Inn Restaurant*, 687 Main St (Ⓣ604/256-0028).

From Lillooet, Hwy 99 heads east for 50km to Hwy 97; you can then either turn south towards Cache Creek (see p.946), or snake your way up north to the gold fields of the Cariboo.

The Cariboo

The Cariboo is the name given to the broad, rolling ranching country and immense forests of British Columbia's interior plateau, which extend north of Lillooet between the Coast Mountains to the west and Cariboo Mountains to the east. The region contains by far the dullest scenery in the province, and what little interest it offers – aside from fishing and boating on thousands of remote lakes – comes from its **gold-mining** heritage. Initially exploited by fur traders to a small degree, the region was fully opened up following the discovery of gold in 1858 in the lower Fraser Valley. The building of the **Cariboo Wagon Road**, a stagecoach route north out of Lillooet, spread gold fever right up the Fraser watershed as men leapfrogged from creek to creek, culminating in the big finds at Williams Creek in 1861 and Barkerville a year later.

Much of the old Wagon Road is today retraced by lonely **Highway 97** (the Cariboo Hwy), which runs through hour after hour of straggling pine forests and past the occasional ranch and small, marsh-edged lake – scenery that strikes you as pristine and pastoral for a while but which soon leaves you in a tree-weary stupor. If you're forced to stop over, there are innumerable lodges, ranches and motels on or just off the highway, and you can pick up copious material on the region at the Vancouver tourist office or infocentres en route.

Clinton and Williams Lake

A compact little village surrounded by green pastures and tree-covered hills, **CLINTON** – originally 47 Mile House but renamed after a British duke – marks the beginning of the heart of Cariboo country. The town has a couple of **bed and breakfasts**, a **campsite**, *Clinton Pines Campground*, 1204 Caribbo Ave (ⓣ250/459-0030; ⓦwww.clintonpines.com; $14–20) and a **motel** – the *Nomad* (ⓣ250/459-2214 or 1-888/776-6623, ⓔnomad@bcwireless.com; ❷).

The three tiny settlements beyond Clinton at 70, 100 and 150 Mile House are echoes of the old roadhouses built by men who were paid by the mile to blaze the Cariboo Wagon Road – which is doubtless why 100 Mile House is well short of one hundred miles from the start of the road. 100 Mile House has a year-round **infocentre** at 422 Cariboo Hwy 97 South (May–Sept daily 9am–6pm; Oct–April Mon–Fri 9am–4pm; ⓣ250/395-5353 or 1-877/511-5353, ⓦwww.southcaribootourism.com) for details of the fishing, riding and other local outdoor pursuits. There are a handful of **motels** in or a few kilometres away from town, the biggest in-town choice being the *Red Coach Inn*, 170 Hwy 97 North (ⓣ250/395-2266 or 1-800/663-8422, ⓔredcoachinn@btinternet.net; ❹). The central *Imperial* is smaller and cheaper (ⓣ250/395-2471; ❷).

WILLIAMS LAKE, 14km north of 150 Mile House and still 238km south of Prince George, is a busy and drab transport centre that huddles in the lee of a vast crag on terraces above the lake of the same name. It has plenty of motels, B&Bs, boat launches and swimming spots south of the town – but it's hardly a place you'd want to spend any time, unless you're dead-beat after driving or around on the first weekend in July for its famous **rodeo**. The year-round **infocentre** is at 1148 Broadway South (May–Sept daily 9am–5pm; Oct–April Mon–Fri 9am–4pm; ⓣ250/392-5025, ⓦwww.williamslakechamber.com).

Bella Coola

Highway 20 branches west from Williams Lake, a part-paved, part-gravel road that runs 456km to **BELLA COOLA**, a wilderness-enveloped village in a superb setting likely to gain an ever-greater tourist profile in the wake of the recent visitor-oriented ferry service from Port Hardy on Vancouver Island (see p.933). Most of the road ploughs through the interminable forest or opening ranching country of the Cariboo Plateau, but there are services, campsites and the odd hotel at regular intervals and the last very worthwhile 100km or so traverses the high and stunningly spectacular peaks of the Coast Mountains and **Tweedsmuir Provincial Park**.

Just outside the park – which at a million hectares is BC's largest – you encounter the notorious "Hill", a hugely winding and precipitous stretch of hwy barely tamed by the various upgradings over the years. Until 1953 there was no road link here at all. Instead there was a sixty-kilometre gap in the mountain stretch, a missing link the state refused to bridge. In response the locals of Bella Coola took it upon themselves to build the road on their own, completing their so-called Freedom Road in three years.

One of the park's chief sights are the **Hunlen Falls**, 260m of plunging water, though it's struggle to see them – you need to leave the road near Atnarko River (midway through the park) and take the rough road the 13km to the trailhead for the falls and Turner Lake. From here it's another 16km of walking, with an elevation gain of 2000m. This is typical of a trail system that is still relatively undeveloped, and there are few day-hikes or easy trails from the highway; an exception is the 8km round trip to a series of pretty lakes from a trailhead 16km west of the Atnarko River campsites (see below).

Bella Coola itself was formerly the domain of the Bella Coola, or Nuxalk, an aboriginal people who prospered thanks to the surfeit of salmon in local rivers and were visited by Alexander Mackenzie as early as 1793. Indeed, Mackenzie's arrival here on July 22 marked the conclusion of his successful attempt to become the first man to cross North America. White visitors nicknamed the settlement the "Friendly Village" after the welcome they received from its inhabitants. In 1869 the Hudson's Bay Company opened a trading post, though permanent white settlement only began in 1894.

One house belonging to a company clerk is now all that remains of the post. Besides the small **Bella Coola Museum** in the old schoolhouse and surveyor's cabin (June–Sept Sun–Fri 10am–5pm; $2.50) and glorious scenery, Bella Coola is hardly stacked with sights. Norwegian settlers, however, perhaps drawn by the fjord-like scenery nearby, were notable early pioneers, and half of today's non-aboriginal inhabitants trace their ancestry to 120 Norwegians led here from Minnesota in 1894 by a pastor determined to found a Utopian society (visit Ⓦwww.nordicfolks.com for more background to the story).

Language, heritage and buildings here – notably the square-logged barns – all show a Scandinavian touch. **Hagensborg**, a village with accommodation (see below) 18km east of Bella Coola, preserves a particularly strong Nordic flavour. About 10km from the village, roughly midway to Bella Coola, are the **Thorsen Creek Petroglyphs**, a hundred or so rock drawings; the infocentre should be able to fix you up with a guide to explore the site.

Practicalities

No buses serve Bella Coola, and beyond the village there is no onward road route: unless you fly out, you'll have to either head back the way you came or pick up the **Discovery Coast Passage** boats to Port Hardy that stop off at the port; see box on p.934 for full details of this service. If you want to indulge in a plane in or out of town, contact Pacific Coastal Airlines (Ⓣ250/982-2225, Ⓦwww.pacific-coastal.com) for daily flights to Vancouver and Port Hardy on the northern tip of Vancouver Island. The airport is at Hagensborg.

Bella Coola's **infocentre** is on the Mackenzie Hwy near town (Mon–Fri daily 9.30am–4.30pm; Ⓣ250/799-5638, Ⓦwww.bellacoola.ca). The ferry service will probably result in the more hotels and restaurants opening: currently **accommodation** is provided by the *Bella Coola Valley Inn* (Ⓣ250/799-5316 or 1-888/799-5316, Ⓦwww.bellacoolavalleyinn.com; ❸), closest hotel to the ferry terminal, and the *Bella Coola Motel* (Ⓣ250/799-5323, Ⓔmotel@bellacoolavalley.com; ❸) at the corner of Burke and Clayton – both places are downtown.

In Hagensborg there's also the *Bay Motor Hotel* on Hwy 20, 14km east of Bella Coola and 1km from the airport (Ⓣ250/982-2212 or 1-888/982-2212, Ⓦwww.baymotorhotel.ca; ❸). For a few dollars more you can also stay here at *Brockton Place* on Hwy 20 16km east of Bella Coola (Ⓣ250/982-2298; ❸) or camp in the heart of the village at *Gnome's Home Campground & RV Park* (Ⓣ250/982-2504, Ⓦwww.gnomeshome.ca; $15–18; April–Oct); Bella Coola itself currently has no dedicated campsite, though the *Bella Coola Motel* offers 20 tent and RV sites at $10–18. In Tweedsmuir park there is just one option: the *Tweedsmuir Lodge* (Ⓣ250/982-2402, Ⓦwww.tweedsmiurparklodge.com; ❻), 60km east of Bella Coola on the Atnarko River. It has ten lodge rooms and chalets, two with kitchenettes. There are also two simple BC provincial **campgrounds** on the north side of the river (June–Sept; $14).

Along Highway 97: north of Williams Lake

North of Williams Lake on Hwy 97, the **Fraser River** re-enters the scenic picture and, after a dramatic stretch of canyon, reinstates more compelling hills and snatches of river meadows. This also marks the start, however, of some of the most concerted **logging operations** in all British Columbia, presaged by increasing numbers of crude pepper-pot kilns used to burn off waste wood. By **QUESNEL**, home of the "world's largest plywood plant", you're greeted with scenes out of an environmentalist's nightmare: whole mountainsides cleared of trees, hill-sized piles of sawdust, and unbelievably large lumber mills surrounded by stacks of logs and finished timber that stretch literally as far as the eye can see. If you're stuck for accommodation (there are a dozen or so hotels) or tempted by any of the many mill tours, contact the **infocentre** in Le Bourdais Park at 703 Carson Ave (May–Oct daily (9am–6pm; Oct–April Tues–Sat 9am–4pm; ⓣ250/992-8716 or 1-800/992-4922, ⓦwww.northcariboo.com).

Barkerville

Most people who take the trouble to drive Hwy 97 detour from Quesnel to **Barkerville Provincial Historic Park**, 90km to the east in the heart of the Cariboo Mountains, the site of the Cariboo's biggest gold strike and an invigorating spot in its own right, providing a much-needed jolt to the senses after the sleepy scenery to the south (June–Sept daily 8am–8pm; $8 entry only, $23.50 for entry, theatre and stagecoach ride). In 1862 a Cornishman named Billy Barker idly staked a claim here and after digging down a metre or so was about to pack up and head north. Urged on by his mates, however, he dug another couple of spadefuls and turned up a cluster of nuggets worth $600,000. Within months Barkerville, as it was later dubbed, had become the largest city in the region, and rode the boom for a decade until the gold finally ran out. Today 125 buildings have been restored and are filled with costumed staff, and the main administrative building has displays on mining methods and the gold rush, together with propaganda on their importance to the province.

If you want to **stay** under cover up here, there are two options: the *St George Hotel* (ⓣ250/994-0008 or 1-888-246-7690, ⓦwww.stgeorgehotel.bc.ca; ❻), a restored 1890s heritage building on the site, or *Kelly House B&B* (ⓣ250/994-3328, ⓦwww.kellyhouse.ca; ❹), also at the heart of Barkerville. In **WELLS**, 8km west of the park, are the *Hubs Motel* (ⓣ250/994-3313; ❷); the *Wells Hotel*, 2341 Pooley St (ⓣ250/994-3427 or 1-800/860-2299, ⓦwww.wellshotel.com; ❹), a restored 1933 heritage country inn with licensed café and breakfast included; and the *White Cap Motor Inn* (ⓣ250/994-3489 or 1-800/377-2028, ⓦwww.whitecapinn.com; ❸) – the last also has RV and camping spaces for $17. Failing this you can **camp** at the linked 168-pitch *Government Hill*, *Forest Rose* and *Lowhee* campsites at Barkerville Provincial Park adjacent to the old town (reservations possible, see p.758; $14–17; June–Sept). Wells has an **infocentre** 4120 Pooley Street, part of a small museum (daily mid-May–Aug 9am–6/7pm; ⓣ250/994-3237 or 1-877/451-WELLS, ⓦwww.wellsbc.com).

If you're continuing from Quesnel north to Prince George and beyond, turn to Chapter 11, "The North", beginning on p.991.

Vancouver Island

The proximity of **VANCOUVER ISLAND** to Vancouver makes it one of western Canada's premier tourist destinations, though its popularity is slightly out of proportion to what is, in most cases, a pale shadow of the scenery on offer on the region's mainland. The largest of North America's west-coast islands, it stretches almost 500km from north to south, but has a population of almost 750,000, mostly concentrated around **Victoria**, whose small-town feel belies its role as British Columbia's second metropolis and provincial capital. Victoria is also the most British of Canadian cities in feel and appearance, something it shamelessly plays up to attract its two million – largely American – visitors annually. While Victoria makes a convenient base for touring the island – and, thanks to a superlative museum, merits a couple of days in its own right – little else here, or in any of the island's other sizeable towns, is enough to justify an overnight stop (the countryside is another matter).

For most visitors Vancouver Island's main attraction is the great outdoors and, increasingly, **whale-watching**, an activity which can be pursued from Victoria, **Tofino**, **Ucluelet**, **Telegraph Cove** and several other places up and down the island. The scenery is a mosaic of landscapes, principally defined by a central spine of snowcapped mountains that divide it decisively between the rugged and sparsely populated wilderness of the west coast and the more sheltered lowlands of the east. Rippling hills characterize the northern and southern tips, and few areas are free of the lush forest mantle that supports one of BC's most lucrative logging industries. Apart from three minor east–west roads (and some rough logging and gravel roads), all the urban centres are linked by a good hwy running along almost the entire length of the east coast.

Once beyond the main towns of **Duncan** and **Nanaimo**, the northern two-thirds of the island is distinctly underpopulated. Locals and tourists alike are lured by the beaches at **Parksville** and **Qualicum**, while the stunning seascapes of the unmissable **Pacific Rim National Park**, protecting the central portion of the island's west coast, and **Strathcona Provincial Park**, which embraces the heart of the island's mountain fastness, are the main destinations for most visitors. Both of these parks offer the usual panoply of outdoor activities, with hikers being particularly well served by the national park's **West Coast Trail**, which is a tough and increasingly popular long-distance path. A newer, but less dramatic (and less busy) trail, the **Juan de Fuca Trail** runs to the south of the park. Shuttle buses and scheduled bus services from Victoria to points in the park, together with a wonderful approach by **boat** from Port Alberni, offer a choice of beguiling alternative itineraries for exploring the region. Another **boat trip** on a smaller working vessel from the tiny settlements of Tahsis and Gold River to the north is also becoming deservedly popular. Lovely, but much shorter ferry rides, will also take you from the ferry terminal north of Victoria to various of the **Southern Gulf Islands**, each dulcet little retreats with plenty of places to stay, good restaurants, galleries, craftspeople and an easy-going way of life.

For a large number of travellers, however, Vancouver Island is little more than a necessary pilgrimage on a longer journey north. Thousands annually make the trip to **Port Hardy**, linked by bus to Victoria, at the northern tip, to pick up the ferry that follows the so-called **Inside Passage**, a breathtaking trip up the British Columbia coast to Prince Rupert. More are likely to pick up on the

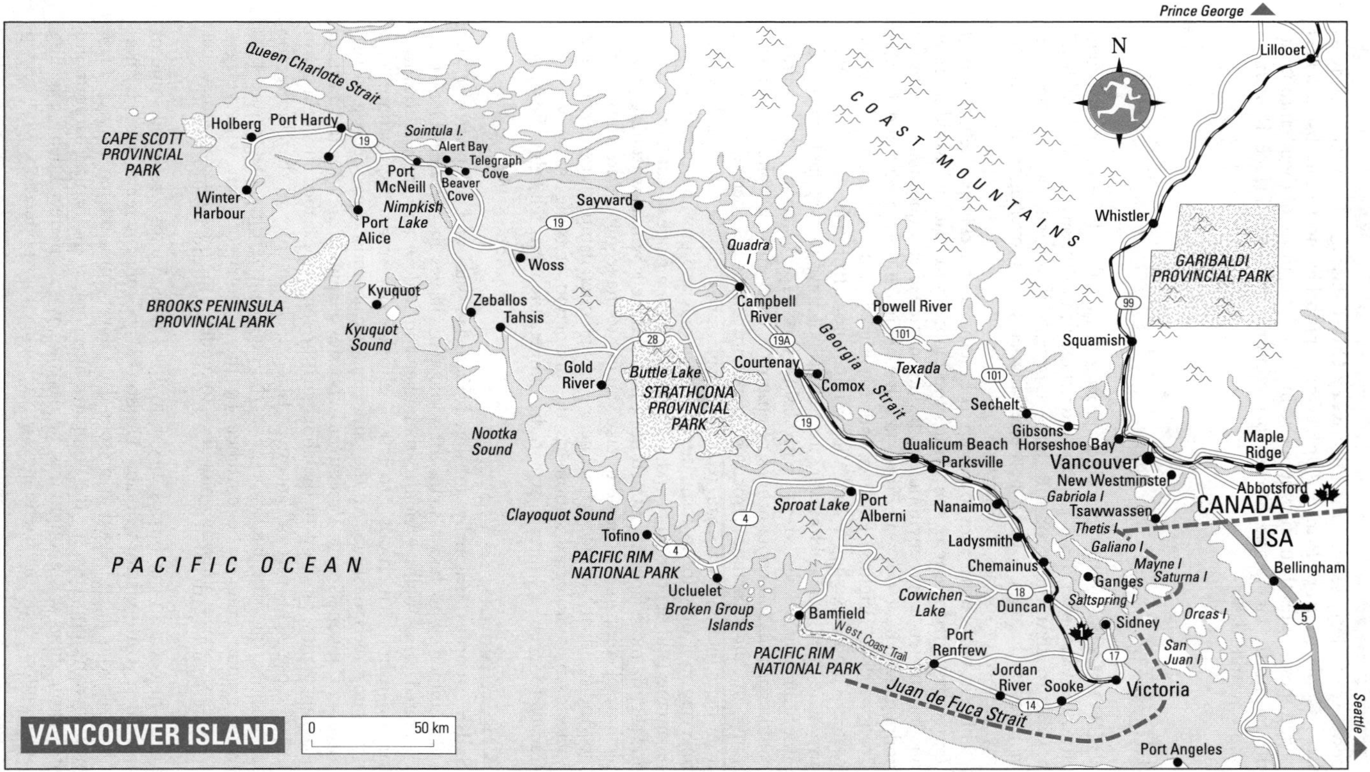

VANCOUVER ISLAND

0 50 km

Prince George
Seattle
N
COAST MOUNTAINS
GARIBALDI PROVINCIAL PARK
Lillooet
Whistler
Squamish
Maple Ridge
Abbotsford
CANADA
USA
Bellingham
Horseshoe Bay
Vancouver
New Westminster
Tsawwassen
Gibsons
Sechelt
Powell River
Texada I
Georgia Strait
Quadra I
Campbell River
Courtenay
Comox
Qualicum Beach
Parksville
Nanaimo
Gabriola I
Thetis I
Galiano I
Mayne I
Saturna I
Ladysmith
Chemainus
Ganges
Saltspring I
Duncan
Sidney
Orcas I
San Juan I
Victoria
Sooke
Jordan River
Port Renfrew
Port Angeles
Juan de Fuca Strait
West Coast Trail
PACIFIC RIM NATIONAL PARK
Bamfield
Cowichen Lake
Port Alberni
Sproat Lake
Broken Group Islands
Ucluelet
Tofino
Clayoquot Sound
STRATHCONA PROVINCIAL PARK
Buttle Lake
Gold River
Nootka Sound
Tahsis
Zeballos
Woss
Sayward
Kyuquot
Kyuquot Sound
BROOKS PENINSULA PROVINCIAL PARK
Port Alice
Nimpkish Lake
Port McNeill
Beaver Cove
Telegraph Cove
Alert Bay
Sointula I.
Port Hardy
Holberg
Winter Harbour
CAPE SCOTT PROVINCIAL PARK
Queen Charlotte Strait
PACIFIC OCEAN
1
5
14
17
18
19
19A
28
4
99
101

newer scenic ferry service, the **Discovery Coast Passage**, from Port Hardy to Bella Coola, south of Prince Rupert. You'll probably meet more backpackers plying these routes than anywhere else in the region, many of them en route to the far north, taking the ferries that continue on from Prince Rupert to Skagway and Alaska.

Victoria

VICTORIA is British Columbia's provincial capital and the region's second city after Vancouver. It's a popular excursion from Vancouver, and though it's possible to come here for the day – especially if you take a seaplane from Vancouver's harbour – you'd be better advised to stay overnight and give the city the two or so days it deserves.

This said, Victoria has a lot to live up to. Leading US travel magazine *Condé Nast Traveler* has voted it one of the world's top ten cities to visit, and world number one for ambience and environment. It's not named after a queen and an era for nothing. Much of the waterfront area has an undeniably quaint and likeable English feel – "Brighton Pavilion with the Himalayas for a backdrop," said the writer Rudyard Kipling – and Victoria has more British-born residents than anywhere in Canada. However, its tourist potential is exploited chiefly for American visitors, served up with lashings of fake Victoriana and chintzy commercialism, and ersatz echoes of empire at every turn. Despite the seasonal influx, and the sometimes atrociously tacky attractions designed to part tourists from their money, it's a small, relaxed and pleasantly sophisticated place, worth lingering in if only for its inspirational museum. It also provides plenty of pubs, restaurants (and the odd club) and serves as a base for a range of outdoor activities and slightly more far-flung attractions. Chief of these is **whale-watching**, with a plethora of companies on hand to take you out to the teeming waters around the city. And as a final lure the weather here – though often damp – is extremely mild; Victoria's meteorological station has the distinction of being the only one in Canada to record a winter in which the temperature never fell below freezing.

A brief history of Victoria

Salish peoples originally inhabited Victoria's site, and in particular the Lekwammen, who had a string of some ten villages in the area. Here they cultivated camas bulbs – vital to their diet and trade – and applied advanced salmon-fishing methods to the shoals of migrating salmon in net-strung reefs offshore. At the time the region must have been a virtual paradise. Captain George Vancouver, who was mapping the North American coast apparently ignorant of the aboriginal presence, described his feelings on first glimpsing this part of Vancouver Island: "The serenity of the climate, the innumerable pleasing landscapes, and the abundant fertility that nature puts forth, require only to be enriched by the industry of man with villages, mansions, cottages and other buildings, to render it the most lovely country that can be imagined."

The first step in this process began in 1842 when Victoria received some of its earliest **white visitors**, notably Hudson's Bay Company representative James Douglas, who disembarked at present-day Clover Point during a search for a new local headquarters for the company. One look at the natural harbour and its surroundings was enough: this, he declared, was a "perfect Eden", a feeling only reinforced by the friendliness of the indigenous population, who helped

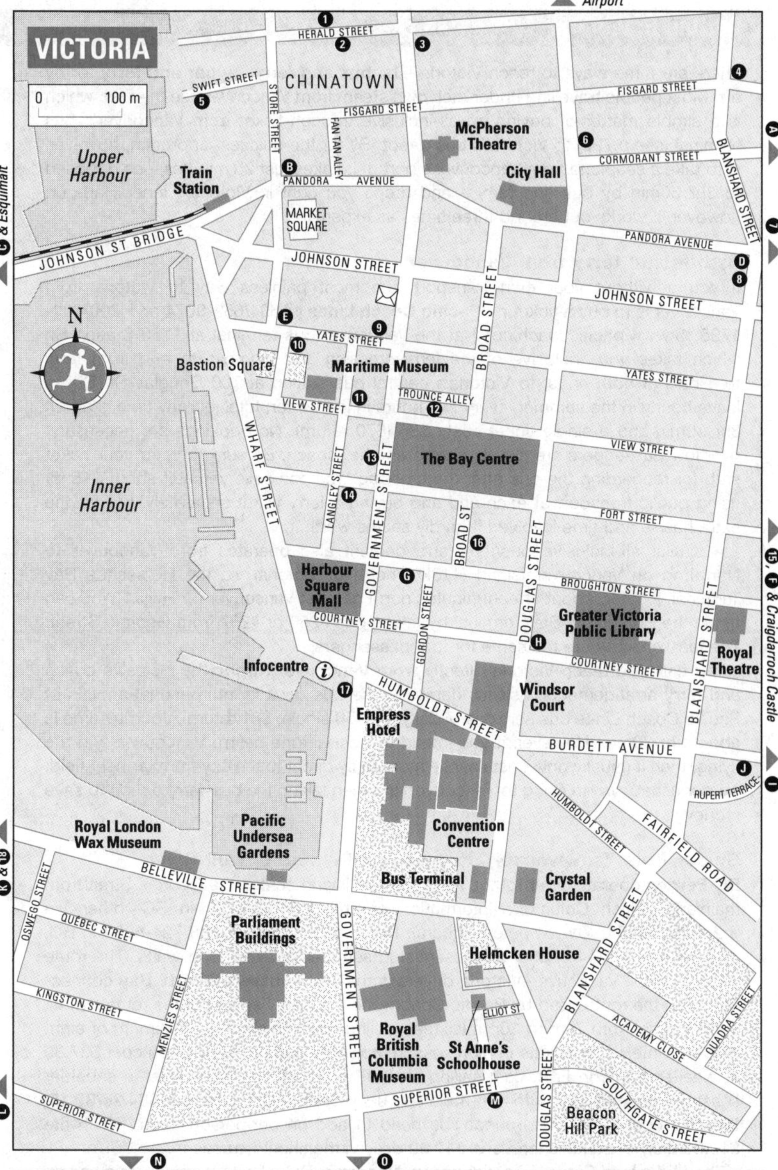

ACCOMMODATION

Abigail's Hotel	I	Ryan's	L
Cherry Bank Hotel	J	Selkirk Guest House	C
Heathergate House	N	Shamrock Suites on the Park	M
James Bay Inn	O	Strathcona Hotel	H
Laurel Point Inn	K	Swans Suite Hotel & Brewpub	B
Magnolia Hotel & Spa	G	Turtle Refuge Hostel	A
Ocean Island Backpacker's Inn	D	Victoria Youth Hostel	E
Prior House	F		

RESTAURANTS, BARS & CAFÉS

Barb's Fish and Chips	18	Milestone's	17
Blethering Place	7	Murchie's	13
Brasserie L'Ecole	3	Pagliacci's	16
Canoe	5	Re-Bar	11
Da Tandoor	15	The Reef	9
Demitasse Coffee Bar	8	Sally's	6
Earl's	4	Swans Brewpub	B
Herald Street Café	1	Taj Mahal	2
Il Terrazzo	10	The Tapa Bar	12
		The Temple	14

Getting to Victoria

There are three ways to reach Victoria – by **bus and ferry**, by **car and ferry**, or by **air**. Most people travelling under their own steam from Vancouver use the first, which is a simple matter of buying an all-inclusive through-ticket from Vancouver's bus terminal (see p.795) to Victoria's bus depot. By far the quickest approach, however, is to take a seaplane from Vancouver's port: this takes just 25 minutes – as opposed to 3hr 30min by bus and ferry – and drops you right in Victoria's Inner Harbour; however, it works out around three times as expensive.

By bus and ferry from Vancouver

If you're without your own transport, the most painless way to Victoria from Vancouver is to buy a ticket on **Pacific Coach Lines** (☎604/662-8074 or 1-800/661-1725, ⓦwww.pacificcoach.com) at the Vancouver bus terminal at 1150 Station St, which takes you, inclusive of the ferry crossing and journeys to and from ferry terminals at both ends, to Victoria's central bus station at 700 Douglas St. Buses leave hourly in the summer, every two hours in the winter; total journey time is about 3hr 30min and a single ticket costs $36 ($70 return). No bookings are necessary: overflow passengers are simply put on another coach. Be sure to keep your ticket stub for reboarding the bus after the crossing. You can save yourself about $15 by using public transport at each end and buying a ferry ticket separately, but for the extra hassle and time involved it hardly seems worth it.

A similar all-inclusive bus/ferry arrangement also operates from Vancouver **to Nanaimo** on Vancouver Island (113km north of Victoria) via the Horseshoe Bay Terminal, located about fifteen minutes north of West Vancouver on Hwy 1. You can reach the Horseshoe Bay Terminal by taking bus #250 or #257 from Georgia Street. The ferry charges are the same for foot passengers.

You can also reach Victoria directly **from Vancouver Airport** by inclusive coach and ferry arrangements: ask for details at the bus desk in international arrivals of Pacific Coach Lines bus services (7 daily; $41.50 single, $81 return). Journey time is about 3hr 30min. However, if you intend to visit Victoria before Vancouver, and are flying, then it usually only costs a little more to fly direct to the city from farther afield: it's not usually worth flying to Vancouver and then taking the bus-ferry option to save money.

By car from Tsawwassen, Horseshoe Bay and Powell River

BC Ferries operates four routes to Vancouver Island across the Georgia Strait from mainland British Columbia (information on ☎1-888/223-3779 in BC, otherwise ☎250/386-3431, ⓦwww.bcferries.com). Reservations (on ☎1-888/724-5223 in BC, otherwise ☎604/444-2890) are essential in summer to avoid long waits. The route used by most Vancouver–Victoria drivers is the **Tsawwassen–Swartz Bay** connection, also the route used by Pacific Coach Lines' buses. Ferries ply the route almost continuously from 7am to 10pm (sixteen sailings daily in summer, minimum of eight daily in winter). Car tickets in high season (from late June to early Sept) cost $37.80 at weekends (noon Fri to last sailing on Sun) or $35.75 on weekdays; in shoulder season (from mid-March to mid-June and early Sept to Oct) fares are $34.20/32.15. Bicycles cost $2.50 year-round. You need to add on per-person fares, which are $10.80 daily in peak season and $10.30 daily in the shoulder season.

The Mid-Island Express **Tsawwassen–Nanaimo** (Duke Point terminal), midway up the island, has eight or so departures daily on the two-hour crossing. More boats

him build **Fort Camouson**, named after an important aboriginal landmark (the name was later changed to **Fort Victoria** to honour the British queen). The aboriginal peoples from up and down the island settled near the fort,

cover the **Horseshoe Bay–Nanaimo** (Departure Bay terminal) route, a 95-minute journey from a terminal about fifteen minutes' drive from West Vancouver. Fares for both these routes are the same as for Tsawwassen to Swartz Bay. The fourth route is **Powell River–Comox**, Powell River being some 160km northwest of Vancouver on the Sunshine Coast.

By air from Vancouver

Flying into Victoria **from Vancouver** Airport is an expensive option. Open return fares typically run to around $150, excursion fares (with restrictions) around $100. It's more fun and more direct to fly from Vancouver harbour to Victoria harbour **by helicopter** or float plane: Harbour Air (ⓣ250/384-2215 or 1-800/665-0212, ⓦwww.harbour-air.com) and West Coast Air (ⓣ250/388-4521 or 1-800/347-2222, ⓦwww.westcoastair.com) fly in 35min from just west of Canada Place in Vancouver (see p.792 for details) for a one-way price of $74 ($148 return). Helijet Airways (ⓣ604/273-1414, ⓦwww.helijet.com) flies either from the helipad east of Canada Place or from Vancouver Airport for $140 one-way, less if you book in advance.

By ferry from the US

Washington State Ferries, at 2499 Ocean Ave, Sidney (in Victoria ⓣ250/381-1551; in Sidney ⓣ250/656-1531; in Seattle ⓣ206/464-6400; in Washington State ⓣ1-888/808-7977; ⓦwww.wsdot.wa.gov/ferries) runs ferries from **Anacortes**, ninety minutes north of Seattle, to Sidney, thirty minutes (and 30km) north of Victoria (summer 2 daily in each direction, winter 1 daily; 3hr–3hr 30min). One of the two summer departures goes via Orcas Island and Friday Harbor on the San Juan Islands. Passenger fares for the full trip are around US$15.60, a car and driver US$41.90. Car reservations are required from Orcas and Friday Harbor and can be made by calling at least a day in advance (ⓣ360/378-4777 in Friday Harbor).

Black Ball Transport, 430 Belleville St, Victoria (in BC ⓣ250/386-2202 or 1/800-972-6509; in WA ⓣ360/457-4491 or 1-800/833-6388; ⓦwww.cohoferry.com) operates a ferry across the Juan de Fuca Strait from **Port Angeles** right to Victoria's Inner Harbour (1–4 daily; 95min). Passenger fares are US$11, plus US$42.50 for a car and US$5 for a bicycle. Reservations are not accepted. Car drivers should call ahead in summer to have some idea of how long they'll have to wait. For foot passengers, and day-trippers in particular, a speedier option is **Victoria Express**'s seasonal service from Port Angeles to Victoria's Inner Harbour (late June to Aug 3 daily; late May to late June & Sept to mid-Oct 2 daily; 55min; in Canada ⓣ250/361-9144; in the US ⓣ360/452-8088 or ⓣ1-800/633-1589; ⓦwww.victoriaexpress.com). The fare is US$12.50 one-way, US$25 return; bicycles or canoes cost $5 one-way or return. There is also a service between Victoria and Friday Harbour (US$35 one-way).

The 300-passenger-only **Victoria Clipper** catamaran travels between Pier 69 in downtown **Seattle** and Victoria's Inner Harbour (mid-May to mid-Sept 4 daily; early May and late Sept 2 daily; rest of year 1 daily) in around 3hr, sometimes less (250 Bellevue St, Victoria; in Victoria ⓣ250/382-8100; in Seattle ⓣ206/448-5000; elsewhere in North America ⓣ1-800/888-2535; ⓦwww.victoriaclipper.com). Ticket prices in summer are US$84 single and US$139 return in peak season (June–Aug & various other holiday weekends) and from US$69/116 off season.

attracted by the new trading opportunities it offered. Soon they were joined by British pioneers, brought in to settle the land by a Bay subsidiary, the Puget Sound Agricultural Company, which quickly built several large company farms

Reserving provincial campsites

Tent and RV pitches at certain **campsites** in British Columbia's provincial parks (Ⓦwlapwww.gov.bc.ca/bcparks) can be reserved in advance. Not all parks accept reservations and some parks have more than one campsite. To make **reservations**, call Discover Camping (Ⓣ1-800/689-9025 or 604/689-9025 in greater Vancouver; March to mid-Sept Mon–Fri 7am–7pm, Sat & Sun 9am–5pm) or go to Ⓦwww.discovercamping.ca. Reservations can be made from three months to 48 hours in advance. A non-refundable **booking fee** of $6.36 per night (to a maximum of $19.08 for three or more nights) is charged (rates include tax). Payment in advance is by Visa or MasterCard only; payment for extra nights once you're at a campsite is in cash only. You can stay in up to a maximum of fourteen days in any single BC provincial park.

to accommodate settlers. In time, the harbour became the busiest West Coast port north of San Francisco and a major base for the British navy's Pacific fleet, a role it now fulfills for the bulk of Canada's modern **navy**.

Boom time came in the 1850s following the mainland gold strikes, when Victoria's port became an essential stopoff and supplies depot for prospectors heading across the water and into the interior. Military and bureaucratic personnel moved in to ensure order, bringing morals and manners of Victorian England with them. Alongside there grew a rumbustious shantytown of shops, bars and brothels, with one bar run by "Gassy" Jack Deighton, unwittingly soon to become one of Vancouver's founders.

Though the gold-rush bubble soon burst, Victoria carried on as a military, economic and political centre, becoming the capital of the newly created British Columbia in 1866 – years before the founding of Vancouver. British values were cemented in stone by the **Canadian Pacific Railway**, which built the *Empress Hotel* in 1908 in place of a proposed railway link that never came into being. Victoria's planned role as Canada's western rail terminus was surrendered to Vancouver, and with it any chance of realistic growth or industrial development. These days the town survives quite well almost entirely on the backs of tourists (four million a year), the civil-service bureaucracy and – shades of the home country – retirees in search of a mild-weathered retreat. Its population today is around 350,000, almost exactly double what it was just thirty years ago.

Arrival, information and transport

Victoria International Airport (Ⓣ250/953-7500, Ⓦwww.Victoriaairport.com) is 26km north of downtown on Hwy 17 near the Sidney ferry terminal. Hwy 17 runs south and takes you to the city outskirts where it becomes Douglas Street, which runs to the heart of downtown. The Airporter shuttle bus heads downtown (where it stops at major hotels) every half-hour between about 4.30am and 1am; a single fare for the 45-minute journey is $14 (Ⓣ250/386-2525 or 1-877/386-2525, Ⓦwww.victoriaairporter.travel.bc.ca). They can also arrange pick-ups to the airport.

The **bus terminal** is downtown at 700 Douglas St and Belleville St, close to the Royal British Columbia Museum. Pacific Coach Lines' buses (Ⓣ250/385-4411, Ⓦwww.pacificcoach.com) from Vancouver or Vancouver airport drop you here, and it is the base for Greyhound (Ⓣ250/388-5248 or 1-800/663-8390, Ⓦwww.greyhound.com) as well as onward connections on Vancouver Island provided by Laidlaw Coach Lines (Ⓣ250/385-4411 or 1-800/318-0818, Ⓦwww.grayline.ca/victoria). Victoria's **train station**, at the northern end of

Wharf Street, is useful only if you are taking the one daily service on Via Rail (ⓣ1-888/842-7245, ⓦwww.viarail.ca) to or from Nanaimo and points north (journey time to Nanaimo is 2hr 25min).

Victoria's busy **infocentre** is at 812 Wharf St, in front of the *Empress Hotel* on the harbour (daily: May–Sept 8.30am–6.30pm; Oct–April 9am–5pm; ⓣ250/953-2033, ⓦwww.tourismvictoria.com). The staff can help you book whale-watching and other tours (see box, p.880), and provide a huge range of general information.

The most enjoyable means of transport are the tiny Inner Harbour **ferries** that run around the harbour. Stops include Fisherman's Wharf, Ocean Pointe Resort and West Bay Marina, but they're worth taking just for the ride: try an evening mini-cruise around the harbour (buy tickets on ferries in the Inner Harbour or book at the infocentre). You're unlikely to need to take a local **bus** if you stick to the downtown area, but if you do venture out, most services run from the corner of Douglas and Yates streets. The fare within the large central zone is $2 – tickets and the DayPass ($6) are sold at the infocentre, 7-Eleven stores and other marked outlets, or you can pay on board if you have the exact fare. For 24-hour recorded information on city transport, call the Busline (ⓣ250/382-6161, lost property 995-5637, ⓦwww.bctransit.com).

Accommodation

Victoria fills up quickly in the summer, and most of its budget **accommodation** is well known and heavily patronized. Top-price hotels cluster around the Inner Harbour area; **hostels** and more downmarket alternatives are scattered all over, though the largest concentration of cheap **hotels** and **motels** is around the Gorge Road and Douglas Street areas northwest of downtown. Reservations are virtually obligatory in all categories, though the infocentre's accommodation service (ⓣ1-800/663-3883) will root out a room if you're stuck. They are more than likely to offer you **B&B** accommodation, of which the town has a vast selection; prices for many are surprisingly elevated, though owners of many of the more far-flung places will pick you up from downtown. Victoria's commercial **campsites** are full to bursting in summer, with most space given over to RVs. Few of these are convenient for downtown – given that you'll have to travel, you might as well head for one of the more scenic provincial park sites. Most are on the Trans-Canada Hwy to the north, or on Hwy 14 east of Victoria.

Hotels, motels and B&Bs

Abigail's Hotel 960 McClure St ⓣ250/388-5363 or 1-800-561-6565, ⓦwww.abigailshotel.com. A very classy, small hotel in a fine building with log fires, voluminous duvets, Jacuzzis and a good breakfast. If you want to treat yourself, this is the place. All rooms are non-smoking. Situated on the corner of Quadra St, a block east of Blanshard St and within easy walking distance of the city centre. ❽

Cherry Bank Hotel 825 Burdett Ave ⓣ250/385-5380 or 1-800/998-6688, ⓦwww.bctravel.com/cherrybankhotel.html. Reservations are essential at this deservedly popular and pleasantly eccentric 26-room budget hotel (note the rotating mermaid on the roof), which has excellent rooms and breakfast included. First choice at this price. ❸

James Bay Inn 270 Government St at Toronto St ⓣ250/384-7151 or 1-800/836-2649, ⓦwww.jamesbayinn.bc.ca. This 45-room hotel vies with the *Cherry Bank* as Victoria's best reasonably priced option, though rates have climbed in the last couple of years. The Edwardian building was the home of painter Emily Carr. Simple rooms at varying prices, with a restaurant and pub in the basement. Two blocks south of the Parliament Buildings. ❻

Laurel Point Inn 680 Montréal St ⓣ250/386-8721 or 1-800/663-7667, ⓕ386-9547, ⓦwww.laurelpoint.com. Don't be put off by the size of this 200-room resort-style hotel. All the rooms have a balcony and good harbour view, thanks to a position on a well-landscape promontory (with a Japanese garden) on the Inner Harbour. The contemporary aesthetic is simple and clean, and a far cry from the chinzy look of many of Victoria's hotels. There are two wings, north and south – you want to be in the southern one, designed by Arthur Erickson (see p.819) in 1989. Here, the rooms are all pale wood and dark marble, with Japanese-style sliding doors, Asian works of art and airy, stylish bathrooms. ⑥

Shamrock Suites on the Park 675 Superior St at the corner of Douglas ⓣ250/385-8768 or 1-800/294-5544, ⓕ250/385-1837. The *Shamrock* lies a block from the Royal BC Museums close to Beacon Hill Park. It has just sixteen units, upgraded from simple motel status to "suites" following a renovation in 2002. Prices have gone up, but the studios and one-bedroom suites are roomy and come with kitchenettes at no extra cost: some rooms have park views. A continental breakfast is included in the rates between July & Sept. ⑤

Strathcona Hotel 919 Douglas St ⓣ250/383-7137 or 1-800/663-7476, ⓦwww.strathconahotel.com. Large, modern hotel where rooms include baths and TVs. There's a British-style pub and restaurant downstairs with booming live and DJ music which may not be to all tastes. ④

Swans Suite Hotel & Brewpub 506 Pandora Ave ⓣ250/361-3310 or 1-800/668-7926, ⓣ361-3491, ⓦwww.swanshotel.com). Brewpub aside, the appeal of the 30 rooms here is the setting, a converted 1880s grain store that means many of the suites and larger rooms are quirky, loft-style spaces, often on a split level and with exposed beams and bold, original artwork. The one- and two-bedroom suites take up to six people, making them perfect for families, and there are fully equipped kitchens and dining and living rooms. Doubles ⑦, suites ⑨

The Magnolia Hotel & Spa 623 Courtney St ⓣ250/381-0999 or 1-877/624-6654, ⓕ381-0988-3838, ⓦwww.magnoliahotel.com. One of the new wave of Victorian lodgings, this 63-room boutique hotel lays on the character thick, the small lobby setting the period Edwardian tone, though the effect, especially in the high-quality rooms (the best have harbour views and fireplaces) and superb bathrooms, is never stuffy. The Aveda Spa is one of the best in the city. ⑦

Bed and breakfasts

Heathergate House 122 Simcoe St ⓣ250/383-0068 or 1-888/683-0068, ⓦwww.heathergatebb.com. This small B&B offers three rooms plus a separate two-bed cottage within walking distance of the Inner Harbour and the sights. All rooms are en suite. There's a private floor for guests with a lounge and TV room. ⑤

Prior House 620 St Charles St ⓣ250/592-8847 or 1-877/924-3300, ⓦwww.priorhouse.com. A very smart five-room B&B; once the home of Victoria's lieutenant governor – ask for his suite, complete with bathroom with chandelier. About 2.5km east of downtown in the smart Rockland area, so it's better if you have transport. ⑦

Ryan's 224 Superior St ⓣ250/389-0012 or 1-877/389-0012, ⓦwww.ryansbb.com. A very pretty 1892 heritage building south of the Royal BC Museum and a five-minute walk to downtown; all seven rooms are nicely decorated and have private bathrooms. ⑦

Selkirk Guest House 934 Selkirk Ave ⓣ250/389-1213 or 1-800/974-6638, ⓦwww.selkirkguesthouse.com. Fine historic waterfront home dating from 1909 northwest of the Inner Harbour: take bus #14 from Douglas St (to within two blocks) or cross the Johnston Bridge and follow the water past Bay St and Banfield Park: then take Arcadia, a right turn from Craigflower Rd to Selkirk Ave. It's well placed for bike and walking trails (it's on the Galloping Goose Trail) and you can rent boats and canoes. Dorm places cost $20 and there's a choice of four other good double rooms $80–110 with breakfast at $5. ④

University residences, hostels and campsites

Ocean Island Backpacker's Inn 791 Pandora Ave at Blanshard St ⓣ250/385-1788 or 1-888/888-4180, ⓦwww.oceanisland.com. A good, reasonably central location in the northeast corner of downtown. Facilities include private and shared rooms, Internet access, a music room with instruments, no curfew, free morning coffee, laundry room, free bike storage, linen and towels provided and limited parking at $4 a day. The restored 1893 heritage building has a wide variety of dorms and rooms (singles and doubles with and without bathroom) on a sliding scale depending on the time of year, the day of the week (more on Fri and Sat) and whether you have a HI card. The following prices are Fri and Sat rates and assume you do not have card (subtract $1–3 if you do): dorm beds cost $19 from mid-Oct to mid-March up to $24 in July and Aug. Private doubles cost from $25 to $68. Weekly and monthly rates are available on dorms and rooms.

Turtle Refuge Hostel 1608 Quadra St at corner of Pandora ⓣ250/386-4471 or 1-866/5-HOSTEL,

ⓦwww.turtlerefuge.com. Central residential home (also known as the *Backpackers' Lodge*) with 25 dorm beds, two doubles and two four-bed family rooms. There's a communal kitchen, laundry, no curfew, parking, luggage storage and free morning coffee. Dorm beds cost $17.50, doubles $40 plus $10 for each extra person.

University of Victoria Corner of Sinclair and Finnerty Rd ⓣ250/721-8395, ⓦwww.hfcs.uvic.ca. Good, if plain rooms (single or double) on the university campus are available May–Sept when not required for students or conferences. Shared bathroom, laundry and kitchen facilities. Good-value four-room suites with bathroom, kitchen and living room are also available. For a small extra fee guests have access to the university pool and other sports facilities. It is a half-hour car or bus (#4 or 14) ride to downtown. Singles $44 (with breakfast), doubles $55.

Victoria Youth Hostel (HI) 516 Yates and Wharf sts ⓣ250/385-4511 or 1-888/883-0099, ⓦwww.hihostels.ca. Large, modern, welcoming and extremely well-run place just a few blocks north of the Inner Harbour. The bunk rooms, though, can be noisy: the reception, rather ominously, sells earplugs. The notice boards are packed with useful information on the city. Members $17–20, nonmembers $21.28–24.28. Open Mon–Thurs 7.30am–midnight, Fri–Sun 7am–2am.

Campsites

Fort Victoria RV and Park Campground 340 Island Hwy 1A ⓣ250/479-8112, ⓦwww.fortvicrv.com. Closest site to downtown, located 6km north of Victoria off the Trans-Canada Hwy. Take bus #14 (for Craigflower) from the city centre; it stops right by the gate. Large 300-pitch site mainly for RVs but with a few tent sites; free hot showers. $25 for two people.

Goldstream Provincial Park 2930 Trans-Canada Hwy ⓣ604/689-9025 or 1-800-689-9025, ⓦwww.discovercamping.ca. Bus #50 from Douglas St downtown. Although 20km north of the city off Hwy 1, this site is set in old-growth forests of cedar and Douglas fir and is Victoria's best camping option. Flush toilets and free hot showers, with plenty of hiking, swimming and fishing opportunities. $22 per site.

Thetis Lake Trans-Canada Hwy at 1938 West Park Lane ⓣ250/478-3845, ⓔthetislake@shaw.ca. Runs a close second to Goldstream Provincial Park's campsites for the pleasantness of its setting, and is only 10km north of downtown. Family-oriented, with 147 sites, as well as laundry and coin-operated showers. $16 per two people.

The City

The Victoria that's worth bothering with is very small: almost everything worth seeing, as well as the best shops and restaurants, is within walking distance of the **Inner Harbour** area and the Old Town district behind it. On summer evenings this area is alive with strollers and buskers, and a pleasure to wander as the sun drops over the water. Foremost among the daytime diversions are the **Royal British Columbia Museum** and the **Empress Hotel**. Most of the other trumpeted attractions are dreadful, and many charge entry fees out of proportion to what's on show. If you're tempted by the Royal London Wax Museum, the Pacific Undersea Gardens, Miniature World, English Village, Anne Hathaway's Thatched Cottage or any of Victoria's other dubious commercial propositions, details are available from the infocentre. Otherwise you might drop by the modest **Maritime Museum** and think about a trip to the celebrated **Butchart Gardens**, some way out of town, but easily accessed by public transport or regular all-inclusive tours from the bus terminal. If you're around for a couple of days you should also find time to walk around **Beacon Hill Park**, a few minutes' walk from downtown to the south.

The best of the area's beaches are well out of town, around three or four miles on Hwy 14 and Hwy 1, but for idling by the sea drop down to the pebble shore along the southern edge of Beacon Hill Park. For some local swimming, the best option by far is **Willows Beach** on the Esplanade in Oak Bay, 2km east of Victoria; take bus #1 to Beach and Dalhousie Road. Other good stretches of sand can be found on Dallas Road and at Island View Beach.

Festivals in Victoria

Summer brings out the buskers and free entertainment in Victoria's people-places – James Bay, Market Square and Beacon Hill Park in particular. Annual highlights include:

TerrifVic Jazz Party April. A showcase for about a dozen top international bands held over four days.

Jazz Fest June. More than 100 assorted lesser-known bands perform in Market Square.

Canada Day July 1. Celebration of Canada's national day concentrated in and around the Inner Harbour and include fireworks, food, music and other cultrual events.

Victoria International Festival July & Aug. Victoria's largest general arts jamboree.

Folk Fest Last week of July. Multicultural arts extravaganza.

First People's Festival Early Aug. Celebration of the cultures of Canada's aboriginal peoples.

Canadian International Dragon Boat Festival Mid-Aug. Over 100 international teams take part in dragon-boat races on the Inner Harbour.

Classic Boat Festival Aug 30–Sept 1. Dozens of wooden antique boats on display.

Royal Victoria Marathon Early Oct. Marathon and half-marathon around the city streets and surroundings held on the Canadian Thanksgiving weekend.

Fringe Festival Sept. Avant-garde performances of all kinds.

Great Canadian Beer Festival Second week of Nov. Selections of beer from some of the province's best microbreweries can tasted at the Victoria Conference Centre, 720 Douglas St.

Merrython Fun Run Mid-Dec. A 10km run through downtown Victoria.

The Royal British Columbia Museum

The Royal British Columbia Museum (daily 9am–5pm, National Geographic IMAX Theatre daily 9am–8pm; museum $14, IMAX Theatre $10.50, combined ticket $22.50, IMAX double feature $16.25; ⓦwww.rbcm.gov.bc.ca) is a short stroll along the waterfront from the infocentre at 675 Belleville St. Founded in 1886, it is arguably the **best museum in Canada**, and regularly rated, by visitors and travel-magazine polls, as one of North America's top ten. All conceivable aspects of the province are examined, but the aboriginal peoples section is probably the definitive collection of a much-covered genre, while the natural-history sections – huge re-creations of natural habitats, complete with sights, sounds and smells – are mind-boggling in scope and imagination. Allow at least two trips to take it all in.

From virtually the first thing you see – a huge stuffed mammoth – you can tell that thought, wit and a lot of money have gone into the museum. Much of the cash must have been sunk into its most popular display, the **Open Ocean**, a self-contained, in-depth look at the sea and the deep-level ocean. Groups of ten are admitted into a series of tunnels, dark rooms, lifts and mock-ups of submarines at thirty-minute intervals. You take a time-coded ticket and wait your turn, so either arrive early or reckon on seeing the rest of the museum first. Though rather heavy-handed in its "we're-all-part-of-the-cosmic-soup" message, it's still an object lesson in presentation and state-of-the-art museum dynamics. It's also designed to be dark and enclosed, and signs wisely warn you to stay out if you suffer even a twinge of claustrophobia.

The **first floor** contains dioramas, full-scale reconstructions of some of the many natural habitats found in British Columbia. The idea of re-creating shorelines, coastal rainforests and Fraser Delta landscapes may sound far-fetched, yet all are incredibly realistic, down to dripping water and cool, dank atmospheres. Audiovisual displays and a tumult of information accompany the exhibits (the beaver film is worth hunting down), most of which focus attention on the province's 25,600km of coastline, a side of British Columbia usually overlooked in favour of its interior forests and mountains.

Upstairs on the **second floor** is the mother of all the tiny museums of bric-a-brac and pioneer memorabilia in BC. Arranged eccentrically from the present day backwards, it explores every aspect of the province's social history over two centuries in nitpicking detail. Prominently featured are part of an early twentieth-century town, complete with cinema and silent films, plus comprehensive displays on logging, mining, the gold rush, farming, fishing and lesser domestic details; all the artefacts and accompanying information are presented with impeccable finesse.

Up on the mezzanine **third floor** is a superb collection of **aboriginal peoples' art, culture and history**. It's presented in gloomy light against muted wood walls and brown carpet, which creates a solemn atmosphere in keeping with the tragic nature of many of the displays. The collection divides into two epochs – before and after the coming of Europeans – tellingly linked by a single aboriginal carving of a white man, starkly and brilliantly capturing the initial wonder and weirdness of the new arrivals. The whole collection takes a thoughtful and oblique approach, taking you to the point where smallpox virtually wiped out in one year a culture that was eight millennia in the making. A section on land and reservations is left for last – the issues are contentious even today – and even if you're succumbing to museum fatigue, the arrogance and duplicity of the documents on display will shock you. The highlights in this section are many, but try to make a point of seeing the short film *In the Land of the War Canoes* (1914), the **Bighouse** (a facsimile of a meeting hall) and its chants, and the audiovisual display on aboriginal myths and superstition.

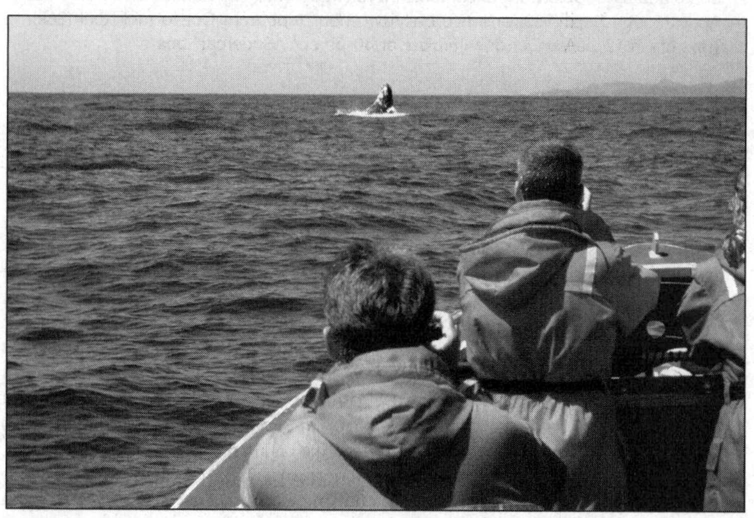

△ Whale-watching off Victoria

Whale-watching from Victoria

The waters around Victoria are not as **whale**-rich as those around Tofino on the west coast of Vancouver Island, but there's still a very good chance of spotting the creatures. Three pods of orcas (**killer whales**) live in the seas around southern Vancouver Island, around a hundred animals in all, so you may see these, though **minke** are the most common whale spotted, with occasional **greys** and **humpbacks** also present. Few outfits offer guaranteed sightings, and many cover themselves by preparing you for the fact that if you don't see whales you stand a good chance of seeing Dall's **porpoises**, harbour or elephant **seals** and California and Steller **sea lions**.

While there are many outfits to choose from, they offer almost identical trips at the same prices, typically around $70 to $90 for a three-hour outing. There's usually a naturalist, or at least a knowledgeable crew member, to fill you in on what you're seeing (or not). The only real variables are the **boats** used, so you need to decide whether you want a rigid-hull cruiser (covered or uncovered), which is comfortable and sedate (and usually the most expensive at around $90), a catamaran ($75–90), or a high-speed aluminium-hull inflatable known as a "zodiac" ($70–90), which is infinitely more exhilarating, but can offer a sometimes bumpy ride and lacks toilets on board. The two companies below have been around longer than most; the infocentre (p.875) has details on others.

Seacoast Expeditions Located across the Inner Harbour at the Boardwalk Level, Ocean Pointe Resort, 45 Songhees Rd (ⓣ250/383-2254 or 1-800/386-1525, ⓦwww.seacoastexpeditions.com) – a ten-minute walk across the Johnson Street bridge or a three-minute harbour ferry crossing (it also has a shuttle-bus pick-up from downtown hotels). Victoria's founding whale-watching company, Seacoast has been in the business over a decade and offers one trip daily in April & Oct, four three-hour trips daily in May, June and Sept, and five daily in July & Aug ($89, $69 in autumn and winter).

Five Star Charters 706 Douglas St (ⓣ250/388-7223 or 1-800/634-9617, ⓦwww.5starwhales.com). Has been in business since 1985 and in the past claimed the highest percentage of whale sightings out of all the tour operators (thanks to spotter boats and a good network of contacts). It runs three daily three-hour trips from mid-April through Sept ($89) and two daily two-hour trips from Oct to mid-April ($69). Trips are in 12-passenger open cruiser or 40-person "Supercat" boats.

The **National Geographic Theatre** in the museum plays host to a huge IMAX screen and a changing programme of special-format films. Outside the museum, there's also **Thunderbird Park**, a strip of grass with a handful of totem poles.

Helmcken House and around

Helmcken House (May–Oct daily 10am–5pm; rest of year Mon & Thurs–Sun 11am–4pm; $5) stands strangely isolated off Belleville Street, directly adjacent to the museum. The oldest house in BC still on its original site, built in 1852, it is a predictable heritage offering that showcases the home, furnishings and embroidery talents of the Helmcken family. Dr John Helmcken was Fort Victoria's doctor and local political bigwig, and his house is a typical monument to stolid Victoria values. Upstairs it contains various attic treasures and some fearsome-looking medical tools. It's probably only of interest, however, if you've so far managed to avoid any of Canada's many thousands of similar houses. If you do visit, pick up the free guided tapes and hear "voices from history" (those of actors and actresses) that give a more personalized slant on the building.

Just behind the house there's another old white-wood building, the **St Anne's Pioneer Schoolhouse**, originally purchased by a Bishop Demers for four sisters of the Order of St Ann, who in 1858 took it upon themselves to leave their Québec home to come and teach in Victoria. Built between 1843 and 1858, it's believed to be the oldest building in Victoria still in use.

The Parliament Buildings

The huge Victorian pile of the **Parliament Buildings** (daily 9am–5pm; guided tours, but times vary according to parliament business; ⓣ250/387-3046 or 1-800/663-7867 in BC), one block west of the museum at 501 Belleville St, is old and imposing in the manner of a large and particularly grand British town hall. Beautifully lit at night by some three hundred tiny bulbs (though locals grumble about the cost), the domed building is fronted by the sea and well-kept gardens – a pleasant enough ensemble, though it doesn't really warrant the manic enthusiasm visited on it by hordes of summer tourists. You're more likely to find yourself taking time out on the front lawns, distinguished by a perky statue of Queen Victoria and a giant sequoia, a gift from the state of California. Designed by the 25-year-old Francis Rattenbury, who was also responsible for the nearby *Empress Hotel*, the building was completed in 1897, at a cost of $923,000, in time for Queen Victoria's jubilee. Figures from Victoria's grey bureaucratic past are duly celebrated, the main door guarded by statues of Sir James Douglas, who chose the site of the city, and Sir Matthew Baillie Begbie (aka the "Hanging Judge"), responsible for law and order during the heady days of gold fever. Sir George Vancouver keeps an eye on proceedings from the top of the dome. Free tours start to the right of the main steps and are led by guides who are chirpy and full of anecdotes. Look out for the dagger that killed Captain Cook, and the gold-plated dome, painted with scenes from Canadian history.

Beacon Hill Park

The best park within walking distance of the town centre is **Beacon Hill Park**, south of the Inner Harbour and a few minutes' walk up the road behind the museum. Victoria is sometimes known as the "City of Gardens", and at the right times of the year this park shows why. Victoria's biggest green space, it has lots of paths, ponds, big trees and quiet corners, and plenty of views over the **Juan de Fuca Strait** to the distant Olympic Mountains of Washington State (especially on the park's southern side). These pretty straits, incidentally, are the focus of some rather bad feeling between Victoria and the US for the city has a dark secret: it dumps raw sewage into the strait, excusing itself by claiming it's quickly broken up by the sea's strong currents. Washington State isn't so sure, and there have been plenty of arguments over the matter and, more to the point for city elders, economically damaging convention boycotts by American companies. Either way, it's pretty bad PR for Victoria and totally at odds with the city's image.

The gardens in the park are by turns well tended and wonderfully wild and unkempt, a far cry from its earliest days, when it was known by the local Salish as Meeacan, their word for a belly, as the hill was thought to resemble the stomach of large man lying on his back. The park was a favoured retreat of celebrated Victorian artist Emily Carr. They also claim the **world's tallest totem pole**, as well as the "Mile Zero" marker of the Trans-Canada Hwy and – that ultimate emblem of Englishness – a cricket pitch. Some of the trees are massive old-growth timbers that you'd normally only see on the island's unlogged west coast. Come here in spring and you'll catch swaths of daffodils

The Butchart Gardens

If you're into things horticultural you'll want to make a trek out to the celebrated and much-hyped **Butchart Gardens**, 22km north of Victoria at 800 Benvenuto Ave, Brentwood Bay on Hwy 17 towards the Swartz Bay ferry terminal (daily: mid-June–Aug 9am–10.30pm, first two weeks of Sept & Dec 9am–9pm; rest of the year 9am–sunset; rates $13 in early Jan, then on a sliding scale through the year to $23 between mid-June and Sept; ⓣ250/652-4422 or 652-5256 for recorded information, ⓦwww.butchartgardens.com). The gardens are renowned among visitors and locals alike for the stunning **firework displays** that usually take place each Sat evening in July and Aug. There is also a restaurant and various other commercial enterprises, with musical entertainment well to the fore. The gardens are also illuminated during the late-evening opening hours between mid-June and the end of Sept.

The gardens were started in 1904 by Jenny Butchart, wife of a mine-owner and pioneer of Portland Cement in Canada and the US, her initial aim being to landscape one of her husband's quarries. The garden now covers fifty breathtaking acres, comprising rose, Japanese and Italian gardens and lots of decorative details. About half a million visitors a year tramp through the foliage, which includes over a million plants and seven hundred different species. At the same time, the amount of space actually given over to gardens may strike you as slightly disproportionate to the space allotted to the car park, gift shop and restaurant.

To get here by public transport take **bus** #75 for "Central Saanich" from downtown. Otherwise, there are regular summer **shuttles** (May–Oct daily, hourly in the morning, half-hourly in the afternoon; ⓣ250/388-5248) from the main bus terminal, where tickets ($4) are obtainable not from the main ticket office but a separate Gray Lines desk.

and blue camas flowers, the latter a floral monument to Victoria's earliest aboriginal inhabitants, who cultivated the flower for its edible bulb. Some 30,000 other flowers are planted in the gardens annually.

The Empress Hotel

A town is usually desperate when one of its key attractions is a hotel, but in the case of Victoria the **Empress Hotel** is so physically overbearing and plays such a part in the town's tourist appeal that it demands some sort of attention. You may be unlikely to stay here – rooms are expensive – but it's worth wandering through the huge lobbies and palatial dining areas for a glimpse of well-restored colonial splendour. In a couple of lounges there's a fairly limp "Smart Casual" dress code – no dirty jeans, running shoes, short shorts or backpacks – but elsewhere you can wander freely. If you want to **take tea**, which is why most casual visitors come, enter the Tea Lounge by the hotel's side entrance (the right, or south side); there you can enjoy scones, biscuits, cakes and, of course, tea over six courses but you have to abide by the dress code and be prepared for an enormous outlay. In other lounges like the *Bengal* (see below) you can ask for just tea and scones.

The hotel's **Crystal Lounge** and its lovely Tiffany-glass dome form the most opulent area on view, but the marginally less ornate entrance lounge is the top place for the charade of afternoon tea, and indulging can be a bit of a laugh. There's also a reasonably priced bar and restaurant downstairs, **Kipling's**, and the attractive **Bengal Lounge**, complete with tiger-skin over the fireplace, where you can have a curry and all the trimmings for about $15. For a bigger treat, take dinner amidst the Edwardian splendour of *The Empress Dining Room*.

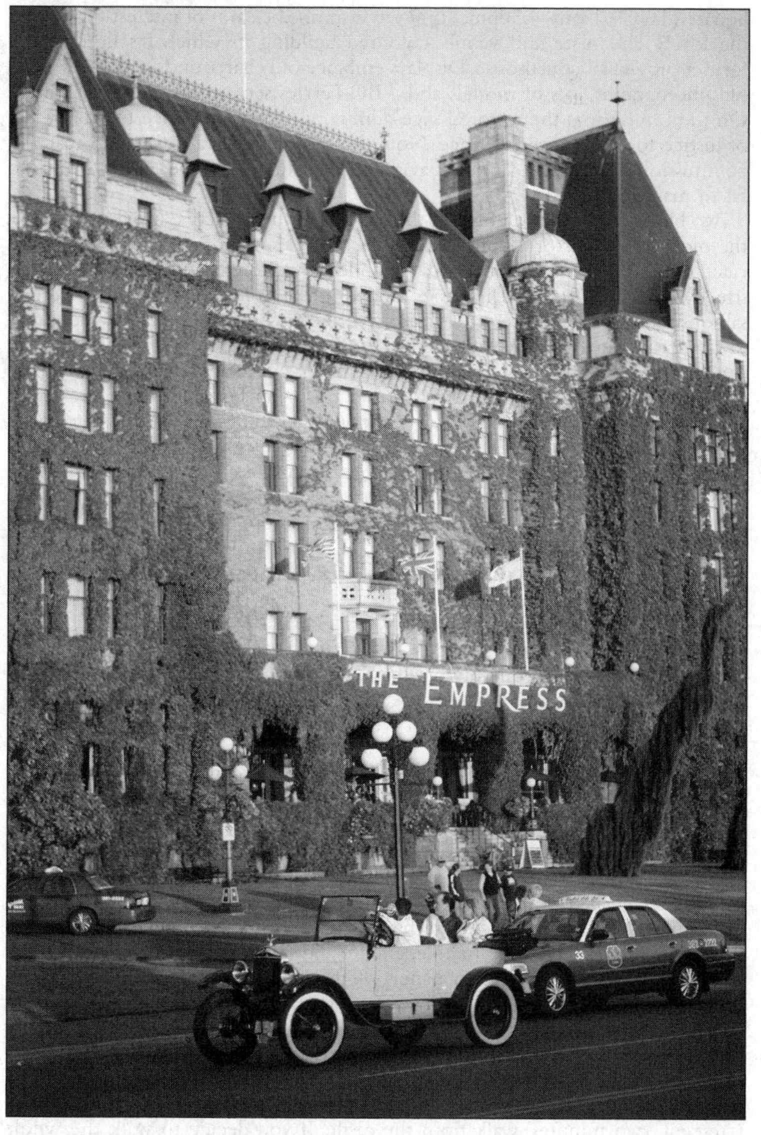

△ The Empress Hotel

The old town

The oldest part of Victoria focuses on **Bastion Square**, original site of Fort Victoria, from which it's a short walk to Market Square, a nice piece of old-town rejuvenation, and the main downtown shopping streets. Bastion Square's former saloons, brothels and warehouses have been spruced up and turned into offices, cafés and galleries. The modest **Maritime Museum** at 28 Bastion

Square (daily 9.30am–4.30pm; $6; Ⓦ www.mmbc.bc.ca) is of interest mainly for the lovely chocolate and vanilla coloured building in which it's housed, the former provincial courthouse. Displays embrace old charts, uniforms, ships' bells, old photographs, lots of models and a BC Ferries section on the second floor. On the top floor is the restored vice-admiralty courtroom, once the main seat of justice for the entire province. Note the old open elevator built to reach it, commissioned by Chief Justice Davie in 1901, supposedly because he was too fat to manage the stairs.

Two blocks away to the north of the square lies the attractive **Market Square**, the old heart of Victoria but now a collection of some 65 speciality shops and cafés around a central courtyard (bounded by Store, Pandora and Johnson streets). This area boomed in 1858 following the gold rush, providing houses, saloons, opium dens, stores and various salacious entertainments for thousands of chancers and would-be immigrants. On the Pandora Avenue side of the area was a ravine, marked by the current sunken courtyard, beyond which lay **Chinatown** (now centred slightly further north on Fisgard Street), the oldest on North America's west coast. Here, among other things, 23 factories processed 90,000 pounds of opium a year for what was then a legitimate trade and – until the twentieth century – one of BC's biggest industries.

As for the **shopping streets**, it's worth looking out for E.A. Morris, a wonderful old cigar and tobacco shop next to Murchie's coffee shop at 1110 Government St, and Roger's Chocolates, 913 Government St, whose whopping Victoria creams (among other things), are regularly dispatched to Buckingham Palace for royal consumption.

Other attractions

Outside the Inner Harbour, Victoria has a scattering of **minor attractions** that don't fit into any logical tour of the city – and at any rate are only quick-stop diversions – the most compelling of which is Craigdarroch Castle.

Craigdarroch Castle and the Art Gallery of Greater Victoria

Craigdarroch Castle (daily: mid-June to early Sept 9am–7pm; rest of year 10am–4.30pm; $11.50; Ⓦ www.craigdarrochcastle.com) is perched on a hilltop at 1050 Joan Crescent in Rockland, one of Victoria's more prestigious neighbourhoods. It was built by Robert Dunsmuir, a caricature of a Victorian politician, strike-breaker, robber baron and coal tycoon, who was forced to put up this gaunt Gothic pastiche to lure his wife away from Scotland. Only the best was good enough, from the marble, granite and sandstone of the superstructure to the intricately handworked panels of the ceilings over the main hall and staircase. The dastardly Dunsmuir never enjoyed his creation: he died in 1889, two years after the castle was begun and a year before it was finished. Among the 39 rooms there's the usual clutter of Victoriana and period detail, in particular some impressive woodwork and stained and leaded glass. To get here by **bus** take the #11-University or #14-University from downtown to the foot of Joan Crescent, two minutes' walk from the castle. If you decide to walk the whole way, allow 45 minutes from the Inner Harbour.

The **Art Gallery of Greater Victoria** (daily 10am–5pm, Thurs till 9pm; $8, but may be higher for some exhibitions; Ⓦ www.aggv.bc.ca) is near Craigdarroch Castle at 1040 Moss St, just off Fort St. It's of little interest unless you're partial to contemporary Canadian paintings and the country's best collection of Japanese art; the building, housed in the 1890 Spencer Mansion, boasts the only complete Shinto shrine outside Japan. It does, however, have a small permanent collection of Emily Carr's work (see p.810) as well as a temporary exhibition, usually interesting, that changes every six weeks. To get here by **bus**, take the #10-Haultain, #11-Uplands/Beacon Hill or #14-University from downtown.

The Emily Carr House, Point Ellice and Craigflower Manor

Ten rooms are open to the public at **Emily Carr House** (May & Sept Tues–Sat 11am–4pm, June–Aug daily 11am–4pm; 10am–5pm; $5.35; Ⓦwww.emilycarr.com), two blocks from the Inner Harbour at 207 Government St. This was the early home of British Columbia's best-known artist, born here during a blizzard in 1871 in the old wooden bed still visible in what would become her bedroom. The building was constructed in 1864, and has been painstakingly restored to its former state. Fans of the artist may want to pay homage, but the works on the walls are copies.

The 1861 Victorian-Italianate **Point Ellice House and Gardens** (guided tours May–Sept daily 10am–4pm; $5.35; Ⓣ250/380-6506, Ⓦwww.pointellicehouse.ca) at 2616 Pleasant St is magnificently re-created but less enticing than Craigdarroch Castle because of its slightly shabby surroundings. These can be overlooked, however, if you make a point of arriving by sea, taking one of the little Harbour Ferry services to the house (10min) from the Inner Harbour. The restored Victorian-style gardens here are a delight on a summer afternoon. The interior – one of the best of its kind in western Canada – retains its largely Victorian appearance thanks partly to the reduced circumstances of the O'Reilly family, whose genteel slide into relative poverty over several generations (they lived here from 1861 to 1974) meant that many furnishings were simply not replaced. Tea is served on the lawns in the summer; it's a good idea to book ahead. Bus #14-University will get you here from downtown if you don't fancy the approach by water.

In its day, **Craigflower Manor and Farmhouse** (May–Oct daily 10am–5pm; $5; Ⓣ250/387-4697) on Admiral's Rd about 9km and fifteen minutes' drive from downtown, was among the earliest of Victoria's farming homesteads, marking the town's transition from trading post to permanent community. It was built in a mock-Georgian style in 1856, apparently from timbers salvaged from the first four farmhouses built in the region. Its owner was Kenneth McKenzie, a Hudson's Bay Company bailiff, who recruited fellow Scottish settlers to form a farming community on Portage Inlet. The house was to remind him of Scotland, and soon became the foremost social centre in the fledgling village – mainly visited by officers because McKenzie's daughters were virtually the only white women on the island. As with Point Ellice House, reservations for tea are recommended. Take **bus** #14-Craigflower from downtown.

Eating, drinking and nightlife

Although clearly in Vancouver's culinary shadow, Victoria still has many **restaurants**, some extremely good, offering greater variety – and higher prices – than you'll find in most other BC towns. **Pubs** tend to be plastic imitations of British equivalents, with one or two worthy exceptions, as do the numerous **cafés** that pander to Victoria's self-conscious afternoon-tea ritual. Good snacks and pastry shops abound, while at the other extreme there are budget-busting establishments if you want a one-off treat or a change from the standard Canadian menus that await you on much of the rest of the island.

Nocturnal diversions are for the most part tame: highbrow tastes, though, are surprisingly well catered for, and there's a smattering of **bars**, as well as **live music** venues and **clubs** to keep you happy for the limited time you're likely to spend in the city. **Jazz** is particularly popular; for information, contact the Victoria Jazz Society, 250-727 Johnson St (Ⓣ250/388-4423, Ⓦwww.vicjazz.bc.ca). **Listings** appear in the main daily newspaper, the *Times-Colonist*, and in a variety of free magazines distributed to shops, cafés and hotels, including the excellent *Monday* magazine (Ⓦwww.mondaymag.com), published every Thursday. **Tickets** for most offerings are available from the city's main performance space, the McPherson Playhouse, 3 Centennial Square, Pandora and Government sts (Ⓣ250/386-6121 or 1-888-717-6121, Ⓦwww.rmts.bc.ca).

Cafés, tea and snacks

Barb's Fish and Chips 310 St Lawrence St, Fisherman's Wharf, off Kingston St Ⓣ250/384-6515. A much-loved floating shack that offers classic home-cut chips, fish straight off the boat and oyster burgers and chowder to boot; the small bathtub-size ferries from the Inner Harbour drop you close by.

Blethering Place 2250 Oak Bay Ave Ⓣ250/598-1413 or 1-888/598-1413. Along with the *Empress Hotel*, this is known as a place to indulge in the tea-taking custom. Scones, cakes and dainty sandwiches are served up against the background of hundreds of toby jugs and royal-family memorabilia – perhaps a tad overrated.

Demitasse Coffee Bar 320 Blanshard St near Pandora Ave. A popular, elegantly laid-back hole-in-the-wall café with excellent coffee, salads, bagels, lunch-time snacks and an open fire in season.

Empress Hotel 721 Government St Ⓣ250/348-8111. Try tea in the lobby, with tourists and locals alike on their best behaviour amidst the chintz and potted plants. A strict dress code allows no dirty jeans, anoraks or sportswear.

Murchie's 1110 Government St. The best place for basic tea, coffee and cakes in the centre of Victoria's shopping streets.

Re-Bar 50 Bastion Square at Langley St. A great place that serves teas, coffees (charcoal-filtered water) and health food at lunch (usually organically grown), but most remarkable for its extraordinary range of fresh-squeezed juices in strange combinations, smoothies, "power tonics" and frighteningly healthy wheatgrass drinks ("Astro Turf": a blend of carrot, beet, garlic and wheatgrass).

Sally's 714 Cormorant St near Douglas St. Funky little café that's very popular with locals and local office workers despite its location on the northern edge of downtown. Drop by if you're up this way, but don't come specially.

Restaurants

Brasserie l'Ecole 1715 Government St Ⓣ250/475-6260, Ⓦwww.lecole.ca. This multi-award-winning restaurant serves the best French country cooking in town, with classic moules, frites, steaks, local fish and other staples, all made with immaculate and well-sourced local ingredients. Menus change daily. The dining room is pleasantly small and intimate, much like the wine list, which doesn't dazzle with big names, just decent, unpretentious wines to match the cooking. And prices won't hurt, either, with main courses from about $18. Tues–Sat 5.30–11pm.

Canoe 450 Swift St Ⓣ250/361-1940, Ⓦwww.canoebrewpub.com. In a short time, this restaurant and brewpub has become one of Victoria's most popular places to eat and drink. It setting is impressive – this was once Victoria's power station, and the interior retains an old industrial feel, with sturdy walls and vast beams. Outside, the patio is superb, with views towards the harbour and the Johnson Street bridge, and the atmosphere lively and convivial. Best of all, the food is excellent, whether you take the more ambitious and refined restaurant offerings such as wild salmon or Moroccan-style tagine stews upstairs (mains from $11) or the simple bar snacks and pub food (oysters, pizzas, burgers) downstairs (from $5). And the beer, of course, is excellent. Sun–Fri 11am–midnight, Sat 11am–1am.

Da Tandoor 1010 Fort St Ⓣ250/384-6333. Tandoori specialist that is, with the *Taj Mahal*, the best of Victoria's half-dozen or so Indian restaurants offering good food at good prices (mains from $9) and a wonderfully over-the-top interior. Daily 5–10pm.

Earl's 1703 Blanshard St and Fisgard St Ⓣ250/386-4323. You'll find an *Earl's* in many Canadian towns, but the restaurants are none the worse for being part of a chain: good – not fast – food, with a lively, pleasant interior and friendly service. Always reliable, and fair prices, with mains from just $9. Mon–Thurs & Sun 11.3am–10pm, Fri & Sat 11.30am–11pm.

Herald Street Café 546 Herald St Ⓣ250/381-1441. An excellent and stylish old favourite for Italian food with a Northwest twist. Pricey (some mains cost almost $40, others begin at $17), but generally good value, plus there's a relaxed atmosphere and lots of pleasant modern art on the walls. Well worth the walk from the Inner Harbour. Daily 5–10pm, brunch Sat & Sun 11am–3pm.

Il Terrazzo 555 Johnson St, Waddington Alley ⓣ250/361-0028. Smooth, laid-back ambience with lots of red brick and plants and a summer patio that provides the setting for good North American versions of Italian food. With *Pagliacci's* (see below), this is the best place in town for Italian food. However, it comes at a price, with mains costing between about $14 and $37. Mon–Sat 11.30am–3pm, daily 5–10pm (closed Sat for lunch Oct–April).

Milestone's 812 Wharf St ⓣ250/381-2244. Popular mid-priced place for burgers, pastas, steaks and the like, slap-bang on the Inner Harbour beneath the infocentre, so expect lots of bustle, passing trade and good views. Prices are keen, with mains starting at $8 and running to around $25. Mon–Thurs 11am–10pm, Fri 11am–11pm, Sat 10am–11pm, Sun 9am–10pm.

Pagliacci's 1011 Broad St between Fort and Broughton ⓣ250/386-1662. The best restaurant in Victoria if you want a fast, furious atmosphere, live music, good Italian food and excellent desserts. Prices are good, too, with mains from $12. A rowdy throng begins to queue almost from the moment the doors are open. Mon–Thurs 11.30am–10pm, Fri & Sat 11.30am–11pm, Sun 10am–10pm.

The Reef 533 Yates St ⓣ250/388-5375, ⓦwww.thereefrestaurant.com. It's a long way from home, but the Caribbean cooking here is authentic, especially the classic jerk sauce, a spicy Caribbean staple, added to meats, and chicken in particular. There are several jerk dishes, plus prawn and fish dishes (good grilled blue marlin) and some innovative salads. Reckon on between $11–20 for main courses. Settle down later in the evening to listen to DJ-spun sounds and a mellow lounge atmosphere. Mon–Thur 11am–midnight, Fri–Sun 11am–1am.

Taj Mahal 679 Herald St ⓣ250/383-4662. Housed in a mini Taj Mahal and a bit of a walk from the centre, this restaurant serves good Indian food with chicken, lamb and tandoori specialities. Main courses cost from around $14–19. daily 5–9.30pm.

The Tapa Bar 620 Trounce Alley ⓣ250/383-0013. This buzzy place has inexpensive tapas (plates from $7) – try the excellent *gambas al ajillo* (prawns in a pugent garlic sauce), wines by the glass and a long list of martinis. Mon–Thur 11.30am–11pm, Fri–Sat 11am–midnight, Sun 11am–10pm.

The Temple 525 Fort St ⓣ250/383-2313, ⓦwww.thetemple.ca. The chic, sleek main dining room here has a wraparound bar (in glowing glass) and a double chaise lounge-bed for reclining couples and an imposing fireplace (the more intimate Velvet Room has a couple of cosier tables). There's a DJ later in the evening, but the emphasis remains on good Pacific Northwest cooking and a seasonal menu, with small dishes from around $8, more substantial ones up to $20 or more. Mon–Fri 11.30am–2.30pm, daily for dinner from 5pm.

Bars and pubs

Bartholomew's Bar and Rockefeller Grill At *Executive House Hotel*, 777 Douglas St. This is an upbeat pub with a steady diet of local bands. For the same sort of place, try *Steamers*, 570 Yates St, where you'll catch enthusiastic local bands most nights, and most types of music from reggae to Celtic.

Big Bad John's 919 Douglas St. Next to the *Strathcona Hotel* this is Victoria's most atmospheric bar by far with bare boards, a fog of smoke, and authentic old banknotes and IOUs pasted to the walls. It also hosts occasional live bands and singers, usually of a country-music persuasion.

D'Arcy McGee's 1127 Wharf St. It was only a matter of time before Victoria acquired an "Irish pub". This one has a prime site on the edge of Bastion Square, offers predictable food and beer, and has excellent occasional live Irish music.

Spinnakers Gastro Brew Pub 308 Catherine St near Esquimalt Rd. Thirty-eight beers, including several home-brewed options, a restaurant, live music, occasional tours of the brewery and good harbour views draw a mixed and relaxed clientele. Bus #23 to Esquimalt Rd.

Swans Brewpub 506 Pandora Ave at Store St. This pretty and highly popular hotel-café-brewery, housed in a 1913 warehouse, is the place to watch Victoria's young professionals at play. Several foreign and six home-brewed beers on tap, with the *Neptune Soundbar* nightclub in the basement.

Clubs and live music

Esquimalt Inn 856 Esquimalt Rd. A long-established venue with country bands most nights and occasional jam sessions. Take bus #23.

Evolution 502 Discovery St. One of Victoria's more interesting clubs and discos, thanks to plenty of techno, rave and alternative sounds.

Hermann's Jazz Club 753 View St. Dimly lit club thick with 1950s atmosphere that specializes in Dixieland but has occasional excursions into fusion and blues.

Legends 919 Douglas St. The biggest, best and noisiest of the live-music venues, this club occupies the garish, neon-lit basement of the *Strathcona Hotel*. Varied live bands, including the occasional big name, and dancing nightly.

Listings

American Express 1213 Douglas St (Mon–Fri 8.30am–4.30pm, Sat 10am–4pm; ⓣ250/385-8731).
Bike rental Cycle BC Rentals at 950 Wharf St and 747 Douglas St (ⓣ250/885-2453 or 1-866/380-2453, ⓦwww.cyclebc.ca) rents a big range of bikes (from $7 an hour, $20 daily) plus scooters, kayaks, rowing boats, motor boats and motor bikes.
Bus information Airporter shuttle bus from Victoria Airport (ⓣ250/386-2525 or 1-877/386-2525, ⓦwww.akalairporter.travel.bc.ca). For services to Vancouver, there's Pacific Coast Lines (ⓣ604/662-8074 in Vancouver or 250/385-4411 at the Victoria bus terminal, ⓦwww.pacificcoach.com); for services on the island, Laidlaw (ⓣ250/385-4411, 388-5248 or 1-800/318-0818, ⓦwww.grayline.ca/victoria). Both operate from the bus terminal at 700 Douglas St and Belleville St, which also has an office for Greyhound (ⓣ250/388-5248 or 1-800/663-8390, ⓦwww.greyhound.com).
Car rental Avis, 62B-1001 Douglas St (ⓣ250/386-8468 or 1-800/879-2847) and Victoria Airport (ⓣ250/656-6033); Budget, 757 Douglas St (ⓣ250/953-5300 or 1-800/668-9833); National, 767 Douglas St (ⓣ250/386-1213 or 1-800/227-7368).
Doctor and dentist Most hotels have a doctor or dentist on call. Otherwise contact Cresta Dental Centre in the Tillicum Street Mall at 3170 Tillicum Rd, Burnside St (ⓣ250/384-7711). The Tillicum Mall Medical Clinic at the same address (ⓣ250/381-8112) accepts walk-in patients.
Equipment rental Sports Rent, 1950 Government St at Discovery (ⓣ250/385-7368, ⓦwww.sportsrentbc.com). Rents a colossal range of equipment, including bikes, rollerblades, all camping, hiking, climbing and diving gear.
Ferries BC Ferries (ⓣ250/386-3431 or 1-888-223-3779, ⓦwww.bcferries.com); Black Ball Transport (ⓣ250/386-2202 or 360/457-4491 in Port Angeles, ⓦwww.cohoferry.com); Victoria Clipper (ⓣ250/382-8100, 206/448-5000 or 1-800/888-2535, ⓦwww.victoriaclipper.com); Washington State Ferries (ⓣ250/382-1551 or 1-800/542-7052, ⓦwww.wsdof.wa.gov/ferries).
Hospital Victoria General Hospital, 35 Helmcken Rd (ⓣ250/727-4212).
Post office Main office, 714 Yates St at Douglas (ⓣ250/953-1352, 1-800/267-1177 in Canada). Mon–Fri 8.30am–5pm.
Taxis Blue Bird Cabs (ⓣ382-4235); Empress Cabs (ⓣ250/381-2222); Victoria Taxi (ⓣ250/383-7111).
Train information VIA Rail, 450 Pandora Ave (ⓣ250/383-4324 or 1-800/561-8630 in Canada and 1-800/561-3949 in the US, ⓦwww.viarail.ca).
Weather Victoria Environment Canada Weatherline (ⓣ250/656-3978).

The Southern Gulf Islands

Scattered between Vancouver Island and the mainland lie several hundred tiny islands, most no more than lumps of rock, a few large enough to hold permanent populations and warrant a regular ferry service. Two main clusters are accessible from Victoria: the **Southern Gulf Islands** and the San Juan Islands, both part of the same archipelago, except that the San Juan group is in the United States.

You get a good look at the Southern Gulf Islands on the seaplanes from Vancouver (see p.872) or on the ferry from Tsawwassen – twisting and threading through their coves and channels, the ride sometimes seems even a little too close for comfort. The coastline makes for superb **sailing**, and an armada of small boats crisscrosses between the islands for most of the year. Hikers and campers are also well served, and **fishing**, too, is good, with some of the world's biggest salmon having met their doom in the surrounding waters. The climate is mild, though hardly "Mediterranean" as claimed in the tourist blurbs, and the vegetation is particularly lush. There's also an abundance of marine wildlife (sea lions, orcas, seals, bald eagles, herons, cormorants). All this has made the Gulf Islands the dream idyll of many people from Washington State and BC, whether they're artists, writers, pensioners or dropouts from the mainstream. For full details of what they're all up to, grab a copy of the local listings, the *Gulf Islander*, distributed on the islands and the ferries.

Planning a visit

BC Ferries (Ⓣ250/386-3431 or 1-888/223-3779, Ⓦwww.bcferries.com) sails to five of the Southern Gulf Islands – **Saltspring**, **Pender**, **Saturna**, **Mayne** and **Galiano** – from Swartz Bay, 33km north of Victoria on Hwy 17. (A few other North Gulf Islands, notably Gabriola, can be reached from Chemainus and Nanaimo; see p.899 and p.901). Reckon on at least two crossings to each daily, but be prepared for all boats to be jammed solid during the summer. Visit the website or pick up the company's *Southern Gulf Islands* timetable, widely available on boats and in the mainland infocentres, which is invaluable if you aim to exploit the many inter-island connections. All the ferries take cars, bikes and motorbikes, though with a car you'll need to make a **reservation**. Bear in mind that there's next to no public transport on the islands, so what few taxis there are can charge more or less what they wish. It costs only around $2.50 to take bikes on board, and **cycling** can be a great way to see the islands: most are small (if hilly), with few roads.

For the San Juans you'll have to pass through US and Canadian immigration, but you can get good stopover deals on ferries between Sidney on Vancouver Island and Anacortes on the Washington mainland. Foot passengers travel free between the four main San Juan islands.

Aim to have your **accommodation** worked out well in advance in summer. **Campers** should have few problems finding sites, most of which are located in the islands' provincial parks, though at peak times you'll want to arrive before noon to ensure a pitch – there are reservations in some parks (see p.758 for details of booking places). For help with B&Bs, use the *BC Approved Accommodation Guide* and the BC tourism website (see Ⓦwww.hellobc.com).

Salt Spring Island

SALT SPRING (pop. 9500), sometimes Saltspring, is the biggest, most populated and most visited of the islands – its population triples in summer – though if you're without transport think twice about coming here on a day-trip as getting around is pretty tough. It's served by Harbour Air seaplanes from Vancouver (see p.872) and has three ferry terminals: **Fulford Harbour** in the south, with sailings from Victoria's Swartz Bay (ten daily, more in summer; 35min; foot passengers $7.05/6.80 return, cars $23/19.60); **Vesuvius Bay** in the northwest, with sailings from Crofton, near Duncan, on Vancouver Island (13 daily; 20min; same fares); and **Long Harbour**, midway down the east coast, which connects to points on the BC mainland, notably Tsawwassen, usually via other islands.

Long Harbour is also the main terminal for inter-island travel. In the past the Saltspring Island Bus service has connected the ferry terminals with **GANGES**,

Fares on BC Ferries

BC Ferries charges a wide range of **fares** for the numerous connections from Vancouver Island and the mainland to the Gulf Islands (many of which have more than one ferry terminal). Rates are generally lower **off season**, which most years means early Sept to late June. One or two routes also have cheaper fares midweek. In the following accounts we've given high-season and low-season fares for foot passengers and cars, separated by slashes, as in "foot passengers $6.25/6 return, cars $20/17.25". Note that larger vehicles incur higher fares and that at the time of writing 'fuel supplements' of around $1 for passengers and $2 for cars were being added to many fares.

Gulf Islands Water Taxi

The **Gulf Islands Water Taxi** (ⓣ250/537-2510, ⓦwww.saltspring.com/watertaxi) has been a feature of island life since 1978, complementing the BC Ferries service and carrying visitors, schoolchildren, fishermen and others on two scheduled routes from the Visitors' Dock below the Oystercatcher Bar & Grill in Ganges. The **first route** runs Salt Spring (Ganges Harbour) to Galiano (Sturdies Bay) and on to Mayne Island (Miners Bay); currently Sept–June 2 daily 6.50am & 4.30pm from Salt Spring; $25 round trip between any two points, $15 one-way, no extra charge for bicycles. Prices and departure details are the same on the **second route**: from Salt Spring (Ganges Harbour) to Saturna (Lyall Harbour) to Horton Bay and on to Pender (Port Washington). An "Island Hopping" **third route** operates in summer (Wed & Sat 9am & 3pm from Ganges) calling at Galiano and Mayne. **Reservations** are recommended for all services, which are timetabled so that you can realistically make short day or sightseeing trips to other islands from Salt Spring.

the island's main village, on the east coast 5km from Long Harbour, but check with the Victoria or local infocentre (see below) for the latest.

Most enjoyment on Salt Spring, as with the other Gulf Islands, is to be had from sinking back into its laid-back approach to life: grabbing a coffee at a café overlooking the water, browsing galleries, cycling the backroads, hiking the odd easy trail, and so on. If you're here to slum it on a **beach**, the best strips are on the island's more sheltered east side – Beddis Beach in particular, off the Fulford to Ganges Road – as well as at Vesuvius Bay in the northwest and at Drummond Park near Fulford in the south. Beddis can be seen en route to one of the best parks in the Gulf Islands, the **Ruckle Provincial Park**, a swath of lovely forest, field and maritime scenery tucked in the island's southeast corner 10km east of Fulford Harbour. It has 15km of trails, most leaving from trailheads at Beaver Point, the rocky headland that marks the end of the access road – the best path marches north from here along the coast of tiny coves and rocky headlands to Yeo Point. The park also has an outstanding campsite at the end of the access road (see opposite). **Mount Maxwell Provincial Park** lies midway up the west coast; the eponymous mountain provides a tremendous 588-metre viewpoint. The park is accessed on Cranberry Road, which strikes west midway down the island off the main Ganges to Fulford Road.

Between April and October, head for the **Saturday Market** (Sat 8.30am–3pm; ⓦwww.saltspringmarket.com), in Ganges' Centennial Park, for food and crafts. Community spirit reaches a climax during the annual **Artcraft** crafts fair (late June to mid-Sept), held in Ganges' Mahon Hall, that displays the talents of the island's many dab-handed creatives. The other main focus for cultural events is the **ArtSpring** centre, 100 Jackson in Ganges (ⓦwww.artspring.ca), which hosts a summer performing arts festival (July & Aug).

Practicalities

Ganges, close to Long Harbour on the east coast, is armed with a small **infocentre** at 121 Lower Ganges Rd (Mon–Thurs 10am–4pm; ⓣ250/537-5252, ⓦwww.saltspringtoday.com) and a rapidly proliferating assortment of galleries, tourist shops and holiday homes.

Ganges' infocentre is the place to check out the island's relatively plentiful **accommodation**. Try the lovely *Salt Spring Forest Retreat*, set amidst ten peaceful acres on the eastern side of the island, 5km south of Ganges and just over 1km from Beddis Beach, at 640 Cusheon Lake Rd (ⓣ250/537-4149,

Ⓦ www.saltspringforestretreat.com; ❸). Otherwise you can choose from the hundred or more, often rather expensive, **B&B** options (whose owners can arrange to pick you up from the ferry), or one of the so-called "resorts" – usually a handful of houses with camping, a few rooms to rent and little else. Each of the ferry terminals also has a range of mid-price **motels**, notably the *Harbour House Hotel*, 121 Upper Ganges Rd, Ganges (Ⓣ250/537-5571 or 1-888/799-5571, Ⓔharbourhouse@saltspring.com; ❹); and the 28-unit *Seabreeze Inn* in a park-like setting above Ganges Harbour at 101 Bittancourt Rd (Ⓣ250/537-4145 or 1-800/434-4112, Ⓦwww.seabreezeinns.com; ❺). The island's best **campsite** is in Ruckle Provincial Park – a magnificent, waterfront, 78-pitch site ($14 in summer, $9 in winter; day-use parking $3) at Beaver Point, reached by following Beaver Point Road from the Fulford Harbour ferry terminal (10km). Note that there are no reservations; it is first-come, first-served.

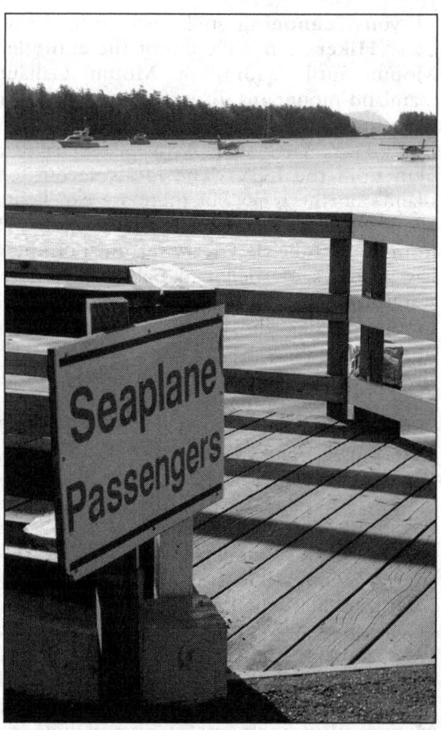

△ The dock for Salt Spring Island

In Ganges, there are numerous **cafés** and coffee shops for high-quality sandwiches: for something more ambitious, try the appealing *Treehouse Café-Restaurant*, 106 Purvis Lane (Ⓣ250/537-5379), which serves breakfast, lunch and dinner and has places to sit outside and low-key live (often acoustic) music most nights of the week. For a treat, the place to go is *House Piccolo*, 108 Hereford Ave, Ganges (Ⓣ250/537-1844, dinner only), which serves high-quality European and Scandinavian food and has won *Wine Spectator* magazine awards.

Galiano Island

Long and finger-shaped, **Galiano** (pop. 1040) is just 27km from north to south and barely five kilometres wide, but it remains one of the more promising islands to visit if you want variety and a realistic chance of finding somewhere to stay. There are two ferry terminals: **Sturdies Bay** in the southeast, which takes boats from the mainland (foot passengers $11, cars $41.50), and **Montague Harbour** on the west coast, which handles the Vancouver Island crossings from Swartz Bay (foot passengers $7.35/7.05, cars $25.35/22.20). You can also get here with the Gulf Islands Water Taxi and there are inter-island BC Ferries connections (1–4 daily) from Salt Spring via Pender and Mayne. Go Galiano Island Shuttle (Ⓣ250/539-0202, Ⓦwww.gogaliano.com) provides a taxi service.

If you're **canoeing**, stick to the calmer waters, cliffs and coves off the west coast. **Hikers** can walk almost the entire length of the east coast, or climb Mount Sutil (323m) or Mount Galiano (342m) for views of the mainland mountains. To reach the trailhead for the latter, take Burrill south from the ferry at Sturdies Bay and along Bluff Road through the forest of Bluffs Park. A left fork, Active Pass Drive, takes you to the trailhead (total 5km from the ferry). The locals' favourite **beach** is at Coon Bay at the island's northern tip, but there are excellent marine landscapes and beaches elsewhere, notably at **Montague Harbour Provincial Marine Park**, 10km from the Sturdies Bay ferry terminal on the west side of the island. The park has stretches of shell and pebble foreshore, a café, shop, three-kilometre waterfront trail to Gray Peninsula (though you can easily do your own foreshore walks) and, more to the point, a glorious provincial **campsite** ($17 in summer, $9 in winter; 15 walk-in reservable tent sites, and 25 drive-in sites, of which eight are reservable). Booking is essential in summer; see phone number on p.867 for details.

The **infocentre** is a booth at Sturdies Bay at 2590 Sturdies Bay Rd (July & Aug daily 9am–5/6pm; ⓣ250/539-2233 or 1-866/539-2233, ⓦwww.galianoisland.com). Galiano Bicycle Rental is at 36 Burrill Rd in Sturdies Bay (ⓣ250/539-9906; $23 for 4hr, $28/day). You can **rent kayaks** or join guided kayak tours at Galiano Island Kayaking at the marina at Montague Harbour (ⓣ250/539-2442, ⓦwww.seakayak.ca; from $28 for 3hr).

For a comfortable **stay** in peaceful and elegant surroundings (close to Montague Harbour Provincial Marine Park), try the excellent twelve-room *Woodstone Country Inn* (ⓣ250/539-2022 or 1-888/339-2022, ⓦwww.woodstoneinn.com; ❻) on Georgeson Bay Rd, 4km from the ferry; breakfast and afternoon tea are included in the price. Right at Studies Bay is the very pleasant ten-room *Galiano Inn & Spa*, 134 Madrona Drive (ⓣ250/539-3388, ⓦwww.galianoinn.com; ❻); rates include gourmet breakfast. For a romantic stay, head for one of the three rooms at the *Bellhouse Inn*, 29 Farmhouse Rd (ⓣ1-800/970-7464, ⓦwww.bellhouseinn.com; ❻), an historic waterfront farmhouse set in beautiful grounds with sandy beach and great ocean views; breakfast is included. A good choice on the island's quieter northern end are the seven log cabins of the *Bodega Ridge Lodge & Cabins*, 120 Monastee Rd off Porlier Pass Drive and Cook Drive (ⓣ250/539-2677, ⓦwww.bodegaridge.com; ❻), set in acres of woods and meadows with sea views and complete with kitchens and wood-burning stoves. For **food and drink** – and to meet locals – the island's main pub, the *Hummingbird Inn* (ⓣ250/539-5472) is about 2km from Sturdies Bay at 47 Sturdies Bay Rd. Food is reasonable at the *Hummingbird*, likewise at *La Bérengerie* (ⓣ250/539-5392; ❸), a genteel restaurant about the same distance from Montague Harbour on the corner of Montague and Clanton roads that usually rents three B&B rooms upstairs.

North and South Pender

The somnolent bridge-linked islands of **North** and **South Pender** muster about a two thousand people between them, many of whom will try to entice you into their studios to buy local arts and crafts. Otherwise you can swim, snooze or walk on one of the many tiny **beaches** – there's public ocean access at some twenty points around the island. Two of the best are Hamilton Beach near Browning Beach on the east coast of North Pender and Mortimer Spit just south of the bridge that links the two islands. The latter is also the place to pick up trails to Mount Norman and Beaumont Provincial Marine Park.

Ferries come to North Pender from Swartz Bay (up to 7 daily; 40min direct or 2hr via Galiano and/or Mayne; foot passengers $7.35/7.05, cars $25.35/22.20) and Tsawwassen (foot-passengers $11.25/11 one-way; cars $41.50/35.25). The **infocentre** booth is just up the hill from the ferry terminal in **Otter Bay** on North Pender's west coast at 2332 Otter Bay Rd (mid-May to early Sept daily 9am–6pm, later hours in July & Aug; ⓣ250/629-6541), home to the Otter Bay Marina, where you can rent **bikes** and buy maps for a tour of the islands' rolling, hilly interior. There's a handful of **B&Bs**, and a small wooded **campsite** at Prior Centennial Provincial Park, 6km south of the Otter Bay ferry terminal (March–Sept; $14). For the only **hotel**-type rooms, try the twelve-room *Inn on Pender Island*, prettily situated in 7.5 acres of wooded country near Prior Park at 4709 Canal Rd, North Pender (ⓣ250/629-3353 or 1-800/550-0172, ⓦwww.innonpender.com; ④), or the *Poets Cove Resort & Spa*, a plush resort at 9801 Spalding Rd, South Pender (ⓣ250/629-3212 or 1-888/512-7638, ⓦwww.poetscove.com; ⑧), which has a pool, marina, bistro-pub, restaurant, store, tennis, harbour views, canoe, boat and bike rentals, and a choice of rooms or cabins. Alternatively, try the three fully equipped self-catering cottages 500m sharp left from the ferry at *Arcadia by the Sea*, 1325 MacKinnon Rd, North Pender (ⓣ250/629-3221 or 1-877/470-8439, ⓦwww.arcadiabythesea.com; ⑤; May–Sept), with tennis court, outdoor pool and private decks.

Mayne Island

Mayne is the first island to your left (Galiano is on your right) if you're crossing from Tsawwassen to Swartz Bay – which is perhaps as close as you'll get, since it's the quietest and most difficult to reach of the islands served by ferries. One-way tickets from Tsawwassen (via Galiano/Montague Harbour) in high season cost foot passengers $11.25/11, cars $41.50/35.25. It also has few places to stay, which may be as good a reason as any for heading out here – particularly if you have a bike to explore the quiet country roads which snake over the island. Best of several **beaches** is Bennett Bay, a sheltered strip with warm water and good sand. It's reached by heading east from the island's principal community at Miner's Bay (5min from the ferry terminal at Village Bay on the west coast) to the end of Fernhill Road and then turning left onto Wilks Road. If you want a **walk**, try the 45-minute climb up Mount Parke in the eponymous regional park; it starts near the Fernhill Centre on Montrose Road.

Village Bay – don't be fooled by the name: there's no village – has a summer-only **infocentre** booth (daily 9am–6pm; no phone, ⓦwww.mayneislandchamber.ca) that should be able to fill you in on the limited but expanding number of **hotel** and **B&B** possibilities. Try the *Blue Vista Cottage Resort*, eight fully equipped cabins overlooking Bennett Bay at 563 Arbutus Drive, 6km from the ferry (ⓣ250/539-2463 or 1-877/535-2424, ⓦwww.bluevistaresort.com; ④), with ferry pick-up, sandy beach, park-like setting and bike, canoe and kayak rental. The *Tinkerer's B&B* on Miner's Bay at 417 Sunset Place off Georgina Point Rd (ⓣ250/539-2280; ④; May–Oct), 2.4km from the ferry, is nicely offbeat: it rents bikes, provides hammocks and offers "demonstrations of medicinal herb and flower gardens". The best **food** around is at the waterfront *Oceanwood Country Inn*, 2km south of the ferry at 630 Dinner Bay Rd (ⓣ250/539-5074, ⓦwww.oceanwood.com; ⑦; March–Nov), which also has twelve smart rooms, sauna, oceanfront hot tub and a superb, quiet garden setting.

Saturna Island

Saturna, to the south, has daily **ferries** from Swartz Bay on Vancouver Island (2–3 daily; foot passengers $7.05/6.80 return, vehicles $23/19.60) and from Tsawwassen but only via Mayne. The island boasts some good **beaches**, the best being at Russell Reef and Winter Cove Marine Park (no campsite) on its northwest tip. There's walking, wildlife and good views to the mainland from Mount Warburton Pike (497m) and on Brown Bridge in the southwest of the island.

Saturna is another **B&B** hideaway: try the three-room waterfront *Lyall Harbour B&B* (Ⓣ250/539-5577 or 1-877/473-9343, Ⓦwww.lyallharbour.com; ④), 500m from the ferry at 121 East Point Rd in Saturna Point, home to a shop and modest **infocentre** (May–Sept daily 8am–6pm; no phone, Ⓦwww.saturnatourism.bc.ca). A slightly larger place to stay is the *East Point Resort*, East Point Rd (Ⓣ250/539-2975, Ⓦwww.eastpointresort.com; ⑤; March–Dec), situated in a park-like setting near a gradually sloping sandy beach; the six cabins are fully equipped and you can choose between one- and two-bedroom units – note that in July and August there's generally a minimum stay of a week. There are no campgrounds and only one or two **places to eat**, notably the pub-restaurant at the modern, waterfront *Saturna Lodge*, 130 Payne Rd (Ⓣ250/539-2254, Ⓦwww.saturna-island.bc.ca; ⑥; May–Oct), which also has seven rooms to rent; rates include breakfast.

Highway 14: Victoria to Port Renfrew

Highway 14 runs west from **Victoria** to **Port Renfrew** and is lined with numerous beaches and provincial parks, most – especially those close to the city – heavily populated during the summer months. The 107km route is covered in summer by the West Coast Trail Bus (see opposite), a private service originally for hikers walking the West Coast Trail and Juan de Fuca Trail (see opposite) but also popular for the ride alone.

Victoria city buses go as far as **SOOKE** (38km; take #50 to Western Exchange and transfer to #61), and you can also cycle here on the Galloping Goose cycle trail. Sooke is the last place of any size, so stock up on supplies if you're continuing west. It's best known for its excellent art galleries, a clutch of good restaurants and **All Sooke Day** in mid-July, when lumberjacks from all over the island compete in various tests of forestry expertise. Check out the small **Sooke Regional Museum** (daily 9am–5pm, July & Aug until 6pm; donation), across the Sooke River Bridge at 2070 Phillips and Sooke streets, to bone up on the largely logging-dominated local history. The **infocentre** lies in the same building (daily 9/10am–6pm; Ⓣ250/642-6351, Ⓦwww.sooke.museum.bc.ca). Sooke has a surfeit of **accommodation**, with a bias towards comfortable B&Bs. Quite a few people make the trip here just for the **food** at *Sooke Harbour House*, 1528 Whiffen Spit (Ⓣ250/642-3421, Ⓦwww.sookeharbourhouse.com; ⑧), one of the finest restaurants on the West Coast; it's expensive, but has a surprisingly casual atmosphere. It also has 28 top-notch **rooms**, with prices ranging from a prohibitive $375 to $572 (lower off season). A far less expensive place to eat in the village centre is the cosy *Mom's*, 2036 Shields Rd.

The mostly empty beaches beyond Sooke are largely grey pebble and driftwood, but none the worse for that. The first key stop, 20km beyond Sooke, is **French Beach Provincial Park** (day-use parking $3). An info-board here fills in the natural history background of the foreshore and rich Douglas fir and

West Coast Trail Bus

The **West Coast Trail Bus**, or West Coast Trail Express (ⓣ250/477-8700 or 1-888/999-2288, ⓦwww.trailbus.com), provides an invaluable complement to Laidlaw's relatively limited scheduled bus services on Vancouver Island. **Reservations** are required for services between May 1 and June 15 and September 15–30. They are also highly recommended for all other services. Cancellations require 10 days' notice.

It offers a shuttle service (May–Sept only; days vary; call for details) from Victoria to **Gordon River** ($43), **Port Renfrew** ($43), **Pachena Bay** ($64) and **Bamfield** ($64), thus providing access to the trailheads of the West Coast Trail and to points in the Pacific Rim National Park such as Bamfield that would otherwise be difficult to reach without your own transport. It also provides **inter-town shuttles** between most combinations of these destinations – and others such as **Nanaimo** (connections to Pachena Bay and Bamfield; $64) and **Port Alberni** (to Pachena Bay and Bamfield; $43). **Departure points** are as follows: Victoria (700 Douglas St); Nanaimo (Departure Bay ferry terminal); Port Alberni (7-Eleven store on 3rd St); Pachena Bay (trailhead car park); Bamfield (Trails Motel); Gordon River (trailhead office); Port Renfrew (at the road intersection by the Port Renfrew Hotel by the Lighthouse Pub sign).

Another service serving the Juan de Fuca Trail runs from Victoria to Port Renfrew ($43) **along Hwy 14** with stops at Sooke (at the Payless Gas station), French Beach ($27), Jordan River ($37), China Beach ($37), Sombrio Beach ($37) and Parkinson Creek ($37). Pickups, unless specified, are the same as for the West Coast bus or at the junction of the individual trailheads with Hwy 14. Transport between the trailheads costs $20.

Sitka forest, and there are maps of trails and the highlights on the road farther west. There's good walking on the fairly wild and windswept beach, and a 69-pitch provincial park campsite (summer $14, winter $9) on the grass immediately away from the shore. About 3km beyond, the 25 log cabins of *Point No Point*, 10828 West Coast Rd (ⓣ250/646-2020, ⓦwww.pointnopointresort.com, ❻), make a tremendous place to overnight near the water.

Sandy, signposted trails lead off the road to beaches over the next 9km, including **Jordan River**, a one-shop, one-hamburger-stall (*Shakies*) logging community known for its good surf, which you can admire from the waterfront *Breakers* cafe. Just beyond is the best of the beaches on this coast, part of **China Beach Provincial Park** (no camping), reached after a fifteen-minute walk from the road through rainforest. The West Coast Trail Bus (see box, above) makes stops at all these parks and beaches on request.

Port Renfrew

The road is partly gravel from China Beach on – past Mystic and Sombrio beaches to **PORT RENFREW**, a logging community that's gained from being the western starting point of the **West Coast Trail** (see box, above). A second trail, the **Juan de Fuca Marine Trail**, also starts from near Port Renfrew, running east towards Victoria for about 50km. This does not have the complicated booking procedure of the West Coast Trail, but the scenery is also less striking and the going far easier for the less experienced or more safety conscious walker. Car parks and hwy access points are also dotted along its length, allowing you to enjoy strolls or day-hikes. Beyond China Beach is the start of the **Juan de Fuca Provincial Park**, designed to protect the beaches and coastal rainforest strip explored by the trail (day-use parking $5, front-country camping $14, backcountry camping $5).

Accommodation in town is still pretty limited: try the four cottages on the San Juan River at *Gallaugher's West Coast Fish Camp* off Beach Rd at 5222 Heritage Drive (Ⓣ250/647-5535, Ⓔgallaughers@shaw.ca; ❺; May–Oct) or *Trailhead Resort* on Parkinson Rd (Ⓣ250/647-5468, Ⓦwww.trailhead-resort.com; ❹), which has six rooms. **Eat** at the *Lighthouse Neighbourhood Pub* on Parkenson Rd, where lunch comes in at between $8 and $16. South of the village on a logging road (6km) is the Juan de Fuca trailhead at **Botanical Beach**, a sandstone shelf and tidal-pool area that reveals a wealth of marine life at low tide.

If you're driving and don't want to retrace your steps, think about taking the gravel logging roads from the village on the north side of the San Juan River to either Shawnigan Lake or the Cowichan Valley. They're marked on most maps, but it's worth picking up the **detailed map** of local roads put out by the Sooke Combined Fire Organization (ask at the Victoria infocentre). Heed all warnings about logging trucks.

Highway 1: Victoria to Nanaimo

If you leave Victoria with high hopes of Vancouver Island's lauded scenery, **Highway 1** – the final, western leg of the Trans-Canada – will come as a disappointing introduction to what you can expect along most of the island's southeast coast. After a lengthy sprawl of suburbs, blighted by more billboards than you'd see in supposedly less scenic cities, the landscape becomes suddenly wooded and immensely lush; unfortunately the beauty is constantly interrupted by bursts of dismal motels and other hwy junk.

Buses operated by Laidlaw make the trip between Victoria and Nanaimo (up to 6 daily). One **train** a day (more in summer) also covers this route – and beyond to Courtenay – but it's a usually a single-carriage job and gets booked solid in summer. It also stops at every stump.

Goldstream Provincial Park

Thetis Lake Regional Park, appearing on the right 11km out of Victoria, is good for swimming, with forested trails and sandy beaches on two lakes backed by high cliffs; there's a busy beach near the car park, which is quieter round the shore, or beyond at the bottom of the hill at Prior Lake. Prettier still is **Goldstream Provincial Park**, 5km beyond Langford and 20km from Victoria city centre, where you'll find an ancient forest of Douglas fir and western red cedar and a large provincial park **campsite** with good facilities and a visitor centre (day-use parking $3, summer frontcountry camping $22, winter $9). There's also a network of marked **trails** to hilltops and waterfalls designed for anything between five minutes and an hour's walking. Try the paths towards Mount Finlayson (3hr hard walk if you go all the way to the summit) for views of the ocean – views you also get if you carry on up the highway, which soon meets Saanich Inlet, a bay with a lovely panorama of wooded ridges across the water. Look out for the Malahat Summit (31km from Victoria) and Gulf Islands (33km) viewpoints.

A scenic diversion off the main road takes you 7km to **Shawnigan Lake**, fringed by a couple of provincial parks; West Shawnigan Park on the lake's northwest side has a safe beach and swimming possibilities. If you're biking or are prepared to tackle pretty rough roads, note the logging road that links the north end of the lake to Port Renfrew on the west coast (check access restrictions at the Victoria infocentre).

Duncan

DUNCAN, 60km north of Victoria, begins inauspiciously, with a particularly scrappy section of hwy spoiling what would otherwise be an exquisitely pastoral patch of country. Still, the town's aboriginal centre – the Quw'utsun Cultural Centre – merits a brief stop, unlike the Glass Castle, a messy affair made from glass bottles off the road to the south, and the even sillier "World's Largest Hockey Stick", arranged as a triumphal arch into the town centre.

Duncan's **infocentre** is at 381A Trans-Canada Hwy opposite the supermarket on the main road (mid-May to mid-Sept daily 9am–5pm, longer hours in July & Aug; ⓣ250/746-4636 or 1-888/303-3337, ⓦwww.duncancc.bc.ca), close to the **bus station**, which has up to six daily connections to and from Victoria (1hr 10min). Duncan is not a place you want to consider staying in – though there are plenty of motels and campsites– but for **meals** you could try the excellent *Arbutus Café*, 195 Kenneth St, at Jubilee (ⓣ250/746-5443), which is much frequented by locals keen for the usual Italian- and Pacific Rim-influenced food. Or try the *Doghouse* (ⓣ250/746-4614) at the corner of Trunk Road and Hwy 1, in business since 1955 and known for their low prices (dinner from $7) and fish and chips in particular. You could also visit the local vineyards; one of the best is the **Vigneti Zanatta Winery**, 5039 Marshall Rd, Glenora (call for tour details on ⓣ250/748-2338, ⓦwww.zanatta.ca), which has been in business for over forty years; as well as their wine, you can buy meals at the lovely (but expensive) restaurant.

Quw'utsun Cultural Centre

Out of Victoria, the first real reason to pull over is Duncan's **Quw'utsun Cultural** Centre, 200 Cowichan Way (May to early Sept Mon–Fri 10am–5pm, Sat & Sun 9am–9pm; rest of year closes 4pm daily; ⓦwww.quwutsun.ca), on your left off the hwy in the unmissable wooden buildings next to Malaspina College. Duncan has long been the self-proclaimed "City of Totems", reference to a rather paltry collection of poles – arranged mostly alongside the main road – that belong to the local Cowichan tribes, historically British Columbia's largest aboriginal group. The tribes, about 3000 strong locally, still preserve certain traditions, and it's been their energy – along with cash from the civic authorities, attuned as ever to potentially lucrative tourist attractions – that has put up the poles and pulled the project together. Much of the heavily worked commercial emphasis is on shifting aboriginal crafts, especially the ubiquitous lumpy jumpers for which the area is famous, but there is a good twenty-minute film and tour of the centre and (for a varying admission) you can usually expect to find historical displays and demonstrations of dancing, knitting, carving, weaving and even native cooking.

British Columbia Forestry Discovery Centre

Vancouver Island is one of the most heavily logged areas in Canada, and the **BC Forest Discovery Centre**, 1km north of Duncan on Hwy 1 (daily: mid-May to early Sept 10am–5pm; mid-April–mid-May & early Sept to the end of Sept 10am–4pm; $11; ⓦwww.bcforestrymusuem.com), is run to preserve artefacts from its lumbering heritage; but with industry bigwigs as museum trustees, you can't help feeling it's designed to be something of a palliative in the increasingly ferocious controversy between loggers and environmentalists. Nonetheless, it does a thorough job on trees, and if the forestry displays in Victoria's museum have whetted your appetite, you'll have a good couple of hours rounding off your arboreal education. The entrance is marked by a small black steam engine

Old-growth forests: going, going, gone...

While Vancouver Island isn't the only place in North America where environmentalists and the forestry industry are at loggerheads, some of the most bitter and high-profile confrontations have taken place here. The island's wet climate is particularly favourable to the growth of thick **temperate rainforest**, part of a belt that once stretched from Alaska to northern California. The most productive ecosystem on the planet, **old-growth** virgin Pacific rainforest contains up to ten times more biomass per acre than its more famous tropical counterpart – and, though it covers a much smaller area, it is being felled at a greater rate and with considerably less media outrage. Environmentalists estimate that British Columbia's portion of the Pacific rainforest has already been reduced by two-thirds; all significant areas will have been felled, they predict, within about ten or fifteen years. The powerful logging industry claims two-thirds survive, but even the Canadian government – largely in thrall to and supportive of the industry – concedes that only a small percentage of the BC rainforest is currently protected.

What is clear is that the government wants a very firm lid kept on the whole affair. In 1990 it commissioned a report into **UK public opinion** on the issue; the UK takes half of all British Columbia's plywood exports, three-quarters of all its lumber shipments to Europe, and a third of all Canada's paper pulp output. It observed that "UK public opinion appears to be highly uncritical of Canadian forestry, largely because awareness of the subject is low... [there is] a reassuringly romantic and simplistic image of Canadian forestry based on a lumberjack in a checked shirt, felling a single tree." The report concluded that "media attention and coverage of Canadian forestry management issues should not be sought". Despite the increased awareness of environmental issues generally, it's still hard to see that UK and other European opinions or perceptions of the Canadian lumber industry have changed much since.

No such apathy or ignorance exists in British Columbia, however. The controversy over logging often pits neighbour against neighbour, for some 250,000 in the province depend directly or indirectly on the industry, and big multinationals dominate the scene. **Employment** is a major rallying cry here, and the prospect of job losses through industry regulation is usually enough to override objections. The trend towards **automation** only adds fuel to the argument: by volume of wood cut, the BC forestry industry provides only half as many jobs as in the rest of Canada, which means, in effect, that twice as many trees have to be cut down in BC to provide the same number of jobs.

In the meantime, however, ninety percent of timber is still lifted from the rainforest instead of from managed stands, clear-cutting of old-growth timber is blithely described by the vast McMillan company as "a form of harvesting", and independent audits suggest that companies are failing to observe either their cutting or replanting quotas. The provincial government has pledged to improve forestry practices, but only a tiny percentage of the province lies within reserves with a degree of environmental protection.

and a massive piece of yellow logging machinery. Ranged over a hundred-acre site next to a scenic lake, the well-presented displays tell everything you want to know about trees and how to cut them down. The narrow-gauge **steam train** round the park is a bit gimmicky (ends 5.30pm), but a good way of getting around; check out the forest dioramas and the artefacts and archive material in the **Log Museum** in particular. There's also the usual array of working blacksmiths, sawmills, a farmstead, an old logging camp, and a few as-yet-underforested patches where you can take time out. The centre forms part of the **Cowichan and Chemainus Valleys Ecomuseum**, a vaguely defined park that takes in much of the surrounding area intended to preserve the logging heritage of the area – a curiously ill-defined concept that appears to be largely a PR exercise on the part of the logging companies. Ask for details of tours and maps from the Duncan infocentre.

The Cowichan Valley

Striking west into the hills from Hwy 1 north of Duncan, Hwy 18 enters the **Cowichan Valley** and fetches up at the 32-kilometre long Lake Cowichan, the largest freshwater lake on the island. Rather than drive, however , the nicest way up the valley is to walk the **Cowichan Valley Footpath**, following the river 18km from Glenora (a hamlet southwest of Duncan at the end of Robertson Road) to Lake Cowichan Village on the lake's eastern shore. You could do the trip in a day, camp en route, or turn around at Skutz Falls and climb up to the Riverbottom Road to return to Duncan, which would be a half-day walk.

A road, rough in parts, circles **Lake Cowichan** (it's 75km round the lake by road – allow 2hr) and offers access to a gamut of outdoor pursuits, most notably fishing; the area is touted, with typical smalltown hyperbole, as the "Fly-Fishing Capital of the World". The water gets warm enough for summer swimming (the aboriginal name for the area, *Kaatza*, means the "land warmed by the sun"), and there's also ample hiking in the wilder country above. At Youbou on the north shore you can visit the **Heritage Mill**, a working sawmill (tours May–Sept); this area boasts some of the most "productive" forest in Canada, thanks to the lake's mild microclimate, and lumber is the obvious mainstay of the local economy. On the road up to the lake from Duncan you pass the **Valley Demonstration Forest**, another link in the industry's public-relations weaponry, with signs and scenic lookouts explaining the intricacies of forest management.

For details of the area's many tours, trails and outfitters contact the **infocentre** at Lake Cowichan Village, 125 South Shore Rd (Mon–Sat 9am–5pm, Sun 1–4pm, longer hours in summer; ⓣ250/749-3244, ⓦwww.cowichanlakecc.ca). Good, cheap **campsites** line the shore, which despite minimal facilities can be quite busy in summer – don't expect to have the place to yourself. There's a municipal site, Lakeview Park, 3km west of the village at 885 Lakeview Rd (ⓣ250/749-6681, ⓦwww.town.lakecowichan.bc.ca; $20; May–Oct), but the biggest and best is at Gordon Bay Provincial Park (day-use parking $3, summer camping $22, winter $9) on the south shore 14km from Lake Cowichan Village on South Shore Road, a popular family place but with a quiet atmosphere and a good sandy **beach**. There are also plenty of hotels, motels and the like in all the lakeside settlements.

Chemainus

CHEMAINUS is the "Little Town That Did", as the billboards for miles around never stop telling you. Its mysterious achievement was the creation of its own tourist attraction, realized when the closure of the local antiquated sawmill in 1982 – it employed 400 and was once amongst the world's largest – threatened the place with almost overnight extinction, despite the opening of a modern, more efficient mill which employed just 150. In 1983 the town's worthies commissioned an artist to paint a huge **mural**, *Steam Donkey at Work*, recording the area's local history. This proved so successful that some 35 panels quickly followed, drawing some 375,000 visitors annually to admire the artwork and tempting them to spend money in local businesses as they did. As murals go, these are surprisingly good, and if you're driving it's worth the short, well-signed diversion off Hwy 1. You might also want to drop in on the **Chemainus**

Valley Museum, 9799 Waterwheel Crescent (daily 10am–4pm, closed mid-Dec–mid-Feb; donation), a community-run museum of local history with displays on logging, mills and pioneer life. Ironically enough, the opening of the modern sawmill has done nothing to deter the welcome influx of resident painters and craftspeople attracted by the murals, a knock-on effect that has done much to enliven the village's pleasant – if occasionally over-twee – community feel.

Buses detour here on the run to Nanaimo, and the **train** drops you slap-bang next to a mural. There's an **infocentre** in town at 9796 Willow St (June–Aug daily 9am–5pm; rest of year Mon–Fri 10am–4pm; ⓣ250/246-3944, ⓦwww.chemainus.bc.ca). If you fancy **staying** – the village's cosy waterside setting is nicer than either Duncan or Nanaimo – it's worth booking ahead, as increasing popularity means the local **hotel** and half-a-dozen or so B&Bs are in heavy demand in summer. For motel accommodation, try the *Fuller Lake Chemainus Motel*, 9300 Trans-Canada Hwy (ⓣ250/246-3282 or 1-888/246-3255, ⓦwww.chemainus-fullerlakemotel.com; ❹). The best **B&B** is the pretty and whimsically decorated *Bird Song Cottage*, 9909 Maple St (ⓣ250/246-9910, ⓦwww.birdsongcottage.com; ❺). For a **campsite** there is the *Country Maples RV Resort*, 9010 Trans-Canada Hwy (ⓣ250/246-2078, ⓦwww.holidaytrailsresorts.com; $27–34; April–Oct) in sixty acres of open and wooded parkland 16km north of Duncan above the Chemainus River, with showers, laundry and pool. About 5km south of the village on the river is the quiet *Bald Eagle Campground*, 8705 Chemainus Rd (ⓣ250/246-9457 or 1-866/246-9457; $18–22). All manner of little cafés, shops and tearooms have sprung up across the village: for **food**, try the *Willow Street Café*, 9749 Willow St, in the newer part of town, with cheap, varied snacks, or the *Waterford* for full meals (lunch from $7, dinner from $15–25) five minutes north of the village centre at 9875 Maple St (ⓣ250/246-1046).

You can pick up a **ferry** from Chemainus to the small islands of **Kuper** and **Thetis** (both $6.90/6.35 for foot passengers, $16.70/14.25 for cars).

Ladysmith

LADYSMITH's claim to fame is based solely on an accident of geography, as it straddles the 49th Parallel, the latitude that divides mainland Canada and the US. Canada held on to Vancouver Island only after some hard bargaining in the buildup to the 1846 Oregon Treaty, even though the boundary's logic ought to put much of it in the States. Ladysmith was originally named Oyster Bay, but was rechristened by Robert Dunsmuir (see below) at the time of the Boer War battle for Ladysmith (many streets bear the name of Boer War generals). There's little to the place other than the usual motels and garages, though a recent attempt to spruce up the older buildings – built as a dormitory town for Nanaimo's miners – won it a Western Canada Award of Excellence. Ladysmith's scenic profile, it has to be said, would be considerably higher were it not for a huge sawmill and a waterfront that is usually hopelessly jammed with lumber. The **infocentre** is a booth at 132 Roberts St (July & Aug daily 9am–5pm; rest of year Mon–Fri 9am–4pm; ⓣ250/245-2112, ⓦwww.ladysmithcofc.com) and has walking maps of the village's "heritage centre". The volunteer-run **Black Nugget Museum**, 12 Gatacre St (currently open only Thurs 5–8pm or by appointment on ⓣ250/245-4846; $2), is a restored 1881 hotel stuffed with predictable memorabilia of coal mining and pioneers. If you stop off, check out **Transfer Beach Park** on the harbour, where the water's said to be the warmest in the Pacific north of San Francisco.

For **accommodation**, make for the fourteen-unit *Holiday House Motel*, 540 Esplanade St (Ⓣ250/245-2231, Ⓔhhmotel@island.net; ②), overlooking Ladysmith's waterfront; the *Seaview Marine Resort*, 1111 Chemainus Rd (Ⓣ250/245-3768 or 1-800/891-8832, Ⓦwww.chemainus.com; ⑤), just off the hwy 6km south of town (and 8km north of Chemainus) with five fully equipped self-catering one- and two-bedroom cottages on the ocean. The best **food** option is the oldest "English-style pub" in BC, the *Crow and Gate* off the main road 19km north of the town on Yellow Point Road.

Nanaimo

With a population of about 75,000, **NANAIMO**, 113km from Victoria, is Vancouver Island's second biggest city, the terminal for **ferries** from Horseshoe Bay and Tsawwassen on the mainland, and a watershed between the island's populated southeastern tip and its wilder, more sparsely peopled countryside to the north and west. In BC, only Vancouver and Kelowna are expanding faster. This said, the town is unexceptional, though the setting, as ever in BC, is eye-catching – particularly around the harbour, which bobs with yachts and rusty fishing boats and, if you've come from Victoria, allows the first views across to the big mountains on the mainland. If you are going to stop here, more than likely it'll be for **Petroglyph Park** or the town's increasingly famous **bungee-jumping** zone. If not, the Nanaimo Parkway provides a 21-kilometre bypass around the town.

Coal first brought white settlers to the region, many of whom made their fortunes here, including the Victorian magnate **Robert Dunsmuir**, who was given £750,000 and almost half the island in return for building the Victoria–Nanaimo railway – an indication of the benefits that could accrue from the British government to those with the pioneering spirit. Five bands of Salish natives originally lived on the site, which they called *Sney-ne-mous*, or "meeting place", from which the present name derives. It was they who innocently showed the local black rock to Hudson's Bay agents in 1852. The old mines are now closed, and the town's pockets are padded today by forestry, deep-sea fishing, tourism and – most notably – by six deep-water docks and a booming port.

Nanaimo, like any self-respecting BC town, lays on a fair few festivals, best known of which is the annual **Bathtub Race** or **Silly Boat Race**, in which bathtubs are raced (and sunk, mostly) across the 55km to Vancouver. The winner, the first to reach Vancouver, receives the silver Plunger Trophy from the Loyal Nanaimo Bathtub Society. It's all part of the four-day Marine Festival held over the third weekend of July. More highbrow is the late May to early June **Nanaimo Festival**, a cultural jamboree that takes place in and around Malaspina College, 900 Fifth St. The town's other minor claim to fame is the **Nanaimo bar**, a glutinous chocolate confection made to varying recipes and on sale everywhere.

Arrival and information

The Nanaimo-Collishaw **airport** is 15km south of downtown on Hwy 19 and is connected by regular shuttle buses to the town centre. Seaplane connections to Vancouver with Harbour Air and Baxter Aviation (see p.911) land close to downtown below Front St on the harbourfront.

Nanaimo's **bus terminal** (Ⓣ250/753-4371) is some way from the harbour on the corner of Comox and Terminal, with six daily Laidlaw buses to Victoria, two to Port Hardy and three or four to Port Alberni, for connections to Tofino and Ucluelet. **BC Ferries** (Ⓣ250/386-3431 or 1-888/223-3779, Ⓦwww.bcferries.bc.ca) sail from **Departure Bay** (Ⓣ250/753-1261), 2km north of downtown, to Horseshoe Bay on the mainland (summer hourly 7am–9pm, off-season every 2hr; foot passengers $10.55 one-way, cars $35.75/33). To reach downtown from Departure Bay take the Seaporter shuttle (Ⓣ250/753-2118; $14.98) or Hammond Bay bus #2 to the north end of Stewart Ave. A newer and more convenient terminal, **Duke Point** (Ⓣ250/722-0181), just south of town, handles ferries from Tsawwassen. Nanaimo lies on the Victoria–Courtenay **train** line and sees two trains daily, northbound around 11am, southbound at 3pm; the **train station** is a little west of downtown, off Selby and near the corner of Fitzwilliam. From the station, turn left and take the latter (and Bastion).

You'll find a typically overstocked **infocentre** north of the centre off the main hwy in Beban Park at Beban House, 2290 Bowen Rd (May–Sept daily 9am–8pm; Oct–April Mon–Fri 9am–5pm; Ⓣ250/756-0106 or 1-800/663-7337, Ⓦwww.tourismnanaimo.com). They'll phone around and help with accommodation referrals, and shower you with pamphlets. There are also details of the many **boat rides** and **tours** you can make to local sawmills, canneries, nature reserves and fishing research stations. There is a smaller downtown office at 82 Commercial St (Ⓣ250/754-8531), but it keeps unreliable hours.

Accommodation

Hotels

Buccaneer Inn 1577 Stewart Ave Ⓣ250/753-1246 or 1-877/282-6337, Ⓦwww.thebuccaneerinn.com. A reliable, if unexciting choice whose main appeal is a convenient location three blocks south of the Departure Bay ferry terminal. ❸–❻

Fairwinds Schooner Cove Resort Hotel and Marina 3521 Dolphin Drive (Ⓣ250/468-7691 or 1-800/663-7060, Ⓦwww.fairwinds.ca. Convenient for the bus terminal, or, for out-of-town comfort. Located 26km north of town near Nanoose Bay. ❺

Howard Johnson Harbourside Hotel 1 Terminal Ave Ⓣ250/753-2241 or 1-800/663-7322, Ⓦwww.hojonanaimo.com. Good, reliable rooms in a chain hotel, with the attraction of a pleasant waterfront setting. ❺

Hostels and campsites

Cambie Hostel 63 Victoria Crescent Ⓣ250/754-5323 or 1-877/754-5323, Ⓦwww.cambiehostels.com. A bigger hostel than Nicol Street with fifty beds in small dorm rooms, and some doubles at $50 ($47 Oct–April). The hostel also has a very cheap cafe, bakery and bar. Dorm beds $23.50 or $18.50 Oct–April. ❶

Nanaimo International Hostel, or **Nicol Street Hostel**, 65 Nicol St (Ⓣ250/753-1188, Ⓦwww.nanaimohostel.com. Nanaimo's cheapest beds are at this central, private mini-hostel; dorm beds from $12. Located seven blocks south of the bus terminal and one block south of the Harbour Park Shopping Centre off Hwy 1. A handful of camping spots ($10) on the lawn (with ocean views) are also available, plus bike rental, laundry, kitchen and Internet access. ❶

Newcastle Island Provincial Park (see p.758; $14 in summer, $9 in winter), has the only pitches (18 in all, so arrive early) within walking distance of town, apart from the *Nicol Street Hostel* (see above). Other sites are spread along the main road to the north and south. ❶

The town and parks

In downtown Nanaimo itself, only two sights warrant the considerable amount of energy used to promote them. The **Nanaimo** District **Museum**, just off the main harbour area at 100 Cameron St by the Harbour Park Mall (May to early Sept daily 10am–5pm; Oct–April Tues–Sat 10am–5pm; $2), houses a collection that runs the usual historical gamut of pioneer, logging, mining, native peoples and natural history displays. The best features are the reconstructed coal mine and the interesting insights into the town's cosmopolitan population – a mix of Polish, Chinese, aboriginal peoples and British citizens – who all see themselves today as some of the island's "friendliest folk". The museum is also responsible for the **Bastion**, two blocks north at the corner of Bastion and Front streets, a wood-planked tower built by the Hudson's Bay Company in 1853 as a store and a stronghold against native attack, though it was never used during such an attack. It's the oldest (perhaps the only) such building in the west. These days it houses a small **museum** of Hudson's Bay memorabilia (same hours as for the Nanaimo District Museum); its silly tourist stunt, without which no BC town would be complete, is "the only ceremonial cannon firing west of Ontario" (summer only, daily at noon). This is marginally more impressive than the town's claim to have the most retail shopping space per capita in the country.

Nanaimo's outskirts are not pretty, nor, if you keep to the road through town, is the main strip of malls and billboards on and around downtown. Big efforts are being made to spruce the place up, however, not least in the town's 25 or so gardens and small parks. Many of these hug the shore, perfectly aligned for a seafront breath of air. The **Harbourfront Walkway** allows you to stroll 3km along the seafront. Also popular is the Swyalana Lagoon, an artificial tidal lagoon built on a renovated stretch of the downtown harbour in Maffeo Sutton Park. It's become a popular swimming, snoozing and picnic area. Farther afield, **Piper's Lagoon Park** offers a windblown, grassy spit, with lots of trails, flowers, rocky bluffs and good sea views; it's off Hammond Bay Road north of the city centre. For beaches you could head for **Departure Bay**, again north of the centre off Stewart Avenue. Plenty of local shops rent out a range of marine gear, as well as bikes and boats.

For the wildest of the local parks, head due west of town to **Westwood Lake Park**, good for a couple of hours' lonely hiking and some fine swimming. Tongue-twisting **Petroglyph Provincial Park**, off Hwy 1, 3km south of downtown, showcases aboriginal peoples' carvings of the sort found all over BC (particularly along coastal waterways), many of them thousands of years old. Often their meaning is vague, but they appear to record important rituals and events. There are plenty of figures – real and mythological – carved into the local sandstone here, though their potential to inspire wonder is somewhat spoilt by more recent graffiti, traffic noise and the first thin edge of Nanaimo's urban sprawl.

Nanaimo's other major claim to fame is as home of North America's first legal public bungee-jumping site. The **Bungy Zone Adrenalin Centre** is 13km south of the town at 35 Nanaimo River Rd (daily 11.30am–6/8pm; ⓣ250/753-5867 or 1-888/668-7874, ⓦwww.bungyzone.com; jumps from $95): look out for the signed turn off Hwy 1. It's become so popular that variations have been added to the standard 42-metre plunge off the bridge, all slightly less terrifying than the bungee jump. The "Flying Fox" is a line to which you are fixed extending in a deep arc along the canyon – expect to hit speeds of 100kph; "Rap Jumping" involves a rapid mountaineering rappel straight down from the bridge; while the "Ultimate Swing" lets you jump off the bridge and swing in a big arc at speeds of up to 140kph. There's provision for **camping** here (with showers, laundry and tents for rent), and if you call in advance you should be able to book free shuttles to the site from Victoria and Nanaimo.

Eating and drinking

Where **eating** is concerned, get your obligatory Nanaimo bar, or other cheap edibles, at the food stands in the **Public Market**, which is near the ferry terminal on Stewart Avenue (daily 9am–9pm). For meals try *Gina's*, a left turn off the north end of Front St at 47 Skinner St (ⓣ250/753-5411) – it's an unmissable Mexican outfit perched on the edge of a cliff and painted bright pink with an electric blue roof. The town's best **seafood** choice is the *Bluenose Chowder House*, 1340 Stewart Ave (ⓣ250/754-6611; closed Mon), also party to a nice outside terrace. Front Street has a choice of places, most with the benefit of terraces or patios looking out to sea: at the plaza at 90 Front St is *Javawocky* (Ⓣ250/753-1688), a good little café, while for fuller snacks or steaks and seafood you should try the *Globe Bar & Grille*, 25 Front St (Ⓣ250/754-4910). For a **drink** (and/or food), there's the *Longwood Brewpub*, 5775 Turner Rd (Ⓣ250/729-8225).

Newcastle and Gabriola islands

Barely a stone's throw offshore from Nanaimo lies **Newcastle Island**, and beyond it the larger bulk of Gabriola Island, both incongruously graced with palm trees: they're beneficiaries of what is supposedly Canada's mildest climate. Ferries (Ⓣ250/391-2300, Ⓦwww.scenicferries.com) make the ten-minute crossing to the former hourly (10am–7pm; foot passengers $5 one-way) from Maffeo Sutton Park (the wharf behind the Civic Arena) to **Newcastle Island Provincial Park**, which has a fine stretch of sand, tame wildlife, no cars, and lots of walking (18km of trails in all) and picnic possibilities. It'll take a couple of hours to walk the 7.5-kilometre trail that encircles the island.

There are about fifteen daily crossings to **Gabriola Island** (6km, 20min; foot passengers $6.80/6.55, cars $16.70/14.50), a much quieter place that's home to about 2000 people, many of them artists and writers. Author Malcolm Lowry, he of *Under the Volcano* fame, immortalized the island in a story entitled *October Ferry to Gabriola Island*. Gabriola also offers several **beaches** – the best are Gabriola Sands' Twin Beaches at the island's northwest end and Drumbeg Provincial Park – and lots of scope for scuba diving, bird-watching (eagles and sea birds), beachcombing and easy walking, plus the added curiosity of the **Malaspina Galleries**, a series of caves and bluffs near Gabriola Sands sculpted by wind, frost and surf.

Both islands have numerous **B&Bs** and several **campsites**, though if you're thinking of staying the night it's as well to check first with the Nanaimo infocentre or Gabriola's own office at 575 North Rd (July & Aug daily 9am–6pm; mid-May to June & Sept to mid-Oct Sat & Sun 9am–5pm; rest of year closed; Ⓣ250/247-9332 or 1-888/284-9332, Ⓦwww.gabriolaisland.org). You can buy snacks on Newcastle from various concessions, notably the restored 1931 Pavilion building, but if you're camping take supplies with you.

From Nanaimo to Port Alberni

North of Nanaimo Hwy 1 is replaced by **Highway 19**, a messy stretch of road spotted with billboards and a rash of motels, marinas and clapboard houses. Almost every last centimetre of the coast is privately owned, this being the chosen site of what appears to be every British Columbian's dream holiday home. Don't expect, therefore, to be able to weave through the houses, wooden huts and boat launches to reach the tempting beaches that flash past below the highway. For sea and sand you have to hang on for **Parksville**, 37km north of Nanaimo, and its quieter near-neighbour **Qualicum Beach**.

Parksville marks a major parting of the ways: while Hwy 19 continues up the eastern coast to Port Hardy, **Highway 4**, the principal trans-island route, pushes west to **Port Alberni** and on through the tremendously scenic Mackenzie Mountains to the Pacific Rim National Park (see p.909). Laidlaw runs up to three **buses** daily from Nanaimo to Port Alberni, where there are connecting services for Ucluelet and Tofino in the national park.

Parksville

The approach to **PARKSVILLE** from the south is promising, taking you through lovely wooded dunes, with lanes striking off eastwards to hidden beaches and a half-dozen secluded **campsites**. Four kilometres on is the best of the beaches, stretched along 2km of **Rathtrevor Beach Provincial Park** (the tide goes out a kilometre here to reveal vast swathes of sand). In summer this area is madness – there's more beach action here than just about anywhere in the country – and if you want to lay claim to some of the park's **camping** space (summer $22, winter $9; day-use parking $5) expect to start queuing first thing in the morning or take advantage of the provincial park reservations service (see box, p.758). The public sand here stretches for 2km and sports all the usual civilized facilities of Canada's tamed outdoors: cooking shelters, picnic spots and walking trails.

The dross starts beyond the bridge into Parksville, and its eight blocks of motels and garages. The worst of the development has been kept off the promenade, however, which fronts **Parksville Beach**, whose annual **Sandfest** draws 30,000 visitors a day in July to watch the World Sandcastle Competition. The beach offers lovely views across to the mainland and boasts Canada's warmest sea water – up to 21°C (70°F) in summer. Though busy, it's as immaculately kept as the rest of the town – a tidiness that bears witness to the reactionary civic pride of Parksville's largely retired permanent population. You'll see some of these worthy burghers at play during August, when the town hosts the World Croquet Championships.

For local **information**, Parksville's Chamber of Commerce is clearly signed off the hwy in downtown at 1275 East Island Hwy (June to early Sept daily 9am–8pm; rest of year generally Mon–Fri 9am–5pm; Ⓣ250/248-3613, Ⓦwww.chamber.parksville.bc.ca). Ask for details of the many **hiking** areas and other nearby refuges from the beaches' summer maelstrom, and **fishing**, which is naturally another of the region's big draws.

If you must **stay**, camping offers the best locations. There are a multitude of cheapish generic **motels** in town and "resort complexes" out along the beaches, though summer vacancies are few and far between. South of Rathtrevor Beach Provincial Park, try the big *Tigh-Na-Mara Resort Hotel*, 1095 East Island Hwy (Ⓣ250/248-2072 or 1-800/663-7373, Ⓦwww.tigh-na-mara.com; ❻), with log cottages and oceanfront apartments, forest setting, beach, indoor pool and self-catering units. More upmarket is the *Beach Acres Resort*, 1015 East Island Hwy (Ⓣ250/248-3424 or 1-800/663-7309, Ⓦwww.beachacresresort.com; ❼), set in 57 acres of woodland with its own pool, sandy beach, and forest or ocean-view cabins. Much cheaper is the *Sea Edge Motel*, 209 West Island Hwy (Ⓣ250/248-8377 or 1-800/667-3382, Ⓦwww.seaedge.com; ❺), with its own stretch of beach. One of the cheapest motels is the *Skylite*, 459 East Island Hwy (Ⓣ250/248-4271 or 1-800/667-1886, Ⓦwww.skylitemotel.com; ❹).

Qualicum Beach

QUALICUM BEACH, claims its Chamber of Commerce, "is to the artist of today what Stratford-on-Avon was to the era of Shakespeare" – a bohemian enclave of West Coast artists and writers that has also been dubbed the "Carmel of the North" after the town in California. Both estimations obviously pitch things ridiculously high, but compared with Parksville the area has more greenery and charm, and it's infinitely less commercialized, though it probably has just as many summer visitors. More a collection of dispersed houses than a town, at least near the water, Qualicum's seafront is correspondingly wilder and more picturesque, skirted by the road and interrupted only by an **infocentre** at 2711 West Island Hwy, the obvious white building midway on the strand (daily 9am–6pm; longer hours in summer; ⓣ250/752-9532, ⓦwww.qualicum.bc.ca), and a well-sited **hotel**, the *Sand Pebbles Inn* (ⓣ250/752-6974 or 1-877/556-2326, ⓦwww.spebbles.com; ❺). A cluster of **motels** also sits at its northern end, where the road swings inland. There's plenty of other local accommodation: contact the infocentre for details. Keep heading north and the road becomes quieter and edged with occasional **campsites**.

Highway 4 to Port Alberni

If you've not yet ventured off the coastal road from Victoria, the short stretch of **Highway 4** to Port Alberni offers the first real taste of the island's beauty. The first worthwhile stop is **Englishman River Falls Provincial Park**, 3km west of Parksville (exit at Errington Rd) and then another 8km south off the highway. Named after an early immigrant who drowned here, the park wraps around the Englishman River, which tumbles over two main sets of waterfalls. A thirty-minute trail takes in both falls, with plenty of swimming and fishing pools en route. The popular year-round provincial park campsite (summer $17, winter $9; day-use parking $3) is on the left off the approach road before the river, secreted amongst cedars, dogwoods – BC's official tree – and lush ferns.

Back on the main highway, another 8km brings you to the **Little Qualicum Hatchery**, given over to chum, trout and chinook salmon, and just beyond it turn right for the **Little Qualicum Falls Provincial Park**, on the north side of Hwy 4, 19km west of Parksville, which is claimed by some to be the island's loveliest small park. A magnificent forest trail follows the river as it drops several hundred metres through a series of gorges and foaming waterfalls. A half-hour stroll gives you views of the main falls, but for a longer hike try the five-hour Wesley Ridge Trail. There's a sheltered provincial park campsite (summer $17, winter $9; day-use parking $3) by the river and a recognized swimming area on the river at its southern end.

Midway to Port Alberni, the road passes **Cameron Lake** and then an imperious belt of old-growth forest. At the lake's western end, it's well worth walking ten minutes into **McMillan Provincial Park** (no campsite) to reach the famous **Cathedral Grove**, a beautiful group of huge Douglas firs, some of them reaching 70m tall, 2m thick; they are up to a thousand years old. The park is the gift of the large McMillan timber concern, whose agents have been responsible for felling similar trees with no compunction over the years. Wandering the grove will take only a few minutes but, just to the east, at the Cameron Lake picnic site, is the start of the area's main **hike**. The well-maintained trail was marked out by railway crews in 1908 and climbs to the summit of **Mount Arrowsmith** (1817m), a long, gentle twenty-kilometre pull through alpine meadows that takes between six and nine hours. The mountain is also one of the island's newer and fast-developing ski areas.

Port Alberni

Self-proclaimed "Gateway to the Pacific" and – along with half of Vancouver Island – "Salmon Capital of the World", **PORT ALBERNI** is a dispersed town more or less dominated by the sights and smells of its huge lumber mills. Despite its relative ugliness, it's also an increasingly popular site for exploring the centre and west coast of the island, and a busy fishing port, situated at the end of the impressive fjord-like Alberni Inlet, Vancouver Island's longest inlet. Various logging and pulp-mill tours are available, but the town's main interest to travellers is as a forward base for the Pacific Rim National Park. If you've ever wanted to hook a salmon, though, this is probably one of the easier places to do so and there are any number of boats and guides ready to help out.

Arrival and information

Laidlaw (see p.874) runs five **buses** daily from Nanaimo to Port Alberni; the terminal is on Victoria Quay at 5065 Southgate. Laidlaw runs connections from here on to Ucluelet and Tofino. Several other companies from Victoria (see p.874) make connections to Bamfield for the West Coast Trail (see p.926).

For help and information on fishing charters, hiking options, minor summer events, or tours of the two local pulp mills, call in at the **infocentre**, unmissable as you come into town at 2533 Redford St, RR2, Site 215 Comp 10 (July & Aug Mon–Fri 9am–6pm, Sat & Sun 9am–5pm; rest of year Mon–Fri 9am–5pm, Sat & Sun 10am–2/4pm; ⓣ250/724-6535, ⓦwww.avcoc.com), off Hwy 4 east of town – look out for the big yellow mural.

Accommodation

Given the early departure of the MV *Lady Rose* (see box, p.908), there's a good chance you may have to **stay** overnight in Port Alberni. Contact the infocentre for a list of the constantly changing B&B outlets.

The Best Western Barclay 4277 Stamp Ave ⓣ250/724-7171 or 1-800/563-6590, ⓦwww.bestwesternbarclay.com. A reliable choice with and outdoor pool. ❼

Bluebird 3755 3rd Ave ⓣ250/723-1153, ⓦwww.bluebirdmotel.net. Closest to the quay. It only has fifteen rooms, so be sure to book in advance. ❸

Coast Hospitality Inn 3835 Redford St ⓣ250/723-8111, ⓦwww.coasthotels.com. A more memorable central hotel – not terribly cheap, but probably the town's best mid-price bet. ❺

Edelweiss B&B 2610-12th Ave ⓣ250/723-5940. An excellent B&B choice. It is not particularly central, but does have very welcoming hosts. ❸

Somass Motel & RV 5279 River Rd ⓣ250/724-3236 or 1-800/927-2217, ⓦwww.somass-motel.ca. Also a reliable choice, but smaller than the *Best Western*. ❹

Campsites

China Creek Marina and Campground 2011 Bamfield Road ⓣ250/723-2657. A big 250-site campground, 15km south of town on Alberni Inlet, which has a wooded, waterside location and sandy, log-strewn beach. Sites range from $16–25 (May–Sept).

The town and around

You might want to check out the industry-backed **Forestry Visitor Centre** (summer daily 9.30am–5.30pm, rest of year Fri–Sun 11am–4pm; ⓣ250/720-2108) on the colourful harbour quay. From here in summer a small steam train runs from the old train station at the corner of Kingsway and Argyle for about half an hour along the waterfront to the **McLean Mill National Historic Site** (site open daily year-round; mill building and steam train mid-June to early Sept Wed & Thurs 10am–5pm; site donation; mill $7; train $24 round-trip, includes mill admission; ⓦwww.alberniheritage.com), an old steam-operated mill at 5633 Smith Rd, which you might also reach by bike or on foot on the twenty-kilometre Log Trail from the infocentre. The mill forms part of a loosely affiliated collection of historic and other local sights, the Alberni Heritage Network (ⓦwww.albernidesign.net), including the **Maritime Discovery Centre** on the waterfront (late June to early Sept 10am–5pm; donation suggested), a museum with plenty of hands-on displays for children devoted to the town's maritime heritage.

For hot-weather swimming, locals head out to **Sproat Lake Provincial Park**, 8km north of town on Hwy 4. It's a hectic scene in summer, thanks to a

Boats from Port Alberni

One of the great trips in British Columbia is aboard the **MV Lady Rose**, a small, fifty-year-old Scottish-built freighter that plies between Port Alberni, Kildonan, Bamfield, Ucluelet and the Broken Group Islands (see p.920). Primarily a conduit for freight and mail, it also takes up to a hundred passengers, many of whom use it as a drop-off for canoe trips or the West Coast Trail at Bamfield. You could easily ride it simply for the exceptional scenery – huge cliffs and tree-covered mountains – and for the abundant wildlife (sea lions, whales, eagles, depending on the time of year). Passengers started as something of a sideline for the company that runs the boat, but such has been the boat's popularity that another boat has been added to the "fleet" – the 200-passenger **MV Frances Barkley** – and reservations for trips are now virtually essential. Remember to take a sweater and jacket and wear sensible shoes, for these are still primarily working boats, and creature comforts are few.

The basic year-round **schedule** is as follows: the boat leaves from the Argyle Pier, 5425 Argyle St at the Alberni Harbour Quay, Port Alberni (Tues, Thurs & Sat 8am). After a stop at **Kildonan** ($18 one-way, $35 return), it arrives in **Bamfield** ($28/55) at 12.30pm. It starts its return journey at 1.30pm, reaching Port Alberni at 5.30pm. From Oct–May the boat stops on advance request at the Broken Group Islands.

From June to mid-Sept, there are additional sailings to the **Broken Group Islands** (Mon, Wed & Fri, departs Port Alberni 8am). At 11am, the boat docks at Sechart ($28/55), site of the highly recommended *Sechart Whaling Station Lodge* (ⓣ250/723-8313, ⓦwww.ladyrosemarine.com), the only place to stay on the archipelago if you're not wilderness camping. Cost per night is $125 per person, $190 for two people sharing a room, including all meals; $15 and $20 less if you stay two or more days. The boat continues to **Ucluelet** ($30/$60), arriving at 12.30pm. The return journey starts from Ucluelet at 2pm, calling at Sechart (3.30pm) before arriving back at Port Alberni at 7pm.

From July 2 to Sept 3 there is an additional sailing (Sun only) on the route from Port Alberni (8am) to Bamfield (1.30pm) and back, with an outbound stop at Sechart at 11am.

For information and **reservations**, contact Lady Rose Marine Services, 5425 Argyle St, Port Alberni (year-round ⓣ250/723-8313 or April–Sept ⓣ1-800/663-7192, ⓦwww.ladyrosemarine.com). It also offers canoe and kayak **rentals** ($35/day, double kayak $50/day, includes lifejackets, paddles, pumps and spray skirts) as well as transportation of the same to the Broken Group Islands. The Toquart Connector Water Taxi (contact the above numbers of ⓣ250/720-7358) runs between the *Sechart Lodge*, Sechart, Bamfield and the Broken Group Islands for between $35 and $65 per person. Other boats to these destinations can occasionally be picked up from Tofino and Ucluelet.

fine beach, picnic area and a pair of good campsites ($15; April–Oct), one on the lake, the other north of the hwy about 1km away. Of peripheral interest, you can take a guided tour of the world's largest fire-fighting planes or follow the short trails that lead to a few ancient petroglyphs on the park's eastern tip.

Sproat Lake marks the start of the superb scenery that unfolds over the 100km of Hwy 4 west of the town. Only heavily logged areas detract from the grandeur of the Mackenzie Range and the majestic interplay of trees and water. Go prepared, however, as there's no fuel or shops for about two hours of driving.

Eating

Eating possibilities are numerous. For coffee, good breakfasts and snacks down by the dock, try the Blue Door Café at 5415 Argyle St, an old-fashioned place much-patronized by locals. For lunch, make for the *Swale Rock Café* 5328

Argyle St (☎250/723-0777), and for seafood check out the waterfront *Clockworks* Harbour Quay (☎250/723-8862). The *Canal*, 5093 Johnson St (☎250/724-6555), serves reliable Greek food, and for cheap lunches there's the *Paradise Café*, 4505 Gertrude St (☎250/724-5050), and several deli-bakeries scattered around town.

Pacific Rim National Park

The **Pacific Rim National Park** – the single best reason to visit Vancouver Island – is a stunning amalgam of mountains, coastal rainforest, wild beaches and unkempt marine landscapes that stretches intermittently for 130km between the towns of Tofino in the north and Port Renfrew to the south. It divides into three distinct areas: **Long Beach**, which is the most popular; the **Broken Group Islands**, hundreds of islets only really accessible to sailors and canoeists; and the **West Coast Trail**, a tough but increasingly popular long-distance footpath. The whole area has also become a magnet for surfing and **whale-watching** enthusiasts, and dozens of small companies run charters out from the main centres to view the migrating mammals. By taking the MV *Lady Rose* from Port Alberni (see box, p.906) to Bamfield or Ucluelet or back, and combining this with shuttle buses or Laidlaw buses from Victoria, Port Alberni and Nanaimo, a wonderfully varied combination of itineraries is possible around the region.

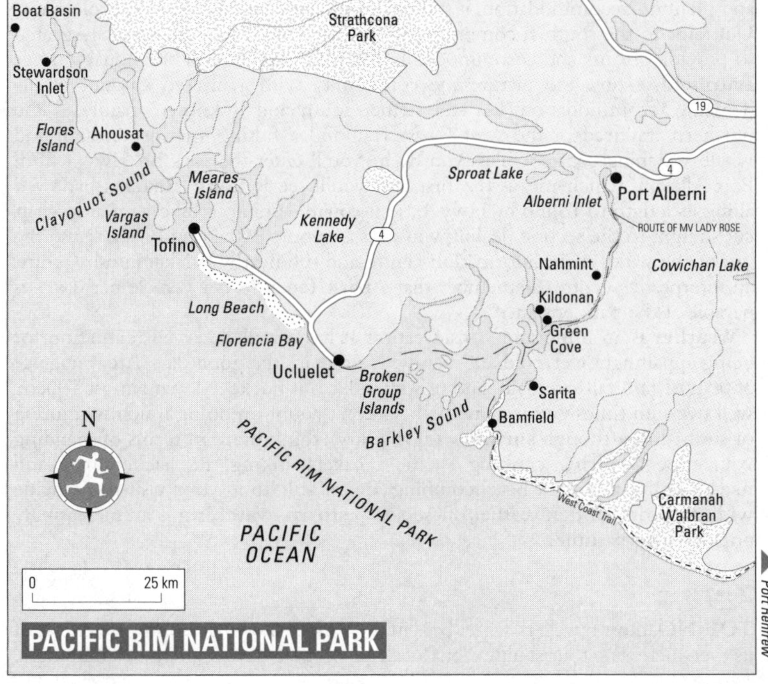

Whales

The Pacific Rim National Park is amongst the world's best areas for **whale-watching**, thanks to its location on the main migration routes, food-rich waters and numerous sheltered bays. People come from all over the world for the spectacle, and it's easy to find a boat going out from Tofino, Ucluelet or Bamfield, most charging around $60–80 a head for the trip depending on duration (usually 2–3hr). Regulations prohibit approaching within 100m of an animal but, though few locals will admit it, there's no doubt that the recent huge upsurge in boat tours has begun to disrupt the **migrations**. The whales' 8000-kilometre journey – the longest known migration of any mammal – takes them from their breeding and calving lagoons in Baja, Mexico, to summer feeding grounds in the Bering and Chukchi seas off Siberia. The northbound migration takes from Feb–May, with the peak period of passage between March & April. A few dozen animals occasionally abort their trip and stop off the Canadian coast for summer feeding (notably at Maquinna Marine Park, 20min by boat from Tofino). The return journey starts in August, hitting Tofino and Ucluelet in late Sept and early Oct. **Mating** takes place in Mexico during Dec, after which the males turn immediately northwards, to be followed by females and their young in Feb. Even if you don't take a boat trip, you stand a faint chance of seeing whales from the coast as they dive, when you can locate their tails, or during fluking, when the animals surface and "blow" three or four times before making another five-minute dive. There are telescopes at various points along Long Beach, the best-known viewpoints being Schooner Cove, Radar Hill, Quistis Point and Combers Beach near Sea Lion Rocks.

Lying at the north end of Long Beach, **Tofino**, once essentially a fishing village, is now changing in the face of tourism, but with its natural charm, scenic position and plentiful accommodation, it still makes the best base for general exploration. **Ucluelet** to the south is comparatively less attractive, but almost equally geared to providing tours and accommodating the park's 800,000 or so annual visitors. **Bamfield**, a tiny and picturesque community with a limited amount of in-demand accommodation, lies still farther south and is known mainly as the northern trailhead of the West Coast Trail and a fishing, marine research and whale-watching centre. Unless you fly in, you'll enter the park on Hwy 4 from Port Alberni, which means the first part you'll see is **Long Beach** (shadowed along its length to Tofino by Hwy 4), so if you're dashing in by car for a day-trip, cut straight to the section dealing with this area on p.916. Long Beach is also the site of the park's main information centre and the nearby Wickaninnish Centre, an interpretive centre. Remember that a **park fee** – $8 per vehicle per day – is payable at the park entrance.

Weather is an important consideration: it has a well-deserved reputation for being appallingly wet, cold and windy – and that's the good days. An average of 300cm of rain falls annually, and in some places it buckets down almost 700cm, well over ten times Victoria's rainfall. So don't count on doing much swimming or sunbathing (though **surfing**'s a possibility): think more in terms of spending your time admiring crashing Pacific breakers, hiking the backcountry and maybe doing a spot of beachcombing. Better still, time your visit to coincide with the worst of the weather off-season – **storm-watching** is an increasingly popular park pastime.

Tofino

TOFINO, most travellers' target base in the park, is showing the adverse effects of its ever-increasing tourist influx, but locals are keeping development to a minimum, clearly realizing they have a vested interest in preserving the salty, waterfront charm that brought them – and visitors – here in the first place. Crowning a narrow spit, the fishing village has a superb situation, bounded on three sides by tree-covered islands and water, a location that graces it with magnificent views and plenty of what the tourist literature refers to as "aquaculture". As a service centre it fulfils most functions, offering food, accommodation and a wide variety of boat and sea-plane tours, most of which have a **whale-watching**, surfing (Canada's best surf is close at hand) and fishing angle or provide a means to travel out to **islands and hot springs** close by. Sleepy in off-season, the place erupts into a commercial frenzy during the summer. Hippies, surfer types and easy-going family groups are the most visible visitors – though there's little to do in town other than walk its few streets, enjoy the views and soak up the casual atmosphere.

You might drop in to the small **Whale Centre** at 411 Campbell St (March–Oct daily 9am–8pm; free; ⓣ250/725-2132), one of many places to book whale-watching tours, but also home to exhibits and artefacts devoted to local seafaring and trading history, whales and aboriginal peoples' culture. Another notable place around town is the **Eagle Aerie Gallery**, 350 Campbell St at the corner of Second St (ⓦwww.royhenryvickers.com), a gallery housed in a traditional long-house-style building with a beautiful cedar interior.

Two fine beaches lie within walking distance to the southeast of the town: **Mackenzie Beach** and **Chesterman's Beach** (for access to the latter take Lynn Rd right just beyond the *Dolphin Motel* as you leave town), the former one of the warmer spots locally, the latter home to a fair number of out-of-town accommodation possibilities (see below). Beyond Chesterman lies Frank Island, a tempting proposition at low tide, but sadly private property. The quietest beach around these parts, though, is **Templar**, a miniature strip of sand: ask at the infocentre for directions.

Arrival and information

Tofino is easily reached by Laidlaw **bus** (ⓣ250/385-4411 or 1-800/318-0818) from Port Alberni (2 daily; 3hr) and Nanaimo (1 daily; 4hr 30min), with a single early-morning connection from Victoria, changing at Nanaimo (6hr 30min). The bus depot is on 1st Street near the junction with Neil Street. There is also a daily mini-bus shuttle, the Tofino Bus, 564 Campbell St (ⓣ250/725-2871 or 1-866/986-3466, ⓦwww.tofinobus.com), from Victoria or Nanaimo at the Departure Bay ferry terminal (connecting with the ferry from Horseshoe Bay). It runs via Port Alberni (4541 Margaret St) and Ucluelet (Murray's Grocery, 1738 Peninsula St). The fare from Victoria is $53 and tickets must be booked by phone.

Some small **airlines** have added Tofino to their schedules, including Craig Air (ⓣ250/247-1000 or 1-877/886-3466, ⓦwww.craigair.com), a small operations that runs from Vancouver between one and three times daily (1hr; $169 one-way) and serves local lodges and communities. Baxter Aviation (ⓣ250/754-1066 or 604/683-6525 in Vancouver or 1-800/661-5599, ⓦwww.baxterair.com) also runs connecting flights to Tofino and Ucluelet from Vancouver harbour, Victoria, Seattle and many other smaller centres.

Tofino's **infocentre** at 121 Third St at the corner of Campbell St (April–Sept daily 9am–8/9pm; Oct–March Mon–Fri 9am–4pm; ⓣ250/725-3414, ⓦwww.tourismtofino.com) can give you the exhaustive lowdown on all the logistics of boat and plane tours.

Accommodation

The infocentre may be able to get you into one of the village's ever-expanding roster of **hotels**, **motels** and **B&B**, should you be unwise enough to turn up in Tofino without reservations in high summer. There are two main concentrations of accommodation options: in Tofino itself or a couple of kilometres east of town on or near Lynn Road, which overlooks Chesterman Beach. Out of town across the water (accessed by water taxi) there are also the desirable but expensive self-contained units at the *Hot Springs Lodge* (Ⓣ250/724-8570; ⑥), the main accommodation at Hot Springs Cove (see p.915); book early. Otherwise you can try one of the near-town **campsites** (don't forget that there is a park campsite at Long Beach; see p.918) or the **private hostels** that now seem to spring up overnight and disappear just as quickly, though local reports suggest some of these places can be pretty unsalubrious. The infocentre website Ⓦwww.tourismtofino.com has a full listing of B&Bs.

Hotels and motels

Cable Cove Inn 201 Main St Ⓣ250/725-4236 or 1-800/663-6449, Ⓦwww.cablecoveinn.com. Stay in high style in one of six smart rooms at the westernmost edge of town that come complete with Jacuzzis, fireplaces and four-poster beds. ⑦

Dolphin Motel 1190 Pacific Rim Hwy Ⓣ250/725-3377, Ⓦwww.dolphinmotel.ca. Fourteen rooms with coffee-maker and fridge or self-catering units 3km south of town; 5min walk to Chesterman Beach. ④

Duffin Cove and Resort 215 Campbell St Ⓣ250/725-3448 or 1-888/629-2903, Ⓦwww.duffin-cove-resort.com. Thirteen nice cabins and suites (for one to eight people) with kitchens and seaview balconies just south of the *Cable Cove Inn* at the western edge of town overlooking the Clayoquot Sound. ⑧

Maquinna Lodge 120 1st St Ⓣ250/725-3261 or 1-800/665-3199, Ⓕ250/725-3433. Central town location at the corner of Main and 1st St, containing 32 renovated rooms, some overlooking Tofino Harbour and Meares Island. ⑤

Middle Beach Lodge 400 Mackenzie Beach Ⓣ250/725-2900, Ⓦwww.middlebeach.com. Extremely nice, secluded 64-room lodge south of town and west of Chesterman Beach with big stone fireplace, deep old chairs and the gentle splash of waves on tiny Templar Beach to lull you to sleep. ⑥

Ocean Village Beach Resort 555 Hellesen Drive Ⓣ250/725-3755, Ⓦwww.oceanvillageresort.com. A resort just north of Long Beach, 2km from town on the main road, with good accommodation, ocean views, kitchen units and indoor pool. ⑦

Schooner Motel 311 Campbell St Ⓣ250/725-3478, Ⓦwww.schoonermotel.net. Overlooking Tofino Inlet and Meares Island in the town centre, this 18-room motel has some rooms complete with kitchen. ④

Tofino Motel 542 Campbell St Ⓣ250/725-2055, Ⓦwww.tofinomotel.com. A 13-room motel on the eastern edge of town including rooms with balconies offering views of the sea and neighbouring islands. ⑤

Tofino Swell Lodge 341 Olsen Rd Ⓣ250/725-3274, website? Ⓕ725-3346. On the eastern edge of town near Crab Dock, this excellent seven-room lodge on the waterfront looking out to Meares Island has kitchen or plain sleeping units. ④

Wickaninnish Inn Osprey Lane at Chesterman Beach Ⓣ250/725-3100 or 1-800/333-4604, Ⓦwww.wickinn.com. If you're feeling like a splurge (rooms start at $440, less off season), shell out for this superb $8.5–million 45-room inn, situated on a rocky promontory at the western end of Chesterman Beach. All rooms are large and have ocean views, fireplaces and baths big enough for two. As well as the obvious local attractions, storm-watching here is a growing wintertime activity. ⑧

Bed and Breakfasts

Brimar 1375 Thornberg Crescent Ⓣ250/725-3410 or 1-800/714-9373, Ⓦwww.brimarbb.com. At the south end of Chesterman Beach, off Lynn Rd, these three rooms have good Pacific Ocean views and come with a full breakfast. ⑥

Cedar Street Guest House 290 Cedar St Ⓣ250/725-3996, Ⓦwww.cedarstreetguesthouse.com. Two suites on a quiet side street in town with a shared kitchenette. ⑤

Chesterman Beach B&B 1345 Chesterman Beach Rd Ⓣ250/725-3725, Ⓦwww.chestermanbeach.net. Three luxurious oceanfront suites on the beach with private entrance and bathrooms, one of which, the Garden Cottage, has a lovely private garden. ⑧

Clayoquot Vista Guesthouse 608 Pfeiffer Crtescent Ⓣ250/725-2686, Ⓦwww.clayoquotvista.com. Two rooms on the lower level of owners' home close to town and with views to Meares Island and beyond. ⑤

Cobblewood Guest House Suites 1115 Fellowship Rd Ⓣ250/725-2742, Ⓦwww.alberni.net/cobblewood. Three rooms among the cedars off Hwy 4 with kitchenettes and private decks. ⑤

Gull Cottage 1254 Lynn Rd ⓣ250/725-3177, ⓦwww.gullcottagetofino.com. A few minutes' walk to the beach, at the west end of Lynn Rd, this Victorian-era home has three rooms (private bathrooms) and a hot tub in the woods. ❻

The Tide's Inn B&B 160 Arnet Rd ⓣ250/725-3765, ⓦwww.tidesinntofino.com. An easy walk south of town (walk down 1st Ave and turn right) on the waterfront with good views of Clayoquot Sound. ❻

Wilp Gybuu (Wolf House) 311 Leighton Way ⓣ250/725-2330, ⓦwww.tofinobedandbreakfast.com. Three rooms in a walkable location south of town close to *The Tide's Inn*. Sea views, good breakfast and private en-suite bathroom. ❺

Hostels

Hummingbird International Hostel At Ahousaht on Flores Island ⓣ250/670-6979, ⓦwww.hummingbird-hostel.com. As well as the hummingbirds you stand a good chance here of seeing whales, bald eagles and sea otters, with the opportunity to hike trails and bathe in natural sulphur springs. Dorm beds cost from $25, private doubles from $75. Add on the cost of a 35-minute water-taxi or boat connection (from $16 each way; departures from First St dock at 10.30am & 4pm, returning 8.30am & 1pm). ❸

Whalers on the Point Guesthouse (HI) 81 West St ⓣ250/725-3443, ⓦwww.tofinohostel.com. Best hostel in town, HI-affiliated, near the west end of Main St with fabulous ocean views. Including tax, beds are $25 per person in high season (May–Sept), $2 less the rest of the year. Private doubles cost $76–86, or $46–51 in low season. Add on $2 for one-night stays from mid-June to mid-Sept. Facilities include kitchen, games room, sauna, bike rental and storage, surf and wet-suit lockers, and a shuttle service to Long Beach. Reservations are essential. Check-in 8am–2pm & 4–10pm. ❸

Campsites

Bella Pacifica Campground Pacific Rim Hwy ⓣ250/725-3400, ⓦwww.bellapacifica.com. Sites with hot showers, flush toilets and laundry 2km south of town, with wilderness and oceanfront sites, private nature trails to Templar Beach and walk-on access to Mackenzie Beach. Reservations recommended. Feb–Nov. $32–35.

Crystal Cove Beach Resort Mackenzie Beach ⓣ250/725-4213, ⓦwww.crystalcove.cc. 72 sites with flush toilets, laundry and showers and some cabins; 3km south of town in a pretty secluded cove and also 1km from Mackenzie Beach with one- and two-bedroom smart log cabins with kitchens and ocean views. Reservations recommended. $39–49. Cabins ❻

Mackenzie Beach Resort 1101 Pacific Rim Hwy ⓣ250/725-3439, ⓦwww.mackenziebeach.com. Located on a fine sandy beach 2km south of Tofino and 10min walk from Long Beach; indoor pool, Jacuzzi, hot showers and kayak rentals. Some walk-in beachfront tent sites. $45–52.

Eating and drinking

For **food**, just about everyone in town clusters around the heaving tables of the *Common Loaf Bake Shop* (ⓣ250/725-3915) behind the bank at 180 1st St, deservedly the most popular choice for coffee and snacks. In the evening the home-made dough is turned into pizzas instead of bread and rolls. Also good for snacks, breakfast and lunch, and with great coffee, is *Caffè Vincent*, 441 Campbell St (ⓣ/250/725-2599): it also offers **internet access**. For smoothies, deli food, snacks, wraps and an all-day breakfast, visit *Breakers Delicatessan* at 430 Campbell St (ⓣ250/725-2558).

One of the best views in town is available at the *Sea Shanty*, 300 Main St (ⓣ250/725-2902), a restaurant that offers **outdoor dining** overlooking the harbour and the chance of some tremendous sunsets on fine evenings. Excellent Pacific Rim fusion food is available at the intimate and sleek *RainCoast Café*, 101-120 Fourth St (ⓣ250/725-2215; dinner only). Equally elevated (mainly fish and seafood) cuisine can be found at breakfast, lunch and dinner at the award-winning *Schooner Restaurant on the Sound*, 331 Campbell St (ⓣ250/725-3444), a romantic place set in pretty gardens with tremendous views of the Tofino Inlet. For an even bigger treat, head out of town to *The Pointe Restaurant* at the *Wickaninnish Inn* (ⓣ250/725-3100; see hotel listings opposite), which is the area's best upmarket restaurant, on account of both its food and its views – but you'll drop over $150 for a full gourmet nine-course special with wine.

Tofino activities

Whale-watching

Ucluelet to the south may claim to be the "whale-watching capital of the world", but **whales** – the main reason a lot of people are here – are just as easily seen from Tofino. As in Victoria, there are plenty of operators, most costing about the same and offering similar **excursions**: all you have to do is decide what sort of boat you want to go out on – zodiacs (inflatables), which are bouncier, more thrilling and potentially wetter, or rigid-hull cruisers (covered or uncovered), which are more sedate. See the box on p.910 for more whale-watching tips. Remember that if you take tours to Meares Islands, Hot Springs Cove and elsewhere, especially in spring or autumn, you stand a good chance of seeing whales en route anyway – some operators try to combine whale-watching and excursions. Reckon on spending from around $70 for two- or three-hour trip in a zodiac and $90 on a rigid-hull.

Operators to try in Tofino include: Clayoquot Connections, 606 Campbell St (☎250/725-3919, Ⓦwww.clayconnect.com), which offers a relatively inexpensive ($25) tour of the harbour and Meares Island; Ocean Outfitters, 421 Main St (☎250/725-2866 or 1-877/90-OCEAN, Ⓦwww.oceanoutfitters.bc.ca), which offers a wide range of tours on rigid or zodiac boats; Jamie's Whaling Station, 606 Campbell St (☎250/725-3919 or 1-800/667-9913, Ⓦwww.jamies.com; mid-Feb–Oct), the longest-running such venture in Tofino (founded in 1982), which also offers a choice of zodiac boats or the twenty-metre Lady Selkirk, which comes with heated cabin. If you don't see whales, Jamie's offers vouchers which can be used on another trip. See p.910 for more general information. Also long-established (since 1986) is zodiac specialist Remote Passages at the bottom end of Wharf St (☎250/725-3330 or 1-800/666-9833, Ⓦwww.remotepassages.com).

Fishing, surfing, kayaking and more

Many of the above companies double up as **fishing** charters, though for a more long-established specialist operator contact Smiley Seas Charters, 210 Campbell St (May–Sept; ☎250/725-2557, Ⓦwww.smileyseas.com), which is quite happy to have novices aboard. Tofino is quickly becoming the **surfing** capital of Canada, thanks to some enormous Pacific waves, though floating driftwood and big lumps of lumber caught up in the waves can be a hazard. For information, board rental and all other equipment, contact Live to Surf, well east of the town centre at 1180 Tofino Hwy (☎250/725-4464, Ⓦwww.livetosurf.com). It rents boards from $25 and many other items, as well as offering lessons (from $55 for 2hr, excluding equipment). If you want to go out in a **kayak** (no experience required) contact Tofino Sea Kayaking, 320 Main St (☎250/725-4222 or 1-800/863-4664, Ⓦwww.tofino-kayaking.com), which offers day-trips or longer tours with lodge accommodation or wilderness camping. Nine holes of **golf** are available at the local course near the airport (☎250/725-3332), while guided **hikes** and easy nature rambles in the forest and along the seashore are offered by several companies; contact the infocentre for details.

Best place for a **beer** and **dancing** is the pub downstairs at the *Maquinna Lodge*, 120 First St, the place to be on Friday and Saturday nights.

Trips from Tofino: Clayoquot Sound

After wandering Tofino's handful of streets, most people head south to explore Long Beach, or put themselves at the mercy of the many boat and plane operators serving the stretch of ocean and landscapes around Tofino known as **Clayoquot Sound**. The name has gained tremendous resonance over the last few years, largely because it has been the focus for some of the most bitterly fought battles against loggers by environmentalists and aboriginal campaigners. It stretches for some

65km from Kennedy Lake to the south of Tofino to the Hesquiat Peninsula 40km to the north, embracing three major islands – Meares, Vargas and Flores – and numerous smaller islets and coastal inlets. More importantly, it is the largest surviving area of low-altitude temperate **rainforest** in North America. Quite incredibly the BC government gave permission to logging companies in 1993 to fell two-thirds of this irreplaceable and age-old forest. The result was the largest outbreak of **civil disobedience** in Canadian history, resulting in eight hundred arrests, as vast numbers congregated at a peace camp in the area and made daily attempts to stop the logging trucks. The stand-off resulted in partial victory, with the designation of new protected areas and limited recognition of the Nuu-chah-nulth band's moral and literal rights to the land. The region remains in a precarious position, however, and if it's happened once you can be pretty sure that, where forestry interests are concerned, it'll happen again.

There are five main destinations in this region for boat and float-plane trips. The nearest is **Meares Island**, easily visible to the east of Tofino and just fifteen minutes away by boat. A beautiful island swathed in lush temperate rainforest, this was one of the areas earmarked for the lumberjack's chainsaw, despite its designation as a Nuu-chah-nulth park in 1985. At present its ancient cedars and hemlock are safe, and visible on the Meares Island Big Cedar Trail (3km), which meanders among some of the biggest trees you'll ever see, many of them more than a thousand years old and up to 6m across – big enough to put a tunnel through. **Vargas Island**, the next nearest target, lies just 5km from Tofino to the north, and is visited for its beauty, beaches, kayaking and swimming possibilities. **Flores Island**, 20km to the northwest, is accessed by boat or plane and, like Vargas Island, is partly protected by partial provincial park status. At the aboriginal peoples' community of Ahousaht you can pick up the Ahousaht Wild Side Heritage Trail ($20 fee unless staying at the Hummingbird hostel on the island; see "Accommodation" p.913), which runs for 16km through idyllic beach and forest scenery to the Mount Flores viewpoint (886m). This is also a chance to encounter aboriginal culture and people at first hand, with **tours** accompanied by local guides available: see the Tofino infocentre or call ⓣ250/725-3309 for details and information on trail conditions.

Perhaps the best, and certainly one of the most popular trips from Tofino, is the 37-kilometre boat or plane ride to **Hot Springs Cove**, site of one of only a handful of hot springs on Vancouver Island. This takes an hour by water-taxi (ⓣ250/726-8631; from $65) or 15 minutes by float plane with one of the town's float-plane operators (from $90), though the most cost-effective way of seeing the island is to take a day tour with one of Tofino's many operators, who throw in whale-watching en route (from $85). A thirty-minute trek from the landing stage brings you to the springs, which emerge at a piping 43°C and run, as a creek, to the sea via a small waterfall and four pools, becoming progressively cooler. Be prepared for something of a crowd in summer when swimming costumes can be optional. An expensive hotel, the *Hot Springs Lodge* – a way to beat other punters by getting in an early morning or late-night dip – sits on the cove near the landing stage (see "Accommodation" p.913).

Finally, a forty-kilometre trip north takes you to **Hesquiat Peninsula**, where you land at or near Refuge Cove, site of a Hesquiat aboriginal village. Locals offer tours here and some lodgings: ask for the latest details at the Tofino infocentre.

Tofino's infocentre is also the place to pick up information on **tours**; otherwise, contact Sea Trek Tours, 455 Campbell St (ⓣ250/725-4412 or 1-800/811-9155) or the whale-watching companies listed under "Activities" opposite, most of which also offer boat tours to the above destinations.

Long Beach

The most accessible of the park's components, **Long Beach** is just what it says: a long tract of wild, windswept sand and rocky points stretching for about 30km south from Tofino to Ucluelet. Around 19km can be hiked unbroken from Schooner Bay in the west to Half Moon Bay in the east.The snow-covered peaks of the Mackenzie Range rise up over 1200m, providing a scenic backdrop, while behind the beach grows a thick, lush canopy of coastal rainforest. The white-packed sand itself is the sort of primal seascape that is all but extinct in much of the world, scattered with beautiful, sea-sculpted driftwood, smashed by surf, broken by crags, and dotted with islets and rock pools oozing with marine life.

It's worth realizing that Long Beach, while a distinct beach in itself, also rather loosely refers to several other beaches to either side, the relative merits of which are outlined opposite. If you haven't done so already, driving or biking Hwy 4 along the beach area is the best time to call in at the Pacific Rim National Park **Information Centre** (daily mid-March to mid-June 10.30am–6pm; mid-June to Aug 8am–8pm; Sept to mid-Oct 10am–6pm; ⓣ250/726-4212, ⓦwww.parkscanada.gc.ca or ⓦwww.pc.gc.ca), located right off Hwy 4 3km northwest of the Ucluelet–Tofino–Port Alberni road junction. Remember that you need to pay a **park fee** of $6.90 per person to be in the park.

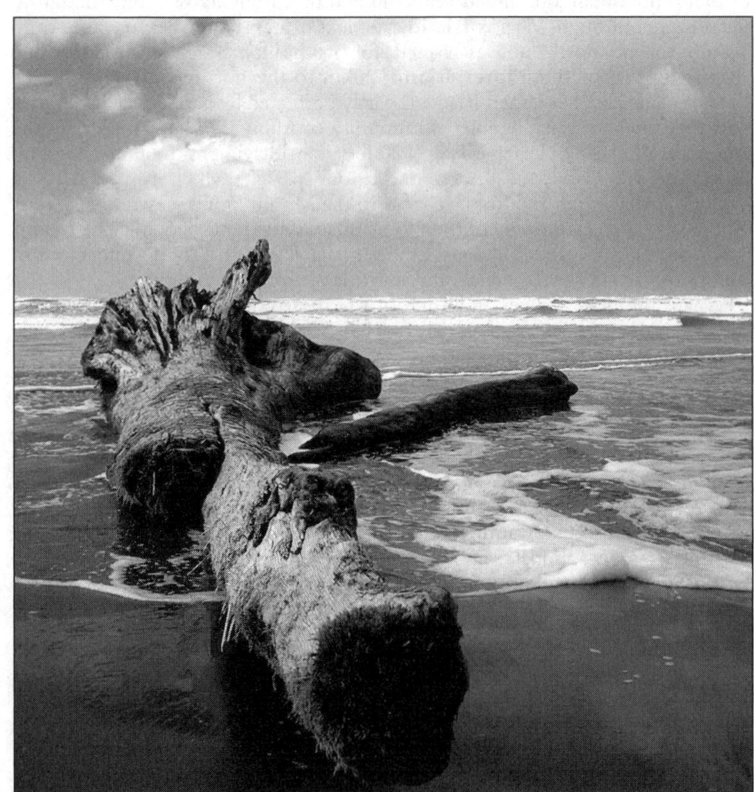

△ Driftwood on Long Beach

Long Beach walks

With an eye on the weather and tide, you can **walk** more or less anywhere on and around Long Beach. Various trails and roads drop to the beach from the main Hwy 4 road to Tofino. At the same time there are nine official trails, most of them short and very easy, so you could tackle a few in the course of a leisurely drive or cycle along the road. All the paths are clearly marked from Hwy 4, but it's still worth picking up a *Hiker's Guide* from the infocentre. From east to west you can choose from the following: The linked trails **1** and **2**, the **Willowbrae Trail** (2.8km round trip), are accessed by turning left at the main Hwy 4 junction and driving or biking 2km towards Ucluelet. A level wooded trail then leads from the trailhead towards the beach, following the steps of early pioneers who used this route before the building of roads between Tofino and Ucluelet. Just before the sea it divides, dropping steeply via steps and ramps, to either the tiny Half Moon Bay or the larger, neighbouring Florencia Bay to the north.

All other walks are accessed off Hwy 4 to Tofino, turning right (north) at the main Hwy 4 junction. The gentle **3 Gold Mine Trail** (3km round trip), signed left off the road, leads along Lost Shoe Creek, a former gold-mining area (look out for debris), to Florencia Beach. For walks **4**, **5** and **6**, take the turn left off the hwy for the Wickaninnish Centre. The **4 South Beach Trail** (1.5km round trip) leaves from behind the centre, leading above forest-fringed shores and coves before climbing to the headlands for a view of the coast and a chance to climb down to South Beach, famous for its big rock-crashing breakers and the sound of the water ripping noisily through the beach pebbles. The **5 Wickaninnish Trail** (5km) follows the South Beach Trail for a while and then at the top of the first hill is signed left, passing through rainforest – once again this is the route of the old pioneer trail – before ending at the parking area above Florencia Beach to the east. The **6 Shorepine Bog Trail** (800m) is a wheelchair-accessible boardwalk trail (accessed on the left on the access road to the centre) that wends through the fascinating stunted bog vegetation; trees which are just a metre or so tall here can be hundreds of years old.

Moving farther west towards Tofino along Hwy 4, the **7 Rain Forest Trails** are two small loops (1km each round trip), one on each side of the road, that follow a boardwalk through virgin temperate rainforest: each has interpretive boards detailing forest life cycle and forest "inhabitants" respectively. Farther down the road on the right at the Combers Beach parking area, a road gives access to the gentle **8 Spruce Fringe Trail** (1.5km loop). This graphically illustrates the effects of the elements on spruce forest, following a log-strewn beach fringe-edged with bent and bowed trees before entering more robust forest farther from the effects of wind and salt spray. It also crosses willow and crab-apple swamps to a glacial terrace, the site of a former shoreline, past the airport turn-off. The final walk, the **9 Schooner Beach Trail** (1km one-way), leads left off the road through superb tranches of rainforest to an extremely scenic beach at Schooner Cove. This might be the end of the official trails, but don't fail to climb to the viewpoint on **Radar Hill** off to the right as you get closer to Tofino.

Scenery aside, Long Beach is noted for its **wildlife**, the BC coastline reputedly having more marine species than any other temperate area in the world. As well as the smaller stuff in tidal pools – starfish, anemones, snails, sponges and suchlike – there are large mammals like whales and sea lions, as well as thousands of migrating birds (especially in Oct & Nov), notably pintails, mallards, black brants and Canada geese. Better weather brings out lots of beachcombers (Japanese glass fishing floats are highly coveted), clam diggers, anglers, surfers, canoeists, windsurfers and divers, though the water is usually too cold to venture in without a wet suit, and rip currents and rogue lumps of driftwood crashed around by the waves can make swimming dangerous. Surf guards patrol the Long Beach day-use area in July and August. And finally, try to resist the temptation to pick up shells as souvenirs – it's against park regulations.

Beaches near Long Beach

As this is a national park, some of Long Beach and its flanking stretches of coastline have been very slightly tamed for human consumption, but in a most discreet and tasteful manner. The best way to get a taste of the area is to walk the beaches or forested shorelines themselves – there are plenty of hidden coves – or to follow any of nine very easy and well-maintained **hiking trails** (see box, p.917). If you're driving or biking along Hwy 4, which backs the beaches all the way, there are distinct areas to look out for. Moving west, the first of these is the five-kilometre **Florencia Beach** (1.5km from the Hwy; access by trails 1, 2, 3 and 5; see p.917), also known as Wreck Beach and formerly the home of hippie beach dwellers in driftwood shacks before the park's formation. This is something of a local favourite, with relatively few people and good rock pools.

Farther along Hwy 4 you come to a turn-off (Long Beach Road) for the **Wickaninnish Centre** (mid-March to mid-Oct daily 10.30am–6pm; ⓣ250/726-4701) on a headland at the start of Long Beach, not to be confused with the similarly named well-known hotel and restaurant closer to Tofino (confusingly, the centre also has a restaurant). Wickaninnish was a noted nineteenth-century aboriginal chief, and arbitrator between Europeans and aboriginal fur traders. His name left no doubt as to his number-one status, as it means "having no one in front of him in the canoe". The centre is the departure point for several trails (see box, p.917), has telescopes for whale-spotting and a variety of films, displays and exhibits relating to the park and ocean. Around 8km beyond the Long Beach Road turn-off is the entrance to the Green Point park **campsite** (see below) and additional access to Long Beach, while 4km beyond that lies the turn-off on the right to Tofino's small airstrip. Around here the peninsula narrows, with **Grice Bay** coming close to the road on the right (north side), a shallow inlet known in winter for its countless wildfowl. Beyond the airstrip turn-off comes a trail to Schooner Cove (see box, p.917) and 3.5km beyond that a 1.5-kilometre turn-off to Kap'yong, or **Radar Hill** (96m), the panoramic site of a wartime radar station. By now Tofino is getting close, and 4.5km farther on (and a couple of kilometres outside the park boundary) you come to **Cox Bay Beach**, **Chesterman Beach** and **Mackenzie Beach**, all accessed from Hwy 4. Cox and Chesterman are known for their breakers; Mackenzie for its relative warmth if you want to chance a dip.

Practicalities

Long Beach's **Pacific Rim National Park Information Centre** is just off Hwy 4, 3km north of the T-junction for Tofino and Ucluelet. It provides a wealth of material on all aspects of the park, and in summer staff offer guided walks and interpretive programmes (daily mid-March to mid-June 10.30am–6pm; mid-June–Aug 8am–8pm; Sept to mid-Oct 10am–6pm; ⓣ250/726-4212, ⓦwww.parkscanada.gc.ca). For year-round information, call the Park Administration Office (ⓣ250/726-7721). For more Long Beach information, viewing decks with telescopes and lots of well-presented displays, head for the **Wickaninnish Centre**, Long Beach Road (mid-March to early Oct daily 10.30am–6pm; ⓣ250/726-4701).

There is one park **campsite**, the *Green Point*, set on a lovely bluff overlooking the beach (from $20.80 for the 94 drive-in sites; washrooms but no showers; $6.90 for firewood; 20 primitive walk-in sites $15.85). However, it's likely to be full every day in July and August, and it's first-come, first-served for the walk-in sites (reservations are taken up to three months in advance for the drive-in sites), so you may have to turn up for several days before getting a spot. There's usually a waiting-list system, however, whereby you're given a number and instructions as to when you should be able to return. The nearest commercial sites and conventional accommodation are in Tofino and Ucluelet.

Ucluelet

UCLUELET, 8km south of the main Hwy 4 Port Alberni junction, means "People of the Sheltered Bay", from the aboriginal word *ucluth* – "wind blowing in from the bay". It was named by the Nuu-chah-nulth, who lived here for centuries before the arrival of whites who came to exploit some of the world's richest fishing grounds immediately offshore. Today the port is still the third largest in BC by volume of fish landed, a trade that gives the town a slightly dispersed appearance and an industrial fringe – mainly lumber and canning concerns – and makes it a less appealing, if nonetheless popular base for anglers, whale-watchers, water-sports enthusiasts and tourists headed for Long Beach to the north.

If you want a breath of air in town, the nearest trails are at **Terrace Beach**, just east of the town off Peninsula Road before the lighthouse. A longer and more coherent trail, the **Wild Pacific Trail**, opened in 1999, though then it consisted of just 2.7km of path. However, the track is planned in seven phases, more of which are being completed annually. Currently, phases three and four have been accomplished, running along the rugged cliffs and shoreline northwest of the town. When the track is finished it will stretch 14km and link with Halfmoon Bay near Florencia Bay and Long Beach in the national park. The trail starts at the end of Coast Guard Road, passing the nearby Amphirite Point Lighthouse (great views of the ocean and perfect for storm-watching) and the He-Tin-Kis Park, where a boardwalk enables you to complete this first section as a loop. Other completed phases have pushed the track from Big Beach Park to the bike path just outside Ucluelet itself.

Practicalities

Buses and **boats** call at Ucluelet from Port Alberni and Tofino – a local transit bus generally makes the road trip twice a day en route to and from Tofino and/or Port Alberni, with one Laidlaw connection daily from Port Alberni to Nanaimo and Victoria. Boats from Port Alberni usually dock here three days a week (see p.908). There's plenty of accommodation (though less than Tofino), much of it spread on or just off Peninsula Road, the main approach to and through town from Hwy 4 (see below). A car or bike is useful here, as there's relatively little in the small central area, though location isn't vital unless you want to be near the sea. For full details, plus information on the many whale-watching, fishing and other tours, visit the **infocentre** at 2791 Pacific Rim Hwy (daily 10am–6pm, shorter hours in winter; ⓣ250/726-4600, ⓦwww.pacificrimvisitor.com).

Many companies are on hand to offer whale-watching, fishing and sightseeing **tours**. The longest-established outfit in the region is here, Subtidal Adventures, 1950 Peninsula Rd at the corner of Norah Rd (ⓣ250/726-7336 or 1-877/444-1134, ⓦwww.subtidaladventures.com). It runs all the usual boat trips in zodiacs or a ten-metre former coastguard rescue vessel, and do a nature tour to the Broken Group Islands with a beach stop.

Hotels and B&Bs

Canadian Princess Resort 1943 Peninsula Rd ⓣ250/726-7771 or 1-800/663-7090, ⓦwww.canadianprincess.com (March–Sept). The most unusual is also the most popular. Just west of the centre, with on-shore rooms or good-value one- to six-berth cabins (the smallest rooms share bathrooms) in a 175-metre 932 west-coast steamer moored in the harbour. You can also book upmarket whale-watching and fishing trips here in big, comfortable cabin cruisers and it has a restaurant and bar open to nonresidents. ❹–❽

Island West Fishing Resort 160 Hemlock St ⓣ250/726-4624, ⓦwww.islandwestresort.com. Overlooking the boat basin and marina, it has a pub on site for drinks and food and also organizes fishing charters and tours. ❹

Little Beach Resort 1187 Peninsula Rd ⓣ250/726-4202, ⓔlittlebeachresort@telus.net;, On the prettier outskirts, with quiet self-contained one- and two-bedroom suites with kitchenettes and just a few steps from Little Beach with great views to the south. ❸–❻

Ocean's Edge B&B 855 Barkley Crescent ⓣ250/726-7099, ⓦwww.oceansedge.bc.ca. On the end of Peninsula Rd by the lighthouse, a three-room place in old-growth forest with views and private entrance and bathroom. ❺

Pacific Rim Motel 1755 Peninsula Rd ⓣ250/726-7728. Relatively inexpensive, a place between the harbour and small centre near the corner of Bay St. ❹

Surf's Inn Backpackers' Lodge 1874 Peninsula Rd ⓣ250/726-4426, ⓦwww.surfsinn.ca;, A key inexpensive choice, centrally located in a restored family home overlooking the seafront. Single beds cost $24 and there are family and private double rooms from $55. ❶

Campsites

Public Campsite 260 Seaplane Base Rd (first right off Peninsula Rd after the *Canadian Princess*) ⓣ250/726-4355, ⓦwww.islandwestresort.com; $17–35; April–Oct. Overlooks the harbour to the west of the centre and has washroom and shower facilities. The central *Island West Fishing Resort* (see opposite) also has an RV campsite. It is also the base for a wide range of tour and charter operators.

Eating and drinking

Blueberries 1627 Peninsula Rd ⓣ250/726-7707. It serves coffee and snacks, breakfast, lunch and dinner (from $10–20), is licensed, and has an outdoor patio with sea views.

Boat Basin Restaurant 1971 Harbour Crescent ⓣ250/726-4644. On the marina and a little more upscale, with dinner from about $20. Dinner only from 4pm.

Smiley's 1992 Peninsula Rd ⓣ250/726-4213. The best place to sample the fresh seafood. A no-frills, no-decor diner popular with locals (eat in or take out), and to work off the meal there's five-pin bowling and billiards here as well.

The Broken Group Islands

The only way for the ordinary traveller to approach these hundred or so islands, speckled across Barkley Sound between Ucluelet and Bamfield, is by sea plane, chartered boat or boat tours from Port Alberni or Ucluelet (see p.919 and below); boats dock at Sechart, where you can stay at the former whaling station (see opposite). Immensely wild and beautiful, the islands have the reputation for tremendous wildlife (seals, sea lions and whales especially), the best **canoeing** in North America, and some of the continent's finest **scuba diving**. You can hire canoes and gear – contact the *Lady Rose* office in Port Alberni or Tofino Sea Kayaking at 320 Main St, Tofino (ⓣ250/725-4222), and then take them on board the *Lady Rose* to be dropped off en route (check current arrangements). You need to know what you're doing, however, as there's plenty of dangerous water and you should pick up the relevant marine chart (Canadian Hydrographic Service Chart: Broken Group 3670), available locally or from the CHS in Sidney (ⓣ250/363-6358). Divers can choose from among fifty shipwrecks claimed by the reefs, rough waters and heavy fogs that beset the aptly named islands. Note that the sheer number of people now visiting the islands, and the state in which they leave some of the campsites, official and otherwise, means that measures are being considered to introduce a quota system: contact the park information centre for latest details.

Nuu-chah-nulth whale hunts

All the peoples of the Northwest coast are famed for their skilfully constructed canoes, but only the **Nuu-chah-nulth** – whose name translates roughly as "all along the mountains" – used these fragile cedar crafts to pursue whales, an activity that was accompanied by elaborate ritual. Before embarking on a whaling expedition the whalers not only were to be trained in the art of capturing these mighty animals but also to be purified through a rigorous programme of fasting, sexual abstinence and bathing. Whalers also visited forest shrines made up of a whale image surrounded by human skulls or corpses and carved wooden representations of deceased whalers – the dead were thought to aid the novice in his task and to bring about the beaching of dead whales near the village.

When the whaler was on the chase, his wife would lie motionless in her bed; it was thought that the whale would become equally docile. His crew propelled the canoe in total silence until the moment of the harpooning, whereupon they frantically back-paddled to escape the animal's violent death throes as it attempted to dive, only to be thwarted by a long line of floats made from inflated sea-lion skins. After exhausting itself, the floating whale was finally killed and boated back to the village, where its meat would be eaten and its blubber processed for its highly prized oil.

The *Sechart Whaling Station Lodge* (book by calling ⓣ250/723-8313 or 1-800/663-7192; ❼) is a potentially magical base for exploring and the only place to **stay** if you're not wilderness camping on the archipelago. Access is via the MV *Lady Rose*, which docks nearby (see p.908 for detailed schedule to the islands). Seven rough **campsites** also serve the group, but water is hard to come by; pick up the park leaflet on camping and freshwater locations.

Bamfield

BAMFIELD is a quaint spot, half-raised above the ocean on a wooden boardwalk, accessible by unpaved road from Port Alberni 102km to the north, by boat – the MV *Lady Rose* – or gravel road from Lake Cowichan 113km to the east. Shuttle **buses** run along the Port Alberni road route if you're without transport and don't want to take the boat: for details, see the "West Coast Trail" box, p.895, and the box feature on p.926. The village is best known as the northern starting point of this trail (the trailhead is 5km away at Pachena Bay), but its population jumps to well over 2000 in the summer with the arrival of divers, canoeists, kayakers and fishermen, the last attracted by its suitability as a base for salmon fishing in the waters of Alberni Inlet and Barkley Sound. Plenty of services have sprung up in the more downbeat part of the village away from the boardwalk to meet visitors' demands, with lots of tours, fishing charters, stores and galleries, but only relatively limited accommodation (see p.922).

Bamfield began life, like so many communities in Canada, as a fur-trading and fishing settlement. The Pacific Cable Board then chose it as the eastern terminus for its trans-Pacific cable, one of the great communication breakthroughs of the late 19th century. The Bamfield cable station opened in 1902, the year in which a 6000-kilometre cable was laid to Fanning Island, a tiny atoll in the mid-Pacific, which was linked in turn to Fiji, New Zealand and Australia.

Despite the influx the village retains its charm, with the boardwalk accessing one side of Bamfield Inlet (the open sea, the other), so that the bay below the boardwalk is a constant hum of activity as boats ply across the water. Trails lead down from the boardwalk to a series of nice small beaches. The village is a good place to join in the activities, bird-watch, walk, beachcomb, sit in cafés or simply relax in a quiet corner with a book. For a short stroll, wander to **Brady's Beach** or the Cape Beale Lighthouse and Keeha and Tapaltos beaches some way beyond. And if you just want to tackle the stage to the trailhead of the West Coast Trail and return to Bamfield in a day, you can walk the 10km (round trip) to the **Pachena Lighthouse**, starting from the Ross Bible Camp on the Ohiaht First Nation campsite at Pachena Beach. After that, the route becomes the real thing.

Information and accommodation

Bamfield's **infocentre** booth is in Centennial Park (ⓣ250/728-3006, ⓦwww.bamfieldcommunity.com & ⓦwww.bamfieldchamber.com), but is open daily (9am–7/8pm) only in July and August. The village has only limited and mainly expensive **accommodation**, including the modest *McKay Bay Lodge* (ⓣ250/728-3323, ⓦwww.bamfield-travel.com; ❺; May–Oct), which overlooks the harbour and is good for families and fishing enthusiasts. Another option is the excellent *Woods End Landing Cottages*, 168 Wild Duck Rd, which has six secluded and high-quality self-contained log cottages sleeping up to four people on a two-acre waterfront site with great opportunities for outdoor activities, bird-watching, scuba diving and kayaking (ⓣ250/728-3383, ⓦwww.woodsend.travel.bc.ca; ❼). Less expensive is the five-room *Imperial Eagle Lodge*, 168 Wild Duck Rd (ⓣ250/728-3430, ⓦwww.imperialeaglelodge.com; ❻), which has a spectacular garden setting and fine harbour views plus hiking, fishing and other outdoor activities; breakfast is included in the room price.

If you're **camping**, try the Ohiaht First Nation Pachena Bay band, which occasionally offers a campsite (ⓣ250/728-1287, ⓔpachena@island.net; call for reservations, which are essential, and for latest prices) at Pachena Beach.

Northern Vancouver Island

It's a moot point where the **north of Vancouver Island** starts, but if you're travelling on Hwy 19 the landscape's sudden lurch into more unspoilt wilderness after Qualicum Beach makes as good a watershed as any. The scenery north of Qualicum Beach is uneventful but restful on the eye, and graced with ever-improving views of the mainland. Along Hwy 19 is the hamlet of Buckley Bay, which consists of little more than a ferry terminal to **Denman** and **Hornby islands** (16 sailings daily; 10min; foot passengers $6.05/5.75 return; a car $14.50/12.60 return).

Few of the towns along Hwy 19 amount to much, and you could bus, drive or hitch the length of Vancouver Island to Port Hardy and take the **Inside Passage** ferry up to Prince Rupert – the obvious and most tantalizing itinerary – without missing a lot. Alternatively, you could follow the main hwy only as far as **Courtenay**, and from there catch a ferry across to the mainland. If you have the means, however, try to get into the wild, central interior, much of it contained within **Strathcona Provincial Park**.

Denman and Hornby islands

Denman and **Hornby Islands** are two outposts that have been described, with some justification, as the "undiscovered Gulf Islands". Big-name celebrities have recently bought property here, complementing a population made up of artists, craftspeople and a laid-back (if wary) mishmash of alternative types. Ferries drop you on Denman on the west coast a few moments' walk from Denman Village: to get to Hornby you need to head 11km across Denman on Denman Road to another terminal at Gravelly Bay, where a fifteen-minute crossing drops you at Hornby's Shingle Spit dock. Most of what happens on Hornby, however, happens at **Tribune Bay** on the far side of the island, 10km away – try hitching a lift from a car coming off the ferry if you're without transport. There's no public transport on either island, so you'll need a car or bike to explore.

Highlights on Denman, the less retrogressive of the islands, are the beaches of the Sandy Island Provincial Marine Park, an island off the northwest tip (take Northwest Rd from the village), and the 800-metre loop trail of Boyle Point Park at the southernmost tip (just beyond the Gravelly Bay ferry terminal) to the Chrome Island Lighthouse. A left turn off Denman Road about 4km, or a third of the way to the terminal, brings you to Fillongley Provincial Park, where there's a provincial campsite (see below), forest trails and a pretty stretch of coastline.

On sleepy Hornby you want to be looking at the **Helliwell Bay Provincial Park** at the island's southern tip (take Helliwell Road from Tribune Bay) and its trails, the best a six-kilometre (1hr–1hr 30min) loop to Helliwell Bluffs, offering plenty of opportunities to see eagles, herons, spring wild flowers and lots of aquatic wildlife. Whaling Station Bay and Tribune Bay Provincial Park have very good beaches (and there's a nudist beach at Little Tribune Bay just to the south of the latter), with a campsite (see below) at Tribune Bay.

Practicalities

Accommodation is in short supply on both islands, and it's virtually essential in summer to have prebooked rooms. On Denman the main options are the *Sea Canary Bed & Breakfast*, 3305 Kirk Rd (Ⓣ250/335-2949 or 1-877/336-2949; ④), close to the ferry terminal (turn left on Northwest Rd then left again on Kirk) with three guestrooms, and the *Hawthorn House Bed and Breakfast*, 3375 Kirk Rd (Ⓣ250/335-0905; ⑤), a restored 1904 heritage building also with three rooms. There's a small (ten-site), rural provincial park **campsite** at Fillongley Provincial Park, close to old-growth forest and pebbly beach 4km across the island from the ferry on the east shore facing the Lambert Channel (summer $17, winter $9). Other B&Bs come and go: try Ⓦwww.denmanisland.com for new arrivals.

Hornby has marginally more **rooms** and **campsites**: *Sea Breeze Lodge*, Big Tree 3–2, Fowler Rd (Ⓣ250/335-2321, Ⓦwww.seabreezelodge.com; ⑧), with fifteen waterfront cottages with sea views, and camping at *Bradsdadsland Waterfront Campsite*, 1980 Shingle Spit Rd (Ⓣ250/335-0757, Ⓦwww.bradsdadsland.com; tents $35–50; April–Oct), 3.3km from the ferry terminal. *Ford's Cove Marina* at Ford's Cove, 12km from the ferry at Government Wharf (Ⓣ250/335-2169; cottages generally let weekly, tents $20–26) has six fully equipped cottages, grocery store and camp and RV sites. There's also the big *Tribune Bay Campsite*, Shields Road (Ⓣ250/335-2359, Ⓦwww.tribunebay.com; $22–27; April–Oct), a wooded site close to a sandy beach and with hot showers, restaurant and bike rental.

Eating places on Denman are concentrated near the ferry, the best being the *Denman Island Store and Café*. At the ferry dock on Hornby is *The Thatch*, a tourist-oriented restaurant, pub and deli with great views. Across at Tribune Bay the Co-op (no street address) is the hub of island life, with virtually everything you'll need in the way of food and supplies (Ⓣ250/335-1121). There's a café, *Jan's*, and a bike-rental outlet here, the Off-Road Bike Shop, which rents bikes in summer. For further **information** on Hornby, including accommodation, call Ⓣ250/335-0506 or visit Ⓦwww.hornbyisland.com.

△ Hikers on the West Coast Trail

Courtenay

Back along Hwy 19 beyond Buckley Bay is a short stretch of wild, pebbly beach, and then the Comox Valley, open rural country that's not as captivating as the brochures might lead you to expect. Of three settlements here – Comox, Cumberland and **COURTENAY** – only the last is of real interest for all but the most committed Vancouver Island devotee, and only then for its quaint (but tiny) downtown area and as a ferry link to Powell River on the mainland. The terminal is a good twenty minutes' drive from the town down back roads – hitching is almost impossible, so you have to take a taxi or hold out for the #11 bus from 4th Ave and Cliffe. Courtenay is connected to Nanaimo and Victoria by **bus** (4 daily), and is the terminus for **trains** from Victoria (1 daily). If you get stranded in town, there are plenty of **motels** along the strip on the southern approach, close to the black steam engine and **infocentre** at 2040 Cliffe Ave (daily 9am–5pm, longer hours in summer; ⓣ250/334-3234 or 1-888/357-4471, ⓦwww.comoxvalleychamber.com). The best **camping** is 20km north of Courtenay at Miracle Beach Provincial Park – a vast, but very popular, tract of sand ($22 in summer, $9 in winter; day-use parking $5).

The **Comox Valley** scores higher inland, on the eastern fringes of Strathcona Provincial Park (see p.928) and the **skiing** areas of Forbidden Plateau and Mount Washington, 25km northwest of Comox. There's plenty of **hiking and mountain biking** in summer, when the Forbidden Plateau lifts operate at weekends. A great day-hike on Mount Washington is the five-hour walk on well-marked trails from the ski area across Paradise Meadows to Moat Lake or Circlet Lake. For details of tougher walks (Battleship Lake, Lady Lake), ask at the infocentre. Access to the trailheads is by minor road from Courtenay.

Campbell River

Of the hundred or so Canadian towns that claim to be "Salmon Capital of the World", **CAMPBELL RIVER**, 46km north of Courtenay, is probably the one that comes closest to justifying the boast. Fish and fishing dominate the place to a ludicrous degree, and you'll soon be heartily sick of pictures of grinning anglers holding impossibly huge chinook salmon. Massive shoals of these monsters are forced into the three-kilometre channel between the town and the mainland, making the job of catching them little more than a formality. The town grew to accommodate fishermen from the outset, centred around a hotel built in 1904 after word spread of the colossal fish that local Cape Mudge natives were able to pluck from the sea. Today about sixty percent of all visitors come to dangle a line in the water. Others come for the scuba diving, while for the casual visitor the place serves as the main road access to the wilds of Strathcona Provincial Park or an overnight stop en route for the morning departures of the MV *Uchuck III* from Gold River (see p.929).

If you want to **fish**, hundreds of shops and guides are on hand to help out and hire equipment. It'll cost about $25 a day for the full kit, and about $60 and upwards for a morning's guidance. Huge numbers of people, however, fish ($2 plus licence) from the 182-metre **Discovery Pier**, Canada's first saltwater fishing pier. If you merely want to know something about salmon before they end up on a plate, drop in on the **Quinsam Salmon Hatchery**, 5km west of town on the road to Gold River (daily 8am–4pm).

Campbell River's well-stocked **infocentre** is at 1235 Shopper's Row (daily 9am–6pm; ⓣ250/287-4636, ⓦwww.visitorinfo.incampbellriver.com). Four Laidlaw **buses** run daily to Victoria, but there's only one, occasionally two, a day north to Port Hardy and towns en route. Airlines big and small also **fly** here (see Vancouver "Listings" on p.844 for details). The **bus terminal** is on the corner of Cedar and 13th near the Royal Bank (ⓣ250/287-7151). **Accommodation** is no problem, with numerous motels, Campbell River being a resort first and foremost: try the carving-stuffed *Campbell River Lodge and Fishing Resort,* a kilometre north of the town centre at 1760 North Island Hwy (ⓣ250/287-7446 or 1-800/663-7212, ⓦwww.campbellriverinns.com; ④). The place to **camp** locally lies 5km west of town at the *Parkside Campground*, 6301 Gold River Hwy (ⓣ250/830-1428, ⓦwww.parksidecampingrv.com; $20–25; May–Oct).

Cheap **places to eat** abound, mainly of the fast-food variety, and in the pricier restaurants there's no prize for spotting the main culinary emphasis.

Quadra Island

Quadra Island and its fine beaches and museum are fifteen minutes away from Campbell River and make a nice respite from the fish, though the famous fishing lodge here has been host to such big-name fisherfolk over the years as John Wayne, Kevin Costner and Julie Andrews. Ferries run roughly hourly from the well-signed terminal out of town ($6.05 return for foot passengers, $12.60 return for a car). The main excuse for the crossing is the **Kwagiulth Museum and Cultural Centre**, in Cape Mudge Village south of the terminal near the island's southern tip (take Cape Mudge Rd). The island's other, and main community, Heriot Bay, is on the east coast. The centre is home to one of the country's most noted collections of aboriginal regalia (ⓣ250/285-3733). As elsewhere in Canada, the masks, costumes and ritual objects were confiscated by the government in 1922 in an attempt to stamp out one of the natives' most potent ceremonies, and only came back in the 1980s on condition they would be locked up in a museum. The museum has around three hundred articles, and you should also ask directions to the petroglyphs in the small park across the road.

While on the island you could also laze on its beaches, walk its **trails** – Mortle Lake (5km loop) and Newton Lake from Granite Bay (8km round-trip) – or

The West Coast Trail

One of North America's classic walks, the **West Coast Trail** starts 5km south of Bamfield (see p.921) and traverses exceptional coastal scenery for 77km to Port Renfrew. It's no stroll, and though becoming very popular – quotas operate to restrict numbers – it still requires experience of longer walks, proper equipment and a fair degree of fitness. Many people, however, do the first easy stage as a day-trip from Bamfield. Reckon on five to eight days for the full trip; carry all your own food, camp where you can, and be prepared for rain, treacherous stretches, thick soaking forest and almost utter isolation.

As originally conceived, the trail had nothing to do with promoting the great outdoors. Mariners long ago dubbed this area of coastline the "graveyard of the Pacific", and when the SS *Valencia* went down with all hands here in 1906 the government was persuaded that constructing a trail would at least give stranded sailors a chance to walk to safety along the coast (trying to penetrate the interior's rainforest was out of the question). The path followed a basic telegraph route that linked Victoria with outlying towns and lighthouses, and was kept open by linesmen and lighthouse keepers until the 1960s, when it fell into disrepair. Early backpackers reblazed the old trail; many thousands now make the trip annually, and the numbers, so far as quotas allow, are rising (see below). The trail passes through the land of the Pacheenaht First Nation near Port Renfrew then passes through Ditidaht First Nation country before ending at Bamfield in the traditional territory of the Ohiaht First Nation. Wardens from each of these tribes work in association with Parks Canada to oversee the trail's management and the care of traditional native villages and fishing areas.

Weather is a key factor in planning any trip; the trail is really only passable between June & Sept (July is the driest month), which is also the only period when it's patrolled by wardens and the only time locals are on hand to ferry you (for a fee) across some of the wider rivers en route. However, you should be prepared for dreadful weather and poor trail conditions at all times. Take cash with you to pay for ferries and nominal fees for camping on native land.

Practicalities

Pre-planning is essential if you wish to walk the trail, as Parks Canada has a **quota system** and reservation–registration–orientation procedures to protect the environment. Numbers are limited to around 8000 a year while the path is open (mid-April/May to end-Sept). A total of sixty people are allowed onto the trail each day: 26 starting at Port Renfrew centre (trailhead is 5km north of the town; trailhead infocentre ☎250/647-5434; daily in season 9am–6pm), 26 at Bamfield-Pachena Bay (trail starts 5km south of Bamfield; infocentre ☎250/728-3234, daily in season 9am–6pm) and eight from Nitinat Village. These are the *only* allowed entrance and exit points from the trail, except in exceptional circumstances.

Note that the quota system does not apply in the shoulder season (May to mid-June & last two weeks of Sept), as Parks Canada found the quotas were not being taken up. However, it still makes sense to reserve the necessary West Coast Trail (WTC) Overnight Use Permit – effectively your passport to the trail and its ferry crossings – in these periods.

Reservations can be made from April of the year you wish to walk for June departures, May 1 for July departures, June 1 for Aug departures and July 1 for Sept walks. The phones start ringing on the first of the month, so move fast. To make bookings, call ☎250/387-1642 or 1-800/435-5622 (Mon–Fri 7am–9pm). Be ready to nominate the location from which you wish to start, the date of departure, two alternative start dates, credit card details and the number in your party. July and August are the most popular months.

It **costs** $25 to make a reservation (payment by Visa or MasterCard). This is nonrefundable, though you may change your date of departure if spaces are available on another day. Another $110 per person is payable as a user fee, paid in person at the beginning of the trail. Allow another $20 or so to pay for each of the two ferry crossings (at Gordon River and Nitinat narrows) along the route (paid at the WCT centres at the orientation sesssion – see below: the WTC Overnight Permit is your receipt for these crossings). The total you'll pay is around $155. Standby hikers pay the same rates minus the booking fee. You must then register in person at the park centre at Bamfield or Port Renfrew between 9am and 12.30pm on the day you have booked to start your walk. (You may want to arrive the night before – if so, be sure to book accommodation in Bamfield if you're starting there.) If you miss this deadline your place is forfeited and will be given to someone on the **waiting list**.

Of the 52 places available each day at Pachena Bay and Gordon river, a minimum of ten (five at each departure point) are available on a first-come, first-served basis. Unless you're very lucky this still doesn't mean you can just turn up and expect to start walking. You must first register in person at either the Port Renfrew or Bamfield centre. Here you'll be given a waiting-list number and told when to come back, which could be in anything between two and ten days.

Finally you must attend compulsory 90-minute **orientation** sessions at the trailhead infocentre, where you will receive your permit and a briefing on conditions, safety issues and so forth. Gordon River sessions are at 9.30am, noon, 1.30pm and 3.30pm; at Pachena Bay they take place at 9.30am, 1.30pm and 3.30pm. Reservations are not required.

Further **information** regarding the trail, path conditions and preplanning can be obtained from the Parks Canada offices near Port Renfrew at the trailhead (Ⓣ250/647-5434), or from the infocentres in Tofino, Ucluelet, Long Beach or Port Alberni. Updated details are also given at Ⓦwww.parkscanada.gc.ca or Ⓦwww.pc.gc.ca/pn-np/bc/pacificrim. An increasing amount of literature and **route guides** are appearing on the trail every year, available directly, online or by mail order from most BC bookshops (see "Listings" for Vancouver p.844). Two of the best are *The West Coast Trail* by Tim Leaden (Douglas and McIntyre; $12.95) and the more irreverent *Blisters and Bliss: A Trekker's Guide to the West Coast Trail* by Foster, Aiteken and Dewey (B&B Publishing Victoria; $10.95). The recommended **trail map** is the 1:50,000 *West Coast Trail, Port Renfrew–Bamfield*, complete with useful hints for walking the trail, available locally or direct from the Ministry of the Environment, 553 Superior St, Victoria (Ⓣ250/387-1441).

Access to and from the trailheads is also an important consideration. Several small shuttle-bus companies have sprung up to run people to the trailheads, mostly from Victoria to Bamfield via Nanaimo, not all of which are likely to survive (see box feature on p.895 or consult the Victoria infocentre for latest updates). For the northern trailhead at Bamfield, the most exhilarating and reliable access is via the MV *Lady Rose* or other boats from Port Alberni (see p.895 for full details). Otherwise the West Coast Trail Express, 3954 Bow Rd, Victoria (May to early Oct; Ⓣ250/477-8700, Ⓦwww.tofinobus.com) runs a daily shuttle bus in each direction between Victoria and Pachena Bay/Bamfield via Duncan, Nanaimo; to Port Renfrew and back from Victoria; and between Bamfield and Port Renfrew (see p.895 for prices and more details). Pick-ups are possible from these points, but reservations are essential to secure a seat from any departure point. It also has a daily service to Port Renfrew.

climb Chinese Mountain (3km round-trip) in its rugged northern reaches for some cracking views. There's swimming in a warm, sheltered bay off a rocky beach at **Rebecca Spit Provincial Park**, a 1.5-kilometre spit near Drew Harbour 8km east of the ferry terminal, but the water's warmer still and a trifle sandier at the more distant **Village Bay Park**.

Around seven places offer **accommodation**, including the *Heriot Bay Inn & Marina* on Heriot Bay Rd (ⓣ250/285-3322, ⓦwww.heriotbayinn.com; ❹–❻, camping $15–22), which has cottages, 13 camping and RV sites, and the superb *Tsa-Kwa-Luten Lodge*, 1 Lighthouse Rd (ⓣ250/285-2042 or 1-800/665-7745, ⓦwww.capemudgeresort.com; ❻; campsites at $30–40), a waterfront lodge by the Cape Mudge Lighthouse. Based on a long house, and with a predominantly aboriginal decorative scheme and design, it was built by local aboriginal people amid forest on high bluffs overlooking Discovery Passage. There is a restaurant, cottage and lodge units, and many facilities including sauna, Jacuzzi, laundry and access to numerous tours and outdoor activities. The island's only official **campsite** is at the *Heriot Bay Inn* (see above).

Cortes Island

If you've taken the trouble to see Quadra Island, then you should push on to the still quieter **Cortes Island** (ⓦwww.cortesisland.com), 45 minutes from Quadra on a second ferry (5 daily; foot passenger $7.25/6.55 return, car $16.50/14.25), an island with a deeply indented coastline at the neck of Desolation Sound, among North America's finest sailing and kayaking areas. Life here is very relaxed indeed, with the main community at **Manson's Landing**, 15km from the ferry terminal at Whaletown.

Boating aside, the island is known for its superlative clams and oysters, exported worldwide, and for one of Canada's leading holistic centres, the Hollyhock Retreat Centre on Highland Road (ⓣ250/935-6576 or 1-800/933-6339, ⓦwww.hollyhock.bc.ca), where you can sign up for all manner of body- and soul-refreshing courses and stay in anything from a tent, dorm or private cottage. Other **accommodation** includes the *Old Floathouse* (ⓣ250/935-6631) at the *Gorge Harbour Marina Resort* (ⓣ250/935-6433) on Hunt Rd, 5km from the ferry, where you can also stay (❹), camp ($15–17) and rent boats and scooters. For something less expensive, join the locals on the nice terrace at the *Cortes Café* in Manson's Landing.

Places to make for around the island include the small **Smelt Bay Provincial Park**, 25km south of the ferry, which has a provincial campsite (summer $14, winter $9) and opportunities to swim, fish, canoe and walk, and the nearly adjacent **Manson's Landing Provincial Park** (good beaches) and **Hague Lake Provincial Park**, signed from Manson's Landing, with several looped trails such as Sutil Point accessible from different points on the road. If you're in a canoe or boat then you can also make for a couple of marine parks (Von Donop and Mansons Landing) and any number of delightful small bays, lagoons and beaches.

Strathcona Provincial Park

Vancouver Island's largest protected area, and the oldest park in British Columbia, **Strathcona Provincial Park** (established in 1911) is one of the few places on the island where the scenery approaches the grandeur of the mainland mountains. The island's highest point, Golden Hinde (2220m) is here, and it's also a place where there's a good chance of seeing rare indigenous wildlife (the Roosevelt elk, marmot and black-tailed deer are the most notable examples).

Only two areas have any sort of facilities for the visitor – **Forbidden Plateau** on the park's eastern side, approached from Courtenay, and the more popular **Buttle Lake** region, accessible from Campbell River via Hwy 28. The rest of the park is unsullied wilderness, but fully open to backpackers and hardier walkers. Be sure to pick up the blue *BC Parks* pamphlet (available from the infocentre at Campbell River and elsewhere): it has a good general map and gives lots of information, such as the comforting fact that there are no grizzly bears in the park.

You'll see numerous pictures of **Della Falls**, around Campbell River, which (at 440m) are Canada's highest (and amongst the world's highest), though unfortunately it'll take a two-day trek and a canoe passage if you're going to see them.

The approach to the park along Hwy 28 is worth taking for the scenery alone; numerous short trails and nature walks are signposted from rest stops, most no more than twenty-minutes' stroll from the car. **Elk Falls Provincial Park**, noted for its gorge and waterfall, is the first stop, ten minutes out of Campbell River. It also has a large provincial park **campsite** (summer $14, winter $9; backcountry camping $5). On the access road and lakeshore proper, good **shorter trails** include the 500-metre stroll to Lupin Falls, an impressive cataract; the Karst Creek Trail (2km loop), which runs through a strange limestone landscape of sinkholes and vanishing streams; Bedwell Lake at the lake's southern end, a steep (600-metre ascent) ten-kilometre round-trip trail to the eponymous lake and high meadows (allow 2hr each way); and Upper Myra Falls (3km each way), which climbs from near the end of the road to a viewpoint over the Myra waterfall.

Fifteen **information** shelters around the lake provide some trail and wildlife information. Buttle Lake has two provincial **campsites** with basic facilities – one alongside the park centre at Buttle Lake, the other at Ralph River (both summer $14, winter $9) on the extreme southern end of Buttle Lake, accessed by the road along the lake's eastern shore. Both have good **swimming** areas nearby. Backcountry camping costs $5. The park's only commercial **accommodation** is provided by the *Strathcona Park Lodge* (Ⓣ250/286-3122, Ⓦwww.strathcona.bc.ca; ❹–❼), just outside the Buttle Lake entrance, a mixture of hotel and outdoor-pursuits centre. You can **rent canoes**, **bikes** and other outdoor equipment, and sign up for any number of organized tours and activities.

Gold River and Tahsis

There's not a lot happening at **GOLD RIVER**, a tiny logging community 89km west of Campbell River – founded in 1965 in the middle of nowhere to service a big pulp mill 12km away at Muchalat Inlet (it closed in 1998). The place only has one hotel and a couple of shops – but the ride over on Hwy 28 is superb, and there's the chance to explore the sublime coastline by boat, the main reason for the settlement's increasing number of visitors. Year-round, the **MV Uchuck III**, a converted World War II US minesweeper, takes mail, cargo and passengers to logging camps and settlements up and down the surrounding coast on a variety of routes (see box, p.932)

Boat aside, one of the area's two minor attractions is **Quatsino Cave**, the deepest vertical cave in North America, parts of which are open to the public – for details ask at the infocentre; the other is the **Big Drop**, a stretch of Gold River white water known to kayakers worldwide. The local **infocentre** is at the corner of Hwy 28 and Scout Lake Rd (mid-May to mid-Sept daily 9.30am–4/5pm; Ⓣ250/283-2418 or 283-7500, Ⓦwww.village.goldriver.bc.ca).

Hiking in Strathcona

Hiking, it hardly needs saying, is superb in Strathcona, with a jaw-dropping scenic combination of jagged mountains – including Golden Hinde (2220m), the island's highest point – lakes, rivers, waterfalls and all the trees you could possibly want. Seven marked **trails** fan out from the Buttle Lake area, together with six shorter nature walks, most less than 2km long, amongst which the Lady Falls and Lupin Falls trails stand out for their waterfall and forest views (see main text). All the longer trails can be tramped in a day, though the most popular, the **Elk River Trail** (10km), which starts from Drum Lake on Hwy 28, lends itself to an overnight stop. Popular with backpackers because of its gentle grade, the path ends up at Landslide Lake, an idyllic camping spot. The other highly regarded trail is the **Flower Ridge** walk, a steep 14-kilometre round-trip (extendable by 10km) which starts at the southern end of Buttle Lake and involves a very stiff 1250-metre elevation gain. The same lung-busting ascent is called for on the **Crest Mountain Trail** (10km round trip), a trail into high mountain country accessed from Hwy 28 at the park's western edge.

In the Forbidden Plateau area, named after a native legend that claimed evil spirits lay in wait to devour women and children who entered its precincts, the most popular trip is the **Forbidden Plateau Skyride** to the summit of Wood Mountain where there's a two-kilometre trail to a viewpoint over Boston Canyon. Backcountry camping is allowed throughout the park, and the backpacking is great once you've hauled up onto the summit ridges above the tree line. For serious exploration, buy the relevant topographic maps (1:50,000 -92F/11 *Forbidden Plateau* and -92F/12 *Buttle Lake* at MAPS BC, Ministry of Environment and Parks, Parliament Buildings, Victoria.

Accommodation is in short supply: the only large place is the *Ridgeview Motor Inn,* located in a panoramic spot above the village at 395 Donner Court (Ⓣ250/283-2277 or 1-800/989-3393, Ⓦwww.ridgeview-inn.com; ❹).

Note that there are also two beautiful roads north from Gold River, both rough, but worth the jolts for the scenery. One provides an alternative approach to **TAHSIS**, another logging community 70km northwest of Gold River, which has one basic **motel** with a restaurant and pub if you need to break your journey; advance summer reservations are needed at the twelve-room *Tahsis Motel*, Head Bay Rd (Ⓣ250/934-6318, Ⓦwww.tahsismotel.com; ❸); or try *Fern's Place B&B*, 379 North Maquinna (Ⓣ250/934-7851, Ⓦwww.fernsplace.biz; ❸).

North to Port McNeill and beyond

The main hwy north of Campbell River cuts inland and climbs through increasingly rugged and deserted country, particularly after Sayward, the one main community en route. Near Sayward is the marvellously oddball **Valley of a Thousand Faces**: 1400 famous faces painted onto cedar logs, the work of a Dutch artist, and more interesting than it sounds (May–Aug daily 10am–4pm; donation). With a car, you could strike off south from here to **Schoen Lake Provincial Park**, located 12km off Hwy 19 on a rough road south of Woss village and featuring a couple of forest trails and a small, ten-pitch, well-kept campsite ($10). Sayward has one **motel**, the *Fisherboy Park*, 400m off Hwy 19 at 1546 Sayward Rd (Ⓣ250/282-3204, Ⓦwww.fisherboypark.com; ❸), which also has 36 tent and RV sites ($12-18). **PORT McNEILL**, 180km north of Campbell River and the first real town along Hwy 19, is little more than a motel and logging centre and not somewhere to spend longer than necessary. If you get stuck here, the infocentre's at 351

Shelley Crescent (July–Aug 9am–5pm; rest of year hours variable; ⓣ250/956-3131, ⓦwww.portmcneill.net).

Telegraph Cove

By contrast, tiny **TELEGRAPH COVE**, 8km south of Port McNeill and reached by a rough side road, is likeable place, though not quite the best of BC's so-called "boardwalk villages", as its growing popularity, and the fact that it is now pretty much owned by a single company, has given it a slightly artificial and commercialized air that is not evident in somewhere like Bamfield (see p.921). The whole community is raised on wooden stilts over the water, a sight that's made it rather too popular with tourists for its own good. This is not to take away from its role as one of the island's premier **whale-watching** spots, the main attraction here being the pods of orcas (killer whales) that calve locally. Some nineteen of these families live or visit Robson Bight, 20km down the Johnstone Strait, which was established as an ecological reserve in 1982 (the whales like the gravel beaches, where they come to rub). This is the world's most accessible and predictable spot to see the creatures – around a ninety percent chance in season. The best outfit for a trip to see them is the founding whale company here, Stubbs Island Charters at the dock at the end of the boardwalk through the old village (ⓣ250/928-3185, 928-3117 or 1-800/665-3066, ⓦwww.stubbs-island.com). The first whale-watching company in BC, it runs 3hr 30min trips (2 daily at 9am & 1pm May–mid-July & late Aug–early Oct; 3 daily at 9am, 1pm & 5.30pm mid-July–late Aug; $79), but they're very popular, so call well in advance to be sure of a place.

In summer you can buy food at a café, boardwalk pub and resort (see below), but otherwise the only provision for visitors is an incongruous modern building with shop, ice-cream counter and coffee bar. The only **accommodation** is the large wooded *Telegraph Cove Resorts* (ⓣ250/928-3131 or 1-800/200-4665, ⓦwww.telegraphcoveresort.com; ❻, camping $20–25; May–Oct), a short walk from the village; reservations are essential in summer. It has seventeen rooms and 121 RV/tent sites with showers, laundry, restaurant, boat rentals and access to guides, charters and whale-watching tours. The *Hidden Cove Lodge* (ⓣ250/956-3916, ⓦwww.hiddencovelodge.com; ❼) at Lewis Point, a secluded cove on Johnstone Strait 7km from Telegraph Cove, has eight superb lodge units, but they go very quickly. The big *Alder Bay Resort* 6km off Hwy 19 en route for Telegraph Cove from Port McNeill provides grassy tent sites with ocean views (ⓣ250/956-4117, ⓦwww.alderbayresort.com; reservations recommended; $18–28; May–Sept).

Alert Bay

The breezy fishing village of **ALERT BAY**, on Cormorant Island, is reached by numerous daily ferries from Port McNeill just 8km away (foot passenger $7.10/6.85 return, car $18.05/15.60). The fifty-minute crossing in the migrating season provides a good chance of seeing whales en route. Despite the predominance of the non-indigenous industries (mainly fish processing), half the population of the island are aboriginal 'Namgis, and a day visit here offers the opportunity to get to grips with something of their history and to meet those who are keeping traditions alive. The **infocentre** (late June–Aug daily 9am–6pm; rest of year Mon–Fri 9am–5pm; ⓣ250/974-5024, ⓦwww.alertbay.bc.ca) is at 116 Fir St to your right as you come off the ferry. Also off to the right from the terminal are the totems of a 'Namgis Burial Ground; you're asked to view from a respectful distance.

Boats from Gold River

Like the MV *Lady Rose* out of Port Alberni, the **MV Uchuck III** boat trips started as a sideline. Very quickly, however, it has become far more of a commercial enterprise, with glossy pamphlets and extra summer sailings, though it's none the worse for that – you just have to book ahead to make sure of a place. For information and **reservations**, contact Nootka Sound Service Ltd (ⓣ250/283-2515 or 250/283-2325, ⓦwww.mvuchuck.com).

There are **three basic routes**, all of them offering wonderful windows onto the wilderness and wildlife (whales, bears, bald eagles and more) of the region's inlets, islands and forested mountains. The dock is at the end of Hwy 28, about 15km southwest of Gold River. There are scheduled halts, but also usually unscheduled calls at logging camps and the like.

The **Nootka Sound Day Trip** ($60 or $35 one-way to Friendly Cove) leaves Gold River every Wed and Sat at 10am July to mid-Sept. It returns at 4pm on Wed and 5.30pm on Sat, when there is a three-hour stop at Friendly Cove, or Kyuquot (the aboriginal name), the latter involving a $12 landing fee, proceeds from which go to the Mowachaht Band for the redevelopment of the aboriginal site. During the ninety-minute or three-hour halt aboriginal guides offer guided tours around their ancestral home. The previous stop, at Friendly Cove, is equally historic, for it was here that Captain Cook made his first-known landing on the west coast in 1778, from which, among other things, was to spring the important sea-otter fur trade. Whites named the area and people here "Nootka", though locals today say *nootka* was merely a word of warning to Cook and his crew, meaning "circle around" to avoid hitting offshore rocks. If you're equipped with provisions and wish to stay over, there are **cabins** and a **campsite** here, but call first to confirm arrangements (ⓣ250/283-2054).

The second trip, the **Kyuquot Adventure** ($260 single, $395 double), is a two-day overnight cruise, departing every Thurs year-round (April–Oct 7am; Nov–March 6am). It takes you much farther north up the coast, returning to Gold River at 4 or 5pm on Friday afternoon: accommodation is included, as is breakfast – though you make it yourself from food supplied – and you can buy Thursday's evening meal on board or onshore at Kyuquot.

The third trip, the **Zeballos Adventure** (single $215, double $335), is also a two-day trip, departing every Mon at 9am (April–Oct) and returning at 4pm on Tues. It combines a stop in Tahsis (see main text) and Friendly Cove (see above) and an overnight stay (with breakfast) in the coastal community of Zeballos.

A 25 percent deposit is required for these trips, refundable in full up until two weeks before departure. People on all trips should bring warm and waterproof clothing. There's a coffee shop on board for drinks and hot snacks. **Kayakers** should note that they can be deposited by lift into the sea at most points en route by prior arrangement.

Bear left from the terminal out of the main part of the village to reach the excellent **U'Mista Cultural Centre** on Front Street (mid-May to early Sept daily 9am–5pm; Oct to mid-May Mon–Fri 9am–5pm; $6.50; ⓣ250/974-5403, ⓦwww.umista.ca), a modern building based on old models, which houses a collection of potlatch items and artefacts. It also shows a couple of award-winning films, and you might also come across local kids being taught native languages, songs and dances. More local artefacts are on show in the library and small museum, open most summer afternoons, at 199 Fir St. For years the village also claimed the world's tallest fully carved **totem pole** (other contenders, say knowing villagers, are all pole and no carving), though much to local chagrin Victoria raised a pole in 1994 that the *Guinness Book of Records* has recognized as 2.1m taller. Also worth a look is the wildlife and weird swamp habitat at **Gator Gardens** behind the bay, accessible via several trails and boardwalks.

Sointula

SOINTULA village is a wonderful aberration. It's located on Malcolm Island, accessible by ferry en route from Port McNeill to Alert Bay (25min; foot passenger $7.10/6.85 return, car $18.05/15.60) and directly from Alert Bay (35min; foot passenger $4.50 one-way, car $7.50). The fishing village would be a good place to wander at any time, thanks to its briney maritime appeal, but what gives added lustre is the fact that it contains a tiny fossil Finnish settlement. An early cult community, it was founded with Finnish pioneers as a model co-operative settlement in 1901 by Matti Kurrika, a curious mixture of guru, dramatist and philosopher. In 1905 the experiment collapsed, but 100 Finns from the original settlement stayed on. Their descendants survive to this day, and you'll still hear Finnish being spoken on the streets. You can wander local beaches, explore the island interior by logging road, or spend a few minutes in the **Sointula Finnish Museum**, which is located on 1st Street just to the left after disembarking the ferry; you'll probably need to call someone (Ⓣ250/973-6353 or 973-6764) to come and open up and show you around.

There are two **B&Bs**: *430-2nd St Bed & Brekky*, 430-2nd St (Ⓣ250/973-6345, Ⓦwww.sointula430-2ndstbb.com; ④) – with inevitable Finnish sauna and the two-room *Sea 4 Miles*, 2km from the ferry at 145 Kaleva Rd (Ⓣ250/973-6486, Ⓦwww.sointulacottages.com; ④).

Port Hardy

Dominated by big-time copper mining, a large fishing fleet and the usual logging concerns, **PORT HARDY**, a total of 485km from Victoria and 230km from Campbell River, is best known among travellers as the departure point for ships plying one of the more spectacular stretches of the famous **Inside Passage** to Prince Rupert (and thence to Alaska) and the more recently introduced **Discovery Coast Passage** (see box, p.934). If you have time to kill waiting for boats, which leave from Bear Cove 10km away from the town centre, you could drop into the modest and occasionally open **town museum** at 7110 Market St (donation) or visit the **Quatse River Salmon Hatchery** (Mon–Fri 8/9am–4.30pm) on Hardy Bay Rd, just off Hwy 19 almost opposite the *Pioneer Inn*.

If possible, though, time your arrival to coincide with one of the Inside Passage **sailings** (see box, p.934) that leave every other day in summer and once or twice weekly in low season. **Bus** services aren't really scheduled to do this for you, with a Laidlaw bus generally timetabled to meet each *incoming* sailing from Prince Rupert. A Laidlaw bus (Ⓣ250/949-7532 in Port Hardy, Ⓣ250/385-4411 or 388-5248 in Victoria) also leaves Victoria daily (currently 11.45am), sometimes with a change in Nanaimo, arriving at the Port Hardy ferry terminal in the evening (currently 9.50pm) to connect with the ferry next morning; in summer an extra service departs from Victoria on the morning before ferry sailings. You can **fly** from Vancouver International Airport to Port Hardy (the airport is 12km south of the town) with Pacific Coastal Airlines (Ⓣ250/273-8666, Ⓦwww.pacific-coastal.com) from $148 one-way.

The Port Hardy **ferry terminal** is visible from town but is actually 10km away at Bear Cove, where buses stop before carrying on to terminate opposite the **infocentre**, 7250 Market St (year-round Mon–Fri 9am–5pm; early June to late Sept 8am–8pm; ⓣ250/949-7622, ⓦwww.ph-chamber.bc.ca). The infocentre can give you all the details about Port Hardy's tiny **museum** (see above) and the immense wilderness of **Cape Scott Provincial Park**, whose interior is accessible only by foot and which is supposed to have some of the most consistently bad weather in the world (and some of the most voracious biting insects). As a short taster you could follow the forty-minute hike from the small campsite and trailhead at San Josef River to some sandy beaches.

The Inside Passage

One of Canada's great trips, the **Inside Passage** aboard BC Ferries' *Queen of the North*, between Port Hardy and Prince Rupert on the British Columbia mainland, is a cheap way of getting what people on the big cruise ships are getting: 274 nautical miles of mountains, islands, waterfalls, glaciers, sea lions, whales, eagles and some of the grandest coastal scenery on the continent. By linking up with the Greyhound bus network or the VIA Rail terminal at Prince Rupert, it also makes a good leg in any number of convenient itineraries around British Columbia. Some travellers will have come from Washington State, others will want to press on from Prince Rupert to Skagway by boat and then head north into Alaska and the Yukon (see p.1023 for details on the Alaska Marine ferries). A lot of people simply treat it as a cruise, and sail north one day and return south to Port Hardy the next. If nothing else, the trip's a good way of meeting fellow travellers and taking a break from the interminable trees of the BC interior.

The boat carries 750 passengers and 160 cars and runs every two days, departing at 7.30am on **odd-numbered days** in Aug, **even-numbered days** in June, July, Sept and the first half of Oct. The journey takes around fifteen hours, arriving in Prince Rupert about 10.30pm, sometimes with a stop at Bella Bella. Be aware that from about Oct 15 to May 25 the sailings are less frequent in both directions and are predominantly at night (they leave Port Hardy in the late afternoon), which rather defeats the sightseeing object of the trip. On board there are cafeterias, restaurants and a shop (among other services); at the last, pick up the cheap and interesting *BC Ferries Guide to the Inside Passage* for more on the trip.

The cost from mid-June to mid-Sep (peak) is $116 single for a foot passenger (May & Oct $83; Nov–April $62), $275 for a car (May & Oct $193; Nov–April $146); reservations are **essential** throughout the summer season if you're taking a car or want a cabin. Bookings can be made by phone or online (ⓣ1-888/223-3779 toll-free in BC, ⓣ250/386-3431 from elsewhere, ⓦwww.bcferries.com), or by post to BC Ferry Corporation, 1112 Fort St, Victoria, BC, V8V 4V2. Include name and address; number in party; length, height and type of car; choice of day-room or cabin; and preferred date of departure and alternatives. Full payment is required up front. **Day cabins** can be reserved by foot passengers, and range from around $24 for two berths with basin, to $45 on the Promenade with two berths, basin and toilet. If you are making the return trip only you can rent **cabins overnight**, saving the hassle of finding accommodation in Port Hardy, but if you do you are obliged to take the cabin for the following day's return trip as well: cabins are not available as an alternative to rooms in town, so don't think you can rent a cabin overnight and then disappear next morning at Prince Rupert. Two-berth overnight cabins range from $75 with basin only to $145 for shower, basin and toilet. Reports suggest BC Ferries are not happy for passengers to roll out sleeping bags in the lounge area. If you're making a return trip and want to leave your car behind, there are several supervised lock-ups in Port Hardy. You can leave vehicles at the ferry terminal, but there have been incidents of vandalism in recent years so neither BC Ferries nor the Port Hardy infocentre recommend this. Note, again, that it is vital to book accommodation at

Increasingly popular, but demanding (allow eight hours plus), is the historic **Cape Scott Trail**, part of a complex web of trails hacked from the forest by early Danish pioneers. Around 28km has been reclaimed from the forest, opening a trail to the cape itself.

If you stay in town overnight, leave plenty of time to reach the ferry terminal – sailings in summer are usually around 7.30am. North Island Transportation provides a shuttle service between the ferry and the town's

your final destination before starting your trip; both Port Hardy and Prince Rupert hotels are very busy on days when the boat arrives.

The Discovery Coast Passage

The huge success of the Inside Passage sailing amongst visitors led BC Ferries to introduce the **Discovery Coast Passage**, a trip it candidly admits will only pay as a result of tourists. The route offers many of the scenic rewards of the Inside Passage, but over a shorter and more circuitous route between Port Hardy and **Bella Coola**, where you pick up the occasionally steep and tortuous road (Hwy 20) through the Coast Mountains to Williams Lake (see p.865) – it goes nowhere else. En route, the boat stops at McLoughlin Bay, Shearwater, Klemtu and Ocean Falls. If the route takes off as BC Ferries hope, you can expect visitor facilities to develop at these places – you can disembark at all of them – but at present the only places to stay overnight are campsites at McLoughlin Bay and a resort, hotels, cabins and B&B at Shearwater. Bella Coola is better equipped, and will probably become more so as the route becomes better known. BC Ferries is offering inclusive ferry and accommodation **packages** – even renting fishing tackle so you can fish over the side – and these too may mature as the service finds its feet.

There are **departures** roughly every couple of days between early June and the end of Sept, currently leaving Port Hardy at 9.30am on Tues and Thurs and at 9.30pm on Sat and returning from Bella Coola on Mon, Wed and Fri. There's a slight catch, however, for while the early morning departures offer you plenty of scenery, some arrive at McLoughlin Bay at 7.30pm and Bella Coola at 6.30am in the morning, meaning that the very best bit of the trip – along the inlet to Bella Coola – is in the middle of the night. The Thurs departures are quicker (they only stop once, at Ocean Falls) and make Bella Coola the same day, arriving at 10.30pm, so the problem is lessened. Alternatively take the 9.30pm departures and wake at McLoughlin Bay at 7.30am with a further daylight trip towards Bella Coola, arriving at 7.30am the next morning – read the timetables carefully. Making the trip southbound from Bella Coola gets round the problem, though there are similar staggered departure and arrival times (services currently leave Mon, Wed and Fri at 7.30 or 8am, arriving Port Hardy 9.30pm on the Mon departure, 7.45am on Wed sailing and 9am on the Fri boat), with overnight and same-day journeys and a variety of stopping points depending on the day you travel. Unlike the Inside Passage, there are **no cabins**: you sleep in aircraft-style reclining seats and – for the time being – sleeping bags seem OK on the floor: check for the latest on freestanding tents on the decks.

Reservations can be made through BC Ferries (see Inside Passage, opposite, for details). **Prices** for a foot passenger are $120 one-way to Bella Coola (plus a $18.30 fuel supplement), $72.50 to all other destinations. If you want to camp or stop over and hop on and off, the boat fares between any two of McLoughlin Bay, Ocean Falls and Klemtu are $24.50 (plus $4 fuel) and $45 ($7.15) from any of these to Bella Coola. Cars cost $241 from Port Hardy to Bella Coola (plus a $36.55 fuel supplement), $155 to all other destinations (and $88 for the single-leg options). To take a **canoe** or **kayak** costs $12.75 stowage from Port Hardy to Bella Coola. Bicycles cost $6.50.

airport, main hotels and the **bus station** at 7210 Market St just south of Hastings St and the infocentre, whence it departs ninety minutes before each sailing (Ⓣ250/949-6300 for information or to arrange a pick-up from hotel or campsite); otherwise call a **taxi** (Ⓣ250/949-8000).

Accommodation and eating

Many travellers to Port Hardy are in RVs, but there's still a huge amount of pressure on hotel **accommodation** in summer, and it's absolutely vital to call ahead if you're not camping or haven't worked your arrival to coincide with one of the ferry sailings. Note that the ferry from Prince Rupert docks around 10.30pm, so you don't want to be hunting out rooms late at night with dozens of others.

There are **rooms** out of town at the *Airport Inn*, 4030 Byng Rd (Ⓣ250/949-9424 or 1-888-218-2224, Ⓦwww.airportinn-porthardy.com; ❸), but if you prefer one of the cheap central choices, make for the *Thunderbird Inn*, 7050 Rupert St and Granville (Ⓣ250/949-7767 or 1-877-682-0222, Ⓦwww.thunderbirdinn.com ❹), with nice views of the harbour but occasional noisy live music. Five minutes south of town at 4965 Byng Rd, in a park-like setting near the river, is the *Pioneer Inn* (Ⓣ250/949-7271 or 1-800/663-8744, Ⓔpioneer@island.net; ❺), which has 36 rooms and RV sites ($23). Other hotels are the *Glen Lyon Inn* by the marina at 6435 Hardy Bay Rd (Ⓣ250/949-7115, Ⓦwww.glenlyoninn.com; ❹) and the large forty-room *Quarterdeck Inn*, 6555 Hardy Bay Rd (Ⓣ250/902-0455 or 1-877/902-0459, Ⓦwww.quarterdeckresort.net; ❺), the town's most comfortable hotel; otherwise contact the infocentre for details of the town's five or so B&B options. To **camp**, there is the *Quatse River Campground* at 5050 Hardy Rd (Ⓣ250/949-2395, Ⓔquatse@island.net; $16–20), with 62 spruce-shaded sites almost opposite the *Pioneer Inn*, 5km from the ferry dock. Or go for the larger 80-site *Sunny Sanctuary Campground* 1km north of Ferry Junction and Hwy 19 by the river and ocean at 8080 Goodspeed Rd (Ⓣ250/949-8111, Ⓔsunnycam@island.net; $15–26).

For **eating** here there's a bevy of budget outlets, so you should be able to fill up for well under $10. Granville and Market streets have the main restaurant concentrations: try the *Stink Creek Café* off Granville at 7030 Market St (Ⓣ250/949-8117); the pub-restaurants of the *Glen Lyon* and *Quarterdeck* (see above), both popular; or *Snuggles*, next to the *Pioneer Inn*, which aims at a cosy English pub atmosphere, with live music and steaks, salads and salmon grilled over an open fire. The cafeteria-coffee shop in the *Pioneer* does filling breakfasts and other snacks. For something with more class, *Malone's Oceanside Bistro* in the former North Island Mall, 9300 Trustee Rd (Ⓣ250/949-3050) is a popular family place with fish, seafood and Greek specialities. Despite the dubious-looking 1970s décor, the *Sportsman's*, opposite the infocentre at the corner of Market and Hastings streets (Ⓣ250/949-7811) offers good steaks and Italian specials.

Travel details

Trains

Vancouver to: Edmonton via Kamloops (3 weekly; 25hr); Jasper (June–Sept daily except Wed; Oct–May 3 weekly; 19hr).
Victoria to: Courtenay via Nanaimo (1 round trip daily; 4hr 35min).

Buses

Nanaimo to: Port Alberni (4 daily; 1hr 20min); Port Hardy (1 daily; 6hr 50min); Tofino (1–2 daily; 4hr 30min); Ucluelet (1–2 daily; 3hr 10min); Victoria (7 daily; 2hr 20min).
Port Alberni to: Nanaimo (4 daily; 1hr 20min); Tofino via Ucluelet (1–2 daily; 3hr).
Vancouver to: Banff (4 daily; 14hr 5min); Bellingham (8–10 daily; 1hr 45min); Cache Creek (2 daily; 5hr 40min); Calgary (4 daily; 16hr); Calgary via Kamloops (6 daily; 13hr); Calgary via Penticton, Nelson and Cranbrook (2 daily; 24hr); Calgary via Princeton and Kelowna (2 daily; 18hr); Chilliwack, for Harrison Hot Springs (10 daily; 1hr 45min); Edmonton via Jasper (3 daily; 16hr 30min); Kamloops (8 daily; 5hr); Kelowna (6 daily; 5hr 30min); Nanaimo (8 daily; 5hr); Pemberton (3 daily; 3hr 10min); Penticton (3 daily; 5hr 20min); Powell River (2 daily; 5hr 10min); Prince George via Cache Creek and Williams Lake (2 daily; 13hr); Salmon Arm (6 daily; 7hr 5min); Seattle, US (8–10 daily; 3hr 15min); Sea-Tac Airport, US (8–10 daily; 4hr 10min); Squamish (6 daily; 1hr 15min); Vernon (6 daily; 6hr); Victoria (8 daily; 5hr); Whistler (6 daily; 2hr 30min).
Victoria to: Bamfield (1–3 daily; 6–8hr); Campbell River (5 daily; 5hr); Nanaimo (7 daily; 2hr 20min); Port Hardy (1 daily; 9hr 45min); Port Renfrew (2 daily; 2hr 30min); Vancouver (8–10 daily; 4hr); Vancouver Airport direct (3 daily; 3hr 30min).

Ferries

Bella Coola to: Port Hardy (2–3 weekly; 21hr).
Chemainus to: Thetis Island and Kuper Island (minimum of 10 round trips daily; 35min).
Courtenay to: Powell River (4 daily; 1hr 15min).
Nanaimo to: Gabriola Island (17 daily; 20min); Vancouver/Horseshoe Bay Terminal (8 daily; 1hr 35min); Vancouver/Tsawwassen Terminal (8 daily; 2hr).
Northern Gulf Islands Denman Island to Hornby Island (minimum 12 round trips daily; 10min); Quadra Island to Cortes Island (Mon–Sat 6 daily, Sun 5 daily; 45min); Vancouver Island (Buckley Bay) to Denman Island (18 round trips daily; 10min); Vancouver Island (Campbell River) to Quadra Island (17 round trips daily; 10min).
Port Hardy to: Bella Coola (1 every two days; 15hr 30min–22hr); Prince Rupert (1 every two days; 15hr).
Powell River to: Courtenay-Comox (4 round trips daily; 1hr 15min); Texada Island (10 round trips daily; 35min).
Southern Gulf Islands Vancouver Island (Crofton) to Saltspring Island/Vesuvius Bay (14 round trips daily; 20min); Vancouver Island (Swartz Bay) to Saltspring Island/Fulford Harbour (10 round trips daily; 35min).
Sunshine Coast to: Horseshoe Bay–Snug Cove (15 round trips daily; 20 minutes); Horseshoe Bay–Langdale (8 round trips daily; 40min); Jervis Inlet/Earls Cove–Saltery Bay (8–9 round trips daily; 50min).
Vancouver to: Nanaimo from Horseshoe Bay Terminal (8 daily; 1hr 35min); from Tsawwassen Terminal (8 daily; 2hr); Victoria (Swartz Bay Terminal) from Tsawwassen (hourly summer 7am–9pm; rest of the year minimum 8 daily 7am–9pm; 1hr 35min).
Victoria to: Anacortes and San Juan Islands, US, from Victoria's Inner Harbour (1–2 daily; 2hr 30min); Seattle, US, from Inner Harbour (1–2 daily; 2hr 30min); Vancouver (Tsawwassen) from Swartz Bay (hourly summer 7am–10pm; rest of the year minimum 8 daily; 1hr 35min).

Flights

Vancouver to: Calgary (20 daily; 1hr 15min); Castlegar (1–2 daily; 1hr 20min); Cranbrook (1–2 daily; 2hr 30min); Edmonton (14 daily; 1hr 30min); Kamloops (4–5 daily; 1hr); Kelowna (7–9 daily; 1hr); Montréal (8 daily; 5hr 35min); Ottawa (10 daily; 4hr 40min); Penticton (3–5 daily; 50min); Prince George (5–8 daily; 1hr 10min); Toronto (15 daily; 4hr 55min); Victoria (14 daily; 25min); Winnipeg (8 daily; 2hr 40min).
Victoria to: Calgary (4 daily; 1hr 40min); Vancouver (14 daily; 25min).

10

The BC Interior

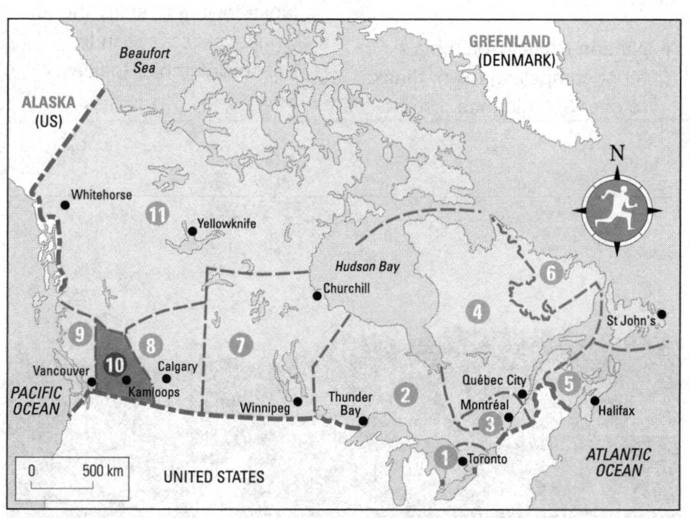

CHAPTER 10 Highlights

* **Wells Gray Provincial Park** This vast tract of wilderness has scenery that is the equal of the Canadian Rockies. See p.952

* **The Kootenays** A pristine region of lakes, mountains, forests, hot springs and charming old-world villages. See p.971

* **Nelson** British Columbia's most compelling town, thanks to over 350 glorious historic buildings and a thriving cultural and alternative life-style scene. See p.980

* **Osoyoos** Beware the rattle-snakes slithering through the surreal, scrub-covered landscape of Canada's only desert. See p.966

* **Fernie** Stay in this scenic, funky town and enjoy the longest ski season in the British Columbia Rockies. See p.985

△ Helmcken Falls in Wells Gray Provincial Park

10

The BC Interior

It says something about the magnificence of **British Columbia's interior** that you can enter it from Vancouver or the Rockies and find a clutch of landscapes every bit as spectacular as those you've just left. Some people will travel inland from Vancouver, others across country from the Rockies or the US. Unfortunately, whatever your approach, both major routes through the region confine you to some of its least interesting areas. The most obvious and quickest line east or west, the **Trans-Canada Highway** (Hwy 1) isn't worth considering in its entirety unless you're keen to cross the region in a hurry: little west of Revelstoke compares to what you might find further north or south. Nor does **Highway 3**, rumbling along just north of the US border, offer a convincing reason for sticking to it religiously.

The best option would be to take a meandering course towards the outstanding **Kootenay** region in the province's southeastern corner – an idyllic assortment of mountains and lakes and several towns that are fun to stay in – perhaps by way of **the Okanagan**, located in BC's arid centre, an almost Californian enclave of orchards, vineyards, warm lakes and resort towns, whose beaches and scorching summers suck in hordes of holidaymakers from all over Canada and the western US. From here you could push north to **Kamloops**, a far from exciting town but transport hub for the region and a jumping-off point for the magnificent **Wells Gray Provincial Park** or the Yukon. The other major option would be to head south to take in the better parts of Hwy 3 west of Osoyoos, also reasonably easily reached directly from Vancouver, and which includes a corner of **desert** and the spectacular ridges of the **Cascades** and **Coast Mountains**.

Vancouver to Kamloops

Two major routes connect **Vancouver and Kamloops**, the latter an unexceptional town in an extraordinary landscape but almost unavoidable as the junction of major routes in the region. These days anyone in any sort of hurry takes the **Coquihalla Highway** (Hwy 5). The scenery is unexceptional in the early part, but things look up considerably in the climb to the Coquihalla Pass (1244m), when forests, mountains and crashing rivers make a dramatic reappearance – compromised somewhat by old mines, clear-cuts (hillsides completely cleared of trees) and road-building scars. There's only a single exit, at the supremely missable town of Merritt, and after **Hope**, (150km east of Vancouver) there are literally no services for the next 182km to Kamloops. Come stocked up with fuel and food, and be prepared to pay a toll at the top of the pass – a

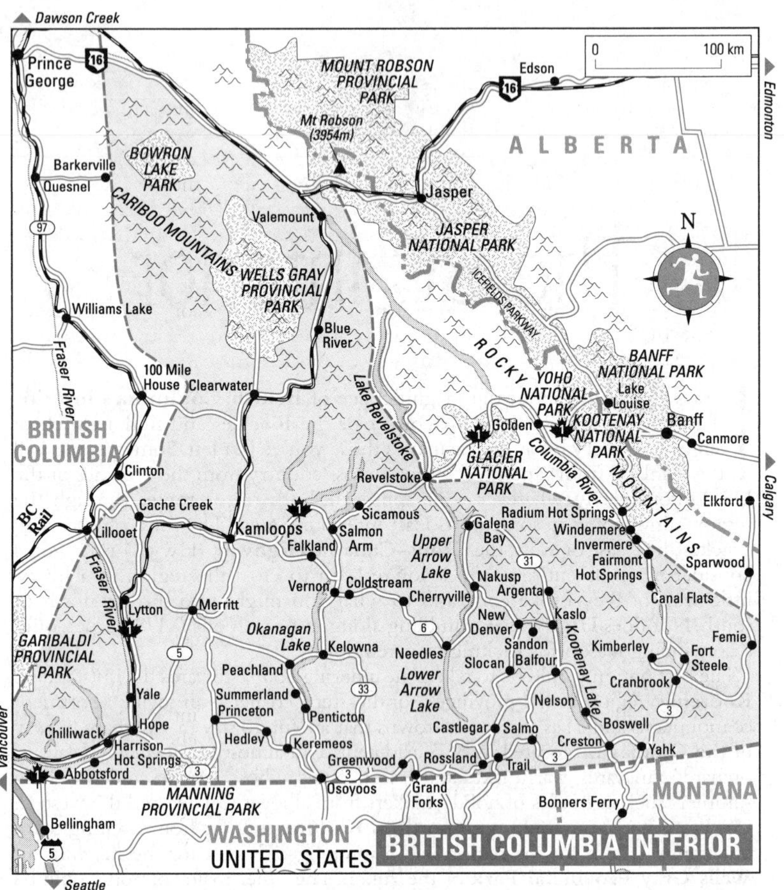

wind- and snow-whipped spot that must offer some of the loneliest employment opportunities in the province.

The older, slower and more scenic route from Vancouver is on the **Lougheed Highway** (Hwy 7) or by VIA Rail, both of which follow a more meandering course along the Thompson River and then the lower reaches of the **Fraser River**. For the first stretch you might also take the less busy but not exactly scintillating Hwy 7, which follows the north shore of the Fraser River from Vancouver and passes **Harrison Hot Springs** en route to Hope.

Highway 7 to Hope

Flanked by dreary malls at first, the 150km drive on Hwy 7 from Vancouver to Hope cheers up considerably as the countryside opens up after the small town of **MISSION**, 30km into the journey. If you have the time, you might want to make a quick stop at **Xá:ytem**, BC's oldest aboriginal dwelling site (late June to

Sept daily 10am–4pm; rest of the year by appointment; Ⓣ604/820-9725, Ⓦwww.xaytem.ca), located by the hwy just before the east side of Mission. People have lived here for as long as nine thousand years, and an ongoing archeological dig has uncovered numerous lithic artefacts including arrowheads and stones used for cutting and chopping – some were made from obsidian from Oregon, an indication of early trade routes. A Stó:lo long house serves as the site's interpretation centre, and inside you can learn more about the excavations.

After Mission, the hwy snakes through pretty farmland to **HARRISON HOT SPRINGS**, 129km from Vancouver and located on the southern edge of Harrison Lake. While aboriginal peoples who believed in the healing properties of the springs came here centuries ago, the springs were not popularized until they were "discovered" by gold prospectors in 1858; soon after the town became BC's first resort. Today, tourism remains Harrison Hot Spring's main industry, as you'll see from the number of modern apartment buildings and motels lining the lake. This said, it remains a scenic spot, thanks to the beautiful mountain views, mercifully free of too much neon and tat. The lake itself is 60km long – making it one of the province's largest lakes – and its waters are very clean, but also very cold. The only swimming option is in the artificial lagoon on the lake's shore, but if you want to play in the lake, boats, windsurfers and jet-skis can be hired from the deck in front of the upmarket but rather ugly *Harrison Hot Springs Resort*. If you're here the weekend after Labour Day, make a point of seeing the incredible sand sculptures on the beach that are created for the **World Championship Sand Sculpture** competition. To reach the **springs** themselves, it's a short walk along the shore and past the *Harrison Hot Springs Resort* – but they are a scalding hot 73°C at the source. In order to make the spring water suitable for soaking, the waters are cooled and redirected to the **Harrison Hot Springs Public Pool** (Mon–Thurs 9am–9pm, Fri 9am–10pm, Sat 8am–10pm, Sun 8am–9pm; $9) back in town at the intersection of Hot Springs Road and the Esplanade. If you are comfortable changing into your birthday suit to experience free hot springs in a series of tubs in a remote setting, **Clear Creek Hot Springs** can be reached by driving 50km north up the east side of Harrison Lake and then a further 30km on a series of extremely rough logging roads. If your car isn't up to the challenge, you might have to journey the last 10km on foot. For detailed directions, ask at the **visitor centre** (early Oct to May 10am–4pm weekends; June–Sept Thurs–Mon 9.30am–5.30pm; Ⓣ604/796-3425, Ⓦwww.harrison.ca) located in an old logging-camp bunkhouse on Hot Springs Road. You can also ask here for a map of the Agassiz-Harrison Mills **Circle Farm Tour** (Ⓦwww.district.kent.bc.ca), which takes you to fifteen local farms, including a hazelnut orchard, a cheese-maker's, a Coho salmon farm and a corn barn, all situated within a 25km radius.

While there is no Greyhound service to Harrison Hot Springs, local buses link the town with Chilliwack (Mon–Fri 6 daily, Sat & Sun 4 daily; Ⓦwww.busonline.ca; $3). For **accommodation**, one of the cheapest **motels** is the *Bungalow*, 511 Lillooet Ave (Ⓣ604/796-3536, Ⓦwww.bungalowmotel.com; ❸), with self-contained lakeside cabins and an ice-cream bar to boot. *Harrison Heritage House and* Kottage at 312 Lillooet Ave (Ⓣ604/796-9552 or 1-800/331-8099, Ⓦwww.bbharrison.com; ❺) is a pricey but beautiful **B&B** in one of the village's few heritage buildings, and also has three cheaper riverside cottages (❸). The *Harrison Hot Springs Resort & Spa* (Ⓣ604/796-2244 or 1-800/663-2266, Ⓦwww.harrisonresort.com; ❻), a favourite of Clark Gable's in the 1950s, is a friendly place with indoor and outside pools piped from the springs. For **camping** there are several private campsites around but it's best to head for nearby *Sasquatch Provincial Park* (reservations possible, see p.758; $14, day-use parking $5). **Eating** options are mostly along the Esplanade by the lake and you can settle for a variety of cuisines, including the Teutonic slant of the *Black Forest Steak and Schnitzel House* at no. 180 (ⓣ604/796-9343), with dinner main courses $14–22. The *Crazy Fish Bistro*, 310 Hot Springs Rd (ⓣ604/796-2280), can cater to those who are not so crazy about fish, but the salmon dinner ($18) is a good catch for those who are. For a treat, indulge yourself at the *Copper Room* at the *Harrison Hot Springs Resort* with a feast of rack of lamb ($39).

Hope

Reputedly christened by pioneers with a grounding in Dante, **HOPE** – as in "Abandon all hope..." – is a pleasant mountain-ringed town 158km east of Vancouver that achieved a certain fame as the place wasted in spectacular fashion by Sylvester Stallone at the end of *First Blood*, the first Rambo movie. Despite the number of roads that converge here – the Trans-Canada, Hwy 3 and the Coquihalla – it remains a remarkably unspoilt stopover. In the past it was rivers, not roads that accounted for the town's growth: the Fraser (Simon Fraser himself passed through in 1808) and two of its major tributaries, the Skagit and Coquihalla, meet at the townsite. The aboriginal villages here were forced to move when a Hudson's Bay post was established in 1848, the status quo being further disturbed when the gold rush hit in 1858.

The **visitor centre** (daily July & Aug 8am–8pm; May, June & Sept 8am–6pm; rest of year Mon–Fri 10am–4pm; ⓣ604/869-2021, ⓦwww.hopebc.ca) is the building next to the restored home gold mill at 919 Water Ave. The town **museum** (May–Sept daily 10am–4pm; donation suggested) is in the same building, and offers the usual hand-me-downs of Hope's erstwhile old-timers. Time permitting, drop by **Memorial Park** downtown, where trees ravaged by rot have been given a new lease of life by local chainsaw sculptors; there were around thirty at last count. Nearby, the **Christ Church National Historic Site**, built in 1861, is one of BC's oldest churches still on its original site.

Hiking, fishing, canoeing and even gold panning are all popular time-wasters around the hundreds of local lakes and rivers, details of which are available from the visitor centre. Of the hikes, the **Rotary Trail** (3km) from the end of 7th Sreett to the confluence of the Fraser and Coquihalla rivers is popular, as is the more demanding **Mount Hope Loop and Lookout Trail** (4km), with a view worth the climb (ask at the visitor centre for directions). Another popular walking expedition is the dark jaunt through the five colossal **Othello-Quintette Tunnels** (closed Nov–April) of the Hope-Midway Kettle Valley Railway, opened in 1916 but abandoned in 1959 after countless avalanches, mudslides and rock falls. The tunnels are reached by a short trail from the **Coquihalla Canyon Provincial Park** parking area (parking is $1 an hour or $3 a day), 6km northeast of town off Coquihalla Hwy. This was one of the backcountry locations used during the filming of *First Blood*, and offers spectacular views over the cliffs and huge sand bars of the Coquihalla Gorge. **Kawkawa Lake**, 3km northeast of Hope town centre on Kawkawa Lake Road, is another popular mountain retreat, endowed with plenty of relaxing and swimming opportunities.

Practicalities

Most of what happens in Hope happens on Hwy 1, here known as Water Avenue. The Greyhound **bus terminal** (corner of Fort St and 3rd Ave with an office in the Midtown Laundromat) is a critical juncture for bus travellers heading west to Vancouver, north to Kamloops or east to Penticton and the Okanagan. Cheap **motels** proliferate along Old Hope Princeton Way. On the banks of the Coquihalla River, *Kw'o:kw'e:hala Eco Vacation Retreat*, 8km east of town at 67400 Tunnels Rd (Ⓣ604/869-3799, Ⓦwww.eco-retreat.com; ❻), offers exclusive getaways in restored historic cabins; you could easily kill a few days here, melting in the wood-fired sauna or burning off the gourmet organic meals with a burst of hiking or tubing down the river. In town, the *Best Continental Motel*, 860 Fraser Ave (Ⓣ604/869-9726, Ⓔbcmhope@hotmail.com; ❹), lies a block back from the main hwy and is handy for the bus depot; or try the *Skagit Motor Inn*, 62030 Flood Hope Rd (Ⓣ604-869-5220 or 1-800/869-5228, Ⓦwww.skagit-motor-inn.com; ❹), which offers functional rooms in a peaceful setting. **Campsites**, too, are numerous, but most are some way from downtown. The town site is at *Coquihalla Campground* (Ⓣ604/869-7119 or 1-888/869-7118, Ⓔhopecamp@uniserve.com; $20–28; April–Oct), in a park setting off Hwy 3 and reached via 7th Avenue. The top of the pile is the *Othello Tunnels Campground & RV Park*, 8km east of Hope at 67851 Othello Rd, (Ⓣ604/869-9448 or 1-877/869-0543, Ⓦwww.othellotunnels.com; $20–26; March–Oct), with a rainbow trout fishing pond that delights the kids.

Food facilities and late-night entertainment are limited in what is, despite Vancouver's proximity, still a small-time town. For snacks, try the buzzing *Blue Moose Coffee House* at 322 Wallace St. For more substantial fare, try the Korean and Japanese cuisine at *Kimchi*, 821A 6th Ave (Ⓣ604/869-0070; closed Sun), with udon and sushi meals from $8.

The Fraser Canyon

Veering north from Hope, the Trans-Canada runs up the Fraser Canyon, squeezed here by the high ridges of the Cascade and Coast ranges into one of British Columbia's grandest waterways. Though it's now a transport corridor – the Canadian Pacific Railway and Canadian National Railway also pass this way – the **Fraser Canyon** was long regarded as impassable; to negotiate it, the Trans-Canada is forced to push through seven tunnels, hug the Fraser's banks, and at times cling perilously to rock ledges hundreds of metres above the swirling waters.

Simon Fraser

The Fraser River is named after **Simon Fraser** (1776–1862), one of North America's most remarkable early explorers, who as an employee of the North West Company established western Canada's first white settlements: Fort McCleod (1805), Fort St James (1806), Fort Fraser (1806) and Fort George (1807). Having traced the route taken by fellow explorer Alexander Mackenzie across the continent, he set out in 1808 to establish a route to the Pacific and secure it for Britain against the rival claims of the US. Instead he travelled the entire 1300-kilometre length of a river – the Fraser – under the mistaken impression he was following the Columbia. "We had to pass where no man should venture," he wrote, making most of the journey on foot guided by local natives, pushing forward using ladders, ropes and improvised platforms to bypass rapids too treacherous to breach by boat. Reaching the river's mouth, where he would have glimpsed the site of present-day Vancouver, he realized his error and deemed the venture a commercial failure, despite the fact he had successfully navigated one of the continent's greatest rivers for the first time. Few people, needless to say, felt the need to follow Fraser's example until the discovery of **gold** near Yale in 1858; prospectors promptly waded in and panned every tributary of the lower Fraser until new strikes tempted them north to the Cariboo.

YALE, about 25km north of Hope, opens the canyon with a ring of plunging cliffs. Sitting at the river's navigable limit, it was once a significant site for Canada's aboriginal peoples, providing an important point of departure for the canoes of the Stó:lo ("People of the River"). A Hudson's Bay Company post, The Falls, appeared here in the 1840s, later renamed in honour of James Murray Yale, commander of the HBC post at Fort Langley. Within a decade it became the largest city in North America west of Chicago and north of San Francisco; during the 1858 gold rush, when it marked the beginning of the infamous Cariboo Wagon Road, Yale's population mushroomed to over 20,000.

Today Yale is a small town of about 200, though a visit to the **Yale Heritage Site** (April–Oct daily 10am–5pm; $5; ⓣ604/863-2324) on the corner of Hwy 1 and Douglas St, offers an exhaustive account of the town's golden age. You might also want to pay homage at **Lady Franklin Rock**, the vast river boulder which blocked the passage of steamers beyond Yale – all goods heading north to the goldfields had to transfer at this point to wagon trains bound for the Cariboo Wagon Road. Ask locals for directions. If you fancy a longer walk, take Hwy 1 a kilometre south out of the village for the trailhead of the **Spirit Cave Trail**, a three-hour walk with fine views of the mountains. For **rooms**, the *Fort Yale Motel* (ⓣ604/863-2216, ⓦwww.fortyalemotel.com; ❸) at the entrance to the Canyon is the only motel in town. The heritage-listed *Teague House B&B* (ⓣ1-800/363-7238; ❸) has a communal kitchen and operates whitewater rafting trips down the Fraser River (ⓣ604/863-2336, ⓦwww.fraserraft.com). If you're **camping**, though, you might want to backtrack 10km towards Hope on Hwy 1 to the *Emory Creek Campground*, a large, peaceful wooded site with river walks and camping sites from May to October ($16).

Hell's Gate and Lytton

Around 20km north of Yale on Hwy 1 is the famous **HELL'S GATE**, where – in a gorge almost 180m deep – the huge swell of the Fraser is squeezed into a 38-metre channel of foaming water that crashes through the rocks with awe-inspiring ferocity. For a good view of the canyon, travel 10km north of Yale on Hwy 1 to the **Alexandra Bridge Provincial Park**, where an old section of the hwy drops to the Alexandra Bridge for some startling panoramas. Eight kilometres further there's a certain amount of resort-like commercialism to negotiate to get down to the river and an "Air-Tram" (cable car) to pay for (daily mid-April to mid-May & early Sept to mid-Oct 10am–4pm, mid-May to early Sept 9.30am–5.30pm; $15; ⓣ604/867-9277, ⓦwww.hellsgateairtram.com). Close by there are also displays on the various provisions made to help migrating **salmon** complete their journeys, which have been interrupted over the years by the coming of the road and railway beside the Fraser. The river is one of the key runs for Pacific salmon, and every summer and autumn they fill the river as they head for tributaries and upstream lakes to spawn (see p.954).

LYTTON, situated 50km north of Hell's Gate, marks the start of BC's arid interior. Lying at the junction of the Fraser and Thompson rivers, it is a small lumber town and a main centre for **whitewater rafting**, the most notorious stretch being along the Thompson River from Spences Bridge to Lytton, home to rapids with intimidating names like *Jaws of Death* and *Witch's Cauldron*. Various companies run several trips a week from May to August; contact *Kumsheen Rafting Resort*, 5km east of Lytton on Hwy 5 (ⓣ1-800/663-6667, ⓦwww.kumsheen.com). For a full list of adventure operators and information

△ Whitewater rafting on the Thompson River

on walking tours drop into the **visitor centre**, 400 Fraser St (June to early Sept daily 9am–5pm, call for times rest of year; (Ⓣ250/455-2523, Ⓦwww.lytton.ca). To **stay** locally, the *Kumsheen Rafting Resort* offers lovely antique-furnished tent-cabins (❹) as well as camping and RV sites from $20 and has an outdoor pool and restaurant. For something central, try the *Totem Motel and Lodge*, 320 Fraser St (Ⓣ250/455-2321, Ⓦwww.totemmotellytton.com; ❹). The Skihist Provincial Park, 6km east of town, has camping sites ($17) with views of the Thompson River canyon.

Cache Creek

CACHE CREEK, 337km from Vancouver and 84km west of Kamloops, has a reputation as a hitchhiker's black hole and indeed is the sort of sleepy place you could get stuck in for days. Cache Creek is known as the "Arizona of Canada" for its extraordinary rocky landscapes and baking summer climate, which settles a heat-wasted somnolence on its dusty streets. The parched, windswept mountains roundabout are anomalous volcanic intrusions in the regional geology, producing a legacy of hard rock and semi-precious stones – including jade – that attract climbers and rock hounds. There's not much else to do here; you can watch semi-precious stones being worked at several places, or check out **Hat Creek Ranch** (May–Sept daily 9am–5pm; $8; Ⓣ1-800/782-0922, Ⓦwww.hatcreekranch.com), a collection of original buildings including a log stopping house, the last remaining of its type, and a reconstruction of a Shuswap village. It's located ten minutes north of Cache Creek by the junction of hwys 97 and 99 (the original Cariboo Wagon Rd). If you're stranded, try one of about a dozen **motels**, such as the *Bonaparte* on Hwy 97 North (Ⓣ1-888/922-1333; ❸), with a large heated pool. The nearest **campsite**, complete with laundry, hot showers and heated outdoor pool, is the *Brookside* (Ⓣ250/457-6633, Ⓦwww.brooksidecampsite.com; $15; April–Oct), located 1km east of town on the main highway.

Kamloops

Almost any trip in southern British Columbia brings you sooner or later to **KAMLOOPS**, a sprawling town 355km northeast of Vancouver and 110km west of Salmon Arm which has been a transport centre from time immemorial. Its name derives from the Shuswap word for "meeting of the rivers" and today marks the meeting point of the Trans-Canada and Yellowhead (South) hwys, the region's principal transcontinental roads, as well as the junction of the Canadian Pacific and Canadian National railways. One of the larger towns in interior southern British Columbia (pop. 84,000), it's a bland and unobjectionable place that is yet to shake off its Wild West heritage. If you're on public transport, there's no particular need to spend any time here; if you're camping or driving, however, it makes a convenient provisions stop, especially for those heading north on Hwy 5 or south on the Coquihalla Hwy, neither of which has much in the way of facilities.

Arrival and information

The **visitor centre**, 1290 West Trans-Canada Hwy (daily mid-May to mid-Oct 9am–5pm, rest of year Mon–Fri 9am-5pm; ⓣ250/374-3377 or 1-800/662-1994, ⓦwww.tourismkamloops.com), is a good 6km west of downtown, close to the Aberdeen Mall. In the summer, there is a visitor centre downtown at 103-340 Victoria St (mid-June to Aug Mon–Fri 11am–3pm).

The **Greyhound terminal** (ⓣ250/374-1212), on Notre Dame Avenue off Hwy 1, is a crucial interchange for buses to all parts of the province; to head into town, jump on the "Crosstown" bus that leaves from outside the station. Kamloops also has a key regional **airport**, located 6km northwest of the centre on Tranquille Road. It is connected to downtown by a BC Transit bus or the airport shuttle (ⓣ250/314-4803; $10-14). The town is also served by three weekly **trains** in each direction from Edmonton and Vancouver, via Jasper. The VIA Rail station is located 11km north of Kamloops off Hwy 5 on CNR Yard Access Road (ⓣ1-888/842-7245, ⓦwww.viarail.ca).

Accommodation

Kamloops' huge volume of **accommodation** is aimed at the motorist and consists of thick clusters of motels, most of which blanket the town's eastern margins on Hwy 1 or out on Columbia Street West.

Executive Inn 540 Victoria St ⓣ250/372-2281 or 1-800/663-2837, ⓦwww.kamloops.com/executive. Make for this central hotel if you want top-of-the-range comfort after a long journey, with an in-house casino and restaurant. ⑤

Fountain Motel 506 Columbia St ⓣ250/374-4451 or 1-888/253-1569, ⓦwww.fountain.kamloops.com. This is a basic and budget option, closer to town. ③

Plaza Heritage Hotel 405 Victoria St ⓣ250/377-8075, ⓦwww.plazaheritagehotel.com. With 66 delightful 1920s-style rooms restored to their former grandeur. ④

Silver Sage Tent and Trailer Park 771 Athabasca St East ⓣ250/828-2077. The nearest campsite, but if you've got a car aim for the far more scenic facilities at Paul Lake Provincial Park ($20–25) (see opposite).

Thriftlodge 2459 Trans-Canada ⓣ250/374-2488 or 1-800/661-7769, ⓦwww.thriftlodge.kamloops.com. This is probably the cheapest of all, but it's about the last building on eastbound Hwy 1 out of town. ③

The town and around

Kamloops is determinedly functional and rough-edged and not a place to spend a happy day wandering, but its downtown does have a modern 2400-work **art**

gallery at 465 Victoria St at 5th, that showcases Canadian artists and in particular, those from British Columbia (Mon–Wed, Fri & Sat 10am–5pm, Thurs 10am–9pm, Sun noon–4pm; $5; ⓣ250/377-2400, ⓦwww.kag.bc.ca).

The **Kamloops Museum**, 207 Seymour St (Tues–Sat 9.30am–4.30pm; donation suggested) is one of the more interesting provincial offerings, with illuminating archive photographs, artefacts, period set-pieces and a particularly well-done section on the Shuswap. For a more complete picture of local First Nations history and traditions, call at the **Secwepemc Museum & Heritage Park**, just over the bridge on Hwy 5 (Mon–Fri 8am–4pm; ⓣ250/828-9801, ⓦwww.secwepemc.org; $6) or attend the **Kamloops Pow Wow**, held the first weekend in August ($10 a day; ⓣ250/828-9738).

For country and western diehards, the **Kamloops Cowboy Festival** in mid-March delivers three days and nights of cowboy poetry, cowboy music and even cowboy church (ⓣ1-888/763-2224, ⓦwww.bcchs.com; $10 a day).

Perhaps the most interesting thing about Kamloops is its surroundings, dominated by strange, bare-earthed brown hills that locals like to say represent the northernmost point of the Mojave Desert. There's no doubting the almost surreal touches of near-desert, which are particularly marked in the bare rock and clay outcrops above the bilious waters of the Thompson River and in the bleached scrub and failing stands of pines that spot the barren hills. A good way to see the scenery is to take a seventy-minute ride on the **Kamloops Heritage Railway**, a restored steam-powered heritage train that hisses and whistles its way through the countryside (July & Aug Fri–Mon; $14; ⓣ250/374-2141, ⓦwww.kamrail.com). It leaves from 510 Lorne St.

Most other scenic diversions lie a short drive out of town, and the visitor centre (see opposite) has full details of every last local bolt hole, with a special bias towards the dozen-plus golf courses and two hundred or so trout-stuffed lakes that dot the hinterland. The nearest and most popular lake on a hot summer's day is the 402-hectare **Paul Lake Provincial Park**, northeast of town on a good paved road (take Hwy 5 north for 5km and then Paul Lake Road east for 17km), with swimming and a provincial campsite ($14). For the chance to get up close and personal with Canadian critters such as grizzly bear, wolf, moose and cougar,– albeit with the animals languishing safely behind a fence – visit the **British Columbia Wildlife Park**, a zoo and animal rehabilitation centre 15km east of Kamloops at 9077 Dallas Drive (June–Sept 9am–6pm, rest of year 9am–4.30pm; $12; ⓣ250/573-3242, ⓦwww.bczoo.org).

North American ginseng has become one of the region's prime crops and the opulent **Sunmore Ginseng Spa** at 925 McGill Place (ⓣ250/372-2814, ⓦwww.sunmore.com) offers pampering sessions to weary travellers using ginseng-based beauty products. One-hour treatments such as the ginseng body wrap start at $100. Next door to the spa is a ginseng factory with free tours and a showroom.

Eating and drinking

Kamloops has plenty of options for filling your tank. Competition is fierce along Victoria Street where you'll have no problem finding a caffeine hit and a good **meal**. There are some lively **bars** here too, but it's worth venturing a few blocks up for the cowboy drinking establishments that Kamloops is famous for.

Brownstone 118 Victoria St ⓣ250/851-9939. For a culinary treat, this fine dining establishment in a 1904 heritage building is apparently good enough for Harrison Ford and Jennifer Lopez (mains $18–36). Closed Sun & Mon.

Cactus Jacks 417 Seymour St ⓣ250/374-7289. Down your beer with the local cowboys and cowgirls at this bona fide western bar with mechanical bull riding every Wed night and line dancing on Fri.

Chapters Viewpoint at the *Panorama Inn* 610 Columbia St West ⓣ250/374-3224. Serves good steaks, salads and seafood against a panoramic backdrop (mains $15–29).

Peter's Pasta at 149 Victoria St ⓣ250/372-8514. For fresh and reliable Italian fare (mains $10–18), slurp your linguine at this always-packed restaurant. Closed Sun & Mon.

Swiss Pastries & Café 359 Victoria St. Snack food is served in generous portions at this popular café, which really is run by Swiss people and does good muesli, cappuccino, pastries and excellent sandwiches.

Zach's Exotic Coffee Shop 377 Victoria St. Pours the best coffee in town and it is attached to a popular little confectionery store called *Zach's Old-Style Sweet Shoppe*.

Highway 5 north of Kamloops

Northbound **Highway 5** (here known as the Yellowhead South Hwy) heads upstream along the broad North Thompson River as it courses through high hills and rolling pasture between Kamloops and **Clearwater** and beyond. It is one of the most scenically astounding road routes in this part of the world, and follows the river as it carves through the Monashee Mountains from its source near **Valemount**, to the final meeting with the main Yellowhead Hwy (Hwy 16) at Tête Jaune Cache, a total distance of 338km. The entire latter half of the journey is spent sidestepping the immense **Wells Gray Provincial Park**, one of the finest protected areas in British Columbia.

Greyhound **buses** cover the route on their run between Kamloops and Prince George via Clearwater (daily in each direction), as do VIA Rail **trains**, which connect Kamloops with Jasper via Clearwater (3 weekly in each direction). To get into Wells Gray without your own transport, however, you'd have to hitch from Clearwater up the 63-kilometre main access road – a feasible proposition at the height of summer, but highly unlikely at any other time. This access road will be enough for most casual visitors to get a taste of the park – you could run up and down it and see the sights in a day – but note that there are some less-travelled gravel roads into other sectors of the park from **Blue River**, 112km north of Clearwater on Hwy 5, and from the village of **100 Mile House**, on Hwy 97 west of the park.

Clearwater

CLEARWATER is a dispersed logging and ranching community 125km north of Kamloops that's invisible from Hwy 5, and unless you need a place to stay or

Sun Peaks

It may not receive half the attention that is lavished on Whistler, but BC's second-largest winter destination, **Sun Peaks Resort**, 53km northeast of Kamloops along Hwy 5 and Sun Peaks Road has some pretty impressive statistics of its own: 117 runs, eleven lifts and 40km of cross-country trails spread across three mountains (Nov–April; day lift pass $60; ⓣ1-800/807-3257, ⓦwww.sunpeaksresort.com). Come summer, Sun Peaks attracts the cycling, hiking and golf lovers, and the ever-increasing accommodation options range from the budget *Sun Peaks International Hostel* (ⓣ250/578-0057, ⓦwww.sunpeakshostel.com; ❷) to the luxurious *Delta Sun Peaks Hotel* (ⓣ1-866/552-5516, ⓦwww.deltahotels.com; ❼). The resort's rapid expansion has not been without controversy, however, with protests from some members of the Secwepemc First Nation over what they claim to be an "illegal land grab".

arrive by rail there's no need to drop down to it at all. Everything you need apart from the odd shop is on or just off the junction between the hwy and the slip road to the village, including the **Greyhound bus stop** and the excellent **visitor centre** (May daily 10am–4pm; June to early Oct daily 9am–6pm; Ⓣ250/674-2646, Ⓦwww.clearwaterbcchamber.com) that has information on all aspects of Wells Gray Provincial Park.

Camping aside, Clearwater is the most realistic place **to stay** along Hwy 5 if you're planning on doing Wells Gray. The lovely *Half Moon Hostel*, about 4km north of town and just off Clearwater Valley Road at 625 Greer Rd (Ⓣ250/674-4199, Ⓦwww.halfmoonhostel.com; ❷) has dorm beds for $25 a night and organizes tours into the park. One block from the visitor centre, the big *Clearwater Valley Resort & KOA Campground*, 373 Clearwater Valley Rd (Ⓣ250/674-3909, Ⓦwww.clearwatervalley.com), on the corner of the Yellowhead Hwy and the Wells Grey Park Rd, is a combination of rooms (❸), cabins (❷), camping and RV sites ($20–35; March–Oct), with a heated pool and a restaurant. Grander and larger is the 64-room *Clearwater Lodge* (Ⓣ250/674-3080 or 1-888/383-2388, Ⓦwww.clearwaterlodge.bcresorts.com; ❹) also with a swimming pool, near the Hwy 5 turn-off for the park. A number of **campsites** lie more or less within walking distance of the visitor centre: the best, and on the lake, is the *Dutch Lake Resort and RV Park* (Ⓣ250/674-3351 or 1-888/884-4424, Ⓦwww.dutchlake.com; cabins ❸, pitch $19–31; mid-April to mid-Oct). Don't forget though, that there are three simple provincial park campsites within the park (see p.953).

For **food**, the big *Wells Gray Inn* at 228 East Yellowhead Hwy (Ⓣ250/674-2214 or 1-800/567-4088, Ⓦwww.wellsgrayinn.ca; ❹) has a good on-site restaurant and grill (mains $12–40). A local favourite is the *Flower Meadow Bakery and Café* at 444 Clearwater Valley Rd (Ⓣ250/674-3654, closed Sun), with good coffee, home-made bread and lunchtime soup and sandwich deals ($8). If you plan to spend the day exploring Wells Gray Park, you can stock up on picnic supplies at the supermarket at 74 Young St.

Blue River and Valemount

Clearwater is by far the best base for forays into Wells Gray, but you may find the **accommodation** options at Blue River and Valemount useful, though the latter is a whopping 225km north of Clearwater on Hwy 5. **BLUE RIVER**, a slip of a place 100km north of Clearwater, has far fewer possibilities, with its cheapest option being the *Blue River Motel* with one- and two-bedroom units two blocks off the hwy on Spruce Street (Ⓣ250/673-8387, Ⓔreservations@wiegele.com; ❷). For **camping**, try the *Blue River Campground and RV Park*, Myrtle Lake Rd and Cedar St (Ⓣ250/673-8203, Ⓦwww.bluerivercampground.ca; $16–30; May to mid-Oct; ❶), which also has tepees and cabins and offers canoe rentals and a variety of fishing, canoeing and horse-riding tours.

In **VALEMOUNT** there's a seasonal visitor centre at Cranberry Lake Rd on Hwy 5 (mid-May to June Mon–Fri 3pm–7pm; Sat–Sun noon–7pm; July–Aug daily 8am–8pm; Ⓣ250/566-9893, Ⓦwww.valemount.org) and around thirty motels and more than a dozen campsites. One block off the hwy on 5th Avenue are a bunch of **motels**, including *Yellowhead* (Ⓣ250/566-4411, Ⓦwww.yellowheadmotel.com; ❹), and the *Canoe Mountain Lodge* (Ⓣ250/566-9171, Ⓦwww.canoemountainlodge.com; ❸). At 360 Loseth Rd, 1km north of Valemount, is the modern *Irvins Park and Campground* (Ⓣ250/566-4781; $18–30; April–Oct), mainly aimed at RVs. For **camping**, head 500m north of Valemount to *Wilderness Creek Camping* (Ⓣ250/566-4098; $15).

From the Yellowhead Hwy junction north of Valemount it's 270km on to Prince George (see p.997) and 77km east to the BC-Alberta border.

Wells Gray Provincial Park

WELLS GRAY PROVINCIAL PARK is the equal of any of the Rocky Mountain national parks to the east: if anything, its wilderness is probably more extreme – so untamed, in fact, that many of its peaks remain unclimbed and unnamed. Wildlife sightings are common – especially if you tramp some of the wilder trails, where encounters with black bears, grizzlies and mountain goats are a possibility, not to mention glimpses of smaller mammals such as timber wolves, coyotes, weasels, martens, minks, wolverines and beavers. Seeing the park is straightforward, at least if you have transport and only want a superficial – but still rewarding – glimpse of the interior. A 63-kilometre **access road** strikes into the park from Hwy 5 at Clearwater, culminating in Clearwater Lake – there's no further wheeled access. Various trails long and short, together with campsites, viewpoints and easily seen waterfalls, are dotted along the road, allowing you to see just about all the obvious scenic landmarks with a car in a day.

Accommodation in or near the park includes the log cabins at *Wells Gray Ranch* (ⓣ250/674-2792, ⓦwww.wellsgrayranch.com; ❺; mid-May to mid-Oct) just within the park entrance (26km from Hwy 5) on Wells Gray Park Rd, offering organized horseriding and canoeing trips; or the slightly larger but equally lonely *Helmcken Falls Lodge* (ⓣ250/674-3657, ⓦwww.helmckenfalls.com; ❻; Dec–March & mid-April to Oct) also in the park itself (35km from Hwy 5), which offers similar facilities and activities at slightly higher prices.

Activities in Wells Gray Provincial Park

With some 250km of maintained trails and dozens of other lesser routes, the 540,000-hectare park is magnificent for **hiking**. We've outlined short walks and day-hikes from the park's access road, but serious backpackers can easily spend a week or more on the backcountry hikes, most of which are in the southern third of the park and link together for days of wild hiking and wilderness camping. The longest one-way trail connects Clearwater Lake to Kostal Lake trail (26km) and begins on the main Wells Gray Park Road, just across from Clearwater Lake campsite. Steep switchbacks, muddy conditions, thick brush and large deadfall as well as tramping across sharp lava flow and loose rock make the going slow on many of the park's remoter trails. For all the backcountry hikes you need a map and a compass, your own food and water supplies and plenty of insect repellent. Make sure you pick up a free *BC Parks* map-pamphlet at the Clearwater visitor centre, and if you're thinking of doing any backcountry exploration you'll want to invest in their more detailed maps and guides. **Cross-country skiing** is also possible, but there are only a few groomed routes in the park.

Another of the park's big attractions is **canoeing** on Clearwater and Azure lakes, the former at the end of the access road, which can be linked with a short portage to make a fifty-plus-kilometre dream trip for paddlers; you can rent canoes for long- or short-haul trips from *Clearwater Lake Tours* situated on the south end of Clearwater Lake, 71km from Hwy 5 in Clearwater (ⓣ250/674-2121). For excellent guided interpretive hikes in the park, contact *Go-Outdoors* (ⓣ250/674-0204). In addition, several local operators run **tours** featuring **white-water rafting**, horse riding, fishing, boating and even float-plane excursions around the park – the Clearwater visitor centre has the inside story on all of these.

Both the lodge and ranch above have tent pitches ($10–15), but there's far better roadside **camping** along the park access road at the park's three provincial campsites (all $14; May–Oct). Many other campsites ($5) dot the shores of the park's major lakes and *Clearwater Lake Tours* operates a water-taxi service which can drop you off at any site on Clearwater Lake and pick you up at a prearranged time.

Sights and hikes along the access road

Even if you're not geared up for the backcountry, the **access road** to the park from Clearwater opens up a medley of waterfalls, walks and viewpoints that make a detour extremely worthwhile. The road is paved for the first 42km into the park boundary, but the remaining 36km to Clearwater Lake is gravel. Most of the sights are well signed.

About 10km north of Clearwater, a short walk from the car park (you can't miss the signs) brings you to the 61-metre **Spahats Falls**, the first of several mighty cascades along this route. You can watch the waters crashing down through layers of pinky-red volcanic rock from a pair of observation platforms, which also provide an impressive and unexpected view of the Clearwater Valley way down below. A few hundred metres further up the road, a 15km gravel lane peels off into the **Wells Gray Recreation Area**; a single trail from the end of the road strikes off into alpine meadows. About 15km further up the main access road, a second 4WD track branches east to reach the trailhead for **Battle Mountain** (19km), with the option of several shorter hikes like the Mount Philip Trail (5km) en route.

Green Mountain Lookout, reached by a rough, winding road to the left just after the park entrance, offers one of the most enormous roadside panoramas in British Columbia: as far as you can see, there's nothing but an almighty emptiness of primal forest and mountains.

The next essential stop is **Dawson Falls**, a broad, powerful cascade (91m wide and 18m high) just five-minutes' walk from the road – signed "Viewpoint". Beyond, the road crosses an ugly iron bridge and shortly after meets the start of the **Murtle River Trail** (14km one-way), a particularly good walk if you want more spectacular waterfalls.

Immediately afterwards, a dead-end side road is signed to **Helmcken Falls**, the park's undisputed highlight. The site is heavily visited, and it's not unknown for wedding parties to come up here to get dramatic matrimonial photos backed by the luminous arc of water plunging into a black, carved bowl fringed with vivid carpets of lichen and splintered trees, the whole ensemble framed by huge plumes of spray wafting up on all sides. At 137m, the falls are two and a half times the height of Niagara Falls.

Continuing north, the park access road rejoins the jade-green Clearwater River, passing picnic spots and short trails that wend down to the bank for close-up views of one of the province's best white-water-rafting stretches. Next up is **Ray Farm**, home to John Bunyon Ray, who in 1912 was the first homesteader in this area; it now consists of picturesquely ruined, wooden shacks scattered in a lush clearing. The last attraction before the end of the road is Bailey's Creek where, in August and September, the robust chinook salmon attempt to jump the rapids before giving up and spawning a kilometre downstream. The park road ends at **Clearwater Lake**, where there are a couple of boat launches, a provincial campsite ($14; May–Oct) and a series of short trails.

Salmon Arm and the Shuswap

Given the variety of routes across southern BC, there's no knowing when you might find yourself in **SALMON ARM**, 108km east of Kamloops. The town – the largest of the somewhat bland resorts spread along **Shuswap Lake**'s 1000km of navigable waterways – has relatively little to recommend it. This said, if you fancy fishing, swimming, water-skiing or houseboating, you could do worse than relax for a couple of days in one of the area's 32 provincial parks or small lakeside villages – Chase, Sorrento, Eagle Bay and others.

Depending on the season, you can also watch one of Canada's most famous **salmon-spawning runs** near Salmon Arm, or indulge in a little **bird-watching**,

Spawn to be wild

At times it seems impossible to escape the **salmon** in British Columbia. Whether it's on restaurant menus, in rivers or in the photographs of grinning fishermen clutching their catch, the fish is almost as much a symbol of the region as its mountains and forests. Five different species inhabit the rivers and lakes of western Canada: **pink**, **coho**, **chum**, **chinook** and **sockeye**.

Though they start and finish their lives in fresh water, in between salmon spend about four years in the open sea. Mature fish make their epic migrations from the Pacific to **spawn** in the BC rivers of their birth between June and Nov, swimming about 30km a day; some chinook travel more than 1400km up the Fraser beyond Prince George, which means almost fifty days' continuous swimming upstream. Though the female lays as many as four thousand eggs, only about six percent of the offspring survive; on the Adams River near Salmon Arm, for example, it's estimated that of four billion sockeye eggs laid in a typical year, one billion survive to become fry (hatched fish about 2cm long), of which 75 percent are eaten by predators before becoming smolts (year-old fish), and only five percent of these then make it to the ocean. In effect, each pair of spawners produces about ten mature fish; of these, eight are caught by commercial fisheries and only two return to reproduce.

These are returns that clearly put the salmon's survival and British Columbia's lucrative **fishing industry** on a knife edge. Caught, canned and exported, salmon accounts for two-thirds of BC's $1 billion annual revenues from fishing – the largest of any Canadian province, and its third-ranking money-earner after forestry and energy products. Commercial fishing suffered its first setback in British Columbia as long ago as 1913, when large rockslides at Hell's Gate in the Fraser Canyon disrupted many of the spawning runs. Although fish runs were painstakingly constructed to bypass the slides, new pressures have subsequently been heaped on the salmon by fish farms, mining, logging, urban and agricultural development, and the dumping of industrial and municipal wastes. An increasingly important line of defence, **hatcheries** have been built on rivers on the mainland and Vancouver Island to increase the percentage of eggs and fry that successfully mature. Meanwhile, overfishing remains a major concern, although a significant step was taken in 1992 when a moratorium was placed on large-scale drift nets. Since then, various measures have been implemented by the Canadian and BC governments including the closure of the Fraser and Thompson rivers to all salmon fishing in 1999. However, Greenpeace estimates that 764 stocks of salmon in BC and Yukon are either extinct or at risk of becoming extinct. There is also concern about parasitic sea lice spreading from open netcage salmon farms to wild stock and of farm-fed Atlantic salmon (the preferred species for BC farms) escaping from pens and undermining wild populations through interbreeding and competition for resources.

for the bay here is one of the world's last nesting areas of the western grebe. To get anything out of Salmon Arm proper, you'll have to pull off the main drag, which is formed by the Trans-Canada itself, and head to the village a little to the south.

The lake and the surrounding region take their name from the Shuswap natives, the northernmost of the great Salishan family and the largest single tribe in British Columbia. The name of the town harks back to a time when it was possible to spear salmon straight from the lake, and fish were so plentiful that they were shovelled onto the land as fertilizer. Shuswap Lake still provides an important sanctuary for hatched salmon fry before they make their long journey down the Thompson and Fraser rivers to the sea, and the Fraser River system is the continent's greatest salmon habitat. Therefore, one of the few reasons you might make a special journey to the Salmon Arm area is to watch the huge migrations of **spawning salmon** that take place around October. Up to two million fish brave the run from the Pacific up to their birthplace in the Adams River. During the spawning time, humans also make their way here in droves; around 250,000 visitors come during the peak week alone. The spectacle takes place yearly, but is most marked on four-yearly cycles (2010 is the next "big" year). This short stretch of river is protected by the **Roderick Haig-Brown Provincial Park**, reached from Salmon Arm by driving 46km west on the Trans-Canada to Squilax and then 5km north on a side road where the park is signposted. If you're thinking of dangling a line, pick up the *Fishing in Shuswap* leaflet from the visitor centre in Salmon Arm, and don't forget to get a licence at the same time.

Practicalities

Greyhound **buses** serve Salmon Arm from Vancouver (7 daily), Calgary (4 daily), Kelowna and Vernon (4 daily) and Penticton (3 daily). The bus terminal is at the West Village Mall on Hwy 1, and the **visitor centre** (Mon–Fri 9am–5pm, mid-May to Sept daily 8am–6pm; ⓣ250/832-2230 or 1-877/725-6667) is at 200 Trans-Canada Hwy SW or contact Columbia

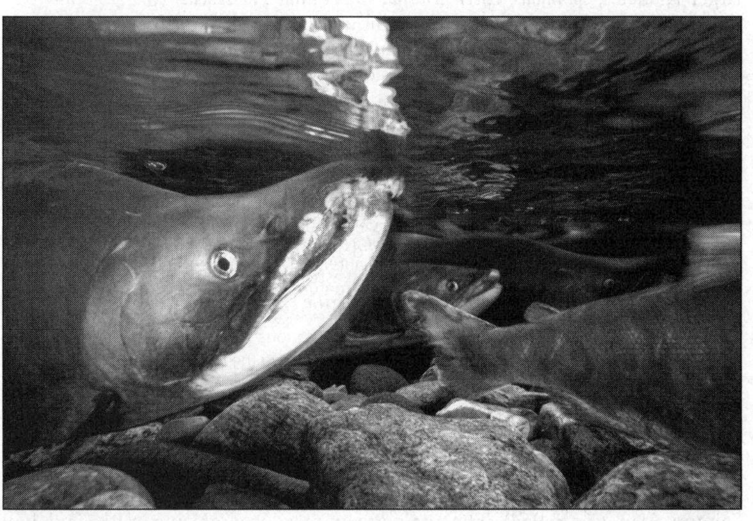

△ Marine sockeye salmon

Shuswap Regional District (Ⓣ250/832-8194 or 1-888/248-2773, Ⓦwww.csrd.bc.ca) for information on the whole region.

One of the most convenient of Salmon Arm's many **motels** is the clean and functional *Village Motel* (Ⓣ250/832-3955; ②) at 620 Trans-Canada Hwy. More upmarket, and still close to the highway, is the *Best Western Salmon Arm Inn*, 61 10th St SW (Ⓣ250/832-9793 or 1-877-778-6777, Ⓦwww.bestwestern.com; ⑥). There is also an HI-affiliated **hostel**, the *Squilax General Store and Caboose Hostel* (Ⓣ250/675-2977; ②) in Chase on the waterfront just off the Trans-Canada. The hostel building is the old General Store, while the 24 dorm beds (members $17, non-members $21) are in converted railway carriages. If you are coming by Greyhound bus, the driver will usually drop you on request at the hostel. Just 7km east of Chase, the lakeside *Quaaout Resort and Conference Centre* on Little Shuswap Rd (Ⓣ250/679-3090, Ⓦwww.quaaout.com; ⑤) is owned and run by the Little Shuswap Indian Band; it has 72 plush rooms, tepees for those who prefer to rough it, a sweat lodge and a restaurant serving native dishes such as 'bird in clay' ($37). Of several **campsites**, the obvious first choice is the *Salmon Arm KOA*, 3km east of town in a big wooded site, whose excellent facilities include a heated swimming pool (Ⓣ250/832-6489 or 1-800/562-9389, Ⓦwww.sakoa.com; $30; May–Oct). For beds or tent space, the *Salmon River Motel and RV Park*, 1km west of downtown at 910 40th St SW (Ⓣ250/832-3065; motel ②, March–Dec; RV $25, April–Oct), is also good. For **food** and drink, make for the *Hideaway Pub & Bistro*, not far from the Greyhound depot at 995 Lakeshore Drive, which does pub food like wings ($3) and ribs ($8).

For a decidedly alternative form of accommodation, head east along the Trans-Canada to **SICAMOUS**, a pleasant waterfront village that attracts the summer boating crowds and is known for its many upmarket **houseboats**. A few rent by the night, but most tend to be let weekly by about half-a-dozen local agencies on the marina and scattered around the village. Agencies you might try include *Bluewater Houseboats* (Ⓣ250/836-2255 or 1-800/663-4024, Ⓦwww.bluewaterhouseboats.ca; $895–6395 a week; April–Oct), one of the larger agencies; *Sicamous Creek Marina & Admiral Houseboats* (Ⓣ250/836-4611 or 1-866/704-4611, Ⓦwww.admiralhouseboats.com; $1795–3295 a week; April–Oct); or the *Twin Anchors Houseboat Association* (Ⓣ250/836-2450 or 1-800/663-4026, Ⓦwww.twinanchors.com; $6690–12,350 a week; April–Oct), with more than 100 boats. Prices might look terrifying, but boats accommodate up to 22 people.

For **information** there's a visitor centre at 110 Finlayson St by the Government Dock (Mon–Fri 9am–5pm; July & Aug daily; Ⓣ250/836-3313, Ⓦwww.sicamouschamber.bc.ca). To **eat and drink** locally, head for the *Brother's Neighbourhood Pub* at 420 Main St, which serves steaks, burgers and pasta ($7–14). For ordinary pub food (mains $6–12) served in the extraordinary surrounds of a seven-storey-high refurbished sawmill waste burner, head 15km north to Malakwa, to the *Burner Bar and Grille* at 4260 Oxbow Frontage (Ⓣ250/836-4600).

Highway 97 east of Kamloops

Passing through landscapes of Eden-like clarity and beauty, **Highway 97** is a far better entrance to (or exit from) the Okanagan than the dreary road to Salmon Arm (see p.954). The grass-green meadows, grazing cattle and low wooded hills here are the sort of scenery pioneers must have dreamed of; most of the little hamlets en route make charming spots to stay, and if you have time and transport any number of minor roads lead off to small lakes.

The hwy peels off the Trans-Canada 26km east of Kamloops, its first good stops being **MONTE LAKE**, served by the excellent *Heritage Campsite & RV Park* (Ⓣ250/375-2434; April–Nov; $18–22). **Westwold**, 5km beyond, is a dispersed ranching community of clean, old wooden houses and large pastures that present a picture of almost idyllic rural life. **FALKLAND**, 13km beyond, is an unassuming place with a rustic village atmosphere. Country lanes lead north and east from here to **Bolean Lake** (10km), **Pillar Lake** (13km) and to **Pinaus Lake** (10km).

The O'Keefe Ranch

Some 12km short ofVernon, near the junction with the west-side Okanagan Lake road, stands the **Historic O'Keefe Ranch**, a collection of early pioneer buildings and a tidy little museum that's well worth a half-hour's pause (Ⓣ250/542-7868, Ⓦwww.okeeferanch.bc.ca; May, June & Sept to mid-Oct daily 9am–5pm; July & Aug 9am–8pm; $10). In addition to a proficient summary of nineteenth-century frontier life, the museum contains an interesting section on the role of aboriginal peoples in the two world wars. Some 25 percent of eligible men immediately volunteered for service – a tour of duty that did little to resolve their national dilemma, which the museum sums up pithily with the observation that they belong to that "unhappy group who lost the old but are unable to obtain the new".

The Okanagan

The vine- and orchard-covered hills and warm-water lakes of the **Okanagan**, located in south-central British Columbia, are in marked contrast to the rugged beauty of the region's more mountainous interior, and have made the region not only one of Canada's most favoured fruit-growing areas but also one of its most popular summer-holiday destinations. However, unless you want (occasionally)

The legend of Okanagan Lake

When travelling through the Okanagan Valley, you'll find it hard to avoid **Ogopogo**, the famed lake monster of Okanagan Lake, whose smiling dragon-like face appears on all manner of postcards, billboards and bumper stickers – someone even thought to sell small bags of green jellybeans as his 'droppings'. Its name comes from a 1920s music-hall song – "his mother was an earwig, his father a whale; a little bit of head and hardly any tail; and Ogopogo was his name" – but the myth is much older. The aboriginal Salish peoples believed in such a creature, and referred to it as **N'ha-a-itk**, meaning "Lake Demon" or "Devil of the Lake". Legend has it that the Salish people warned early white settlers of the lake monster, who apparently was a demon-possessed man punished by the gods for murdering a tribal brother. To appease him, the Salish would sacrifice animals whenever crossing near **Rattlesnake Island**, around which the monster supposedly lurked. The early white settlers feared the reptile as well, setting up armed patrols along the shores in case of an attack. Nowadays, holiday-makers would be thrilled to spot BC's version of the Loch Ness monster, and numerous sightings are claimed every year.

rowdy beach life or enjoy mixing with families on their annual holiday, you'll probably want to ignore the area altogether in summer. Three main centres – **Vernon**, **Kelowna** and **Penticton**, ranging from north to south along the hundred-kilometre-long **Okanagan Lake** – together contain the lion's share of the province's interior population. All have fairly unpleasant downtown cores that embrace concrete, cars and unbridled construction, with an array of accommodation and tacky attractions for the summer hordes. As ever in BC, however, things improve immeasurably if you can slip away from the towns and head for the hills or quieter stretches of lakeshore.

The almost year-round Californian lushness that makes this "the land of beaches, peaches, sunshine and wine" means that, in the relative peace of **off season**, you can begin to experience the region's considerable charms: fruit trees in blossom, quiet lakeside villages and free wine tastings in local vineyards. Plus, you can also expect room rates to be up to fifty percent less in the off season. Kelowna is the biggest and probably best overall base at any time of the year, but Greyhound **buses** ply Hwy 97 on their way between Osoyoos and Kamloops or Salmon Arm.

Vernon

The beach scene is less frenetic in **VERNON** (pop. 38,000) than elsewhere in the Okanagan. Located at the junction of Hwys 6 and 97 near the northern edge of Okanagan Lake, the town attracts fewer of the bucket-and-spade brigade, though the emphasis on fruit and the great outdoors is as strong as ever, and the main hwy through town is bumper-to-bumper with motels, fast-food joints and ever-more garish neon signs. It's easier to find a place to stay here than in Kelowna (see opposite) – but there are also fewer reasons for wanting to do so.

Downtown Vernon centres on 30th Avenue (known as Main Street) and despite numerous listed buildings, is a charmless, downtrodden thoroughfare dominated by impatient traffic. At the southern entrance to town, sprawling **Polson Park** is a green sanctuary, but for beaches you should head 8km south of Vernon to **Kalamalka Provincial Park**, which sits on a stunning blue-green lake. The most popular **beach** on Kalamalka Lake is Kal Beach, fringed by trees, convenient parking just across the railway, and with a large pub with a terrace at its eastern end. **Kin Beach** on Okanagan Lake west on Okanagan Landing Road is another good spot.

Other outdoor recreation (but not camping) is on hand at **Silver Star Mountain Resort** (Nov–April day lift pass $65; ⓣ250-542-0224, ⓦwww.skisilverstar.com), a steep 22-kilometre drive to the northeast on 48th Avenue off Hwy 97, where in summer a **ski lift** (June–Sept daily 10am–5pm; $9) trundles to the top of Silver Star Mountain (1915m) for wide views and meadow-walking opportunities; the most-used trail wends from the summit back to the base area. This is also a popular mountain biking route and bicycle hire is available on the mountain from $40 a day. For guided summer interpretive hikes as well as winter snowshoeing trips, contact Outdoor Discoveries (ⓣ250/545-7446, ⓦwww.outdoordiscoveries.com). A shuttle bus services the mountain on demand (ⓣ250/938-0321, ⓦwww.allcanadianescapes.com).

On the other side of the valley, Paraglide Canada offer an eagle's-eye view of the area with tandem rides from the top of **Vernon Mountain** (ⓣ250/503-1962, ⓦwww.paraglidecanada.com; from $160).

Heading **south from Vernon**, be sure to take Mission Road to Commonage Road into Cars Landing on the western shore of Okanagan Lake – a quiet detour that offers something of the beauty for which the area is frequently praised, but which can be somewhat obscured by the commercialism of towns to the south. From the road, weaving through woods and small bays, the lake looks enchanting.

Practicalities

Vernon's **visitor centre** is well south of the centre at 701 Hwy 97 (May–Aug daily 8.30am–6pm; Sept–May Mon–Fri 8.30am–4.30pm; ⓣ250/542-1415, ⓦwww.vernontourism.com), along with a seasonal office north of town on the main hwy at 6326 Hwy 97 N. The **Greyhound station** is on the corner of 30th St and 31st Ave (ⓣ250/545-0527) with connections to Calgary and Vancouver.

The most pleasant place to stay if money isn't too much of an issue is the *Best Western Vernon Lodge*, 3914 32nd St (ⓣ250/545-3385 or 1-800/663-9400, ⓦwww.rpbhotels.com; ❺), nine blocks from Main Street on Hwy 97 with 127 air-conditioned rooms; or *Tiki Village*, 2408 34th St (ⓣ250/503-5566, ⓦwww.tikivillagevernon.com; ❺), fifteen minutes' walk southwest of downtown with thirty rooms, an outdoor pool and on-site Japanese restaurant. There's a **hostel** at Silver Star Mountain, the *Same Sun Backpacker Ski Lodge,* 9898 Pinnacles Rd (ⓣ250/545-8933, ⓦwww.samesun.com; ❷), with dorm beds $27 a night. **Campsites** near town all get busy during the high season, and the nicer option is the more rural *Ellison Provincial Park,* 16km off to the southwest on Okanagan Lake (reservations possible, see p.758; $17; March–Nov), with a beach and hiking trails.

There are plenty of **eating** choices, especially amongst the many cafés and sandwich places. Downtown, try *Portillo* at 2706 30th Ave (ⓣ250/545-9599) for good coffee, sandwiches, pastries and live music most nights. At 2915 30th Ave, *Eclectic Med* (ⓣ250/558-4646) has an extensive menu that is eclectic indeed, with Mediterranean, North African and Asian mains from $16–36. *Sir Winston's* at 2705 32nd St is the downtown **pub** of choice.

Kelowna

If you want a summer suntan, big crowds and cheek-by-jowl nightlife – none of which you'd readily associate with the British Columbian interior – then **KELOWNA** ("grizzly bear" in the Salish dialect) – is the place to come. Compared with other interior towns, Kelowna (pop.109,000) ranks as a sprawling metropolis, and to the unsuspecting visitor its approaches come as a very unpleasant surprise – particularly the appalling conglomeration of motels, garages and fast-food outlets on Hwy 97 at the north end of town.

That said, the lakefront and beaches, though heavily developed, aren't too bad, and off-season Kelowna's **downtown** can make a good respite from mountains and forests. Remarkable jumps in population have taken place over the last few years, mostly due to its popularity with retirees.

Arrival and information

Kelowna has a major regional **airport** situated 12km north of the town on Hwy 97; there are regular shuttles and local buses to the centre. The inconveniently located Greyhound **bus terminal** is at the east end of town in the Orchard Park Mall 5km from the centre at 2366 Leckie Rd on the corner of Harvey (Hwy 97), and sees off two buses daily to Calgary, Banff and Cache Creek and three to Kamloops (ⓣ250/860-3835). Buses #3, #7 and #19 run to downtown. The **visitor centre** (May–Sept daily 8am–8pm; Sept–May Mon–Fri 8am–5pm, Sat &

Sun 10am–5pm; ⓣ250/861-1515 or 1-800/663-4345, ⓦwww.tourismkelowna.com), five blocks back from the lake at 544 Harvey, has all the information you could possibly need. To **rent a bike**, try Sports Rent at 3000 Pandosy St or hook up with Monashee Adventure Tours, 1591 Highland Drive North (ⓣ1-888/762-9253, ⓦwww.monasheeadventuretours.com), for cycling tours to wineries and other parts of the Okanagan. A popular cycling route, the **Kettle Valley Railway Trail**, took a beating in the forest fires that ravaged the outskirts of Kelowna in 2003 (some 238 homes were also destroyed in the blaze), but it is on the way to being rebuilt. There's plenty of action on the lake for **water sports** aficionados; seadoos and boats can be rented for $50 an hour from Kelowna Marina at the end of Queensway Ave (ⓣ250/861-8001).

Accommodation

There are a staggering number of motels and campsites in and around town. However, **accommodation** can still be a major headache in the height of summer unless you can get to one of the **motels** on northbound Hwy 97 early in the morning, but it's a neon- and traffic-infested area well away from downtown and the lake (prices drop the further out you go). For something more low-key, there are countless bed and breakfast options. Kelowna's hostels fill quickly in the summer. If you're camping, all sites are pretty expensive, and in high season some places may only accept reservations for three days or more.

Hotels, motels and B&Bs

Grand Okanagan Lakeside Resort 1310 Water St ⓣ250/763-4500 or 1-800/465-4651, ⓦwww.grandokanagan.com. This is the money-no-object top choice in town. 8

Okanagan House 1449 Lambert Ave ⓣ250/712-1132 or 1-800/561-7653, ⓦwww.okanaganhouse.ca. Located in a tranquil suburban location just east of town, this welcoming B&B offers in-house massage and has a gallery displaying local art. 5

Prestige Hotel 1675 Abbott St ⓣ250/860-7900 or 1-877/737-8443, ⓦwww.prestigehotelsandresorts.com. Across from the City Park and Okanagan Lake, this is one of the best options in town. 6

Royal-Anne at 348 Bernard Ave ⓣ250/763-2277 or 1-888/811-3400, ⓦwww.royalannehotel.com. This popular and functional hotel is located right in the heart of the downtown action. 6

Travelodge Kelowna 1627 Abbott St ⓣ250/763-7771 or 1-800/663-2000, ⓦwww.travelodge.com. A few doors down from the *Prestige*, you could do worse than this busy, central option. 5

Hostels

Kelowna International Hostel 2343 Pandosy St near Guisachan Rd and the hospital ⓣ250/763-6024, ⓦwww.kelowna-hostel.bc.ca. Beds cost $13–15 at this charming, intimate hostel south of downtown. The owner will pick you up from the bus station or airport.

SameSun International Motel-Hostel 245 Harvey St just east of Abbott St ⓣ250/763-9814 or 1-877/562-2783, ⓦwww.samesun.com. From the bus station take bus #10 to Queensway. This enormous hostel just across from the beach has thirty private rooms and one hundred dorm beds at $27.

University of British Columbia Okanagan 3180 College Way ⓣ250/762-5445. The university lets out their campus rooms from May through Aug and is a good option if the hostels are full.

Camping

Bear Creek Provincial Park 9km west of town on Westside Road off Hwy 97 on the west side of the lake; $22; March–Nov. A good option if you want to be further away from the crowds, this campground has showers and most facilities.

Fintry Provincial Park 34km north of town. On the site of a former orchard, this campground doesn't skimp on facilities. Sites from $22; April–Oct.

Hiawatha RV Park 3795 Lakeshore Rd ⓣ250/861-4837 or 1-888/784-7275, ⓦwww.hiawatharvpark.com. Reasonably close to the action and backing onto Lakeshore Road, this campsite has a separate tenting area, laundry, heated pool and free hot showers. Sites from $39–47; April–Oct.

Willow Creek Family Campground 3316 Lakeshore Rd ⓣ250/762-6302, ⓦwww.willowcreekcampground.ca. Also fairly central, this campground boasts a grassy tenting area flanking a sandy beach. Sites from $29–38; open year-round.

The town and around

The main attractions in downtown Kelowna are the public beach off **City Park**, a green space that fronts downtown, and the strips along Lakeshore Road south of Kelowna's famed pontoon bridge, which tend to attract a younger, trendier crowd – **Rotary Beach** here is a windsurfers' hangout, and **Gyro Park**, just north, is where the town's teenagers practise their preening. Across the bridge and 2km and 14km respectively up the lake's west bank, **Bear Creek** and **Fintry Provincial Parks** are lovely spots with great beaches and campsites, but they are also horrendously popular.

Kelowna owes its prosperity primarily to one man, Father Pandosy, a French priest who founded a mission here in 1859 and planted a couple of apple trees two years later. Much of Canada's **fruit** is now grown in the area – including virtually all the apricots, half the pears and plums, and a third of the country's apples. The visitor centre can point you to dozens of fruit and food tours, but if you feel like sampling the more hedonistic fruits of Father Pandosy's labours, consider visiting one of the local **vineyards**, all of them known for their open-handed generosity with free samples after a tour of the premises. You can choose from a variety of whites and reds as the valley's microclimates and soil types allow neighbouring vineyards to produce completely different wines. At one time most were crisp, fruity German-style white wines and dessert wines, but now successful red wines and drier whites are emerging. There's even organic

△ Vineyard by Okanagan Lake

champagne at **Summerhill Pyramid Winery**, 4870 Chute Lake Rd (tours daily on the hour 11am–2pm; ⓣ250/764-8000 or 1-800/667-3538; ⓦwww.summerhill.bc.ca), in a beautiful spot with a top-notch restaurant and wines that are aged in a replica Egyptian pyramid; or try **Cedar Creek Estate Winery**, voted Canada's winery of the year in 2005 and 2006, at 5445 Lakeshore Rd (daily May–Oct 10am–6pm, Nov–April 11am–5pm; tours by appointment; ⓣ250/764-8866, ⓦwww.cedarcreek.bc.ca); or **Mission Hill Family Estate**, on the west side of the lake at 1730 Mission Hill Rd in a building that wouldn't look out of place in Tuscany (daily 9am–5pm; tours every half hour, $5; ⓣ250/768-6448, ⓦwww.missionhillwinery.com). A number of local companies run half or full day **wine tours** of the region; ask for a list at the visitor centre or contact the highly regarded Wildflower Trails and Winery Tours (ⓣ250/979-1211, ⓦwww.wildflowersandwine.com). All of the wineries join together in May and late September to lay on the region's annual spring and autumn **wine festivals** (ⓣ250/861-6654, ⓦwww.owfs.com) when free wine tastings, gourmet dinners, grape stomps and vineyard picnics take place to lure the connoisseur and beginner alike. More background can be found at the **Wine Museum**, 1304 Ellis St (Mon–Fri 10am–6pm, Sat 10am–5pm, Sun 11am–5pm), which is basically a glorified shop with a few exhibits.

Kelowna has a growing arts scene, and is justifiably proud of its six-block **cultural district**, centred around Cawston Avenue and Water Street; the main attractions here are the Rotary Centre for the Arts, 421 Cawston Ave, with a gallery, theatre, studios and café (daily 8am–8pm; ⓣ250/717-5304, & ⓦwww.rotarycentreofthearts.com), and the small but impressive Kelowna Art Gallery at 1315 Water St (Tues–Sat 10am–5pm, Sun 1–4pm, Thurs until 9pm; ⓣ250/762-2226; ⓦwww.kelownaartgallery.com; $4, free Thurs 3–9pm).

Getting away from Kelowna's crowds isn't easy, but the closest you'll come to shaking them off is by climbing **Knox Mountain**, the high knoll that overlooks the city to the north, just five minutes' drive (or a 30min walk) from downtown. It offers lovely views over the lake and town, particularly at sunset, and there's a wooden observation tower to make the most of the panorama.

Come winter, the focus moves 54km southeast of Kelowna off Hwy 33 to **Big White Ski Resort** (Nov–April; day lift pass $65; ⓣ250/765-8888, ⓦwww.bigwhite.com). The dry winters make this something of a powder paradise; with 16 lifts and 118 runs – over half of which cater to intermediate skiers – its claim to fame is Canada's largest totally ski-in/ski-out resort. There are more accommodation options here, including one hostel, the *Same Sun Big White Lodge* (ⓣ250/765-7920; ⓦwww.samesun.com) with dorms from $25 a night.

Eating, drinking and nightlife

Most **eating** places are crammed into the downtown area and cater to a range of tastes and budgets.

Bohemian Cafe and Catering Co 524 Bernard Ave. Usually packed with gossiping girlfriends, this cavernous hangout does hearty breakfasts and lunches for around $7.

Bouchons Bistro 105-1180 Sunset Drive ⓣ250/763-6595. This fine-dining restaurant serves French cuisine such as duck confit, rabbit and steak medallions (mains $20–33).

Flashbacks 1268 Ellis St (Fri & Sat only). Perennial downtown weekend favourite is the spot to go to for a good boogie.

Fresco 1560 Water St ⓣ250/868-8805; closed Jan & Mon. Widely considered the best restaurant in the Okanagan, *Fresco* prides itself on using local, seasonal produce (mains $26–36).

Grateful Fed Psyche Deli 509 Bernard Ave. Hosting live music at nights, the walls of this lively establishment are plastered with retro music paraphernalia.
Rosie's Pub 1352 Water St. If you're in town to sink a beer and people-watch, make for this lakeside terrace heaving with sun-struck revellers.
Siam Orchard 279 Bernard Ave ⓣ250/860-5600; closed Mon. Follow the crowds here for terrific value Thai (the vegetarian phad Thai is a bargain at $7.50).

Penticton

PENTICTON (pop.33,000) 68km south of Kelowna, is a corruption of the Salish phrase *pen tak tin* – "a place to stay forever"; while this is not a sobriquet the most southerly of the Okanagan's big towns deserves, it is far more laid back and inviting than Kelowna. Its summer daily average of ten hours of sunshine ranks it higher than Honolulu, making tourism its biggest industry after fruit (this is "Peach City"). That, along with Penticton's proximity to Vancouver and the US, keeps prices high and ensures that the town and beaches are swarming with water-sports jocks, cross-country travellers, RV skippers and lots of happy families. Off the beaches there's some festival or other playing virtually every day of the year to keep the punters entertained, the key ones being the **Wine Festival** in May and late September and the **Peach Festival** in August.

Most leisure pastimes in Penticton take place on or near Okanagan Lake, just ten blocks from the town centre. **Okanagan Beach** is the closest sand to downtown and is usually covered in oiled bodies for most of its one-kilometre stretch; **Skaha Beach**, 4km south of town on Skaha Lake, is a touch quieter and trendier – both close at midnight, and sleeping on them is out of the question. The favourite method of cooling off in the summer is by **floating** down the Okanagan River Channel to Skaha Lake in an inflatable boat or tube; the route takes between two and four hours depending on the current and is popular with posturing teenagers working hard on their skin cancer; Cayote Cruises, 215 Riverside Drive (ⓣ250/492-2116), rent out tubes and offer a return shuttle for $11.

If you're determined to sightsee, the **museum** at 785 Main St has a panoply of predictable Canadiana (Mon–Sat 10am–5pm; donation suggested) and you can take tours around the SS *Sicamous* (May–Sept daily 9am–9pm; Oct–April daily 9am–5pm; $5), a beached **paddlesteamer** off Lakeshore Drive on the Kelowna side of town. Just off Main Street there's the **Art Gallery of South Okanagan**, 199 Front St, which often carries high-quality shows (Tues–Fri 10am–5pm, Sat & Sun noon–5pm; $2, free on Saturdays) and backs onto lovely Japanese gardens. More tempting perhaps, and an ideal part of a day's stopover, is a trip to the **Tin Whistle Brewery**, 954 West Eckhardt Ave (drop-in tours and tastings year-round; Mon–Sat 11am–5pm; ⓣ250/770-1122), which offers three English-type ales and a celebrated Peaches and Cream beer (summer only). If your taste is for wine rather than beer, head for the **Red Rooster Winery**, 891 Naramata Rd (daily 10am–6pm; tours 1pm & 3pm; ⓣ250/492-2424, ⓦwww.redroosterwinery.com), with an on-site art gallery housing a replica of *The Baggage Handler*, a controversial sculpture known to locals as "Frank"; it was banished from its original home in a downtown Penticton traffic circle after locals took offence to its nudity – one incensed vandal even had the guts to hack off Frank's privates. For another unique experience, **Elephant Island Winery**, 2730 Aikens Loop, Naramata, 15km north of town (ⓣ250/496-5522, ⓦwww.elephantislandwine.com), makes highly regarded fruit wines. If you are vineyard hopping and want to avoid drink driving, Top Cat Tours offer **guided trips**, with lunch included (ⓣ250/493-7385, ⓦwww.topcattours.com).

Winters in Penticton centre 33km west of the town at the **Apex Mountain Resort** (Nov to early April; day lift pass $53; ⓣ877/777-2730, ⓦwww.apexresort.com;), where experienced downhill **skiers** go weak at the knees at the selection of black diamond mogul runs. It has five lifts and 67 runs (many of these become hiking, cycling and horseriding trails in the summer).

Practicalities

Penticton **airport** (ⓣ250/493-2900, ⓦwww.cyyf.org) is eight-kilometres south of downtown. Arriving by Greyhound, you'll pull in to the **bus depot** just off Main St between Robinson and Ellis sts (ⓣ250/493-4101); Penticton is a major intersection of routes, with buses bound for Vancouver (4 daily), Kamloops (3 daily), Nelson and points east (1 daily). The downtown area is small and easy to negotiate, particularly after a visit to the big **visitor centre** at 533 Railway St (June–Sept daily 8am–8pm, rest of year Mon–Fri 9am–6pm, Sat & Sun 10am–5pm; ⓣ250/493-4055 or 1-800/663-5052, ⓦwww.tourismpenticton.ca) on the north side of town – it has an adjacent BC Wine Information Centre, where bottles cost the same as they do at the vineyards. For used books, **guides and maps**, visit *The Bookshop*, 238–242 Main St. **Bicycles** can be rented at *Freedom The Bike Shop*, 533 Main St (ⓣ250/493-0683). For **rock climbing** on the famed Skaha Bluffs, hook up with Skaha Rock Adventures, 113–437 Martin St (ⓣ250/493-1765, ⓦwww.skaharockclimbing.com).

Although Penticton boasts a brimful of **accommodation**, it doesn't make finding a room in summer any easier. Most of the cheaper **motels** line the messy southern approach to the town along Hwy 97. Two of the best and more central choices are the luxurious *Penticton Lakeside Resort*, 21 Lakeshore Drive West (ⓣ250/493-8221 or 1-800/663-9400, ⓦwww.pentictonlakesideresort.com; ⑦), and *Days Inn Conference Centre*, with 105 rooms at 152 Riverside Drive (ⓣ250/493-6616, ⓦwww.daysinnpenticton.ca; ⑥). If location doesn't matter too much, try the *Waterfront Inn*, 3688 Parkview St (ⓣ250/492-8228 or 1-800/563-6006, ⓦwww.waterfrontinn.net; ⑥; May to mid-Oct) just across from Skaha Lake beach. The HI-affiliated **hostel** is at 464 Ellis St (ⓣ250/492-3992 or 1-866/782-9736, ⓦwww.hihostels.ca) in an old bunkhouse downtown that has 47 beds in dorms (members $20, non-members $24) and private rooms. To get here, walk one block south from the bus station and the hostel is on the left.

Recommended **campsites** are *South Beach Gardens*, 3815 Skaha Lake Rd (ⓣ250/492-0628, ⓦwww.southbeachgardens.net; $28–35; April–Sept), or *Wright's Beach Camp*, south of town on Hwy 97 right on Lake Skaha (ⓣ250/492-7120, ⓦwww.wrightsbeachcamp.com; $30–43; May–Oct). If you want to camp away from town, make for the *Camp-Along Tent and Trailer Park*, 6km south of the town off Hwy 97 in an apricot orchard overlooking Skaha Lake (ⓣ250/497-5584 or 1-800/968-5267, ⓦwww.campalong.com; $24–40; April–Oct). The nicest campground of all is in the *Okanagan Lake Provincial Park* (March–Oct; $22), approximately 22km north of Penticton, with sites overlooking the lake.

For its size, Penticton has an impressive range of **eating** options. For something low-key try the funky *Fibonacci Rostery and Café*, 219 Main St, serving organic coffee and vegetarian wraps. Flying the flag for bohemian Penticton, *The Dream Cafe*, 67 Front St (ⓣ250/490-9012, ⓦwww.thedreamcafe.ca) has oodles of atmosphere and delectable Indian, Middle Eastern and Asian-inspired cuisine (mains $7.50–16) and also hosts quality live music events. *Theo's* at 687 Main St (ⓣ250/492-4019) is a friendly, crowded and highly rated Greek place that does big portions (mains $13–27). For something more upmarket, search out *Salty's Beach House*, 988 Lakeshore Drive (ⓣ250/493-5001), a restaurant that's very popular but eccentric, with a South Seas setting of palm trees and fishing nets and a spicy menu of Caribbean, Thai, Indonesian and Malaysian food (mains around $18). For **drinks**, make for the perennially popular *Barking Parrot* in the *Penticton Lakeside Resort*, with unbeatable views and live music on the outdoor patio.

Highway 3: the border towns

Unless you're crossing the US–Canada border locally, British Columbia's slightly tawdry necklace of border towns between Hope (see p.944) and the Alberta border along **Highway 3** is as good a reason as any for taking a more northerly route across the province. Few of the towns amount to much; if you have to break the journey, aim to do it in **Salmo** or **Castlegar**, towns on which some of the Kootenays' charm has rubbed off. Things are more interesting around **Osoyoos** and **Keremeos**, where the road enters a parched desert landscape after climbing from Hope through the gripping mountain scenery of the Coastal Ranges, passing en route through **Manning Provincial Park**.

If you're crossing over **the border** hereabouts, incidentally, don't be lulled by the remote customs posts into expecting an easy passage: if you don't hold a Canadian or US passport you can expect the sort of grilling you'd get at major entry points.

Manning Provincial Park

One of the few parks in the Coast and Cascade ranges, **Manning Provincial Park** parcels up a typical assortment of mountain, lake and forest scenery about 60km south of Princeton and 64km east of Hope and is conveniently bisected by Hwy 3. Even if you're just passing through it's time well spent walking at least one of the short **trails** off the road, the best of which is the 700-metre Sumallo Grove loop, located 10km east of the park's west portal. The most popular drive within the park is the fifteen-kilometre side road to **Cascade Lookout**, a viewpoint overlooking an amphitheatre of mountains; a gravel road carries on another 6km from here to **Blackwall Peak**, the starting point for the **Heather Trail** (10km one-way), renowned for its swaths of summer wild flowers. Other manageable day-hikes leave the south side of the main highway, the majority accessed from the Lightning Lake Road. In the winter, the park is a good for downhill and cross country **skiing** as well as snowshoeing.

For park information and trail leaflets, ask at the front desk of the *Manning Park Resort* (Ⓣ250/840-8822 or 1-800/330-3321, Ⓦwww.manningparkresort.com; ❻), on Hwy 3 almost exactly midway between Princeton and Hope (64km), which has cabins, chalets and hotel rooms. There are also four provincial **campsites** ($14–22; reservations possible, see p.758) on and off the highway, those close to the road being *Coldspring, Hampton* and *Mule Deer*. A fourth, *Lightning Lake*, has free hot showers and flush toilets, but you'll need to reserve a site in advance.

Highway 3 from Princeton

Lacklustre low hills ripple around **PRINCETON**'s dispersed collection of mostly drab houses. If you need to stay here, the **visitor centre** (daily 9am–5pm; Ⓣ250/295-3103, Ⓦwww.princetonbc.info), is at 105 Hwy 3 East. **HEDLEY**, about 20km further on, is an old gold-mining hamlet that today is little more than a single street with great scenery and a couple of motels. The **visitor centre** is part of a small but interesting **museum** with archive photos and mining memorabilia at 712 Daly St (mid-May to Aug daily 9am–5pm; rest of year Thurs–Mon 9am–4pm; donation suggested; ⓣ250/292-8422, ⓔhedleymuseum@uniserve.net). Pick up details of the self-guided walking tour around the village's period buildings. To **stay**, try the *Colonial Inn Bed & Breakfast* (ⓣ250/292-8131, ⓦwww.colonialinnbb.ca; ❹), an historic 1930s house built by the Kelowna Exploration Gold Mining Company to wine and dine potential investors; it has just five rooms and sixteen RV sites ($25). The *Gold House B&B* 200m off Hwy 3 at 644 Colonial Rd (ⓣ250/292-8418 or 1-866/676-4653, ⓦwww.thegoldhouse.com; ❸), is equally historic, having been the 1904 Gold Assay Office. **Eat** and **drink** at *The Hitching Post*, 916 Scott Ave (ⓣ250/292-8413; closed Tues), in a downtown heritage building, serving generous portions of seafood, steak and ribs with dishes from $5–28.

Beyond Hedley and 21km east of Princeton, off the highway, lies **Bromley Rock Provincial Park**, a lovely picnic stop looking down on the white water of the Similkameen River. It also has seventeen campsites ($14). West of the village is the *Stemwinder Provincial Park* **campsite** ($14; April–Oct), a small, pine-tree dotted site with 27 pitches. Further on, on the way to Keremeos, is another of British Columbia's extremely picturesque patches of road; for much of the way it follows the ever-narrowing Similkameen Valley.

Keremeos

Highway 3 meanders eventually to pretty little **KEREMEOS**, whose aboriginal name supposedly means "where the three winds meet" – a reference to the stiff breezes that are channeled through the hills hereabouts. The local landscape lurches suddenly into a far more beautiful rural mode, thanks mainly to a climate that blesses the region with the longest growing season in the country – hence the tag "Fruit Stand Capital of Canada". Keremeos, whose attractive situation rivals Nelson's (see p.980), spreads over a dried-up lake bed, with hills and mountains rising from the narrow plain on all sides. Lush, irrigated orchards surround the town, offset in spring by huge swaths of flowers across the valley floor, and depending on the season you can pick up fruit and vegetables from stands dotted more or less everywhere: cherries, apricots, peaches, pears, apples, plums and grapes all grow in abundance. If you're not tempted by the food, however, you may be by the **wine tastings** at the organic **St Laszlo Vineyards** (9am-9pm, ⓣ250/499-2856), 1km east of town on Hwy 3.

Keremeos itself is a rustic, two-street affair that's almost unspoilt by neon or other urban clutter. There are a couple of **motels** locally: the cheaper is the *Similkameen Motel* (ⓣ250/499-5984; ❷), 1km west of the centre in open country surrounded by lawns and orchards; but the nicer is *The Elk* (ⓣ250/499-2043 or 1-888/499-7773; ❹), also with landscaped gardens. The *Pasta Trading Post* on 629 7th Ave is a wonderful place to **eat** locally grown organic produce, with mains ranging from $5–20 (closed Tues). They also have comfortable **rooms** upstairs (ⓣ250/499-2933, ⓦwww.pastatradingpost.com; ❹).

Osoyoos

Beyond Keremeos the road climbs 46km, eventually unfolding a dramatic view, far below, of **OSOYOOS** – meaning "gathered together" – and a sizeable lake surrounded by bare, ochre hills. Descending, you enter one of Canada's strangest landscapes – a bona fide desert of half-bare, scrub-covered hills, sand, lizards, cactus, snakes (23 types of invertebrate here are found nowhere else in the world) and Canada's lowest average rainfall (around 25cm per year). Temperatures are regularly 10°C higher than in Nelson, less than a morning's drive away, enabling exotic fruit like bananas and pomegranates to be grown and prompting Osoyoos to declare itself the "Spanish Capital of Canada".

The town is otherwise distinguished by its position beside **Lake Osoyoos** (Canada's warmest freshwater lake, at 24°C) in the Okanagan Valley; Hwy 97, which passes through the town as an ugly strip, is the main route into the Okanagan region. In summer the place comes alive with swimmers and boaters and with streams of American RVs slow-tailing their way northwards to where the real action is.

A visit to the **Desert Centre** (mid-April to mid-Oct daily 10am–4.30pm; $6; ⓣ250/1-877/899-0897, ⓦwww.desert.org), on Hwy 97 just north of town, is a good way to learn a little more about the region's oddball environment. There are tours over a 1.5km boardwalk through a small area of desert, a fascinating ecosystem of some one hundred rare plants, including tiny cacti and sage, as well as three hundred animals from rattlesnakes to pocket gophers that are now all under serious threat. For a similar experience that packs a bonus cultural punch, visit the recently upgraded **Nk'Mip Desert Culture Centre,** 1000 Rancher Creek Rd on Hwy 3 just east of town (Nov–April Mon–Sat 9.30am–4pm; May–Oct daily 9.30am–4.30pm; $12; ⓣ250/495-7901, ⓦwww.nkmipdesert.com), run by the Osoyoos Indian Band and featuring a reconstruction of a native village and 2km of trails through a desert landscape that has an unnerving number of "rattlesnake alert" signs. On the same property is a nine-hole golf course, a campground and RV park, the swanky *Spirit Ridge Resort and Spa* (ⓣ250/495-2684, ⓦwww.spiritridge.ca; ❽) and **Nk'Mip Cellars**, Canada's first aboriginal-owned winery (daily 9am–5pm, tours 11am, 1 & 3pm; Nov–April 10am–5pm, tours 1pm; ⓣ250/495-2985, ⓦwww.nkmipcellars.com).

The relative lack of crowds (summer excepted) and strange scenery might persuade you to do your beach-bumming in Osoyoos, though you may be pushed to find space in any of the town's twenty or so **hotels** and **motels** during high season; a good choice is the *Avalon*, 9106 Main St (ⓣ250/495-6334 or 1-800/264-5999, ⓦwww.avaloninn.ca; ❺). A more expensive option is the *Best Western Sunrise Inn,* 5506 Main St (ⓣ250/495-4000 or 1-877/878-2200, ⓦwww.bestwesternosoyoos.com; ❻), with an indoor pool and restaurant. For more choice and help, contact the **visitor centre** at the corner of Hwys 3 and 97 (ⓣ250/495-3366, ⓦwww.destinationosoyoos.com), with the **Greyhound stop** (ⓣ250/495-7252) outside. You're more likely to get a place in one of the half-dozen local **campsites** – try the *Nk'Mip Campground and RV Park* on 45th St 1km from Hwy 3 East (ⓣ250/495-7279; $27-35) or the popular and picturesque *Hayes Point Provincial Park*, 2km south of town on 32nd Ave off Hwy 97 (ⓣ1-800/689-9025, ⓦwww.discovercamping.ca; $22). Local **eateries** are almost entirely fast food, but the *Wildfire Grill*, 8526 Main St (ⓣ250/495-2215; closed Sun & Mon), is a fine dining favourite (mains around $18). For a caffeine fix, join the locals at *Garage Gallery & Coffee Company*, 8111 Main St, with free Internet use for customers.

Moving on from Osoyoos involves a major decision if you're travelling by car or bike: continue east on Hwy 3, or strike north on Hwy 97 through the Okanagan to the Trans-Canada Hwy. Twice-daily Greyhound buses plow north through the Okanagan; one bus leaves daily for Vancouver (8h 30min) while another heads east towards Nelson (5hrs) in the Kootenays.

Grand Forks

GRAND FORKS, 126km east of Osoyoos, is not grand at all – it's very small and little more than a perfunctory transit settlement built on a river flat. Several Greyhound **buses** drop in daily, probably the biggest thing to happen to the place. The **visitor centre** is at 7362 5th St (Sept–May Mon–Fri 8.30am–4.30pm; June–Aug daily 8.30am–6pm; Ⓣ250/442-2833, Ⓦwww.grandforkschamber.com). The history of Doukhobor settlers (see box opposite) is charted at the small **Hardy Mountain Doukhobor Village Historic Site** (June–Aug daily 9am–6pm; $2) on Hardy Mountain Rd. For a further taste of all things Russian, sample the home-made Eastern European (and Mexican) fare at the *Borscht Bowl* at 258 Market Ave (Ⓣ250/442-5977) – its namesake dish comes in different sizes ($5–7). About 25km north of town, 19km long **Christina Lake** – which claims some of BC's warmest water – is a modestly unspoilt summer resort with lots of swimming, boating and camping opportunities (two other BC lakes make similar claims for their waters). A dozen or so motels and campsites sprout along its shore, mostly at the lake's southern end.

Rossland

Picturesque **ROSSLAND**, which relies on the lead and zinc smelter in nearby **Trail** for employment, was founded on gold mining – some $125 million-worth of which was gouged from the surrounding hills around the year 1900 (that's $2 billion-worth at today's prices). If you're into mining heritage, a tour of the **Le Roi Gold Mine** – once one of the world's largest, with 100km of tunnels – and the adjoining **Rossland Historical Museum** will entertain you with fascinating technical and geological background (mid-May to mid-Sept daily 9am–5pm; mine tours May, June & Sept every 1hr 30min, July & Aug every 30min; museum & mine $8, just museum $4; Ⓣ1-800/448-7444, Ⓦwww.rosslandmuseum.ca).

The **visitor centre** (mid-May to Sept daily 9am–5pm; Ⓣ250/362-7722 or 1-888/448-7444, Ⓦwww.rossland.com), in the museum at the junction of the town's two main roads (Hwy 3B & Hwy 22), is useful for details of the **Nancy Greene Provincial Park**, nestled in the Monashee Mountains, and which has a ten-pitch campsite (no showers; May–Sept; $10) northwest of town. The town's major draw is the **Red Mountain Resort** (mid-Dec to early April; day lift pass $52; Ⓣ1-800/663-0105, Ⓦwww.redresort.com); a training ground for the Canadian national ski team, it has over 1,500 acres of skiable terrain and is also excellent for mountain biking in the summer (there are over a hundred kilometres of trails). **Rent bikes** and pick up information at *Revolution Cycles and Service*, 2133 Columbia Ave (Ⓣ250/362-5688). There's a **hostel**, the *Mountain Shadow Hostel* at 2125 Columbia Ave (Ⓣ250/362-7160, Ⓦwww.mshostel.com; dorm beds $20), and several resort hotels; or try the upmarket twelve-unit *Ram's Head Inn*, 3km west of Rossland on Hwy 3B (Ⓣ250/362-9577 or 1-877/267-4323, Ⓦwww.ramshead.bc.ca; ⑤), with hot tubs and bike rental.

Rossland has a few nice places to **eat**: the locals' choice is the *Sunshine Café* (breakfast & lunch only; closes 3pm) on Columbia (the main street) or sample the award-winning desserts ($7) at the more upmarket *Gypsy at Red* at the base of the ski hill at 4430 Red Mountain Rd (Ⓣ250/362-3347; lunch Thurs–Sun and dinner daily); for a protein fix, sink your teeth into the Angus sirloin steak ($23).

Castlegar

Some 27km north of Trail on Hwy 22, **CASTLEGAR** is a strange diffuse place with no obvious centre, probably because roads and rivers – this is where the

Kootenay meets the Columbia – make it more a transport hub than a community. In the early 1900s it was famous for its immigrant **Doukhobor** or "Spirit Wrestler" population (see box below). Much of the community's heritage has been collected in the **Doukhobor Village Museum** (May–Sept daily 10am–5pm; $8; ⓣ250/365-6622, ⓦwww.doukhobor-museum.org) at 112 Heritage Way, just off the main road on the right after you cross the big suspension bridge over the Kootenay River. A Doukhobor descendant is on hand to take you through the museum, which houses a winsome display of farm machinery, handmade tools, superb archive photographs and traditional Russian clothing. For a further taste of Doukhobor culture, visit the evocative **Zuckerberg Island Heritage Park** (ⓣ250/365-6440) off 7th Ave, named after a local teacher of Doukhobors who built a log Russian Orthodox Chapel House and other buildings and memorials here after coming to the town in 1931; it is reached by a ninety-metre pedestrian suspension bridge.

Castlegar's **visitor centre** (July & Aug daily 8am–7pm; rest of year Mon–Fri 9am–5pm; ⓣ250/365-6313, ⓦwww.castlegar.com) is at 1995 6th Ave off the main road as you come into town from Grand Forks. The town has the major regional **airport** for the Kootenays region; the landing strip is alongside Hwy 3A. There are some half-dozen places to stay in and around town: the best **motel** – small, and with a nice view and an RV site ($20) – is the *Cozy Pines* on Hwy 3 on the western edge of town at 2118 Crestview Crescent (ⓣ250/365-5613, ⓦwww.cozypines.com; ❷). Closer in is the modern and

The Doukhobors

The **Doukhobors** were members of a southern Russian sect who fled their home country in 1899 after being persecuted for their religious and political views. The so-called "Spirit Wrestlers" – the name was coined by a Russian Orthodox archbishop who argued that they were in conflict with the Holy Spirit – were fiercely pacifist, rejected secular government and ignored the liturgy and procedures of the organized church, believing that God resided in each individual, rather than in a building or institution.

The flight from Russia was aided by the Quakers, whose pacifist and other ideals closely tallied with those of the Doukhobors, and by the novelist Leo Tolstoy, whose beliefs also chimed with those of the sect. Around 7500 left in the first wave, bringing their pacifist-agrarian lifestyle to western Canada, and to Saskatchewan in particular. Initially the authorities were sympathetic to their beliefs, and granted religious, educational and housing concessions. In 1905, however, sect members refused to swear an oath of allegiance to the dominion government and subsequently, between 1908 and 1913 followed their leader, Peter Verigin, to southern BC.

By the 1920s the province had around ninety Doukhobor settlements, each with a communal population of around sixty. They arrived in Castlegar in 1908, establishing at least 24 villages in the area, each with Russian names meaning things like "the beautiful", "the blessed" or "consolation". Accomplished farmers, they laboured under the motto "Toil and a Peaceful Life", creating highly successful orchards, farms, sawmills and packing plants. Although their way of life waned after the death of Verigin in 1924, killed by a bomb planted in his railway carriage, the Doukhobors' considerable industry and agricultural expertise transformed the Castlegar area; many locals still practise the old beliefs – Doukhobor numbers are around 15,000 across the region (though those with Doukhobor roots total about 30,000) – and Russian is still spoken. These days there's also a breakaway radical sect, the Freedomites, or Sons of Freedom, infamous for their eye-catching demonstrations – of which fires and nude parades are just two – against materialism and other morally dubious values.

attractive *Best Western Fireside Motor Inn*, 1810 8th Ave at the junction of hwys 3 and 22 (Ⓣ250/365-2128 or 1-800/499-6399, Ⓦwww.bestwestern.com; ④). About 3km west of town on Hwy 3 is the *Castlegar RV Park and Campground*, (Ⓣ250/365-2337, Ⓦwww.castelgarrvpark.com; $16–24; April–Oct), with wireless Internet, free hot showers, laundry and restaurant. There are also regional and provincial park **campsites** in the vicinity: *Pass Creek Regional Park*, which has a nice, sandy beach (Ⓣ250/365-3386; $15; April–Sept), 2km west off Hwy 3a at the Kootenay River Bridge; and the *Syringa Provincial Park* (reservations possible, see p.758; $17; April–Oct), 19km north of Hwy 3 at Castlegar on the east side of Lower Arrow Lake. For cheap **eating**, *Gabriel's Restaurant* (Ⓣ250/365-6028) at 1432 Columbia Ave serves light meals from pasta dishes ($11) to ribs ($23).

Salmo

Despite the large volume of traffic converging on it along Hwy 3 and Hwy 6, tiny **SALMO**, 43km east of Castlegar, somehow manages to retain a pioneer feel with its tidy wooden buildings. The Chamber of Commerce (Mon–Fri 10am–4pm, plus Sat & Sun same hours July & Aug; Ⓣ250/357-2596, Ⓦwww.salmo.net) is at 4th St and Railway Ave. In August, 10,000 ravers, hippies and world-class DJs descend on the Salmo River Ranch, 6km east of town, for the five-day **Shambala Music Festival** (Ⓣ250/352-7623, Ⓦwww.shambhalamusicfestival.com). In winter there's **skiing** 2km east of town at the Salmo ski area.

Buses usually pull in here for a long rest stop. If you need to overnight, use either of the two central motels: the *Reno*, 123 Railway Ave (Ⓣ250/357-9937, Ⓦwww.renomotel.ca; ④), one block east of the bus terminal, or the slightly cheaper *Salcrest*, 110 Motel Ave (Ⓣ250/357-9557; ③), at the junction of hwys 3 and 6. For **camping**, try the *Selkirk Motel and RV Sites* (Ⓣ250/357-2346 or 1-888/368-6336; $12–16; units ①; May–Oct), 4km west of town at 307 2nd Relief Rd. For **food**, *Charlie's Pizza and Spaghetti House* (Ⓣ250/357-9335) is an old-style diner on 4th Street serving hunger-crushing breakfasts as well as wraps and burgers (dinner mains $12–18). Just up the road, the *Silver Dollar Pub* is the town's favourite **bar**, with pool tables, a jukebox and lots of good ol' boys in an atmospheric wooden interior.

A classic stretch of scenic road, Hwy 3 climbs south from Salmo and then east to the fruit-growing plains around Creston via **Kootenay Pass** (1774m). This is one of the highest main roads in the country – it's frequently closed by bad weather – and, beyond about 13km out of Salmo, it has no services until Creston, so check your petrol before setting out. If you're cycling, brace yourself for a fifty-kilometre uphill slog, but the reward is an unexpected and stunning lake at the pass, where there's a pull-off picnic area and views of high peaks in the far distance.

Creston and around

Don't stop in prosperous little **CRESTON**, 83km east of Salmo near the broad mountain-flanked floodplain of the Kootenay River, unless you're a bird-watcher. In recent years, Creston has found itself on the map no thanks to **Bountiful**, a community of 1200 polygamists, fundamentalist Mormons who reside southeast of downtown near the US border, in a sprawling collection of drab houses. The sect members do not take well to tourists coming to gawk at their lifestyle, nor the publicity generated by claims of widespread sexual abuse.

If you're passing through downtown Creston, you might want to pause for the **Stone House Museum**, 219 Devon St (May–Sept daily 10am–3.30pm, by appointment the rest of the year; $3; ⓣ250/428-9262), known for its replica Kuntenai (Ktunaxa) canoe. Similar canoes, with their down-pointed ends, are only found elsewhere in the world in parts of eastern Russia, underlining the fact that millennia ago migrations took place across the Bering Straits into North America. If you're not driving, another temptation is the **Columbia Brewery**, 1220 Erickson St (ⓣ250/428-9344, tours in summer), whose Kokanee beers you'll find in most of the region's bars and restaurants.

The **visitor centre** is at 1607 Canyon St (daily July & Aug 9am–5pm, Mon–Fri Sept–June 9am–4pm; ⓣ250/428-4342, ⓦwww.crestonbc.com or www.crestonvalley.com): use it if by mischance you need **accommodation**. The cheapest option in town is the central but sparse *Snoring Sasquatch Hostel*, 221 11th Ave North (ⓣ250/428-4660, ⓦwww.crestonhostel.com; ❶), with dorm beds $18 a night; motels on the town's fringes offer more salubrious alternatives. If you want coffee, snacks or picnic provisions, a good place to **eat** is the *Creston Valley Bakery*, 113 10th Ave or the *Other Side Café*, 1021 Canyon St, which serves hearty vegetarian and Asian fusion dishes for around $8.

Probably the best reason to spend time locally is the 7000-hectare **Creston Valley Wildlife Management Area** (ⓣ250/402-6900, ⓦwww.crestonwildlife.ca), located 10km northwest of town off Hwy 3. Creston overlooks a broad section of valley and lowlands – home to the idly meandering Kootenay River. Over the years the river has repeatedly burst its banks, creating a rich alluvial plain beloved by farmers, and producing the lush medley of orchards and verdant fields that fringe Creston. The flood plain and its wetlands – the so-called "Valley of the Swans" – have created a haven for birds and waterfowl. This area has one of the world's largest nesting osprey populations, while a total of 250 species have been recorded in the confines of the Creston Management Area (not to mention otters, moose and other animals). For full details of the area visit the sanctuary's Wildlife Centre (May–Oct daily 9am–5pm; $3).

For details of the trip east of Creston, see p.984.

The Kootenays

The Kootenays is one of the most attractive and unvisited parts of British Columbia, and one of the most loosely defined. It consists essentially of two major north–south valleys – the Kootenay and the Columbia, which are largely taken up by **Kootenay Lake** and **Upper** and **Lower Arrow Lakes** – and three intervening mountain ranges – the Purcells, Selkirks and Monashees, whose once-rich mineral deposits formed the kernel of the province's early mining industry. **Nelson** is the key town, slightly peripheral to the Kootenays' rugged core, but a lovely place, and one of the few provincial towns that offers real attractions in its own right. Scattered lakeside hamlets, notably **Kaslo** and **Nakusp**, make excellent bases for excursions into mountain scenery which has a pristine quality rarely found elsewhere. Water-based activities – canoeing and fishing in particular – are excellent, and you can also explore the ramshackle mining heritage of near-ghost towns like **Sandon** and **New Denver**. Many of these towns and villages also have more than their fair share of artists, painters, writers, healers and New Age enthusiasts, lending the region considerable cultural and alternative-lifestyle lustre.

Getting around the region is tricky without **private transport**, which is a shame because the roads here are amongst the most scenic in a province noted for its scenery. The most **scenic routes** – and these are some of the loveliest drives in the province – are Hwy 31A from Kaslo to New Denver, Hwy 6 south of New Denver in the Slocan Valley and Hwy 6 from New Denver to Vernon. Given no time constraints, your best strategy would be to enter from Creston and exit via Vernon, which sets you up for the Okanagan.

Highway 3A to Kootenay Bay

Starting from just north of Creston, **Highway 3A** picks a slow, twisting course up the eastern shore of **Kootenay Lake** to the free car ferry at Kootenay Bay. Apart from the ample scenic rewards of the lake and the mountains beyond it, the hwy is almost completely empty for all of its 79km, and none of the villages marked on maps amount to anything more than scattered houses hidden in the woods. The only noteworthy sight is the **Glass House** (May, June, Sept & Oct daily 9am–5pm; July & Aug 8am–8pm; $6; ⓣ250/223-8372), midway up the lake 7km south of **BOSWELL**, which ranks highly on the list of Canada's more bizarre offerings. Constructed entirely from embalming bottles, the house was built by a Mr David Brown in 1952 after 35 years in the funeral business – "to indulge", so the wonderfully po-faced pamphlet tells you, "a whim of a peculiar nature". The retired mortician travelled widely, visiting friends in the funeral profession until he'd collected 600,000 bottles to build his lakeside retirement home. The family continued to live here until curious tourists took the upper hand. Nearby **accommodation** is provided by the seven-unit *Kootenay Lake Lodge Resort*, 12622 Hwy 3A (ⓣ250/223-8181, ⓦwww.kootenaylakelodge.com; ❹), a rustic log lodge with private beach, wood-fired cedar baths and RV sites; and the lakeside *Mountain Shores Resort and Marina* (ⓣ250/223-8258, ⓦwww.mtnshores.com; ❸; April–Sept), a combination of twelve motel-type rooms, cottages and **campsites** (from $25) with a heated outdoor pool.

At **GRAY CREEK**, a few kilometres onward, check out the superb **Gray Creek Store**, which boasts the once-in-a-lifetime address of 1979 Chainsaw Avenue and claims, with some justification, to be "The Most Interesting Store You've Ever Seen". The shop basically *is* Gray Creek – it's the sort of place you go to get your chainsaw fixed and where real lumberjacks come for their red-checked shirts. There is one lakeside **campsite** nearby: the small *Lockhart Beach* provincial park campsite ($14; May–Sept) with RV and tent sites 13km south of Gray Creek and 20km south of Kootenay Bay (see below). A bit more exotic, *Tipi Camp* (ⓣ250/227-9555 or 1-866/800-2267, ⓦwww.tipicamp.bc.ca; June–Sept) is situated on Pilot Peninsula, reached by a twice daily twenty-minute boat taxi from Gray Creek. To stay in a teepee you need your own bedding, and it costs $85 a night, including water taxi and vegetarian meals. From Gray Greek, the Gray Greek Forest service road (July–Oct) leads 85km east to Kimberley (see p.987), not a short cut by any means, but scenic and adventurous driving nonetheless. Be sure to be stocked up on supplies before setting off.

CRAWFORD BAY and **KOOTENAY BAY** are names on the map that refer in the flesh to the most fleeting of settlements, the latter also being the **ferry terminal** for boats to Balfour on the west shore. Crawford Bay, 3.5km from the terminal, boasts the Kootenay Forge (ⓦwww.kootenayforge.com), an old-world forge, where in summer you can often watch blacksmiths working and a number of other artisan shops from traditional broom-makers to weavers. The area has also long been famous for the **Yasodhara Ashram**, 527 Walkers Landing Rd (ⓣ250/227-9224 or 1-800/661-8711, ⓦwww.yasodhara.org; ❹), a spiritual retreat centre. As a place to **stay**, this side of the ferry crossing is a touch brighter. The *Wedgewood Manor Country Inn* (ⓣ250/227-9233 or

1-800/862-0022, Ⓔwedgwood@netidea.com; ❹; April to mid-Oct), a 1910 heritage building set amidst fifty acres of gardens and estate, is an extremely pleasant place to stay, but you'll have to book well in advance. The local **campsite** is the nicely wooded *Kokanee Chalets, Motel, Campground & RV Park* on Hwy 3A (Ⓣ250/227-9292 or 1-800/448-9292, Ⓦwww.kokaneechalets .com; mid-April to mid-Oct); as well as tent and RV sites ($20–29) it also has motel and chalet rooms around seven minutes' walk from the beach (❸).

The nine-kilometre, forty-minute **ferry crossing** is beautiful. The Kootenay Lake ferry (free; Ⓣ250/229-4215) leaves every fifty minutes from June to September, and every two hours the rest of the year.

Balfour and Ainsworth Hot Springs

BALFOUR is a fairly shoddy and dispersed collection of motels, garages and cafés – albeit in verdant surroundings – designed to catch the traffic rolling on and off the Kootenay Lake ferry. RV **campsites** line the road south to Nelson for about 2km, but a much better option is the campsite at Kokanee Creek (reservations possible, see p.758, $22; May–Sept), about 10km beyond Balfour with a sandy beach, a mosquito problem and an interpretive centre with advice on trails (May–Sept daily 9am–9pm; Ⓣ250/825-4723). The handiest **motel** for the ferry is the *Balfour Beach Inn and Motel*, 8406 Busk Rd (Ⓣ250/229-4235, Ⓦwww.balfourbeachinn.com; ❹), with a heated indoor pool but convenient also for the small pebbly beach just north of the terminal.

About 16km north of Balfour on Hwy 31, **AINSWORTH HOT SPRINGS** is home to some one hundred residents, making it a town by local standards. The tasteful *Ainsworth Hot Springs Resort* (Ⓣ250/229-4212 or 1-800/668-1171, Ⓦwww.hotnaturally.com; ❺) is ideal if you want to stay over while taking in the scalding water of the **mineral springs,** They include a wonderful network of hot spring caves (daily 10am–9.30pm; day-pass $11, single visit $7.50), and despite the lovely views and the health-giving properties of the waters, local opinion rates the Nakusp Hot Springs (see p.977) rather more highly. Note that you don't need to stay in the resort to sample the springs. The nicest local **motel** is the eight-room *Mermaid Lodge and Motel* (Ⓣ250/229-4969 or 1-888/229-4963, Ⓦwww.themermaidlodge-motel.com; ❷) alongside the springs and pools. Cave enthusiasts might want to take a guided tour of **Cody Caves Provincial Park** (Ⓦwww.codycaves.ca) 12km up a rough gravel side road off Hwy 3 3km north of town. From the end of the road it's a twenty-minute walk to the caves, whose kilometre or more of galleries can be seen by tour only: contact Hiad Venture Corporation (Ⓣ250/353-7364; $15).

Kaslo and around

KASLO, 70km north of Nelson and 25km north of Ainsworth Hot Springs, must rate as one of British Columbia's most attractive and friendliest little villages. Huddled at the edge of Kootenay Lake and dwarfed by towering mountains, its half-dozen streets are lined with picture-perfect wooden homes and flower-filled gardens. It started life as a sawmill in 1889 and turned into a boom town – there were 27 bars, compared with two today – with the discovery of silver in 1893; diversification, and the steamers that plied the lakes, saved it from the cycle of boom and bust that ripped the heart out of so many similar towns. Today Kaslo remains an urbane and civilized community whose thousand or so citizens work hard at keeping it that way, supporting a cultural centre, art galleries, rummage sales – even a concert society.

Kaslo's main attraction is the SS *Moyie* at 324 Front St, the oldest surviving **sternwheeler** in North America (ⓣ250/353-7323, ⓦwww.klhs.bc.ca; tours April to mid-Oct daily 9am–5pm; $5), which ferried people, ore and supplies along the mining routes from 1898 until the relatively recent advent of reliable roads. Similar steamers were the key to the Kootenays' early prosperity, their shallow draught and featherweight construction allowing them to nose into the lakes' shallowest waters. Inside is a collection of antiques, artefacts and photographs from the steamer's heyday. Drop in on Kaslo's thriving **arts centre**, the Langham Cultural Society, on A Avenue opposite the post office (ⓣ250/353-2661), for theatrical performances and art exhibitions. The building, which dates from 1893, began life as a hotel-cum-brothel for miners and was also used as an internment centre for Japanese-Canadians during World War II. If you're around in August, the **Kaslo Jazz Festival** (ⓣ250/353-7548, ⓦwww.kaslojazzfest.com) has some top-notch acts that perform on a floating stage on Kootenay Lake.

Kaslo makes an ideal base for tackling the Purcell Wilderness Conservancy and for pottering around some of the charming lakeshore communities. The visitor centre can advise on getting to **Argenta** (pop.150), 35km north, a former refugee settlement of Quakers who in 1952 came from California, alienated by growing militarism, to start a new life; it's also the western trailhead for the difficult 61km **Earl Grey Pass Trail** over the Purcell Mountains to Invermere (p.988). This area, incidentally, offers a good chance of seeing **ospreys**: the Kootenays' hundred or so breeding pairs represent the largest concentration of the species in North America.

Practicalities

Getting to Kaslo without your own transport is difficult; shuttle buses run every Wednesday morning to Nelson, leaving outside the senior's hall on 4th and Front Street, but these are not reliable year on year (ⓣ1-877/843-2877, ⓦwww.busonline.ca). Finding your way around Kaslo, however, is no problem, nor is getting information – everyone is disarmingly helpful – and there's also a **visitor centre** (March–Oct daily 9am–5pm; ⓣ250/353-2525, ⓦwww.kaslo.com) at 324 Front St. More or less opposite, Kaslo Kayaking (ⓣ250/353-9649, ⓦwww.kaslokayaking.ca) rents **kayaks** and offers lessons and guided tours to view aboriginal petroglyphs on lakeside cliffs. Ask at the visitor centre for information on **bicycle** rentals and updated local trails. Kootenay Mountain Holidays (ⓣ250/353-7122, ⓦwww.skihikebc.com) can guide you on wilderness adventures by foot.

The best central **accommodation** is *Beach Gables* at 243 Front St (ⓣ250/353-2111; ❸), with uninterrupted lake views and two themed rooms. Also downtown is the large *Kaslo Motel*, 330 D Ave (ⓣ250/353-2431 or 1-877/353-2431, ⓦwww.kaslomotel.ca; ❷). Or there is a welcoming **hostel**, the *Kootenay Lake Hostel*, 232 B Ave (ⓣ250/353-2551, ⓦwww.kaslohostel.com; ❷), with dorm beds for $20, bike and kayak rentals and a large communal kitchen and lounge area. For most other alternatives, head towards the marina just north of the centre where en route you'll find, amongst others, the *Sunny Bluffs Cabins & Camp*, 434 North Marine Drive (ⓣ250/353-2277; ❷), offering cabins and camping sites ($19). Several more interesting accommodation possibilities are available farther up and down the lake, many with private lakeside beaches and lovely settings. The most notable is the *Lakewood Inn* (ⓣ250/353-2395, ⓦwww.lakewoodinn.com; ❸; tent and RV sites $18–23; April to mid-Oct), offering fully-equipped lakeside log cabins, trailers ($35–50) and camping sites with private beach and boat rentals; it's 6km north of Kaslo on Kohle Road. Kaslo has a municipal **campsite** ($14–19) on the flat ground by the lake at the end of Front Street. *Mirror Lake Campground* (☎250/353-7102, Ⓦwww.mirrorlake.kaslobc.com; $17; mid-April to mid-Oct), beautifully situated 2km south of town on the main road to Ainsworth, has 100 sites and more facilities.

For **food** and **drink** in Kaslo try the rightly renowned *Treehouse Restaurant*, 419 Front St, the town's social hub, where you can eat superbly (main courses $6–15) and easily strike up conversations. An intimate place for coffee and snacks is the *Silver Spoon Bakery* at 310 Front St (closed Tues). For smoothies, soups and a range of healthy bites, try *Sunnyside Naturals*, 404 Front St but expect service in "Kootenay Time". The *Fisherman's Tale Pub* with a deck and good views on the marina at 551 Rainbow Drive is an appealing place to kick back with a beer, and also does a range of standard pub food, including pizza, steak and ribs (mains $10–21).

Highway 31A and the Slocan Valley

After Kaslo you can either rattle north along a mostly gravel road to link with the Trans-Canada Hwy at Revelstoke, a wild and glorious 150-kilometre drive with a free ferry crossing at **GALENA BAY**, 50km south of Revelstoke, or you can stay in the Kootenays and shuffle west on the fabulously scenic **Highway 31A** through the Selkirk Mountains to the **Slocan Valley**. The latter road ascends from Kaslo alongside the Kaslo River, a crashing torrent choked with branches and fallen trees and hemmed in by high mountains and cliffs of dark rock. Near its high point the road passes a series of massively picturesque lakes: **Fish Lake** is deep green and has a nice picnic spot at one end; **Bear Lake** is equally pretty; and **Beaver Pond** is an amazing testament to the beaver's energy and ingenuity.

Sandon

The ghost town of **SANDON**, one of five in the region, is located 13km south of Hwy 31A, up a signed gravel side road that climbs through scenery of the utmost grandeur. Unfortunately, nowadays Sandon is a little too much ghost and not enough town to suggest how it might have looked in its silver-mining heyday, when it had 24 hotels, 23 saloons, an opera house, thriving red-light district and 5000 inhabitants (it even had electric light well before Victoria or Vancouver). It's slightly dilapidated, rather than evocative, state is due mainly to a flood, which swept away the earlier boardwalk settlement in 1955, leaving a partly inhabited rump that clutters along Carpenter Creek. Pop into the old City Hall, built in 1900, for a walking tour pamphlet ($1) from the **visitor centre** (May–Oct daily 10am–6pm), then head for the **museum** (May–Oct Wed–Sun 9.30am–5.30pm, $2) in the old general store with photos and domestic and commercial artefacts from the town's heyday.

New Denver

After the Sandon turn-off Hwy 31A drops into the **Slocan Valley**, a minor but still spectacular lake-bottomed tributary between the main Kootenay and Columbia watersheds. It meets Hwy 6 at **NEW DENVER** (pop 600), formerly known as Eldorado after its mineral riches. Born of the same silver-mining boom as Kaslo, and with a similarly pretty lakeside setting and genuine pioneer feel, New Denver is, if anything, quieter than its neighbour. The clapboard houses are in peeling, pastel-painted wood, and the tree-lined streets are mercifully free of neon, fast food and most evidence of tourist passage.

Well signposted from the highway, the moving **Nikkei Internment Memorial Centre** at 306 Josephine St (May–Sept daily 9.30am–5pm; rest of

Hikes from Sandon

The side-trip to Sandon is enhanced if you manage a couple of local **hikes**. Idaho Peak (2280m) is a must, being one of the most accessible and spectacular walks in the area. A twelve-kilometre gravel access road leads into alpine pastures and a car park; from there it's a steep three-kilometre round trip to the summit of Mount Idaho and back, with emerging views all the way to the breathtaking panorama at the Forest Service lookout point. Or, hike all or part of the **KNS Historic Trail** (14km one way) from the site to New Denver; the trail follows the course of the 1895 Kaslo–New Denver–Slocan ore-carrying railway, past old mine works and eventually to fine views of the New Denver Glacier across the Slocan Valley to the west. Coupled with leaflets from the visitor centre, the walk vividly documents the area's Wild West mining history, harking back to an era when the district – known as "Silvery Slocan" – produced the lion's share of Canada's silver.

year by appointment; $6; ⓣ250/358-7288) is the only museum in Canada dedicated to the 22,000 Nikkei (Canadians of Japanese ancestry) who, in 1942, were forcibly relocated from the coast to remote internment camps in the interior after Pearl Harbor. Beautiful Japanese gardens now surround the wooden shacks and outhouses that the Nikkei were forced to build themselves. Although the majority of Nikkei were Canadian citizens, they were all labelled "enemy aliens" and stripped of their possessions, homes and businesses. It wasn't until 1988 that former prime minister Brian Mulroney finally apologized to Japanese–Canadians and awarded them token monetary compensation.

The **visitor centre** in New Denver is at 202 6th Ave (late June–Aug daily 8.30am–5pm; ⓣ250/358-2719, ⓦwww.newdenver.ca or www.slocanlake.com). As a stopover it's appealing but not quite as enticing as Kaslo; its most exotic **accommodation** possibility is the *Villa Dome Quixote* 602 6th Ave (ⓣ250/358-7242, ⓦwww.domequixote.com; ❸), an ecologically-sound domed lodge with ten rooms. *Glacier View Cabins*, 426 8th Ave (ⓣ250/358-7277, ⓦwww.glaciercabins.com; ❸), offers five individual cabins just off Hwy 6 in town; while the *Valhalla Inn*, 509 Slocan Ave (ⓣ250/358-2228, ⓦwww.valhallainn.biz; ❷) has 28 rooms in a beach-hut-type motel with pub and restaurant. For **camping**, the *New Denver Municipal Campground* (ⓣ250/358-2316; $15–19; May–Sept) is unexceptional despite a waterfront location on the south side of the village. Four kilometres north of town on Hwy 6 is the *Rosebery Provincial Park* campsite ($14; April–Sept) on the banks of Wilson Creek, a lightly forested site with lake and mountain views. For **food** in the village try 6th Avenue, where at no. 210 you'll find the relaxed *Apple Tree Sandwich Shop* and the bistro *Panini* at no. 306. There's more accommodation and a campsite at Silverton, another tiny former mining village just 4.5km south of New Denver on Hwy 6.

Slocan and the Slocan Valley

Southbound out of New Denver, Hwy 6 follows the tight confines of the **Slocan Valley** for another 100km of ineffable mountain and lake landscapes. Be certain to stop at the **Slocan Lake Viewpoint**, 6km out of New Denver, where a short path up a small cliff provides stupendous views. The 125,000-acre **Valhalla Provincial Park** wraps up the best of the landscapes on the western side of Slocan Lake; a wilderness area with very few developed facilities. Most of it is out of reach unless you boat across the water, though there are three options that penetrate it from the hamlet of **SLOCAN**, another former mining village at the south end of the lake. The canter around the lake (8km) from

Slocan to the west shore is a popular local hike. The best longer **trails** within the park are Gwillim Lakes (11.6km; elevation gain 701m) and Mulvey Basin (9.7km; 765m elevation gain), but both require access drives on forestry roads of 20km of more: pick up detailed directions at the New Denver or Slocan visitor centres. You can also contact the Valhalla Wilderness Society, 307 6th Ave, New Denver (Ⓣ250/358-2333), a local pressure group who campaigned hard for the establishment of the park. Note that gravel roads lead up from Hwy 6 to the more accessible heights of **Kokanee Glacier Provincial Park** to the east (p.983). For more on the area, contact Slocan's **visitor centre**, 1020 Griffin Rd at the *Springer* Creek Campground (daily July & Aug 11.30am–7.30pm Ⓣ250/355-2277 or 355-2266, Ⓔspringr@telus.net).

For a further taste of the local outdoors, **floating** down the Slocan River is a lazy way to spend a summer's day. For **kayak** or **canoe** rentals as well as guided **white-water rafting** trips, contact *Smiling Otter Wilderness Adventures* (Ⓣ250/355-2373, Ⓦwww.smilingotter.com). The Slocan Rail Trail is a popular fifty-kilometre **cycling** route from Slocan to Crescent Valley at the junction of Hwys 6 and 3A; for bike rental and shuttle service to and from the trail contact the *Spoke 'n' Dog B&B and Cycling*, 6285 McKean Rd, Winlaw (Ⓣ250/226-6752; Ⓦwww.spokendog.com; ④).

As elsewhere in the Kootenays, getting around is difficult without your own transport, but a **minibus** shuttles between Nelson and Slocan three times a day and to Nakusp via Slocan twice a week (Ⓣ1-877/843-2877). Valla Ventures (Ⓣ250/358-7775) operate a water taxi service from Slocan to access points in the Valhalla Provincial Park. If you need **accommodation**, there are about half-a-dozen options, most in rustic settings with mountain or lake views. For a truly unique experience in remote surrounds, try the off-grid, straw-built **hostel**, *Little Slocan Lodge,* 7km west of town at 8185 Little Slocan Forest Service Rd, with communal kitchen, free shuttle pick-up from Slocan, live music nights, camping for $10 and dorm beds $24 (Ⓣ250/355-2900 or 1-800/505-6788; Ⓦwww.littleslocanlodge.com; ③). You could also try *Lemon Creek Lodge* (Ⓣ250/355-2403, Ⓦwww.lemoncreeklodge.com; ③, campsite $14–21), 7km south of Slocan on Kennedy Road – it has great **food** and rents out bikes and kayaks. In addition to a provincial **campsite** at Little Slocan Lake ($5; May–Oct), there's the *Springer Creek RV Park and Campground* (Ⓣ250/355-2266; $10–22; May–Oct) in Slocan.

Highway 6: New Denver to Vernon

Highway 6 may not be the most direct east-west route through British Columbia, but it's certainly one of the most dramatic, and the one to think about if you're heading towards Revelstoke to the north or the Okanagan to the west. From New Denver it initially strikes north and after 30km passes **Summit Lake**, a perfect jewel of water, mountain and forest that's served by the new *Summit Lake Provincial Park* **campsite** ($17; May–Sept). A road runs south from here into the mountains and to a small **ski** area (Dec–March, day lift pass $18; Ⓣ250/265-3312, Ⓦwww.skisummitlake.com).

Nakusp

Some 16km beyond Summit Lake and 47km north of New Denver, lakefront **NAKUSP** is, like Kaslo and Nelson, a rare thing in British Columbia: a town with enough charisma to make it worth visiting for its own sake. The setting is par for the course in the Kootenays, with a big lake – **Upper Arrow Lake**, part of the Columbia River system – and the snowcapped Selkirk Mountains to the east

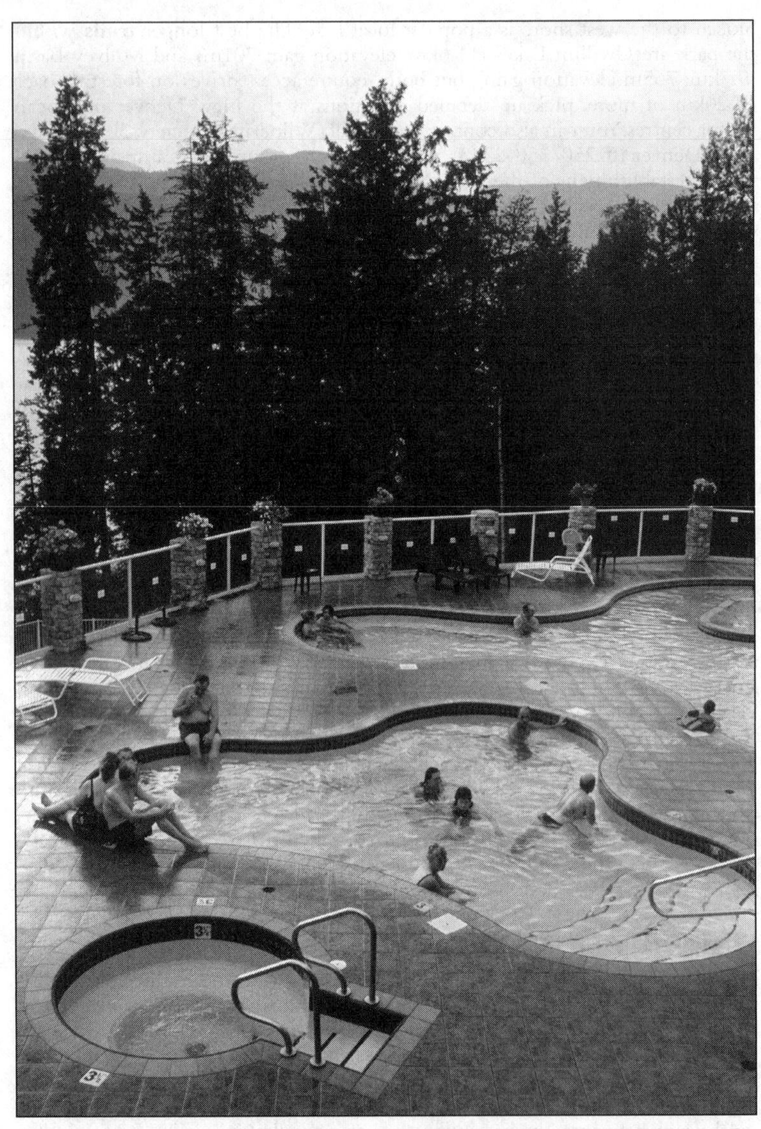

△ Halcyon Hot Springs near Nakusp

providing the majestic backdrop. The nearby hot springs are the main attraction, but you could happily wander around the town for an hour or so, or boat or swim off the public **beach**. The helpful **visitor centre**, based in the fake paddle-steamer building at 92 West St and 6th Ave just off the main street (May–Sept Mon–Sat 9am–5pm, July & Aug Sun 10am–5pm, Nov–May Mon–Wed 9am–3pm; ⓣ250/265-4234 or 1-800/909-8819, ⓦwww.nakusphotsprings.com), can provide details on local fishing, boating and hiking possibilities, and – for those driving

Hot springs near Nakusp

There are some undeveloped hot springs within striking distance of Nakusp if you have a car. To reach the intimate **Halfway Hot Springs**, take Hwy 23 north out of Nakusp for 25km and then after crossing the St Leon Creek bridge, take the first right onto Halfway Road and follow the road for 11km until you see a trail off to the left. The piping hot springs are about 300 metres down on the banks of the river. If you stay on Hwy 23 for 32km north of Nakusp, you'll reach the delightful **Halcyon Hot Springs** (daily 8am–10/11pm; $9, day pass $14.50), which was first commercialized in 1888, its waters bottled and sent to England. Today, there are four pools here of varying temperatures, all of which face Upper Arrow Lake and the mountain peaks beyond. Camping is also available for $20. The resort here, the *Halycon Springs Resort* (ⓣ250/265-3554 or 1-888/689-4699, ⓦwww.halcyonhotsprings.com; ❻), is one of the region's best – but its eleven chalets and cabins are expensive. However, there are tent and RV sites for $32–50. Driving one kilometre north of Halcyon will bring you to the natural pools at **Coyote Springs** (ⓣ250/265-2155, ⓔmedicinewaters@telusnet; $10), with three cabins and camping possible on site.

onwards – timings for the Galena Bay and Fauquier ferries. BC Transit provides **buses** to and from Nelson with connections for Trail and Castlegar, but only a couple of times a week (call ⓣ1-877/843-2877 for latest details).

If you're only going to try the hot springs experience once, **Nakusp Hot Springs**, a well-signposted complex 13km northeast of town, is the place to do it (daily: June–Sept 9.30am–10pm; Oct–May 10am–9.30pm; $6, day-pass $9; ⓣ250/265-4528); it's not unusual for late-night informal parties to develop around the two outdoor pools.

For a **place to stay** in or near Nakusp, Hwy 6 west along the lake is dotted with cabins, resorts and campsites. In downtown itself try the *Selkirk Inn*, 210 6th Ave West (ⓣ250/265-3666 or 1-800/661-8007, ⓦwww.selkirkin-nakusp.com; ❸), or *Kuskanax/Tenderfoot Lodge*, 515 Broadway (ⓣ250/265-3618 or 1-800/663-0100, ⓦwww.kuskanax.kootenays.com; ❸), which is equally central but a bit more upmarket and has a recommended Canadian-fare **restaurant** with salmon and steak mains for $17. The *Leland Hotel*, 96 4th Ave SW (ⓣ250/265-4221; ❷) is situated right on the lake and claims to be the oldest operating hotel in BC. For **hostel** accommodation, the lovely *Hotsprings Guesthouse,* one kilometre north of town on Hwy 23N and on the lakeshore, has dorm beds for $25 (ⓣ250/265-3069, ⓦwww.enjoynakusp.com; ❷). For breakfast and snacks, head for the *Broadway Deli Bistro*, 408 Broadway, and join the locals for inexpensive food to go at *The Hut Drive Inn* or *What's Brewing* for coffee, muffins and more, both also on Broadway. Campers would do best to aim for the lovely *Nakusp Hot Springs* **campsite**, near the hot springs at 1701 Canyon Rd (ⓣ250/265-4528 or 1-800/909-8819; $10–22); non-campers could try the adjoining seven-unit *Cedar Chalets* (ⓣ250/265-4505, ⓦwww.nakusphotspringschalets.com; ❷). Another out-of-town campsite is the *McDonald Creek Provincial Park* site ($15; May–Oct), 10km south of Nakusp on Hwy 6, and complete with lakeside beaches. Or make for the *Summit Lake Provincial Park* site ($17), 13km southeast on Hwy 6 at the crest of land between Slocan Lake and Upper Arrow Lake.

From Nakusp, you can either continue along Hwy 6 or branch off up **Highway 23**, which heads 100km north to Revelstoke (see p.773), a spectacular journey involving a free ferry crossing halfway at **Galena Bay** (hourly sailings each way).

Fauquier to Vernon

Highway 6 doglegs south from Nakusp for 57 delightful kilometres to the ferry crossing at **FAUQUIER**. This hamlet consists of a handful of buildings including a garage, a store and the only **motel** (with a restaurant) for kilometres – the *Arrow Lake Motel* (Ⓣ250/269-7622; ❷), bang on the lakeside door near the ferry at 101 Oak St, but call ahead to check that it's open. There's a **campsite** off Hwy 6 at the northern entrance to the hamlet, the *Tukaluk* (Ⓣ250/269-7355), with twenty sites for $15–18.

The **free ferry** across Lower Arrow Lake to Needles takes about five minutes (departs half-hourly 5am–10pm; intermittent shuttle throughout the night). **NEEDLES** amounts to no more than a ramp off the ferry on the other side. There's an unofficial **campsite** at Whatshan Lake, 3km off the hwy just after Needles, but otherwise Hwy 6 is a gloriously empty ribbon as it burrows through the staggering Monashee Mountains. After cresting Monashee Pass (1198m), the hwy begins the long descent through the **Coldstream Valley** towards the Okanagan. Snow dusts the mountains here almost year-round, crags loom above the meadows that increasingly break the forest cover, and beautiful flower-filled valleys wind down to the highway. The first sign of life in over 100km is the *Gold Panner* **campsite** (Ⓣ250/547-2025, Ⓦwww.goldpannercampground.com; $16; April–Oct), 55km east of Vernon and a good spot to overnight or to explore the utter wilderness of **Monashee Provincial Park** to the north. The park is reached by rough road from **CHERRYVILLE**, a hamlet 10km further west.

LUMBY, another 22km beyond, is scarcely more substantial, although **rooms** at the *Twin Creeks Motel* (Ⓣ250/547-9221; ❸) might be worth considering if it's late, given that the Okanagan lodgings ahead could well be packed. The village also boasts a simple riverside **campsite** at 2215 Shield Ave run by the local Lions Club (Ⓣ250/547-2005 or 547-6346 off season; $15; May–Oct) and there's a seasonal **visitor centre** on the hwy at 1882 Vernon St (July & Aug 9am–5pm; Ⓣ250/547-2300, Ⓦwww.monasheetourism.com). Beyond the village, the road glides through lovely pastoral country, with orchards, verdant meadows, low, tree-covered hills, and fine wooden barns that look like inverted longboats. Vernon (see p.958) is a short drive away.

Nelson and around

NELSON – reachable on Hwy 6 south of Slocan (see p.976) and Hwy 3A 34km west of Balfour (see p.973) – is one of British Columbia's best towns, and one of the few interior settlements in which you could happily spend two or three days; longer, if you use it as a base for touring the Kootenays by car. The elegant town (pop.10,000) is home to more than its share of baby-boomers, the dreadlocked, and refugees from the 1960s and later mainstream, a hangover that's nurtured a friendly, civilized and close-knit community, a healthy cultural scene and a liveliness – manifest in alternative cafés, nightlife and secondhand-clothes shops – that you'll be hard pushed to find elsewhere in the province outside Vancouver. The town's Chinese medicine school as well as the Kootenay School of the Arts attract students from all over North America and there are, apparently, more artists and craftspeople here per head than any other town in Canada – and this is without the many similar types who live in the dozens of smaller outlying villages and isolated homesteads for which Nelson provides a natural central focus. It's a young place permeated with immense civic pride, which was given a further boost by the filming here of *Roxanne*, Steve Martin's spoof version of *Cyrano de Bergerac*. Producers chose the town for its idyllic lakeside setting and 350-plus homes from the late nineteenth to the early twentieth-century, factors which for once live up to the Canadian talent for hyperbole – in this case a claim to be "Queen of the Kootenays" and "Heritage Capital of Western Canada".

Arrival and information

Nelson is served by Greyhound **buses** (Ⓣ250/352-3939, Ⓦwww.greyhound.ca) that run west to Kelowna (for connections to Vancouver, the Okanagan and Kamloops) and east to Cranbrook (connections to Calgary via Banff or Fort Macleod). The Greyhound depot is on the lakeshore, just below the town proper in the Chahko-Mika Mall at 1112 Lakeside Drive. There are also weekly minibus services to Kaslo and Nakusp (Ⓣ1-877/843-2877, Ⓦwww.busonline.ca for details).

If you need **car rental**, Rent-a-Wreck has an outlet in town at 524 Nelson Ave (Ⓣ250/352-5122), and Budget has an office in the *Prestige Lakeside Resort* at 701 Lakeside Drive (Ⓣ250/505-7368). For **boat rental**, contact *Captain Erik's Watertoys* (Ⓣ250/551-5502), also with an office in the *Prestige*. For **bike rental**, visit *Gerick Cycle and Sports*, 702 Baker St (Ⓣ250/354-4622), which also has trail maps and information on the many **mountain-biking** routes carved out by enthusiasts locally; *The Sacred Ride* at 213 Baker St and *Boomtown Sports* at 510 Hall St also rent out bikes.

The **visitor centre** is on the northeast edge of the downtown grid at 225 Hall St at the corner of Lake St (June–Aug daily 8.30am–6pm; Sept–May Mon–Fri 8.30am–5pm; Ⓣ250/352-3433 or 1-877/663-5706, Ⓦwww.discovernelson.com).

Accommodation

Nelson has a reasonable spread of **accommodation**; among the central choices are three hostels and some charming boutique hotels. There is also a wide range of B&B options, with more than a dozen at last count and rising. Most of the motels are on Hwy 31A at the north end of town or over the Nelson Bridge on the north side of the lake.

Hotels and motels

Hume Hotel 422 Vernon St Ⓣ250/352-5331 or 1-877/568-0888, Ⓦwww.humehotel.com. This charming, 1898 four-storey hotel is the best central, mid-range hotel choice. It has cosy, old-world rooms (some with views) and complimentary breakfast in the downstairs restaurant. ④

Mountain Hound Inn 612 Baker St Ⓣ250/352-6490. A wonderfully restored boutique hotel located in the thick of the action. ④

North Shore Inn 687 Hwy 3A Ⓣ250/352-6606 or 1-800/593-6636, Ⓦwww.nshoreinn.com. On the north side of town, this 30-unit motel offers good value. ③

Prestige Lakeside Resort 701 Lakeshore Drive Ⓣ250/352-7222 or 1-877/737-8443. Ⓦwww.prestigeinn.com. This is the most luxurious hotel in town, part of Nelson's rather crass ongoing lakefront redevelopment; it has a spa, gym, marina, shops and all the other resort trimmings. ⑥

B&Bs

Inn the Garden 408 Victoria St Ⓣ250/352-3226 or 1-800/596-2337, Ⓦwww.innthegarden.com. A restored Victoria home one block south of Baker Street, this B&B has both charm and location. ③

Stanley House 420 Railway St Ⓣ250/352-3777, Ⓦwww.stanleyhousebb.com. There are three ornate rooms in this 1908 Victorian home. ④

Hostels

Back Country Hostel 198 Baker St Ⓣ250/352-2151, Ⓦwww.thebackcountryhostel.com. This lively hostel has dorm beds for $21, a noisy pub downstairs and generally attracts a younger and rowdier crowd.

Dancing Bear Inn between Kootenay St and Hwy 3A at 171 Baker St Ⓣ250/352-7573, Ⓦwww.dancingbearinn.com. Beautifully renovated, this 43-bed HI-affiliated place is by far the nicest hostel in Nelson. The staff are particularly knowledgeable and passionate about the area.

Dorm beds (maximum of six to a room) are $18 for HI members, $22 for non-members.

New Grand Hotel and Hostel 616 Vernon St ⓣ250/352-7211 or 1-888/722-2258, ⓦwww.newgrandhotel.ca. This establishment has retro-style hotel rooms and dorm beds for $19.

Camping

City Tourist Park cnr High Street and Willow ⓣ250/352-9031. Though it's small, this campground is just 800 metres east of downtown. Despite some trees, it has the definite feel of an urban site. Sites range from $17–23 from mid-May to early Oct.

Kokanee Creek Provincial Park 20km northeast of town on Hwy 3A. With 168 pitches on a forested site, this campsite offers access to sandy beaches and nature trails; mosquitoes can be a problem though. Campsite ($22).

The Town

Nelson forms a 24-odd block tree-shaded grid of streets laid over the hilly slopes that edge down to the westernmost shores of Kootenay Lake. Most homes are immaculately kept and vividly painted, and even the commercial **buildings** along the parallel main east-west streets – Baker and Vernon – owe more to the vintage architecture of Seattle and San Francisco than to the drab Victoriana and worse of much of eastern Canada. If you want to add purpose to your wanderings, pick up the *Heritage Walking Tour* or the *Heritage Motoring Tour* pamphlets from the **visitor centre**, which takes you around the sort of houses (26 in all on the walking tour) that many Canadians dream of retiring to. Highlights are the courthouse on Ward Street and City Hall (at the corner of Ward and Vernon), both designed by F.M. Rattenbury, also responsible for Victoria's *Empress Hotel* and Parliament Buildings. Also check out the old railway station and the *Hume Hotel*.

If walking tours aren't your thing, perhaps the town's **shops** may be, particularly those of its artists and craftspeople. In summer they club together to present **Artwalk**, a crawl round about a hundred of the town's artists' studios and little galleries (see the visitor centre for more details). If you don't want to walk in town, take the restored **Streetcar 23** (weekends May to mid-June, daily mid-June to Sept; $3), a tram that runs the length of the lakeshore waterfront from a point about 200 metres north of the visitor centre on Hall St. Particularly good galleries include the *Craft Connection*, a cooperative owned by a dozen local craftspeople at 441 Baker St (ⓣ250/352-3006), and the *Mermaid Gallery*, 410 Kootenay St (ⓣ250/352-2330), selling paintings, jewellery and pottery. For second-hand books and CDs – and a great little café-restaurant – make for *Packrat Annie's* at 411 Kootenay St. Another shop worth a stop is *Still Eagle*, 557 Ward St, the province's first hemp store, where even cat toys are made from hemp. On a similar theme, *Holy Smoke*, 512 Hendryx St, sells marijuana paraphernalia and adopts a liberal attitude to the wacky weed that riles the local law enforcers.

For the most part the area owes its development to the discovery of copper and silver ore on nearby Toad Mountain at the end of the nineteenth century. Even though the mines declined fairly quickly, Nelson's diversification into gold and lumber, and its roads, railway and waterways, saved it from mining's usual downside. Today mining is back on the agenda as old claims are re-explored, and the town's **Mining Museum** (daily 9am–3pm; free), is next to the visitor centre for those interested.

The **Touchstone's Nelson: Museum of Art and History**, 502 Vernon St (Mon–Sat 9am–5pm; ⓣ250/352-9813, ⓦwww.nelsonmuseum.ca), is housed in the former City Hall building and hosts art exhibitions and Nelson's historical archives. Back outside, walk to **Lakeside Park** near the Nelson Bridge, where there are surprisingly good sandy **beaches**, picnic areas and waterfront paths.

For a workout with the sweetest of rewards, the one-hour climb to **Pulpit Rock**, starting on the north side of the lake, offers an eagle's eye view over Nelson. If you're in town between May and mid-October, make it a point to stop by the Saturday **farmers' and artisans' market**, known as the Cottonwood Falls Market, near the old railway station in Cottonwood Falls Park (9.30am–3pm). Organic fruit, vegetables, delicious breads and local arts and crafts are all for sale. The local ski hill, **Whitewater Winter Resort** – 12km south of Nelson off Hwy 6 – may be lacking in size, but it more than makes up for it in powder (Dec–April; day lift pass $44; ⓣ250/354-4944 or 1-800/666-9420, ⓦwww.skiwhitewater.com), and boasts some good steep terrain, eleven cross-country trails and two chairlifts.

Eating, drinking and nightlife

Nelson's choice of **restaurants** is broad, and you can't go wrong just wandering around and choosing something that looks tempting.

All Seasons Café 620 Herridge Lane ⓣ250/352-0101. In a restored heritage home, this top-flight restaurant is one of the Kootenays' best dining experiences. It serves superb West Coast (or what it calls "left-coast") food and boasts a wine list that has won a prestigious *Wine Spectator* Award of Excellence (mains $19–33). Open daily for dinner from 5pm.

El Taco 306 Victoria St. For Mexican fare you can down with a glass of sangria, tuck into one of the tasty burritos, quesadillas and taco mains (from $4–9).

The Full Circle 101-402 Baker St. For superb breakfasts (average $11) follow the locals to this cafe.

Fusion 301 301 Baker St. This swanky tapas bar has a buzzing outdoor patio and also dishes up creative mains ($12–18).

Kootenay Co-Op 295 Baker St. If you're shopping for your own meals, this supermarket can satisfy all your organic and wholefood needs.

Max & Irma's Kitchen 515 Kootenay St ⓣ250/352-2332. If you want a simple pizza, for around $14 the thin-crust choice comes from the wood-fired oven. Closed Sun.

Mike's Place side of the *Hume Hotel*, 422 Vernon St. If you're looking for a drink, this usually packed spot sells the full range of Nelson Brewing Company beers (the brewery was founded in 1893); top tipple is the flagship Old Brewery Ale (OBA). There's usually dancing from 9pm (Fri–Sat) at the adjoining *Taffy Jack's* nightclub. The *Hume's* more elegant bar, *The Library*, as its name suggests, offers a quieter drinking experience.

Oso Negro 604 Ward St. A block up from Baker, this invariably crowded café is a good option for coffee and snacks. It roasts its own coffee beans and provides great people-watching opportunities.

Outer Clove 353 Stanley St ⓣ250/354-1667. For novelty value you could do worse than spoil your breath at this restaurant where virtually everything from decor to dessert features garlic (it's better than it sounds); tasty mains range between $9 and $17. Closed Sun.

RezAvoir 198 Baker St. Younger locals and backpackers head to this bar for its hip-hop and reggae nights.

Royal Pub and Grill 330 Baker St. A good choice for **live music** from good local and regional bands.

Kokanee Glacier Provincial Park

Nelson is one of several possible jumping-off points for the tremendous **Kokanee Glacier Provincial Park**, straddling the Slocan Range of the Selkirk Mountains. The easiest approach is to drive 19km northeast of Nelson on Hwy 3A and then follow the road left for 16km up Kokanne Glacier Road to one of the park entrances at Gibson Lake parking lot. Here you'll also find the trailhead for the 2.5km jaunt around the lake. A trail from Gibson Lake also leads 4km uphill to the lovely Kokanee Lake, where it levels out and continues 3km to Kaslo Lake. Two kilometres further you reach backcountry campsites and *Kokanee Glacier Cabin* (ⓦwww.alpineclubofcanada.ca for booking information). Other approaches to the park are from Hwy 31 10km north of Ainsworth, driving 13km up Woodbury Creek into the park; from Hwy 6 some 14km north of Slocan, where you drive 13km up Enterprise

Creek; and from Hwy 6 8km south of Slocan, where you follow a road up Lemon Creek for 16km. For more information on the park, call ⓣ250/354-6333.

Highway 95: north to Radium Hot Springs

Heading north from Creston and the Kootenays, **Highway 95** travels through scenery as spectacular as anything in the big Rockies parks to the north. The route follows the broad valley bottom of the **Columbia River**, bordered on the east by the Rockies and on the west by the marginally less breathtaking **Purcell Mountains**. Hwys 93 and 95 meet near **Cranbrook**, where you can make for either of two US border crossings, double back eastwards on Hwy 3 to Fernie, Crowsnest Pass and Alberta, or head north for Radium Hot Springs and the entrance to Kootenay National Park (see p.776). Greyhound **buses** ply all these routes, with most connections at Cranbrook.

East of Creston

Some 42km east of Creston (see p.970), buses drop off at the garage in the quaint and unspoilt village of **YAHK**, no more than a few houses and antique shops nestled amidst the trees; for a good, quiet stop-over try the *Cozy Quilt Motel*, 8849 Hwy 3/95 (ⓣ250/424-5558 or 1-877/717-5558, ⓦwww.cozyquilt.ca; ❸), or you can camp at *Yahk Provincial Park* ($14; May to mid-Sept) east of town or the private *Riverside Campground* (ⓣ250/424-5454; $14; April to mid-Oct) south of Yahk on the Moyie River; it has a store for groceries and other basics. Hwy 95 branches off from Hwy 3 here and heads south for the US border (11km). Incidentally, the hwy crosses a **time zone** between Yahk and Moyie – clocks go forward one hour.

Following Hwy 3/95 northbound you reach the tiny community of **MOYIE** on the edge of lovely **Moyie Lake**. There are local **campsites** here, including the excellent one at **Moyie Lake Provincial Park** (reservations possible, see p.758; $22; May–Sept), with short trails and sandy swimming beach – reach it by taking Munro Lake Road west off Hwy 3/95 for a kilometre from the northernmost point of Moyie Lake.

Cranbrook

The regional service and ex-forestry town of **CRANBROOK**, 30km north of Moyie Lake and 106km east of Creston, despite a location that marks it out as a transport hub, is one of the most dismal in the province. A strip of motels and marshalling yards dominates a soulless downtown area. The Greyhound **bus terminal** (ⓣ250/426-3331) is behind *Pizza Hut* at 1229 Cranbrook St. Bus services run east to Fernie, Sparwood and southern Alberta (2 daily); west to Nelson, Castlegar and Vancouver (3 daily); north to Kimberley, Radium, Banff and Calgary (1 daily).

The only sight to speak of is the worthwhile **Canadian Museum of Rail Travel** (mid-April to mid-Oct 10am–6pm; rest of year Tues–Sat 10am–5pm; tours $5.25–11.95; ⓣ250/489-3918, ⓦwww.trainsdeluxe.com) at 57 Van Horne St, which centres around the restored luxurious passenger cars of Canadian trains, including the *Trans-Canada Limited*, which chugged across the country in the Roaring Twenties, linking Montréal with Vancouver.

If you stick to Hwy 93/95 out of Cranbrook for 18km, you'll come to **Fort Steele Heritage Town** (daily July–Aug 9.30am–6.30pm, Sept–Oct & May–June 9.30am–5.30pm, Nov–April 10am–4pm; ⓣ250/417-6000, ⓦwww.fortsteel.bc.ca; $12.50), an impressively reconstructed c.1900 village of some 55 buildings in a superb mountain-ringed setting.

The **visitor centre**, 2279 Cranbrook St (year-round Mon–Fri 8.30am–5pm, weekends 9am–5pm; ⓣ250/426-5914, 489-5261 or 1-800/222-6174, ⓦwww.cranbrookchamber.com), was burned down by animal-rights activists in 1999 because of its stuffed-animal display, but not to be defeated they have reopened on the same spot with a new **Wildlife Museum** filled with stuffed road-kill.

If you need to stay in Cranbrook, one of the top **accommodation** options in town is the *Heritage Inn* at 803 Cranbrook St North (ⓣ250/489-4301 or 1-800/663-2708, ⓦwww.heritageinn.net; ❺), a large, modern hotel on the main road. A cheaper option is the *Lazy Bear Lodge* (ⓣ250/426-6086 or 1-888/808-6086, ⓦwww.lazybear-lodge.ca; ❸), on Hwy 3 at 621 Cranbrook St N. The town's *Mount Baker RV Park*, at Baker Park on 14th Ave and 1st St (ⓣ1-877/501-2288; $20–30), is the closest **campsite**, though it's a good deal less appealing than the *Jimsmith Lake Provincial Park*, 4km southwest of town, but which has no showers (June–Sept; $14). The strip offers plenty of cheap **eating** options; make for *Allegra* at 1225 B Cranbrook St North (ⓣ250/426-8812; closed Sun & Mon), which serves Mediterranean cuisine (mains $13–24).

Highway 3 east of Cranbrook

Highway 93 leaves Hwy 95 between Fort Steele (see above) and Cranbrook, following Hwy 3 as far as Elko before branching off south for the United States border (91km). An unsullied hamlet of around half a dozen homes, **ELKO**, 65km east of Cranbrook, is gone in a flash, but you might want to stop and camp at the excellent Kikomun Creek Provincial Park **campsite** (reservations possible, see p.758; $22; May–Sept), on the eastern shore of the artificial Lake Koocanusa and signed off Hwy 93 3km west of town. Hwy 3 offers colossal **views** of the Rockies and the fast-flowing, ice-clear Elk River.

Fernie

FERNIE, 32km north of Elko, is a pleasant place of tree-lined streets, boutique shops and small wooden houses surrounded by a ring of knife-edged mountains. The commercial centre of the Elk Valley (logging and open pit coal mining form the economic backbone of the town), Fernie's appeal as a recreation centre has brought in a more liberal demographic that is reflected in the number of art galleries, health food shops and hemp stores lining the main street. The increasing popularity of the ski resort locally has led to a certain amount of lackluster development along the highway.

The **visitor centre** (daily 9am–5pm; ⓣ250/423-6868, ⓦwww.fernie.com or www.ferniechamber.com) stands alongside a reconstructed wooden oil derrick 2km north of town on Hwy 3 at 102 Commerce Rd. There is another visitor centre downtown in the **museum** on the corner of 2nd Ave and 4th St (daily 9.30am–5pm; ⓣ250/423-7016). Pick up details of the heritage walking tour of downtown, whose best buildings cluster along 2nd Avenue between 3rd and 7th streets, monuments to the rebuilding of town following a destructive fire in 1908. **Mount Fernie Provincial Park** has plenty of **hiking** and **biking** trails, picnic areas and a pleasant forty-pitch campsite 2km west of town off Hwy 3 on Park Road (reservations possible, see p.758; $14; mid-May to mid-Sept). For a challenging hike, try the full-day **Three Sisters Trail**, which starts from the visitor centre on Hwy 3. A couple of local outfitters will take you on day or overnight hiking tours or on white-water **rafting** trips down the Elk or Bull rivers; for the latter try the Canyon Raft Company (Ⓣ1-888/423-7226, Ⓦwww.canyonraft.com).

Fernie's population doubles in the winter, as skiers flock to the **Fernie Alpine Resort** (Nov–May; day lift pass $69; Ⓣ250/423-4655, Ⓦwww.skifernie.com), 5km west of town and 2km off the main highway. It claims the longest ski season in the BC Rockies, has a whopping 107 trails and gets an average of nine metres of snowfall annually. In the summer, the area is a magnet for mountain bikers and hikers.

In town, the 64-room *Park Place Lodge*, 742 Hwy 3 (Ⓣ1-800/381-7275, Ⓦwww.parkplacelodge.com; ⑤), with an indoor pool, is the place to **stay** or, failing that, one of two good **hostels**: either the basic, ninety-bed, HI-affiliated *Raging Elk Hostel*, a converted motel one block south of Hwy 3 between 8th and 9th streets at 892 6th Ave (Ⓣ250/423-6811, Ⓦwww.ragingelk.com; ③), with dorm beds $23; or the *SameSun Budget Lodge* on Hwy 3 (Ⓣ250/423-4492 or 1-877/562-2783, Ⓦwww.samesun.com; ④), with an outdoor pool and dorm beds for $23.

Eating in Fernie is concentrated along 2nd Avenue, the main drag. Good coffee and a quick snack can be had at *Freshies* at 561 2nd Ave; while breakfasts are scrumptious at the hip *Blue Toque Diner* in the Arts Station next to the gallery and theatre at 601 1st Ave with gourmet omelettes for $7. For dinner, the *Curry Bowl* at 931 7th Ave serves a range of outstanding Asian fusion dishes (mains $11–13) and also has a wide selection of beers, including the locally-brewed Fernie Griz. For **drinks**, the *Royal Hotel*, 501 1st Ave, has a pool table and live music as well as a fine dining restaurant *Mojo Risin'* (Ⓣ250/423-7743), with carnivorous and vegan mains from $13–27.

Elkford

The remainder of Hwy 3 in British Columbia is largely despoiled by mining; Sparwood is 29km beyond Fernie and the road crests the Continental Divide 19km east of Sparwood at **Crowsnest Pass** (see p.681). Far more scenic is the drive north from Sparwood on Hwy 43, which heads upstream beside the Elk River for 35km to **ELKFORD**. Nestled against a wall of mountains to the east and more gentle hills to the west, the village claims to be the "wilderness capital of British Columbia" – a high-pitched punt, but close to the mark if you're prepared to carry on up either of two rough gravel roads to the north. The more westerly road follows the Elk a further 70km to **Elk Lakes Provincial Park** close to the Continental Divide, one of the wildest road-accessible spots in the province (camping costs $5 at the simple campsite at the main trailhead at the end of the road). The slightly better route to the east heads 55km into the heart of unbeatable scenery below 2792-metre **Mount Armstrong**. Both areas offer excellent chances of spotting wildlife like cougars, deer, moose, elk or members of North America's largest population of bighorn sheep.

Before entering either area, however, it's essential to pick up maps and information at the Elkford **visitor centre** (year-round Mon–Fri 8.30am–5pm; Ⓣ1-877/355-9453, Ⓦwww.tourismelkford.ca), located at 4A Front St on your right as you are entering town. It can also give directions to nearby **Josephine Falls**, a few minutes' walk from the parking area on Fording Mine Road. Whether you're staying here or pushing on north, a tent is helpful: for **accommodation** in town, try the *Elkford Motor Inn*, 808 Michel Rd, next to the shopping centre (Ⓣ250/865-2211 or 1-800/203-7723, Ⓔelkfordmi@elkvalley.net; ③) or the

Hi Rock Inn, 2 Chauncey St (ⓣ250/865-2226 or 1-866/865-2226, ⓦwww.hirockinn.com; ❸). **Camping** can be had at Elkford's municipal campsite (ⓣ250/865-2650; $15; May–Oct) and at the wilderness campsites around Elk Lakes ($5; June–Sept).

Kimberley

KIMBERLEY, a few kilometres north of Cranbrook on Hwy 95A, is Canada's second highest city (1117m), and in many ways one of its silliest, thanks to a tourist-tempting ruse in the 1970s to transform itself into a Bavarian village. The result is a masterpiece of kitsch that's almost irresistible: buildings have been given a plywood-thin veneer of authenticity, piped Bavarian music dribbles from shops with names like *The Yodelling Woodcarver*, and even the fire hydrants have been painted to look like miniature replicas of Happy Hans, Kimberley's lederhosened mascot. The ploy might seem absurd, but there's no doubting the economic rewards that have accrued from the influx of tourists and European immigrants – Germans included – who've provided an authentic range of cafés and restaurants and a variety of family-oriented summer and winter activities.

Most of the Teutonic gloss is around the **Bavarian Platzl** on Spokane Street in the small downtown area. If nothing else, you can leave Kimberley safe in the knowledge that you have seen "**Canada's Biggest Cuckoo Clock**", a fraudulent affair which amounts to little more than a large wooden box that twitters inane music.

Practicalities

For full details of Kimberley's many events, call in on the **visitor centre** (daily 9am–8pm; ⓣ250/427-3666, ⓦwww.kimberleychamber.ca) at 270 Kimberley Ave. If you need **accommodation**, try the central *Château Kimberley*, 78 Howard St (ⓣ250/427-1500 or 1-866/488-8886, ⓦwww.Chateau-kimberley.com; ❺), a boutique hotel just west of the plaza. *Same Sun Budget Lodge* is a hotel connected to the *Ozone Pub* (pub food and live entertainment some nights, noon–2.30am) on the Platzl with **hostel beds** ($22) at 275 Spokane St (ⓣ250/427-7191 or 1-877/562-2783, ⓦwww.samsun.com; ❷) and a winter shuttle service to the ski hill. The nearest **campsite**, the *Kimberley Riverside Campground* (ⓣ1-877/999-2929, ⓦwww.kimberleycampground.com; $17–27; May–Oct), is 7km south of the town centre then 3km west on St Mary's River Road and has modern facilities including a new pool. Drop in to the twee but excellent *Chef Bernard* café and **restaurant** opposite the clock at 170 Spokane St (ⓣ250/427-4820), where the owner – heartily sick of Bavaria – often plays Irish fiddle music as a mark of defiance. He has **rooms** available upstairs (❷). A favourite cheap place for lunch and breakfast and good vegetarian dishes for

Kimberley activities

If you're around from early Dec through April, and feel the need to escape Kimberley's kitsch for **skiing** and other winter activities, head for the **Kimberley Alpine Resort** (ⓣ250/427-4881 or 1-800/258-7669 for accommodation packages, ⓦwww.skikimberley.com), 4km west of town. The resort has eight lifts and 67 runs, the longest of which covers more than 6km. Passes cost $54 for the day, $44 for the afternoon and $20 for a night skiing session.

Kimberley also boasts one of Canada's most popular **golf** courses, Trickle Creek on Jerry Sorenson Way (ⓣ250/427-3389; $108 for eighteen holes with a cart), but you'll have to book ahead if you want to play here.

around $8 is the *Snowdrift Cafe* at 110 Spokane St. Farther afield is the *Old Bauernhaus*, about fifteen-minutes' walk from the town centre towards the ski area off Dewdney Road at 280 Norton Ave (Ⓣ250/427-5133; dinner only, closed Tues & Wed). The Bavarian food is good (a hearty schnitzel meal costs $18), but the draw here is the location, a 350-year-old post-and-beam building dismantled and brought from its original site in southern Bavaria.

Highway 95 north to Fairmont Hot Springs

Back on Hwy 93/95, the Columbia Valley's scenery picks up as the Rockies begin to encroach and the blanket of trees opens up into pastoral river meadows. First stop is **Wasa**, 30km north of Kimberley, whose lake, protected by the *Wasa Lake Provincial Park*, is warm enough for summer swimming. A few kilometres after **Skookumchuck** the road curves around the **Dutch Creek Hoodoos**, fantastically eroded river bluffs that were created, according to Ktunaxa legend, when a vast wounded fish crawling up the valley expired at this point; as its flesh rotted, the bones fell apart to create the hoodoos.

Some 28km north of Skookumchuck is the Whiteswan Lake Road turn-off for **Whiteswan Lake Provincial Park**, a handkerchief-sized piece of unbeatable scenery at the end of a twenty-kilometre gravel logging road; the park has five **campsites** ($14; May–Sept) but few trails, as its main emphasis is on boating and trout fishing. Three of the campsites are at Whiteswan Lake itself, the other two at Alces Lake; also keep an eye open for the undeveloped **Lussier Hot Springs** at the entrance of the park (17.5km from the main road), reached by a steep downhill trail. The same access road, called the Lussier River Road after it passes the park, continues another 30km from Alces Lake to **Top of the World Provincial Park**, a far wilder and very beautiful alpine region with good hiking trails. You need to be completely self-sufficient – the five walk-in campsites ($5; June–Sept), reached by an easy six-kilometre trail (200m elevation gain) from the parking area at the end of the road, offer water and firewood and spaces for twenty in the Fish Lake cabin ($15; June–Sept).

FAIRMONT HOT SPRINGS spills over the Columbia's flat flood plain, less a settlement than an ugly modern upmarket resort that feeds off the appeal of the hot springs themselves. The pools were commandeered from the Ktunaxa (Kootenay) in 1922 for exploitation as a tourist resource; the calcium springs (daily 8am–10pm; $7) were particularly prized by the whites because they lack the sulphurous stench of many BC hot dips. However, the locals have now opened some cheaper, makeshift pools above the resort, which are proving very popular with tourists. If you don't fancy coughing up around $109–299 to stay in a room at the swish resort, you could try its big **campsite** (Ⓣ250/345-6311 or 1-800/663-4979, Ⓦwww.fairmonthotsprings.com; $22–43), one minute from the pools but only if you're in an RV – they don't want tents – or the *Spruce Grove Resort* (Ⓣ250/345-6561, Ⓦwww.sprucegroveresort.com; ❸, tents $22; May–Oct), near the river 2km south of Fairmont with rooms and a riverside campsite and an outdoor pool.

Invermere

About 16km north of Fairmont Hot Springs, on the western shore of Windermere Lake, **INVERMERE** is a feel-good summer resort with the usual range of aquatic temptations. However, droves of anglers, boaters and beach bums mean summer vacancies may be in short supply, in which case call the central **visitor centre** near the junction of Hwy 93 and Hwy 95 (Mon–Fri 8am–4pm; June to early Sept daily 9am–5pm; Ⓣ250/342-6316, Ⓦwww.columbiavalleychamber.com) for B&B

If you're continuing north of Invermere into the **Kootenay National Park** and the Rockies, see p.776. From Invermere, if you're crossing the Crowsnest Pass into southern Alberta for **Waterton Lakes National Park**, see p.686.

possibilities, or head for one of the town's handful of **motels** – the *Lee-Jay*, 1015 13th St (Ⓣ250/342-9227, Ⓦwww.leejaymotel.com; ③), is the most reasonable and three of their rooms have kitchen units. The *Best Western Invermere Inn* at the heart of downtown at 1310 7th Ave is the smartest with an outdoor hot tub and fitness room, (Ⓣ250/342-9246 or 1-800/661-8911, Ⓦwww.invermereinn.com; ⑥). The nearest provincial **campsite**, with vehicle and tent sites, is 7km north at *Dry Gulch Provincial Park* ($17; May to mid-Sept). For **food**, the popular *Blue Dog Café* on 7th Ave is particularly good for vegetarians and wholefood aficionados, serving up lentil burgers and falafels ($8.50).

From Invermere the minor Toby Creek Road climbs west into the mountains to the burgeoning **Panorama ski resort** (18km), with nine lifts and over 120 groomed runs (Nov to late April, day lift pass $65), or Panorama Mountain Village (central reservations Ⓣ1-800/663-2929, Ⓦwww.panoramaresort.com), whose slick facilities include the Greywolf golf course (May–Oct) and a range of accommodation. In summer, the chief appeal of the area is hiking, particularly if you continue up the road toward the less tainted **Purcell Wilderness Conservancy Provincial Park** (the road stops 9km short of the park), one of the few easily accessible parts of the Purcell Mountains. If you have a tent and robust hiking inclinations, you could tackle the 61km **trail** through the area to Argenta (see p.516) on the northern end of Kootenay Lake, an excellent cross-country route that largely follows undemanding valleys except when crossing the Purcell watershed at Earl Grey Pass (2256m).

Radium Hot Springs (see p.783) is a little way north of Invermere.

Travel details

Trains

Kamloops to: Vancouver (3 weekly; 9hr 40min).

Buses

Cranbrook to: Kamloops (1 daily; 9hr 15min); Kelowna (2 daily; 9hr 40min); Kimberley (2 daily; 30min); Nelson (2 daily; 4hr 10min); Vancouver (3 daily; 16hr 50min).
Kamloops to: Kelowna (5 daily; 3hr 40min); Vancouver (8 daily; 5hr); Vernon (5 daily; 1hr 50min).
Kelowna to: Castlegar (2 daily; 4hr 30min); Cranbrook (2 daily; 10hr); Nelson (2 daily; 5hr 25min); Penticton (4 daily; 1hr 10min); Vancouver (7 daily; 5hr 30min).
Nelson to: Fernie (2 daily; 6hr); Kamloops (1 daily; 8hr 35min); Kelowna (2 daily; 5hr 20min); Vancouver (2 daily; 12hr).

Flights

Castlegar to: Vancouver (3 daily; 1hr 20min).
Cranbrook to: Vancouver (5 daily; 1hr 50min).
Kamloops to: Prince George (2 daily; 1hr 5min); Vancouver (5 daily; 1hr).
Kelowna to: Prince George (Mon-Fri 1 daily; 1hr 10min); Vancouver (11 daily; 1hr); Victoria (1 daily; 1hr 20min).
Penticton to: Vancouver (2 daily; 1 hr 4min).

Travel details

Buses

Flights

The North

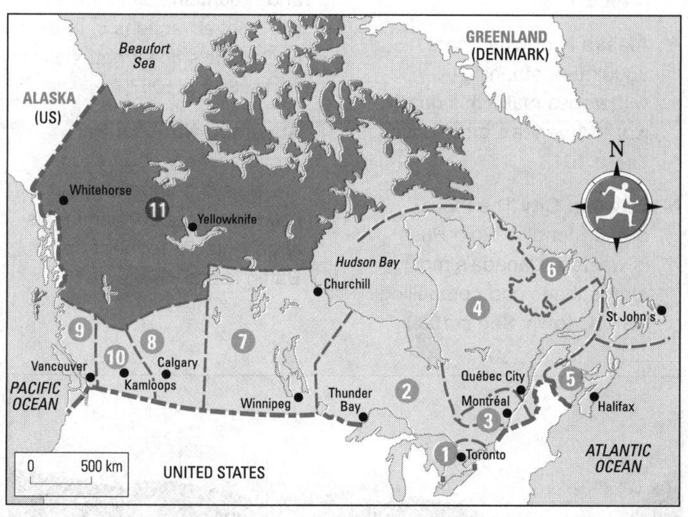
Beaufort Sea
GREENLAND (DENMARK)
ALASKA (US)
N
Whitehorse
11
Yellowknife
Hudson Bay
Churchill
6
4
St John's
9
8
7
10
Calgary
Vancouver
Kamloops
PACIFIC OCEAN
Winnipeg
Thunder Bay
2
Québec City
Montréal
5
3
Halifax
1
Toronto
ATLANTIC OCEAN
0 500 km
UNITED STATES

CHAPTER 11

Highlights

* **The Skeena Valley** Glorious wildlife-rich river and estuary flanked by soaring mountains. See p.992

* **Haida Gwaii** A superb archipelago of wild islands whose natural profusion has earned them the title of the Canadian Galapagos. See p.1000

* **Alaska Highway** Some 2500km of stunning wilderness make this one of North America's great drives. See p.1018

* **Dawson City** The focus of the Klondike Gold Rush is western Canada's most atmospheric and compelling historic town. See p.1036

* **Dempster Highway** The only public road in North America to cross the Arctic Circle offers a fascinating insight into the tundra and other landscapes of the far north. See p.1045

* **Nahanni National Park** Magnificent gorges, waterfalls and mountain scenery are the chief attractions in one of Canada's finest national parks. See p.1057

* **Auyuittuq National Park** Arctic scenery and culture are always compelling, but nowhere more so than in this largely glacial redoubt on Baffin Island. See p.1077

△ Float plane in Nahanni National Park

The North

Although much of Canada still has the flavour of the "last frontier", it's only when you embark on the push north to the Yukon that you know for certain you've left mainstream North American life behind. In the popular imagination, **the north** figures as a perpetually frozen wasteland blasted by ferocious gloomy winters, inhabited – if at all – by hardened characters who make do without civilization. In truth, it's a region where months of summer sunshine offer almost limitless opportunities for outdoor activities and an incredible profusion of flora and fauna; a country within a country, the character of whose settlements has often been forged by the mingling of white settlers and **aboriginal peoples**. The indigenous hunters of the north are as varied as in the south, but two groups predominate: the **Dene**, people of the northern forests who traditionally occupied the Mackenzie River region from the Alberta border to the river's delta at the Beaufort Sea; and the Arctic **Inuit** (literally "the people"), once known as the Eskimos or "fish eaters", a Dene term picked up by early European settlers and now discouraged.

The north is as much a state of mind as a place. People "north of 60" – the 60th Parallel – claim the right to be called **northerners**, and maintain a kinship with Alaskans, but those north of the **Arctic Circle** – the 66th Parallel – look with light-hearted disdain on these "southerners". All mock the inhabitants of the northernmost corners of Alberta and such areas of the so-called Northwest, who, after all, live with the luxury of being able to get around their backcountry by road. To any outsider, however, in terms of landscape and overall spirit the north begins well south of the 60th Parallel. Accordingly, this chapter includes not just the territories of the "true north" – **Yukon**, **Nunavut** and parts of the western Arctic and **Northwest Territories** – but also northern **British Columbia** and **Alberta**, regions of both provinces that are considerably starker and more remote than areas further south.

The two roads into the Yukon strike through northern **British Columbia**: the **Alaska Highway** heads up from the eastern side of the province, connecting

Regional Information

Tourism British Columbia ⓣ1-800/663-6000, ⓦwww.hellobc.com.

Northern BC ⓣ1-800/663-8843, ⓦwww.nbctourism.bc.ca.

Tourism Yukon ⓣ867/667-5340, ⓦwww.touryukon.com.

NWT Arctic Tourism ⓣ1-800/661-0788, ⓦwww.nwttravel.nt.ca.

Nunavut Tourism ⓣ867/979-6551 or 1-866/686-2888, ⓦwww.nunavuttourism.com.

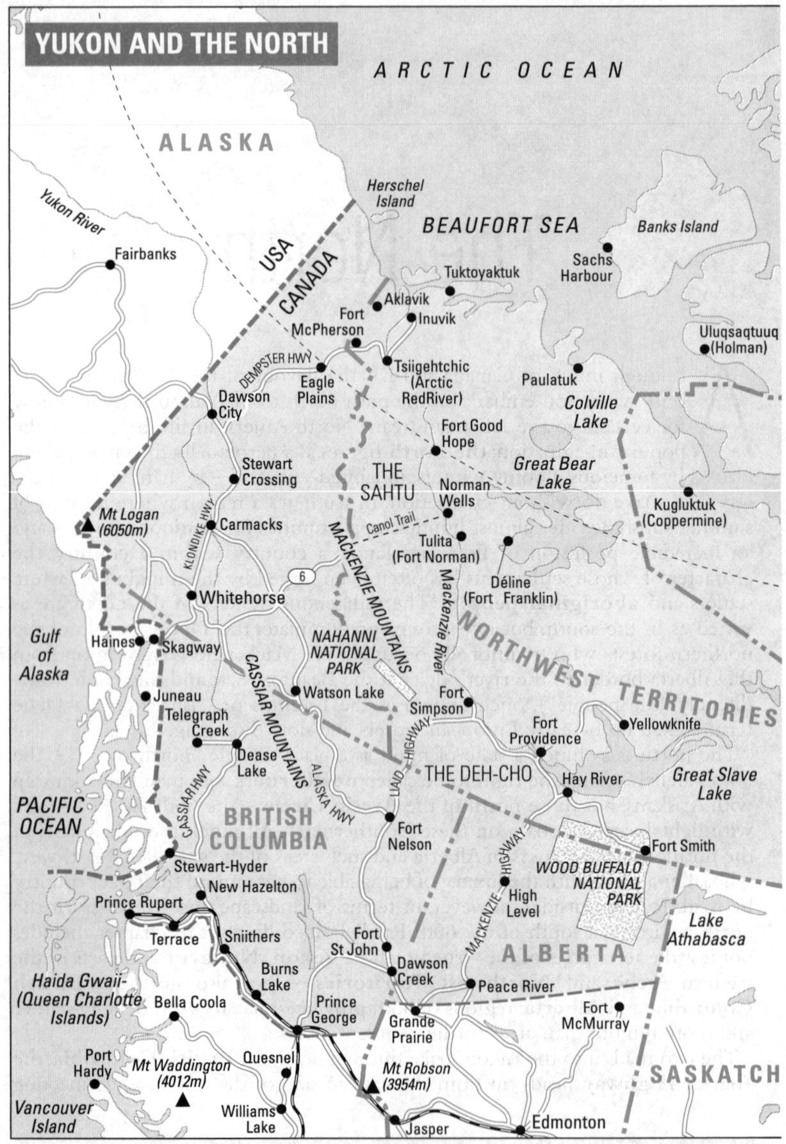

11 THE NORTH

Dawson Creek to Fairbanks in Alaska, and to the west is the adventurous **Stewart-Cassiar Highway**, from near **Prince Rupert** to **Watson Lake**, on the Yukon border. Though the Stewart-Cassiar's passage through the Coast Mountains offers perhaps the better landscapes, it's the Alaska Hwy – serviced by daily Greyhound **buses** and plentiful motels and campsites – that is more travelled, starting in the rolling wheatlands of the Peace River country before

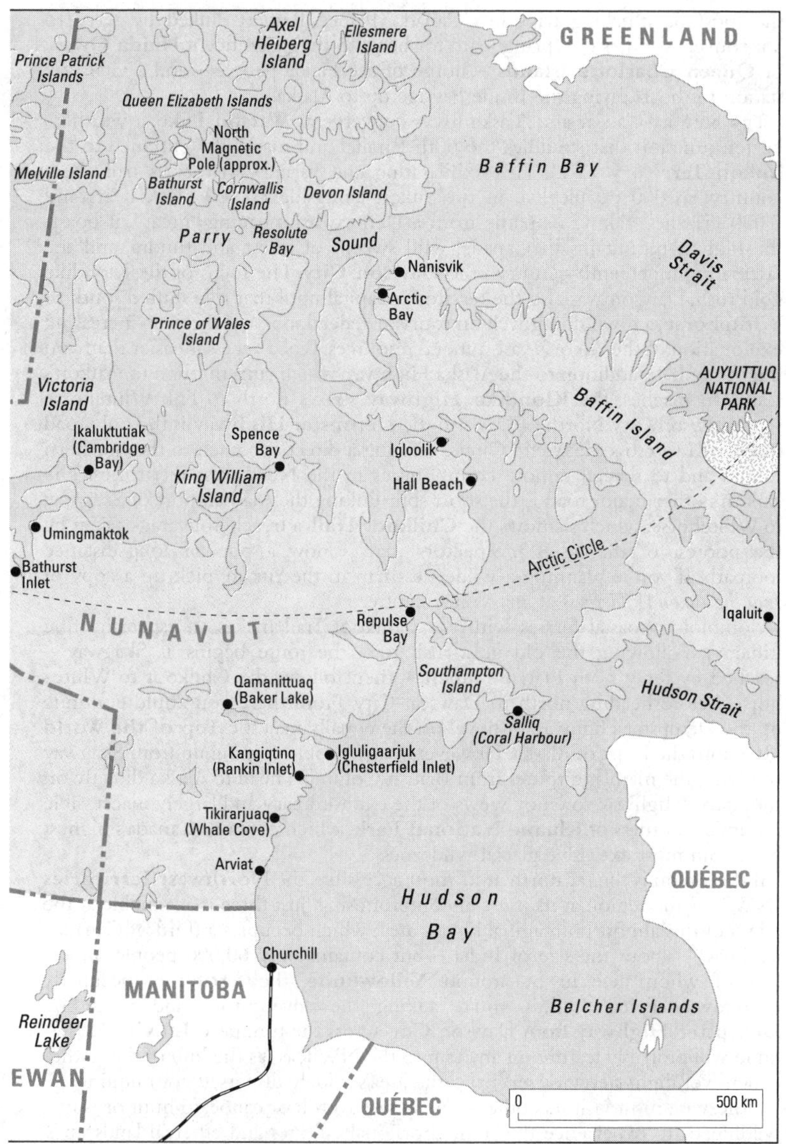

curving into the spruce forests and sawtooth ridges of the northern Rockies. While the scenery is superb, most towns on both roads are battered and perfunctory places built around lumber mills, oil and gas plants and mining camps, though increasingly they are spawning motels and restaurants to serve the surge of summer visitors out to capture the thrill of driving the frontier hwys. Equally popular are the **sea journeys** offered along northern British Columbia, among the most breathtaking trips in Canada. Prince Rupert, linked by ferry to Vancouver Island, is the springboard for boats to the magnificent **Haida Gwaii**, or **Queen Charlotte Islands** – home of the Haida people – and a vital way station for boats plying the Inside Passage up to Alaska.

The Stewart-Cassiar and Alaska hwys converge at **Watson Lake**, a weather-beaten junction that straddles the 60th Parallel and marks the entrance to the **Yukon Territory** (YT). This exhilarating and varied territory is truly bear country: 31,000 people live in the Yukon alongside 10,000 black bears and 7,000 grizzlies. Taking its name from a Dene word meaning "great", it boasts the highest mountains in Canada, wild sweeps of forest and tundra, and the fascinating nineteenth-century relic **Dawson City**. The focus of the Klondike gold rush, Dawson was also the territory's capital until that role shifted south to **Whitehorse**, a town doing well on tourism, federal jobs and the ever-increasing exploitation of the Yukon's vast mineral resources. Road access is easier than you might think. In addition to the Alaska Highway, which runs through the Yukon's southern reaches, the **Klondike Highway** strikes north to link Whitehorse with Dawson City. North of Dawson the **Dempster Highway** is the only road in Canada to cross the Arctic Circle, offering a direct approach to the northern tundra and to several remote communities in the Northwest Territories. The Yukon's other major road is the short spur linking the Alaskan port of Skagway to Whitehorse, which shadows the **Chilkoot Trail**, a treacherous track taken by the poorest of the 1898 prospectors that is now a popular long-distance footpath. If you're planning a wilderness trip in the Yukon, pick up a copy of *Into the Yukon Wilderness* at any visitor centre.

Combining coastal ferries with the Chilkoot Trail makes an especially fine itinerary. Following the old gold-rush trail, the route begins at Skagway – reached by ferry from Prince Rupert – then follows the Chilkoot to White-horse, before heading north to Dawson City. From there you could continue up the Dempster Highway, or travel on the equally majestic **Top of the World** Hwy into the heart of Alaska. However, many people coming up from Skagway or plying the mainland routes from British Columbia head to Alaska directly on the Alaska Highway, to enjoy views of the extraordinary and largely inaccessible mountain vastness of **Kluane National Park**, which contains Canada's highest peaks and most extensive glacial wilderness.

If the Yukon is the far north at its most accessible, the **Northwest Territories** (NWT) is the region at its most uncompromising. Just three roads nibble at the edges of this almost unimaginably vast area, which occupies a third of Canada's landmass – about the size of India – but contains only 60,000 people, almost half of whom live in or around **Yellowknife**, the territories' peculiarly overblown capital. Unless you're taking the adventurous and rewarding **Dempster Highway** from Dawson City across the tundra to **Inuvik**, Yellow-knife will probably feature on any trip to the NWT, as it's the hub of the (rather expensive) flight network servicing the area's widely dispersed communities.

Otherwise most visitors come to the NWT to fish or canoe, to hunt or watch wildlife, or to experience the Inuit aboriginal cultures and ethereal landscapes. More for convenience than any political or geographical reasons, the NWT was formally divided into eight regions. Since 1999 a new two-way division has applied: the eastern portion of the NWT was renamed **Nunavut**, a separate entity administered by and on behalf of the region's aboriginal peoples. One effect has been the **renaming** of most settlements with Inuit names, though in many cases the old English-language names appear in much literature. Nunavut and the "old" western NWT issue their own tourist material, and you should obtain a copy of their respective *Arctic Nunavut Travel Planner* and *Explorers'*

The aurora borealis

The **aurora borealis**, or "**Northern Lights**", is a beautiful and ethereal display of light in the upper atmosphere that can be seen over large areas of northern Canada. The night sky appears to shimmer with dancing curtains of colour, ranging from luminescent monotones – most commonly green or a dark red – to fantastic veils that run the full spectrum. The display becomes more animated as it proceeds, twisting and turning in patterns called "rayed bands". As a finale, a corona sometimes appears, in which rays seem to flare in all directions from a central point.

Named after the Roman goddess of dawn, the aurora was long thought to be produced by sunlight reflected from polar snow and ice, or refracted light produced in the manner of a rainbow. Certain Inuit peoples believed the lights were the spirits of animals or ancestors; others thought they represented wicked forces. Old-time gold prospectors thought they might be vapours given off by ore deposits. Research still continues into the phenomenon, and while the earth's geomagnetic field certainly plays some part in the creation of the aurora, its source would appear to lie with the sun – auroras become more distinct and are seen spread over a larger area two days after intense solar activity, the time it takes the "solar wind" to arrive. This wind is composed of fast-moving electrically charged ions. When these hit the earth's atmosphere they respond to the earth's magnetic field and move towards the poles. En route they strike atoms and molecules of gas in the upper atmosphere, causing them to become temporarily charged or ionized. These molecules then release the charge, or energy, usually in the form of light. Different colours are emitted depending on the gases involved: oxygen produces green hues (or orange at higher altitudes), nitrogen occasionally violet colours.

You should be able to see the Northern Lights as far south as Prince George in British Columbia, over parts of northern Alberta (where on average they're visible some 160 nights a year) and over much of the Northwest Territories, Nunavut and northern Manitoba. They are at their most dazzling **from December to March**, when nights are longest and the sky darkest, though they are potentially visible all year round. Look out for a faint glow on the northeastern horizon after dusk, and then – if you're lucky – for the full show as the night deepens.

Guide brochures. These summarize accommodation options, airline connections, many of the available tours – costing anything from $50 to $5000 or more – and the plethora of outfitters who provide the equipment and backup essential for any but the most superficial trip to the region.

Prince George

Lying some 780km north of Vancouver, and 380km northwest of Jasper, rough-edged **PRINCE GEORGE** (pop. 78,000) is the general area's services and transport centre. Forestry, in the form of pulp mills, kilns, planers, plywood plants and allied chemical works, is at the core of its industrial landscape – if you ever wanted the inside story on the lumber business, this is where to find it.

The town is a disorienting open-plan network of roads and sporadic houses between Hwy 97 and a sprawling downtown area at the junction of the Fraser and Nechako rivers. Simon Fraser established a North West Trading Company post here in 1805. As a commercial nexus it quickly altered the lives of the local **Carrier Sekani** people, who abandoned their semi-nomadic migration from winter to summer villages in favour of a permanent settlement alongside the fort. Little changed until 1914 when the arrival of the Grand Trunk Railway – later the Canadian National – spawned an influx of pioneers and loggers. The town was connected by road to Dawson Creek and the north as late as 1951, and saw the arrival of the Pacific Great Eastern Railway in 1958, two developments that give some idea of how recent the opening up of the far north has been.

As far as **sightseeing** is concerned, Canfor run free **tours** (June–Aug) around some of its big mills and processing plants; to reserve a place, contact Tourism Prince George at one of their two **visitor centre** locations at 101-1300 1st Ave (daily May–Sept 8am–8pm, Oct–April 8.30am–5pm; ⓣ250/562-3700 or 1-800/668-7646, ⓦwww.tourismpg.com) or 2800 Hwy 16 (May–Sept daily 8am–8pm). The city's numerous **parks** provide a welcome respite from Canfor's tree graveyards; the small but central Connaught Hill Park has 360 degree views over the city, while just north of downtown, Cottonwood Island Nature Park has longer trails for stretching your legs.

A good **motel** on the Hwy 97 strip is the big *Spruceland Inn* (ⓣ250/563-0102 or 1-800/663-3295; ❸) at 1391 Central St at the junction of Hwy 97 and 15th Ave. At the nearby *Esther's Inn* (ⓣ250/562-4131 or 1-800/663-6844, ⓦwww.esthersinn.com; ❸), one block off the hwy at 1151 Commercial Drive (10th Ave), the price includes a swimming pool, water slides and Jacuzzi. Closer to downtown is the comfortable 200-room *Ramada Hotel Downtown Prince George*, 444 George St (ⓣ250/563-0055 or 1-800/830-8833, ⓦwww.ramadaprincegeorge.com; ❺). All the campsites are some way out, the best being the big *Blue Spruce RV & Campground* about 5km west at Kimball Road on Hwy 16 (ⓣ250/964-7272 or 964-4060, ⓔbluespruncervpark@shaw.ca; $18.50–25; April to mid-Oct), which includes a heated outdoor pool. For **food** that rises above chain restaurant standards, try *White Goose Bistro*, 1205 3rd Ave (ⓣ250/561-1002; closed Sun), specializing in Italian and French

Transport to and from Prince George

By air, Air Canada Jazz (ⓣ1-888/247-2262, ⓦwww.flyjazz.ca) and WestJet, (ⓣ1-888/538-5696, ⓦwww.westjet.com) fly to Prince George from Vancouver; the airport is 18km east of downtown and linked by regular shuttles. The town is linked three times weekly by VIA Rail **trains** (ⓣ1-800/561-8630, ⓦwww.viarail.ca) to Jasper, Edmonton and beyond eastbound (a highly scenic journey), and Prince Rupert westbound (for the Haida Gwaii/Prince Charlotte Islands and Inside Passage ferries). The train station is downtown at 1300 1st Ave (ⓣ1-888/842-7245, ⓦwww.viarail.ca); if you're heading for motels or the bus terminal use a taxi from either Prince George Taxi (ⓣ250/564-4444); or Emerald Taxi Ltd (ⓣ250/563-3333).

Prince George is also a staging post for **Greyhound** routes to the north, and integral to the main road routes to Dawson Creek (for the Alaska Hwy) and Prince Rupert (for the Stewart-Cassiar Hwy). The Greyhound **bus terminal**, well south of downtown at 1566 12th Ave (ⓣ250/564-5454 or 1-800/661-1202, ⓦwww.greyhound.ca), is close to a handful of the town's many hotels and motels. There are three buses a week to Whitehorse in the Yukon (via Dawson Creek), three daily to Vancouver, and two daily to Prince Rupert.

cuisine – the popular duck in cherry red wine sauce is $21; or for no-fuss Italian, *Cimo*, 601 Victoria St (☎250/564-7975; closed Sun), has an extensive choice of pasta dishes ($12–14). If you fancy a **drink**, *BX Pub*, at the corner of Carnie Street and 5th Avenue, attracts a young crowd.

For the route from Prince George north and east to Dawson Creek, and the Alaska Highway, see p.1018.

Prince George to Prince Rupert

To make the 735-kilometre journey west from Prince George to **Prince Rupert**, you can use either Hwy 16 (the Yellowhead Hwy) or the parallel VIA Rail railway; neither is terribly scenic by BC standards until you reach the glorious river and mountain landscapes of the **Skeena Valley** 150km before Prince Rupert. Most people make this trip as a link in a much longer journey, either to pick up **ferries** north to Alaska or south to Port Hardy on Vancouver Island, or to pick up the start of the Stewart-Cassiar Hwy, a rough wilderness road that cuts north from the Skeena Valley to meet the Alaska Hwy at Watson Lake over the Yukon border. Unless you fly, it's also the only way to reach Haida Gwaii/the Queen Charlotte Islands, accessible by ferry or plane from Prince Rupert. The best place to pause during the journey is near **Hazelton**, approximately 450km from Prince George, where you can visit a little cluster of aboriginal villages. Hitchhiking is strongly discouraged along Hwy 16, where the grisly workings of a serial killer, or killers, have lent it the title "Highway of Tears"; over the past three decades, eight women have been murdered and dozens more have gone missing while hitchhiking along the stretch between Prince George and Prince Rupert.

West of Prince George

Riding out of Prince George you're confronted quickly with the relentless monotony of the Interior Plateau's rolling forests, an arboreal grind broken only by the occasional lake and the grey silhouettes of distant low-hilled horizons. The pine beetle, which has infested many of the lodgehole pine trees in the BC interior, has made particular inroads along the stretch heading towards **BURNS LAKE**, 229km to the west. The road travels past vast swaths of red and grey forest, all ravaged by a beetle that has been thriving in increasingly mild winters. Burns Lake is the gateway to the northern end of **Tweedsmuir Provincial Park**, considered to be one of the epicenters of the epidemic. There is a **visitor centre** at 540 Hwy 16 West (daily June–Sept 9am–6pm, Jan–May Mon–Fri 9am–4.30pm; ☎250/692-5737, ⓦwww.bldchamber.ca) which can provide information on the twenty or so **accommodation** options in the area.

Beyond Burn's Lake the scenery picks up still more, as if preparing for the mountains in the distance, though the run of villages continues to offer little but places to fill either the tank or the stomach. If you need to **stay** in this region, aim for the *Two Rivers Lodge* (☎250/846-5679, ⓦwww.tworiverslodge.ca; ❸), on the banks of the Bulkley River, just 150m out of the unspoiled hamlet of **TELKWA**, 10km east of Smithers. As long as you're here, be sure to take a few minutes to stroll up Telkwa's riverfront street of heritage buildings and its handsome brown-and-white, wood-planked **pioneer museum**.

SMITHERS (pop. 5500), the largest community after Prince George (370km to the east), is a picturesque outdoor adventure hub. The sizable Swiss population has made their mark on the Alpine-themed downtown core, focused on Main

Street at the crossroads of Hwy 16. There is a **visitor centre** nearby at 1411 Court St (daily mid-May to Aug 9am–6pm; Sept to mid-May Mon–Fri 9am–5pm; ⓣ250/847-5072 or 1-800/542-6673, ⓦwww.tourismsmithers.com), good for free Internet and information about adventure sports activities nearby, including fishing, kayaking and horse riding. There is mountain biking and hiking in the **Babine Mountains Provincial Park** and downhill and cross-country **skiing** 20km from town on Hudson Bay Mountain (Dec to mid-April; day lift pass $36; ⓣ250/665-4299, ⓦwww.skismithers.com; for cross-country skiing contact Bulkley Valley Nordic Centre ⓣ250/847-3828, ⓦwww.bvnordic.ca). As far as indoor attractions are concerned, there is a joint **art gallery** and **museum** at the corner of Main St and Hwy 16 with a lovingly-tended exhibit on Smithers' brief brush with notoriety in 1911 when a local invented the egg carton (Mon–Sat 9am–5pm; ⓔbvmuseum@nucleus.com).

Smithers is serviced three times weekly by VIA Rail's "Skeena" **train** at 3815 Railway Ave. Greyhound **buses** run twice daily in each direction along Hwy 16 – the station is just west of downtown at 4011 Hwy 16 (ⓣ250/847-2204). There is also an **airport** five kilometres west on Hwy 16, with regular Air Canada Jazz flights.

If you're overnighting here – and there's plenty of **accommodation** – ignore the brace of motels on the road and settle for the big white-timbered *Hudson Bay Lodge* (ⓣ250/847-4581 or 1-800/663-5040, ⓦwww.hblodge.com; ❹) just east of the downtown core on Hwy 16; it has a great restaurant, *Pepper Jack's*, which has schnitzel and fondue theme nights (mains $15–30). For hostel accommodation, try the spotless *Smithers Hostel and Guesthouse* at 1766 Main St, with kitchen facilities, free Internet and dorm beds for $25 (ⓣ250/847-4862, ⓦwww.smithershostel.com; ❷). For camping and RV, the *Riverside Park and Municipal Campground* occupies an idyllic spot northwest of Main Street on the banks of the Bulkley River (ⓣ250/847-3494; $10–21). For something to **eat**, *Schimmel's* at 1172 Main St (ⓣ250/847-9044; closed Sun & Mon) packs a European punch, with great coffee, artisan breads, soups, pizzas, tarts and home-made gelato (mains $5–6.50).

The Skeena Valley

Just beyond Smithers, the **Skeena River** (the "River of the Mists") carves a beautiful valley through the Coast Mountains, an important trade route for aboriginal peoples and stern-wheelers before the coming of the railway in 1912. For a couple of hours the road and railway run past an imposing backdrop of snowcapped peaks half-reflected in the mist-wraithed estuary. Out on the water there's a good chance of seeing the ripples of beavers and sea otters, not to mention bald eagles perched on the river's immense logjams. Dark valleys peel off the main river's majestic course, suggestive of a deep, untrodden wilderness, and delicate threads of waterfalls are repeatedly visible though the trees.

Shortly after Hwy 16 meets the river crashing down from the north near Hazelton and New Hazelton, a couple of minor roads strike off to four nearby **villages**, where something of the culture of the indigenous Gitxsan peoples has been preserved, along with new examples of totem carving and other crafts. 'Ksan and Kispiox, home to the best totems and long houses, are a few kilometres off Hwy 16 on the minor High Level Road (Hwy 62) out of New Hazelton; just north of 'Ksan a road links west to Gitwangak and Gitanyow (formerly Kitwancool), or they can be reached by continuing west on Hwy 16 a few kilometres and heading north on Hwy 37 (the Stewart-Cassiar Hwy).

The most easterly of the west coast aboriginal peoples, the Gitxsan – "people of the river of the mists" – traditionally lived off fish and game rather than agriculture, and were consummate artists and carvers. In 1958, the Gitxsan opened the first aboriginal museum in Canada followed in 1970 by an entire reconstructed traditional Gitxsan village at **'Ksan**. This is the village to concentrate on – aboriginal women act as guides around seven cedar long houses and numerous totem poles, giving a commentary on the carvings, clothes, buildings and masks on show (tours daily April–Sept 9am–5pm; museum same summer hours plus Oct–March Mon–Fri 9.30am–4.30pm; tours $10, museum $5; Ⓣ250/842-5544 or 1-877/842-5518, Ⓦwww.ksan.org).

Kispiox, 13km north of Hazelton, is the ancient Gitxsan home of the Frog, Wolf and Fireweed clans, and was given its name by the old Department for Indian Affairs. It means "place of loud talkers" but locals not surprisingly prefer the traditional name, which is Anspayaxw, meaning "the hidden place". The highlights here are fifteen riverside totems. **Gitwangak** to the west, just 500m north of the Hwy 16 and Hwy 37 junction, means "the place of rabbits", and it too, has some impressive totems, as does **Gitanyow** – "people of a small village" – 21km north on Hwy 37, whose eighteen poles include the 140-year-old "Hole in the Sky" totem. You can sometimes watch poles being repaired at one of two carving sheds around the village.

The nearest **visitor centre** for the villages is near New Hazelton at the junction of hwys 16 and 62 (mid-May to mid-Sept daily 8am–8pm; Ⓣ250/842-6071 or 842-6571 year-round, Ⓔtourism@newhazelton.ca), but you should also spend a few minutes looking round the evocative old Victorian streets of old **Hazelton** 6km to the northwest on Hwy 62. **Accommodation** is limited to a handful of motels in New Hazelton, one of the cheapest being the *Bulkley Valley Motel*, 4444 Hwy 16 (Ⓣ250/842-6817; ❷). Kispiox also has a handful of bed and breakfasts. The closest to the village is the two-room *Trakehnerhof Bed and Breakfast*, Salmon River Rd (Ⓣ250/842-5400, Ⓦwww.trakehnerhof.ca; ❸), on the banks of the Skeena River with a spa and sauna. For camping, the *River's Edge Campground*, Kispiox Valley Rd (Ⓣ250/842-5822; pitch/RV $15/20), is 7km outside the village on the Kispiox River and attracts many fishing enthusiasts.

Some 142km before Prince Rupert, Hwy 16 passes through **TERRACE** (pop. 18,000), the commercial centre of the Skeena Valley. There is a **visitor centre** on the hwy at 4511 Keith Ave (daily June–Aug 8am–5pm, rest of year Mon–Fri 8.30am–4.30pm; Ⓣ250/635-2063, Ⓦwww.terracetourism.bc.ca), but few reasons to stop in the town itself. In winter there is **skiing** 35km west off Hwy 16 at **Shames Mountain** (mid-Dec to mid-April; day lift pass $39; Ⓣ250/635-3773, Ⓦwww.shamesmountain.com), with 22 trails and a hefty annual snow dump of twelve metres. Terrace is also a good jumping off point for the 250-year-old lava flows at **Nisga'a Memorial Lava Bed Provincial Park**, situated 80km to the north. There is a **campground** here ($14; mid-May to mid-Sept) and a visitor centre (mid-June to Sept daily 10am–6pm) that can arrange volcano tours.

Prince Rupert

There's a bracing tang of salt and fish in the air in **PRINCE RUPERT**, a distinctive port on Kaien Island – linked by bridge to the mainland – that comes as an invigorating relief after the run out of Prince George. A stunning place when the mist lifts, it looks out over an archipelago of islands and is ringed by mountains that tumble to the sea along a beautiful fjord-cut coastline. A crowd of cars, backpackers and RVs washes daily through its streets off the **Alaska**, **Queen Charlotte** and **Port Hardy ferries**, complementing

Ferries from Prince Rupert

Ferry terminals for both BC Ferries (for Port Hardy and the Queen Charlotte Islands) and the Alaska Marine Hwy (for Skagway and Alaska Panhandle ports) are at **Fairview Dock**, 2km southwest of town at the end of Hwy 16. Walk-on tickets for foot passengers are rarely a problem at either terminal, but advance reservations are essential if you're taking a car or want a cabin for any summer crossing. A town bus passes the terminal every two or three hours for incoming sailings, but for outbound sailings it's probably best to grab a **taxi** from downtown (⑦250/624-2185). In 2006, ferry services were severely disrupted after the *Queen of the North* sank 135km south of Prince Rupert. A new ferry is due to be running in 2007 and the schedule below reflects a return to normal services.

To Haida Gwaii / the Queen Charlotte Islands

BC Ferries operates the MV *Queen of Prince Rupert* to **Skidegate** on the Queen Charlotte Islands (mid-May to Sept: six weekly; rest of year: three weekly). The crossing takes between 6hr 30min and 8hr depending on weather, and costs $30.20 one-way for foot passengers ($26.45 low season: late Sept to mid-May), plus $112.15/$97.40 for cars and $6 for bikes. Two-berth cabins cost $50. Return ferries from Skidegate sometimes provide a connection with the Inside Passage boat to Port Hardy on Vancouver Island (see below). For **reservations** or timetable information, contact BC Ferries on ⑦250/386-3431 or 1-888/223-3779 anywhere in BC, or in Prince Rupert on ⑦250/624-9627, ⓦwww.bcferries.com.

To Port Hardy

Ferries **to Port Hardy** leave every other day in summer and three times every two weeks in winter for a stunning cruise that lasts fifteen to twenty-five hours, depending on the weather. One-way fares are: in peak season (mid-May to Sept) $127.20 for passengers, $297.10 extra for a car, $6.50 extra for a bicycle; in shoulder season (Oct, mid-Dec to early Jan, early March to mid-May) $99.20/$229.10/$6.50; and in low season (Nov to mid-Dec, early Jan to early March) $78.20/$180.10/$6.50. Two-berth cabins cost $65. To take on a car in the summer, you'll need to have booked at least two months in advance (see also Port Hardy, p.933).

To Alaska

Ferries run by **Alaska Marine Highway** (⑦250/627-1744 or 1-800/642-0066) go to **Skagway** in Alaska, via (some or all) Ketchikan, Wrangell, Petersburg, Sitka, Hyder, Stewart, Juneau, Haines and Hollis and other minor halts. Frequency is three times a week in the summer and twice a week in winter. Schedules and fares are complicated, given the many possible permutations of route and port, but can be sourced from ⓦwww.alaska.gov/ferry or by calling the central reservations number in Juneau (⑦1-800/642-0066) or the Anchorage office (⑦907/272-7116). One-way adult passenger fare from Prince Rupert to Skagway starts at around US$184, with US$34 extra to bring a bicycle and US$403 for a car. Two- or four-berth cabins can also be booked: reckon on two-berth cabin from Prince Rupert to Haines or Skagway costing US$150. Boats stop frequently en route, with the chance to go ashore for a short time, though longer stopovers must be arranged when buying a through-ticket. For all Alaskan sailings turn up at least an hour before departure to go through US customs and immigration procedures if you're a foot passenger, and three hours if you have a car, and note that though the journey takes two days there are various restrictions on the fresh food you can take on board.

the seafront's vibrant activity, and adding to the coffers of a town that's clearly on the up and up. In the summer, **cruise ships** make four-hour pit stops here, spewing up to 2000 passengers ashore at a time to gorge on fish and chips and take sightseeing tours. There's plenty of outdoor and indoor attractions here, and it's an amiable enough spot to while away a day while you're waiting for a boat.

Arrival and information

The **Greyhound station** is in the centre of town at 822 3rd Ave and 8th St (Ⓣ250/624-5090, Ⓦwww.greyhound.ca) and handles two buses daily for the 10-hour ride to Prince George ($105 one-way). The VIA Rail **train station** is on the waterfront at Fairview Dock and the ticket office is in the BC Ferries building on Hwy 16 (open 2hr either side of departures and arrivals; Ⓣ1-888/842-7245, Ⓦwww.viarail.ca). Trains to Prince George for connections to Edmonton via Jasper leave on Tuesday, Thursday and Sunday at 8am, arriving in Prince George at 8.30pm. If you're thinking of taking the train right through, note that you have to stay overnight in Prince George, as there are no through-trains to Jasper or Edmonton. The local **airport** is on Digby Island just across the harbour, with ferry connections to the BC and Alaska Marine ferry terminals (see box opposite) and shuttle bus connections to downtown (Ⓣ250/622-2222), which leave and drop off at the *Howard Johnson Highliner Plaza Hotel* at 815 1st Ave West. Air Canada Jazz (Ⓣ1-888/247-2262, Ⓦwww.aircanada.com) flies to Vancouver, as does Hawkair (Ⓣ1-866-429-5247, Ⓦwww.hawkair.net). North Pacific Sea Planes (Ⓣ250/627-1341 or 1-800/689-4234, Ⓦwww.northpacificseaplanes.com) run 45-minute flights to Sandspit, Masset and Queen Charlotte on Haida Gwaii/the Queen Charlotte Islands (see p.1006) leaving east of town from the Seal Cove seaplane base on Bellis Road. Many people reach Prince Rupert by **ferry**. For **car rentals**, contact National (Ⓣ250/624-5318, Ⓦwww.nationalcar.ca) at the *Howard Johnson Highliner Plaza Hotel*; Hertz at 207 3rd Ave (Ⓣ250/627-9166, Ⓦwww.hertz.ca); or Car to Go (Ⓣ250/627-1525 or 1-800/227-8646, Ⓦwww.car-to-go.com). Prince Rupert's **visitor centre** is in the Atlin Terminal on Cow Bay Road (Ⓣ250/624-5637 or 1-800/667-1994, Ⓦwww.tourismprincerupert.com), a little to the north in an older part of the town known as Cow Bay, a small and funky waterfront enclave that also boasts some attractive cafés, galleries and restaurants.

Accommodation

The town has two **hostels**; the quickly filled *Pioneer Hostel* is around the corner from the museum and visitor centre at 167 3rd Ave (Ⓣ250/624-2334, Ⓦwww.citytel.net/pioneer; ❷) and has bright but basic rooms (dorm beds $20, private doubles $48) and shared bathrooms. The newer, 32-bed *Black Rooster Roadhouse* at 501 6th Ave (Ⓣ250/627-5337 or 1866/371-5337, Ⓦww.blackrooster.ca, ❷) is a spacious affair with a kitchen, free Internet and dorm beds for $20.

The nearest **motel** to the ferry terminals is the *Totem Lodge*, 1335 Park Ave (Ⓣ250/624-6761 or 1-800/550-0178, Ⓦwww.totemlodge.com ❹); Park Avenue is a continuation of 2nd Avenue, which runs south to the terminals from downtown. Perhaps the best all-round central choice, especially if you can secure a room with a sea view, is the *Inn on the Harbour*, 720 1st Ave (Ⓣ250/624-9107 or 1-800/663-8155, Ⓦwww.innontheharbour.com; ❹). The *Pacific Inn*, 909 3rd Ave West (Ⓣ250/627-1711 or 1-888/663-1999, Ⓦwww.pacificinn.bc.ca; ❹), is a big and good-value motel, but if you want to go top-of-the-range try the large *Crest Hotel*, 222 1st Ave (Ⓣ250/624-6771 or 1-800/663-8150, Ⓦwww.cresthotel.bc.ca; ❻). Farther afield, the *Parkside Resort*, 101 11th Ave

△ Chatham Sound, Prince Rupert

(Ⓣ250/624-9131 or 1-888/575-2288, Ⓦwww.parksideresortmotel.com; ❷), is a smart-looking hotel with good rates about 1km out of town and is likely to have room when downtown places are full.

The only big local **campsite** is the rather unattractive *A Prince Rupert RV Campground*, 1750 Park Ave (Ⓣ250/624-5861; $19–30; April–Sept), 1km west of town and 1km from the ferry terminals; it has tent sites but is usually full of RVs. Otherwise the *Parkside Resort* (see above) has some sites ($12–18) that few people know about, and there's also the rural *Prudhomme Lake* provincial campsite ($14; May–Sept; for information on reserving provincial campsites in British Columbia see p.758), with forested lakeside sites 16km east of town on Hwy 16.

The Town

Although you wouldn't know to look at it, Prince Rupert's port is one of the world's largest deep-water terminals, and handles a huge volume of trade (grain, coal and fish in particular). In the past the region was the focal point of trade between aboriginal peoples to the north and south, one reason why the Hudson's Bay Company built a post at Fort Simpson, 30km north of the present townsite. For information on how the terminus of Canada's second **transcontinental rail link** came to be Prince Rupert, visit the **Kwinitsa Station Railway Museum** housed in the old 1911 station near the waterfront on Bill Murray Way (July–Aug daily 9am–5pm; donation suggested; Ⓣ250/627-1915).

Prince Rupert's excellent **Museum of Northern British Columbia** (daily mid-May to Sept 9am–5pm; Oct to mid-May Tues–Sat 9am–5pm; $5; Ⓣ250/624-3207, Ⓦwww.museumofnorthernbc.ca) is on 1st Ave and McBride St at the northern end of the town's tight downtown zone. It's housed in an impressive reproduction First Nation cedar longhouse and is particularly strong on the culture and history of the local Tsimshian. The museum also boasts a clutch of wonderful silent archive films on topics ranging from fishing to the building of the railway – ideal ways to whittle away a wet afternoon, of which storm-lashed Prince Rupert ("City of Rainbows") has plenty. There are also tours, performances and feasts offered in the summer and a carving shed across the road where you can watch artists at work.

For a whiff of the city's fishy past, you can tour the oldest salmon cannery village on the West Coast at the **North Pacific Historic Fishing Village**, 20km south of Prince Rupert near Port Edward at 1889 Skeena Drive, (May–Aug Mon–Sat 10am–7.30pm, Sun 10am–5pm, Sept reduced hours; $12; ⓣ250/628-3538, ⓦwww.cannery.ca). Abandoned as a cannery in 1968, you can now amble along the creaking boardwalks and view the old processing facilities and workers' cottages.

While you're in town, check out some of the local **tours** or **boat trips**, many of which are inexpensive and provide a good way to see the offshore islands and wildlife. Seashore Charters (ⓣ250/624-5645, ⓦwww.seashorecharters.com), with an office in the Atlin Terminal, is a good outfit, offering kayaking and whale-watching tours as well as half-day archaeological and cultural trips to **Pike Island** to view ancient village sites and aboriginal petroglyphs. A very popular trip locally is to **Khuzeymateen Grizzly Bear Sanctuary** (contact BC Parks on ⓣ250/847-7320 for information on one- to ten-day tours), a remote coastal valley 45km northeast of Prince Rupert created in 1994 to protect BC's largest-known coastal population of **grizzly bears**. In British Columbia, the damage done to grizzly habitats by logging, mining, hunting and other concerns – notably the slaughter of the animals for body parts in dubious Asian remedies – is one of the keenest environmental issues in the province. In the summer, several local tour operators run full-day and multi-day boat tours to view the grizzlies in action; Palmerville (ⓣ250/624-8243, ⓦwww.palmerville.bc.ca) runs half-day tours with access via floatplane (from $400) and also offers rustic accommodation in a floating cabin just outside the sanctuary.

A little out of town, beyond the museum, **Mount Hays** gives a bird's-eye view of the harbour and the chance to spot bald eagles. To reach the steep track that provides the only route to the top, take the Wantage Road turn-off on Hwy 16 just out of town. It's three hours to the top but you get fairly good views after clambering just a short way up the track. For a less energetic **walk**, take the five-kilometre interpretive loop trail through old growth rainforest to **Butze Rapids** – unique reversing tidal rapids; the trailhead is about 5km east of town along Hwy 16.

Eating and drinking

Fresh fish is the obvious thing to **eat** locally, preferably at a town institution, the *Green Apple*, a shack that serves a mean halibut and chips for around $8; it's at 301 McBride St (ⓣ250/627-1666; closed Sun) just before Hwy 16 turns into town. For something more upmarket, locals flock to the *Cow Bay Café*, 205 Cow Bay Rd (ⓣ250/627-1212; closed Sun & Mon), which does a roaring trade on the waterfront and serves some of the best meals in town (mains $15–20). Also in Cow Bay is *Cowpuccinos*, a café that's the centre of Prince Rupert's alternative scene. The restaurant in the *Crest Hotel* does great seafood, burgers and steaks (mains $10–37) and its outdoor deck offers spectacular harbour views on a sunny day. The *Breakers* pub just across the bridge at 117 George Hills Way (ⓣ250/624-5990) is a popular and inexpensive place to sink a beer and also serves decent food, with main courses from $17–27. For the chicest **bar** north of Vancouver, drop into *Rain,* at 737 2nd Ave West (ⓣ250/627-8272, closed Sun), which not only has an extensive wine and cocktail list, but also whips up superb and creative food (main meals $12–21).

Kermode or 'spirit' bears of Princess Royal Island

At first glance, you could easily mistake it for a polar bear, or an albino black bear. But the elusive kermode or 'spirit' bear is actually a white-furred genetic variation of the black bear. A recessive gene passed down from both parents gives it its white fur, and according to local aboriginal legend, its existence serves to remind us of the Ice Age. The kermode is unique to the rugged temperate rainforest along British Columbia's central coast, its habitat concentrated in the fifteen million acres stretching from Bella Coola to Prince Rupert (also known as the Great Bear Rainforest). Despite ongoing pressure from conservationists to preserve its habitat, the kermode remains under threat from logging, hunting and mining. The highest number of kermode bears can be found on Princess Royal Island, where one in ten black bears are born with white fur. No humans live on the island, which is 200km south of Prince Rupert. Access is by boat or float plane only, with one-day wildlife-viewing boat tours (Ⓣ250/841-2522, Ⓦwww.gitgaat.net) operating out of Hartley Bay, a remote community of 180 Gitga'at people 140km south of Prince Rupert. Best viewing months are between August and October, when the bears gather around the creeks to feed on the spawning salmon. Hartley Bay is accessed by air or water from Prince Rupert. Northco Corp Ferry Service (Ⓣ250/624-3337 or 622-8067) runs twice weekly leaving from the terminal on Cow Bay Road behind the *Crest Hotel* in Prince Rupert (four hours; $45 one-way), while North Pacific Sea Planes (Ⓣ250/627-1341) operates a daily, one-hour flight ($143 one-way). For accommodation in Hartley Bay, try the five-room *Squirrel's Den Inn* at 120 Hayimiisaxaa Way (Ⓣ250/841-2727, Ⓔchillart@telus.net; ❺ including meals), or contact *King Pacific Lodge*, a luxury wilderness retreat on a barge moored in Barnard Harbour on Princess Royal Island, one hour by boat from Hartley Bay (Ⓣ604/987-5452, Ⓦwww.kingpacificlodge.com; May–Sept; ❽ including meals). Further down the coast, Klemtu Tourism also run kermode-viewing tours to Princess Royal Island (Ⓣ250/839-2346, Ⓦwww.klemtutourism.com).

Haida Gwaii – the Queen Charlotte Islands

Ranged in a gentle arc some 150km off the Prince Rupert coast, **Haida Gwaii**, until recently better known as the **Queen Charlotte Islands**, consist of a triangular-shaped archipelago of two major islands – **Graham** and **Moresby** – and two hundred islets that make an enticing diversion from the heavily travelled sea route up through BC. The islands are something of a cult amongst travellers and environmentalists, partly for their scenery, flora and fauna and almost legendary remoteness from the mainstream, but also because they've achieved a high profile in the battle between the forestry industry and ecology activists. At the forefront of the battle are the **Haida**, widely acknowledged as the region's most artistically-prolific aboriginal groups, who have made the islands their home for over 10,000 years (see box, p.1008). Their culture, and in particular the chance to visit their many **deserted villages**, forms an increasing part of the islands' attraction, but many people also come here to sample the immensely rich **flora and fauna**, a natural profusion that's earned them the title of the "Canadian Galapagos".

Haida Gwaii was one of only two areas in western Canada to escape the last Ice Age, which elsewhere altered the evolutionary progress, and which has resulted in the survival of many so-called **relic species**. Species unique to the islands include a fine yellow daisy, the world's largest **black bears**, and subspecies of pine marten, deer mouse, hairy woodpecker, saw-whet owl and Stellar's jay. There are also more **eagles** here than anywhere else in the region, as well as the world's largest population of Peale's peregrine falcons and the elusive **black-footed albatross** – whose wingspan exceeds that of the largest eagles. Fish, too, are immensely plentiful, and there's a good chance of spotting whales, otters, sea lions and other aquatic mammals.

Haida Gwaii practicalities

The islands can be accessed either by air or ferry from Prince Rupert. Ferries from Prince Rupert (see box, p.1002 for details) dock at tiny Skidegate near Queen Charlotte on **Graham Island**, the northern of the group's two main collections of islands. Most of the archipelago's five thousand or so inhabitants live either in Queen Charlotte or at Masset to the north, leaving the southern cluster of islands across Skidegate Channel – known for convenience as **Moresby Island** – a virtually deserted primal wilderness but for the small community at Sandspit (see p.1012). Regular twenty-minute ferry crossings on the MV *Kwuna* connect Moresby Island to Skidegate (7.30am–10.30pm, 12 daily; $6 foot passengers, $17.50 cars, bicycles free).

You can also **fly** to the islands from Prince Rupert, landing at Sandspit, which has the islands' only airstrip (seaplanes can land elsewhere). Air Canada Jazz (Ⓣ1-888/247-2262, Ⓦwww.flyjazz.ca) flies here daily from Vancouver and Pacific Coastal Airlines (Ⓣ1-800/663-2872, Ⓦwww.pacificcoastal.com) flies to Masset from Vancouver daily in the summer and three times weekly in the winter. Eagle Transit (Ⓣ250/559-4461 or 1-877/747-4461, Ⓦwww.qcislands.net/eagle) operates a **taxi** service and **airport shuttle**. You could also fly from Prince Rupert with North Pacific Sea Planes (Ⓣ250/627-1341 or 1-800/689-4234, Ⓦwww.northpacificseaplanes.com), which flies daily to Masset on the north of Graham Island, Sandspit three times a week and to Queen Charlotte on demand. For flights and tours around Haida Gwaii, contact South Moresby Air Charters (Ⓣ250/559-4222 or 1-888/551-4222, Ⓦwww.smair.com) in Queen Charlotte, who'll take you out to the deepest of the backwoods.

For **bicycle** hire, try Wings on Wheels (Ⓣ250/626-3233), based on Main Street in Masset. **Car rental** rates here are expensive, and unless you have a car, bike or canoe, you could be in for a long and expensive trip that shows you very little of what you came for. Budget (Ⓣ250/637-5688 or 1-800/557-3228) has offices in Queen Charlotte and Sandspit airport, but in summer you'll need to have booked in advance to secure a car. Thrifty (Ⓣ250/637-2299) has an office at Sandspit airport. Rates at Rustic Rentals (Ⓣ250/559-4641 or 1-877/559-4557) and Extreme West RV Rentals (Ⓣ250/559-4255) in Queen Charlotte may be a touch lower than the main companies. If you're planning to drive logging roads (most of the roads on the islands are controlled by logging companies) ask at the visitor centres for latest access details. To see the **Haida villages**, virtually all of which are on inaccessible parts of Moresby, you'll need to take a boat, and if you want to see SGang Gwaay in a day, you'll need to take a pricey tour by seaplane.

Graham Island

Most casual visitors stick to **Graham Island**, where the bulk of the island's roads and accommodation are concentrated along the eastern side of the island, between **Queen Charlotte** in the south and **Masset** some 108km to the north. These settlements and the villages in between – Skidegate, Tl'ell and Port

The Haida

The **Haida** are widely considered to have the most highly developed culture and sophisticated art tradition of British Columbia's aboriginal peoples. Extending from Haida Gwaii (the Queen Charlotte Islands) to southern Alaska, their lands included major stands of red cedar, the raw material for their huge dugout **canoes**, intricate **carvings** and refined **architecture**. Haida trade links were built on the reputation of their skill – to own a Haida canoe, for example, is a major status symbol. Renowned as traders and artists, the Haida were also feared **warriors**, paddling into rival villages and returning with canoes laden with goods and slaves. Their skill on the open sea make them the "Vikings" of North America.

Socially the Haida divided themselves into two main groups, the **Eagles** and the **Ravens**, which were further divided into hereditary kin groups named after their original village location. Marriage within each major group – or *moiety* – was considered incestuous, so Eagles would always seek Raven mates and vice versa. Furthermore, descent was traced through the **female line**, which meant that a chief could not pass his property on to his sons because they would belong to a different *moiety* – instead his inheritance passed to his sister's sons.

Haida **villages** were an impressive sight, their vast cedar-plank houses dominated by fifteen-metre totem poles displaying the kin group's unique animal crest or other mythical creatures, all carved in elegant fluid lines. Entrance to each house was through the gaping mouth of a massive carved figure; inside, supporting posts were carved into the forms of the crest animals and most household objects were similarly decorative. Equal elaboration attended the many Haida ceremonies, one of the most important of which was the **memorial potlatch**, serving to mark the end of mourning for a dead chief and the validation of the heir's right to succession. The dead individual was laid out at the top of a carved pole in front of his house, past which the visiting chiefs would walk wearing robes of finely woven and patterned mountain-goat wool and immense headdresses fringed with long sea-lion whiskers and ermine skins. A space at the top of each headdress was filled with eagle feathers, which floated down onto the witnesses as the chiefs sedately danced.

After **European contact** the Haida population was devastated by smallpox and other epidemics. In 1787, there were approximately 10,000 Haida scattered across the archipelago. Their numbers were then reduced from around 6000 in 1835 to 588 by 1915. Consequently they were forced to leave many of their traditional villages and today gather largely at two sites, Old Masset (pop. 650) and Skidegate (Haida pop. 1000). At other locations the homes and totems fell into disrepair and artefacts were taken by collectors and museums. **SGang Gwaay**, a remote village at the southern tip of Haida Gwaii, remained relatively untouched; UNESCO has now declared it a World Heritage Site.

These days the Haida number around 3000, and are highly regarded in the North American art world; Bill Reid, Freda Diesing and Robert Davidson are amongst the best-known figures, and scores of other Haida artists produce a mass of carvings and jewellery for the tourist market. They also play a powerful role in the islands' social, political and cultural life, having been vocal in the formation of sites such as the Gwaii Haanas National Park Reserve and Heritage Site (p.1013) and Duu Guusd Tribal Park (p.1011), the latter established to protect old aboriginal villages on Graham Island's northwest coast.

Clements – lie along Hwy 16, the principal road, and shelter in the lee of the islands, away from a mountainous and indented rocky west coast that boasts the highest combined seismic, wind and tidal energy of any North American coastline (producing treacherous seas and a tidal range of eight metres). Much of the east coast consists of beautiful half-moon, driftwood-strewn beaches and a string of provincial parks where you can appreciate the milder climes produced by the Pacific's Japanese Current, a warming stream that contributes to the island's lush canopy of thousand-year-old spruce and cedar rainforests. On the downside, though, it drenches both sides of the island with endless rainstorms, even in summer. Make sure you pack a raincoat.

Queen Charlotte

The island's second-largest settlement, **QUEEN CHARLOTTE** (pop. 1047), is a picturesque fishing village and frontier administrative centre about 5km west of the Skidegate ferry terminal. The village takes its name from the ship of Captain George Dixon, the British explorer who sailed to Haida Gwaii in 1787, thirteen years after first European contact was probably made by the Spaniard Juan Perez. Until fairly recently, when the logging industry went into steep decline, most of its residents earned a living from the timber companies, whose felling exploits have cleared most of the hills around the port. For a fine overview of the place, try the stroll to the top of **Sleeping Beauty Mountain**, which is reached by a rough track from Crown Forest Road near Honna Road. Farther afield, you can drive to **Rennell Sound**, a west coast inlet with shingle beaches: take the main logging road north from the town for 22km and then turn left and follow the steep gravel road for 14km. The **Rennell Sound Recreation Site** offers paths through stands of primal rainforest to isolated sandy beaches and a couple of campsites with a total of ten beachfront wilderness pitches (free).

Otherwise the town is the major place to sign up for any number of outdoor activities; contact the **visitor centre**, 3220 Wharf St (daily May to early Oct 9am–6pm; reduced hours in winter; ⓣ250/559-8316, ⓦwww.qcinfo.ca). Be sure to pick up the invaluable and free *Guide to the Queen Charlotte Islands*. The centre is also the place to organize **tours** to the Gwaii Haanas National Park Reserve and Haida Heritage Site (see p.1013) as well as fishing, sailing, sightseeing and canoeing trips. Enquire, too, about the free basic campsites on Graham and Moresby islands.

Practicalities

Accommodation is scarce and demand is high in summer, so call ahead to make bookings. The first-choice hotel is probably the twelve-room ★ *Premier Creek Lodging*, 3101 3rd Ave (ⓣ250/559-8451 or 1-888/322-3388, ⓦwww.qcislands.net/premier; ❸), a restored 1910 heritage building overlooking the harbour and Bearskin Bay; it has a small **hostel** at the back with a kitchen and dorm beds for $23 and also offers car and bike rentals. There's a cheaper but extremely basic hostel about 2km out of town, *The Bunkhouse*, 924 3rd Ave (ⓣ250/559-8383 or 1-888/559-8383, ⓦwww.islandsretreat.com; ❶), with twelve dorm beds at $12 (mattresses not provided), as well as twelve tent sites for $7. Then there's the unique five-room *Gracie's Place*, 3113 3rd Ave (ⓣ250/559-4262 or 1-888/244-4262, ⓦwww.graciesplace.ca; ❷), with characterful landlady, oceanview rooms and antique furniture, or intimate *Dorothy & Mike's Guest House*, 3127 2nd Ave (ⓣ250/559-8439, ⓦwww.qcislands.net/doromike; ❷), with a deck with harbour views and full cooking facilities. Overlooking Bearskin Bay is the *Sea Raven Motel*, 3301 3rd Ave (ⓣ250/559-4423 or 1-800/665-9606, ⓦwww.searaven.com; ❸), which has its own dining room with a view. If you're **camping**, try the *Haydn Turner Park* ($10) in the community park at the western end of town, or the *Kagan Bay Forest Service Campground*, a handful of lovely beachfront pitches on Honna Forest Service Road 5km west of the town (free).

For **food**, locals make for the central *Ocean View Restaurant* (Ⓣ250/559-8503) next door to the *Sea Raven Motel* which serves a wide selection of main courses from $9 to $22. For great coffee, sandwiches ($6), sweet treats and Internet, try the *Purple Onion Deli* at 3207 Wharf St; or cross the road for the equally welcoming *Queen B's*, a fine breakfast and lunch hangout serving savoury snacks ($5–16) and decorated with local art. Upstairs is *Sips Martini Bar* (Thurs–Sat), a relaxed wine bar with live music and delicious bites ($7–11).

Skidegate

The ferries dock at Skidegate Landing 2km to the south of **SKIDEGATE** (pop. 1000). You can browse through the more accessible aspects of Haida culture at the new and impressive **Haida Heritage Centre at Qay'llnagaay**, located at Second Beach around 500m east of the ferry terminal (open year-round, call for times; $12 including tour; Ⓣ250/559-4643, Ⓦwww.haidaheritagecentre.com). The centre – a series of long houses fronted by totem poles – includes a canoe house, a restaurant, a performance space, an art and carving studio and a museum which, among other things, contains a comprehensive collection of the Haida's treasured argillite carvings. Argillite is a form of black slate-like rock found only on Haida Gwaii, and only in one site, whose location west of Queen Charlotte is kept a closely guarded secret. Also check out the platform here for viewing grey whales during their migrations (April–June). Ask at the museum about the **seafood feasts** held by the Haida Repatriation Committee in July and August and open to everyone for $50. At the canoe house you can view the famous *Loo Taas* ("Wave Eater") canoe, carved by Haida artist Bill Reid. It was made for the '86 Expo in Vancouver and was the first Haida canoe carved since 1909. About one kilometre up the road in Skidegate village, you can see another of Bill Reid's creations, the Dogfish Totem that fronts a long house. Further along, there's a carving long house where you may be able to watch craftspeople at work. Next door is the office of the **Haida Gwaii Watchmen**. Bands of Haida "watchmen" were formed in the 1970s to protect aboriginal sites from vandalism and theft, and survive to this day. A popular walk in the area is the **Spirit Lake Trail**, which winds through old growth forest and around two lakes; the trailhead is opposite the George Brown Recreation Centre on Hwy 16.

Tl'ell and Port Clements

If you blink you'll miss the ranching community of **TL'ELL** (pop. 369), 36km north of Skidegate. Stop here and walk down to the sea, where you can stroll for hours on deserted wind-sculpted dunes; from here it is ninety kilometres along the unbroken beach to Rose Point, at the northeast tip of Graham Island. Tl'ell is a community favoured by craftspeople and alternative types – pop into the little café, grocery store, bakery or handful of **galleries**, the latter concentrated along Richardson Road. There's a bunch of bed and breakfasts in the area. Just north of Richardson Ranch on the main road is the pleasantly rustic *Cacilia's B&B* (Ⓣ250/557-4664, Ⓦwww.qcislands.net/ceebysea; ③), a renovated log house set behind the dunes on Hecate Strait. **Bikes** and **kayaks** are usually available for rent here.

Tl'ell is at the southern border of the **Naikoon Provincial Park**, an enclave that extends over Graham Island's northeast corner and designed to protect fine beach, dune and dwarf-woodland habitats. **Campers** should head for the *Misty Meadows Campground* ($15; May–Sept) just south of the Tl'ell River Bridge and 500m north of the **park headquarters** (Ⓣ250/557-4390) (backcountry camping is allowed throughout the park). About 8km beyond, look out for the picnic site and trails at the southern tip of **Mayer Lake**, one of the nicer spots to pull over. The most popular hike is to the **shipwreck of the Pesuta**, which ran aground here in 1927; the trail starts at the picnic site just north of the Tl'ell River Bridge.

The road cuts inland for **PORT CLEMENTS** (pop. 516), 21km northwest of Tl'ell. In the past it was famous for the **Golden Spruce** tree, a 300-year-old bleached albino tree, sacred to the Haida; in 1997 a vandal chopped it down. A rare genetic mutation allowed the tree's needles to be bleached by sunlight and geneticists and foresters are currently trying to produce another tree. A 20-minute trail along the banks of the Yakoun River leads to a viewpoint where you can see where the mighty sitka spruce once stood; the trailhead is six kilometres south of town along Bayview Drive, and ten kilometres further south, look out for the 200-year-old partially carved abandoned **Haida canoe** protruding from the bushes.

The one official **motel** is the twelve-room *Golden Spruce*, 2 Grouse St (ⓣ250/557-4325 or 1-877/801-4653, ⓦwww.qcislands.net/golden; ❸). For **camping**, the *Sunset RV and Campground* ($10–15; June–Sept) is at the south end of Bayview Drive. For **food and drink**, the main option is the *Yakoun River Inn* on Bayview Drive (ⓣ250/557-4440), with meals around $15.

About 20km north of town on the road for Masset, look out for the signed **Pure Lake Provincial Park**, where on summer days the waters of Pure Lake should be warm enough for swimming.

Masset

MASSET, 40km north of Port Clements, is the biggest place on the islands, a scattered, rather ugly town – it is a former military base – of some 1000 people, most of whom are employed in the fishing industry. Many visitors are here to bird-watch at the **Delkatla Wildlife Sanctuary**, a saltwater marsh north of the village – contact Delkatla Bay Birding Tours (ⓣ250/626-5015) for guided visits – which supports 113 bird species, or to walk the trails around Tow Hill 26km to the east (see p.1012). Others come to wander the neighbouring village of Old Massett – with an extra "t" – 2km to the west, the administrative centre for the Council of the Haida First Nation and where some six hundred aboriginal people still live and work. Visitors should show respect when visiting totem sites, craft houses and community homes. Many locals are involved in producing crafts for tourists, or organizing wilderness tours, but some are restoring and adding to the dozen or so totems still standing locally (it's possible to visit various canoe and carving sheds). For more **information** on where to see carving and on the village in general, visit the Old Massett Council office on Eagle Rd (Mon–Fri 9am–5pm; ⓣ250/626-3337), where you should also enquire about permission to visit the **Duu Guusd Tribal Park**, established by the Haida to protect villages on the coast to the northwest. Two villages here are still active, and the park is used as a base for the Haida Gwaii Rediscovery Centre, which offers courses to children on Haida culture and history.

The Masset **visitor booth**, at 1455 Old Beach Rd (July & Aug daily 9am–5pm; ⓣ250/626-3982, ⓦwww.massetbc.com), has full details of wildlife and bird-watching possibilities. The **airport** lies two kilometres east of town. For **accommodation**, try the central, 18-room *Engelhard's Oceanview Lodge*, 1970 Harrison Ave (ⓣ250/626-3388, ⓦwww.engelhardsoceanviewlodge.ca; ❺), with a prime position on Masset Inlet. For a true escape, *Rapid Richie's Rustic Rentals* is a collection of off-grid beach cabins nestled in rainforest (ⓣ250/626-5472, ⓦwww.beachcabins.com; ❷), 16km from Masset along Tow Hill Road. The only nearby **campsite** is the *Hidden Island RV and Resort* (ⓣ250/626-5286 or 1-866/303-5286, ⓦwww.hidden-island-resort.ca; $15–23.50) on Tow Hill

Rd, 2km north of town alongside the wildlife sanctuary, with a licensed restaurant serving fish and chips ($10–16). Further afield there's the *Agate Beach* (Ⓔpark@mhtv.ca; $14; May–Sept) in Naikoon Provincial Park, a park site near trails and sandy beaches, 26km east of Masset off the secondary road towards Tow Hill (see below). For a pleasant place to **eat**, join the locals at *Haida Rose*, 415 Frog St (Ⓣ250/626-3310), which does coffee, pastries, soup and sandwiches, or try the handful of **bars** on Collison Avenue and Main Street.

Heading away from the village, follow Tow Hill Road – peppered with quaint cafes, a gallery and bed and breakfasts – to **Tow Hill**, 28km east; three trails begin by the Hiellen River at the foot of Tow Hill itself, where there is the nearby *Agate Beach* campground. The easiest hike is the one-kilometre **Blow Hole Trail**, which drops down to striking rock formations and basalt cliffs by the sea. From here you can follow another path to the top of Tow Hill (109m) for superb views of deserted sandy beaches stretching into the hazy distance – on a clear day you can see Alaska approximately 75km away. The third track, the **Cape Fife Trail**, is a longer (10km one way) hike to the east side of the island where there is a small, basic cabin (free). Naikoon means "point", a reference to Rose Spit, the twelve-kilometre spit that extends from the park and Graham Island's northeasterly tip. It's an ecological and wildlife reserve of beaches, dunes, marsh and stunted forest, but it's also a sacred Haida site, for it was here, according to legend, that the Haida's Raven clan were first tempted from a giant clamshell by a solitary raven.

Moresby Island

Moresby Island is all but free from human contact except for deserted Haida villages (one of which contains the world's largest stand of totems), forestry roads and the small logging community of **Sandspit** (pop. 460). The latter lies 15km from the **Alliford Bay** terminal for the inter-island ferry link with Skidegate on Graham Island. Seaplanes fly to Alliford Bay from Prince Rupert on demand. Sandspit's **visitor centre** is in the airport terminal building (May–Sept daily 8am–5pm; Ⓣ250/637-5362).

Most locals here and on Graham Island work in Moresby's forests, and the **forestry** issue has divided the community for years between the Haida and environmentalists and the lumber workers. At stake are the islands' temperate rainforests and the traditional sites of the Haida, themselves politically shrewd media manipulators who've sent representatives to Brazil to advise local aboriginal peoples there on their own rainforest programmes. They've also occasionally provided the muscle to halt logging on the islands. On the other hand, the forests provide jobs and some of the world's most lucrative timber: a single good sitka trunk can be worth up to $60,000. Currently a compromise has been reached and most of Moresby has National Park Reserve status (established in 1987). If you're intending to drive any of the logging roads, however – and most of the handful of roads here *are* logging roads – drive with extreme care and check in with the visitor centre for updated logging activity before setting out. If you're determined enough you can canoe, mountain bike or backpack the interior of northern Moresby Island, but you need to know what you're doing and be prepared to lug plenty of supplies.

Sandspit's **accommodation** includes a few intermittently open B&Bs and the reliable *Moresby Island Guest House* on 385 Alliford Bay Rd overlooking the ocean at Shingle Bay, 1km south of the airport (Ⓣ250/637-5300, Ⓦwww.moresbyisland-bnb.com; ❸); or if you don't mind being a stone's throw from the runway, the 20-room *Sandspit Airport Inn*, 2 Airport Rd (Ⓣ250/637-5334, Ⓦwww.sandspitadventures.ca; ❺), has an on-site restaurant serving basic pub grub (mains $9–13). For tenting, try the *501 RV/Tent Park* at 501 Beach Rd (May–Sept; ⓣ250/637-5473, ⓔrvpark@island.net; $10–20), but many people choose to sleep on the spit's beaches: Gray Bay, 21km southeast of Sandspit, has primitive and peaceful **campsites** near gravel and sand beaches (for more details, contact the Teal Jones forestry offices on Beach Road; ⓣ250/637-5323).

Gwaii Haanas National Park Reserve and Haida Heritage Site

Gwaii Haanas National Park Reserve and Haida Heritage Site is a 90km-long archipelago that embraces 138 islands, some 500 Haida archeological sites, five former Haida villages and 1750km of coastline across the south of the island group. An agreement signed with the federal government in 1993 gave the Haida joint control of this region, and afforded protection to their ancient villages, traditional lands and resources, but many land claims to the region remain unresolved. You need money, time and effort to see the park. There are no roads, and access is by boat or chartered planes only. Joining a tour is the easiest way to visit, although experienced sea kayakers and boaters often travel here independently.

Visits to a variety of ancient **Haida sites** and their totems and ruined dwellings are described here in order of distance (and therefore time and expense) from Sandspit. Closest is **K'uuna Llnagaay** (**Skedans**), accessible on day-trips by boat from Moresby Camp on the Cumshewa Inlet, 46km south of Sandspit; access to

△ Totem Heritage Site poles in the Haida

the camp is by logging road). Farther afield are **T'aanuu Llnagaay**, **Hlk'yah Gaawga** (**Windy Bay**) – one of the main battlegrounds in the fight to protect the region in the 1980s – and **Gandll K'in Gwaayaay** (**Hot Spring Island**), whose series of outdoor thermal pools make it one of the most popular destinations. The finest site of all is the one that's furthest away: **SGang Gwaay** (**Ninstints**) lies close to the southern tip of the archipelago, whose Haida residents left around 1880 in the wake of smallpox epidemics. Today, it contains the most striking of the ruined Haida villages, its long houses and many mortuary totems declared a UNESCO World Heritage Site in 1981. In accordance with the wishes of the Haida, little attempt is made to preserve ancient village sites and, within decades, many of these decaying totem poles may have returned to nature.

Park practicalities

The easiest way into the park is with a **tour**; contact the Queen Charlotte visitor centre or see Ⓦwww.pc.gc.ca/gwaiihaanas for full details. Queen Charlotte Adventures (Ⓣ250/559-8990, Ⓦwww.qcislands.net/qciadven) and Moresby Explorers (Ⓣ250/637-2215, Ⓦwww.moresbyexplorers.com) both offer good one-day and multi-day boat trips into the park. If you want to see SGang Gwaay in one day, the only option is with South Moresby Air Charters (Ⓣ250/559-4222 or 1-888/551-4222) whose full-day joint flight and boat tours start from $310.

To visit the reserve as an **independent traveller**, you must make an advance reservation or obtain a stand-by space. Reservations can be made by calling Ⓣ1-800/HELLOBC or 250/387-1642. There is a $15 per person reservation fee. If you choose not to make a reservation, then six stand-by places daily are available on a first-come, first-serve basis from the Parks Canada office at the Haida Centre at Qay'llnagaay in Skidegate. There are also **fees** to visit the park: $20 per person per day and $120 for a season's pass.

An **orientation session** is mandatory for all independent visitors entering Gwaii Haanas (those on guided tours are exempt). Sessions take place at the Haida Heritage Centre at Qay'llnagaay in Skidegate and at Sandspit airport, but it is worth contacting **Parks Canada** for updated times and locations of orientation (Ⓣ250/559-8818). Sessions last around ninety minutes and cover topics such as public safety, no-trace camping, natural and cultural heritage and the Haida Gwaii Watchmen Programme. Apart from some restricted areas, which you are informed of during orientation, you can **camp** where you wish in the reserve; fees for camping are included in the park's general entrance fee. There are two **accommodation** options just outside the park's southern boundary; 10km from SGang Gwaay UNESCO site is the *Gwaii Haanas Guest House* (Ⓣ250/559-8638, Ⓦwww.gwaiihaanas.com; ❼), with four rooms in a family homestead (boat or floatplane access only) that lies in ancient rainforest with ocean views, organic food, sea kayak rentals, guided boat tours, bird-watching and other outdoor activity possibilities; or 12km west of SGang Gwaay is the equally delightful and rustic *Rose Harbour Guest House* (Ⓣ250/559-2326, Ⓦwww.roseharbour.com; ❹), at the site of an old whaling station. It offers organized tours.

The Stewart-Cassiar Highway

The 733km of the **Stewart-Cassiar Highway** (Hwy 37) – from the Skeena Valley east of Prince Rupert to Watson Lake just inside the Yukon – are some of the wildest and most beautiful of any road in British Columbia. Though less famous than the Alaska Hwy, the road is increasingly travelled by those who want to capture some of the adventure that was found on the wilder reaches of its better-known neighbour in the 1950s and 1960s.

Some stretches are still gravel, and the petrol and repair facilities, let alone food and lodgings, are extremely patchy: don't contemplate the journey unless your vehicle's in top condition, with two spare tyres and spare fuel containers. The road also provides a shorter route from Prince George to the Yukon than the Alaska Hwy.

If you're ready to drive the distances involved, you'll also probably be prepared to explore the highway's two main side roads to **Stewart** and **Telegraph Creek**, and possibly the rough roads and trails that lead into two wilderness parks midway up the hwy – the **Mount Edziza Provincial Park** and the **Spatsizi Plateau Wilderness Park**. If you can't face the highway's entire length, take the side-trip to Stewart, which offers exceptional sea and mountain **scenery**, as well as the chance to cross into Alaska at **Hyder** to indulge in its vaunted alcoholic border initiation.

In summer Stewart is added to the itinerary of certain sailings of the Alaska Marine Hwy **ferry** service (see box, p.1002) – albeit infrequently – so with careful planning you could travel overland to Stewart, or ride a boat to Ketchikan and thence to either Skagway or Prince Rupert.

Stewart and Hyder

The Stewart-Cassiar Hwy starts near Gitwangak, one of several aboriginal villages off Hwy 16 (see p.1001). Some hint of the sense of adventure required comes when you hit a section (47km beyond **Cranberry Junction**), where the road doubles up as an airstrip – planes have right of way. Almost immediately after you leave Hwy 16, though, the road pitches into the mesmerizing high scenery of the Coast Ranges, a medley of mountain, lake and forest that reaches a crescendo after 156km around **Meziadin Junction**, where Hwy 37A branches off; near here is the first formal place to **stay** – the 62-pitch *Meziadin Lake Provincial Park* **campsite** (May–Oct, $14) 67km east of Stewart and 156km north of Gitwangak.

Some 67km west of Meziadin Junction lies **STEWART**, Canada's most northerly ice-free port. Here a series of immense glaciers culminates in the dramatic appearance of the unmissable **Bear Glacier**, a vast sky-blue mass of ice that comes down virtually to the hwy and has the strange ability to glow in the dark. Stewart itself, 37km west of the glacier, is a shrivelled mining centre (pop. 550) that sits at the end of the Portland Canal, the world's fourth longest fjord, a natural boundary between British Columbia and Alaska that encircles the town with peaks (the ferry ride in from Prince Rupert through some of the west coast's wildest scenery is sensational). Dominating its rocky amphitheatre is **Mount Rainey**, whose cliffs represent one of the greatest vertical rises from sea level in the world. Scenery aside, the main thing to see in town is the **Stewart Historical Museum** housed in the former fire hall at Columbia and 6th Avenue (May–Sept, daily 10am–5pm, $5; ⓣ250/636-2568), its exhibits devoted largely to stuffed wildlife and the town's logging and mining heritage. You might also want to take Salmon Glacier Road out 5km beyond Hyder in Alaska to Fish Creek, where from the special viewing platform above the artificial spawning channel you may be lucky enough to see **black bears** catching some of the world's largest chum salmon.

The town's **visitor centre** is housed at 222 5th Ave near Victoria (mid-May to mid-Sept daily 9am–6pm; ⓣ250/636-9224 or 1-888/366-5999, ⓦwww.stewart-hyder.com). As for **hotels**, the *King Edward Hotel*, 405 5th Ave

(Ⓣ250/636-2244 or 1-800/663-3126, Ⓦwww.kingedwardhotel.com; ❸) has basic rooms and offers units with kitchenettes in its *King Edward Motel* (❺) on the other side of the street. The *Ripley Creek Inn* on the estuary at 306 5th Ave (Ⓣ250/636-2344 or 636-2701, Ⓦwww.ripleycreekinn.homestead.com; ❷) has eleven rooms in the main lodge building and other rooms in linked buildings, including a former brothel from 1928. The nearest **campsite** is the *Rainey Creek Campground* on the edge of town on 8th Avenue (Ⓣ250/636-2537 or 1-888-366-5999; $12–20; May–Sept), and the tenting area (excluding RVs) is located across Rainey Creek, a pleasant little stream. Starting here is the **Rainey Creek Nature Walk**, one of the area's easiest hikes. It shadows the creek for 2.5km to the northern end of town (return to the centre on Railway St). The *King Edward Hotel* is the town's main **pub**, **restaurant** and **coffee shop** – it's where the locals eat (the heaving king crab feast for $40 is enough for two people) – while visitors tend to prefer the pleasantly polished *Bitter Creek Café* (part of the *Ripley Creek Inn* complex on 5th Avenue a block west of the *King Edward*), which offers an outside deck and a mouth-watering dinner menu that includes pistachio-crusted halibut ($20). For bread and baked snacks, duck into the bakery and deli next door to the *Bitter Creek*.

Most people come to **HYDER** (pop. 70), Stewart's oddball twin, simply to drink in one or both of its two bars. It's a ramshackle place, barely a settlement at all, just 3km from Stewart across the border in Alaska. You'll encounter none of the usual border formalities since there's nothing beyond the end of the road but 800km of wilderness. People use Canadian currency, the police are of the Mountie variety and the phone system (and Ⓣ250 area code) are also Canadian. At the *Glacier Inn* the tradition is to pin a dollar to the wall in case you return broke and need a drink, and then toss back a shot of hard liquor and receive an "I've Been Hyderized" card. The result is many thousands of tacked dollars: "the world's most expensive wallpaper". It sounds a bit of a tourist carry-on, but if you arrive out of season there's a genuine amiability about the place that warrants its claims to be the "The Friendliest Ghost Town in Alaska". The town's two bars are often open 23 hours a day and a couple of **motels** are on hand if you literally can't stand any more: the *Sealaska Inn*, Premier Avenue (Ⓣ250/636-9006, Ⓦwww.sealaskainn.com; ❸) – which has one of the two bars in question – and the preferable *Grand View Inn* (Ⓣ250/636-9174, Ⓦwww.grandviewinn.net; ❸). They're both cheaper than their Stewart equivalents, and as you're in Alaska there's no room tax to pay. If you want something to soak up the alcohol, make for the *Sealaska Inn Restaurant* (Ⓣ250/636-2486) for the artery-clogging deep-fried halibut ($14). The community's little **visitor centre** is on the right as you come into town (June to early Sept daily except Wed 9am–1pm).

Iskut and Dease Lake

For several hundred kilometres beyond the Stewart junction there's nothing along the Stewart-Cassiar other than the odd garage, rest area, campsite, trailhead and patches of burnt or clear-cut forest etched into the Cassiar and Skeena mountains. In places, though, you can still see traces of the incredible 3060km Dominion Telegraph line that used to link the Dawson City gold fields with Vancouver, and glimpse a proposed railway extension out of Prince George that was abandoned as late as 1977. At **BELL II**, 95km north of Meziadin Junction in a mountain-hemmed river valley, the *Bell II Lodge* (Ⓣ604/639-8455 or 1-800-530-2167, Ⓦwww.bell2lodge.com; ❺) offers a lounge, coffee shop, petrol station, sauna and hot tub as well as 22 chalet rooms.

ISKUT, an aboriginal village 130km north of Bell II, arranges tours into the adjacent wilderness parks, which are also accessible by float plane from Dease

Lake itself. For information, contact the Iskut Band Office (Ⓣ250/234-3331) or local stores and garages. Local **accommodation** amounts to the six-room *Red Goat Lodge* (Ⓣ1-888/733-4628, Ⓔredgoatlodge@aol.com; ❸, tents $13; late May to mid-Sept) with a 26-pitch campground 3km south of the village; the four-room *Bike, Hike & Paddle Touring Co*, 6km south of Iskut on Eddontenajon Lake (Ⓣ250/234-3456, Ⓦwww.bikehikepaddle.com), which has activity and accommodation packages from $150 (July–Oct only); and *Todagin Guest Ranch* (radio contact only; ❷), 30km south of Iskut, with three cabins and numerous outdoor activities.

DEASE LAKE, 65km north of Iskut, has two **motels**, the 46-room *Northway Motor Inn* on Boulder Ave (Ⓣ250/771-5341 or 1-866/888-2588, Ⓔnorthwaymotorinn@stikine.net; ❸) and the eight-room *Arctic Divide Inn & Motel* on the hwy (Ⓣ250/771-3119, Ⓔarcticdivide@stikine.net; ❸), still 246km from the junction with the Alaska Hwy to the north. You can **camp** at the *Boya Lake Provincial Park*, a lovely 45-site lakeside campground 150km north of Dease Lake ($14).

The road from Dease Lake is wild and beautiful, the 240km to the Yukon border passing through some of the most miraculous scenery of what is already a superb journey. Much of this area was swamped with gold-hungry pioneers during the **Cassiar Gold Rush** of 1872–80. In 1877 Alfred Freedman plucked one of the world's largest pure gold nuggets – a 72-ounce monster – from a creek east of present-day **CASSIAR** (133km from the junction with the Alaska Hwy to the north). These days the mining has a less romantic allure, being concentrated in an open-pit **asbestos mine** 5km from the village. Most of the world's high-grade asbestos once came from here, and poisonous-looking piles of green chrysotile asbestos tailings are scattered for kilometres around. The mine closed in 1992, transforming the community into a virtual ghost town at a stroke.

Telegraph Creek

For a taste of what is possibly a more remarkable landscape than you see on the Stewart-Cassiar, it's worth driving the potentially treacherous 113-kilometre side road from Dease Lake to **TELEGRAPH CREEK** (allow 2hr in good conditions). This delightful riverbank town has a look and feel reckoning back to the early twentieth century, when it was a major telegraph station and trading post for the gold-rush towns to the north. The road navigates some incredible gradients and bends, twisting past canyons, old lava beds and touching on several **aboriginal villages**, notably at Tahltan River, where salmon are caught and cured in traditional smokehouses and sold to passing tourists. If you're lucky you might see a Tahltan bear dog, a species now virtually extinct; only ankle high, and weighing less than fifteen pounds, these tiny animals were able to keep a bear cornered by barking and darting around until a hunter came to finish it off. Telegraph Creek itself is a lesson in how latter-day pioneers live on the north's last frontiers: it's home to a friendly mixture of city exiles, hunters, trappers and ranchers, but also a cloistered bunch of **religious fundamentalists** who have eschewed the decadent mainstream for wilderness purity. Such groups are growing in outback British Columbia, a phenomenon that's creating friction with the easygoing types who first settled the backwoods. Mining companies have been attracted by the recent gold discovery, so ways of life may change soon for all concerned.

Much of the village revolves around the General Delivery – a combined café (the *Riversong*), grocery and garage – and small adjoining **motel**, the *Stikine River Song Lodge* (Ⓣ250/235-3196, Ⓦwww.stikineriversong.com; ❸), whose

If you're continuing north on the Stewart-Cassiar Hwy to **Watson Lake** and the Alaska Hwy junction, turn to p.1022.

rooms include kitchenettes. Enquire at the café for details of rafting and other trips into the backcountry.

The Alaska Highway: Dawson Creek to Whitehorse

Dawson Creek is the launching pad for the Alaska Hwy. While it may not be somewhere you'd otherwise stop, it's almost impossible to avoid a night here whether you're approaching from Edmonton and the east or from Prince George on the scenically more uplifting **John Hart Highway** (Hwy 97). The route from Prince George leads you out of British Columbia's upland interior to the so-called Peace River country, a region that belongs in look and spirit to the Albertan prairies. There's some 409km of driving between Prince George and Dawson Creek along the John Hart Hwy, and two daily Greyhound **buses** make the journey.

The best part of the **Alaska Highway** – a distance of about 1500km – winds through northern British Columbia from Dawson Creek to Whitehorse, the capital of the Yukon; only 320km of the hwy is actually in Alaska. Don't be fooled by the string of villages emblazoned across the area's maps, for there are only two towns worthy of the name en route – **Fort St John** and **Fort Nelson** – the rest are no more than a garage, a store and perhaps a motel. **Watson Lake**, on the Yukon border, is the largest of these lesser spots, and also marks the junction of the Alaska and Stewart-Cassiar hwys. All the way down the road, though, it's vital to book accommodation during July and August.

Driving the Alaska Hwy is no longer the adventure of days past – that's now provided by the Stewart-Cassiar and Dempster hwys and the Deh-Cho route (see p.1054). Food, fuel and lodgings are found at between forty- and eighty-kilometre intervals, though cars still need to be in good shape. You should drive with headlights on at all times, and take care when passing or being passed by heavy trucks. It goes without saying that wilderness – anything up to 800km of it on each side – begins at the edge of the hwy and unless you're very experienced, you shouldn't contemplate off-road exploration. Any number of free guides and pamphlets are available at visitor centres along the route to take you through to Fairbanks, but *The Milepost* (Ⓦwww.themilepost.com), the road's bible, is, for all its mind-numbing detail, the only one you need buy.

From 1201 Alaska Ave in Dawson Creek, a **Greyhound bus** heads out in the morning and plies the road all the way to Whitehorse; it currently runs daily (except Sat) from mid-May to mid-October, and on Monday, Wednesday and Friday the rest of the year. The twenty-hour trip finishes at around 5am, with only occasional half-hour meal stops, but covers the road's best scenery in daylight.

Dawson Creek

Except for a small museum next to the town's eye-catching red grain hopper, and taking the obligatory photograph of the cairn marking Mile Zero of the

History of the Alaska Highway

The **Alaska Hwy** runs northeast from Mile Zero at Dawson Creek through the Yukon to Mile 1520 in Fairbanks, Alaska. Built as a military road, it's now an all-weather hwy travelled by bus services and thousands of tourists out to recapture the thrill of the days when it was known as the "junkyard of the American automobile". It's no longer a driver's Calvary, but the scenery and the sense of pushing through wilderness on one of the continent's last frontiers remain as alluring as ever: around 360,000 people a year make the journey.

As recently as 1940 there was no direct land route to the Yukon or Alaska other than trails passable only by experienced trappers. When the Japanese invaded the Aleutian Islands during World War II, however, they both threatened the traditional sea routes to the north and seemed ready for an attack on mainland Alaska – the signal for the building of the joint US–Canadian road to the north. A proposed coastal route from Hazelton in British Columbia was deemed too susceptible to enemy attack (it's since been built as the Stewart-Cassiar Hwy), while an inland route bypassing Whitehorse and following the Rockies would have taken five years to build. This left the so-called **Prairie Route**, which had the advantage of following a line of air bases through Canada into Alaska – a chain known as the **Northwest Staging Route**. In the course of the war, some 8000 planes were transported along this route from Montana to Edmonton and then to Fairbanks, where they were picked up by Soviet pilots and flown into action on the Siberian front.

Construction of the hwy began on **March 9, 1942**, the start of months of misery for the 20,000 mainly US soldiers shanghaied to ram a road through mountains, mud, mosquito-ridden bogs, icy rivers and forest during some of the harshest extremes of weather. Incredibly, crews working on the eastern and western sections met at Contact Creek, British Columbia, in September 1942, and completed the last leg to Fairbanks in October – an engineering triumph that had taken less than a year but cost around $140 million. The first full convoy of trucks to make Fairbanks managed an average 25kph during one of the worst winters in memory.

By 1943 the hwy already needed virtual rebuilding, and for seven years workers widened the road, raised bridges, reduced gradients, bypassed swampy ground and started to remove some of the vast bends that are still being ironed out – the reason why it's now only **1488 miles** (2394km) to the old Mile 1520 post in Fairbanks. All sorts of ideas have been put forward to explain the numerous curves: that they were to stop Japanese planes using the road as a landing strip, that they simply went where bulldozers could go at the time, or even at one point that they followed the trail of a rutting moose. Canada took over control of the road in 1946, but civilian traffic was barred until 1948. Within months of its opening so much traffic had broken down and failed to make the trip that it was closed for a year.

Although the road is now widely celebrated, there are sides to the story that are glossed over. Many of its toughest sections, for example, were assigned to African-American GIs, few of whom have received credit for their part in building the hwy – you'll look in vain for African-American faces amongst the white officers in the archive photos of ribbon-cutting ceremonies. Another often overlooked fact is the road's effect on aboriginal peoples on the route, scores of whom died from epidemics brought in by the workers. Yet another was the building of the controversial "Canadian Oil" or **Canol pipeline** in conjunction with the road, together with huge dumps of poisonous waste and construction junk. Wildlife en route was also devastated by trigger-happy GIs taking recreational pot shots as they worked; the devastation of big game populations was part of the reason for the creation of the Kluane Game Sanctuary, the forerunner of the Yukon's Kluane National Park.

Alaska Hwy, there's almost nothing to do in **DAWSON CREEK** (pop. 12,000). Contact the **visitor centre** at the museum, 900 Alaska Ave (April–May Mon–Sat 9am–6pm, May–Sept daily 8am–7pm, Sept–Oct Mon–Sat 9am–5pm, Oct–April Tues–Sat 10am–5pm; ⓣ250/782-9595 or 1-866/645-3022, ⓦwww.tourismdawsoncreek.com), for information about **motels**, most of which are concentrated on the Alaska Hwy northeast of town. One of the nicer places is the *Ramada Limited Dawson Creek*, 1748 Alaska Ave (ⓣ250/782-8595 or 1-800/663-2749, ⓦwww.ramada.ca; ❹), with views of countryside rather than the highway. The most attractive nearby **campsite** is the *Mile 0 RV Park and Campground* (ⓣ250/782-2590; $13–19; May to mid-Sept), about 1km west of the town centre at the junction of Hwy 97 North and Hwy 97 South opposite 20th Street on the Alaska Hwy. For something to **eat**, *Caruso's* at 1025 Alaska Ave (ⓣ250/782-4938) has a mix of Asian and Western cuisine (mains around $10) and does a popular lunch buffet. Join the locals at 10th Street's *Alaska Pub*, an attractive old wooden building adorned with taxidermied animals.

Dawson Creek to Prophet River

You need to adapt to a different notion of distance on a 2500-kilometre drive: points of interest on the Alaska Hwy are a long way apart, and pleasure comes in broad changes in scenery, the sighting of a solitary moose, or in the passing excitement of a lonely bar. It takes forty minutes before the benign ridged prairies around Dawson Creek drop suddenly into the broad, flat-bottomed valley of the Peace River, a canyon whose walls are scalloped with creeks, gulches and deep muddy scars. Just across the river is **FORT ST JOHN**, a charmless oil boom town dotted with flare stacks.

PINK MOUNTAIN, 226km on from Dawson, with the *Pink Mountain Campsite* (ⓣ250/772-5133, $15–22) and its adjoining service station is a good place to stop for a caffeine fix and basic groceries. Thereafter the road offers immense **views** of utter wilderness in all directions, the trees as dense as ever, but noticeably more stunted than farther south and nearing the limit of commercial viability. Look out for the bright "New Forest Planted" signs, more often than not a token riposte from the loggers to the ecology lobby, as they are invariably backed by a graveyard of sickly looking trees. If you're **camping**, look out for two provincial sanctuaries over the remaining 236km to Fort Nelson. Around 60km north of Pink Mountain is the *Buckinghorse River Provincial Park* campsite (May–Sept, $10); another 69km farther is the *Prophet River Provincial Recreation Area* with a campsite (May–Sept; $9) overlooking the river. This is good bird-watching country, but it's also good bear country, so be careful.

Fort Nelson

One of the highway's key stopoffs, **FORT NELSON** (pop. 5000), is 381km north of Fort St John. Everything in town, except a small **museum** devoted to the highway's construction, speaks of a frontier supplies depot, the latest in a long line of trading posts attracted to a site that is fed by four major rivers and stands in the lee of the Rockies. Dour buildings stand in a battered sprawl around a windswept grid and much of life here seems to revolve around exploitation of its huge natural gas deposits – the town has the world's second-largest gas-processing plant and the huge storage tanks to prove it.

The **visitor centre** is at 5500 50th Ave (daily late May to early Sept, 8am–8pm; ⓣ250/774-6400, ⓦwww.northernrockies.org). The town's **motels** are all much the same and you'll be paying the inflated rates which characterize the north. On the town's southern approaches the *Bluebell Inn*, 3907 50th Ave South (ⓣ250/774-6961 or 1-800/663-5267, ⓦwww.bluebellinn.ca; ❹), is better looking than many of the run-of-the-mill places. To **camp**, make for the *Westend Campground* (ⓣ250/774-2340; $25) on the hwy next to the museum. It has grassy tent sites, pay showers, laundry and store. If you're looking for somewhere to eat and quaff a beer, try the busy *Dan's Neighbourhood Pub* at 4204 50th Ave North, where there's a good variety of beers to wash down some decent bar food (main courses $10–27).

Fort Nelson to Liard Hot Springs

This stretch is the Alaska Hwy at its best. Landscapes divide markedly around Fort Nelson, where the hwy arches west from the flatter hills of the Peace River country to meet the northern Rockies above the plains and plateau of the Liard River. Within a short time, once the road has picked up the river's headwaters, you're in some of the most grandiose scenery in British Columbia. The area either side of the road is some of the world's wildest – twenty million acres of nothing – and experts say that only parts of Africa surpass the region for the variety of mammals present and the pristine state of its ecosystems. Services and motels become scarcer, but those that exist – though often beaten-up looking places – make atmospheric and often unforgettable stops.

The first worthwhile stopoff, a kilometre off the hwy on a gravel road, is **Tetsa River Provincial Park**, about 77km west of Fort Nelson, which has a nice and secluded campsite ($14; May to mid-Sept) and appealing short hikes through the trees and along the river. Next up is **Stone Mountain Provincial Park**, 139km west of Fort Nelson, with a campsite ($14; May–Oct) which gives access to a short trail (10min) to two hoodoos (rock columns) claimed by myth to be the heads of two devils; a longer trail, the Flower Springs Lake Trail (6km), leads to a delightful upland mountain lake. Other accommodation and services include the *Rocky Mountain Lodge* (ⓣ250/232-7000, ⓦwww.karo-ent.com/rockymt.htm; ❷), 165km on from Fort Nelson with lovely views of the mountains and an adjacent **campsite** ($10).

Toad River, 195km from Fort Nelson, has perhaps the best motel of all on this lonely stretch, the *Toad River Lodge* (ⓣ250/232-5401, ⓦwww.karo-ent.com/toadriv.htm; ❸), with rooms and cabins offering superlative views of thickly forested and deeply cleft mountains on all sides. Note that it also has a grocery store, petrol station and sites for tents ($15) and RVs ($25). About 3km to its north is the *Poplars Campground and Café*, with four log cabins and fully serviced tent and RV sites (ⓣ250/232-5465; ❸, tent sites $14, RV sites $25; May to mid-Sept). Turn right off the hwy 9km north of Toad River and you come to the *Stone Mountain Safaris Lodge* (ⓣ250/232-5469, ⓦwww.stonemountainsafaris.com; ❺), with four rooms and riding, hunting and hiking possibilities.

Muncho Lake, 260km from Fort Nelson, is the next big natural feature, and sits at the heart of a large provincial park whose ranks of bare mountains provide a foretaste of the barren tundra of the far north. There's a small motel and campsite at the lake's southern end, but it's worth hanging on for the popular *Muncho Lake Provincial Park Campground* ($14; May–Sept), midway up the lake on its eastern side, or the fine *Northern Rockies Lodge-Highland Glen Lodge and Campground* (ⓣ250/776-3481 or 1-800/663-5269, ⓦwww.northern-rockies-lodge.com; ❺) for a choice of log cabins or camping and RV sites ($25).

About 70km beyond the lake is the excellent *Liard Hot Springs Lodge* (ⓣ250/776-7349, ⓦwww.liardhotsprings.ca; ❺) ("Liard" comes from the French for poplar or cottonwood tree, a ubiquitous presence in these parts.) It also has RV ($26–32) and tent sites ($12) and is across the road from one of the most popular spots on the entire Alaska Hwy, the **Liard Hot Springs**, (ⓣ1-800/776-7000, $5) whose **two**

thermal pools (Alpha and Beta) are amongst the best and hottest in BC. They're reached by a short wooden boardwalk across steaming marsh, and are otherwise unspoilt apart from a wooden changing room and the big high-season crowds. As the marsh never freezes, it attracts moose and grizzlies down to drink and graze, and some 250 plant species grow in the mild microhabitat nearby, including fourteen species of orchid, as well as lobelias, ostrich ferns and other rare boreal forest plants. The nearby *Liard River Hotsprings Provincial Park* **campsite** is one of the region's most popular; bookings are possible through the provincial park central reservation line (May–Aug \$17; Sept–April \$14); see box on p.758.

Watson Lake and beyond

Beyond the Liard Hot Springs the Alaska Hwy follows the Liard River, settling into about 135km of unexceptional scenery before **WATSON LAKE**, just over the Yukon border (though the road trips back and forth across the border seven times before hitting the town). It's neither attractive nor terribly big, but shops, motels and garages have sprung up here to service the traffic congregating off the Stewart-Cassiar and Campbell hwys to the north and south.

Even if you're just passing through it's well worth pulling off to look at the **Alaska Highway Interpretive Centre** (daily May–Sept 8am–8pm; ⓣ250/536-7469), which as well as providing information on the Yukon also describes the highway's construction through archive photos and audiovisual displays. It also acts as the local **visitor centre** and is situated on the hwy behind the famous **Sign Post Forest**. This last bit of gimmickry was started in 1942 by homesick GI Carl K. Lindley, who erected a sign pointing the way and stating the mileage to his home in Danville, Illinois. Since then the signs have just kept on coming, and at last count numbered around thirty thousand. You might also want to dip briefly into the **Northern Lights Centre** (mid-May to mid-Sept, six shows daily 1pm–8.30pm; \$10; ⓣ867/536-7827, ⓦwww.northernlightscentre.ca), a planetarium and science centre that explores the myths, folklore and science behind phenomena such as the aurora borealis (see box, p.997).

It's still 441km from Watson Lake to Whitehorse and a lot of people wisely stop here overnight to recuperate. Countless small government-run **campsites** are dotted along the length of the hwy beyond the village; the closest is a rustic site 4km west of the Sign Forest (\$12; May–Oct). If you decide to **stay in town** the *Gateway Motor Inn* (ⓣ867/536-7744; ④), which is open 24 hours a day, and the *Cedar Lodge Motel* (ⓣ867/536-7406, ⓦwww.cedarlodge.yk.net; ③) are both good choices.

West of Watson Lake

West of Watson Lake the road picks up more fine mountain scenery, running for hour after hour past snowcapped peaks and thick forest. About 10km before **TESLIN**, 263km west of Watson, look out for the *Dawson Peaks Resort and RV Park* (ⓣ867/390-2244, or 1-866/402-2244, ⓦwww.dawsonpeaks.ca; May–Sept; ③), which not only has cabins, a campsite (\$12) and RV sites (\$18–22), but also boasts one of the highway's better **restaurants** (pasta, steak and salmon mains \$14–23); fishing and boat rentals are also available. Teslin itself was founded as a trading post in 1903 and now has one of the region's largest aboriginal populations, many of whom still live by hunting and fishing. The **George Johnston Museum** (mid-May to Sept daily 9am–7pm; \$3; ⓣ867/390-2550, ⓦwww.gjmuseum.yk.net) is on the right on the way into the village and has a good collection of local Tlingit artefacts.

Whitehorse

WHITEHORSE is the likeable capital of the Yukon and home to more than 23,000 of the region's 31,000 inhabitants. It's also the centre of the Yukon's mining and forestry industries and a busy, welcoming stop for thousands of summer visitors. The town owes its existence to the **Yukon River**, a 3000-kilometre artery that rises in BC's Coast Mountains and flows through the heart of the Yukon and Alaska to the Bering Sea. The river's flood plain and strange escarpment above the present town were long a resting point for Dene peoples, but the spot burgeoned into a full-blown city when thousands of stampeders arrived in the spring of 1898. Having braved the Chilkoot Pass (see box, p.1024) to meet the Yukon's upper reaches, men and supplies then had to pause on the shores of Lineman or Bennett Lake before navigating the **Miles Canyon** and White Horse rapids southeast of the present town. After the first few boats through had been reduced to matchwood, the Mounties laid down rules allowing only experienced boatmen to take craft through – the writer Jack London, one such boatman, made $3000 in the summer of 1898, when more than seven thousand boats set off from the lakes. The prospectors eventually constructed an eight-kilometre wooden tramway around the rapids, and in time raised a shantytown at the canyon and tramway's northern head in order to catch their breath before the river journey to Dawson City.

The completion of the **White Pass and Yukon Railway** (WP&YR) to Whitehorse put this tentative settlement on a firmer footing – almost at the same time as the gold rush petered out. In the early years of the twentieth century the town's population dwindled quickly from about 10,000 to about 400. The town's second boom arrived with the construction of the Alaska Hwy, a kick-start that swelled the town's population almost overnight, and has stood it in good stead ever since.

Arrival, information and tours

Whitehorse's **airport** is on the bluff above the town, 5km west of downtown; taxis (Ⓣ867/667-4111 or 393-6543) are around $15 to the centre, and the Whitehorse Transit Hillcrest bus ($2) runs downtown hourly during the day. If you're taking the bus to the airport, pick it up at the Qwanlin Mall at the northern end of 3rd Avenue. The Greyhound **bus terminal** is at 2191 2nd Ave (Ⓣ867/667-2223 or 1-800/661-8747, Ⓦwww.greyhound.ca) at the extreme eastern end of downtown. Buses to and from other destinations, notably those in Alaska, arrive and leave from a variety of destinations. See the box on p.1030 for full details of all transport links to and from the town.

Whitehorse's large and very helpful downtown **visitor centre** is on 2nd Ave and Hanson St (mid-May to Sept daily 8am–8pm; rest of year Mon–Fri 9am–5pm; Ⓣ867/667-3084, Ⓦwww.touryukon.com or Ⓦwww.visitwhitehorse.com). Staff can point you in the direction of tour operators based in Whitehorse (or see Ⓦwww.explorenorth.com). Visiting drivers should note that they can pick up a three-day free parking **pass** from City Hall, 2121 2nd Ave (Ⓣ867/667-6401). For information on the Yukon's aboriginal cultures, stop by the office of the **Yukon First Nations Tourism Association** in the White Pass and Yukon Route Train Depot at 1-1109 1st Ave (Mon–Fri 9am–5pm; Ⓣ867/667-7698, Ⓦwww.yfnta.org) and pick up a copy of the *Yukon's First Nations Guide*. Almost as useful as these centres is Mac's Fireweed, 203 Main St (Ⓣ867/668-2434, Ⓦwww.yukonbooks.com), which has a full range of Yukon books, guides, maps, nautical charts and pamphlets you probably won't find

Skagway to Whitehorse: walking the Chilkoot Trail

No single image better conjures the human drama of the 1898 gold rush than the lines of prospectors struggling over the **Chilkoot Trail**, a 53-kilometre path over the Coast Mountains between **Dyea**, north of Skagway in Alaska, and **Bennett Lake** on the BC border south of Whitehorse. Before the rush, Dyea was a small village of Chilkat Tlingit, who made annual trade runs over the trail to barter fish oil, clamshells and dried fish with the Tutchone, Tagish and other interior Dene peoples in exchange for animal hides, skin clothing and copper. The Chilkat jealously guarded access to the **Chilkoot Pass** (1122m) – the key to the trail and one of only three glacier-free routes through the Coast Mountains west of Juneau. Sheer numbers and a show of force from a US gunboat, however, opened the trail to stampeders, who used it as a link between the ferries at the Pacific Coast ports and the Yukon River, which they then rode to the gold fields at Dawson City.

For much of 1897, the pass and border were disputed by the US and Canada until the Canadian NWMP (Northwest Mounted Police) established a storm-battered shack at the summit and enforced the fateful "ton of goods" entry requirement. Introduced because of chronic shortages in the gold fields, this obliged every man entering the Yukon to carry a ton of provisions – and, though it probably saved many lives in the long run, the rule laid enormous hardship on the back of the would-be prospectors. Weather conditions and the trail's fifty-degree slopes proved too severe even for horses or mules, so that men had to carry supplies on their backs over as many as fifty journeys to move their "ton of goods". Many died in avalanches or lost everything during a winter when temperatures dropped to -51°C and 25m of snow fell. Even so, the lure of gold was enough to drag some 22,000 men over the pass.

Preparation

These days most people off the ferries from Prince Rupert and the Alaska Panhandle make the fantastic journey across the mountains by train, car or bus **from Skagway to Whitehorse.** This route parallels that taken by the restored White Pass & Yukon Route **railway** (WP&YR; mid-May to mid-Sept 1 daily; train from Skagway to White Pass, then connecting bus to Whitehorse; US$95; ⓣ907/983-2217 or 1-800/343-7373, ⓦwww.whitepassrailroad.com), originally built to supersede the Chilkoot Trail.

Increasing numbers, however, are **walking** the old trail, which has been laid out and preserved by Parks Canada as a long-distance hikers' route. Its great appeal lies not only in the scenery and natural habitats – which embrace coastal rainforest, tundra and subalpine boreal woodland – but also in the numerous artefacts like old huts, rotting boots, mugs and broken bottles still scattered where they were left by the prospectors. The trail is well marked, regularly patrolled and generally fit to walk between June and September, though throughout June you can expect snow on the trail. Most people hike the trail in **three or four days** and if you're moderately fit it shouldn't be a problem, but there are dangers from bears, avalanches, drastic changes in weather and exhaustion – there's one twelve-kilometre stretch, for example, for which you're advised to allow twelve hours. Almost everyone hikes from south to north. Although there are three warming huts on the trail, these aren't designed for sleeping in, and you'll be making use of the nine approved **campsites** spaced at intervals along the trail: no backcountry camping is allowed.

elsewhere. For **exchange**, plus reservations for ferries and **tickets** for local events, contact Thomas Cook, 2101A 2nd Ave (Mon–Fri 8.30am–5.30pm; ⓣ867/668-2867). There's a 45-minute **downtown walking tour** offered by the Yukon Historical & Museums Association (June–Aug Mon–Sat 9am, 11am,

Reservations and permits

Order an advance **information pack** by calling the **reservation system** (☎867/667-3910 or 1-800/661-0486 between 8.30am and 4pm), or by visiting either Ⓦwww.pc.gc.ca/chilkoot or the government offices in central Whitehorse – at 300 Main St, (2nd floor, suite 205; open Mon–Fri 8am–noon & 1–4.30pm). There is no facility for booking online. Throughout the hiking season, the number of hikers crossing the Chilkoot Pass into Canada is limited to fifty per day, of which 42 places can be booked in advance ($12) by calling the reservation system. The remaining eight places are offered on a first-come, first-served basis after 1pm on the day before you plan to start the trail; to register, aim for the **Skagway Trail Center**, on Broadway at 2nd Avenue (late May to early Sept daily 8am–5pm; ☎907/983-9234). The busy season is July and the first two weeks of August; outside this time you probably don't need to make a reservation.

While you do not need a permit for day hikes on the Chilkoot Trail (parking is available near the trailhead in Dyea by the public restrooms), all other hikers need to go to the Skagway Trail Center to buy a **permit** ($55), sign a register (for customs purposes) and consult the weather forecast. You'll need to carry **identification**, which means a birth certificate for North Americans (a driver's licence is not acceptable) and a passport for everyone else. You may be required to deal with Canadian customs at the Chilkoot Pass ranger station but more likely you'll do it after your hike at the Alaska–Canada border post at Fraser or in Whitehorse.

If you've made an advance reservation, you'll already have Parks Canada's *Chilkoot Trail* **map** (otherwise $6 from the Trail Center or the Parks Canada office at the SS *Klondike* in Whitehorse).

Transport and supplies

Dyea Dave (☎907/209-5051), Frontier Excursions (☎907/983-2512) and Klondike Tours and Taxis (☎907/983-2400) all run shuttle buses (US$10) from Skagway to **Dyea**, the start of the trail some 14km northwest of Skagway. The trail finishes at **Bennett**, where you can order Alpine Aviation (☎867/668-7725, Ⓦwwwalpineaviationyukon.com) to take you by seaplane to Whitehorse ($215 or $135 each for four people). Alternatively you can walk the 12km to the hwy at Log Cabin (there's a marked short cut off the trail which avoids Bennett but there is no signage once you reach the railway tracks) and meet up with Dyea Dave, Frontier Excursions or Klondike Tours and Taxis who also make pick-ups at the end of the trail (call to confirm; US$25); or catch the daily service run by Yukon Alaska Tourist Tours (☎867/668-5944 or 4414, Ⓦwww.yatt.ca; call to confirm; US$14–40) from Log Cabin to either Whitehorse or Skagway; or return to Skagway on the **WP&YR railroad**. In June, July and August the railroad offers the Chilkoot Trail Hikers Service (departs 1pm Alaska time Sat, Sun & Mon; US$50–60 one-way to Fraser, US$80–90 to Skagway), which comprises either a railcar or one carriage of the Lake Bennett Excursion that's specially designated for smelly hikers. Remember to buy your tickets before you set off on the trail or you'll have a $15 fee added to the ticket price; and note that for customs reasons the train doesn't stop at Log Cabin.

Remember to take wet-weather gear, matches, some method of water treatment, sunscreen, sunglasses, a flashlight and **nine metres of rope** so that you can sling your food, toothpaste and any scented items over the bear poles at each campsite. Early in the season when there's plenty of snow about, consider **gaiters**, which can be rented in Skagway.

1pm & 3pm; $4), which departs from Donnenworth House, 3126 3rd Ave (☎867/667-4704). Or you could try the variety of free summer strolls organized by the Yukon Conservation Society, 302 Hawkins St (July & Aug daily; ☎867/668-5678, Ⓦwww.yukonconservation.org), two- to six-hour walks that

delve into local and natural history, and the Yukon's geology, flora and fauna.

Of the several self-guided walks in and around town, you could walk all the way round **Schwatka Lake** from Whitehorse, beginning from the bridge by the SS *Klondike,* or the 5km paved, river-hugging Millennium Trail; both of these trails take you past the **Whitehorse Fishway**, Nisultin Drive (June–August 9am–9pm; ⓣ867/633-5965), the world's longest fish ladder, complete with interpretive displays and three underwater windows where you can watch the chinook salmon 'climb' the ladder to bypass a hydroelectric dam as they swim upstream to their spawning ground. Another popular two-kilometre trail goes from the Robert Lowe Bridge (straddling the Miles Canyon) to **Canyon City**, a ghost town from the gold rush era. Several **river tours** shoot the **Miles Canyon** 9km south of Whitehorse. The building of the hydroelectric dam has tamed the rapids' violence and replaced them with Schwatka Lake and the two-hour narrated trip on the MV *Schwatka* (daily May–Sept 2pm; June–Aug also 6pm; $25; ⓣ867/668-4716,

Ⓦwww.yukonrivercruises.com) gives a better view of the river's potential ferocity and the canyon's sheer walls than the viewpoints off the road. Board at the dock above the dam about 3km down Canyon Road. For a river tour to Canyon City on a replica gold-rush raft, contact Gold Rush Float Tours, corner of 1st Ave and Main St (June–Aug daily tours 10am and 2pm; $60; Ⓣ867/668-4836, Ⓦwww.subarctic.ca).

Transport, equipment and rentals

Car rental agencies have desks or courtesy phones at the airport and occasionally a downtown office: Budget, 4178 4th Ave (Ⓣ867/667-6200 or 1-800/268-8900, Ⓦwww.budgetyukon.com) and Norcan, 213 Range Rd (Ⓣ867/668-2137, 1-800/661-0445 or 1-800/227-7368, Ⓦwww.norcan.yk.ca), are companies to try, but remember they may have restrictions on taking cars on gravel roads if you're thinking of heading north on the Dempster Hwy.

Canoes, paddles and life-jackets plus **bikes** can be rented from the Kanoe People, on the river across the tram line at Strickland Street and 1st Avenue (Ⓣ867/668-4899, Ⓦwww.kanoepeople.com), who can also set you up with everything you need for guided or non-guided trips of anything from two hours to twenty days, including the paddle to Dawson (700km, but lots of people do it). Guided day-trips begin at $150. Bike rentals start at $30 for a day and $180 weekly. Canoe and kayaks start from $35 daily and $180 weekly. About 75m away, you'll get similar rates on bikes and canoes, plus lots of fishing, camping and other equipment rentals from Up North Adventures, 103 Strickland St, (Ⓣ867/667-7035, Ⓦwww.upnorth.yk.ca), which also offers horse riding and hiking excursions and winter tours that involve dog-sledding, ice-fishing and snowshoeing.

Should you need to buy **outdoor equipment**, the town is full of dedicated stores; the largest is *Coast Mountain Sports*, 208A Main St (Ⓣ867/667-4074).

Accommodation

Whitehorse has a surprising amount of **accommodation**, but in high summer much of it is booked up well in advance. If you arrive without a reservation, contact the visitor centre or try the string of **hotels** on Main Street between 1st and 5th avenues. For **B&Bs**, visit Ⓦwww.yukonbandb.com. The town has two good private **hostels** and while the Wal-Mart car park is free for RVs, Whitehorse is not bereft of far nicer **RV sites** and **campgrounds**.

Hotels and B&Bs

Airport Chalet 91634 Alaska Hwy Ⓣ867/668-2166. This is directly opposite the airport and serviceable enough for its purposes. There is Internet access in the lobby and a basic restaurant. ❹

Casey's 608 Wood St, between 6th and 7th Ave Ⓣ867/668-7481, Ⓦwww.caseybandb.com. Downtown location with good breakfasts; kitchen and laundry facilities are available. ❹

Edgewater Hotel 101 Main St Ⓣ867/667-2572 or 1-877/484-3334, Ⓦwww.edgewaterhotelwhitehorse.com. Good, high-priced hotel in the downtown area, with a bar and two popular restaurants on site. ❻

High Country Inn 4051 4th Ave Ⓣ867/667-4471, Ⓦwww.highcountryinn.yk.ca. A pleasant and easygoing hotel at the far western end of 4th Ave, a 10min walk from downtown, with a wide variety of excellent room deals and weekly rates. Also has a popular bar-patio. ❻

Historical Guest House B&B 505 Wood St, corner of 5th Ave Ⓣ867/668-3907, Ⓦwww.yukongold.com. This two-storey log home two blocks east of Main St was built in 1907 for Sam McGee and his family, the protagonist of a Robert Service poem (see p.1042). Modern facilities have been added in a new wing; it has two double rooms with private bathrooms. ❹

Midnight Sun Bed & Breakfast 6188 6th Ave, at the corner of Cook St Ⓣ867/667-2255, 1-866/284-4448, Ⓦwww.midnightsunbandbyukon.com. This large home on the northern edge of town has a guest lounge and four comfortable en-suite rooms. ❺

Westmark Whitehorse Hotel 201 Wood St ⓣ867/393-9700 or 1-800/544-0970, ⓦwww.westmarkhotels.com. If you want to see Whitehorse in style, this is the smartest and most expensive hotel in town. It has 181 rooms, a gift shop and restaurant. Deals are often available in the off-season. ❻

Hostels and campsites

Beez Kneez Bakpakers Hostel [sic] 408 Hoge St ⓣ867/456-2333, ⓦwww.bzkneez.com. Cosy and friendly place at the western end of downtown (near the junction with 4th Ave and Robert Service Way), with a kitchen, laundry, Internet access, free bicycle use and dorm rooms and private doubles from $25 per person.

Hide on Jeckell Hostel 410 Jeckell St, near the junction with 4th Ave ⓣ867/633-4933, ⓦwww.hide-on-jeckell.com. One block farther west than its rival, and marginally the better choice, with the same facilities and same prices: four dorm rooms and two private doubles.

Robert Service campground ⓣ867/668-3721, ⓦwww.robertservicecampground.com. About 2km and twenty minutes' walk down South Access Rd, past the SS *Klondike* on the river path. It's set on the banks of the Yukon River and is specifically for tents and backpackers ($14 plus $3 for firewood). It becomes very busy in summer; if it's full you could always pitch your tent in the woods above the lake which is situated past the dam beyond the campsite or otherwise along the bluff above town by the airport. Open mid-May to mid-Sept.

Wolf Creek campsite The nearest Yukon government campsite ($12), located off the Alaska Hwy 16km south of town. It has just eleven tents sites (and 40 RV sites) and there are no services, but wood and water are available.

The town and around

Although greater Whitehorse spills along the Alaska Hwy for several kilometres, the old **downtown** core is a forty-block grid centred on Main Street and mostly sandwiched between 2nd and 4th avenues. Though now graced only with a handful of pioneer buildings, the place still retains the dour integrity and appealing energy of a frontier town, and at night the baying of timber wolves and coyotes is a reminder of the wilderness immediately beyond the city limits. Nonetheless, the tourist influx provides a fair amount of action in the bars and cafés, and the streets are more appealing and lively than in many northern towns.

The main thing to see is the **SS Klondike** (May–Sept daily, tours every half-hour Mon–Sat 8.30am–6pm, Sun 10am-5pm; $6; ⓣ867/667-4511), one of only two surviving paddle steamers in the Yukon, now rather sadly beached at the western end of 2nd Avenue at 300 Main St, though it has been beautifully restored to the glory of its 1930s heyday. More than 250 stern-wheelers once plied the river, taking 36 hours to make the 700-kilometre journey to Dawson City, and five days to make the return trip against the current.

Elsewhere in town you could pop in to the **MacBride Museum**, housed in a sod-roofed log cabin at 1st Ave and Wood St (May–Aug daily 9am–7pm; call for winter hours; $6; ⓣ867/667-2709, ⓦwww.macbridemuseum.com), for the usual zoo of stuffed animals, an old WP&YR engine, pioneer and gold-rush memorabilia, as well as hundreds of marvellous archive photos and a display on the Asiatic peoples who crossed the Bering Straits to inhabit the Americas. The **Old Log Church Museum**, 3rd Ave and Elliott St (mid-May to early Sept daily 10am–6pm; $3; ⓣ867/668-2555), is a modest museum devoted to the pre-contact life of the region's aboriginal peoples, whaling, missionaries, the gold rush and early exploration. For **free beer**, there are tours and tastings at the Yukon Brewing Co brewery just north of Wal-Mart at 102 Copper Rd (daily in summer 11am–6pm, tours at 11.30am & 3.30pm; free; ⓣ867/668-4183). You may find it easier to resist the widely touted Frantic Follies **stage shows** at the *Westmark Whitehorse Hotel*, however (late May to early Sept; $20; ⓣ867/668-2042, ⓦwww.franticfollies.com). These vaudeville acts of the banjo-plucking and frilly-knickered-dancing variety have been playing in town for around three decades.

Whitehorse has a thriving arts scene and **Arts Underground**, 15-305 Main St, on the lower level of the Hougen Centre (Mon–Fri 9am–5.30pm, Sat 11am–5pm; ⓣ867/667-6058, ⓦwww.artsunderground.com) is a good place to view, buy and get the inside scoop on local artists. Northwest of downtown, the gallery at the **Yukon Arts Centre,** Yukon Place, 300 College Drive (Tues–Fri noon–6pm; Sat & Sun noon–5pm; ⓣ867/667-8575, ⓦwww.yukonartscentre.org) exhibits the work of regional and international artists.

Outside downtown, two of the most tempting attractions are up on the bluff above the town on the Alaska Hwy, close to the airport. One is the excellent **Yukon Transportation Museum** (mid-May to Aug daily 10am–6pm; $6, or joint ticket with Beringia Interpretive Centre $9; ⓣ867/668-4792); its displays, murals, historical videos, memorabilia and vehicles embrace everything from dog-sledding, early aviation and the construction of the Alaska Hwy, to the Canol pipeline, the gold rush and the White Pass and Yukon Railway. Right next door is the dynamic **Yukon Beringia Interpretive Centre** (May & Sept daily 9am–6pm, June–Aug daily 8.30am–7pm; $6; ⓣ867/667-8855, ⓦwww.beringia.com). Beringia was the vast subcontinent that existed some 24,000 years ago when the Yukon and Alaska were joined by a land bridge across the Bering Sea to Arctic Russia. The centre's interactive exhibits, films and other displays explore the aboriginal history of the time. The people who crossed this land bridge ultimately colonized the most distant reaches of present-day North and South America. It also looks at the flora, fauna and geology of that period with the help of paleontological and archeological exhibits, including the skeletal remains of a 12,000-year-old mammoth.

Eating and drinking

Alpine Bakery 411 Alexander St ⓣ867/668-6871. The bread, pizza slices, soups, cakes and freshly squeezed juices are all made from organic ingredients at this popular bakery. Closed Sun & Mon.

Capital Hotel 103 Main St ⓣ867/667-2565. This cavernous drinking hole pulls in a young crowd and has live music every night.

The Cellar *Edgewater Hotel*, 101 Main St ⓣ867/667-2572. If you're feeling flush, this is one of the town's best restaurants, serving solid staples such as ribs, steaks, salmon, Arctic char and lobster (mains $24–45). The *Edge Bar and Grill* in the same hotel has similar food but is less formal (mains $10–24). Closed Sun & Mon.

Chocolate Claim 305 Strickland. A welcoming café for soups, sandwiches coffee, cakes and, of course, chocolate. Closed Sun.

Deli 203 Hanson St ⓣ867/667-6077, Grab a sandwich and a home-made cake or stock up on European meats and cheeses. Closed Mon.

Giorgio's Cuccina 206 Jarvis St & 2nd Ave ⓣ867/668-4050. Italian dishes (main courses from $18) served in a setting with ancient Roman decorative flourishes.

Klondike Rib and Salmon 2nd Ave & Steele St ⓣ867/667-7554. An informal place for good fish and chips and northern specialties such as caribou, bison and musk ox (mains $15–29). Closed late Sept to mid-May.

Talisman Café *River View Hotel* 102 Wood St ⓣ867/667-7342. Friendly and laid-back, this is a good inexpensive option and serves a range of full meals (average $10).

Yukon Mining Company *High Country Inn,* 4051 4th Ave ⓣ867/667-4471. Popular and lively, this pub-eatery has local brews by Chilkoot Brewing Company and barbecued food on the outdoor deck in summer (mains $7–29).

Kluane Country

Kluane Country is the pocket of southwest Yukon on and around a scenically stunning 491-kilometre stretch of the Alaska Hwy from Whitehorse to **Beaver Creek** at the border with Alaska. *Kluane* comes from a Southern Tutchone

Transport in the Yukon

Whitehorse provides the main **transport** links not only to most other points in the Yukon, but also to Alaska and the Northwest Territories. Public transport will get you to surprisingly remote places, but times and schedules can change, so ask at the visitor centre or call numbers directly for latest information. We have arranged the information below alphabetically by destination from Whitehorse, unless stated. Note that may of the longer routes (such as Whitehorse to Inuvik) are also plied by local airlines.

Distances from Whitehorse

Anchorage 1165km
Beaver Creek 457km
Burwash Landing 285km
Carcross 74km
Dawson City 1471km
Edmonton 2054km
Fairbanks 980km
Fort Nelson 988km
Haines 415km
Haines Junction 158km
Inuvik 1226km
Prince George 1880km
Seattle 2831km
Tok 639km
Vancouver 2702km
Watson Lake 455km

Transport options from Whitehorse

Alaska Highway For westbound journeys, Alaska Direct Bus Lines (☎867/668-4833 or 1-800/770-6652) runs services from Whitehorse (Sun, Wed & Fri 6am) to reach Haines Junction (arrives 8am; US$65), Beaver Creek (arrives 12pm; US$100) and points in between such as Burwash Landing (US$70). See Vancouver (opposite) for details of Greyhound buses to Teslin, Watson Lake and points east on the Alaska Highway.

Anchorage, Alaska Alaska Direct Bus Lines (☎867/668-4833 or 1-800/770-6652) runs to Tok (see opposite) on Sun, Wed & Fri, continuing to Anchorage. Cost from Whitehorse is US$210.

Atlin (via Tagish and Carcross). The Atlin Express (☎250/651-7617) leaves Mon, Wed & Fri at 12.15pm from the Greyhound bus terminal, arriving at 3.45pm at the *Atlin* Inn. Cost is $28 one-way, $42 return.

Carcross See Atlin and Skagway.

Carmacks See Dawson City.

Dawson City At the time of publication, there was no regular bus service between Whitehorse and Dawson City. Up North Adventures (☎867/667-7035, Ⓦwww.upnorth.yk.ca) can take passengers from May to September when they make weekly runs to pick up canoes and customers ($150 one way), and stop in Carmacks ($100), Pelly Crossing and Mayo. Otherwise, PK's Get Outa Here Trailhead Service (☎867/633-5346, Ⓦwww.pkstrailheadservice.com) runs excellent three-day return camping trips for budget travellers (from $150).

Fairbanks from Dawson City The Parks Hwy Express (☎1-888/600-6001, Ⓦwww.alaskashuttle.com) leaves the Dawson visitor centre at 8am on Sun, Wed & Fri, arriving at 6.15pm. Cost is US$155.

Fairbanks from Whitehorse Alaska Direct Bus Lines (☎867/668-4833 or 1-800/770-6652) leaves Tok (connections from Whitehorse – see below) on Sun, Wed & Fri at 2.30pm, arriving 7.30pm at 501 Cushman St. Cost from Whitehorse is US$180.

Haines Junction Bernie's Deliveries (☎867/634-2682) runs Mon–Fri, leaving Whitehorse at 6pm and Haines Junction at 1pm ($45 each way); no same-day return, so overnight stay required. Call for availability and departure location. You can also use the Alaska Direct Bus Lines (☎867-668-4833 or 1-800/770-6652) service to Tok (see opposite), which departs at 6am from 509 Main St on Sun, Wed & Fri, arriving at 8am. Cost is US$65 one-way. It returns through Haines Junction at 10pm.

Inuvik MGM Services (ⓣ867/777-4295, 678-0129 or 678-0139, ⓦwww.mgmbusservices.ca) runs a bus down the Dempster Hwy from Inuvik to Whitehorse ($250 one-way) via Dawson City ($200 one-way), leaving Inuvik at 8am, arriving in Dawson City around 5pm and in Whitehorse approximately five hours later. Call for departures and availability; minimum of eight passengers required.

Inuvik from Dawson City See above.

Skagway The best way to reach Skagway and points in between is to take a Yukon Alaska Tourist Tour (mid-May to early Sept daily 8am; ⓣ867/633-5710 or 1-866/626-7383 in Whitehorse, 907/983-2115 in Skagway; one-way/return by bus US$40/65; one-way/return bus-train combination US$95/$109; ⓦwww.yatt.ca) which departs from the old White Pass railway building. Pick-ups at Carcross, Log Cabin and Fraser are possible and arrive in Skagway at 11.20am (Alaska time) at Sgt Preston's Trading Post. The return tours leave Skagway at 3.30pm (Alaska time), arriving back in Whitehorse at 7.30pm (Yukon time). Gray Lines' Alaskon Express (May–Sept daily; US$45 each way; bus-train combination US$95 each way; ⓣ867/668-3225) run a similar service between Whitehorse and Skagway. The White Pass & Yukon Route rail/bus combination (May–Sept daily; one-way US$95; ⓣ907/983-2217, ⓦwww.wpyr.com) departs Whitehorse at 1.30pm and arrives in Skagway four hours later. Three to four times a week, Alaska Direct Bus Lines (ⓣ867/668-4833 or 1-800/770-6652) does the run between Whitehorse and Skagway. Cost is US$65 each way.

Tok Alaska Direct Bus Lines (ⓣ867/668-4833 or 1-800/770-6652) leaves 509 Main St, Whitehorse, on Sun, Wed & Fri at 6am, arriving in Tok at 2.30pm. Cost is US$125. Connections the same days to Anchorage and Fairbanks (see opposite).

Vancouver via Alaska Hwy, Watson Lake and Dawson Creek. Greyhound buses (ⓣ867/667-2223 or 1-800/661-8747, ⓦwww.greyhound.ca) leave the Whitehorse Greyhound bus depot Mon–Sat at 1.30pm for Watson Lake and Dawson Creek, where you can pick up connections for Edmonton (total journey time 28hr from Whitehorse; $206) and Vancouver (40hr; $270).

Watson Lake See Vancouver.

Airlines in the Yukon

The Yukon has several **airlines** that operate scheduled services, and several more that offer tours and charter flights only. The idea of chartering a small plane may sound expensive and far-fetched, but often the prices are not prohibitive – at least by the standards of land transportation costs in the region — especially if you can get a group of people together.

Air Canada Arrivals & departures ⓣ867/668-4466, reservations and schedules 1-888/247-2262, ⓦwww.aircanada.ca. Flies four times daily between Vancouver and Whitehorse.

Air North ⓣ867/668-2228, ⓦwww.flyairnorth.com. From Whitehorse: to Vancouver (daily, twice on Tues & Thurs); Dawson City & Old Crow (6 weekly); Inuvik & Fairbanks (3 weekly); Calgary & Edmonton (4 weekly). Also from Dawson City: to Inuvik & Fairbanks (3 weekly); Old Crow & Whitehorse (6 weekly). Also from Inuvik to Old Crow (1 weekly). All routes also operate in reverse.

First Air ⓣ1-800/267-1247, ⓦwww.firstair.ca. From Whitehorse: to Yellowknife (3 weekly).

Charter airlines Alkan Air ⓣ867/668-2107, ⓦwww.alkanair.com; Alpine Aviation ⓣ867/668-7725, ⓦwww.alpineaviationyukon.com; Atlin Air Charters ⓣ250/651-0025, ⓦwww.atlin.net/AtlinAir.

Condor ⓣ1-800/524-6975, ⓦwww.condor.com. In the summer runs a weekly service from Frankfurt in Germany to Whitehorse.

aboriginal word meaning a "place of many fish." The area teems with fish, particularly **Kluane Lake**, the Yukon's highest and largest stretch of water. These days, though, the name is associated more with the all-but-impenetrable wilderness of Canada's largest mountain park, the **Kluane National Park** – a region that contains the country's highest mountains, the second most extensive non-polar ice fields in the world, and the greatest diversity of plant and animal species in the far north. The park's main centre is **Haines Junction** at the intersection of the Alaska Hwy and the Haines Road. Although motels and campsites regularly dot the Alaska Hwy, the only other settlements of any size are **Destruction Bay** and **Burwash Landing** on Kluane Lake. Gray Line's **Alaskon Express** as well as **Alaska Direct** buses (see box, p.1030) ply the length of the Alaska Hwy, which is also very popular with hitchhikers.

Haines Junction

A blunt and ugly modern place, but with a fine mountain-circled setting, **HAINES JUNCTION** (pop. 789) is the biggest service centre between Whitehorse (160km away) and Tok in Alaska, boasting plenty of shops, a handful of overnight possibilities and lots of tour and rental companies for river-rafting, canoeing, fishing, hiking, cycling, horse riding and glacier flights in Kluane National Park. It's the national park's eastern headquarters – the park covers a vast tract west of the Alaska Hwy well to the north and south of the village. The combined **Parks Canada** (Ⓣ867/634-7207, Ⓦwww.parkscanada.gc.ca/kluane) and Yukon government **visitor centre** is in the Kluane National Park Reserve Building on Logan Street just off the north side of the Alaska Hwy (mid-May to mid-Sept daily 8am–8pm; Ⓣ867/634-2345).

For cheap and central **accommodation**, local tour operator Paddle Wheel Adventures at 113 Auriol St (Ⓣ867/634-2683, Ⓦwww.paddlewheeladventures.com; ❷) rents out two small but delightful cabins, complete with bunk beds and cooking facilities. One of the newer motels in town, the *Alcan Motor Inn* (Ⓣ867/634-2371, Ⓦwww.yukonweb.com/tourism/alcan; ❺), on the junction of Haines Road and the Alaska Hwy, has rooms with kitchenettes. Or try the *Raven Hotel & Gourmet Dining* (Ⓣ867/634-2500, Ⓦwww.yukonweb.com/tourism/raven; ❻), a central place with a restaurant that includes a German breakfast in its room rate. Foodies will love its elegant evening meals, rated some of the Yukon's best (try the elk for something different), but you're looking at around $80 a head for three courses. The simple *Pine Lake* **campsite** ($12; May–Oct) with a nice sandy beach and swimming is 7km east of the village signed off the Alaska Hwy, or there's the bigge and more central *Kluane RV Kampground* in town (Ⓣ867/634-2709; $15–$24.50; May–Sept), which has wooded RV and tent sites, laundry and a souvenir store. The best general place **to eat** is the popular *Village Bakery & Deli* on Logan St across from the visitor centre.

Kluane National Park

Created in 1972 using land from the earlier Kluane Game Sanctuary, **KLUANE NATIONAL PARK** contains some of the Yukon's greatest but most inaccessible scenery within its 21,980 square kilometres, and for the most part, you'll only see and walk the easterly margins of this UNESCO World Heritage Site from points along the Alaska Hwy (no road runs into the park). Together with the neighbouring Wrangell-St Elias National Park in Alaska, the park protects the **St Elias Mountains**, though from the hwy the peaks you see rearing up to the south are part of the subsidiary Kluane Range. Beyond them, and largely invisible from the road, are St Elias's monumental **Icefield Ranges**, which contain Mount St Elias

(5488m) and **Mount Logan** (5950m) – Canada's highest point – as well as Mount Denali (Mt McKinley) (6193m), part of the Alaska Range and the highest point in North America. These form the world's second highest coastal range (after the Andes). Below them, and covering more than half the park, is a huge base of mile-deep glaciers and ice fields, the world's second largest non-polar ice field (after Greenland) and just one permanent resident, the legendary ice worm. Global warming, however, is taking its toll on the ice fields, with levels dropping by approximately 1.8 metres a year. Unless you're prepared for full-scale expeditions, this interior is off limits, though from around $175 you can take plane and helicopter **tours** over the area – information on these and other guided tours is available from the Whitehorse and Haines Junction visitor centres.

At the edge of the ice fields a drier, warmer range encourages a green belt of meadow, marsh, forest and fen that provide sanctuary for a huge variety of **wildlife** such as grizzlies, moose, mountain goats and a 4000-strong population of white **Dall sheep**. These margins also support the widest spectrum of **birds** in the far north, some 150 species in all, including easily seen raptors such as peregrine falcons, bald eagles and golden eagles, together with smaller birds like arctic terns, mountain bluebirds, tattlers and hawk owls.

Trails (see box below) offer the chance to see some of these creatures, but the only **campsite** within the park that is accessible from the hwy is at *Kathleen*

Walking in Kluane National Park

Kluane has only fifteen maintained **trails** but experienced walkers will enjoy wilderness routes totaling about 250km, most of which follow old mining roads or creek beds and require overnight rough camping. Several signposted day and multi-day hike trailheads can be accessed from the highway, each mapped on pamphlets available from Haines Junction's visitor centre where enthusiastic staff also organize popular guided day-walks during the summer.

Six trails start from points along Haines Road immediately south of Haines Junction. The path nearest to the town (7 km south) and the most popular walk is the fifteen-kilometre round trip **Auriol Trail**. The trailhead for the classic **King's Throne** walk (5km one-way) lies 27km south of Haines Junction. It's fairly steep, but offers spectacular views of Kathleen Lake; if you overcome vertigo and continue past the maintained trail to the summit of the mountain, you'll be rewarded with views of the ice fields. The well maintained **Rock Glacier Trail,** 50km south of Haines Junction, is a twenty-minute jaunt to a view of Dezadeash Lake. For a longer trek, the **Mush Lake Road** route (trailhead 52km south of Haines Junction) is 22km one-way and part of the 85km of the Cottonwood Trail. North of Haines Junction, paths strike out from the Tachal Dhal (Sheep Mountain) visitor centre on Kluane Lake. The **Sheep Mountain Ridge** (11.5km) is steep and a hard slog, but offers good chances of seeing the area's Dall sheep. The longer **Slim's River West Trail** (22.5km one-way) is a difficult hike but lets you see the edges of the park's ice field interior. Backcountry permits ($9 per night) are required for those planning **overnight** or multi-day hikes - register at the Haines Junction or Tachal Dhal visitor centres where you can also pick up a mandatory bear-proof food canister. Seventeen kilometres north of Haines Junction and just outside the park boundaries on the Alaska Hwy, the **Spruce Beetle Walk** is a two-kilometre interpretive loop trail that takes in a patch of forest devastated by the spruce beetle. Thriving in the balmier winters provided by global warming, these persistent little borers operate like a slow motion forest fire and have infested and killed an estimated forty percent of the mature spruce trees in Kluane Country since the early 1990s. Look out for red pine needles - this is a sign of infestation - while grey trees without needles have well and truly succumbed.

Lake, on the Haines Road 27km south of Haines Junction ($12) – though there is hotel and camping accommodation along the Alaska Hwy.

Kluane Lake

The Kluane region might keep its greatest mountains out of sight, but it makes amends by laying on the stunning **Kluane Lake** along some 60km of the Alaska Hwy. About 75km northwest of Haines Junction, and hot on the heels of magnificent views of the St Elias Mountains, the huge lake (some 400 square kilometres) is framed on all sides by snow-covered peaks whose sinister glaciers feed its ice-blue waters. It's not part of the national park, but there's still a second park visitor centre at its southern tip, the **Tachal Dhal (Sheep Mountain) Information Kiosk** (mid-May to early Sept daily 9am–5pm). About 12km before the kiosk is the *Kluane Bed & Breakfast* (ⓣ867/841-4250, ⓦwww.kluanecabins.com; ❸), with a self-contained chalet and four cabins on the lakeshore.

If you want to boat or fish try one of the rental facilities at the two main settlements along the shores, Destruction Bay and Burwash Landing, each of which also has a small selection of accommodation to supplement the odd lodges and campsites along the Alaska Hwy. In the smaller **Destruction Bay**, named when a previous road construction camp was destroyed by a storm in 1942, bed down at the *Talbot Arm Motel* (ⓣ867/841-4461; ❹) with restaurant, café, store, petrol station and RV sites ($12). The best overall local **campsite** is the lovely Yukon government-run *Congdon Creek* ($12) site off the Alaska Hwy, 12km south of Destruction Bay, which also offers the start of hiking trails. At **Burwash Landing**, 15km beyond, there's a tiny 1944 Oblate mission church, Our Lady of the Holy Rosary. The Kluane Museum (mid-May to early Sept 9am–8pm, $4; ⓣ867/841-5561), has displays on Yukon wildlife and aboriginal history, while the *Burwash Landing Resort* (ⓣ867/841-4441; ❸), has a restaurant, store, fishing trips and a big, unserviced campsite (free; May–Sept). Five kilometres farther south, the *Cottonwood Park Campground* offers more facilities, including a hot tub, a small convenience store, a log cabin for rent and tent pitches for $16 (ⓦwww.yukonweb.com/tourism/cottonwood/; mid May to mid-Oct).

Moving 42km on from Burwash, the *Kluane Wilderness Village* (ⓣ867-841-4141, ⓦwww.karo-ent.com/kluanewv.htm, ❸), also with RV sites ($24–28), is the last major indoor **accommodation** possibility before Beaver Creek.

Beaver Creek and the US border

BEAVER CREEK, Canada's westernmost settlement (pop. 109), is the last stop before Alaska. The customs post is a couple of kilometres up the road and the border is open 24 hours a day. For full details on crossing the border, and what to expect on the other side, visit the **Yukon Visitor Information Centre,** 1202 Alaska Hwy, (mid-May to early Sept daily 8am–8pm; ⓣ867/862-7321).

You may wish to **stay** at Beaver Creek, either at the *Westmark Inn* (ⓣ867/862-7501 or 1-800/544-0970, ⓦwww.westmarkhotels.com; ❺; May–Sept), which also offers hostel-type rooms for $59; or the characterful twenty-room *Ida's Motel and Restaurant* (ⓣ867/862-7223; ❹), a distinctive building across the highway. The *Westmark* has a large, serviced **campsite** (May–Sept, $12), though they're happier to see RVs ($17) than backpackers (try free camping in the woods). There's a good but small Yukon-government-run site located 10km south at the *Snag Junction* ($12; May–Oct).

Those not pushing deeper into Alaska but looping to Dawson City have a great journey ahead: just before Tok, the **Taylor Highway** (Hwy 5) bears northeast off the Alaska Hwy back towards the Yukon border, passing through relatively unexceptional scenery until it hits the US–Canadian border at Little Gold Creek (open daily 9am–9pm). From here, the 105km road to Dawson on the **Top of the World Highway** offers sensational views (see p.1045).

North Klondike Highway: Whitehorse to Dawson City

Most people approach Dawson City on the Klondike Hwy from Whitehorse, a wonderful, lonely, 536km paved road running through almost utter wilderness. The hwy loosely follows the original winter **overland route** to the gold fields first utilized in 1902; it took fortune seekers five days to compete the chilly journey in horse-drawn stages, with the trip costing an extortionate $125 per person (passengers were also expected to carry enough overproof rum to keep the drivers sufficiently lubricated). Roadhouses – complete with stables, storehouses and cabins – once dotted the road at thirty-to-forty-kilometre intervals. Nowadays, the drive takes little more than six hours, but you could easily stretch that out by allowing for frequent stops and a detour along the **Silver Trail** to explore the historic silver mining towns of Mayo and Keno.

Whitehorse to Pelly Crossing

Eight kilometres from Whitehorse, take the turn-off for Hot Springs Road, which brings you ten kilometres later to the topnotch **Takhini Hot Springs** (June to early Sept daily 8am–10pm; rest of year Thurs–Sun only – call for hours; $7; ⓣ867/633-2706, ⓦwww.takhinihotsprings.yk.ca). The water in the large pool is a toasty 36°C. You can camp here ($14.50–25) and if you don't want to pay for the privilege of a hot soak, use the public pool at the outflow point in the stream below, which the locals have built.

Back on the highway, the road carves through a wide dry valley covered with small pine, spruce and poplar trees as well as sporadic bursts of purple fireweed flowers. Some 40km north of Whitehorse, the road bypasses the 50km-long **Lake Laberge**, immortalized in Robert Service's poem *The Cremation of Sam McGee.* There is a government campground ($12) and beach here and the lake is popular with the boating set. **Fox Lake** is another 24km on and soon after the road passes through the first of many forest fire-ravaged areas. The unfolding miles of black skeleton trunks from a 1998 blaze reveals just how slowly the trees in these parts recover. Twenty or so kilometres later, **Braeburn Lodge** (ⓣ867/456-2867), opposite the airstrip, is a good place to fork out $7 for one of the massive, sickly sweet **cinnamon buns** that have become de rigueur along this stretch. Rearing up from the roadside 56km later is the ramshackle ruins of **Montague House**, an old roadhouse and one of the last remaining relics of the overland trail.

CARMACKS (pop. 450), 34km further, has two petrol stations, a **visitor centre** on the eastern side of the hwy as you enter town (daily June–Aug 9am–7pm; ⓣ867/863-6271, ⓦwww.carmacks.ca) and a handful of accommodation options. The riverside *Coal Mine Campground* (ⓣ867/863-6363; $12) is at the junction of the Klondike Hwy and the **Robert Campbell Highway**, the latter a scenic gravel road that winds 590km east to Watson Lake. Just after the bridge leaving Carmacks, the **Tage Cho Hudan Interpretive Centre** (Mon–Fri 8.30am–4.30pm, Sat 10am–4pm; ⓣ867/863-5830) has indoor and outdoor exhibits that reveal something of the traditional lifestyle of the Northern Tutchone people.

A further 25km north of Carmacks, it's worth stopping briefly at the lookout for the formidable **Five Finger Rapids**, formed by five huge pillars which divide the Yukon River into narrow channels. The rapids look benign from above, but many a stampeder lost his belongings and life here, and canoeists still lose their nerve here today. A steep one-kilometre trail leads down from the lookout to the water's edge. Some 80km along the road at **PELLY CROSSING** (pop. 280) look out for *Penny's Place*, whose burgers, ice cream and coffee are a favourite among hungry travellers. For camping, try the free *Pelly River Crossing Campground* before the bridge on the riverfront.

The Silver Trail

The village of **STEWART CROSSING** (pop. 40), 60km north of Pelly Crossing, sits at the junction of the **Silver Trail**, a hwy which strikes off northeast for three historic silver mining towns that sprung up following the discovery of silver on Keno Hill in 1919. The first 62km of road is paved and there is a **visitor kiosk** (mid-May to Sept) just after the turn-off for the Silver Trail.

MAYO (pop. 450), 56km along, has a **visitor centre** on the corner of Centre Street and Second Avenue (mid-June to early Sept; ⓣ867/996-2926), in the same building as a **museum** that gives a good overview of the area's history and geology. There are two motels here: the central, nine-room *North Star* at 212 Fourth Ave (ⓣ867/996-2231; ❹), and the 12-room *Bedrock*, 2km north of town (ⓣ867/996-2290, ⓦwww.bedrockmotel.yk.ca; ❹), with tent ($10) and RV sites ($15–20).

Some 24km on, there is nothing to see at **ELSA** where there has been some resumption in mining activity, but it is worth pushing 41km on to the end of the road to tiny **KENO CITY** (pop. 25), a weathered collection of characterful wooden buildings whose highlights include a mining museum (daily June–Sept 10am–6pm; ⓣ867/995-2792, ⓦwww.kinocity.info), an alpine centre and a house constructed with 32,000 beer bottles (the owner thought it would be good insulation). There is also a campground here, the *Keno City Campground* ($10, ask at the mining museum), a number of good hiking trails, and panoramic views of the Ogilvie and Wernecke mountains from the signpost on Keno Hill.

Stewart Crossing to Dawson City

The scenery picks up considerably after Stewart Crossing for the last stretch of the Klondike Hwy, with wide views of sweeping valleys, rounded mountains and dense boreal forest. Some 40km before Dawson City is the turn-off for the **Dempster Highway** (see p.1045). Just before Dawson City, the road wanders through low but steeply sided hills covered in spruce, aspen and dwarf firs, and then picks up a small, ice-clear river – the **Klondike** itself. Gradually the first small spoil heaps appear on the hills to the south, and then suddenly the entire valley bottom turns into a devastated landscape of vast boulders and abandoned workings. The desolate tailings continue for several kilometres until the Klondike flows into the much broader **Yukon River** and the town of Dawson City, previously hidden by hills, comes suddenly into view.

Dawson City

Few episodes in Canadian history have captured the imagination like the **Klondike gold rush**, and few places have remained as evocative of their past as **DAWSON CITY** (pop. 1772), the stampede's tumultuous capital. For a few months in 1898 this former patch of moose pasture became one of the wealthiest and most famous places on earth, as something like 100,000 people struggled across huge tracts of wilderness to seek their fortunes in the richest gold field of all time.

An ever-increasing number of tourists and backpackers are drawn here to explore the boardwalks, rutted dirt streets and dozens of false-fronted wooden houses; others come to canoe the Yukon or travel down the Dempster or Top of the World hwys into Alaska and the Northwest Territories. After decades of decline Parks Canada is restoring the town, now deservedly a **National Historic Site**. That said, in a spot where permafrost buckles buildings, snow falls in August, and temperatures touch -60°C during winters of almost perpetual gloom, there's little real chance of Dawson losing the gritty, weather-worn feel of a true frontier town. Small-time prospecting still goes on, and there are one or two rough-and-ready bars whose hardened locals take a dim view of sharing their haunt, let alone their gold, with coachloads of tourists.

You could easily spend a couple of days or more here: one day exploring the town, the other touring the old Klondike creeks to the east. If at all possible prime yourself beforehand with the background to one of the most colourful chapters in Canada's history: Pierre Berton's widely available bestseller *Klondike – The Last Great Gold Rush 1896–1899* is a superbly written introduction both to the period and to the place.

Arrival and information

Dawson City's **airport**, 19km southeast of the town on the Klondike Hwy, is used by charter Alkan Air with services to Inuvik (NWT), Old Crow, Mayo and Whitehorse, and by Air North with services to Fairbanks, Whitehorse, Inuvik, Old Crow, Watson Lake and Juneau. Buses to Alaska generally arrive and depart from behind the visitor centre. See the box on p.1030 for full details of **transport links** to and from Dawson. Tickets for Air North flights and an **airport shuttle** service can be arranged at Gold City Tours on Front Street (Ⓣ867/993-5175). For further details of tours and general information, contact the impressive

△ Remains of gold mining equipment in Dawson City

The Klondike gold rush

Gold rushes in North America during the nineteenth century were nothing new, but none generated quite the delirium of the **Klondike gold rush** in 1898. Over a million people are estimated to have left home for the Yukon gold fields, the largest single one-year mass movement of people in the century. Of these, about 100,000 made it to the Yukon, about 30,000 panned the creeks, 4000 found something and a couple of dozen made – and invariably lost – huge fortunes.

The discovery of gold in 1896 on the Klondike, a tributary of the Yukon River, was the culmination of twenty years of prospecting in the Yukon and Alaska. A Hudson's Bay fur trader first noticed gold in 1842, and the first substantial report was made by an English missionary in 1863, but as the exploitation of gold was deemed bad for trade in both furs and religion, neither report was followed up. The first mining on any scale took place in 1883 and gradually small camps sprang up along almost 3200km of river at places like Forty Mile, Sixty Mile and Circle City. All were established before the Klondike strike, but were home to only a few hundred men, hardened types reared on the earlier Californian and British Columbian gold rushes.

The discovery of the gold that started the stampede is inevitably shrouded in myth and countermyth. The first man to prospect near the Klondike River was **Robert Henderson**, a dour Nova Scotian and the very embodiment of the lone pioneer. In early 1896 he found 8¢ worth of gold in a pan scooped from a creek in the hills above present-day Dawson City. This was considered an excellent return at the time, and a sign to Henderson that the creek would make worthwhile yields. He panned out about $750 with four companions and then returned downriver to pick up supplies.

Henderson then set about finding a route up the Klondike to meet the creek he'd prospected, and at the mouth of the Klondike met **George Washington Carmack** and a couple of his aboriginal friends, known as **Skookum Jim** and **Tagish Charley**. Henderson told Carmack of his hopes for the area, and then – with a glance at the aboriginal pair – uttered the phrase that probably cost him a fortune, "There's a chance for you George, but I don't want any damn Siwashes [aboriginal people] staking on that creek." Henderson wandered off into the hills, leaving Carmack, rankled by the remark, to prospect a different set of creeks – the right ones, as it turned out. On the eve of August 16, Skookum Jim found $4 of gold in a pan on **Bonanza Creek**, a virtually unprecedented amount at the time. Next day Carmack staked the first claim, and rushed off to register the find as Henderson prospected almost barren ground on the other side of the hills.

By the end of August all of Bonanza had been staked by a hundred or so old-timers from camps up and down the Yukon. Almost all the real fortunes had been secured by the winter of 1896, when the snows and frozen river effectively sealed the region from the outside world. The second phase occurred after the thaw when a thousand

Tourism Yukon–Parks Canada **visitor centre** (mid-May to mid-Sept daily 8am–8pm; ⓣ867/993-5566 or 993-7200, ⓦwww.dawsoncity.ca) on Front Street, at the junction with King Street; the place also has a **Parks Canada** desk (June–Sept 9am–4.30pm, ⓣ1-888/773-8888, ⓦwww.parkscanada.gc.ca) and shows good archival and contemporary films throughout the day. It also organizes **walking tours** (June to mid-Sept several daily; $6) that take in the *SS Keno* paddle steamer and the town's heritage buildings.

Another way of exploring the surroundings of Dawson is to take a Gray Line **cruise** on the 110-passenger catamaran *Yukon Queen*, which in summer runs daily on the Yukon River to Eagle, Alaska, offering a day-long round trip of 170km for around $200. Gray Line also run tours to the gold fields, rafting trips down the Klondike River and day-long bus tours along the Dempster Hwy to

or so miners from the West Coast arrived drawn by vague rumours emanating from the north of a big find. The headlong rush that was to make the Klondike unique, however, followed the docking in July 1897 of the *Excelsior* in **San Francisco** and the *Portland* in **Seattle**. Few sights could have been so stirring a proof of the riches up for grabs as the battered Yukon miners who came down the gangplanks dragging bags, boxes and sacks literally bursting with gold. The press were waiting for the *Portland*, which docked with two tons of gold on board, all taken by hand from the Klondike creeks by just a few miners. The rush was now on in earnest.

Whipped up by the media and the outfitters of Seattle and San Francisco, thousands embarked on trips that were to claim hundreds of lives. The most common route – the "poor man's route" – was to take a boat from a West Coast port to **Skagway**, climb the dreaded **Chilkoot Pass** to pick up the Yukon River at Whitehorse and then boat the last 700 kilometres to **Dawson City**. The easiest and most expensive route lay by boat upstream from the mouth of the Yukon in western Alaska. The most dangerous and most bogus were the "All Canadian Route" from **Edmonton** and the overland trails through the northern wilderness.

The largest single influx came with the melting of the ice on the Yukon in **May 1898** – 21 months after the first claim – when a vast makeshift armada drifted down the river. When they docked at Dawson City, the boats nestled six deep along a three-kilometre stretch of the waterfront. For most it was to have been a fruitless journey, every inch of the creeks having long been staked – yet in most accounts of the stampede it is clear that this was a rite of passage as much as a quest for wealth.

As for the gold, it's the smaller details that hint at the scale of the Klondike gold rush: the miner's wife, for example, who could wander the creek by her cabin picking nuggets from the stream bed as she waited for her husband to come home; or the destitutes during the Great Depression who could pan $40 a day from the dirt under Dawson's boardwalks; or the $1000 panned during rebuilding of the Orpheum Theatre in the 1940s, all taken in a morning from under the floorboards where it had drifted from miners' pockets half a century before; or the $200 worth of dust panned nightly from the beer mats of a Dawson saloon during 1897.

By about 1899 the rush was over, not because the gold had run out, but because the most easily accessible gold had been taken from the creeks. It had been the making of Alaska; the cities of Tacoma, Portland, Victoria and San Francisco all felt its impact; Edmonton sprang from almost nothing; and Vancouver's population doubled in a year. It was also the first of a string of mineral discoveries in the Yukon and the far north, a region whose vast and untapped natural resources are increasingly the subject of attention from multinational corporations as rapacious and determined as their grizzled predecessors.

Tombstone National Park; tickets are available from the office on Front Street (Ⓣ867/993-5599). First Nations-owned Fishwheel Charter Services (Ⓣ867/993-6237) run intimate, two-hour motor boat tours up the Yukon River that take in a visit to a traditional fish camp; in the winter, dog-sledding and guided camping trips are offered. Trans North Helicopters (Ⓣ867/993-5494, Ⓦwww.tntaheli.com) and Fireweed Helicopters (Ⓣ867/993-5800) run **helicopter trips** over the gold fields, the Klondike Valley and Midnight Dome, while Klondike Air Tours (Ⓣ867/993-5009 or 993-5001) flies tourists to and from the Arctic Circle. If you're planning a **canoe** trip, the *Dawson City River Hostel* and the *Trading Post* store on Front Street rents out canoes. Both can give you information on good trips from Dawson City, including the float down the Yukon River to the abandoned gold mining town of Fortymile.

Distances from Dawson City

Anchorage 828km
Beaver Creek 415km
Burwash Landing 587km
Carcross 610km
Dawson Creek 2007km
Destruction Bay 798km
Fairbanks 631km
Fort Nelson 1524km
Haines 927km
Haines Junction 671km
Inuvik 766km
Keno 285km
Prince George 2416km
Skagway 716km
Tok 300km
Vancouver 3191km
Watson Lake 991km
Whitehorse 536km

Accommodation

In July and August it's pretty much essential to book **accommodation** in advance. Rates are high in the half-dozen or so mid-range places, most of which look the part of old-fashioned wood- and false-fronted hotels. Prices in all places drop considerably outside the high summer period. Note, though, that many places close their doors between September and mid-May.

Hotels and B&Bs

Aurora Inn 5th Ave & Harper ⓣ867/993-6860, ⓦwww.aurorainn.ca. A colourful exterior, cheerful staff and eighteen immaculate rooms make this one of the best picks in town. ❻

Bedside Manner B&B At 931 5th Ave ⓣ867/993-6948. On a quiet residential street, this is Dawson City's cheapest B&B, with five themed rooms, two shared bathrooms and a hot tub. ❷

Bombay Peggy's 2nd Ave & Princess St ⓣ867/993-6969, ⓦwww.bombaypeggys.com. Ten very comfortable rooms in a central, heritage house of former ill-repute. ❻

Dawson City Bunkhouse Near the corner of Front St and Princess St ⓣ867/993-6164, ⓦwww.bunkhouse.ca. A good, if noisy place (often known just as "The Bunkhouse") with a choice between rooms with shared bathrooms or private facilities. Open June to early-Sept. ❸

Downtown Hotel 2nd Ave & Queen St ⓣ867/993-5346 or 1-800/764-0514 in BC and YK, ⓦwww.downtown.yk.net. One of the town's plusher wooden-fronted hotels. ❻

Eldorado 3rd Ave & Princess St ⓣ867/993-5451 or 1-800/661-0518, ⓦwww.eldoradohotel.ca. Much the same as the *Downtown*, with 52 central rooms (some kitchenettes). ❻

Fifth Ave B&B On 5th Ave near the museum ⓣ867/993-5941 or 1-866/631-5237, ⓦwww.5thavebandb.com. A spacious house with shared kitchen; optional en suite. Look out for the electric-blue exterior. ❹

Klondike Kate's Cabins & Rooms 3rd Ave & King St ⓣ867/993-6527, ⓦwww.klondikekates.com. Renovated, pretty and popular cabins. Open mid-May to Sept. ❺

Westmark Inn Dawson 5th Ave & Harper St ⓣ867/993-5542 or 1-800/544-0970, ⓦwww.westmarkhotels.com. Part of an upmarket northern chain, and the town's swishest hotel. Open mid-May to early Sept. ❻

White Ram Manor B&B 7th Ave & Harper St ⓣ867/993-5772, ⓦwww.bbcanada.com/whiterammanor. A distinctive pink house that has a hot tub and outside deck. ❹

Whitehouse Cabins Front St ⓣ867/993-5576, ⓦwww.whitehousecabins.com. Six cabins with kitchenettes on the waterfront at the northern end of the street beyond the *George Black* ferry. Open May to Sept. ❹

Yurt ⓣ867/993-4440. Across the river, a kilometre up the hwy and turn left. These two fully-furnished yurts may be basic, but the owners haven't skimped on wireless Internet. Open May to Aug. ❷

Hostel

Dawson City River Hostel (HI) ⓣ867/993-6823, ⓦwww.yukonhostels.com. Across the river from downtown; first left after you jump the free ferry. An HI-affiliated collection of bunks in smart log cabins with a good view over Dawson and the river. There are bunk rooms (two to six people; $16 for HI members, $19 for non-members), tent sites ($12 for individuals,

$8.50 per person for multiple-occupancy tents), family and private double rooms (from $39), wood-fired showers and stoves, canoe and bike rentals and bus transfers to Whitehorse on demand. No electricity. Cash only. Open May–Oct.

Campsites

Gold Rush Campground At 5th and York in town ⓣ867/993-5247. A bleak, fully serviced but busy place designed for RVs ($18–36; May–Sept).

Klondike River Campground A Yukon government site ($12) on the Klondike Hwy 15km east of town. While it's a bit quieter than the *Yukon River Campground* site, it's not as pleasant.

Yukon River Campground The main town campsite for tents ($12), located on the west bank of the Yukon on the right about 500m after the free *George Black* seven-minute ferry crossing (see p.1045). There are no showers – the most central in town are the Wash House at 2nd Ave and Queen St. There are also showers at the municipal swimming pool by the museum.

The Town

You should start any wander on **Front Street**, the leading edge of a street grid that runs parallel to the Yukon River. The town has a wealth of **heritage buildings** – there are 35 National Historic Sites, seven of which you can enter, usually as part of a tour ($6 each or $28 for all seven). The buildings are easily seen on your own, however, as are the cabins that belonged to two chroniclers of the gold rush, poet **Robert Service** and the better-known **Jack London**. The local **museum** is also good for an hour, and you might want to dabble in the casino – though it's the atmospheric streets of Dawson that are most compelling.

Opposite the visitor centre on Front Street is the **Western Arctic Information Centre**, an essential port of call if you are heading north on the Dempster Hwy (see p.1045) and, next to that, the dramatic-looking **Dänojà Zho**, or "Long Time Ago House", also known as Tr'ondëk Hwëch'in Cultural Centre (daily June–Sept 10am–6pm; by appointment rest of year; $5; ⓣ867/993-6768 or 867/633-6519, ⓦwww.trondek.com), which uses exhibits, guides, videos and live demonstrations to explore the traditional and present-day culture of the Tr'ondëk Hwëch'in, the region's original aboriginal inhabitants.

The heritage buildings

Fuelled by limitless avarice, between 1898 and 1900 Dawson exploded into a full-blown metropolis of 30,000 people – the largest city in the Canadian West and the equal of places like Seattle and San Francisco in its opportunities for vice, decadence and good living. There were opera houses, theatres, cinemas (at a time when motion-picture houses were just three years old), steam heating, three hospitals, restaurants with French chefs, and bars, brothels and dance halls that generated phenomenal business. Showgirls charged miners $5 – payable in gold – for a minute's dance; slow dances were charged at a higher rate. Cleaners panning the bars' sawdust floors after hours were clearing $50 in gold dust a night. Rules of supply and demand also made Dawson an expensive town, with a single two-metre frontage fetching as much in rent in a month as a four-bedroom apartment in New York cost for two years.

Only a few of the many intact **heritage buildings** around the town date from the earliest days of the rush, dozens having been lost to fire and to permafrost, whose effects are seen in some of the most appealing of the older buildings: higgledy-piggledy collapsing ruins of rotting wood, weeds and rusting corrugated iron. Most of these, thankfully, have been deliberately preserved in their tumbledown state. Elsewhere, restoration projects are in full flow, partly financed by profits from the town casino. Permafrost precluded the construction of brick buildings with deep foundations, so restoration engineers have had to work doubly hard to save what are generally all-wood buildings, most notably the **Palace Grand Theatre** (1899) on the corner of 3rd Ave and King St. The theatre was originally built from the hulks of two beached paddle steamers and tours run daily in summer ($6).

Nearby, on the corner of King Street and 3rd Avenue, there's the 1901 **post office**; opposite is **Madame Tremblay's Store**. On 3rd Avenue and Princess Street, **Harrington's Store** has a "Dawson as They Saw It" exhibition of photos (June–Sept daily 9am–4.30pm; free); near the same junction stands **Billy Bigg's Blacksmith Shop**; elsewhere is the cream-and-brown clapboard **Anglican Church**, built in 1902 with money collected from the miners. At 4th Avenue and Queen Street is **Diamond Tooth Gertie's Gambling Hall**, founded by one of the town's more notorious characters, and still operating as the first legal casino in Canada (opened after restoration in 1971) – it's also the world's northernmost casino (for details, see "Nightlife" opposite).

Also check out the **Firefighters Museum** in City Hall across from the *George Black* ferry on Front Street where a guide takes you on a tour of old fire tenders, water pumps and other old firefighting equipment. In a town built almost entirely of wood, these were once vital to Dawson's survival: the town all but burnt to the ground twice in the space of a year in 1898–99. One of the town's more obvious old wooden constructions is the **SS Keno** riverboat ($6), moored on the river just down from the visitor centre. Open for viewing, it was built in 1922 and ran up and down the Stewart River carrying ore from the mines around Mayo. Not all boats were as lucky as the *Keno*, and a good short hike just out of town will take you to a **ships' graveyard**. The improvements to transport links, chiefly the completion of the Klondike Hwy, made many riverboats redundant. Some were beached downstream, where their overgrown carcasses can still be seen with a little effort. Cross the river on the free *George Black* ferry on Front Street and walk through the campsite and then a farther ten minutes along the waterfront to reach the ruins of seven boats.

The Dawson City Museum

The **Dawson City Museum & Historical Society**, 595 5th Ave and Church St (mid-May to Sept daily 10am–6pm; $7), has an adequate historical run-through of the gold rush from the first finds. Fascinating old diaries and newspaper cuttings vividly document the minutiae of pioneer life and events such as the big winter freeze of 1897–98 when temperatures reputedly touched -86°C. The museum also shows some of the hundreds of old films that were discovered under the floorboards of a Dawson building a few years back. Its highlight is the wistful, award-winning, black-and-white film *City of Gold*, a wonderful documentary which first drew the attention of the federal government to Dawson's decline in the 1950s. You might also take a **tour** of the museum building (summer daily 11am & 3pm), the former Territorial Administration Building (1901).

The Robert Service and Jack London cabins

The cabins of Dawson's two literary lions, Robert Service and Jack London, are only about 100 metres apart on 8th Aveue, about ten minutes' walk from Front Street. Parks Canada offer tours of these and a third home, that of local writer Pierre Berton, but they are just as easily seen on your own.

Most Canadians hold **Robert Service** (1874–1958) in high esteem and he has a place, deserved or not, in the pantheon of Canadian literature. Verses like *The Shooting of Dan McGrew* and *The Cremation of Sam McGee* (see "Contexts", p.1043) combine strong narrative and broad comedy to evoke the myth of the North. Born in Preston, England, in 1874, the poet wrote most of his gold-rush verse before he'd even set foot in the Yukon: he was posted by his bank employers to Whitehorse in 1904 and only made Dawson in 1908. He retired a rich man on the proceeds of his writing – he outsold Kipling – spending his last years mainly in France, where he died in 1958. His **cabin** (June–Sept free daily viewing 3pm–4.30pm, tours 10.30am–1.30pm) is probably cosier and better decorated than it was, but it still gives an idea of how most people must have lived once Dawson was reasonably established. During the summer people come here to pay homage and join a **tour** which includes a short reading of one or two Service poems (July–Sept daily 10.30am & 1.30pm; $6 for cabin and recital).

The unexceptional-looking **Berton House Writers' Retreat** almost opposite the Service cabin was built in 1901, and bought by mining recorder, Frank Berton, for $500 in 1920. It was the Berton family home until they left Dawson, with son and future writer Pierre, in 1932. It was acquired by the Yukon Arts Council with a donation of $50,000 from Pierre Berton himself, and was restored and reopened in 1996 as a private retreat for Canadian writers.

Jack London's Cabin home two blocks south on 8th Avenue at Grant is an unpersuasive piece of reconstruction (logs from the original were separated and half of them used to build a cabin in Jack London Square in Oakland, California). London knew far more than Service of the real rigours of northern life, having spent time in 1897 as a ferryman on Whitehorse's Mile's Canyon before moving north to spend about a year holed up on Henderson's Creek above the Klondike River. He returned home to California penniless, but loaded with a fund of material that was to find expression in books like *The Call of the Wild*, *White Fang* and *A Daughter of the Snows*. Alongside the hut there's a good little museum of pictures and memorabilia (hut and museum mid-May to mid-Sept daily 10am–6pm; $2). Talks about London's life and work are presented here in summer (noon & 3pm).

Eating, drinking and nightlife

For **eating** there are numerous cafés around town, including several good snack places on Front Street – probably the most popular is *River West Bistro*, a place with good coffee, soups, sandwiches and cakes. The excellent *Klondike Kate's*, at 3rd and King, is the friendliest and most laid-back place in town for staples like breakfasts and straightforward dinners (main meals $18–23). The popular *Sourdough Joe's* on Front St, with an outdoor patio that overflows on a warm night, does a roaring trade in greasy fish-and-chips. *Mama Cita's* on 2nd Ave and Queen St does heaving Mediterranean plates and good pizzas (☎867/993-2370; mains $14–44, closed Mon, Oct–April). Otherwise, most dining goes on in the restaurants attached to the town's bigger hotels: three of the best are the *Jack London Grill* (closed Dec) in the *Downtown Hotel* at 2nd Ave and Queen St; the *Bonanza Dining Room* in the *Eldorado* at 3rd Ave and Princess St, and the *Aurora Inn Restaurant* at 5th Ave and Harper St (open mid-May to mid-Sept); all serve seafood, pasta, steak and stir-fry mains for around $20.

Nightlife revolves around drinking in the main hotel bars, or spending an hour or so at *Diamond Tooth Gertie's Gambling Hall* at 4th Ave and Queen Street Canada's oldest legal gambling hall (mid-May to mid-Sept daily 7pm–2am; $6); you need to be over 19 to gamble and all proceeds from here and several other town sights go to the restoration of Dawson. Three times a night, a singer and can-can girls grace the stage for some over-the-top knicker-flashing, tap-dancing and titillating audience interaction. If you want a taste of a real northern **bar**, try the *Westminster* on 2nd Ave: it's full of grizzled characters and most certainly not the place for a quiet drink or the faint-hearted. It hosts live music most nights. Other hotel bars provide more sedate alternatives, among which the lounge at *Bombay Peggy's* hotel on 2nd Ave and Princess St stands out for its fine atmosphere. The *Sourdough Saloon* at the *Downtown Hotel*, 2nd Ave and Queen St is popular with locals and visitors alike, and known for a cocktail that involves a real pickled human toe.

Listings

Books and guides Maximilian's ☎867/993-5486, on the corner of Front & Queen.
Currency exchange and ATM At the CIBC bank ☎867/993-5447, on Queen St, between Front & 2nd.
Internet access Free at the public library on 5th and Queen. (June to mid-Aug Tues–Sat 10am–8pm; mid-Aug to May Tues–Thurs noon–7.30pm, Fri noon–5.30pm, Sat 10am–5.30pm)
Post office On 3rd Ave between King and Queen St (Mon–Fri 8.30am–5.30pm, Sat 11.30am–2.30pm).

Around Dawson

While in Dawson, make a point of seeing the two creeks where it all started and where most of the gold was mined – **Bonanza and Eldorado**, both over 20km away from the town site along rough roads to the southeast. These days, no big working mine survives in the region, though most of the claims are still owned and definitely out of bounds to amateurs. Another popular local excursion is to **Midnight Dome**, the gouged-out hill behind the town, while farther afield numerous RVs, cyclists and hitchhikers follow the **Top of the World Highway**, which runs on beyond the Alaskan border to link with the Alaska Hwy at Tetlin Junction.

Bonanza and Eldorado creeks

To reach **Bonanza Creek**, follow the Klondike Hwy – the continuation of Front Street – for 4km to the junction with Bonanza Creek Road. The road threads through scenes of apocalyptic piles of boulders and river gravel for some 12km until it comes to a simple cairn marking **Discovery Claim**, the spot staked by George Carmack after pulling out a nugget the size of his thumb, or so the story goes. Every 150m along the creek in front of you – the width of a claim – was to yield some 3000kg of gold, or about $25 million worth at 1900 prices.

At Discovery Claim the road forks again, one spur running east up **Eldorado Creek**, if anything richer than Bonanza, the other following Upper Bonanza Road to the summit of **King Solomon's Dome**, where you can look down over smaller scarred rivulets like Hunker and Dominion creeks, before returning in a loop to the Klondike Hwy via Hunker Road.

As time went by and the easily reached gold was exploited, miners increasingly consolidated claims, or sold out to large companies who installed dredges capable of clawing out the bedrock and gravel. Numerous examples of these industrial dinosaurs litter the creeks, but the largest and most famous is the 1912 **No. 4 Dredge** at Claim 17 BD ("Below Discovery") off Bonanza Creek Rd, an extraordinary piece of industrial archeology that from the start of operations in 1913 until 1966 dug up as much as 25kg of gold a day. Modern mines are lucky to produce a quarter of that amount in a week.

Without a car or bike you'll have to join up with one of the various **gold-field tours** (from about $35 for a 3hr 30min tour) run by either Gray Line or Gold Bottom Mine Tours on Front Street (Ⓣ867/993-5750, Ⓦwww.goldbottom.com). The only place where you can pan for free is on Claim 6 in Bonanza Creek – 1km down from Discovery Claim. Gold Bottom Creek at the still-operating Gold Bottom Mine also offers a creek panning experience for $10. Alternatively, nearby you can pan flakes from a water trough for $6 at Claim 33 and for $7 at Guggieville, both with a guarantee of finding gold, because it's been put there (ask at the visitor centre for directions).

Midnight Dome and Top of the World Highway

The **Midnight Dome** is the distinctive hill that rears up behind Dawson City, half-covered in stunted pines and half-eaten away by landslips. From its summit at midnight on June 21 you can watch the sun dip to the horizon before rising again straight away – Dawson being only 300km south of the Arctic Circle. The Midnight Dome Road runs 8km to its summit (884m) from the Klondike Hwy just out of the town proper. Without a car it's an extremely steep haul (ask at the visitor centre for details of the trail), but more than worth the slog for the massive views over Dawson, the gold fields, the Yukon's broad meanders and the ranks of mountains stretching away in all directions. At the summer solstice there's a race to the top and lots of drink-sodden and fancy-dress festivities down in Dawson.

Another popular hike is to **Moosehide**, an aboriginal summer settlement about 7km north of Dawson City, but before entering the village you'll need to obtain a permit from the Tr'ondëk Hwëch'in office next door to the visitor centre on Front Street (Mon–Fri 9am–5pm; Ⓣ867/993-5385); access to the settlement is by foot or boat only.

You can snatch further broad vistas from the **Top of the World Highway** (Hwy 9), a good summer-only gravel road reached across the Yukon by the *George Black* **ferry** from Front Street (mid-May to mid-Sept daily 24hr; rest of year 7am–11pm, depending on whether or not the river is frozen; free; Ⓣ867/993-5441). After only 5km the road reaches a great panorama over the area and after 14km, another **viewpoint** looks out over the Yukon Valley and the **Ogilvie Mountains** straddling the Arctic Circle. In late summer, many people pile out of their cars around here to pick **wild blueberries** from roadside bushes. Thereafter the road runs above the tree line as a massive belvedere and can be seen switchbacking over barren ridges way into the distance. It hits the **Alaska border** 108km from Dawson, where you can cross only when the customs post is open (mid-May to mid-Sept 9am–9pm). Alaska/Yukon Trails (Ⓣ1-800/770-7275, Ⓦwww.alaskashuttle.com) runs a bus service on demand between Dawson City and Fairbanks, but you should be able to hitch easily in summer because it's much-travelled as a neat way of linking with the Alaska Hwy at Tok for the roads to Fairbanks and Anchorage or the loop back to Whitehorse. Be prepared to do only about 50kph, and ask at the Dawson visitor centre about local difficulties and fuel availability.

The Dempster Highway

Begun in 1959 to service northern oilfields, and completed over twenty years later – by which time all the accessible oil had been siphoned off – the 741-kilometre **Dempster Highway** between Dawson City and Inuvik in the Northwest

Territories is the only road in Canada to cross the **Arctic Circle**, offering a tremendous journey through a superb and ever-changing spectrum of landscapes. It's hard to resist the temptation of crossing into the Arctic 445km north of Dawson City, a section that takes you over the most captivating stretch of the highway. However, the Dempster is a **gravel road** and the journey north to Inuvik takes anything between twelve and fifteen hours by car in good conditions. It's an increasingly travelled route – which locals say means four cars an hour – but is not a journey to be undertaken lightly. Inuvik, too, is an ugly disappointment, but then this road is very much about the journey rather than the destination.

Note that all distances given below (unless stated) are from **Kilometre 0** of the highway, which is at the junction of the North Klondike Hwy 40km east of Dawson City, almost the only way to locate things on the road.

Dempster Highway practicalities

If you're **cycling** or motorbiking – both increasingly popular ways of doing the trip – you need to be prepared for rough camping, and should call at the **Western Arctic-NWT Information Centre** on Front St in Dawson City (mid-May to mid-Sept 9am–8pm; ⓣ867/993-6167 or 1-800/661-0750) for invaluable information from the staff. If you're without your own transport you might pick up a **lift** here, or take the **bus service** run by MGM Services, which only operates on demand (see p.1031).

The first **fuel** is at the start of the hwy at the *Klondike River Lodge* (ⓣ867/993-6893; ❹); the next is 365km north at the year-round *Eagle Plains Hotel* at Eagle Plains. Then it's Fort McPherson, 193km beyond Eagle Plains; thereafter there's nothing until Inuvik, so for emergencies take a jerrycan (you rent them at the *Klondike River Lodge*) and make sure that you have two spare tyres and your car's mechanics are sound – the only maintenance facilities are at Eagle Plains. It's worth checking on ⓣ1-800/661-0750 that the two **ferry** services on the route at Peel River (539km; free on demand, spring to late autumn daily 9.30am–12.30am, then ice bridge) and Tsiigehtchic, formerly Arctic Red River (609km; same details) are running.

Just as important, make sure you have lots of **drinking water**: the only place you'll find any that isn't out of a stream is at Eagle Plains.

To the Arctic Circle and beyond

After the millions of lodgepole pines in this part of the world, it's almost time for a celebration when you pass what are reputedly Canada's most northerly pines (8km). Beyond them you'll see occasional trappers' cabins: the hunting of mink, wolverine and lynx is still lucrative.

Some 72km north of Dawson is one of the highway's three rudimentary Yukon government campsites (shelter only), at **Tombstone Mountain Territorial Park** (31 RV/tent sites; $12), a magnificent, 2000-square-kilometre park packed with wildlife and archaeological sites where there's an interpretive centre (mid-May to mid-Sept 9am–9pm) offering guided nature walks and trail information.

At **Hart River** (80km) you may see part of the 1200-strong Hart River Woodland **caribou herd**; unlike the barren-ground herds farther north these caribou have sufficient fodder to graze one area instead of making seasonal migrations. Golden eagles and ptarmigan are also common on willow-lined streams like Blackstone River (93km), as are tundra birds like Lapland longspurs, lesser golden plovers, mew gulls and long-tailed jaegers. At Moose Lake (105km), **moose** can often be seen feeding, along with numerous species of waterfowl such as northern shoveller, American widgeon and the arctic tern, whose Arctic to Antarctic migration is the longest of any bird.

Chapman Lake (120km) marks the start of the northern **Ogilvie Mountains**, a region that has never been glaciated and so preserves numerous relic species of plant and insect, and provides an important early wintering range for the Porcupine Caribou herd; as many as 40,000 caribou cross the hwy in mid-October – they take four days and have right of way. The road crosses the Ogilvie Mountains at **North Fork Pass** (1289m), the highest elevation on the highway, at 139km. Unique butterfly species breed at Butterfly Ridge (155km), close to some obvious caribou trails which cross the region, and it should also be easy to spot Dall sheep, cliff swallows and bald eagles.

Beyond, the hwy goes up to **Eagle Plain** and almost unparalleled access to the subarctic **tundra**, which in summer and autumn is a beautiful medley of colours, the vegetation having been coaxed to riotous life by hours of perpetual daylight. At **Engineer Creek** (194km) – good for fishing – is another basic Yukon government-run campsite (fifteen RV/tent sites; $12), but the only orthodox accommodation on the Dempster within the Yukon is the 32-room *Eagle Plains Hotel* at 369km (ⓣ867/993-2453, ⓔeagleplains@yknet.yk.ca; ❻; camping $10). It has fuel, a garage with mechanic, tyres, lounge and a restaurant.

The **Arctic Circle** (405km) is marked on the Dempster by a battered roadside cairn, and the former summer home of one of the north's premier eccentrics, one Harry Waldron, the self-proclaimed "Keeper of the Arctic Circle". In his late 60s, Harry was wont to sit in a rocking chair in a tuxedo with a glass of champagne and regale all-comers with snippets of Robert Service. An ex-highway worker, he started his act of his own accord, but proved so popular that he was paid by the Yukon government to sit and do his spiel.

Beyond is a Yukon government-run campsite at **Rock River** (447km; seventeen RV sites/three tent sites; $12), and then the road climbs into the **Richardson Mountains** to meet the border of the NWT (465km) before the less-than-arresting flats of the Peel Plateau and Mackenzie River and the run to Inuvik. Note the **time change** at the Yukon–NWT border: NWT time is one hour ahead of Yukon time.

The tiny Gwich'in Dene village of **FORT MCPHERSON** is at 574km, or 115km south of Inuvik, soon after crossing the Peel River. Here, there is a service station and the *Peel River Inns North* (ⓣ867/952-2373, ❼) with eight rooms and a grocery store next door. Nearby is also the unserviced NWT government **campsite**, the *Nutuiluie Territorial Campground*, 10km south of Fort McPherson (23 sites; shelter, toilets and water; $12; June–Sept). It has a small **visitor centre** (daily June to early Sept).

The minuscule settlement of **TSIIGEHTCHIC** (formerly Arctic Red River), at 609km and 80km south of Inuvik, was founded as a mission in 1868 – a red-roofed mission church from 1931 still stands – acquiring a Hudson's Bay post soon after. Since 1996 it has been known by its Dene aboriginal name, which means "mouth of the red-coloured river". On the (relatively) short run on to Inuvik (see p.1048), there's another eleven-site campsite at **VADZAIH VAN TSHIK**, at 692km ($12; water, shelter and toilets).

The Western Arctic

The **Western Arctic** region centres on the planned government-built town of **Inuvik** and encompasses the mighty delta of the **Mackenzie River** – North

America's second longest river – and reaches across the Beaufort Sea to the border with Nunavut. The region also includes part of Victoria Island and Banks Island, the most westerly of Canada's Arctic islands. The delta ranks as one of the continent's great **bird** habitats, with swans, cranes and big raptors amongst the many hundreds of species that either nest or overfly the region during the spring and autumn migration cycles. It also offers the chance of seeing pods of **beluga whales** and other big sea mammals, while local **Inuit** guides on Banks Island should be able to lead you to possible sightings of musk ox, white fox and polar bears.

After Inuvik and the two villages on the short NWT section of the Dempster – Fort McPherson and Tsiigehtchic – the area's other four settlements are **fly-in communities** reached from Inuvik. Two of them, **Aklavik** and **Tuktoyaktuk**, are near – by NWT standards – and are the places to fly out to if you want a comparatively accessible taste of aboriginal northern culture. **Sachs Harbour** (on Banks Island) and **Paulatuk** lie much farther afield, and are bases for more arduous tours into the delta and Arctic tundra. Inuvik, along with Yellowknife and Fort Smith, is one of the key centres of the accessible north, and one of the main places from which to take or plan tours farther afield. **Tour companies** run a wide variety of boat and plane tours to all four destinations (see box below). Having come this far it's well worth taking one of the shorter tours to the fly-in communities for a taste of Arctic life, and to enjoy the superb bird's-eye view of the delta.

Inuvik

INUVIK – "the place of man" – is the farthest north you can drive on a public hwy in North America, unless, that is, you wait for the winter freeze and follow the ice road carved across the frozen sea to the north. Canada's first planned town north of the Arctic Circle, Inuvik is a battered spot begun in 1954 as an

Tours from Inuvik

Most people who come to Inuvik take a **tour** of some description, and despite the remoteness of the Northwest Territories and the isolated nature of its communities, it is remarkably simple – if occasionally rather expensive – to find **tour operators** who offer a wide range of cultural, natural history and other trips. A full list of operators can be found in the *Explorers' Guide to Canada's Northwest Territories* or by visiting the excellent ⓦwww.nwttravel.nt.ca. You can call for further information on ⓣ1-800/661-0788.

Day-trips from Inuvik include tours to the tundra, to Hershel Island, to a traditional bush camp, boat tours on the Mackenzie River, beluga whale-watching, flights over the Mackenzie Delta and trips to the fly-in communities by plane. **Arctic Nature Tours** (ⓣ867/777-3300 or 1-866/TOUR-TUK, ⓦwww.arcticnaturetours.com), with over twenty years' experience of the region, is the main operator and has a special bias towards wildlife: trips include tours to the Babbage River, which if the timing is right also takes in a bird's eye view of the Porcupine caribou herd, and bird and wildlife visits to Hershel Island – a Yukon territorial park in the Beaufort Sea that is still a prime hunting and fishing ground for Inuvialuit. The company also offers guided trips out to Tuktoyaktuk and can arrange tours with guides based in Aklavik, Paulatuk and Ikahuk. Other companies, such as **Midnight Express** (ⓣ867/777-4829), offer boat trips on the Mackenzie River; Arctic Chalet (ⓣ867/777-3535, ⓦwww.arcticchalet.com) organizes dog-sledding excursions and **Western Arctic Adventures & Equipment** (ⓣ867/777-2594) hires out canoes and kayaks.

administrative centre to replace Aklavik, a settlement to the west wrongly thought to be doomed to envelopment by the Mackenzie's swirling waters and shifting mud flats. Finished in 1961, it's a strange melting pot of around 3500 people, with Dene, Métis and Inuvialuit living alongside the trappers, pilots, scientists and frontier entrepreneurs drawn here in the 1970s when a boom followed the oil exploration in the delta. Today the local economy also relies on government jobs, services and the town's role as a supply and communication centre for much of the western Arctic.

Wandering the town provides an eye-opening introduction to the vagaries of northern life, from the strange stilted buildings designed to prevent their heat melting the **permafrost** (which would have disastrous effects on foundations, assuming any could be dug), to the strange pipes, or "utilidors", which snake round the streets carrying water, power and sewage lines – again, to prevent problems with permafrost (the average temperature here is a very chilly -9.7°C). There are also the all-too-visible signs of the **alcoholism** that affects this and many northern communities.

On a happier note, the influence of Inuvialuit people in local political and economic life has increased, to the extent that the **Western Claims Settlement Act** of 1984 saw the government cede titles to various lands in the area, returning control that had been lost to the fur trade, the church, oil companies and national government. A potent symbol of the church's local role in particular resides in the town's most-photographed building, the **Igloo Church**, or Our Lady of Victory (ⓣ867/777-2236), a rather incongruous cultural mix. It's on Mackenzie Road, the main street which runs west to east through town, but isn't always open; ask at the rectory for a glimpse inside and for the paintings by local Inuvialuit artist, Mona Thrasher. Just behind the church, on the corner of Gwich'in Road and Breynat Street, is the **Inuvik Community Greenhouse** (9am–5pm; ⓣ867/777-3267, ⓦwww.inuvikgreenhouse.com), the most northern greenhouse in Northern America, blooming with flowers and fruit and vegetables that would otherwise not survive in the harsh climate. It is housed in a converted hockey arena and hosts a small community market on Saturday. The best place in town to pick up unique pieces by Northern artists – including one-off carvings and clothing made from polar bear, wolf or muskox – is at the not-for-profit **Inuvialuit Regional Corporation Craft Shop**, 3rd Floor 107 Mackenzie Rd (ⓣ867/777-2737). For 56 days from late June, Inuvik revels in 24 hours of sunshine and it is well worth timing your trip to coincide with the **Great Northern Arts Festival** (mid-July; ⓦwww.gnaf.ca) – ten fabulous days of exhibitions and performances courtesy of local and international artists.

Practicalities

Flights from Whitehorse, Dawson City, Old Crow, Fairbanks and other points south (see box, p.1030) operate to Inuvik's **airport** (ⓣ867/777-2467), 12km south of town. Additionally, First Air (ⓣ1-800/267-1247, ⓦwww.firstair.ca) has numerous northern connections, including four flights weekly from Edmonton. Smaller local airlines also use the airport for flights to the "fly-in" communities around Inuvik (see p.1051). A **taxi** (ⓣ867/777-5050) to or from the airport, should cost around $25–30. If you've flown here and want to **rent a car**, then Arctic Chalet Car Rental, 25 Carn St (ⓣ867/777-3535, ⓦwww.arcticchalet.com); Beaufort Delta Rentals, 171 Industrial Rd, (ⓣ867/777-5304, (ⓔnorthwind@northwestel.net) and Norcan, 60 Franklin Rd (ⓣ867/777-2346 or 1-877/298-1338, ⓔinuvik@norcan.yk.ca) all have counters at the airport; however, only the latter allows for drop-offs with Whitehorse the only option.

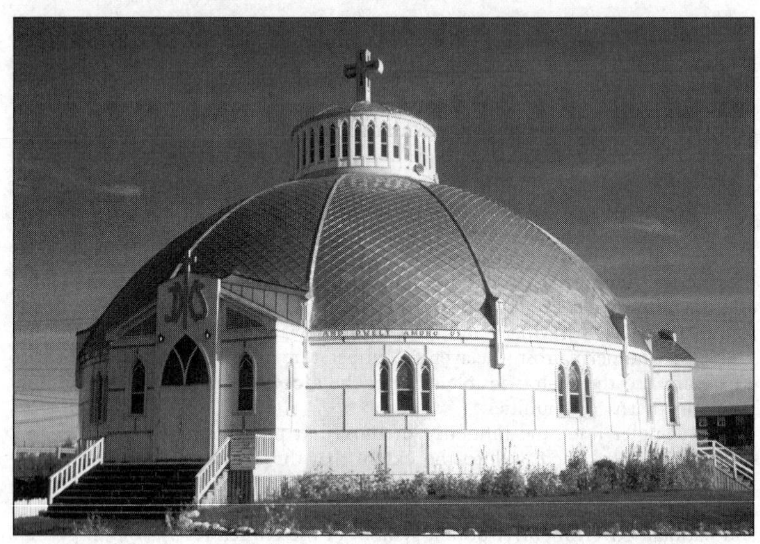

△ Igloo Church in the Inuit town of Inuvik

MGM Services operates a charter **bus** service within Inuvik and the surrounding communities and also runs on demand from Inuvik to Whitehorse (see p.1031); the **Dempster Highway** is open year-round except for brief periods during the November freeze and April thaw.

For information on Inuvik and the region, contact the **Western Arctic Visitor Centre** (daily: July & Aug 9am–8pm, mid-May or June to early Sept 10am–6pm; ⓣ867/777-4727, ⓦwww.nwttravel.nt.ca), located near the entrance to town at the eastern end of Mackenzie Road at the junction with Loucheux, a ten-minute walk from the centre. For town information, visit 2 Firth St (ⓣ867/777-8618, ⓦwww.inuvik.ca & www.inuvikinfo.com). For information on parks and protected areas in the region, contact **Parks Canada** (ⓣ867/777-8800, ⓦwww.parkscanada.gc.ca). In town you can also dig out more background to the area and access the Internet at the **Inuvik Centennial Library**, 100 Mackenzie Rd, (Mon–Thurs 10am–9pm, Fri 10am–6pm, Sat & Sun 1pm–5pm; ⓣ867/777-8620, ⓦwww.inuvik.net/icl), and pick up **maps**, guides, books and charts at the Boreal Bookstore (ⓣ867/777-3748) at 75 Mackenzie Rd.

Accommodation and eating

The best option for budget travellers is the excellent *Arctic Chalet*, a set of cabins, most with kitchenettes, in a natural setting beside a lake, 3km from the centre of town off the approach road at 25 Carn St (ⓣ867/777-3535, ⓦwww.arcticchalet.com; ❷). There are three co-owned **hotels** in town that are similarly pricey: the big *Eskimo Inn* (ⓣ867/777-2801; ❻) in downtown at 133 Mackenzie Rd; the *Finto Motor Inn* (ⓣ867/777-2647; ❻), to the east at 288 Mackenzie Rd next door to the Western Arctic Visitor Centre, with a good restaurant; and the central and newly-renovated *Mackenzie Hotel* (ⓣ867/777-2861; ❼) at 185 Mackenzie Rd. All are online at ⓦwww.inuvikhotels.com. For an alternative downtown hotel, try the *Nova Inn*, 300 Mackenzie Rd (ⓣ867/777-6682, ⓦwww.novahotels.ca; ❻). There are also usually two or three B&B options in town: check with the visitor centre for latest details. The nearest local **campsite**, the *Happy Valley* at the northwest end of town on Franklin Rd off Mackenzie Rd (Ⓣ867/777-3652; $10–20; June–Sept), overlooks the delta and Twin Lakes. The simple and peaceful *Juk Park* site (Ⓣ867/777-3613; $15–20; June-Sept) with pretty views of the delta, is quieter but 6km out of town on the way to the airport.

Eating possibilities are largely confined to hotel dining rooms where you can gorge on arctic char and musk ox; the best is probably *The Peppermill* at the *Finto Motor Inn*, serving wild arctic char for $27 and musk ox burgers for $14, followed by the *Green Briar Dining Room* in the *Mackenzie Hotel.* For coffee, soup and sandwiches, try the *Café Gallery* at 90 Mackenzie St. *The Mad Trapper Pub*, 124 Mackenzie Rd (Mon–Sat 11am–2am), is a locals' hangout that puts on live music, while the *Cabin Lounge* in the *Finto* is a more relaxed and cosy affair.

The fly-in communities

Accessible only by air except in winter, when incredible snow roads are ploughed across the frozen delta, the region's four **fly-in communities** are close to some fascinating and relatively accessible Arctic landscapes, wildlife and cultures. All are served by Inuvik-based **Aklak Air** (Ⓣ867/777-3777, Ⓦwww.inuvialuit.com/aklak) or **Daazraii North-Wright Airways** (Ⓣ867/777-2220), and have simple grocery stores, though their prices make it wise to take in at least some of your own supplies. Some have hotels, but you should be able to camp close to all four; ask permission first at the village head office. The best way to see them is with a tour company from Inuvik (see box, p.1048), but even if you're going under your own steam it's still worth checking with the tour companies for discounted flight-only deals.

Aklavik

AKLAVIK (pop. 730), 50km west of Inuvik on the western bank of the Mackenzie delta, means "Place of the Barren Lands Grizzly Bear". A Hudson's Bay post aimed at the trade in muskrat fur was established here in 1918, though for generations before the region had been the home of Inuvialuit families who once traded and frequently clashed with the Gwich'in of Alaska and the Yukon. Today both live together in a town that melds modern and traditional, and whose inhabitants are proud not to have jumped ship when they were invited to leave their sinking town for Inuvik in the 1950s. Most are happy to regale you with stories of the mysterious "Mad Trapper of Rat River", a crazed drifter (supposedly a former Chicago gangster) who reputedly killed trappers for the gold in their teeth. Questions should really have been asked when he arrived in Fort McPherson and purchased unusually large numbers of guns and ammunition. He then built a cabin-cum-fortress on the delta and shot the constable sent to figure out what was going on. A seven-man posse armed with guns and fistfuls of dynamite were then forced to retreat after a fifteen-hour siege. After fleeing and shooting a Mountie, he grabbed world headlines briefly in 1931 as he managed to elude capture for forty days in the dead of a brutal winter. He was eventually shot on the Eagle River, surrounded by seventeen men and buzzed by a bomb-carrying light plane; he's buried in town in unconsecrated ground. The Hudson's Bay post is still around, together with a former mission church, now a small museum.

For local **information** contact the hamlet office (Ⓣ867/978-2351). **Flights** from Inuvik operate daily ($175 return). There are three stores in town – but no restaurant – and a seven-room B&B boarding house, *Bessie's* (Ⓣ867/978-2461; ❻). You can prepare your own meals here or pay extra for half or full board.

Tuktoyaktuk

TUKTOYAKTUK, or simply Tuk (pop. around 1000), sits on a sandspit on the Beaufort coast about 137km north of Inuvik. It acts as a springboard for oil workers and tourists, both considered outsiders who have diluted the traditional ways of the whale-hunting Karngmalit (or Mackenzie Inuit). The Karngmalit have lived and hunted in small family groups on this fascinating but inhospitable shore for centuries. The settlements name means "Looks Like Caribou", as this was once a hunting ground for *tuktu*, or caribou. Half the families were wiped out in the early twentieth century by an influenza epidemic introduced by outsiders. The Hudson's Bay Company, inevitably, arrived in 1937. Many locals still hunt, fish and trap, but government, tourism and the oil business now pay most wages. This is the most popular tour outing from Inuvik, with trips starting at about $280, a sum worth paying just to enjoy the scenic low-altitude flight up here. Most casual visitors come to see pods of beluga and great bowhead whales, or to look at the world's largest concentration of **pingoes**, 1400 volcano-like hills thrown up by frost heaves across the delta's otherwise treeless flats.

Tuk's only **hotels** are the *Hotel Tuk Inn* (ⓣ867/977-2381; ❼), on the main street near the ocean, and the *Pingo Park Lodge* (ⓣ867/977-2155; ❻); both have restaurants. The Northern supermarket sells groceries. You should be able to **camp** near the beach, but ask first. **Flights** from Inuvik operate three times daily ($280 return). Inuvik's main tour companies come out here, but if you want a local guide, Arctic Tour Company (ⓣ867/977-2230, ⓔrtgruben@permafrost.com) or Ookpik Tours (ⓣ867/977-2170, ⓔookpiktours@yahoo.ca) offer cultural, boat or dog-sledding tours in summer or winter. For further **information** on the settlement, contact the community office (ⓣ867/977-2493).

Paulatuk and Ikahuk

PAULATUK (pop. 318), 400km east of Inuvik, is one of NWT's smallest permanent communities. Situated on a spur between the Beaufort and an inland lake, the settlement was started by the Roman Catholic Mission in 1935 as a communal focus for the semi-nomadic Karngmalit, who despite such paternalism have fought off the adverse effects of missionaries and trader-introduced alcoholism to hang on to some of their old ways. Hunting, fishing and trapping still provide their economic staples, along with handicrafts aimed at the tourists out here mainly for the chance to watch or hunt big game. Key sites for the former activity are the cliffs of the Cape Parry Bird Sanctuary and the **Tuktut National Park** on the Parry Peninsula to the west, a calving ground for the migrating Bluenose caribou herd. Local operators will take you out to both areas, and in spring run trips to look for polar bears on the Amundsen Gulf. The village's name means "place of coal", a reference to the coal seams to the northeast, where the (literally) Smoking Hills take their name from the smouldering coal ignited years ago and is still burning. Aklak Air **flights** operate three times weekly from Inuvik ($850 return). There is one place to **stay**: the ten rooms in the *Parks Canada Visitor Centre Hotel* (ⓣ867/580-3051 or 580-3054; ❽), with common kitchen facilities and a small store. For further **information** on the settlement, contact the hamlet office (ⓣ867/580-3531).

The only settlement on Bank's Island, 520km northeast of Inuvik in the Arctic Ocean, is **IKAHUK** ("Place Where One Crosses Over") or **SACHS HARBOUR** (pop. 119). It was only permanently settled in the late 1920s, and only then by just three Inuvialuit families. Today it supports a handful of self-sufficient Inuit families who survive largely by outfitting hunters and trapping musk ox for food and underfur (*qiviut*), which is spun and woven into

Love in a cold climate

Polar bears and **grizzlies** rarely cross paths in the wild, and when they do, an icy standoff or territorial blows are more likely to ensue than a frigid love affair. But for two particular lonesome predators, steam must have risen on the ice flows around Banks Island, because in spring 2006, a big game hunter from the United States bagged an animal with the creamy fur of a polar bear and the humped back and long claws of a grizzly. This polar-grizzly bear hybrid excited biologists: while the two have been known to interbreed in zoos, this was the first documented case in the wild. Names being bandied around for the new super-predator include 'pizzly', 'grolar bear' and the far more dignified 'nanulak' – a fusion of the Inuit words for polar bear (nanuk) and grizzly (aklak).

clothes that are sold locally. The island is known as one of the north's finest trapping areas, the abundance of white foxes in particular having long attracted the Inuit and other hunters. There's still an abundance of wildlife, including the world's largest grouping of musk ox. If you're feeling bloodthirsty and have $30,000 to spare, contact Kuptana's Outfitters, which specialize in polar bear hunts between January and April. There are also five **rooms** available at *Kuptana's Guest House* (ⓣ867/690-4151; ❼ including meals). Ask first and you should be able to **camp** by the beach. There is no restaurant in the town, just a small grocery store. Two Aklak Air **flights** operate from Inuvik twice a week ($1057 return). For further **information** on the settlement, contact the community office (ⓣ867/690-4351).

The Sahtu

The **Sahtu** embraces the Mackenzie River south of its delta as far as Fort Norman and the great swathe of land across to and including **Great Bear Lake** to the east, the world's eighth largest lake. There's no year-round road access: you either fly in, canoe the Mackenzie – no mean feat – or sign up with **fishing** and hunting charters that boat or fly you into the backcountry, home to some of North America's finest fishing lodges and lakes. Great Bear Lake, to name but one, holds world records for most classes of arctic char and lake trout (the top trout overall – weighing in at 30kg – was caught in 1991). In 1994 a road was built to Wrigley, 225km northwest of Fort Simpson (see p.1056), and plans to push it through to Inuvik will be a long time in the making. In the meantime, most tours operate out of the area's nominal capital at **Norman Wells**, on the banks of the Mackenzie in the lee of the Franklin Mountains, which separate the river and Great Bear Lake. The **Sahtu** has just three other lonely communities: **Fort Good Hope** on the Mackenzie north of Norman Wells; **Déline** (formerly Fort Franklin) on Great Bear Lake, a self-sufficient Dene community of hunters and trappers; and **Colville Lake**, north of Great Bear Lake, a spot which amounts to little more than a few log cabins in the woods.

Norman Wells and the Canol Heritage Trail

Ramshackle **NORMAN WELLS** (pop. 848) once owed its economic well-being to **oil**: the local Dene long knew this region as Le Gohlini – "where the oil is". Explorer Alexander Mackenzie first noticed a yellow liquid seeping from the rocks in 1789, but the black gold was only rediscovered in 1919 after Dene locals led geologists to the same spot. Drilling and refinement on an industrial scale began in 1932 and increased in World War II when the American government sponsored the building of the **Canol Pipeline** to supply the Alaska Hwy – now long abandoned, though for a while the town continued to pump about 30,000 barrels a day through a pipeline to Zama, Alberta. Though the pipeline was abandoned in 1945, oil fields in the area remain important, producing around 10 million barrels of crude oil per year. You can follow the oil and Canol story in the **Norman Wells Historical Centre** (July & Aug daily noon–6pm, but check current opening; free; ⓣ867/587-2415), filled with photographs, modest displays and odd memorabilia. Alongside, the settlement's uniquely ecumenical **church** does double duty: Catholics sit on one side, Protestants on the other. These days the Canol's old route has become the **Canol Heritage Trail** an increasingly popular **long-distance wilderness footpath**. Logistics are a problem. Covering the 372-km wilderness trail from Norman Wells to the Canol Road above Ross River in the Yukon can take three to four weeks and it ranks among the world's tougher treks. The mountains east of Norman Wells contain some of the NWT's bleaker and more spectacular ranges, and good outdoor skills are a must unless you sign up for a tour.

Practicalities

For **flights**, Canadian North (ⓣ867/587-2361 in Norman Wells or 1-800/661-1505, ⓦwww.canadiannorth.com) flies daily to Norman Wells from Inuvik and Yellowknife, Edmonton and Calgary. Within the area North-Wright Air flies to Inuvik (ⓣ867/587-2288 or 1-800/661-0702, ⓦwww.north-wrightairways.com) and offers sightseeing flights.

The **airport** is a twenty-minute walk from the centre of the village, which amounts to a bank, post office, four motels, supermarket and plenty of tumble-down housing. The local **visitor centre** is on the corner of Forestry Rd and Mackenzie Drive (ⓣ867/587-3700). The *Mackenzie Valley Hotel* (ⓣ867/587-2511, ⓦwww.mackenzievalleyhotel.com; ❺) has its own restaurant. If you want to spend time on the river, try Mountain River Outfitters (ⓣ867/587-2698, ⓦwww.mountainriver.nt.ca), which runs **day-trips** to Fort Good Hope and the Arctic Circle (mid-June to mid-Sept), provides support for hikers on the Canol trail and also **rents canoes** and other outdoor equipment. For details of the many fishing-charter companies, enquire locally or obtain the *Explorers' Guide* (see box, p.1-57) from a Canadian national tourist office before you leave home.

The Deh-Cho Trail

Northern Alberta and the adjoining southern portion of the NWT were first opened up to trade courtesy of the mighty rivers that flow through these parts. Traders, particularly the Hudson's Bay Company, used routes along the Peace,

Hay, Slave, Liard and Mackenzie rivers to maintain remote outposts and foster commercial relations with the natives. Some of these far-flung communities have survived to the present day, and the circuit of roads that connect them has become known as the **Deh-Cho Trail,** which is furiously promoted by local tourist forces (Ⓦwww.dehchotravel.com) in a bid to lure travellers away from the Alaska Highway.

The southern parts of this 1,800-km loop weave their way through an all but uninhabited landscape of rippling hills, rivers, lakes, lonely farms and open prairie. However, most of the route passes through a monotonous mantle of the boreal forest and after hours of motoring through it, the region's very modest communities appear as exceptional highlights. In truth, they offer very few attractions worthy of a stop. The sheer untrammelled wilderness is a Godsend for adventurers, especially **fishers** or **boaters.** It's easy to break personal catch records in pristine waters that are replete with healthy stocks of trout and grayling. Kayakers and canoers will find extraordinary rapids and waterfalls, and long-distance lake and river systems invite expeditions. But for most outdoor enthusiasts, the main reason to travel the Deh-Cho Trail is to reach a trio of side-trips off it: the impressive wilderness of **Nahanni National Park**; the bison and crane sanctuary **Wood Buffalo National Park** (see p.1062); and the rough-edged **Yellowknife** (see p.1964), one of Canada's most accessible and reliable places to enjoy the Northern Lights (see p.997).

Officially, the Deh-Cho loop incorporates the initial leg of the **Alaska Highway** (see p.1018) before branching off near Fort Nelson (see p.1020) onto the **Liard Highway**. This a long, largely gravel road passing within sight of Nahnni National Park and close to **Fort Simpson**, from where the **Mackenzie Highway** (Hwy 1) pushes its way East and then South beyond the Alberta border (as Hwy 35) to **Peace River.** A number of hwys there allow you to complete the loop back to BC.

Daily long-haul Greyhound (Ⓦwww.greyhound.ca) **buses** run up the eastern side of the Deh-Cho Trail, connecting Edmonton with Yellowknife, via Peace River and Hay River. These bus services are supplemented by the Hay River-based Frontier Coachlines, 16 102nd St (Ⓣ867/874-2566), which runs buses to Fort Providence, Yellowknife, Fort Smith and Fort Simpson. Because the roads barely merit travelling for their own sake, **flying** is a tempting time-saving option, though it is expensive unless you organize flights well in advance. If you decide to **drive**, remember to fuel up at virtually every community you pass and, if you are going to camp, prepare for the unwelcome nocturnal attention of bears.

The Liard Highway

Beginning 35 km north of Fort Nelson, the **Liard Highway** – or BC Hwy 77 which becomes NWT Hwy 7 – pushes north through a mundane wilderness of boreal forest to the regional center **Fort Simpson**. En route it passes the hamlet of **Fort Liard** (fuel available) and offers great views of Nahanni National Park from the roadside **Blackstone Territorial Park** (campsites $15) where there's also a couple of short hiking trails. The road conditions are generally very good even though the highway's surface is gravel for much of its length. Icy winter conditions pose a threat as do bison that can wander onto the road at any time of year.

Fort Simpson

All means of access and facilities – including tour operators and outfitters – for the Nahanni National Park reside in busy **FORT SIMPSON** (pop. 1269), 150km to the east at the confluence of the Liard and Mackenzie, two of North America's greatest rivers. This spot has been inhabited for 9000 years by the Slavey peoples and their ancestors, making this the longest continually inhabited region in the NWT. The North West Company established a fur post here in 1804 which was renamed Fort Simpson in 1821, but equal to its fur-trading potential was the settlement's role as a staging point for supply boats using the Mackenzie. The inevitable missions arrived in 1858 and 1894, which were so often the bane of indigenous communities. Recently the area has become an important base for oil exploration projects along the Mackenzie; a major regional administrative centre; and a bustling summer base for visitors organising trips and tours and to the interior. Most of the town's resources is found along the main street, **100th Street**, effectively a continuation of the main road through town. Before this hwy was built, the main street was the nearly parallel Mackenzie Drive on the lakefront. At its southern end you'll find the site of the old Hudson's Bay Company post and an area known as the "Flat" or the Papal Grounds, whose tepee and other developments dates from the papal visit here on September 20, 1987 (this area was inhabited until disastrous floods in 1963). A light plane and float-plane airstrip lies just to the northwest of downtown, while the bulk of the outfitters' offices are gathered north of the strip at the top of Mackenzie Drive.

Practicalities

You can get to Fort Simpson by **air** twice a day from Yellowknife using either Air Tindi (Ⓣ867/669-8260 or 1-888/545-6794, Ⓦwww.airtindi.com) or First Air (Ⓣ613/839-3340 or 1-800/267-1247, Ⓦwww.firstair.ca); the latter also provides a service to Whitehorse. The main **airport** is 12km south of town. The **visitor centre** (May–Sept daily 11am–7pm, Oct–April Mon–Fri 1pm–5pm; summer Ⓣ867/695-3182, winter Ⓣ867/695-3005, Ⓦwww.fortsimpson.com) lies at the south entrance to town.

If you're hoping to **stay** in town, be sure to book ahead. The town's hotels are on, or just off 100th Street and include the *Nahanni Inn* (Ⓣ867/695-2201; ❻), a standard motel with coffee shop and dining room; the smaller *Maroda Motel* (Ⓣ867/695-2602; ❻), a couple of blocks south, half of whose units have fully equipped kitchenettes. Finally, 4km southeast of town along the Mackenzie Highway, there's the idyllic *Bannockland B&B* (Ⓣ867/695-3337, Ⓦwww.bbcanada.com/1831.html; ❺). The five rooms have private bathrooms and share a cosy lounge; free pickup is offered from the airport. To **eat**, try the dining room of the *Nahanni Inn*, or the *Sub-Arctic* opposite the visitor centre on 100th Street. The local **campsite** – operated on a first-come, first-served basis, but large enough to always have space –is just to the southwest of the Papal Grounds with lots of space, showers and firewood. The cost is $15 nightly for tent sites, $20 for electrical hook-ups.

The Mackenzie Highway

Though it takes its name from the lightly-used leg that runs parallel to the Mackenzie River, the **Mackenzie Highway** is far more important for the section that hooks south through northern Alberta – providing the vital link for travellers driving between Edmonton, Yellowknife and Wood Buffalo Park – to

Nahanni National Park

With gorges deeper than the Grand Canyon and waterfalls twice the height of Niagara, the vast **Nahanni National Park** (Ⓦwww.pc.gc.ca/pn-np/nt/nahanni/index_e.asp) ranks as one of the finest national parks in North America and one of the most rugged wilderness areas anywhere in the world. Located close to the Yukon border in the heart of the Mackenzie Mountains, it surrounds the **South Nahanni River**, a renowned 322-kilometre stretch of water whose white-water torrents, pristine mountains and 1200-metre-deep canyons have attracted the world's most eminent explorers and the ultimate thrill-seeking canoeists (the river is one of the best white-water runs in the world). Unless you fit one of these categories, however, or can afford to fork out for **guided trips** by boat or sightseeing by air – well worth the money, even if you're only out in the wilderness for a short time – there's no way of getting close to the best areas, even by backpacking: the park is totally roadless and totally wild. Also note that the popularity of trips means that there's a **reservation** and **fee** system for people wishing to use the river: the day-use fee is $19.80, the reservation fee for overnight trips $125, and there are strict quotas on numbers visiting the park, so check the latest details whether you intend to visit independently or with a tour. For full information, contact the **Nahanni National Park Reserve Office** (Ⓣ867/695-3151, Ⓔnahanni.info@pc.gc.ca) or visitor centre in Fort Simpson.

As for **tours**, the sky's the limit. Operators in Fort Simpson cater to all levels of demand, from day-trippers wanting air tours of the big set-pieces to self-contained canoers and walkers on month-long expeditions who require no more than a drop-off or pick-up by air. Even self-sufficient explorers should note that it saves considerable time, hassle and money to take a three- or four-week tour with a licensed outfitter in Fort Simpson.

For day-trips to the spectacular **Virginia Falls**, the most popular day outing in the park (usually with 2hr on the ground), contact Wolverine Air (Ⓣ867/695-2263 or 1-888/695-2263, Ⓦwww.wolverineair.com) which will take groups of three people for a 5 hour flight in a float-plane to Nahanni for $1200, with stops at Virginia Falls and at the idyllic Little Doctor Lake at the edge of the mountain range. Simpson Air (Ⓣ867/695-2505, Ⓦwww.simpsonair.com), whose offices are almost next door to Wolverine on the southwest edge of town – offer a slightly cheaper service but very similar trips. Simpson air also offers a flight in conjunction with a cabin rental on Little Doctor Lake – two or three days in romantic seclusion cost $1500 for two; a week $2400. Which of the day trips you choose is likely to depend most availability. Advance bookings are highly recommended, but if you are in a party of less than three and turn up on spec, contact the airlines and ask to be put on a waiting list – they will contact you if they find others to fill a trip.

For rafting on the rivers, from one ($3860) to three ($5700) weeks contact Nahanni River Adventures (Ⓣ867/668-3180 or 1-800/297-692, Ⓦwww.nahanni.com). Other outfits include Nahanni Wilderness Adventure (Ⓣ403/678-3374 or 1-888/897-5223, Ⓦnahanniwild.com). Various other tours of the region – that run into hundreds, rather than thousands of dollars – and accommodation in a pleasant backcountry lodge is offered by North Nahanni Naturalist Lodge (Ⓣ1-867/695-2116 or 1-888/880-6665, Ⓦwww.nnnlodge.ca).

its "mile zero" at **Peace River**. Though generally in excellent condition, this road begun after World War II is about as dull as northern drives get: the hwy plows through a tight corridor of seemingly endless evergreens in which views rarely open out and little tempts you to get out and stretch your legs. The notable exception are the short and well-marked trails that head to occasional highway-side waterfalls that have led local tourism promoters to hopefully dub the hwy the Waterfall Route.

The only stop of interest on the stretch of the Mackenzie Hwy between Fort Simpson (see p.1056) and the junction with Hwy 3 to Yellowknife is **Sambaa Deh Falls Territorial Park**; 150km east of Fort Simpson. You can camp (sites $15) here and from the campground, its' a ten-minute hike on an unmarked trail that heads upstream beside the river to a broad-shouldered, pounding waterfall. More impressive is the waterfall further downstream – in view of the hwy and the campground turnoff – where waters plummet dramatically into a narrow gorge.

More waterfalls dot the road beyond the junction with Hwy 3 to Yellowknife, where the Mackenzie Hwy is paved for its remaining 186km journey to the Alberta border. The most impressive of these falls are the 33m-high **Alexandra Falls**, located 72km shy of the Alberta. In 2003 Ed Lucero plunged his kayak over these falls and, in surviving, made Alexandra the world's highest falls successfully negotiated by kayak.

Practicalities

Services along the Mackenzie are few and far between. You can pitch a tent or park an RV for $15/$20 at **Lady Evelyn Falls Territorial Park** near Kakiska and the junction to Hwy 3; at Louise Falls, by Alexandra Falls, as well as at the **60th Parallel Visitors' Center** (mid-May to mid-Sept 8.30am–8.30pm, ⓣ867/920-1021) which lies hard on the Alberta border. The only motel is the basic Twin Falls Inn (ⓣ867-984-3711; $90) in the village of Enterprise; its restaurant Winnie's serves most of the meals in town. A better selection of food and accommodation can be had 43km away at **Hay River** – the gateway to both the **Great Slave Lake**, the third largest in North America, and to **Fort Smith** and **Wood Buffalo National Park** (see p.1062).

South of Alberta's provincial border the Mackenzie Hwy becomes **Highway-35** and a string of campsites provides the only **accommodation** en-route to the town of **High Level**. The aboriginal hamlets of Meander River, Steen River and Indian Cabins offer only food and fuel. Located 191km from the NWT border, High Level has a glut of hotels, yet from here south to Manning – the next motel cluster – only a couple of basic campsites and the odd wind-blown store disturb the peace. Official tenting spots are *Notikewin Provincial* (ⓣ780/554-1348; $15; May–Oct), 30km east of Hwy 35 on Hwy 692 – look for the junction 37km north of Manning, and the 49-site *Twin Lakes Provincial Recreation Area* (ⓣ780/554-1348; $15; May–Sept), a total of 65km north of Manning on Hwy 35.

Hay River

HAY RIVER (pop. 3876) is a typical no-nonsense northern town. Well situated on Great Slave Lake at the mouth of the Hay River, it's been inhabited for thousands of years by Dene people. White settlers had put it on the map by 1854, but the inevitable Hudson's Bay Company trading post only arrived in 1868, and it wasn't until the 1940s – when the Mackenzie Hwy was completed, oil and gas exploration began in earnest, and the railway arrived in order to carry zinc ore from local mines – that the town became an important transport centre. It's now also one of the most important **ports** in the north, shipping freight up the Mackenzie in huge barges to provide a precarious lifeline for High Arctic communities as far away as Inuvik and Tuktoyaktuk. If you're stuck in town, the best way to kill time is to wander the wharves where piles of supplies compete for space with tugs, barges, huge dredges and the town's big fishing fleet.

The town divides into the New Town on the west bank of the Hay River – home to most of the motels, restaurants and key buildings – and the somewhat moribund Vale Island across a bridge to the north. Vale Island centres on Mackenzie Drive and is home to the wharves, airport, the remnants of the old town (badly damaged by flooding in 1963), the campsite and a series of passable and popular **beaches** (the last a total of 7km from the centre of New Town). The best sand is near the campsite on the northeast side of the island at the end of 106th Avenue.

Practicalities

In addition to Greyhound and Frontier Coachlines bus services (see p.1055) Hay River is also connected to the outside world via regular flights to Yellowknife with Buffalo Airways, First Air and Canadian North; the latter also provides three flights per week to Edmonton. The **visitor centre** (mid-May to mid-Sept daily 9am–9pm; ⓣ867/874-3180) is on Hwy 2 south of the New Town centre on the corner with McBryan Drive. There's ample **accommodation**, much of it less expensive than elsewhere in the north. An economical but very pleasant choice is the beach-side *Harbour House Bed & Breakfast* (ⓣ867/874-2233; ❹) on Vale Island. But if you'd rather be close to downtown try the *Migrator Hotel*, 912 Mackenzie Hwy (ⓣ867/874-6792; ❺), just north of downtown, between New Town and the Vale Island bridge and five minutes' walk from the town centre. For the most comfort after a long haul, try the downtown *Ptarmigan Inn*, 10 J. Gagnier St (ⓣ867/874-6781 or 1-800/661-0842, ⓦwww.ptarmiganinn.com; ❻), which has a fitness centre, sauna, and sports bar. For **food** try *Salt 'n' Pepper*, 66 Woodland Drive (ⓣ867/875-4100), which is open until 10pm most nights and specialises in good, and inexpensive Cantonese food. You can **camp** near the beach on Vale Island at the *Hay River Campground* ($15; mid-May to mid-Sept).

High Level

You're only going to stop in **HIGH LEVEL** – 191km south of the NWT border and 250km north of Peace River – if you want a place to bed down. The huge stock of motel accommodation here means that room rates are very reasonable, with most motels charging around $70; but beware, many of the town's thousand guest rooms are block-booked far in advance by seasonal workers employed in the region's logging, oil and gas industries. If you do end up over-nighting here, it's worth popping into the **tourist office** (summer daily 9am–5pm; rest of year Mon–Fri 9am–5pm; ⓣ780/926-4811) alongside Hwy 35 at the southern edge of town. The small museum ($1) in the back of the same building is provides insight into the pioneering history of the area – a story told via vintage photographs and the reconstructed interiors of a trapper's cabin and a general store.

Most of the town's rooms overlook Hwy 35, with the cheapest among them usually at the 75-unit *Four Winds Hotel* (ⓣ780/926-3736; ❷), while the *Stardust Motor Inn*, 9704 97th St (ⓣ780/926-4222; ❺) is a good bit smarter, even if few real extra facilities are offered. Top-flight in town, but with barely more expensive rates, is the *Super 8*, 9502-114 Ave (ⓣ780/841-3448; ❻) which boasts a pool, high-speed Internet access and complimentary breakfast. The best option for **campers** is the forty-site *Aspen Ridge Campground* (April–Oct; ⓣ780/926-4540; sites $15), 3km south of the centre on the main road (Hwy 35). Most motels have adjoining **restaurants** with the sort of filling pan-North American specials you'd probably crave after a day of logging or rough-necking.

Among them the *Flamingo Inn*, 9802 97th St, is particularly popular, though most locals agree the steaks at the *Stardust Steakhouse,* in the Stardust Motor Inn are the best in town.

Peace River

If you're travelling under your own steam you'll probably end up staying overnight in **PEACE RIVER**, 486km from Edmonton. The largest town in the region, it has a handful of standard **motels**: probably the best choice – for convenience, value and quality – is the large *Traveller's Motor Hotel,* on the northern edge of downtown at 9510 100th St (Ⓣ780/624-3621 or 1-800/661-3227, Ⓦwww.travellershotel.com; ❹). Located a block north, the **tourist office** operates out of the old station building at 9309 100th St (summer daily 10am–6pm; Ⓣ780/624-2044). For **campers** there's the 84-site *Peace River Lion's Club* campsite with showers (Ⓣ780/624-2120; $13; May–Oct) at Lion's Club Park on the west side of the river. As for **restaurants**, the *Su Casa Café* tucked away on 3-9720 94th St, near the river, has Mexican meals; the *Sunflower Cafe,* 4 100th St, serves soups and sandwiches.

Fort Smith and Wood Buffalo National Park

Beginning near Hay River (see p.1058), lonely Hwy 5 is the only overland route to **Fort Smith**, which in turn is the only conceivable base for exploring the adjacent **Wood Buffalo National Park**. The drive's an easy 280km haul through boreal forest and swampy muskeg, with the last 150km running within park boundaries on the park's only paved road. Traffic along the way is extraordinarily light, since there's not much to draw anyone to either Fort Smith nor, for all its massive expanse, Wood Buffalo – hardly a top-flight park by Canada's extraordinary standards. Even so it's easy to spend an enjoyable couple of days touring both, investigating the few footpaths, and watching bison that are easily seen at the roadsides, more often than not wallowing in dust to escape the same ferocious local mosquitoes that force visitors to use repellent liberally. Even Fort Smith, modest as it is, is a likeable base to soak up some Northern atmosphere, including in its good local history museum.

Fort Smith

Located just over Alberta's northern border in the Northwest Territories **FORT SMITH** (pop. 2514) developed along one of the major water routes to the north and is virtually the only settlement for several hundred kilometres East and north. Its site was particularly influenced by the need to avoid a violent set of rapids, an interruption to waterborne transport that required a 25-km portage. The Dene natives' name for the area, not surprisingly, was Thebacha, meaning "along the rapids". In 1872 the Hudson's Bay Company built a post, Fort Fitzgerald, at the rapids' southern end. Two years later Fort Smith was established at their northern limit. In time the settlement became the administrative capital of the NWT, a function it fulfilled until the federal government promoted Yellowknife to the role in 1967.

The disappearance of government jobs has left its mark on the town, as has the opening of the all-weather road between Hay River and Yellowknife, which captured a lot of the freight that used to pass through the region by boat. Nonetheless, there are a handful of things to see around town before visiting the park. The **Northern Life Museum**, 110 King St (daily June–Aug 10am–7pm; Sept–May 10am–5pm; free; ⓣ867/872-2859), is worth a look for its excellent collection of traditional artefacts, crafts, fur-trading memorabilia and archive photographs. If the small amount of traditional art here whets your appetite, then ask at the Visitor Information Centre for the names and numbers of local artists. Of the eight or so commercial artists with workshops in town, Sonny MacDonald (ⓣ867/872-5935) is one of the most interesting for his inventive carvings based on natural themes. While in town you might also want to glance at the old **Fort Smith Mission Historic Park**, on the corner of Mercredi Ave and Breynat St, former home to the region's bishop, who for years took on many of Fort Smith's bureaucratic responsibilities.

If you fancy a short **hike** or two and a chance to see some of the region's famous white pelicans then try exploring the series of rapids beside town and upstream. All are linked by the Trans Canada Trail, but can be visited from trail-heads that start beside the road to Fort Fitzgerald southeast of town. A map is available from the visitor information centre though the trails themselves are easy enough to follow. **Mountain Rapids** – about 8km southeast of Fort Smith – are of particular interest as the location of a white pelican colony; while **Pelican Rapids** – 12km from Fort Smith and a 45-min walk through dense vegetation from the road – are most memorable for to their thundering bulk. They're readily viewed at close quarters from tongues of granite Canadian shield that jut into the centre of the watercourse.

Arrival and Information

The easiest access to Fort Smith and the park is **by plane**, but isn't cheap with prices of around $260 from Yellowknife and almost twice that from Edmonton. Fort Smith airport is 5km west of town on McDougal Road. If you need a taxi from the airport or around town call Portage Cabs (ⓣ867/872-3333), and for **car rental** contact J&M Enterprises, on Portage Avenue (Mon–Sat 8am–6pm; ⓣ867/872-2221). Frontier Coachlines (see p.1055) runs three per week **buses** from Hay River – timed to connect with Greyhound services from Edmonton.

Fort Smith's Visitor **Information Centre**, 108 King St (daily 9am–10pm; ⓣ867/872-3065, ⓦwww.virtualfortsmith.com or www.town.fort-smith.nt.ca) is in the recreation complex, beside the Northern Life Museum. The excellent **National Park Visitor Centre** and headquarters is a short distance west at 149 McDougal Rd (mid-Jun to early Sept Mon–Fri 9am–noon & 1pm–5pm, Sat & Sun 1pm–5pm; late Sept to mid-June Mon–Fri 9am–noon & 1pm–5pm; ⓣ867/872-7900 or 872-2349, ⓦwww.parkscanada.gc.ca/buffalo). Further **maps and guides** can be found among the cluster of shops at the intersection of McDougal Road and Portage Avenue in the well-stocked North of 60 Books (ⓣ867/872-2606).

Accommodation and eating

It's advisable to prebook **accommodation** in summer. The town's hotels are similar in terms of quality, though the larger *Pelican Rapids Inn*, 152 McDougal Rd (ⓣ867/872-2789; ❻), built in 1997, is fractionally more convenient at the centre of downtown and is home to the town's only **restaurant**. The alternative is the *Portage Inn*, 72 Portage Rd (ⓣ867/872-2276, ⓔportageinn@auroranet.nt.ca; ❺), where all units have kitchenettes. Lower prices can be found in the *Thebacha B&B River Trails North*, 53 Portage Ave (ⓣ867/872-2060, ⓦwww.taigatour.com; ❹), which has two doubles and two singles (no smoking and no alcohol). There's a public **campground** in *Queen Elizabeth Territorial Park* alongside the Slave River on the northern edge of town; sites cost $20.

Wood Buffalo National Park

Straddling the border between Alberta and the Northwest Territories, **WOOD BUFFALO NATIONAL PARK** is bigger than Switzerland, making it Canada's largest national park and the world's second-largest protected environment (the largest is in Greenland). Though wild and vast in extent, the park is limited to low hills, lakes, grasslands, boreal forest, salt plains and marsh. These drain into the Peace and Athabasca rivers and then into Lake Claire, forming one of the world's largest freshwater deltas in the process. To the casual visitor the landscape is likely to be a disappointment – there are no real "sights" or scenic set pieces to compare with, say, the Rockies – but for dedicated naturalists, or those who are prepared to spend time (and money) letting the landscapes get under their skin, the park holds much of interest, embracing North America's finest karst (limestone) scenery, classic swaths of coniferous forest and rare salt-plain habitats.

The park was created in 1922 to protect an estimated 1500 wood bison, but since then it has also become a vital refuge for around fifty other species of mammal, including black and grizzly bear and lynx. Moreover, the Peace–Athabasca river

The Wood Bison of Wood Buffalo

The largest land mammal in North America, the **Wood Bison** – commonly called the Wood Buffalo – is the longer-legged, darker and more robust relative of the plains bison. Like the plains bison, the wood bison were also mercilessly hunted to the brink of extinction, albeit a a couple of decades later in the 1890s which helped prompt the creation of **Wood Buffalo National Park**. Soon after its designation, local herds were bolstered in a dubious way by the introduction of some 6000 plains bison whose grazing lands in a former National Park near Wainright, Alberta, were appropriated for a firing range.

As a result, most of the bison in Wood Buffalo National Park today are hybrids, but an even more contentious consequence was the spread of tuberculosis and brucellosis – already rampant in the plains herd – to animals throughout the park. This has created a long-simmering row between conservationists and Alberta's beef lobby, with some (government) scientists asserting that the only way to prevent the spread of the diseases (which they claim are highly infectious) to elk and to Alberta's valuable beef herds is to kill all the bison off. Scientists opposed to this plan point out that the herd has been infected since the 1920s, yet the disease has survived by internal regulation and natural balance; with animals showing no outward signs of the diseases or of suffering. Furthermore, there has never been an instance of disease transferring itself to humans. Most locals, who are largely opposed to the cull, argue that killing or inoculating every animal would be a daunting task, given the immensity of the animals' range, and that, if even one was missed, the whole cull would be fruitless as disease would presumably erupt afresh when the herd regenerated.

Despite some attempts to small-scale culling and vaccination in the 1950s, there's been little recent action. However, the two disease-free northern herds (the only wild pure-bred Wood Bison) – that range around the Mackenzie Bison Sanctuary (which surrounds much of Hwy 3 to Yellowknife) and the Liard Hwy near Fort Simpson (see p.1056) – are kept that way by constant vigilance in a bison no-go area: any bison found here, disease free or not, are shot. Meanwhile, as a long-term management solution is debated, the park's buffalo – now around 6000 in all – continue to nibble contentedly.

delta in the park's southeast corner boasts 227 species of wildfowl – no fewer than four major migration routes cross the area. The world's only river rookery of rare **white pelicans** is here and the park is the last refuge of the critically endangered **whooping crane** – re-discovered in a remote part of the park in 1954 after it was assumed that hunters supplying the decorative demands of European aristocrats had made them extinct. Though there were only 21 of the majestic birds in the park in 1954, there are over 230 today – about half the total world population (most of the others being in captivity). Each boasts a 2.4-metre wingspan and nests far from any human contamination on the park's northern fringes. The presence of the cranes, not to mention that of bison and the various rare and unspoiled habitats, saw the park declared a UNESCO World Heritage Site in 1983. A further claim to fame for the park is as the most northerly breeding site for **garter snakes**. Able to hibernate in the warm cracks in the limestone bedrock during the winter, in spring these snakes join dozens of others for mating to create an unforgettable writhing mass.

Exploring the park

The best way to absorb the landscape of Wood Buffalo National Park is probably from the air or on a tour (see below), or by paddling a canoe around the almost limitless Athabasca and Peace river system that was once the main route for trade from the south. The easiest and cheapest way to see some of the park independently is to spend a long day driving a clockwise loop through the northeastern corner of the park from Fort Smith. Completing this loop relies on the use of a sandy dirt road called Parson's Lake Road. It is essential that you check on both its current condition and its suitability for your vehicle at the park visitor centre in Fort Smith.

To follow this loop, drive southwest from Fort Smith on Hwy 5, turning off at 8km to the south, following the road to Peace Point. Possible stops along here include the **Salt River Day Use Area** (after 15km), where you can hike the 750m Karstland Loop that acts as an introduction to both the local geology and the straightforward 16.5km day hike that also starts here. Stop at a small roadside parking lot about 3km southwest along the road from the Salt River Day Use Area to reach the scenic highlight of this loop: **Grosbeak Lake** – a bleak salt lake flecked with salt-etched rocks on the southern side of the loop. It can be visited in an hour-long roundtrip hike. The intersection of the main park road with the **Parson's Lake Road** comes after another 10km. This 57km-long, sandy and often impassable road is the best place to see bison, with good chances of spotting bears along the way too. The road finishes in a junction with a dirt road (close to Hwy 5) which you can follow to the **Salt Plains Lookout** for fantastic views of the park and the chance to wander across these remarkable plains. From here the 30km back to Fort Smith on the sealed Hwy 5 quickly completes the loop.

The best way to see the park and its wildlife is to sign up for a **tour**. The only licensed operator is Taiga Tour Company (ⓣ867/872-2060, ⓦwww.taigatour.com), which offers a full spectrum of paddling and birding tours from $934 per person including three nights' accommodation. Eleven-day expeditions can be arranged by snowmobile, dog sled or canoe. Cheaper and far quicker are the **sightseeing flights** offered by Northwestern Air (ⓣ1-877/872-2216, ⓦwww.nwal.ca) and Reliance Airways (ⓣ867/872-4004, ⓦwww.relianceairways.ca). Prices start at around $60 per person for half an hour.

Staying in the park

If you want to overnight in the park choose between the park's only serviced **campground** (sites $14) at Pine Lake, backcountry camping, or staying in a cabin at the remote Sweetgrass Station. Camping at Pine Lake is the easiest option, and gives you access to its day use area, pleasant beach and lakeshore hiking trails. Backcountry camping is allowed anywhere in the park that's at least 1500m from Pine Lake or any road or trail. Be sure to get advice about good spots and precautions from the park visitor centre first.

The park's most-visited backcountry destination is the meadowland and delta habitat at **Sweetgrass Station**, 12km south of the Peace River. Built in 1954 to cull and vaccinate diseased bison (see box, p.1062), the area is a prime spot from which to watch bison and admire the wildlife of the Lake Claire region. You can stay in the cabin (bunks) here free of charge, but must first register with the park visitor centre in Fort Smith. Drinking water comes from the river and needs to be boiled and treated. To get here you'll need to canoe or pay heftily for a charter flight with Northwestern Air or Reliance Airways (see p.1063).

Yellowknife

Nothing about **YELLOWKNIFE** – named after the copper knives of aboriginal Slavey people – can hide the fact that it's a city that shouldn't really be here. Already surreally inappropriate in a region of virtual wilderness, it's also not really worth the 640km round-trip drive from the Mackenzie Hwy to see. But since it's the main transport hub for flights throughout the NWT and Nunavut you might find yourself passing though; if so, there are plenty of diversions for a day or two, as well as a mind-boggling selection of canoe routes and fishing spots.

Yellowknife's high-rise core of offices and government buildings exists to administer the NWT and support a population of some 20,000 in a region whose resources – despite the recent discovery of diamonds to the north – should by all rights support only a small town. Even the Hudson's Bay Company closed its trading post here as early as 1823 on the grounds of economics and, except for traces of gold found by prospectors on the way to the Klondike in 1898, the spot was a forgotten backwater until the advent of commercial gold and uranium mining in the 1930s. This prompted the growth of the **Old Town** on an island and rocky peninsula on Great Slave Lake, and then in 1947 the **New Town** on the sandy plain behind it. In 1967, the year a road to the outside world was completed (Edmonton is 1524km away by car), Yellowknife replaced Ottawa as the seat of government for the NWT. Oiled by bureaucratic profligacy and the odd gold mine, the city has blossomed ever since, if that can be said for so dispersed and unprepossessing a place.

Much of Yellowknife's accessible hinterland is an ideal playground for paddlers and naturalists, or for hunters on the trail of the region's 400,000-strong herd of caribou. Yellowknife itself has its high points if you manage to be in town during one of its **festivals**. One of the most intriguing is the **Caribou Carnival** (Ⓦwww.cariboucarnival.com) in late March, whose attractions include dog-sled racing, bingo on ice, igloo building, flour packing and – best of all – "ugliest truck" competitions. **Raven Mad Daze**, a midsummer celebration taking place each June 21, is celebrated with lots of street events, drinking and high spirits through 24 hours of daylight. More cerebral and fascinating is the mid-July **Folk on the Rocks** (Ⓦwww.folkontherocks.com), when folk singers from across Canada and the US meet Inuit and Dene folk singers, folk dancers and the famous Inuit "throat singers" in an amazing medley of world music.

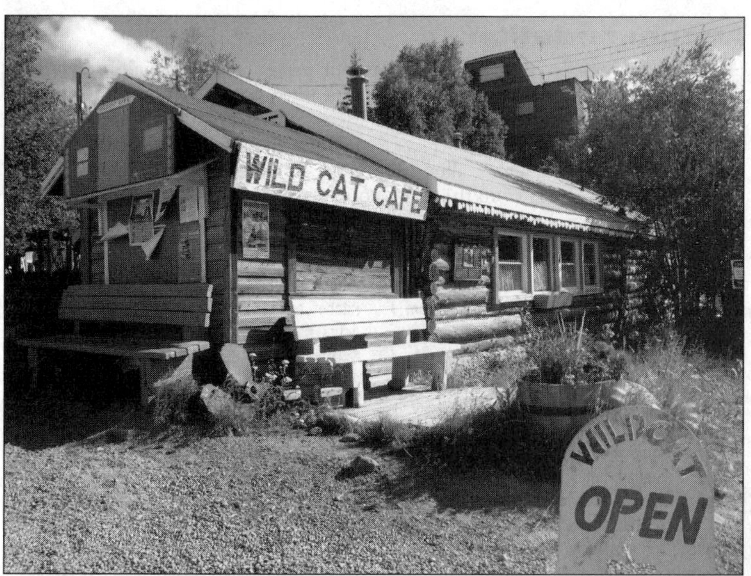

△ Cafe in Yellowknife

Arrival and information

There are regular Canadian North and First Air **flights** to Edmonton, with Canadian North also flying to Calgary. Meanwhile numerous smaller airlines serve most NWT and many Nunavut destinations. Yellowknife's **airport** is 5km west of the city on Hwy 3. **Car rental** companies at or near the airport include Budget, 20 Old Airport Rd (ⓣ867/920-2776); elsewhere try National, downtown at 5118 50th St (ⓣ867/873-3424). **Taxis** to downtown from the airport cost around $14: call City Cab (ⓣ867/873-4444) or Diamond (ⓣ867/873-6666). Three **buses** run weekly by Frontier Coachlines (ⓣ867/872-2031) shuttle from Hay River via Fort Smith (around $80 one-way).

The **Northern Frontier Regional Visitors Centre** is on the edge of Frame Lake just north of the Northern Heritage Centre at 4807 49th St (June–Aug daily 8.30am–6pm; rest of year Mon–Fri 9am–5pm, Sat & Sun noon–4/5pm; ⓣ867/873-4262 or 1-877/881-4262, ⓦwww.northernfrontier.com). The **post office** is at 4902 50th St and the **Stanton Regional Hospital** is off Old Airport Rd at Range Lake Rd (ⓣ867/920-4111). For the **police**, call ⓣ867/669-1111. To rent camping gear, canoes, snowmobiles, fishing tackle and other **outdoor equipment**, contact Narwhal Northern Adventures, 101 5103-51st Ave (ⓣ867/873-6443, ⓔnarwal@ssimicro.com), who have served as canoe-trip and rental experts for over 25 years. Yellowknife is, along with Inuvik, the headquarters of most of the far north's **outfitters and tour operators**. Many outfits run fishing, wildlife, Arctic sightseeing, canoeing, kayaking, boating and other trips, most ranging from one- or two-day outings up to full-blown three-week mini-expeditions to unimaginably wild areas. You'll find a comprehensive listing in the *Explorers' Guide* brochure, obtainable from national tourist offices before your trip. If you decide you want adventure on the spur of the moment, contact the regional visitors centre.

Accommodation

Hotels in the city have plenty of rooms, but prices are high, making it worth looking up one of the dozen or so **B&Bs** if you're on a budget. The only **campsite** is the fully serviced *Fred Henne Territorial Park* (ⓣ867/920-2472; tents $15; RVs $20) by Long Lake off Hwy 3 north of the airport. Trails run to town from here via Frame Lake: allow about an hour – or you can follow the Prospectors' Trail north from the site, a good way to get a taste of the wilderness that encircles Yellowknife.

Blue Raven B&B 37 Otto Drive ⓣ867/873-6328, ⓔtmacfoto@arctic.data.ca. Cosy three-room B&B, with simple modern rooms and grand views from its wonderful sun deck of the Great Slave Lake from its location high on the bluff at the edge of the Old Town. Excellent cooked breakfasts. ❹

Château Nova 4401 50th Ave ⓣ867/873-9700 or 1-877/839-1236, ⓦwww.Chateaunova.com. Quality mid-range hotel on the fringe of downtown with fairly standard hotel rooms, though the historic photos of Yellowknife's early days dotting their walls are a nice touch. Facilities include in-room broadband and a gym, hot tub and sauna. ❻

Captain Ron's 8 Lessard Drive ⓣ867/873-3746. Old Town lakeshore B&B near the *Wildcat Café* (see opposite), where some of the simple, TV-less rooms share bathrooms; all have access to the reading lounge with fireplace. ❺

Embleton House 5203 52nd St ⓣ867/873-2892 or 1-866/873-2066, ⓦwww.bbcanada.com/embletonhouse. Friendly B&B in a quiet district two blocks from downtown. Rooms range from modest doubles with shared bath to a suite with kitchen and skylight for watching the northern lights. ❹

Explorer Hotel 4825 49th Ave ⓣ867/873-3531 or 1-800/661-0892, ⓦwww.explorerhotel.nt.ca. Facility-laden, high-rise business hotel decorated in contemporary earth-tones. Amenities include broadband, gym and free airport shuttle. Many rooms have kitchenettes. ❼

Red Coach Inn 4115 Franklin Ave ⓣ867/873-8511, ⓔredcoachinn@theedge.ca. The cheapest beds in town are usually in this permafrost-battered motel – much improved since its 2006 renovation – midway between the Old Town and downtown. Most rooms have a kitchenette. ❹

Yellowknife Inn 5010 49th St ⓣ867/873-2601 or 1-800/661-0580, ⓦwww.yellowknifeinn.com. Swish downtown hotel that's handy, particularly in winter, for its attachment to the Centre Square Mall with its selection of shops and restaurants. ❼

The City

Visitors are steered carefully down the main street, Franklin Avenue (50th Avenue), and down the long hill from the New Town to quaint Old Town cabins such as the **Wildcat Café** (see opposite); in operation since 1937. Elsewhere the old town is a shakedown of pitted and buckled roads (the result of permafrost) and a few quaintly battered buildings on the aptly-named Ragged Ass Road and Willow Road. These are more or less the only remnants of the old times – though if you venture to the outskirts you'll find shanty settlements and scenes of poverty that take the lustre off the high-rises of the city centre.

Just west of New Town's core lies the **Prince of Wales Northern Heritage Centre** (June–August daily 10.30am–5.30pm; Sept–May Mon–Fri 10.30am–5pm, Sat & Sun noon–5pm; free; ⓣ867/873-7551, ⓦwww.pwnhc.ca), three blocks from downtown on Frame Lake. Yellowknife's key sight, the modern centre peddles a more sanitized view of northern history and aboriginal culture than is on offer in parts of the Old Town, offering extensive displays of northern artefacts, Inuit carvings and persuasive dioramas of local wildlife and habitats. The centre's South Gallery has displays on aboriginal people; the North Gallery features life in the north after the arrival of Europeans. The Aviation Gallery is devoted to the planes and pilots who for years played (and play) a vital part in keeping the north alive. The centre also houses the NWT Archives, a collection of maps, books, photographs and documents devoted to the region. Just northwest of the centre, also on Frame Lake, stands the $25-million **Northwest Territories Legislative Assembly**, opened in 1993 to house the Territories' 24-strong Legislative Assembly. It's an impressive piece of architecture, much of it open to public view (tours June–Aug Mon–Fri 10.30am, 1.30pm & 3.30pm, Sun 1.30pm; Sept–May Mon–Fri 10.30am; free; ⓣ867/669-2230 or 1-800/661-0784, ⓦwww.assembly.gov.nt.ca).

Shops around town sell a variety of northern aboriginal crafts that are expensive, but cheaper than you'll find in southerly cities; most are beautiful products of a living culture – even if the culture is not at its healthiest in the city itself. Close to town you can walk the trails around Frame Lake and from the campsite on Long Lake (see opposite). Or, you can drive out on the **Ingraham Trail**, an 81-km hwy that was to be the start of a major NWT "Road to Resources" but which was abandoned in the 1960s. There are plenty of boat launches, picnic sites and campsites en route, as well as short walking trails like the **Cameron River Falls** (48km from Yellowknife) and lakeside beaches where the hardier of the city's population brave the water.

Eating and drinking

Though generally good, many of Yellowknife's **restaurants** are a little pricey, so if you're on a budget, a couple of ethnic food places offer a good alternative to the grubby diners on 50th Street. If you are splashing out, look out for uniquely Northern items like caribou, musk ox and arctic char. Most of the hotels have good dining rooms and much of the **nightlife** revolves around their lounges, notably the plush nightclub at the *Explorer*.

Black Knight Pub 4910 49th St. British-themed bar that's become a popular spot for its great range of malts, reasonable bar food and adjoining nightclub.

Bullocks Bistro 3534 Weaver Drive. ⓣ867/873-3474. Fish and chips meets fine dining in this informal, yet fairly high-end eatery. You'll only find simply prepared local whitefish, cod pike and trout on the menu (mains $10–20), along with some delicious chowders. Reservations recommended.

Gold Range Hotel 5010 50th St. Widely considered one of the great northern bars, the dingy, rough and raucous "Strange Range" is where you'll meet the most interesting and dubious types in town. It claims to sell the second-largest amount of beer per customer of any bar in Canada; to line your stomach visit the adjoining greasy-spoon bistro; which has surprisingly good pan-fried white fish on Fri.

Javaroma 5201 50th Ave. Successfully formulaic coffeehouse with good fresh bagels, pastries and sandwiches and of course a medley of styles of coffee on offer. The only free Wifi hotspot in town.

L'Heritage 5019 49th St ⓣ867/873-9561. The town's premier gourmet restaurant where a French country atmosphere – white linen table clothes, candlelight and polished wood – serves as a backdrop to clever renditions of local foods. Musk ox, bison, deer and elk all appear on the menu (mains $20–37), usually beside unusual sauces: fruit and brandy; bourbon and berries. The game meat fondue is good way to try a range of what's on offer.

Le Frolic 5019 49th St ⓣ867/669-9853 French bistro and watering hole with a giant selection of wines many tapas-style dishes meant for sharing and buffalo burgers too. Mains run $18–25 and include panfried pickerel from the Great Slave Lake.

Mainstreet Donair & Falafel 4905 Franklin Ave ⓣ867/766-3910. Great Middle-Eastern snack food joint: takeaway or perch at the counter; either way make a beeline for the deliciously garlicky chicken swarma ($7.25).

Vietnamese Noodle House 4609 Franklin Ave. Great big inexpensive but tasty noodle concoctions doled out in basic surrounds – a block out of downtown en-route to the Old Town.

Wildcat Café 3904 Wiley Rd ⓣ867/873-8850. Atmospheric and endlessly busy little café in a log cabin; operating since 1937. Expect to share tables as part of the sociable experience while you enjoy a taste of the region in the form of mid-priced fish dishes – or the excellent caribou medallions in zesty horseradish sauce. Open June–Sept.

Nunavut

Home to only around 26,500 people, **Nunavut** (meaning "Our Land" in the **Inuit** language) covers almost two million square kilometres – a fifth of Canada's land surface and an area five times the size of California, stretching west from Hudson Bay then north through the great "Barrenlands" of the interior to the Arctic islands in the north. From its western edge to the tip of Baffin Island in the east is 2000km (the distance from Washington DC to Denver). From north to south it's even farther – 2500km, or the distance from London to Moscow.

Long an amorphous political entity administered not as a semi-autonomous province but by the federal government, the Northwest Territories was formally superseded on April 1, 1999 by a land treaty which divided the old territories in two and created a new central and eastern Arctic territory termed Nunavut, which is now firmly established as a political and physical entity. The deal followed fifteen years of low-profile but effective negotiating and campaigning and produced the largest land deal in Canadian history, in which the Inuit got back their homeland (valued at $1.15 billion) in return for renouncing all their claims to the remainder of the NWT. One practical effect of this new political division has been the **renaming** of most settlements with Inuit names, though in many cases English-language names have continued to stick; both are given in this book, with the more common appellation given preference.

Nunuvut is the land of vast caribou migrations, musk ox, polar bears and endless empty horizons of fish-filled lakes and rivers. Most of the region's communities are formed of indigenous Inuit people and lie on the arc of Hudson Bay's western coast, from **Arviat** in the south through **Whale Cove** (Tikirarjuaq, "long point"), **Rankin Inlet** (Kangiqtinq, "deep bay") – the area's main transport and administrative centre – to **Chesterfield Inlet** (Igluligaarjuk, "place with a few igloos") and **Coral Harbour** (Salliq, "large flat island") in the north. In all of these places you will find an almost unchanged way of life; the local arts and handicrafts are outstanding, and in places you can hear the old drummers and "throat singers" traditionally responsible for handing down the stories and myths of the Inuit. The entire region has just 21km of highway, with the capital at **Iqaluit** on Baffin Island home to nearly one-fifth of the province's population.

Exploring this region is hugely rewarding, but far from easy. The landscapes are sublime – huge expanses of flower-filled tundra, ice fields, open sea, frozen sea, deep valleys and beautiful vast horizons – but often inhospitable. Access is invariably by plane and therefore expensive. Whatever your interest or activity, the best way to see the area is with one of the many tour companies. Besides breathtaking landscapes, there's also wildlife, fishing, whale-watching and a plethora of often exotic or high-adventure outdoor activities, not to mention a wide spectrum of living cultural treasures, from Inuit printmakers and carvers to traditional drummers and "throat" singers.

The region's major centres are covered in the following pages, but it's good to know **flight details** and where **accommodation** is available in the smaller communities. Note that **hotel prices** in the north are invariably per person, not per room, so double all rates if you are two people sharing a double room. Rates sometimes include meals, so are not as steep as they first appear.

Rankin Inlet (Kangiqtinq) and around

Although you'll find an old way of life and sublime Arctic scenery in the region, don't expect much in the way of charming villages: communities are often poor,

For comprehensive **information**, Nunavut puts out its own heavyweight visitors' guide, the annual *Canada's Arctic Nunavut Travel Planner* (free), an essential accessory to any visit, full of all the information you are likely to need for casual visits or fully fledged expeditions with tour operators and outfitters (all of whom are listed). Information is also available at ⓣ1-866/686-2888, ⓦwww.nunavuttourism.com.

roads pitted, houses strung out and dilapidated, and the streets festooned with telephone and electric cables. The region currently has just one paved road – from the airport at **RANKIN INLET** to the settlement's "downtown". And remember that villages often aren't communities at all in the usual sense: Rankin Inlet, for example, was only founded in 1955 when the North Rankin Nickel Mine opened. Three years later the government, shocked at conditions of local Inuit, "moved" people here from their nomadic homes in the wilderness; the resulting settlement, **Itivia** (now all but vanished), 1km from Rankin, was a disaster made even worse by the closure of the nickel mine in 1962. Only a craft-producing initiative and recent tourism saved the day. Things to do include hiking, fishing and bird-watching in the Ijiraliq (Meliadine) river valley, 5km from the settlement, and seeing a Thule site with stone tent rings, meat caches, kayak racks and underground winter houses.

First Air (ⓣ1-800/267-1247, ⓦwww.firstair.ca) has direct **flights** to Rankin Inlet from Iqaluit via Coral Harbour and connecting services from Ottawa and Montréal via Iqaluit on Baffin Island. Calm Air (ⓣ1-800/839-2256, ⓦwww.calmair.com) flies scheduled services from Churchill in Manitoba to Rankin Inlet and most other Keewatin villages. Outfitters and small charter firms here and in all the communities are available to fly or guide you into the interior or out into Hudson Bay for fishing and naturalist trips. Rankin Inlet boasts the small regional **Kivalliq Regional Visitor Centre**, housed at the airport, and a post office at the 65-room *Siniktarvik Hotel & Conference Centre* (ⓣ867/645-2807; ❽). Among the other accommodation is *Tara's Bed & Breakfast* (ⓣ867/645-3478, ⓔtarasbb@arctic.ca; ❼) and the well-equipped and friendly B&B *Nanuq Lodge* (ⓣ867/645-2650, ⓦwww.nanuqlodge.com; ❼), which has Internet and a small library of books of local interest.

CORAL HARBOUR or Salliq ("a large flat island in front of the mainland"; pop. 759) is the only settlement on Southampton Island and one of the best places to see walrus (on nearby Goats Island), as well as the beautiful Kirchoffer Falls and Thule archeological sites at "Native Point". **Accommodation** is found at the small *Leonie's Place* (ⓣ867/925-9751 or 925-8810, ⓔ925-8606; ❼ per person with all meals) or the *Esungark Hotel* (ⓣ867/925-9926 or 925-9969, ⓦwww.coralharbourhotel.com; ❼ per person) at the Katudgevik Co-op. There are **flights** here on Calm Air three times weekly, and on First Air once weekly, from Iqaluit via Rankin Inlet.

Arviat (pop. 1676), 240km southwest of Rankin Inlet (connected by daily Calm Air flights from Rankin Inlet), means the "place of the bowhead whale" and is particularly known for its crafts and the McConnell River Migratory Bird Sanctuary, home to thousands of nesting waterfowl. For more information on the community call the summer-only Margaret Aniksak Visitors' Centre (ⓣ867/857-2698). The settlement's **accommodation** comprises the *Padlei Inns North* (ⓣ867/857-2919, ⓦwww.innsnorth.com or www.arviathotel.com; ❼ per person) and *The Bayside B&B* (ⓣ867/857-2653, ⓔbayside2@attcanada.ca; ❼); rates at the latter include three meals a day, though a kitchen facility is available.

At **WHALE COVE** or Tikirarjuaq ("long point"; pop. 331), a traditional hunting, crafts and fishing community 80km south of Rankin Inlet, there's the six-room *Issatik Hotel Inns North* (Ⓣ867/896-9956 or 1-888-866-6784, Ⓦwww.whalecovehotel.com; ❼ per person with all meals). The similar **CHESTERFIELD INLET**, or Igluligaarjuk ("place with a few igloos"; pop. 364), is the oldest settlement in the region; it has daily flights from Rankin Inlet to the south, and one hotel, the *Tangmavik* (Ⓣ867/898-9190 or 1-888/866-6784, Ⓦwww.chesterfieldinlet.com; ❼ per person with all meals).

Baker Lake (Qamanit'uaq)

Some 260km west of Rankin Inlet at the mouth of the Thelon River lies **BAKER LAKE** (or Qamanit'uaq which means "far inland" or "huge widening of a river"; pop. 1453), the Arctic's only inland Inuit community, which marks

The Inuit

"They be like to Tartars, with long blacke haire, broad faces, and flatte noses, and tawnie in colour, wearing Seale skinnes... The women are marked in the faces with blewe streakes downe the cheekes, and round about the eies."
An officer on Frobisher's 1576 search for the Northwest Passage

Distinct from all other Canadian aboriginal peoples by virtue of their culture, language and Asiatic physical features, the **Inuit** are the dominant people of a **territory** that extends all the way from northern Alaska to Greenland. Though increasingly confined to reserves, they once led a **nomadic** existence in one of the most hostile environments on earth, dwelling in domed **igloos** during the winter and **skin tents** in the summer, and moving around using **kayaks** (*umiaks*) or **dog sleds** (*komatik*). The latter were examples of typical Inuit adaptability – the runners were sometimes made from frozen fish wrapped in sealskin and, in the absence of wood, caribou bones were used for crossbars.

Their prey – caribou, musk ox, seals, walruses, narwhals, beluga whales, polar bears, birds and fish – provided oil for heating and cooking, hides for clothing and tents, harpoon lines, ivory and dog harnesses. Using harpoons, bows and arrows and spears, ingenious hunting methods were devised; to catch caribou, for example, huge **inuksuits**, piles of rocks resembling the human form, were used to steer the herd into a line of armed hunters.

The Inuit **diet** was composed totally of flesh, and every part of the animal was eaten, usually raw, from the eyeballs to the heart. Delicacies included the plaited and dried intestines of seals and whole sealskins stuffed with small birds and left to putrefy until the contents had turned to the consistency of cheese. All food was shared and the successful hunter had to watch his catch being distributed amongst other families in the group, in accordance with specific relationships, before his own kin were allowed the smallest portion. **Starvation** was common – it was not unusual for whole villages to perish in the winter – and consequently **infanticide**, particularly of females, was employed to keep population sizes down. Elderly people who could not keep up with the travelling group were abandoned, a fate that also befell some offenders against the social code, though the usual way of resolving conflict was the **song-duel**, whereby the aggrieved would publicly ridicule the behaviour of the other, who was expected to accept the insults with good grace.

Making **clothes**, most often of caribou hide, was a task assigned to women and was as essential to survival as a man's ability to hunt. Older women also **tattooed** the faces of the younger ones by threading a sinew darkened with soot through the face to make lines that radiated from the nose and mouth. Women were usually betrothed at birth and married at puberty, and both polygamy and polyandry were frequent – though female infanticide made it rare for a man to have more than two spouses.

both Canada's geographic centre. It has long been a meeting place for members of different Inuit groups and provides a point of access into the **tundra** that characterizes the vastness of the region. This is a subtle landscape that's worth more than its "Barrenland" label suggests, particularly in summer, when the thaw brings to life thousands of tiny streams and lakes, and some three hundred species of wild flowers amidst the lichens and grasses that provide fodder for huge herds of musk ox and caribou. Millions of wildfowl can also be seen, and the huge skies and flat horizons are also one of the best places in Canada to see the **aurora borealis** (see box, p.997). Also be sure to take in the **Inuit Camp,** which includes a demonstration by Inuit families of the activities, such as hunting, trapping and weaving, that might have taken place in a Caribou Inuit camp.

It was a woman who often served as the **shaman,** or *angakok*, who maintained the group's communion with supernatural spirits. The deity who features most regularly in Inuit myth is a goddess called **Sedna**, who was mutilated by her father. Her severed fingers became seals and walruses and her hands became whales, but Sedna lived on as the mother and protector of all sea life, capable of withholding her bounty if strict taboos were not adhered to. These taboos included keeping land and sea products totally separate – so seals could never be eaten with caribou and all caribou clothing had to be made before the winter seal hunt.

Sporadic **European contact** dates back to the Norse settlement of Greenland, and early missionaries visited some Inuit, but it wasn't until the early nineteenth century that the two cultures met in earnest. By 1860 commercial **whalers** had begun wintering around the north of Hudson Bay, employing Inuit as crew and hunters for their food in return for European goods. Even then, the impact on the Inuit was not really deleterious until the arrival of **American whalers** in Canadian waters in 1890, when the liberal dispensing of alcohol and diseases such as smallpox and veneral disease led to a drastic decline in population.

By the early decades of the twentieth century **fur traders** were encouraging the Inuit to stop hunting off the coast and turn inland using firearms and traps. The accompanying **missionaries** brought welcome medical help and schools, but put an end to multiple marriages, shamanism and other traditional practices. More changes came when Inuit were employed to build roads, airfields and other military facilities during World War II and to construct the line of radar installations known as Distant Early Warning during the Cold War era. As well as bringing new jobs, this also focused government attention on the plight of the Inuit.

The consequent largesse was not wholly beneficial: subsidized housing and welfare payments led many Inuit to abandon their hunting camps and settle in **permanent communities**, usually located in places strategic to Canada's sovereignty in the Arctic. Without knowledge of the English and French languages, these Inuit were left out of all decision-making and often lived in a totally separate part of towns that were administered by outsiders. Old values and beliefs were all but eroded by television and radio, and high levels of depression, alcoholism and violence became the norm. The 1982 ban on European imports of sealskins created mass **unemployment**, and although hunting still provides the basics of subsistence, the high cost of ammunition and fuel makes commercial-scale hunting uneconomical.

All is not gloom, however. Inuit co-operatives are increasingly successful and the production of **soapstone carvings** – admittedly a commercial adulteration of traditional Inuit ivory art – is very profitable. Having organized themselves into politically active groups and secured such **land claims** as Nunavut, the Inuit are slowly rebuilding an ancient culture that was shattered in under half a century.

Calm Air has daily flights here from Rankin Inlet. For **accommodation** there are the two rather bleak aircraft-hanger-like structures of *Iglu Hotel* (Ⓣ867/793-2801, Ⓦwww.bakerlakehotel.com; ❼ per person with all meals) within which there's also the restaurant with its mediocre cafeteria food; alternatives include the small number of rooms and cabins offered by the *Baker Lake Lodge* (Ⓣ867/793-2905; ❺ per person including pick-up from the airport), and the Inuit-owned *Nunamiut Lodge* (Ⓣ867/793-2127; ❻), which has pretty lake views. There's also a small community campsite. The summer-only Akumalik **visitors' centre** (hours vary; Ⓣ867/793-2456) occupies a reconstructed 1936 Hudson's Bay Company post in the original lakeside building, successor to the 1916 post that originally brought about the settlement's development. A short walk east along the shore is the **Inuit Heritage Centre** (July & Aug hours vary; Ⓣ867/793-2598).

△ Kiawak Ashoona, an Inuit carver

The Northwest Passage

Traversed in its entirety fewer than fifty times, the fabled **Northwest Passage** around the American continent exerts a continuing romantic allure – and, in the wake of oil discoveries in the far north, an increasingly economic one too. The world's most severe maritime challenge, it involves a 1500-kilometre traverse from north of Baffin Island to the Beaufort Sea above Alaska. Some 50,000 icebergs constantly line the eastern approaches and thick pack ice covers the route for nine months of the year, with temperatures rising above freezing only in July and August. Perpetual darkness reigns for four months of the year, and thick fog and blizzards can obscure visibility for the remaining eight months. Even with modern technology navigation is extremely difficult; little is known of Arctic tides and currents; sonar is confused by submerged ice; and the featureless tundra of the Arctic islands provides the only few points of visual or radar reference.

John Cabot can hardly have been happy with his order from Henry VII in 1497 to blaze the northwest trail, the first recorded instance of such an attempt. The elusive passage subsequently excited the imagination of the world's greatest adventurers, men such as Sir Francis Drake, Jacques Cartier, Sir Martin Frobisher, James Cook and **Henry Hudson** – cast adrift by his mutinous crew in 1611 when the Hudson Bay turned out to be an icebound trap rather than the passage.

Details of a possible route were pieced together over the centuries, though many paid with their lives in the process, most famously **Sir John Franklin**, who vanished into the ice with 129 men in 1845. Many rescue parties set out to find Franklin's vessels, HMS *Erebus* and HMS *Terror*, and it was one searcher, **Robert McClure**, who – in the broadest sense – made the first northwest passage in 1854. Entering the passage from the west, he was trapped for two winters, and then sledged to meet a rescue boat coming from the east. The **first sea crossing** was achieved by the Norwegian **Roald Amundsen** in 1906, but only after a three-year voyage. The first single-season traverse was made by a Canadian Mountie, **Henry Larsen**, in 1944 – his schooner, the *St Roch*, is now enshrined in Vancouver's Maritime Museum. More recently, huge ice-breakers have explored the potential of cracking a commercial route mainly for the export of oil from the Alaskan and Beaufort fields, and for the exploitation of minerals in Canada's Arctic north.

The Arctic Coast

Canada's last frontier, the Arctic Coast encompasses the country's northern mainland coast from the Mackenzie to Baffin Island, and – as "coast" is a relative term in a region where the sea is often frozen – numerous islands too, most notably a large part of Victoria Island. It is a barren, ice-carved and wind-scoured landscape of chill lakes and low hills with not a tree to be seen. Braving this setting which is also nearly completely dark and frozen for nine months of the year is a permanent population of a few hundred. As recently as fifty years ago, the Inuit (see box, p.1070) here had known little or no contact with the outside world. Few explorers encountered them, and even the most determined of Western agencies – the church and the trading companies – have failed to compromise a people who are still extraordinarily isolated by climate, distance and culture. Today, however, few of the Inuit live according to the ways of popular myth. Except on the odd trapping party, for example, igloos have been replaced by government-built homes, and the bone tools, sledges and kayaks of a generation ago have been superseded by rifles, snow bikes and light aircraft.

You have to be fairly determined to reach any of the region's eight communities (five on the coast, three on islands), let alone explore the hauntingly beautiful ice fields and tundra. Those that forge their way are usually looking to spot wildlife, fish, or, more dubiously, to hunt for musk ox, caribou and polar bears, a practice the government defends by claiming "It's done the Inuit way, using dog teams, on a demanding safari over land and sea ice". It also provides much-needed income for the Inuit, who have the right to sell the limited number of permits. Most visitors base themselves either at **Kugluktuk** (formerly **Coppermine**) or at Victoria Island's **Ikaluktutiak** (formerly **Cambridge Bay**), the transport and service capital. Each main Arctic coast community, remarkably, has **accommodation**, but reservations are vital and prices predictably steep. You need to come prepared: in some cases meals must be booked in advance. Basic groceries are usually available at stores, but there are no banks. As ever, various **tour operators** run trips to and from the main centres; for information, send for the *Nunavut Travel Planner* before you go (see p.1069).

Cambridge Bay (Ikaluktutiak)

CAMBRIDGE BAY (pop.1413) or Ikaluktutiak– the "fair fishing place" – lies to the north of the Arctic Circle on the southern shore of **Victoria Island**, Canada's second largest island. As ever in the high Arctic, you need motivation to come here, for accommodation, food and flights are all hideously expensive. Today it's the regional centre for the Kitikmeot communities and an important staging point for tours or for heading still deeper into the hinterland. It also operates as the administrative focus for the region's western lands, despite being a full 1300km from Nunavut's capital at Iqaluit. Over the centuries the region was a summer gathering place for the Copper Inuit (so called by the whites because they made many of their tools and weapons from copper), attracted here by the abundance of good hunting, notably seals, caribou and arctic char. The last two are local staples to this day. Kitikmeot Meats processes caribou and musk for export and the Ikaluktutiak Co-op runs a fishery that supplies arctic char nationwide (both concerns are open to the public for direct sales). The Hudson's Bay Company arrived in 1921, late by Canadian standards, and purchased the *Maud*, explorer Roald Amundsen's schooner, for use as a supplies and trading ship. This little piece of Arctic history was used for years before being left to sink into disrepair and ultimately into the harbour, where its hulk can still be seen in the bay.

The region's main **tourist office** is the Arctic Coast Visitors Centre (Mon–Fri 9am–5pm, ⓣ867/983-2842), an attractive modern building overlooking the bay. It has displays on the art, history and culture of the Copper and Netsilik Inuit, as well as exhibits of maps and documents that shed light on the age-old search for the Northwest Passage (see box, p.1073). A library of northern books and videos is also available, and there are pamphlets on self-guided walks around the community. **Scheduled flights** arrive on Canadian North (ⓣ867/979-6828 or 1-800/661-1505, ⓦwww.canadian.com) from Yellowknife; First Air flies between all the settlements except Bathurst Inlet and Umingmaktok, which can be reached by charter aircraft only.

As regards **accommodation**, there's the 25-room *Arctic Islands Lodge* (ⓣ867/983-2345 or 1-888/866-6784, ⓦwww.cambridgebayhotel.com; ❼ per person). There are also one- and two-bedroom apartments, a coffee shop and restaurant where meals cost another $30 to $60 per day. The smaller *Green Row Executive Suites* (ⓣ867/983-3456, ⓦwww.greenrow.ca; ❻) has eighteen central, self-contained suites with kitchenettes. You can **camp** at Freshwater Creek, 5km away, and – if you're self-catering – buy supplies at the Northern store. You should also be able to camp on the shoreline of the bay, but ask first, and make sure you are well away from, and out of sight of, any houses.

Kugluktuk (Coppermine)

KUGLUKTUK (pop. 1267) lies west of Cambridge Bay on the Canadian "mainland", sitting astride the **Coppermine River** close to the westernmost point of Nunavut (the river lends Kugluktuk its name, which means "place of rapids"). Yellowknife is 600km away to the south. The Coronation Gulf, a relatively narrow sea passage, separates the mainland coast from Victoria Island at this point, a vital through-route on the Northwest Passage. The river has long been of primary importance in the region. Copper Inuit, so called because they fashioned tools and weapons from copper, converged at its mouth for a millennium to fish and hunt. Today hunting and fishing still play a part in generating local income, though tourism and oil and gas exploration also contribute to local coffers. The river, which rises in the wilderness 360km north of Yellowknife, has also provided a "convenient" way of accessing the far north. It was used by Samuel Hearne, for example, the first white to reach the region, who paddled here on the orders of the Hudson's Bay Company to seek out the source of the copper being traded by the Inuit at company posts to the south. Today the river provides one of the continent's great **canoe trips**, most canoeists (or rafters) joining tours or chartering a plane from Yellowknife to the river's headwaters. The 325-kilometre trip downstream takes around ten days. The trip, among other things, offers sensational opportunities for watching wildlife, but you can also strike lucky with wildlife by walking or taking short tours from Kugluktuk itself. The most popular walk (20km one-way) is to the **Bloody Falls**, so called because a party of Inuit were massacred here following an argument with a group of Dene guides accompanying Hearne (relations between the two aboriginal groups were traditionally poor). If you don't fancy the walk, or only want to go one way – it's tough going in places – you can arrange a boat to take you or pick you up – organise this at the information centre (below).

Access by **air** is provided through First Air from Yellowknife and other "local" communities. **Information** is available in summer from the Heritage Visitors Centre (July & Aug daily 8.30am–5pm, other times on request; ⓣ867/982-3232). There are two **accommodation** options. The central *Coppermine Inn* (ⓣ867/982-3333, ⓔ867/982-3340; ❼ per person) has motel rooms or self-contained units; breakfast, lunch and dinner if you want them should be reserved in advance (you can take meals individually). Alternatively, there's the smaller *Enokhok Inn* (ⓣ867/982-3197, ⓔ867/982-4291; ❼ per person including meals). **Camping** is possible at Kukluktuk Park. As for **eating**, nonresidents can use the *Coppermine Inn*, but you need to book meals a day in advance.

Uluqsaqtuuq (Holman)

One of the region's more northerly communities, **ULUQSAQTUUQ**, or Holman (pop. 300), lies on the western side of Victoria Island – so strictly speaking just outside Nunavut's borders. Most people are here to fish for trout and arctic char or, remarkably, for the novelty of playing golf on one of the world's most northerly courses. The settlement is situated in a scenic open cove, the half-moon Queen's Bay, backed by massive two-metre bluffs and escarpments. It developed almost by default, when a Hudson's Bay Company post was moved here from Prince Albert Sound in 1939. Inuit had previously summered here in the search for caribou, but the post encouraged some to settle and sell white-fox furs with the Hudson's Bay traders. Today two groups of Inuit – the Copper and Inuvialuit – live here, the region forming part of a designated

Inuvialuit settlement area. The community has become especially well-known for its crafts, notably clothing and traditional tools, but most particularly prints and silk-screened items, a tradition that goes back fifty years, to when an Oblate missionary, the Reverend Henri Tardi, came here and taught locals various printing techniques.

You can buy crafts around the settlement, or at the gift shop in the hamlet's only **accommodation**, the *Arctic Char Inn* (Ⓣ867/396-3501 or 396-3531, Ⓔ867/396-3705; ❼ per person), which has just eight rooms at $185 per person per night. You can **camp** at Okpilik Lake, but should be able to pitch a tent just about anywhere if you ask at the hamlet office. The *Arctic Char Inn* is the only place to **eat**, but there is a Northern groceries store almost opposite for supplies.

Baffin Island

Baffin Island comprises half a million square kilometres of Arctic vastness, whose main attraction is **Auyuittuq National Park Reserve** on the Cumberland Peninsula, Canada's northernmost accessible national park. With a treeless landscape, mountains towering over 1500m, icy glacial streams and 24-hour daylight from May to July, hiking in Auyuittuq offers one of the most majestic experiences in Canada. However, with temperatures rising to a mere 6°C from June to August, it's a brutal environment that will appeal only to the truly adventurous; expensive though they are, **package tours** are definitely recommended if this is your first venture into such a forbidding place. Be sure to bring all necessary gear with you, as the island supplies arrive just once a year.

Iqaluit (Frobisher Bay)

The main gateway to Baffin Island – and capital of Nunavut – is the rapidly growing **Iqaluit**, whose name means simply "fish" and whose population of four thousand plus is predominantly Inuit. The Nunavut Tourism office is here (Ⓣ867/979-6551 or 1-866/686-2888, Ⓦwww.nunavuttourism.com), as is the Unikkaarvik (Baffin Regional) **Visitor Centre** (July & Aug Mon–Fri 10am–6pm, Sat & Sun 10am–6pm & 1–4pm other times on request; Ⓣ867/979-4636). So, too, are many of the **tour operators** who run trips into the interior. Things to see include the St Jude's Anglican church – an igloo-shaped affair like the one in Inuvik – and the collection of Inuit art and artefacts in the **Nunatta Sunakkutaangit Museum** (call for latest times; Ⓣ867/979-5537).

Getting to Baffin Island is only feasible by **air**. First Air (Ⓣ1-800/267-1247 or 613/839-3340, Ⓦwww.firstair.ca) and Canadian North (Ⓣ1-800/661-1505 or 867/979-6828, Ⓦwww.canadiannorth.com) makes the trip from Montréal (1–2 daily; 3hr) and from Ottawa (4 weekly; 4hr). Ticket **prices** can get as low as $500 return, but are usually nearer $700. First Air also links Yellowknife to Iqaluit (5 weekly; 3hr 50min) for around $800 return. Remember to ask about cheap pass deals and other prebooked flight deals if you're making international flights into Canada: these are often much cheaper bought beforehand in conjunction with the carrier you're using to fly to the country. Consult the *Nunavut Travel Planner* or website (see p.1069) or contact the Iqaluit visitor centre for details of flights and other **information** on outfitters, guides and accommodation. However, hiking maps should be bought in advance from maps specialists and regional topographic maps distributors: listed at Ⓦmaps.nrcan.gc.ca/distribution_e.php.

In summer many of the Inuit families of Iqaluit abandon their homes in favour of tents, and your best bet may well be to join them, although there are no fixed campsites. Iqaluit has around eight **accommodation** options, including B&B choices which tend to open and close from year to year. The big main **hotels** charge more or less similar rates – around $145 per person per night – for similar facilities: *The Navigator Inn* (Ⓣ867/979-6201, Ⓦwww.evaz.ca/navigator_inn.htm; ❻), *Discovery Lodge* (Ⓣ867/979-4433, Ⓦwww.discoverylodge.com; ❻) and the recently renovated *Frobisher Inn* (Ⓣ867/979-2222, Ⓦwww.frobisherinn.com; ❻).

In addition to flights to Pangnirtung (for the Auyuittuq park; see below), there are scheduled flights on First Air from Iqaluit to Baffin Island's various small communities, as well as chartered sightseeing flights. Each of the following remoter settlements has single and highly expensive hotels: Arctic Bay, Cape Dorset, Clyde River, Hall Beach, Igloolik, Pond Inlet, Resolute and Sanikiluaq.

Auyuittuq National Park Reserve

Straddling the Arctic Circle in the northeast of Baffin Island, **Auyuittuq National Park Reserve** is one of the most spectacular destinations in the Canadian north. The heart of the park is the massive **Penney Ice Cap**, a remnant of the ice sheet that extended over most of Canada east of the Rockies about 18,000 years ago, and the major **hiking route** is the 110-km Pangnirtung/Aksayuk Pass, which cuts through the mountains between Cumberland Sound and the Davis Strait. *Auyuittuq* is Inuit for "the land that never melts", but despite the unrelenting cold there is abundant life here: in summer the sparse tundra plants burst into green, the wild flowers are blooming and the amazing array of wildlife includes lemmings, polar bears, caribou, arctic hares and foxes, snow geese, peregrines, narwhals, walruses, bowhead and beluga whales, as well as harp, ringed and bearded seals.

There is a daily one-hour First Air flight during the summer from Iqaluit to **Pangnirtung**, the gateway to Auyuittuq National Park. In Pangnirtung there is an established free **campsite**, *Pisuktinee Tungavik*, and a church that occasionally lets you sleep on the floor for a donation if you are desperate. The only commercial **places to stay** are the 25-room *Auyuittuq Lodge* (Ⓣ867/473-8955, Ⓔpanglodge@qiniq.ca; ❻) and newer two-room *Kilabuk Lodge* (Ⓣ867/473-8229; ❻), where you can take meals or cook your own. The former has good but expensive meals and they usually allow exhausted hikers to use their showers for a few dollars.

The only transport for the 25km from Pangnirtung to the south entrance of the park is by **freighter canoe**, which the Inuit also charter for fishing, whale-watching and sightseeing trips. The rates on these "canoes" – which are like small fishing boats with outboard motors – are set by the Inuit co-operative, and work out at around $130 for two people one-way, plus $35–60 for each additional person. The boats can only pass through the Pangnirtung Fjord after the ice break-up in July; at other times you have to walk. Arrangements for a canoe pick-up should be possible by radio from the few emergency shelters in the park, but be warned that one summer all the batteries were stolen, so you may have to arrange your pick-up before being dropped off.

Services within the park are extremely limited and the **weather** is highly unpredictable. Snowstorms, high wind and rain occur frequently, and deaths from hypothermia have been known even in the height of summer. All-weather hiking gear is essential, and a walking stick or ski pole is necessary to assist you with the ice-cold stream crossings which occur every 200–300m and can still be waist-high in July. There is no wood for fuel, as the park is located kilometres north of the tree line, so a camping stove is also essential. You can get **information** from Auyuittuq National Park Reserve, Pangnirtung, NT, X0A 0R0 (☎867/473-2500, Ⓦwww.pc.gc.ca/pn-np/nu/auyuittuq/index_e.asp).

Travel details

Trains

Prince George to: Edmonton via Jasper (3 weekly; 8hr 15min); Prince Rupert (3 weekly; 13hr); Vancouver (mid-June to Oct 1 daily; rest of year 3 weekly; 13hr 30min).
Prince Rupert to: Prince George (3 weekly; 13hr).

Buses

Dawson City to: Inuvik (mid-June to early Sept 2–3 weekly; 12hr); Whitehorse (late June to Sept 3 weekly; Oct & March to early June 2 weekly; rest of year 1 weekly; 7hr 30min).
Dawson Creek to: Edmonton (2 daily; 9hr); Prince George (2 daily; 6hr 30min); Whitehorse (mid-May to mid-Oct 1 daily except Sun; rest of year 3 weekly; 21hr).
Hay River to: Fort Resolution (3 weekly; 6hr); Fort Smith (3 weekly; 7hr); Peace River (daily except Mon; connections for Edmonton and Grande Prairie; 8hr); Yellowknife (3 weekly; 12hr).
Prince George to: Dawson Creek (2 daily; 6hr 30min); Edmonton via Jasper (2 daily; 9hr 45min); Prince Rupert (2 daily; 11hr); Vancouver via Williams Lake and Cache Creek (2 daily; 13hr).
Whitehorse to: Dawson City (June–Sept 3 weekly; Oct & March to early June 2 weekly; rest of year 1 weekly; 7hr 30min); Dawson Creek (mid-May to mid-Oct 1 daily except Sun; rest of year 3 weekly; 21hr); Skagway (mid-May to mid-June 1 daily except Wed & Sun; 4hr).

Flights

Listed below are only the main direct scheduled flights operated by the big carriers; for details on the many small provincial companies operating within the north, turn to each relevant town account.
Inuvik from: Calgary (3 weekly; 5hrs); Yellowknife (1 daily; 2hr 35min).
Iqaluit from: Edmonton (2 weekly; 6hrs) Montréal (1–2 daily; 3hr); Ottawa (4 weekly; 4hr); Yellowknife (5 weekly; 3hr 50min).
Whitehorse from: Vancouver (3 daily; 2hr 20min).
Yellowknife from: Calgary (1–3 daily; 3hr 20min); Cambridge Bay (3 weekly; 1hr 30min); Edmonton (2–3 daily; 1hr 35min); Fort Smith (1 daily; 1hr 30min); Inuvik (1 daily; 2hr 35min); Norman Wells (1 daily; 1hr 15min); Resolute (2 weekly; 3hr 20min).

Contexts

Contexts

History of Canada

Fully unified as late as 1949, **Canada** is a country of intertwining histories rather than a single national thread. Not only does each of its provinces maintain a considerable degree of autonomy, but each grouping of native peoples can claim a heritage that cannot be fully integrated into the story of white Canada. Such a complex mosaic militates against generalization, although Canadians themselves continue to grapple with the nature of their own identity. What follows is an attempt to identify key events and themes.

The beginnings

The ancestors of the **aboriginal peoples** of North America first entered the continent around 25,000 years ago, when vast glaciers covered most of the northern continents, keeping the sea level far below that of today. It seems likely that North America's first human inhabitants crossed the land bridge linking Asia with present-day Alaska – they were probably Siberian hunter-nomads travelling in pursuit of mammoths, hairy rhinos, bison, wild horses and sloths, the Ice Age animals that made up their diet. These people left very little to mark their passing, apart from some simple graves and the grooved, chipped-stone spear-heads that earned them the name **Fluted Point People**. In successive waves the Fluted Point People moved down through North America, across the isthmus of Panama, until they reached the southernmost tip of South America. As they settled, so they slowly developed distinctive cultures and languages, whose degree of elaboration depended on the resources of their environment.

About 3000 BC another wave of migration passed over from Asia to North America. This wave was made up of the first group of **Inuit** migrants who – because the sea level had risen and submerged the land bridge under today's Bering Strait – made their crossings either in skin-covered boats or on foot over the winter ice. Within the next thousand years the Inuit occupied the entire northern zone of the continent, moving east as far as Greenland and displacing the earlier occupants. These first Inuits – called the **Dorset Eskimos** after Cape Dorset, on Baffin Island in the Northwest Territories, where archeologists first identified their remains in the 1920s – were assimilated or wiped out by the next wave of Inuit. These crossed into the continent 3000 years ago, creating the **Thule** culture – so called after the Greek word for the world's northernmost extremity. The Thule people were the direct ancestors of today's Inuit.

The aboriginal peoples

Before the Europeans arrived, the aboriginal peoples – numbering around 300,000 – were divided into three main language groups: **Algonkian**, **Athapascan** (principally in the north and west) and **Inuktitut** (Inuit). Within these groups existed a multitude of cultures. None of these people had a written language, the wheel was unknown to them and their largest draught animal, prior to the introduction of the horse, was the dog. However, over the centuries, each of the tribes developed techniques that enabled them to cope with the problems of survival posed by their environments.

Immediately prior to the arrival of the Europeans, Canada was divided into a number of cultural zones. In the extreme north lived the nomadic **Inuit** (see box, p.1070), whose basic unit was the family group, small enough to survive in the precarious conditions. The necessarily small-scale nature of Inuit life meant that they developed no political structures and gathered together in larger groups only if the supply of food required it – when, for example, the arctic char were running upriver from the sea to spawn, or the caribou were migrating. Immediately to the south of the Inuit, in a zone stretching from the Labrador coast across the Canadian Shield to northern British Columbia, lived the tribes of the **northern forests**. This was a harsh environment, too, and consequently these peoples spent most of their time in small nomadic bands following the game on which they depended. Indeed, variations between the tribes largely resulted from the type of game they pursued: the **Naskapi** fished and hunted seals on the Labrador coast; the **Chipewyan**, occupying the border country between the tundra and forest to the west of Hudson Bay, mainly hunted caribou; the **Wood Cree**, to the south of the Chipewyan, along the Churchill River, hunted deer and moose; and the **Tahltan** of British Columbia combined hunting with seasonal fishing. Like the Inuit, the political structures of these tribes were rudimentary and, although older men enjoyed a certain respect, there were no "chiefs" in any European sense of the term. In fact, decisions were generally made collectively with the opinions of successful hunters – the guarantors of survival – carrying great weight, as did those of their **shaman**, whose main function was to satisfy the spirits that they believed inhabited every animate and inanimate object around them.

The southern zone of Canada, stretching from the St Lawrence River along the northern shores of the Great Lakes to southern British Columbia, was climatically much kinder, and it's in this region that Canada's native peoples developed their most sophisticated cultures. Here, along the banks of the St Lawrence and the shores of the Great Lakes, lived the **Iroquois-speaking** peoples, divided into three tribal confederacies: the **Five Nations**, the **Huron** (see p.159) and the **Neutrals**. All three groups cultivated corn (maize), beans and squash in an agricultural system that enabled them to lead a settled life – often in communities of several hundreds. Iroquois society was divided into matriarchal clans, whose affairs would be governed by a female elder. The clan shared a long house and when a man married (always outside his own clan), he would go to live in the long house of his wife. Tribal chiefs (sachems) were male, but they were selected by the female elders of the tribe and they also had to belong to a lineage through which the rank of sachem descended. Once selected a sachem had to have his rank confirmed by the federal council of the inter-tribal league: in the case of the Five Nations this consisted of sachems from the Seneca, Cayuga, Onondaga, Oneida and Mohawk tribes. Iroquoian society had its bellicose side, too. An assured winter supply of food enabled the Iroquois to indulge in protracted inter-tribal warfare: in particular, the Five Nations were almost always at war with the Hurons.

To the west of the Iroquois, between lakes Superior and Winnipeg, lived the **Ojibwa**, forest hunters who learned to cultivate maize from the Iroquois and also harvested the wild rice that grew on the fringes of the region's lakes. Further west still, on the prairies, lived the peoples of the **Blackfoot Confederation**: the **Piegan**, **Blackfoot** and **Blood** tribes. The economy of this latter grouping was based on the buffalo (or bison): its flesh was eaten; its hide provided clothes and shelter; its bones were made into tools; its sinews were ideal for bow strings; and its hooves were melted down to provide glue. In the late seventeenth century, the hunting techniques of these prairie peoples were transformed by the arrival of the horse, which had made its way – either wild or by trade – from Mexico, where it had been introduced by the Spanish conquistadors. The horse made the bison easy prey and, as with the Iroquois, a ready food supply spawned the development of a militaristic culture centred on the prowess of the tribes' young braves.

On the **Pacific coast**, tribes such as the **Tlingit** and **Salish** were dependent on the ocean, which provided them with a plentiful supply of food. There was, however, little cohesion within tribes and people from different villages – even though of the same tribe – would at times be in conflict with each other. Yet these tribes had a rich ceremonial and cultural life, as exemplified by the excellence of their woodcarvings, whose most conspicuous manifestations were the **totem poles** (or, more accurately, house posts), which reached colossal sizes in the nineteenth century.

The coming of the Europeans

The first recorded contact between Europeans and the native peoples of North America occurred in around 1000 AD, when a **Norse** expedition sailing from Greenland landed somewhere on the Atlantic seaboard, probably in Newfoundland (see p.534 for more). It was a fairly short-lived stay – according to the Icelandic sagas, the Norse were forced to withdraw from the area they called Vinland because of the hostility of the natives.

In 1492 Ferdinand and Isabella of Spain were finally persuaded to underwrite **Christopher Columbus**'s expedition in search of the westward route to Asia. Columbus bumped into the West Indies instead, but his "discovery" of islands that were presumed to lie off India encouraged other European monarchs to sponsor expeditions of their own. In 1497, **John Cabot**, supported by the English king Henry VII, sailed west and sighted Newfoundland and Cape Breton. On his return, Cabot reported seeing multitudes of cod off Newfoundland, and his much-publicized comments effectively started the **Newfoundland** cod fishery. In less than sixty years, up to four hundred **fishing** vessels from Britain, France and Spain were making annual voyages to the Grand Banks fishing grounds around the island. Soon some of the fishermen established shore bases to cure their catch in the sun, and then they started to over-winter here – which was how settlement of the island began.

By the end of the sixteenth century the cod trade was largely controlled by the British and French, and Newfoundland became an early cockpit of English–French rivalries, a colonial conflict that continued until England secured control of the island in the 1713 Treaty of Utrecht.

New France

Meanwhile, in 1535, **Jacques Cartier**, on a voyage paid for by the French crown, made his way down the St Lawrence, also hoping to find Asia. Instead he stumbled upon the Iroquois, first at Stadacona, on the site of Québec City, and later at Hochelaga, today's Montréal. At both places, the Frenchman had a friendly reception, but the Iroquois attitude changed after Cartier seized one of their *sachems* and took him back to France. For a time the Iroquois were a barrier to further exploration up the St Lawrence, but subsequently they abandoned their riverside villages (possibly as a result of an epidemic brought about by contact with Europeans diseases), enabling French traders to move up the river buying **furs**, an enterprise pioneered by seasonal fishermen.

The development of this trade aroused the interest of the French king, who in 1603 commissioned **Samuel de Champlain** to chart the St Lawrence.

Two years later Champlain founded **Port Royal** (see p.425) in today's Nova Scotia, which became the capital of **Acadie** (Acadia), a colony whose agricultural preoccupations were soon far removed from the main thrust of French colonialism along the St Lawrence. It was here, on a subsequent expedition in 1608, that Champlain established the settlement of Québec City at the heart of **New France**, and, to stimulate the fur trade, allied the French with those tribes he identified as likely to be his principal suppliers. In practice this meant siding with the Huron against the Five Nations, a decision that intensified their traditional hostility. Furthermore, the fur trade destroyed the balance of power between the tribes: first one and then another would receive, in return for their pelts, the latest type of musket as well as iron axes and knives, forcing enemies back to the fur trade to redress the military balance. One terrible consequence of such European intervention was the **extermination of the Huron people** in 1648 by the Five Nations, armed by the Dutch merchants of the Hudson River.

As pandemonium reigned among the native peoples, the pattern of life in **New France** was becoming well established. On the farmlands of the St Lawrence a New World feudalism was practised by the land-owning seigneurs and their habitant tenants, while the fur territories – entered at Montréal – were extended deep into the interior. Many of the fur traders adopted native dress, learnt aboriginal languages, and took wives from the tribes through which they passed, spawning the mixed-race people known as the **Métis**. The furs they brought back to Montréal were shipped downriver to Québec City whence they were shipped to France. But the white population in the French colony remained relatively small – there were only 18,000 New French in 1713. In the context of a growing British presence, this represented a dangerous weakness.

The rise of the British

In 1670 Charles II of England had established the **Hudson's Bay Company** and given it control of a million and a half square miles adjacent to its namesake bay, a territory named Rupert's Land, after the king's uncle. Four years later the British captured the Dutch possessions of the Hudson River Valley – thereby trapping New France. Slowly the British closed the net: in 1713, they took control of Acadia, renaming it **Nova Scotia** (New Scotland), and in 1755 they deported its French-speaking farmers. When the Seven Years War broke out in 1756, the French attempted to outflank the British by using the Great Lakes route to occupy the area to the west of the British colonies and then, with the help of their native allies, pin them to the coast. In the event the British won the war by exploiting their naval superiority: a large force under the command of **General James Wolfe** sailed up the St Lawrence in 1759 and, against all expectations, successfully scaled the Heights of Abraham to capture Québec City. Montréal fell a few months later – and at that point the French North American empire was effectively finished, though they held onto Louisiana until Napoleon sold it off in 1803.

For the native peoples, the ending of the Anglo–French conflict was a mixed blessing. If the war had turned the tribes into sought-after allies, it had also destroyed the traditional inter-tribal balance of power and subordinated native to European interests. A recognition of the change wrought by the end of the war inspired the uprising of the Ottawas in 1763, when **Pontiac**, their chief, led an unsuccessful assault on Detroit, hoping to restore the French position and halt the progress of the English settlers. Moved largely by a desire for a stable economy, the response of the British Crown was to issue a proclamation which confirmed the legal right of the natives to their lands and set aside the territory to the west of the Appalachian Mountains and the Great Lakes as "**Indian Territory**". Although colonial governors were given instructions to remove trespassers on "Indian Land", in reality the proclamation had little practical effect until the twentieth century, when it became a cornerstone of native peoples' attempts to seek compensation for the illegal confiscation of their land.

The other great problem the British faced in the 1760s was how to deal with the French-speaking **Canadiens** of the defunct New France – the term Canadiens used to distinguish local settlers from those born in France, most of whom left the colony after the British conquest. Initially the British government hoped to anglicize the province, swamping the French-speaking population with English-speaking Protestants. In the event, large-scale migration failed to materialize immediately, and the second English governor of Québec, **Sir Guy Carleton**, realized that – as discontent grew in the American colonies – the loyalty of the Canadiens was of vital importance.

Carleton's plan to achieve this was embodied in the 1774 **Québec Act**, which made a number of concessions to the region's French speakers: Catholics were permitted to hold civil appointments, the seigneurial system was maintained, and the Roman Catholic Church allowed to collect tithes. Remarkably, all these concessions were made at a time when Catholics in Britain were not politically emancipated.

The migrations

The success of this policy was seen during the **American War of Independence** (1775–83) – and later during the Anglo-American War of 1812. The Canadiens refused to volunteer for the armed forces of the Crown, but equally they failed to respond to the appeals of the Americans – no doubt calculating that their survival as a distinctive cultural group was more likely under the British than in an English-speaking United States.

In the immediate aftermath of the American War of Independence, the population of what was left of British North America expanded rapidly, both in "Canada" – which then covered the present-day provinces of Québec and Ontario – and in the separate colonies of New Brunswick, Nova Scotia, Prince Edward Island and Newfoundland. The first large wave of migration came from the United States as 40,000 **United Empire Loyalists** (see p.459 for more on this group) made their way north to stay within British jurisdiction. Of these, all but 8000 moved to Nova Scotia and New Brunswick, the rest going to the western edge of Québec, where they laid the foundations of the future province of Ontario. Between 1783 and 1812 the population of Canada, as defined at the time, trebled to 330,000, with a large part of the increase being the product of revanche du berceau (revenge of the cradle) – an attempt, encouraged by the Catholic clergy, to outbreed the English-speaking population.

However, tensions between Britain and the United States still deterred potential colonists, a problem resolved by the **War of 1812**. Neither side was strong enough to win, but by the Treaty of Ghent in 1814 the Americans recognized the legitimacy of British North America, whose border was established along the **49th parallel** west from Lake of the Woods to the Rockies. Immigration now boomed, especially in the 1840s, when economic crises and shortages in Britain as well as the Irish famine pushed it up to levels that even the fertile Canadiens could not match. Between 1815 and 1850 over 800,000 immigrants poured into British North America. Most headed for "Upper Canada", later called Ontario, which received 66,000 migrants in 1832 alone.

Faced with this human tide, the surveyors charted new townships as quickly as possible, but they simply couldn't keep pace with demand. One result was that many native peoples were dispossessed in direct contravention of the 1763 proclamation. By 1806 the region's native peoples had lost 4.5 million acres.

The division and union of Canada

Throughout this period economic expansion was largely generated by the English-speaking merchants who now controlled the Montréal-based fur trade, organized as the **North West Company**. Seeking political changes that would enhance their economic power, they wanted their own legislative assembly and the universal application of English law, which of course would not have been acceptable to the French-speakers.

In 1791, through the **Canada Act**, the British government imposed a compromise, dividing the region into **Upper** and **Lower Canada**, which broadly separated the two groups along the line of the Ottawa River. In Lower Canada, the French-based legal system was retained, as was the right of the Catholic Church to collect tithes, while in Upper Canada, English common law was introduced. Each of the new provinces had an elective assembly, though these shared their limited powers with an appointed assembly and executive councils appointed by the governor of each province. This arrangement allowed the assemblies to become the focal points for vocal opposition, but ultimately condemned them to impotence. At the same time, the merchant elite built up chains of influence and power around the appointed provincial governments: in Upper Canada this grouping was called the "**Family Compact**", in Lower Canada the "**Château Clique**".

By the late 1830s considerable opposition had developed to these cliques. In Upper Canada the **Reform Movement** led by **William Lyon Mackenzie** demanded a government accountable to a broad electorate, and the expansion of credit facilities for small farmers. In 1837 both Mackenzie and **Louis-Joseph Papineau**, the reform leader in Lower Canada, were sufficiently frustrated to attempt open rebellion. Neither was successful and both were forced into exile in the United States, but the rebellions did bring home to the British Government the need for effective reform, prompting the **Act of Union** of 1840, which united Lower and Upper Canada with a single assembly.

The rationale for this arrangement was the belief that the French-Canadians were incapable of handling elective government without Anglo-Saxon guidance. Nevertheless, the assembly provided equal representation for Canada East and West – in effect the old Lower and Upper Canadas. A few years later, this new assembly achieved **responsible government** almost accidentally. In 1849 the Reform Party, which had a majority of the seats, passed an Act compensating those involved in the 1837 rebellions. The Governor-General, Lord Elgin, disapproved, but he didn't exercise his veto – so, for the first time, a Canadian administration acted on the vote of an elected assembly, rather than imperial sanction.

The Reform Party, which pushed through the compensation scheme, included both French- and English-speakers and mainly represented small farmers and businessmen opposed to the power of the cliques. In the 1850s this grouping became the Canadian **Liberal Party**, but the coalition fell apart in the 1860s with the emergence of "Clear Grit" Liberals in Canada West. The Grits argued for "Representation by Population" – in other words, instead of equal representation for the two halves of Canada, they wanted constituencies based on the total population. As the English-speakers outnumbered the French, the "Rep by

Poppers" slogan seemed a direct threat to many of the institutions of French Canada. As a consequence, many French-Canadians transferred their support to the **Conservative Party**, while the radicals of Canada East, the **Rouges**, developed a more nationalist creed.

The Conservative Party comprised a number of elements, including the rump of the merchant elite who were so infuriated by their loss of control that they burnt the Montréal parliament building to the ground in 1849. Some of this group campaigned to break the imperial tie and join the United States, but, when the party fully emerged in 1854, the old "Compact Tories" were much less influential than a younger generation of moderate conservatives. The lynchpin of this younger group was **John A. Macdonald**, who was to form the first federal government in 1868. Such moderates sought, by overcoming the democratic excesses of the "Grits" and the nationalism of the "Rouges", to weld together an economic and political state that would not be absorbed into the increasingly powerful United States.

Confederation

In the mid-1860s "Canada" had achieved responsible party government, but British North America was still a collection of **self-governing colonies**. In the east, Newfoundland was almost entirely dependent on its cod fishery, Prince Edward Island had a prosperous agricultural economy, and both Nova Scotia and New Brunswick had boomed on the backs of their shipbuilding industry. Far to the west, on the Pacific coast, lay fur-trading British Columbia, which had just beaten off American attempts to annex the region during the Oregon crisis, finally resolved in 1846, when the international frontier was fixed along a westward extension of the original 49th parallel. Not that this was the end of British Columbia's problems: in 1858 gold was discovered beside the Fraser River and, in response to the influx of American prospectors, British Columbia was hastily designated a Crown Colony – a process that was repeated in 1895 when gold was discovered in the Yukon's Klondike. Between Canada West and British Columbia stretched thousands of miles of prairie and forest, the old Rupert's Land that was still under the extremely loose authority of the Hudson's Bay Company.

Also in the 1860s, the American Civil War raised fears of a US invasion of an incoherently structured British North America, at the same time as "Rep by Poppers" agitation was making the status of the French-speaking minority problematic. These issues prompted a series of conferences to discuss the issue of **Confederation**, and after three years of intense debate the British Parliament passed the British North America Act of 1867. In effect this was a constitution for the new **Dominion of Canada**, providing for a federal parliament to be established at Ottawa; for Canada East and West to become the provinces of Québec and Ontario respectively; and for each province to retain a regional government and assembly. All of the existing colonies joined the Confederation except British Columbia, which waited until 1871; Prince Edward Island, till 1873; and Newfoundland, which remained independent until 1949.

The consolidation of the west

Having settled the question of a constitution, the Dominion turned its attention to the west. In 1869, the territory of the Hudson's Bay Company was bought for £300,000 and the **Northwest Territories**, as the area then became known, reverted to the Crown until Canada was ready to administer them. Predictably, the wishes of its population – primarily Plains Indians and 5000 **Métis** – were given no heed. The Métis, whose main settlement was near the site of modern-day Winnipeg, were already alarmed by the arrival of Ontario settlers and were even more alarmed when government land surveyors arrived to divide the land into lots that cut right across their holdings. Fearful of their land rights, the Métis formed a provisional government under the leadership of **Louis Riel** and prepared to resist the federal authorities (see p.624).

In the course of the rebellion, Riel executed a troublesome Ontario Orangeman by the name of Thomas Scott, an action which created uproar in Ontario. Despite this, the federal government negotiated with a Métis delegation and appeared to meet all their demands, although Riel was obliged to go into exile in the States. As a result of the negotiations, Ottawa created the new province **of Manitoba** to the west of Ontario in 1870, and set aside 140 acres per person for the Métis – though land speculators and lawyers ensured that fewer than twenty percent of those eligible actually got their land.

Dispossession was also the fate of the **Plains Indians**. From 1871 onwards a series of treaties were negotiated, offering native families 160-acre plots and a whole range of goods and services if they signed. By 1877 seven treaties had been agreed (eventually there were eleven), handing over to the government all of the southern prairies. However, the promised aid did not materialize and the native peoples found themselves confined to small, infertile reservations.

The federal government's increased interest in the area – spurred by the **Cypress Hills Massacre** of Assiniboine natives in 1873 (see p.607) – was underlined by the arrival in 1874 of the first 275 members of the newly formed Northwest Mounted Police, the **Mounties** (for more, see p.595). One of their first actions was to expel the American whiskey traders who had earned the region the nickname 'Whoop-up Country'. Once the police had taken charge, Ottawa passed the **Second Indian Act** of 1880, making a Minister of Indian Affairs responsible for the native peoples. The minister and his superintendents exercised a near dictatorial control, so that almost any action that a native person might wish to take, from building a house to making a visit off the reservation, had to be approved by the local official, and often the ministry in Ottawa too. The Act laid down that every aboriginal applicant for "enfranchisement" as an ordinary Canadian citizen had to pass through a three-year probation period. They were also to be examined to see if they had attained a sufficient level of "civilization". If "enfranchised," the individual was counted as a so-called "non-status Indian", as opposed to the "status Indians" of the reservations. These distinctions persist today: with status Indians, of whom there are around 600,000, divided up into around six hundred aboriginal bands. Some bands number fewer than 100 inhabitants and others more than 5000, but all now have at least a degree of self-government as well as local fishing, hunting and land rights. Both status and non-status Indians can vote, but the former were only granted this right in 1960.

During the 1870s, most of the **Métis** had moved west into the territory that was to become the province of **Saskatchewan** in 1905. Here they congregated along the Saskatchewan River in the vicinity of Batoche, but once again federal surveyors caught up with them and, in the 1880s, began to divide the land into the familiar gridiron pattern. In 1885, the Métis rose in **revolt** and, after the return of Riel, formed a provisional government. In March they successfully beat off a detachment of Mounted Police, encouraging the neighbouring Cree to raid a Hudson's Bay Company Store. It seemed that a general native insurrection might follow, born of the desperation that accompanied the treaty system, the starvation which went with the disappearance of the buffalo, and the ravages of smallpox. The government dispatched a force of 7000 with Gatling guns and an armed steamer, and after two preliminary skirmishes the Métis and the Cree were crushed absolutely. Riel, despite his obvious insanity, was found guilty of treason and hanged in November 1885.

The defeat of the Métis opened a new phase in the development of the west. In 1886 the first **train** ran **from Montréal to Vancouver** and settlers swarmed onto the prairies, pushing the population up from 250,000 in 1890 to 1,300,000 in 1911. Clifford Sifton, Minister of the Interior, encouraged the large-scale immigration from Eastern Europe of what he called "stalwart peasants in sheepskin coats". These Ukrainians, Poles, Czechs and Hungarians ploughed up the grasslands and turned central Canada into a vast granary, leading the Dominion into the "wheat boom" of the early twentieth century.

Native peoples from 1900 to today

For Canada's **native peoples** the early years of the twentieth century were grim. Herded onto small reservations under the authoritarian control of the ministry, they were subjected to a concerted campaign of **Europeanization** – ceremonies such as the sun dance and the potlatch were banned, and they were obliged to send their children to boarding schools for ten months of the year. Deprived of their traditions and independence, they lapsed into poverty, alcoholism and apathy. In the late 1940s, the academic Frederick Tisdall estimated that no fewer than 65,000 reservation aboriginals were "chronically sick" from starvation. In addition, the Inuit were drawn into increasing dependence on the Hudson's Bay Company, who encouraged them to concentrate on hunting for furs rather than food, while the twin agencies of the Christian missions and the Royal Canadian Mounted Police worked to incorporate the Inuit into white culture. All over Canada, a major consequence of the disruption of the traditional way of native life was the spread of disease, especially TB, which was fifteen to twenty times more prevalent amongst the aboriginal population than amongst whites.

In 1951, a new **Indian Act** increased both the autonomy of tribal bands and federal subsidies, but nonetheless aboriginal people remained well behind the rest of Canadian society in all the key economic indicators. In 1969, the average income of a Canadian family was $8874, whilst 88 percent of aboriginal families earned $3000 or less, with fifty percent earning less than $1000. In that same year, partly as a result of native lobbying, all Indian agents were withdrawn from reservations, and aboriginal political organizations started receiving government funding. Increasingly, these organizations focused on the need for full recognition of their aboriginal rights and renegotiation of the treaties that had created the reservations in the first place.

The early 1980s saw the foundation of the **Assembly of First Nations** (AFN), which championed "Status Indians" in a number of legal actions over treaty rights and opposed federal plans to abolish the whole notion of "Status Indians". Many of these treaty cases were based on breaches of the 1763 proclamation, whose terms stated that native land rights could only be taken away by direct negotiation with the Crown. One recent Grand Chief of the AFN, **Ovide Mercredi** – a lawyer and former human-rights commissioner – announced that his objective was to secure equal status between the AFN and the provincial governments, a stance indicative of the growth in native self-confidence, despite the continuing impoverishment of the reservations. The political weight of the AFN was made clear in the constitutional talks that took place over the establishment of an **Inuit homeland** in the Northwest

Territories, a complex negotiation resulting in an agreement to create two self-governing territories in 1999 (see p.1068). But not all of Canada's natives, who comprise around three percent of Canada's population, see negotiation as their salvation: the action of armed Mohawks to prevent a golf course being built on tribal burial grounds at **Oka** in Québec (p.275) displayed an almost uncontainable anger against the dominant whites, and divided sympathies across the country. In the event, the Oka militants paved the way for more conciliatory voices to hold sway in the AFN, but the balance of power between those native peoples committed to negotiation as distinct from those favouring direct action is delicate. As a result, the AFN ploughs on with negotiations that rarely hit the headlines against a backdrop lit by occasional bursts of unrestrained native rage, often to do with fishing rights.

More positively, there has been a resurgence in native fine and applied art, and aboriginal ceremonies, like the summer powwows, have started to attract large crowds and adequate media attention. Aboriginal theatre groups have sprung up right across Canada and there's now a public television channel for indigenous people, the **Aboriginal Peoples Television Network** (APTN; ⓦwww.aptn.ca), which went on air in 1999.

Québec and the future of Canada

Just as Canada's native peoples drew inspiration from the worldwide national liberation movements of the late 1950s and 1960s, so did the **Québecois**. Ever since the conquest of 1760, francophones had been deeply concerned about *la survivance*, the continuation of their language and culture. Periodically this anxiety had been heightened, notably during both world wars, when the Québecois opposed the introduction of conscription because it seemed to subordinate their interests to those of Britain. Nevertheless, despite these difficulties, the essentially conservative Québecois political–religious establishment almost always recommended accommodation with the British and later the federal authorities. This same establishment upheld the traditional values of Catholic rural New France, a consequence of which was that Québec's industry and commerce developed under anglophone control. Thus, in early twentieth-century Montréal, a francophone proletariat worked in the factories of anglophone owners, an anglophone dominance that was compounded by the indifference of Canada's other provinces to French-Canadian interests, spurring the development of a new generation of Québec **separatists**.

Held in Montréal, **Expo '67** was meant to be a confirmation of Canada's arrival as an industrial power of the first rank. However, when France's President de Gaulle used the event as a platform to announce his advocacy of a "free Québec", he ignited a row that has dominated the political agenda ever since. That same year, **René Lévesque** formed the **Parti Québécois** (PQ), with the ultimate goal of full independence, hence the slogan Maîtres chez nous ("masters in our own house"), but in 1968 this was offset by the election of a determinedly federalist French-Canadian, **Pierre Trudeau**, as prime minister: the scene was set for a showdown.

The PQ represented the constitutional wing of a social movement that, at its most militant extreme, embraced the activities of the short-lived **Front de la Libération du Québec** (FLQ). In 1970 the FLQ kidnapped and murdered Pierre Laporte, the province's Minister of Labour, an action which provoked Trudeau into putting the troops onto the streets of Montréal. This reaction was to benefit the PQ, a modernizing party of the social-democratic left, which came to power in 1976 and set about using state resources to develop economic interests such as the Québec hydroelectric plant on James Bay. It also reformed education – including controversial legislation to make Québec unilingual – and pressed ahead with plans for a referendum on secession. But when the referendum came, in 1980, sixty percent of Québec's electorate voted "non" to separation, partly because the 1970s had witnessed a closing of the opportunity gap between the francophone and anglophone communities. This did not, however, end the affair.

In 1985, Québec's PQ government was defeated by **Robert Bourassa**'s Liberals, not so much reflecting a shift in francophone feeling but more Bourassa's espousal of the bulk of the nationalist agenda and what many felt to be the PQ's poor economic track record. The Liberals held power in Québec until 1994, when the PQ bounced back into office, promising to hold another independence referendum. They seemed well set. Polls regularly rated support at around sixty percent, but in 1995 the PQ lost again in a **second referendum** that rejected independence by just 50,000 votes. Despite all the subsequent bluster, this was a political disaster for the PQ, and, with the momentum lost, subsequent polls indicated that the separatist bubble had well and truly burst. Consequently, although the PQ continued in office for the next few years, they never had the political strength to call another referendum and they were ousted by the province's Liberals in 2003 and kept out of power again in 2007. One of the key reasons for the PQ's failure was its inability to define the precise nature of Québec sovereignty and how future relations with the rest of Canada would be conducted, though this remains a very vexed subject that sets many Canadians frothing at the mouth.

Into the twenty-first century

To say that the rest of Canada has become exasperated with the interminable discussions over the future of Québec would be an understatement – and never more so than during the **Meech Lake** conference of 1990, which conspicuously failed to agree on a new decentralized constitution. The conference was convened by the Conservative **Brian Mulroney**, who had become the country's premier in 1984. Mulroney had other pressing problems, too, though admittedly nothing as fractious as Québec. To begin with, the NAFTA free trade agreement between the US and Canada, which Mulroney pushed through parliament, came into effect in 1989, destroying the country's protective tariffs and thereby exposing its industries to undercutting and causing thousands of redundancies. There was also the collapse of the North Atlantic cod fishery, which brought Nova Scotia and Newfoundland to the brink of economic ruin, whilst falls in wheat prices hurt the Prairies. Efforts were made to deal with these issues, but few were satisfied and during Mulroney's second term (1988–93), the premier became a byword for incompetence, his party commonly accused of large-scale corruption. As a result, the 1993 federal elections almost wiped out the Conservatives and, equipped with a huge majority, the new Liberal administration, under **Jean Chrétien**, once Trudeau's Minister of Finance, set about rebuilding federal prestige. A cautious politician, Chrétien had some success, his pragmatic approach to politics proving sufficiently popular to see him re-elected for a second term in 1997 and a third in 2000, albeit with reduced majorities. However, much of Chrétien's electoral success was down to the **balkanization** of the Canadian political scene. The Liberals were the only party with any claim to a national presence – with the right-wing Canadian Alliance (formerly the Reform Party), for instance, dominating much of the west, but simply failing to show in the east. Neither were Canadians as a whole politically enthused: in the 2000 federal election, only sixty percent turned out to vote and of these the Liberals only secured the support of 39 percent.

In 2003, Chrétien announced his retirement, and his Liberals appointed a new leader, the politically formidable and very competent **Paul Martin**. Facing the prospect of further electoral defeats, Canada's two rightist parties – the Canadian Alliance and the Progressive Conservatives – belatedly managed to swallow their differences, uniting to form the **Conservative Party**, but were still unable to defeat the Liberals in the **federal elections of 2004**. The new Liberal administration, with Martin as premier, did not, however, have an overall majority and its political weakness made the government shaky. The Martin regime did manage to pass several progressive measures – 2005 saw the passage of the Civil Marriage Act sanctioning same-sex marriages, the Kelowna Accord dedicated to improving the lot of Canada's native peoples, and an injection of funds into the public health care system – but allegations of **corruption** swirled around the Prime Minister and the Liberals lost a vote of confidence in late 2005. Shortly afterwards. the **federal elections of 2006** produced a narrow victory for the Conservatives with **Stephen Harper** as the new Prime Minister. At time of writing, it's too early to say how the new regime will face up, but mercifully the new government seems to be tacking to the centre ground rather than the right.

The natural environment

Canada has just about every **natural habitat** going, from ice-bound polar islands in the far north to sun-drilled pockets of desert along the US border. Between these extremes the country's mountains, forests and grasslands support an incredible variety and profusion of **wildlife** – any brief account can only scratch the surface of what it's possible to see. National and provincial parks offer the best starting places, and we've listed some of the outstanding sites for spotting particular species. However, don't expect to see the big attractions like bears and wolves easily; despite the enthusiasm of guides and tourist offices, these are encountered only rarely.

Flora and fauna checklist

This is by no means an exhaustive list of all Canada's flora and fauna – simply an indication of the places and the seasons that you are most likely to see certain species and types of wildlife.

Bears Black bears: Glacier National Park, BC and Banff, Jasper and Kananaskis Country, AB. Grizzlies: Glacier National Park, BC and Khutzeymateen Estuary, north of Prince Rupert, BC. *August.*

Bison Wood Buffalo National Park, AB.

Butterfly migrations Point Pelee and Long Point, Lake Erie, ON. *Spring and autumn.*

Caribou Dempster Hwy, YT. *Autumn.*

Cranes and pelicans Last Mountain Lake, SK. *Late August.*

Dall's sheep Sheep Mountain, Kluane National Park, YT. *Summer.*

Desert species Cacti, sagebrush, rattlesnakes and kangaroo rats: around Osoyoos, BC. *Summer.*

Eagles and owls Boundary Bay, south of Vancouver, BC. *Winter.*

Elk Banff, Jasper and Kananaskis Country, AB. *Summer.*

Orchids Bruce Peninsula National Park, ON. *Spring and summer.*

Polar bears Near Churchill, MB. *Autumn.*

Prairie species Hawks, coyotes and rattlesnakes: in the Milk River region, AB. *May and June.*

Salmon Adams River sockeye salmon run near Salmon Arm, BC. *October.*

Sea birds Gannets, murres and black kittiwakes around Cape St Mary's, NFL. Waterfowl and sea birds in the Queen Charlotte Islands, BC. Northern gannets on Bonaventure Island, Gaspé Peninsula, QC. *June and July.*

Sea otters and sea lions Off Pacific Rim National Park, Vancouver Island, BC. *Spring and summer.*

Seals Queen Charlotte Islands, BC. *Summer.*

Snow geese Cap-Tourmente, QC. *Autumn.*

Whales Beluga, fin, humpback, blue and minke whales: near Tadoussac, QC and Bay of Fundy, NB. Killer whales (orcas): Robson Bight in Johnstone Strait, Vancouver Island, BC. All in summer. Grey whales: Pacific Rim National Park, Vancouver Island, BC. *Spring and summer.*

Wild flowers Numerous woodland species on Vancouver Island and the Gulf Islands, BC and at Mount Revelstoke National Park, BC. *Late spring to summer.*

Eastern forests

Canada's **eastern forests** divide into two main groups – the Carolinian forest of southwestern Ontario, and the Great Lakes-St Lawrence forest extending from the edge of the Carolinian forest to Lake Superior and the Gulf of St Lawrence.

The **Carolinian forest** forms a narrow belt of largely deciduous hardwood trees similar to the broad-leaved woodlands found over much of the eastern United States. Trees are often typical of more southerly climes – Kentucky coffee tree, tulip tree, sassafras, sycamore, chinquapin oak, shagbark hickory and more ordinary staples like beech, sugar maple, basswood and swamp oak. None of these are rare in the US, but in Canada they grow only here, thanks to the region's rich soils and relatively warm, sheltered climate.

A good deal of the Carolinian flora and fauna is coming under increasing threat from southern Ontario's urban and agricultural sprawl. These days much of the original forest has shrunk to a mosaic of fragments protected by national and provincial parks. The forests are most often visited by tourists for the astounding October colours, but if you're looking for **wildlife** you might also catch Canada's only marsupial, the **opossum**, or other southern species like the **fox squirrel** (introduced on Lake Erie's Pelee Island); the **eastern mole**, which occurs only in Essex County on Lake Erie's north shore; and the **eastern vole**, found only in a narrow band around Lake Erie.

Naturalists are equally drawn here for the **birds**, many of which are found nowhere else in Canada, especially during seasonal migrations, when up to one hundred species can easily be seen in a day. Most noteworthy of the more unusual species is the **golden swamp warbler**, a bird of almost unnaturally colourful plumage. More common visitors are hooded and Kentucky warblers, blue-winged and golden-winged warblers, gnatcatchers and virtually every species of eastern North American hawk. Sharp-shin hawks are common, and during autumn migrations of up to 70,000 broad-winged hawks might be seen in a single day near Port Stanley on Lake Erie's north shore.

In the wetlands bordering the forests, particularly at Long Point on Lake Erie, you can search out **reptiles** found nowhere else in the country. Most impressive is the water-loving fox snake, a harmless animal that often reaches well over a metre in length, but is often killed because of its resemblance to the rattlesnake and venomous copperhead – neither of which is found in the region. Also present, but in marked decline, are several **turtle** species, especially Blanding's, wood, spotted and spiny softshell.

Occurring in one of the most densely populated parts of Canada, the mixed conifer forests of the **Great Lakes-St Lawrence** area have been heavily logged and severely affected by urbanization. Most of the trees are southern species – beech and sugar maple, red and white pines – but are mixed with the eastern hemlock, spruce, jack pine, paper birch and balsam fir typical of more northerly forests. Ironically, widespread human disturbance has, if anything, created a greater diversity of forest types, which makes this region second only to southern British Columbia in the number of bird species it supports. It also provides for large numbers of **white-tailed deer**, a rare beneficiary of logging as it prefers to browse along the edges of clearings. In the evergreen stands on the north shore of the St Lawrence there are also large numbers of Canada's smallest mammal, the **pygmy shrew**. These tiny animals must eat their own weight in food daily and can't rest for more than an hour or so – they'd starve to death if they tried to sleep through the night.

Grassland

Contrary to the popular image of Canada's interior as a huge prairie of waving wheat, true **grassland** covers only ten percent of the country. Most is concentrated in the southernmost reaches of Alberta and Saskatchewan, with tiny spillovers in Manitoba and British Columbia – areas which lie in the Rockies' rain shadow and are too dry to support forest.

Two grassland belts once thrived in the region, **tall-grass prairie** in the north and **shortgrass** in the south. Farming has now not only put large areas of each under crops, but also decimated most of the large mammals that roamed the range – pronghorns, mule deer, white-tailed deer and elk – not to mention their predators, such as wolves, grizzlies, coyotes, foxes, bobcats and cougars.

The most dramatic loss from the grasslands, though, has been **bison** (or buffalo), the continent's largest land mammal. Once numbering an estimated 45 million, bison are now limited to just a few free-roaming herds in Canada. They're extraordinarily impressive animals – the average bull stands six feet at the shoulder and weighs over a ton – and early prairie settlers were so struck with their size that they believed bison, not the climate, had been responsible for clearing the grasslands.

Once almost as prevalent as the bison, but now almost as rare, is the **pronghorn**, a beautiful tawny-gold antelope species. Capable of speeds of over 100kph, it's the continent's swiftest land mammal, so you'll generally see nothing but its distinctive white rump disappearing at speed. Uniquely adapted for speed and stamina, the pronghorn has long legs, a heart twice the size of similar-sized animals, and an astonishingly wide windpipe. It also complements its respiratory machinery by running with its mouth open to gulp maximum amounts of air. Though only the size of a large dog, it has larger eyes than those of a horse, a refinement that spots predators several kilometres away. These days, however, wolves and coyotes are more likely to be after the prairie's new masters – countless small rodents such as gophers, ground squirrels and jackrabbits.

Birds have had to adapt not only to the prairie's dryness but also, of course, to the lack of extensive tree cover, and most species nest on the ground; many are also able to survive on reduced amounts of water and rely on seed-centred diets. Others confine themselves to occasional ponds, lakes and "sloughs", which are important breeding grounds for ducks, grebes, herons, pelicans, rails and many more. Other birds typical of the grassland in its natural state are the marbled godwit, the curlew and raptors such as the **prairie falcon**, a close relation of the peregrine falcon that's capable of diving speeds of up to 290kph.

Boreal forest

The **boreal forest** is Canada's largest single ecosystem, bigger than all the others combined. Stretching in a broad belt from Newfoundland to the Yukon, it fills the area between the eastern forests, grasslands and the northern tundra, occupying a good slice of every province except British Columbia. Only certain **trees** thrive in this zone of long, cold winters, short summers and acidic soils: although the cover is not identical countrywide, expect to see billions of white and black spruce (plus red spruce in the east), balsam fir, tamarack (larch) and jack pine, as well as such deciduous species as birch, poplar and aspen – all of which are ideal for wood pulp, making the boreal forest the staple resource of the country's **lumber industry**.

If you spend any time in the backcountry you'll also come across **muskeg**: neither land nor water, this porridge-like bog is the breeding ground of choice for pestilent hordes of mosquitoes and blackflies – and Canada has 1.3 million square kilometres of it. It also harbours mosses, scrub willow, pitcher plant, leatherleaf, sundew, cranberry and even the occasional orchid.

The boreal forest supports just about every animal recognized as distinctively Canadian: moose, beaver, black bear, wolf and lynx, plus a broad cross-section of small mammals and creatures such as deer, caribou and coyote from transitional forest-tundra and aspen-parkland habitats to the north and south. **Wolves** are still numerous in Canada, but hunting and harassment has pushed them to the northernmost parts of the boreal forest. Their supposed ferocity is more myth than truth; intelligent and elusive creatures, they rarely harm humans, and it's unlikely you'll see any – though you may well hear their howling if you're out in the sticks. **Lynx** are even more elusive. One of the northern forest's most elegant animals, this big cat requires a 150- to 200-square-kilometre range, making Canada's northern wilderness one of the world's few regions capable of sustaining a viable population. Nocturnal hunters, lynx feed on deer and moose but favour the hare, a common boreal creature that is to the forest's predators what the lemming is to the carnivores of the tundra.

Beavers, on the other hand, are commonly seen all over Canada. You may catch them at dawn or dusk, heads just above the water as they glide across lakes and rivers. Signs of their legendary activity include log jams across streams and ponds, stumps of felled saplings resembling sharpened pencils, and dens which look like domed piles of mud and sticks.

Lakes, streams and marshy muskeg margins are all favoured by **moose**. A lumbering animal with magnificent spreading antlers, it is the largest member of the deer family and is found over most of Canada, but especially near swampy ground, where it likes to graze on mosses and lichens. It's also a favourite with hunters, and few northern bars are without their moose head – perhaps the only place you'll see this solitary and reclusive species.

Forest wetlands also offer refuge for **ducks and geese**, with **loons**, grebes and songbirds attracted to their surrounding undergrowth. Canada's three species of ptarmigan – willow, rock and white-tailed – are also common, and you'll see plenty of big **raptors**, including the great grey owl, Canada's largest owl. Many boreal birds migrate, and even those that don't, such as hawks, jays, ravens and grouse, tend to move a little way south, sometimes breaking out into southern Canada in mass movements known as "irruptions". Smaller birds, like chickadees, waxwings and finches, are particularly fond of these sporadic forays.

Mountain forests

Mountain forests cover much of western Canada and, depending on location and elevation, divide into four types: West Coast, Columbia, montane and subalpine.

The **West Coast**'s torrential rainfall, mild maritime climate, deep soils and long growing season produce Canada's most impressive forests and its biggest trees. Swaths of luxuriant temperate **rainforest** cover much of Vancouver Island and the Pacific coast, dominated by Sitka spruce, western red cedar, Pacific silver fir, western hemlock, western yew and, biggest of all, **Douglas fir**, some of which tower 90 metres high and are 1200 years old. However, these conifers make valuable timber, and much of this forest is under severe threat from logging. Some of the best stands – a fraction of the original – have been preserved on the Queen Charlotte Islands and in Vancouver Island's Pacific Rim National Park. Below the luxuriant, dripping canopy of the big trees lies an **undergrowth** teeming with life. Shrubs and bushes such as salal, huckleberry, bunchberry, salmonberry and twinberry thrive alongside mosses, ferns, lichens, liverworts, skunk cabbage and orchids. All sorts of animals can be found here, most notably the **cougar** and its main prey, the Columbian blacktail **deer**, a subspecies of the mule deer. **Birds** are legion, and include a wealth of woodland species such as the Townsend's warbler, Wilson's warbler, orange-crowned warbler, junco, Swainson's thrush and golden-crowned kinglet. Rarer birds include the rufous **hummingbird**, which migrates from its wintering grounds in Mexico to feed on the forest's numerous nectar-bearing flowers.

The **Columbia forest** covers the lower slopes (400–1400m) of British Columbia's interior mountains and much of the Rockies. **Trees** here are similar to those of the West Coast's warmer and wetter rainforest – western red cedar, western hemlock and Douglas fir – with Sitka spruce, which rarely thrives away from the coast, the notable exception. The undercover, too, is similar, with lots of devil's club (a particularly vicious thorn), azaleas, black and red twinberry, salmonberry and redberry alder. Mountain lily, columbine, bunchberry and heart-leaf arnica are among the common flowers. Few mammals live exclusively in the forests with the exception of the **red squirrel**, which makes a meal of conifer seeds, and is in turn preyed on by hawks, owls, coyotes and weasels, among others. Bigger predators roam the mountain forest, however, most notably the **brown bear**, a western variant of the ubiquitous **black bear**. Aside from the coyote, the tough, agile black bear is one of the continent's most successful carnivores and the one you're most likely to see around campsites and rubbish dumps. Black bears have adapted to a wide range of habitats and food sources, and their only natural enemies – save wolves, which may attack young cubs – are hunters, who bag some 30,000 annually in North America. Scarcer but still hunted is the famous **grizzly bear**, a far larger and potentially dangerous creature distinguished by its brownish fur and the ridged hump on its back. Now extinct in many of its original habitats, the grizzly is largely confined to the remoter slopes of the Rockies and West Coast ranges, where it feeds mainly on berries and salmon. Like other bears, grizzlies are unpredictable and readily provoked – see p.703 for tips on avoiding unpleasant encounters.

Montane forest covers the more southerly and sheltered reaches of the Rockies and the dry plateaux of interior British Columbia, where spindly Douglas fir, western larch, ponderosa pine and the **lodgepole pine** predominate. Like its eastern counterpart, the jack pine, the lodgepole requires intense heat before opening and releasing its seeds, and huge stands of these trees grew in the aftermath of the forest fires which accompanied the building and running of the railways. Plentiful voles and small rodents attract **coyotes**, whose yapping – an announcement of territorial claims – you'll often hear at night close to small towns. Coyotes are spreading northwards into the Yukon and Northwest Territories and eastwards into Ontario and Québec, a proliferation that continues despite massive extermination campaigns, prompted by the coyotes' taste for livestock. Few predators have the speed to keep up with coyotes – only the stealthy **cougar**, or wolves hunting in tandem, can successfully bring them down. Cougars are now severely depleted in Canada, and the British Columbia interior and Vancouver Island are the only regions where they survive in significant numbers. Among the biggest and most beautiful of the carnivores, they seem to arouse the greatest bloodlust in hunters. Ponderosa and lodgepole pines provide fine cover for **birds** like goshawks, Swainson's hawks and lesser species such as ruby-crowned kinglets, warblers, pileated woodpeckers, nuthatches and chickadees. In the forest's lowest reaches the vegetation and birds are those of the southern prairies – semi-arid regions of sagebrush, prickly pear and bunch grasses, dotted with lakes full of common **ducks** such as mallard, shoveler and widgeon. You might also see the cinnamon teal, a red version of the more common green-wing teal, a bird whose limited distribution draws bird-watchers to British Columbia on its own account.

Subalpine forest covers mountain slopes from 1300m to 2200m throughout the Rockies and much of British Columbia, supporting lodgepole, whitebark and limber pines, alpine fir and Engelmann spruce. It also contains a preponderance of **alpine larch**, a deciduous conifer whose vivid autumnal yellows dot the mountainsides to beautiful effect. One of the more common animals of this zone is the **elk**, or wapiti, a powerful member of the deer family, which can often be seen summering in large herds above the tree line. Elk court and mate during the autumn, making a thin nasal sound called "bugling". Respect their privacy, as rutting elk have notoriously unpredictable temperaments. Small herds of **mule deer** migrate between forests and alpine meadows, using small glands between their hooves to leave a scent for other herd members to follow. They're named after their distinctive ears, designed to provide early warning of predators. Other smaller animals which are also attracted to the subalpine forest include the golden-mantled ground squirrel, and birds such as **Clark's nutcracker**, both tame and curious creatures which often gather around campsites in search of scraps.

Alpine zones

Alpine zones occur in mountains above the tree line, which in Canada means parts of the Rockies, much of British Columbia and large areas of the Yukon. Plant and animal life varies hugely between summer and winter, and according to terrain and exposure to the elements – sometimes it resembles that of the tundra, at others it recalls the profile of lower forest habitats.

In spring, alpine meadows are carpeted with breathtaking displays of **wild flowers**: clumps of Parnassus grass, lilies, anemones, Indian paintbrushes, lupins and a wealth of yellow flowers such as arnica, cinquefoil, glacier lily and wood betony. These meadows make excellent pasture, attracting elk and mule deer in summer, as well as full-time residents such as **Dall's sheep**, the related **bighorn** and the incredible **mountain goat**, perhaps the hardiest of Canada's bigger mammals. Staying close to the roughest terrain possible, mountain goats are equipped with short, stolid legs, flexible toes and nonskid soles, all designed for clambering over near-vertical slopes, grazing well out of reach of their less agile predators.

Marmots, resembling hugely overstuffed squirrels, take things easier and hibernate through the worst of the winter and beyond. In a good year they can sleep for eight months, prey only to grizzly bears, which are strong enough and have the claws to dig down into their dens. In their waking periods they can be tame and friendly, often nibbling contentedly in the sunnier corners of campsites. When threatened, however, they produce a piercing and unearthly whistle. (They can also do a lot of damage: some specialize in chewing the radiator hoses of parked cars.) The strange little **pika**, a relative of the rabbit, is more elusive but keeps itself busy throughout the year, living off a miniature haystack of fodder which it builds up during the summer.

Birds are numerous in summer, and include rosy finches, pipits and blue grouse, but few manage to live in the alpine zone year-round. One which does is the white-tailed **ptarmigan**, a plump, partridge-like bird which, thanks to its heavily feathered feet and legs, is able to snowshoe around deep drifts of snow;

its white winter plumage provides camouflage. Unfortunately, ptarmigans can be as slow-moving and stupid as barnyard chickens, making them easy targets for hunters and predators.

Coastlines

Canada has three **coastlines**: the Atlantic, the Pacific and the Arctic (dealt with under "Tundra"). Each boasts a profusion of maritime, dunal and intertidal life; the Pacific coast, warmed by the Japanese current, actually has the greatest number of species of any temperate shore. Few people are very interested in the small fry, however – most come for the big mammals, and **whales** in particular.

Grey whales are most common in the Pacific, and are often easily spotted from mainland headlands in the February to May and September to October periods as they migrate between the Arctic and their breeding grounds off Mexico. Once hunted close to the point of extinction, they've now returned in large numbers, and most West Coast harbours have charter companies offering whale-watching tours. **Humpback whales** are another favourite, largely because they're curious and follow sightseeing boats, but also because of their surface acrobatics and long, haunting "songs". They too were hunted to near-extinction, and though protected by international agreement since 1966 they still number less than ten percent of their original population. Vancouver Island's inner coast supports one of the world's most concentrated populations of **killer whales** or **orcas**. These are often seen in family groups or "pods" travelling close to shore, usually on the trail of large fish – which on the West Coast means **salmon**. The orca, however, is the only whale whose diet also runs to warm-blooded animals – hence the "killer" tag – and it will gorge on walrus, seal and even minke, grey and beluga whales.

Another West Coast inhabitant, the **sea otter**, differs from most marine mammals in that it keeps itself warm with a thick soft coat of fur rather than with blubber. This brought it to the attention of early Russian and British fur traders, and by the beginning of the twentieth century it was virtually extinct. Reintroduced in 1969 to Vancouver Island's northwest coast, they are now breeding successfully at the heart of their original range. With binoculars, it's often easy to spot these charming creatures lolling on their backs, cracking open sea urchins or mussels with a rock and using their stomachs as anvils; they often lie bobbing asleep, entwined in kelp to stop them floating away. Northern **fur seals** breed on Alaska's Pribilof Islands but are often seen off the British Columbian coast during their migrations. Like their cousin, the northern **sea lion**, a year-round resident, they are "eared seals", who can manage rudimentary shuffling on land thanks to short rear limbs which can be rotated for forward movement. They also swim with strokes from front flippers, as opposed to the slithering, fishlike action of true seals.

The **Atlantic**'s colder waters nurture fewer overall species than the Pacific coast, but many birds and larger mammals – especially **whales** – are common to both. One of the Atlantic region's more distinctive creatures is the **harp seal** (or saddleback), a true seal species that migrates in late winter to breeding grounds off Newfoundland and in the Greenland and White seas. Most pups are born on the pack ice, and for about two weeks sport fluffy white coats that have been highly prized by the fur trade for centuries. Until the late 1960s tens of thousands of young seals died annually in an unsupervised slaughter whose methods – clubbing and skinning alive – brought about outrage on an international scale (see p.508).

Tundra

Tundra extends over much of northern Yukon, the Northwest Territories and Nunavut, stretching between the boreal forest and the polar seas. Part grassland and part wasteland, it's a region distinguished by high winds, bitter cold and **permafrost**, a layer of perpetually frozen subsoil which covers over thirty percent of Canada. The tundra is not only the domain of ice and emptiness, however: long hours of summer sunshine and the melting of topsoil nurture a carpet of wild flowers and many species of birds and mammals have adapted to the vagaries of climate and terrain.

Vegetation is uniformly stunted by poor drainage, acidic soils and permafrost, which prevents the formation of deep roots and locks nutrients in the ice. **Trees** like birch and willow can grow, but they spread their branches over a wide area, rarely rising over a metre in height. Over 99 percent of the remaining vegetation consists of perennials like **grasses** and sedges, small flowering annuals, mosses, lichens and shrubs. Most have evolved ingenious ways of protecting themselves against the elements: Arctic cotton grass, for example, grows in large insulated hummocks in which the interior temperature is higher than the air outside; others have large, waxy leaves to conserve moisture or catch as much sunlight as possible. **Wild flowers** during the short, intense spring can be superlative, covering seemingly inert ground in a carpet of purple mountain saxifrage, yellow Arctic poppy, indigo clusters of Arctic forget-me-not and the pink buds of Jacob's ladder.

Tundra grasses provide some of the first links in the food chain, nourishing mammals such as white **Arctic ground squirrels**, also known as parkas, as their fur is used by the Inuit to make parka jackets. Vegetation also provides the staple diet of **lemmings**, amongst the most remarkable of the Arctic fauna. Instead of hibernating these creatures live under the snow, busily tucking away on shoots in order to double their weight daily – the intake they need merely to survive. They also breed almost continuously, which is just as well for they are the mainstay of a long list of predators. Chief of these are **Arctic white foxes**, ermines and weasels, though birds, bears and Arctic wolves may also hunt them in preference to larger prey. Because they provide a staple diet to so many, lemming populations have a marked effect on the life cycles of numerous creatures.

A notable exception is the **caribou**, a member of the reindeer family and the most populous of the big tundra mammals. Caribou are known above all for their epic migrations, frequently involving thousands of animals, which start in March when the herds leave their wintering grounds on the fringes of the boreal forest for calving grounds to the north. The exact purpose of these migrations is still a matter of conjecture. They certainly prevent the overgrazing of the tundra's fragile mosses and lichens, and probably also enable the caribou to shake off some of the wolves that would otherwise shadow the herd (wolves have to find southerly dens at this time to bear their own pups). The timing of treks also means that calving takes place before the arrival of biting insects, which can claim as many calves as predators – an adult caribou can lose as much as a litre of blood a week to insects.

The tundra's other large mammal is the **musk ox**, a vast, shaggy herbivore and close cousin of the bison. The musk ox's Achilles' heel is a tendency to form lines or circles when threatened – a perfect defence against wolves, but not against rifle-toting hunters, who, until the introduction of conservation measures, threatened to be their undoing. Canada now has some of the world's largest free-roaming herds, although – like the caribou – they're still hunted for food and fur by the Inuit.

Tundra **birds** number about a hundred species and are mostly migratory. Three-quarters of these are **waterfowl**, which arrive first to take advantage of streams, marshes and small lakes created by surface meltwater: Arctic wetlands provide nesting grounds for numerous swans, geese and ducks, as well as the **loon**, which is immortalized on the back of the Canadian dollar coin. The red-necked **phalarope** is a particularly specialized visitor, able to feed on aquatic insects and plankton, though not as impressive in its abilities as the migratory **Arctic tern**, whose 32,000-kilometre round trip from the Antarctic is the longest annual migration of any creature on the planet. The handful of non-migratory birds tend to be scavengers like the raven, or predators like the **gyrfalcon**, the world's largest falcon, which preys on Arctic hares and ptarmigan. Jaegers, gulls, hawks and owls largely depend on the lemming: the snowy owl, for example, synchronizes its returns to southern Canada with four-year dips in the lemming population.

Fauna on the Arctic **coast** has a food chain that starts with plankton and algae, ranging up through tiny crustaceans, clams and mussels, sea cucumbers and sea urchins, cod, ringed and bearded seals, to beluga whales and **polar bears** – perhaps the most evocative of all tundra creatures, but still being killed in their hundreds for "sport" despite almost thirty years of hunting restrictions. Migrating **birds** are especially common here, notably near Nunaluk Spit on the Yukon coast, which is used as a corridor and stopover by millions of loons, swans, geese, plovers, sandpipers, dowitchers, eagles, hawks, guillemots and assorted songbirds.

Books

Most of the following books should be readily available in bookshops or online (eg www.amazon.com), though you may have a little more difficulty tracking down those few titles we mention which are currently out of print, signified o/p. The same caution applies to those books which are only published in Canada and in these cases we've given the name of the publisher in brackets after the title. Titles marked with the symbol are especially recommended.

Travel and guides

Ranulph Fiennes *The Headless Valley* (o/p). Tales of 1970s derring-do from Fiennes, a noted adventurer, who white-water rafted down the South Nahanni and Fraser rivers of British Columbia and the old NWT.

John Gimlette *Theatre of Fish: Travels Through Newfoundland and Labrador.* Apparently following in the footsteps of his great grandfather, Gimlette reaches parts of the province few have travelled in this lively, entertaining journal that is, at times, perhaps a little too colloquial for its own (stylistic) good. Published in 2005.

Anna Jameson *Winter Studies and Summer Rambles in Canada.* Originally published in 1839, these tart observations of early Toronto's colonial society are marked by a sense of wonderment at the vastness of Canada's untamed wilderness.

Paul Kane *Wanderings of an Artist among the Indians of North America.* Kane, one of Canada's better-known landscape artists, spent two and a half years travelling from Toronto to the Pacific Coast and back in the 1840s. His witty, racy account of his wanderings makes a delightful read.

David McFadden *Trip Around Lake Ontario.* Part of a trilogy detailing the author's recent circumnavigation of lakes Ontario, Erie and Huron written in a deceptively simple style. Last version published in 1997.

Gary and Joannie McGuffin *Canoeing Across Canada* (o/p). Reflections on a 6000-mile journey along the country's rivers and backwaters. The McGuffins obviously like a watery challenge and their latest book, *Wilderness Paddling*, was published in 2007.

Susanna Moodie *Roughing It in the Bush, or Forest Life in Canada* (McClelland & Stewart, Canada). Intriguing narrative written in 1852, describing an English couple's slow ruin as they attempt to create a new life in southeastern Ontario.

Jan Morris *O Canada: Travels in an Unknown Country* (o/p) Musings from this well-known travel writer after a coast-to-coast Canadian trip. Comprises a series of finely judged and beautifully written essays on each of Canada's principal cities. Published in 1992, some of Morris's observations are inevitably outmoded, but the book is still an excellent primer.

Grey Owl *Three Complete & Unabridged Works – Men of the Last Frontier; Pilgrims of the Wild & The Adventures of Sajo and Her Beaver People.* First published in the 1930s, these three books – now often packaged in one volume – romantically describe life in the wilds of Canada at the time when exploitation was changing the land forever. Grey Owl's love of animals and the wilderness are inspiring and his forward-thinking, ecological views are particularly startling. Also in print is Grey Owl's *Tales of an Empty Cabin*.

Duncan Pryde *Nununga: Ten Years of Eskimo Life*. Less a travel book than a social document from a Glaswegian who left home at eighteen in the 1950s to spend ten years with the Inuit.

Elizabeth Simcoe (ed. Mary Innis) *Mrs Simcoe's Diary*. The wife of Upper Canada's first lieutenant governor and an early resident of York (Toronto), not only did Mrs Simcoe provide detailed observations of the landscape and the city's fledging way of life, but she was also an astute political observer, offering pinprick portraits of major historical figures like the Mohawk chief, Joseph Brant.

Specialist guides

Neil G. Carey *A Guide to the Queen Charlotte Islands* (Group West, o/p). An authoritative guide to islands which are difficult to explore and ill-served by back-up literature. Published in 1998.

Doug Eastcott *Backcountry Biking in the Canadian Rockies*. The essential and definitive guide to all things mountain-bike in the Rockies, with over 200 trails accompanied by accurate sketch maps and helpful elevation profiles. Last edition published in 2000.

Ben Gadd *The Canadian Rockies* (Key Porter Books). Widely available in western Canada's larger bookshops, this is a lovingly produced and painstakingly detailed handbook of walks, flora, fauna, geology and anything else remotely connected with the Rockies. Latest version published in 2007.

Brian Patton and Bart Robinson The *Canadian Rockies Trail Guide*. An essential guide for anyone wishing to do more than simply scratch the surface of the Rockies' walking possibilities. Latest version published in 2007.

Archie Shutterfield *The Chilkoot Trail: a Hiker's Historical Guide* (o/p). A pithy accompaniment to the Chilkoot Trail that should be read in conjunction with Pierre Berton's *Klondike*.

Culture, art and society

Kevin Bazzana *Wondrous Strange: the Life and Art of Glenn Gould*. Scholarly, well-researched Gould reader giving the low-down of every facet of the man and his music – in 500-odd pages. Gould fans will love it.

John Bently-Mays *Emerald City: Toronto Visited* (o/p). Thoughtful critical essays about Toronto, its architecture and its inhabitants.

Hugh Brody *Maps and Dreams*. Brilliantly written account of the lives and lands of the Beaver natives of northwest Canada. For further acute insights into the ways of the far north see also the same author's *Living Arctic* (o/p) and *The People's Land: Eskimos and Whites in the Eastern Arctic* (o/p).

David Cruise & Alison Griffiths *The Great Adventure: How the Mounties conquered the West*. Contemporary accounts of the Mounties' first major expedition into the West from the strange assortment of men who made up this legendary force.

Beatrice Culleton *April Raintree* (Pemmican, Canada). Heart-rending account of the enforced fostering of Métis children in Manitoba during the 1950s.

Don Dumond *The Eskimos and Aleuts*. Anthropological and archeological tour de force on the prehistory, history and culture of northern peoples: backed up with fine maps, drawings and photographs.

Christian F. Feest *Native Arts of North America*. This attractively illustrated book covers every aspect of North American native art in revealing detail. Everything you've ever wanted to know – and probably a good bit more.

Paul Fleming *The North American Indians in Early Photographs* (o/p). Stylized poses don't detract from a plaintive record of a way of life that has all but vanished.

Glenn Gould *The Solitude Trilogy*. These CDs comprise three extraordinary sound documentaries made by Gould for CBC (who also recorded his music) concerning life in the extreme parts of Canada. A fascinating insight into harsh lifestyles in the words of the people themselves.

Glenn Gould (ed. Tim Page) *The Glenn Gould Reader*. Sometimes chatty, sometimes pompous, Gould's voice and erudition shine through this collection of essays, articles and letters written from early adulthood to the end of his short life.

Mark Kurlansky *Cod: A Biography of the Fish that Changed the World*. This fascinating book tracks the life and times of the cod and the generations of fishermen who have lived off it. There are sections on over-fishing and the fish's breeding habits along with cod recipes. Naturally enough, the Newfoundland cod fishery features prominently and you won't get a more balanced view as to what went wrong – and why the fishery was closed.

Barry Lopez *Arctic Dreams: Imagination and Desire in a Northern Landscape*. Extraordinary, award-winning book combining natural history, physics, poetry, earth sciences and philosophy in a dazzling portrait of the far north.

Alan D. McMillan *Native Peoples and Cultures of Canada*. Comprehensive account of Canada's native groups from prehistory to current issues of self-government and land claims. Well written, though more an academic textbook than a leisure-time read. Published in 1995.

Dennis Reid *A Concise History of Canadian Painting*. Not especially concise, but a thorough trawl through Canada's leading artists, with bags of biographical detail and lots of black-and-white (and a few colour) illustrations of major works. Goes as far as the early 1980s.

Mike Tooby (ed) *The True North – Canadian Landscape Painting 1896–1939*. A fascinating and well-illustrated book exploring how Canadian artists have treated the country's challenging landscapes.

Harold Towne and David P. Silcox *Tom Thomson: The Silence in the Storm* (McClelland & Stewart, Canada). A study of the career and inspirations of Tom Thomson, one of Canada's best-known artists.

William White (ed) *The Complete Toronto* Dispatches, *1920–1924* (Charles Scribners Sons, o/p). Ernest Hemingway's first professional writing job was with *The Toronto Star* as both a local reporter and as a European correspondent. This is a collection of his dispatches for the paper.

Biography

Anahareo *Grey Owl and I* (P. Davies, o/p). The story of Grey Owl's Iroquois wife, their fight to save the beaver from extinction and her shock at discovering that her husband was in fact an Englishman. Good insights into the changing life of Canada's natives in the twentieth century.

Lovat Dickson *Wilderness Man.* The fascinating story of Archie Belaney, the Englishman who became famous as his adopted persona, Grey Owl. Written by his English publisher and friend, who was one of many that did not discover the charade until after Grey Owl's death.

Richard Gwyn *Smallwood: the Unlikely Revolutionary* (McClelland & Stewart, o/p). Detailed biography of Joey Smallwood, the Newfoundland premier who pushed his island into Confederation in 1949. Gwyn's exploration of island corruption and incompetence is incisive and intriguing in equal measure.

James MacKay *Robert Service: Vagabond of Verse* (o/p). Not the first, but certainly the most substantial biography discussing this prominent Canadian poet's life and work. Published in 1995.

Peter F. Ostwald *Glenn Gould: The Ecstasy and Tragedy of Genius.* A biography by a psychiatrist (100% Freud-free) of Canada's most famous musician. The eccentric pianist comes across as a rather inhuman egotist but with a talent to make this sufferable to many of his followers.

History

Fred Anderson *Crucible of War: The Seven Years' War and the Fate of the British Empire in British North America, 1754–1766.* Lucid and extraordinarily well-researched account of this crucial period in the development of North America. At 800-odd pages, it's perhaps a little too detailed for many tastes, but it's a fascinating read. Included is the story of the fall of Fort William Henry, as celebrated in the film, *The Last of the Mohicans.*

Owen Beattie and John Geiger *The Fate of the Franklin Expedition 1845–48.* An account both of the doomed expedition to find the Northwest Passage and the discovery of artefacts and bodies still frozen in the northern ice; worth buying for the extraordinary photos alone.

Carl Benn *The Iroquois in the War of 1812.* In 1812, the United States was at war with Canada and one of its armies invaded and briefly occupied York (Toronto). The role played by the Five Nations and Iroquois peoples in the war was pivotal to Canada's survival, and the ramifications of the War of 1812 affected the aboriginal people of Ontario for years to come.

Pierre Berton *Klondike: the Last Great Goldrush 1896–1899.* Exceptionally readable account from one of Canada's finest and most approachable writers of the characters and epic episodes of the Yukon gold rush. Other Berton titles include *The Arctic Grail*, describing the quest for the North Pole and the Northwest Passage from 1818 to 1919; *The Last Spike: the Great Railway 1881–1885*, an account of the history and building of the transcontinental railway; *Flames across the Border*, a detailed account of the US attack on Canada in 1813–1814; and *Vimy*, an account of the World War I battle fought mainly by Canadians which Berton sees as a turning point in the nation's history.

Gerald Friesen *The Canadian Prairies: a History*. Stunningly well-researched and detailed account of the development of Central Canada. A surprisingly entertaining book that's particularly good on the culture of the Métis and Plains Indians. First published in 1984, paperback 1987.

Harold Innis *The Fur Trade in Canada: An Introduction to Canadian Economic History*. The words "dramatic, sweeping and engaging" are not usually associated with books on economic history, but in this case they fit the bill. Innis's study is invaluable for the insight it gives to pre-European Canada, and its trading customs with Ontario's native peoples.

Kenneth McNaught *The Penguin History of Canada*. Concise analysis of the country's economic, social and political history. First published in 1970 and updated in 1988.

Peter C. Newman *Caesars of the Wilderness*. Highly acclaimed and readable account of the rise and fall of the Hudson's Bay Company.

George Woodcock *A Social History of Canada* (o/p). Erudite and incisive book about the peoples of Canada and the country's development. Woodcock was the most perceptive of Canada's historians and his work has the added advantage of being very readable. Also by the author is *The Canadians*, a lavishly illustrated and brilliantly lucid attempt to summarize the Canadian experience. Last printed in 1990.

Fiction

Margaret Atwood *Surfacing*. Canada's most eminent novelist is not always easy reading, but her analysis, particularly of women and society, is invariably witty and penetrating. In *Surfacing* the remote landscape of northern Québec plays an instrumental part in an extreme voyage of self-discovery. Regeneration through exploration of the past is also the theme of *Cat's Eye* and *Lady Oracle*, while the collection of short stories *Wilderness Tips* sees women ruminating over the bastards in their lives. *Alias Grace* is a dark and sensual tale centred around the true story of one of Canada's most notorious female criminals of the 1840s. Atwood's *The Blind Assassin* is a "Canadian dynastic epic" and won the UK's prestigious Booker Prize in 2000.

Lynn Coady *Saints of Big Harbour*. Forceful novel set in rural Nova Scotia dealing with a dysfunctional family – all alcohol and violence. Hardly cheerful stuff, but the characters are immaculately portrayed.

Robertson Davies For many years the leading figure of Canada's literary scene, Davies died in 1995 at the age of 82. Amongst his considerable output are big, dark and complicated webs of familial and social history which include wonderful evocations of the semi-rural Canada of his youth. A good place to start is *What's Bred in the Bone*, part of *The Cornish Trilogy*, whose other titles are *The Rebel Angels* and *The Lyre of Orpheus*. Similarly intriguing is *Fifth Business*, the first part of *The Deptford Trilogy*.

Timothy Findley *Headhunter*. A sombre novel that brings aspects of Conrad's *Heart of Darkness* to contemporary Rosedale, a haute bourgeois Toronto neighbourhood.

William Gibson *Virtual Light* and *Idoru* are arguably the best books from the master of cyberdom. The impact of technologies on human experience and the overlapping of artifice and reality are his significant themes.

Hammond Innes *Campbell's Kingdom*. A melodrama of love and oil-drilling in the Canadian Rockies – though the landscape's less well evoked than in *The Land God Gave to Cain*, the story of one man's search for "gold and truth" in Labrador.

Margaret Laurence *A Jest of God* and *The Stone Angel*. Manitoba-born Laurence epitomized the new vigour that swept through the country's literature during the Sixties – though the best of her fiction was written in England. Most of her books are set in the fictional prairie backwater of Manawaka, and explore the loneliness and frustration of women within an environment of stifling small-town conventionality.

Stephen Leacock *Sunshine Sketches of a Little Town*. Whimsical tale of Ontario small-town life; the best of a series based on Leacock's (1869-1944) summertime stays in Orillia.

Jack London *Call of the Wild* and *White Fang*. London spent over a year in the Yukon gold fields during the Klondike gold rush. Many of his experiences found their way into his vivid – if sometimes overwrought – tales of the northern wilderness. These are the pick.

Malcolm Lowry *Hear Us O Lord from Heaven thy Dwelling Place*. Lowry spent almost half his writing life (1939–54) in log cabins and beach houses he built for himself around Vancouver. *Hear Us O Lord* is a difficult read to say the least: a fragmentary novella which, amongst other things, describes a disturbing sojourn on Canada's wild Pacific coast.

Ann-Marie MacDonald *Fall on Your Knees*. Entertaining, epic-style family saga from this Toronto-based writer with an astute eye for characters and a fine storytelling touch. The novel follows the fortunes of four sisters from Halifax, against a backdrop which sweeps from World War II to the New York jazz scene.

Alistair MacLeod *No Great Mischief*. This forceful, evocative novel tells the tale of a family of Gaelic-speaking Nova Scotians from Cape Breton. Some of the episodes are brilliantly written – others less so – but it was undoubtedly one of the best Canadian novels of the 1990s.

Anne Michaels *Fugitive Pieces*. This debut novel from an award-winning poet concerns survivors from the Nazis who emigrate to Canada. Their relationship deepens but memory and the past are never far away. A beautiful work.

W.O. Mitchell *Who Has Seen the Wind*. Canada's equivalent of *Huckleberry Finn* is a folksy story of a young boy coming of age in small-town Saskatchewan, with great offbeat characters and fine evocations of prairie life.

L.M. Montgomery *Anne of Green Gables*. Growing pains and bucolic bliss in a children's classic from 1908. Bound to appeal to little girls of all ages; set on Prince Edward Island.

Brian Moore *Black Robe*. Moore emigrated to Canada from Ireland in 1948 and stayed long enough to gain citizenship before moving on to California. *Black Robe* – the story of a missionary's journey into native territory – is typical of the author's preoccupations with Catholicism, repression and redemption.

Alice Munro *Lives of Girls and Women; The Progress of Love; The Beggar Maid; Friend of My Youth; Dance of the Happy Shades; Who Do You Think You Are?; Something I've Been Meaning to Tell You; Runaway; The Moons of Jupiter;* and *Hateship, Friendship, Courtship, Loveship and Marriage*. Amongst the world's finest living short-story writers, Munro deals primarily with the lives of women in the semi-rural and Protestant backcountry of southwest Ontario. Unsettling emotions are never far beneath the surface. Among her more recent works, *Open Secrets* focuses on stories set in two small Ontario towns from the days of the early settlers to the present. Otherwise, start with *Who Do You Think You Are?*

New Oxford Book of Canadian Short Stories in English ed. Margaret Atwood and Robert Weaver. A broad selection which delves beyond the better-known names of Alice Munro and Margaret Atwood, with space being given to diaspora writers. While the intention is to celebrate Canadian writing, some of the works offer a distinctly negative view of the country. Published in 1997.

Howard Norman *The Haunting of L.* Curious novel of psychosis, deception and sexual shenanigans mostly set in the far north – Churchill, Manitoba to be exact. The writing is a tad patchy, but the best sections are disconcerting and effecting in equal measure.

Michael Ondaatje *In the Skin of a Lion.* This is the novel that introduces readers to the characters that appear in the more famous *The English Patient.* It's a highly charged work spanning the period between the end of World War I and the Great Depression in Toronto.

Oxford Book of Canadian Ghost Stories (ed. Alberto Manguel o/p). Over twenty stories, including W.P. Kinsella's *Shoeless Joe Jackson Comes to Iowa* – the inspiration for the fey *Field of Dreams.*

Oxford Companion to Canadian Literature (ed. William Toye & Eugene Benson, o/p). At almost 1200 pages, this was the last word on the subject when it was published in 1998, though it is more useful as a work of reference than as a primer for the country's literature.

E. Annie Proulx *The Shipping News.* The 1994 Pulitzer Prize-winner is a rambling, inconclusive narrative of a social misfit who finds love and happiness of sorts in small-town Newfoundland. Superb descriptions of sea, weather and all things fishy (as distinct from some very average characterization) make it a possible primer for a visit to the province.

Mordecai Richler French-Canadian, working-class and Jewish – Yiddishkeit is Richler's bag. He is the laureate of the minority within a minority within a minority. All his novels explore this relation with broad humour and pathos. In *The Apprenticeship of Duddy Kravitz*, his best-known work, Richler uses his early experiences of Montréal's working-class Jewish ghetto in an acerbic and slick cross-cultural romance built around the ambivalent but tightly drawn figure of Kravitz. Richler's pushy and ironic prose is not to all tastes, but you might also try *Solomon Gursky Was Here* or his later *Barney's Version*, a rip-roaring comic portrait of a reckless artist *manqué*. Richler died in 2001.

Carol Shields *Happenstance*; *The Stone Diaries*; *Larry's Party.* Winner of the Pulitzer Prize, Shields is much lauded for the detail she finds in the everyday. There are moments of great beauty and sensitivity in these books which chronicle the experiences of bourgeois North American suburbia with unnerving frankness.

Elizabeth Smart *By Grand Central Station I Sat Down and Wept.* A cult masterpiece which lyrically details the writer's love affair with the English poet George Barker.

Susan Swan *The Wives of Bath.* At a Toronto girls' school in the Sixties, the protagonist, Mouse, struggles with notions of feminine beauty as her best friend struggles with gender identity. A wry novel written in a genre the author described as "sexual gothic".

Audrey Thomas *The Wild Blue Yonder*. A collection of witty tales about male–female relationships by a renowned Canadian short-story writer. Published in 1991.

Jane Urquhart *The Underpainter*. A painful book concerning the life of a narcissistic painter who uses and leaves his muse but ultimately finds the demands of art destroy his humanity.

Guy Vanderhaeghe *The Last Crossing*. A thoroughly researched account of the last of the Canadian Wild West, largely set in Saskatchewan and cleverly told from several points of view.

John Wyndham *The Chrysalids*. A science-fiction classic built around a group of telepathic children and their adventures in post-Holocaust Labrador.

Poetry

Elizabeth Bishop *The Complete Poems*. Though American by birth, Bishop spent much of her youth in Nova Scotia. Many of her early poems feed off her Canadian childhood and her fascination with the country's rough landscapes.

Leonard Cohen *Stranger Music: Selected Poems & Songs*. A fine collection from a Sixties survivor who enjoyed high critical acclaim as a poet before emerging as a husky-throated crooner of bedsit ballads. See also his *Beautiful Losers*, one of the most aggressively experimental Canadian novels of the Sixties.

New Oxford Book of Canadian Verse ed. Margaret Atwood (o/p). In the 1970s, Canadian poets found an increasingly distinctive voice, though few (except Atwood herself) went on to make much of an international impact. Atwood's own sharp, witty examinations of nationality and gender are among the best in this anthology, though there is much more of merit too. Published in 1985.

Robert Service *The Best of Robert Service*. Service's Victorian ballads of pioneer and gold-rush life have a certain charm and they capture the essence of the gold-rush period. Amongst them the *Songs of a Sourdough* collection of 1907 is perhaps the most memorable.

Language

Language

Language

Canada has two official **languages** – English and French – plus numerous native tongues. Tensions between the two main language groups play a prominent part in the politics of Canada, but the native languages are more or less ignored except in the country's more remote areas, particularly in the Northwest Territories and Nunavut, where **Inuktitut**, the language of the Inuit, is spoken widely

In a brief glossary such as this there is no space to get to grips with the complexities of aboriginal languages, and very few travellers would have any need of them anyway: most natives (including those in Québec) have a good knowledge of English, especially if they deal with tourists in any capacity.

Québecois French

Québecois French differs from its European source in much the same way as North American English differs from British English. Thus, although Québecois French vocabulary, grammar and syntax are very near European French, speech can pose a few problems. If you plan to be spending much time in French-speaking Canada, consider investing in the *Rough Guide to French*, a pocket guide in a handy A–Z format.

Tracing its roots back to seventeenth-century vernacular French, Québecois has preserved features that disappeared long ago in France itself and it has also been affected by its close contact with English. The end result is a dialect that – frankly – is a source of amusement to many French people and bafflement for those educated in the French language back in Europe, not to mention other parts of Canada. Within Québec itself there are marked regional differences of pronunciation, so much so that Montréalers find it hard to understand northern Québecois.

The Québecois are extremely sympathetic when visiting English-speakers make the effort to speak French – and most are much more forthcoming with their knowledge of English when talking to a Briton or American than to a Canadian. Similarly easy-going is the attitude towards the formal vous (you), which is used less often in Québec; you may even be corrected when saying S'il vous plaît with the suggestion that S'il te plaît is more appropriate. Another popular phrase that you are likely to come across is pas de tout ("not at all"), which in Québec is pronounced pan toot, completely different from the French '*pa du too*'. The same goes for *c'est tout?* ("is that all?"), pronounced *say toot*; you're likely to hear this when buying something in a shop.

With **pronunciation** there's little point trying to mimic the local dialect – generally, just stick to the classic French rules.

French pronunciation

French isn't an easy language for English-speakers to **pronounce**, despite the number of words shared with English, but learning the bare essentials is not difficult. Differentiating words is the initial problem in understanding spoken French; it's very hard to get people to slow down. If, as a last resort, you get them to write it down, you may find you can identify half the words anyway.

Vowels

a as in h**a**t
au as in **o**ver
e as in g**e**t
é between g**e**t and g**a**te
è between g**e**t and g**u**t
eu as in h**u**rt
i as in mach**i**ne
o as in h**o**t
ô as in **o**ver
ou as in f**oo**d
u is a pursed-lip version of tr**u**e

The following are extra-tricky nasal sounds:
an/am and *en/em* like **Don**caster said through your nose
in/im like **an**xious
on/om like **Don**caster said with a heavy cold
un/um like **un**derstand

Consonants

Consonants are pronounced much as in English, except:
ç is an English **s**
ch is an English **sh**
h is silent
ll as in ba**y**onet
r is growled rather than trilled
th is like an English **t**
w is an English **v**

French words and phrases

The basics

good morning/ afternoon/hello	bonjour
good evening	bonsoir
good night	bonne nuit
goodbye	au revoir
yes	oui
no	non
please	s'il vous/te plaît
thank you (very much)	merci (beaucoup)
you're welcome	bienvenue/de rien/je vous en prie
OK	d'accord
How are you?	Comment allez-vous?/ Ça va?
Fine, thanks	Très bien, merci
Do you speak English?	Parlez-vous anglais?
I don't speak French	Je ne parle pas français
I don't understand	Je ne comprends pas
I don't know	Je ne sais pas
Excuse me (in a crowd)	Excusez-moi
Sorry	Pardon/désolé(e)
I'm English	Je suis anglais(e)
Scottish/Welsh	écossais(e)/gallois(e)
Irish/American	irlandais(e)/ américain(e)
Australian	australian(e)
I live in…	Je demeure à…
Wait a minute!	Un instant!
here/there	ici/là
good/bad	bon/mauvais
big/small	grand/petit
cheap/expensive	bon marché/cher
early/late	tôt/tard
hot/cold	chaud/froid
near/far	près (pas loin)/loin
vacant/occupied	libre/occupé
quickly/slowly	vite/lentement
loudly/quietly	bruyant/tranquille
with/without	avec/sans

more/less	plus/moins
enough/no more	assez/ça suffit
Mr	Monsieur
Mrs	Madame
Miss	Mademoiselle

Numbers

1	un/une
2	deux
3	trois
4	quatre
5	cinq
6	six
7	sept
8	huit
9	neuf
10	dix
11	onze
12	douze
13	treize
14	quatorze
15	quinze
16	seize
17	dix-sept
18	dix-huit
19	dix-neuf
20	vingt
21	vingt-et-un
22	vingt-deux
30	trente
40	quarante
50	cinquante
60	soixante
70	soixante-dix
80	quatre-vingts
90	quatre-vingt-dix
100	cent
101	cent-et-un
110	cent-dix
200	deux cents
1000	mille
2000	deux milles

Days

Monday	lundi
Tuesday	mardi
Wednesday	mercredi
Thursday	jeudi
Friday	vendredi
Saturday	samedi
Sunday	dimanche
morning	le matin
afternoon	l'après-midi
evening	le soir
night	la nuit
yesterday	hier
today	aujourd'hui
tomorrow	demain
tomorrow morning	demain matin

Months

January	janvier
February	février
March	mars
April	avril
May	mai
June	juin
July	juillet
August	août
September	septembre
October	octobre
November	novembre
December	décembre

Time

minute	minute
hour	heure
day	jour
week	semaine
month	mois
year	année
now	maintenant
later	plus tard
What time is it?	Quelle heure est-il?
It's 9.00	Il est neuf heures
1.05	une heure cinq
2.15	deux heures et quart
5.45	six heures moins quart
9.40	dix heures moins vingt
10.30	dix heures et demie
noon	midi
midnight	minuit

Questions and directions

Where?	Où?
When?	Quand?
What?	Quoi?
What is it?	Qu'est-ce que c'est?
How much/many?	Combien?
Why?	Pourquoi?
It is/there is	C'est/Il y a
Is it/is there...?	Est-ce que/Y a-t-il...?
How do I get to...?	Où se trouve...?
How far is it to...?	À quelle distance est-il à...?
Can you give me a lift to...?	Pouvez-vous me conduire jusqu'à...?
Can you tell me when to get off?	Pouvez-vous me dire quand descendre?
What time does it open?	À quelle heure ça ouvre?
How much does it cost?	Combien cela coûte-t-il?
How do you say it in French?	Comment ça se dit en français?

Accommodation

Is there a campsite nearby?	Y a-t-il un camping près d'ici?
tent	tente
cabin	chalet
hostel	auberge de jeunesse
hotel	hôtel
Do you have anything cheaper?	Avez-vous quelque chose de meilleur marché?
full board	tout compris
Can I see the room?	Puis-je peux voir la chambre?
I'll take this one	Je vais prendre celle-ci
I'd like to book a room	J'aimerais réserver une chambre
I have a booking	J'ai une réservation
Can we camp here?	Pouvons-nous camper ici?
How much is it?	C'est combien?
It's expensive	C'est cher
Is breakfast included?	Est-ce que le petit déjeuner est compris?
I'm looking for a nearby hotel	Je cherche un hôtel près d'ici
Do you have a room?	Avez-vous une chambre?
for one/two/three people	pour une/deux/trois personne(s)
for one/two/three nights	pour une/deux/trois nuit(s)
for one week	pour une semaine
with a double bed	avec un lit double
with a shower/bathtub	avec douche/salle de bain
hot/cold water	eau chaude/froide

Travelling

bus	autobus
train	train
plane	avion
car	voiture
taxi	taxi
bicycle	vélo
ferry	traversier
ship	bâteau
hitch-hiking	faire du pouce
on foot	à pied
bus station	terminus d'autobus
train station	gare centrale
ferry terminal	quai du traversier
port	port
A ticket to...	Un billet pour...
one-way/return	aller-simple/aller-retour
Can I book a seat?	Puis-je réserver un siège?
What time does it leave?	Il part à quelle heure?
When is the next train to...?	Quand est le prochain train pour...?
Do I have to change?	Dois-je transférer?
Where does it leave from?	D'où est-ce qu'il part?
How many kilometres?	Combien de kilomètres?
How many hours?	Combien d'heures?
Which bus do I take to get to...?	Quel autobus dois-je prendre pour aller à...?

Next stop	Le prochain arrêt
Where's the road to...?	Où est la route pour...?

Some signs

Entrance/Exit	Entrée/Sortie
Free admission	Entrée Libre
Gentlemen/Ladies	Messieurs/Dames
WC	Toilette
Vacant/Engaged	Libre/Occupé
Open/Closed	Ouvert/Fermé
Arrivals/Departures	Arrivées/Départs
Closed for holidays	Fermé pour les vacances
Pull/Push	Tirez/Poussez
Out of order	Hors d'usage/Brisé
To let	À louer
Platform	Voie
Cash desk	Caisse
Go/Walk	Marchez
Stop	Arrêtez
Customs	Douanes
Do not touch!	Défense de toucher!
Danger!	Danger!
Beware!	Attention!
First aid	Premiers soins
Ring the bell	Sonnez
No smoking	Défense de fumer

Driving

turn to the left/ right	tournez à gauche/ droite
straight ahead	tout droit
car park	terrain de stationnement
no parking	défense de stationner/ stationnement interdit
tow-away zone	zone de remorquage
cars towed at owner's expense	remorquage à vos frais
one-way street	sens unique
dead end	cul-de-sac
no entry	défense d'entrer
slow down	ralentir
proceed on flashing green light	attendez le feu vert clignotant
turn on headlights!	allumez vos phares!
no overtaking	défense de dépasser
passing lane only	voie réservée au dépassement
speed	vitesse
self-service	libre-service
full service	service complet
Fill the tank with...	Faîtes le plein avec...
...regular	...de l'essence ordinaire
...super	...du super
...unleaded	...du sans plomb
Check the oil	Vérifiez l'huile
battery	la batterie
radiator	le radiateur
plugs	bougies d'allumage
tyre pressure	pression des pneus
Pump up the tyres	Gonflez les pneus

A French menu reader

Basic terms and ingredients

butter	beurre
hot	chaud
sour cream	crème fraiche
dessert	dessert
iced	frappé
cold	froid
cheese	fromage
starters	hors d'oeuvre
vegetables	legumes
eggs	oeufs
bread	pain
fish	poisson
pepper	poivre
salad	salade
salt	sel
sugar	sucre
tart or pie	tourte
a slice	tranche
meat	viande

Snacks

a sandwich...	un sandwich/ une baguette...
...with ham	...de jambon
...with cheese	...de fromage
...with sausage	...de saucisson
with garlic	à l'ail
with pepper	au poivre
grilled cheese and ham sandwich	croque-monsieur
fried eggs	oeufs au plat
boiled eggs	oeufs à la coque
hard-boiled eggs	oeufs durs
scrambled eggs	oeufs brouillés
plain omelette	omelette nature
cheese omelette	omelette au fromage

Soups and starters

plate of cold meats	assiette anglaise
shellfish soup	bisque
fish soup	bouillabaisse
broth or stock	bouillon
clear soup	consommé
raw vegetables with dressing	crudités
thick soup, usually vegetable	potage

Meat and poultry

lamb	agneau
steak	bifteck
beef	boeuf
duck	canard
horsemeat	cheval
cutlets	côtelettes
leg of lamb	cuisson
turkey	dindon
snails	escargots
liver	foie
game	gibiers
leg of venison	gigot
ham	jambon
bacon	lard
pork	porc
chicken	poulet
sausage	saucisse
veal	veau

Fish and seafood

anchovies	anchois
eels	anguilles
plaice	carrelet
prawns	cervettes roses
herring	hareng
lobster	homard
monkfish	lotte de mer
mackerel	maquereau
cod	morue
mussels	moules
salmon	saumon
sole	sole
trout	truite

Cooking methods

rare (steak)	saignant
medium done (steak)	a point
well done (steak)	bien cuit
baked	au four
boiled	bouilli
fried/deep fried	frit/friture
smoked	fumé
grilled	grillé
stewed	mijoté
breaded	pané
roasted	rôti
lightly cooked in butter	sauté

Vegetables and grains

garlic	ail
asparagus	asperges
carrots	carottes
mushrooms	champignons
cauliflower	choufleur
cucumber	concombre
lettuce	laitue
onions	oignons
peas	petits pois
leek	poireau

potatoes	pommes (de terre)
rice	riz
tomato	tomate

Fruit and nuts

almonds	amandes
pineapple	ananas
peanut	cacahouète
cherries	cérises
lemon	citron
strawberries	fraises
raspberries	framboises
chestnuts	marrons
hazelnut	noisette
grapefruit	pamplemousse
pear	poire
apple	pomme
plum	prune
prune	pruneau
grapes	raisins

Sweets and desserts

pancakes with sugar	crêpes au sucre
pancakes with lemon	crêpes au citron
pancakes with honey	crêpes au miel
pancakes with jam/jelly	crêpes à la confiture
thin pancakes with orange juice and liqueur	crêpes suzettes
ice cream	glace
small, shell-shaped sponge cake	madeleine
frozen mousse, sometimes ice cream	parfait
bite-sized cakes or pastries	petits fours

Drinks

coffee	café
tea	thé
milk	lait
orange juice	jus d'orange
sweetened lemon juice	citron pressé
beer	bière
red wine	vin rouge
white wine	vin blanc
very dry	brut
dry	sec
sweet	demi-sec
very sweet	doux
fruit spirit/liquor	eaux de vie

Travel store

ROUGH GUIDES Complete Listing

UK & Ireland
Britain
Devon & Cornwall
Dublin **D**
Edinburgh **D**
England
Ireland
The Lake District
London
London **D**
London Mini Guide
Scotland
Scottish Highlands & Islands
Wales

Europe
Algarve **D**
Amsterdam
Amsterdam **D**
Andalucía
Athens **D**
Austria
Baltic States
Barcelona
Barcelona **D**
Belgium & Luxembourg
Berlin
Brittany & Normandy
Bruges **D**
Brussels
Budapest
Bulgaria
Copenhagen
Corfu
Corsica
Costa Brava **D**
Crete
Croatia
Cyprus
Czech & Slovak Republics
Denmark
Dodecanese & East Aegean Islands
Dordogne & The Lot
Europe
Florence & Siena
Florence **D**
France
Germany
Gran Canaria **D**
Greece
Greek Islands
Hungary
Ibiza & Formentera **D**
Iceland
Ionian Islands
Italy
The Italian Lakes
Languedoc & Roussillon
Lanzarote & Fuerteventura **D**
Lisbon **D**
The Loire Valley
Madeira **D**
Madrid **D**
Mallorca **D**
Mallorca & Menorca
Malta & Gozo **D**
Menorca
Moscow
The Netherlands
Norway
Paris
Paris **D**
Paris Mini Guide
Poland
Portugal
Prague
Prague **D**
Provence & the Côte D'Azur
Pyrenees
Romania
Rome
Rome **D**
Sardinia
Scandinavia
Sicily
Slovenia
Spain
St Petersburg
Sweden
Switzerland
Tenerife & La Gomera **D**
Turkey
Tuscany & Umbria
Venice & The Veneto
Venice **D**
Vienna

Asia
Bali & Lombok
Bangkok
Beijing
Cambodia
China
Goa
Hong Kong & Macau
Hong Kong & Macau **D**
India
Indonesia
Japan
Kerala
Laos
Malaysia, Singapore & Brunei
Nepal
The Philippines
Rajasthan, Dehli & Agra
Singapore
Singapore **D**
South India
Southeast Asia
Sri Lanka
Taiwan
Thailand
Thailand's Beaches & Islands
Tokyo
Vietnam

Australasia
Australia
Melbourne
New Zealand
Sydney

North America
Alaska
Baja California
Boston
California
Canada
Chicago
Colorado
Florida
The Grand Canyon
Hawaii
Honolulu **D**
Las Vegas **D**
Los Angeles
Maui **D**
Miami & South Florida
Montréal
New England
New Orleans **D**
New York City
New York City **D**
New York City Mini Guide
Orlando & Walt Disney World® **D**
Pacific Northwest
San Francisco
San Francisco **D**
Seattle
Southwest USA
Toronto
USA
Vancouver
Washington DC
Washington DC **D**
Yellowstone & The Grand Tetons
Yosemite

Caribbean & Latin America
Antigua & Barbuda **D**
Argentina
Bahamas
Barbados **D**
Belize
Bolivia
Brazil
Cancùn & Cozumel **D**
Caribbean
Central America
Chile
Costa Rica
Cuba
Dominican Republic
Dominican Republic **D**
Ecuador
Guatemala
Jamaica
Mexico
Peru
St Lucia **D**
South America
Trinidad & Tobago
Yúcatan

Africa & Middle East
Cape Town & the Garden Route
Dubai **D**
Egypt
Gambia
Jordan

D: Rough Guide **DIRECTIONS** for short breaks

Available from all good bookstores

Kenya
Marrakesh **D**
Morocco
South Africa, Lesotho & Swaziland
Syria
Tanzania
Tunisia
West Africa
Zanzibar

Travel Specials
First-Time Africa
First-Time Around the World
First-Time Asia
First-Time Europe
First-Time Latin America
Travel Health
Travel Online
Travel Survival
Walks in London & SE England
Women Travel
World Party

Maps
Algarve
Amsterdam
Andalucia & Costa del Sol
Argentina
Athens
Australia
Barcelona
Berlin
Boston & Cambridge
Brittany
Brussels
California
Chicago
Chile
Corsica
Costa Rica & Panama
Crete
Croatia
Cuba
Cyprus
Czech Republic
Dominican Republic
Dubai & UAE
Dublin
Egypt
Florence & Siena
Florida
France
Frankfurt
Germany
Greece
Guatemala & Belize
Iceland
India
Ireland
Italy
Kenya & Northern Tanzania
Lisbon
London
Los Angeles
Madrid
Malaysia
Mallorca
Marrakesh
Mexico
Miami & Key West
Morocco
New England
New York City
New Zealand
Northern Spain
Paris
Peru
Portugal
Prague
Pyrenees & Andorra
Rome
San Francisco
Sicily
South Africa
South India
Spain & Portugal
Sri Lanka
Tenerife
Thailand
Toronto
Trinidad & Tobago
Tunisia
Turkey
Tuscany
Venice
Vietnam, Laos & Cambodia
Washington DC
Yucatán Peninsula

Dictionary Phrasebooks
Croatian
Czech
Dutch
Egyptian Arabic
French
German
Greek
Hindi & Urdu
Italian
Japanese
Latin American Spanish
Mandarin Chinese
Mexican Spanish
Polish
Portuguese
Russian
Spanish
Swahili
Thai
Turkish
Vietnamese

Computers
Blogging
eBay
iPhone
iPods, iTunes & music online
The Internet
Macs & OS X
MySpace
PCs and Windows
PlayStation Portable
Website Directory

Film & TV
American Independent Film
British Cult Comedy
Chick Flicks
Comedy Movies
Cult Movies
Film
Film Musicals
Film Noir
Gangster Movies
Horror Movies
Kids' Movies
Sci-Fi Movies
Westerns

Lifestyle
Babies
Ethical Living
Pregnancy & Birth
Running

Music Guides
The Beatles
Blues
Bob Dylan
Book of Playlists
Classical Music
Elvis
Frank Sinatra
Heavy Metal
Hip-Hop
Jazz
Led Zeppelin
Opera
Pink Floyd
Punk
Reggae
Rock
The Rolling Stones
Soul and R&B
Velvet Underground
World Music (2 vols)

Popular Culture
Books for Teenagers
Children's Books, 5-11
Conspiracy Theories
Crime Fiction
Cult Fiction
The Da Vinci Code
His Dark Materials
Lord of the Rings
Shakespeare
Superheroes
The Templars
Unexplained Phenomena

Science
The Brain
Climate Change
The Earth
Genes & Cloning
The Universe
Weather

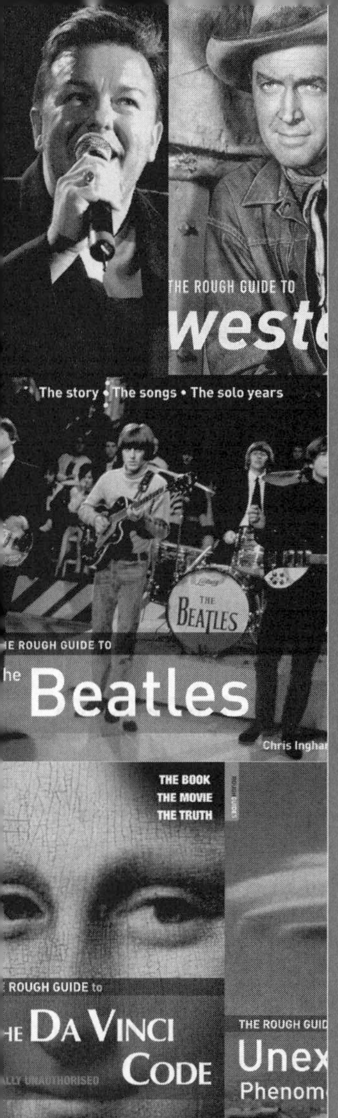
THE ROUGH GUIDE TO
weste
The story • The songs • The solo years
THE BEATLES
E ROUGH GUIDE TO
he Beatles
Chris Inghar
THE BOOK
THE MOVIE
THE TRUTH
ROUGH GUIDE to
HE DA VINCI CODE
THE ROUGH GUID
Unex
Phenom

ROUGH
GUIDES

The filth • the fury • the fa
The songs • the singers • the stories • the soul
OUGH GUIDE to
unk
THE ROUGH GUIDE to
Soul and R&B

THE ROUGH GUIDE to
The Rolling Stones

THE ROUGH
Blo

HUT TO HUT HIKING
in British Columbia
All trips in the great mountain wilderness of Wells Gray Park
Excellent Service / Fair Prices
WELLS GRAY ADVENTURES
We specialize in family trips.
Hiking & Canoeing from 1 to 14 days
Tel: Canada 250-587-6444 info@skihike.com
www.skihike.com

worldchoice
Creating dreams –
exceeding expectations...
visit experienceholidays.co.uk
Experience Holidays
The Art of Travel
Canada • Alaska • United States of America
Southern Africa • Australia • New Zealand
Worldchoice 1613, Royal Bank of Scotland Trust account 10057449.

NOTES

NOTES

NOTES

NOTES

NOTES

Small print and Index

A Rough Guide to Rough Guides

Published in 1982, the first Rough Guide – to Greece – was a student scheme that became a publishing phenomenon. Mark Ellingham, a recent graduate in English from Bristol University, had been traveling in Greece the previous summer and couldn't find the right guidebook. With a small group of friends he wrote his own guide, combining a highly contemporary, journalistic style with a thoroughly practical approach to travelers' needs.

The immediate success of the book spawned a series that rapidly covered dozens of destinations. And, in addition to impecunious backpackers, Rough Guides soon acquired a much broader and older readership that relished the guides' wit and inquisitiveness as much as their enthusiastic, critical approach and value-for-money ethos.

These days, Rough Guides include recommendations from shoestring to luxury and cover more than 200 destinations around the globe, including almost every country in the Americas and Europe, more than half of Africa and most of Asia and Australasia. Our ever-growing team of authors and photographers is spread all over the world, particularly in Europe, the USA and Australia.

In the early 1990s, Rough Guides branched out of travel, with the publication of Rough Guides to World Music, Classical Music and the Internet. All three have become benchmark titles in their fields, spearheading the publication of a wide range of books under the Rough Guide name.

Including the travel series, Rough Guides now number more than 350 titles, covering: phrasebooks, waterproof maps, music guides from Opera to Heavy Metal, reference works as diverse as Conspiracy Theories and Shakespeare, and popular culture books from iPods to Poker. Rough Guides also produce a series of more than 120 World Music CDs in partnership with World Music Network.

Visit www.roughguides.com to see our latest publications.

Rough Guide travel images are available for commercial licensing at www.roughguidespictures.com

Rough Guide credits

Text editors: Anna Owens, Steven Horak
Layout: Ankur Guha
Cartography: Animesh Pathak, Katie Lloyd-Jones
Picture editor: Jj Luck
Production: Vicky Baldwin
Proofreader: Mary Beth Maioli
Photographers: Tim Draper, Enrique Uranga
Cover design: Chloë Roberts
Editorial: London Kate Berens, Claire Saunders, Ruth Blackmore, Polly Thomas, Alison Murchie, Karoline Densley, Andy Turner, Keith Drew, Edward Aves, Nikki Birrell, Alice Park, Sarah Eno, Lucy White, Jo Kirby, Samantha Cook, James Smart, Natasha Foges, Róisín Cameron, Emma Gibbs, Joe Staines, Duncan Clark, Peter Buckley, Matthew Milton, Tracy Hopkins, Ruth Tidball; **New York** Andrew Rosenberg, AnneLise Sorensen, Amy Hegarty, April Isaacs, Ella Steim, Joseph Petta, Sean Mahoney
Design & Pictures: **London** Scott Stickland, Dan May, Diana Jarvis, Mark Thomas, Harriet Mills, Nicole Newman; **Delhi** Umesh Aggarwal, Ajay Verma, Jessica Subramanian, Pradeep Thapliyal, Sachin Tanwar, Anita Singh, Madhavi Singh, Karen D'Souza
Production: Aimee Hampson
Cartography: **London** Maxine Repath, Ed Wright; **Delhi** Jai Prakash Mishra, Rajesh Chhibber, Ashutosh Bharti, Rajesh Mishra, Jasbir Sandhu, Karobi Gogoi, Amod Singh, Alakananda Bhattacharya, Swati Handoo
Online: **New York** Jennifer Gold, Kristin Mingrone; **Delhi** Manik Chauhan, Narender Kumar, Rakesh Kumar, Amit Kumar, Amit Verma, Rahul Kumar, Ganesh Sharma, Debojit Borah
Marketing & Publicity: **London** Liz Statham, Niki Hanmer, Louise Maher, Jess Carter, Vanessa Godden, Vivienne Watton, Anna Paynton, Rachel Sprackett; **New York** Geoff Colquitt, Megan Kennedy, Katy Ball; **Delhi** Reem Khokhar
Editorial Coordinator: Emma Traynor
Manager India: Punita Singh
Series Editor: Mark Ellingham
Reference Director: Andrew Lockett
PA to MD and Publishing Director: Helen Phillips
Publishing Director: Martin Dunford
Commercial Manager: Gino Magnotta
Managing Director: John Duhigg

Publishing information

This sixth edition published July 2007 by
Rough Guides Ltd,
80 Strand, London WC2R 0RL
345 Hudson St, 4th Floor,
New York, NY 10014, USA
14 Local Shopping Centre, Panchsheel Park,
New Delhi 110017, India
Distributed by the Penguin Group
Penguin Books Ltd,
80 Strand, London WC2R 0RL
Penguin Group (USA)
375 Hudson Street, NY 10014, USA
Penguin Group (Australia)
250 Camberwell Road, Camberwell,
Victoria 3124, Australia
Penguin Books Canada Ltd,
10 Alcorn Avenue, Toronto, Ontario,
Canada M4V 1E4
Penguin Group (NZ)
67 Apollo Drive, Mairangi Bay, Auckland 1310,
New Zealand

Cover concept by Peter Dyer.

Typeset in Bembo and Helvetica to an original design by Henry Iles.

Printed in Italy by LegoPrint S.p.A

1160pp includes index

A catalogue record for this book is available from the British Library

ISBN: 978-1-84353-787-8

1 3 5 7 9 8 6 4 2

Help us update

We've gone to a lot of effort to ensure that the sixth edition of **The Rough Guide to Canada** is accurate and up to date. However, things change – places get "discovered", opening hours are notoriously fickle, restaurants and rooms raise prices or lower standards. If you feel we've got it wrong or left something out, we'd like to know, and if you can remember the address, the price, the time, the phone number, so much the better. We'll credit all contributions, and send a copy of the next edition (or any other Rough Guide if you prefer) for the best letters. Everyone who writes to us and isn't already a subscriber will receive a copy of our full-colour thrice-yearly newsletter. Please mark letters: "**Rough Guide Canada Update**" and send to: Rough Guides, 80 Strand, London WC2R 0RL, or Rough Guides, 345 Hudson St, 4th Floor, New York, NY 10014. Or send an email to **mail@roughguides.com**
Have your questions answered and tell others about your trip at
www.roughguides.atinfopop.com

Acknowledgements

Phil Lee would like to thank his editor, Anna Owens, for her help with this new edition – a mammoth task for anyone. Special thanks also to Diane Helinski and Rey Stephen of Ontario Tourism; Kathleen Crotty of Newfoundland & Labrador Tourism; Randy Brooks of Nova Scotia Tourism; and Carol Horne of Tourism PEI. Also to my stepdaughter, Emma Rees, for being such a chum in the depths of a Toronto winter.

Tim Jepson would like to thank his editors; Lucy Hyslop; James and Vicky Ballentyne; Air Canada; Charlotte Fraser and Fairmont Hotels; Claire Griffin and Four Seasons hotels; and Kathleen Eccles.

Christian Williams would like to thank the Canadians of central Canada for being such a friendly and hospitable bunch and to CBC for making prairie journeys feel shorter. In particular praise is due to Daryl Demoskoff at Tourism Saskatchewan for his immense support; to Marie-Claude for her stellar performance at the sushi counter; and to Katrin for flirting with the Mounties at all the right times. At Rough Guides thanks goes to Andrew Rosenberg and Steven Horak for managing the project so well in the face of many competing demands and to Anna Owens for stepping in late in the day to nonetheless perform an admirable editorial job. Thanks also to my co-authors for their support and encouragement.

The editor thanks the authors and contributors for doing such great work; additional thanks to Katie Lloyd-Jones, Animesh Pathak, Jj Luck, Ankur Guha, Madhavi Singh, Umesh Aggarwal, Scott Stickland, Andrew Rosenberg and Steven Horak.

Readers' letters

Thanks to all the readers who have taken the time to write in with comments and suggestions (and apologies if we've inadvertently omitted or misspelt anyone's name):

Friederike Albrecht, Christian Asseburg, Vera Bakstad, Brendan Bracken, Tim Burford, Doug Campbell, Christine Chenetti, Chris Clayton, Gordon Craig, Haruna Dankaro, Brad Darch, Ulrike Döll, Beni Downing, Ulrike Ehnes, Dwight Elliot, Carole Embrey, Andrea Fahrmeyer, Paulo Filipe, Ute Frank, Sandra Ganahl, Marie-Helene Gauthier, Lida Ghaemi, Suzette Gibson, Philip Grout, Alice Gwinnell, Jennifer Haak, Dawn Harilstad, Greg Harper, Stephen Hart, Bill Hawkins, Michael Herbert, Brian Hislop, Simon Hollows, June Hornby, Bernadette Hyland, Iain & Clare Inglis, Dale Jarvis, Claude Jouhannet, Craig Kelley, Arnelle Kendall, Ian Kilroy, Norbert Kipp, Jocelyn Labbe, Johane Larouche, Stephen Loose, Gloria Marsh, Kerry Marshall, Genevihve Mathieu, Giles Mercer, Bernadette & Michael Mossley, Jason Murphy, Henry Parkinson, Roger Peabody, Joan Pederson, Stephanie Pelletier, Piergiorgio Pescali, Andreas Pittner, Dee Powell, John Rowling, Keith Rohman, Carol & John Rowling, Anke Rowold, Frank & Sheila Ryan, Julie Sanderson, Ernie Savage, David Saville, Frank Sierowski, Richard Skermer, Mike Smallenberg, Mikaël Smoth, Julia Speh, Corina Stofer, Chantal Tarif, Geoff Taylor, Geoff Thomason, Alexis Thornely, Mark Tillmanns, Lynn Ulrey, Belinda Walker, Darrel Warman, Serena Webber, Alan Weeks, Geoff Wood, Andrew Young

Photo credits

All photos © Rough Guides except the following:

Title page

Cattle Drive, Alberta © Robert McGouey/Alamy

Full page

Cape Breton Highlands National Park, Nova Scotia © David Noton Photography/Alamy

Introduction

Totem pole, Vancouver © B&Y Photography/ Alamy

Inuit parka and gloves © Chris Coe/Axiom

Great Bear Rainforest © John Schwieder/Alamy

CN Rail train and grain elevator, Saskatchewan © Darwin Wiggett /All Canada Photos/Getty Images

Prince Edward Island © Shaun Lowe/ iStockphoto.com

Vieux-Montréal © Bill Brooks/Alamy

Things not to miss

01 Dawson City, Yukon © Gary Cook/Alamy

02 Ice-climbing, Jasper © Real World People/ Alamy

03 Polar bear, Churchill © Murray Cohen/iStock .com

04 Wells Gray © Daryl Benson/Masterfile

05 Lunenburg © Vladone/iStock.com

06 Bay of Fundy © Rüdiger Baun/iStock.com

07 Witless Bay, Newfoundland © Danita Delimont/Alamy

08 Coast line, Pacific Rim National Park © All Canada Photos/Getty Images

09 Whistler, BC © britishcolumbiaphotos.com/ Alamy

10 Grey Wolf © Art Wolfe/Stone/Getty Images

13 Parliament Buildings, Ottawa © Vladone/ iStock.com

15 Valley of Ten Peaks, Banff National Park, Alberta © Philip & Karen Smith/Stone Getty Images

16 Mount Robson, BC © Karolek/Alamy

18 Kaskawulsh glacier in Kluane National Park, Yukon © Hemis/Alamy

19 Aurora borealis © Jason Verschoor/iStock.com

20 The Laurentians © First Light/Getty Images

21 Cow and Calf Moose, Algonquin Park, Ontario © First Light/Getty Images

22 Skidegate, Graham Island, British Columbia, 1928 (oil on canvas); by Emily Carr © Art Gallery of Ontario, Toronto, Canada; Gift of the J.S.McLean Collection by Canada Packers Inc 1990 Bridgeman Art Library

23 St John's Harbour © Jason Hollett/iStock.com

24 Empress Hotel, Victoria © Arco Images/Alamy

25 Calgary Stampede © Robert McGouey/Alamy

26 Chinatown, Toronto © Bruce Burkhardt/Corbis

27 Haida Gwaii © Jason Verschoor/iStock.com

28 Icefields Parkway © Robert McGouey/Alamy

29 Whale-watching, British Columbia © Arco Images/Alamy

30 Prince Edward Island © Denis Tangney/iStock .com

31 Skiing, Horseshoe Ski Resort © Elena Elisseeva/iStock.com

Black and whites

p.106 Bruce Penninsula National Park Islands © Gordon Wood/Alamy

p.116 Georgian Bay Islands © Janusz Wrobel/ Alamy

p.169 Algonquin Park, Muskoka, Ontario © Henry Georgi/Aurora photolibrary.com

p.185 Parliament building, Ottawa © Chris Coe/Axiom

p.207 American Indian enterprise © Janusz Wrobel/Alamy

p.211 Manitoulin island Lighthouse © Don Johnston/Alamy

p.228 Abbey Saint Benoit Du Lac, Quebec © Frank Vetere/Alamy

p.278 Le P'tit Train du Nord Bike path © Megapress/Alamy

p.285 Mont Tremblant Village, Quebec © Preston Schlebusch/The Image Bank/Getty Images

p.292 Ice hotel, Québec © Arco Images/Alamy

p.327 Ile d'Orleans House Québec City © JTB Photo Communications, Inc./Alamy

p.339 Reserve Frannique © Alt-6 Alamy

p.349 Gaspé Peninsula Perce, Quebec © Andre Jenny/Alamy

p.365 Tadoussac ferry © Martin Paquin/Alamy

p.374 Homes in Val-Jalbert © Alt-6/Alamy

p.390 Harbour, Blue Rocks, Nova Scotia © Chris Coe/Axiom

p.403 Bagpiper at the Citadel © Chris Coe/Axiom

p.414 Churches, Mahone Bay © Chris Coe/Axiom

p.235 Cape Breton © Jan Butchofsky-Houser/ Corbis

p.448 Beaverbrook Art Gallery © Danita Delimont/Corbis

p.464 Cape Enrage © xela/Alamy

p.479 Charlottetown © Rubens Abboud/Alamy

p.492 L'Anse aux Meadows © Wolfgang Kaehler/ Alamy

p.505 St John's Port entrance © imagebroker/ Alamy

p.514 Iceberg at Witless Bay © George Blonsky/ Alamy

p.522 Bonavista Peninsula, Newfoundland © David Noton Photography/Alamy

p.531 Fjord in Gros Morne National Park © Tom Till/Alamy

p.543 Fishing houses at Red Bay © Wolfgang Kaehler/Alamy

p.554 Polar bear, Cape Churchill © Steve Bloom Images/Alamy

p.569 Forks Market, Winnipeg © Terrance Klassen/Alamy
p.579 Grain elevator © Christian Williams
p.581 Manitoba Stampede © Christian Williams
p.569 RCMP Academy © Christian Williams
p.603 Grasslands National Park © John E. Marriott/Alamy
p.621 Canadian Plains First Nations Men © Tim Graham/Alamy
p.638 Polar bear warning, Churchill © Christian Williams
p.644 Downtown Banff © Christian Williams
p.655 Edmonton's historic district © nagelestock.com/Alamy
p.669 Downtown Calgary © Christian Williams
p.677 Royal Tyrrell Museum © Christian Williams
p.702 Banff Spring Hotel © Christian Williams
p.731 Moraine Lake © Christian Williams
p.742 Athabasca Glacier, Icefields Parkway © Jon Arnold Images/Alamy
p.765 Lake O'Hara © John Sylvester/Alamy
p.778 Kootenay National Park © John E Marriott/Alamy
p.786 Inside Passage Ferry © Arco Images/Alamy
p.794 Vancouver skyline © Jurgen Vogt/Image Bank/Getty Images
p.848 Sunshine Coast © Howard Kingsnorth/Taxi/Getty Images
p.879 Whale-watching off Victoria © ulco de jong/iStock.com
p.891 Salt-Spring Island ©Ulana Switucha/Alamy
p.916 Long Beach © Keith Douglas/Alamy
p.924 West Coast Trail © Tim Thompson/Corbis
p.940 Helmcken Falls © Gunter Marx/Alamy
p.947 Rafting the Thompson River © Gunter Marx/Alamy
p.955 Marine Sockeye salmon © Bruce Coleman Inc./Alamy
p.961 Vineyard, Okanagan Lake © Cephas Picture Library/Alamy
p.978 Halcyon Hot Springs near Natusp © britishcolumbiaphotos.com/Alamy
p.992 Nahanni National Park © Christian Williams
p.1004 Chatham Sound, Prince Rupert © Robert Harding Picture Library Ltd/Alamy
p.1013 Totem poles at Haida Heritage Centre © Gunter Marx/Alamy
p.1037 Dawson City © Gary Cook/Alamy
p.1050 Inuit Church, Inuvik © Robert Harding Picture Library Ltd/Alamy
p.1065 Café in Yellowknife© Christian Williams
p.1072 Kiawak Ashoona, Inuit carver © Bryan & Cherry Alexander Photography/Alamy

Skiing and snowboarding colour section

Whistler, BC © Rob Howard/Corbis
Skiing at Lake Louise © First Light/Getty Images
Ice-skating, Ottawa © Publiphoto Diffusion Inc./Alamy
Mont Tremblant Resort, Québec © All Canada Photos/Getty Images
Snowboarders standing on ridge © Mike Powell/Allsport Concepts/Getty Images
Mont Tremblant, Québec © Drew Hadley/Alamy
Heliskiing, BC © Karl Weatherly/Corbis

Canadian art colour section

Indian Encampment on Lake Huron, c.1845 (oil on canvas) by Paul Kane © Art Gallery of Ontario, Toronto, Canada/The Bridgeman Art Library
Lake and Mountains, 1928 (oil on canvas) by Lawren Stewart Harris © Art Gallery of Ontario, Toronto, Canada/The Bridgeman Art Library
Western Forest, c.1931 (oil on canvas) by Emily Carr © Art Gallery of Ontario, Toronto, Canada/The Bridgeman Art Library
Round Lake, Mud Bay, 1915 (oil on panel), Thomas John Thomson © Art Gallery of Ontario, Toronto, Canada/The Bridgeman Art Library

National parks colour section

Waterton Lakes National Park, Southern Alberta © Darby Sawchuk/Alamy
Ellesmere Island National Park © David Noton Photography/Alamy
Yoho National Park © 2006 Alexander Kolomietz/iStock.com
Kayaking at sunset © Charles Tearle/iStock.com
Sitka deer among Haida poles © Danita Delimont/Alamy
Grizzly bear © John Schwieder/Alamy
Dall's sheep © John E. Marriott/Alamy

Index

Map entries are in colour.

C

D

I INDEX

I

J

K

M

N

INDEX

S

Note that St and Ste are alphabetized under "Saint"

T

U

INDEX

INDEX

Map symbols

maps are listed in the full index using colored text

International border
Province/U.S. state border
Chapter division boundary
Expressway
Trans-Canada Highway
Yellowhead Highway
U.S. interstate
U.S. highway
Highway
Secondary highway
Local road
Pedestrianised road
Steps
Path
Railway
Ferry route
Cable car
Wall
River
Dam
Bridge
Gate
Mountain range
Mountain peak
Waterfall
Viewpoint
Lighthouse

Campsite
Subway station
Bus stop
Helijet
Airport
Boat
Point of interest
Restaurant
Accommodation
Picnic site
Parking
Ski area
Tourist Information
Hospital/medical centre
Post office
Golf course
Statue
Tower
Monument
Monastery
Church (regional maps)
Building
Church (town maps)
Cemetery
Park
Forest
Beach

SELMA AND DALLAS COUNTY LIBRARY
We're